Safety Symbols

ANIMAL SAFETY Never injure an animal. Follow your teacher's instructions for handling specific animals or preserved specimens. Wash your hands with soap and water when finished handling animals or preserved specimens.

APRON Wear an apron when using any substance that could cause harm if spilled on you. Stand whenever possible to avoid spilling in your lap.

BREAKAGE Use caution when handling items that may break, such as glassware and thermometers. Always store test tubes in a test tube rack.

CHEMICAL SAFETY Always wear goggles when working with chemicals. Stand whenever possible when working with chemicals to avoid spilling on your lap. Tell your teacher immediately if you spill chemicals on yourself, the table, or floor. Never taste any substance or chemical in the lab. Always wash your hands after working with chemicals.

DISPOSAL Follow your teacher's instructions for disposing of all waste materials, including chemicals, specimens, or broken glass.

ELECTRICAL SAFETY Keep electrical cords away from water to avoid shock. Do not use cords with frayed edges. Unplug all equipment when done.

FIRE SAFETY Put on safety goggles before lighting flames. Remove loose clothing and tie back hair. Never leave a lit object unattended. Extinguish flames as soon as you finish heating.

FUMES Always work in a well-ventilated area. Bring fumes up to your nose by wafting with your fingers instead of sniffing.

GENERAL SAFETY Always follow the safety rules and ask your teacher if you are unsure about something. If you are designing your own experiment, get your teacher's approval on your plan before you start. Think about which safety rules you must follow in your experiment.

GLOVES Always wear gloves to protect your skin from possible injury when working with substances that may be harmful or when working with animals.

HAND WASHING Wash your hands with soap and water after working with soil, chemicals, animals, or preserved specimens.

HEATING SAFETY Wear goggles and never leave any substance while it is being heated. Use tongs, hot pads, or test tube holders to hold hot objects. Point any materials being heated away from you and others. Place hot objects such as test tubes in test tube racks while cooling.

HOT/GLOVE Always wear gloves such as oven mitts when handling larger hot materials.

POISON Never touch, taste, or inhale chemicals. Most chemicals are toxic in high concentrations. Wear goggles and wash your hands.

SAFETY GOGGLES Always wear safety goggles when working with chemicals, heating any substance, or using a sharp object or any material that could fly up and injure you or others.

SHARP OBJECTS Use scissors, knives, or razor tools with care. Wear goggles when cutting something with scalpels, knives, or razor tools. Always cut away from yourself.

Michigan

McDougal Littell

Biology

Stephen
Nowicki

Acknowledgments for Michigan Student Guide

PHOTOGRAPHY Cover *bottom left* © Ingo Arndt/naturepl.com; *top left* © William Fowle/Electron Microscopy Center, Northeastern University; *all others* © Getty Images; **title page** *bottom left* © Ingo Arndt/naturepl.com; *top left* © William Fowle/Electron Microscopy Center, Northeastern University; *all others* © Getty; **back cover** © Bruce Coleman Inc./Alamy Images Images; **MI3** © Jim Wallace/Duke University Photography; **MI8** © Doug Perrine/naturepl.com; **MI9** *left* © OSF/Photolibrary. com; **MI11** *left* © Don W. Fawcett/Photo Researchers, Inc.; **MI12** Photos by Atison Phumchoosri; **MI15** *left* © Michael & Patricia Fogden/Corbis; **MI16** © Dennis MacDonald/Alamy Images; **MI18** © Dr. Gopal Murti/Visuals Unlimited; **MI19** *left* © Larry Michael/naturepl.com; **MI20** © Anette Linnea Rasmussen/ShutterStock; **MI21** *left* © Joseph Sohm/Corbis; **MI23** © Dwight Kuhn; **MI26** © D. Philips/Photo Researchers, Inc.; **MI27** *left* © Chris Stewart/San Francisco Chronicle/Corbis; *right* © Dan Dry/University of Chicago; **MI28** © Michael Neugebauer/mine@netway.at; **MI29** *left* © age fotostock/SuperStock; **MI31** *top* © Biophoto Associates/Photo Researchers, Inc.; **MI32** *bottom right* © U.S. Grains Council; **MI34** *left* © Albert Tousson/Phototake; **MI29, MI31, MI32** Photographs by Sharon Hoogstraten

ILLUSTRATIONS Illustration by Argosy **MI11, MI13, MI15, MI17, MI21; MI32;** Illustration by Peter Bull **MI40;** Illustration by Stephen Durke **MI10;** Illustration by Garth Glazier **MI25;** Illustration by Patrick Gnan **MI46;** Illustration by Keith Kasnot **MI45;** Illustration by Debbie Maizels **MI44;** Illustration by Six Red Marbles **MI9;** Illustration by Inklink Studio/Sparks Arts & Literary Agents **MI42–MI43;** Illustration by Tata Interactive **MI19;** Illustration by Bart Vallecoccia **MI34, MI38;** Illustration by Richard Bonson/Wildlife Art Ltd. **MI41;** Illustration by Myke Taylor/Wildlife Art Ltd. **MI39**

Printed in Canada.

ISBN-13: 978-0-547-05597-8   ISBN-10: 0-547-05597-8

1 2 3 4 5 6 7 8 TBQC 10 09 08 07

Internet Web Site: http://www.mcdougallittell.com

Stephen Nowicki, Ph.D.

Stephen Nowicki grew up with a strong interest in music and at one time wanted to be a classical musician. A biology course in college sparked his excitement for biology, leading him to a double major in both biology and music. Nowicki obtained both his bachelor's and master's degrees from Tufts University. He received his doctorate in neurobiology and behavior from Cornell University in 1985.

Nowicki is now Dean of the Natural Sciences, as well as Bass Fellow and Professor in the departments of Biology, Psychology, and Neurobiology at Duke University. He has taught at Duke since 1989, where he directed a complete redesign of the introductory biology program. Nowicki's research interests center on animal behavior and how communication systems evolve. His work combines both field studies and laboratory experiments. He uses birdsong as a model system and studies topics such as the structure, function, and evolution of animal communication systems. In the past, Nowicki and his students have studied behavior in a wide variety of organisms, including insects, lobsters, lizards, squirrels, and primates.

Nowicki's research has been published in more than 70 articles in scientific journals, including *Science, Nature,* and *Animal Behavior.* He also coauthored the book *The Evolution of Animal Communication: Reliability and Deception in Signaling Systems.* In addition, he is the author of a video lecture series based on the introductory biology course he taught at Duke. He serves regularly on proposal review panels for the National Science Foundation.

Outside of his professional interests, Nowicki enjoys music. He has played the trombone since the fourth grade, and played for two seasons with the Duke University Pep Band at basketball games. Juggling and cooking are other hobbies that Nowicki enjoys in his free time. Nowicki is married to Susan Peters, who also studies animal communication, and they have one son, Schuyler. Nowicki and his family live in Durham, North Carolina.

Content Reviewers

Mark Baustian, Ph.D.
President
West Hill Biological Resources
Spencer, NY

John Beaver, Ph.D.
Professor Emeritus
College of Education and Human Services
Western Illinois University
Macomb, IL

Elizabeth A. De Stasio, Ph.D.
Associate Professor and Raymond H. Herzog
  Professor of Science
Department of Biology
Lawrence University
Appleton, WI

Dan Franck, Ph.D.
Botany Education Consultant
Chatham, NY

Linda Graham, Ph.D.
Professor of Botany
Department of Botany
University of Wisconsin
Madison, WI

David Harbster, M.A. in Biology Education
Professor of Biology
Paradise Valley Community College
Phoenix, AZ

C. Leon Harris, Ph.D.
Professor Emeritus
Department of Biological Sciences
State University of New York at Plattsburgh
Plattsburgh, NY

Anthony Ippolito, Ph.D.
Visiting Assistant Professor
Department of Biological Sciences
DePaul University
Chicago, IL

Sönke Johnsen, Ph.D.
Assistant Professor
Department of Biology
Duke University
Durham, NC

Paula Lemons, Ph.D.
Assistant Professor of the Practice
Department of Biology
Duke University
Durham, NC

Lori Marino, Ph.D.
Senior Lecturer
Neuroscience and Behavioral Biology Program
Emory University
Atlanta, GA

Louise McCullough, M.D./Ph.D.
Director of Stroke Research
Department of Neurology
University of Connecticut Health Center
Farmington, CT

Elizabeth Panter, R.D.
Dietitian
Clinical Nutrition Department
Johns Hopkins Bayview Medical Center
Baltimore, MD

Sheila Patek, Ph.D.
Assistant Professor
Department of Integrative Biology
University of California
Berkeley, CA

Adam Savage, B.S., M.F.A.
Science Consultant
Chicago, IL

F. Daniel Vogt, Ph.D.
Professor
Department of Biological Sciences
State University of New York at Plattsburgh
Plattsburgh, NY

Jerry Waldvogel, Ph.D.
Associate Professor
Department of Biological Sciences
Clemson University
Clemson, SC

Safety Reviewer

Juliana Texley, Ph.D.
Former K–12 Science Teacher and School
  Superintendent
Boca Raton, FL

Program Consultant

Laine Gurley, Ph.D.
Biology Teacher
Rolling Meadows High School
Rolling Meadows, IL

Michigan Teacher Reviewers

Dr. Michele Cook
Cadillac High School
Cadillac, MI

Megan Fenech
Plymouth High School
Canton, MI

Cheryl Hach
Kalamazoo Area Mathematics
and Science Center
Kalamazoo, MI

Marc Krugielki
North Branch High School
North Branch, MI

Mary Z. Lindow
Battle Creek Area Mathematics
and Science Center
Battle Creek, MI

LaMoine L. Motz, Ph.D
Oakland County Schools
OSMTech Center
Waterford, MI

Nicole Norris
Corunna High School
Corunna, MI

Kevin J. Richard
Glen Lake High School
Maple City, MI

Tom Wessels
Traverse Bay Area Intermediate
School District
Traverse City, MI

Mark Bradley Willis
Hart High School
Hart, MI

Teacher Reviewers and Lab Evaluators

Elaine Armstrong
Battle Ground High School
Battle Ground, WA

Amy Bell
Arcadia High School
Phoenix, AZ

Jerry Bell
Desert Vista High School
Phoenix, AZ

Bonnie Brenner
Niles West High School
Niles, IL

Jason Campbell
Schaumburg High School
Schaumburg, IL

Christopher Dignam
Lane Tech High School
Chicago, IL

Jennifer Ellberg
Maine West High School
Des Plaines, IL

Charles Ellwood
Pebblebrook High School
Mableton, GA

Barry Feldman
Corona del Sol High School
Tempe, AZ

Gerry Foster
Desert Vista High School
Phoenix, AZ

Riley Greenwood
Valley Center High School
Valley Center, KS

Michelle Hadden
La Joya High School
Avondale, AZ

Randy Hein
Floyd Central High School
Floyds Knobs, IN

Stephen Hobbs
Seton Catholic High School
Chandler, AZ

Janet Jones
Sullivan High School
Chicago, IL

Karen Klafeta
Morton East High School
Cicero, IL

Robert Kolenda
Neshaminy High School
Langhorne, PA

Wanda Miller
Martinsburg High School
Martinsburg, WV

Birgit Musheno
Desert Vista High School
Phoenix, AZ

Kenneth Nealy
Windsor Public Schools
Windsor, CT

Lonnie Newton
Arvada West Senior High
Arvada, CO

Palak Patel
Wheaton North High
School
Wheaton, IL

Yvonne Perry
Douglas County High
School
Douglasville, GA

Tracy Rader
Fulton Jr-Sr High School
Indianapolis, IN

Kathey Roberts
Lakeside High School
Hot Springs, AR

Cassandra Ross
Redan High School
Stone Mountain, GA

Lori Ruter
Lake Norman High School
Mooresville, NC

James Rutkowski
Erie School District
Erie, PA

Sara Sagmeister
Maine South High School
Park Ridge, IL

Jackie Snow
Lee's Summit North High
School
Lee's Summit, MO

Laura Spitznogle
Williamsville East High
School
East Amherst, NY

Jason Wikman
Charlotte High School
Punta Gorda, FL

Michigan

Overview of Michigan Student Edition

Michigan Table of Contents   MI8

Michigan Student Guide   MI33

Overview of Michigan Biology High School
Content Expectations   MI34
Michigan Biology High School Content Expectations   MI35
Prerequisite Knowledge Content Expectations   MI47

Look for the Michigan Standards symbol throughout the book. It tells you which standards are covered in each section.

Mackinac Bridge, Michigan © Ilene MacDonald/Alamy

Unit 1 Introducing Biology   1

1 Biology in the 21st Century
2 Chemistry of Life

Unit 2 Cells   67

3 Cell Structure and Function
4 Cells and Energy
5 Cell Growth and Division

Unit 3 Genetics   165

6 Meiosis and Mendel
7 Extending Mendelian Genetics
8 From DNA to Proteins
9 Frontiers of Biotechnology

Unit 4 Evolution   295

10 Principles of Evolution
11 The Evolution of Populations
12 The History of Life

Unit 5 Ecology   393

13 Principles of Ecology
14 Interactions in Ecosystems
15 The Biosphere
16 Human Impact on Ecosystems

Unit 6 Classification and Diversity   515

17 The Tree of Life
18 Viruses and Prokaryotes
19 Protists and Fungi

Unit 7 Plants   609

20 Plant Diversity
21 Plant Structure and Function
22 Plant Growth, Reproduction, and Response

Unit 8 Animals   693

23 Invertebrate Diversity
24 A Closer Look at Arthropods
25 Vertebrate Diversity
26 A Closer Look at Amniotes
27 Animal Behavior

Unit 9 Human Biology   849

28 Human Systems and Homeostasis
29 Nervous and Endocrine Systems
30 Respiratory and Circulatory Systems
31 Immune System and Disease
32 Digestive and Excretory Systems
33 Protection, Support, and Movement
34 Reproduction and Development

MICHIGAN TABLE OF CONTENTS

UNIT 1

MICHIGAN

Introducing Biology

Chapter 1 Biology in the 21st Century   2

1.1	The Study of Life	4
1.2	Unifying Themes of Biology	7
	DATA ANALYSIS *Qualitative and Quantitative*	12
1.3	Scientific Thinking and Processes	13
1.4	Biologists' Tools and Technology	19
1.5	Biology and Your Future	24

QUICK LAB	Life Under a Microscope	22
INVESTIGATION	Manipulating Independent Variables	18
OPTIONS FOR INQUIRY	Lab: Manipulating Plant Growth	28
	Lab: Biology in the News	29
	Online: **Animated** BIOLOGY, WebQuest, Data Analysis	29

MICHIGAN   STANDARDS-BASED ASSESSMENT   *B1.1B, B1.1E, B3.4B, B5.1A, B1.2h, B2.3e*   33

Moray eel and cleaner shrimp, *p. 7*

Chapter 2   Chemistry of Life   34

2.1	Atoms, Ions, and Molecules	36
2.2	Properties of Water	40
2.3	Carbon-Based Molecules	44
	DATA ANALYSIS *Identifying Variables*	49
2.4	Chemical Reactions	50
2.5	Enzymes	54

QUICK LAB	Chemical Bonding	51
INVESTIGATION	Enzymatic Activity	57
OPTIONS FOR INQUIRY	Lab: Testing pH	58
	Lab: Enzymes	59
	Online: **Animated** BIOLOGY, Virtual Lab, WebQuest	59

MICHIGAN   STANDARDS-BASED ASSESSMENT   *L2.p1B, B1.1E, B2.2D, B2.2F, B2.5A, B2.2c*   63

UNIT 1 BIOZINE

When Knowledge and Ethics Collide   64

Technology   Genetic Testing
Careers   Geneticist

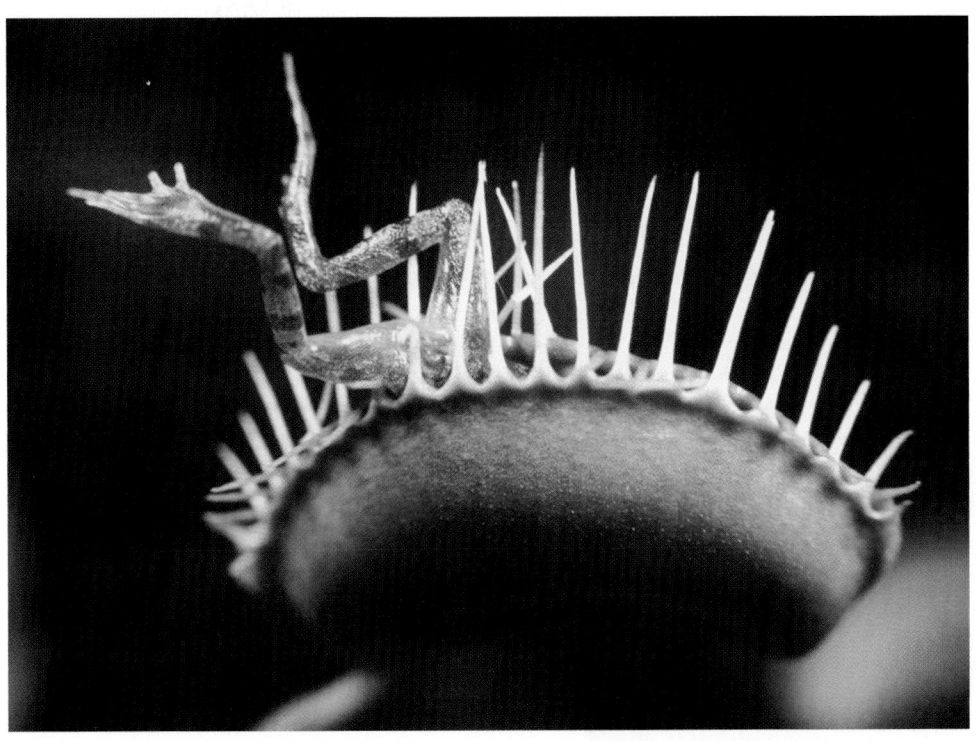

Venus flytrap and frog, *pp. 34–35*

VIRTUAL LAB
Chapter 2   Calorimetry

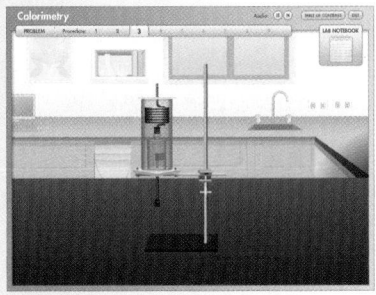

Animated BIOLOGY

Chapter 1   Cells Through Different Microscopes, Experimental Design
Chapter 2   Hydrogen Bonding, Energy and Chemical Reactions, Atoms and Bonding

WEBQUEST
Chapter 1   Bioethics
Chapter 2   Prions and Public Health

Interactive Review

REVIEW Key Concepts, Vocabulary Games, Concept Maps, Animated Biology, Online Quiz

BIOZINE

INTERNET MAGAZINE
Explore today's world of biology online at ClassZone.com.

UNIT 2
MICHIGAN

Cells

Content Expectations Focus

In Unit 2, you will learn about different types of cells, the structure and function of their specialized parts, energy use in cells, and cell division. The following standards receive primary coverage:

Standard B2: Organization and Development of Living Systems

B2.1 Transformation of Matter and Energy in Cells

Chapter 3 Cell Structure and Function — 68

3.1	Cell Theory	70
3.2	Cell Organelles	73
	DATA ANALYSIS *Defining Variables*	80
3.3	Cell Membrane	81
3.4	Diffusion and Osmosis	85
3.5	Active Transport, Endocytosis, and Exocytosis	89

QUICK LAB	Modeling the Cell Membrane	83
INVESTIGATION	Diffusion Across a Membrane	88
OPTIONS FOR INQUIRY	Lab: Comparing Cells	92
	Lab: Modeling the Cell	93
	Online: *Animated* BIOLOGY, WebQuest, BioZine	93

MICHIGAN STANDARDS-BASED ASSESSMENT *B1.2i, B2.2f, B2.4g, B2.5g, B2.5h, B2.5i* — 97

Chapter 4 Cells and Energy — 98

4.1	Chemical Energy and ATP	100
4.2	Overview of Photosynthesis	103
4.3	Photosynthesis in Detail	108
4.4	Overview of Cellular Respiration	113
	DATA ANALYSIS *Interpreting Graphs*	116
4.5	Cellular Respiration in Detail	117
4.6	Fermentation	122

QUICK LAB	Fermentation	124
INVESTIGATION	Rates of Photosynthesis	106
OPTIONS FOR INQUIRY	Lab: Cellular Respiration	126
	Lab: Investigating Fermentation in Foods	127
	Online: *Animated* BIOLOGY, Virtual Lab, WebQuest	127

MICHIGAN STANDARDS-BASED ASSESSMENT *B1.1B, B2.1A, B2.1B, B2.5D* — 131

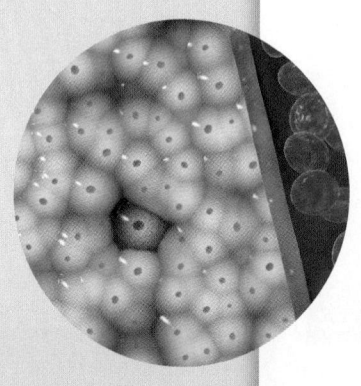
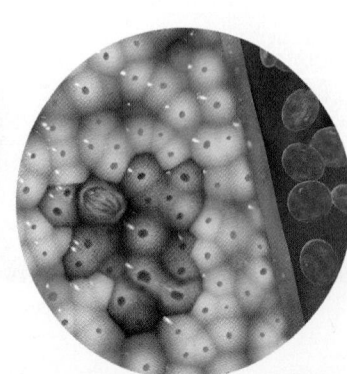
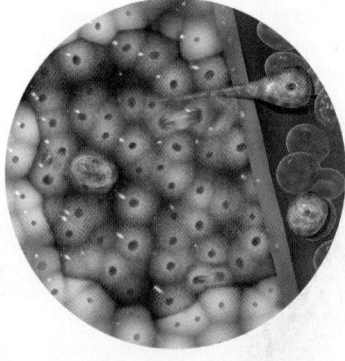

Cancer cells, *p. 146*

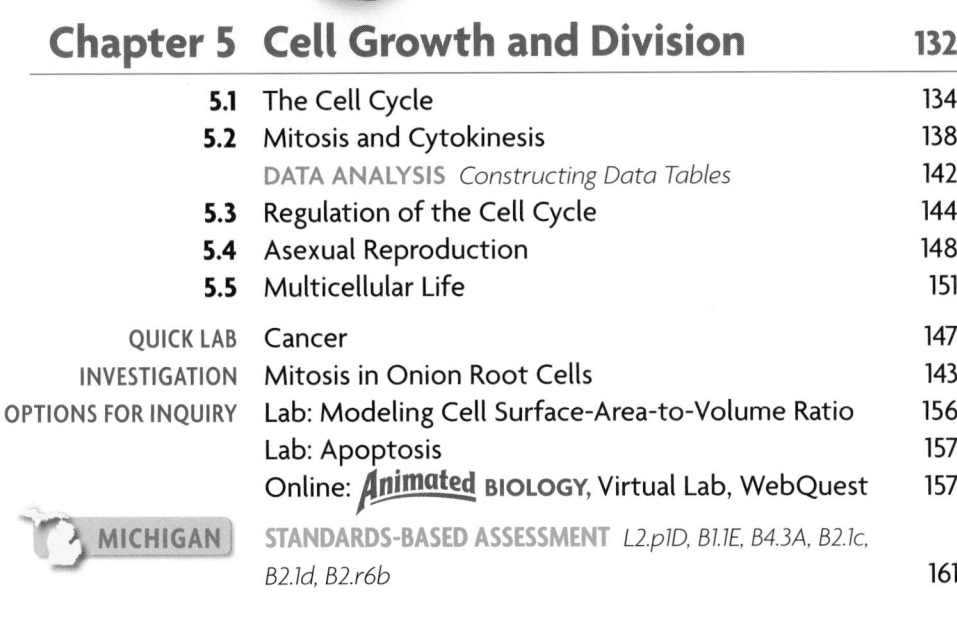

Chapter 5 Cell Growth and Division

		132
5.1	The Cell Cycle	134
5.2	Mitosis and Cytokinesis	138
	DATA ANALYSIS *Constructing Data Tables*	142
5.3	Regulation of the Cell Cycle	144
5.4	Asexual Reproduction	148
5.5	Multicellular Life	151
QUICK LAB	Cancer	147
INVESTIGATION	Mitosis in Onion Root Cells	143
OPTIONS FOR INQUIRY	Lab: Modeling Cell Surface-Area-to-Volume Ratio	156
	Lab: Apoptosis	157
	Online: **Animated** BIOLOGY, Virtual Lab, WebQuest	157

 **MICHIGAN** STANDARDS-BASED ASSESSMENT *L2.p1D, B1.1E, B4.3A, B2.1c, B2.1d, B2.r6b* 161

UNIT 2 BIOZINE

Stem Cell Research— Potential Solutions, Practical Challenges 162

Technology Somatic Cell Nuclear Transfer
Careers Cell Biologist

Vesicles in a cell, *p. 77*

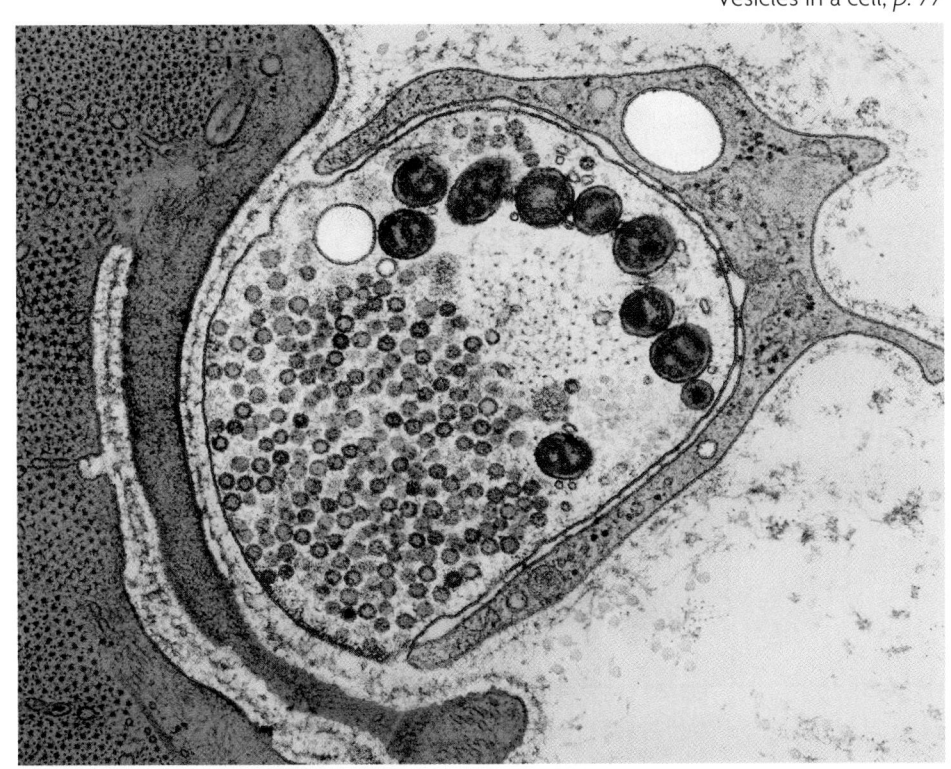

CLASSZONE.COM

VIRTUAL LAB

Chapter 4 Carbon Dioxide Transfer Through Snails and Elodea

Chapter 5 Investigating Bacterial Growth

Animated BIOLOGY

Chapter 3 Cell Organelles, Get Through a Cell Membrane

Chapter 4 Photosynthesis, Cellular Respiration, Mirror Processes

Chapter 5 Mitosis, Binary Fission, Mitosis Stage Matching Game

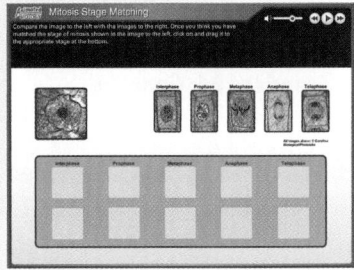

WEBQUEST

Chapter 3 Organelle Dysfunction

Chapter 4 Energy and Athletic Training

Chapter 5 Skin Cancer

Interactive ← Review

REVIEW Key Concepts, Vocabulary Games, Concept Maps, Animated Biology, Online Quiz

BIO ZINE

INTERNET MAGAZINE
Explore today's world of biology online at ClassZone.com.

Genetics

Chapter 6 Meiosis and Mendel 166

6.1	Chromosomes and Meiosis	168
	DATA ANALYSIS *Interpreting Bar Graphs*	172
6.2	Process of Meiosis	173
6.3	Mendel and Heredity	177
6.4	Traits, Genes, and Alleles	180
6.5	Traits and Probability	183
6.6	Meiosis and Genetic Variation	189
QUICK LAB	Using a Testcross to Determine Genotype	185
INVESTIGATION	Allele Combinations and Punnett Squares	188
OPTIONS FOR INQUIRY	Lab: Modeling Meiosis	192
	Lab: Probability Practice	193
	Online: **Animated** BIOLOGY, Virtual Lab, WebQuest	193

MICHIGAN STANDARDS-BASED ASSESSMENT *L4.p2A, B1.1E, B4.3A, B4.1c, B4.1d, B4.3c* 197

Chapter 7 Extending Mendelian Genetics 198

7.1	Chromosomes and Phenotype	200
7.2	Complex Patterns of Inheritance	204
7.3	Gene Linkage and Mapping	209
	DATA ANALYSIS *Constructing Bar Graphs*	210
7.4	Human Genetics and Pedigrees	212
QUICK LAB	Sex-Linked Inheritance	202
INVESTIGATION	Codominance	208
OPTIONS FOR INQUIRY	Lab: Pedigree Analysis	218
	Lab: Incomplete Dominance	219
	Online: **Animated** BIOLOGY, WebQuest, Data Analysis	219

MICHIGAN STANDARDS-BASED ASSESSMENT *B4.3c, B4.1c, B4.1d, B4.1e, B4.2d, B4.3f* 223

Content Expectations Focus

In Unit 3, you will learn about sources of genetic variation, how the genetic makeup of an individual is determined, how the genetic code is eventually translated into proteins, and how biotechnology can change an organism's DNA. The following standards receive primary coverage:

Standard B4: Genetics

Royal blue and green betta fish, *p. 205*

Chapter 8 From DNA to Proteins   **224**

8.1	Identifying DNA as the Genetic Material	226
8.2	Structure of DNA	230
	DATA ANALYSIS *Interpreting Histograms*	234
8.3	DNA Replication	235
8.4	Transcription	239
8.5	Translation	243
8.6	Gene Expression and Regulation	248
8.7	Mutations	252
QUICK LAB	Replication	238
INVESTIGATION	Extracting DNA	229
OPTIONS FOR INQUIRY	Lab: UV Light and Skin Cancer	256
	Lab: Modeling Transcription	257
	Online: **Animated** BIOLOGY, WebQuest, Data Analysis	257
MICHIGAN	STANDARDS-BASED ASSESSMENT *B2.2D, B4.2C, B4.3B, B4.2f, B4.2g, B4.4b*	261

Chapter 9 Frontiers of Biotechnology   **262**

9.1	Manipulating DNA	264
9.2	Copying DNA	269
9.3	DNA Fingerprinting	272
9.4	Genetic Engineering	275
9.5	Genomics and Bioinformatics	280
	DATA ANALYSIS *Constructing Histograms*	282
9.6	Genetic Screening and Gene Therapy	284
QUICK LAB	Modeling Plasmids and Restriction Enzymes	278
INVESTIGATION	Modeling Forensics	268
OPTIONS FOR INQUIRY	Lab: Modeling Genetic Engineering	286
	Lab: Genetic Screening	287
	Online: **Animated** BIOLOGY, Virtual Lab, WebQuest	287
MICHIGAN	STANDARDS-BASED ASSESSMENT *B4.2B, B4.2C, B4.2h, B5.3f, B4.r2i*	291

UNIT 3 BIOZINE Medical Technology— The Genetic Forefront   **292**

Technology Biochips
Careers Cancer Geneticist

Online BIOLOGY
CLASSZONE.COM

VIRTUAL LAB
Chapter 6 Breeding Mutations in Fruit Flies
Chapter 9 Gel Electrophoresis, Bacterial Transformation

Animated BIOLOGY
Chapter 6 Meiosis, Genotypes and Phenotypes, Mendel's Experiment
Chapter 7 Human Chromosomes, Tracking Traits
Chapter 8 DNA Replication, Build a Protein
Chapter 9 Restriction Enzymes, Polymerase Chain Reaction

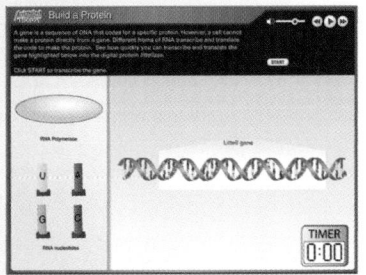

WEBQUEST
Chapter 6 Selective Breeding
Chapter 7 Genetic Heritage
Chapter 8 Transgenic Organisms
Chapter 9 Animal Cloning

Interactive Review
REVIEW Key Concepts, Vocabulary Games, Concept Maps, Animated Biology, Online Quiz

BIOZINE
INTERNET MAGAZINE
Explore today's world of biology online at ClassZone.com.

UNIT 4

MICHIGAN

Content Expectations Focus

The focus of Unit 4 includes the basic principles of evolution and natural selection, how populations evolve, and the history of life on Earth. The following standards receive primary coverage:

Standard B5: Evolution and Biodiversity

Evolution

Chapter 10 Principles of Evolution 296

10.1	Early Ideas About Evolution	298
10.2	Darwin's Observations	302
10.3	Theory of Natural Selection	304
	DATA ANALYSIS *Interpreting Line Graphs*	308
10.4	Evidence of Evolution	310
10.5	Evolutionary Biology Today	316

QUICK LAB	Piecing Together Evidence	313
INVESTIGATION	Predator-Prey Pursuit	315
OPTIONS FOR INQUIRY	Lab: Using Patterns to Make Predictions	320
	Lab: Adaptations in Beaks	321
	Online: **Animated** BIOLOGY, WebQuest, Data Analysis	321

MICHIGAN STANDARDS-BASED ASSESSMENT *B5.1A, B1.2i, B2.4d, B5.1e, B5.1f* 325

Chapter 11 The Evolution of Populations 326

11.1	Genetic Variation Within Populations	328
11.2	Natural Selection in Populations	330
11.3	Other Mechanisms of Evolution	335
	DATA ANALYSIS *Identifying Patterns*	339
11.4	Hardy-Weinberg Equilibrium	340
11.5	Speciation Through Isolation	344
11.6	Patterns in Evolution	347

QUICK LAB	Genetic Drift	337
INVESTIGATION	Natural Selection in African Swallowtails	334
OPTIONS FOR INQUIRY	Lab: Investigating an Anole Lizard Population	352
	Lab: Exploring Adaptations	353
	Online: **Animated** BIOLOGY, WebQuest, Data Analysis	353

MICHIGAN STANDARDS-BASED ASSESSMENT *B5.1d, B5.3A, B5.3B, B5.3C, B5.1g, B5.2c* 357

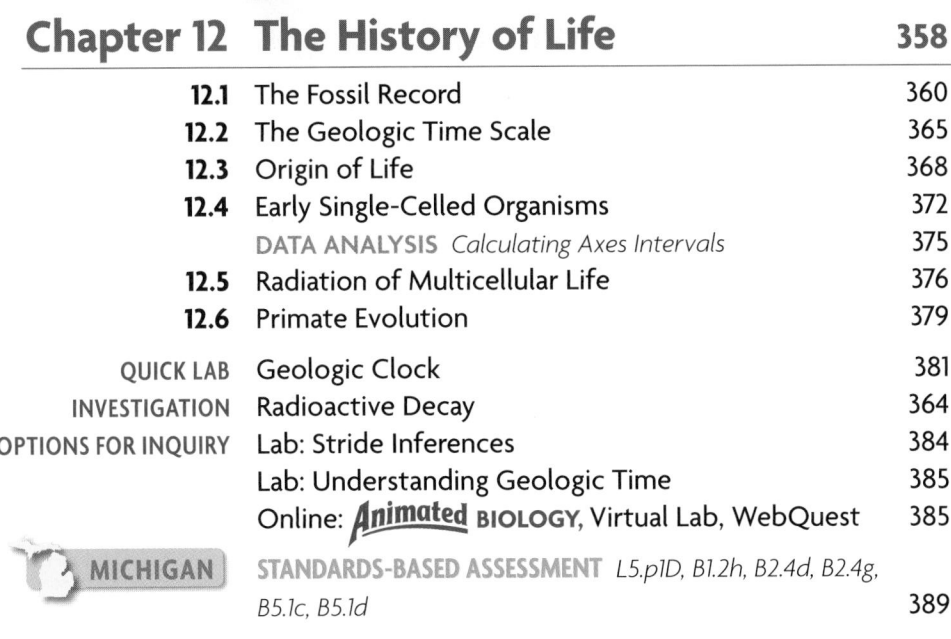

Chapter 12 The History of Life   358

12.1	The Fossil Record	360
12.2	The Geologic Time Scale	365
12.3	Origin of Life	368
12.4	Early Single-Celled Organisms	372
	DATA ANALYSIS *Calculating Axes Intervals*	375
12.5	Radiation of Multicellular Life	376
12.6	Primate Evolution	379

QUICK LAB	Geologic Clock	381
INVESTIGATION	Radioactive Decay	364
OPTIONS FOR INQUIRY	Lab: Stride Inferences	384
	Lab: Understanding Geologic Time	385
	Online: *Animated* BIOLOGY, Virtual Lab, WebQuest	385

 **MICHIGAN**   STANDARDS-BASED ASSESSMENT   *L5.p1D, B1.2h, B2.4d, B2.4g, B5.1c, B5.1d*   389

UNIT 4 BIOZINE

Drug-Resistant Bacteria— A Global Health Issue   390

Technology New Drug Delivery System
Careers Evolutionary Biologist

Tarsiers, *p. 379*

Online BIOLOGY
CLASSZONE.COM

VIRTUAL LAB
Chapter 12 Comparing Hominoid Skulls

Animated BIOLOGY
Chapter 10 Natural Selection Principles, Simulate Natural Selection

Chapter 11 Mechanisms of Evolution, Founder Effect, Evolutionary Arms Race

Chapter 12 Endosymbiosis, Geologic Time Scale

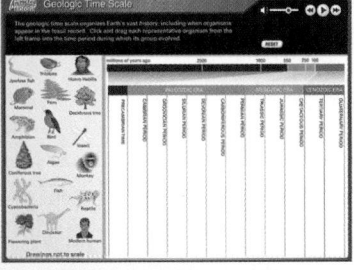

WEBQUEST
Chapter 10 Dinosaur Descendants
Chapter 11 Speciation in Action
Chapter 12 Geologic Dating

Interactive Review

REVIEW Key Concepts, Vocabulary Games, Concept Maps, Animated Biology, Online Quiz

BIOZINE
INTERNET MAGAZINE
Explore today's world of biology online at ClassZone.com.

Ecology

Chapter 13 Principles of Ecology — 394

13.1	Ecologists Study Relationships	396
	DATA ANALYSIS *Populations and Samples*	401
13.2	Biotic and Abiotic Factors	402
13.3	Energy in Ecosystems	406
13.4	Food Chains and Food Webs	408
13.5	Cycling of Matter	412
13.6	Pyramid Models	417

QUICK LAB	Quadrat Sampling	399
INVESTIGATION	Abiotic Factors and Plant Growth	405
OPTIONS FOR INQUIRY	Lab: Random Sampling	420
	Lab: Build a Terrarium	421
	Online: *Animated* BIOLOGY, Virtual Lab, WebQuest	421

MICHIGAN STANDARDS-BASED ASSESSMENT *L3.p1A, L3.p2A, L3.p2c, B1.1C, B3.2B, B3.3b* — 425

Chapter 14 Interactions in Ecosystems — 426

14.1	Habitat and Niche	428
14.2	Community Interactions	431
14.3	Population Density and Distribution	436
14.4	Population Growth Patterns	440
	DATA ANALYSIS *Reading Combination Graphs*	442
14.5	Ecological Succession	445

QUICK LAB	Survivorship Curves	438
INVESTIGATION	Modeling Predation	435
OPTIONS FOR INQUIRY	Lab: Limiting Nutrients for Algae	448
	Lab: Making a Local Field Guide	449
	Online: *Animated* BIOLOGY, WebQuest, Data Analysis	449

MICHIGAN STANDARDS-BASED ASSESSMENT *L3.p2A, L3.p2B, B3.4A, B3.5B, B2.2g, B3.5e* — 453

Content Expectations Focus

In Unit 5, ecology is defined as the study of interactions among living and nonliving things in an ecosystem. You will learn about various types of interactions and how scientists study them, how Earth is divided into biomes, and how humans can impact ecosystems within these biomes. The following standards receive primary coverage:

**Standard B3:
Interdependence of Living Systems and the Environment**

Industrial pollution,
p. 491

Chapter 15   The Biosphere   454

15.1	Life in the Earth System	456
15.2	Climate	458
	DATA ANALYSIS *Constructing Combination Graphs*	461
15.3	Biomes	462
15.4	Marine Ecosystems	468
15.5	Estuaries and Freshwater Ecosystems	471
QUICK LAB	Microclimates	460
INVESTIGATION	Winter Water Chemistry	475
OPTIONS FOR INQUIRY	Lab: Modeling Biomes	476
	Lab: Heating and Cooling Rates of Water and Soil	477
	Online: **Animated** BIOLOGY, WebQuest, Data Analysis	477

MICHIGAN   STANDARDS-BASED ASSESSMENT *L3.p2B, L3.p2C, L3.p3A, L3.p3B, L3.p4A*   481

Chapter 16   Human Impact on Ecosystems   482

16.1	Human Population Growth and Natural Resources	484
16.2	Air Quality	488
16.3	Water Quality	494
	DATA ANALYSIS *Discrete and Continuous Data*	497
16.4	Threats to Biodiversity	498
16.5	Conservation	502
QUICK LAB	Modeling Biomagnification	496
INVESTIGATION	Acid Rain	493
OPTIONS FOR INQUIRY	Lab: Water Quality Testing	506
	Lab: Contamination of Groundwater	507
	Online: **Animated** BIOLOGY, WebQuest, Data Analysis	507

MICHIGAN   STANDARDS-BASED ASSESSMENT *L3.p2B, L3.p3C, L3.p4A, B1.1E, B3.4C, B3.5C*   511

UNIT 5 BIOZINE

Global Warming— Changing the Planet   512

Technology Deep Sea Sediment Coring
Careers Oceanographer

Online BIOLOGY
CLASSZONE.COM

VIRTUAL LAB
Chapter 13 Estimating Population Size

Animated BIOLOGY
Chapter 13 Distribution of Producers, Build a Food Web

Chapter 14 Survive within a Niche, What Limits Population Growth?

Chapter 15 Lake Turnover, Where Do They Live?

Chapter 16 Human Population Growth, Global Warming, Human Effects on a Food Web

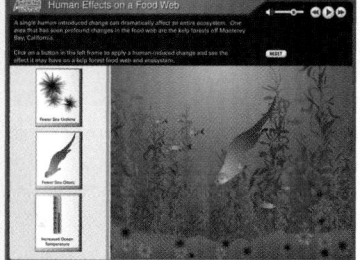

WEBQUEST
Chapter 13 Keystone Species
Chapter 14 Environmental Stress
Chapter 15 Explore an Ecosystem
Chapter 16 Invasive Species

Interactive Review
REVIEW Key Concepts, Vocabulary Games, Concept Maps, Animated Biology, Online Quiz

BIOZINE
INTERNET MAGAZINE
Explore today's world of biology online at ClassZone.com.

Classification and Diversity

Chapter 17 The Tree of Life   516

17.1	The Linnaean System of Classification	518
17.2	Classification Based on Evolutionary Relationships	524
	DATA ANALYSIS *Transforming Data*	529
17.3	Molecular Clocks	530
17.4	Domains and Kingdoms	533
QUICK LAB	Construct a Cladogram	525
INVESTIGATION	Creating a Dichotomous Key for Limpet Shells	522
OPTIONS FOR INQUIRY	Lab: Modeling DNA Hybridization	536
	Lab: Defining Species	537
	Online: *Animated* BIOLOGY, WebQuest, BioZine	537
MICHIGAN	STANDARDS-BASED ASSESSMENT *B2.4A, B1.2i, B2.4d, B5.r2d*	541

Chapter 18 Viruses and Prokaryotes   542

18.1	Studying Viruses and Prokaryotes	544
	DATA ANALYSIS *Choosing Data Representation*	546
18.2	Viral Structure and Reproduction	547
18.3	Viral Diseases	552
18.4	Bacteria and Archaea	555
18.5	Beneficial Roles of Prokaryotes	559
18.6	Bacterial Diseases and Antibiotics	563
QUICK LAB	Examining Bacteria in Yogurt	560
INVESTIGATION	Leaf Print Bacteria	562
OPTIONS FOR INQUIRY	Lab: Using Bacteria to Break Down Oil	566
	Lab: Modeling Viruses	567
	Online: *Animated* BIOLOGY, Virtual Lab, WebQuest	567
MICHIGAN	STANDARDS-BASED ASSESSMENT *L2.p1A, L3.p2B, B1.1E, B2.3c, B2.4h, B2.4i*	571

Content Expectations Focus

Unit 6 first introduces the way in which scientists classify living things. Next it begins the exploration of diversity of living things with viruses and prokaryotes, followed by protists and fungi. This unit reinforces and extends the following standards:

Standard B2: Organization and Development of Living Systems

Standard B3: Interdependence of Living Systems and the Environment

Standard B5: Evolution and Biodiversity

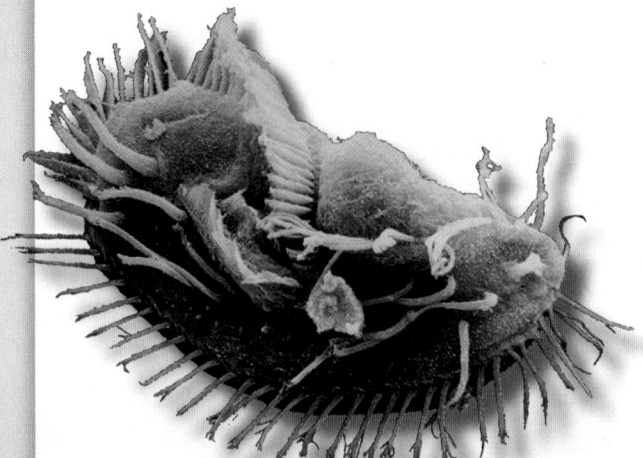

Oxytricha, an animal-like protist, *p. 575*

Chapter 19 Protists and Fungi   572

19.1	Diversity of Protists	574
19.2	Animal-like Protists	577
19.3	Plantlike Protists	581
	DATA ANALYSIS *Analyzing Experimental Design*	586
19.4	Funguslike Protists	587
19.5	Diversity of Fungi	589
19.6	Ecology of Fungi	596

QUICK LAB	Investigating Motion in Protists	579
INVESTIGATION	Exploring Mushroom Anatomy	595
OPTIONS FOR INQUIRY	Lab: Quantifying Mold Growth	600
	Lab: Algae in Products	601
	Online: **Animated** BIOLOGY, WebQuest, Data Analysis	601

 MICHIGAN STANDARDS-BASED ASSESSMENT *L2.p4A, L3.p2C, L4.p1A, B2.4A, B3.2C, B2.4d*   605

UNIT 6 BIOZINE

Pandemics—Is the Next One on the Way?   606

Technology Dissecting a Virus
Careers Epidemiologist

Online BIOLOGY
CLASSZONE.COM

VIRTUAL LAB
Chapter 18 Testing Antibacterial Products

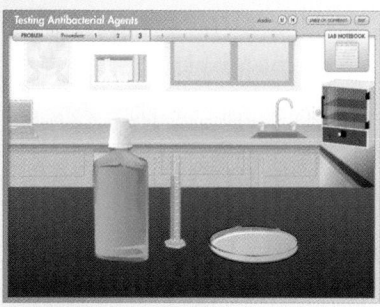

Animated BIOLOGY

Chapter 17 Molecular Clock, Build a Cladogram

Chapter 18 Viral Infections, What Would You Prescribe?

Chapter 19 Protist Movement, Algae Concentrations, Protist and Fungus Life Cycles

WEBQUEST

Chapter 17 Classify a Sea Cucumber

Chapter 18 Antibiotics in Agriculture

Chapter 19 Sickening Protists

Interactive ((+)) Review

REVIEW Key Concepts, Vocabulary Games, Concept Maps, Animated Biology, Online Quiz

BIOZINE

INTERNET MAGAZINE
Explore today's world of biology online at ClassZone.com.

White oak, *p. 519*

Plants

Chapter 20 Plant Diversity   610

20.1	Origins of Plant Life	612
20.2	Classification of Plants	617
20.3	Diversity of Flowering Plants	624
	DATA ANALYSIS *Mean, Median, and Mode*	628
20.4	Plants in Human Culture	629
QUICK LAB	Classifying Plants as Vascular or Nonvascular	620
INVESTIGATION	Habitat Clues	623
OPTIONS FOR INQUIRY	Lab: Comparing Monocots and Dicots	632
	Lab: Investigating Medicinal Plants	633
	Online: **Animated** BIOLOGY, WebQuest, BioZine	633
MICHIGAN	STANDARDS-BASED ASSESSMENT *L3.p2D, B1.1B, B1.1E, B3.5E*	637

Chapter 21 Plant Structure and Function   638

21.1	Plant Cells and Tissues	640
21.2	The Vascular System	643
21.3	Roots and Stems	648
	DATA ANALYSIS *Identifying the Importance of Repeated Trials*	649
21.4	Leaves	652
QUICK LAB	Chlorophyll Fluorescence	654
INVESTIGATION	Density of Stomata	647
OPTIONS FOR INQUIRY	Lab: Photosynthesis and Red Leaves	656
	Lab: Connecting Form to Function	657
	Online: **Animated** BIOLOGY, Virtual Lab, WebQuest	657
MICHIGAN	STANDARDS-BASED ASSESSMENT *B1.1B, B1.1E, B2.1A, B2.4g, B2.5B, B2.5f*	661

Content Expectations Focus

In Unit 7, you will first learn about the origins and diversity of plant life. Plant physiology is the next focus followed by plant life cycles and responses. This unit reinforces and extends the following standards:

Standard B2: Organization and Development of Living Systems

Standard B3: Interdependence of Living Systems and the Environment

Double samaras, *p. 673*

Chapter 22 Plant Growth, Reproduction, and Response   **662**

22.1	Plant Life Cycles	664
22.2	Reproduction in Flowering Plants	668
22.3	Seed Dispersal and Germination	673
	DATA ANALYSIS *Identifying Experimental Design Flaws*	674
22.4	Asexual Reproduction	678
22.5	Plant Hormones and Responses	680
QUICK LAB	A Closer Look at Flowers	669
INVESTIGATION	Seed Germination	676
OPTIONS FOR INQUIRY	Lab: Investigating Plant Hormones	684
	Lab: Fruit Dissection	685
	Online: **Animated** BIOLOGY, Virtual Lab, WebQuest	685

MICHIGAN   STANDARDS-BASED ASSESSMENT *B1.1B, B1.1E, B2.1A, B2.5B, B2.5f, B2.4g*   689

UNIT 7 BIOZINE Genetically Modified Foods— Do Potential Problems Outweigh Benefits?   **690**

Technology Gene Gun
Careers Research Engineer

Prickly pear cactus, *p. 678*

Online BIOLOGY
CLASSZONE.COM

VIRTUAL LAB
Chapter 21 Plant Transpiration
Chapter 22 Exploring Plant Responses

Animated BIOLOGY
Chapter 20 Plant and Pollinator Matching Game
Chapter 21 Movement Through a Plant, Name That Tree
Chapter 22 Seed Dispersal

WEBQUEST
Chapter 20 Endangered Plants
Chapter 21 Plant Adaptations
Chapter 22 Plants in Space

Interactive Review
REVIEW Key Concepts, Vocabulary Games, Concept Maps, Animated Biology, Online Quiz

BIOZINE
INTERNET MAGAZINE
Explore today's world of biology online at ClassZone.com.

UNIT 8

MICHIGAN

Animals

Content Expectations Focus

Unit 8 begins by discussing the common characteristics of all animals. Animal diversity, including invertebrate and vertebrate diversity, is explored. Then the focus shifts to animal behavior. The following standards receive primary coverage:

Standard B2: Organization and Development of Living Systems

B2.4 Cell Specialization

Unit 8 also reinforces and extends on the following standards:

Standard B3: Interdependence of Living Systems and the Environment

Chapter 23 Invertebrate Diversity 694

23.1	Animal Characteristics	696
23.2	Animal Diversity	699
23.3	Sponges and Cnidarians	705
23.4	Flatworms, Mollusks, and Annelids	710
23.5	Roundworms	716
23.6	Echinoderms	718
	DATA ANALYSIS *Analyzing Scatterplots*	721
QUICK LAB	Anatomy of a Clam	714
INVESTIGATION	Feeding *Hydra*	709
OPTIONS FOR INQUIRY	Lab: Anatomy of a Sea Star	722
	Lab: Anatomy of an Annelid	723
	Online: *Animated* BIOLOGY, WebQuest, BioZine	723

MICHIGAN STANDARDS-BASED ASSESSMENT *L2.p1D, L2.p1E, B1.1C, B2.4A, B2.4C, B2.4d* 727

Chapter 24 A Closer Look at Arthropods 728

24.1	Arthropod Diversity	730
24.2	Crustaceans	735
24.3	Arachnids	740
	DATA ANALYSIS *Constructing Scatterplots*	742
24.4	Insect Adaptations	743
24.5	Arthropods and Humans	747
QUICK LAB	Comparing Arthropods	733
INVESTIGATION	Hatching Brine Shrimp	739
OPTIONS FOR INQUIRY	Lab: Daphnia and Heart Rate	750
	Lab: Inside a Crayfish	751
	Online: *Animated* BIOLOGY, Virtual Lab, WebQuest	751

MICHIGAN STANDARDS-BASED ASSESSMENT *B2.3C, B2.4B, B2.4C, B5.3A, B1.1h, B5.1e* 755

Chapter 25 Vertebrate Diversity 756

25.1	Vertebrate Origins	758
25.2	Fish Diversity	763
25.3	A Closer Look at Bony Fish	768
	DATA ANALYSIS *Constructing Scatterplots*	770
25.4	Amphibians	773
25.5	Vertebrates on Land	778
QUICK LAB	Frog Development	776
INVESTIGATION	Fish Reproduction	772
OPTIONS FOR INQUIRY	Lab: Anatomy of a Bony Fish	780
	Lab: Vanishing Amphibian—an Indicator Species	781
	Online: *Animated* BIOLOGY, WebQuest, Data Analysis	781

MICHIGAN STANDARDS-BASED ASSESSMENT *L4.p1A, B1.2C, B2.4A, B2.4B, B2.4C, B5.1c* 785

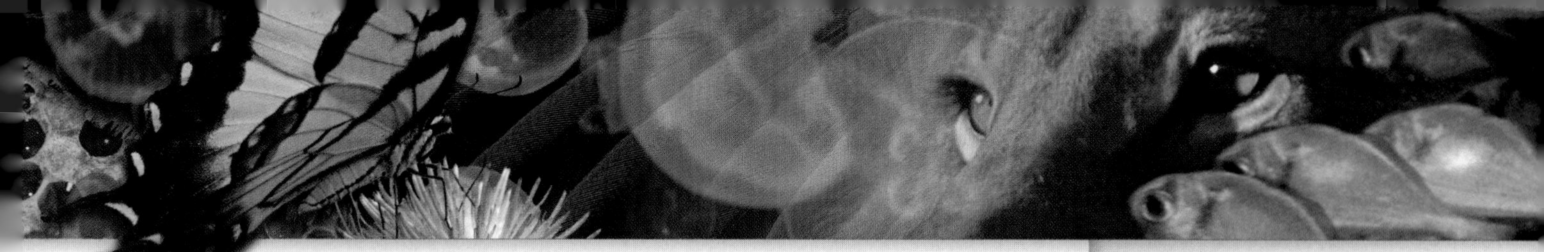

Chapter 26   A Closer Look at Amniotes   786

26.1	Amniotes	788
	DATA ANALYSIS *Choosing Graphs*	792
26.2	Reptiles	793
26.3	Birds	798
26.4	Mammals	805
QUICK LAB	Comparing Feathers	802
INVESTIGATION	A Bird's Airframe	804
OPTIONS FOR INQUIRY	Lab: The Parts of an Egg	810
	Lab: Migration and Range	811
	Online: **Animated** BIOLOGY, WebQuest, Data Analysis	811

MICHIGAN   STANDARDS-BASED ASSESSMENT   *B1.1B, B1.1C, B2.4A, B2.4B, B2.4C*   815

Chapter 27   Animal Behavior   816

27.1	Adaptive Value of Behavior	818
27.2	Instinct and Learning	822
27.3	Evolution of Behavior	827
27.4	Social Behavior	831
	DATA ANALYSIS *Constructing Bar Graphs*	836
27.5	Animal Cognition	837
QUICK LAB	Human Behavior	824
INVESTIGATION	Using an Ethogram to Describe Animal Behavior	830
OPTIONS FOR INQUIRY	Lab: Pill Bug Behavior	840
	Lab: Animal Cognition	841
	Online: **Animated** BIOLOGY, Virtual Lab, WebQuest	841

MICHIGAN   STANDARDS-BASED ASSESSMENT   *B1.2C, B2.6A, B3.2B, B5.3A, B1.1f, B2.3d*   845

UNIT 8 BIOZINE   The Loss of Biodiversity   846

Technology Bioremediation
Careers Conservation Biologist

Pill bugs, *p. 840*

Online BIOLOGY
CLASSZONE.COM

VIRTUAL LAB

Chapter 24 Insects and Crime Scene Analysis

Chapter 27 Interpreting Bird Response

Animated BIOLOGY

Chapter 23 Digestive Tract Formation, Shared Body Structures

Chapter 24 Molting Cicada, Insect Metamorphosis, What Type of Arthropod?

Chapter 25 Gas Exchange in Gills, Frog Metamorphosis, What Type of Fish Is It?

Chapter 26 Bird Flight, Beak Shape and Diet

Chapter 27 Spider Mating Habits, Animal Cognition, Behavioral Costs and Benefits

WEBQUEST

Chapter 23 Parasites

Chapter 24 Field Guide

Chapter 25 Fisheries on the Brink

Chapter 26 Sea Turtles

Chapter 27 Animal Cognition

Interactive Review

REVIEW Key Concepts, Vocabulary Games, Concept Maps, Animated Biology, Online Quiz

BIOZINE

INTERNET MAGAZINE
Explore today's world of biology online at ClassZone.com.

Human Biology

Chapter 28 Human Systems and Homeostasis   850

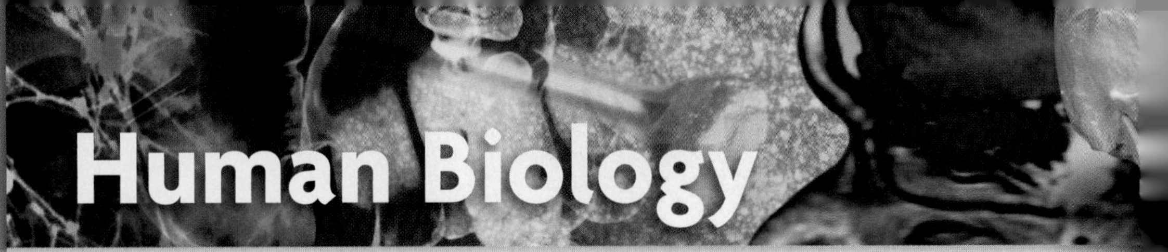

28.1	Levels of Organization	852
28.2	Mechanisms of Homeostasis	858
28.3	Interactions Among Systems	862
	DATA ANALYSIS *Interpreting Inverse Relationships*	865
QUICK LAB	Negative Feedback Loop	861
INVESTIGATION	Homeostasis and Exercise	857
OPTIONS FOR INQUIRY	Lab: Examining Human Cells	866
	Lab: Hormones and Homeostasis	867
	Online: *Animated* BIOLOGY, WebQuest, BioZine	867

MICHIGAN   STANDARDS-BASED ASSESSMENT *B1.1B, B2.3B, B2.3D, B2.5B, B2.3C, B2.3e*   871

Chapter 29 Nervous and Endocrine Systems   872

29.1	How Organ Systems Communicate	874
29.2	Neurons	876
29.3	The Senses	880
29.4	Central and Peripheral Nervous Systems	885
29.5	Brain Function and Chemistry	891
	DATA ANALYSIS *Correlation or Causation*	895
29.6	The Endocrine System and Hormones	896
QUICK LAB	The Primary Sensory Cortex	886
INVESTIGATION	The Stroop Effect	884
OPTIONS FOR INQUIRY	Lab: Reaction Time	902
	Lab: Brain-Based Disorders	903
	Online: *Animated* BIOLOGY, WebQuest, Data Analysis	903

MICHIGAN   STANDARDS-BASED ASSESSMENT *L2.p1C, B1.1B, B2.2f, B2.3d, B2.3f, B2.3g*   907

Chapter 30 Respiratory and Circulatory Systems   908

30.1	Respiratory and Circulatory Functions	910
30.2	Respiration and Gas Exchange	914
30.3	The Heart and Circulation	917
30.4	Blood Vessels and Transport	922
	DATA ANALYSIS *Forming a Null Hypothesis*	925
30.5	Blood	926
30.6	Lymphatic System	930
QUICK LAB	Blood Cells	928
INVESTIGATION	Carbon Dioxide and Exercise	921
OPTIONS FOR INQUIRY	Lab: Making and Using a Respirometer	932
	Lab: Stimuli and Heart Rate	933
	Online: *Animated* BIOLOGY, Virtual Lab, WebQuest	933

MICHIGAN   STANDARDS-BASED ASSESSMENT *B1.1E, B2.3d, B2.3e*   937

Content Expectations Focus

In Unit 9, you will learn about how your body systems work together to maintain a stable internal environment. Structures and functions of all the major body systems are addressed. This unit reinforces and extends the following standards:

Standard B2: Organization and Development of Living Systems

Standard B3: Interdependence of Living Systems and the Environment

Standard B5: Evolution and Biodiversity

Chapter 31   **Immune System and Disease**   **938**

31.1	Pathogens and Human Illness	940
31.2	Immune System	945
	DATA ANALYSIS *Identifying Experimental Design Flaws*	947
31.3	Immune Responses	950
31.4	Immunity and Technology	955
31.5	Overreactions of the Immune System	957
31.6	Diseases that Weaken the Immune System	960
QUICK LAB	How Pathogens Spread	943
INVESTIGATION	Observing Normal and Diseased Tissue	949
OPTIONS FOR INQUIRY	Lab: Modeling T Cell Activation	964
	Lab: What Is an Autoimmune Disease?	965
	Online: *Animated* BIOLOGY, WebQuest, Data Analysis	965

MICHIGAN   STANDARDS-BASED ASSESSMENT *B1.1E, B1.2h, B2.2f, B2.3C, B2.3d*   **969**

Chapter 32   **Digestive and Excretory Systems** **970**

32.1	Nutrients and Homeostasis	972
32.2	Digestive System	977
32.3	Absorption of Nutrients	982
	DATA ANALYSIS *Identifying Outliers*	985
32.4	Excretory System	986
QUICK LAB	Villi in the Small Intestine	983
INVESTIGATION	Testing a Digestive Enzyme	981
OPTIONS FOR INQUIRY	Lab: Antacid Effectiveness	992
	Lab: Digesting Milk	993
	Online: *Animated* BIOLOGY, WebQuest, Data Analysis	993

MICHIGAN   STANDARDS-BASED ASSESSMENT *B1.1B, B2.2f, B2.3C, B2.3d, B2.3e*   **997**

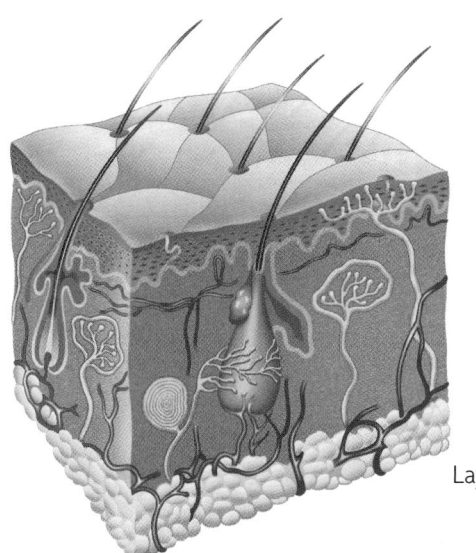

Layers of skin, *p. 883*

Online BIOLOGY
CLASSZONE.COM

VIRTUAL LAB
Chapter 30 Blood Typing

Animated BIOLOGY

Chapter 28 Human Organ Systems, Keep an Athlete Running

Chapter 29 Nerve Impulse Transmission, Reflex Arc, Diagnose a Hormone Disorder

Chapter 30 How You Breathe, How the Heart Pumps Blood, Build the Circulatory and Respiratory Systems

Chapter 31 Vaccines and Active Immunity, Destroy the Invaders

Chapter 32 Digestive System, Run the Digestive System

Chapter 33 Muscle Contraction, What Kind of Joint Is It?

Chapter 34 Embryonic Development, Human Aging, Developmental Timeline

WEBQUEST

Chapter 28 Hypothermia

Chapter 29 Drug Addiction

Chapter 30 Asthma

Chapter 31 HIV and AIDS

Chapter 32 Obesity

Chapter 33 Muscular Dystrophy

Chapter 34 Healthy Diet, Healthy Baby

Interactive Review

REVIEW Key Concepts, Vocabulary Games, Concept Maps, Animated Biology, Online Quiz

BIOZINE
INTERNET MAGAZINE
Explore today's world of biology online at ClassZone.com.

Human Biology *continued*

Chapter 33 Protection, Support, and Movement 998

33.1	Skeletal System	1000
33.2	Muscular System	1006
33.3	Integumentary System	1013
	DATA ANALYSIS *Analyzing Trends in Data*	1014
QUICK LAB	Muscles and Bones of the Skull	1011
INVESTIGATION	Muscle Fatigue	1012
OPTIONS FOR INQUIRY	Lab: Muscles in Action	1016
	Lab: Bone and Muscle Cells	1017
	Online: **Animated** BIOLOGY, WebQuest, Data Analysis	1017
MICHIGAN	STANDARDS-BASED ASSESSMENT *B1.1B, B2.3C, B2.3d, B2.3e*	1021

Chapter 34 Reproduction and Development 1022

34.1	Reproductive Anatomy	1024
34.2	Reproductive Processes	1027
34.3	Fetal Development	1034
	DATA ANALYSIS *Interpreting Graphs*	1038
34.4	Birth and Development	1040
QUICK LAB	Human Sex Cells	1031
INVESTIGATION	Hormones in the Human Menstrual Cycle	1033
OPTIONS FOR INQUIRY	Lab: Development of an Embryo	1044
	Lab: Effects of Chemicals on Reproductive Organs	1045
	Online: **Animated** BIOLOGY, WebQuest, Data Analysis	1045
MICHIGAN	STANDARDS-BASED ASSESSMENT *L4.pIA, B1.IE, B4.3A, B2.2f, B2.3C, B2.3d*	1049

Sperm and egg, *p. 1031*

UNIT 9 BIOZINE

Brain Science— We Are Wired to Learn! 1050

Technology Scanning the Brain
Careers Neuroscientist

Student Resources R1

Lab Handbook	R2
Math and Data Analysis Handbook	R14
Vocabulary Handbook	R18
Note-taking Handbook	R22
Appendices	R25
Glossary	R40
Index	R75

Biology Online

BIOZINE at ClassZone.com

This online companion to the BioZine pages in your textbook keeps you up to date with cutting-edge advances in biology. The BioZine provides the latest information about biology topics, issues, and technology. It also features news feeds, opinion polls, and much more about careers in biology.

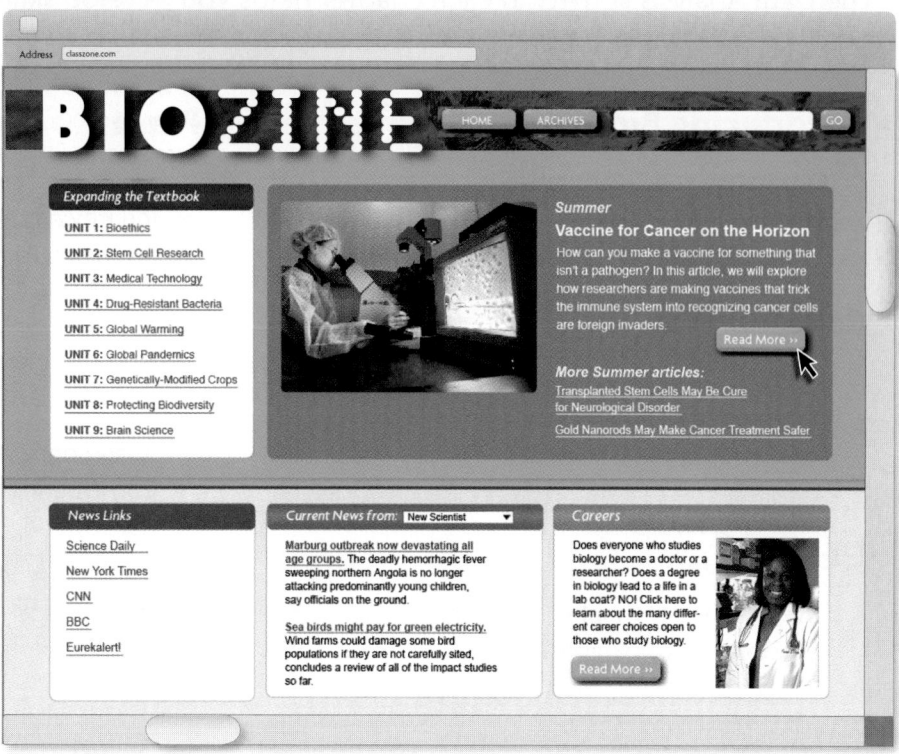

BIOZINE Features in the Pupil Edition

UNIT 1 When Knowledge and Ethics Collide   64
Technology: Genetic Testing
Careers: Geneticist

UNIT 2 Stem Cell Research—Potential Solutions, Practical Challenges   162
Technology: Somatic Cell Nuclear Transfer
Careers: Cell Biologist

UNIT 3 Medical Technology— The Genetic Forefront   292
Technology: Biochips
Careers: Cancer Geneticist

UNIT 4 Drug-Resistant Bacteria— A Global Health Issue   390
Technology: New Drug Delivery System
Careers: Evolutionary Biologist

UNIT 5 Global Warming— Changing the Planet   512
Technology: Deep Sea Sediment Coring
Careers: Oceanographer

UNIT 6 Pandemics—Is the Next One on the Way?   606
Technology: Dissecting a Virus
Careers: Epidemiologist

UNIT 7 Genetically Modified Foods— Do Potential Problems Outweigh Benefits?   690
Technology: Gene Gun
Careers: Research Engineer

UNIT 8 The Loss of Biodiversity   846
Technology: Bioremediation
Careers: Conservation Biologist

UNIT 9 Brain Science—We Are Wired to Learn!   1050
Technology: Scanning the Brain
Careers: Neuroscientist

Data Analysis

The Data Analysis activity in each chapter helps you develop skills you need to analyze data from scientific investigations.

Introducing Biology

Qualitative and Quantitative	12
Identifying Variables	49

Cells

Defining Variables	80
Interpreting Graphs	116
Constructing Data Tables	142

Genetics

Interpreting Bar Graphs	172
Constructing Bar Graphs	210
Interpreting Histograms	234
Constructing Histograms	282

Evolution

Interpreting Line Graphs	308
Identifying Patterns	339
Calculating Axes Intervals	375

Ecology

Populations and Samples	401
Reading Combination Graphs	442
Constructing Combination Graphs	461
Discrete and Continuous Data	497

Classification and Diversity

Transforming Data	529
Choosing Data Representation	546
Analyzing Experimental Design	586

Plants

Mean, Median, and Mode	628
Identifying the Importance of Repeated Trials	649
Identifying Experimental Design Flaws	674

Animals

Analyzing Scatterplots	721
Constructing Scatterplots	742
Constructing Scatterplots	770
Choosing Graphs	792
Constructing Bar Graphs	836

Human Biology

Interpreting Inverse Relationships	865
Correlation or Causation	895
Forming a Null Hypothesis	925
Identifying Experimental Design Flaws	947
Identifying Outliers	985
Analyzing Trends in Data	1014
Interpreting Graphs	1038

Jane Goodall and chimpanzee

Quick Labs

Explore key concepts and develop basic lab skills using these Quick Labs.

Introducing Biology

Life Under a Microscope Observing	22
Chemical Bonding Modeling	51

Cells

Modeling the Cell Membrane Modeling	83
Fermentation Designing Experiments	124
Cancer Observing	147

Genetics

Using a Testcross Inferring	185
Sex-Linked Inheritance Predicting	202
Replication Modeling	238
Modeling Plasmids and Restriction Enzymes Modeling	278

Evolution

Piecing Together Evidence Inferring	313
Genetic Drift Modeling	337
Geologic Clock Modeling	381

Ecology

Quadrat Sampling Sampling	399
Survivorship Curves Interpreting Data	438
Microclimates Observing	460
Modeling Biomagnification Modeling	496

Classification and Diversity

Construct a Cladogram Classifying	525
Examining Bacteria in Yogurt Observing	560
Investigating Motion in Protists Observing	579

Plants

Classifying Plants as Vascular or Nonvascular Classifying	620
Chlorophyll Fluorescence Analyzing	654
A Closer Look at Flowers Dissecting	669

Animals

Anatomy of a Clam Observing	714
Comparing Arthropods Comparing	733
Frog Development Observing	776
Comparing Feathers Observing	802
Human Behavior Observing	824

Human Biology

Negative Feedback Loop Modeling	861
The Primary Sensory Cortex Designing Experiments	886
Blood Cells Observing	928
How Pathogens Spread Modeling	943
Villi in the Small Intestine Designing Experiments	983
Muscles and Bones of the Skull Interpreting Graphics	1011
Human Sex Cells Observing	1031

Chapter Investigations

Connect content to the scientific process with design-your-own investigations or guided inquiry with real-world applications.

Unit 1 Introducing Biology

1 Manipulating Independent Variables Measuring, Modeling 18

2 Enzymatic Activity Identifying Variables, Observing, Measuring, Collecting Data, Interpreting Data 57

Unit 2 Cells

3 Diffusion Across a Membrane Designing Experiments, Analyzing Data 88

4 Rates of Photosynthesis Designing Experiments, Analyzing, Calculating, Graphing, Inferring 106

5 Mitosis in Onion Root Cells Observing, Collecting Data, Concluding 143

Unit 3 Genetics

6 Allele Combinations and Punnett Squares Calculating, Analyzing 188

7 Codominance Inferring, Predicting 208

8 Extracting DNA Observing, Analyzing 229

9 Modeling Forensics Modeling, Analyzing, Concluding, Predicting 268

Unit 4 Evolution

10 Predator-Prey Pursuit Modeling, Observing, Predicting 315

11 Natural Selection in African Swallowtails Modeling, Graphing, Interpreting Data 334

12 Radioactive Decay Analyzing, Interpreting Data, Modeling 364

Unit 5 Ecology

13 Abiotic Factors and Plant Growth Designing Experiments, Collecting Data 405

14 Modeling Predation Modeling, Analyzing Data 435

15 Winter Water Chemistry Designing Experiments, Collecting Data, Analyzing Data 475

16 Acid Rain Designing Experiments, Hypothesizing, Collecting Data, Analyzing Data 493

Chapter Investigations

Hydra (LM; magnification 20×)

Unit 6 Classification and Diversity

17 Creating a Dichotomous Key for Limpet Shells Observing, Identifying, Classifying   522

18 Leaf Print Bacteria Observing, Evaluating Outcomes   562

19 Exploring Mushroom Anatomy Observing, Predicting, Inferring   595

Unit 7 Plants

20 Habitat Clues Observing, Analyzing, Classifying   623

21 Density of Stomata Observing, Collecting Data, Analyzing Data   647

22 Seed Germination Observing, Measuring, Collecting, Interpreting Data 676

Unit 8 Animals

23 Feeding *Hydra* Observing, Collecting Data   709

24 Hatching Brine Shrimp Designing Experiments, Collecting Data, Analyzing, Predicting   739

25 Fish Reproduction Modeling   772

26 A Bird's Airframe Observing, Measuring, Analyzing   804

27 Using an Ethogram to Describe Animal Behavior Observing, Graphing Data   830

Unit 9 Human Biology

28 Homeostasis and Exercise Observing, Collecting Data   857

29 The Stroop Effect Observing, Collecting Data, Inferring   884

30 Carbon Dioxide and Exercise Observing, Measuring, Analyzing   921

31 Observing Normal and Diseased Tissue Observing, Analyzing   949

32 Testing a Digestive Enzyme Analyzing Data   981

33 Muscle Fatigue Collecting Data, Analyzing Data, Graphing   1012

34 Hormones in the Human Menstrual Cycle Graphing, Interpreting Graphs 1033

Table of Contents

Additional Inquiry Opportunities

The Options for Inquiry pages at the end of each chapter give you a choice of two hands-on labs and three online activities.

Michigan Standards for both investigations are listed in the left column.

Online Activities include:
- Virtual Labs
- Animated Biology
- WebQuests
- Data Analysis

CHAPTER 8   **OPTIONS FOR INQUIRY**

Use these inquiry-based labs and online activities to deepen your understanding of DNA.

MICHIGAN STANDARDS

B4.2g Describe the processes of replication, transcription, and translation and how they relate to each other in molecular biology.

B4.4b Explain that gene mutation in a cell can result in uncontrolled cell division called cancer. Also know that exposure of cells to certain chemicals and radiation increases mutations and thus increases the chance of cancer.

DESIGN YOUR OWN INVESTIGATION

UV Light and Skin Cancer

Exposure to the ultraviolet (UV) radiation in sunlight can lead to skin cancer caused by mutations in the DNA of skin cells. The most common type of damage from UV light is the formation of thymine dimers, or pairs of thymine bases bonded together. These mutations interfere with both replication and transcription. Sunscreens receive ratings based on the amount of protection from UV radiation they provide. The higher the sun protection factor (SPF), the more radiation the lotion blocks.

MATERIALS
- 3 different kinds of sunscreen
- sunlight or UV light box
- 12 UV beads

UV beads

SKILLS Collecting Data, Defining Operational Variables

PROBLEM Which sunscreen blocks more UV rays?

PROCEDURE
1. Choose either three different brands of sunscreen or three samples of the same brand with different SPFs.
2. Design an experiment using the UV beads to test the effectiveness of each of the sunscreens. Remember to include a control group and multiple trials.
3. Identify the independent and dependent variables and any constants in your procedure.
4. Once your teacher has approved your experimental design, carry out your procedure. Record your results in a data table.

ANALYZE AND CONCLUDE
1. **Analyze** What can you conclude about the effectiveness of the sunscreens?
2. **Apply** Identify the operational definition of your variable in this experiment.
3. **Evaluate** What was the importance of having a control in this procedure?
4. **Experimental Design** Identify sources of unavoidable error and reasons for inconsistent results.

EXTEND YOUR INVESTIGATION
Exposure to high levels of UV radiation during the teenage years is a major risk factor for skin cancer, but the cancer itself generally does not develop until many years later. Use what you have learned about mutations to propose a reasonable explanation for why skin cancer usually appears later in life.

INVESTIGATION

Modeling Transcription

During the process of transcription, a strand of mRNA that complements the base sequence on a strand of DNA is made.

SKILL Modeling

MATERIALS
- metric ruler
- 60 cm piece of wide ribbon
- scissors
- construction paper of 5 colors
- marker
- stapler

PROBLEM How can you model transcription?

PROCEDURE
1. Cut two pieces of ribbon, each about 30 cm long.
2. Choose five colors of construction paper to represent each of the bases in DNA and RNA.
3. Write out a sequence of 12 bases on a strand of DNA. Cut out corresponding squares of construction paper for each base. Use the marker to label each base.
4. Staple each base along the edge of one piece of ribbon so that they are an equal distance apart. This piece represents a single strand of DNA in the nucleus.
5. Write out the set of complementary bases that will make up the strand of mRNA. Cut out corresponding squares of construction paper for each base. Use the marker to label each base.
6. Staple each base in the correct order along the edge of the second piece of ribbon.

ANALYZE AND CONCLUDE
1. **Compare** How is your model similar to the process of transcription?
2. **Apply** Explain what happens when mRNA leaves the nucleus of a eukaryotic cell.
3. **Evaluate** How would you continue to model translation using the materials in this lab?
4. **Experimental Design** What are some limitations of the model you used in this lab?

Online BIOLOGY
CLASSZONE.COM

ANIMATED BIOLOGY
Build a Protein
Can you build a protein from a DNA code? Use enzymes, nucleotides, ribosomes, and transfer RNA to synthesize protein.

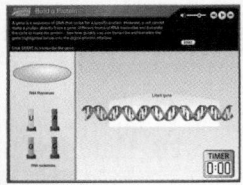

WEBQUEST
What do *Bt* corn and a fluorescent mouse have in common? They both produce proteins with genes from other organisms. In this WebQuest, you will learn more about transgenic organisms. Explore the potential benefits and risks involved when one organism is engineered to produce a protein from another organism

DATA ANALYSIS ONLINE
Erwin Chargaff showed that the proportion of certain base pairs always had a consistent relationship, although the amount of each might vary across species. This idea that A = T and C = G is known as Chargaff's rules. Graph the percentage of bases in four different species to put Chargaff's rules to the test.

Labs These additional inquiry activities offer labs of all types, including Design Your Own and dissections.

Michigan

Michigan Student Guide

Overview of Michigan Biology High
School Content Expectations   **MI34**

Michigan Biology High School Content
Expectations   **MI35**

Prerequisite Knowledge Content
Expectations   **MI47**

MICHIGAN STUDENT GUIDE

Mackinac Bridge, Michigan © Ilene MacDonald/Alamy

Overview of the Michigan Biology High School Content Expectations

MICHIGAN

Biology High School Content Expectations This page shows you how to read the Content Expectations that you will find in the beginning of each section of your textbook. Starting on page MI35, you will find a listing of all the Michigan Biology High School Content Expectations covered in this book. You will also see where the Content Expectations are addressed and examples of how they are tested.

Section Opener

You can tell which standards are covered in a section of your textbook by looking at the section opener.

The Performance Expectations listed in this box are the main standards covered in the section.

Additional Performance Expectations may also be touched upon. This is not a comprehensive list.

1.1 The Study of Life

KEY CONCEPT Biologists study life in all its forms.

MAIN IDEAS
- Earth is home to an incredible diversity of life.
- All organisms share certain characteristics.

VOCABULARY

biosphere, p. 4
biodiversity, p. 5
species, p. 5
biology, p. 5

organism, p. 5
cell, p. 5
metabolism, p. 6
DNA, p. 6

MICHIGAN STANDARDS

L2.p1A Distinguish between living and nonliving systems. (prerequisite)
L5.p1A Define a species and give examples. (prerequisite)

Connect It's a warm summer evening. Maybe you're laughing and joking while waiting to eat at a family barbecue. As you sit down for dinner, mosquitoes flying around have the same idea. But their dinner is you, not the barbecue. Probably the most attention that you pay to mosquitoes is when you take careful aim before smacking them. Biologists have a somewhat different view of mosquitoes, unless of course they are the ones being bitten. But in those times of logic and reason, a biologist can see a mosquito as just one example of the great diversity of life found on Earth.

MAIN IDEA

Earth is home to an incredible diversity of life.

In Yellowstone National Park, there are pools of hot water as acidic as vinegar. It might be difficult to believe, but those pools are also full of life. Life is found in the darkness at the deepest ocean floors and in thousands-of-years-old ice in Antarctica. Not only are living things found just about anywhere on Earth but they also come in a huge variety of shapes and sizes. Plants, for example, include tiny mosses and giant redwood trees on which moss can grow. There are massive animals such as the blue whale, which is the largest animal living on Earth. There are tiny animals such as the honeypot ant in **FIGURE 1.1**, which can store so much food for other ants that it swells to the size of a grape.

The Biosphere

All living things and all the places they are found on Earth make up the **biosphere**. Every part of the biosphere is connected, however distantly, with every other part of the biosphere. The biosphere includes land environments such as deserts, grasslands, and different types of forests. The biosphere also includes saltwater and freshwater environments, as well as portions of the atmosphere. And different types of plants, animals, and other living things are found in different areas of the biosphere. Even the inside of your nose, which is home to bacteria and fungi, is a part of the biosphere.

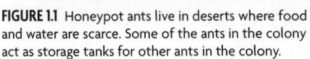

FIGURE 1.1 Honeypot ants live in deserts where food and water are scarce. Some of the ants in the colony act as storage tanks for other ants in the colony.

4 Unit 1: Introducing Biology

Michigan Merit Examination (MME) The MME is Michigan's high school test. The MME is given to eleventh grade students during the spring. The MME includes three parts. The first of these parts is a college entrance exam. The second part tests important job skills, such as reading and mathematics. The third part of the MME tests your knowledge of math, science, social studies, and persuasive writing. The science portion will take about an hour to complete, and it consists of about 65 multiple-choice questions.

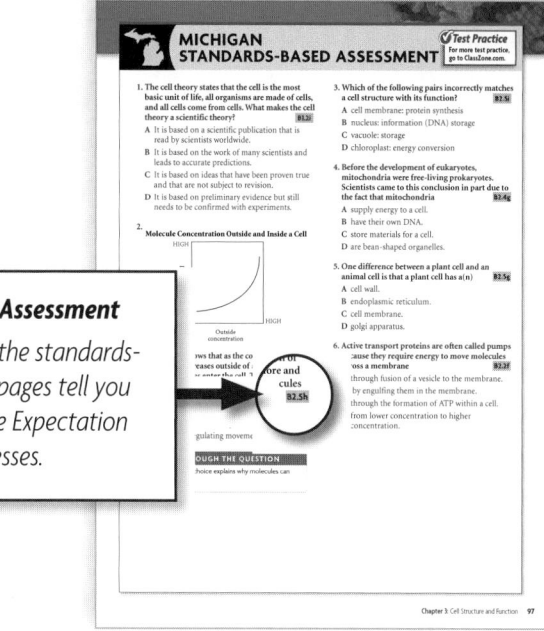

Standards-Based Assessment

Small numbers on the standards-based assessment pages tell you which Performance Expectation the question addresses.

Michigan Biology High School Content Expectations

The Michigan Board of Education divides the scientific processes and facts that you need to know into four levels. Only the second level, essential knowledge, will be covered on the MME.

- **Prerequisite Knowledge**
  These standards include information that you should have learned before reaching high school. Without this knowledge, you will have a difficult time learning the new material. These standards are listed in this student handbook.

- **Essential Knowledge (MME)**
  Essential knowledge standards cover new information in biology. This is the knowledge you will need to pass your MME. These standards are listed in this student handbook.

- **Core Knowledge and Recommended Knowledge**
  These standards include detailed information that you have not learned before. Core and recommended knowledge standards are not listed in the student handbook because you will not need them to pass your MME. However, you may need to know these standards for classroom tests, so they are listed in the sections of the textbook where they are covered.

How Do I Identify the Knowledge Level?

You can tell what level of knowledge a standard belongs to by looking at its standard number and letter(s).

- **Any uppercase letter** in a standard number means the standard covers prerequisite or essential knowledge.

- **Any lowercase letter** in a standard number means that it covers core or recommended knowledge.

MICHIGAN STUDENT GUIDE

Standard B1: Inquiry, Reflection, and Social Implications

Students will understand the nature of science and demonstrate an ability to practice scientific reasoning by applying it to the design, execution, and evaluation of scientific investigations. Students will demonstrate their understanding that scientific knowledge is gathered through various forms of direct and indirect observations and the testing of this information by methods including, but not limited to, experimentation. They will be able to distinguish between types of scientific knowledge (e.g., hypotheses, laws, theories) and become aware of areas of active research in contrast to conclusions that are part of established scientific consensus. They will use their scientific knowledge to assess the costs, risks, and benefits of technological systems as they make personal choices and participate in public policy decisions. These insights will help them analyze the role science plays in society, technology, and potential career opportunities.

WHAT IT MEANS TO YOU

Learning how to think scientifically can help you in many aspects of your life. At some point, you'll likely want to read a scientific report to decide whether a certain product is safe or to help form an opinion about an issue during an election year. Understanding how to read scientific data and being familiar with scientific processes can help you to make informed decisions.

B1.1 Scientific Inquiry

Science is a way of understanding nature. Scientific research may begin by generating new scientific questions that can be answered through replicable scientific investigations that are logically developed and conducted systematically. Scientific conclusions and explanations result from careful analysis of empirical evidence and the use of logical reasoning. Some questions in science are addressed through indirect rather than direct observation, evaluating the consistency of new evidence with results predicted by models of natural processes. Results from investigations are communicated in reports that are scrutinized through a peer review process.

B1.1A Generate new questions that can be investigated in the laboratory or field.

B1.1B Evaluate the uncertainties or validity of scientific conclusions using an understanding of sources of measurement error, the challenges of controlling variables, accuracy of data analysis, logic of argument, logic of experimental design, and/or the dependence on underlying assumptions.

B1.1C Conduct scientific investigations using appropriate tools and techniques (e.g., selecting an instrument that measures the desired quantity—length, volume, weight, time interval, temperature—with the appropriate level of precision).

B1.1D Identify patterns in data and relate them to theoretical models.

B1.1E Describe a reason for a given conclusion using evidence from an investigation.

SAMPLE QUESTION

A fish species is introduced to a park pond. Which hypothesis best describes why the population increased the first three years, but leveled off at the fourth year?   **B1.1E**

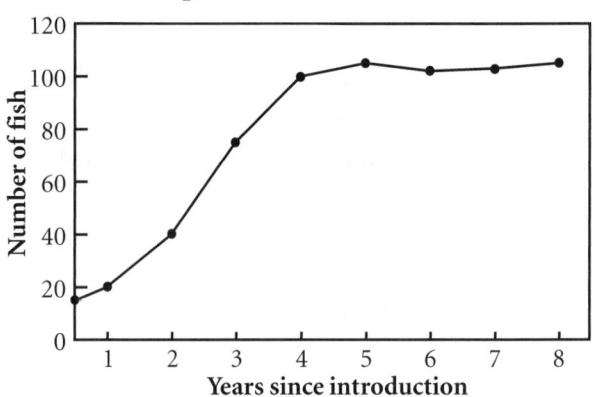

Fish Population in Birch Park Pond

A At first, the population reproduced quickly, and then it stopped reproducing at year four.

B At first, the population had many deaths, but then few deaths occurred after year four.

C At first, the population did not have any disease, but then a disease killed the entire population.

D At first, there was no competition and many resources, but by year four competition increased.

Answer: D

B1.2 Scientific Reflection and Social Implications

The integrity of the scientific process depends on scientists and citizens understanding and respecting the "Nature of Science." Openness to new ideas, skepticism, and honesty are attributes required for good scientific practice. Scientists must use logical reasoning during investigation design, analysis, conclusion, and communication. Science can produce critical insights on societal problems from a personal and local scale to a global scale. Science both aids in the development of technology and provides tools for assessing the costs, risks, and benefits of technological systems. Scientific conclusions and arguments play a role in personal choice and public policy decisions. New technology and scientific discoveries have had a major influence in shaping human history. Science and technology continue to offer diverse and significant career opportunities.

B1.2A Critique whether or not specific questions can be answered through scientific investigations.

B1.2B Identify and critique arguments about personal or societal issues based on scientific evidence.

B1.2C Develop an understanding of a scientific concept by accessing information from multiple sources. Evaluate the scientific accuracy and significance of the information.

B1.2D Evaluate scientific explanations in a peer review process or discussion format.

B1.2E Evaluate the future career and occupational prospects of science fields.

WHAT IT MEANS TO YOU

Technology is more than computers, robots, and microwaves. It also plays an important role in the study of biology and other sciences. We use technology, such as microscopes, to study life. Other kinds of technology help us to live longer. Medicines and vaccines are kinds of technology that help keep us healthy. But it's also true that technology would not exist without science. Scientists spend a lot of time researching and developing new technologies, and many of these new developments help them to carry out other types of research.

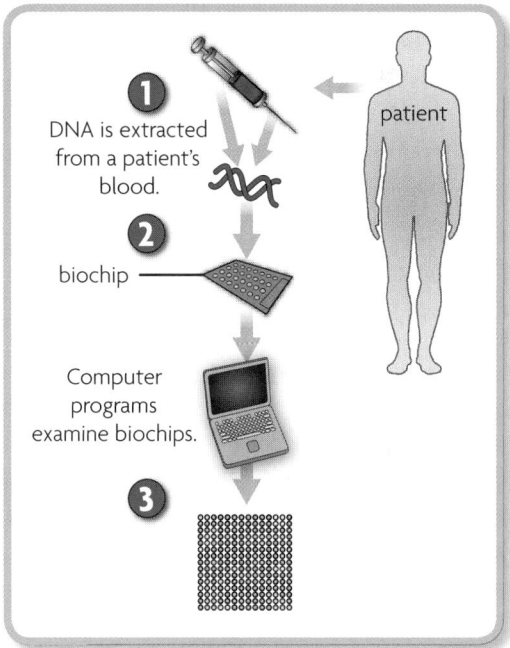

1. DNA is extracted from a patient's blood.
2. biochip
   Computer programs examine biochips.
3. patient

SAMPLE QUESTION

Students hypothesized that water pollution affects the growth of fish. In an experiment, they added the same amount of food to ponds polluted by fertilizer and industrial waste. They measured fish growth and found that most fish grow slowly in these environments. Which best explains why this experiment did not support their hypothesis? **B1.2D**

A They do not know how quickly fish grow in normal conditions.

B They found that fish grow slower when water is polluted.

C They measured the same fish each time.

D They added the same type of food to each environment.

Answer: A

MICHIGAN STUDENT GUIDE

Standard B2: Organization and Development of Living Systems

Students describe the general structure and function of cells. They can explain that all living systems are composed of cells and that organisms may be unicellular or multicellular. They understand that cells are composed of biological macromolecules and that the complex processes of the cell allow it to maintain a stable internal environment necessary to maintain life. They make predictions based on these understandings.

B2.1 Transformation of Matter and Energy in Cells

In multicellular organisms, cells are specialized to carry out specific functions such as transport, reproduction, or energy transformation.

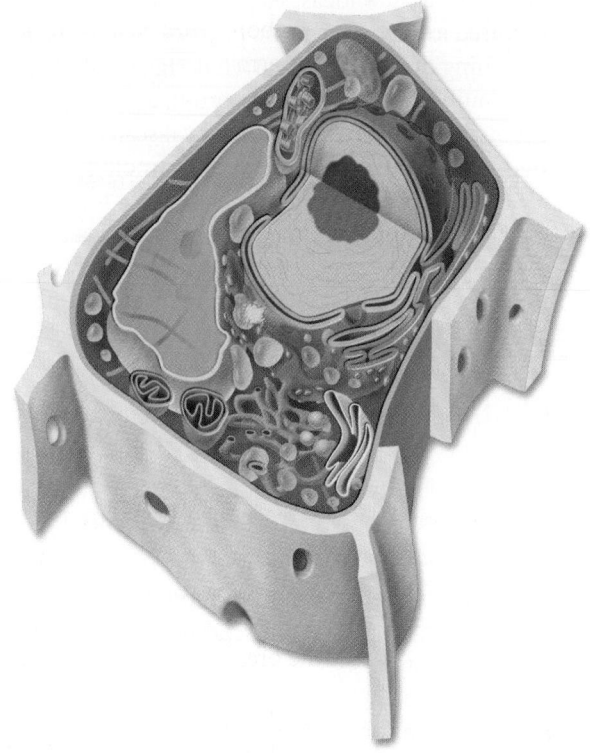

B2.1A Explain how cells transform energy (ultimately obtained from the sun) from one form to another through the processes of photosynthesis and respiration. Identify the reactants and products in the general reaction of photosynthesis.

B2.1B Compare and contrast the transformation of matter and energy during photosynthesis and respiration.

B2.1C Explain cell division, growth, and development as a consequence of an increase in cell number, cell size, and/or cell products.

SAMPLE QUESTION

The process shown in this chemical equation is photosynthesis. Which of the following supplies the energy needed for photosynthesis to occur? **B2.1A**

$$6CO_2 + 6H_2O \rightarrow \rightarrow \rightarrow \rightarrow C_6H_{12}O_6 + 6O_2$$

A sugar

B chloroplasts

C electrons

D the Sun

Answer: D

WHAT IT MEANS TO YOU

All living things are made up of one or more cells. In fact, your body is made of millions of cells that together carry out all of your life functions. As you read these words, muscle cells allow your eyes to scan the page. Nerve cells transmit chemical and electrical signals from your eyes to your brain. Your cells and the many parts of your cells allow this to happen.

STANDARD	CHAPTERS	PAGES
B2.1A	4, 5, 6	103–115, 117–125,
B2.1B		144–147, 173–176
B2.1C		

B2.2 Organic Molecules

There are four major categories of organic molecules that make up living systems: carbohydrates, fats, proteins, and nucleic acids.

B2.2A Explain how carbon can join to other carbon atoms in chains and rings to form large and complex molecules.

B2.2B Recognize the six most common elements in organic molecules (C, H, N, O, P, S).

B2.2C Describe the composition of the four major categories of organic molecules (carbohydrates, lipids, proteins, and nucleic acids).

B2.2D Explain the general structure and primary functions of the major complex organic molecules that compose living organisms.

B2.2E Describe how dehydration and hydrolysis relate to organic molecules.

B2.3 Maintaining Environmental Stability

The internal environment of living things must remain relatively constant. Many systems work together to maintain stability. Stability is challenged by changing physical, chemical, and environmental conditions as well as the presence of disease agents.

B2.3A Describe how cells function in a narrow range of physical conditions, such as temperature and pH (acidity), to perform life functions.

B2.3B Describe how the maintenance of a relatively stable internal environment is required for the continuation of life.

B2.3C Explain how stability is challenged by changing physical, chemical, and environmental conditions as well as the presence of disease agents.

STANDARD	CHAPTERS	PAGES
B2.2A B2.2B B2.2C B2.2D B2.2E	2	36–48
B2.3A	2	54–56
B2.3B	28	858–865
B2.3C	18, 28, 31	563–565, 862–865, 940–944, 957–963

MICHIGAN STUDENT GUIDE

SAMPLE QUESTION

Sugars are examples of   `B2.2A`

A lipids.
B proteins.
C nucleic acids.
D carbohydrates.

Answer: D

B2.4 Cell Specialization

In multicellular organisms, specialized cells perform specialized functions. Organs and organ systems are composed of cells and function to serve the needs of cells for food, air, and waste removal. The way in which cells function is similar in all living organisms.

B2.4A Explain that living things can be classified based on structural, embryological, and molecular (relatedness of DNA sequence) evidence.

B2.4B Describe how various organisms have developed different specializations to accomplish a particular function and yet the end result is the same (e.g., excreting nitrogenous wastes in animals, obtaining oxygen for respiration).

B2.4C Explain how different organisms accomplish the same result using different structural specializations (gills vs. lungs vs. membranes).

B2.5 Living Organism Composition

All living or once-living organisms are composed of carbohydrates, lipids, proteins, and nucleic acids. Carbohydrates and lipids contain many carbon-hydrogen bonds that also store energy.

B2.5A Recognize and explain that macromolecules such as lipids contain high energy bonds.

B2.5B Explain how major systems and processes work together in animals and plants, including relationships between organelles, cells, tissues, organs, organ systems, and organisms. Relate these to molecular functions.

B2.5C Describe how energy is transferred and transformed from the Sun to energy-rich molecules during photosynthesis.

B2.5D Describe how individual cells break down energy-rich molecules to provide energy for cell functions.

STANDARD	CHAPTERS	PAGES
B2.4A	17	518–537
B2.4B	23, 24, 25, 26	696–704, 740–741, 763–767, 788–805
B2.4C		
B2.5A	2	44–53
B2.5B	28	852–857
B2.5C	2, 4, 12, 13	50–53, 100–112, 372–375, 406–407
B2.5D	4	100–102

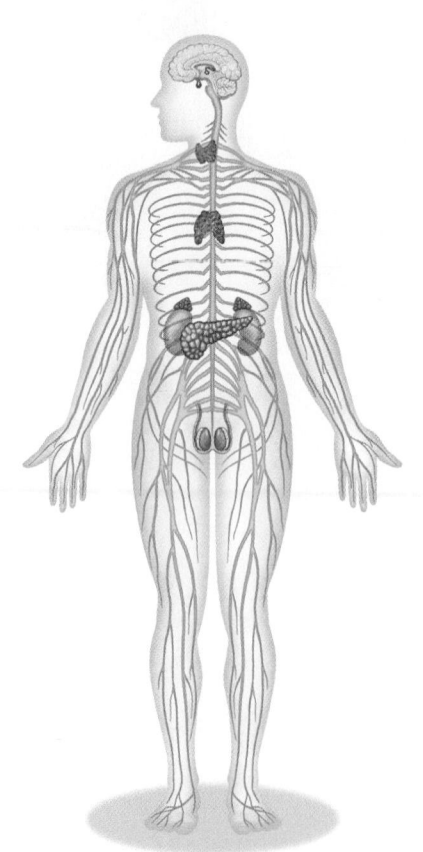

SAMPLE QUESTION

Eukaryotes can be single-celled or multicellular. Prokaryotes, however, can only be single-celled. Which statement explains another difference between prokaryotes and eukaryotes? **B2.5B**

A All eukaryotes have more than one million base pairs, while prokaryotes have significantly fewer base pairs.

B All eukaryotes reproduce sexually, while prokaryotes reproduce asexually.

C All eukaryotes undergo cellular respiration, while prokaryotes undergo photosynthesis.

D All eukaryotes have DNA enclosed in nuclei, while prokaryotes have their DNA free-floating in the cytoplasm.

Answer: D

Standard B3: Interdependence of Living Systems and the Environment

Students describe the processes of photosynthesis and cellular respiration and how energy is transferred through food webs. They recognize and analyze the consequences of the dependence of organisms on environmental resources and the interdependence of organisms in ecosystems.

B3.1 Photosynthesis and Respiration

Organisms acquire their energy directly or indirectly from sunlight. Plants capture the Sun's energy and use it to convert carbon dioxide and water to sugar and oxygen through the process of photosynthesis. Through the process of cellular respiration, animals are able to release the energy stored in the molecules produced by plants and use it for cellular processes, producing carbon dioxide and water.

B3.1A Describe how organisms acquire energy directly or indirectly from sunlight.

B3.1B Illustrate and describe the energy conversions that occur during photosynthesis and respiration.

B3.1C Recognize the equations for photosynthesis and respiration and identify the reactants and products for both.

B3.1D Explain how living organisms gain and use mass through the processes of photosynthesis and respiration.

WHAT IT MEANS TO YOU

All living things need energy to survive. Some living things, such as plants, use sunlight or chemicals to make sugars that store chemical energy. Other living things, such as you, get energy when you eat plants or other animals. Cells in your body break down molecules in the food you eat. These food molecules give you energy.

STANDARD	CHAPTERS	PAGES
B3.1A	4, 13	103–125 406–407,
B3.1B		417–419
B3.1C		
B3.1D		

SAMPLE QUESTION

Which of the following is necessary in order for plants to undergo photosynthesis? **B3.1A**

A nitrogen

B ATP

C carbon dioxide

D oxygen

Answer: C

B3.2 Ecosystems

The chemical elements that make up the molecules of living things pass through food webs and are combined and recombined in different ways. At each link in an ecosystem, some energy is stored in newly made structures, but much is dissipated into the environment as heat. Continual input of energy from sunlight keeps the process going.

B3.2A Identify how energy is stored in an ecosystem.

B3.2B Describe energy transfer through an ecosystem, accounting for energy lost to the environment as heat.

B3.2C Draw the flow of energy through an ecosystem. Predict changes in the food web when one or more organisms are removed.

STANDARD	CHAPTERS	PAGES
B3.2A	13	406–407, 417–419
B3.2B		
B3.2C	13	408–411
B3.3A	13	408–411

B3.3 Element Recombination

As matter cycles and energy flows through different levels of organization of living systems—cells, organs, organisms, and communities—and between living systems and the physical environment, chemical elements are recombined in different ways. Each recombination results in storage and dissipation of energy into the environment as heat. Matter and energy are conserved in each change.

B3.3A Use a food web to identify and distinguish producers, consumers, and decomposers and explain the transfer of energy through trophic levels.

energy lost

energy transferred

SAMPLE QUESTION

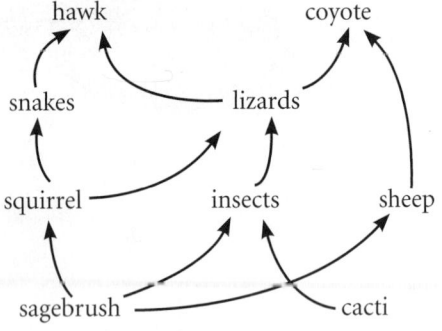

This food web shows the relationships between organisms in an ecosystem. In this food web, which term best describes the role of the snake? **B3.3A**

A producer

B consumer

C herbivore

D decomposer

Answer: B

B3.4 Changes in Ecosystems

Although the interrelationships and interdependence of organisms may generate biological communities in ecosystems that are stable for hundreds or thousands of years, ecosystems always change when climate changes or when one or more new species appear as a result of migration or local evolution. The impact of the human species has major consequences for other species.

B3.4A Describe ecosystem stability. Understand that if a disaster such as flood or fire occurs, the damaged ecosystem is likely to recover in stages of succession that eventually result in a system similar to the original one.

B3.4B Recognize and describe that a great diversity of species increases the chance that at least some living organisms will survive in the face of cataclysmic changes in the environment.

B3.4C Examine the negative impact of human activities.

STANDARD	CHAPTERS	PAGES
B3.4A	14	445–447
B3.4B	16	498–501
B3.4C	16	484–505
B3.5A	14	436–441
B3.5B		
B3.5C		

B3.5 Populations

Populations of living things increase and decrease in size as they interact with other populations and with the environment. The rate of change is dependent upon relative birth and death rates.

B3.5A Graph changes in population growth, given a data table.

B3.5B Explain the influences that affect population growth.

B3.5C Predict the consequences of an invading organism on the survival of other organisms.

SAMPLE QUESTION

Which situation would most efficiently increase the size of a field mouse population?   B3.5B

A decreased death rates and emigration

B decreased death rates and immigration

C increased death rates and immigration

D increased death rates and emigration

Answer: B

MICHIGAN STUDENT GUIDE

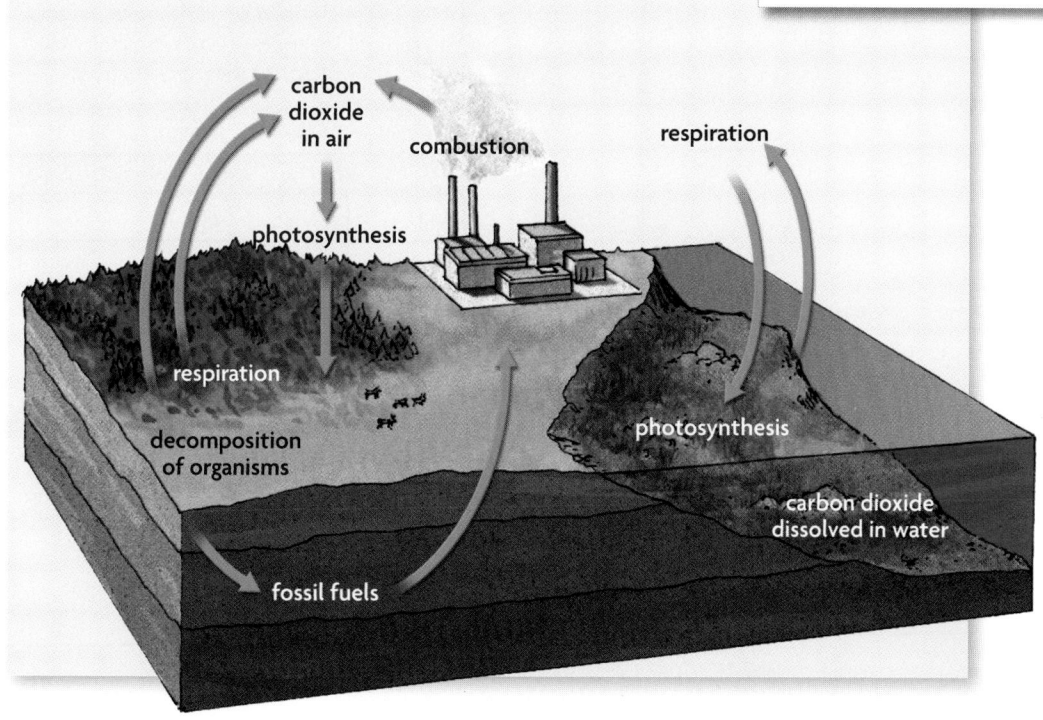

Standard B4: Genetics

Students recognize that the specific genetic instructions for any organism are contained within genes composed of DNA molecules located in chromosomes. They explain the mechanism for the direct production of specific proteins based on inherited DNA. Students diagram how occasional modifications in genes and the random distribution of genes from each parent provide genetic variation and become the raw material for evolution.

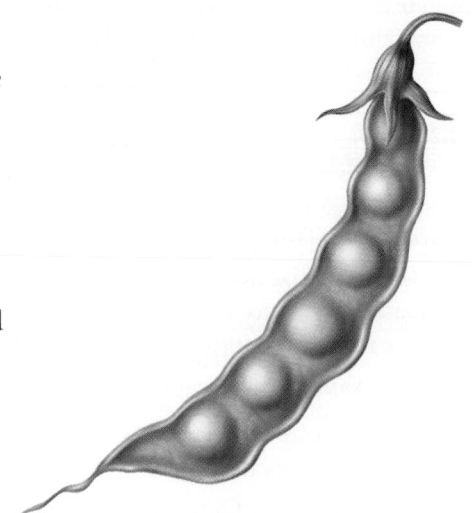

B4.1 Genetics and Inherited Traits

Hereditary information is contained in genes, located in the chromosomes of each cell. Cells contain many thousands of different genes. One or many genes can determine an inherited trait of an individual, and a single gene can influence more than one trait. Before a cell divides, this genetic information must be copied and apportioned evenly into the daughter cells.

B4.1A Draw and label a homologous chromosome pair with heterozygous alleles highlighting a particular gene location.

B4.1B Explain that the information passed from parents to offspring is transmitted by means of genes that are coded in DNA molecules. These genes contain the information for the production of proteins.

SAMPLE QUESTION

A pea plant has a genotype of RRYy. Female gametes, or egg cells, are produced through meiosis. What are the possible genetic combinations that could be present in a single egg produced by this plant? **B4.1B**

A *RR* only

B *Yy* only

C *Ry* and *rY*

D *RY* and *Ry*

Answer: D

WHAT IT MEANS TO YOU

If the DNA in one of your cells were stretched out and lined up end-to-end, it would measure longer than two meters. When you were just one little cell, you had a complete set of DNA. You got half of your DNA from your mother and half from your father. Because you share much of the same DNA, you might look similar to your parents. You can use technology and probability to explain how offspring inherit traits from their parents.

STANDARD	CHAPTERS	PAGES
B4.1A	6	180–182
B4.1B	8	248–251

B4.2 DNA

The genetic information encoded in DNA molecules provides instructions for assembling protein molecules. Genes are segments of DNA molecules. Inserting, deleting, or substituting DNA segments can alter genes. An altered gene may be passed on to every cell that develops from it. The resulting features may help, harm, or have little or no effect on the offspring's success in its environment.

B4.2A Show that when mutations occur in sex cells, they can be passed on to offspring (inherited mutations), but if they occur in other cells, they can be passed on to descendant cells only (noninherited mutations).

B4.2B Recognize that every species has its own characteristic DNA sequence.

B4.2C Describe the structure and function of DNA.

B4.2D Predict the consequences that changes in the DNA composition of particular genes may have on an organism (e.g., sickle cell anemia, other).

B4.2E Propose possible effects (on the genes) of exposing an organism to radiation and toxic chemicals.

STANDARD	CHAPTERS	PAGES
B4.2A	8	252–255
B4.2B	8, 9	226–229, 272–273
B4.2C	8, 9	226–242, 269–271
B4.2D	8, 9	252–255, 275–279
B4.2E	5	144–147
B4.3A B4.3B	5, 6, 7, 22	134–141, 168–176, 189–191, 200–203, 664–667
B4.3C	11	328–329

B4.3 Cell Division — Mitosis and Meiosis

Sorting and recombination of genes in sexual reproduction results in a great variety of possible gene combinations from the offspring of any two parents.

B4.3A Compare and contrast the processes of cell division (mitosis and meiosis), particularly as those processes relate to production of new cells and to passing on genetic information between generations.

B4.3B Explain why only mutations occurring in gametes (sex cells) can be passed on to offspring.

B4.3C Explain how it might be possible to identify genetic defects from just a karyotype of a few cells.

SAMPLE QUESTION

Genes that are located on different parts of homologous chromosomes can end up in the same gamete due to   B4.3

A genetic linkage.

B independent assortment.

C crossing over.

D external fertilization.

Answer: B

MICHIGAN STUDENT GUIDE

Standard B5: Evolution and Biodiversity

Students recognize that evolution is the result of genetic changes that occur in constantly changing environments. They can explain that modern evolution includes both the concepts of common descent and natural selection. They illustrate how the consequences of natural selection and differential reproduction have led to the great biodiversity on Earth.

B5.1 Theory of Evolution

The theory of evolution provides a scientific explanation for the history of life on Earth as depicted in the fossil record and in the similarities evident within the diversity of existing organisms.

B5.1A Summarize the major concepts of natural selection (differential survival and reproduction of chance inherited variants, depending on environmental conditions).

B5.1B Describe how natural selection provides a mechanism for evolution.

B5.3 Natural Selection

Evolution is the consequence of natural selection, the interactions of (1) the potential for a population to increase its numbers, (2) the genetic variability of offspring due to mutation and recombination of genes, (3) a finite supply of the resources required for life, and (4) the ensuing selection from environmental pressure of those organisms better able to survive and leave offspring.

B5.3A Explain how natural selection acts on individuals, but it is populations that evolve. Relate genetic mutations and genetic variety produced by sexual reproduction to diversity within a given population.

B5.3B Describe the role of geographic isolation in speciation.

B4.3C Give examples of ways in which genetic variation and environmental factors are causes of evolution and the diversity of organisms.

WHAT IT MEANS TO YOU

All of the living things in your environment have adaptations that arose through natural selection. The wings of birds, the compound eyes of ants, and the shapes of leaves are all traits that are advantageous in certain environments. As traits are selected for, and others are selected against, the genetic make-up of species changes over time.

STANDARD	CHAPTERS	PAGES
B5.1A	10	304–307
B5.1B	10, 29	304–307, 880–884
B5.3A	11, 24	330–343, 747–749
B5.3B B5.3C	11	328–338, 344–346

SAMPLE QUESTION

Herbicides are used to keep weeds from growing in farm fields and gardens. After many years, farmers might find that a weed species is no longer affected by a particular herbicide. This occurred because the herbicide **B4.3C**

A killed most of the plants in the population.

B caused mutations in the plant species' gene pool.

C caused another plant species to go extinct.

D selected for plants that were able to survive and reproduce.

Answer: D

Prerequisite Knowledge Content Expectations

In order to pass your MME, you'll need to know the biology concepts taught this year. You will also need to remember science concepts you learned before this year. Here is a list of prerequisite standards that you will be tested on when you take the MME.

L2.p1 Cells

All organisms are composed of cells, from just one cell to many cells. Water accounts for more than two-thirds of the weight of a cell, which gives cells many of their properties. In multicellular organisms, specialized cells perform specialized functions. Organs and organ systems are composed of cells and function to serve the needs of organisms for food, air, and waste removal. The way in which cells function is similar in all living organisms.

L2.p1A Distinguish between living and nonliving systems.

L2.p1B Explain the importance of both water and the element carbon to cells.

L2.p1C Describe growth and development in terms of increase in cell number, cell size, and/or cell products.

L2.p1D Explain how the systems in a multicellular organism work together to support the organism.

L2.p1E Compare and contrast how different organisms accomplish similar functions (e.g., obtain oxygen for respiration, and excrete waste).

L2.p2 Cell Function

Cells carry out the many functions needed to sustain life. They grow and divide, thereby producing more cells. Food is used to provide energy for the work that cells do and is a source of the molecular building blocks from which needed materials are assembled.

L2.p2A Describe how organisms sustain life by obtaining, transporting, transforming, releasing, and eliminating matter and energy.

L2.p2B Describe the effect of limiting food to developing cells.

L2.p3 Plants as Producers

Plants are producers; they use the energy from light to make sugar molecules from the atoms of carbon dioxide and water. Plants use these sugars, along with minerals from the soil, to form fats, proteins, and carbohydrates. This food can be used immediately, incorporated into the cells of a plant as the plant grows, or stored for later use.

L2.p3A Explain the significance of carbon in organic molecules.

L2.p3B Explain the origins of plant mass.

L2.p3C Predict what would happen to plants growing in low carbon dioxide atmospheres.

L2.p3D Explain how the roots of specific plants grow.

L2.p4 Animals as Consumers

All animals, including humans, are consumers; they obtain food by eating other organisms or their products. Consumers break down the structures of the organisms they eat to obtain the materials they need to grow and function. Decomposers, including bacteria and fungi, use dead organisms or their products for food.

L2.p4A Classify different organisms based on how they obtain energy for growth and development.

L2.p4B Explain how an organism obtains energy from the food it consumes.

L2.p5 Common Elements

Living systems are made of complex molecules that consist mostly of a few elements, especially carbon, hydrogen, oxygen, nitrogen, and phosphorous.

L2.p5A Recognize the six most common elements in organic molecules (C, H, N, O, P, S).

L2.p5B Identify the most common complex molecules that make up living organisms.

L2.p5C Predict what would happen if essential elements were withheld from developing cells.

L3.p1 Populations, Communities, and Ecosystems

Organisms of one species form a population. Populations of different organisms interact and form communities. Living communities and the nonliving factors that interact with them form ecosystems.

L3.p1A Provide examples of a population, community, and ecosystem.

L3.p2 Relationships Among Organisms

Two types of organisms may interact with one another in several ways; they may be in a producer/consumer, predator/prey, or parasite/host relationship. Or one organism may scavenge or decompose another. Relationships may be competitive or mutually beneficial. Some species have become so adapted to each other that neither could survive without the other.

L3.p2A Describe common relationships among organisms and provide examples of producer/consumer, predator/prey, or parasite/host relationship.

L3.p2B Describe common ecological relationships between and among species and their environments (competition, territory, carrying capacity, natural balance, population, dependence, survival, and other biotic and abiotic factors).

L3.p2C Describe the role of decomposers in the transfer of energy in an ecosystem.

L3.p2D Explain how two organisms can be mutually beneficial and how that can lead to interdependency.

L3.p3 Factors Influencing Ecosystems

The number of organisms and populations an ecosystem can support depends on the biotic resources available and abiotic factors, such as quantity of light and water, range of temperatures, and soil composition.

L3.p3A Identify the factors in an ecosystem that influence fluctuations in population size.

L3.p3B Distinguish between the living (biotic) and nonliving (abiotic) components of an ecosystem.

L3.p3C Explain how biotic and abiotic factors cycle in an ecosystem (water, carbon, oxygen, and nitrogen).

L3.p3D Predict how changes in one population might affect other populations based upon their relationships in a food web.

L3.p4 Human Impact on Ecosystems

All organisms cause changes in their environments. Some of these changes are detrimental, whereas others are beneficial.

L3.p4A Recognize that, and describe how, human beings are part of Earth's ecosystems. Note that human activities can deliberately or inadvertently alter the equilibrium in ecosystems.

L4.p1 Reproduction

Reproduction is a characteristic of all living systems; because no individual organism lives forever, reproduction is essential to the continuation of every species. Some organisms reproduce asexually. Other organisms reproduce sexually.

L4.p1A Compare and contrast the differences between sexual and asexual reproduction.

L4.p1B Discuss the advantages and disadvantages of sexual vs. asexual reproduction.

L4.p2 Heredity and Environment

The characteristics of organisms are influenced by heredity and environment. For some characteristics, inheritance is more important. For other characteristics, interactions with the environment are more important.

L4.p2A Explain that the traits of an individual are influenced by both the environment and the genetics of the individual. Acquired traits are not inherited; only genetic traits are inherited.

L5.p1 Survival and Extinction

Individual organisms with certain traits in particular environments are more likely than others to survive and have offspring. When an environment changes, the advantage or disadvantage of characteristics can change. Extinction of a species occurs when the environment changes and the characteristics of a species are insufficient to allow survival. Fossils indicate that many organisms that lived long ago are extinct. Extinction of species is common; most of the species that have lived on the Earth no longer exist.

L5.p1A Define a species and give examples.

L5.p1B Define a population and identify local populations.

L5.p1C Explain how extinction removes genes from the gene pool.

L5.p1D Explain the importance of the fossil record.

L5.p2 Classification

Similarities among organisms are found in anatomical features, which can be used to infer the degree of relatedness among organisms. In classifying organisms, biologists consider details of internal and external structures to be more important than behavior or general appearance.

L5.p2A Explain, with examples, that ecology studies the varieties and interactions of living things across space while evolution studies the varieties and interactions of living things across time.

UNIT 1

Introducing Biology

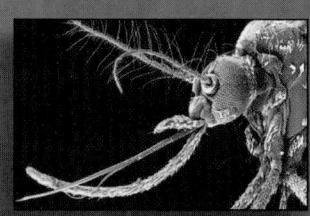

CHAPTER 1
Biology in the 21st Century   2

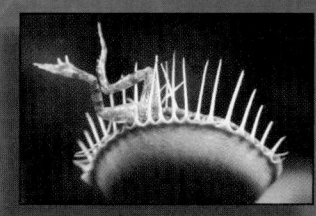

CHAPTER 2
Chemistry of Life   34

INTERNET MAGAZINE
When Knowledge and Ethics Collide   64
  TECHNOLOGY Genetic Testing
  CAREER Geneticist

CHAPTER

1 Biology in the 21st Century

KEY CONCEPTS

1.1 The Study of Life
Biologists study life in all its forms.

1.2 Unifying Themes of Biology
Unifying themes connect concepts from many fields of biology.

1.3 Scientific Thinking and Processes
Science is a way of thinking, questioning, and gathering evidence.

1.4 Biologists' Tools and Technology
Technology continually changes the way biologists work.

1.5 Biology and Your Future
Understanding biology can help you make informed decisions.

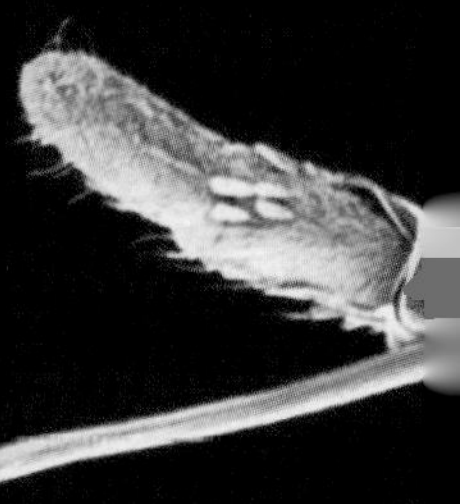

Online BIOLOGY CLASSZONE.COM

Animated BIOLOGY

View animated chapter concepts.
• Cells Through Different Microscopes
• Experimental Design

BIOZINE

Keep current with biology news.
• Featured stories
• News feeds
• Careers

 RESOURCE CENTER

Get more information on
• Biodiversity
• Scientific Tools and Technology

colored SEM; magnification 200×

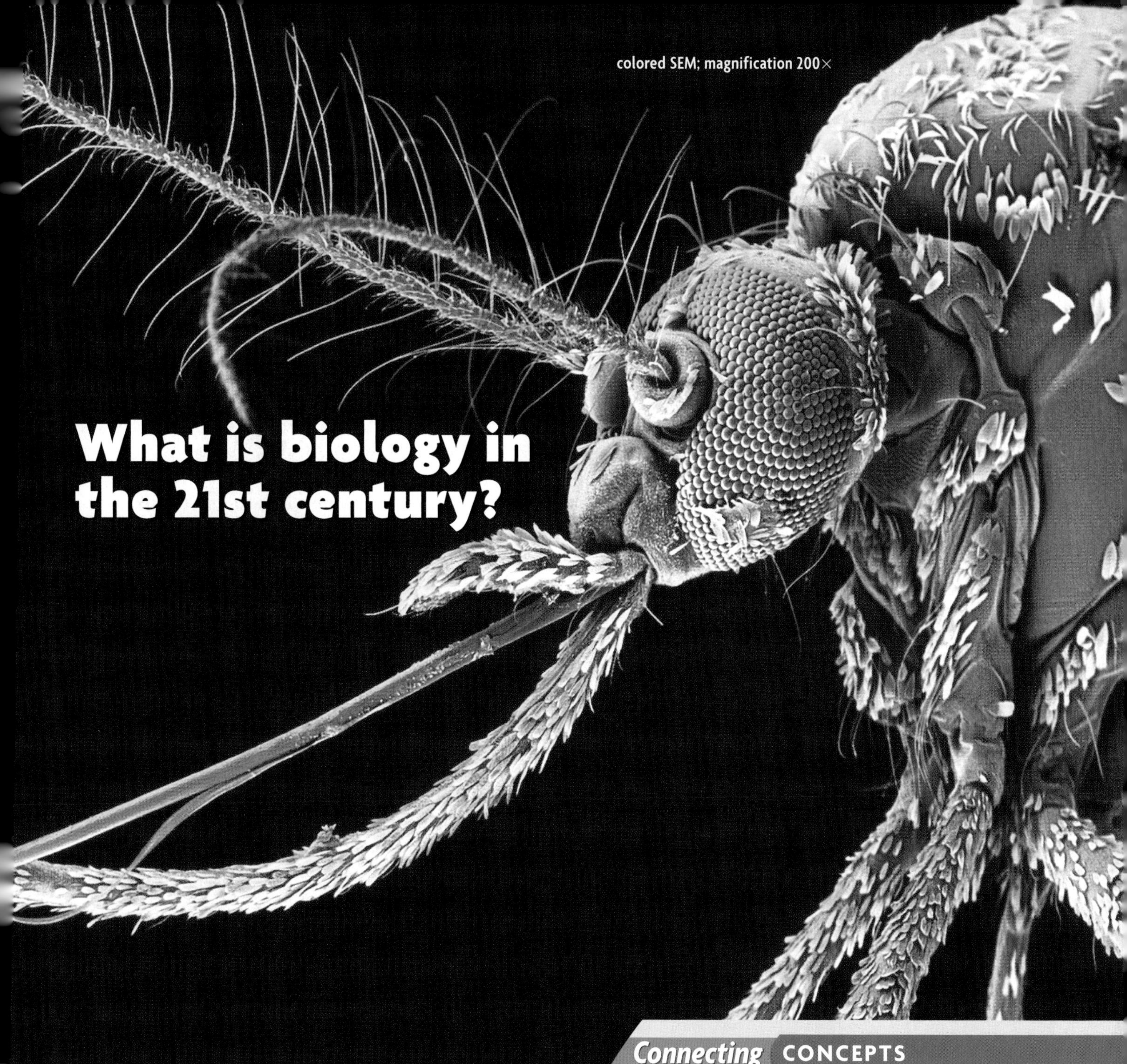

What is biology in the 21st century?

Biology has always been the study of life, but our knowledge of living things and our use of technology to study them is always changing. For example, the above image of a yellow fever mosquito was made with a scanning electron microscope. Why bother with a mosquito? Because even in the 21st century, mosquitoes can carry viruses for which we have no defense.

Connecting CONCEPTS

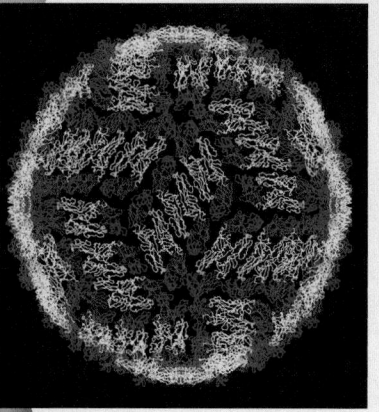

Computer Models Scientists use computer models, such as the virus model shown in the image to the left, to study things that could not otherwise be investigated. For example, the chemical structure of a virus's outer coat cannot be seen, even with an electron microscope. But by using computer models, scientists can better understand viruses and how to attack them.

1.1 The Study of Life

KEY CONCEPT Biologists study life in all its forms.

▶ MAIN IDEAS

- Earth is home to an incredible diversity of life.
- All organisms share certain characteristics.

VOCABULARY

biosphere, p. 4
biodiversity, p. 5
species, p. 5
biology, p. 5

organism, p. 5
cell, p. 5
metabolism, p. 6
DNA, p. 6

MICHIGAN STANDARDS

L2.p1A Distinguish between living and nonliving systems. (prerequisite)
L5.p1A Define a species and give examples. (prerequisite)

Connect It's a warm summer evening. Maybe you're laughing and joking while waiting to eat at a family barbecue. As you sit down for dinner, mosquitoes flying around have the same idea. But their dinner is you, not the barbecue. Probably the most attention that you pay to mosquitoes is when you take careful aim before smacking them. Biologists have a somewhat different view of mosquitoes, unless of course they are the ones being bitten. But in those times of logic and reason, a biologist can see a mosquito as just one example of the great diversity of life found on Earth.

▶ MAIN IDEA

Earth is home to an incredible diversity of life.

In Yellowstone National Park, there are pools of hot water as acidic as vinegar. It might be difficult to believe, but those pools are also full of life. Life is found in the darkness at the deepest ocean floors and in thousands-of-years-old ice in Antarctica. Not only are living things found just about anywhere on Earth but they also come in a huge variety of shapes and sizes. Plants, for example, include tiny mosses and giant redwood trees on which moss can grow. There are massive animals such as the blue whale, which is the largest animal living on Earth. There are tiny animals such as the honeypot ant in **FIGURE 1.1**, which can store so much food for other ants that it swells to the size of a grape.

The Biosphere

All living things and all the places they are found on Earth make up the **biosphere.** Every part of the biosphere is connected, however distantly, with every other part of the biosphere. The biosphere includes land environments such as deserts, grasslands, and different types of forests. The biosphere also includes saltwater and freshwater environments, as well as portions of the atmosphere. And different types of plants, animals, and other living things are found in different areas of the biosphere. Even the inside of your nose, which is home to bacteria and fungi, is a part of the biosphere.

FIGURE 1.1 Honeypot ants live in deserts where food and water are scarce. Some of the ants in the colony act as storage tanks for other ants in the colony.

Biodiversity

Across the biosphere, the variety of life is called biological diversity, or **biodiversity.** Biodiversity generally increases from Earth's poles to the equator. This means that greater biodiversity is found in warmer areas. Why is biodiversity greater closer to the equator? More living things are able to survive in consistently warm temperatures than in areas that have large temperature changes during a year. Because more living things, especially plants, can survive in warm areas, those areas provide a larger, more consistent food supply for more species.

VISUAL VOCAB

Across the **biosphere,** the variety of life is called **biodiversity.**

Biodiversity is **greater** closer to the equator.

biosphere = everywhere life exists

There are several different ways *species* can be defined. One definition of **species** is a particular type of living things that can reproduce by interbreeding among themselves. About 2 million different living species have been identified, but biologists estimate that tens of millions of species remain to be discovered. Over half of the known species are insects, but no one knows how many insect species actually exist.

Every year, biologists discover about 10,000 new species. In contrast, some scientists estimate that over 50,000 species die out, or become extinct, every year. Occasionally, however, a species thought to be extinct is found again. For example, the ivory-billed woodpecker was thought to have become extinct in 1944, but a team of scientists reported seeing it in Arkansas in 2004.

Apply Describe biodiversity in terms of species.

TAKING NOTES

Use a two-column chart to help you summarize vocabulary terms and concepts.

term or concept	meaning

⦿ MAIN IDEA
All organisms share certain characteristics.

Biology is the scientific study of all forms of life, or all types of organisms. An **organism** is any individual living thing. All organisms on Earth share certain characteristics, but an actual definition of life is not simple. Why? The categories of living and nonliving are constructed by humans, and they are not perfect. For example, some things, such as viruses, fall into a middle range between living and nonliving. They show some, but not all, of the characteristics of living things.

Cells All organisms are made up of one or more cells. A **cell** is the basic unit of life. In fact, microscopic, single-celled organisms are the most common forms of life on Earth. A single-celled, or unicellular, organism carries out all of the functions of life, just as you do. Larger organisms that you see every day are made of many cells, and are called multicellular organisms. Different types of cells in a multicellular organism have specialized functions, as shown in **FIGURE 1.2**. Your muscle cells contract and relax, your stomach cells secrete digestive juices, and your brain cells interpret sensory information. Together, specialized cells make you a complete organism.

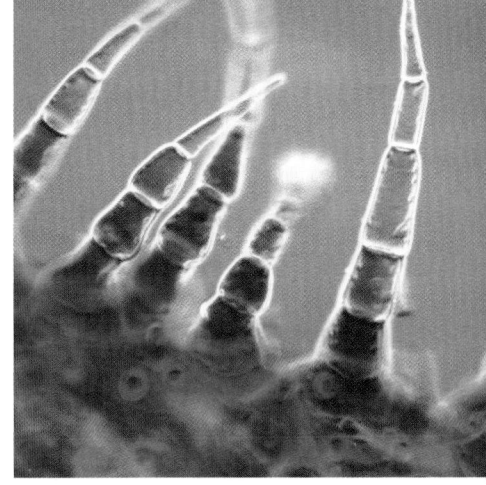

FIGURE 1.2 Cells can work together in specialized structures, such as these leaf hairs that protect a leaf from insects. (LM; magnification 700×)

FIGURE 1.3 Reproductive strategies differ among species. The male gold-specs jawfish protects unhatched eggs by holding them in his mouth.

Connecting CONCEPTS

Cells and Energy You will read in **Chapter 4** about different processes used by cells to capture and release energy—photosynthesis, chemosynthesis, and cellular respiration.

Need for energy All organisms need a source of energy for their life processes. Energy is the ability to cause a change or to do work. The form of energy used by all living things, from bacteria to ferrets to ferns, is chemical energy. Some organisms use chemicals from their environment to make their own source of chemical energy. Some organisms, such as plants, algae, and some bacteria, absorb energy from sunlight and store some of it in chemicals that can be used later as a source of energy. Animals get their source of energy by eating other organisms. In all organisms, energy is important for **metabolism,** or all of the chemical processes that build up or break down materials.

Response to environment All organisms must react to their environment to survive. Light, temperature, and touch are just a few of the physical factors, called stimuli, to which organisms must respond. Think about how you respond to light when you leave a dimly lit room and go into bright sunlight. One of your body's responses is to contract the pupils of your eyes. Your behavior might also change. You might put on sunglasses or raise your hand to shade your eyes. Other organisms also respond to changes in light. For example, plants grow toward light. Some fungi need light to form the structures that you know as mushrooms.

Reproduction and development Members of a species must have the ability to produce new individuals, or reproduce. When organisms reproduce, they pass their genetic material to their offspring. In all organisms, the genetic material is a molecule called deoxyribonucleic acid (dee-AHK-see-RY-boh-noo-KLEE-ihk), or **DNA.**

Single-celled organisms can reproduce when one cell divides into two cells. Both new cells have genetic information that is identical to the original cell. Many multicellular organisms, such as the gold-specs jawfish in **FIGURE 1.3,** reproduce by combining the genetic information from two parents. In both cases, the instructions for growth and development of organisms, from bacteria to people, are carried by the same chemicals— DNA and ribonucleic acid (RNA). The process of development allows organisms to mature and gain the ability to reproduce.

Summarize What characteristics are shared by all living things?

1.1 ASSESSMENT

ONLINE QUIZ
ClassZone.com

REVIEWING ▶ MAIN IDEAS

1. How are **species** related to the concept of **biodiversity**?

2. How do the characteristics of living things contribute to an **organism's** survival?

CRITICAL THINKING

3. **Apply** Describe the relationship between **cells** and organisms.

4. **Synthesize** How does biodiversity depend on a species' ability to reproduce?

Connecting CONCEPTS

5. **Human Biology** You respond automatically to many different stimuli, such as loud noises. Why might a quick response to a sound be important?

1.2 Unifying Themes of Biology

KEY CONCEPT Unifying themes connect concepts from many fields of biology.

▶ MAIN IDEAS

- All levels of life have systems of related parts.
- Structure and function are related in biology.
- Organisms must maintain homeostasis to survive in diverse environments.
- Evolution explains the unity and diversity of life.

VOCABULARY

system, p. 7
ecosystem, p. 7
homeostasis, p. 9
evolution, p. 10
adaptation, p. 10

MICHIGAN STANDARDS

B1.1i Distinguish between scientific explanations that are regarded as current scientific consensus and the emerging questions that active researchers investigate.

L2.p1D Explain how the systems in a multicellular organism work together to support the organism. (prerequisite)

Connect What do you think about when you hear the term *theme*? Maybe you think about the music at the start of your favorite TV show. Maybe you think about the colors and organization of a computer desktop. In both cases, that theme shows up over and over again. In biology, you will see something similar. That is, some concepts come up time after time, even in topics that might seem to be completely unrelated. Understanding these themes, or concepts, can help you to connect the different areas of biology.

▶ MAIN IDEA
All levels of life have systems of related parts.

Think about the separate parts of a car—tires, engine, seats, and so on. Even if you have a complete set of car parts, you might not have a functioning car. Only when all of the parts that make up a car are put together in the correct way do you have a working car. A car is a system. A **system** is an organized group of related parts that interact to form a whole. Like any other system, a car's characteristics come from the arrangement and interaction of its parts.

Systems exist on all scales in biology, from molecules that cannot be seen, to cells that can be seen only with a microscope, to the entire biosphere. In just one heart muscle cell, for example, many chemicals and processes interact in a precise way so that the cell has energy to do its work. Moving up a level, heart muscle, valves, arteries, and veins help form a system in your body—the circulatory system.

Two organisms that interact can also be a system, as you can see in **FIGURE 1.4.** On a larger scale, you are a part of a biological system—an ecosystem—that has living and nonliving parts. An **ecosystem** is a physical environment with different species that interact with one another and with nonliving things. When you hear the term *ecosystem*, you might think about a large region, such as a desert, a coral reef, or a forest. But an ecosystem can also be a very small area, such as an individual tree.

FIGURE 1.4 The moray eel and the cleaner shrimp are parts of a system in which both organisms benefit. The shrimp cleans the eel's mouth and gets food and protection in return.

Often, different biologists study different systems. For example, a person studying DNA might focus on very specific chemical interactions that take place in a cell. A person studying behavior in birds might focus on predator–prey relationships in an ecosystem. However, more and more biologists are working across different system levels. For example, some scientists study how chemicals in the brain affect social interactions.

Connect Describe how your biology class could be considered a system.

▶ MAIN IDEA
Structure and function are related in biology.

Think about a car again. In a car, different parts have different structures. The structure of a car part gives the part a specific function. For example, a tire's function is directly related to its structure. No other part of the car can perform that function. Structure and function are also related in living things. What something does in an organism is directly related to its shape or form. For example, when you eat, you probably bite into food with your sharp front teeth. Then you probably chew it mostly with your grinding molars. All of your teeth help you eat, but different types of teeth have different functions.

Structure and function are related at the level of chemicals in cells. For example, membrane channels and enzymes are both proteins, but they have very different structures and functions. A channel is a protein molecule that extends through the membrane, or outer layer, of a cell. It has a structure like a tube that allows specific chemicals to pass into and out of a cell. Enzymes are protein molecules that make chemical processes possible in living things. These proteins have shapes that allow them to attach to only certain chemicals and then cause the chemicals to react with each other.

Different types of cells also have different functions that depend on their specialized structures. For example, cells in your brain process information. They have many branches that receive information from other cells. They also have long extensions that allow them to send messages to other cells. Red blood cells are very different. They are much smaller, disk-shaped, and are

Connecting CONCEPTS

Biochemistry Proteins are a type of molecule found in all living things. Proteins have many different functions, which you will read about in **Chapter 2.**

FIGURE 1.5 The snout beetle (below) has specialized prongs and pads on its tarsi (right) that allow it to easily walk on both smooth and rough surfaces. (colored SEMs; magnifications: beetle 30×; tarsus 100×)

specialized to carry oxygen. Their structure allows them to fit through even the smallest blood vessels to deliver oxygen throughout your body. Of course, a cell from your brain cannot take the place of one of your red blood cells.

Structure and function are also related on the level of the organism. For example, your foot structure allows you to walk easily on rough, fairly level surfaces. Walking on a surface such as ice is more difficult, and walking up a wall is impossible for you. The beetle in **FIGURE 1.5** is different. Its tarsi, or "feet," have sharp prongs that can grip smooth or vertical surfaces, as well as soft pads for walking on rough surfaces. The beetle's tarsus has a different structure and function than your foot has, but both are specialized for walking.

Infer Do you think heart muscle has the same structure as arm muscle? Explain.

▶ MAIN IDEA
Organisms must maintain homeostasis to survive in diverse environments.

Temperature and other environmental conditions are always changing, but the conditions inside organisms usually stay quite stable. How does the polar bear in **FIGURE 1.6** live in the arctic? How can people be outside when the temperature is below freezing, but still have a stable body temperature around 37°C (98.6°F)? Why do you shiver when you are cold, sweat when you are hot, and feel thirsty when you need water?

Homeostasis (HOH-mee-oh-STAY-sihs) is the maintenance of constant internal conditions in an organism. Homeostasis is important because cells function best within a limited range of conditions. Temperature, blood sugar, acidity, and other conditions must be controlled. Breakdowns in homeostasis are often life-threatening.

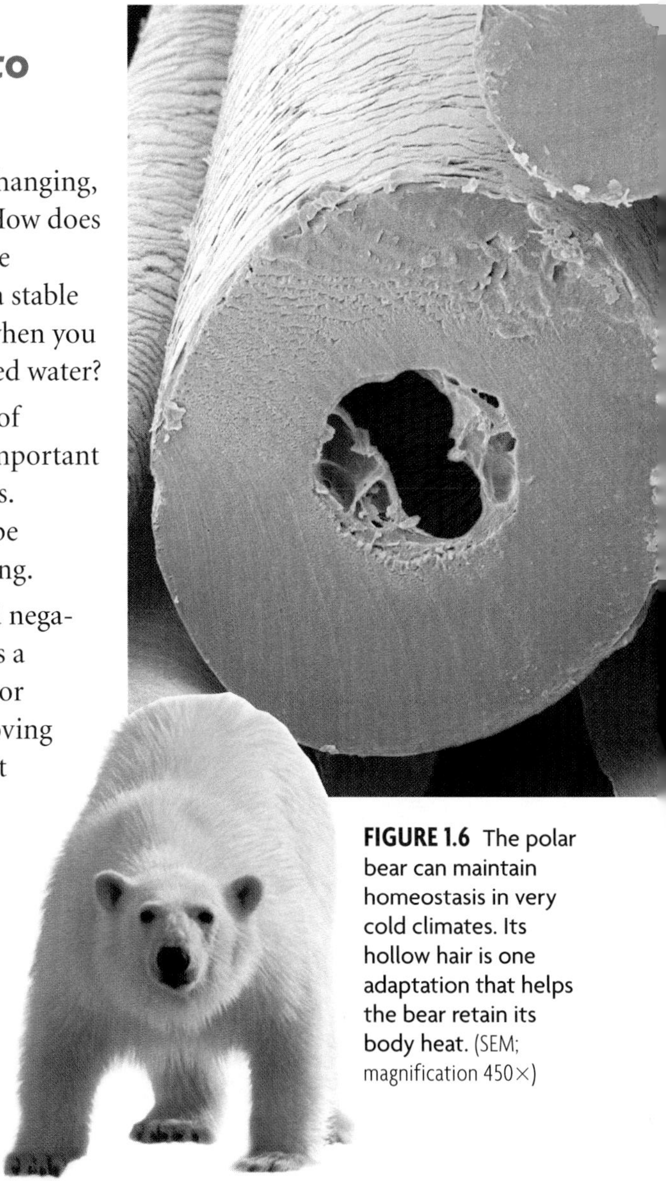

Homeostasis is usually maintained through a process called negative feedback. In negative feedback, a change in a system causes a response that tends to return that system to its original state. For example, think about how a car's cruise control keeps a car moving at a constant set speed. A cruise control system has sensors that monitor the car's speed and then send that information to a computer. If the car begins to go faster than the set speed, the computer tells the car to slow down. If the car slows below the set speed, the computer tells the car to speed up. Similarly, if your body temperature drops below normal, systems in your body act to return your temperature to normal. Your muscles cause you to shiver, and blood vessels near your skin's surface constrict. If your body temperature rises above normal, different responses cool your body.

Behavior is also involved in homeostasis. For example, animals regulate their temperature through behavior. If you feel cold, you may put on a jacket. Reptiles sit on a warm rock in sunlight if they get too cold, and they move into shade if they get too warm.

Summarize What is homeostasis, and why is it important?

FIGURE 1.6 The polar bear can maintain homeostasis in very cold climates. Its hollow hair is one adaptation that helps the bear retain its body heat. (SEM; magnification 450×)

▶ MAIN IDEA
Evolution explains the unity and diversity of life.

Connecting CONCEPTS

Evolution The processes of evolution, natural selection, and adaptation are described in more detail in **Unit 4**.

Evolution is the change in living things over time. More specifically, evolution is a change in the genetic makeup of a subgroup, or population, of a species. The concept of evolution links observations from all levels of biology, from cells to the biosphere. A wide range of scientific evidence, including the fossil record and genetic comparisons of species, show that evolution is continuing today.

Adaptation

One way evolution occurs is through natural selection of adaptations. In natural selection, a genetic, or inherited, trait helps some individuals of a species survive and reproduce more successfully than other individuals in a particular environment. An inherited trait that gives an advantage to individual organisms and is passed on to future generations is an **adaptation.** Over time, the makeup of a population changes because more individuals have the adaptation. Two different populations of the same species might have different adaptations in different environments. The two populations may continue to evolve to the point at which they are different species.

Consider the orchid and the thorn bug in **FIGURE 1.7**. Both organisms have adapted in ways that make them resemble other organisms. The orchid that looks like an insect lures other insects to it. The insects that are attracted to the orchid can pollinate the flower, helping the orchid to reproduce. The thorn bug's appearance is an adaptation that makes predators less likely to see and eat it.

FIGURE 1.7 Through evolution, some orchids (left) have flowers that look like insects and some insects, such as the thorn bug (right), look like parts of plants.

This adaptation allows the thorn bug to survive and reproduce. In different environments, however, you would find other orchid and insect species that have different adaptations.

Adaptation in evolution is different from the common meaning of adaptation. For example, if you say that you are adapting to a new classroom or to a new town, you are not talking about evolution. Instead, you are talking about consciously getting used to something new. Evolutionary adaptations are changes in a species that occur over many generations due to environmental pressures, not through choices made by organisms. Evolution is simply a long-term response to the environment. The process does not necessarily lead to more complex organisms, and it does not have any special end point. Evolution continues today, and it will continue as long as life exists on Earth.

Unity and Diversity

Evolution is a unifying theme of biology because it accounts for both the diversity and the similarities, or the unity, of life. As you study biology, you will see time after time that organisms are related to one another. When you read about cells in Unit 2 and genetics in Unit 3, you will see that all organisms have similar cell structures and chemical processes. These shared characteristics result from a common evolutionary descent.

Humans and bacteria have much more in common than you may think. Both human and bacterial genetics are based on the same molecules—DNA and RNA. Both human and bacterial cells rely upon the same sources of energy, and they have similar cell structures. Both human and bacterial cells have membranes made mostly of fats that protect the inside of the cell from the environment outside the cell.

Now think about the vast number of different types of organisms. All of the species now alive are the result of billions of years of evolution and adaptation to the environment. How? Natural selection of genetic traits can lead to the evolution of a new species. In the end, this genetic diversity is responsible for the diversity of life on Earth.

Analyze **How does evolution lead to both the diversity and the unity of life?**

1.2 ASSESSMENT

ONLINE QUIZ ClassZone.com

REVIEWING ▶ MAIN IDEAS

1. Describe a biological **system.**
2. Give an example of how structure is related to function in living things.
3. Why is **homeostasis** essential for living things?
4. What is the relationship between **adaptation** and natural selection?

CRITICAL THINKING

5. **Analyze** How are structure and function related to adaptation?
6. **Apply** How is the process of natural selection involved in **evolution**?

Connecting CONCEPTS

7. **Cells** Do you think homeostasis is necessary at the level of a single cell? Explain.

Types of Data

Scientists collect two different types of data: qualitative data and quantitative data.

Qualitative data Qualitative data are descriptions in words of what is being observed. They are based on some quality of an observation, such as color, odor, or texture.

Quantitative data Quantitative data are numeric measurements. The data are objective—they are the same no matter who measures them. They include measurements such as mass, volume, temperature, distance, concentration, time, or frequency.

EXAMPLE

Suppose that a marine biologist observes the behavior and activities of dolphins. She identifies different dolphins within the group and observes them every day for a month. She records detailed observations about their behaviors. Some of her observations are qualitative data, and some are quantitative data.

Qualitative data examples
• Dolphin colors range from gray to white.
• Dolphins in a pod engage in play behavior.
• Dolphins have smooth skin.

Quantitative data examples
• There are nine dolphins in this pod.
• Dolphins eat the equivalent of 4–5 percent of their body mass each day.
• The sonar frequency most often used by the dolphins is around 100 kHz.

Notice that the qualitative data are descriptions. The quantitative data are objective numerical measurements.

IDENTIFY DATA TYPES

Suppose that you are a biologist studying jackals in their natural habitat in Africa. You observe their behaviors and interactions, and take photographs of their interactions to study later. Examine the photograph of the jackals shown to the right.

1. **Analyze** Give three examples of qualitative data that could be obtained from the photograph of the jackals.

2. **Analyze** Give three examples of quantitative data that could be obtained from the photograph of the jackals.

1.3 Scientific Thinking and Processes

KEY CONCEPT Science is a way of thinking, questioning, and gathering evidence.

▶ MAIN IDEAS

- Like all science, biology is a process of inquiry.
- Biologists use experiments to test hypotheses.
- A theory explains a wide range of observations.

VOCABULARY

observation, p. 13
data, p. 14
hypothesis, p. 14
experiment, p. 16

independent variable, p. 16
dependent variable, p. 16
constant, p. 16
theory, p. 16

MICHIGAN STANDARDS

B1.1A Generate new questions that can be investigated in the laboratory or field.
B1.2h Describe the distinctions between scientific theories, laws, hypotheses, and observations.

Connect What does the study of fungus have in common with the study of human heart disease? How is research in a laboratory similar to research in a rain forest? Biologists, like all scientists, ask questions about the world and try to find answers through observation and experimentation. How do your daily observations help answer questions that you have about the world?

▶ MAIN IDEA

Like all science, biology is a process of inquiry.

Science is a human process of trying to understand the world around us. There is no one method used by all scientists, but all scientific inquiry is based on the same principles. Scientific thinking is based on both curiosity and skepticism. Skepticism is the use of critical and logical thinking to evaluate results and conclusions. Scientific inquiry also requires evidence. One of the most important points of science is that scientific evidence may support or even overturn long-standing ideas. To improve our understanding of the world, scientists share their findings with each other. The open and honest exchange of data is extremely important in science.

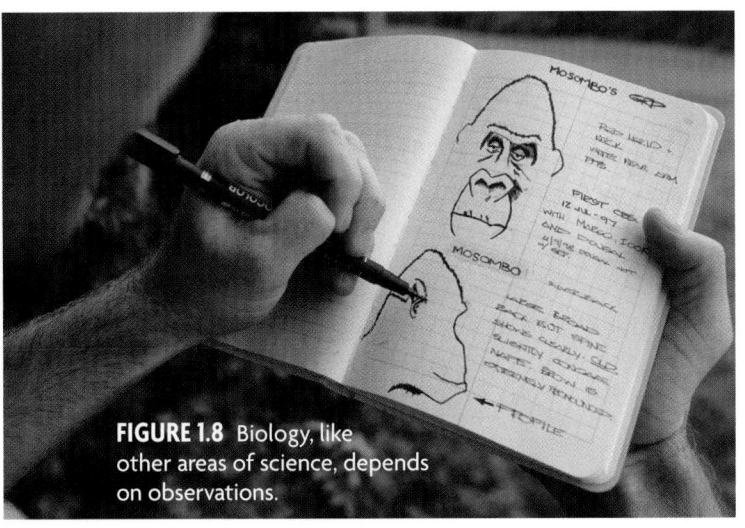
FIGURE 1.8 Biology, like other areas of science, depends on observations.

Observations, Data, and Hypotheses

All scientific inquiry begins with careful and systematic observations. Of course, **observation** includes using our senses to study the world, but it may also involve other tools. For example, scientists use computers to collect measurements or to examine past research results. Much early biological research was based on observing, describing, and categorizing the living world. By themselves, description and categorization are not as common in research today due to advances in technology, but they are still very important in biology. For example, how could someone study the interactions of gorillas without observing and describing their behavior, as in **FIGURE 1.8**?

Scientific questions often come from observations, whether the observations are one's own or someone else's. Observations can also be recorded as **data** that can be analyzed. Scientists collect two general types of data: qualitative data and quantitative data. As you learned on page 12, qualitative data are descriptions of a phenomenon that can include sights, sounds, and smells. This type of data is often useful to report what happens but not how it happens. In contrast, quantitative data are characteristics that can be measured or counted, such as mass, volume, and temperature. Anything that is expressed as a number, from time to a rating scale on a survey, is quantitative data that can be used to explore how something happens.

Scientists use observations and data to form a hypothesis. A **hypothesis** (plural, *hypotheses*) is a proposed answer for a scientific question. A hypothesis must be specific and testable. You probably form and test many hypotheses every day, even though you may not be aware of it. Suppose you oversleep. You needed to get up at 7 A.M., but when you wake up you observe that it is 8 A.M. What happened? Did the alarm not go off? Was it set for the wrong time? Did it go off but you slept through it? You just made three hypotheses to explain why you overslept—the alarm did not go off, the alarm was set for the wrong time, or the alarm went off but you did not hear it.

Testing Hypotheses

A hypothesis leads to testable predictions of what would happen if the hypothesis is valid. How could you use scientific thinking to test a hypothesis about oversleeping? If you slept late because the alarm was set for the wrong time, you could check the alarm to find out the time for which it was set. Suppose the alarm was actually set for 7 P.M. In this case, your hypothesis would be supported by your data, and you could be certain that the alarm was set for the wrong time.

For scientists, just one test of a hypothesis is usually not enough. Most of the time, it is only by repeating tests that scientists can be more certain that their results are not mistaken or due to chance. Why? Biological systems are highly variable. By repeating tests, scientists take this variability into account and try to decrease its effects on the experimental results.

After scientists collect data, they use statistics to mathematically analyze whether a hypothesis is supported. There are two possible outcomes of statistical analysis.

- **Nonsignificant** The data show no effect, or an effect so small that the results could have happened by chance.
- **Statistically significant** The data show an effect that is likely not due to chance.

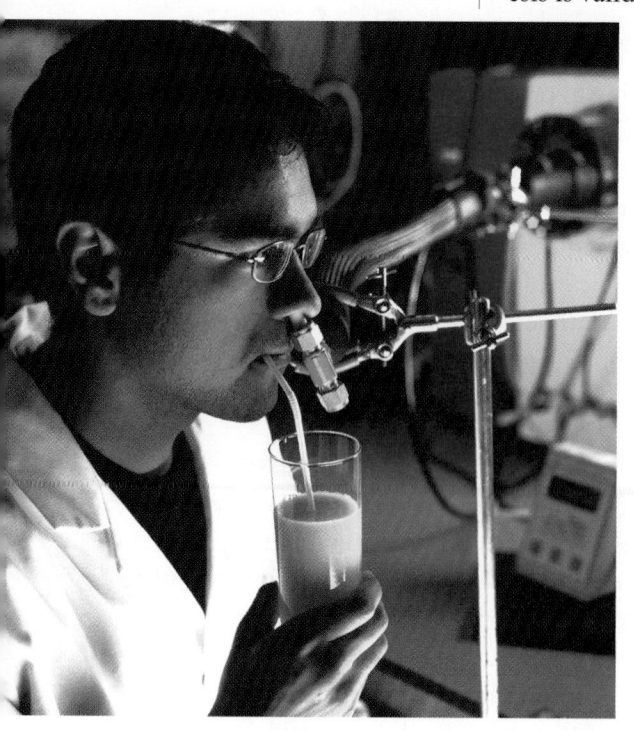

FIGURE 1.9 In this experiment, a scientist studies how chemicals are detected in the mouth and nose to produce taste.

When data do not support a hypothesis, it is rejected. But these data are still useful because they often lead to new hypotheses.

Experimental methods and results are evaluated by other scientists in a process called peer review. How was an experiment done and how were the data analyzed? Do the data support the conclusions of the experiment?

FIGURE 1.10 Scientific Thinking

Science is a cycle. The steps are shown in a certain order, but the cycle does not begin or end at any one point, and the steps may take place in various orders.

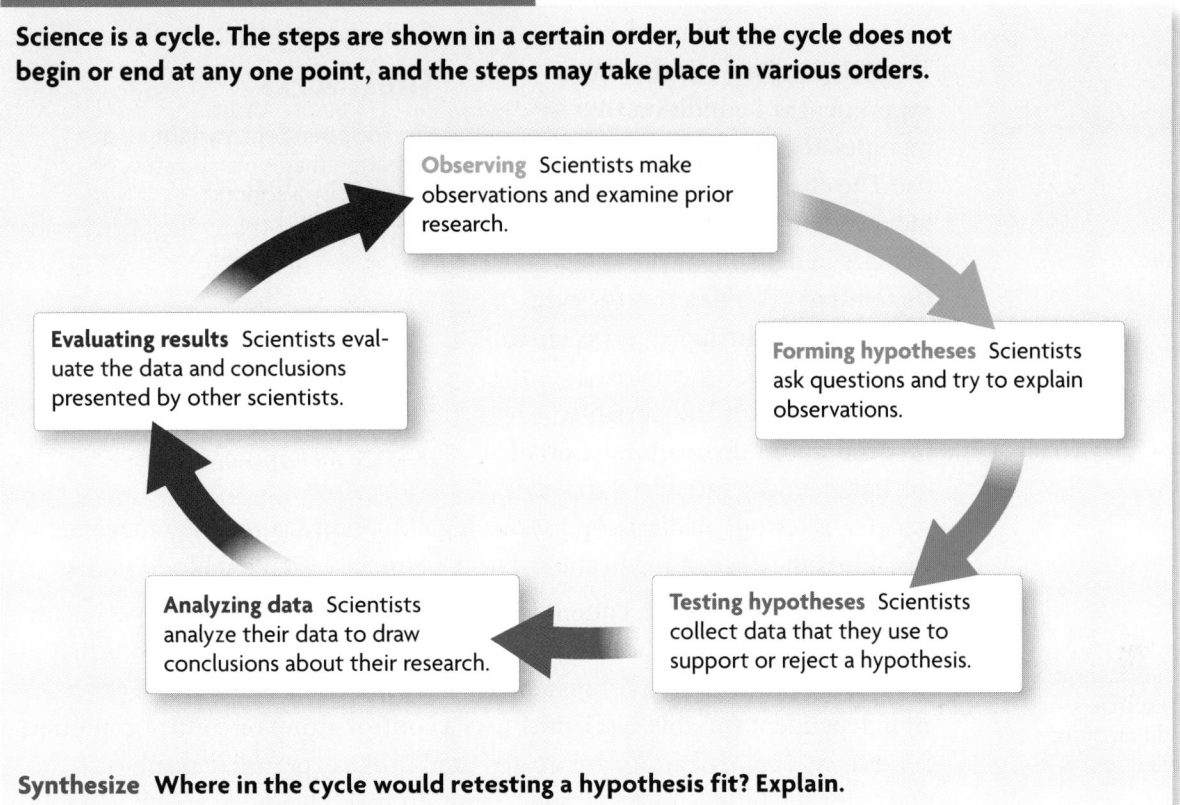

Observing Scientists make observations and examine prior research.

Forming hypotheses Scientists ask questions and try to explain observations.

Testing hypotheses Scientists collect data that they use to support or reject a hypothesis.

Analyzing data Scientists analyze their data to draw conclusions about their research.

Evaluating results Scientists evaluate the data and conclusions presented by other scientists.

Synthesize Where in the cycle would retesting a hypothesis fit? Explain.

Is there bias in the experimental design or in the conclusions? Only after this review process is complete are research results accepted. Whether the results support an existing theory or disagree with earlier research, they are often used as a starting point for new questions. In **FIGURE 1.10**, you see the cycle of observing, forming hypotheses, testing hypotheses, analyzing data, and evaluating results that keeps scientific inquiry going.

Synthesize Why is there no one correct process of scientific investigation?

▶ MAIN IDEA

Biologists use experiments to test hypotheses.

You have read about the importance of observations in science. Observational studies help biologists describe and explain something in the world. But in observational studies, scientists try not to interfere with what happens. They try to simply observe a phenomenon. One example involves the endangered white stork. The number of white storks has decreased sharply over the last 50 years. To help protect the storks, biologists have studied the migration patterns of the birds. What can observational studies tell a biologist about stork populations and migration? The studies can show changes in migration path and distance. They can show where storks breed and how many eggs they lay. Observational studies can answer all of these questions. But there is one question that observations cannot answer: What causes any changes that might be observed? The only way to answer that question is through an experiment.

Scientific experiments allow scientists to test hypotheses and find out how something happens. In **experiments,** scientists study factors called independent variables and dependent variables to find cause-and-effect relationships.

The **independent variable** in an experiment is a condition that is manipulated, or changed, by a scientist. The effects of manipulating an independent variable are measured by changes in dependent variables. **Dependent variables** are observed and measured during an experiment; they are the experimental data. Changes in dependent variables "depend upon" the manipulation of the independent variable. Suppose a scientist is testing medications to treat high blood pressure. The independent variable is the dose of medication. The dependent variable is blood pressure.

VISUAL VOCAB

The **independent variable** is a condition that is manipulated, or changed, by a scientist.

independent variable
⟨affects⟩
dependent variable

Dependent variables are observed and measured during an experiment; they are the experimental data.

Ideally, only one independent variable should be tested in an experiment. Thus, all of the other conditions have to stay the same. The conditions that do not change during an experiment are called **constants.** To study the effects of an independent variable, a scientist uses a control group or control condition. Subjects in a control group are treated exactly like experimental subjects except for the independent variable being studied. The independent variable is manipulated in experimental groups or experimental conditions.

Constants in the blood pressure medication experiment include how often the medication is given, and how the medication is taken. To control the experiment, these factors must remain the same, or be held constant. For example, the medication could be tested with 0, 25, 50, or 100 milligram doses, twice a day, taken by swallowing a pill. By changing only one variable at a time—the amount of medication—a scientist can be more confident that the results are due to that variable.

Infer How do experiments show cause-and-effect relationships?

VOCABULARY

In common usage, the term *constant* means "unchanging." In experimental research, a constant is a condition or factor that is controlled so that it does not change.

▶ MAIN IDEA

A theory explains a wide range of observations.

Many words have several different meanings. Depending on the context in which a word is used, its meaning can change completely. For example, the word *right* could mean "correct," or it could refer to a direction. Similarly, the word *theory* has different meanings. Usually, the word *theory* in everyday conversation means a speculation, or something that is imagined to be true. In science, the meaning of *theory* is very different.

Recall that a hypothesis is a proposed answer for a scientific question. A **theory** is a proposed explanation for a wide range of observations and experimental results that is supported by a wide range of evidence. Eventually, a theory may be broadly accepted by the scientific community. Natural selection is a scientific theory. It is supported by a large amount of data, and it explains many observations of life on Earth. Theories are not easily accepted in science, and by definition they are never proved. Scientific hypotheses and theories may be supported or refuted, and they are always subject to change. New theories that better explain observations and experimental results can replace older theories.

Theories can change based on new evidence. One example of how scientific understanding can change involves the cause of disease. Until the mid-1800s, illnesses were thought to be related to supernatural causes or to imbalances of the body's "humours," or fluids. Then scientific research suggested that diseases were caused by microscopic organisms, such as bacteria. The germ theory of disease was born, but it has changed over the years. For example, an early addition to the germ theory stated that it must be possible to grow a disease-causing microorganism in a laboratory.

Now, we know that viruses and prions do not completely fit the germ theory of disease because they are not living organisms. A virus has some of the characteristics of life, but it cannot reproduce itself without infecting a living cell. Prions are even less like organisms—they are just misfolded proteins. The link between prions and disease was not even suggested until the early 1980s, but much evidence points to prions as the cause of mad cow disease and, in humans, Creutzfeldt–Jakob disease.

The details of germ theory have changed as our knowledge of biology has grown, but the basic theory is still accepted. Scientists are always willing to revise theories and conclusions as new evidence about the living world is gathered. Science is an ongoing process. New experiments and observations refine and expand scientific knowledge, as you can see in **FIGURE 1.11**. Our understanding of the world around us has changed dramatically over the past few decades, and the study of biology has changed and expanded as well.

Summarize **What is a scientific theory?**

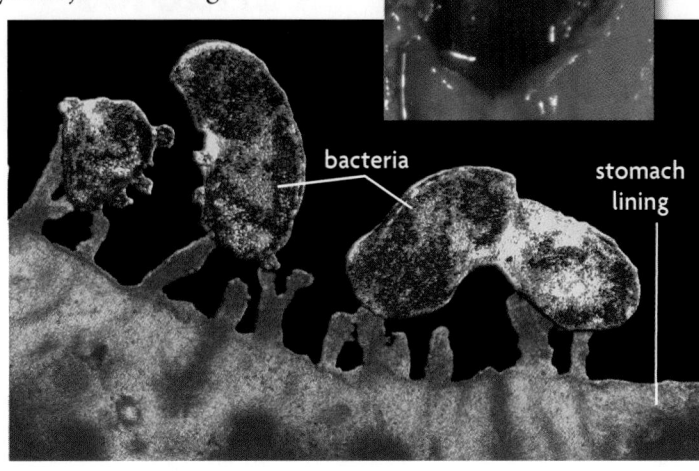

FIGURE 1.11 For many years, scientific evidence indicated that stomach ulcers (top) were caused by stress. Then, new evidence showed that the ulcers are actually caused by a type of bacteria called *Helicobacter pylori* (bottom). (colored TEM; magnification 10,000×)

To learn more about scientific methods, go to scilinks.org.
Keycode: MLB001

1.3 ASSESSMENT

ONLINE QUIZ
ClassZone.com

REVIEWING ▶ MAIN IDEAS

1. What role do **hypotheses** play in scientific inquiry?
2. What is the difference between an **independent variable** and a **dependent variable**?
3. How is the meaning of **theory** in science different from the everyday use of the term?

CRITICAL THINKING

4. **Compare and Contrast** How are hypotheses and theories related?
5. **Apply** Give examples of different ways in which **observations** are used in scientific inquiry.

Connecting CONCEPTS

6. **Scientific Process** Why is the statement "All life is made of cells" an example of a theory? Explain.

MATERIALS

- 4 graduated cylinders with gelatin
- 4 marbles
- metric ruler
- 10 mL water
- 2 10-mL graduated cylinders
- 10 mL detergent (10%)
- 10 mL detergent (30%)
- 10 mL detergent (50%)

OR

- 10 mL detergent (pH 4)
- 10 mL detergent (pH 7)
- 10 mL detergent (pH 10)

PROCESS SKILLS

- **Measuring**
- **Modeling**

B1.1C Conduct scientific investigations using appropriate tools and techniques (e.g., selecting an instrument that measures the desired quantity—length, volume, weight, time interval, temperature—with the appropriate level of precision).

B2.2F Explain the role of enzymes and other proteins in biochemical functions (e.g., the protein hemoglobin carries oxygen in some organisms, digestive enzymes, and hormones).

Manipulating Independent Variables

Some chemicals, called enzymes, help break down substances into smaller molecules. Some laundry detergents contain enzymes that help break down protein stains in clothing. In this investigation, you will test how different conditions affect the activity of the enzymes in laundry detergent.

PROBLEM How is enzyme activity affected by changes in conditions?

PROCEDURE

1. Obtain four graduated cylinders filled with gelatin. One of the cylinders is for the control condition. The other three are for the experimental conditions.

2. Decide which variable you would like to test.
   - pH (pH is a measurement of acidity, and a lower pH means that a substance is more acidic)
   - detergent concentration

3. The dependent variable is the amount of gelatin broken down by the enzyme in the detergent. Measure the dependent variable by placing a marble on top of the gelatin and measuring how far the marble sinks into the gelatin.

4. Identify the independent variable in your experiment. Form a hypothesis that explains the effect of the independent variable on the dependent variable.

5. Pour 10 mL of water onto the gelatin in one graduated cylinder. This graduated cylinder represents the control condition. Pour 10 mL of each different detergent solution into each of the other graduated cylinders. These graduated cylinders represent the experimental conditions.

6. Place a marble on the top of the gelatin in each graduated cylinder. Wait five minutes, then measure the distance that the marble has sunk into the gelatin.

7. Construct a data table like the one shown below, and record your data.

TABLE 1. EFFECT OF DETERGENT ON GELATIN	
Condition	**Distance (cm)**
Water	
Solution 1	
Solution 2	
Solution 3	

ANALYZE AND CONCLUDE

1. **Analyze** Use a bar graph to plot your data. What trends exist in your data? Explain whether your results supported your hypothesis.

2. **Communicate** Share the results of your experiment with other groups in your class. Did other groups that manipulated the same independent variable obtain similar results? Why or why not?

EXTEND YOUR INVESTIGATION

Some areas have "hard" water, or water with a high mineral content. Other areas have "soft" water, or water with a low mineral content. Design an experiment to test the effect of the mineral content of water on detergent activity.

1.4 Biologists' Tools and Technology

KEY CONCEPT Technology continually changes the way biologists work.

MAIN IDEAS

- Imaging technologies provide new views of life.
- Complex systems are modeled on computers.
- The tools of molecular genetics give rise to new biological studies.

VOCABULARY

microscope, p. 19
gene, p. 23
molecular genetics, p. 23
genomics, p. 23

MICHIGAN STANDARDS

B4.2h Recognize that genetic engineering techniques provide great potential and responsibilities.

Connect Can you imagine life without cars, computers, or cell phones? Technology changes the way we live and work. Technology also plays a major part in the rapid increase of biological knowledge. Today, technology allows biologists to view tiny structures within cells and activity within a human brain. Technology allows biologists to study and change genes. What will technology allow next?

MAIN IDEA

Imaging technologies provide new views of life.

Until the late 1600s, no one knew about cells or single-celled organisms. Then the microscope was invented. Scientists suddenly had the ability to study living things at a level they never knew existed. Thus, the microscope was the first in a long line of technologies that have changed the study of biology.

Microscopes

A **microscope** provides an enlarged image of an object. Some of the most basic concepts of biology—such as the fact that cells make up all organisms—were not even imaginable before microscopes. The first microscopes magnified objects but did not produce clear images. By the 1800s, most microscopes had combinations of lenses that provided clearer images. Today's light microscopes, such as the one in **FIGURE 1.12** that you might use, are still based on the same principles. They are used to see living or preserved specimens, and they provide clear images of cells as small as bacteria. Light microscopes clearly magnify specimens up to about 1500 times their actual size, and samples are often stained with chemicals to make details stand out.

Electron microscopes, developed in the 1950s, use beams of electrons instead of light to magnify objects. These microscopes can be used to see cells, but they produce much higher magnifications, so they can also show much smaller things. Electron microscopes can clearly magnify specimens more than 100,000 times their actual size. They can even be used to directly study individual protein molecules. However, electron microscopes, unlike light microscopes, cannot be used to study living organisms because the specimens being studied have to be in a vacuum.

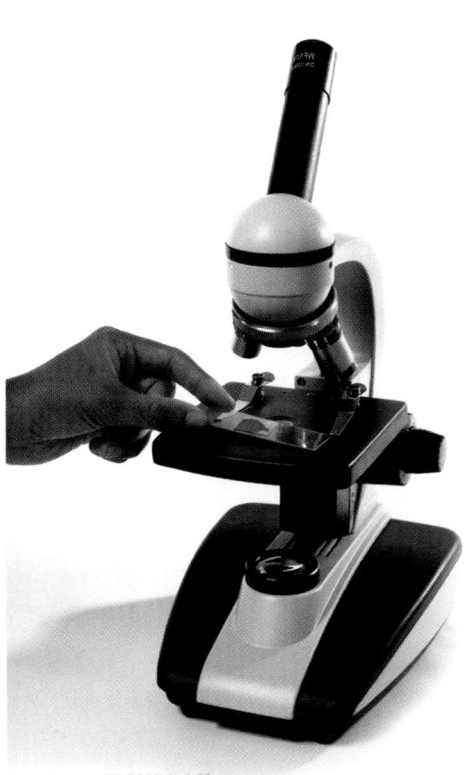

FIGURE 1.12 Biologists use microscopes to study cells, which are too small to be seen with the naked eye.

There are two main types of electron microscopes.

- A scanning electron microscope (SEM) scans the surface of a specimen with a beam of electrons. Usually, the specimen's surface is coated with a very thin layer of a metal that deflects the electrons. A computer forms a three-dimensional image from measurements of the deflected electrons.
- A transmission electron microscope (TEM) transmits electrons through a thin slice of a specimen. The TEM makes a two-dimensional image similar to that of a light microscope, but a TEM has a much higher magnification.

Often, SEM and TEM images are colorized with computers so that certain details are easier to see, as shown in **FIGURE 1.14**. Any time you see an SEM or TEM image in color, it has been given that color artificially.

Medical Imaging

Imaging technology is not limited to microscopes. In fact, technology used to study tissues inside living humans is commonly used in research and medicine. For example, doctors or dentists have probably taken x-ray images of you several times. An x-ray image is formed by x-rays, which pass through soft tissues, such as skin and muscle, but are absorbed by bones and teeth. Thus, x-ray images are very useful for looking at the skeleton but not so useful for examining soft tissues such as ligaments, cartilage, or the brain.

What if a doctor wants to examine ligaments in a person's knee? Another imaging technology called magnetic resonance imaging (MRI) is used. MRI uses a strong magnetic field to produce a cross-section image of a part of the body. A series of MRI images can be put together to give a complete view of all of the tissues in that area, as you can see in **FIGURE 1.13**. Advances in technology have led to new uses for MRI. For example, a technique called functional MRI (fMRI) can show which areas of the brain are active while a person is doing a particular task.

Compare and Contrast How do SEMs and TEMs produce different images of the same specimen?

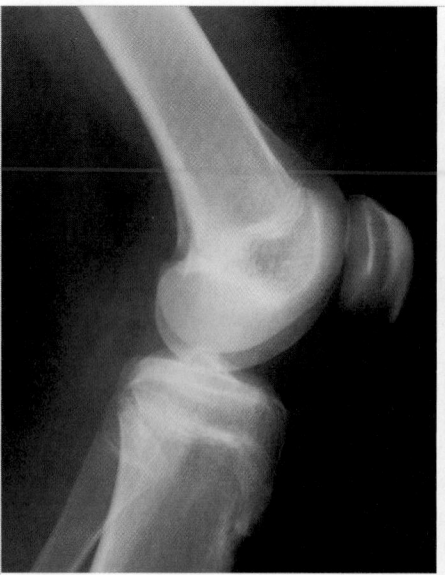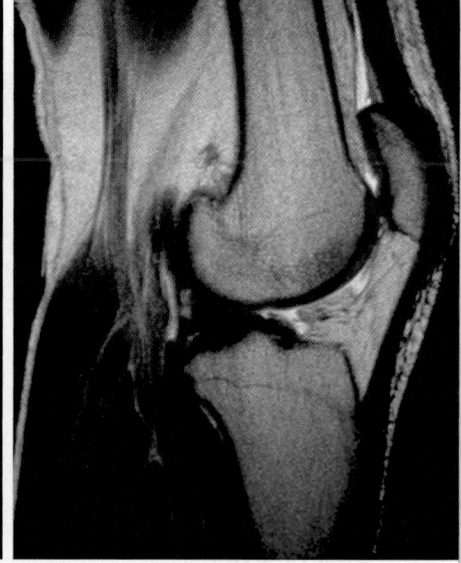

FIGURE 1.13 An x-ray of the human knee (left) shows dense tissues, such as bone, in detail. An MRI of the human knee (right) shows both soft and dense tissues in detail.

Connecting CONCEPTS

Imaging Biologists use several types of micrographs, or images from microscopes. Whenever you see a micrograph in this book, LM stands for "light micrograph," SEM stands for "scanning electron micrograph," and TEM stands for "transmission electron micrograph."

FIGURE 1.14 Comparing Micrographs

Different types of microscopes provide different views and magnifications, such as in these images of guard cells surrounding a stoma, or pore, in a leaf.

Animated BIOLOGY
View a set of cells through different microscopes at ClassZone.com.

LIGHT MICROGRAPH (LM)

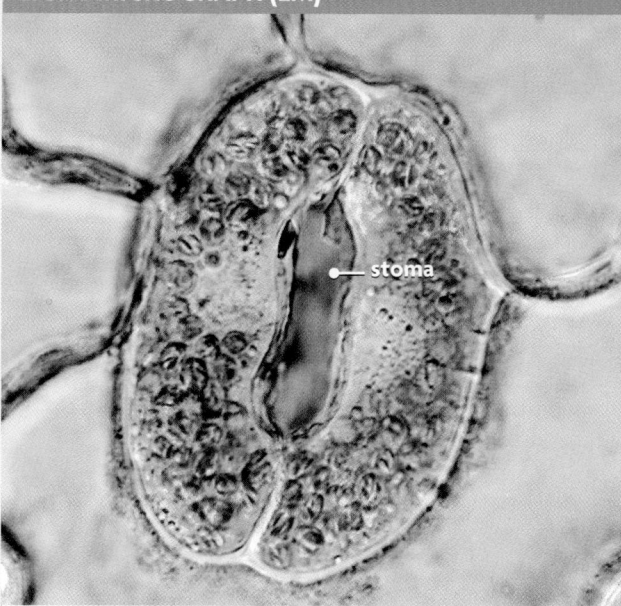

A light micrograph shows a two-dimensional image of a specimen. This light micrograph shows the actual color of the specimen. (LM; magnification 2000×)

TRANSMISSION ELECTRON MICROGRAPH (TEM)

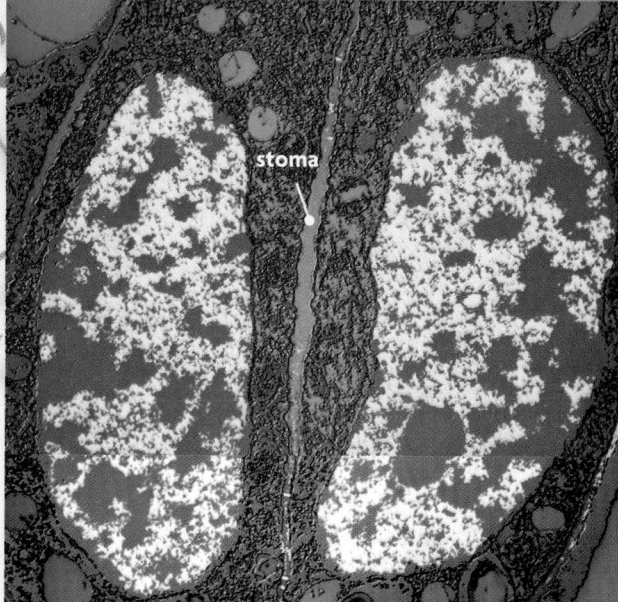

A TEM shows a two-dimensional image of a thin slice of a specimen. A TEM is colorized by computer. The bottom part of the image shows the original black-and-white image. (colored TEM; magnification 5000×)

SCANNING ELECTRON MICROGRAPH (SEM)

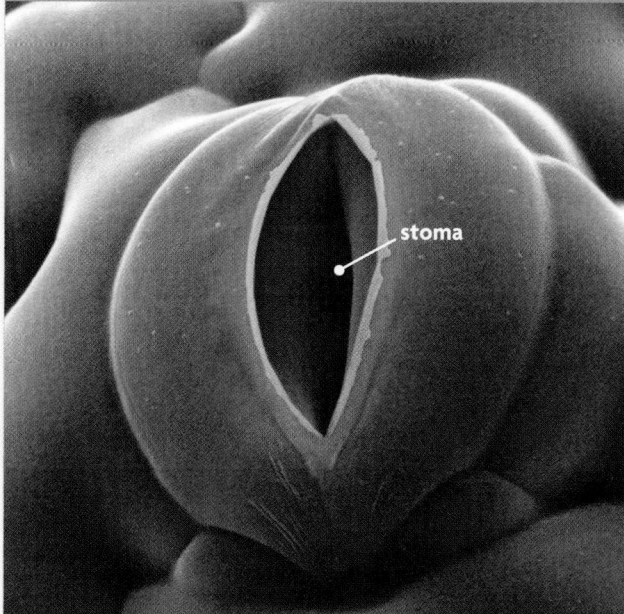

An SEM shows a three-dimensional image of a specimen's surface. An SEM is colorized by computer. The bottom part of the image shows the original black-and-white image. (colored SEM; magnification 1500×)

CRITICAL VIEWING What type of microscope would be best for showing details inside a cell? Why?

OBSERVING

Life Under a Microscope

Using a microscope properly is an important skill for many biologists. In this lab, you will review microscope skills by examining a drop of water from the surface of a local pond.

PROBLEM What types of organisms can be found in pond water?

PROCEDURE

1. Make a wet mount slide. Place a drop of pond water in the center of a microscope slide and carefully put a cover slip over the water. For more information on making a wet mount, see page R8.

2. View the pond water sample under low power on the microscope. Use the coarse focus knob to bring the sample into focus. Draw and label any organisms that you see in the sample.

3. View the slide under high power. Use the fine focus knob to bring portions of the sample into focus. Draw and label any organisms, including details of their structures, that you see in the sample.

ANALYZE AND CONCLUDE

1. **Connect** Describe how organisms in the sample exhibit the characteristics of living things.

2. **Compare and Contrast** Make a table to compare and contrast the characteristics of organisms in the sample of pond water.

MATERIALS
- 1 drop pond water
- eyedropper
- microscope slide
- cover slip
- microscope

▶ **MAIN IDEA**

Complex systems are modeled on computers.

Normal heartbeat

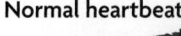
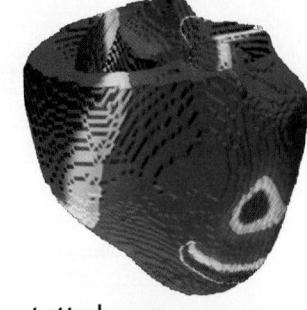

Heart attack

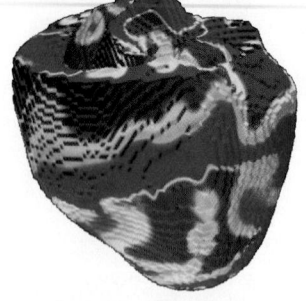

FIGURE 1.15 This computer-generated model shows that heart activity (red) is tightly regulated during a normal heartbeat. During a heart attack, heart activity is widespread and disorganized.

Computer-based technology has greatly expanded biological research. As computers have become faster and more powerful, biologists have found ways to use them to model living systems that cannot be studied directly. A computer model simulates the interactions among many different variables to provide scientists with a general idea of how a biological system may work.

Computers can model complex systems within organisms. For example, computer models are used to study how medicines might affect the body or, as you can see in **FIGURE 1.15**, the effects of a heart attack. Scientists have even used computer models to find out how water molecules travel into and out of cells. The scientists made a computer program that took into account more than 50,000 virtual atoms in a virtual cell. The computer model showed that water molecules must spin around in the middle of a channel, or a passage into the cell, to fit through the channel. Water molecules had a specific fit that other molecules could not match.

Computer models can also help biologists study complex systems on a much larger scale. Epidemiology, which is the study of how diseases spread, depends on computer models. For example, computer models can predict how fast and how far the flu might spread in a city. A model can calculate the number of people who might get sick, and suggest where in the city the illness began. This study cannot be done with people and cities. Computer models are used when actual experiments are not safe, ethical, or practical.

Infer **What are some reasons why biologists use computer models?**

▶ MAIN IDEA
The tools of molecular genetics give rise to new biological studies.

Computer-based technologies, such as those shown in **FIGURE 1.16**, have led to major changes in biology. But perhaps the greatest leap forward in our knowledge of life has happened in genetics. In just 40 years, we have gone from learning how the genetic code works, to changing genes, to implanting genes from one species into another. What is a gene? A **gene** is nothing more than a segment of DNA that stores genetic information. Our understanding of the DNA molecule has led to many technologies that were unimaginable when your parents were in high school—genetically modified foods, transgenic plants and animals, even replacement of faulty genes. These advances come from molecular genetics. **Molecular genetics** is the study and manipulation of DNA on a molecular level. Molecular genetics is used to study evolution, ecology, biochemistry, and many other areas of biology.

Entirely new areas of biology have arisen from combining molecular genetics with computer technology. For example, computers are used to quickly find DNA sequences. Through the use of computers, the entire DNA sequences, or genomes, of humans and other organisms have been found. **Genomics** (juh-NOH-mihks) is the study and comparison of genomes both within and across species. Here again, biologists need to use computers.

All of the information from genomics is managed by computer databases. By searching computer databases, a process called data mining, a biologist can find patterns, similarities, and differences in biological data. Suppose a biologist identifies a molecule that prevents the growth of cancerous tumors. The biologist could use computer databases to search for similar molecules.

This is the cutting edge of biology today. Where will biology be when your children are in high school?

Connect What does the term *genetics* mean to you? Why?

FIGURE 1.16 Robots are used to speed up research into the human genome (top). Computers are used to sequence human DNA (bottom).

Connecting CONCEPTS

Genetics You will learn much more about these and other genetics topics in **Unit 3**.

1.4 ASSESSMENT

ONLINE QUIZ
ClassZone.com

REVIEWING ▶ MAIN IDEAS

1. How do light **microscopes** differ from electron microscopes?
2. Why is computer modeling used in biological studies?
3. How does **molecular genetics** add to our understanding of **genes**?

CRITICAL THINKING

4. **Apply** Viruses are smaller than cells. What types of microscopes could be used to study them? Explain.
5. **Synthesize** Provide an example of how technology has helped biologists gain a better understanding of life.

Connecting CONCEPTS

6. **Evolution Genomics** can be used to study the genetic relationships among species. Why might genomics be important for evolution research? Explain.

1.5 Biology and Your Future

KEY CONCEPT Understanding biology can help you make informed decisions.

MAIN IDEAS

- Your health and the health of the environment depend on your knowledge of biology.
- Biotechnology offers great promise but also raises many issues.
- Biology presents many unanswered questions.

VOCABULARY

biotechnology, p. 26
transgenic, p. 26

MICHIGAN STANDARDS

B1.2A Critique whether or not specific questions can be answered through scientific investigations.

B1.2B Identify and critique arguments about personal or societal issues based on scientific evidence.

Connect Should brain imaging technology be used to tell if someone is lying? Is an endangered moth's habitat more important than a new highway? Would you vote for or against the pursuit of stem cell research? An informed answer to any of these questions requires an understanding of biology and scientific thinking. And although science alone cannot answer these questions, gathering evidence and analyzing data can help every decision maker.

MAIN IDEA

Your health and the health of the environment depend on your knowledge of biology.

Decisions are based on opinions, emotions, education, experiences, values, and logic. Many of your decisions, now and in the future, at both personal and societal levels, involve biology. Your knowledge of biology can help you make informed decisions about issues involving endangered species, biotechnology, medical research, and pollution control, to name a few. How will your decisions affect the future of yourself and others?

Biology and Your Health

What you eat and drink is directly related to your health. But you may not think twice about the possibility of contaminated food or water, or a lack of vitamins in your diet. Not long ago, diseases caused by vitamin deficiencies were still fairly common. The first vitamins were identified less than 100 years ago, but today the vitamins found in foods are printed on labels.

TAKING NOTES

Use a mind map to take notes about the importance of studying biology.

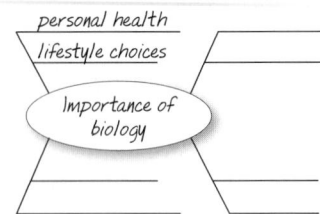

Even today we still face food-related causes of illness. For example, you might hear about an outbreak of food poisoning, and mad cow disease was only recognized in the late 1980s. Of perhaps greater concern to you are food allergies. Many people suffer from severe, even life-threatening, allergies to foods such as peanuts and shellfish. Beyond questions about the sources of food are questions and concerns about what people eat and how much they eat. For example, scientists estimate that more than 60 percent of adults in the United States are overweight or obese. The health consequences of obesity include increased risks of diabetes, stroke, heart disease, breast cancer, colon cancer, and other health problems. Biology can help you to better understand all of these health-related issues.

An understanding of biology on many different levels—genetic, chemical, and cellular, for example—can help you make any number of lifestyle choices that affect your health. Why is it important to use sunscreen? What are the benefits of exercise? What are the effects of using alcohol, illegal drugs, and tobacco? Cigarette smoke does not just affect the lungs; it can also change a person's body chemistry, as you can see in **FIGURE 1.17**. Lower levels of monoamine oxidase in the brain can affect mood, and lower levels in the liver could contribute to high blood pressure.

Biology and the World Around You

In 1995, some middle school students from Minnesota were walking through a wetland and collecting frogs for a school project. The students stopped to look at the frogs, and what they saw shocked them. Many of the frogs had deformities, including missing legs, extra legs, and missing eyes. What caused the deformities? Scientists investigated that question by testing several hypotheses. They studied whether the deformities could have been caused by factors such as a chemical in the water, ultraviolet radiation, or some type of infection.

Why would frog deformities such as that in **FIGURE 1.18** provoke such scientific interest? The frogs are a part of an ecosystem, so whatever affected them could affect other species in the area. If the deformities were caused by a chemical in the water, might the chemical pose a risk to people living in the area? In other regions of the United States, parasites caused similar deformities in frogs. Might that parasite also be present in Minnesota? If so, did it pose a risk to other species?

Scientists still do not know for sure what caused the frog deformities in Minnesota. No parasitic infection was found, so that hypothesis was rejected. However, evidence indicates that the water contained a chemical very similar to a chemical in frogs that helps control limb development. It is not known whether the chemical is the result of pollution or if it occurs naturally.

Suppose that the chemical comes from a factory in the area. Is it reasonable to ban the chemical? Should the factory be closed or fined? In any instance like this, political, legal, economic, and biological concerns have to be considered. What is the economic impact of the factory on the area? Is there any evidence of human health problems in the area? Is there a different chemical that could be used? Without an understanding of biology, how could you make an informed decision related to any of these questions?

These are the types of questions that people try to answer every day. Biologists and other scientists research environmental issues such as pollution, biodiversity, habitat preservation, land conservation, and natural resource use, but decisions about the future are not in the hands of scientists. It is up to everyone to make decisions based on evidence and conclusions from many different sources.

Connect How might biology help you to better understand environmental issues?

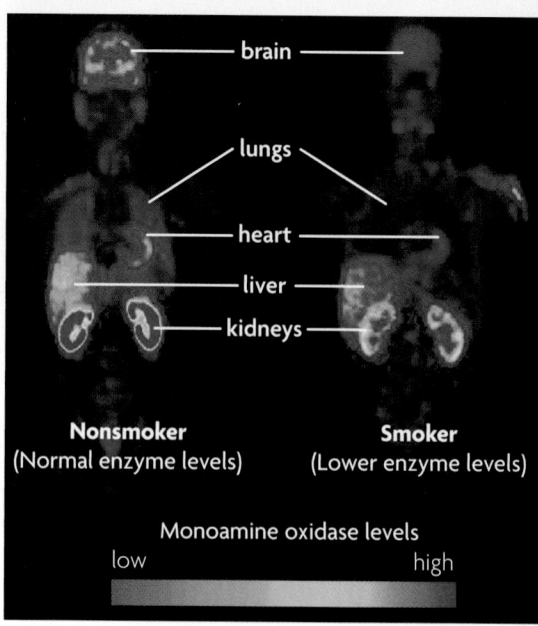

FIGURE 1.17 As compared with nonsmokers, smokers have much lower levels of an enzyme called monoamine oxidase throughout their bodies.

FIGURE 1.18 Deformities in frogs can be an indication of chemical pollution in an ecosystem.

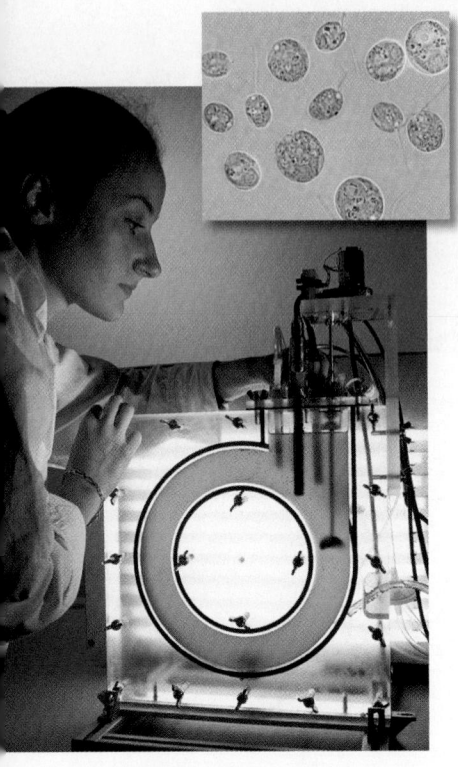

MAIN IDEA

Biotechnology offers great promise but also raises many issues.

Biotechnology is the use and application of living things and biological processes. Biotechnology includes a very broad range of products, processes, and techniques. In fact, some forms of biotechnology have been around for centuries, such as the use of microorganisms to make bread and cheese. Today, biotechnology is used in medicine, agriculture, forensic science, and many other fields. For example, people wrongly convicted of crimes have been freed from prison when DNA testing has shown that their DNA did not match DNA found at crime scenes. Biotechnology has great potential to help solve a variety of modern problems, such as the search for alternative energy sources like the algae shown in **FIGURE 1.19**. However, along with the advances in biotechnology come questions about its uses.

Benefits and Biological Risks

All domestic plants and animals are the result of centuries of genetic manipulation through selective breeding. Today, genetic manipulation can mean the transfer of genetic information from one organism to a very different organism. Organisms that have genes from more than one species, or have altered copies of their own genes, are called **transgenic** organisms. Transgenic bacteria can make human insulin to treat people with diabetes. Transgenic sheep and cows can make human antibodies and proteins. When you hear about genetically modified foods, you are hearing about transgenic organisms.

Genetically modified foods have many potential benefits. Crop plants are changed to increase the nutrients and yield of the plants and to resist insects. Insect-resistant crops could reduce or end the need for chemical pesticides. However, the long-term effects of genetically modified crops are not fully known. Is it safe to eat foods with genetically modified insect resistance? What if genetically modified plants spread undesirable genes, such as those for herbicide resistance, to wild plants? Around the world, the benefits and risks of biotechnology are debated. Understanding these benefits and risks requires knowledge of ecosystems, genetic principles, and even the functions of genes.

Benefits and Ethical Considerations

Another form of biotechnology is human genetic screening, which is the analysis of a person's genes to identify genetic variations. Genetic screening can indicate whether individuals or their potential offspring may be at risk for certain diseases or genetic disorders. Genetic screening has the potential for early diagnosis of conditions that can be treated before an illness occurs.

Genetic screening also raises ethical concerns. For example, who should have access to a person's genetic information? Some people are concerned that insurance companies might refuse health insurance to someone with a gene that might cause a disease. Suppose genetic screening reveals that a child might have a genetic disorder. How should that information be used? Genetic screening has the potential to eliminate some disorders, but what should be

FIGURE 1.19 Biotechnology is being used in the search for alternative energy sources, as shown in this bioreactor that uses algae (inset) to produce hydrogen gas. (LM; magnification 400×)

Connecting CONCEPTS

Genetics You will learn more about genetic screening and how it is used in **Chapter 9.**

26 Unit 1: Introducing Biology

considered a disorder? Of greater concern is the possibility that people might use genetic screening to choose the characteristics of their children. Is it ethical to allow people to choose to have only brown-eyed male children who would be at least six feet tall?

Predict How might genetically modified crops affect biodiversity?

◗ MAIN IDEA
Biology presents many unanswered questions.

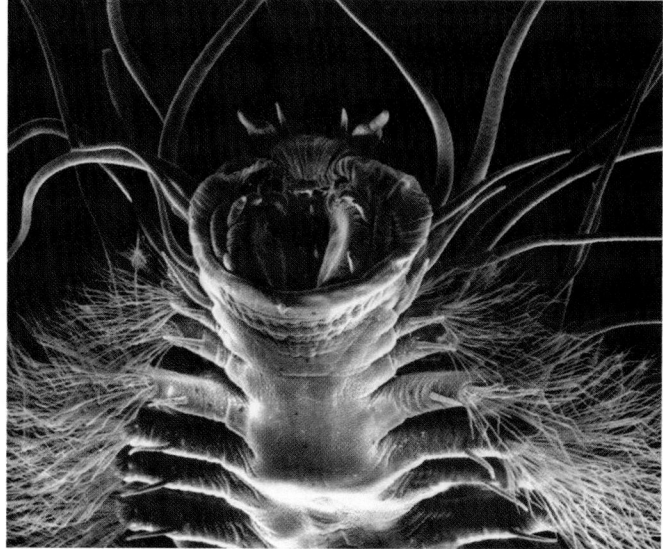

About 50 years ago, the structure of DNA was discovered. By 2003, the entire human DNA sequence was known. Over the last 50 years, our biological knowledge has exploded. But even today there are more questions than answers. Can cancer be prevented or cured? How do viruses mutate? How are memories stored in the brain? One of the most interesting questions is whether life exists on planets other than Earth. Extreme environments on Earth are home to living things like the methane worms in **FIGURE 1.20**. Thus, it is logical to suspect that other planets may also support life. But even if life exists elsewhere in the universe, it may be completely different from life on Earth. How might biological theories change to take into account the characteristics of those organisms?

A huge number of questions in biology are not just unanswered—they are unasked. Before the microscope was developed, no one investigated anything microscopic. Before the middle of the 20th century, biologists did not know for sure what the genetic material in organisms was made of. As technology and biology advance, who knows what will be discovered in the next 20 years?

Evaluate Do you think technology can help answer all biological questions? Explain your views.

FIGURE 1.20 Methane worms live in frozen methane gas at the bottom of the Gulf of Mexico. Because some organisms can live in such extreme environments, some scientists hypothesize that life exists, or once existed, on the planet Mars. (SEM; magnification 20×)

1.5 / ASSESSMENT

ONLINE QUIZ
ClassZone.com

REVIEWING ◗ MAIN IDEAS

1. Give three examples of ways in which biology can help inform everyday decisions.

2. What are some of the potential benefits and potential risks of **biotechnology**?

3. What are some of the unanswered questions in biology?

CRITICAL THINKING

4. **Synthesize** Scientists disagree on whether genetically modified foods are safe to eat. What type of scientific evidence would be needed to show that a genetically modified food is unsafe?

5. **Connect** How might your study of biology help inform you about your lifestyle choices?

Connecting CONCEPTS

6. **Ecology** What effects might genetically modified plants and animals have on an ecosystem if they breed with wild plants and animals?

Use these inquiry-based labs and online activities to deepen your understanding of biology and scientific experiments.

MICHIGAN STANDARDS

B1.1A Generate new questions that can be investigated in the laboratory or field.

B1.1h Design and conduct a systematic scientific investigation that tests a hypothesis. Draw conclusions from data presented in charts or tables.

DESIGN YOUR OWN INVESTIGATION

Manipulating Plant Growth

The direction in which plants grow is affected by conditions such as light, gravity, and contact with an object. In this lab, you will design your own experiment to determine how changing an independent variable affects a dependent variable.

SKILLS Designing Experiments, Observing, Collecting Data, Analyzing Data, Inferring

PROBLEM How does changing an external condition affect plant growth?

MATERIALS

- 3 bean plants
- 10 cm masking tape
- permanent marker
- light source
- 3 wooden sticks
- 1 m string
- metric ruler
- water
- 250-mL beaker

PROCEDURE

1. Label three bean plants A, B, and C.

2. Decide which condition you will test: light, gravity, or contact with an object.

3. Design your experiment and identify your independent variable. Use one plant as the control condition. Use the other two plants as experimental conditions. For example, gravity can be tested by placing an experimental plant on its side.

4. Identify the constants in your experiment, such as the amount of water you will give the plants.

5. Determine the operational definition for the dependent variable; that is, decide how you will measure the dependent variable. For example, it could be the number of leaves facing in a certain direction each day.

6. Record your observations once a day for five days in a table like the one shown below. Remember to wash your hands after handling the plants.

7. Have your teacher approve your procedure. Carry out your experiment.

TABLE 1. EFFECT OF _____ ON PLANT GROWTH			
Day	Plant A Growth (mm)	Plant B Growth (mm)	Plant C Growth (mm)
1			
2			

ANALYZE AND CONCLUDE

1. **Analyze** How did your independent variable affect plant growth? How did you measure the dependent variable? Do the data support your hypothesis? Explain.

2. **Infer** Why is it important to have control groups and constants in an experiment?

3. **Communicate** Share your results with other groups. How did different independent variables affect plant growth? Did your results agree with the results of other groups that tested the same variable? If not, what might have caused that difference?

4. **Design Experiments** Review the design of your experiment. What changes could you make to the procedure to reduce the variability in your data?

5. **Ask Questions** From your data, what new questions do you have about plant growth?

Biology in the News

Every day, newspapers print articles related to biology. Maybe someone has reported a previously unknown species, such as the Goodman's mouse lemur, discovered on the island of Madagascar in 2005. Maybe it's a story about the effect of a low-fat diet on the risk of developing cancer. Some articles discuss biology-related questions or problems, such as the use of a mercury-based preservative in certain vaccines. What biology news stories interest you?

SKILL Researching

PROBLEM What types of biology-based problems are reported in the news?

PROCEDURE

1. Find a news story about a biology-based problem in the newspaper or from one of the news feeds in the BioZine at ClassZone.com. Because medical research is the most common topic discussed in news articles, find an article about a different topic in biology.

2. Read the article and answer the following questions:

   - What is the topic of the article?
   - What is the problem, discovery, or event?
   - What is being decided?
   - Who are the people involved in making the decision?
   - What are all of the possible consequences of the decision?
   - What factors may be influencing the decision?
   - What new questions are raised as a result of the discovery, situation, or research?
   - How is knowledge of biology useful for understanding this topic?

Goodman's mouse lemur was discovered in 2005.

Online BIOLOGY
CLASSZONE.COM

ANIMATED BIOLOGY
Experimental Design

How do you test a hypothesis? Use items in a lab to design a valid experiment for a sample hypothesis, and identify all of the factors in your investigation.

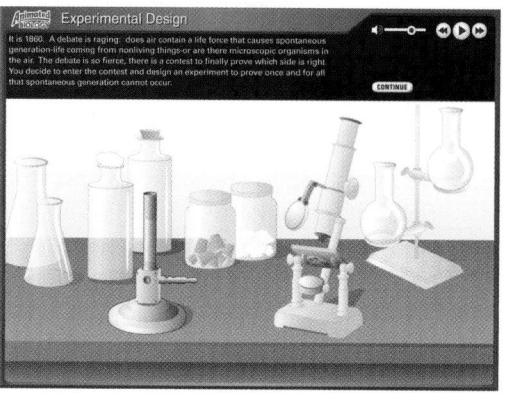

WEBQUEST

Is it always ethical to conduct scientific research, ask for a person's DNA, or use all of the biotechnology that we have? In this WebQuest, you will explore bio-ethics. First, learn how scientists think ethically. Then, explore a situation and determine for yourself if it was handled in an ethical manner.

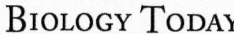

BIOLOGY TODAY

Scientist Suspected of Bioethics Violations

DATA ANALYSIS ONLINE

Earth has a great, ever-changing diversity of life. The types and numbers of organisms have changed over time. Graph the estimated number of different categories of marine organisms over the past 550 million years to analyze the trends in Earth's biodiversity.

1.1 The Study of Life

Biologists study life in all its forms. Everywhere that organisms are found on Earth is considered to be the biosphere. The biosphere includes millions of diverse species. Organisms are made of one or more cells, need energy for all of their functions, respond to their environment, and reproduce by passing on their genetic information to offspring.

1.2 Unifying Themes of Biology

Unifying themes connect concepts from many fields of biology. Life is based on interrelated systems, from chemical processes within cells to interactions among different species in an ecosystem. Individual organisms depend on the relationship between structure and function, and on the ability to maintain homeostasis. Over billions of years, evolution and adaptation have given rise to all of the species on Earth.

1.3 Scientific Thinking and Processes

Science is a way of thinking, questioning, and gathering evidence. Scientists test hypotheses, or proposed explanations, through observation and experimentation. In a scientific experiment, a scientist controls constants, manipulates independent variables, and measures dependent variables. A scientific theory explains a wide range of observations and experimental results. A theory is supported by a wide range of evidence, and it is widely accepted by the scientific community.

1.4 Biologists' Tools and Technology

Technology continually changes the way biologists work. Imaging technologies have had a major influence on biology. Microscopes, from the light microscope to today's electron microscopes, allow biologists to study tiny details of cells. The development of fast, powerful computers has given scientists the ability to model aspects of life that cannot be studied directly. Technology also allows the study, comparison, and manipulation of genes at the molecular level.

1.5 Biology and Your Future

Understanding biology can help you make informed decisions. An understanding of biology can help you to make important decisions about your own health and lifestyle, as well as decisions that will shape the world around you. The development of biotechnology and genetic manipulation is just one issue in biology that will affect you and the rest of society in the coming years.

Synthesize Your Notes

Content Frame Identify relationships between the characteristics of living things and the unifying themes of biology. Use your notes to make content frame organizers like the one below to summarize the relationships.

Characteristic	Theme	Example
Cells	Systems	Cells work together in multicellular organisms.
	Structure and Function	

Concept Map Use concept maps like the one below to visualize general relationships among topics in biology.

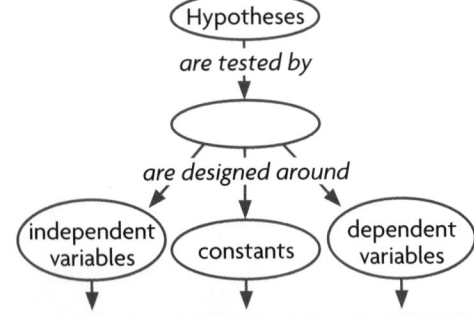

Chapter Assessment

Chapter Vocabulary

1.1
biosphere, p. 4
biodiversity, p. 5
species, p. 5
biology, p. 5
organism, p. 5
cell, p. 5
metabolism, p. 6
DNA, p. 6

1.2
system, p. 7
ecosystem, p. 7

homeostasis, p. 9
evolution, p. 10
adaptation, p. 10

1.3
observation, p. 13
data, p. 14
hypothesis, p. 14
experiment, p. 16
independent variable, p. 16
dependent variable, p. 16
constant, p. 16
theory, p. 16

1.4
microscope, p. 19
gene, p. 23
molecular genetics, p. 23
genomics, p. 23

1.5
biotechnology, p. 26
transgenic, p. 26

Reviewing Vocabulary

Compare and Contrast

Describe one similarity and one difference between the two terms in each of the following pairs.

1. biosphere, ecosystem
2. hypothesis, theory
3. independent variable, constant

Write Your Own Questions

Think about the relationship between each word pair below. Then write a question about the first term that uses the second term as the answer. For the pair *organism, cell,* the question could be "What is the basic building block of all organisms?" Answer: the cell

4. evolution, adaptation
5. observation, data
6. DNA, gene

Greek and Latin Word Origins

7. The prefix *bio-* means "life." How does this meaning relate to the definitions of terms in the chapter that contain the prefix *bio-*?

8. The prefix *homeo-* comes from a Greek word that means "same." The suffix *-stasis* comes from a Greek word that means "stoppage," or "standstill." How are these definitions related to the meaning of *homeostasis*?

Reviewing MAIN IDEAS

9. In general, greater biodiversity exists closer to Earth's equator than in areas closer to Earth's poles. What does this mean in terms of the number of species that are found in these regions?

10. Briefly describe the basic characteristics that all living things on Earth have in common.

11. Give an example of how structure and function are related in an organism.

12. How does negative feedback act to maintain homeostasis in living things?

13. Evidence shows that hippos and whales are closely related organisms. How might evolution and adaptation account for similarities and differences between them?

14. Explain how scientists use observations and data to develop a hypothesis.

15. How does the manipulation of an independent variable during a scientific experiment allow a scientist to find a cause-and-effect relationship between variables?

16. What is the difference between a hypothesis and a theory?

17. Briefly describe why the development of the microscope was important in biology.

18. How can an understanding of biology play a role in your health? in the health of your environment?

19. Describe an example of biotechnology, including its benefits and risks.

Critical Thinking

20. Predict Many medications used to treat human illnesses are based on substances found in other organisms. How might a decrease in biodiversity affect medical discoveries and treatments?

21. Synthesize In 1973, the insecticide called DDT was banned in the United States due to concerns that it was toxic to fish and that it may have affected birds. There is little scientific evidence that DDT is directly harmful to humans. How could banning DDT be beneficial to human health?

22. Synthesize Birds and mammals have complex circulatory systems that pump and carry blood to all parts of their bodies. Insects have much simpler circulatory systems. Select two unifying themes of biology from Section 1.2, and describe how they apply to the circulatory systems of animals.

23. Evaluate Suppose a scientist is investigating plant growth. During the experiment, both the type of light and the type of plant are manipulated. The scientist concludes that the results are caused only by changes in the light. Is this an appropriate conclusion? Why or why not?

24. Compare and Contrast Describe the similarities and differences among images from light microscopes, scanning electron microscopes, and transmission electron microscopes.

Interpreting Visuals

Use the diagram below to answer the next two questions.

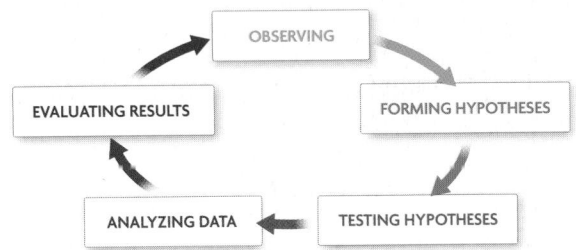

25. Apply Observing is shown at only one point during the cycle. At what other points during the cycle is observing necessary? Explain.

26. Analyze As shown, the cycle of scientific thinking goes in one step-by-step direction. Where could you add arrows to the diagram to show a more complete description of the scientific process? Explain.

Analyzing Data

Use the information below to answer the next three questions.

Suppose a team of scientists is studying the migration of animal species in Africa. One of the scientists takes the photograph below.

27. Apply Give three examples of qualitative data that could be collected during this research.

28. Apply Give three examples of quantitative data that could be collected during this research.

29. Synthesize Suppose the scientists wanted to change the number of species present in this study. Could this manipulation be done? If so, how? If not, why not?

Connecting CONCEPTS

30. Write an Analogy Earlier in the chapter, a car's cruise control system was used as an analogy for negative feedback and homeostasis in an organism. Think of your own analogy to describe one of the other unifying themes of biology. Write a paragraph using that analogy to explain that theme. Be sure to also describe any ways in which your analogy does not fit the theme.

31. Synthesize The yellow fever mosquito shown on page 3 is just one type of mosquito that can pass disease-causing viruses to people. Mosquitoes can also carry other diseases such as malaria, Dengue fever, and West Nile virus. And even if mosquitoes do not carry dangerous viruses, they are certainly pests. On the other hand, mosquitoes are a source of food for many types of animals. Suppose you developed a way to rid Earth of mosquitoes. Do you think it should be used? Why or why not?

MICHIGAN
STANDARDS-BASED ASSESSMENT

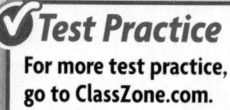

✓ **Test Practice**
For more test practice,
go to ClassZone.com.

1. A proposed explanation for a wide range of observations and experimental results that is supported by a large amount of evidence is a scientific **B1.2h**

   A hypothesis.

   B theory.

   C conclusion.

   D law.

2. **Effect of Fertilizer in Two Soils**

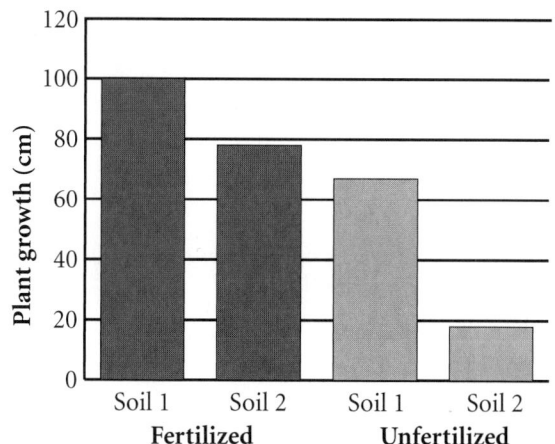

   A scientist wants to know how a certain fertilizer affects the growth of tomato plants growing in two different soils. What conclusion can be drawn from the graph shown here? **B1.1E**

   A Soil 1 and Soil 2 are the same.

   B The fertilizer has a greater effect in Soil 1.

   C The fertilizer has a greater effect in Soil 2.

   D Soil 1 absorbed more fertilizer than Soil 2.

   THINK THROUGH THE QUESTION

   Conclusions based on scientific research must be supported by the data collected. Conclusions are very specific to the data, so statements that appear to be very general are unlikely to be the right answers.

3. Students hypothesized that water pollution affects the growth of fish. In an experiment, they added the same amount of food to ponds polluted by fertilizers and industrial waste. They measured fish growth and found that most fish grow slowly in each of these environments. What part of their experiment did they forget to include? **B1.1B**

   A a group to serve as a control

   B a hypothesis to test

   C a theory to explain their results

   D a procedure to follow

4. Which of the following is the *best* example of biodiversity? **B3.4B**

   A In Sri Lanka, over 30 species of tree frog are in danger of becoming extinct.

   B Atlantic salmon may swim 500 miles against a river current just to spawn.

   C Sequoia National Park has more than 1200 plant species.

   D Birds have feathers with different colors.

5. Finch species in the Galapagos Islands have a wide variety of beak shapes. The theory of natural selection suggests that these differences arose because **B5.1A**

   A changes occurred over a short period of time.

   B finches with certain beak shapes survived in greater numbers.

   C conscious decisions let certain finches survive.

   D individual finches adapted to their environment.

6.

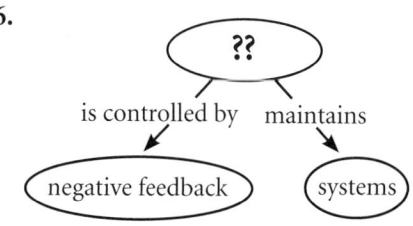

   Which of the following best completes this concept map? **B2.3e**

   A biodiversity

   B homeostasis

   C evolution

   D adaptation

CHAPTER
2 Chemistry of Life

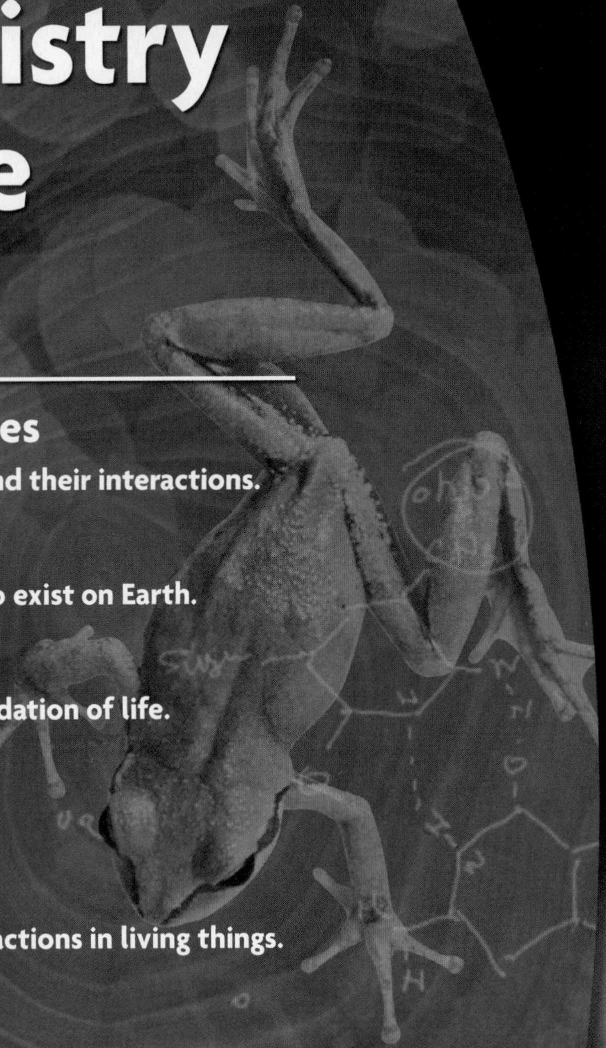

KEY CONCEPTS

2.1 Atoms, Ions, and Molecules
All living things are based on atoms and their interactions.

2.2 Properties of Water
Water's unique properties allow life to exist on Earth.

2.3 Carbon-Based Molecules
Carbon-based molecules are the foundation of life.

2.4 Chemical Reactions
Life depends on chemical reactions.

2.5 Enzymes
Enzymes are catalysts for chemical reactions in living things.

Online BIOLOGY CLASSZONE.COM

Animated BIOLOGY

View animated chapter concepts.
• Hydrogen Bonding
• Energy and Chemical Reactions
• Calorimetry
• Atoms and Bonding

BIOZINE

Keep current with biology news.
• News feeds
• Careers
• Polls

 RESOURCE CENTER

Get more information on
• Elements of Life
• Acids, Bases, and pH

How can this plant digest a frog?

L ike other carnivores, the Venus flytrap eats animals to get nutrients that it needs to make molecules such as proteins and nucleic acids. Other chemical compounds made by the plant's cells enable the Venus flytrap to digest the animals that it eats. These chemicals are similar to the chemicals that allow you to digest the food that you eat.

Connecting CONCEPTS

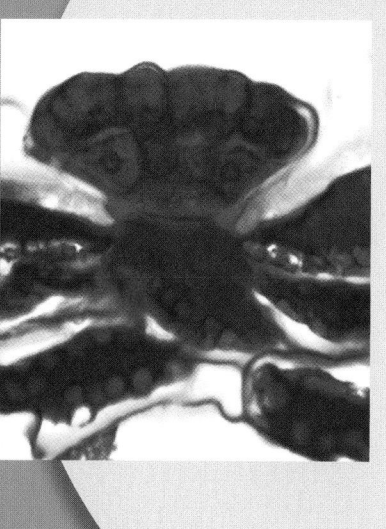

Cell Function The Venus flytrap has specialized cells on the surfaces of its leaves. Some of these cells allow the plant to snap shut on its prey within 0.5 seconds. Other cells, such as those that appear purple in this light micrograph, secrete digestive chemicals that allow the plant to consume its prey. (LM; magnification 500×)

2.1 Atoms, Ions, and Molecules

KEY CONCEPT All living things are based on atoms and their interactions.

MAIN IDEAS

- Living things consist of atoms of different elements.
- Ions form when atoms gain or lose electrons.
- Atoms share pairs of electrons in covalent bonds.

VOCABULARY

atom, p. 36
element, p. 36
compound, p. 37
ion, p. 38

ionic bond, p. 38
covalent bond, p. 39
molecule, p. 39

Review
cell, organism

MICHIGAN STANDARDS

B2.4f Recognize and describe that both living and nonliving things are composed of compounds, which are themselves made up of elements joined by energy-containing bonds, such as those in ATP.

TAKING NOTES

Use a main idea web to help you make connections among elements, atoms, ions, compounds, and molecules.

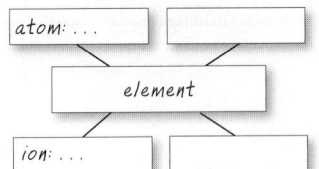

Connect The Venus flytrap produces chemicals that allow it to consume and digest insects and other small animals, including an unlucky frog. Frogs also produce specialized chemicals that allow them to consume and digest their prey. In fact, all organisms depend on many chemicals and chemical reactions. For this reason, the study of living things also involves the study of chemistry.

MAIN IDEA

Living things consist of atoms of different elements.

What do a frog, a skyscraper, a car, and your body all have in common? Every physical thing you can think of, living or not, is made of incredibly small particles called atoms. An **atom** is the smallest basic unit of matter. Millions of atoms could fit in a space the size of the period at the end of this sentence. And it would take you more than 1 trillion (1,000,000,000,000, or 10^{11}) years to count the number of atoms in a single grain of sand.

Atoms and Elements

Although there is a huge variety of matter on Earth, all atoms share the same basic structure. Atoms consist of three types of smaller particles: protons, neutrons, and electrons. Protons and neutrons form the dense center of an atom—the atomic nucleus. Electrons are much smaller particles outside of the nucleus. Protons have a positive electrical charge, and electrons have a negative electrical charge. Neutrons, as their name implies, are neutral—they have no charge. Because an atom has equal numbers of positively charged protons and negatively charged electrons, it is electrically neutral.

An **element** is one particular type of atom, and it cannot be broken down into a simpler substance by ordinary chemical means. An element can also refer to a group of atoms of the same type. A few familiar elements include the gases hydrogen and oxygen and the metals aluminum and gold. Because all atoms are made of the same types of particles, what difference among atoms makes one element different from other elements? Atoms of different elements differ in the number of protons they have. All atoms of a given element have a specific number of protons that never varies. For example, all hydrogen atoms have one proton, and all oxygen atoms have eight protons.

The electrons in the atoms of each element determine the properties of that element. As **FIGURE 2.1** shows, electrons are considered to be in a cloud around the nucleus. The simplified models of a hydrogen atom and an oxygen atom on the left side of **FIGURE 2.2** illustrate how electrons move around the nucleus in regions called energy levels. Different energy levels can hold different numbers of electrons. For example, the first energy level can hold two electrons, and the second energy level can hold eight electrons. Atoms are most stable when they have a full outermost energy level.

Of the 91 elements that naturally occur on Earth, only about 25 are found in organisms. Just 4 elements—carbon (C), oxygen (O), nitrogen (N), and hydrogen (H)—make up 96 percent of the human body's mass. The other 4 percent consists of calcium (Ca), phosphorus (P), potassium (K), sulfur (S), sodium (Na), and several other trace elements. Trace elements are found in very small amounts in your body, but you need them to survive. For example, iron (Fe) is needed to transport oxygen in your blood. Chromium (Cr) is needed for your cells to break down sugars for usable energy.

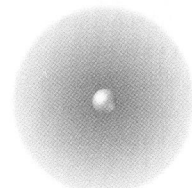

FIGURE 2.1 The exact position of electrons cannot be known. They are somewhere in a three-dimensional electron cloud around the nucleus.

FIGURE 2.2 Representing Atoms

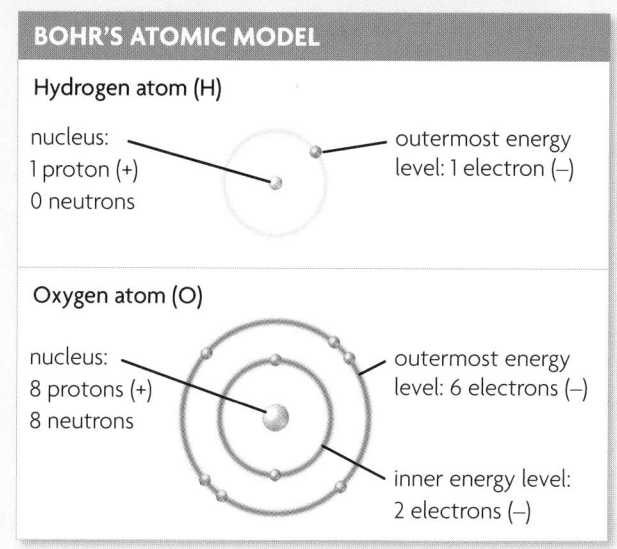

BOHR'S ATOMIC MODEL

Hydrogen atom (H)

nucleus:
1 proton (+)
0 neutrons

outermost energy level: 1 electron (−)

Oxygen atom (O)

nucleus:
8 protons (+)
8 neutrons

outermost energy level: 6 electrons (−)

inner energy level: 2 electrons (−)

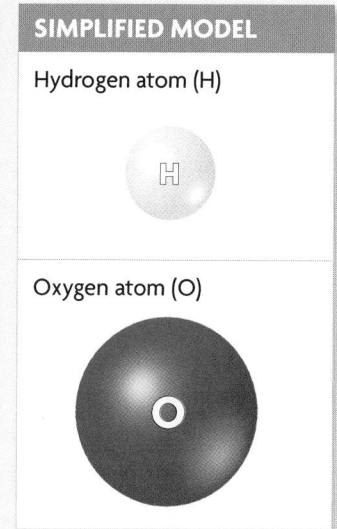

SIMPLIFIED MODEL

Hydrogen atom (H)

Oxygen atom (O)

The model of the atom developed by Niels Bohr (left) shows that an atom's electrons are located outside the nucleus in regions called energy levels. Different types of atoms have different numbers of electrons and energy levels.

Often, atoms are shown as simplified spheres (right). Different types of atoms are shown in different sizes and colors.

Apply How many electrons would need to be added to fill the outermost energy level of hydrogen? of oxygen?

Compounds

The atoms of elements found in organisms are often linked, or bonded, to other atoms. A **compound** is a substance made of atoms of different elements bonded together in a certain ratio. Common compounds in living things include water (H_2O) and carbon dioxide (CO_2). A compound's properties are often different from the properties of the elements that make up the compound. At temperatures on Earth, for example, hydrogen and oxygen are both gases. Together, though, they can form water. Similarly, a diamond is pure carbon, but carbon atoms are also the basis of sugars, proteins, and millions of other compounds.

Contrast How are elements different from compounds?

● MAIN IDEA
Ions form when atoms gain or lose electrons.

An **ion** is an atom that has gained or lost one or more electrons. An ion forms because an atom is more stable when its outermost energy level is full; the gain or loss of electrons results in a full outermost energy level. An atom becomes an ion when its number of electrons changes and it gains an electrical charge. This charge gives ions certain properties. For example, compounds consisting only of ions—ionic compounds—easily dissolve in water.

Some ions are positively charged, and other ions are negatively charged. The type of ion that forms depends on the number of electrons in an atom's outer energy level. An atom with few electrons in its outer energy level tends to lose those electrons. An atom that loses one or more electrons becomes a positively charged ion because it has more protons than electrons. In contrast, an atom with a nearly full outer energy level tends to gain electrons. An atom that gains one or more electrons becomes a negatively charged ion because it has more electrons than protons.

Ions play large roles in organisms. For example, hydrogen ions (H^+) are needed for the production of usable chemical energy in cells. Calcium ions (Ca^{2+}) are necessary for every muscle movement in your body. And chloride ions (Cl^-) are important for a certain type of chemical signal in the brain.

Ions usually form when electrons are transferred from one atom to another. For example, **FIGURE 2.3** shows the transfer of an electron from a sodium atom (Na) to a chlorine atom (Cl). When it loses its one outer electron, the sodium atom becomes a positively charged sodium ion (Na^+). Its second energy level, which has eight electrons, is now a full outermost energy level. The transferred electron fills chlorine's outermost energy level, forming a negatively charged chloride ion (Cl^-). Positive ions, such as Na^+, are attracted to negative ions, such as Cl^-. An **ionic bond** forms through the electrical force between oppositely charged ions. Salt, or sodium chloride (NaCl), is an ionic compound of Na^+ and Cl^-. Sodium chloride is held together by ionic bonds.

Apply **What determines whether an atom becomes a positive ion or a negative ion?**

Connecting CONCEPTS
Cell Structure and Function
Several different ions are transported across cell membranes during cell processes. You will learn how this transport occurs in **Chapters 3** and **4**.

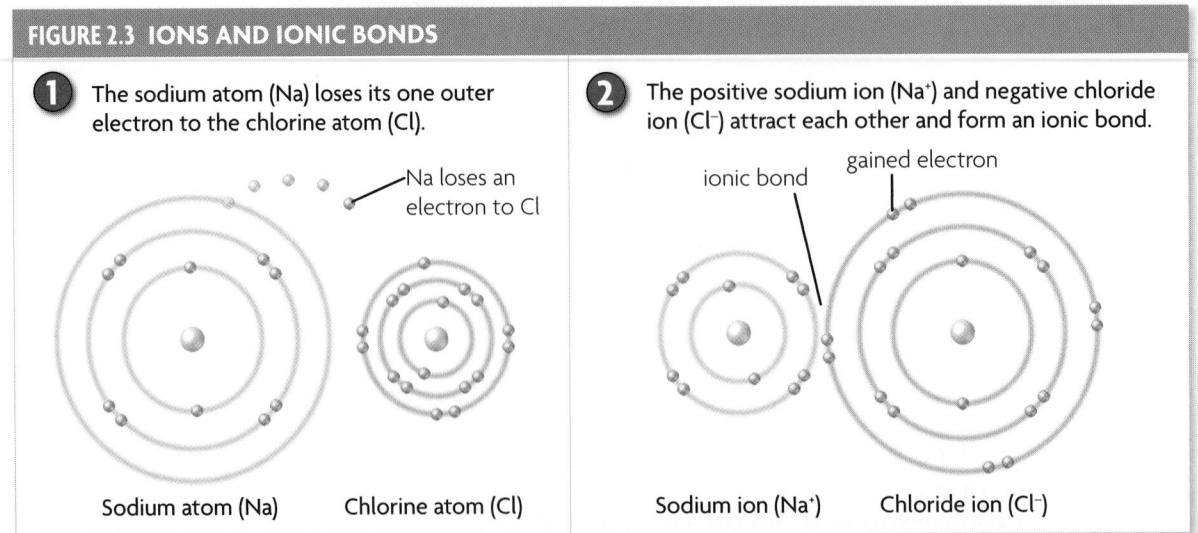

FIGURE 2.3 IONS AND IONIC BONDS

1 The sodium atom (Na) loses its one outer electron to the chlorine atom (Cl).

Na loses an electron to Cl

Sodium atom (Na)   Chlorine atom (Cl)

2 The positive sodium ion (Na^+) and negative chloride ion (Cl^-) attract each other and form an ionic bond.

ionic bond   gained electron

Sodium ion (Na^+)   Chloride ion (Cl^-)

▶ MAIN IDEA

Atoms share pairs of electrons in covalent bonds.

Not all atoms easily gain or lose electrons. Rather, the atoms of many elements share pairs of electrons. The shared pairs of electrons fill the outermost energy levels of the bonded atoms. A **covalent bond** forms when atoms share a pair of electrons. Covalent bonds are generally very strong, and depending on how many electrons an atom has, two atoms may form several covalent bonds to share several pairs of electrons. **FIGURE 2.4** illustrates how atoms of carbon and oxygen share pairs of electrons in covalent bonds. All three atoms in a molecule of carbon dioxide (CO_2) have full outer energy levels.

VOCABULARY

The prefix *co-* means "together," and *valent* comes from a Latin word that means "power" or "strength."

FIGURE 2.4 COVALENT BONDS

A carbon atom needs four electrons to fill its outer energy level. An oxygen atom needs two electrons to fill its outer energy level. In carbon dioxide, carbon makes a double bond, or shares two pairs of electrons, with each oxygen atom.

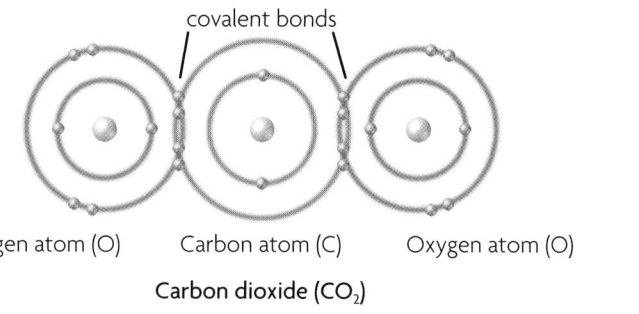

covalent bonds

Oxygen atom (O)   Carbon atom (C)   Oxygen atom (O)

Carbon dioxide (CO_2)

A **molecule** is two or more atoms held together by covalent bonds. In the compound carbon dioxide, each oxygen atom shares two pairs of electrons (four electrons) with the carbon atom. Some elements occur naturally in the form of diatomic, or "two-atom," molecules. For example, a molecule of oxygen (O_2) consists of two oxygen atoms that share two pairs of electrons. Almost all of the substances that make up organisms, from lipids to nucleic acids to water, are molecules held together by covalent bonds.

Summarize What happens to electrons in outer energy levels when two atoms form a covalent bond?

2.1 ASSESSMENT

ONLINE QUIZ
ClassZone.com

REVIEWING ▶ MAIN IDEAS

1. What distinguishes one **element** from another?

2. Describe the formation of an **ionic compound.**

3. What is the difference between an **ionic bond** and a **covalent bond**?

CRITICAL THINKING

4. **Compare and Contrast** How does a **molecule** differ from an **atom**?

5. **Apply** Explain why a hydrogen atom can become either an **ion** or a part of a molecule.

Connecting CONCEPTS

6. **Chemistry** A sodium atom has one outer electron, and a carbon atom has four outer electrons. How might this difference be related to the types of compounds formed by atoms of these two elements?

Properties of Water

KEY CONCEPT Water's unique properties allow life to exist on Earth.

▶ **MAIN IDEAS**

- Life depends on hydrogen bonds in water.
- Many compounds dissolve in water.
- Some compounds form acids or bases.

VOCABULARY

hydrogen bond, p. 41
cohesion, p. 41
adhesion, p. 41
solution, p. 42
solvent, p. 42

solute, p. 42
acid, p. 42
base, p. 42
pH, p. 42

Review
ion, molecule

MICHIGAN STANDARDS

L2.p1B Explain the importance of both water and the element carbon to cells. (prerequisite)

B2.3B Describe how the maintenance of a relatively stable internal environment is required for the continuation of life.

Connect When you are thirsty, you need to drink something that is mostly water. Why is the water you drink absolutely necessary? Your cells, and the cells of every other living thing on Earth, are mostly water. Water gives cells structure and transports materials within organisms. All of the processes necessary for life take place in that watery environment. Water's unique properties, which are related to the structure of the water molecule, are important for living things.

▶ **MAIN IDEA**

Life depends on hydrogen bonds in water.

How do fish survive a cold winter if their pond freezes? Unlike most substances, water expands when it freezes. Water is less dense as a solid (ice) than as a liquid. In a pond, ice floats and covers the water's surface. The ice acts as an insulator that allows the water underneath to remain a liquid. Ice's low density is related to the structure of the water molecule.

Water and Hydrogen Bonds

Water is a polar molecule. You can think about polar molecules in the same way that you can think about a magnet's poles. That is, polar molecules have a region with a slight positive charge and a region with a slight negative charge. Polar molecules, such as the water molecule shown in **FIGURE 2.5,** form when atoms in a molecule have unequal pulls on the electrons they share. In a molecule of water, the oxygen nucleus, with its eight protons, attracts the shared electrons more strongly than do the hydrogen nuclei, with only one proton each. The oxygen atom gains a small negative charge, and the hydrogen atoms gain small positive charges. Other molecules, called nonpolar molecules, do not have these charged regions. The atoms in nonpolar molecules share electrons more equally.

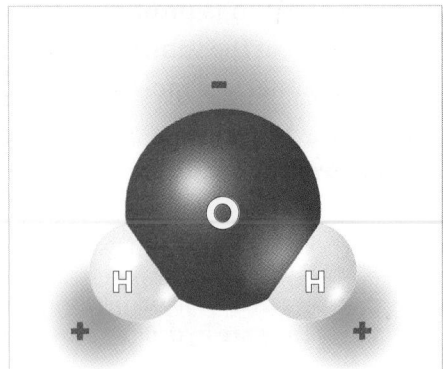

FIGURE 2.5 In water molecules, the oxygen atom has a slightly negative charge, and the hydrogen atoms have slightly positive charges.

Opposite charges of polar molecules can interact to form hydrogen bonds. A **hydrogen bond** is an attraction between a slightly positive hydrogen atom and a slightly negative atom, often oxygen or nitrogen. Hydrogen bonding is shown among water molecules in **FIGURE 2.6**, but these bonds are also found in many other molecules. For example, hydrogen bonds are part of the structures of proteins and of DNA, which is the genetic material for all organisms.

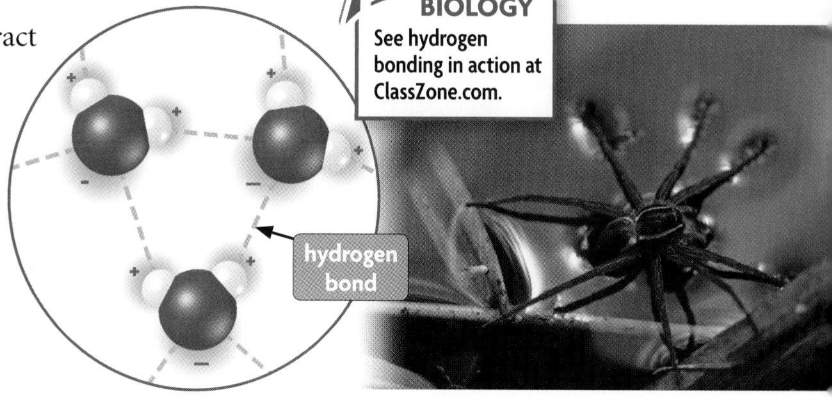

Animated BIOLOGY
See hydrogen bonding in action at ClassZone.com.

hydrogen bond

FIGURE 2.6 Water's surface tension comes from hydrogen bonds (left) that cause water molecules to stick together.

Properties Related to Hydrogen Bonds

Individual hydrogen bonds are about 20 times weaker than typical covalent bonds, but they are relatively strong among water molecules. As a result, a large amount of energy is needed to overcome the attractions among water molecules. Without hydrogen bonds, water would boil at a much lower temperature than it does because less energy would be needed to change liquid water into water vapor. Water is a liquid at the temperatures that support most life on Earth only because of hydrogen bonds in water. Hydrogen bonds are responsible for three important properties of water.

- **High specific heat** Hydrogen bonds give water an abnormally high specific heat. This means that water resists changes in temperature. Compared to many other compounds, water must absorb more heat energy to increase in temperature. This property is very important in cells. The processes that produce usable chemical energy in cells release a great deal of heat. Water absorbs the heat, which helps to regulate cell temperatures.

- **Cohesion** The attraction among molecules of a substance is **cohesion.** Cohesion from hydrogen bonds makes water molecules stick to each other. You can see this when water forms beads, such as on a recently washed car. Cohesion also produces surface tension, which makes a kind of skin on water. Surface tension keeps the spider in **FIGURE 2.6** from sinking.

- **Adhesion** The attraction among molecules of different substances is called **adhesion.** In other words, water molecules stick to other things. Adhesion is responsible for the upward curve on the surface of the water in **FIGURE 2.7** because water molecules are attracted to the glass of the test tube. Adhesion helps plants transport water from their roots to their leaves because water molecules stick to the sides of the vessels that carry water.

FIGURE 2.7 The water's surface (left, dyed red) is curved down because water has greater adhesion than cohesion. The surface of the mercury (right) is curved up because mercury has greater cohesion than adhesion.

Compare How are hydrogen bonds similar to ionic bonds?

▶ MAIN IDEA
Many compounds dissolve in water.

Molecules and ions cannot take part in chemical processes inside cells unless they dissolve in water. Important materials such as sugars and oxygen cannot be transported from one part of an organism to another unless they are dissolved in blood, plant sap, or other water-based fluids.

Many substances dissolve in the water in your body. When one substance dissolves in another, a solution forms. A **solution** is a mixture of substances that is the same throughout—it is a homogeneous mixture. A solution has two parts. The **solvent** is the substance that is present in the greater amount and that dissolves another substance. A **solute** is a substance that dissolves in a solvent.

The amount of solute dissolved in a certain amount of solvent is a solution's concentration. One spoonful of a drink mix in water has little flavor because it has a low concentration. But a solution with four spoonfuls in the same amount of water tastes stronger because it has a higher concentration.

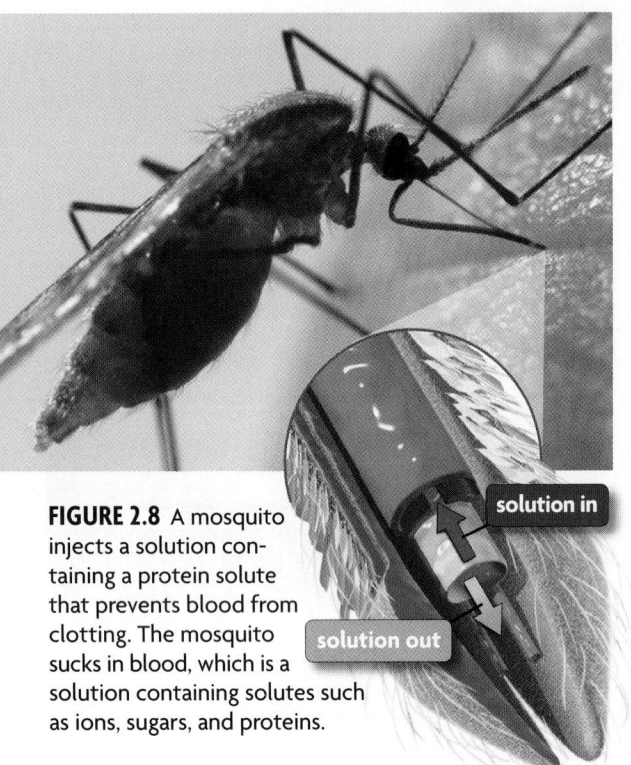

FIGURE 2.8 A mosquito injects a solution containing a protein solute that prevents blood from clotting. The mosquito sucks in blood, which is a solution containing solutes such as ions, sugars, and proteins.

solution in

solution out

The liquid part of your blood, called plasma, is about 95 percent water. Therefore, the solvent in plasma is water and all of the substances dissolved in it are solutes. Most of these solutes, such as sugars and proteins, dissolve in the water of blood plasma because they are polar. Polar molecules dissolve in water because the attraction between the water molecules and the solute molecules is greater than the attraction among the molecules of the solute. Similarly, ionic compounds, such as sodium chloride, dissolve in water because the charges of the water molecules attract the charges of the ions. The water molecules surround each ion and pull the compound apart.

Nonpolar substances, such as fats and oils, rarely dissolve in water. Nonpolar molecules do not have charged regions, so they are not attracted to polar molecules. Polar molecules and nonpolar molecules tend to remain separate, which is why we say, "Oil and water don't mix." But nonpolar molecules will dissolve in nonpolar solvents. For example, some vitamins, such as vitamin E, are nonpolar and dissolve in fat in your body.

Connect What are the solvent and solutes in a beverage you drink?

> **MAIN IDEA**
Some compounds form acids or bases.

Some compounds break up into ions when they dissolve in water. An **acid** is a compound that releases a proton—a hydrogen ion (H^+)—when it dissolves in water. An acid increases the concentration of H^+ ions in a solution. **Bases** are compounds that remove H^+ ions from a solution. When a base dissolves in water, the solution has a low H^+ concentration. A solution's acidity, or H^+ ion concentration, is measured by the **pH** scale. In **FIGURE 2.9** you can see that pH is usually between 0 and 14. A solution with a pH of 0 is very acidic, with a high H^+ concentration. A solution with a pH of 14 is very basic, with a low H^+ concentration. Solutions with a pH of 7 are neutral—neither acidic nor basic.

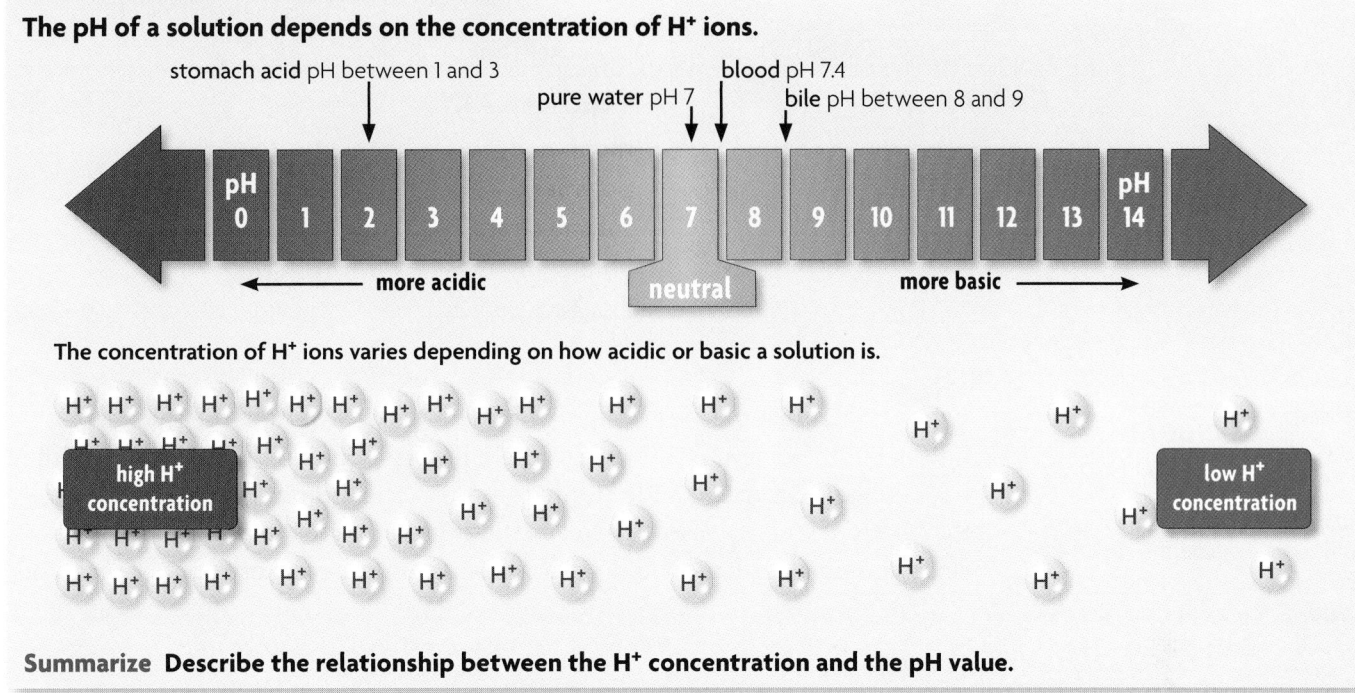

FIGURE 2.9 Understanding pH

The pH of a solution depends on the concentration of H⁺ ions.

stomach acid pH between 1 and 3

pure water pH 7

blood pH 7.4

bile pH between 8 and 9

pH 0 | 1 | 2 | 3 | 4 | 5 | 6 | 7 | 8 | 9 | 10 | 11 | 12 | 13 | pH 14

← more acidic

neutral

more basic →

The concentration of H⁺ ions varies depending on how acidic or basic a solution is.

high H⁺ concentration

low H⁺ concentration

Summarize Describe the relationship between the H⁺ concentration and the pH value.

Most organisms, including humans, need to keep their pH within a very narrow range around neutral (pH 7.0). However, some organisms need a very different pH range. The azalea plant thrives in acidic (pH 4.5) soil, and a microorganism called *Picrophilus* survives best at an extremely acidic pH of 0.7. For all of these different organisms, pH must be tightly controlled.

One way pH is regulated in organisms is by substances called buffers. A buffer is a compound that can bind to an H⁺ ion when the H⁺ concentration increases, and can release an H⁺ ion when the H⁺ concentration decreases. In other words, a buffer "locks up" H⁺ ions and helps to maintain homeostasis. For example, the normal pH of human blood is between 7.35 and 7.45, so it is slightly basic. Just a small change in pH can disrupt processes in your cells, and a blood pH greater than 7.8 or less than 6.8, for even a short time, is deadly. Buffers in your blood help prevent any large changes in blood pH.

Apply Cells have higher H⁺ concentrations than blood. Which has a higher pH? Why?

Connecting CONCEPTS

Human Biology In the human body, both the respiratory system and the excretory system help regulate pH. You will learn about human systems and homeostasis in **Chapter 28.**

2.2 ASSESSMENT

ONLINE QUIZ
ClassZone.com

REVIEWING ▶ MAIN IDEAS

1. How do polar molecules form **hydrogen bonds**?
2. What determines whether a compound will dissolve in water?
3. Make a chart that compares **acids** and **bases.**

CRITICAL THINKING

4. **Compare and Contrast** How do polar molecules differ from non-polar molecules? How does this difference affect their interactions?
5. **Connect** Describe an example of **cohesion** or **adhesion** that you might observe during your daily life.

Connecting CONCEPTS

6. **Cellular Respiration** When sugars are broken down to produce usable energy for cells, a large amount of heat is released. Explain how the water inside a cell helps to keep the cell's temperature constant.

2.3 Carbon-Based Molecules

KEY CONCEPT Carbon-based molecules are the foundation of life.

MAIN IDEAS

- Carbon atoms have unique bonding properties.
- Four main types of carbon-based molecules are found in living things.

VOCABULARY

monomer, p. 45
polymer, p. 45
carbohydrate, p. 45
lipid, p. 46
fatty acid, p. 46

protein, p. 47
amino acid, p. 47
nucleic acid, p. 48

Review
atom, molecule, covalent bond

Connect Car manufacturers often build several types of cars from the same internal frame. The size and style of the cars might differ on the outside, but they have the same structure underneath. Carbon-based molecules are similar, but they are much more varied. There are millions of different carbon-based molecules, but they form around only a few simple frames composed of carbon atoms.

MAIN IDEA

Carbon atoms have unique bonding properties.

Carbon is often called the building block of life because carbon atoms are the basis of most molecules that make up living things. These molecules form the structure of living things and carry out most of the processes that keep organisms alive. Carbon is so important because its atomic structure gives it bonding properties that are unique among elements. Each carbon atom has four unpaired electrons in its outer energy level. Therefore, carbon atoms can form covalent bonds with up to four other atoms, including other carbon atoms.

As **FIGURE 2.10** shows, carbon-based molecules have three fundamental structures—straight chains, branched chains, and rings. All three types of molecules are the result of carbon's ability to form four covalent bonds. Carbon chains can bond with carbon rings to form very large, very complex molecules. These large molecules can be made of many small molecules that are bonded together. In a sense, the way these molecules form is similar to the way in which individual links of metal come together to make a bicycle chain.

FIGURE 2.10 CARBON CHAINS AND RINGS

Straight chain	Branched chain	Ring

Straight chain

A simplified structure can also be shown as:

CH_3—CH_2—CH_2—CH=CH_2

Pentene

Branched chain

Hexane

Ring

Vanillin

In many carbon-based molecules, small molecules are subunits of an entire molecule, like links in a chain. Each subunit in the complete molecule is called a **monomer.** When monomers are linked, they form molecules called polymers. A **polymer** is a large molecule, or macromolecule, made of many monomers bonded together. All of the monomers in a polymer may be the same, as they are in starches, or they may be different, as they are in proteins.

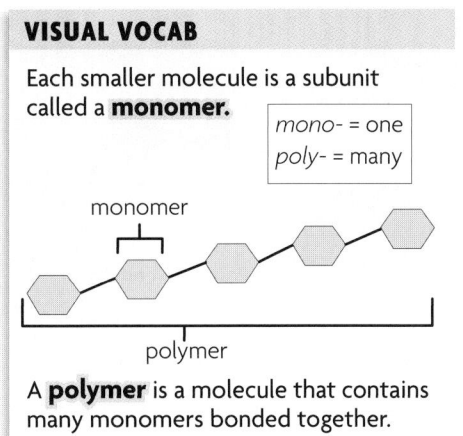

Each smaller molecule is a subunit called a **monomer.**

mono- = one
poly- = many

monomer

polymer

A **polymer** is a molecule that contains many monomers bonded together.

Synthesize **Write your own analogy for the formation of a polymer from monomers.**

▶ MAIN IDEA

Four main types of carbon-based molecules are found in living things.

All organisms are made of four types of carbon-based molecules: carbohydrates, lipids, proteins, and nucleic acids. These molecules have different structures and functions, but all are formed around carbon chains and rings.

Carbohydrates

Fruits and grains are in different food groups, but they both contain large amounts of carbohydrates. **Carbohydrates** are molecules composed of carbon, hydrogen, and oxygen, and they include sugars and starches. Carbohydrates can be broken down to provide a source of usable chemical energy for cells. Carbohydrates are also a major part of plant cell structure.

The most basic carbohydrates are simple sugars, or monosaccharides (MAHN-uh-SAK-uh-RYDZ). Many simple sugars have either five or six carbon atoms. Fruits contain a six-carbon sugar called fructose. Glucose, one of the sugars made by plant cells during photosynthesis, is another six-carbon sugar. Simple sugars can be bonded to make larger carbohydrates. For example, two sugars bonded together make the disaccharide you know as table sugar, shown in **FIGURE 2.11.** Many glucose molecules can be linked to make polysaccharides (PAHL-ee-SAK-uh-RYDZ), which are polymers of monosaccharides.

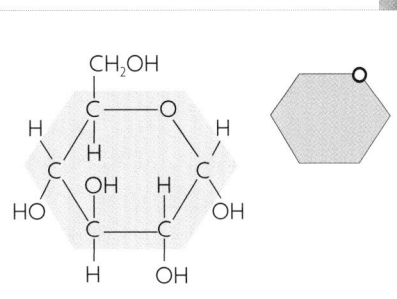

Glucose ($C_6H_{12}O_6$) can be ring shaped and is often shown as a simplified hexagon.

Starches, glycogen, and cellulose are polysaccharides. Starches and glycogen are similar, but they differ from cellulose because their glucose monomers are bonded together differently. Most starches are branched chains of glucose molecules. Starches are made and stored by plants, and they can be broken down as a source of energy by plant and animal cells. Glycogen, which is made and stored in animals, is more highly branched than plant starches.

TAKING NOTES

Use a content frame to help you understand monomers and polymers in carbon-based molecules.

Monomer	Polymer	Example	Function

FIGURE 2.11 Household sugar (sucrose) is a disaccharide, or two-sugar molecule, of glucose (inset) and fructose.

FIGURE 2.12 CARBOHYDRATE STRUCTURE

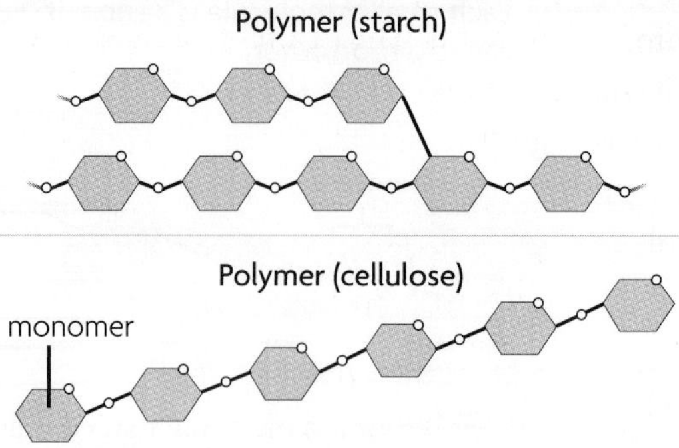

Polymer (starch)

Starch is a polymer of glucose monomers that often has a branched structure.

Polymer (cellulose)

monomer

Cellulose is a polymer of glucose monomers that has a straight, rigid structure.

Connecting CONCEPTS

Cell Structure A cell wall made of cellulose surrounds the membrane of plant cells. You will learn more about cell walls in **Chapter 3**.

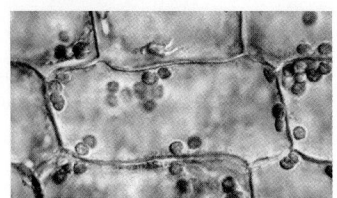

Cellulose is somewhat different from starch and glycogen. Its straight, rigid structure, shown in **FIGURE 2.12**, makes the cellulose molecule a major building block in plant cell structure. Cellulose makes up the cell wall that is the tough outer covering of plant cells. You have eaten cellulose in the stringy fibers of vegetables such as celery, so you know that it is tough to chew and break up.

Lipids

Lipids are nonpolar molecules that include fats, oils, and cholesterol. Like carbohydrates, most lipids contain chains of carbon atoms bonded to oxygen and hydrogen atoms. Some lipids are broken down as a source of usable energy for cells. Other lipids are parts of a cell's structure.

Fats and oils are two familiar types of lipids. They store large amounts of chemical energy in organisms. Animal fats are found in foods such as meat and butter. You know plant fats as oils, such as olive oil and peanut oil. The structures of fats and oils are similar. They both consist of a molecule called glycerol (GLIHS-uh-RAWL) bonded to molecules called fatty acids. **Fatty acids** are chains of carbon atoms bonded to hydrogen atoms. Two different types of fatty acids are shown in **FIGURE 2.13**.

Many lipids, both fats and oils, contain three fatty acids bonded to glycerol. They are called triglycerides. Most animal fats are saturated fats, which means they have the maximum number of hydrogen atoms possible. That is, every place that a hydrogen atom can bond to a carbon atom is filled with a hydrogen atom, and all carbon–carbon bonds are single bonds. You can think of the fatty acid as being "saturated" with hydrogen atoms. In contrast, fatty acids in oils have fewer hydrogen atoms because there is at least one double bond between carbon atoms. These lipids are called unsaturated fats because the fatty acids are not saturated with hydrogen atoms. Fats and oils are very similar, but why are animal fats solid and plant oils liquid? The double bonds in unsaturated fats make kinks in the fatty acids. As a result, the molecules cannot pack together tightly enough to form a solid.

FIGURE 2.13 Fatty acids can be either saturated or unsaturated.

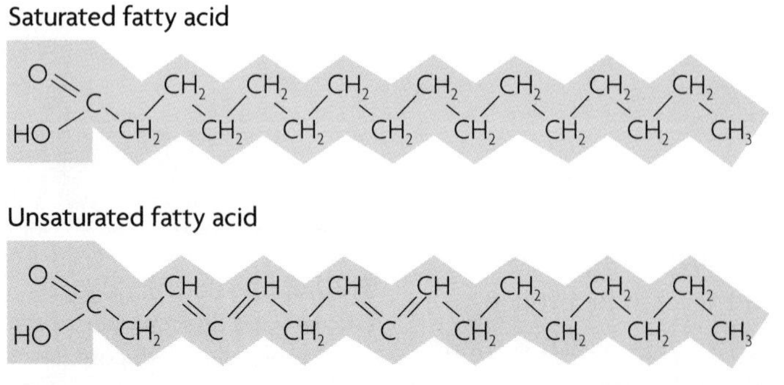

Saturated fatty acid

Saturated fats contain fatty acids in which all carbon–carbon bonds are single bonds.

Unsaturated fatty acid

Unsaturated fats have fatty acids with at least one carbon–carbon double bond.

All cell membranes are made mostly of another type of lipid, called a phospholipid (FAHS-foh-LIHP-ihd). A phospholipid consists of glycerol, two fatty acids, and a phosphate group (PO_4^-) that is part of the polar "head" of the molecule. The fatty acids are the nonpolar "tails" of a phospholipid. Compare the structure of a phospholipid to the structure of a triglyceride in **FIGURE 2.14**.

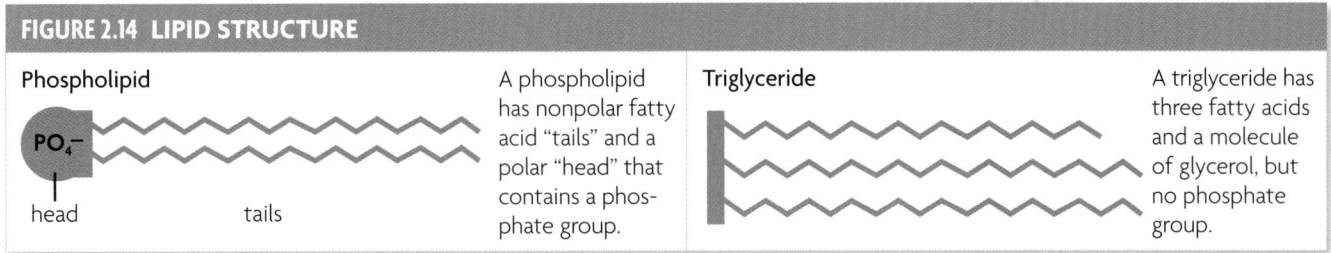

FIGURE 2.14 LIPID STRUCTURE

Phospholipid

PO₄⁻

head   tails

A phospholipid has nonpolar fatty acid "tails" and a polar "head" that contains a phosphate group.

Triglyceride

A triglyceride has three fatty acids and a molecule of glycerol, but no phosphate group.

Cholesterol (kuh-LEHS-tuh-RAWL) is a lipid that has a ring structure. You may hear about dangers of eating foods that contain a lot of cholesterol, such as eggs, but your body needs a certain amount of it to function. For example, cholesterol is a part of cell membranes, and your body uses it to make chemicals called steroid hormones. Cholesterol-based steroids have many functions. Some regulate your body's response to stress. Others, such as testosterone and estrogen, control sexual development and the reproductive system.

Proteins

Proteins are the most varied of the carbon-based molecules in organisms. In movement, eyesight, or digestion, proteins are at work. A **protein** is a polymer made of monomers called amino acids. **Amino acids** are molecules that contain carbon, hydrogen, oxygen, nitrogen, and sometimes sulfur. Organisms use 20 different amino acids to build proteins. Your body can make 12 of the amino acids. The others come from foods you eat, such as meat, beans, and nuts.

Look at **FIGURE 2.15** to see the amino acid serine. All amino acids have similar structures. As **FIGURE 2.16** shows, each amino acid monomer has a carbon atom that is bonded to four other parts. Three of these parts are the same in every amino acid: a hydrogen atom, an amino group (NH_2), and a carboxyl group (COOH). Amino acids differ only in their side group, or the R-group.

Amino acids form covalent bonds, called peptide bonds, with each other. The bonds form between the amino group of one amino acid and the carboxyl group of another amino acid. Through peptide bonds, amino acids are linked into chains called polypeptides. A protein is one or more polypeptides.

FIGURE 2.15 Serine is one of 20 amino acids that make up proteins in organisms.

OH
|
H   CH₂   O
 \ | //
  N — C — C
 / | \
H   H   OH

FIGURE 2.16 AMINO ACID AND PROTEIN STRUCTURE

All amino acids have a carbon atom bonded to a hydrogen atom, an amino group (NH_2), and a carboxyl group (COOH). Different amino acids have different side groups (R).

H   R   O
 \ | //
  N — C — C
 / | \
H   H   OH

Monomer (amino acid)

O   R   O
|| | ||
—C—N—C—C—N—
    | | |
    H   H   H

peptide bonds

Peptide bonds form between the amino group of one amino acid and the carboxyl group of another amino acid.

Polymer (protein)

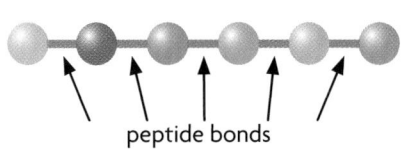

peptide bonds

A polypeptide is a chain of precisely ordered amino acids linked by peptide bonds. A protein is made of one or more polypeptides.

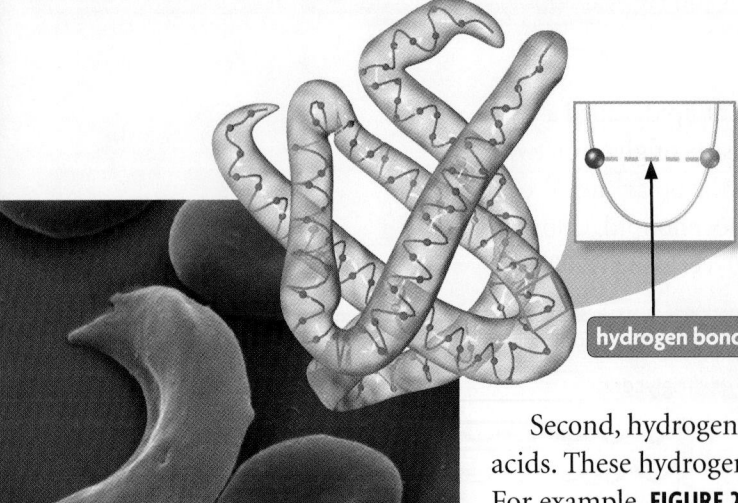

hydrogen bond

FIGURE 2.17 Hemoglobin in red blood cells transports oxygen. The structure of hemoglobin depends on hydrogen bonds between specific amino acids. Just one amino acid change causes red blood cells to have the curved shape characteristic of sickle cell anemia. (colored SEM; magnification 3500×)

scilinks.org

For more information on carbon-based molecules, visit scilinks.org.
Keycode: MLB002

Proteins differ in the number and order of amino acids. The specific sequence of amino acids determines a protein's structure and function. Two types of interactions between the side groups of some amino acids are especially important in protein structure. First, some side groups contain sulfur atoms. The sulfur atoms can form covalent bonds that force the protein to bend into a certain shape.

Second, hydrogen bonds can form between the side groups of some amino acids. These hydrogen bonds cause the protein to fold into a specific shape. For example, **FIGURE 2.17** shows the structure of one of the four polypeptides that makes up hemoglobin, the protein in your red blood cells that transports oxygen. Each of the four polypeptides contains an iron atom that bonds to an oxygen molecule. The four polypeptides are folded in a way that puts the four oxygen-carrying sites together in a pocketlike structure inside the molecule. If a protein has incorrect amino acids, the structure may change in a way that prevents the protein from working properly. Just one wrong amino acid of the 574 amino acids in hemoglobin causes the disorder sickle cell anemia.

Nucleic Acids

Detailed instructions to build proteins are stored in extremely long carbon-based molecules called nucleic acids. **Nucleic acids** are polymers that are made up of monomers called nucleotides. A nucleotide is composed of a sugar, a phosphate group, and a nitrogen-containing molecule called a base. There are two general types of nucleic acids: DNA and RNA.

Nucleic acids differ from the other types of carbon-based molecules. Carbohydrates, lipids, and proteins have a large number of structures and functions. Nucleic acids have just one function. They work together to make proteins. DNA stores the information for putting amino acids together to make proteins, and RNA helps to build proteins. DNA is the basis of genes and heredity, but cannot do anything by itself. Instead, the structure of DNA—the order of nucleotides—provides the code for the proper assembly of proteins. You will learn more about nucleic acids and how they build proteins in Unit 3.

Apply **What is the relationship between proteins and nucleic acids?**

2.3 ASSESSMENT

ONLINE QUIZ
ClassZone.com

REVIEWING ▶ MAIN IDEAS

1. What is the relationship between a **polymer** and a **monomer**?

2. Explain how both **nucleic acids** and **proteins** are polymers. Be sure to describe the monomers that make up the polymers.

CRITICAL THINKING

3. **Compare and Contrast** How are **carbohydrates** and **lipids** similar? How are they different?

4. **Infer** Explain how the bonding properties of carbon atoms result in the large variety of carbon-based molecules in living things.

Connecting CONCEPTS

5. **Biochemistry** Why might **fatty acids, amino acids,** and nucleic acids increase the hydrogen ion (H$^+$) concentration of a solution? Explain your answer.

Independent and Dependent Variables

In an experiment, a scientist determines the effect one variable has on another. A scientist changes, or manipulates, the **independent variable** and measures or observes the **dependent variables.** Therefore, data from an experiment are measurements of dependent variables. Changes in dependent variables "depend upon" the independent variable.

EXAMPLE
A scientist studied the effect of jogging on the number of Calories used. (The Calories in food are kilocalories, or 1000 calories.) People jogged for three different lengths of time—10 minutes, 20 minutes, and 30 minutes. The number of Calories used was measured, recorded, and plotted on a graph like the one shown on the right. What are the independent and dependent variables?

- The independent variable is the length of time spent jogging (10 minutes, 20 minutes, or 30 minutes).
- The dependent variable is the number of Calories used while jogging—the number of Calories "depends on" time.

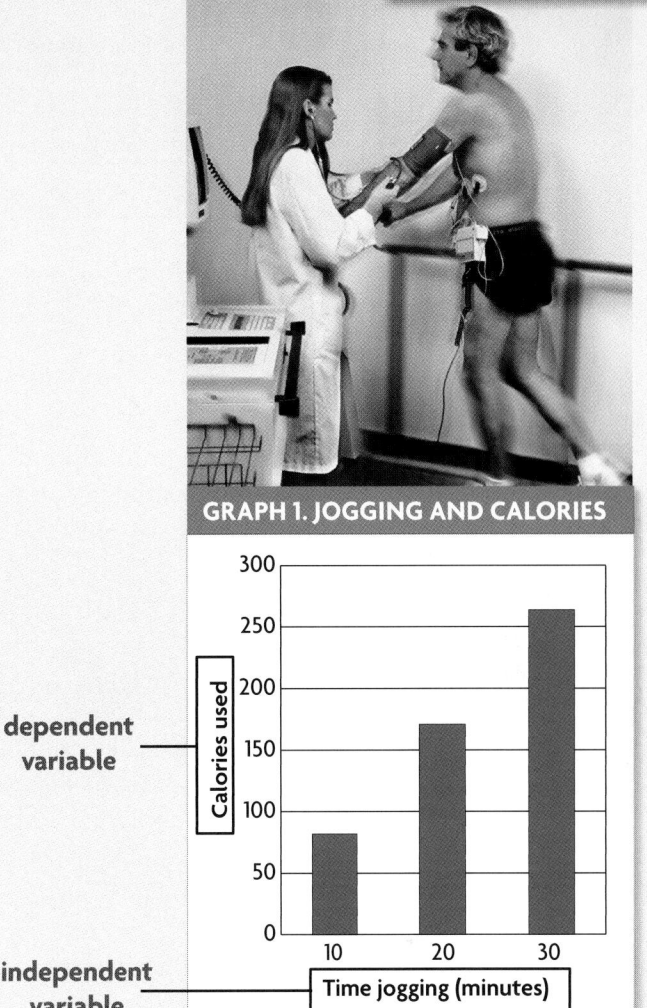

GRAPH 1. JOGGING AND CALORIES

dependent variable

Calories used

independent variable

Time jogging (minutes)

IDENTIFY VARIABLES
A company that makes nutritional products is developing a new type of protein drink for athletes. A scientist at the company is studying the pH at which a digestive enzyme best breaks down the different proteins in the drink. The scientist uses the following experimental procedure:

- Five test tubes each contain 2 mL of the protein drink.
- Five different solutions contain the digestive enzyme, but each solution has a different pH—1.5, 2.0, 2.5, 3.0, and 3.5. One enzyme solution is added to each test tube of protein drink.
- Protein levels are measured in each of the five test tubes.

1. **Identify** What are the independent and dependent variables in the experiment? Explain your answers.

2. **Apply** Time is often used as a dependent variable in experiments. Describe how time could be used as a dependent variable in this experiment.

Chemical Reactions

KEY CONCEPT Life depends on chemical reactions.

▶ MAIN IDEAS

- Bonds break and form during chemical reactions.
- Chemical reactions release or absorb energy.

VOCABULARY

chemical reaction, p. 50
reactant, p. 50
product, p. 50
bond energy, p. 51
equilibrium, p. 51

activation energy, p. 53
exothermic, p. 53
endothermic, p. 53

Review
atom, molecule

MICHIGAN STANDARDS

B2.5A Recognize and explain that macromolecules such as lipids contain high energy bonds.
B2.5C Describe how energy is transferred and transformed from the Sun to energy-rich molecules during photosynthesis.

Connect When you hear the term *chemical reaction,* what comes to mind? Maybe you think of liquids bubbling in beakers. You probably do not think of the air in your breath, but most of the carbon dioxide and water vapor that you breathe out are made by chemical reactions in your cells.

▶ MAIN IDEA

Bonds break and form during chemical reactions.

Plant cells make cellulose by linking simple sugars together. Plant and animal cells break down sugars to get usable energy. And all cells build protein molecules by bonding amino acids together. These are just a few of the chemical reactions in living things. **Chemical reactions** change substances into different substances by breaking and forming chemical bonds.

Reactants, Products, and Bond Energy

Your cells need the oxygen molecules that you breathe in. Oxygen (O_2) plays a part in a series of chemical reactions that provides usable energy for your cells. These reactions, which are described in detail in Chapter 4, break down the simple sugar glucose ($C_6H_{12}O_6$). The process uses oxygen and glucose and results in carbon dioxide (CO_2), water (H_2O), and usable energy. Oxygen and glucose are the reactants. **Reactants** are the substances changed during a chemical reaction. Carbon dioxide and water are the products. **Products** are the substances made by a chemical reaction. Chemical equations are used to show what happens during a reaction. The overall equation for the process that changes oxygen and glucose into carbon dioxide and water is

$$6O_2 + C_6H_{12}O_6 \longrightarrow 6CO_2 + 6H_2O$$

Reactants   Direction   Products

The reactants are on the left side of the equation, and the products are on the right side. The arrow shows the direction of the reaction. This process, which is called cellular respiration, makes the carbon dioxide and water vapor that you breathe out. But for carbon dioxide and water to be made, bonds must be broken in the reactants, and bonds must form in the products. What causes bonds in oxygen and glucose molecules to break? And what happens when new bonds form in carbon dioxide and water?

FIGURE 2.18 The breakdown of glucose provides chemical energy for all activities, including speed skating.

Chemical Bonding

You use energy to put things together, but chemical bonding is different. Energy is added to break bonds, and energy is released when bonds form.

PROBLEM How is chemical bonding similar to the interaction between two magnets?

PROCEDURE

1. Bring the magnets close to each other until they snap together.
2. Pull the magnets away from each other.

ANALYZE AND CONCLUDE

1. **Infer** How is bond formation represented by the snapping sound?
2. **Apply** How is bond energy related to your separation of the magnets?

MATERIALS
2 flat magnets

First, energy is added to break bonds in molecules of oxygen and glucose. **Bond energy** is the amount of energy that will break a bond between two atoms. Bonds between different types of atoms have different bond energies. A certain amount of energy is needed to break bonds in an oxygen molecule. A different amount of energy is needed to break bonds in a glucose molecule.

Energy is released when bonds form, such as when molecules of water and carbon dioxide are made. When a bond forms, the amount of energy released is equal to the amount of energy that breaks the same bond. For example, energy is released when hydrogen and oxygen atoms bond to form a water molecule. The same amount of energy is needed to break apart a water molecule.

Chemical Equilibrium

Some reactions go from reactants to products until the reactants are used up. However, many reactions in living things are reversible. They move in both directions at the same time. These reactions tend to go in one direction or the other depending on the concentrations of the reactants and products. One such reaction lets blood, shown in **FIGURE 2.19**, carry carbon dioxide. Carbon dioxide reacts with water in blood to form a compound called carbonic acid (H_2CO_3). Your body needs this reaction to get rid of carbon dioxide waste from your cells.

$$CO_2 + H_2O \rightleftharpoons H_2CO_3$$

The arrows in the equation above show that the reaction goes in both directions. When the carbon dioxide concentration is high, as it is around your cells, the reaction moves toward the right and carbonic acid forms. In your lungs, the carbon dioxide concentration is low. The reaction goes in the other direction, and carbonic acid breaks down.

When a reaction takes place at an equal rate in both directions, the reactant and product concentrations stay the same. This state is called equilibrium. **Equilibrium** (EE-kwuh-LIHB-ree-uhm) is reached when both the reactants and products are made at the same rate.

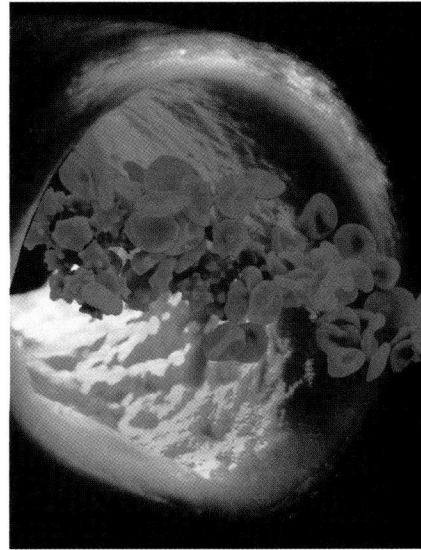

FIGURE 2.19 Blood cells and plasma transport materials throughout the body. Carbonic acid dissolves in the blood so that carbon dioxide can be transported to the lungs. (composite colored SEM; magnification 1000×)

Apply Explain why concentration is important in a chemical reaction.

FIGURE 2.20 Energy and Chemical Reactions

Energy is required to break bonds in reactants, and energy is released when bonds form in products. Overall, a chemical reaction either absorbs or releases energy.

Animated BIOLOGY
Watch exothermic and endothermic reactions at ClassZone.com.

ACTIVATION ENERGY

When enough activation energy is added to the reactants, bonds in the reactants break and the reaction begins.

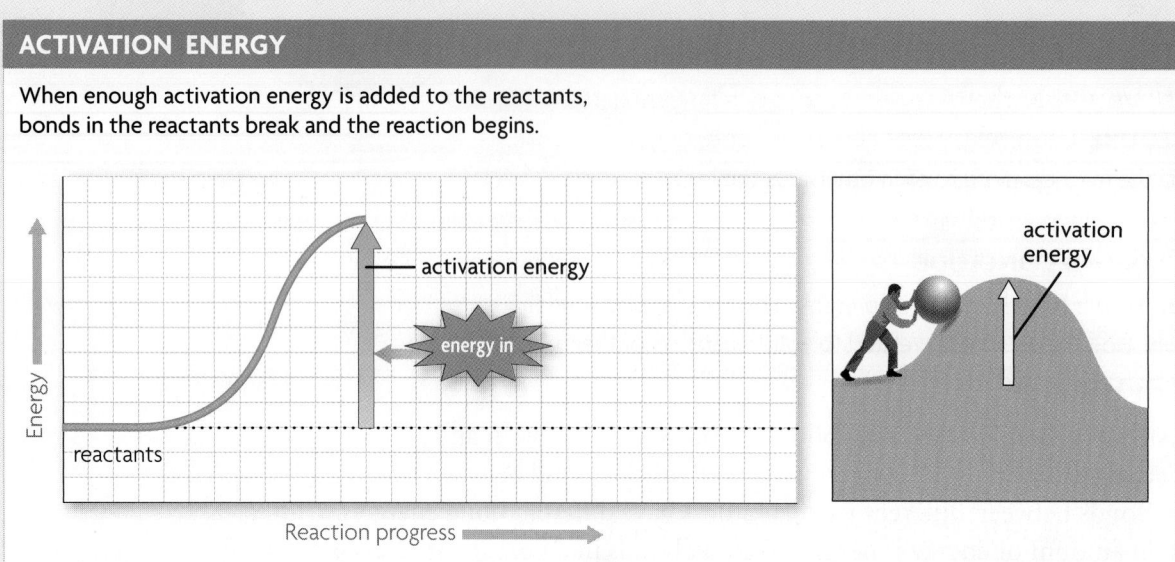

EXOTHERMIC REACTION Energy Released

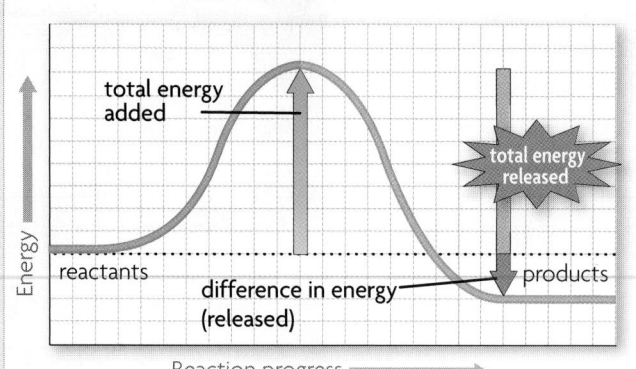

The products in an exothermic reaction have a lower bond energy than the reactants, and the difference in bond energy is released to the surroundings.

ENDOTHERMIC REACTION Energy Absorbed

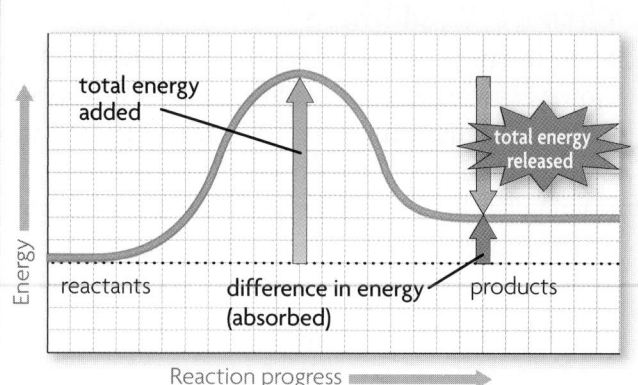

The products in an endothermic reaction have a higher bond energy than the reactants, and the difference in bond energy is absorbed from the surroundings.

CRITICAL VIEWING **Is the amount of activation energy related to whether a reaction is exothermic or endothermic? Why or why not?**

► MAIN IDEA
Chemical reactions release or absorb energy.

All chemical reactions involve changes in energy. Energy that is added to the reactants breaks their chemical bonds. When new bonds form in the products, energy is released. This means that energy is both absorbed and released during a chemical reaction. Some chemical reactions release more energy than they absorb. Other chemical reactions absorb more energy than they release. Whether a reaction releases or absorbs energy depends on bond energy.

Some energy must be absorbed by the reactants in any chemical reaction. **Activation energy** is the amount of energy that needs to be absorbed for a chemical reaction to start. Activation energy is like the energy you would need to push a rock up a hill. Once the rock is at the top of the hill, it rolls down the other side by itself. A graph of the activation energy that is added to start a chemical reaction is shown at the top of **FIGURE 2.20**.

An **exothermic** chemical reaction releases more energy than it absorbs. If the products have a lower bond energy than the reactants, the reaction is exothermic. The excess energy—the difference in bond energy between the reactants and products—is often given off as heat or light. Some animals, such as squids and fireflies, give off light that comes from exothermic reactions, as shown in **FIGURE 2.21**. Cellular respiration, the process that uses glucose and oxygen to provide usable energy for cells, is also exothermic. Cellular respiration releases not only usable energy for your cells but also heat that keeps your body warm.

An **endothermic** chemical reaction absorbs more energy than it releases. If products have a higher bond energy than reactants, the reaction is endothermic. Energy must be absorbed to make up the difference. One of the most important processes for life on Earth, photosynthesis, is endothermic. During photosynthesis, plants absorb energy from sunlight and use that energy to make simple sugars and complex carbohydrates.

VOCABULARY

The prefix *exo-* means "out," and the prefix *endo-* means "in." Energy "moves out of" an exothermic reaction, and energy "moves into" an endothermic reaction.

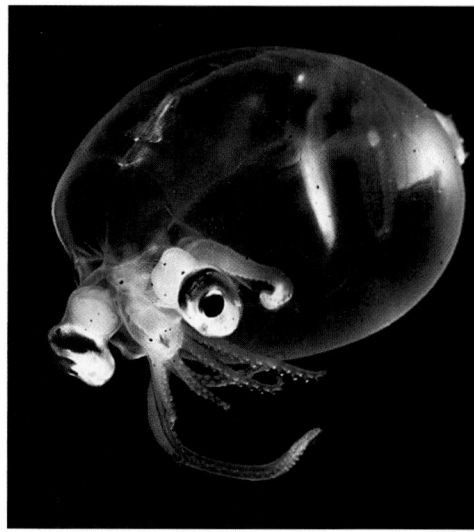

FIGURE 2.21 The glow of the bugeye squid comes from an exothermic reaction that releases light.

Analyze How is activation energy related to bond energy?

2.4 ASSESSMENT

ONLINE QUIZ
ClassZone.com

REVIEWING ► MAIN IDEAS

1. Hydrogen peroxide (H$_2$O$_2$) breaks down into water (H$_2$O) and oxygen (O$_2$). Explain why this is a **chemical reaction.** What are the **reactants** and the **products** in the reaction?

2. How do **endothermic** and **exothermic** reactions differ?

CRITICAL THINKING

3. **Infer** The process below is exothermic. What must be true about the **bond energies** of the reactants and the products? Explain.

$$6O_2 + C_6H_{12}O_6 \longrightarrow 6CO_2 + 6H_2O$$

4. **Evaluate** Why might it not always be possible to determine the reactants and the products in a reaction? Explain your answer in terms of chemical **equilibrium.**

Connecting CONCEPTS

5. **Biochemistry** A chemical reaction can start when enough **activation energy** is added to the reactants. Do you think the activation energy for chemical reactions in living things is high or low? Explain your answer.

Chapter 2: Chemistry of Life 53

2.5 Enzymes

KEY CONCEPT Enzymes are catalysts for chemical reactions in living things.

▶ MAIN IDEAS

- A catalyst lowers activation energy.
- Enzymes allow chemical reactions to occur under tightly controlled conditions.

VOCABULARY

catalyst, p. 54

enzyme, p. 55

substrate, p. 56

Review
chemical reaction, activation energy, protein, hydrogen bond

MICHIGAN STANDARDS

B2.2f Explain the role of enzymes and other proteins in biochemical functions (e.g., the protein hemoglobin carries oxygen in some organisms, digestive enzymes, and hormones).

B2.3A Describe how cells function in a narrow range of physical conditions, such as temperature and pH (acidity), to perform life functions.

Connect Just how can a Venus flytrap digest a frog? It happens through the action of proteins called enzymes. Enzymes help to start and run chemical reactions in living things. For example, enzymes are needed to break down food into smaller molecules that cells can use. Without enzymes, a Venus flytrap couldn't break down its food, and neither could you.

▶ MAIN IDEA

A catalyst lowers activation energy.

Remember what you learned about activation energy in Section 2.4. Activation energy for a chemical reaction is like the energy that is needed to push a rock up a hill. When enough energy is added to get the rock to the top of a hill, the rock can roll down the other side by itself. Activation energy gives a similar push to a chemical reaction. Once a chemical reaction starts, it can continue by itself, and it will go at a certain rate.

Often, the activation energy for a chemical reaction comes from an increase in temperature. But even after a chemical reaction starts, it may happen very slowly. The reactants may not interact enough, or they may not be at a high enough concentration, to quickly form the products of the reaction. However, both the activation energy and rate of a chemical reaction can be changed by a chemical catalyst, as shown in **FIGURE 2.22**. A **catalyst** (KAT-l-ihst) is a substance that decreases the activation energy needed to start a chemical reaction and, as a result, also increases the rate of the chemical reaction.

FIGURE 2.22 CATALYSTS AND ACTIVATION ENERGY

Under normal conditions, a certain amount of activation energy is needed to start a chemical reaction. A catalyst decreases the activation energy needed.

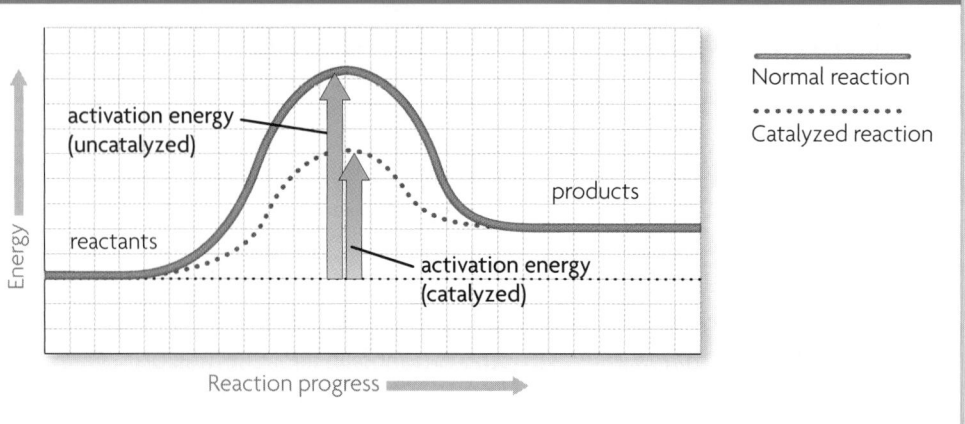

Compare the activation energies and the reaction rates in the graph in **FIGURE 2.22.** Under normal conditions, the reaction requires a certain amount of activation energy, and it occurs at a certain rate. When a catalyst is present, less energy is needed and the products form faster. Although catalysts take part in chemical reactions, catalysts are not considered to be either reactants or products because catalysts are not changed or used up during a reaction.

Summarize Describe two functions of catalysts in chemical reactions.

● MAIN IDEA
Enzymes allow chemical reactions to occur under tightly controlled conditions.

Chemical reactions in organisms have to take place at an organism's body temperature. Often, reactants are found in low concentrations. Because the reactions must take place very quickly, they usually need a catalyst. **Enzymes** are catalysts for chemical reactions in living things. Enzymes, like other catalysts, lower the activation energy and increase the rate of chemical reactions. In reactions that are reversible, such as the carbon dioxide and carbonic acid reaction described in Section 2.4, enzymes do not affect chemical equilibrium. This means that enzymes do not change the direction of a reaction—they just change the amount of time needed for equilibrium to be reached.

Enzymes are involved in almost every process in organisms. From breaking down food to building proteins, enzymes are needed. For example, amylase is an enzyme in saliva that breaks down starch into simpler sugars. This reaction occurs up to a million times faster with amylase than without it. Enzymes are also an important part of your immune system, as shown in **FIGURE 2.23**.

Almost all enzymes are proteins. These enzymes, like other proteins, are long chains of amino acids. Each enzyme also depends on its structure to function properly. Conditions such as temperature and pH can affect the shape and function, or activity, of an enzyme. Enzymes work best in a small temperature range around the organism's normal body temperature. At only slightly higher temperatures, the hydrogen bonds in an enzyme may begin to break apart. The enzyme's structure changes and it loses its ability to function. This is one reason why a very high fever is so dangerous to a person. A change in pH can also affect the hydrogen bonds in enzymes. Many enzymes in humans work best at the nearly neutral pH that is maintained within cells of the human body.

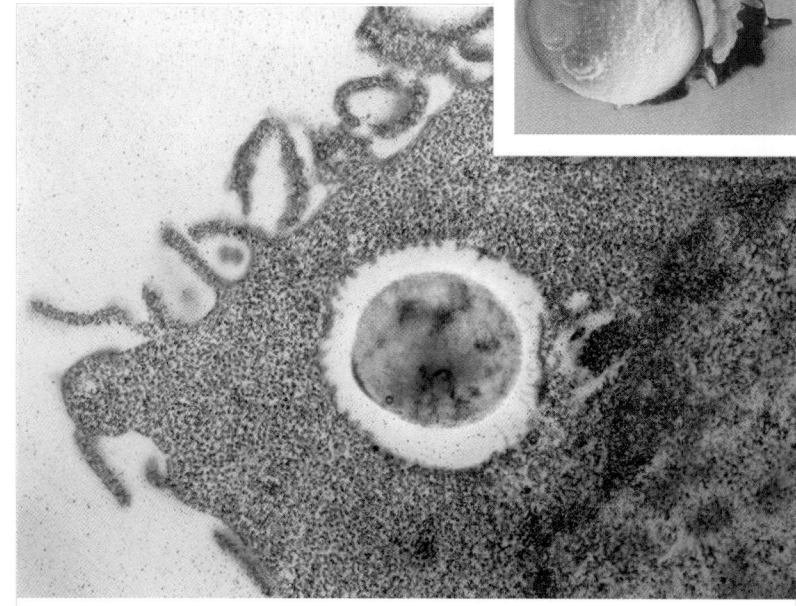

FIGURE 2.23 The inset micrograph (top) shows a white blood cell engulfing an invading pathogen. The larger micrograph shows a pathogen after it has been captured. Once inside a white blood cell, enzymes are used to destroy the pathogen. (inset image: colored SEM; magnification about 3000×; large image: colored TEM; magnification 11,000×)

Biochemistry The order of amino acids determines the structure and function of an enzyme. An enzyme's structure often depends on hydrogen bonds between amino acids.

Enzyme structure is important because each enzyme's shape allows only certain reactants to bind to the enzyme. The specific reactants that an enzyme acts on are called **substrates.** For example, amylase only breaks down starch. Therefore, starch is the substrate for amylase. Substrates temporarily bind to enzymes at specific places called active sites. Like a key fits into a lock, substrates exactly fit the active sites of enzymes. This is why if an enzyme's structure changes, it may not work at all. This idea of enzyme function, which is called the lock-and-key model, is shown below.

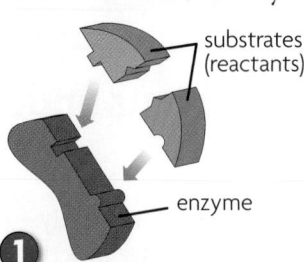
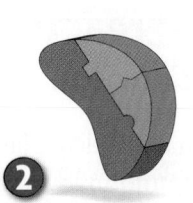
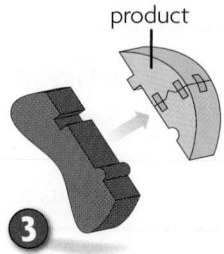

① Substrates bind to an enzyme at certain places called active sites.

② The enzyme brings substrates together and weakens their bonds.

③ The catalyzed reaction forms a product that is released from the enzyme.

The lock-and-key model helps explain how enzymes work. First, enzymes bring substrate molecules close together. Because of the low concentrations of reactants in cells, many reactions would be unlikely to take place without enzymes bringing substrates together. Second, enzymes decrease activation energy. When substrates bind to the enzyme at the enzyme's active site, the bonds inside these molecules become strained. If bonds are strained, or stretched slightly out of their normal positions, they become weaker. Less activation energy is needed for these slightly weakened bonds to be broken.

The lock-and-key model is a good starting point for understanding enzyme function. However, scientists have recently found that the structures of enzymes are not fixed in place. Instead, enzymes actually bend slightly when they are bound to their substrates. In terms of a lock and key, it is as if the lock bends around the key to make the key fit better. The bending of the enzyme is one way in which bonds in the substrates are weakened.

Apply How does the structure of an enzyme affect its function?

2.5 ASSESSMENT

ONLINE QUIZ ClassZone.com

REVIEWING ▶ MAIN IDEAS

1. How does a **catalyst** affect the activation energy of a chemical reaction?

2. Describe how the interaction between an **enzyme** and its **substrates** changes a chemical reaction.

CRITICAL THINKING

3. **Infer** Some organisms live in very hot or very acidic environments. Would their enzymes function in a person's cells? Why or why not?

4. **Predict** Suppose that the amino acids that make up an enzyme's active site are changed. How might this change affect the enzyme?

Connecting CONCEPTS

5. **Homeostasis** Organisms need to maintain homeostasis, or stable internal conditions. Why is homeostasis important for the function of enzymes?

MATERIALS

- 5 test tubes
- test tube rack
- marker
- 7 10-mL graduated cylinders
- 4 mL each of solutions of pH 3, 5, 7, 9, and 11
- 2 mL 60% catalase solution
- 1 mL 3% hydrogen peroxide solution
- metric ruler

PROCESS SKILLS

- **Identifying Variables**
- **Observing**
- **Measuring**
- **Collecting Data**
- **Interpreting Data**

MICHIGAN STANDARDS

B1.1B Evaluate the uncertainties or validity of scientific conclusions using an understanding of sources of measurement error, the challenges of controlling variables, accuracy of data analysis, logic of argument, logic of experimental design, and/or the dependence on underlying assumptions.

B1.1C Conduct scientific investigations using appropriate tools and techniques (e.g., selecting an instrument that measures the desired quantity—length, volume, weight, time interval, temperature—with the appropriate level of precision).

Enzymatic Activity

Enzymes are necessary for many processes, including digestion and fighting disease. Conditions such as temperature and pH must be tightly controlled so that enzymes can function properly. In this lab, you will study an enzyme called catalase that helps break down hydrogen peroxide into water and oxygen.

PROBLEM How does pH affect enzymatic activity?

PROCEDURE

1. Label 5 test tubes pH 3, pH 5, pH 7, pH 9, pH 11. Place them in the test tube rack.

2. Add 4 mL of the appropriate pH solution to each test tube. Be sure to use a different graduated cylinder for each of the solutions.

3. Add 2 mL of the catalase enzyme solution to each of the test tubes. Gently swirl the test tubes to mix the solutions. Allow the test tubes to sit for 5 minutes.

4. Design a data table that has rows labeled with the independent variable and columns labeled with the dependent variable. Read step 6 to determine whether the foam height is the independent variable or the dependent variable.

5. Add 1 mL of the hydrogen peroxide solution to each test tube. Allow 5 minutes for the solutions to react. Foam should appear on the solution tops.

Caution: Avoid skin contact with hydrogen peroxide.

6. Measure the distance in millimeters from the bottom of each test tube to the top of the foam in the test tube. Record your measurements in your data table.

ANALYZE AND CONCLUDE

1. **Identify Variables** What are the independent and dependent variables? What is the operational definition of the dependent variable?

2. **Analyze** Choose a type of graph to appropriately display your data. Construct your graph.

3. **Analyze** How is the enzymatic activity of catalase related to pH? What does this tell you about the pH of your cells?

4. **Infer** The activity of an enzyme depends upon its structure. What do your results suggest about the effect of pH on the structure of catalase? Explain.

5. **Experimental Design** Why is it important that each test tube have the same amount of each solution? What other sources of experimental error may have existed?

6. **Apply** Gelatin recipes that include fruit often say not to use pineapple. Gelatin is mostly protein. Pineapple contains an enzyme that is often used in meat tenderizers. What effect might pineapple have on gelatin? Why?

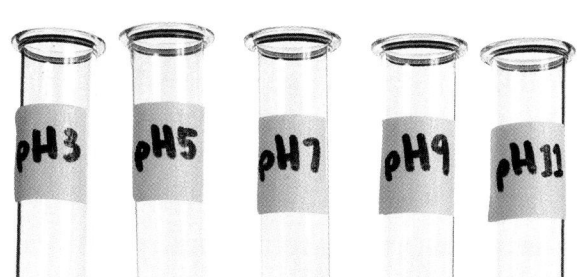

Use these inquiry-based labs and online activities to deepen your understanding of the importance of chemistry in biology.

INVESTIGATION

Testing pH

Universal indicator paper changes color depending on the pH of the solution being tested. Many substances around your home are acids and have a low pH. Others are bases and have a high pH. In this lab you will use pH indicator paper to investigate the pH of several common substances.

SKILLS Observing, Analyzing, Inferring

PROBLEM How acidic or basic are household substances?

PROCEDURE

1. Use a different graduated cylinder to pour 5 mL of each of the six solutions into each of six test tubes.

2. Test the pH of each known solution with a different strip of pH indicator paper. Use the color scale on the indicator paper package to estimate the pH of each solution. Record the pH of the known solutions.

3. Construct a pH scale ranging from 0 (very acidic) to 14 (very basic), with 7 (neutral) in the center. Label your pH scale with the known solutions.

4. Test the pH of both unknown solutions with different strips of pH indicator paper, and record the pH of each.

5. Add labels for the unknown solutions to the pH scale that you made in step 3.

MATERIALS

- 6 test tubes
- test tube rack
- 6 10-mL graduated cylinders
- lemon juice
- vinegar
- mouthwash
- window cleaner
- 2 unknown solutions
- pH indicator paper

ANALYZE AND CONCLUDE

1. **Identify** Find out from your teacher what the unknown solutions are. Is the pH of any of the solutions different than you might have expected? Why or why not?

2. **Apply** What is the pH range of the solutions you tested? Are any of them very acidic or basic? What does this indicate about many common substances found in the home?

3. **Analyze** Describe the hydrogen ion concentrations in each of the six solutions.

EXTEND YOUR INVESTIGATION

Use red cabbage juice as a pH indicator to test the six solutions that you tested earlier. Is the red cabbage juice as accurate as the pH indicator paper? Explain.

INVESTIGATION

Enzymes

As in all organisms, enzymes are critical for chemical reactions in humans. One reaction produces melanin, which gives skin a dark color. Melanin helps protect skin cells from ultraviolet radiation—the greater the exposure to ultraviolet radiation, the greater the production of melanin. Melanin is made from the amino acid tyrosine by an enzyme called tyrosinase. Without tyrosinase, the reaction cannot take place. This causes a condition called albinism.

SKILL Communicating

PROBLEM What happens if an enzyme is missing or defective?

RESEARCH

Research the effect of one of the following enzyme deficiencies:

• phenylketonuria
• galactosemia
• lactose intolerance

For the enzyme deficiency that you have selected:

1. Identify the enzyme involved and its function.
2. Examine how a person's health is affected by this enzyme deficiency.
3. Find out how the deficiency is diagnosed.
4. Describe the effects of not treating the deficiency.

People who are lactose intolerant often replace regular milk with soymilk.

Online BIOLOGY
CLASSZONE.COM

VIRTUAL LAB
Calorimetry

How much energy is in the food you eat? In this interactive lab, you will burn different food items and measure the number of Calories each releases.

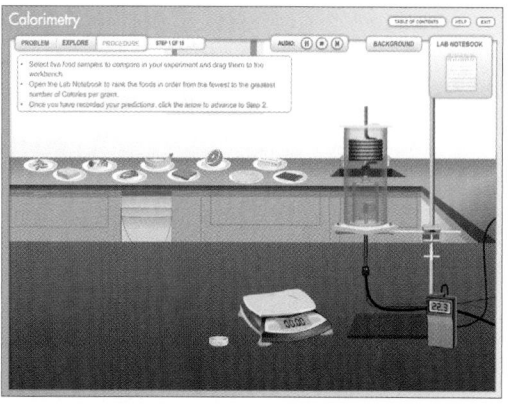

ANIMATED BIOLOGY
Atoms and Bonding

Build atoms from a bank of protons, neutrons, and electrons. Then explore how two or more atoms interact to form compounds.

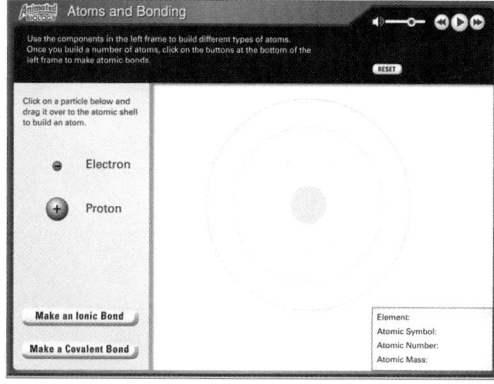

WEBQUEST

Prions are misfolded proteins that cause mad cow disease and, in humans, new variant Creutzfeldt-Jakob disease. In this WebQuest, you will learn about prions and how they infect people and other animals. Determine if the drastic steps taken to prevent the spread of prions actually keep people safe.

2.1 Atoms, Ions, and Molecules

All living things are based on atoms and their interactions. All matter is composed of atoms that interact. Atoms can become ions by gaining or losing electrons. Compounds and molecules form when atoms form bonds.

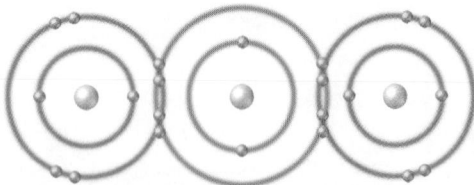

Carbon dioxide

2.2 Properties of Water

Water's unique properties allow life to exist on Earth. Water is a polar molecule. The slightly charged regions of water molecules form hydrogen bonds that give water properties such as cohesion and adhesion. Many substances dissolve in water to form solutions.

Polar water molecule

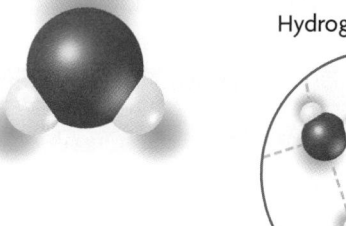

Hydrogen bonding

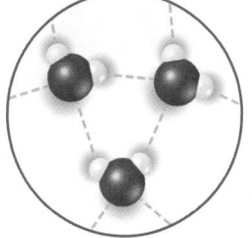

2.3 Carbon-Based Molecules

Carbon-based molecules are the foundation of life. The four main types of carbon-based molecules in living things are carbohydrates, lipids, proteins, and nucleic acids. The molecules have different functions that are based on their different structures.

2.4 Chemical Reactions

Life depends on chemical reactions. A chemical reaction changes reactants into products. Bonds break in the reactants, and new bonds form in the products. Chemical reactions either release energy (exothermic reactions) or absorb energy (endothermic reactions).

2.5 Enzymes

Enzymes are catalysts for chemical reactions in living things. Enzymes increase the rate of reactions and decrease the activation energy for reactions. Each enzyme catalyzes a specific reaction, and a change in an enzyme's structure changes its function.

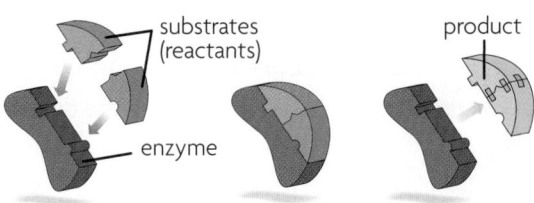

substrates (reactants) · product · enzyme

Synthesize Your Notes

Supporting Main Ideas Use your notes to make a detailed version of the graphic organizer shown below. Make organizers for each key concept in the chapter. Be sure to include important details and to mark important vocabulary terms.

Atoms and their interactions
→ Ions—formed when atoms gain or lose electrons
→ Compounds—
→ Molecules—

Concept Map Use concept maps like the one on the right to visualize the relationships among chapter concepts.

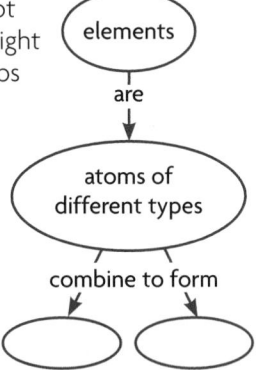

elements → are → atoms of different types → combine to form →

Chapter Assessment

Chapter Vocabulary

2.1 atom, p. 36
element, p. 36
compound, p. 37
ion, p. 38
ionic bond, p. 38
covalent bond, p. 39
molecule, p. 39

2.2 hydrogen bond, p. 41
cohesion, p. 41
adhesion, p. 41
solution, p. 42
solvent, p. 42

solute, p. 42
acid, p. 42
base, p. 42
pH, p. 42

2.3 monomer, p. 45
polymer, p. 45
carbohydrate, p. 45
lipid, p. 46
fatty acid, p. 46
protein, p. 47
amino acid, p. 47
nucleic acid, p. 48

2.4 chemical reaction, p. 50
reactant, p. 50
product, p. 50
bond energy, p. 51
equilibrium, p. 51
activation energy, p. 53
exothermic, p. 53
endothermic, p. 53

2.5 catalyst, p. 54
enzyme, p. 55
substrate, p. 56

Reviewing Vocabulary

Vocabulary Connections

The vocabulary terms in this chapter are related to each other in various ways. For each group of words below, write a sentence or two to clearly explain how the terms are connected. For example, for the terms *covalent bond* and *molecule,* you could write "A molecule is made of atoms connected by covalent bonds."

1. atom, ion

2. hydrogen bond, cohesion

3. solution, solvent

4. acid, base, pH

5. exothermic, endothermic

6. catalyst, enzyme

Word Origins

7. The word *atom* comes from the Greek word *atomos,* which means "indivisible." Describe the relationship between the Greek term and your understanding of atoms.

8. The *p* in *pH* stands for the German word *Potenz,* which means "power" or "potential." The *H* represents hydrogen ions (H^+). How are these related to the definition of pH?

9. The prefix *mono-* means "one" and the prefix *poly-* means "many." Some lipids are monounsaturated and others are polyunsaturated. Explain the difference between the fatty acids in these different types of lipids.

Reviewing **MAIN IDEAS**

10. Explain how the combination of electrons, protons, and neutrons results in the neutral charge of an atom.

11. Potassium ions (K^+) have a positive charge. What happens to a potassium atom's electrons when it becomes an ion?

12. Some types of atoms form more than one covalent bond with another atom. What determines how many covalent bonds two atoms can make? Explain.

13. How is hydrogen bonding among water molecules related to the structure of the water molecule?

14. Explain the difference between solvents and solutes.

15. Describe the relationship between hydrogen ions (H^+) and pH. How is pH related to a solution's acidity?

16. Carbon forms a very large number of compounds. What characteristic of carbon atoms allows the formation of all of these compounds? Explain.

17. Identify and explain examples of monomers and polymers in carbohydrates, proteins, and nucleic acids.

18. Explain the relationship between a protein's structure and its ability to function.

19. What are the components of a chemical reaction?

20. Explain the difference between exothermic and endothermic reactions.

21. Describe the effect of a catalyst on activation energy and reaction rate.

22. What is the role of enzymes in organisms?

Critical Thinking

23. Compare and Contrast How are phospholipids similar to lipids such as triglycerides? How are they different?

24. Compare and Contrast Briefly describe the similarities and differences between hydrogen bonds and ionic bonds. Which type of bond do you think is stronger? Why?

25. Infer Suppose that you have a cold. What characteristics must cold medicine have that allow it to be transported throughout your body? Explain.

26. Predict Homeostasis involves the maintenance of constant conditions in an organism. What might happen to a protein if homeostasis is disrupted? Why?

27. Compare and Contrast Describe the structures and functions of starch and cellulose. How are the molecules similar? How are they different?

28. Apply Suppose you had a friend who wanted to entirely avoid eating fats. What functions of lipids could you describe to convince that person of the importance of fats to his or her health?

29. Infer The human body can reuse some of the enzymes found in raw fruits and vegetables. Why is this not the case for cooked fruits and vegetables?

Interpreting Visuals

The diagram below shows the lock-and-key model of enzyme function. Use it to answer the next three questions.

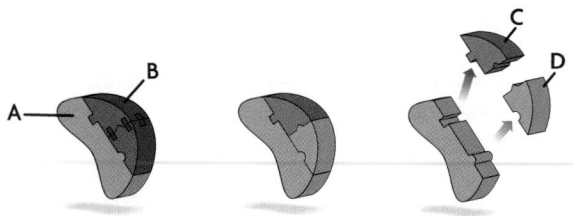

30. Summarize Briefly explain what is happening at each step of the process. Be sure to identify each of the substances (A–D) shown in each step of the process.

31. Apply How does Substance A affect the amount of activation energy needed by the process? Explain.

32. Synthesize Describe the importance of buffers in solutions in allowing the process shown above to take place.

Analyzing Data

Use the graph below to answer the next three questions.

ENERGY IN A CHEMICAL REACTION

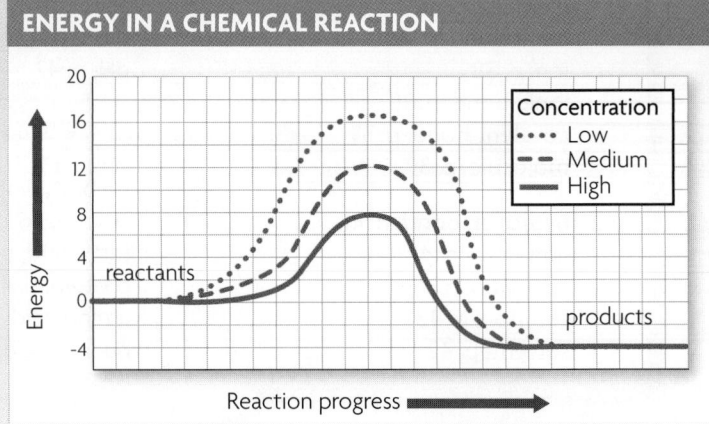

33. Apply Suppose the graph was constructed from data collected during an experiment. What were the independent and dependent variables in the experiment? Explain.

34. Analyze How much activation energy is needed to start the chemical reaction represented by each line on the graph? How much energy is released from each reaction?

35. Apply Explain whether each of the chemical reactions shown on the graph is endothermic or exothermic.

Connecting CONCEPTS

36. Write About Chemical Equilibrium Carbon dioxide reacts with water in blood plasma to form carbonic acid. The equation for this reaction is shown on page 51. Suppose that you are a molecule of carbon dioxide. Describe the chemical reactions that take place when you enter the blood and when you leave the blood. Explain what determines how these reactions occur. Be sure to include all terms from the chapter that are related to the chemical reaction.

37. Apply The Venus flytrap shown in the photograph on page 35 uses enzymes to digest its prey. Describe how pH, solutions, and chemical reactions all play important roles inside the trap of this carnivorous plant.

MICHIGAN
STANDARDS-BASED ASSESSMENT

✓ **Test Practice**
For more test practice,
go to ClassZone.com.

1.

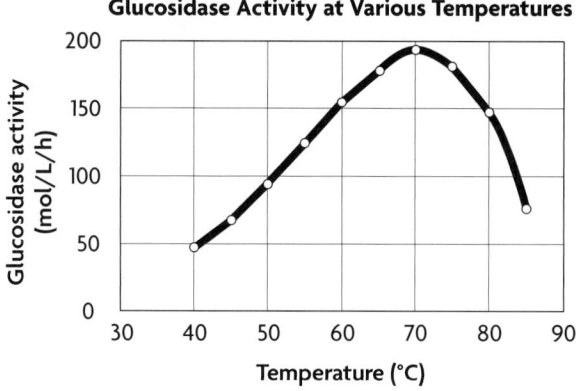

Glucosidase Activity at Various Temperatures

Glucosidase activity (mol/L/h) vs Temperature (°C)

This graph shows the activity of an enzyme called glucosidase. What can you conclude from these data? **B1.1E**

A Glucosidase breaks down glucose substrates.

B Glucosidase functions best around 70°C.

C Glucosidase does not function below 70°C.

D Glucosidase is not affected by temperature.

THINK THROUGH THE QUESTION

The type of enzyme in this question is unimportant. Instead, focus on the data in the graph. To help you answer the question, note at which point the slope of the graph changes.

---

2. Proteins are long molecules that are built from various combinations of **B2.2C**

A carbohydrates.

B nucleic acids.

C lipids.

D amino acids.

3.

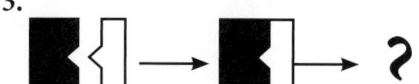

The diagram shows how an enzyme (black) binds to a substrate (white) during a chemical reaction. When this reaction is complete, the **B2.2D**

A enzyme's shape will be different.

B surrounding temperature will have increased.

C hydrogen ion concentration will have decreased.

D substrate will be a different molecule.

4. An animal's stomach contains enzymes that break down food into smaller molecules that the animal's cells can use. Enzymes perform this function by **B2.2F**

A participating in chemical reactions.

B increasing the temperature.

C changing the ionic concentration.

D lowering the pH.

5. A macromolecule such as a lipid is characterized by having **B2.5A**

A ionic bonds.

B polar bonds.

C low-energy bonds.

D high-energy bonds.

6. A spider is able to walk on water without sinking due to water's **L2.p1B**

A cohesion.

B high specific heat.

C adhesion.

D solvency.

BIOZINE

at CLASSZONE.COM

INTERNET MAGAZINE

Go online for the latest biology news and updates on all BioZine articles.

Expanding the Textbook

News Feeds

- Science Daily
- CNN
- BBC

Careers

Bio Bytes

Opinion Poll

Strange Biology

Scientists can change an organism's genes. Should they?

When Knowledge and Ethics Collide

Our ability to change living things grows as we learn more about life. But sometimes biotechnology makes us question whether we should change organisms just because we can. Maybe the technology is dangerous or maybe it challenges our values. Consider the greenish pig above. A gene from a fluorescent jellyfish was added to its genome by genetic engineering. Genetic engineering holds great promise for medicine. But how and when should we alter an organism's genes?

What is Bioethics?

A short answer is that bioethics is the study of the moral questions that are raised as a result of biology research and its applications. But what do questions of ethics have to do with biology? It might seem better to leave questions about values in a philosophy or social studies class. However, today's cutting-edge research often prompts discussions about some of our most basic values. In the end, you might find that biology class is the best place to consider any number of ethical questions.

Ethical questions require all of us to make decisions about "the right thing to do." Often, the right thing to do is very clear. The decision benefits ourselves, our families, and our society, and it follows the accepted values of society. However, many times a decision about an ethical issue is not so obvious. It is in these cases when strong feelings on different sides of an ethical question can produce conflicts—in ourselves, our families, and our society. Can we rely upon biology, or any other scientific field, for our decisions?

For better or for worse, science can only provide us with information. The knowledge that comes from scientific research is very useful, and often necessary, in helping people arrive at decisions, but science only provides part of the answer to ethical questions. All of the advances in science have given us the ability to do many wondrous things. But bioethics asks us to question whether we should actually do all of those things.

We can add new genes to an organism's DNA. We can clone animals. We can extend human life expectancies. We can test people for genetic diseases. But should we, as a society, do all of these things? And who should decide whether we use all of our technological advances? Should these decisions be left to researchers? to universities? to corporations? Should the government make laws to cover bioethical issues? In the end, any decision based on a bioethical question will likely come down to a combination of scientific knowledge, personal values, and law.

TECHNOLOGY

Genetic Testing

Genetic testing is used in many ways. We can identify disease-causing genes, determine the guilt or innocence of crime suspects, and reunite families that have been separated. But should genetic testing be used by employers to make decisions about employees?

Suppose that a company secretly obtained and tested DNA samples from some of its employees. Because of rising medical insurance claims, the company wanted to know if the employees had a gene that increased their risk for developing a certain medical condition. Does this seem like a plot for a television show? It isn't. In 2002, a company had to pay more than $2 million in damages for testing the DNA of employees without their knowledge.

Consider another case. In 2005 a basketball player named Eddy Curry missed the end of the season due to a potential heart problem. His team wanted to use a genetic test to find out if he had a life-threatening condition. Curry refused because the test results could have ended his career. The team refused to let him play. Both the team and Curry made choices. Who do you think was right?

Read More >> *at* CLASSZONE.COM

Bioethics and Society

Many bioethics issues place an individual's right to privacy against the right of a company to conduct business, against the need of a community to have access to health information, or against the need of scientists to share research. In March of 2000, for example, Iceland's government sold the genetic and medical records of its 275,000 citizens to a Swiss drug manufacturer for $200 million. The money helped Iceland's economy, and any medications or tests for genetic diseases that result from the medical records will be provided for free to all Icelanders.

CAREERS

Geneticist in Action

DR. CHARMAINE ROYAL

TITLE Professor, Pediatrics, Howard University

EDUCATION Ph. D., Human Genetics, Howard University

Many bioethicists focus on the ethical implications of technology. Dr. Charmaine Royal, however, is concerned with the ethics of experimental design and the applications and implications of biological research. Dr. Royal, who is a geneticist at the Human Genome Center of Howard University, points out that some scientists in the past tried to use genetic research to justify treating non-Caucasians as inferior. She also notes that although there is no biological basis for any meaningful differences among races, many African-Americans are still suspicious of genetic research. Many, for example, have been discriminated against when an insurance company or a prospective employer finds out they have sickle cell anemia, which is a relatively common genetic disorder in African-Americans.

Dr. Royal, who is Jamaican, wants to ensure that African-Americans are included and treated fairly in research studies, and that they receive the benefits of genetic screening and genetic counseling. In 1998 Dr. Royal helped start the African-American Hereditary Prostate Cancer Study, the first large-scale genetic study of African-Americans to be designed and carried out by an almost entirely African-American research team.

Read More >> *at* CLASSZONE.COM

However, the government's actions could also be considered to be very troubling. Even though the citizens were given the option to not be included in the database, were the Icelanders' rights to privacy over their genetic records violated? Does anyone other than the individual have the right to be given access to this very personal information?

As biotechnology continues to advance, you will face new bioethics questions throughout your lifetime. Will you be ready?

Health insurance applicants are screened for preexisting conditions, such as HIV. If a condition is found, companies might offer insurance to a person at a higher cost. Should insurance companies be allowed to do genetic screening to detect whether people have genes that might increase their risk of developing cancer or alcoholism? If not, should healthy people have to pay more to make up for higher costs the company has to pay for people who refuse to be screened? From the company's point of view, its responsibility is to make a profit for its shareholders. With genetic testing, the company can protect itself from potentially large costs. As you can see, a company's policy based on its ethics may differ from what others see as ethical.

Science alone cannot answer bioethics questions. When these questions arise, we all need to weigh the issues for ourselves. As biotechnology continues to advance, you will face new bioethics questions throughout your lifetime. Will you be ready?

Questions to Consider

- Should scientists do all of the things that technology has made it possible for them to do?
- Who should decide how biotechnology is used?
- Should scientific knowledge and personal beliefs play equal or unequal roles in decisions about biotechnology?

Read More >> *at* CLASSZONE.COM

UNIT 2
Cells

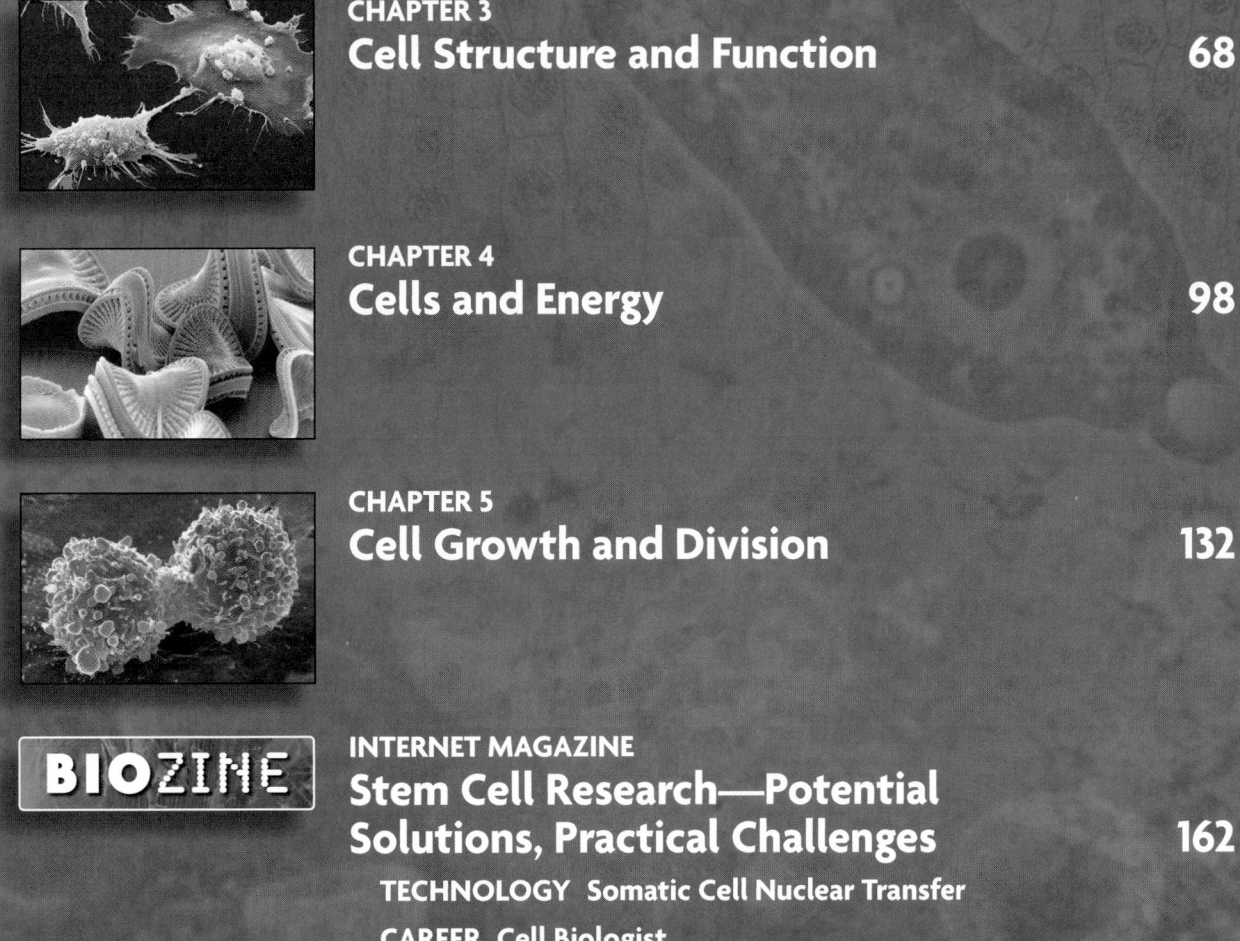

CHAPTER 3
Cell Structure and Function   68

CHAPTER 4
Cells and Energy   98

CHAPTER 5
Cell Growth and Division   132

BIOZINE

INTERNET MAGAZINE
**Stem Cell Research—Potential
Solutions, Practical Challenges**   162
   TECHNOLOGY Somatic Cell Nuclear Transfer
   CAREER Cell Biologist

CHAPTER

3 Cell Structure and Function

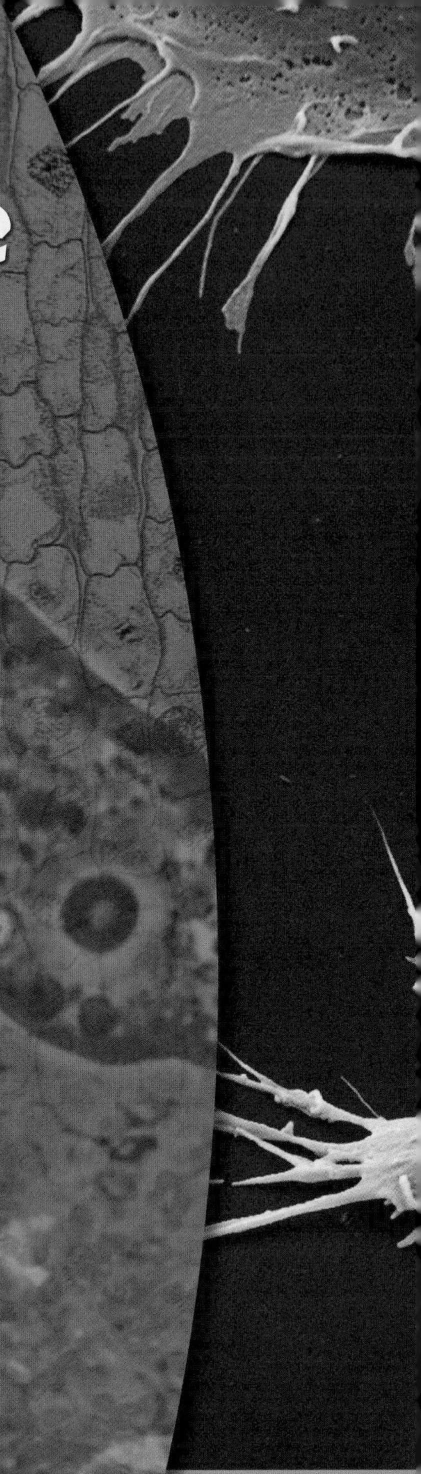

KEY CONCEPTS

3.1 Cell Theory
Cells are the basic unit of life.

3.2 Cell Organelles
Eukaryotic cells share many similarities.

3.3 Cell Membrane
The cell membrane is a barrier that separates a cell from the external environment.

3.4 Diffusion and Osmosis
Materials move across membranes because of concentration differences.

3.5 Active Transport, Endocytosis, and Exocytosis
Cells use energy to transport materials that cannot diffuse across a membrane.

Online BIOLOGY CLASSZONE.COM

Animated BIOLOGY

View animated chapter concepts.
- Cell Organelles
- Get Through a Cell Membrane

BIOZINE

Keep current with biology news.
- Featured stories
- News feeds
- Careers

RESOURCE CENTER

Get more information on
- Prokaryotic and Eukaryotic Cells
- Diffusion and Osmosis

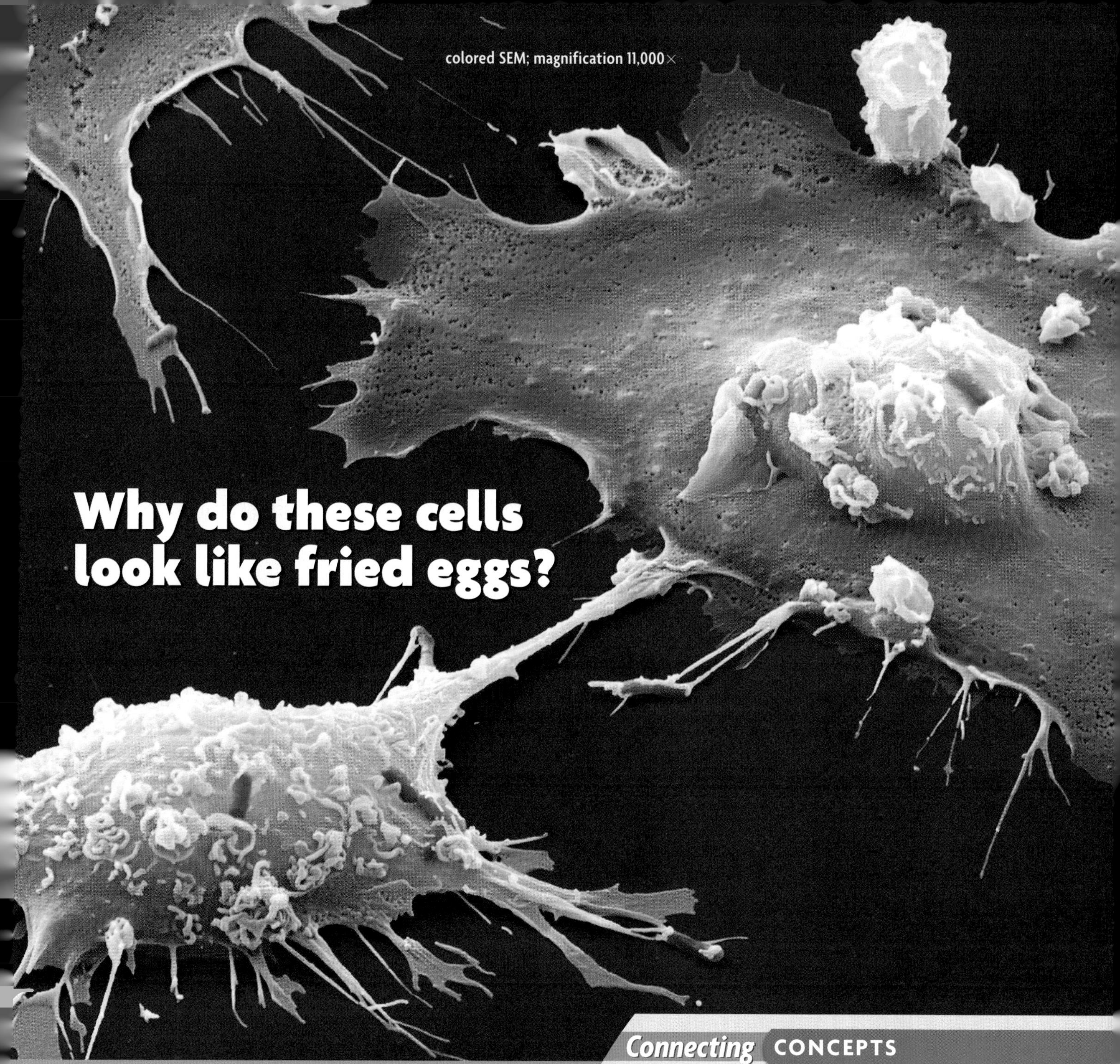

Why do these cells look like fried eggs?

Connecting CONCEPTS

M acrophages (large tan cells) take in and digest foreign material, such as invading bacteria (small red cells). They play an important role in your immune system. Many macrophages travel the body, recognize foreign material, engulf it, and break it down using chemicals. They have an adaptable internal skeleton that helps them move and stretch out their "arms" to capture invading particles.

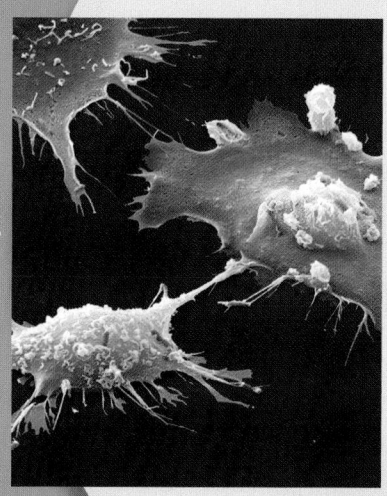

Technology The scanning electron microscope (SEM) uses electrons to create greatly magnified, three-dimensional images of surface structures. Samples must be carefully prepared to withstand the vacuum and to prevent shriveling. This means that any cell or organism you see in an SEM image is dead. In addition, images are generated in black and white (left). The picture above is artificially colored to highlight specific parts.

Chapter 3: Cell Structure and Function **69**

3.1 Cell Theory

KEY CONCEPT Cells are the basic unit of life.

MAIN IDEAS

- Early studies led to the development of the cell theory.
- Prokaryotic cells lack a nucleus and most internal structures of eukaryotic cells.

VOCABULARY

cell theory, p. 71
cytoplasm, p. 72
organelle, p. 72
prokaryotic cell, p. 72
eukaryotic cell, p. 72

MICHIGAN STANDARDS

B1.2i Explain the progression of ideas and explanations that leads to science theories that are part of the current scientific consensus or core knowledge.

B2.5g Compare and contrast plant and animal cells.

Connect You and all other organisms are made of cells. As you saw on the previous page, a cell's structure is closely related to its function. Today we know that cells are the smallest unit of living matter that can carry out all processes required for life. But before the 1600s, people had many other ideas about the basis of life. Like many breakthroughs, the discovery of cells was aided by the development of new technology—in this case, the microscope.

MAIN IDEA

Early studies led to the development of the cell theory.

Almost all cells are too small to see without the aid of a microscope. Although glass lenses had been used to magnify images for hundreds of years, the early lenses were not powerful enough to reveal individual cells. The invention of the compound microscope in the late 1500s was an early step toward this discovery. The Dutch eyeglass maker Zacharias Janssen, who was probably assisted by his father, Hans, usually gets credit for this invention.

A compound microscope contains two or more lenses. Total magnification, the product of the magnifying power of each individual lens, is generally much more powerful with a compound microscope than with a single lens.

TAKING NOTES

As you read, make an outline using the headings as topics. Summarize details that further explain those ideas.

I. Main Idea
   A. Supporting idea
      1. Detail
      2. Detail
   B. Supporting idea

Discovery of Cells

In 1665, the English scientist Robert Hooke used the three-lens compound microscope shown in **FIGURE 3.1** to examine thin slices of cork. Cork is the tough outer bark of a species of oak tree. He observed that cork is made of tiny, hollow compartments. The compartments reminded Hooke of small rooms found in a monastery, so he gave them the same name: cells. The plant cells he observed, shown in **FIGURE 3.2** (top), were dead. Hooke was looking only at cell walls and empty space.

Around the same time, Anton van Leeuwenhoek, a Dutch tradesman, was studying new methods for making lenses to examine cloth. As a result of his research, his single-lens microscopes were much more powerful than Hooke's crude compound microscope. In 1674, Leeuwenhoek became one of the first people to describe living cells when he observed numerous single-celled organisms swimming in a drop of pond water. Sketches of his "animalcules" are pictured in **FIGURE 3.2** (bottom).

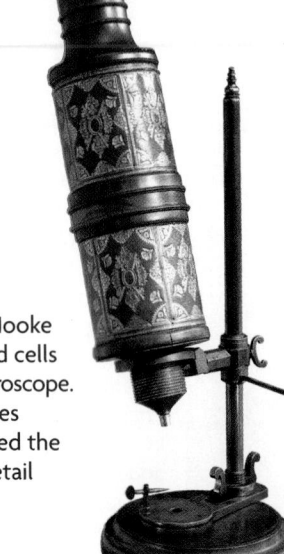

FIGURE 3.1 Hooke first identified cells using this microscope. Its crude lenses severely limited the amount of detail he could see.

As people continued to improve the microscope over the next century and a half, it became sturdier, easier to use, and capable of greater magnification. This combination of factors led people to examine even more organisms. They observed a wide variety of cell shapes, and they observed cells dividing. Scientists began to ask important questions: Is all living matter made of cells? Where do cells come from?

Cell Theory

The German scientist Matthias Schleiden also used compound microscopes to study plant tissue. In 1838, he proposed that plants are made of cells. Schleiden discussed the results of his work with another German scientist, Theodor Schwann, who was struck by the structural similarities between plant cells and the animal cells he had been studying. Schwann concluded that all animals are made of cells. Shortly thereafter, in 1839, he published the first statement of the cell theory, concluding that all living things are made of cells and cell products. This theory helped lay the groundwork for all biological research that followed. However, it had to be refined over the years as additional data led to new conclusions. For example, Schwann stated in his publication that cells form spontaneously by free-cell formation. As later scientists studied the process of cell division, they realized that this part of Schwann's idea was wrong. In 1855, Rudolf Virchow, another German scientist, reported that all cells come from preexisting cells. These early contributors are shown in **FIGURE 3.3**.

This accumulated research can be summarized in the cell theory, one of the first unifying concepts developed in biology. The major principles of the **cell theory** are the following:

- All organisms are made of cells.
- All existing cells are produced by other living cells.
- The cell is the most basic unit of life.

FIGURE 3.2 Hooke observed the cell walls of dead plant cells (top). In contrast, Leeuwenhoek observed and drew microscopic life, which he called animalcules, in pond water (bottom).

Summarize **Explain the three major principles of cell theory in your own words.**

FIGURE 3.3 Contributors to Cell Theory

HOOKE
1665 Hooke was the first to identify cells, and he named them.

LEEUWENHOEK
1674 Because he made better lenses, Leeuwenhoek observed cells in greater detail.

SCHLEIDEN
1838 Schleiden was the first to note that plants are made of cells.

SCHWANN
1839 Schwann concluded that all living things are made of cells.

VIRCHOW
1855 Virchow proposed that all cells come from other cells.

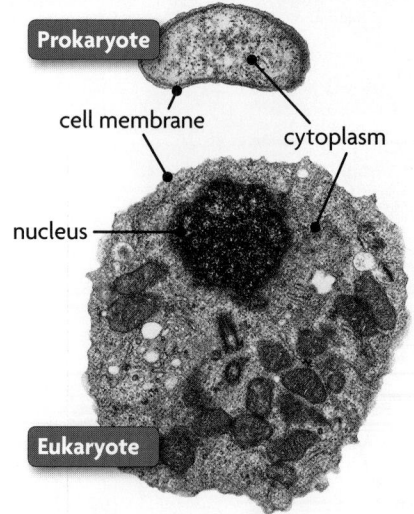

Prokaryote

cell membrane

cytoplasm

nucleus

Eukaryote

FIGURE 3.4 In prokaryotic cells, such as this bacterium (top), DNA is suspended in the cytoplasm. In eukaryotic cells, such as this mammalian cell (bottom), the nuclear envelope separates DNA from the cytoplasm. (colored TEMs; magnifications: mammalian cell 20,000×; bacterium 19,000×)

Connecting CONCEPTS

Prokaryotes You will learn more about prokaryotes in **Chapter 18,** which discusses their requirements to sustain life, their role in the ecosystem, and, their role in human disease.

▶ **MAIN IDEA**

Prokaryotic cells lack a nucleus and most internal structures of eukaryotic cells.

The variety of cell types found in living things is staggering. Your body alone is made of trillions of cells of many different shapes, sizes, and functions. They include long, thin nerve cells that transmit sensory information, as well as short, blocky skin cells that cover and protect the body. Despite this variety, the cells in your body share many characteristics with one another and with the cells that make up every other organism. In general, cells tend to be microscopic in size and have similar building blocks. They are also enclosed by a membrane that controls the movement of materials into and out of the cell.

Within the membrane, a cell is filled with cytoplasm. **Cytoplasm** is a jellylike substance that contains dissolved molecular building blocks—such as proteins, nucleic acids, minerals, and ions. In some types of cells, the cytoplasm also contains **organelles,** which are structures specialized to perform distinct processes within a cell. Most organelles are surrounded by a membrane. In many cells, the largest and most visible organelle is the nucleus, which stores genetic information.

As shown in **FIGURE 3.4,** cells can be separated into two broad categories based on their internal structures: prokaryotic cells and eukaryotic cells.

- **Prokaryotic cells** (pro-KAR-ee-AHT-ihk) do not have a nucleus or other membrane-bound organelles. Instead, the cell's DNA is suspended in the cytoplasm. All prokaryotes are microscopic single-celled organisms.

- **Eukaryotic cells** (yoo-KAR-ee-AHT-ihk) have a nucleus and other membrane-bound organelles. The nucleus, the largest organelle, encloses the genetic information. Eukaryotes may be multicellular or single-celled organisms.

VISUAL VOCAB

Prokaryotic cells do not have a nucleus or other membrane-bound organelles.

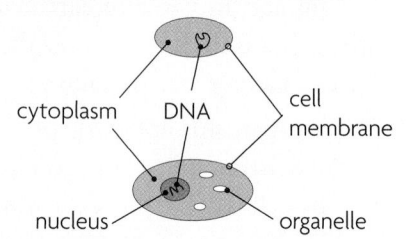

cytoplasm   DNA   cell membrane

nucleus   organelle

Eukaryotic cells have a nucleus and other membrane-bound organelles.

Summarize **What characteristics are shared by most cells?**

3.1 ASSESSMENT

ONLINE QUIZ
ClassZone.com

REVIEWING ▶ MAIN IDEAS

1. How did improvements in the microscope help scientists form the **cell theory**?

2. How do **prokaryotic** and **eukaryotic cells** differ?

CRITICAL THINKING

3. **Analyze** Today, scientists can study human cells grown in petri dishes. Explain how this technique builds on the work of early scientists.

4. **Compare** In what way are cells similar to atoms?

Connecting CONCEPTS

5. **Medicine** Suppose a certain poison kills human cells by blocking pores in the nuclear membrane. Explain why it would or would not kill bacteria.

3.2 Cell Organelles

KEY CONCEPT Eukaryotic cells share many similarities.

▶ MAIN IDEAS

- Cells have an internal structure.
- Several organelles are involved in making and processing proteins.
- Other organelles have various functions.
- Plant cells have cell walls and chloroplasts.

VOCABULARY

cytoskeleton, p. 73	**mitochondrion,** p. 77
nucleus, p. 75	**vacuole,** p. 77
endoplasmic reticulum, p. 76	**lysosome,** p. 78
ribosome, p. 76	**centriole,** p. 78
Golgi apparatus, p. 76	**cell wall,** p. 79
vesicle, p. 77	**chloroplast,** p. 79

MICHIGAN STANDARDS

B2.4g Explain that some structures in the modern eukaryotic cell developed from early prokaryotes, such as mitochondria, and in plants, chloroplasts.

B2.5g Compare and contrast plant and animal cells.

Connect Your body is highly organized. It contains organs that are specialized to perform particular tasks. For example, your skin receives sensory information and helps prevent infection. Your intestines digest food, your kidneys filter wastes, and your bones protect and support other organs. On a much smaller scale, your cells have a similar division of labor. They contain specialized structures that work together to respond to stimuli and efficiently carry out other necessary processes.

▶ MAIN IDEA

Cells have an internal structure.

Like your body, eukaryotic cells are highly organized structures. They are surrounded by a protective membrane that receives messages from other cells. They contain membrane-bound organelles that perform specific cellular processes, divide certain molecules into compartments, and help regulate the timing of key events. But the cell is not a random jumble of suspended organelles and molecules. Rather, certain organelles and molecules are anchored to specific sites, which vary by cell type. If the membrane was removed from a cell, the contents wouldn't collapse and ooze out in a big puddle. How does a cell maintain this framework?

Each eukaryotic cell has a **cytoskeleton,** which is a network of proteins that is constantly changing to meet the needs of a cell. It is made of small protein subunits that form long threads, or fibers, that crisscross the entire cell, as shown in **FIGURE 3.5**. Three main types of fibers make up the cytoskeleton and allow it to serve a wide range of functions.

- Microtubules are long hollow tubes. They give the cell its shape and act as "tracks" for the movement of organelles. When cells divide, microtubules form fibers that pull half of the DNA into each new cell.
- Intermediate filaments, which are somewhat smaller than microtubules, give a cell its strength.
- Microfilaments, the smallest of the three, are tiny threads that enable cells to move and divide. They play an important role in muscle cells, where they help the muscle contract and relax.

FIGURE 3.5 The cytoskeleton supports and shapes the cell. The cytoskeleton includes microtubules (green) and microfilaments (red). (epifluorescence microscopy; magnification 750×)

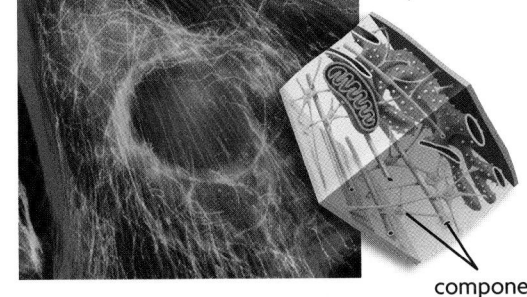

components of the cytoskeleton

FIGURE 3.6 Cell Structure

Animated BIOLOGY
Explore cell organelles at ClassZone.com.

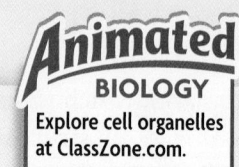

Eukaryotic cells have highly organized structures, including membrane-bound organelles. Plant and animal cells share many of the same types of organelles, but both also have organelles that are unique to their needs.

PLANT CELL

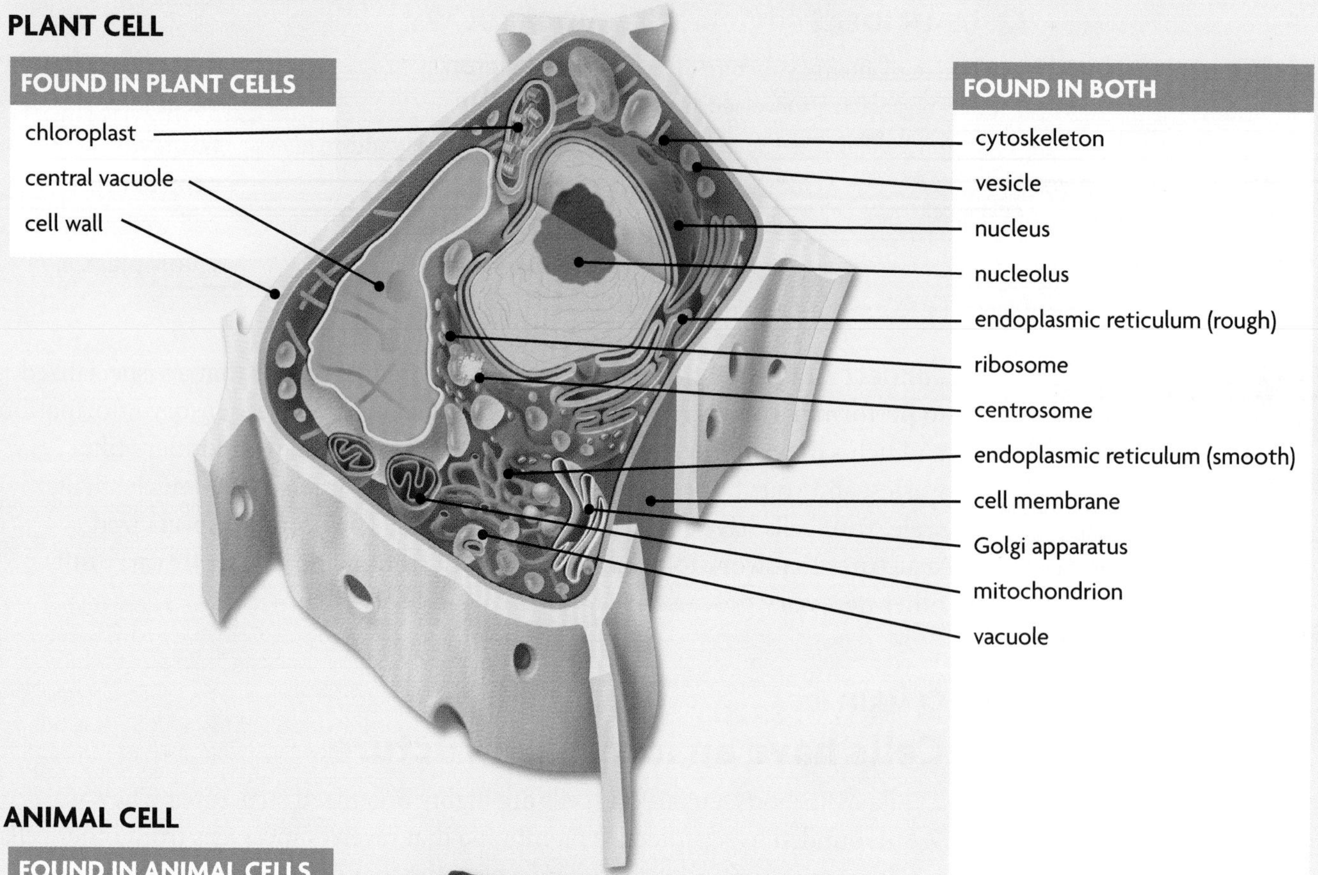

FOUND IN PLANT CELLS
chloroplast
central vacuole
cell wall
FOUND IN BOTH
cytoskeleton
vesicle
nucleus
nucleolus
endoplasmic reticulum (rough)
ribosome
centrosome
endoplasmic reticulum (smooth)
cell membrane
Golgi apparatus
mitochondrion
vacuole

ANIMAL CELL

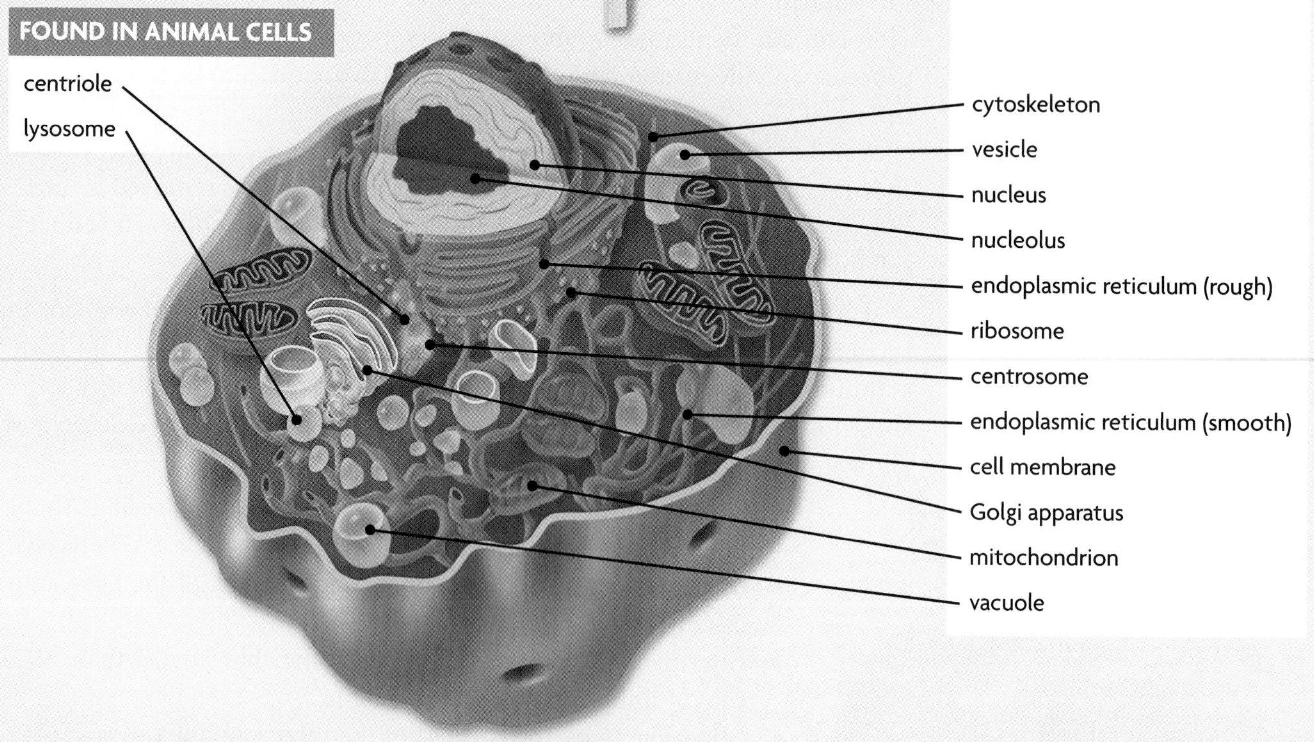

FOUND IN ANIMAL CELLS
centriole
lysosome
cytoskeleton
vesicle
nucleus
nucleolus
endoplasmic reticulum (rough)
ribosome
centrosome
endoplasmic reticulum (smooth)
cell membrane
Golgi apparatus
mitochondrion
vacuole

CRITICAL VIEWING **What differences do you observe between animal and plant cells?**

Cytoplasm, which you read about in Section 3.1, is itself an important contributor to cell structure. In eukaryotes, it fills the space between the nucleus and the cell membrane. The fluid portion, excluding the organelles, is called cytosol and consists mostly of water. The makeup of cytoplasm shows that water is necessary for maintaining cell structure. This is only one of many reasons that water is an essential component for life, however. Many chemical reactions occur in the cytoplasm, where water acts as an important solvent.

The remainder of this chapter highlights the structure and function of the organelles found in eukaryotic cells. As **FIGURE 3.6** shows, plant and animal cells use many of the same types of organelles to carry out basic functions. Both cell types also have organelles that are unique to their needs.

Infer **What problems might a cell experience if it had no cytoskeleton?**

TAKING NOTES

Make a chart to correlate each organelle with its function.

Organelle	Function
Nucleus	stores DNA
Ribosome	

▶ MAIN IDEA

Several organelles are involved in making and processing proteins.

Much of the cell is devoted to making proteins. Proteins are made of 20 types of amino acids that have unique characteristics of size, polarity, and acidity. They can form very long or very short protein chains that fold into different shapes. And multiple protein chains can interact with each other. This almost limitless variety of shapes and interactions makes proteins very powerful. Proteins carry out many critical functions, so they need to be made correctly.

Nucleus

The **nucleus** (NOO-klee-uhs) is the storehouse for most of the genetic information, or DNA (deoxyribonucleic acid), in your cells. DNA contains genes that are instructions for making proteins. There are two major demands on the nucleus: (1) DNA must be carefully protected, and (2) DNA must be available for use at the proper times. Molecules that would damage DNA need to be kept out of the nucleus. But many proteins are involved in turning genes on and off, and they need to access the DNA at certain times. The special structure of the nucleus helps it meet both demands.

The nucleus is composed of the cell's DNA enclosed in a double membrane called the nuclear envelope. Each membrane in the nuclear envelope is similar to the membrane surrounding the entire cell. As **FIGURE 3.7** shows, the nuclear envelope is pierced with holes called pores that allow large molecules to pass between the nucleus and cytoplasm.

The nucleus also contains the nucleolus. The nucleolus is a dense region where tiny organelles essential for making proteins are assembled. These organelles, called ribosomes, are a combination of proteins and RNA molecules. They are discussed on the next page, and a more complete description of their structure and function is given in Chapter 8.

Connecting CONCEPTS

Biochemistry Recall from **Chapter 2** that certain amino acids within a protein molecule may form hydrogen bonds with other amino acids. These bonds cause the protein to form a specific shape.

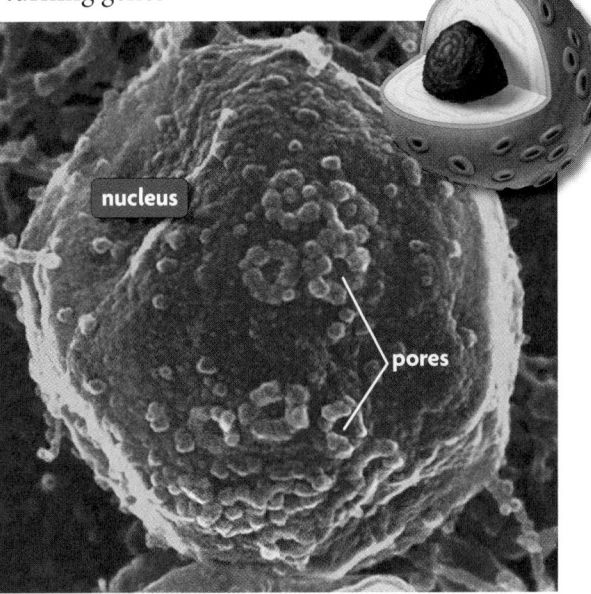

FIGURE 3.7 The nucleus stores and protects DNA. (colored SEM; magnification 90,000×)

nucleus

pores

Endoplasmic Reticulum and Ribosomes

A large part of the cytoplasm of most eukaryotic cells is filled by the endoplasmic reticulum, shown in **FIGURE 3.8**. The **endoplasmic reticulum** (EHN-duh-PLAZ-mihk rih-TIHK-yuh-luhm), or the ER, is an interconnected network of thin folded membranes. The composition is very similar to that of the cell membrane and nuclear membranes. The ER membranes form a maze of enclosed spaces. The interior of this maze is called the lumen. Numerous processes, including the production of proteins and lipids, occur both on the surface of the ER and inside the lumen. The ER must be large enough to accommodate all these processes. How does it fit inside a cell?

The ER membrane has many creases and folds. If you have ever gone camping, you probably slept in a sleeping bag that covered you from head to foot. The next morning, you stuffed it back into a tiny little sack. How does the entire sleeping bag fit inside such a small sack? The surface area of the sleeping bag does not change, but the folds allow it to take up less space. Likewise, the ER's many folds enable it to fit within the cell.

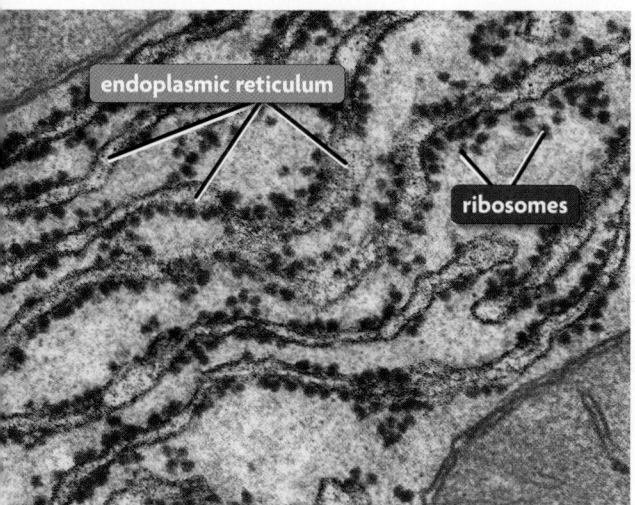
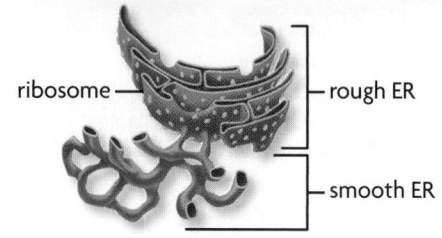

FIGURE 3.8 The endoplasmic reticulum aids in the production of proteins and lipids. (colored TEM; magnification about 20,000×)

endoplasmic reticulum

ribosomes

ribosome — rough ER

— smooth ER

In some regions, the ER is studded with **ribosomes** (RY-buh-SOHMZ), tiny organelles that link amino acids together to form proteins. Ribosomes are both the site of protein synthesis and active participants in the process. Ribosomes are themselves made of proteins and RNA. After assembly in the nucleolus, ribosomes pass through the nuclear pores into the cytoplasm, where most protein synthesis occurs.

Surfaces of the ER that are covered with ribosomes are called rough ER because they look bumpy when viewed with an electron microscope. As a protein is being made on these ribosomes, it enters the lumen. Inside the lumen, the protein may be modified by having sugar chains added to it, which can help the protein fold or give it stability.

Not all ribosomes are bound to the ER; some are suspended in the cytoplasm. In general, proteins made on the ER are either incorporated into the cell membrane or secreted. In contrast, proteins made on suspended ribosomes are typically used in chemical reactions occurring within the cytoplasm.

Surfaces of the ER that do not contain ribosomes are called smooth ER. Smooth ER makes lipids and performs a variety of other specialized functions, such as breaking down drugs and alcohol.

Golgi Apparatus

From the ER, proteins generally move to the Golgi apparatus, shown in **FIGURE 3.9**. The **Golgi apparatus** (GOHL-jee) consists of closely layered stacks of membrane-enclosed spaces that process, sort, and deliver proteins. Its membranes contain enzymes that make additional changes to proteins. The Golgi apparatus also packages proteins. Some of the packaged proteins are stored within the Golgi apparatus for later use. Some are transported to other organelles within the cell. Still others are carried to the membrane and secreted outside the cell.

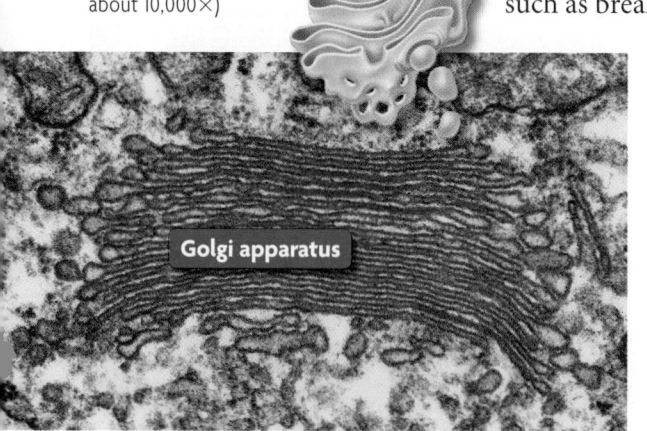

FIGURE 3.9 The Golgi apparatus modifies, packages, and transports proteins. (colored TEM; magnification about 10,000×)

Golgi apparatus

Vesicles

Cells need to separate reactants for various chemical reactions until it is time for them to be used. **Vesicles** (VEHS-ih-kuhlz), shown in **FIGURE 3.10**, are a general name used to describe small membrane-bound sacs that divide some materials from the rest of the cytoplasm and transport these materials from place to place within the cell. Vesicles are generally short-lived and are formed and recycled as needed.

After a protein has been made, part of the ER pinches off to form a vesicle surrounding the protein. Protected by the vesicle, the protein can be safely transported to the Golgi apparatus. There, any necessary modifications are made, and the protein is packaged inside a new vesicle for storage, transport, or secretion.

Compare and Contrast How are the nucleus and a vesicle similar and different in structure and function?

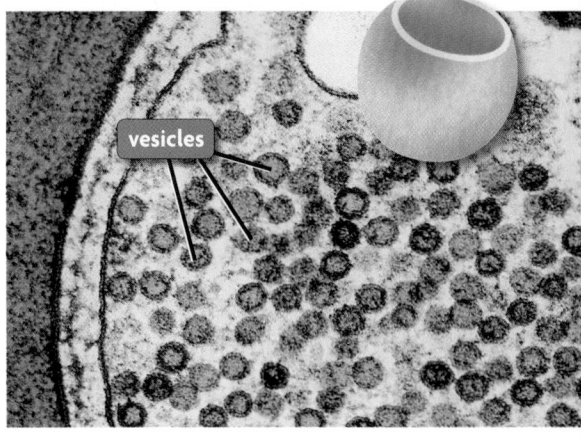

FIGURE 3.10 Vesicles isolate and transport specific molecules. (colored SEM; magnification 20,000×)

vesicles

▶ MAIN IDEA

Other organelles have various functions.

Mitochondria

Mitochondria (MY-tuh-KAHN-dree-uh) supply energy to the cell. Mitochondria (singular, *mitochondrion*) are bean shaped and have two membranes, as shown in **FIGURE 3.11**. The inner membrane has many folds that greatly increase its surface area. Within these inner folds and compartments, a series of chemical reactions takes place that converts molecules from the food you eat into usable energy. You will learn more about this process in Chapter 4.

Unlike most organelles, mitochondria have their own ribosomes and DNA. This fact suggests that mitochondria were originally free-living prokaryotes that were taken in by larger cells. The relationship must have helped both organisms to survive.

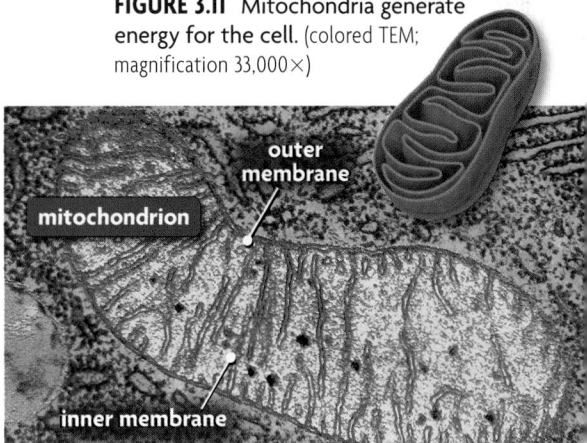

FIGURE 3.11 Mitochondria generate energy for the cell. (colored TEM; magnification 33,000×)

outer membrane

mitochondrion

inner membrane

Vacuole

A **vacuole** (VAK-yoo-OHL) is a fluid-filled sac used for the storage of materials needed by a cell. These materials may include water, food molecules, inorganic ions, and enzymes. Most animal cells contain many small vacuoles. The central vacuole, shown in **FIGURE 3.12**, is a structure unique to plant cells. It is a single large vacuole that usually takes up most of the space inside a plant cell. It is filled with a watery fluid that strengthens the cell and helps to support the entire plant. When a plant wilts, its leaves shrivel because there is not enough water in each cell's central vacuole to support the leaf's normal structure. The central vacuole may also contain other substances, including toxins that would harm predators, waste products that would harm the cell itself, and pigments that give color to cells—such as those in the petals of a flower.

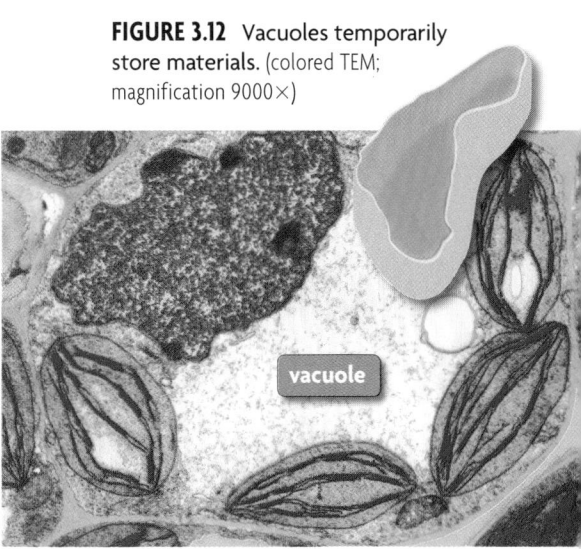

FIGURE 3.12 Vacuoles temporarily store materials. (colored TEM; magnification 9000×)

vacuole

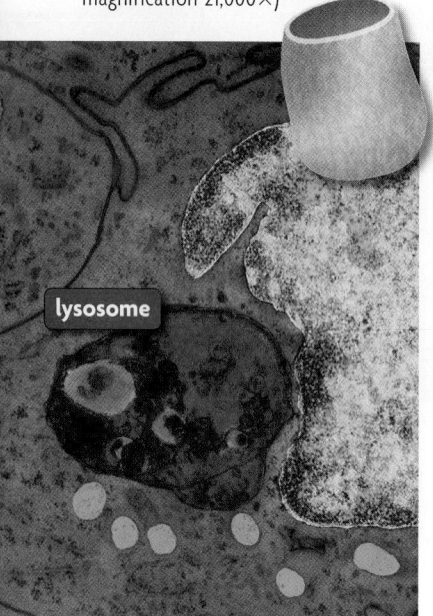

FIGURE 3.13 Lysosomes digest and recycle foreign materials or worn-out parts. (colored TEM; magnification 21,000×)

lysosome

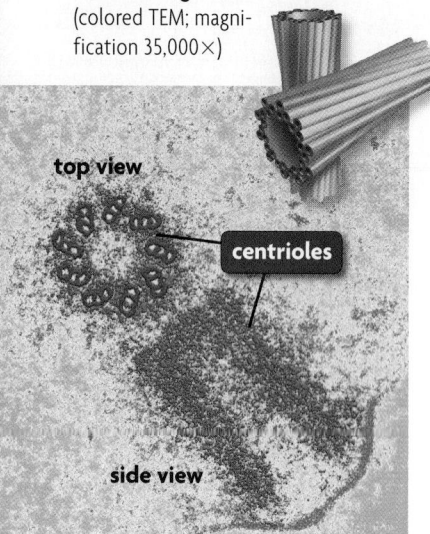

FIGURE 3.14 Centrioles divide DNA during cell division. (colored TEM; magnification 35,000×)

top view

centrioles

side view

Lysosomes

Lysosomes (LY-suh-SOHMZ), shown in **FIGURE 3.13**, are membrane-bound organelles that contain enzymes. They defend a cell from invading bacteria and viruses. They also break down damaged or worn-out cell parts. Lysosomes tend to be numerous in animal cells. Their presence in plant cells is still questioned by some scientists, but others assert that plant cells do have lysosomes, though fewer than are found in animal cells.

Recall that all enzymes are proteins. Initially, lysosomal enzymes are made in the rough ER in an inactive form. Vesicles pinch off from the ER membrane, carry the enzymes, and then fuse with the Golgi apparatus. There, the enzymes are activated and packaged as lysosomes that pinch off from the Golgi membrane. The lysosomes can then engulf and digest targeted molecules. When a molecule is broken down, the products pass through the lysosomal membrane and into the cytoplasm, where they are used again.

Lysosomes provide an example of the importance of membrane-bound structures in the eukaryotic cell. Because lysosomal enzymes can destroy cell components, they must be surrounded by a membrane that prevents them from destroying necessary structures. However, the cell also uses other methods to protect itself from these destructive enzymes. For example, the enzymes do not work as well in the cytoplasm as they do inside the lysosome.

Centrosome and Centrioles

The centrosome is a small region of cytoplasm that produces microtubules. In animal cells, it contains two small structures called centrioles. **Centrioles** (SEHN-tree-OHLZ) are cylinder-shaped organelles made of short microtubules arranged in a circle. The two centrioles are perpendicular to each other, as shown in **FIGURE 3.14**. Before an animal cell divides, the centrosome, including the centrioles, doubles and the two new centrosomes move to opposite ends of the cell. Microtubules grow from each centrosome, forming spindle fibers. These fibers attach to the DNA and appear to help divide it between the two cells.

Centrioles were once thought to play a critical role in animal cell division. However, experiments have shown that animal cells can divide even if the centrioles are removed, which makes their role more questionable. In addition, although centrioles are found in some algae, they are not found in plants.

Centrioles also organize microtubules to form cilia and flagella. Cilia look like little hairs; flagella look like a whip or a tail. Their motion forces liquids past a cell. For single cells, this movement results in swimming. For cells anchored in tissue, this motion sweeps liquid across the cell surface.

Compare In what ways are lysosomes, vesicles, and the central vacuole similar?

▶ MAIN IDEA
Plant cells have cell walls and chloroplasts.

Plant cells have two features not shared by animal cells: cell walls and chloroplasts. Cell walls are structures that provide rigid support. Chloroplasts are organelles that help a plant convert solar energy to chemical energy.

Cell Walls

In plants, algae, fungi, and most bacteria, the cell membrane is surrounded by a strong **cell wall,** which is a rigid layer that gives protection, support, and shape to the cell. The cell walls of multiple cells, as shown in **FIGURE 3.15,** can adhere to each other to help support an entire organism. For instance, much of the wood in a tree trunk consists of dead cells whose cell walls continue to support the entire tree.

Cell wall composition varies and is related to the different needs of each type of organism. In plants and algae, the cell wall is made of cellulose, a polysaccharide. Because molecules cannot easily diffuse across cellulose, the cell walls of plants and algae have openings, or channels. Water and other molecules small enough to fit through the channels can freely pass through the cell wall. In fungi, cell walls are made of chitin, and in bacteria, they are made of peptidoglycan. The unique characteristics and functions of these materials will be discussed in Chapters 18 and 19.

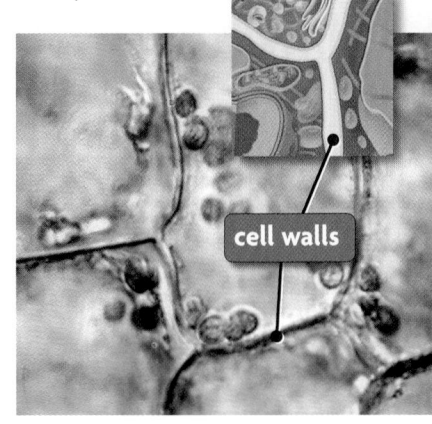

FIGURE 3.15 Cell walls shape and support individual cells and entire organisms. (LM; magnification 3000×)

cell walls

Chloroplasts

Chloroplasts (KLAWR-uh-PLASTS) are organelles that carry out photosynthesis, a series of complex chemical reactions that convert solar energy into energy-rich molecules the cell can use. Photosynthesis will be discussed more fully in Chapter 4. Like mitochondria, chloroplasts are highly compartmentalized. They have both an outer membrane and an inner membrane. They also have stacks of disc-shaped sacs within the inner membrane, shown in **FIGURE 3.16.** These sacs, called thylakoids, contain chlorophyll, a light-absorbing molecule that gives plants their green color and plays a key role in photosynthesis. Like mitochondria, chloroplasts also have their own ribosomes and DNA. Scientists have hypothesized that they, too, were originally free-living prokaryotes that were taken in by larger cells.

Both chloroplasts and mitochondria are present in plant cells, where they work together to capture and convert energy. Chloroplasts are found in the cells of certain other organisms as well, including green algae.

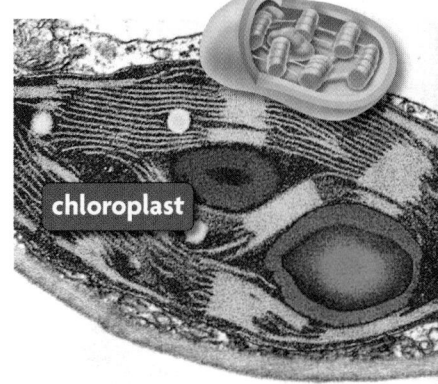

FIGURE 3.16 Chloroplasts convert solar energy into chemical energy through photosynthesis. (colored TEM; magnification 41,500×)

chloroplast

Analyze **Would it be accurate to say that a chloroplast makes energy for a plant cell? Explain your answer.**

3.2 ASSESSMENT

ONLINE QUIZ ClassZone.com

REVIEWING ▶ MAIN IDEAS

1. What are the functions of the **cytoskeleton**?

2. Describe the structure of the **nucleus.**

3. Explain the structure and function of the **mitochondrion.**

4. What function does the **cell wall** perform in a plant?

CRITICAL THINKING

5. **Compare** What similarities do mitochondria and **chloroplasts** share?

6. **Compare** Describe how the **endoplasmic reticulum,** mitochondrion, and **Golgi apparatus** are structurally similar.

Connecting CONCEPTS

7. **Health** Medicine, alcohol, and many drugs are detoxified in liver cells. Why do you think the liver cells of some people who abuse alcohol and drugs have an increased amount of smooth ER?

DATA ANALYSIS
ClassZone.com

Operational Definitions

The **operational definition** of a dependent variable is a description of what is to be observed and measured in an experiment, and what that measurement represents. It is important for scientists to include in their reports the operational definition of the dependent variable so that different scientists repeating the experiment will collect and record data in exactly the same way.

EXAMPLE

Students wanted to determine if the rate of photosynthesis was greater in summer or fall. They collected leaves from many trees in both summer and fall and counted the number of chloroplasts with chlorophyll.

Chloroplasts are organelles that can have a variety of pigments. Only chloroplasts that contain chlorophyll, a type of pigment, can carry out photosynthesis. The rate of photosynthesis increases as the number of chloroplasts with chlorophyll increases.

In this experiment, the number of chloroplasts with chlorophyll is what is being measured. The operational definition is the number of chloroplasts with chlorophyll in the leaf. This number represents the rate at which a plant can carry out photosynthesis.

TABLE 1. CHLOROPLASTS WITH CHLOROPHYLL		
Tree	Leaf Chloroplasts with Chlorophyll (no./cell)	
	Summer	Fall
Birch	192	44
Linden	182	32
Maple	183	28
Weeping willow	177	35

FORM AN OPERATIONAL DEFINITION

Some studies suggest that drinking cranberry juice may help prevent the development of urinary tract infections caused by bacterial cells, which are prokaryotes. Researchers hypothesize that a chemical in cranberry juice may stop the bacteria from attaching to cells in the wall of the urinary bladder. Researchers grew the eukaryotic bladder cells in culture and exposed them to a solution containing bacteria. The cells were then treated with a solution of different juices or water to determine if the juices interfered with bacterial attachment. The results are shown in the graph.

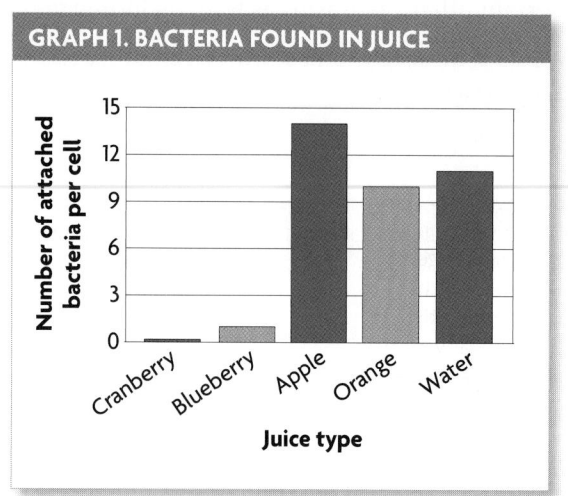
GRAPH 1. BACTERIA FOUND IN JUICE

1. **Apply** What is the operational definition of the dependent variable in this experiment?
2. **Conclude** Which juices may be effective in preventing urinary tract infections?

3.3 Cell Membrane

KEY CONCEPT The cell membrane is a barrier that separates a cell from the external environment.

▶ MAIN IDEAS

- Cell membranes are composed of two phospholipid layers.
- Chemical signals are transmitted across the cell membrane.

VOCABULARY

cell membrane, p. 81
phospholipid, p. 81
fluid mosaic model, p. 82
selective permeability, p. 83
receptor, p. 84

MICHIGAN STANDARDS

B2.5h Explain the role of cell membranes as a highly selective barrier (diffusion, osmosis, and active transport).

Connect Think about how the products you buy are packaged—a pint of berries, perhaps, or a tube of toothpaste. The berries are probably in a plastic container that has holes to allow air circulation. The toothpaste is in a tube strong enough to be squeezed without ripping. Both containers protect their contents, but they do so in different ways. Like these products, the cell needs protection, but it must also be able to respond to its surroundings. It is constantly taking in and getting rid of various molecules. The structure of the cell membrane allows it to perform all those functions.

▶ MAIN IDEA

Cell membranes are composed of two phospholipid layers.

The **cell membrane,** or the plasma membrane, forms a boundary between a cell and the outside environment and controls the passage of materials into and out of a cell. The cell membrane consists of a double layer of phospholipids interspersed with a variety of other molecules. A **phospholipid** (FAHS-foh-LIHP-ihd) is a molecule composed of three basic parts:

- a charged phosphate group
- glycerol
- two fatty acid chains

Together, the glycerol and the phosphate groups form the "head" of a phospholipid; the fatty acids form the "tail." Because the head bears a charge, it is polar. Recall that water molecules are also polar. Therefore, the polar head of the phospholipid forms hydrogen bonds with water molecules. In contrast, the fatty acid tails are nonpolar and cannot form hydrogen bonds with water. As a result, the nonpolar tails are attracted to each other and repelled by water.

Because the membrane touches the cytoplasm inside the cell and the watery fluid outside the cell, the properties of polar heads and nonpolar tails cause the phospholipids to arrange themselves in layers, like a sandwich.

VISUAL VOCAB

A **phospholipid** is composed of three basic parts:

- charged phosphate group
- glycerol
- two fatty acid chains

Connecting CONCEPTS

Biochemistry Recall from **Chapter 2** that a hydrogen bond is a weak chemical bond that forms between a slightly positive hydrogen atom and a negatively charged region of another molecule.

The polar heads are like the bread. They form the outer surfaces of the membrane, where they interact with the watery environment both outside and inside a cell. The nonpolar tails are like the filling. They are sandwiched between the layers of polar heads, where they are protected from the watery environment.

FIGURE 3.17 shows other molecules embedded within the phospholipid layers. They give the membrane properties and characteristics it would not otherwise have. These molecules serve diverse functions. Here are a few examples:

- Cholesterol molecules strengthen the cell membrane.
- Some proteins extend through one or both phospholipid layers and help materials cross the membrane. Other proteins are key components of the cytoskeleton. Different cell types have different membrane proteins.
- Carbohydrates attached to membrane proteins serve as identification tags, enabling cells to distinguish one type of cell from another.

FIGURE 3.17 Cell Membrane

The cell membrane is made of two phospholipid layers embedded with other molecules, such as proteins, carbohydrates, and cholesterol.

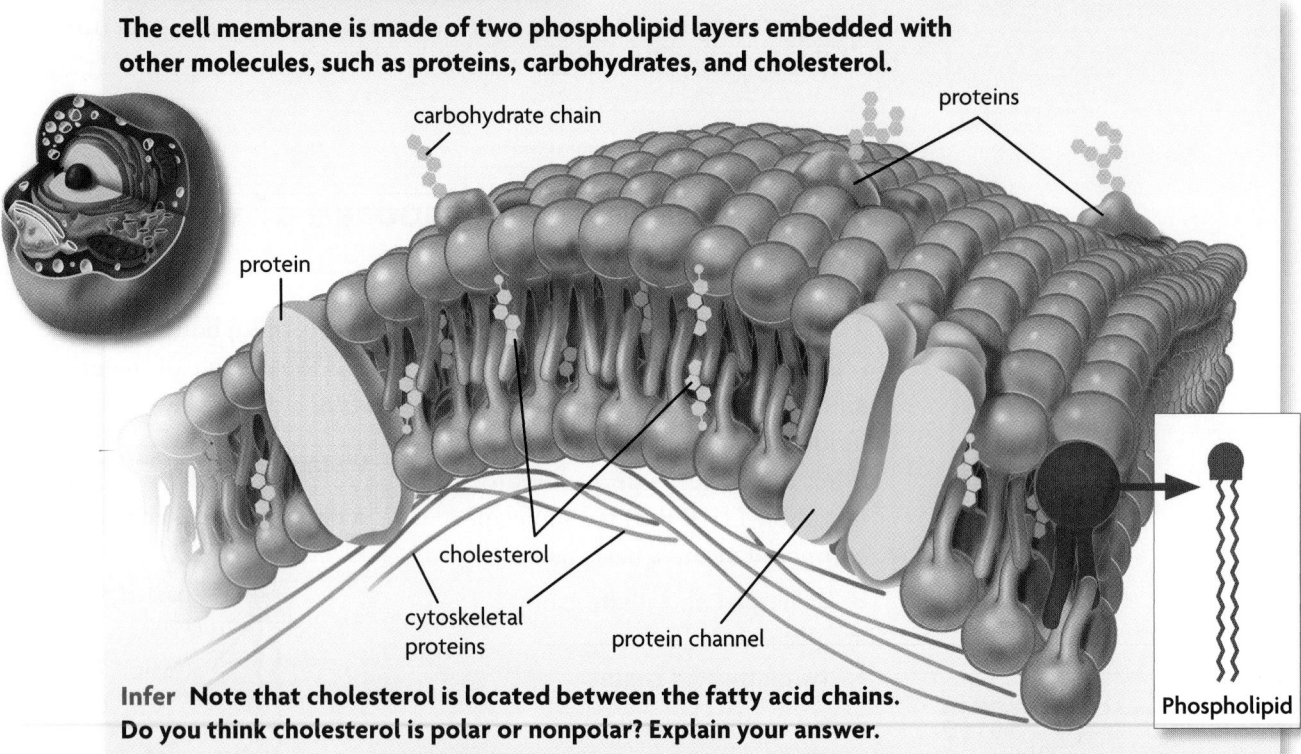

carbohydrate chain

proteins

protein

cholesterol

cytoskeletal proteins

protein channel

Phospholipid

Infer Note that cholesterol is located between the fatty acid chains. Do you think cholesterol is polar or nonpolar? Explain your answer.

Fluid Mosaic Model

Scientists have developed the **fluid mosaic model,** which describes the arrangement of the molecules that make up a cell membrane. This model of cell membrane structure takes its name from two characteristics. First, the cell membrane is flexible, not rigid. The phospholipids in each layer can move from side to side and slide past each other. As a result, the membrane behaves like a fluid, similar to a film of oil on the surface of water. However, proteins embedded in the membrane do not flip vertically. If one part of a protein is outside the membrane, it will stay outside the membrane. Second, the variety of molecules studding the membrane is similar to the arrangement of colorful tiles with different textures and patterns that make up a dynamic mosaic.

Modeling the Cell Membrane

The cell membrane regulates what moves into and out of the cell.

PROBLEM How does the cell membrane regulate what moves into and out of the cells?

PROCEDURE

1. Bundle the swabs as shown.

2. Make a receptor from one pipe cleaner. It should extend through the bunch of swabs and have a region that would bind to a signal molecule. Use the other pipe cleaner to make a carbohydrate chain. Insert the chain into the "membrane" of the bunch of swabs.

3. Cut the drinking straw in half and insert both halves into the bunch of swabs.

ANALYZE AND CONCLUDE

1. **Explain** How do the swabs represent the polar and nonpolar characteristics of the cell membrane?

2. **Apply** In this model, the swabs and proteins can be moved around. Explain whether this is an accurate representation of actual cell membranes.

MATERIALS

- 50 cotton swabs
- 1 thick medium-sized rubber band
- 2 pipe cleaners, each a different color
- 1 drinking straw
- scissors

Selective Permeability

The cell membrane has the property of **selective permeability,** which means it allows some, but not all, materials to cross. Selective permeability is illustrated in **FIGURE 3.18.** The terms *semipermeable* and *selectively permeable* also refer to this property. As an example, outdoor clothing is often made of semipermeable fabric. The material is waterproof yet breathable. Molecules of water vapor from sweat are small enough to exit the fabric, but water droplets are too large to enter.

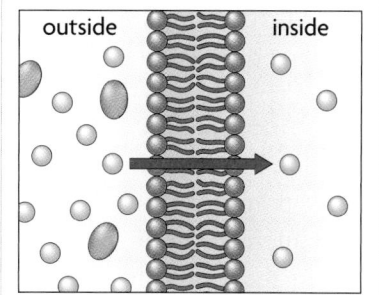

FIGURE 3.18 A selectively permeable membrane allows some, but not all, molecules to cross.

Selective permeability enables a cell to maintain homeostasis in spite of unpredictable, changing conditions outside the cell. Because a cell needs to maintain certain conditions to carry out its functions, it must control the import and export of certain molecules and ions. Thus, even if ion concentrations change drastically outside a cell, these ions won't necessarily interfere with vital chemical reactions inside a cell.

Molecules cross the membrane in several ways. Some of these methods require the cell to expend energy; others do not. How a particular molecule crosses the membrane depends on the molecule's size, polarity, and concentration inside versus outside the cell. In general, small nonpolar molecules easily pass through the cell membrane, small polar molecules are transported via proteins, and large molecules are moved in vesicles.

Connect Describe a semipermeable membrane with which you are already familiar.

Connecting CONCEPTS

Homeostasis Recall from Chapter 1 that homeostasis must be maintained in all organisms because vital chemical reactions can take place only within a limited range of conditions.

Chemical signals are transmitted across the cell membrane.

Recall that cell membranes may secrete molecules and may contain identifying molecules, such as carbohydrates. All these molecules can act as signals to communicate with other cells. How are these signals recognized?

A **receptor** is a protein that detects a signal molecule and performs an action in response. It recognizes and binds to only certain molecules, which ensures that the right cell gets the right signal at the right time. The molecule a receptor binds to is called a ligand. When a receptor and a ligand bind, they change shape. This change is critical because it affects how a receptor interacts with other molecules. Two major types of receptors are present in your cells.

Intracellular Receptor

A molecule may cross the cell membrane and bind to an intracellular receptor, as shown in **FIGURE 3.19**. *Intracellular* means "within, or inside, a cell." Molecules that cross the membrane are generally nonpolar and may be relatively small. Many hormones fit within this category. For example, aldosterone can cross most cell membranes. However, it produces an effect only in cells that have the right type of receptor, such as kidney cells. When aldosterone enters a kidney cell, it binds to an intracellular receptor. The receptor-ligand complex enters the nucleus, interacts with the DNA, and turns on certain genes. As a result, specific proteins are made that help the kidneys absorb sodium ions and retain water, both of which are important for maintaining normal blood pressure.

Membrane Receptor

A molecule that cannot cross the membrane may bind to a receptor in the cell membrane, as shown in **FIGURE 3.20**. The receptor then sends the message to the cell interior. Although the receptor binds to a signal molecule outside the cell, the entire receptor changes shape—even the part inside the cell. As a result, it causes molecules inside the cell to respond. These molecules, in turn, start a complicated chain of events inside the cell that tells the cell what to do. For instance, band 3 protein is a membrane receptor in red blood cells. When activated, it triggers processes that carry carbon dioxide from body tissues to the lungs.

Contrast How do intracellular receptors differ from membrane receptors?

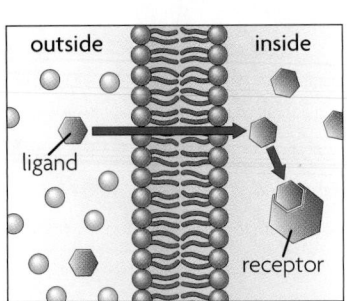

FIGURE 3.19 Intracellular receptors are located inside the cell. They are bound by molecules that can cross the membrane.

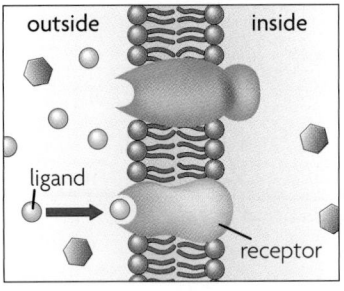

FIGURE 3.20 Membrane receptors bind to molecules that cannot enter the cell. When bound, the receptor transmits the signal inside the cell by changing shape.

3.3 ASSESSMENT

ONLINE QUIZ
ClassZone.com

REVIEWING ▶ MAIN IDEAS

1. Why do **phospholipids** form a double layer?

2. Explain how membrane **receptors** transmit messages across the **cell membrane.**

CRITICAL THINKING

3. **Compare** Describe the similarities between enzymes and receptors.

4. **Infer** If proteins were rigid, why would they make poor receptors?

Connecting CONCEPTS

5. **Human Biology** Insulin helps cells take up sugar from the blood. Explain the effect on blood sugar levels if insulin receptors stopped working.

3.4 Diffusion and Osmosis

KEY CONCEPT Materials move across membranes because of concentration differences.

▶ MAIN IDEAS
- Diffusion and osmosis are types of passive transport.
- Some molecules diffuse through transport proteins.

VOCABULARY
passive transport, p. 85
diffusion, p. 85
concentration gradient, p. 85
osmosis, p. 86
isotonic, p. 86
hypertonic, p. 86
hypotonic, p. 87
facilitated diffusion, p. 87

MICHIGAN STANDARDS

B2.5h Explain the role of cell membranes as a highly selective barrier (diffusion, osmosis, and active transport).

Connect If you have ever been stuck in traffic behind a truck full of pigs, you know that "unpleasant" fails to fully describe the situation. That is because molecules travel from the pigs to receptors in your nose, which your brain interprets as a really bad odor. Or perhaps you have tie-dyed a T-shirt and have seen dye molecules spread throughout the pot of water, turning it neon green or electric blue. Why does that happen? Why don't the molecules stay in one place?

▶ MAIN IDEA
Diffusion and osmosis are types of passive transport.

Cells almost continually import and export substances. If they had to expend energy to move every molecule, cells would require an enormous amount of energy to stay alive. Fortunately, some molecules enter and exit a cell without requiring the cell to work. As **FIGURE 3.21** shows, **passive transport** is the movement of molecules across a cell membrane without energy input from the cell. It may also be described as the diffusion of molecules across a membrane.

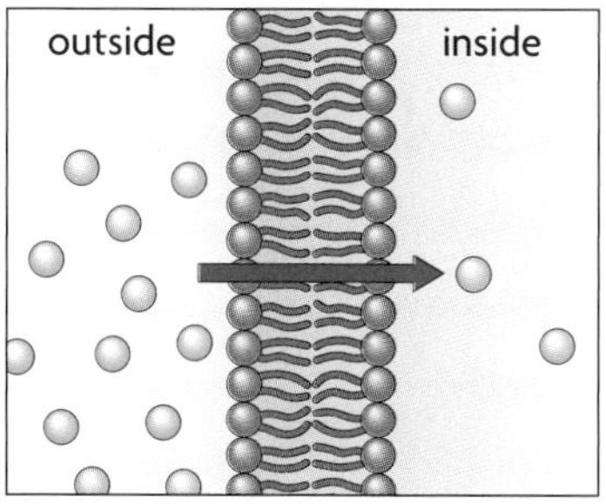

FIGURE 3.21 Passive transport is the movement of molecules across the membrane from areas of higher concentration to areas of lower concentration. It does not require energy input from the cell.

Diffusion
Diffusion is the movement of molecules in a fluid or gas from a region of higher concentration to a region of lower concentration. It results from the natural motion of particles, which causes molecules to collide and scatter. Concentration is the number of molecules of a substance in a given volume, and it can vary from one region to another. A **concentration gradient** is the difference in the concentration of a substance from one location to another. Molecules diffuse down their concentration gradient—that is, from a region of higher concentration to a region of lower concentration.

In the tie-dye example, dye molecules are initially at a high concentration in the area where they are added to the water. Random movements of the dye and water molecules cause them to bump into each other and mix. Thus, the dye molecules move from an area of higher concentration to an area of lower concentration. Eventually, they are evenly spread throughout the solution. This means the molecules have reached a dynamic equilibrium. The concentration of dye molecules is the same throughout the solution (equilibrium), but the molecules continue to move (dynamic).

Connecting CONCEPTS

Human Biology As you will learn in **Chapter 30**, diffusion plays a key role in gas exchange in the lungs and other body tissues.

FIGURE 3.22 Diffusion results from the natural motion of particles.

In cells, diffusion plays an important role in moving substances across the membrane. Small lipids and other nonpolar molecules, such as carbon dioxide and oxygen, easily diffuse across the membrane. For example, most of your cells continually consume oxygen, which means that the oxygen concentration is almost always higher outside a cell than it is inside a cell. As a result, oxygen generally diffuses into a cell, without the cell's expending any energy.

Osmosis

Water molecules, of course, also diffuse. They move across a semipermeable membrane from an area of higher water concentration to an area of lower water concentration. This process is called **osmosis.** It is important to recognize that the higher the concentration of dissolved particles in a solution, the lower the concentration of water molecules in the same solution. So if you put 1 teaspoon of salt in a cup of water and 10 teaspoons of salt in a different cup of water, the first cup would have the higher water concentration.

A solution may be described as isotonic, hypertonic, or hypotonic relative to another solution. Note that these terms are comparisons; they require a point of reference, as shown in **FIGURE 3.23.** For example, you may be taller than your coach or taller than you were two years ago, but you are never just taller. Likewise, a solution may be described as isotonic only in comparison with another solution. To describe it as isotonic by itself would be meaningless.

① A solution is **isotonic** to a cell if it has the same concentration of dissolved particles as the cell. Water molecules move into and out of the cell at an equal rate, so the cell's size remains constant.

② A **hypertonic** solution has a higher concentration of dissolved particles than a cell. This means water concentration is higher inside the cell than outside. Thus, water flows out of the cell, causing it to shrivel or even die.

FIGURE 3.23 Effects of Osmosis

Osmosis is the diffusion of water across a semipermeable membrane from an area of higher water concentration to an area of lower water concentration.

① ISOTONIC SOLUTION

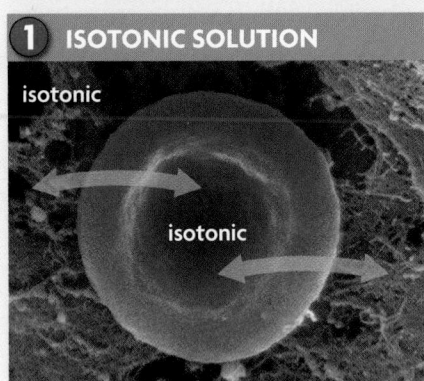

A solution is isotonic to a cell if it has the same concentration of solutes as the cell. Equal amounts of water enter and exit the cell, so its size stays constant.

② HYPERTONIC SOLUTION

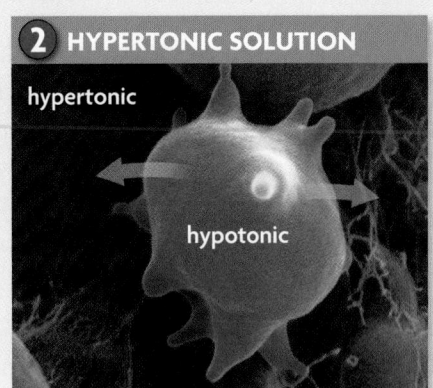

A hypertonic solution has more solutes than a cell. Overall, more water exits a cell in hypertonic solution, causing the cell to shrivel or even die.

③ HYPOTONIC SOLUTION

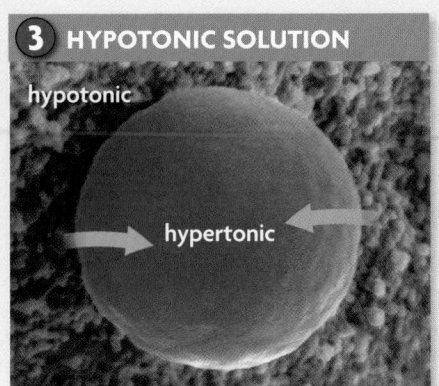

A hypotonic solution has fewer solutes than a cell. Overall, more water enters a cell in hypotonic solution, causing the cell to expand or even burst.

Apply How would adding salt to the isotonic solution above affect the cell?

colored SEMs; magnification 4500×

3 A **hypotonic** solution has a lower concentration of dissolved particles than a cell. This means water molecules are more concentrated outside the cell than inside. Water diffuses into the cell. If too much water enters a cell, the cell membrane could potentially expand until it bursts.

Some animals and single-celled organisms can survive in hypotonic environments. Their cells have adaptations for removing excess water. In plants, the rigid cell wall prevents the membrane from expanding too much. Remember from Section 3.2 that pressure exerted on the cell wall by fluid inside the central vacuole provides structural support for each cell and for the plant as a whole.

Apply What will happen to a houseplant if you water it with salt water (a hypertonic solution)?

⊙ MAIN IDEA
Some molecules diffuse through transport proteins.

Some molecules cannot easily diffuse across a membrane. They may cross more easily through transport proteins—openings formed by proteins that pierce the cell membrane. **Facilitated diffusion** is the diffusion of molecules across a membrane through transport proteins. The word *facilitate* means "to make easier." Transport proteins make it easier for molecules to enter or exit a cell. But the process is still a form of passive transport. The molecules move down a concentration gradient, requiring no energy expenditure by the cell.

There are many types of transport proteins. Most types allow only certain ions or molecules to pass. As **FIGURE 3.24** shows, some transport proteins are simple channels, or tunnels, through which particles such as ions can pass. Others act more like enzymes. When bound, the protein changes shape, allowing the molecule to travel the rest of the way into the cell.

Summarize Explain why transport proteins are needed in the cell membrane.

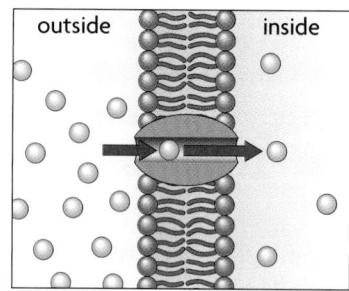

FIGURE 3.24 Facilitated diffusion enables molecules that cannot directly cross the phospholipid bilayer to diffuse through transport proteins in the membrane.

3.4 / ASSESSMENT

ONLINE QUIZ
ClassZone.com

REVIEWING ⊙ MAIN IDEAS

1. Explain what a **concentration gradient** is and what it means for a molecule to diffuse down its concentration gradient.

2. Explain why **facilitated diffusion** does not require energy from a cell.

CRITICAL THINKING

3. **Apply** A cell is bathed in fluid. However, you notice that water is flowing out of the cell. In what kind of solution is this cell immersed: **isotonic, hypotonic,** or **hypertonic**?

4. **Compare** How are receptors and transport proteins similar?

Connecting CONCEPTS

5. **Health** When a person becomes dehydrated due to the loss of fluids and solutes, saline solution (water and salts) is infused into the bloodstream by medical personnel. Why is saline solution used instead of pure water?

MATERIALS

- 2 vinegar-soaked chicken eggs
- water
- balance
- 2 disposable plastic cups
- distilled water
- 5% NaCl solution
- 20% NaCl solution
- 50% glucose solution
- 10 cm masking tape
- marker
- 500-mL beaker
- 20 cm piece of plastic wrap
- 2 rubber bands

PROCESS SKILL

- **Designing Experiments**
- **Analyzing Data**

B1.1C Conduct scientific investigations using appropriate tools and techniques (e.g., selecting an instrument that measures the desired quantity—length, volume, weight, time interval, temperature—with the appropriate level of precision).

B2.5h Explain the role of cell membranes as a highly selective barrier (diffusion, osmosis, and active transport).

Diffusion Across a Membrane

In this investigation, you will determine whether different solutions are hypotonic, isotonic, or hypertonic relative to the inside of a chicken egg. Your teacher has already soaked the eggs in vinegar, which removes calcium from the shell. This allows the egg to act as a single cell encased in a selectively permeable membrane.

PROBLEM Are the tested solutions hypotonic, isotonic, or hypertonic to the egg?

PROCEDURE

1. Choose two solutions you want to test in your experiment to determine whether they are hypotonic, isotonic, or hypertonic relative to the chicken egg. Select from distilled water, 5% NaCl, 20% NaCl, and 50% glucose solutions.

2. Identify the variables you will measure and the constants you will maintain during the investigation. Examples of constants include the amount of solution used for each egg.

3. Design a data table, such as the example shown below, to organize your results.

4. Thoroughly rinse each egg and find its mass. Place each egg in a separate plastic cup.

5. Cover each egg with one of the solutions you are testing. Label the cups with the solution names.

6. Cover each cup with plastic wrap, securing it with a rubber band. Soak the eggs overnight.

7. The next day, find the mass of each egg and note any changes in appearance.

TABLE 1. CHANGES IN EGG MASS		
	Name of Solution 1	**Name of Solution 2**
Initial mass of egg (g)		
Mass of egg after soaking in solution (g)		

ANALYZE AND CONCLUDE

1. **Apply** What is the operational definition of the dependent variable in this lab?

2. **Analyze** How did you conclude whether the solutions you tested were hypotonic, isotonic, or hypertonic?

3. **Identify** What were the independent and dependent variables in your experiment? What was held constant?

4. **Calculate** Calculate the change in the mass of the eggs. Explain how this may relate to your findings.

5. **Predict** What effect would eating too much salt have on the human body?

6. **Experimental Design** List possible reasons for any inconsistent results you may have observed.

3.5 Active Transport, Endocytosis, and Exocytosis

KEY CONCEPT Cells use energy to transport materials that cannot diffuse across a membrane.

MAIN IDEAS

- Proteins can transport materials against a concentration gradient.
- Endocytosis and exocytosis transport materials across the membrane in vesicles.

VOCABULARY

active transport, p. 89
endocytosis, p. 90
phagocytosis, p. 90
exocytosis, p. 91

MICHIGAN STANDARDS

B2.2f Explain the role of enzymes and other proteins in biochemical functions (e.g., the protein hemoglobin carries oxygen in some organisms, digestive enzymes, and hormones).

B2.5h Explain the role of cell membranes as a highly selective barrier (diffusion, osmosis, and active transport).

Connect You have seen that a cell membrane controls the passive transport of materials into and out of a cell. However, a cell needs many substances that cannot simply diffuse across the membrane. The cell has several ways to take in or get rid of these materials. These processes, such as active transport, endocytosis, and exocytosis, all need energy from the cell.

MAIN IDEA

Proteins can transport materials against a concentration gradient.

You just learned that some transport proteins let materials diffuse into and out of a cell down a concentration gradient. Many other transport proteins, often called pumps, move materials against a concentration gradient. **Active transport** drives molecules across a membrane from a region of lower concentration to a region of higher concentration. This process, shown in **FIGURE 3.25**, uses transport proteins powered by chemical energy. Cells use active transport to get needed molecules regardless of the concentration gradient and to maintain homeostasis.

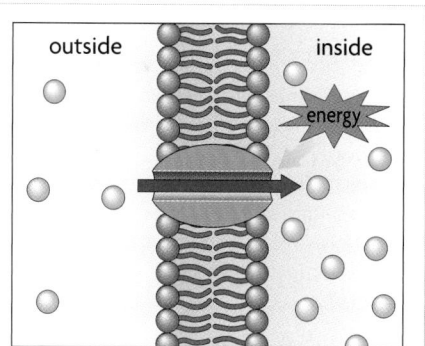

FIGURE 3.25 During active transport, a cell uses energy to move substances against a concentration gradient—that is, from a lower to a higher concentration.

Before we discuss active transport proteins, let's look at transport proteins in general. All transport proteins span the membrane, and most change shape when they bind to a target molecule or molecules. Some transport proteins bind to only one type of molecule. Others bind to two different types. Some proteins that bind to two types of molecules move both types in the same direction. Others move the molecules in opposite directions.

Connecting CONCEPTS

Human Biology As you will learn in **Chapter 32**, active transport is a necessary part of nutrient absorption.

FIGURE 3.26 Just as a cell uses energy in the process of active transport, this boy uses energy to pump air against a concentration gradient.

The key feature of active transport proteins is that they can use chemical energy to move a substance against its concentration gradient. Most use energy from a molecule called ATP, either directly or indirectly. For example, nerve cells, or neurons, need to have a higher concentration of potassium ions and a lower concentration of sodium ions than the fluid outside the cell. The sodium-potassium pump uses energy directly from the breakdown of ATP. It pumps three sodium ions out of the cell for every two potassium ions it pumps in. The proton pump, another transport protein, uses energy from the breakdown of ATP to move hydrogen ions (or protons) out of the cell. This action forms a concentration gradient of hydrogen ions (H^+), which makes the fluid outside the cell more positively charged than the fluid inside. In fact, this gradient is a form of stored energy that is used to power other active transport proteins. In plant cells, this gradient causes yet another protein to transport sucrose into the cell—an example of indirect active transport.

Synthesize **In what ways are active transport proteins similar to enzymes?**

▶ **MAIN IDEA**

Endocytosis and exocytosis transport materials across the membrane in vesicles.

A cell may also use energy to move a large substance or a large amount of a substance in vesicles. Transport in vesicles lets substances enter or exit a cell without crossing through the membrane.

Endocytosis

Endocytosis (EN-doh-sy-TOH-sihs) is the process of taking liquids or fairly large molecules into a cell by engulfing them in a membrane. In this process, the cell membrane makes a pocket around a substance. The pocket breaks off inside the cell and forms a vesicle, which then fuses with a lysosome or a similar type of vesicle. Lysosomal enzymes break down the vesicle membrane and its contents (if necessary), which are then released into the cell.

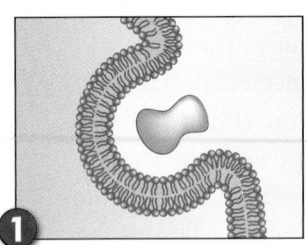

1 During endocytosis, the cell membrane folds inward and fuses together, surrounding the substance in a pocket.

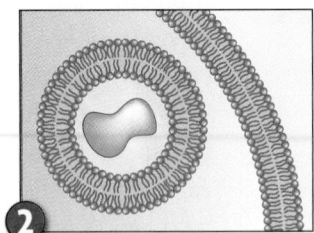

2 The pocket pinches off inside the cell, forming a vesicle.

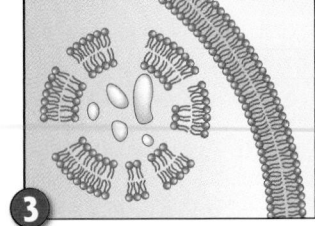

3 The vesicle fuses with a lysosome or a similar vesicle, where enzymes break down the membrane and its contents.

Phagocytosis (FAG-uh-sy-TOH-sihs) is a type of endocytosis in which the cell membrane engulfs large particles. The word literally means "cell eating." Phagocytosis plays a key role in your immune system. Some white blood cells called macrophages help your body fight infection. They find foreign materials, such as bacteria, and engulf and destroy them.

Exocytosis

Exocytosis (EHK-soh-sy-TOH-sihs), the opposite of endocytosis, is the release of substances out of a cell by the fusion of a vesicle with the membrane. During this process, a vesicle forms around materials to be sent out of the cell. The vesicle then moves toward the cell's surface, where it fuses with the membrane and lets go of its contents.

Connecting CONCEPTS

Endocrine System As you will learn in **Chapter 29**, thyroid hormones play an important role in controlling your growth and development. These hormones are released into the blood by exocytosis.

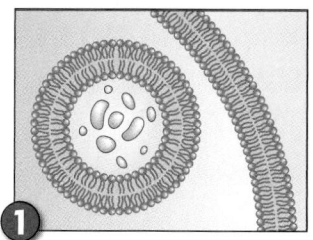

1 The cell forms a vesicle around material that needs to be removed or secreted.

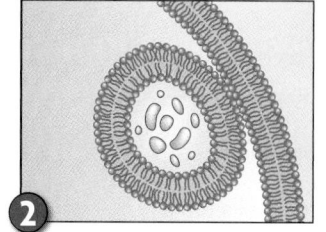

2 The vesicle is transported to the cell membrane.

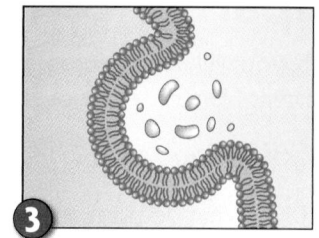

3 The vesicle membrane fuses with the cell membrane and releases the contents.

Exocytosis happens all the time in your body. In fact, you couldn't think or move a muscle without it. When you want to move your big toe, for example, your brain sends a message that travels through a series of nerve cells to reach your toe. This message, or nerve impulse, travels along each nerve cell as an electrical signal, but it must be converted to a chemical signal to cross the tiny gap that separates one nerve cell from the next. These chemicals are stored in vesicles within the nerve cells. When a nerve impulse reaches the end of a cell, it causes the vesicles to fuse with the cell membrane and release the chemicals outside the cell. There they attach to the next nerve cell, which triggers a new electrical impulse in that cell.

NSTA SCi**LINKS**
scilinks.org

For more information about active transport, go to scilinks.org.
Keycode: MLB003

Hypothesize **What might happen if vesicles in your neurons were suddenly unable to fuse with the cell membrane?**

3.5 ASSESSMENT

ONLINE QUIZ
ClassZone.com

REVIEWING ▶ MAIN IDEAS

1. How do transport proteins that are pumps differ from those that are channels?

2. How do **endocytosis** and **exocytosis** differ from diffusion?

THINKING CRITICALLY

3. **Apply** Small lipid molecules are in high concentration outside a cell. They slowly cross the membrane into the cell. What term describes this action? Does it require energy?

4. **Apply** Ions are in low concentration outside a cell. They move rapidly into the cell via protein molecules. What term describes this action? Does it require energy?

Connecting CONCEPTS

5. **Diffusion** Suppose molecules were unable to diffuse into and out of cells. How might life be different if cells had to use **active transport** to move every substance? Explain your reasoning.

Use these inquiry-based labs and online activities to deepen your understanding of cell structure.

INVESTIGATION

MICHIGAN STANDARDS

B2.5g Compare and contrast plant and animal cells.

B2.5h Explain the role of cell membranes as a highly selective barrier (diffusion, osmosis, and active transport).

Comparing Cells

In this lab, you will use a microscope to examine and compare cells from different organisms.

SKILLS Observing, Comparing, Drawing

PROBLEM What do plant and animal cells have in common?

PROCEDURE

1. Refer to page R8 if you need to review instructions on using a microscope and making a wet mount.

2. Construct a table to organize your observations and drawings.

3. Peel a thin slice of onion and place it on the slide.

4. Carefully add a drop of methylene blue to the onion. Avoid getting the stain on your clothes. Place one side of a cover slip against the methylene blue, and gently lower it, being careful not to trap air bubbles.

5. Examine the onion under the microscope at low and high power, and draw what you see. Large structures such as the nucleus, cell membrane, and cell wall should be visible. Label as many cell structures as you can.

6. Repeat steps 2 through 4 for the celery and the elodea.

7. Examine prepared slides of human cheek cells under the microscope at low and high power. Draw what you see, and label as many structures as you can.

ANALYZE AND CONCLUDE

1. **Compare** What characteristics do all of the cells have in common? List as many as you can.

2. **Contrast** Identify the unique characteristics of each cell type.

3. **Connect** What type of cells did you examine, eukaryotic or prokaryotic? Explain your answer.

4. **Infer** Why do you think it was necessary to add methylene blue to the slides?

MATERIALS

- 3 microscope slides
- razor tool
- thinly sliced onion pieces
- methylene blue stain
- eyedropper
- 3 plastic cover slips
- microscope
- thinly sliced celery stalk
- elodea leaf
- prepared slides of human cheek cells

INVESTIGATION

Modeling the Cell

The diversity of life on Earth is enormous, although all living things are made from the same basic structural unit, the cell. In your body alone, there are trillions of cells. In this activity, you will make a model of a cell.

SKILL Modeling

PROBLEM What components make up a cell?

MATERIALS

- 2 resealable plastic sandwich bags
- gelatin jigglers
- a small round balloon
- a permanent marker
- coffee stirring straws
- drinking straws cut in half
- different sizes of erasers
- slices of two colors of sponges
- tiny beads

PROCEDURE

1. Use the materials to construct a detailed model of a cell.

2. Be sure to include at least the following components in your model: cell membrane, cytoplasm, nucleus, cytoskeleton, ribosomes, mitochondria, Golgi apparatus, and centrioles.

3. Use both sandwich bags in constructing your model.

4. Tightly seal your cell after it has been completed.

ANALYZE AND CONCLUDE

1. **Apply** Make a table to list which materials you chose to represent the various cell structures and to explain your choices.

2. **Analyze** What is the significance of the double bag?

3. **Connect** What substance represents the cytoplasm? Explain why your choice is suitable.

Online BIOLOGY
CLASSZONE.COM

ANIMATED BIOLOGY
Get Through a Cell Membrane

Many substances, including sugars and wastes, cannot diffuse through a cell membrane. Use a set of proteins and vesicles to move materials into and out of a cell to keep it healthy and in balance with the environment.

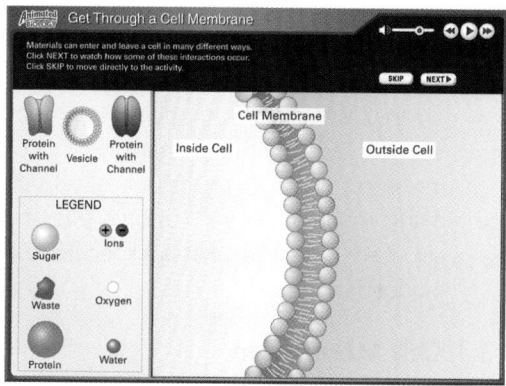

WEBQUEST

Cell organelles interact with many substances to keep cells alive and well. In this WebQuest, you will explore what happens when an organelle does not function as it should. Review a patient's symptoms, research them, and diagnose her illness. Explore how the health of an entire person can depend on just one organelle.

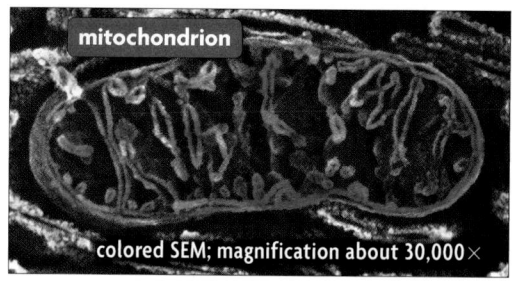

mitochondrion

colored SEM; magnification about 30,000×

BIOZINE

Stories about cell biology—such as "Higher CO_2 Levels Increase Productivity In Plants" and "Stem Cells Help Mend Broken Hearts"— are often in the headlines. Catch the latest news about cell biology in the BioZine.

3.1 Cell Theory

Cells are the basic unit of life. The contributions of many scientists led to the discovery of cells and the development of the cell theory. The cell theory states that all organisms are made of cells, all cells are produced by other living cells, and the cell is the most basic unit of life.

3.2 Cell Organelles

Eukaryotic cells share many similarities. They have a nucleus and other membrane-bound organelles that perform specialized tasks within the cell. Many of these organelles are involved in making proteins. Plant and animal cells share many of the same types of organelles, but both also have organelles that are specific to the cells' unique functions.

3.3 Cell Membrane

The cell membrane is a barrier that separates a cell from the external environment. It is made of a double layer of phospholipids and a variety of embedded molecules. Some of these molecules act as signals; others act as receptors. The membrane is selectively permeable, allowing some but not all materials to cross.

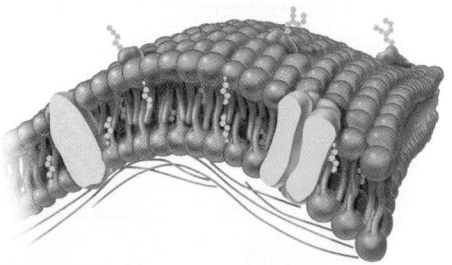

3.4 Diffusion and Osmosis

Materials move across membranes because of concentration differences. Diffusion is the movement of molecules in a fluid or gas from a region of higher concentration to a region of lower concentration. It does not require a cell to expend energy; therefore, it is a form of passive transport. Osmosis is the diffusion of water. Net water movement into or out of a cell depends on the concentration of the surrounding solution.

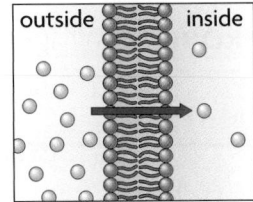

outside   inside

Passive transport

3.5 Active Transport, Endocytosis, and Exocytosis

Cells use energy to transport materials that cannot diffuse across a membrane. Active transport is the movement of molecules across a membrane from a region of lower concentration to a region of higher concentration—against a concentration gradient. The processes of endocytosis and exocytosis move substances in vesicles and also require energy.

Endocytosis

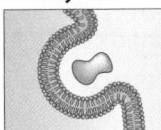 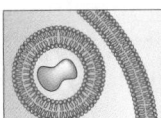 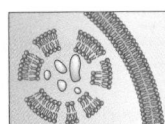

Exocytosis

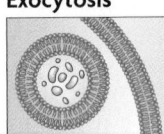 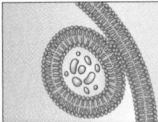 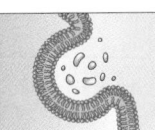

Synthesize Your Notes

Main Idea Web Plant and animal cells, though similar, each have some unique features. Identify how these cell types differ by placing plant cell characteristics on the left side of the main idea web and animal cell characteristics on the right.

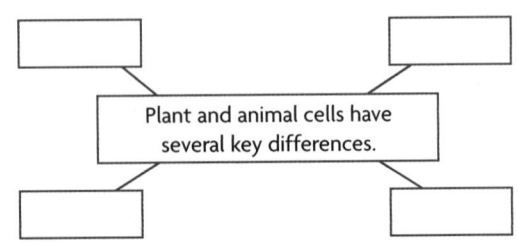

Plant and animal cells have several key differences.

Concept Map Fill in the concept map to summarize what you know about forms of transport.

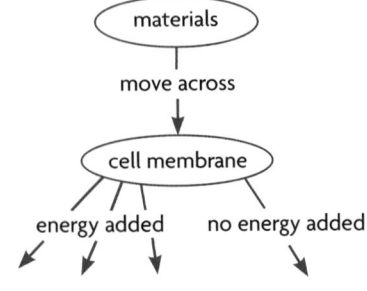

materials
↓
move across
↓
cell membrane
energy added   no energy added

active transport
passive transport
diffusion
endocytosis
materials
exocytosis
osmosis
cell membrane

Chapter Assessment

Reviewing Vocabulary

Labeling Diagrams

In your notebook, write the vocabulary term that matches each numbered item below.

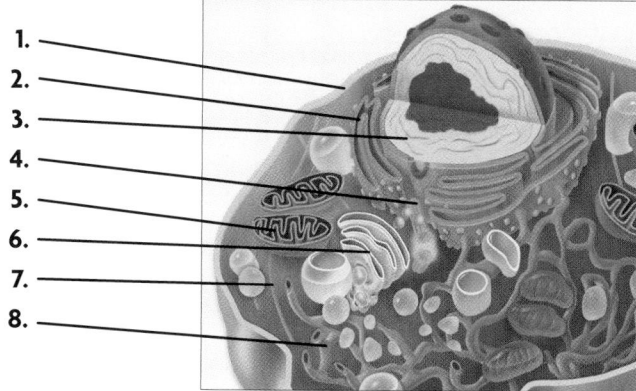

1.
2.
3.
4.
5.
6.
7.
8.

Compare and Contrast

Describe one similarity and one difference between the two terms in each of the following pairs.

9. eukaryotic, prokaryotic

10. cell wall, cell membrane

11. diffusion, facilitated diffusion

Greek and Latin Word Origins

12. The word *organelle* is the diminutive, or "tiny," form of the Latin word for organs of the body. How is an organelle like a tiny organ?

13. The Greek word *karuon* means "nut." The prefix *pro-* means "before," and the prefix *eu-* means "true." Thus, *prokaryote* means "before nut" and *eukaryote* means "true nut." How do these meanings relate to structural differences between these two cell types?

Reviewing MAIN IDEAS

14. According to the cell theory, what is required for an object to be considered alive?

15. What role do membranes play in prokaryotic cells? in eukaryotic cells?

16. How do the cytoskeleton and the cytoplasm contribute to a cell's shape?

17. You know that many organelles are involved in protein production. Briefly explain where proteins are made, modified, and packaged within a cell.

18. Explain what mitochondria do and why evidence suggests that they might have descended from free-living prokaryotes in the evolutionary past.

19. If you were looking through a microscope at an unknown cell, how might you determine whether it was a plant cell or an animal cell?

20. Cells are surrounded by a watery fluid, and they contain watery cytoplasm. Explain how the structure of the lipid bilayer is related to these two watery environments.

21. How are cells able to respond to signal molecules that are too large to enter the cytoplasm?

22. How do transport proteins make it easier for certain molecules to diffuse across a membrane?

23. Under what conditions would a molecule need to be actively transported across a membrane?

24. Do you think that endocytosis and exocytosis can occur within the same cell? Explain your reasoning.

Critical Thinking

25. Summarize How was the development of cell theory closely tied to advancements in technology?

26. Analyze What structural differences suggest that eukaryotic cells evolved from prokaryotic cells?

27. Synthesize If vesicles are almost constantly pinching off from the ER to carry proteins to the Golgi apparatus, why does the ER not shrink and finally disappear?

28. Compare and Contrast You know that both vesicles and vacuoles are hollow compartments used for storage. How do they differ in function?

29. Infer When cells release ligands, they are sent through the blood stream to every area of the body. Why do you think that only certain types of cells will respond to a particular ligand?

30. Provide Examples What are two ways in which exocytosis might help a cell maintain homeostasis?

31. Compare How is facilitated diffusion similar to both passive transport and active transport?

Interpreting Visuals

Use the diagram to answer the next three questions.

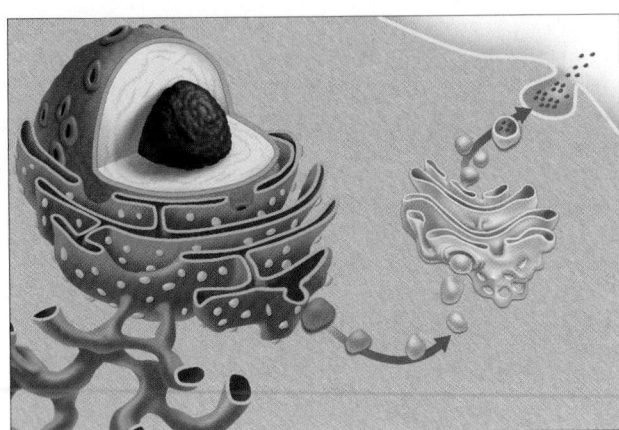

32. Apply What process is occurring in the diagram, and how do you know?

33. Predict If the transport proteins that carry amino acids into this cell stopped working, how might the process shown be affected?

34. Infer What might you conclude about the membrane structure of the final vesicle and the cell membrane?

Analyzing Data

Use the text and table below to answer the next three questions. Reactive oxygen species, or ROS, are clusters of highly reactive oxygen atoms that can damage the body. As people age, the amount of ROS in the body increases, causing a condition called oxidative stress. In one study, researchers studied how the number of mitochondria might be involved in this situation.

- Muscle tissue was obtained from patients.
- Radioactive probes labeled the mitochondria.
- A machine counted the mitochondria per cell.

AGE AND MUSCLE CELL MITOCHONDRIA		
Patient	**Age**	**Mitochondria per Muscle Cell**
1	47	2026
2	89	2987
3	65	2752
4	38	1989

35. Apply If the independent variable in this study is age, what is the operational definition of the dependent variable?

36. Analyze What do the data show about the relationship between age and number of mitochondria?

37. Infer What might the relationship between age and number of mitochondria indicate about the increase in ROS levels?

Connecting CONCEPTS

38. Write an Analogy The cell membrane regulates what can enter and exit a cell. In eukaryotes, it encloses a complex group of organelles that carry out special jobs. Make an analogy to describe the cell membrane and the variety of organelles and processes that take place inside it. Explain any limitations of your analogy.

39. Connect On page 69 of this chapter, you saw a picture of macrophages eating up bacteria. Identify the ways in which the cytoskeleton helps the macrophage carry out this job.

MICHIGAN STANDARDS-BASED ASSESSMENT

✓ **Test Practice**
For more test practice,
go to ClassZone.com.

1. The cell theory states that the cell is the most basic unit of life, all organisms are made of cells, and all cells come from cells. What makes the cell theory a scientific theory? **B1.2i**

   A It is based on a scientific publication that is read by scientists worldwide.

   B It is based on the work of many scientists and leads to accurate predictions.

   C It is based on ideas that have been proven true and that are not subject to revision.

   D It is based on preliminary evidence but still needs to be confirmed with experiments.

2.

   Molecule Concentration Outside and Inside a Cell

   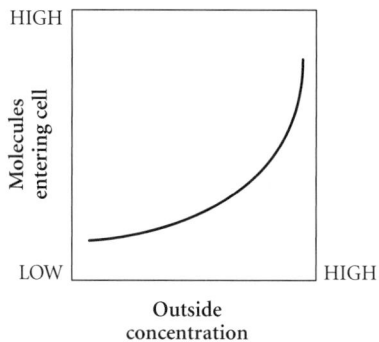

   This graph shows that as the concentration of molecules increases outside of a cell, more and more molecules enter the cell. These molecules are able to enter the cell because the **B2.5h**

   A molecules are polar.

   B cytoplasm is warm.

   C cell membrane is semipermeable.

   D nucleus is regulating movement.

   THINK THROUGH THE QUESTION

   Which answer choice explains why molecules can enter a cell?

3. Which of the following pairs incorrectly matches a cell structure with its function? **B2.5i**

   A cell membrane: protein synthesis

   B nucleus: information (DNA) storage

   C vacuole: storage

   D chloroplast: energy conversion

4. Before the development of eukaryotes, mitochondria were free-living prokaryotes. Scientists came to this conclusion in part due to the fact that mitochondria **B2.4g**

   A supply energy to a cell.

   B have their own DNA.

   C store materials for a cell.

   D are bean-shaped organelles.

5. One difference between a plant cell and an animal cell is that a plant cell has a(n) **B2.5g**

   A cell wall.

   B endoplasmic reticulum.

   C cell membrane.

   D golgi apparatus.

6. Active transport proteins are often called pumps because they require energy to move molecules across a membrane **B2.2f**

   A through fusion of a vesicle to the membrane.

   B by engulfing them in the membrane.

   C through the formation of ATP within a cell.

   D from lower concentration to higher concentration.

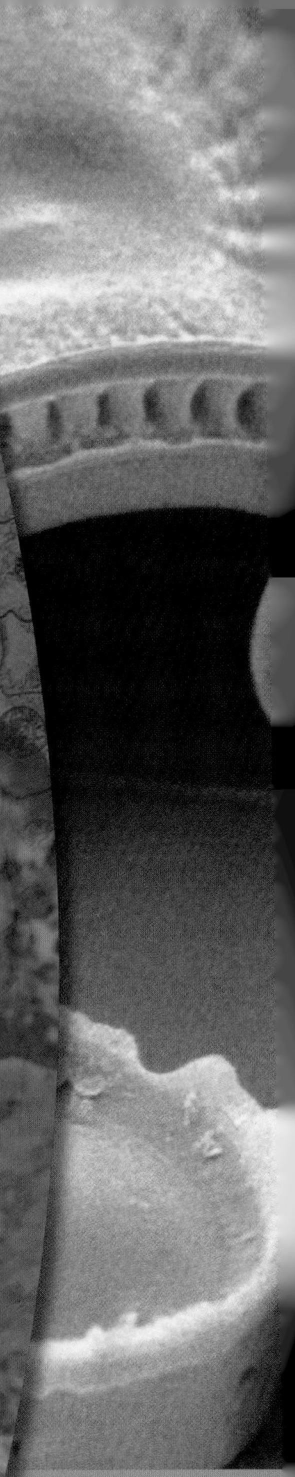

4 Cells and Energy

KEY CONCEPTS

4.1 Chemical Energy and ATP
All cells need chemical energy.

4.2 Overview of Photosynthesis
The overall process of photosynthesis produces sugars that store chemical energy.

4.3 Photosynthesis in Detail
Photosynthesis requires a series of chemical reactions.

4.4 Overview of Cellular Respiration
The overall process of cellular respiration converts sugar into ATP using oxygen.

4.5 Cellular Respiration in Detail
Cellular respiration is an aerobic process with two main stages.

4.6 Fermentation
Fermentation allows the production of a small amount of ATP without oxygen.

Online BIOLOGY · CLASSZONE.COM

Animated BIOLOGY

View animated chapter concepts.
• Photosynthesis
• Cellular Respiration
• Carbon Dioxide Transfer Through Snails and Elodea
• Mirror Processes

 BIOZINE

Keep current with biology news.
• News feeds
• Careers
• Bio Bytes

 **RESOURCE CENTER**

Get more information on
• Chemosynthesis
• Photosynthesis
• Fermentation

colored SEM; magnification 5000×

What does it mean for a cell to be immortal?

The photograph above shows a lung cancer cell undergoing cell division. Unlike healthy cells, cancer cells can divide without limit—they are what scientists call *immortal*. This property is useful to scientists who culture cancer cells for research purposes. However, cancer cells are very dangerous in the body, where they may form tumors and invade tissues.

Connecting CONCEPTS

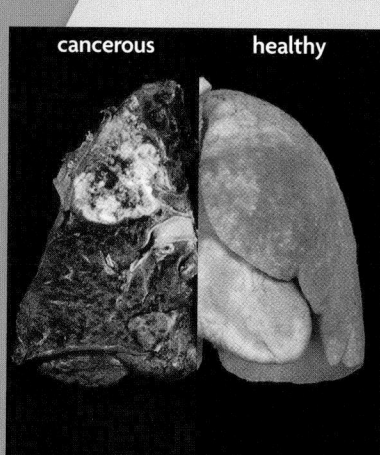

cancerous   healthy

Human Biology These photographs show half of a cancerous lung and half of a healthy lung. Gases diffuse across the surfaces of a healthy lung, so the membrane surfaces must be thin and moist. Exposure to substances such as tobacco smoke can cause changes in the lung cells. Cilia are destroyed, and the lung lining becomes thicker. The lungs can no longer clean themselves, so they are more susceptible to cancer-causing agents.

5.1 The Cell Cycle

KEY CONCEPT Cells have distinct phases of growth, reproduction, and normal functions.

▶ MAIN IDEAS
- The cell cycle has four main stages.
- Cells divide at different rates.
- Cell size is limited.

VOCABULARY
cell cycle, p. 134
mitosis, p. 135
cytokinesis, p. 135

MICHIGAN STANDARDS

L2.p1C Describe growth and development in terms of increase in cell number, cell size, and/or cell products. (prerequisite)

B2.r6b Explain that complex interactions among the different kinds of molecules in the cell cause distinct cycles of activities, such as growth and division. Note that cell behavior can also be affected by molecules from other parts of the organism, such as hormones. (recommended)

Connect Many of life's little chores such as sweeping and dusting, are quietly satisfying and rather fun. Washing dishes by hand, however, is never fun, which is why some clever person made the dishwasher. This handy invention soaks, washes, and rinses your dishes to a spot-free, sanitary sparkle. You unload the dishes, and the machine is ready to start the cycle all over again. A cell goes through a cycle, too. This cycle of growth, DNA synthesis, and division is essential for an organism to grow and heal. If it goes out of control, abnormal cell growth may occur, resulting in cancer cells like those shown on the previous page.

▶ MAIN IDEA
The cell cycle has four main stages.

Just as all species have life cycles, from tiny chihuahuas to massive beluga whales, cells also have a life cycle. The **cell cycle** is the regular pattern of growth, DNA duplication, and cell division that occurs in eukaryotic cells. **FIGURE 5.1** shows its four main stages: gap 1, synthesis, gap 2, and mitosis. Gap 1, synthesis, and gap 2 together make up what is called interphase.

The stages of the cell cycle get their names from early studies of cell division. Scientists' observations were limited by the microscopes of the time. When a cell was not actively dividing, they could not see activity in it. Thus, they originally divided the cell cycle into two parts: interphase, when the cell appeared to be at rest, and mitosis, when the cell was dividing. Improved techniques and tools later allowed scientists to detect the copying of DNA (DNA synthesis), and they changed their description of the cell cycle to include the synthesis stage. Since they still could not see anything happening during the other parts of interphase, scientists named the periods between mitosis and synthesis "gap 1" and "gap 2." Eventually, scientists learned that, during interphase, cells carry out their normal functions and undergo critical growth and preparation for cell division.

FIGURE 5.1 Cells grow and copy their DNA during interphase. They also carry out cell-specific functions in G₁ and G₂. During M stage, both the nucleus (in mitosis) and cytoplasm (in cytokinesis) are divided.

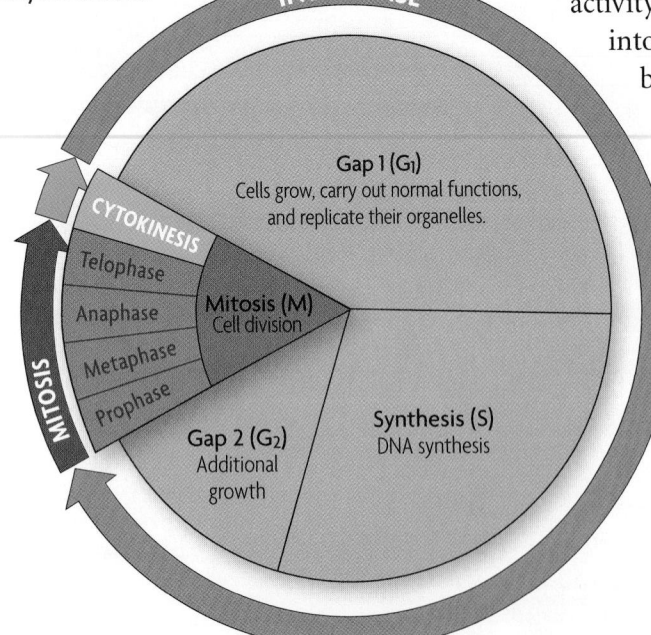

INTERPHASE

CYTOKINESIS

MITOSIS

Gap 1 (G₁)
Cells grow, carry out normal functions, and replicate their organelles.

Telophase
Anaphase
Metaphase
Prophase

Mitosis (M)
Cell division

Gap 2 (G₂)
Additional growth

Synthesis (S)
DNA synthesis

Gap 1 (G₁)

The first stage of the cell cycle is gap 1 (G_1). During G_1, a cell carries out its normal functions. If it is a skeletal muscle cell, it contracts to move joints. If it is an adrenal cell, it secretes hormones such as adrenaline. If it is an intestinal cell, it absorbs nutrients. During G_1, cells also increase in size, and organelles increase in number. A cell spends most of its time in the G_1 stage, although the length of this stage varies by cell type.

During G_1, the cell must pass a critical checkpoint before it can proceed to the synthesis stage. Just as it would be dangerous for you to run a marathon if you had not slept or eaten for several days, it would also be dangerous for your cells to continue dividing if certain conditions were not met. For instance, most animal cells need enough nutrition, adequate size, and relatively undamaged DNA to divide successfully. They also need specific signals from other cells, telling them whether more cell division is needed.

Synthesis (S)

The second stage of the cell cycle is the synthesis (S) stage. *Synthesis* means "the combining of parts to make a whole." During the S stage, the cell makes a copy of its nuclear DNA. In eukaryotes, DNA is located in the nucleus. During interphase, it is loosely organized and appears grainy in photographs. By the end of the S stage, the cell nucleus contains two complete sets of DNA.

Gap 2 (G₂)

Gap 2 (G_2) is the third stage of the cell cycle. During G_2, cells continue to carry out their normal functions, and additional growth occurs. Like G_1, this stage includes a critical checkpoint. Everything must be in order—adequate cell size, undamaged DNA—before the cell goes through mitosis and division.

Mitosis (M)

Mitosis (M), the fourth stage of the cell cycle, includes two processes: mitosis and cytokinesis. **Mitosis** (my-TOH-sihs) is the division of the cell nucleus and its contents. During mitosis, the nuclear membrane dissolves, the duplicated DNA condenses around proteins and separates, and two new nuclei form. Lastly, **cytokinesis** (sy-toh-kuh-NEE-sihs) is the process that divides the cell cytoplasm. The result is two daughter cells that are genetically identical to the original cell.

> **VISUAL VOCAB**
>
> **Mitosis** is the division of the cell nucleus and its contents.
>
> - parent cell
> - mitosis
> - cytokinesis
> - daughter cells
>
> **Cytokinesis** divides the cell cytoplasm.

The stages of the cell cycle and the proteins that control it are similar in all eukaryotes. For example, scientists have demonstrated that some of the molecules that regulate checkpoints in the yeast cell cycle can work in human cells, too. Such similarities suggest that eukaryotes share a common ancestry.

Predict What might happen if the G_2 checkpoint stopped working in cells?

TAKING NOTES

Construct your own cycle diagram to take notes about processes such as the cell cycle.

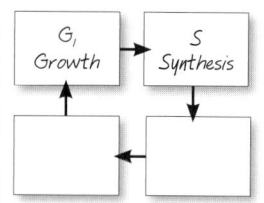

Connecting **CONCEPTS**

DNA replication As you will learn in **Chapter 8**, DNA synthesis is also called DNA replication. During this process, the DNA molecule unzips and each strand is used as a pattern for a new DNA strand.

Multicellular organisms use cell division for growth and repair.

FIGURE 5.2 CELL LIFE SPAN

CELL TYPE	APPROXIMATE LIFE SPAN
Skin cell	2 weeks
Red blood cell	4 months
Liver cell	300–500 days
Intestine—internal lining	4–5 days
Intestine—muscle and other tissues	16 years

Source: Spaulding et al., *Cell* 122:1.

Connecting CONCEPTS

Lymphocytes As you will learn in **Chapter 31**, lymphocytes are a part of your immune system. There are two major types of lymphocytes, B and T cells. Both types recognize specific antigens.

▶ MAIN IDEA
Cells divide at different rates.

Rates of cell division vary widely, as shown in **FIGURE 5.2**. The prokaryotic cell cycle is similar but not identical to that of eukaryotic cells. Recall that prokaryotes do not have the membrane-bound organelles and cytoskeleton found in eukaryotes. Thus, prokaryotic cells typically divide much faster than do eukaryotic cells.

The rate at which your cells divide is linked to your body's need for those cells. In human cells, the S, G_2, and M stages together usually take about 12 hours. The length of the G_1 stage differs most from cell type to cell type. The rate of cell division is greater in embryos and children than it is in adults. Their cell cycle is shorter, and many of their organs are still developing. But the rate of cell division also varies within different tissues of the adult body. The internal lining of your digestive tract receives a lot of wear and tear. As a result, cells that line your stomach and intestine are replaced every few days. In contrast, cells that make up the rest of your intestine (mainly smooth muscle) and many of your internal organs, such as lungs, kidney, and liver, divide only occasionally, in response to injury or cell death.

Cells that divide only rarely are thought to enter a stage that some scientists call G_0. In G_0, cells are unlikely to divide, although they continue to carry out their normal functions. Some cells, such as neurons, appear to stay permanently in the G_0 stage. However, some data suggest that neurons actually can divide, and this question continues to be actively researched. Other cells, such as lymphocytes, a type of white blood cell, may remain in G_0 for years until they recognize an invader. Once the invader binds to a lymphocyte receptor, the lymphocyte goes through rapid cell divisions to help fight infection.

Infer Do you think a skin cell would have a long or short G_1 stage? Explain why.

▶ MAIN IDEA
Cell size is limited.

Cells have upper and lower size limits. If cells were too small, they could not contain all of the necessary organelles and molecules. For instance, a cell with too few mitochondria would not have enough energy to live. Nor can cells grow beyond a certain size, even if surrounded by plenty of nutrients. The upper limit on cell size is due to the ratio of cell surface area to volume. Recall that oxygen, nutrients, and wastes move across the cell membrane, or the surface of the cell. These materials must be transported in adequate amounts and with adequate speed to keep the inside of the cell functioning. But as a cell increases in size, its volume increases faster than its surface area, as shown in **FIGURE 5.3**. Therefore, a further increase in size could result in a surface area too small for the adequate exchange of materials.

FIGURE 5.3 Ratio of Surface Area to Volume in Cells

As a cell grows, its volume increases more rapidly than its surface area. When the surface area–to–volume ratio is too small, the cell cannot move materials into and out of the cell at a sufficient rate or in sufficient quantities.

Relative size	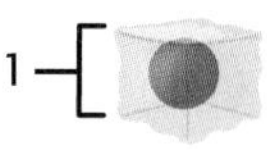	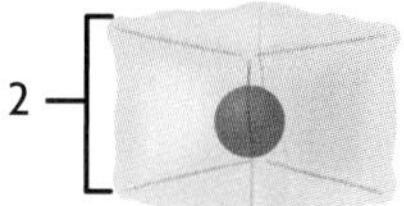	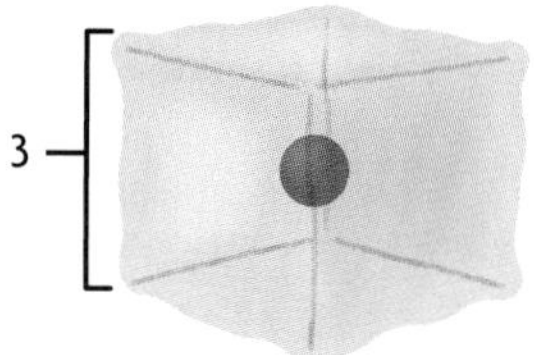
Surface area (length × width × number of sides)	6	24	54
Volume (length × width × height)	1	8	27
Ratio of surface area to volume	$\frac{6}{1} = 6:1$	$\frac{24}{8} = 3:1$	$\frac{54}{27} = 2:1$

Compare Which cell has the largest surface area? Which cell has the largest surface area to volume ratio?

Some cells, however, must be large. A neuron running down a giraffe's neck to its legs may be several meters long, for instance. But it is not shaped like a cube or a sphere. Instead, it is extremely long and thin. This structure gives the neuron a large surface area with a relatively small increase in volume.

To maintain a suitable cell size, growth and division must be coordinated. If a cell more than doubled its size before dividing, the daughter cells would be larger than the original cell. If this happened each generation, cells would quickly become too large to live. Similarly, if a cell did not double its size before dividing, the daughter cells would be smaller than the original cell. If this happened each generation, cells would quickly become too small to live.

NSTA
scilinks.org
SCILINKS
For more information about mitosis, go to scilinks.org.
Keycode: MLB005

Connect Which has the larger ratio of surface area to volume, a tennis ball or a soccer ball? Explain your reasoning.

5.1 ASSESSMENT

ONLINE QUIZ
ClassZone.com

REVIEWING ▶ MAIN IDEAS

1. During which stage of the **cell cycle** is the DNA copied?

2. Which stages of the cell cycle generally require about the same amount of time in all human cells?

3. What limits the maximum size of a cell?

CRITICAL THINKING

4. **Infer** Suppose you were to draw a diagram representing the cell cycle of a neuron. Explain where and how you would represent G_0.

5. **Predict** Suppose you treat cells with chemicals that block **cytokinesis.** Describe what you think the cells would look like.

Connecting CONCEPTS

6. **Scientific Process** Predict how the rate of cell division would differ between single-celled algae living in a sunny, nutrient-rich pond versus algae living in a shady, nutrient-poor pond. How could you test your prediction?

5.2 Mitosis and Cytokinesis

KEY CONCEPT Cells divide during mitosis and cytokinesis.

▶ MAIN IDEAS

- Chromosomes condense at the start of mitosis.
- Mitosis and cytokinesis produce two genetically identical daughter cells.

VOCABULARY

chromosome, p. 138	**telomere**, p. 139
histone, p. 139	**prophase**, p. 140
chromatin, p. 139	**metaphase**, p. 140
chromatid, p. 139	**anaphase**, p. 140
centromere, p. 139	**telophase**, p. 140

MICHIGAN STANDARDS

B2.r6b Explain that complex interactions among the different kinds of molecules in the cell cause distinct cycles of activities, such as growth and division. Note that cell behavior can also be affected by molecules from other parts of the organism, such as hormones. (recommended)

B4.3A Compare and contrast the processes of cell division (mitosis and meiosis), particularly as those processes relate to production of new cells and to passing on genetic information between generations.

Connect When you were a child, perhaps you attended a birthday party where goody bags were handed out. Whoever stuffed the bags had to make sure that each bag had exactly the same number of erasers, candies, and stickers. Otherwise, some ill-mannered child (not you, of course) might have raised a fuss if an item was missing. In a similar way, your cells must receive a full set of DNA—no more, no less—to work properly. Dividing DNA is a complicated task because the DNA is so long and stringy. Mitosis is an amazing process that efficiently sorts two sets of DNA and divides them between two nuclei.

▶ MAIN IDEA
Chromosomes condense at the start of mitosis.

DNA is a double-stranded molecule made of four different subunits called nucleotides. A **chromosome** is one long continuous thread of DNA that consists of numerous genes along with regulatory information. Your body cells have 46 chromosomes each. If stretched out straight and laid end to end, the DNA in just one of your cells would be about 3 meters (10 feet) long. How does it fit inside the nucleus of a microscopic cell?

DNA wraps around proteins that help organize and condense it. During interphase, or when a cell is not dividing, DNA is loosely organized—it looks a bit like spaghetti. During mitosis, however, your chromosomes are tightly condensed, as shown in **FIGURE 5.4**. These changes in DNA's organization allow a cell to carry out its necessary functions. During all of interphase, proteins must access specific genes for a cell to make specific proteins or to copy the entire DNA sequence. During mitosis, the duplicated chromosomes must condense to be divided between two nuclei.

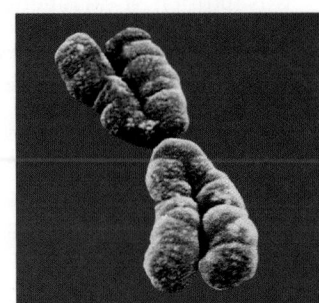

FIGURE 5.4 This duplicated chromosome is tightly condensed. (colored SEM; magnification about 5000×)

If chromosomes remained stringy during mitosis, they could become entangled. Perhaps a cell would get two copies of one chromosome and no copies of a different one. **FIGURE 5.5** shows the process that converts a chromosome from a linear strand of DNA to its highly condensed form. The key to this process is the association between DNA and proteins.

Connecting CONCEPTS

Biochemistry As you will learn in **Chapter 8**, a nucleotide is made of three parts: a sugar, a phosphate group, and a nitrogen-containing molecule called a base. When the sugars and phosphate groups bond, they form the backbones of the long chains called nucleic acids.

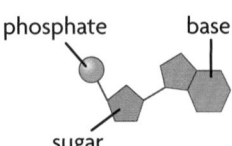

phosphate   base

sugar

FIGURE 5.5 Chromosome Structure

DNA condenses tightly during the early stages of mitosis.

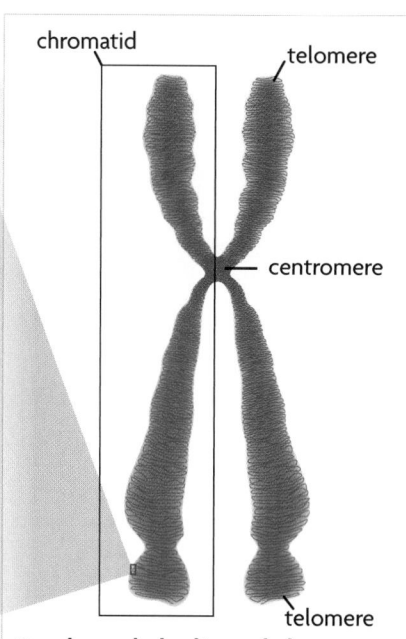

DNA double helix
Each continuous, double-stranded DNA molecule makes one chromosome.

DNA and histones
DNA wraps at regular intervals around proteins called histones, forming chromatin.

Chromatin
Interactions between parts of the histones further compact the DNA.

Supercoiled DNA
The chromatin coils more and more tightly around organizing proteins.

Condensed, duplicated chromosome
The condensed, duplicated chromosomes can be aligned and separated during mitosis.

Infer Overall, DNA has a negative charge. Look at the histone proteins in the figure. What type of overall charge do you think they have? Explain.

At almost all times during the cell cycle, each of your chromosomes is associated with a group of proteins called **histones.** DNA wraps around histones at regular intervals, similar to beads on a string. Parts of the histones interact with each other, further compacting the DNA. At this stage—the "spaghetti" stage—the loose combination of DNA and proteins is called **chromatin.** The word "loose" describes how much the DNA strand folds back on itself; it does not mean the DNA is loosely wrapped around the histones.

As a cell progresses into mitosis, chromatin further condenses. It continues to coil more and more tightly around organizing proteins, finally forming small thick rods. Recall that each chromosome has already been copied during the previous S stage. Thus, the chromosome looks similar to an "X" in which the left and right halves are two identical DNA double helixes. One half of a duplicated chromosome is called a **chromatid** (KROH-muh-tihd). Together, the two identical chromatids are called sister chromatids. Sister chromatids are held together at the **centromere** (SEHN-truh-MEER), a region of the condensed chromosome that looks pinched.

In addition, the ends of DNA molecules form structures called **telomeres** (TEHL-uh-meers), which are made of repeating nucleotides that do not form genes. They prevent the ends of chromosomes from accidentally attaching to each other, and they help prevent the loss of genes. A short section of nucleotides is lost from a new DNA molecule each time it is copied. It is important that these nucleotides are lost from telomeres, not from the genes themselves.

Apply What is the relationship between a molecule of DNA and a chromosome?

TAKING NOTES

Use a main idea web to help you study the makeup and organization of chromosomes.

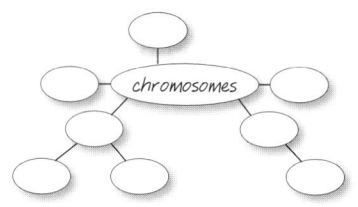

▶ MAIN IDEA
Mitosis and cytokinesis produce two genetically identical daughter cells.

The combined processes of mitosis and cytokinesis produce two genetically identical daughter cells. Follow along in **FIGURE 5.7** as you read about the process in more detail below.

Interphase

Interphase plays an important role in preparing the cell to divide. It provides critical time for the duplication of organelles and for DNA replication. By the end of interphase, an individual cell has two full sets of DNA, or chromosomes, and is large enough to divide.

Mitosis

MITOSIS

Mitosis divides a cell's nucleus into two genetically identical nuclei, each with its own single, full set of DNA. This process occurs in all of your body cells—except those that form eggs or sperm—and prepares them for cytokinesis. Although mitosis and cytokinesis are continuous processes, scientists have divided them into phases to make them easier to understand and discuss. The four main phases of mitosis are prophase, metaphase, anaphase, and telophase. Cytokinesis begins during late anaphase or telophase.

① During **prophase,** chromatin condenses into tightly coiled chromosomes. Each consists of two identical sister chromatids. The nuclear envelope breaks down, the nucleolus disappears, and the centrosomes and centrioles begin to migrate to opposite sides of the cell. Organized microtubules called spindle fibers grow from the centrioles and radiate toward the center of the cell.

② In **metaphase,** the spindle fibers attach to a protein structure on the centromere of each chromosome and align the chromosomes along the cell equator, around the middle of the cell.

③ During **anaphase,** sister chromatids separate from each other. The spindle fibers begin to shorten, which pulls the sister chromatids away from each other and toward opposite sides of the cell.

④ In **telophase,** a complete set of identical chromosomes is positioned at each pole of the cell. The nuclear membranes start to form, the chromosomes begin to uncoil, and the spindle fibers fall apart.

Cytokinesis

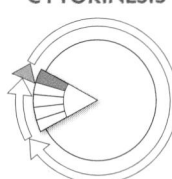

Cytokinesis divides the cytoplasm into two cells and completes a full stage of the cell cycle. Cytokinesis differs in animal and plant cells. In animal cells, the membrane forms a furrow, or trench, that is pulled inward by tiny filaments, like a drawstring. Gradually, the membrane pinches closed, forming a separate cell around each nucleus.

FIGURE 5.6 The nucleus and chromosomes go through dramatic changes in a dividing cell.

Parent cell

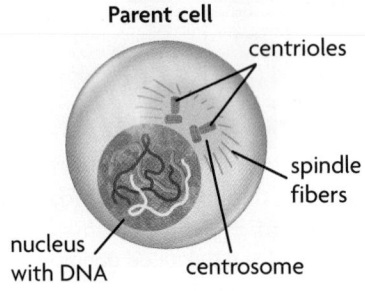

centrioles
spindle fibers
nucleus with DNA
centrosome

Connecting CONCEPTS

Cells As you will learn in **Chapter 6**, your body has two major cell types. Germ cells develop into eggs or sperm. Somatic cells make up the rest of your body.

FIGURE 5.7 The Cell Cycle in Detail

Following interphase, mitosis divides duplicated chromosomes between two nuclei. Cytokinesis divides the cytoplasm. In this diagram, the mitosis stage is greatly expanded to highlight its four major phases. (micrographs; magnification about 100×)

Animated BIOLOGY
Watch mitosis in action at ClassZone.com.

INTERPHASE

The cell copies its DNA and grows in preparation for division. The DNA is loosely organized during interphase.

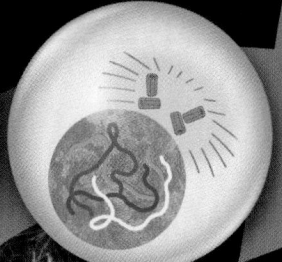

MITOSIS

Mitosis divides a cell's nucleus into two nuclei, each with an identical set of DNA.

1 Prophase DNA and proteins condense into tightly coiled chromosomes. The nuclear envelope breaks down, centrioles begin to move to opposite poles, and spindle fibers form.

2 Metaphase Spindle fibers attach to each chromosome. They align the chromosomes along the cell equator.

CYTOKINESIS

Cytokinesis divides cytoplasm between two daughter cells, each with a genetically identical nucleus. The cells enter interphase and begin the cycle again.

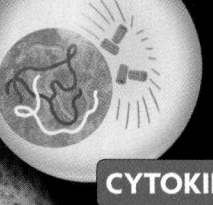

3 Anaphase Chromatids separate to opposite sides of the cell. Cytokinesis usually begins in late anaphase or telophase.

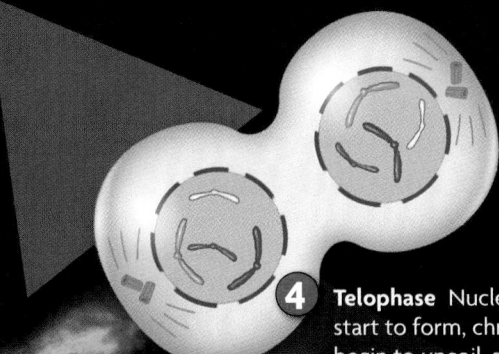

4 Telophase Nuclear membranes start to form, chromosomes begin to uncoil, and the spindle fibers fall apart.

CRITICAL VIEWING How many chromosomes does the cell have at the start of mitosis? How many does it have after cytokinesis?

DATA ANALYSIS

CONSTRUCTING DATA TABLES

Scientists use data tables to record their data. Data tables are organized by the independent and dependent variables. Usually the independent variable is listed in the left column, and the other columns list the dependent variables. Each separate observation is listed in its own row. When measurements are taken using units, they are listed in the column headings in parentheses. All tables should have numbers and titles.

TABLE 1. EFFECT OF HORMONES ON CELL DIVISION

independent variable →

dependent variable →

Concentration of Hormone Solution (%)	Size of Cell Clump After 24 Hours (mm)
0	3
25	4
50	8
75	9
100	9

↑ observations

Table 1 shows data from a hypothetical experiment in which growth hormones were added to clumps of cells in a laboratory, and the growth of the cell clumps was measured.

1. **Display Data** Suppose a scientist decided to measure the effect of temperature on cell division in *chlorella*, a type of green algae. Set up a table that could be used to record the results for the number of daily doublings of the cells: 20°C, 3 doublings; 30°C, 7 doublings; 40°C, 12 doublings; 50°C, 0 doublings.

2. **Apply** Label the independent and dependent variables on your table.

During cytokinesis in plant cells, the membrane cannot pinch inward because of the cell wall. Instead, a cell plate forms between the two nuclei. It is made by the Golgi apparatus, which supplies the new plasma membrane. A new wall then grows as cellulose and other materials are laid down. Typically, cytoplasm is divided evenly between daughter cells in both plant and animal cells.

The formation of new cells is critical in both multicellular and single-celled organisms. Single-celled organisms use cell division to reproduce, whereas multicellular organisms use it for growth, development, and repair.

Contrast How does cytokinesis differ in animal and plant cells?

5.2 ASSESSMENT

ONLINE QUIZ
ClassZone.com

REVIEWING ▶ MAIN IDEAS

1. Draw what a **chromosome** looks like during **metaphase.** Identify the **chromatids** and the **centromere.**

2. Briefly explain why the daughter cells resulting from mitosis are genetically identical to each other and to the original cell.

CRITICAL THINKING

3. **Contrast** How do **prophase** and **telophase** differ?

4. **Apply** Using a light microscope, you observe a cell that has no nucleus. What features would you look for to determine whether it is a eukaryotic cell undergoing mitosis or a prokaryotic cell?

Connecting CONCEPTS

5. **Protein Synthesis** For a cell to make proteins, enzymes must access its genes. When **histones** are modified with acetyl groups (-$COCH_3$), their positive charge is neutralized, so they wrap DNA less tightly. How might this affect the rate of protein synthesis?

MATERIALS
- slides of onion root cells
- microscope

PROCESS SKILLS
- **Observing**
- **Collecting Data**
- **Concluding**

MICHIGAN STANDARDS

L2.p1C Describe growth and development in terms of increase in cell number, cell size, and/or cell products. (prerequisite)

B4.3A Compare and contrast the processes of cell division (mitosis and meiosis), particularly as those processes relate to production of new cells and to passing on genetic information between generations.

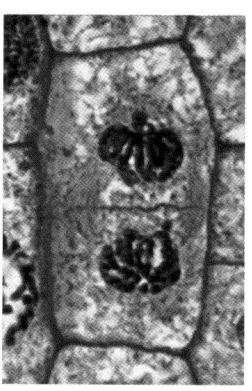

This onion cell lays down a cell plate (middle) that will form new cell membranes and the cell wall. (LM, magnification about 800×)

Mitosis in Onion Root Cells

In this lab, you will examine cells from onion root tissue under the microscope and identify the different stages of cell division. You will also determine how much time is spent in each stage of the cell cycle.

PROBLEM   How much time do cells spend in each part of the cell cycle?

PROCEDURE

1. Obtain a slide of onion root cells. Examine the slide under the microscope using the low-power lens.

2. Find examples of cells in each stage of the cell cycle, including interphase and the stages of mitosis—prophase, metaphase, anaphase, and telophase. Draw and label each cell. Label structures within the cell.

3. Select a random area of the slide to study using the high-power lens.

4. Identify and record the stage of each cell in the view. Make a data table, like the one shown below, and record your data.

5. Repeat step 3 two more times.

6. Calculate the percentage of cells in each part of the cell cycle for each sample.

TABLE 1. STAGES OF THE CELL CYCLE											
Sample	Total Cells	Interphase		Prophase		Metaphase		Anaphase		Telophase	
	No.	No.	%	No.	%	No.	%	No.	%	No.	%
1											
2											
3											

ANALYZE AND CONCLUDE

1. **Analyze** What patterns exist in your data? In which stage of the cell cycle are most of the cells you examined? How do these data support what you know about the cell cycle?

2. **Calculate** Find the average percentage of cells in each stage of the cell cycle among the three samples. Assume that a cell takes 24 hours to complete one cell cycle. Calculate how much time is spent in each stage of the cell cycle. (**Hint:** Multiply the percentage of cells in each stage, as a decimal, by 24 hours.)

3. **Apply** The cells in the root of an onion are actively dividing. How might the numbers you count here be different than if you had examined cells from a different part of the plant?

4. **Predict** A chemical company is testing a new product that it believes will increase the growth rate of food plants. Suppose you are able to view the slides of onion root tips that have been treated with the product. If the product is successful, how might the slides look different from the slides you viewed in this lab? Draw some examples of what the treated slides might look like.

EXTEND YOUR INVESTIGATION

Design an experiment that would test the product described in question 4. Assume the product is a liquid that can be added to the soil in which the plant is growing.

5.3 Regulation of the Cell Cycle

KEY CONCEPT Cell cycle regulation is necessary for healthy growth.

▶ MAIN IDEAS

- Internal and external factors regulate cell division.
- Cell division is uncontrolled in cancer.

VOCABULARY

growth factor, p. 144
apoptosis, p. 145
cancer, p. 146
benign, p. 146
malignant, p. 146

metastasize, p. 146
carcinogen, p. 146

MICHIGAN STANDARDS

L2.p1C Describe growth and development in terms of increase in cell number, cell size, and/or cell products. (prerequisite)

B2.1C Explain cell division, growth, and development as a consequence of an increase in cell number, cell size, and/or cell products.

Connect Have you ever watched a movie in which people play with the elements of nature? They might bring back dinosaurs or make a newfangled robot. And have you noticed that these movies are always scary? That's because things go out of control. The robots take over, or the dinosaurs start eating humans. If cell growth goes out of control in your body, the result can be even scarier. Cancer is uncontrolled cell growth and results from many factors that affect the cell cycle. So how does your body regulate all the millions of cell divisions happening in your body?

▶ MAIN IDEA

Internal and external factors regulate cell division.

Both external and internal factors regulate the cell cycle in eukaryotic cells. External factors come from outside the cell. They include messages from nearby cells and from distant parts of the organism's body.

Internal factors come from inside the cell and include several types of molecules found in the cytoplasm. Both types of factors work together to help your body control the process of cell division.

External Factors

External factors that help regulate the cell cycle include physical and chemical signals. One example of a physical signal is cell–cell contact. Most mammal cells grown in the laboratory form a single layer on the bottom of a culture dish, as shown in **FIGURE 5.8**. Once a cell touches other cells, it stops dividing. The exact reason for this phenomenon is unknown. One hypothesis is that receptors on neighboring cells bind to each other and cause the cells' cytoskeletons to form structures that may block the signals that trigger growth.

Many cells also release chemical signals that tell other cells to grow. For example, **growth factors** are a broad group of proteins that stimulate cell division. Growth factors bind to receptors that activate specific genes to trigger cell growth. In general, cells grow and divide in response to a combination of different growth factors, not just one.

FIGURE 5.8 Normal animal cells (top) respond to external factors and stop dividing when they touch each other. Cancer cells (bottom) fail to respond and form clumps.

Normal cell growth

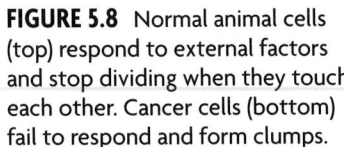

Cancerous cell growth

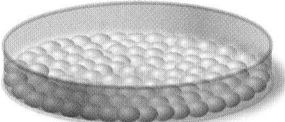

Some growth factors affect many different types of cells. For example, platelets are sticky fragments of bone marrow cells. They form clots that help stop bleeding. Platelets store a type of growth factor that helps your body repair wounds by triggering the growth of many different cell types. Other growth factors have more specific targets. For instance, erythropoietin (ih-RIHTH-roh-poy-EE-tihn) stimulates the production only of cells that will become red blood cells. Red blood cells carry oxygen. If you moved from the coast to the mountains, your blood oxygen levels would be lower because the air pressure is lower at higher altitudes. The decrease in blood oxygen levels would cause your body to produce more erythropoietin. That factor would increase the number of red blood cells and raise your blood oxygen levels.

Various hormones may also stimulate the growth of certain cell types. In particular, growth hormone results in bone growth and also affects your protein and fat metabolism.

Internal Factors

When external factors bind to their receptors, they can trigger internal factors that affect the cell cycle. Two of the most important and well-studied internal factors involved in the eukaryotic cell cycle are kinases and cyclins. A kinase is an enzyme that, when activated, transfers a phosphate group from one molecule to a specific target molecule. This action typically increases the energy of the target molecule or changes its shape. Your cells have many types of kinases, and they are almost always present in the cell. Those kinases that help control the cell cycle are activated by cyclins. Cyclins are a group of proteins that are rapidly made and destroyed at certain points in the cell cycle. These two factors help a cell advance to different stages of the cell cycle when cells bind to each other.

Apoptosis

Just as some cells need to grow and divide, other cells need to die. **Apoptosis** (AP-uhp-TOH-sihs) is programmed cell death. It occurs when internal or external signals activate genes that help produce self-destructive enzymes. Many questions remain about this process. What is known is that the nucleus of an apoptotic cell tends to shrink and break apart, and the cell is recognized by specialized cells in the immune system. These cells very tidily gobble up the apoptotic cell and recycle its chemical parts for use in building other molecules. **FIGURE 5.9** shows a classic example of apoptosis. In the early stages of development, human embryos have webbing between their fingers and toes, or digits. Before a baby is born, those cells typically go through apoptosis. Most babies are born with little unwebbed fingers and toes they love to put in their mouths.

Predict **Suppose a child was born whose receptors for growth hormone did not work properly. How do you think this would affect the child's development?**

FIGURE 5.9 Human embryos have webbed digits early in their development. The cells between the digits undergo apoptosis during later stages of development. As a result, the baby is born with unwebbed fingers and toes.

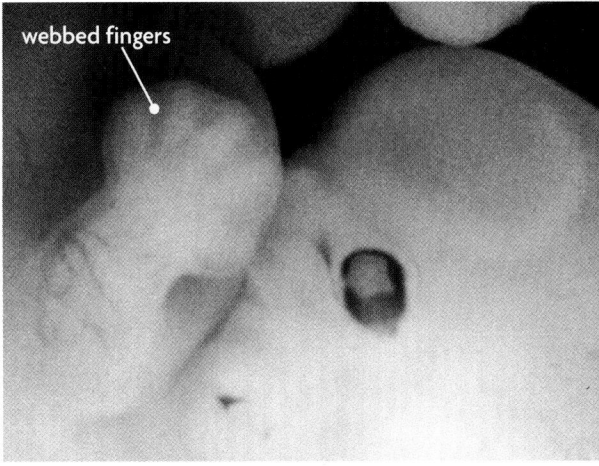
webbed fingers

Cell division is uncontrolled in cancer.

Cancer is the common name for a class of diseases characterized by uncontrolled cell division. It arises when regulation of the cell cycle breaks down. Unlike healthy cells, cancer cells grown in a culture dish continue to divide, even when surrounded by neighboring cells. Cancer cells can also continue to divide in the absence of many of the growth factors required for division in healthy cells. As a result, they divide much more often than do healthy cells.

Cancer cells form disorganized clumps called tumors. In a **benign** tumor, the cancer cells typically remain clustered together. This means the tumor may be relatively harmless and can probably be cured by removing it. However, if a tumor is **malignant,** some of the cancer cells can break away, or **metastasize** (mih-TAS-tuh-SYZ), from the tumor. These breakaway cells can be carried in the bloodstream or lymph system to other parts of the body, as shown in **FIGURE 5.10,** where they can form more tumors, called metastases. Once a tumor metastasizes, it is much more difficult to entirely rid the body of tumors.

But why are tumors harmful? Cancer cells do not perform the specialized functions needed by the body. In the lung, for example, cancer cells do not exchange oxygen and carbon dioxide. In the brain, they do not transmit the carefully ordered electrical messages needed to interpret information. Therefore, the body has large clumps of rapidly dividing cells that require lots of food and a hearty blood supply but that contribute nothing to the body's function. In addition, a growing tumor can exert great pressure on surrounding organs. For instance, a tumor growing inside the skull will cramp the brain for space, and some regions will be unable to function properly. If cancer cells continue to grow unchecked, they will eventually kill the organism.

Cancer cells come from normal cells that have suffered damage to the genes that help make proteins involved in cell-cycle regulation. Most cancer cells carry mutations, or errors, in two types of genes. One type, called oncogenes, accelerate the cell cycle. The second type act as cell-cycle brakes. Mutations in these genes can be inherited. For instance, some breast cancers appear to be caused by inherited errors in specific genes. Other mutations can be caused by exposure to radiation or chemicals. For example, some skin cancers are due to DNA damage caused by ultraviolet radiation from sunlight. Substances known to produce or promote the development of cancer are called **carcinogens** (kahr-SIHN-uh-juhnz). These include tobacco smoke and certain air pollutants, which are both associated with lung cancer. Some mutated forms of oncogenes are even carried by viruses; one such virus can cause cervical cancer.

FIGURE 5.10 Cancer cells form tumors that may metastasize to other parts of the body.

normal cell   cancer cell   bloodstream

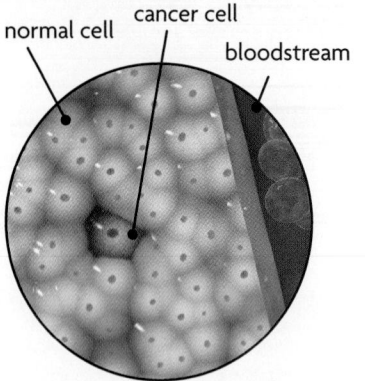

1. A healthy cell may become a cancer cell if certain genes are damaged.

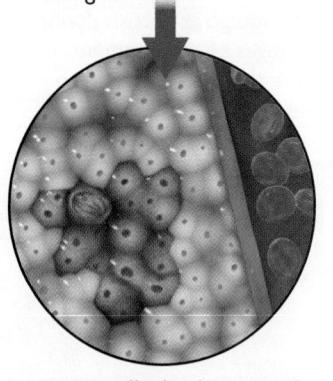

2. Cancer cells divide more often than do healthy cells and may form disorganized clumps called tumors.

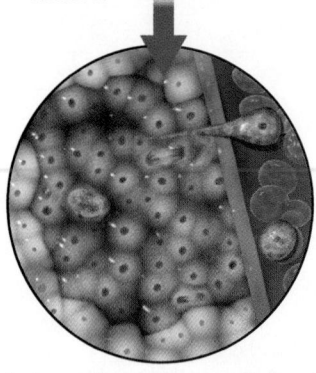

3. Sometimes, cancer cells break away from the tumor. They can be carried in the bloodstream to other parts of the body, where they form new tumors.

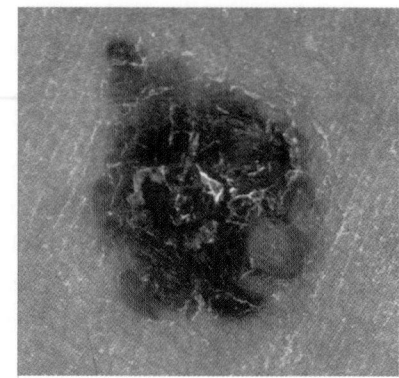

FIGURE 5.11 This cancerous mole is an example of a skin cancer, which may metastasize quickly.

QUICK LAB OBSERVING

Cancer

In this lab, you will compare normal cells with cancerous cells and observe the differences between them.

PROBLEM How do normal and cancerous cells compare?

PROCEDURE

1. Examine the slides of normal cells under the microscope. Draw and describe your observations.
2. Repeat step 1 with slides of cancer cells.

ANALYZE AND CONCLUDE

1. **Compare** How does the structure of the normal cells compare with the structure of the cancerous cells for each of the slides you viewed?
2. **Infer** Cancer cells not only appear different from normal cells but they also divide more rapidly. Why do you think chemotherapy, a common treatment for cancer, results in the loss of hair?

MATERIALS

- microscope
- slides of normal cells
- slides of cancerous cells

Standard cancer treatment often involves both radiation and chemotherapy. Radiation therapy is the use of radiation to kill cancer cells and shrink tumors. It works by damaging a cell's DNA so much that the cell cannot divide. Radiation is usually localized—that is, its use is targeted to a specific region—because it can also hurt healthy cells. Chemotherapy uses certain drugs, often in combination, to kill actively dividing cells. Like radiation, it kills both cancerous and healthy cells. However, chemotherapy is systemic—drugs travel throughout the entire body.

Medical researchers use laboratory-grown cancer cells in their search for cancer treatments. Much of what is known about the cell cycle has come from studies that use cancer cells. The most famous cancer cells used for research are called HeLa cells. HeLa cells were originally obtained in 1951 from a cervical tumor removed from a woman named Henrietta Lacks. This cell line continues to be grown and studied in laboratories all over the world.

Analyze HeLa cells are also used to study cell signaling processes. What might be a disadvantage of using cancer cells to study processes occurring in healthy cells?

5.3 ASSESSMENT

ONLINE QUIZ
ClassZone.com

REVIEWING ▶ MAIN IDEAS

1. Describe what a **growth factor** is and how it influences the cell cycle.
2. Explain how **cancer** cells differ from healthy cells.

CRITICAL THINKING

3. **Contrast** How do **benign** and **malignant** tumors differ?
4. **Hypothesize** Suppose chromosomes in a skin cell are damaged by ultraviolet radiation. If the damaged genes do not affect cell cycle regulation, do you think the cell will become cancerous? Explain.

Connecting CONCEPTS

5. **Cell Organelles** Some anticancer drugs prevent microtubules from forming spindle fibers. Why do you think these drugs might be effective treatments for cancer?

5.4 Asexual Reproduction

KEY CONCEPT Many organisms reproduce by cell division.

MAIN IDEAS

- Binary fission is similar in function to mitosis.
- Some eukaryotes reproduce through mitosis.

VOCABULARY

asexual reproduction, p. 148
binary fission, p. 148

MICHIGAN STANDARDS

L4.p1A Compare and contrast the differences between sexual and asexual reproduction. (prerequisite)

L4.p1B Discuss the advantages and disadvantages of sexual vs. asexual reproduction. (prerequisite)

Connect In this flashy world of ours, you may think that the humble bacterium would have little chance of finding a mate. No dazzling smile, no fancy hair products, no shiny car, and—if we are brutally honest—not even a brain. With all of these limitatio\ns, it may seem that our bacteria friends would be destined to die out. And yet, bacteria are found in abundance and live just about everywhere on Earth. How can there be so many bacteria?

MAIN IDEA

Binary fission is similar in function to mitosis.

Reproduction is a process that makes new organisms from one or more parent organisms. It happens in two ways—sexually and asexually. Sexual reproduction involves the joining of two specialized cells called gametes (eggs and sperm cells), one from each of two parents. The offspring that result are genetically unique; they have a mixture of genes from both parents. In contrast, **asexual reproduction** is the creation of offspring from a single parent and does not involve the joining of gametes. The offspring that result are, for the most part, genetically identical to each other and to the single parent.

Connecting CONCEPTS

Cell Structure Recall from **Chapter 3** that many scientists hypothesize that mitochondria and chloroplasts were originally free-living prokaryotes. One piece of evidence that supports this hypothesis is the fact that these two organelles replicate much as bacteria do, through fission.

Binary Fission and Mitosis

Most prokaryotes reproduce through binary fission. **Binary fission** (BY-nuh-ree FIHSH-uhn) is the asexual reproduction of a single-celled organism by division into two roughly equal parts. Binary fission and mitosis have similar results. That is, both processes form two daughter cells that are genetically identical to the parent cell. However, the actual processes are different in several important ways.

As you already learned, prokaryotes such as bacteria do not have nuclei. And although they do have DNA, they have much less of it than do most eukaryotes. Also, most of a bacterium's DNA is in the form of one circular chromosome, and bacteria have no spindle fibers.

VISUAL VOCAB

Binary fission is the asexual reproduction of a single-celled organism by division into two roughly equal parts.

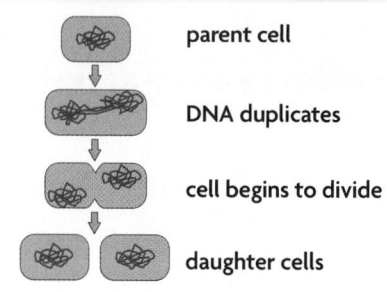

parent cell

DNA duplicates

cell begins to divide

daughter cells

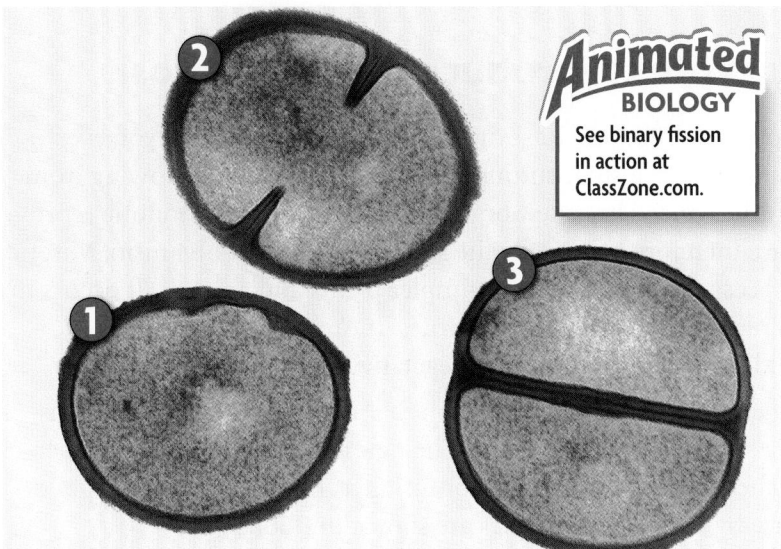

Animated
BIOLOGY
See binary fission in action at ClassZone.com.

FIGURE 5.13 Binary fission is shown in this micrograph of three individual bacteria, each at a different stage of binary fission. First, a cell elongates (1), and the DNA is replicated. Next, the cell membrane pinches inward (2). Finally, the membrane meets, and a new cell wall is laid down, forming two separate cells (3). (colored TEM; magnification 60,000×)

Binary fission, shown in **FIGURE 5.13**, starts when the bacterial chromosome is copied. The two chromosomes are both attached to the cell membrane. As the cell grows and gets longer, the chromosomes move away from each other. When the cell is about twice its original size, it undergoes cytokinesis. The membrane pinches inward, and a new cell wall is laid down between the two chromosomes, which completes the separation into two daughter cells.

Advantages and Disadvantages of Asexual Reproduction

Very often, whether something is helpful or harmful depends on the situation. In favorable environments that do not change much, asexual reproduction can be more efficient than sexual reproduction. Recall that asexual reproduction results in genetically identical offspring. If they are well suited to the environment, genetic variation could be more harmful than helpful. In other words, if it ain't broke, don't fix it.

However, asexual reproduction may be a disadvantage in changing conditions. Genetically identical offspring will respond to the environment in the same way. If population members lack traits that enable them to reproduce, the entire population could die off. In contrast, sexual reproduction increases genetic diversity, which raises the chance that at least a few individuals will survive or even thrive in changing conditions.

Keep in mind, however, that the act of asexual reproduction itself is not more efficient; rather, the associated costs of sexual reproduction are greater. For example, all asexually reproducing organisms can potentially reproduce. Suppose two organisms each have ten offspring. If one organism reproduces asexually, all ten offspring can have offspring of their own. If the other organism reproduces sexually, having five females and five males, only the five females can bear offspring. In addition, sexually reproducing organisms must attract a mate. This effort involves not only the time and energy needed to find a mate but also many structures, signals, and behaviors that have evolved to attract mates. Organisms that reproduce asexually do not have these costs.

Summarize How is asexual reproduction an advantage in some conditions?

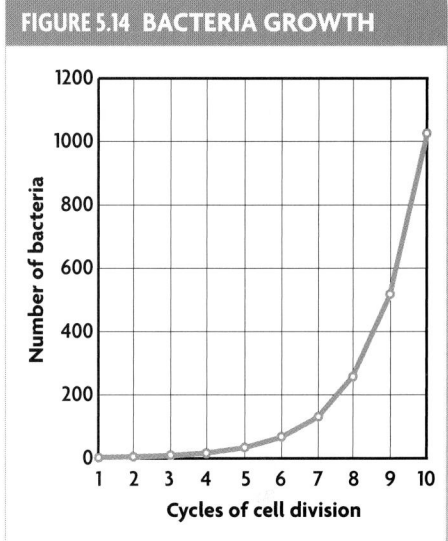

FIGURE 5.14 BACTERIA GROWTH

One bacterium can result in a total of 1024 cells after only 10 rounds of cell division.

Connecting CONCEPTS

Evolution As you will learn in **Chapter 18**, the misuse of antibiotics has resulted in multidrug-resistant bacteria. The bacteria not killed by antibiotics can reproduce quickly, passing the genes for antibiotic resistance on to their offspring.

▶ **MAIN IDEA**

Some eukaryotes reproduce through mitosis.

Some eukaryotes also reproduce asexually, through mitosis. Have you ever grown a new plant from a stem cutting? Or seen a new sea star growing from the arm of another one? These new organisms are the result of mitotic reproduction and are therefore genetically the same as the parent organism. Mitotic reproduction is especially common in simpler plants and animals. It occurs in both multicellular and unicellular eukaryotes. It can take several forms, including budding, fragmentation, and vegetative reproduction.

In budding, a small projection grows on the surface of the parent organism, forming a separate new individual. The new organism may live independently or attached as part of a colony. For instance, hydras and some types of yeast reproduce by budding. Examples are shown in **FIGURE 5.15**.

In fragmentation, a parent organism splits into pieces, each of which can grow into a new organism. Flatworms and sea stars both reproduce by fragmentation. Many plants, including strawberries and potatoes, reproduce via vegetative reproduction. In general, vegetative reproduction involves the modification of a stem or underground structures of the parent organism. The offspring often stay connected to the original organism, through structures called runners, for example.

Many organisms can reproduce both asexually and sexually. The form of reproduction may depend on the current conditions. The sea anemone can reproduce in many ways. It can reproduce asexually by dividing in half, by breaking off small pieces from its base, or by budding. It can also reproduce sexually by making eggs and sperm. Some species of anemone have males and females. In other anemone species, the same organism can produce both eggs and sperm cells.

FIGURE 5.15 Yeast and hydras can reproduce by budding.
(colored SEMs; magnifications: yeast 2400×; hydra about 30×)

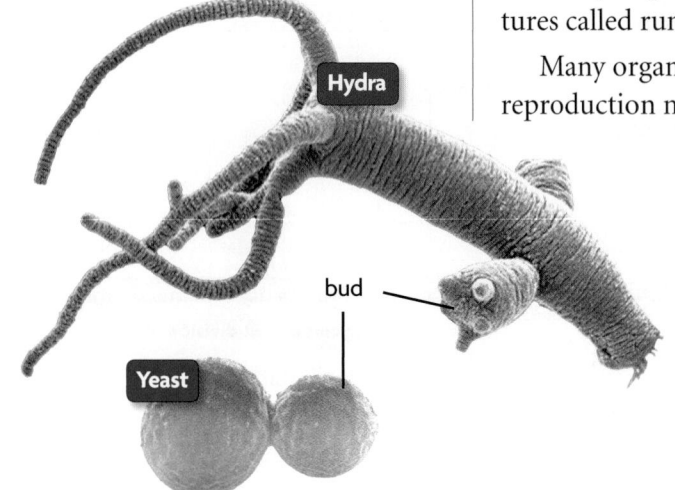

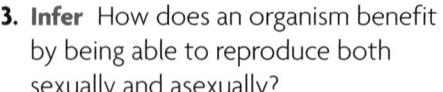

Synthesize How might the asexual reproduction of genetically identical plants be useful to humans? How could it prove harmful to our food supply?

5.4 | ASSESSMENT

ONLINE QUIZ
ClassZone.com

REVIEWING ▶ MAIN IDEAS

1. Explain how mitosis differs from **binary fission.**

2. Briefly explain why cutting a flatworm into pieces would not kill it.

CRITICAL THINKING

3. **Infer** How does an organism benefit by being able to reproduce both sexually and asexually?

4. **Apply** Yeasts are growing in two dishes. You treat one dish with a chemical that blocks DNA replication but forget to label it. How can you identify the treated dish?

Connecting CONCEPTS

5. **Ecology** Two populations live in the same habitat and compete for food. The first group is larger and uses **asexual reproduction**; the second reproduces sexually. What could happen to cause the second group to outnumber the first?

5.5 Multicellular Life

KEY CONCEPT Cells work together to carry out complex functions.

MAIN IDEAS

- Multicellular organisms depend on interactions among different cell types.
- Specialized cells perform specific functions.
- Stem cells can develop into different cell types.

VOCABULARY

tissue, p. 151
organ, p. 151
organ system, p. 151
cell differentiation, p. 152

stem cell, p. 153

Review
homeostasis

MICHIGAN STANDARDS

L2.p1D Explain how the systems in a multicellular organism work together to support the organism. (prerequisite)

B2.1d Describe how, through cell division, cells can become specialized for specific function.

Connect Each of us enters this world as a screaming infant. At first, the ability to eat solid foods or take a step draws forth great praise. These general skills rapidly lose their wonder, however, and by the time you reach the age of 18, everyone wants to know what you plan to do with yourself. Will you build houses or design clothing or treat patients? What will your specialty be? Cells, too, undergo specialization to carry out the complex functions required by the body.

MAIN IDEA
Multicellular organisms depend on interactions among different cell types.

Within multicellular organisms, cells communicate and work together in groups that form increasingly larger, more complex structures. This arrangement progresses from cells to tissues to organs to organ systems, as shown in **FIGURE 5.16. Tissues** are groups of cells that work together to perform a similar function. Groups of tissues that work together to perform a specific function or related functions are called **organs.** For instance, plants have photosynthetic tissues made of chlorophyll-containing cells. Conductive tissues transport sugars, water, and minerals to and from other parts of the plant. Protective tissues help prevent water loss. Together, these and other tissues form a leaf, the plant's food-producing organ.

Organs that carry out similar functions are further grouped into **organ systems.** In plants, the shoot system is above the ground. It includes stems that support the plant, leaves that capture radiant energy, and flowers that aid reproduction. Beneath the ground, the root system has different types of roots and root hairs that anchor the plant and absorb water and minerals.

As organ systems work together, they help an organism maintain homeostasis. For example, plants need to maintain a certain level of water within their cells, or they will wilt and die. They absorb water through their roots and expel it as water vapor through openings in their leaves called stomata. Stomata are controlled by special cells called guard cells, which close the stomata when a plant's water intake cannot keep up with its water loss.

Connecting CONCEPTS

Homeostasis As you learned in **Chapter 1,** homeostasis is the maintenance of a stable internal environment. Both an organism's physiology and its behavior help it achieve homeostasis.

Apply Suppose your family goes out of town and forgets to ask your neighbor to water the plants. Do you think the plants' stomata will be open or closed? Explain.

FIGURE 5.16 Levels of Organization

Cells work together in groups that form larger, specialized structures.

CELL	TISSUE	ORGAN	SYSTEMS
Vessel elements are tube-shaped cells. (colored SEM; magnification 200×)	Vessel elements and tracheids form xylem. (colored SEM; magnification 200×)	Xylem and other tissues form roots that absorb water and nutrients.	

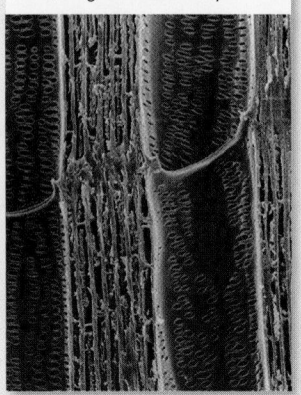
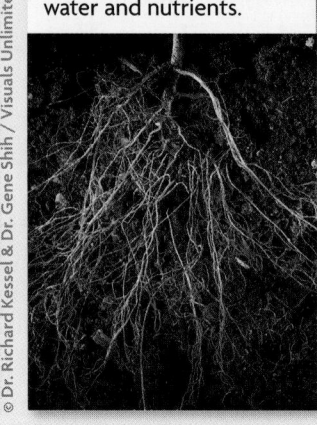
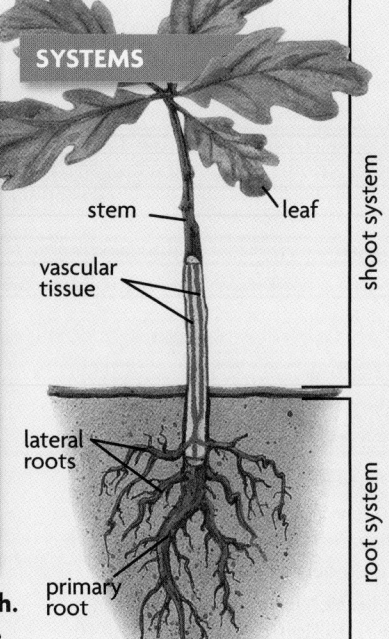

© Dr. Richard Kessel & Dr. Gene Shih / Visuals Unlimited

stem — leaf
vascular tissue
lateral roots
primary root

shoot system
root system

Apply Draw a simple sketch of the middle photograph. Label the vessel elements. Identify what you think are the tracheids and label them.

▶ MAIN IDEA
Specialized cells perform specific functions.

It is easy to see that a skin cell can divide to make a new skin cell, or that a single bacterium can generate another bacterium. But how does a complex organism like you develop? Your body began as a single fertilized egg. If the egg simply divided to make lots of identical cells, it would not form a baby. To form the intricate structures that make up your body and the bodies of countless organisms around you, cells must specialize.

Cell differentiation is the process by which unspecialized cells develop into their mature forms and functions. While almost every cell in your body has a full set of DNA, each type of cell uses only the specific genes it needs to carry out its function. That is, a cell differentiates among the genes and uses only certain ones. You can think of your DNA as a cookbook. When you want to make a specific dish, you select that recipe and carry out its instructions. If you need to make a dessert, you might bake turtle brownies. If you need to make a main course, you might roast apple-stuffed pork chops or fix a hearty lentil stew. The dishes are very different, but they all come from the same cookbook.

A cell's location within the embryo helps determine how it will differentiate. In plant cells, the first division of a fertilized egg is unequal, or asymmetric, and produces two cells—the apical cell and the basal cell. The apical cell forms most of the embryo, including the growth point for stems and leaves. The major role of the basal cell is to provide nutrients to the embryo; it also creates the growth point for the roots. Plant cells cannot easily migrate because of the cell wall, but they adapt to changing conditions and continue to develop throughout their lifetime. As the plant grows, new cells continue to differentiate based on their location. For example, cells on the outer layer of a leaf may become epidermal cells that secrete a waxy substance that helps prevent water loss. Cells on the lower leaf surface may become guard cells that control the exchange of water, air, and carbon dioxide.

In animals, an egg undergoes many rapid divisions after it is fertilized. The resulting cells can migrate to a specific area, and the cells quickly begin to differentiate. The early animal embryo generally takes the shape of a hollow ball. As the embryo develops, part of the ball folds inward, forming an inner layer and creating an opening in the outer cell layer. A middle layer of cells then forms between the other two.

FIGURE 5.17 Cell Differentiation

Cell differentiation in the developing animal embryo is based on location.

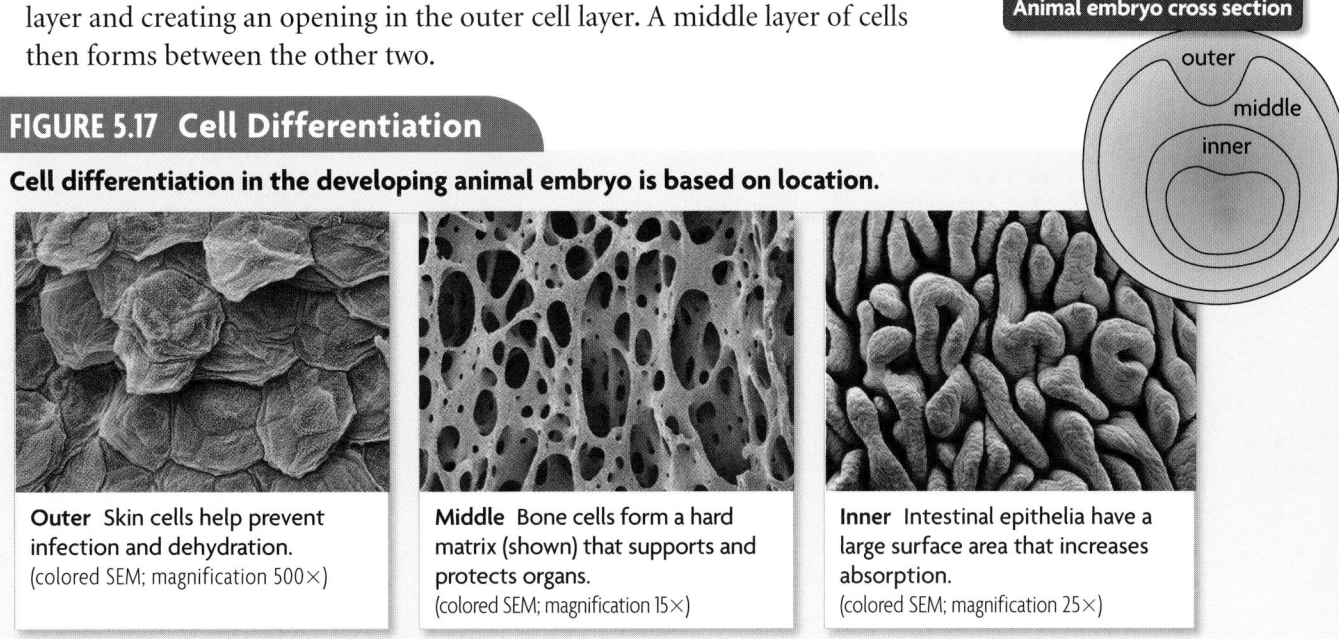

Outer Skin cells help prevent infection and dehydration.
(colored SEM; magnification 500×)

Middle Bone cells form a hard matrix (shown) that supports and protects organs.
(colored SEM; magnification 15×)

Inner Intestinal epithelia have a large surface area that increases absorption.
(colored SEM; magnification 25×)

As shown in **FIGURE 5.17**, in vertebrates, the outer cell layer differentiates to form the outer layer of skin and elements of the nervous system such as the brain and spinal cord. The middle cell layer forms bones, muscles, kidneys, and the inner layer of skin. The inner cell layer forms internal organs such as the pancreas, lungs, and digestive system lining.

Analyze Why is regulation of the differentiation process during the early stages of development so critical?

⊙ MAIN IDEA
Stem cells can develop into different cell types.

Stem cells are a unique type of body cell that have the ability to (1) divide and renew themselves for long periods of time, (2) remain undifferentiated in form, and (3) develop into a variety of specialized cell types. When a stem cell divides, it forms either two stem cells or one stem cell and one specialized cell.

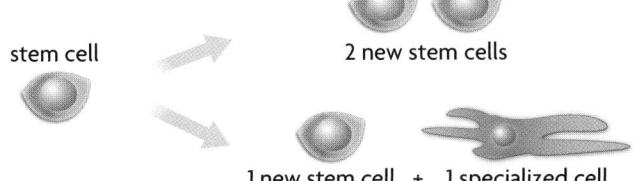

stem cell

2 new stem cells

1 new stem cell + 1 specialized cell

Stem Cell Classification

Stem cells can be categorized by their ability, or potential, to develop into the differentiated cell types of different tissues, as shown in **FIGURE 5.18.** In general, the more differentiated a stem cell already is, the fewer the types of cells it can form.

- Totipotent stem cells can grow into any other cell type. Only a fertilized egg and the cells produced by the first few divisions of an embryo are totipotent.
- Pluripotent stem cells can grow into any cell type except for totipotent stem cells.
- Multipotent stem cells can only grow into cells of a closely related cell family.

VOCABULARY

Potent comes from a Latin word meaning "to be able." The addition of prefixes defines the level of power or ability.
toti- = all
pluri- = more, several
multi- = many

FIGURE 5.18 STEM CELL CLASSIFICATION

Class	totipotent	pluripotent	multipotent
Type of cell	fertilized egg 	embryonic stem cell 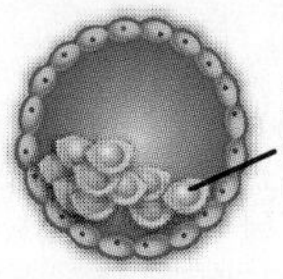 inner cell mass	adult stem cell (example from blood) 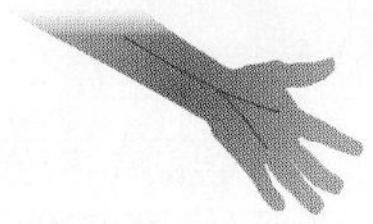
Can give rise to	all cells	almost any cell	closely related cells
Example	new organism	neurons, skin, muscle, kidney, cartilage, bone, liver, pancreas	red blood cells, platelets, white blood cells

Stem cells are also classified by their origin, as either adult or embryonic. Adult stem cells have been studied for decades, but the ability to grow human embryonic stem cells was not developed until 1998. Since that time, embryonic stem cells have attracted great attention because of their potential to form almost any cell type. Both adult and embryonic stem cells offer unique advantages and challenges to researchers.

Adult Stem Cells

Adult stem cells are partially undifferentiated cells located among the specialized cells of many organs and tissues. They are found all over the body, in the brain, liver, bone marrow, skeletal muscle, dental pulp, and even fat. These stem cells are also found in children and in umbilical cord blood, so the term *somatic stem cell* is more accurate although less frequently used.

A major advantage of adult stem cells is that they can be taken from a patient, grown in culture, and put back into the patient. Thus, the risk of transplant rejection by a patient's immune system is very low. This method also avoids many ethical issues associated with using embryonic stem cells.

Adult stem cells currently pose many disadvantages as well. They are few in number, difficult to isolate, and sometimes tricky to grow. They may also contain more DNA abnormalities than do embryonic stem cells. For years, much evidence suggested that adult stem cells were multipotent. This would mean that a stem cell from fat would produce only fat cells, never muscle cells. Newer data suggest otherwise. Adult stem cells treated with the right combination of molecules may give rise to a completely different type of tissue. This process, called transdifferentiation, remains an active area of research.

Embryonic Stem Cells

Most embryonic stem cells come from donated embryos grown in a clinic. These embryos are the result of in vitro fertilization, a process by which eggs are fertilized outside a woman's body. The stem cells are taken from a cluster of undifferentiated cells in the three-to-five-day-old embryo.

These cells, called the inner cell mass, do not have the characteristics of any specific cell type. Because they are pluripotent, they can form any of the 200 cell types of the body. They can also be grown indefinitely in culture. These qualities have given many people hope that many now devastating diseases will be treatable or even curable in the future.

Embryonic stem cells also have a downside. If these cells are used in treatment, a patient's body might reject them as foreign material. The stem cells could potentially grow unchecked in a patient's body and form a tumor. The use of embryonic stem cells also raises many ethical questions. The most common method of getting embryonic stem cells, **FIGURE 5.19**, currently involves destruction of the embryo, which some people consider ethically unacceptable.

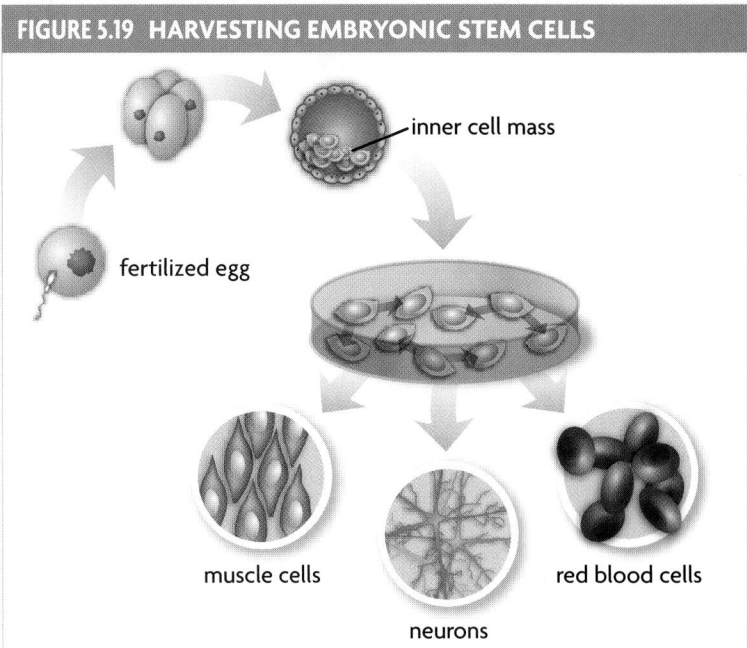

FIGURE 5.19 HARVESTING EMBRYONIC STEM CELLS

inner cell mass

fertilized egg

muscle cells

neurons

red blood cells

First, an egg is fertilized by a sperm cell in a petri dish. The egg divides, forming an inner cell mass. These cells are then removed and grown with nutrients. Scientists try to control how the cells specialize by adding or removing certain molecules.

Research and Treatment Hope

Stem cells have long been used to treat patients with leukemia and lymphoma, and they offer hope for treating many other diseases as well. For instance, some patients might be cured of diabetes if nonworking cells in the pancreas were replaced with healthy, growing cells. Similarly, damaged organs, such as the heart, might be strengthened by an injection of healthy cells. Research, such as the testing of new drugs, might also benefit. The current research system requires a lot of time and money. Many of the most innovative drugs have little chance of reaching the patient. Potentially, these new compounds could be tested on large numbers of specific cell types grown from stem cells.

Compare and Contrast **List treatment benefits and risks of both types of stem cells.**

5.5 ASSESSMENT

REVIEWING ▶ MAIN IDEAS

1. How does communication between cells help maintain homeostasis?

2. Explain why **cell differentiation** is an important part of the development of a multicellular organism.

3. What are the defining characteristics of **stem cells**?

CRITICAL THINKING

4. **Compare** Describe how **tissues, organs,** and **organ systems** are similar.

5. **Evaluate** Explain which factor you think is most important in deciding whether stem-cell research should be legal and government-funded.

Connecting CONCEPTS

6. **Animal Behavior** Choose an animal and give an example of how its behavior reflects its need to maintain homeostasis.

Use these inquiry-based labs and online activities to deepen your understanding of cell growth and development.

B1.1C Conduct scientific investigations using appropriate tools and techniques (e.g., selecting an instrument that measures the desired quantity—length, volume, weight, time interval, temperature—with the appropriate level of precision).

L2.p1C Describe growth and development in terms of increase in cell number, cell size, and/or cell products. (prerequisite)

INVESTIGATION

Modeling Cell Surface Area–to–Volume Ratio

A cell's surface area–to–volume ratio affects the amount of material that can diffuse across the membrane and throughout the cell. You will make cell models to determine how this ratio changes as cell size increases.

SKILLS Modeling, Inferring

PROBLEM Which cell has the greatest surface area–to–volume ratio?

MATERIALS
- plastic knife
- phenolphthalein agar
- metric ruler
- 250-mL beaker
- 100-mL graduated cylinder
- 100 mL sodium hydroxide solution
- timer
- plastic spoon
- paper towel

PROCEDURE

1. Make three model cells by using the knife to cut three cubes from the phenolphthalein agar. Cell A should be 3 cm on each side, cell B should be 2 cm on each side, and cell C should be 1 cm on each side. Use the ruler to make exact measurements.

2. Calculate the area of one side of each cell. Calculate the total surface area of each cell. Record your data in Table 1. (**Hint:** Multiply the area of one side by the number of sides.)

3. Calculate the volume of each cell. Record your data in the table. (**Hint:** Multiply the length by the width by the height of the cube.)

4. Calculate the ratio of surface area to volume for each cell. For example, for cell A, the ratio would be 54 cm^2:27 cm^3 = 2:1 = 2. Record your data.

5. Put the model cells in the beaker. Carefully cover them with sodium hydroxide solution, which turns the agar pink. Soak the cells in solution for four minutes. Use a spoon to turn the cells repeatedly throughout that time.

6. Remove the cells from solution and dry them on the paper towel.

7. Use the knife to cut each cube in half. Measure the distance from the edge of the cell to the inner edge of the pink line. This shows how far the sodium hydroxide diffused.

TABLE 1. CALCULATIONS OF CELL SIZE				
Cell	Area of One Side (cm^2)	Total Surface Area (cm^2)	Volume of Cell (cm^3)	Surface Area–to–Volume Ratio
A				
B				
C				

ANALYZE AND CONCLUDE

1. **Analyze** How does the surface area–to–volume ratio change as cell size increases? How might this affect the diffusion of materials throughout a cell?

2. **Apply** Identify which cell turned pink in the greatest proportion, and explain how this relates to cell size.

3. **Apply** How does a cell's surface area–to–volume ratio affect its ability to stay alive?

Apoptosis

In this lab, you will research the role of apoptosis in a developmental process.

SKILL Communicating

PROBLEM What role does apoptosis play as organisms develop?

RESEARCH

1. Use the Internet to research one of the following processes:

   - the development of neural connections in the human brain
   - the development and maintenance of the human immune system
   - the metamorphosis of a tadpole into an adult frog

2. Explain the role of apoptosis in your topic in a typed, one-page summary. In your answer, clearly identify the state of the organism before the apoptotic changes, the state of the organism following apoptosis, and what would be the result if apoptosis failed to occur.

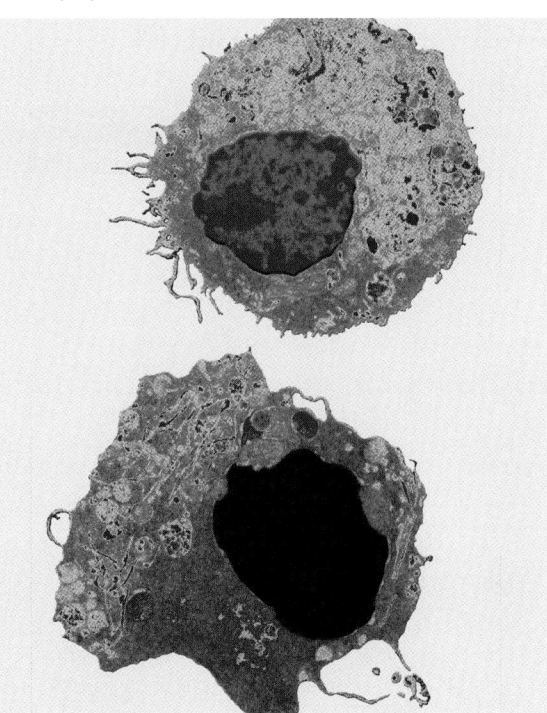

The top image is a normal white blood cell. The bottom image shows an apoptotic white blood cell with a darkened nucleus and disintegrating cytoplasm. (colored TEMs; magnification about 10,000×)

Online BIOLOGY
CLASSZONE.COM

VIRTUAL LAB
Investigating Bacterial Growth
Not all bacteria thrive in the same environmental conditions. In this interactive lab, you will determine which strains of bacteria grow in an environment with oxygen and which strains grow without oxygen.

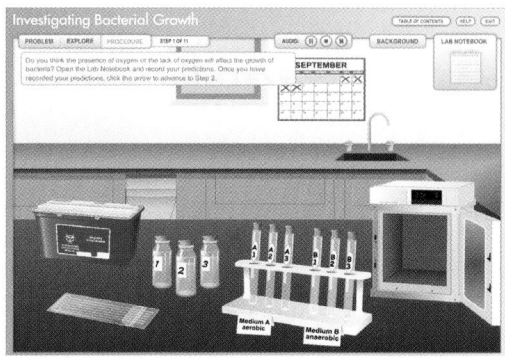

ANIMATED BIOLOGY
Mitosis Stage Matching Game
How well can you recognize the stages of mitosis? Test your skills by categorizing images showing different phases of mitosis.

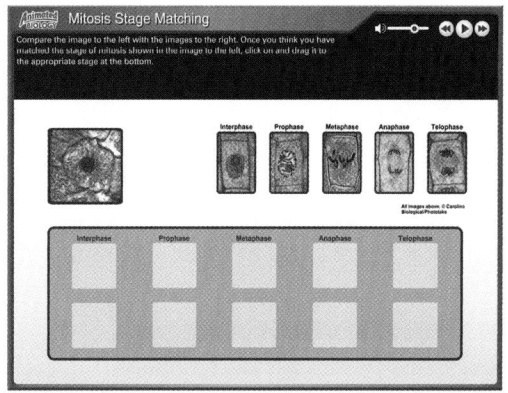

WEBQUEST
Cancer occurs when the cell cycle breaks down. In this WebQuest, you will learn about the most common cancer in the United States—skin cancer. Explore its causes, how cells become cancerous, and why prevention is truly the best medicine.

5.1 The Cell Cycle

Cells have distinct phases of growth, reproduction, and normal functions. The cell cycle has four main stages: G_1, S, G_2, and M. The length of the cell cycle can vary, resulting in different rates of cell division. This variability is based on the body's need for different cell types. Cells also divide because they need a sufficient surface area–to–volume ratio to move materials into and out of the cell.

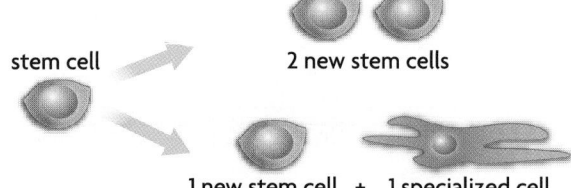

5.2 Mitosis and Cytokinesis

Cells divide during mitosis and cytokinesis. Mitosis divides the nucleus into two genetically identical nuclei in a four-phase process: prophase, metaphase, anaphase, telophase. In prophase, the duplicated chromosomes condense tightly. Cytokinesis actually divides the cell cytoplasm.

5.3 Regulation of the Cell Cycle

Cell cycle regulation is necessary for healthy growth. Cell growth and division are regulated by both external factors, such as hormones and growth factors, and internal factors, such as cyclins and kinases. When proper regulation of cell growth is disrupted, a cell may become cancerous. Cancer cells grow more rapidly than do normal cells and form clumps called tumors that may metastasize to other regions of the body.

5.4 Asexual Reproduction

Many organisms reproduce by cell division. Most prokaryotes reproduce through a process called binary fission, in which a cell divides into two approximately equal parts. Some eukaryotes reproduce through mitosis. The offspring that result from asexual reproduction are genetically identical to the parent organism, except when mutations occur. Whether being identical is an advantage or a disadvantage depends on the environment.

5.5 Multicellular Life

Cells work together to carry out complex functions. Within multicellular organisms, cells form tissues, tissues form organs, and organs form organ systems. The cells differentiate to perform specific functions. Much of this specialization is determined by a cell's location within the developing embryo. Stem cells are a special type of cell that continue to divide and renew themselves for long periods of time.

stem cell → 2 new stem cells

1 new stem cell + 1 specialized cell

Synthesize Your Notes

Concept Map Use a concept map like the one below to summarize what you know about mitosis.

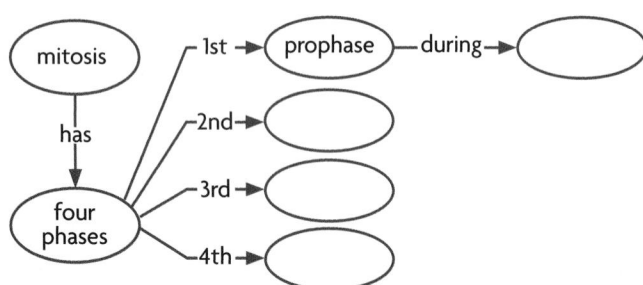

Venn Diagram Draw a Venn diagram like the one below to summarize the similarities and differences between embryonic and adult stem cells.

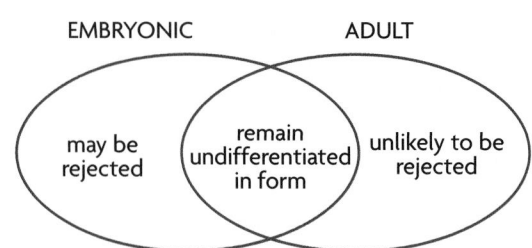

Chapter Assessment

Chapter Vocabulary

5.1   cell cycle, p. 134
mitosis, p. 135
cytokinesis, p. 135

5.2   chromosome, p. 138
histone, p. 139
chromatin, p. 139
chromatid, p. 139
centromere, p. 139
telomere, p. 139

prophase, p. 140
metaphase, p. 140
anaphase, p. 140
telophase, p. 140

5.3   growth factor, p. 144
apoptosis, p. 145
cancer, p. 146
benign, p. 146
malignant, p. 146
metastasize, p. 146
carcinogen, p. 146

5.4   asexual reproduction, p. 148
binary fission, p. 148

5.5   tissue, p. 151
organ, p. 151
organ system, p. 151
cell differentiation, p. 152
stem cell, p. 153

Reviewing Vocabulary

Visualize Vocabulary

For each term below, draw a simple picture that represents the meaning of the word. Here is an example for *mitosis*.

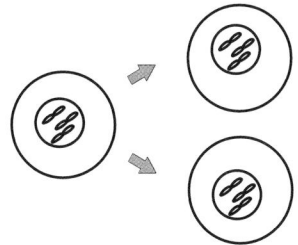

1. prophase

2. metaphase

3. anaphase

4. telophase

5. cytokinesis

6. centromere

7. telomere

Word Origins

8. The prefix *pro-* means "earlier than" or "prior to." Explain how this meaning relates to the word *prophase*.

9. The prefix *telo-* means "distant, far, or end." How does this meaning relate to the words *telophase* and *telomere*?

10. The term *mitosis* comes from the Greek root *mitos,* which means "thread." How does this meaning relate to the process of mitosis?

Reviewing MAIN IDEAS

11. The cell cycle has four main stages—G_1, S, G_2, and M. What occurs in the cell during each stage?

12. Compare the rates of cell division occurring in your neurons and your hair follicles.

13. What is the relationship between a cell's surface area and its volume?

14. You know that a chromosome is a very long, continuous strand of DNA. How do proteins help condense chromosomes?

15. Describe what happens in each main phase of mitosis— prophase, metaphase, anaphase, and telophase.

16. How does the process of cytokinesis differ from the process of mitosis?

17. Increased levels of cyclin help trigger a cell to divide. Do you think a growth factor would increase or decrease cyclin levels? Explain.

18. Describe how uncontrolled cell division is dangerous in organisms.

19. List one similarity and one difference between binary fission and mitosis.

20. You pull a leaf from a plant and place it in a cup of water. After a week, roots start to grow from the leaf. What type of reproduction has occurred, and what role does mitosis play in it?

21. Briefly describe how cell differentiation occurs in the developing animal embryo.

22. List three characteristics of all stem cells.

23. Synthesize How do regulatory proteins of the cell cycle help maintain homeostasis?

24. Hypothesize Plants often grow in the direction of a sunny window, yet plant cells cannot easily migrate due to their rigid cell walls. How do you think plants grow toward light?

25. Analyze A scientist wants to use asexually reproducing vegetables to increase crop yields. He plans to distribute budding potatoes and teach farmers how to separate them into new plants. What are some potential benefits and risks that could result from this situation?

26. Analyze The rates of DNA mutations in bacteria are known to increase when they are under stressed environmental conditions. Why do you think this is important for an organism that reproduces asexually?

27. Apply Suppose an organism usually has 24 chromosomes in its nucleus. How many chromatids would it have just after the S phase of the cell cycle?

28. Predict If a mutation made histone proteins bind less tightly to DNA, how might the cell cycle be affected?

Interpreting Visuals

Use the picture of onion root cells shown below to answer the next three questions.

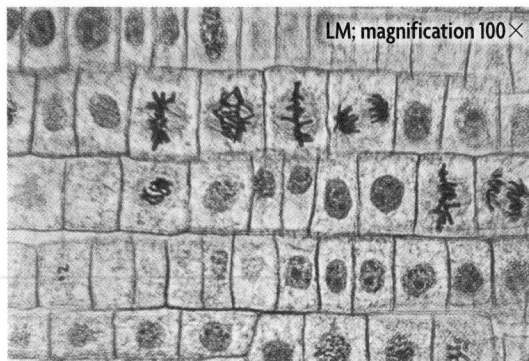

LM; magnification 100✕

29. Apply In what stage of the cell cycle are most of these cells? Explain.

30. Apply Which cells are newly formed and which are slightly older?

31. Synthesize If this onion were immersed in salt water, how would the cells undergoing mitosis be affected? (Hint: Think about the process of osmosis.)

Analyzing Data

The graph below shows the five-year survival rate, expressed as percentages, of patients diagnosed with cancer from 1985 through 1997. This data is for all types of invasive cancers and includes males and females of all races. Use the graph to answer the next two questions.

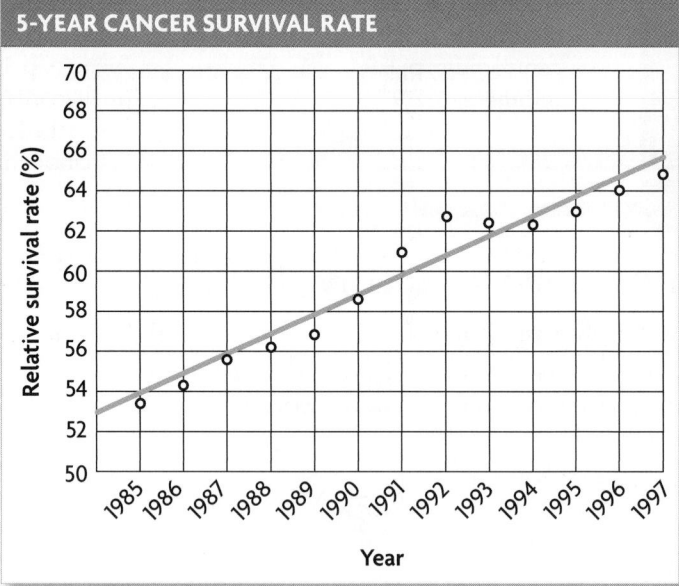

5-YEAR CANCER SURVIVAL RATE

Source: The National Cancer Institute

32. Analyze Which points do not follow the best-fit line for the data?

33. Interpret What is the trend in the data of cancer survival during the span of time given?

Connecting CONCEPTS

34. Write a Narrative Imagine that you are a single chromosome about to undergo replication and mitosis. Describe what will happen to you from the S phase through mitosis. Be creative. Use humor and first-person point of view. Come up with sounds or perspectives that illustrate what is happening. Be sure to include all details of the process and related terms.

35. Design an Experiment Cancer cells, such as those shown on page 133, are frequently grown in labs for research uses. Suppose you wanted to determine whether a certain substance was a carcinogen. Outline an experimental plan to describe what questions you would want to answer, what experiments you would perform, and what the different possible results would suggest.

 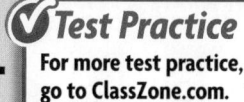
1. Scientists searching for new anticancer drugs treat a cell culture with a certain compound. Following treatment, they notice that the culture has stopped growing. Untreated cells from the same culture, however, have continued to grow. These results could indicate that the compound blocks the normal cell cycle. What else could have caused these results? **B1.1E**

   A The compound had degraded.

   B The compound prevented cells from mutating.

   C The compound killed the treated cells.

   D The compound had no effect.

THINK THROUGH THE QUESTION

The untreated cells serve as a control in this experiment. Therefore, differences between the treated and untreated cells should be the result of the drug. If the drug has no effect, the two groups of cells should be the same.

---

2. After being scraped or cut, the skin is able to heal. What biological process *best* accounts for the replacement of skin cells? **B4.3A**

   A mitosis

   B meiosis

   C asexual reproduction

   D cementation

3.

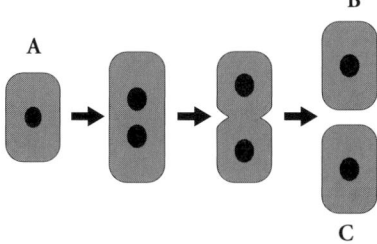

   In this diagram, cell A is undergoing mitosis. If cell A has 6 chromosomes, how many chromosomes will the resulting cells B and C have? **B2.1c**

   A none

   B 3 each

   C 6 each

   D 12 each

4. What is the main function of messenger RNA? **B2.r6b**

   A to build proteins out of amino acids

   B to transfer genetic code into the cytoplasm

   C to copy DNA during mitosis

   D to activate polymers that initiate fission

5.

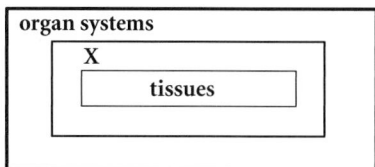

   This figure represents some levels of structural and functional organization in multicellular organisms. Which term fits in the box marked "X"? **L2.p1D**

   A cells

   B organelles

   C organs

   D organisms

6. Stem cells can form many kinds of cells. In contrast, most body cells cannot form different types of cells. For example, skin cells can only make skin cells, and nerve cells only make nerve cells. Which statement best explains why skin cells will never become nerve cells? **B2.1d**

   A Each type of cell gets a different message from the central DNA, which is stored in DNA cells.

   B Each type of cell has only the part of the DNA necessary for making that type of cell.

   C Each cell type is determined by messages sent from the brain, which directs development.

   D Both types of cells have the same DNA, but each cell uses only part of the DNA message.

BIOZINE *at* CLASSZONE.COM

INTERNET MAGAZINE

Go online for the latest biology news and updates on all BioZine articles.

Expanding the Textbook

News Feeds

- Science Daily
- CNN
- BBC

Careers

Bio Bytes

Opinion Poll

Strange Biology

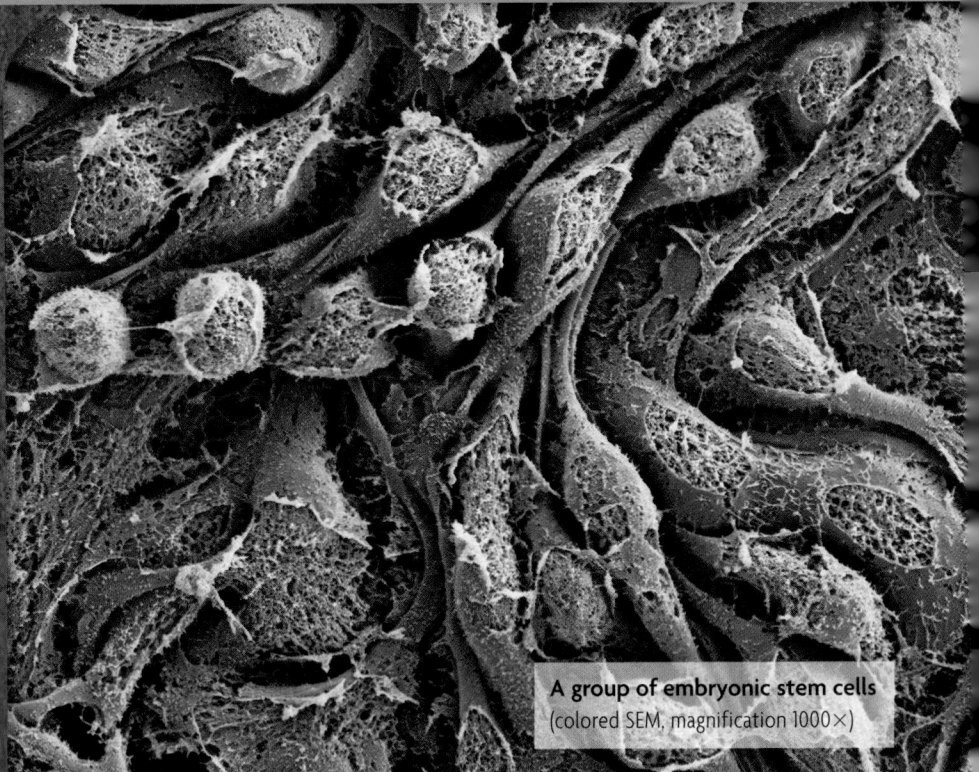

A group of embryonic stem cells
(colored SEM, magnification 1000×)

Stem Cell Research— Potential Solutions, Practical Challenges

A news program asks viewers to vote online: "Should stem cell research be banned? Yes or no?" Some people claim that stem cell therapy will revolutionize medicine. Others believe that some types of stem cell research violate ethical standards and are not justified by the potential benefits. Between these two positions exists a wide range of ideas about what is or is not acceptable. Would you know how to vote?

Using Stem Cells

Stem cells are undifferentiated cells that can regenerate themselves and develop into specialized types of cells. Stem cell research offers the hope of understanding basic cell processes and treating or even curing many dreaded diseases. However, a lot of technical challenges must be overcome before stem cell therapy is a realistic option, and ethical issues continue to surround stem cell research.

Potential Benefits

Stem cell research offers many potential benefits.

- Studying adult stem cells may help scientists better understand how tissues develop and what goes wrong when those tissues become diseased.

- A better understanding of the properties of stem cells may give scientists more information about how cancer cells replace themselves and thus helps scientists develop more targeted cancer therapies.

- Stem cells could be used to grow human tissues to test the effects of drugs and chemicals.

- Stem cells may be used to replace healthy cells that are killed by radiation treatment for cancer.

- Stem cells may be used to replace tissues. For example, chemotherapy kills blood-producing cells in bone marrow. Many chemotherapy patients have marrow taken before treatment that is later reinjected into the patient after treatment. However, the marrow could have cancer cells. The use of blood-producing stem cells in place of bone marrow transplants would remove this danger.

TECHNOLOGY

Somatic Cell Nuclear Transfer

Somatic cell nuclear transfer (SCNT), also called therapeutic cloning, is a method for obtaining stem cells that has been used to clone animals. The process is still under development, however, and it has not yet been used to produce human stem cells. SCNT offers the hope of using a patient's own DNA to produce stem cells that can form many types of specialized cells. The use of stem cells that are genetically identical to a patient would decrease that person's risk of cell rejection and the need for drugs to suppress the immune system. Many SCNT studies have been done in mice; the diagram to the right shows how the SCNT process might be applied in human cells.

1 An unfertilized egg is taken from a female's body, and the nucleus—containing the DNA—is removed. A cell is then taken from a patient's body. The nucleus is removed and inserted into the egg.

2 The egg is given a mild electrical stimulation, which makes it divide. The DNA comes from the patient's nucleus, and the materials needed for division come from the egg.

3 The stem cells could then be cultured and caused to differentiate into any tissue or organ needed by the patient.

human egg cell

DNA

body cell from patient

1

The egg cell DNA is extracted and discarded.

The DNA from the body cell is extracted to be used, and the rest is discarded.

2

heart cells

red blood cells

3

spinal cord cells

insulin producing cells

neurons

An organ or tissue can be transplanted into a patient without rejection.

Once a stem cell line is established, in theory it can continue to grow indefinitely. Researchers could use these cell lines without having to harvest more stem cells. The cell lines also could be frozen and shipped to other researchers around the world.

Read More >> *at* CLASSZONE.COM

Technical Challenges

Adult stem cells have been used therapeutically for years in the form of bone marrow transplants. Nevertheless, many technical challenges must still be overcome before stem cells can be used to treat a wide range of disorders. Examples are highlighted below.

Supply Stem cells can be taken from a variety of sources, including an embryo, a patient, a patient's relative, or an established stem cell line. Each source presents unique challenges. Established cell lines may seem like the obvious choice, but some scientists are concerned that these cells have built up a lot of mutations as they have undergone thousands of divisions.

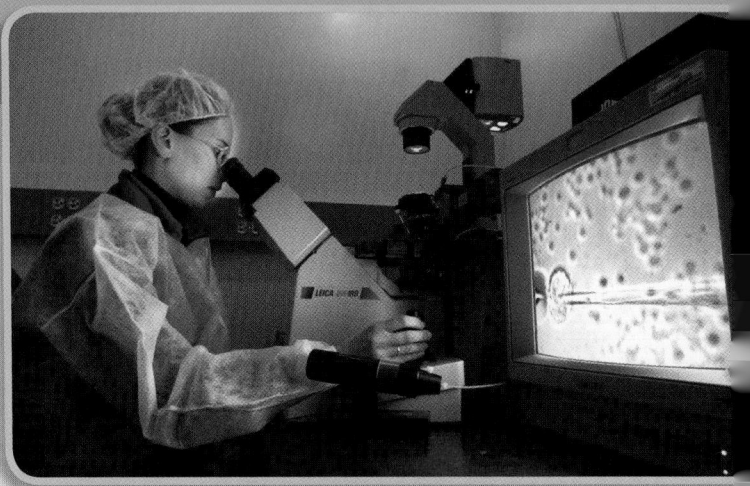

This researcher is micro-injecting mouse stem cells into fertilized mouse eggs to be used in drug research.

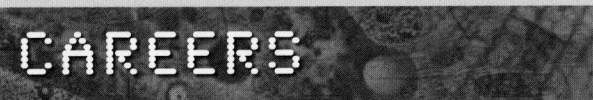

Cell Biologist in Action

DR. GAIL MARTIN	
TITLE Professor, Anatomy, University of California, San Francisco	
EDUCATION Ph. D., Molecular Biology, University of California, Berkeley	

In 1974 Dr. Gail Martin was working at the University College in London when she made a huge advance. She developed a way to grow stem cells in a petri dish. These fragile cells were hard to work with, so Dr. Martin's breakthrough removed a big obstacle to stem cell research. Seven years later, she made another key discovery while working in her own laboratory at the University of California at San Francisco (UCSF) in her native United States—how to harvest stem cells from mouse embryos. Her work has helped other scientists develop ways to harvest stem cells from human embryos and explore their use in treating disorders.

   Dr. Martin likes to point out that her work shows how small advances in basic biology can pay off years later in unexpected ways. She states that many people focus on cures for specific diseases, not realizing that these cures "may come from basic research in seemingly unrelated areas. What is really going to be important 20 years from now isn't clear."

Read More >> *at* CLASSZONE.COM

Transplantation into the target area The delivery of stem cells to targeted tissues can be complex, especially if the tissues are deep inside the body. And once delivered, stem cells must "learn" to work with other cells. For instance, inserted cardiac cells must beat in unison with a patient's heart cells to be effective.

Prevention of rejection Stem cells may be rejected if a patient's body sees them as foreign. This problem can remain even when certain identifying proteins are removed from the cells' membranes. The development of SCNT technology in humans could help solve this problem so that patients would not have to take drugs to suppress their immune system.

Suppression of tumor formation By their very nature, stem cells remain undifferentiated and continue to divide for long periods of time. When transplanted into an organism, many embryonic stem cells tend to form tumors. This risk must be removed before they can be used therapeutically.

Unanswered Questions

Stem cell research and therapy do not only involve questions of what we can do. They also involve questions about what we should do, who should benefit, and who should pay.

- Should human embryos be a source of stem cells?
- How can scientists protect their work when patent laws vary from country to country?
- How should stem cell research be funded?
- How can the benefits of stem cell research best be shared by all people, regardless of income?
- Should insurance cover costly stem cell procedures?

Read More >> *at* CLASSZONE.COM

UNIT 3

Genetics

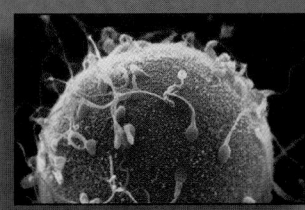

CHAPTER 6
Meiosis and Mendel   166

CHAPTER 7
Extending Mendelian Genetics   198

CHAPTER 8
From DNA to Proteins   224

CHAPTER 9
Frontiers of Biotechnology   262

BIOZINE

INTERNET MAGAZINE
**Medical Technology—
The Genetic Forefront**   292

TECHNOLOGY Biochips
CAREER   Cancer Geneticist

Meiosis and Mendel

KEY CONCEPTS

6.1 Chromosomes and Meiosis

Gametes have half the number of chromosomes that body cells have.

6.2 Process of Meiosis

During meiosis, diploid cells undergo two cell divisions that result in haploid cells.

6.3 Mendel and Heredity

Mendel's research showed that traits are inherited as discrete units.

6.4 Traits, Genes, and Alleles

Genes encode proteins that produce a diverse range of traits.

6.5 Traits and Probability

The inheritance of traits follows the rules of probability.

6.6 Meiosis and Genetic Variation

Independent assortment and crossing over during meiosis result in genetic diversity.

Online BIOLOGY CLASSZONE.COM

Animated BIOLOGY

View animated chapter concepts.
- Meiosis
- Genotypes and Phenotypes
- Breeding Mutations in Fruit Flies
- Mendel's Experiment

BIOZINE

Keep current with biology news.
- Featured stories
- News feeds
- Strange Biology

RESOURCE CENTER

Get more information on
- Chromosomes
- Gregor Mendel
- Sexual Reproduction
- Heredity

colored SEM; magnification 1300×

What makes you who you are?

Connecting CONCEPTS

The human egg and sperm cells (above) are the result of meiosis, a process that reduces chromosome number by half. Millions of sperm could potentially fertilize the egg, but only one actually succeeds. The fusion of egg and sperm triggers a series of events that lead to the development of a healthy new organism who will display features of both the mother and the father.

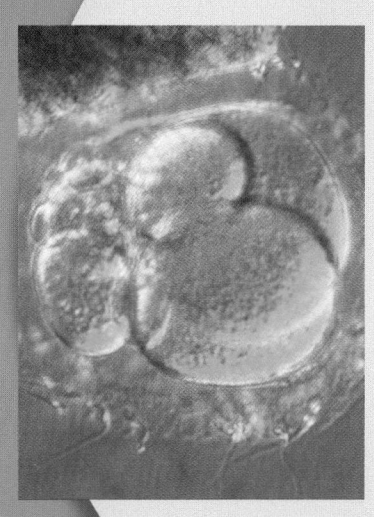

Receptors This micrograph (left) shows a four-cell human embryo surrounded by a matrix of proteins and sugars. This matrix originally surrounded the egg and acted as a receptor for sperm cells from organisms of the same species. For example, a cow sperm cannot bind to a mouse egg. When a sperm passes through the matrix and binds to the egg membrane, the matrix hardens, which blocks other sperm from binding. (colored LM; magnification 450×)

6.1 Chromosomes and Meiosis

KEY CONCEPT Gametes have half the number of chromosomes that body cells have.

MAIN IDEAS

- You have body cells and gametes.
- Your cells have autosomes and sex chromosomes.
- Body cells are diploid; gametes are haploid.

VOCABULARY

somatic cell, p. 168
gamete, p. 168
homologous chromosome, p. 169
autosome, p. 169
sex chromosome, p. 169

sexual reproduction, p. 170
fertilization, p. 170
diploid, p. 170
haploid, p. 170
meiosis, p. 170

MICHIGAN STANDARDS

L4.p1A Compare and contrast the differences between sexual and asexual reproduction. (prerequisite)

B4.3A Compare and contrast the processes of cell division (mitosis and meiosis), particularly as those processes relate to production of new cells and to passing on genetic information between generations.

TAKING NOTES

Make a two-column table to keep track of the vocabulary in this chapter.

Term	Definition
somatic cell	
gamete	

Connect Perhaps you are familiar with the saying, "Everything old is new again." This phrase usually indicates that a past style is again current. However, it applies equally well to you. The fusion of a single egg and sperm cell resulted in the complex creature that is you. There's never been anyone quite like you. And yet the DNA that directs your cells came from your mother and father. And their DNA came from their mother and father, and so on and so on. In this chapter, you will examine the processes that went into making you who you are.

MAIN IDEA
You have body cells and gametes.

You have many types of specialized cells in your body, but they can be divided into two major groups: somatic cells and germ cells. **Somatic cells** (soh-MAT-ihk), also called body cells, make up most of your body tissues and organs. For example, your spleen, kidneys, and eyeballs are all made entirely of body cells. DNA in your body cells is not passed on to your children. Germ cells, in contrast, are cells in your reproductive organs, the ovaries or the testes, that develop into gametes. **Gametes** are sex cells—ova, or eggs, in the female, and spermatozoa, or sperm cells, in the male. DNA in your gametes can be passed on to your children.

Each species has a characteristic number of chromosomes per cell. This number is typically given for body cells, not for gametes. Chromosome number does not seem to be related to the complexity of an organism. For example, yeast have 32 chromosomes, which come in 16 pairs. The fruit flies commonly used in genetic experiments have 8 chromosomes, which come in 4 pairs. A fern holds the record for the most chromosomes—more than 1200. Each of your body cells contains a set of 46 chromosomes, which come in 23 pairs. These cells are genetically identical to each other unless mutations have occurred. As you learned in Chapter 5, cells within an organism differ from each other because different genes are expressed, not because they have different genes.

Identify Which cell type makes up the brain?

MAIN IDEA
Your cells have autosomes and sex chromosomes.

Suppose you had 23 pairs of gloves. You would have a total of 46 gloves that you could divide into two sets, 23 right and 23 left. Similarly, your body cells have 23 pairs of chromosomes for a total of 46 that can be divided into two sets: 23 from your mother and 23 from your father. Just as you use both gloves when it's cold outside, your cells use both sets of chromosomes to function properly.

Together, each pair of chromosomes is referred to as a homologous pair. In this context, *homologous* means "having the same structure." **Homologous chromosomes** are two chromosomes—one inherited from the mother, one from the father—that have the same length and general appearance. More importantly, these chromosomes have copies of the same genes, although the two copies may differ. For example, if you have a gene that influences blood cholesterol levels on chromosome 8, you will have one copy from your mother and one copy from your father. It is possible that one of these copies is associated with high cholesterol levels, while the other is associated with low cholesterol levels. For convenience, scientists have assigned a number to each pair of homologous chromosomes, ordered from largest to smallest. As **FIGURE 6.1** shows, the largest pair of chromosomes is number 1, the next largest pair is number 2, and so forth.

Collectively, chromosome pairs 1 through 22 make up your **autosomes,** chromosomes that contain genes for characteristics not directly related to the sex of an organism. But what about the 23rd chromosome pair?

Most sexually reproducing species also have **sex chromosomes** that directly control the development of sexual characteristics. Humans have two very different sex chromosomes, X and Y. How sex is determined varies by species. In all mammals, including humans, an organism's sex is determined by the XY system. An organism with two X chromosomes is female. An organism with one X and one Y chromosome is male. Sex chromosomes make up your 23rd pair of chromosomes. Although the X and Y chromosomes pair with each other, they are not homologous. The X chromosome is the larger sex chromosome and contains numerous genes, including many that are unrelated to sexual characteristics. The Y chromosome is the sex chromosome that contains genes that direct the development of the testes and other male traits. It is the smallest chromosome and carries the fewest genes.

Summarize Are homologous chromosomes identical to each other? Explain.

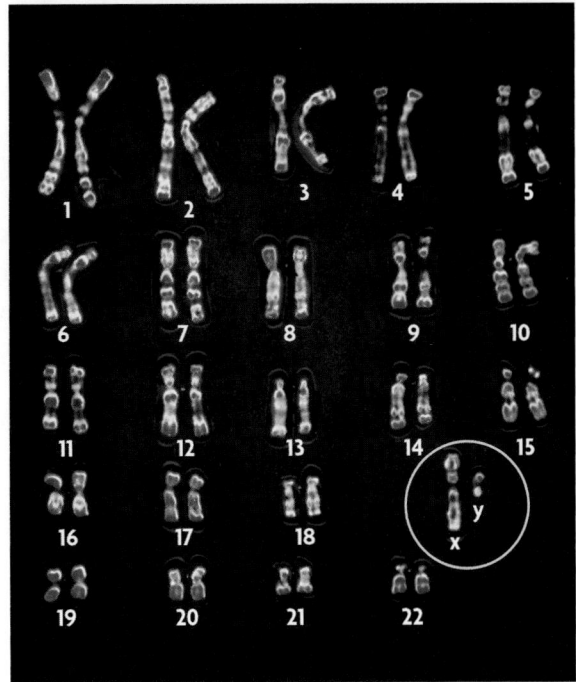

FIGURE 6.1 Human DNA is organized into two sets of 23 chromosomes. Each set contains 22 autosomes and 1 sex chromosome. Females have two X chromosomes. Males have an X and a Y chromosome (circled). (colored LM; magnification 4400×)

"The parents are both geneticists."

MAIN IDEA
Body cells are diploid; gametes are haploid.

Sexual reproduction involves the fusion of two gametes that results in off-spring that are a genetic mixture of both parents. The actual fusion of an egg and a sperm cell is called **fertilization.** When fertilization occurs, the nuclei of the egg and sperm cell fuse to form one nucleus. This new nucleus must have the correct number of chromosomes for a healthy new organism to develop. Therefore, the egg and sperm cell need only half the usual number of chromosomes—one chromosome from each homologous pair.

Diploid and Haploid Cells
Body cells and gametes have different numbers of chromosomes. Your body cells are diploid. **Diploid** (DIHP-LOYD) means a cell has two copies of each chromosome: one copy from the mother, and one copy from the father. Diploid cells can be represented as $2n$. In humans, the diploid chromosome number is 46.

Gametes are not diploid cells; they are haploid cells, represented as n. **Haploid** (HAP-LOYD) means that a cell has only one copy of each chromosome. Each human egg or sperm cell has 22 autosomes and 1 sex chromosome. In the egg, the sex chromosome is always an X chromosome. In the sperm cell, the sex chromosome can be an X chromosome or a Y chromosome. The reason for this difference will be discussed in the following sections.

Maintaining the correct number of chromosomes is important to the survival of all organisms. Typically, a change in chromosome number is harmful. However, increasing the number of sets of chromosomes can, on occasion, give rise to a new species. The fertilization of nonhaploid gametes has played an important role in plant evolution by rapidly making new species with more than two sets of chromosomes. For example, some plants have four copies of each chromosome, a condition called tetraploidy ($4n$). This type of event has occurred in many groups of plants, but it is very rare in animals.

Meiosis
Germ cells in your reproductive organs undergo the process of meiosis to form gametes. **Meiosis** (my-OH-sihs) is a form of nuclear division that divides a diploid cell into haploid cells. This process is essential for sexual reproduction. The details of meiosis will be presented in the next section. But **FIGURE 6.2** highlights some differences between mitosis and meiosis in advance to help you keep these two processes clear in your mind.

VISUAL VOCAB

Diploid cells have two copies of each chromosome: one copy from the mother and one from the father.

Body cells are diploid ($2n$).

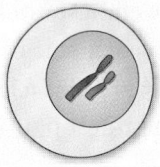

Gametes (sex cells) are haploid (n).

Haploid cells have only one copy of each chromosome.

VOCABULARY

Diploid comes from the Greek word *diplous*, which means "double". *Haploid* comes from the Greek word *haplous*, which means "single."

Connecting CONCEPTS

Plant Life Cycles As you will learn in **Chapter 22**, all plants complete their life cycle by alternating between two phases: diploid and haploid. During the diploid phase, plants make spores. During the haploid phase, plants make gametes.

FIGURE 6.2 Comparing Mitosis and Meiosis

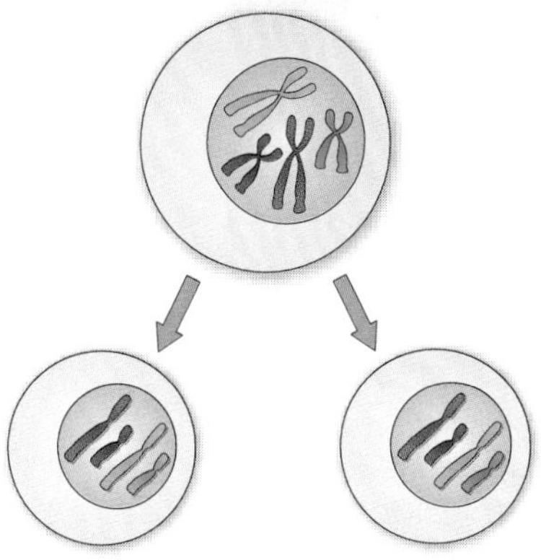

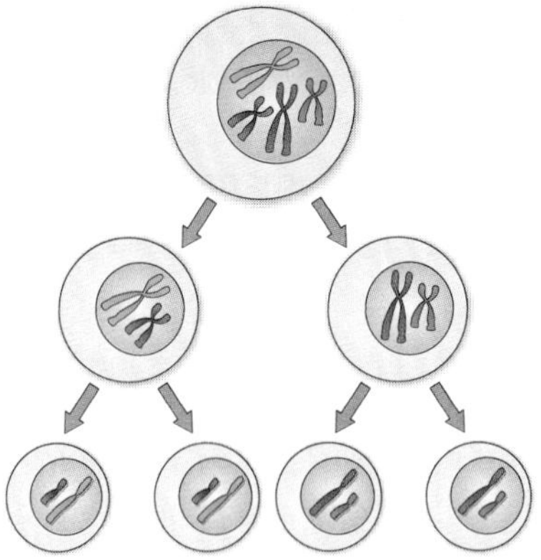

MITOSIS		MEIOSIS	
	Produces genetically identical cells	Produces genetically unique cells	
	Results in diploid cells	Results in haploid cells	
	Takes place throughout an organism's lifetime	Takes place only at certain times in an organism's life cycle	
	Involved in asexual reproduction	Involved in sexual reproduction	

Compare Using the diagrams above, explain how you think the process of meiosis differs from mitosis.

In Chapter 5 you learned about mitosis, another form of nuclear division. Recall that mitosis is a process that occurs in body cells. It helps produce daughter cells that are genetically identical to the parent cell. In cells undergoing mitosis, DNA is copied once and divided once. Both the parent cell and the daughter cells are diploid. Mitosis is used for development, growth, and repair in all types of organisms. It is also used for reproduction in asexually reproducing eukaryotes.

In contrast, meiosis occurs in germ cells to produce gametes. This process is sometimes called a "reduction division" because it reduces chromosome number by half. In cells undergoing meiosis, DNA is copied once but divided twice. Meiosis makes genetically unique haploid cells from a diploid cell. These haploid cells then undergo more processing in the ovaries or testes, finally forming mature gametes.

Apply Why is it important that gametes are haploid cells?

6.1 ASSESSMENT

ONLINE QUIZ ClassZone.com

REVIEWING ▶ MAIN IDEAS

1. Where are germ cells located in the human body?

2. What is the difference between an **autosome** and a **sex chromosome**?

3. Is the cell that results from **fertilization** a **haploid** or **diploid** cell? Explain.

CRITICAL THINKING

4. **Infer** Does mitosis or **meiosis** occur more frequently in your body? Explain your answer.

5. **Analyze** Do you think the Y chromosome contains genes that are critical for an organism's survival? Explain your reasoning.

Connecting CONCEPTS

6. **Telomeres** The ends of DNA molecules form telomeres that help keep the ends of chromosomes from sticking to each other. Why might this be especially important in germ cells, which go through meiosis and make haploid **gametes**?

DATA ANALYSIS
ClassZone.com

Genetic Data

Bar graphs use bars to show data. In a bar graph, the independent variable is usually graphed on the *x*-axis and the dependent variable is usually graphed on the *y*-axis. Both axes are labeled with the name and unit of the variable.

EXAMPLE

The bar graph below contains data about the frequency of some genetic disorders in the human population. Each of the disorders listed is the result of nondisjunction, the failure of two chromosomes to separate properly during meiosis. This results in one extra chromosome or one less chromosome being passed on to the offspring.

For each syndrome on the *x*-axis, the bar extends vertically on the *y*-axis to represent the incidence per 100,000 births. For example, out of 100,000 births, 111 children are born with Down syndrome.

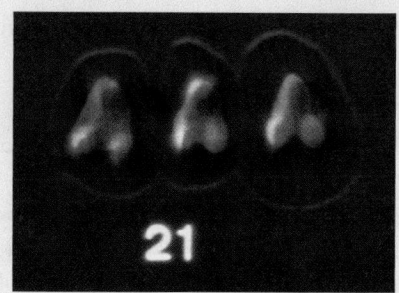

In most cases, Down syndrome results from having an extra chromosome 21.
(colored LM; magnification 2000×)

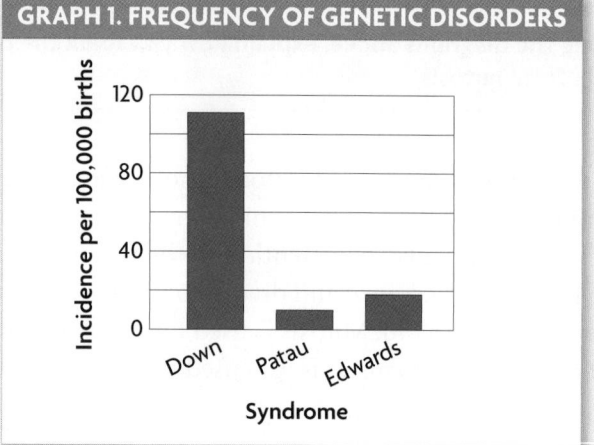

GRAPH 1. FREQUENCY OF GENETIC DISORDERS

Source: U.S. National Library of Medicine

INTERPRET A BAR GRAPH

The bar graph below contains data about the diploid number of chromosomes in different organisms.

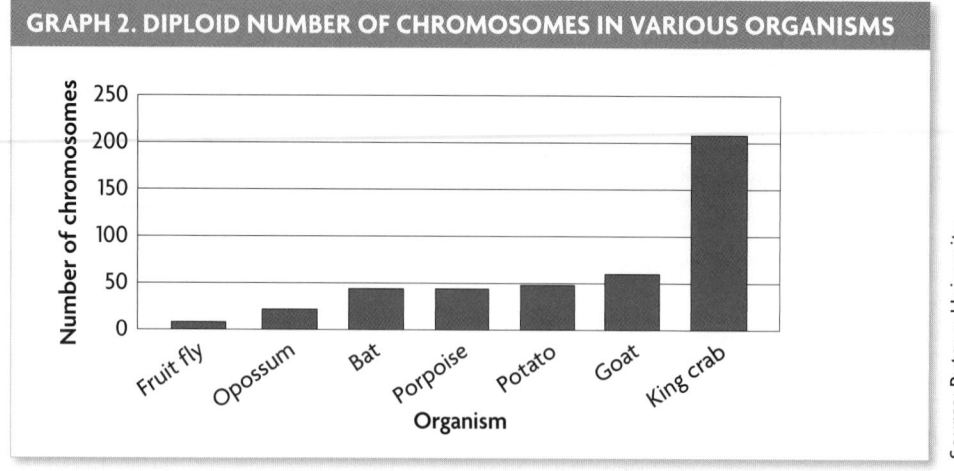

GRAPH 2. DIPLOID NUMBER OF CHROMOSOMES IN VARIOUS ORGANISMS

Source: Rutgers University

1. **Analyze** Which organism has the greatest number of chromosomes? The least?

2. **Evaluate** Does chromosome number appear to correlate to the type of organism? Explain.

3. **Hypothesize** Do you think there is an upper limit to chromosome number? Explain.

Process of Meiosis

KEY CONCEPT During meiosis, diploid cells undergo two cell divisions that result in haploid cells.

▶ MAIN IDEAS

- Cells go through two rounds of division in meiosis.
- Haploid cells develop into mature gametes.

VOCABULARY

gametogenesis, p. 176

sperm, p. 176

egg, p. 176

polar body, p. 176

MICHIGAN STANDARDS

B4.3A Compare and contrast the processes of cell division (mitosis and meiosis), particularly as those processes relate to production of new cells and to passing on genetic information between generations.

Connect Sometimes division is difficult, such as splitting the bill at a restaurant or dividing people into teams for basketball. Luckily, understanding how meiosis divides chromosomes between cells is not that hard. Meiosis begins with a diploid cell that has already undergone DNA replication. The cell copies the chromosomes once and divides them twice, making four haploid cells.

▶ MAIN IDEA

Cells go through two rounds of division in meiosis.

Meiosis is a form of nuclear division that creates four haploid cells from one diploid cell. This process involves two rounds of cell division—meiosis I and meiosis II. Each round of cell division has four phases, which are similar to those in mitosis. To keep the two processes distinct in your mind, focus on the big picture. Pay attention to how meiosis reduces chromosome number and creates genetic diversity.

Homologous Chromosomes and Sister Chromatids

To understand meiosis, you need to distinguish between homologous chromosomes and sister chromatids. As **FIGURE 6.3** shows, homologous chromosomes are two separate chromosomes: one from your mother, one from your

Connecting CONCEPTS

Mitosis As you learned in **Chapter 5**, a condensed, duplicated chromosome is made of two chromatids. Sister chromatids separate during anaphase in mitosis.

TAKING NOTES

Draw a Venn diagram like the one below to summarize the similarities and differences between meiosis I and meiosis II.

Meiosis I — Meiosis II

divides homologous chromosomes / chromosomes condense / divides sister chromatids

father. Homologous chromosomes are very similar to each other, since they have the same length and carry the same genes. But they are not copies of each other. In contrast, each half of a duplicated chromosome is called a chromatid. Together, the two chromatids are called sister chromatids. Thus, *sister chromatids* refers to the duplicated chromosomes that remain attached (by the centromere). Homologous chromosomes are divided in meiosis I. Sister chromatids are not divided until meiosis II.

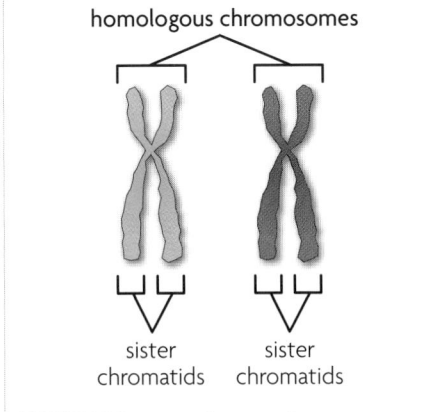

homologous chromosomes

sister chromatids   sister chromatids

FIGURE 6.3 Homologous chromosomes (shown duplicated) are two separate chromosomes—one inherited from the mother, and one from the father.

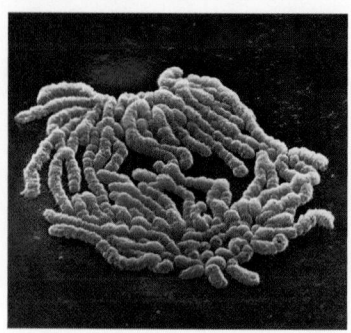

FIGURE 6.4 Homologous chromosomes separate during anaphase I. (colored SEM; magnification 2200×)

Meiosis I

Before meiosis begins, DNA has already been copied. Meiosis I divides homologous chromosomes, producing two haploid cells with duplicated chromosomes. Like mitosis, scientists describe meiosis in terms of phases, illustrated in **FIGURE 6.5** below. The figure is simplified, showing only four chromosomes.

1 **Prophase I** Early in meiosis, the nuclear membrane breaks down, the centrosomes and centrioles move to opposite sides of the cell, and spindle fibers start to assemble. The duplicated chromosomes condense, and homologous chromosomes pair up. They appear to pair up precisely, gene for gene, down their entire length. The sex chromosomes also pair with each other, and some regions of their DNA appear to line up as well.

2 **Metaphase I** The homologous chromosome pairs are randomly lined up along the middle of the cell by spindle fibers. The result is that 23 chromosomes—some from the father, some from the mother—are lined up along each side of the cell equator. This arrangement mixes up the chromosomal combinations and helps create and maintain genetic diversity. Since human cells have 23 pairs of chromosomes, meiosis may result in 2^{23}, or 8,388,608, possible combinations of chromosomes.

3 **Anaphase I** Next, the paired homologous chromosomes separate from each other and move toward opposite sides of the cell. The sister chromatids remain together during this step and throughout meiosis I.

4 **Telophase I** The nuclear membrane forms again in some species, the spindle fibers disassemble, and the cell undergoes cytokinesis. The end result is two cells that each have a unique combination of 23 duplicated chromosomes coming from both parents.

FIGURE 6.5 Meiosis

Meiosis I divides homologous chromosomes.

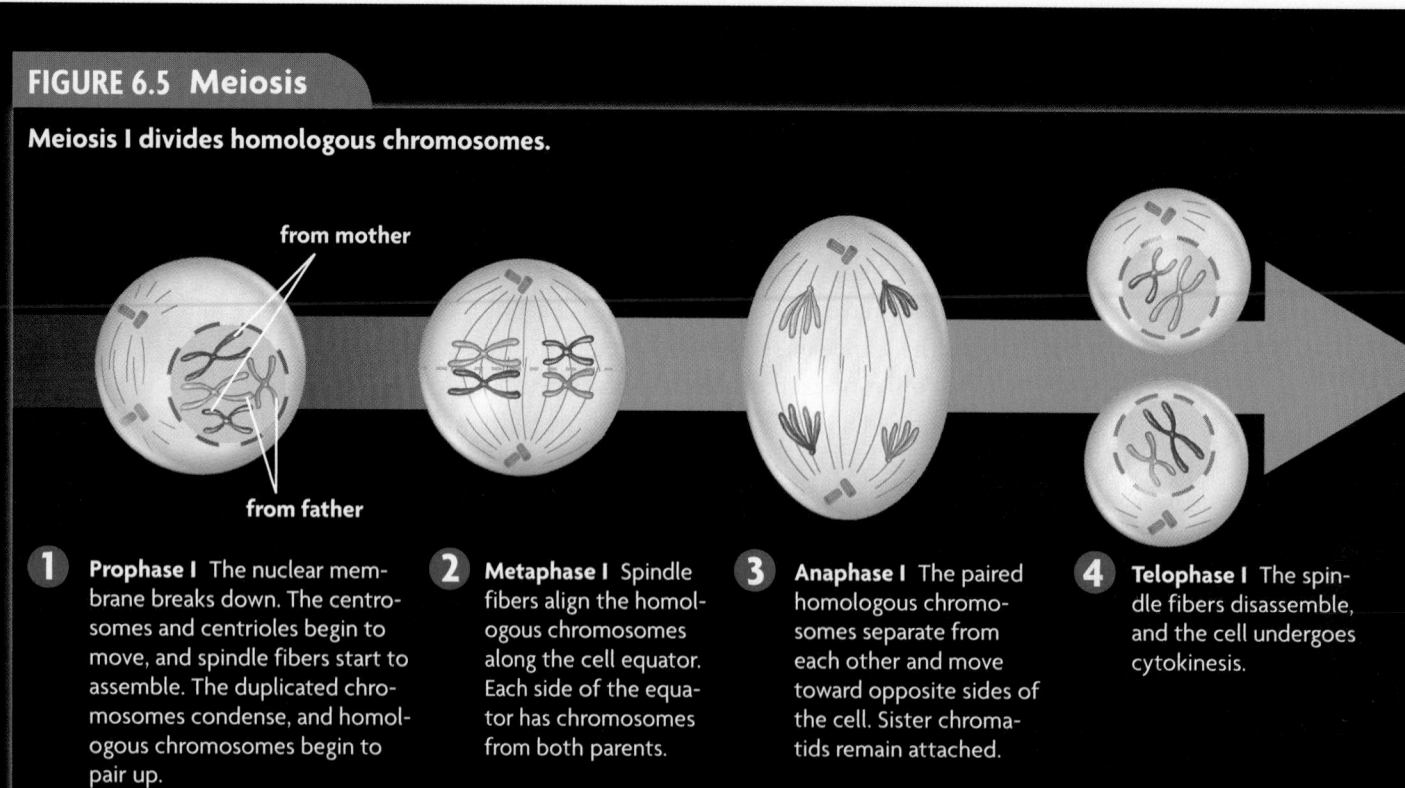

from mother

from father

1 **Prophase I** The nuclear membrane breaks down. The centrosomes and centrioles begin to move, and spindle fibers start to assemble. The duplicated chromosomes condense, and homologous chromosomes begin to pair up.

2 **Metaphase I** Spindle fibers align the homologous chromosomes along the cell equator. Each side of the equator has chromosomes from both parents.

3 **Anaphase I** The paired homologous chromosomes separate from each other and move toward opposite sides of the cell. Sister chromatids remain attached.

4 **Telophase I** The spindle fibers disassemble, and the cell undergoes cytokinesis.

Meiosis II

Meiosis II divides sister chromatids, and results in undoubled chromosomes. The following description of this process applies to both of the cells produced in meiosis I. Note that DNA is not copied again between these two stages.

5 **Prophase II** The nuclear membrane breaks down, centrosomes and centrioles move to opposite sides of the cell, and spindle fibers assemble.

6 **Metaphase II** Spindle fibers align the 23 chromosomes at the cell equator. Each chromosome still has two sister chromatids at this stage.

7 **Anaphase II** Next, the sister chromatids are pulled apart from each other and move to opposite sides of the cell.

8 **Telophase II** Finally, nuclear membranes form around each set of chromosomes at opposite ends of the cell, the spindle fibers break apart, and the cell undergoes cytokinesis. The end result is four haploid cells with a combination of chromosomes from both the mother and father.

Now that you've seen how meiosis works, let's review some key differences between the processes of meiosis and mitosis.

- Meiosis has two cell divisions. Mitosis has only one cell division.
- During meiosis, homologous chromosomes pair up along the cell equator. During mitosis, homologous chromosomes never pair up.
- In anaphase I of meiosis, sister chromatids remain together. In anaphase of mitosis, sister chromatids separate.
- Meiosis results in haploid cells. Mitosis results in diploid cells.

Contrast **What is the major difference between metaphase I and metaphase II?**

Connecting CONCEPTS

Cytokinesis As you learned in **Chapter 5**, cytokinesis is the division of the cell cytoplasm. This process is the same in cells undergoing either mitosis or meiosis.

Animated BIOLOGY
Watch meiosis in action at ClassZone.com.

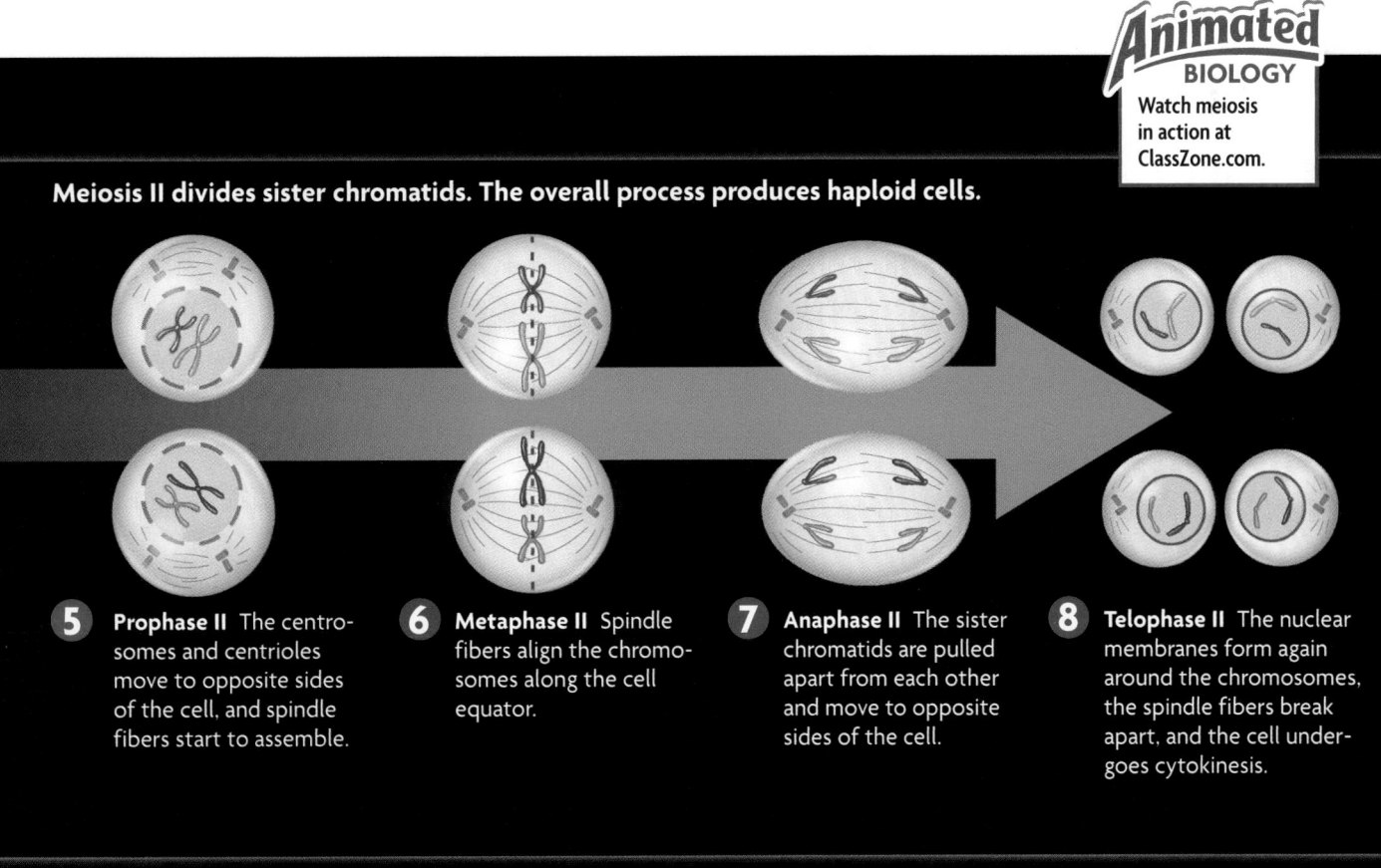

Meiosis II divides sister chromatids. The overall process produces haploid cells.

5 **Prophase II** The centrosomes and centrioles move to opposite sides of the cell, and spindle fibers start to assemble.

6 **Metaphase II** Spindle fibers align the chromosomes along the cell equator.

7 **Anaphase II** The sister chromatids are pulled apart from each other and move to opposite sides of the cell.

8 **Telophase II** The nuclear membranes form again around the chromosomes, the spindle fibers break apart, and the cell undergoes cytokinesis.

▶ MAIN IDEA

Haploid cells develop into mature gametes.

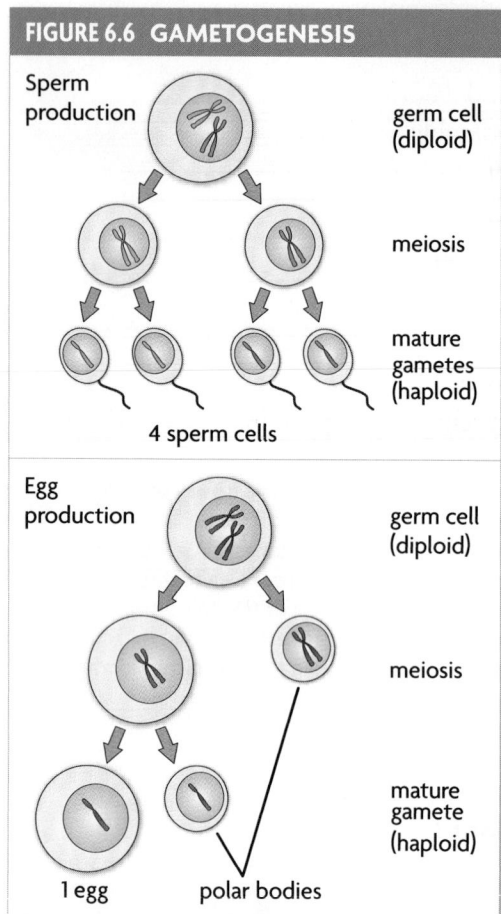

FIGURE 6.6 GAMETOGENESIS

Sperm production

germ cell (diploid)

meiosis

mature gametes (haploid)

4 sperm cells

Egg production

germ cell (diploid)

meiosis

mature gamete (haploid)

1 egg   polar bodies

NSTA SCiLINKS
scilinks.org
For more about meiosis, go to scilinks.org.
Keycode: MLB006

Haploid cells are the end result of meiosis. Yet these cells are incapable of fertilization until they go through more changes to form mature gametes. **Gametogenesis** (guh-MEE-tuh-JEHN-ih-sihs) is the production of gametes. As **FIGURE 6.6** shows, gametogenesis includes both meiosis and other changes that produce a mature cell. The final stages of gametogenesis differ between the sexes.

The **sperm** cell, the male gamete, is much smaller than the **egg,** the female gamete. The sperm cell's main contribution to an embryo is DNA. Yet it must swim to an egg to fertilize it, so the ability to move is critical. Sperm formation starts with a round cell and ends by making a streamlined cell that can move rapidly. During this process, significant changes occur. DNA is tightly packed and much of the cytoplasm is lost, forming a compact head. The sperm cell develops a whiplike flagellum and connecting neck region packed with mitochondria that drive the cell. Other changes also take place, such as the addition of new proteins to the cell membrane.

The formation of an egg is a complicated process, as you will read about in greater detail in Chapter 34. It begins before birth, inside the developing body of a female embryo, and is not finished until that egg is fertilized by a sperm many years later. The process includes periods of active development and long periods of inactivity.

An egg not only gives its share of DNA to an embryo but also contributes the organelles, molecular building blocks, and other materials an embryo needs to begin life. Only one of the four cells produced by each round of meiosis actually makes an egg. One cell—the egg—receives most of the organelles, cytoplasm, and nutrients. Many molecules are not evenly distributed throughout the egg's cytoplasm. This unequal distribution of molecules helps cells in the developing embryo to specialize. The other cells produced by meiosis become **polar bodies,** cells with little more than DNA that are eventually broken down. In many species, including humans, the polar body produced by meiosis I does not undergo meiosis II.

Apply   Briefly explain how a sperm cell's structure is related to its function.

6.2   ASSESSMENT

ONLINE QUIZ
ClassZone.com

REVIEWING ▶ MAIN IDEAS

1. How do homologous chromosomes differ from sister chromatids?

2. Explain why an **egg** is so much larger than a **sperm** cell.

CRITICAL THINKING

3. **Predict** If, during metaphase I, all 23 maternal chromosomes lined up on one side of the cell, would genetic diversity increase? Explain.

4. **Contrast** List the key differences between meiosis I and II.

Connecting CONCEPTS

5. **Cell Biology** Both mitosis and meiosis are types of nuclear division, but they result in different cell types. Describe how the steps of meiosis I differ from those of mitosis.

6.3 Mendel and Heredity

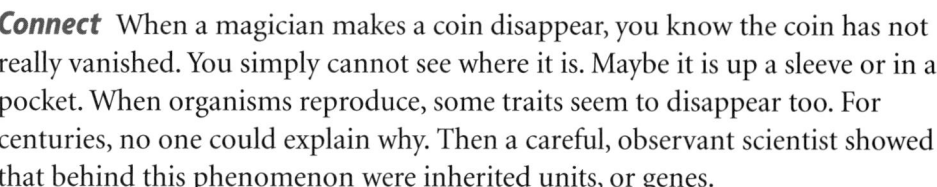

KEY CONCEPT Mendel's research showed that traits are inherited as discrete units.

MAIN IDEAS

- Mendel laid the groundwork for genetics.
- Mendel's data revealed patterns of inheritance.

VOCABULARY

trait, p. 177
genetics, p. 177
purebred, p. 178

cross, p. 178
law of segregation, p. 179

MICHIGAN STANDARDS

B1.2i Explain the progression of ideas and explanations that leads to science theories that are part of the current scientific consensus or core knowledge.

B4.1d Explain the genetic basis for Mendel's laws of segregation and independent assortment.

Connect When a magician makes a coin disappear, you know the coin has not really vanished. You simply cannot see where it is. Maybe it is up a sleeve or in a pocket. When organisms reproduce, some traits seem to disappear too. For centuries, no one could explain why. Then a careful, observant scientist showed that behind this phenomenon were inherited units, or genes.

MAIN IDEA
Mendel laid the groundwork for genetics.

When we think of how offspring resemble or differ from their parents, we typically refer to specific traits. **Traits** are distinguishing characteristics that are inherited, such as eye color, leaf shape, and tail length. Scientists recognized that traits are hereditary, or passed from one generation to the next, long before they understood how traits are passed on. **Genetics** is the study of biological inheritance patterns and variation in organisms.

The groundwork for much of our understanding of genetics was laid in the middle of the 1800s by an Austrian monk named Gregor Mendel, shown in **FIGURE 6.7**. Scientists of the time commonly thought parents' traits were blended in offspring, like mixing red and white paint to get pink paint. But this idea failed to explain how certain traits remained without being "diluted." Mendel, a shrewd mathematician, bred thousands of plants, carefully counting and recording his results. From his data, Mendel correctly predicted the results of meiosis long before chromosomes were discovered. He recognized that traits are inherited as discrete units from the parental generation, like different colored marbles mixed together that can still be picked out separately. By recognizing that organisms inherit two copies of each discrete unit, what we now call genes, Mendel also described how traits were passed between generations.

Connect Give two examples of traits not listed above.

MAIN IDEA
Mendel's data revealed patterns of inheritance.

Mendel studied plant variation in a monastery garden. He made three key choices about his experiments that played an important role in the development of his laws of inheritance: control over breeding, use of purebred plants, and observation of "either-or" traits that appeared in only two alternate forms.

FIGURE 6.7 Gregor Mendel is called "the father of genetics" for discovering hereditary units. The significance of his work went unrecognized for almost 40 years.

Gregor Mendel

FIGURE 6.8 MENDEL'S PROCESS

Mendel controlled the fertilization of his pea plants by removing the male parts, or stamens.

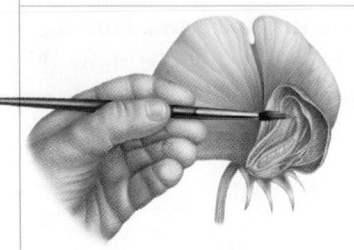

He then fertilized the female part, or pistil, with pollen from a different pea plant.

VOCABULARY

In Latin, the word *filius* means "son" and *filia* means "daughter."

Experimental Design

Mendel chose pea plants for his experiments because they reproduce quickly, and he could easily control how they mate. The sex organs of a plant are in its flowers, and pea flowers contain both male and female reproductive organs. In nature, the pea flower typically self-pollinates; that is, the plant mates with itself. If a line of plants has self-pollinated for long enough, that line becomes genetically uniform, or **purebred.** As a result, the offspring of purebred parents inherit all of the parent organisms' characteristics. Mendel was able to mate plants with specific traits by interrupting the self-pollination process. As you can see in **FIGURE 6.8,** he removed the male parts of flowers and fertilized the female parts with pollen that contained sperm cells from a different plant. Because he started with purebred plants, Mendel knew that any variations in offspring resulted from his experiments.

Mendel chose seven traits to follow: pea shape, pea color, pod shape, pod color, plant height, flower color, and flower position. All of these traits are simple "either-or" characteristics; they do not show intermediate features. The plant is tall or short. Its peas are wrinkled or round. What Mendel did not know was that most of the traits he had selected were controlled by genes on separate chromosomes. The selection of these particular traits played a crucial role in enabling Mendel to identify the patterns he observed.

Results

In genetics, the mating of two organisms is called a **cross.** An example of one of Mendel's crosses is highlighted in **FIGURE 6.9.** In this example, he crossed a purebred white-flowered pea plant with a purebred purple-flowered pea plant. These plants are the parental, or P, generation. The resulting offspring, called the first filial—or F_1—generation, all had purple flowers. The trait for white flowers seemed to disappear. When Mendel allowed the F_1 generation to self-fertilize, the resulting F_2 generation produced both plants with purple flowers and plants with white flowers. Therefore, the trait for white flowers had not disappeared; it had been hidden, or masked.

FIGURE 6.9 Mendel's Experimental Cross

Traits that were hidden when parental purebred flowers were crossed reappeared when the F_1 generation was allowed to self-pollinate.

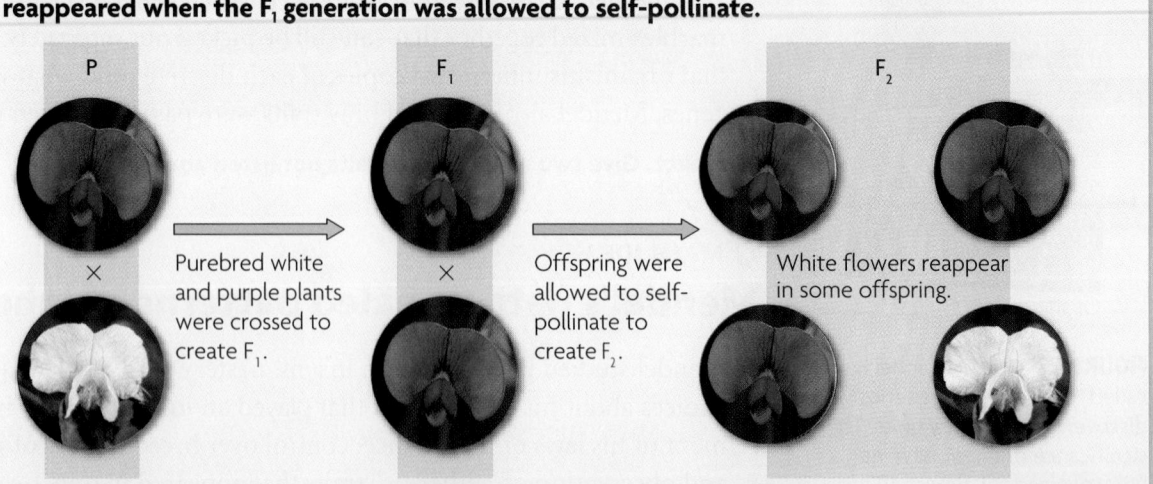

P

Purebred white and purple plants were crossed to create F_1.

F_1

Offspring were allowed to self-pollinate to create F_2.

F_2

White flowers reappear in some offspring.

Mendel did not cross only two plants, however; he crossed many plants. As a result, he was able to observe patterns. He noticed that each cross yielded similar ratios in the F_2 generation: about three-fourths of the plants had purple flowers, and about one-fourth had white flowers. A ratio is a comparison that tells how two or more things relate. This ratio can be expressed as 3:1 (read "three to one") of purple:white flowers. As you can see in **FIGURE 6.10**, Mendel's data show this approximately 3:1 ratio for each of his crosses.

FIGURE 6.10 MENDEL'S MONOHYBRID CROSS RESULTS			
F$_2$ TRAITS	**DOMINANT**	**RECESSIVE**	**RATIO**
Pea shape	5474 round	1850 wrinkled	2.96:1
Pea color	6022 yellow	2001 green	3.01:1
Flower color	705 purple	224 white	3.15:1
Pod shape	882 smooth	299 constricted	2.95:1
Pod color	428 green	152 yellow	2.82:1
Flower position	651 axial	207 terminal	3.14:1
Plant height	787 tall	277 short	2.84:1

Source: Mendel, *Abhandlungen* (1865).

Conclusions

From these observations, Mendel drew three important conclusions. He demonstrated that traits are inherited as discrete units, which explained why individual traits persisted without being blended or diluted over successive generations. Mendel's two other key conclusions are collectively called the **law of segregation,** or Mendel's first law.

- Organisms inherit two copies of each gene, one from each parent.
- Organisms donate only one copy of each gene in their gametes. Thus, the two copies of each gene segregate, or separate, during gamete formation.

Section 6.5 covers Mendel's second law, the law of independent assortment.

Infer **Explain why Mendel's choice of either-or characteristics aided his research.**

Connecting CONCEPTS

Meiosis As you learned in **Section 6.2,** during meiosis, homologous chromosomes pair up in prophase I and are separated in anaphase I. The overall process produces haploid cells that have a random assortment of chromosomes.

6.3 ASSESSMENT

ONLINE QUIZ
ClassZone.com

REVIEWING ▶ MAIN IDEAS

1. Mendel had no understanding of DNA as the genetic material, yet he was able to correctly predict how **traits** were passed between generations. What does Mendel's work in **genetics** show about the value of scientific observation?

2. Why is it important that Mendel began with **purebred** plants?

CRITICAL THINKING

3. **Analyze** Mendel saw purple flowers in the F_1 generation, but both purple and white flowers in the F_2. How did this help him see that traits are inherited as discrete units?

4. **Evaluate** If Mendel had examined only one trait, do you think he would have developed the **law of segregation**? Explain.

Connecting CONCEPTS

5. **Scientific Process** You have learned that scientific thinking involves observing, forming hypotheses, testing hypotheses, and analyzing data. Use examples from Mendel's scientific process to show how his work fit this pattern.

6.4 Traits, Genes, and Alleles

KEY CONCEPT Genes encode proteins that produce a diverse range of traits.

▶ MAIN IDEAS

- The same gene can have many versions.
- Genes influence the development of traits.

VOCABULARY

gene, p. 180
allele, p. 180
homozygous, p. 180
heterozygous, p. 180
genome, p. 181

genotype, p. 181
phenotype, p. 181
dominant, p. 181
recessive, p. 181

Connect Most things come in many forms. Bread can be wheat, white, or rye. Cars can be two-door, four-door, hatchback, or convertible. Even the variety of potatoes cannot be counted on two hands. Genes, too, come in many forms.

▶ MAIN IDEA

The same gene can have many versions.

As you have learned, Mendel's discrete units of heredity are now called genes. But what are genes? You can think of a **gene** as a piece of DNA that provides a set of instructions to a cell to make a certain protein. This definition is not precise, but it gives you the main idea. Each gene has a locus, a specific position on a pair of homologous chromosomes. Just as a house is a physical structure and an address tells where that house is located, you can think of the locus as the "address" that tells where a gene is located on a chromosome.

Most genes exist in many forms. In Mendel's experiments, the effects of these different forms were easy to see: yellow or green, round or wrinkled. An **allele** (uh-LEEL) is any of the alternative forms of a gene that may occur at a specific locus. Your cells have two alleles for each gene, one on each of the homologous chromosomes on which the locus for that gene is found. Each parent gives one allele. The two alleles may be the same, or they may be different. The term **homozygous** (HOH-moh-ZY-guhs) describes two of the same alleles at a specific locus. For example, both might code for white flowers. The term **heterozygous** (HEHT-uhr-uh-ZY-guhs) describes two different alleles at a specific locus. Thus, one might code for white flowers, the other for purple flowers.

Compare and Contrast Distinguish between the terms *locus* and *allele*.

VISUAL VOCAB

Homozygous alleles are identical to each other.

homozygous alleles

wrinkled   wrinkled

heterozygous alleles

wrinkled   round

Heterozygous alleles are different from each other.

▶ MAIN IDEA

Genes influence the development of traits.

You may have heard about the Human Genome Project. Its goal was to find out the sequence of the 3 billion nucleotide pairs that make up a human's genome. A **genome** is all of an organism's genetic material. Unless you have an identical twin, you have a unique genome that determines all of your traits. Some of your traits can be seen, such as the color of your eyes. Other traits cannot be seen, such as the exact chemical makeup of your eyeball.

In genetics, we often focus on a single trait or set of traits. A genome is all of an organism's genes, but a **genotype** (JEHN-uh-TYP) typically refers to the genetic makeup of a specific set of genes. The genotype of a pea plant includes both of the genes that code for flower color, even if one of these genes is masked. In contrast, the physical characteristics, or traits, of an individual organism make up its **phenotype** (FEE-nuh-TYP). A pea plant with purple flowers has a phenotype for purple flowers. The plant might have a hidden gene for white flowers, but that does not matter to its phenotype.

Dominant and Recessive Alleles

If an organism is heterozygous for a trait, which allele will be expressed? That is, if a plant has one allele for purple flowers and one for white flowers, what color will the flowers be? As Mendel learned, one allele may be dominant over another allele. A **dominant** allele is the allele that is expressed when two different alleles or two dominant alleles are present. A **recessive** allele is the allele that is only expressed when two copies are present. In Mendel's experiments, the allele for purple flowers was dominant to the allele for white flowers. All F_1 plants were purple even though they had only one allele for purple flowers.

VISUAL VOCAB
A **dominant** allele is expressed when two different alleles are present.

genotype   phenotype

wrinkled—recessive   —round dominant

genotype   phenotype

wrinkled—recessive   —wrinkled recessive

A **recessive** allele is expressed only when two copies are present.

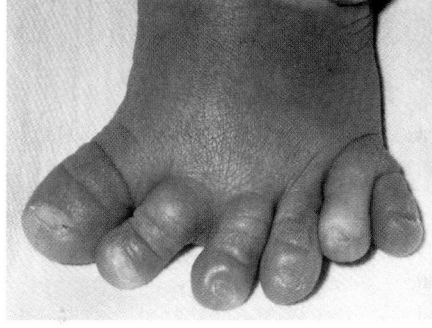

FIGURE 6.11 Polydactyly is the condition of having more than the typical number of fingers or toes. The allele for polydactyly is dominant.

Sometimes the word *dominant* is misunderstood. A dominant allele is not necessarily better or stronger than a recessive allele. It does not necessarily occur most often in the population. An allele is dominant in a heterozygote simply because it is expressed and the other allele is not.

Alleles are often represented on paper with individual letters. An organism's genotype for a trait can be shown with two letters—one per allele. Uppercase letters are used for dominant alleles, and lowercase letters are used for recessive alleles. For example, the dominant allele for height in pea plants is written as *T*, for tall. The recessive allele for short plants is written as *t*.

Connecting CONCEPTS

Exceptions to Mendel's Laws Mendel's theory of inheritance cannot explain all patterns of inheritance. As you will learn in **Chapter 7**, incomplete dominance, codominance, polygenic traits, and environmental influences all provide exceptions.

A plant's genotype might be homozygous dominant (*TT*), heterozygous (*Tt*), or homozygous recessive (*tt*).

Animated
BIOLOGY
Explore how genotype affects phenotype at ClassZone.com.

FIGURE 6.12 Both the homozygous dominant and heterozygous genotypes result in smooth, or inflated, pods (top). Only the homozygous recessive genotype results in constricted pods (inset).

Alleles and Phenotype

Because some alleles are dominant over others, two genotypes can produce the dominant phenotype. For example, smooth pods and constricted pods in pea plants, shown in **FIGURE 6.12**, are phenotypes. A plant with smooth pods could have a homozygous dominant (*SS*) or heterozygous (*Ss*) genotype. In contrast, a plant with constricted, or compressed, pods could only have a homozygous recessive (*ss*) genotype.

What actually makes one allele dominant over another? The answer is very complicated. It depends on the nature of the protein that is, or is not, made. Let's look at a fairly simple example. Pigment gives cells color. If *P* directs flower cells to make pigment, the flower may look purple. If *p* directs the cells not to make pigment, the flower looks white. So *P* codes for pigment to be present, but *p* codes for nothing, the absence of pigment. As a result, *P* has to be dominant. Even if the flower has only one *P* allele (*Pp*), that one allele tells its cells to make pigment, and the flower has color. Flower pigment is only one example. Many factors make one allele dominant over another.

As you know, most plants are not simply tall or short. Most flowers are not just white or purple. Most traits occur in a range. Other factors also affect traits. A lack of sunshine or vital nutrients could stunt a plant's growth. How does genetics account for these issues? Mendel studied traits that follow simple dominant-recessive patterns of inheritance, and each trait was the result of a single gene. In general, however, inheritance is much more complex. Most alleles are not simply dominant or recessive; some are codominant. Many traits are influenced by multiple genes. The environment also interacts with genes and affects their expression. These complexities are discussed in Chapter 7.

Contrast **Explain the difference between genotype and phenotype.**

6.4 ASSESSMENT

ONLINE QUIZ
ClassZone.com

REVIEWING ▶ MAIN IDEAS

1. How are the terms **gene,** locus, and **allele** related?

2. Explain why an organism's genotype may be **homozygous** dominant, homozygous recessive, or **heterozygous,** but never heterozygous recessive.

CRITICAL THINKING

3. **Apply** Suppose you are studying a fruit fly's DNA and you discover a gene for antenna length on chromosome 2. What word describes its location, and where would it be found in other fruit flies' DNA?

4. **Predict** If a **recessive** allele helps an organism reproduce, but the **dominant** allele hinders reproduction, which will be more common in a population?

Connecting CONCEPTS

5. **Human Biology** Cystic fibrosis is a recessive disease that causes the production of abnormally thick, life-threatening mucus secretions. What is the **genotype** of a person with cystic fibrosis: *CC*, *Cc*, or *cc*? Explain.

6.5 Traits and Probability

KEY CONCEPT The inheritance of traits follows the rules of probability.

▶ MAIN IDEAS

- Punnett squares illustrate genetic crosses.
- A monohybrid cross involves one trait.
- A dihybrid cross involves two traits.
- Heredity patterns can be calculated with probability.

VOCABULARY

Punnett square, p. 183
monohybrid cross, p. 184
testcross, p. 185
dihybrid cross, p. 186
law of independent assortment, p. 186
probability, p. 187

MICHIGAN STANDARDS

L4.p2A Explain that the traits of an individual are influenced by both the environment and the genetics of the individual. Acquired traits are not inherited; only genetic traits are inherited. (prerequisite)
B4.1e Determine the genotype and phenotype of monohybrid crosses using a Punnett Square.

Connect If you have tried juggling, you know it can be a tricky thing. Keeping three flaming torches or juggling clubs in motion at the same time is a lot to handle. Trying to keep track of what organism has which genotype and which gamete gets which allele can also be a lot to juggle. Fortunately, R. C. Punnett developed a method to graphically keep track of all of the various combinations.

▶ MAIN IDEA

Punnett squares illustrate genetic crosses.

Shortly after Mendel's experiments became widely known among scientists, a poultry geneticist named R. C. Punnett, shown in **FIGURE 6.13**, developed the Punnett square. A **Punnett square** is a grid system for predicting all possible genotypes resulting from a cross. The axes of the grid represent the possible gamete genotypes of each parent. The grid boxes show all of the possible genotypes of offspring from those two parents. Because segregation and fertilization are random events, each combination of alleles is as likely to be produced as any other. By counting the number of squares with each genetic combination, we can find the ratio of genotypes in that generation. If we also know how the genotype corresponds to the phenotype, we can find the ratio of phenotypes in that generation as well.

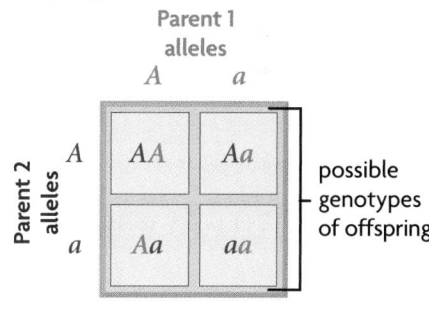

VISUAL VOCAB

The **Punnett square** is a grid system for predicting possible genotypes of offspring.

Let's briefly review what you've learned about meiosis and segregation to examine why the Punnett square is effective. Both parents have two alleles for each gene. These alleles are represented on the axes of the Punnett square. During meiosis, the chromosomes—and, therefore, the alleles—are separated.

FIGURE 6.13 R. C. Punnett developed the Punnett square as a way to illustrate genetic crosses.

Each gamete gets one of the alleles. Since each parent contributes only one allele to the offspring, only one allele from each parent is written inside each grid box. Fertilization restores the diploid number in the resulting offspring, which is why each grid box has two alleles, one from the mother and one from the father. Since any egg has the same chance of being fertilized by any sperm cell, each possible genetic combination is equally likely to occur.

Explain What do the letters on the axes of the Punnett square represent?

▶ MAIN IDEA
A monohybrid cross involves one trait.

Thus far, we have studied **monohybrid crosses,** crosses that examine the inheritance of only one specific trait. Three example crosses are used below and on the next page to illustrate how Punnett squares work and to highlight the resulting ratios—for both genotype and phenotype.

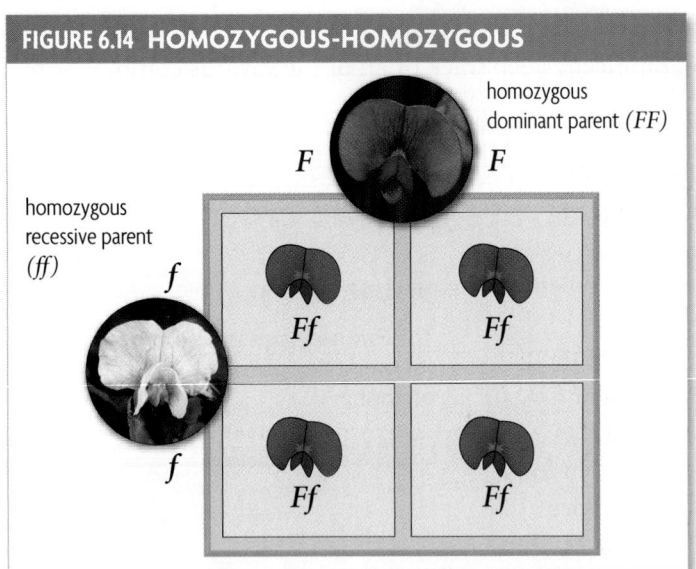

FIGURE 6.14 HOMOZYGOUS-HOMOZYGOUS

homozygous dominant parent *(FF)*

homozygous recessive parent *(ff)*

FIGURE 6.15 HETEROZYGOUS-HETEROZYGOUS

heterozygous parent *(Ff)*

heterozygous parent *(Ff)*

Homozygous-Homozygous
Suppose you cross a pea plant that is homozygous dominant for purple flowers with a pea plant that is homozygous recessive for white flowers. To determine the genotypic and phenotypic ratios of the offspring, first write each parent's genotype on one axis: *FF* for the purple-flowered plant, *ff* for the white-flowered plant. Every gamete from the purple-flowered plant contains the dominant allele, *F*. Every gamete from the white-flowered plant contains the recessive allele, *f*. Therefore, 100 percent of the offspring have the heterozygous genotype, *Ff*. And 100 percent of the offspring have purple flowers, because they all have a copy of the dominant allele, as shown in **FIGURE 6.14.**

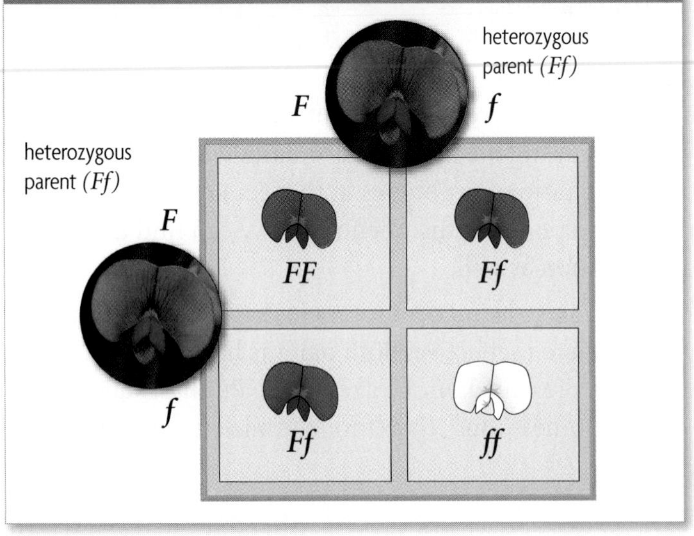

Heterozygous-Heterozygous
Next, in **FIGURE 6.15,** you can see a cross between two purple-flowered pea plants that are both heterozygous *(Ff)*. From each parent, half the offspring receive a dominant allele, *F*, and half receive a recessive allele, *f*. Therefore, one-fourth of the offspring have a homozygous dominant genotype, *FF*; half have a heterozygous genotype, *Ff*; and one-fourth have a homozygous recessive genotype, *ff*. Both the *FF* and the *Ff* genotypes result in purple flowers. Only the *ff* genotype results in white flowers. Thus, the genotypic ratio is 1:2:1 of homozygous dominant:heterozygous:homozygous recessive. The phenotypic ratio is 3:1 of purple:white flowers.

Heterozygous-Homozygous

Finally, suppose you cross a pea plant that is heterozygous for purple flowers (*Ff*) with a pea plant that is homozygous recessive for white flowers (*ff*). As before, each parent's genotype is placed on an axis, as shown in **FIGURE 6.16.** From the homozygous parent with white flowers, the offspring each receive a recessive allele, *f*. From the heterozygous parent, half the offspring receive a dominant allele, *F*, and half receive a recessive allele, *f*. Half the offspring have a heterozygous genotype, *Ff*. Half have a homozygous recessive genotype, *ff*. Thus, half the offspring have purple flowers, and half have white flowers. The resulting genotypic ratio is 1:1 of heterozygous:homozygous recessive. The phenotypic ratio is 1:1 of purple:white.

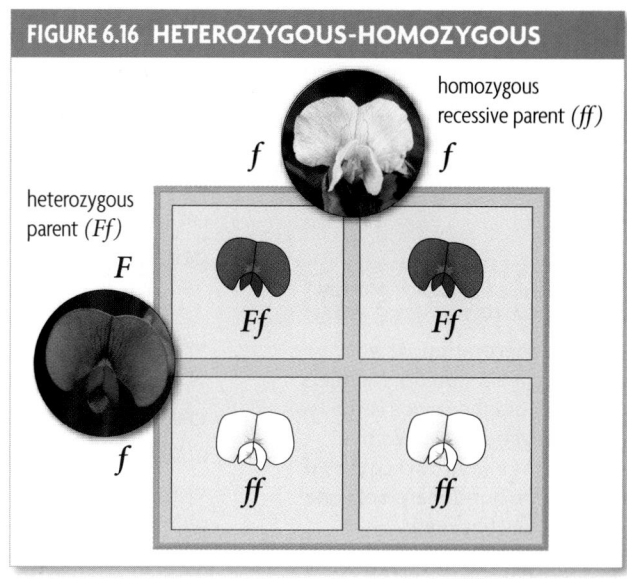

FIGURE 6.16 HETEROZYGOUS-HOMOZYGOUS

homozygous recessive parent *(ff)*

heterozygous parent *(Ff)*

Suppose we did not know the genotype of the purple flower in the cross above. This cross would allow us to determine that the purple flower is heterozygous, not homozygous dominant. A **testcross** is a cross between an organism with an unknown genotype and an organism with the recessive phenotype. The organism with the recessive phenotype must be homozygous recessive. The offspring will show whether the organism with the unknown genotype is heterozygous, as above, or homozygous dominant.

Apply From an *FF* × *Ff* cross, what percent of offspring would have purple flowers?

QUICK LAB   INFERRING

Using a Testcross

Suppose you work for a company that sells plant seeds. You are studying a plant species in which the dominant phenotype is pink flowers (*PP* or *Pp*). The recessive phenotype is white flowers (*pp*). Customers have been requesting more plants with pink flowers. To meet this demand, you need to determine the genotypes of some of the plants you are currently working with.

PROBLEM What is the genotype of each plant?

PROCEDURE

1. Suppose you are presented with Plant A of the species you are studying, which has pink flowers. You want to determine the genotype of the plant.

2. You cross Plant A with Plant B of the same species, which has white flowers and a known genotype of *pp*.

3. The resulting cross yields six plants with pink flowers and six plants with white flowers. Use Punnett squares to determine the genotype of Plant A.

MATERIALS
- pencil
- paper

ANALYZE AND CONCLUDE

1. **Apply** What is the genotype of Plant A? Explain how you arrived at your answer.

2. **Apply** What are the possible genotypes and phenotypes of offspring if Plant A is crossed with a plant that has a genotype of *PP*?

3. **Calculate** What ratio of dominant to recessive phenotypes would exist if Plant A were crossed with a plant that has a genotype of *Pp*?

4. **Evaluate** Is Plant A the best plant, in terms of genotype, that you can work with to produce as many of the requested seeds as possible? Why or why not? Which genotype would be best to work with?

● MAIN IDEA
A dihybrid cross involves two traits.

All of the crosses discussed so far have involved only a single trait. However, Mendel also conducted **dihybrid crosses,** crosses that examine the inheritance of two different traits. He wondered if both traits would always appear together or if they would be expressed independently of each other.

Mendel performed many dihybrid crosses and tested a variety of different combinations. For example, he would cross a plant with yellow round peas with a plant with green wrinkled peas. Remember that Mendel began his crosses with purebred plants. Thus, the first generation offspring (F_1) would all be heterozygous and would all look the same. In this example, the plants would all have yellow round peas. When Mendel allowed the F_1 plants to self-pollinate, he obtained the following results: 9 yellow/round, 3 yellow/wrinkled, 3 green/round, 1 green/wrinkled.

Mendel continued to find this approximately 9:3:3:1 phenotypic ratio in the F_2 generation, regardless of the combination of traits. From these results, he realized that the presence of one trait did not affect the presence of another trait. His second law of genetics, the **law of independent assortment,** states that allele pairs separate independently of each other during gamete formation, or meiosis. That is, different traits appear to be inherited separately.

The results of Mendel's dihybrid crosses can also be illustrated with a Punnett square, like the one in **FIGURE 6.17**. Drawing a Punnett square for a dihybrid cross is the same as drawing one for a monohybrid cross, except that the grid is bigger because two genes, or four alleles, are involved. For example, suppose you cross two plants with yellow, round peas that are heterozygous for both traits (*YyRr*). The four allele combinations possible in each gamete—*YR*, *Yr*, *yR*, and *yr*—are used to label each axis. Each grid box can be filled in using the same method as that used in the monohybrid cross. A total of nine different genotypes may result from the cross in this example. However, these nine genotypes produce only four different phenotypes. These phenotypes are yellow round, yellow wrinkled, green round, and green wrinkled, and they occur in the ratio of 9:3:3:1. Note that the 9:3:3:1 phenotypic ratio results from a cross between organisms that are heterozygous for both traits. The phenotypic ratio of the offspring will differ (from 9:3:3:1) if one or both of the parent organisms are homozygous for one or both traits.

Analyze In FIGURE 6.17, the boxes on the axes represent the possible gametes made by each parent plant. Why does each box have two alleles?

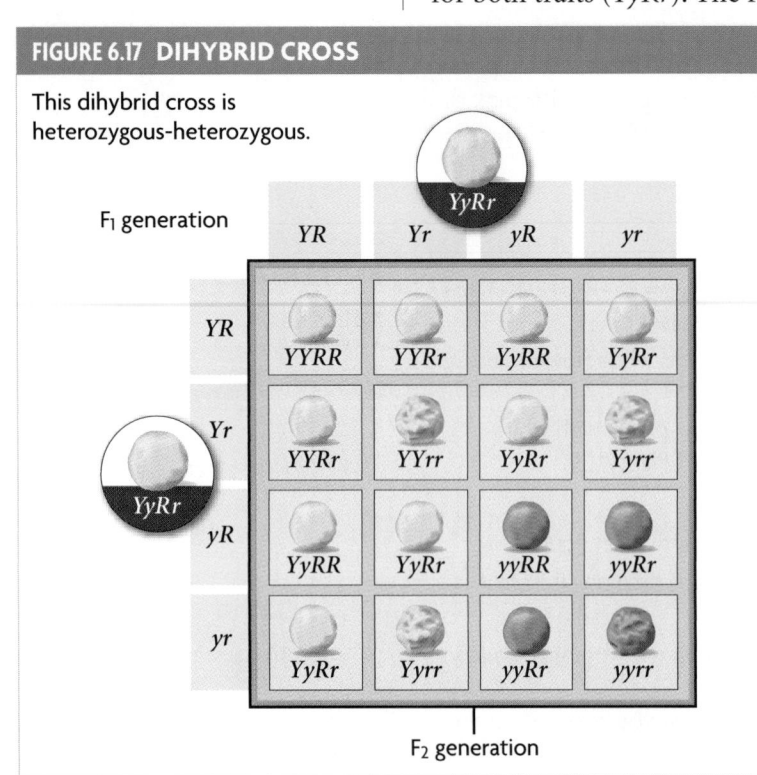

FIGURE 6.17 DIHYBRID CROSS

This dihybrid cross is heterozygous-heterozygous.

F_1 generation

YyRr

	YR	Yr	yR	yr
YR	YYRR	YYRr	YyRR	YyRr
Yr	YYRr	YYrr	YyRr	Yyrr
yR	YyRR	YyRr	yyRR	yyRr
yr	YyRr	Yyrr	yyRr	yyrr

YyRr

F_2 generation

▶ MAIN IDEA
Heredity patterns can be calculated with probability.

Probability is the likelihood that a particular event will happen. It predicts the average number of occurrences, not the exact number of occurrences.

$$\text{Probability} = \frac{\text{number of ways a specific event can occur}}{\text{number of total possible outcomes}}$$

Suppose you flip a coin. The number of total possible outcomes is two: heads up or tails up. The probability that it would land heads up is 1/2, or one out of two. The probability that it would land tails up is also 1/2.

Next, suppose you flip two coins. How one coin lands does not affect how the other coin lands. To calculate the probability that two independent events will happen together, multiply the probability of each individual event. The probability that both coins will land heads up, for example, is 1/2 × 1/2 = 1/4.

These probabilities can be applied to meiosis. Suppose a germ cell undergoes meiosis in a plant that is heterozygous for purple flowers. The number of total possible outcomes is two because a gamete could get a dominant or a recessive allele. The probability that a gamete will get a dominant allele is 1/2. The probability that it will get a recessive allele is also 1/2.

If two plants that are heterozygous for purple flowers fertilize each other, the probability that both egg and sperm have a dominant allele is 1/2 × 1/2 = 1/4. So, too, the probability that both have a recessive allele is 1/4. There is also a 1/4 chance that a sperm cell with a dominant allele will fertilize an egg with a recessive allele, or that a sperm cell with a recessive allele will fertilize an egg with a dominant allele. These last two combinations are basically the same. In either case, the resulting plant will be heterozygous. Thus, the probability that a pea plant will be heterozygous for this trait is the sum of the probabilities: 1/4 + 1/4 = 1/2.

Apply **Explain how Mendel's laws relate to probability.**

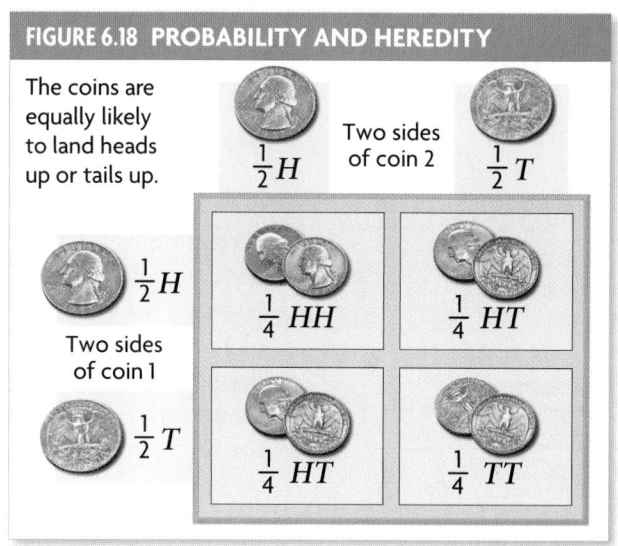

FIGURE 6.18 PROBABILITY AND HEREDITY

The coins are equally likely to land heads up or tails up.

$\frac{1}{2}H$ Two sides of coin 2 $\frac{1}{2}T$

Two sides of coin 1

$\frac{1}{2}H$

$\frac{1}{2}T$

$\frac{1}{4}HH$ $\frac{1}{4}HT$

$\frac{1}{4}HT$ $\frac{1}{4}TT$

6.5 ASSESSMENT

ONLINE QUIZ
ClassZone.com

REVIEWING ▶ MAIN IDEAS

1. What do the grid boxes in a **Punnett square** represent?

2. Why does the expected genotypic ratio often differ from the expected phenotypic ratio resulting from a **monohybrid cross**?

3. How did Mendel's **dihybrid crosses** help him develop his second law?

CRITICAL THINKING

4. **Calculate** What would be the phenotypic ratios of the offspring resulting from the following cross: *YYRr × YyRr*?

5. **Predict** If you are working with two tall pea plants and know that one is *Tt*, how could you determine the genotype of the other plant?

Connecting CONCEPTS

6. **Adaptation** You have seen that one-quarter of offspring resulting from two heterozygous parents are homozygous recessive. Yet for some genes, the recessive allele is more common in the population. Explain why this might be.

MATERIALS
- paper
- pencil
- calculator

PROCESS SKILLS
- **Calculating**
- **Analyzing**

MICHIGAN STANDARDS

B4.1c Differentiate between dominant, recessive, codominant, polygenic, and sex-linked traits.
B4.1e Determine the genotype and phenotype of monohybrid crosses using a Punnett Square.

Allele Combinations and Punnett Squares

Corn is bred for traits that improve its usefulness for specific purposes. For example, it may be bred to grow in various climates, to produce more corn, or to be better tasting. These traits depend on the alleles inherited by the corn plant. Suppose that you are studying the color and texture of kernels on a cob. Kernels can be either purple (*R*), which is the dominant color, or yellow (*r*), which is the recessive color. Kernels can also be smooth (*T*), which is the dominant texture, or wrinkled (*t*), which is the recessive texture. In this lab, you will predict the inheritance of alleles for two particular traits in a dihybrid cross by using a Punnett square.

PROBLEM What is the inheritance pattern for a dihybrid cross?

PROCEDURE

1. Suppose you want to cross two corn plants with the following genotypes: Plant A with *Rrtt* and Plant B with *RrTT*.

2. Create a Punnett square like the one below to predict the possible genotypes of the offspring for this dihybrid cross.

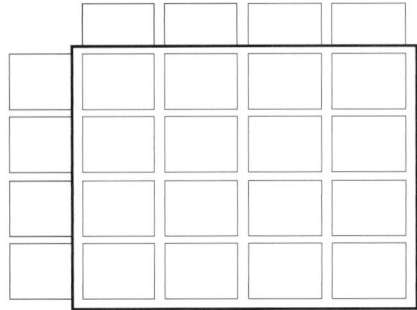

3. To fill in the Punnett square, place the four combinations of Plant A's alleles in the narrow boxes at the top.

4. Place the four combinations of Plant B's alleles in the narrow boxes on the left.

5. Complete the Punnett square by crossing the alleles of the two plants.

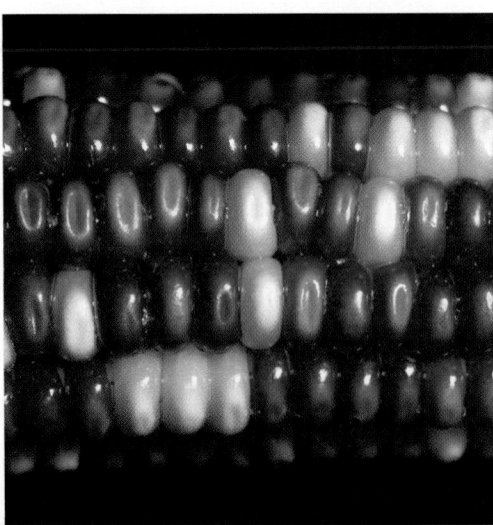

ANALYZE AND CONCLUDE

1. **Apply** List the genotypes and phenotypes produced by this cross.

2. **Calculate** What is the genotypic ratio resulting from this cross? The phenotypic ratio?

3. **Calculate** If the genotypes for kernel texture of two plants are *tt* and *tt*, what is the probability of their having offspring that have smooth kernels? Why?

4. **Predict** Suppose corn plant C has a known genotype of *RRTT*. Could corn plants with cobs that had some yellow and wrinkled kernels be produced by crossing Plant C with a plant with a genotype of your choice? Why or why not?

6.6 Meiosis and Genetic Variation

KEY CONCEPT Independent assortment and crossing over during meiosis result in genetic diversity.

▶ MAIN IDEAS

- Sexual reproduction creates unique gene combinations.
- Crossing over during meiosis increases genetic diversity.

VOCABULARY

crossing over, p. 190
genetic linkage, p. 191

MICHIGAN STANDARDS

B4.3A Compare and contrast the processes of cell division (mitosis and meiosis), particularly as those processes relate to production of new cells and to passing on genetic information between generations.

B4.3e Recognize that genetic variation can occur from such processes as crossing over, jumping genes, and deletion and duplication of genes.

Connect A surprising number of people make their living as Elvis impersonators. They wear slicked-up hairdos, large sunglasses, and big white jumpsuits. They mimic his voice, his dancing, and his phrases. They copy every possible detail, but they still do not come close to being the King. For Elvis, like all people, was unique, or one of a kind. And this uniqueness arises more from the events of meiosis—from the tiny shufflings of chromosomes and the crossing over of DNA segments—than from our hairstyles or our clothing.

▶ MAIN IDEA

Sexual reproduction creates unique gene combinations.

The major advantage of sexual reproduction is that it gives rise to a great deal of genetic variation within a species, as shown in **FIGURE 6.19**. This variation results largely from (1) the independent assortment of chromosomes during meiosis and (2) the random fertilization of gametes.

Recall that homologous chromosomes pair up randomly along the cell equator during meiosis I. In other words, it's a matter of chance which of the two chromosomes from any homologous pair ends up on a given side of the cell equator. As you've learned, human cells have 23 pairs of chromosomes, and each pair lines up independently. As a result, gametes with 2^{23}, or about 8 million, different combinations of chromosomes can be produced through meiosis from one human cell.

Now, think about the fact that sexual reproduction produces offspring through the random combination of gametes. In humans, for example, a sperm cell with one of 2^{23} (about 8 million) chromosome combinations fertilizes an egg cell, which also has one out of 2^{23} chromosome combinations. Since any sperm cell can fertilize any egg, the total number of possible combinations is the product of $2^{23} \times 2^{23}$, or more than 70 trillion. In other words, any human couple can produce a child with one of about 70 trillion different combinations of chromosomes.

FIGURE 6.19 This photograph shows only a small sample of the great genetic potential for variety in the human population.

Connecting CONCEPTS

Evolution As you will learn in **Chapter 10**, natural selection is a mechanism by which individuals that have inherited beneficial adaptations produce more offspring on average than do other individuals. The rabbit-eared bandicoot (below) has adaptations that enable it to survive and reproduce in regions of Australia.

Independent assortment and fertilization play key roles in creating and maintaining genetic diversity in all sexually reproducing organisms. However, the number of possible chromosome combinations varies by species. The probability that a bald eagle or a rabbit-eared bandicoot will inherit a specific allele is determined in the same way that it is for a pea plant.

Sexual reproduction creates unique combinations of genes. This results in organisms with unique phenotypes. The offspring of sexual reproduction have a mixture of both parents' traits. For example, rabbit-eared bandicoot offspring all share many traits for the things that make them bandicoots, but they may also differ in many ways. Some may be colored more like the mother, others more like the father. Some may dig deeper burrows or hunt more skillfully; others may in time produce more milk for their own offspring or have more litters. Having some of these traits may allow one bandicoot to reproduce in conditions where another bandicoot could not.

Calculate Fruit fly gametes each have four chromosomes, representing 2^4, or 16, possible chromosome combinations. How many chromosome combinations could result from fertilization between a fruit fly egg and a sperm cell?

▶ MAIN IDEA
Crossing over during meiosis increases genetic diversity.

It is clear that independent assortment creates a lot of variation within a species. Another process, called crossing over, occurs during meiosis and helps create even greater variation. **Crossing over** is the exchange of chromosome segments between homologous chromosomes during prophase I of meiosis I. At this stage, each chromosome has been duplicated, the sister chromatids are still connected to each other, and homologous chromosomes have paired with each other. When homologous chromosomes are in this position, some of the chromatids are very close to each other. Part of one chromatid from each chromosome breaks off and reattaches to the other chromosome, as shown in **FIGURE 6.20**. Crossing over happens any time a germ cell divides. In fact, it can occur many times within the same pair of homologous chromosomes.

FIGURE 6.20 Crossing Over

Crossing over exchanges segments of DNA between homologous chromosomes.

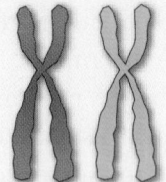
1 Two homologous chromosomes pair up with each other during prophase I in meiosis.

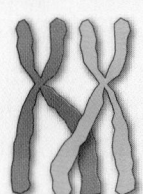
2 In this position, some chromatids are very close to each other and segments cross.

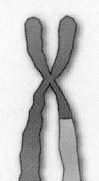
3 Some of these segments break off and reattach to the other homologous chromosome.

Synthesize Draw the four chromosomes that would result after the above chromosomes go through meiosis.

Because crossing over results in new combinations of genes, it is also called recombination. The term *recombination* generally refers to any mixing of parental alleles, including recombination events, other than crossing over.

Now that you know about crossing over, let's look again at some of Mendel's results and conclusions. As you know from his research, genes located on separate chromosomes assort independently. This independence is caused by the random assortment of chromosomes during meiosis. But you also know that a single chromosome can have hundreds of genes. What happens when two genes are both on the same chromosome? Will they display independent assortment as well? Or will they travel together as a unit?

The answer to these questions is, "It depends." Recall that each gene has its own locus, or place on a chromosome. As **FIGURE 6.21** shows, some genes on the same chromosome are close together; others are far apart. The farther apart two genes are located, the more likely they are to be separated when crossing over happens. Thus, genes located close together tend to be inherited together, which is called **genetic linkage.** Linked genes will be inherited in the same predicted ratios as would a single gene. In contrast, genes that are far apart are more likely to assort independently. For example, the alleles for flower and seed color are located on the same chromosome in pea plants, but they are not near each other. Because they are so far apart, Mendel observed independent assortment for these traits.

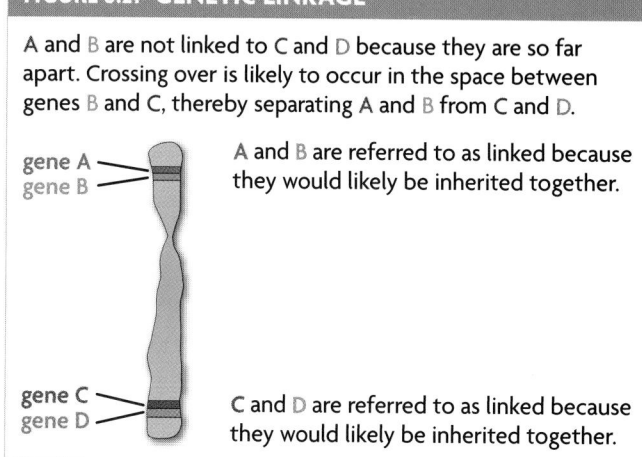

FIGURE 6.21 GENETIC LINKAGE

A and B are not linked to C and D because they are so far apart. Crossing over is likely to occur in the space between genes B and C, thereby separating A and B from C and D.

gene A
gene B

A and B are referred to as linked because they would likely be inherited together.

gene C
gene D

C and D are referred to as linked because they would likely be inherited together.

Genetic linkage has let scientists calculate the physical distance between two genes. By exploring relationships between many genes, scientists have been able to build a linkage, or genetic, map of many species. This research tool will be discussed in more detail in Chapter 7.

Predict **Suppose two genes are very close together on a chromosome. Are the genes likely to be separated by crossing over? Explain.**

6.6 ASSESSMENT

ONLINE QUIZ
ClassZone.com

REVIEWING ▶ MAIN IDEAS

1. Briefly explain how sexual reproduction generates new allele combinations in offspring.

2. How does **crossing over** contribute to genetic diversity?

CRITICAL THINKING

3. **Infer** You know that you get half your DNA from your mom, half from your dad. Does this mean you got one-quarter of your DNA from each of your grandparents? Explain your reasoning.

4. **Synthesize** Suppose you know two genes exist on the same chromosome. How could you determine whether they are located close to each other?

Connecting CONCEPTS

5. **Mitosis** Mitosis creates daughter cells that are genetically identical to the parent cell. If crossing over occurred between sister chromatids during mitosis, would it increase genetic diversity? Explain.

Use these inquiry-based labs and online activities to deepen your understanding of meiosis.

INVESTIGATION

B4.1d Explain the genetic basis for Mendel's laws of segregation and independent assortment.

B4.3A Compare and contrast the processes of cell division (mitosis and meiosis), particularly as those processes relate to production of new cells and to passing on genetic information between generations.

Modeling Meiosis

In this lab, you will make a model of meiosis that will be reusable as a study tool.

SKILLS Modeling, Analyzing

PROBLEM How does a diploid cell divide to form haploid cells?

MATERIALS
- 4 white pipe cleaners
- 2 2-cm pieces hook-and-loop tabs
- colored markers
- notebook paper

PROCEDURE

1. Construct a pair of homologous chromosomes. Use pipe cleaners to make the chromosomes and hook-and-loop tabs to represent the centromere that holds the sister chromatids together. The homologous chromosomes should have bands of color that represent the different genes carried on those chromosomes. The pair should be heterozygous for each of the genes. For example, if you choose to make a thick band of dark blue to represent an allele for eye color on one chromosome in the homologous pair, you should make a matching band in light blue on the other chromosome in the pair.

2. Lay out the chromosomes on notebook paper and model the four steps of meiosis I. Then remove the chromosomes and sketch the position of the chromosomes at the end of meiosis I on your paper.

3. Cut the sheet of paper in half to represent cytokinesis. Make sure that each half of the notebook paper, or cell, has one homologous chromosome.

4. Model the four steps of meiosis II in both cells.

5. Remove the chromosomes. Sketch the position of the chromosomes in both cells at the end of meiosis II.

6. Cut the cells in half again to show cytokinesis. Each cell should have one chromosome.

ANALYZE AND CONCLUDE

1. **Predict** Explain how your results would differ if the homologous chromosomes had been homozygous for each of the genes.

2. **Evaluate** Which aspects of meiosis are not represented in your model? What changes could you make to show these processes?

3. **Synthesize** Refer to your model to explain why meiosis is also called "reduction division." Use the words *diploid* and *haploid* in your explanation.

EXTEND YOUR INVESTIGATION

Nondisjunction describes what happens when homologous chromosomes fail to separate during meiosis I or when sister chromatids fail to separate during meiosis II. On chromosome 21, it can lead to Down syndrome. Research the effects of having three copies of chromosome 21.

INVESTIGATION

Probability Practice

In this lab, you will model the distribution of alleles, calculate the probabilities of specific allele combinations, and compare them to those that Gregor Mendel found in his work.

SKILL Calculating Probabilities

PROBLEM What is the probability that certain genotypes and phenotypes will occur?

MATERIALS
- 2 coins
- 4 cm masking tape
- marker
- one folded 3" × 5" index card with a monohybrid cross on it (e.g., Aa × aa, or AA × Aa)

PROCEDURE

1. Using the coins, tape, and marker, label a set of two coins to simulate the cross listed on your group's index card. Use a capital letter to represent a dominant allele and a lowercase letter to represent a recessive allele. One coin should have the mother's gametes. The other coin should have the father's gametes.

2. Flip the two coins simultaneously. The two coins together make up the genetic material of the zygote. Record the genotype of the offspring.

3. Repeat step 2 for a total of 50 trials. Calculate what percentage of "offspring" had each possible genotype and phenotype. Show your data and calculations to your teacher before moving on.

ANALYZE AND CONCLUDE

1. **Analyze** The crosses below show the predicted phenotypes of the offspring based on Mendel's laws. Compare your genetic cross results (phenotypes) to those of Mendel. Explain possible reasons for any differences you observe in data.
   - *AA* × *aa* : 100% dominant
   - *aa* × *aa* : 100% recessive
   - *Aa* × *aa* : 50% dominant, 50% recessive

2. **Apply** Did the genotype of any one trial depend upon the results of another? Explain.

3. **Synthesize** Explain how meiosis accounts for the distribution of alleles to gametes.

Online BIOLOGY
CLASSZONE.COM

VIRTUAL LAB
Breeding Mutations in Fruit Flies
How are mutations expressed in fruit flies? In this interactive lab, you will cross purebred fruit flies to determine the pattern of inheritance for a set of mutant alleles.

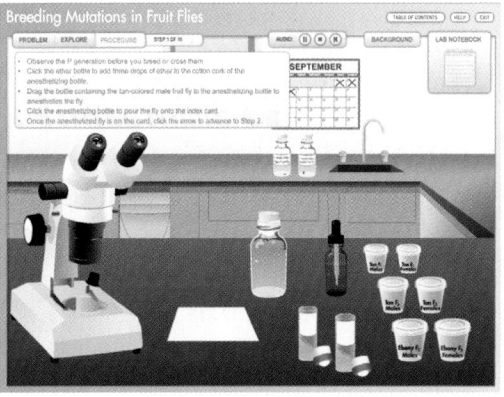

ANIMATED BIOLOGY
Mendel's Experiment
Recreate some of Mendel's experiments with virtual pea plants. Then use your skills to breed a specific type of pea on a tight budget.

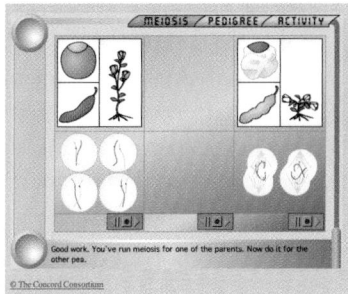

WEBQUEST
Dogs come in many shapes and sizes. How did this variety come about? In this WebQuest you will learn about selective breeding. Find out how dog breeders enhance certain traits, and how breeding can expose genetic disorders. Finally, describe how you might breed dogs to enhance a specific trait.

6.1 Chromosomes and Meiosis

Gametes have half the number of chromosomes that body cells have. Your body cells have 23 pairs of homologous chromosomes, making 46 total chromosomes. Gametes have only one chromosome from each homologous pair—23 chromosomes in all.

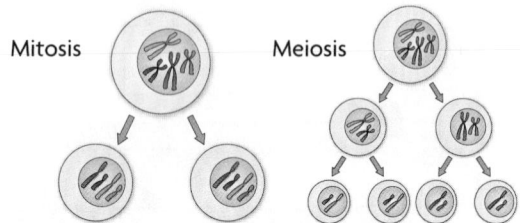

6.2 Process of Meiosis

During meiosis, diploid cells undergo two cell divisions that result in haploid cells. In meiosis I, homologous chromosomes pair up along the cell equator and are divided into separate cells. In meiosis II, sister chromatids are divided into separate cells, making a total of four haploid cells that are genetically unique.

6.3 Mendel and Heredity

Mendel's research showed that traits are inherited as discrete units. His large amount of data, control over breeding, use of purebred plants, and observation of "either-or" traits allowed him to see patterns in the inheritance of traits. He concluded that organisms inherit two copies of each gene and that organisms donate only one copy of each gene in their gametes.

6.4 Traits, Genes, and Alleles

Genes encode proteins that produce a diverse range of traits. Every diploid organism has two alleles for each gene: one from the mother, one from the father. These two alleles may be the same (homozygous) or different (heterozygous). One allele may be dominant over another.

6.5 Traits and Probability

The inheritance of traits follows the rules of probability. Punnett squares are a grid system that help predict all possible genotypes resulting from a cross. When Mendel performed two-trait crosses, he discovered that different traits appear to be inherited separately—the law of independent assortment. The patterns of inheritance that he observed can be predicted using mathematical probabilities.

6.6 Meiosis and Genetic Variation

Independent assortment and crossing over during meiosis result in genetic diversity. Independent assortment produces unique combinations of parental chromosomes. Crossing over between homologous chromosomes creates a patchwork of genes from both parents. Genetic linkage describes genes that are close together and tend to be inherited as a unit.

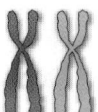

Synthesize Your Notes

"Y" Diagram Use a "Y" diagram to summarize what you know about meiosis I and II.

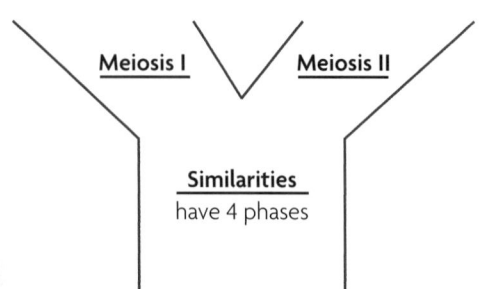

Cycle Diagram Fill in a cycle diagram like the one below to show the relationship between diploid and haploid cells.

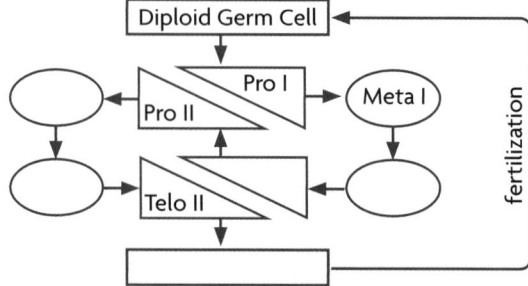

Chapter Assessment

Reviewing Vocabulary

Visualize Vocabulary

For each term below, use simple shapes, lines, or arrows to illustrate its meaning. Below each picture, write a short caption. Here's an example for *diploid:*

1. gene
2. fertilization
3. crossing over
4. genetic linkage
5. haploid

Diploid cells have two copies of each chromosome.

Greek Word Origins

6. The word *meiosis* comes from a Greek word meaning "to diminish," or make less. How does this word's origin relate to its meaning?

7. The word *haploid* comes from the Greek word *haplous,* which means "single." *Diploid* comes from the Greek word *diplous,* which means "double." Explain how these two terms' meanings relate to their origins.

8. The Greek prefix *homo-* means "one and the same." How does this relate to the words *homologous* and *homozygous*?

Compare and Contrast

Describe one similarity and one difference between the two terms in each of the following pairs.

9. monohybrid cross, dihybrid cross

10. heterozygous, homozygous

11. genotype, phenotype

Reviewing MAIN IDEAS

12. Each of your cells has a set of chromosomes, including autosomes and sex chromosomes. Explain the main differences between these two types of chromosomes.

13. A fruit fly has diploid cells with 8 chromosomes. Explain how many chromosomes are in its haploid gametes.

14. Meiosis is a continuous process, but we can think of it as taking place in two stages, meiosis I and meiosis II. Describe the products of each stage. How do the products of meiosis I differ from those of meiosis II?

15. The foundation for our modern study of genetics began with Gregor Mendel, who studied pea plants. What were Mendel's two main conclusions about how traits are passed between generations?

16. How did Mendel's use of purebred plants—for example, purebred white- and purebred purple-flowered peas—contribute to his understanding of inheritance?

17. How does the homozygous condition differ from the heterozygous condition? In your answer, use the terms *gene, homologous chromosome,* and *allele.*

18. What does each of the following parts of a Punnett square represent: (a) the entries on each axis of the grid and (b) the entries in the four squares within the grid?

19. How did the results of Mendel's dihybrid crosses lead him to formulate the law of independent assortment?

20. How does crossing over during meiosis I increase genetic diversity?

Critical Thinking

21. Hypothesize Could a mutation in one of an individual's somatic cells be passed on to the individual's offspring? Explain your answer.

22. Predict Consider a species with a 2n, or diploid, chromosome number of 4. If gametes were formed by mitosis, rather than meiosis, what would happen to the chromosome number of the offspring of these organisms over generations? Explain.

23. Contrast Draw a pair of homologous chromosomes before and after duplication. Use your drawings to explain how homologous chromosomes and sister chromatids differ.

24. Synthesize Mendel's law of independent assortment states that allele pairs separate independently of each other during meiosis. How does this law relate to crossing over and genetic linkage?

25. Infer Imagine that you are studying the trait of flower petal shape in a species of plant. Petal shape is determined by a single gene with two alleles. You make a cross of two plants with unknown genotypes, both with smooth petals, and get the following F₁ offspring phenotypes: 23 wrinkled and 77 smooth. What conclusions can you draw about the inheritance of this trait? In your answer, include the probable genotypes of each parent, and which allele is likely dominant.

26. Analyze In a particular species of butterfly, the genes for two different traits, antenna shape and antenna color, are located on the same chromosome. As a result, crosses between these butterflies do not obey one of Mendel's laws. Which law does not apply, and why?

Interpreting Visuals

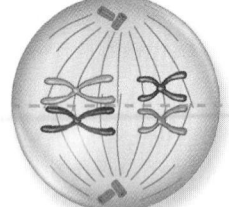

The drawing to the right shows a cell at a certain point during meiosis. Use the drawing to answer the next two questions.

27. Identify What stage of meiosis is shown above? Defend your answer.

28. Apply Is the above cell diploid or haploid? Explain.

Analyzing Data

During meiosis, pairs of homologous chromosomes separate independently of the others, and gametes receive one of the two chromosomes from each pair. The number of possible chromosome combinations for a species is 2n, where n = the number of homologous pairs. The graph below shows the number of possible chromosome combinations for a variety of species. Use it to answer the next two questions.

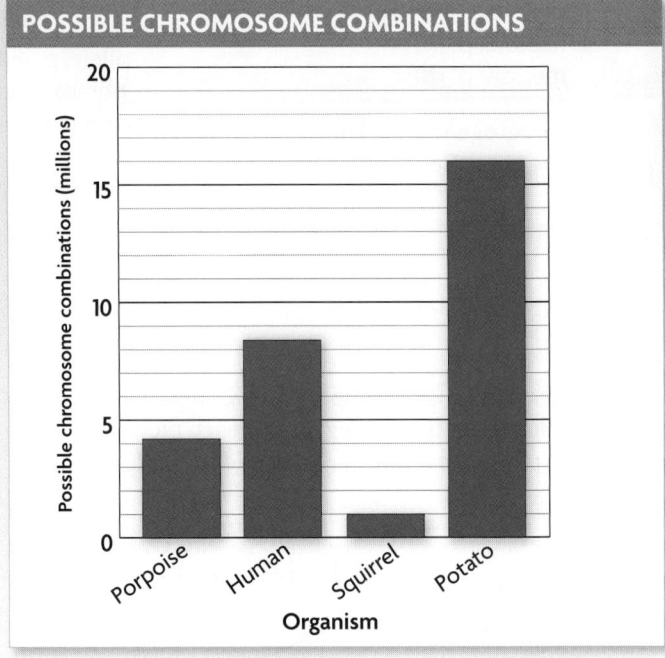

Source: Rutgers University

29. Summarize List the organisms in the above graph, in order, from least to most possible chromosome combinations.

30. Infer What can you infer from the graph about the number of homologous chromosomes in squirrels compared with potatoes?

Connecting CONCEPTS

31. Write a Diary Entry Put yourself in Mendel's shoes. It is the mid-1800s. DNA and genes have not been identified, and the mechanisms of heritability are not understood. Write a diary entry (or letter) about one of Mendel's crosses from his perspective. Describe the results of the cross and ideas that may have come from the results.

32. Synthesize Look again at the picture of the egg and sperm cells on page 167. Each of these sperm cells is genetically unique. What are the sources of variation that make each one different from the others?

MICHIGAN
STANDARDS-BASED ASSESSMENT

✓ **Test Practice**
For more test practice,
go to ClassZone.com.

1. **Researchers crossed two types of mice together, type A and type B. In the resulting offspring, half of the DNA comes from type A and half comes from type B. Why?** **B1.1E**

   A X-inactivation occurs with 50/50 chance in each cell.

   B The offspring get their DNA from the sperm and their cytoplasm from the egg.

   C Each parent contributes one set of chromosomes to each offspring.

   D The offspring make binary divisions during development.

2. **The exchange of chromosome segments between homologous chromosomes results in** **B4.3e**

   A increased genetic variation.

   B decreased genetic variation.

   C increased mortality.

   D decreased mortality.

3. **In peas, the gene for green pod color (G) is dominant to the gene for yellow pod color (g). If a heterozygous plant (Gg) is crossed with another heterozygous plant (Gg), what genotype will likely be the most common among the offspring?** **B4.1c**

   A *GG*

   B *Gg*

   C *gg*

   D *GGgg*

   THINK THROUGH THE QUESTION

   If necessary, take the time to draw out a Punnett square to answer this question. Remember that the Gg genotype is the same as the gG genotype.

4. **Genes that are on two different chromosomes are said to exhibit independent assortment because these chromosomes** **B4.1d**

   A are physically unconnected to the spindle.

   B are replicated independently of each other.

   C become aligned on opposite poles of the cell.

   D end up in the same gamete by random chance.

5. **An individual's traits are influenced by** **L4.p2A**

   A genotype only.

   B phenotype only.

   C genotype and environment.

   D phenotype and environment.

6.

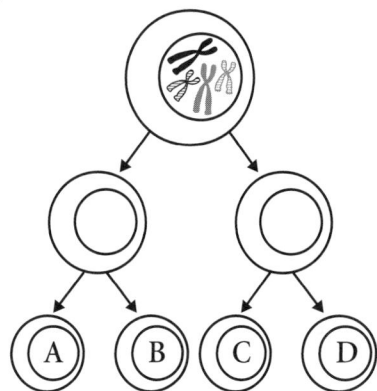

If the process of meiosis shown here proceeds normally, how many chromosomes will cells A, B, C, and D have? **B4.3A**

A 2 each

B 4 each

C 6 each

D 8 each

CHAPTER

7

Extending Mendelian Genetics

KEY CONCEPTS

7.1 Chromosomes and Phenotype
The chromosomes on which genes are located can affect the expression of traits.

7.2 Complex Patterns of Inheritance
Phenotype is affected by many different factors.

7.3 Gene Linkage and Mapping
Genes can be mapped to specific locations on chromosomes.

7.4 Human Genetics and Pedigrees
A combination of methods is used to study human genetics.

Online   BIOLOGY   CLASSZONE.COM

 **Animated**
BIOLOGY
View animated chapter concepts.
• Human Chromosomes
• Tracking Traits

 BIOZINE
Keep current with biology news.
• News feeds
• Bio Bytes
• Polls

↗ **RESOURCE CENTER**
Get more information on
• Phenotype Complexity
• Gene Mapping
• Pedigrees

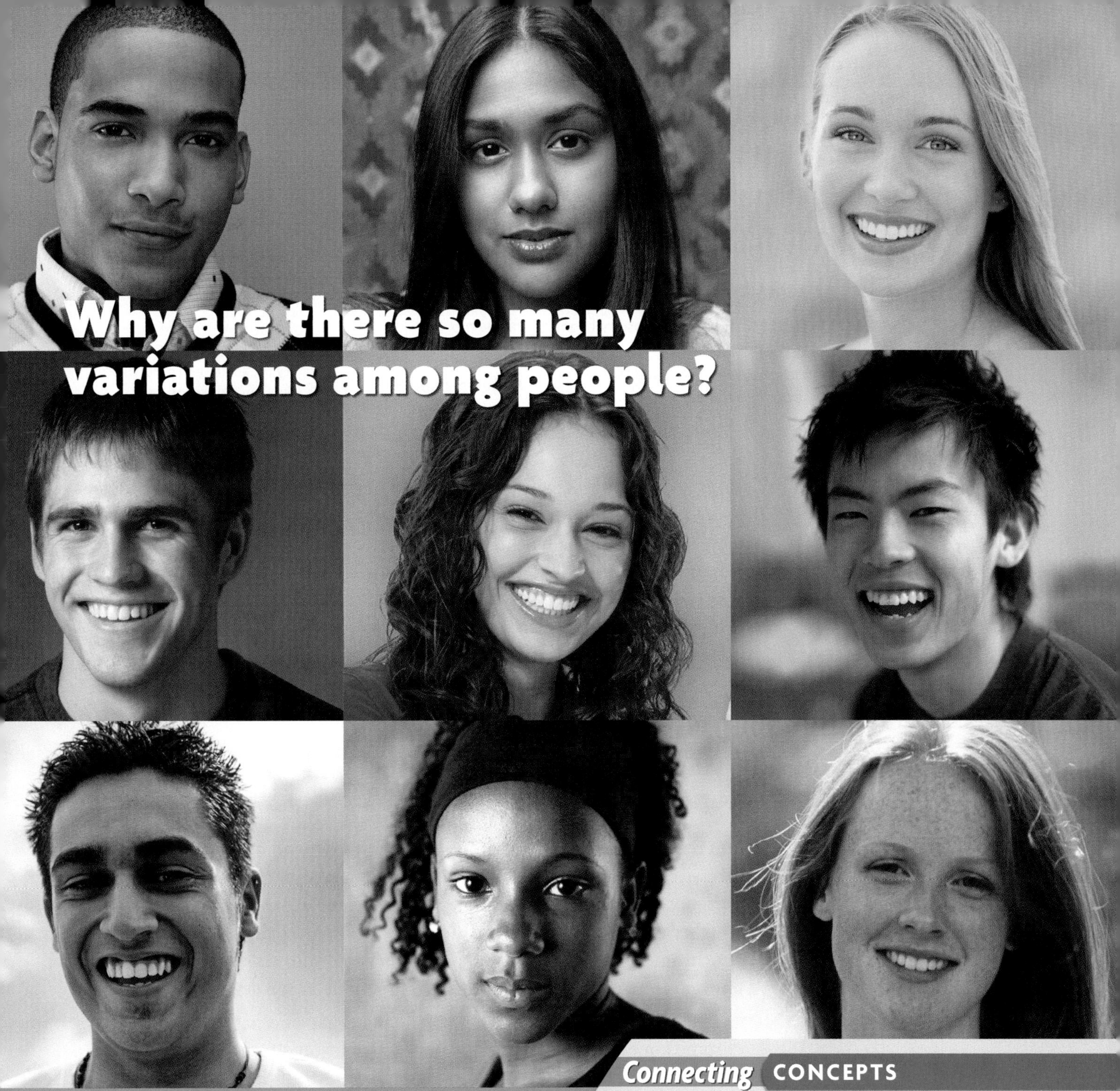

Why are there so many variations among people?

Connecting CONCEPTS

It will come as no surprise to you, but you are not a pea plant. But, Mendel's principles apply to you just as they apply to other organisms. About 99.9 percent of everyone's DNA is identical. So how can a 0.1 percent difference in DNA lead to the wide range of human traits? In many organisms, genetics is more than dominant and recessive alleles.

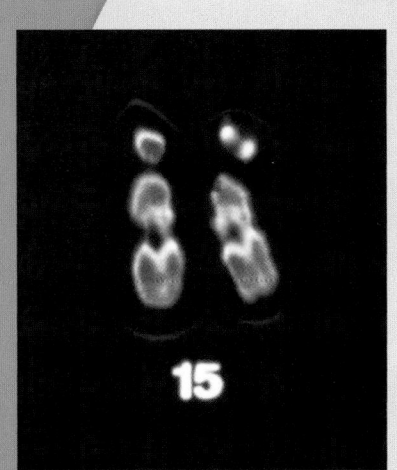

Multiple Gene Traits Two genes for human eye color are located on chromosome 15, shown at the left. One reason for the large variations in phenotype in many species is that most traits are produced by several genes that interact with each other. Eye color in humans is a trait controlled by more than one gene. And the alleles of those genes have different dominant and recessive relationships. (colored LM; magnification 13,000×)

7.1 Chromosomes and Phenotype

KEY CONCEPT The chromosomes on which genes are located can affect the expression of traits.

▶ MAIN IDEAS

- Two copies of each autosomal gene affect phenotype.
- Males and females can differ in sex-linked traits.

VOCABULARY

carrier, p. 201
sex-linked gene, p. 201
X chromosome inactivation, p. 203

Review
dominant, recessive, phenotype, allele, gene, autosome, sex chromosome, trait

L4.p2A Explain that the traits of an individual are influenced by both the environment and the genetics of the individual. Acquired traits are not inherited; only genetic traits are inherited. (prerequisite)

B4.1c Differentiate between dominant, recessive, codominant, polygenic, and sex-linked traits.

Connect The next time you are in a crowd of people, take a moment to look at the variety of traits around you. Hair color and texture, eye color and shape, height, and weight are all influenced by genetics. Can dominant and recessive alleles of one gene produce so many subtle differences in any of those traits? In most cases, the answer is no. But the dominant and recessive relationship among alleles is a good place to start when learning about the complexities of genetics.

▶ MAIN IDEA

Two copies of each autosomal gene affect phenotype.

You read in Chapter 6 how some genetic traits depend on dominant and recessive alleles. But many factors affect phenotype, including the specific chromosome upon which a gene is located. Gene expression is often related to whether a gene is located on an autosome or on a sex chromosome. Recall that sex chromosomes determine an organism's sex. Autosomes are all of the other chromosomes, and they do not play a direct role in sex determination.

You also know that sexually reproducing organisms have two of each chromosome. Each pair consists of one chromosome from each of two parents. Both chromosomes have the same genes, but the chromosomes might have different alleles for those genes. And, as Mendel observed, different alleles can produce different phenotypes, such as white flowers or purple flowers.

All of the traits that Mendel studied are determined by genes on autosomes. In fact, most traits in sexually reproducing organisms, including humans, are the result of autosomal genes. Look at **FIGURE 7.1**. Is your hair curly or straight? What about your parents' hair? The genes that affect your hair texture—curly hair or straight hair—are autosomal genes.

Many human genetic disorders are also caused by autosomal genes. The chance of a person having one of these disorders can be predicted, just as Mendel could predict the phenotypes that would appear in his pea plants. Why? Because there are two copies of each gene on autosomes—one on each homologous chromosome—and each copy can influence phenotype.

FIGURE 7.1 Hair texture is just one example of a trait that is controlled by autosomal genes.

Disorders Caused by Recessive Alleles

Some human genetic disorders are caused by recessive alleles on autosomes. Two copies of the recessive allele must be present for a person to have the disorder. These disorders often appear in offspring of parents who are both heterozygotes. That is, each parent has one dominant, "normal" allele that masks the one disease-causing recessive allele.

For example, cystic fibrosis is a severe recessive disorder that mainly affects the sweat glands and the mucus glands. A person who is homozygous for the recessive allele will have the disease. Someone who is heterozygous for the alleles will not have the disease, but is a carrier. A **carrier** does not show disease symptoms, but can pass on the disease-causing allele to offspring. In this way, alleles that are lethal, or deadly, in a homozygous recessive individual can remain in a population's gene pool. This inheritance pattern is shown in **FIGURE 7.2**.

Disorders Caused by Dominant Alleles

Dominant genetic disorders are far less common than recessive disorders. One example is Huntington's disease. Huntington's disease damages the nervous system and usually appears during adulthood. Because the disease is caused by a dominant allele, there is a 50 percent chance that a child will have it even if only one parent has one of the alleles. If both parents are heterozygous for the disease, there is a 75 percent chance that any of their children will inherit the disease. Because Huntington's disease strikes later in life, a person with the allele can have children before the disease appears. In that way, the allele is passed on in the population even though the disease is fatal.

Connect How are Mendel's observations related to genes on autosomes?

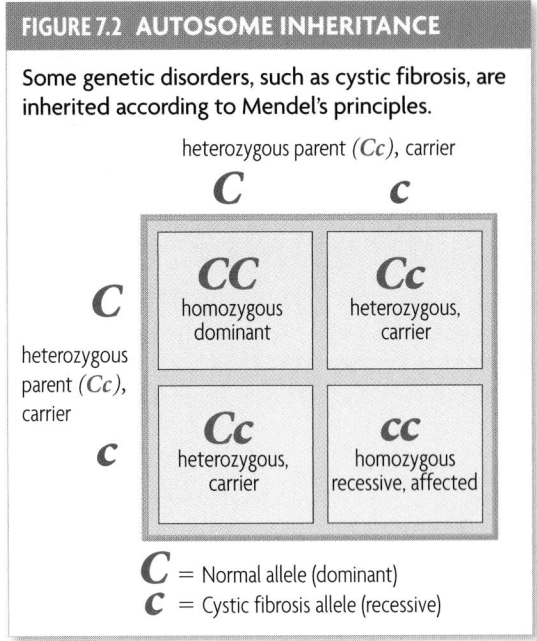

FIGURE 7.2 AUTOSOME INHERITANCE

Some genetic disorders, such as cystic fibrosis, are inherited according to Mendel's principles.

heterozygous parent *(Cc)*, carrier

heterozygous parent *(Cc)*, carrier

C = Normal allele (dominant)
c = Cystic fibrosis allele (recessive)

▶ MAIN IDEA

Males and females can differ in sex-linked traits.

Mendel figured out much about heredity, but he did not know about chromosomes. As it turns out, he only studied traits produced by genes on autosomes. Now, we know about sex chromosomes, and we know that the expression of genes on the sex chromosomes differs from the expression of autosomal genes.

Sex-Linked Genes

Genes that are located on the sex chromosomes are called **sex-linked genes.** Recall from Chapter 6 that many species have specialized sex chromosomes called the X and Y chromosomes. In mammals and some other animals, individuals with two X chromosomes—an XX genotype—are female. Individuals with one X and one Y—an XY genotype—are male. As **FIGURE 7.3** shows, a female can pass on only an X chromosome to offspring, but a male can pass on either an X or a Y chromosome.

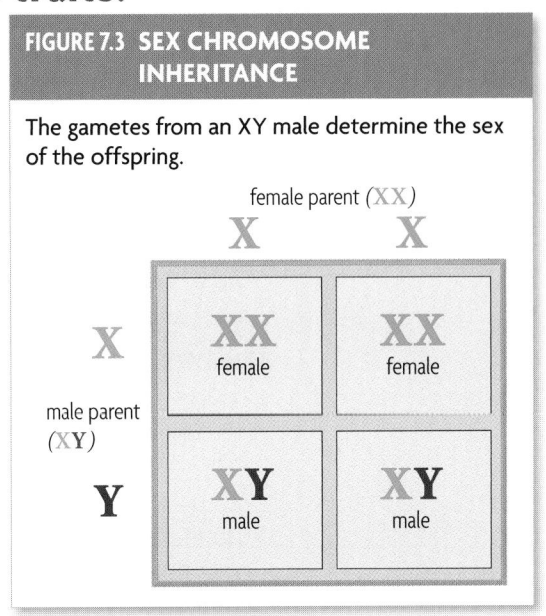

FIGURE 7.3 SEX CHROMOSOME INHERITANCE

The gametes from an XY male determine the sex of the offspring.

female parent *(XX)*

male parent *(XY)*

TAKING NOTES

Use a two-column chart to compare and contrast the expression of autosomal and sex-linked genes.

autosomes	sex chromosomes

Genes on the Y chromosome are responsible for the development of male offspring, but the X chromosome actually has much more influence over phenotype. The X chromosome has many genes that affect many traits. Scientists hypothesize that the Y chromosome may have genes for more than sex determination, but there is little evidence to support this idea.

In many organisms, including humans, the Y chromosome is much smaller and has many fewer genes than the X chromosome. Evidence suggests that over millions of years of evolution, the joining of the X and Y chromosomes during meiosis has resulted in segments of the Y chromosome being transferred to the X. You will read more about specific sex-linked genes and their locations on the human X and Y chromosomes in Section 7.4.

Expression of Sex-Linked Genes

Because the X and Y chromosomes have different genes, sex-linked genes have a pattern of expression that is different from autosomal genes. Remember, two copies of an autosomal gene affect a trait. What happens when there is only one copy of a gene, as is the case in an XY male? Because males have only one copy of each type of sex chromosome, they express all of the alleles on both chromosomes. In males, there are no second copies of sex-linked genes to mask the effects of another allele. This means that even if all of the alleles of sex-linked genes in a male are recessive, they will be expressed.

QUICK LAB PREDICTING

Sex-Linked Inheritance

The relationship between genotype and phenotype in sex-linked genes differs from that in autosomal genes. A female must have two recessive alleles of a sex-linked gene to express a recessive sex-linked trait. Just one recessive allele is needed for the same trait to be expressed in a male. In this lab, you will model the inheritance pattern of sex-linked genes.

PROBLEM How does probability explain sex-linked inheritance?

PROCEDURE

1. Use the tape and marker to label two coins with the genetic cross shown on your group's index card. One coin represents the egg cell and the other coin represents the sperm cell.

2. Flip the two coins and record the genotype of the "offspring."

3. Repeat step 2 until you have modeled 50 genetic crosses. Make a data table to record each genetic cross that you model.

4. Calculate the genotype and phenotype probabilities for both males and females. Calculate the frequency of male offspring and female offspring.

MATERIALS

- 2 coins
- masking tape
- marker
- index card with genetic cross

ANALYZE AND CONCLUDE

1. **Analyze** Do all of the females from the genetic cross show the recessive trait? Do all of the males show the recessive trait? Why or why not?

2. **Apply** Make a Punnett square that shows the genetic cross. Do the results from your Punnett square agree with those from your experiment? Why or why not?

FIGURE 7.4 The female calico cats have two X chromosomes with different alleles for fur color. Both alleles are expressed in a random pattern. The male cat has only one X chromosome, and its allele for fur color is expressed across the entire body.

X^O = Orange fur allele
X^o = Black fur allele

In mammals, the expression of sex-linked genes in females is also different from the way in which genes on other chromosomes are expressed. In each cell of female mammals, one of the two X chromosomes is randomly "turned off" by a process called **X chromosome inactivation.** Because of X chromosome inactivation, females are a patchwork of two types of cells—one type with an active X chromosome that came from the mother, and a second type with an active X chromosome that came from the father.

Colorful examples of X chromosome inactivation are seen in female tortoiseshell cats and female calico cats. The female calico cats shown in **FIGURE 7.4** have white fur, as well as alleles for black or orange fur on their X chromosomes. Those alleles are expressed randomly in cells across the cat's body. As a result, its coat is a mixture of color splotches. It is truly a patchwork of cells. Because the male cats only have one X chromosome, they have white fur and one sex-linked gene for either orange or black fur.

Infer Why are males more likely than females to have sex-linked genetic disorders?

Connecting CONCEPTS

Mitosis Recall from **Chapter 5** that DNA coils to form chromosomes. In XX females, one of the two X chromosomes in each cell is "inactivated" by becoming even more tightly coiled.

7.1 | ASSESSMENT

ONLINE QUIZ
ClassZone.com

REVIEWING ▶ MAIN IDEAS

1. How are autosomal traits, including recessive genetic disorders that are carried in a population, related to Mendel's observations of heredity?

2. Describe how **sex-linked genes** are expressed differently in males and in females.

CRITICAL THINKING

3. **Apply** How might a scientist determine whether a trait is sex-linked by observing the offspring of several genetic crosses?

4. **Compare and Contrast** How is the expression of sex-linked genes both similar to and different from the expression of autosomal genes?

Connecting CONCEPTS

5. **Meiosis** Scientists hypothesize that over millions of years, the Y chromosome has lost genes to the X chromosome. During what stages of meiosis might the Y chromosome have transferred genes to the X chromosome? Explain.

7.2 Complex Patterns of Inheritance

KEY CONCEPT Phenotype is affected by many different factors.

▶ MAIN IDEAS

- Phenotype can depend on interactions of alleles.
- Many genes may interact to produce one trait.
- The environment interacts with genotype.

VOCABULARY

incomplete dominance, p. 204
codominance, p. 205
polygenic trait, p. 206

Review
allele, phenotype, genotype

Connect Suppose you have blue and yellow paints to paint a room. You paint the walls yellow, let them dry, then paint the walls blue. The blue paint masks the yellow paint, so you could say that the blue paint is "dominant." You could also combine the paints in other ways. You could paint the room in blue and yellow stripes, or you could mix the colors and paint the room green. You can think of different alleles as different paint colors, but in genetics there are many more paint colors—alleles—and many more ways that they are combined.

▶ MAIN IDEA

Phenotype can depend on interactions of alleles.

Although Mendel's basic theory of heredity was correct, his research could not have explained all of the continuous variations for many traits. For example, many traits result from alleles with a range of dominance, rather than a strict dominant and recessive relationship.

The pea flowers that Mendel observed were either white or purple. One allele was dominant, but dominance does not mean that one allele "defeats" the other. Usually, it means that the dominant allele codes for a certain protein and the recessive allele codes for a variation of the protein that has little or no effect. In Mendel's pea flowers, a heterozygous plant makes enough of the purple color that only one dominant allele is needed to give the flowers a purple color. But in many cases, a phenotype comes from more than just one gene, and many genes in a population have more than just two alleles.

Incomplete Dominance

Sometimes, alleles show **incomplete dominance,** in which a heterozygous phenotype is somewhere between the two homozygous phenotypes. Neither allele is completely dominant nor completely recessive. One example of incomplete dominance is the four-o'clock plant. When plants that are homozygous for red flowers are crossed with plants that are homozygous for white flowers, the offspring have pink flowers. The pink color is a third, distinct phenotype. Neither of the original phenotypes of the plants in the parent's generation can be seen separately in the F_1 generation offspring.

Connecting CONCEPTS

Principles of Genetics Recall from **Chapter 6** that a homozygote has two identical alleles of a gene, and a heterozygote has two different alleles of a gene.

FIGURE 7.5 Incomplete Dominance

PHENOTYPE	GENOTYPE	PHENOTYPE	GENOTYPE	PHENOTYPE	GENOTYPE
green	B_1B_1	steel blue	B_2B_2	royal blue	B_1B_2

The green betta fish is homozygous for the green color allele.	The steel blue betta fish is homozygous for the blue color allele.	The royal blue betta fish is heterozygous for the two color alleles.

Another example of incomplete dominance is the color of betta fish shown in **FIGURE 7.5**. When a green fish (B_1B_1) is crossed with a steel blue fish (B_2B_2), all of the offspring have the heterozygous genotype (B_1B_2). These offspring will be a royal blue color that comes from the phenotypes from both alleles. The alleles of this gene follow a pattern of incomplete dominance. What happens when two royal blue betta fish are crossed? Some offspring (25 percent) will be green (B_1B_1), some (50 percent) will be royal blue (B_1B_2), and some (25 percent) will be steel blue (B_2B_2).

VOCABULARY

When alleles are neither dominant nor recessive, such as with incomplete dominance, uppercase letters with either subscripts or superscripts are used to represent the different alleles.

Codominance

Sometimes, both alleles of a gene are expressed completely—neither allele is dominant nor recessive. In this case, alleles show **codominance,** in which both traits are fully and separately expressed. Suppose a plant that is homozygous for red flowers is crossed with a plant that is homozygous for white flowers. In incomplete dominance, the offspring have pink flowers. Codominant alleles are different. Instead of what looks like an intermediate phenotype, both traits are expressed. The flowers will have some red areas and some white areas.

One trait that you likely know about—human ABO blood types—is an example of codominance. And, because the blood types come from three different alleles in the human population, this trait is also considered a multiple-allele trait. The multiple alleles, shown in **FIGURE 7.6**, are called I^A, I^B, and i. Both I^A and I^B result in a protein, called an antigen, on the surface of red blood cells. Allele i is recessive and does not result in an antigen. Someone with a genotype of I^Ai will have type A blood, and someone with a genotype of I^Bi will have type B blood. But remember that the I^A and I^B alleles are codominant.

FIGURE 7.6 CODOMINANCE

PHENOTYPE (BLOOD TYPE)		GENOTYPES
A	antigen A 	I^AI^A or I^Ai
B	 antigen B	I^BI^B or I^Bi
AB	both antigens 	I^AI^B
O	no antigens 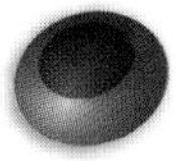	ii

People with both codominant alleles (I^AI^B) have both antigens, so they have type AB blood. People with an *ii* genotype have red blood cells without either antigen, and they have type O blood. Two heterozygous people, one with type A blood (I^Ai) and one with type B blood (I^Bi), can have offspring with any of the four blood types, depending on the alleles that are passed on.

Apply How can two people with type B blood have a child with type O blood?

▶ MAIN IDEA

Many genes may interact to produce one trait.

As you have seen, some variations in phenotype are related to incomplete dominance, codominance, and multiple alleles. But most traits in plants and animals, including humans, are the result of several genes that interact.

Polygenic Traits

Traits produced by two or more genes are called **polygenic traits.** Human skin color, for example, is the result of four genes that interact to produce a continuous range of colors. Similarly, human eye color, which is often thought of as a single gene trait, is polygenic. As **FIGURE 7.7** shows, at least three genes with complicated patterns of expression play roles in determining eye color. For example, the green allele is dominant to blue alleles, but it is recessive to all brown alleles. These genes do not account for all eye color variations, such as changes in eye color over time, the continuous range of eye colors, and patterns of colors in eyes. As a result, scientists hypothesize that still undiscovered genes affect eye color.

> **VISUAL VOCAB**
>
> Traits that are produced by two or more genes are called **polygenic traits.**
>
> many   genes
>
> **poly** **genic**

Epistasis

Another polygenic trait is fur color in mice and in other mammals. In mice, at least five different genes interact to produce the phenotype. Two genes give the mouse its general color, one gene affects the shading of the color, and one gene determines whether the mouse will have spots. But the fifth gene involved in mouse fur color can overshadow all of the others. In cases such as this, one gene, called an epistatic gene, can interfere with the expression of other genes.

FIGURE 7.7 Eye Color

At least three different genes interact to produce the range of human eye colors, such as in the examples on the right.

GENE NAME	DOMINANT ALLELE	RECESSIVE ALLELE
BEY1	brown	blue
BEY2	brown	blue
GEY	green	blue

Order of dominance: brown > green > blue.

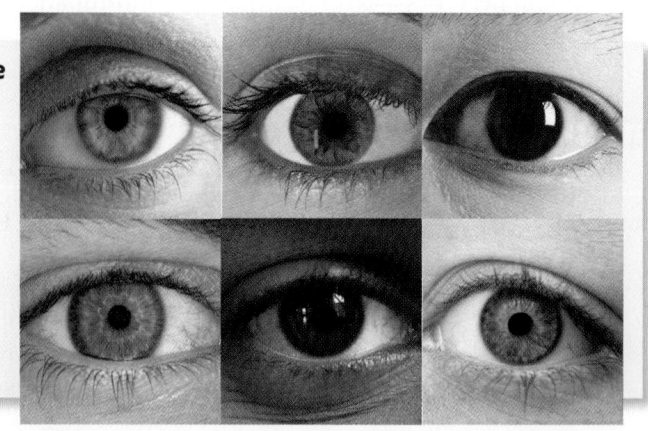

In albinism, a single epistatic gene interferes with the expression of other genes. Albinism, as you can see in **FIGURE 7.8**, is characterized by a lack of pigment in skin, hair, and eyes. A mouse that is homozygous for the alleles that prevent the coloration of fur will be white, regardless of the phenotypes that would normally come from the other four genes. A person with the alleles for albinism will have very light skin, hair, and eyes, regardless of the other genes he or she has inherited.

Contrast **How do multiple-allele traits differ from polygenic traits?**

FIGURE 7.8 Albinism in mammals, such as this hedgehog, is caused by an epistatic gene that blocks the production of pigments.

○ **MAIN IDEA**

The environment interacts with genotype.

Phenotype is more than the sum of gene expression. For example, the sex of sea turtles depends both on genes and on environment. Female turtles make nests on beaches and bury their eggs in the sand. Eggs that mature in warmer temperatures develop into female turtles. Eggs that mature in cooler temperatures develop into male turtles.

Genes and environment also interact to determine human traits. Think about height. Genes give someone a tendency to be either short or tall, but they do not control everything. An interesting question for the interaction between genes and environment is "Are identical twins always identical?" Studies of identical twins have shown that the environment during early development can have long-lasting effects. One twin might get more nutrients than the other because of its position in the mother's uterus. This difference can result in height and size differences that last throughout the twins' lives. Also, twins raised in environments with different nutrition and health care often differ in height and other physical traits. In the end, phenotype is usually a mixture of genes and environment.

scilinks.org *SciLINKS*
Find out more about dominant and recessive traits at scilinks.org.
Keycode: MLB007

Connect **Sunlight can cause a person's hair to become lighter in color. Is this an example of an interaction between genes and the environment? Why or why not?**

7.2 ASSESSMENT

ONLINE QUIZ ClassZone.com

REVIEWING ○ **MAIN IDEAS**

1. How is **incomplete dominance** expressed in a phenotype?

2. Why might **polygenic traits** vary more in phenotype than do single-gene traits?

3. Explain how interactions between genes and the environment can affect phenotype.

CRITICAL THINKING

4. **Synthesize** How is **codominance** the same as having no dominant and recessive relationship at all between two alleles?

5. **Compare and Contrast** How are codominant alleles and incompletely dominant alleles similar? How are they different?

Connecting **CONCEPTS**

6. **Principles of Genetics** Why can parents who are heterozygous for type A and type B blood have children with any of the four human blood types? Use a Punnett square to support your answer.

MATERIALS
- paper
- pencil

PROCESS SKILLS
- **Inferring**
- **Predicting**

MICHIGAN STANDARDS

B4.1c Differentiate between dominant, recessive, codominant, polygenic, and sex-linked traits.

B4.2D Predict the consequences that changes in the DNA composition of particular genes may have on an organism (e.g., sickle cell anemia, other).

Codominance

Codominant alleles are both expressed in a person's phenotype. A heterozygote will have the traits associated with both alleles. In this lab, you will explore codominance by analyzing the results of tests for sickle cell disease within a family.

BACKGROUND

Sickle cell disease is caused by a change in the gene for hemoglobin, which is the oxygen-carrying protein in red blood cells. Individuals who are homozygous for the sickle cell allele often cannot endure exercise. Individuals who are heterozygous for the allele can have sickle cell attacks under extreme conditions. Normal individuals ($Hb^S Hb^S$) have only normal hemoglobin. Homozygous sickle cell individuals ($Hb^s Hb^s$) have only sickle cell hemoglobin. Heterozygous individuals ($Hb^S Hb^s$) have both normal hemoglobin and sickle cell hemoglobin.

Jerry Smith collapsed while running a race for his track team. A doctor said that he had a sickle cell attack. Genetic tests were run on several family members. The test results are shown below. An X indicates that form of hemoglobin in red blood cells.

PROBLEM How can you determine the genotypes of people in a family?

TABLE 1. FAMILY PHENOTYPES		
Subject	Normal Hemoglobin	Sickle Cell Hemoglobin
Jerry Smith	X	X
Jerry's brother	X	
Jerry's younger sister	X	X
Jerry's youngest sister	X	
Jerry's father	X	
Jerry's grandfather	X	
Jerry's grandmother	X	X

PROCEDURE

1. Use the background information and the genetic test results to answer questions 1–4.
2. Use the background information and a Punnett square to help you answer question 5.

ANALYZE AND CONCLUDE

1. **Analyze** Are any of Jerry's siblings homozygous for the sickle cell allele? Are any of Jerry's siblings heterozygous for sickle cell disease?
2. **Analyze** What genotype is Jerry's father?
3. **Analyze** What genotypes are Jerry's grandparents?
4. **Infer** What is the genotype of Jerry's mother? Explain.
5. **Predict** If Jerry marries a female who is heterozygous for the sickle cell allele, what would be the possible genotypes and phenotypes of their children, according to your Punnett square?

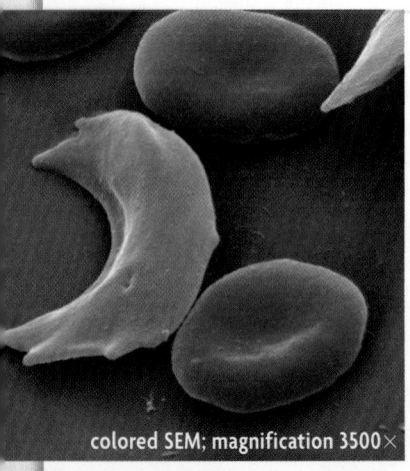

colored SEM; magnification 3500×

7.3 Gene Linkage and Mapping

KEY CONCEPT Genes can be mapped to specific locations on chromosomes.

> **MAIN IDEAS**
> - Gene linkage was explained through fruit flies.
> - Linkage maps estimate distances between genes.

VOCABULARY

linkage map, p. 210

Review
chromosome,
crossing over

MICHIGAN STANDARDS

B1.2i Explain the progression of ideas and explanations that leads to science theories that are part of the current scientific consensus or core knowledge.
B4.1c Differentiate between dominant, recessive, codominant, polygenic, and sex-linked traits.

Connect If you leave a banana out on a table until it is very ripe, you might see some of the most useful organisms for genetic research—fruit flies—buzzing around it. In your kitchen, fruit flies are pests. In the laboratory, early experiments with fruit flies showed not only that genes are on chromosomes but also that genes are found at specific places on chromosomes.

> **MAIN IDEA**
Gene linkage was explained through fruit flies.

Gene linkage, which you read about in Chapter 6, was first described by William Bateson and R. C. Punnett, who invented the Punnett square. Punnett and Bateson, like Mendel, studied dihybrid crosses of pea plants. But their results differed from the 9:3:3:1 phenotype ratios that Mendel observed. The results suggested that some genes were linked together. But how could genes be linked and still follow Mendel's law of independent assortment?

American scientist Thomas Hunt Morgan, who worked with fruit flies (*Drosophila melanogaster*), found the answer. At first, Morgan was just looking for an organism to use in genetic research. He found fruit flies very useful because he could quickly and cheaply grow new generations of flies. He observed among fruit flies easily identifiable variations in eye color, body color, and wing shape. Knowing these variations, Morgan and his students set up experiments similar to Mendel's dihybrid crosses. They chose one type of fly with traits associated with the wild type, or most common phenotype. They crossed the wild type flies with mutant flies, or flies with a different, less common phenotype. You can see examples of fruit flies in **FIGURE 7.9.**

Morgan's results, like those of Punnett and Bateson, did not always follow the 9:3:3:1 ratio predicted by Mendel. But the results did differ in a noticeable pattern. Some traits appeared to be inherited together. Morgan called these traits linked traits, and they appeared to fall into four groups. As it turns out, fruit flies have four pairs of chromosomes. Each of the four groups of linked traits identified by Morgan matches one of the chromosome pairs. Morgan concluded that linked genes were on the same chromosome. The chromosomes, not the genes, assort independently during meiosis. Because the linked genes were not inherited together every time, Morgan also concluded that chromosomes must exchange homologous genes during meiosis.

Wild type

Mutant

FIGURE 7.9 The wild type fruit fly (top) shows the most common phenotype. The mutant fruit fly (bottom) has no wings, white eyes, and a different body color.

Synthesize How did Morgan's research build upon Mendel's observations?

CONSTRUCTING BAR GRAPHS

Scientists tested the reaction of fruit flies to stress by exposing them to bright light—a source of stress for *Drosophila*. The scientists timed how long it took for half of the flies in each group to reach food, which they called a "half-time." Three strains of flies were tested—wild type 1, wild type 2, and a mutant eyeless type—under control conditions and with bright light. The data are shown in Table 1.

1. **Graph Data** Construct a bar graph that shows the data in the table. Recall that the independent variable is on the *x*-axis and the dependent variable is on the *y*-axis.

2. **Analyze** How did the condition of bright light affect the flies? Were all strains affected to the same degree? Why or why not?

TABLE 1. *DROSOPHILA* RESPONSES TO LIGHT

Strain	Condition	Half-Time (min)
Wild type 1	control	4.0
Wild type 1	bright light	12.5
Wild type 2	control	4.5
Wild type 2	bright light	12.0
Eyeless	control	4.5
Eyeless	bright light	5.0

Source: V. Min, B. Condron, Journal of Neuroscience Methods, 145.

▶ **MAIN IDEA**

Linkage maps estimate distances between genes.

The probability that two genes on a chromosome will be inherited together is related to the distance between them. The closer together two genes are, the more likely it is that they will be inherited together. The farther apart two genes are, the more likely it is that they will be separated during meiosis.

One of Morgan's students, Alfred Sturtevant, hypothesized that the frequency of cross-overs during meiosis was related to the distance between genes. This meant that the closer together two genes were, the more likely they were to stay together when cross-overs took place. Sturtevant identified three linked traits in fruit flies—body color, eye color, and wing size—and then crossed the fruit flies. He recorded the percentage of times that the phenotypes did not appear together in the offspring. This percentage represented the frequency of cross-overs between chromosomes.

From the cross-over frequencies, Sturtevant made **linkage maps,** which are maps of the relative locations, or loci, of genes on a chromosome. On a linkage map, one map unit is equal to one cross-over for each 100 offspring, or one percentage point. You can see an example of a linkage map in **FIGURE 7.10**.

Making a linkage map is fairly easy if all of the cross-over frequencies for the genes being studied are known. Suppose the following data were collected.

- Gene A and gene B cross over 6.0 percent of the time.
- Gene B and gene C cross over 12.5 percent of the time.
- Gene A and gene C cross over 18.5 percent of the time.

According to Sturtevant's conclusions, genes A and B are 6 map units apart because they cross over 6 percent of the time. Similarly, genes B and C are 12.5 map units apart because they cross over 12.5 percent of the time. But where are the genes located in relation to each other on the chromosome?

Connecting CONCEPTS

Crossing Over Recall from Chapter 6 that segments of non-sister chromatids can be exchanged during meiosis.

FIGURE 7.10 Gene Linkage in *Drosophila*

Linkage maps show the relative locations of genes.

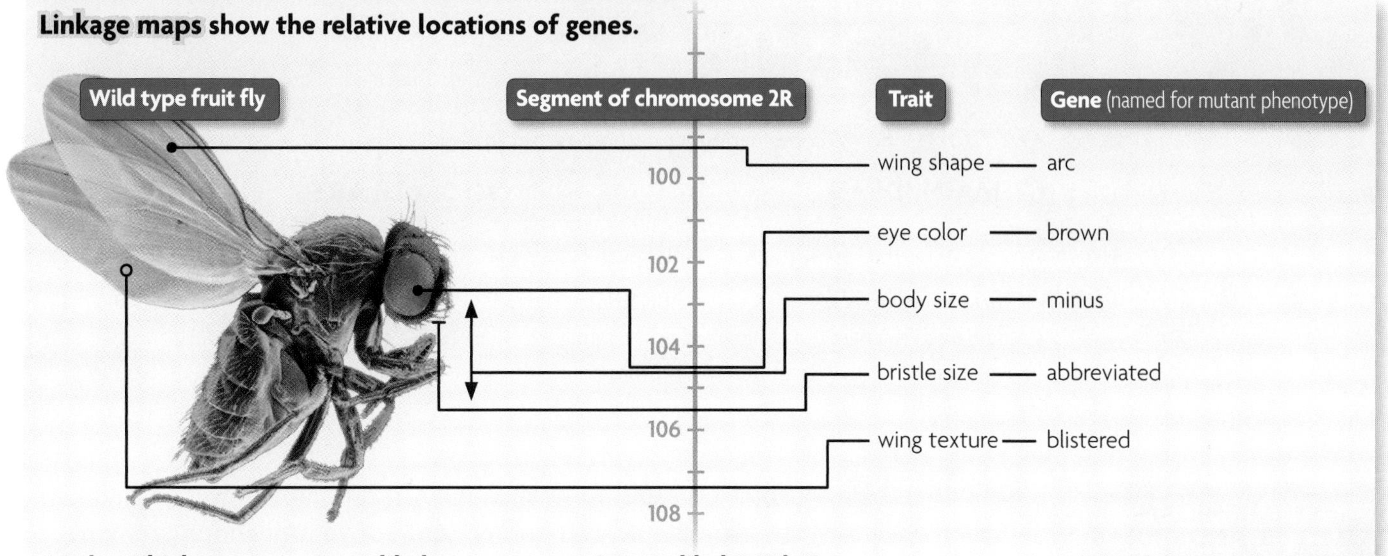

Wild type fruit fly	Segment of chromosome 2R	Trait	Gene (named for mutant phenotype)

100 — wing shape —— arc

102 — eye color —— brown

104 — body size —— minus

— bristle size —— abbreviated

106 — wing texture —— blistered

108

Apply Which genes are most likely to cross over? Least likely? Why?

(colored SEM; magnification 20×)

Think about gene A as a point on a line. Gene B is either to the left or to the right of gene A. The same is true of the relationship between genes B and C. But if you only know the distances between genes A and B, and between genes B and C, you cannot determine the order of all three genes. You must also know the distance between genes A and C. As shown in **FIGURE 7.11**, the map distances between genes A and B and between genes B and C equal the map distance between genes A and C. Therefore, gene B must be located between genes A and C. If the map distance between genes A and C were 6.5 map units instead of 18.5 map units, then gene A would be between genes B and C.

Although linkage maps show the relative locations of linked genes, the maps do not show actual physical distances between genes. Linkage maps can give you a general idea about distances between genes, but many factors affect gene linkage. As a result, two pairs of genes may be the same number of map units apart, but they may not have the same physical distance between them.

Summarize How can a linkage map be made from observations of traits?

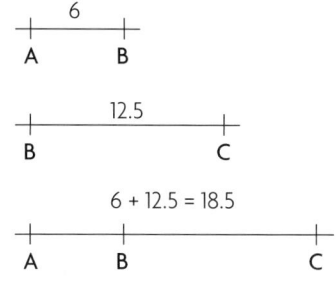

FIGURE 7.11 The order of genes on a chromosome can be determined if all of their cross-over frequencies are known.

7.3 ASSESSMENT

ONLINE QUIZ ClassZone.com

REVIEWING ▶ MAIN IDEAS

1. Summarize the importance of comparing wild type and mutant fruit flies in genetic research.

2. How is a **linkage map** related to cross-overs that take place during meiosis?

CRITICAL THINKING

3. **Compare and Contrast** How are linked genes similar to sex-linked genes? How are they different?

4. **Apply** Draw a linkage map based on the following cross-over percentages for three gene pairs: A – B = 8%, B – C = 10%, and A – C = 2%.

Connecting CONCEPTS

5. **Scientific Process** Punnett, Bateson, and Morgan found phenotype ratios that differed from Mendel's results. Explain how these differences led to new hypotheses and new investigations in genetics.

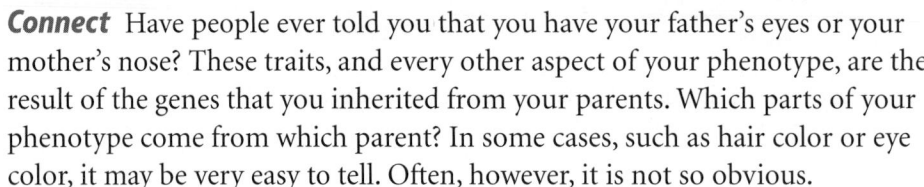

7.4 Human Genetics and Pedigrees

KEY CONCEPT A combination of methods is used to study human genetics.

▶ MAIN IDEAS

- Human genetics follows the patterns seen in other organisms.
- Females can carry sex-linked genetic disorders.
- A pedigree is a chart for tracing genes in a family.
- Several methods help map human chromosomes.

VOCABULARY

pedigree, p. 214
karyotype, p. 217

Review
phenotype, allele, sex-linked gene, genotype

MICHIGAN STANDARDS

B4.1c Differentiate between dominant, recessive, codominant, polygenic, and sex-linked traits.

B4.3C Explain how it might be possible to identify genetic defects from just a karyotype of a few cells.

Connect Have people ever told you that you have your father's eyes or your mother's nose? These traits, and every other aspect of your phenotype, are the result of the genes that you inherited from your parents. Which parts of your phenotype come from which parent? In some cases, such as hair color or eye color, it may be very easy to tell. Often, however, it is not so obvious.

▶ MAIN IDEA

Human genetics follows the patterns seen in other organisms.

Fruit flies and pea plants may seem boring and simple, but the basic principles of genetics were worked out using those organisms. Humans follow the same patterns of heredity. First, meiosis independently assorts chromosomes when gametes are made for sexual reproduction. Second, human heredity involves the same relationships between alleles—dominant and recessive interactions, polygenic traits, and sex-linked genes, among others.

The inheritance of many traits is very complex. A single trait may be controlled by several genes that interact. As you read in Section 7.2, eye color is controlled by at least three different genes. And, although several genes affect height, a person's environment during growth and development plays a large role in his or her adult height. What might seem like an obvious phenotype is rarely as simple as it looks.

Nonetheless, single-gene traits are very helpful in understanding human genetics. One such trait is the shape of a person's hairline. A hairline with a downward point, such as a widow's peak shown in **FIGURE 7.12**, is a dominant trait. A straight hairline is a recessive trait. The inheritance of this trait follows the same dominant and recessive pattern as the traits in Mendel's pea plants. Many genetic disorders, such as Huntington's disease, hemophilia, and Duchenne's muscular dystrophy, are also caused by single genes that follow a dominant and recessive pattern. In fact, much of what is known about human genetics comes from studying genetic disorders.

FIGURE 7.12 The widow's peak, or pointed hairline, is a phenotype produced by a dominant autosomal gene.

Apply Why can the genetics of pea plants and fruit flies be applied to humans?

MAIN IDEA

Females can carry sex-linked genetic disorders.

Recall from Section 7.1 that some genetic disorders are caused by autosomal genes. A carrier of an autosomal disorder does not show the disease but can pass on the disease-causing allele. Both males and females can be carriers of an autosomal disorder.

In contrast, only females can be carriers of sex-linked disorders. Several genetic disorders are caused by genes on the X chromosome, as you can see in **FIGURE 7.13**. Recall that males have an XY genotype. A male who has a gene for a disorder located on the X chromosome will not have a second, normal allele to mask it. One copy of the allele is enough for males to have the disorder. There are no male carriers of sex-linked disorders, because any male who has the gene displays the phenotype. Females can be carriers, because they may have a normal allele that gives them a normal phenotype. The likelihood of inheriting a sex-linked disorder depends both on the sex of the child and on which parent carries the disorder-causing allele. If only the mother has the allele and is a carrier, a child has a 50 percent chance of inheriting the allele. A daughter who inherits it will not show the phenotype, but a son will.

The British royal family provides a historical example of a sex-linked disorder. Queen Victoria (1819–1901) was a carrier of a recessive sex-linked allele for a disorder called hemophilia, which is a lack of proteins needed for blood to clot. People with hemophilia do not stop bleeding easily. Queen Victoria passed the allele to her son, who had hemophilia. He passed it to his daughter, who was a carrier, and so on. Members of royal families tended to marry into royal families in other countries, and by the early 1900s the royal families of several countries, including Russia and Spain, also had the allele for hemophilia. The allele in all of these people is traced back to Queen Victoria.

Contrast How can carriers differ between autosomal and sex-linked disorders?

FIGURE 7.13 Comparing the X and Y Chromosomes

The X chromosome has about 1100 known genes, including many that cause genetic disorders. The Y chromosome is about one-third the size of the X and has only about 250 known genes.

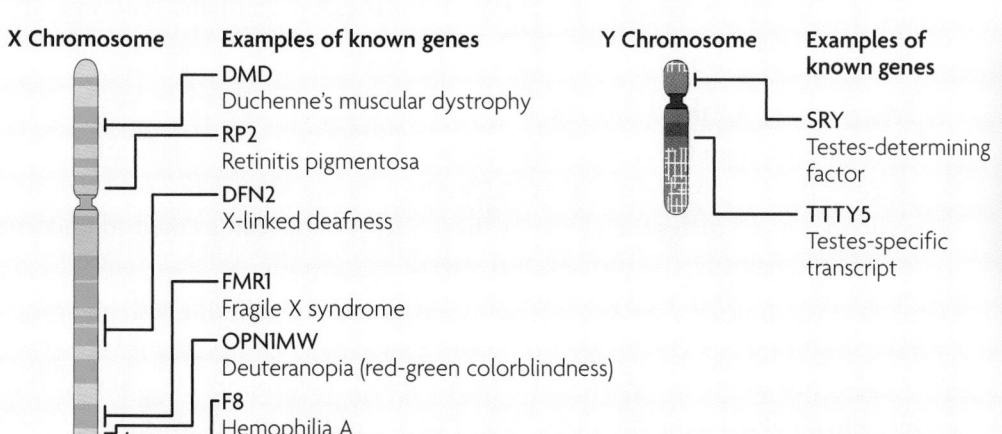

X Chromosome

Examples of known genes
- DMD
  Duchenne's muscular dystrophy
- RP2
  Retinitis pigmentosa
- DFN2
  X-linked deafness
- FMR1
  Fragile X syndrome
- OPN1MW
  Deuteranopia (red-green colorblindness)
- F8
  Hemophilia A

Y Chromosome

Examples of known genes
- SRY
  Testes-determining factor
- TTTY5
  Testes-specific transcript

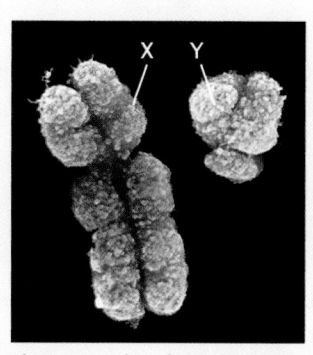

These X and Y chromosomes are duplicated and condensed. (colored SEM; magnification about 15,000×)

A pedigree is a chart for tracing genes in a family.

Connecting CONCEPTS

Genetic Screening DNA testing is a direct method of studying genetic disorders. You will learn more about DNA tests and genetic screening in **Chapter 9.**

If two people want to know their child's chances of having a certain genetic disorder, they cannot rely upon their phenotypes. The parents also need to know their genotypes. A **pedigree** chart can help trace the phenotypes and genotypes in a family to determine whether people carry recessive alleles. When enough family phenotypes are known, genotypes can often be inferred.

A human pedigree shows several types of information. Boxes represent males and circles represent females. A shaded shape means that a person shows the trait, a white shape means that the person does not, and a shape that is half-shaded and half-white means that a person is a carrier. Lines connect a person to his or her mate, and to their children.

Using phenotypes to figure out the possible genotypes in a family is like putting pieces of a puzzle together. You have to use clues and logic to narrow the possibilities for each person's genotype. One particular clue, for example, can tell you whether the gene is on an autosome or on a sex chromosome. If approximately the same number of males and females have the phenotype, then the gene is most likely on an autosome. If, however, the phenotype is much more common in males, then the gene is likely on the X chromosome.

Tracing Autosomal Genes

It is fairly easy to trace genotypes through a pedigree when you know that you are dealing with a trait controlled by an autosomal gene. Why? A person who does not show the phenotype must have a homozygous recessive genotype. Any other genotype—either heterozygous or homozygous dominant—would produce the phenotype. Use the following steps to work your way through a pedigree for a gene on an autosome. The inheritance of an autosomal trait, such as the widow's peak described earlier, is shown on the top of **FIGURE 7.14.**

- People with a widow's peak have either homozygous dominant (*WW*) or heterozygous (*Ww*) genotypes.
- Two parents without a widow's peak are both homozygous recessive (*ww*), and cannot have children who have a widow's peak.
- Two parents who both have a widow's peak can have a child who does not (*ww*) if both parents are heterozygous for the dominant and recessive alleles (*Ww*).

Tracing Sex-Linked Genes

When a gene is on the X chromosome, you have to think about the inheritance of the sex chromosomes as well as dominant and recessive alleles. Also, recall that more males than females show a sex-linked trait in their phenotype, and that females can be carriers of the trait.

One example of a sex-linked trait is red-green colorblindness. Three genes for color vision are on the X chromosome, so a male with even one recessive allele of one of the three genes is at least partially colorblind. He will pass that allele to all of his daughters, but cannot pass the allele to any sons. A pedigree for colorblindness, which is sex-linked, is shown on the bottom of **FIGURE 7.14.**

FIGURE 7.14 Interpreting Pedigree Charts

Figuring out genotypes from phenotypes requires you to use a process of elimination. You can often determine which genotypes are possible, and which ones are not.

☐ Male without phenotype

▨ Male with phenotype

◩ Male carrier

○ Female without phenotype

● Female with phenotype

◐ Female carrier

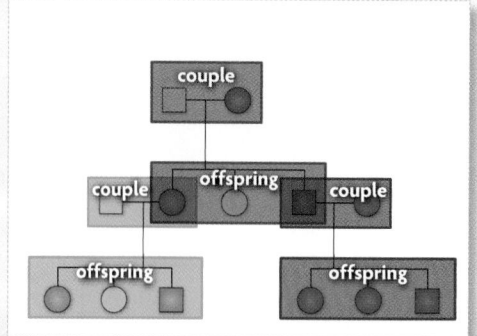

TRACING AUTOSOMAL GENES: WIDOW'S PEAK

Parental generation

☐ 1 — ● 2
ww   Ww

W = Dominant
w = Recessive

• Male 1 must be *ww* and female 2 must be heterozygous (*Ww*), because they have a daughter (5) with the recessive trait.

F_1 generation

☐ 3   ● 4   ○ 5   ▨ 6   ○ 7
ww   Ww   ww   Ww   WW or Ww

• Children 4 and 6 have the widow's peak trait. They must be heterozygous, because they can inherit only one dominant allele.

F_2 generation

● 8   ○ 9   ▨ 10   ● 11   ● 12   ▨ 13
Ww   ww   Ww   WW or Ww   WW or Ww   WW or Ww

• Children 8 and 10 have the widow's peak trait. They must be heterozygous, because they can inherit only one dominant allele.

TRACING SEX-LINKED GENES: COLORBLINDNESS

Parental generation

☐ 1 — ◐ 2
$X^M Y$ $X^M X^m$

X^M = Dominant
X^m = Recessive

• Male 1 must be $X^M Y$ and female 2 must be a carrier ($X^M X^m$) because they have two colorblind sons.

F_1 generation

☐ 3   ◐ 4   ○ 5 ?   ▨ 6   ▨ 7   ○ 8 ?
$X^M Y$ $X^M X^m$ $X^M X^M$ or $X^M X^m$ $X^m Y$ $X^m Y$ $X^M X^M$ or $X^M X^m$

• Female 4 must be a carrier ($X^M X^m$) because she has a colorblind son. Males 6 and 7 must be $X^m Y$. Females 5 and 8 are not colorblind, but it is not possible to determine whether they are carriers.

F_2 generation

○ 9 ?   ☐ 10   ○ 11 ?   ▨ 12   ◐ 13   ◐ 14   ☐ 15
$X^M X^M$ or $X^M X^m$ $X^M Y$ $X^M X^M$ or $X^M X^m$ $X^m Y$ $X^M X^m$ $X^M X^m$ $X^M Y$

• Children 13 and 14 must be carriers because their father is colorblind. Females 9 and 11 are not colorblind, but it is not possible to determine whether they are carriers.

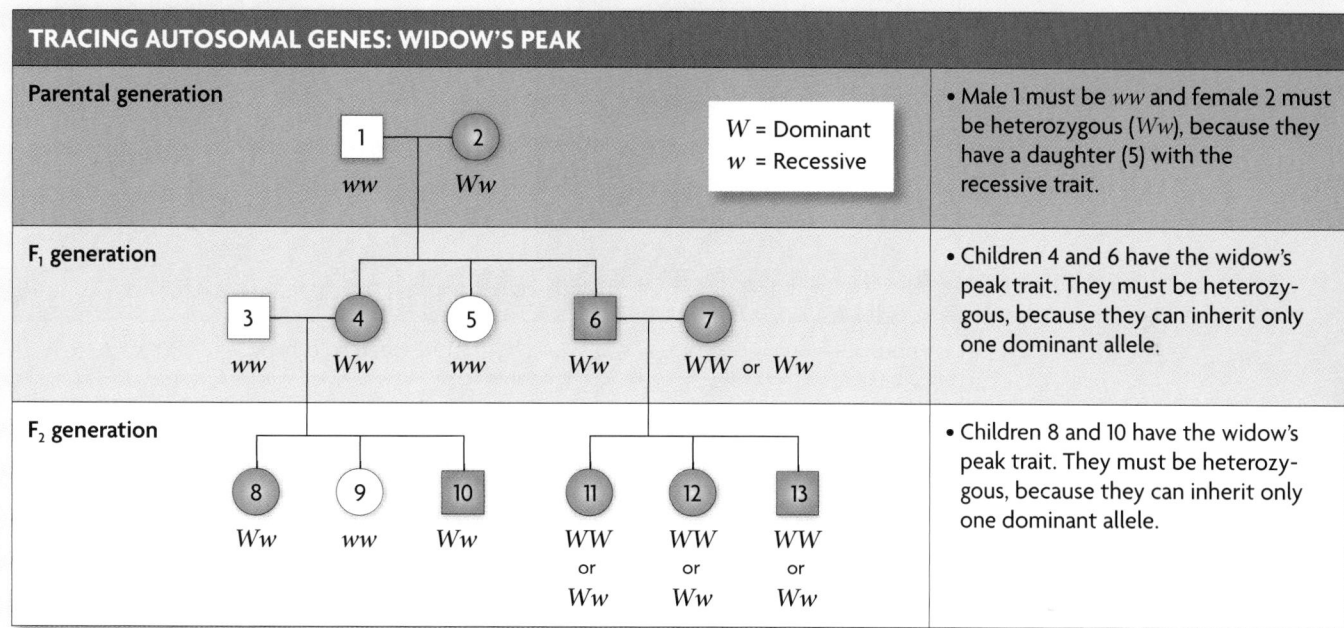

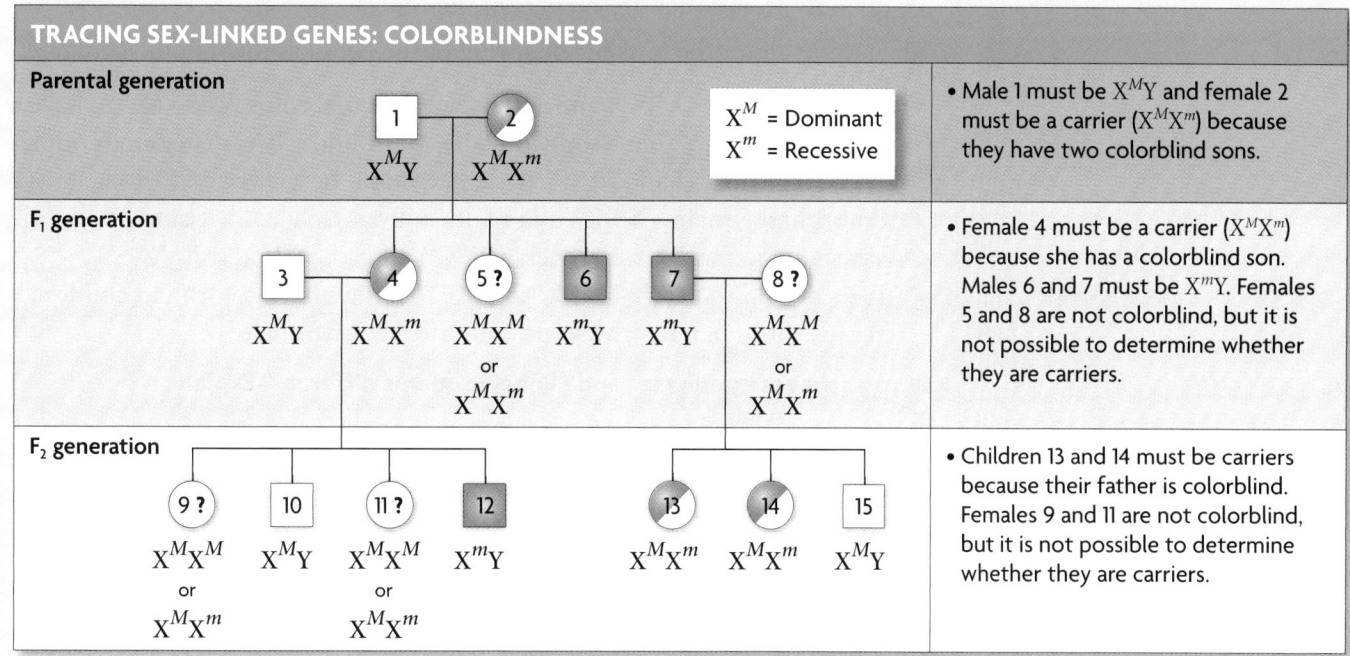

CRITICAL VIEWING Explain why it is not possible to identify all of the genotypes in the pedigree charts above. What information would you need to identify the genotypes of those people?

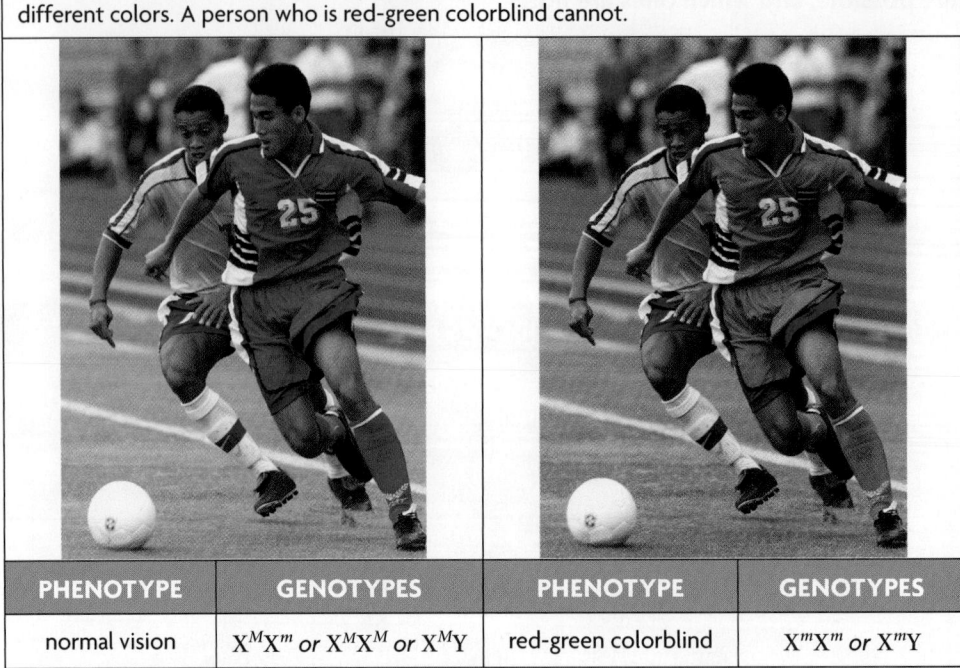

FIGURE 7.15 RED-GREEN COLORBLINDNESS

A person with normal color vision can easily distinguish between different colors. A person who is red-green colorblind cannot.

PHENOTYPE	GENOTYPES	PHENOTYPE	GENOTYPES
normal vision	X^MX^m or X^MX^M or X^MY	red-green colorblind	X^mX^m or X^mY

The steps below can be applied to any sex-linked trait. By using a process of elimination, you can often figure out the possible genotypes for a given phenotype. First, think about the individuals shown in the pedigree chart.

- Colorblind females must be homozygous recessive (X^mX^m).
- Males who are colorblind must have the recessive allele (X^mY).
- Females who are heterozygous for the alleles (X^MX^m) do not show the phenotype, but they are carriers of the trait.

Then think about the possible offspring of the people shown in the pedigree.

- A female carrier (X^MX^m) and a male with normal color vision (X^MY) have a 50 percent chance that a son would be colorblind (X^mY). The same couple has a 50 percent chance that a daughter would be a carrier (X^MX^m).
- Colorblind females (X^mX^m) and males with normal color vision (X^MY) will have daughters who are carriers (X^MX^m) and colorblind sons (X^mY).
- Two colorblind parents (X^mX^m and X^mY) always have colorblind children because both parents always pass on the recessive allele.

Contrast How are pedigrees and Punnett squares different? Explain.

▶ MAIN IDEA
Several methods help map human chromosomes.

The human genome, or all of the DNA in a human cell, is so large that mapping human genes is difficult. As a result, a combination of several methods is used. Pedigrees are useful for studying genetics in a family. Scientists can even gather a large number of pedigrees from people who are not related to look for inheritance patterns.

Other methods more directly study human chromosomes. A **karyotype** (KAR-ee-uh-TYP), for example, is a picture of all of the chromosomes in a cell. In order to study the chromosomes, chemicals are used to stain them. The chemical stains produce a pattern of bands on the chromosomes, as shown in **FIGURE 7.16**. The sizes and locations of the bands are very consistent for each chromosome, but the bands differ greatly among different chromosomes. Therefore, different chromosomes can be easily identified in a karyotype.

Karyotypes can show changes in chromosomes. Chromosome changes can be dramatic, such as when a person has too many chromosomes. In Down syndrome, for example, a person has an extra copy of at least part of chromosome 21. In XYY syndrome, a male has an extra Y chromosome. Other times, a karyotype reveals the loss of part of a chromosome. In the figure, you can see a deletion of a large part of chromosome 1. Scientists also use karyotypes to estimate the distances between genes on a chromosome. A karyotype can help show the possible location of a gene on a chromosome.

Chromosome mapping can be done directly by searching for a particular gene. All of the chromosomes are cut apart into smaller pieces. Then this library of chromosome parts is searched to find the gene. Although many genes and their locations have been identified through this process, it is a slow and inefficient method. The large-scale mapping of all of the genes on human chromosomes truly began with the Human Genome Project, which you will read more about in Chapter 9.

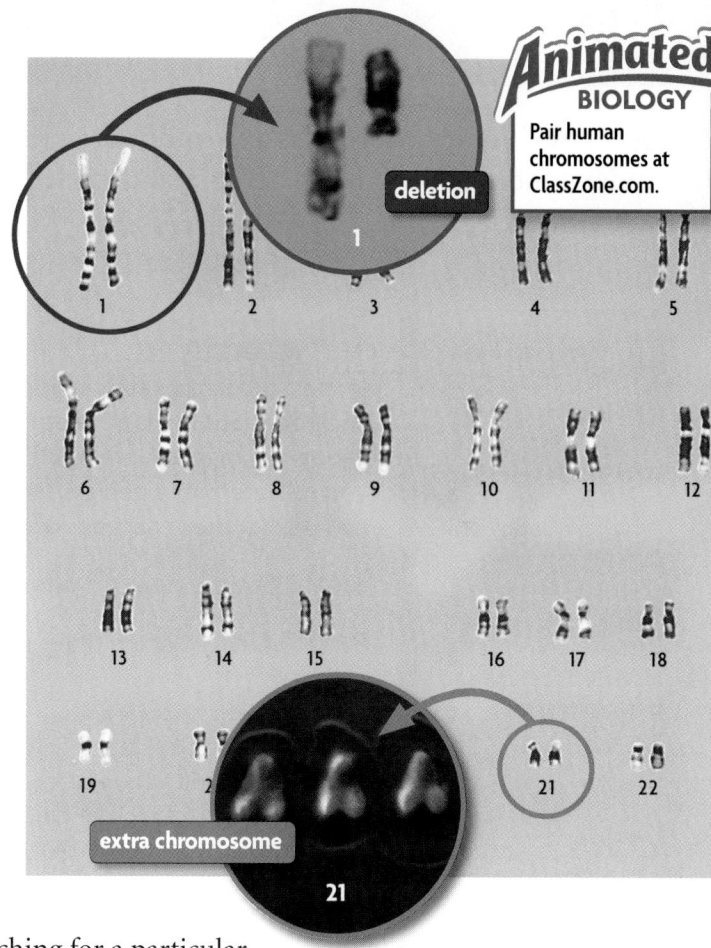

FIGURE 7.16 A karyotype can help show chromosomal disorders, such as the deletion in chromosome 1 (top inset) and the extra chromosome 21 in Down syndrome (bottom inset). (LM; magnifications: deletion 8000×; colored LM, extra chromosome 11,000×)

Apply **Why must a combination of methods be used to study human genetics?**

7.4 ASSESSMENT

ONLINE QUIZ ClassZone.com

REVIEWING ▷ MAIN IDEAS

1. How can Mendel's principles be used to study human traits?
2. Is a person who is homozygous recessive for a recessive genetic disease a carrier? Explain.
3. Describe how phenotypes can be used to predict genotypes in a **pedigree.**
4. What is a **karyotype,** and how can it be used to study human chromosomes?

CRITICAL THINKING

5. **Apply** Suppose a colorblind male and a female with no recessive alleles for colorblindness have children. What is the probability they will have a colorblind son? a colorblind daughter?
6. **Contrast** How do pedigrees for autosomal genes differ from pedigrees for sex-linked genes?

Connecting CONCEPTS

7. **Principles of Genetics** Explain why Mendel's principles of inheritance can be applied to all sexually reproducing species.

Use these inquiry-based labs and online activities to deepen your understanding of human genetics and complex patterns of inheritance.

INVESTIGATION

Pedigree Analysis

In most human genetics studies, scientists do not know the genotypes of people involved, so possible genotypes must be inferred from pedigrees. In this lab, you will interpret a pedigree to determine genotypes and predict the genotypes of future offspring.

MATERIALS
Pedigree Datasheet

SKILLS Inferring, Calculating Probabilities

PROBLEM What are the genotypes of the people in the pedigree?

PROCEDURE

1. Read the following background information and pedigree.

   People fall into three categories for the ability to taste a bitter chemical called 6-n-propylthiouracil (PROP). People who can taste PROP find it very unpleasant. Scientists hypothesize that these people, called supertasters, are homozygous for the trait ($T_1 T_1$). People who are heterozygous ($T_1 T_2$), called medium tasters, taste PROP as being somewhat bitter. Nontasters ($T_2 T_2$) do not taste the bitterness at all.

2. On your datasheet, fill in the possible genotypes for each person, including the phenotypes for those people who are medium tasters.

ANALYZE AND CONCLUDE

1. **Calculate** What is the probability that Jack will be a supertaster? What is the probability that Jill will be a supertaster? Explain your answers.

2. **Analyze** Is the gene for being a supertaster autosomal or sex-linked? Explain your answer based on the pedigree chart.

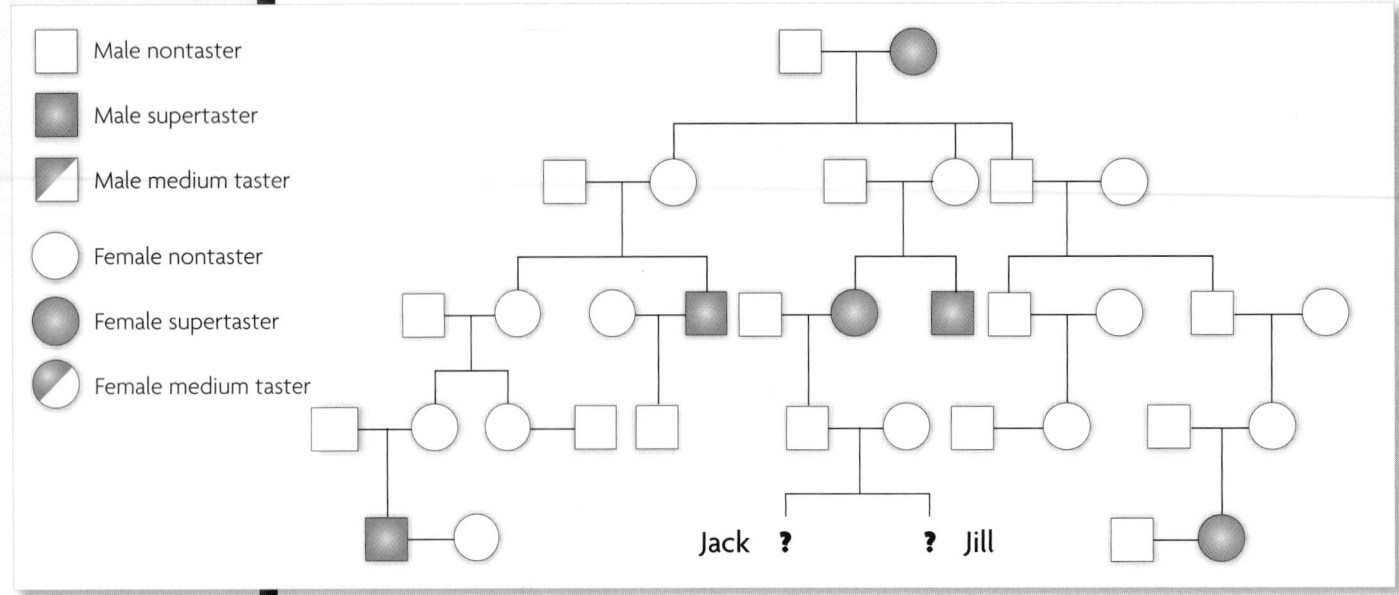

Male nontaster
Male supertaster
Male medium taster
Female nontaster
Female supertaster
Female medium taster

Jack ?   ? Jill

INVESTIGATION

Incomplete Dominance

When alleles are incompletely dominant, neither allele is completely dominant nor completely recessive. A heterozygous individual has an intermediate phenotype. In this lab, you will explore incomplete dominance by examining the human trait of hair texture.

SKILL Predicting

PROBLEM What is the genotype of each family member?

MATERIALS
- paper
- pencil

PROCEDURE

Use the information below to answer the questions that follow.

TABLE 1. FAMILY PHENOTYPES	
Individual	**Hair Texture**
Kathy's father	straight
Kathy's mother	curly
Kathy	wavy
Kathy's brother	wavy

ANALYZE AND CONCLUDE

1. **Apply** If I^s is the allele for straight hair and I^c is the allele for curly hair, then what are the genotypes of each individual in Kathy's family? Explain your answer using Punnett squares.

2. **Predict** If Kathy married a man with straight hair and they had children, what type of hair texture (straight, curly, wavy) might their children have? Explain your answer using Punnett squares.

3. **Predict** If Kathy married a man with curly hair and they had children, what type of hair texture might their children have? Explain your answer using Punnett squares.

4. **Predict** If Kathy married a man with wavy hair and they had children, what type of hair texture might their children have? Explain your answer using Punnett squares.

ANIMATED BIOLOGY
Tracking Traits

Make Punnett squares and a pedigree chart to track genotypes and phenotypes from one generation to the next. Then determine the probability of trait expression in the offspring.

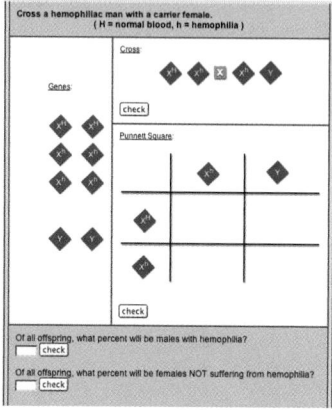

WEBQUEST

How can you track your ancestry when your family history is lost? Complete this WebQuest to find out. Learn how mitochondrial DNA and the DNA on the Y chromosome hold clues about someone's heritage. Find out how far back scientists can track a person's—or a whole population's—ancestry.

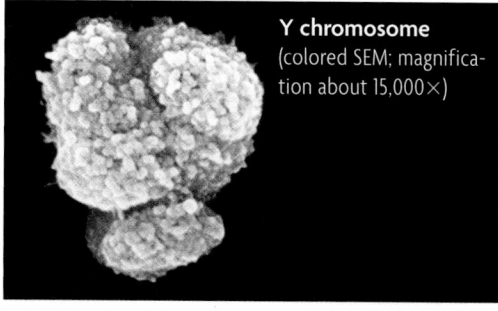

Y chromosome
(colored SEM; magnification about 15,000×)

DATA ANALYSIS ONLINE

Height is strongly influenced by genetics. However, the average height of men and women in the United States has increased over the past 150 years. Graph average heights over time and hypothesize why we are getting taller.

7.1 Chromosomes and Phenotype

The chromosomes on which genes are located can affect the expression of traits. Two alleles of autosomal genes interact to produce phenotype. Genes on the sex chromosomes are expressed differently in males and females of many species. In humans, males are XY and females are XX. Males only have one copy of each gene found on the sex chromosomes, so all of those genes are expressed in their phenotype.

7.2 Complex Patterns of Inheritance

Phenotype is affected by many different factors. Phenotype is rarely the result of a simple dominant and recessive relationship between two alleles of a gene. Often, there are more than two possible alleles of a gene. Incomplete dominance produces an intermediate phenotype. Codominance results in both alleles being fully and separately expressed. Many traits are polygenic, or controlled by several genes. Interactions between genes and the environment also affect phenotype.

7.3 Gene Linkage and Mapping

Genes can be mapped to specific locations on chromosomes. Studies of wild type and mutant fruit flies led to a new understanding of genetics. Linked genes are often inherited together. During meiosis, linked genes can be separated from each other when parts of chromosomes are exchanged. By studying the frequency of cross-overs between chromosomes, a linkage map can be made that shows the relative order of genes on a chromosome.

7.4 Human Genetics and Pedigrees

A combination of methods is used to study human genetics. Although most traits do not follow a simple dominant and recessive pattern, single-gene traits are important in the study of human genetics. Several genetic disorders are caused by a single gene with dominant and recessive alleles. Carriers are people who have an allele for a genetic disorder but do not express the allele in their phenotype. The patterns of genetic inheritance can be studied in families by pedigree analysis. Pedigree analysis is an indirect method of investigating human genotypes. Karyotypes can show large changes in chromosomes.

Synthesize Your Notes

Main Idea Web Use a main idea web like the one shown below to organize your notes. Make connections among the genetics concepts in the chapter, such as chromosomes and gene expression.

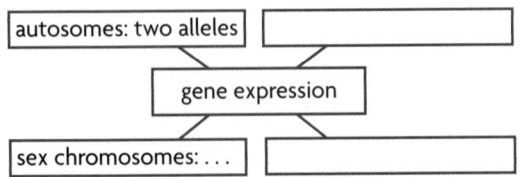

Concept Map Make a concept map like the one shown below to synthesize your knowledge of Mendelian genetics with more complex patterns of inheritance.

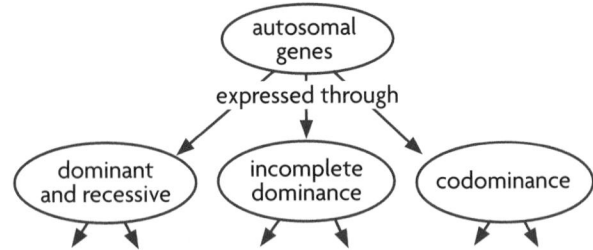

Chapter Assessment

Chapter Vocabulary

7.1 carrier, p. 201 sex-linked gene, p. 201 X chromosome inactivation, p. 203	**7.2** incomplete dominance, p. 204 codominance, p. 205 polygenic trait, p. 206	**7.3** linkage map, p. 210 **7.4** pedigree, p. 214 karyotype, p. 217

Reviewing Vocabulary

Compare and Contrast

Describe one similarity and one difference between the two terms in each of the following pairs.

1. sex-linked gene, carrier
2. incomplete dominance, codominance
3. linkage map, karyotype

Visualize Vocabulary

For each term below, use simple shapes, lines, or arrows to illustrate the meaning. Below each picture, write a short caption. Here's an example for *linkage map*.

A linkage map shows the order of genes on a chromosome.

4. polygenic trait
5. pedigree
6. X chromosome inactivation

Word Origins

Use the definitions of the word parts to answer the next two questions.

Word Part	Meaning
poly-	many
co-	together; the same amount
genic	produced by genes

7. How are the word parts *poly-* and *genic* related to the meaning of the term *polygenic trait*?
8. How is the prefix *co-* related to the meaning of the term *codominant*?

Reviewing MAIN IDEAS

9. Explain why disorders caused by dominant alleles on autosomes are less common than those caused by recessive alleles on autosomes.

10. Describe how the expression of sex-linked genes can differ between males and females.

11. How do codominance and incomplete dominance differ from a simple dominant and recessive relationship between alleles?

12. Humans have a tremendous range of hair, eye, and skin colors. How does the polygenic nature of these traits explain the wide range of phenotypes?

13. Give two examples that demonstrate how the environment can interact with genotype to affect an organism's phenotype.

14. How did Morgan's research with fruit flies explain Punnett's and Bateson's observations of pea plants?

15. Explain how linked genes and cross-over frequencies are used to make linkage maps.

16. What are two main ways in which human genetics follows the genetic patterns seen in other organisms?

17. Under what circumstances could two individuals with no symptoms of a recessive genetic disease have children that do have the disease?

18. What are one similarity and one difference between patterns for autosomal and sex-linked genes on a pedigree chart?

19. What is a karyotype, and how can it be used to study human chromosomes and to map human genes?

Critical Thinking

20. Analyze Can a person be a carrier for a dominant genetic disorder? Explain.

21. Apply Both men and women can be colorblind, but there are approximately 100 times more colorblind men than women in the world. Explain why men are more likely to be colorblind than women.

22. Apply Suppose two plants with light purple, or lavender, flowers are crossed. About 25 percent of the offspring have white flowers, 25 percent have purple flowers, and 50 percent have lavender flowers. Which of the following could explain these results: codominance, incomplete dominance, or multiple alleles? Explain.

23. Apply Copy the chart below into your notebook. Following the provided example, fill in the chart to show the number of possible genotypes given 2, 3, or 4 alleles.

Number of Alleles	Number of Possible Genotypes
2 (A, B)	3 (AA, AB, BB)
3 (A, B, C)	
4 (A, B, C, D)	

24. Apply Some members of David's family have an autosomal recessive disease. David does not have the disease; neither do his parents, nor his two brothers. His maternal grandfather has the disease, his paternal grandmother has the disease, and his sister has the disease. Draw a pedigree chart to represent the genotypes of all grandparents, parents, and children. Next to each person, write his or her possible genotype.

25. Synthesize Why are studies of identical twins important in helping understand interactions between environment and genotype? Explain.

Interpreting Visuals

Copy into your notebook the pedigree chart to the right to answer the next two questions. Use A as the dominant allele, and use a as the recessive allele.

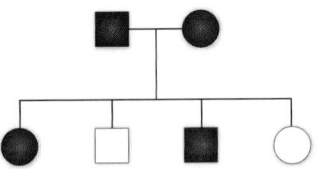

26. Analyze Is this trait most likely recessive or dominant? Explain.

27. Analyze What is the genotype of each individual in the pedigree chart? Explain your answers.

Analyzing Data

A scientist studies four linked traits in fruit flies and observes the frequency with which the traits cross over. The bar graph below shows the cross-over frequencies among genes A, B, C, and D. Use the graph to answer the next three questions.

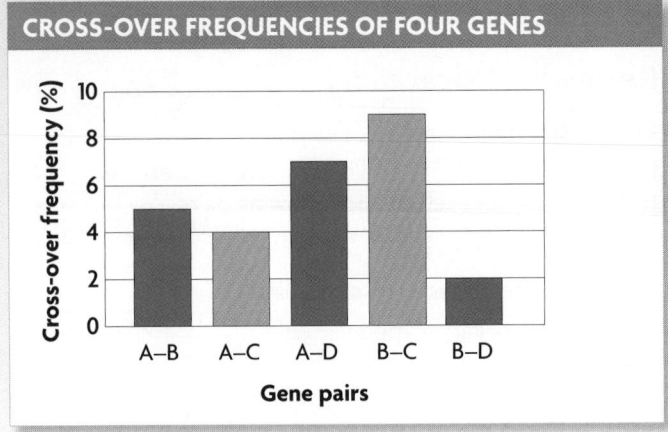

CROSS-OVER FREQUENCIES OF FOUR GENES

28. Evaluate Which two genes are least likely to be inherited together? How do you know?

29. Evaluate Which two genes are most likely to be inherited together? How do you know?

30. Apply Explain why a bar graph is an appropriate type of graph to use to display these data.

Connecting CONCEPTS

31. Write Ad Copy Imagine that you are starting a business that will make pedigree charts for people who want to map particular family traits. Your ad should be written in simple language that all readers will understand. Your ad should also demonstrate that you possess the necessary understanding of human genetics for a successful pedigree chart-making business.

32. Synthesize Look again at the tremendous range of human phenotypes in the photographs on pages 198–199. How is human genetics similar to and different from the genetics of Mendel's pea plants?

MICHIGAN
STANDARDS-BASED ASSESSMENT

✓ **Test Practice**
For more test practice,
go to ClassZone.com.

1. A genotyped pedigree of 239 people shows evidence of an inheritable recessive disease. One female, however, doesn't fit the pattern of inheritance demonstrated by all of the other family members. What is *most* likely true of this individual? **B4.2d**

A She had been treated for the disease.

B She accumulated additional mutations.

C She is immune to the disorder.

D She was genotyped incorrectly.

THINK THROUGH THE QUESTION

Consider both what a pedigree chart shows and what it doesn't show. Phenotypes are shown on a pedigree, but genotypes are inferred from the phenotypes.

---

2. A method used to identify genetic defects by chemically staining chromosomes is called a **B4.3C**

A gel electrophoresis.

B pedigree.

C karyotype.

D gene knockout.

3.

Genes on a pair of chromosomes often cross over during meiosis, as shown in the diagram. The discovery of crossing over added to Mendel's law of independent assortment, which stated that genes assort independently of one another. What did cross-overs indicate? **B4.1d**

A Crossing over allows for more than two alleles of a gene.

B Chromosomes assort independently, not genes.

C Mendel's principles could be applied to asexual reproduction.

D Crossing over explains incomplete dominance.

4. A scientist studying two traits in mice knows that each trait is determined by one gene and that both genes are on the same chromosome. If the two traits are not always inherited together by the offspring of the mice, what must be true? **B4.3f**

A The genes are not near the centromere.

B The genes are far enough apart to allow crossing over.

C The sister chromatids are unlinked.

D The genes must be on different arms of the chromosome.

5.

Fruit Fly Dihybrid Cross				
Eeww\eeWw	*eW*	*ew*	*eW*	*ew*
Ew				
Ew				
ew			■	
ew				
Red eyes is dominant (E); white eyes is recessive (e).				
Normal wings is dominant (W); short wings is recessive (w).				

A fruit fly with red eyes and short wings is crossed with a fruit fly with white eyes and normal wings. According to the cross shown in the diagram, what is the expected phenotype of fruit flies in the shaded box? **B4.1e**

A white eyes and normal wings

B white eyes and clipped wings

C red eyes and normal wings

D red eyes and clipped wings

6. The allele that causes Duchenne's muscular dystrophy is X-linked recessive. The symbol for the dominant allele is X_F. The symbol for the recessive allele is X_f. If an X_FX_F female and an X_fY male have children, what percentage of their male offspring would be expected to have Duchenne's muscular dystrophy? **B4.1c**

A 0%

B 50%

C 75%

D 100%

KEY CONCEPTS

8.1 Identifying DNA as the Genetic Material

DNA was identified as the genetic material through a series of experiments.

8.2 Structure of DNA

DNA structure is the same in all organisms.

8.3 DNA Replication

DNA replication copies the genetic information of a cell.

8.4 Transcription

Transcription converts a gene into a single-stranded RNA molecule.

8.5 Translation

Translation converts an mRNA message into a polypeptide, or protein.

8.6 Gene Expression and Regulation

Gene expression is carefully regulated in both prokaryotic and eukaryotic cells.

8.7 Mutations

Mutations are changes in DNA that may or may not affect phenotype.

Online BIOLOGY CLASSZONE.COM

Animated BIOLOGY	BIOZINE	RESOURCE CENTER
View animated chapter concepts.	Keep current with biology news.	Get more information on
• DNA Replication	• Featured stories	• DNA
• Build a Protein	• News feeds	• RNA
	• Strange Biology	• Mutations

Why is this mouse glowing?

This mouse's eerie green glow comes from green fluorescent protein (GFP), which glows under ultraviolet light. Scientists put a gene from a glowing jellyfish into a virus that was allowed to infect a mouse egg. The jellyfish gene became part of the mouse's genes. As a result, the mouse cells produce the same protein. Researchers hope to track cancer cells using GFP.

Connecting CONCEPTS

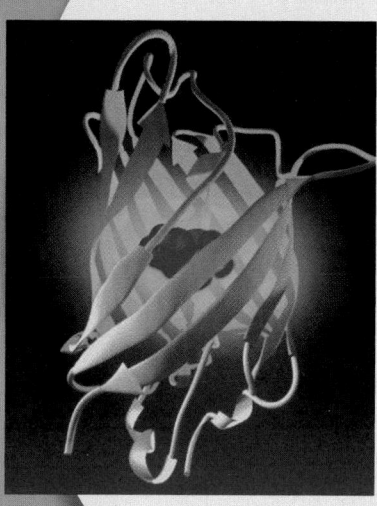

Translation This computer model of GFP shows the amino acids (purple) in the center of the protein that make the protein glow. The genetic code is universal, which means that a gene from one organism can be correctly translated into a protein in another organism. Although the gene for GFP comes from a jellyfish, GFP has been made in bacteria, yeast, slime mold, plants, fruit flies, zebrafish, and mammals.

8.1 Identifying DNA as the Genetic Material

KEY CONCEPT DNA was identified as the genetic material through a series of experiments.

▶ **MAIN IDEAS**

- Griffith finds a "transforming principle."
- Avery identifies DNA as the transforming principle.
- Hershey and Chase confirm that DNA is the genetic material.

VOCABULARY

bacteriophage, p. 228

Review
deoxyribonucleic acid (DNA), gene, enzyme

MICHIGAN STANDARDS

B1.2i Explain the progression of ideas and explanations that leads to science theories that are part of the current scientific consensus or core knowledge.

B4.2C Describe the structure and function of DNA.

TAKING NOTES

Make a table to keep track of the experiments discussed in this section and how they contributed to our understanding of DNA.

Experiment	Results
Griffith's mice	A transferable material changed harmless bacteria into disease-causing bacteria

Connect Some people think a complicated answer is better than a simple one. If they have a head cold, for instance, they may use all sorts of pills, syrups, and sprays, when they simply need rest, water, and warm chicken soup. In the early 1900s, most scientists thought DNA's structure was too repetitive for it to be the genetic material. Proteins, which are more variable in structure, appeared to be a better candidate. Starting in the 1920s, experiments provided data that did not support this idea. By the 1950s, sufficient evidence showed that DNA—the same molecule that codes for GFP in the glowing mouse—carries genetic information.

▶ **MAIN IDEA**

Griffith finds a "transforming principle."

In 1928 the British microbiologist Frederick Griffith was investigating two forms of the bacterium that causes pneumonia. One form is surrounded by a coating made of sugar molecules. Griffith called these bacteria the S form because colonies of them look smooth. The second form of bacteria do not have a smooth coating and are called the R, or rough, form. As you can see in **FIGURE 8.1**, when Griffith injected the two types of bacteria into mice, only the S type killed the mice. When the S bacteria were killed with heat, the mice were unaffected. Therefore, only live S bacteria would cause the mice to die.

FIGURE 8.1 Griffith's Experiments

The S form of the bacterium is deadly; the R form is not.

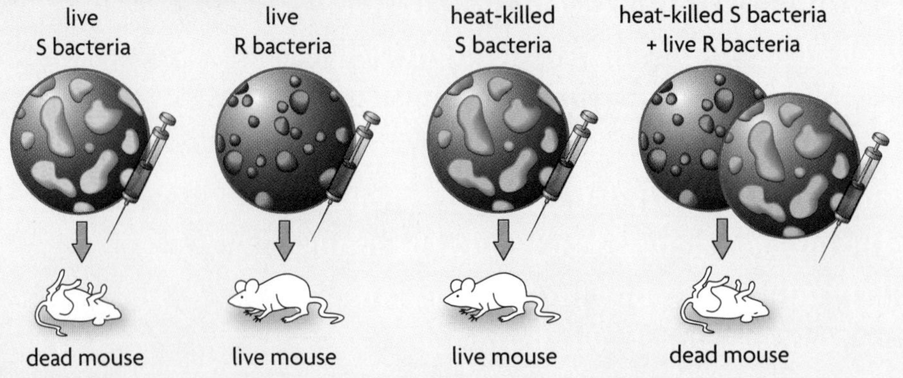

live S bacteria	live R bacteria	heat-killed S bacteria	heat-killed S bacteria + live R bacteria
dead mouse	live mouse	live mouse	dead mouse

Griffith next injected mice with a combination of heat-killed S bacteria and live R bacteria. To his surprise, the mice died. Even more surprising, he found live S bacteria in blood samples from the dead mice. Griffith concluded that some material must have been transferred from the heat-killed S bacteria to the live R bacteria. Whatever that material was, it contained information that changed harmless R bacteria into disease-causing S bacteria. Griffith called this mystery material the "transforming principle."

Infer **What evidence suggested that there was a transforming principle?**

Connecting CONCEPTS

Microbiology Much of our knowledge of the chemical basis of genetics has come from the study of bacteria. You will learn much more about bacteria in **Chapter 18.**

● MAIN IDEA

Avery identifies DNA as the transforming principle.

What exactly is the transforming principle that Griffith discovered? That question puzzled Oswald Avery and his fellow biologists. They worked for more than ten years to find the answer. Avery's team began by combining living R bacteria with an extract made from S bacteria. This procedure allowed them to directly observe the transformation of R bacteria into S bacteria in a petri dish.

Avery's group next developed a process to purify their extract. They then performed a series of tests to find out if the transforming principle was DNA or protein.

- **Qualitative tests** Standard chemical tests showed that no protein was present. In contrast, tests revealed that DNA was present.
- **Chemical analysis** As you can see in **FIGURE 8.2,** the proportions of elements in the extract closely matched those found in DNA. Proteins contain almost no phosphorus.
- **Enzyme tests** When the team added to the extract enzymes known to break down proteins, the extract still transformed the R bacteria to the S form. Also, transformation occurred when researchers added an enzyme that breaks down RNA (another nucleic acid). Transformation failed to occur only when an enzyme was added to destroy DNA.

FIGURE 8.2 Avery's Discoveries

CHEMICAL ANALYSIS OF TRANSFORMING PRINCIPLE

	% Nitrogen (N)	% Phosphorus (P)	Ratio of N to P
Sample A	14.21	8.57	1.66
Sample B	15.93	9.09	1.75
Sample C	15.36	9.04	1.69
Sample D	13.40	8.45	1.58
Known value for DNA	15.32	9.05	1.69

Source: Avery, O. T. et al., *The Journal of Experimental Medicine* 79:2.

Analyze **How do the data support the hypothesis that DNA, not protein, is the transforming principle?**

Oswald Avery

In 1944 Avery and his group presented this and other evidence to support their conclusion that DNA must be the transforming principle, or genetic material. The results created great interest. However, some scientists questioned whether the genetic material in bacteria was the same as that in other organisms. Despite Avery's evidence, some scientists insisted that his extract must have contained protein.

Summarize **List the key steps in the process that Avery's team used to identify the transforming principle.**

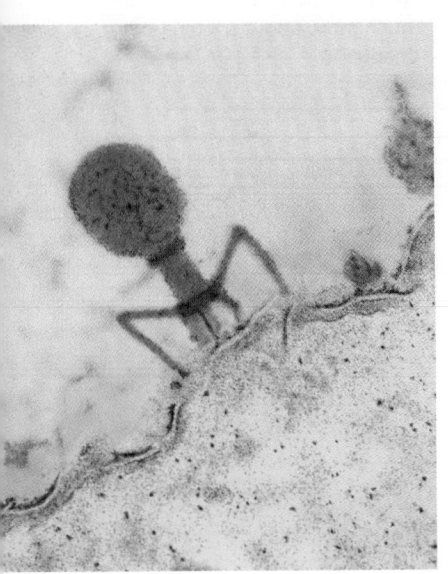

FIGURE 8.3 This micrograph shows the protein coat of a bacteriophage (orange) after it has injected its DNA into an *E. coli* bacterium (blue). (colored TEM; magnification 115,000×)

▶ MAIN IDEA

Hershey and Chase confirm that DNA is the genetic material.

Conclusive evidence for DNA as the genetic material came in 1952 from two American biologists, Alfred Hershey and Martha Chase. Hershey and Chase were studying viruses that infect bacteria. This type of virus, called a **bacteriophage** (bak-TEER-ee-uh-FAYJ), or "phage" for short, takes over a bacterium's genetic machinery and directs it to make more viruses.

Phages like the ones Hershey and Chase studied are relatively simple—little more than a DNA molecule surrounded by a protein coat. This two-part structure of phages offered a perfect opportunity to answer the question, Is the genetic material made of DNA or protein? By discovering which part of a phage (DNA or protein) actually entered a bacterium, as shown in **FIGURE 8.3**, they could answer this question once and for all.

Hershey and Chase thought up a clever procedure that made use of the chemical elements found in protein and DNA. Protein contains sulfur but very little phosphorus, while DNA contains phosphorus but no sulfur. The researchers grew phages in cultures that contained radioactive isotopes of sulfur or phosphorus. Hershey and Chase then used these radioactively tagged phages in two experiments.

- **Experiment 1** In the first experiment, bacteria were infected with phages that had radioactive sulfur atoms in their protein molecules. Hershey and Chase then used an ordinary kitchen blender to separate the bacteria from the parts of the phages that remained outside the bacteria. When they examined the bacteria, they found no significant radioactivity.

- **Experiment 2** Next, Hershey and Chase repeated the procedure with phages that had DNA tagged with radioactive phosphorus. This time, radioactivity was clearly present inside the bacteria.

From their results, Hershey and Chase concluded that the phages' DNA had entered the bacteria, but the protein had not. Their findings finally convinced scientists that the genetic material is DNA and not protein.

Apply How did Hershey and Chase build upon Avery's chemical analysis results?

8.1 ASSESSMENT

ONLINE QUIZ
ClassZone.com

REVIEWING ▶ MAIN IDEAS

1. What was "transformed" in Griffith's experiment?

2. How did Avery and his group identify the transforming principle?

3. Summarize how Hershey and Chase confirmed that DNA is the genetic material.

CRITICAL THINKING

4. **Summarize** Why was the **bacteriophage** an excellent choice for research to determine whether genes are made of DNA or proteins?

5. **Analyze** Choose one experiment from this section and explain how the results support the conclusion.

Connecting CONCEPTS

6. **Mendelian Genetics** Describe how Mendel's studies relate to the experiments discussed in this section.

MATERIALS

- balance
- 10 g raw wheat germ
- laboratory spatula
- test tube
- test tube rack
- 10 mL warm distilled water
- 2 eyedroppers
- 4 10-mL graduated cylinders
- 20 mL detergent solution
- 3 g meat tenderizer
- 20 mL salt solution
- 10 mL cold isopropyl alcohol
- glass stirring rod

PROCESS SKILLS

- **Observing**
- **Analyzing**

B1.1f Predict what would happen if the variables, methods, or timing of an investigation were changed.

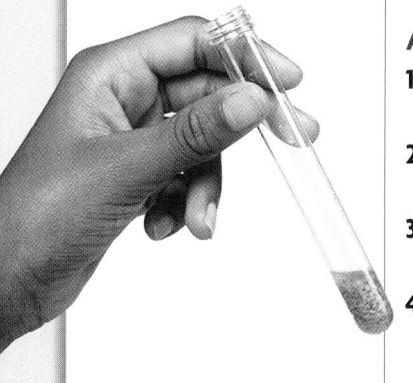

Extracting DNA

Oswald Avery wrote in a scientific article, "At a critical concentration . . . of alcohol the active material separates out in the form of fibrous strands that wind themselves around the stirring rod." In this lab, you can observe the same thing Avery observed as you extract DNA from wheat germ. This procedure is a simplified version of the one scientists commonly use to extract DNA today.

PROBLEM How do you extract the DNA from plant cells?

PROCEDURE

1. Place a small amount of wheat germ in a test tube. The wheat germ should be about 1 cm high in the test tube.

2. Add enough distilled water to wet and cover all of the wheat germ.

3. Add 25–30 drops of detergent solution to the test tube. For 3 minutes, gently swirl the test-tube contents. Avoid making bubbles.

4. Add 3 g of meat tenderizer.

5. Add 25–30 drops of salt solution to the test tube. Swirl for 1 minute.

6. Tilt the test tube at an angle as shown. Slowly add alcohol so that it runs down the inside of the test tube to form a separate layer on top of the mixture in the tube. Add enough alcohol to double the total volume in the tube. Let the test tube stand for 2 minutes.

7. Watch for stringy, cloudy material to rise from the bottom layer into the alcohol layer. This is the DNA.

8. Use the glass stirring rod to remove some DNA. Be careful to probe only the alcohol layer.

9. Draw in your lab report what the mixture and DNA looked like in steps 2–7. Be sure to include color, texture, and what happened after a new solution was added.

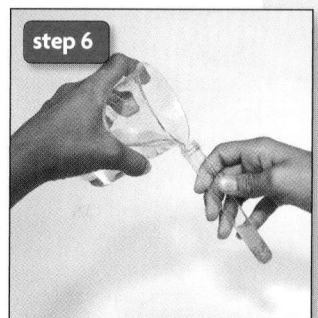
step 6

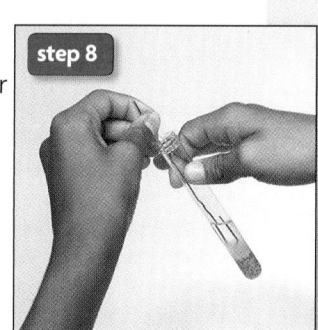
step 8

ANALYZE AND CONCLUDE

1. **Connect** Consider what you know about cell structure and the location of DNA. Suggest a reason for adding detergent solution to the test tube.

2. **Predict** What do you think might happen if the alcohol were added quickly and the two layers mixed?

3. **Infer** Meat tenderizer contains enzymes that break down proteins. What do you think is the purpose of adding meat tenderizer in this procedure?

4. **Connect** In what type of real-life situation would the extraction of DNA be useful?

EXTEND YOUR INVESTIGATION

Determine a method to calculate what percentage of the wheat germ consists of DNA.

8.2

Structure of DNA

KEY CONCEPT DNA structure is the same in all organisms.

▶ MAIN IDEAS

- DNA is composed of four types of nucleotides.
- Watson and Crick developed an accurate model of DNA's three-dimensional structure.
- Nucleotides always pair in the same way.

VOCABULARY

nucleotide, p. 230
double helix, p. 232
base pairing rules, p. 232

Review
covalent bond, hydrogen bond

MICHIGAN STANDARDS

B1.2i Explain the progression of ideas and explanations that leads to science theories that are part of the current scientific consensus or core knowledge.

B4.2C Describe the structure and function of DNA.

Connect The experiments of Hershey and Chase confirmed that DNA carries the genetic information, but they left other big questions unanswered: What exactly is this genetic information? How does DNA store this information? Scientists in the early 1950s still had a limited knowledge of the structure of DNA, but that was about to change dramatically.

▶ MAIN IDEA

DNA is composed of four types of nucleotides.

Since the 1920s, scientists have known that the DNA molecule is a very long polymer, or chain of repeating units. The small units, or monomers, that make up DNA are called **nucleotides** (NOO-klee-oh-TYDZ). Each nucleotide has three parts.

- A phosphate group (one phosphorus with four oxygens)
- A ring-shaped sugar called deoxyribose
- A nitrogen-containing base (a single or double ring built around nitrogen and carbon atoms)

Connecting CONCEPTS

Biochemistry The nucleotides in a strand of DNA all line up in the same direction. As a result, DNA has chemical polarity, which means that the two ends of the DNA strand are different. The 5′ carbon is located at one end of the DNA strand, and the 3′ carbon is located at the other end. When the two strands of DNA pair together, the 5′ end of one strand aligns with the 3′ end of the other strand.

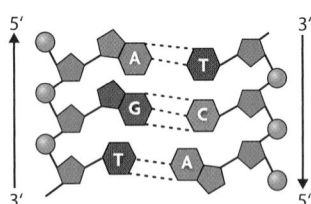

One molecule of human DNA contains billions of nucleotides, but there are only four types of nucleotides in DNA. These nucleotides differ only in their nitrogen-containing bases.

VISUAL VOCAB

The small units, or monomers, that make up a strand of DNA are called **nucleotides.** Nucleotides have three parts.

phosphate group   nitrogen-containing base

deoxyribose (sugar)

The four bases in DNA are shown in **FIGURE 8.4**. Notice that the bases cytosine (C) and thymine (T) have a single-ring structure. Adenine (A) and guanine (G) have a larger, double-ring structure. The letter abbreviations refer both to the bases and to the nucleotides that contain the bases.

For a long time, scientists hypothesized that DNA was made up of equal amounts of the four nucleotides, and so the DNA in all organisms was exactly the same. That hypothesis was a key reason that it was so hard to convince scientists that DNA was the genetic material. They reasoned that identical molecules could not carry different instructions across all organisms.

FIGURE 8.4 The Four Nitrogen-Containing Bases of DNA

PYRIMIDINES = SINGLE RING			PURINES = DOUBLE RING		
Name of Base	Structural Formula	Model	Name of Base	Structural Formula	Model
thymine	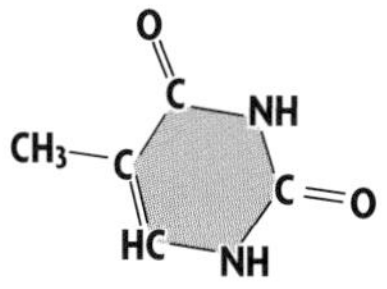	 T	adenine	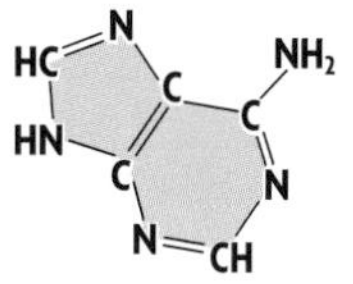	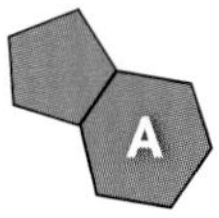 A
cytosine	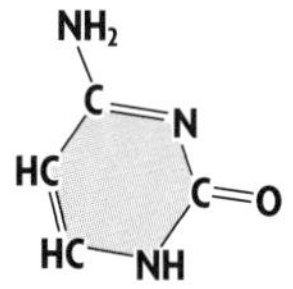	 C	guanine	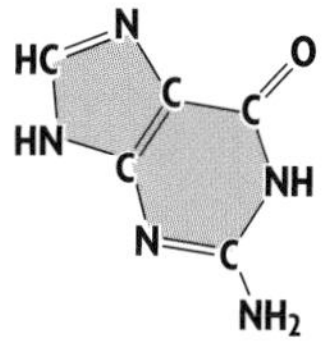	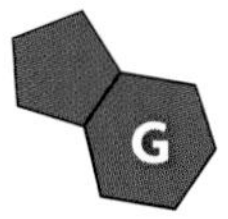 G

Compare Which base is most similar in structure to thymine?

By 1950 Erwin Chargaff changed the thinking about DNA by analyzing the DNA of several different organisms. Chargaff found that the same four bases are found in the DNA of all organisms, but the proportion of the four bases differs somewhat from organism to organism. In the DNA of each organism, the amount of adenine approximately equals the amount of thymine. Similarly, the amount of cytosine roughly equals the amount of guanine. These A = T and C = G relationships became known as Chargaff's rules.

VOCABULARY

An amine is a molecule that contains nitrogen. Notice that the four DNA bases end in -ine and all contain nitrogen.

Summarize What is the only difference among the four DNA nucleotides?

⊙ MAIN IDEA
Watson and Crick developed an accurate model of DNA's three-dimensional structure.

The breakthrough in understanding the structure of DNA came in the early 1950s through the teamwork of American geneticist James Watson and British physicist Francis Crick. Watson and Crick were supposed to be studying the structure of proteins. Both men, however, were more fascinated by the challenge of figuring out DNA's structure. Their interest was sparked not only by the findings of Hershey, Chase, and Chargaff but also by the work of the biochemist Linus Pauling. Pauling had found that the structure of some proteins was a helix, or spiral. Watson and Crick hypothesized that DNA might also be a helix.

X-Ray Evidence

At the same time, Rosalind Franklin, shown in **FIGURE 8.5,** and Maurice Wilkins were studying DNA using a technique called x-ray crystallography. When DNA is bombarded with x-rays, the atoms in DNA diffract the x-rays in a pattern that can be captured on film. Franklin's x-ray photographs of DNA showed an X surrounded by a circle. Franklin's data gave Watson and Crick the clues they needed. The patterns and angle of the X suggested that DNA is a helix consisting of two strands that are a regular, consistent width apart.

Rosalind Franklin

FIGURE 8.5 Rosalind Franklin (above) produced x-ray photographs of DNA that indicated it was a helix. Her coworker, Maurice Wilkins, showed the data without Franklin's consent to Watson and Crick, which helped them discover DNA's structure.

FIGURE 8.6 James Watson (left) and Francis Crick (right) used a model to figure out DNA's structure. Their model was influenced by data from other researchers, including an x-ray image (far right) taken by Rosalind Franklin. When x-rays bounce off vertically suspended DNA, they form this characteristic x-shaped pattern.

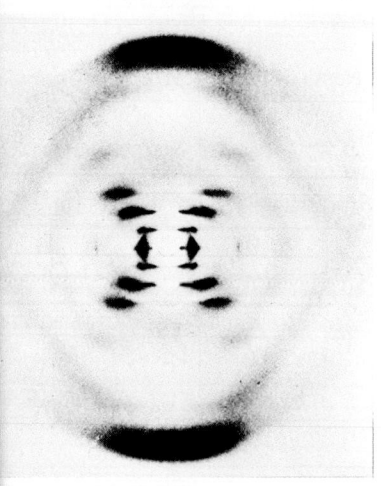

James Watson and Francis Crick

The Double Helix

Back in their own laboratory, Watson and Crick made models of metal and wood to figure out the structure of DNA. Their models placed the sugar-phosphate backbones on the outside and the bases on the inside. At first, Watson reasoned that A might pair with A, T with T, and so on. But the bases A and G are about twice as wide as C and T, so this produced a helix that varied in width. Finally, Watson and Crick found that if they paired double-ringed nucleotides with single-ringed nucleotides, the bases fit like a puzzle.

In April 1953 Watson and Crick published their DNA model in a paper in the journal *Nature*. **FIGURE 8.6** shows their **double helix** (HEE-lihks) model, in which two strands of DNA wind around each other like a twisted ladder. The strands are complementary—they fit together and are the opposite of each other. That is, if one strand is ACACAC, the other strand is TGTGTG. The pairing of bases in their model finally explained Chargaff's rules.

Apply How did the Watson and Crick model explain Chargaff's rules?

▶ MAIN IDEA

Nucleotides always pair in the same way.

Connecting CONCEPTS

Chemical Bonds Recall from **Chapter 2** that a covalent bond is a strong bond in which two atoms share one or more pairs of electrons. Hydrogen bonds are much weaker than covalent bonds and can easily be broken.

The DNA nucleotides of a single strand are joined together by covalent bonds that connect the sugar of one nucleotide to the phosphate of the next nucleotide. The alternating sugars and phosphates form the sides of a double helix, sort of like a twisted ladder. The DNA double helix is held together by hydrogen bonds between the bases in the middle. Individually, each hydrogen bond is weak, but together, they maintain DNA structure.

As shown in **FIGURE 8.7**, the bases of the two DNA strands always pair up in the same way. This is summarized in the **base pairing rules:** thymine (T) always pairs with adenine (A), and cytosine (C) always pairs with guanine (G). These pairings occur because of the sizes of the bases and the ability of the

FIGURE 8.7 Base Pairing Rules

The base pairing rules describe how nucleotides form pairs in DNA. T always pairs with A, and G always pairs with C.

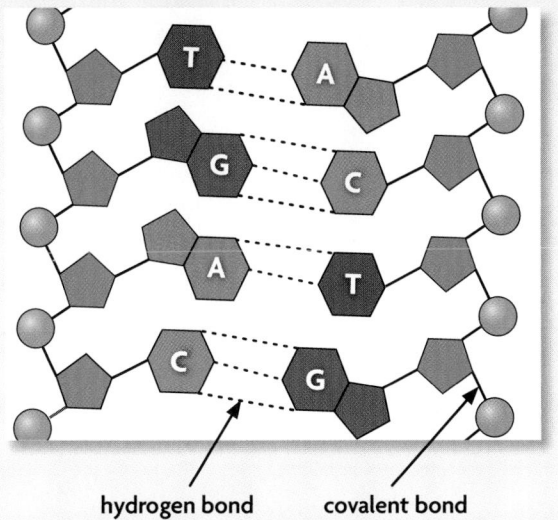

hydrogen bond   covalent bond

This ribbonlike part represents the phosphate groups and deoxyribose sugar molecules that make up DNA's "backbone."

The nitrogen-containing bases bond in the middle to form the rungs of the DNA ladder.

Synthesize Which base pairs do you think are held more tightly together? Why?

bases to form hydrogen bonds with each other. Due to the arrangement of their molecules, A can form unique hydrogen bonds with T, and C with G. Notice that A and T form two hydrogen bonds, whereas C and G form three.

You can remember the rules of base pairing by noticing that the letters C and G have a similar shape. Once you know that C and G pair together, you know that A and T pair together by default. If a sequence of bases on one strand of DNA is CTGCTA, you know the other DNA strand will be GACGAT.

Apply What sequence of bases would pair with the sequence TGACTA?

8.2 ASSESSMENT

ONLINE QUIZ ClassZone.com

REVIEWING ▶ MAIN IDEAS

1. How many types of **nucleotides** are in DNA, and how do they differ?

2. How are the **base pairing rules** related to Chargaff's research on DNA?

3. Explain how the **double helix** model of DNA built on the research of Rosalind Franklin.

CRITICAL THINKING

4. **Infer** Which part of a DNA molecule carries the genetic instructions that are unique for each individual: the sugar-phosphate backbone or the nitrogen-containing bases? Explain.

5. **Predict** In a sample of yeast DNA, 31.5% of the bases are adenine (A). Predict the approximate percentages of C, G, and T. Explain.

Connecting CONCEPTS

6. **Evolution** The DNA of all organisms contains the same four bases (adenine, thymine, cytosine, and guanine). What might this similarity indicate about the origins of life on Earth?

DATA ANALYSIS
ClassZone.com

Frequency Distributions

A **histogram** is a graph that shows the frequency distribution of a data set. First, a scientist collects data. Then, she groups the data values into equal intervals. The number of data values in each interval is the frequency of the interval. The intervals are shown along the *x*-axis of the histogram, and the frequencies are shown on the *y*-axis.

EXAMPLE

The histogram at right shows the frequency distribution of the ages of winners of the Nobel Prize in Medicine at the time of winning. Francis Crick was 46 and James Watson was 34 when they were jointly awarded a Nobel Prize in Medicine in 1962.

According to the histogram, the most winners have been between 50 and 59 years old at the time of winning. Only five scientists have been between the ages of 80 and 89 at the time of winning a Nobel Prize in Medicine.

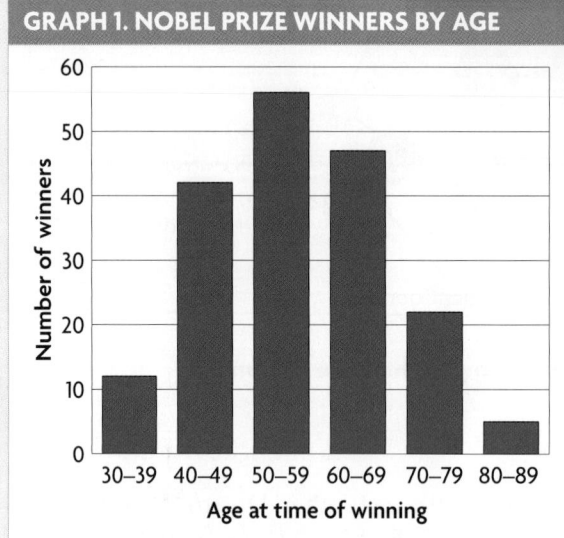

GRAPH 1. NOBEL PRIZE WINNERS BY AGE

ANALYZE A HISTOGRAM

The histogram below categorizes data collected based on the number of genes in 11 species.

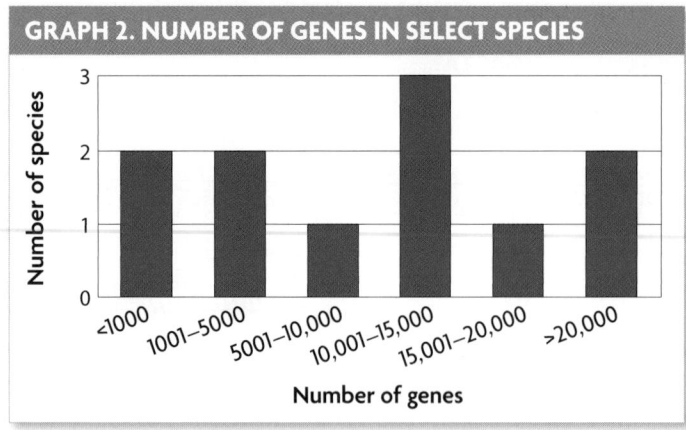

GRAPH 2. NUMBER OF GENES IN SELECT SPECIES

1. **Identify** How many species had between 10,001 and 15,000 genes?

2. **Analyze** Are the data in graph 2 sufficient to reveal a trend in the number of genes per species? Explain your reasoning.

8.3 DNA Replication

KEY CONCEPT DNA replication copies the genetic information of a cell.

▶ **MAIN IDEAS**
- Replication copies the genetic information.
- Proteins carry out the process of replication.
- Replication is fast and accurate.

VOCABULARY

replication, p. 235
DNA polymerase, p. 236

Review
base pairing rules, S phase

MICHIGAN STANDARDS

B4.2C Describe the structure and function of DNA.
B4.2g Describe the processes of replication, transcription, and translation and how they relate to each other in molecular biology.

Connect Do you know that some of your cells are dying right now? You may live to the ripe old age of 100, but most of your cells will have been replaced thousands of times before you blow out the candles on that birthday cake. Every time that cells divide to produce new cells, DNA must first be copied in a remarkable process of unzipping and zipping by enzymes and other proteins. The next few pages will take you through that process.

▶ **MAIN IDEA**

Replication copies the genetic information.

One of the powerful features of the Watson and Crick model was that it suggested a way that DNA could be copied. In fact, Watson and Crick ended the journal article announcing their discovery with this sentence: "It has not escaped our notice that the specific pairing we have postulated immediately suggests a possible copying mechanism for the genetic material."

Recall that the bases that connect the strands of DNA will pair only in one way, according to the rules of base pairing. An A must bind with a T, and a C must bind with a G. If the base sequence of one strand of the DNA double helix is known, the sequence of the other strand is also known. Watson and Crick realized that a single DNA strand can serve as a template, or pattern, for a new strand. This process by which DNA is copied during the cell cycle is called **replication.**

Suppose all of your classmates took off their shoes, placed their left shoe in a line, and tossed their right shoe into a pile. You could easily pick out the right shoes from the pile and place them with the matching left shoes. The order of the shoes would be preserved. Similarly, a new strand of DNA can be synthesized when the other strand is a template to guide the process. Every time, the order of the bases is preserved, and DNA can be accurately replicated over and over again.

Replication assures that every cell has a complete set of identical genetic information. Recall that your DNA is divided into 46 chromosomes that are replicated during the S phase of the cell cycle. So your DNA is copied once in each round of the cell cycle. As a result, every cell has a complete set of DNA.

Connecting CONCEPTS

Cell Biology In **Chapter 5** you learned that the cell cycle has four main stages. DNA is replicated during the S (synthesis) stage.

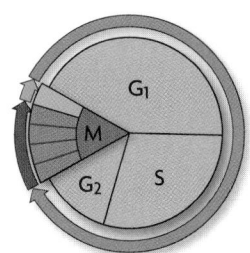

The fact that cells throughout the body have complete sets of DNA is very useful for forensic scientists. They can identify someone from nearly any cell in the body. A few cells from a drop of blood or from saliva on a cigarette butt are all detectives need to produce a DNA "fingerprint" of a criminal suspect.

Apply How does replication ensure that cells have complete sets of DNA?

▶ MAIN IDEA

Proteins carry out the process of replication.

Connecting CONCEPTS

Biochemistry You read in **Chapter 2** that many proteins are enzymes that function as catalysts. Enzymes decrease the activation energy and increase the rate of chemical reactions. DNA polymerase catalyzes the reaction that bonds two nucleotides together.

Although people may say that DNA copies itself, the DNA itself does nothing more than store information. Enzymes and other proteins do the actual work of replication. For example, some enzymes start the process by unzipping the double helix to separate the strands of DNA. Other proteins hold the strands apart while the strands serve as templates. Nucleotides that are floating free in the nucleus can then pair up with the nucleotides of the existing DNA strands. A group of enzymes called **DNA polymerases** (PAHL-uh-muh-rays) bond the new nucleotides together. When the process is finished, the result is two complete molecules of DNA, each exactly like the original double strand.

VISUAL VOCAB

DNA polymerases are enzymes that form bonds between nucleotides during replication.

The ending *-ase* signals that this is an enzyme.

DNA polymer | ase

This part of the name tells what the enzyme does—makes DNA polymers.

The Replication Process

The following information describes the process of DNA replication in eukaryotes, which is similar in prokaryotes. As you read, follow along with each step illustrated in **FIGURE 8.8**.

1 Enzymes begin to unzip the double helix at numerous places along the chromosome, called origins of replication. That is, the hydrogen bonds connecting base pairs are broken, the original molecule separates, and the bases on each strand are exposed. Unlike unzipping a jacket, this process proceeds in two directions at the same time.

2 Free-floating nucleotides pair, one by one, with the bases on the template strands as they are exposed. DNA polymerases bond the nucleotides together to form new strands that are complementary to each template strand. DNA replication occurs in a smooth, continuous way on one of the strands. Due to the chemical nature of DNA polymerase, replication of the other strand is more complex. It involves the formation of many small DNA segments that are joined together. This more complex process is not shown or described in detail here.

3 Two identical molecules of DNA result. Each new molecule has one strand from the original molecule and one new strand. As a result, DNA replication is called semiconservative because one old strand is conserved, and one complementary new strand is made.

Infer How does step 3 of replication show that DNA acts as a template?

TAKING NOTES

Use a cycle diagram to take notes about processes such as replication.

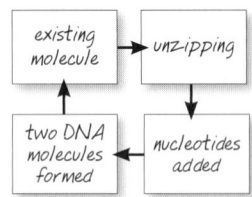

FIGURE 8.8 Replication

When a cell's DNA is copied, or replicated, two complete and identical sets of genetic information are produced. Then cell division can occur.

Animated BIOLOGY
See DNA replication in action at ClassZone.com.

1 A DNA molecule unzips as nucleotide base pairs separate. Replication begins on both strands of the molecule at the same time.

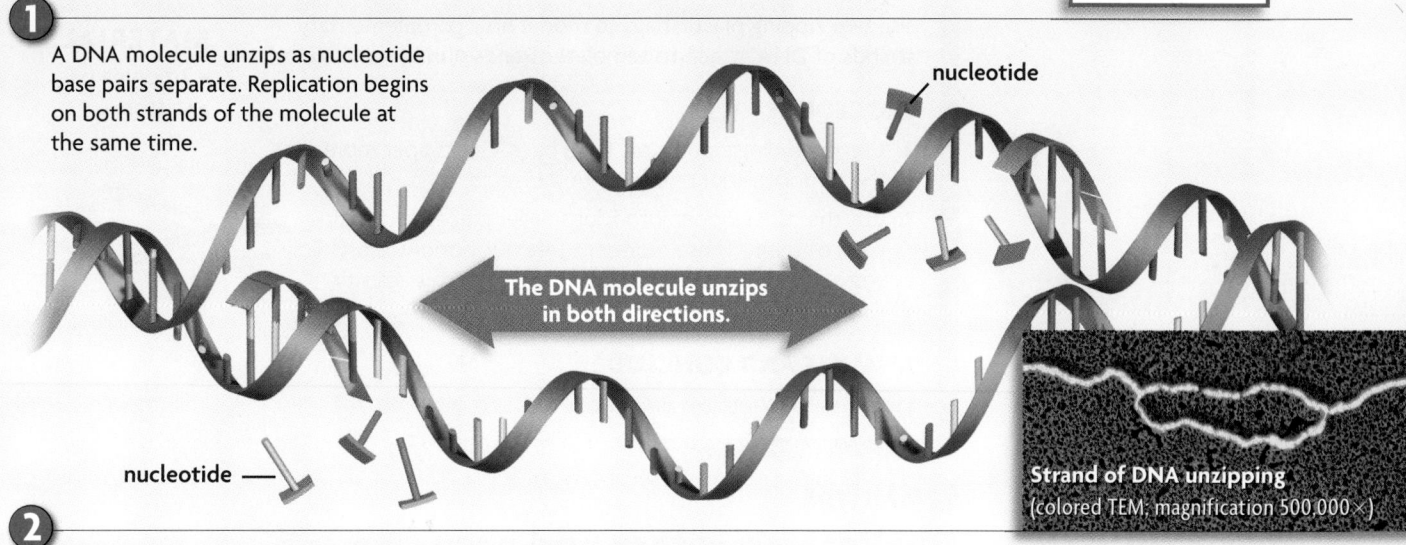

nucleotide

The DNA molecule unzips in both directions.

nucleotide —

Strand of DNA unzipping
(colored TEM; magnification 500,000×)

2 Each existing strand of the DNA molecule is a template for a new strand. Free-floating nucleotides pair up with the exposed bases on each template strand. DNA polymerases bond these nucleotides together to form the new strands. The arrows show the directions in which new strands form.

DNA polymerase

new strands

nucleotide

DNA polymerase

3 Two identical double-stranded DNA molecules result from replication. DNA replication is semiconservative. That is, each DNA molecule contains an original strand and one new strand.

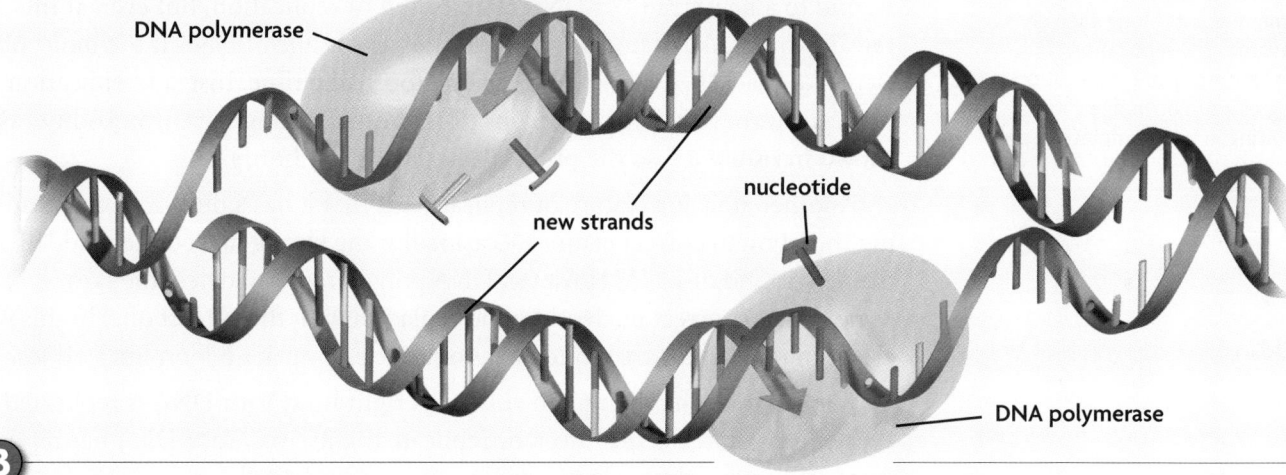

original strand   new strand

Two molecules of DNA

CRITICAL VIEWING   How is each new molecule of DNA related to the original molecule?

Replication

Use two zipping plastic bags to model how complementary strands of DNA attach to template strands during replication.

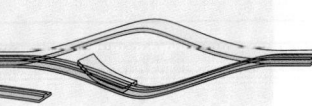

PROCEDURE

1. Cut the sliding zippers off both bags. One zipper represents the template strands of a DNA molecule.

2. Cut the other zipper into four smaller pieces and unzip each of them. These represent free nucleotides. Don't worry about which nucleotide is which in this activity.

3. Use the pieces to model replication as shown on page 237.

ANALYZE AND CONCLUDE

Evaluate What are the limitations of this model?

▶ MAIN IDEA

Replication is fast and accurate.

FIGURE 8.9 Eukaryotic chromosomes have many origins of replication. The DNA helix is unzipped at many points along each chromosome. The replication "bubbles" grow larger as replication progresses in both directions, resulting in two complete copies.

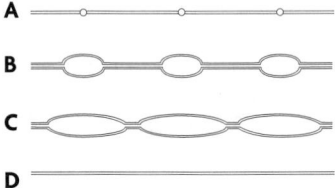

In every living thing, DNA replication happens over and over again, and it happens remarkably fast. In human cells, about 50 nucleotides are added every second to a new strand of DNA at an origin of replication. But even at this rate, it would take many days to replicate a molecule of DNA if the molecule were like a jacket zipper, unzipping one tooth at a time. Instead, replication proceeds from hundreds of origins of replication along the chromosome, as shown in **FIGURE 8.9**, so the process takes just a few hours.

Another amazing feature of replication is that it has a built-in "proofreading" function to correct errors. Occasionally, the wrong nucleotide is added to the new strand of DNA. However, DNA polymerase can detect the error, remove the incorrect nucleotide, and replace it with the correct one. In this way, errors in replication are limited to about one error per 1 billion nucleotides.

Replication is happening in your cells right now. Your DNA is replicated every time your cells turn over, or replicate themselves. Your DNA has replicated trillions of times since you grew from a single cell.

Infer Why does a cell need to replicate its DNA quickly?

8.3 ASSESSMENT

ONLINE QUIZ
ClassZone.com

REVIEWING ▶ MAIN IDEAS

1. Explain the function of **replication.**

2. Explain how DNA serves as its own template during replication.

3. How do cells help ensure that DNA replication is accurate?

CRITICAL THINKING

4. **Summarize** Describe two major functions of **DNA polymerases.**

5. **Infer** Why is it important that human chromosomes have many origins of replication?

Connecting CONCEPTS

6. **Cell Biology** DNA is replicated before both mitosis and meiosis. How does the amount of DNA produced in a cell during mitosis compare with that produced during meiosis?

Transcription

KEY CONCEPT Transcription converts a gene into a single-stranded RNA molecule.

▶ MAIN IDEAS

- RNA carries DNA's instructions.
- Transcription makes three types of RNA.
- The transcription process is similar to replication.

VOCABULARY

central dogma, p. 239
RNA, p. 239
transcription, p. 240
RNA polymerase, p. 240

messenger RNA (mRNA), p. 240
ribosomal RNA (rRNA), p. 240
transfer RNA (tRNA), p. 240

MICHIGAN STANDARDS

B4.2C Describe the structure and function of DNA.
B4.2g Describe the processes of replication, transcription, and translation and how they relate to each other in molecular biology.

Connect Suppose you want to play skeeball at a game center, but the skeeball lane only takes tokens. You only have quarters. Do you go home in defeat? Stand idly by as someone else becomes high scorer? No, you exchange your quarters for tokens and then proceed to show the other players how it's done. In a similar way, your cells cannot make proteins directly from DNA. They must convert the DNA into an intermediate molecule called RNA, or ribonucleic acid. That conversion process, called transcription, is the focus of this section.

▶ MAIN IDEA

RNA carries DNA's instructions.

Soon after his discovery of DNA structure, Francis Crick defined the **central dogma** of molecular biology, which states that information flows in one direction, from DNA to RNA to proteins. The central dogma involves three processes, as shown in **FIGURE 8.10**.

- Replication, as you just learned, copies DNA (blue arrow).

- Transcription converts a DNA message into an intermediate molecule, called RNA (red arrow).

- Translation interprets an RNA message into a string of amino acids, called a polypeptide. Either a single polypeptide or many polypeptides working together make up a protein (green arrow).

In prokaryotic cells, replication, transcription, and translation all occur in the cytoplasm at approximately the same time. In eukaryotic cells, where DNA is located inside the nuclear membrane, these processes are separated both in location and time. Replication and transcription occur in the nucleus, while translation occurs in the cytoplasm. In addition, the RNA in eukaryotic cells goes through a processing step before it can be transported out of the nucleus. Unless otherwise stated, the rest of this chapter describes how these processes work in eukaryotic cells.

RNA acts as an intermediate link between DNA in the nucleus and protein synthesis in the cytoplasm. Like DNA, **RNA,** or ribonucleic acid, is a chain of nucleotides, each made of a sugar, a phosphate group, and a nitrogen-containing base. You can think of RNA as a temporary copy of DNA that is used and then destroyed.

FIGURE 8.10 The central dogma describes the flow of information from DNA to RNA to proteins. It involves three major processes, shown in a eukaryotic cell below.

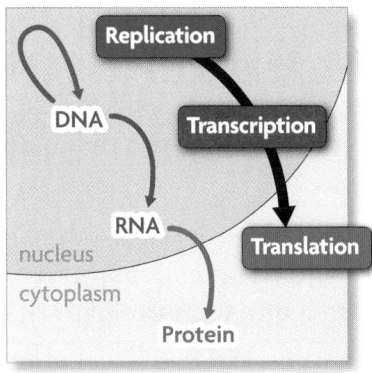

Connecting CONCEPTS

DNA Structure As you learned in Section 8.2, nucleotides are made of a phosphate group, a sugar, and a nitrogen-containing base. In DNA, the four bases are adenine, cytosine, guanine, and thymine. In RNA, uracil (below) replaces thymine and pairs with adenine.

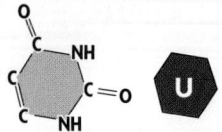

RNA differs from DNA in three significant ways. First, the sugar in RNA is ribose, which has one additional oxygen atom not present in DNA's sugar (deoxyribose). Second, RNA has the base uracil in place of thymine. Uracil, like thymine, forms base pairs with adenine. Third, RNA is a single strand of nucleotides, in contrast to the double-stranded structure of DNA. This single-stranded structure allows some types of RNA to form complex three-dimensional shapes. As a result, some RNA molecules can catalyze reactions much as enzymes do.

Contrast How do DNA and RNA differ?

▶ MAIN IDEA

Transcription makes three types of RNA.

Transcription is the process of copying a sequence of DNA to produce a complementary strand of RNA. During the process of transcription, a gene—not an entire chromosome—is transferred into an RNA message. Just as replication is catalyzed by DNA polymerase, transcription is catalyzed by **RNA polymerases,** enzymes that bond nucleotides together in a chain to make a new RNA molecule. RNA polymerases are very large enzymes composed of many proteins that play a variety of roles in the transcription process. **FIGURE 8.11** shows the basic steps of transcription in eukaryotic cells.

1 With the help of other proteins and DNA sequences, RNA polymerase recognizes the transcription start site of a gene. A large transcription complex consisting of RNA polymerase and other proteins assembles on the DNA strand and begins to unwind a segment of the DNA molecule, until the two strands separate from each other.

2 RNA polymerase, using only one strand of DNA as a template, strings together a complementary strand of RNA nucleotides. RNA base pairing follows the same rules as DNA base pairing, except that uracil, not thymine, pairs with adenine. The growing RNA strand hangs freely as it is transcribed, and the DNA helix zips back together.

3 Once the entire gene has been transcribed, the RNA strand detaches completely from the DNA. Exactly how RNA polymerase recognizes the end of a transcription unit is complicated. It varies with the type of RNA.

Transcription produces three major types of RNA molecules. Not all RNA molecules code for proteins, but most play a role in the translation process. Each type of RNA molecule has a unique function.

- **Messenger RNA (mRNA)** is an intermediate message that is translated to form a protein.
- **Ribosomal RNA (rRNA)** forms part of ribosomes, a cell's protein factories.
- **Transfer RNA (tRNA)** brings amino acids from the cytoplasm to a ribosome to help make the growing protein.

Remember that the RNA strand must be processed before it can exit the nucleus of a eukaryotic cell. This step occurs during or just after transcription. However, we will next examine translation and then return to processing.

Analyze Explain why transcription occurs in the nucleus of eukaryotes.

VOCABULARY

The word *transcribe* means "to make a written copy of." *Transcription* is the process of transcribing. A *transcript* is the copy produced by transcription.

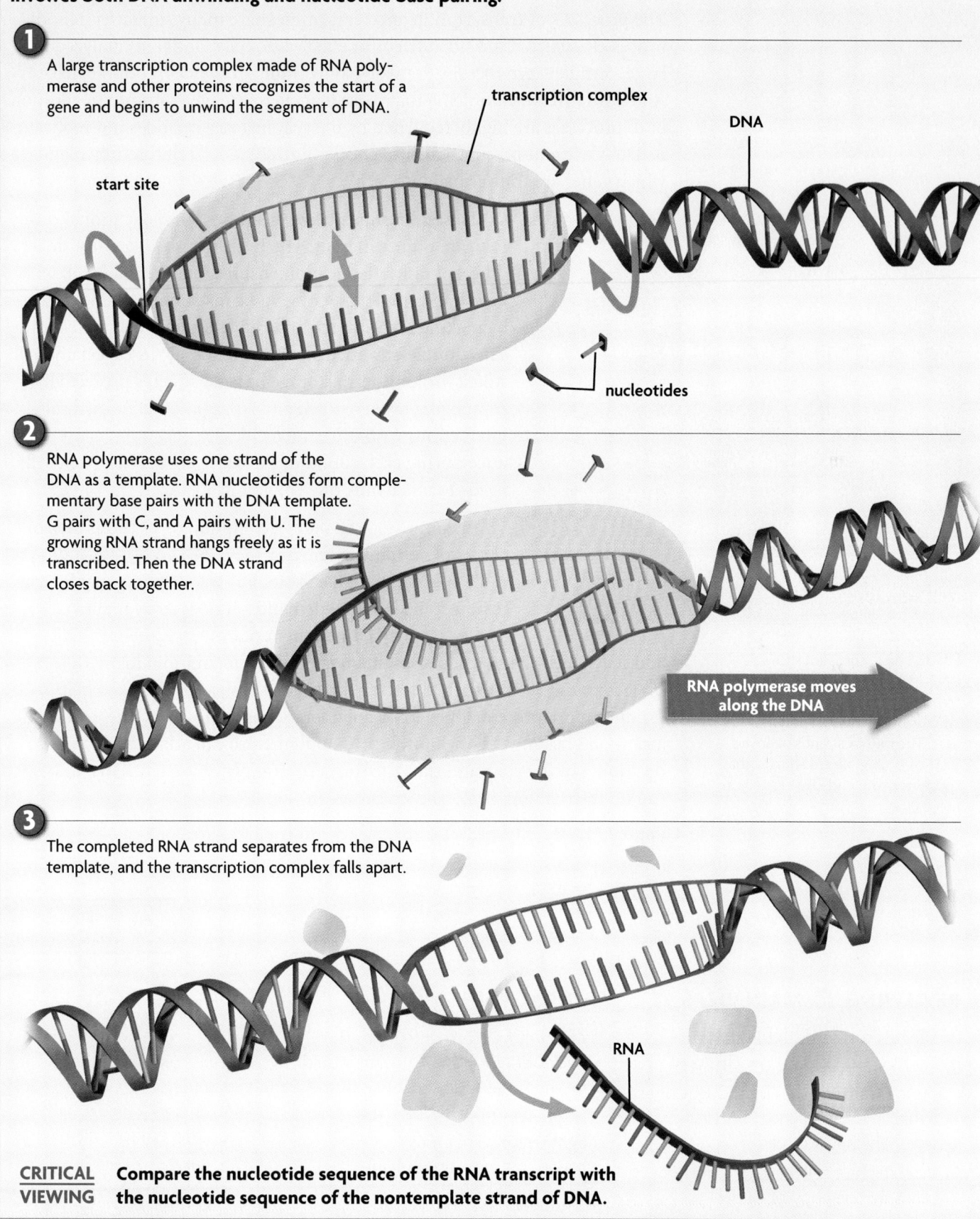

FIGURE 8.11 Transcription

Transcription produces an RNA molecule from a DNA template. Like DNA replication, this process takes place in the nucleus in eukaryotic cells and involves both DNA unwinding and nucleotide base pairing.

1 A large transcription complex made of RNA polymerase and other proteins recognizes the start of a gene and begins to unwind the segment of DNA.

transcription complex

DNA

start site

nucleotides

2 RNA polymerase uses one strand of the DNA as a template. RNA nucleotides form complementary base pairs with the DNA template. G pairs with C, and A pairs with U. The growing RNA strand hangs freely as it is transcribed. Then the DNA strand closes back together.

RNA polymerase moves along the DNA

3 The completed RNA strand separates from the DNA template, and the transcription complex falls apart.

RNA

CRITICAL VIEWING Compare the nucleotide sequence of the RNA transcript with the nucleotide sequence of the nontemplate strand of DNA.

▶ MAIN IDEA

The transcription process is similar to replication.

The processes of transcription and replication share many similarities. Both processes occur within the nucleus of eukaryotic cells. Both are catalyzed by large, complex enzymes. Both involve unwinding of the DNA double helix. And both involve complementary base pairing to the DNA strand. In addition, both processes are highly regulated by the cell. Just as a cell does not replicate its DNA without passing a critical checkpoint, so, too, a cell carefully regulates which genes are transcribed into RNA.

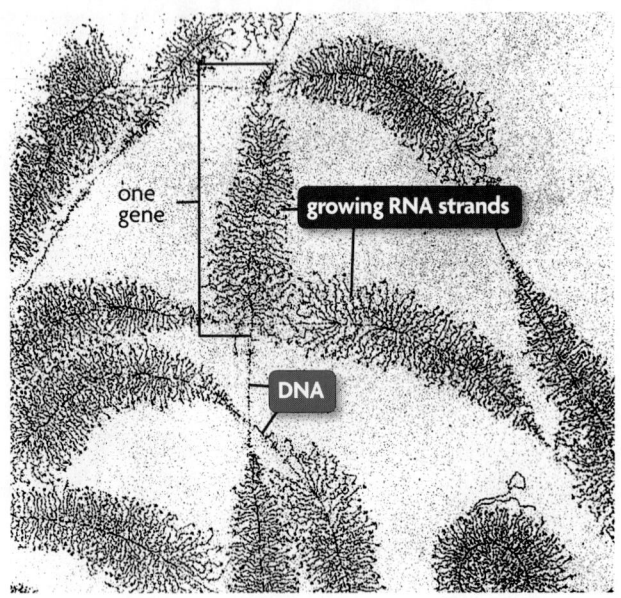

FIGURE 8.12 This TEM shows DNA in a eukaryotic cell being transcribed into numerous mRNA strands by many RNA polymerases. The mRNA strands near the start of each gene are shorter than those near the end. (TEM; magnification 13,000×)

The end results of transcription and replication, however, are quite different. The two processes accomplish very different tasks. Replication ensures that each new cell will have one complete set of genetic instructions. It does this by making identical sets of double-stranded chromosomes. This double-stranded structure makes DNA especially well suited for long-term storage because it helps protect DNA from being broken down and from potentially harmful interactions with other molecules. Replication occurs only once during each round of the cell cycle because each cell needs to make only one copy of its DNA.

In contrast, a cell may need hundreds or thousands of copies of certain proteins, or the rRNA and tRNA molecules needed to make proteins. Transcription enables a cell to adjust to changing demands. It does so by making a single-stranded complement of only a segment of DNA and only when that particular segment is needed. In addition, many RNA molecules can be transcribed from a single gene at the same time to help produce more protein. Once RNA polymerase has transcribed one portion of a gene and has moved on, another RNA polymerase can attach itself to the beginning of the gene and start the transcription process again. This process can occur over and over again, as shown in **FIGURE 8.12**.

Compare How are the processes of transcription and replication similar?

8.4 ASSESSMENT

ONLINE QUIZ
ClassZone.com

REVIEWING ▶ MAIN IDEAS

1. What is the **central dogma**?

2. Why can the **mRNA** strand made during **transcription** be thought of as a mirror image of the DNA strand from which it was made?

3. Why might a cell make lots of **rRNA** but only one copy of DNA?

CRITICAL THINKING

4. **Apply** If a DNA segment has the nucleotides AGCCTAA, what would be the nucleotide sequence of the complementary **RNA** strand?

5. **Synthesize** What might geneticists learn about genes by studying RNA?

Connecting CONCEPTS

6. **Cell Cycle** You know that a healthy cell cannot pass the G_2 checkpoint until all of its DNA has been copied. Do you think that a cell must also transcribe all of its genes into RNA to pass this checkpoint? Explain.

Translation

KEY CONCEPT Translation converts an mRNA message into a polypeptide, or protein.

MAIN IDEAS

- Amino acids are coded by mRNA base sequences.
- Amino acids are linked to become a protein.

VOCABULARY

translation, p. 243
codon, p. 243
stop codon, p. 244
start codon, p. 244
anticodon, p. 245

Review
peptide bond

MICHIGAN STANDARDS

B4.2f Demonstrate how the genetic information in DNA molecules provides instructions for assembling protein molecules and that this is virtually the same mechanism for all life forms.

B4.2g Describe the processes of replication, transcription, and translation and how they relate to each other in molecular biology.

Connect As you know, translation is a process that converts a message from one language into another. For example, English words can be translated into Spanish words, into Chinese characters, or into the hand shapes and gestures of sign language. Translation occurs in cells too. Cells translate an RNA message into amino acids, the building blocks of proteins. But unlike people who use many different languages, all cells use the same genetic code.

MAIN IDEA

Amino acids are coded by mRNA base sequences.

Translation is the process that converts, or translates, an mRNA message into a polypeptide. One or more polypeptides make up a protein. The "language" of nucleic acids uses four nucleotides—A, G, C, and T in DNA; or A, G, C, and U in RNA. The "language" of proteins, on the other hand, uses 20 amino acids. How can four nucleotides code for 20 amino acids? Just as letters are strung together in the English language to make words, nucleotides are strung together to code for amino acids.

Connecting CONCEPTS

Biochemistry Recall from **Chapter 2** that amino acids are the building blocks of proteins. Although there are many types of amino acids, only the same 20 types make up the proteins of almost all organisms.

Triplet Code

Different words have different numbers of letters. In the genetic code, however, all of the "words," called codons, are made up of three letters. A **codon** is a three-nucleotide sequence that codes for an amino acid. Why is the genetic code read in units of three nucleotides? Well, we can't entirely answer that question, but consider the possibilities. If one nucleotide coded for one amino acid, RNA could code for only four amino acids. If two nucleotides coded for one amino acid, RNA could code for 16 (4^2) amino acids— still not enough. But if three nucleotides coded for one amino acid, RNA

VISUAL VOCAB

A **codon** is a sequence of three nucleotides that codes for an amino acid.

codon for methionine (Met)   codon for leucine (Leu)

A U G C U U

Segment of mRNA

could code for 64 (4^3) amino acids, plenty to cover the 20 amino acids used to build proteins in the human body and most other organisms.

FIGURE 8.13 Genetic Code: mRNA Codons

The genetic code matches each mRNA **codon** with its amino acid or function.

Suppose you want to determine which amino acid is encoded by the CAU codon.

1 Find the first base, C, in the left column.

2 Find the second base, A, in the top row. Find the box where these two intersect.

3 Find the third base, U, in the right column. CAU codes for histidine, abbreviated as His.

		Second base							
		U		**C**		**A**		**G**	
First base **U**	UUU UUC	phenylalanine (Phe)	UCU UCC	serine (Ser)	UAU UAC	tyrosine (Tyr)	UGU UGC	cysteine (Cys)	U C
	UUA UUG	leucine (Leu)	UCA UCG		UAA UAG	STOP STOP	UGA UGG	STOP tryptophan (Trp)	A G
C	CUU CUC	leucine (Leu)	CCU CCC	proline (Pro)	CAU CAC	**histidine** (His)	CGU CGC	arginine (Arg)	U C
	CUA CUG		CCA CCG		CAA CAG	glutamine (Gln)	CGA CGG		A G
A	AUU AUC	isoleucine (Ile)	ACU ACC	threonine (Thr)	AAU AAC	asparagine (Asn)	AGU AGC	serine (Ser)	U C
	AUA AUG	methionine (Met)	ACA ACG		AAA AAG	lysine (Lys)	AGA AGG	arginine (Arg)	A G
G	GUU GUC	valine (Val)	GCU GCC	alanine (Ala)	GAU GAC	aspartic acid (Asp)	GGU GGC	glycine (Gly)	U C
	GUA GUG		GCA GCG		GAA GAG	glutamic acid (Glu)	GGA GGG		A G

Third base

Apply Which amino acid would be encoded by the mRNA codon CGA?

FIGURE 8.14 Codons are read as a series of three nonoverlapping nucleotides. A change in the reading frame changes the resulting protein.

Reading frame 1

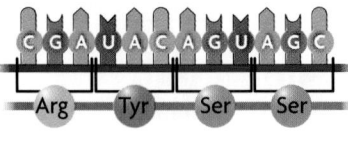

Reading frame 2

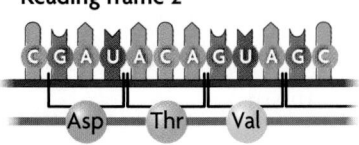

As you can see in **FIGURE 8.13,** many amino acids are coded for by more than one codon. The amino acid leucine, for example, is represented by six different codons: CUU, CUC, CUA, CUG, UUA, and UUG. There is a pattern to the codons. In most cases, codons that represent the same amino acid share the same first two nucleotides. For example, the four codons that code for alanine each begin with the nucleotides GC. Therefore, the first two nucleotides are generally the most important in coding for an amino acid. As you will learn in Section 8.7, this feature makes DNA more tolerant of many point mutations.

In addition to codons that code for amino acids, three **stop codons** signal the end of the amino acid chain. There is also one **start codon,** which signals the start of translation and the amino acid methionine. This means that translation always begins with methionine. However, in many cases, this methionine is removed later in the process.

For the mRNA code to be translated correctly, codons must be read in the right order. Codons are read, without spaces, as a series of three nonoverlapping nucleotides. This order is called the reading frame. Changing the reading frame completely changes the resulting protein. It may even keep a protein from being made if a stop codon turns up early in the translation process. Therefore, punctuation—such as a clear start codon—plays an important role in the genetic code. **FIGURE 8.14** shows how a change in reading frame changes the resulting protein. When the mRNA strand is read starting from the first nucleotide, the resulting protein includes the amino acids arginine, tyrosine, and two serines. When the strand is read starting from the second nucleotide, the resulting protein includes aspartic acid, threonine, and valine.

Common Language

The genetic code is shared by almost all organisms—and even viruses. That means, for example, that the codon UUU codes for phenylalanine when that codon occurs in an armadillo, a cactus, a yeast, or a human. With a few minor exceptions, almost all organisms follow this genetic code. As a result, the code is often called universal. The common nature of the genetic code suggests that almost all organisms arose from a common ancestor. It also means that scientists can insert a gene from one organism into another organism to make a functional protein.

Calculate **Suppose an mRNA molecule in the cytoplasm had 300 nucleotides. How many amino acids would be in the resulting protein?**

▶ MAIN IDEA

Amino acids are linked to become a protein.

Let's take a step back to look at where we are in the process of making proteins. You know mRNA is a short-lived molecule that carries instructions from DNA in the nucleus to the cytoplasm. And you know that this mRNA message is read in sets of three nucleotides, or codons. But how does a cell actually translate a codon into an amino acid? It uses two important tools: ribosomes and tRNA molecules, as illustrated in **FIGURE 8.15.**

Recall from Chapter 3 that ribosomes are the site of protein synthesis. Ribosomes are made of a combination of rRNA and proteins, and they catalyze the reaction that forms the bonds between amino acids. Ribosomes have a large and small subunit that fit together and pull the mRNA strand through. The small subunit holds onto the mRNA strand, and the large subunit holds onto the growing protein.

The tRNA acts as a sort of adaptor between mRNA and amino acids. You would need an adaptor to plug an appliance with a three-prong plug into an outlet with only two-prong openings. Similarly, cells need tRNA to carry free-floating amino acids from the cytoplasm to the ribosome. The tRNA molecules fold up in a characteristic L shape. One end of the L is attached to a specific amino acid. The other end of the L, called the anticodon, recognizes a specific codon. An **anticodon** is a set of three nucleotides that is complementary to an mRNA codon. For example, the anticodon CCC pairs with the mRNA codon GGG.

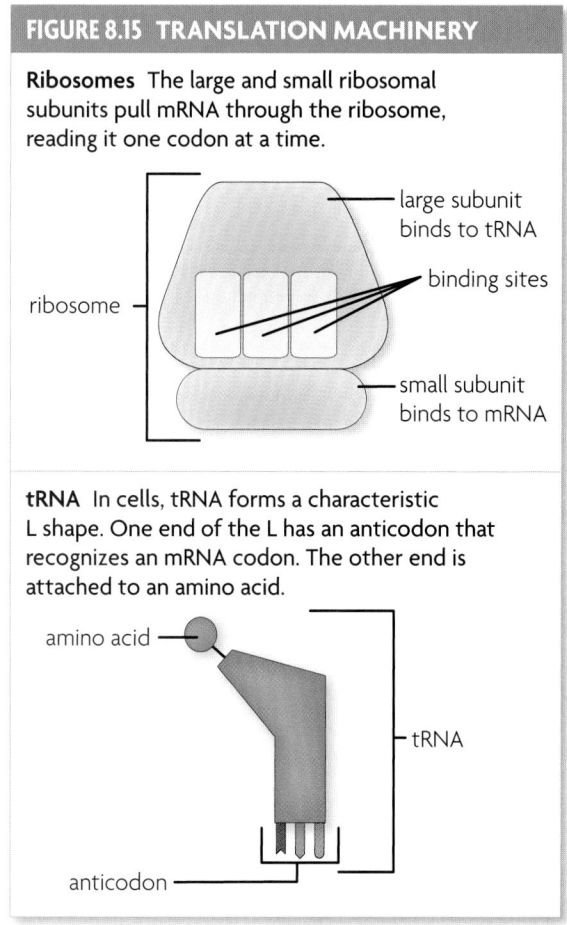

FIGURE 8.15 TRANSLATION MACHINERY

Ribosomes The large and small ribosomal subunits pull mRNA through the ribosome, reading it one codon at a time.

large subunit binds to tRNA

binding sites

ribosome

small subunit binds to mRNA

tRNA In cells, tRNA forms a characteristic L shape. One end of the L has an anticodon that recognizes an mRNA codon. The other end is attached to an amino acid.

amino acid

tRNA

anticodon

FIGURE 8.16 Translation

**Translation converts an mRNA transcript into a polypeptide.
The process consists of three repeating steps.**

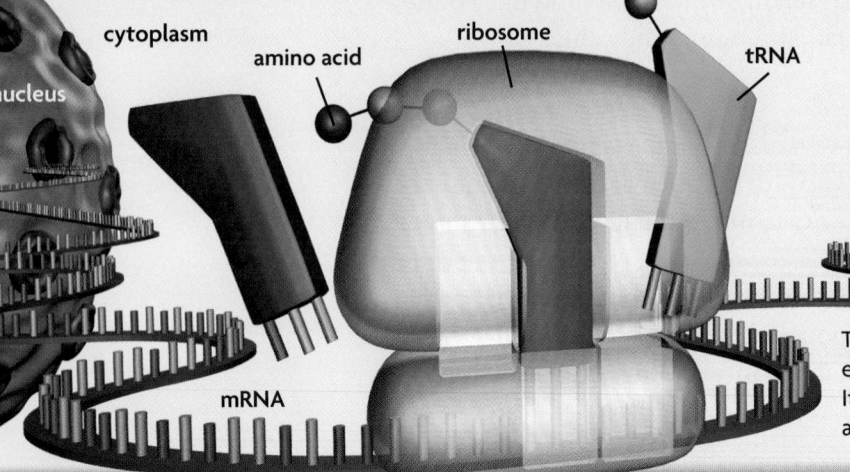

cytoplasm

amino acid

ribosome

tRNA

nucleus

mRNA

Translation occurs in the cytoplasm of both eukaryotic (illustrated) and prokaryotic cells. It starts when a tRNA carrying a methionine attaches to a start codon.

1

The exposed codon in the first site attracts a complementary tRNA bearing an amino acid. The tRNA anticodon pairs with the mRNA codon, bringing it very close to the other tRNA molecule.

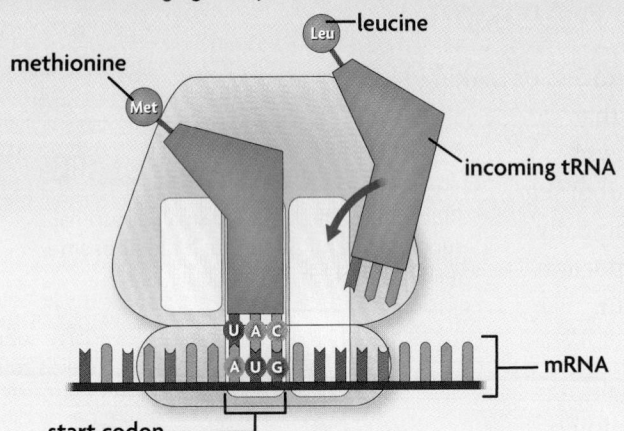

leucine

methionine

Met

Leu

incoming tRNA

U A C
A U G

mRNA

start codon

2

The ribosome forms a peptide bond between the two amino acids and breaks the bond between the first tRNA and its amino acid.

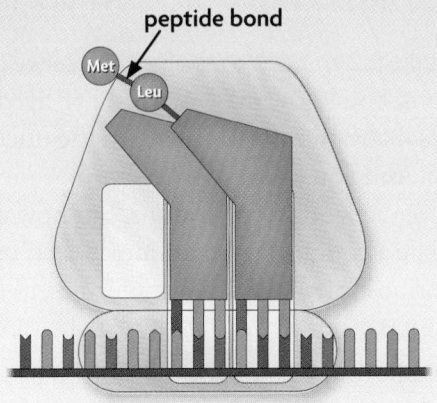

peptide bond

Met

Leu

3

The ribosome pulls the mRNA strand the length of one codon. The first tRNA is shifted into the exit site, where it leaves the ribosome and returns to the cytoplasm to recharge. The first site is again empty, exposing the next mRNA codon.

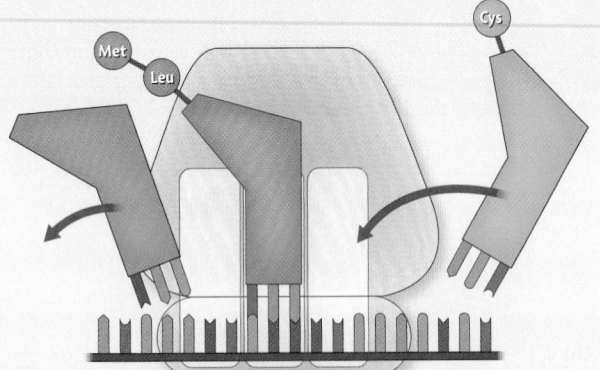

Met

Leu

Cys

The ribosome continues to translate the mRNA strand until it reaches a stop codon. Then it releases the new protein and disassembles.

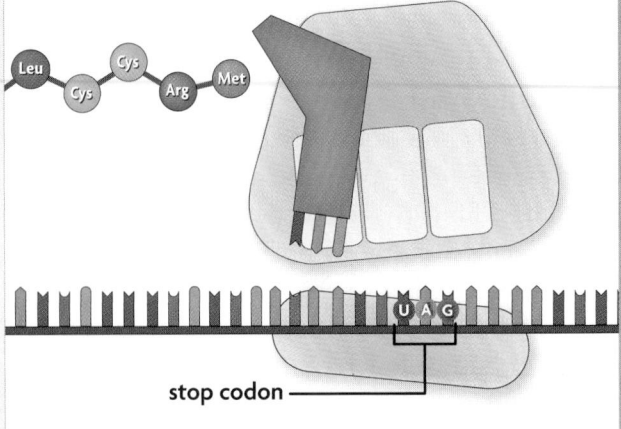

Leu

Cys

Cys

Arg

Met

U A G

stop codon

CRITICAL VIEWING   **The figure above shows how the first two amino acids are added to a growing protein. Draw a series of sketches to show how the next two amino acids are added.**

Translation, shown in **FIGURE 8.16,** has many steps and takes a lot of energy from a cell. It happens in the cytoplasm of both prokaryotic and eukaryotic cells. Before translation can begin, a small ribosomal subunit must bind to an mRNA strand in the cytoplasm. Next, a tRNA with methionine attached binds to the AUG start codon. This binding signals a large ribosomal subunit— which has three binding sites for tRNA molecules—to join. The ribosome pulls the mRNA strand through itself one codon at a time. As the strand moves, the start codon and its complementary tRNA molecule shift into the second site inside the large subunit. This shift leaves the first site empty, which exposes the next mRNA codon. The illustration shows the process in one ribosome, but in a cell many ribosomes may translate the same gene at the same time.

1 The exposed codon attracts a complementary tRNA molecule bearing an amino acid. The tRNA anticodon pairs with the mRNA codon. This action brings the new tRNA molecule very close to the tRNA molecule occupying the second site.

2 Next, the ribosome helps form a peptide bond between the two amino acids. The ribosome then breaks the bond between the tRNA molecule in the second site and its amino acid.

3 The ribosome pulls the mRNA strand the length of one codon. The tRNA molecule in the second site is shifted into the third site, which is the exit site. The tRNA leaves the ribosome and returns to the cytoplasm to be charged with another amino acid. The tRNA molecule that was in the first site shifts into the second site. The first site is again empty, exposing the next mRNA codon.

Another complementary tRNA molecule is attracted to the exposed mRNA codon, and the process continues. The ribosome moves down the mRNA strand, attaching new amino acids to the growing protein, until it reaches a stop codon. Then it lets go of the new protein and falls apart.

NSTA scilinks.org SC*LINKS*

To learn more about protein synthesis, visit scilink.org.
Keycode: MLB008

Summarize **Explain the different roles of the large and small ribosomal subunits.**

ONLINE QUIZ ClassZone.com

8.5 ASSESSMENT

REVIEWING ▶ MAIN IDEAS

1. Explain the connection between a **codon** and an amino acid.

2. Briefly describe how the process of **translation** is started.

CRITICAL THINKING

3. **Synthesize** Suppose a tRNA molecule had the **anticodon** AGU. What amino acid would it carry?

4. **Hypothesize** The DNA of eukaryotic cells has many copies of genes that code for rRNA molecules. Suggest a hypothesis to explain why a cell needs so many copies of these genes.

Connecting CONCEPTS

5. **Biochemical Reactions** Enzymes have shapes that allow them to bind to a substrate. Some types of RNA also form specific three-dimensional shapes. Why do you think RNA, but not DNA, catalyzes biochemical reactions?

8.6 Gene Expression and Regulation

KEY CONCEPT Gene expression is carefully regulated in both prokaryotic and eukaryotic cells.

▶ MAIN IDEAS
- Prokaryotic cells turn genes on and off by controlling transcription.
- Eukaryotic cells regulate gene expression at many points.

VOCABULARY
promoter, p. 248
operon, p. 248
exon, p. 251
intron, p. 251

MICHIGAN STANDARDS

B4.1B Explain that the information passed from parents to offspring is transmitted by means of genes that are coded in DNA molecules. These genes contain the information for the production of proteins.

B4.2g Describe the processes of replication, transcription, and translation and how they relate to each other in molecular biology.

VOCABULARY

The word *promote* comes from the Latin prefix *pro-*, meaning "forward," and the Latin word *movere*, meaning "to move."

Connect Ours is a world of marvels. So many, in fact, that we may overlook what seem like little ones, such as plumbing. The turn of a handle sends clean water to your sink or shower. One twist and the water trickles out; two twists and it gushes forth. Another turn of the handle and the water is off again. But think about the mess and waste that would result if you couldn't control its flow. In a similar way, your cells have ways to control gene expression. Depending on an organism's needs, a gene can make a lot of protein, a little protein, or none at all.

▶ MAIN IDEA
Prokaryotic cells turn genes on and off by controlling transcription.

The regulation of gene expression allows prokaryotic cells, such as bacteria, to better respond to stimuli and to conserve energy and materials. In general, this regulation is simpler in prokaryotic cells than in eukaryotic cells, such as those that make up your body. DNA in a prokaryotic cell is in the cytoplasm. Transcription and translation can happen at the same time. As a result, gene expression in prokaryotic cells is mainly regulated at the start of transcription.

A gene includes more than just a protein-coding sequence. It may have many other nucleotide sequences that play a part in controlling its expression. The start of transcription is largely controlled by these sequences, including promoters and operators. A **promoter** is a DNA segment that allows a gene to be transcribed. It helps RNA polymerase find where a gene starts. An operator is a DNA segment that turns a gene "on" or "off." It interacts with proteins that increase the rate of transcription or block transcription from occurring.

Bacteria have much less DNA than do eukaryotes, and their genes tend to be organized into operons. An **operon** is a region of DNA that includes a promoter, an operator, and one or more structural genes that code for all the proteins needed to do a specific task. Typically, operons are found only in prokaryotes and roundworms. The *lac* operon was one of the earliest examples of gene regulation discovered in bacteria. It will serve as our example. The *lac* operon has three genes, which all code for enzymes that play a role in breaking down the sugar lactose. These genes are transcribed as a single mRNA transcript and are all under the control of a single promoter and operator. This means that although we're dealing with several genes, they act together as a unit.

The *lac* operon is turned on and off like a switch. When lactose is absent from the environment, the *lac* operon is switched off to prevent transcription of the *lac* genes and save the cell's resources. When lactose is present, the *lac* operon is switched on to allow transcription. How does this happen?

Bacteria have a protein that can bind specifically to the operator. When lactose is absent, this protein binds to the operator, which blocks RNA polymerase from transcribing the genes. Because the protein blocks—or represses—transcription, it is called a repressor protein.

Without lactose (switched off)

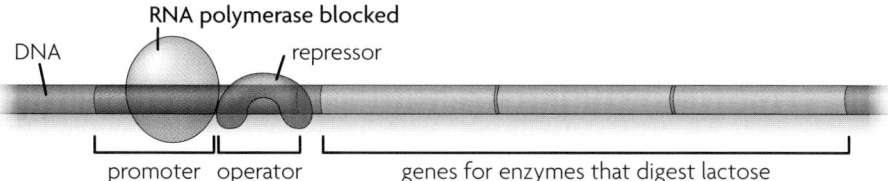

When lactose is present it binds to the repressor, which makes the repressor change shape and fall off the *lac* operon. RNA polymerase can then transcribe the genes in the *lac* operon. The resulting transcript is translated and forms three enzymes that work together to break down the lactose.

With lactose (switched on)

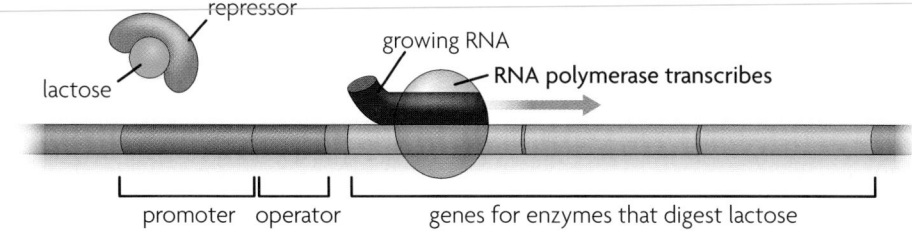

Analyze **Explain how the *lac* operon is turned on or off like a switch.**

▶ MAIN IDEA
Eukaryotic cells regulate gene expression at many points.

You have already learned that every body cell in an organism has the same set of DNA. But your cells are not all the same. Cells differ from each other because different sets of genes are expressed in different types of cells. Eukaryotic cells can control the process of gene expression at many different points because of their internal compartments and chromosomal organization. As in prokaryotic cells, however, one of the most highly regulated steps is the start of transcription. In both cell types, RNA processing is a part of the transcription process. In eukaryotic cells, however, RNA processing also includes the removal of extra nucleotide segments from an mRNA transcript.

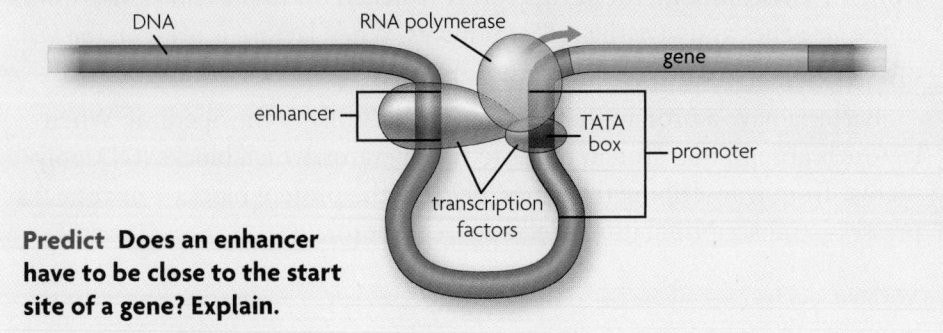

FIGURE 8.17 Starting Transcription

Transcription factors that bind to **promoters** and other DNA sequences help RNA polymerase recognize the start of a gene in a eukaryotic cell.

DNA

RNA polymerase

gene

enhancer

TATA box

promoter

transcription factors

Predict Does an enhancer have to be close to the start site of a gene? Explain.

Starting Transcription

The start of transcription in eukaryotic cells is controlled by many elements that work together in complex ways. These elements include regulatory DNA sequences and proteins called transcription factors, as shown in **FIGURE 8.17**. They occur in different combinations in different types of cells. The interplay between these elements results in specialized cells and cell responses.

Eukaryotes have many types of regulatory DNA sequences. These sequences are recognized by transcription factors that bind to the DNA strand and help RNA polymerase know where a gene starts. Some DNA sequences, such as promoters, are close to the start of a gene. Others are far away from the genes they affect. However, DNA can loop and bend, bringing these sequences with their transcription factors into close contact with the others.

Each gene has a unique combination of regulatory sequences. Some are found in almost all eukaryotic cells. For example, most eukaryotic cells have a seven-nucleotide promoter (TATAAAA) called the TATA box. Eukaryotic cells also have other types of promoters that are more specific to an individual gene. DNA sequences called enhancers and silencers also play a role by speeding up or slowing down, respectively, the rate of transcription of a gene.

Some genes control the expression of many other genes. Regulation of these genes is very important because they can have a large effect on development. One such gene codes for a protein called sonic hedgehog. This protein was first found in fruit flies, but many other organisms have very similar proteins that serve a similar function. Sonic hedgehog helps establish body pattern. When missing in fruit flies, the embryos are covered with little prickles and fail to form normal body segments.

mRNA Processing

Another important part of gene regulation in eukaryotic cells is RNA processing, which is shown in **FIGURE 8.18**. The mRNA produced by transcription is similar to a rough cut of a film that needs a bit of editing. A specialized nucleotide is added to the beginning of each mRNA molecule, which forms a cap. It helps the mRNA strand bind to a ribosome and prevents the strand from being broken down too fast. The end of the mRNA molecule gets a string of A nucleotides, called the tail, that helps the mRNA molecule exit the nucleus.

Connecting CONCEPTS

Animals As you will learn in **Chapter 23**, most animals have homeobox genes. These genes are among the earliest that are expressed and play a key role in development. The micrograph below shows the expression of homeobox genes in a fruitfly embryo.

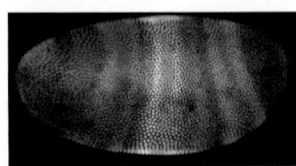

FIGURE 8.18 mRNA Processing

An mRNA molecule typically undergoes processing during or immediately after DNA transcription.

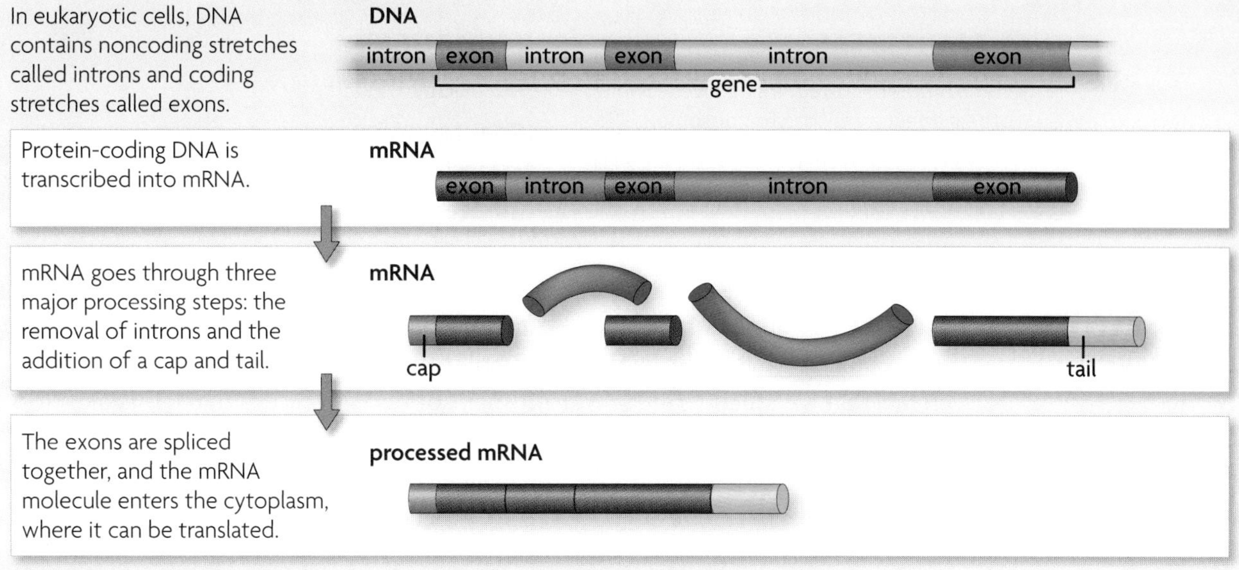

In eukaryotic cells, DNA contains noncoding stretches called introns and coding stretches called exons.

DNA

intron | exon | intron | exon | intron | exon
— gene —

Protein-coding DNA is transcribed into mRNA.

mRNA

exon | intron | exon | intron | exon

mRNA goes through three major processing steps: the removal of introns and the addition of a cap and tail.

mRNA

cap

tail

The exons are spliced together, and the mRNA molecule enters the cytoplasm, where it can be translated.

processed mRNA

Connect Where does mRNA processing take place in a eukaryotic cell?

The "extra footage" takes the form of nucleotide segments that are not included in the final protein. In eukaryotes, **exons** are nucleotide segments that code for parts of the protein. **Introns** are nucleotide segments that inter- vene, or occur, between exons. Almost no prokaryotes have introns. Introns are removed from mRNA before it leaves the nucleus. The cut ends of the exons are then joined together by a variety of molecular mechanisms.

The role of introns is not clear. They may regulate gene expression. Or they may protect DNA against harmful mutations. That is, if large regions of DNA are noncoding "junk," then mutations occurring in those regions will have no effect. Some mRNA strands can be cut at various points, resulting in different proteins. As a result, introns increase genetic diversity without increasing the size of the genome.

Apply Which parts of a gene are expressed as protein: introns or exons?

8.6 ASSESSMENT

ONLINE QUIZ
ClassZone.com

REVIEWING ▶ MAIN IDEAS

1. What is a **promoter**?

2. In eukaryotic cells, genes each have a specific combination of regulatory DNA sequences. How do these combinations help cells carry out specialized jobs?

CRITICAL THINKING

3. **Predict** Suppose a bacterium had a mutated repressor protein that could not bind to the *lac* operator. How might this affect regulation of the **operon**?

4. **Summarize** What are the three major steps involved in mRNA processing?

Connecting CONCEPTS

5. **DNA** DNA is loosely organized in areas where RNA polymerase is transcrib- ing genes. What might you infer about a region of DNA that was loosely organized in muscle cells but tightly coiled in lung cells?

8.7 Mutations

KEY CONCEPTS Mutations are changes in DNA that may or may not affect phenotype.

▶ MAIN IDEAS

- Some mutations affect a single gene, while others affect an entire chromosome.
- Mutations may or may not affect phenotype.
- Mutations can be caused by several factors.

VOCABULARY

mutation, p. 252
point mutation, p. 252
frameshift mutation, p. 252
mutagen, p. 255

MICHIGAN STANDARDS

B4.2A Show that when mutations occur in sex cells, they can be passed on to offspring (inherited mutations), but if they occur in other cells, they can be passed on to descendant cells only (non-inherited mutations).

B4.3B Explain why only mutations occurring in gametes (sex cells) can be passed on to offspring.

Connect We all make mistakes. Some may be a bit embarrassing. Others become funny stories we tell our friends later. Still others, however, have far-reaching effects that we failed to see in our moment of decision. Cells make mistakes too. These mistakes, like our own, can have a range of effects. When they occur in DNA, they are called mutations, and cells have evolved a variety of methods for dealing with them.

▶ MAIN IDEA

Some mutations affect a single gene, while others affect an entire chromosome.

You may already know the term *mutation* from popular culture, but it has a specific meaning in biology. A **mutation** is a change in the an organism's DNA. Many types of mutations can occur, as shown in **FIGURE 8.20.** Typically, mutations that affect a single gene happen during replication, whereas mutations that affect a group of genes or an entire chromosome happen during meiosis.

Gene Mutations

A **point mutation** is a mutation in which one nucleotide is substituted for another. That is, an incorrect nucleotide is put in the place of the correct nucleotide. Very often, such a mistake is caught and fixed by DNA polymerase. If it is not, the substitution may permanently change an organism's DNA.

A **frameshift mutation** involves the insertion or deletion of a nucleotide in the DNA sequence. It usually affects a polypeptide much more than does a substitution. Frameshift mutations are so named because they shift the entire sequence following them by one or more nucleotides. To understand how this affects an mRNA strand, imagine a short sentence of three-letter "codons":

THE CAT ATE THE RAT

If the letter *E* is removed, or deleted, from the first "THE," all the letters that follow shift to the left. The sentence now reads:

THC ATA TET HER AT . . .

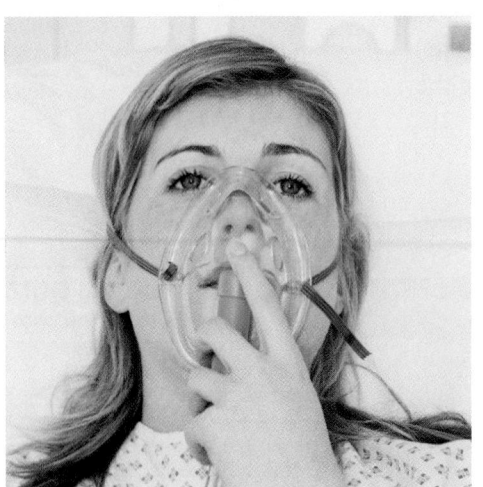
FIGURE 8.19 Cystic fibrosis (CF) is a genetic disease that is most commonly caused by a specific deletion. It causes the overproduction of thick, sticky mucus. Although CF cannot be cured, it is treated in a number of ways, including oxygen therapy (above).

FIGURE 8.20 Types of Mutations

A **mutation** is a change in an organism's DNA.

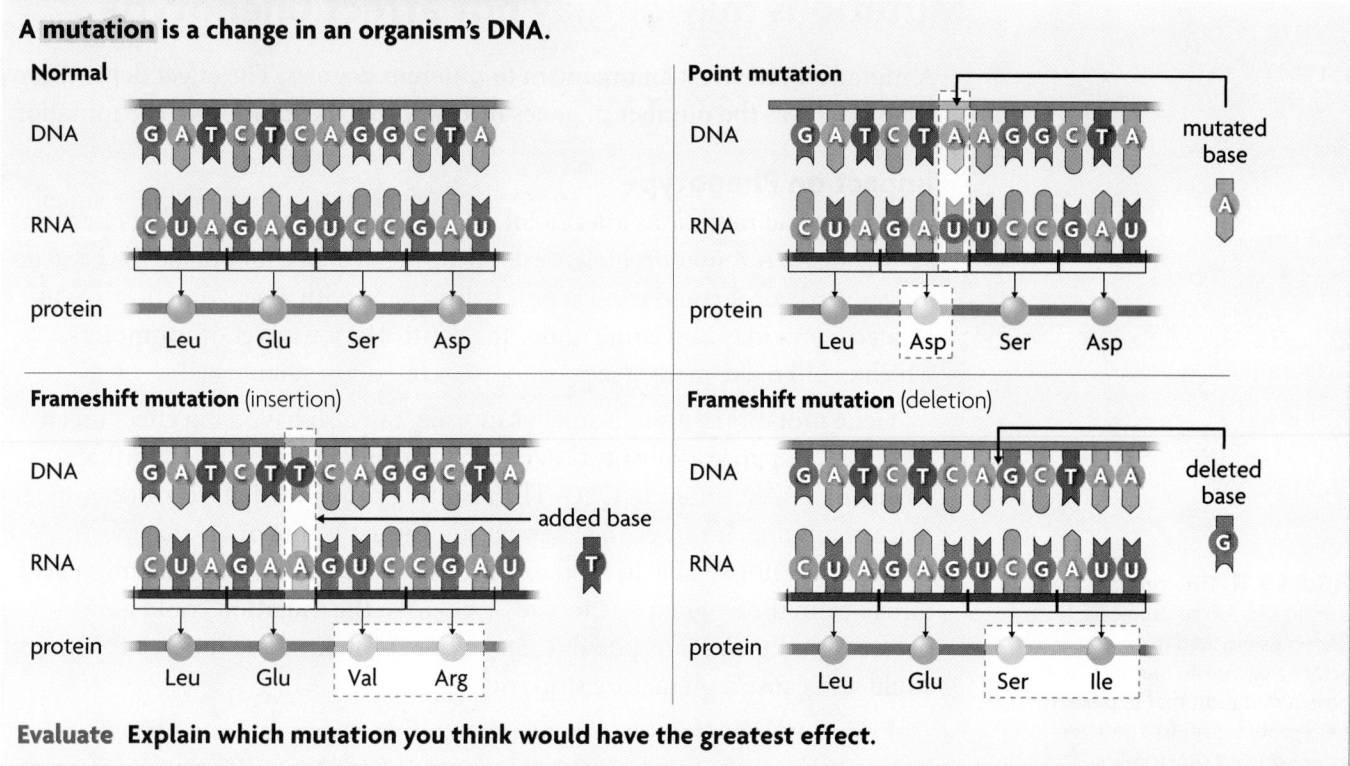

Evaluate Explain which mutation you think would have the greatest effect.

The sentence no longer makes sense. The same would be true if a nucleotide was added, or inserted, and all the letters shifted to the right. In the same way, a nucleotide sequence loses its meaning when an insertion or deletion shifts all the codons by one nucleotide. This change throws off the reading frame, which results in codons that code for different amino acids.

Chromosomal Mutations

Recall that during meiosis, homologous chromosomes exchange DNA segments through crossing over. If the chromosomes do not align with each other, these segments may be different in size. As a result, one chromosome may have two copies of a gene or genes, called gene duplication. The other chromosome may have no copy of the gene or genes. Gene duplication has happened again and again throughout eukaryotic evolution.

Translocation is another type of chromosomal mutation. In translocation, a piece of one chromosome moves to a nonhomologous chromosome. Translocations are often reciprocal, which means that the two nonhomologous chromosomes exchange segments with each other.

Explain How does a frameshift mutation affect reading frame?

Gene duplication

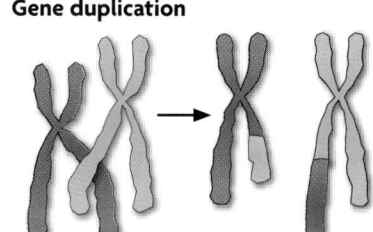

Gene translocation

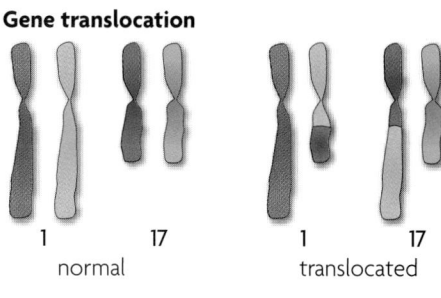

▶ MAIN IDEA

Mutations may or may not affect phenotype.

A mutation can affect an organism to different degrees. The effect depends on factors such as the number of genes involved and the location of the mutation.

Impact on Phenotype

Chromosomal mutations affect a lot of genes and tend to have a big effect on an organism. A mutation may break up a gene, which could make the gene no longer work, or it could make a new hybrid gene with a new function. Translocated genes may also come under the control of a new set of promoters, which could make many genes be more or less active than usual.

Gene mutations, though smaller in scale, can also have a big effect on an organism. Suppose a substitution occurs in a coding region of DNA that changes an AAG codon to CAG. The resulting protein will have a glutamine in place of a lysine. If this change happens in the active site of an enzyme, the enzyme may not be able to bind to its substrate. If the substituted amino acid differs from the original one in size or polarity, the mutation could affect protein folding and thus possibly destroy the protein's function. A substitution could also cause a premature stop codon.

Even a mutation that occurs in a noncoding region can cause problems. For example, such a mutation could disrupt an mRNA splice site and prevent an intron from being removed. A mutation in a noncoding region could also interfere with the regulation of gene expression, keeping a protein from being produced or causing it to be produced all the time.

Many gene mutations, however, do not affect an organism's phenotype. Remember that many codons code for the same amino acid. Therefore, some substitutions have no effect, especially those occurring in the third nucleotide of a codon. If AAG changes to AAA, the resulting protein still has the correct amino acid, lysine. A mutation that does not affect the resulting protein is called silent. Similarly, an incorrect amino acid might have little effect on a protein if it has about the same size or polarity as the original amino acid or if it is far from an active site. If a mutation occurs in a noncoding region, such as an intron, it may not affect the encoded protein at all.

Impact on Offspring

Mutations happen both in body cells and in germ cells. Mutations in body cells affect only the organism in which they occur. In contrast, mutations in germ cells may be passed to offspring. They are the underlying source of genetic variation, which is the basis of natural selection. Mutations in the germ line affect the phenotype of offspring. Often, this effect is so harmful that offspring do not develop properly or die before they can reproduce. Other mutations, though less severe, still result in less adaptive phenotypes. In such cases, natural selection removes these mutant alleles from the population. More rarely, a mutation results in a more beneficial phenotype. These mutations are favored by natural selection and increase in a population.

Apply **Why aren't mutations in body cells passed on to offspring?**

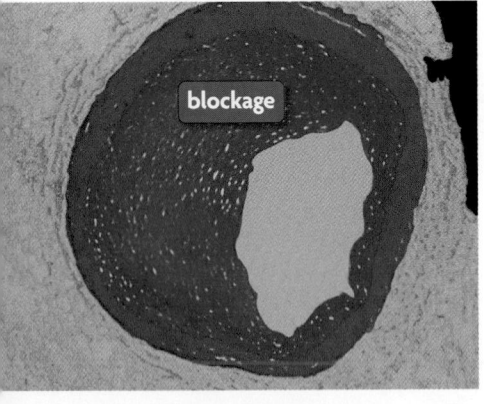

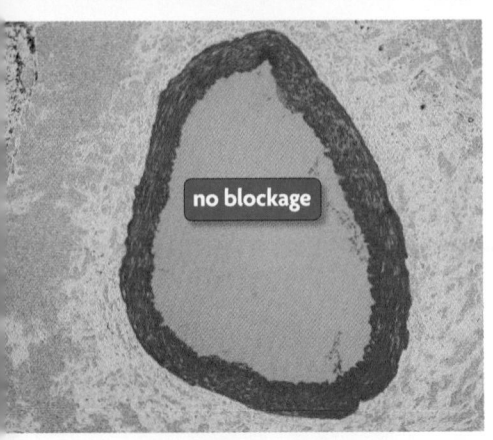

FIGURE 8.21 The coronary artery supplies blood to the heart. If it becomes blocked (top), a heart attack may result. Some people have a mutation that appears to help protect against coronary artery disease (bottom) by increasing their "good" cholesterol levels and decreasing their triglyceride levels. (colored LMs; magnifications: 15×)

◉ MAIN IDEA

Mutations can be caused by several factors.

Mutations are not uncommon, and organisms have many tools to repair them. However, events and substances can make mutations happen faster than the body's repair system can handle.

Replication Errors

As you have learned, DNA polymerase has a built-in proofreading function. Nevertheless, a small number of replication errors are not fixed. They build up over time, and eventually affect how the cell works. For example, many studies suggest that mutations are a significant cause of aging.

Mutagens

Mutagens are agents in the environment that can change DNA. They speed up the rate of replication errors and, in some cases, even break DNA strands. Some mutagens occur naturally, such as ultraviolet (UV) rays in sunshine. Many others are industrial chemicals. Ecologists such as Rachel Carson, shown in **FIGURE 8.22**, warned the public about mutagens.

The human body has DNA repair enzymes that help find and fix mutations. For instance, UV light can cause neighboring thymine nucleotides to break their hydrogen bonds to adenine and bond with each other instead. Typically, one enzyme removes the bonded thymines, another replaces the damaged section, and a third bonds the new segment in place. Sometimes, these enzymes do not work. If these mistakes interfere with regulatory sites and control mechanisms, they may result in cancer. In rare cases, people inherit mutations that make their DNA repair systems less active, which makes these people very vulnerable to the damaging effects of sunlight.

Some cancer drugs take advantage of mutagenic properties by causing similar damage to cancer cells. One type wedges its way between nucleotides, causing so many mutations that cancer cells can no longer function.

Summarize Explain why mutagens can damage DNA in spite of repair enzymes.

Rachel Carson

FIGURE 8.22 Rachel Carson was one of the first ecologists to warn against the widespread use of pesticides and other potential mutagens and toxins.

8.7 ASSESSMENT

ONLINE QUIZ ClassZone.com

REVIEWING ◉ MAIN IDEAS

1. Explain why **frameshift mutations** have a greater effect than do **point mutations.**

2. If GUA is changed to GUU, will the resulting protein be affected? Explain.

3. Explain how **mutagens** can cause genetic **mutations** in spite of your body's DNA repair enzymes.

CRITICAL THINKING

4. **Connect** Some genetic mutations are associated with increased risk for a particular disease. Tests exist for some of these genes. What might be the advantages and disadvantages of being tested?

5. **Infer** How could a mutated gene produce a shorter protein than that produced by the normal gene?

Connecting CONCEPTS

6. **Ecology** How might the presence of a chemical mutagen in the environment affect the genetic makeup and size of a population over time?

Use these inquiry-based labs and online activities to deepen your understanding of DNA.

MICHIGAN STANDARDS

B4.2g Describe the processes of replication, transcription, and translation and how they relate to each other in molecular biology.

B4.4b Explain that gene mutation in a cell can result in uncontrolled cell division called cancer. Also know that exposure of cells to certain chemicals and radiation increases mutations and thus increases the chance of cancer.

DESIGN YOUR OWN INVESTIGATION

UV Light and Skin Cancer

Exposure to the ultraviolet (UV) radiation in sunlight can lead to skin cancer caused by mutations in the DNA of skin cells. The most common type of damage from UV light is the formation of thymine dimers, or pairs of thymine bases bonded together. These mutations interfere with both replication and transcription. Sunscreens receive ratings based on the amount of protection from UV radiation they provide. The higher the sun protection factor (SPF), the more radiation the lotion blocks.

MATERIALS
- 3 different kinds of sunscreen
- sunlight or UV light box
- 12 UV beads

UV beads

SKILLS Collecting Data, Defining Operational Variables

PROBLEM Which sunscreen blocks more UV rays?

PROCEDURE

1. Choose either three different brands of sunscreen or three samples of the same brand with different SPFs.
2. Design an experiment using the UV beads to test the effectiveness of each of the sunscreens. Remember to include a control group and multiple trials.
3. Identify the independent and dependent variables and any constants in your procedure.
4. Once your teacher has approved your experimental design, carry out your procedure. Record your results in a data table.

ANALYZE AND CONCLUDE

1. **Analyze** What can you conclude about the effectiveness of the sunscreens?
2. **Apply** Identify the operational definition of your variable in this experiment.
3. **Evaluate** What was the importance of having a control in this procedure?
4. **Experimental Design** Identify sources of unavoidable error and reasons for inconsistent results.

EXTEND YOUR INVESTIGATION

Exposure to high levels of UV radiation during the teenage years is a major risk factor for skin cancer, but the cancer itself generally does not develop until many years later. Use what you have learned about mutations to propose a reasonable explanation for why skin cancer usually appears later in life.

Modeling Transcription

During the process of transcription, a strand of mRNA that complements the base sequence on a strand of DNA is made.

SKILL Modeling

MATERIALS

- metric ruler
- 60 cm piece of wide ribbon
- scissors
- construction paper of 5 colors
- marker
- stapler

PROBLEM How can you model transcription?

PROCEDURE

1. Cut two pieces of ribbon, each about 30 cm long.

2. Choose five colors of construction paper to represent each of the bases in DNA and RNA.

3. Write out a sequence of 12 bases on a strand of DNA. Cut out corresponding squares of construction paper for each base. Use the marker to label each base.

4. Staple each base along the edge of one piece of ribbon so that they are an equal distance apart. This piece represents a single strand of DNA in the nucleus.

5. Write out the set of complementary bases that will make up the strand of mRNA. Cut out corresponding squares of construction paper for each base. Use the marker to label each base.

6. Staple each base in the correct order along the edge of the second piece of ribbon.

ANALYZE AND CONCLUDE

1. **Compare** How is your model similar to the process of transcription?

2. **Apply** Explain what happens when mRNA leaves the nucleus of a eukaryotic cell.

3. **Evaluate** How would you continue to model translation using the materials in this lab?

4. **Experimental Design** What are some limitations of the model you used in this lab?

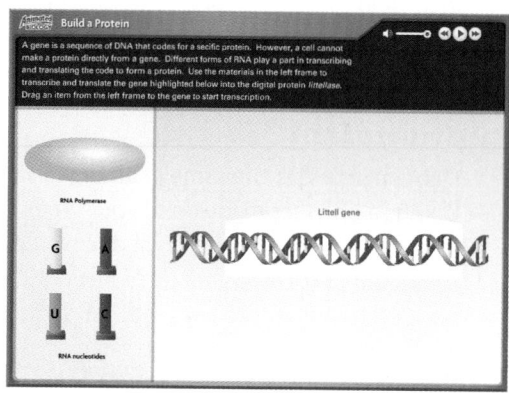

ANIMATED BIOLOGY
Build a Protein

Can you build a protein from a DNA code? Use enzymes, nucleotides, ribosomes, and transfer RNA to synthesize protein.

WEBQUEST

What do *Bt* corn and a fluorescent mouse have in common? They both produce proteins with genes from other organisms. In this WebQuest, you will learn more about transgenic organisms. Explore the potential benefits and risks involved when one organism is engineered to produce a protein from another organism.

DATA ANALYSIS ONLINE

Erwin Chargaff showed that the proportion of certain base pairs always had a consistent relationship, although the amount of each might vary across species. This idea that A = T and C = G is known as Chargaff's rules. Graph the percentage of bases in four different species to put Chargaff's rules to the test.

8.1 Identifying DNA as the Genetic Material

DNA was identified as the genetic material through a series of experiments. Griffith discovered a "transforming principle," which Avery later identified as DNA. Hershey and Chase's experiments with bacteriophages conclusively demonstrated that DNA is the genetic material.

8.2 Structure of DNA

DNA structure is the same in all organisms. DNA is a polymer made up of four types of nucleotides. Watson and Crick discovered that DNA consists of two strands of nucleotides bonded together into a double helix structure. Nucleotides always pair in the same way— C with G, and A with T.

8.3 DNA Replication

DNA replication copies the genetic information of a cell. During replication, a DNA molecule separates into two strands. Each strand serves as a template for building a new complementary strand through a rapid, accurate process involving DNA polymerase and other enzymes.

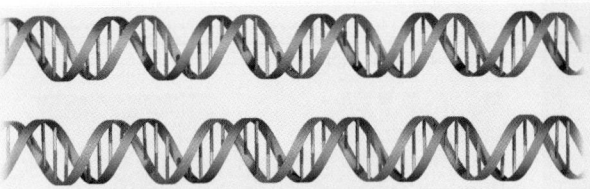

Two identical double-stranded DNA molecules result from replication.

8.4 Transcription

Transcription converts a gene into a single-stranded RNA molecule. The transcription process is similar to DNA replication and makes three types of RNA. Messenger RNA is an intermediate molecule that carries DNA's instructions to be translated.

8.5 Translation

Translation converts an mRNA message into a polypeptide, or protein. This process occurs on ribosomes, which are made of rRNA and proteins. Transfer RNA molecules bring amino acids to the growing protein by selectively pairing with mRNA codons.

8.6 Gene Expression and Regulation

Gene expression is carefully regulated in both prokaryotic and eukaryotic cells. In prokaryotes, transcription is the primary point of control. In eukaryotes, gene expression is controlled at many points, including RNA processing.

8.7 Mutations

Mutations are changes in DNA that may or may not affect phenotype. Some affect a single gene, and others affect an entire chromosome. Mutations may occur naturally, or they may be caused by mutagens. A mutation that does not affect phenotype is called silent. Mutations in sperm or egg cells can be passed to offspring.

Synthesize Your Notes

Summarize How can you summarize the process by which proteins are made? Use your notes to make a detailed version of the graphic organizer below. Include important details about the processes of transcription and translation. Mark important vocabulary terms.

From DNA to Proteins

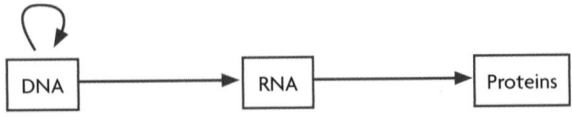

Concept Map Use a concept map like the one below to summarize what you know about mutations.

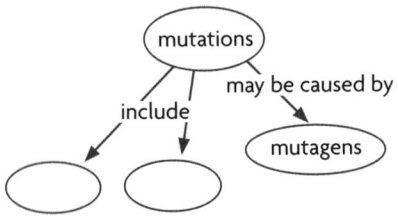

Chapter Assessment

Chapter Vocabulary

8.1 bacteriophage, p. 228

8.2 nucleotide, p. 230
double helix, p. 232
base pairing rules, p. 232

8.3 replication, p. 235
DNA polymerase, p. 236

8.4 central dogma, p. 239
RNA, p. 239
transcription, p. 240
RNA polymerase, p. 240
messenger RNA (mRNA), p. 240
ribosomal RNA (rRNA), p. 240
transfer RNA (tRNA), p. 240

8.5 translation, p. 243
codon, p. 243
stop codon, p. 244

start codon, p. 244
anticodon, p. 245

8.6 promoter, p. 248
operon, p. 248
exon, p. 251
intron, p. 251

8.7 mutation, p. 252
point mutation, p. 252
frameshift mutation, p. 252
mutagen, p. 255

Reviewing Vocabulary

Compare and Contrast

Describe one similarity and one difference between the two terms in each of the following pairs.

1. translation, transcription
2. point mutation, frameshift mutation
3. messenger RNA (mRNA), transfer RNA (tRNA)
4. codon, anticodon

Word Origins

5. The word *codon* was coined in 1962 by putting together the word *code* with the suffix *-on*, which means "a hereditary unit." How do these word parts relate to the meaning of the term *codon*?

Use the word parts in this table to answer the next two questions.

Part	Meaning
-gen	to give birth
muta-	to change
phago-	eating
poly-	many

6. Use the meaning of the word parts to write your own definitions for the following terms: *mutagen, bacteriophage, polypeptide.*
7. Suggest a likely definition for these biology terms: *polygenic, phagocyte.*

Reviewing MAIN IDEAS

8. How did qualitative, chemical, and enzyme tests help Avery identify DNA as the transforming principle?

9. Hershey and Chase confirmed that DNA, not protein, was the genetic material. How do the results of their two experiments support this conclusion?

10. Describe Watson and Crick's double helix model of DNA. Include a labeled drawing of the model.

11. One DNA strand has the nucleotide sequence AACGTA. What is the sequence of the other strand?

12. How do the base pairing rules explain how a strand of DNA acts as a template during DNA replication?

13. What are three main steps in DNA replication?

14. What does it mean to say that there is a "proofreading" function in DNA replication?

15. Describe two differences between DNA and RNA.

16. List the main types of RNA and their functions.

17. Explain how the interaction between mRNA codons and tRNA anticodons codes for a specific amino acid.

18. What role do ribosomes play in translation?

19. Where in the eukaryotic cell do replication, transcription, RNA processing, and translation each occur?

20. How do the promoter and operator work together to control gene expression?

21. Describe mRNA processing in eukaryotic cells.

22. Describe three ways mutations can occur.

Critical Thinking

23. Apply Give one example of how a mutation may affect an organism's traits, and one example of how a mutation may not affect an organism's traits.

24. Synthesize When you eat a serving of black beans, your body breaks down the beans into smaller subunits. How do you think your body uses the nucleotides and amino acids that are found in black beans?

25. Hypothesize If the nucleus was surrounded by a membrane that had fewer pores, how might the rate of protein synthesis be affected, and why?

26. Apply For the DNA sequence TACCAAGTGAAAATT, write the sequence of its RNA transcript and the sequence of amino acids for which it codes.

27. Predict Suppose you genetically altered a gene in a line of eukaryotic cells by inserting only the operator from the bacterial *lac* operon. Do you think that adding lactose to the cell culture would cause the cells to start transcribing the altered gene? Explain your reasoning.

28. Contrast What process did Watson and Crick use to develop their model of DNA, and how did it differ from the controlled experiments used by Griffith, Avery, and Hershey and Chase?

29. Infer Having spent much time in sunlight during youth, an older person develops skin cancer and has the growths removed. Why might the growths keep coming back?

30. Synthesize Watson and Crick learned from Franklin's x-ray crystallography that the distance between the backbones of the DNA molecule was the same for the entire length of the molecule. How did this information, combined with what they knew about the sizes of the four bases, lead to their model of DNA structure?

Interpreting Visuals

Use the diagram to answer the next three questions.

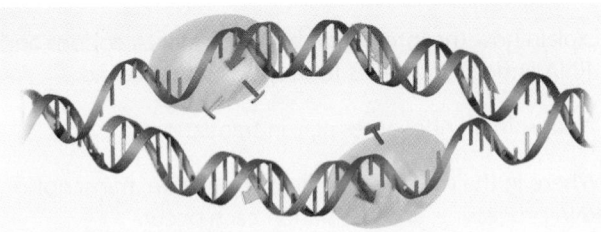

31. Apply What process is taking place in this diagram?

32. Apply What do the arrows on the yellow strands indicate?

33. Predict If you were to extend the diagram in both directions, what would you expect to see?

Analyzing Data

Many factors contribute to breast cancer, including some that are genetic. For example, women with a mutation in the BRCA1 gene have an especially high risk of developing breast cancer. The histogram below shows the total estimated number of new breast cancer cases for women in the United States for 2003. Use the data in the histogram to answer the next two questions.

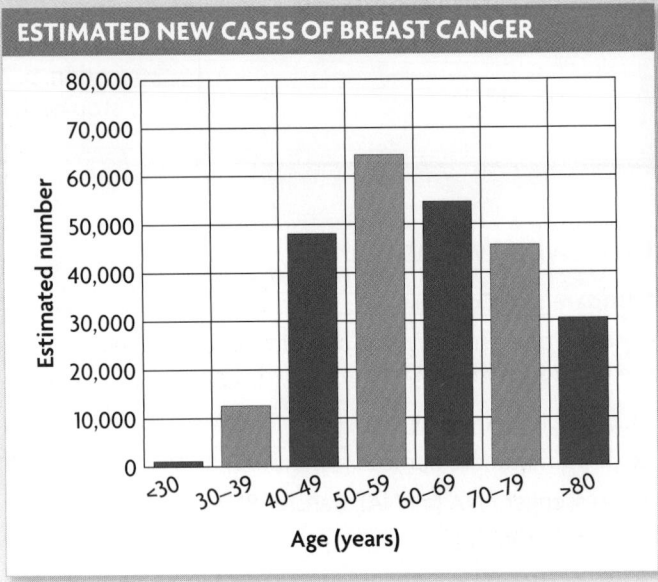

ESTIMATED NEW CASES OF BREAST CANCER

Source: American Cancer Society

34. Analyze In which age group was the incidence of new cases the lowest? the highest?

35. Hypothesize Using the data in this histogram, develop a hypothesis to explain why breast cancer genes are still present in the population.

Connecting CONCEPTS

36. Write an Analogy This chapter used an analogy about exchanging quarters for tokens at a game center to represent the process of transcription. Think of your own analogy for one of the processes you learned about in this chapter. Write a paragraph using that analogy to explain the process. Also, note any limitations of your analogy. (That is, in what ways does it not "fit" the process you're explaining?)

37. Synthesize Look again at the picture of the glowing mouse on page 225. The gene for the protein GFP was inserted into a mouse egg, and then expressed in the mouse. What genetic processes are involved in the expression of this gene?

MICHIGAN
STANDARDS-BASED ASSESSMENT

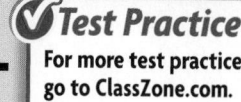

✓ **Test Practice**
For more test practice,
go to ClassZone.com.

1. Before the genetic code could be understood, scientists needed to know that a codon is composed of three nucleotides. This situation is an example of the **B2.2D**

   A fact that codons are the building block of life.

   B cumulative nature of scientific evidence.

   C way that theories can lead to scientific laws.

   D ability of scientists to make hypotheses.

2.

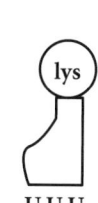

AAACACUAU

tyr
AUA

lys
UUU

his
GUG

   This illustration shows a strand of mRNA and the complementary tRNA molecules that can base pair with the mRNA codons. What is the correct sequence of amino acids? **B4.2g**

   A lys-his-tyr

   B his-tyr-lys

   C tyr-lys-his

   D lys-tyr-his

3. Less than 60% of the DNA sequence of the human GM-CSF gene and the mouse GM-CSF gene is the same. When scientists put the human gene into mice, however, it functions properly. Which statement *best* explains why this happens? **B4.2f**

   A The resulting proteins are similar enough.

   B Mice can make any human protein.

   C The DNA is mutated in the mouse.

   D The differences are at the ends of the protein.

   THINK THROUGH THE QUESTION

   The name of the gene is not important in answering this question. All you need to learn from the names is that the question involves only one type of gene. Don't let a complicated name distract you from answering the real question.

4. A mutant protein that has a proline in place of a histidine generally has different chemical properties from the normal protein. Which statement *best* explains this difference? **B4.3B**

   A Proline and histidine cannot exist in the same protein sequence.

   B Proline and histidine are both rare amino acids.

   C Proline and histidine cannot both be made by the same cell.

   D Proline and histidine interact differently with other amino acids.

5. According to the base-pairing rules in DNA, **B4.2C**

   A T pairs with G, and A pairs with C.

   B T pairs with A, and G pairs with C.

   C T pairs with C, and G pairs with A.

   D U pairs with A, and G pairs with C.

6. Agents in the environment that can change DNA and lead to cancer are called **B4.4b**

   A mutants.

   B mutagens.

   C operons.

   D exons.

9 Frontiers of Biotechnology

KEY CONCEPTS

9.1 Manipulating DNA
Biotechnology relies on cutting DNA at specific places.

9.2 Copying DNA
The polymerase chain reaction rapidly copies segments of DNA.

9.3 DNA Fingerprinting
DNA fingerprints identify people at the molecular level.

9.4 Genetic Engineering
DNA sequences of organisms can be changed.

9.5 Genomics and Bioinformatics
Entire genomes are sequenced, studied, and compared.

9.6 Genetic Screening and Gene Therapy
Genetics provides a basis for new medical treatments.

Online BIOLOGY CLASSZONE.COM

Animated BIOLOGY
View animated chapter concepts.
• Restriction Enzymes
• Polymerase Chain Reaction
• Gel Electrophoresis
• Bacterial Transformation

BIOZINE
Keep current with biology news.
• Featured stories
• News feeds
• Careers

RESOURCE CENTER
Get more information on
• DNA Manipulation Tools
• Genetic Engineering
• Genomics

How can biotechnology reunite families?

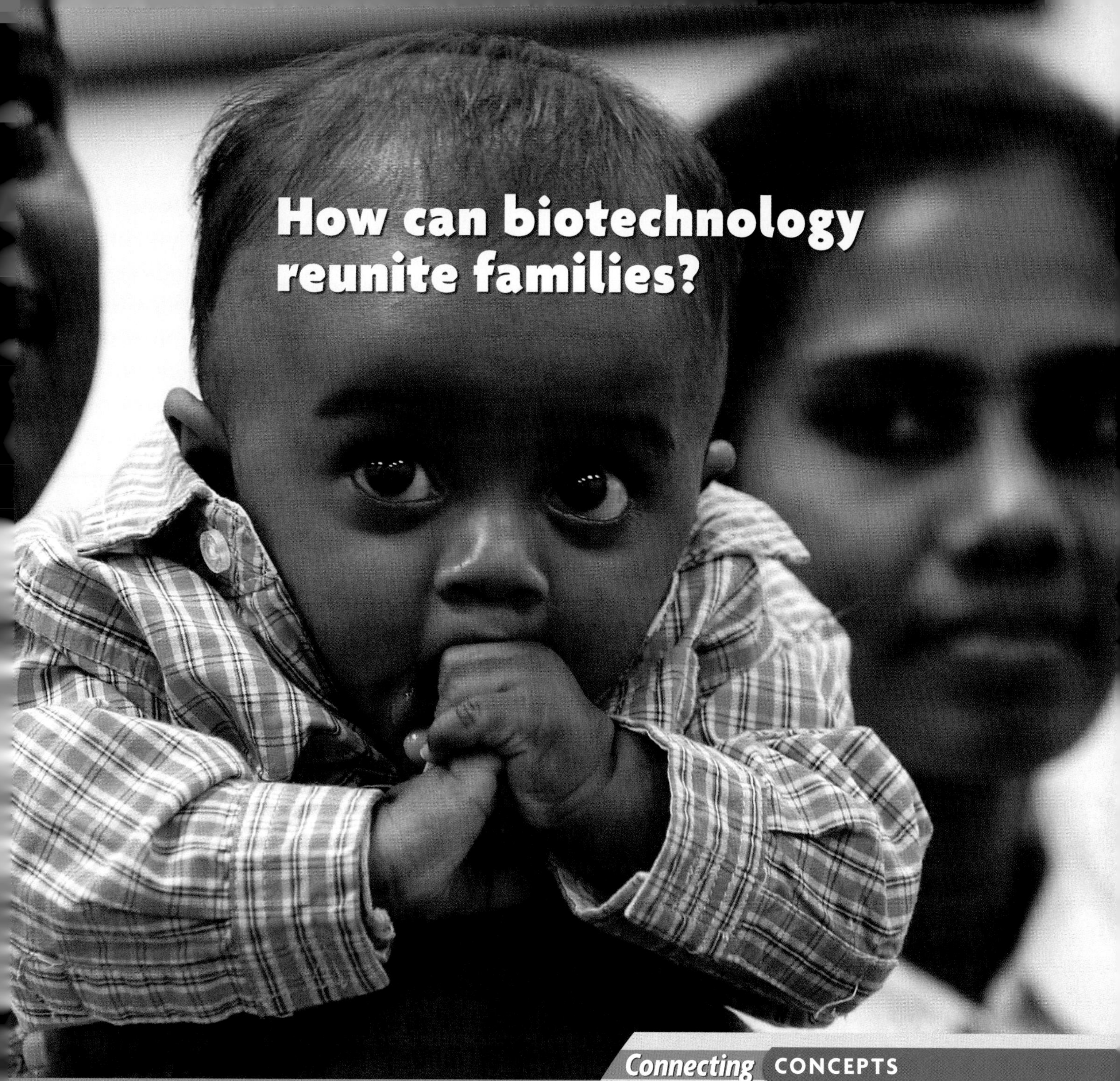

A natural disaster strikes. Families are separated. One application of biotechnology can help bring the families back together. DNA fingerprinting can identify people at the genetic level. And it allowed the child above, called Baby 81 by rescue workers, to be reunited with his parents months after a tsunami, or tidal wave, devastated many parts of Southeast Asia.

Connecting CONCEPTS

Ecology DNA fingerprinting is not just used to identify people and to help fight crime. It can also be used to identify different species. Scientists at the San Diego Zoo use DNA fingerprinting to identify different tortoise species from the Galapagos Islands. Through the help of DNA fingerprinting, the scientists hope to repopulate the islands with native tortoise species.

9.1 Manipulating DNA

KEY CONCEPT Biotechnology relies on cutting DNA at specific places.

MAIN IDEAS

- Scientists use several techniques to manipulate DNA.
- Restriction enzymes cut DNA.
- Restriction maps show the lengths of DNA fragments.

VOCABULARY

restriction enzyme, p. 265
gel electrophoresis, p. 266
restriction map, p. 267

Review
DNA, enzyme, allele, nucleotide

MICHIGAN STANDARDS

B4.4c Explain how mutations in the DNA sequence of a gene may be silent or result in phenotypic change in an organism and in its offspring.

B4.r5b Evaluate the advantages and disadvantages of human manipulation of DNA. (recommended)

Connect Many applications of genetics that are widely used today were unimaginable just 30 years ago. Our use of genetics to identify people is just one example. Biotechnology and genetics are used to produce transgenic organisms and clones. They are used to study diseases and evolution. They are used to produce medical treatments for people with life-threatening illnesses. Through many years of research and a combination of many different methods, advances in biotechnology seem to happen on a daily basis.

MAIN IDEA

Scientists use several techniques to manipulate DNA.

By the middle of the 1950s, scientists had concluded that DNA was the genetic material. Watson and Crick had determined the structure of DNA. Yet the field of genetics as we know it today was just beginning. For example, even the genetic code that you learned about in Chapter 8 was not fully understood until the early 1960s. Since that time, scientists have developed a combination of methods to study DNA and genes.

DNA is a very large molecule, but it is still just a molecule. It is far too small to see, and you cannot pick it up or rearrange it with your hands. Therefore, scientists must be able to work with DNA without being able to see or handle it directly. Chemicals, computers, and bacteria are just a few of the tools that have allowed advances in genetics research.

Artificial nucleotides are used to sequence genes. Artificial copies of genes are used to study gene expression. Chemical mutagens are used to change DNA sequences. Computers analyze and organize the vast amounts of data from genetics research. Enzymes, often from bacteria, are used to cut and copy DNA. Bacteria also provide one of the ways in which genes are transferred between different organisms. Throughout this chapter, you will learn about some of the techniques used in biotechnology, as well as some of its applications. You likely have heard of genetic engineering, DNA fingerprinting, and cloning, but how are they done? In many cases, one of the first steps in biotechnology and genetics research is to precisely cut DNA.

Infer Why might so many different methods be needed to study DNA and genes?

TAKING NOTES

Use a supporting main ideas chart to organize your notes on ways in which DNA is manipulated.

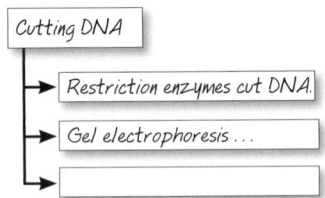

⊙ MAIN IDEA
Restriction enzymes cut DNA.

Why would scientists want to cut DNA? To answer that question, you have to remember that a gene is a sequence of DNA nucleotides, and that a chromosome is one long DNA molecule. A whole chromosome is too large for scientists to study a particular gene easily, so they had to find a way to get much smaller pieces of DNA. Of course, slicing a chromosome into pieces is not as simple as picking up the molecule and cutting it with a pair of scissors. Instead, scientists use enzymes that act as molecular "scissors." These enzymes, which slice apart DNA, come from many different types of bacteria.

Bacterial cells, like your cells, can be infected by viruses. As protection against these invaders, bacteria produce enzymes that cut up the DNA of the viruses. As **FIGURE 9.1** shows, a DNA molecule can be cut apart in several places at once by several molecules of a restriction enzyme, or endonuclease. **Restriction enzymes** are enzymes that cut DNA molecules at specific nucleotide sequences. In fact, any time the enzyme finds that exact DNA sequence, it cuts the DNA molecule. The sequence of nucleotides that is identified and cut by a restriction enzyme is called a restriction site. These enzymes are called restriction enzymes because they restrict, or decrease, the effect of the virus on the bacterial cell.

Each of the hundreds of known restriction enzymes has a different restriction site. Different restriction enzymes will cut the same DNA molecule in different ways. For example, one restriction enzyme may find three of its restriction sites in a segment of DNA. Another restriction enzyme might find six of its restriction sites in the same segment. Different numbers of fragments with different lengths result. As you can see below, two different restriction enzymes can cut the same strand of DNA in very different ways.

FIGURE 9.1 A restriction enzyme (blue peaks) from an *E. coli* bacterium helps protect against viruses by cutting DNA (red). This cutting "restricts" the effect of a virus on a bacterium. (colored 3D atomic force micrograph; magnification 63,000×)

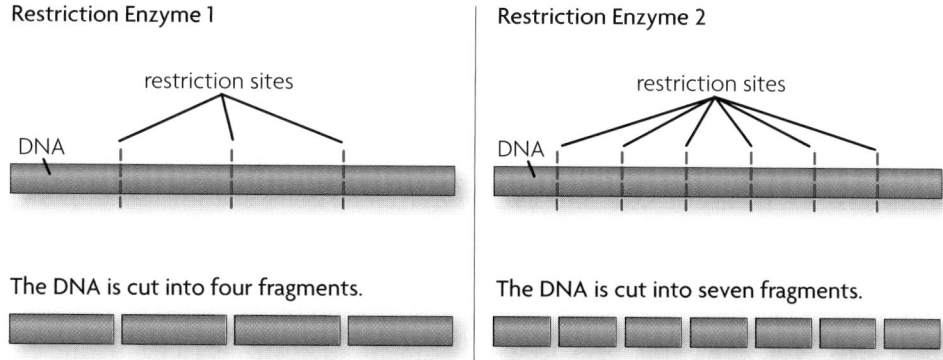

Restriction Enzyme 1

restriction sites

DNA

The DNA is cut into four fragments.

Restriction Enzyme 2

restriction sites

DNA

The DNA is cut into seven fragments.

Restriction enzymes recognize nucleotide sequences that are between four and eight base pairs long, and then cut the DNA within that area. Some enzymes make cuts straight across the two strands of a DNA molecule. These cuts leave behind fragments of DNA that end in what are called "blunt ends."

FIGURE 9.2 Restriction Enzymes Cut DNA

Use virtual restriction enzymes at ClassZone.com.

Some restriction enzymes leave behind nucleotide tails, or "sticky ends," when they cut DNA.

A restriction enzyme called *Taq*I cuts DNA when it finds its restriction site. *Taq*I's restriction site is
TCGA
AGCT

Infer How would the above illustration change if *Taq*I left behind blunt ends rather than sticky ends when it cuts DNA?

Connecting CONCEPTS

DNA Base Pairs Recall from **Chapter 8** that DNA nucleotides match up by complementary base pairing. A always pairs with T, and C always pairs with G.

Other restriction enzymes, as shown in **FIGURE 9.2**, make staggered cuts that leave tails of free DNA bases on each side of the cut. These nucleotide tails of the cut DNA strands are called "sticky ends." Sticky ends are like tiny pieces of Velcro that are ready to hook on to their opposite sides. If two pieces of DNA with sticky ends and complementary base pairs come close to each other, the two segments of DNA will join by hydrogen bonding. Because of this characteristic of DNA, restriction enzymes that leave sticky ends when they cut DNA are often used in biotechnology, as you will learn in Section 9.4.

Summarize How do different restriction enzymes produce different DNA fragments from the same DNA molecule?

▶ MAIN IDEA

Restriction maps show the lengths of DNA fragments.

After a long DNA molecule has been cut by restriction enzymes into many smaller fragments, several different things can be done with the DNA. For example, the DNA sequence of a gene can be studied, or a gene cut out from the DNA can be placed into the DNA of another organism. But before anything else can be done, the DNA fragments have to be separated from one another. The fragments are sorted according to their sizes by a technique called gel electrophoresis (ih-LEHK-troh-fuh-REE-sihs).

In **gel electrophoresis,** an electrical current is used to separate a mixture of DNA fragments from each other. A sample of DNA is loaded into a gel, which is like a thin slab of hard gelatin. A positive electrode is at one end of the gel. At the other end is a negative electrode. Because DNA has a negative charge, the fragments move toward the positive electrode, or the positively charged pole. The gel also has tiny pores running through it. The pores allow small molecules to move quickly. Larger molecules cannot easily move through the gel and they travel more slowly. Therefore, the length of a DNA fragment can be estimated from the distance it travels through a gel in a certain period of time. As shown in **FIGURE 9.3**, DNA fragments of different sizes appear as different bands, or lines, on a gel. The pattern of bands on the gel can be thought of as a map of the original strand of DNA. **Restriction maps** show the lengths of DNA fragments between restriction sites in a strand of DNA.

The bands on a gel indicate only the lengths of DNA fragments. Alone, they do not give any information about the DNA sequences of the fragments. Even though restriction maps do not directly show the makeup of a fragment of DNA, the maps are very useful in genetic engineering, which you will read about in Section 9.4. They can also be used to study gene mutations. How? First, a mutation may add or delete bases between restriction sites, which would change the lengths of DNA fragments on a gel. Second, a mutation may change a restriction site, and the DNA would not be cut in the same places.

Suppose, for example, that when a normal allele of a gene is cut by a restriction enzyme, five DNA fragments appear as five different bands on a gel. Then, when a mutant allele of the same gene is cut with the same enzyme, only three bands appear. Comparisons of restriction maps can help diagnose genetic diseases, as you will see in Section 9.6. A restriction map from a person's DNA can be compared with a restriction map from DNA that is known to be normal. If the restriction maps differ, it is an indication that the person has inherited a disease-causing allele of the gene.

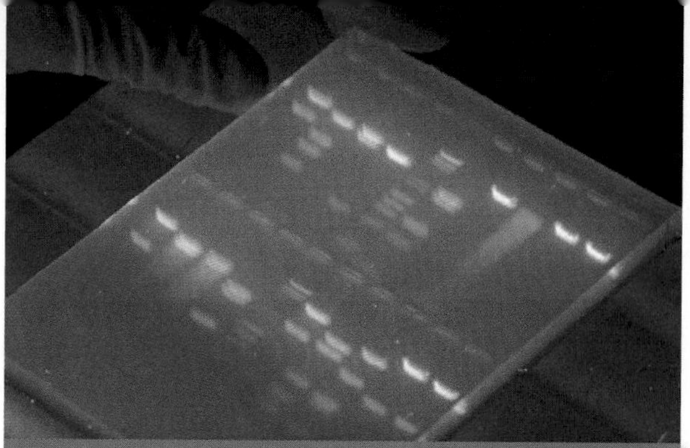

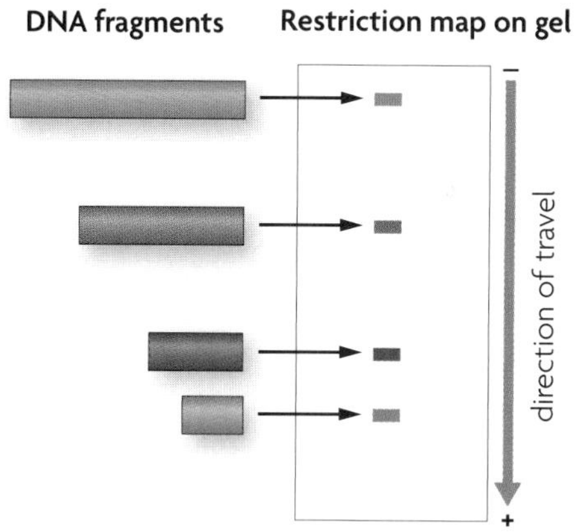

Synthesize **How are restriction enzymes used in making restriction maps?**

FIGURE 9.3 GEL ELECTROPHORESIS

A segment of DNA is cut with a restriction enzyme into fragments of different lengths.

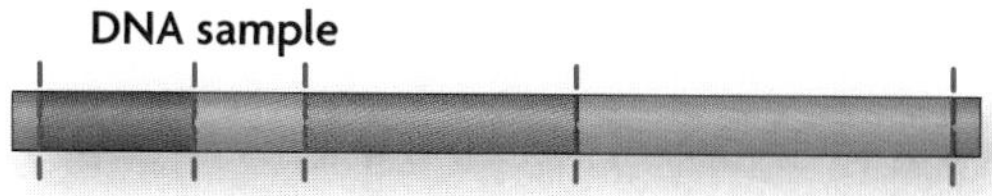

DNA sample

Different sizes of DNA fragments show up as bands on a gel. Smaller fragments move farther down the gel.

DNA fragments   Restriction map on gel

direction of travel

ONLINE QUIZ
ClassZone.com

REVIEWING ▶ MAIN IDEAS

1. List four different ways in which scientists can manipulate DNA.

2. What determines how DNA will be cut by a **restriction enzyme**?

3. How does **gel electrophoresis** separate DNA fragments from each other?

CRITICAL THINKING

4. **Apply** Suppose you cut DNA. You know that you should find four DNA fragments on a gel, but only three appear, and one fragment is very large. Explain what happened.

5. **Synthesize** What is the relationship between restriction sites and a **restriction map**?

Connecting CONCEPTS

6. **Mutations** Would a mutation in a gene always be detectable by using restriction maps? Why or why not?

MATERIALS

- Gel Electrophoresis Datasheet
- scissors
- foam tray
- metric ruler
- plastic soap dish (rectangular)
- 2 100-mL graduated cylinders
- 60 mL 1% agarose solution (warm to the touch)
- aluminum foil strips cut to the width of the soap dish
- 2 wires with alligator clips on both ends
- 50 mL 3% baking soda solution
- 5 small test tubes
- test tube rack
- 5 pipettes
- 5 "DNA" samples
- 10 mL graduated cylinder
- 10 mL glycerol
- 5 9-volt batteries

PROCESS SKILLS

- **Modeling**
- **Analyzing**
- **Concluding**
- **Predicting**

B1.1E Describe a reason for a given conclusion using evidence from an investigation.

B4.2C Describe the structure and function of DNA.

Modeling Forensics

In newspapers, on television, and in movies, you often hear about DNA evidence being used to solve crimes. Scientists use a method called gel electrophoresis to separate DNA molecules on the basis of their size. In this lab, you will build a gel electrophoresis apparatus and use it to separate simulated DNA samples to determine a suspect's identity.

PROBLEM Which "DNA" sample matches DNA found at a crime scene?

PROCEDURE

1. Use the instructions on the Gel Electrophoresis Datasheet to make the agarose gel and to construct your gel electrophoresis apparatus. Have your teacher check your experimental set-up before you continue.

2. In each of five different test tubes place 6 drops each of the different "DNA" samples. Add 2 drops of glycerol to each tube and gently mix.

3. Use a different pipette to fill each well of the gel with a few drops of one of the samples. The samples should sink into the wells. Do not overfill the wells.

4. Carefully connect the five batteries in a series, as shown on the datasheet. Attach the free ends of the wires to the positive and negative ends of the battery series.

   Caution: Keep electrical equipment from getting wet.

5. Allow the gel to run for at least 30 minutes. Observe and record what happens. Make drawings of your observations.

ANALYZE AND CONCLUDE

1. **Observe** Summarize your observations of what happened to the samples that you ran through the gel.

2. **Analyze** Which samples matched? How do you know?

3. **Apply** How is the analysis of DNA useful for identification of a crime suspect?

4. **Conclude** Gel electrophoresis sorts DNA by the sizes of different fragments. Does the method tell you anything about genes in the DNA? Explain.

5. **Predict** Suppose that you place a mixture of DNA fragments in a single gel electrophoresis well. The fragments have base pair lengths of 300, 5000, 700, 1000, and 500. Make a sketch of how the fragments would appear in the gel after they have been separated by gel electrophoresis. Explain your answer.

EXTEND YOUR INVESTIGATION

How might the separation of the samples be affected by changing the concentration of agarose? Design an experiment to test your hypothesis.

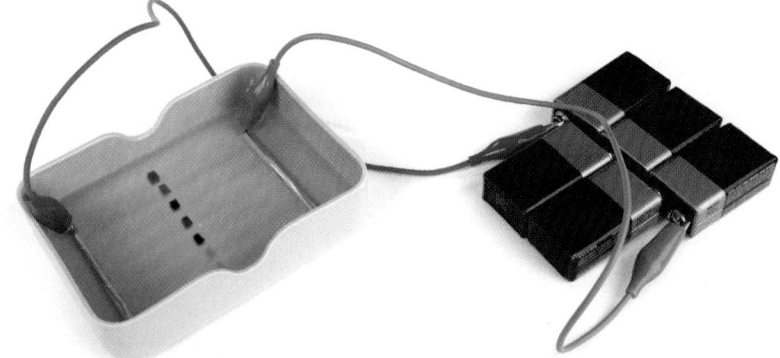

9.2 Copying DNA

KEY CONCEPT The polymerase chain reaction rapidly copies segments of DNA.

▶ MAIN IDEAS

- PCR uses polymerases to copy DNA segments.
- PCR is a three-step process.

VOCABULARY

polymerase chain reaction (PCR), p. 269
primer, p. 271

Review
DNA polymerase, replication

Connect Forensic scientists use DNA from cells in a single hair at a crime scene to identify a criminal. Doctors test a patient's blood to quickly detect the presence of bacteria that cause Lyme disease. Scientists compare DNA from different species to determine how closely the species are related. However, the original amount of DNA from any of these sources is far too small to accurately study. Samples of DNA must be increased, or amplified, so that they can be analyzed.

▶ MAIN IDEA

PCR uses polymerases to copy DNA segments.

How do scientists get an amount of DNA that is large enough to be studied and manipulated? They copy the same segment of DNA over and over again. **Polymerase chain reaction (PCR)** is a technique that produces millions—or even billions—of copies of a specific DNA sequence in just a few hours. As the name indicates, the DNA polymerase enzymes that you learned about in Chapter 8 play key roles in this process.

Kary Mullis, who invented PCR, is shown in **FIGURE 9.4**. While working for a California biotechnology company in 1983, Mullis had an insight about how to copy DNA segments. He adapted the process of DNA replication that occurs in every living cell into a method for copying DNA in a test tube. Under the right set of conditions, DNA polymerases copy DNA in a test tube just as they do inside cells. However, in cells several other enzymes are needed before the polymerases can do their job. For example, before a cell can begin to copy its DNA, enzymes called helicases unwind and separate DNA molecules. Instead of using these enzymes, Mullis used heat to separate the DNA strands.

Unfortunately, heat also broke down the *E. coli* polymerases that Mullis first used. Then came Mullis's second stroke of genius: Why not use polymerases from a bacterium that lives in temperatures above 80°C (176°F)? By using this enzyme, Mullis was able to raise the temperature of the DNA to separate the strands without destroying the DNA polymerases. Here again, just as with restriction enzymes that you read about in Section 9.1, a major advance came from applying an adaptation found in nature to biotechnology. Mullis introduced PCR to the world in 1985, and in 1993 he won the Nobel Prize in chemistry for his revolutionary technique.

Compare and Contrast How are replication and PCR similar? different? Explain.

FIGURE 9.4 Kary Mullis came up with the idea for PCR while on a surfing trip in 1983. He won the Nobel Prize in chemistry in 1993.

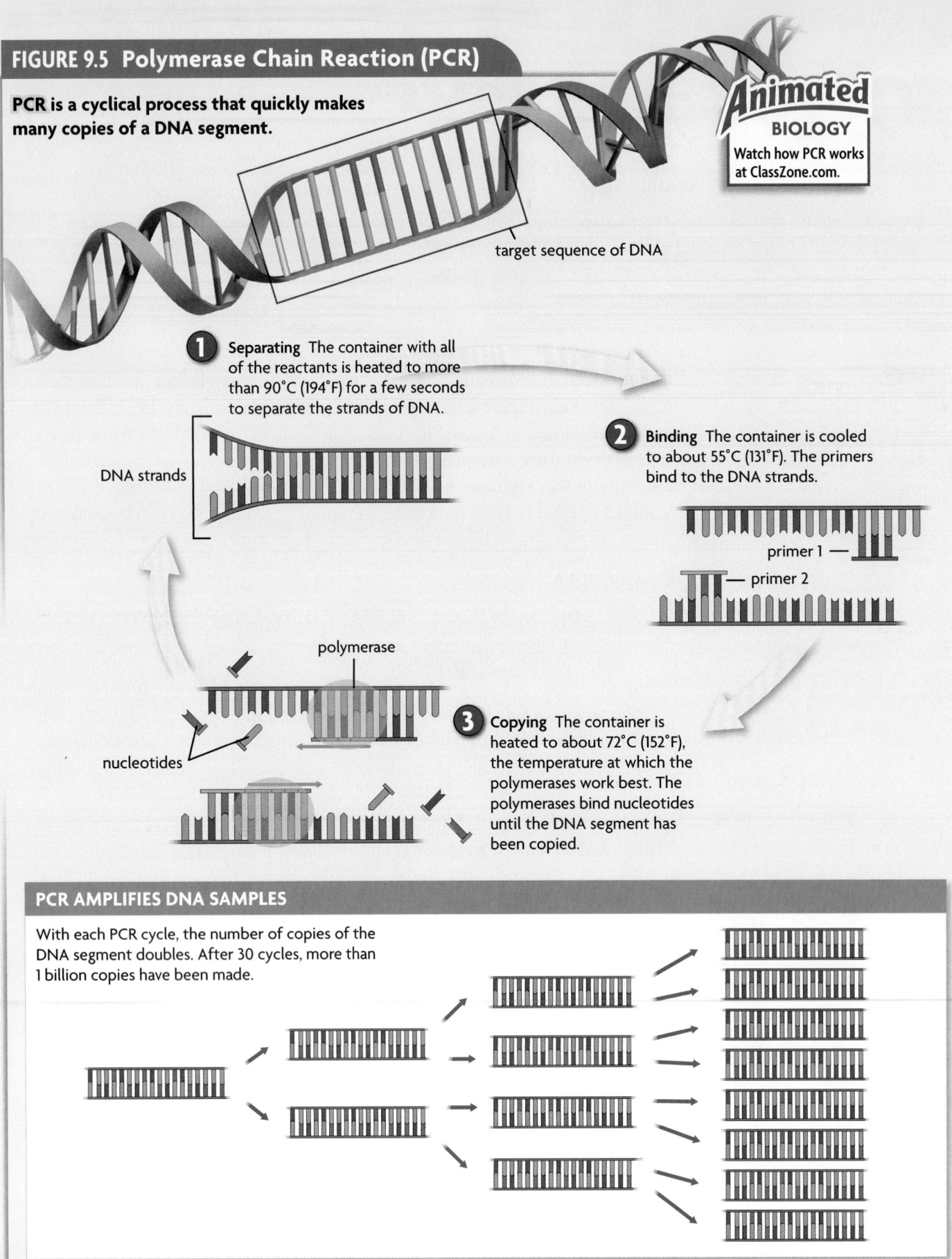

FIGURE 9.5 Polymerase Chain Reaction (PCR)

PCR is a cyclical process that quickly makes many copies of a DNA segment.

Animated BIOLOGY
Watch how PCR works at ClassZone.com.

target sequence of DNA

1 **Separating** The container with all of the reactants is heated to more than 90°C (194°F) for a few seconds to separate the strands of DNA.

DNA strands

2 **Binding** The container is cooled to about 55°C (131°F). The primers bind to the DNA strands.

primer 1

primer 2

polymerase

nucleotides

3 **Copying** The container is heated to about 72°C (152°F), the temperature at which the polymerases work best. The polymerases bind nucleotides until the DNA segment has been copied.

PCR AMPLIFIES DNA SAMPLES

With each PCR cycle, the number of copies of the DNA segment doubles. After 30 cycles, more than 1 billion copies have been made.

CRITICAL VIEWING   How many copies of DNA will exist after one more PCR cycle? After three more cycles?

PCR is a three-step process.

PCR is a surprisingly simple process. It uses just four materials: the DNA to be copied, DNA polymerases, large amounts of each of the four DNA nucleotides (A, T, C, and G), and two primers. A **primer** is a short segment of DNA that acts as the starting point for a new strand. If DNA polymerases build new DNA strands, why are primers needed for PCR? DNA polymerases can add nucleotides to strands that have already been started, but they cannot start the strands. In PCR, two primers are used to start the copying of DNA close to the desired segment. The two primers are like bookends for the DNA strand. They limit the length of the copied DNA to one small segment of the strand.

PCR has three main steps, as shown in **FIGURE 9.5**. All of the steps of the cycle take place in the same container but at different temperatures. The main function of the first two PCR cycles is to produce the small segment of DNA that is desired. By making a copy of the desired segment, many copies of that tiny piece of DNA can be made, rather than copying an entire chromosome.

1 Separating The container with all of the reactants is heated to separate the double-stranded DNA into single strands.

2 Binding The container is cooled and the primers bind to their complementary DNA sequences. One primer binds to each DNA strand. The primers bind on opposite ends of the DNA segment being copied.

3 Copying The container is heated again and the polymerases begin to build new strands of DNA. Added nucleotides bind to the original DNA strands by complementary base pairing. The polymerases continue attaching nucleotides until the entire DNA segment has been copied.

Each PCR cycle doubles the number of DNA copies. The original piece of DNA becomes two copies. Those two copies become four copies. And the cycle is repeated over and over to quickly copy enough DNA for study. After only 30 cycles of PCR, for example, the original DNA sequence is copied more than 1 billion times. This doubling is why the process is called a chain reaction.

Infer Why is it necessary to keep changing the temperature in the PCR process?

> **VOCABULARY**
>
> The term *primer* comes from a Latin word that means "first." In PCR, a primer is the starting point for the DNA copying process.

> *Connecting* CONCEPTS
>
> **Replication** Look back at the process of DNA replication in **Chapter 8** to compare PCR with replication.

9.2 ASSESSMENT

ONLINE QUIZ
ClassZone.com

REVIEWING ▶ MAIN IDEAS

1. Briefly describe the function of **polymerase chain reaction (PCR).**

2. Summarize the cycle involved in the PCR process.

CRITICAL THINKING

3. **Synthesize** Describe how heating double-stranded DNA separates the strands. Why does heating also inactivate DNA polymerases from many organisms?

4. **Analyze** Explain two reasons why **primers** are important in PCR.

Connecting CONCEPTS

5. **Human Genetics** Many human genetic diseases are caused by recessive alleles of genes. How might PCR be important in the diagnosis of these illnesses?

9.3 DNA Fingerprinting

KEY CONCEPT DNA fingerprints identify people at the molecular level.

▶ MAIN IDEAS

- A DNA fingerprint is a type of restriction map.
- DNA fingerprinting is used for identification.

VOCABULARY

DNA fingerprint, p. 272

Review
restriction enzyme, gel electrophoresis, restriction map

MICHIGAN STANDARDS

B4.2B Recognize that every species has its own characteristic DNA sequence.

B4.r5b Evaluate the advantages and disadvantages of human manipulation of DNA. (recommended)

Connect You hear about it in the news all the time. DNA evidence is used to convict a criminal, release an innocent person from prison, or solve a mystery. A couple of decades ago, the lines and swirls of someone's fingertip were a detective's best hope for identifying someone. Now, investigators gather biological samples and analyze DNA for another kind of evidence: a DNA fingerprint.

▶ MAIN IDEA

A DNA fingerprint is a type of restriction map.

Unless you have an identical twin, your complete set of DNA, or your genome, is unique. This variation in DNA among people is the basis of DNA fingerprinting. A **DNA fingerprint** is a representation of parts of an individual's DNA that can be used to identify a person at the molecular level.

A DNA fingerprint is a specific type of restriction map, which you learned about in Section 9.1. First, a DNA sample is cut with a restriction enzyme. Then the DNA fragments are run through a gel and the pattern of bands on the gel is analyzed. As you can see in **FIGURE 9.6**, a DNA fingerprint can show relationships among family members. The children (C) have similar DNA fingerprints to one another, but they are not identical. Also, their DNA fingerprints are combinations of the DNA fingerprints of the parents (M and F).

The greatest differences in DNA among people are found in regions of the genome that are not parts of genes. As a result, DNA fingerprinting focuses on noncoding regions of DNA, or DNA sequences outside genes. Noncoding DNA sequences often include stretches of nucleotides that repeat several times, one after another, as shown in **FIGURE 9.7**. Each person's DNA differs in the numbers of copies of the repeats. For example, one person may have seven repeats in one location, and another person may have three in the same place. To get to the specific regions of DNA that can be identified through DNA fingerprinting, the DNA is cut in known locations with restriction enzymes.

The differences in the number of repeats are found by separating the DNA fragments with gel electrophoresis. When there are more repeats, a DNA fragment is larger. The pattern of DNA fragments on a gel represents the uniqueness of a person's DNA. Individuals might have some of the fragments in common, but it is very unlikely that all of them would be the same.

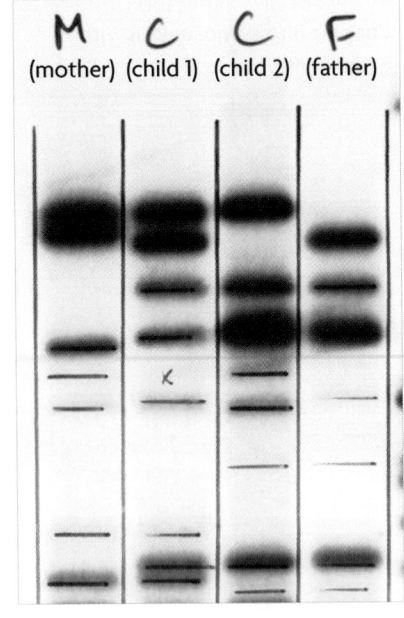

FIGURE 9.6 DNA fingerprints can be compared to identify people. Both children share some bands with each parent.

M C C F
(mother) (child 1) (child 2) (father)

Synthesize Does a DNA fingerprint show a person's genotype? Why or why not?

FIGURE 9.7 DNA Fingerprinting

A DNA fingerprint shows differences in the number of repeats of certain DNA sequences.

This DNA sequence of 33 bases can be repeated many times in a sample of a person's DNA.

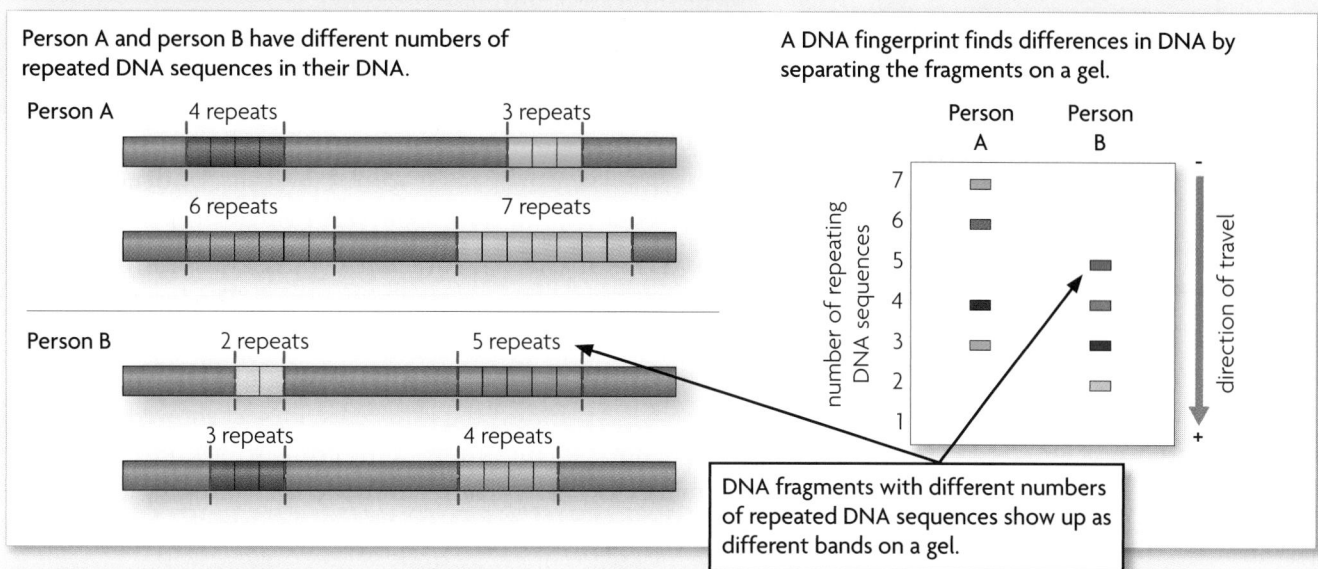

Person A and person B have different numbers of repeated DNA sequences in their DNA.

A DNA fingerprint finds differences in DNA by separating the fragments on a gel.

Person A — 4 repeats — 3 repeats — 6 repeats — 7 repeats

Person B — 2 repeats — 5 repeats — 3 repeats — 4 repeats

DNA fragments with different numbers of repeated DNA sequences show up as different bands on a gel.

Infer How would the DNA fingerprints change if a different restriction enzyme cut the DNA in the middle of one of the repeated DNA sequences?

◉ MAIN IDEA

DNA fingerprinting is used for identification.

DNA fingerprinting to identify people has become a reliable and widely used process since the 1990s. Why? The specific nucleotide sequences that are repeated can be found in everyone. More importantly, from one person to another, the number of repeat sequences can differ greatly, even among brothers and sisters.

DNA Fingerprints and Probability

Identification with DNA fingerprinting depends on probability. Suppose that 1 in every 500 people has three copies of the repeat at location A. This means any person has a 1-in-500 chance of having a matching DNA fingerprint for that region of a chromosome. By itself, the number of repeats in one location cannot be used for identification, because too many people would match.

But then suppose that 1 in every 90 people has six copies of the repeat sequence at location B, and 1 in every 120 people has ten copies of the repeat sequence at location C. Individual probabilities are multiplied by each other to find the total probability. Therefore, when the three separate probabilities are multiplied, suddenly the chance that two people have the same DNA fingerprint is very small.

$$\frac{1}{500} \times \frac{1}{90} \times \frac{1}{120} = \frac{1}{5,400,000} = 1 \text{ chance in 5.4 million people}$$

Connecting CONCEPTS

Genome Recall from **Chapter 6** that a genome is the entire set of DNA in a cell. You will learn more about genome research in **Section 9.5**.

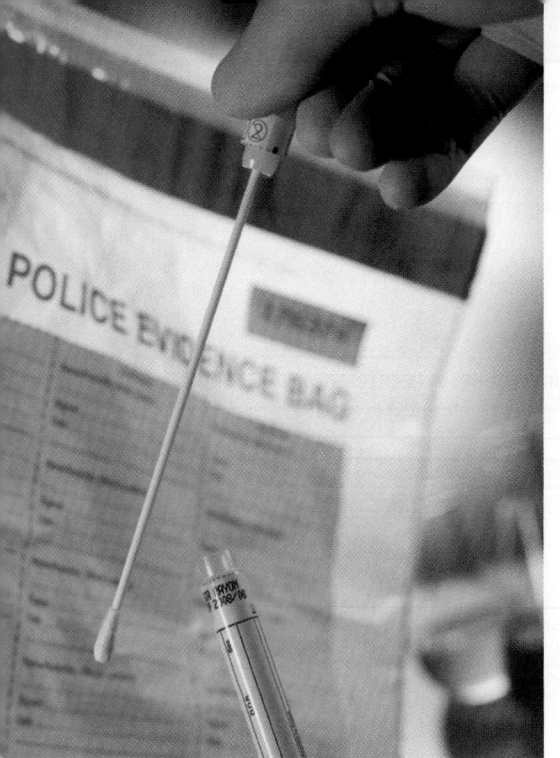

Usually, DNA fingerprinting compares at least five regions of the genome. That way it is more certain that the pattern of DNA fragments in the fingerprint is unique. The more regions of DNA that are studied, the less likely it becomes that another person would have the same DNA fingerprint. For this reason, DNA fingerprinting is considered very reliable for identification purposes.

Uses of DNA Fingerprinting

DNA fingerprints are often used in legal cases. Because PCR can make a large sample of DNA even when there is a very small sample to start with, DNA fingerprints can be made from a few cells. Evidence, such as that shown in **FIGURE 9.8**, can come from just a single drop of blood.

Sometimes, DNA fingerprints are used against a suspect, but other times they are used to prove someone's innocence. The Innocence Project at Benjamin Cardozo Law School in New York City has used DNA evidence to help free more than 170 wrongfully convicted people. Through DNA fingerprinting, the Innocence Project showed that DNA from those people did not match DNA from the crime scenes. Proving a person's guilt through DNA fingerprinting is harder than proving a person's innocence. For example, a DNA sample can become contaminated with other DNA if it is not handled carefully. Investigators must also consider questions such as "What is the chance that another person has the same DNA fingerprint?" and "What probability is low enough to be acceptable?" Are chances of 1 in 100,000 low enough? One in 1 million? In fact, there is no legal standard for this probability of a random DNA fingerprint match.

The same DNA fingerprinting methods are also used for identification purposes outside of the courtroom. DNA fingerprints can prove family relationships, such as paternity and the kinship necessary for immigration requests. But DNA fingerprinting is not limited to human identification. Genetic comparisons through DNA fingerprinting are used to study biodiversity and to locate genetically engineered crops. And, as you saw at the beginning of the chapter, researchers are using DNA fingerprinting to identify tortoises native to the Galapagos Islands.

FIGURE 9.8 DNA collected at crime scenes is used as evidence in many legal cases.

To find out more about DNA fingerprinting, go to scilinks.org. Keycode: MLB009

Summarize How does identification by DNA fingerprinting depend on probability?

9.3 ASSESSMENT

ONLINE QUIZ ClassZone.com

REVIEWING ▶ MAIN IDEAS

1. On what, in a person's DNA, is a **DNA fingerprint** based?

2. Describe two ways in which DNA fingerprinting is used.

CRITICAL THINKING

3. **Compare and Contrast** How are DNA fingerprints and restriction maps similar? different? Explain.

4. **Synthesize** Briefly describe how restriction enzymes, gel electrophoresis, and PCR are used in DNA fingerprinting.

Connecting CONCEPTS

5. **Mutations** Why might non-coding regions of DNA outside of genes be more variable than coding regions of DNA?

9.4 Genetic Engineering

KEY CONCEPT DNA sequences of organisms can be changed.

▶ MAIN IDEAS

- Entire organisms can be cloned.
- New genes can be added to an organism's DNA.
- Genetic engineering produces organisms with new traits.

VOCABULARY

clone, p. 275
genetic engineering, p. 276
recombinant DNA, p. 276
plasmid, p. 276

transgenic, p. 277
gene knockout, p. 279

Review
restriction enzyme

MICHIGAN STANDARDS

B4.2h Recognize that genetic engineering techniques provide great potential and responsibilities.
B4.r5b Evaluate the advantages and disadvantages of human manipulation of DNA. (recommended)

Connect Glowing mice are used in cancer research. Glowing plants are used to track genetically modified crops. And, in 1999, British researchers introduced glowing yeast cells that locate water pollution. The scientists put a gene for a fluorescent protein into yeast. Under normal conditions, the yeast cells do not glow. But they do glow when certain chemicals are present. The glow identifies areas that need to be cleaned. New biotechnology applications seem to be developed on a daily basis. What advances will you see during your lifetime?

▶ MAIN IDEA

Entire organisms can be cloned.

The term *cloning* might make you think of science fiction and horror movies, but the process is quite common in nature. A **clone** is a genetically identical copy of a gene or of an organism. For example, some plants clone themselves from their roots. Bacteria produce identical genetic copies of themselves through binary fission. And human identical twins are clones of each other.

People have cloned plants for centuries. The process is fairly easy because many plants naturally clone themselves and because plants have stem cell tissues that can develop into many types of cells. Some simple animals, such as sea stars, can essentially clone themselves through a process called regeneration. Mammals, however, cannot clone themselves.

FIGURE 9.9 The cat named CC—for Copy Cat or Carbon Copy—is the first successful clone of a cat (right). The original cat is on the left.

To clone a mammal, scientists swap DNA between cells with a technique called nuclear transfer. First, an unfertilized egg is taken from an animal, and the egg's nucleus is removed. Then the nucleus of a cell from the animal to be cloned is implanted into the egg. The egg is stimulated and, if the procedure is successful, the egg will begin dividing. After the embryo grows for a few days, it is transplanted into a female. In 1997 a sheep named Dolly became the first clone of an adult mammal. The success of Dolly led to the cloning of adult cows, pigs, and mice. Now, a biotechnology company has even said that it can clone people's pets.

But pet owners who expect cloning to produce an exact copy of their furry friend will likely be disappointed. As you can see from the cat called CC in **FIGURE 9.9**, a clone may not look like the original, and it will probably not behave like the original, either. Why? Because, as you have learned, many factors, including environment, affect the expression of genes.

Cloning brings with it some extraordinary opportunities. For example, scientists are studying how to use organs from cloned mammals for transplant into humans. This use of cloning could save an enormous number of lives each year. Cloning could even help save endangered species. Cells from endangered species could be taken and used to produce clones that would increase the population of the species.

Cloning is also controversial for a few reasons. The success rate in cloning mammals is very low. It takes hundreds of tries to produce one clone, and sometimes the clone is not as healthy as the original. For example, Dolly seemed to develop and grow normally, but she also had health problems. She seemed to age quickly and did not live as long as a typical sheep, possibly because she was cloned from an adult sheep and had "old DNA." There are also ecological concerns about cloning. Cloned animals in a wild population would reduce biodiversity because the clones would be genetically identical.

Apply Given the opportunity, would you have a pet cloned? Explain your answer based on your knowledge of genetics, biotechnology, and cloning.

Connecting CONCEPTS

Biodiversity In **Chapter 1**, you learned that biodiversity can be defined as the number of different species in an area. You will learn much more about genetic diversity within a species in **Unit 4**.

▶ MAIN IDEA
New genes can be added to an organism's DNA.

Genetic research relies on cloning, but not the cloning of organisms. Instead, it is the cloning of individual genes. A clone of a gene is a copy of that one segment of DNA. In some cases, scientists insert cloned genes from one organism into a different organism. This changing of an organism's DNA to give the organism new traits is called **genetic engineering.** Genetic engineering is possible because the genetic code is shared by all organisms.

Genetic engineering is based on the use of recombinant DNA technology. **Recombinant DNA** (ree-KAHM-buh-nuhnt) is DNA that contains genes from more than one organism. Scientists are trying to use recombinant DNA in several different ways. For example, recombinant DNA could be used to produce crop plants that make medicines and vitamins. Scientists hope that large amounts of medicines will one day be made through this process, which has been called "pharming." Scientists are also studying ways of using recombinant DNA to make vaccines to protect against HIV, the virus that causes AIDS.

Bacteria are commonly used in genetic engineering. One reason is because bacteria have tiny rings of DNA called plasmids. **Plasmids,** as shown in **FIGURE 9.10**, are closed loops of DNA that are separate from the bacterial chromosome and that replicate on their own within the cell.

Bacterium

plasmid

bacterial chromosome

FIGURE 9.10 A plasmid is a closed loop of DNA in a bacterium that is separate from the bacterial chromosome. (colored TEM; magnification 48,000×)

VISUAL VOCAB

Recombinant DNA is DNA that combines genes from more than one organism.

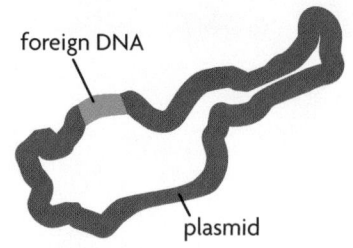

foreign DNA

plasmid

Foreign DNA is inserted into **plasmids** to make recombinant DNA.

FIGURE 9.11 Making Recombinant DNA

Foreign DNA can be inserted into a plasmid to make recombinant DNA.

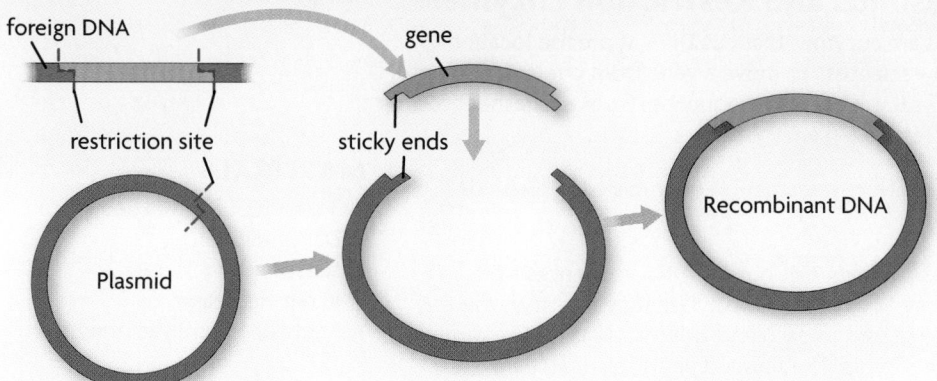

A plasmid and the foreign DNA with the gene are cut with the same restriction enzyme.

The sticky ends of the plasmid and the foreign gene match.

The plasmid and the foreign gene are bonded together to form recombinant DNA.

Apply Why are sticky ends important for making recombinant DNA?

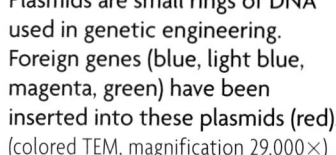

Plasmids are small rings of DNA used in genetic engineering. Foreign genes (blue, light blue, magenta, green) have been inserted into these plasmids (red). (colored TEM, magnification 29,000×)

Recombinant DNA is found naturally in bacteria that take in exogenous DNA (or DNA from a different organism) and add it to their own. Scientists adapted what happens in nature to make artificial recombinant DNA. First, a restriction enzyme is used to cut out the desired gene from a strand of DNA. Then plasmids are cut with the same enzyme. The plasmid opens, and when the gene is added to the plasmid, their complementary sticky ends are bonded together by a process called ligation. The resulting plasmid contains recombinant DNA, as shown in **FIGURE 9.11.**

Summarize How does genetic engineering rely on a shared genetic code?

◉ MAIN IDEA
Genetic engineering produces organisms with new traits.

After a gene is added to a plasmid, the genetically engineered plasmids can be put into bacteria. In a way, bacteria are turned into tiny gene factories that make copy after copy of the plasmid. As a result, the transformed bacteria make many copies of the new gene. The bacteria will express the new gene and make that gene's product. The bacteria with the recombinant plasmid are called transgenic. A **transgenic** organism has one or more genes from another organism inserted into its genome. For example, the gene for human insulin can be put into plasmids. The plasmids are inserted into bacteria. The transgenic bacteria make human insulin that is collected and used to treat people with diabetes.

Genetic Engineering in Plants
Genetic engineering of plants is directly related to genetic engineering of bacteria. To change a plant's DNA, a gene is inserted into a plasmid and the plasmid is inserted into bacteria. After the bacteria infect the plant, the new gene becomes a part of the plant's DNA and is expressed like any other gene.

VOCABULARY

The prefix *trans-* means "across," and the root *genic* means "referring to genes." When genes are transferred across different organisms, transgenic organisms are produced.

Modeling Plasmids and Restriction Enzymes

Restriction enzymes are enzymes that cut DNA at precise locations. These enzymes allow scientists to move a gene from one organism into another. In this lab, you will use DNA sequences from a datasheet to simulate the use of restriction enzymes.

PROBLEM How do different restriction enzymes cut a plasmid?

PROCEDURE

1. Make models of 3 plasmids. Cut out the DNA sequences from the copies of Figure 1 on the datasheet. Use tape to attach the appropriate piece of yarn to each end where indicated. The yarn represents the entire plasmid. The finished plasmid should be a circle.

2. Use the scissors to cut a plasmid at the correct sites for *EcoR*I.

3. Use the sequences for sites of *Hind*III and *Sma*I to repeat step 3 with the other two plasmids.

ANALYZE AND CONCLUDE

1. Apply How many DNA fragments would you get if you cut the same plasmid with both *EcoR*I and *Sma*I ?

2. Infer Why might scientists use different restrictions enzymes to cut out different genes from a strand of DNA?

MATERIALS

• 3 copies of Plasmid Sequence Datasheet
• scissors
• 10 cm clear tape
• 3 sets of 5 5-cm yarn pieces

This technique has allowed scientists to give plants new traits, such as resistance to frost, diseases, and insects. For instance, a gene known as *Bt* makes a natural pesticide in some organisms. After *Bt* is added to crop plants, smaller amounts of chemical pesticides are needed to protect the crop from insects. Some genetically engineered crops, which are also called genetically modified (GM), are now common in the United States. These crops include *Bt* potatoes and corn, and they are even more important in developing countries. By increasing crop yields, more food is produced more quickly and cheaply.

Genetic Engineering in Animals

In general, transgenic animals are much harder to produce than GM plants because animals are more resistant to genetic manipulation. To produce a transgenic animal, a researcher must first get a fertilized egg cell. Then the foreign DNA is inserted into the nucleus and the egg is implanted back into a female. However, only a small percentage of the genetically manipulated eggs mature normally. And only a portion of those that develop will be transgenic. That is, only a small number will have the foreign gene as a part of their DNA. But those animals that are transgenic will have the gene in all of their cells—including reproductive cells—and the transgenic trait will be passed on to their offspring.

Transgenic mice are often used as models of human development and disease. The first such animal was called the oncomouse. This mouse always develops cancer, because a gene that controls cell growth and differentiation

was mutated. Researchers use the oncomouse to study both cancer and anti-cancer drugs. Other types of transgenic mice are used to study diabetes, brain function and development, and sex determination.

In another type of genetic manipulation, some mice have genes that have been purposely "turned off." These mice, called **gene knockout** mice, are made by disrupting the function of a gene. Knockout mice are very useful for studying gene function and genetic diseases because a researcher can observe specific changes in gene expression and traits. For example, scientists are using a gene knockout mouse to study obesity, as you can see in **FIGURE 9.12**.

FIGURE 9.12 The knockout mouse (left) does not have a functional gene for a protein called leptin, which helps to control food intake. Researchers are using this type of mouse to study obesity.

Concerns About Genetic Engineering

Scientists have genetically engineered many useful organisms by transferring genes between species to give individuals new traits. At the same time, there are concerns about possible effects of genetically engineered organisms on both human health and the environment. And at an even more basic level, some people wonder whether genetic engineering is ethical in the first place.

Questions have been raised about GM crops, even though scientists have not yet found negative health effects of GM foods. Critics say that not enough research has been done, and that some added genes might cause allergic reactions or have other unknown side effects. Scientists also have concerns about the possible effects of GM plants on the environment and on biodiversity. For example, what would happen if genetically engineered *Bt* plants killed insects that pollinate plants, such as bees and butterflies? In some instances, transgenic plants have cross-pollinated with wild type plants in farming regions. Scientists do not yet know what long-term effect this interbreeding might have on the natural plants. In addition, all organisms in a transgenic population have the same genome. As a result, some scientists worry that a decrease in genetic diversity could leave crops vulnerable to new diseases or pests.

Infer Why is it important that a transgenic trait is passed on to the transgenic organism's offspring?

9.4 ASSESSMENT

ONLINE QUIZ
ClassZone.com

REVIEWING ▶ MAIN IDEAS

1. Why is the offspring of asexual reproduction a **clone**?

2. What are **plasmids,** and how are they used in **genetic engineering**?

3. Describe two applications of **transgenic** organisms.

CRITICAL THINKING

4. **Compare and Contrast** How is the cloning of genes different from the cloning of mammals?

5. **Summarize** How are restriction enzymes used to make both **recombinant DNA** and transgenic organisms?

Connecting CONCEPTS

6. **Ecology** Do you think cloning endangered species is a good idea? What effect might this have on an ecosystem?

9.5 Genomics and Bioinformatics

KEY CONCEPT Entire genomes are sequenced, studied, and compared.

▶ MAIN IDEAS

- Genomics involves the study of genes, gene functions, and entire genomes.
- Technology allows the study and comparison of both genes and proteins.

VOCABULARY

genomics, p. 280
gene sequencing, p. 280
Human Genome Project, p. 281
bioinformatics, p. 282
DNA microarray, p. 282
proteomics, p. 283

Review
genome, mRNA

MICHIGAN STANDARDS

B4.r2i Explain how recombinant DNA technology allows scientists to analyze the structure and function of genes. (recommended)
B4.r5b Evaluate the advantages and disadvantages of human manipulation of DNA. (recommended)

Connect Humans and chimpanzees are identical in 98 to 99 percent of their DNA. How do scientists know this? They have sequenced all of the DNA in both species. Recent technologies are allowing scientists to look at huge amounts of genetic information at once. What might tomorrow's discoveries tell us about evolution, gene expression, and medical treatments?

▶ MAIN IDEA

Genomics involves the study of genes, gene functions, and entire genomes.

A gene, as you know, is a single stretch of DNA that codes for one or more polypeptides or RNA molecules. A genome is all of an organism's genetic information. **Genomics** is the study of genomes, which can include the sequencing of all of an organism's DNA. Scientists compare genomes both within and across species to find similarities and differences among DNA sequences. Comparing DNA from many people at one time helps researchers to find genes that cause disease and to understand how medications work. Biologists who study evolution can learn when closely related species diverged from each other. Scientists can also learn about interactions among genes and find out how an organism's genome makes the organism unique.

TAKING NOTES

Use a mind map to organize your notes on genomics.

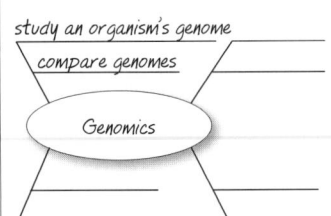

DNA Sequencing

All studies of genomics begin with **gene sequencing,** or determining the order of DNA nucleotides in genes or in genomes. An early sequencing method was developed in the 1970s by British scientist Frederick Sanger. The Sanger method is somewhat similar to PCR, which you read about in Section 9.2.

A radioactive primer is added to a single strand of DNA. Polymerase then builds a short segment of a new DNA strand. The lengths of the new strands are controlled so that they can be separated by gel electrophoresis. Based on the pattern of DNA fragments on the gel, the DNA sequence of the original strand can be put together like the pieces of a puzzle.

You might be surprised to learn that humans do not have the largest genome—the most DNA—among organisms. Scientists have determined the DNA sequences for the genomes of several species, including the ones listed in **FIGURE 9.13**. In some cases, the genomes are used to study basic questions about genes and genetics. In other cases, a genome is sequenced because that organism is used as a model in medical research. In all cases, the genomes of organisms that have been sequenced, including bacteria, insects, plants, and mammals, give us important clues toward finding out how genes function.

Yeast, for example, are very useful for scientists who study gene regulation. Genes that control development in the fruit fly are very similar to those genes in humans. The genomes of several plants have been sequenced so that scientists can learn ways to improve crop yields and to increase the resistance of those crops to disease and weather. The genomes of rats and mice are quite similar to the human genome. As a result, both of these species are used as models for human diseases and gene function.

FIGURE 9.13 COMPARING GENOME SIZES	
Organism	Approximate Total DNA (millions of base pairs)
E. coli	4.6
Yeast	12.1
Fruit fly	165
Banana	873
Chicken	1200
Human	3000
Vanilla	7672
Crested newt	18,600
Lungfish	139,000

Source: University of Nebraska

The Human Genome Project

The genomes of yeast and fruit flies are easier to sequence than the human genome. This difficulty is not due to the number of genes that humans have. In fact, while there is still a debate about the exact number of human genes, scientists agree it is surprisingly small. It is estimated that there are somewhere between 30,000 and 40,000 genes in the human genome. But think about the amount of DNA that each of us has in our cells. The human genome has at least 3 billion base pairs. This means that there is an average of about one gene in each sequence of 100,000 bases. Now just try to imagine the huge task of finding out the exact order of all of those DNA bases. In 1990 an international effort began to do exactly that.

The two main goals of the **Human Genome Project** are (1) to map and sequence all of the DNA base pairs of the human chromosomes and (2) to identify all of the genes within the sequence. The first goal was accomplished in 2003 when scientists announced that they had sequenced the human genome. However, the Human Genome Project only analyzed the DNA from a few people. Knowing those few complete DNA sequences is only the first step in understanding the human genome.

Today, scientists continue to work on identifying genes, finding the locations of genes, and determining the functions of genes. The complete sequencing of a human genome was a giant step, but much more work still needs to be done. For example, some scientists are working on a project called the HapMap to study how DNA sequences vary among people. The goal of the HapMap is to develop a method that will quickly identify genetic differences that may play a part in human diseases.

Synthesize How is genomics related to genes and DNA?

FIGURE 9.14 Computer analysis of DNA was necessary in sequencing the human genome.

CONSTRUCTING HISTOGRAMS

To construct a histogram a scientist will count the number of data points in each category and then graph the number of times that category occurs. The categories are shown on the x-axis and the frequencies are shown on the y-axis. The data table to the right shows the ranges of base pair lengths for the 24 human chromosomes (chromosomes 1–22, the X chromosome, and the Y chromosome). The data are organized by these ranges.

TABLE 1. HUMAN CHROMOSOME SIZES	
Millions of Base Pairs	Number of Human Chromosomes
0–50	2
51–100	6
101–150	8
151–200	6
201–250	2

Source: U.S. Department of Energy Office of Science

1. **Graph Data** Construct a histogram that shows the frequency of base pair lengths for the 24 human chromosomes.
2. **Interpret** Which range of base pair length is most common for human chromosomes?
3. **Analyze** Summarize the overall trend for human chromosome length shown in the histogram.

▶ MAIN IDEA

Technology allows the study and comparison of both genes and proteins.

You have learned about specific genes that produce specific traits. But you also know that genes act as more than simple, separate units. They interact and affect each other's expression. Most biological processes and physical traits are the result of the interactions among many different genes.

Bioinformatics

Genes are sequenced, genomes are compared, and proteins are analyzed. What happens to the huge amounts of data that are produced? These data can be analyzed only if they are organized and searchable. **Bioinformatics** is the use of computer databases to organize and analyze biological data. Powerful computer programs are needed to compare genomes that are billions of base pairs in length, especially if the genomes differ by only a small amount.

Bioinformatics gives scientists a way to store, share, and find data. It also lets researchers predict and model the functions of genes and proteins. Because bioinformatics links different areas of research, it has become vital to the study of genes and proteins. For example, a scientist can now search databases to find the gene that is the code for a known protein.

DNA Microarrays

DNA microarrays are tools that allow scientists to study many genes, and their expression, at once. A microarray is a small chip that is dotted with all of the genes being studied. The genes are laid out in a grid pattern. Each block of the grid is so small that a one-square-inch chip can hold thousands of genes.

Connecting CONCEPTS

Computer Models Recall from Chapter 1 how computer models are used to investigate biological systems that cannot be studied directly. Computer models are often used in genetics and genomics.

Complementary DNA (cDNA) labeled with a fluorescent dye is added to the microarray. A cDNA molecule is a single-stranded DNA molecule that is made from an mRNA molecule. The mRNA acts as a template for the cDNA. Therefore, a cDNA molecule is complementary to an mRNA molecule and is identical to a gene's DNA sequence. The cDNA binds to its complementary DNA strand in the microarray by the same base pairing that you learned about in Chapter 8.

Anywhere cDNA binds to DNA in the microarray shows up as a glowing dot because of the dye. A glowing dot in the microarray is a match between a cDNA molecule and the DNA on the chip. Therefore, a glowing dot shows which genes are expressed and how much they are expressed. Microarrays, as shown in **FIGURE 9.15**, help researchers find which genes are expressed in which tissues, and under what conditions. For example, DNA microarrays can compare gene expression in cancer cells with gene expression in healthy cells. Scientists hope that this method will lead to cancer treatments that target the faulty genes.

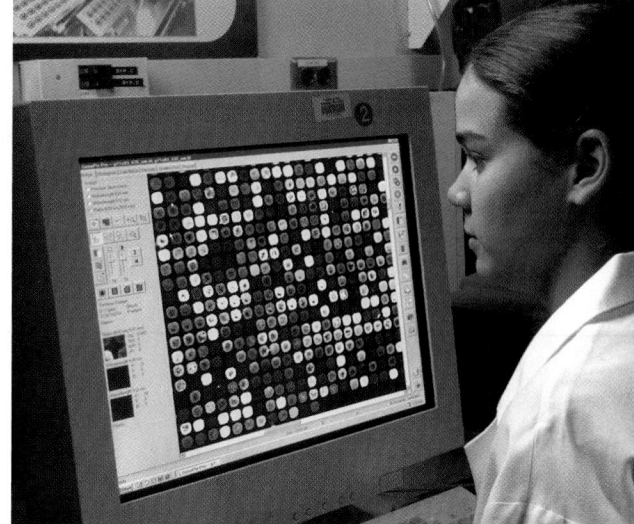

FIGURE 9.15 Gene expression can be studied with microarrays. The red dots show genes that are expressed after exposure to a toxic chemical.

Proteomics

You have read how genomics is the study of genomes. **Proteomics** (PROH-tee-AH-mihks) is the study and comparison of all the proteins that result from an organism's genome. Proteomics also includes the study of the functions and interactions of proteins. Identifying and studying proteins is more difficult than identifying and studying genes. A single gene, depending on how its mRNA is edited, can code for more than one polypeptide. Different proteins are found in different tissues, depending on gene expression. And, often, the functions of proteins have to be studied within a biological system.

Proteomics has potential benefits for many areas of biology. Shared evolutionary histories among organisms are studied by comparing proteins across species. Proteomics allows scientists to learn about proteins involved in human diseases. By better understanding the proteins that might play a part in cancer, arthritis, or heart disease, scientists might be able to develop new treatments that target the proteins. Proteomics even has the potential to help doctors match medical treatments to a patient's unique body chemistry.

Apply How is bioinformatics a form of data analysis?

9.5 ASSESSMENT

ONLINE QUIZ
ClassZone.com

REVIEWING ▶ MAIN IDEAS

1. Describe the goals of the **Human Genome Project.**
2. Why is **bioinformatics** important in genetic research?

CRITICAL THINKING

3. **Apply** Describe the difference between **gene sequencing** and DNA fingerprinting.
4. **Compare and Contrast** How is the study of specific genes different from the study of a genome?

Connecting CONCEPTS

5. **Cell Biology** How might **genomics** and **proteomics** help researchers predict how a medical treatment might affect cells in different tissues?

Genetic Screening and Gene Therapy

KEY CONCEPT Genetics provides a basis for new medical treatments.

▶ MAIN IDEAS

- Genetic screening can detect genetic disorders.
- Gene therapy is the replacement of faulty genes.

VOCABULARY

genetic screening, p. 284
gene therapy, p. 285

Review
pedigree, genetic engineering

MICHIGAN STANDARDS

B4.r5b Evaluate the advantages and disadvantages of human manipulation of DNA. (recommended)
B5.3f Demonstrate and explain how biotechnology can improve a population and species.

Connect Anyone could be a carrier of a genetic disorder. Genetic screening is used to help people figure out whether they are at risk for passing on that disorder. If they are at risk, what do they do? Do they not have children? Do they have children and hope that a child does not get the disorder? What would you do?

▶ MAIN IDEA

Genetic screening can detect genetic disorders.

Every one of us carries alleles that produce defective proteins. Usually, these genes do not affect us in a significant way because we have other alleles that make up for the deficiency. But about 10 percent of people will find themselves dealing with an illness related to their genes at some point in their lives.

Genetic screening is the process of testing DNA to determine a person's risk of having or passing on a genetic disorder. Genetic screening often involves both pedigree analysis, which you read about in Chapter 7, and DNA tests. Because our knowledge of the human genome is still limited, it is not yet possible to test for every possible defect. Often, genetic screening is used to look for specific genes or proteins that indicate a particular disorder. Some tests can detect genes that are related to an increased risk of developing a disease, such as a gene called BRCA1 that has been linked to breast cancer. There are also tests for about 900 genetic disorders, including cystic fibrosis and Duchenne's muscular dystrophy (DMD). In DMD, it is quite easy to see differences in DNA tests between people with and without the disorder, as shown in **FIGURE 9.16**.

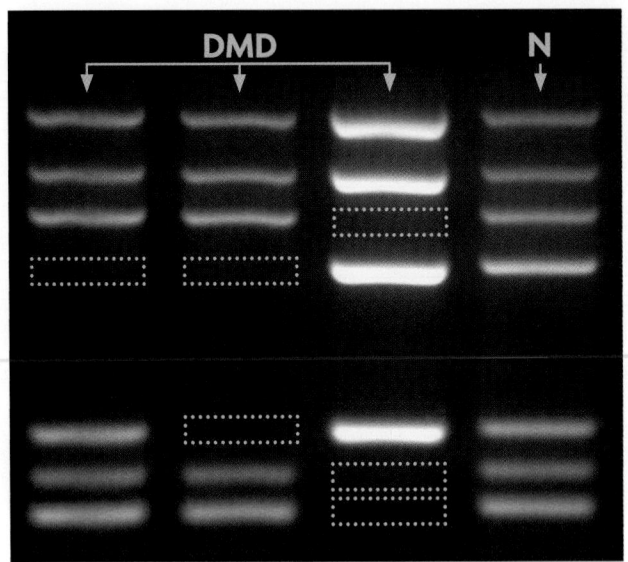

FIGURE 9.16 Genetic screening can be used to detect Duchenne's muscular dystrophy (DMD). Notice the missing bands on the gel (boxes) for three people with DMD as compared with a person without the disorder (N).

Genetic screening can help save lives. It can also lead to some difficult choices. Suppose a person has a family history of cancer and is tested for a gene that may lead to an increased risk of cancer. Is that information helpful or harmful? If a person has a chance of being a carrier of a genetic disorder, should screening be required? As genetic screening becomes more common, more questions like these will need to be answered.

Infer Why might genetic screening raise ethical concerns about privacy?

Gene therapy is the replacement of faulty genes.

A defective part in a car or in a computer can be easily replaced. If someone has a faulty gene that causes a disorder, is it possible to replace the gene? The goal of gene therapy is to do exactly that. **Gene therapy** is the replacement of a defective or missing gene, or the addition of a new gene, into a person's genome to treat a disease.

For any type of gene therapy to work, researchers such as Dr. Betty Pace, shown in **FIGURE 9.17**, must first get the new gene into the correct cells of a patient's body. Once in the body, the gene has to become a part of the cells' DNA. One method of gene therapy that scientists have tried is to take a sample of bone marrow stem cells and "infect" them with a virus that has been genetically engineered with the new gene. Then the stem cells are put back into the patient's bone marrow. Because they are stem cells, they divide and make more blood cells with the gene.

FIGURE 9.17 Dr. Betty Pace, director of the Sickle Cell Disease Research Center at the University of Texas at Dallas, is studying potential gene therapy treatments for sickle cell disease.

The first successful trial of gene therapy took place in 1990. The treatment was used on two children with a genetic autoimmune disorder, and the children are now adults leading normal lives. However, much of gene therapy is still experimental. For example, researchers are studying several different methods to treat cancer with gene therapy. One experimental approach involves inserting a gene that stimulates a person's immune system to attack cancer cells. Another method is to insert "suicide" genes into cancer cells. These genes activate a drug inside those cells so that only the cancer cells are killed.

Gene therapy has many technical challenges. First, the correct gene has to be added to the correct cells. And even after researchers have figured out how to transfer the desired gene, the gene's expression has to be regulated so that it does not make too much or too little protein. Scientists must also determine if the new gene will affect other genes. The many trials have produced few long-lasting positive results. But because of its great potential, research on gene therapy continues.

Synthesize How does gene therapy rely on genetic screening?

9.6 ASSESSMENT

ONLINE QUIZ
ClassZone.com

REVIEWING ▶ MAIN IDEAS

1. How does **genetic screening** use both old and new methods of studying human genetics?

2. Briefly describe the goals and methods of **gene therapy.**

CRITICAL THINKING

3. **Compare and Contrast** How is gene therapy similar to, and different from, making a transgenic organism?

4. **Synthesize** How are restriction enzymes and recombinant DNA important for gene therapy?

Connecting CONCEPTS

5. **Cell Specialization** How is the type of cell into which a new gene is inserted important in gene therapy?

Use these inquiry-based labs and online activities to deepen your understanding of biotechnology and genetic engineering.

INVESTIGATION

MICHIGAN STANDARDS

B4.2h Recognize that genetic engineering techniques provide great potential and responsibilities.

B4.r5b Evaluate the advantages and disadvantages of human manipulation of DNA. (recommended)

Modeling Genetic Engineering

Scientists use restriction enzymes to make recombinant DNA. Genes are placed into plasmids that are put into bacteria. The plasmids transform the bacteria to produce the new gene product. In this lab, you will model a genetic engineering process. You will insert the human factor VIII gene into a plasmid. This gene produces a protein that causes blood to coagulate. People with mutations in this gene can suffer from hemophilia, a bleeding disease.

MATERIALS
- DNA Sequence Datasheet
- scissors
- 20 cm clear tape
- red and yellow colored pencils

SKILL Modeling

PROBLEM How can a plasmid's DNA be changed?

PROCEDURE

1. Cut out the plasmid DNA sequences from the datasheet. Color the DNA sequences yellow.

2. Use tape to attach the sequences to each end where indicated. The completed plasmid should be circular in shape.

3. Make a human factor VIII gene using the DNA sequences from the datasheet. The gene should be a straight fragment. Color the sequence red.

4. Use the datasheet to choose the appropriate restriction enzymes to cut the plasmid and the human factor VIII gene. Cut the plasmids and the gene with the scissors at the proper places.

5. Construct a new plasmid that contains the human factor VIII gene. Use tape to hold the completed plasmid together.

ANALYZE AND CONCLUDE

1. **Analyze** What characteristic would bacteria implanted with the new plasmid have? Explain.

2. **Apply** What might be the purpose of inserting the human factor VIII gene into a plasmid?

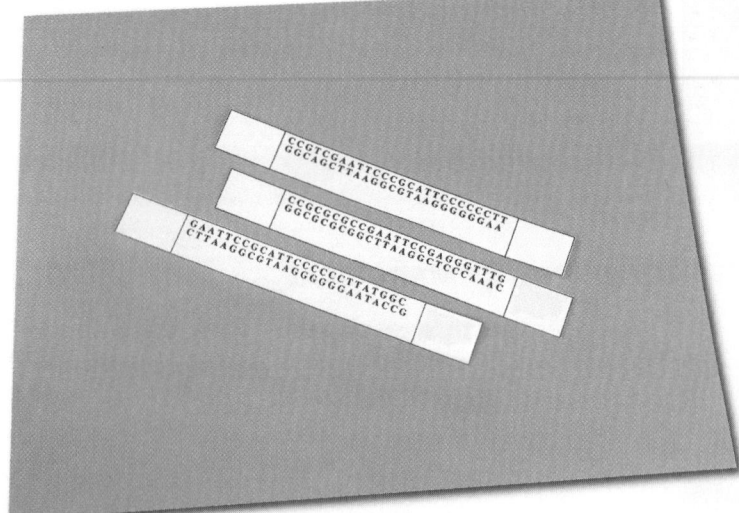

Genetic Screening

A combination of pedigree analysis and DNA testing is used to screen for genetic diseases. In this investigation, you will use a pedigree and a restriction map to determine who in a family is a carrier of a genetic disorder.

SKILL Analyzing

PROBLEM Which members of the family are carriers of the genetic disorder?

MATERIALS

- paper
- pencil

PROCEDURE

1. Copy the pedigree into your notebook.

2. Look at the gel below. The letters on the gel correspond to the letters of people on the pedigree. Write on your pedigree the alleles that each person has, as shown by the lengths of DNA fragments on the gel. (**Hint:** Person E has two copies of one allele.)

3. Person E's phenotype is given. Determine the phenotypes of the other people—non-carrier or carrier—and show them on the pedigree with the shading conventions you learned in Chapter 7.

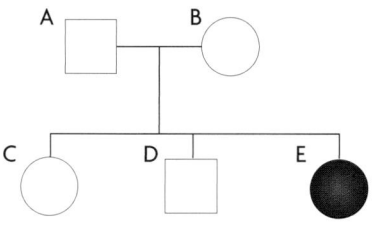

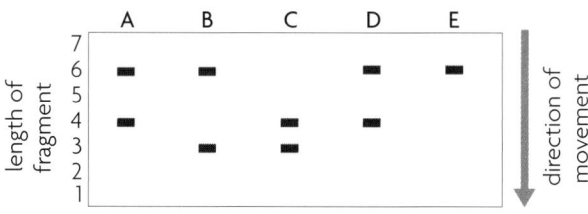

ANALYZE AND CONCLUDE

1. **Analyze** How many people are carriers?

2. **Infer** Is the disorder sex-linked or is it related to a gene on an autosome? Explain.

VIRTUAL LAB
Gel Electrophoresis

How do you use DNA to identify a person? In this virtual lab, you will use gel electrophoresis to make the DNA fingerprint of a person who committed a crime.

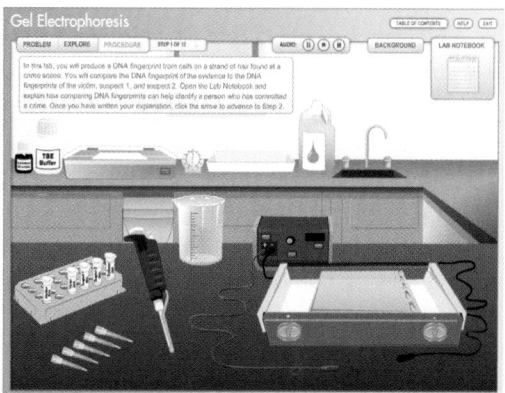

VIRTUAL LAB
Bacterial Transformation

How do genetic engineers make recombinant DNA? In this interactive lab, you will put a new gene into the DNA of a bacterium.

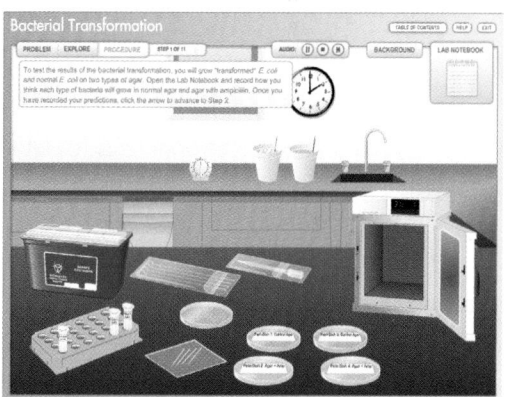

WEBQUEST

Should animal cloning projects be funded? Complete this WebQuest to learn how scientists clone animals, and review the risks and benefits of making animal clones. Then make a recommendation regarding the best use of funds for animal cloning projects.

9.1 Manipulating DNA

Biotechnology relies on cutting DNA at specific places. Bacterial enzymes called restriction enzymes are used to cut DNA. Each restriction enzyme cuts DNA at a specific DNA sequence. After DNA is cut with a restriction enzyme, the fragments of DNA can be separated using gel electrophoresis. A restriction map of the DNA is made based on the lengths of the fragments.

9.2 Copying DNA

The polymerase chain reaction rapidly copies segments of DNA. The polymerase chain reaction (PCR) is based on the process of DNA replication. By combining the DNA to be copied, DNA nucleotides, primers, and specific polymerase enzymes, a desired segment of DNA can be copied in the laboratory.

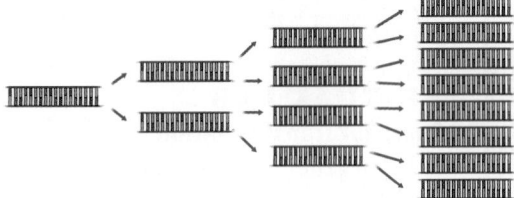

9.3 DNA Fingerprinting

DNA fingerprints identify people at the molecular level. DNA has many repeating base sequences. The number of repeats differs from person to person. DNA fingerprinting uses restriction enzymes and gel electrophoresis to detect these differences. By using DNA fingerprinting on several regions of DNA, one particular person can be identified.

9.4 Genetic Engineering

DNA sequences of organisms can be changed. Clones, or identical genetic copies, of many organisms can be made. Organisms can also be implanted with genes that give them new traits. Often, genes are inserted into plasmids to make recombinant DNA. Genetically engineered plasmids are inserted into bacteria, producing a transgenic organism. Transgenic bacteria, plants, and animals are used in several different ways.

Recombinant DNA

9.5 Genomics and Bioinformatics

Entire genomes are sequenced, studied, and compared. Through DNA sequencing, the genomes of several organisms, including humans, have been found and studied. Genomic data are organized and analyzed through bioinformatics. DNA microarrays are used to study interactions among genes in a genome. In addition, genomics has led to the study and comparison of proteins through proteomics.

9.6 Genetic Screening and Gene Therapy

Genetics provides a basis for new medical treatments. Genetic screening is used to test people for genes that are linked to genetic disorders. One method to correct these faulty genes or to replace missing genes is gene therapy. Gene therapy is experimental, but has the potential to cure many diseases.

Synthesize Your Notes

Two-Column Chart Use your notes to make two-column charts for the processes described in the chapter. On one side of the chart, define and explain the process. On the other side, draw a sketch of the process.

Cutting DNA	Process
Restriction enzymes cut DNA at specific places.	

Concept Map Use concept maps like the one below to visualize the relationships among different biotechnologies.

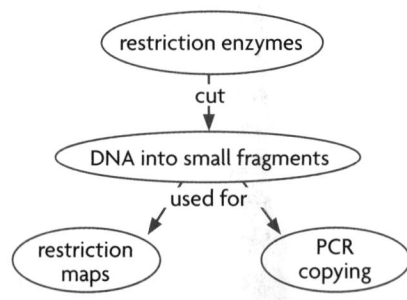

Chapter Assessment

Chapter Vocabulary

9.1 restriction enzyme, p. 265
gel electrophoresis, p. 266
restriction map, p. 267

9.2 polymerase chain reaction
(PCR), p. 269
primer, p. 271

9.3 DNA fingerprint, p. 272

9.4 clone, p. 275
genetic engineering, p. 276
recombinant DNA, p. 276
plasmid, p. 276
transgenic, p. 277
gene knockout, p. 279

9.5 genomics, p. 280
gene sequencing, p. 280
Human Genome Project, p. 281
bioinformatics, p. 282
DNA microarray, p. 282
proteomics, p. 283

9.6 genetic screening, p. 284
gene therapy, p. 285

Reviewing Vocabulary

Label Diagrams

In your notebook, write the vocabulary term that matches each item that is pointed out below.

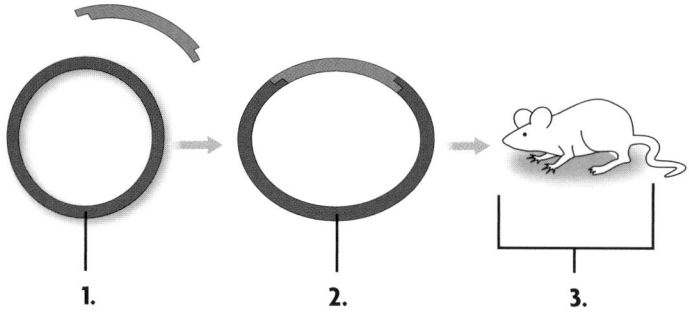

1.   **2.**   **3.**

Keep It Short

For each vocabulary term below, write a short, precise phrase that describes its meaning. For example, a short phrase to describe *PCR* could be "DNA copying tool."

4. genetic screening

5. genomics

6. DNA fingerprint

7. clone

Word Origins

8. The prefix *electro-* means "electricity." The suffix *-phoresis* means "transmission" or "carrying." How do these meanings relate to the meaning of the term *electrophoresis*?

9. The suffix *-ics* means "science or study of." What is studied in *genomics?* in *proteomics?* in *bioinformatics?*

Reviewing MAIN IDEAS

10. Why can restriction enzymes be thought of as molecular "scissors"?

11. Explain what gel electrophoresis shows about DNA, and how it is used to separate DNA.

12. PCR requires DNA polymerase from bacteria that live in hot springs. Why can't DNA polymerase from organisms that live in cooler temperatures be used in PCR?

13. Briefly describe the three main steps of PCR.

14. What parts of DNA molecules are the basis of the differences detected by DNA fingerprinting?

15. Why is probability important in DNA fingerprinting?

16. What is the role of nuclear transfer in the process of cloning an animal?

17. Describe the general process used to make bacteria that have recombinant DNA. Include the terms *restriction enzyme* and *plasmid* in your answer.

18. How are gene knockout mice useful in determining the function of genes?

19. How does genomics rely on DNA sequencing?

20. Explain why computer databases are important in genomics and proteomics.

21. How are pedigree analysis and DNA testing used together in genetic screening?

22. What is gene therapy, and how might it be used as a treatment for cancer or for genetic disorders?

Critical Thinking

23. Analyze How are DNA microarrays related to genomics?

24. Compare and Contrast How are restriction maps and DNA fingerprints similar? How are they different? Explain your answers.

25. Compare and Contrast A plant can send out a runner that will sprout a new plant that is a clone of the "parent." Single-celled organisms divide in two, forming two clones. How is the cloning of an animal similar to and different from the cloning that happens in nature?

26. Synthesize Some fruits and vegetables are the result of crossing different species. A tangelo, for example, results from crossing a tangerine with a grapefruit. How are the genetic engineering processes of making transgenic organisms similar to and different from crossbreeding?

27. Apply Identical twins are technically clones of each other but can differ in both appearance and behavior. How is it possible that two people with the same genome could be different?

28. Synthesize Transgenic bacteria can be used to make human insulin. Explain how bacteria can produce a human protein.

Interpreting Visuals

The gel below shows two different restriction maps for the same segment of DNA. One of the maps is for a normal gene (N) and the other is for a disease gene (D). Use the information in the gel to answer the next two questions.

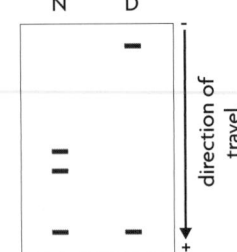

29. Analyze Which restriction map (N or D) has the smallest fragment of DNA? Which has the largest fragment? Explain your answers.

30. Interpret What do the restriction maps tell you about differences between a normal allele (N) and a disease (D) allele? Explain.

Analyzing Data

Ten of the most commonly modified crops include rice, potatoes, maize, papayas, tomatoes, corn, soybeans, wheat, alfalfa, and sugar cane. The histogram below shows how many times these crops have been modified. Among the 15 countries studied from 2001 through 2003, for example, different researchers modified rice a total of 37 times. Use the data to answer the next two questions.

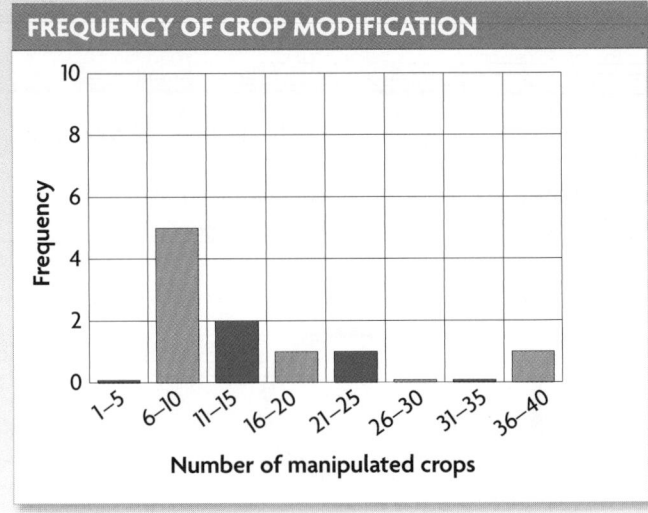

FREQUENCY OF CROP MODIFICATION

Source: Cohen, *Nature Biotechnology*, 23:1.

31. Analyze What is the most common range of genetic modifications for crop plants? The least common?

32. Calculate What percentage of crop types fall in the range of 11–15 genetic modifications?

Connecting CONCEPTS

33. Write an Informational Pamphlet Suppose that you work for a biotechnology company that specializes in DNA fingerprinting to help reunite families that have been separated. Write a pamphlet that describes how DNA fingerprinting works. Explain why the results of DNA fingerprinting can be trusted.

34. Synthesize Look again at the picture of Baby 81 on page 263. After reading this chapter, you know that DNA fingerprinting is just one part of biotechnology. Choose a topic from the chapter, such as genetic engineering or PCR. Discuss how that topic is related to Mendel's work on heredity, and how it is related to the structure and function of DNA.

MICHIGAN STANDARDS-BASED ASSESSMENT

✓ Test Practice
For more test practice, go to ClassZone.com.

1.

DNA Production over Time

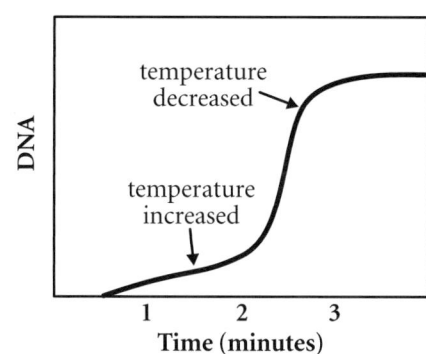

This graph shows the amount of DNA over time during a polymerase chain reaction (PCR). Changes that take place during PCR are shown with arrows. Based upon the graph, it can be inferred that **B1.1E**

A one PCR cycle takes about three minutes.

B polymerase doesn't function at high temperatures.

C polymerase needs one minute to begin working well.

D temperature is not an important factor.

2. Transgenic bacteria that is used to make human insulin is an example of **B4.r2i**

A tRNA.

B PCR.

C frameshift mutation.

D recombinant DNA.

3. In order to determine the relationship between two species, a scientist might use **B4.2B**

A DNA microarrays.

B cloning.

C gene therapy.

D DNA fingerprinting.

4. Some scientists want to genetically engineer apples to produce the insecticide pyrethrin. In order to ensure that all offspring from the original tree also produce apples with the chemical, they must be sure that the gene that produces pyrethrin is in the cells of what tissue? **B4.2h**

A root

B leaf

C stem

D seed

THINK THROUGH THE QUESTION

To answer this question you don't need to know the details used in the example, such as insecticides and the names of chemicals. Instead, focus on the main point of the question, which addresses genetic engineering and reproduction.

---

5. A scientist wants to insert a gene into a plasmid as shown in this diagram. In order to open the plasmid to insert the gene, the scientist must use **B4.2C**

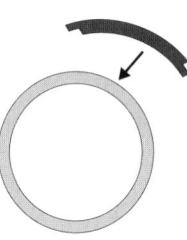

A restriction mapping.

B PCR.

C restriction enzymes.

D restriction sites.

6. *Bt* soybeans are transgenic. These soybean plants express a bacterial gene that codes for a natural pesticide. This is an example of **B5.3f**

A mutation.

B gene sequencing.

C proteomics.

D genetic engineering.

BIOZINE

INTERNET MAGAZINE

at **CLASSZONE.COM**

Go online for the latest biology news and updates on all BioZine articles.

Expanding the Textbook

News Feeds

- 🔊 Science Daily
- 🔊 CNN
- 🔊 BBC

Careers

Bio Bytes

Opinion Poll

Strange Biology

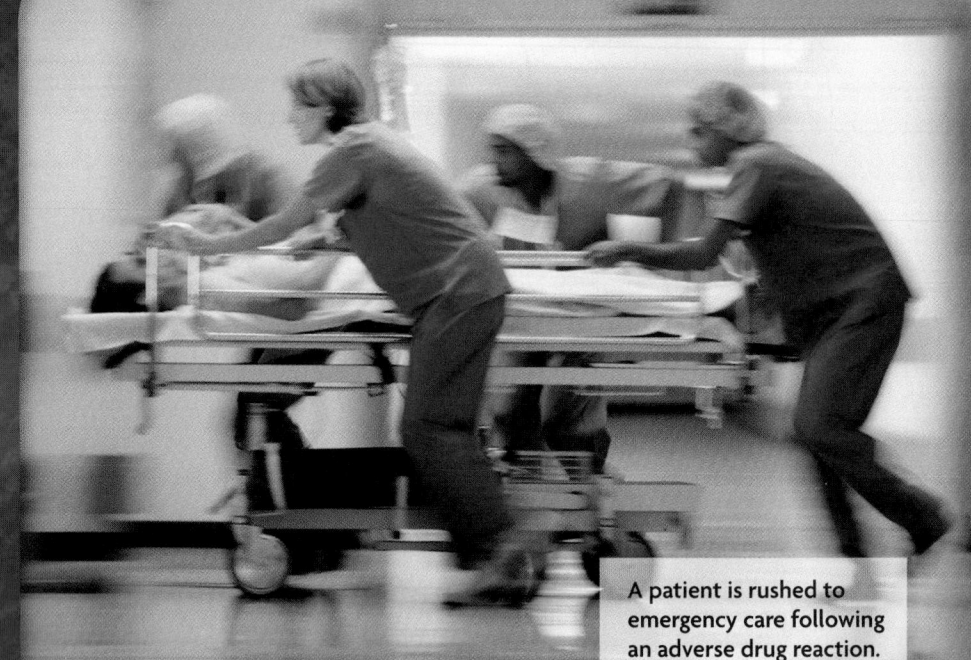

A patient is rushed to emergency care following an adverse drug reaction.

Medical Technology— The Genetic Forefront

A college student comes down with the flu. Worried about missing class, he goes to an emergency clinic and is given a prescription for an antiviral flu drug. Thirty minutes after taking the first pill, he is gasping for breath and his heart is racing. He is rushed to the hospital, where doctors tell him he has had an adverse reaction to his antiviral medication.

A Cure Worse than the Disease

Usually, medications cause only mild side effects, such as drowsiness, headaches, or nausea. Occasionally, patients are allergic to medicines and break out in hives or go into shock. But sometimes reactions to drugs are more serious. In the United States, about 2.2 million patients per year are hospitalized because of adverse drug reactions, and 100,000 die. Of course, no doctor intends for a drug's side effects to be worse than the disease it is meant to cure. Nonetheless, the current process of prescribing drugs based on medical and family history is one of trial and error.

Customized Drugs

An emerging field called pharmacogenomics is about to revolutionize the prescription process. Pharmacogenomics is the study of how genetic variations can cause different people to react in different ways to the same drugs. In most cases, for example, genetics determines the way in which—and the speed at which—a person's body breaks down a medication. If a person's body metabolizes a drug too quickly, the drug may not be effective. If the drug is metabolized too slowly, a standard dose may be too much.

In the future, a patient in need of a prescription could have a blood test, and health care workers could run the blood test results through a computer using biochip, or microarray, technology. In hours, a patient's doctor could have enough information about the person's genetic background to predict how the patient would respond to a certain drug and decide whether the dose should be changed. Individuals may even be able to have their genomes mapped and put onto cards that they can take to every doctor visit. Biochip technology is not yet available in most doctors' offices, but some oncologists (cancer specialists) are already screening patients for particular genotypes before prescribing medications.

Gene Therapy

While pharmacogenomics can provide doctors with more information about their patients, gene therapy may someday provide them with another tool. Some diseases, such as Alzheimer's disease and hemophilia, have a strong genetic basis. Researchers hope to replace disease-causing alleles with normal ones.

TECHNOLOGY

Biochips

To provide truly individualized medicine, doctors would have to analyze a patient's DNA using biochip technology. A biochip is a solid surface to which tiny strands of DNA are attached. It allows thousands of biological reactions to occur within a few seconds. When this type of screening becomes clinically feasible, it will take several steps.

1 DNA will be extracted from the patient's blood.

2 A biochip will be used to map the patient's genome. Computer software could scan the genome looking for single nucleotide polymorphisms (called SNPs, or "snips"), places where human DNA is more variable.

3 A doctor will then compare the patient's genomic results with the latest available medical research.

Ideally, the resulting prescription should be customized to the patient. If a patient has a variation that is found in a small percentage of the population, however, the doctor is unlikely to have enough data about possible reactions.

Read More >> *at* **CLASSZONE.COM**

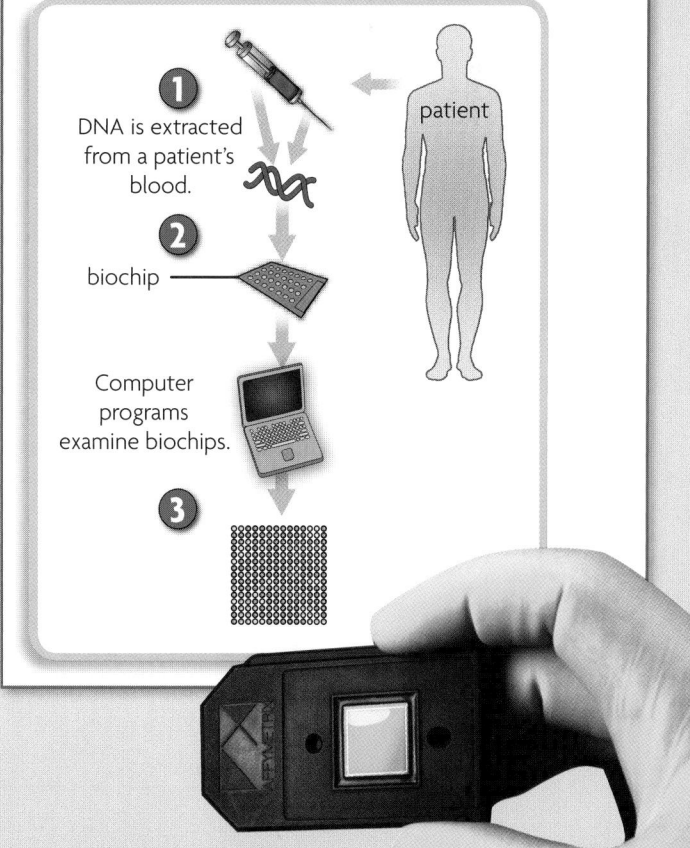

1 DNA is extracted from a patient's blood.

patient

2 biochip

Computer programs examine biochips.

3

CAREERS

Cancer Geneticist in Action

DR. OLUFUNMILAYO OLOPADE

TITLE Director, Center for Clinical Cancer Genetics, University of Chicago

EDUCATION M.D., University of Ibadan, Nigeria

Breast cancer occurs in many different forms. It has been most widely studied in Caucasian women but takes a very different form in women of African ancestry. Breast cancer hits women of African ancestry earlier and more aggressively than it does Caucasian women. Dr. Olufunmilayo Olopade wants to learn why. Working with scientists in her native Nigeria, Dr. Olopade compared gene expression in samples of cancer tissue from African women with samples of cancer tissue from Canadian women. She found that cancer cells from the African women often lacked estrogen receptors. This finding means that many of the standard treatments are not effective for this group of women.

Dr. Olopade's work will have a huge impact on breast cancer screening and treatment in women of African ancestry. "Cancer doesn't start overnight," she says. "We can develop strategies for preventing it."

Read More >> *at* **CLASSZONE.COM**

The field of gene therapy is developing slowly because it requires researchers to accomplish several feats. First, they must alter an existing virus—or some other agent that can carry genetic material—so it no longer causes disease; then they insert normal human DNA into it. Next, they must test this virus to make sure that it is safe for humans. Finally, they must test the therapy itself, to see if the virus can carry human DNA to the cells that need it. Much of this research is still being done in animals, but there have been a few successful gene therapy trials in humans.

Other Uses

New uses for DNA technology offer both solutions and hard choices. Some of the more difficult questions involve the following kinds of projects:

- Researchers can alter the DNA of viruses to make them harmless and then use the harmless version of the virus as a vaccine.
- Scientists are developing transgenic animals that can be used as medical supply factories. For example, researchers hope to breed pigs that have organs that could be used for human transplants.
- Researchers are engineering crops that contain vaccines that could be administered orally. These vaccines would be easier to grow and distribute in developing countries than are current vaccines.

A scientist examines different types of genetically modified rice plants.

Unanswered Questions

The Human Genome Project has generated a lot of excitement about its potential use for pharmaco-genomic applications. However, many challenges must be addressed before pharmacogenomics can have widespread clinical application.

- Many of the current studies of patients' responses to different drugs have conflicting results, probably due to small sample sizes, different criteria for measuring a good response, and different population groups.
- Patients' responses to a drug may be caused by many genes. Scientists will need to study the effect of multiple genes to determine response.
- Genotype testing may increase short-term health-care costs, which raises questions about who will pay and who will have access to the technology.

Read More >> *at* **CLASSZONE.COM**

UNIT 4
Evolution

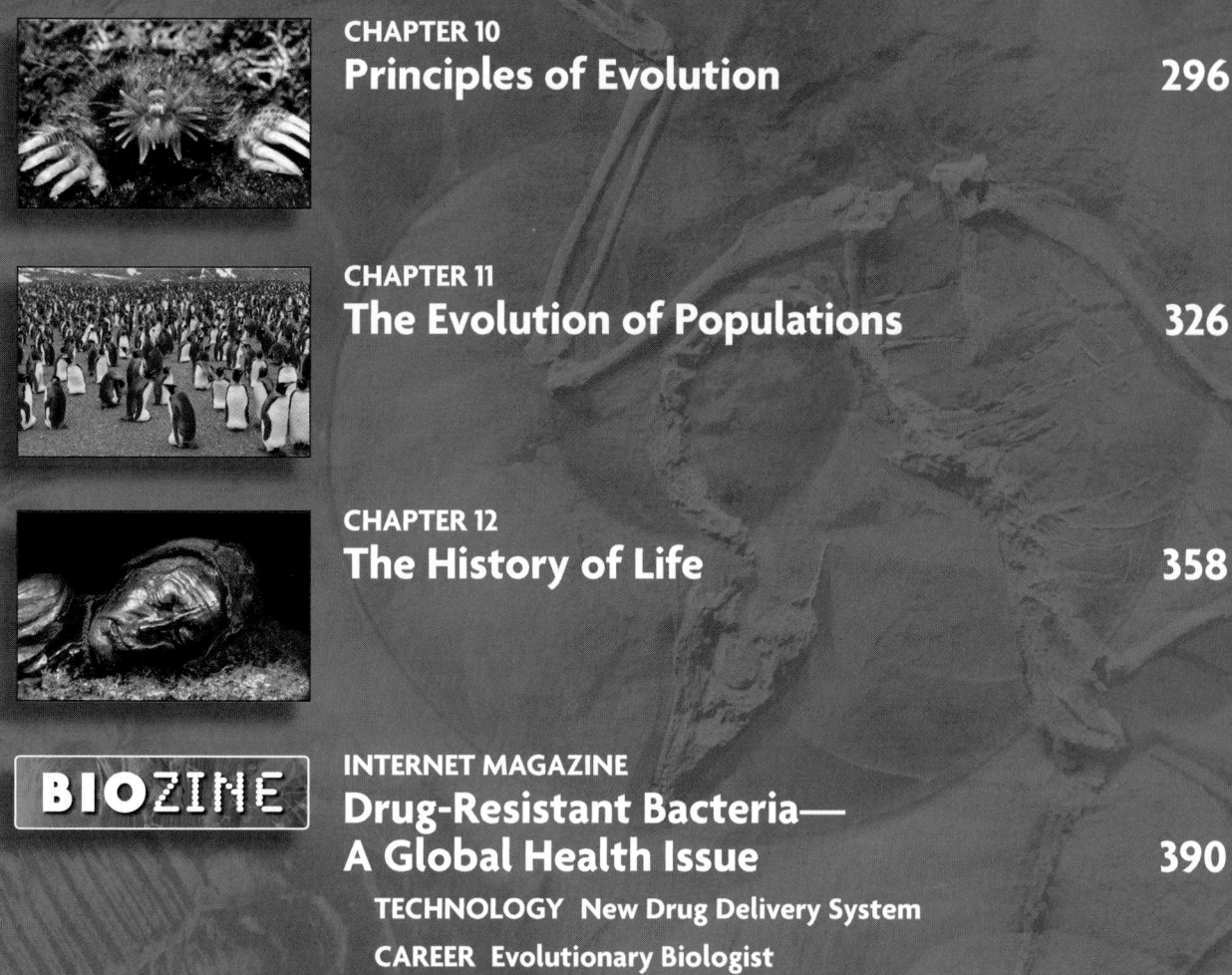

CHAPTER 10
Principles of Evolution 296

CHAPTER 11
The Evolution of Populations 326

CHAPTER 12
The History of Life 358

BIOZINE

INTERNET MAGAZINE
Drug-Resistant Bacteria—
A Global Health Issue 390
TECHNOLOGY New Drug Delivery System
CAREER Evolutionary Biologist

10 Principles of Evolution

KEY CONCEPTS

10.1 Early Ideas About Evolution
There were theories of biological and geologic change before Darwin.

10.2 Darwin's Observations
Darwin's voyage provided insights into evolution.

10.3 Theory of Natural Selection
Darwin proposed natural selection as a mechanism for evolution.

10.4 Evidence of Evolution
Evidence of common ancestry among species comes from many sources.

10.5 Evolutionary Biology Today
New technology is furthering our understanding of evolution.

Online BIOLOGY CLASSZONE.COM

Animated BIOLOGY
View animated chapter concepts.
- Natural Selection Principles
- Simulate Natural Selection

BIOZINE
Keep current with biology news.
- Featured stories
- Strange Biology
- Careers

RESOURCE CENTER
Get more information on
- Charles Darwin
- Artificial Selection
- Genetic Tools to Study Evolution

How could evolution lead to this?

The star-nosed mole has a pink snout that is especially good at finding food. The snout's 22 fingerlike rays can touch up to 12 objects in just one second. The mole also uses strong paddle-shaped feet for burrowing, and its large ear openings give it excellent hearing. These special traits make up for its poor vision—which it doesn't really need underground.

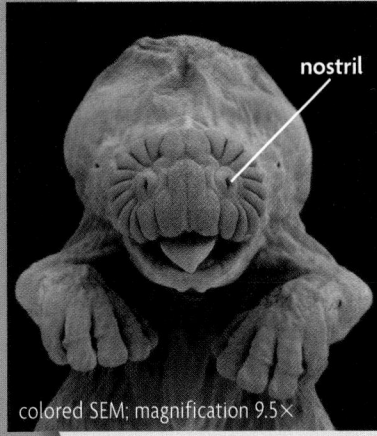

nostril

colored SEM; magnification 9.5×

Genetics The pink rays that sprout around the star-nosed mole's nostrils develop differently from the body parts of any other animal. After the mole is born, the rays spring forward to form their "star." Scientists are researching whether the mole has a unique set of genes for development. In this chapter, you will learn how genes are involved in evolution.

10.1 Early Ideas About Evolution

KEY CONCEPT There were theories of biological and geologic change before Darwin.

▶ **MAIN IDEAS**

- Early scientists proposed ideas about evolution.
- Theories of geologic change set the stage for Darwin's theory.

VOCABULARY

evolution, p. 298
species, p. 298
fossil, p. 300
catastrophism, p. 301
gradualism, p. 301
uniformitarianism, p. 301

Review
hybridization

MICHIGAN STANDARDS

B1.2i Explain the progression of ideas and explanations that leads to science theories that are part of the current scientific consensus or core knowledge.

B2.4d Analyze the relationships among organisms based on their shared physical, biochemical, genetic, and cellular characteristics and functional processes.

TAKING NOTES

Create a chart with a column for each scientist mentioned in this section and a second column for his contribution to evolutionary theory.

Scientist	Contribution
Linnaeus	
Buffon	

Connect Why are there so many kinds of living things, such as the strange looking star-nosed mole? Earth is home to millions of species, from bacteria to plants to ocean organisms, that look like something from science fiction. The search for reasons for Earth's great biological diversity was aided in the 1800s, when Charles Darwin proposed his theory of evolution by natural selection. But long before Darwin, evolution had been the focus of talk among scholars.

▶ **MAIN IDEA**

Early scientists proposed ideas about evolution.

Although Darwin rightly deserves much of the credit for evolutionary theory as we know it today, he was not the first person to come up with the idea. **Evolution** is the process of biological change by which descendants come to differ from their ancestors. This concept had been discussed for more than 100 years when Darwin proposed his theory of how evolution works. Today, evolution is a central theme in all fields of biology.

The 1700s were a time of great advances in intellectual thought. Many fields of science came out with new ways of looking at the world. Four scientists in particular are important. They not only made valuable contributions to biology in general but they also laid the foundations upon which Darwin would later build his ideas. **FIGURE 10.1** highlights the work of some of these early scientists.

Carolus Linnaeus In the 1700s, the Swedish botanist Carolus Linnaeus developed a classification system for all types of organisms known at the time. Although Linnaeus used his system to group organisms by their similarities, the system also reflects evolutionary relationships. This system is still in use by scientists today. Years into his career, Linnaeus abandoned the common belief of the time that organisms were fixed and did not change. He proposed instead that some might have arisen through hybridization—a crossing that he could observe through experiments with varieties, or species, of plants. A **species** is a group of organisms so similar to one another that they can reproduce and have fertile offspring.

Georges Louis Leclerc de Buffon Buffon, a French naturalist of the 1700s, challenged many of the accepted ideas of the day. Based on evidence of past life on Earth, he proposed that species shared ancestors instead of arising separately. Buffon also rejected the common idea of the time that Earth was only 6000 years old. He suggested that it was much older. This argument was similar to that of Charles Lyell, a geologist whose work helped inspire Darwin's writings. You will read more about Lyell later in this section.

Erasmus Darwin Born in 1731, Charles Darwin's grandfather was a respected English doctor and a poet. He proposed that all living things were descended from a common ancestor and that more-complex forms of life arose from less-complex forms. This idea was expanded upon 65 years later by his grandson.

Jean-Baptiste Lamarck In 1809, the year of Darwin's birth, a French naturalist named Lamarck proposed that all organisms evolved toward perfection and complexity. Like other scientists of the time, he did not think that species became extinct. Instead, he reasoned that they must have evolved into different forms.

Lamarck proposed that changes in an environment caused an organism's behavior to change, leading to greater use or disuse of a structure or organ. The structure would become larger or smaller as a result. The organism would pass on these changes to its offspring. For example, Lamarck thought that the long necks of giraffes evolved as generations of giraffes reached for leaves higher in the trees. Lamarck's idea is known as the inheritance of acquired characteristics.

Connecting CONCEPTS

Scientific Process Recall from **Chapter 1** that in every scientific field, knowledge is built upon evidence gathered by earlier scientists.

FIGURE 10.1 Early Naturalists

Evolutionary thought, like all scientific inquiry, draws heavily upon its history. The published works of these scientists contributed important ideas prior to Darwin's theory.

1735 *Systema Naturae*	1749 *Histoire Naturelle*	1794–1796 *Zoonomia*	1809 *Philosophie Zoologique*
Carolus Linnaeus proposed a new system of organization for plants, animals, and minerals, based upon their similarities. 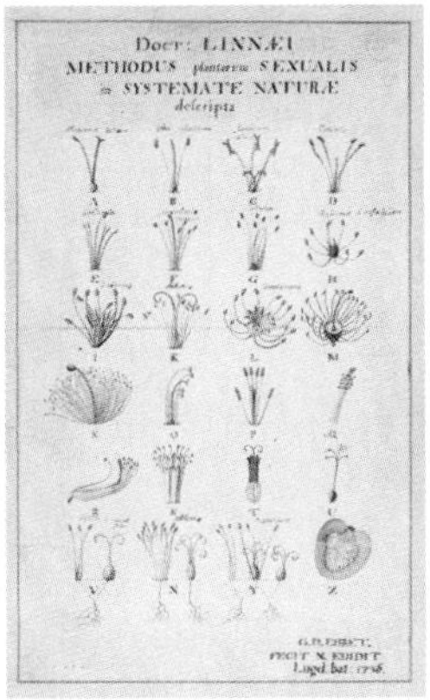	**Georges Buffon** discussed important ideas about relationships among organisms, sources of biological variation, and the possibility of evolution. 	**Erasmus Darwin** considered how organisms could evolve through mechanisms such as competition. 	**Jean-Baptiste Lamarck** presented evolution as occurring due to environmental change over long periods of time. 

Summarize Explain why Darwin cannot be considered the first scientist to consider evolution.

Lamarck did not propose how traits were passed on to offspring, and his explanation of how organisms evolve was flawed. However, Darwin was influenced by Lamarck's idea that changes in physical characteristics could be inherited and were driven by environmental changes over time.

Compare What common idea about organisms did these scientists share?

▶ MAIN IDEA

Theories of geologic change set the stage for Darwin's theory.

The age of Earth was a key issue in the early debates over evolution. The common view was that Earth was created about 6000 years earlier, and that since that time, neither Earth nor the species that lived on it had changed.

French zoologist Georges Cuvier did not think that species could change. However, he did think that they could become extinct, an idea considered radical by many of his peers. Cuvier had observed that each stratum, or rock layer, held its own specific type of fossils. **Fossils** are traces of organisms that existed in the past. He found that the fossils in the deepest layers were quite different from those in the upper layers, which were formed by more recent deposits of sediment. Cuvier explained his observations in the early 1800s with the theory now known as catastrophism, shown in **FIGURE 10.2**.

Connecting CONCEPTS

Earth Science Cuvier based his thinking on what we know as the Law of Superposition. It states that in a sequence of layered rocks, a given layer was deposited before any layer above it.

FIGURE 10.2 Principles of Geologic Change

Ideas from geology played a role in Darwin's developing theory.

CATASTROPHISM	GRADUALISM	UNIFORMITARIANISM
Volcanoes, floods, and earthquakes are examples of catastrophic events that were once believed responsible for mass extinctions and the formation of all landforms.	Canyons carved by rivers show gradual change. Gradualism is the idea that changes on Earth occurred by small steps over long periods of time.	Rock strata demonstrate that geologic processes, which are still occurring today, add up over long periods of time to cause great change.

Compare and Contrast How are these three theories similar, and what are their differences?

The theory of **catastrophism** (kuh-TAS-truh-FIHZ-uhm) states that natural disasters such as floods and volcanic eruptions have happened often during Earth's long history. These events shaped landforms and caused species to become extinct in the process. Cuvier argued that the appearance of new species in each rock layer resulted from other species' moving into the area from elsewhere after each catastrophic event.

In the late 1700s, the Scottish geologist James Hutton proposed that the changes he observed in landforms resulted from slow changes over a long period of time, a principle that became known as **gradualism** (GRAJ-oo-uh-LIHZ-uhm). He argued that the laying down of soil or the creation of canyons by rivers cutting through rock were not the result of large-scale events. Rather, they resulted from slow processes that had happened in the past. This idea has become so important to evolution that today the term *gradualism* is often used to mean the gradual change of a species through evolution.

One of the leading supporters of the argument for an ancient Earth was the English geologist Charles Lyell. In *Principles of Geology*, published in the 1830s, Lyell expanded Hutton's theory of gradualism into the theory of **uniformitarianism** (YOO-nuh-FAWR-mih-TAIR-ee-uh-NIHZ-uhm). This theory states that the geologic processes that shape Earth are uniform through time. Lyell observed processes that made small changes in Earth's features. He inferred that similar changes had happened in the past. Uniformitarianism combines Hutton's idea of gradual change over time with Lyell's observations that such changes have occurred at a constant rate and are ongoing. Uniformitarianism soon replaced catastrophism as the favored theory of geologic change. Lyell's theory greatly affected the scientific community—particularly a young English naturalist named Charles Darwin.

VOCABULARY

The names of these geologic theories can be broken down into familiar words.

- *Catastrophe* means "sudden disaster."
- *Gradual* means "moving or changing slowly."
- *Uniform* means "always staying the same."

VISUAL VOCAB

Uniformitarianism proposes that present geologic processes are the key to the past.

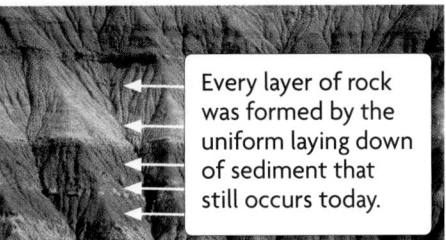

Every layer of rock was formed by the uniform laying down of sediment that still occurs today.

Connecting CONCEPTS

Scientific Process Recall from **Chapter 1** that in science, the term *theory* describes a well-supported explanation that incorporates observations, inferences, and tested hypotheses.

Compare What important concepts about Earth did Hutton and Lyell agree upon?

10.1 ASSESSMENT

ONLINE QUIZ
ClassZone.com

REVIEWING ▷ MAIN IDEAS

1. Briefly describe two ideas about **evolution** that were proposed by scientists in the 18th century.

2. What ideas in Lyell's theory of **uniformitarianism** were important for evolutionary theory?

CRITICAL THINKING

3. **Contrast** What are the key differences between the theories of **gradualism** and **catastrophism**?

4. **Apply** Why are the ideas that Earth undergoes change and is billions of years old important for evolutionary theory?

Connecting CONCEPTS

5. **Genetics** How can you use the concept of genetic inheritance to disprove Lamarck's idea of the inheritance of acquired characteristics?

10.2 Darwin's Observations

KEY CONCEPT   Darwin's voyage provided insights into evolution.

▶ **MAIN IDEAS**

- Darwin observed differences among island species.
- Darwin observed fossil and geologic evidence supporting an ancient Earth.

VOCABULARY

variation, p. 302
adaptation, p. 302

Connect Lyell's views of gradual geologic change greatly influenced Darwin's thinking. In 1831, the ship HMS *Beagle* set sail from England to map the coast of South America and the Pacific islands. Hired at first to keep the captain company, Darwin was interested in observing the land and its inhabitants. During the voyage, he read Lyell's *Principles of Geology*. When the ship reached South America, Darwin spent most of his time ashore, where he found much evidence supporting Lyell's views.

▶ **MAIN IDEA**

Darwin observed differences among island species.

Darwin, shown in **FIGURE 10.3**, was struck by the variation of traits among similar species that he observed in all his travels. In biology, **variation** is the difference in the physical traits of an individual from those of other individuals in the group to which it belongs. Variation can occur either among members of different species (*inter*specific variation) or among individuals of the same species (*intra*specific variation). Darwin noted that the species found on one island looked different from those on nearby islands and that many of the islands' species looked different from those on the nearest mainland.

The differences between species on different islands was especially noticeable in the Galápagos Islands, an island chain off the coast of Ecuador in South America. Some differences seemed well suited to the animals' environments and diets, as shown in **FIGURE 10.4**. For example, saddle-backed tortoises, which have long necks and legs, lived in areas with a lot of tall plants. Domed tortoises, with their shorter necks and legs, lived in wet areas rich in mosses and short plants. Similarly, finches with strong, thick beaks lived in areas with a lot of large, hard-shelled nuts, while those species of finch with more delicate beaks were found where insects or fruits were widely available.

These observations led Darwin to realize that species may somehow be able to adapt to their surroundings. An **adaptation** is a feature that allows an organism to better survive in its environment. Adaptations can lead to genetic change in a population over time.

FIGURE 10.3 Darwin spent more than 20 years compiling evidence before publishing in 1859 his ideas on how evolution works.

Connect **What adaptations did Darwin see in the finches of the Galápagos Islands?**

FIGURE 10.4 Adaptations Within Species

Galápagos tortoises (*Geochelone elephantopus*) are evidence that species can adapt to their environments.

Domed tortoises have short necks and legs, and live in areas with low vegetation.

Saddle-backed tortoises have a high shell edge, allowing them to stretch their long necks.

Explain Why do these tortoises of the same species look different?

Galápagos Islands

> **MAIN IDEA**

Darwin observed fossil and geologic evidence supporting an ancient Earth.

On his voyage, Darwin found fossil evidence of species changing over time. In Argentina, he found fossils of huge animals, such as *Glyptodon*, a giant armadillo. The fact that these fossils looked like living species suggested that modern animals might have some relationship to fossil forms. These fossils suggested that, in order for such changes to occur, Earth must be much more than 6000 years old.

During his voyage, Darwin also found fossil shells of marine organisms high up in the Andes mountains. Darwin later experienced an earthquake during his voyage and saw firsthand the result: land that had been underwater was moved above sea level. This experience explained what he saw in the Andes. Darwin's observations on his voyage supported Lyell's theory that daily geologic processes can add up to great change over a long period of time. Darwin later extended the ideas of an old Earth and slow, gradual change to the evolution of organisms.

Infer What could account for fossils of marine organisms being found on top of modern-day mountain ranges?

10.2 ASSESSMENT

ONLINE QUIZ
ClassZone.com

REVIEWING ▶ MAIN IDEAS

1. What accounts for the **variation** Darwin observed among island species?

2. What did Darwin learn from the fossils that he observed on his voyage?

CRITICAL THINKING

3. **Apply** Explain how wings are an **adaptation** for birds.

4. **Synthesize** How did Darwin's observations support Lyell's theory of an ancient Earth undergoing continual geologic change?

Connecting CONCEPTS

5. **Ecology** Some birds in the Galápagos Islands build nests in trees, while others hide eggs in rock crevices. What could account for this difference in nesting behaviors?

10.3 Theory of Natural Selection

KEY CONCEPT Darwin proposed natural selection as a mechanism for evolution.

▶ MAIN IDEAS

- Several key insights led to Darwin's idea for natural selection.
- Natural selection explains how evolution can occur.
- Natural selection acts on existing variation.

VOCABULARY

artificial selection, p. 304
heritability, p. 304
natural selection, p. 305
population, p. 306

fitness, p. 307

Review
phenotype,
competition

MICHIGAN STANDARDS

B5.1A Summarize the major concepts of natural selection (differential survival and reproduction of chance inherited variants, depending on environmental conditions).

B5.1e Explain how natural selection leads to organisms that are well suited for the environment (differential survival and reproduction of chance inherited variants, depending upon environmental conditions).

Connect Although Darwin began his voyage thinking that species could not change, his experiences during the five-year journey altered his thinking. Variation of similar species among islands, fossil evidence, and geologic events convinced him that evolution occurs. But he had yet to determine *how* evolution could happen.

▶ MAIN IDEA

Several key insights led to Darwin's idea for natural selection.

After his voyage, Darwin spent more than 20 years conducting research while thinking about how evolution occurs. Although he had traveled the world, Darwin also found great insight in his home country of England. One important influence of Darwin's was the work of farmers and breeders.

Artificial Selection

Darwin noticed a lot of variation in domesticated plants and animals. The populations of domesticated species seemed to show variation in traits that were not shown in their wild relatives. Through selection of certain traits, breeders could produce a great amount of diversity. The process by which humans change a species by breeding it for certain traits is called **artificial selection.** In this process, humans make use of the genetic variation in plants and animals by acting as the selective agent. That is, humans determine which traits are favorable and then breed individuals that show those traits.

To explore this idea, Darwin turned to the hobby of breeding pigeons. Although Darwin had no knowledge of genetics, he had noticed certain traits being selected in animals such as livestock and pets. Humans had been breeding pigeons for thousands of years, producing pigeons, such as those in **FIGURE 10.5,** that showed many different traits. In order for artificial—or natural—selection to occur, the trait must be heritable. **Heritability** (HER-ih-tuh-BIHL-uh-tee) is the ability of a trait to be passed down from one generation to the next.

Darwin compared what he learned about breeding to his ideas on adaptation. In artificial selection, features such as reversed neck feathers, large crops, or extra tail feathers are favored over generations only if these traits are liked by breeders. However, if a feature is not desirable or "useful," it might be selected against. During artificial selection humans act as the selective agent. In nature, however, the environment creates the selective pressure that determines if a trait is passed on or not.

Darwin used this line of thinking for his theory of natural selection. **Natural selection** is a mechanism by which individuals that have inherited beneficial adaptations produce more offspring on average than do other individuals. In nature, the environment is the selective agent. Therefore, in nature, characteristics are selected only if they give advantages to individuals in the environment as it is right now. Furthermore, Darwin reasoned, breeds are not produced perfectly all at once. He knew it sometimes took many generations for breeders to produce the varieties he had observed.

Struggle for Survival

Another important idea came from English economist Thomas Malthus. Malthus had proposed that resources such as food, water, and shelter were natural limits to population growth. That is, human populations would grow geometrically if resources were unlimited. Instead, disease and a limited food supply kept the population smaller.

FIGURE 10.5 Artificial Selection of Pigeon Traits

For thousands of years, new varieties of organisms, such as pigeons, have resulted from selective breeding for particular traits.

neck feathers

crop

tail feathers

ARTIFICIALLY BRED PIGEONS

Jacobins are bred for their reversed neck feathers.

Croppers are bred for their inflatable crop.

Fantails are bred to have many tail feathers.

Connect **What other species of organisms are often subjects of artificial selection?**

Darwin reasoned that a similar struggle took place in nature. Resources were limited, and organisms had more offspring than could ever survive. Why did some individuals, and not others, survive?

Darwin found his answer in the variation he had seen within populations. A **population** is all the individuals of a species that live in an area. Darwin had noticed in the Galápagos Islands that in any population, such as the tortoises or the finches, some individuals had variations that were particularly well-suited to their environment. He proposed that these adaptations arose over many generations. Darwin called this process of evolution "descent with modification."

Explain How did Malthus's economic theory influence Darwin?

▶ MAIN IDEA

Natural selection explains how evolution can occur.

Charles Darwin was not the only person to develop a theory to explain how evolution may take place. An English naturalist named Alfred Russel Wallace independently developed a theory very similar to Darwin's. Both Darwin and Wallace had studied the huge diversity of plants and animals in the tropics, and both studied the fossil record. In 1858, the ideas of Darwin and Wallace were presented to an important group of scientists in London. The next year, Darwin published his ideas in the book *On the Origin of Species by Means of Natural Selection.*

There are four main principles to the theory of natural selection: variation, overproduction, adaptation, and descent with modification.

- **Variation** The heritable differences, or variations, that exist in every population are the basis for natural selection. The differences among individuals result from differences in the genetic material of the organisms, whether inherited from a parent or resulting from a genetic mutation.
- **Overproduction** While having many offspring raises the chance that some will survive, it also results in competition between offspring for resources.
- **Adaptation** Sometimes a certain variation allows an individual to survive better than other individuals it competes against in its environment. More successful individuals are "naturally selected" to live longer and to produce more offspring that share those adaptations for their environment.
- **Descent with modification** Over time, natural selection will result in species with adaptations that are well suited for survival and reproduction in an environment. More individuals will have the trait in every following generation, as long as the environmental conditions continue to remain beneficial for that trait.

A well-studied example of natural selection in jaguars is shown in **FIGURE 10.6**. About 11,000 years ago, many species faced extinction. Large cats, including jaguars, faced a shortage of food due to the changing climate of that time. There were fewer mammals to eat, so the jaguars had to eat reptiles. In the jaguar population, there were variations of jaw and tooth size that became

VOCABULARY

The term *descent* is used in evolution to mean the passing of genetic information from generation to generation.

TAKING NOTES

Write a sentence in your own words that summarizes each of the four principles of natural selection.

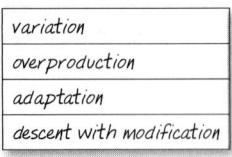

| variation |
| overproduction |
| adaptation |
| descent with modification |

important for survival. Like many other species, jaguars can produce more offspring than can be supported by the environment. Jaguars with the biggest jaws and teeth could prey more easily on the shelled reptiles. Because jaw size and tooth size are heritable traits and were beneficial, large jaws and teeth became adaptations for this population. The jaguars' descendants showed modifications, or changes, over time.

In biology, the term **fitness** is a measure of the ability to survive and produce more offspring relative to other members of the population in a given environment. After the change in climate, jaguars that had larger teeth and jaws had a higher fitness than other jaguars in the population. Jaguars that ate less didn't necessarily all die or stop producing altogether; they just reproduced a little less. Today, large teeth and jaws are considered typical traits of jaguars.

Compare and Contrast What are the similarities and differences between natural selection and artificial selection?

FIGURE 10.6 The Principles of Natural Selection

Certain traits become more common in a population through the process of natural selection.

Animated BIOLOGY
Watch the principles of natural selection in action at ClassZone.com.

jaguar 1
jaguar 2

OVERPRODUCTION

A jaguar may produce many offspring, but not all of young will survive due to competition for resources.

VARIATION

Some jaguars, such as jaguar 1 shown here, may be born with slightly larger jaws and teeth due to natural variation in the population. Some variations are heritable.

jaguar skull 1
jaguar skull 2

ADAPTATION

Jaguars with larger jaws and teeth are able to eat shelled reptiles. These jaguars are likely to survive longer and leave more offspring than jaguars that can eat only mammals.

DESCENT WITH MODIFICATION

Because large teeth and jaws are heritable traits, they become more common characteristics in the population.

Summarize How did large jaws and teeth become typical characteristics of jaguars?

INTERPRETING LINE GRAPHS

Scientists used mice to study whether exercise ability can improve in animals over several generations. In this experiment, mice were artificially selected for increased wheel-running behavior. The mice that were able to do the most wheel running were selected to breed the next generation. The control group represents generations of mice that were allowed to breed randomly.

- The x-axis shows the different generations of mice from Generation 1 to Generation 9.
- The y-axis shows the number of revolutions the mice ran on the wheel per day.
- The solid blue line represents the control group, in which generations of mice were allowed to breed randomly.
- The dotted orange line represents the generations of mice that were artificially selected based on their wheel-running activity. This is the experimental group.

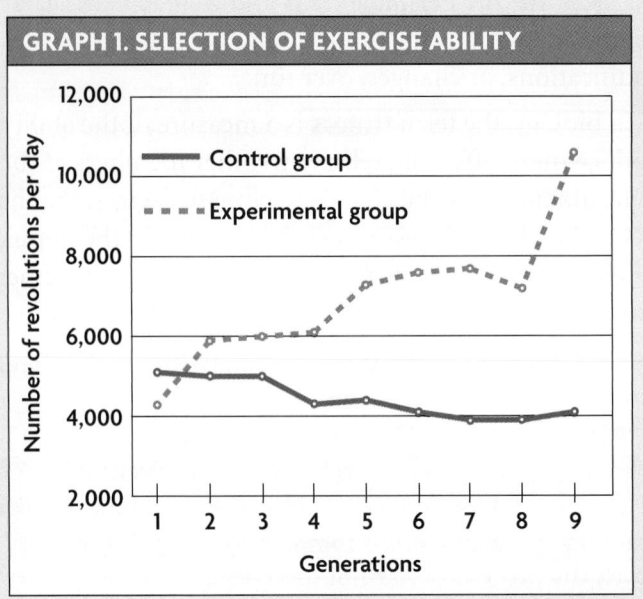

GRAPH 1. SELECTION OF EXERCISE ABILITY

Source: Swallow et. al, *Behavior Genetics* 28:3.

1. **Interpret** What is the difference in results between the mice in the control group and the mice in the experimental group?

2. **Predict** Use the trend in the data to make a general prediction about the number of revolutions on the wheel per day for mice in Generation 10 of the experimental group.

▶ MAIN IDEA
Natural selection acts on existing variation.

Natural selection acts on phenotypes, or physical traits, rather than on genetic material itself. New alleles are not made by natural selection—they occur by genetic mutations. Natural selection can act only on traits that already exist.

Changing Environments

Ecologists Peter and Rosemary Grant observed an example of natural selection acting on existing traits within a population of medium ground finches on one of the Galápagos Islands. A drought in 1977 suddenly reduced the amount of small, soft seeds that the finches preferred. However, there were still plenty of large, tough-shelled seeds. Because the large-beaked finches in the population were able to crack the large, tough seeds, they did not starve. The next year, the Grants noted a big increase of large-beaked hatchlings. In contrast, most of the finches with small beaks had died.

Darwin's theory predicted exactly what the Grants observed. A trait that was already in the population became favorable for survival because of a change in the environment, and thus was passed on to future generations.

As an environment changes, different traits will become beneficial. The numbers of large-beaked finches on this Galápagos Island kept rising until 1984, when the supply of large seeds went down after an unusually wet period. These conditions favored production of small, soft seeds and small-beaked birds. With evolution, a trait that is an advantage today may be a disadvantage in the future.

Adaptations as Compromises

One mistake people make about natural selection is to think that adaptive characteristics passed down over a long time result in individuals that are perfectly suited to their surroundings. This is not the case. For example, some structures may take on new functions. Pandas have a structure in their wrist that acts like a thumb. As pandas eat bamboo shoots, they hold the shoots as you would hold a carrot. However, a close look at the paw reveals that it has six digits: five digits that resemble your fingers, plus a small thumblike structure. The panda's "thumb," shown in **FIGURE 10.7**, is actually an enlarged wrist bone. The ancestors of today's pandas had five full digits like today's bears, but those early pandas with bigger wrist bones had an advantage in eating bamboo. Because of its size and position, this bone functions like a human thumb. It is not considered a true thumb, because it does not have separate bones and joints as a human thumb does. It is also not a typical wrist bone, as the bone is clearly longer than needed to function for the wrist. Instead, it functions both as a wrist bone and a thumb.

FIGURE 10.7 A panda's wrist bone also functions like a thumb.

Explain Why is the panda's "thumb" considered an adaptive compromise?

To learn more about natural selection, visit scilinks.org.
Keycode: MLB010

10.3 ASSESSMENT

ONLINE QUIZ ClassZone.com

REVIEWING ▶ MAIN IDEAS

1. What did Darwin hope to learn about **artificial selection** by studying pigeons?

2. What are the four principles of **natural selection**?

3. Why must there be variation in the **population** in order for natural selection to occur?

CRITICAL THINKING

4. **Evaluate** Explain why the phrase "survival of the fittest" does not accurately reflect Darwin's concept of evolutionary **fitness.**

5. **Synthesize** Why is it said that natural selection acts on phenotypes rather than on the genetic material of organisms?

Connecting CONCEPTS

6. **Ecology** You have learned that the environment affects how organisms change over generations. How would you explain a species that remains the same for millions of years?

10.4 Evidence of Evolution

KEY CONCEPT Evidence of common ancestry among species comes from many sources.

MAIN IDEAS

- Evidence for evolution in Darwin's time came from several sources.
- Structural patterns are clues to the history of a species.

VOCABULARY

biogeography, p. 311
homologous structure, p. 312
analogous structure, p. 313
vestigial structure, p. 314

MICHIGAN STANDARDS

B5.1f Explain, using examples, how the fossil record, comparative anatomy, and other evidence supports the theory of evolution.

Connect How genetic inheritance works was not known while Darwin was working on his theory of natural selection. However, Darwin documented natural selection from every angle available at the time. His thoroughness was important. It left no doubt in the minds of scientists that all organisms have a past history. Today, the concept of evolution ties together all fields of biology.

MAIN IDEA

Evidence for evolution in Darwin's time came from several sources.

Darwin found evidence from a wide range of sources to support his argument for evolution. The most important and convincing support came from fossils, geography, embryology, and anatomy.

Fossils

Even before Darwin, scholars studying fossils knew that organisms changed over time. Scientists who study fossils study more than just the fossil itself. They also think about its age, its location, and what the environment was like when the organism it came from was alive.

In the late 1700s, geologists wondered why certain types of fossils were found in some layers of rock and not others. Later studies suggested that the fossil organisms in the bottom, or older, layers were more primitive than those in the upper, or newer, layers. Geologists were interested in fossil sequences as a record of events such as earthquakes that disturb rock strata, not as proof of evolution. However, these and other findings in the fossil record supported Darwin's concept of descent with modification.

Geography

Recall that during the *Beagle* expedition Darwin saw that island plants and animals looked like, but were not identical to, species on the South American continent. He extended this observation, proposing that island species most closely resemble species on the nearest mainland. He hypothesized that at some point in the past, some individuals from the South American mainland had migrated to the islands.

FIGURE 10.8 This trilobite, an early marine invertebrate that is now extinct, was found in this loose rock bed in Ohio. Although far from modern-day oceans, this site is actually the floor of an ancient sea.

FIGURE 10.9 Variation in Galápagos Finches

Finches on certain Galápagos Islands live in different environments and have beaks of different sizes and shapes.

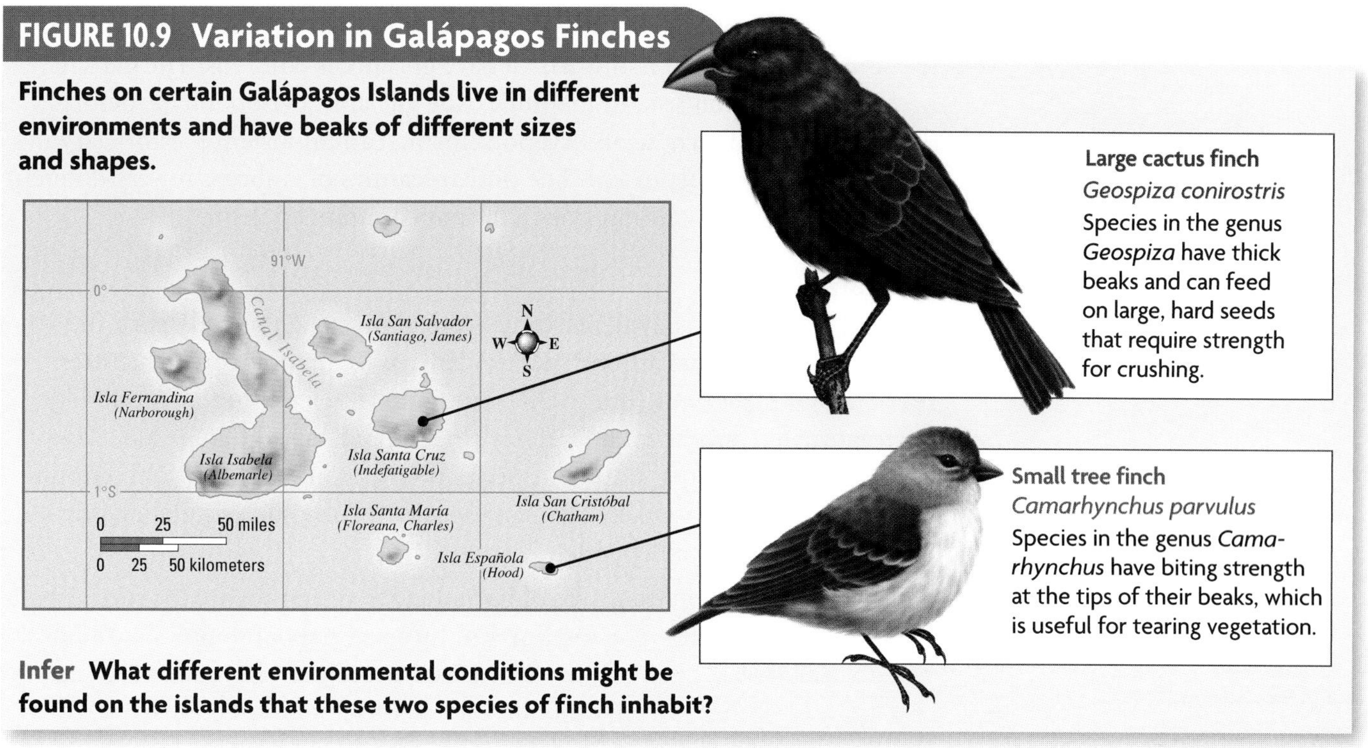

Large cactus finch
Geospiza conirostris
Species in the genus *Geospiza* have thick beaks and can feed on large, hard seeds that require strength for crushing.

Small tree finch
Camarhynchus parvulus
Species in the genus *Camarhynchus* have biting strength at the tips of their beaks, which is useful for tearing vegetation.

Infer What different environmental conditions might be found on the islands that these two species of finch inhabit?

Different ecosystems on each island—with different plants, climates, and predators—had favored different traits in these migrants. Over time, these new traits became well established in the separate island populations, since the islands were too far apart for mating to occur.

One clear example of local adaptation is found in what are now known as Darwin's finches. The finches from the Galápagos Islands, shown in **FIGURE 10.9,** have distinct-looking beaks, as well as different habits, diets, and behaviors that evolved after generations of adaptation to specific island habitats. However, they all share a common ancestor from the South American mainland.

Since Darwin's time, the same pattern of evolution on islands has been studied in many living things, such as fruit flies and honeycreepers on the Hawaiian Islands. Darwin was the first scientist to establish this relationship between island and mainland species. Today this is an important principle of **biogeography,** the study of the distribution of organisms around the world.

Embryology

A study proposing a relationship between crabs, which can walk, and barnacles, which are fixed in one place as adults, fascinated Darwin. He had collected barnacles for many years and had noted that immature crabs and barnacles, called larvae, were similar. As **FIGURE 10.10** shows, barnacle and crab larvae both swim and look alike, but the adult animals look and behave very differently.

FIGURE 10.10 Although adult crabs and barnacles look and behave very differently, they can look identical as larvae. This suggested to Darwin that they share a common ancestor.

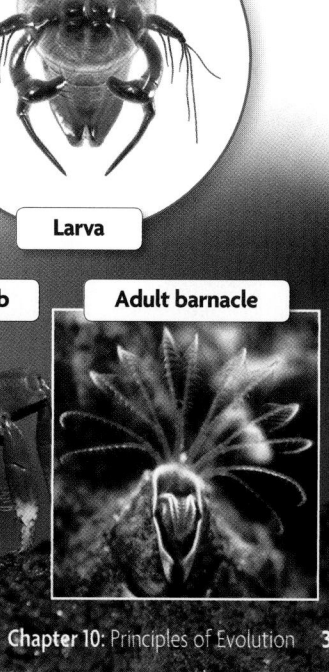

Larva

Adult crab

Adult barnacle

Like larvae, embryos of vertebrates can be hard to tell apart. For example, fish, birds, reptiles, and mammals all have gill slits as embryos. The gill slits become gills in adult fish. In mammals, the gill slits develop into structures of ears and throats. These observations formed an important part of Darwin's evidence for common descent. The similar features of embryos in very different organisms suggest evolution from a distant common ancestor.

Anatomy

Some of Darwin's best evidence came from comparing the body parts of different species. Chief among such evidence were homologous structures. **Homologous structures** (huh-MAHL-uh-guhs) are features that are similar in structure but appear in different organisms and have different functions. Their appearance across different species offers strong evidence for common descent. It would be unlikely for many species to have such similar anatomy if each species evolved independently.

The most common examples of homologous structures are the forelimbs of tetrapod vertebrates. The forelimbs of humans, bats, and moles are compared in **FIGURE 10.11.** In all of these animals, the forelimbs have several bones that are very similar to each other despite their different functions. Notice also how the same bones vary in different animals. Homologous structures are different in detail but similar in structure and relation to each other.

In using homologous structures as evidence of evolution, Darwin posed a logical question: If each of these groups descended from a different ancestor, why would they share these homologous structures? A simple answer is that they share a common ancestor.

VOCABULARY

A tetrapod is a four-limbed animal. *Tetra-* means "four," and *-pod* means "foot."

FIGURE 10.11 Homologous Structures

Homologous structures, though they often have differing functions, are the result of a common ancestor.

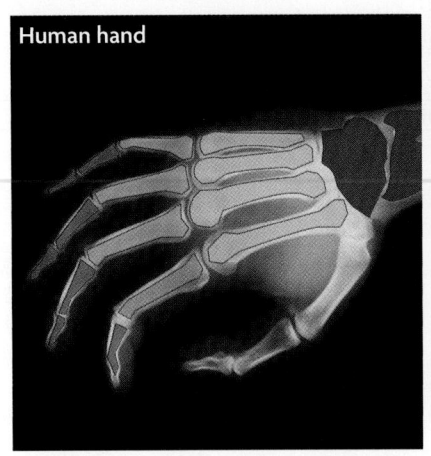
Human hand

Bat wing

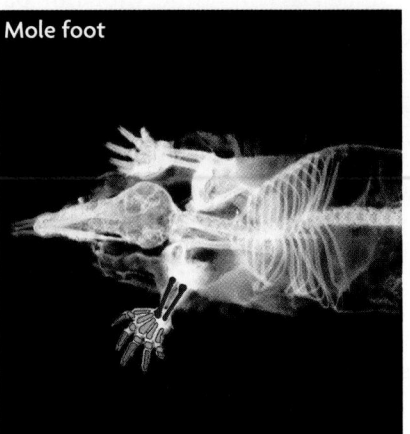
Mole foot

Notice that each of these homologous structures uses the same bones in relation to the others.

Apply What body part of a dolphin is homologous to the structures shown above?

The idea of common descent provides a logical explanation for how homologous structures appeared in diverse groups. Having similar structures doesn't always mean two species are closely related, however. Some structures found in different species have the same functions but did not evolve from a common ancestor.

Suppose two organisms have similar needs caused by the environment. For example, two different organisms need to be able to fly. Both can develop similar adaptations using different body parts. Think about the wings of bats and the wings of flying insects. Clearly these organisms differ in more ways than they are similar. Insects are arthropods, while bats are mammals. The wings of bats and insects are called analogous structures, as shown in **FIGURE 10.12. Analogous structures** (uh-NAL-uh-guhs) are structures that perform a similar function—in this case, flight—but are not similar in origin. Bat wings have bones. In contrast, insect wings do not have bones, only membranes. The similar function of wings in bats and flying insects evolved separately. Their ancestors faced similar environmental challenges and came upon similar solutions.

Analyze Using the terms *homologous* and *analogous,* identify which group of structures provides evidence for a common ancestor. Explain.

FIGURE 10.12 ANALOGOUS STRUCTURES

Analogous structures evolved separately and are not evidence of a common ancestor. A bat's wing has bones, whereas insect wings do not.

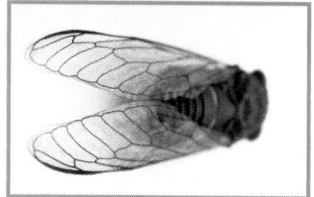

QUICK LAB INFERRING

Piecing Together Evidence

Evolutionary biologists and paleontologists rarely get all of the pieces of what they are studying. In this activity, you will receive pieces of "evidence" about a picture in order to make observations, inferences, and predictions about it.

PROBLEM How are inferences modified when new information is obtained?

MATERIALS
picture cut into strips

PROCEDURE

1. Using the three strips that your teacher has provided, write down all observations and inferences that you can make about this picture.

2. Make a prediction about the picture's topic, using your observations as supporting evidence for your prediction.

3. Record observations, inferences, and a prediction for each remaining strip of "evidence" that you receive from your teacher.

ANALYZE AND CONCLUDE

1. **Analyze** What inferences did you modify as you gathered more evidence from your teacher?

2. **Provide Examples** What type of evidence might paleontologists find that would allow them to see the big picture of a species' evolutionary past?

FIGURE 10.13 Vestigial structures, such as the wings of an ostrich, are organs or structures that are greatly reduced from the original ancestral form and have little or no current use.

▶ MAIN IDEA

Structural patterns are clues to the history of a species.

Some organisms have structures or organs that seem to lack any useful function, or at least are no longer used for their original purpose. For example, snakes have tiny pelvic bones and stumplike limbs, even though snakes don't walk. Underdeveloped or unused features are called vestigial structures. **Vestigial structures** (veh-STIHJ-ee-uhl) are remnants of organs or structures that had a function in an early ancestor. As vertebrates, snakes share a common ancestor with tetrapods such as lizards and dogs. The tiny pelvic bones and hind limbs in many snakes are homologous to the pelvic bones of tetrapods.

The wings of ostriches are another example of vestigial structures. Ostriches have wings that they use for balance but not to fly, as shown in **FIGURE 10.13**. Over generations, their increasingly large bodies and powerful long legs may have been enough to avoid predators. If ostriches that lived long ago could escape by running or by kicking viciously, their large wings would no longer have been useful. Thus, the genes coding for large wings were not preserved over generations.

Examples of vestigial structures are found in many organisms. In humans, the appendix is an example of a vestigial structure. The appendix is a remnant of the cecum, which makes up a large part of the large intestine in plant-eating mammals. It helps to digest the cellulose in plants. As omnivores, humans do not eat much cellulose. The human appendix does not have the ability to digest cellulose. In fact, it performs no known function at all.

Vestigial structures did not get smaller in one individual organism. It took many generations for those organs to shrink. Today, biologists consider vestigial structures among the most important examples demonstrating how evolution works.

Summarize What are vestigial structures, and how do they demonstrate common ancestry?

10.4 ASSESSMENT

ONLINE QUIZ
ClassZone.com

REVIEWING ▶ MAIN IDEAS

1. Describe the four sources of evidence for evolution upon which Darwin based his ideas on common descent.

2. Why are **vestigial structures** considered critical evidence of evolution?

CRITICAL THINKING

3. **Hypothesize** Describe how some of the Galápagos finch species, which traditionally were seed eaters, evolved over generations to prefer insects over seeds.

4. **Apply** How can a bat's wing be considered both a **homologous structure** and an **analogous structure**?

Connecting CONCEPTS

5. **Human Biology** Wisdom teeth are a third set of molars that usually appear in humans between the ages of 17 and 25, and often need removing because they crowd out other teeth. Explain why wisdom teeth are vestigial structures.

MATERIALS
- piece of fabric
- bag of paper pieces

PROCESS SKILLS
- **Modeling**
- **Observing**
- **Predicting**

MICHIGAN STANDARDS

B1.1f Predict what would happen if the variables, methods, or timing of an investigation were changed.

L3.p2A Describe common relationships among organisms and provide examples of producer/consumer, predator/prey, or parasite/host relationship. (prerequisite)

Predator-Prey Pursuit

In this lab you will act like an owl in search of field mice. Your group will "consume" all the field mice that you see until only 25 percent of the population remains. These remaining field mice will then reproduce. These organisms pass an important trait for survival to their offspring—the ability to blend in with their surroundings. You will continue the process for several generations of mice, with some being consumed and others surviving to pass on their traits.

PROBLEM How does a population change as a result of natural selection?

PROCEDURE

1. Spread out the fabric habitat given to you on the tabletop.
2. Count out 20 pieces of paper of each of the five different colors for a total of 100 pieces. This will be your initial population of field mice.
3. One person should spread the pieces out randomly over the entire fabric habitat, making sure that none of the pieces cover the others. The remaining members of the group should not watch this process.
4. The other members of the group are now owls. They should pick up the pieces as they see them, one by one, until a total of 25 percent of the field mice remain in the habitat. Be sure to count carefully.
5. Carefully shake off the habitat to remove the surviving mice (a total of 25 pieces).
6. Group the survivors by color and record the numbers in your data table.
7. Next, assume that each survivor has three offspring. Place three additional pieces of the same color with each survivor.
8. Mix up the new set of pieces and have a different person spread them over the habitat. Note that there should again be 100 total pieces.
9. Repeat the entire process two more times, making a total of three generations of field mice being preyed upon.

OBSERVATIONS

TABLE 1. INFLUENCE OF SELECTIVE PREDATION ON FIELD MICE POPULATIONS					
	Color 1	Color 2	Color 3	Color 4	Color 5
Number at start	20	20	20	20	20
Number after first predation					
Number after first reproduction					

ANALYZE AND CONCLUDE

1. **Compare** How do the original population and the survivor populations compare?
2. **Predict** How do you think the data would have changed if the experiment were continued until a total of five generations of field mice were preyed upon?
3. **Apply** Name one animal in real life that uses camouflage to avoid predators. What habitat is it most likely to survive in? What possible traits would give it a further advantage over members of its own species?

10.5 Evolutionary Biology Today

KEY CONCEPT New technology is furthering our understanding of evolution.

▶ **MAIN IDEAS**

- Fossils provide a record of evolution.
- Molecular and genetic evidence support fossil and anatomical evidence.
- Evolution unites all fields of biology.

VOCABULARY

paleontology, p. 316

Connect Darwin had spent many years collecting evidence of evolution from different fields of science before publishing his results. Since that time, technology has greatly advanced. Scientists can now examine evidence only dreamed about in the 1800s. In particular, the relatively new fields of genetics and molecular biology have added strong support to Darwin's theory of natural selection. They have shown how hereditary variation occurs.

▶ **MAIN IDEA**

Fossils provide a record of evolution.

Paleontology (PAY-lee-ahn-TAHL-uh-jee), the study of fossils or extinct organisms, continues to provide new information and support current hypotheses about how evolution occurs. The fossil record is not complete, because most living things do not form into fossils after they die, and fossils have not been looked for in many areas of the world. However, no fossil evidence that contradicts evolution has ever been found.

In Darwin's time, paleontology was still a new science. Darwin worried about the lack of transitional fossils between groups of organisms. Since Darwin's time, however, many transitional forms have been discovered between species. Many of the large gaps in the fossil record have been filled in. The fossil record today includes many thousands of species that show the change in forms over time that Darwin outlined in his theory. These "missing links" demonstrate the evolution of traits within groups as well as the common ancestors between groups.

Although scientists classify organisms into groups, the mix of traits in transitional species often makes it difficult to tell where one group ends and another begins. One example of transitional species in the evolution of whales is shown in **FIGURE 10.14**. *Basilosaurus isis* had a whalelike body but also still had the limbs of land animals.

Infer Why are fossils such as *Basilosaurus isis* considered transitional fossils?

FIGURE 10.14 This skeleton of *Basilosaurus isis* was found in a desert in Egypt in 2005. It lived 40 million years ago and has characteristics of both land and marine animals.

⏵ MAIN IDEA

Molecular and genetic evidence support fossil and anatomical evidence.

As with homologous traits, very different species have similar molecular and genetic mechanisms. Because all living things have DNA, they share the same genetic code and make most of the same proteins from the same 20 amino acids. DNA or protein sequence comparisons can be used to show probable evolutionary relationships between species.

DNA sequence analysis As you learned in Chapter 8, the sequences of nucleotides in a gene change over time due to mutations. DNA sequence analysis depends on the fact that the more related two organisms are, the more similar their DNA will be. Because there are thousands of genes in even simple organisms, DNA contains a huge amount of information on evolutionary history.

Pseudogenes Sequences of DNA nucleotides known as pseudogenes also provide evidence of evolution. Pseudogenes are like vestigial structures. They no longer function but are still carried along with functional DNA. They can also change as they are passed on through generations, so they provide another way to figure out evolutionary relationships. Functioning genes may be similar in organisms with similar lifestyles, such as a wolf and a coyote, due to natural selection. Similarities between pseudogenes, however, must reflect a common ancestor.

Homeobox genes As you will learn in Chapter 23, homeobox genes control the development of specific structures. These sequences of genes are found in many organisms, from fruit flies to humans. They also indicate a very distant common ancestor. Evidence of homeobox gene clusters are found in organisms that lived as far back as 600 million years ago.

Protein comparisons Similarities among cell types across organisms can be revealed by comparing their proteins, a technique called molecular fingerprinting. A unique set of proteins are found in specific types of cells, such as liver or muscle cells. Cells from different species that have the same proteins most likely come from a common ancestor. For example, the proteins of light-sensitive cells in the brain of an ancient marine worm, as shown in **FIGURE 10.15,** were found to closely resemble those of cells found in the vertebrate eye. This resemblance shows a shared ancestry between worms and vertebrates. It also shows that the cells of the vertebrate eye originally came from cells in the brain.

> **VOCABULARY**
>
> A pseudogene is a DNA sequence that resembles a gene but seems to have no function. *Pseudo-* means "false" or "deceptive."

FIGURE 10.15 The eye spots of this marine worm have light-sensitive cells with a molecular fingerprint similar to that of a vertebrate eye.

Explain How have protein comparisons helped determine ancestral relationships between organisms?

FIGURE 10.16 Evidence of Whale Evolution

The evidence that whales descended from hoofed mammals is supported by scientific research in several different fields of biology.

Modern-day whale

Vestigial Evidence

Many modern whale species have vestigial pelvic and leg bones. They also have vestigial nerves for the sense of smell, and small muscles devoted to external ears that no longer exist.

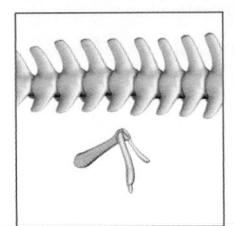

Embryological Evidence

Whale embryos have features such as hind leg buds and nostrils that resemble those of land animals. Nostrils are at the end of the whale's snout early in development but travel to the top of the head to form one or more blowholes before birth.

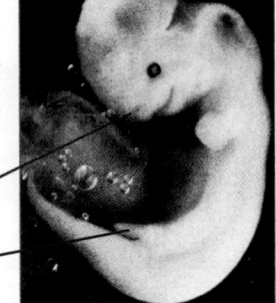

nostril

hind leg bud

Molecular Evidence

The DNA sequences of milk protein genes in whales and ungulates are very similar, as demonstrated by the DNA fragments below.

Hippopotamus	TCC TGGCA GTCCA GTGGT
Humpback whale	CCC TGGCA GTGCA GTGCT

Fossil Evidence

There are many transitional fossils that have characteristics of both land mammals and whales. These are a few examples.

Dorudon 40 million years ago

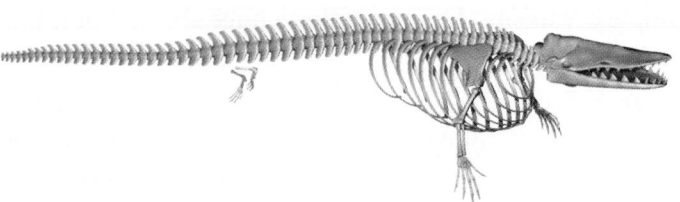

Tiny hind legs were useless on land, and a shorter neck and longer tail makes *Dorudon* similar to modern-day whales. Its ankle joints closely resemble those of modern ungulates.

Ambulocetus natans 50 million years ago

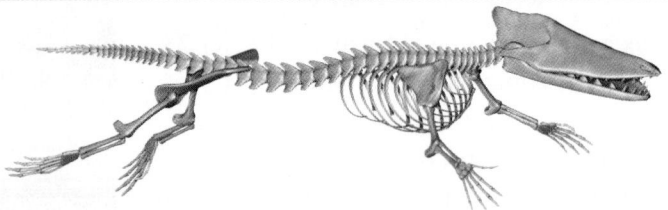

With a name that means "the walking whale that swims," *Ambulocetus natans* was an amphibious fish eater the size of a sea lion.

Pakicetus 52 million years ago

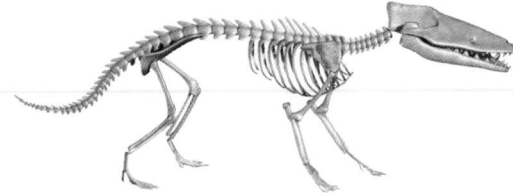

Pakicetus had a whale-shaped skull and teeth adapted for hunting fish. However, with ear bones that are in between those of land and aquatic mammals, it could not hear well underwater or make deep dives.

CRITICAL VIEWING Whales are divided into two groups: tooth whales, such as the orca pictured above, and baleen whales, such as the humpback whale pictured on the next page. Which would you predict is most closely related to *Dorudon*? Explain.

MAIN IDEA

Evolution unites all fields of biology.

Despite the advances talked about in this section, scientists are still actively studying evolution through natural selection. The theory of natural selection combined with genetics is sometimes called the modern synthesis of evolutionary theory. The 21st century is an exciting time to study evolutionary biology. New tools are providing more data than ever before. When you consider the number of proteins in a single organism, the amount of data that can be gathered through molecular evidence alone is overwhelming. New discoveries are limited only by the time and resources of scientists.

FIGURE 10.17 Baleen whales, such as this humpback whale, have evolved a highly specialized adaptation for catching microscopic food. Molecular techniques have allowed scientists to discover the whale's relationship with hoofed animals.

Scientists from many fields of science are shedding new light on the mechanisms and patterns of evolution. In some cases, modern tools add to what has been discovered through fossil evidence. For example, you have read that fossil evidence suggests that early ancestors of whales were hoofed land mammals. As shown in **FIGURE 10.16**, comparisons of milk protein genes confirm this relationship and even provide evidence that the hippopotamus is the closest living land animal related to whales.

The field of evolutionary biology is growing fast. The basic principles of evolution are used in fields such as medicine, geology, geography, chemistry, and ecology. For instance, the idea of common descent helps biologists understand where new diseases come from, as well as how to best manage endangered species. As much as we know about life on Earth, there is so much more waiting to be discovered. As the great geneticist Theodosius Dobzhansky (1900–1975) once noted, "Nothing in biology makes sense except in the light of evolution."

Infer How can the idea of a common ancestor help us understand new diseases?

10.5 ASSESSMENT

ONLINE QUIZ ClassZone.com

REVIEWING ▶ MAIN IDEAS

1. How has our knowledge of the fossil record changed since Darwin proposed his theory of natural selection?

2. How has genetics, combined with **paleontology,** added to our understanding of evolution?

3. What are some of the fields of science to which evolutionary biology contributes?

CRITICAL THINKING

4. **Apply** Describe how similar protein comparisons of cells in two species can suggest a close evolutionary relationship.

5. **Synthesize** You have discovered the fossil remains of three organisms. One is mammalian, one is reptilian, and the third has both mammalian and reptilian features. What techniques could you apply to determine the relationship between these organisms?

Connecting CONCEPTS

6. **Genetics** Researchers have found that a gene controlling reproduction is linked to the gene for the number of digits an organism has. How does this help explain why many vertebrates have five digits per limb, despite the fact that there is no fitness benefit in having five rather than six or four?

Use these inquiry-based labs and online activities to deepen your understanding of evolution.

INVESTIGATION

Using Patterns to Make Predictions

Scientists who study evolution and other processes in biology do not always have a complete set of information. They often form hypotheses and make predictions based on a limited number of observations and measurable data. In this lab, you will make your own prediction about an unknown using a set of observations.

MATERIALS
cube for each group

SKILLS Predicting, Inferring, Analyzing, Drawing Conclusions

PROBLEM How do predictions change with new observations?

PROCEDURE

1. Observe the large cube your teacher has set out in the center of the room. Note the arrangement of the numbers and the colors of the sides.

2. Write your observations about the cube in your notebook.

3. Record what you predict will be found on the bottom section of the cube.

4. Split into groups of three or four students and get a different cube from your teacher. Do not look at the bottom side of the cube.

5. As a group, look for patterns on the cube. Observe the names and the numbers on the cube. If you need help determining the patterns, obtain a hint card from your teacher. Record any patterns you observe in your notebook.

6. Use the patterns that you have observed to predict the following information on the bottom section of the cube: the gender of the name, the number on the upper right corner, and the number on the bottom left corner. Use all three of these predictions as clues to predict the name on the bottom of the cube.

7. Write your group's prediction on a piece of paper and hand it to your teacher.

ANALYZE AND CONCLUDE

1. **Analyze** What patterns did you observe on each cube?

2. **Predict** Describe what you think is on the bottom of the first cube. Describe what you think is on the bottom of the second cube.

3. **Infer** How did you determine the name on the bottom of the second cube?

4. **Synthesize** After completing this exercise, what do you now know about the way scientists make their hypotheses?

EXTEND YOUR INVESTIGATION

In your group, create a cube with sides that follow patterns. Trade cubes with another group and repeat steps 5 through 7.

Adaptations in Beaks

Differences in tools can affect the feeding efficiency, and therefore the survival, of a species. Similarly, beak variations in birds can influence their survival.

SKILL Inferring

MATERIALS

- aluminum pie plate
- petri dishes
- sunflower seeds
- forceps
- clothespins
- tongs
- chopsticks
- stopwatch

PROBLEM How do adaptations affect natural selection?

PROCEDURE

1. Gather a pan of seeds, four petri dishes, and four different tools, or "beaks."
2. Choose one member of the group to be the recorder and timer. The other members will be the "birds."
3. Create a data table with space to record three trials of each tool and an average of all of the trials.
4. Run three timed trials of 30 seconds each for each tool. Pick up as many seeds as you can during the 30 seconds and place them in a petri dish. At the end of each trial, count the number of seeds "eaten."
5. After the third trial, calculate the average for the "beak," and record the average in your data table.

ANALYZE AND CONCLUDE

1. **Conclude** Overall, which "beak" or "beaks" were most successful?
2. **Infer** Describe the beak of a bird that could have evolved to successfully eat these seeds. Which beak would not be suited to these particular seeds? Draw a rough sketch of each beak type.
3. **Apply** Use the terms *beak, seeds, natural selection, adaptation,* and *success* to describe what happened in the lab.

CLASSZONE.COM

ANIMATED BIOLOGY
Natural Selection
Watch a population evolve—or not. Discover how populations can evolve through natural selection, and how each principle is important to the entire mechanism.

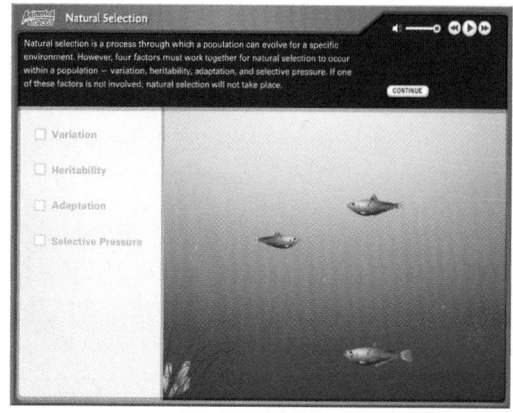

WEBQUEST

Are there living descendants of *Tyrannosaurus rex,* one of the most ferocious dinosaurs? Complete this WebQuest to find out. Explore the fossil evidence of a lineage extending from one group of dinosaurs, and determine which animals can call the *T. rex* their ancestor.

DATA ANALYSIS ONLINE
Bill depth in Darwin's finches is selected for mainly by the size and hardness of available seeds, but other factors can also affect bill depth. Graph and compare how bill depth in a species differs on one island with more competition and another island with less.

10.1 Early Ideas About Evolution

There were theories of biological and geologic change before Darwin. Early biologists suggested that different species might have shared ancestors, and geologists observed that new species appeared in the fossil record. Charles Lyell proposed the theory of uniformitarianism to explain how present observations explain past events.

10.2 Darwin's Observations

Darwin's voyage provided insights into evolution. Darwin observed variation between island species on his voyage, such as with the Galápagos tortoises. He noticed that species have adaptations that allow them to better survive in their environments. He also observed fossil evidence of species changing over time.

10.3 Theory of Natural Selection

Darwin proposed natural selection as a mechanism for evolution. Natural selection is a mechanism by which individuals that have inherited beneficial adaptations produce more offspring on average than do other individuals. Natural selection is based upon four principles: overproduction, variation, adaptation, and descent with modification.

10.4 Evidence of Evolution

Evidence of common ancestry among species comes from many sources. Fossil evidence is a record of change in a species over time. The study of biogeography showed that species could adapt to different environments. Two species that exhibit similar traits during development likely have a common ancestor. Vestigial and homologous structures also point to a shared ancestry.

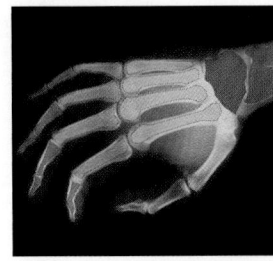 

10.5 Evolutionary Biology Today

New technology is furthering our understanding of evolution. Modern techniques, such as DNA sequence analysis and molecular fingerprinting, continue to provide new information about how evolution occurs. Evolution is a unifying theme of all the fields of biology today.

Synthesize Your Notes

Main Idea Web Use a main idea web to summarize the four principles of natural selection.

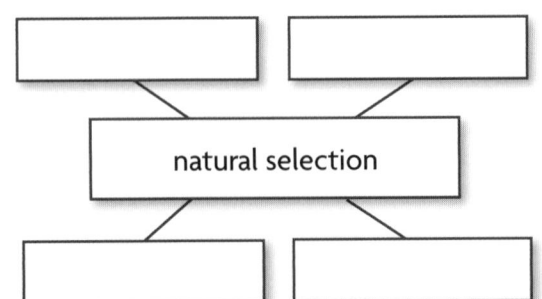

Concept Map Use a concept map like the one below to summarize what you know about evolutionary evidence.

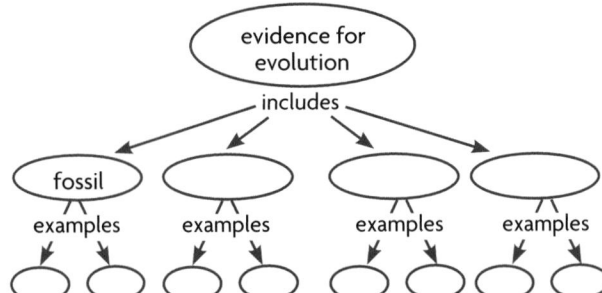

Chapter Assessment

Reviewing Vocabulary

Vocabulary Connections

The vocabulary terms in this chapter are related to each other in various ways. For each group of words below, write a sentence or two to clearly explain how the terms are connected. For example, for the terms *variation* and *natural selection,* you could write "Natural selection depends on heritable variations."

1. catastrophism, gradualism

2. population, variation

3. adaptation, evolution

4. vestigial structure, analogous structure

5. fossil, paleontology

Greek and Latin Word Origins

6. The term *homologous* comes from the Greek word *homos,* which means "the same." Explain how this meaning relates to *homologous structures.*

7. The term *vestigial* come from the Latin word *vestigium,* which means "track or footprint." Explain how this meaning relates to *vestigial structures.*

Reviewing MAIN IDEAS

8. Describe one idea about evolution that was proposed before Darwin published his theory of natural selection.

9. Briefly explain how the geologist Charles Lyell influenced Darwin's ideas about how evolution works.

10. What insights did Darwin gain from observing island organisms such as the Galápagos tortoises and finches?

11. On his voyage, Darwin observed fossils of extinct organisms that resembled living organisms. He also found shells of marine organisms high up in the mountains. How did these observations provide evidence that Earth is very old?

12. Thomas Malthus was an economist who proposed that resources such as food, water, and shelter are natural limits to human population growth. Explain how Darwin extended this idea in his theory of natural selection.

13. Why is heritability important for both natural and artificial selection?

14. Natural selection is based on four main principles: variation, overproduction, adaptation, and descent with modification. Briefly explain how each of these principles is necessary for natural selection to occur.

15. Explain what is meant by the sentence "Natural selection can act only on existing traits."

16. Evidence of evolution comes from diverse sources, such as fossils, geography, embryology, and anatomy. Briefly describe one example of evidence for evolution from each of these sources.

17. Give an example of a vestigial structure and explain how vestigial structures are significant to evolution.

18. Paleontology is the study of fossils or extinct organisms. Explain how this field is important to evolutionary biology.

19. How are genes and proteins similar to homologous structures when determining evolutionary relationships among species?

20. Explain what the following quote by Theodosius Dobzhansky means: "Nothing in biology makes sense except in the light of evolution."

Critical Thinking

21. Compare Jean-Baptiste Lamarck hypothesized that changes in an environment led to an organism's greater or lesser use of a body part. Although his hypothesis was wrong, what ideas related to evolution did Lamarck and Charles Darwin share?

22. Apply Both birds and crocodiles build nests, care for their young, and "sing" to defend territory and attract mates. They inherited these behaviors from a common ancestor. Are these homologous or analogous behaviors? Explain.

23. Analyze The turkey vulture and the California condor both feed upon dead animals, known as carrion. Neither species of bird has feathers on its head. Explain how natural selection may have played a role in the featherless heads of these carrion eaters.

24. Synthesize The Labrador retriever, a breed of dog, has been artificially selected for certain traits. However, these dogs are also prone to having weak hips. Use concepts from the chapter and your knowledge of genetics to explain how this situation may have arisen.

Interpreting Visuals

Use the following diagram, which shows the evolution of the wild mustard plant, to answer the next three questions.

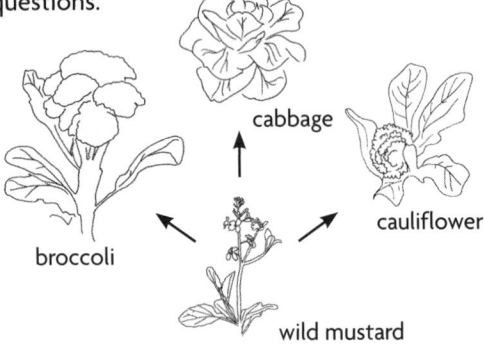

25. Infer Traits of the wild mustard plant have been emphasized by artificial selection to produce different vegetables. In some varieties, the flower heads were emphasized; in other vegetables, it is the leaves or the stems that are to be eaten. Which traits were emphasized to produce cauliflower? cabbage?

26. Apply Describe a procedure humans may have used to produce broccoli, which has small flowers and thick stems.

27. Predict What would a protein comparison of broccoli, cabbage, and cauliflower confirm about their relationships to each other?

Analyzing Data

One hundred million seabirds use the island of Gaugh, in the South Atlantic Ocean, as a critical nesting ground. Non-native carnivorous mice eat the helpless seabird chicks at a rate of about 1 million per year. Prior to the arrival of the mice, no natural predators existed on the island, so the birds did not evolve any defense mechanisms. Scientists estimate the current population of the mice at 700,000. The graph below displays a projection of seabird casualties and changes in the size of the mouse population.

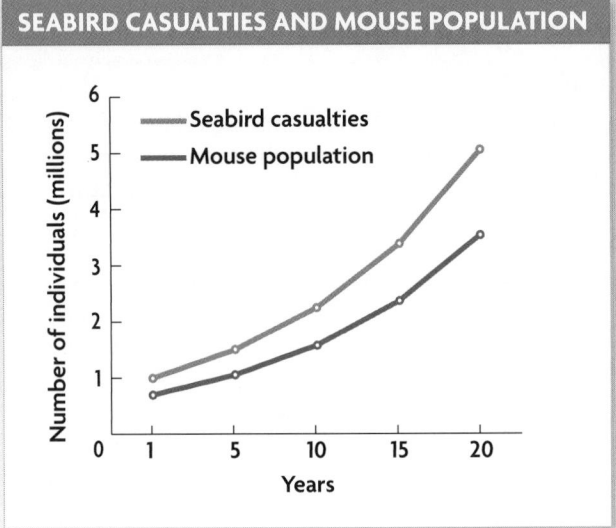

28. Interpret What does the graph show about seabird casualties and the mouse population over a 20-year period?

29. Predict Imagine some seabirds began defending their nests from the mice, and that this behavior is heritable. What changes might such a graph show over the next 20 years? Explain.

Connecting CONCEPTS

30. Write a Scenario Imagine a way in which seabirds could adapt to the mouse population and avoid predation upon their chicks. Then consider how, after many generations, the mouse population could counter this defense and again limit the seabird population. What are possible adaptations that could lead to this co-evolution of mice and seabirds?

31. Synthesize Look again at the picture of the star-nosed mole. Its claws are well adapted for breaking through soil. How could natural selection have played a role in this trait becoming common among star-nosed moles?

MICHIGAN STANDARDS-BASED ASSESSMENT

☑ *Test Practice*
For more test practice,
go to ClassZone.com.

1. **The similarity in forelimb structure of humans, bats, and moles is evidence that they** **B2.4d**

   A share a common ancestor.

   B are members of the same genus.

   C use their forelimbs in similar ways.

   D evolved from each other.

2. **The theory of evolution provides a scientific explanation for which of the following?** **B5.1f**

   A the fossil record

   B a stable climate

   C geologic change

   D global warming

3. **Darwin based his ideas about natural selection on various observations, including variations in island species, fossils, and geologic evidence. Since that time, many other scientists have carried out comparative studies in anatomy, embryology, and DNA sequencing. The work of these other scientists has supported and broadened Darwin's ideas. This scenario is an example of** **B1.2i**

   A how different fields of science often yield conflicting information.

   B how scientific theories are developed and modified in light of new information.

   C how the work of many scientists is frequently redundant.

   D how additional information can be interpreted to fit existing theories.

4. **An herbicide killed 99% of a weed population. Which of the following is the *best* biological explanation for why some weeds were able to survive?** **B5.1e**

   A Some individuals were able to evolve before the spraying.

   B Genetic variation in the population allowed some weeds to survive.

   C The spray caused some individuals to mutate, and they were able to survive and reproduce.

   D Each individual occupied a different ecological niche and so some were unaffected.

5. **In a population, natural selection acts on** **B5.1A**

   A phenotypic variation.

   B genotypic variation.

   C recessive alleles.

   D dominant alleles.

6.

   Which of the following is the best explanation for the presence of light-colored lizards in the White Sands region of New Mexico, when darker lizards live in the surrounding areas? **B5.1e**

   A Light-colored lizards are more likely to survive and reproduce in the White Sands region.

   B Light-colored lizards are replacing all of the darker lizards, regardless of the environment.

   C Mutations in the White Sands region resulted in more lizards having a lighter color.

   D Light-colored lizards prefer the White Sands environment, and darker lizards dislike it.

CHAPTER

11 The Evolution of Populations

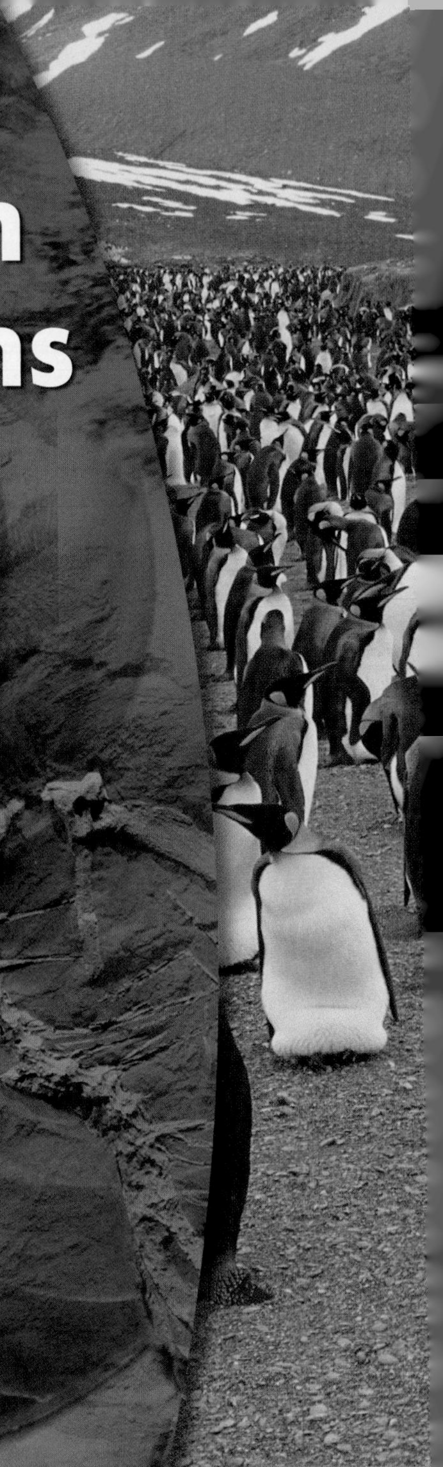

KEY CONCEPTS

11.1 Genetic Variation Within Populations
A population shares a common gene pool.

11.2 Natural Selection in Populations
Populations, not individuals, evolve.

11.3 Other Mechanisms of Evolution
Natural selection is not the only mechanism through which populations evolve.

11.4 Hardy-Weinberg Equilibrium
Hardy-Weinberg equilibrium provides a framework for understanding how populations evolve.

11.5 Speciation Through Isolation
New species can arise when populations are isolated.

11.6 Patterns in Evolution
Evolution occurs in patterns.

Online BIOLOGY CLASSZONE.COM

Animated BIOLOGY
View animated chapter concepts.
- Mechanisms of Evolution
- Evolutionary Arms Race
- Founder Effect

BIOZINE
Keep current with biology news.
- News feeds
- Polls
- Bio Bytes

RESOURCE CENTER
Get more information on
- Selective Pressures
- Mechanisms of Evolution
- Hardy-Weinberg Equilibrium
- Coevolution

How does a population of penguins evolve?

Every year, king penguins return to breed in the same colony in which they were born. These colonies help penguins to guard, protect, and defend their young. By ensuring the success of their young, penguins pass on their genes to future generations. Variation in these genes is the basis for the evolution of populations.

Connecting **CONCEPTS**

Homeostasis King penguins breed in harsh, cold conditions on sub-Antarctic islands. They have special adaptations that allow them to maintain a stable body temperature. One of the most difficult challenges for a penguin during this time is keeping the newly laid egg warm by balancing it on his feet. The egg is kept insulated by a thick roll of skin and feathers called a brood pouch.

11.1 Genetic Variation Within Populations

KEY CONCEPT A population shares a common gene pool.

MAIN IDEAS
- Genetic variation in a population increases the chance that some individuals will survive.
- Genetic variation comes from several sources.

VOCABULARY
gene pool, p. 328
allele frequency, p. 328

Review
phenotype, gene, allele, meiosis, gamete

MICHIGAN STANDARDS

B4.4a Describe how inserting, deleting, or substituting DNA segments can alter a gene. Recognize that an altered gene may be passed on to every cell that develops from it and that the resulting features may help, harm, or have little or no effect on the offspring's success in its environment.

B5.1g Illustrate how genetic variation is preserved or eliminated from a population through natural selection (evolution) resulting in biodiversity.

TAKING NOTES

Use mind maps to show relationships among related terms and concepts.

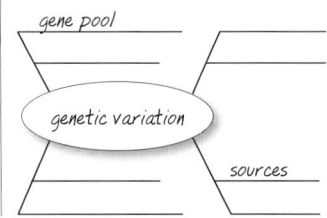

Connect You may think that if you've seen one penguin, you've seen them all. However, penguins can differ in body size, feather patterns, and many other traits. Just like humans, penguins are genetically different from one another. What is the nature of genetic variation in populations? And how is this variation measured by biologists?

MAIN IDEA

Genetic variation in a population increases the chance that some individuals will survive.

Body size and feather patterns in penguins are each examples of phenotypes. A phenotype is a trait produced by one or more genes. In a population, there may be a wide range of phenotypes. For example, some penguins may be short and rounded. Others could be tall and slim.

Natural selection acts on different phenotypes in a population. However, in order to have different phenotypes, a population must have genetic variation. A population with a lot of genetic variation likely has a wide range of phenotypes. The greater the variation in phenotypes, the more likely it is that some individuals can survive in a changing environment. For example, if an unusually cold winter occurs, short, rounded penguins might be able to stay warm more easily. But if there is a shortage of food, tall, slim penguins might be better divers, allowing them to catch more fish.

Genetic variation is stored in a population's **gene pool**—the combined alleles of all of the individuals in a population. Different combinations of alleles in a gene pool can be formed when organisms mate and have offspring. Each allele exists at a certain rate, or frequency. An **allele frequency** is a measure of how common a certain allele is in the population. As shown in **FIGURE 11.1,** you can calculate allele frequencies. First count the number of times an allele occurs in a gene pool. Then divide by the total number of alleles for that gene in the gene pool.

Analyze What is the relationship between allele frequencies and a gene pool?

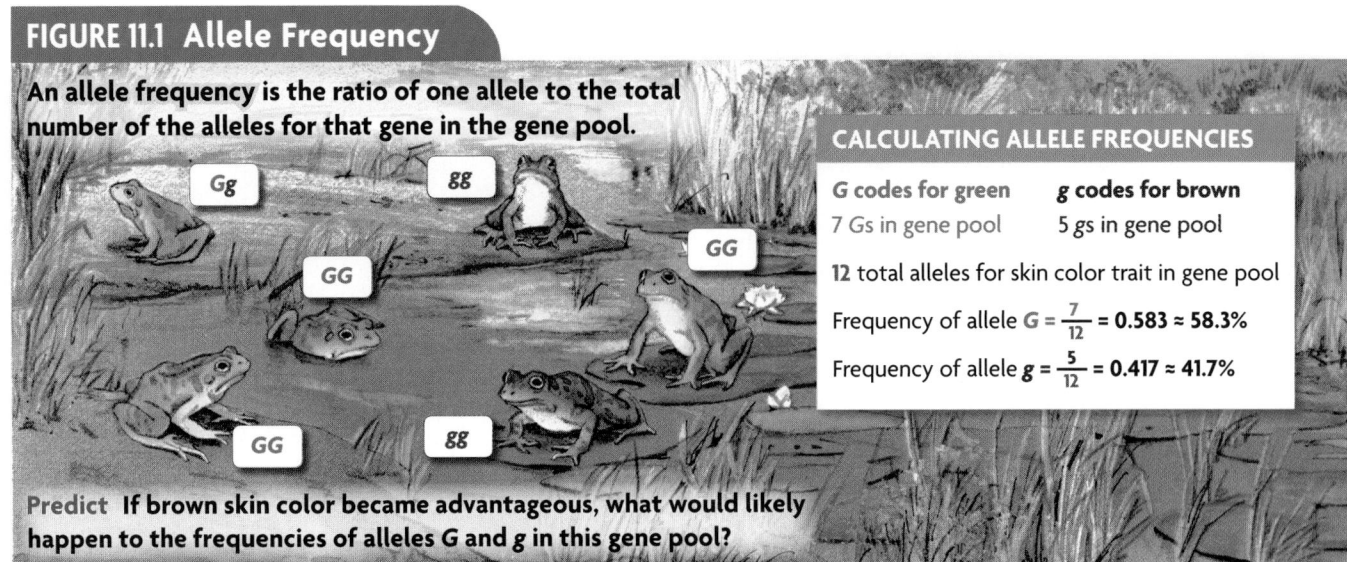

FIGURE 11.1 Allele Frequency

An allele frequency is the ratio of one allele to the total number of the alleles for that gene in the gene pool.

CALCULATING ALLELE FREQUENCIES

G codes for green	g codes for brown
7 Gs in gene pool	5 gs in gene pool

12 total alleles for skin color trait in gene pool

Frequency of allele $G = \frac{7}{12} = 0.583 \approx 58.3\%$

Frequency of allele $g = \frac{5}{12} = 0.417 \approx 41.7\%$

Predict If brown skin color became advantageous, what would likely happen to the frequencies of alleles *G* and *g* in this gene pool?

▶ MAIN IDEA

Genetic variation comes from several sources.

Genetic variation comes from two main sources: mutation and recombination.

- **Mutation** A mutation is a random change in the DNA of a gene. This change can form a new allele. Mutations in reproductive cells can be passed on to offspring. This increases the genetic variation in the gene pool. Because there are many genes in each individual and many individuals in a population, new mutations form frequently in gene pools.

- **Recombination** New allele combinations form in offspring through a process called recombination. Most recombination occurs during meiosis—the type of cell division needed for sexual reproduction. When gametes are made, each parent's alleles are arranged in new ways. This shuffling of alleles results in many different genetic combinations.

Some biologists are studying hybridization as another source of genetic variation. Hybridization is the crossing of two different species that share common genes. Research suggests that this process occurs within many groups of animals, including birds and mammals, when similar species live in the same area and individuals cannot easily find mates of their own species.

Infer Why aren't mutations in nonreproductive cells sources of genetic variation?

Connecting CONCEPTS

Genetics Recall from **Chapter 8** that mutations on noncoding regions of DNA do not affect phenotypes. Only mutations on coding regions of DNA can affect an organism's phenotype.

11.1 / ASSESSMENT

ONLINE QUIZ
ClassZone.com

REVIEWING ▶ MAIN IDEAS

1. Why does genetic variation increase the chance that some individuals in a population will survive?

2. Describe two main sources of genetic variation.

CRITICAL THINKING

3. **Analyze** In what way is a **gene pool** representative of a population?

4. **Apply** If a certain trait's **allele frequency** is 100 percent, describe the genetic variation for that trait in the population.

Connecting CONCEPTS

5. **Genetics** How does crossing over during meiosis provide a source of genetic variation? Draw a diagram to show this process.

11.2 Natural Selection in Populations

KEY CONCEPT Populations, not individuals, evolve.

> **MAIN IDEAS**
> - Natural selection acts on distributions of traits.
> - Natural selection can change the distribution of a trait in one of three ways.

VOCABULARY

normal distribution, p. 330
microevolution, p. 331
directional selection, p. 331
stabilizing selection, p. 332
disruptive selection, p. 333

Review
natural selection

MICHIGAN STANDARDS

B5.3A Explain how natural selection acts on individuals, but it is populations that evolve. Relate genetic mutations and genetic variety produced by sexual reproduction to diversity within a given population.

Connecting CONCEPTS

Genetics As you learned in **Chapter 7**, single-gene traits are expressed in either one distinct form or another. However, the range of phenotypes common for most traits is the result of polygenic traits, which are controlled by multiple genes.

Connect How do you describe a person's appearance? Perhaps you use height, hair color, and eye color. These traits are often used in descriptions because these traits vary widely among humans. In this section you will learn about how natural selection can act upon such variation.

> **MAIN IDEA**
> ## Natural selection acts on distributions of traits.

Any time you stand in a large crowd of people, you are likely to observe a wide range of heights. Imagine organizing this crowd across a football field according to each individual's height, with very short people at one end, people of average height in the middle, and very tall people at the other end. You would soon notice a pattern in the distribution for the human height trait. Relatively few people would be at each extreme height, very short or very tall. A majority of people would be in the middle due to their medium height.

This type of distribution, in which the frequency is highest near the mean value and decreases toward each extreme end of the range, is called a **normal distribution.** When these frequency values are graphed, the result is a bell-shaped curve like the one you see in **FIGURE 11.2.**

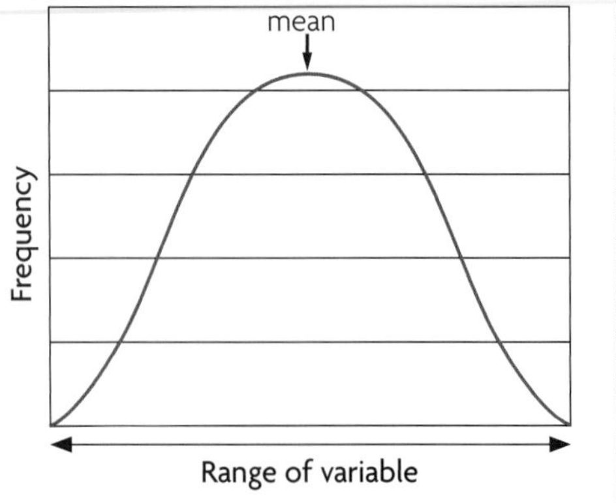

For some traits, all phenotypes provide an equal chance of survival. The distribution for these traits generally shows a normal distribution. Phenotypes near the middle of the range tend to be most common, while the extremes are less common. However, environmental conditions can change and a certain phenotype may become an advantage. Nature favors individuals with this phenotype. These individuals are able to survive and reproduce at higher rates than individuals with less favorable phenotypes. Therefore, alleles associated with favorable phenotypes increase in frequency.

Synthesize What other types of data might follow a normal distribution?

FIGURE 11.2 NORMAL DISTRIBUTION

mean

Frequency

Range of variable

Natural selection can change the distribution of a trait in one of three ways.

Microevolution is the observable change in the allele frequencies of a population over time. Microevolution occurs on a small scale—within a single population. One process that can lead to microevolution is natural selection. Natural selection can change the distribution of a trait along one of three paths: directional, stabilizing, or disruptive selection. Such changes can have major effects on how a population looks and behaves.

Directional Selection

A type of selection that favors phenotypes at one extreme of a trait's range is called **directional selection.** Directional selection causes a shift in a population's phenotypic distribution. An extreme phenotype that was once rare in a population becomes more common. As shown in **FIGURE 11.3,** during directional selection, the mean value of a trait shifts in the direction of the more advantageous phenotype.

The rise of drug-resistant bacteria provides a classic example of this type of selection. Before antibiotics were developed in the 1940s, a trait for varying levels of drug resistance existed among bacteria. At the time, there was no advantage to having drug resistance. But once antibiotics came into use, the resistant bacteria had a great advantage.

The early success of antibiotics in controlling infectious diseases led to overuse of these drugs. This overuse favored even more resistant phenotypes. New drugs were then developed to fight the resistant bacteria. This resulted in the evolution of "superbugs" that are highly resistant to many drugs. Today, over 200 types of bacteria show some degree of antibiotic resistance.

Connecting **CONCEPTS**

Bacteria Although many bacteria are helpful to other organisms, some do cause disease. You will learn more about how bacteria can evolve and become resistant to antibiotics in **Chapter 18.**

FIGURE 11.3 Directional Selection

Directional selection occurs when one extreme phenotype is favored by natural selection.

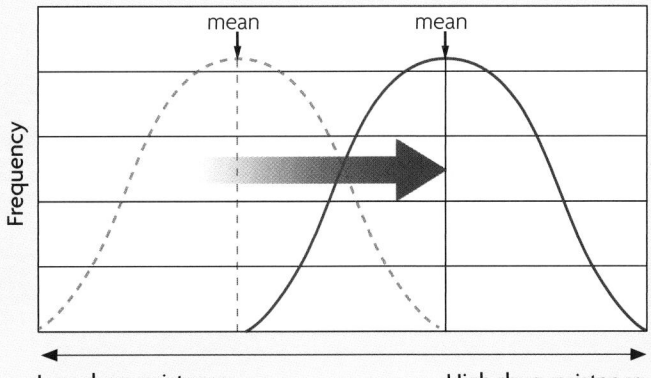

- ➡ Antibiotic drugs put pressure on bacteria populations.
- ---- Normal distribution
- —— Distribution after directional selection

Frequency

Low drug resistance — High drug resistance

Today, scientists continue to research new drugs developed to treat infection-causing bacteria such as *Enterococcus faecalis,* which is resistant to many antibiotics.

FIGURE 11.4 The gall fly and the goldenrod have a parasitic relationship. The fly benefits by receiving shelter and food during its larval stage, while the goldenrod is harmed, growing more slowly than a gall-free goldenrod.

Stabilizing Selection

The gall fly and its predators provide an excellent example of stabilizing selection. During **stabilizing selection,** the intermediate phenotype is favored and becomes more common in the population. That is, the distribution becomes stable at the intermediate phenotype rather than shifting toward one of the extremes. In the case of gall flies, something in nature selects against phenotypes at both extremes of the trait's range.

Gall flies lay their eggs in developing shoots of the tall goldenrod. The fly larvae produce a chemical that causes the plant tissue to swell around them. **FIGURE 11.4** shows the resulting mass of plant tissue, called a gall. The gall serves as a home where the larvae can develop. There is a range of phenotypes for body size in gall-fly larvae. Each body size causes a certain size gall to form, and each of the two main predators of gall flies specializes on a specific gall size.

- Downy woodpeckers attack larger galls and feed on the larvae inside.
- The parasitic wasp lays its own eggs inside small galls. After the wasp larvae emerge from the eggs, they eat the gall-fly larvae.

In this situation, selective pressure from predators works against fly phenotypes that produce galls at both extremes, large and small. As a result, flies that produce middle-sized galls become more common. As you can see in **FIGURE 11.5,** over time, stabilizing selection results in a higher frequency of flies that produce middle-sized galls.

Stabilizing selection increases the number of individuals with intermediate phenotypes. Notice, however, that selection against both extremes decreases the genetic diversity of the gall fly population. Flies that produce small and large galls become less common. In some populations, these extreme phenotypes may be lost altogether.

FIGURE 11.5 Stabilizing Selection

Stabilizing selection occurs when intermediate phenotypes are favored by natural selection.

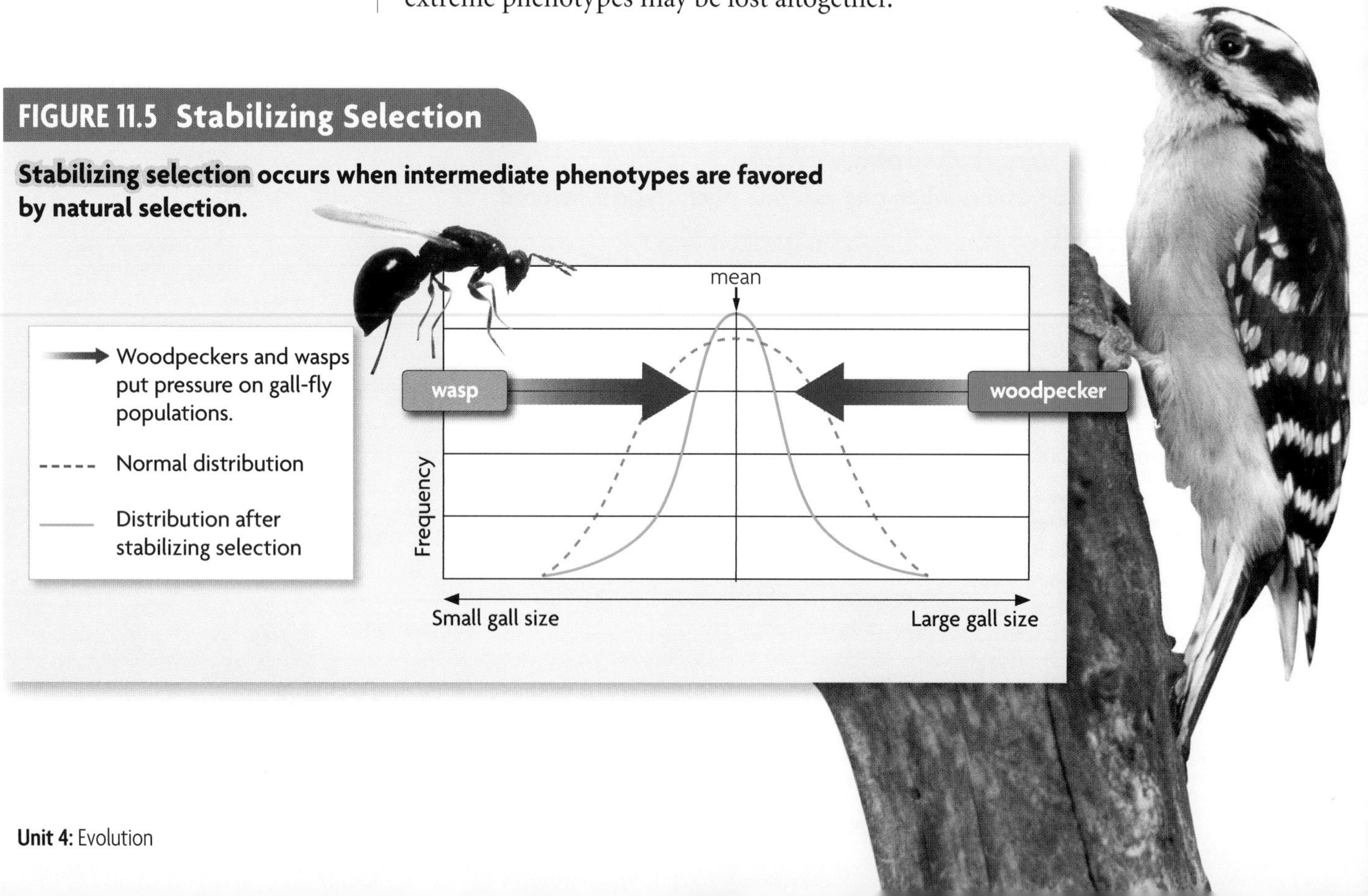

→ Woodpeckers and wasps put pressure on gall-fly populations.

---- Normal distribution

—— Distribution after stabilizing selection

mean

wasp

woodpecker

Frequency

Small gall size   Large gall size

Disruptive Selection

Disruptive selection occurs when both extreme phenotypes are favored, while individuals with intermediate phenotypes are selected against by something in nature. As you can see in **FIGURE 11.6,** the middle of the distribution is disrupted. One example of this type of selection involves feather color in male lazuli buntings, a bird species native to North America.

Young male lazuli buntings vary widely in the brightness of their feathers, ranging from dull brown to bright blue. Dominant adult males are those with the brightest blue feathers on their heads and backs. These birds have their pick of the best territories. They also are most successful at attracting females. However, for young buntings, the brightest blue and dullest brown males are more likely to win mates than males with bluish brown feathers are.

Research suggests that dominant adult males are aggressive toward young buntings that they see as a threat, including bright blue and bluish brown males. The dullest brown birds can therefore win a mate because the adult males leave them alone. Meanwhile, the bright blue birds attract mates simply because of their color.

Both extreme phenotypes are favored in this situation, while intermediate forms are selected against. The bluish brown males are not as well adapted to compete for mates because they are too blue to be left alone by adult males, but not blue enough to win a mate based on color alone. By favoring both extreme phenotypes, disruptive selection can lead to the formation of new species.

Apply **If bluish brown coloring became advantageous for young males, what type of selection would likely occur in a lazuli bunting population?**

FIGURE 11.6 Disruptive Selection

Disruptive selection occurs when both extreme phenotypes are favored by selection.

mean

Frequency

Brown · Blue

→ Dominant adult males put pressure on young males in the bunting population.

- - - - - Normal distribution

——— Distribution after disruptive selection

Adult male lazuli bunting

11.2 ASSESSMENT

ONLINE QUIZ
ClassZone.com

REVIEWING ▶ MAIN IDEAS

1. In terms of phenotypes, describe what is meant by the phrase "distribution of traits."

2. What are the three ways in which natural selection can change a distribution of traits?

CRITICAL THINKING

3. **Predict** How might the extinction of downy woodpeckers affect the phenotypic distribution of gall flies?

4. **Predict** How might overfishing of large pink salmon select for smaller body size in subsequent generations?

Connecting CONCEPTS

5. **Genetics** For polygenic traits, a smooth curve results when the range of phenotypes is plotted against frequency. If you were to plot the frequencies of two phenotypes of a single-gene trait, you would end up with a double bar graph. Explain why.

MATERIALS

- 15 small pieces of colored paper: 5 yellow, 5 orange, 5 red (These have been premarked by your teacher.)
- extra paper of each color

PROCESS SKILLS

- **Modeling**
- **Graphing**
- **Interpreting Data**

L3.p2A Describe common relationships among organisms and provide examples of producer/consumer, predator/prey, or parasite/host relationship. (prerequisite)

B5.3A Explain how natural selection acts on individuals, but it is populations that evolve. Relate genetic mutations and genetic variety produced by sexual reproduction to diversity within a given population.

Natural Selection in African Swallowtails

African swallowtails are nonpoisonous butterflies that mimic the colors of poisonous butterflies. Predators learn which butterflies are poisonous and avoid eating butterflies resembling those that made them sick. In this lab, you will use colored paper to model natural selection in African swallowtails.

PROBLEM How can natural selection change the distribution of a trait?

PROCEDURE

1. Divide your group into birds and butterflies. Birds, close your eyes. Butterflies, place the 15 pieces of paper randomly on the table with the markings face up.

2. The pieces of paper with an *X* written on them represent poisonous butterflies; those with *ST* represent swallowtails, which are not poisonous. Butterflies, record the number of swallowtails of each color in your notebook, using a table similar to Table 1.

TABLE 1. NUMBER OF SWALLOWTAILS (MIMICS) OF EACH COLOR			
	Yellow	Orange	Red
Original population			
Trial 1			
Trial 2			
Trial 3			

3. Butterflies, flip the pieces of paper over and tell the birds to open their eyes.

4. Birds, draw up to 6 pieces of paper (total) from the table to represent predation. If you "ate" any poisonous butterflies, do not draw another piece of paper that color for the rest of the activity. (Note: You may not always be able to draw 6.)

5. Birds, close your eyes. Butterflies, repopulate by duplicating every piece of paper that remains. Write *X* and *ST* on the appropriate new pieces of paper.

6. Butterflies, record the number of swallowtails on the table.

7. Repeat steps 3–6 two more times to complete three trials.

ANALYZE AND CONCLUDE

1. **Graph Data** Draw a line graph with three lines, one for each color. Put the trial number on the x-axis (including the original population) and the number of swallowtails on the y-axis. What trends can you identify in the data?

2. **Graph Data** Draw two bar graphs: one for the original population and one for the last trial. Set up your graphs with color on the x-axis (yellow, orange, and red) and number of swallowtails on the y-axis. How do these graphs differ?

3. **Analyze** What type of distribution best describes the original population?

4. **Apply** What type of selection (directional, stabilizing, or disruptive) is demonstrated in this activity? What caused this type of selection to occur?

5. **Predict** Suppose the poisonous butterflies were all orange. What type of selection would have likely occurred in the swallowtail population?

11.3 Other Mechanisms of Evolution

KEY CONCEPT Natural selection is not the only mechanism through which populations evolve.

▶ MAIN IDEAS

- Gene flow is the movement of alleles between populations.
- Genetic drift is a change in allele frequencies due to chance.
- Sexual selection occurs when certain traits increase mating success.

VOCABULARY

gene flow, p. 335
genetic drift, p. 336
bottleneck effect, p. 336
founder effect, p. 336
sexual selection, p. 338

Review
homozygous, heterozygous

MICHIGAN STANDARDS

B5.2c Trace the relationship between environmental changes and changes in the gene pool, such as genetic drift and isolation of subpopulations.

Connect Have you ever wondered why many male birds, such as cardinals, are brightly colored while females of the same species are dull brown? Such bright coloring may not make sense in terms of natural selection, since the male birds are more likely to be seen by predators. However, natural selection is not the whole story. There are other factors that can lead to the evolution of populations.

▶ MAIN IDEA
Gene flow is the movement of alleles between populations.

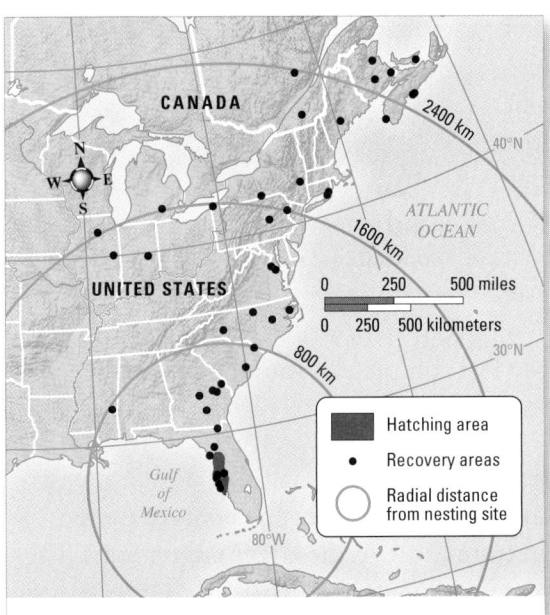

FIGURE 11.7 This map shows the locations where young banded eagles were found during the first summer after hatching.

Bird-banding studies have shown that certain birds leave their nesting areas once they are able to fly. As shown in **FIGURE 11.7**, bald eagles banded as nestlings have been tracked during the same summer more than 2500 kilometers away. These eagles have possibly joined a new population.

When an organism joins a new population and reproduces, its alleles become part of that population's gene pool. At the same time, these alleles are removed from the gene pool of its former population. The movement of alleles from one population to another is called **gene flow.** For many animals, gene flow occurs when individuals move between populations. Gene flow can occur in fungi and plant populations when spores or seeds are spread to new areas.

Gene flow increases the genetic variation of the receiving population. Gene flow between neighboring populations keeps their gene pools similar. However, the less gene flow that occurs between two populations, the more genetically different the two populations can become. A lack of gene flow also increases the chance that the two populations will evolve into different species.

Predict How does gene flow affect neighboring populations?

▶ MAIN IDEA

Genetic drift is a change in allele frequencies due to chance.

Imagine a patch of 100 flowers growing in a field. Fifty are white and fifty are purple. If you randomly pick flowers from this patch to create a bouquet, you would expect about half white and half purple flowers. The more flowers you randomly pick, the more likely you are to get these proportions. However, the fewer flowers you pick, the more likely you are to have a bouquet that is not representative of the patch. It might even be all one color.

A similar situation can occur in small populations. Small populations, like small sample sizes, are more likely to be affected by chance. Due to chance alone, some alleles will likely decrease in frequency and become eliminated. Other alleles will likely increase in frequency and become fixed. These changes in allele frequencies that are due to chance are called **genetic drift.** Genetic drift causes a loss of genetic diversity in a population.

Two processes commonly cause populations to become small enough for genetic drift to occur. Each of these processes results in a population with different allele frequencies than the original population.

Bottleneck Effect

The **bottleneck effect** is genetic drift that occurs after an event greatly reduces the size of a population. One example of the bottleneck effect is the overhunting of northern elephant seals during the 1800s. By the 1890s, the population was reduced to about 20 individuals. These 20 seals did not represent the genetic diversity of the original population. Since hunting has ended, the population has grown to over 100,000 individuals. However,

VISUAL VOCAB

The **bottleneck effect** describes the effect of a destructive event that leaves only a few survivors in a population.

Initial population | Bottleneck effect | Surviving population

it has very little genetic variation. Through genetic drift, certain alleles have become fixed while others have been lost completely from the gene pool.

Founder Effect

As shown in **FIGURE 11.8**, the **founder effect** is genetic drift that occurs after a small number of individuals colonize a new area. The gene pools of these populations are often very different from those of the larger populations. The founder effect can be studied in human populations such as Old Order Amish communities. These communities were founded in North America by small numbers of migrants from Europe. For example, the Amish of Lancaster County, Pennsylvania, have a high rate of Ellis–van Creveld syndrome. Although this form of dwarfism is rare in other human populations, it has become common in this Amish population through genetic drift. Geneticists have traced this syndrome back to one of the community's founding couples.

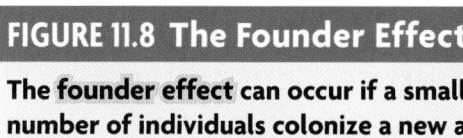

FIGURE 11.8 The Founder Effect

The founder effect can occur if a small number of individuals colonize a new area.

A bird carries a few seeds to a new location. These seeds "found" a new population.

Animated BIOLOGY
See the founder effect in action at ClassZone.com.

The gene pool for a population of flowers has genetic diversity that results in red, yellow, and blue phenotypes.

Alleles for yellow flower color increase in the new small population through genetic drift.

Effects of Genetic Drift

Genetic drift can cause several problems for populations. One problem is that the population loses genetic variation. With little genetic variation, a population is less likely to have some individuals that will be able to adapt to a changing environment. Another problem is that alleles that are lethal in homozygous individuals may be carried by heterozygous individuals, and become more common in the gene pool due to chance alone.

Apply Why is genetic drift more likely to occur in smaller populations?

QUICK LAB MODELING

Genetic Drift

Use a deck of cards to represent a population of island birds. The four suits represent different alleles for tail shape. The allele frequencies in the original population are 25% spade, 25% heart, 25% club, and 25% diamond tail shapes.

PROBLEM How does genetic drift occur?

PROCEDURE

MATERIALS
• deck of cards

1. Shuffle the cards and hold the deck face down. Turn over 40 cards to represent the alleles of 20 offspring produced by random matings in the initial population.

2. Separate the 40 cards by suit. Find the allele frequencies for the offspring by calculating the percentage of each suit.

3. Suppose a storm blows a few birds to another island. They are isolated on this island and start a new population. Reshuffle the deck and draw 10 cards to represent the alleles of five offspring produced in the smaller population.

4. Repeat step 2 to calculate the resulting allele frequencies.

ANALYZE AND CONCLUDE

1. **Analyze** Compare the original allele frequencies to those calculated in steps 2 and 4. How did they change?

2. **Analyze** Did step 1 or 3 demonstrate genetic drift?

3. **Evaluate** Does this activity demonstrate evolution? Why or why not? Does it demonstrate natural selection? Explain.

FIGURE 11.9 Male frigate birds inflate an air sac in their chest to attract females. This trait has evolved through sexual selection.

VOCABULARY

Intra is Latin for "within." Intrasexual selection occurs within one sex.

Inter is Latin for "between." Intersexual selection occurs between both sexes.

▶ **MAIN IDEA**

Sexual selection occurs when certain traits increase mating success.

Mating can have an important effect on the evolution of populations. Both sexes benefit from having offspring that survive. However, the cost of reproduction often differs for males and females.

- Males produce many sperm continuously, making the value of each sperm relatively small. They can make many investments at little cost.
- Females are much more limited in the number of offspring they can produce in each reproductive cycle. Each investment they make is more valuable, and they want a good return.

In many species, this difference in reproductive cost makes females choosy about mates. **Sexual selection** occurs when certain traits increase mating success. There are two types of sexual selection:

- Intrasexual selection involves competition among males, such as the head-butting of bighorn sheep. Whoever wins the competition wins the female.
- Intersexual selection occurs when males display certain traits that attract the female, such as peacocks fanning out their tails.

Traits that increase mating success are not always adaptive for the survival of the individual. As shown in **FIGURE 11.9**, bright red air sacs likely make male frigate birds very easy to spot by predators. How could such an exaggerated trait evolve?

Research has shown that some showy traits may be linked with genes for good health and fertility. Other traits are present in males that can offer better care for offspring or defense from predators. Therefore, females may use showy traits as signs of quality and health in males. These traits, such as the red air sacs of male frigate birds, can become very exaggerated over time through sexual selection.

Apply Male Irish elks, which are now extinct, had 12-foot-wide antlers. Describe how sexual selection could have caused such an exaggerated trait to evolve.

11.3 ASSESSMENT

ONLINE QUIZ
ClassZone.com

REVIEWING ▶ MAIN IDEAS

1. How does **gene flow** affect neighboring populations?
2. Name two processes through which **genetic drift** can occur.
3. How does **sexual selection** occur?

CRITICAL THINKING

4. **Analyze** Would a population of 10 individuals or 100 individuals be more vulnerable to genetic drift? Why?
5. **Infer** What impact can the **bottleneck effect** have on populations that have rebounded after near extinction?

Connecting CONCEPTS

6. **Genetics** Ellis–van Creveld syndrome is a recessive trait. Explain why it has become common in the Amish of Lancaster County while remaining very rare in other human populations.

Patterns in Sexual Selection

Identifying patterns in data from graphs and charts is essential for making future predictions and hypotheses.

EXAMPLE

The data in the graph below were collected during an experiment involving widowbirds in Kenya. The biologist was trying to determine the relationship between tail feather length and reproductive success in males of this species. The average number of nesting sites was used to measure reproductive success and was recorded for four groups of birds. Tail feathers were artificially shortened in one group, two groups were used as control groups, and tail feathers were artificially lengthened in the fourth group.

- Look at the bar representing the group with shortened tail feathers. Notice that this group averaged less than 0.5 nests.
- Next, notice that the bars for the two control groups show that these groups both averaged less than one nest.
- Now, look at the bar representing lengthened tail feathers. Notice that birds in this group averaged almost two nests.
- Finally, look for trends and patterns. The data show a trend that males with longer tail feathers have greater reproductive success: on average, they had more nesting sites.

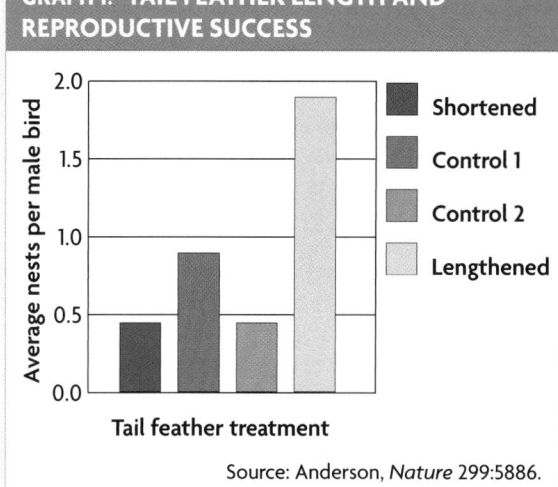

GRAPH 1. TAIL FEATHER LENGTH AND REPRODUCTIVE SUCCESS

Source: Anderson, *Nature* 299:5886.

IDENTIFY PATTERNS

The graph at the right shows sexual selection patterns in guppies. Three experiments were run to determine if female guppies prefer males with specific tail sizes. In each experiment, female guppies were given the choice of two males to mate with, each having a different tail size: large versus small, large versus medium, and medium versus small.

1. **Analyze** What tail sizes were compared in each experiment?

2. **Analyze** What is the relationship between tail size in male guppies and female preference for mates?

3. **Infer** Why might the difference in preference be larger in Experiment 1 than in Experiment 2?

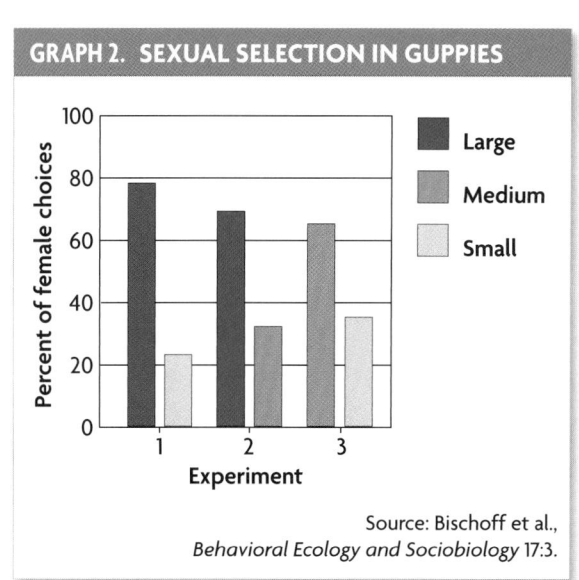

GRAPH 2. SEXUAL SELECTION IN GUPPIES

Source: Bischoff et al.,
Behavioral Ecology and Sociobiology 17:3.

Hardy-Weinberg Equilibrium

KEY CONCEPT Hardy-Weinberg equilibrium provides a framework for understanding how populations evolve.

▶ MAIN IDEAS

- Hardy-Weinberg equilibrium describes populations that are not evolving.
- The Hardy-Weinberg equation is used to predict genotype frequencies in a population.
- There are five factors that can lead to evolution.

VOCABULARY

Hardy-Weinberg equilibrium, p. 340

Review
equilibrium, dominant, recessive, homozygous, heterozygous

MICHIGAN STANDARDS

B4.1c Differentiate between dominant, recessive, codominant, polygenic, and sex-linked traits.
B5.3A Explain how natural selection acts on individuals, but it is populations that evolve. Relate genetic mutations and genetic variety produced by sexual reproduction to diversity within a given population.

Connecting CONCEPTS

Genetics The Hardy-Weinberg model and its equation are based on Mendelian genetics, which you learned about in **Chapter 6.** As you will soon see, the equation is derived from a simple Punnett square in which p is the frequency of the dominant allele and q is the frequency of the recessive allele.

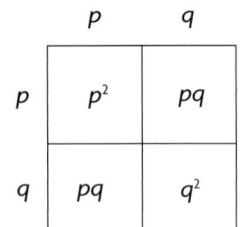

	p	q
p	p^2	pq
q	pq	q^2

Connect Many things affect how populations evolve. Natural selection may favor yellow butterflies over orange ones. But if a population of butterflies is small, genetic drift may also play a role. Studying populations in nature can be tricky. It can be hard to figure out what is causing a population to change. Therefore, biologists use models to learn more about how populations change over time.

▶ MAIN IDEA

Hardy-Weinberg equilibrium describes populations that are not evolving.

Biologists often compare their data to a model to study how a population is changing. One important model is based on the research of a British mathematician named Godfrey Hardy and a German physician named Wilhelm Weinberg. In 1908, Hardy and Weinberg showed that genotype frequencies in a population stay the same over time as long as certain conditions are met. They also showed that these frequencies can be predicted. Hardy and Weinberg identified five conditions needed for a population to stay in equilibrium. Populations that meet these conditions are not evolving. They are said to be in **Hardy-Weinberg equilibrium.**

- **Very large population** No genetic drift can occur.
- **No emigration or immigration** No gene flow can occur.
- **No mutations** No new alleles can be added to the gene pool.
- **Random mating** No sexual selection can occur.
- **No natural selection** All traits must equally aid in survival.

Real populations rarely meet all five conditions. However, Hardy-Weinberg equilibrium is still a very important concept. Biologists can compare real data to data predicted by the model. Then they can learn more about how the population is evolving. The model also gives a framework for testing the factors that can lead to evolution.

Summarize How are models used by population biologists?

▶ MAIN IDEA

The Hardy-Weinberg equation is used to predict genotype frequencies in a population.

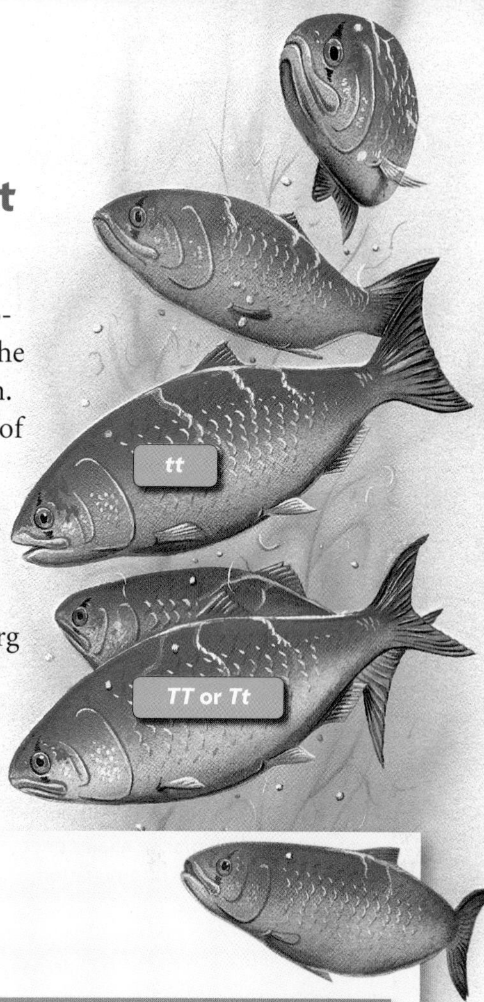

For traits in simple dominant-recessive systems, biologists can predict genotype frequencies using the Hardy-Weinberg equation. Values predicted by the equation are those that would be present if the population is in equilibrium. If p equals the frequency of the dominant allele and q equals the frequency of the recessive allele, the equation can be written as follows:

$$p^2 + 2pq + q^2 = 1$$

Population biologists compare predicted genotype frequencies with actual frequencies. If they are the same, the population is in Hardy-Weinberg equilibrium for that trait. If the genetic data do not match the equation, the population is not in equilibrium; it is evolving.

tt

TT or Tt

FIGURE 11.10 Using the Hardy-Weinberg Equation

Use the Hardy-Weinberg equation to calculate predicted genotype frequencies for this population.

In a population of 1000 fish, 640 have forked tail fins and 360 have smooth tail fins. Tail fin shape is determined by two alleles: *T* is dominant for forked and *t* is recessive for smooth.

VARIABLES

- p = **frequency of allele *T*** (dominant allele)
- q = **frequency of allele *t*** (recessive allele)
- p^2 = **frequency of fish with *TT*** (homozygous dominant genotype)
- $2pq$ = **frequency of fish with *Tt*** (heterozygous genotype)
- q^2 = **frequency of fish with *tt*** (homozygous recessive genotype)

1 Find q^2, the frequency of smooth-finned fish (recessive homozygotes).

$$q^2 = \frac{360 \text{ smooth-finned fish}}{1000 \text{ fish in population}} = 0.36$$

2 To find the predicted value of q, take the square root of q^2.

$$q = \sqrt{0.36} = 0.6$$

3 Use the equation $p + q = 1$ to find the predicted value of p. Rearrange the equation to solve for p.

$$p = 1 - q$$
$$p = 1 - 0.6 = 0.4$$

> These are the predicted allele frequencies: $p = 0.4$ and $q = 0.6$.

4 Calculate the predicted genotype frequencies from the predicted allele frequencies.

$$p^2 = 0.4^2 = 0.16 \longrightarrow \text{16\% of fish have forked fins (TT)}$$
$$2pq = 2 \times (0.4) \times (0.6) = 0.48 \longrightarrow \text{48\% of fish have forked fins (Tt)}$$
$$q^2 = 0.6^2 = 0.36 \longrightarrow \text{36\% of fish have smooth fins (tt)}$$

Analyze Through genetic analysis, scientists have found the genotype frequencies of the same fish population to be *TT* = 0.50, *Tt* = 0.14, *tt* = 0.36. What can you infer by comparing these data with the values predicted by the Hardy-Weinberg equation?

FIGURE 11.11 Factors That Can Lead to Evolution

Animated BIOLOGY
Explore the ways that populations can evolve at ClassZone.com.

There are five factors that can lead to evolution at the population level.

INITIAL POPULATION

Here are the alleles associated with body color in a hypothetical population.

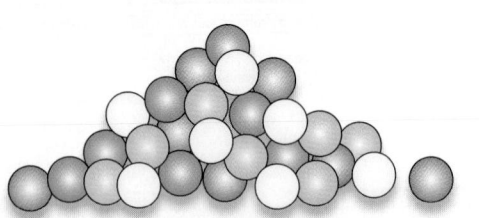

GENETIC DRIFT

After a bottleneck event, only orange and blue alleles remained in the small population. Through genetic drift, orange alleles increase in frequency.

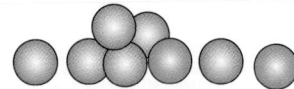

GENE FLOW

Green alleles increase in frequency because of immigration; orange alleles decrease in frequency because of emigration.

arriving

leaving

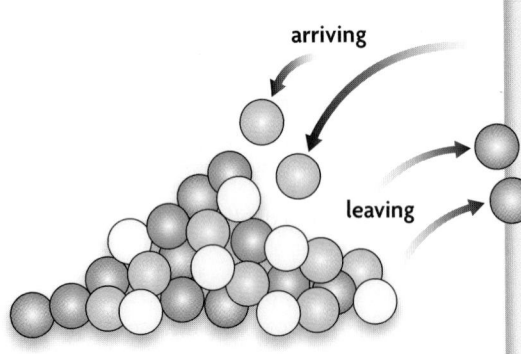

MUTATION

A new allele, associated with red body color, is formed through mutation. This could affect sexual selection if red body color improves mating success. It could affect natural selection if red body color increases the chance for survival.

new allele

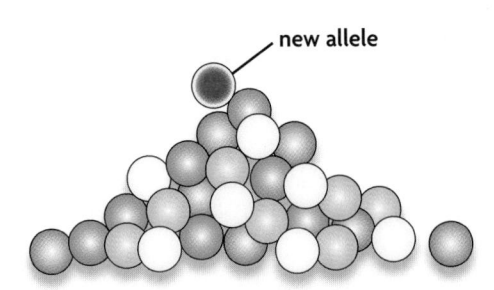

SEXUAL SELECTION

Blue alleles are associated with blue body color, which improves mating success. Blue alleles therefore increase in frequency.

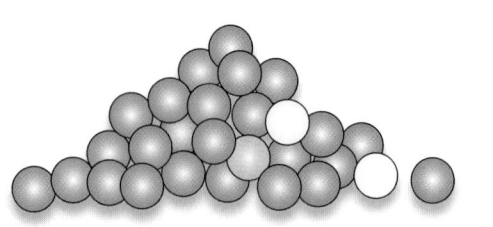

NATURAL SELECTION

White alleles are associated with white body color, which allows individuals to blend in with their environment and avoid predation. White alleles therefore increase in frequency.

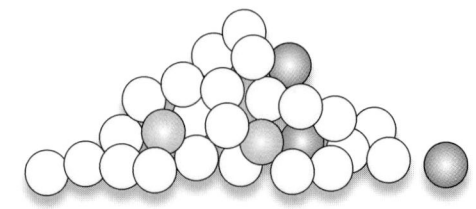

CRITICAL VIEWING Describe a scenario in which more than one factor could influence this population at the same time.

▶ MAIN IDEA

There are five factors that can lead to evolution.

The conditions needed for Hardy-Weinberg equilibrium are not common in nature. Some parts of a population's environment may stay the same over time. However, other things will likely change. Perhaps a flood carries part of a population to a new place. This population may then go through genetic drift. A mutation may create a new allele that allows some individuals to run faster and get away from predators. The frequency of this allele may then increase in the gene pool as it is passed on to future generations.

In nature, populations evolve, or change in response to their environments. Populations that are not in Hardy-Weinberg equilibrium are evolving. In their studies, Hardy and Weinberg concluded that evolution should be expected in all populations almost all of the time. Their model shows that there are five factors that can lead to evolution. These factors are illustrated in **FIGURE 11.11**.

- **Genetic drift** Allele frequencies can change due to chance alone.
- **Gene flow** The movement of alleles from one population to another changes the allele frequencies in each population.
- **Mutation** New alleles can form through mutation. Mutations create the genetic variation needed for evolution.
- **Sexual selection** Certain traits may improve mating success. Alleles for these traits increase in frequency.
- **Natural selection** Certain traits may be an advantage for survival. Alleles for these traits increase in frequency.

Evolution is continuous. Environments are always changing, though often very slowly relative to a human's lifetime. Evolution is a response to these changes. As environments change, populations either adapt or go extinct. When a population becomes extinct, a different species can take its place, and the cycle continues.

Infer **Why do real populations rarely reach Hardy-Weinberg equilibrium?**

11.4 / ASSESSMENT

REVIEWING ▶ MAIN IDEAS

1. What conditions are necessary for populations to remain in **Hardy-Weinberg equilibrium**?

2. What can be predicted using the Hardy-Weinberg equation?

3. What are the five factors that can lead to evolution?

CRITICAL THINKING

4. **Analyze** Why is phenotypic variation necessary for natural selection and sexual selection?

5. **Apply** Based on what you read in Section 11.3, is it likely that a population of peacocks would be in Hardy-Weinberg equilibrium? Why or why not?

Connecting CONCEPTS

6. **Genetics** How are the concepts of dominant, recessive, heterozygous, and homozygous related to the Hardy-Weinberg equation?

11.5 Speciation Through Isolation

KEY CONCEPT New species can arise when populations are isolated.

> **MAIN IDEAS**

- The isolation of populations can lead to speciation.
- Populations can become isolated in several ways.

VOCABULARY

reproductive isolation, p. 344
speciation, p. 344
behavioral isolation, p. 345

geographic isolation, p. 346
temporal isolation, p. 346

MICHIGAN STANDARDS

B5.1d Explain how a new species or variety originates through the evolutionary process of natural selection.

B5.3C Give examples of ways in which genetic variation and environmental factors are causes of evolution and the diversity of organisms.

Connect You have learned that gene flow helps to keep neighboring populations similar. The more gene flow that exists between populations, the more similar the populations will be. However, the less gene flow there is between two populations, the more likely the two populations are to become different. What happens if no gene flow occurs between two populations? This is one way that new species can arise.

> **MAIN IDEA**

The isolation of populations can lead to speciation.

If gene flow between two populations stops for any reason, the populations are said to be isolated. As these populations adapt to their environments, their gene pools may change. Random processes like mutation and genetic drift can also change gene pools. All of these changes add up over many generations. With time, isolated populations become more and more genetically different. Members of the two populations may also begin to look and behave differently from one another.

Reproductive isolation occurs when members of different populations can no longer mate successfully with one another. Sometimes members of the two populations are not physically able to mate with each other. In other cases, they cannot produce offspring that survive and reproduce. Reproductive isolation between populations is the final step of becoming separate species. The rise of two or more species from one existing species is called **speciation.**

FIGURE 11.12 illustrates a recent experiment that shows how one mutation can result in reproductive isolation. Scientists studied the *ds2* gene of fruit flies. This gene affects how well fruit flies can deal with cold temperatures. Fruit flies living in tropical areas, where competition for food is high, have a tropical allele. Fruit flies living in cooler regions, where competition for food is less, have a temperate allele. The *ds2* gene also affects chemical scents called pheromones. Fruit flies use these scents to attracts mates of their own species.

Connecting CONCEPTS

Genetics Fruit flies (*Drosophila melanogaster*) are very common in genetic research, as you may recall from **Unit 3**. Their popularity is based on several factors: they are easy to breed, they are common, and they have well understood genetic structures.

FIGURE 11.12 Reproductive Isolation

Reproductive isolation occurs when members of isolated populations are no longer able to mate with each other successfully.

① Scientists used lab fruit flies that are genetically similar. They developed a technique that allowed them to replace the *ds2* gene in each lab fruit fly with either the tropical or temperate allele.

Tropical fruit flies have a tropical *ds2* allele.

Temperate fruit flies have a temperate *ds2* allele.

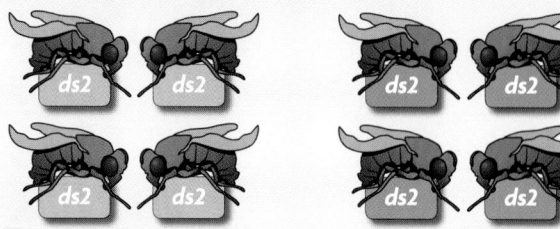

② Laboratory males that received the tropical allele were attracted to females that received the tropical allele. Males that received the temperate allele were attracted to females that received the temperate allele.

Synthesize Explain why fruit flies with a specific *ds2* allele prefer to mate with fruit flies with the same allele.

This experiment shows how speciation may have occurred in natural fruit fly populations. Fruit flies migrating north from Africa to areas where there is less competition for food faced colder temperatures. A mutation in the *ds2* gene may have produced the temperate allele. This allele allows fruit flies to survive in cooler climates. Because the *ds2* gene also affects phero-mones, mating behaviors changed. Fruit flies with the temperate allele and fruit flies with the tropical allele mated together less and less often. Eventually, these populations became reproductively isolated.

Summarize Why is reproductive isolation considered to be the final stage in speciation?

▶ MAIN IDEA
Populations can become isolated in several ways.

Several kinds of barriers can prevent mating between populations, leading to reproductive isolation. These include behavioral, geographic, and temporal barriers.

Behavioral Barriers

Chemical scents, courtship dances of birds, and courtship songs of frogs are sexual signals used to attract mates. Changes in these signals can prevent mating between populations. **Behavioral isolation** is isolation caused by differences in courtship or mating behaviors. Over 2000 species of fireflies are isolated in this way. Male and female fireflies produce patterns of flashes that attract mates of their own species. For example, *Photuris frontalis* emits one flash every second, *P. hebes* emits one flash every 2 seconds, and *P. fairch-ildi* produces a double flash every 5.5 seconds.

FIGURE 11.13 GEOGRAPHIC BARRIER

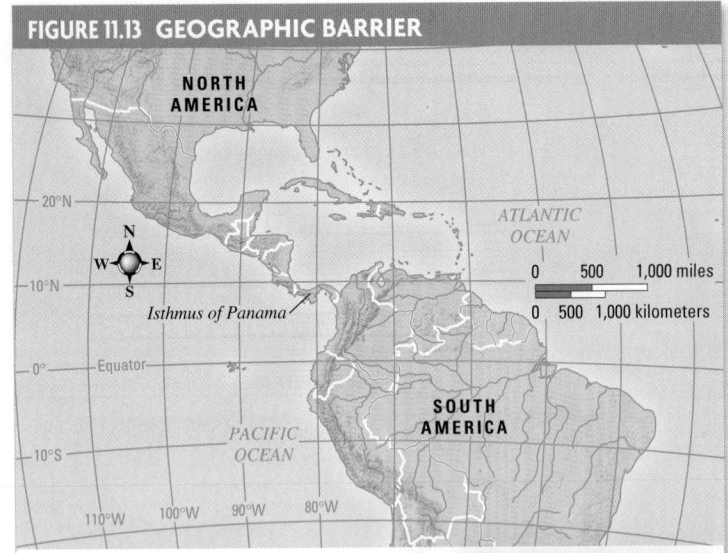

Although snapping shrimp in the Atlantic and Pacific oceans look similar, they are distinct species that have evolved through geographic isolation.

Geographic Barriers

The most commonly studied type of isolation is geographic isolation. **Geographic isolation** involves physical barriers that divide a population into two or more groups. These barriers can include rivers, mountains, and dried lakebeds. As shown in **FIGURE 11.13**, the formation of the Isthmus of Panama created a barrier for many marine species. Marine organisms could no longer easily cross between the Atlantic and Pacific oceans. Over time, the isolated populations became genetically different. Several species of snapping shrimp have evolved through geographic isolation. These species appear almost identical to one another. However, when males and females from opposite sides of the isthmus are placed together, they snap at each other instead of courting. Because they will no longer mate, these shrimp are classified as different species.

Temporal Barriers

Barriers can also involve timing. **Temporal isolation** exists when timing prevents reproduction between populations. Some members of a population may show signs of courtship at different times if there is a lot of competition for mates. Reproductive periods may change to a different time of the year or a different part of the day. These differences in timing can lead to speciation. For example, two tree species that grow on the Monterey peninsula in California are very closely related. However, they have different pollination periods. The Monterey pine sheds its pollen in February, while the Bishop pine sheds its pollen in April. These pine species have likely evolved through temporal isolation.

VOCABULARY

Temporal comes from the Latin word *tempus*, meaning "time."

To learn more about speciation, visit scilinks.org.
Keycode: MLB011

Compare and Contrast What are the differences and similarities between behavioral isolation and temporal isolation?

11.5 ASSESSMENT

ONLINE QUIZ
ClassZone.com

REVIEWING ▶ MAIN IDEAS

1. How can **reproductive isolation** lead to **speciation**?

2. What are three types of barriers that can lead to reproductive isolation?

CRITICAL THINKING

3. **Apply** Why are the flash patterns of fireflies considered to be **behavioral isolation**?

4. **Synthesize** How did **geographic isolation** affect the diversity Darwin observed in Galápagos finches?

Connecting CONCEPTS

5. **Scientific Process** What could have been used as a control group in the fruit fly experiment described on page 345?

11.6 Patterns in Evolution

KEY CONCEPT Evolution occurs in patterns.

▶ MAIN IDEAS

- Evolution through natural selection is not random.
- Species can shape each other over time.
- Species can become extinct.
- Speciation often occurs in patterns.

VOCABULARY

convergent evolution, p. 348
divergent evolution, p. 348
coevolution, p. 349
extinction, p. 350
punctuated equilibrium, p. 351
adaptive radiation, p. 351

MICHIGAN STANDARDS

L5.p1C Explain how extinction removes genes from the gene pool. (prerequisite)

B5.1d Explain how a new species or variety originates through the evolutionary process of natural selection.

Connect Even before the process of speciation is complete, individuals of an emerging new species are under pressure to survive. Adaptive traits are preserved in a population through natural selection. However, sudden changes in the environment can end the existence of a species. The rise and fall of species over time reveal clear evolutionary patterns.

▶ MAIN IDEA

Evolution through natural selection is not random.

In science, the terms *chance* and *random* relate to how easily an outcome can be predicted. Because mutations and genetic drift cannot be predicted, they are called random events. These random events are sources of genetic diversity. However, natural selection, which acts on this diversity, is not random. Individuals with traits that are better adapted for their environment have a better chance of surviving and reproducing than do individuals without these traits.

You have learned about directional, stabilizing, and disruptive selection. In each of these modes of selection, the effects of natural selection add up over many generations. In other words, natural selection pushes a population's traits in an advantageous direction. As you can see in **FIGURE 11.14**, alleles associated with these traits add up in the population's gene pool.

Remember, however, that having direction is not the same as having purpose or intent. The environment controls the direction taken by natural selection. When the environment changes, different traits may become advantageous. The response of species to environmental challenges and opportunities is not random.

FIGURE 11.14 PATTERNS IN NATURAL SELECTION

In this hypothetical population, green body color is favored by natural selection. With each generation, alleles associated with green body color increase in frequency. Over time, more and more individuals in the population will have the advantageous phenotype.

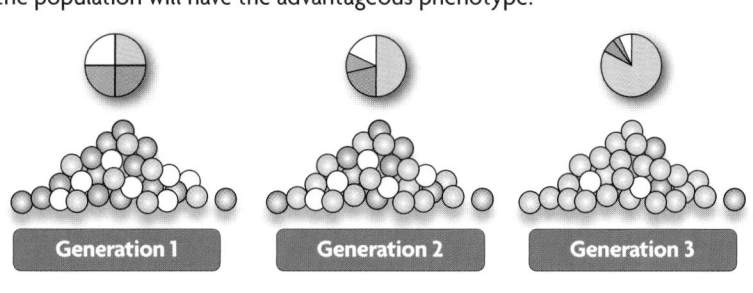

Generation 1   Generation 2   Generation 3

Convergent Evolution

Different species often must adapt to similar environments. Evolution toward similar characteristics in unrelated species is called **convergent evolution.** Analogous structures, such as wings on birds and insects, are common examples of convergent evolution. Another example is the tail fin of fish and marine mammals, as shown in **FIGURE 11.15**. Sharks, which are fish, and dolphins, which are mammals, are separated by about 300 million years of evolution. Separately, they have both evolved similar tail fins to propel themselves through the water. However, the tail fins of sharks and other fish are vertical, while those of dolphins are horizontal.

Divergent Evolution

When closely related species evolve in different directions, they become increasingly different through **divergent evolution.** The evolution of the red fox and the kit fox is an example of this trend. Though closely related, the two species have different appearances that have resulted from adapting to different environments. The red fox lives in temperate regions, usually in forests. Its dark reddish coat helps it to hide from predators. The sandy-colored coat of the kit fox allows it to blend in with its desert surroundings. Kit foxes also have large ears relative to their body size. This adaptation helps them to keep cool in the desert heat.

Infer Are the shells of turtles and snails examples of convergent or divergent evolution? Explain.

FIGURE 11.15 Convergent and Divergent Evolution

Natural selection is not random. It can have direction, and its effects are cumulative through generations.

CONVERGENT EVOLUTION

Dolphins, which are mammals, and sharks, which are fish, have evolved similar tail fins, as each has adapted to similar environmental conditions.

Dolphin   Shark

DIVERGENT EVOLUTION

The kit fox and red fox evolved from a common ancestor while adapting to different environments.

Kit fox   Red fox

Ancestor

Analyze How do convergent and divergent evolution illustrate the directional nature of natural selection?

MAIN IDEA
Species can shape each other over time.

Species interact with each other in many different ways. For example, they may compete for the same food source or be involved in a predator-prey relationship. Most of these interactions do not involve evolutionary changes. However, sometimes the evolutionary paths of two species become connected.

Beneficial Relationships Through Coevolution

The bull-thorn acacia is a plant species with branches covered in hollow thorns. Although the thorns protect the plant from being eaten by large animals, small herbivores such as caterpillars can fit between them. To the rescue comes *Pseudomyrmex ferrugineus,* a species of stinging ants. As shown in **FIGURE 11.16**, these ants live inside the thorns and feed on the plant's nectar. The ants protect the plant by stinging animals that try to eat the leaves.

Although this relationship may seem to be a simple cooperation between two species, it is much more than that. The acacia and the ants share an evolutionary history. The hollow thorns and nectar-producing leaves of the acacia and the stinging of the ants have evolved due to the relationship between the two species. Close relatives of these species that are not involved in this type of relationship do not have these traits. Such specialized relationships form through coevolution. **Coevolution** is the process in which two or more species evolve in response to changes in each other.

FIGURE 11.16 The relationship between this ant and the acacia plant has developed through coevolution. The ant lives inside the hollow thorn and protects the acacia by stinging any potential predators.

Evolutionary Arms Races

Coevolution can also occur in competitive relationships. These interactions can lead to "evolutionary arms races," in which each species responds to pressure from the other through better adaptations over many generations.

For example, many plants produce defense chemicals to discourage herbivores from eating them. Natural selection then favors herbivores that can overcome the effects of the chemicals. After many generations, most herbivores have some level of resistance and are again able to safely eat the plant. Natural selection then favors plants that have evolved even more potent chemicals. In another case, the thick shells and spines of murex snails are an adaptive response to predation by crabs. In turn, crabs have evolved powerful claws strong enough to crack the snails' shells.

Predict **What do you think will happen in future generations of crabs and snails?**

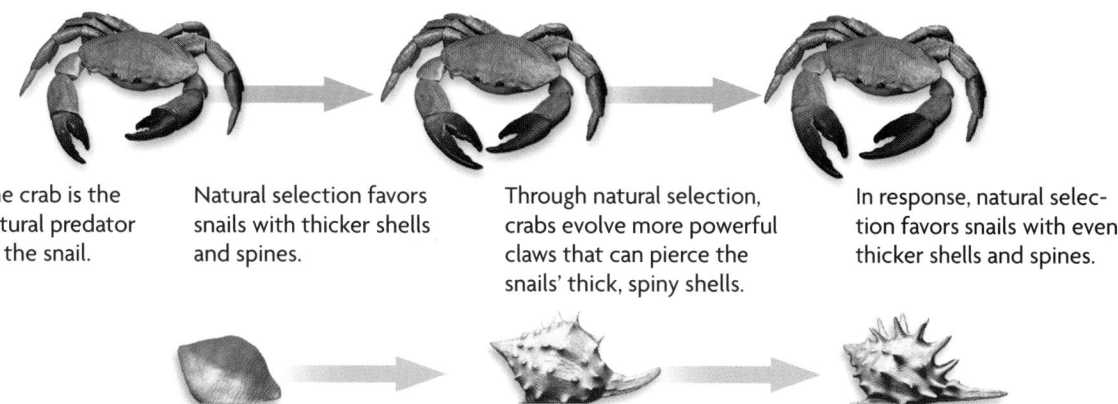

The crab is the natural predator of the snail.

Natural selection favors snails with thicker shells and spines.

Through natural selection, crabs evolve more powerful claws that can pierce the snails' thick, spiny shells.

In response, natural selection favors snails with even thicker shells and spines.

FIGURE 11.17 Native to Portugal and Spain, the Iberian lynx is the world's most endangered feline. The World Wildlife Federation estimates that there may be fewer than 200 individuals remaining in the wild.

Species can become extinct.

Just as birth and death are natural events in the life of an individual, the rise and fall of species are natural processes of evolution. The elimination of a species from Earth is called **extinction.** Extinction often occurs when a species as a whole is unable to adapt to a change in its environment. Biologists divide extinction events into two categories—background extinctions and mass extinctions. Although they differ in degree, the effect of both is the same: the permanent loss of species from Earth.

Background Extinctions

Extinctions that occur continuously but at a very low rate are called background extinctions. They are part of the cycle of life on Earth. Background extinctions occur at roughly the same rate as speciation. Unlike catastrophic mass extinctions, background extinction events usually affect only one or a few species in a relatively small area, such as a rain forest or a mountain range. They can be caused by local changes in the environment, such as the introduction of a new predator species or a decrease in food supply. From a human perspective, such extinctions seem to occur randomly but at a fairly constant rate.

Mass Extinctions

Mass extinctions are much more rare than background extinctions. However, as illustrated in **FIGURE 11.18,** they are much more intense. These events often operate at the global level. Therefore, they destroy many species—even entire orders or families. Mass extinctions are thought to occur suddenly in geologic time, usually because of a catastrophic event such as an ice age or asteroid impact. The fossil record confirms that there have been at least five mass extinctions in the last 600 million years.

Compare and Contrast What are the differences and similarities between background extinctions and mass extinctions?

FIGURE 11.18 EXTINCTION RATES THROUGH TIME

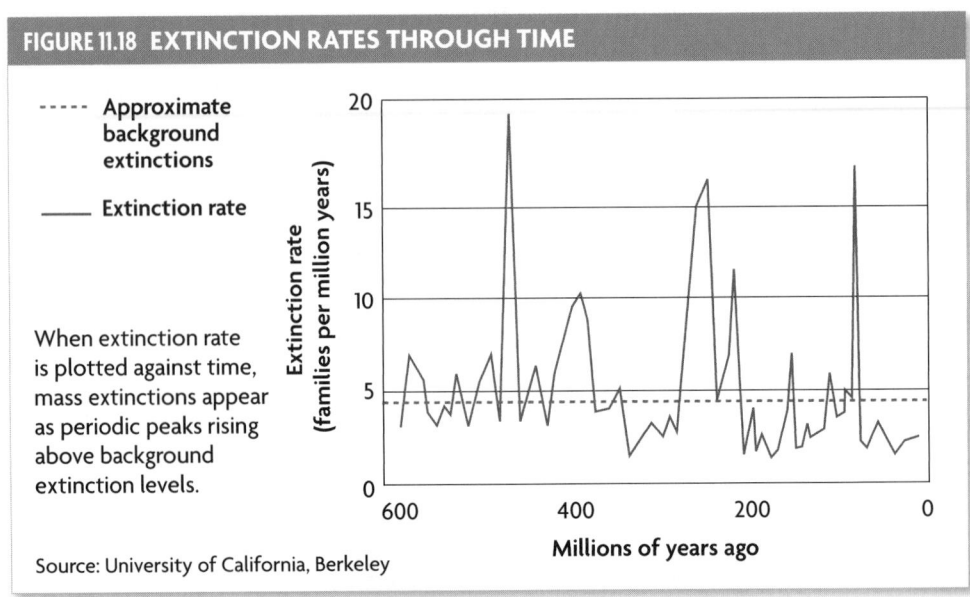

----- Approximate background extinctions

—— Extinction rate

When extinction rate is plotted against time, mass extinctions appear as periodic peaks rising above background extinction levels.

Source: University of California, Berkeley

▶ MAIN IDEA
Speciation often occurs in patterns.

Paleontologists have long noticed a repeating pattern in the history of life, reflected in the fossil record. Bursts of evolutionary activity are followed by long periods of stability. This pattern is described by the theory of **punctuated equilibrium,** which states that episodes of speciation occur suddenly in geologic time and are followed by long periods of little evolutionary change. Niles Eldredge and Stephen Jay Gould originally proposed this theory in 1972. It was written as a revision of Darwin's idea that new species arise through gradual transformations of ancestral species.

The diversification of one ancestral species into many descendent species is called **adaptive radiation.** These descendent species are usually adapted to a wide range of environments. One example of adaptive radiation is the radiation of mammals following the mass extinction at the end of the Cretaceous period 65 million years ago.

Although mammals had evolved for about 150 million years before the end of the Cretaceous period, they barely resembled the mammals we know today. The earliest mammals were tiny, usually insect eaters, and mostly nocturnal. These characteristics allowed them to coexist with the dinosaurs. The extinction of the dinosaurs left environments full of opportunities for other types of animals. In the first 10 million years following the dinosaurs' extinction, more than 4000 mammal species had evolved, including whales, bats, rodents, and primates.

VISUAL VOCAB

Adaptive radiation is the rapid evolution of many diverse species from ancestral species.

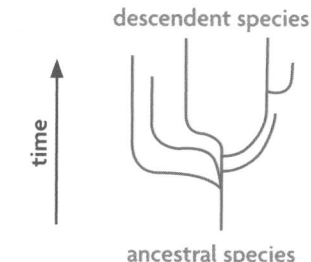

descendent species

time

ancestral species

Connecting CONCEPTS

Ecology Early mammals were able to coexist with dinosaurs because mammals and dinosaurs had different niches, or roles in the ecosystem. You will learn more about the concept of niches in **Chapter 14.**

Synthesize The adaptive radiation of mammals followed the extinction of the dinosaurs. How do these events support the theory of punctuated equilibrium?

11.6 / ASSESSMENT

 ONLINE QUIZ
ClassZone.com

REVIEWING ▶ MAIN IDEAS

1. Explain what it means to say that natural selection is not random.

2. How does **coevolution** shape two species over time?

3. What are some of the causes of background and mass **extinctions**?

4. What pattern is described by the theory of **punctuated equilibrium**?

CRITICAL THINKING

5. **Synthesize** Defensive chemicals are usually found in unripe fruit but not in ripe fruit. In terms of coevolution, why might this be?

6. **Infer** If analogous structures are often examples of **convergent evolution,** what types of structures would likely be examples of **divergent evolution**?

Connecting CONCEPTS

7. **Human Biology** Through mutation, HIV can accumulate resistance to drugs developed for treatment. Describe the relationship between HIV and the humans who develop these drugs in terms of an evolutionary arms race.

Use these inquiry-based labs and online activities to deepen your understanding of evolution.

MICHIGAN STANDARDS

B5.3A Explain how natural selection acts on individuals, but it is populations that evolve. Relate genetic mutations and genetic variety produced by sexual reproduction to diversity within a given population.
B5.3B Describe the role of geographic isolation in speciation.

INVESTIGATION

Investigating an Anole Lizard Population

Curly-tailed lizards will eat any brown anole lizards that fit into their mouths. In this activity, you will model the effect of curly-tailed lizards on an anole population.

SKILL Modeling

PROBLEM Is this population evolving?

PROCEDURE

1. Obtain 10 large and 10 small paper clips to represent the initial population of anoles. Spread them out in front of your group. Large anoles may have genotype *BB* (large ribbed paper clip) or *Bb* (large smooth paper clip). Small anoles have genotype *bb* (small paper clip). Keep extra paper clips in the "extras" cup.

2. Copy and fill out Table 1 below for population stage 1.

MATERIALS
- 10 large paper clips (mix of smooth and ribbed), 10 small paper clips
- "extras" cup containing 20 additional large paper clips (10 smooth, 10 ribbed)
- graph paper

TABLE 1. EFFECT OF CURLY-TAILED LIZARDS ON A POPULATION OF BROWN ANOLE LIZARDS									
Population Stage	Number of Anoles				Genotype Frequencies			Allele Frequencies	
	Total	*BB*	*Bb*	*bb*	*BB*	*Bb*	*bb*	*B*	*b*
1 (Generation 1)									
2 (Generations 1 + 2)									
3 (Generations 1 + 2 + 3)									
4 (Generations 1 + 2 + 3 + 4)									

3. Three small anoles are eaten by curly tails. Put 3 small paper clips in the "extras" cup.

4. Mix up the paper clips that remain in your population and randomly pull 3 aside. These represent the genotypes that get passed on to the next generation.

5. Take 3 paper clips from the cup—one to match each paper clip that you pulled aside in step 4. The new paper clips represent the new generation. Join the 3 pairs with the rest of the population, bringing the population total back up to 20.

6. Fill in the information for this population stage in the next row of Table 1.

7. Repeat steps 3–6 until you have produced generation 4.

8. Draw two line graphs, one each for each allele frequency—*B* and *b*. Put population stage (1 through 4) on the *x*-axis and allele frequency (from 0 to 1) on the *y*-axis.

ANALYZE AND CONCLUDE

1. **Analyze** What happens to the frequency of each allele over the four generations?

2. **Analyze** Is this population evolving, or is it in Hardy-Weinberg equilibrium? Explain.

3. **Predict** Which of the five conditions required for equilibrium are met and which are not?

INVESTIGATION

Exploring Adaptations

A toolbox has a wide variety of tools, each designed to perform a specific task. But what if the ideal tools are not available? In this activity, you will relate this problem to the natural process of adaptation.

SKILL Drawing Analogies

MATERIALS

- wooden block
- one wood screw
- ruler

PROBLEM What purposes do adaptations serve?

PROCEDURE

1. Obtain a wooden block and a wood screw from your teacher.

2. Find a way to insert the screw into the block of wood as far as possible. Use any device, method, or object to do this other than a tool designed for this purpose. Be sure not to do anything that could cause damage or injury.

3. After trying for five minutes, measure the length of the screw that remains outside of the wood block. Subtract this length from the total length of the screw to determine how far you were able to insert the screw into the wood.

ANALYZE AND CONCLUDE

1. **Summarize** List the objects you used and the strategies you tried to accomplish this task.

2. **Analyze** Which of your methods worked best?

3. **Evaluate** Compare your results and strategies with those of another group. Evaluate the effectiveness of each strategy.

4. **Contrast** How do adaptations differ from traits that you can acquire through a lifetime, such as bigger muscles from strength training?

5. **Apply** A woodpecker has adaptations for chipping wood and getting insects from cracks in tree bark. How might its beak, tongue, neck, and feet be different from those of other birds?

ANIMATED BIOLOGY

Evolutionary Arms Race

Can you keep tuberculosis in check? See how the bacteria that cause tuberculosis have evolved resistance to a number of antibiotics.

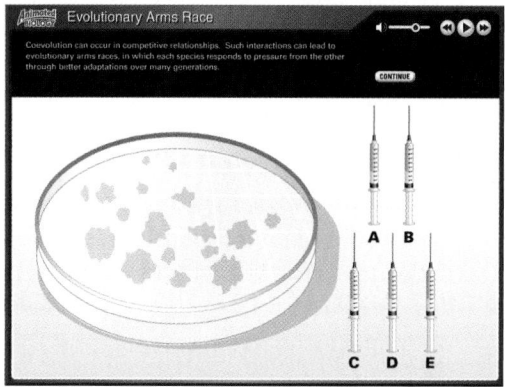

WEBQUEST

Speciation is an ongoing process, still active today. Complete this WebQuest to explore a butterfly population and a walking stick population that are each diverging into new species.

DATA ANALYSIS ONLINE

T. Dobzhansky and N.P. Spassky studied genetic drift in sample fruit fly populations. Graph the allele frequencies of the initial populations and the frequencies recorded at each stage of the experiment. Then determine if the populations are evolving.

Interactive Review @ CLASSZONE.COM

11.1 Genetic Variation Within Populations

GG

gg

A population shares a common gene pool. Genetic variation in a gene pool can be measured through allele frequencies. Genetic variation increases the chance that some members of a population will be able to adapt to their environment.

11.2 Natural Selection in Populations

Populations, not individuals, evolve. Natural selection acts on distributions of traits in a population. Directional selection occurs when one extreme phenotype is advantageous for survival. If intermediate phenotypes are advantageous, they become more common through stabilizing selection. In the process of disruptive selection, extreme phenotypes are selected for.

11.3 Other Mechanisms of Evolution

Natural selection is not the only mechanism through which populations evolve. Gene flow is the movement of alleles between populations. Changes in allele frequencies due to chance alone can occur through genetic drift. If certain traits increase mating success, those traits can become more common through sexual selection.

11.4 Hardy-Weinberg Equilibrium

Hardy-Weinberg equilibrium provides a framework for understanding how populations evolve. A population in Hardy-Weinberg equilibrium is not evolving. The conditions required for this equilibrium are rarely met in nature. However, Hardy-Weinberg equilibrium provides a framework for understanding the factors that can lead to evolution. It is therefore very useful to population biologists.

11.5 Speciation Through Isolation

New species can arise when populations are isolated. Reproductive isolation occurs when members of two populations are no longer able to mate successfully. It is the final stage in speciation—the rise of two or more species from one existing species. Isolation can be due to behavioral, geographic, or temporal barriers.

Isthmus of Panama

0   500   1,000 miles
0   500 1,000 kilometers

11.6 Patterns in Evolution

Evolution occurs in patterns. Evolution through natural selection can have direction, and its effects add up over many generations. The evolutionary paths of two or more species can become connected through the process of coevolution. Extinction and speciation events also appear in patterns in the fossil record.

Synthesize Your Notes

Two-Column Chart Make a two-column chart to synthesize your notes about the three modes of natural selection.

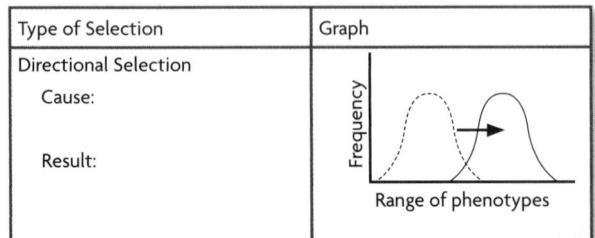

Type of Selection	Graph
Directional Selection Cause: Result:	Frequency Range of phenotypes

Concept Map Use concept maps to summarize factors that can lead to evolution.

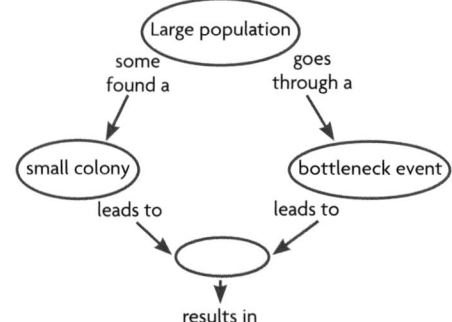

Chapter Assessment

Reviewing Vocabulary

Visualizing Vocabulary

For each term below, use simple shapes, lines, or arrows to illustrate their meaning. Below each picture, write a short caption. Here's an example for *founder effect*.

A small group of individuals starts a population that is subject to genetic drift.

1. gene flow

3. divergent evolution

2. geographic isolation

4. punctuated equilibrium

Keep It Short

For each vocabulary word below, write a short, precise phrase that describes its meaning. For example, a short phrase to describe *extinction* could be "gone forever."

5. gene pool

8. convergent evolution

6. reproductive isolation

9. coevolution

7. speciation

10. adaptive radiation

Reviewing MAIN IDEAS

11. Would a population with a lot of genetic variation or little genetic variation be more likely to have individuals that can adapt to a changing environment? Explain your answer.

12. Describe two major sources of genetic variation.

13. A certain trait in a population is not under any selective pressure. Draw a curve showing the likely phenotypic distribution for this trait.

14. Over many generations, certain insect species have become more and more resistant to insecticides. What type of natural selection is this an example of, and how does it differ from the other types?

15. Describe how gene flow can increase genetic variation within two neighboring populations.

16. How are the effects of genetic drift similar to the effects of having a small sample size in a scientific experiment?

17. Give an example of how sexual selection can cause extreme phenotypes in a population.

18. What are the conditions necessary for a population to stay in Hardy-Weinberg equilibrium?

19. How can a lack of gene flow between populations lead to speciation?

20. Describe three types of barriers that can cause populations to become reproductively isolated from each other.

21. Explain why mutation and genetic drift are random events, while natural selection is not.

22. Speciation is the rise of two or more species from one existing species. What process keeps the number of total species on Earth from growing exponentially through speciation?

23. What is the relationship between speciation and the theory of punctuated equilibrium?

Critical Thinking

24. Apply About 40 species of Hawaiian honeycreeper birds have likely descended from a common ancestor. These species occupy many different niches on the islands and they exhibit a variety of beak types, songs, and nesting behaviors. Describe how reproductive isolation and adaptive radiation likely played a role in the many species of honeycreepers in Hawaii today.

25. Apply How could gene flow affect a population that was founded by a small number of individuals?

26. Analyze What type of selection produces a distribution of phenotypes opposite to that produced by stabilizing selection? Explain your answer.

27. Analyze Explain how the process of genetic drift is completely due to chance.

28. Analyze Why must allele frequencies in a gene pool always add up to 100 percent?

29. Compare and Contrast What are the differences and similarities between natural selection and sexual selection?

Interpreting Visuals

Below is a frequency distribution for beak size in a hypothetical population of birds. Use this graph to answer the next three questions.

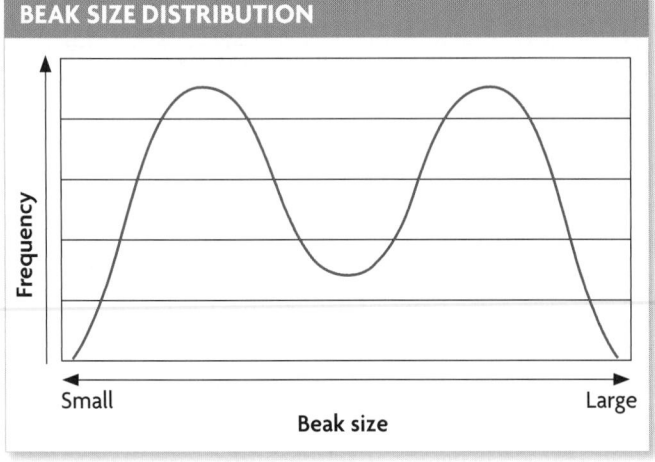

BEAK SIZE DISTRIBUTION

30. Analyze What type of selection is demonstrated by the data in this graph? Explain your answer.

31. Analyze Which phenotypes are the most common in this population?

32. Synthesize Describe a scenario that could realistically lead to this pattern of selection in a bird population.

Analyzing Data

Below is a graph showing the relationship between female chimpanzee rank and the survival of offspring. Use the graph to answer the next three questions.

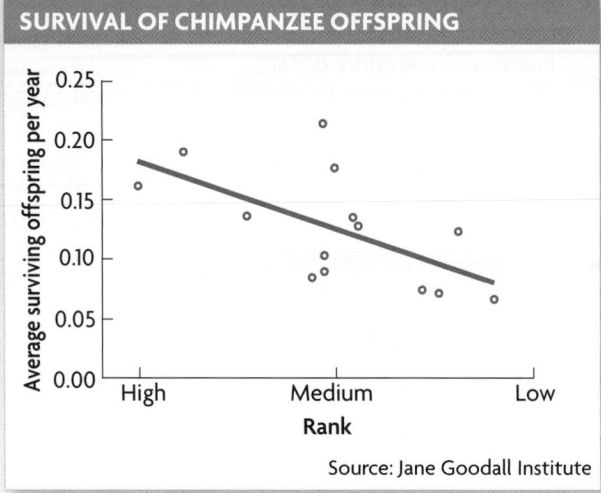

SURVIVAL OF CHIMPANZEE OFFSPRING

Source: Jane Goodall Institute

33. Analyze What is the relationship between female rank and the survival of her offspring?

34. Analyze Is there a level of rank that prevents a female chimp from reproducing? Explain.

35. Infer What can you infer by studying the scale of the *y*-axis on this graph?

Connecting CONCEPTS

36. Write a Proposal The explosive growth of nonnative species is a major global issue. A few individuals from one area act as founders of new populations on other continents or in other oceans. This is causing many native populations to decline. Human activities such as global commerce and travel are directly causing these destructive founding populations. Write a proposal to an international committee on the environment regarding this issue. Include in your proposal the significance of the changes to native populations, using terms and concepts from the chapter.

37. Infer Hemoglobin, an oxygen-carrying protein found in the red blood cells of vertebrates, helps to circulate oxygen from the lungs to all parts of the body. In penguins, the blood has a very high concentration of hemoglobin. Penguin muscles have a high concentration of myoglobin, which also stores oxygen. What might be a reason for these adaptations?

MICHIGAN STANDARDS-BASED ASSESSMENT

✔ *Test Practice*
For more test practice, go to ClassZone.com.

1. An isolated population of bats goes through 100 generations with no immigration. However, genetic variation within the population increases. What *best* explains the cause of this increase? **B5.3A**

   A Reproductive isolation results in variation.

   B Natural selection acts on the genotypes.

   C Sexual selection has been disrupted.

   D Random mutations can occur each generation.

2. The fossil record indicates that bursts of evolutionary activity are often followed by long periods of stability. These bursts of evolutionary activity *most* likely include **B5.1d**

   A background extinctions.

   B mass extinctions.

   C episodes of speciation.

   D genetic equilibrium.

3.

Habitat Conditions		
	Old Habitat	New Habitat
Temp (°C)	14–22	15–21
Light level	low	low
Soil pH	5.3	5.4
Rainfall (cm/week)	4.2	2.2

   Seeds from a plant species are introduced into a new habitat. The chart shows the environmental conditions in the old and new habitats. Based on this information, what is *most* likely to happen to the new population over the course of many generations? **B5.3C**

   A Individuals will require more sunlight.

   B Individuals will require higher temperatures.

   C Individuals that can survive with 2.2 cm/week of rainfall will become more common.

   D Individuals that can survive with 2.2 cm/week of rainfall will become less common.

4. Due to severe flooding, 95 percent of a ground-nesting ant population dies. This event is different from natural selection in that any resulting change in allele frequencies is **B5.2c**

   A harmful to the population.

   B beneficial to the population.

   C random.

   D directional.

5.

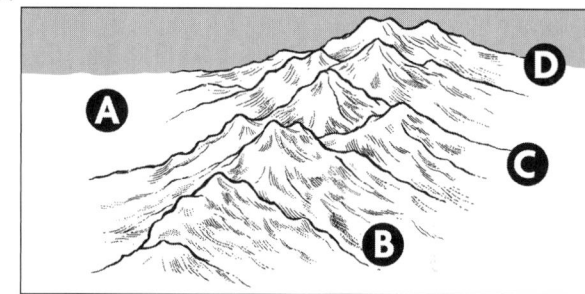

   The map shows the location of four populations of a bee species. Over time, population A is *most* likely to evolve into a new species due to **B5.3B**

   A geographic isolation.

   B temporal isolation.

   C convergent evolution.

   D adaptive radiation.

6. The Irish potato famine in the 1840s was caused by a fungus that infected the potato crop. This potato population was *most* likely vulnerable to infection due to a lack of **B5.1g**

   A genetic drift in the population.

   B sexual selection in the population.

   C organisms in the population.

   D genetic variation in the population.

   ### THINK THROUGH THE QUESTION

   Read each of the answer choices carefully. Which of these choices would make a population less likely to survive in a changing environment?

12 The History of Life

KEY CONCEPTS

12.1 The Fossil Record
Fossils are a record of life that existed in the past.

12.2 The Geologic Time Scale
The geologic time scale divides Earth's history based on major past events.

12.3 Origin of Life
The origin of life on Earth remains a puzzle.

12.4 Early Single-Celled Organisms
Single-celled organisms existed 3.8 billion years ago.

12.5 Radiation of Multicellular Life
Multicellular life evolved in distinct phases.

12.6 Primate Evolution
Humans appeared late in Earth's history.

Online BIOLOGY CLASSZONE.COM

Animated BIOLOGY
View animated chapter concepts.
• Endosymbiosis
• Comparing Hominoid Skulls
• Geologic Time Scale

BIOZINE
Keep current with biology news.
• Featured stories
• News feeds
• Polls

RESOURCE CENTER
Get more information on
• Earth's Ancient Past
• Geologic Dating Methods
• History of Life

What can fossils teach us about the past?

This man, known only as Tollund Man, died about 2200 years ago in what is now Denmark. Details such as his skin and hair were preserved by the acid of the bog in which he was found. A bog is a type of wetland that accumulates peat, the deposits of dead plant material. Older remains from bogs can add information to the fossil record, which tends to consist of mostly hard shells, teeth, and bones.

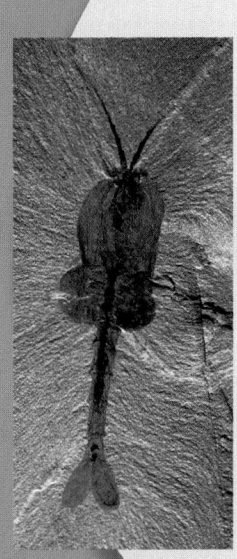

Arthropods This fossil of an extinct lobsterlike arthropod was discovered at a site where some of the world's oldest fossils are found—the Burgess Shale, in British Columbia, Canada. Arthropods are a large group of invertebrates that have segmented body parts and jointed legs. Fossils found at the Burgess Shale site offer a glimpse of what life was like during the Cambrian period, more than 500 million years ago. These fossils are special due to their great age and their remarkable state of preservation. In this chapter, you will read more about how fossils are preserved and about the time period during which this ancient arthropod lived.

12.1 The Fossil Record

KEY CONCEPT Fossils are a record of life that existed in the past.

▶ MAIN IDEAS

- Fossils can form in several ways.
- Radiometric dating provides an accurate estimate of a fossil's age.

VOCABULARY

relative dating, p. 362
radiometric dating, p. 362
isotope, p. 362
half-life, p. 362

MICHIGAN STANDARDS

L5.p1D Explain the importance of the fossil record. (prerequisite)

B5.1c Summarize the relationships between present-day organisms and those that inhabited the Earth in the past (e.g., use fossil record, embryonic stages, homologous structures, chemical basis).

Connect Tollund Man and the arthropod found in the Burgess Shale site are both traces of Earth's history of life, although they lived about 500 million years apart. They were also preserved as fossils in different ways. In this section, you will learn about types of fossils, how fossils form, and how they can help us understand the history of life on Earth.

▶ MAIN IDEA

Fossils can form in several ways.

Fossils are far more diverse than the giant dinosaur skeletons we see in museums. The following are some of the processes that make fossils. **FIGURE 12.1** shows examples of fossils produced in different ways.

- **Permineralization** occurs when minerals carried by water are deposited around a hard structure. They may also replace the hard structure itself.
- **Natural casts** form when flowing water removes all of the original bone or tissue, leaving just an impression in sediment. Minerals fill in the mold, recreating the original shape of the organism.
- **Trace fossils** record the activity of an organism. They include nests, burrows, imprints of leaves, and footprints.
- **Amber-preserved fossils** are organisms that become trapped in tree resin that hardens into amber after the tree gets buried underground.
- **Preserved remains** form when an entire organism becomes encased in material such as ice or volcanic ash or immersed in bogs.

FIGURE 12.1 The fossil record includes fossils that formed in many different ways.

Permineralized skeleton of a *Velociraptor* dinosaur

Natural cast of a crinoid, a marine animal

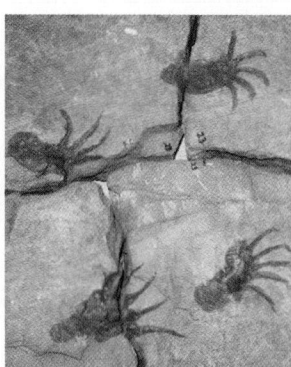

Trace fossils of footprints from a *Dimetrodon* dinosaur

Amber-preserved wasp

Ice-preserved 5000-year-old remains of a man found in the Italian Alps

FIGURE 12.2 The Process of Permineralization

The process of permineralization requires rapid burial in an area with water and continuous sedimentation.

An organism dies in a location, such as a riverbed, where sediments can rapidly cover its body.

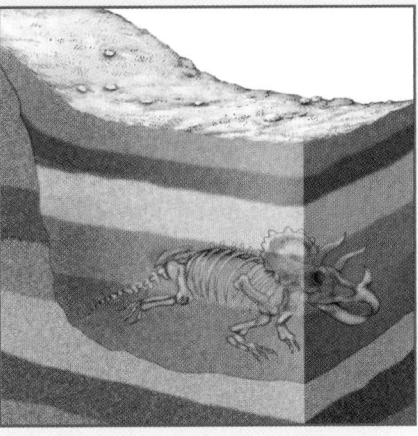

Over time, pressure from additional sediment compresses the body, and minerals slowly replace all hard structures, such as bone.

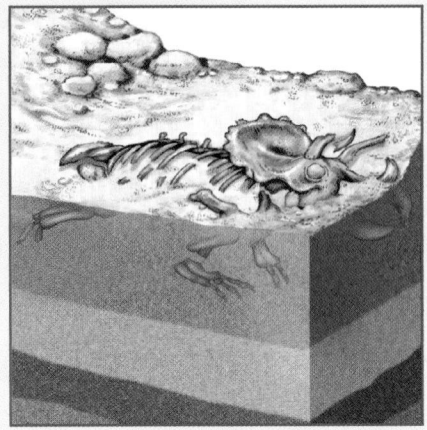

Earthquakes or erosion may expose the fossil millions of years after formation, or it may be uncovered by paleontologists, hikers, or road-building crews.

Infer What conditions could occur that would prevent an organism from being preserved through permineralization?

Most fossils form in sedimentary rock, which is made by many layers of sediment or small rock particles. The best environments for any type of fossilization include wetlands, bogs, and areas where sediment is continuously deposited, such as river mouths, lakebeds, and floodplains.

The most common fossils result from permineralization. Several circumstances are critical for this process, as shown in **FIGURE 12.2.** The organism must be buried or encased in some type of material—such as sand, sediment, mud, or tar—very soon after death, while the organism's features are still intact. After burial, groundwater trickles into tiny pores and spaces in plants, bones, and shells. During this process, the excess minerals in the water are deposited on the remaining cells and tissues. Many layers of mineral deposits are left behind, creating a fossilized record by replacing organic tissues with hard minerals. The resulting fossil has the same shape as the original structure and may contain some original tissue.

With such specific conditions needed for fossilization, it is easy to see why only a tiny percentage of living things that ever existed became fossils. Most remains decompose or are destroyed before they can be preserved. Even successful fossilization is no guarantee that an organism's remains will be added to the fossil record. Natural events such as earthquakes and the recycling of rock into magma can destroy fossils that took thousands of years to form.

Summarize Why are so few complete fossils discovered?

TAKING NOTES

Make a cause-and-effect chain of the conditions required for fossilization. Fill in important details.

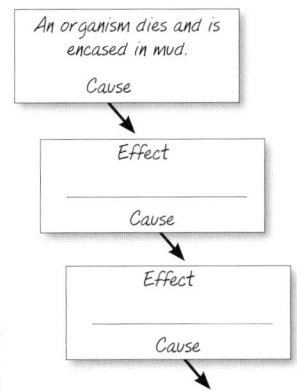

MAIN IDEA

Radiometric dating provides an accurate estimate of a fossil's age.

Connecting CONCEPTS

Chemistry of Life Recall from **Chapter 2** that all atoms of a given element have the same number of protons. Isotopes are named for the total number of protons and neutrons in their nuclei.

● neutrons ● protons

CARBON-12
NUCLEUS
6 protons
6 neutrons

CARBON-14
NUCLEUS
6 protons
8 neutrons

Recall from Chapter 10 that geologists in the 1700s had realized that rock layers at the bottom of an undisturbed sequence of rocks were deposited before those at the top, and therefore are older. The same logic holds true for the fossils found in rock layers. **Relative dating** estimates the time during which an organism lived by comparing the placement of fossils of that organism with the placement of fossils in other layers of rock. Relative dating allows scientists to infer the order in which groups of species existed, although it does not provide the actual ages of fossils.

To estimate a fossil's actual, or absolute, age, scientists use **radiometric dating**—a technique that uses the natural decay rate of unstable isotopes found in materials in order to calculate the age of that material. **Isotopes** are atoms of an element that have the same number of protons but a different number of neutrons. Most elements have several isotopes. For example, the element carbon (C) has three naturally occurring isotopes. All carbon isotopes have six protons. Isotopes are named, however, by their number of protons plus their number of neutrons. Thus, carbon-12 (^{12}C) has six neutrons, carbon-13 (^{13}C) has seven neutrons, and carbon-14 (^{14}C) has eight neutrons. More than 98 percent of the carbon in a living organism is ^{12}C.

Some isotopes have unstable nuclei. As a result, their nuclei undergo radioactive decay—they break down—over time. This releases radiation in the form of particles and energy. As an isotope decays, it can transform into a different element. The decay rate of many radioactive isotopes has been measured and is expressed as the isotope's half-life, as shown in **FIGURE 12.3**. A **half-life** is the amount of time it takes for half of the isotope in a sample to decay into a different element, or its product isotope. An element's half-life is not affected by environmental conditions such as temperature or pressure. Both ^{12}C and ^{13}C are stable, but ^{14}C decays into nitrogen-14 (^{14}N), with a half-life of roughly 5700 years.

Radiocarbon Dating

The isotope ^{14}C is commonly used for radiometric dating of recent remains, such as those of Tollund Man shown at the beginning of this chapter. Organisms absorb carbon through eating and breathing, so ^{14}C is constantly being resupplied. When an organism dies, its intake of carbon stops, but the decay of ^{14}C continues. The fossil's age can be estimated by comparing the ratio of a stable isotope, such as ^{12}C, to ^{14}C. The longer the organism has been dead, the larger the difference between the amounts of ^{12}C and ^{14}C there will be. ^{14}C has a half-life of roughly 5700 years. This means that after 5700 years, half of the ^{14}C in a fossil will have decayed into ^{14}N, its decay product. The other half remains as ^{14}C. After 11,400 years, or two half-lives, 75 percent of the ^{14}C will have decayed.

FIGURE 12.3 DECAY OF ISOTOPES		
Isotope (parent)	**Product (daughter)**	**Half-life (years)**
rubidium-87	strontium-87	48.8 billion
uranium-238	lead-206	4.5 billion
chlorine-36	argon-36	300,000
carbon-14	nitrogen-14	5730

FIGURE 12.4 Radiometric Dating Using Carbon-14

Radiometric dating uses the natural decay rate of unstable isotopes to calculate the age of a fossil.

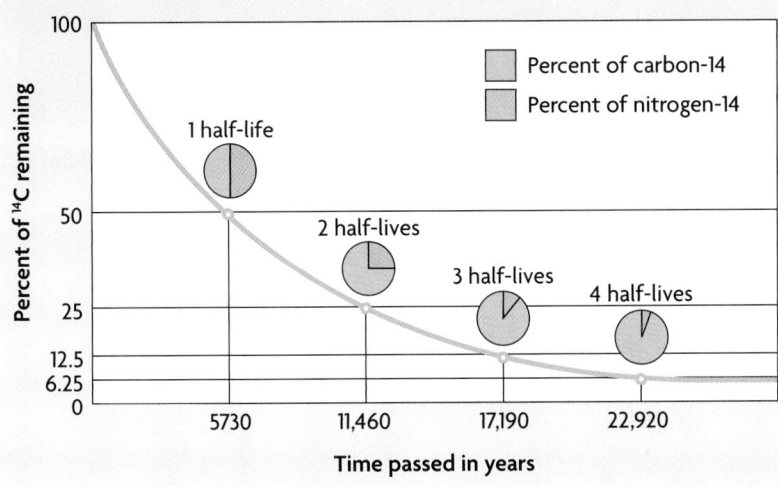

One-quarter of the original ^{14}C remains. Radioactive decay of ^{14}C is shown in **FIGURE 12.4**. Carbon-14 dating can be used to date objects only up to about 45,000 years old. If the objects are older than that, the fraction of ^{14}C will be too small to accurately measure. Older objects can be dated using isotopes with longer half-lives.

Determining Earth's Age

Scientists have used radiometric dating to determine the age of Earth. Because Earth constantly undergoes erosion and rock recycling, rocks on Earth do not remain in their original state. Unlike Earth, meteorites—which are mostly pieces of rock and iron that have fallen to Earth's surface from space—do not get recycled or undergo erosion. Meteorites are thought to have formed at about the same time as Earth. Therefore, meteorites provide an unspoiled sample for radiometric dating. Uranium-to-lead isotope ratios in many meteorite samples consistently estimate Earth's age at about 4.5 billion years.

Summarize Why are meteorites helpful for determining the age of Earth?

12.1 ASSESSMENT

REVIEWING ▷ MAIN IDEAS

1. What types of evidence of ancient life can be preserved as fossils?

2. Why is a uranium **isotope** often used rather than ^{14}C in **radiometric dating** to determine the age of Earth?

CRITICAL THINKING

3. **Apply** Considering that millions of species have lived on Earth, why are there relatively few fossils?

4. **Contrast** Explain the difference between **relative dating** and absolute dating.

Connecting CONCEPTS

5. **Earth Science** When mountains form, the order of rock layers can be disturbed. How could radiometric dating be used to sort out the relative ages of such rock layers?

MATERIALS

- 10 pennies
- graph paper
- 3 pencils of different colors

PROCESS SKILLS

- **Analyzing**
- **Interpreting Data**
- **Modeling**

MICHIGAN STANDARDS

L5.p1D Explain the importance of the fossil record. (prerequisite)

B5.1c Summarize the relationships between present-day organisms and those that inhabited the Earth in the past (e.g., use fossil record, embryonic stages, homologous structures, chemical basis).

Radioactive Decay

In this lab, you will model how scientists determine the age of a fossil. Whereas the scientist pictured is measuring the decay of carbon from a sample of bone, you will model the decay of a fictitious radioactive isotope called "tailsium."

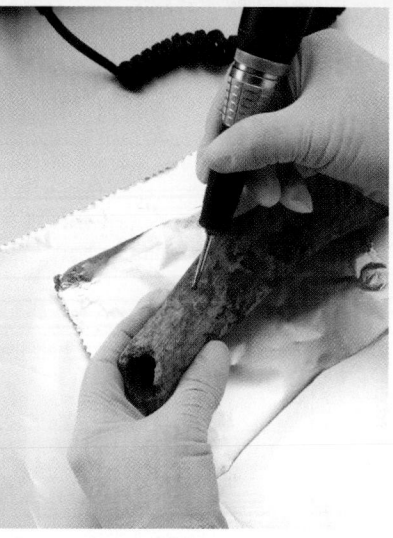

PROBLEM How is the half-life of an unstable isotope used to determine the age of a material?

PROCEDURE

1. Arrange your pennies so that they are all tails-side-up. These pennies represent 10 atoms of "tailsium," a radioactive isotope.

2. Pick up all 10 tailsium atoms and drop them on the table. The pennies that fall heads-side-up represent atoms of a more stable element, "headsium." Put the headsium atoms off to the side. Count the number of tailsium atoms. Record that value in a table under toss 1.

3. Pick up only the tailsium atoms and drop them again. Put the newly formed headsium atoms off to the side with the other headsium atoms. Count the number of tailsium atoms and record this value in your table.

4. Repeat step 3 until there is no more tailsium, or until you have run 10 tosses.

5. Share your results with your class. Using the class data, determine the average number of tailsium atoms that remained after each toss.

ANALYZE AND CONCLUDE

1. **Graph Data** Graph your group results along with the average for the class on the same sheet of graph paper. The number of tosses should be on the *x*-axis, and the number of tailsium atoms remaining should be on the *y*-axis.

2. **Calculate** Using the class average, calculate an average half-life for tailsium. This is the number of tosses it took for half of the pennies to "decay" to headsium.

3. **Analyze** Below is the ideal rate of decay for tailsium. Graph these data on the same axes as your other graphs, using a different colored pencil to differentiate between the data sets. Which data set was closer to the ideal rate of decay, your group's data or the class average? Explain.

TABLE 1. IDEAL RATE OF TAILSIUM DECAY											
Time	Start	1	2	3	4	5	6	7	8	9	10
# tailsium atoms	10	5	2.5	1.25	0.625	0.313	0.156	0.078	0.039	0.019	0

4. **Apply** Assume that there are 20 years between tosses. According to your data from the penny lab, how old would a material be that had 3 tailsium atoms and 7 headsium atoms? How old would it be according to the class data?

12.2 The Geologic Time Scale

KEY CONCEPT The geologic time scale divides Earth's history based on major past events.

MAIN IDEAS
- Index fossils are another tool to determine the age of rock layers.
- The geologic time scale organizes Earth's history.

VOCABULARY
index fossil, p. 365
geologic time scale, p. 367
era, p. 367
period, p. 367

epoch, p. 367
Review
mass extinction,
adaptive radiation

MICHIGAN STANDARDS

L5.p1D Explain the importance of the fossil record. (prerequisite)
B5.1c Summarize the relationships between present-day organisms and those that inhabited the Earth in the past (e.g., use fossil record, embryonic stages, homologous structures, chemical basis).

Connect As you just read, radiometric dating has shown that Earth is very old. It formed about 4.5 billion years ago. Scientists have divided this vast amount of time into manageable units based on major geologic changes.

MAIN IDEA
Index fossils are another tool to determine the age of rock layers.

You have learned that both relative dating and radiometric dating can help scientists determine the age of rock layers. Scientists who are trying to determine the age of a rock layer almost always use two or more methods to confirm results. Index fossils provide an additional tool to determine the age of fossils or the strata in which they are found. **Index fossils** are fossils of organisms that existed only during specific spans of time over large geographic areas.

Using index fossils for age estimates of rock layers is not a new idea. In the late 1700s, English geologist William Smith discovered that certain rock layers contained fossils unlike those in other layers. Using these key fossils as markers, Smith could identify a particular layer of rock wherever it was exposed.

The shorter the life span of a species, the more precisely the different strata can be correlated. The best index fossils are common, easy to identify, found widely around the world, and only existed for a relatively brief time. The extinct marine invertebrates known as fusulinids (FYOO-zuh-LY-nihdz), shown in **FIGURE 12.5**, are one example of an index fossil. They were at one time very common but disappeared after a mass extinction event about 248 million years ago. The presence of fusulinids indicates that a rock layer must be between 248 million and 360 million years old. Fossil fusulinids are useful for dating fossils of other organisms in strata because the presence of both organisms in one layer shows that they lived during the same time period.

Apply **Could a rock layer with fusulinid fossils be 100 million years old? Explain.**

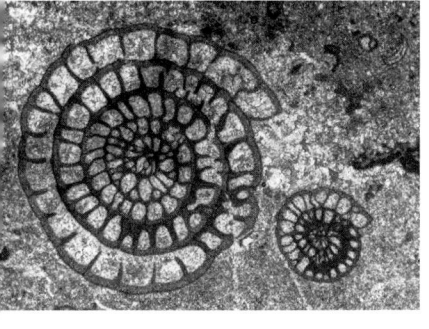

FIGURE 12.5 Fusulinids, tiny fossils usually less than 2 millimeters wide, make good index fossils. They are very abundant in marine sediment, widely distributed, and existed during a specific period of time.

FIGURE 12.6 Geologic Time Scale

X = Major extinction

Millions of years ago (mya)

100
250
550
1000
2000

CENOZOIC ERA

QUATERNARY PERIOD (NEOGENE)
1.8 mya–present This period continues today and includes all modern forms of life.

TERTIARY PERIOD (PALEOGENE)
65–1.8 mya Mammals, flowering plants, grasslands, insects, fish, and birds diversified. Primates evolved.

Primate

MESOZOIC ERA

CRETACEOUS PERIOD
145–65 mya Dinosaur populations peaked and then went extinct. Birds survived to radiate in the Tertiary period. Flowering plants arose.

JURASSIC PERIOD
213–145 mya Dinosaurs diversified, as did early trees that are common today. Oceans were full of fish and squid. First birds arose.

TRIASSIC PERIOD
248–213 mya Following the largest mass extinction to date, dinosaurs evolved, as did plants such as ferns and cycads. Mammals and flying reptiles (pterosaurs) arose.

Mononykus

PALEOZOIC ERA

PERMIAN PERIOD
286–248 mya Modern pine trees first appeared, and Pangaea supercontinent was formed as major landmasses joined together.

CARBONIFEROUS PERIOD
360–286 mya Coal-forming sediments were laid down in vast swamps. Fish continued to diversify. Life forms included amphibians, winged insects, early conifers, and small reptiles.

Pine tree

DEVONIAN PERIOD
410–360 mya Fish diversified. First sharks, amphibians, and insects appeared. First trees and forests arose.

SILURIAN PERIOD
440–410 mya Earliest land plants arose. Melting of glaciers allowed seas to form. Jawless and freshwater fishes evolved.

Jawless fish

ORDOVICIAN PERIOD
505–440 mya Diverse marine invertebrates evolved, as did the earliest vertebrates. Massive glaciers formed, causing sea levels to drop and a mass extinction of marine life to occur.

CAMBRIAN PERIOD
544–505 mya All existing animal phyla developed over a relatively short period of time known as the Cambrian Explosion.

Trilobite

PRECAMBRIAN TIME

This time span makes up the vast majority of Earth's history. It includes the oldest known rocks and fossils, the origin of eukaryotes, and the oldest animal fossils. (colored SEM; magnification 50×)

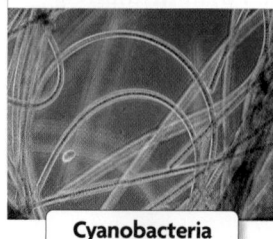
Cyanobacteria

▶ MAIN IDEA

The geologic time scale organizes Earth's history.

The **geologic time scale,** shown in **FIGURE 12.6,** is a representation of the history of Earth. It organizes Earth's history by major changes or events that have occurred, using evidence from the fossil and geologic records. Scientists worked out the entire geologic time scale during the 1800s and early 1900s. Although they are still being changed a little bit here and there, the main divisions of geologic time have stayed the same for over a hundred years.

The time scale is divided into a series of units based on the order in which different groups of rocks and fossils were formed. The geologic time scale consists of three basic units of time.

- **Eras** last tens to hundreds of millions of years and consist of two or more periods.
- **Periods** are the most commonly used units of time on the geologic time scale, lasting tens of millions of years. Each period is associated with a particular type of rock system.
- **Epochs** (EHP-uhks) are the smallest units of geologic time and last several million years.

The names of the eras came from early ideas about life forms preserved as fossils. *Paleozoic* means "ancient life," *Mesozoic* means "middle life," and *Cenozoic* means "recent life." Within the eras, the boundaries between many of the geologic periods are defined by mass extinction events. These events help to define when one period ends and another begins. The largest adaptive radiations tend to follow large mass extinctions. Recall that adaptive radiation happens when a group of organisms diversifies into several species. Those species adapt to different ecological niches because mass extinctions make many niches available. Over generations, the adaptive traits favored within these newly opened niches may become common for that population of organisms, and speciation may occur.

Summarize **Why do adaptive radiations often occur after mass extinctions?**

> **Connecting CONCEPTS**
>
> **Adaptive Radiation** Recall from **Chapter 11** that *adaptive radiation* refers to the change of a single species into several forms that are each adapted to a specific environmental niche.

12.2 / ASSESSMENT

ONLINE QUIZ ClassZone.com

REVIEWING ▶ MAIN IDEAS

1. How are **index fossils** used to date rock layers?
2. What is the usefulness of categorizing Earth's history into the **geologic time scale**?

CRITICAL THINKING

3. **Infer** The most common index fossils are shells of invertebrates. Give two reasons why this is so.
4. **Analyze** Scientists have inferred that there have been at least five mass extinctions in Earth's history. How would fossil evidence support this inference?

Connecting CONCEPTS

5. **Scientific Process** French physicist Henri Becquerel discovered radioactivity in 1896, after geologists had developed the geologic time scale. How did Becquerel's discovery help later geologists as they refined the time scale?

12.3 Origin of Life

KEY CONCEPT The origin of life on Earth remains a puzzle.

▶ MAIN IDEAS

- Earth was very different billions of years ago.
- Several sets of hypotheses propose how life began on Earth.

VOCABULARY

nebula, p. 368
ribozyme, p. 370

MICHIGAN STANDARDS

B1.2h Describe the distinctions between scientific theories, laws, hypotheses, and observations.
L2.p1A Distinguish between living and nonliving systems. (prerequisite)

Connect By studying the geologic time scale, it is clear that the farther back in Earth's history we go, the tougher it is to piece together what life at that time was like. Hypotheses of how Earth formed and life began have been proposed and researched. But as with any branch of science, questions still remain.

▶ MAIN IDEA

Earth was very different billions of years ago.

For centuries, many of history's greatest minds have wondered about the origin of Earth and its living things. Despite differences over the details of Earth's origins, most scientists agree on two key points: (1) Earth is billions of years old, and (2) the conditions of the early planet and its atmosphere were very different from those of today.

Today, the most widely accepted hypothesis of Earth's origins suggests that the solar system was formed by a condensing **nebula,** a cloud of gas and dust in space, as shown in **FIGURE 12.7.** This hypothesis is supported by computer models and observations made with the Hubble Space Telescope. It suggests that about 4.6 billion years ago, the Sun formed from a nebula. Over time, most of the material in the nebula pulled together due to gravity. Materials that remained in the nebula's disk circled the newly formed Sun. Over millions of years, repeated collisions of this space debris built up into the planets of our solar system.

Earth was most likely violent and very hot for its first 700 million years, a time now called the Hadean eon. Many asteroids, meteorites, and comets struck the planet, releasing enormous amounts of heat. Meanwhile, the radioactive decay of elements trapped deep within Earth released heat as well. This intense heat kept the materials making up Earth in a molten state. Over time, these materials separated into Earth's layers. Hydrogen, carbon monoxide, and nitrogen gas were released from the interior. They combined to form an atmosphere containing compounds such as ammonia, water vapor, methane, and carbon dioxide. Most scientists agree that free oxygen was not abundant until about 2 billion years ago, after the first forms of life had begun to evolve.

Toward the end of the Hadean eon, between 4 and 3.8 billion years ago, impacts became less frequent. That allowed Earth to cool down. Solar radiation and lightning produced energy for reactions on Earth and in the early atmosphere. The continents began to form. Water vapor condensed and fell as rain that collected in pools and larger bodies of water.

FIGURE 12.7 One hypothesis proposes that the Sun and planets formed from a rotating disk of gas and dust about 4.6 billion years ago.

Once liquid water was present, organic compounds could be formed from inorganic materials. All living matter is organic, as are the building blocks of life such as sugars and amino acids. However, you'll see below that the leap that resulted in life on Earth required conditions other than just the presence of water.

Summarize Describe the nebular hypothesis of Earth's origin.

▶ MAIN IDEA
Several sets of hypotheses propose how life began on Earth.

Since the 1950s, scientists have proposed several hypotheses to explain how life began on Earth. These hypotheses have looked at early organic molecules, how cell structures might have evolved, and early genetic material.

Organic Molecule Hypotheses
There are two general hypotheses about how life-supporting molecules appeared on early Earth.

Miller-Urey experiment In 1953 Stanley Miller and Harold Urey designed an experiment to test a hypothesis first proposed in the 1920s. Earlier scientists had proposed that an input of energy from lightning led to the formation of organic molecules from inorganic molecules present in the atmosphere of early Earth. Miller and Urey built a system to model conditions on early Earth, as shown in **FIGURE 12.8.** They demonstrated that organic compounds could be made by passing an electrical current, to simulate lightning, through a closed system that held a mixture of gases. These gases—methane (CH_4), ammonia (NH_3), hydrogen (H_2), and water vapor (H_2O)—were thought to be present in the early atmosphere. The Miller-Urey experiment produced a variety of organic compounds, such as amino acids. Later, scientists suggested different compounds were present in the early atmosphere. However, similar experiments using more recent estimates of conditions on early Earth have also produced organic molecules, including amino acids and nucleotides.

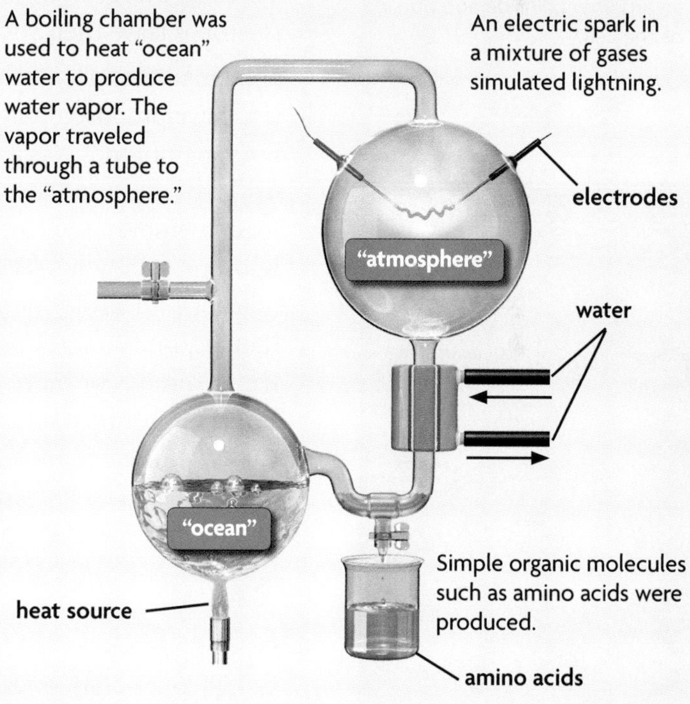

Meteorite hypothesis Analysis of a meteorite that fell near Murchison, Australia, in 1969 revealed that organic molecules can be found in space. More than 90 amino acids have been identified from this meteorite. Nineteen of these amino acids are found on Earth, and many others have been made in experiments similar to the Miller-Urey study. This evidence suggests that amino acids could have been present when Earth formed, or that these organic molecules may have arrived on Earth through meteorite or asteroid impacts.

FIGURE 12.8 Miller-Urey Experiment

A laboratory model is used to represent the conditions of early Earth. This experiment demonstrated that organic molecules can be made from inorganic molecules.

A boiling chamber was used to heat "ocean" water to produce water vapor. The vapor traveled through a tube to the "atmosphere."

An electric spark in a mixture of gases simulated lightning.

electrodes

"atmosphere"

water

"ocean"

heat source

Simple organic molecules such as amino acids were produced.

amino acids

Early Cell Structure Hypotheses

There are several hypotheses of how the first cells may have formed. One concerns how organic molecules could have been brought together, and another addresses how cell membranes may have formed.

Iron-sulfide bubbles hypothesis In the 1990s, biologists William Martin and Michael Russell noted that hot iron sulfide rising from below the ocean floor combines with the cooler ocean water to form chimneylike structures made of many compartments. Russell modeled this process in the laboratory by injecting warm sodium sulfide into a cool iron-rich solution. Iron sulfide bubbles quickly formed, making a similar chimney structure within minutes.

Russell proposed that around 4 billion years ago, biological molecules combined in the compartments of these chimneys. The compartment walls concentrated the basic organic molecules in a small space. Thus, the walls of the compartments, Russell proposed, acted as the first cell membranes. Once the right ingredients came together, the first organic cell membranes could form. These membranes would have let early microbes leave their rocky compartments.

FIGURE 12.9 Hydrothermal vents produce sulfur that mixes with ocean water to make compartments of rock. These structures may have created conditions necessary for early life to form.

Lipid membrane hypothesis Several scientists have proposed that the evolution of lipid membranes was a crucial step for the origin of life. Lipid molecules spontaneously form membrane-enclosed spheres, called liposomes, shown in **FIGURE 12.10**. In 1992 biochemist Harold Morowitz tested the idea that at some point liposomes were formed with a double, or bilayer, lipid membrane. These liposomes could then form around a variety of organic molecules, such as amino acids, fatty acids, sugars, and nucleotides. The liposomes would act as membranes that separated these organic molecules from the environment. These cell-like structures would later give rise to the first true cells.

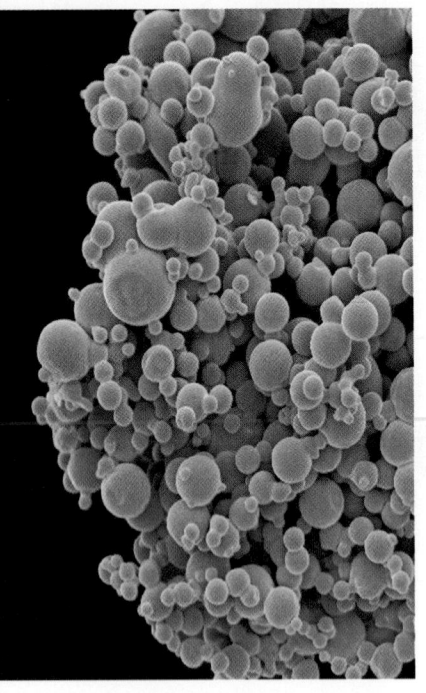

FIGURE 12.10 Liposomes have a lipid membrane that is similar to the membrane of a living cell.
(colored SEM; magnification 1500×)

RNA as Early Genetic Material

A hypothesis that has gained much support in recent years proposes that RNA, rather than DNA, was the genetic material that stored information in living things on early Earth. In the 1980s, Thomas Cech from the University of Colorado and Sidney Altman from Yale University independently discovered that RNA can catalyze reactions. **Ribozymes** are RNA molecules that can catalyze specific chemical reactions. As **FIGURE 12.11** shows, ribozymes can catalyze their own replication and synthesis. RNA can copy itself, chop itself into pieces, and from these pieces make even more RNA. Unlike RNA, DNA needs enzymes to replicate itself.

FIGURE 12.11 RNA AND DNA

RNA, in the form of a ribozyme, is able to replicate itself without the help of additional enzymes.

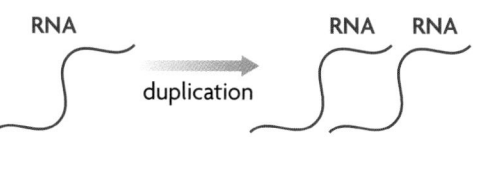

DNA requires many enzymes to replicate. Helicase enzymes separate the DNA strand and polymerase enzymes add nucleotides to the DNA strands.

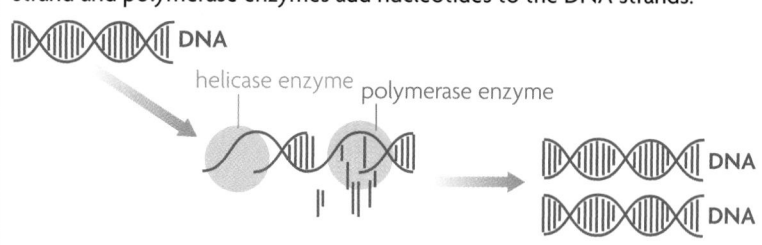

Along with the discovery of ribozymes, several other types of evidence support the RNA hypothesis. Short chains of RNA will form from inorganic materials in a test tube. If zinc is added as a catalyst, longer chains will grow. Also, RNA will fold into different shapes depending upon its sequence of nucleotides. Thus, it can perform more functions than DNA. But RNA does not catalyze chemical reactions as well as proteins do, nor does it store genetic information as well as DNA does. Over time, RNA may have become less important for these functions.

Perhaps the earliest replicating RNA molecule gained simple membranes over many generations through natural selection. Membranes might protect chemical reactions and make them work more efficiently. RNA molecules that made copies of themselves in a double-stranded form, similar to DNA, might eventually have been selected because fewer mutations would occur. Since DNA is more stable than RNA, it may have replaced RNA as the genetic material. Currently, there are several hypotheses about how RNA could have led to life as we know it today. Laboratory experiments in which RNA molecules survive and self-replicate support the idea of early cells being based on RNA. This model of the origins of life on Earth is sometimes called the RNA world.

Synthesize **Could cell structures or RNA have been present before organic molecules existed on Earth? Explain.**

12.3 / ASSESSMENT

ONLINE QUIZ
ClassZone.com

REVIEWING ▶ MAIN IDEAS

1. Describe the environmental conditions that are thought to have existed during the Hadean eon.

2. Describe two different hypotheses of the origin of early cell structure.

CRITICAL THINKING

3. **Evaluate** The theory of impact frustration proposes that life may have started several times during the Hadean eon, but was interrupted by space debris hitting Earth. What makes this theory difficult to test?

4. **Contrast** How are the two organic molecule hypotheses different?

Connecting CONCEPTS

5. **Protein Synthesis** RNA is hypothesized to be the earliest form of genetic material because it can store information, catalyze its own replication, and catalyze other reactions. Which two of these functions can DNA not do? Which two can proteins not do?

Early Single-Celled Organisms

KEY CONCEPT Single-celled organisms existed 3.8 billion years ago.

▶ MAIN IDEAS

- Microbes have changed the physical and chemical composition of Earth.
- Eukaryotic cells may have evolved through endosymbiosis.
- The evolution of sexual reproduction led to increased diversity.

VOCABULARY

cyanobacteria, p. 372
endosymbiosis, p. 373

Review
prokaryote, anaerobic, eukaryote, aerobic, asexual reproduction, sexual reproduction

MICHIGAN STANDARDS

B2.4g Explain that some structures in the modern eukaryotic cell developed from early prokaryotes, such as mitochondria, and in plants, chloroplasts.

L4.p1A Compare and contrast the differences between sexual and asexual reproduction. (prerequisite)

Connect By 3.8 billion years ago, the seas of the early Earth were full of organic molecules. As you have read, the leap from free-floating molecules to the first true cells has yet to be discovered. But once the first cells arose, they forever changed Earth's environment.

▶ MAIN IDEA

Microbes have changed the physical and chemical composition of Earth.

Single-celled organisms changed Earth's surface by depositing minerals. They changed the atmosphere by giving off oxygen as a by-product of photosynthesis. However, before photosynthesis evolved, the first prokaryotes would have been anaerobic, living without oxygen. Many of these early prokaryotes probably got their energy from organic molecules.

Scientists have found evidence that photosynthetic life evolved more than 3.5 billion years ago, since that is the age of the oldest known fossils. These fossils are of a group of marine **cyanobacteria** (SY-uh-noh-bak-TEER-ee-uh), which are bacteria that can carry out photosynthesis. Like all early life forms, each cyanobacterium was a single prokaryotic cell. Recall from Chapter 3 that prokaryotic cells have no membrane-bound organelles.

Some cyanobacteria live in colonies and form stromatolites (stroh-MAT-l-yts). Stromatolites are domed, rocky structures made of layers of cyanobacteria and sediment. There are many stromatolite fossils, but some are living communities, as shown in **FIGURE 12.12**. Fossils of stromatolites as old as 3.5 billion years have been found. Communities of photosynthesizing cyanobacteria in stromatolites released oxygen as a by-product. Higher oxygen levels in the atmosphere and the ocean allowed the evolution of aerobic prokaryotes, which need oxygen to live.

Apply How are stromatolites evidence of Earth's early life?

FIGURE 12.12 Stromatolites, like these found in Australia, are made by cyanobacteria. Cyanobacteria are considered to have been among the first organisms on early Earth.

▶ MAIN IDEA

Eukaryotic cells may have evolved through endosymbiosis.

The fossil record shows that eukaryotic organisms had evolved by 1.5 billion years ago. Unlike a prokaryote, a eukaryote has a nucleus and other membrane-bound organelles. Eukaryotic cells were all aerobic. While the first eukaryotes were made of only one cell, later eukaryotic organisms became multicellular, or made of many cells. All cells in multicellular organisms today are eukaryotic.

One hypothesis of eukaryote evolution, proposed more than a hundred years ago, did not get much attention until the 1970s. Biologist Lynn Margulis of the University of Massachusetts found evidence to support the theory of endosymbiosis. **Endosymbiosis** (EHN-doh-SIHM-bee-OH-sihs) is a relationship in which one organism lives within the body of another, and both benefit from the relationship.

The theory of endosymbiosis suggests that early mitochondria and chloroplasts were once simple prokaryotic cells that were taken up by larger prokaryotes around 1.5 billion years ago. Instead of being digested, some of the smaller prokaryotes may have survived inside the larger ones as illustrated in **FIGURE 12.13**. This relationship would have had its advantages. If it took in a prokaryote that acted as a mitochondrion, the larger cell got energy in the form of ATP. If it took in a prokaryote that acted as a chloroplast, the larger cell could use photosynthesis to make sugars. In exchange, the mitochondria and the chloroplasts found a stable environment and nutrients.

Margulis based her theory on several factors. Unlike other organelles, mitochondria and chloroplasts have their own DNA and ribosomes. They can copy themselves within the cell in which they are found. Mitochondria and chloroplasts are also about the same size as prokaryotes, their DNA forms a circle, and their gene structures are similar to that of prokaryotes.

Analyze What evidence supports the theory of endosymbiosis?

VOCABULARY

Endosymbiosis can be broken down into *endo-*, meaning "within," *sym-*, meaning "together," and *biosis*, meaning "way of life."

FIGURE 12.13 Endosymbiosis

The theory of endosymbiosis proposes that the mitochondria found in eukaryotic cells descended from ancestors of infection-causing bacteria. Likewise, chloroplasts are considered descendants of cyanobacteria.

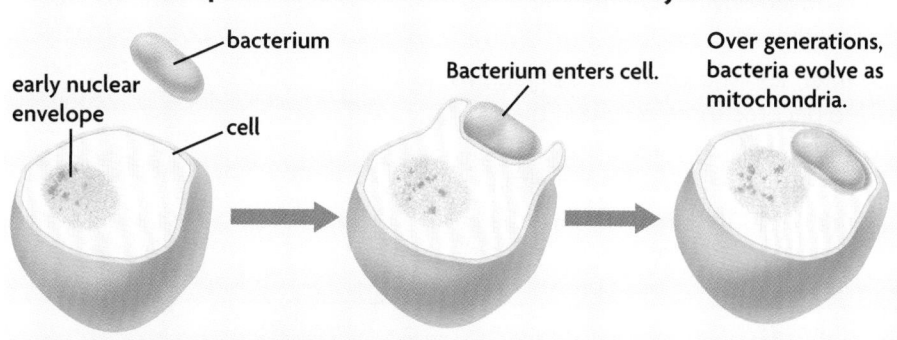

early nuclear envelope · bacterium · cell

Bacterium enters cell.

Over generations, bacteria evolve as mitochondria.

Animated BIOLOGY

Watch endosymbiosis in action at ClassZone.com.

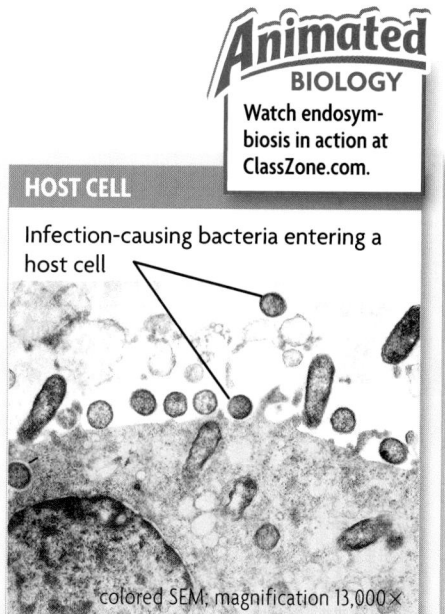

HOST CELL

Infection-causing bacteria entering a host cell

colored SEM; magnification 13,000×

Chapter 12: The History of Life   **373**

▶ MAIN IDEA

The evolution of sexual reproduction led to increased diversity.

The first prokaryotes and eukaryotes could only reproduce asexually. Some time later, eukaryotic cells began to reproduce sexually. Of the groups of organisms that reproduce asexually today, only a few—such as bacteria and certain groups of mites—appear to have ancient asexual origins.

Recall from Chapter 5 that in asexual reproduction, a single parent produces offspring that are genetically identical to itself. Asexual reproduction lets organisms have many offspring quickly. Sexual reproduction, on the other hand, needs two parents. Both parents give genes to their offspring. This means that individuals must use time and energy to find a mate, and each parent passes on only half of its genes to offspring.

The evolution of sexual reproduction is still an active area of research. The disadvantages of sexual reproduction—needing a partner and passing on only half of a set of genes—seem clear. One advantage to sexual reproduction, however, is genetic variation. Sexual reproduction allows new combinations of genes to come together. This process may mask harmful mutations, and in some cases it may also bring beneficial mutations together.

Sexual reproduction may also have resulted in an increase in the rate of evolution by natural selection. Sexual reproduction creates more genetic variation, which lets a population adapt quickly to new conditions. Over a long time, early eukaryotes may have gained variations that made living closely together, and eventually cooperating, beneficial. Thus, sexual reproduction may have been the first step in the evolution of multicellular life.

Infer How can mutations be beneficial to organisms?

Connecting CONCEPTS

Genetics Recall from **Chapter 6** that recombination is an important source of genetic variation. Sexual reproduction results in many different phenotypes through the process of producing gametes and during crossing-over in meiosis.

12.4 ASSESSMENT

ONLINE QUIZ
ClassZone.com

REVIEWING ▶ MAIN IDEAS

1. How did early **cyanobacteria** affect the physical and chemical conditions on Earth?

2. How does the theory of **endosymbiosis** account for the evolution of eukaryotes?

3. How does sexual reproduction increase diversity among living things?

CRITICAL THINKING

4. **Apply** How does sexual reproduction increase the chances that some individuals will survive changed environmental conditions?

5. **Infer** For photosynthetic organisms to become more common than those that get energy from eating organic molecules, what environmental conditions must have changed?

Connecting CONCEPTS

6. **Scientific Process** According to the theory of endosymbiosis, mitochondria were once independent organisms. Do you think it's possible that mitochondria might now be able to exist independently if removed from a cell? Describe how you could investigate this.

Generation Times of Bacteria

Determining the correct scales of axes on graphs is important so that all data points can be plotted. The scale can also influence the reader's perception of the results. If the intervals are too far apart, the slope of the graph will seem steep—indicating a fast rate or a large change in the data. If the intervals are too small, the graph will be flatter, with change that seems small or nonexistent.

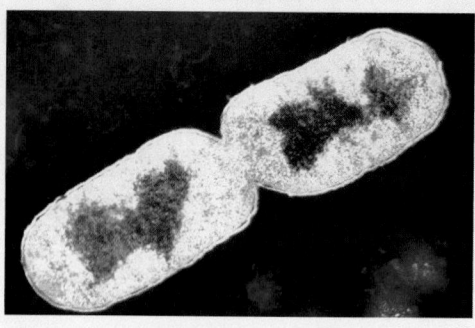

***E. coli* bacteria dividing** (colored SEM; magnification 32,000×)

EXAMPLE

Some species that reproduce asexually have the benefit of short generation times. They may be able to adapt more quickly to changing environmental conditions. Bacteria populations, for instance, can quickly become resistant to antibiotics. Individual bacteria that survive antibiotic treatment will pass the gene for resistance to their offspring when they reproduce.

The population of bacteria doubles with each generation. The following are the steps used to determine axis intervals of the line graph of the growth of *Escherichia coli* over 5 generations:

- Calculate the difference between the smallest and largest values of the variable and divide the difference by the number of data points. For the *E. coli* data, 85 − 17 = 68. Divided by 5, this equals 13.6.
- Round the result to the nearest convenient number, such as 2, 5, or 10. For *E. coli,* the interval was rounded down to 12.
- Use the rounded number as the interval.
- Begin the scale on the axis at zero (or at one interval lower than the lowest value if the values to be graphed are much larger than the interval).
- End the scale above the highest value. For *E. coli,* the scale ranges from 0 to 96.

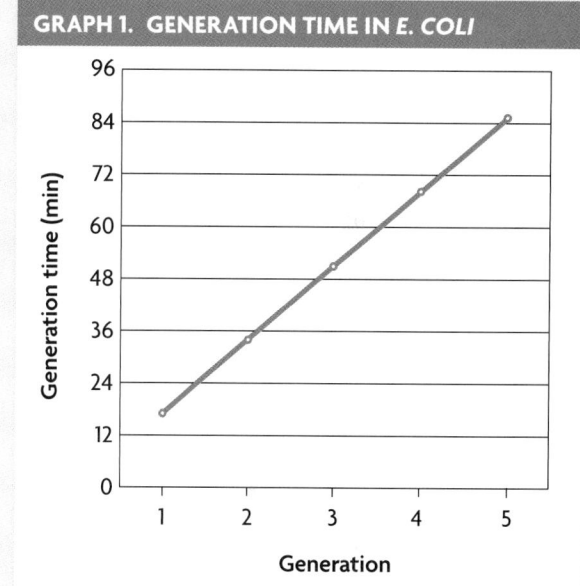

GRAPH 1. GENERATION TIME IN *E. COLI*

CALCULATE AXES INTERVALS

1. **Graph Data** Calculate the intervals for the *y*-axis and *x*-axis for a graph that compares the generation times of all three of the bacteria species listed below. Draw the axes, plot the data, and label each of the three plotted lines. Be sure to title your graph and label your axes.

TABLE 1. GENERATION TIMES FOR COMMON BACTERIA					
Bacteria	**Generation 1 Time (min)**	**Generation 2 Time (min)**	**Generation 3 Time (min)**	**Generation 4 Time (min)**	**Generation 5 Time (min)**
	10 bacteria	**20 bacteria**	**40 bacteria**	**80 bacteria**	**160 bacteria**
E. coli	17	34	51	68	85
B. megaterium	25	50	75	100	125
S. lactis	48	96	144	192	240

2. **Analyze** Using your graph for *E. coli* as an example, explain how changing the axes of a graph can influence how data are interpreted.

12.5 Radiation of Multicellular Life

KEY CONCEPT Multicellular life evolved in distinct phases.

▶ MAIN IDEAS

- Life moved onto land during the Paleozoic era.
- Reptiles radiated during the Mesozoic era.
- Mammals radiated during the Cenozoic era.

VOCABULARY

Paleozoic, p. 376
Cambrian explosion, p. 376
Mesozoic, p. 377
Cenozoic, p. 378

MICHIGAN STANDARDS

B5.1c Summarize the relationships between present-day organisms and those that inhabited the Earth in the past (e.g., use fossil record, embryonic stages, homologous structures, chemical basis).

Connect Due to early photosynthetic organisms, oxygen levels in Earth's atmosphere began to increase dramatically about 2 billion years ago. As multicellular organisms evolved, the new environment produced new ecological opportunities for organisms.

▶ MAIN IDEA

Life moved onto land during the Paleozoic era.

The trend toward multicellular organisms was one of the most important transitions in the history of life. One hypothesis suggests that it was an advantage for early one-celled organisms to increase in size by becoming multicellular. Cells that cooperated could compete more effectively for energy, by processes such as cooperative feeding. At some point, increased dependence on neighboring cells would have led the cells to function as a colony.

Multicellular organisms first appeared during the **Paleozoic** (PAY-lee-uh-ZOH-ihk) era, which began 544 million years ago. Members of every major animal group evolved within only a few million years. The era ended 248 million years ago with a mass extinction. More than 90 percent of marine animal species and 70 percent of land animal species of that time became extinct. In between these remarkable events, multicellular animals radiated, the first vertebrates evolved, and early plants moved onto land.

The earliest part of the Paleozoic era, the Cambrian period, is often called the **Cambrian explosion.** During the Cambrian explosion, a huge diversity of animal species evolved. At the start of the Paleozoic era, all life was found in the ocean. Among the earliest vertebrates was a group of jawless fishes. Marine invertebrates, such as the trilobites, were especially abundant. This highly diverse group of arthropods had thousands of species, though almost half of these species died in the mass extinction event at the end of the Cambrian period. Many other animals from this time period are also extinct. The best-known of these are found at the Burgess Shale site in British Columbia, where many fossils were well preserved.

The middle of the Paleozoic era was a time of great diversity as life moved onto land. The number and variety of plant groups greatly increased. Four-legged vertebrates, such as amphibians, became common. Most of the coal used in the United States formed during the Carboniferous period of this era, illustrated in **FIGURE 12.14**. The decomposed remains of millions of organisms were buried in sediment and changed over time into coal and the petroleum that fuels our cars today.

Summarize Why is the Cambrian period also called the Cambrian explosion?

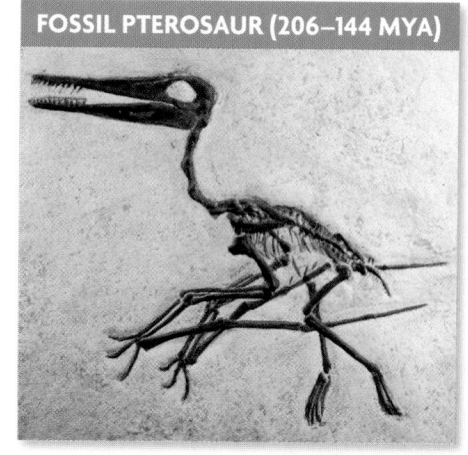
FOSSIL PTEROSAUR (206–144 MYA)

▶ MAIN IDEA
Reptiles radiated during the Mesozoic era.

The **Mesozoic** (MEHZ-uh-ZOH-ihk) era began 248 million years ago and ended 65 million years ago. Called the Age of Reptiles because the dinosaurs roamed Earth during this era, the Mesozoic also featured birds and flowering plants. The oldest direct ancestor of mammals first appeared during this era. By the era's end, mammals—particularly marsupials, whose young develop in a pouch—had evolved numerous key traits that improved their chances of survival during the mass extinction at the end of the era.

FIGURE 12.15 This illustration depicts a scene from the Jurassic period of the Mesozoic era. Fossils of pterosaurs (above) have been found in groups, suggesting that they may have lived in colonies.

The Mesozoic era is divided into three periods: the Triassic, the Jurassic, and the Cretaceous. Life took off slowly in the early Triassic, as organisms that survived earlier extinction events explored new environments. On land, the earliest crocodiles and dinosaurs arose. The fossil record shows that the first mammals also evolved during this time. An extinction event near the end of the Triassic destroyed many animal families. This mass extinction allowed the radiation of the dinosaurs in the Jurassic period, illustrated in **FIGURE 12.15**.

Although life had moved onto land, it was abundant under water as well. Ichthyosaurs (IK-thee-uh-SAWRZ), a specialized group of predatory marine reptiles, dominated the oceans. Sharks and bony fishes continued to evolve more complex forms.

The peak in dinosaur diversity, the Cretaceous period, also saw the rise of the first marsupial mammals. The period ended in the most famous of the mass extinctions, when a massive meteorite struck Earth. This impact sent enormous amounts of dust and debris into the atmosphere. Scientists think this airborne debris kept much of the Sun's light from reaching Earth, which in turn caused a change in climate and reduced photosynthesis. Without plants to eat, dinosaurs became extinct.

Analyze How had life on Earth changed from the beginning of the Paleozoic era to the end of the Mesozoic?

▶ **MAIN IDEA**

Mammals radiated during the Cenozoic era.

HORSE ANCESTOR (55 MYA)

FIGURE 12.16 This illustration depicts a scene from the Tertiary period of the Cenozoic era. This ancestor of modern-day horses (above) was the size of a small dog.

The **Cenozoic** era (SEE-nuh-ZOH-ihk) began 65 million years ago and continues today. It is divided into two periods, the Tertiary (65–1.8 million years ago), illustrated in **FIGURE 12.16**, and the Quaternary (1.8 million years ago until today). During the Tertiary, placental mammals and monotremes—a small group of mammals that lay eggs—evolved and diversified. Their adaptive radiation rivaled that of the marsupials in the Mesozoic. The most dramatic radiation of the mammals, however, occurred with the placentals. Today, this group numbers roughly 4000 species. During the Tertiary period, birds, ray-finned fishes, and flowering plants also underwent dramatic radiations.

The earliest ancestors of modern humans evolved near the end of the Tertiary. However, *Homo sapiens,* anatomically modern humans, did not appear until about 100,000 years ago, very recently in Earth's history. The evolution of primates is covered in the next section.

Infer Why is the Cenozoic era sometimes referred to as the Age of Mammals?

Connecting CONCEPTS

Mammals Placental mammals include all mammals except monotremes, which lay eggs, and marsupials, which rear their underdeveloped young in a pouch. You will learn more about mammals in **Chapter 26.**

NSTA scilinks.org SCI LINKS

For more about the rise of mammals, go to scilinks.org. Keycode: MLB012

12.5 ASSESSMENT

ONLINE QUIZ
ClassZone.com

REVIEWING ▶ MAIN IDEAS

1. What important events occurred during the **Paleozoic** era?

2. What were some of the key appearances and radiations in the **Mesozoic** era?

3. What two groups of mammals evolved during the **Cenozoic** era?

CRITICAL THINKING

4. **Contrast** Examine the illustrations of the Paleozoic, Mesozoic, and Cenozoic eras in this section. What differences can you see in plant and animal diversity across these eras?

5. **Infer** How does a great diversity of organisms increase the chances that some will survive a major change in the environment?

Connecting CONCEPTS

6. **Ecology** How do you think the evolution of flowering plants affected the evolution and radiation of birds?

12.6 Primate Evolution

KEY CONCEPT Humans appeared late in Earth's history.

▶ MAIN IDEAS

- Humans share a common ancestor with other primates.
- There are many fossils of extinct hominids.
- Modern humans arose about 200,000 years ago.

VOCABULARY

primate, p. 379
prosimian, p. 379
anthropoid, p. 380

hominid, p. 380
bipedal, p. 381

Connect In terms of the geologic time scale, the evolution of humans has occurred only very recently. Many fossils of our early ancestors consist of partial skeletons from which details must be inferred through careful study. Though far from complete, this fossil record offers a fascinating glimpse of our past.

▶ MAIN IDEA

Humans share a common ancestor with other primates.

The common ancestor of all primates probably arose before the mass extinction that closed the Cretaceous period 65 million years ago. **Primates** make up a category of mammals with flexible hands and feet, forward-looking eyes—which allows for excellent three-dimensional vision—and enlarged brains relative to body size. Primates also have arms that can rotate in a circle around their shoulder joint, and many primates have thumbs that can move against their fingers. Primates include lemurs, monkeys, apes, and humans. In addition to sharing similar physical traits, primates share strong molecular similarities.

Primate Evolution

Similar to other groups of related organisms, the relationship among the primate groups forms a many-branched tree. At the tree's base is the common ancestor of all primates. Just above this base, the tree splits into two main subgroups: the prosimians and the anthropoids. **Prosimians** (proh-SIHM-ee-uhnz) are the oldest living primate group, and most are small and active at night. This group of nocturnal animals includes the lemurs, the lorises, and the tarsiers, like the ones shown in **FIGURE 12.17**. Tarsiers have been called living fossils, as their physical traits have changed little since their appearance in the fossil record more than 40 million years ago.

TAKING NOTES

Make a concept map of primate classification. Add more shapes as needed.

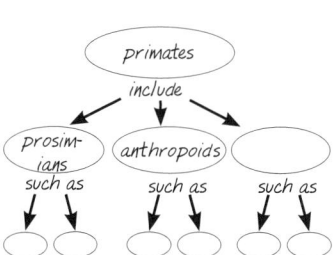

FIGURE 12.17 Prosimians, such as these tarsiers, are the oldest living primate group. They are active at night and have large eyes and ears.

Anthropoids (AN-thruh-POYDZ), the humanlike primates, are further subdivided into the New World monkeys, Old World monkeys, and hominoids, as shown in **FIGURE 12.18.** New World monkeys, which are native to the Americas, all live in trees. Many species have prehensile, or grasping, tails, an adaptation that allows them to hang by their tails from tree branches while feeding. Some Old World monkeys also spend time in trees, but most travel and forage on the ground as well. They have larger brains than do New World monkeys and a greater ability to manipulate objects.

The hominoids can be further divided into the lesser apes (gibbons), the great apes (orangutans, chimpanzees, and gorillas), and the hominids. **Hominids** walk upright, have long lower limbs, thumbs that oppose—or work against—the other four fingers, and relatively large brains. This group includes all of the species in the human lineage, both modern and extinct.

FIGURE 12.18 Evolutionary Relationships of Primates

Primates are divided into two groups: anthropoids and prosimians. Anthropoids are divided into hominoids and monkeys. The last division is between the apes and hominids, which include humans.

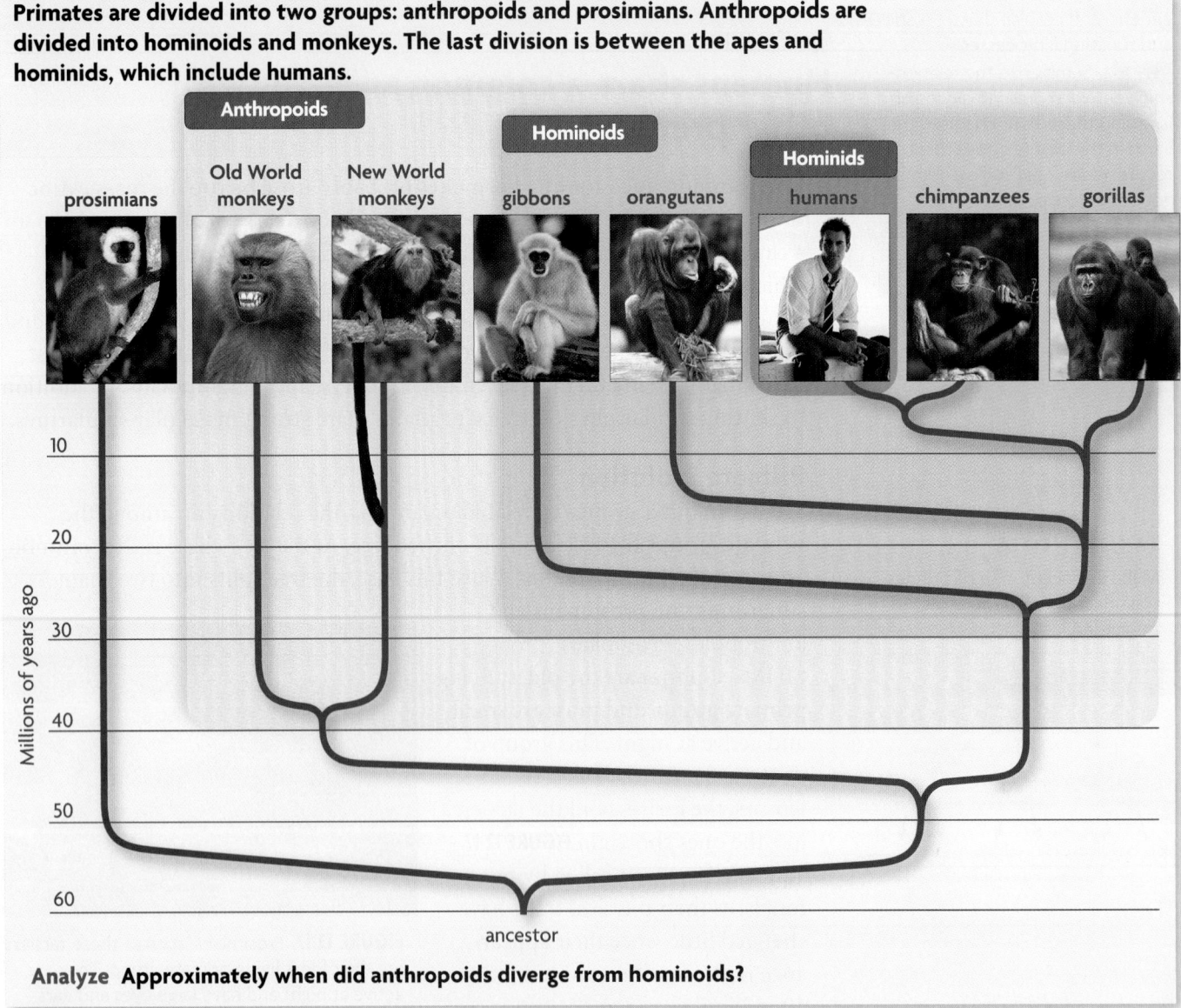

Analyze Approximately when did anthropoids diverge from hominoids?

Walking Upright

Many hypotheses have been proposed to explain the evolutionary success of the hominids. Enlarged brain size and the ability to make and use tools were for many years among the most accepted ideas. However, fossil discoveries have revealed that another trait came before tool use and the large brains—walking upright on two legs. Upright posture and two-legged walking required changes in skeletal anatomy. These changes can be found in intermediate fossils between hominoids that walked only on all fours and early hominids that walked on two legs. Animals that can walk on two legs are called **bipedal** (by-PEHD-l). This trait has important adaptive advantages. It allows higher reach into tree branches while foraging, and perhaps most importantly, it frees the hands for foraging, carrying infants and food, and using tools.

> **VISUAL VOCAB**
>
> **Bipedal** is an adjective that describes two-legged or upright walking. *Bi-* means "two," and *ped* means "foot."

Connect **What is another common animal that is bipedal?**

QUICK LAB MODELING

Geologic Clock

One way to understand the relative length of time in Earth's history is to compare its age to a clock face. Precambrian time goes from 12 noon to about 10:30 P.M. The time span from early human ancestors—more than 5 million years ago—to *Homo sapiens* covers less than a second on our 12-hour clock!

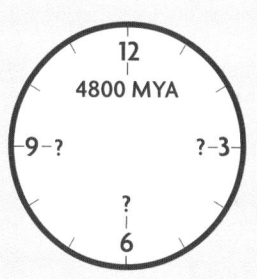

PROBLEM How do different geologic time periods compare?

PROCEDURE

1. Draw a large circle and mark the 12, 3, 6, and 9 positions of a clock face. Use the scale 1 hour = 400 million years ago, and label the four positions with the appropriate number of years, starting with 12 o'clock = 4800 million years ago. (Example: the three o'clock position = 3600 million years ago.)

2. Using the geological time scale, label Precambrian time and the three eras on your clock, along with the approximate time frames in which they occurred.

3. Label the following events on your clock in the appropriate positions, also filling in the approximate time frames they occurred: formation of Earth, oldest rocks, first stromatolites, first aerobic prokaryotes, first eukaryotes, first fishes, first flowering plants, first dinosaurs, first birds, and earliest hominids.

MATERIALS
- paper
- pencil

ANALYZE AND CONCLUDE

1. **Synthesize** How are eras and periods related? Where would the periods fit in this diagram?

2. **Calculate** Using your scale of 1 hour = 400 million years, how many millions of years in Earth's history would 1 minute represent?

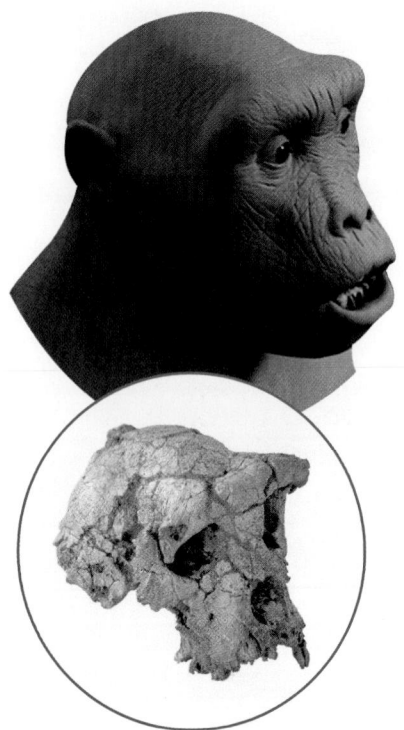

FIGURE 12.19 Computer technology allowed scientists to piece together 7-million-year-old skull fragments found in Africa. The three-dimensional reconstruction suggests that this may be the oldest known hominid ancestor of *Homo sapiens;* it has been named *Sahelanthropus tchadensis.*

▶ **MAIN IDEA**

There are many fossils of extinct hominids.

Most hominid species are classified into two groups: the genus *Australopithecus* (aw-STRAY-loh-PIHTH-ih-kuhs) and the genus *Homo.* The australopithecines were a long-lived and successful genus. *Australopithecus afarensis* (AF-uh-REHN-sihs), who lived 3 to 4 million years ago in Africa, is one of the better known species of early humans. Although its brain was much smaller than that of a modern human—about the size of a modern-day chimpanzee's brain—*A. afarensis* had very humanlike limbs.

The earliest member of the genus *Homo* was *Homo habilis.* Nicknamed "handy man" because of the crude stone tools associated with its skeletons, *H. habilis* lived 2.4–1.5 million years ago in what are now Kenya and Tanzania. This species may have lived alongside the australopithecine species for about 1 million years. *H. habilis* is the earliest known hominid to make stone tools. The brain of *H. habilis* was much larger than that of any of the australopithecines, and it more closely resembled the modern human brain in shape.

Another hominid species was *H. neanderthalensis,* commonly called Neanderthals for the Neander Valley in Germany, where their fossils were first found. This group lived from 200,000 to 30,000 years ago in Europe and the Middle East. Some evidence suggests that *H. neanderthalensis* coexisted with modern *Homo sapiens.* Did the two species live side by side? Or did they engage in a fierce competition for resources, causing the extinction of the Neanderthals by the better-adapted *H. sapiens*? This puzzle has not yet been solved.

Observations from the fossil record demonstrate a trend toward increased brain size in the human lineage. Although brain size can only be loosely related to intelligence, the combination of modern-day humans' physical and cultural adaptations has no doubt contributed to our success as a species.

Hypothesize **What type of evidence could indicate that *H. sapiens* and *H. neanderthalensis* coexisted?**

▶ **MAIN IDEA**

Modern humans arose about 100,000 years ago.

Fossil evidence reveals that the first appearance of *Homo sapiens,* the species name of modern humans, dates to roughly 100,000 years ago in what is now Ethiopia. Many of their features are different than those of humans today. After becoming a distinct species, *H. sapiens* clearly did not stop evolving.

The Role of Culture

Human evolution is influenced by culture. Tools are among key markers of culture in human evolution, although they are used by some other animals as well. A comparison of tools from their first appearance some 2.5 million years ago, through their association with later *Homo* fossil sites, shows a steady trend of increasing sophistication and usefulness.

FIGURE 12.20 Examples of Hominid Skulls

Hominid evolution shows a progression in brain size.

4–3 MILLION YEARS AGO	2.4–1.5 MILLION YEARS AGO	200,000–30,000 YEARS AGO	200,000 YEARS AGO–PRESENT
Australopithecus afarensis	*Homo habilis*	*Homo neanderthalensis*	*Homo sapiens*
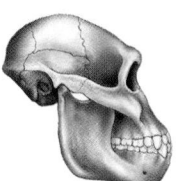	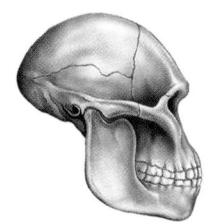	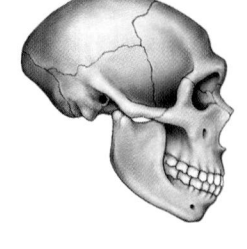	
Australopithecus afarensis had a brain volume of 430 cm³.	*Homo habilis* had a brain volume of about 700 cm³.	*Homo neanderthalensis'* brain volume may have reached 1500 cm³.	Modern *Homo sapiens* have a brain volume average of about 1300 cm³.

Contrast What characteristics besides brain size differ among the species shown?

The Evolution of the Human Brain

Human evolution would not have advanced as it did without an enlarging skull and brain size, as shown in **FIGURE 12.20**. One recent study has demonstrated that genes controlling the size and complexity of the human brain evolved faster than analogous genes in nonhuman primates. Researchers compared the DNA sequences for more than 200 genes affecting brain development in humans, Old World monkeys, rats, and mice. They found that these genes evolved at a much faster rate in the two primates than in the two rodents and that brain-related genes in humans evolved faster than did those in the monkeys. The results of the study support the hypothesis that the rapid evolution of large brain size posed an especially strong selective advantage among the hominids.

Connecting CONCEPTS

Classification A genus is a closely related group of species. You will learn more about categories for classification in **Chapter 17**.

Synthesize When might having an increasingly larger brain size no longer be a selective advantage?

12.6 ASSESSMENT

ONLINE QUIZ
ClassZone.com

REVIEWING ▶ MAIN IDEAS

1. What characteristics shared by humans and other **primates** suggest they have a common ancestor?

2. According to the fossil record, what other *Homo* species was present when modern humans arose?

3. From the **hominid** fossils described, what common trends can be found?

CRITICAL THINKING

4. **Apply** Explain why, according to the fossil record, it is not correct to say that humans evolved from chimpanzees.

5. **Infer** Scientists can often identify whether a fossil skull was from a **bipedal** primate. What characteristics of a skull might help them make this determination?

Connecting CONCEPTS

6. **Anatomy** Consider the skull illustrations above. Besides size, how did skull structure change as hominids evolved? What features are considered more apelike than humanlike?

Use these inquiry-based labs and online activities to deepen your understanding of the history of life on Earth.

DESIGN YOUR OWN INVESTIGATION

Stride Inferences

Paleontologists can use fossilized footprints to gain information about an entire organism, even if that organism is now extinct. But how much can they learn? In this investigation, you will measure the length of your classmates' feet, their legs, and their strides—walking and running—to see if there are any relationships between these variables.

SKILLS Measuring, Calculating, Interpreting Data

PROBLEM What relationship exists between foot length, leg length, and stride length?

MATERIALS
- meter stick
- calculator (optional)
- graph paper

PROCEDURE

1. Determine a procedure to measure foot length, leg length, and height of each person in your group.

2. Design a procedure for measuring both walking stride length and running stride length. Remember that repeated trials increase the validity of results.

3. Create a data table to organize the following information: foot length, leg length, height, stride length walking, and stride length running. Each person in your group will have these values measured and recorded.

4. Have your teacher approve your design. Then collect and record your data.

5. Each person in the group should make a bar graph of their own data for each of the following pairs of variables: foot length and leg length, foot length and height, leg length and height, stride length walking and leg length, and stride length walking and running. In addition, graph the average values.

ANALYZE AND CONCLUDE

1. **Analyze** Which of the above pairs of variables has a positive correlation? (As one increases, so does the other.) Which has a negative correlation? (As one increases, the other decreases.) Which pairs of variables have no clear relationship?

2. **Experimental Design** What steps in your design helped to avoid bias in your data collection?

3. **Experimental Design** What possible sources of error may have existed in your design? How could you change your experimental design to make the results more valid?

4. **Apply** Paleontologists have studied dinosaur footprints left as fossils in rock. What sort of information can they measure directly by looking at the footprints of these ancient animals? What information can they infer even if there are no fossilized skeletons?

INVESTIGATION

Understanding Geologic Time

The history of Earth has spanned the past 4.6 billion years. During that time, the oceans and the atmosphere have formed, life has begun, and species have evolved and become extinct. The geologic time scale can be broken into eras, periods, and epochs, which your teacher has modeled for you around your classroom. In this exercise you will learn about major events in the history of Earth and explore how these events have led to the world we know today.

SKILL Modeling

MATERIALS

- Geologic Time Scale datasheet

PROBLEM How do past events contribute to the changing populations of life on Earth?

PROCEDURE

1. Your teacher will assign you an event to record on the geologic time scale that is displayed around the room.

2. Use your textbook to determine the appropriate place for the event you were assigned.

3. Once everyone has recorded their event on the geologic time scale, walk around the room, taking note of the major events in each era and period on the datasheet you were provided.

ANALYZE AND CONCLUDE

1. **Analyze** In what eon, era, period, and epoch are we living today?

2. **Calculate** What fraction of the total distance does the Quaternary period cover on the geologic time scale? (**Hint:** The time scale is 46 feet [14 m] long and each foot [30.5 cm] equals 100 million years.)

EXTEND YOUR INVESTIGATION

Choose one period of the geologic time scale and investigate it more. Learn about the era in which it occurred, providing specific examples of organisms, important events, and a physical description of Earth at that time. Write a summary of the period with an illustration. Post your summary near the appropriate flag.

Online BIOLOGY
CLASSZONE.COM

VIRTUAL LAB
Comparing Hominoid Skulls

How are modern humans similar to chimps and australopithecines. How are they different? In this interactive lab, you will examine hominoid skulls to determine the sequence in which select traits evolved.

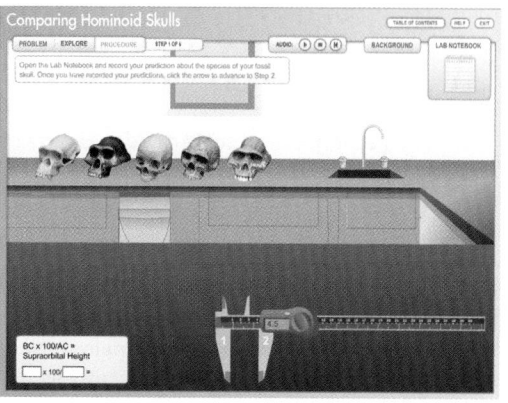

ANIMATED BIOLOGY
Geologic Time Scale

Which came first—flowering plants or coniferous trees? Use your knowledge of the history of life to place organisms in the correct order along a geologic time scale.

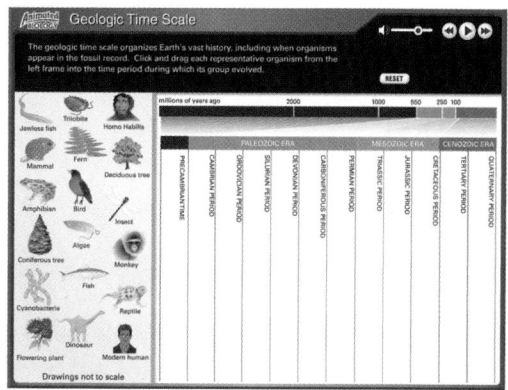

WEBQUEST

How do scientists decide which type of geologic dating to use for a sample? In this WebQuest, you will decide which method would be best to date two different types of fossil samples.

12.1 The Fossil Record

Fossils are a record of life that existed in the past. Fossils can form in several different ways. The age of a fossil or rock can be determined by radiometric dating, which uses radioactive isotopes to determine the age of a fossil or the rock in which it is found. Through radiometric dating, scientists have estimated that Earth is about 4.5 billion years old.

12.2 The Geologic Time Scale

The geologic time scale divides Earth's history based on major past events. Index fossils can be used along with radiometric dating to determine the age of a fossil or rock.

12.3 Origin of Life

The origin of life on Earth remains a puzzle. There are several hypotheses about how early organic molecules appeared on Earth and about how early cells may have formed. The discovery of ribozymes, RNA molecules that can catalyze reactions without the help of proteins, led to the hypothesis that RNA arose before DNA as the first genetic material on Earth.

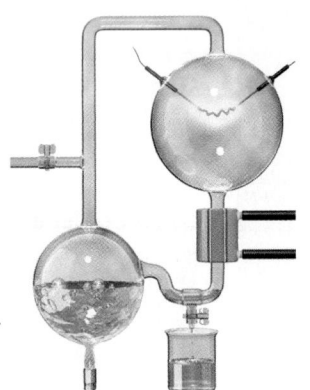

12.4 Early Single-Celled Organisms

Single-celled organisms existed 3.8 billion years ago. The first organisms on Earth were most likely anaerobic prokaryotes. The theory of endosymbiosis proposes that the first eukaryotic cells arose from a large prokaryote engulfing a smaller prokaryote.

12.5 Radiation of Multicellular Life

Multicellular life evolved in distinct phases. During the Paleozoic era, members of every major animal group evolved within only a few million years. During the Mesozoic era, dinosaurs, flowering plants, and birds inhabited the earth. Mammals also arose during this time. During the Cenozoic era, mammals diversified, as did birds, fishes, and flowering plants. Modern humans did not appear until 100,000 years ago.

12.6 Primate Evolution

Humans appeared late in Earth's history. Humans share a common ancestor with other primates. Primates include all mammals with flexible hands and feet, forward-looking eyes, and enlarged brains relative to their body size. The hominids include all species in the human lineage, both modern and extinct. Hominids walk upright, have long lower limbs, opposable thumbs, and relatively large brains. There are many fossils of extinct hominids.

Synthesize Your Notes

Timeline Make a timeline noting the history of hominid evolution. Add details about characteristics of each hominid that is on your diagram.

TERTIARY PERIOD   QUATERNARY PERIOD

Concept Map Use a concept map to summarize hypotheses about the origin of life on Earth.

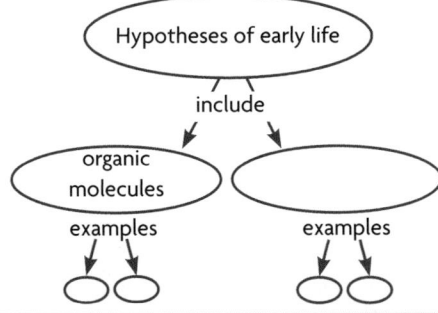

Chapter Assessment

Chapter Vocabulary

12.1 relative dating, p. 362
radiometric dating, p. 362
isotope, p. 362
half-life, p. 362

12.2 index fossil, p. 365
geologic time scale, p. 367
era, p. 367
period, p. 367
epoch, p. 367

12.3 nebula, p. 368
ribozyme, p. 370

12.4 cyanobacteria, p. 372
endosymbiosis, p. 373

12.5 Paleozoic, p. 376
Cambrian explosion, p. 376
Mesozoic, p. 377
Cenozoic, p. 378

12.6 primate, p. 379
prosimian, p. 379
anthropoid, p. 380
hominid, p. 380
bipedal, p. 381

Reviewing Vocabulary

Compare and Contrast

Describe one similarity and one difference between the two terms in each of the following pairs.

1. relative dating, radiometric dating
2. isotope, half-life
3. era, period
4. cyanobacteria, endosymbiosis
5. Paleozoic, Cambrian explosion
6. primate, hominid

Keep It Short

Write a short, precise phrase that describes the meaning of each vocabulary term below. For example, a short phrase to describe *geologic time scale* could be "organizes life's history."

7. index fossil
8. epoch
9. ribozyme
10. bipedal

Greek and Latin Word Origins

11. *Nebula* is a Latin word that means "cloud." Explain why you think astronomers chose this word as a name for what they were observing in outer space.

12. The prefix *iso-* means "the same." How does this meaning relate to the definition of *isotope*?

Reviewing MAIN IDEAS

13. Fossils can form in several ways, one of which is by permineralization. Describe the process of permineralization and give an example of the type of fossil that may result.

14. Give an example of how the concept of half-life is used in radiometric dating.

15. How are index fossils used in relative dating?

16. The geologic time scale organizes the history of Earth into eras, periods, and epochs. How are these units of time related to one another?

17. The Miller-Urey experiment and the meteorite hypothesis both suggest how the molecules that can support life might have appeared on early Earth. What is the main difference between these two hypotheses? Explain.

18. What are two ways that cyanobacteria have changed the physical or chemical composition of Earth?

19. What evidence exists to support the endosymbiotic origins of eukaryotic cells?

20. One evolutionary advantage of sexual reproduction is that it creates more genetic variation in a population than asexual reproduction. Why might this be an advantage?

21. The earliest part of the Paleozoic era is called the Cambrian period. What was the Cambrian explosion?

22. In which era did mammals, dinosaurs, and birds appear on Earth? What happened to these groups in the following era?

23. Humans, apes, monkeys, and lemurs are all examples of primates. What characteristics do all primates share?

Critical Thinking

24. Calculate A sample is dated using uranium-235 (half-life 704,000,000 years), and it has 1/4 of the original amount of uranium. How old is the sample?

25. Apply Why is it likely that autotrophs appeared on Earth before any aerobes, organisms that depended on oxygen?

26. Predict Astronomers determine the composition of the atmosphere around another planet by examining the light that travels from that planet to Earth. Would finding a lot of oxygen in the atmosphere of another planet strongly suggest that it supported life? Explain.

27. Evaluate Thirteen of the 20 amino acids used to make proteins in modern-day cells were made by Miller-Urey's simulation of early Earth's conditions. How does this result support Miller and Urey's hypothesis?

Interpreting Visuals

The chart below shows when some human ancestors lived and traits that they had. Use the chart to answer the next three questions.

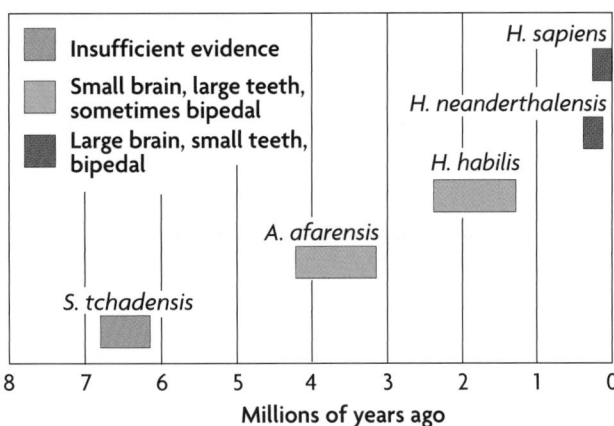

28. Summarize In one or two sentences, summarize the information in the chart.

29. Infer *Sahelanthropus tchadensis* was pictured on page 382 as a three-dimensional computer reconstruction. Although skull fragments have been found of this species, the chart above shows that there is not enough evidence to describe the traits of *S. tchadensis*. Explain why this might be so. Consider the scientific process in your explanation.

30. Analyze Some scientists suggest that *Homo habilis* should be classified as *Australopithecus habilis*. Based upon the information in the chart, explain why this might be the case.

Analyzing Data

Both graphs show the rate of decay of chlorine-36, which changes into argon-36. Use the graphs to answer the next two questions.

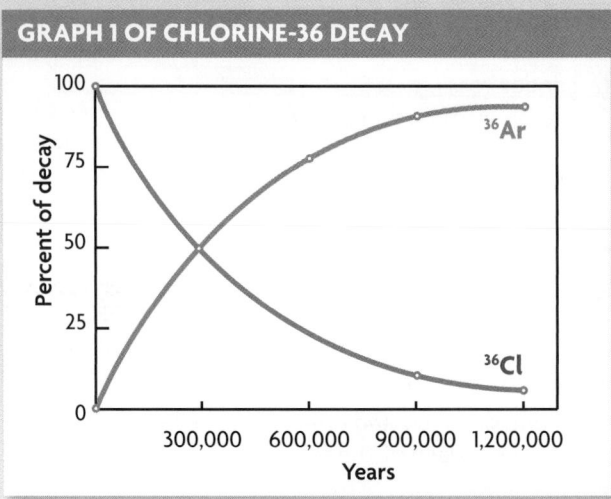

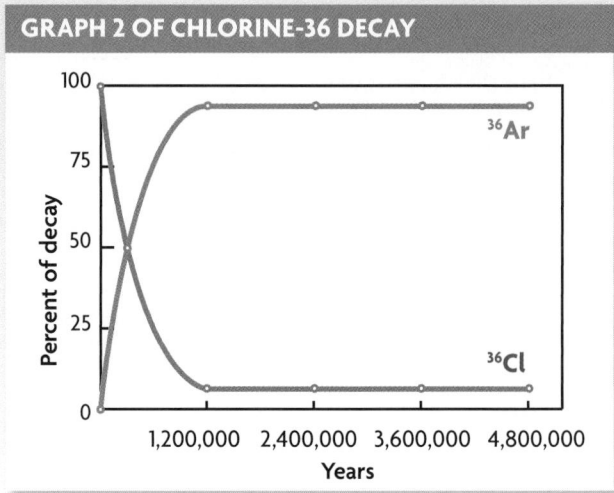

31. Analyze Which graph better shows the concept that the percentage change of ^{36}Cl and ^{36}Ar slows down dramatically over time? Explain.

32. Analyze From which graph can you more accurately determine the half-life in years of ^{36}Cl? Explain.

Connecting CONCEPTS

33. Write a Detailed Description Choose one of the periods in geological time and describe it in detail. Be sure to include vivid details about the organisms of the period.

34. Connect The time that the Tollund Man on page 359 lived was determined by radiocarbon dating. Why can't ^{14}C be used to date the Burgess Shale fossil shown on the same page?

MICHIGAN STANDARDS-BASED ASSESSMENT

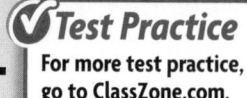

Test Practice
For more test practice, go to ClassZone.com.

1. There are several different ideas that propose how life may have begun on Earth. Scientists have built models and performed experiments to prove or disprove these ideas. A term used in science that means "an idea that is tested for validity" is **B1.2h**

   A theory.

   B law.

   C observation.

   D hypothesis.

2.

Percent of Native Bird Fossils in Hawaii			
Excavated Section	¹⁴C Dating (years before present)	% Bones from Non-native Species	% Bones from Native Species
I	390	100.0	0.0
II	770	98.8	1.2
III	4340	9.2	90.8
IV	7750	0.0	100.0

   The table above shows the fossil evidence of birds in a section of cave wall in Hawaii. What information does this fossil evidence provide that would otherwise never have been known? **L5.p1D**

   A A catastrophic event occurred between 770 and 4340 years ago.

   B Native species out-competed non-native species.

   C Most native species died out over 800 years ago.

   D The disappearance of non-native species is a function of time.

3. Like modern plants, early photosynthetic organisms used light as the energy source for synthesizing sugar. Based on this fact, what substance had to be available to these organisms in the environment of early Earth? **B2.4d**

   A nitrogen

   B ATP

   C oxygen

   D carbon dioxide

4. **Number of Genera over Time**

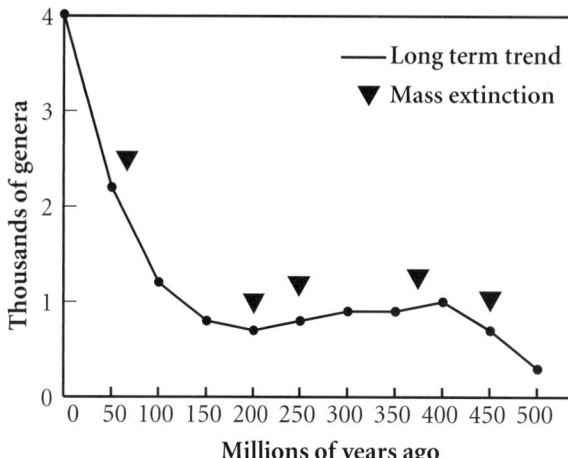

   The graph above shows the estimated number of genera over time, with major extinction events indicated by arrows. Given that genera are made up of closely related species, what can be understood from these data? **B5.1c**

   A The number of species always increases.

   B Mass extinctions wipe out all species.

   C Some species survive during mass extinctions.

   D A mass extinction is not likely to happen again.

5. As the oxygen content of Earth's atmosphere increased, what would have *best* allowed populations of anaerobic prokaryotes to adapt? **B5.1d**

   A genetic mutation

   B sexual selection

   C competition

   D sexual reproduction

6. In the evolution of eukaryotes, cells that contained mitochondria-like organelles had an advantage because they **B2.4g**

   A could make use of photosynthesis.

   B could make use of more available energy.

   C had more DNA.

   D were protected from bacterial invasion.

THINK THROUGH THE QUESTION

This question is really just asking how mitochondria help a cell.

Go online for the latest biology news and updates on all BioZine articles.

Expanding the Textbook

News Feeds

- Science Daily
- CNN
- BBC

Careers

Bio Bytes

Opinion Poll

Strange Biology

Could a scraped knee land you in the hospital?

Drug-Resistant Bacteria—A Global Health Issue

A bicyclist falls, scrapes his knees, and within a few days is unable to walk. Soccer players with turf burns suddenly find themselves in the hospital with skin infections that require intravenous antibiotics. Why are these young, healthy athletes developing such serious infections?

Staph Infections

These athletes were infected by *Staphylococcus aureus*, or "staph." Staph is a common bacteria that most people carry on the surface of their skin and in their nose. To cause an infection, staph bacteria must get inside your body. The scrapes athletes commonly get provide an ideal entrance.

Serious problems caused by staph infections used to be rare. Doctors would prescribe antibiotics, such as penicillin, which killed the staph bacteria. Ordinary staph infections can still be treated this way. But the athletes in our examples did not have ordinary infections. These athletes' scrapes were infected by methicillin-resistant *Staphylococcus aureus* (MRSA) bacteria. This strain of bacteria is only one of many that has evolved resistance to antibiotics.

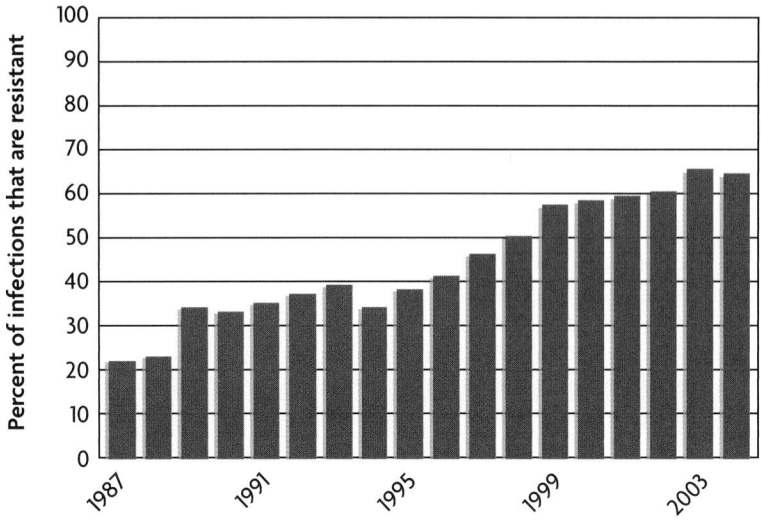

MRSA on the Rise

Source: NNIS System and Centers for Disease Control and Prevention

Drug-Resistant Bacteria

Bacteria that can survive antibiotic treatment are called drug-resistant bacteria. Some bacteria have resistance for one particular antibiotic, some have resistance for several, and a few cannot be treated with any known antibiotic.

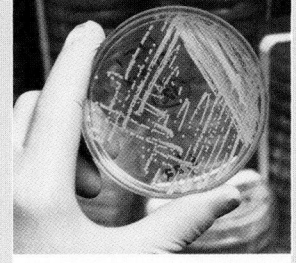

This petri dish contains *Staphylococcus aureus* bacteria.

MRSA can resist an entire class of antibiotics. Patients who have an MRSA infection must often be treated with what doctors call "the drug of last resort," vancomycin. Vancomycin is a drug that must be given intravenously. Not surprisingly, doctors began to see cases of vancomycin-resistant *Staphylococcus aureus* (VRSA) in 1997.

Staph isn't the only type of bacteria that is making a comeback with drug-resistant strains. For example, antibiotics developed to treat tuberculosis increased the survival rate of this disease to 98 percent. But now, drug-resistant strains of tuberculosis are killing 2.5 million people per year. Drug-resistant strains of cholera and bubonic plague also have been reported.

How Does Drug Resistance Evolve?

When you take antibiotics for a bacterial infection, billions of bacteria may be killed right away. However, there are likely to be a few that survive. Antibiotics kill the less resistant bacteria, leaving behind the more resistant bacteria to survive and reproduce. When resistant bacteria reproduce, the genes that make them resistant are passed on to their offspring; and bacteria reproduce rapidly. In six hours, one cell can produce as many as 500,000 offspring.

In addition to their ability to reproduce quickly, populations of bacteria evolve rapidly through another process as well. Bacteria use plasmids—small loops of DNA—to transfer genetic material between individual cells. This transfer of plasmids between cells is called conjugation. Some plasmids pass on resistance for one particular antibiotic. Others can transfer resistance for several antibiotics at once.

What characteristics do resistant bacteria pass on to their offspring? Some have cell walls that antibiotics cannot easily pass through. Others have pumps that remove antibiotics once they enter the cell. Some can even produce enzymes that attack the antibiotic drugs themselves.

Fighting Back

Some scientists are trying to develop ways to treat patients without killing the bacteria that are making them sick. Instead, they target the toxins produced by bacteria. If the bacteria are not harmed by the treatment, no selective pressure is produced. Scientists hope that by using this approach, bacteria will be slower to evolve defense mechanisms against the antibiotics. Other scientists hope to fight back by using bacteria's ancient rival, bacteriophages, which are viruses that infect bacteria.

CAREERS

Evolutionary Biologist in Action

DR. RICHARD LENSKI	
TITLE Professor, Microbial Ecology, Michigan State University	
EDUCATION Ph. D., Zoology, University of North Carolina, Chapel Hill	

If you want to observe evolution in action, you must find populations that reproduce quickly. Dr. Richard Lenski, a professor at Michigan State University, has done just that. Dr. Lenski studies populations of *E. coli* bacteria, which he grows in flasks filled with a sugary broth. These bacteria produce about seven generations each day. Dr. Lenski has now observed more than 30,000 generations of *E. coli*.

The rapid rate of *E. coli* reproduction allows Dr. Lenski to watch evolution take place. Dr. Lenski can subject each generation of bacteria to the same environmental stresses, such as food shortages or antibiotics. He can then compare individuals from more recent generations with their ancestors, which he keeps in his laboratory freezer. By comparing generations in this way, Dr. Lenski can study how the population has evolved.

When Dr. Lenski began his research in 1988, watching evolution in action was still new. Now, many evolutionary biologists are following in his footsteps.

Read More >> *at* CLASSZONE.COM

TECHNOLOGY

New Drug Delivery System

Researcher at the University of South Florida decided to take on one of the most difficult bacterial infections of all, methicillin-resistant staph. They have developed a new class of antibiotics along with a new way to deliver it to the bacteria.

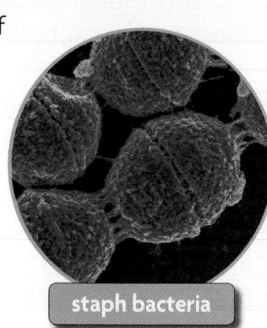
staph bacteria

- Antibiotics are bonded to nano-sized plastic balls. (One nanometer is one millionth of a millimeter.)

- The "nanoballs" are dissolved in water, and the solution is released into the patient's bloodstream. When the nanoballs reach the bacteria, the bacteria eat them.

- Nanoballs release antibiotics inside bacterial cells.

Because the bacteria are "eating" the nanoballs, cell wall adaptations that once kept antibiotics out are no longer an obstacle.

Read More >> *at* CLASSZONE.COM

Unanswered Questions

Some important research questions involving drug-resistant bacteria include the following:

- Can plasmids or bacteriophages be used in vaccines to fight bacteria?

- Are bacteria being exposed to antibiotics in sewage systems and evolving resistant strains there?

- How do antibacterial soaps and household cleaners contribute to the evolution of drug-resistant bacteria?

- Can drug-resistant bacteria be transferred from domestic animals to humans through food?

Read More >> *at* CLASSZONE.COM

UNIT 5

Ecology

CHAPTER 13
Principles of Ecology   394

CHAPTER 14
Interactions in Ecosystems   426

CHAPTER 15
The Biosphere   454

CHAPTER 16
Human Impact on Ecosystems   482

BIOZINE

INTERNET MAGAZINE
**Global Warming—
Changing the Planet**   512

TECHNOLOGY Deep Sea Sediment Coring

CAREER Oceanographer

13 Principles of Ecology

KEY CONCEPTS

13.1 Ecologists Study Relationships
Ecology is the study of the relationships among organisms and their environment.

13.2 Biotic and Abiotic Factors
Every ecosystem includes both living and nonliving factors.

13.3 Energy in Ecosystems
Life in an ecosystem requires a source of energy.

13.4 Food Chains and Food Webs
Food chains and food webs model the flow of energy in an ecosystem.

13.5 Cycling of Matter
Matter cycles in and out of an ecosystem.

13.6 Pyramid Models
Pyramids model the distribution of energy and matter in an ecosystem.

Online BIOLOGY CLASSZONE.COM

Animated BIOLOGY

View animated chapter concepts.
• Distribution of Producers
• Estimating Population Size
• Build a Food Web

BIOZINE

Keep current with biology news.
• Featured stories
• News feeds
• Careers

RESOURCE CENTER

Get more information on
• Chemosynthesis
• Food Webs
• Cycles in Ecosystems
• Energy in Ecosystems

How does this bird interact with its ecosystem?

Anhingas live in freshwater marshes and swamps of the southeastern United States. While they are primarily consumers of fish, an anhinga's diet may also include aquatic insects and invertebrates. The anhinga and the fish are just two of the many organisms that interact in this complex wetland ecosystem.

Connecting CONCEPTS

Vertebrates Unlike other water birds, anhingas do not have oil glands to waterproof their feathers. Without the buoyancy of waterproof feathers, anhingas are effective underwater divers and swimmers. Because they cannot fly when their feathers are waterlogged, anhingas are often seen perched above water, drying their wings in the sun.

13.1 Ecologists Study Relationships

KEY CONCEPT Ecology is the study of the relationships among organisms and their environment.

▶ **MAIN IDEAS**

- Ecologists study environments at different levels of organization.
- Ecological research methods include observation, experimentation, and modeling.

VOCABULARY

ecology, p. 396
community, p. 397
ecosystem, p. 397
biome, p. 397

Review
organism, population

MICHIGAN STANDARDS

L3.p1A Provide examples of a population, community, and ecosystem. (prerequisite)

L5.p2A Explain, with examples, that ecology studies the varieties and interactions of living things across space while evolution studies the varieties and interactions of living things across time. (prerequisite)

Connect Water birds such as anhingas, along with a variety of other plants and animals, rely on the presence of wetlands for their survival. How might the loss of wetland areas affect these aquatic species? Learning about organisms and how they interact with one another, with other species, and with their environment is what the study of ecology is all about.

▶ **MAIN IDEA**

Ecologists study environments at different levels of organization.

Over their life cycle, Pacific salmon are the main food source for more than 140 species of wildlife, including grizzly bears, as shown in **FIGURE 13.1.** If they are not eaten, their bodies return vital nutrients back into the river system, some of which are used by plants to grow. In addition to their role in the health of river systems, salmon are also important to the Pacific Northwest's economy. Today, many species of wild Pacific salmon are threatened with extinction due to competition from hatchery fish, blocked river paths, and loss of spawning grounds. As salmon populations decline, how are other species affected? What effect would the loss of salmon have on a local and a global scale? These are the types of questions ecologists are trying to answer.

FIGURE 13.1 Salmon are a primary food source for many species, including grizzly bears. If salmon disappeared, species dependent on them would also suffer.

What Is Ecology?

Ecology is the study of the interactions among living things, and between living things and their surroundings. The word *ecology* comes from the Greek word *oikos,* which means "house." This word origin makes sense if you think of Earth as home and all organisms as members of Earth's household. Ernst Haeckel, a German biologist, coined the term *ecology* in 1866 to encourage biologists to consider the ways organisms interact. Until that time, most scientists studied a plant or an animal as though it existed in isolation—as if it did not affect its surroundings, and its surroundings did not affect it.

Levels of Organization

Ecologists study nature on different levels, from a local to a global scale. These levels, shown in **FIGURE 13.2**, reveal the complex relationships found in nature.

- **Organism** An organism is an individual living thing, such as an alligator.
- **Population** A population is a group of the same species that lives in one area, such as all the alligators that live in a swamp.
- **Community** A **community** is a group of different species that live together in one area, such as groups of alligators, turtles, birds, fish, and plants that live together in the Florida Everglades.
- **Ecosystem** An **ecosystem** includes all of the organisms as well as the climate, soil, water, rocks, and other nonliving things in a given area. Ecosystems can vary in size. An entire ecosystem may live within a decaying log, which in turn may be part of a larger wetland ecosystem.
- **Biome** A **biome** (BY-ohm) is a major regional or global community of organisms. Biomes are usually characterized by the climate conditions and plant communities that thrive there.

Ecologists study relationships within each level of organization and also between levels. For example, researchers may study the relationships within a population of alligators, as well as the relationships between alligators and turtles in a community.

Apply What level of organization describes a flock of pigeons in a park?

TAKING NOTES

Use a diagram to take notes on the levels of organization.

Levels of Organization

- organism
- population
- community
- ecosystem
- biome

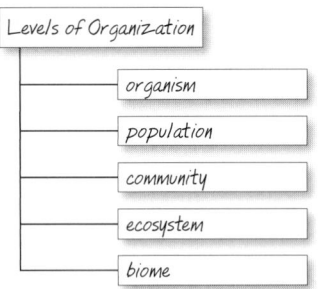

Biome

Savanna

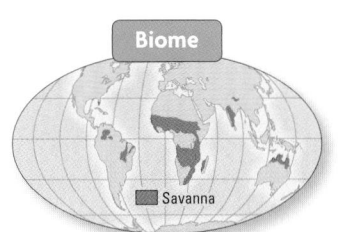

Ecosystem

FIGURE 13.2 Levels of Organization

The Florida Everglades is an example of the subtropical savanna biome. Many organisms live in this aquatic ecosystem.

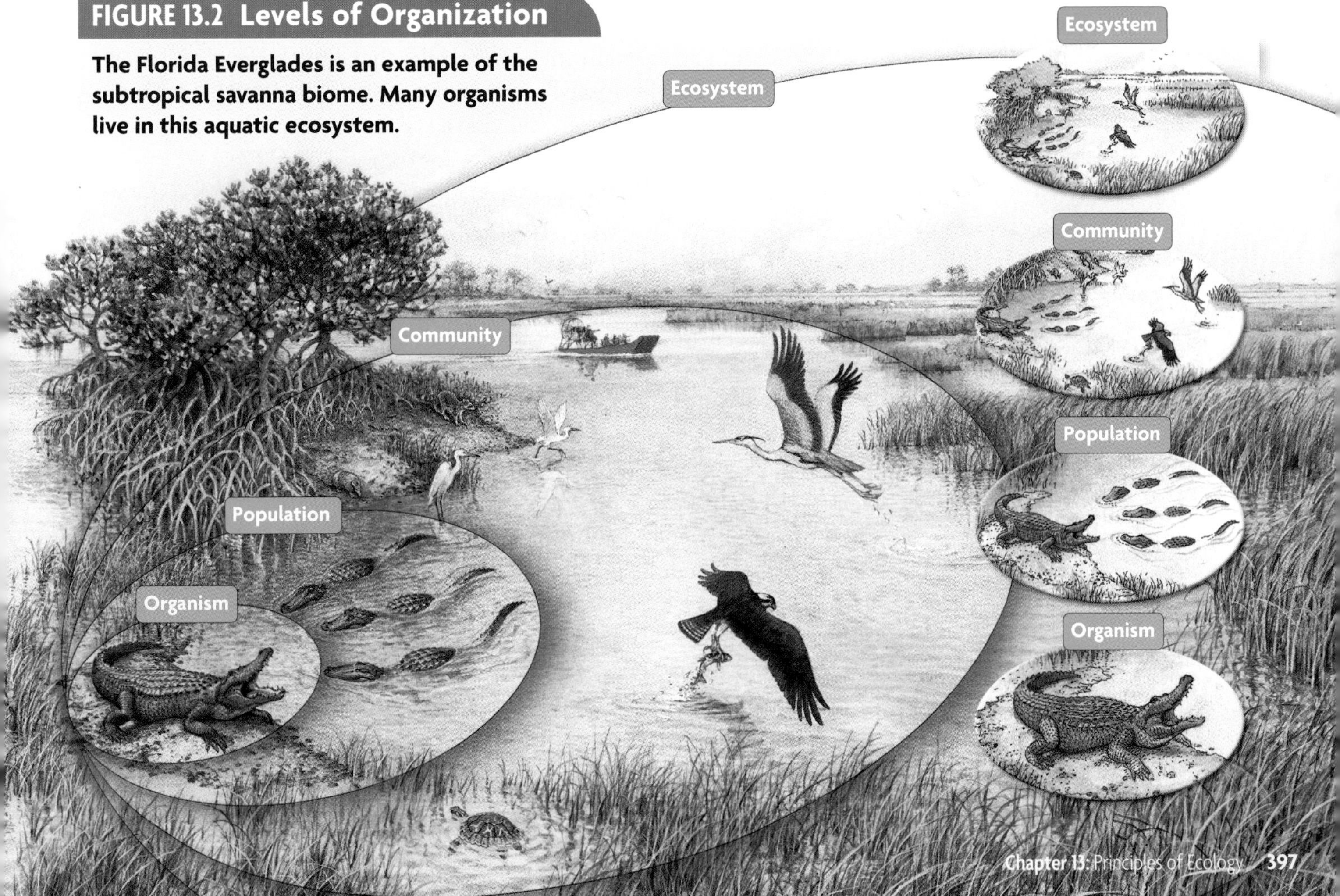

Ecosystem

Community

Community

Population

Population

Organism

Organism

Ecological research methods include observation, experimentation, and modeling.

Scientists rely on a variety of methods and tools to conduct research. Tools can range from a simple tape measure used to find an organism's size to a sophisticated computer system used to create a model of an entire ecosystem.

Observation

Observation is the act of carefully watching something over time. Such observations may occur over short or long periods of time. Long-term studies are a key part of a scientist's toolkit because most environmental changes happen over a long period of time. For example, studies of prairie-dog populations are helping scientists to determine which locations are most appropriate for the reintroduction of the black-footed ferret. The black-footed ferret is an endangered species that relies on the prairie dog as its main food source.

One way that scientists monitor and observe populations is by conducting surveys. Visual surveys may be direct or indirect.

- Direct surveys are used for species that are easy to follow. In these surveys, scientists watch animals either with the naked eye or with tools such as binoculars or scopes.
- Indirect surveys are used for species that are difficult to track. In these surveys, scientists search for other signs of its presence, such as feces or a recent kill.

Radio telemetry is another method used by scientists to monitor populations. Scientists fit an animal with a radio collar that emits a signal and then use the signal to track the animal's movement, as shown in **FIGURE 13.3**. This practice is especially useful when studying a species that has a broad range, such as the coyote.

In addition to observing the activities of a species, scientists may want to determine its population size. Rather than count every individual organism in a large study area, scientists often sample the population instead. Mark-recapture is a method used by scientists to estimate the population size of mobile organisms. For example, to monitor prairie-dog populations, scientists capture and mark prairie dogs with ear tags and then release them back into the wild. When scientists later repeat the survey, the captured prairie dogs will include both marked and unmarked animals. Scientists calculate the ratio of marked to unmarked animals and use this value to estimate the total population size.

To monitor plant populations, scientists use a method called quadrat sampling. In this method, quadrats, or rectangular frames, are randomly placed on the study site. To determine plant population numbers, scientists identify and count the number of plants within each randomly selected plot. The total number of counted plants is then plugged into a mathematical formula to determine the plant population of the entire study site.

FIGURE 13.3 Much of the data gathered by ecologists results from long hours of observation in the field. This ecologist is using radio telemetry to track coyotes.

Apply How might a scientist use observation to study a population of mountain goats? Explain your answer.

Quadrat Sampling

Ecologists often use quadrats—square or rectangular grids—to collect data about population numbers in an ecosystem. In this lab, you will use a quadrat to collect data on three "species."

PROBLEM What is the population size of each species?

PROCEDURE

1. Obtain a quadrat frame. Measure, calculate, and record the area of the quadrat.

2. Stand at the edge of the area you will sample and randomly throw your quadrat.

3. Move your quadrat so that it does not overlap with any other quadrat. Each different object represents a different species. Count how many individuals of each species are in your quadrat and record your data in a data table. Repeat this procedure three times.

4. Combine your data with that of your classmates. Find the average number of each species for all of the samples. Obtain the area of the sampling plot from your teacher. Calculate how many quadrats would fit in the area of the sampling plot. Multiply this by the average number of each species found in one quadrat to estimate the population of each species.

MATERIALS
- quadrat
- meter stick
- calculator
- objects to count

ANALYZE AND CONCLUDE

1. **Analyze** Compare your population estimate for each species to the actual number that your teacher provides. Is the estimate accurate? Why or why not?

2. **Evaluate** How can you ensure that your estimate of population size will be as accurate as possible?

Experimentation

Scientists may perform experiments in the lab or in the field. There are benefits and drawbacks to each type of experiment. While a lab experiment gives the researcher more control, the artificial setting does not reflect the complex interactions that occur in nature. A field experiment, on the other hand, gives a more accurate picture of how organisms interact in a natural setting. However, in a field study, it is more difficult to determine cause and effect due to the large number of factors at work in nature.

A lab experiment is conducted in a controlled, indoor environment. This isolation helps scientists to focus each experiment on a very specific part of an ecosystem, such as a single organism. For example, to find out how climate change affects the growth rates of plants, scientists can grow plants in a lab and adjust temperature settings. Working in a lab allows scientists to control variables in a way that would not be possible in the field.

A field experiment is performed where the organisms live. Like lab experiments, field experiments also have controls and manipulated variables. For example, to determine how browsing by deer affects plant and small-animal communities, scientists might fence off large study plots to keep out the deer. By monitoring the fenced and unfenced plots over a period of time, scientists can determine whether deer significantly change the areas in which they browse for food.

Connecting CONCEPTS

Scientific Method As you learned in **Chapter 1**, all fields of science, including ecology, use the scientific method to investigate and answer scientific questions. Applied ecology uses the principles of ecology along with the scientific method to solve environmental problems.

Contrast **What is the difference between a lab experiment and a field experiment?**

FIGURE 13.4 Ecologists use data transmitted by GPS receivers worn by elephants to develop computer models of the animals' movements.

scilinks.org

To learn more about ecology, go to scilinks.org.
Keycode: MLB013

Modeling

Sometimes the questions scientists wish to ask cannot be easily answered through observation or experimentation. Instead, scientists use computer and mathematical models to describe and model nature. Scientists can manipulate different model variables to learn about organisms or whole ecosystems in ways that would not be possible in a natural setting.

Although they are used to test hypothetical situations, models are created with the use of real data. For example, in Kenya, scientists are using satellite technology to track the movement of elephants, as shown in **FIGURE 13.4**. These data, in turn, can be used to create a model to study how changes to the ecosystem might affect elephant movement patterns. Before putting the model to use, scientists can test it by inserting actual data values. Such testing allows scientists to make sure that the values predicted by the model are similar to actual observations in the field.

In the United States, scientists developed a computer software program to create a virtual model of the Greater Yellowstone ecosystem. A variety of data were used to create this model, including

- the movements of elk, bison, bear, and wolf populations
- the location of different vegetation, such as meadows and forests
- the amount of snow
- the activities of geysers and other geothermal landforms

The combination of these data together with computer-generated maps creates a virtual ecosystem that scientists can use to model how one variable affects another. This type of modeling program sometimes plays a role in the development of wildlife conservation plans. Computer programs modeled population dynamics with and without the presence of the gray wolf. These programs were used to study how the reintroduction of gray wolves into Yellowstone might affect other species within the park and the surrounding area. By understanding how different organisms and factors within an ecosystem interact, wildlife managers are able to make well-informed decisions.

Contrast How does modeling differ from experimentation?

13.1 ASSESSMENT

ONLINE QUIZ
ClassZone.com

REVIEWING ▶ MAIN IDEAS

1. What are the five different levels of organization studied by ecologists?

2. Describe the three general methods used by ecologists to study organisms.

CRITICAL THINKING

3. **Apply** What ecological research methods would you use to study bird migration? Explain your choices.

4. **Apply** How might an ecologist use modeling to study fire in a forest **ecosystem**? What might be some key variables used to create the model?

Connecting CONCEPTS

5. **Evolution** Ernst Haeckel was greatly influenced by the writings of Charles Darwin. How do the principles of **ecology** relate to understanding how adaptations occur?

Quadrats and Population Size

One part of studying a population is to record its size. Often, it is possible to count all of the individuals in a population of organisms, such as large mammals or trees. With smaller organisms or more numerous populations, the population must be estimated based on representative samples. A **sample** is a portion of the population that is defined and counted.

QUADRAT SAMPLING

EXAMPLE

One method used to estimate populations is to count the number of individuals within a known sample area. To sample plants, quadrats are randomly placed over a large area and the number of individuals of the same species within the quadrat is counted. The number of quadrats sampled depends on the size of the entire area under study. In the example shown here, a scientist used quadrats to estimate the population of shrubs in a field. A simple equation can be used to find the population estimate: $T = NA$

Quadrat sampling is most often used to survey plant populations. This method can be used to identify species, calculate species' frequency, and monitor changes in plant communities over time.

$T = NA$

T = Total population estimate

$$N = \frac{\text{Total number of individuals counted}}{\text{Number of quadrats}}$$

$$A = \frac{\text{Total area}}{\text{Area of quadrat}}$$

In the example, each darkly shaded area represents a quadrat. Six shrubs were counted in five quadrats. The area of each quadrat is 1 m². The total area of the sampling plot is 200 m².

$T = NA$

$$T = \frac{6}{5} \cdot \frac{200 \text{ m}^2}{1 \text{ m}^2}$$

$T = 1.20 \cdot 200 = 240$

T = 240 individuals = estimated population of shrubs in the field

ESTIMATE A POPULATION FROM A SAMPLE
For each example, calculate the estimated population. Use the formula and show all of your work.
1. **Calculate** A scientist uses a quadrat of 2 m² to estimate the population of daisies in a field. She counts 173 individuals in 15 quadrats. The total area of the field is 250 m².
2. **Calculate** A scientist uses a 0.25 m² quadrat to sample a population of dandelions in a garden that is 500 m². The number of dandelions counted in 10 quadrats is 63.

13.2 Biotic and Abiotic Factors

KEY CONCEPT Every ecosystem includes both living and nonliving factors.

► MAIN IDEAS

- An ecosystem includes both biotic and abiotic factors.
- Changing one factor in an ecosystem can affect many other factors.

VOCABULARY

biotic, p. 402
abiotic, p. 402
biodiversity, p. 403
keystone species, p. 403

MICHIGAN STANDARDS

L3.p2B Describe common ecological relationships between and among species and their environments (competition, territory, carrying capacity, natural balance, population, dependence, survival, and other biotic and abiotic factors). (prerequisite)

L3.p3B Distinguish between the living (biotic) and nonliving (abiotic) components of an ecosystem. (prerequisite)

FIGURE 13.5 The underwater roots of mangrove trees camouflage young coral-reef fish from predators.

Connect A vegetable garden is a small ecosystem, and its success depends on many factors. You can probably list several without too much thought. You might think of sunlight, fertilizer, or insects to pollinate the plants' flowers. Gardeners usually don't think of themselves as scientists, but they must take into account how these factors affect their plants in order for the plants to flourish.

► MAIN IDEA

An ecosystem includes both biotic and abiotic factors.

All ecosystems are made up of living and nonliving components. These parts are referred to as biotic and abiotic factors.

- **Biotic** (by-AHT-ihk) factors are living things, such as plants, animals, fungi, and bacteria. Each organism plays a particular role in the ecosystem. For example, earthworms play a key role in enriching the soil.

- **Abiotic** (AY-by-AHT-ihk) factors are nonliving things such as moisture, temperature, wind, sunlight, and soil. The balance of these factors determines which living things can survive in a particular environment.

In the Caribbean Sea, scientists found that coral reefs located near saltwater marshes have more fish than do reefs farther out at sea. As shown in **FIGURE 13.5**, the key biotic factor is the mangrove trees that live in the marshes. The trees provide food and shelter for newly hatched fish, protecting them from predators. After the fish mature, they swim to the reefs. Abiotic factors that affect the growth of mangrove trees include low levels of oxygen in the mud where they grow and changing levels of salinity, or saltiness, due to daily tidal changes.

An ecosystem may look similar from one year to the next, with similar numbers of animals and plants. However, an ecosystem is always undergoing some changes. For example, a long period of increased precipitation might allow one plant species to grow better than others. As the plant continues to grow, it may crowd out other plant species, changing the community's composition. Though the total number of plants in the community may remain the same, the species have changed. As these cyclic changes occur, an ecosystem falls into a balance, which is known as approximate equilibrium.

Contrast What is the difference between biotic and abiotic factors?

▶ MAIN IDEA

Changing one factor in an ecosystem can affect many other factors.

An ecosystem is a complex web of connected biotic and abiotic factors. You may not always think of yourself as part of the ecosystem, but humans, like other species, rely on the environment for survival. All species are affected by changes to the biotic and abiotic factors in an ecosystem.

Biodiversity

The relationships within an ecosystem are very complicated. If you attached a separate string between a forest tree and each of the living and nonliving things in the ecosystem that influenced it, and did the same for each of those living and nonliving things, the forest would quickly become a huge web of strings. The web would also reveal the biodiversity in the forest. **Biodiversity** (BY-oh-dih-VUR-sih-tee) is the assortment, or variety, of living things in an ecosystem. An area with a high level of biodiversity, such as a rain forest, has a large assortment of different species living near one another. The amount of biodiversity found in an area depends on many factors, including moisture and temperature.

Some areas of the world have an unusually large amount of biodiversity in comparison to other locations. For example, tropical rain forests, which are moist and warm environments, cover less than 7 percent of Earth's ground surface. However, they account for over 50 percent of the planet's plant and animal species. This large amount of biodiversity emphasizes the importance of conserving such areas. Tropical rain forests are one of several areas referred to as hot spots. These hot spots, located across the globe, are areas that are rich in biodiversity, but are threatened by human activities.

Keystone Species

The complex relationships in ecosystems mean that a change in a single biotic or abiotic factor—a few broken strings in the web—can have a variety of effects. The change may barely be noticed, or it may have a deep impact. In some cases, the loss of a single species may cause a ripple effect felt across an entire ecosystem. Such an organism is called a keystone species. A **keystone species** is a species that has an unusually large effect on its ecosystem.

One example of a keystone species is the beaver. By felling trees to construct dams, beavers change free-flowing stream habitats into ponds, wetlands, and meadows. This modification leads to a cascade of changes within their ecosystem.

Connecting CONCEPTS

Biodiversity The discovery of potential medicines and new species are two reasons why it is important to maintain biodiversity. In **Chapter 16**, you will learn how human activities impact biodiversity and how the loss of biodiversity affects us all.

VISUAL VOCAB

Like a keystone that holds up an arch, a **keystone species** holds together a dynamic ecosystem.

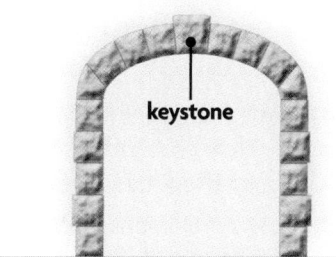

keystone

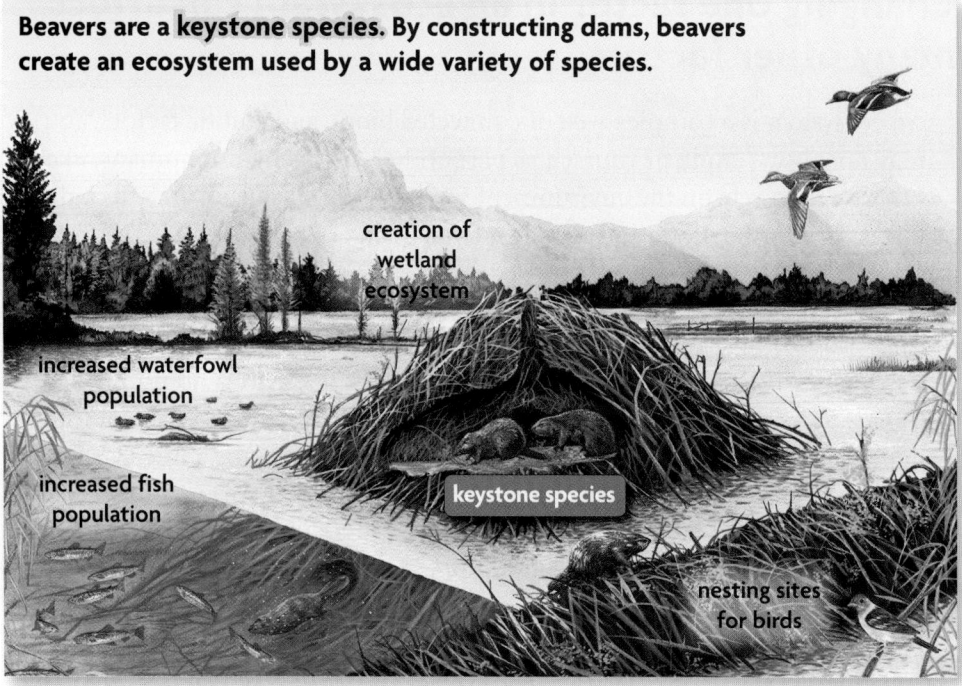

FIGURE 13.6 Keystone Species

Beavers are a **keystone species.** By constructing dams, beavers create an ecosystem used by a wide variety of species.

creation of wetland ecosystem

increased waterfowl population

increased fish population

keystone species

nesting sites for birds

As **FIGURE 13.6** shows, beavers cause changes that create an ecosystem used by a variety of different species, leading to an overall increase in biodiversity.

- A greater number and wider variety of fish are able to live in the still waters of the pond.
- The fish attract fish-eating birds, such as herons and kingfishers.
- Insects inhabit the pond and the dead trees along the shore, attracting insect-eating birds, such as great-crested flycatchers, that nest in the tree cavities.
- Waterfowl nest among the shrubs and grasses along the pond's edge.
- Animals that prey on birds or their eggs are also attracted to the pond.

Keystone species form and maintain a complex web of life. Whatever happens to that species affects all the other species connected to it.

Connect Explain why the Pacific salmon, introduced in Section 13.1, could be considered a keystone species.

13.2 ASSESSMENT

ONLINE QUIZ
ClassZone.com

REVIEWING ▶ MAIN IDEAS

1. Select an ecosystem that is familiar to you and describe the **biotic** and **abiotic** factors that exist there.

2. How would the removal of a **keystone species** affect an ecosystem's **biodiversity**?

CRITICAL THINKING

3. **Predict** Explain how a change in an abiotic factor such as sunlight would affect biodiversity.

4. **Analyze** Humans are sometimes described as being a keystone species. Does this label fit? Why or why not?

Connecting CONCEPTS

5. **Evolution** What role might an abiotic factor such as temperature play in the evolution of a species?

MATERIALS
- 4 radish seedlings
- 4 cups
- ruler
- cheesecloth
- sand
- gravel
- potting soil
- household-plant liquid fertilizer
- plastic wrap in a variety of colors
- graduated cylinder

PROCESS SKILLS
- **Designing Experiments**
- **Collecting Data**

L3.p2B Describe common ecological relationships between and among species and their environments (competition, territory, carrying capacity, natural balance, population, dependence, survival, and other biotic and abiotic factors). (prerequisite)
L3.p3B Distinguish between the living (biotic) and nonliving (abiotic) components of an ecosystem. (prerequisite)

Abiotic Factors and Plant Growth

Many factors affect plant growth. Is it possible to test some in a laboratory setting? In this investigation you will choose an abiotic factor and attempt to test how (or if) it affects the growth of radish seedlings.

PROBLEM How do abiotic factors affect plant growth?

PROCEDURE

1. Choose an abiotic factor to test on the growth of radish seedlings. Possible factors include amount of sunlight, amount of water, soil type, light color available to plants, or amount of fertilizer.

2. Determine a way to vary the factor you have chosen. Be sure to include at least three different settings of your variable and to keep all other factors constant. Write out a procedure for your investigation.

3. Obtain 4 plants. Label one "Control" and the remaining three "A," "B," and "C."

4. Measure the height of your control and variable plants over a period of seven days. Use the same method to repeat measurements each day. Be sure to keep plants watered.

5. Record all data you generate in a well-organized data table.

ANALYZE AND CONCLUDE

1. **Operational Definitions** On the basis of your procedure, how are you defining plant growth?

2. **Identify Variables** What are your independent and dependent variables? What are your constants? What is your control?

3. **Graph Data** Make a bar graph to present the data you obtained on plant growth.

4. **Conclude** By studying your data, what can you conclude about how (or if) your variable affects the growth of radish seedlings?

5. **Conclude** Is your experiment a failure if your variable did not apparently affect the growth? Explain.

6. **Experimental Design** What possible sources of error may have occurred in your experiment? Why might they have occurred?

EXTEND YOUR INVESTIGATION

How would you design an experiment to determine whether a specific biotic factor influences plant growth?

13.3 Energy in Ecosystems

KEY CONCEPT Life in an ecosystem requires a source of energy.

▶ MAIN IDEAS

- Producers provide energy for other organisms in an ecosystem.
- Almost all producers obtain energy from sunlight.

VOCABULARY

producer, p. 406
autotroph, p. 406
consumer, p. 406

heterotroph, p. 406
chemosynthesis, p. 407

Review
photosynthesis

MICHIGAN STANDARDS

B3.2A Identify how energy is stored in an ecosystem.
B3.2B Describe energy transfer through an ecosystem, accounting for energy lost to the environment as heat.

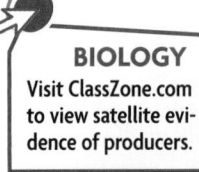

BIOLOGY
Visit ClassZone.com to view satellite evidence of producers.

FIGURE 13.7 This satellite image uses chlorophyll abundance to show the distribution of producers in the Western Hemisphere. Dark green areas are heavily forested, while yellow areas have limited vegetation.

Connect In the previous section, you learned that every ecosystem includes biotic and abiotic factors. Another important part of an ecosystem is the flow of energy. This energy is needed to fuel life processes, such as breathing and growing. Where does this energy come from, and what role does it play within an ecosystem?

▶ MAIN IDEA

Producers provide energy for other organisms in an ecosystem.

All organisms must have a source of energy in order to survive. However, not all organisms obtain their energy by eating other organisms.

- **Producers** are organisms that get their energy from nonliving resources, meaning they make their own food. Their distribution is shown in **FIGURE 13.7.** Producers are also called **autotrophs** (AW-tuh-TRAHFS). In the word *autotroph,* the suffix *-troph* comes from a Greek word meaning "nourishment." The prefix *auto-* means "self."

- **Consumers** are organisms that get their energy by eating other living or once-living resources, such as plants and animals. Consumers are also called **heterotrophs** (HEHT-uhr-uh-TRAHFS). In the word *heterotroph,* the prefix *hetero-* means "different."

All ecosystems depend on producers, because they provide the basis for the ecosystem's energy. Even animals that eat only meat rely on producers. One such species is the gray wolf. Gray wolves are consumers that eat elk and moose. Elk and moose are consumers that eat plants, such as grasses and shrubs. Plants are producers that make their own food. If the grasses and shrubs disappeared, the elk and moose would either have to find some other producer to eat or they would starve. The wolves would also be affected because they eat elk and moose. Although the wolves do not eat plants, their lives are tied to the grasses and shrubs that feed their prey. Likewise, all consumers are connected in some way to producers.

Most producers need sunlight to make food. These producers depend directly on the sun as their source of energy. For this reason, all the consumers connected to these producers depend indirectly on the sun for their energy.

Predict How would a long-term drought affect producers and consumers?

▶ MAIN IDEA

Almost all producers obtain energy from sunlight.

Most producers on Earth use sunlight as their energy source. Photosynthesis is the two-stage process that green plants, cyanobacteria, and some protists use to produce energy. Chemical reactions form carbohydrates from carbon dioxide and water. Oxygen is released as a waste product.

Photosynthesis in plants begins when energy from the sun hits chloroplasts and is absorbed by chlorophyll. In the first stage of photosynthesis, energy from sunlight is converted to chemical energy. In the second stage, this chemical energy is used to change carbon dioxide into carbohydrates, such as glucose. Plants use these carbohydrates as an energy source to fuel cellular respiration.

Not all producers depend on sunlight for their energy. Scientists were stunned in 1977 when they first visited deep-sea vents on the bottom of the ocean. There they found thriving ecosystems in places where super-heated water shoots up from the ocean floor. Studies showed that tiny prokaryotes were making their own food from minerals in the water. They had no need for sunlight. **Chemosynthesis** (KEE-moh-SIHN-thih-sihs) is the process by which an organism forms carbohydrates using chemicals, rather than light, as an energy source. A series of reactions changes the chemicals into a usable energy form. Different reactions occur depending on which chemicals are present.

In addition to deep-sea vents, chemosynthetic organisms are also found in sulfur-rich salt marsh flats and in hydrothermal pools, such as those in Yellowstone National Park, shown in **FIGURE 13.8**. In this case, chemical energy is used to change carbon dioxide (CO_2), water (H_2O), hydrogen sulfide (H_2S), and oxygen (O_2) into an energy-rich sugar molecule. Sulfuric acid (H_2SO_4) is released as a waste product.

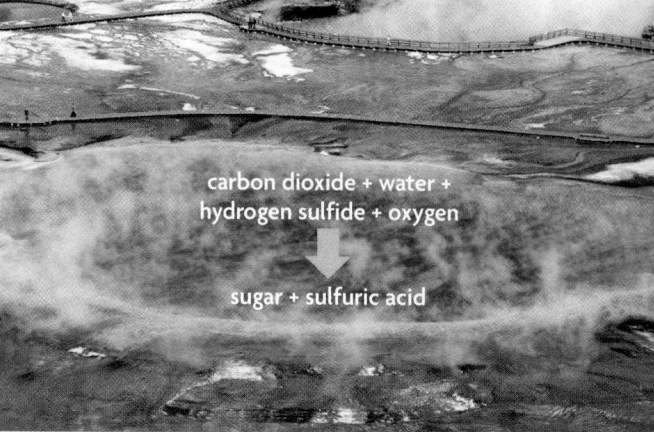

carbon dioxide + water + hydrogen sulfide + oxygen

sugar + sulfuric acid

FIGURE 13.8 Chemosynthetic bacteria thrive in many of Yellowstone National Park's hydrothermal pools.

Contrast How do photosynthesis and chemosynthesis differ?

13.3 ASSESSMENT

ONLINE QUIZ ClassZone.com

REVIEWING ▶ MAIN IDEAS

1. How does the stability of an ecosystem depend on its **producers**?

2. What are the two processes used by producers to obtain energy?

CRITICAL THINKING

3. **Hypothesize** Few producers live deep below a lake's surface. Suggest an explanation for this pattern.

4. **Infer** Could producers survive without **consumers**? Explain why or why not.

Connecting CONCEPTS

5. **History of Life** How might chemosynthetic organisms help scientists to understand how life developed on Earth?

Food Chains and Food Webs

KEY CONCEPT Food chains and food webs model the flow of energy in an ecosystem.

▶ MAIN IDEAS

- A food chain is a model that shows a sequence of feeding relationships.
- A food web shows a complex network of feeding relationships.

VOCABULARY

food chain, p. 408	**decomposer,** p. 409
herbivore, p. 409	**specialist,** p. 409
carnivore, p. 409	**generalist,** p. 409
omnivore, p. 409	**trophic level,** p. 409
detritivore, p. 409	**food web,** p. 411

MICHIGAN STANDARDS

L3.p2A Describe common relationships among organisms and provide examples of producer/consumer, predator/ prey, or parasite/host relationship. (prerequisite)

L3.p2C Describe the role of decomposers in the transfer of energy in an ecosystem. (prerequisite)

Connect As we have seen, energy flows through an ecosystem in one direction—from producers to consumers. However, since an ecosystem can have hundreds or even thousands of different species, determining the relationship between species can be quite tricky. Food chains and food webs are used to model these relationships.

▶ MAIN IDEA

A food chain is a model that shows a sequence of feeding relationships.

The simplest way to look at energy flow in an ecosystem is through a food chain. A **food chain** is a sequence that links species by their feeding relationships. Rather than describe every potential relationship, this model chain only follows the connection between one producer and a single chain of consumers within an ecosystem. For example, in a desert ecosystem, a desert cottontail eats grass. The food chain is, therefore, grass–desert cottontail. If another consumer such as a Harris's hawk eats a desert cottontail, the food chain gets longer: grass–desert cottontail–Harris's hawk, as shown in **FIGURE 13.9**.

FIGURE 13.9 Food Chain

Energy flows through a food chain.

GRAMA GRASS	DESERT COTTONTAIL	HARRIS'S HAWK

Grama grass, a producer, obtains its energy through photosynthesis.	The desert cottontail, a consumer, obtains its energy by eating the seeds of plants, such as grama grass.	The Harris's hawk, a consumer, obtains its energy by eating other animals, such as desert cottontails.

Types of Consumers

As you read in Section 13.3, consumers are organisms that eat other organisms. All consumers, however, are not alike.

- **Herbivores,** such as desert cottontails, are organisms that eat only plants.
- **Carnivores** are organisms that eat only animals. Harris's hawks are carnivores that eat desert cottontails.
- **Omnivores** are organisms that eat both plants and animals. Kangaroo rats are omnivores that eat both seeds and insects.
- **Detritivores** (dih-TRY-tuh-vOHRZ) are organisms that eat detritus, or dead organic matter. A millipede is a detritivore that feeds on particles of detritus on the ground.
- **Decomposers** are detritivores that break down organic matter into simpler compounds. Fungi, for example, are decomposers. Decomposers are important to the stability of an ecosystem because they return vital nutrients back into the environment.

Food chains are especially helpful in describing feeding relationships among extremely selective eaters, known as specialists. A **specialist** is a consumer that primarily eats one specific organism or feeds on a very small number of organisms.

Specialists are very sensitive to changes in the availability of prey. For example, the Florida snail kite, shown in **FIGURE 13.10,** is a specialist that depends on the apple snail as its main source of food. In the early 1900s, apple snails became less common in Florida as a result of land development. Florida snail kite populations declined suddenly, and in 1967, the bird was listed as an endangered species. Currently, the snails and the birds continue to survive in lower numbers in protected areas, such as the Everglades.

Most species do not rely on a single source of food. These species are called generalists. **Generalists** are consumers that have a varying diet. For example, the diet of a gray wolf may include a number of animals, including elk, moose, white-tailed deer, beavers, and even mice.

VOCABULARY

Most words for consumers come from Latin words.
- *Vorāre* means "to swallow or devour."
- *Herba* means "vegetation."
- *Carnus* means "flesh."
- *Omnis* means "all."
- *Dētrere* means "to wear away."

FIGURE 13.10 Florida snail kites are specialists that rely on apple snails as their primary food source.

Trophic Levels

Trophic levels are the levels of nourishment in a food chain. For example, the producer–herbivore–carnivore chain has three trophic levels. Carnivores are at the highest trophic level. Herbivores are at the second trophic level. Producers are at the first, or bottom, trophic level. Energy flows up the food chain from the lowest trophic level to the highest.

- Primary consumers are herbivores because they are the first consumer above the producer trophic level.
- Secondary consumers are carnivores that eat herbivores.
- Tertiary consumers are carnivores that eat secondary consumers.

Omnivores, such as humans that eat both plants and animals, may be listed at different trophic levels in different food chains. When a person eats a salad, the trophic levels in the food chain are producer–omnivore. When a person eats a steak, the trophic levels are producer–herbivore–omnivore.

Connect What is the connection between food chains and trophic levels?

FIGURE 13.11 Food Web

A food web shows the network of feeding relationships between trophic levels within an ecosystem. The food web in a coral reef can be quite complex because many organisms feed on a variety of other species.

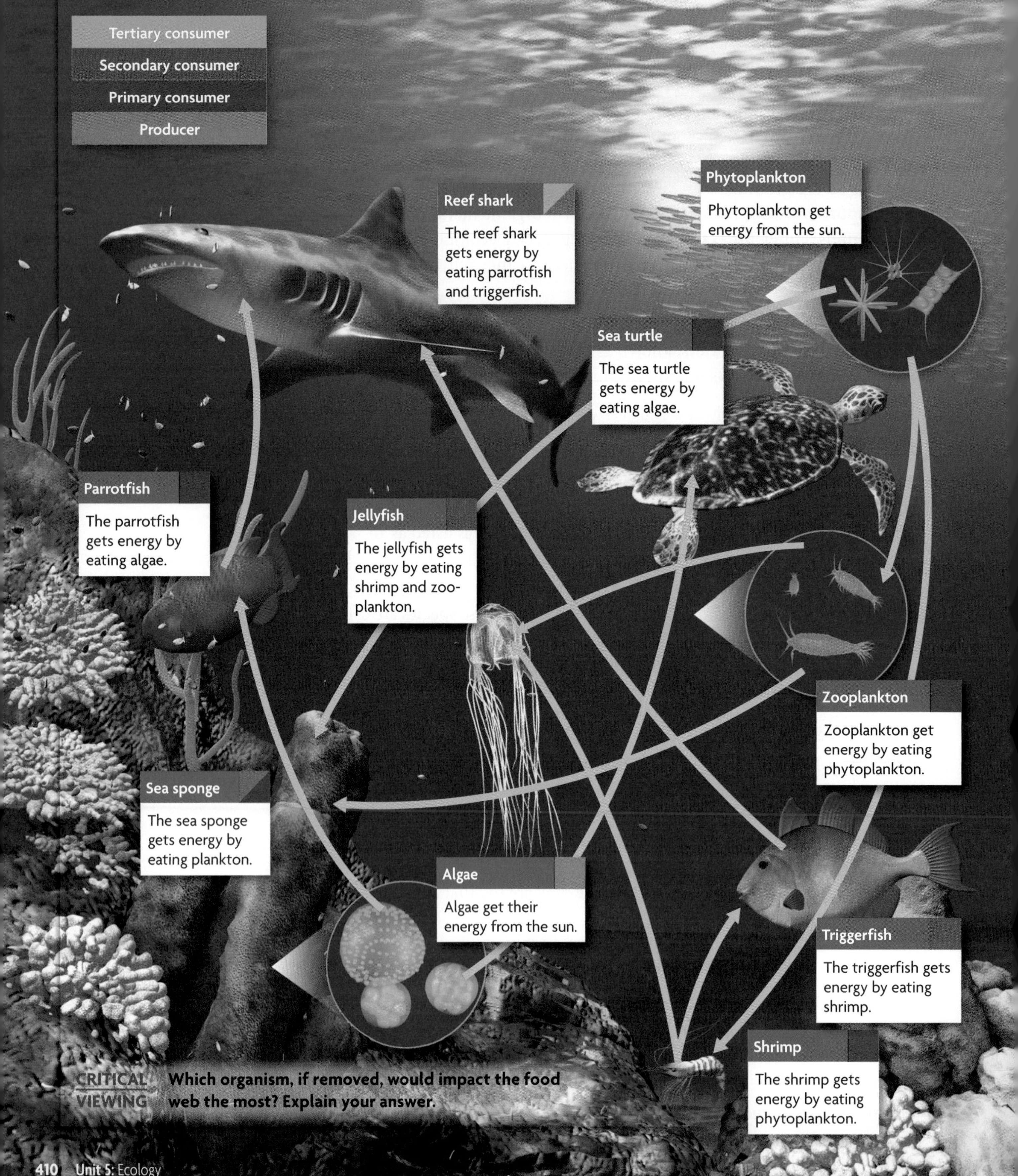

- Tertiary consumer
- Secondary consumer
- Primary consumer
- Producer

Reef shark
The reef shark gets energy by eating parrotfish and triggerfish.

Phytoplankton
Phytoplankton get energy from the sun.

Sea turtle
The sea turtle gets energy by eating algae.

Parrotfish
The parrotfish gets energy by eating algae.

Jellyfish
The jellyfish gets energy by eating shrimp and zoo-plankton.

Zooplankton
Zooplankton get energy by eating phytoplankton.

Sea sponge
The sea sponge gets energy by eating plankton.

Algae
Algae get their energy from the sun.

Triggerfish
The triggerfish gets energy by eating shrimp.

Shrimp
The shrimp gets energy by eating phytoplankton.

CRITICAL VIEWING   Which organism, if removed, would impact the food web the most? Explain your answer.

▶ MAIN IDEA
A food web shows a complex network of feeding relationships.

Generalists may be involved in many food chains, depending on which links are in the chain. Each of the organisms in those links, in turn, may be part of many other food chains. As a result, scientists use food webs to describe these interconnections. A **food web** is a model that shows the complex network of feeding relationships and the flow of energy within and sometimes beyond an ecosystem. At each link in a food web, some energy is stored within an organism, and some energy is dissipated into the environment.

Coral reefs are often referred to as rain forests of the sea, due to the abundance and diversity of species found there. The complex connections in a coral reef ecosystem, illustrated in **FIGURE 13.11,** are created by the feeding relationships within the food web.

The stability of any food web depends on the presence of producers, as they form the base of the food web. In the case of a marine ecosystem such as a coral reef, algae and phytoplankton are two of the producers that play this important role.

An organism may have multiple feeding relationships within a food web. For example, reef sharks are generalists that eat several different food items. When a reef shark eats a parrotfish, it is a secondary consumer, because a parrotfish is a primary consumer that eats algae. However, a reef shark is a tertiary consumer when it eats a triggerfish. This difference in trophic levels occurs because a triggerfish is a secondary consumer that feeds on shrimp. The shrimp, in turn, is a primary consumer that eats phytoplankton. Food webs like this one emphasize both the complicated nature of feeding relationships and the flow of energy within an ecosystem.

Analyze **How might the introduction of a new predator affect the flow of energy through a food web?**

Connecting CONCEPTS

Marine Ecosystems Coral reefs are ecosystems that are rich in diversity. In **Chapter 15** you will learn about the complex relationships found in these underwater ecosystems.

13.4 / ASSESSMENT

ONLINE QUIZ
ClassZone.com

REVIEWING ▶ MAIN IDEAS

1. Why are **food chains** especially useful for describing the relationships of **specialists**?

2. What happens to energy as it flows through a **food web**?

CRITICAL THINKING

3. **Compare and Contrast** Only a small percentage of all consumers are specialists. What danger does a specialist face that a **generalist** does not?

4. **Predict** How might the stability of an ecosystem be affected if all of the **decomposers** were suddenly removed?

Connecting CONCEPTS

5. **Pollution** How might an oil spill in the ocean affect an aquatic food web? What might happen to the food web on land located near the spill? Explain your answers.

13.5 Cycling of Matter

KEY CONCEPT Matter cycles in and out of an ecosystem.

▶ **MAIN IDEAS**

- Water cycles through the environment.
- Elements essential for life also cycle through ecosystems.

VOCABULARY

hydrologic cycle, p. 412
biogeochemical cycle, p. 413
nitrogen fixation, p. 415

L3.p3C Explain how biotic and abiotic factors cycle in an ecosystem (water, carbon, oxygen, and nitrogen). (prerequisite)
B3.3b Describe environmental processes (e.g., the carbon and nitrogen cycles) and their role in processing matter crucial for sustaining life.

Connect Since life in most ecosystems requires a constant inflow of energy from the sun, Earth is an open system in terms of energy. However, in terms of matter, such as oxygen and carbon, Earth is a closed system. Today's Earth has roughly the same amount of carbon as it had billions of years ago, meaning that the same carbon atoms that make up your body may once have been part of a tree, or gases spewed by a volcano, or even part of a dinosaur.

▶ **MAIN IDEA**

Water cycles through the environment.

Matter changes form, but it does not disappear. It can be used over and over again in a continuous cycle. If you crush a rock, for example, it does not vanish. Instead, it turns into sand and other bits of minerals. Although matter may change form over time, the total amount of matter remains the same.

As you learned earlier, a major part of life on Earth is water, which has a cycle of its own. The **hydrologic cycle** (HY-druh-LAHJ-ihk), also known as the water cycle, is the circular pathway of water on Earth from the atmosphere, to the surface, below ground, and back. Part of that pathway involves humans and other organisms, which all have bodies made mostly of water.

As shown in **FIGURE 13.12**, precipitation, such as rain or snow, falls to Earth. Some of this precipitation seeps into the ground, some drops into ponds, streams, lakes, or other waterways, and some forms puddles or other temporary pools. Depending on the type of soil and rocks surrounding it and also on its location, groundwater may empty directly into oceans. Sometimes water flows first into lakes, swamps, or wetlands, but these—along with rivers, streams, and other freshwater sources—also feed into oceans.

In addition, some droplets of water quickly reenter the atmosphere through evaporation. Since oceans cover over 70 percent of Earth's surface, about 85 percent of Earth's evaporation occurs between the oceans and the atmosphere. On land, water vapor is released by plants during transpiration, which is evaporation that occurs between plant leaves and the atmosphere. The cycle is completed as water vapor in the atmosphere condenses and forms clouds, returning water to the surface once again in the form of precipitation.

Analyze If the total amount of water on Earth does not change, why are there concerns about global water shortages?

Connecting CONCEPTS

Properties of Water The presence of water is necessary for life on Earth. All organisms depend on the simple structure of the water molecule. As you learned in **Chapter 2**, water has several unique properties. Water's high specific heat helps keep cells at the right temperature to carry out life processes.

FIGURE 13.12 Hydrologic Cycle

The hydrologic cycle is the circular pathway of water on Earth.

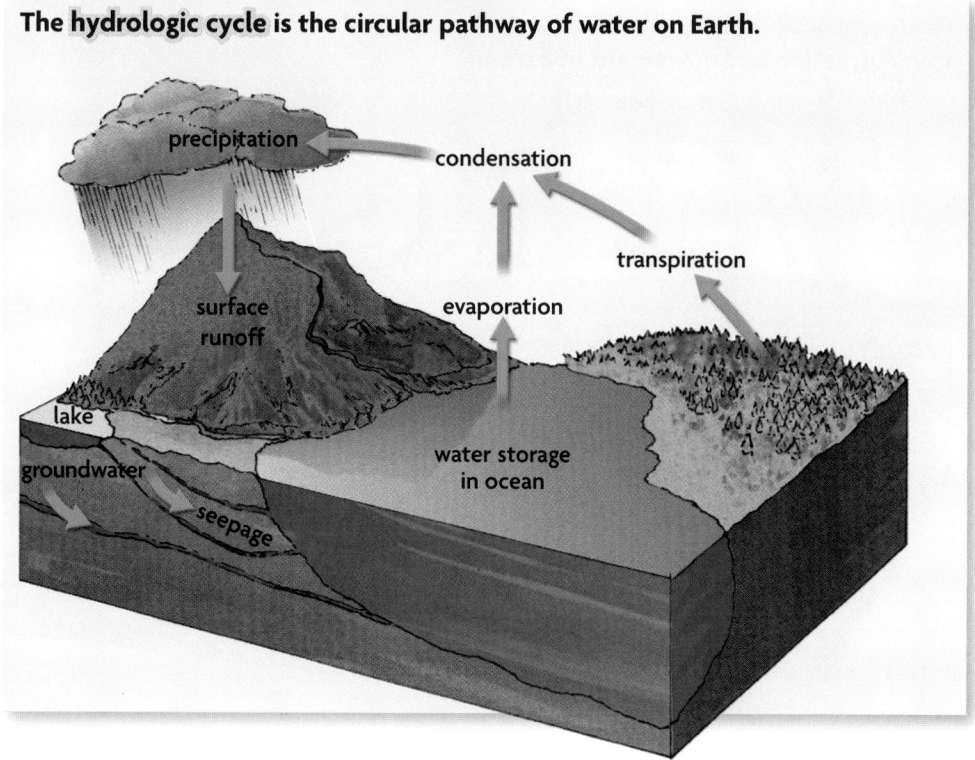

▶ MAIN IDEA

Elements essential for life also cycle through ecosystems.

Many elements are essential to the structure and function of organisms. Elements are basic chemical substances, such as the oxygen and hydrogen found in the chemical compound of water. Additional elements important to life include carbon, nitrogen, phosphorus, and sulfur. As you learned in Chapter 2, oxygen, carbon, nitrogen, and hydrogen make up 96 percent of the mass of the human body. This is just one reason why the cycling of these elements is so important. All of these elements cycle through ecosystems, just as water does.

A **biogeochemical cycle** (BY-oh-JEE-oh-KEHM-ih-kuhl) is the movement of a particular chemical through the biological and geological, or living and nonliving, parts of an ecosystem. Just as water changes from solid form (ice or snow) to liquid form (rain) or gaseous form (water vapor), other substances may also change state as they move through their cycles.

The Oxygen Cycle

Plants, animals, and most other organisms need oxygen for cellular respiration. As shown in **FIGURE 13.13**, plants release oxygen as a waste product during photosynthesis. In turn, humans and other organisms take in this oxygen and release it as carbon dioxide through respiration. Oxygen is also indirectly transferred through an ecosystem by the cycling of other nutrients, including carbon, nitrogen, and phosphorus.

Apply Explain how deforestation might affect the oxygen cycle.

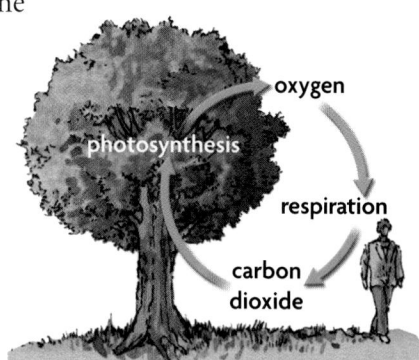

FIGURE 13.13 In the oxygen cycle, oxygen flows into the atmosphere as a byproduct of photosynthesis. Organisms take in this oxygen and release it as carbon dioxide through respiration.

FIGURE 13.14 Carbon Cycle

Photosynthesis and respiration account for much of the transformation and movement of carbon.

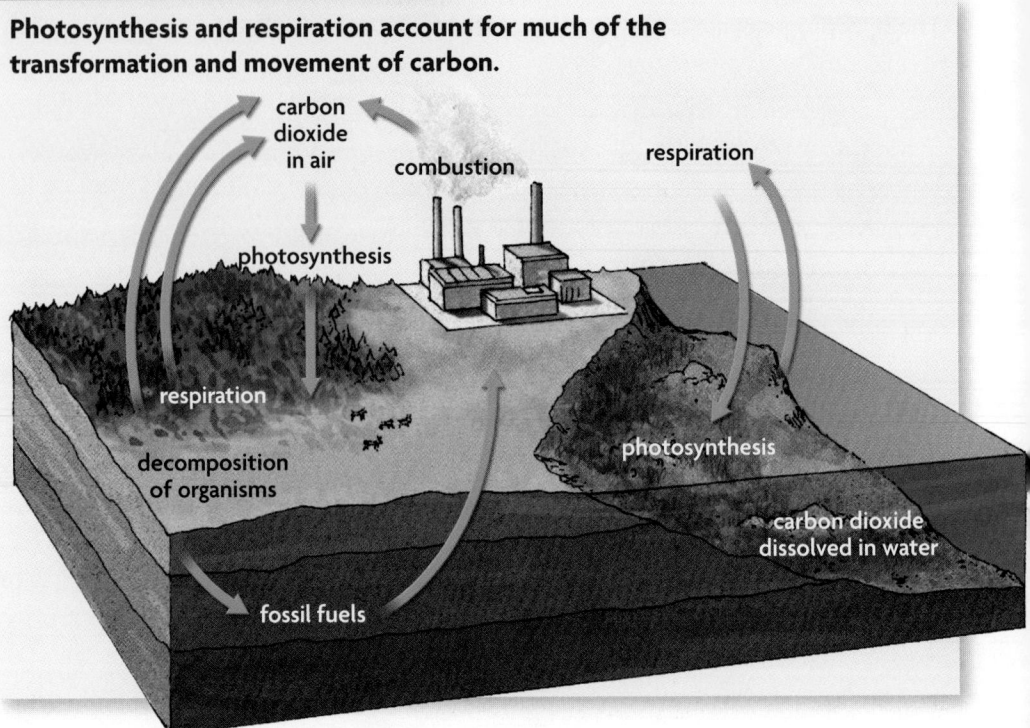

The Carbon Cycle

Carbon is the building block of life—it is key to the structure of all organisms on our planet. It is an essential component of carbohydrates, proteins, fats, and all the other organic molecules that make up your body. Carbon continually flows from the environment to living organisms and back again in the carbon cycle, shown in **FIGURE 13.14.**

Carbon exists in the abiotic world in several forms. Carbon can be found in solid, liquid, and gaseous states. Sources of carbon include

- carbon dioxide (CO_2) gas in the atmosphere
- bicarbonate (HCO_3^-) dissolved in water
- fossil fuels, which are underground deposits of oil, natural gas, and coal
- carbonate rocks, such as limestone
- dead organic matter, such as humus, in the soil

The simplest transfer of carbon occurs between plants and animals. Plants use energy from the sun to convert carbon dioxide from the air into organic material that becomes a part of the plant's structure. The carbon then moves through the biotic world as one organism eats another.

Carbon is returned to the atmosphere as carbon dioxide by respiration or through the decomposition of dead organisms. The burning of fossil fuels and wood, as well as emissions from factories and automobiles, adds to carbon dioxide in the atmosphere. Another source of atmospheric carbon is methane, which is emitted from wetlands, landfills, and livestock.

Not all carbon molecules move freely through the cycle. Areas that store carbon over a long period of time are called carbon sinks. One example is forest land, where large amounts of carbon are stored in the cellulose of wood.

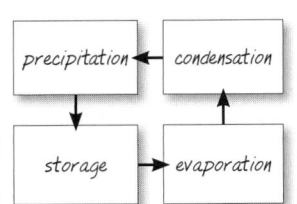

The Nitrogen Cycle

About 78 percent of Earth's atmosphere is made of nitrogen gas. However, most organisms can use nitrogen only in the form of ions such as ammonium (NH_4^+) or nitrate (NO_3^-). As shown in **FIGURE 13.15,** much of the nitrogen cycle takes place underground.

Certain types of bacteria convert gaseous nitrogen into ammonia (NH_3) through a process called **nitrogen fixation.** A few types of cyanobacteria fix nitrogen in aquatic ecosystems. On land, some nitrogen-fixing bacteria live in small outgrowths, called nodules, on the roots of plants such as beans and peas. Other nitrogen-fixing bacteria live freely in the soil. The ammonia released by these bacteria is transformed into ammonium by the addition of hydrogen ions found in acidic soil. Some ammonium is taken up by plants, but most is used by nitrifying bacteria as an energy source. Through the process called nitrification, these bacteria change ammonium into nitrate.

Nitrates released by soil bacteria are taken up by plants, which convert them into organic compounds such as amino acids and proteins. Nitrogen continues along the cycle as animals eat plant or animal matter. When decomposers break down animal excretions or dead animal and plant matter, nitrogen is returned to the soil as ammonium, in a process called ammonification.

Denitrifying bacteria use nitrate as an oxygen source, releasing nitrogen gas into the atmosphere as a waste product. Some nitrogen also enters the soil as a result of atmospheric fixation by lightning. Lightning's energy breaks apart nitrogen molecules in the atmosphere. Nitrogen recombines with oxygen in the air, forming nitrogen oxide. The combination of nitrogen oxide with rainwater forms nitrates, which are absorbed by the soil.

FIGURE 13.15 Nitrogen Cycle

Much of the nitrogen cycle occurs underground, where bacteria transform ammonium into nitrates, which are used by plants to make amino acids.

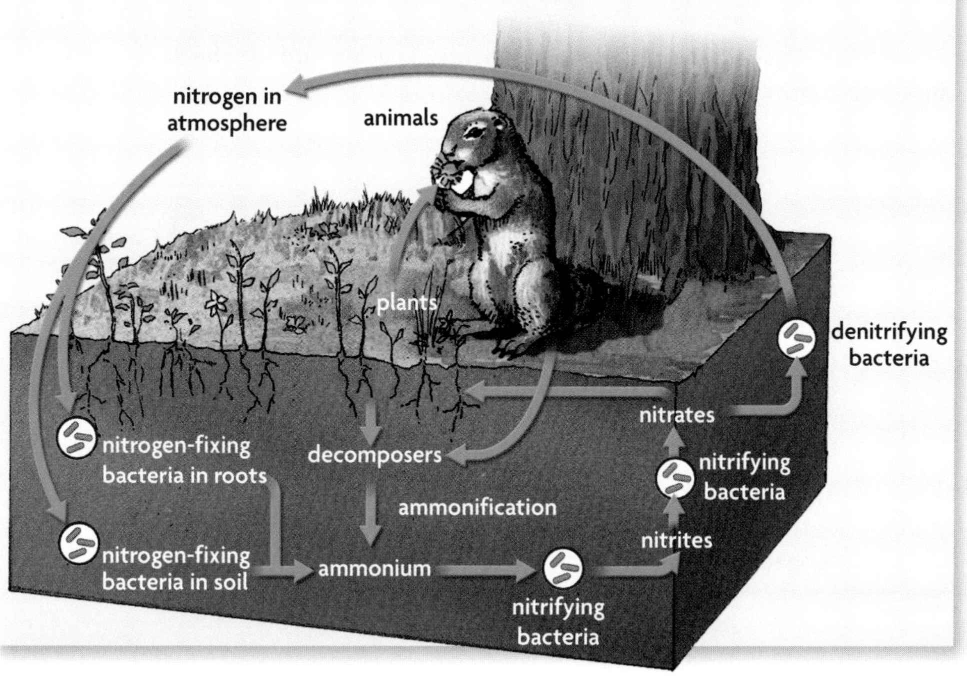

The Phosphorus Cycle

Unlike the other cycles, the phosphorus cycle does not include an atmospheric portion. Instead, most of the cycle takes place at and below ground level, as shown in **FIGURE 13.16**.

FIGURE 13.16 Phosphorus Cycle

The phosphorus cycle occurs on a local, rather than global, scale. Its cycle is limited to water, soil, and ocean sediment.

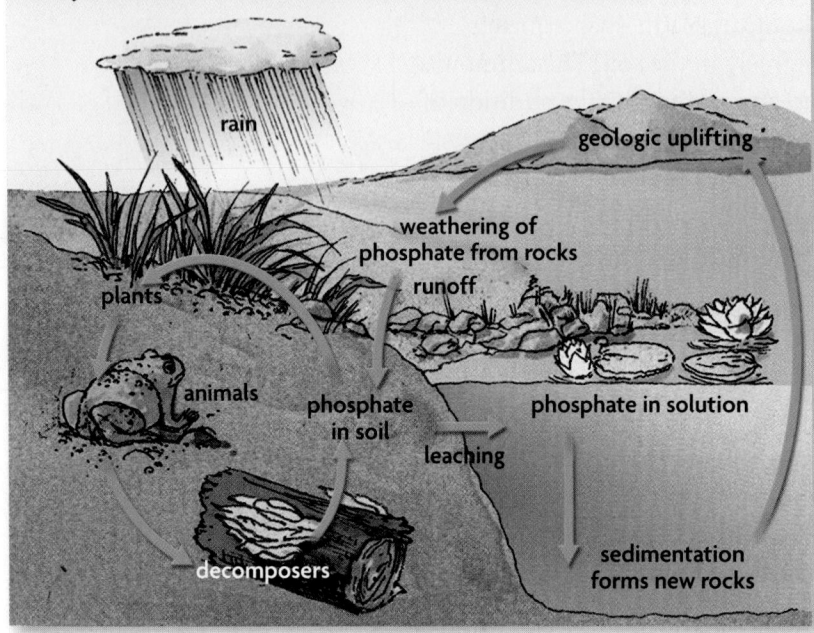

The phosphorus cycle begins when phosphate is released by the weathering of rocks. Plants and some fungi found near plant roots are able to take up phosphate. Phosphorus moves from producers to consumers through the food web. When the producers and consumers die, decomposers break down the organisms. This process releases phosphorus back into the soil or water for use by producers. Some phosphorus may leach into groundwater from the soil. This groundwater may flow into a lake or other body of water, where the phosphorus becomes locked in sediments at the bottom. Over many thousands of years, these sediments eventually become rock again, and the cycle starts again as phosphate is released by the weathering of these newly formed rocks.

Mining and agricultural runoff also add to the overall amount of phosphorus in the environment. The excessive flow of phosphorus into an aquatic ecosystem from sewage and agricultural runoff can cause significant problems. Phosphorus is a limiting factor for the growth of plants. Large amounts of phosphorus within an aquatic environment can lead to algal blooms. These blooms crowd out other plant species and negatively impact wildlife populations as well.

Summarize Choose one of the biogeochemical cycles, and list the key processes involved in the cycling of the element.

13.5 ASSESSMENT

ONLINE QUIZ
ClassZone.com

REVIEWING ▶ MAIN IDEAS

1. How does the **hydrologic cycle** move water through the environment?

2. What are four elements that cycle through ecosystems, and why are they important?

CRITICAL THINKING

3. **Apply** Why might farmers plant legumes such as peas to improve the nitrogen levels in their soil?

4. **Synthesize** Explain the importance of decomposers to the overall **biogeochemical cycle.**

Connecting CONCEPTS

5. **Evolution** How might Earth's biogeochemical cycles help scientists to understand the early history of life on Earth?

13.6 Pyramid Models

KEY CONCEPT Pyramids model the distribution of energy and matter in an ecosystem.

▶ MAIN IDEAS

- An energy pyramid shows the distribution of energy among trophic levels.
- Other pyramid models illustrate an ecosystem's biomass and distribution of organisms.

VOCABULARY

biomass, p. 417
energy pyramid, p. 418

MICHIGAN STANDARDS

B3.2A Identify how energy is stored in an ecosystem.
B3.2B Describe energy transfer through an ecosystem, accounting for energy lost to the environment as heat.

Connect You have seen that ecosystems have a structure, with large numbers of producers supporting several levels of consumers. Ecologists often model this structure as a pyramid, in terms of both matter and energy. The pyramids can represent the general flow of energy through an ecosystem, from producers to consumers. They can also represent the mass or numbers of organisms at each trophic level.

▶ MAIN IDEA

An energy pyramid shows the distribution of energy among trophic levels.

Ecosystems get their energy from sunlight. Sunlight provides the energy for photosynthesis, and that energy flows up the food chain. However, along the way, some of the energy is dissipated, or lost. Producers use energy from sunlight to make food. Herbivores eat the plants, but burn some energy in the process. This energy is given off as heat, and the heat escapes into space. Carnivores then eat the herbivores, but again lose energy as heat. In other words, each level in the food chain contains much less energy than the level below it. Fortunately, the Sun pumps new energy into the system and allows life to continue.

Loss of Available Energy

Each meal that you consume is packed with energy in the form of proteins, fats, and carbohydrates. Your body uses this energy for many purposes such as movement and growth. The majority of the food you consume is used to keep your body at its normal temperature. Your body is very inefficient at converting what you consume into useful energy, so there will always be some material that is not used. Unused material is simply excreted as waste.

Energy in an ecosystem works in much the same way, only on a larger scale. **Biomass** is a measure of the total dry mass of organisms in a given area. When a consumer incorporates the biomass of a producer into its own biomass, a great deal of energy is lost in the process as heat and waste. The conversion of biomass from a producer into biomass of the consumer is inefficient.

Consider the simple producer-to-consumer food chain of grass–prairie dog. Photosynthesis traps energy as carbohydrates, which can be thought of as a high-quality form of energy. A hungry prairie dog then eats the grass.

Connecting CONCEPTS

Cellular Respiration As you learned in **Chapter 4**, the processes of cellular respiration use ATP to maintain your body's functions. While the chemical reactions of metabolism are relatively efficient, there will always be some loss of available energy.

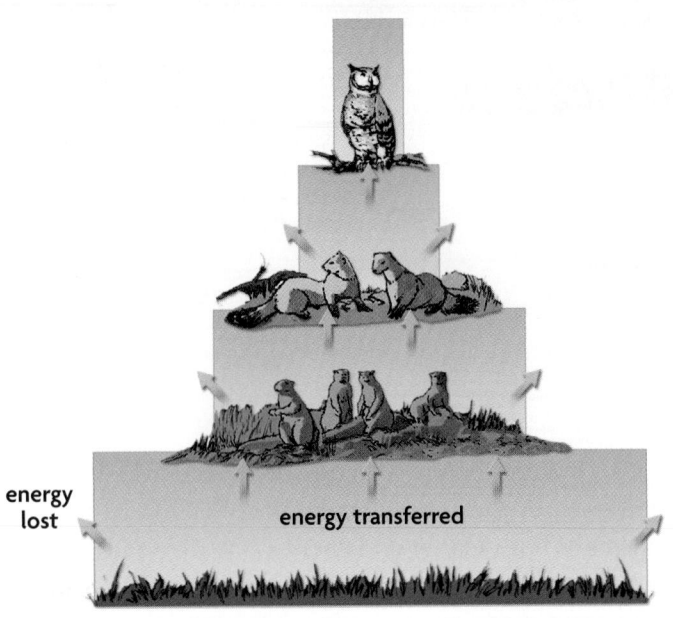

energy lost · energy transferred

FIGURE 13.17 An energy pyramid illustrates the energy flow between trophic levels in an ecosystem. Between each tier, up to 90 percent of the energy is lost as heat into the atmosphere.

Some of the energy is used by the animal to grow. The remaining energy may be used to fuel cellular respiration or remains undigested. The dissipation, or loss, of energy between trophic levels may be as much as 90 percent, meaning that only 10 percent of the available energy is left to transfer from one trophic level to another.

Energy Pyramids

Because energy is lost at each stage of a food chain, the longer the chain is, the more energy is lost overall. The total energy used by producers far exceeds the energy used by the consumers they support. This concept can be illustrated with an energy pyramid. An **energy pyramid** is a diagram that compares energy used by producers, primary consumers, and other trophic levels. The pyramid, therefore, illustrates how available energy is distributed among trophic levels in an ecosystem. The unit of measurement used to describe the amount of energy at each trophic level in an energy pyramid is the kilocalorie (kcal).

A typical energy pyramid has a very large section at the base for the producers, and sections that become progressively smaller above. For example, in a prairie ecosystem, as illustrated in **FIGURE 13.17**, energy flows from grass at the producer level, to prairie dogs at the primary consumer level, to black-footed ferrets at the secondary consumer level, to a great horned owl at the tertiary consumer level.

Connect **Draw an energy pyramid for the desert food chain introduced in Section 13.4. Use arrows to illustrate the flow of energy.**

FIGURE 13.18 The biomass pyramid depicts the total dry mass of organisms found at each trophic level.

▶ **MAIN IDEA**
Other pyramid models illustrate an ecosystem's biomass and distribution of organisms.

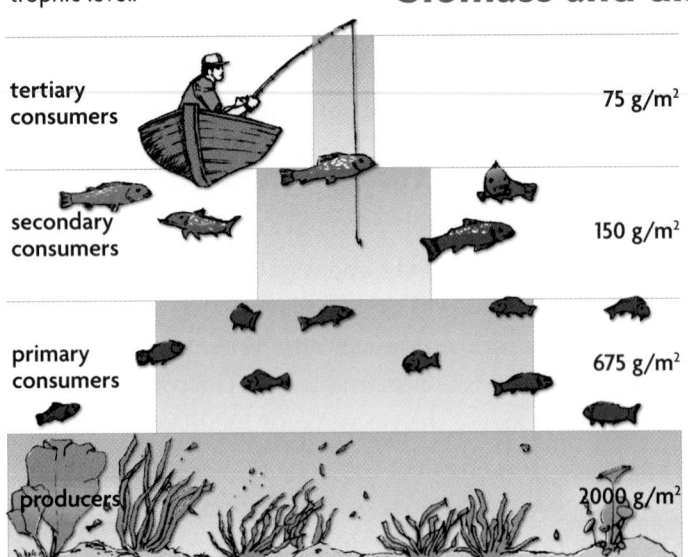

tertiary consumers — 75 g/m²

secondary consumers — 150 g/m²

primary consumers — 675 g/m²

producers — 2000 g/m²

A biomass pyramid is a diagram that compares the biomass of different trophic levels within an ecosystem. Unlike an energy pyramid, which represents energy use, a biomass pyramid provides a picture of the mass of producers needed to support primary consumers, the mass of primary consumers required to support secondary consumers, and so on.

In a pond ecosystem, such as the one illustrated in **FIGURE 13.18**, a biomass pyramid shows that the total dry mass (given in grams per square meter, or g/m²) of algae within the pond is far greater than the dry mass of fish. This example illustrates yet again the important role producers play in maintaining a stable ecosystem.

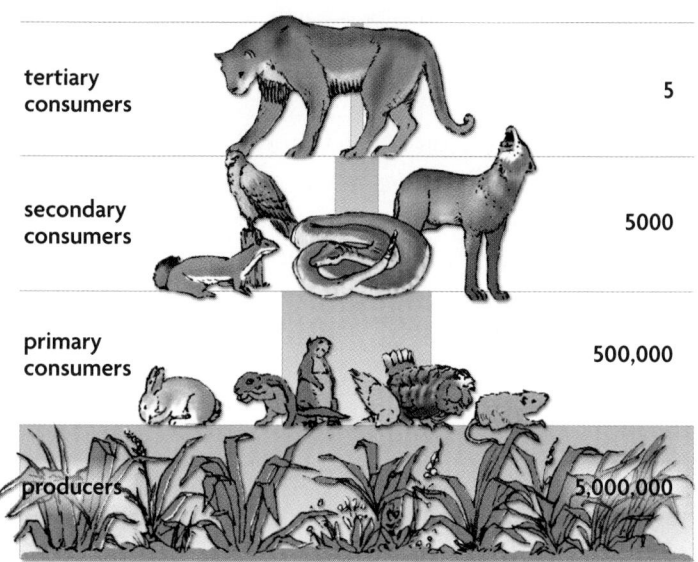

tertiary
consumers   5

secondary
consumers   5000

primary
consumers   500,000

producers   5,000,000

FIGURE 13.19 In a pyramid of numbers, each tier represents the actual number of individual organisms present in each trophic level.

   A pyramid of numbers shows the numbers of individual organisms at each trophic level in an ecosystem. For example, a pyramid of numbers depicting a mountainous habitat, as shown in **FIGURE 13.19**, might include organisms such as grasses, snowshoe hares, gophers, coyotes, snakes, and mountain lions. This type of pyramid is particularly effective in showing the vast number of producers required to support even a few top level consumers.

   In certain situations, both biomass pyramids and pyramids of numbers may occur in an inverted, or upside down, formation. Consider, for example, a pyramid of numbers based on a single tree. This single tree would be greatly outnumbered by the primary and secondary consumers, such as insects and birds, that live within it. In this case, the upper tiers of the pyramid of numbers would be much larger than the bottom tier representing the single tree.

Apply **If a scientist wanted to compare the exact number of organisms at each trophic level within a desert ecosystem, which pyramid model would he or she use?**

13.6 ASSESSMENT

ONLINE QUIZ
ClassZone.com

REVIEWING ▶ MAIN IDEAS

1. How does an **energy pyramid** help to describe energy flow in a food web?

2. What is the difference between a **biomass** pyramid and a pyramid of numbers?

CRITICAL THINKING

3. **Apply** How would you draw a pyramid of numbers for a dog with fleas? What shape would the pyramid take?

4. **Calculate** If each level in a food chain typically loses 90 percent of the energy it takes in, and the producer level uses 1000 kcal of energy, how much of that energy is left after the third trophic level?

Connecting CONCEPTS

5. **Nutrition** Why is an herbivorous diet more energy efficient than a carnivorous diet? Explain your answer.

Use these inquiry-based labs and online activities to deepen your understanding of ecological principles.

MICHIGAN STANDARDS

L3.p3D Predict how changes in one population might affect other populations based upon their relationships in a food web. (prerequisite)

INVESTIGATION

Random Sampling

In this activity, you will use random sampling to calculate the number of big bluestems, a typical tall-grass species, found in a restored prairie.

SKILL Sampling

PROBLEM How many big bluestems are in the field?

PROCEDURE

1. Cut 14 equal-sized paper squares.
2. Letter seven of the squares A through G. Number seven of the squares 1 through 7. Place the lettered squares and numbered squares in separate containers.
3. In your notebook, draw a data table like the one below. Include 12 rows in your table.
4. The pictured grid is your study plot. It is part of a larger grassland. The study plot measures 7 meters on each side, and each grid segment measures 1 meter by 1 meter. A single big bluestem plant is represented by each dot.
5. Determine which segment you will count by taking one square from each container without looking. Locate the letter-number combination on the grid and count the number of big bluestem plants. Record this number in your data table. Place each square back in its container.
6. Repeat step 5 until you have collected data for 12 different grid segments. Do not count the same segment twice.

MATERIALS

- ruler
- scissors
- paper
- 2 containers
- Calculation datasheet
- calculator

CALCULATE Complete the calculation datasheet to estimate the population size.

TABLE 1. RANDOM SAMPLE DATA		
Grid Letter	Grid Number	No. of Big Bluestems in Grid Segment

ANALYZE AND CONCLUDE

1. **Experimental Design** Why were paper squares used to determine which grid segment to count? Why didn't you just choose ten grid segments on your own?
2. **Evaluate** How could you change the procedure to reduce your percent error?
3. **Analyze** What are the advantages of using random sampling to estimate population size? What are the disadvantages?

INVESTIGATION

Build a Terrarium

In this activity, you will construct a miniature self-sustaining ecosystem and monitor its stability.

SKILL Modeling

PROBLEM How does an ecosystem change or maintain its equilibrium over time?

MATERIALS

- glass jar with lid
- gravel
- potting soil
- large sealable plastic bags
- water
- measuring cup
- ruler
- small plants
- light source

PROCEDURE

1. Cover the bottom of the jar with a layer of gravel about 2 centimeters deep.

2. Place 2 cups of potting soil and 1/2 cup of water in the plastic bag. Seal the bag and mix well until the soil is moist.

3. Add the moistened soil into the jar over the gravel layer.

4. Select and plant the small plants in the soil. Cover the jar with the lid and tighten it shut.

5. Observe and record changes in your terrarium over time.

ANALYZE AND CONCLUDE

1. **Operational Definitions** What criteria did you use to select the size and number of plants for your terrarium?

2. **Identify Variables** What are the key variables involved in maintaining your ecosystem?

3. **Observe** How did your terrarium ecosystem change over time?

4. **Conclude** Was your terrarium a success? Explain.

VIRTUAL LAB

Estimating Population Size

How does a scientist count a mobile population? In this interactive lab, capture, mark, then recapture individual animals to estimate the size of a sample population.

ANIMATED BIOLOGY

Build a Food Web

Build a food web. Use your knowledge of producers and consumers to place a set of organisms in a food web.

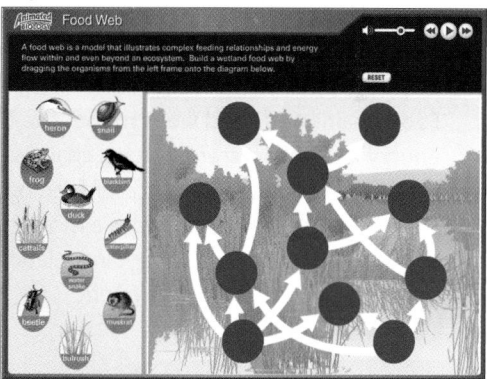

WEBQUEST

A sea otter is playful, fun to watch, and very critical to its ecosystem. In this WebQuest, you will explore its role as a keystone species within the aquatic environment of the California coast. Learn what happened after sea otters were almost wiped out. Finally, think of ways you can protect sea otter populations and the ecosystems in which they live.

Interactive ⟨⟩ Review @ CLASSZONE.COM

KEY CONCEPTS | Vocabulary Games | Concept Maps | Animated Biology | Online Quiz

13.1 Ecologists Study Relationships

Ecology is the study of the relationships among organisms and their environment. Ecologists study environments at different levels of organization. Ecologists use methods such as observation, experimentation, and modeling to study ecological principles.

13.2 Biotic and Abiotic Factors

keystone

Every ecosystem includes both living and nonliving factors. Changing one factor in an ecosystem can affect many other factors. The removal of a keystone species may lead to changes in an ecosystem's biodiversity.

13.3 Energy in Ecosystems

Life in an ecosystem requires a source of energy. Producers provide energy for other organisms in an ecosystem. Most producers obtain their energy from sunlight through photosynthesis. Other producers obtain their energy through a process called chemosynthesis.

13.4 Food Chains and Food Webs

Food chains and food webs model the flow of energy in an ecosystem. A food chain is a simple model that shows a sequence of feeding relationships. A food web provides a more complex picture of the network of feeding relationships among organisms in an ecosystem.

13.5 Cycling of Matter

Matter cycles in and out of an ecosystem. The hydrologic cycle is the circular pathway of water through the environment. Elements essential for life on Earth, such as oxygen, carbon, nitrogen, and phosphorus, also cycle through ecosystems.

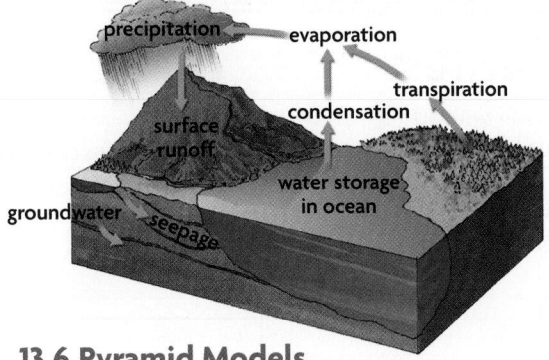

13.6 Pyramid Models

Pyramids model the distribution of energy and matter in an ecosystem. An energy pyramid shows the distribution of energy in a food chain. Energy flows upward from producers to consumers. Between each tier of the energy pyramid, energy is lost as heat. Sometimes only 10 percent of the original energy is transferred to the next trophic level. A biomass pyramid shows the total mass of organisms at each trophic level, while a pyramid of numbers shows the actual number of organisms present in each trophic level.

energy transferred

energy lost

Synthesize Your Notes

Energy Pyramid Add labels and organisms that belong in each trophic level to this energy pyramid.

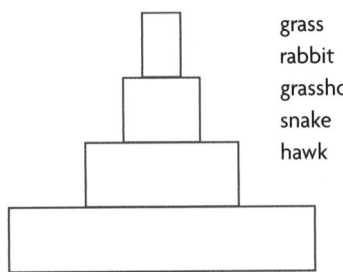

grass   producer
rabbit   primary consumer
grasshopper   secondary consumer
snake   tertiary consumer
hawk

Concept Map Use a concept map to summarize what you know about food webs.

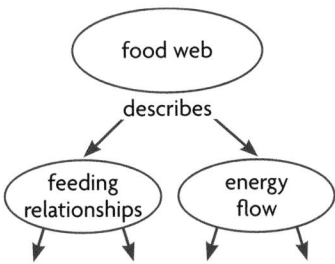

Chapter Assessment

Chapter Vocabulary

13.1 ecology, p. 396
community, p. 397
ecosystem, p. 397
biome, p. 397

13.2 biotic, p. 402
abiotic, p. 402
biodiversity, p. 403
keystone species, p. 403

13.3 producer, p. 406
autotroph, p. 406

consumer, p. 406
heterotroph, p. 406
chemosynthesis, p. 407

13.4 food chain, p. 408
herbivore, p. 409
carnivore, p. 409
omnivore, p. 409
detritivore, p. 409
decomposer, p. 409
specialist, p. 409
generalist, p. 409

trophic level, p. 409
food web, p. 411

13.5 hydrologic cycle, p. 412
biogeochemical cycle, p. 413
nitrogen fixation, p. 415

13.6 biomass, p. 417
energy pyramid, p. 418

Reviewing Vocabulary

Find an Opposite

Pair each of the words listed below with a different vocabulary term that has an opposing definition. Then, write one sentence describing a difference.

1. abiotic factor

2. producer

3. heterotroph

4. carnivore

5. specialist

Greek and Latin Word Origins

Use the definitions of the word parts to answer the following questions.

Part	Meaning
bio-	life
eco-	home
syn-	together, joined
vore	eat

6. Explain why the root *vore* is used in the appropriate vocabulary terms.

7. Six vocabulary terms include the prefix *bio-*. Describe how they are all related.

8. Use the meaning of *eco-* to write your own definition of *ecosystem*.

9. *Photo-* means "light," and *chemo-* means "chemical." Explain why *photosynthesis* and *chemosynthesis* both include the prefix *syn-*.

Reviewing MAIN IDEAS

10. How can an individual organism simultaneously be part of a population, community, ecosystem, and biome?

11. What are the major differences between observation, experimentation, and modeling?

12. List some biotic and abiotic factors you would expect to find in a city park.

13. What is a keystone species and how might the removal of it affect the stability of and biodiversity within its ecosystem?

14. What would happen to a forest ecosystem if a fire killed most of its producers?

15. Describe one similarity and one difference between photosynthesis and chemosynthesis.

16. An acorn is eaten by a squirrel, which is eaten by an owl. What model best describes this simple relationship, and how does it show energy flow?

17. How is a food web related to energy flow within an ecosystem?

18. Describe the main processes involved in the hydrologic cycle.

19. Give an example of one biogeochemical cycle and explain how it is important to living things.

20. How does an energy pyramid show the flow of energy in an ecosystem?

21. A biomass pyramid and a pyramid of numbers are two ways of modeling the flow of matter in an ecosystem. What is the main difference between the two?

Critical Thinking

22. Apply At what level of organization would a scientist study the interaction between seals and polar bears in the Arctic? Explain your answer.

23. Apply Explain which biotic factors used by the beaver are related to its role as a keystone species.

24. Evaluate Scientists used to say that all living things depend on the sun. Explain why this statement is no longer valid.

25. Analyze How might a drought affect a grassland food web? Which trophic level would the drought affect the most? Explain your answer.

26. Synthesize Humans have changed many ecosystems on Earth. Compare different types of consumers, and predict which types would be more likely to adapt to these changes and which would not. Explain your answers.

27. Synthesize Use the information you learned about carbon-based molecules to explain a human's need to participate in the biogeochemical cycles.

28. Connect What role do decomposers play in the nitrogen cycle?

29. Predict In a pyramid of numbers, the highest organism has the smallest number of individuals in a community. What might happen if this organism increased its numbers significantly? Explain the effect this increase would have on the other members of the community.

Interpreting Visuals

Use the energy pyramid below to answer the following questions.

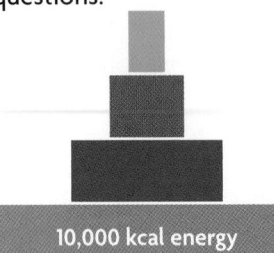

10,000 kcal energy

30. Apply Use the energy pyramid to describe the flow of energy within an ecosystem. Identify which tier represents producers, primary consumers, and so on.

31. Calculate If 90 percent of the energy is lost as heat between trophic levels, approximately how much energy is available to the secondary consumers in this energy pyramid? Show your calculations.

Analyzing Data

Use the equation $T = N \times A$ to estimate the population size in questions 32–33. Show all of your work.

32. Calculate A scientist wants to estimate the population of mushrooms on a forest floor with an area of 300 m². Each quadrat is 2 m². She counts 13 mushrooms in 20 quadrats. What is the population of mushrooms in the forest?

33. Calculate A scientist uses quadrats to sample the population of strawberry cactus plants in a section of the Chihuahuan desert that is 150 m². He counts 5 cacti in 10 quadrats. Each quadrat is 2 m². What is the population of strawberry cacti in the desert?

34. Analyze What are the advantages and disadvantages of using random sampling to obtain an estimate of the population size?

35. Evaluate A scientist uses quadrats to determine the population size of lupines in a field 500 m² in size. She uses ten 1 m² quadrats. Is this an adequate sample size? Explain your answer.

36. Apply Scientists often use tables of random numbers to determine where to place quadrats on their study site. Why might they do this? Why can't they choose where to place the quadrats?

37. Apply A scientist wants to determine the population size of whiptail lizards within a 15-acre area. What sampling method should she use? How can she ensure that she obtains an accurate estimate of the lizard population? Explain your answer.

Connecting CONCEPTS

38. Write About Your Own Ecosystem Imagine you built a large greenhouse in your home to create your own ecosystem. What types of organisms would you include? How would you ensure that the biogeochemical cycles were in place? Describe in detail an ecosystem you would like to have in your home. Be sure to include the biotic and abiotic factors in your explanation of how the ecosystem would sustain itself.

39. Make a Food Web Read the description of anhingas on page 395 and draw a partial food web of a freshwater marsh ecosystem. Include producers and consumers in your web.

MICHIGAN
STANDARDS-BASED ASSESSMENT

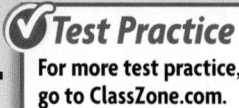
✓ **Test Practice**
For more test practice,
go to ClassZone.com.

1. A scientist wants to measure the size of a cactus population in a desert valley. What method should she use? **B1.1C**

   A mark-recapture sampling

   B quadrat sampling

   C computer modeling

   D radio telemetry

2.

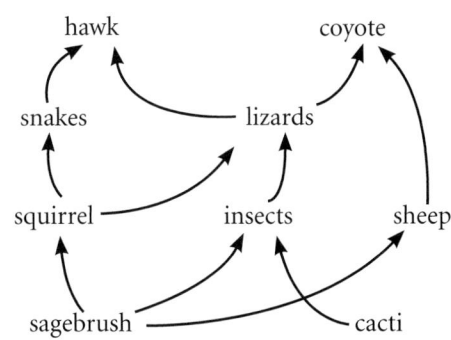

   This food web shows the relationships between organisms in an ecosystem. Which type of organism *not* shown in this food web is important to the stability of the ecosystem? **L3.p2C**

   A producer

   B consumer

   C herbivore

   D decomposer

3. A group of penguins that live together in the same colony is an example of a(n) **L3.p1A**

   A community.

   B ecosystem.

   C population.

   D abiotic factor.

4.

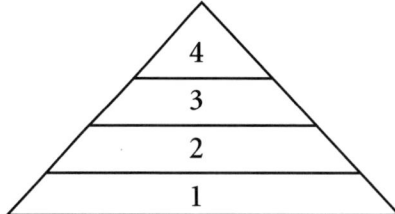

   In which direction does energy flow through this energy pyramid? **B3.2B**

   A 4, 3, 2, 1

   B 1, 2, 3, 4

   C 2, 1, 3, 4

   D 3, 4, 2, 1

THINK THROUGH THE QUESTION

Remember that an energy pyramid shows the amount of energy in each trophic level, with producers at the bottom of the pyramid, and consumers at the top.

---

5. Which of the following groups is most important for bringing energy into an ecosystem? **L3.p2A**

   A consumers

   B producers

   C decomposers

   D generalists

6. In the carbon cycle, through what process does carbon move from an abiotic resource into organic matter? **B3.3b**

   A immigration

   B combustion

   C respiration

   D photosynthesis

14 Interactions in Ecosystems

KEY CONCEPTS

14.1 Habitat and Niche
Every organism has a habitat and a niche.

14.2 Community Interactions
Organisms interact as individuals and as populations.

14.3 Population Density and Distribution
Each population has a density, a dispersion, and a reproductive strategy.

14.4 Population Growth Patterns
Populations grow in predictable patterns.

14.5 Ecological Succession
Ecological succession is a process of change in the species that make up a community.

Online BIOLOGY CLASSZONE.COM

Animated BIOLOGY

View animated chapter concepts.
• Survive Within a Niche
• What Limits Population Growth?

BIOZINE

Keep current with biology news.
• News feeds
• Strange Biology
• Bio Bytes

RESOURCE CENTER

Get more information on
• Symbiotic Relationships
• Succession

Why are these zebras fighting?

For the zebra, life on the African savannah is about survival. Whether escaping the ambush of a pride of lions, walking vast distances to drink fresh water, or competing for the right to mate with females, only the best adapted zebras will survive and pass on their genes. The interactions among organisms, and between organisms and their environment, make ecosystems function.

Connecting CONCEPTS

Adaptation The zebra's stripes are not just for show. They are an adaptation that protect zebras against predators. As the herd moves, the stripes of all the zebras blend together, creating a kind of camouflage that makes it difficult for a predator to pick out just one.

14.1 Habitat and Niche

KEY CONCEPT Every organism has a habitat and a niche.

▶ **MAIN IDEAS**

- A habitat differs from a niche.
- Resource availability gives structure to a community.

VOCABULARY

habitat, p. 428
ecological niche, p. 428
competitive exclusion, p. 429
ecological equivalent, p. 430

MICHIGAN STANDARDS

B2.2g Propose how moving an organism to a new environment may influence its ability to survive and predict the possible impact of this type of transfer.

B3.5C Predict the consequences of an invading organism on the survival of other organisms.

Connect The ways in which a zebra interacts with its environment and other organisms are only a small part of the ecology of the African plains. To understand what individuals, populations, and communities need to survive, ecologists study the interactions among species and between species and their environment. Why does a zebra fit so well into the African savannah?

▶ **MAIN IDEA**

A habitat differs from a niche.

On the vast plains of Africa, tall grasses grow among trees and shrubs, and small pools of water surrounded by thirsty animals dot the landscape. This challenging environment is the home of the African lion, shown in **FIGURE 14.1.** Here, lions stalk through tall grass to hunt zebras and antelope, find places to rest in the shade of trees, and never stray far from valuable pools of water. These are just a few of the environmental features that make up the lion's habitat. A **habitat** can be described as all of the biotic and abiotic factors in the area where an organism lives. These factors include all aspects of the environment, including the grass, the trees, and the watering holes.

Each species interacts with its environment in a different way. Within an ecosystem, each species has an ecological niche. An **ecological niche** (nihch) is composed of all of the physical, chemical, and biological factors that a species needs to survive, stay healthy, and reproduce.

You can think of a habitat as *where* a species lives and a niche as *how* it lives within its habitat. A niche includes

- **Food** The type of food a species eats, how a species competes with others for food, and where it fits in the food web are all part of its niche.
- **Abiotic conditions** A niche includes the range of conditions, such as air temperature and amount of water, that a species can tolerate.
- **Behavior** The time of day a species is active as well as where and when it reproduces are factors in the niche of a species.

FIGURE 14.1 A lion must hunt and kill its prey in order to survive on the African savannah. Its role as a top predator is part of the lion's niche.

Looking closely at all of these factors, we can see that while an antelope may use the tall grasses of the African plains as a food resource, a lion may use the same grasses as camouflage for hunting. A lion uses the antelope as a food resource and hunts primarily during low-light times like dawn or dusk. In order to avoid the intense heat of the savannah, lions often spend afternoons in the shade. These examples are only a few parts of the lion's ecological niche, but they help to give a picture of how a lion fits into the African savannah.

Connect **What are some of the abiotic and biotic factors of your habitat?**

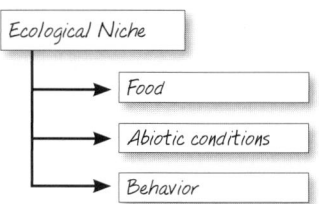
▶ MAIN IDEA
Resource availability gives structure to a community.

As you learned in Chapter 10, the ability of an individual to survive and reproduce is the driving force behind natural selection. A species needs resources such as food, water, and shelter to be successful in its habitat. The organism that is best suited to obtain these resources is most likely to survive and reproduce. But what if two species are competing over limited resources?

Competitive Exclusion

We have already seen that many species can share similar habitats and that they may use some of the same resources, as shown in **FIGURE 14.2**. But when two species use the same resources in the same ways, one species will always be better adapted to the environment. The principle of **competitive exclusion** states that when two species are competing for the same resources, one species will be better suited to the niche, and the other species will be pushed into another niche or become extinct.

The North American gray squirrel was introduced to Great Britain in the late 1800s. The native European red squirrel was forced to compete with the newcomer for the same food resources, habitat, and space. In this case the gray squirrel was better adapted to the niche and pushed out its smaller competitor. Currently, the red squirrel population is declining due to competition with its larger, more aggressive cousin. But competitive exclusion can also result in other outcomes.

FIGURE 14.2 Even though bees and butterflies both use these flowers for food, they occupy different niches. Many species with similar niches can coexist.

- **Niche partitioning** The two squirrel species could have naturally divided different resources based on competitive advantages. If one type of squirrel ate nuts from the tops of trees while others ate nuts from the ground, the niche would have been divided.

- **Evolutionary response** The two species of squirrel could have experienced divergent evolution. Selection for larger teeth might have allowed one type of squirrel to become better at cracking large nuts, while selection for smaller teeth might have allowed the other to eat small seeds.

FIGURE 14.3 Ecological Equivalents

Animated
BIOLOGY
Explore survival
in a niche at
ClassZone.com.

Ecological equivalents are two species that occupy similar niches in geographically separate areas.

Madagascar

South America

The mantella frog (left) and the poison dart frog (right) have evolved similar defense mechanisms. The bright coloration of each is a warning to predators. Each frog secretes a highly poisonous toxin through its skin that makes it an unpleasant meal for a predator.

Synthesize Explain how natural selection resulted in the evolution of two similar frog species in two similar niches.

Connecting CONCEPTS

Amphibians Amphibians were the first vertebrates to move out of the water and onto land. In **Chapter 25**, you will learn more about amphibians.

Ecological Equivalents

The competitive exclusion principle involves species competing for resources in the same community. In different communities, ecological equivalents occur in very similar niches. In mathematics, numbers that are equal are called equivalents. Similarly, **ecological equivalents** are species that occupy similar niches but live in different geographical regions. Pictured in **FIGURE 14.3**, the mantella frog of Madagascar and the poison dart frog of South America have much the same niche in similar habitats. They both have brightly colored skin that secretes a highly poisonous toxin to ward off predators. Both prey on similar insects and live in a similar habitat, but because they live in different regions of the world, they never compete for the same resources.

Apply Are these frogs experiencing competitive exclusion? Explain.

14.1 ASSESSMENT

 **ONLINE QUIZ**
ClassZone.com

REVIEWING ▶ MAIN IDEAS

1. What are the three parts of an organism's **ecological niche**?

2. What does the principle of **competitive exclusion** say will happen when two species compete for the same resource?

CRITICAL THINKING

3. **Predict** If a group of mantella frogs were transported to the ecosystem of the poison dart frogs, what might happen to the two species' populations?

4. **Analyze** A bison and an elk live in the same **habitat** and feed on the same grasses. Does this mean that the competitive exclusion principle does not apply? Explain.

Connecting CONCEPTS

5. **Exotic Species** Considering the competitive exclusion principle, why may it be harmful to transport a species, such as a rabbit, to another habitat where it currently does not exist?

14.2 Community Interactions

KEY CONCEPT Organisms interact as individuals and as populations.

MAIN IDEAS

- Competition and predation are two important ways in which organisms interact.
- Symbiosis is a close relationship between species.

VOCABULARY

competition, p. 431
predation, p. 431
symbiosis, p. 432
mutualism, p. 432

commensalism, p. 432
parasitism, p. 432

Review
community

MICHIGAN STANDARDS

L3.p2B Describe common ecological relationships between and among species and their environments (competition, territory, carrying capacity, natural balance, population, dependence, survival, and other biotic and abiotic factors). (prerequisite)

L3.p2D Explain how two organisms can be mutually beneficial and how that can lead to interdependency. (prerequisite)

Connect Each day, two hot dog vendors sell virtually identical products to anyone who is hungry. They may be on different sides of the street, but they are still trying to sell hot dogs to the same hungry consumers. A vendor selling hot pretzels may also be trying to sell to the same customers, but with a slightly varied product. Just like these vendors, organisms constantly compete with one another.

MAIN IDEA

Competition and predation are two important ways in which organisms interact.

Two birds may fight over territories. A fish may prey on insects floating on the water. These are just two examples of the many interactions between species in an ecosystem.

Competition

Competition occurs when two organisms fight for the same limited resources. There are two different types of competition: interspecific competition and intraspecific competition.

Even though they may have different niches, two species may still use similar resources. Interspecific competition occurs when two different species compete for a limited resource, such as space. In a lawn, for example, grass, dandelions, and many other plants all compete for nutrients and water.

Competition also occurs among members of the same species. This is known as intraspecific competition. Individuals of a particular species struggle against one another for limited resources. You can observe intraspecific competition during the spring breeding season of birds. A typical male will share a particular territory with males of different bird species but will not tolerate another male of its own species in the same area.

Predation

Another way species interact with one another is through predation. **Predation** is the process by which one organism captures and feeds upon another organism. Many organisms, such as the snake in **FIGURE 14.4**, have become highly adapted to hunting and killing their prey.

FIGURE 14.4 Snakes are predators that swallow their prey whole. The hollow fangs of this timber rattlesnake inject venom to paralyze and kill its prey.

The timber rattlesnake, for example, is a predator that preys on small animals such as mice, voles, rabbits, and squirrels. Lying silent, hidden among leaf litter on the forest floor, the rattlesnake has found a niche as an ambush predator. A swift bite from the snake's fangs injects its venom. The venom attacks the nervous system and eventually paralyzes the prey. The snake swallows the paralyzed animal whole.

Herbivores can also be considered predators. The deer that eats grass in fields and leaves from trees is preying on the plants.

Evaluate How does natural selection shape predator–prey relationships?

▶ MAIN IDEA
Symbiosis is a close relationship between species.

A honeybee buzzes away from a flower with its reward of nectar. Small pollen grains have become attached to the bee's back. When the bee arrives at the next flower, the pollen fertilizes the egg of the next plant. In this way, a relationship, or symbiosis, between the bee and the flower has evolved. **Symbiosis** is a close ecological relationship between two or more organisms of different species that live in direct contact with one another. There are three major types of symbiosis: mutualism, commensalism, and parasitism.

Mutualism
Mutualism is an interspecies interaction in which both organisms benefit from one another. The relationship between the lesser long-nosed bat and the saguaro cactus is another example of mutualism. During the spring, bats help pollinate the cacti through the indirect transfer of pollen as they fly from one cactus to another to feed on flower nectar. When the fruit ripens in the summer, bats become fruit eaters, as shown in **FIGURE 14.5**. The cactus benefits when bats spread its indigestible seeds across the desert.

Commensalism
Another type of symbiotic relationship is commensalism. **Commensalism** is a relationship between two organisms in which one receives an ecological benefit from another, while the other neither benefits nor is harmed. Right now you may be a part of a commensal relationship. Buried deep in the hair follicles of your eyelashes are microscopic mites that feed on the secretions and dead skin cells of your body. These harmless organisms are called demodicids, and they have found their highly specialized niche in your hair follicles.

Parasitism
Parasitism is a symbiotic relationship involving a species that directly harms its host. **Parasitism** is a relationship similar to predation in that one organism benefits while the other is harmed. But unlike a predator, which quickly kills and eats its prey, a parasite benefits by keeping its host alive for days or years. For example, the braconid wasp lays its eggs inside a caterpillar. When the larvae hatch, they eat the caterpillar from the inside out, consuming the nutrients they need to grow into adults.

TAKING NOTES

Mutualism, commensalism, and parasitism are distinct types of symbiosis. Add details with examples of your own.

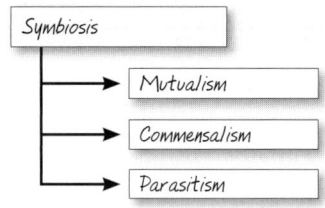

FIGURE 14.5 Symbiotic Relationships

The interactions between species in an ecosystem can take many different forms. A symbiotic relationship involves interactions between organisms of different species that live in direct contact.

- (—) Organism is harmed
- (0) Organism is not affected
- (+) Organism benefits

Parasitism

(—) **Hornworm caterpillar** The host hornworm will eventually die as its organs are consumed by wasp larvae.

(+) **Braconid wasp** Braconid larvae feed on their host and release themselves shortly before reaching the pupae stage of development.

Commensalism

(0) **Human** Our eyelashes are home to tiny mites that feast on oil secretions and dead skin. Without harming us, up to 20 mites may be living in one eyelash follicle.

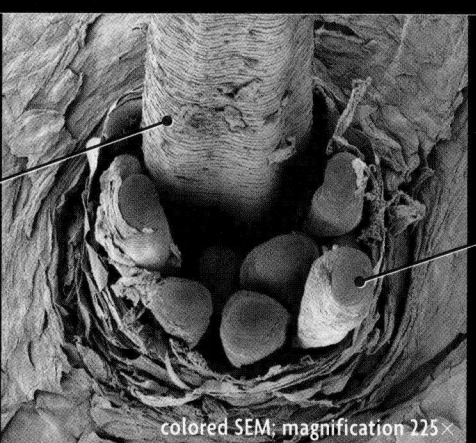

colored SEM; magnification 225×

(+) **Demodicids** Eyelash mites find all they need to survive in the tiny follicles of eyelashes. Magnified here 225 times, these creatures measure 0.4 mm in length and can be seen only with a microscope.

Mutualism

(+) **Lesser long-nosed bat** The bat depends on night-blooming cacti as its primary source of food. Cacti are a rich source of fruit and nectar, staples of the bat's diet.

(+) **Saguaro cactus** As the bat feeds on the cactus' fruit, it also ingests the seeds. These indigestible seeds are dispersed to new locations as the bat flies across the desert.

CRITICAL VIEWING How might the symbiotic relationship change if eyelash mites destroyed hair follicles?

FIGURE 14.6 Human Parasites: Inside and Out

Humans can get parasites in many ways. Leeches attach to the exposed skin of humans. By penetrating human skin, hookworms find their home in the digestive tract.

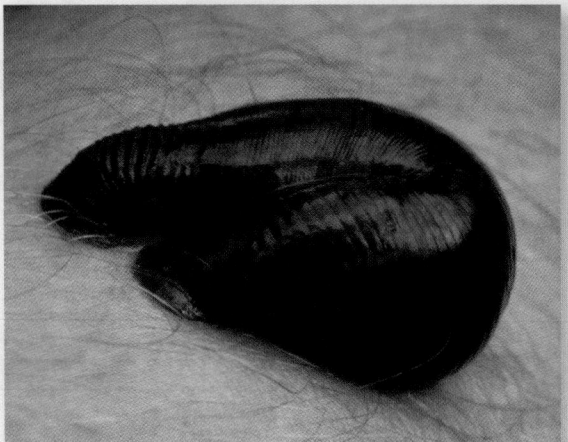

Many leeches feed on the blood of a host organism. Freshwater leeches such as this one can grow to lengths of 12 cm or more.

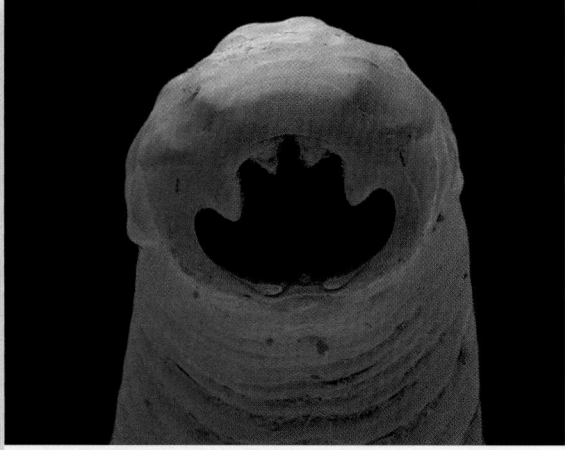

Hookworms are endoparasites with sharp teeth that attach to the intestinal wall of a host organism and absorb nutrients for food. (colored SEM; magnification 200×)

Hypothesize Why is it important for ectoparasites to stay undetected by their hosts?

Connecting CONCEPTS

Invertebrates Leeches and hookworms are classified as invertebrates. In **Chapter 23,** you will learn more about invertebrate diversity.

The needs of a parasite are met by a host—the victim of the parasite. There are two different ways that parasites can use their host. An ectoparasite makes its home on the exterior of an organism, attaching itself to the outside of the host and usually feeding on its fluids. Common ectoparasites include fleas, ticks, and leeches, such as the one seen in **FIGURE 14.6.** Many types of ectoparasites are also known to carry a wide variety of diseases that can affect their host. Parasites can also be found inside of living organisms. Endoparasites live in the tissues and organs of a host where, safely hidden, they feed on the nutrients ingested by their host. Large endoparasites, such as tapeworms and hookworms, and smaller protozoan endoparasites can kill their host if not treated.

Connect What type of symbiosis is the relationship between a dog and its owner?

14.2 ASSESSMENT

ONLINE QUIZ
ClassZone.com

REVIEWING ▶ MAIN IDEAS

1. During the fall spawning of salmon, grizzly bears fight over space on the banks of a river. What type of **competition** is this?

2. Describe and give examples of the three types of **symbiosis.**

CRITICAL THINKING

3. **Compare and Contrast** How are **predation** and **parasitism** similar? How do they differ?

4. **Synthesize** After a lion has made a kill, birds will sometimes arrive to pick at the leftover carcass. Which are the predators: the birds, the lion, or both? Why?

Connecting CONCEPTS

5. **Animal Behavior** You have probably heard the saying "There is safety in numbers." Why might traveling in a large group be beneficial to prey species?

MATERIALS
- 21 × 27 cm² grid paper
- 400 uncooked rice grains
- toothpick

PROCESS SKILLS
- **Modeling**
- **Analyzing Data**

MICHIGAN STANDARDS

B1.1h Design and conduct a systematic scientific investigation that tests a hypothesis. Draw conclusions from data presented in charts or tables.

L3.p2A Describe common relationships among organisms and provide examples of producer/consumer, predator/prey, or parasite/host relationship. (prerequisite)

Modeling Predation

In this lab, you will model predation and the effects of changes in the environment on organisms. Blue herons are large birds that live in aquatic habitats and feed on fish, frogs, salamanders, lizards, small snakes, and dragonflies. You will model a lake filled with fish.

PROBLEM How do changes in environmental factors affect the predation habits of the blue heron?

PROCEDURE

1. Spread 200 rice grains over the grid. The grid represents the lake from which the heron feeds, and the rice grains represent fish.

2. A blue heron will catch an average of two fish per hour during daylight. To model the heron hunting for fish, close your eyes and lower the end of the toothpick slowly down onto the grid.

3. Remove the grains that are in the square touching the toothpick. Count the grains.

4. Rearrange the remaining grains on the grid, and repeat steps 2 and 3 five more times to model one day's worth of feeding for the heron. Count the total number of grains removed, and record this number in a data table like the one shown below.

5. Repeat steps 2–4 five more times to represent six total days of feeding by the heron.

6. Return all of the removed rice grains to the grid. Runoff containing large amounts of nitrates causes an algal bloom in the lake. When the algae die and decomposition occurs, the oxygen level in the lake becomes very low, causing fish to die. Remove 150 grains from the grid. Repeat steps 2–5. Make a second data table and record your data.

7. Return all of the removed grains to the grid. The fish in the lake spawn during the spring. To model this, add another 200 grains to the grid. Repeat steps 2–5. Make a third data table and record your data.

TABLE 1. NUMBER OF FISH CAUGHT PER DAY						
Day	1	2	3	4	5	6
No. of Fish Caught						

ANALYZE AND CONCLUDE

1. **Graph Data** Construct a graph to represent your data.

2. **Analyze** How was the amount of food caught by a heron related to changes in biotic and abiotic factors?

3. **Infer** How might abundant amounts of food allow herons to reproduce more often?

4. **Predict** How would the populations of amphibians and small reptiles be affected if the fish population in the lake remained low for an extended period of time?

14.3

Population Density and Distribution

KEY CONCEPT Each population has a density, a dispersion, and a reproductive strategy.

▶ MAIN IDEAS

- Population density is the number of individuals that live in a defined area.
- Geographic dispersion of a population shows how individuals in a population are spaced.
- Survivorship curves help to describe the reproductive strategy of a species.

VOCABULARY

population density, p. 436
population dispersion, p. 437
survivorship curve, p. 438

MICHIGAN STANDARDS

L3.p2B Describe common ecological relationships between and among species and their environments (competition, territory, carrying capacity, natural balance, population, dependence, survival, and other biotic and abiotic factors). (prerequisite)

B3.5d Describe different reproductive strategies employed by various organisms and explain their advantages and disadvantages.

Connecting CONCEPTS

Gene Flow Recall that in **Chapter 11** you learned about gene flow and geographic isolation. Population dispersion patterns influence the rate of gene flow among and between species.

Connect If you have ever traveled from a rural area into a city, you may have noticed a change in population density. Cities have more dense populations, while rural areas have more widely dispersed populations. Scientists measure species populations in a similar way. What can we learn from population data?

▶ MAIN IDEA

Population density is the number of individuals that live in a defined area.

The wandering albatross may fly over open ocean waters for days or weeks at a time without ever encountering another bird. In contrast to this solitary lifestyle, elephant seals may gather in groups of a thousand or more on California beaches. By collecting data about a population in a particular area, scientists can calculate the density of a population. **Population density** is a measurement of the number of individuals living in a defined space.

Calculating an accurate population density can tell scientists a great deal about a species. When scientists notice changes in population densities over time, they work to determine whether the changes are the result of environmental factors or are simply due to normal variation in the life history of a species. In this way a wildlife biologist can work to make changes that will help to keep the population healthy. One way to calculate population density is to create a ratio of the number of individuals that live in a particular area to the size of the area. This formula is simplified as follows:

$$\frac{\text{\# of individuals}}{\text{area (units}^2)} = \text{population density}$$

For example, if scientists sampling a population of deer counted 200 individuals in an area of 10 square kilometers, the density of this deer population would be 20 deer per square kilometer.

Connect What might a decrease in the density of a deer population over a specific time period tell scientists about the habitat in the area?

FIGURE 14.7 Dispersion Patterns

Dispersion patterns help us understand species interactions by showing how populations group together.

CLUMPED DISPERSION

Many species of fish swim together in large groups called schools. By moving as a large mass, individuals have an advantage in avoiding predators.

UNIFORM DISPERSION

Nesting sites of the gannet show uniform distances for protection of eggs from other males. Territorial organisms generally display uniform dispersion.

RANDOM DISPERSION

The three-toed tree sloth, a solitary animal, spends most of its life in the canopy of tropical forests. The sloth has almost no competitors and has few natural predators.

▶ MAIN IDEA

Geographic dispersion of a population shows how individuals in a population are spaced.

Other information can be gained from population density measurements. Patterns of geographical dispersion give us ideas of how individuals of the same species interact and how different species interact with one another.

Population dispersion is the way in which individuals of a population are spread in an area or a volume. **FIGURE 14.7** shows the three types of population dispersion.

- **Clumped dispersion** Individuals may live close together in groups in order to facilitate mating, gain protection, or access food resources.

- **Uniform dispersion** Territoriality and intraspecies competition for limited resources lead to individuals living at specific distances from one another.

- **Random dispersion** Individuals are spread randomly within an area or a volume.

VISUAL VOCAB

Population dispersion is the way in which individuals of a population are spread in an area or a volume.

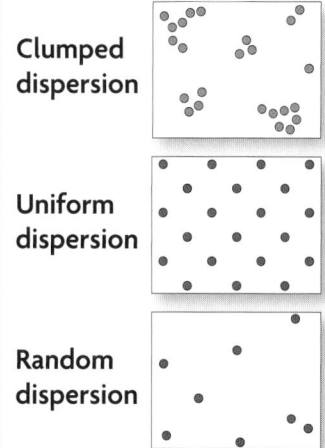

Clumped dispersion

Uniform dispersion

Random dispersion

Infer What type of intraspecies interaction might cause uniform dispersion?

Survivorship Curves

In this lab, you will make a type 1 survivorship curve using data from the obituary section of a newspaper.

MATERIALS
- obituary section of a newspaper
- graph paper

PROBLEM What is the trend in data for type 1 survivorship curves?

PROCEDURE

1. Obtain the obituary section of the newspaper.

2. Create a data table like the one at right that extends to include five-year age groups up to 91–95 years.

3. For 35 obituaries, place a tally next to the age group in which the individual died.

4. Subtract the number of individuals that died from the number of remaining survivors, and record the answer in the third column of your data table. Calculate the percent surviving in each age group by dividing the number of survivors by 35 and multiplying by 100. Repeat this step for all age groups.

TABLE 1. SURVIVORSHIP DATA

Age (years)	Deaths	Survivors	% Surviving
0–5	I	35 – 1 = 34	97
6–10	I	34 – 1 = 33	94
11–15	0	33 – 0 = 33	94
16–20	IIII	33 – 4 = 29	83
21–25	I	29 – 1 = 28	80

ANALYZE AND CONCLUDE

1. **Graph Data** Draw a survivorship curve by plotting the age group on the x-axis, and the percent survivors on the y-axis.

2. **Analyze** Explain the trend in the data.

▶ MAIN IDEA

Survivorship curves help to describe the reproductive strategy of a species.

The California red-legged frog of the western United States is an amphibian that reproduces by laying 2000 to 5000 eggs in late winter and early spring. In one to two weeks, these eggs hatch, and over the next four to seven months, the tadpoles grow into frogs. If so many eggs are laid, why is this frog a threatened species in much of the western United States?

Many predators feed on the eggs of the red-legged frog, so of the thousands of eggs laid, only a small number of offspring will survive to adulthood. This type of reproductive strategy is to produce a lot of offspring. Species use many other reproductive strategies as well. Survivorship curves illustrate how offspring survival from birth to death fits in with the survival strategies of a particular species.

A **survivorship curve** is a generalized diagram showing the number of surviving members over time from a measured set of births. By measuring the number of offspring born in a year and following those offspring through until death, survivorship curves give information about the life history of a species. For example, we will begin with 100 coyotes born in year zero. After one year, 10 of those baby coyotes died from disease or predation. Of the original 100, 90 are left. During year two, 4 more coyotes die, leaving 86 of the original 100. In year three, 3 more die, leaving 83 of the original 100. The number of individuals surviving from year to year decreases, but a substantial portion of the group will live a full life and reproduce. In **FIGURE 14.8,** you can see the three basic patterns of animal survivorship curves.

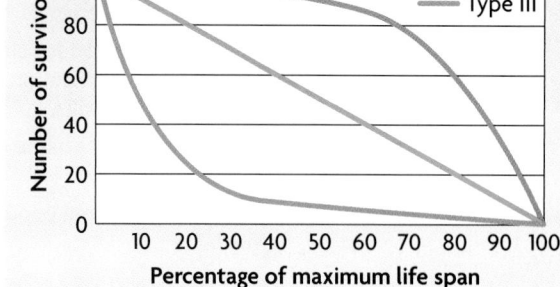

FIGURE 14.8 SURVIVORSHIP CURVES

Type I The graph shows a type I survivorship curve in orange. Type I survivorship represents a life history that is common among large mammals, including humans. The curve shows a low level of infant mortality and a population that generally will survive until old age. A behavior that most organisms showing type I survivorship share is parental care for the young. Most infant organisms are unable to care for themselves. By protecting their young, parents are better able to ensure that their offspring stay alive until they can survive on their own.

Type II Organisms such as birds, small mammals, and some reptiles show a survivorship rate that is roughly equal at all ages of an organism's life. At all times, these species have equal chances of living and dying, whether from disease or as a result of predation. A type II survivorship curve is shown in green on the graph.

Type III Organisms with type III survivorship (shown in blue) have a very high birth rate and also a very high infant mortality rate. Species with type III survivorship are generally invertebrates, fish, amphibians, and plants. Many of their offspring will die from predation, but inevitably a few will survive to adulthood and be able to pass their genes on to the next generation. Though the California red-legged frogs are threatened largely because of habitat loss and pollution, the frogs are also targets of high levels of predation at an early age, making recovery for this species especially difficult.

For more information about populations and communities, go to scilinks.org.
Keycode: MLB014

Synthesize Is there any connection between survivorship curves and reproductive strategies? Explain.

14.3 / ASSESSMENT

ONLINE QUIZ
ClassZone.com

REVIEWING ◉ MAIN IDEAS

1. A shoreline mussel species has a **population density** of one organism per square meter. Will all mussels be found one meter apart? Explain.

2. Draw and label a diagram showing the three **population dispersion** patterns.

3. How do **survivorship curves** show three types of reproductive strategies?

CRITICAL THINKING

4. **Analyze** What might be the advantages of having a clumped dispersal pattern?

5. **Infer** An organism has ten offspring. Two of these offspring die each year over a five-year period. Is the organism more likely to be a bird or an insect? Explain.

Connecting CONCEPTS

6. **Abiotic Factors** On the African savannah, what types of abiotic factors may lead to high population density and clumped dispersion patterns?

14.4 Population Growth Patterns

KEY CONCEPT Populations grow in predictable patterns.

MAIN IDEAS
- Changes in a population's size are determined by immigration, births, emigration, and deaths.
- Population growth is based on available resources.
- Ecological factors limit population growth.

VOCABULARY
immigration, p. 440
emigration, p. 440
exponential growth, p. 441
logistic growth, p. 441
carrying capacity, p. 442
population crash, p. 442
limiting factor, p. 443
density-dependent limiting factor, p. 443
density-independent limiting factor, p. 444

MICHIGAN STANDARDS

L3.p3A Identify the factors in an ecosystem that influence fluctuations in population size. (prerequisite)

B3.5B Explain the influences that affect population growth.

VOCABULARY

The word *immigrate* comes from the Latin word *immigrare*, meaning "to go into," and the word *emigrate* comes from the Latin word *emigrare*, meaning "to move."

Connect That banana you left in your backpack did not go unnoticed. After one week, you open your bag and dozens of tiny insects swarm out. The smell of rotting fruit follows close behind. Only a week ago, the population of fruit flies in your backpack was zero. Just before you opened it, the population had grown to several dozen. How did this population grow so quickly?

MAIN IDEA

Changes in a population's size are determined by immigration, births, emigration, and deaths.

The size of a population is usually changing. If resources such as food and water are abundant, or plentiful, a population may grow. On the other hand, if resources are in short supply, the population may decrease in size. Hopefully, the normal fruit fly population in your backpack is zero. But if an abundance of resources, such as an overripe banana, becomes available, the population will increase dramatically. However, when the resources are removed, the fruit fly population in your backpack will once again return to zero. Four factors affect the size of a population.

- **Immigration** When one or two fruit flies found the banana, they immigrated into your backpack. **Immigration** is the movement of individuals into a population from another population.
- **Births** Additional fruit flies were born in your backpack. Births increase the number of individuals in a population.
- **Emigration** After you opened your backpack, some fruit flies flew out and left to find other rotting fruit. **Emigration** is the movement of individuals out of a population and into another population.
- **Deaths** You might have squashed a couple of unlucky fruit flies as you were opening your backpack. The size of a population decreases when individuals die.

Apply When a population is declining, what two factors are likely outpacing what other two factors?

MAIN IDEA
Population growth is based on available resources.

Population growth is a function of the environment. The rate of growth for a population is directly determined by the amount of resources available. A population may grow very rapidly, or it may take a bit of time to grow. There are two distinct types of population growth.

Exponential Growth

When resources are abundant, a population has the opportunity to grow rapidly. This type of growth, called **exponential growth,** occurs when a population size increases dramatically over a period of time. In **FIGURE 14.9,** you can see that exponential growth appears as a J-shaped curve.

Exponential growth may occur when a species moves to a previously uninhabited area. For example, in 1859 an Australian landowner returning home from England brought 24 European rabbits to the country for the purpose of sport hunting. The rabbits were introduced into an environment that had abundant space and food and no predators fast enough to catch them. The initial population of 24 rabbits grew exponentially and spread across the country. After many attempts to control the population, today there are between 200 million and 300 million rabbits in Australia.

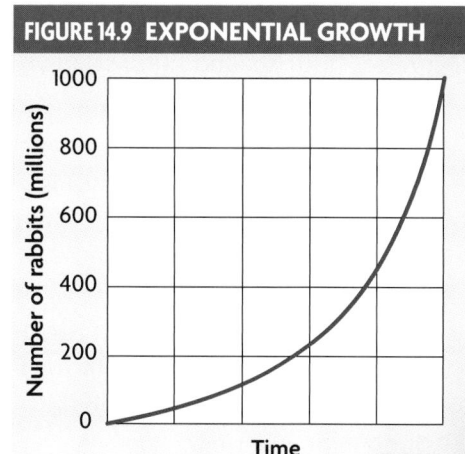

FIGURE 14.9 EXPONENTIAL GROWTH

Number of rabbits (millions) — Time

FIGURE 14.10 In Australia during the early 1900s, the introduced European rabbit population exhibited exponential growth.

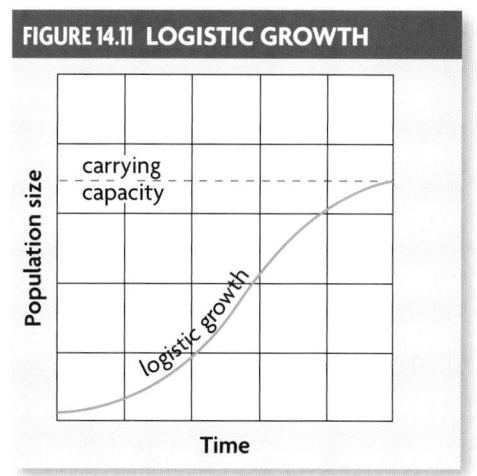

Logistic Growth

Most populations face limited resources and thus show a logistic growth rate. During **logistic growth,** a population begins with a period of slow growth followed by a brief period of exponential growth before leveling off at a stable size. A graph of logistic growth takes the form of an S-shaped curve and can be seen in **FIGURE 14.11,** which models a population's change in size over time. During initial growth, resources are abundant, and the population is able to grow. Over time, resources begin to deplete, and growth starts to slow. As resources become limited, the population levels off at a size the environment can support.

FIGURE 14.11 LOGISTIC GROWTH

Population size — carrying capacity — logistic growth — Time

Carrying Capacity

The environment determines how many individuals of the species can be supported based on natural cycles and species diversity. An environment, therefore, has a carrying capacity for each species living in it. The **carrying capacity** of an environment is the maximum number of individuals of a particular species that the environment can normally and consistently support.

In nature, a carrying capacity can change when the environment changes. Consider a population of grasshoppers that feed on meadow grasses. If a fire burns part of the meadow, the insects' food resources diminish, and the carrying capacity declines. But during years with plentiful rain, the meadow grasses flourish, and the carrying capacity rises.

The actual size of the population usually is higher or lower than the carrying capacity. Populations will rise and fall as a result of natural changes in the supply of resources. In this way, the environment naturally controls the size of a population.

Population Crash

When the carrying capacity for a population suddenly drops, the population experiences a crash. A **population crash** is a dramatic decline in the size of a population over a short period of time. There are many reasons why a population might experience a crash.

DATA ANALYSIS

READING COMBINATION GRAPHS

Combination graphs show two sets of data on the same graph. One set of data may be shown as a bar graph, while the other set may be shown as a line graph. The two data sets must share the same independent variable on the x-axis. Scientists can then interpret the data to determine if a relationship exists between the variables.

This combination graph displays data about fish kill events, during which many fish died at once, and average monthly rainfall in Florida from 1991–2001.

- The y-axis on the left side represents the total number of fish kill events.
- The y-axis on the right side represents average monthly rainfall during that time.
- The x-axis shows the month of data collection.

The graph shows that in January there were four fish kill events and an average of 2.7 inches of rain.

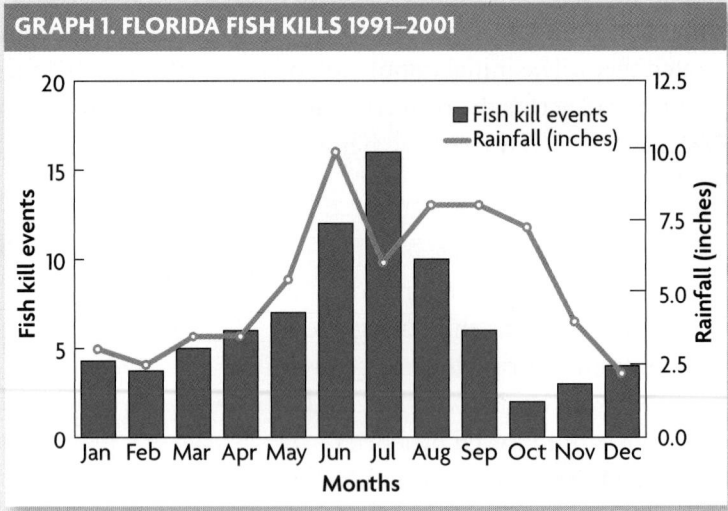

GRAPH 1. FLORIDA FISH KILLS 1991–2001

Source: The University of Florida Extension Information Circular 107. Used by permission.

1. **Analyze** An increase in fish kills and a decrease in rainfall occurs in what months?
2. **Analyze** Describe the trend in the fish kill events throughout the year. Describe the trend in rainfall data throughout the year.
3. **Hypothesize** What relationship might exist between fish kill events and rainfall?

For example, in 1944, 29 reindeer were introduced to St. Matthew Island off the coast of Alaska. At the time of the introduction, the entire island was covered with a rich mat of lichens. Plenty of good food allowed the reindeer herd to grow at an exponential rate. By the summer of 1963, the island population had grown to 6000 reindeer. However, over the winter, large amounts of snow fell on food resources that had already become greatly depleted by the large herd. By the spring of 1964, only 50 reindeer remained. The population crash on St. Matthew Island came as the result of two factors that limited resources: the harsh winter and the scarcity of food.

Predict What would have eventually happened to the reindeer herd if the winter had not made foraging so difficult? Explain.

▶ MAIN IDEA

Ecological factors limit population growth.

Many factors can affect the carrying capacity of an environment for a population of organisms. The factor that has the greatest effect in keeping down the size of a population is called the **limiting factor.** There are two categories of limiting factors—density dependent and density independent.

Density-Dependent Limiting Factors

Density-dependent limiting factors are limiting factors that are affected by the number of individuals in a given area. Density-dependent limiting factors include many different types of species interactions.

Competition Members of populations compete with one another for resources such as food and shelter. As a population becomes denser, the resources are used up, limiting how large the population can grow.

Predation The population of a predator can be limited by the available prey, and the population of prey can be limited by being caught for food. On Isle Royale in Michigan, changes in wolf and moose populations, shown in **FIGURE 14.13**, provide an example. As the moose population grows, so does the wolf population. But at a certain point, the wolves eat so many moose that there are not enough left to feed all the wolves. The result is a decrease in the wolf population. Over time, the two populations rise and fall in a pattern, shown in **FIGURE 14.13**.

Parasitism and disease Parasites and diseases can spread more quickly through dense populations. The more crowded an area becomes, the easier it is for parasites or diseases to spread. The parasites or diseases can then cause the size of the population to decrease.

Analyze How does the wolf population on Isle Royale affect the carrying capacity of the moose population?

FIGURE 14.12 Taking down prey as large as a moose requires that the members of a pack work together. As many as ten wolves may take hours or even days to wear down this moose.

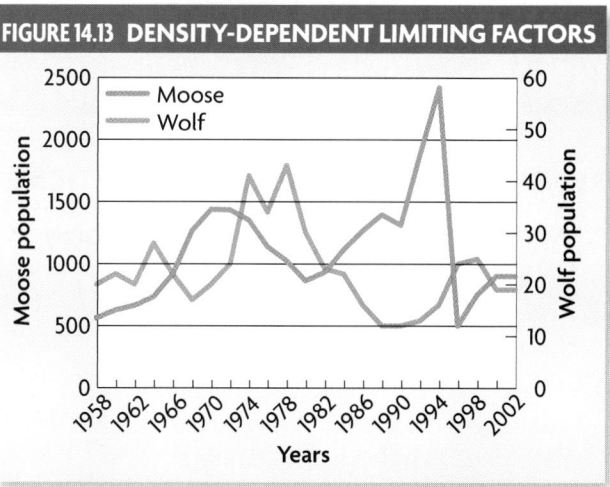

FIGURE 14.13 DENSITY-DEPENDENT LIMITING FACTORS

Source: Isle Royale Research Data

Density-Independent Limiting Factors

Density-independent limiting factors are the aspects of the environment that limit a population's growth regardless of the density of the population.

Unusual weather Weather can affect the size of a population regardless of its density. For example, along the western coast of the United States, a lack of southerly winds can prevent nutrient-poor warm water from being replaced, as it normally is, with nutrient-rich cold water. The lack of nutrients in the water along the coast can prevent phytoplankton, which form the base of the marine ecosystem, from growing in their usual large numbers. In turn, zooplankton, tiny organisms that feed on phytoplankton, have smaller populations. The effects are felt all the way up the food chain, with smaller populations of fish and birds.

FIGURE 14.14 The storm surge accompanying a hurricane can cause dangerous flooding.

Natural disasters Volcanoes, tsunamis, tornados, and hurricanes, shown in **FIGURE 14.14**, can wipe out populations regardless of density. For example, the large wave of a tsunami can damage fragile coral reefs, knock down entire mangrove forests, and destroy sea turtle nesting beaches.

Human activities Destruction of a wetland habitat along the Platte River in Nebraska has threatened an important feeding ground for the sandhill crane. Urbanization in this area is depleting the resources these migratory birds need during their trek to nesting grounds in northern Canada and in Alaska. By clearing forests, filling wetlands, and polluting the air, land, and water, humans threaten habitats and the organisms that live in them. As we will discuss in Chapter 16, human influence as a limiting factor has had a profound effect on populations. For example, the introduction of nonnative species has caused population crashes in many parts of the world where biodiversity is an important part of the ecosystem's functioning.

Apply A population of algae in a pond is limited in size by the amount of sunlight that strikes the pond's surface. Is sunlight a density-dependent or density-independent limiting factor for the algae population?

14.4 ASSESSMENT

ONLINE QUIZ
ClassZone.com

REVIEWING ▶ MAIN IDEAS

1. What four factors determine the growth rate of a population?

2. How does **carrying capacity** affect the size of a population?

3. What is the main difference between a **density-dependent limiting factor** and a **density-independent limiting factor**? Give examples of each.

CRITICAL THINKING

4. **Apply** What might cause **exponential growth** to occur only for a short period when a new species is introduced to a resource-filled environment?

5. **Synthesize** How might density-dependent limiting factors be affected by a flood or some other natural disaster?

Connecting CONCEPTS

6. **Symbiosis** Give an example of how a symbiotic relationship could cause a population crash.

14.5 Ecological Succession

KEY CONCEPT Ecological succession is a process of change in the species that make up a community.

▶ MAIN IDEA

• Succession occurs following a disturbance in an ecosystem.

VOCABULARY

succession, p. 445
primary succession, p. 446
pioneer species, p. 446
secondary succession, p. 447

MICHIGAN STANDARDS

L3.p2B Describe common ecological relationships between and among species and their environments (competition, territory, carrying capacity, natural balance, population, dependence, survival, and other biotic and abiotic factors). (prerequisite)

B3.4A Describe ecosystem stability. Understand that if a disaster such as flood or fire occurs, the damaged ecosystem is likely to recover in stages of succession that eventually result in a system similar to the original one.

FIGURE 14.15 The path of a lava flow, like this one on the island of Hawaii (left), leaves behind nothing but solid rock. Over time, primary succession will turn this harsh landscape into a fertile ecosystem (right).

Connect It begins with a dirty sock. Then a discarded homework assignment. But this is only the start. If you have ever spent a Saturday afternoon cleaning your bedroom, you may have wondered how a perfectly clean room could manage to become such a cluttered mess. A clean room becoming cluttered is a gradual process much like the process that rebuilds damaged ecosystems.

▶ MAIN IDEA

Succession occurs following a disturbance in an ecosystem.

After an ecosystem experiences a devastating catastrophe and begins to regrow, the space re-forms itself through a process known as succession. **Succession** is the sequence of biotic changes that regenerate a damaged community or create a community in a previously uninhabited area.

The Hawaiian Islands began to form more than 70 million years ago. Over time, volcanic eruptions like the one shown in **FIGURE 14.15** created these islands in the middle of the Pacific Ocean. Eventually, the bare volcanic rock began to break down into soil, which provided a place for plants to grow. As time passed, the process of succession created unique tropical ecosystems. Succession from bare rock to such highly diverse vegetation takes a great deal of time.

445

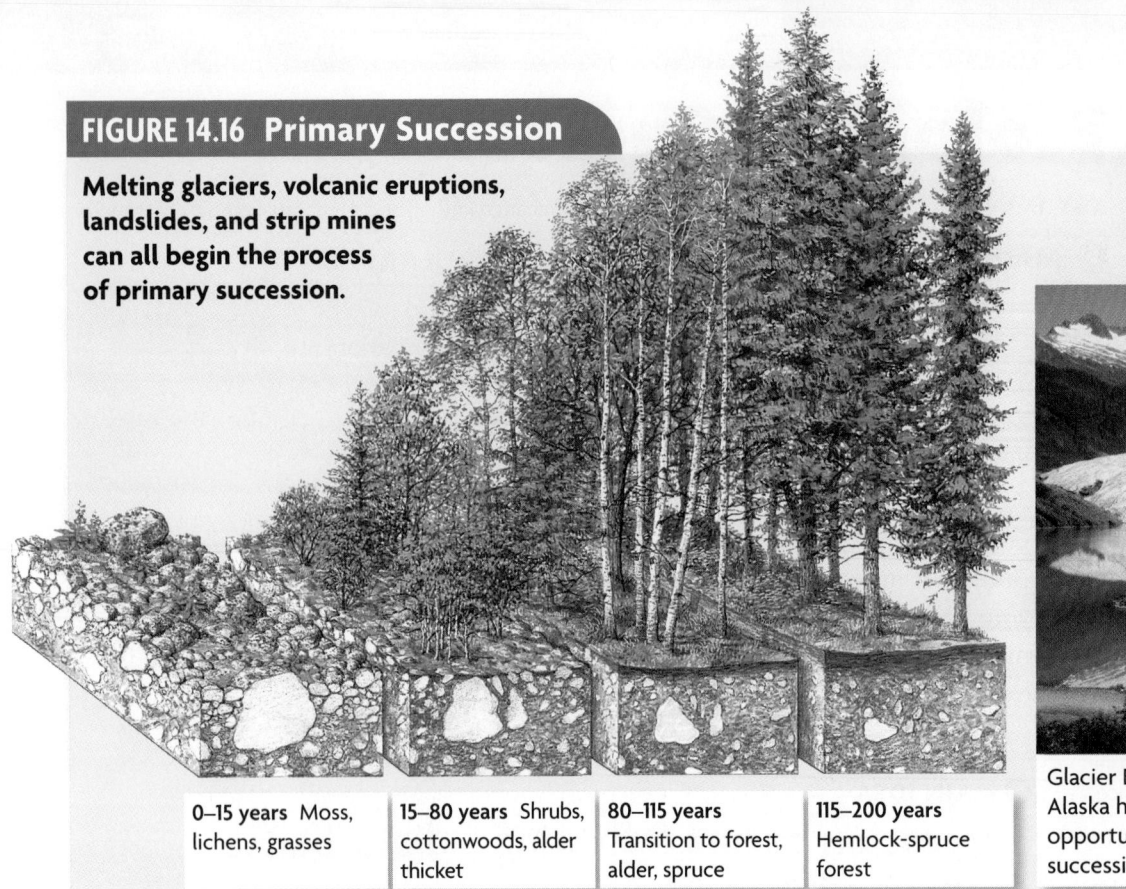

FIGURE 14.16 Primary Succession

Melting glaciers, volcanic eruptions, landslides, and strip mines can all begin the process of primary succession.

| **0–15 years** Moss, lichens, grasses | **15–80 years** Shrubs, cottonwoods, alder thicket | **80–115 years** Transition to forest, alder, spruce | **115–200 years** Hemlock-spruce forest |

Glacier Bay National Park in Alaska has given scientists an opportunity to witness primary succession as the glacier recedes.

Apply What function might the mosses and lichens serve in primary succession?

Primary Succession

One of the best ways to understand succession is to watch it progress. **Primary succession** is the establishment and development of an ecosystem in an area that was previously uninhabited. The first organisms that live in a previously uninhabited area are called **pioneer species.** Typical examples of pioneer species are lichens and some mosses, which can break down solid rock into smaller pieces. The process of primary succession, which is illustrated in **FIGURE 14.16,** follows this basic pattern:

- Bare rock is exposed by a retreating glacier or is created when lava cools. Wind, rain, and ice begin to break down the surface of the rock, forming cracks and breaking the rock into smaller pieces.
- Lichen and moss spores are blown in by wind. As they grow, they break up the rock further. When they die, their remains mix with the rock pieces to form a thin layer of soil.
- Over time, seeds are blown into the area or are dropped by birds. Small flowers and hardy shrubs grow from these seeds. These new plants provide a habitat for small animals, break up the rock with their roots, and add material to the soil when they die.
- As the soil continues to grow thicker, small trees take root, and different animals move into the area. These trees provide shade.
- Different tree species take root in the shade and eventually replace the original trees, which need direct sunlight to thrive.

Connecting CONCEPTS

Symbiosis A lichen is actually two completely different species. Fungus and algae form a symbiotic relationship in which the fungi collects water, while the algae uses chlorophyll to conduct photosynthesis and synthesize food for the lichen community.

FIGURE 14.17 Secondary Succession

Following a flood or a fire, a community is given a chance for new life. Plants remaining after the disturbance reestablish the ecosystem.

0–2 years Horseweed, crabgrass, asters

2–18 years Grass, shrubs, pine seedlings

18–70 years Pine forest and young hardwood seedlings

70–100 years Oak-hickory forest

Fire is important in helping forests return nutrients to the soil. Secondary succession uses these nutrients to grow.

Analyze Why does secondary succession take less time than primary succession?

Secondary Succession

Succession does not always begin from bare rock. More often, a disturbance, such as a fire or hurricane, halts the progress of succession or destroys an established community. **Secondary succession,** which is illustrated in **FIGURE 14.17,** is the reestablishment of a damaged ecosystem in an area where the soil was left intact. Plants and other organisms that remain start the process of regrowth. There is no end to secondary succession. Small disturbances, such as a tree falling, start the process again and again. The dynamic processes of succession are always changing the face of an ecosystem.

Connect Where might succession occur in the ocean?

14.5 ASSESSMENT

ONLINE QUIZ
ClassZone.com

REVIEWING ▶ MAIN IDEAS

1. How is **primary succession** different from **secondary succession**?

2. Why are **pioneer species** so important for primary succession?

CRITICAL THINKING

3. **Infer** Does the process of primary succession take longer in tropical or arctic areas? Explain.

4. **Predict** During **succession,** what might become the limiting factor for sun-loving mosses as taller plants begin to grow?

Connecting CONCEPTS

5. **Niche** At what point during primary succession does an ecosystem provide the fewest habitats for organisms? Explain your reasoning.

Use these inquiry-based labs and online activities to deepen your understanding of ecosystems.

INVESTIGATION

Limiting Nutrients for Algae

All organisms require sufficient nutrients to grow. In many ecosystems, two important limiting nutrients, nitrogen and phosphorus, may limit plant growth.

SKILL Interpreting Data

PROBLEM Are nitrogen and phosphorus limiting nutrients for algae growth?

PROCEDURE

1. Mark the three jars *control*, *A*, and *B*, and add pond water until each is two-thirds full.

2. Add 40 to 50 mL of algae culture to each jar.

3. Add 4 or 5 drops of the trisodium phosphate solution to jar A. This is a source of phosphorous. Swirl to mix.

4. Add 4 or 5 drops of the ammonium sulfate or urea solution to jar B. This is a source of nitrogen. Swirl to mix.

5. Cap the jars and place them in a sunny window.

6. Design a data table to record your observations.

7. Predict how algae levels will change in each jar after seven days.

8. Observe every day for seven days. Record your observations.

ANALYZE AND CONCLUDE

1. **Observe** After seven days, how did the appearances of the three jars differ? How did their smells differ?

2. **Evaluate** Use your data to determine whether your results support your prediction.

3. **Conclude** Explain how you know whether phosphorus or nitrogen was a limiting nutrient.

4. **Experimental Design** In what way did your experiment fall short in revealing limiting nutrients for algae?

5. **Application** Based on what you learned in this experiment, which nutrients would you add to a vegetable garden?

MATERIALS

- 3 baby food jars with lids
- glass marking pencil
- 200 mL pond water
- 3 eyedroppers
- 50 mL algae culture
- 5 drops 10% trisodium phosphate solution
- 5 drops 10% ammonium sulfate or urea solution
- 50-mL graduated cylinder

EXTEND YOUR INVESTIGATION

Excess nutrients in waterways can cause an environmental problem called eutrophication. Sources of excess nutrients include sewage treatment runoff, agriculture runoff, industrial waste, storm water runoff, and atmospheric fallout. Do research on eutrophication and the effects of excess amounts of nitrogen and phosphorus on algae growth.

INVESTIGATION

Making a Local Field Guide

Field guides contain descriptions and pictures of plant, insect, and animal species. In this activity, you will observe specimens near your home or school to create your own local field guide.

SKILL Observing

PROBLEM What plant and animal species can you identify in your region?

MATERIALS

- several field guides appropriate to the plants and animals in your area
- hand lens
- blank notebook
- pencil
- colored pencils
- camera (optional)

PROCEDURE

1. Find an area near your home or school with as many different species as possible, such as an open field or a pond. Choose a category of species from your teacher's list, and find as many different species in that category as you can.

2. Draw pictures in your notebook or take photographs of each species.

3. Use field guides to identify each species. Write down both the common and scientific names, and note any interesting species information.

4. Make a field-guide page for each species you identified in your local ecosystem. Include the drawing or photograph of each species, along with its common and scientific names, when and where you collected it, and interesting information about it.

5. Compile your field guide in a binder or folder. Give your guide a title and a table of contents.

ANALYZE AND CONCLUDE

1. **Analyze** How diverse is the ecosystem you studied? Compare the species richness you observed with what your classmates discovered.

2. **Conclude** Summarize what you learned about the ecosystem you surveyed. How did creating your own field guide affect your understanding of the ecosystem?

Online BIOLOGY
CLASSZONE.COM

ANIMATED BIOLOGY
What Limits Population Growth?
Apply a limiting factor within a sample environment and see how the populations of organisms react.

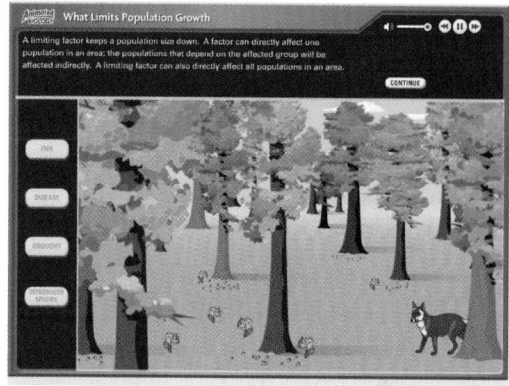

WEBQUEST

In this WebQuest, you will examine how Hurricane Hugo affected endangered Puerto Rican parrots. Explore how healthy parrot populations weathered hurricanes in the past, then determine if the current population recovered from the hurricane.

DATA ANALYSIS ONLINE

By 1900, most bison in Yellowstone Park had been wiped out. Between 1902 and 1968, scientists gathered data on the reemerging bison population. Make a graph of the data to analyze how the population grew and when the population reached its carrying capacity.

KEY CONCEPTS | Vocabulary Games | Concept Maps | Animated Biology | Online Quiz

14.1 Habitat and Niche

Every organism has a habitat and a niche.
Each organism in an ecosystem has an ecological niche, which includes the type of food it consumes, its behavior, and its habitat—the place where it lives. Competitive exclusion prevents two species from sharing the same niche. In different geographical regions, ecological equivalents may have similar ecological niches.

14.2 Community Interactions

Organisms interact as individuals and as populations. Interactions between species include competition and predation. Interactions shape ecosystem dynamics. Parasitism, commensalism, and mutualism are symbiotic relationships involving two species living in direct contact with one another.

14.3 Population Density and Distribution

Each population has a density, a dispersion, and a reproductive strategy. The distribution of a population can be measured by population density. Species can have clumped, uniform, or random dispersion patterns. Survivorship curves describe the reproductive strategies of different species.

Clumped dispersion	Uniform dispersion	Random dispersion

14.4 Population Growth Patterns

Populations grow in predictable patterns.
Population growth accommodates changes in population size due to births and deaths as well as immigration and emigration. Populations experiencing exponential growth increase dramatically over time. When resources become a limiting factor, a population will grow logistically until it reaches the environmental carrying capacity, or the maximum population size the environment can support. Density-dependent limiting factors affect dense populations, but density-independent limiting factors affect populations regardless of density.

14.5 Ecological Succession

Ecological succession is a process of change in the species that make up a community.
Succession refers to the progression of plants and animals that repopulate a region after an ecological disturbance. Primary succession begins in a previously uninhabited area, such as bare rock exposed by the receding of a glacier or created by a volcanic eruption. Secondary succession occurs in a previously inhabited area that is damaged by an ecological disturbance, such as a fire or a flood.

Synthesize Your Notes

Concept Map Use a concept map to display the differences between exponential and logistic growth.

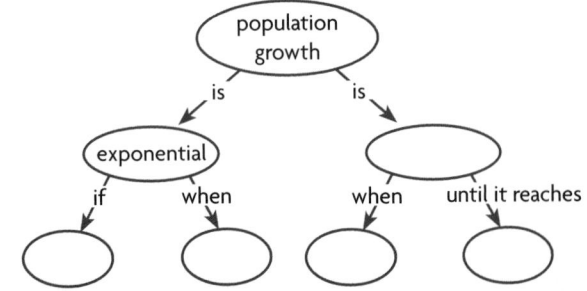

Main Idea Chart Use the main idea chart to explain and give examples of density-independent and density-dependent limiting factors.

Density Independent	Density Dependent

Chapter Assessment

Chapter Vocabulary

14.1 habitat, p. 428
ecological niche, p. 428
competitive exclusion, p. 429
ecological equivalent, p. 430

14.2 competition, p. 431
predation, p. 431
symbiosis, p. 432
mutualism, p. 432
commensalism, p. 432
parasitism, p. 432

14.3 population density, p. 436
population dispersion, p. 437
survivorship curve, p. 438

14.4 immigration, p. 440
emigration, p. 440
exponential growth, p. 441
logistic growth, p. 441
carrying capacity, p. 442
population crash, p. 442
limiting factor, p. 443

density-dependent limiting
factor, p. 443
density-independent limiting
factor, p. 444

14.5 succession, p. 445
primary succession, p. 446
pioneer species, p. 446
secondary succession, p. 447

Reviewing Vocabulary

Category Clues

For each clue in the category group, list the appropriate vocabulary words from the chapter.

Category: Types of Symbiosis

1. two-way benefit
2. host is harmed
3. no effect on host

Category: Types of Dispersion

4. a herd
5. no pattern
6. territories

Category: Population Growth

7. quick growth
8. sudden decrease in size
9. number environment can sustain

Word Origins

10. *Niche* is an English word with a French origin. In general, it means "a special place." How does this meaning relate to the ecological definition of the word?

11. *Habitat* comes from a Latin word meaning "it inhabits." Connect this meaning with the definition in Section 14.1.

Reviewing MAIN IDEAS

12. A deer is a large herbivore that usually lives in a forest. What is the deer's habitat, and what is its niche?

13. How does competitive exclusion differ from ecological equivalents?

14. A brown bear is an omnivore. Explain how a brown bear and a squirrel can be in interspecific competition and have a predatory–prey relationship.

15. The remora fish has an adaptation that allows it to attach to a shark, and it feeds on scraps of food left over from the shark's meal. What type of symbiotic relationship is this? Explain.

16. If you were to add two goldfish into a fish tank that already contains three goldfish, explain what happens to the population density of the fish tank.

17. Explain how the three types of survivorship curves align with different reproductive strategies.

18. If a large number of individuals immigrated into a population of bison, what two things could happen to return the population to its original size?

19. Why does a population that experiences exponential growth have a high chance of having a population crash?

20. How might the carrying capacity of an environment for a particular species change in response to an unusually long and harsh winter? Why?

21. Describe and give examples of two limiting factors that affect a dense population.

22. Why is succession considered an ongoing process?

Critical Thinking

23. Apply A bee gathers nectar from a flower by using a strawlike appendage called a proboscis. While on the flower, grains of pollen attach to the bee's back. When the bee travels to another flower, the pollen fertilizes the new plant. What type of symbiosis is this?

24. Predict A population of prairie dogs is experiencing high immigration and birthrates, but resources are beginning to deplete. What could eventually happen to this population? Give two possibilities.

25. Synthesize A species of beetle is in a period of exponential growth, but a competing species has started sharing the same space. Is the competing species an example of a density-dependent or a density-independent limiting factor? Explain.

26. Evaluate Imagine that scientists introduced a disease into the rabbit population of Australia, and the rabbit population crashed. Was the crash caused by a density-dependent or density-independent limiting factor? Justify your answer.

27. Apply Each year, thousands of California market squid swim up from the ocean depths and lay millions of eggs along California shorelines. The squid then die, leaving their offspring to fend for themselves. Draw and label a graph that illustrates a likely survivorship curve of the California market squid.

Analyzing a Diagram

Use the diagram below to answer the next two questions.

28. Apply What part of the diagram depicts pioneer species? Explain your answer.

29. Infer What could happen in the ecosystem shown that could make it revert to an earlier stage of succession?

Analyzing Data

Use the graph to answer the next three questions.

The combination graph below shows changes in the sizes of bee and mite populations in one area of the Midwest. The mites live as parasites on the bees.

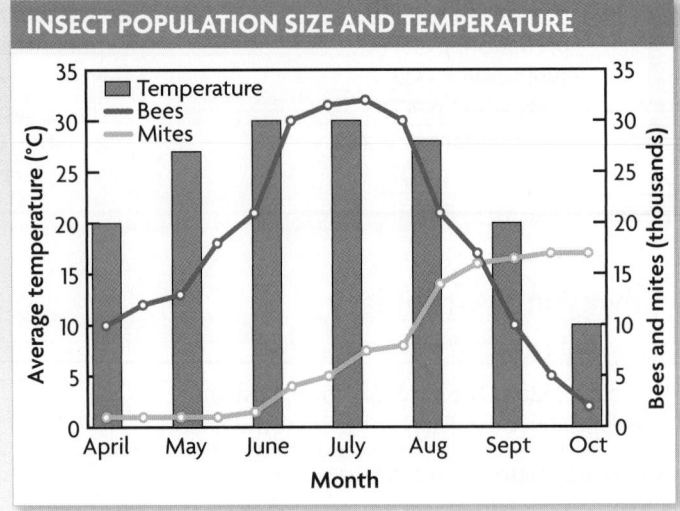

30. Interpret A decrease in the number of bees occurs during which months?

31. Analyze Describe the trends in the bee and mite populations from April through October.

32. Hypothesize What might explain the relationship between the bee and mite population numbers?

Connecting CONCEPTS

33. Write Ad Copy Imagine that you are an advertising agent trying to encourage a new species to move into an environment. Design an advertisement using the concepts from the chapter. Keep in mind that a population will not want to move to a new area without abundant resources. Choose a target species and make sure that your advertisement answers the following questions: What resources and environmental factors would make this species want to move? What abiotic and biotic factors does it need? Include several vocabulary terms from the chapter.

34. Apply The two zebras on page 427 are competing for the right to mate with females. Are they engaging in intraspecific or interspecific competition? Explain your answer.

MICHIGAN
STANDARDS-BASED ASSESSMENT

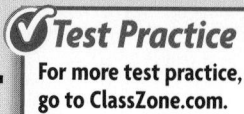

✓ **Test Practice**
For more test practice,
go to ClassZone.com.

1. Archaeologists find that the disappearance of a large mammal occurred shortly after the arrival of hominids in a certain region. What most likely occurred between these two species? **L3.p2A**

   A dispersion

   B predation

   C commensalism

   D parasitism

2. Officials attempt to control the spread of an exotic wildflower species by introducing its natural predator, a beetle. Unexpectedly, the beetle population grows exponentially and begins to eat local crops. What best accounts for this unexpected population explosion? **B3.5B**

   A Adaptive radiation allowed the beetle population to evolve faster.

   B The beetle population has few predators in the new habitat.

   C The wildflower and the local crops are genetically similar kinds of plants.

   D The beetle has different nutritional requirements in the new habitat.

3.

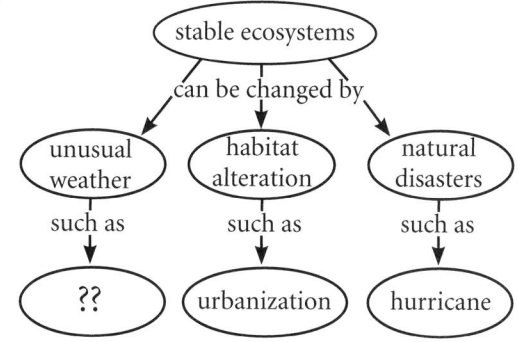

   Which of these best completes this concept map? **B3.4A**

   A acid rain

   B pollution

   C an earthquake

   D extended drought

   THINK THROUGH THE QUESTION

   Keep in mind that unusual weather is a natural part of ecosystem function.

4. A population of rodents becomes stranded on a remote island. Eventually, the population reaches the island's carrying capacity. At this point, the birth and death rates are **L3.p2B**

   A relatively equal.

   B crashing.

   C density independent.

   D density dependent.

5.

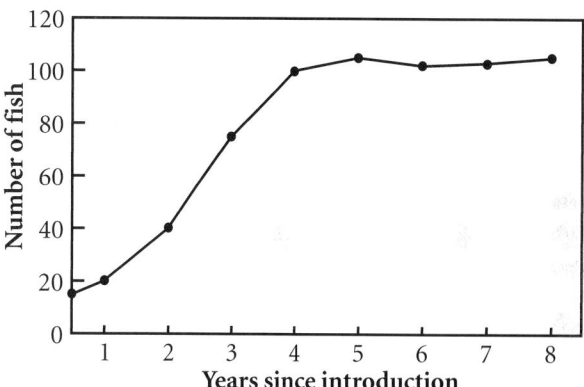

   Fish Population in Birch Park Pond

   A fish species is introduced to a park pond. Which statement best describes the population growth of these fish shown in the graph? **B3.5e**

   A The population stopped growing because the fish stopped reproducing.

   B The population stopped growing because this species of fish lives less than one year.

   C The population grew until disease caused the population to level off.

   D The population grew until it reached the pond's carrying capacity.

6. In many parts of the United States, native plants that once grew on the forest floor have been replaced by garlic mustard, an invasive species that thrives in cool forest understories. This situation is an example of **B2.2g**

   A parasitism between species.

   B primary succession between species.

   C predation between species.

   D competition between species.

15 The Biosphere

KEY CONCEPTS

15.1 Life in the Earth System
The biosphere is one of Earth's four interconnected systems.

15.2 Climate
Climate is a key abiotic factor that affects the biosphere.

15.3 Biomes
Biomes are land-based, global communities of organisms.

15.4 Marine Ecosystems
Marine ecosystems are global.

15.5 Estuaries and Freshwater Ecosystems
Freshwater ecosystems include estuaries as well as flowing and standing water.

Online BIOLOGY CLASSZONE.COM

Animated BIOLOGY

View animated chapter concepts.
• Lake Turnover
• Where Do They Live?

BIOZINE

Keep current with biology news.
• Strange Biology
• News feeds
• Careers

RESOURCE CENTER

Get more information on
• Biosphere
• Biomes
• Aquatic Ecosystems

What species would you expect to find in a rain forest?

Connecting **CONCEPTS**

Not all rain forests are teeming with monkeys and macaws. The temperate rain forest of the Pacific Northwest is inhabited by an entirely different community of plants and animals than is found in tropical rain forests. Location, climatic conditions, and other abiotic factors determine what species you will find in a particular area.

Plant Evolution Ferns, which are abundant in the temperate rain forest, first appeared during the early Carboniferous period (360 to 320 million years ago). These plants diversified before the evolution of flowering plants. Instead of reproducing through pollen, ferns reproduce through spores. The early evolution of ferns makes them among the oldest plants still in existence today.

15.1 Life in the Earth System

KEY CONCEPT The biosphere is one of Earth's four interconnected systems.

▶ MAIN IDEAS

- The biosphere is the portion of Earth that is inhabited by life.
- Biotic and abiotic factors interact in the biosphere.

VOCABULARY

biosphere, p. 456
biota, p. 456
hydrosphere, p. 456
atmosphere, p. 456

geosphere, p. 456

Review
biotic, abiotic

L3.p2A Describe common relationships among organisms and provide examples of producer/consumer, predator/prey, or parasite/host relationship. (prerequisite)

L3.p3B Distinguish between the living (biotic) and nonliving (abiotic) components of an ecosystem. (prerequisite)

Connect You've probably seen many photos of tropical rain forests, complete with monkeys and brightly colored frogs. But did you know that there are also temperate rain forests? They get just as much rain but have cooler temperatures and different types of plants and animals. These are just two of the biomes found within the biosphere.

▶ MAIN IDEA

The biosphere is the portion of Earth that is inhabited by life.

The **biosphere** is the part of Earth where life exists. All of Earth's ecosystems, taken together, form the biosphere. If you could remove all the nonliving parts of the biosphere—all the water, air, rocks, and so on—you would be left with the biota. The **biota** is the collection of living things that live in the biosphere.

The biosphere is one of Earth's four major interconnected systems. The other three Earth systems are

- the **hydrosphere,** all of Earth's water, ice, and water vapor
- the **atmosphere,** the air blanketing Earth's solid and liquid surface
- the **geosphere,** the features of Earth's surface—such as the continents, rocks, and the sea floor—and everything below Earth's surface

You need to look at how all four Earth systems interact to really understand how an ecosystem works. For example, a plant growing in a swamp depends on the soil in which it grows just as much as on the water in the swamp. It uses carbon dioxide from the atmosphere to make sugars, and it gives off excess oxygen, slightly changing the air around it. One plant growing in one swamp has a small effect on the Earth system as a whole. But all living things together throughout the planet's history have had a vast effect.

Connect Is the air in your classroom part of the biosphere or the biota? Explain.

VISUAL VOCAB

The **biosphere** includes living organisms and the land, air, and water on Earth where living things reside.

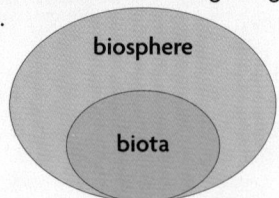

The collection of living things in the biosphere may also be called the **biota.**

TAKING NOTES

Use a diagram to take notes on the biosphere.

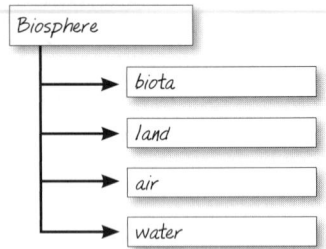

MAIN IDEA

Biotic and abiotic factors interact in the biosphere.

Just as one ecosystem is connected to another, all four Earth systems are also connected. A change in one sphere can affect the others. If plants are removed from a riverbank, for example, rain may flow more easily from the land to the water. This increased flow would likely carry more sediment and therefore make the river water murkier, as shown in **FIGURE 15.1**. The murky water might block sunlight, affecting the growth of aquatic plants. This change might in turn prevent these plants from taking up carbon dioxide and releasing oxygen.

James Lovelock, an atmospheric scientist from the United Kingdom, proposed the Gaia hypothesis to explain how biotic and abiotic factors interact in the biosphere. This hypothesis considers Earth itself a kind of living organism. Its atmosphere, geosphere, and hydrosphere are cooperating systems that yield a biosphere full of life. He called this living planet Gaia after the Greek goddess of Earth. In the early 1970s, Lynn Margulis, a microbiologist from the United States, added to the hypothesis, specifically noting the ties between the biosphere and other Earth systems. For example, when carbon dioxide levels increase in the atmosphere, plants grow more quickly. As their growth continues, they remove more and more carbon dioxide from the atmosphere. The atmospheric carbon dioxide level drops, and plant growth slows. This give-and-take, known as a feedback loop, helps maintain a fairly constant level of carbon dioxide in the atmosphere.

Sometimes, people mistakenly believe that the Gaia hypothesis suggests that Earth is a thinking being that regulates the geosphere, the atmosphere, and the hydrosphere. This is obviously not the case. Rather, the Gaia hypothesis recognizes the extensive connections and feedback loops between the living and nonliving parts of the planet. Many scientists are now devoting their careers to organizing new fields of study, such as geobiology and geomicrobiology, to examine these intriguing relationships.

Summarize Explain the Gaia hypothesis in your own words.

FIGURE 15.1 Deforestation, or the removal of forests, along the Mahajamba Bay in Madagascar has led to erosion along the waterway, clogging the water with silt and soil.

15.1 / ASSESSMENT

ONLINE QUIZ
ClassZone.com

REVIEWING ▶ MAIN IDEAS

1. What is the relationship between the **biota** and the **biosphere**?

2. How does the Gaia hypothesis explain the interaction between biotic and abiotic factors in the biosphere?

CRITICAL THINKING

3. **Apply** A frog jumps into a pond and it's skin absorbs water. What spheres has the water moved through?

4. **Predict** How might a rise in global temperatures affect the biosphere?

Connecting CONCEPTS

5. **Predator-Prey** Explain how feedback loops, such as those described in the Gaia hypothesis, might apply to predator-prey relationships.

15.2 Climate

KEY CONCEPT Climate is a key abiotic factor that affects the biosphere.

MAIN IDEAS
- Climate is the prevailing weather of a region.
- Earth has three main climate zones.

VOCABULARY
climate, p. 458
microclimate, p. 458

Review
biosphere

MICHIGAN STANDARDS

L3.p2B Describe common ecological relationships between and among species and their environments (competition, territory, carrying capacity, natural balance, population, dependence, survival, and other biotic and abiotic factors). (prerequisite)

L3.p3B Distinguish between the living (biotic) and nonliving (abiotic) components of an eco-system. (prerequisite)

FIGURE 15.2 The cavity in this log provides a humid microclimate that supports the growth of mushrooms.

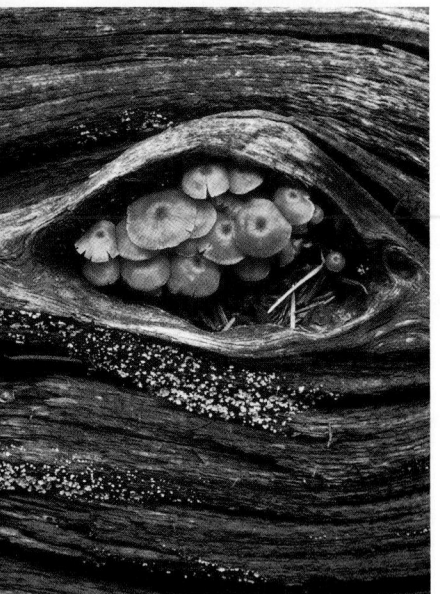

Connect Although you might sometimes check the local weather report to see if you'll need an umbrella, you are already familiar with the general climate where you live. If you live in the Midwest, you know that winter means cold temperatures, while if you live in the Southwest, winter temperatures are much milder. The long-term weather patterns of an area help determine which plants and animals you will find living there.

MAIN IDEA
Climate is the prevailing weather of a region.

The weather of an area may change from day to day, and even from hour to hour. In contrast, the **climate** is the long-term pattern of weather conditions in a region. Climate includes factors such as average temperature and precipitation and relative humidity. It also includes the seasonal variations an area experiences, such as rainy or dry seasons, cold winters, or hot summers.

The key factors that shape an area's climate include temperature, sunlight, water, and wind. Among these abiotic factors, temperature and moisture play a large role in the shaping of ecosystems. Descriptions of a specific region's climate take these abiotic factors into consideration. For example, a specific region such as a desert may be described as hot and dry, while a rain forest may be described as warm and moist.

Even within a specific region, climate conditions may vary dramatically. A **microclimate** is the climate of a small specific place within a larger area. A microclimate may be as small as a hole in a decaying log where mushrooms grow, as pictured in **FIGURE 15.2**, or as large as a city neighborhood. San Francisco, for example, is characterized by frequent fog and cool temperatures. However, not far beyond the city limits, and even within other sections of the city itself, the weather may be quite different.

Microclimates can be very important to living things. The same grassy meadow, for example, may be home to both frogs and grasshoppers. The frogs may tend toward areas that are moist, often at the base of the grasses, while the grasshoppers may prefer drier sites and cling to the tops of the grass blades. Each of these locations is a microclimate.

Analyze Where in a forest might you find different microclimates?

▶ MAIN IDEA
Earth has three main climate zones.

Scientists use average temperature and precipitation levels to categorize a region's climate. Using this system, Earth can be divided into three main climate zones, as shown in **FIGURE 15.3**. These three zones are the polar, tropical, and temperate climates. The polar climate is found at the far northern and southern regions of Earth. The tropical zone surrounds the equator. The temperate zone is the wide area in between the polar and tropical zones.

Influence of Sunlight

What determines an area's climate? The answer begins with the Sun. The Sun's rays are most intense, and therefore hottest, on the portion of the planet that sunlight strikes most directly. Earth's surface is heated unevenly due to its curved shape. The area of Earth that receives the most direct radiation from the Sun all year is the region at and around the equator, where the tropical climate zone is found. Near the north and south poles, or polar climate zones, the Sun's rays strike Earth's surface at a lower angle, diffusing their heat over a larger area.

Earth's tilt on its axis also plays a role in seasonal change. As Earth orbits the Sun, different regions of the planet receive higher or lower amounts of sunlight. When the North Pole is at its maximum tilt away from the Sun, it is winter in the Northern Hemisphere and summer in the Southern Hemisphere. When the North Pole reaches its maximum tilt toward the Sun, the opposite is true.

Connecting CONCEPTS

Seasons At the March and September equinoxes, both hemispheres receive equal amounts of sunlight. At the June solstice, the Northern Hemisphere enters summer and the Southern Hemisphere enters winter. The opposite is true at the December solstice.

FIGURE 15.3 Climate Zones

The uneven heating of Earth by the Sun results in three different climate zones.

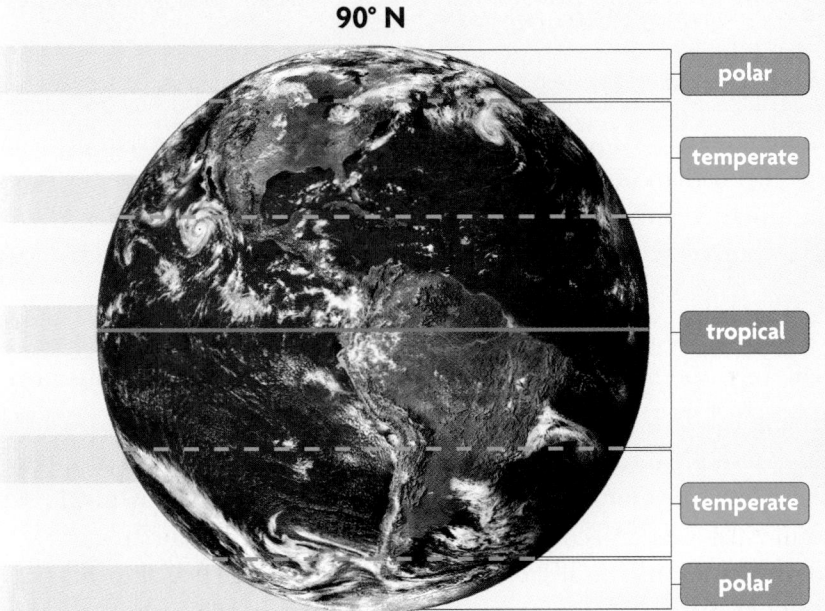

90° N

- polar
- temperate
- tropical
- temperate
- polar

POLAR CLIMATE

The polar climate zone is located in far northern and far southern reaches of the planet, where the temperature is typically cold and often below freezing.

TROPICAL CLIMATE

The tropical climate zone, which surrounds the equator, runs from the tropic of Cancer to the tropic of Capricorn and is characterized by warm, moist conditions.

TEMPERATE CLIMATE

The temperate climate zone is located in the broad area lying between the polar and tropical climate zones. This zone experiences summer and winter seasons of about equal length.

Apply What is the relationship between sunlight and climate zone?

Microclimates

Determine the temperature of inside and outside areas of your school to identify different microclimates.

PROBLEM Where are different microclimates in and around your school grounds?

PROCEDURE

1. Identify one place inside and one place outside your school where microclimates may exist.

2. Place a thermometer at each location. Wait at least five minutes before recording the temperature.

MATERIALS
- thermometer
- stopwatch

ANALYZE AND CONCLUDE

Compare the temperatures you collected with those recorded by your classmates at different locations.

Western slope

Eastern slope

FIGURE 15.4 The western slope of the Sierra Nevada, which faces the prevailing winds, receives precipitation throughout the year. Due to the rain shadow, the eastern slope of the Sierras is much drier.

Air and Water Movement

When the Sun heats Earth, it warms not only the land and the rocks but also the water and the air. This heating causes movements in both water and air. Warm air and warm water are less dense than cooler air and water, and therefore they rise. Since the tropics near the equator are especially warm, the warm air here rises and the cooler air from areas to the north or south moves in to take its place. As the warm air rises, it cools. Since cold air holds less moisture than warm air does, a large amount of precipitation drops as rain. This large amount of precipitation, along with warm temperatures, defines the tropical rain forest regions found near the equator. The movement of air also leads to movement in water, forming currents. The rotation of Earth, water temperatures, and salinity levels also interact to form currents.

Landmasses

Landmasses also shape climates. For example, areas closer to bodies of water have a different climate from areas farther away because land tends to heat and cool more quickly than water. Thus, coastal areas tend to have smaller changes in temperature than areas farther inland. Farther inland, areas experience a much larger range of seasonal high and low temperatures.

Water evaporates from open bodies such as lakes or oceans faster than it does from soil or through plant transpiration. As a result, coastal sites in general have higher humidity and receive more precipitation than inland areas.

Mountains also may have a large effect on an area's climate. As warm, moist air nears a mountain, it rises and cools. This cooling of air results in precipitation on the side of the mountain range facing the wind. On the downwind side of the mountains, drier and cooler air produces a rain shadow, or area of decreased precipitation. The Sierra Nevada mountain range in California, shown in **FIGURE 15.4,** is one example of this phenomenon. While the western slope receives a large amount of precipitation, the Great Basin to the east of the mountains is dry.

CONSTRUCTING COMBINATION GRAPHS

Climatograms are combination graphs that represent weather data for a specific location or biome over a period of time. Refer to the Data Analysis Feature on page 442 to recall what a combination graph looks like.

1. **Graph Data** Plot the average precipitation as a bar graph, and plot the average temperature as a line graph.

2. **Analyze** How would you describe the temperature change throughout the year in this location?

3. **Identify** During which month is the precipitation level lowest for this location?

4. **Analyze** Is there a relationship between temperature and precipitation in Albuquerque, New Mexico? If so, explain how they are related.

5. **Explain** What is the benefit of using a combination graph to illustrate an area's climate?

TABLE 1. AVERAGE CLIMATE IN ALBUQUERQUE, NM		
Month	**Precipitation (mm)**	**Temperature (°C)**
January	12.4	2.1
February	11.2	5.2
March	15.5	8.9
April	12.7	13.1
May	15.2	18.2
June	16.5	23.8
July	32.3	25.8
August	43.9	24.5
September	27.2	20.6
October	25.4	14.1
November	15.7	6.9
December	12.4	2.3

Source: National Oceanic and Atmospheric Administration

Adaptations to Climate

Many organisms have adaptations that allow them to survive in a specific climate. The water-holding frog shown in **FIGURE 15.5** is a dramatic example. It lives in the dry grasslands and deserts of inland Australia, where the rainy season comes only once a year. Dry periods can last 10 months or more. The frog survives the dry season by burrowing underground, where water evaporates more slowly. Moisture loss is further reduced by a cocoonlike structure formed from the frog's shed skin. When rains soak the ground, the frogs crawl out of their burrows to mate, and the females lay eggs in water puddles that form in depressions along the ground. Within a matter of weeks, the eggs hatch into tadpoles, and the tadpoles change into frogs. This frog must move through its life cycle very quickly because the water evaporates quickly once the rains end. If the tadpoles are not ready to leave the ponds, they will die.

Connect Describe the climate where you live.

FIGURE 15.5 Water-holding frogs crawl out of their burrows to mate during the rainy season.

15.2 ASSESSMENT

ONLINE QUIZ
ClassZone.com

REVIEWING ▶ MAIN IDEAS

1. What is the difference between **climate** and weather?

2. What are the three different climate zones, and where are they located?

CRITICAL THINKING

3. **Connect** Where might there be **microclimates** in your area?

4. **Infer** Would areas along the shores of the Great Lakes have warmer summers and colder winters than other inland areas? Explain.

Connecting CONCEPTS

5. **Niches** Would you expect an area with several microclimates to have more or fewer ecological niches? Explain your answer.

15.3 Biomes

KEY CONCEPT Biomes are land-based, global communities of organisms.

▶ MAIN IDEAS

- Earth has six major biomes.
- Polar ice caps and mountains are not considered biomes.

VOCABULARY

canopy, p. 464
grassland, p. 464
desert, p. 464
deciduous, p. 465
coniferous, p. 465

taiga, p. 465
tundra, p. 466
chaparral, p. 466

Review
biome

L3.p2B Describe common ecological relationships between and among species and their environments (competition, territory, carrying capacity, natural balance, population, dependence, survival, and other biotic and abiotic factors). (prerequisite)

Connecting CONCEPTS

Levels of Organization Recall from **Chapter 13** that a biome is a major community of organisms, usually characterized by the climate conditions and plant communities that live there.

Connect You wouldn't find a cactus in a tropical rain forest or a penguin in a desert. Individual plant and animal species have adaptations that let them thrive only in certain biomes. In this section, you will learn about the major biomes of the world and the characteristics of each.

▶ MAIN IDEA

Earth has six major biomes.

The global distribution of biomes is shown in **FIGURE 15.6.** Characteristics of each biome are given in **FIGURE 15.7.** As you will see, these broad biome types can be divided into even more specific zones. For example, the grassland biome can be further separated into zones of temperate and tropical grassland.

A variety of different ecosystems are found within a biome. However, because a biome is characterized by a certain set of abiotic factors, ecosystems located across the globe in the same biome—the tropical rain forest of Brazil or Madagascar, for example—tend to have similar plant and animal species.

FIGURE 15.6 World Biomes

A biome is defined by its climate and by the plant communities that live there.

Biomes
- Tropical rain forest
- Grassland
- Desert
- Temperate forest
- Taiga
- Tundra

Non-Biome Areas
- Mountain zones
- Polar ice

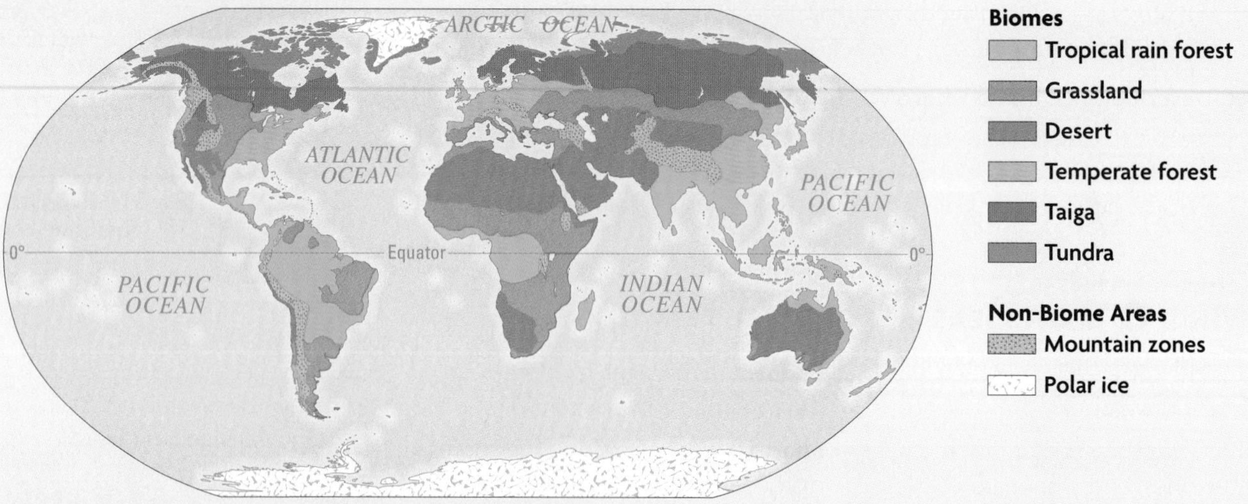

Identify Which biomes are found in North America?

FIGURE 15.7 Biomes

TROPICAL

Tropical rain forest
- Warm temperatures and abundant rainfall occur all year.
- Vegetation includes lush thick forests.
- Animals that live within the thick cover of the upper-most branches of rain forest trees use loud vocalizations to defend their territory and attract mates.

GRASSLAND

Tropical grassland
- Temperatures are warm throughout the year, with definite dry and rainy seasons.
- Vegetation includes tall grasses with scattered trees and shrubs.
- Hoofed animals, such as gazelles and other herbivores, dominate this biome.

Temperate grassland
- This biome is dry and warm during the summer; most precipitation falls as snow during the winter.
- Vegetation includes short or tall grasses, depending on the amount of precipitation.
- Many animals live below ground to survive the dry and windy conditions in this biome.

DESERT

Desert
- This biome has a very dry climate.
- Plants, such as cacti, store water or have deep root systems.
- Many animals are nocturnal; they limit their activities during the day.

TEMPERATE

Temperate deciduous forest
- Temperatures are hot in the summer and cold in the winter; precipitation is spaced evenly over the year.
- Broadleaf forest dominates this biome, and deciduous trees lose their leaves in the winter.

Temperate rain forest
- This biome has one long wet season and a relatively dry summer.
- Evergreen conifers, which retain their leaves (needles) year-round, dominate this biome.
- While some species remain active in the winter, others migrate to warmer climates or hibernate.

TAIGA

Taiga
- This biome has long, cold winters and short, warm, humid summers.
- Coniferous trees dominate this biome.
- Mammals have heavy fur coats to withstand the cold winters.

TUNDRA

Tundra
- Subzero temperatures are the norm during the long winter, and there is little precipitation.
- The ground is permanently frozen; only mosses and other low-lying plants survive.
- Animal diversity is low.

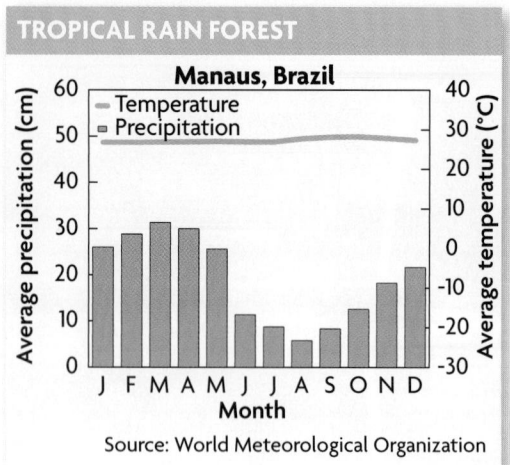

TROPICAL RAIN FOREST

Manaus, Brazil

Source: World Meteorological Organization

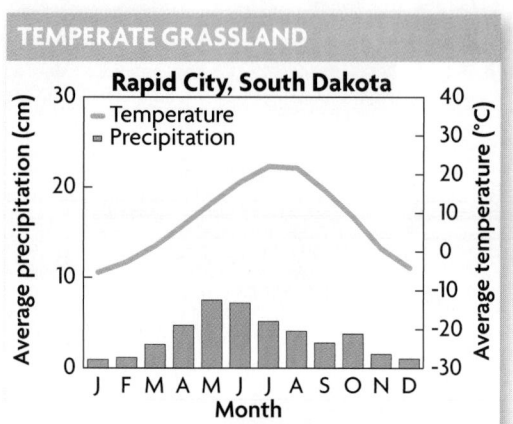

TEMPERATE GRASSLAND

Rapid City, South Dakota

Source: National Oceanic Atmospheric Administration

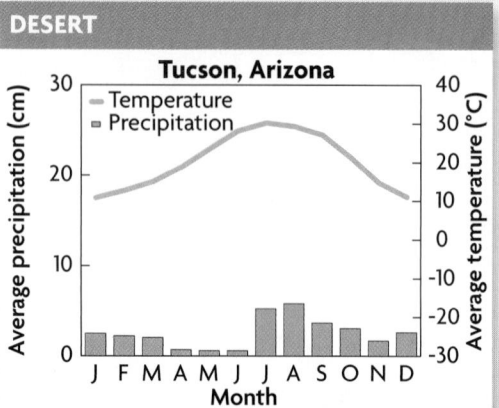

DESERT

Tucson, Arizona

Source: National Oceanic Atmospheric Administration

Tropical Rain Forest Biome

A tropical rain forest has warm temperatures and abundant precipitation throughout most, if not all, of the year. This climate typically produces lush, thick forests that can completely shade the forest floor. The limiting factor for plants that live on the forest floor is sunlight. In fact, as little as 1 percent of the sunlight that strikes the uppermost branches of the trees, called the **canopy,** may make it through to the ground. The soil is very thin and low in nutrients. Most organisms that live in this biome inhabit branches of the upper canopy. Some plants, called epiphytes, grow above the ground on the branches of trees. A few of these, such as some figs, sprout and develop on branches and then send down long lengths of roots that grow into the ground below.

Grassland Biomes

Grassland biomes occur in a variety of climates. A **grassland** is an area where the primary plant life is grass. Tropical grasslands are found in the tropical climate zones of South America, Africa, and Australia. Temperate grasslands are found in the temperate climate zones of South Africa, eastern Europe, and central North America.

Tropical grasslands, also called savannas, are covered with grass plants that may stand 1–2 meters (3–7 ft) in height. Some grasslands have scattered trees or shrubs, but the trees are never as thick and lush as in the tropical rain forests. The limiting factor in the savanna is rainfall. For five months or more each year, precipitation averages at most 10 centimeters (4 in.) a month; often there is much less. During the rainy season, however, water can replenish lakes, rivers, streams, and wetlands and form temporary ponds. This biome is home to plants and animals that have adapted to the extreme shifts in moisture.

Temperate grasslands receive 50–90 centimeters (20–35 in.) of annual precipitation, most occurring as rain in the late spring and early summer. Summers may be warm or quite hot, depending on the latitude of the grassland. Under such arid conditions, fast-spreading fires are common. Some plants in temperate grasslands have adapted to fire by producing fire-resistant seeds that require the fire's heat to start germination.

Desert Biome

Desert biomes receive less than 25 centimeters (10 in.) of precipitation annually, and are always characterized by a very dry, or arid, climate. There are four different types of deserts: hot, semiarid, coastal, and cold.

In hot deserts, such as the Sonoran Desert in Arizona, the daily summer temperature may easily top 38°C (100°F). At night, however, the temperature can drop by 10 degrees Celsius or more. During the winter, the temperature may be as low as 0°C (32°F). The precipitation falls as rain in hot deserts.

Semiarid deserts, like hot deserts, have long and dry summers and low amounts of rain in the winter. In comparison with hot deserts, however, temperatures are cooler and rarely exceed 38°C. Coastal deserts are characterized by cool winters followed by relatively long, warm summers. Temperatures range from a maximum of 35°C (95°F) in the summer to –4°C (25°F) in the winter. In cold deserts, such as the Great Basin of the western United States, precipitation falls evenly throughout the year and often occurs as snow in the winter. Summer temperatures range between 10°C (50°F) at night to 24°C (75°F) during the day, and winter temperatures can drop below freezing.

Plants use a variety of strategies to survive a desert's heat and lack of moisture. The reduced surface area of a cactus's spines helps it to retain more water by avoiding moisture loss from transpiration. Many desert plants have the ability to conserve or store water over a long period of time. Some desert plants, such as mesquite, have extremely long root systems that absorb water by reaching down to the water table. Desert plants also have heat- and drought-resistant seeds.

Contrast How do rainfall amounts differ in deserts and in tropical rain forests?

Temperate Forest Biomes

A key feature of temperate biomes is their distinguishable seasons. The growing season occurs during the warmer temperatures from mid-spring to mid-fall and depends upon the availability of water.

The **temperate deciduous forest** typically receives about 75–150 centimeters (30–59 in.) of precipitation spread over the entire year as rain or snow. This biome is characterized by hot summers and cold winters. **Deciduous** trees have adapted to winter temperatures by dropping their leaves and going dormant during the cold season. Trees, such as oaks, beeches, and maples, along with shrubs, lichens, and mosses, make up the main vegetation.

The **temperate rain forest** does not receive precipitation evenly spaced across the year. Instead, it has one long wet season and a relatively dry summer, during which fog and low-lying clouds provide the needed moisture. Precipitation in the temperate rain forest averages over 250 centimeters (98 in.) per year. Evergreen conifers, such as spruces, Douglas firs, and redwoods, dominate this biome. **Coniferous** trees retain their needles all year. Mosses, lichens, and ferns are plant species found on the forest floor.

Taiga Biome

The **taiga** (TY-guh), also known as the boreal forest, is located in cooler climates. Winters are long and cold, often lasting six months or more. The average winter temperature is below freezing. Summers are short, typically with only two to three months of frost-free days. However, they may be quite humid and warm, sometimes reaching 21°C (70°F). Precipitation in the taiga is 30–85 centimeters (12–33 in.) per year, which is similar to that in the arid temperate grasslands. Coniferous forest is dominant in the taiga.

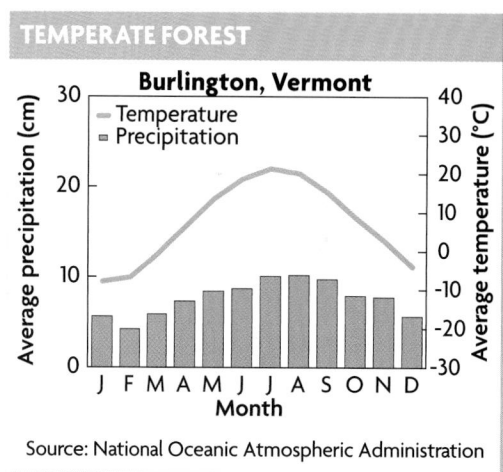

TEMPERATE FOREST

Source: National Oceanic Atmospheric Administration

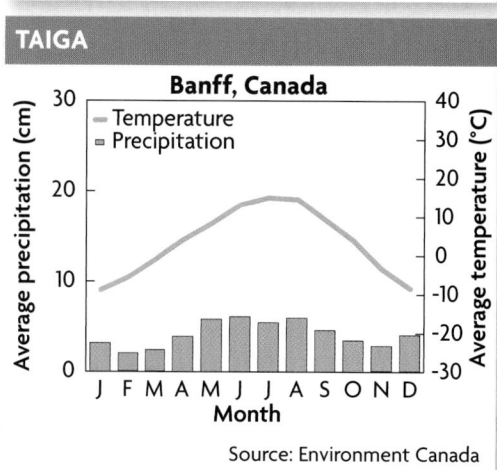

TAIGA

Source: Environment Canada

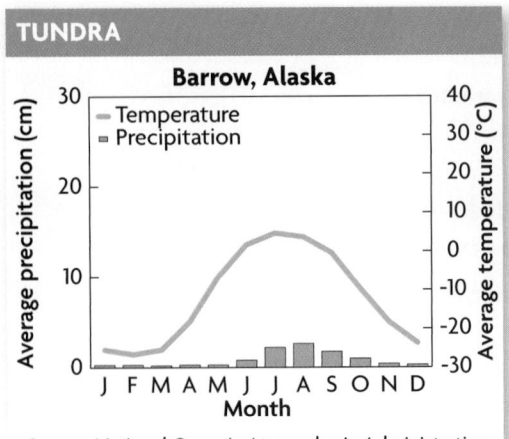

TUNDRA

Barrow, Alaska

Average precipitation (cm) / Average temperature (°C)

— Temperature
▪ Precipitation

J F M A M J J A S O N D
Month

Source: National Oceanic Atmospheric Administration

Tundra Biome

Often described as bleak, the **tundra** is located beyond the taiga in far northern latitudes. Winter lasts as long as 10 months a year. The average winter temperature is below freezing. The ground below the surface is always frozen. This frozen ground is known as permafrost. Summers last just 6 to 10 weeks. Precipitation is meager, averaging less than 13 centimeters (5 in.) annually.

In addition to limited precipitation, permafrost captures and holds moisture, making very little available to plants. Therefore, the tundra is quite barren. Only mosses, other tiny, low-lying plants, and a few scattered shrubs are able to survive. Trees and most flowering plants do not grow here.

Minor Biomes

In addition to the six major biomes, there are also some other biomes that occur globally, but on a smaller scale. One example is chaparral, shown in **FIGURE 15.8**. **Chaparral** (SHAP-uh-RAL), also called Mediterranean shrubland, is characterized by its hot, dry summers and cool, moist winters. Over the year, temperatures in the chaparral range from 10°C (50°F) to 40°C (104°F). Annual precipitation ranges from 38–102 centimeters (15–40 in.), and occurs mostly during the winter as rain. The dominant plants in the chaparral are small-leaved evergreen shrubs. This biome is found in small areas across the globe, including the central and southern coast of California in the western United States, the coast of Chile in South America, the Mediterranean Sea coast in Europe, the southern and western coasts of Australia, and the southwestern tip of South Africa. Because of the fairly hot climate, the plants in this biome exhibit some of the same adaptations to heat as those found in the desert biome. Many plants have shallow root systems that let them take in as much water as possible when it rains. The leaves of shrubs have thick cuticles that help in water retention. Many plant species, such as sage and rosemary, give off a strong smell. These aromatic oils are also highly flammable, and promote fire. As in temperate grasslands, chaparral plants have adapted to the presence of fire, and some plants need fire in order for their seeds to germinate.

Connect **What biome includes the area where you live?**

FIGURE 15.8 In the United States, chaparral is found along the central and southern coasts of California. This biome is characterized by hot, dry summers and cool, moist winters.

MAIN IDEA
Polar ice caps and mountains are not considered biomes.

Polar ice caps are ice-covered areas that have no soil and do not have a specific plant community. In mountains, the climate and the animal and plant communities change depending on elevation. Because of these characteristics, polar caps and mountains are not categorized as biomes.

Polar ice caps occur around the poles at the top and bottom of Earth. In the Northern Hemisphere, the polar ice cap includes parts of Greenland and permanently frozen portions of the Arctic Ocean and surrounding islands. In the Southern Hemisphere, the polar ice cap includes the glacier-covered continent of Antarctica. At the ice caps, ice and snow cover the surface all year. Very few plants or fungi are able to survive the harsh conditions found in the polar regions. Some species found in Antarctica include mosses and lichens. Most animals in this region depend on the sea for their food. Animals such as polar bears, shown in **FIGURE 15.9,** have layers of fat that keep them warm in the cold polar conditions. Different animals are found in the northern and southern polar regions. For example, polar bears are found only in the north, while penguins are found only in the south.

Mountains are often rich with life. Different communities of species have adapted to the variety of ecosystems found at different mountain elevations. As you move up a mountain, the different communities that you see are similar to the biomes found in different latitudes across the globe. For example, you may begin a hike in a grassland at the base of the mountain, continue upward through a coniferous forest, and finally reach a desolate tundralike zone at the mountain's top. While the life zones found on mountains are similar across biomes, their species of plants and animals differ as a result of the different abiotic factors that shape each biome.

FIGURE 15.9 A polar bear's thick layer of fat, or blubber, keeps it well insulated from the cold as it rests on an ice floe or swims in Arctic waters to catch food.

Summarize Explain why neither polar ice caps nor mountains are considered biomes.

15.3 / ASSESSMENT

ONLINE QUIZ
ClassZone.com

REVIEWING ▶ MAIN IDEAS

1. List and describe the six major biome types.

2. What are some characteristics of mountains and polar ice caps?

CRITICAL THINKING

3. **Predict** How might stopping fires change a temperate **grassland**?

4. **Infer** Polar bears have white fur but black skin underneath. Consider the climate in which the bears live. What might be the adaptive advantage of the bears' black skin?

Connecting CONCEPTS

5. **Animal Behavior** Male birds that migrate the earliest to their summer nesting sites can usually secure the best territories. What limiting factor keeps birds from arriving too early in the **taiga**?

Marine Ecosystems

KEY CONCEPT Marine ecosystems are global.

▶ MAIN IDEAS

- The ocean can be divided into zones.
- Coastal waters contain unique habitats.

VOCABULARY

intertidal zone, p. 468　　**zooplankton,** p. 469

neritic zone, p. 468　　**phytoplankton,** p. 469

bathyal zone, p. 469　　**coral reef,** p. 470

abyssal zone, p. 469　　**kelp forest,** p. 470

plankton, p. 469

MICHIGAN STANDARDS

L3.p3A Identify the factors in an ecosystem that influence fluctuations in population size. (prerequisite)

L3.p3D Predict how changes in one population might affect other populations based upon their relationships in a food web. (prerequisite)

FIGURE 15.10 Organisms that live in tidal pools, such as this one off the Washington coast, are adapted to habitats with constantly changing salt and moisture levels.

Connect If you've ever been to the ocean, you are already familiar with some ocean zones. If you walked on the beach at the edge of the surf, you were in the intertidal zone. If you went into the water, you were swimming in the neritic zone. In this section, you will learn about these and other zones that divide the ocean. You will also read about the unique habitats found along the ocean's coasts.

▶ MAIN IDEA

The ocean can be divided into zones.

The oceans are a global expanse of water containing a large variety of living things that dwell from coastline shallows to the great depths of the deep-sea vents.

Ocean Zones

Scientists use several systems to divide the ocean into different zones. The simplest division of the ocean separates the water of the open sea, or pelagic zone, from the ocean floor, which is called the benthic zone.

The presence of light is also used to differentiate between areas of the ocean. The photic zone is the portion of the ocean that receives plentiful sunlight. In contrast, the aphotic zone refers to the depths of the ocean where sunlight does not reach.

In a third system, as shown in **FIGURE 15.11,** the ocean is separated into zones using distance from the shoreline and water depth as dividing factors.

The **intertidal zone** is the strip of land between the high and low tide lines. If you have ever walked on the beach, you have been in the intertidal zone. Organisms in this zone, such as those that inhabit tidal pools, must tolerate a variety of conditions that result from changing water levels. Organisms must contend with changes in temperature, amount of moisture, and salinity. The sea anemone, for example, opens up when underwater during high tide. It avoids drying out during low tide by closing up.

The **neritic zone** (nuh-RIHT-ihk) extends from the intertidal zone out to the edge of the continental shelf. The depth of the neritic zone may range from a few centimeters at low tide to more than 200 meters deep.

FIGURE 15.11 Ocean Zones

The ocean is divided into four major zones.

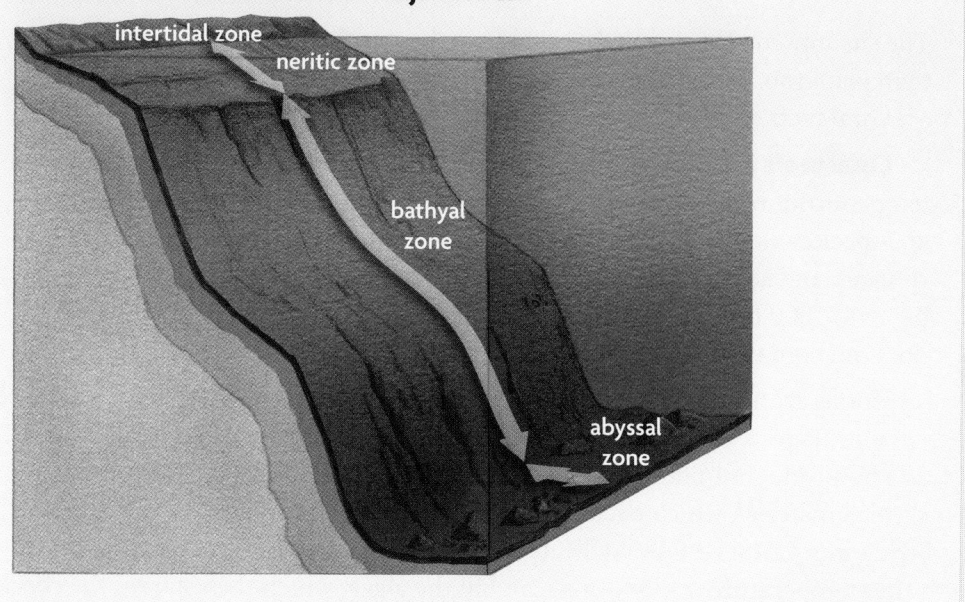

intertidal zone
neritic zone
bathyal zone
abyssal zone

The **bathyal zone** (BATH-ee-uhl) extends from the edge of the neritic zone to the base of the continental shelf. The bathyal zone lies between the depths of 200 and 2000 meters. This zone is characterized by water that is turbid, or murky, due to the accumulation of silt. Fish that have adapted to living in areas of high pressure live in the bathyal zone. Burrowing animals thrive in this zone.

The **abyssal zone** (uh-BIHS-uhl) lies below 2000 meters and is in complete darkness. While deep-sea vents support a large number of organisms, the total number of species found in this zone is much smaller than the number found in the neritic zone. Since there is no light, photosynthetic organisms do not exist. Chemosynthetic organisms are the base of the food webs at the deep-sea vents. Many organisms that live in the abyssal zone make their own light, much as a firefly produces its glow. This light is often used to attract mates and prey.

Life in the Neritic Zone

Although the neritic zone represents less than one-tenth of the total ocean area, it contains 40 times more biomass than the rest of the ocean. Much of the biomass consists of organisms called plankton. **Plankton** are tiny free-floating organisms that live in the water. These organisms include both animals and protists. **Zooplankton** is another term for animal plankton. **Phytoplankton** are photosynthetic plankton, which include microscopic protists such as algae.

Marine phytoplankton, especially blue-green algae and other types of algae, are critical to life on the planet. These organisms carry out the bulk of photosynthesis on Earth, and therefore provide most of the oxygen. According to many estimates, 70 percent or more of the oxygen in every breath you take can be traced back to marine phytoplankton. In addition to their role in oxygen production, phytoplankton also form the base of the oceanic food web.

Hypothesize What other adaptations might organisms have in the abyssal zone?

VOCABULARY

In the word *bathyal*, the prefix *bathy-* comes from a Greek word meaning "deep." In the word *abyssal*, the word part *abyss* comes from a Greek word meaning "bottomless."

Connecting CONCEPTS

Invertebrates Some invertebrates, such as sea stars and lobsters, are plankton during their larval stage. You will learn more about the life stages of invertebrates in **Chapter 23.**

MAIN IDEA
Coastal waters contain unique habitats.

The shallow coastal waters that make up the neritic zone contain much more than plankton. Two highly diverse habitats found within these coastal waters are coral reefs and kelp forests.

Coral reefs are found within the tropical climate zone. In this area, water temperatures remain warm all year. A single coral reef may be home to 50 to 400 species of corals, along with hundreds of other species, including fishes, sponges, and sea urchins. Studies indicate that the biomass in coral reefs may be up to 1000 times greater than the biomass in a similar area of ocean that does not contain a reef.

Corals are animals that have a mutualistic relationship with algae. The coral provides a home for the algae, and algae provide nutrients for the coral as a by-product of photosynthesis. Coral reefs are made mostly of coral skeletal material, which packs together over thousands of years into solid structures. Coral reefs are delicate. A change in conditions, such as increased water temperature or pollution, can kill the algae, which then starves the coral. With global ocean temperatures on the rise, coral reefs are in decline around the world.

Ecologists are trying to reintroduce these diverse communities in some areas by making artificial reefs, shown in **FIGURE 15.12**, where organisms can find shelter. In addition, some shipwrecks and sunken oil rigs have become artificial reefs that can support fishes and other species associated with coral reefs.

In contrast to coral reefs, **kelp forests** exist in cold, nutrient-rich waters, such as those found in California's Monterey Bay. These forests are composed of large communities of kelp, a seaweed. Kelp grows from the ocean floor up to the water's surface, sometimes extending up to a height of over 30 meters (about 100 ft). Kelp forests are areas of high productivity that provide habitat and food sources to many marine species ranging from tiny invertebrates to large mammals, such as sea lions.

Compare What are the similarities between coral reefs and kelp forests?

FIGURE 15.12 Ecologists are working to rebuild coral reef ecosystems by building artificial reefs, such as this network of cables, onto which corals can adhere.

scilinks.org
To learn more about coral reefs, visit scilinks.org.
Keycode: MLB015

15.4 ASSESSMENT

ONLINE QUIZ
ClassZone.com

REVIEWING ▶ MAIN IDEAS

1. What criteria do scientists use to divide the ocean into different zones?

2. What conditions account for the development of highly diverse habitats in coastal waters?

CRITICAL THINKING

3. **Connect** A red tide occurs when a bloom of **plankton** causes a reddish discoloration of coastal ocean waters. What might cause such an increase in plankton populations?

4. **Predict** What might organisms that inhabit the **abyssal zone** eat?

Connecting CONCEPTS

5. **Food Webs** How might the disappearance of coastal habitats affect an oceanic food web?

15.5 Estuaries and Freshwater Ecosystems

KEY CONCEPT Freshwater ecosystems include estuaries as well as flowing and standing water.

MAIN IDEAS

- Estuaries are dynamic environments where rivers flow into the ocean.
- Freshwater ecosystems include moving and standing water.
- Ponds and lakes share common features.

VOCABULARY

estuary, p. 471
watershed, p. 473
littoral zone, p. 474
limnetic zone, p. 474
benthic zone, p. 474

Review
ecosystem

MICHIGAN STANDARDS

L3.p2C Describe the role of decomposers in the transfer of energy in an ecosystem. (prerequisite)

L2.p4A Classify different organisms based on how they obtain energy for growth and development. (prerequisite)

Connect You rely on aquatic ecosystems more than you might realize. Many of the fish and shellfish that you might eat depend, at least for a part of their lives, on estuaries. But more importantly for you, freshwater ecosystems provide the water that you need to survive.

MAIN IDEA

Estuaries are dynamic environments where rivers flow into the ocean.

An **estuary** is a partially enclosed body of water formed where a river flows into an ocean. The San Francisco and Chesapeake bays are estuaries. So are the Louisiana bayous, Florida Bay in the Everglades, and many other harbors, sounds, and inlets around the world.

The distinctive feature of an estuary is the mixture of fresh water from a river with salt water from the ocean. The river carries high levels of nutrients from inland areas. The tidal movements of water in the ocean also bring in large volumes of organic matter and a variety of marine species from the ocean. Large numbers of species thrive in this rich mixture of fresh water and salt water.

Estuaries are highly productive ecosystems, on a level comparable to tropical rain forests and coral reefs. Photosynthetic organisms thrive in estuaries throughout the year, providing the basis for the aquatic food web. Estuaries also have thriving detritivore communities that decompose the enormous amounts of dead plant and animal matter that build up in the estuary's waters. These decomposers return vital nutrients back to the ecosystem. Estuaries also provide the necessary habitat for a number of endangered and threatened species. For example, the brown pelican, the Morro Bay kangaroo rat, and a plant called the Morro manzanita are all threatened or endangered species that depend on the Morro Bay estuary in California, shown in **FIGURE 15.13**.

FIGURE 15.13 An estuary occurs where a river flows into the ocean. Estuaries are high in biodiversity and provide habitat for a number of different species.

FIGURE 15.14 The Tejo Estuary in Portugal is an important stop-over point for migratory birds such as these greater flamingos.

Connecting CONCEPTS

Keystone Species Recall from **Chapter 13** that a keystone species is a species that has a large effect on its ecosystem. Migratory birds in the Delaware Bay depend on horseshoe crab eggs as a main food source. This dependence illustrates the importance of the horseshoe crab in its estuarine ecosystem.

Estuary Characteristics

The large number of phytoplankton and zooplankton in an estuary support a variety of species. Populations of fish and crustaceans depend on plankton as their primary food source. In turn, birds and other secondary consumers eat fish and crustaceans. Humans also rely on estuaries as a food source. In fact, 75 percent of the fish we eat depend on estuary ecosystems, making estuaries an important resource for the commercial fishing industry.

Estuaries provide a protected refuge for many species. Reefs and barrier islands along an estuary's boundary with the ocean protect estuary species from storms and the ocean's strong currents and waves. In an estuary's calm waters, many aquatic species lay eggs, and their young mature there before venturing into the ocean. The use of estuaries as spawning grounds explains why these areas are often called nurseries of the sea. Estuaries are also a key part of the migration paths of many bird species, as shown in **FIGURE 15.14**. Birds rely on estuaries as a refuge from the cold weather that occurs in the northern parts of their range during certain parts of the year.

Changing conditions in estuaries present challenges for species that live there. For example, in order to withstand changing salinities, some organisms have glands that remove the excess salt that builds up in their bodies. This adaptation helps organisms cope with an estuary's changing salinity level. Salt levels may lower with the tide and during periods of drought or heavy rainfall.

Threats to Estuary Ecosystems

Estuaries are made up of a variety of ecosystems, including salt marshes, mud flats, open water, mangrove forests, and tidal pools. When estuaries are lost to land development and other human activities, these ecosystems and the organisms that live within them are also lost.

The removal of estuaries also makes coastal areas more vulnerable to flood damage from catastrophic storms such as hurricanes. Estuaries act as a buffer between the ocean and coastal land. In some coastal areas of the United States, over 80 percent of the original estuary habitat has been lost to land development.

Analyze What characteristics make an estuary such a productive ecosystem?

MAIN IDEA

Freshwater ecosystems include moving and standing water.

Rivers and streams are the flowing bodies of fresh water that serve as paths through many different ecosystems. Rivers and streams, along with lakes and ponds, originate from watersheds. A **watershed** is a region of land that drains into a river, a river system, or another body of water.

Freshwater Ecosystems

If you have ever paddled down a river in a canoe, you have probably witnessed the change in shoreline ecosystems, perhaps with a forest along one stretch and sand dunes along another. Along its course, a river may vary in many ways. For example, the speed of its flow is greater in narrow areas than in wide ones. The river bottom may be alternately sandy, gravel-covered, or rock-strewn. The water level may differ across seasons. In some areas, spring brings about the melting of snow and causes river water levels to rise. Humans also affect water levels by damming rivers or by draining water for irrigation or drinking water.

Unlike rivers and streams, wetlands have very little water flowing through them. A wetland is an area of land that is saturated by ground or surface water for at least part of the year. Bogs, marshes, and swamps are different types of wetlands that are identified by their plant communities. Common wetland plants include cattails, duckweed, and sedges.

Like estuaries, wetlands are among the most productive ecosystems on Earth. They provide a home for a large number of species, some of which are only found in wetlands. Wetlands also help maintain a clean water supply. A wetland filters dirty water and renews underground stores of water.

Adaptations of Freshwater Organisms

The particular variety of freshwater organisms found in a body of water depends on a number of factors. These factors include water temperature, oxygen levels, pH, and the water flow rate. Each type of freshwater ecosystem is home to species with adaptations suited to its conditions. In fast-moving rivers, for example, trout are adapted to swim against the current. They have streamlined bodies that can slice through the water easily. Some aquatic insects, such as the stonefly, have hooks on their bodies. The stonefly uses the hooks to attach itself to a solid surface in fast-running water to avoid being swept away. Similarly, tadpoles that live in fast-running water often have sucker mouths that they use to attach to a surface while feeding. These tadpoles also have streamlined bodies with long tails and low fins that help them to move in the fast water. Tadpoles that live in pools or in slower moving water often lack sucker mouths and have more rounded bodies and higher fins.

FIGURE 15.15 As the Colorado River travels southward from Colorado to Mexico, it flows through different ecosystems, including forests and deserts.

Predict **What effect would the construction of a dam have on a river ecosystem?**

Animated
BIOLOGY
Watch how the water and nutrients in a lake turn over at ClassZone.com.

FIGURE 15.16 In the spring and fall, the water in a lake turns over, bringing nutrients from the bottom of the lake to the top.

▶ **MAIN IDEA**

Ponds and lakes share common features.

Although they are much smaller in size than oceans, freshwater ponds and lakes are also divided into zones. Scientists use the terms *littoral, limnetic,* and *benthic* to identify and separate these zones.

- The freshwater **littoral zone** is similar to the oceanic intertidal zone, and it is located between the high and low water marks along the shoreline. The waters of the littoral zone are well-lit, warm, and shallow. A diverse set of organisms, including water lilies, dragonflies, and snails, live in this zone.
- The **limnetic zone** (also called the pelagic zone) refers to the open water located farther out from shore. This zone is characterized by an abundance of plankton communities, which support populations of fish.
- The **benthic zone** is the lake or pond bottom, where less sunlight reaches. Decomposers, such as bacteria, live in the mud and sand of the benthic zone.

During the summer and the winter, the water temperature within a lake is stratified, which means that different layers of the lake have different temperatures. In the summer, water is warmer near the surface and colder at the bottom of the lake. These warm and cold regions are separated by a thin zone called the thermocline.

All of the water within a lake "turns over" periodically. This happens because water is most dense at 4°C (39°F). When water reaches this temperature, it will sink beneath water that is either warmer or cooler. In autumn, colder air temperatures cool the surface layer of water to 4°C, causing it to sink and mix with the water underneath. During the winter, the surface layer of water cools to less than 4°C. In the spring, when the surface water warms to 4°C, it sinks and mixes with the layers of water below. In both autumn and spring, the underlying water flows upward and switches places with the surface water. This upwelling brings nutrients such as bits of decaying plants and animals from the benthic zone to the surface, where they are eaten by surface-dwelling organisms.

Analyze **What is the significance of lake turnover to the lake ecosystem?**

15.5 ASSESSMENT

ONLINE QUIZ
ClassZone.com

REVIEWING ▶ MAIN IDEAS

1. What are the characteristics of an **estuary** ecosystem?

2. What abiotic factors might affect a river ecosystem?

3. How is a lake different from the ocean? How is it the same?

CRITICAL THINKING

4. **Compare and Contrast** How are coastal wetlands different from and similar to estuaries?

5. **Predict** If an oil spill wipes out most of the producers in an estuary, how might the food web in the surrounding area be affected?

Connecting CONCEPTS

6. **Adaptation** Many fish species and other aquatic animals have colorations that closely resemble the rocks or silt found on the bottom of their aquatic habitat. What types of ecological advantages might such an adaptation give an aquatic species?

MATERIALS

- 2 plastic bowls
- sample water and sediment
- 500 mL beaker
- Elodea leaves
- wax paper
- plastic food wrap
- large rubber band
- warm water bath
- cold water bath
- 2 thermometers
- dissolved oxygen kits
- pH strips

PROCESS SKILLS

- **Designing Experiments**
- **Collecting Data**
- **Analyzing Data**

MICHIGAN STANDARDS

B1.1B Evaluate the uncertainties or validity of scientific conclusions using an understanding of sources of measurement error, the challenges of controlling variables, accuracy of data analysis, logic of argument, logic of experimental design, and/or the dependence on underlying assumptions.

B1.1C Conduct scientific investigations using appropriate tools and techniques (e.g., selecting an instrument that measures the desired quantity—length, volume, weight, time interval, temperature—with the appropriate level of precision).

Winter Water Chemistry

Seasonal changes in temperature cause changes in lake ecosystems and the organisms that live there. Chemical cycles can vary from winter to summer, and the presence of ice on the surface of a lake also can alter oxygen levels. In this lab, you will design an experiment that models the conditions of lake water in the summer and in the winter. You will collect data from both models to determine how a layer of surface ice can affect lake water chemistry.

PROBLEM How does a layer of winter ice affect the chemistry of lake water?

DESIGN YOUR EXPERIMENT

1. Using the materials listed, design an experiment to determine differences between lake water chemistry in winter conditions and in summer conditions. Keep in mind that dissolved oxygen and pH are two variables that are influenced by lake surface ice.

2. Write a procedure to explain how you will set up your experiment, and which variable you will test. Identify a control group and experimental group, the data you will collect, and how often you will collect it.

3. Have your experimental design approved by your teacher.

4. Design a table to organize your results.

5. Conduct your experiment.

ANALYZE AND CONCLUDE

1. **Graph Data** Determine the best way to present how the variable in the experimental group changed over time. Determine whether you should draw a line graph or a bar graph, and then construct that type of graph.

2. **Analyze Data** How did the variable in each experimental group change over time? Why did these changes occur? What differences occurred between the two set-ups? What accounts for these differences?

3. **Experimental Design** What discrepancies exist between your simulation of summer and winter water conditions and real conditions? How might these discrepancies affect your results?

4. **Communicate** Discuss your results with other groups. Are the trends in their results similar to yours? If not, compare your experimental designs. Can any differences in experimental design or procedure account for differences in results? As a class, discuss what factors in this experiment are most important to obtaining accurate results.

5. **Apply** Review your data. How would the changes in the chemistry of the water affect aquatic organisms?

EXTEND YOUR INVESTIGATION

Design an experiment in which you would track the changes in these variables in a real lake over a year. Include information on how you would measure the effects of the changes on the organisms living in the lake. What other variables, besides dissolved oxygen and pH, would you want to track as part of this experiment?

Use these inquiry-based labs and online activities to deepen your understanding about the biosphere.

MICHIGAN STANDARDS

L3.p2B Describe common ecological relationships between and among species and their environments (competition, territory, carrying capacity, natural balance, population, dependence, survival, and other biotic and abiotic factors). (prerequisite)

L3.p3B Distinguish between the living (biotic) and nonliving (abiotic) components of an ecosystem. (prerequisite)

INVESTIGATION

Modeling Biomes

You have already learned about the characteristics of Earth's different biomes, including temperature ranges and how much water and light they receive. In this lab, you will model several biomes.

SKILL Modeling

PROBLEM What types of plants grow in certain biomes?

PROCEDURE

1. Choose two of the following biomes to model: desert, grassland, or tropical rain forest.

2. Choose which soil you will use in each biome and which seeds you will plant in each. Decide how much light and water each biome will receive each day. Determine how you will measure which type of plant grows in each biome.

3. Determine what type of data you need to collect and how often you need to collect it; construct a data table to record the data you collect.

MATERIALS

- cardboard container
- scissors
- stapler
- plastic or aluminum tray
- sandy soil
- potting soil
- 30 wheatgrass seeds
- 10 lima bean seeds
- 5 sunflower seeds
- permanent marker
- masking tape
- water
- light source
- refrigerator
- metric ruler

ANALYZE AND CONCLUDE

1. **Analyze** How did seed growth differ between the biomes? Which seeds were the most and least successful? Under which conditions did these situations occur?

2. **Experimental Design** What other variables could you control to make your model biomes as realistic as possible?

3. **Synthesize** How would you model an aquatic biome such as a wetland or a lake?

Heating and Cooling Rates of Water and Soil

Water and soil have many different qualities. One quality is the rate at which each substance heats up and cools down. In this lab, you will compare the heating and cooling rates of water and soil.

SKILL Comparing

MATERIALS

- marker
- 2 clear plastic cups
- ruler
- soil
- water at room temperature
- 2 thermometers
- lamp

PROBLEM What are the heating and cooling rates of water and soil?

PROCEDURE

1. Mark a line 3 centimeters from the bottom of each cup. Fill one cup to the line with water and the other with soil.

2. Design a table in which to record your data.

3. Place a thermometer into the contents of each cup. Allow the thermometer to sit in each cup for 3 minutes, then take an initial temperature reading. Record your data in your data table.

4. Put the cups side by side under a lamp. Do not allow the lamp bulb to touch the water. Keep all electrical cords away from the water. After 15 minutes, record the temperature in each cup.

5. Turn off the lamp and move the cups away from the lamp to simulate shade. After 15 minutes, record the temperature in each cup.

ANALYZE AND CONCLUDE

1. **Analyze Data** Which substance had the faster rate of heating? Which had the faster rate of cooling?

2. **Apply** How do the heating and cooling rates of water and soil affect aquatic and land ecosystems?

3. **Connect** How do the differences in heating and cooling rates affect climates of coastal cities?

ANIMATED BIOLOGY
Where Do They Live?

Species have adapted to life in specific ocean zones. Use their adaptations as well as other clues to place organisms in the appropriate ocean environments.

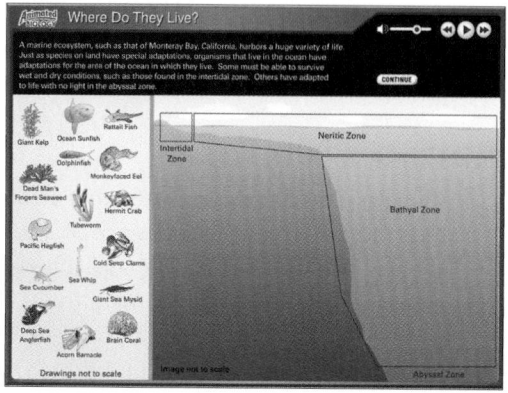

WEBQUEST

In this chapter you read overviews of the major ecosystems on Earth. Use this WebQuest to focus on one ecosystem and dig further. Explore the organisms, geology, soils, climate, and other characteristics specific to that environment. Then compare that ecosystem with your observations of the one in which you live.

DATA ANALYSIS ONLINE

Amphibians are found all over the world, but they are not evenly distributed. Some areas have many more types of amphibians than others. Graph the number of known amphibian species by region and analyze the distribution.

15.1 Life in the Earth System

The biosphere is one of Earth's four interconnected systems. The biosphere includes living organisms, called the biota, and the land, air, and water on Earth where the biota live. Biotic and abiotic factors interact in the biosphere, and a change in one Earth system can affect the others.

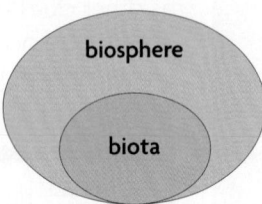

15.2 Climate

Climate is a key abiotic factor that affects the biosphere. Factors that influence an area's climate include temperature, sunlight, water, and wind. The three main climate zones on Earth are polar, tropical, and temperate. The polar zone is located at the far northern and far southern reaches of the planet. The tropical zone surrounds the equator. The temperate zone is located in the broad area between the polar and tropical zones.

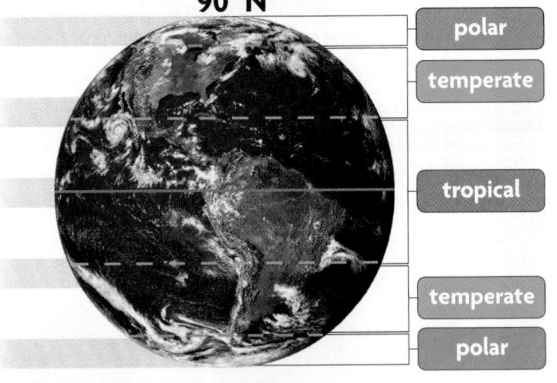

90° N

polar
temperate
tropical
temperate
polar

15.3 Biomes

Biomes are land-based, global communities of organisms. Earth has six major biomes. These biomes include tropical rain forest, grassland, desert, temperate forest, taiga, and tundra. Polar ice caps and mountains are not considered biomes.

15.4 Marine Ecosystems

Marine ecosystems are global. Scientists use different criteria to separate the ocean into different zones. One system separates the ocean into zones using distance from the shoreline and water depth as dividing factors. The neritic zone contains 40 times more biomass than the open ocean. Coral reefs are found in the warm, shallow waters of the tropical climate zone. Kelp forests thrive in cold, nutrient-rich waters.

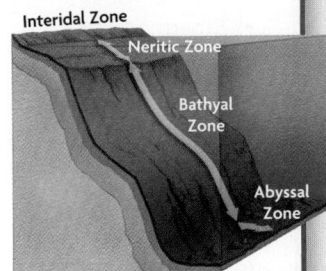

Interidal Zone
Neritic Zone
Bathyal Zone
Abyssal Zone

15.5 Estuaries and Freshwater Ecosystems

Freshwater ecosystems include estuaries as well as flowing and standing water. An estuary is a partially enclosed body of water that exists where a river flows into an ocean. A variety of organisms are adapted to the constant change in salinity found in an estuarine ecosystem. Freshwater ecosystems include rivers and streams, wetlands, and lakes and ponds.

Synthesize Your Notes

Concept Map Use a concept map to summarize what you know about climate zones.

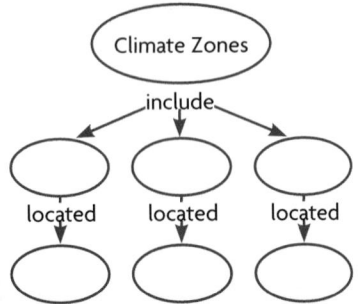

Climate Zones
include
located   located   located

Supporting Main Ideas Use a diagram like the one below to summarize what you know about biomes.

Earth has six major biomes.

Tropical rain forests are warm and have abundant precipitation year-round.

Chapter Assessment

Chapter Vocabulary

15.1 biosphere, p. 456
biota, p. 456
hydrosphere, p. 456
atmosphere, p. 456
geosphere, p. 456

15.2 climate, p. 458
microclimate, p. 458

15.3 canopy, p. 464
grassland, p. 464

desert, p. 464
deciduous, p. 465
coniferous, p. 465
taiga, p. 465
tundra, p. 466
chaparral, p. 466

15.4 intertidal zone, p. 468
neritic zone p. 468
bathyal zone, p. 469
abyssal zone, p. 469

plankton, p. 469
zooplankton, p. 469
phytoplankton, p. 469
coral reef, p. 470
kelp forest, p. 470

15.5 estuary, p. 471
watershed, p. 473
littoral zone, p. 474
limnetic zone, p. 474
benthic zone, p. 474

Reviewing Vocabulary

Compare and Contrast

Describe one similarity and one difference between the two terms in each of the following pairs.

1. biosphere, biota
2. zooplankton, phytoplankton
3. hydrosphere, atmosphere
4. climate, microclimate
5. taiga, tundra
6. neritic, intertidal
7. kelp forest, coral reef

Greek and Latin Word Origins

8. The term *plankton* comes from the Greek word *planktos*, which means "wandering." Explain how this meaning relates to plankton.

9. The term *climate* comes from the Greek word *klima*, which means "surface of the earth." Explain how this meaning relates to the definition of *climate*.

10. The term *estuary* comes from the Latin word *æstus*, which means "tide" or "surges." Using this meaning, explain how it relates to what an estuary is.

11. The term *littoral* comes from the Latin word *litoralis*, meaning "shore." Explain how this meaning relates to the definition of *littoral zone*.

12. The term *deciduous* comes from the Latin word *decidere*, which means "to fall off." How is this meaning related to the definition of *deciduous*?

Reviewing MAIN IDEAS

13. Explain the difference between the terms *biota*, *biosphere*, and *biome*.

14. After a forest fire wipes out plants growing on a hill, rainwater washes soil down into a stream, and the stream fills with silt. In this example, what are the interactions between biotic and abiotic factors?

15. If the temperature in an area drops five degrees between one day and the next, has the climate of the area changed? Explain.

16. What is the connection between sunlight, the curved shape of Earth, and Earth's three main climate zones?

17. Earth has six major biomes—tropical rain forest, grassland, desert, temperate forest, taiga, and tundra. Why are two different deserts, each on a separate continent, considered to be the same biome?

18. Why are polar caps and mountains not considered biomes?

19. Briefly compare the four ocean zones—intertidal, neritic, bathyal, and abyssal—based on their distance from the shoreline and their water depth.

20. Where, in terms of water depth, would you expect to find a coral reef? a kelp forest?

21. Estuaries occur where rivers flow into the ocean. What conditions in estuaries make them suitable as nurseries for organisms that live out in the open ocean as adults?

22. The ecosystem of a river upstream in the mountains and downstream in a valley can be very different. Describe the adaptations of an upstream organism and an organism that lives downstream in the same river.

23. Apply A deer drinks water from a stream, and then later it breathes out some of the water as vapor into the air. Through which three Earth spheres has this water moved?

24. Infer How would Earth's three main climate zones be different if Earth's axis were not tilted in relation to the Sun? (**Hint:** The tropical climate zone would likely be the most similar to how it is now.)

25. Infer Do you think it is possible for a biome to change from one type into another? Explain a situation in which this might happen.

26. Connect Why does the health of an entire coral reef ecosystem depend on algae?

27. Analyze Describe two reasons why it is critical to protect estuary ecosystems.

Interpreting Visuals

Use the diagram of a rocky intertidal zone to answer the next three questions.

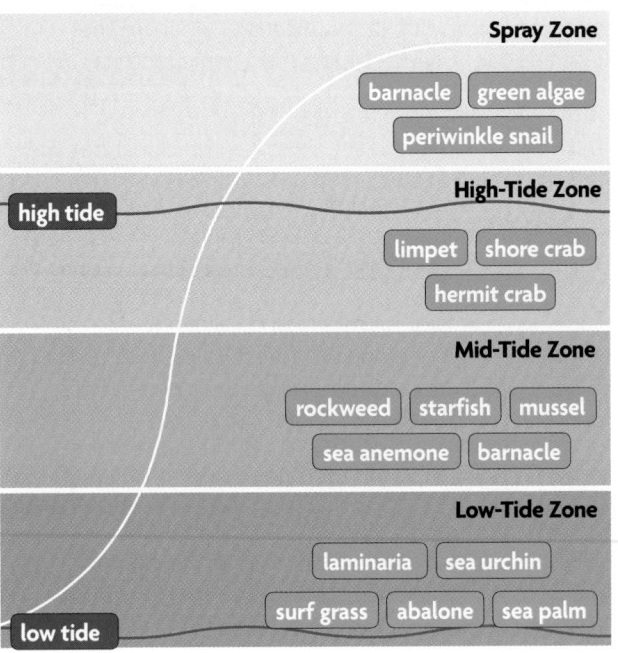

28. Predict How do you think the organisms above the high-tide mark are able to obtain the water they need to survive?

29. Compare What adaptations are necessary for a species to survive in the spray zone compared with a species in the low-tide zone?

30. Hypothesize Why do you think there aren't any fish shown in the diagram? Why wouldn't fish be a major part of the rocky intertidal zone?

Analyzing Data

Below is a climatogram for the city of Portland, Oregon. Use the graph to answer the next four questions.

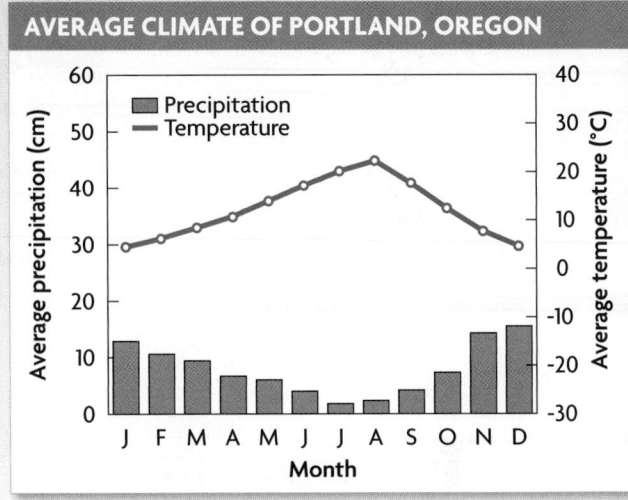

Source: National Oceanic Atmospheric Administration

31. Analyze Which month receives the highest amount of rain? the highest temperature?

32. Summarize Describe in one or two sentences the climate of Portland throughout the year.

33. Analyze A family is planning to vacation in Portland. Many of their planned activities occur outdoors. If they wish to avoid rain, in which month should they travel?

34. Connect Based on the data in the graph, which biome is Portland a part of? Explain your choice.

Connecting CONCEPTS

35. Write a Policy The majority of the wetlands in the United States have been drained and used for development. A company has submitted a proposal to purchase an area of 100 acres of wetland that it plans to develop. If you were an official in the area, how would you respond to this proposal? What would you say to a local environmental group that opposes the proposal? What might be a possible compromise? Use information from the chapter to convince your fellow elected officials to take your position.

36. Synthesize Reread the information about the temperate rain forest at the beginning of the chapter. Using your knowledge of climate, biomes, and evolution, explain why different species are found in temperate and tropical rain forests.

MICHIGAN
STANDARDS-BASED ASSESSMENT

✓ **Test Practice**
For more test practice,
go to ClassZone.com.

1.

Thompson, Canada

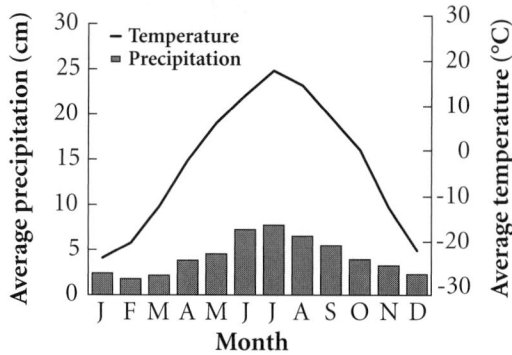

This graph shows the average monthly temperature and precipitation for a location in Canada. What can you conclude from these data? **B1.1E**

A An increase in temperature causes an increase in precipitation.

B An increase in precipitation causes an increase in temperature.

C Temperature and precipitation both peak in the month of July.

D It never rains more than 5 cm per month.

2. Over thousands of years, the plant life in a region gradually changes from plants with lush green foliage to hardy, deep-rooted plants adapted to dry conditions. This shift is most likely the result of a change in **L3.p2B**

A predators.

B climate.

C sunlight.

D weather.

3. Tropical rain forests have the greatest number of species of any biome. However, the alteration of rain forest habitats into farmland threatens to decrease this **L3.p4A**

A biomass.

B biosphere.

C bioindicator.

D biodiversity.

4. The Yucatan rain forest and the Sahara desert exist at the same latitudes in the tropical zone, but the Yucatan is humid and the Sahara is dry. Which of the following statements best accounts for this difference? **L3.p3B**

A Climate patterns affect their rainfall differently.

B Plant life adds moisture to the rain forest air.

C The sun is hotter in deserts, drying out the air.

D The weather is less predictable in deserts.

5.

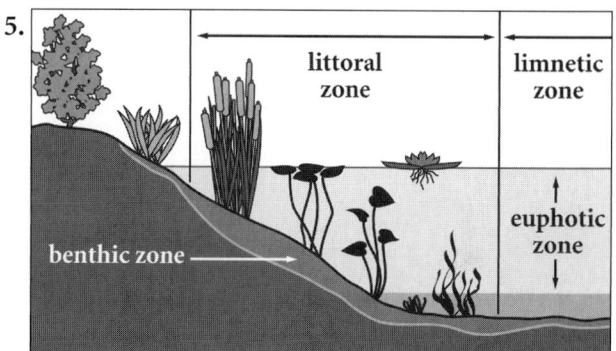

This diagram shows the zones that exist in freshwater lakes. In the benthic zone, dead organic material is converted into nutrients that can be used by other organisms. What type of organisms carry out this conversion? **L3.p2C**

A decomposers

B consumers

C carnivores

D producers

6. High concentrations of sediment in the water can block out sunlight needed by aquatic plants for photosynthesis. This condition will most likely result in **L3.p3A**

A increased concentrations of nitrogen.

B decreased concentrations of nitrogen.

C increased concentrations of oxygen.

D decreased concentrations of oxygen.

THINK THROUGH THE QUESTION

Think about what is produced and what is consumed during photosynthesis. If rates of photosynthesis decrease, the products of photosynthesis will decrease in the ecosystem.

16 Human Impact on Ecosystems

KEY CONCEPTS

16.1 Human Population Growth and Natural Resources

As the human population grows, the demand for Earth's resources increases.

16.2 Air Quality

Fossil fuel emissions affect the biosphere.

16.3 Water Quality

Pollution of Earth's freshwater supply threatens habitat and health.

16.4 Threats to Biodiversity

The impact of a growing human population threatens biodiversity.

16.5 Conservation

Conservation methods can help protect and restore ecosystems.

Online BIOLOGY CLASSZONE.COM

Animated BIOLOGY

View animated chapter concepts.
• Human Population Growth
• Global Warming
• Human Effects on a Food Web

BIOZINE

Keep current with biology news.
• Featured stories
• News feeds
• Polls

RESOURCE CENTER

Get more information on
• Global Warming
• Introduced Species
• Sustainable Development

What happened to this forest?

Connecting **CONCEPTS**

This once lush hillside has been destroyed by acid rain. Emissions from a nearby steel plant release chemical compounds that change the natural pH of rain, forming acid rain. Not only does acid rain damage leaves and branches, but because it lowers soil pH, it can damage plant root systems and kill useful microorganisms that release nutrients from dead organic material.

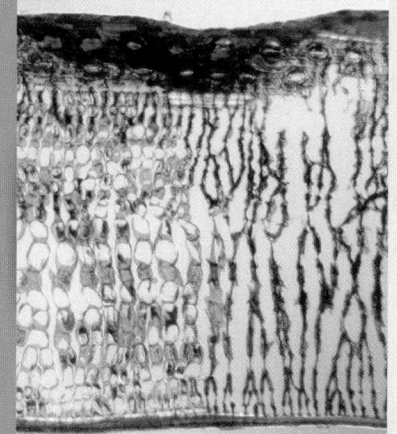

Plant Cells The acidity of rain affects plants at the cellular level. As you can see in this cross-section of a leaf, the plant cells on the left are healthy, but the cells on the right have been greatly damaged by water with a lowered pH. Acid rain destroys cell walls and can damage or even kill plants. (LM; magnification 30×)

16.1 Human Population Growth and Natural Resources

KEY CONCEPT As the human population grows, the demand for Earth's resources increases.

▶ MAIN IDEA

- Earth's human population continues to grow.
- The growing human population exerts pressure on Earth's natural resources.
- Effective management of Earth's resources will help meet the needs of the future.

VOCABULARY

nonrenewable resource, p. 485
renewable resource, p. 485
ecological footprint, p. 487

Review
carrying capacity, population, limiting factor

Animated BIOLOGY

Watch human population growth over time at ClassZone.com.

FIGURE 16.1 WORLD POPULATION

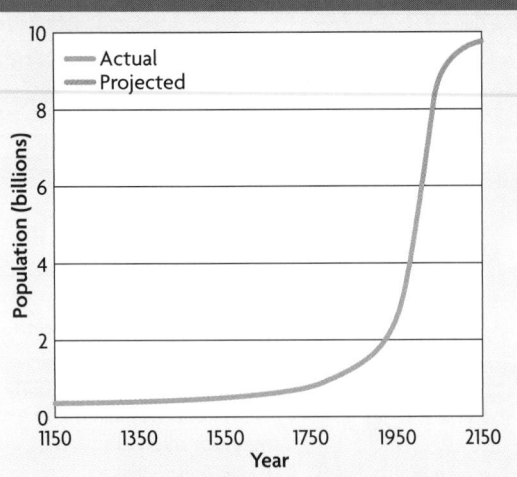

Source: United Nations, World Population Prospects, Population Reference Bureau

Connect Humans depend upon Earth's nutrient and energy cycles. We harness Earth's energy to power our televisions, radios, streetlights, automobiles, airplanes—and everything else in our homes and cities. Your cotton T-shirt and this paper page came from plants that depend on Earth's nutrient cycles. The water you drink comes from water sources replenished by the hydrologic cycle. We do not just use Earth's cycles, we are a part of Earth's cycles. Everything we eat, drink, and use comes from Earth. But the overuse of resources and the production of waste can cause disruptions in the energy and nutrient cycles of Earth.

▶ MAIN IDEA

Earth's human population continues to grow.

How many people can Earth support? In other words, what is the carrying capacity for humans on Earth? Recall that carrying capacity refers to the maximum population size that an environment can consistently support.

Earth's Carrying Capacity

Our predictions of Earth's human carrying capacity have changed over time. In the late 1700s, a young economist named Thomas Malthus wrote a controversial essay in which he claimed that the human population was growing faster than Earth's resources could support. Today, scientists use his observations and predictions when they are describing the concept of an ecosystem's carrying capacity. In Malthus's lifetime, the world population was around 1 billion. The graph in **FIGURE 16.1** shows how population size has changed over time. Today's human population of more than 6 billion has exceeded many earlier predictions. In the future, will Earth support 10 billion people, 20 billion, or even 50 billion people? Although we do not know of a fixed limit to the number of people that Earth can support, some limit must exist—Earth cannot support an infinite number of people.

Technology and Human Population

Recall that the carrying capacity of an environment can change as the environment changes. As humans have modified their environment through agriculture, transportation, medical advances, and sanitation, the carrying capacity of Earth has greatly increased.

Technologies developed by humans have allowed Earth to support many more people than Malthus could ever have imagined. Gas-powered farm equipment, for example, made possible the production of huge quantities of food—much more than could be produced by human and animal power. Medical advances have also contributed to population growth. For example, infant mortality rates in the United States have dropped steadily over the last 70 years. In 1940, more than 40 infants died for every 1000 births. In 2002, only 7 infants died in 1000 births. Antibiotics and antiseptic cleaners have lowered infant mortality and the spread of diseases.

For a moment, think about how much we depend on technology. How have human lives changed with the help of plumbing to bring fresh water into homes and to take human waste out of homes? What if there were no transportation to move food and materials around the globe? What if there were no medicines? How many people could Earth support without electricity or gas, or if all construction had to be done by hand? Technological advances have allowed for continued human population growth.

Connect What technologies do you depend on each day?

TAKING NOTES

Use a diagram to summarize how technology has helped the human population grow.

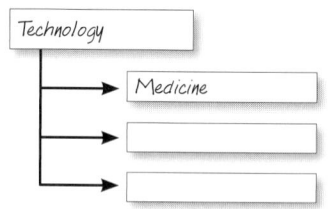

● MAIN IDEA

The growing human population exerts pressure on Earth's natural resources.

Two resources, oil and coal, currently support the majority of our country's energy use. Oil and coal are the result of natural processes. Over millions of years, natural processes transformed dead organisms into the concentrated carbon substances we use today as oil and coal. Oil and coal are **nonrenewable resources** because they are used faster than they form. In 2006, the human population was using oil at a rate of about 77 million barrels per day, and world oil use continues to rise. The growing use of this limited resource will lead to energy crises in the decades ahead unless technologies are developed to use other forms of energy.

Not all resources are nonrenewable. Resources that cannot be used up or can replenish themselves over time are called **renewable resources.** For example, wind energy—captured by wind turbines such as those shown in **FIGURE 16.2**—and solar energy are renewable resources because they cannot be used up by humans. Other resources, such as those that come from plants and animals, can be used up, but because they could last indefinitely through regrowth and reproduction, they are renewable. As long as these resources are replenished faster than they are used, they are considered renewable. But if renewable resources are not used carefully, they can become nonrenewable.

FIGURE 16.2 Giant wind turbines such as these capture renewable energy from Earth's natural processes.

Drinking water is a renewable resource, but pollution and overuse threaten its supply. Pesticides, industrial waste, and other contaminants have been found in water sources that supply tens of millions of people across the United States with fresh water. Groundwater is also being extracted from aquifers faster than it is replaced.

As Earth's human population continues to grow, the management of renewable and nonrenewable resources will play an important role. Today, the United States uses more resources and produces more waste than any other country on Earth. Each year, the United States generates about 230 million tons of garbage. That is about 4.2 pounds per day, per person, or almost 1 ton per year. What would happen if each of Earth's 6 billion humans generated 1 ton of garbage each year?

Analyze **Explain how a renewable resource such as water could become a nonrenewable resource.**

Connecting CONCEPTS

Hydrologic Cycle In **Chapter 13**, you learned how the hydrologic cycle moves water through Earth's atmosphere and back to Earth's surface. This cycling of water from resources such as lakes, rivers, and aquifers sustains the needs of the surrounding ecosystem.

▶ MAIN IDEA
Effective management of Earth's resources will help meet the needs of the future.

Management of Earth's resources affects both current and future generations. The responsible use of Earth's resources can help to maintain these resources for future generations.

The story of Easter Island is a cautionary tale of destruction caused by careless use of resources. When humans first landed on Easter Island between A.D. 400 and 700, it was thickly forested on rich soil, with many bird species. The human colony grew quickly over the next 1000 years, building the stone monuments for which the island is now famous. The island inhabitants cut down the forests for lumber and for building boats. The trees were cut down faster than they could grow back. Eventually, Easter Island was left with no trees, as shown in **FIGURE 16.3.** Without trees, there was no wood for shelter or boats, the rich soil washed away, and habitat for the island's animal populations was lost. Without boats, there was no offshore fishing. With no food and island resources nearly gone, the Easter Island human population crashed and the Easter Islanders disappeared.

The Easter Islanders' use of trees was unsustainable. In other words, the islanders used trees to meet their short-term needs. But this resource could not be maintained into the future, and its use had negative long-term effects. In contrast, sustainable use of resources means using resources in such a way that they will be available for future generations.

FIGURE 16.3 Today, the barren landscapes of Easter Island are an eerie reminder of the fate of the island's ancient inhabitants.

Ecological Footprint

Humans need natural resources to survive, but the way resources are used threatens the welfare of the human population. Earth's carrying capacity depends on how much land is needed to support each person on Earth. The amount of land necessary to produce and maintain enough food and water, shelter, energy, and waste is called an **ecological footprint.** The size of an ecological footprint depends on a number of factors. These include the amount and efficiency of resource use, and the amount and toxicity of waste produced.

As shown in **FIGURE 16.4**, individuals and populations vary in their use of resources and production of waste, and therefore in the size of their ecological footprints. The average U.S. citizen's ecological footprint covers an area larger than 24 football fields (9.7 hectares) and is one of the largest in the world. But the ecological footprint of individuals in developing nations is growing, and nations such as China and India have populations that are more than three times the size of the U.S. population. Individuals in the United States may have a large footprint, but other nations have a lot more "feet."

As the world population continues to grow, we face many challenging decisions. Waste production and management is an issue that will become more important as we move into the future. Should we have rules to regulate resource use and waste production? If so, how much resource use and waste production should individuals and populations be allowed? How much land needs to be maintained for agriculture, how much for living space, and how much for other uses? How much fresh water should be used for crop irrigation and how much reserved for humans to drink? Our welfare, and the welfare of future generations, depends on sustainable management of Earth's resources.

Analyze Why is our ecological footprint related to an area of land?

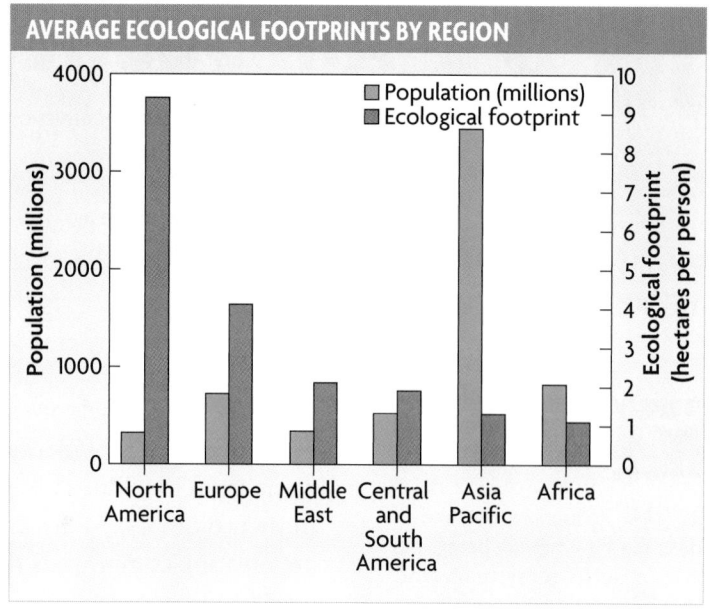

Source: Global Footprint Network

FIGURE 16.4 Different regions of the world have varying levels of impact on their environment. This graph shows the average ecological footprint of individuals around the world.

scilinks.org

To learn more about Earth's human population, go to scilinks.org.
Keycode: MLB016

ONLINE QUIZ
ClassZone.com

REVIEWING ▶ MAIN IDEAS

1. Give three examples of how technology has influenced human population growth.

2. What is the difference between **renewable** and **nonrenewable resources**?

3. Describe how a population can use resources in a sustainable way.

CRITICAL THINKING

4. **Connect** What factors can limit the growth of the human population?

5. **Synthesize** How could the Easter Islanders have prevented their population crash?

Connecting CONCEPTS

6. **Carrying Capacity** The progressive increase in Earth's human carrying capacity came from advances in technology. What density-independent and density-dependent limiting factors may prevent the human population from continued growth?

Air Quality

KEY CONCEPT Fossil fuel emissions affect the biosphere.

▶ MAIN IDEA

- Pollutants accumulate in the air.
- Air pollution is changing Earth's biosphere.

VOCABULARY

pollution, p. 488
smog, p. 488
particulate, p. 488

acid rain, p. 489
greenhouse effect, p. 490
global warming, p. 492

MICHIGAN STANDARDS

L3.p4A Recognize that, and describe how, human beings are part of Earth's ecosystems. Note that human activities can deliberately or inadvertently alter the equilibrium in ecosystems. (prerequisite)

B3.4C Examine the negative impact of human activities.

Connect Fossil fuels are an important part of modern society. Consider that every time you ride in a car, you are being transported by energy that originally came from the Sun. This energy was absorbed by ancient organisms and stored in their biomass. Today, as humans burn these fuels in the form of gas and oil, we are creating compounds that pollute Earth's biosphere. Without this energy our lives would be very different, but how does air pollution from fossil fuels affect the biosphere?

▶ MAIN IDEA

Pollutants accumulate in the air.

Although it is sometimes easy to forget, humans are an important part of the biosphere. Our actions have direct and indirect effects on Earth's natural cycles. Each year humans add synthetic chemicals and materials to the Earth. Many of them cannot be integrated into normal ecosystem functions. The addition of these materials to the environment is called pollution. **Pollution** describes any undesirable factor, or pollutant, that is added to the air, water, or soil. Pollution can take the form of microscopic air particles, or waste products from factories and sewers, or household chemicals that are poured down the kitchen sink. The harmful effects of pollutants can be immediate or delayed, but these effects may add up over time and can disrupt the function of ecosystems.

Smog and Ozone

The most common air pollution comes from the waste products produced by burning fossil fuels such as gas and oil. Chemical compounds released through this process can combine to form a haze of matter called smog, shown in **FIGURE 16.5**. **Smog** is a type of air pollution caused by the interaction of sunlight with pollutants produced by fossil fuel emissions. There are several components of smog, including particulate matter and ground-level ozone. **Particulates** are microscopic bits of dust, metal, and unburned fuel, 1–10 microns in size, that are produced by many different industrial processes. Once in the air, some particulates may stay in the atmosphere for weeks before they settle to the ground. Fine particulates can be inhaled and can cause many different types of health problems.

FIGURE 16.5 The hazy fog over the city of Los Angeles is largely produced by automobile emissions and industrial processes. Smog is a growing problem in many areas of the United States.

The second component of smog is ground-level ozone. In the presence of sunlight, two types of chemicals react to produce ground-level ozone (O_3). Nitrogen oxides are produced during fossil fuel combustion, and these chemicals give smog a yellowish color. Ozone is formed when nitrogen dioxide (NO_2) reacts with oxygen (O_2) present in the atmosphere. In this reaction, one oxygen from an NO_2 molecule is transferred to an O_2 molecule, forming ozone (O_3). The ozone produced by reactions of nitrogen oxide and oxygen tends to stay close to the ground, where it can be harmful to human health and ecosystem functions. Although ozone is harmful to organisms, it also plays an important, protective role in the Earth's upper atmosphere. High concentrations of ozone in the stratosphere, also known as the ozonosphere or ozone layer, act as a shield protecting Earth's biosphere against harmful ultraviolet rays found in sunlight.

Acid Rain

The chemicals produced by the burning of fossil fuels become part of the ecosystem and can change the products of natural cycles. For example, nitrogen oxides and sulfur oxides from fossil fuel emissions can lead to the formation of acid rain. **Acid rain** is a type of precipitation produced when pollutants in the water cycle cause rain pH to drop below normal levels.

VISUAL VOCAB

Acid rain is a type of precipitation produced when pollutants in the water cycle cause rain pH to drop below normal levels.

Acid rain
pH 4.6

Normal rain
pH 5.6

H+ ions

During the water cycle, rain falls through Earth's atmosphere and interacts with carbon dioxide molecules. As it falls, water molecules react with carbon dioxide molecules to form a weak carbonic acid, which then breaks apart, leaving lone hydrogen ions. This is normal. All rain that falls is slightly acidic, with a pH around 5.6. When pollutants such as nitrogen oxides and sulfur oxides become a part of the water cycle, acid rain is the result. Reactions between these chemicals and the oxygen and water normally present in the atmosphere create sulfuric and nitric acids that can cause pH levels to fall below 5.6.

Acid rain falls in many areas of the United States and has a major effect on ecosystems. By decreasing pH levels in lakes and streams, acid rain threatens water supplies and species habitat. Acid rain can cause a decline in growth rates, as shown in **FIGURE 16.6**. It can also cause leaves and bark to break down more quickly and make trees more vulnerable to disease and weather.

Synthesize As the human population continues to increase and use more fossil fuels, why might acid rain become a bigger problem?

Connecting CONCEPTS

pH Recall from **Chapter 2** that the pH is a measure of the concentration of H+ ions in a solution. Concentrations of H+ ions in acid rain are very high, giving the rain a lower pH level.

FIGURE 16.6 The wide growth rings of this tree indicate a healthy environment. The smaller growth rings illustrate how acid rain directly impacts plant growth.

▶ MAIN IDEA
Air pollution is changing Earth's biosphere.

Earth's atmosphere naturally includes molecules of carbon dioxide that play an important part in keeping the biosphere at a temperature that can support life. The levels of atmospheric carbon dioxide rise and fall over time as a normal part of the climate cycles of Earth. Collections of data from arctic ice cores allow scientists to look deep into Earth's atmospheric history. They have discovered that cycles of rising and falling carbon dioxide levels follow known patterns of periodic warming and cooling. The relationship between changes in global average temperatures and carbon dioxide levels is shown in **FIGURE 16.7**. We know that high levels of carbon dioxide are typical of Earth's warmer periods, while low levels are associated with cool climates, eventually leading to periods of extreme cold called ice ages.

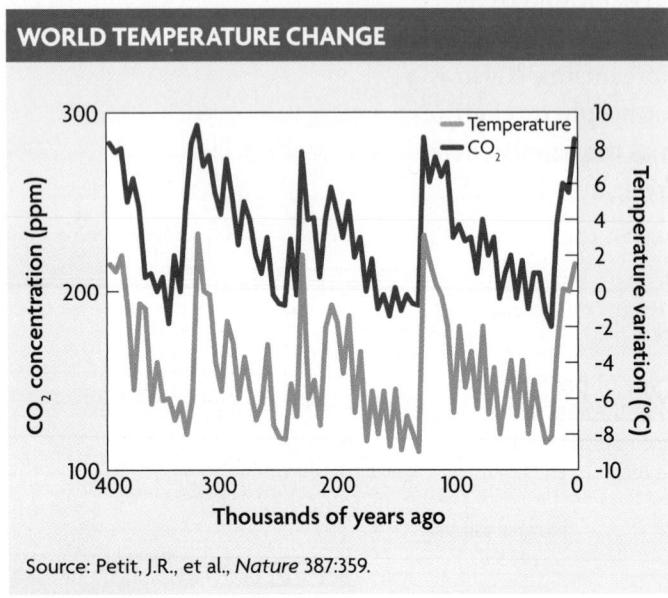

WORLD TEMPERATURE CHANGE

Source: Petit, J.R., et al., *Nature* 387:359.

FIGURE 16.7 Scientists have found that changes in Earth's temperature correspond with fluctuations in global carbon dioxide levels.

The Greenhouse Effect

Earth gets nearly all of its energy from the wavelengths of both visible and invisible light emitted by the Sun. When the Sun's waves reach Earth, some are absorbed by Earth's atmosphere, but many of these rays pass through the atmosphere and reach Earth's surface. Some of this energy is absorbed by Earth's surface, but it is later reradiated as invisible infrared radiation—heat. After being reradiated from Earth's surface, this energy could travel away from Earth, be lost into space, and leave an extremely cold Earth that could never sustain life. But Earth is not cold and does have life. So what keeps Earth's temperature from dropping to extreme freezing conditions?

To answer this question, think about the greenhouses that scientists and gardeners use to grow plants. Greenhouses use glass that allows sunlight to pass radiation through and provide energy for plant growth. The glass also prevents infrared radiation from escaping. This infrared radiation keeps the inside of the greenhouse warm. This same phenomenon occurs in a car, causing the inside to heat up when the windows are closed.

In the same way that greenhouse glass creates an environment for plants to grow, the chemical composition of Earth's atmosphere plays an important role in maintaining an environment that is suitable for life. Earth's atmosphere contains gases called greenhouse gases that act as insulators and slow the loss of heat through the atmosphere. Water vapor, carbon dioxide, and methane are three of the most common greenhouse gases found in the atmosphere. Greenhouse gases absorb wavelengths of infrared radiation. This process is called the greenhouse effect and is illustrated in **FIGURE 16.8**. The **greenhouse effect** occurs when carbon dioxide, water, and methane molecules absorb energy reradiated by Earth's surface and slow the release of this energy from Earth's atmosphere.

FIGURE 16.8 Greenhouse Effect

Water vapor, carbon dioxide, and methane can be found all through Earth's atmosphere. These greenhouse gases act as a blanket that slows the release of energy and helps to keep Earth at a temperature that can support life.

1 Short, high-energy wavelengths of light emitted from the Sun penetrate Earth's atmosphere.

3 Greenhouse gases in the atmosphere absorb many of the longer wavelengths of infrared radiation.

carbon dioxide (CO_2)

methane (CH_4)   water (H_2O)

2 Energy from the Sun is absorbed by Earth and reradiated as infrared radiation, or heat.

4 The molecules rerelease infrared radiation, which is absorbed again by other molecules, Earth's surface, or lost in outer space.

GLOBAL WARMING

As automobile use and industry have grown, so have the levels of carbon dioxide and other greenhouse gases in the atmosphere. This graph shows average global temperature changes (blue) against atmospheric carbon dioxide levels (green) measured at Mauna Loa Observatory in Hawaii.

Global Temperature And Carbon Dioxide Levels Over Time

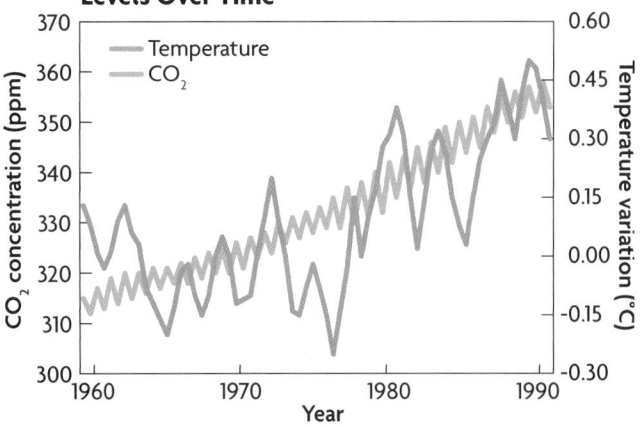

— Temperature
— CO_2

CO_2 concentration (ppm)

Temperature variation (°C)

Year

Source: University of California, Scripps Institute of Oceanography/ Hadley Centre for Climate Prediction and Research

CRITICAL VIEWING How would an increase in atmospheric greenhouse gases contribute to an increase in average global temperatures?

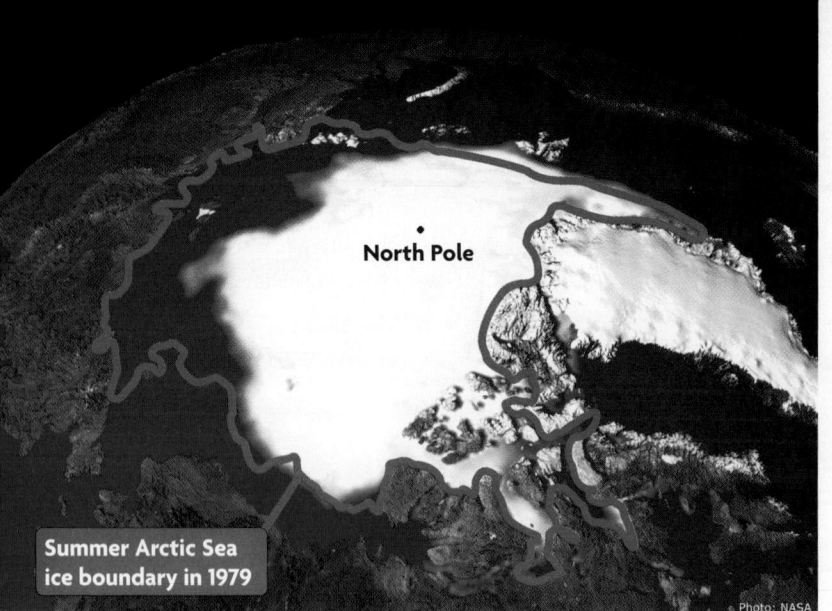

North Pole

Summer Arctic Sea ice boundary in 1979

Photo: NASA

FIGURE 16.9 Over the past 20 years, increasing global temperatures have decreased summer ice pack around the North Pole by about 20 percent.

Global Warming

Over the past 100 years, the average global temperature has risen 0.6°C (1.2°F), with the most dramatic change occurring over the past 40 years. What is causing this rise in temperature? Global temperature fluctuations are a normal part of Earth's climate cycle. But major changes in temperature generally occur over tens of thousands of years, not over 100 years.

The trend of increasing global temperatures is known as **global warming.** From a variety of evidence, scientists can infer that the changes in temperature are the result of increased levels of greenhouse gases such as carbon dioxide, water, and methane. There is no doubt that the growth of industry and use of automobiles has increased the emission of greenhouse gases over the past 100 years. Scientists may disagree on how much this human impact is influencing global warming, but most agree that we must take steps to slow the warming process.

Scientists do not know how these atmospheric changes will affect the global biosphere. What they do know is that evidence shows global warming is already threatening ecosystems around the world. Ecological disasters, such as increased flooding, stronger tropical storms, and the loss of biodiversity, are just a few of the threats that may be caused by global warming. As shown in **FIGURE 16.9,** the polar ice pack is melting at a rapid pace, which may eventually affect global weather patterns. These changes may be part of a slow warming process, or they may be the beginning of a rapid global climate change. The future of global warming is uncertain, but scientists predict that average temperatures on Earth could increase anywhere from 1.4 to 5.8°C (2.2 to 10°F) by the year 2100, a change that could have dramatic effects on Earth's biosphere, and change the planet that we call home.

Connect How might global warming affect seasonal temperature changes?

16.2 / ASSESSMENT

ONLINE QUIZ
ClassZone.com

REVIEWING ▶ MAIN IDEAS

1. Name and describe two ways in which **pollution** affects ecosystems.

2. How does the **greenhouse effect** keep Earth warm?

3. Explain how a build-up of carbon dioxide in the atmosphere could increase Earth's global temperature.

CRITICAL THINKING

4. **Predict** Describe how **acid rain** falling in a forest could disrupt the trophic structure of the ecosystem.

5. **Connect** Greenhouse gases are found close to Earth's surface and high above in the atmosphere. Name two important functions of greenhouse gases at Earth's surface.

Connecting CONCEPTS

6. **Food Webs** Ocean producers such as phytoplankton are an important part of food webs, but they need a specific temperature to survive. How might increased water temperatures affect these ocean food webs?

MATERIALS

- 4 potted radish seedlings
- sharpened pencil
- marker
- water, pH 6
- water, pH 5
- water, pH 4
- water, pH 3
- 250-mL beaker
- metric ruler

PROCESS SKILLS

- **Designing Experiments**
- **Hypothesizing**
- **Collecting Data**
- **Analyzing Data**

MICHIGAN STANDARDS

L3.p4A Recognize that, and describe how, human beings are part of Earth's ecosystems. Note that human activities can deliberately or inadvertently alter the equilibrium in ecosystems. (prerequisite)
B3.4C Examine the negative impact of human activities.

Acid Rain

In this lab, you will determine the effects of acid rain on plant growth. You will use water with different levels of acidity to water plants and monitor how it affects plant growth over a two-week period.

PROBLEM How does acid rain affect plant growth?

DESIGN YOUR EXPERIMENT

1. Write a procedure to explain how you will set up and conduct an experiment to test how acid rain affects plant growth. Identify the independent and dependent variables and constants you will maintain. For example:

   - What amount of water will you use to water the plants?
   - How often will you water the plants?
   - How will you measure the effects of acid rain on plant growth, both quantitatively and qualitatively?
   - How often will you collect data?

2. Form a hypothesis about the effects of acidic water on plant growth.
3. Design a data table to organize your results.
4. Have your teacher approve your experimental design.
5. Obtain your materials. Set up and conduct your experiment.

ANALYZE AND CONCLUDE

1. **Analyze** What were the independent and dependent variables in your experiment? What variables were held constant?
2. **Graph Data** Determine the best way to graph the data you collected. Determine whether a line graph or bar graph is appropriate, and construct that type of graph.
3. **Analyze Data** Write a summary statement that describes the results of your experiment. Include the qualitative data as well as the quantitative data. Is your hypothesis supported by the data you collected? Why or why not?
4. **Experimental Design** Identify possible sources of unavoidable experimental error in your design. List possible reasons for inconsistent results you may have observed.
5. **Apply** How does acid rain appear to affect plant growth?

EXTEND YOUR INVESTIGATION

Measure the pH of rain in your area. Based on the results of your experiment, what could you conclude about how the pH of rain might affect the growth of plants?

16.3 Water Quality

KEY CONCEPT Pollution of Earth's freshwater supply threatens habitat and health.

MAIN IDEA
- Water pollution affects ecosystems.
- Biomagnification causes accumulation of toxins in the food chain.

VOCABULARY
indicator species, p. 494
biomagnification, p. 495

Review
pollution

MICHIGAN STANDARDS

L3.p4A Recognize that, and describe how, human beings are part of Earth's ecosystems. Note that human activities can deliberately or inadvertently alter the equilibrium in ecosystems. (prerequisite)
B3.4C Examine the negative impact of human activities.

Connect When you swallow a pill, your body only uses a part of the medicine in the pill and gets rid of the rest as waste, which is flushed away. Scientists have detected traces of many prescription drugs in freshwater supplies. Several fish species that live in fresh waters have been exposed to the female hormone, estrogen. Some of the male fish have begun showing female characteristics. These "gender-bending" fish are only one effect of water pollution. What other pollutants can be found in our water?

MAIN IDEA
Water pollution affects ecosystems.

Pollution can have a major impact on water ecosystems. Chemical contaminants, raw sewage, trash, and other waste products are only a few pollutants that make their way into rivers, lakes, and aquifers all over the world.

Runoff from farms and cities may contain toxic chemicals and debris that can disrupt the chemical balance of freshwater lakes and streams and put entire freshwater ecosystems at risk. For example, detergents and fertilizers used in fields can affect a lake ecosystem by stimulating plant and algae overgrowth. A buildup of algae, such as the one shown in **FIGURE 16.10**, can drastically lower the levels of dissolved oxygen, leading to the dying off of fish populations. A lack of oxygen can also keep detritivores from breaking down waste materials. Over time, lakes and ponds slowly begin to fill in through a process called eutrophication.

FIGURE 16.10 A buildup of algae in lakes such as this one is the direct result of pollution. Eventually, the process of eutrophication will lead to the disappearance of the lake.

One way in which scientists can determine the health of an ecosystem is through the study of natural indicator species. An **indicator species,** also known as a bioindicator, is a species that provides a sign, or indication, of the quality of the ecosystem's environmental conditions. The gender-bending fish discussed above is an example of an aquatic indicator species. Frogs are sometimes considered an indicator species for water quality. Because the skin of tadpoles and adults is water-permeable, they come into direct contact with pollutants that can cause deformities such as extra arms and legs, as well as body tumors. Terrestrial ecosystems have indicator species as well, but the environmental impacts on these species are shown in different ways. Aquatic indicator species show the direct effects of pollution.

The Forster's tern, a bird species native to coastal regions of the United States, has provided scientists with clues about pollution in the San Francisco Bay. This indicator species occupies a niche at the top of this ecosystem's food web. An important part of the tern's diet is fish it catches in the San Francisco Bay. By studying the tissues of dead tern chicks, scientists are finding large amounts of chemical contaminants such as mercury and PCBs, or polychlorinated biphenyls. These chemicals can harm developing eggs and can cause problems in the nervous system of adult birds. The high levels of these pollutants found in birds could lead to a decrease in the tern population and disrupt the balance of this aquatic ecosystem.

Apply **If the population of an indicator species is increasing, what might you infer about the conditions of the ecosystem?**

▶ MAIN IDEA

Biomagnification causes accumulation of toxins in the food chain.

The high death rates in young Forster's terns are due to high levels of toxic compounds found in the parents. How did these chemicals get into the adult birds?

Some pollutants are water-soluble, which means that they dissolve in water and will exit an organism through its wastes. Other pollutants are fat-soluble and stay in the body fat of an organism. Fat-soluble pollutants can also move from one organism to another in a process known as biomagnification. In **biomagnification,** a pollutant moves up the food chain as predators eat prey, accumulating in higher concentrations in the bodies of predators. Scientists measure pollutants in parts per million (ppm). The illustration in **FIGURE 16.11** shows how biomagnification moves small traces of a pollutant to higher concentrations further up the food chain.

After a pesticide is sprayed onto fields, large amounts of the chemical are washed into ponds and lakes, where phytoplankton pick up the chemical from their environment. The phytoplankton contain very small concentrations of the chemical, but when zooplankton feed on phytoplankton, they are also eating the chemical. Because the zooplankton eat many phytoplankton, higher levels of the chemical build up in the zooplankton. Secondary consumers such as small fish eat zooplankton and collect larger concentrations in their own body fat. Larger fish eat the chemical-laden fish, and the amount of the chemical in their fat builds up as they eat more and more. The increase in contamination is dramatic and causes the consumer at the top of the food chain, often a large predator such as an eagle or hawk, to receive the most concentrated dose of the pollutant.

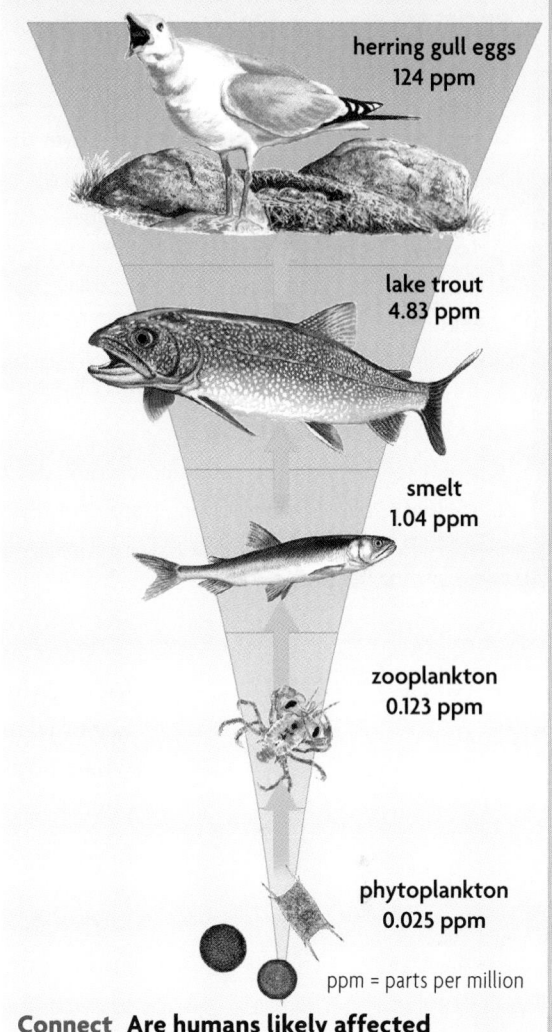

FIGURE 16.11 **Biomagnification**

The movement of fat-soluble pollutants through a food chain results in higher concentrations in the top consumer.

herring gull eggs
124 ppm

lake trout
4.83 ppm

smelt
1.04 ppm

zooplankton
0.123 ppm

phytoplankton
0.025 ppm

ppm = parts per million

Connect **Are humans likely affected by biomagnification? If so, what foods might be dangerous?**

Connecting CONCEPTS

Energy Pyramid In **Chapter 13,** you learned how energy is lost as it moves up through trophic levels. In comparison, the process of biomagnification increases toxic material as it moves up the trophic structure.

Modeling Biomagnification

In this lab, you will model biomagnification. Small cups represent smelt, a fish that feeds on zooplankton. Medium-sized cups represent trout, which feed on smelt. The large cup represents an eagle, which feeds on trout.

PROBLEM   How are contaminants magnified up the food chain?

PROCEDURE

1. Label the cups, smelt, trout, and eagle according to size. Punch holes in the bottom of each cup with the pencil. Cover the holes with masking tape.

2. Fill each of the cups halfway with salt. Add 4 beads to each small cup.

3. Hold each of the small cups over the beaker and remove the tape. Allow the salt to flow through the holes into the beaker.

4. Pour the remaining contents of two small cups into one medium cup. Pour the contents of the other two small cups into the second medium cup. Repeat step 3 with the medium-sized cups.

5. Pour the remaining contents of both of the medium cups into the large cup.

ANALYZE AND CONCLUDE

1. **Analyze**   What do the beads represent in this model of biomagnification?

2. **Evaluate**   Why is the following statement true: "Carnivores at the top of the food chain tend to be most affected by pollutants released into the environment"?

MATERIALS

- 4 small paper cups
- 2 medium paper cups
- 1 large paper cup
- marker
- sharpened pencil
- 10 cm masking tape
- 400 mL salt
- 16 beads
- 500-mL beaker

Biomagnification has the most serious effect on species near the top of the food chain. For example, the beluga whale is a top predator that lives in cold ocean waters and feeds on a wide variety of fish species. Studies of a beluga whale population in eastern Canada have shown such extreme levels of toxic chemicals that some whale carcasses have been treated as hazardous waste.

As top level consumers, humans can also be affected by biomagnification. Scientists have recently found small amounts of PCBs in the blood of new-born babies. Exposure to fat-soluble toxins such as PCBs during pregnancy and nursing can be dangerous to the developing fetus, and may also affect growth and development in young children.

Compare   Why would tertiary consumers have higher concentrations of toxins than primary consumers?

16.3 / ASSESSMENT

ONLINE QUIZ
ClassZone.com

REVIEWING ▶ MAIN IDEAS

1. What does an **indicator species** tell us about the health of an ecosystem?

2. How do PCBs affect bird populations through **biomagnification**?

CRITICAL THINKING

3. **Compare**   How are the concepts of carrying capacity and indicator species related?

4. **Synthesize**   Would a buffalo or a mountain lion be more affected by biomagnification? Why?

Connecting CONCEPTS

5. **Energy Pyramid**   How does the biomagnification "pyramid" compare with the energy pyramid?

DATA ANALYSIS
ClassZone.com

Types of Quantitative Data

Collecting data is a fundamental part of the scientific process. Before you design and carry out an experiment, it is important to understand the two different types of quantitative data: discrete and continuous.

Discrete data Data that cannot be broken down into smaller units and have meaning, such as the number of frogs in a pond, are called discrete data. Bar graphs are usually used for discrete data.

Continuous data Data that have fractional values—that are not whole numbers—are called continuous data. The length and mass of a frog are continuous data. Continuous data are usually shown on a line graph. The values of points that were not actually measured in an experiment can be inferred from the graph.

EXAMPLE

Frogs are commonly used as a biological indicator for water quality. A classroom of students wishes to test how water quality affects growth rates in frogs. Frogs hatch from eggs into tadpoles and then slowly mature into adult frogs.

Students compared hatching rates in frog eggs over an eight-day period. Eggs were raised in one of two water samples, a sample from a known polluted pond, and a sample from an unpolluted pond. These data are discrete because a certain number of eggs hatched. There were no half or quarter tadpoles.

After hatching, students measured tadpole growth in both polluted and unpolluted water over the next five days. These data are continuous because they can be broken down further and data points between measurements can be inferred.

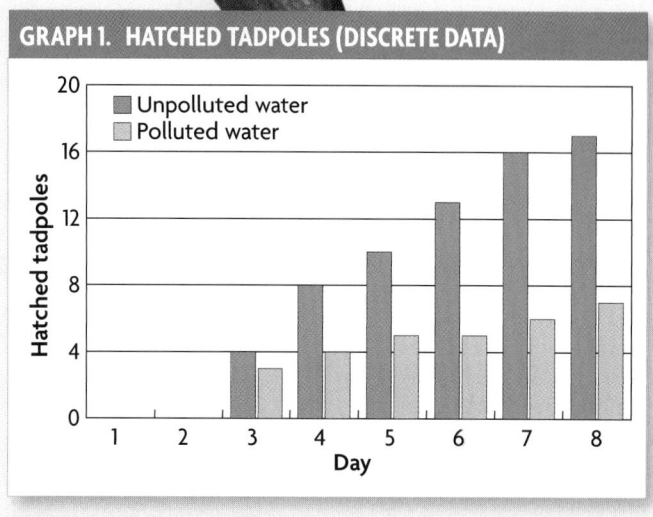

GRAPH 1. HATCHED TADPOLES (DISCRETE DATA)

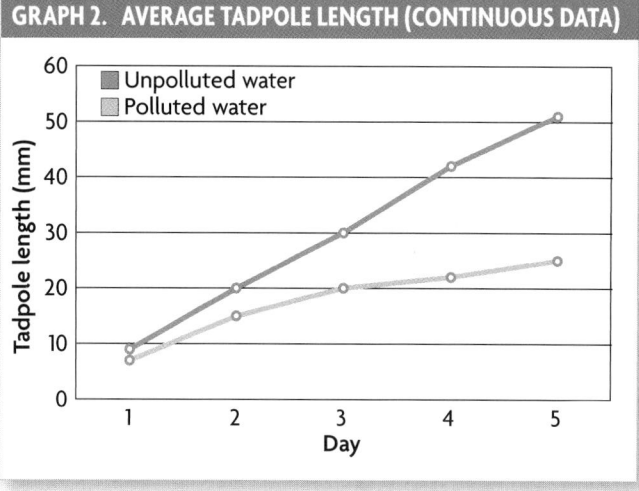

GRAPH 2. AVERAGE TADPOLE LENGTH (CONTINUOUS DATA)

IDENTIFY DISCRETE AND CONTINUOUS DATA

For each example, identify whether the data are discrete or continuous.

1. **Apply** A student collects data each spring and summer for five years about populations of endangered frogs in a wetland by counting the number of individual frogs in quadrats.

2. **Classify** The EPA compiles data about the mass of recycled aluminum (millions of tons) for every year since 1990.

3. **Analyze** Since 1860, the National Oceanic and Atmospheric Association has collected data about the change in Earth's surface temperature and the concentration of carbon dioxide in the atmosphere.

16.4

Threats to Biodiversity

KEY CONCEPT The impact of a growing human population threatens biodiversity.

▶ MAIN IDEA

- Preserving biodiversity is important to the future of the biosphere.
- Loss of habitat eliminates species.
- Introduced species can disrupt stable relationships in an ecosystem.

VOCABULARY

habitat fragmentation, p. 499
introduced species, p. 500

Review
biodiversity

MICHIGAN STANDARDS

L3.p4A Recognize that, and describe how, human beings are part of Earth's ecosystems. Note that human activities can deliberately or inadvertently alter the equilibrium in ecosystems. (prerequisite)

B3.4C Examine the negative impact of human activities.

Connect Imagine yourself taking a walk down your favorite street. But instead of bright colors and interesting sights, you see only one type of everything. There is one type of tree, one type of flower, and one type of car. At school all of your friends look exactly like you, lunch is the same every day, and everyone listens to the same music. We rarely think of the diversity we experience each day. The diversity of Earth makes our planet unique and maintains the stability of ecosystems.

▶ MAIN IDEA

Preserving biodiversity is important to the future of the biosphere.

Ecosystems are constantly changing, and populations are always adjusting to these changes. Many times, human actions alter ecosystems in ways that harm a population and threaten biodiversity. The loss of habitat and the growing pollution problem are affecting animal and plant populations around the world. The value of biodiversity is not just measured in dollars. Biodiversity ensures the future of Earth.

Biodiversity is the diverse world of living things—the wide array and assortment of species that are found in any ecosystem. A decrease in an ecosystem's biodiversity will have a ripple effect through the entire ecosystem, affecting all species. Biodiversity is the foundation of much of our world.

Many medical and technological advancements come from nature. Nearly half of prescribed medicines are derived from plants. On the technological front, scientists in many fields continue to get inspiration from nature. For example, an adhesive from a mussel is being used as the pattern for a new coating for medical implants.

The loss of biodiversity has long-term effects. When a species goes extinct, it is gone forever. In many cases, all that remains of extinct species is a few dead specimens in a museum that can give little information other than where they were discovered. A loss of biodiversity can reduce an ecosystem's stability and make it more difficult for the ecosystem to handle future change.

FIGURE 16.12 Rare frog species of the Sri Lankan rain forests, such as this Knuckles leaf nesting frog, are in danger of becoming extinct due to habitat destruction.

For example, as the nation of Sri Lanka has modernized, the natural resources of the island have become increasingly depleted. Ninety-five percent of the island's rain forests have been lost, and with them more than 19 different frog species have gone extinct. In addition, numerous other species, such as the rare frog species shown in **FIGURE 16.12**, are endangered. The loss of even a single species can harm the overall stability of an island ecosystem.

Biodiversity is highest in the rain forest biomes of the world, and it is these areas that are most threatened. Currently, about 1 percent of this biome is lost each year to logging or to clearing for agricultural use. Preserving the rain forests of the world will do a great deal to protect and preserve the biodiversity of our planet.

Connect Why is biodiversity highest in tropical rain forests?

Connecting CONCEPTS

Carbon Cycle Rain forests around the world play an integral role in Earth's carbon cycle, storing large amounts of carbon in their structures.

▶ MAIN IDEA
Loss of habitat eliminates species.

One way to protect species is to monitor and manage their numbers, and to ensure they have adequate habitat for survival. Governments and organizations around the world are developing programs to protect species that are threatened by overhunting, overcollecting, and habitat loss.

As the human population moves into what was formerly wilderness, people are moving into the territory of many different species of wildlife. In many parts of the world, the loss of habitat can put species in danger of becoming extinct. Historically, for example, wetland habitats were viewed as breeding grounds for disease and as "wasted land." Between the 1780s and the 1980s, more than 53 percent of wetland habitat in the United States was eliminated. This destruction displaced large numbers of wildlife and disrupted migration patterns for many species of water birds.

Efforts to ensure adequate habitat must take into account the life history of the organism, including mating habits and migration patterns. Ecologists have become particularly worried about habitat fragmentation. **Habitat fragmentation** occurs when a barrier forms that prevents an organism from accessing its entire home range. Often, habitat fragmentation is caused by the building of roadways or the harvesting of forests. Bears, deer, raccoons, and opossums are just a few of the animals that find their home ranges fragmented as urban sprawl increases. To try to fix this growing problem, some states are building underpasses and overpasses so that wildlife can avoid busy roadways. Corridors such as the one shown in **FIGURE 16.13** help to maintain continuous tracts of habitat for those species that move between different areas.

Connect Why is wetland habitat important for migrating birds?

FIGURE 16.13 By providing a safe way to cross barriers such as roads and highways, land bridges such as this one in Canada allow animals to move safely from one part of their habitat to the next.

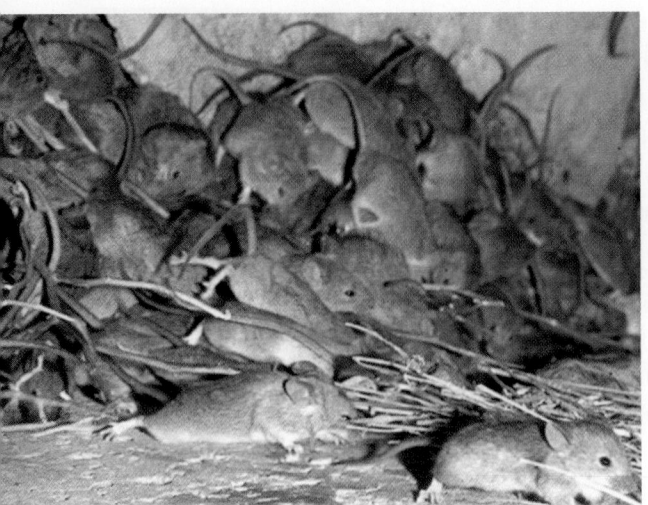

FIGURE 16.14 Mice plagues in Australia and China can cost farmers millions of dollars in lost crops.

Introduced species can disrupt stable relationships in an ecosystem.

Introduced species have a direct impact on the biodiversity and natural flow of energy in an ecosystem. An **introduced species** is any organism that was brought to an ecosystem as the result of human actions. Introduced species can pose a great threat to the stability of an ecosystem if they prey on or crowd out native species. In some instances, introduced species can cause economic damage. Just as native species interact with one another and their habitat, nonnative or introduced species are active and sometimes disruptive in their new ecosystems.

Invasive species are successful in environments under many different circumstances. If an environment has a niche that the invasive species can exploit, or if the invasive species is a better competitor in a particular niche, native species may be pushed out. Invasive species are also successful if there is a lack of predators to keep the population stable.

Effect on Native Species

The Florida Everglades is a dynamic ecosystem where unique plants and animals have evolved for tens of thousands of years. The climate is similar to that of a tropical jungle, and the Everglades can support a great diversity of organisms. One species that has been introduced to this region originally came from the tropical jungles of Southeastern Asia. The Burmese python, shown in **FIGURE 16.15**, came to the United States as a pet species. Growing more than 6 meters (20 ft) in length, this massive snake can be difficult to care for. Irresponsible owners have released many of the snakes back into the wild. A large number of Burmese pythons have been captured and removed from Everglades National Park, and officials say that there is a good chance that a breeding population is present. As a constrictor species, the Burmese python feeds on small animals such as rats, birds, raccoons, and even dogs. Threats to endangered bird species in the park worry officials. As the python population begins to grow, endangered species protected in the Everglades could be affected.

FIGURE 16.15 Introduced species such as the Burmese python are growing in numbers in places like the Florida Everglades.

Introduced animals are not the only problem. Plant species such as kudzu, another native of southeastern Asia, are invasive in the United States and are choking out native species of plants across the southeastern United States. The kudzu plant, shown in **FIGURE 16.16,** was introduced in 1876 as an ornamental tropical houseplant enjoyed for its fragrant flowers and large leaves. It was planted as field cover to prevent soil loss from erosion, but it rapidly began to spread out of the fields. Currently, kudzu is a classified as a problematic weed species in much of the eastern United States. Kudzu is a hardy plant, at home in virtually any soil, and it can grow up to 18 meters (60 ft) in a single growing season. This growth rate makes it difficult to control. Very few plant species can survive in an environment once kudzu is introduced. By blanketing trees and shrubs with its large leaves, kudzu deprives other plants of the sunlight they need to survive. The plant is resistant to most types of herbicides and can live for many years.

FIGURE 16.16 After a few months of being left in a single place, this car has become covered with kudzu. Fast-growing kudzu can destroy natural habitats in just a few years.

Economic Damage

Invasive species can have a major impact on humans as well as ecosystems. The common house mouse is an introduced species to the Australian continent. During the late 1700s, mice came from Europe as stowaways on British cargo ships. Today, mice are considered a major pest species in Australia and have caused widespread economic damage. Every four or five years, mice populations increase exponentially. Seasons of heavy rainfall lead to bumper crops of corn and grain, causing a dramatic rise in mouse populations and leading to huge numbers of mice moving from one food source to another. It was estimated that during the 1993–1994 season, the mouse population in Australia cost farmers about $65 million in lost revenue. Mice continue to be a problem throughout the region.

Predict How might a species of carnivorous fish introduced into a lake have a negative impact on the lake ecosystem?

16.4 ASSESSMENT

ONLINE QUIZ
ClassZone.com

REVIEWING ▶ MAIN IDEAS

1. Give two reasons why biodiversity is important to humans.

2. How does **habitat fragmentation** affect migrating bird populations?

3. What types of damage can **introduced species** cause?

CRITICAL THINKING

4. **Analyze** How could continued habitat fragmentation reduce biodiversity?

5. **Connect** How might the introduction of a mouse predator help with the mouse problem in Australia? What problems might it cause?

Connecting CONCEPTS

6. **Population Growth** Using your knowledge of populations, describe what will eventually happen to mouse populations in Australia as they run out of food.

16.5 Conservation

KEY CONCEPT Conservation methods can help protect and restore ecosystems.

▶ MAIN IDEA

- Sustainable development manages resources for present and future generations.
- Conservation practices focus on a few species but benefit entire ecosystems.
- Protecting Earth's resources helps protect our future.

VOCABULARY

sustainable development, p. 502
umbrella species, p. 503

Review
ecosystem, habitat, keystone species

MICHIGAN STANDARDS

L3.p4A Recognize that, and describe how, human beings are part of Earth's ecosystems. Note that human activities can deliberately or inadvertently alter the equilibrium in ecosystems. (prerequisite)
B3.4C Examine the negative impact of human activities.

Connect When Rachel Carson's book *Silent Spring* was published in 1962, the wheels were set in motion for the creation of the modern environmental movement. The book, which described how the pesticide DDT was affecting wildlife, brought about a public uproar and helped lead to a ban on the use of DDT in the United States. Since then, a variety of measures have been put into place, both to restore Earth's biosphere and to protect it from further degradation.

▶ MAIN IDEA

Sustainable development manages resources for present and future generations.

To ensure that Earth can continue to support, or sustain, a growing human population, it is important to secure the future of the Earth's ecosystems. This way of thinking is known as sustainable development. **Sustainable development** is a practice in which natural resources are used and managed in a way that meets current needs without hurting future generations.

Sustainable development covers a wide range of resource management methods. Concerns about the condition of the environment have led to changes in methods of harvesting natural resources. In the timber industry, for example, old growth forests are being lost at a fast rate due to a method called clear cutting. By cutting down large sections of wooded areas and removing entire forest ecosystems, lumber companies serve a growing need for building supplies. Today, with the raised awareness of forest ecosystem

FIGURE 16.17 Forests of bamboo in China grow quickly and can provide an abundant supply of wood to support the growing demand for building materials.

safety, several companies are choosing to cut selected trees rather than clear-cutting forests. This practice encourages rapid regrowth of trees, and makes sure there is only minimal impact to the forest ecosystem. When choosing where and when to harvest trees, foresters must consider how the soil, water, and wildlife of the area will be affected and change their harvest strategy accordingly.

Global fisheries are also in need of sustainable development practices. Overfishing has depleted fish populations worldwide. Fish stocks are not as hardy as they once were. One reason for this is that the fish that are caught represent the healthy, reproducing age groups of the fish population. By removing the reproducing individuals from the population, the fishing industry is actually hurting itself. Without fish to reproduce now, there will be no fish for the future. In addition, unsustainable fishing techniques damage marine and coastal environments. A number of techniques can be adopted by fisheries to make the industry sustainable:

Connecting CONCEPTS

Natural Selection Recall from **Chapter 11** that in natural selection the environment favors certain traits over others. In a fish's environment, nets used by humans catch fish that are large and slow. Fish that may be smaller and faster have a distinct advantage, thus leading to a genetic shift in the population.

- **Rotation** Rotating catches between different species gives the "off" species time to recover their numbers following a harvest.
- **Fishing gear review** The gear used to catch fish can damage the sea floor and often unintentionally catches other species. Reviewing and possibly banning certain fishing gear could help avoid damaging the sea floor and prevent ecologically important organisms from being killed.
- **Harvest reduction** Slowing the harvests of deep-water species that grow very slowly allows them more time to recover their populations.
- **Fishing bans** Creating and enforcing fishing bans in certain areas helps to replenish populations within that area, which may lead to greater fish numbers in nearby locations.

Connect **What important services do forests provide? How might their destruction have an effect on humans?**

FIGURE 16.18 The West Indian manatee is an umbrella species whose protection helps to re-establish marine habitats.

⦿ MAIN IDEA
Conservation practices focus on a few species but benefit entire ecosystems.

Laws written to protect individual species also help to protect their habitats. The Endangered Species Act in the United States, for example, is designed to protect individual species that are near extinction by establishing protection for the organism and its environment. When a single species within an ecosystem is placed on a list of endangered species, many other species within the ecosystem also benefit. The listed species is often called an **umbrella species** because its protection means a wide range of other species will also be protected. Such is the case with the West Indian manatee. These aquatic mammals, shown in **FIGURE 16.18,** live in the waters of the Gulf of Mexico and Atlantic Ocean along the coast of the southeastern United States. Their range extends as far west as Texas and as far north as Virginia.

The manatee was placed on the endangered species list in 1967. Its listing resulted from a variety of factors including loss of habitat, overhunting, and deaths due to collisions with powerboats. Today, the situation for manatees is difficult, and fewer than 3000 manatees remain in the United States. To promote their survival, local, state, and federal agencies are working to develop policies to protect their habitat. When developing recovery plans for an endangered species, scientists must consider many factors. For example, since manatees rely on seagrass as their main food source, areas rich in this resource must also be protected. By protecting waterways from pollution, restoring damaged areas, and limiting boating, the marine ecosystem that is the natural habitat for manatees is also protected. As a result, entire ecosystems can benefit from efforts to save a single species from extinction.

Apply **What factors might scientists consider when developing a recovery plan for the endangered grizzly bear of western North America?**

⊙ MAIN IDEA

Protecting Earth's resources helps protect our future.

All living things, including humans, share Earth and its resources, and the value of the services our planet provides is priceless. The cycling of nutrients and the regulation of water provide essential resources that are almost impossible for humans to manufacture. If we were to put a human economic value on it, the total value of the services Earth's natural ecosystems provide has been estimated to be over $30 trillion a year.

Global warming, pollution, and the loss of biodiversity are only a few of the direct threats our planet is facing. To prevent further loss of the valuable resources of Earth, public actions are helping to preserve and protect the future of our planet.

Protecting Natural Resources

The Environmental Protection Agency was created as part of the National Environmental Policy Act in 1970. Its creation paved the way for the development of policies and regulations to protect the environment across the United States. Laws such as the Clean Air Act, Clean Water Act, and Endangered Species Act have had a major impact on the environment. The Clean Air Act, signed into law in 1970, has helped to increase air quality across the nation. It regulates emissions from industrial factories and automobiles. In 1970, only 36 percent of the lakes and waterways in the United States were considered safe for swimming. Since the Clean Water Act was signed in 1972, regulations against pollution and an increased public awareness have helped to double the number of waterways that are safe today. Since 1973, when the Endangered Species Act was signed, breeding pairs of the bald eagle, once in danger of extinction, grew from 791 pairs to almost 6500 pairs in 2000.

Setting aside areas as public land is another way that governments can protect ecosystems. The Yosemite Grant of 1864 was the United States' first step to protect nature from development. This grant established what would

FIGURE 16.19 Yosemite Falls in California is the tallest waterfall in the United States, and is just one of the wonders that the founders of the National Park System hoped to preserve.

eventually become Yosemite National Park, part of which is shown in **FIGURE 16.19**. The success of this grant eventually led to the formation of the National Park Service. The management of multiple-use areas and wilderness areas balances recreation for visitors with protection of the natural ecosystem. Today, grassroots environmental organizations are working with local governments and private citizens to purchase and restore areas of land across the country to increase the amount of suitable habitat for wildlife.

A Sustainable Earth

As we have seen, humans represent an integral part of Earth's ecosystems and are subject to the same limitations as other species living on the planet. However, unlike other organisms, we have a much larger impact on our environment because of our population size and the fact that we are found over the entire globe. At the same time, we have the ability and technology to change the extent of our impact on Earth's biosphere and ultimately control our destiny.

FIGURE 16.20 Each year on Arbor Day, people around the world plant trees and play an important role in rebuilding ecosystems for future generations.

- We have the ability to control how fast our population grows, through controlling birth rates.
- We can develop technology to produce more food and produce less waste.
- Most importantly, we have the ability to change our practices and take action to protect and maintain ecosystems. In some cases, we can reduce or even eliminate the pressures we place on the planet's biogeochemical processes.

No places on Earth are untouched by humans. While we may not have directly visited each square inch of the planet, human-caused pollutants, invasive species, or ecosystem alterations have reached the world over. Yet our economies, and our very lives, depend on a healthy, thriving, sustainable Earth.

Connect **How could you reduce the amount of waste produced by your school?**

16.5 / ASSESSMENT

ONLINE QUIZ ClassZone.com

REVIEWING ▶ MAIN IDEAS

1. Give two examples of **sustainable development.**

2. Describe how the protection of an **umbrella species** can be beneficial to an ecosystem.

3. How do governmental actions help to preserve natural habitats and protect resources?

CRITICAL THINKING

4. **Connect** What can humans do to minimize the impact of urban sprawl on wildlife?

5. **Evaluate** Could the West Indian manatee be considered a keystone species? Justify your answer.

Connecting CONCEPTS

6. **Nutrient Cycling** Natural ecosystems provide important cleansing and recycling functions to humans. What specific products do Earth's natural cycles provide for humans?

Use these inquiry-based labs and online activities to deepen your understanding of human impact on ecosystems.

MICHIGAN STANDARDS

L3.p4A Recognize that, and describe how, human beings are part of Earth's ecosystems. Note that human activities can deliberately or inadvertently alter the equilibrium in ecosystems. (prerequisite)

B3.4C Examine the negative impact of human activities.

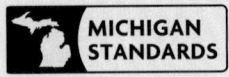

INVESTIGATION

Water Quality Testing

The United States Environmental Protection Agency (EPA) regulates the drinking water that comes from public water systems. In this lab, you will test two water samples to determine if they meet EPA standards.

SKILLS Measuring, Comparing

PROBLEM Which sample meets EPA standards?

MATERIALS

- 2 plastic cups
- marker
- 2 100-mL graduated cylinders
- 100 mL water sample A
- 100 mL water sample B
- 2 chlorine test strips
- 2 copper test strips
- 2 iron test strips
- 2 nitrate test strips
- 2 nitrite test strips

PROCEDURE

1. Label one cup water sample A and the second cup water sample B. Fill each cup half full with the corresponding water sample.
2. Read the instructions for each type of testing strip and then collect data on both water samples. Record your data in a chart like the one below.

TABLE 1. TEST RESULTS AND EPA STANDARDS FOR DRINKING WATER

Possible Contaminant	EPA Maximum Level (mg/L)	Sample A	Sample B
Chlorine	4		
Copper	1.3		
Iron*	0.3		
Nitrate	100		
Nitrite	1		

*EPA Recommended Standard

ANALYZE AND CONCLUDE

1. **Analyze** Compare the results of your tests with the EPA standards listed in Table 1. Does either of the water samples not meet the recommended standards? What conclusions can you reach about the water samples based on your results? (**Note:** Check to make sure you are comparing the same units between your tests and the EPA standards.)
2. **Apply** Suppose you collect and analyze a water sample that receives runoff from a large area of farmland. Predict how the quality of the water may be affected. Assume that you test for the same contaminants listed in the table above.

EXTEND YOUR INVESTIGATION

Research how exposure to high levels of the toxins listed above can affect human health.

INVESTIGATION

Contamination of Groundwater

Leakage of toxic chemicals from underground storage tanks (USTs) is the leading threat to the security of the U.S. drinking water supply. This contamination can have devastating effects on nearby ecosystems. In this activity, you will work to map an area and locate a UST contaminated area.

SKILL Modeling

PROBLEM How much land can be contaminated by a leaking UST?

MATERIALS

- shoebox containing hidden water balloon
- 1 m string
- 10 cm masking tape
- toothpick
- craft stick
- graph paper
- ruler

PROCEDURE

1. Obtain a container with a water balloon (UST) buried in surrounding kitty litter.

2. Using string and masking tape, section the container into quadrats about 2.5 cm × 2.5 cm. Copy the quadrats onto graph paper and label with a grid system.

3. Systematically, gently insert the craftstick in each grid to locate all quadrats the UST sits inside.

4. Sketch on your map the location of the UST.

5. Insert a toothpick to break the UST to determine the number of quadrats contaminated.

ANALYZE AND CONCLUDE

1. **Conclude** what effect might a leaking UST have on an ecosystem?

2. **Predict** what other problems might result when a UST must be removed from the ground?

CLASSZONE.COM

ANIMATED BIOLOGY

Human Effects on a Food Web

Humans can have a profound effect on the organisms in an ecosystem. Apply a human-induced change to a food web and see how the change ripples through the system.

WEBQUEST

Invasive species are a leading cause of extinctions of native species around the world. In this WebQuest, you will explore an invasive species in your area. Determine if the species has a harmful effect within your local environment and what can be done to control its damage.

Northern pike

DATA ANALYSIS ONLINE

Humans introduced trout into wilderness lakes of the Sierra Nevada in California for sport fishing. Since the fish were introduced, the number of mountain yellow-legged frogs has declined significantly. Graph frog density in lakes with no trout and in lakes from which trout were removed over time to see if the fish do affect frog population size.

KEY CONCEPTS | Vocabulary Games | Concept Maps | Animated Biology | Online Quiz

16.1 Human Population Growth and Natural Resources

As the human population grows, the demand for Earth's resources increases. The human population has grown tremendously due to advancements in technology. But a large population puts pressure on nonrenewable resources such as fossil fuels as well as on renewable resources such as water. Balancing the needs of our population with the resources of our environments will help to reduce our ecological footprint to sustainable levels.

16.2 Air Quality

Fossil fuel emissions affect the biosphere. Pollution is the addition of undesirable factors to the air, water, and soil. Fossil fuel emissions from industrial processes are causing an increase in smog and acid rain, which both threaten Earth's ecosystems. Carbon dioxide, methane, and other greenhouse gases slow the release of energy from Earth's atmosphere. But increased fossil fuel emissions appear to be contributing to rapid climate change in a process called global warming.

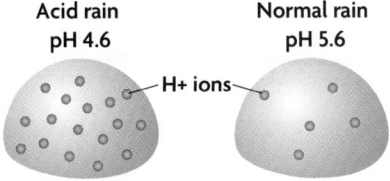

Acid rain
pH 4.6

Normal rain
pH 5.6

H+ ions

16.3 Water Quality

Pollution of Earth's freshwater supply threatens habitat and health. Indicator species help us understand the effects of pollution on an ecosystem. The process of biomagnification is a threat to both humans and ecosystems, as toxins accumulate at the top of food chains.

16.4 Threats to Biodiversity

The impact of a growing human population threatens biodiversity. The biodiversity of a region helps keep ecosystems stable. Habitat fragmentation and destruction are threatening biodiversity. Nonnative species can have a negative effect on ecosystems by pushing out native species and using up resources.

16.5 Conservation

Conservation methods can help protect and restore ecosystems. To protect Earth's natural resources for future generations, we need to plan for sustainable development. In addition, the protection of umbrella species and the positive support of government and industry can help to ensure Earth is protected for future generations.

Synthesize Your Notes

Concept Map Use a concept map like the one below to display the effects of pollution.

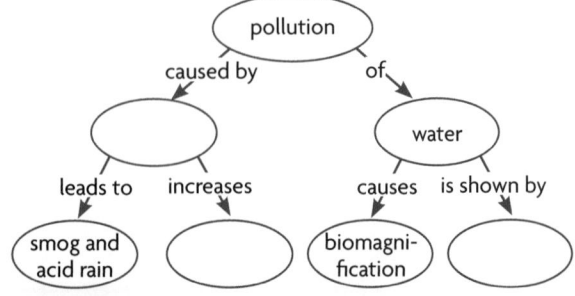

pollution

caused by · of

water

leads to · increases · causes · is shown by

smog and acid rain

biomagnification

Process Diagram Use the process diagram like the one below to explain the greenhouse effect.

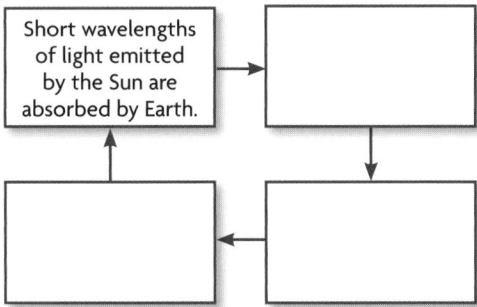

Short wavelengths of light emitted by the Sun are absorbed by Earth.

Chapter Assessment

Chapter Vocabulary

16.1 nonrenewable resource, p. 485
renewable resource, p. 485
ecological footprint, p. 487

16.2 pollution, p. 488
smog, p. 488
particulate, p. 488
acid rain, p. 489
greenhouse effect, p. 490
global warming, p. 492

16.3 indicator species, p. 494
biomagnification, p. 495

16.4 habitat fragmentation, p. 499
introduced species, p. 500

16.5 sustainable development, p. 502
umbrella species, p. 503

Reviewing Vocabulary

Compare and Contrast

Describe one similarity and one difference between the two terms in each of the following pairs.

1. renewable resource, nonrenewable resource
2. smog, acid rain
3. greenhouse effect, global warming
4. indicator species, umbrella species

Word Origins

5. The word *sustain* comes from the Latin words *sub-*, which means "below," and *tenere*, which means "to hold." Explain how these meanings relate to the term *sustainable development*.

6. The term *biomagnification* is comprised of the prefix *bio-*, which means "life," and the word *magnify*, which comes from a Latin word meaning "great" or "large." Explain how the meanings of the word parts make up the meaning of the term.

7. The word *umbrella* comes from the Latin word *umbra*, which means "shadow." How does the everyday meaning of the word *umbrella* relate to the ecological meaning of the term *umbrella species*?

Draw Cartoons

For each vocabulary term below, draw a cartoon that will best summarize the definition.

8. ecological footprint
9. global warming
10. introduced species

Reviewing MAIN IDEAS

11. Earth's human carrying capacity has exceeded many earlier predictions. How has technology affected human population growth?

12. The United States uses more resources and produces more waste than any other country. How is this resource use reflected in the ecological footprint of the United States?

13. What are the major causes of smog and acid rain? What are the effects of each type of pollution?

14. Since the 1970s, human activity has released approximately 150 billion tons of carbon dioxide into the atmosphere. How could the increase in atmospheric carbon dioxide impact the greenhouse effect?

15. Which organism is most likely to have accumulated toxins through biomagnification: plankton, a small plankton-eating fish, or a large fish that eats smaller fish? Explain.

16. How could the extinction of a single species, such as a predatory bird, affect an entire ecosystem?

17. In what ways can an introduced species impact an ecosystem it has colonized?

18. The North American grizzly bear is considered an umbrella species. Explain how the protection of the grizzly bear may affect the larger ecosystem to which the bear belongs.

19. Analyze Assuming all other factors are the same, the more meat in a person's diet, the larger that person's ecological footprint. Why might this be the case?

20. Connect Nationwide, automobiles are the major source of carbon monoxide, carbon dioxide, nitrogen oxides, particulate matter, and cancer-causing toxins. What can you do to decrease your fossil fuel use?

21. Evaluate An ecological footprint is a measure of the impact of the resources we use on the environment. Explain how buying a carton of milk relates to your ecological footprint.

22. Infer Frogs are commonly used as an indicator species in aquatic habitats. Could a large predator such as a bear or an eagle be used as an indicator species? Explain.

23. Synthesize Explain how a predator insect species, introduced to help control insect pests, could become a threat to an ecosystem.

Interpreting Visuals

Use the simple food web outlined below to answer the next three questions.

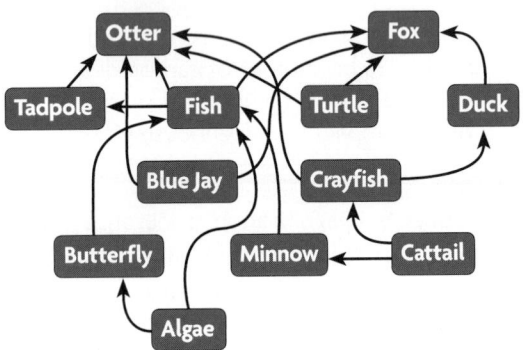

24. Apply Which of these organisms is likely to be most affected by biomagnification of toxins? Explain your answer.

25. Predict This food web includes both aquatic and terrestrial organisms. Imagine that a new road separates the aquatic environment from the nearby terrestrial environment. Do you think the turtle or the duck would be more affected by this habitat fragmentation? Explain.

26. Predict Imagine that an introduced species results in the local extermination of crayfish. How might this change affect the larger ecosystem?

Analyzing Data

This circle graph shows the components of the ecological footprint for a resident of a North American city. Use the graph to answer the next two questions.

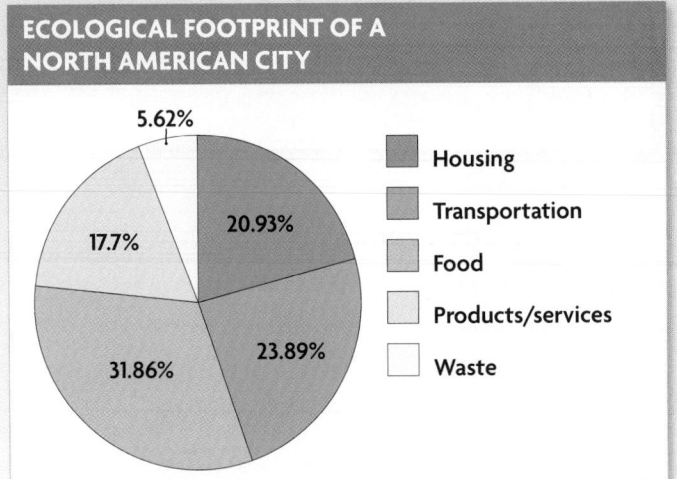

ECOLOGICAL FOOTPRINT OF A NORTH AMERICAN CITY

5.62%

20.93%

17.7%

23.89%

31.86%

■ Housing
■ Transportation
■ Food
□ Products/services
□ Waste

27. Apply Does the circle graph show discrete or continuous data? Explain.

28. Analyze In order of biggest to smallest impact, list the components of human activity that make up the average ecological footprint, according to this graph.

Connecting CONCEPTS

29. Write a Scenario Imagine that successful efforts in sustainable development have made global resource use and waste production fully sustainable by the year 2099. Write a few paragraphs that describe what a sustainable world might look like in 2099. Include information about resource use, waste production, pollution, biodiversity, and conservation.

30. Connect Look again at the damaged forest ecosystem on page 483. The emissions produced in this region have led to the rapid decline in the biodiversity of this area. How might this decline affect the resources of local animal populations?

MICHIGAN STANDARDS-BASED ASSESSMENT

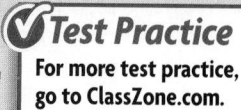
☑ **Test Practice**
For more test practice, go to ClassZone.com.

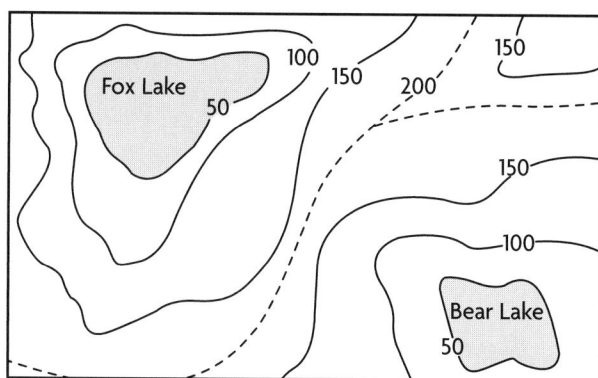

1. This topographic map shows the Fox Lake and Bear Lake watersheds, or regions that drain into these lakes. The watershed boundary, shown with a dashed line, determines which lake water will flow into. According to the map, this boundary follows   **B1.1E**

A the highest elevation points between the lakes.

B the lowest elevation points between the lakes.

C a river that likely flows between the lakes.

D exactly halfway between the two lakes.

2. Which of the following *most* directly played a role in the human population growth of the 20th century?   **L3.p4A**

A improved transportation, which increased immigration

B satellite technology, which increased global communication

C improved public health, which decreased death rates

D readily available contraception, which decreased birth rates

3. The nonnative zebra mussel was first found in a lake near Detroit in 1988. By 1989, it had colonized all Great Lakes waterways. Which scenario is *most* likely true regarding the introduction of this species?   **B3.5C**

A Native fish naturally eat zebra mussels.

B The higher biodiversity leads to healthier lakes.

C They compete with native mussels for food and other resources.

D Native mussel populations are growing rapidly.

4.

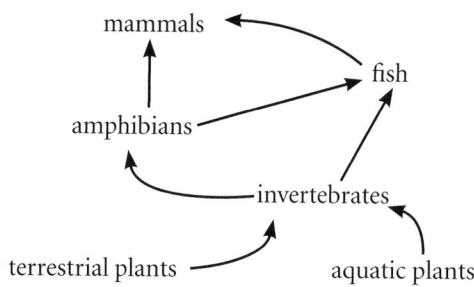

Through the process of biomagnification, certain pollutants build up at each link of a food web. In a polluted river, at what link in the food web above would pollutant concentrations be the highest?   **L3.p3C**

A aquatic plants

B fish

C invertebrates

D mammals

5. Which situation would *most* efficiently decrease the size of a field mouse population?   **L3.p2B**

A decreased death rates and emigration.

B decreased birth rates and immigration.

C increased death rates and immigration.

D increased death rates and emigration.

> **THINK THROUGH THE QUESTION**
>
> As you look at the answer choices, think carefully about how each factor—birth rates, death rates, immigration, and emigration—affect population size.

6. CO_2 is important in our atmosphere because it is required for photosynthesis and it traps some heat, keeping Earth warm. However, human-produced CO_2 is a problem because it   **B3.4C**

A leads to higher global temperatures.

B disrupts the natural cycling of other greenhouse gases.

C adds too much CO_2 to the oceans.

D causes uncontrolled photosynthesis.

BIOZINE
INTERNET MAGAZINE
at CLASSZONE.COM

Go online for the latest biology news and updates on all BioZine articles.

Expanding the Textbook

News Feeds

- 🔊 Science Daily
- 🔊 CNN
- 🔊 BBC

Careers

Bio Bytes

Opinion Poll

Strange Biology

As global temperatures rise and arctic ice melts, polar bears are losing important hunting grounds.

Global Warming— Changing the Planet

Polar bears are beginning to drown. In the summer, the area of arctic sea ice on which these carnivores hunt seals has declined 10 to 15 percent as worldwide temperatures rise. As this ice is lost, polar bears must swim as far as 100 kilometers (about 60 mi) to find their prey. Some of these polar bears do not make it. If global warming is changing the shape of one of Earth's coldest regions, how will it affect the rest of our planet?

Ecosystems at Risk

In the 21st century, the average global temperature is expected to rise about 0.22°C (0.4°F) per decade. This may seem like a small change, but this change is magnified in the seasonal temperature changes of a region. In some parts of the world, such as the Arctic, the temperature is changing much faster. Average annual temperatures in Alaska have risen 3.3°C (5.9°F) since 1949. Sea ice area has been shrinking over the past 100 years, and the ice has become 40 percent thinner in the past several decades, leaving coastal land vulnerable to erosion.

Good and Bad News?

In the rest of the world, the impact of global warming on Earth's species may not be as bad. Many animal species, such as birds and butterflies, can move to cooler areas as the climate warms. But the microorganisms that cause infectious diseases, such as malaria and yellow fever, are also spreading toward the poles. Plant species are moving as well, but many are not able to move as quickly as the climate is expected to change.

Researchers are also finding that changing temperatures can affect animals in surprising ways. The sex of some reptiles, for example, is partially determined by the temperature of the developing egg. A consistent warming trend could cause some reptiles to become extinct by creating entire generations that are all the same sex. Migratory birds and marine mammals also face challenges. For example, birds that wait until their normal migration time to fly north in the spring may arrive too late, missing the best weeks for laying eggs and catching the insects they need to raise their young. In addition, marine mammals face challenges in their own food webs. Several researchers are predicting that the productivity of phytoplankton, the algae on which ocean food webs are based, may decline in some areas. A change of this sort could cause a domino effect in marine food webs. If phytoplankton levels decline, fish will have less food and will be less numerous. If fish are less numerous, marine mammals and birds will have less to eat too.

TECHNOLOGY

Deep Sea Sediment Coring

Analyzing ocean floor sediments can provide scientists with data about how plants and animals were affected during past climate changes. The process of collecting deep sea sediments is expensive and time-consuming, but the results of this research give scientists a look at what life in the oceans was like millions of years ago.

To study these ancient organisms, scientists need sediment samples that are hundreds of meters long. To obtain these, they must use drills similar to the drills used by the oil and gas industry. Taking these samples requires many hours and can be dangerous if the seas are rough or full of ice. Once scientists have obtained the cores, they first split the core in half lengthwise. One half is sampled for fossils of ancient organisms. This is the "working half." The other half, the "archive half," is saved and stored away so that future scientists who may develop other questions can have access to this difficult-to-obtain material.

By carefully dissecting the working half of the sample, scientists discover microscopic fossils of marine animals. Scientists know that these ancient animals were very sensitive to slight changes in temperature and chemistry. These microfossils can tell scientists how Earth's climate has changed over millions of years.

Read More >> *at* CLASSZONE.COM

These "working half" cores will be carefully dissected and analyzed to better understand Earth's changing climate.

Computer modeling programs such as this one work to predict the effects of global warming by simulating different temperature increases.

The news may not be all bad. Global warming is caused by increased levels of carbon dioxide in the atmosphere. Many plants, including crops such as cotton, soybeans, wheat, and rice, can benefit from the increase in CO_2. They can absorb the CO_2 and yield more at harvest time as a result. On the other hand, in warmer weather crops may also be more at risk from insect pests and from severe storms or droughts.

Unanswered Questions

Scientists have little doubt that Earth's climate is changing. Unfortunately, it is impossible to predict exactly how any particular ecosystem will be affected by global warming. However, biologists and climatologists are collecting data about processes including solar radiation, precipitation, evaporation, the transfer of heat energy by winds and by ocean currents, and the ways in which plants affect climate. Then, by using computer models that interpret this information, they can begin to answer questions about how global warming will affect Earth.

- Does global warming cause the number of tropical storms and hurricanes to increase?

- Could global warming alter certain ocean currents, changing Earth's temperatures further?

- How quickly might the polar ice caps melt?

- How have global climate changes affected Earth's ecosystems in the past?

Read More >> *at* **CLASSZONE.COM**

CAREERS

Oceanographer in Action

RUTH CURRY
TITLE Oceanographer, Woods Hole Oceanographic Institution
EDUCATION B.S., Geology, Brown University

For Ruth Curry, spending time on the ocean waves has nothing to do with surfing or vacationing. She spends her time studying the ocean currents that affect our lives each day. Ruth Curry is an oceanographer at the Woods Hole Oceanographic Institute, an organization of scientists who research and study how the ocean affects the global environment.

Curry's research focuses on the North Atlantic circulation and the currents that carry warm waters from tropical regions northward. As these warm waters reach higher latitudes, they release heat that warms the air above them and warms the climate of western Europe. As warm water cools, its density increases and it sinks to the bottom of the ocean. There it begins a southward journey back to the tropics. This conveyor belt of water plays an important role in maintaining Earth's climate. Normally, the salinity, or saltiness, of ocean water stays about the same. But changes in global temperatures are melting large sheets of ice in Greenland, which is introducing large amounts of fresh water into the ocean. This fresh water is diluting the ocean water, making it less salty. A decrease in salinity makes ocean waters less dense and prevents them from sinking to the bottom of the ocean. Eventually, the melting of ice sheets in Greenland could cause the North Atlantic currents to slow and eventually stop, leading to dramatic changes in the Northern Hemisphere's climate.

Read More >> *at* **CLASSZONE.COM**

UNIT 6

Classification and Diversity

CHAPTER 17
The Tree of Life   516

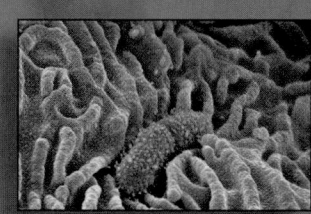

CHAPTER 18
Viruses and Prokaryotes   542

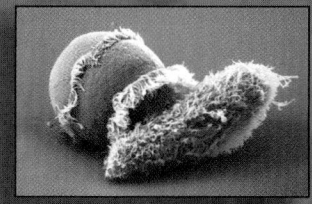

CHAPTER 19
Protists and Fungi   572

BIOZINE   INTERNET MAGAZINE
**Pandemics—Is the Next
One on the Way?**   606
    TECHNOLOGY Dissecting a Virus
    CAREER Epidemiologist

CHAPTER

17 The Tree of Life

KEY CONCEPTS

17.1 The Linnaean System of Classification
Organisms can be classified based on physical similarities.

17.2 Classification Based on Evolutionary Relationships
Modern classification is based on evolutionary relationships.

17.3 Molecular Clocks
Molecular clocks provide clues to evolutionary history.

17.4 Domains and Kingdoms
The current tree of life has three domains.

 Online BIOLOGY CLASSZONE.COM

Animated BIOLOGY
View animated chapter concepts.
• Molecular Clock
• Build a Cladogram

BIOZINE
Keep current with biology news.
• Featured stories
• News feeds
• Strange Biology

RESOURCE CENTER
Get more information on
• Modern Classification
• Molecular Clocks

How would you classify this organism?

Connecting CONCEPTS

Pangolins, native to Africa and Asia, are not closely related to any other living mammals. Their backs and tails are covered with large scales similar in arrangement to dinosaur bone plates. Pangolins do not have teeth. Instead, they have an organ similar to a bird's gizzard. Due to these unique traits, pangolins are classified into their own group within class Mammalia.

Evolution The pangolin's long snout and tongue, sharp claws for digging, and the absence of teeth are all adaptations to an ant-eating lifestyle. Anteaters and aardvarks have similar traits. However, these animals are not closely related. Instead, pangolins, anteaters, and aardvarks display convergent evolution. Their similar characteristics arose independently as natural selection acted upon species with similar diets.

17.1

The Linnaean System of Classification

KEY CONCEPT Organisms can be classified based on physical similarities.

► MAIN IDEAS

- Linnaeus developed the scientific naming system still used today.
- Linnaeus' classification system has seven levels.
- The Linnaean classification system has limitations.

VOCABULARY

taxonomy, p. 518
taxon, p. 518
binomial nomenclature, p. 519
genus, p. 519

Review
species

MICHIGAN STANDARDS

B1.2i Explain the progression of ideas and explanations that leads to science theories that are part of the current scientific consensus or core knowledge.

B2.4A Explain that living things can be classified based on structural, embryological, and molecular (relatedness of DNA sequence) evidence.

TAKING NOTES

Use a main idea web to take notes about the Linnaean system of classification.

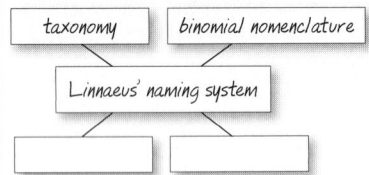

VOCABULARY

Taxonomy comes from the Greek *taxis,* which means "arrangement," and *nomie,* which means "method."

Connect The pangolin shown on the previous page may not look like any other animal that you are familiar with. However, scientists classify pangolins as mammals—the same group of animals that includes dogs, cats, mice, and humans. All female mammals have the ability to produce milk. Unlike pangolins, most mammals have hair. Scientists use key characteristics such as these to classify all living things.

► MAIN IDEA

Linnaeus developed the scientific naming system still used today.

Before Swedish botanist Carolus Linnaeus introduced his scientific naming system, naturalists named newly discovered organisms however they wanted. In fact, they often named organisms after themselves. Because they had no agreed-upon way to name living things, it was difficult for naturalists to talk about their findings with one another. This all changed in the 1750s, when Linnaeus devised a system that standardized the way organisms are classified and named.

Taxonomy

Taxonomy is the science of naming and classifying organisms. Taxonomy gives scientists a standard way to refer to species and organize the diversity of living things. Linnaean taxonomy classifies organisms based on their physical and structural similarities. Organisms are placed into different levels in a hierarchy—a multilevel scale in which each level is "nested" in the next-higher level. In other words, each level is included in a larger, more general level, which in turn is included in an even larger, more general level.

A group of organisms in a classification system is called a **taxon** (plural, *taxa*). The basic taxon in the Linnaean system is the species. In this system, species are most commonly defined as a group of organisms that can breed and produce offspring that can reproduce. Linnaeus' system gives each species a scientific name. With few changes, this method of naming is still used today.

Scientific Names

Binomial nomenclature (by-NOH-mee-uhl NOH-muhn-KLAY-chuhr) is a system that gives each species a two-part scientific name using Latin words. The first part of the name is the genus. A **genus** (plural, *genera*) includes one or more physically similar species that are thought to be closely related. For example, the genus *Quercus* includes more than 500 species of oak trees. Genus names are always capitalized. They are written in italics or underlined.

VISUAL VOCAB

Binomial nomenclature is a standard naming system that gives each species a two-part name using Latin words.

two — bi; name — nomial; naming — nomen; system — clature

bi → (1) *Genus* (2) *species*

The second part of the name is the species descriptor. It can refer to a trait of the species, the scientist who first described it, or its native location. Like the genus, the species descriptor is written in italics or underlined. However, it is always lowercase. The species descriptor is never written alone because, as **FIGURE 17.1** shows, the same word may be used in different genera. *Quercus alba* is the scientific name for white oak trees (*alba* means "white"), but *Tyto alba* is the scientific name for barn owls.

You may wonder why biologists use scientific names. It may seem easier to use terms such as *white oak* instead of remembering two-part Latin names. However, scientific names are helpful in a number of ways. First, genera such as *Quercus* contain hundreds of species. Many of these species have very similar common names. Scientific names allow scientists to talk about particular species without confusion. Also, remember that biology is studied all over the world. One species may have many different common names. In fact, a species may have several different common names within a single country. *Armidillidium vulgare* is the scientific name for pill bugs. However, this species is also called roly-poly, sow bug, and potato bug. Scientific names allow scientists around the world to communicate clearly about living things.

Contrast **Describe the difference between a genus and a species.**

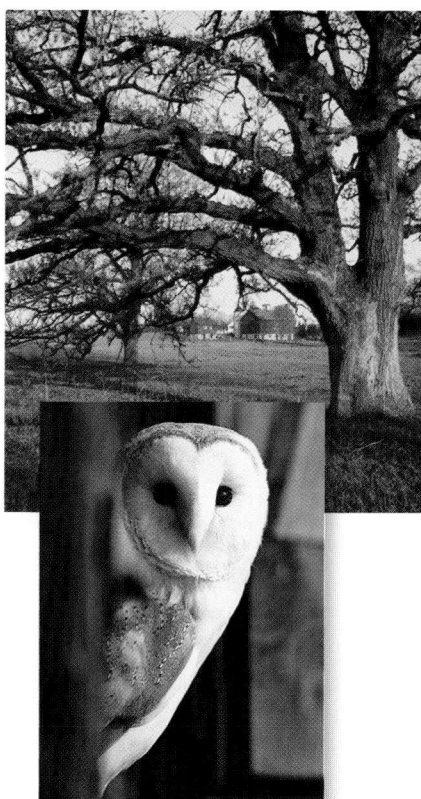

FIGURE 17.1 The white oak (*Quercus alba*) and the barn owl (*Tyto alba*) belong to different genera. The species parts of their scientific names are both *alba*, meaning "white."

FIGURE 17.2 SCIENTIFIC AND COMMON NAMES

COMMON NAMES	SCIENTIFIC NAME	
	Genus	**species**
Roly-poly, pill bug, sow bug, potato bug	*Armadillidium*	*vulgare*
Dandelion, Irish daisy, lion's tooth	*Taraxacum*	*officinale*
House sparrow, English sparrow	*Passer*	*domesticus*
Mountain lion, cougar, puma	*Puma*	*concolor*
Red maple, scarlet maple, swamp maple	*Acer*	*rubrum*

MAIN IDEA

Linnaeus' classification system has seven levels.

Connecting CONCEPTS

Domains The tree of life has been updated since Linnaeus' time. Scientists now classify organisms into an even broader category, called the domain, above the kingdom level. You will learn more about domains and kingdoms in **Section 17.4.**

The Linnaean system of classification has seven levels, or taxa. From the most general to the most specific, these levels are kingdom, phylum (the term *division* is often used instead of *phylum* for plants and fungi), class, order, family, genus, and species. Each level in Linnaeus' system is nested, or included, in the level above it. A kingdom contains one or more phyla, a phylum contains one or more classes, and so forth. The classification of the gray wolf, *Canis lupis,* is shown in **FIGURE 17.3**. Moving down, the levels represent taxa that become more and more specific, until you reach the species level at the bottom.

FIGURE 17.3 The Linnaean Classification System

Linnaean taxonomy classifies living things into a hierarchy of groups called taxa. The classification of the gray wolf is illustrated here.

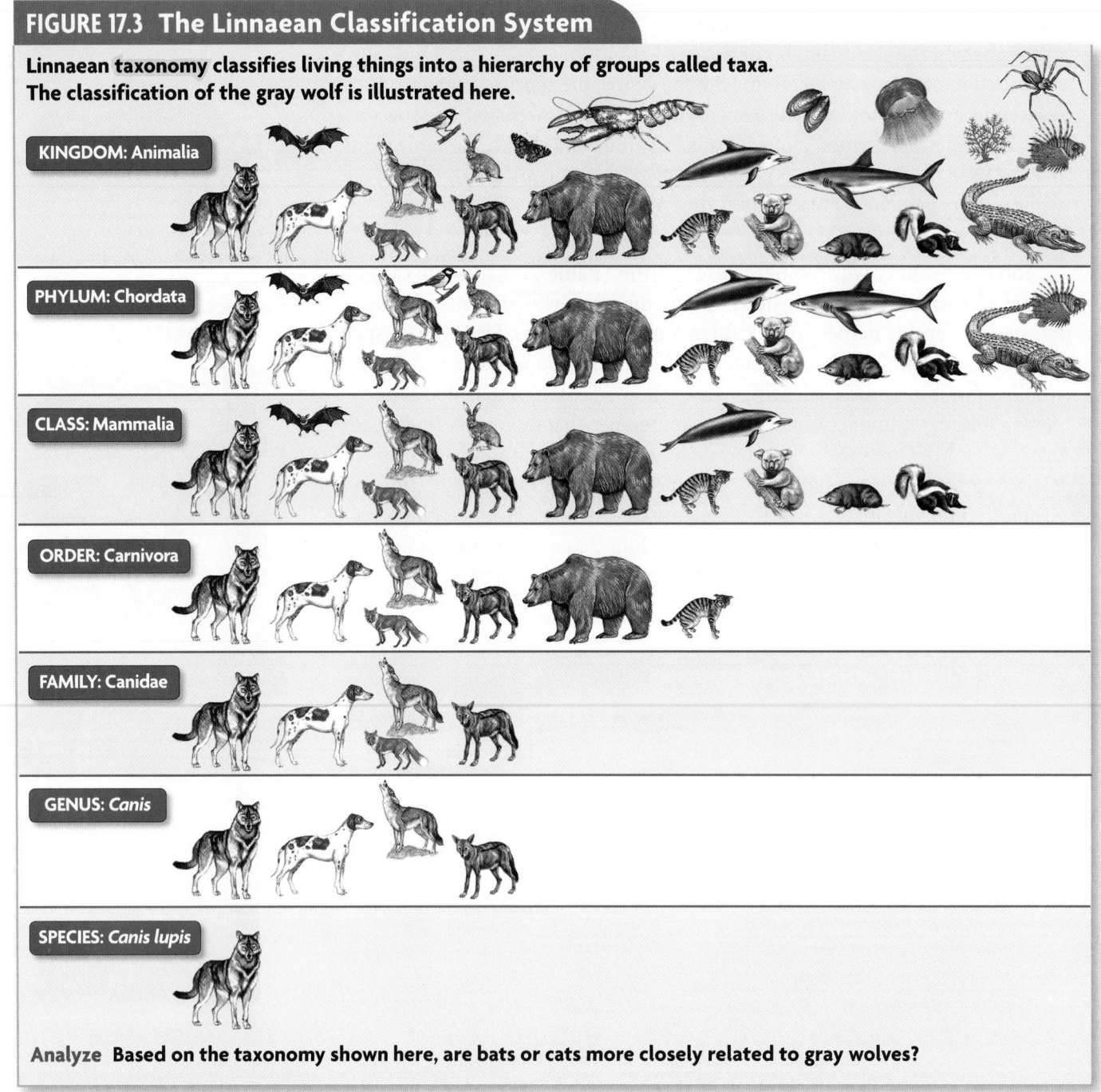

KINGDOM: Animalia

PHYLUM: Chordata

CLASS: Mammalia

ORDER: Carnivora

FAMILY: Canidae

GENUS: *Canis*

SPECIES: *Canis lupis*

Analyze Based on the taxonomy shown here, are bats or cats more closely related to gray wolves?

The top level represents all of the species in kingdom Animalia. As you move down, the levels show examples of species from phylum Chordata, class Mammalia, order Carnivora, family Canidae, genus *Canis*, and the species *Canis lupis*. Each level is included in all of the more general levels above it.

Notice that gray wolves are in the same genus, *Canis*, as dogs and coyotes. Because the Linnaean system is a nested hierarchy, wolves, dogs, and coyotes also belong to the same family, order, class, phylum, and kingdom. Foxes do not belong to the *Canis* genus, but they do belong to Canidae—the same family as wolves, dogs, and coyotes. Therefore, foxes also belong to the same order, class, phylum, and kingdom as wolves, dogs, and coyotes.

Apply **If two species belong to the same order, what other levels in the Linnaean system must they have in common?**

FIGURE 17.4 This red panda (*Ailurus fulgens*) is more closely related to raccoons than to giant pandas.

◉ MAIN IDEA

The Linnaean classification system has limitations.

Linnaeus created his classification system before technology allowed us to study organisms at the molecular level. His system focuses on physical similarities alone. Remember that physical similarities between two species are not always a result of the species' being closely related. Unrelated species can evolve similar traits through convergent evolution. Linnaeus' system does not account for similarities that evolved this way. So today, scientists use genetic research to help classify living things. Genetic similarities between two species are more likely than physical similarities to be due to a common ancestor.

For example, the giant panda and the raccoon have similar ears and snouts. Because of these similarities, they have been placed in the same family in the Linnaean system. However, molecular biologists have found that the giant panda is more closely related to members of the bear family than it is to raccoons. Furthermore, the red panda, shown in **FIGURE 17.4**, is more closely related to the raccoon than to the giant panda.

Infer **Why is the common name *red panda* misleading in terms of classification based on relatedness?**

Connecting CONCEPTS

Classification Refer to the **Appendix** for a complete list of the kingdoms and their phyla.

NSTA
scilinks.org
SC*I*INKS

To learn more about taxonomy, go to scilinks.org.
Keycode: MLB017

ONLINE QUIZ
ClassZone.com

REVIEWING ◉ MAIN IDEAS

1. What is **binomial nomenclature**?

2. Name each **taxon** in the Linnaean system of classification, from most general to most specific.

3. What are some limitations of the Linnaean classification system?

CRITICAL THINKING

4. **Compare** How is a scientific name similar to an address that includes city and state?

5. **Apply** Which two species are more closely related: *Ursus maritimus, Ursus americanus,* or *Bufo americanus?* Explain your answer.

Connecting CONCEPTS

6. **History of Science** During his voyages, Darwin collected thousands of organisms, which he classified using the Linnaean classification system. How did this system help him share his findings with other naturalists?

MATERIAL

set of or photographs
of limpet shells

PROCESS SKILLS

- **Observing**
- **Identifying**
- **Classifying**

B2.4A Explain that living
things can be classified
based on structural, embryological, and molecular
(relatedness of DNA
sequence) evidence.

B2.4d Analyze the
relationships among
organisms based on their
shared physical,
biochemical, genetic, and
cellular characteristics and
functional processes.

Creating a Dichotomous Key for Limpet Shells

Limpets are marine invertebrates found along rocky shorelines around the world. The flattened shape of a limpet's shell allows it to withstand the impact of waves, and its muscular foot allows it to cling tightly to rocks. Although biologists today classify limpets by using traits of the entire organism, for this activity you will construct a dichotomous key based on shell characteristics.

Dichotomous keys are used to identify objects or organisms that have already been described by another scientist. As its name implies (*di-* means "two"), a dichotomous key is made up of paired statements. Each pair of statements divides the objects to be classified into two categories. This means that each object must fit into one category or the other, but not both. At the right is a simple example of a dichotomous key that identifies five common beans. As you proceed from step to step, the classification is narrowed down until all five beans are identified.

SAMPLE DICHOTOMOUS KEY FOR BEANS	
1.a. If the bean is round .... it is a garbanzo bean.	
1.b. If the bean is oblong .... go to step 2.	
2.a. If the bean is white ..... it is a white northern bean.	
2.b. If the bean is dark-colored .... go to step 3.	
3.a. If the bean is a solid color .... go to step 4.	
3.b. If the bean is speckled .... it is a pinto bean.	
4.a. If the bean is black .... it is a black bean.	
4.b. If the bean is reddish-brown .... it is a kidney bean.	

PROBLEM What characteristics can you use to make a dichotomous key for limpet shells?

PROCEDURE

1. Identify some characteristics of each limpet shell. Characteristics may include margin (edge) variation, shape, color, and features on the shell.

2. Construct a dichotomous key, using the above sample for beans as a guide. Start with a general characteristic that separates your limpets into two groups. (**Example:** Keyhole limpets have a hole at the highest point of their shell; true limpets do not.)

3. Continue making paired statements that become more detailed.

   - Each pair of statements must contain only two choices, and these choices must refer to the same characteristic. (**Example:** Do not compare size and color in the same pair of statements.) Every limpet that has not yet been identified must fit one of the two choices.

   - Do not use vague terms such as *big* and *little*. Be as specific as possible.

   - Each statement must either identify a limpet or lead to another step in the key.

4. Trade dichotomous keys with another student or group in your class. Check to make sure you can identify each limpet using your classmates' key.

 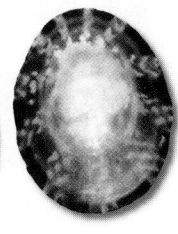

Cellana testudinaria
Common turtle limpet

Collisella striata
Striate limpet

Patelloida saccharina
Sugar limpet

Fissurella nodosa
Knobbed keyhole limpet

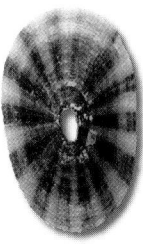

Fissurella maxima
Giant keyhole limpet

Cellana radiata
Rayed limpet

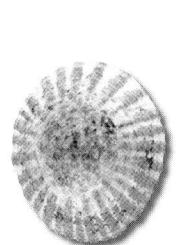 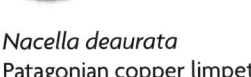

Nacella deaurata
Patagonian copper limpet

 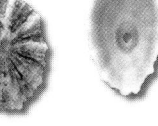

Fissurella barbadensis
Barbados keyhole limpet

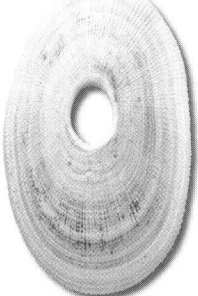

Megathura crenulata
Great keyhole limpet

ANALYZE AND CONCLUDE

1. **Summarize** How did you organize the limpet shells?

2. **Analyze** What different categories did other groups use to organize the shells?

3. **Identify Problems** What problems arose as you constructed your key?

4. **Infer** If you were given the actual shells, what additional characteristics could you have used to make your key?

5. **Apply** Two outcomes are said to be mutually exclusive if they cannot both occur at the same time. For example, heads and tails are mutually exclusive outcomes of flipping a coin. Why is it important that the paired statements in a dichotomous key describe mutually exclusive characteristics?

17.2 Classification Based on Evolutionary Relationships

KEY CONCEPT Modern classification is based on evolutionary relationships.

MAIN IDEAS
- Cladistics is classification based on common ancestry.
- Molecular evidence reveals species' relatedness.

VOCABULARY
phylogeny, p. 524
cladistics, p. 525
cladogram, p. 525

derived character, p. 525

Review
taxon

MICHIGAN STANDARDS

B2.4d Analyze the relationships among organisms based on their shared physical, biochemical, genetic, and cellular characteristics and functional processes.

B5.r2d Interpret a cladogram or phylogenetic tree showing evolutionary relationships among organisms. (recommended)

Connect If you've ever observed bats in a zoo or in the night sky, you've likely noticed that they have several features in common with birds, such as wings. However, bats are actually more closely related to rodents and primates than they are to birds. Today, scientists agree that species should be classified based on evolutionary relationships rather than just physical similarities.

MAIN IDEA
Cladistics is classification based on common ancestry.

Similar traits between species are often the result of sharing a common ancestor, such as the ancestor shared by dogs and wolves. However, scientists now know that similar traits, such as the wings of bats and birds, can also evolve in species that are adapting to similar environmental conditions. As you read in Chapter 11, this process is called convergent evolution.

To classify species according to how they are related, scientists must look at more than just physical traits. Modern classification is based on figuring out evolutionary relationships using evidence from living species, the fossil record, and molecular data. The evolutionary history for a group of species is called a **phylogeny** (fy-LAHJ-uh-nee).

Phylogenies can be shown as branching tree diagrams. In a way, these diagrams are like family trees. The branches of a family tree show how family members are related to each other. The branches of an evolutionary tree show how different groups of species are related to each other.

FIGURE 17.5 The glyptodon (*Glyptotherium arizonae*), illustrated here, was the size of a small car and lived more than 10,000 years ago. It is the common ancestor to about 20 modern armadillo species, including the nine-banded armadillo (*Dasypus novemcinctus*).

Glyptodon

Armadillo

Cladistics

The most common method used to make evolutionary trees is called cladistics. **Cladistics** (kluh-DIHS-tihks) is classification based on common ancestry. The goal of cladistics is to place species in the order in which they descended from a common ancestor. A **cladogram** is an evolutionary tree that proposes how species may be related to each other through common ancestors.

At the root of the words *cladistics* and *cladogram* is the word *clade*. A clade is a group of species that shares a common ancestor. For example, the glyptodon in **FIGURE 17.5** is the common ancestor of about 20 modern species of armadillos. Together, the glyptodon and all of its descendants form a clade.

Through the course of evolution, certain traits change in some species of a clade but stay the same in other species. Therefore, each species in a clade has some traits that have not changed from its ancestors, such as the similar shells of glyptodons and modern armadillos. However, each species also has traits that have changed over evolutionary time.

The traits that can be used to figure out evolutionary relationships among a group of species are those that are shared by some species but are not present in others. These traits are called **derived characters.** As you will soon see, cladograms are made by figuring out which derived characters are shared by which species. The more closely related species are, the more derived characters they will share. A group of species that shares no derived characters with the other groups being studied is called an outgroup.

VOCABULARY

The word *derived* comes from the Latin *de-*, meaning "from," and *rivus*, meaning "stream." Therefore, *derived* refers to something that has "flowed" from a source. The term *derived characters* refers to characters that have evolved in a species since sharing a common ancestor.

QUICK LAB   CLASSIFYING

Construct a Cladogram

You can think of a cladogram as an evolutionary family tree in which things that are more closely related share more characteristics. As an analogy, processes that have evolved due to new technologies can be organized using cladistics. In this lab, you will fill in a cladogram for methods of transportation.

PROBLEM How can methods of transportation be organized using a cladogram?

PROCEDURE

1. Copy the cladogram axes on the right into your notebook.
2. Think about the characteristics of the following methods of transportation: bicycle, car, motorcycle, airplane, and on foot.
3. Complete your cladogram by filling in each method of transportation listed in step 2 on the appropriate line at the top.

ANALYZE AND CONCLUDE

1. **Identify** What "derived characters" are used in this cladogram?
2. **Analyze** Which mode of transportation may be considered an "outgroup"—a group that has none of the characteristics labeled on the cladogram?
3. **Connect** A species that has evolved a new trait is not better than a species without that trait. Each species is just adapted to a certain way of life. When might riding a bike have an advantage over flying in an airplane?

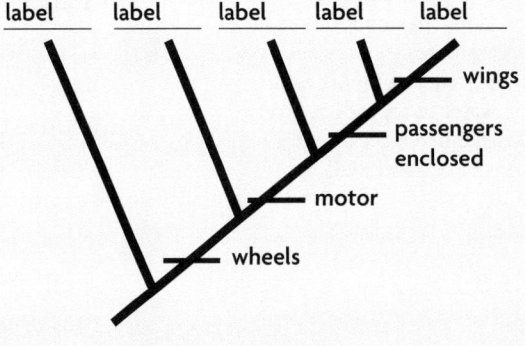

Interpreting a Cladogram

The main features of a cladogram are shown in **FIGURE 17.6.** Tetrapods are vertebrates that have four limbs—amphibians, reptiles, birds, and mammals. Some tetrapods, such as snakes and marine mammals, no longer have the four limbs that their known ancestors had. However, they are still members of the tetrapoda clade because they share a common ancestor.

Derived characters In a cladogram, groups of species are placed in order by the derived characters that have added up in their lineage over time. This order is hypothesized to be the order in which they descended from their common ancestor. Derived characters are shown as hash marks between the branches of the cladogram. All species above a hash mark share the derived character it represents.

Nodes Each place where a branch splits is called a node. There are five nodes on the tetrapod cladogram. The first node is where the amphibian branch splits off from the rest of the cladogram. Nodes represent the most recent common ancestor shared by a clade. Therefore, the first node of the tetrapod cladogram represents a common ancestor for the whole tetrapod clade.

Identifying clades You can identify clades by using the "snip rule." Whenever you "snip" a branch under a node, a clade falls off. In this cladogram, if you were to "snip" below the node where turtles and tortoises branch off, you would be left with the reptilia clade. This clade includes turtles and tortoises, lizards and snakes, crocodiles and alligators, and birds. As you can see, each clade is nested within the clade that forms just before it. There are five clades in the tetrapod cladogram. Crocodiles, alligators, and birds belong to all five clades.

1 All of the organisms in this cladogram belong to the tetrapoda clade (brown). They all share the derived character of four limbs.

2 An embryo protected by a fluid-filled sac is a derived character for all organisms in the amniota clade (blue). Because amphibians do not produce an amniotic sac, the amphibian branch splits off from rest of the branches before the mark that represents this trait.

3 Organisms in the reptilia clade (yellow) have a common ancestor that had four legs, produced protected eggs, and had a skull with openings behind the eyes. The third node in the cladogram represents this common ancestor. Because mammal skulls do not have these openings, they are not part of the reptilia clade.

4 Organisms in the diapsida clade (green) have openings in the side of the skull. The skulls of turtles and tortoises do not have these openings, so they are not part of the diapsida clade.

5 Lizards and snakes branch off of the cladogram next. Their skulls do not have certain openings in the jaw that are found in crocodiles, alligators, and birds. This is the derived character shared by all organisms in the archosauria clade (pink). Feathers and toothless beaks separate crocodiles and alligators from birds within the archosauria clade.

Contrast **What is the difference between a clade and a taxon?**

FIGURE 17.6 Cladogram for Tetrapods

A **cladogram** presents hypothesized evolutionary relationships among a group of species based on common ancestry and derived characters.

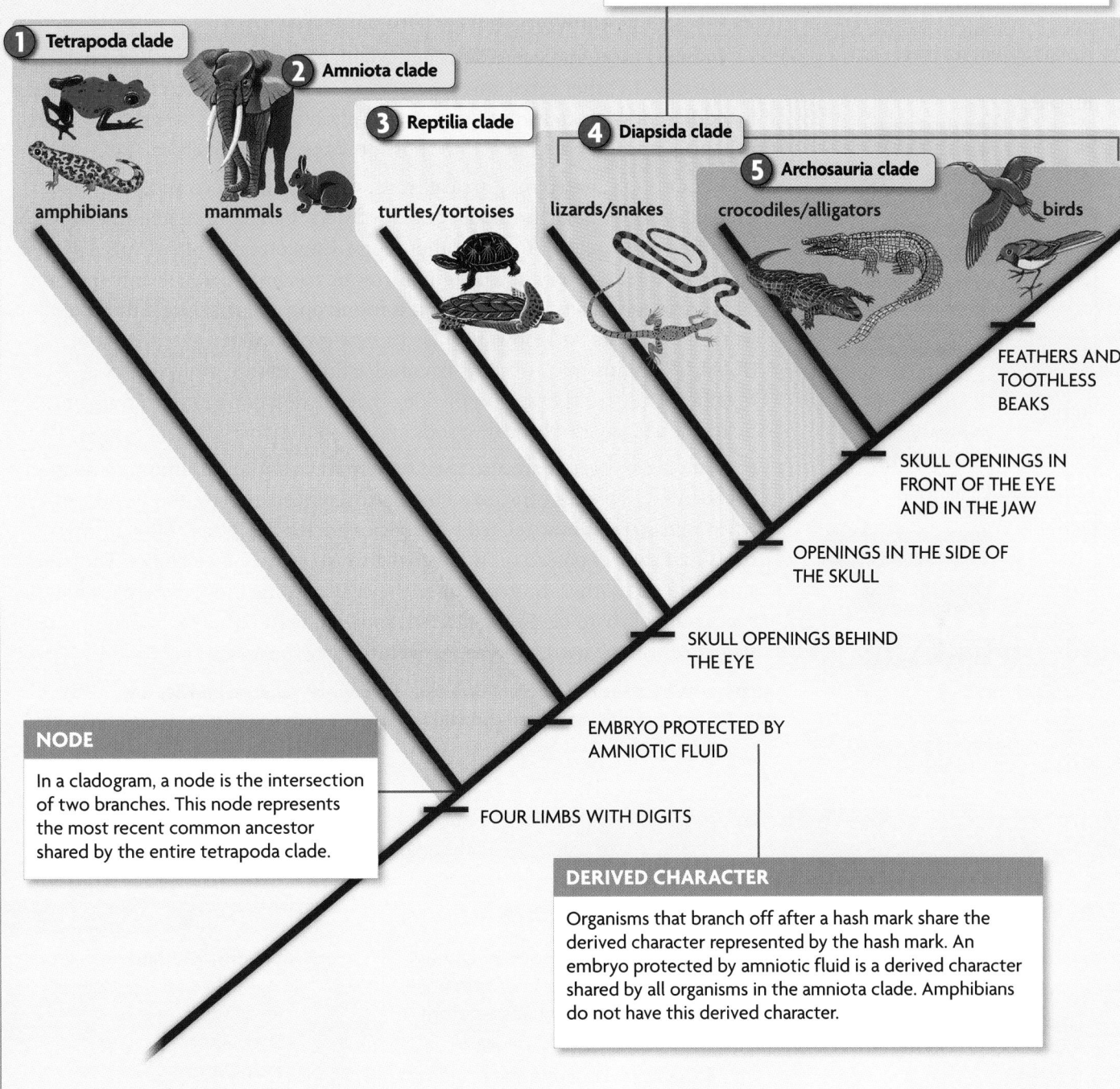

CLADE

A clade is a group of organisms that share certain traits derived from a common ancestor. In this cladogram, a clade looks like the letter V, including all the branches that extend from the right end of the V. The diapsida clade includes lizards and snakes, crocodiles and alligators, and birds.

1 **Tetrapoda clade**

2 **Amniota clade**

3 **Reptilia clade**

4 **Diapsida clade**

5 **Archosauria clade**

amphibians

mammals

turtles/tortoises

lizards/snakes

crocodiles/alligators

birds

FEATHERS AND TOOTHLESS BEAKS

SKULL OPENINGS IN FRONT OF THE EYE AND IN THE JAW

OPENINGS IN THE SIDE OF THE SKULL

SKULL OPENINGS BEHIND THE EYE

EMBRYO PROTECTED BY AMNIOTIC FLUID

FOUR LIMBS WITH DIGITS

NODE

In a cladogram, a node is the intersection of two branches. This node represents the most recent common ancestor shared by the entire tetrapoda clade.

DERIVED CHARACTER

Organisms that branch off after a hash mark share the derived character represented by the hash mark. An embryo protected by amniotic fluid is a derived character shared by all organisms in the amniota clade. Amphibians do not have this derived character.

CRITICAL VIEWING   Which groups of animals belong to the amniota clade? Which belong to the archosauria clade?

▶ MAIN IDEA
Molecular evidence reveals species' relatedness.

FIGURE 17.7 Based on structural similarities, scientists previously classified segmented worms and arthropods as sister taxa. The discovery of a hormone found only in roundworms and arthropods has led scientists to propose a new phylogeny for these taxa.

BEFORE

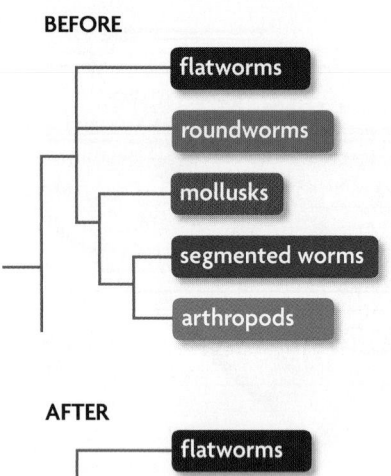

AFTER

You have learned how physical characteristics, such as protected eggs, can be used to build evolutionary trees. In this example, a protected egg is a derived character shared by all species in the amniota clade. Today, new technology allows biologists to compare groups of species at the molecular level. Molecular evidence, such as a certain DNA sequence, can be used as a derived character if it is shared among certain groups of species.

In many cases, molecular data agree with classification based on physical similarities. In other cases, this type of data leads scientists to classify species in a different way. An evolutionary tree is always a work in progress. With new evidence, trees can be changed to show how species are likely related.

For example, based on physical traits, most biologists considered segmented worms and arthropods (crabs, lobsters, insects, and their relatives) to be more closely related to each other than to any other group of species. However, the discovery of a certain hormone has provided new information. This hormone affects molting, and it is found only in arthropods and roundworms. Biologists have now proposed a new evolutionary tree, shown in **FIGURE 17.7**. In this tree, roundworms and arthropods are grouped closer together. This tree is based on the idea that the hormone evolved only once, in an ancestor shared by arthropods and roundworms.

Proteins and genes are also used to help learn about evolutionary relationships. In fact, DNA is considered by many scientists to have the "last word" when figuring out how related two species are to each other. After all, any traits that can get passed on to offspring must have a genetic basis. The more similar to each other the genes of two species are, the more closely related the species are likely to be. In the next section, you will see how DNA and protein sequences can be used to measure evolutionary time itself.

Analyze Why does DNA often have the "last word" when scientists are constructing evolutionary relationships?

17.2 / ASSESSMENT

ONLINE QUIZ
ClassZone.com

REVIEWING ▶ MAIN IDEAS

1. What is the goal of **cladistics**?

2. What role does molecular evidence play in determining how closely two species are related to each other?

CRITICAL THINKING

3. **Compare and Contrast** Discuss some similarities and differences between the Linnaean system of classification and cladistics.

4. **Analyze** Describe the relationship between clades and shared **derived characters.**

Connecting CONCEPTS

5. **Scientific Method** Recall that a hypothesis is a possible explanation for a set of observations. Why are **cladograms** considered to be hypotheses?

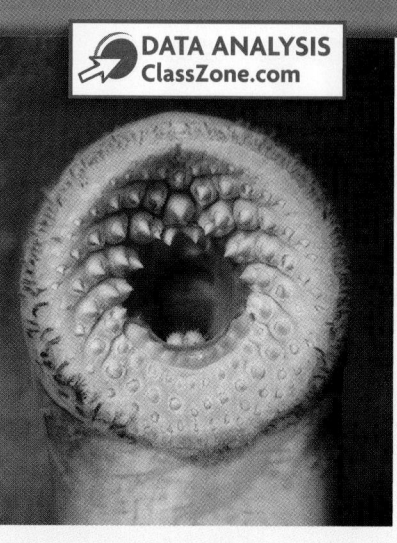

DATA ANALYSIS
ClassZone.com

Amino Acid Differences Among Species

Researchers rarely publish raw data by itself. Instead, data are usually analyzed in some way. This is because certain types of observations and patterns can be made clearer when data are presented in different ways. For example, data that show change or difference may be best represented as percentage difference.

EXAMPLE

Cytochrome C is a protein that functions in cellular respiration. A sequence of 104 amino acids make up the cytochrome C protein. Scientists have compared this sequence of amino acids in humans with the sequence in a variety of other species. The number of amino acid differences between cytochrome C in humans and in other species has been used to help determine species' relatedness.

Lampreys such as this one are jawless fish with a round sucking mouth.

Look at the data table at the right. Notice that the cytochrome C of chimpanzees most closely resembles that of humans, while the cytochrome C of lampreys, a type of jawless fish, has more differences. To more clearly represent how different they are, these data can be transformed into percentage differences. To calculate the percentage difference of cytochrome C between humans and lampreys, follow this procedure.

1. First, transform the number of amino acid differences into a fraction of the total number of amino acids that make up the cytochrome C protein (104).

$$\frac{20 \text{ differences}}{104 \text{ total amino acids}}$$

2. Next, perform the division.

20 ÷ 104 = 0.1923

3. Transform this number into a percentage by multiplying by 100.

0.1923 × 100 = 19.23% difference

TABLE 1. AMINO ACID DIFFERENCES COMPARED WITH HUMAN CYTOCHROME C	
Organism	**Number of Differences**
Chimpanzee	0
Rhesus monkey	1
Whale	10
Turtle	15
Bullfrog	18
Lamprey	20
Tuna	21

Source: M. Dayhoff, *Atlas of Protein Sequence and Structure*.

TRANSFORM DATA

1. **Calculate** Use the procedure outlined above to find percentage differences in cytochrome C between humans and the following animals: tunas, bullfrogs, turtles, whales, rhesus monkeys, and chimpanzees.

2. **Apply** What do the transformed data suggest about how related each type of animal is to humans?

3. **Infer** What percentage of the human cytochrome C protein is the same as that of whales?
   Hint: 100 percent − percentage difference = percentage similarity.

17.3 Molecular Clocks

KEY CONCEPT Molecular clocks provide clues to evolutionary history.

MAIN IDEAS

- Molecular clocks use mutations to estimate evolutionary time.
- Mitochondrial DNA and ribosomal RNA provide two types of molecular clocks.

VOCABULARY

molecular clock, p. 530
mitochondrial DNA, p. 532
ribosomal RNA, p. 532

MICHIGAN STANDARDS

B2.4A Explain that living things can be classified based on structural, embryological, and molecular (relatedness of DNA sequence) evidence.
B2.4d Analyze the relationships among organisms based on their shared physical, biochemical, genetic, and cellular characteristics and functional processes.

Connect Have you ever played the game telephone? One person whispers a message to another person, who repeats it to yet another person, and so on. By the time it reaches the final person, the message has changed. In a similar way, DNA changes slightly each time it is passed from generation to generation.

MAIN IDEA

Molecular clocks use mutations to estimate evolutionary time.

In the early 1960s, biochemists Linus Pauling and Emile Zuckerkandl proposed a new way to measure evolutionary time. They compared the amino acid sequences of hemoglobin from a wide range of species. Their findings show that the more distantly related two species are, the more amino acid differences there are in their hemoglobin. Using this data, they were able to calculate a mutation rate for part of the hemoglobin protein.

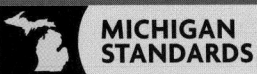

***Connecting* CONCEPTS**

Human Biology Hemoglobin is an oxygen-carrying protein that is found in the blood cells of all vertebrates, including humans. You will learn more about hemoglobin in **Chapter 30.**

Molecular Evolution

Molecular clocks are models that use mutation rates to measure evolutionary time. Recall that mutations are nucleotide substitutions in DNA, some of which cause amino acid substitutions in proteins. Pauling and Zuckerkandl found that mutations tend to add up at a constant rate for a group of related species. As shown in **FIGURE 17.8,** the rate of mutations is the "ticking" that powers a molecular clock. The more time that has passed since two species have diverged from a common ancestor, the more mutations will have built up in each lineage, and the more different the two species will be at the molecular level.

FIGURE 17.8 MOLECULAR EVOLUTION

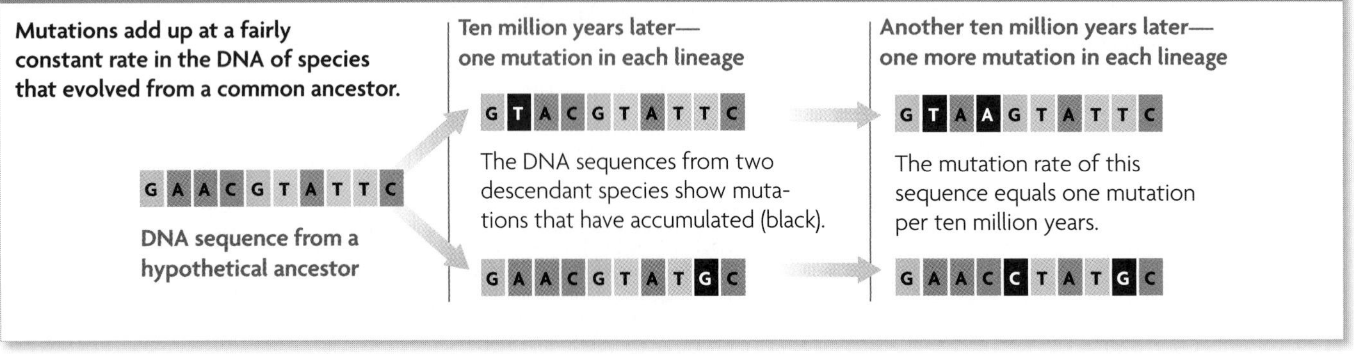
Mutations add up at a fairly constant rate in the DNA of species that evolved from a common ancestor.
G A A C G T A T T C
DNA sequence from a hypothetical ancestor
Ten million years later—one mutation in each lineage
G T A C G T A T T C
The DNA sequences from two descendant species show mutations that have accumulated (black).
G A A C G T A T G C
Another ten million years later—one more mutation in each lineage
G T A A G T A T T C
The mutation rate of this sequence equals one mutation per ten million years.
G A A C C T A T G C

Linking Molecular Data with Real Time

To estimate mutation rates, scientists must find links between molecular data and real time. Often this link comes from the timing of a geologic event that is known to have separated the species they are studying. If scientists know when the species began to diverge from a common ancestor, they can find the mutation rate for the molecule they are studying. For example, scientists know that marsupials of Australia and those of South America diverged about 200 million years ago, when these two continents split.

A link can also come from fossil evidence. Pauling and Zuckerkandl compared their molecular data with the first appearance of each type of organism in the fossil record. Using these dates, they confirmed that the number of amino acid differences increases with the evolutionary time between each group of species. The number of amino acid differences between human hemoglobin and the hemoglobin of several other types of organisms is shown in **FIGURE 17.9.** Human hemoglobin is most different from species that diverged earliest in evolutionary time.

Infer **Why is the hemoglobin of humans more different from that of sharks than that of birds?**

FIGURE 17.9 LINKING MOLECULAR AND FOSSIL DATA

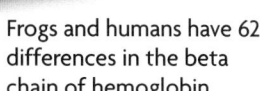

Learn how a molecular clock works at ClassZone.com.

Animal species that evolved longer ago compared with humans have more amino acid differences in the beta chain of their hemoglobin.

ANIMAL	AMINO ACID DIFFERENCES COMPARED WITH HUMANS	APPEARANCE IN FOSSIL RECORD (millions of years ago)
Mouse	16	70
Horse	18	70
Bird	35	270
Frog	62	350
Shark	79	450

Analyze **Which two animals in this table are least related to humans?**

Frogs and humans have 62 differences in the beta chain of hemoglobin.

▶ MAIN IDEA

Mitochondrial DNA and ribosomal RNA provide two types of molecular clocks.

Different molecules have different mutation rates. For example, some sequences of DNA accumulate mutations relatively quickly in a lineage, while others have very low mutation rates. Depending on how closely two species are related, scientists choose a molecule with an appropriate mutation rate to use as a molecular clock.

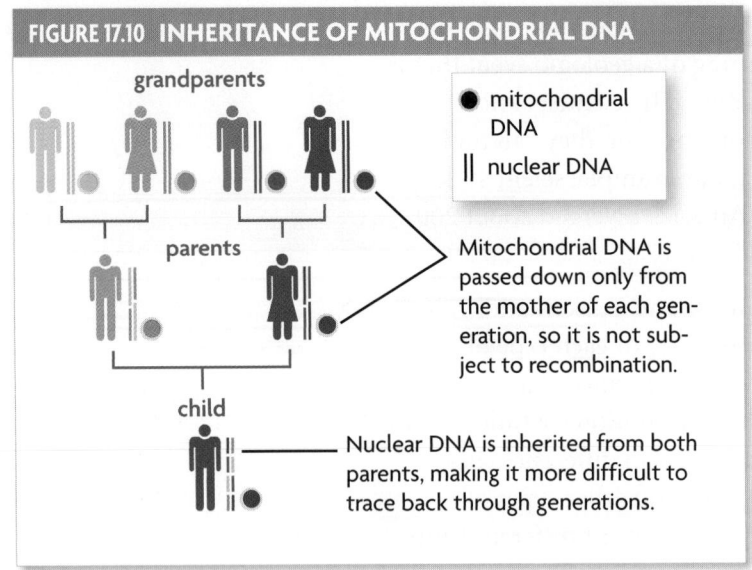

FIGURE 17.10 INHERITANCE OF MITOCHONDRIAL DNA

grandparents

● mitochondrial DNA
|| nuclear DNA

parents

Mitochondrial DNA is passed down only from the mother of each generation, so it is not subject to recombination.

child

Nuclear DNA is inherited from both parents, making it more difficult to trace back through generations.

Mitochondrial DNA

Mitochondrial DNA (mtDNA) is DNA found only in mitochondria, the energy factories of cells. The mutation rate of mtDNA is about ten times faster than that of nuclear DNA, which makes mtDNA a good molecular clock for closely related species. Furthermore, as shown in **FIGURE 17.10**, mtDNA is always inherited from the mother because the mitochondria in a sperm cell are lost after fertilization. This type of inheritance is different from that of nuclear DNA, which is a combination of DNA from both parents. Scientists use the fact that mtDNA is passed down unshuffled to trace mutations back through many generations in a single species. In fact, mutations in mtDNA have been used to study the migration routes of humans over the past 200,000 years.

Ribosomal RNA

Ribosomes, the organelles that manufacture proteins in cells, contain **ribosomal RNA** (rRNA). Ribosomal RNA is useful for studying distantly related species, such as species that are in different kingdoms or phyla. When studying the relationships among species over longer time scales, it is best to use a molecule that has a lower mutation rate. Ribosomal RNA has conservative regions that accumulate mutations at a low rate relative to most DNA. Over long periods of geologic time, mutations that do build up in the rRNA of different lineages are relatively clear and can be compared. American microbiologist Carl Woese first used rRNA to establish that archaea diverged from the common ancestor they share with bacteria almost 4 billion years ago. As you will learn in the next section, these findings supported a restructuring of the tree of life at its highest level.

Summarize Why is rRNA useful for studying more distantly related species?

VOCABULARY

In this context, the word *conservative* means "resistant to change." Because ribosomes play such a crucial role in cell function, even small changes can be very disruptive and damaging to the cell. Therefore, most mutations in rRNA do not accumulate within the genome.

17.3 ASSESSMENT

ONLINE QUIZ
ClassZone.com

REVIEWING ▶ MAIN IDEAS

1. How are **molecular clocks** used to measure evolutionary time?
2. What are the benefits of **mitochondrial DNA** and **ribosomal RNA** as molecular clocks?

CRITICAL THINKING

3. **Explain** How do rates of mutation "power" molecular clocks?
4. **Apply** What molecular clock might be useful to examine the evolutionary relationship between several phyla in the kingdom Plantae? Explain your answer.

Connecting CONCEPTS

5. **History of Life** The theory of endosymbiosis explains how eukaryotic cells may have evolved from prokaryotic cells. According to this theory, explain why mitochondria have their own DNA, separate from nuclear DNA.

17.4 Domains and Kingdoms

KEY CONCEPT The current tree of life has three domains.

MAIN IDEAS
- Classification is always a work in progress.
- The three domains in the tree of life are Bacteria, Archaea, and Eukarya.

VOCABULARY
Bacteria, p. 534
Archaea, p. 534
Eukarya, p. 534

Review
prokaryote, eukaryote

MICHIGAN STANDARDS

B1.2i Explain the progression of ideas and explanations that leads to science theories that are part of the current scientific consensus or core knowledge.

B2.4A Explain that living things can be classified based on structural, embryological, and molecular (relatedness of DNA sequence) evidence.

Connect Have you ever swum in a pond? Every drop of pond water is teeming with single-celled organisms. At one time, scientists classified these organisms as either plants or animals. However, classification schemes change. Single-celled eukaryotes such as these pond dwellers now have a kingdom of their own.

MAIN IDEA
Classification is always a work in progress.

The tree of life is a model that shows the most current understanding of how living things are related. Some new discoveries confirm parts of the tree that were once based on similarities in form alone. But as **FIGURE 17.11** shows, new findings can also lead scientists to change how they classify certain organisms.

- The two-kingdom system was accepted by biologists until 1866, when German biologist Ernst Haeckel proposed moving all single-celled organisms to the kingdom Protista.
- In 1938, American biologist Herbert Copeland argued that the prokaryotes deserved their own kingdom, called Monera. Prokaryotes are single-celled organisms that do not have membrane-bound nuclei or organelles.
- In 1959, American ecologist Robert Whittaker proposed that because of how they feed, fungi should be placed into their own kingdom apart from plants. The kingdom Fungi includes molds and mushrooms.
- In 1977, rRNA research by Carl Woese revealed two genetically different groups of prokaryotes. His findings led scientists to split the kingdom Monera into two kingdoms, called Bacteria and Archaea.

Connecting CONCEPTS

Fungi Fungi are heterotrophs that feed by absorbing dead organic materials from the environment. This is one characteristic that distinguishes fungi from plants, which are autotrophs, or organisms that make their own food. You will learn more about fungi in **Chapter 19.**

FIGURE 17.11 HISTORY OF THE KINGDOM SYSTEM

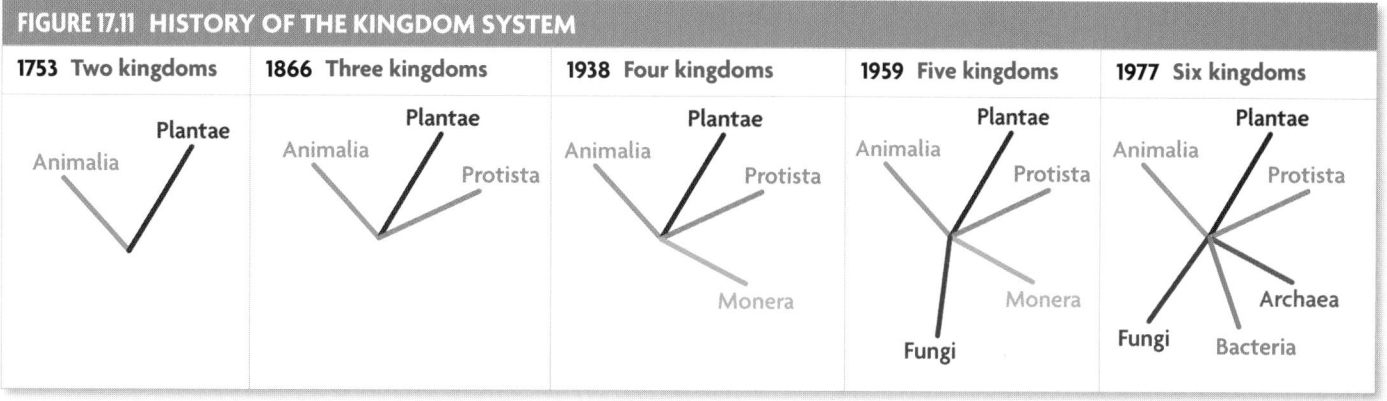

Woese's discovery did more than split the kingdom Monera. The two groups of prokaryotes that he studied have very different cell wall chemistry. In terms of genes, these two groups are more different from each other than animals are from plants, fungi, and protists. Based on these differences, Woese proposed that all life be divided into three domains. These domains are above the kingdom level.

Analyze Why did Woese propose classifying bacteria and archaea into separate domains, rather than just separate kingdoms?

▶ MAIN IDEA

The three domains in the tree of life are Bacteria, Archaea, and Eukarya.

Most biologists now accept Woese's domain system. This system more clearly shows the great diversity of prokaryotes in the tree of life by dividing them into two domains. These domains are called Bacteria and Archaea. All eukaryotes are placed into a third domain, called Eukarya.

Bacteria

The domain **Bacteria** includes single-celled prokaryotes in the kingdom Bacteria. The domain Bacteria is one of the largest groups of organisms on Earth. In fact, there are more bacteria in your mouth than there are people that have ever lived! Bacteria can be classified by many traits, such as their shape, their need for oxygen, and whether they cause disease.

Archaea

Like bacteria, organisms in the domain **Archaea** (ahr-KEE-uh) are single-celled prokaryotes. However, the cell walls of archaea and bacteria are chemically different. Archaea, like those in **FIGURE 17.12**, are known for their ability to live in extreme environments, such as deep sea vents, hot geysers, Antarctic waters, and salt lakes. All archaea are classified in the kingdom Archaea.

Eukarya

The domain **Eukarya** (yoo-KAR-ee-uh) is made up of all organisms with eukaryotic cells. Eukaryotic cells have a distinct nucleus and membrane-bound organelles. Eukarya may be single-celled, such as most protists. They can also be colonial, such as some algae, or multicellular, like you. The domain Eukarya includes the kingdoms Protista, Plantae, Fungi, and Animalia.

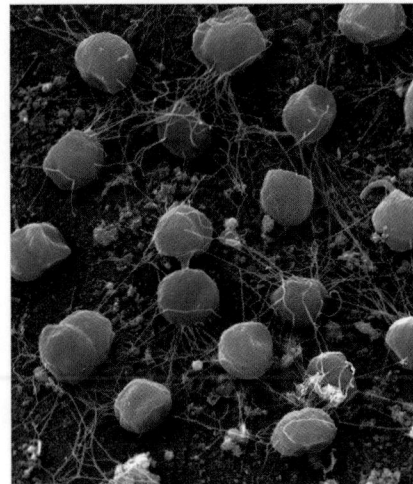

FIGURE 17.12 This archaean species, *Pyrococcus furiosus*, can be found in undersea hot vents and in the sand surrounding sulfurous volcanoes. These organisms live without oxygen and can grow in temperatures higher than the boiling point of water. (colored SEM; magnification 6500×)

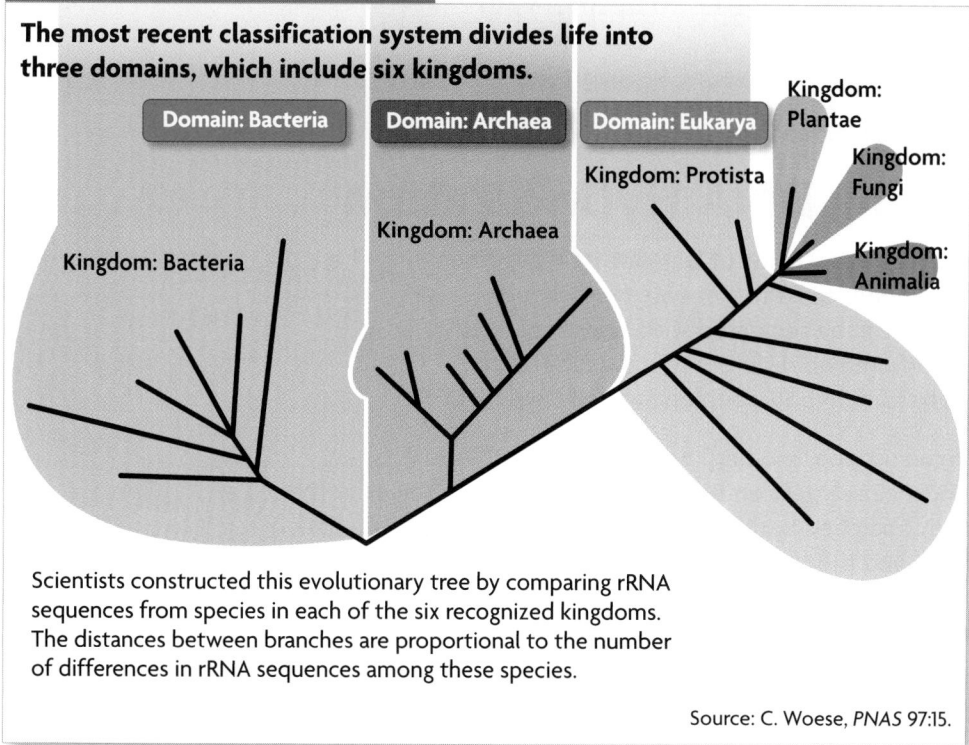

FIGURE 17.13 Tree of Life

The most recent classification system divides life into three domains, which include six kingdoms.

Domain: Bacteria

Kingdom: Bacteria

Domain: Archaea

Kingdom: Archaea

Domain: Eukarya

Kingdom: Protista

Kingdom: Plantae

Kingdom: Fungi

Kingdom: Animalia

Scientists constructed this evolutionary tree by comparing rRNA sequences from species in each of the six recognized kingdoms. The distances between branches are proportional to the number of differences in rRNA sequences among these species.

Source: C. Woese, *PNAS* 97:15.

Connecting CONCEPTS

Kingdoms and Phyla See the **Appendix** for a detailed description of each kingdom and its phyla.

Classifying Bacteria and Archaea

Some scientists think that bacteria and archaea have no true species. This is because many of these organisms transfer genes among themselves outside of typical reproduction. This sharing of genes blurs the lines between "species" as we define them in the Linnaean system. One study found that almost a quarter of the genes in the bacterium *Thermotoga maritima* are similar to archaean genes. Our understanding of how to classify prokaryotes is just beginning. You will learn more about these organisms in Chapter 18.

Analyze Why are protists, plants, fungi, and animals classified into the same domain but into different kingdoms?

17.4 ASSESSMENT

ONLINE QUIZ
ClassZone.com

REVIEWING ▶ MAIN IDEAS

1. Why is the classification of life considered a work in progress?

2. What kingdoms are included in each of the three domains in the modern tree of life?

CRITICAL THINKING

3. **Apply** If you come across an unusual single-celled organism, what parts of the cell would you study in order to classify it into one of the three domains?

4. **Analyze** Explain, using the traditional definition of species, why it is difficult to classify some **bacteria** and **archaea** at the species level.

Connecting CONCEPTS

5. **History of Life** The Archaea lineage may include the first life on Earth, which began under much different environmental conditions from those present today. What characteristics of archaea help to support this statement?

Use these inquiry-based labs and online activities to deepen your understanding of classification.

INVESTIGATION

Modeling DNA Hybridization

Remember that two strands of DNA are held together by hydrogen bonds to form a double helix. Double-stranded DNA can be separated with heat. Separated DNA strands from two different species can then be combined to form hybrid double-stranded DNA.

Scientists can use the "melting" point of hybrid DNA to estimate how closely related two different species are to each other. The more mismatched bases there are, the fewer hydrogen bonds there will be, and the more easily the strands from the different species will separate when heated. In this lab, you will use DNA fragments from five hypothetical species to estimate how related the species are.

MATERIALS

- DNA Hybridization Sequences
- 5 different colored pencils

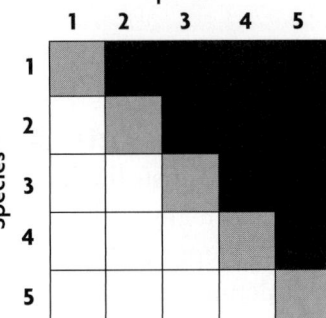

SKILL Modeling

PROBLEM How is DNA hybridization used to study species relatedness?

PROCEDURE

1. Copy the grid shown here into your notebook.
2. Recall the base-pairing rules for DNA:
   - A pairs with T, forming two hydrogen bonds.
   - C pairs with G, forming three hydrogen bonds.

   If adjoining bases do not form one of these pairs, no hydrogen bonds form.
3. Using the DNA sequence fragments, put the strands from the original species (same color) together. Count the number of hydrogen bonds that would form for each species' DNA fragment. Record this number in your grid. Notice that these counts will go in the gray diagonal boxes of the grid.
4. Form hybrid DNA fragments for each possible combination of species by matching the strands up with the arrows pointing in opposite directions. Count and record the number of hydrogen bonds holding each hybrid together. Notice that each of these counts will be recorded in one of the white boxes of the grid.

ANALYZE AND CONCLUDE

1. **Analyze** Which DNA hybrid had the most hydrogen bonds? Which had the fewest?
2. **Analyze** Which species is the least related to the other four species?
3. **Synthesize** How has DNA technology changed the way scientists classify some organisms?

INVESTIGATION

Defining Species

The biological species concept is often used to define species. According to this definition, a species is a group of individuals that can mate and produce offspring that are able to reproduce. However, this definition has limitations. For example, a liger is the offspring of a male lion and a female tiger. Some female ligers have been able to reproduce. This ability blurs the line between lions and tigers as species, as defined by the biological species concept.

SKILL Evaluating

PROBLEM What are some different ways to define species?

PROCEDURE

1. Research the definition of one of the species concepts listed below.
   - morphological species concept
   - paleontological species concept
   - ecological species concept
   - phylogenetic species concept

2. Write two paragraphs evaluating the species concept you have chosen. Be sure to include answers to the following questions:
   - How are species defined by this concept?
   - What are the advantages and limitations of the concept?
   - In what types of scientific research might this concept be the most useful?
   - Would this concept be more appropriate than the biological species concept in classifying bacteria and archaea?

The liger shown here, named Patrick, lives in the Shambala Preserve in California. He has a mane like a lion and stripes like a tiger.

ANIMATED BIOLOGY

Build a Cladogram

How are crocodiles related to birds? Use derived characters to build a cladogram of taxa within the archosauria clade.

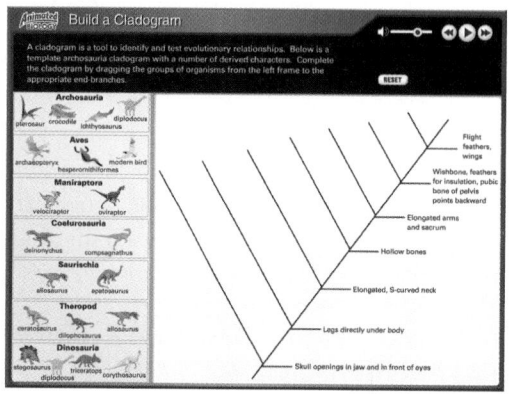

WEBQUEST

How do you classify a sea cucumber, an animal that looks like a water balloon? Complete this WebQuest to find out. Discover the evolutionary history of these animals and examine the traits that define them. Explore how sea cucumbers fit in the tree of life.

BIOZINE

Stories about the diversity of life— such as "New Species Found in New York's Central Park" and "Parasitic Fungus Drives Ant to Self-Destruction"—are often in the headlines. Read the latest news about the diversity of life in the BioZine.

17.1 The Linnaean System of Classification

Organisms can be classified based on physical similarities. The Linnaean system of classification groups organisms based on shared physical or structural characteristics. This system is a nested hierarchy with seven taxa, or levels. The most specific level in this system is a species. Species are named according to binomial nomenclature, which gives each species a two-part scientific name using Latin words.

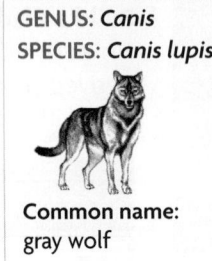

GENUS: *Canis*
SPECIES: *Canis lupis*

Common name:
gray wolf

17.2 Classification Based on Evolutionary Relationships

Modern classification is based on evolutionary relationships. Cladistics is a common method used to group species based on the order in which they diverged from a common ancestor. These evolutionary relationships can be presented in a branching diagram called a cladogram. Cladograms are constructed by identifying which derived characters are shared by which species in the group being analyzed.

Glyptodon

Armadillo

17.3 Molecular Clocks

Molecular clocks provide clues to evolutionary history. Mutations tend to accumulate at a constant rate for a group of related species. The longer that two species are separated after diverging from a common ancestor, the more different the two species will be at the molecular level. Biologists use molecular clocks by linking molecular data to real time. They can then measure the rate of evolution for these species. Ribosomal RNA and mitochondrial DNA provide two types of molecular clocks, used to measure evolution at different time scales.

17.4 Domains and Kingdoms

The current tree of life has three domains. The domains are based on fundamental differences at the cellular level. Within these domains are a total of six kingdoms. The Bacteria and Archaea domains include all organisms in the Bacteria and Archaea kingdoms, respectively. Bacteria and archaea are unicellular prokaryotes, but the genetic and cellular differences between these groups are greater than the differences between any other two kingdoms. The domain Eukarya includes all organisms with eukaryotic cells—kingdoms Protista, Fungi, Plantae, and Animalia.

Tree of life

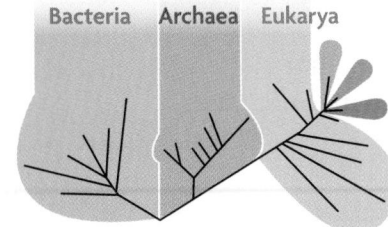

Bacteria Archaea Eukarya

Synthesize Your Notes

Main Idea Web Use a main idea web to take notes about cladograms.

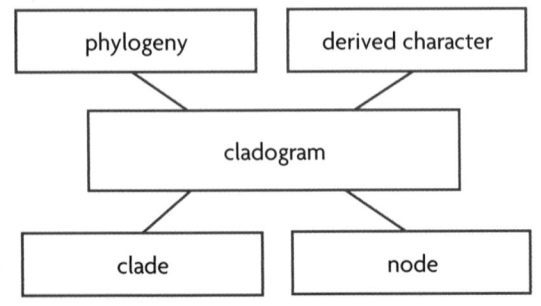

phylogeny | derived character

cladogram

clade | node

Concept Map Summarize what you know about taxonomy using a concept map.

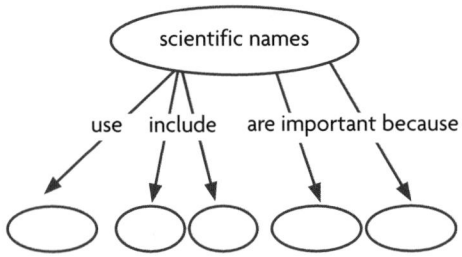

scientific names

use   include   are important because

Chapter Assessment

Reviewing Vocabulary

Vocabulary Connections

For each group of words below, write a sentence or two to clearly explain how the terms are connected. For example, for the terms *taxonomy* and *taxon,* you could write "In Linnaean taxonomy, each level of classification is called a taxon."

1. binomial nomenclature, genus, species

2. Bacteria, Archaea, Eukarya

3. molecular clock, mitochondrial DNA, ribosomal RNA

Write Your Own Questions

Think about the relationship between each pair of terms below. Then write a question about the first term that uses the second term as the answer. For the pair *taxonomy, taxon,* the question could be "In Linnaean taxonomy, what is each level of classification called?" Answer: taxon

4. phylogeny, cladistics

5. cladogram, derived characters

Greek and Latin Word Origins

6. *Klados* is Greek for "branch," and *-gram* is a suffix meaning "something written or drawn." Explain how this meaning relates to *cladogram.*

7. The prefix *archaeo-* comes from the Greek word *arkhaio,* which means "ancient" or "primitive." Explain how this meaning relates to *Archaea.*

Reviewing MAIN IDEAS

8. The scientific name for humans is *Homo sapiens.* What genus do humans belong to?

9. Why is it important for biologists to include scientific names when reporting their research to other biologists around the world?

10. Name the seven levels of organization in Linnaean taxonomy, from the most general to the most specific.

11. Current technology allows scientists to examine organisms at the molecular level. How has this technology exposed limitations in Linnaean taxonomy?

12. What basic idea does cladistics use to classify groups of organisms?

13. Two species with similar adaptations are found to have key differences at the molecular level. Scientists conclude that these species are not as closely related as previously thought. Why should the molecular evidence outweigh physical similarities that the species share?

14. A particular DNA sequence accumulated three mutations over 10,000 years. After how much time would you expect this sequence to have accumulated six more mutations? Explain.

15. Mutations accumulate more slowly in ribosomal RNA than in mitochondrial DNA. Which of these molecules would provide a better molecular clock for studying the evolution of species from different kingdoms?

16. The original Linnaean system of classification had two kingdoms. Biologists now use six kingdoms. What does this change suggest about the nature of classification?

17. What distinguishes the three domains in the tree of life from one another?

18. **Apply** Are species in the same family more or less closely related than species in the same class? Explain your answer.

19. **Synthesize** Scientists have used mtDNA as a molecular clock to trace human evolution and early migration routes. Explain why mtDNA would be more useful in this research than rRNA.

20. **Apply** Refer to the cladogram on page 527. Are crocodiles and alligators more closely related to snakes or to birds? Explain your answer using the terms *common ancestor* and *derived characters*.

21. **Compare and Contrast** What types of evidence are used for classifying organisms in the Linnaean classification system? What types of evidence are used for classifying organisms based on evolutionary relationships?

22. **Evaluate** What is the significance of grouping the six kingdoms into three domains? How does the domain model more clearly represent the diversity of prokaryotes than a system with the six kingdoms as its broadest divisions?

Interpreting Visuals

Use the cladogram, which classifies species A, B, C, and D, to answer the next three questions.

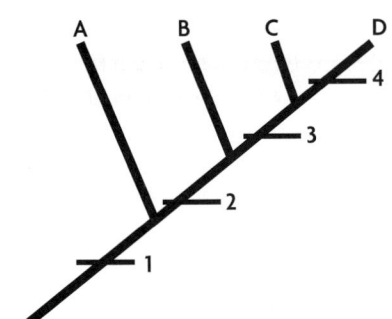

23. **Apply** What represents the derived characters that were used to construct this cladogram?

24. **Analyze** Where are the nodes in this cladogram, and what do they represent?

25. **Analyze** How many clades are represented in this cladogram?

Analyzing DATA

The family Ursidae contains all bear species. The data below show the number of species in each of the five genera of this family. Use this data to answer the next three questions.

GENERA OF THE FAMILY URSIDAE	
Genus Names	**Number of Species**
Ailuropoda	1
Helarctos	1
Melursus	1
Tremarctos	1
Ursus	4

Source: University of Michigan Museum of Zoology

26. **Analyze** How many species belong to family Ursidae?

27. **Transform Data** Transform the number of species in each genus to a percent of the total number of bear species in family Ursidae.

28. **Analyze** What do the transformed data show that raw data do not show?

Connecting CONCEPTS

29. **Write a Letter** Imagine that you are a modern-day molecular biologist. Write a letter to Linnaeus explaining how advances in technology have affected the way that scientists classify living organisms. Describe the parts of his classification system that are still used in the same way today. Also describe the aspects of his system that have changed over the years.

30. **Compare and Contrast** The pangolin on page 517 shares many physical traits, such as a long snout, with anteaters and aardvarks. However, these traits are known to have evolved separately in each of these groups of species. Write a paragraph that compares how Linnaeus and a modern taxonomist would likely classify pangolins. Include in your paragraph the kinds of additional information that a modern taxonomist might look for in order to classify the pangolin.

MICHIGAN STANDARDS-BASED ASSESSMENT

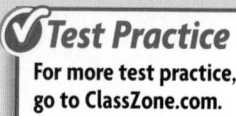
✓ **Test Practice**
For more test practice,
go to ClassZone.com.

1. In the past 150 years, the classification of life has changed through the addition and restructuring of kingdoms and domains. This system is always changing because **B1.2i**

   A scientific study keeps producing more data.

   B evolution keeps producing unique organisms.

   C extinctions change evolutionary relationships.

   D humans increase the rate of speciation.

2. Birds and snakes share a common ancestor from over 250 million years ago, but now they show many physical differences. These differences are *most* directly the result of

   A coevolution between species.

   B molecular clocks ticking at different rates.

   C the long-term accumulation of mutations.

   D differences in the alleles of the ancestor.

3.

   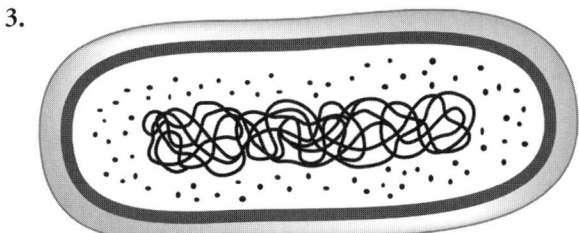

   Scientists isolate this organism from marsh water. Based on this illustration, the organism would *most* likely be classified as a **B2.4A**

   A protist.

   B bacterium.

   C plant.

   D fungus.

4. Mammals are multicellular organisms with about 3 billion base pairs in their genome. Yeasts are single-celled organisms with about 13 million base pairs in their genome. Both of these groups are classified as eukaryotes because they **B2.4d**

   A have over one million base pairs.

   B can reproduce sexually.

   C utilize aerobic respiration.

   D have a similar basic cellular structure.

   THINK THROUGH THE QUESTION

   Do not get confused by extra information provided in this question. Focus on the definition of eukaryotes. The number of base pairs is not relevant to this question.

5.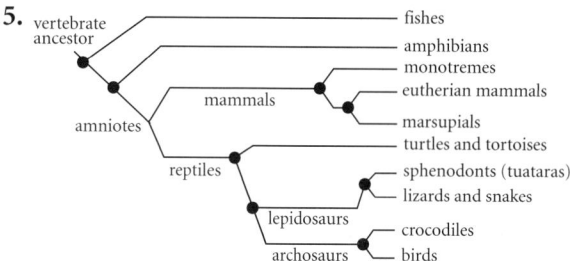

   According to the phylogenetic tree above, crocodiles are most closely related to **B5.r2d**

   A lizards and snakes.

   B fishes.

   C all reptiles.

   D birds.

6.

ginger	atgcgccgatccttacgtcgaatcggaac
corn	acgcaccgatacttacgtcgattcgggac
orchid	acgcgccgatacttacgtcgaatcgggac
lily	acgcgccgatacttccgtcgaatctggac

   The DNA sequences above show a conserved gene among four related plants. The highlighted differences are *most* directly the result of **B2.4d**

   A crossing over.

   B adaptation.

   C mutation.

   D meiosis.

CHAPTER
18 Viruses and Prokaryotes

KEY CONCEPTS

18.1 Studying Viruses and Prokaryotes
Infections can be caused in several ways.

18.2 Viral Structure and Reproduction
Viruses exist in a variety of shapes and sizes.

18.3 Viral Diseases
Some viral diseases can be prevented with vaccines.

18.4 Bacteria and Archaea
Bacteria and archaea are both single-celled prokaryotes.

18.5 Beneficial Roles of Prokaryotes
Prokaryotes perform important functions for organisms and ecosystems.

18.6 Bacterial Diseases and Antibiotics
Understanding bacteria is necessary to prevent and treat disease.

 BIOLOGY CLASSZONE.COM

BIOLOGY

View animated chapter concepts.
• Viral Infections
• Testing Antibacterial Products
• What Would You Prescribe?

BIOZINE

Keep current with biology news.
• News feeds
• Careers
• Polls

 RESOURCE CENTER

Get more information on
• Research Applications
• Vaccines
• Bacteria
• Archaea

How are bacteria helpful to humans?

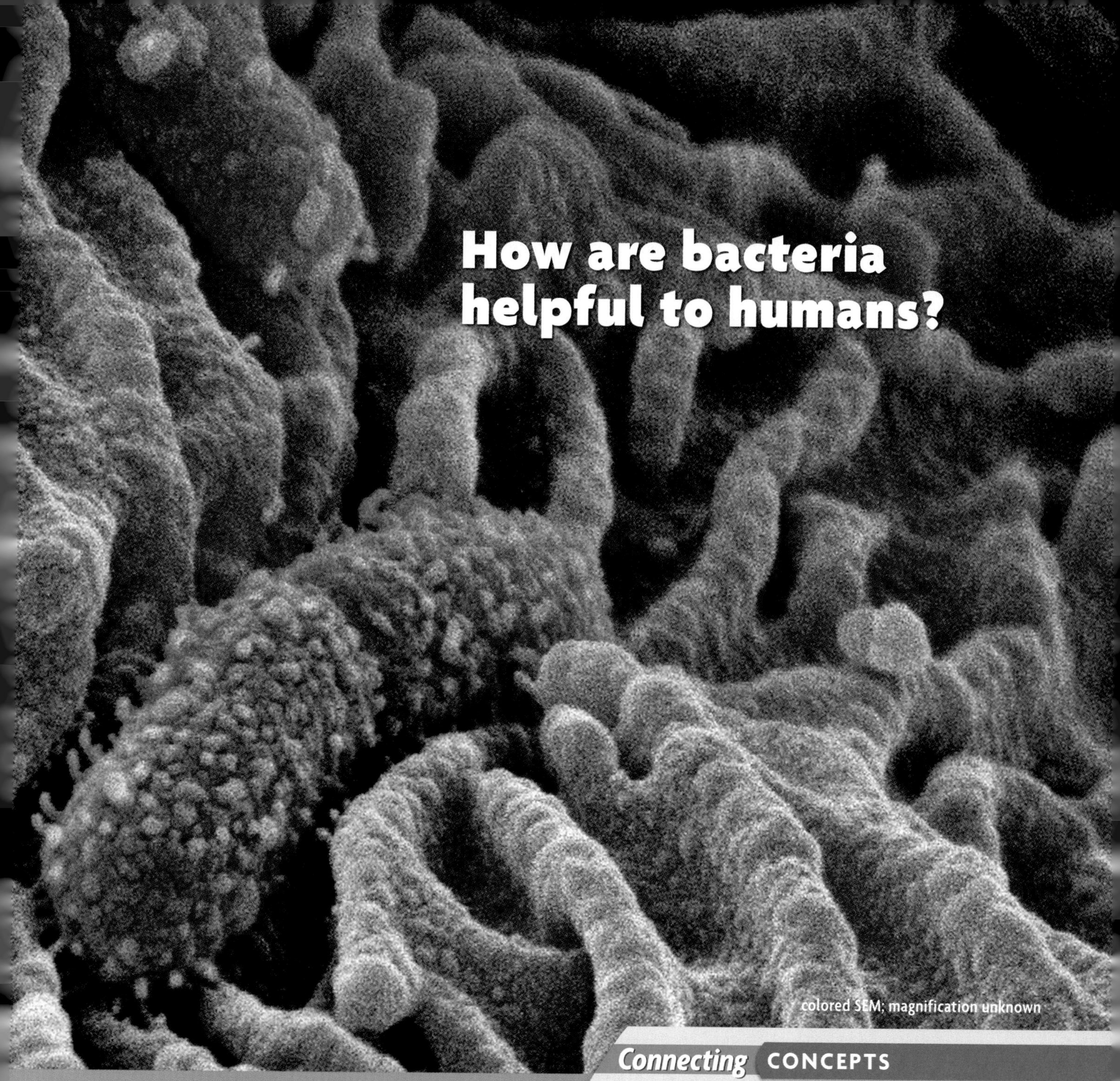

colored SEM; magnification unknown

These bacteria live in the lining of an esophagus, the tube that leads from your mouth to your stomach. Only a few years ago, it was thought that nothing could survive in an esophagus, but the entire digestive tract is home for many types of bacteria. Being a home to bacteria isn't bad, though. Some doctors hypothesize that these bacteria may protect us from some throat and stomach cancers.

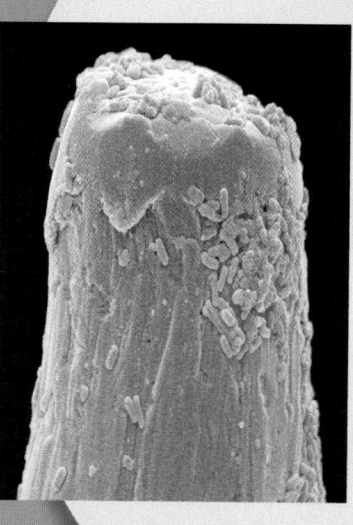

Biotechnology Hundreds of bacteria can fit on the tip of a pin, as shown at left. About the same number of bacteria will fit on a silicon chip. Scientists have made a device that can collect signals from bacteria joined to silicon chips. These bacteria have been specially altered to glow when near pollutants. The chips then measure the amount of light emitted—the more light, the more pollution present. (colored SEM; magnification 1100×)

Chapter 18: Viruses and Prokaryotes **543**

18.1 / Studying Viruses and Prokaryotes

KEY CONCEPT Infections can be caused in several ways.

▶ **MAIN IDEA**
- Viruses, bacteria, viroids, and prions can all cause infection.

VOCABULARY

virus, p. 544
pathogen, p. 544
viroid, p. 544

prion, p. 545

Review
prokaryote, archaea

MICHIGAN STANDARDS

L2.p1A Distinguish between living and nonliving systems. (prerequisite)

B2.4i Recognize that while viruses lack cellular structure, they have the genetic material to invade living cells.

Connect Bacteria are everywhere, including in and on your own body—such as the bacteria that live in our digestive tracts. The relationship between you and the microorganisms in your body is usually mutually beneficial. Under certain conditions, however, normally harmless microorganisms can cause disease, and some types of microorganisms are particularly nasty—they always make you sick.

▶ **MAIN IDEA**

Viruses, bacteria, viroids, and prions can all cause infection.

You are probably familiar with the terms *virus* and *bacteria,* but you may not know exactly what they are. A **virus** is an infectious particle made only of a strand of DNA or RNA surrounded by a protein coat. Bacteria, on the other hand, are one-celled microorganisms that can also cause infection. Any living organism or particle that can cause an infectious disease is called an infectious agent, or **pathogen.**

In Chapter 1, you learned that all living things share certain key characteristics: the abilities to reproduce, to use nutrients and energy, to grow and develop, and to respond to their environments. They also contain genetic material that carries the code of life. Prokaryotes—such as the bacterium shown in **FIGURE 18.1**—are clearly living things, since they have each of the traits of life. But are viruses living things? Like living cells, viruses respond to their environment. Viruses have genes and can reproduce. Unlike cells, however, viruses cannot reproduce on their own. Instead, they need living cells to help them reproduce and make proteins. Viruses are also much smaller than most cells, as you can see in **FIGURE 18.2**. While viruses have key traits similar to living cells, they also have many differences. In fact, viruses are not even given a place in the Linnaean system of biological classification.

A viroid has even less in common with living things than do viruses. **Viroids** are infectious particles that cause disease in plants. Viroids are made of single-stranded RNA without a protein coat. They are passed through seeds or pollen. Viroids have had a major economic impact on agriculture because they can stunt the growth of plants.

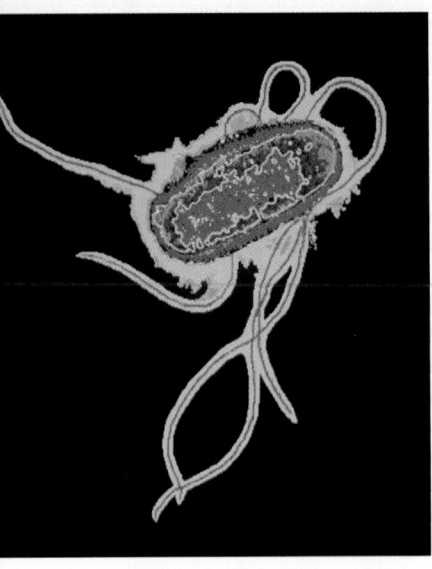

FIGURE 18.1 Prokaryotes, such as this *Escherichia coli* bacterium, are single cells that have all of the characteristics of living things. (colored TEM; magnification 6000×)

FIGURE 18.2 Relative Sizes of Cells and Infectious Particles

Although eukaryotic and prokaryotic cells can be microscopic, they are large in comparison to viruses, viroids, and prions.

1 nanometer (nm) = one billionth of a meter

100 nm

eukaryotic cells
10,000–100,000 nm

prokaryotic cells
200–10,000 nm

viruses
50–200 nm

viroids
5–150 nm

prion
2–10 nm

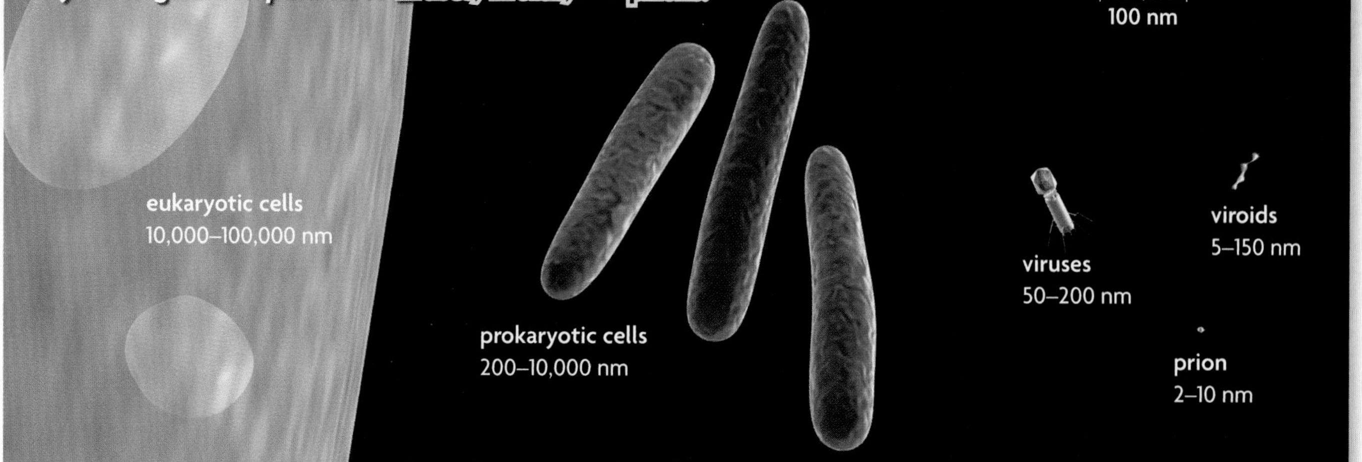

Infer Why are viroids and prions sometimes called subviral particles?

At the boundary between living and nonliving, perhaps the strangest entity of all is the prion. A **prion** (PREE-ahn) is an infectious particle made only of proteins that can cause other proteins to fold incorrectly. When proteins misfold, the protein will not work properly. Prions are unusual in that they are infectious yet have no genetic material. They play a part in certain diseases of the brain such as mad cow disease, known to scientists as bovine spongiform encephalopathy, or BSE. Humans may become infected with BSE when they eat meat from animals that are infected. Food safety laws in the United States, however, try to reduce the risk of infection. Creutzfeld-Jakob (KROYTS-fehlt YAH-kawp) disease (CJD), another brain disease that affects humans, is also associated with prions. Prion diseases can incubate for a long time with no effect on their host. However, once symptoms appear, they worsen quickly and are always fatal, because the body has no immune response against a protein.

Synthesize Why are viruses, viroids, and prions not included in the Linnaean system of biological classification?

TAKING NOTES

Use a two-column chart to take notes on viruses, viroids, and prions.

Main Idea	Detail
Virus	
Viroid	
Prion	

18.1 ASSESSMENT

ONLINE QUIZ
ClassZone.com

REVIEWING ▶ MAIN IDEAS

1. What are the main differences between living cells and **viruses**?

2. Viruses, **viroids, prions,** and some bacteria can all be considered **pathogens.** What do all pathogens have in common?

CRITICAL THINKING

3. **Infer** Prions were not widely known to be infectious agents until the 1980s. Give two reasons why this might be so.

4. **Apply** An RNA-based disease spreads through pollen. Is it likely due to a virus, viroid, or prion? Explain.

Connecting CONCEPTS

5. **Medicine** To multiply, viruses must take over the functions of the cells they infect. Why does this make it difficult to make effective antiviral drugs?

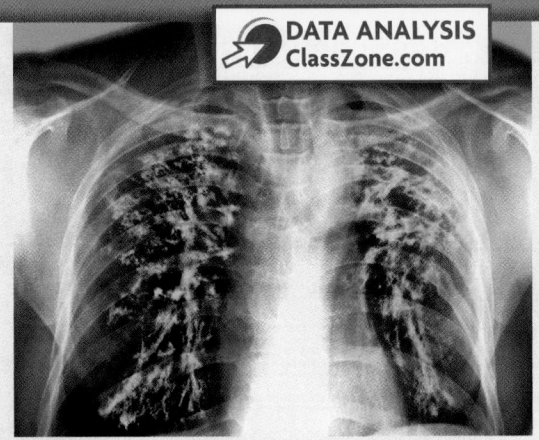

DATA ANALYSIS
ClassZone.com

Trends in Infectious Disease

Collecting data on the spread of infectious disease in a population is an important part of monitoring trends and determining a course of treatment. Different methods of displaying data, such as bar graphs or line graphs, often convey different information. Recall from page 497 in Chapter 16 the difference between discrete and continuous data.

Lungs infected by tuberculosis

TABLE 1. STATES WITH MOST TB CASES IN 2005

State	Number of Cases
California	2900
Texas	1535
New York	1294
Florida	1094
Illinois	596
Georgia	510
New Jersey	485
Virginia	355
North Carolina	329
Pennsylvania	325

TABLE 2. RATE OF TB FOR U.S. RESIDENTS

Year	TB Cases per 100,000 Persons
1955	46.6
1960	30.7
1965	25.2
1970	18.1
1975	15.7
1980	12.2
1985	9.3
1990	10.3
1995	8.7
2000	5.8
2005	4.8

Source: Centers for Disease Control and Prevention

CHOOSE DATA REPRESENTATION

The tables above show two sets of data describing tuberculosis (TB) infection in the United States.

1. **Connect** For each of the tables above, identify whether the data are continuous or discrete.

2. **Graph Data** Determine which type of graph would best represent each set of data and construct the graph for each set.

3. **Analyze** What trend did your graph show in rates of tuberculosis cases in the United States between the years 1955 and 2005?

4. **Analyze** Which table gives a more complete picture of TB infection in the United States? Explain.

5. **Predict** What trend do you expect the rate of TB cases to show in 2010?

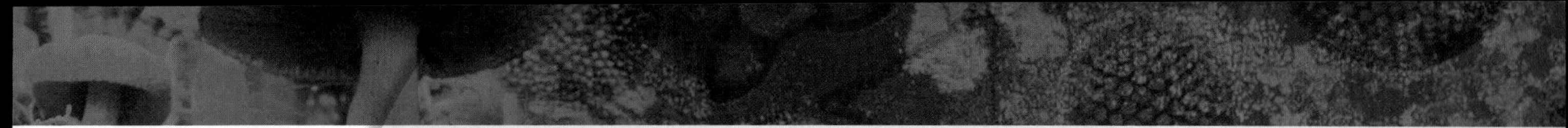

18.2 Viral Structure and Reproduction

KEY CONCEPT Viruses exist in a variety of shapes and sizes.

▶ MAIN IDEAS
- Viruses differ in shape and in ways of entering host cells.
- Viruses cause two types of infections.

VOCABULARY
capsid, p. 547
bacteriophage, p. 549
lytic infection, p. 551
lysogenic infection, p. 551
prophage, p. 551

Review
endocytosis, lipid

MICHIGAN STANDARDS

B2.4h Describe the structures of viruses and bacteria.
B2.4i Recognize that while viruses lack cellular structure, they have the genetic material to invade living cells.

Connect Just like the computer viruses that you hear about in the news, viruses that affect living things pass from one host to the next. While computer viruses pass through networks from one computer to another, human viruses pass from person to person. Also like computer viruses, viruses of living things can be simple or complex in structure, and have several different ways to get into their hosts.

▶ MAIN IDEA
Viruses differ in shape and in ways of entering host cells.

The idea that infectious agents cause certain diseases was a fairly new concept in 1892 when Russian scientist Dmitri Ivanovsky made a surprising observation. He was studying tobacco mosaic disease, named for the scar pattern left on affected leaves of tobacco or tomato plants. Mosaic disease, shown in **FIGURE 18.3**, was thought to be caused by a bacterium. But so far no one had been able to prove it. Ivanovsky passed extracts of diseased tobacco leaves through filter pores small enough to strain out bacteria and found that the extracts could still pass on the disease. Was this a new bacterium? Or was it some unknown type of organism?

In 1898, Dutch microbiologist Martinus Beijerinck built upon Ivanovsky's work. He showed that the disease agent passed through agar gel. He proposed that tiny particles within the extracts caused infection, and he called the particles *viruses,* from the Latin for "poison." The observations of Ivanovsky and Beijerinck laid the groundwork for more discoveries. Scientists began finding that many diseases of unknown causes could be explained by viruses.

The Structure of Viruses
Viruses have an amazingly simple basic structure. A single viral particle, called a *virion,* is made up of genetic material surrounded by a protein shell called a **capsid.** Capsids can have different shapes. In some viruses, the capsid itself is surrounded by a lipid envelope. A lipid envelope is the protective outer coat of a virus, from which spiky structures of proteins and sugars may stick out.

Healthy leaf

Infected leaf

FIGURE 18.3 These pictures compare a healthy leaf and a leaf infected by tobacco mosaic virus (TMV). TMV was the first virus identified by scientists.

Some viruses attach to host cells by these spikes. The spikes are such an obvious trait of some viruses that they can be used for identification.

Viruses can only reproduce after they have infected host cells. Viruses are simply packaged sets of genes that move from one host cell to another. Unlike bacteria and other living parasites, a virus has no structures to maintain—no membranes or organelles needing ATP, oxygen, or glucose. All it carries into the cell is what it needs to reproduce—its genes.

The structure and shape of viruses play an important role in how they work. Each type of virus can infect only certain hosts. A virus identifies its host by fitting its surface proteins to receptor molecules on the surface of the host cell, like a key fitting a lock. Some viruses are able to infect several species, while other viruses can infect only a single species. Common viral shapes are shown in **FIGURE 18.4**.

FIGURE 18.4 Viral Shapes

The different proteins that make up a viral capsid give viruses a variety of shapes.

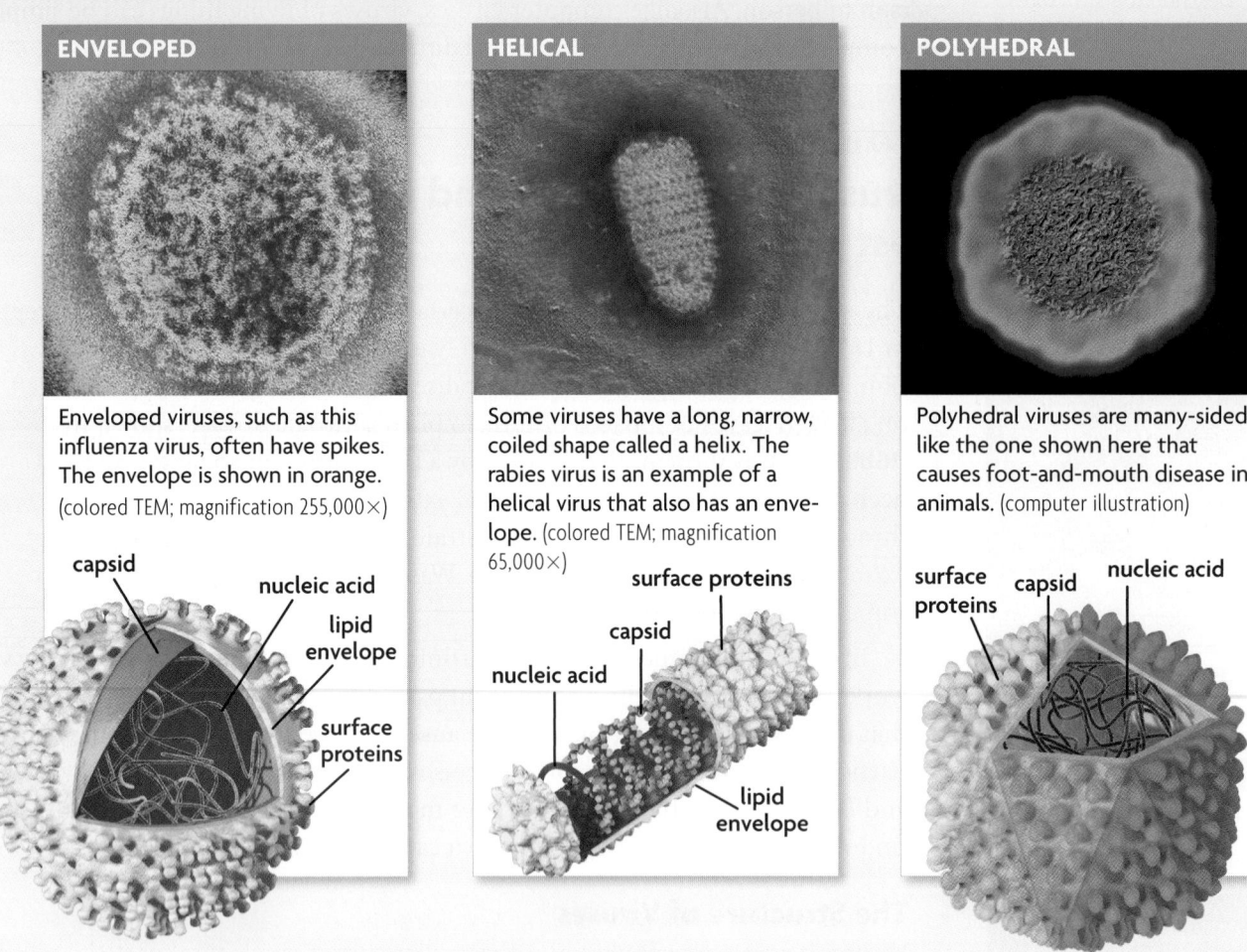

ENVELOPED

Enveloped viruses, such as this influenza virus, often have spikes. The envelope is shown in orange. (colored TEM; magnification 255,000×)

capsid
nucleic acid
lipid envelope
surface proteins

HELICAL

Some viruses have a long, narrow, coiled shape called a helix. The rabies virus is an example of a helical virus that also has an envelope. (colored TEM; magnification 65,000×)

surface proteins
capsid
nucleic acid
lipid envelope

POLYHEDRAL

Polyhedral viruses are many-sided, like the one shown here that causes foot-and-mouth disease in animals. (computer illustration)

surface proteins
capsid
nucleic acid

Compare and Contrast What are the similarities and differences between the three types of viruses shown above?

In some viruses, capsids form a 20-sided polyhedral. Rod-shaped and strandlike viruses often have capsids shaped in coils, like a spring or helix.

In contrast to prokaryotes and eukaryotes, in which DNA is always the main genetic material, a virus can have either DNA or RNA but never both. The genetic material of viruses can be single-stranded or double-stranded, and linear, circular, or segmented.

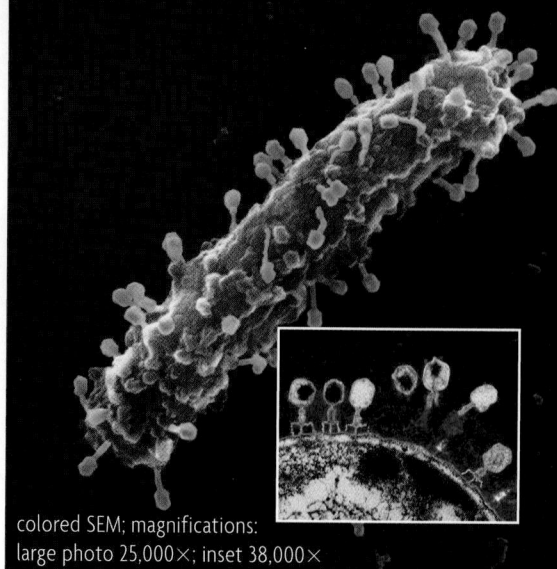

colored SEM; magnifications:
large photo 25,000×; inset 38,000×

Viruses that Infect Bacteria

One group of viruses is the bacteriophages, often called simply "phages." **Bacteriophages** (bak-TEER-ee-uh-FAYJ-ihz) are viruses that prey on bacteria. One example is the T-bacteriophage that infects *Escherichia coli,* the bacteria commonly found in the intestines of mammals. The T-bacteriophage shown in **FIGURE 18.5** has a 20-sided capsid connected to a long protein tail with spiky footlike fibers. The capsid contains the genetic material. The tail and its spikes help attach the virus to the host cell. After attachment, the bacteriophage's tail releases an enzyme that breaks down part of the bacterial cell wall. The tail sheath contracts, and the tail core punches through the cell wall, injecting the phage's DNA. The phage works like a syringe, injecting its genes into the host cell's cytoplasm, where its DNA is found.

FIGURE 18.5 The SEM above shows bacteriophages attacking an *E. coli* bacterium. While injecting their genetic material into the bacterium, the protein coats remain outside the cell (inset). The unique structure of a bacteriophage is shown below.

Viruses that Infect Eukaryotes

Viruses that prey on eukaryotes differ from bacteriophages in their methods of entering the host cell. For example, these viruses may enter the cells by endocytosis. Recall from Chapter 3 that endocytosis is an active method of bringing molecules into a cell by forming vesicles, or membrane-bound sacs, around the molecules. If the viruses are enveloped, they can also enter a host cell by fusing with the plasma membrane of the host cell and releasing the capsid into the cell's cytoplasm. HIV is a virus that enters cells in this way. Once inside the cell, eukaryotic viruses target the nucleus of the cell.

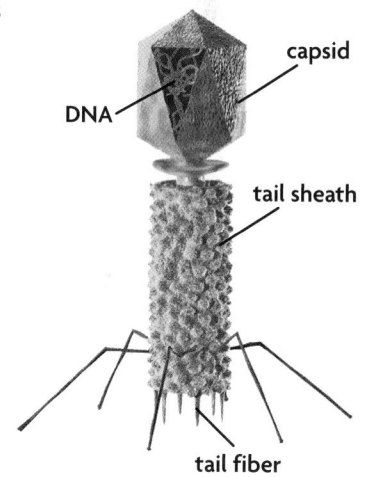

capsid
DNA
tail sheath
tail fiber

Summarize Describe how the structures of a bacteriophage are well-suited for their functions.

▶ MAIN IDEA

Viruses cause two types of infections.

The ways in which viruses enter and leave a cell may vary, but two basic pathways of infection are similar for all viruses. These pathways are shown for the most studied viruses, the bacteriophages, in **FIGURE 18.6**.

Once inside the host cell, phages follow one of two general paths in causing disease. In one path, the phage behaves like a bad houseguest. It takes over the household, eats all of the food in the refrigerator, and then blows up the house when it leaves. The other path of infection is somewhat more subtle. Instead of destroying the house, the phage becomes a permanent houseguest. Neither path is good for the host.

FIGURE 18.6 General Pathways of Viral Infection

A **lytic infection** results in the lysis, or breaking apart, of the host cell and release of new viral particles. A **lysogenic infection** does not destroy the host cell.

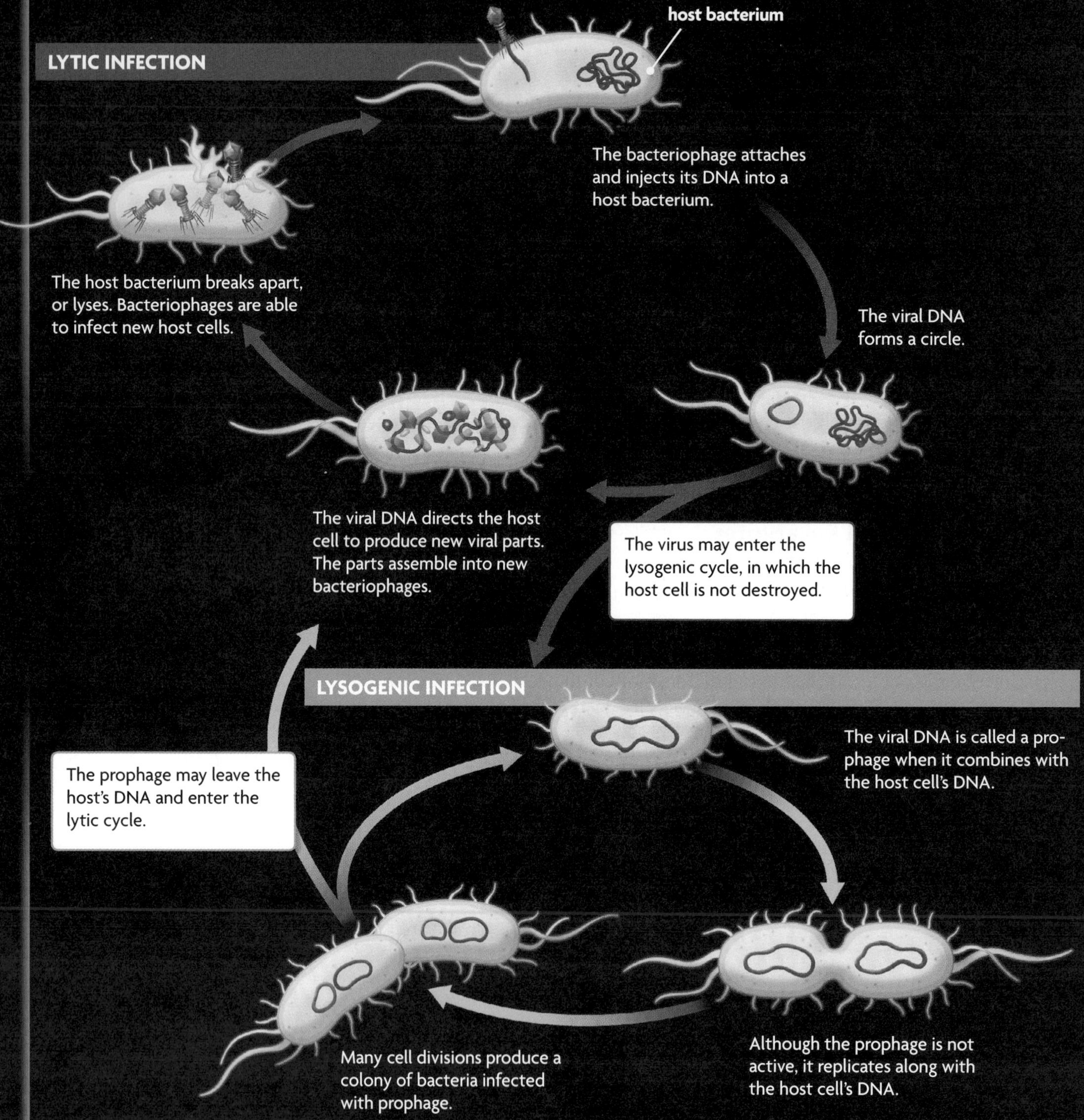

Animated BIOLOGY
Examine the two ways in which viruses infect host cells at ClassZone.com.

LYTIC INFECTION

host bacterium

The bacteriophage attaches and injects its DNA into a host bacterium.

The host bacterium breaks apart, or lyses. Bacteriophages are able to infect new host cells.

The viral DNA forms a circle.

The viral DNA directs the host cell to produce new viral parts. The parts assemble into new bacteriophages.

The virus may enter the lysogenic cycle, in which the host cell is not destroyed.

LYSOGENIC INFECTION

The prophage may leave the host's DNA and enter the lytic cycle.

The viral DNA is called a prophage when it combines with the host cell's DNA.

Many cell divisions produce a colony of bacteria infected with prophage.

Although the prophage is not active, it replicates along with the host cell's DNA.

CRITICAL VIEWING Why are no capsids or tail sheaths made during a lysogenic infection?

Lytic Infection

A **lytic infection** (LIHT-ihk) is an infection pathway in which the host cell bursts, releasing the new viral offspring into the host's system, where each then infects another cell.

- When the viral DNA enters the host cell, it takes over control of the host's own DNA, turning on the genes necessary to copy the viral genes.
- Under direction of the viral genes, the host's DNA undergoes transcription and translation, and produces capsids and enzymes. The enzymes then help in the copying of the virus's DNA.
- Using energy from the host cell, the capsids and viral DNA assemble into new virions. Viral enzymes dissolve the host cell membrane, releasing the new virus particles into the host's bloodstream or tissues—and destroying the host cell in the process.

Lysogenic Infection

In a **lysogenic infection** (LY-suh-JEHN-ihk), a phage combines its DNA into the host cell's DNA.

- After entering the host cell, the viral DNA combines with the host's DNA, forming a new set of genes called a prophage. A **prophage** is the phage DNA inserted into the host cell's DNA. In organisms other than bacteria, this stage is called a provirus.
- The prophage is copied and passed to daughter cells, with the host's own DNA, when the host cell undergoes mitosis. Although this process doesn't destroy the cell, it can change some of the cell's traits.
- After the cell has been copied, the prophage faces two possible paths. A trigger, such as stress, can activate the prophage, which then uses the cell to produce new viruses. Or the prophage can remain as a permanent gene.

Connect Using the analogy of viral infections resembling houseguests, explain which describes a lytic and which describes a lysogenic infection.

VOCABULARY

The term *lytic* comes from the Greek word *lutikos*, meaning "able to loosen." The word *lysis* is often used in biology to describe a cell breaking apart.

For more information on viruses, visit scilinks.org.
Keycode: MLB018

18.2 / ASSESSMENT

ONLINE QUIZ
ClassZone.com

REVIEWING ▶ MAIN IDEAS

1. Name and describe the main parts of a typical virus.
2. What are the differences between a **lytic infection** and a **lysogenic infection**? Include the effects of each type of infection on the cells of the host organism in your answer.

CRITICAL THINKING

3. **Apply** Researchers studying infection can often grow bacteria more easily than they can grow viruses. What conditions must scientists provide for viruses to multiply?
4. **Classify** A wart is caused by a virus that may lie dormant for years before any symptoms appear. Does this resemble a lytic or lysogenic infection? Explain.

Connecting CONCEPTS

5. **Evolution** If the virus is a foreign invader, how is it possible for the proteins of its **capsid** to match the receptors on the host cell's surface? Consider natural selection in your answer.

18.3 Viral Diseases

KEY CONCEPT Some viral diseases can be prevented with vaccines.

MAIN IDEAS
- Viruses cause many infectious diseases.
- Vaccines are made from weakened pathogens.

VOCABULARY
epidemic, p. 553
vaccine, p. 553
retrovirus, p. 553

MICHIGAN STANDARDS

B2.4h Describe the structures of viruses and bacteria.
B2.4i Recognize that while viruses lack cellular structure, they have the genetic material to invade living cells.

Connect Why do we worry about catching a cold or the flu every winter? Cold weather itself does not cause us to get sick, but spending time close to other people can. For most people, winter means spending more time indoors. Cold and flu viruses then easily transfer to hands from doorknobs and other objects. That's why frequently washing your hands can help keep you healthy.

MAIN IDEA
Viruses cause many infectious diseases.

As you have read, viruses follow two pathways of infection once they encounter their target cells. But to enter the host's body in the first place, the virus must first pass a major obstacle.

First Defenses
In vertebrates, the first obstacle a virus must pass is the skin, but in other organisms it might be an outer skeleton or a tough cell wall. Viruses can penetrate the skin only through an opening such as a cut or scrape. Or they can take another route—the mucous membranes and body openings. It's no accident that some of the most common points of entry for infection are the mouth, nose, genital area, eyes, and ears.

Once inside the body, the virus finds its way to its target organ or tissue. However, the targeted cells don't just open the door to this unwanted guest. Body cells have receptors that guard against foreign intruders. These receptors act almost like locks. When the virus arrives at the host cell, it uses its own surface proteins as keys to trick the cell into allowing it to enter.

Examples of Viral Infections
Viruses can cause symptoms that range from merely bothersome to life-threatening. Below are a few of the many human illnesses caused by viruses.

The common cold The most familiar viral disease is the common cold. More than 200 viruses are known to cause this seasonal nuisance. One such cold virus is shown in **FIGURE 18.7**. With so many viruses, it's not easy to find a cure. In fact, cold viruses can mutate as they move from one person to another. Although they're unpleasant to have, colds usually last only about one week.

Connecting CONCEPTS

Cells Recall from **Chapter 3** that receptors are proteins that detect chemical signals and perform an action in response. In the case of a host-specific infection, these normally helpful receptors provide little protection to the cell.

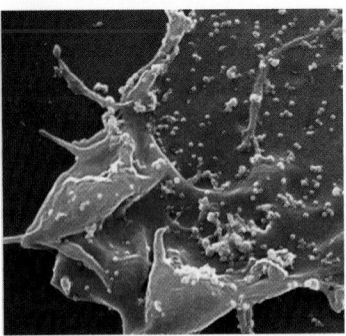

FIGURE 18.7 Cold virus particles (yellow) on the surface of a cell culture (blue). (colored SEM; magnification 10,000×)

Influenza Winter usually causes concern about the influenza, or "flu" virus—and with good reason. The flu spreads quickly and can result in frequent local epidemics. An **epidemic** is a rapid outbreak of an infection that affects many people. In the United States, up to 20 percent of the population is infected with the flu each year.

At this time, only three influenza subtypes infect humans; other subtypes may infect horses, pigs, whales, and seals. More than fifteen subtypes infect birds, and are all referred to as avian influenza, or bird flu. Sometimes a mutation enables a virus to jump from one species to another, making the spread of infection difficult to control. The high mutation rate of surface proteins on viral capsids makes it necessary for a new influenza vaccine to be made every year. A **vaccine** (vak-SEEN) is a substance that stimulates the body's own immune response against invasion by microbes.

SARS Severe acute respiratory syndrome (SARS) is another viral respiratory disease. It has symptoms similar to influenza, such as fever and coughing or difficulty in breathing. SARS is a relatively recent concern. It first appeared in Asia in late 2002. By the following summer, it had spread to other countries. SARS continues to be monitored globally by the World Health Organization.

HIV Human immunodeficiency virus, or HIV, is a retrovirus. *Retro-* means "backward," which describes how retroviruses work. Usually, DNA is used to make an RNA copy in a cell, but a **retrovirus** is a virus that contains RNA and uses an enzyme called reverse transcriptase to make a DNA copy. Double-stranded DNA then enters the nucleus and combines with the host's genes as a lysogenic infection. The viral DNA can remain dormant for years as a pro-virus, causing no symptoms to its human host.

When the virus becomes active, it directs the formation of new viral parts. The new viruses leave, either by budding or bursting through cell membranes, and infect new cells. This stage of the disease is a lytic infection that destroys white blood cells of the host's immune system, as shown in **FIGURE 18.9**. The loss of white blood cells ultimately causes AIDS, acquired immune deficiency syndrome. Once a person's immune system is affected, he or she may be unable to fight off even the common microorganisms that humans encounter every day. HIV's unusually high mutation rate has made it a challenge to treat. The combined use of several antiviral drugs—medications that treat viral infection—has proved somewhat effective in slowing the spread of the virus once a person is infected.

Analyze **How do retroviruses work differently from other viruses?**

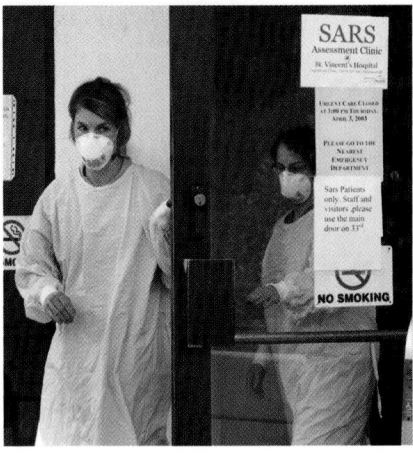

FIGURE 18.8 Nurses in Canada walk outside an emergency SARS clinic, which was opened to deal with an outbreak.

Connecting CONCEPTS

HIV Certain types of white blood cells of the human immune system are targeted by HIV to cause AIDS. You will learn more about HIV transmission and how this virus targets the immune system in **Chapter 31**.

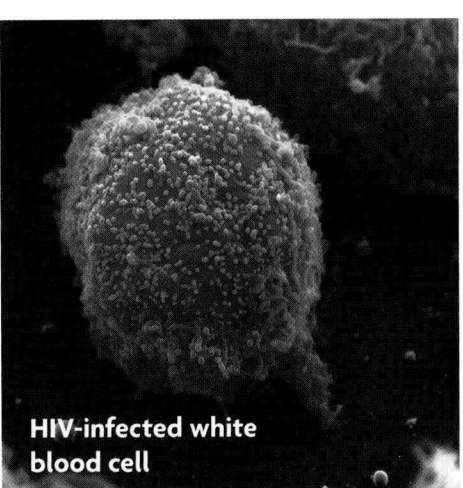

HIV-infected white blood cell

FIGURE 18.9 This scanning electron micrograph (SEM) shows the HIV virus as purple dots on an infected white blood cell. Destruction of white blood cells weakens the immune system and causes AIDS. (colored SEM; magnification: 3500×)

FIGURE 18.10 Viral Diseases

VIRAL INFECTION	SYMPTOMS OF DISEASE	TRANSMISSION OF DISEASE	U.S. VACCINE RECOMMENDATION
Chickenpox	rash, itchy skin, fever, fatigue	contact with rash, droplet inhalation	for children between 12 and 18 months
Hepatitis A	yellow skin, fatigue, abdominal pain	contact with contaminated feces	for people traveling to infected locations and protection during outbreaks
Mumps	painful swelling in salivary glands, fever	droplet inhalation	for children between 12 and 15 months and again at 4 to 6 years
Rabies	anxiety, paralysis, fear of water	bite from infected animal	for veterinarians and biologists in contact with wildlife
West Nile	fever, headache, body ache	bite from infected mosquito	no available vaccine

▶ MAIN IDEA

Vaccines are made from weakened pathogens.

Chances are good that you have had vaccinations. In the United States, children are vaccinated at an early age against diseases such as measles, mumps, rubella (MMR), and chickenpox. Every year, millions of people are vaccinated against influenza. How does a simple shot provide protection against disease?

A vaccine is made from the same pathogen—disease-causing agent—that it is supposed to protect against. Vaccines consist of weakened versions of the virus, or parts of the virus, that will cause the body to produce a response. The immune system is triggered by the surface proteins of a pathogen. In the host's body, the vaccine works by preparing the host's immune system for a future attack. Vaccines can prevent some bacterial and some viral infections, including the viral diseases shown in **FIGURE 18.10**. Whereas bacterial diseases can also be treated with medicine once they occur, viral diseases are not easily treated. Vaccination is often the only way of controlling the spread of viral disease.

Vaccines cause a mild immune response. If the body is invaded again, it will be able to start an immune defense before the virus can cause damage.

Apply Before the chickenpox vaccination was available, children were often purposely exposed to the virus at a young age. What was the reason for doing this?

Connecting CONCEPTS

Human Biology Vaccines help build up the immune system to prepare for exposure to a pathogen by recognizing its surface proteins. You will learn more about the immune system in **Chapter 31**.

18.3 / ASSESSMENT

ONLINE QUIZ
ClassZone.com

REVIEWING ▶ MAIN IDEAS

1. Name and describe two infectious viruses and a body's first defense against infection.

2. Briefly describe how a **vaccine** can prevent some viral infections.

CRITICAL THINKING

3. **Infer** If a vaccine is in short supply, why is it often recommended that older adults and children get vaccinated first?

4. **Apply** Why might getting a flu vaccination sometimes cause you to get a mild case of the flu?

Connecting CONCEPTS

5. **Human Biology** People infected with HIV, the virus that causes the disease AIDS, can become unable to fight off infections by organisms that normally do not harm people. Why is this so?

18.4 Bacteria and Archaea

KEY CONCEPT Bacteria and archaea are both single-celled prokaryotes.

▶ MAIN IDEAS

- Prokaryotes are widespread on Earth.
- Bacteria and archaea are structurally similar but have different molecular characteristics.
- Bacteria have various strategies for survival.

VOCABULARY

obligate anaerobe, p. 555
obligate aerobe, p. 555
facultative aerobe, p. 555
plasmid, p. 556
flagellum, p. 556
conjugation, p. 558
endospore, p. 558

MICHIGAN STANDARDS

B2.4h Describe the structures of viruses and bacteria.

Connect Humans not only share the environment with prokaryotes—for many species, we *are* the environment. Up to 500 types of prokaryotes can live in the human mouth. In fact, you may have as many as 25 different types in your mouth right now. One milliliter of saliva can contain up to 40 million bacterial cells.

▶ MAIN IDEA

Prokaryotes are widespread on Earth.

Prokaryotes, which include bacteria and archaea, are the most widespread and abundant organisms on Earth. Consider that humans are one species with about 6 billion individuals. In contrast, scientists estimate there are more than 1 billion (10^9) types of bacteria and more than 10^{30} individual prokaryotic cells on, above, and under Earth's surface. Bacteria and archaea are an important part of every community they inhabit. These tiny organisms live in just about every habitat on Earth, including the air we breathe. Prokaryotes have been found living inside rocks, in deserts, and in polar ice caps. One gram of soil may contain as many as 5 billion bacterial cells from up to 10,000 types of bacteria.

Prokaryotes can be grouped based on their need for oxygen. Prokaryotes that cannot live in the presence of oxygen are called obligate anaerobes. An **obligate anaerobe** (AHB-lih-giht AN-uh-ROHB) is actually poisoned by oxygen. As you have learned, archaea are prokaryotes that can live in extreme environments. The archaea that produce methane gas are obligate anaerobes. They live in marshes, at the bottom of lakes, and in the digestive tracts of herbivores such as deer, sheep, and cows, as shown in **FIGURE 18.11**. These microorganisms release nutrients from plants that animals are unable to digest on their own.

In contrast, some prokaryotes need the presence of oxygen in their environment. Organisms that need oxygen in their environment are called **obligate aerobes** (AHB-lih-giht AIR-OHBZ). This group includes several familiar pathogens, such as those that cause the diseases tuberculosis and leprosy. There are also prokaryotes that can survive whether oxygen is present in the environment or not. This type of prokaryote is called a **facultative aerobe** (FAK-uhl-TAY-tihv AIR-OHB).

FIGURE 18.11 A "window" made into a cow's rumen, the first of its four stomachs, allows scientists to study digestion. Anaerobic bacteria live mutualistically within a cow's stomach. The bacteria have shelter and nutrients, and break down plant material for the cow to digest.

Evaluate **Bacteria are often associated with illness. Why is this a misconception?**

Bacteria and archaea are structurally similar but have different molecular characteristics.

TAKING NOTES

Create a Venn diagram to compare bacteria and archaea using information from this section.

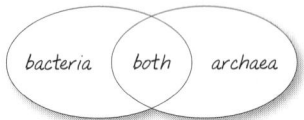

Members of domain Bacteria and domain Archaea comprise all of Earth's prokaryotes. Domain Bacteria is the more diverse and widespread of the two domains, while many archaea are found in Earth's extreme environments. Some archaea are even able to grow at temperatures greater than 100°C (212°F). Bacteria and archaea have many structural similarities but important genetic and biochemical differences.

Structural Comparisons

Even under the microscope, archaea look very similar to bacteria. For example, both archaea and bacteria are small, single-celled organisms that have cell walls and plasma membranes. Archaea come in many shapes, while the three most common forms of bacteria are shown in **FIGURE 18.12**. Bacteria are often named based upon their shapes. Rod-shaped bacteria are called *bacilli*. Spiral-shaped bacteria are called *spirilla* or *spirochetes*, and spherical bacteria are called *cocci*.

Prokaryotes do not have any membrane-bound organelles, such as a nucleus containing double-stranded DNA. Instead, their DNA is in the form of a circle and is surrounded by cytoplasm. Prokaryotes may also have plasmids. A **plasmid** is a small piece of genetic material that can replicate separately from the prokaryote's main chromosome.

Most prokaryotes can move on their own. Many bacteria and archaea move by gliding or using flagella. A **flagellum** (fluh-JEHL-uhm) is a long, whiplike structure outside of a cell that is used for movement. The flagella of prokaryotes are attached to the plasma membrane and cell wall. They may be at one end of an organism, or they may have different arrangements over the entire cell. Although similar in appearance, the flagella of bacteria and archaea are structurally different from each other. In addition, their flagella are both structurally different from the flagella of eukaryotes. You will learn more about the flagella of eukaryotes in Chapter 19.

Many prokaryotes also contain structures called pili that are thinner, shorter, and often more numerous than flagella. Pili help prokaryotes stick to surfaces and to other prokaryotes. A typical prokaryote is shown in **FIGURE 18.13**.

FIGURE 18.12 The most common shapes of bacteria are rods, spirals, and spheres. Many bacteria are named after these shapes. Some examples are shown at right.

(colored SEMs; magnifications: *lactobacilli* magnification unknown; *spirochaeta* 5000×; *enterococci* 7000×)

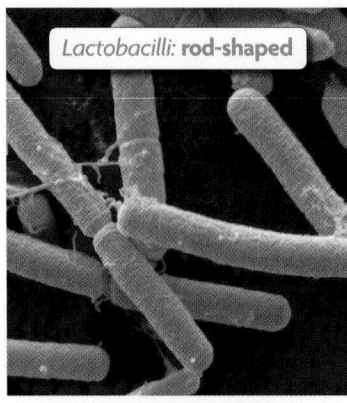
Lactobacilli: **rod-shaped**

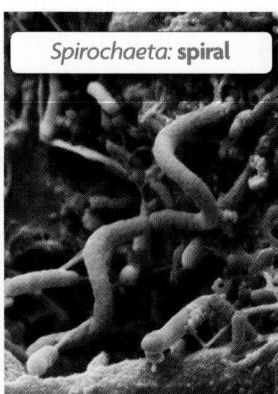
Spirochaeta: **spiral**

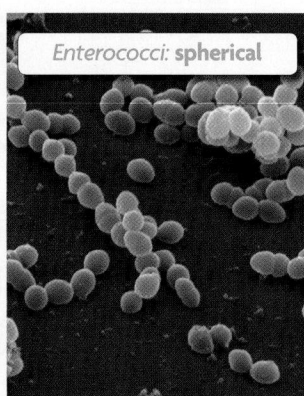
Enterococci: **spherical**

FIGURE 18.13 Prokaryote Structure

This diagram shows the typical structure of a prokaryote. Archaea and bacteria look very similar, although they have important molecular differences.

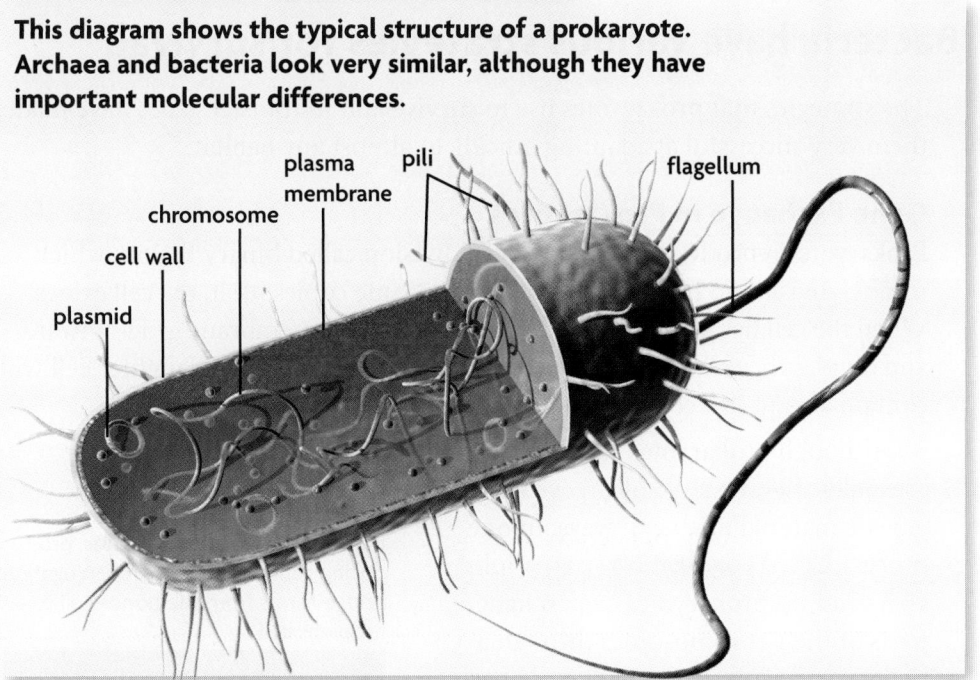

Molecular Comparisons

It was not until molecular analysis techniques were available that the many differences between bacteria and archaea became clear. Despite their similarities in function and appearance, bacteria and archaea are not closely related. Molecular evidence suggests that archaea have at least as much in common with eukaryotes as they do with bacteria. For example, archaea cell walls and membranes are chemically different from those of bacteria. The membranes of archaea contain lipids that are not found in any other type of organism on Earth, and bacteria have a polymer called peptidoglycan (PEHP-tih-doh-GLY-cuhn) in their cell walls, which archaea do not.

The amount of peptidoglycan in their cell walls is an important characteristic of bacteria. Bacteria are often classified into one of two groups based on this difference, as shown in **FIGURE 18.14**. A staining method called a Gram stain is used to tell the two groups apart. The Gram stain is important for diagnosing infectious bacterial diseases, and it sometimes helps determine the type of medicine a doctor chooses to fight infection. Because of their cell wall differences, archaea are often not affected by medicine used to treat bacterial infection.

Contrast Archaea were first named archaeabacteria, a term that you may still find in some books and articles. What are two differences between archaea and bacteria?

FIGURE 18.14 GRAM STAINING

A staining technique called a Gram stain is used to identify types of bacteria. This stain identifies the amount of a polymer, called peptidoglycan, that is present. The result is either gram positive or gram negative. (LMs; magnifications 500×)

Gram-negative bacteria have a thin layer of peptidoglycan and stain red.

Gram-positive bacteria have a thicker peptidoglycan layer and stain purple.

GRAM NEGATIVE

GRAM POSITIVE

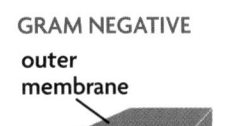

Bacteria have various strategies for survival.

The strategies that prokaryotes use to survive and to transfer genes have made them very successful at adapting quickly to almost any habitat.

Gene Exchange in Prokaryotes

Prokaryotes reproduce by a type of cell division called binary fission, which means "division in half." While the chromosome copies itself, the cell grows. When the cell has about doubled in size, its plasma membrane grows inward and divides the cell into two equal-sized daughter cells. Each daughter cell will contain a complete copy of the parent cell's genes.

Although prokaryotes reproduce asexually, they are still able to exchange genetic material in several ways. In one process, called **conjugation** (KAHN-juh-GAY-shuhn), prokaryotes can exchange parts of their chromosomes through a hollow bridge of pili formed to connect two or more cells.

Surviving Harsh Conditions

During conditions unfavorable for survival, some bacteria can produce an **endospore,** a specialized cell with a thick, protective wall. To form an endospore, the bacterium copies its chromosome and produces a wall around the copy. This thick wall around the bacterial DNA helps it survive harsh conditions such as drying out, temperature change, and disinfectants. Endospores can last for centuries. Some have even been found in Egyptian mummies!

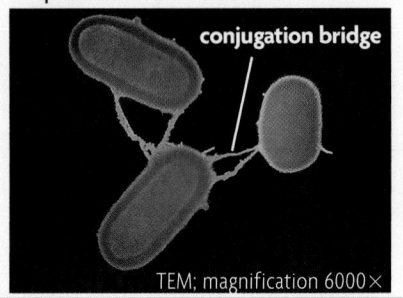

VISUAL VOCAB

In **conjugation,** genetic material transfers between prokaryotes, producing genetic variation. A conjugation bridge forms from the donor cell to a recipient cell.

conjugation bridge

TEM; magnification 6000×

Connect Why are disinfectants alone not enough to kill all types of bacteria?

18.4 ASSESSMENT

ONLINE QUIZ
ClassZone.com

REVIEWING ▶ MAIN IDEAS

1. What are the three most common shapes of bacteria?

2. Why are bacteria and archaea classified into different domains?

3. Prokaryotes will take up foreign DNA. How is this characteristic used in genetic engineering?

CRITICAL THINKING

4. **Infer** Scientists estimate that only 1 percent of prokaryotes can be grown in the lab. What does this suggest about our knowledge of bacteria and archaea?

5. **Synthesize** Prokaryotes multiply by binary fission, which simply divides a cell in two. Why are mutations and **conjugation** important for natural selection in prokaryotes?

Connecting CONCEPTS

6. **Health** Bacteria in your mouth convert foods containing sugar and starch into acids that can then cause cavities in your teeth. These bacteria will be present even if you brush your teeth, floss, or use mouthwash. So why are these hygiene habits so important?

18.5

Beneficial Roles of Prokaryotes

KEY CONCEPT Prokaryotes perform important functions for organisms and ecosystems.

▶ **MAIN IDEAS**
- Prokaryotes provide nutrients to humans and other animals.
- Prokaryotes play important roles in ecosystems.

VOCABULARY
bioremediation, p. 561

Review
nitrogen fixation

L3.p2B Describe common ecological relationships between and among species and their environments (competition, territory, carrying capacity, natural balance, population, dependence, survival, and other biotic and abiotic factors). (prerequisite)

Connect People usually think bacteria in or on food are harmful, and it is true that food poisoning caused by bacteria can be a serious problem. However, some bacteria are safe in food, and actually provide a taste or texture that many people enjoy. Swiss cheese, sour cream, and butter are just a few products that are made with the help of bacteria. Eating food produced by bacteria is not dangerous, as long as they are the right kind of bacteria!

▶ **MAIN IDEA**

Prokaryotes provide nutrients to humans and other animals.

Prokaryotes, such as the bacteria shown in **FIGURE 18.15,** are a key part of animal digestive systems. A balanced community of prokaryotes in our bodies is important for our health. Prokaryotes have a beneficial relationship, or mutualistic symbiosis, with the host animal and break down food while getting a place to live. They also make vitamins and other compounds, and keep away harmful microbes by filling niches that might otherwise be filled by disease-causing bacteria. In turn, the host animal provides the bacteria with food and a home with a stable pH and temperature.

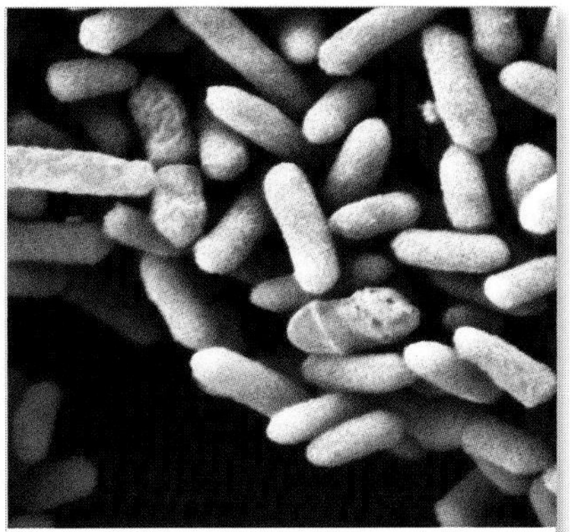

Connecting CONCEPTS

Ecology Recall from **Chapter 14** that *symbiosis* is the close association of two or more species. A *niche* is a specific role an organism plays in its environment.

FIGURE 18.15 These bacteria, found in human intestines, are beneficial to our health. They produce B vitamins and keep out harmful microbes. (colored SEM; magnification: 6300×)

Humans can get nutrients from prokaryotes in other ways as well. Many foods that humans enjoy are fermented by bacteria. Bacteria help ferment, or chemically break down, many dairy products people eat every day, such as yogurt and cheeses. Pickles, soy sauce, sauerkraut, and vinegar also depend on fermentation by prokaryotes to produce their flavors.

Summarize What are two ways in which prokaryotes that live within our bodies are helpful to us?

Examining Bacteria in Yogurt

Some types of bacteria can ferment milk, producing lactic acid in the process. Yogurt is a product of fermentation. It is acidic and stays fresh longer than milk, and it is also digested more easily. In this exercise, you will prepare a microscope slide of yogurt.

PROBLEM What types of bacteria can you observe in yogurt?

PROCEDURE

1. Using a toothpick, place a dab of yogurt on a microscope slide. **Caution:** Do not eat in the laboratory.

2. Mix the yogurt in a drop of water and carefully add a coverslip.

3. Examine the slide with a compound microscope.

4. Record your observations by drawing a picture of what you see through the microscope.

MATERIALS
- toothpick
- dab of yogurt
- microscope slide
- drop of water
- coverslip
- microscope

ANALYZE AND CONCLUDE

1. **Identify** Recall the terms *bacillus, coccus,* and *spirilla* from the previous section. Which type or types of bacteria did you observe in your slides?

2. **Analyze** Many people do not produce lactase, which is an enzyme that breaks down the milk sugar lactose. As a result, lactose-intolerant people have trouble digesting dairy products. Why might they have fewer problems eating yogurt?

▶ MAIN IDEA

Prokaryotes play important roles in ecosystems.

Even though you can't easily see them, prokaryotes play important roles in every ecosystem they occupy. Some, such as cyanobacteria, produce oxygen through photosynthesis. Others help recycle carbon, nitrogen, hydrogen, and sulfur through the ecosystem. The absence of prokaryotes in the environment can disrupt an ecosystem, since other organisms rely on them for survival.

Photosynthesizing prokaryotes include purple and green photosynthetic bacteria and cyanobacteria. Whereas purple and green bacteria use light to make carbohydrates, they do not produce oxygen. Cyanobacteria, however, are similar to plants in how they produce oxygen as a byproduct of photosynthesis. Cyanobacteria are named for their greenish blue (cyan) color. Recall from Chapter 12 that cyanobacteria played an important part on early Earth, supporting the life forms we are familiar with today. Fossil evidence suggests there was very little oxygen on Earth prior to the appearance of cyanobacteria.

Some colonies of photosynthesizing cyanobacteria, as well as other bacteria, are also able to fix nitrogen. Although much of the atmosphere is made up of nitrogen gas (N_2), this is not in a form that plants or animals can use to make amino acids or proteins.

Recall from Chapter 13 that nitrogen fixation is the process of converting atmospheric nitrogen into ammonia (NH_3) and other nitrogen compounds that plants can then use. Prokaryotes supply usable nitrogen to ecosystems ranging from grasslands and forests to the arctic tundra.

Some types of nitrogen-fixing bacteria are free-living, while others live along with other organisms. Legumes, a group of plants including peas, beans, alfalfa, and clover, have a mutualistic relationship with nitrogen-fixing bacteria. These bacteria live in the plant's nodules, small rounded lumps that form the roots, as shown in **FIGURE 18.16**. The bacteria provide usable nitrogen to the plant by capturing nitrogen gas from air trapped in the soil. They combine the nitrogen with hydrogen to produce ammonia. In return, the plant supplies food and shelter to the bacteria.

Scientists have found many ways to use prokaryotes to benefit industry and the environment. One important use of prokaryotes is in **bioremediation** (BY-oh-rih-MEE-dee-AY-shuhn), a process that uses microbes and other living things to break down pollutants. For example, some types of bacteria can digest oil, which is helpful for cleaning up oil spills and other industrial accidents. Workers spray oil-polluted beaches with a fertilizer that helps the bacteria grow.

Bacteria can digest almost any product that humans can make, including poisons. Therefore, they play an important role in recycling and composting. When you hear the term *biodegradable*, it often refers to the ability of bacteria to break down a material. Some of the only materials made by humans that cannot be biodegraded are certain types of plastics.

Apply When there is a toxic chemical spill, sometimes workers will spray bacteria over the contaminated area. Why might they do this?

FIGURE 18.16 Root nodules of this white clover contain nitrogen-fixing bacteria. The symbiotic bacteria convert nitrogen from the atmosphere (N_2) into a form usable by the clover. In return, the plant produces carbohydrates through photosynthesis that the bacteria can consume. (inset colored SEM; magnification 90×)

18.5 / ASSESSMENT

ONLINE QUIZ
ClassZone.com

REVIEWING ▶ MAIN IDEAS

1. Describe two ways bacteria provide nutrients to humans.

2. What are two roles prokaryotes play in the cycling of elements in an ecosytem?

CRITICAL THINKING

3. **Connect** Think of an example in which the use of **bioremediation** either has improved the environment or has the potential to do so.

4. **Synthesize** How do prokaryotes lend stability to an ecosystem?

Connecting CONCEPTS

5. **Ecology** Prokaryotes in cow intestines produce more methane if the cow is fed a diet high in grains rather than grass. Some scientists propose that overfeeding grain to cows contributes to global warming. How did these scientists arrive at this hypothesis, and how could it be tested?

Leaf Print Bacteria

PPFM are pink-pigmented bacteria that grow on plant surfaces. They help plants by stimulating seed germination and plant growth. A unique feature of PPFM bacteria is that they use methanol as their sole source of carbon. Therefore, a simple nutrient mixture that contains only methanol as a carbon source will "select" for PPFM bacteria. This type of mixture is called a selective medium. A mixture that contains many nutrients is called a nonselective medium. In this lab, you will make leaf prints on selective and nonselective media to study the growth of PPFM and other bacteria.

PROBLEM How do populations of bacteria grown on various media differ?

PROCEDURE

1. Obtain two petri dishes, one containing a selective medium (methanol carbon source only) and the other containing a nonselective, nutrient-rich medium.

2. Label the petri dishes with your name, the date, and "selective" or "nonselective."

3. To make the first leaf print, lay one of the leaves on the surface of the selective medium. Use the eraser end of a pencil to gently press the leaf into the medium, as shown below. After making the impression, carefully lift the leaf away from the medium and discard. Close the petri dish.

4. Repeat step 3 using your other leaf and the nonselective medium.

5. Seal the petri dishes with tape. Store them upside down at room temperature.

   Caution: Once the dishes are sealed, they should not be opened again. Follow your teacher's directions for disposal of the petri dishes at the end of the lab.

6. Write a prediction based on what you know about PPFM bacteria and the selective and nonselective media.

7. Observe the dishes over a period of one or two weeks. Record your observations daily. These should be both qualitative (shape, color, and size of colonies) and quantitative (number of colonies). To count colonies, it may help to create a grid on the underside of each petri dish.

8. At the end of the observation period, compare your results with those from the rest of the class.

ANALYZE AND CONCLUDE

1. **Analyze** How many types of bacteria were present on the nonselective medium? the selective medium? What might account for differences between the two?

2. **Analyze** Is PPFM bacteria growth the same on both types of media? Which observations support this conclusion?

3. **Analyze** Do all bacteria grow at the same rate? Which observations support this conclusion?

4. **Infer** Why might bacteria grow faster on the nonselective medium?

EXTEND YOUR INVESTIGATION

Design an experimental procedure to test the hypothesis that different types of PPFM bacteria are found on different plants.

MATERIALS
- petri dish containing a selective medium
- petri dish containing a nonselective medium
- permanent marker
- 2 leaves from the same plant
- pencil with eraser
- transparent tape

PROCESS SKILLS
- **Observing**
- **Evaluating Outcomes**

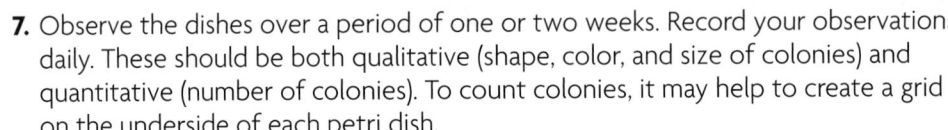

MICHIGAN STANDARDS

B1.1E Describe a reason for a given conclusion using evidence from an investigation.

B2.4h Describe the structures of viruses and bacteria.

18.6

Bacterial Diseases and Antibiotics

KEY CONCEPT Understanding bacteria is necessary to prevent and treat disease.

▶ MAIN IDEAS

- Some bacteria cause disease.
- Antibiotics are used to fight bacterial disease.
- Bacteria can evolve resistance to antibiotics.

VOCABULARY

toxin, p. 563
antibiotic, p. 564

Review
homeostasis

Connect In the early 1900s, most deaths in the United States were caused by infectious diseases, such as bacterial pneumonia and tuberculosis. Thanks to new medicines, infectious diseases were among the least common causes of death by the century's end. In recent years, however, many diseases are making a comeback due to a new problem—antibiotic resistance.

▶ MAIN IDEA

Some bacteria cause disease.

Some bacteria cause disease in plants and animals by disrupting the host organism's homeostasis, or the stability of its internal environment. Bacteria can cause illness to a host in two basic ways: by invading tissues and attacking cells or by making poisons, or toxins, that can be carried by blood to sites throughout the body. A **toxin** is a poison released by an organism.

The disease tuberculosis (TB) is an example of bacteria invading the host's tissues, and using the tissues for nutrients. *Mycobacterium tuberculosis* bacteria multiply in the lungs, killing white blood cells that respond to the invasion. The host's reaction to an invasion by bacteria may itself cause serious problems. In the case of TB, the host responds to the infection by releasing enzymes that cause swelling. That swelling, in turn, damages the host's lungs.

TB is a good example of the changing ecological balance between host and pathogen in an infectious disease. A host is not usually aware of pathogens that its immune system defeats. It is when the host's immune system fails that the host becomes aware of the pathogen's presence. Most healthy people can defeat a potential TB infection, especially if there are not many bacteria present.

Bacteria, such as *Staphylococcus aureus* and *Clostridium botulinum,* shown in **FIGURE 18.17,** can also make their hosts sick through food poisoning. *S. aureus,* which normally lives in nasal passages, can be transferred to food when food handlers don't wash their hands after they blow their nose. This transfer can result in serious food poisoning, known as staph poisoning. Even high temperatures cannot destroy a toxin produced by *S. aureus.* The most common source of food poisoning by *S. aureus,* however, is from foods that were contaminated after they were cooked. If contaminated food is not refrigerated, bacteria can multiply and produce a large amount of toxin.

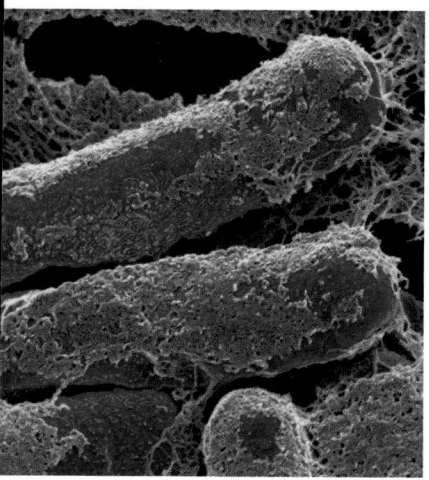

FIGURE 18.17 *Clostridium botulinum* causes a serious illness called botulism. Food contamination by this bacterium often comes from improper home canning. (magnification unknown)

FIGURE 18.18 Common Bacterial Infections

INFECTION	BACTERIUM	SYMPTOMS	CAUSES
Acne	*Propionibacterium*	chronic cysts, blackheads	increased oil production in skin
Anthrax	*Bacillus anthracis*	fever, trouble breathing	inhaling endospores
Lyme disease	*Borrelia burgdorferi*	rash, aching, fever, swelling of joints	bite from infected tick
Tetanus	*Clostridium tetani*	severe muscle spasms, fever, lockjaw	wound contaminated with soil
Tooth decay	*Streptococcus mutans*	tooth cavities	large populations of bacteria in mouth

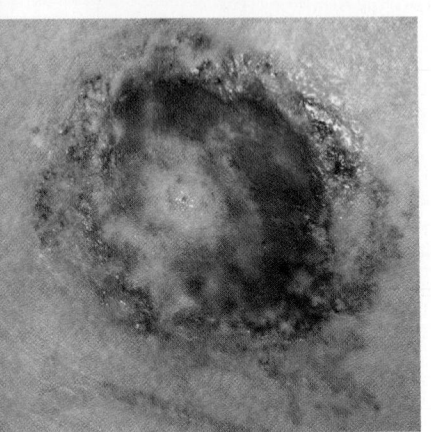

FIGURE 18.19 "Flesh eating" group A *Streptococcus* bacteria are commonly found on skin. They are fairly harmless unless they come in contact with tissues they do not normally colonize, such as muscle or fat. This can occur through open wounds.

Connecting CONCEPTS

Immune System Although antibiotics do not work on viruses, vaccines may work on both viruses and bacteria. This is because vaccines trigger the immune system. You will learn more about how the immune system works in **Chapter 31**.

Staph food poisoning can make you pretty sick, but botulism can kill you. *C. botulinum* produces a deadly toxin. Botulism is usually caused by the eating of improperly canned foods that were contaminated with endospores before being sealed. Bulging cans are a sign that *C. botulinum* may be present.

Normally harmless bacteria can be destructive when introduced to a part of the host that is not adapted to them. Disease can result if these bacteria get into tissues they do not usually colonize through a cut, scrape, or surgical incision. You can see one result of typically harmless *Streptococci*, which we have normally in our mouths and noses—and often on our skin—becoming pathogenic in **FIGURE 18.19**. These are also the bacteria that can cause what is commonly known as strep throat.

Apply **Potato salad left out at a picnic is sometimes a source of food poisoning. Which bacterium mentioned above is the most likely culprit? Explain.**

MAIN IDEA
Antibiotics are used to fight bacterial disease.

If you've ever had a cold, your doctor may have told you that the only cure was to let the cold "run its course." If you had strep throat, however, the doctor would prescribe a powerful antibiotic. Why do you get antibiotics for strep throat but not for the common cold?

Colds and strep throat are treated differently because they are caused by different pathogens. Viruses cause colds, while the bacterium *Streptococcus* causes strep throat. Many types of **antibiotics**—or chemicals that kill or slow the growth of bacteria—work by stopping bacteria from making cell walls.

Antibiotics are produced naturally by some species of bacteria and fungi. They can be used as medicine for humans and other animals without damaging their cells, since animal cells do not have cell walls. Because viruses also lack cell walls, antibiotics do not work on viral infections.

Antibiotics can be effective when used properly, but they should not be the first line of defense against bacterial infection; prevention should. Overuse of antibiotics can completely wipe out the community of intestinal microbes, resulting in illness.

Infer **Why don't antibiotics affect our bodies' own cells?**

MAIN IDEA

Bacteria can evolve resistance to antibiotics.

Although antibiotics should certainly be used when needed, the inappropriate and incomplete use of antibiotics has produced a serious public health issue—multidrug-resistant bacteria. Resistance occurs as a result of natural selection, as individuals who are more resistant are more likely to survive and reproduce. This has led to the evolution of multidrug-resistant strains of "superbugs" that are almost impossible to treat. As you can see in **FIGURE 18.20**, bacteria can acquire genes for resistance through plasmid exchange. This has happened with many bacteria with a wide range of commonly used antibiotics. This problem has arisen due to various factors.

Overuse The potential problem with antibiotics is that they may create a selective pressure that favors the very bacteria they are intended to destroy. Using antibiotics when bacteria are not causing an illness may make some bacteria resistant.

Underuse Failure to take the entire course of antibiotics prescribed for a bacterial infection is one of the main factors leading to drug resistance. If your doctor prescribed a ten-day course of an antibiotic, you must finish the entire prescription. Otherwise, you may not have destroyed all of the bacteria—only the weakest ones.

Misuse A large portion of the antibiotics distributed in the United States are fed to livestock. Antibiotics are often misused in agriculture to increase the animals' rate of growth. However, when antibiotics are added to the food of healthy animals, bacteria within the food—including pathogens—can become resistant to multiple antibiotics.

Connect How can you use "superbugs" as an example of natural selection?

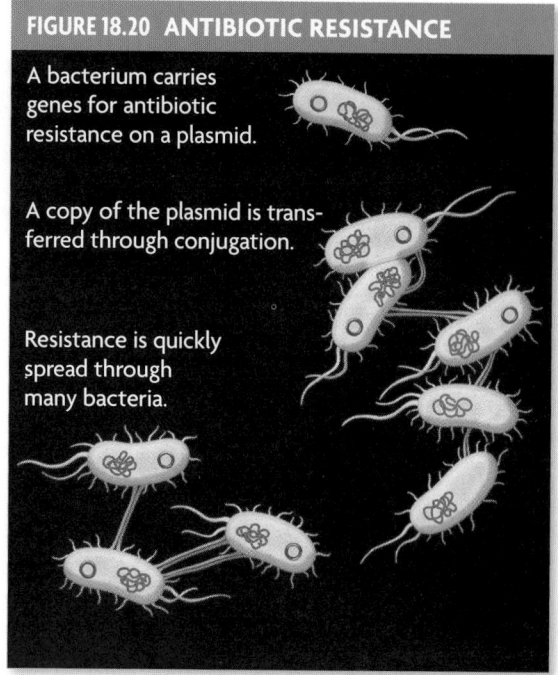

FIGURE 18.20 ANTIBIOTIC RESISTANCE

A bacterium carries genes for antibiotic resistance on a plasmid.

A copy of the plasmid is transferred through conjugation.

Resistance is quickly spread through many bacteria.

18.6 ASSESSMENT

ONLINE QUIZ
ClassZone.com

REVIEWING ▶ MAIN IDEAS

1. What are two ways in which bacteria can cause disease?

2. How can **antibiotics** stop bacterial infections?

3. What is antibiotic resistance, and how does it occur?

CRITICAL THINKING

4. **Apply** Why are antibiotics not effective against viruses?

5. **Synthesize** Evolution is often thought of as taking thousands, or even millions, of years to occur. What are two reasons that antibiotic resistance has been able to evolve in bacteria so quickly?

Connecting CONCEPTS

6. **Ecology** Pesticide resistance occurs in much the same way as antibiotic resistance. How could we apply what we have learned about antibiotic resistance to how pesticides are used in the environment?

Use these inquiry-based labs and online activities to deepen your understanding of viruses and prokaryotes.

DESIGN YOUR OWN INVESTIGATION

Using Bacteria to Break Down Oil

Some types of bacteria have enzymes that can break down oil and are used by scientists to help clean up an oil spill. Some types of drain cleaners contain bacteria that work in the same way to clear drain pipes. In this lab, you will test the effectiveness of different types of enzymatic drain cleaners at breaking down cooking oil.

SKILLS Designing Experiments, Concluding

PROBLEM Which enzymatic drain cleaner is most effective at breaking down oil?

MATERIALS

- 4 10-mL test tubes with caps
- 6 cm masking tape
- marker
- test tube rack
- 5 plastic droppers
- 3 10-mL graduated cylinders
- 2 mL cooking oil
- 2 mL 0.02% tetrazolium indicator solution
- 2 mL each of three types of enzymatic drain cleaner

PROCEDURE

1. Label four test tubes A, B, C, and D.

2. Determine a procedure for your experiment, using small amounts of the materials. Decide which materials and how much of each will be placed in each test tube. You will test the effectiveness of each type of drain cleaner at breaking down cooking oil. Each class group will use a different type of oil. The tetrazolium indicator solution turns pink when oil is broken down.

3. Identify the independent and dependent variables in your experiment. Identify the controls and constants in your experiment. Develop an operational definition of your dependent variable.

4. Get approval from your teacher to carry out your experiment. Wear gloves.

5. Use a separate dropper for the oil, the tetrazolium solution, and each type of drain cleaner. Once they are prepared, place the caps on the test tubes and gently swirl the test tubes to thoroughly mix solutions.

6. Observe your test tubes every day for at least five days. Record your data in a table like the one below. Day 0 represents the observations you make immediately after your test tubes have been prepared.

TABLE 1. DRAIN CLEANER EFFECTIVENESS				
Day	Tube A	Tube B	Tube C	Tube D
0				
1				

ANALYZE AND CONCLUDE

1. **Analyze** Which drain cleaner was most effective at breaking down the oil?

2. **Compare** Compare your results to those of other groups in the class that used different types of cooking oil. Which type of oil was broken down most effectively?

3. **Conclude** Which drain cleaner would you buy? Explain.

INVESTIGATION

Modeling Viruses

The structure of a virus actually helps the virus to enter into a host cell and multiply. In this exercise, you will create a model to help understand how a virus attacks a healthy cell.

SKILL Modeling

PROBLEM How does the shape of a virus relate to how it functions?

MATERIALS

- research materials (books, scientific journals, Internet)
- markers
- pipe cleaners
- clay
- tooth picks
- construction paper
- white paper

PROCEDURE

1. In your group, select one of the following viral illnesses:

   - chickenpox
   - common cold
   - influenza
   - mumps
   - polio
   - measles
   - AIDS
   - West Nile
   - hemorrhagic fever

2. Research the structure of the virus that causes the illness. State the scientific name of the virus (or virus family) that causes the illness.

3. Using the provided craft materials, construct a model of the virus based on the micrographs that you find.

ANALYZE AND CONCLUDE

1. **Analyze** Look at all the models. What differences do you see? How are they similar?

2. **Apply** How does the specific shape of your virus enable it to attack healthy cells?

3. **Evaluate** What characteristics of the virus are not represented by your model?

Online BIOLOGY
CLASSZONE.COM

VIRTUAL LAB
Testing Antibacterial Products
Do antibacterial products really kill germs as they claim? In this interactive lab, you will culture bacteria, and then determine the effectiveness of different germ-killing agents.

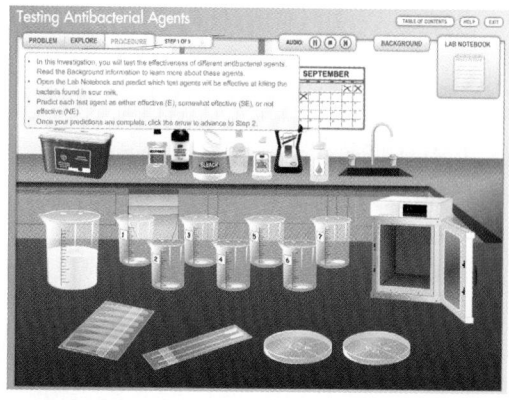

ANIMATED BIOLOGY
What Would You Prescribe?
Is an antibiotic always the best medicine? Review patients' symptoms and diagnoses, then determine if an antibiotic should be used to treat the patients.

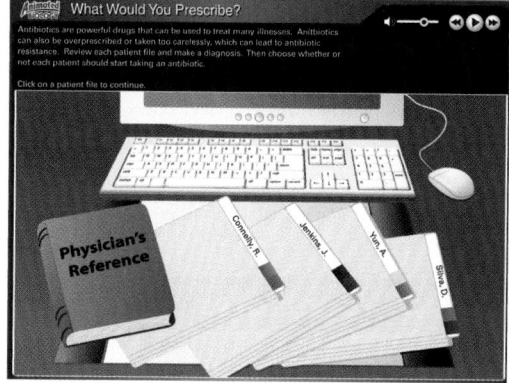

WEBQUEST
Modern agriculture uses antibiotics to keep livestock healthy. Is there a downside to giving livestock antibiotics? Complete this WebQuest to find out. Explore links between antibiotic resistance and antibiotic use in agriculture.

18.1 Studying Viruses and Prokaryotes

Infections can be caused in several ways. Viruses, viroids, and prions have characteristics of both living and nonliving things. Unlike bacteria, viruses cannot reproduce on their own. A virus has genetic material and a protein coat. Viroids have only RNA and no protein coat. Prions are made of only protein.

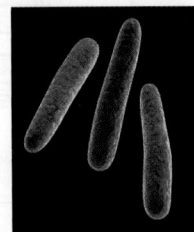

18.2 Viral Structure and Reproduction

Viruses exist in a variety of shapes and sizes. Viruses can be helical like a spring, many-sided, or enveloped. Bacteriophages, or viruses that attack bacteria, have a many-sided capsid with a long protein tail and spiky footlike fibers. There

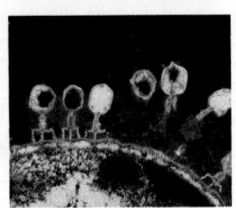

are two basic types of viral infections: lytic and lysogenic. A lytic infection results in the host cells bursting open, while the virions in a lysogenic infection do not immediately destroy the host.

18.3 Viral Diseases

Some viral diseases can be prevented with vaccines. Viruses can enter a body through wounds or body openings such as mouths or noses. Many infectious viruses exist. Examples of illnesses caused by viruses include the common cold, influenza, SARS, and AIDS. Vaccines can prevent some, but not all, viral diseases.

18.4 Bacteria and Archaea

Bacteria and archaea are both single-celled prokaryotes. Prokaryotes are widespread on Earth. Archaea look very similar to bacteria, but many of their structures are made of different compounds. Some prokaryotes can survive harsh conditions by forming endospores. Prokaryotes can transfer genes to each other through conjugation.

18.5 Beneficial Roles of Prokaryotes

Prokaryotes perform important functions for organisms and ecosystems. Prokaryotes that live in an animal's digestive tract help the animal absorb nutrients from the food that it eats. Animals and plants also depend on prokaryotes to fix atmospheric nitrogen. Nitrogen is necessary to make amino acids and proteins. Bioremediation uses prokaryotes to help break down pollutants in the environment.

18.6 Bacterial Diseases and Antibiotics

Understanding bacteria is necessary to prevent and treat disease. Although the majority of bacteria are not pathogenic, some do cause disease. Bacteria can also cause conditions such as food poisoning, chronic acne, Lyme disease, and tooth decay. Antibiotics are used to fight bacterial infection. However, through natural selection, many bacteria have become resistant to commonly used antibiotics.

Synthesize Your Notes

Concept Map Use a concept map like the one below to summarize what you know about infectious agents. Include details about genetic material and types of hosts they infect.

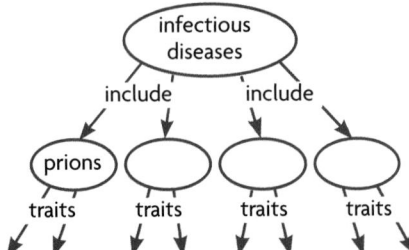

Cycle Diagram Use two cycle diagrams like the one below to summarize lytic and lysogenic infections.

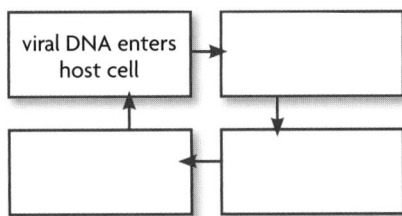

Chapter Assessment

18.1 virus, p. 544
pathogen, p. 544
viroid, p. 544
prion, p. 545

18.2 capsid, p. 547
bacteriophage, p. 549
lytic infection, p. 551
lysogenic infection, p. 551
prophage, p. 551

18.3 epidemic, p. 553
vaccine, p. 553
retrovirus, p. 553

18.4 obligate anaerobe, p. 555
obligate aerobe, p. 555
facultative aerobe, p. 555
plasmid, p. 556
flagellum, p. 556

conjugation, p. 558
endospore, p. 558

18.5 bioremediation, p. 561

18.6 toxin, p. 563
antibiotic, p. 564

Reviewing Vocabulary

Category Clues

For each clue, list the appropriate vocabulary term from the chapter.

Category: Viral Infection

1. protects against infection
2. plant virus
3. host and viral DNA

Category: Bacteria

4. virus of bacteria
5. fights bacterial infection
6. pollution digestion

Greek and Latin Word Origins

7. The term *flagellum* comes from the Latin word *flagrum,* which means "whip." Explain how this meaning relates to flagellum.

8. The term *conjugation* comes from the Latin word *conjugare,* which means "to join together." Using this meaning, explain how it relates to what conjugation is.

9. The term *epidemic* comes from the Greek words *epi-,* which means "upon," and *demos,* which means "people." Explain how these meanings relate to an epidemic.

10. The term *aerobe* means "an organism that requires oxygen to live." The prefixes *a-* or *an-* mean "without, or not." How do these meanings relate to the term *anaerobe*?

Reviewing MAIN IDEAS

11. Viruses, viroids, and prions are not considered to be living things. Which of their traits resemble living organisms, and which traits do not?

12. The flu virus has an envelope with surface proteins that allow it to infect its host cells. What structures help viruses infect bacterial cells? Explain.

13. Explain the differences between the two ways viruses infect their host cells.

14. Children across the United States get "shots," or injections, during their physical exams. Explain what these shots are and why they are recommended for all children.

15. The success of prokaryotes is due to special characteristics they have, such as the ability to form endospores and perform conjugation. Explain how each of these abilities helps prokaryotes survive changing environments.

16. It surprises most people to learn that their lives depend on bacteria. Describe three roles bacteria play in human health and survival.

17. Due to their unique ability to break down an enormous array of substances, prokaryotes play critical roles in ecosystems. Summarize two of these roles.

18. Doctors recommend washing hands before eating to prevent the spread of disease. What is the connection between bacteria and disease?

19. Prokaryotes have the ability to carry genes other than their own. How is this trait important for genetic engineering?

20. Recently, doctors have been advised to limit the use of antibiotics whenever possible. Why is this recommendation important?

Critical Thinking

21. Apply Many bacteria cause food spoilage because they have dietary needs similar to humans. However, some bacteria consume chemicals such as heavy metals, sulfur, petroleum, and mercury. How are these bacteria being used to help humans?

22. Compare and Contrast In the lysogenic infection, viral genes can become a part of the host's cell. In the lytic infection, the host cell is destroyed. What might be the benefit of each type of infection to the virus?

23. Infer New viruses may quickly kill their host after infection, but after many generations viruses tend to weaken and cause fewer deaths. Why might it be a disadvantage for a virus to quickly kill its host?

24. Synthesize Endospore-forming bacteria include those that cause the diseases tetanus, botulism, and anthrax. Endospores themselves, however, do not cause illness and cannot reproduce. Why, then, are endospores such a concern to the food and healthcare industries?

Interpreting Visuals

Use the diagram below to answer the next three questions.

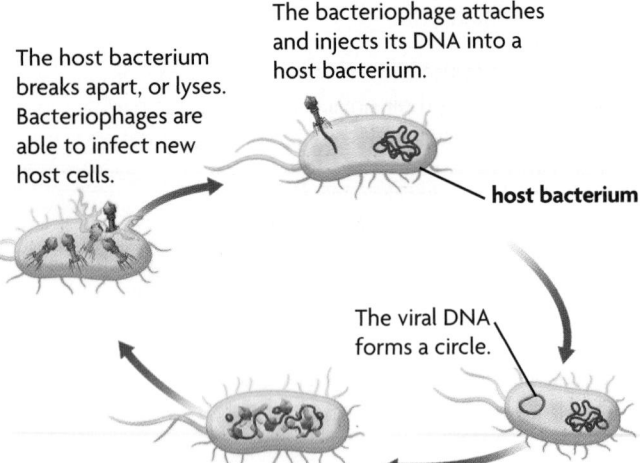

The bacteriophage attaches and injects its DNA into a host bacterium.

The host bacterium breaks apart, or lyses. Bacteriophages are able to infect new host cells.

host bacterium

The viral DNA forms a circle.

The viral DNA directs the host cell to produce new viral parts. The parts assemble into new bacteriophages.

25. Apply What type of viral infection is shown above? Explain your answer.

26. Apply Why is it necessary for the viral genes to enter the host cell?

27. Analyze How would the way that the virion enters the host cell change if the virus were a type that infected animals, and the host cell were eukaryotic rather than prokaryotic?

Analyzing Data

Use the hypothetical data below to answer the next questions.

TYPE OF BACTERIA AND LENGTH	
Type of bacteria	Average length (nm)
Streptococcus	500
Staphylococcus	900
Vibrio	2600
Aquaspirillum	2800

REPLICATION TIME OF STREPTOCOCCUS	
Time (min)	Number of streptococcus cells
0	1
28	2
56	4
84	8

28. Connect For each of the tables above, identify whether the data are continuous or discrete. Explain.

29. Calculate Assuming that nutrients are unlimited, how many *Streptococcus* cells will there be after 112 minutes? Explain.

Connecting CONCEPTS

30. Writing a Pamphlet Scientists agree that a form of the avian flu virus has the potential to cause a worldwide flu epidemic. This type of virus is known to mutate easily and adapt quickly to host changes. Imagine you are a representative from the Centers for Disease Control and are writing a pamphlet to educate citizens about the virus and how it actually causes infection. Using your knowledge of cells and viruses, make a detailed pamphlet that the general public could understand.

31. Synthesize The bacteria in the esophagus shown on page 543 are one of the many types of symbiotic prokaryotes living within our bodies. How might these types of mutualistic relationships have arisen? Consider natural selection in your answer.

MICHIGAN STANDARDS-BASED ASSESSMENT

✓ *Test Practice*
For more test practice, go to ClassZone.com.

1.

Set-up for Antibiotic Testing			
Antibiotic	A	B	C
Infected mice tested	30	15	5
% Effectiveness	83%	25%	100%

Scientists are testing three antibiotics—A, B, and C—on 50 mice with bacterial infections. Their experimental design is shown above. They conclude that they need to do more testing on antibiotic C because **B1.1E**

A it unexpectedly worked better than A and B.

B 100 percent of the mice were cured.

C the sample size was too small.

D it will likely have the worst side effects.

2. Impetigo is a highly contagious skin infection caused by staph or strep bacteria that are normally found on the skin, where they are harmless. This infection is *most* likely to occur when **B2.3C**

A scraped skin provides the bacteria with access to tissues they do not normally contact.

B the bacteria have been genetically altered by scientists doing research.

C the infected person did not receive regularly scheduled vaccinations.

D the bacteria form endospores on the surface of the skin.

3. Some scientists think that measures of an ecosystem's health—such as usable nitrogen levels in the soil—may become more variable as the diversity of organisms on Earth declines. This is because usable soil nitrogen depends on a variety of **L3.p2B**

A animals that return nitrogen to the soil through respiration.

B animals that return nitrogen to the soil after they die.

C bacteria and other decomposers that fix nitrogen into a usable form.

D plants, which produce nitrogen as a byproduct of photosynthesis.

4. The main reason that viruses are not considered to be living things is that they do not **L2.p1A**

A die when exposed to antibiotics.

B reproduce on their own.

C contain a nucleus.

D undergo meiosis before replication.

THINK THROUGH THE QUESTION

All of these answer choices correctly describe viruses, so do not be tricked! Look at each answer choice and try to think of a living organism that fits the characteristic described, making that answer choice wrong.

5. Hepatitis B is a viral disease that attacks cells in the liver. When should a person receive a vaccination against hepatitis B? **B2.4i**

A before being exposed to the virus

B as soon as viral symptoms begin to appear

C after being diagnosed with the disease

D never; the overuse of vaccines leads to antibiotic resistance

6.

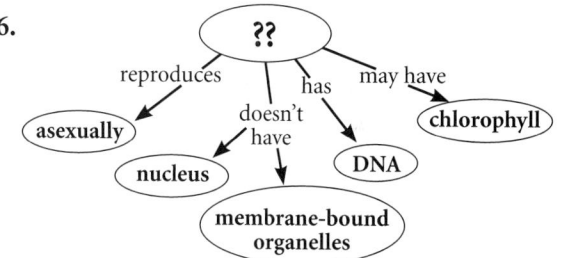

Which of the following is described by this concept map? **B2.4h**

A animal cell

B plant cell

C bacterium

D virus

19 Protists and Fungi

KEY CONCEPTS

19.1 Diversity of Protists
Kingdom Protista is the most diverse of all the kingdoms.

19.2 Animal-like Protists
Animal-like protists are single-celled heterotrophs that can move.

19.3 Plantlike Protists
Algae are plantlike protists.

19.4 Funguslike Protists
Funguslike protists decompose organic matter.

19.5 Diversity of Fungi
Fungi are heterotrophs that absorb their food.

19.6 Ecology of Fungi
Fungi recycle nutrients in the environment.

Online BIOLOGY CLASSZONE.COM

Animated BIOLOGY

View animated chapter concepts.
• Protist Movement
• Algae Concentrations
• Protist and Fungus Life Cycles

BIOZINE

Keep current with biology news.
• Featured stories
• Strange Biology
• Bio Bytes

RESOURCE CENTER

Get more information on
• Protozoa
• Algae
• Slime Molds

When these two protists meet, who is the prey?

colored SEM; magnification 2000×

A lthough they are both protists, the round *Didinium* hunts live paramecia almost exclusively. Paramecia are much longer than this predator, but that doesn't stop *Didinium*. It captures, paralyzes, and reels in paramecia like fish on a line. It then eats its prey whole, expanding its own body just so that its meal will fit.

Connecting CONCEPTS

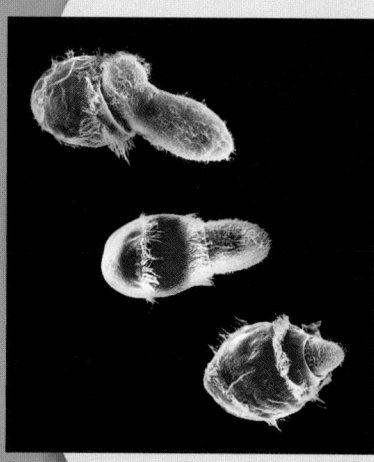

Ecology Most organisms follow one of two basic strategies for finding food, acting as specialists or generalists. *Didinium* is a specialist that eats only paramecia. In fact, when no paramecia are around, *Didinium* just turns into a cyst and waits until more come along. Paramecia are considered generalists, because they will eat anything smaller than themselves.

19.1 Diversity of Protists

KEY CONCEPT Kingdom Protista is the most diverse of all the kingdoms.

▶ **MAIN IDEAS**
- Protists can be animal-like, plantlike, or funguslike.
- Protists are difficult to classify.

VOCABULARY
protist, p. 574

MICHIGAN STANDARDS

B2.4A Explain that living things can be classified based on structural, embryological, and molecular (relatedness of DNA sequence) evidence.
B2.4d Analyze the relationships among organisms based on their shared physical, biochemical, genetic, and cellular characteristics and functional processes.

Connect If you looked at a drop of water from a pond, a roadside puddle, or a bird bath, you might find specimens of both *Didinium* and *Paramecium*. Despite their unique appearances, they are single-celled. That is what makes single-celled protists so amazing—they can carry out all life functions within just one cell. As you will see, one cell can be quite complex.

▶ **MAIN IDEA**

Protists can be animal-like, plantlike, or funguslike.

Large yellow globs of slime seemed to come out of nowhere. They were spreading across lawns and pulsing up telephone poles. Afraid that this was an alien invasion, residents of the Dallas neighborhood called police and firefighters. The firefighters turned their hoses on the blobs, but water only made the invaders grow.

Scientists came to the rescue. What the people in the Dallas neighborhood were seeing on this sunny day in 1973 wasn't an alien life form, but a slime mold. Specifically, it was *Fuligo septica*, shown in **FIGURE 19.1**, a species commonly called dog-vomit slime mold because of its resemblance to—well, dog vomit.

FIGURE 19.1 *Fuligo septica*, commonly known as the dog-vomit slime mold, is just one member of the diverse kingdom Protista.

Slime molds usually don't grow large enough to scare a neighborhood, but they are unusual. Slime molds are one of several groups of living things classified in kingdom Protista, a very diverse kingdom that includes hundreds of phyla. Members of this kingdom are often simply called protists.

A **protist** is a eukaryote that is not an animal, a plant, or a fungus. Protists are generally grouped together because, although they share some features with animals, plants, and fungi, they also lack one or more traits that would place them in any of these three kingdoms. Protists may be single-celled or multicellular, microscopic or very large. They have different ways of moving around and of responding to the environment. Some protists reproduce asexually, whereas others reproduce both asexually and sexually.

TAKING NOTES

Use a three-column chart to take notes about the groups of protists mentioned in this section.

Group	Description	Examples
animal-like		

Protists can be divided informally into three broad categories based on how they get their food. Categorizing protists in this way does not reflect evolutionary relationships, but it is a convenient way to study their diversity.

- **Animal-like protists** Animal-like protists, such as the *Oxytricha* in **FIGURE 19.2**, are heterotrophs—organisms that consume other organisms. However, all animal-like protists are single-celled, while all animals—no matter how simple—are multicellular.
- **Plantlike protists** Plantlike protists, such as the algae *Pediastrum* in **FIGURE 19.2**, make their own food by photosynthesis just as plants do. Although these protists may have chloroplasts, they do not have roots, stems, or leaves. And while all plants are multicellular, plantlike protists may be either single-celled, colonial, or multicellular.
- **Funguslike protists** Funguslike protists, such as slime molds, decompose dead organisms. Because of this trait, these protists were once classified in kingdom Fungi. However, funguslike protists can move during part of their life cycle, whereas fungi cannot. You will learn about fungi later in this chapter.

Apply **What one characteristic do all protists share?**

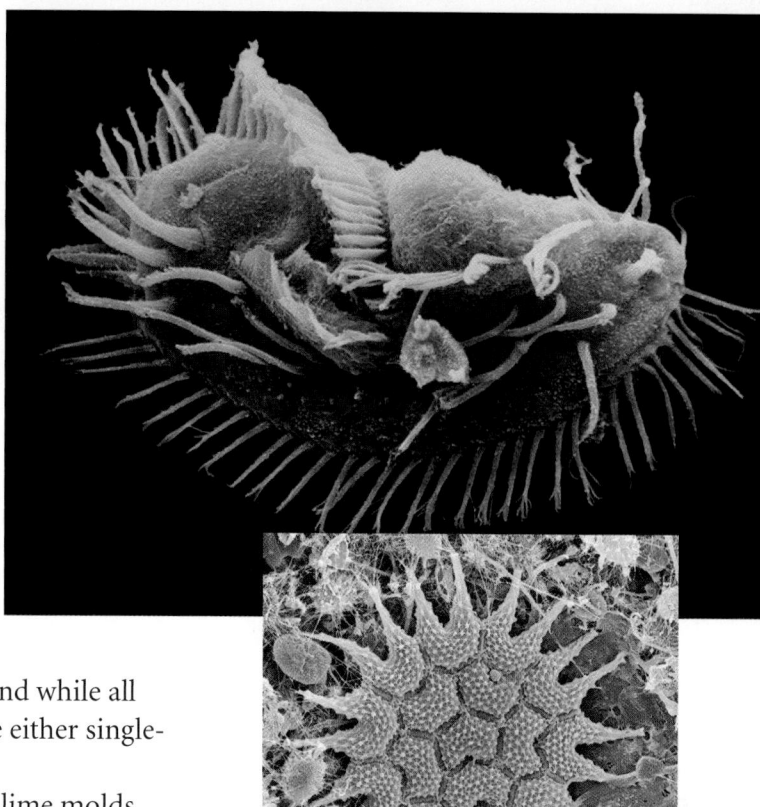

FIGURE 19.2 *Oxytricha* (top) is an example of an animal-like protist. It can move around quickly to find its food. *Pediastrum* (bottom) are algae that live in colonies. Like plants, they use sunlight to make food. (colored SEMs; magnifications unknown)

▶ MAIN IDEA
Protists are difficult to classify.

Recall from Chapter 17 that the three-domain system of classification divides prokaryotes into two domains, Archaea and Bacteria, and places all eukaryotes in one domain, Eukarya. There are four kingdoms within the domain Eukarya: Animalia, Fungi, Plantae, and Protista. The kingdom Protista includes many phyla. These phyla are very different from one another, and most are only distantly related. In fact, many protists are more closely related to members of other kingdoms than to other protists.

Kingdom Protista can be considered the junk-drawer of the kingdoms. It is a kingdom for all the eukaryotes that don't seem to fit in the animal, plant, or fungi definitions. Now that molecular biology techniques have revealed the genetic relationships between groups of organisms, many biologists think the protist kingdom will eventually be divided into several kingdoms within the domain Eukarya. If the genetic differences used to classify fungi, plants, and animals were used as a guide for classifying protists, we'd end up with more than 15 kingdoms of eukaryotes rather than the four we currently use. Until there is a widely accepted division of kingdom Protista into multiple kingdoms, the term *protist* remains useful when studying the group.

Connecting CONCEPTS

Classification Recall from **Chapter 17** that the six-kingdom model is made of two prokaryotic kingdoms and four eukaryotic kingdoms.

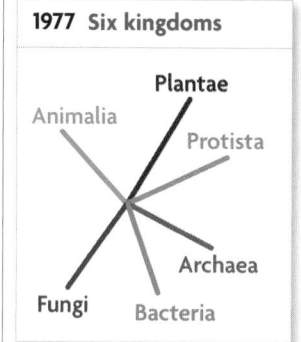

1977 Six kingdoms

Plantae
Animalia
Protista
Archaea
Fungi   Bacteria

FIGURE 19.3 Relationships of Protists to Other Eukaryotes

All protists currently belong to kingdom Protista, but some protists are more closely related to other kingdoms than to members of their own kingdom.

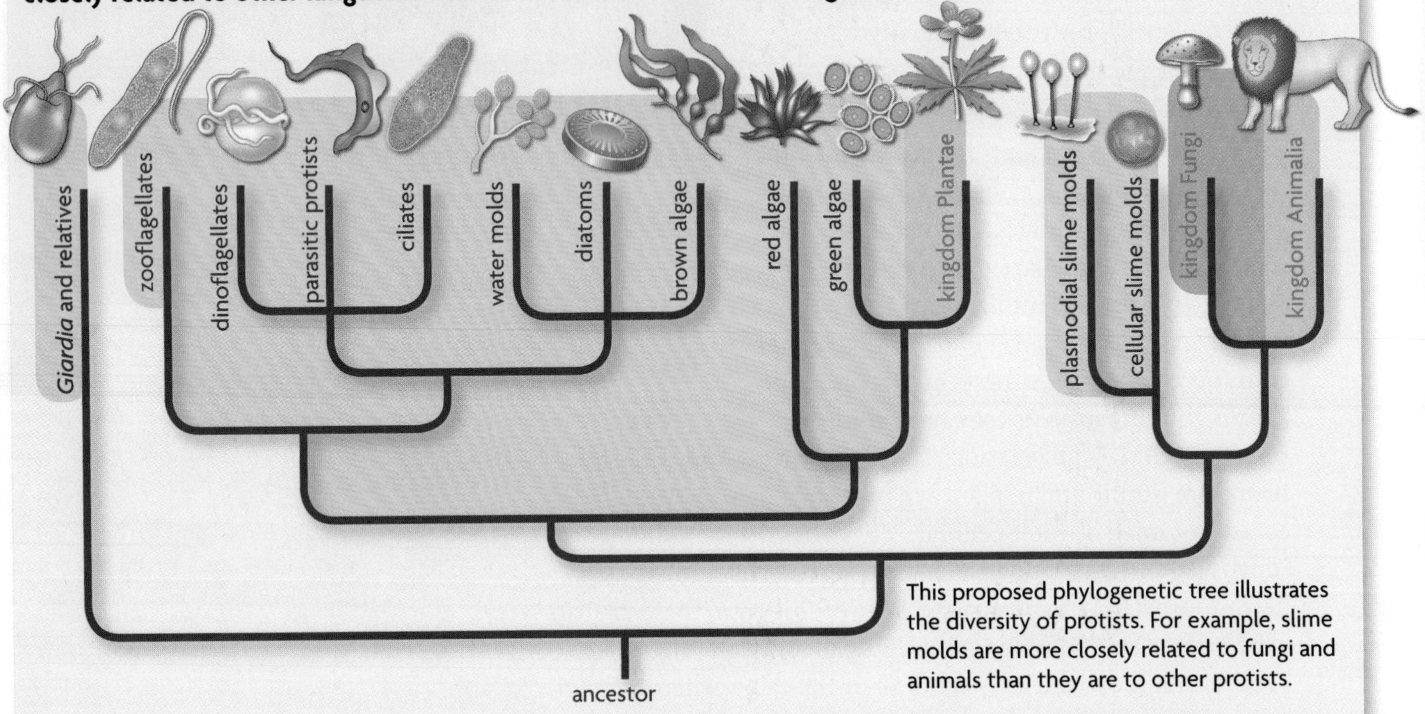

Giardia and relatives · zooflagellates · dinoflagellates · parasitic protists · ciliates · water molds · diatoms · brown algae · red algae · green algae · kingdom Plantae · plasmodial slime molds · cellular slime molds · kingdom Fungi · kingdom Animalia

ancestor

This proposed phylogenetic tree illustrates the diversity of protists. For example, slime molds are more closely related to fungi and animals than they are to other protists.

You can see the genetic relationship of protists to each other and to other kingdoms in **FIGURE 19.3**. For example, a comparison of RNA sequences between plants and green algae indicates that green algae are more closely related to plants than to other algae. Protist classification is a very active area of research, and in the future may provide insight into areas of study such as preventing or treating protist-caused diseases.

Summarize What is the argument for placing protists in more than one kingdom?

19.1 ASSESSMENT

ONLINE QUIZ
ClassZone.com

REVIEWING ▶ MAIN IDEAS

1. Name the three main groups within the kingdom Protista. What characteristics distinguish each group from the other two?

2. Give two reasons why **protists** are difficult to classify.

CRITICAL THINKING

3. **Infer** What observable traits might green algae and plants share that support the molecular evidence that these two groups are closely related?

4. **Contrast** At one time, scientists grouped all single-celled organisms together. What are the main differences between single-celled protists and bacteria or archaea?

Connecting CONCEPTS

5. **Ecology** Organisms that get their food by ingesting it are called heterotrophs, while those that make their own food are called autotrophs. Categorize animal-like, plant-like, and funguslike protists using these two terms.

Animal-like Protists

KEY CONCEPT Animal-like protists are single-celled heterotrophs that can move.

▶ **MAIN IDEAS**

- Animal-like protists move in various ways.
- Some animal-like protists cause disease.

VOCABULARY

protozoa, p. 577
pseudopod, p. 578
cilia, p. 578

Review
flagella, heterotroph, phagocytosis, conjugation

MICHIGAN STANDARDS

B2.3C Explain how stability is challenged by changing physical, chemical, and environmental conditions as well as the presence of disease agents.

B3.r5g Diagram and describe the stages of the life cycle for a human disease-causing organism. (recommended)

Connect Think of all the ways that different animals move. Some walk on two legs, while others walk on four. Some spend most of their time flying, while others can only swim. Just like animals, animal-like protists use different ways to get around.

▶ **MAIN IDEA**

Animal-like protists move in various ways.

The animal-like protists represent the largest number of species in the kingdom Protista. In the early two-kingdom classification system, some protists were classified as animals because they had many animal-like traits. Like animals, they can move around, they consume other organisms, and their cells lack chloroplasts. The key difference between animal-like protists and animals is their body organization: all animal-like protists are unicellular, while animals are multicellular. The term **protozoa** is often used informally to describe the many phyla of animal-like protists. A few common protozoan groups are discussed below.

Protozoa with Flagella

The zooflagellates (zoh-uh-FLAJ-uh-lihts) are animal-like protists that have one or more flagella at some point in their life cycle. Recall from Chapter 18 that flagella are tail-like structures that help unicellular organisms swim. Although the flagella of zooflagellates (phylum Zoomastigophora) look like the flagella of prokaryotes, they are structurally very different. Prokaryotic flagella attach to the surface of the cell. In contrast, eukaryotic flagella, such as those of the zooflagellate shown in **FIGURE 19.4**, are extensions of the cytoplasm. They are made of bundles of small tubes called microtubules and are enclosed by the plasma membrane. Prokaryotic flagella are also much smaller than the flagella of protists. You can easily see protist flagella with the aid of a light microscope, but prokaryotic flagella are invisible at the same magnification.

More than 2000 species of zooflagellates exist. All free-living zooflagellates are heterotrophs. For example, some zooflagellates eat prokaryotes that feed on dissolved organic matter, playing an important role in recycling nutrients through aquatic ecosystems. Other zooflagellates are pathogens, or disease-causing parasites of humans and other animals. Some zooflagellates live inside other organisms in mutualism—a relationship in which both organisms benefit.

FIGURE 19.4 Zooflagellates have flagella that help them move through water. (colored SEM; magnification unknown)

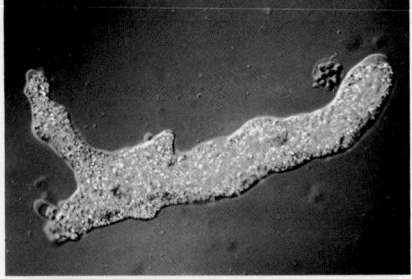

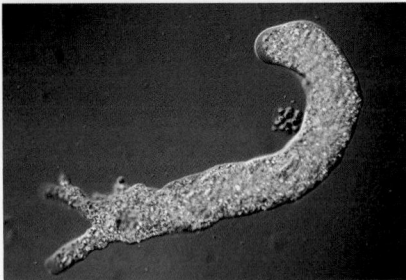

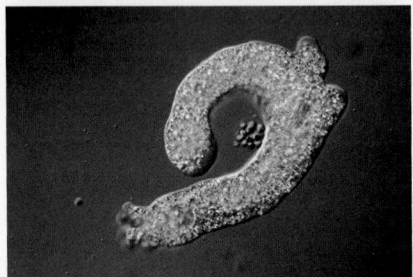

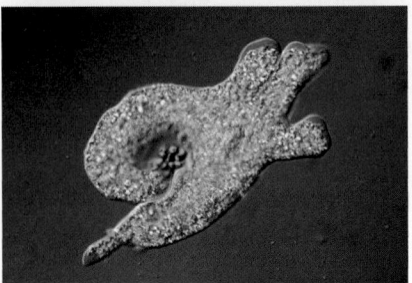

FIGURE 19.5 An amoeba extends a pseudopod to surround and ingest algae cells. (LM; magnification 150×)

Connecting CONCEPTS

Cell Organelles Recall from **Chapter 3** that a vacuole is a fluid-filled sac used for the temporary storage of materials needed by the cell.

Sometimes zooflagellates play a crucial role in another organism's life. For example, termites cannot digest the wood they eat. Inside the gut of a termite is a complex community made of zooflagellates and bacteria that *can* digest wood. The termites get nutrition from the zooflagellate's activity, and the zooflagellates get free meals and a place to live.

Protozoa with Pseudopods

Two groups of protozoa that can easily change shape as they move are the amoebas and the foraminifera.

Amoebas The amoebas (uh-MEE-buhz) are very flexible. Amoebas (phylum Rhizopoda) form pseudopods to move. A **pseudopod** (SOO-duh-PAHD), which means "fake foot," is a temporary extension of cytoplasm and plasma membrane that helps protozoa move and feed. To form a pseudopod, the cell cytoplasm flows outward, forming a bulge. This bulge spreads, anchors itself to the surface it is on, and pulls the rest of the cell toward it. Pseudopod formation uses energy. When the amoeba is not moving or feeding, it does not form pseudopods.

An amoeba's method of getting food is shown in **FIGURE 19.5**. Ingestion takes place by the process of phagocytosis. Recall from Chapter 3 that phagocytosis is the engulfing of solid material by a cell. The amoeba surrounds the food with its pseudopod, and the outer membrane of the amoeba then forms a food vacuole, or sac. Digestive enzymes enter the food vacuole from the surrounding cytoplasm, and digestion takes place.

Amoebas live in fresh water, salt water, and soil. The majority of amoebas are free-living, but some species are parasites. Most amoebas are microscopic. However, *Pelomyxa palustris* is an amoeba that can grow as large as five millimeters in diameter—a huge size for a single-celled organism—and can be seen without a microscope.

Foraminifera Another group of protozoa with pseudopods are members of phylum Foraminifera (fuh-RAM-uh-NIHF-uhr-uh). Foraminifera, sometimes simply called forams, are named for their multichambered shell, shown in **FIGURE 19.6**. The Latin word *foramen* means "little hole." Their shells are made of organic matter, sand, or other materials, depending on the species. Forams make up a large group of marine protozoa that, like amoeba, use pseudopods to move.

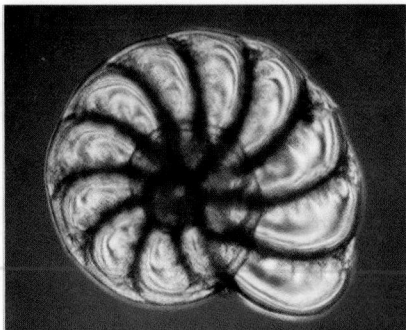

FIGURE 19.6 Pseudopods can extend from pores in a foraminifera's multichambered shell. This shell is smaller than the head of a matchstick. (magnification unknown)

Protozoa with Cilia

This group's name, Ciliates, comes from its most obvious feature—cilia. **Cilia** are short, hairlike structures that cover some or all of the cell surface and help the organism swim and capture food. Cilia are usually much shorter than flagella and found in much greater numbers. Some ciliates have many rows of cilia all over their surface, whereas other ciliates just have clusters of cilia. About 8000 species of ciliates make up the phylum Ciliophora. Some ciliates are parasites that cause disease. However, most ciliates are free-living cells found in fresh water, such as the common pondwater protists in the genus *Paramecium*.

Structures of a paramecium are shown in **FIGURE 19.7**. Food is swept into the oral groove by the cilia, and is sent to the gullet. Eventually the food is digested in food vacuoles. Two organs that act like pumps, called contractile vacuoles, control the amount of water inside the cell. An unusual trait found in paramecia and other ciliates is the presence of two types of nuclei. Each cell has one large macronucleus, but there can be many small micronuclei. The macronucleus controls the cell's structures and activities. The micronuclei contain all of the cell's chromosomes. They function only during conjugation, a process of genetic exchange. Two paramecia unite at the oral grooves and exchange micronuclei. Some species of the genus *Paramecium* have up to 80 micronuclei. Because micronuclei can be exchanged during conjugation, having so many micronuclei allows for a huge amount of genetic variation.

Summarize What functions do the two kinds of nuclei within *Paramecium* perform?

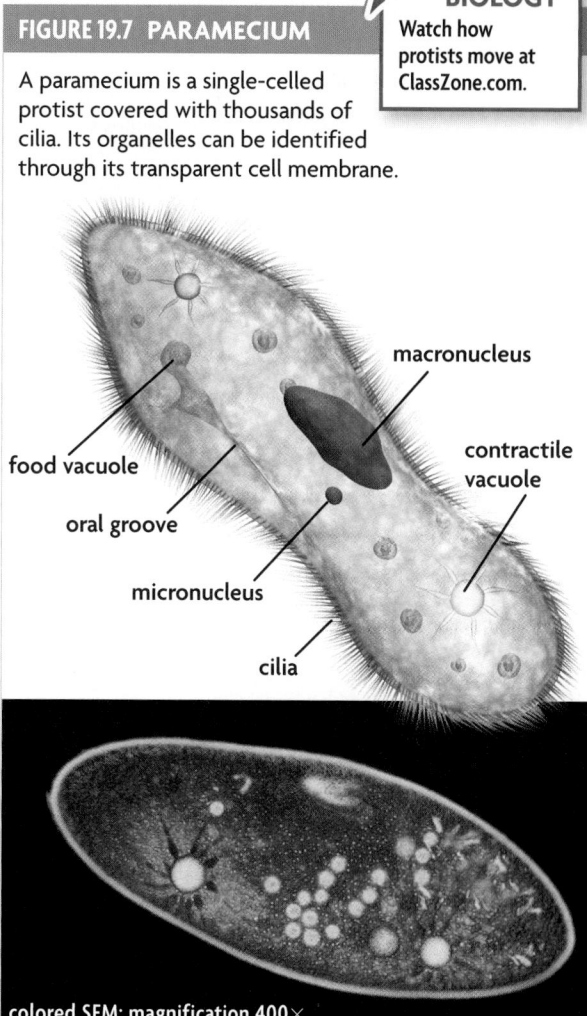

FIGURE 19.7 PARAMECIUM

Animated **BIOLOGY** Watch how protists move at ClassZone.com.

A paramecium is a single-celled protist covered with thousands of cilia. Its organelles can be identified through its transparent cell membrane.

macronucleus
contractile vacuole
food vacuole
oral groove
micronucleus
cilia

colored SEM; magnification 400×

QUICK LAB   OBSERVING

Investigating Motion in Protists

In this investigation you will observe the movement of one or more of the following protists: *Paramecium, Amoeba,* or *Euglena*.

PROBLEM What does a protist's movement look like?

1. Make a wet mount slide of the protist. You may need to add a drop of methylcellulose solution to the wet mount so that you can slow down the organism enough to observe. **Caution:** Do not use a cover slip on the amoeba slide, as you will crush the organism.

2. Observe how the organism moves. Make a series of three drawings that depict the movement of the organism.

3. If time allows, repeat steps 1 and 2 with the other two protists.

ANALYZE AND CONCLUDE

1. **Analyze** Describe the movement of the protist(s) you observed.

2. **Analyze** What structures did the protist that you observed use to move?

3. **Infer** Based on the structures you observed, do you think the species of protist that you observed swims in the water or crawls in the bottom sediments? Explain.

MATERIALS

- 4 eyedroppers
- 4 drops bottled spring water
- 3 microscope slides
- 2 cover slips
- culture of *Paramecium*
- 3 drops methylcellulose solution
- culture of *Amoeba*
- culture of *Euglena*
- microscope

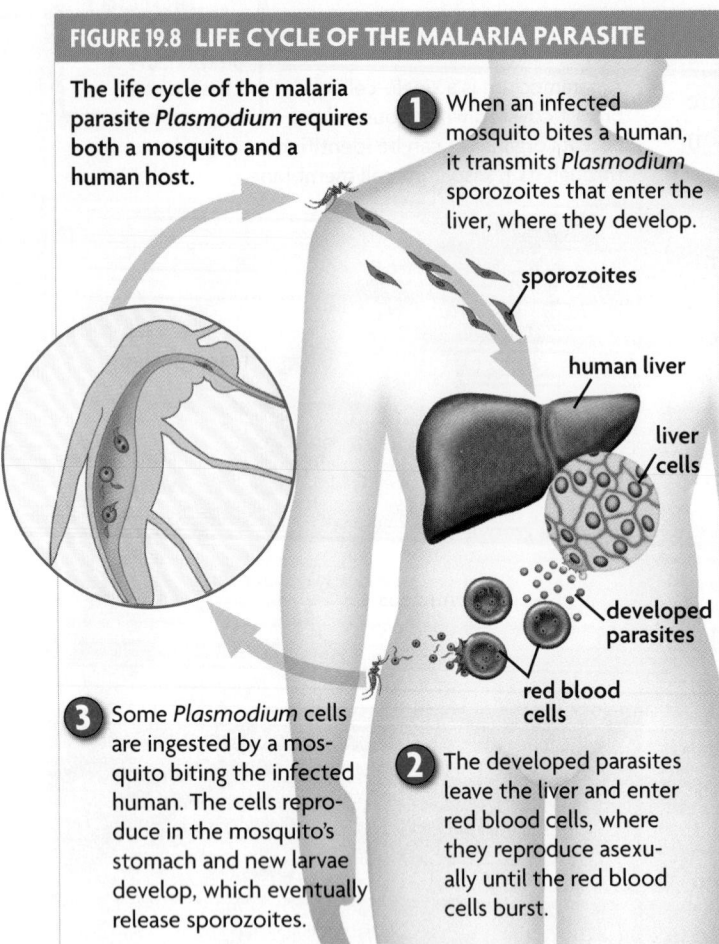

FIGURE 19.8 LIFE CYCLE OF THE MALARIA PARASITE

The life cycle of the malaria parasite *Plasmodium* requires both a mosquito and a human host.

1 When an infected mosquito bites a human, it transmits *Plasmodium* sporozoites that enter the liver, where they develop.

sporozoites

human liver

liver cells

developed parasites

red blood cells

2 The developed parasites leave the liver and enter red blood cells, where they reproduce asexually until the red blood cells burst.

3 Some *Plasmodium* cells are ingested by a mosquito biting the infected human. The cells reproduce in the mosquito's stomach and new larvae develop, which eventually release sporozoites.

⊙ MAIN IDEA

Some animal-like protists cause disease.

Protists cause some of the world's most well-known infectious diseases. The phylum Apicomplexa (A-pih-kuhm-PLEHK-suh) includes about 4000 species, all of which are parasites of animals. Many members of this phylum are known as sporozoans because they form sporozoites—infectious cells that have tough outer coats. Malaria is an example of a disease caused by sporozoans. It is caused by infection with the protozoan *Plasmodium*, shown in **FIGURE 19.8**.

Malaria is passed to humans and other animals through the bite of the *Anopheles* mosquito. Symptoms of malaria include high fever and vomiting. In some cases, the parasite can severely affect kidney and liver function, leading to coma and even death. Although the disease was once on the decline, today more than 1 million people—mostly children in developing countries—die from malaria each year. Mosquitoes have developed resistance to the insecticides that once would kill them, and *Plasmodium* species have become resistant to antimalarial drugs.

Two other parasitic protists that cause disease are the zooflagellates *Trypanosoma* and *Giardia*. In Africa, several species of *Trypanosoma* cause the disease known as sleeping sickness in humans and other mammals. Trypanosomes are transmitted through the bite of the tsetse fly, and can cause coma and death. *Giardia* causes intestinal disease in humans. People can become infected with *Giardia* by drinking water contaminated with feces of infected animals. Campers and hikers must be careful of *Giardia*, as even streams or rivers that appear clean could be contaminated.

Compare How do the parasites *Plasmodium* and *Giardia* each infect humans?

19.2 / ASSESSMENT

REVIEWING ⊙ MAIN IDEAS

1. Name and describe the three basic means of movement used by animal-like protists.

2. Describe how the parasite *Plasmodium* causes disease in humans.

CRITICAL THINKING

3. **Compare and Contrast** In what ways are **cilia** and flagella similar? How are they different?

4. **Infer** Why do amoebas form **pseudopods** only when they need them?

Connecting CONCEPTS

5. **Analogous Structures** The flagella of eukaryotes and prokaryotes serve the same function, but they are structurally very different. What does this suggest about the evolution of flagella?

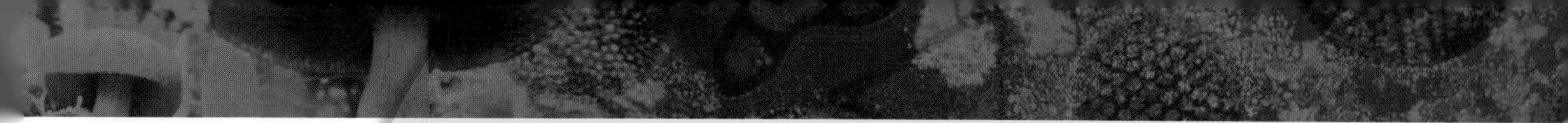

19.3 Plantlike Protists

KEY CONCEPT Algae are plantlike protists.

▶ MAIN IDEAS

- Plantlike protists can be single-celled or multicellular.
- Many plantlike protists can reproduce both sexually and asexually.

VOCABULARY

algae, p. 581

Review
phytoplankton, gamete, plankton, haploid, mitosis, diploid, meiosis

MICHIGAN STANDARDS

B3.2C Draw the flow of energy through an ecosystem. Predict changes in the food web when one or more organisms are removed.

L4.p1A Compare and contrast the differences between sexual and asexual reproduction. (prerequisite)

Connect On your birthday, do you enjoy decorations on your cake, or do you prefer it topped with ice cream? Both cake decorations and ice cream are among the many products that commonly contain substances from seaweeds, types of plantlike protists.

▶ MAIN IDEA

Plantlike protists can be single-celled or multicellular.

Just as animal-like protists were once classified as animals, it is not surprising that many plantlike protists used to be classified as plants. Although many plantlike protists look like plants, they are different in many ways. Unlike plants, plantlike protists do not have roots, stems, leaves, specialized tissues, or the same reproductive structures that plants have. All plants are multicellular, while plantlike protists may be single-celled or multicellular.

Many single-celled plantlike protists are free-living aquatic organisms that, together with photosynthetic bacteria, are known as phytoplankton. Recall from Chapter 15 that phytoplankton form the base of aquatic food chains and provide about half of the oxygen in Earth's atmosphere. Several species of single-celled plantlike protists, such as *Volvox*, shown in **FIGURE 19.9**, live in colonies. Multicellular plantlike protists include the seaweeds or kelps. Some species eat other organisms, but most plantlike protists have chloroplasts and can produce their own food through photosynthesis. Photosynthetic plantlike protists are called **algae.**

From Single-Celled to Multicellular

In the distant past, single-celled organisms combined to become multicellular. It is likely that multicellular algae arose from colonies of algae such as *Volvox*. Members of the order Volvocales include three kinds of forms: single-celled, multicellular forms with every cell acting independently, and multicellular forms in which the cells are specialized. In the evolution from single-celled to multicellular algae, some individual cells in colonies were probably very efficient at certain tasks, such as digesting food or producing gametes. These cells and their offspring would have become more specialized over time, and eventually may have become dependent on each other. Over many generations, colonies could have led to multicellular forms.

FIGURE 19.9 *Volvox* are actually hundreds of individual algae cells that join together to form a colony in the shape of a hollow ball. Offspring form smaller daughter colonies inside the parent colony. (LM; magnification 50×)

colony

daughter colony

FIGURE 19.10 EUGLENA

A euglena has both animal-like structures—such as an eyespot, contractile vacuoles, and flagella—and plantlike structures, such as chloroplasts.

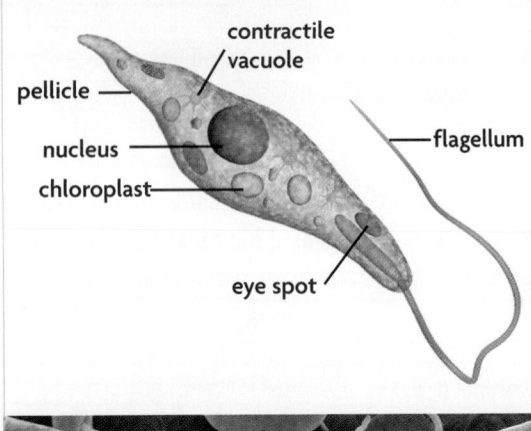

pellicle

contractile vacuole

nucleus

chloroplast

flagellum

eye spot

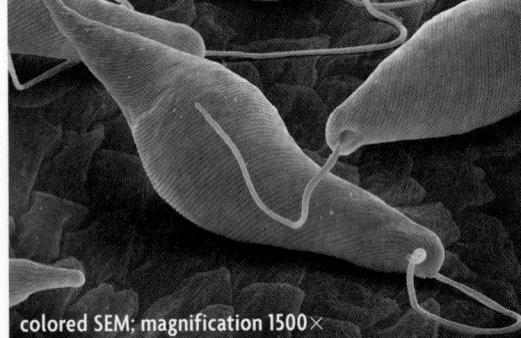

colored SEM; magnification 1500×

VOCABULARY

The name *dinoflagellates* comes from the Greek word *dinos,* meaning "whirling," and the Latin word *flagrum,* meaning "whip." This name describes how dinoflagellates move.

Diversity of Plantlike Protists

Plantlike protists are found in most habitats on Earth. Most are aquatic organisms that live in freshwater and marine ecosystems. Some species live in deserts, while others live in the tundra. Despite their great diversity, plantlike protists have certain features in common, such as the chlorophyll they use for photosynthesis. Also, most plantlike protists have flagella at some point in their life cycle. Although their classification will likely change, for now many biologists group the plantlike protists into several phyla based on their photosynthetic pigments and cell wall structure.

Euglenoids The euglenoids (phylum Euglenophyta) are a large group of single-celled organisms that swim with the aid of one or two flagella. Although most of these species are found in fresh water, some live in ocean environments. Members of this group are both animal-like and plantlike. Like animals, these protists can move around easily. Euglenoids have a pellicle, a flexible coatlike covering on their cell surface. The pellicle allows the cell to change shape. In some species, the pellicle helps the organism to creep across solid surfaces using a type of movement that resembles the inching movement of worms. Although some colorless species of euglenoids eat other organisms, most make their own food through photosynthesis.

Plantlike photosynthetic euglenoids are green, such as the euglena shown in **FIGURE 19.10**. Their bright green color comes from two different chlorophyll pigments, called chlorophyll *a* and *b*. Chlorophyll *a* is found in all photosynthesizing organisms. Chlorophyll *b* is found only in green algae and plants.

Dinoflagellates The dinoflagellates (phylum Dinoflagellata) are single-celled. About 90 percent of dinoflagellates are marine plankton. Recall from Chapter 15 that plankton are often microscopic organisms that live suspended in the water. Some dinoflagellates are freshwater species, and a few species have even been found in snow. About half of all marine dinoflagellates photosynthesize.

Dinoflagellates have two flagella, as shown in **FIGURE 19.11**. One flagellum extends from the rear of the cell and propels it forward. The other is a ribbon-like strand that circles the cell in a groove along its body. This flagellum allows the cell to turn over and change direction. The combination of the two flagella cause this protist to turn in a spiral as it moves forward. Some species also have a covering of stiff plates that form a protective armor.

Some dinoflagellates, such as *Noctiluca,* are bioluminescent; that is, they can produce light through internal chemical reactions. The name *Noctiluca* means "night-light." If you have ever visited the ocean at night, you may have seen these tiny, blue glowing organisms along the surface of the water. They give off light when they are disturbed. The light may act as an alarm to help them avoid being eaten.

Certain other photosynthetic dinoflagellates help build coral reefs through their symbiotic partnership with corals. These dinoflagellates live in the inner tissues of the corals. In return for shelter from the corals, the dinoflagellates provide the corals with nutrients in tropical waters that are usually nutrient-poor.

Some species of dinoflagellates produce toxins. A large population of these dinoflagellates can create what is known as a red tide, due to the reddish color produced by a high density of these species. Red tides, shown in **FIGURE 19.11,** occur when changes in ocean currents bring up nutrients from far below the ocean surface. The higher nutrient levels produce a rapid increase, or bloom, in the dino-flagellate population. A toxic bloom in the waters can kill large numbers of fish. The toxins can also build up in the tissues of shellfish, which then can be dangerous to humans who eat the contaminated seafood.

Diatoms Most diatoms (phylum Bacillariophyta) are easy to recognize when viewed through a microscope. These tiny single-celled algae are covered with delicately patterned glasslike shells. The shells of diatoms serve almost as an external skeleton, helping the cell to hold a rigid shape. Diatom shells, such as those shown in **FIGURE 19.12,** are made of silica, the same brittle substance that is used to make glass. The silica shell is divided into two parts that overlap each other, like the lid of a box.

Like other autotrophs, all diatoms release oxygen into the environment. In fact, diatoms could be considered the world champions of photosynthesis. They play a critical role in the uptake of carbon dioxide on Earth and produce about half of the oxygen we breathe. Diatoms may be freshwater or marine. Many species are phytoplankton. Others live clinging to rocks, plants, soil, and even animals—diatoms have been found growing on crustaceans, turtles, and even whales. Because of their glassy, mineralized shells, diatoms have been well preserved in the fossil record. Some fossil rocks consist almost entirely of diatoms. These diatom skeletons have many industrial uses, such as an ingredient in scrubbing products, because of their rough texture.

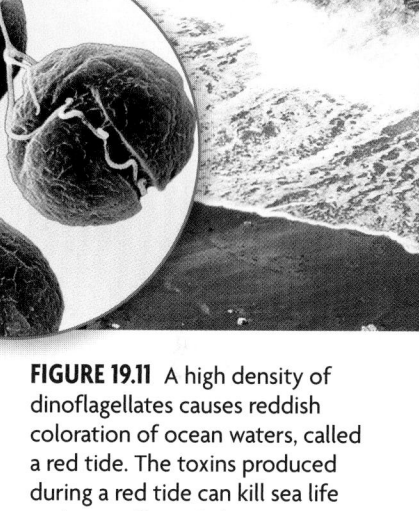

Dinoflagellates

FIGURE 19.11 A high density of dinoflagellates causes reddish coloration of ocean waters, called a red tide. The toxins produced during a red tide can kill sea life and cause illness in humans. (colored SEM; magnification 3000×)

VOCABULARY

The name *diatom* comes from the Greek term *diatomos,* meaning "cut in half." This refers to the appearance of the diatom's overlapping shell.

FIGURE 19.12 DIATOMS

Diatoms are known for their delicate glasslike cell walls, or shells, that can have many shapes. They are common in both freshwater and marine environments.

Animated BIOLOGY

Explore algae diatom concentrations over time at ClassZone.com.

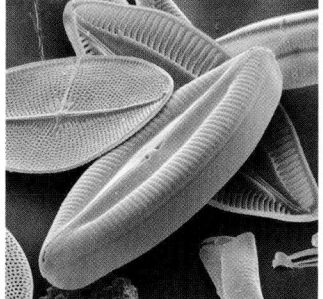

(all colored SEMs; magnification 750×; magnification 250×; magnification unknown)

FIGURE 19.13 Giant kelp are a type of brown algae that form underwater forests. The forests are home to a large variety of marine organisms.

Green algae The green algae (phylum Chlorophyta) may be found in the water or on land, although most species are aquatic. Recall that algae are not considered plants because they do not have roots, stems, or leaves. Like plants, however, green algae are multicellular and contain the photosynthetic pigments chlorophyll *a* and chlorophyll *b*. Both plants and green algae also have accessory pigments called carotenoids. Accessory pigments capture light energy and transfer it to chlorophyll during photosynthesis. Both plants and green algae also have cell walls made of cellulose and store food within their cells as starch. These similarities suggest that green algae were an early ancestor to land plants.

Brown algae The brown algae (phylum Phaeophyta) include the giant kelps, shown in **FIGURE 19.13,** that form thick underwater forests. Brown algae are multicellular and can grow to be extremely large. Some giant kelp can grow up to 100 meters high (about 330 ft). Most brown algae live in marine environments. Brown algae are photosynthetic but have a different form of chlorophyll—chlorophyll *c*—than do plants or green algae. Brown algae share this trait with the diatoms. This observation has led some biologists to propose classifying brown algae and diatoms together in their own kingdom.

Red algae Most red algae are found in the ocean, though a few live in freshwater habitats. Red algae (phylum Rhodophyta) use chlorophyll *a* for photosynthesis, but they get their color from the pigment phycoerythrin. Red algae can grow at deeper depths than other algae because the red pigments allow red algae to absorb the blue light that reaches deepest into the ocean. Some species secrete calcium carbonate, forming thick crusts that look like corals and provide habitats for tiny invertebrates. Red algae provide many products for the food industry. Carrageenan and agar, thickening agents used in products such as ice cream, come from red algae. In Japan, red algae is dried to make nori, a seaweed wrap used for sushi.

Compare and Contrast **What are the similarities and differences between green, brown, and red algae?**

 **MAIN IDEA**

Many plantlike protists can reproduce both sexually and asexually.

Most protists can undergo both sexual and asexual reproduction. All algae can reproduce asexually. Multicellular algae can fragment; each piece is capable of forming a new body. When a single-celled alga, such as the green alga *Chlamydomonas* shown in **FIGURE 19.14,** reproduces asexually, its life cycle is a bit more complex. The dominant phase of the life cycle for this species is haploid. Before reproducing asexually, the haploid parent alga absorbs its flagella and then divides by mitosis. This division may occur two or more times, producing up to eight cells. The daughter cells develop flagella and cell walls. These daughter cells, called zoospores, leave the parent cell, disperse, and grow. The zoospores then grow into mature haploid cells.

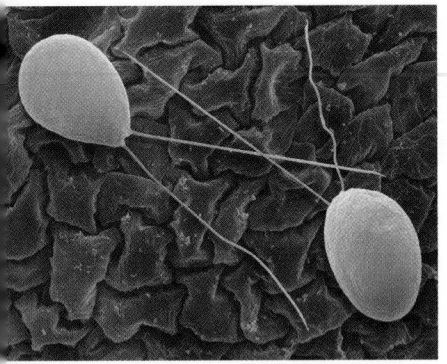

FIGURE 19.14 *Chlamydomonas* are single-celled green algae with two flagella. (colored SEM; magnification 1600×)

FIGURE 19.15 Life Cycle of Single-Celled Green Algae

Some single-celled green algae, such as *Chlamydomonas*, undergo sexual as well as asexual reproduction.

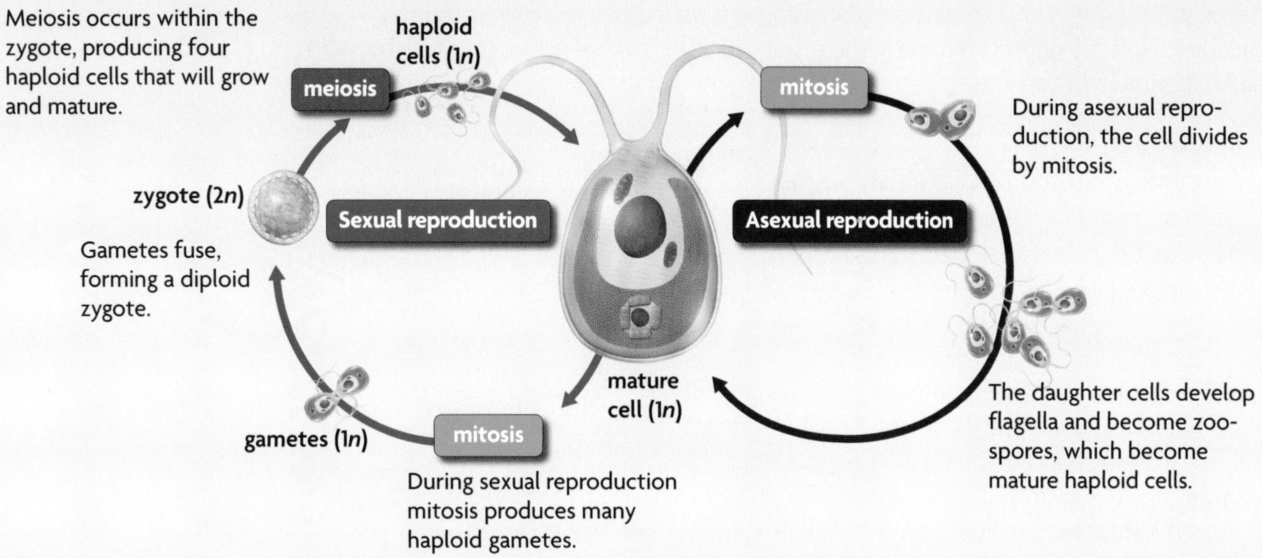

Meiosis occurs within the zygote, producing four haploid cells that will grow and mature.

haploid cells (1*n*)

meiosis

mitosis

During asexual reproduction, the cell divides by mitosis.

zygote (2*n*)

Sexual reproduction

Asexual reproduction

Gametes fuse, forming a diploid zygote.

mature cell (1*n*)

The daughter cells develop flagella and become zoospores, which become mature haploid cells.

gametes (1*n*)

mitosis

During sexual reproduction mitosis produces many haploid gametes.

Sexual reproduction occurs in algae as well. Some species alternate generations so that the offspring from sexual reproduction reproduce asexually, and the next generation then reproduces sexually. In other species, asexual reproduction occurs for several generations until conditions change. For the single-celled *Chlamydomonas*, sexual reproduction is triggered by stress such as lack of moisture or food. As shown in **FIGURE 19.15**, it begins with cells dividing by mitosis to produce one of two types of gametes. Because the gametes look identical in most species of *Chlamydomonas*, they are usually identified as different mating types, labeled + and –. When the gametes come together, they join and form a diploid zygote. The zygote may develop into a zygospore by making a thick wall that can protect it during unfavorable conditions. When favorable conditions return, meiosis occurs, producing four haploid cells.

Apply Explain how sudden population increases, or "blooms," of algae may occur.

19.3 ASSESSMENT

ONLINE QUIZ
ClassZone.com

REVIEWING ▶ MAIN IDEAS

1. Give an example of each of the following: a single-celled, a colonial, and a multicellular plantlike protist.

2. Many plantlike protists, or **algae**, reproduce sexually when conditions are harsh. Why might this be beneficial for a species?

CRITICAL THINKING

3. **Classify** If a multicellular organism contains chlorophyll *c* but no silica, to which phylum does it likely belong?

4. **Analyze** Many biologists argue that the euglenoids should be classified as an animal-like protist rather than a plantlike protist. Explain.

Connecting CONCEPTS

5. **Ecology** Draw a simple food web for a marine ecosystem. Include dinoflagellates, fish and shellfish, diving birds, and humans in your diagram. What might happen if nutrient levels in the water increased?

DATA ANALYSIS
ClassZone.com

Algae Preference of Coral Larvae

Scientists repeating another person's experiment must be able to follow the procedures exactly and obtain the same results in order for the experiment to be valid. Valid experiments must have

- a testable hypothesis
- a control group and an experimental group
- defined independent and dependent variables
- all other conditions held constant
- repeated trials

EXAMPLE

A student performed an experiment to determine whether a certain species of coral larvae prefer to settle on live red algae or dead red algae. She placed live red algae and dead algae in a tank held at 28°C (82°F). In a second tank held at 26°C (79°F), she placed a piece of lettuce as a control because it had a texture similar to the algae. After 24 hours, she counted the number of larvae that settled on each type of algae. The following flaws exist in this experiment:

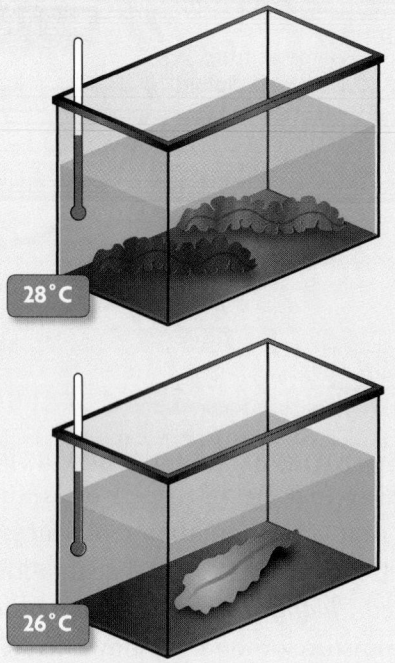

- A controlled variable—temperature—was not held constant.
- The lettuce control was separated from the algae choices.
- There were no repeated trials.

A valid experimental design would have all of the choices in a single aquarium, which makes it easier to maintain constants, and allows accurate observation of which surface types the larvae prefer. At least three aquariums should be used with the same setup so that the results could be compared.

IDENTIFY EXPERIMENTAL DESIGN FLAWS

A student wanted to determine what concentration—low, medium, or high—of a chemical released from brown algae prevented coral larvae from settling and growing on the algae. Each concentration level of the chemical from one brown alga was added to the water of each tank. Tank size, water temperature, and algae species were held constant. A different number and species of larvae were dropped into each tank. After three days, the percent of settled larvae for each concentration of inhibiting chemical was found.

TABLE 1. RESULTS OF INHIBITING CHEMICAL ON LARVAL SETTLEMENT			
Inhibiting Chemical Concentration	**Low**	**Medium**	**High**
Percent of Larvae Settled	85%	40%	1%

1. **Evaluate** What are the design flaws in this experiment? How would you change the experiment to make the results more valid?

2. **Analyze** The student concluded that at all levels the inhibiting chemical affected the rate of settlement of marine larvae. Is this an accurate conclusion based on the data collected? Explain.

19.4 Funguslike Protists

KEY CONCEPT Funguslike protists decompose organic matter.

▶ **MAIN IDEAS**

• Slime molds and water molds are funguslike protists.

VOCABULARY

slime mold, p. 587
water mold, p. 588

Review
decomposer

MICHIGAN STANDARDS

L3.p2C Describe the role of decomposers in the transfer of energy in an ecosystem. (prerequisite)

B5.1e Explain how natural selection leads to organisms that are well suited for the environment (differential survival and reproduction of chance inherited variants, depending upon environmental conditions).

Connect Perhaps you have seen a funguslike protist and didn't recognize it, like the Dallas residents you read about at the start of this chapter. Most funguslike protists don't grow large enough to scare people. In fact, some you can barely see.

▶ **MAIN IDEA**

Slime molds and water molds are funguslike protists.

As decomposers, funguslike protists play an important role in ecosystems by recycling nutrients such as carbon and nitrogen back into the soil. For a long time, funguslike protists were classified as fungi because they are all decomposers and have similar reproductive structures and cycles. However, funguslike protists can move during part of their life cycle, while fungi cannot.

Slime Molds

Slime molds are eukaryotic organisms that have both funguslike and animal-like traits. They can be divided into two phyla: plasmodial slime molds (phylum Myxomycota) and cellular slime molds (phylum Acrasiomycota).

Plasmodial slime molds For most of their life, plasmodial slime molds live as a single mass of cytoplasm that actually is a large single cell with many nuclei, called a plasmodium. They can grow as large as a meter or more in diameter. A plasmodium, shown in **FIGURE 19.16,** moves like a giant amoeba, creeping over the ground as it absorbs bacteria and nutrients from decaying matter. *Fuligo septica,* the dog-vomit slime mold, is typical of this group.

Connecting CONCEPTS

Biogeochemical Cycles Recall from **Chapter 13** that a biogeochemical cycle is the movement of a particular chemical, such as carbon or nitrogen, through the living and nonliving parts of an ecosystem.

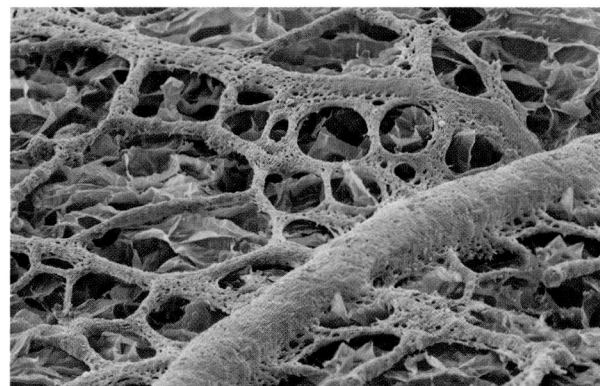
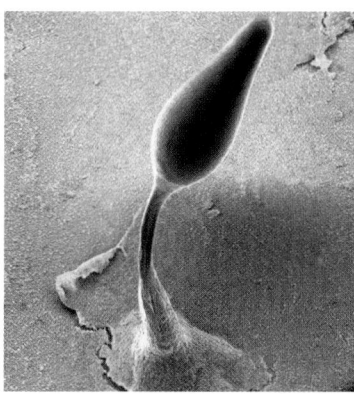

FIGURE 19.16 A plasmodial slime mold (left) in the plasmodium stage resembles a giant amoeba. A cellular slime mold (right) forms a stalk in the spore-producing stage. (colored SEMs; plasmodial slime mold magnification 80×; cellular slime mold magnification 180× © Dr. Richard Kessel & Dr. Gene Shih/Visuals Unlimited)

Plasmodial slime molds are common on the underside of logs and on dead leaves. When food or moisture is in short supply, the plasmodial slime mold stops growing and develops nonmoving reproductive structures that produce spores. Such a structure is a resistant, resting form of the slime mold. When the spores are released, they are often able to move on their own. They may creep like an amoeba, or, if water is present, they can develop up to four flagella per cell. Eventually, the spores swarm together and form a new plasmodium.

Cellular slime molds The cellular slime molds are common in soil. Each spore released by a cellular slime mold becomes a single amoeba-like cell. However, when food is scarce, individual cells can release chemical signals that cause the cells to swarm together. They form a sluglike body that moves as though it were one organism. This form of a cellular slime mold is called a pseudo-plasmodium, meaning "fake plasmodium," because each cell is independent—the membranes of each cell do not fuse. These slime molds are of interest to biologists who study how cells can communicate with each other.

Water Molds

Water molds are funguslike protists (phylum Oomycota) that are made up of branching strands of cells. They are common in freshwater habitats. Like slime molds, many water molds are decomposers. However, some water molds are parasites of plants or fish. For example, if you keep an aquarium, you may have seen a water mold that infects fish. The mold appears first as a cottony coating on the skin and gills but later causes deep wounds.

Perhaps the best known water mold is the downy mildew *Phytophthora infestans*, shown in **FIGURE 19.17**, which causes a disease called potato blight. An outbreak of this disease in Ireland from 1845 to 1849 destroyed almost all of the country's potato crops. As a result, more than 1 million people died of starvation in what became known as the Great Potato Famine.

Infer Many protists have two modes of reproduction. How does having two modes of reproduction affect when and how they reproduce?

FIGURE 19.17 The water mold *Phytophthora infestans* causes disease, including potato blight in many plants. This disease was the cause of a seven-year famine in Ireland in the 1800s. (colored SEM; magnification 100×)

19.4 ASSESSMENT

ONLINE QUIZ
ClassZone.com

REVIEWING ▶ MAIN IDEAS

1. In what ways are **slime molds** and **water molds** similar to fungi?

2. Describe how slime molds help other organisms within an ecosystem obtain nutrients.

CRITICAL THINKING

3. **Compare** Make a three-column chart comparing plasmodial slime molds, cellular slime molds, and water molds.

4. **Analyze** Why doesn't spraying water on slime molds work to destroy them?

Connecting CONCEPTS

5. **Natural Selection** What might be the advantage of being able to switch from living as separate cells to become a coordinated unit acting like a single organism?

19.5

Diversity of Fungi

KEY CONCEPT: Fungi are heterotrophs that absorb their food.

MAIN IDEAS

- Fungi are adapted to absorb their food from the environment.
- Fungi come in many shapes and sizes.
- Fungi reproduce sexually and asexually.

VOCABULARY

chitin, p. 589
hyphae, p. 589
mycelium, p. 590

fruiting body, p. 590
mycorrhizae, p. 591
sporangia, p. 592

MICHIGAN STANDARDS

L3.p2C Describe the role of decomposers in the transfer of energy in an ecosystem. (prerequisite)

Connect What is the largest living thing in the world? The blue whale? A giant redwood tree? Although they are big, both species are tiny compared with a fungus growing in Oregon—a single honey mushroom, *Armillaria ostoyae*. Most of it is underground, but this mushroom could cover more than 1500 football fields. It is thought to be at least 2400 years old. As amazing as it sounds, there are other fungi throughout the world nearly as large.

MAIN IDEA

Fungi are adapted to absorb their food from the environment.

Despite how little most people know about fungi, they are all around us—in soil, water, and even in the air. Many forms live in and on plants and animals. Scientists have named about 70,000 species but estimate there may be a total of 1.5 million fungi species in the world.

Comparing Fungi and Plants

Members of the kingdom Fungi fall into one of three groups—the single-celled yeasts, the molds, and the true fungi. For many years, biologists classified fungi as plants. But there are a few traits that separate these two kingdoms.

- Plants contain chlorophyll and photosynthesize. Fungi do not have chlorophyll and get food by absorbing it from their environment.
- Plants have true roots, leaves, and stems, but fungi do not.
- Plant cell walls are made of the polysaccharide cellulose. Fungal cell walls are made of **chitin** (KYT-uhn), a tough polysaccharide that is also found in the shells of insects and their close relatives.

Anatomy of Fungi

With the exception of the yeasts, fungi are multicellular organisms. The bodies of multicellular fungi are made of long strands called **hyphae** (HY-fee). Hyphae (singular, *hypha*) are shown in **FIGURE 19.18**. Depending on the species, each hypha may consist of a chain of cells or may contain one large, long cell with many nuclei. In both cases, cytoplasm can flow freely throughout the hyphae, and each hypha is surrounded by a plasma membrane and a cell wall of chitin.

FIGURE 19.18 A mushroom is actually just the reproductive, or fruiting, body of a fungus. Most of the fungus grows in the ground, as a mycelium.

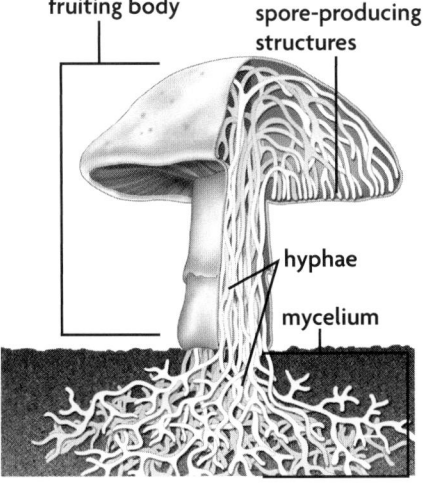

fruiting body

spore-producing structures

hyphae

mycelium

Hyphae often group together in long tangled masses to form a mycelium. A **mycelium** (my-SEE-lee-uhm) is an underground network of hyphae. Under certain conditions, such as a moist environment, a mycelium (plural, *mycelia*) can grow quickly to cover a large area. Mycelia may produce fruiting bodies. A **fruiting body** is a reproductive structure of a fungus that grows above ground. Mushrooms are one type of fruiting body.

Fungi absorb their food from their environment. The food can be from a wide variety of food sources—including tree bark, bread, cheese, and even flesh. As fungi grow, hyphae extend into the food source and release enzymes. These enzymes break down their food so that it can be absorbed across their cell walls. Fungi can take in large amounts of nutrients due to their mycelia, which in turn allows mycelia to grow very quickly.

Contrast How is the way that fungi get their food different from that of any other group of organisms?

▶ MAIN IDEA
Fungi come in many shapes and sizes.

The kingdom Fungi is diverse, and it is commonly divided into four main groups—primitive fungi (phylum Chytridiomycota), sac fungi (phylum Ascomycota), bread molds (phylum Zygomycota), and club fungi (phylum Basidiomycota).

Primitive Fungi
The primitive fungi, or chytrids, are the smallest and simplest group of fungi. They are mostly aquatic, and their spores have flagella, which help propel them through the water. They are the only fungi with flagellated spores. Some primitive fungi are decomposers, while others are parasites of protists, plants, or animals. One explanation for the global decrease of amphibians such as frogs may be due to a parasitic type of chytrid fungi.

Sac Fungi
Yeasts, certain molds such as *Penicillium,* and morels and truffles—which many people consider delicious to eat—are all sac fungi. The sac fungi are a diverse group, but they have one key trait in common. They all form a sac, called an ascus, that contains spores for reproduction. Some examples of sac fungi are shown in **FIGURE 19.19**.

The yeast that makes bread rise is *Saccharomyces cerevisiae*. This yeast is also an important model organism used in molecular biology. As a eukaryote, it has many of the same genes as humans. Because it is single-celled, it is easy to work with in a laboratory.

If you've ever let an orange grow moldy, you've seen *Penicillium chrysogenum*. This mold is usually a deep green color and appears fuzzy. *Penicillium* is also the source for the antibiotic penicillin. In contrast, one dangerous sac fungus is *Aspergillis flavus,* a mold that makes a poison called aflatoxin that can contaminate cereals, nuts, and milk.

FIGURE 19.19 Many sac fungi are sac- or cup-shaped or have cup-shaped indentations. Sac fungi include morels (top), which are prized for their tastiness, and moss cup fungi (bottom), also known as scarlet elf cups.

Bread Molds

The bread molds range from the molds you see on spoiled foods to fungi used to ferment certain foods such as soy sauce. Most members of this phylum get food by decomposing dead or decaying matter. At least one group of symbiotic fungi belongs to this group. **Mycorrhizae** (MY-kuh-RY-zuh) are mutualistic partnerships between fungi and the roots of certain plants. Mycorrhizae help these plants to fix nitrogen—that is, they take inorganic nitrogen from the soil and convert it to nitrates and ammonia, which the plants use.

Club Fungi

The club fungi get their name because their fruiting bodies are club-shaped. This phylum includes mushrooms, puffballs, and bracket, or shelf, fungi. It also includes the rusts and smuts, which are two types of fungi that cause diseases in plants. Puffballs, shown in **FIGURE 19.20**, form dry-looking structures that release their spores when someone or something strikes the mature fruiting body. Bracket fungi are a common sight in forests, where they grow outward from tree trunks, forming a little shelf.

Identify What two organisms share a mutualistic partnership in the formation of mycorrhizae?

FIGURE 19.20 Puffballs release a cloud of spores when the fruiting body matures and bursts.

◗ MAIN IDEA

Fungi reproduce sexually and asexually.

Most fungi reproduce both sexually and asexually through a wide variety of strategies.

Reproduction in Single-Celled Fungi

Yeasts are single-celled fungi. They reproduce asexually, either through simple fission or through a process called budding, shown in **FIGURE 19.21**. Fission is identical to mitosis—the cell's DNA is copied and the nucleus and cytoplasm divide, making two identical daughter cells. During budding, the parent cell forms a small bud of cytoplasm that also contains a copy of the nucleus. When these buds reach a certain size, they detach and form a cell.

Some yeasts undergo sexual reproduction. A diploid yeast cell undergoes meiosis, producing four haploid nuclei. However, the parent cell's cytoplasm does not divide. Recall that a yeast is a type of sac fungi. Instead of the cytoplasm dividing, it produces the characteristic saclike structure of this phylum called an ascus. The haploid nuclei it contains are actually a type of spore. The ascus undergoes budding, releasing each of the haploid spores. Some spores may then reproduce more haploid spores through budding. Others may fuse with other haploid spores to form diploid yeast cells.

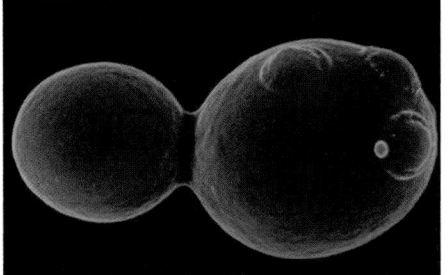

FIGURE 19.21 Yeast can reproduce by budding, the pinching of small cells off the parent cell. (colored SEM; magnification 6000×)

FIGURE 19.22 REPRODUCTIVE STRUCTURES OF FUNGI

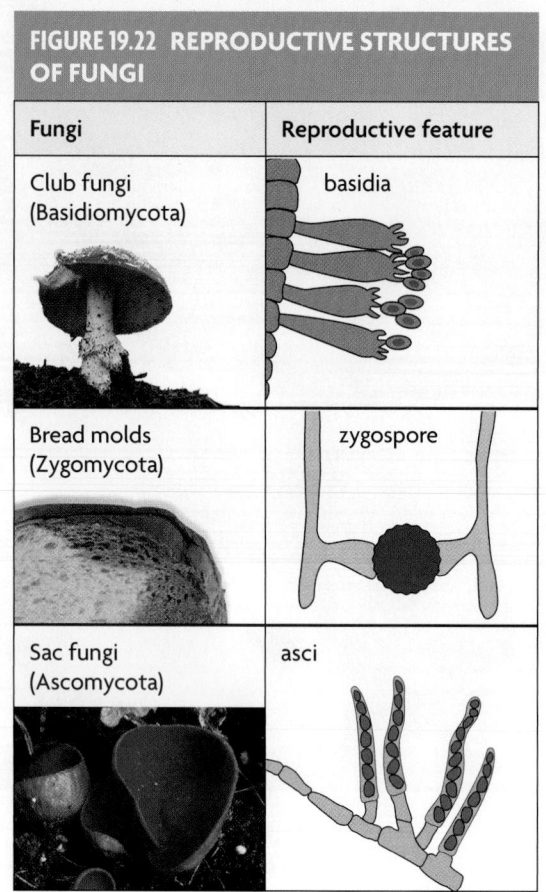

Fungi	Reproductive feature
Club fungi (Basidiomycota)	basidia
Bread molds (Zygomycota)	zygospore
Sac fungi (Ascomycota)	asci

Connecting CONCEPTS

Asexual Reproduction Recall from **Chapter 5** that asexual reproduction is the creation of offspring from a single parent that does not involve the joining of gametes. The offspring are genetically identical to each other and to the parent.

Reproduction in Multicellular Fungi

The multicellular fungi have complex reproductive cycles. Examples of life cycles for two phyla of fungi are shown in **FIGURE 19.23.**

Club fungi Basidiomycota are named for their club-shaped structures called basidia, where spores are produced during sexual reproduction. Basidia are found on the undersides of mushrooms. They form within the leaflike gills that you can easily see. In club fungi, unlike the other phyla, spores are most often formed by sexual reproduction.

- Nuclei within the basidia fuse to form diploid zygotes.
- The zygotes undergo meiosis to form haploid spores.
- The spores drop from the gills and are carried away by wind or by contact with animals.
- If the spores land in a favorable environment, they grow and form haploid hyphae.
- Some cells of the haploid mycelium may fuse with the cells of another haploid mycelium, producing a diploid mycelium underground.
- An environmental cue, such as rain or change in temperature, can trigger the formation of aboveground fruiting bodies such as mushrooms.

Bread molds Members of Zygomycota are also known as zygote fungi because of the structures they form during sexual reproduction. Bread molds reproduce sexually when the food supply is low but can also reproduce asexually when there is plenty of food. They reproduce asexually by producing spores in **sporangia,** spore-forming structures at the tips of their hyphae. The term *sporangium* is used to describe similar reproductive structures of a variety of organisms, including some fungi, mosses, algae, and ferns.

VISUAL VOCAB

Sporangia are structures that produce spores.

spores — sporangia

- As in the club fungi, sexual reproduction in zygote fungi involves hyphae that look alike but are different mating types.
- The two types of hyphae fuse their nuclei to produce a diploid zygospore that can tolerate long periods of extreme conditions.
- When the conditions become favorable, a sporangium grows and produces haploid spores.
- The spores are released and can grow into new hyphae.
- The new hyphae in turn may reproduce asexually, by forming haploid spores in sporangia. Or they may reproduce sexually, by fusing hyphae to produce more zygospores.

FIGURE 19.23 **Typical Life Cycles of Fungi**

Reproduction in fungi can occur in several ways. Although most club fungi reproduce sexually, bread molds can reproduce both sexually and asexually.

LIFE CYCLE OF CLUB FUNGI

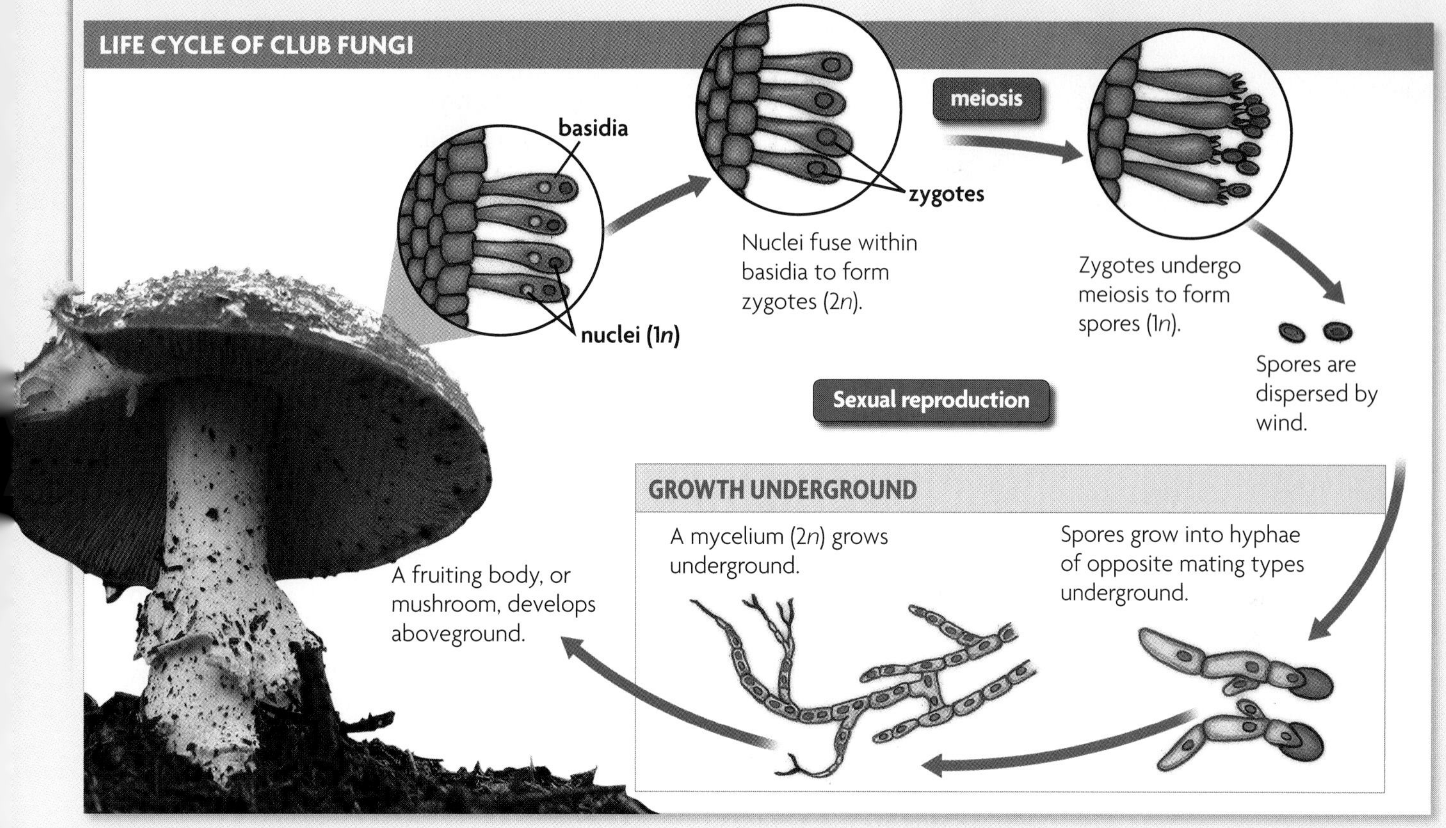

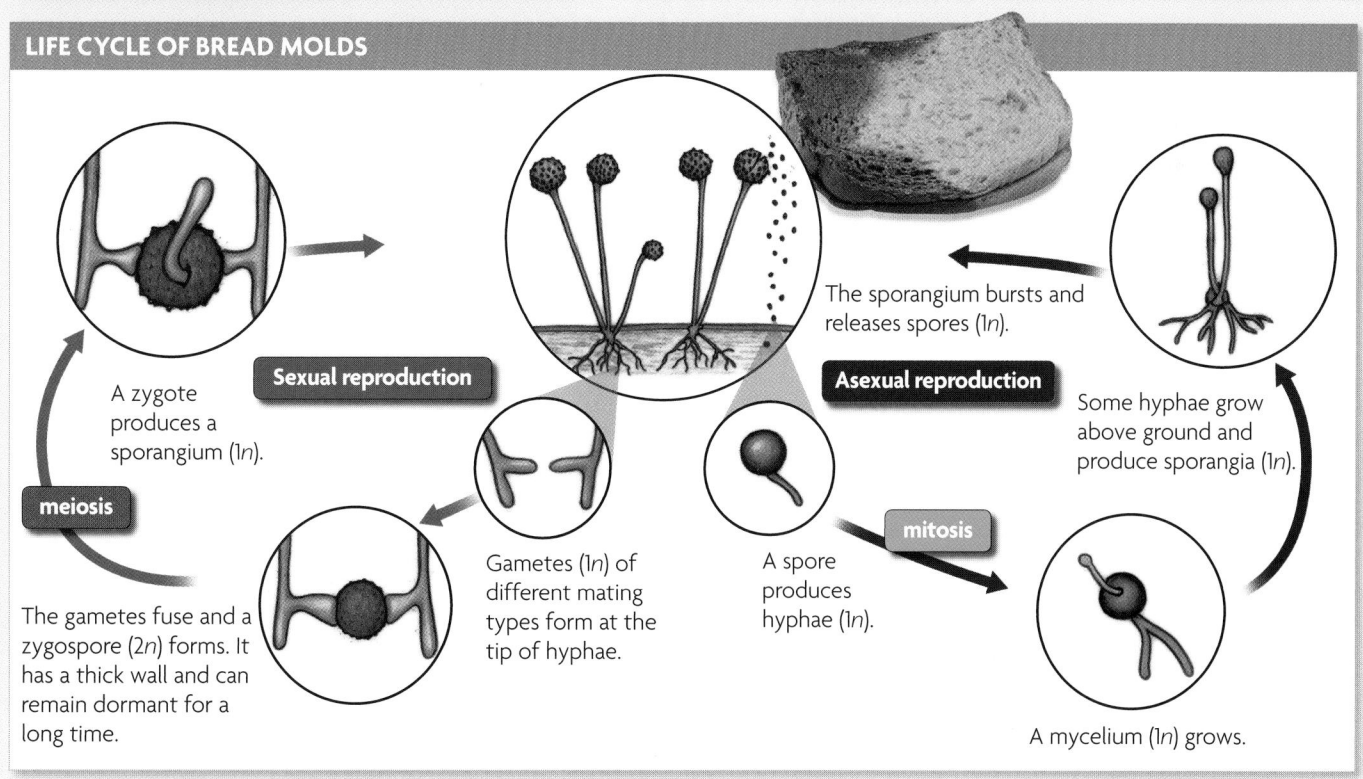

basidia

nuclei (1n)

Nuclei fuse within basidia to form zygotes (2n).

zygotes

meiosis

Zygotes undergo meiosis to form spores (1n).

Spores are dispersed by wind.

Sexual reproduction

GROWTH UNDERGROUND

A mycelium (2n) grows underground.

Spores grow into hyphae of opposite mating types underground.

A fruiting body, or mushroom, develops aboveground.

LIFE CYCLE OF BREAD MOLDS

The sporangium bursts and releases spores (1n).

Sexual reproduction

Asexual reproduction

A zygote produces a sporangium (1n).

Some hyphae grow above ground and produce sporangia (1n).

meiosis

Gametes (1n) of different mating types form at the tip of hyphae.

A spore produces hyphae (1n).

mitosis

The gametes fuse and a zygospore (2n) forms. It has a thick wall and can remain dormant for a long time.

A mycelium (1n) grows.

CRITICAL VIEWING How are the life cycles of club fungi and bread molds similar? How are they different?

ascospore

ascus

FIGURE 19.24 A cross-section of the cup-shaped fruiting body of a sac fungi shows spores encased in an ascus. (colored LM; magnification 170×)

NSTA SCI*LINKS*
scilinks.org
To learn more about fungi, go to scilinks.org.
Keycode: MLB019

Sac fungi Members of Ascomycota are called the sac fungi due to the saclike case, or ascus (plural, *asci*), that forms during sexual reproduction. These reproductive structures are shown in **FIGURE 19.24**. Most asci are found within the fungi's cup-shaped fruiting body. As in club fungi and bread molds, sexual reproduction in multicellular sac fungi involves the joining of two mycelia that are different mating types. The joined hyphae grow into the aboveground fruiting body. An ascus, or sac, develops at the tip of each hypha within the fruiting body. Inside the ascus, haploid spores form. When mature, the cup-shaped fruiting body collapses, and releases the spores.

Like the bread molds, sac fungi usually reproduce asexually when conditions are favorable and reproduce sexually when conditions are harsh. They produce different types of spores during asexual reproduction than they do during sexual reproduction. Spores produced during asexual reproduction are called conidia, which means "dust," because they travel easily through air.

Release of Spores

Fungi release their spores at the tips of their hyphae, high above their food source. This strategy allows the small spores to be carried in air currents to a new location. Some species of fungi go even further and use unusual strategies in releasing their spores. For example, members of the fungal genus *Cordyceps* grow on insects. In some species, the fungi penetrate the insect's brain, causing the insect to climb high into a tree or other vegetation. Eventually, the insect stops climbing and remains fixed in place. The fungus then releases its spores from this greater height.

Spores of fungi are everywhere, and have even been found in the air more than 150 kilometers (93 mi) above the surface of Earth. The great number of spores in the air at any given time is the reason that the growth of mold on our leftover food cannot be avoided, even if the food is refrigerated. Fungal spores are also a source of allergies for many people worldwide.

Hypothesize How might producing spores benefit an organism?

19.5 / ASSESSMENT

ONLINE QUIZ
ClassZone.com

REVIEWING ▶ MAIN IDEAS

1. Describe how fungi use **hyphae** to obtain their food.

2. Describe a typical **fruiting body** of sac fungi, bread mold, and club fungi.

3. **Sporangia** are formed during the life cycle of a typical bread mold. At what stage are they formed?

CRITICAL THINKING

4. **Summarize** Draw a flowchart showing the sequence of steps in the reproduction of yeast, a single-celled fungus.

5. **Infer** The **mycelium** of a fungus grows underground. In what ways might this be helpful for the fungus?

Connecting CONCEPTS

6. **Ecology** Some scientists support using fungi such as *Cordyceps* instead of pesticides to control insect pests in agriculture. What might be some pros and cons of such a plan?

MATERIALS
- mushroom
- plastic knife
- 1/2 sheet of white paper
- plastic cup
- hairspray
- dissecting scope, or magnifying lens

PROCESS SKILLS
- **Observing**
- **Predicting**
- **Inferring**

B5.1e Explain how natural selection leads to organisms that are well suited for the environment (differential survival and reproduction of chance inherited variants, depending upon environmental conditions).

Exploring Mushroom Anatomy

In this lab, you will first identify the main parts of a mushroom. Then you will make a spore print to reveal the color of its spores.

PROBLEM What are the structures of a mushroom?

PROCEDURE

1. Obtain a mushroom from your teacher and look at it carefully. Using the illustration and terms below as a guide, draw a diagram of your mushroom, and label the parts of its anatomy that are present. **Note:** Many mushrooms do not have all of these parts!

   - cap—top part of mushroom
   - scales—rough patches on cap surface
   - gills—radially arranged flat surfaces on the underside of the cap
   - ring—skirt of tissue circling stem
   - stalk—main support of mushroom
   - cup—at the base of the mushroom

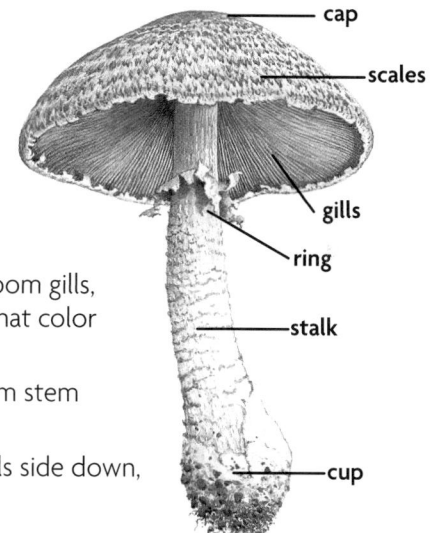

2. Based on your observations of the mushroom gills, make and record your prediction about what color the spores are.

3. Use a plastic knife to cut off the mushroom stem very close to the gills.

4. Put the mushroom cap on white paper, gills side down, and cover with a plastic cup overnight.

5. Carefully remove the cup and the mushroom cap. Thousands of spores should have fallen onto the paper, creating an outline of the gills.

6. Spray the print with hairspray to preserve it.

7. Examine the spore print, using a dissecting scope or magnifying lens if available.

   Note: If the spores are light-colored, hold the paper at an angle toward the light to see them better.

ANALYZE AND CONCLUDE

1. **Analyze** Was your prediction of spore color correct? Why might it be difficult to predict spore color?

2. **Infer** Why do you think the spores are located where they are in the mushroom?

3. **Experimental Design** Why was it necessary to cover the mushroom cap when you left it out overnight?

4. **Predict** Under what type of environmental conditions do you think these spores would be most likely to grow into new mycelia?

5. **Apply** The color of external mushroom parts can vary within one species since they may be affected by environmental conditions. Knowing this, why do you think spore prints are a valuable technique for mushroom identification?

19.6 Ecology of Fungi

KEY CONCEPT Fungi recycle nutrients in the environment.

▶ **MAIN IDEAS**

- Fungi may be decomposers, pathogens, or mutualists.
- Fungi are studied for many purposes.

VOCABULARY

lichen, p. 598

Review
mycorrhizae

MICHIGAN STANDARDS

L2.p4A Classify different organisms based on how they obtain energy for growth and development. (prerequisite)

L3.p2C Describe the role of decomposers in the transfer of energy in an ecosystem. (prerequisite)

Connect Fungi just might be the most overlooked and unappreciated organisms on Earth. Fungi grow on shower curtains, spoil food, and cause illnesses to humans. But humans also eat some fungi and use them to make things that range from bread to antibiotics. Perhaps most importantly, these unusual organisms play a major role in every ecosystem on Earth.

▶ **MAIN IDEA**

Fungi may be decomposers, pathogens, or mutualists.

> Some fungi act as decomposers in the environment. Others act as either pathogens or mutualists to other organisms—including humans.

FIGURE 19.25 Fungi produce enzymes that help break down the complex molecules in wood to simpler molecules that fungi can absorb and use.

Fungi as Decomposers

Fungi and bacteria are the main decomposers in any ecosystem. Fungi, such as those shown in **FIGURE 19.25**, decompose dead and decaying organic matter such as leaves, twigs, logs, and animals. They return nutrients such as carbon, nitrogen, and minerals back into the soil. Because of the large surface area of their mycelia, fungi are well adapted for absorbing their food and can recycle nutrients quickly. This constant cycling of nutrients helps enrich soil with organic compounds. The nutrients can then be taken up by other organisms.

Plants and animals could not survive without the activity of decomposers. The ability of fungi to break down tough plant materials such as lignin and cellulose is especially important in woodland ecosystems. Fungi are the main decomposers of these hard parts of plants, which cannot be used by animals without being first broken down by decomposers.

The decomposing activity of fungi is not always helpful to humans, however. Fungi can damage fruit trees, and they can also cause damage inside wooden houses and boats. Molds and other fungi inside a house can weaken its walls, and their spores can cause respiratory illness. Homeowners should check for and remove molds that are established in their homes.

Fungi as Pathogens

Like bacteria, some fungi can be pathogenic, or disease-causing. A few pathogenic fungi always cause disease. These fungi are called obligate pathogens—the term *obligate* means necessary or obliged. Other fungi are normally harmless, coexisting with other organisms in a delicate ecological balance. However, changes in environmental circumstances can upset this balance and lead to disease. Organisms that normally don't cause a problem until there is a change in the host's homeostasis are called opportunistic pathogens. A change in the host's body provides them an opportunity to grow unchecked and cause infection.

Connecting CONCEPTS

Prokaryotes In biology, the term *obligate* means requiring a particular environment to survive. Recall from **Chapter 18** that prokaryotes can be obligate anaerobes, meaning they cannot have oxygen in their environment. Some bacteria, protists, and fungi can also be obligate pathogens or obligate parasites.

Fungi and humans The overuse and incorrect use of antibiotics is one example of how humans allow pathogens an opportunity to cause infection. Antibiotics can destroy certain beneficial bacteria in the human digestive system, allowing other organisms such as fungi to thrive. Typically harmless fungi also cause disease when the immune system is not functioning at its best. For instance, all healthy humans have populations of the yeast *Candida* that occupy certain parts of the body, such as the skin and mouth. If a human's immune system is damaged, populations may grow and cause disease.

Some fungal pathogens, such as those that cause ringworm and athlete's foot, have fairly mild effects. But several fungi cause severe diseases, such as some lung illnesses, that are hard to cure and can even cause death. Fungal infections are hard to treat because fungi are eukaryotes, and so their cellular structure is very similar to ours. It is difficult to develop medicine that will harm fungal cells but not damage human cells.

Fungi and plants Fungal diseases also affect plants, and they can be especially devastating in agriculture and horticulture. Dutch elm disease is caused by a fungus that is transmitted by elm bark beetles, shown in **FIGURE 19.26.** In the United States, the first cases of Dutch elm disease were reported in Ohio in 1930. Today, the disease has destroyed more than half of the elms in the northern United States. Fungi also destroy a large portion of the world's fruit crops. A disease of peaches called peach scab is caused by a fungus and results in millions of dollars in losses to growers each year. Gray mold is a disease of produce such as strawberries. This fungus can grow even in refrigerated fruit and is a major cause of fruit spoilage during shipment and storage.

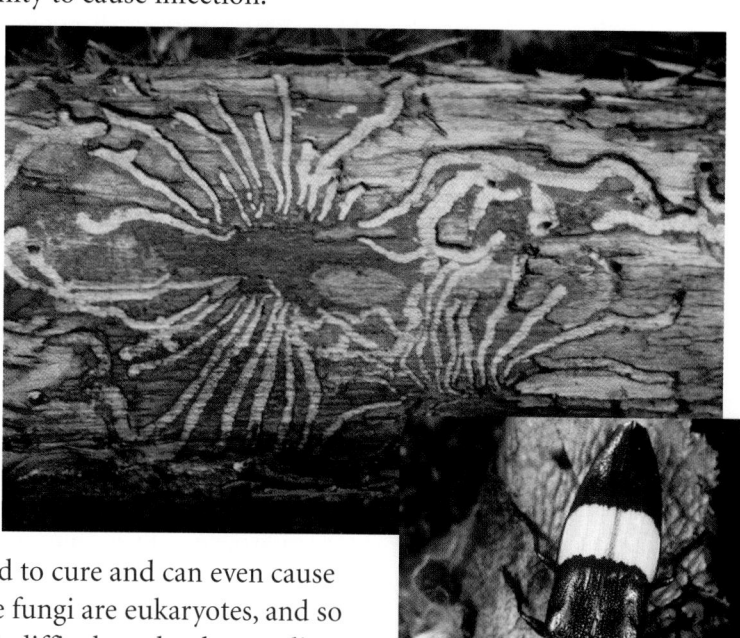

FIGURE 19.26 A fungus is responsible for Dutch elm disease. Adult elm bark beetles tunnel into the bark of elms to lay their eggs. If the trees are diseased, fungus spores stick to the adults as they visit new trees.

Fungal diseases in agriculture are often treated with chemical sprays called fungicides. Today, however, crops that are genetically engineered to resist fungi are becoming more common. Fungal diseases in animals, including those in humans, are usually treated with antifungal medications. These treatments usually come from fungi themselves, which produce them as a defense against other fungi. Like bacteria and protists, however, fungi can develop resistance to treatments if they are overused. These products should be used carefully.

FIGURE 19.27 Lichens

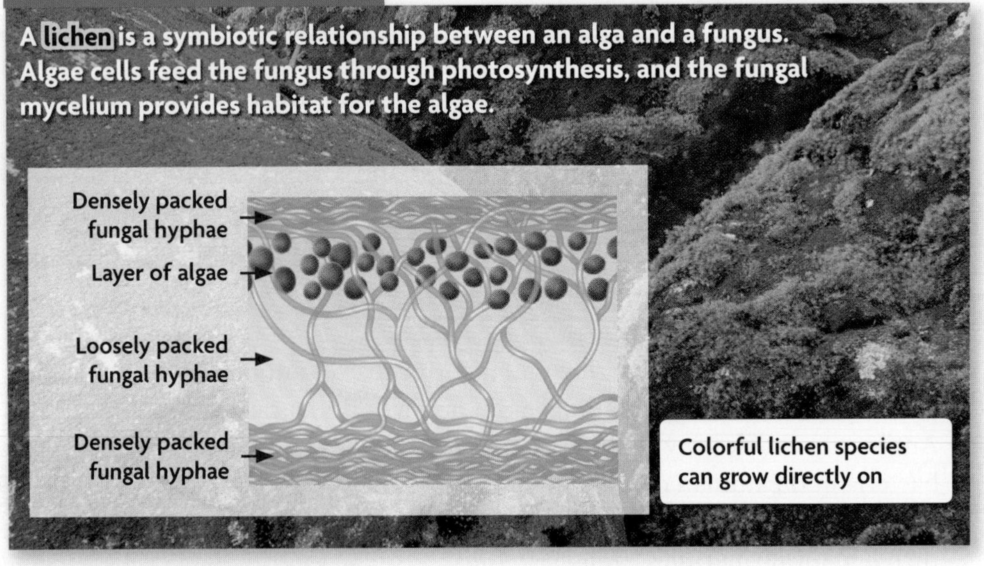

A **lichen** is a symbiotic relationship between an alga and a fungus. Algae cells feed the fungus through photosynthesis, and the fungal mycelium provides habitat for the algae.

Densely packed fungal hyphae

Layer of algae

Loosely packed fungal hyphae

Densely packed fungal hyphae

Colorful lichen species can grow directly on

Fungi as Mutualists

Mutualism is a symbiotic relationship in which both organisms benefit. Fungi form mutualistic relationships with several types of organisms.

Lichens A **lichen** (LY-kuhn) is a mutualistic relationship between a fungus and algae or photosynthetic bacteria. Only certain fungi, algae, or cyanobacteria can combine to form a lichen body. The body itself consists mainly of fungal hyphae that surround and grow into the algal cells, as shown in **FIGURE 19.27**. The algal part of the lichen carries out photosynthesis, making sugars that feed both the alga and the fungus. Lichens (phylum Mycomycota) can grow on almost any solid surface, from tree trunks to soil to rocks. They are common in cool, dry environments. They can also withstand severe temperatures. This characteristic of lichens allows them to live in habitats such as tundra, where fungi could not survive alone.

Lichens play several different roles in the environment and in the lives of humans. For example, they are extremely important during primary succession, because they can live on bare rock. Many species of lichens are sensitive to air pollution and can be used as indicators of air quality. Lichens are also important in nutrient cycling, because they function as both a decomposer and a producer. Lichens produce hundreds of unique chemicals, including pigments used as dyes in traditional cultures and compounds that have antibiotic properties.

Mycorrhizae Mutualistic associations between plant roots and soil fungi are called mycorrhizae. More than 80 percent of the world's plants have mycorrhizae on their roots. Mycorrhizae form when the hyphae of a fungus colonize the roots of a nearby plant. The huge surface area of the fungal mycelium is much larger than the root surface area of the plants, so the mycelium can absorb soil nutrients and water faster than the plant's roots could alone. In return, the fungus benefits because it gets sugars and other nutrients from the plant. Mycorrhizae can boost plant growth and reduce the need for fertilizers, which can cause soil and water pollution. Mycorrhizae also produce chemicals with antibiotic properties that help fight harmful bacteria.

Connecting CONCEPTS

Ecology Recall from **Chapter 14** that primary succession occurs after disruptive events such as fires and volcanic eruptions. The first organisms to recolonize an area, such as lichens, are called pioneer species.

Fungal gardens and insects Some insects also live as partners in a mutualistic symbiosis with fungi. The leafcutter ants of Central and South America, shown in **FIGURE 19.28**, don't just use fungi—they actually grow them. These ants cut tiny pieces of leaf from plants with their jaws. They carry these leaf pieces back to an underground nest area, where they build a garden of leaf pieces. Next, the ants add pieces of the fungus. The fungus breaks down the leaf pieces and absorbs nutrients from them. The ants in turn feed on the fungal mycelium.

Summarize Describe three ways that fungi are important to the environment.

FIGURE 19.28 Leafcutter ants carry leaves back to their nests to provide food for fungi. The ants then eat the growing fungal mycelium.

▶ **MAIN IDEA**
Fungi are studied for many purposes.

Many species of fungi are edible, such as the mushrooms we eat on pizza and the yeast we use to bake bread. In addition, fungi make citric acid, which is used in soft drinks and some candy. Fungi are also useful in the health care industry. Since the discovery of antibiotics in the 1900s, scientists have been researching how pathogens interact with their natural environments. This knowledge is then applied to develop useful medicines. For example, in their natural habitats fungi and bacteria compete for similar resources, such as space and nutrients. This is true whether they live on a forest floor or in a human digestive tract. Over time, fungi have evolved natural defenses against bacteria.

Studies of yeast have produced equally valuable insights. These tiny single-celled organisms are among the most important model systems used in molecular biology. Most yeasts have many of the same genes and proteins found in plants and animals. Insights gained from studies of a yeast's genome can often be applied to multicellular organisms. Yeast are small, grow quickly, and are easy to culture, or raise, in the laboratory.

Summarize What are three ways that fungi benefit humans?

Connecting **CONCEPTS**

Antibiotics Recall from **Chapter 18** that an antibiotic is a chemical that kills or slows the growth of bacteria.

19.6 ASSESSMENT

ONLINE QUIZ ClassZone.com

REVIEWING ▶ MAIN IDEAS

1. How do fungi contribute to the balance of an ecosystem?
2. What are three reasons **lichens** are useful to humans?

CRITICAL THINKING

3. **Compare** Draw a Venn diagram comparing lichens and mycorrhizae. Include terms such as *roots, photosynthesis,* and *mutualism.*
4. **Analyze** Some antifungal medications can damage the patient's own tissues. Why doesn't this problem occur with antibiotics?

Connecting CONCEPTS

5. **Natural Selection** A peach farmer is faced every year with an outbreak of peach scab, a fungal disease of peaches. Every year he sprays his crop carefully with fungicides, but each time these seem less effective than the year before. Why might this be?

Use these inquiry-based labs and online activities to deepen your understanding of protists and fungi observed in everyday life.

MICHIGAN STANDARDS

B1.1C Conduct scientific investigations using appropriate tools and techniques (e.g., selecting an instrument that measures the desired quantity—length, volume, weight, time interval, temperature—with the appropriate level of precision).

B1.2C Develop an understanding of a scientific concept by accessing information from multiple sources. Evaluate the scientific accuracy and significance of the information.

DESIGN YOUR OWN INVESTIGATION

Quantifying Mold Growth

Mold grows in many places. For example, baked goods will eventually grow mold when left out on the counter. In this experiment, you will grow mold on the surface of a slice of bread. You will gather quantitative and qualitative data to study the growth and structure of this mold.

SKILLS Designing Experiments, Analyzing Data

PROBLEM How can you best quantify mold growth on a slice of bread?

MATERIALS
- slice of white bread
- 10 mL water
- eyedropper
- sealable plastic lunch bag
- straw cut into pieces
- scale
- clear plastic grid
- prepared slide (optional)
- microscope (optional)

PROCEDURE

1. Use a piece of bread, water, pieces of straw, and a sandwich bag to design an experiment to determine how much mold grows on a slice of bread.

2. Your experiment should take place over a week. Once you have placed the bread in the bag you will never open the bag again.

3. Choose the quantitative data that your group wishes to record. Examples include mass, or approximate percentage of the bread slice that is covered in mold (using a plastic grid). If you will be recording mass, record the initial mass of the bag with the bread.

4. Have your teacher approve your experimental design, and then set up your experiment.

5. Keeping the bag sealed, record your data every day for a week. Also record a daily qualitative description of the mold growth (color, size, texture, growth pattern, and so on). Wash your hands after you take data. Keep the bag sealed and dispose of it at the end of the week according to your teacher's directions.

ANALYZE AND CONCLUDE

1. **Analyze** Using the quantitative and qualitative data that you recorded, describe how the amount of mold growing on the bread changed each day.

2. **Analyze** Was there a pattern that the mold growth followed or was it random? Explain.

3. **Experimental Design** What are the potential disadvantages with the quantitative method that you decided to use? What are methods that would make your results more accurate?

EXTEND YOUR INVESTIGATION

If a prepared slide of bread mold is available, examine it under the microscope. Draw a sketch of what you see. Label the sketch, referring to the life cycle illustrations on page 593.

Algae in Products

Do you enjoy eating algae? Even if you don't like seaweed-wrapped sushi, you might be surprised to find that you like other products made from algae. Algal products are found in many foods, including ice cream and chocolate milk. Algae contain important nutrients, such as iodine, potassium, magnesium, iron, and selenium. Look through your refrigerator and cabinets at home to see what other household products you can find that contain algae.

SKILL Researching

PROBLEM What products in your home contain algae?

RESEARCH

All of the ingredients listed below come from different types of algae.

- *Carrageenan* is found in the cell walls of some red algae. It is used as a thickener in foods, cosmetics, and medicines.

- *Agar* is another product made from red algae. It is often used as a replacement for gelatin. It is also used in science laboratories to grow bacteria.

- *Alginates,* also called *alginin* or *algin,* are compounds from brown algae that help form smooth, creamy liquids. They also make products more stable over a range of temperatures, making the products last longer.

- *Beta carotene* is a pigment from green algae, as well as other sources. It is used as a yellow-orange food coloring.

1. Find an item in your home that contains algae.
2. How do you think the algal compounds are used in the product that you found?
3. Perform research to describe how the red, brown, or green alga that your product contains grows naturally.
4. How is the algae found in your product farmed in order to produce enough for industry?

Online BIOLOGY
CLASSZONE.COM

ANIMATED BIOLOGY
Protist and Fungus Life Cycles
Build the life cycles of a slime mold, a cup fungus, and a brown algae. Compare and contrast the ways by which these diverse organisms reproduce.

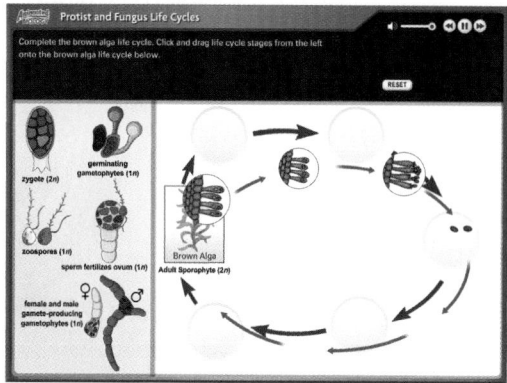

WEBQUEST
Some of the world's most dangerous diseases are caused by protists. In this WebQuest, you will learn more about three of these diseases: sleeping sickness, giardiasis, and malaria. Use your knowledge to diagnose and treat three patients.

DATA ANALYSIS ONLINE
The Mediterranean strain of *Caulerpa taxifolia* is a tropical seaweed that was bred for use in aquariums. It was accidentally released in 1984 into the Mediterranean Sea. Graph the spread of *Cualerpa* from 1984 until 2000 and determine if *Caulerpa* has been successful in its new environment.

19.1 Diversity of Protists

Kingdom Protista is the most diverse of all the kingdoms. It includes organisms that are animal-like, plantlike, and funguslike. Protists may be single-celled or multicellular, and may be microscopic or very large. Protist classification is likely to change in the future, as some protists are more closely related to members of other kingdoms than they are to other protists.

19.2 Animal-like Protists

Animal-like protists are single-celled heterotrophs that can move. Commonly known as protozoa, animal-like protists have various structures that help them move, such as flagella, pseudopods, or cilia. Some animal-like protists can cause diseases such as malaria and sleeping sickness.

19.3 Plantlike Protists

Algae are plantlike protists. Unlike animal-like protists, which are all single-celled, plantlike protists can be either single-celled or multicellular. Most plantlike protists can make their own food through photosynthesis. Plantlike protists are not classified as plants because they do not have roots, stems, leaves, or the specialized tissues and reproductive structures that plants have. However, like many plants, most plantlike protists can reproduce both sexually and asexually.

19.4 Funguslike Protists

Funguslike protists decompose organic matter. These protists have an important role in recycling nutrients through ecosystems. Unlike fungi, funguslike protists can move during part of their life cycle. Funguslike protists include slime molds and water molds.

19.5 Diversity of Fungi

Fungi are heterotrophs that absorb their food. Their bodies are made of long strands, called hyphae, which grow underground in a tangled mass called a mycelium. The parts of fungi that humans normally recognize, such as mushrooms, are actually only the reproductive structures of the fungi, called fruiting bodies.

19.6 Ecology of Fungi

Fungi recycle nutrients in the environment. Some fungi cause illness to humans, such as those that cause athlete's foot and ringworm. Other fungi, such as those that cause Dutch elm disease, cause illness to plants or other organisms. Some fungi share a mutualistic relationship with organisms such as algae to form lichens, or plant roots, which form mycorrhizae. Humans use fungi for foods, medicine, and as model organisms in scientific research.

Synthesize Your Notes

Supporting Main Ideas Use a supporting main ideas diagram to summarize how the three groups of protists get their food.

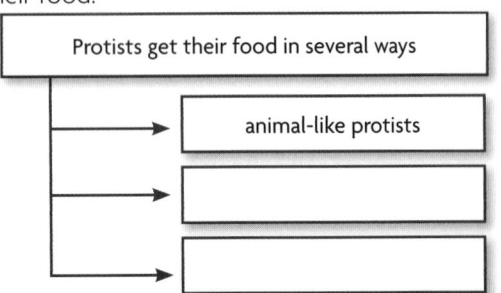

Concept Map Use a concept map like the one below to summarize what you know about the roles of fungi in the environment.

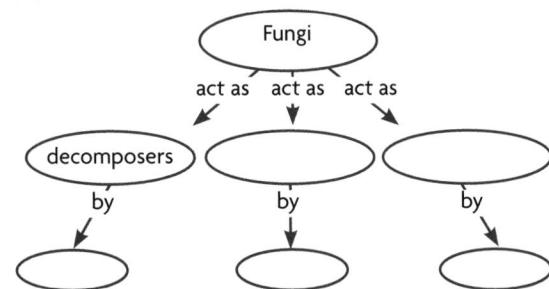

Chapter Assessment

Chapter Vocabulary

19.1 protist, p. 574

19.2 protozoa, p. 577
pseudopod, p. 578
cilia, p. 578

19.3 algae, p. 581

19.4 slime mold, p. 587
water mold, p. 588

19.5 chitin, p. 589
hyphae, p. 589
mycelium, p. 590
fruiting body, p. 590

mycorrhizae, p. 591
sporangia, p. 592

19.6 lichen, p. 598

Reviewing Vocabulary

Compare and Contrast

Describe one similarity and one difference between the two terms in each of the following pairs.

1. pseudopod, cilia
2. slime mold, water mold
3. mycorrhizae, lichen
4. protozoa, algae
5. fruiting body, sporangia
6. hyphae, mycelium

Greek and Latin Word Origins

7. The term *hyphae* comes from the Greek word *huphe*, which means "web." Explain how this meaning relates to hyphae.

8. The term *mycorrhizae* comes from the Greek words *mukes*, which means "fungus," and *rhiza*, which means "root." Explain how these meanings relate to mycorrhizae.

Labeling Diagrams

In your notebook, write the vocabulary term that matches each numbered item below.

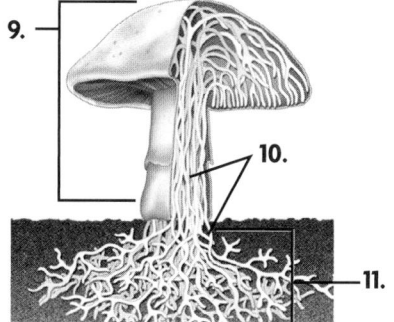

9.
10.
11.

Reviewing MAIN IDEAS

12. Give one characteristic of each type of protist that explains why it is animal-like, plantlike, or funguslike.

13. Explain why the phyla of the kingdom Protista might be regrouped into several kingdoms and what would likely be the basis for this reclassification.

14. What are three types of structures that help some protists move?

15. When does an amoeba form a pseudopod?

16. Name two animal-like protists that cause disease and briefly describe the diseases that they cause.

17. Are protists classified on the basis of being single-celled or multicellular? Give an example to support your answer.

18. How do multicellular algae reproduce asexually?

19. Slime molds have animal-like traits. What might be one reason they are classified with water molds as funguslike protists?

20. Explain how hyphae help a fungus absorb food.

21. The phyla Ascomycota and Basidiomycota are both in the kingdom Fungi. What structures are the basis for placing organisms in one or the other of these phyla?

22. Describe sexual reproduction in yeast, or single-celled fungi.

23. How can the hyphae of bread molds be involved in both asexual and sexual reproduction?

24. Why are yeasts useful to scientific research?

25. How is the decomposing activity of fungi both beneficial and harmful?

Critical Thinking

26. **Analyze** What characteristics of protists prevent them from being classified as animals, plants, or fungi?

27. **Analyze** Amoebas have pseudopods, zooflagellates have flagella, and ciliates have cilia to help them move. Would you expect to find each of these types of protists on land or water? Explain your answer.

28. **Classify** A new plantlike protist has been discovered. It has the following characteristics: two flagella, found in a marine environment, body covering made of cellulose. What phylum would it likely be placed in?

29. **Infer** The prefix *pseudo-* means "false" or "fake." Why is the term *pseudoplasmodium* used to describe one form of a cellular slime mold?

30. **Predict** A grape crop is infected with a fungus. There is a fungicide that targets only this kind of fungus and kills it. But a broad-spectrum fungicide that kills many different kinds of fungi is cheaper, and the farmer decides to use it instead. Explain why the farmer's crops may actually become less healthy.

Interpreting Visuals

Use the diagram below to answer the next two questions.

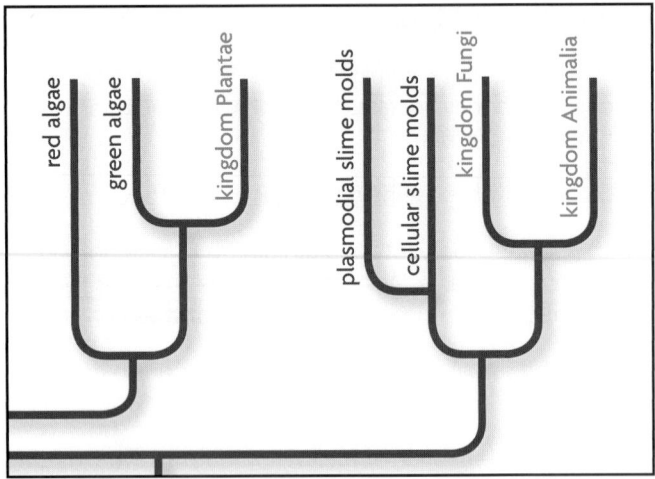

31. **Analyze** What does this diagram suggest about the relationship between fungi and animals, as compared with fungi and plants?

32. **Analyze** Are green algae more closely related to red algae or plants? Explain your answer.

Analyzing Data

Use the text and the data below to answer the next two questions. The following experiment was conducted by two students to determine if adding yeast to a decomposing fruit would speed up the rate of decomposition.

Two 3-cm² pieces of banana were cut. Each was placed in a different plastic bag and the bags were sealed. Each student took one of the banana pieces home.

- Student A placed her banana piece on a bookshelf.
- Student B put some dry yeast on his banana and resealed the bag. He also put his banana piece on a bookshelf.

Both students looked at the banana pieces every day for the next four days and recorded their observations.

PERCENT DECOMPOSITION				
Organism	**Day 1**	**Day 2**	**Day 3**	**Day 4**
Student A's banana	1%	5%	7%	10%
Student B's banana	0%	4%	7%	10%

33. **Experimental Design** What is the main design flaw in this experiment?

34. **Analyze** Does the experimental design clearly indicate the question that the students were trying to answer? Explain.

Connecting CONCEPTS

35. **Write an Argument** Write an argument between two euglenoids in which one wants to be placed with animals and the other wants to be placed with plants. Include the decision of the referee who explains why they can be neither plants nor animals.

36. **Evaluate** Look again at the picture of *Didinium* eating the *Paramecium* on page 573. What might be one advantage and disadvantage to having a specialist feeding strategy? a generalist feeding strategy? Explain your answer.

MICHIGAN
STANDARDS-BASED ASSESSMENT

✓**Test Practice**
For more test practice,
go to ClassZone.com.

1. If fungi and funguslike protists were removed from an ecosystem, the main effect to the ecosystem would likely be   **B3.2C**

   A more space for other organisms to inhabit.

   B less available nutrients for other organisms.

   C more competition for resources between other organisms.

   D less predation upon organisms that fungi prey upon.

2.

   prokaryote: bacteria, archaea   eukaryote: protists, fungi, plants, animals

   The grouping of kingdoms into prokaryotes and eukaryotes is shown in the Venn diagram above. One characteristic that could be placed in the area that overlaps both groups is   **B2.4A**

   A nucleus.

   B organelles.

   C chloroplasts.

   D cell membranes.

3. Protists are often grouped into categories according to whether they are animal-like, plantlike, or funguslike. This broad grouping is based on   **B2.4d**

   A how they move.

   B how they protect themselves.

   C how they obtain food.

   D how they reproduce.

4. Most fungi are decomposers. How do their life processes affect other organisms in the community?   **L3.p2C**

   A Fungi keep other populations under control by preying on weak organisms.

   B Fungi make stored nutrients available to other organisms.

   C Fungi compete with plants for soil nutrients.

   D Fungi compete with plants and animals for space.

   THINK THROUGH THE QUESTION

   If you are having a hard time answering this question in terms of fungi, try to consider it based on the role of decomposers in general.

5.

   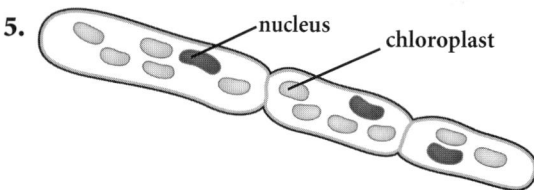

   A researcher discovers a new type of organism. Only some structures, labeled above, can be clearly seen. Based on this information alone, the researcher is able to conclude that the organism   **L2.p4A**

   A is a protist that lives in colonies.

   B is a multicellular protist.

   C can capture energy from the sun.

   D will not prey upon other organisms.

6. Yeast is a single-celled fungus that can reproduce both asexually and sexually. During asexual reproduction, yeast cells do *not* undergo   **L4.p1A**

   A budding.

   B mitosis.

   C meiosis.

   D fission.

BIOZINE

at **CLASSZONE.COM**

INTERNET MAGAZINE

Go online for the latest biology news and updates on all BioZine articles.

Expanding the Textbook

News Feeds

- 📡 Science Daily
- 📡 CNN
- 📡 BBC

Careers

Bio Bytes

Opinion Poll

Strange Biology

Could one of these travelers be carrying a virus that causes the next pandemic?

Pandemics— Is the Next One on the Way?

Imagine that a new virus emerges and people have no immunity. There is no vaccine. If this were to happen, there could be mandatory travel restrictions, quarantines, and social distancing—including staying out of all crowded places. In the United States alone, such an outbreak could kill up to 2 million people. But how can such a virus emerge, and how can we prepare for it?

Pandemics

When a new virus emerges, the species that it infects has had little or no opportunity to evolve immunity. If the virus infects people, there is often little time to produce vaccines. For these reasons, a new virus may be able to spread easily from person to person.

A new virus can cause a pandemic, which is a disease outbreak that affects large areas of the world and has a high fatality rate. The 1918 flu pandemic was the most devastating pandemic recorded in world history. This virus infected nearly one-fifth of the world's population, killing about 50 million people worldwide. It spread mainly along global trade routes and with the movement of soldiers during World War I.

If a new and deadly disease emerges today, a carrier could travel around the world in 24 hours. More than a million people travel internationally by plane every year, easily reaching their destinations before symptoms of any diseases they may be harboring appear.

The "Perfect" Virus

Not every virus is well-suited to cause massive human casualties. For many viruses, humans represent a dead-end infection because they cannot be passed from human to human. For other viruses, victims die too quickly for the virus to reproduce. Quarantines can contain this type of virus relatively easily.

What characteristics would make an emerging virus likely to cause a pandemic? The virus would need to be adapted to humans as hosts and easily spread through casual contact. Victims would also have to survive infection long enough without symptoms to go about their daily business and infect other people. Finally, the most deadly virus would mutate rapidly, foiling the attempts of scientists to develop a vaccine or a drug that targets it.

TECHNOLOGY

Dissecting a Virus

Scientists have long debated how the genetic material of influenza A viruses, RNA, is likely arranged. In 2005 virologist Yoshihiro Kawaoka and his team of researchers at the University of Wisconsin unraveled the mystery using a technique called electron tomography.

Electron tomography is a way to construct a three-dimensional image from a series of electron microscope images taken at different angles. By making slices along flu virus particles that cut them into "top" and "bottom" halves, researchers found that all influenza A viruses have a total of eight RNA strands. As shown at the right, seven strands form a circle just inside the edge of the virus particle, surrounding an eighth strand in the center.

The researchers concluded that all influenza A viruses, including those responsible for regular seasonal outbreaks as well as the avian flu, must share a specific mechanism for packaging their genetic material. By knowing how these viruses package their genetic material, it may be possible to engineer viruses that can be used to mass produce vaccines.

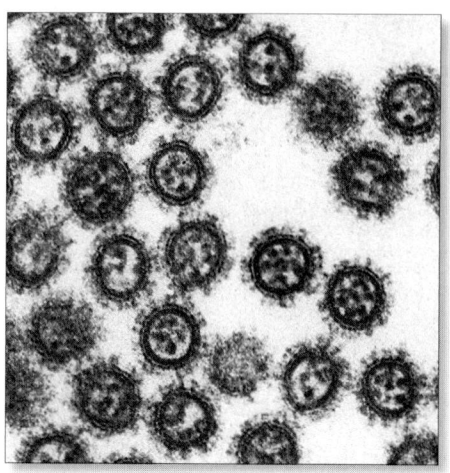

Read More >> *at* CLASSZONE.COM

CAREERS

Epidemiologist in Action

DR. BEN MUNETA	
TITLE Medical Epidemiologist, Indian Health Service	
EDUCATION M.D., Stanford University	

In 1993 a mystery disease began to kill people in the southwestern United States. One of the experts that the Centers for Disease Control (CDC) consulted was Dr. Ben Muneta. Dr. Muneta is an epidemiologist, a scientist who studies the causes, transmission, and control of diseases within a population. He works at the Indian Health Service National Epidemiology Program in Albuquerque, New Mexico.

Dr. Muneta consulted a traditional Navajo healer. From him, Dr. Muneta learned that the disease was associated with extra rainfall, which had caused the pinon trees to produce more nuts than usual. This in turn had led to a population explosion among mice that feed on these nuts.

Using this lead, CDC researchers determined that the disease was caused by hantavirus, a virus spread through the droppings of deer mice. With further research, Dr. Muneta confirmed that some Navajo healers had even predicted the 1993 outbreak.

Read More >> *at* **CLASSZONE.COM**

Diseases that Jump to New Species

Some diseases, called zoonoses, can jump between species. If a virus evolves the ability to jump from a nonhuman animal species to humans, our immune systems will have had little opportunity to evolve defenses. And if this virus exchanges genetic material with another human virus, a new virus that is capable of spreading from person to person may form.

Perhaps the most familiar zoonosis is the avian flu virus. Sometimes called the bird flu, this virus normally infects wild birds such as ducks and geese as well as domestic birds such as chickens. The spread of avian flu does not rely on any human form of transportation, since migrating birds can carry it to other continents.

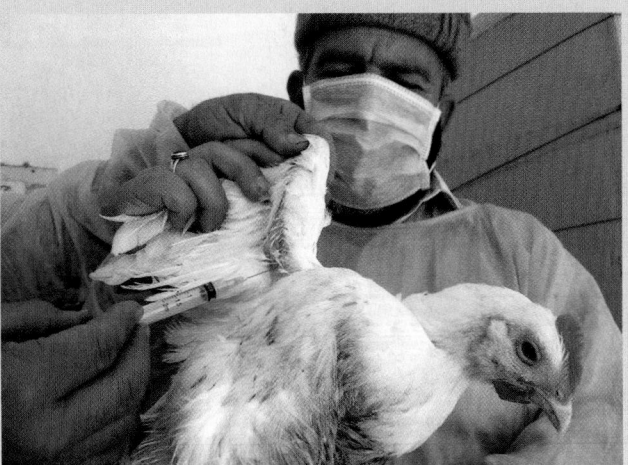

China, Thailand, Russia, Turkey, and Pakistan are among the countries that have confirmed cases of avian flu in poultry farms. Here, a Pakistani health worker vaccinates a healthy chicken.

Avian Flu H5N1

Is avian flu the perfect killer virus? Researchers are currently tracking a form of avian flu called H5N1. Like other flu viruses, H5N1 mutates rapidly. However, mutations are random and may or may not help the virus adapt to new host species.

Unfortunately, a faster, less random way for viruses to mutate exists. Some animals can be infected with viruses from two different species at the same time. For example, if a pig becomes infected by both avian and human flu viruses at the same time, the viruses can exchange genetic information. If this happens, the avian flu can jump the species barrier, becoming a flu virus that can be transmitted from one human to another.

Unanswered Questions

Despite the danger that a new virus represents, no one knows how the virus may mutate or whether it will cause a pandemic. Some of the most important questions include the following:

- How can vaccines be developed quickly enough to stop a disease that can spread in hours or days?
- Can a broad-spectrum antiviral drug be developed that could target more than one flu virus?
- What specific molecular factors allow a virus to jump from one species to another?

Read More >> *at* **CLASSZONE.COM**

UNIT 7

Plants

CHAPTER 20
Plant Diversity   **610**

CHAPTER 21
**Plant Structure
and Function**   **638**

CHAPTER 22
**Plant Growth, Reproduction,
and Response**   **662**

BIOZINE

INTERNET MAGAZINE
**Genetically Modified Foods—
Do Potential Problems
Outweigh Benefits?**   **690**
   TECHNOLOGY Gene Gun
   CAREER Research Engineer

CHAPTER
20 Plant Diversity

KEY CONCEPTS

20.1 Origins of Plant Life
Plant life began in the water and became adapted to land.

20.2 Classification of Plants
Plants can be classified into nine phyla.

20.3 Diversity of Flowering Plants
The largest phylum in the plant kingdom is the flowering plants.

20.4 Plants in Human Culture
Humans rely on plants in many ways.

Online BIOLOGY CLASSZONE.COM

Animated BIOLOGY
View animated chapter concepts.
• Plant and Pollinator Matching Game

BIOZINE
Keep current with biology news.
• Featured stories
• News feeds
• Careers

RESOURCE CENTER
Get more information on
• Plant Evolution
• Plant Classification
• Plant Resources

How have flowering plants come to dominate Earth's landscapes?

From the mosses that live in Antarctica to these flowering protea plants of South Africa, the plant kingdom is diverse. Proteas are native to one region of South Africa, called the Cape floristic region, which can go through long periods of drought. This small region is home to over 9,000 plant species, including at least 6,000 that are found nowhere else on Earth.

Habitat Protea plants are a necessary part of the habitat for Cape sugarbirds, such as the one shown at left. These birds depend on proteas for both food and shelter. They drink the nectar produced inside protea flowers. They build their nests in tangled protea branches and line them with the soft, short hairs that cover protea leaves. During the mating season, male Cape sugarbirds perch on top of the highest protea plants to defend their territories in an effort to attract a mate.

20.1 Origins of Plant Life

KEY CONCEPT Plant life began in the water and became adapted to land.

MAIN IDEAS

- Land plants evolved from green algae.
- Plants have adaptations that allow them to live on land.
- Plants evolve with other organisms in their environment.

VOCABULARY

plant, p. 612
cuticle, p. 614
stomata, p. 614
vascular system, p. 614
lignin, p. 614

pollen grain, p. 614
seed, p. 614

Review
algae, eukaryote, photosynthesis, chlorophyll, herbivore

MICHIGAN STANDARDS

L2.p1E Compare and contrast how different organisms accomplish similar functions (e.g., obtain oxygen for respiration, and excrete waste). (prerequisite)

L3.p2D Explain how two organisms can be mutually beneficial and how that can lead to interdependency. (prerequisite)

Connect The flowering proteas shown on the previous page are not just plants with beautiful flowers. Various birds, rodents, and insects rely on protea nectar and pollen as food sources. Green protea beetles even live inside of protea flowers. Without plants, animal life as we know it would not exist on land.

MAIN IDEA

Land plants evolved from green algae.

All green algae share certain characteristics with plants. **Plants** are multicellular eukaryotes, most of which produce their own food through photosynthesis and have adapted to life on land. Like plants, green algae are photosynthetic eukaryotes. They have chlorophyll that captures energy from sunlight during photosynthesis. Chlorophyll is what makes these algae—and most of the plants that we are familiar with—green. Green algae and plants have the same types of chlorophyll. Another feature both green algae and plants share is that they use starch as a storage product. Most green algae also have cell walls that contain cellulose, a complex carbohydrate that is found in the cell walls of all plants.

Evidence from genetic analysis points to one ancient species of green algae that is the common ancestor of all plants. If it were alive today, this species would be classified as a member of the class Charophyceae, like the algae in **FIGURE 20.1.** Several other important plant characteristics likely originated in charophyceans.

- A multicellular body, which led to the specialization of cells and tissues
- A method of cell division that produces cells with small channels in their walls, which allows cells to communicate with each other chemically
- Reproduction that involves sperm traveling to and fertilizing an egg cell

Today, charophyceans are common in freshwater habitats. Scientists hypothesize that the ancestral charophycean species may have grown in areas of shallow water that dried out from time to time. Natural selection likely favored individuals that could withstand longer dry periods. Eventually, the first true plant species evolved, as shown in **FIGURE 20.2.** True plants have multicellular embryos that remain attached to the female parent as they develop.

FIGURE 20.1 Multicellular green algae of the genus *Chara* can be found in many lakes and ponds. They are charophyceans, which are thought to be the closest living relatives of the common ancestor of all plants.

FIGURE 20.2 Evolution of Plants

Plants have evolved from green algae. An extinct charophycean species is the common ancestor of all plants.

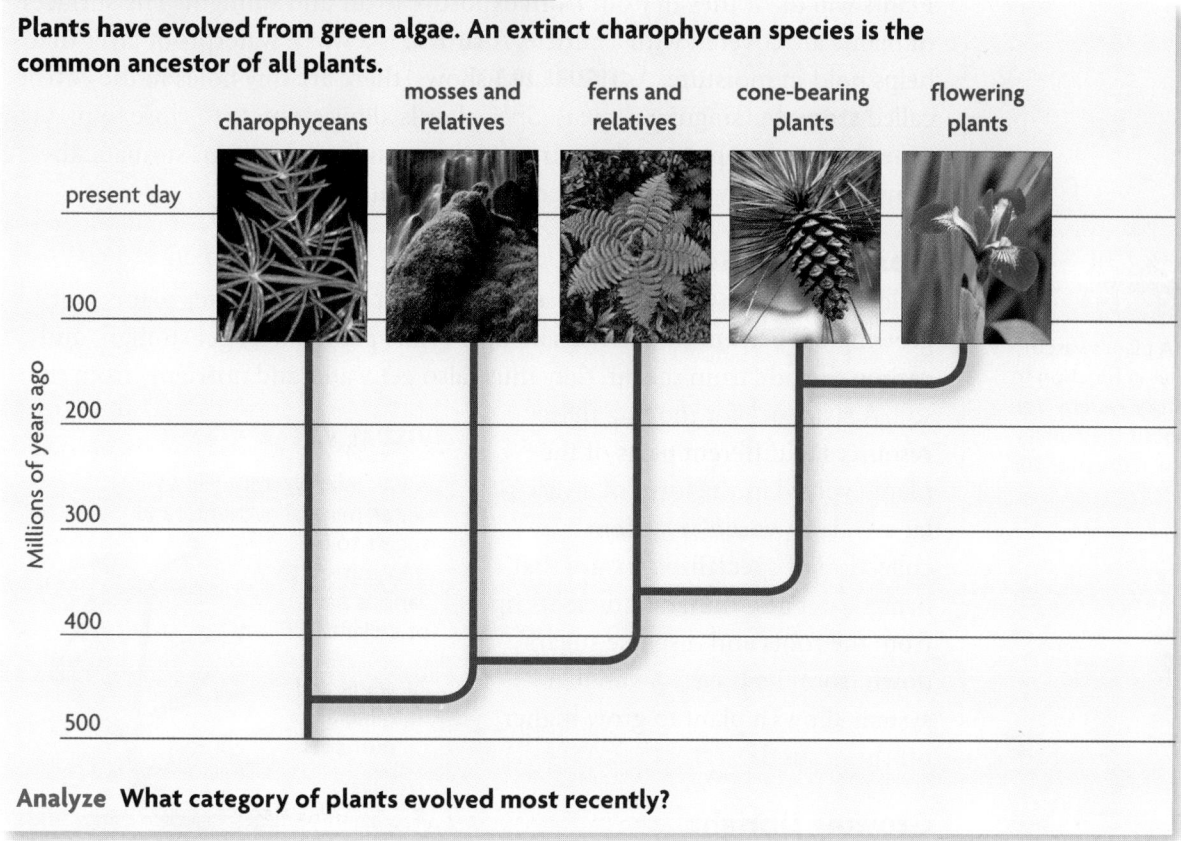

Analyze **What category of plants evolved most recently?**

The earliest plant fossils date to more than 450 million years ago. The first true plants probably grew on the edges of lakes and streams. Like modern-day mosses, they relied on droplets of water that brought sperm to eggs to produce the next generation of plants. They also had a fairly simple structure similar to that of moss, keeping low to the ground to retain moisture. Over time, the descendants of these plants were able to live in even drier areas.

Connecting CONCEPTS

Algae Recall from **Chapter 19** that algae are plantlike protists. Photosynthetic pigments give various types of algae their distinct colors.

Apply **What evidence suggests that green algae are close relatives of land plants?**

▶ MAIN IDEA
Plants have adaptations that allow them to live on land.

Life on land presents different challenges than does life in the water. Unlike land plants, algae are constantly surrounded by water, which is needed for photosynthesis. The buoyancy of water supports the weight of most algae. For algae, water provides a medium through which sperm and spores can travel, allowing for reproduction and dispersal. Finally, water prevents sperm, eggs, and developing offspring from drying out.

The challenges of living on drier land have acted as selective pressures for plant life on Earth. In turn, many land plants have evolved adaptations that allow them to retain moisture, transport water and other resources between plant parts, grow upright, and reproduce without free-standing water.

TAKING NOTES

Use a main idea web to take notes about the challenges of life on land and plants' adaptations to these challenges.

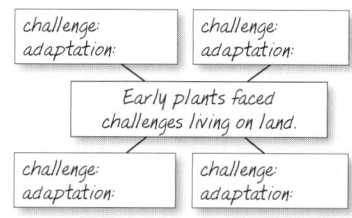

Retaining Moisture

Plants will die if they dry out from exposure to air and sunlight. The surfaces of plants are covered with a cuticle. A **cuticle** is a waxy, waterproof layer that helps hold in moisture. As **FIGURE 20.3** shows, there are tiny holes in the cuticle, called **stomata** (singular, *stoma*). Special cells allow stomata to close to prevent water loss, or to open to allow air to move in and out. Without stomata, the movement of air would be prevented by the cuticle.

Transporting Resources

Taller plants often have more access to sunlight than do shorter plants, but growing tall presents another challenge. While plants must get sunlight and carbon dioxide from the air, they must also get water and nutrients from the soil. A structure for moving these resources to different parts of the plant evolved in the form of a vascular system. A **vascular system** is a collection of specialized tissues that bring water and mineral nutrients up from the roots and disperse sugars down from the leaves. A vascular system allows a plant to grow higher off the ground.

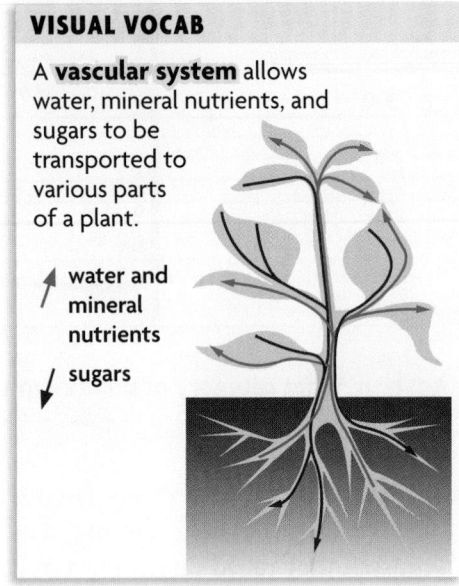

VISUAL VOCAB

A **vascular system** allows water, mineral nutrients, and sugars to be transported to various parts of a plant.

↑ water and mineral nutrients

↓ sugars

Growing Upright

Plant height is also limited by the ability of a plant to support its own weight. Plants need structure to support their weight and provide space for vascular tissues. This support comes from a material called **lignin** (LIHG-nihn), which hardens the cell walls of some vascular tissues. Lignin is also responsible for the strength of wood and provides stiffness to the stems of other plants. As a result, plants can retain their upright structure as they grow toward the sun.

Reproducing on Land

In all plants, eggs are fertilized within the tissue of the parent plant. There, the fertilized egg develops into an embryo, the earliest stage of growth and development for a plant. Some plants reproduce with the help of rainwater or dew, while others do not need free-standing water to reproduce. Pollen and seeds are adaptations that allow seed plants to reproduce completely free of water. A **pollen grain** is a two-celled structure that contains a cell that will divide to form sperm. Pollen can be carried by wind or animals to female reproductive structures. A **seed** is a storage device for a plant embryo. A seed has a hard coat that protects the embryo from drying wind and sunlight. Once a seed encounters the right conditions, the embryo can develop into an adult plant.

Analyze Discuss why the four challenges on this page do not apply to most algae.

Connecting CONCEPTS

Human Biology A plant's vascular system is similar in function to a human's circulatory system. You will learn more about the human circulatory system in **Chapter 30**.

FIGURE 20.3 Adaptations of Land Plants

Land plants have evolved to adapt to the challenges of life on land.

POLLEN AND SEEDS

Pollen can be carried by wind or animals. Each pollen grain contains cells that will divide to form sperm.

Seeds protect and provide nutrients for developing embryos.

pollen   seeds

STOMATA AND CUTICLES

Stomata are small openings in the cuticle that allow for gas exchange between the plant and the atmosphere.

A cuticle is a waxy coating that protects plant leaves from drying out.

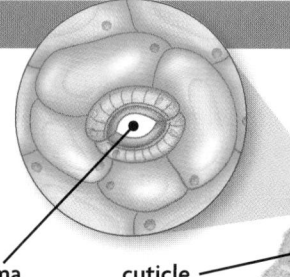

stoma   cuticle

LIGNIN

Tough lignin is found in the cell walls of plant tissues that provide support and conduct fluids.

lignin

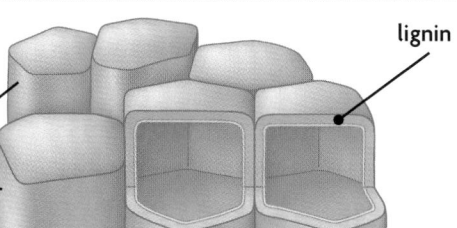

plant cells

VASCULAR SYSTEM

Vascular tissues form "pipelines" that carry resources up and down to different parts of the plant. A vascular system allows plants to grow higher off the ground.

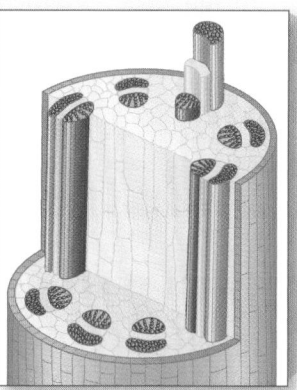

CRITICAL VIEWING   Why is lignin especially important in the cell walls of vascular tissues?

▶ MAIN IDEA
Plants evolve with other organisms in their environment.

Plants have coevolved with other terrestrial organisms for millions of years. Some of these relationships are cooperative, while others have evolved between plant species and the animal species that eat them.

Mutualisms

A mutualism is an interaction between two species in which both species benefit. Some mutualisms exist between plant roots and certain types of fungi and bacteria. Roots provide a habitat for these fungi and bacteria, while the fungi and bacteria help the plant get mineral nutrients from the soil.

Many flowering plants depend on specific animal species for pollination or seed dispersal. In turn, these animals are fed by the plant's pollen, nectar, or fruit. For example, in Madagascar, Darwin noticed a variety of orchids with long, tubular flower parts. He predicted that a nocturnal moth with a tongue 10 to 12 inches long must be the pollinator. That very moth, shown in **FIGURE 20.4**, was discovered 40 years after Darwin's prediction.

Plant-Herbivore Interactions

Plants have a variety of adaptations that discourage animals from eating them. The spines on a cactus and the thorns on a rose stem are examples. Other plants produce defensive chemicals that act as pesticides against plant-eating predators. Natural selection favors herbivores that can overcome the effects of defensive plant adaptations. In turn, natural selection favors plants that produce even sharper spines or thorns or even more toxic chemicals.

Some insects use defensive chemicals produced by plants to their advantage. The larvae of monarch butterflies, for example, feed exclusively on milkweed species. Milkweed plants produce a chemical that makes monarch larvae, adults, and even eggs taste bad to potential predators. In this way, the butterfly has a type of chemical protection as a result of eating milkweed leaves during its development.

FIGURE 20.4 The hawk moth has a tongue that measures between 30 and 35 cm (12–14 in.). It is the pollinator of a night-blooming orchid whose nectar is produced 30 cm down inside the flower.

Synthesize **Describe how defensive chemicals in plant leaves may have evolved.**

20.1 ASSESSMENT

REVIEWING ▶ MAIN IDEAS

1. What characteristics do land **plants** share with green algae?

2. What adaptations allow plants to thrive on dry land?

3. Describe two ways in which plants evolve with other organisms.

CRITICAL THINKING

4. **Synthesize** Describe how a **cuticle** could have evolved through natural selection.

5. **Evaluate** For plants, what are the advantages and disadvantages of growing tall?

Connecting CONCEPTS

6. **Classification** Some scientists think that certain species of green algae should be in the kingdom Plantae. What reasons might these scientists use to defend their position?

20.2

Classification of Plants

KEY CONCEPTS Plants can be classified into nine phyla.

▶ **MAIN IDEAS**

- Mosses and their relatives are seedless nonvascular plants.
- Club mosses and ferns are seedless vascular plants.
- Seed plants include cone-bearing plants and flowering plants.

VOCABULARY

pollination, p. 620
gymnosperm, p. 621
angiosperm, p. 621
cone, p. 621

flower, p. 622
fruit, p. 622

Review
seed, vascular system, pollen

MICHIGAN STANDARDS

B2.4A Explain that living things can be classified based on structural, embryological, and molecular (relatedness of DNA sequence) evidence.

Connecting CONCEPTS

Classification Recall from **Chapter 17** that the term *division* is sometimes used instead of *phylum* for the classification of plants and fungi.

Connect Scientists have described about 300,000 plant species, and many more probably remain to be found. All plants belong to the kingdom Plantae. While modern plants can be classified into nine phyla, DNA analysis continues to reveal new relationships that keep taxonomists updating the plant family tree.

▶ **MAIN IDEA**

Mosses and their relatives are seedless nonvascular plants.

In a damp forest, mosses lend an emerald green color to the landscape. These plants do not produce seeds. They have no vascular systems. Instead, they grow close to the ground or on surfaces such as tree trunks, where they can absorb water and nutrients directly. They also rely on free-standing water to allow their sperm to swim to and fertilize eggs. Mosses belong to Bryophyta, one of the three phyla of nonvascular plants. The other phyla in this category are Hepatophyta, the liverworts, and Anthocerophyta, the hornworts.

Liverworts

Most liverworts live in damp environments and get moisture directly from the surface of the soil. They are often found growing on wet rocks, in greenhouse flowerpots, and in other areas with plenty of moisture. Liverworts can have one of two basic forms: thallose or leafy. The name *liverwort* refers to thallose liverworts, which look like the lobes of a liver flat on the ground. Eggs are produced on umbrella-like structures of the thallose liverwort, shown in **FIGURE 20.5**. Though thallose liverworts may be easier to recognize, leafy liverworts are much more common. Leafy liverworts have stemlike and leaflike structures. These leaflike structures are most often arranged in three rows.

FIGURE 20.5 Thallose liverworts, like the one shown here, can grow from 2 mm to 25 cm in length.

Hornworts

Hornworts are a widespread group of plants that are found in tropical forests and along streams around the world. Hornworts grow low to the ground, and the main plant body has a flat, lobed appearance similar to that of thallose liverworts. Little green horns rising above the flat plant body, as shown in **FIGURE 20.6**, produce spores.

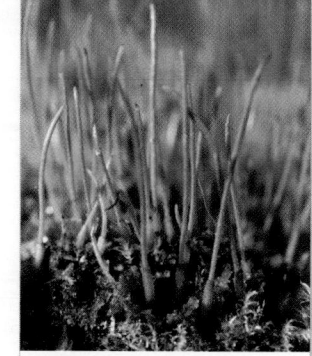

FIGURE 20.6 The stalks of these hornworts are 2 to 5 cm long.

Mosses

Mosses are the most common nonvascular plants. Some look like clumps of grass, others look like tiny trees, and still others look like strands of green yarn. Mosses do not have true leaves. Instead, they have leaflike structures that are just one cell thick. While they lack vascular systems, some moss species do have cuticles, and most of them have stomata. Mosses can anchor themselves to surfaces such as soil, rocks, or tree trunks, as shown in **FIGURE 20.7**, with structures called rhizoids (RY-ZOYDZ).

Mosses are often tolerant of harsh weather conditions and nutrient-poor soils. They can grow in many places where other plants are unable to grow. Some mosses can survive in deserts and tundras by entering a stage of dormancy until water is available. In fact, mosses are often among the first plants to colonize bare land and begin the soil-making process in the early stages of primary succession.

One moss that is commonly used by humans is sphagnum (SFAG-nuhm), which grows in acidic bogs. Sphagnum does not decay when it dies, so thick deposits of this dead moss, called peat, build up over time. Peat can be cut from the ground and burned as fuel. Dried peat can absorb water, and it has antibacterial properties. In fact, dried peat has been used in products such as diapers and bandages. Peat also has an important role in the carbon cycle, as a reservoir that holds carbon in an organic form.

Apply Why can't nonvascular plants grow tall?

***Connecting* CONCEPTS**

Ecology Recall from **Chapter 14** that primary succession is the establishment of an ecosystem in an area that was previously uninhabited. Mosses are common pioneer species that help to break down solid rock into smaller pieces—one of the first steps in producing soil.

FIGURE 20.7 Like all nonvascular plants, mosses need to live in moist environments.

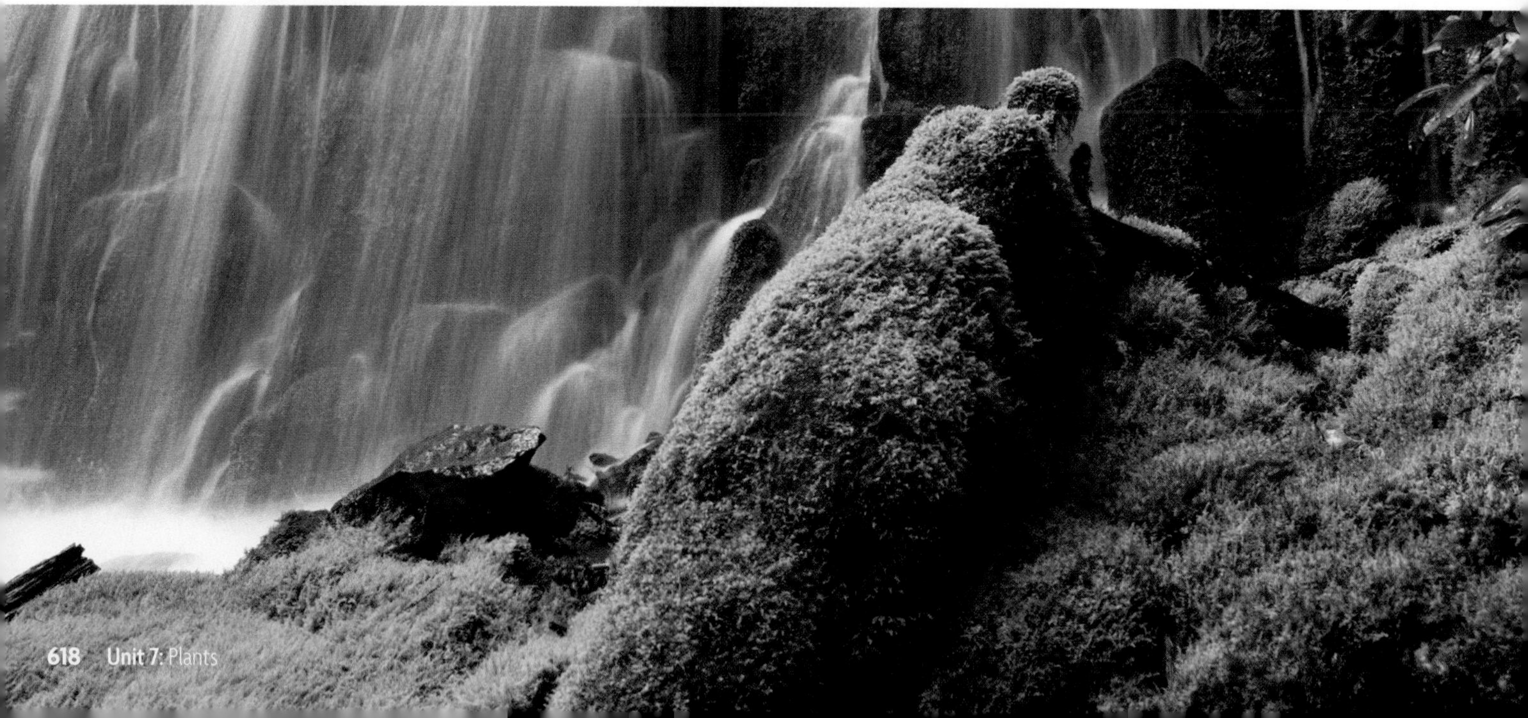

▶ MAIN IDEA

Club mosses and ferns are seedless vascular plants.

About 300 million years ago, during the Carboniferous period, shallow swamps were home to enormous seedless vascular plants. Over time, the dead remains of these plants were pressed and heated underground, where they gradually turned into coal. This is why we call coal a fossil fuel.

Club mosses (phylum Lycophyta) and ferns (phylum Pterophyta) are modern seedless vascular plants. Like nonvascular plants, they depend on water for reproduction. However, a vascular system allows these plants to grow higher above the ground and still get materials they need from the soil.

FIGURE 20.8 Club mosses, such as this *Lycopodium* species, are able to grow up off of the ground because they have vascular systems.

Club Mosses

Club mosses, which are not true mosses, belong to the oldest living group of vascular plants. Some ancient species looked like modern trees, growing more than ten stories tall. These giant plants were wiped out when the Carboniferous climate cooled, but some of the smaller species survived. One common living genus of club moss is *Lycopodium*. Some *Lycopodium* species, such as the one shown in **FIGURE 20.8**, look like tiny pine trees and are sometimes called "ground pines."

Whisk Ferns, Horsetails, and Ferns

Ferns and their relatives, whisk ferns and horsetails, can be grouped together in one phylum. Whisk ferns grow mostly in the tropics and subtropics. Although they lack true roots and leaves, DNA analysis indicates that whisk ferns are closely related to ferns.

Horsetails grow in wetland areas and along rivers and streams. They have tan, scalelike leaves that grow in whorls around a tubular stem. Like club mosses, horsetails were much larger and more common in the Carboniferous period. Because horsetails' cell walls contain a rough compound called silica, colonial settlers used the plant, also called "scouring rush," to scrub pots.

Ferns are the most successful survivors of the Carboniferous period, with about 12,000 species alive today. Most ferns grow from underground stems called rhizomes (RY-zohmz). Their large leaves, shown in **FIGURE 20.9**, are called fronds. Newly forming fronds, called fiddleheads, uncurl as they grow. Some ferns are grown as houseplants. Others, called tree ferns, live in the tropics and can grow over three stories tall.

FIGURE 20.9 FERNS

frond

fiddlehead

Fern leaves are called fronds. Newly-forming fronds, called fiddleheads, uncurl as they grow.

Infer Why do most seedless vascular plants live in moist areas?

Classifying Plants as Vascular or Nonvascular

In this lab, you will examine tissues from several plants to determine whether they are vascular or nonvascular. This is the first step in classifying plants into one of the nine phyla.

PROBLEM Are the plants vascular or nonvascular?

PROCEDURE

1. Observe each slide under the microscope.
2. Make a sketch of each plant tissue you examine.

MATERIALS

- prepared slides of plant tissue
- microscope

ANALYZE AND CONCLUDE

1. **Analyze** In what ways are the plant tissues similar? In what ways are they different?
2. **Analyze** Based on your observations, are the plants vascular or nonvascular? What evidence did you use to determine their identity?
3. **Apply** How does the absence of vascular tissue affect the size (height) of nonvascular plants?

▶ MAIN IDEA

Seed plants include cone-bearing plants and flowering plants.

You may be familiar with seeds as the small plant parts that, when sown and tended, will produce another plant. From an evolutionary viewpoint, seed plants have several great advantages over their ancestors.

- **Seed plants can reproduce without free-standing water.** Seedless plants depend on water through which sperm swim to fertilize an egg. However, seed plants do not depend on water in this way. Seed plants, such as the pine tree in **FIGURE 20.10**, produce pollen. Pollen can be carried by the wind or on the body of an animal pollinator, such as a bee. **Pollination** occurs when pollen meets female reproductive parts of the same plant species. Each pollen grain has a cell that will then divide to form sperm. Fertilization occurs when a sperm meets an egg. The ability to reproduce without free-standing water allows many seed plants to live in drier climates.

- **Seeds nourish and protect plant embryos.** A seed consists of a protective coat that contains a plant embryo and a food supply. A seed can survive for many months, or even years, in a dormant state. During this time, the seed can withstand harsh conditions, such as drought or cold, that might kill an adult plant. When conditions are right, the embryo will begin growing, using the food supply provided by the seed.

- **Seeds allow plants to disperse to new places.** Wind, water, or animals often carry seeds far from the individual plant that produced them. In fact, many seed plants have adaptations that aid in the dispersal of seeds, such as the "wings" that carry maple seeds in the wind. Because seeds can remain dormant, the embryo will not begin to develop until it reaches a suitable environment.

FIGURE 20.10 Seed plants produce pollen. In pine trees such as the one shown here, clouds of pollen are released from male pine cones.

Scientists hypothesize that seed plants evolved as the Earth's climate changed from warm and moist to hot and dry during the Devonian period, 410 to 360 million years ago. Fossil evidence suggests that seed plants evolved about 360 million years ago. Seed plants can be grouped according to whether their seeds are enclosed in fruit.

- A **gymnosperm** (JIHM-nuh-SPURM) is a seed plant whose seeds are not enclosed in fruit.
- An **angiosperm** (AN-jee-uh-SPURM) is a seed plant that has seeds enclosed in some type of fruit.

FIGURE 20.11 Cycads, such as the one shown here, produce seeds on large, protective, female cones.

Most gymnosperms are cone-bearing and evergreen, such as pine trees. A woody **cone** is the reproductive structure of most gymnosperms. It contains hard protective scales. Pollen is produced in male cones, while eggs are produced in female cones. Seeds also develop on the scales of female cones, which protect fertilized eggs. There are three living phyla of gymnosperms: cycads (phylum Cycadophyta), *Ginkgo biloba* (phylum Ginkgophyta), and conifers (phylum Coniferophyta).

Cycads

Cycads look like palm trees with large cones, as shown in **FIGURE 20.11**. Huge forests of cycads grew during the Mesozoic era, 248 million to 65 million years ago. These plants provided food for dinosaurs. In fact, the Jurassic period of this era is commonly called the Age of the Cycads. Today, cycads grow in tropical areas in the Americas, Asia, Africa, and Australia. Many cycad species are endangered because of their slow growth and loss of habitat in these tropical areas.

Ginkgo

Like cycads, ginkgoes were abundant while the dinosaurs lived. Only one species lives today, *Ginkgo biloba*, shown in **FIGURE 20.12**. This species is native to China, and it has survived in part due to its cultivation by Buddhist monks since the year 1100. Because it so closely resembles its fossil ancestors, Darwin called this species a living fossil. In fact, the ginkgo may be the oldest living species of seed plants. Today, it is grown around the world in gardens and used in urban landscaping.

FIGURE 20.12 The name *Ginkgo biloba* refers to the two-lobed leaves of this plant. Ginkgo trees are used commonly in garden landscapes.

FIGURE 20.13 This Ponderosa pine is a typical evergreen conifer with needlelike leaves.

Conifers

By far the most diverse and common gymnosperms alive today are the conifers—familiar trees with needlelike leaves, such as those in **FIGURE 20.13**. Pines, redwood, spruce, cedar, fir, and juniper all belong to this phylum. Conifers supply most of the timber used for paper, cardboard, housing lumber, and plywood. They grow quickly, and large tree farms help produce enough wood to meet demand.

Many conifers are evergreen, or green all year-round. However, a few lose their needles in the winter. Conifers are well adapted to high altitudes, sloping hillsides, and poor soil. These characteristics allow conifers to thrive in mountainous regions.

Conifers tend to grow old and grow tall. Two conifers living in California hold world records. At more than 4700 years of age, one bristlecone pine in California's White Mountains is the oldest known living tree. And a giant sequoia tree in Sequoia National Park is the world's most massive living thing. It has a mass of 1.2 million kilograms, which is about the mass of 40 buses.

Flowering Plants

Angiosperms belong to a phylum of their own (phylum Anthophyta) and are commonly called flowering plants. A **flower** is the reproductive structure of flowering plants. Flowers protect a plant's gametes and fertilized eggs, as woody cones do for most gymnosperms. A **fruit** is the mature ovary of a flower. Fruit can take the form of a juicy peach, the wings attached to a maple seed, or the fluff surrounding dandelion seeds. As you will learn in the next section, flowers and fruits have played a large role in the dominance and diversity of flowering plants today.

Apply What adaptation of seed plants allows sperm to reach and fertilize an egg in the absence of water?

20.2 ASSESSMENT

ONLINE QUIZ
ClassZone.com

REVIEWING ▶ MAIN IDEAS

1. What are the habitat requirements for seedless nonvascular plants?
2. What are the evolutionary advantages of a vascular system?
3. What are the evolutionary advantages of seeds?

CRITICAL THINKING

4. **Infer** In what type of environment might you find nonvascular plants, seedless vascular plants, and seed plants growing together? Explain.
5. **Apply** Consider the characteristics of pollen grains. Why do people with pollen allergies find it difficult to avoid exposure to pollen?

Connecting CONCEPTS

6. **History of Life** According to the fossil record, seed plants date back to 360 million years ago, when the Earth's climate was becoming hotter and drier. What role did this global climate change likely play in the evolution of seed plants?

MATERIALS

- 2 plant samples
- hand lens
- ruler
- razor tool
- forceps
- 2 microscope slides
- 2 cover slips
- microscope

PROCESS SKILLS

- **Observing**
- **Analyzing**
- **Classifying**

B5.1e Explain how natural selection leads to organisms that are well suited for the environment (differential survival and reproduction of chance inherited variants, depending upon environmental conditions).

Habitat Clues

By examining different parts of a plant, you can often tell a lot about its habitat. In this lab, you will examine external features to help you determine the natural habitat of several different plants. You will also examine the epidermal tissue—the "skin" of the plant—which you will learn more about in Chapter 21. This tissue is in direct contact with the air. It has adaptive traits that allow the plant to survive and reproduce in a specific type of environment.

PROBLEM What kinds of adaptations allow plants to live in different habitats?

PROCEDURE

1. Record descriptions for each plant in a data table. Include leaf blade size, shape, thickness, and appearance (dull, shiny, and so on).

2. Using a hand lens, closely examine each plant sample. Look for differences as well as similarities between the plant samples. Record these observations in your data table.

3. Gently bend a leaf from each plant to determine how flexible the leaf is. If the leaf bends quite easily without snapping, then it is flexible. If the leaf is stiff, it may be difficult to bend, or it may snap while you are trying to bend it. Record this information in your table.

4. Carefully prepare a wet mount slide of epidermal tissue from each plant. For some plants, you may be able to tear the leaf at an angle, and then "peel" the leaf apart gently by hand. For others, it will be easier to cut the leaf at an angle with a razor tool. Be very cautious using razors, always cut away from yourself. Forceps may also be helpful for peeling off layers of tissue.

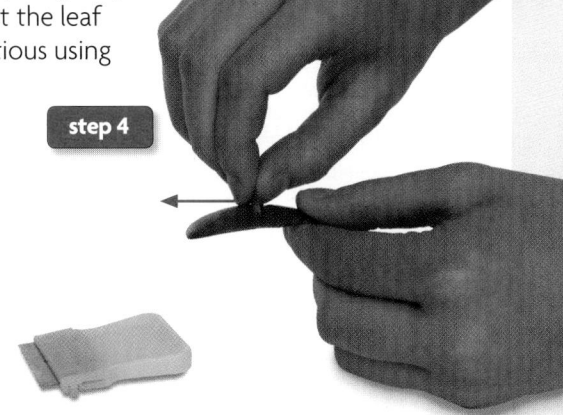

step 4

5. Examine the epidermal tissue under a microscope. Pay close attention to differences between the plant samples. Record your observations for each slide.

ANALYZE AND CONCLUDE

1. **Analyze** What visible characteristics do these plants share? What characteristics are unique for each plant?

2. **Analyze** How is the epidermal tissue from each plant different?

3. **Infer** Based on your observations, what conclusions can you make about the natural habitat of each plant?

4. **Infer** How are stiff leaves and flexible leaves adapted for different habitats?

5. **Apply** Describe a characteristic of a plant that lives in the same area that you do. How might this characteristic help the plant to survive in its habitat?

EXTEND YOUR INVESTIGATION

Research the adaptations of plants that live in one of the following types of environments: aquatic, acidic, or salty.

20.3 Diversity of Flowering Plants

KEY CONCEPT The largest phylum in the plant kingdom is the flowering plants.

▶ MAIN IDEAS

- Flowering plants have unique adaptations that allow them to dominate in today's world.
- Botanists classify flowering plants into two groups based on seed type.
- Flowering plants are also categorized by stem type and lifespan.

VOCABULARY

cotyledon, p. 625
monocot, p. 626
dicot, p. 626
wood, p. 627

Review
fruit, flower, pollination, pollen, lignin

MICHIGAN STANDARDS

B2.4B Describe how various organisms have developed different specializations to accomplish a particular function and yet the end result is the same (e.g., excreting nitrogenous wastes in animals, obtaining oxygen for respiration).

Connecting CONCEPTS

Evolution Recall from **Chapter 11** that mammals also went through a period of adaptive radiation after the mass extinction that killed the dinosaurs 65 million years ago.

FIGURE 20.14 Many trees, including dogwoods, are flowering plants.

Connect Sunflower seeds in the shell aren't just a tasty snack. They are an example of one of the great adaptations of flowering plants. Like all flowering plants, sunflowers produce fruits. Technically, the fruit is the shell surrounding the sunflower seed. As you will soon learn, fruits can take many forms beyond the juicy apple or peach that first comes to mind.

▶ MAIN IDEA

Flowering plants have unique adaptations that allow them to dominate in today's world.

Up until about 65 million years ago, there were far fewer flowering plants than there are today. After the mass extinction event that ended the Cretaceous period, the fossil record reveals that a major shift took place in species that dominated the Earth. Dinosaurs disappeared, as did many seedless plant species. These plant extinctions left open niches into which flowering plants, such as the dogwoods in **FIGURE 20.14**, could radiate and prosper. Their diversification happened quickly in geologic terms and was closely tied to the diversification of land animals such as insects and birds. The same adaptations that were important to the success of flowering plants long ago continue to be important today.

Flowers and Pollination

Flowers allow for more efficient pollination than occurs in most gymnosperms, which rely on wind for pollination. You have probably observed a bee or a butterfly hovering around the center of a flower. These insects and other animals feed on pollen, which is high in protein, or on nectar, a sugary solution produced in the flowers of some plant species. As an animal feeds from a flower, it gets pollen on itself. Then, when it moves to another flower for more food, some of the pollen brushes off onto the new flower. Thus, animal pollinators transfer pollen from flower to flower in a very targeted way. For this reason, flowering plants pollinated by animals don't need to produce nearly as much pollen as do plants that rely on the wind to randomly transfer their pollen.

FIGURE 20.15 Adaptations of Flowering Plants

Flowers and fruits are unique adaptations of all flowering plants.

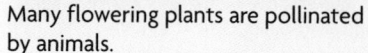
Many flowering plants are pollinated by animals.

Fruits protect the seeds of flowering plants and often play a role in seed dispersal.

Synthesize How is each photograph showing a coevolutionary relationship?

Fruits and Seed Dispersal

The many types of fruits include some very unlike the kinds you see in a grocery store. In biological terms, a fruit is a flower's ripened ovary, which surrounds and protects the seed or seeds. For example, the shells of sunflower seeds and peanuts are fruits. Fruit play an important role in seed dispersal. As shown in **FIGURE 20.15**, the more familiar fleshy fruits are tasty food sources for animals, which digest the fruit tissue but not the seeds. Seeds pass through the animal, and are deposited along with a convenient supply of fecal fertilizer that is helpful during germination. Others take the form of burrs that cling to passing wildlife, or fibers that help spread seeds by wind. You will learn more about flowers, fruits, and seed dispersal in Chapter 22.

Infer Why is pollination by animals more efficient than wind pollination?

⏵ MAIN IDEA

Botanists classify flowering plants into two groups based on seed type.

There are at least 250,000 identified flowering plant species. Compared with other living plant phyla—the three gymnosperm phyla have a total of 720 species—the number of flowering plants is impressive.

Botanists classify flowering plants into two groups based on two basic kinds of seed: seeds with one or two cotyledons. A **cotyledon** (KAHT-uhl-EED-uhn) is an embryonic leaf inside a seed. For this reason, cotyledons are often called "seed leaves." As an embryo develops into a seedling, the seed leaf of some species remains inside the seed coat. In other species, cotyledons break out of the seed and turn green.

FIGURE 20.16 Monocots and Dicots

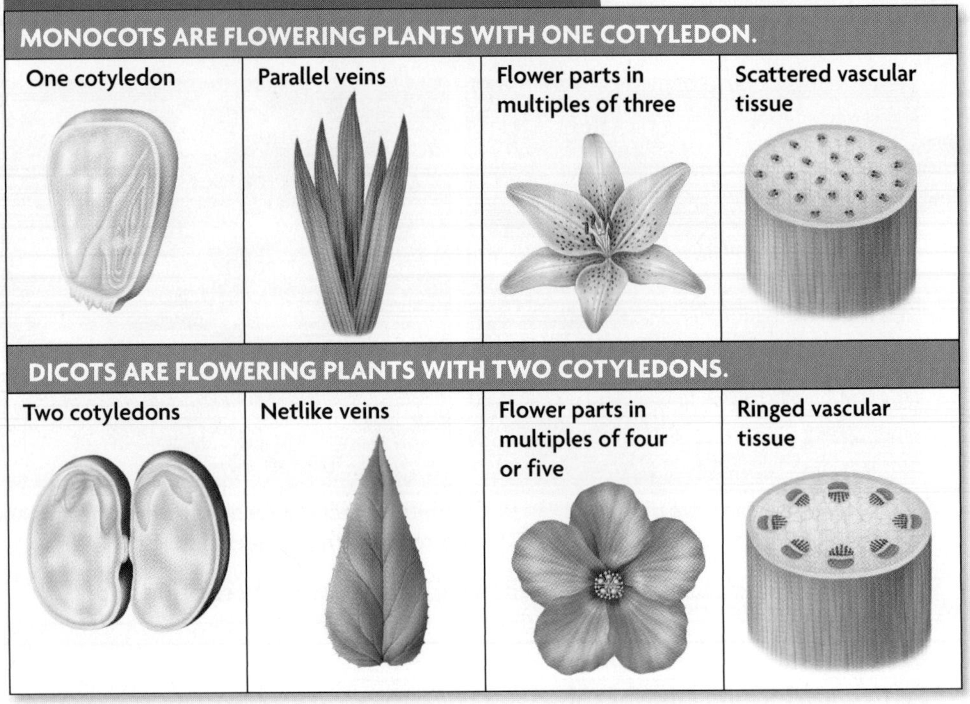

MONOCOTS ARE FLOWERING PLANTS WITH ONE COTYLEDON.

One cotyledon	Parallel veins	Flower parts in multiples of three	Scattered vascular tissue

DICOTS ARE FLOWERING PLANTS WITH TWO COTYLEDONS.

Two cotyledons	Netlike veins	Flower parts in multiples of four or five	Ringed vascular tissue

VOCABULARY

Mono- and *di-* are prefixes meaning "one" and "two." *Cot* is a shortened form of the word *cotyledon.* Therefore, monocots have one cotyledon and dicots have two.

Monocots

Flowering plants whose embryos have one seed leaf are called monocotyledons, or **monocots** (MAHN-uh-KAHTS). As **FIGURE 20.16** shows, monocot plants generally have parallel veins in long, narrow leaves, such as those of an iris or lily. Their flower parts usually occur in multiples of three, and bundles of vascular tissues are scattered throughout the stem. The cereal plants we depend on—corn, wheat, rice—are monocots, as are all other grasses, irises, and lilies.

Dicots

Dicotyledons, or **dicots** (DY-KAHTS), are flowering plants whose embryos have two seed leaves. In contrast to monocots, dicots have leaves with netlike veins. Flower parts in dicots usually occur in multiples of four or five, and bundles of vascular tissue are arranged in rings. Most deciduous trees, which lose their leaves in the fall, are dicots. Peanuts are also dicots. Each "half" of a peanut that has been removed from its shell is a cotyledon.

Predict Would you expect that cotyledons are green inside a seed? Explain.

◯▶ MAIN IDEA
Flowering plants are also categorized by stem type and lifespan.

Flowering plants can also be categorized by stem type and lifespan, as shown in **FIGURE 20.17**. These characteristics help describe mature flowering plants and are commonly used by botanists, gardeners, landscape designers, and horticulturists.

Iris Monocot, herbaceous, perennial

Wheat Monocot, herbaceous, annual

Foxglove Dicot, herbacious, biennial

Oak Dicot, woody, perennial

Big bluestem Monocot, herbaceous, perennial

Herbaceous or Woody Stems

Some flowering plants develop woody stems, while others do not. **Wood** is a fibrous material made up of dead cells that are part of the vascular system of some plants. High concentrations of lignin and cellulose make the cell walls of these cells thick and stiff. Woody plants therefore have stiff stems and branches. Wood also accounts for the thickness of many woody plant stems. Trees, shrubs, and most vines have woody stems. Plants that do not produce wood, such as cucumbers, cacti, and marigolds, are called herbaceous plants.

Three Types of Lifespans

It is also helpful for gardeners to classify plants in terms of their lifespans, since lifespan determines which plants they need to replace each year.

- **Annual** Flowering plants that mature from seeds, produce flowers, and die all in one year are called annuals. Corn and lettuce are common annuals, as are some garden flowers such as zinnias.
- **Biennial** Flowering plants that take two years to complete their life cycle are called biennials. During the first year, a biennial produces a short stem, leaves that grow close to the ground, and underground food reserves. During the second year, these reserves are used to produce a taller stem, leaves, flowers, and seeds. Carrots are common biennial garden plants.
- **Perennial** Any flowering plant that lives for more than two years is a perennial. Most woody plants, including trees, are perennials. The stems and leaves of some herbaceous perennials, such as some grasses and dandelions, die at the end of the fall and grow back in the spring.

Contrast How do the lifespans of annuals, biennials, and perennials differ?

FIGURE 20.17 Flowering plants are the largest and most diverse of the plant phyla. They are commonly categorized according to seed type, stem type, and lifespan.

NSTA SCILINKS
scilinks.org
To learn more about flowering plants, visit scilinks.org.
Keycode: MLB020

20.3 ASSESSMENT

ONLINE QUIZ ClassZone.com

REVIEWING ▶ MAIN IDEAS

1. What adaptations give flowering plants a reproductive advantage over gymnosperms?
2. What are the primary differences between **monocots** and **dicots**?
3. Name three ways in which flowering plants can be categorized.

CRITICAL THINKING

4. **Contrast** In what ways does pollination in gymnosperms differ from pollination in angiosperms?
5. **Apply** How would you take plant lifespan type into account when planning a garden?

Connecting CONCEPTS

6. **Mass Extinctions** The fossil record reveals a mass extinction at the end of the Cretaceous period. Discuss why mass extinctions are commonly followed by a period of adaptive radiation, in this case, of flowering plants.

Measures of Central Tendency

One way to analyze data is to use measures of **central tendency,** which are measures that indicate the center of a data set. The three most common measures of central tendency are the mean, median, and mode. It is often helpful to look at all three of these measures because they may each point out different characteristics of a data set.

The **mean** is calculated by adding all of the data points together and dividing by the number of data points. The mean considers the full range of data, and is therefore affected by **outliers**—data points that vary greatly from all of the other points in the data set.

The **median** is the data point that falls in the middle when all of the data points are ordered from least to greatest. If there is an even number of data points, the median is the average of the two middle numbers. Since outliers do not affect the median, this may be a good measure to use with a data set that includes outliers.

The **mode** is the value that occurs most frequently. It is not affected by outliers. Some data sets have more than one mode. If there are several modes that dominate the data set, it is a good idea to study these data points more closely.

EXAMPLES

A class counted the number of seeds found in some common fruits. These data are shown in Table 1.

- **Oranges** The mean is an appropriate measure to use for this data set because there are no obvious outliers.
- **Watermelons** The mean is affected by an outlier, 582 seeds. The median is a good measure to represent this data set.
- **Apples** The two modes represent a trend in these results that the students may want to investigate further.

TABLE 1. NUMBER OF SEEDS IN VARIOUS FRUIT

Fruit	Number of Seeds per Fruit	Mean	Median	Mode
Oranges	14, 6, 10, 8, 4, 11, 6, 3, 5, 13	8	7	6
Watermelons	582, 133, 207, 87, 164, 290, 98, 155, 196, 278	219	180	none
Apples	6, 7, 6, 4, 4, 4, 3, 6, 4, 6	5	5	4 and 6
Strawberries	171, 208, 230, 171, 159, 182, 217, 238, 165, 179	?	?	?

CHOOSE AN APPROPRIATE MEASURE OF CENTRAL TENDENCY

Use the data for the number of seeds counted in each of 10 strawberries to answer the questions below.

1. **Calculate** Find the mean, median, and mode for this set of data.
2. **Evaluate** Which measure of central tendency best represents this data set? Why?

20.4 Plants in Human Culture

KEY CONCEPTS Humans rely on plants in many ways.

▶ MAIN IDEAS

- Agriculture provides stable food supplies for people in permanent settlements.
- Plant products are important economic resources.
- Plant compounds are essential to modern medicine.

VOCABULARY

botany, p. 629
ethnobotany, p. 629
pharmacology, p. 631
alkaloid, p. 631

MICHIGAN STANDARDS

L3.p4A Recognize that, and describe how, human beings are part of Earth's ecosystems. Note that human activities can deliberately or inadvertently alter the equilibrium in ecosystems. (prerequisite)

VOCABULARY

Ethnobotany comes from the Greek words *ethnos*, which means "people," and *botanē*, which means "plants."

Connect Books are made from plants. The pages are pulverized wood from trees, the ink contains plant oil, and the glue that binds them together is made from petroleum—the ancient leftovers of algae and plants. Humans rely on plants for nearly everything in daily life. Today, crop plants are so important to our economy that their changing prices are reported in the media alongside those of stocks and bonds.

▶ MAIN IDEA

Agriculture provides stable food supplies for people in permanent settlements.

Some of the plants that are considered important by humans have changed over time, but plants have always been used to fill the basic needs of our species: food, shelter, clothing, and medicine. While **botany** is the study of plants, **ethnobotany** explores how people in different cultures use plants.

For most of human history, people survived by hunting and gathering. This requires a very thorough understanding of local botany—plant locations, life cycles, and characteristics. Hunting and gathering also requires people to change locations if resources are diminished by weather, disease, or overuse. People then must become familiar with the resources of the new area.

FIGURE 20.18 Agriculture has become an important part of our global economy. Many river deltas, such as the Sacramento River delta in California, are used for farmland because of their nutrient-rich soils and water.

Teosinte

Modern corn

FIGURE 20.19 An ear of teosinte, the ancestor of modern corn, is shown along with a kernel of modern corn (top). Modern corn evolved through artificial selection. Humans likely selected individual plants that had the most numerous and accessible seeds.

Archaeological evidence suggests that people started intentionally planting for harvest about 10,000 years ago. Over the centuries, ancient farmers "tamed" wild species by a process of artificial selection, as shown in **FIGURE 20.19.** They chose plants with the best traits, saved their seeds, and planted them the next year. Most of the world's staple foods—corn, rice, and wheat—were developed from wild grasses in this way. These farmers became more closely tied to particular areas.

Because farming requires people to stay in one place, agriculture gave rise to more socially complex centers of human populations. A benefit of farming was a more reliable source of food that could support a growing population. Eventually, farmers grew enough excess food to sell it to neighbors as a cash crop. In this way, farming became part of a culture's economy.

Summarize **What does an ethnobotanist study?**

▶ MAIN IDEA
Plant products are important economic resources.

Plant products have been traded among various regions for thousands of years. Spices such as pepper, cinnamon, and cloves were so valuable that they were commonly used as a form of currency during the early Middle Ages. In fact, many of the seafaring explorations to Asia and the Americas during the 1400s and 1500s were prompted by the value of spices, like those shown in **FIGURE 20.20.** Among these explorers, Columbus, Magellan, and da Gama were all in search of a new route to the valuable commodities of the East.

Today, plants are important economic resources on a global scale. The values of rice, corn, wheat, soybeans, coffee, sugar, cotton, and forest products traded in world markets every year are each billions of dollars. Paper, textiles, and lumber are just a few of the plant-derived products that are the basis of industries contributing to our economy.

Connect **What plants were used to make the clothes that you are wearing and the contents of your backpack?**

FIGURE 20.20 Spices have been an economically important resource for at least 4000 years.

⊙ MAIN IDEA
Plant compounds are essential to modern medicine.

The study of drugs and their effects on the body is called **pharmacology.** Many of the drugs used today are derived from plants, and much of the knowledge of these plants comes from traditional cultures. We still use some plants medicinally in the same way they have been used for thousands of years. For instance, the aloe vera gel you can buy to soothe sunburn was used for the same purpose by the Egyptians 3500 years ago.

As shown in **FIGURE 20.21**, scientists continue to look for and find new uses for plants that have been used medicinally for centuries. For example, Native Americans have long used the Pacific yew to treat a variety of conditions. In the 1960s, scientists isolated a compound called taxol from the tree, which has been used as a cancer treatment since 1993. Salicin, which comes from willow trees, is another plant compound that you are likely familiar with. It is the active ingredient in aspirin, the most widely used medicine in the world.

While plant oils and resins are common in traditional medicines, other plant compounds, including gums, steroids, and alkaloids, have found their way into modern medicines. **Alkaloids** are potent plant chemicals that contain nitrogen. In small amounts, many alkaloids are medicinal. By interfering with cell division, some alkaloids—such as taxol—have anti-cancer properties. Two alkaloids produced by the Madagascar periwinkle are used to treat childhood leukemia and Hodgkin's disease. Other alkaloids have been identified to treat conditions ranging from a nasty cough to high blood pressure.

Today, much medical research focuses on the chemical properties of various plant compounds—especially compounds from plants that have been used medicinally in traditional cultures. Chemists also work to develop synthetic drugs based on the structure of these natural compounds, often changing the structures slightly to increase effectiveness and reduce side effects.

Infer Why might certain plant compounds have healing effects in small quantities but be dangerous in larger doses?

FIGURE 20.21 This scientist, standing waist-high in water, is studying a mangrove forest in Thailand. Mangrove forests grow in intertidal zones in the tropics. These diverse ecosystems may hold treatments for a variety of medical conditions.

Connecting CONCEPTS

Cells Some alkaloids help stop the spread of cancer by interfering with mitosis. Recall from **Chapter 5** that mitosis is the phase of the cell cycle when the duplicated chromosomes separate so that two new cells form.

20.4 ASSESSMENT

ONLINE QUIZ
ClassZone.com

REVIEWING ⊙ MAIN IDEAS

1. How has agriculture affected the day-to-day life of humans?

2. In what ways are plants an important part of our culture today?

3. Why is a knowledge of plants so important to **pharmacology**?

CRITICAL THINKING

4. **Analyze** How did the average person's knowledge of plants change in societies that adopted agriculture? Explain your answer.

5. **Connect** Aside from food and medicine, in what ways are plants used in your life?

Connecting CONCEPTS

6. **Human Impact on Ecosystems** Many plants harvested for medicinal purposes grow in rain forests of developing countries. How might this fact affect the ecosystems and economies of these countries?

Use these inquiry-based labs and online activities to deepen your understanding of plant diversity.

INVESTIGATION

Comparing Monocots and Dicots

Several characteristics can be used to distinguish between monocots and dicots. In this activity, you will use these characteristics to classify plants as either monocots or dicots.

MATERIALS
- 2–4 plant samples
- razor tool
- dissecting microscope

SKILLS Observing, Classifying

PROBLEM Is the plant that you are observing a monocot or a dicot?

PROCEDURE

1. Select a plant to classify.
2. Draw a detailed illustration of the plant, including stem, leaves, and flower (if present). Save space to add labels and observations.
3. Examine the leaves of the plant. Draw a sketch of the vein pattern.
4. If the plant has a flower, record the number of petals on your drawing.
5. Using a razor tool, carefully cut off a very thin cross-section of the stem. Examine the cross-section of the stem under a dissecting microscope. Draw what you see next to the stem in your drawing. Record whether the vascular bundles are arranged in a simple ring or several rings, or if they are more scattered throughout the stem cross-section.
6. Record whether the plant has wood or bark.
7. Compare your observations with the characteristics listed in Table 1. Based on this information, classify the plant as a monocot or a dicot, and label it in your drawing.
8. Repeat steps 1–7 for each plant sample.

TABLE 1. CHARACTERISTICS OF MONOCOTS AND DICOTS	
Monocots	**Dicots**
Veins in leaves are parallel.	Veins in leaves are netlike.
Flower parts are usually in multiples of 3.	Flower parts are usually in multiples of 4 or 5.
Vascular bundles in stem are scattered.	Vascular bundles in stem form a ring.
Wood and bark are not common.	Wood and bark are common.

ANALYZE AND CONCLUDE

1. **Analyze** Which characteristics do you think were the easiest to use in classifying the plants as monocots or dicots?
2. **Analyze** List the plants that you were able to classify, and include whether you identified them as monocots or dicots.
3. **Apply** Why do you think that botanists rely on the number of cotyledons to classify flowering plants, rather than using a characteristic such as number of flower parts?

MICHIGAN STANDARDS

B2.4A Explain that living things can be classified based on structural, embryo-logical, and molecular (relatedness of DNA sequence) evidence.

B2.4d Analyze the relationships among organisms based on their shared physical, biochemical, genetic, and cellular character-istics and functional processes.

INVESTIGATION

Investigating Medicinal Plants

Rain forests have great biodiversity, and botanists frequently discover new plants in these ecosystems. One important area of research involves testing the chemical properties of these plants for medical purposes. You have learned that chemicals from the Madagascar periwinkle are used to treat childhood leukemia and Hodgkin's disease. Chemicals from another plant, *Forsteronia refracta,* have been found to stop the growth of breast cancer cells. Each time a new plant is discovered, there is a possibility of finding a new treatment or cure.

SKILL Researching

PROBLEM What medicinal qualities can be found in rain forest plants?

RESEARCH

1. Find another example of a rain forest plant that is being used to produce pharmaceuticals.
2. Record the scientific and common names of the plant.
3. What disease or condition is this plant used to treat?
4. What chemical qualities of the plant make it an effective treatment?
5. Are there any problems associated with harvesting this plant?
6. Why do you think so many medicinal plants are discovered in the rain forests of the world, rather than in other biomes?

The Madagascar periwinkle contains two alkaloids, vinblastine and vincristine, which have been isolated and developed into anti-cancer drugs.

Online BIOLOGY
CLASSZONE.COM

ANIMATED BIOLOGY
Plant and Pollinator Matching Game
What pollinates a saguaro cactus? Examine the adaptive features of flowers and animals, and use them as clues to determine which animal pollinates a particular plant.

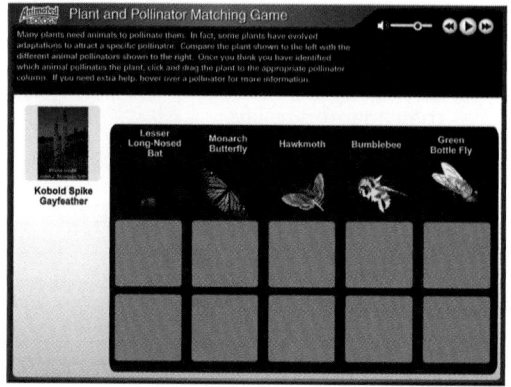

WEBQUEST
When you think of endangered species, you may think of animals. In this WebQuest, you will explore one of more than 700 plant species that are threatened or endangered in the United States. Learn about a plant in your state that is protected by the Endangered Species Act. Explore the threats to the plant and determine how to keep an essential producer from going extinct.

BIOZINE
Stories about plants—such as "Compound in Tropical Plant Used to Treat Cancer" and "Transgenic Corn Boasts Higher Yields, Greater Controversy"—are often in the headlines. Get the latest news about botany in the BioZine.

20.1 Origins of Plant Life

Plant life began in the water and became adapted to land. The common ancestor of plants is an ancient species of green algae. Green algae called charophyceans are the closest living relatives to this common ancestor. Over time, the first true plant species evolved as they adapted to life on land. Land plants have evolved mechanisms to retain moisture, transport resources, grow upright, and reproduce on land. They have also coevolved with other organisms that inhabit dry land.

20.2 Classification of Plants

Plants can be classified into nine phyla. Mosses and their relatives make up three phyla of seedless nonvascular plants. These plants rely on water for reproduction and must grow low to the ground to absorb water and nutrients. Club mosses and ferns make up two phyla of seedless vascular plants. Vascular tissue allows these plants to grow higher above the ground. Seed plants, which include three phyla of cone-bearing plants and one phylum of flowering plants, do not rely on water for reproduction. Sperm of seed plants are produced by pollen grains. Seeds nourish and protect the embryos of these plants.

20.3 Diversity of Flowering Plants

The largest phylum in the plant kingdom is the flowering plants. Flowers and fruit are two adaptations that have allowed flowering plants to become the dominant plant group on Earth today. Flowers often allow for more efficient pollination by animals, while fruit can aid in seed dispersal. Botanists classify flowering plants into two groups based on the number of cotyledons inside the seed. Flowering plants can also be categorized based on stem type and lifespan.

20.4 Plants in Human Culture

Humans rely on plants in many ways. Plants are essential to human existence. All of the food that we eat comes either directly or indirectly from plant life. Agriculture provides stable food supplies for most people today. Many agricultural products are important economic resources on a global scale. Plants also provide us with clothing, paper, textiles, lumber, and medicines.

Synthesize Your Notes

Three-Column Chart Use a three-column chart to take notes about the nine divisions of plants. Use the columns to write the scientific names of each division, the common names, and details about the plants.

Scientific Name	Common Name	Details

Concept Map Use a concept map to review how flowering plants can be classified.

flowering plants

can be classified by

which can be · which can be · which can be

Chapter Assessment

Chapter Vocabulary

20.1 plant, p. 612
  cuticle, p. 614
  stomata, p. 614
  vascular system, p. 614
  lignin, p. 614
  pollen grain, p. 614
  seed, p. 614

20.2 pollination, p. 620
  gymnosperm, p. 621
  angiosperm, p. 621
  cone, p. 621
  flower, p. 622
  fruit, p. 622

20.3 cotyledon, p. 625
  monocot, p. 626
  dicot, p. 626
  wood, p. 627

20.4 botany, p. 629
  ethnobotany, p. 629
  pharmacology, p. 631
  alkaloid, p. 631

Reviewing Vocabulary

Vocabulary Connections

For each group of words below, write a sentence or two to clearly explain how the terms are connected. For example, for the terms *cuticle* and *stomata,* you could write "Together, the cuticle and stomata prevent water loss while allowing for gas exchange."

1. lignin, wood
2. pollen grain, pollination
3. gymnosperm, seed, cone
4. angiosperm, seed, flower, fruit
5. cotyledon, monocot, dicot
6. pharmacology, alkaloid

Greek and Latin Word Origins

7. *Cuticula* is the Latin word for "skin." How does this meaning relate to the definition of *cuticle?*

8. In Greek, the word *stoma* means "mouth." How does this meaning relate to its botanical meaning?

9. In Latin, the word *pollen* means "dust" or "fine flour." How does this meaning relate to its botanical meaning?

10. *Conus* is a Latin word that means "wedge" or "peak." How does this meaning relate to the definition of *cone?*

11. *Fruī* is a Latin verb meaning "to enjoy." How does this meaning relate to the role that various fruits play in human culture?

12. The prefix *mono-* means "one" in Latin, while the prefix *di-* means "two." How do these meanings relate to the words *monocot* and *dicot?*

Reviewing MAIN IDEAS

13. Summarize the evidence supporting the statement that modern plants evolved from an ancient species of green algae.

14. Discuss four major challenges that early plants faced while adapting to life on dry land.

15. The 30-centimeter tongue of the hawk moth is long enough to reach the nectar—and reproductive organs—of the night-blooming orchid. What can be concluded about the evolution of plants from these types of relationships? Explain.

16. Describe the structural features that limit the height of mosses and their relatives.

17. Explain why most seedless vascular plants live in moist environments.

18. What is the main difference between the seeds of cone-bearing plants and the seeds of flowering plants?

19. Summarize two of the adaptations of flowering plants that allow them to flourish in today's world.

20. Describe the system that botanists use to classify flowering plants into two main groups.

21. Compare and contrast annual, biennial, and perennial lifespans.

22. What role does agriculture play in the stability and survival of modern human populations?

23. How can plants play a role in developing modern medicines, even if they are not used as ingredients?

24. Analyze Aquatic plants, which evolved from land plants, have adaptations that allow them to live in the water. Some aquatic plants grow completely submerged in water. What challenges might these plants face that do not apply to plants that live entirely on land?

25. Analyze The sperm of seedless plants are flagellated, while those of seed plants are not. How do the sperm of seed plants reach eggs without flagella?

26. Compare When a plant reproduces, it is important for its offspring to disperse so that they do not compete directly with the parent plant. Compare the structures that allow seedless plants and seed plants to disperse to new locations.

27. Synthesize Some experts predict that the Amazon rain forest will be completely destroyed due to human activities within the next century. What resources would potentially be lost along with this ecosystem?

28. Infer Some types of flowers have special markings on their petals that act as guides to the pollen or nectar for their pollinators. How could such markings have evolved through natural selection?

29. Analyze What evolutionary advantage do the seeds of dandelions have over the seeds of pine trees?

30. Synthesize How might an increase in the use of insecticides affect flowering-plant populations in the area?

Interpreting Visuals

Use the illustration below to answer the next two questions.

31. Analyze What parts of this plant could you examine to determine whether it is a monocot or a dicot?

32. Apply Is this plant likely a monocot or a dicot? Explain your reasoning.

Analyzing Data

Valencia oranges, which likely originated in Spain or Portugal, are now the most widely planted orange variety in the world. Use the data below on the number of California Valencia oranges per tree to answer the next three questions.

CALIFORNIA VALENCIA ORANGES PER TREE
596, 402, 489, 708, 374, 548, 640, 585, 518, 450

Source: California Agricultural Statistics Service

33. Calculate What are the mean, median, and mode for this data set? Round the mean to the nearest whole number.

34. Analyze Does this data set contain outliers? Explain your answer.

35. Evaluate Which measure of central tendency best represents this data set? Explain your answer.

Connecting CONCEPTS

36. Write About Seeds From the viewpoint of a plant embryo, write about the importance of a seed. What does the seed provide for you? In what ways does it help you? What advantages do you have over nonseed plants?

37. Synthesize The flowering proteas of South Africa are adapted to a dry climate that receives as little as 600 mm of rain each year. However, plants must retain moisture in order for photosynthesis to occur. Describe the adaptations that allow these plants to retain moisture in their leaves while still allowing for air to move in and out.

MICHIGAN
STANDARDS-BASED ASSESSMENT

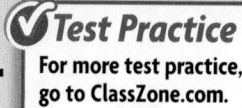

✓**Test Practice**
For more test practice,
go to ClassZone.com.

1. In the 1940s, Barbara McClintock observed patterns of inheritance in corn plants that could not be explained by the current gene theory. The conclusions of her work were not widely accepted for many years until further supported by the work of other scientists. What does this scenario demonstrate about science? **B1.1B**

   A Data that are more than 50 years old should be discarded.

   B Data that do not fit a scientific theory should be discarded.

   C Theories may be modified as additional data lead to new conclusions.

   D The repetition of results by many scientists is not necessary to validate a theory.

2. Many wind-pollinated flowers are small and green, with male reproductive structures that hang outside the flower where wind can easily pick up and carry the pollen. Which is likely to also be true for wind-pollinated flowers? **B5.1e**

   A Colorful petals would not be an advantage.

   B Sweet-smelling petals would be an advantage.

   C They produce less pollen than other flowers.

   D They can thrive in any environment.

3.

Tomato Plant Growth Per Week (cm)		
Plot	Condition	Average Growth
1	full sun	9 cm
2	part sun	7 cm
3	full shade	2 cm

   Gardeners are testing three plots of land with similar soil to find out which is best for growing tomato plants. Which of the following conclusions is *best* supported by their data? **B1.1.E**

   A Plot 1 received the most nutrients.

   B Plot 3 did not receive enough water.

   C Tomato plants grow best in full sun.

   D Tomato plants cannot grow in the shade.

4. The sugar in corn is rapidly converted to starch after the corn has been picked. After picking, corn with the *Sh2* gene was found to have more sugar and less starch than corn without this gene. Which of the following statements is *most* likely to be true about corn with this gene? **B2.5g**

   A It cannot convert sugar to starch.

   B It cannot photosynthesize.

   C It has no chloroplasts.

   D It has no chlorophyll.

> **THINK THROUGH THE QUESTION**
>
> Think about the process by which plants produce sugars. You can eliminate any answer choices that would result in plants with less sugar.

5. The beak shape shown here likely evolved through a process in which birds that could get food most efficiently **L3.p2D**

   A died in the absence of long, tubular flowers.

   B did not have time to find mates.

   C shared food with other individuals.

   D were more likely to survive and reproduce.

6. Rock from the Cretaceous period contains the fossils of a wide variety of dinosaurs and seedless plants. The fossil record after the end of this period includes the fossils of many flowering plants and smaller animals, but no dinosaurs. Which of the following statements is supported by this evidence? **B3.5E**

   A Dinosaurs had begun to die out during the Cretaceous.

   B A mass extinction at the end of the Cretaceous made new niches available for flowering plants.

   C The Cretaceous environment was less favorable to seedless plants than to flowering plants.

   D Dinosaurs evolved around the end of the Cretaceous.

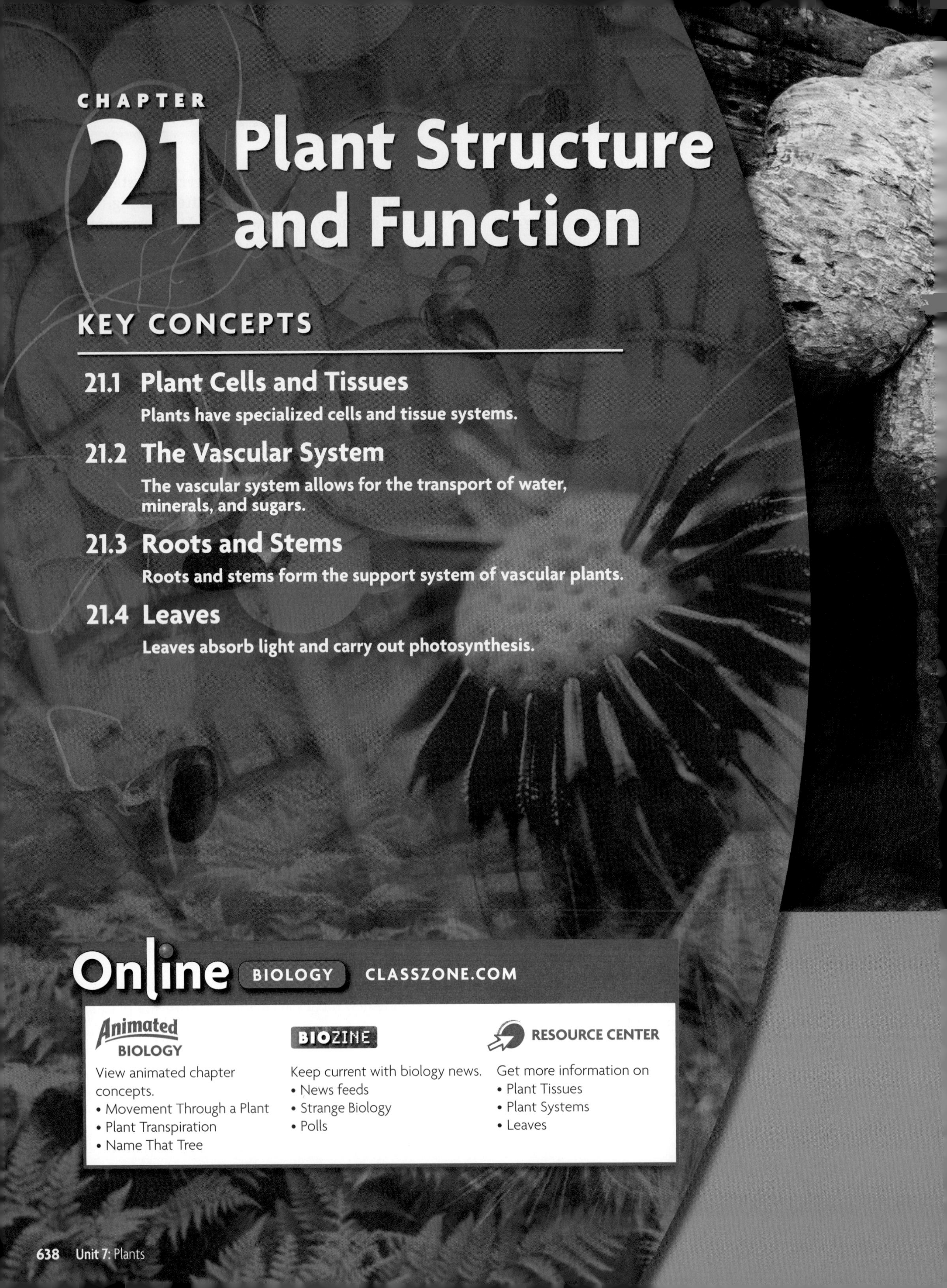

21 Plant Structure and Function

KEY CONCEPTS

21.1 Plant Cells and Tissues
Plants have specialized cells and tissue systems.

21.2 The Vascular System
The vascular system allows for the transport of water, minerals, and sugars.

21.3 Roots and Stems
Roots and stems form the support system of vascular plants.

21.4 Leaves
Leaves absorb light and carry out photosynthesis.

Online BIOLOGY CLASSZONE.COM

Animated BIOLOGY

View animated chapter concepts.
• Movement Through a Plant
• Plant Transpiration
• Name That Tree

BIOZINE

Keep current with biology news.
• News feeds
• Strange Biology
• Polls

RESOURCE CENTER

Get more information on
• Plant Tissues
• Plant Systems
• Leaves

How would this tree compete with other species?

Fig trees (*Ficus*) have a unique way of growing. Many trees of this genus are called strangler figs because their aggressive growth actually strangles other trees. Strangler figs can also wrap around unmoving objects such as these temple walls. Their seeds germinate easily in tree branches or building cracks, and then snakelike roots grow down to the ground.

Connecting CONCEPTS

Competition Besides strangling their host trees, figs can kill by outcompeting other plants for sunlight. Many tropical figs develop aerial roots that extend through the air from the branches to the ground. These roots are commonly called prop roots, and they allow the tree to spread outward for long distances. In fact, the tree canopy of a great banyan fig in Calcutta, India, covers three acres and has 1775 prop roots.

21.1 Plant Cells and Tissues

KEY CONCEPT Plants have specialized cells and tissue systems.

MAIN IDEAS

- Plant tissues are made of three basic cell types.
- Plant organs are made of three tissue systems.

VOCABULARY

parenchyma cell, p. 640
collenchyma cell, p. 640
sclerenchyma cell, p. 641
dermal tissue, p. 642
ground tissue, p. 642

vascular tissue, p. 642
xylem, p. 642
phloem, p. 642

Review
tissue, lignin, vascular system, cuticle

MICHIGAN STANDARDS

B2.5B Explain how major systems and processes work together in animals and plants, including relationships between organelles, cells, tissues, organs, organ systems, and organisms. Relate these to molecular functions.

B2.5f Relate plant structures and functions to the process of photosynthesis and respiration.

Connecting CONCEPTS

Cells Recall from **Chapter 3** that plant cells differ from animal cells in having cell walls, chloroplasts, and large vacuoles. Like animals, plants have different cell types.

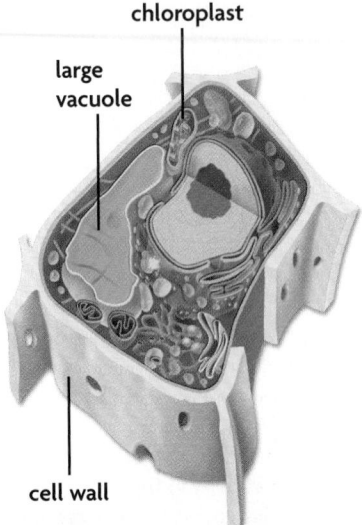

chloroplast

large vacuole

cell wall

Connect You already know that besides roots, plants have stems, or trunks, and leaves. But did you know that these parts are considered the organs of the plant? Just like other organisms, plants have organs that are made of tissues, and tissues that are made of cells. It is easy to remember: plants have three main organs, made up of three tissue systems, mostly made up of three basic cell types.

MAIN IDEA

Plant tissues are made of three basic cell types.

Plant cells are quite different from animal cells. In addition to all of the structures that animal cells have, plant cells have cell walls, plastids, and a large vacuole. Just as with animals, plants are made up of many types of cells that are organized into tissues. Three basic types of plant cells, shown in **FIGURE 21.1**, are parenchyma cells, collenchyma cells, and sclerenchyma cells.

Parenchyma Cells

A **parenchyma cell** (puh-REHNG-kuh-muh)—the most common type of plant cell—stores starch, oils, and water for the plant. You can find parenchyma cells throughout a plant. These cells have thin walls and large water-filled vacuoles in the middle. Photosynthesis occurs in green chloroplasts within parenchyma cells in leaves. Both chloroplasts and colorless plastids in parenchyma cells within roots and stems store starch. The flesh of many fruits we eat is also made of parenchyma cells. Parenchyma cells are sometimes thought of as the least specialized of plant cells, but they have one very special trait. They have the ability to divide throughout their entire lives, so they are important in healing wounds to the plant and regenerating parts. For example, parenchyma cells let you place stem cuttings of many types of plants in water to grow into a complete, new plant.

Collenchyma Cells

A **collenchyma cell** (kuh-LEHNG-kuh-muh) has cell walls that range from thin to thick, providing support while still allowing the plant to grow. These cells are most common in the younger tissues of leaves and shoots. They often form into strands. For example, celery strings are strands of collenchyma cells.

FIGURE 21.1 Basic Plant Cell Types

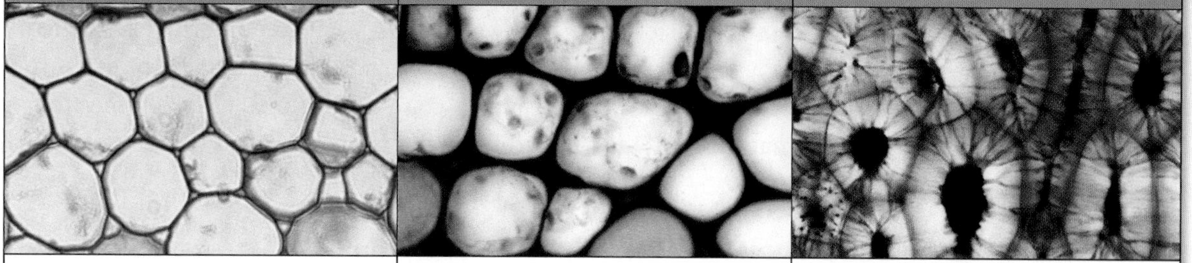

PARENCHYMA	COLLENCHYMA	SCLERENCHYMA
Parenchyma cells have thin and flexible cell walls that can change shape. (LM; magnification 160×)	Collenchyma cells have walls that range from thin to thick. (LM; magnification 250×)	Sclerenchyma cells have very thick and rigid walls that support the plant, even when the cells die. (LM; magnification 400×)

The unique feature of collenchyma cells is that they are flexible. Their cell walls don't contain lignin, so they are stretchy and can change size. As a young leaf grows, collenchyma cells can elongate and still give the leaf structure.

Sclerenchyma Cells

Of the three basic plant cell types, a **sclerenchyma cell** (skluh-REHNG-kuh-muh) is the strongest. These cells have a second cell wall that is hardened by lignin, which makes these cells very tough and durable. But the lignin also makes these cells very rigid. Unlike collenchyma cells, they can't grow with the plant. Therefore, sclerenchyma cells are found in parts of the plant that aren't lengthening anymore. Many sclerenchyma cells, such as those within the vascular system, die when they reach maturity. The cytoplasm and organelles of these dead cells disintegrate, but the rigid cell walls are left behind as skeletal support for the water-conducting tissues or for the plant itself. Sclerenchyma cells form a major part of fruit pits and the hard outer shells of nuts. They are also found in stems and leaf veins and are responsible for the gritty texture of pears. Humans use sclerenchyma cell fibers to make linen and rope.

TAKING NOTES

Make a three-column chart that organizes the relationship between plant cells, where they are found, and their function.

Cell Type	Where	Function
Parenchyma		

Contrast **How are the cell walls of parenchyma, collenchyma, and sclerenchyma cells different from one another?**

MAIN IDEA

Plant organs are made of three tissue systems.

Just as there are three basic types of plant cells, there are three groups of tissue systems in plants: dermal, ground, and vascular tissue systems. Recall from Chapter 5 that a tissue is a group of cells working together to perform a certain function. The tissue systems of plants may consist of simple tissues from the basic cell types: parenchyma, collenchyma, and sclerenchyma. They may also be made of complex tissues that have additional types of cells. Neighboring cells are often connected by plasmodesmata (PLAZ-muh-DEHZ-muh-tuh), strands of cytoplasm that pass through openings in cell walls and connect living cells. Through the plasmodesmata, cells of a plant tissue can share water, nutrients, and chemical signals.

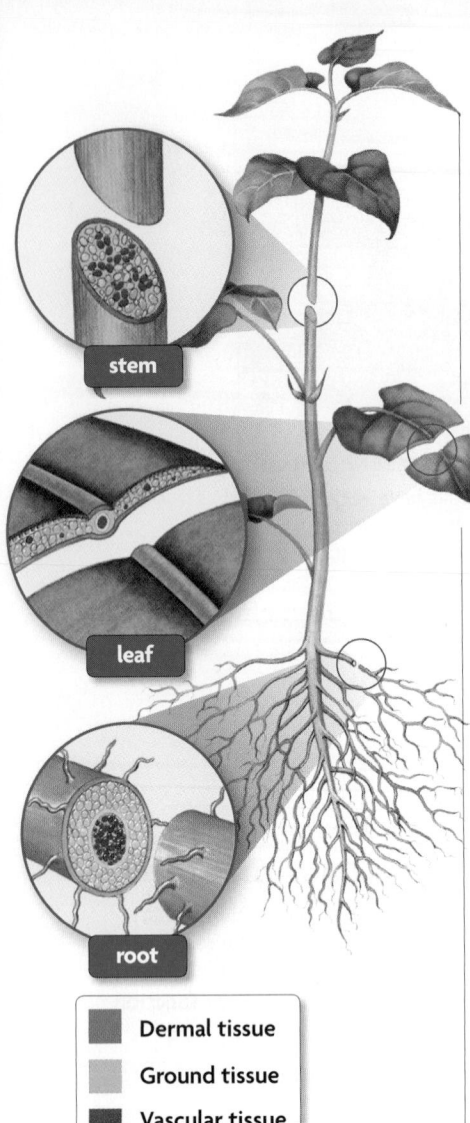

stem

leaf

root

■ Dermal tissue
■ Ground tissue
■ Vascular tissue

FIGURE 21.2 All three types of tissue systems are found throughout a plant.

Dermal Tissue System

Your body is covered with skin. Plants don't have skin, but they do have a system of **dermal tissue,** shown in **FIGURE 21.2,** that covers the outside of a plant and protects it in a variety of ways. Dermal tissue called epidermis is made up of live parenchyma cells in the nonwoody parts of plants. On leaves and some stems, epidermal cells may secrete a wax-coated substance that becomes the cuticle. Dermal tissue made of dead parenchyma cells makes up the outer bark of woody plants.

Ground Tissue System

Dermal tissue surrounds the system of **ground tissue,** which makes up much of the inside of a plant. Ground tissue provides support and stores materials in roots and stems. In leaves, ground tissue is packed with chloroplasts, where photosynthesis makes food for the plant. The ground tissue system consists of all three of the simple tissues—parenchyma tissue, collenchyma tissue, and sclerenchyma tissue—but parenchyma is by far the most common of the ground tissues. The ground tissue of cacti has many parenchyma cells that store water. However, the spines of cacti—which are actually modified leaves—contain mostly rigid sclerenchyma cells in their ground tissue.

Vascular Tissue System

Surrounded by ground tissue, the system of **vascular tissue** transports water, mineral nutrients, and organic compounds to all parts of the plant. Plants can transport necessary fluids and nutrients throughout their systems. A plant's vascular system is made up of two networks of hollow tubes somewhat like our veins and arteries. Each network consists of a different type of vascular tissue that works to move different resources throughout the plant. **Xylem** (ZY-luhm) is the vascular tissue that carries water and dissolved mineral nutrients up from the roots to the rest of the plant. **Phloem** (FLOH-EHM) is the vascular tissue that carries the products of photosynthesis through the plant. You will learn more about the vascular system in the next section.

Identify What tissue system contains the most photosynthesizing cells?

21.1 ASSESSMENT

ONLINE QUIZ
ClassZone.com

REVIEWING ▶ MAIN IDEAS

1. Describe three basic types of cells found within plants.
2. List two functions for each type of tissue system found in plants.

CRITICAL THINKING

3. **Connect** The **dermal tissue** system has been compared to human skin. In what ways does this analogy hold true?
4. **Compare** What structures in the human body provide a function similar to that of **sclerenchyma cells** in plants? Explain.

Connecting CONCEPTS

5. **Cell Biology** Plant cells have distinct differences from animal cells, such as cell walls, large vacuoles, and chloroplasts. How are these differences useful for a plant?

21.2 The Vascular System

KEY CONCEPT The vascular system allows for the transport of water, minerals, and sugars.

▶ MAIN IDEAS

- Water and dissolved minerals move through xylem.
- Phloem carries sugars from photo-synthesis throughout the plant.

VOCABULARY

cohesion-tension theory, p. 643
transpiration, p. 645
pressure-flow model, p. 645

Review
hydrogen bond, cohesion, adhesion, osmosis

MICHIGAN STANDARDS

B2.5B Explain how major systems and processes work together in animals and plants, including relationships between organelles, cells, tissues, organs, organ systems, and organisms. Relate these to molecular functions.
B2.5f Relate plant structures and functions to the process of photosynthesis and respiration.

Connect As you read this, your heart is pumping blood, which carries nutrients to your cells and removes wastes from them. In the world outside, fluids are also moving from tree roots all the way up to the highest leaves. But a tree has no heart to act as a pump. How can it move water up to a height of two, three, even ten stories?

▶ MAIN IDEA
Water and dissolved minerals move through xylem.

Recall that xylem is one of the two types of vascular tissue. Water and dissolved minerals move up from the roots to the rest of the plant through xylem. Xylem contains other types of cells besides the basic cell types. Because it contains other types of cells, xylem tissue is called a complex tissue.

One type of specialized cell in xylem is called a tracheid (TRAY-kee-ihd). Tracheid cells, shown in **FIGURE 21.3**, are long and narrow. Water can flow from cell to cell in tracheids through openings in the thick cell walls. Some types of vascular plants, including most flowering plants, have an additional kind of xylem cell called a vessel element. Vessel elements are shorter and wider than tracheids. Both types of cells mature and die before water moves through them. When a vessel element dies, the cell wall disintegrates at both ends. The cells then connect end to end, forming long tubes.

FIGURE 21.3 Xylem tissue consists of tracheids and vessel elements, conducting and supporting cells that lie end-to-end throughout xylem. Tracheid cells are narrow and long, while vessel elements are wider and shorter. (colored SEM; magnification 250× © Dr. Richard Kessel & Dr. Gene Shih/Visuals Unlimited)

Connecting CONCEPTS

Hydrogen Bonding Recall from **Chapter 2** that a hydrogen bond is an attraction between a slightly positive hydrogen atom and a slightly negative atom. Hydrogen bonds between water molecules produce a force called cohesion that helps water move through a plant.

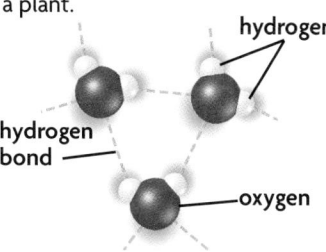
hydrogen
hydrogen bond
oxygen

Amazingly, plants don't use any metabolic energy to move water through xylem. So how do they do it? The **cohesion-tension theory** proposes that the physical properties of water allow the rise of water through a plant. This well-supported theory is based on the strong attraction of water molecules to one another and to other surfaces. The tendency of hydrogen bonds to form between water molecules creates a force called cohesion. However, water molecules are also attracted to the xylem wall due to adhesion, a force made by hydrogen bonds forming between water molecules and other substances. Cohesion and adhesion create tension that moves water upward in xylem.

FIGURE 21.4 Movement of Fluids Through Xylem

Forces responsible for the movement of fluids through xylem are transpiration, cohesion, adhesion, and absorption.

Animated BIOLOGY
See how materials move through a plant at ClassZone.com.

TRANSPIRATION

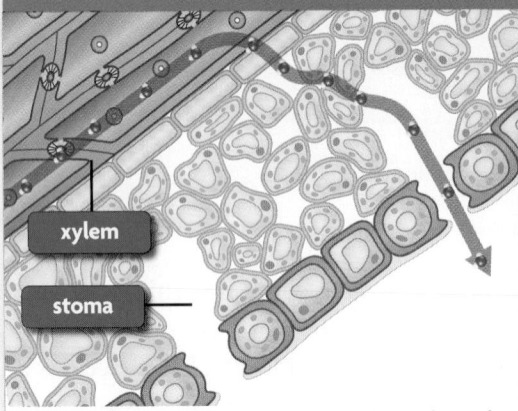

xylem

stoma

Transpiration is the evaporation of water through leaf stomata. It is the major force moving water through plants.

COHESION AND ADHESION

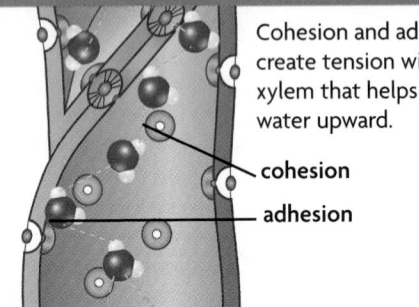

Cohesion and adhesion create tension within xylem that helps move water upward.

cohesion

adhesion

ABSORPTION

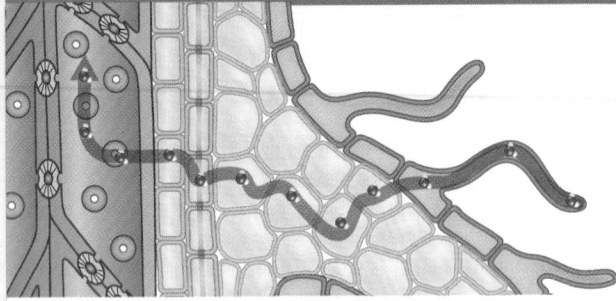

Water and dissolved minerals in the soil are pulled into roots through cell walls, through plasmodesmata (channels), or from cell to cell through their vacuoles.

water vapor

water

CRITICAL VIEWING What process is the main force for the movement of fluids through xylem? Explain.

To understand how cohesion and adhesion affect xylem flow, imagine you are inside the cylinder of a xylem vessel. In the middle, the water molecules float freely, attracted to each other. Toward the edges, though, the molecules are also drawn to the xylem wall. Where the water meets the wall, this attraction draws it upward a bit so that the actual shape of the water surface is slightly concave. You can see this shape if you fill a test tube with water. The tendency of water to rise in a hollow tube is known as capillary action. Capillary action causes water to rise above ground level in the xylem of plants.

For most plants, capillary action is not enough force to lift water to the top branches. Upward force is also provided by the evaporation of water from leaves. The loss of water vapor from plants is called **transpiration.** As leaves transpire, the outward flow of water lowers the pressure in the leaf xylem, creating a vacuum that pulls water upward. This force is responsible for most of the water flow in plants, including lifting water to the tops of trees. The movement of water through xylem is shown in **FIGURE 21.4.**

Apply **How does transpiration affect water movement through a plant?**

VOCABULARY

The term *cohesion* comes from the Latin prefix *co-,* which means "together," and the term *haerere,* which means "to cling."

▶ MAIN IDEA
Phloem carries sugars from photosynthesis throughout the plant.

The second tissue in a plant's vascular system is phloem tissue, shown in **FIGURE 21.5.** Phloem carries plant nutrients, including minerals and sugars, throughout the plant. Phloem moves the products of photosynthesis out of the leaves to stems and roots. Minerals that travel up the xylem can also move into the phloem through specialized parenchyma transfer cells in the leaves.

Unlike xylem, phloem tissue is alive. Phloem is a complex tissue made mostly of cells called sieve tube elements. Their name comes from the small holes in the end walls of their cells. These holes let the phloem fluids, or sap, flow through the plant. As they form, sieve tube elements lose their nuclei and ribosomes. Nutrients can then move from cell to cell. Each sieve tube element is next to a companion cell, and the two cells are connected by many plasmodesmata, or small channels. Because the companion cells keep all their organelles, they perform some functions for the mature sieve tube cells. In some plants, the companion cells help load sugars into the sieve tube cells.

Recall that fluids in xylem always flow away from the roots toward the rest of the plant. In contrast, phloem sap can move in any direction, depending on the plant's need. The **pressure-flow model** is a well-supported theory that explains how food, or sap, moves through a plant. Phloem sap moves from a sugar source to a sugar sink. A source is any part of the plant that has a high concentration of sugars. Most commonly this source is the leaves, but it can also be a place where the sugars have been stored, such as the roots. A sink is a part of the plant using or storing the sugar, such as growing shoots and stems, a fruit, or even the storage roots that will be a sugar source later in the season. The locations of sugar sources and sinks in a plant can change as the plant grows and as the seasons change.

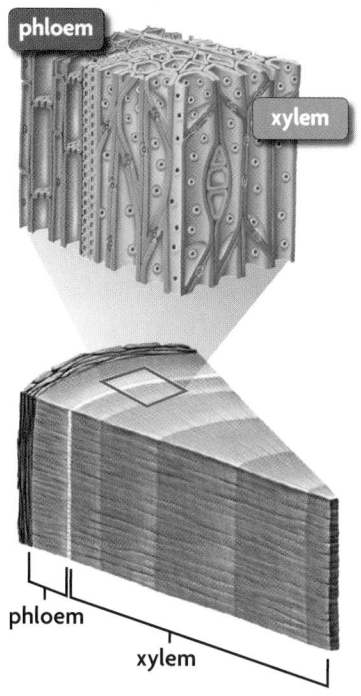

FIGURE 21.5 Fluids move from the roots to the rest of the tree through the xylem. Phloem carries the sugars produced by photosynthesis.

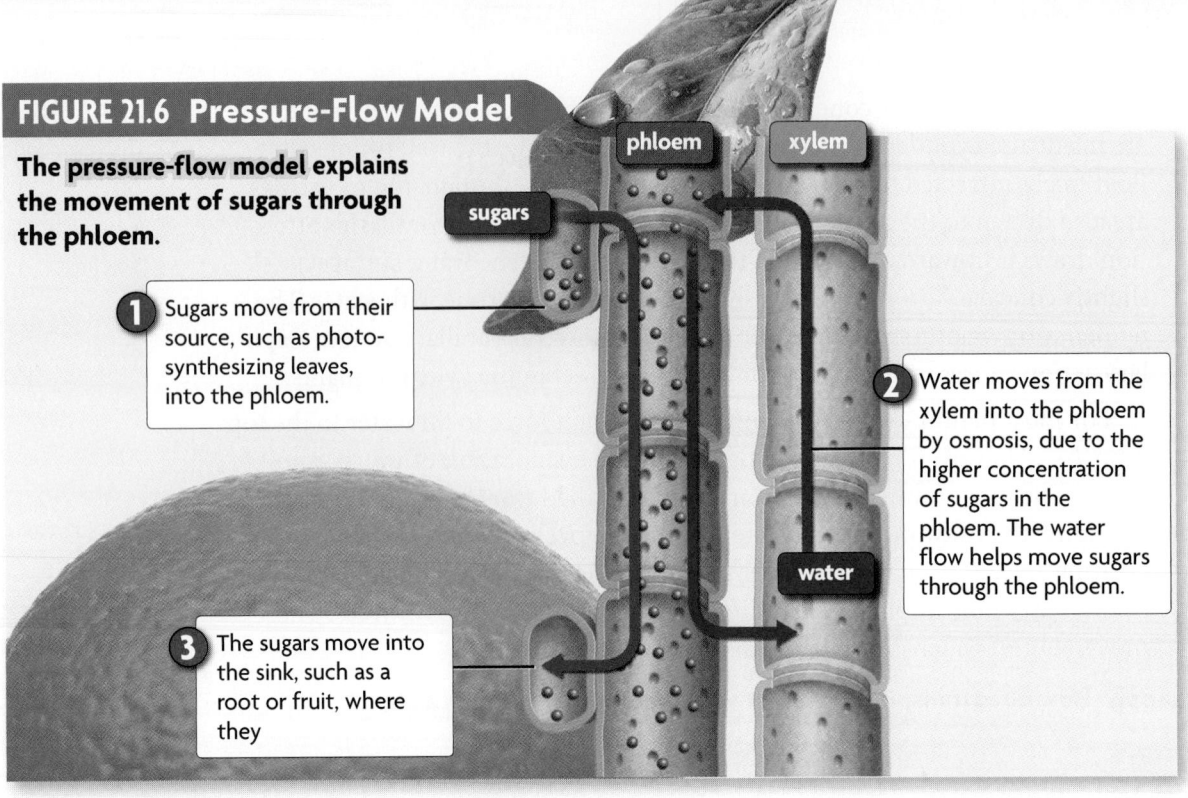

FIGURE 21.6 Pressure-Flow Model

The pressure-flow model explains the movement of sugars through the phloem.

phloem
xylem
sugars

1 Sugars move from their source, such as photo-synthesizing leaves, into the phloem.

2 Water moves from the xylem into the phloem by osmosis, due to the higher concentration of sugars in the phloem. The water flow helps move sugars through the phloem.

water

3 The sugars move into the sink, such as a root or fruit, where they

The pressure changes between sugar sources and sinks, shown in **FIGURE 21.6,** keep nutrients moving through phloem. At a source, many plants use ATP to pump or load sugar into phloem at a high concentration. There-fore, at a source, there is a low concentration of water relative to sugars. Water then flows into the phloem through osmosis, due to the high concentration of sugars. Osmosis requires no energy on the part of the plant. This active loading of sugars and passive flow of water creates high pressure at the sugar source. At the same time, the sugar concentration of the sink end is lessened as sugar is unloaded into the sink. Unloading sugars also uses ATP from the plant. The overall result is higher pressure at the source end and lower pres-sure at the sink end. This difference in pressure keeps the sugary sap flowing in the direction of the sink.

Apply What are two plant parts that can be sugar sources?

Connecting CONCEPTS

Osmosis Recall from **Chapter 3** that osmosis is the diffusion of water molecules across a semi-permeable membrane from an area of high concentration to an area of lower concentration.

21.2 ASSESSMENT

ONLINE QUIZ
ClassZone.com

REVIEWING ▶ MAIN IDEAS

1. How are absorption and **transpiration** involved in the movement of water through the xylem of a plant?

2. Describe how nutrients are moved through the phloem according to the **pressure-flow model.**

CRITICAL THINKING

3. **Infer** Suppose that xylem were located only in the roots and stems of a plant. Would fluids in the xylem still move? Why or why not?

4. **Analyze** How are the specialized cells of xylem and phloem suited for their functions?

Connecting CONCEPTS

5. **Cell Function** Which process requires more energy from the plant, moving water up through the xylem or moving nutrients down through the phloem? Explain.

MATERIALS

- tree leaf
- clear fingernail polish
- 5 cm clear tape
- microscope slide
- compound light microscope

PROCESS SKILLS

- **Observing**
- **Collecting Data**
- **Analyzing Data**

B2.5B Explain how major systems and processes work together in animals and plants, including relationships between organelles, cells, tissues, organs, organ systems, and organisms. Relate these to molecular functions.

B2.5f Relate plant structures and functions to the process of photosynthesis and respiration.

Density of Stomata

In this lab, you will examine the upper and lower leaf surfaces from trees and determine the density of the stomata in the leaves.

PROBLEM How does the density of stomata vary among leaf surfaces?

PROCEDURE

1. Obtain a leaf of a known species.
2. Paint both the upper and lower surfaces of an area of leaf between two veins with clear fingernail polish. Allow the fingernail polish to dry completely.
3. Place a piece of clear tape over the dried nail polish on the lower surface of the leaf. Gently but firmly press the tape to the leaf.
4. Peel the tape from the leaf and place the tape onto the microscope slide. Examine the tape, which has an impression of the leaf cells, under low power and high power of the microscope.
5. Under high power, count the number of stomata in the field of view. Then count the number of epidermal cells in the same field of view. Record your data in a table like the one shown below.
6. Repeat steps 2–5 two more times, using a new leaf of the same species each time, and find the average number of stomata and the average number of cells of your three samples.
7. Repeat steps 3–6 using the upper surface of the leaf.

TABLE 1. STOMATA AND EPIDERMAL CELLS IN THE SURFACES OF A LEAF				
	Lower Leaf Surface		Upper Leaf Surface	
Field of View	Number of Stomata (S)	Number of Epidermal Cells (E)	Number of Stomata (S)	Number of Epidermal Cells (E)
1				
2				
3				
TOTAL				

ANALYZE AND CONCLUDE

1. **Calculate** Find the density of stomata for the lower and upper leaf surfaces of each leaf using the following equation:

$$\textbf{Stomata Density} = \frac{S}{(S + E)} \times 100$$

where S = the average number of stomata and E = the average number of epidermal cells in one surface of the leaf.

2. **Analyze** What is the difference between the density of stomata on the lower surface of the leaf and on the upper surface of the leaf? Form a hypothesis that might explain this difference.

3. **Predict** How might the stomata density be different for a tree in the desert? in the rain forest?

21.3 Roots and Stems

KEY CONCEPT Roots and stems form the support system of vascular plants.

▶ MAIN IDEAS

- Roots anchor plants and absorb mineral nutrients from soil.
- Stems support plants, transport materials, and provide storage.

VOCABULARY

vascular cylinder, p. 648
root hair, p. 648
root cap, p. 648
meristem, p. 648

fibrous root, p. 649
taproot, p. 649
primary growth, p. 651
secondary growth, p. 651

MICHIGAN STANDARDS

B2.5B Explain how major systems and processes work together in animals and plants, including relationships between organelles, cells, tissues, organs, organ systems, and organisms. Relate these to molecular functions.

B2.5f Relate plant structures and functions to the process of photosynthesis and respiration.

Connect Humans reach a certain height and stop growing. Plants, however, can continue growing their entire lives. Woody plants in particular can keep growing in both height and width. Each part of a plant grows in the direction that allows it to reach the resources the plant needs, and each part plays a role in the plant's survival.

▶ MAIN IDEA

Roots anchor plants and absorb mineral nutrients from soil.

Why are roots important? Roots may make up over half of the body of a plant. They anchor the plant to the ground, and from the soil they absorb water and minerals the plant needs.

Parts of a Root

Roots support the plant and absorb, transport, and store nutrients. Like other plant parts, roots contain all three tissue systems—vascular, ground, and dermal. Parts of a root are shown in **FIGURE 21.7.**

In the center of the root is the **vascular cylinder,** which is made of xylem and phloem tissues. The vascular cylinder is surrounded by ground tissue, covered by dermal tissue. A plant absorbs most of its water in the dermal tissue just above the root tips. These cells have tiny projections called **root hairs,** shown in **FIGURE 21.8.** Root hairs find their way through the spaces between soil particles, greatly adding to the surface area available to take up water. Covering the tip of the root is the **root cap,** a small cone of cells that protects the growing part of the root as it pushes through the soil.

Just behind the root cap is where most of the root's growth occurs. Groups of cells that are the source of new cells form tissue called **meristem.** Meristem cells aren't specialized, but when they divide, some of the new cells specialize into tissues. Areas of growth that lengthen the tips of roots and stems are called apical (AY-pik-kul) meristems. Lateral meristems, found all along woody roots and stems, increase the thickness of these plant parts.

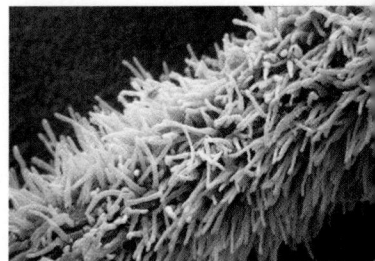

FIGURE 21.8 Root hairs are located above the root tip. (colored SEM; magnification 80×)

FIGURE 21.7 This light micrograph of a root tip cross-section shows some of the parts of a root. (LM; magnification 35×)

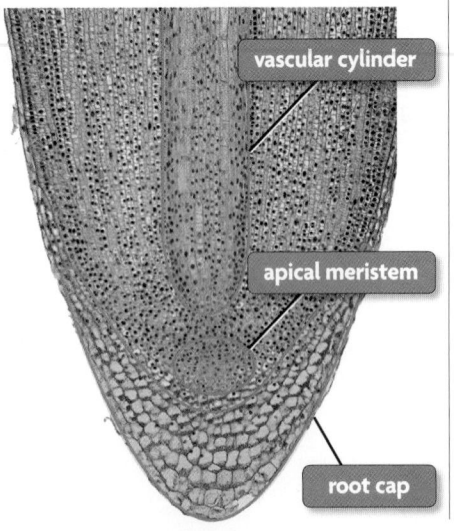

vascular cylinder

apical meristem

root cap

Types of Roots

Roots take one of two basic forms, as shown in **FIGURE 21.9. Fibrous root** systems make fine branches in which most of the roots are the same size. These roots spread like a mat beneath the soil surface, and firmly anchor the plant to the ground. **Taproot** systems have a long, thick, vertical root with smaller branches. Long taproots allow plants to get water from deep in the ground. The thick taproot can also sometimes store food. Radishes, carrots, and beets are examples of taproots that we eat.

Water and Mineral Uptake

All plants require water and certain mineral nutrients for growth, development, and function. Their roots take up nutrients in a process that also results in water absorption. Mineral nutrients are usually dissolved in soil water as ions. For example, nitrogen is often taken up as NO_3^- ions, and iron can be taken up as Fe^{2+} ions. Plants use energy to transport nutrient ions into the roots through active transport. The increased concentration of ions within root cells also causes water to move into the root tip by osmosis.

Some minerals are needed in large amounts. Nitrogen, for example, is an essential mineral needed for nucleic acids, proteins, and chlorophyll. Other minerals serve mostly to catalyze reactions and are needed only in tiny amounts. Magnesium is a mineral involved in the production of chlorophyll. Even though only tiny amounts are needed, these minerals are also necessary for plant health.

Fibrous root

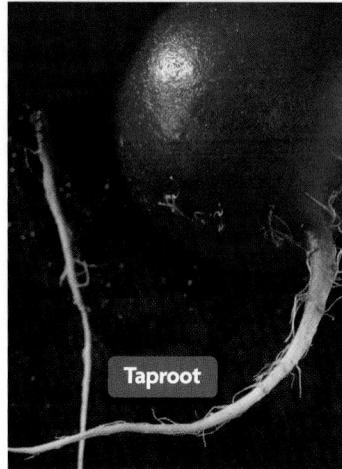

Taproot

FIGURE 21.9 Corn plants have fibrous root systems. Radishes have one large taproot from which much smaller roots may branch.

Explain How do root hairs help roots absorb water?

DATA ANALYSIS

IDENTIFYING THE IMPORTANCE OF REPEATED TRIALS

Scientists need to include repeated trials in experiments in order to draw reliable conclusions. One factor to consider when determining the number of trials in an experiment is how much variation there is among the organisms being tested.

A group of students collected data on the effect of water on the root densities of bean plants. They planted three bean seeds of the same species, each in the same size pot. They used the same type and amount of soil for each plant. Each plant received the same amount of sunlight.

- Plant A received 30 mL of water every day.
- Plant B received 30 mL of water every other day.
- Plant C received 30 mL of water once a week.

Root density, the number of roots per cm^2, was measured in all three plants after 30 days. The graph shows the results of the experiment. The students conclude that this species of bean plant should receive 30 mL of water every other day in order to produce the most roots.

1. **Analyze** Did the students reach a valid conclusion? Why or why not?

2. **Experimental Design** How would you change the experiment to improve the experimental design?

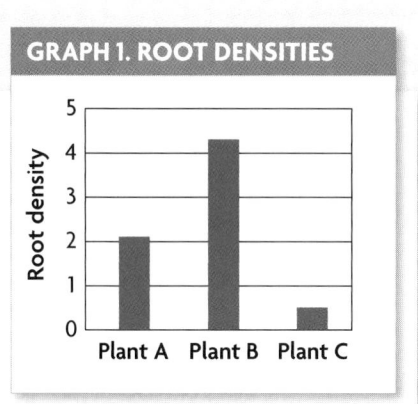

GRAPH 1. ROOT DENSITIES

Baobab trees

Cactus

Potato tubers

Strawberry stolons

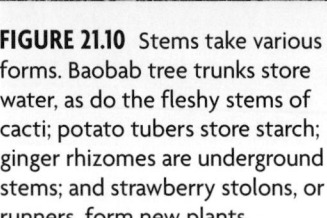

Ginger rhizomes

FIGURE 21.10 Stems take various forms. Baobab tree trunks store water, as do the fleshy stems of cacti; potato tubers store starch; ginger rhizomes are underground stems; and strawberry stolons, or runners, form new plants.

Connecting CONCEPTS

Monocots and Dicots Recall from **Chapter 20** that the pattern of vascular tissue in dicots differs from that in monocots. The cross-section of a monocot stem shows ground tissue with bundles of vascular tissue scattered through it. The cross-section of a herbaceous dicot shows vascular bundles forming a ring.

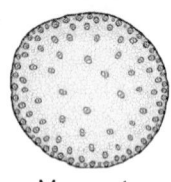
Monocot

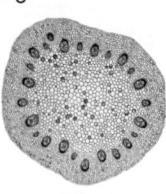
Dicot

▶ **MAIN IDEA**

Stems support plants, transport materials, and provide storage.

You may know that stems support flowers and leaves, giving them better access to pollinators and sunlight. But stems have other functions as well, as you can see in **FIGURE 21.10**. Stems often house a majority of the vascular system and can store food or water. The green stems of cacti, for example, can both photosynthesize and store water. Although most stems grow above ground, potatoes and ginger are examples of stems that can grow underground.

Some stems are herbaceous. Herbaceous plants produce little or no wood. They are usually soft because they do not have many rigid xylem cells. Herbaceous plants may be monocots, such as corn, or dicots, such as beans, and most do not grow taller than two meters. Herbaceous stems are often green and may conduct photosynthesis.

Stems can also be woody. Most plants with woody stems are dicots, such as many broadleaf trees or gymnosperms—pines or fir trees. Tree trunks are an example of woody stems. The oldest part of the xylem, the heartwood, is in the center of a tree trunk. Heartwood no longer conducts water but still provides structure. Sapwood, which is xylem and conducts water, surrounds the heartwood. Phloem produced near the outside of the trunk forms the inner layer of bark. An outer layer of bark provides a protective covering.

Stem Growth

For as long as a plant survives, it is capable of growth. The continued growth of plants is possible because meristems are active throughout the life of the plant. Meristem cells divide to create more cells. Some of the divided cells remain meristem cells for future divisions, while the others become specialized and end up as part of the tissues and organs of a plant.

The pattern of plant growth depends on the location of the meristems within the plant. Growth that increases a plant's length—makes stems grow taller or roots grow longer—is called **primary growth.** This type of growth takes place in apical meristems found at the ends of stems and roots. **Secondary growth** adds to the width in the stems and roots of woody plants. Dicot trees, such as oak and maple, produce a lot of secondary growth over their lifetimes. Secondary growth takes place in lateral meristems in the outer trunk layers.

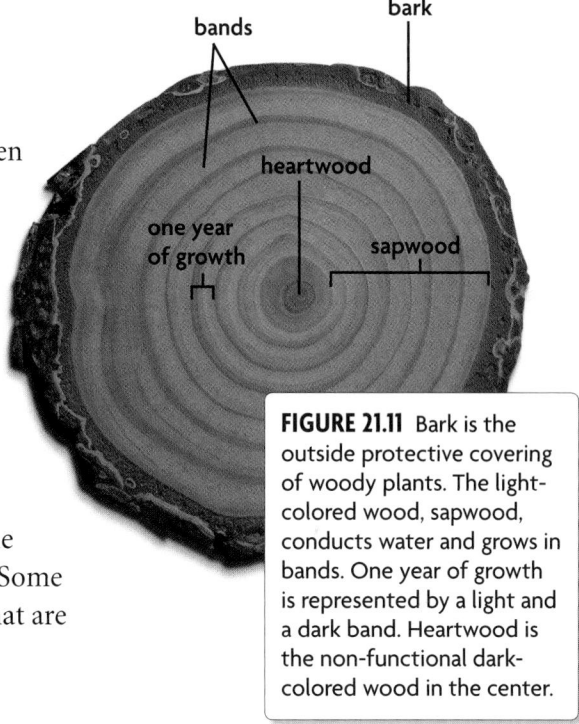

VISUAL VOCAB

Primary growth lengthens roots and stems.

Secondary growth widens roots and stems.

Tree Rings

Secondary growth is also responsible for the formation of tree rings, shown in **FIGURE 21.11.** Tree rings form due to uneven growth over the seasons. In spring, if water is plentiful, new xylem cells are wide and have thin walls. These cells appear light in color. When water becomes more limited in the following months, xylem cells are smaller and have thicker walls, so they appear darker in color.

The age of a tree can be determined by counting these annual rings. One ring represents one year of growth. Each ring includes both the larger, lighter cell bands of spring growth and the smaller, darker cell bands of later season growth. Climate, too, can be inferred from the rings since the rings will be thicker if there were good growing conditions. Some trees live thousands of years and can provide climate data that are not available from any other scientific records.

Summarize **How are tree rings formed?**

FIGURE 21.11 Bark is the outside protective covering of woody plants. The light-colored wood, sapwood, conducts water and grows in bands. One year of growth is represented by a light and a dark band. Heartwood is the non-functional dark-colored wood in the center.

21.3 / ASSESSMENT

ONLINE QUIZ ClassZone.com

REVIEWING ▶ MAIN IDEAS

1. Describe two major functions of roots. Explain why these functions are important to the plant.

2. How do the functions of stems differ from those of roots? How are they similar?

CRITICAL THINKING

3. **Analyze** Some stems, such as ginger rhizomes, grow underground. Why are they considered stems rather than roots?

4. **Apply** What effect could a cold winter with little precipitation have on the **primary growth** and **secondary growth** of a tree?

Connecting CONCEPTS

5. **Earth's History** The principle of uniformitarianism states that processes that can be observed today can be used to explain events that occurred in the past, or "The present is the key to the past." How does this principle relate to tree ring dating?

21.4 Leaves

KEY CONCEPT Leaves absorb light and carry out photosynthesis.

▶ MAIN IDEAS
- Most leaves share some similar structures.
- Most leaves are specialized systems for photosynthesis.

VOCABULARY
blade, p. 652
petiole, p. 652
mesophyll, p. 652
guard cell, p. 653

MICHIGAN STANDARDS

B2.5B Explain how major systems and processes work together in animals and plants, including relationships between organelles, cells, tissues, organs, organ systems, and organisms. Relate these to molecular functions.

B2.5f Relate plant structures and functions to the process of photosynthesis and respiration.

Connect "Leaves of three, let it be." This is a saying of many experienced hikers who know how to avoid poison ivy. Hikers can identify poisonous plants in the same way that people can identify many plants that are safe to eat—by the shapes of their leaves. Plant species have their own unique leaf shapes, specially adapted for light gathering and retaining water in their particular environment.

▶ MAIN IDEA

Most leaves share some similar structures.

Leaves of different species don't all look the same, but most leaves do share some common parts. Leaves grow out from a plant's stem, and they are made up of a few basic parts. The **blade** is usually broad and flat, and it collects the sunlight for the plant. The blade connects to the stem by a thin stalk called the **petiole** (PEHT-ee-ohl). A bud that grows between the petiole and the stem of a plant, called an axillary bud, marks where a leaf ends.

Leaf Tissues

Like roots and stems, leaves have an outer covering of dermal tissue and an internal system of vascular tissue surrounded by ground tissue. The dermal tissue of many leaves is covered by a waxy cuticle that forms a water resistant covering. The cuticle protects the inner tissues and limits evaporation from the plant. Between the two dermal layers of a leaf is parenchyma tissue called **mesophyll** (MEHZ-uh-FIHL). The vascular tissues of xylem and phloem make up the veins that run throughout the mesophyll.

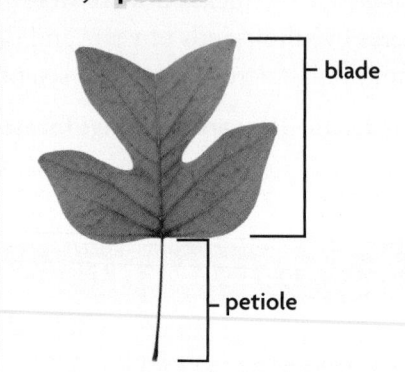

VISUAL VOCAB

The **blade** of a leaf collects sunlight for photosynthesis. It connects to the plant's stem by a **petiole.**

blade

petiole

Stomata and Guard Cells

In most plants, the top and undersides of leaves have different functions. The upper portion of the mesophyll has most of the chloroplasts and is where most photosynthesis takes place. The underside portion of a leaf has stomata and is the site of transpiration and gas exchange.

A pair of **guard cells,** shown in **FIGURE 21.12,** surround each stoma, and can open and close by changing shape. During the day, the stomata of most plants are open, allowing the carbon dioxide (CO_2) necessary for photosynthesis to enter. Potassium ions (K^+) from neighboring cells accumulate in the guard cells. A high concentration of K^+ causes water to flow into the guard cells as well. When the plant is full of water, the two guard cells plump up into a semicircle shape, opening the stoma.

When the stomata are open, water evaporates from the leaves. When the plant is losing water from transpiration faster than it is gaining water at its roots, the guard cells deflate and close the stomata. With the stomata closed, the plant may run low on CO_2 for photosynthesis. The stomata also close at night. Factors such as temperature, humidity, hormonal response, and the amount of CO_2 in the leaves signal the guard cells to open or close.

Leaf Characteristics

It is not always obvious what part of a plant is actually a leaf. As shown in **FIGURE 21.13,** leaves may be simple, with just one blade connected to the petiole, or they may be compound, with many blades on one petiole. The multiple blades are called leaflets. All of the leaflets and their petiole together are actually a single leaf because the axillary bud is at the base of the petiole. There are no buds at the bases of the leaflets. Besides leaf shape, other traits of leaves used to identify plants include the pattern of veins and the leaf edge, or margin.

Summarize What is the function of the guard cells of a plant?

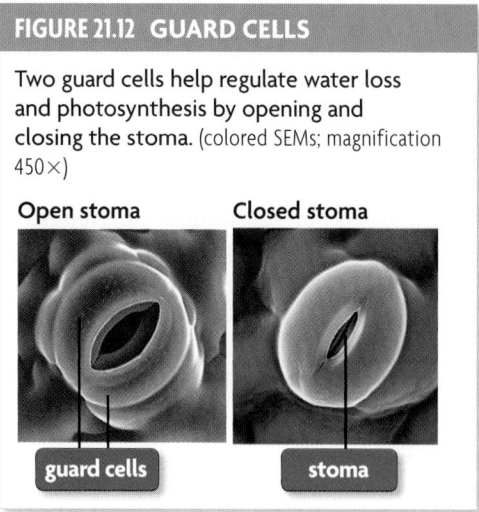

FIGURE 21.12 GUARD CELLS

Two guard cells help regulate water loss and photosynthesis by opening and closing the stoma. (colored SEMs; magnification 450×)

Open stoma   Closed stoma

guard cells   stoma

FIGURE 21.13 Leaf Characteristics

Certain leaf characteristics—such as the leaf type, the vein pattern, and the shape of the leaf margin—can be used to identify plants.

LEAF TYPE

Compound leaf

Simple leaf

Double compound leaf

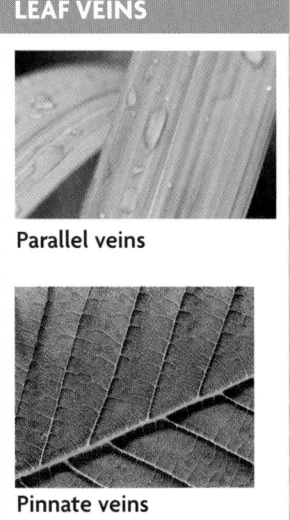

LEAF VEINS

Parallel veins

Pinnate veins

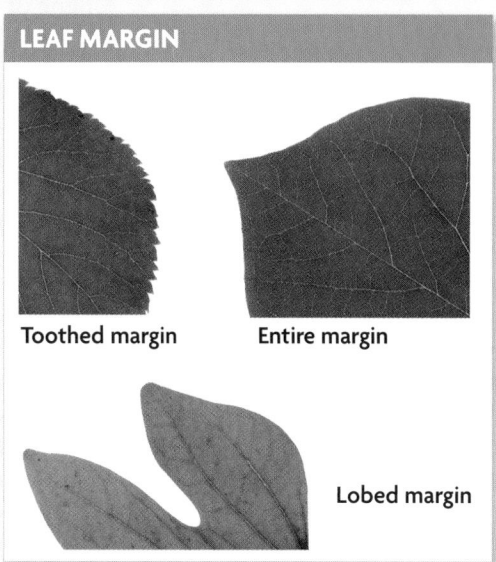

LEAF MARGIN

Toothed margin   Entire margin

Lobed margin

Infer How might compound leaves and leaves with lobed margins be well-suited to windy environments?

Chlorophyll Fluorescence

If you remove chlorophyll molecules from their cells and then expose them to bright light, the energy absorbed from the excited electrons in the chlorophyll will be either lost as heat or released as a dull-colored light as the electrons return to their normal state. This is an example of fluorescence: the absorption of light at one wavelength, and its release at a longer—and lower-energy—wavelength.

PROBLEM How can fluorescence be used to study photosynthesis?

PROCEDURE

1. Use the mortar and pestle to crush a handful of spinach leaves, adding enough methanol to make 10 mL of extract. Use a graduated cylinder to collect and measure the extract.

2. Place the filter paper in the funnel, and hold the funnel over a beaker. A second person should pour the extract through the funnel to filter the extract.

3. Carefully transfer the extract to a test tube, and hold it in front of a lit flashlight. Observe the fluorescence that occurs at a 90-degree angle from the beam of light.

ANALYZE AND CONCLUDE

1. **Identify** What color does the fluorescence appear?

2. **Analyze** Why did the chlorophyll have to be extracted before the fluorescence could be observed?

MATERIALS
- mortar
- pestle
- handful spinach leaves
- 10 mL methanol
- graduated cylinder
- filter paper
- funnel
- beaker
- eyedropper or pipette
- test tube
- test tube rack
- flashlight

▶ MAIN IDEA

Most leaves are specialized systems for photosynthesis.

The leaves of a plant are the main sites for photosynthesis. The broad, flat shape of many leaves allows for light gathering on the upper surface and gas exchange on the underside. Since the undersides of leaves are not exposed to direct sunlight, the plant loses less water while the stomata are open.

Photosynthetic Structures

There are two types of mesophyll cells in leaves, shown in **FIGURE 21.14**. Mesophyll is the photosynthetic tissue of a leaf. Both types of cells in mesophyll have chloroplasts. Just under the dermal layer is a layer of tall, rectangular cells called the palisade mesophyll. These cells absorb much of the light that enters the leaf. Beneath this layer is the spongy mesophyll. Spongy mesophyll has cells that are loosely packed, creating many air spaces. These air spaces connect with the outside of the plant through the stomata, allowing carbon dioxide and oxygen to diffuse in and out of the leaf. Carbohydrates that the plant makes move from mesophyll cells into phloem vessels, which carry the products to tissues throughout the plant.

TAKING NOTES

Use combination notes to describe and sketch each leaf structure mentioned here.

Notes	Sketch
stomata mesophyll	

Leaf Adaptations

Not all leaves are "leafy." Leaves are adapted for photosynthesis in the plant's particular environment. For example, cacti leaves are actually the sharp spines that protect them from predators and help minimize water loss due to transpiration. Other desert plants, such as agave, store water in their leaves. The leaves and stems of many desert plants are protected by very thick cuticles, which minimize the loss of water from the plant.

Similar adaptations are common in coniferous trees in cold, dry climates. Pine needles, for example, are leaves with a small surface area and a thick, waxy epidermis that protects them from cold damage. Tiny sunken areas for the stomata help reduce water loss.

Water loss is not a problem for aquatic plants, however. The undersides of a water lily's leaves are below the water surface. To accommodate gas exchange in an aquatic environment, the water lily has stomata on the upper surface of its leaves. Many aquatic plants also have flexible petioles adapted to wave action.

Many tropical plants have very large, broad leaves. In the crowded rain forest, the challenge is to get enough light and space among all the other plants. Larger leaves mean more light-gathering surface.

A few plants are actually predators. The pitcher plant, for example, has tall, tubular leaves that help lure, trap, and digest insects. These insects provide extra nitrogen for the plant, which is needed because there is little of it in the soil where the plant grows.

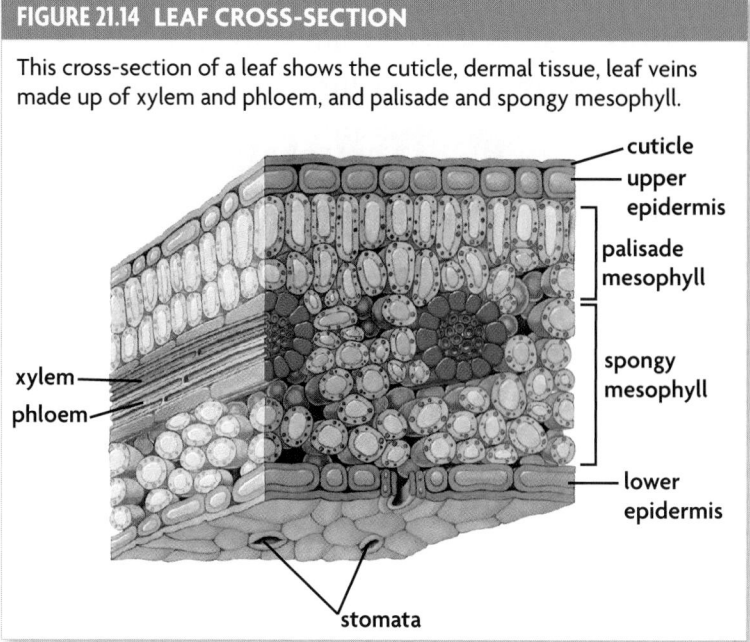

FIGURE 21.14 LEAF CROSS-SECTION

This cross-section of a leaf shows the cuticle, dermal tissue, leaf veins made up of xylem and phloem, and palisade and spongy mesophyll.

- cuticle
- upper epidermis
- palisade mesophyll
- spongy mesophyll
- lower epidermis
- xylem
- phloem
- stomata

For more information on plant adaptations, go to scilinks.org. Keycode: MLB021

Infer Flower petals are also an adaptation of leaves. Their bright colors and fragrance attract animals and insects. Why is attracting other organisms important for some plants?

21.4 ASSESSMENT

ONLINE QUIZ
ClassZone.com

REVIEWING ▶ MAIN IDEAS

1. Describe the functions of the **blade** and **petiole** in a leaf.
2. How do the palisade and spongy **mesophyll** layers help a leaf perform photosynthesis?

CRITICAL THINKING

3. **Infer** The leaves of aquatic plants that are completely underwater have few stomata. Why might this be so?
4. **Apply** Grass blades are leaves that are joined directly to the stem. What structure that is typical of many leaves is missing in grass?

Connecting CONCEPTS

5. **Analogous Structures** The tendrils that allow pea plants to climb up an object are modified leaves, whereas the tendrils of grape vines are modified stems. Explain.

Use these inquiry-based labs and online activities to deepen your understanding of plant structure and function.

INVESTIGATION

Photosynthesis and Red Leaves

How do plants with yellow, purple, or red leaves year-round carry out photosynthesis to produce the food they need to live? In this lab, you will investigate whether a red-leafed plant contains the same pigments for photosynthesis as a green-leafed plant.

SKILLS Observing, Interpreting Data, Drawing Conclusions

PROBLEM What pigments are found in plants that appear red?

PROCEDURE

1. Make a J-shaped hook out of each paper clip. Carefully push the straight end into the bottom of the rubber stoppers. Attach the strip of chromatography paper to the other end of each wire. **Caution:** Do not force the stopper.

2. Place the green leaf on one paper strip, about 2 cm from the bottom. Roll the coin over the leaf until you see a horizontal green line across the strip. Repeat with the red leaf on the other strip of paper.

3. Add alcohol to the test tubes so that the bottom edge of the chromatography paper will be submerged. Lower the papers into the test tubes, making sure that each horizontal line of pigments is NOT submerged in the alcohol.

4. Place the tests tubes in a holder and leave them undisturbed for 15–30 minutes. Record your observations.

5. After the alcohol has traveled to the top of the paper strips, remove the papers from the test tubes. Allow the papers to dry and compare the chromatograms, or records of pigment patterns, for the two leaves. Use the table provided by your teacher to identify the separated pigments.

MATERIALS
- 2 paper clips stretched into a wire
- 2 rubber stoppers
- 2 strips of chromatography paper
- 2 large test tubes
- test tube rack
- green leaf
- red leaf
- coin
- 10-mL graduated cylinder
- 5 mL isopropyl alcohol

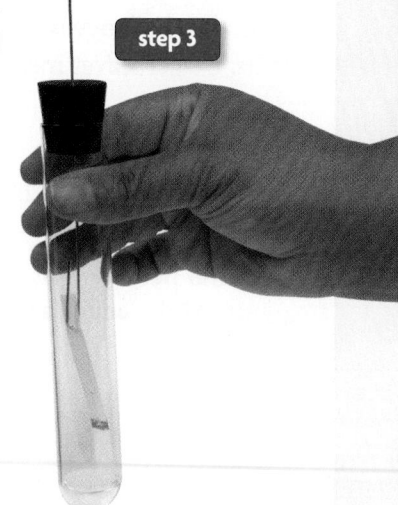

step 3

ANALYZE AND CONCLUDE

1. **Compare and Contrast** Describe the similarities and the differences between the two chromatograms.

2. **Apply** Based on your results, explain how a red-leafed plant photosynthesizes.

3. **Analyze** During the fall, some trees form a plug at the base of their leaf petioles, cutting off water to the leaf. This causes the leaf to stop photosynthesizing. Chlorophyll begins to break down, and the colors of the other pigments present in the leaf begin to show. How do you think a chromatogram of a healthy red leaf would compare with a chromatogram of a tree leaf that just turned red in autumn?

INVESTIGATION

Connecting Form to Function

In this lab, you will examine a slice of the roots, stems, and leaves of a plant and describe how their structures relate to their functions.

SKILL Observing

PROBLEM How are plant structures related to their functions?

MATERIALS
- plant root, stem, and leaf
- razor tool
- 3 slides
- 3 cover slips
- eyedropper
- water
- compound microscope

PROCEDURE

1. Draw a table with three labeled columns: name of plant part, sketch, and function. Label three rows: root, stem, and leaf.

2. Carefully use the razor tool to cut a very thin slice from the root, stem, and leaf of the plant. You must be able to see light through the sliced sections.

3. Prepare a wet mount slide of a slice of each plant organ. Examine each slide under the microscope and sketch the structures that you see. Describe the function of each structure under the third column.

ANALYZE AND CONCLUDE

1. **Compare** What similarities did you observe among the slides of the three plant organs? Explain why these similarities may exist.

2. **Analyze** Which organ had the most vessels? Which organ had the most chloroplasts? Which organ had the most hairs? Is this what you would predict based on the function of these organs? Explain your answer.

Online BIOLOGY

CLASSZONE.COM

VIRTUAL LAB
Plant Transpiration

Is the rate of transpiration always the same? In this interactive lab, you will determine how different environmental conditions affect the rate of transpiration.

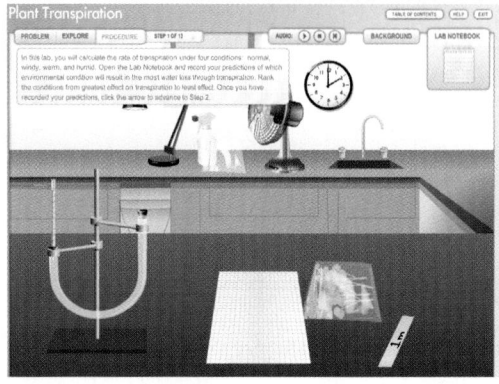

ANIMATED BIOLOGY
Name That Tree

Is that leaf from an oak or a hickory tree? Are those needles from a pine tree or spruce? Choose a mystery leaf, then identify the tree it came from with an interactive dichotomous key.

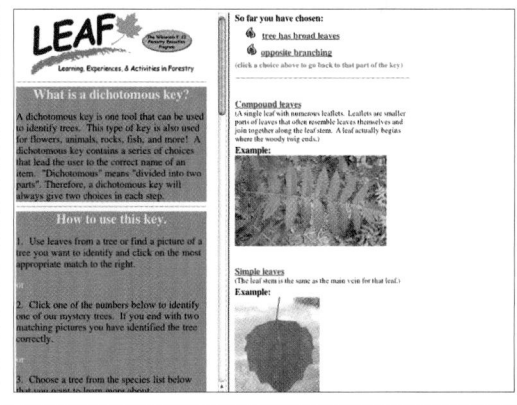

WEBQUEST

How have plants adapted to their surroundings? In this WebQuest, you will learn about various adaptations that plants have developed for specific environments. Then write a description of the adaptations found on a fictitious new plant.

21.1 Plant Cells and Tissues

Plants have specialized cells and tissue systems. There are three basic types of plant cells that differ in cell wall structure. Each of these cell types can make up simple tissues. These tissues, as well as complex tissues, make up tissue systems. A plant has a dermal tissue system that covers the plant, a ground tissue system that makes up most of the inside of the plant, and a vascular tissue system that transports fluids throughout the plant.

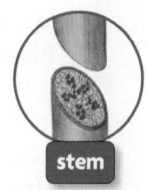
stem

leaf

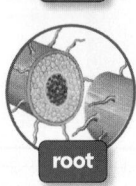
root

21.2 The Vascular System

The vascular system allows for the transport of water, minerals, and sugars. Xylem and phloem are the two main tissues of the vascular system. Water and dissolved minerals move through xylem from the roots of a plant up to the leaves, where it evaporates through leaf stomata. This process is called transpiration. The pressure-flow model is a hypothesis of how sugars from photosynthesis move through the plant within the phloem.

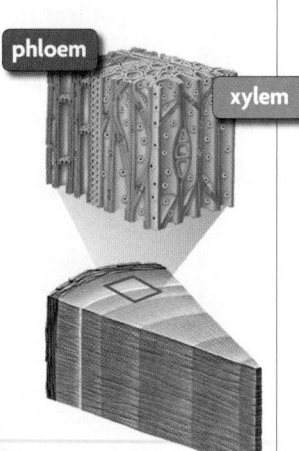
phloem

xylem

21.3 Roots and Stems

Roots and stems form the support system of vascular plants. Roots anchor plants in the soil and absorb water and mineral nutrients for the plant to use. There are two main types of roots: fibrous roots and taproots. Stems provide support for the plant, and house the vascular systems of the plant. They also give leaves and flowers better access to sunlight and to pollinators. Some stems can store food, while other stems are adapted to store water.

21.4 Leaves

Leaves absorb light and carry out photosynthesis. Most leaves are specialized for photosynthesis, with a broad shape, many chloroplasts, and stomata that allow carbon dioxide and oxygen to move into and out of the plant. Certain leaf characteristics, such as the vein pattern and the shape of the leaf, can be used to help identify plants. There are many adaptations of leaves, such as cactus spines, pine needles, and the tubular leaves of a pitcher plant that are used to lure and trap insects for food.

Synthesize Your Notes

Supporting Main Ideas Use a main idea diagram to outline the tissue systems in plants.

Plant organs are made of three tissue systems.

→ ☐

→ ☐

→ ☐

Three-Column Chart Make a three-column chart to summarize the forces involved in the movement of fluids within xylem.

Force	Description	Where in Plant
Transpiration		
Cohesion and adhesion		
Absorption		

Chapter Assessment

Reviewing Vocabulary

Compare and Contrast

Describe one similarity and one difference between the two terms in each of the following pairs.

1. parenchyma cell, sclerenchyma cell
2. ground tissue, vascular tissue
3. xylem, phloem
4. fibrous root, taproot
5. primary growth, secondary growth

Labeling Diagrams

In your notebook, write the vocabulary term that matches each numbered item below.

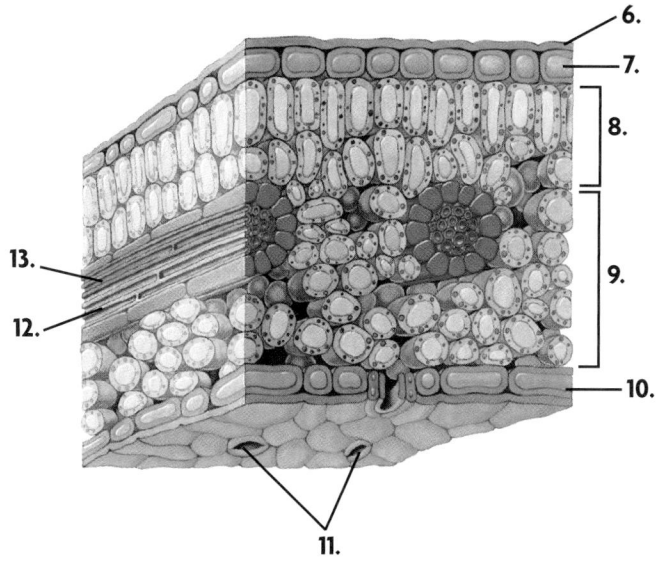

Reviewing MAIN IDEAS

14. Name two roles of parenchyma cells, and briefly explain how these cells are specialized for these roles.

15. Both collenchyma and sclerenchyma cells provide support to a plant. But only one of these cell types can exist in plant parts that are still growing. Identify the cell type and explain the traits that make this so.

16. Describe one similarity and one difference between the dermal tissues in nonwoody and woody parts of a plant.

17. Some ground tissue contains many chloroplasts. Where is this tissue located and why does it contain so many chloroplasts?

18. How is the structure of vascular tissue related to its ability to transport materials in the plant?

19. What must happen to tracheids and vessel elements before they can function in xylem?

20. What processes are responsible for water flowing through xylem from the roots to the tips of leaves?

21. Name three substances that are transported by phloem.

22. What can taproots do that fibrous roots cannot do?

23. Describe similarities between herbaceous stems and woody stems.

24. How do the xylem and phloem in leaves help identify a plant species?

25. Photosynthesis requires carbon dioxide and produces oxygen. How does spongy mesophyll play a role in the diffusion of these gases into and out of the leaves?

Critical Thinking

26. Compare In animals, the term *stem cells* refers to unspecialized or undifferentiated cells that give rise to specialized cells, such as a blood cell. How are meristem cells in plants similar to animal stem cells?

27. Analyze A sugar beet plant develops a large root in the first year of growth and stores sugar in it until the second growing season. But, besides sugar, as much as three-fourths of the root's weight can be water. Why is there so much water in the root?

28. Apply In 1894, naturalist John Muir wrote about white bark pines he saw at Yosemite National Park in California. At high elevations, where there was snow on the ground for six months each year, he studied a tree only three feet tall and six inches in diameter and determined it was 426 years old. How did he know how old the tree was? Why might it be so small when trees of the same species were much larger down the mountain?

29. Infer Many rain forest plants have leaves that taper to tips on the ends. Water from heavy rains drips off the tips of the leaves so that water doesn't collect on the leaves. Why might this be an adaptive advantage for the plant?

30. Synthesize Use what you know about cohesion and adhesion to explain why almost an entire sheet of paper towel can become wet even if only a corner of it is placed in water.

Interpreting Visuals

Use the photograph to answer the next three questions.

31. Apply About how many years old was this tree when it was cut down?

32. Infer What does the pattern of growth rings indicate about the climate and the rate of growth of this tree over the years?

33. Predict Imagine this tree were still growing. If the next year had a spring with much less rain than previous springs and then a summer with a lot of sunshine, what would the next growth ring look like? Explain.

Analyzing Data

An experiment was designed to test the effect of various environmental factors on the successful germination of grass seed. The control group of seeds was planted according to the directions on the seed packet. Each of three additional groups tested one variable. The experimental design and results are shown in the chart below. Use the chart to answer the next three questions.

ENVIRONMENTAL FACTORS THAT AFFECT GRASS SEED GERMINATION				
Environmental Factor	Control Group	Group A	Group B	Group C
Hours daylight	12	6	12	12
Water	100%	100%	50%	100%
Temperature (°C)	24	24	24	12
Seeds planted/ seeds germinated	5/5	5/5	5/1	5/3

34. Infer What does the data suggest about the conditions under which grass seeds will or will not germinate?

35. Evaluate Do the results seem logical? Explain.

36. Analyze If you could change anything in this experimental design, what would it be? Give at least two reasons to support your response.

Connecting CONCEPTS

37. Write an Instruction Manual Imagine that you want to sell plant dissection kits. The kits will include instructions on where to find all of the structures of a plant, such as the different type of cells and tissues, roots, leaves, stomata, stems, phloem, and xylem. You need to write an instruction manual to help people dissect the plant. Write instructions to dissect the plant from the bottom up. Decide whether it is a woody or nonwoody plant.

38. Analyze Strangler figs were transplanted from the tropics to states such as Florida and California because of their unusual growth forms. Considering how they got their common name, why was this perhaps not a good idea?

MICHIGAN STANDARDS-BASED ASSESSMENT

✓ **Test Practice**
For more test practice, go to ClassZone.com.

1. **Tree Ring Growth from 1955 to 2005**

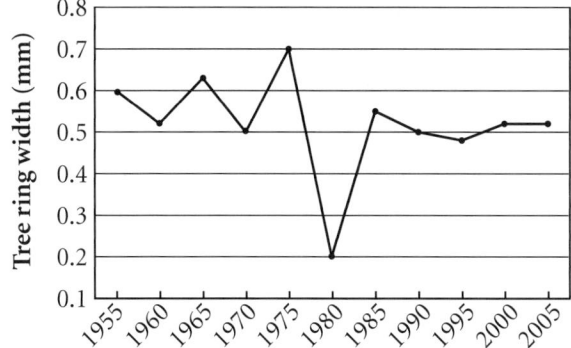

Suppose a tree farmer has collected data about tree ring growth for many years. During that time, only one major drought has occurred. Based on the graph, between which years did the drought most likely occur? **B1.1E**

A 1955–1960

B 1965–1970

C 1975–1980

D 1990–1995

THINK THROUGH THE QUESTION

First, eliminate answer choices that list the years where there is no remarkable change in the graph. Then consider the remaining choices. Would drought have a negative or a positive effect on the width of a tree ring?

---

2. Which plant tissue transports the products of photosynthesis from the leaves to stems and roots? **B2.5f**

A dermal tissue

B ground tissue

C xylem

D phloem

3. Plants capture radiant energy from sunlight and convert it into usable energy in the form of **B2.1A**

A carbon dioxide.

B. protein.

C oxygen.

D sugar.

4. What two structures do plant cells have that animal cells do not have? **B2.4g**

A ribosomes and mitochondria

B mitochondria and cell walls

C chloroplasts and cell walls

D chloroplasts and ribosomes

5. Water and certain mineral nutrients are taken up by a plant's **B2.5B**

A leaves.

B roots.

C stems.

D tissues.

6.

Effect of Nitrogen on Bean Plant Growth				
Trial	0% N	5% N	10% N	15% N
1	1.4 cm	2.2 cm	2.2 cm	3.6 cm
2	0.5 cm	2.6 cm	2.6 cm	2.6 cm
3	1.0 cm	3.6 cm	2.9 cm	3.5 cm

Students recorded data on the effect of different percentages of nitrogen (N) in fertilizer on the growth of bean plants in centimeters. Fertilizer with no nitrogen was included in this experiment because it served as the **B1.1B**

A model for the experiment.

B control for the experiment.

C independent variable for the experiment.

D dependent variable for the experiment.

CHAPTER
22 Plant Growth, Reproduction, and Response

KEY CONCEPTS

22.1 Plant Life Cycles
All plants alternate between two phases in their life cycles.

22.2 Reproduction in Flowering Plants
Reproduction of flowering plants takes place within flowers.

22.3 Seed Dispersal and Germination
Seeds disperse and begin to grow when conditions are favorable.

22.4 Asexual Reproduction
Plants can produce genetic clones of themselves through asexual reproduction.

22.5 Plant Hormones and Responses
Plant hormones guide plant growth and development.

Online BIOLOGY CLASSZONE.COM

Animated BIOLOGY

View animated chapter concepts.
• Exploring Plant Responses
• Seed Dispersal

BIOZINE

Keep current with biology news.
• Featured stories
• News feeds
• Strange Biology

RESOURCE CENTER

Get more information on
• Plant Life Cycles
• Plant Reproduction
• Seeds and Fruits

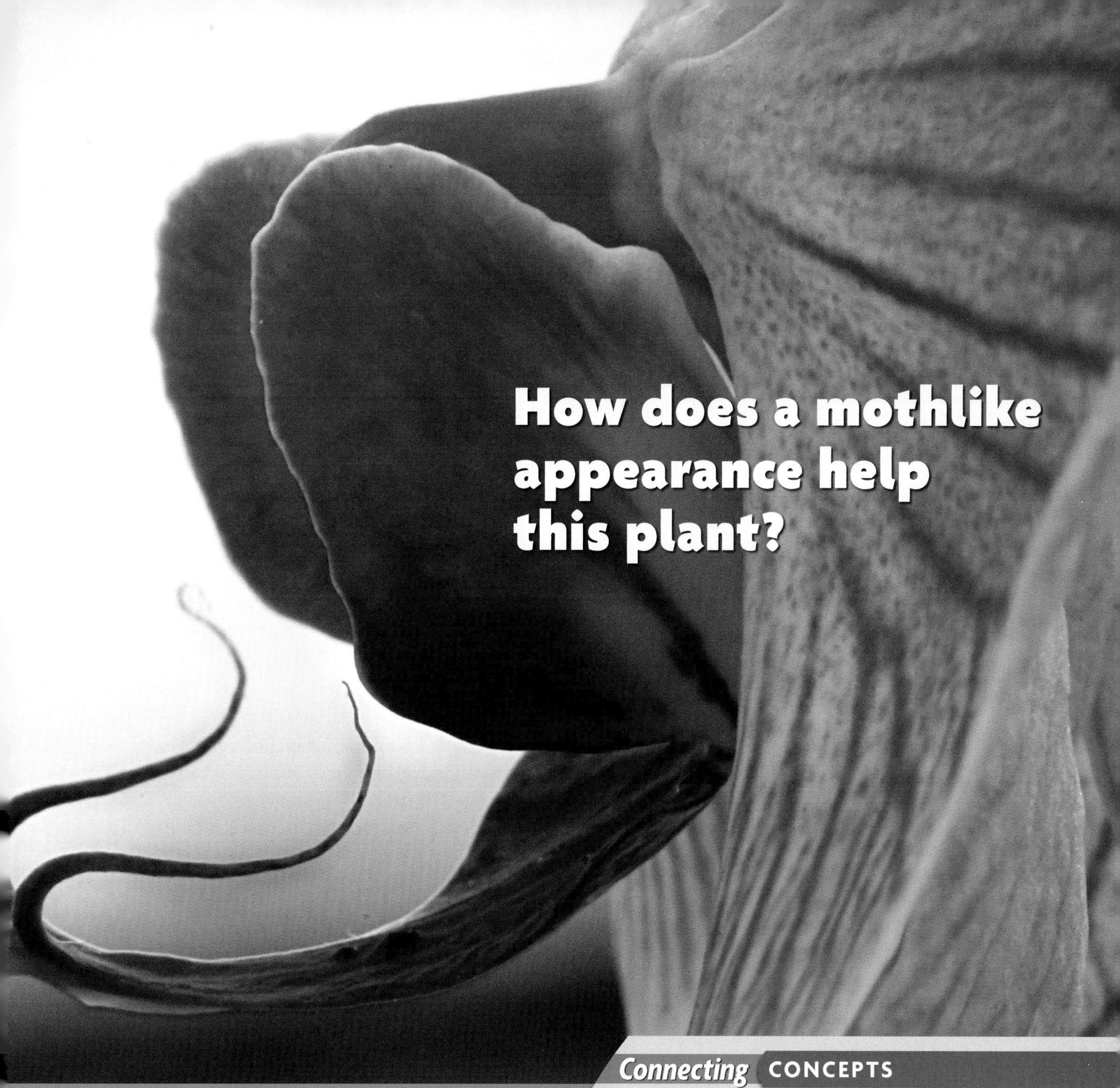

How does a mothlike appearance help this plant?

Connecting CONCEPTS

Some pollinators are attracted to flowers that mimic insects. This orchid belongs to a genus commonly called "moth orchids." Moths may be drawn to this flower and be dusted with pollen grains. The pollen now has a free ticket to the next flower on the moth's route. When pollen comes into contact with the female parts of another flower, the reproductive cycle begins.

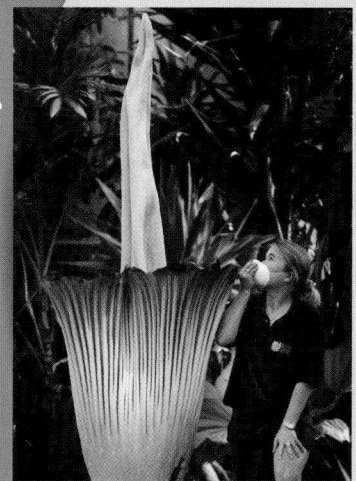

Ecology The titan arum plant, shown at left, produces a flower that smells like carrion, or rotting meat. Beetles that eat carrion are attracted by this odor and often wind up pollinating the flower. This ecological relationship is an example of commensalism. The plant benefits from being pollinated, but the beetles are neither helped nor harmed. Instead, they are tricked by the flower's smell, expecting to find a meal.

22.1 Plant Life Cycles

KEY CONCEPTS All plants alternate between two phases in their life cycles.

▶ MAIN IDEAS

- Plant life cycles alternate between producing spores and gametes.
- Life cycle phases look different among various plant groups.

VOCABULARY

alternation of generations, p. 664
sporophyte, p. 664
gametophyte, p. 664

Review
pollination, meiosis, diploid, haploid, zygote, mitosis, sporangia, flagella

MICHIGAN STANDARDS

B2.5f Relate plant structures and functions to the process of photosynthesis and respiration.

B4.3A Compare and contrast the processes of cell division (mitosis and meiosis), particularly as those processes relate to production of new cells and to passing on genetic information between generations.

Connect The moth orchid flower mimics the shape of its pollinators, which are attracted to what they think is a potential mate. Pollination is a part of sexual reproduction in seed plants. But how do seedless plants, such as moss, reproduce? And what are the common features of all plant life cycles?

▶ MAIN IDEA

Plant life cycles alternate between producing spores and gametes.

Recall that animals produce gametes—sperm and eggs—through meiosis. When a sperm fertilizes an egg, a new diploid organism is produced. Plants also produce gametes, but their reproductive cycle includes a few extra steps. Plants complete their life cycle by alternating between two phases. Together, these phases allow plants to reproduce sexually and disperse to new areas. One phase involves a diploid plant body that produces spores. Remember, diploid cells have two copies of each chromosome ($2n$). The other phase involves a haploid plant body that produces gametes. Haploid cells have one copy of each chromosome ($1n$). This type of life cycle, which alternates between diploid and haploid phases, is called **alternation of generations.**

As shown in **FIGURE 22.1**, the diploid phase of a plant life cycle begins with a fertilized egg, called a zygote. A zygote divides by mitosis and grows into a mature **sporophyte** (SPAWR-uh-FYT), or spore-producing plant. A mature sporophyte has specialized cells that divide by meiosis to produce haploid spores. Recall that cell division by meiosis reduces the number of chromosomes in a cell by one-half.

A spore marks the beginning of the haploid phase of the plant life cycle. A spore divides by mitosis and grows into a mature **gametophyte** (guh-MEE-tuh-FYT), or gamete-producing plant. Specialized parts of a mature gametophyte produce gametes—sperm and eggs—through mitosis. When a sperm meets an egg, fertilization takes place, and the cycle continues with a new sporophyte.

Analyze Why must gametophyte cells divide by mitosis?

FIGURE 22.1 ALTERNATION OF GENERATIONS

Plant life cycles alternate between a sporophyte phase, which produces spores, and a gametophyte stage, which produces gametes.

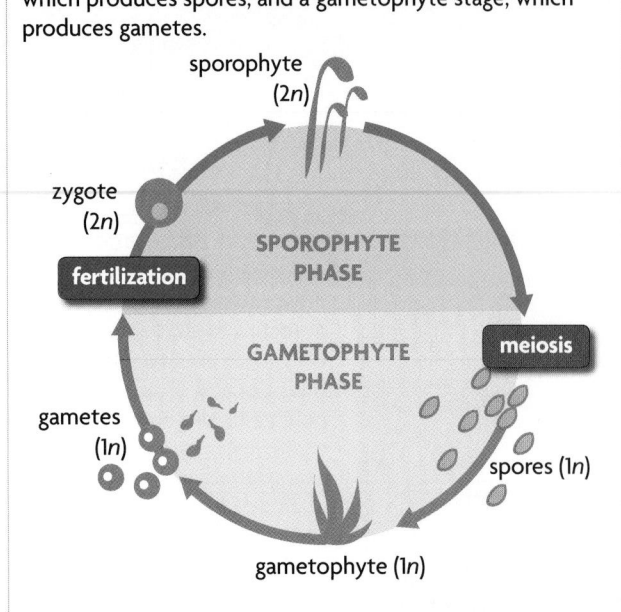

sporophyte ($2n$)

zygote ($2n$)

fertilization

SPOROPHYTE PHASE

GAMETOPHYTE PHASE

meiosis

gametes ($1n$)

spores ($1n$)

gametophyte ($1n$)

MAIN IDEA

Life cycle phases look different among various plant groups.

Different plant groups each have their own version of alternation of generations. The sporophyte and gametophyte generations look different for nonvascular plants, seedless vascular plants, and seed plants.

Life Cycle of Nonvascular Plants: Moss

Nonvascular plants are the only plants in which the gametophyte phase is dominant. In other words, the green, carpetlike plants that you might recognize as moss are gametophytes. If you look very closely, sometimes you can see the moss sporophytes. Moss sporophytes are stalklike structures that grow up from the gametophyte. As you can see in **FIGURE 22.2**, the moss sporophyte looks like a brown stem topped with a tiny cup called a capsule.

The capsule at the tip of the moss sporophyte contains spore-producing sacs called sporangia. When the spores are mature, the capsule opens and releases them. Spores allow seedless plants to disperse to new areas. If a spore lands in a favorable spot for growing, it can grow into a gametophyte.

A moss gametophyte produces gametes in special reproductive structures. Each male structure produces hundreds of sperm with whiplike flagella, and each female structure produces a single egg. When water is present, sperm swim toward an egg. Once a sperm fertilizes an egg, the sporophyte phase begins once again.

TAKING NOTES

Use combination notes to summarize the life cycles of nonvascular, seedless vascular, and seed plants.

type of plant	life cycle

VOCABULARY

The suffix *–phyte* comes from the Greek word *phuton*, meaning "plant."

FIGURE 22.2 MOSS LIFE CYCLE

sporophyte (2*n*)

gametophyte (1*n*)

capsule

spores (1*n*)

The gametophyte of mosses is the carpet-like plant that may be familiar to you. The sporophyte grows up from the gametophyte. A tiny cup called a capsule forms at the tip of each moss sporophyte.

Spores form inside the capsule. When the spores are mature, the capsule opens and releases them. Spores can grow into new gametophytes when the environmental conditions are favorable.

Connecting CONCEPTS

Life Cycles Refer to the **Appendix** for a detailed view of the moss life cycle.

Chapter 22: Plant Growth, Reproduction, and Response **665**

FIGURE 22.3 FERN LIFE CYCLE

sporophyte (2*n*)

sori

The fern sporophyte is the leafy plant that you may be familiar with. Clusters of spore-holding sacs called sori grow on the underside of each fern leaf, or frond.

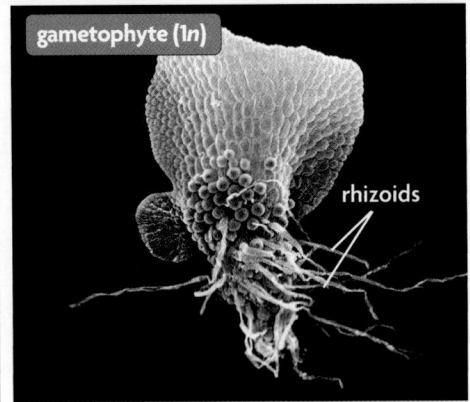

gametophyte (1*n*)

rhizoids

A fern spore can grow into a fern gametophyte, called a prothallus. The prothallus is about the size of your little fingernail. Structures that produce sperm and eggs are located on the bottom of the prothallus. (colored SEM; magnification 110× © Dr. Richard Kessel & Dr. Gene Shih/Visuals Unlimited)

Connecting CONCEPTS

Life Cycles Refer to the **Appendix** for detailed views of fern and conifer life cycles.

Life Cycle of Seedless Vascular Plants: Ferns

The sporophyte is the dominant phase for all vascular plants, including seedless vascular plants such as ferns. This means that the plants you recognize as ferns are sporophytes. If you look at the underside of a fern leaf, called a frond, you might see sori. Sori are clusters of sporangia, which are spore-producing sacs. As shown in **FIGURE 22.3**, sori look like brown dots on the fern frond. Spores are released from the sporangia when they are mature. If a spore lands in a favorable spot for growing, it can develop into a gametophyte.

A fern gametophyte is often called a prothallus. As you can see in **FIGURE 22.3**, a prothallus is a plant body about the size of your little fingernail. It anchors itself to the soil with tiny threadlike structures called rhizoids. The prothallus contains special reproductive structures that produce sperm and eggs.

When free-standing water is present, male structures release sperm. Sperm then swim toward an egg. When a sperm fertilizes an egg, a zygote forms on the prothallus. Remember that the zygote is the beginning of the sporophyte generation. The zygote grows above the prothallus, which eventually rots away. The mature sporophyte is the familiar fern plant. Newly forming fronds are called fiddleheads, and they slowly uncurl as they grow. Eventually, the sporophyte will produce spores on the underside of each frond, and the cycle will begin again.

Life Cycle of Seed Plants: Conifers

The sporophyte is the familiar form for all seed plants. Unlike most seedless plants, seed plants produce two types of spores that develop into male and female gametophytes. Another difference between most seedless plants and seed plants is that the gametophytes of seed plants are microscopic.

A pine tree is a typical conifer sporophyte. If you look closely at a branch of a pine tree, you may notice two different types of cones. This is because cone-bearing plants have male and female cones. Female cones are usually larger and more scaly than male cones. They live and grow for several years. Each scale of a female pine cone has two ovules that produce spores. One spore in each ovule can develop into a microscopic female gametophyte, and the rest will die. Male spores are produced inside of male cones, which only live for a few weeks. Male spores develop into pollen grains, which are the very tiny male gametophytes of seed plants.

As shown in **FIGURE 22.4**, male cones release clouds of pollen in the spring. When a pollen grain lands on a female cone, it sticks. Pollination occurs in a cone-bearing plant when a pollen grain reaches the small opening of an ovule. After pollination, eggs are produced inside the ovule and a pollen tube begins to grow from the pollen grain toward an egg. In pine species, it takes a year for the pollen tube to reach the egg, which is only several millimeters away.

FIGURE 22.4 Conifer Life Cycle

The pine tree is a typical conifer sporophyte. Male and female gametophytes are produced on separate male and female pine cones.

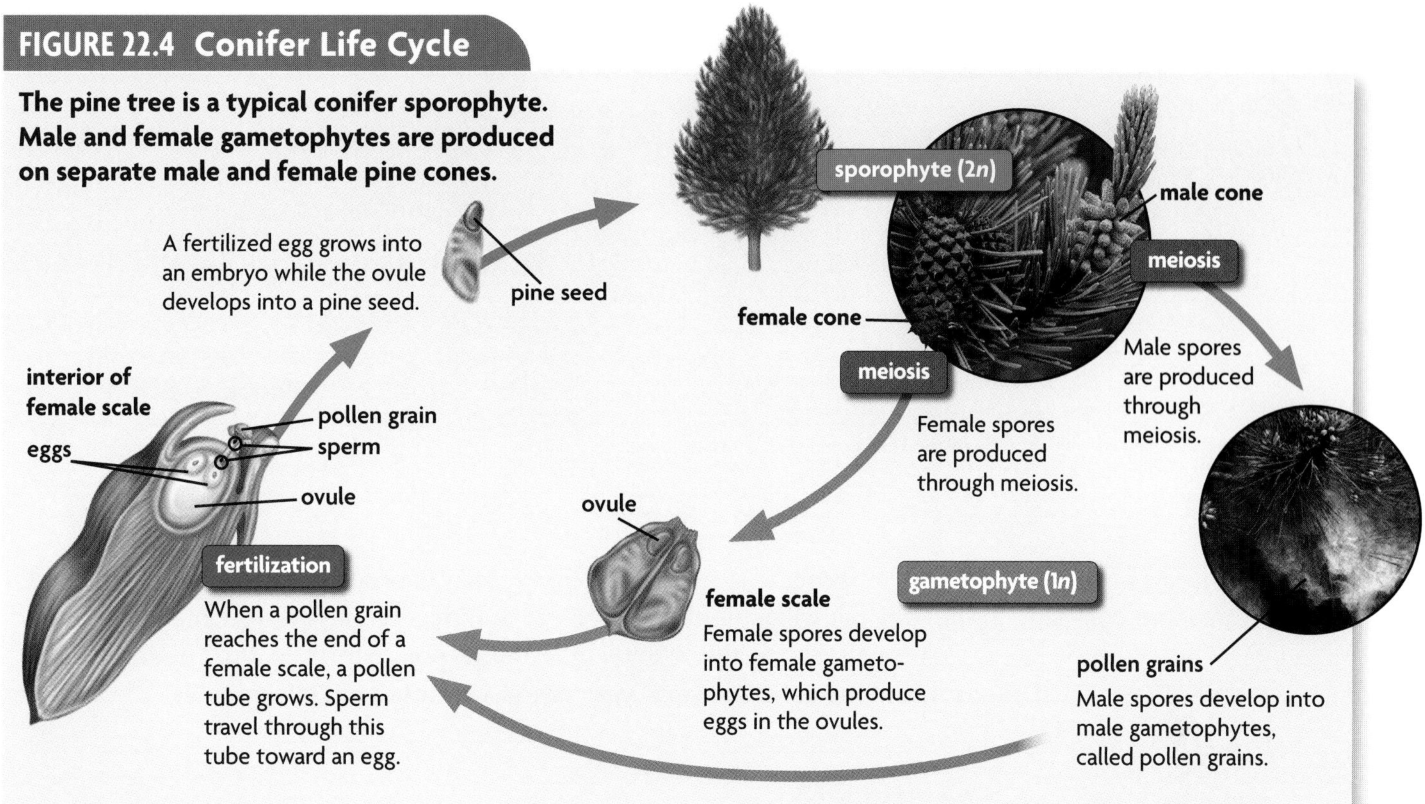

A fertilized egg grows into an embryo while the ovule develops into a pine seed.

pine seed

sporophyte (2n)

male cone

meiosis

female cone

meiosis

Male spores are produced through meiosis.

Female spores are produced through meiosis.

interior of female scale

eggs

pollen grain

sperm

ovule

ovule

fertilization
When a pollen grain reaches the end of a female scale, a pollen tube grows. Sperm travel through this tube toward an egg.

female scale
Female spores develop into female gametophytes, which produce eggs in the ovules.

gametophyte (1n)

pollen grains
Male spores develop into male gametophytes, called pollen grains.

Two sperm also develop inside the pollen grain during this time. Eventually, these sperm travel down the pollen tube toward the egg. The sperm of seed plants do not have flagella, since they do not need to swim through water to reach an egg. One sperm may fertilize an egg, forming a zygote, which will develop into an embryo. Meanwhile, the ovule develops into a protective pine seed. Each scale of a female pine cone can be home to two developing pine seeds. Once the seeds are mature, the scales open up and release them. The life cycle then begins again with a new sporophyte—a pine tree seedling.

Contrast What is the difference between how seedless plants and seed plants disperse to new areas?

22.1 ASSESSMENT

ONLINE QUIZ
ClassZone.com

REVIEWING ▶ MAIN IDEAS

1. What is the main difference between the two types of plant bodies involved in the **alternation of generations**?

2. What is the main difference between the **gametophytes** of nonvascular plants and those of seed plants?

CRITICAL THINKING

3. **Apply** Why do seedless plants require free-standing water for sexual reproduction, while seed plants do not?

4. **Infer** The scales of female pine cones produce a sticky substance. What function might this serve?

Connecting CONCEPTS

5. **Genetics** Draw a diagram to show how cellular division through meiosis results in the haploid spores of plants.

22.2

Reproduction in Flowering Plants

KEY CONCEPTS Reproduction of flowering plants takes place within flowers.

▶ **MAIN IDEAS**

- Flowers contain reproductive organs protected by specialized leaves.
- Flowering plants can be pollinated by wind or animals.
- Fertilization takes place within the flower.

VOCABULARY

sepal, p. 668   **ovary,** p. 668

petal, p. 668   **endosperm,** p. 670

stamen, p. 668   **double fertilization,** p. 670

carpel, p. 668

Review
cotyledon, fruit

REVIEW AT CLASSZONE.COM

Connect When planning a garden, you may choose plants with sweet-smelling flowers that will add splashes of color to the space. But did you know that these same qualities can attract and guide animal pollinators? So don't be surprised if you and the insects in your yard have a similar taste in flowers.

▶ **MAIN IDEA**

Flowers contain reproductive organs protected by specialized leaves.

Look at a bouquet of flowers in various stages of bloom, and you will likely notice that different flower parts are arranged in layers. The outermost layer of a flower is made up of sepals. **Sepals** are modified leaves that protect the developing flower. They are often green but can also be brightly colored. The layer just inside of the sepals is made of up **petals,** which are also modified leaves. Their bright colors often help to attract animal pollinators. Monocot flowers, such as lilies, have sepals and petals that look the same. These structures are often called tepals. Flowering plants that are not pollinated by animals usually have very small sepals and petals, or they have none at all.

Some species have flowers with only male or only female structures, but the flowers of most species have both. A typical flower is illustrated in **FIGURE 22.5.** A **stamen** is the male structure of a flower. Each stamen has a stalk called a filament that supports an anther. Anthers produce pollen grains, the male gametophytes. The innermost layer of a flower is made up of the female structure, called a **carpel.** Most flowers have several carpels fused together, forming a structure called a pistil. Each carpel is made of three parts. The tip, called the stigma, is often covered with a sticky substance that holds pollen grains when they land there. The style is a tube that leads from the stigma to the ovary. Female gametophytes are produced inside the **ovary,** which is found at the base of a flower.

FIGURE 22.5 This lily has both male and female structures. In lilies and other monocots, sepals and petals look similar and are often called "tepals."

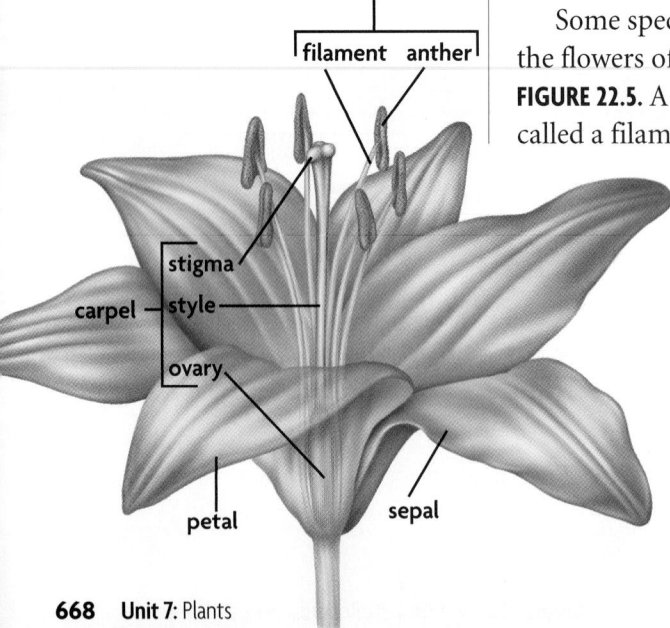

stamen
filament   anther

stigma
carpel — style
ovary
petal   sepal

Compare What parts of conifers have functions similar to stamens?

MAIN IDEA
Flowering plants can be pollinated by wind or animals.

When a pollen grain reaches the stigma of the same plant species, that flower has been pollinated. Pollination is a necessary step of sexual reproduction in flowering plants. You can often tell how a flowering plant is pollinated by looking at its flowers. Wind-pollinated species usually have small or inconspicuous flowers and produce large amounts of pollen. A lot of energy is required to produce so much pollen.

Many flowering plants are pollinated when insects, birds, or other animals visit flowers to collect pollen or nectar as a food source. In the process of feeding, an animal is dusted with pollen grains, as shown in **FIGURE 22.6.** As the animal searches for food in another flower, pollen from the first flower may brush against the stigma of the other flower. Because animal pollinators transfer pollen in this reliable way, pollination by an animal is more efficient than wind pollination. Animal pollinators are important factors in the success and diversity of flowering plants.

Infer Why is pollination more reliable by animals than by wind?

pollen grains

FIGURE 22.6 This honeybee has many tiny hairs on its body (right). When a bee moves around inside of a flower, gathering pollen or nectar, pollen grains stick to these hairs (left). (colored SEM; magnification unknown)

QUICK LAB   DISSECTING

A Closer Look at Flowers
Dissect a flower to discover how its various structures aid in reproduction.

PROBLEM How do the parts of a flower aid in reproduction?

PROCEDURE

1. Locate the outermost layer of flower parts. These are the sepals. Draw and label the sepals to begin your flower diagram. Carefully remove the sepals.

2. Petals form the next layer of flower parts. Draw and label the petals in your drawing. Carefully remove each petal.

3. Now the stamens, the male flower parts, should be exposed. Add the stamens to your drawing and label them. Label an anther and a filament in your drawing. Remove the stamens.

4. The female flower part remains. Most flowers have several carpels fused together, forming a structure called a pistil. Add the carpel or pistil to your drawing. Label the carpel or pistil, stigma, style, and ovary.

MATERIALS
- flower
- colored pencils
- tweezers
- magnifying glass

ANALYZE AND CONCLUDE

1. **Identify** Write the function of the following structures next to their labels in your drawing: sepals, petals, anther, filament, stigma, style, and ovary.

2. **Infer** Do flowers usually contain more stamens or carpels? Why do you think this is?

3. **Infer** What does the position of the anthers relative to the position of the stigmas suggest about how this flower is pollinated?

● MAIN IDEA

Fertilization takes place within the flower.

In flowering plants, as in all vascular plants, the sporophyte is the dominant phase. The parts of a flower that you have just learned about are all part of the sporophyte, while the gametophytes of flowering plants are tiny and enclosed within flower parts. **FIGURE 22.7** illustrates the life cycle of flowering plants.

Production of Male Gametophytes

Recall that anthers produce pollen grains, which are the male gametophytes of seed plants. Cells within the anthers divide by meiosis to produce four male spores. Each spore divides again, by mitosis, producing two haploid cells. These two cells, together with a thick wall that protects them, form a single pollen grain. Wind-pollinated plants have light, fine pollen grains that can be carried far by the wind. Pollen from wind-pollinated plants, such as ragweed, is the source of some outdoor allergies.

Production of Female Gametophytes

One female gametophyte can form in each ovule of a flower's ovary. One cell in the ovule divides by meiosis to produce four female spores. In most flowering plants, three of these spores die. The nucleus of the last spore grows, dividing by mitosis three times, resulting in one spore with eight nuclei. Membranes grow between the nuclei to form seven cells. Together, these seven cells make up the female gametophyte, which is sometimes called an embryo sac. One large, central cell has two haploid nuclei, called polar nuclei. One of the other cells develops into an egg.

Double Fertilization

After pollination, one cell in the pollen grain grows into a pollen tube. This tube extends down the style toward the ovule. The other cell in the pollen grain divides by mitosis, producing two sperm. Both sperm travel down the pollen tube. One sperm fertilizes the egg. The other sperm combines with the polar nuclei in the embryo sac. This cell now has a triploid ($3n$) nucleus. It will become the **endosperm**, a food supply for the developing plant embryo. The process in which one sperm fertilizes an egg and the other forms a triploid cell is called **double fertilization.** Double fertilization only happens in flowering plants and gives them an advantage over cone-bearing plants. Cone-bearing plants produce a food supply for each egg before fertilization. However, if the egg of a flowering plant is not fertilized, the plant does not waste energy making an unneeded food supply.

Connecting CONCEPTS

Meiosis Recall from **Chapter 6** that meiosis is the form of cellular division needed for sexual reproduction. Gametes—sperm and eggs—are haploid, containing half as many chromosomes as somatic cells do.

VISUAL VOCAB

The **endosperm** nourishes the developing plant embryo inside of the seed coat. The prefix *endo-* means "inside," and *sperm* comes from the Greek word *sperma*, which means "seed."

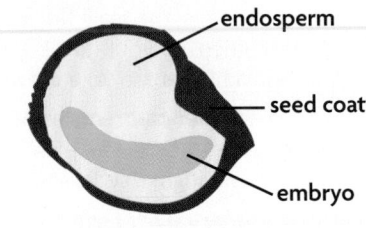

endosperm

seed coat

embryo

Summarize **What is the function of each sperm during double fertilization?**

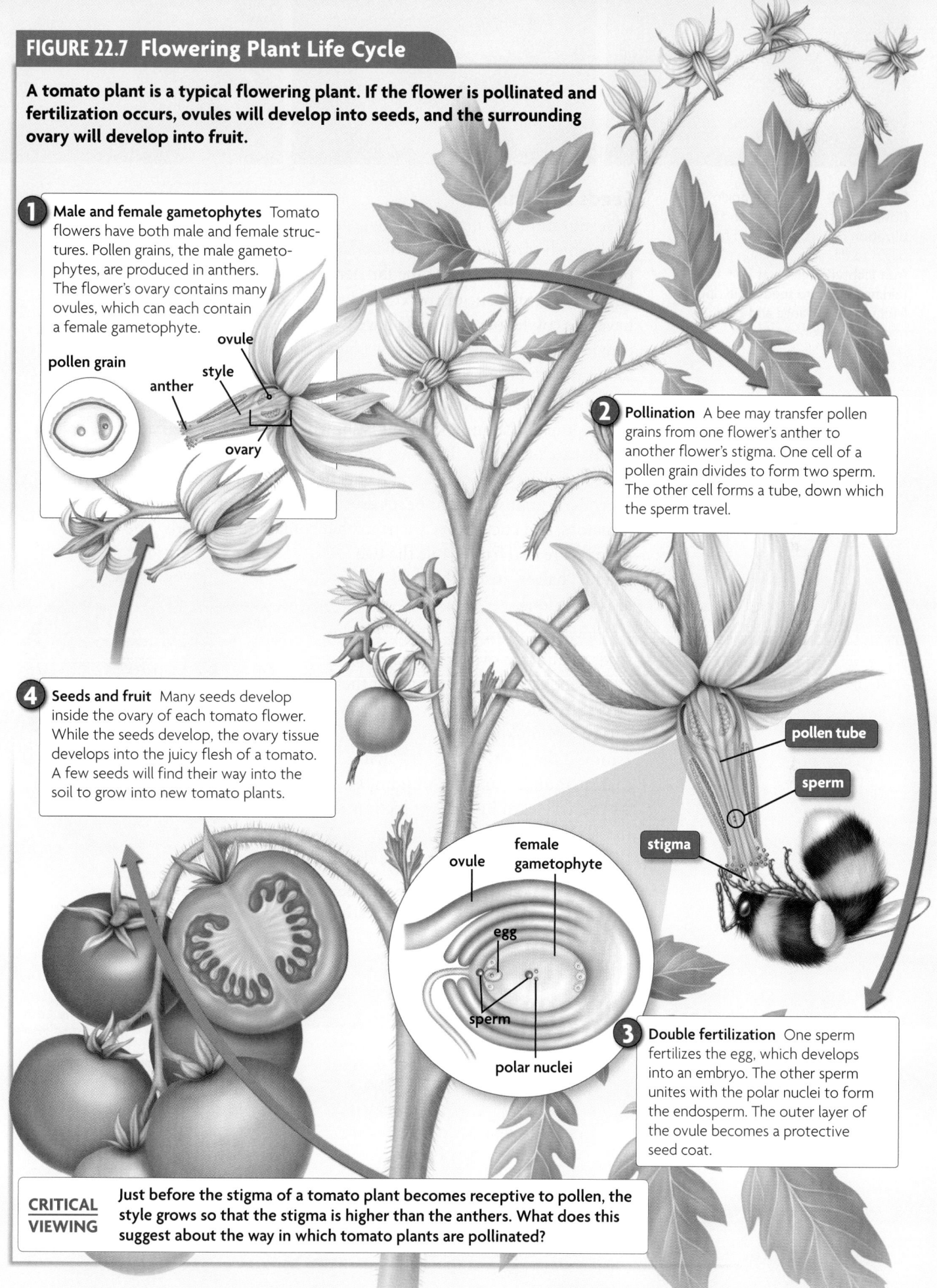

FIGURE 22.7 Flowering Plant Life Cycle

A tomato plant is a typical flowering plant. If the flower is pollinated and fertilization occurs, ovules will develop into seeds, and the surrounding ovary will develop into fruit.

1 Male and female gametophytes Tomato flowers have both male and female structures. Pollen grains, the male gametophytes, are produced in anthers. The flower's ovary contains many ovules, which can each contain a female gametophyte.

pollen grain

ovule

style

anther

ovary

2 Pollination A bee may transfer pollen grains from one flower's anther to another flower's stigma. One cell of a pollen grain divides to form two sperm. The other cell forms a tube, down which the sperm travel.

4 Seeds and fruit Many seeds develop inside the ovary of each tomato flower. While the seeds develop, the ovary tissue develops into the juicy flesh of a tomato. A few seeds will find their way into the soil to grow into new tomato plants.

pollen tube

sperm

stigma

female gametophyte

ovule

egg

sperm

polar nuclei

3 Double fertilization One sperm fertilizes the egg, which develops into an embryo. The other sperm unites with the polar nuclei to form the endosperm. The outer layer of the ovule becomes a protective seed coat.

CRITICAL VIEWING Just before the stigma of a tomato plant becomes receptive to pollen, the style grows so that the stigma is higher than the anthers. What does this suggest about the way in which tomato plants are pollinated?

FIGURE 22.8 After a pumpkin flower (left) is pollinated and fertilization occurs, seeds and fruit begin to develop. The pumpkin fruit (center) is green at first, containing immature seeds. The ripe fruit (right) is orange and contains mature pumpkin seeds.

Seeds and Fruit

At fertilization, the next sporophyte generation begins. The ovule becomes a seed, which contains an embryo and a nutritious endosperm enclosed by a protective seed coat. Using the nutrients provided by the endosperm, the embryo develops one or two cotyledons, or seed leaves. Recall that monocots have one cotyledon and dicots have two cotyledons. Cotyledons sometimes provide nourishment for the new plant before it can begin producing its own food through photosynthesis.

While the seed develops, the surrounding ovary grows into a fruit. The development of a pumpkin fruit is shown in **FIGURE 22.8**. Remember, a fruit is the mature ovary of a flowering plant. You have probably eaten many fruits, such as apples, watermelons, and cherries. Many foods that you think of as vegetables, grains, nuts, or beans are also technically fruits. Sweet peppers, tomatoes, and cucumbers are fruits that contain many seeds. The shells of peanuts are also fruit, while the two peanut "halves" inside the shell are cotyledons.

Flowering plants that produce many seeds within one ovary have larger fruit. Pumpkin plants produce some of the largest fruits on record. If you have ever carved a pumpkin, you have actually removed the fleshy part of the mature ovary that surrounds hundreds of pumpkin seeds. As you will learn in the next section, a fruit aids in the dispersal of seeds to new areas. A seed has the ability to grow into a mature flowering plant.

Contrast **What is the major difference between seeds of flowering plants and seeds of cone-bearing plants?**

22.2 ASSESSMENT

ONLINE QUIZ
ClassZone.com

REVIEWING ▷ MAIN IDEAS

1. What are the functions of the four basic parts found in most flowers?

2. How does pollination occur in flowering plants?

3. What is **double fertilization**?

CRITICAL THINKING

4. **Infer** Why do wind-pollinated plant species generally produce more pollen than animal-pollinated species?

5. **Analyze** In flowering plants, which cells divide by meiosis to produce male and female spores?

Connecting CONCEPTS

6. **History of Life** Would brightly colored flowers and sweet, juicy fruits have been as beneficial to the earliest land plants as they are to modern flowering plants? Explain.

22.3 Seed Dispersal and Germination

KEY CONCEPT Seeds disperse and begin to grow when conditions are favorable.

▶ **MAIN IDEAS**
- Animals, wind, and water can spread seeds.
- Seeds begin to grow when environmental conditions are favorable.

VOCABULARY

dormancy, p. 674
germination, p. 675

MICHIGAN STANDARDS

B2.5f Relate plant structures and functions to the process of photosynthesis and respiration.

Connect It's lunchtime—how about a burrito stuffed with seeds and fruit? This burrito may not sound too appetizing; that is, unless you know that white rice and beans are seeds and tomatoes are fruits. Although burritos are cooked, many seeds and fruits we eat are not. Animals eat seeds and fruits for their nutritional benefits, and plants benefit by getting their seeds dispersed.

▶ **MAIN IDEA**
Animals, wind, and water can spread seeds.

VOCABULARY

The word *disperse* means "to scatter apart," The prefix *dis-* means "apart", and *sperse* comes from the Latin verb *spargere,* which means "to scatter."

FIGURE 22.9 Fruits can take many forms, including burrs, parachute-like structures such as cypselae, and winglike structures such as samaras.

You have learned that cone-bearing plants do not bear fruit, and their seeds are often spread by wind and gravity. The function of fruit in flowering plants is to help disperse seeds. Seed dispersal is important because a plant that grows right next to its parent may compete with it for space, sunlight, water, and nutrients. As shown in **FIGURE 22.9**, fruits come in a variety of different shapes and sizes, each of which is adapted to spread seeds to new areas.

Fleshy fruits, such as apples and berries, attract animals with their fragrant, nutritious offerings. When an animal eats the fruit, it digests the flesh. But the seeds, covered with a tough protective coat, pass through. Eventually, the animal eliminates the seeds from its digestive tract, along with a supply of fecal fertilizer that serves as a sprouting ground for the seedling. Some plants have fruits that can hitchhike a ride with an animal that is passing by. Burrs, for example, can cling to a passing animal and fall off later in a new area.

Seeds dispersed by wind often have fruits that act like parachutes or wings. Clumps of cotton from cottonwood trees are actually fruits with a seed attached. Some plants that grow near water produce fruits that float. Coconuts can travel thousands of miles across oceans and arrive on different islands.

Analyze **Why is it important for a fruit to ripen when its seeds are mature?**

Burrs

Cypselae

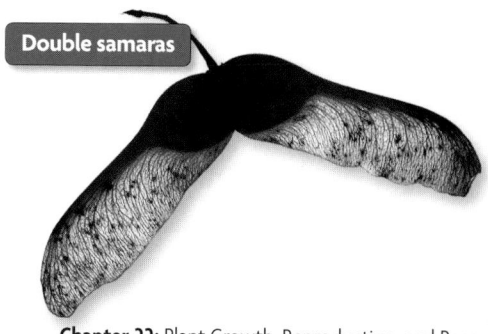

Double samaras

Chapter 22: Plant Growth, Reproduction, and Response **673**

IDENTIFYING EXPERIMENTAL DESIGN FLAWS
Recall that a good experimental design is necessary to obtain valid results. In the experiment described below, a group of students collected data about the effect of water on germination.

- Students planted 2 radish seeds in each of 3 flower pots.
- Each pot contained the same amount and type of soil.
- The pots were placed close to a window, as shown at the right.
- Pot A was given 200 mL of water each day, Pot B was given 100 mL of water each day, and Pot C was given no water. This watering pattern was continued for one full week.
- Every day, students recorded the seeds' progress.
- The students made conclusions about the amount of water that is best for radish seed germination.

1. **Analyze** Which parts of the experimental design are flawed?
2. **Design** How would you change the experimental design to collect valid results?

▶ MAIN IDEA

Seeds begin to grow when environmental conditions are favorable.

After a parent plant releases seeds, it may be days, months, or years until the seeds begin to grow into new plants. In fact, scientists recently found a 2000-year-old seed from a now-extinct species of date palm tree in Israel. After they placed it in the conditions the tree needs to grow, the seed sprouted. How can the living embryo inside a seed last years without food or water?

Dormancy
For 2000 years, the embryo inside the date palm seed was in a state of **dormancy.** When a seed is dormant, the embryo has stopped growing. For some plant species, proper temperature, moisture, oxygen, and light levels are enough to end dormancy.

Other plant species have seeds that stay dormant even during good growing conditions. For example, strawberry seeds remain dormant until their seed coats are weakened in the digestive tract of an animal. This way, the seeds are not only carried far from the parent plant but they are also deposited with their own batch of fertilizer. Other seeds have waterproof seed coats that can only be cracked by winter ice. Then, in the spring, the embryo can begin to grow with less chance of freezing than if it had begun to grow in the fall.

Seed dormancy allows the next generation of plants to grow under favorable conditions. Inside the seed coat, an embryo can withstand extremes that would kill a young seedling. Gardeners contend with seed dormancy all the time. When soil is turned over before planting a garden, fresh air and sunlight can cause the buried seeds of unexpected plants to come out of dormancy.

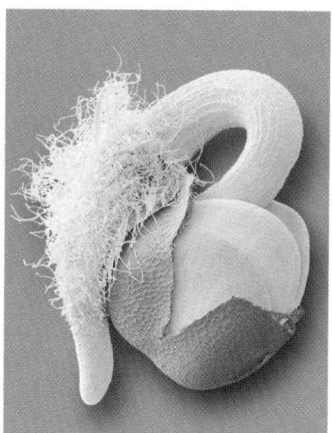

FIGURE 22.10 The embryonic root emerges from the seed.

As the root continues to emerge, root hairs can be seen.

The embryonic shoot and the cotyledons are revealed.

The young plant is completely free of its seed coat.

Germination

Many types of seeds begin to grow when there are certain changes in temperature, moisture, or light levels. During **germination,** the embryo breaks out of the seed coat and begins to grow into a seedling, as shown in **FIGURE 22.10.** Germination begins when the embryo starts to take up water. Water causes the seed to swell and crack the seed coat. As the embryo grows, the embryonic root, called a radicle, breaks through the cracks. Water also activates enzymes inside the seed. Recall that enzymes are proteins that need specific conditions to speed up chemical reactions. These enzymes help to break down material in the endosperm into sugars, which are moved to the growing embryo.

As the embryo continues to grow, a young shoot called the plumule eventually breaks through the surface of the soil. In most monocots, the cotyledon stays underground while the shoot grows upwards. Some species of dicots have cotyledons that stay below ground, but the cotyledons of other dicots emerge above ground with the growing shoot. When leaves emerge from the shoot, they begin to make food through photosynthesis. Once photosynthesis begins, the young plant is called a seedling.

Sequence Which emerges first from a seed, a root or a shoot?

Connecting CONCEPTS

Enzymes Recall from **Chapter 2** that enzymes are catalysts for chemical reactions in living things. Enzymes allow chemical reactions to take place under controlled conditions.

22.3 ASSESSMENT

ONLINE QUIZ
ClassZone.com

REVIEWING ▶ MAIN IDEAS

1. What are three ways that seeds of flowering plants can be dispersed?
2. What is the advantage of most seeds going through a stage of **dormancy** before **germination**?

CRITICAL THINKING

3. **Analyze** How are enzymes involved in the process of germination?
4. **Infer** What is the adaptive advantage to water uptake causing a seed coat to crack?

Connecting CONCEPTS

5. **Adaptations** Some tropical plant species have fruits with air cavities that allow them to float. How might natural selection have led to this adaptation?

MATERIALS

- 2 plastic grids
- 2 petri dishes
- pencil
- forceps
- 7 nonirradiated radish seeds
- 7 irradiated radish seeds
- paper towel
- small container to hold petri dishes
- fluorescent light
- hand lens
- metric ruler

PROCESS SKILLS

- **Observing**
- **Measuring**
- **Collecting**
- **Interpreting Data**

MICHIGAN STANDARDS

B1.1B Evaluate the uncertainties or validity of scientific conclusions using an understanding of sources of measurement error, the challenges of controlling variables, accuracy of data analysis, logic of argument, logic of experimental design, and/or the dependence on underlying assumptions.

B2.5f Relate plant structures and functions to the process of photosynthesis and respiration.

Seed Germination

Germination is the process in which a seed develops into a plant. During this lab, you will observe the emergence of different seedling parts and track their growth. As a class, you will test the effect that different levels of radiation have on the process of germination. Irradiated seeds have been treated with specific levels of radiation; nonirradiated seeds have not been exposed to radiation.

PROBLEM   What effect does radiation have on the process of seed germination?

PROCEDURE

1. Label two plastic grids with your initials, date, and level of radiation. Place one grid in the top of each petri dish. (You may want to put a bit of water between the petri dish and the plastic grid to hold it in place. Make sure you smooth out any air pockets or wrinkles in the plastic.)

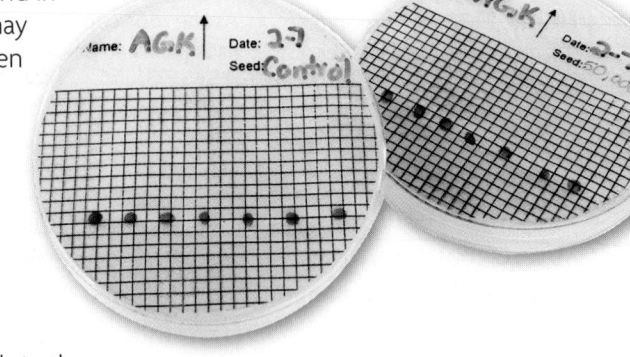

2. Use the forceps to place seven nonirradiated seeds in a row on one of the grid lines of the appropriate petri dish, as shown. Repeat with seven irradiated seeds in the other petri dish.

3. Place a paper towel over the grid in the top of each petri dish. Wet the paper towel thoroughly and cover each dish with its bottom half.

4. Put the petri dishes in a small container. Rest the petri dishes at a slight angle against the side of the container, as shown. Add water to the container to a depth of 2 cm.

5. Place the container holding the petri dishes under a fluorescent light or close to a window.

6. Beginning on the day after you set up the experiment (Day 1), observe the process of seed germination for each seed. Use a hand lens to examine each seed closely. Using two tables similar to Table 1 (one for control and one for irradiated seeds), record the day that these events occur for each seed:

   - the embryo splits from its seed coat
   - the radicle emerges
   - the plumule emerges
   - the cotyledons emerge

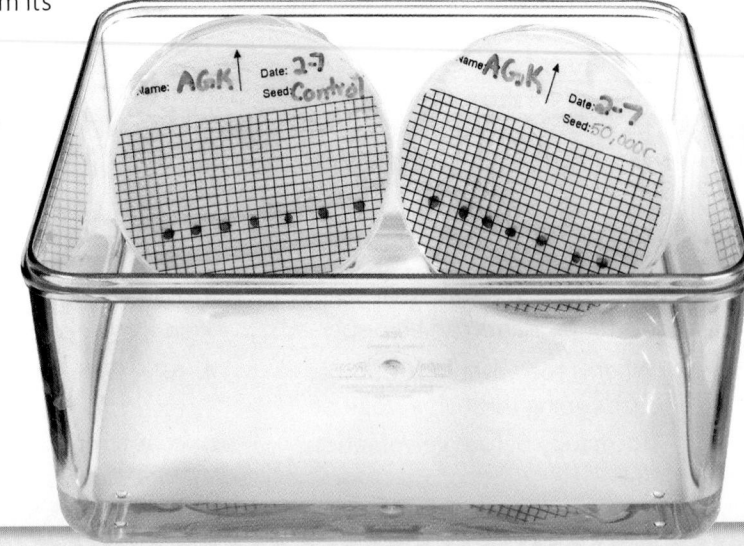

TABLE 1. SEED GERMINATION AND EMERGENCE OF SEEDLING PARTS				
	Newly Split Seed Coats	Newly Emerged Radicles	Newly Emerged Plumules	Newly Emerged Cotyledons
Day 1				
Day 2				
Day 3				
Day 4				

7. Observe the germinating seeds for four days. Be sure to keep the paper towel moist by adding water to the container, as necessary, up to 2 cm deep.

8. On the last day of your experiment, randomly pick three of the germinated seedlings from each dish. Use a ruler to measure the radicle/root length, plumule/stem length, and cotyledon/leaf length of each of these seedlings. Record this data for both sets of seedlings in your notebook.

ANALYZE AND CONCLUDE

1. Analyze Did the seedling structures emerge in the same order in all of your germinating seeds? Describe any variation that you observed.

2. Analyze When you measured seedling structures on the last day of the experiment, did the size of the same structures differ from one seedling to another? If so, what would account for this difference?

3. Calculate What percentage of your nonirradiated seeds germinated? What percentage of your irradiated seeds germinated?

4. Analyze Pool your class data for percent germination (question 3) by finding the average percent germination for level of radiation. What effect did level of radiation have on seed germination?

5. Compare Compare your measurements with the measurements of seedlings that were exposed to a different level of radiation. Did the level of radiation affect the growth rate of the seedlings?

6. Infer You may have noticed that the seeds that germinated increased in size before the seed coats cracked open. What likely caused this increase in size?

7. Infer At what point in the germination process would photosynthesis begin to provide energy for further seedling growth?

EXTEND YOUR INVESTIGATION

Plant the seedlings from each petri dish into two flower plots. Track their development as they grow into mature radish plants.

During germination, the embryo emerges from its seed coat and begins to grow into a seedling.

22.4 Asexual Reproduction

KEY CONCEPTS Plants can produce genetic clones of themselves through asexual reproduction.

▶ MAIN IDEAS

- Plants can reproduce asexually with stems, leaves, or roots.
- Humans can produce plants with desirable traits using vegetative structures.

VOCABULARY

regeneration, p. 678
vegetative reproduction, p. 678

Review
asexual reproduction

MICHIGAN STANDARDS

L4.p1A Compare and contrast the differences between sexual and asexual reproduction. (prerequisite)

L4.p1B Discuss the advantages and disadvantages of sexual vs. asexual reproduction. (prerequisite)

Connecting CONCEPTS

Asexual Reproduction Recall from **Chapter 5** that asexual reproduction is the production of offspring from a single parent. These offspring are produced through mitosis and are genetically identical to the parent.

FIGURE 22.11 The jointed stem of this prickly pear cactus is made of teardrop-shaped pads. A pad that falls to the ground can grow into a full-size plant.

Connect Have you ever noticed that some plants, such as grasses and irises, grow in clumps? If you try to pull up a single iris, you'll likely find that it is connected to others by underground stems. These clumps are often made up of clones, or genetically identical copies, of one individual parent plant.

▶ MAIN IDEA

Plants can reproduce asexually with stems, leaves, or roots.

A combination of sexual and asexual reproduction helps plants to populate a variety of environments. Sexual reproduction gives rise to genetic diversity, which allows a population to adapt to changing conditions. Asexual reproduction allows a well-adapted plant to make many copies of itself. Most plants have a way of cloning themselves through asexual reproduction.

Plants that can grow a new individual from a fragment of a stem, leaf, or root are reproducing by **regeneration.** For example, the prickly pear cactus shown in **FIGURE 22.11** has a jointed stem that looks like teardrop-shaped pads stuck together. If one of these "pads" falls off, it can take root and a new plant will grow.

Vegetative reproduction is a type of asexual reproduction in which stems, leaves, or roots attached to the parent plant produce new individuals. One stunning example of vegetative reproduction is a forest of aspen trees in Utah that would almost cover 100 football fields. The forest is actually 47,000 trunks growing from the roots of one parent plant.

Many plants have structures that are specifically adapted for vegetative reproduction.

- **Stolons** Some plants send out stems that grow horizontally along the ground. These stems are called runners, or stolons. At certain points on a stolon, roots and leaves are produced, and a new plant can grow. Strawberries reproduce almost exclusively in this way.

- **Rhizomes** Other plants, such as irises, can reproduce using horizontal underground stems called rhizomes. New plants grow from buds in the rhizome's joints, even if separated from the parent plant.

- **Tubers** A potato is actually a tuber, an underground stem modified for storage. The "eyes" of a potato are buds that can sprout new plants, as shown in **FIGURE 22.12**.

- **Bulbs** Tulips, daffodils, and onion plants can all reproduce asexually with bulbs. Bulbs are underground stems surrounded by modified leaves adapted for storage, covered with a protective, papery skin. In favorable conditions, bulbs can divide to produce new plants.

Analyze What distinguishes regeneration from vegetative reproduction?

FIGURE 22.12 New potato plants are growing from the "eyes" of this potato tuber.

⊙ MAIN IDEA

Humans can produce plants with desirable traits using vegetative structures.

Plant growers use a process called vegetative propagation to grow plants with desirable qualities, such as seedless fruits or tolerance to frost. Vegetative propagation takes advantage of a plant's ability to grow new individuals from fragments of a parent plant. For example, most apples and oranges that we eat come from propagated branches rather than trees grown from seeds.

Vegetative propagation can be achieved by a few common methods. Many houseplants, including African violets, are reproduced using cuttings from stems or leaves. If the cutting is buried in soil or placed in water, it will produce new roots, as shown in **FIGURE 22.13**. Cuttings are an easy way for horticulturists to produce new houseplants for sale to nurseries.

Fruit and nut tree growers usually use trees that have been produced by grafting, or joining vegetative structures from two or more plants together. Grafting involves making an incision in the bark of one tree and attaching to it either a branch or a bud from another tree. Growers can graft a bud from a tree that produces the desired fruit or nut onto the trunk of a tree that has other desired qualities, such as disease resistance.

FIGURE 22.13 This plant cutting has grown roots after being placed in water for several weeks. Many types of houseplants can be propagated in this way.

Analyze What is a benefit of producing houseplants through asexual reproduction?

22.4 ASSESSMENT

⟳ **ONLINE QUIZ** ClassZone.com

REVIEWING ⊙ MAIN IDEAS

1. How can a combination of sexual and asexual reproduction be beneficial for plant populations?

2. How do humans use plants' ability to reproduce asexually?

CRITICAL THINKING

3. **Compare and Contrast** What are the differences and similarities between stolons and rhizomes?

4. **Infer** What is a benefit of using propagated branches to grow fruits?

Connecting CONCEPTS

5. **Genetics** How does the genotype of an offspring produced through asexual reproduction compare with the parent plant's genotype?

22.5 Plant Hormones and Responses

KEY CONCEPT Plant hormones guide plant growth and development.

▶ MAIN IDEAS

- Plant hormones regulate plant functions.
- Plants can respond to light, touch, gravity, and seasonal changes.

VOCABULARY

hormone, p. 680
gibberellin, p. 680
ethylene, p. 681
cytokinin, p. 681
auxin, p. 681

tropism, p. 681
phototropism, p. 682
thigmotropism, p. 682
gravitropism, p. 682
photoperiodism, p. 683

MICHIGAN STANDARDS

B2.2f Explain the role of enzymes and other proteins in biochemical functions (e.g., the protein hemoglobin carries oxygen in some organisms, digestive enzymes, and hormones).

Connect If you have houseplants, you've seen how they grow toward the sunlight streaming through the window. But without eyes, how do plants know where the light is? Plant hormones are involved in this process, which is only one of many ways that plants can respond to their environment.

▶ MAIN IDEA
Plant hormones regulate plant functions.

A **hormone** is a chemical messenger produced in one part of an organism that stimulates or suppresses the activity of cells in another part. In humans and other animals, hormones control functions vital to survival and reproduction. Hormones direct and regulate many of the same functions in plants. However, most plant hormones are very different chemicals from those in animals.

Some plant hormones are released in response to normal changes in the environment where the plant grows. Other hormones are released due to internal changes, as part of a plant's life cycle. Hormones have an influence when they move from the cells that secrete them to the cells for which they are targeted. Target cells have receptors that recognize the hormone. Most plant cells have receptors for many different hormones. When a hormone meets the right receptor, it triggers a response. Plant hormones are divided into several different groups based on their functions and chemical properties.

Gibberellins
Gibberellins (jihb-uh-REHL-ihnz) are plant hormones that produce dramatic increases in size. They are involved in ending seed dormancy, starting germination, and promoting the rapid growth of young seedlings. Gibberellins are also responsible for the large size of many fruits and the rapid upward growth of some flower stalks. For example, the agave shown in **FIGURE 22.14** can send a flowering stalk up to 12 meters (40 ft) tall in a few weeks. Grape growers often spray their vines with a gibberellin solution, which makes the fruits grow larger and elongates the stems in the bunches, making room for more grapes.

FIGURE 22.14 An agave plant only flowers one time, when the plant is at least 15 years old. Gibberellins trigger its flower stalk to shoot up over the course of a few weeks.

Ethylene

Put an apple in an airtight container for a day, and it will get soft and start to look rotten. The apple is being ripened abnormally fast by its own production of **ethylene** (EHTH-uh-LEEN), a plant hormone that causes ripening and is naturally produced by fruits. Commercial growers can use ethylene to their advantage. Fruits such as apples that are shipped long distances must be kept in rooms where the ethylene is filtered out, or they may become overripe during the journey. Some fruits, such as the tomatoes in **FIGURE 22.5**, are picked before they are ripe. Once they reach their destination, they are exposed to ethylene gas, which makes them turn a ripe-tomato red. They may not taste so ripe, though, because this artificial ripening process does not bring out the same sugars that a vine-ripened tomato has.

Cytokinins

Cytokinins (SY-tuh-KY-nihnz) are plant hormones that stimulate cytokinesis, which is the final stage of cell division. They are produced in growing roots and developing seeds and fruits. They are also involved in the growth of side branches. This sideways growth is called lateral growth. Commercial florists make use of another property of cytokinins—they slow the aging process of some plant organs. For example, leaves dipped in a cytokinin solution stay green much longer than normal.

FIGURE 22.15 Many tomatoes are picked before they are ripe and treated with ethylene before they are sold at grocery stores. These tomatoes may not taste as sweet as vine-ripened tomatoes.

Auxins

Auxins (AWK-sihnz) are plant hormones involved in the lengthening of plant cells produced in the apical meristem, or growing tip. Auxins stimulate growth of the primary stem, preventing growth of new branches. Gardeners can use this property of auxins to control branching patterns by cutting off the tip of a growing stem. With no growing tip, there is less auxin in the stem, and side branches are encouraged to grow. Conversely, high concentrations of auxins can prevent plant growth altogether, particularly in the roots. For this reason, auxins are a common ingredient in herbicides, chemicals used to kill unwanted plants.

The lengthening of cells triggered by auxins also controls some forms of **tropism,** the movement of a plant in response to an environmental stimulus. For example, if a stimulus such as light hits one side of a stem, auxins will build up in the cells on the shaded side of the stem. These cells then elongate, or grow longer, causing the stem to bend toward the light. As you will soon learn, auxins have different effects in the cells of different plant organs.

TAKING NOTES

Use a main idea web to take notes about four major plant hormones.

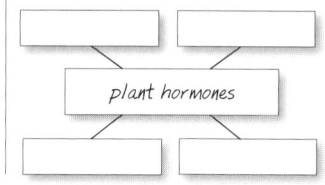

Apply **If you started your own plant nursery, explain two ways in which you could use different plant hormones to your advantage.**

Auxins build up on the shaded side of plant stems, causing these cells to lengthen. The lengthening of these cells causes the stem to bend in the direction of the light source.

FIGURE 22.16 Phototropism is the process in which plants grow toward a light source. Here, the stems and leaves of a houseplant bend toward a nearby window.

Connecting CONCEPTS

Physical Science Recall that gravity is the force that objects exert on each other because of their mass. Gravity is the force responsible for things falling to the ground.

▶ **MAIN IDEA**

Plants can respond to light, touch, gravity, and seasonal changes.

If you've ever touched a hot pan in the kitchen, you likely responded by pulling your hand away quickly. And if you've ever been outside on a very hot summer day, you may have responded by moving to a shady spot. While plants cannot uproot themselves and change locations, they have other ways of responding to their environment.

Phototropism

When light hits a plant stem, it causes auxins to build up on the shaded side. Remember that in a stem, auxins cause cell elongation. As described earlier, cell lengthening on the shaded side of a stem causes the stem to bend toward the light. This tendency of a plant to grow toward light is called **phototropism.** If you grow a plant in a space with only one small light source, that plant will lean toward the light through the process of phototropism, as shown in **FIGURE 22.16**. Let's say you turn that plant around so that it's pointing away from the light. If you come back in a few days, you will likely find the plant growing in the direction of the light again.

Thigmotropism

Many plants also have a response to touch, called **thigmotropism.** This quality is apparent in climbing plants and vines. Tendrils emerge from the leaf base of these plants and grow in coils around anything they touch. In these curling "fingers," contact with an object triggers the same sort of cell growth that is found with other tropisms. Plants are sensitive to many kinds of touchlike stimuli. For example, a plant regularly exposed to winds on a hillside will grow as if it is being pushed in the direction of the wind. Repeatedly touching a young plant can even stunt its growth.

Gravitropism

When a seed germinates underground, the root grows downward into the soil, and the shoot grows upward toward the soil surface. This up-and-down growth of a plant is called **gravitropism,** because the plant is responding to Earth's gravitational pull. Downward growth is positive gravitropism because the growth is in the direction that gravity pulls. Upward growth is negative gravitropism because it is growth against the force of gravity.

Auxins play a part in gravitropism, which is more complex than phototropism. Root growth is stimulated by low levels of auxin, but is slowed down by high levels of auxin. Auxins build up on the lower side of horizontally growing roots so that the upper side grows faster and the root grows downward. At the same time, high levels of auxin, which stimulate shoot growth, build up in the lower side of the stem. This buildup causes the stem to grow upward.

Rapid Responses

Some plants have very rapid responses that do not involve growth. These rapid responses are often adaptations that help to protect plants from predators. For example, the mimosa, or sensitive plant, quickly folds its leaves together a few seconds after being touched. A few plants are quick enough to capture insects for a meal. The Venus flytrap shown in **FIGURE 22.17** can close its leaves on an unsuspecting insect in less than a second. Scientists recently discovered that when the leaves are touched, water rushes to the cells at their bases, changing their curvature and snapping the trap shut.

Photoperiodism

What triggers a shrub to flower or a tree to drop its leaves? Plants take signals from the changing lengths of day and night throughout the year, in a response called **photoperiodism.** Some plants keep very accurate clocks when it comes to the amount of daylight or darkness in a 24-hour period. In fact, some plants that flower while the days are short, such as poinsettias, will not bloom if there is one extra minute of light in the evening.

Shorter days and longer nights during the fall help trigger the leaves of many deciduous trees to change color. This response is part of the preparation for winter, when these trees enter a stage of dormancy. Winter dormancy in plants is functionally similar to the hibernation of many animals during the winter months. With less rainfall and less direct sunlight, it is more energy-efficient for these plants to shut down and rely on reserved sugars than it is for them to photosynthesize. Leaves therefore begin to die in the fall. Chlorophyll, the pigment that gives leaves their green color, breaks down. Once the chlorophyll is gone, the remaining leaf pigments become visible and new pigments are produced. Water and nutrients are drawn out of the leaves for the rest of the tree to use during the winter, and the leaves eventually fall off of the tree.

Apply What stimulus causes each of the following tropisms: phototropism, gravitropism, thigmotropism?

FIGURE 22.17 When the leaves of a Venus flytrap are touched, water rushes to the cells of the leaf bases, causing the leaves to rapidly bend inward.

To learn more about plant responses, visit scilinks.org.
Keycode: MLB022

22.5 ASSESSMENT

ONLINE QUIZ
ClassZone.com

REVIEWING ▶ MAIN IDEAS

1. Describe two plant **hormones** that regulate plant growth and development.

2. Name and describe five ways in which plants can respond to their environment.

CRITICAL THINKING

3. **Apply** A vine grows sideways, twisting along a railing. What type of **tropism** is this plant exhibiting?

4. **Apply** If you want full, bushy plants, which part of the plant would you trim to control **auxin** production in your favor?

Connecting CONCEPTS

5. **Adaptations** Many trees in temperate climates lose their leaves before the long, cold winter. How is this ability an adaptation for these trees?

Use these inquiry-based labs and online activities to deepen your understanding of seeds and fruit.

DESIGN YOUR OWN INVESTIGATION

Investigating Plant Hormones

Ethylene is a plant hormone that is released by the cells of ripening fruit. As ethylene is released, new pigments are revealed as chlorophyll is broken down, causing the fruit skin to change color. The cell walls begin to break down, making the fruit softer. Finally, complex sugars break down into simple sugars, which make the fruit smell and taste sweet. These properties make fruit more appealing to eat. In this activity, you will design an experiment to determine the effects that ethylene produced by ripe fruit can have on unripe fruit.

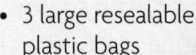

MATERIALS
- 3 unripe bananas from the same bunch
- several pieces of various ripened fruit (apple, pear, peach, and so on)
- 3 large resealable plastic bags

SKILL Observing

PROBLEM How can hormones produced by ripened fruit affect unripe fruit?

PROCEDURE

1. Using the materials provided, design a procedure that will test the effect of ripened fruit on unripe bananas. Be sure to include a control group in your design.

2. Have your experimental design checked by your teacher.

3. Record observations, such as color, texture, firmness, and smell, over a five-day period.

4. Compare your results with the results of other classmates.

ANALYZE AND CONCLUDE

1. **Summarize** What changes took place in each plastic bag over the five-day period?

2. **Analyze** Draw conclusions about the production of ethylene based on your results.

3. **Experimental Design** Why was it important that the bananas in your experiment were from the same bunch?

4. **Experimental Design** Identify some possible sources of unavoidable experimental error in your design.

5. **Infer** Why is fruit ripening an important phase in the reproduction of flowering plants?

EXTEND YOUR INVESTIGATION

Do some research to find out what kinds of fruit are often harvested before they are ripe.

INVESTIGATION

Fruit Dissection

In this lab, you will accurately represent the inside of a fruit and its seeds with a scientific illustration.

SKILL Illustrating

PROBLEM How can you represent the sizes and proportions of structures in a scientific illustration?

MATERIALS

- pea pod
- scalpel
- dissecting tray
- metric ruler
- tweezers
- paper towel
- dissecting microscope

PROCEDURE

1. Carefully open the pea pod with a scalpel. **Caution:** Always cut away from your body.
2. Draw and label the inside of the pea pod so that the size of the peas (seeds) relative to the size of the pod (fruit) is accurate.
3. Use tweezers to remove one pea from the pod. Use a paper towel to clean the outside of the pea. Carefully cut the pea in half lengthwise.
4. Examine the inside of the pea under the microscope.
5. Draw a cross-section of the pea. Label the seed parts that are visible under the microscope.

ANALYZE AND CONCLUDE

1. **Analyze** What accounts for genetic differences between peas in the same pod?
2. **Analyze** How many eggs were likely fertilized in the ovary that developed into your pea pod?
3. **Infer** Pods burst at the seam when they are mature. What function might this bursting serve?
4. **Synthesize** Why is it important for scientific illustrations to be drawn with correct proportions?

Online BIOLOGY
CLASSZONE.COM

VIRTUAL LAB
Exploring Plant Responses

How do plants respond to different stimuli? In this interactive lab, you will test for plant reactions to light, gravity, and touch.

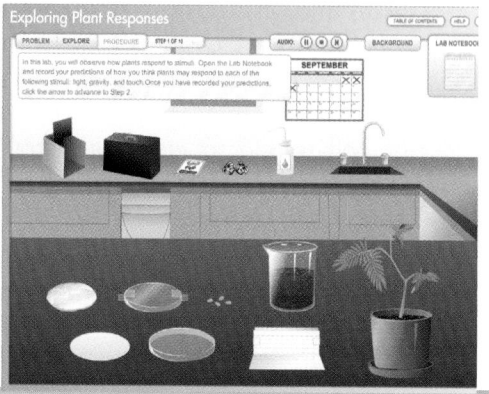

ANIMATED BIOLOGY
Seed Dispersal

Some glide through the air and others drop straight to the ground. Plants have adapted many methods to get their seeds from one place to another. Use physical characteristics to determine how seeds are spread.

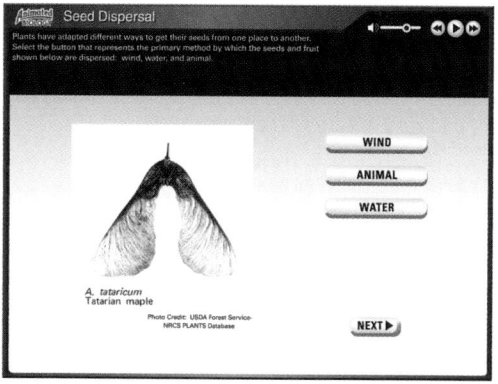

WEBQUEST

We often take for granted that shoots grow up and roots grow down. But what would happen if you took a plant into space? Complete this WebQuest to find out. Learn how plants respond to conditions in outer space and why these experiments are important to the future of space exploration.

22.1 Plant Life Cycles

All plants alternate between two phases in their life cycles. This type of life cycle is called alternation of generations, and it involves a diploid (2*n*) and a haploid (1*n*) phase. The diploid phase, called the sporophyte, produces haploid spores through meiosis. A spore develops into a gametophyte, which is also haploid. The gametophyte produces gametes—sperm and eggs—by mitosis. A fertilized egg can develop into a new sporophyte. Sporophyte and gametophyte phases look different among nonvascular, seedless vascular, and seed plants.

22.2 Reproduction in Flowering Plants

Reproduction of flowering plants takes place within flowers. Flowers contain reproductive organs surrounded by specialized leaves called sepals and petals. Brightly colored petals can attract animal pollinators. A flower is pollinated when a pollen grain reaches the tip of the female reproductive structure. One cell in the pollen grain grows into a pollen tube and the other cell divides to form two sperm. In a process called double fertilization, one sperm fertilizes an egg, produced in the flower's ovary, while the other helps produce the endosperm, which will nourish the developing embryo.

22.3 Seed Dispersal and Germination

Seeds disperse and begin to grow when conditions are favorable. The function of fruit in flowering plants is to help disperse seeds. Many seeds go through a stage of dormancy, or nongrowth, until environmental conditions are favorable for growing. Germination is the process by which the embryo breaks out of the seed coat and begins to grow into a seedling.

22.4 Asexual Reproduction

Plants can produce genetic clones of themselves through asexual reproduction. Some plants can grow a new individual from a fragment of a stem, a leaf, or a root in a process called regeneration. Vegetative reproduction involves new individuals growing from a stem, a leaf, or a root attached to the parent plant. Humans can produce plants with desirable traits by propagating plants asexually.

22.5 Plant Hormones and Responses

Plant hormones guide plant growth and development. Four major groups of plant hormones are gibberellins, ethylene, cytokinins, and auxins. Auxins are involved with the lengthening of plant cells that controls several forms of tropism, including responses to light and gravity. Some types of plants can also respond to touch and seasonal changes in the lengths of day and night.

Synthesize Your Notes

Concept Map Summarize what you know about plant responses using a concept map.

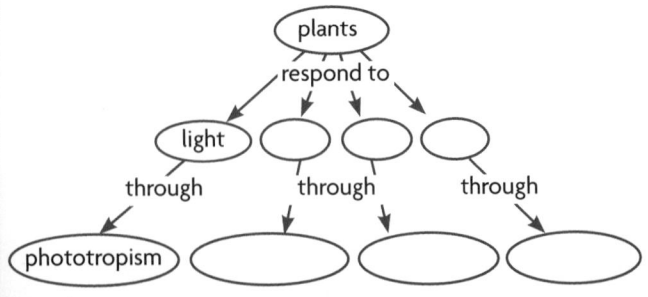

Cycle Diagram Draw a cycle diagram to show the alternation of generations in flowering plants. Include sketches of the sporophyte and gametophytes, using labels specific to flowering plants.

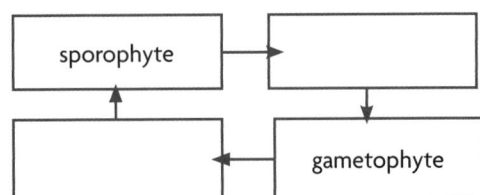

Chapter Assessment

Chapter Vocabulary

22.1 alternation of generations, p. 664
sporophyte, p. 664
gametophyte, p. 664

22.2 sepal, p. 668
petal, p. 668
stamen, p. 668
carpel, p. 668

ovary, p. 668
endosperm, p. 670
double fertilization, p. 670

22.3 dormancy, p. 674
germination, p. 675

22.4 regeneration, p. 678
vegetative reproduction, p. 678

22.5 hormone, p. 680
gibberellin, p. 680
ethylene, p. 681
cytokinin, p. 681
auxin, p. 681
tropism, p. 681
phototropism, p. 682
thigmotropism, p. 682
gravitropism, p. 682
photoperiodism, p. 683

Reviewing Vocabulary

Label Diagrams

In your notebook, write the vocabulary term that matches each item that is pointed out below.

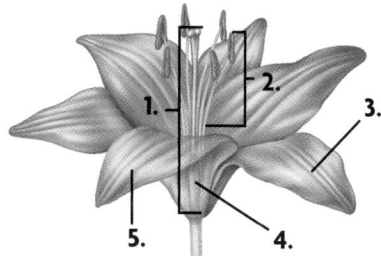

Word Origins

6. The prefix *endo-* means "inside," and the Greek word *sperma* means "seed." How do these meanings relate to the word *endosperm*?

7. How does the word *dormancy* relate to the French verb *dormir*, which means "to sleep"?

8. How does the Latin verb *germinare*, which means "to sprout," relate to the meaning of *germination*?

9. The prefix *trop-* means "a turning." How does this relate to the meaning of the word *tropism*?

Category Clues

For each clue, list the appropriate vocabulary term from the chapter.

Category: Plant Responses

10. response to light

11. response to touch

12. response to gravity

13. response to amount of daylight or darkness

Reviewing MAIN IDEAS

14. What types of cellular division are involved in the alternation of generations?

15. What is a major difference between the gametophyte generations of moss and pine trees?

16. How can brightly colored petals aid in the reproduction of flowering plants?

17. What characteristic might be a clue that a flower is wind-pollinated? Explain your answer.

18. Name the two structures in the female gametophyte that are fertilized in the process of double fertilization.

19. How does seed dispersal aid in the survival of plant offspring?

20. People may enjoy a spring season with relatively little rain. How might this type of spring weather affect seeds that were dispersed during the previous fall?

21. Discuss the role of enzymes in the development of an embryo during germination.

22. How can the ability to produce both sexually and asexually allow plant species to populate a variety of environments?

23. Why is plant propagation an efficient way for people to produce new plants?

24. A well-known disease of rice plants causes rice seedlings to grow to several times their normal size and then die. Which of the major plant hormones is likely involved in this disease? Explain your answer.

25. Name four types of stimuli to which plants are capable of responding.

Critical Thinking

26. Compare and Contrast What are some differences and similarities between the life cycle of a seedless plant and that of a seed plant, such as a conifer?

27. Infer Female pine cones have scales that open, close, and then open again. These three phases correspond with three specific events in the conifer reproductive cycle. What three events might trigger these phases in female cones?

28. Predict Most people cook potatoes soon after they buy them at the store. What will happen to a potato that is left sitting on the kitchen counter for a few weeks? Explain your answer.

29. Infer A homeowner is planting a new garden and buys some plant seeds. The plant shop owner offers to sell her regular seeds or specially treated seeds that will germinate faster. How may these special seeds have been treated?

30. Analyze A kiwi fruit was purchased at the store, but it was not ripe enough to eat. It was placed in a sealed container along with an apple. Several days later, the kiwi was ripe. Explain how this likely happened.

31. Analyze Four-o'clock flowers bloom late in the day, as their name suggests. The flowers stay open all night and close the following morning. What type of response is the flower demonstrating? Explain your answer.

Interpreting Visuals

Use this cartoon to answer the next two questions.

"I'll say he's busy. He has hundreds of frequent flower miles"

source: www.CartoonStock.com

32. Apply Name the process that these bees have carried out for flowering plants.

33. Summarize Describe how this process occurs as bees fly from flower to flower.

Analyzing Data

Students are testing the effect of light on the germination of millet seeds. The setup for their experiment is shown in the table below. Students observe and track seed development for one week. Use the data to answer the next four questions.

MILLET SEED EXPERIMENT SETUP

	Tray A	Tray B
Seeds	50	50
Water	25 mL per day	25 mL per day
Location	on a shelf beneath a grow light	on a shelf in a dark refrigerator

34. Analyze What are the dependent and independent variables in this experiment?

35. Analyze What is the control in this experiment?

36. Evaluate Which part of the experimental design is flawed?

37. Experimental Design What changes would you make to the experimental design to collect valid results?

Connecting CONCEPTS

38. Write a Blog Imagine that you are a seed that is about to come out of dormancy. Write a blog describing your experiences as you germinate. Be sure to include the following terms: *dormancy, germinate, seed coat, radicle, plumule, cotyledons,* and *seedling.*

39. Analyze Look at the moth orchid shown in the chapter opener on page 663. Does this photograph show the gametophyte or sporophyte generation? Explain your answer.

MICHIGAN STANDARDS-BASED ASSESSMENT

✔ **Test Practice**
For more test practice, go to ClassZone.com.

1. A strawberry grower divides a large field into three sections: the first bordering a grove of trees, the second in the middle, and the third bordering an interstate. Each section is treated with a different insecticide to determine effectiveness. Which of the following is not a design flaw of this experiment? **B1.1B**

   A No part of the field was used as a control.

   B Fumes from the interstate might kill pests in the third section.

   C The same type of strawberries were grown in each section.

   D The trees might harbor animals that eat pests in the first section.

2. Which of the following scenarios is using sexual reproduction to increase genetic variation? **L4.p1A**

   A A researcher grafts the branch of a pear tree onto a drought-resistant apple tree.

   B A gardener slices the "eyes" off of potatoes and plants them to yield a new crop.

   C A flower lover cuts the leaves from a violet and plants them in soil to grow more violets.

   D A farmer uses pollen from tall pea plants to fertilize short pea plants.

3.

Enzyme Activity at Different Temperatures	
Temperature (°C)	Enzyme Activity (units/mL)
25	6
20	8
15	14
10	27
5	36
0	30

Suppose that scientists are studying the activity of enzymes that are involved in ending seed dormancy. Which statement is best supported by their data? **B1.1E**

   A The enzyme is ineffective below 0°C.

   B Temperature does not affect enzyme activity.

   C Enzyme activity peaks at around 5°C.

   D The enzyme is most active in warm weather.

4. The plant life cycle involves a diploid sporophyte stage that produces haploid spores. Which of the following statements is true? **B4.3A**

   A Haploid spores are produced through meiosis.

   B Haploid spores are produced through mitosis.

   C Diploid spores are produced through meiosis.

   D Diploid spores are produced through mitosis.

5.

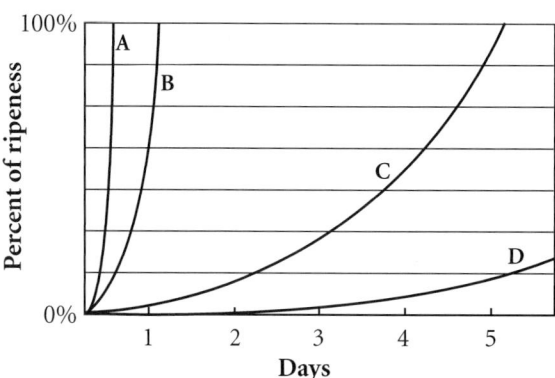

Scientists are developing a molecule that will slow down the rate of fruit ripening to a few days. Based on the graph, which molecule do you think they would choose? **B1.1E**

   A A

   B B

   C C

   D D

6. According to one hypothesis, auxins may cause a change in pH that results in the cell wall becoming more flexible. Then, the cell lengthens due to pressure from an organelle. Which organelle is *most* likely exerting this pressure? **B2.5B**

   A vacuole

   B ribosome

   C nucleus

   D chloroplast

THINK THROUGH THE QUESTION

Think about the properties and functions of each organelle listed as a possible answer. Which of these is most likely to expand in size?

BIOZINE

INTERNET MAGAZINE

at **CLASSZONE.COM**

Go online for the latest biology news and updates on all BioZine articles.

Expanding the Textbook

News Feeds

- 🔊 Science Daily
- 🔊 CNN
- 🔊 BBC

Careers

Bio Bytes

Opinion Poll

Strange Biology

Although these tomatoes are labeled, genetically modified foods are not required to be labeled in the United States. However, they must meet the same standards of safety as traditionally grown foods.

Genetically Modified Foods—Do Potential Problems Outweigh Benefits?

There is a food fight going on, and you may need to choose a side. Genetically modified (GM) foods have been on the market since the early 1990s, and today most foods in U.S. grocery stores have GM ingredients. But the wide availability of GM food also raises concerns on topics ranging from health to the environment. Should you be worried about eating GM foods?

New Technology, Old Idea

GM plants have genes that have been genetically engineered, or artificially introduced into the plant's genome. This technology gives plants a new characteristic. For instance, many crop plants are commonly engineered for disease resistance. Some examples of crops that have GM varieties on the market are wheat, rice, corn, soybeans, potatoes, squash, papayas, tomatoes, and cantaloupes.

Genetic engineering is a fairly new process, but plants have been modified through careful breeding for thousands of years. Many people knowledgeable about genetics argue that genetic engineering of crops is just a faster and more precise method of selective breeding.

The Green Revolution

In the 1960s, scientist Norman Borlaug and a team of researchers used cross-breeding techniques to develop a new strain of wheat. The new strain produced two to three times as much wheat as traditional varieties, and resisted many types of insects and diseases. Widely planted, these new varieties changed Mexico from an importer of wheat to an exporter within 20 years. Borlaug and his team began shipping the new strain of wheat to India and Pakistan, and both countries quickly doubled their

wheat production. Known as the Green Revolution, this scientific advance improved crop yields drastically worldwide. For his work, Borlaug received the Nobel Prize in 1970. Today, Borlaug and many others view genetic engineering of crops as the next wave of the Green Revolution.

Plants can be genetically modified to produce larger fruits.

Benefits of GM crops

One benefit of GM crops is the potential of improved nutrition. For example, half of the world's population relies on rice as the main part of their diet. Rice lacks vitamin A, however, and vitamin A deficiency can cause blindness and sometimes death. Researchers developed a new strain of rice, called "golden rice." Unlike regular rice, golden rice is high in vitamin A. Golden rice could prevent millions of deaths of young children in developing countries every year.

TECHNOLOGY

Gene Gun

Genetic engineers use various ways to insert new genes into host cells. For plant cells, which have thick cell walls, one of the best ways to put foreign DNA into the cell is to actually shoot it through the plant tissue using a gene gun.

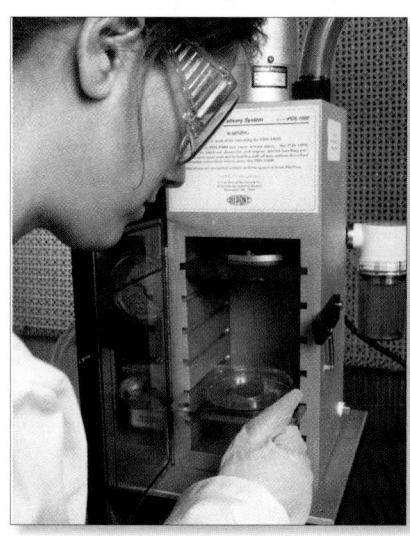

1. A researcher coats gold or tungsten particles with DNA and places them on the end of a microscopic plastic bullet.

2. The plastic bullet is placed in the gene gun and directed toward the target plant tissue.

3. A burst of helium propels the bullet to the end of the gun. The gold particles containing the DNA are released while the bullet remains in the gun.

4. Particles enter the cytoplasm of some of the cells in the target tissue. DNA is released from the gold particles and moves into the plant cell's nucleus, where it ultimately combines with the cell's DNA.

Read More >> *at* CLASSZONE.COM

CAREERS

Research Engineer in Action

DR. TONG-JEN FU
TITLE Research Engineer, Food and Drug Administration
EDUCATION Ph. D., Chemical Engineering, Pennsylvania State University

Dr. Tong-Jen Fu is a research engineer with the U.S. Food and Drug Administration (FDA), where she evaluates the methods currently used by scientists to determine the allergic potential of GM foods. She and other researchers are trying to understand exactly what makes substances in food cause allergic reactions.

One of the concerns of GM food is its potential to increase allergies in humans. Many proteins can potentially be an allergen—that is, cause an allergic reaction in some people. Since genetic engineering introduces new proteins into crops, concerns have been raised that unexpected allergies may arise. GM foods could trigger allergies by including proteins already known to cause a reaction, or by introducing completely new allergy-causing proteins—such as those from bacteria—into the food supply.

Researchers use extensive safety tests to determine whether a genetically modified food is likely to cause an allergic reaction. If any of these tests has a positive reaction, the GM food is not likely to be commercially produced. These tests include checking the amino acid sequences of introduced proteins against those of known allergens and testing whether the introduced proteins are resistant to digestion.

Read More >> *at* CLASSZONE.COM

Other promising uses of genetic engineering include growing fruits and vegetables that produce vaccines in their tissues. This would make shipment, storage, and administration of medicine easier worldwide.

Some benefits of GM crops are well established. They include benefits to farmers, such as crops that take less time, water, and land to grow, and plants that can withstand drought, cold temperature, insect damage, or that grow in poor soils.

There are also benefits to the environment, such as crops that lessen the need for pesticide, herbicide, or fertilizer applications. Even the consumer benefits with GM produce that stays fresh longer.

Potential Hidden Costs of GM Crops

Not everyone is enthusiastic about genetically modified foods. Opponents argue that it is impossible to predict exactly how the new crops—sometimes called "Frankenfoods"—will affect ecosystems. For example, the bacterial gene *Bt* is commonly inserted into GM plants. It produces an insecticidal toxin that is harmless to people. But will insects become resistant to *Bt*? Insect-repelling GM plants may speed the evolution of pesticide-resistant pests.

Another concern is that weeds can become stronger by cross-breeding with GM crops. When herbicide-resistant genes are inserted into crop plants, the weeds are easily killed by herbicides while the crops remain unaffected. But pollen from plants can be carried by the wind for long distances, and seeds from GM crops could be accidentally dispersed outside their intended locations, causing the rise of "superweeds."

Unanswered Questions

Genetically modified crops are no longer considered new, but some questions about them remain. Many of the most important research questions concern the long-term effects of GM crops on human health and the environment. Specific questions include

- Will the levels of various vitamins in genetically modified crops differ from those found in their traditionally grown relatives?

- Could GM crops, such as those engineered to produce medicines, have adverse effects on wildlife?

Read More >> *at* CLASSZONE.COM

UNIT 8
Animals

CHAPTER 23
Invertebrate Diversity   **694**

CHAPTER 24
A Closer Look at Arthropods   **728**

CHAPTER 25
Vertebrate Diversity   **756**

CHAPTER 26
A Closer Look at Amniotes   **786**

CHAPTER 27
Animal Behavior   **816**

BIOZINE

INTERNET MAGAZINE
The Loss of Biodiversity   **846**
  TECHNOLOGY Bioremediation
  CAREER Conservation Biologist

CHAPTER

23 Invertebrate Diversity

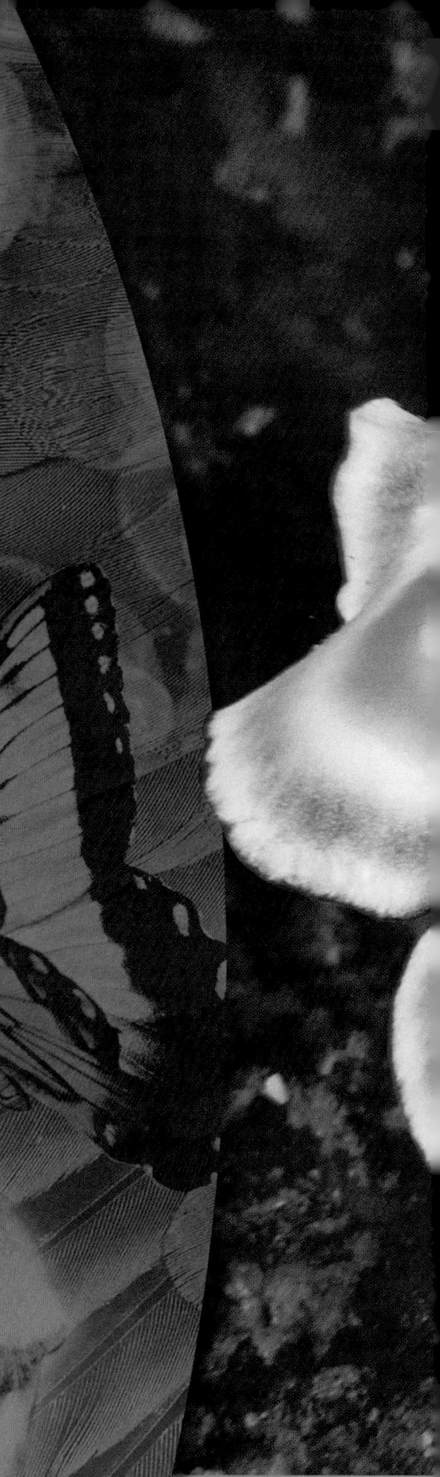

KEY CONCEPTS

23.1 Animal Characteristics

Animals are diverse but share common characteristics.

23.2 Animal Diversity

More than 95 percent of all animal species are invertebrates.

23.3 Sponges and Cnidarians

Sponges and cnidarians are the simplest animals.

23.4 Flatworms, Mollusks, and Annelids

Flatworms, mollusks, and annelids belong to closely related phyla.

23.5 Roundworms

Roundworms have bilateral symmetry and shed their outer skeleton to grow.

23.6 Echinoderms

Echinoderms are on the same evolutionary branch as vertebrates.

Online BIOLOGY CLASSZONE.COM

Animated BIOLOGY

View animated chapter concepts.
• Digestive Tract Formation
• Shared Body Structures

BIOZINE

Keep current with biology news.
• News feeds
• Bio Bytes
• Polls

 RESOURCE CENTER

Get more information on
• Sponges and Cnidarians
• Worms
• Mollusks

How is this sea slug similar to a spider?

B oth sea slugs and spiders are invertebrates. Invertebrates, which are animals without backbones, account for the vast majority of animals on Earth. You are surrounded by invertebrates on a daily basis, whether you are aware of them or not. Invertebrates exist in a wide variety of shapes and sizes and live in many different habitats—including your body!

Connecting CONCEPTS

Adaptation Because adult sea slugs do not have shells, they must use other methods to avoid being eaten. Some sea slugs eat sponges. Sponges (left) have chemicals that make them taste bad. Sea slugs have the ability to overcome the foul taste and are able to incorporate the chemicals into their body. These chemicals, in turn, give the sea slugs a bad taste, helping them to avoid predation.

23.1 Animal Characteristics

KEY CONCEPT Animals are diverse but share common characteristics.

MAIN IDEAS

- Animals are the most physically diverse kingdom of organisms.
- All animals share a set of characteristics.

VOCABULARY

collagen, p. 697
homeotic, p. 698
homeobox, p. 698

MICHIGAN STANDARDS

B2.4C Explain how different organisms accomplish the same result using different structural specializations (gills vs. lungs vs. membranes).

B2.4d Analyze the relationships among organisms based on their shared physical, biochemical, genetic, and cellular characteristics and functional processes.

FIGURE 23.1 Animal body plans vary widely in shape and size, from microscopic rotifers (colored SEM; magnification 80×) to blue whales 24 meters in length.

Connect We are animals. So are jellyfish, squid, cockroaches, tapeworms, sea stars, and the family dog. Animals live in nearly every environment on Earth, from high in the atmosphere to the deepest sea trench. While they come in a huge variety of shapes and sizes, they all share a common ancestry and a set of common physical and genetic characteristics.

MAIN IDEA

Animals are the most physically diverse kingdom of organisms.

More than 1 million species of animals have been described so far, and scientists predict that tens of millions more have yet to be discovered. Animals are a remarkably diverse group of organisms. They range in size from blue whales twice the length of a school bus to rotifers smaller than the period at the end of this sentence. As shown in **FIGURE 23.1**, some look like soft tubes, and others have muscular bodies inside hard shells, or soft tissues over hard internal skeletons. Some animals have many specialized tissues and organs, and others have no distinct tissues at all.

Rotifer

Giraffe

Red leaf beetle

Steller's jay

Tube worm

Blue whale

Animals are found nearly everywhere on Earth, including places where plants and fungi do not live. They are the dominant herbivores, predators, and detritivores in most ecosystems. Some walk, burrow, swim, fly, or slide along on mucus trails in search of food. Others spend their whole adult lives fixed to a single spot, endlessly straining water to collect microscopic particles of food.

Connect What ecological factors determine where certain animals are found?

Connecting CONCEPTS

Niches Recall from **Chapter 14** that an ecological niche includes all of the factors a species needs to survive, thrive, and reproduce.

◉ MAIN IDEA
All animals share a set of characteristics.

Given the huge physical diversity among animals, what characteristics distinguish animals from other organisms? All animals share a set of derived characters, or heritable features, that set them apart from other eukaryotes. These characteristics suggest that all animals are the descendants of a single common ancestor.

All Animals Are Multicellular Heterotrophs
Animals must eat. Their cells lack the chloroplasts that let photosynthetic organisms make their own food. All animals are heterotrophs, meaning they eat other organisms to gain the nutrients they need to survive. Any organic compound an animal uses in cellular respiration has to come from an outside source. Single-celled protists also eat other organisms. But because even the simplest animal is built of many specialized cells, all animals can ingest and process larger food particles than a single cell can engulf.

Animals are not the only eukaryotes that are both heterotrophic and multicellular. Fungi are also multicellular and use organisms for food. But cells of fungi do not have the same diversity of functions that animal cells have. Although animals and fungi share hetero-trophic ancestors, it is likely that they evolved the trait of multicellularity independently.

Animal Cells Are Supported by Collagen
Unlike the cells of plants and fungi, animal cells lack rigid cell walls. Therefore, animals are the only multicellular organisms with no cellular structure to support their cells. What component carries out these functions in animals?

Collagen (KAHL-uh-juhn), shown in **FIGURE 23.2**, is a three-stranded protein unique to animals. Animal body parts that contain collagen include skin, bone, ligaments, fingernails, and hair. Individual collagen proteins combine with one another to form ropelike fibers that are both strong and flexible. These fibers form an extracellular network that many animal cells use for support. Unlike a cell wall, the collagen network does not glue cells in place, so it is possible for cells to move within the animal's body. Collagen also forms an integral part of the jointed skeleton that many animals use to move their entire bodies.

TAKING NOTES

Use a diagram to take notes on the unique characteristics of animals.

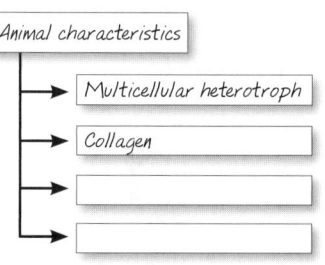

Animal characteristics
- Multicellular heterotroph
- Collagen

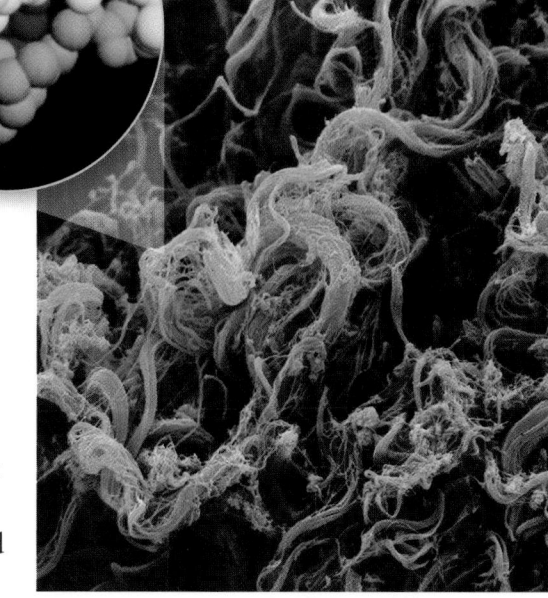

FIGURE 23.2 This molecular model and SEM show the triple-stranded structure of collagen, a strong and flexible protein that is unique to animals. (colored SEM; magnification 3000×)

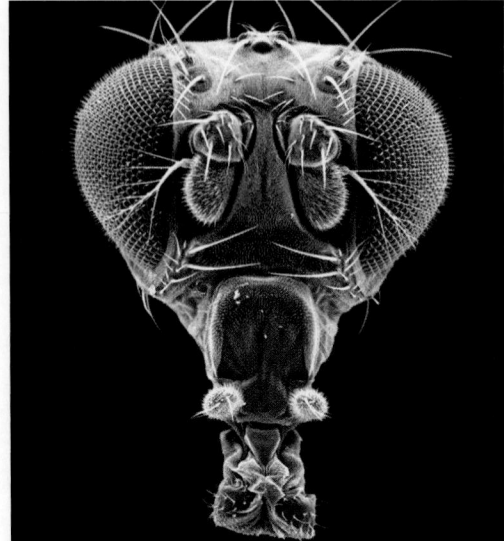

FIGURE 23.3 In the wildtype fly (top), the antennae develop normally. In the mutant fly (bottom), a mutation causes legs to form in place of the antennae. (SEMs; magnification 70×)

Animals Are Diploid and Usually Reproduce Sexually

Animals are the only multicellular organisms that do not alternate between free-living diploid and haploid stages. In all animal species, the individuals that reproduce are diploid (meaning they have one set of chromosomes from each parent), and they produce offspring that are also diploid. Some kinds of animals can reproduce both asexually and sexually. For example, a *Hydra* can clone itself by budding. These species have male and female sexual organs and also reproduce sexually. A few animals have become completely asexual. All whiptail lizards, for example, are females, and all their offspring are clones of the mother. But these animals evolved from sexual species, and their asexual habits are derived characters.

Most Animals Have *Hox* Genes

Most of the animals that scientists have studied so far share a group of genes called homeotic genes. **Homeotic** (HOH-mee-AH-tihk) genes are a class of genes that control early development in animals. Every homeotic gene has a specific sequence of 180 nucleotides called **homeobox** (HOH-mee-uh-BAHKS), or *Hox*, genes. *Hox* genes define the head-to-tail pattern of development in animal embryos. Homeotic genes create segments in a larva or embryo that develop into specific organs and tissues. The *Hox* genes within these segments determine the position of cell differentiation and development by switching certain genes "on" or "off."

A mutation in a homeotic gene leads to the development of a body structure in the wrong position. For example, the effect of a mutation in a homeotic gene, *Antennapedia,* determines whether an insect body segment will grow antennae or legs. As shown in **FIGURE 23.3**, in the wildtype fly (top), antennae develop normally. In the fly with a mutation in its homeotic genes (bottom), legs develop where the antennae should be. However, the rest of the fly develops normally. Although the misplaced legs look normal in structure, they are not functional for the fly. Flies with homeotic mutations usually do not live very long.

Analyze How are homeotic and *Hox* genes related?

23.1 ASSESSMENT

ONLINE QUIZ
ClassZone.com

REVIEWING ▶ MAIN IDEAS

1. In what ways are animals physically diverse? Give three examples.

2. List and describe the derived characters that all animals share.

CRITICAL THINKING

3. **Apply** How does the structure of animal cells allow animals to move?

4. **Hypothesize** Animals are heterotrophs. How might this have contributed to such great animal diversity?

Connecting CONCEPTS

5. **Genetics** How does the genome of an offspring resulting from sexual reproduction differ from that of an offspring resulting from asexual reproduction?

23.2 Animal Diversity

KEY CONCEPT More than 95 percent of all animal species are invertebrates.

▶ MAIN IDEAS

- Each animal phylum has a unique body plan.
- Animals are grouped using a variety of criteria.
- A comparison of structure and genetics reveals the evolutionary history of animals.

VOCABULARY

vertebrate, p. 699
invertebrate, p. 699
phylum, p. 699
bilateral symmetry, p. 701

radial symmetry, p. 701
protostome, p. 702
deuterostome, p. 702

MICHIGAN STANDARDS

B2.4A Explain that living things can be classified based on structural, embryological, and molecular (relatedness of DNA sequence) evidence.

B2.4d Analyze the relationships among organisms based on their shared physical, biochemical, genetic, and cellular characteristics and functional processes.

Connecting CONCEPTS

Classification Recall from **Chapter 17** that in the Linnaean system of classification, phylum is the first level below kingdom. As you learned earlier, all animals are classified in the kingdom Animalia.

Connect When you think of an animal, something familiar such as a dog or a snake probably comes to mind. Both of these animals are vertebrates, a group that represents one small subset of animals. However, most animals are invertebrates and look nothing like your mental picture. To understand the vast diversity of animal life, biologists look for unique characteristics that help them sort animals into distinct groups and arrange those groups into a family tree.

▶ MAIN IDEA

Each animal phylum has a unique body plan.

A **vertebrate** (VUR-tuh-briht) is an animal with an internal segmented backbone. Vertebrates are the most obvious animals around us, and we are vertebrates, too. But vertebrates make up less than five percent of all known animal species. All other animals are invertebrates. **Invertebrates** (ihn-VUR-tuh-brihts) are animals without backbones. Early animal classifications divided all animals into vertebrates and invertebrates. But because invertebrates are not defined by a set of shared derived characters, the division is considered outdated. Many invertebrates are not closely related to one another.

Animal Phyla

Scientists now use shared characters to divide animals into more than 30 major groups. Each group, or **phylum** (FY-luhm) (plural, *phyla*), of animals is defined by structural and functional characteristics that are different from every other animal group. Each animal phylum has a unique body plan and represents a different way that a multicellular animal is put together.

Every animal phylum has a unique set of anatomical characteristics. These unique characteristics are true of both the largest and smallest phyla. Some phyla, such as mollusks, have tens of thousands of species, ranging from land snails to marine octopuses. Others are much less diverse. Phyla such as Arthropoda contain species that look very different from one another. In other phyla, such as Nematoda, all of the species look very similar. The relative amount of invertebrate species per group is shown in **FIGURE 23.4**.

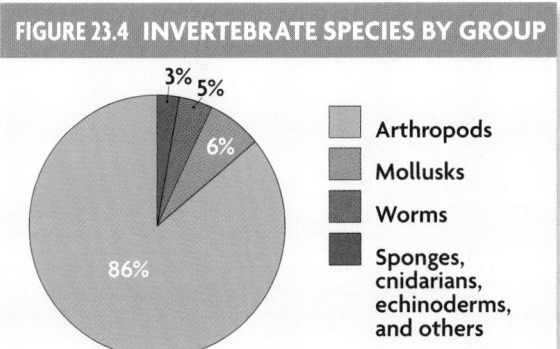

FIGURE 23.4 INVERTEBRATE SPECIES BY GROUP

3% 5%
6%
86%

- Arthropods
- Mollusks
- Worms
- Sponges, cnidarians, echinoderms, and others

Homeobox Genes and Body Plans

If you take a look at the animals that you might see on a walk through the park, you may notice how different their body plans are. The swimming fish in a park pond have sets of fins, the flying birds have pairs of wings, and the squirrels chasing one another have four legs.

Differences in body plans result from differences in the expression of homeobox genes. As shown in **FIGURE 23.5**, homeobox genes tell embryonic cells which part of the body they are going to become, such as the head, middle, or tail. These instructions start a chain reaction that turns on all other genes that define the adult form—where limbs go, how many eyes will develop, the location of the gut, and so on. For this reason, a mutation in a *Hox* gene can change an animal's entire body plan. Scientists think that mutations in these genes led to the vast diversity of animal species.

All the animal phyla now known first appeared during the Cambrian explosion. How did so many unique body plans appear in such a short time? The trigger may have been an increase in oxygen levels in the atmosphere that began about 700 million years ago. As oxygen levels rose, eukaryotic organisms could become more active and begin to occupy different niches within more complex ecosystems.

The Cambrian explosion was only possible because animals had already evolved *Hox* genes. These genes became a toolkit that changed animal bodies through duplication and loss. For example, a sponge is a simple animal that has at least one *Hox* gene, while an arthropod has eight. This difference suggests that over time, mutations have caused the original *Hox* gene to be copied repeatedly, forming a series of similar genes along a chromosome. Every time a gene is duplicated, one of the copies can keep doing its original job in the organism, leaving the other free to mutate and take on new roles.

Analyze How are *Hox* genes related to the diversity of body plans?

FIGURE 23.5 *Hox* Gene Expression

The genes that determine a fruit fly's body plan are variations of the same genes that determine a human's, but they are expressed in different patterns.

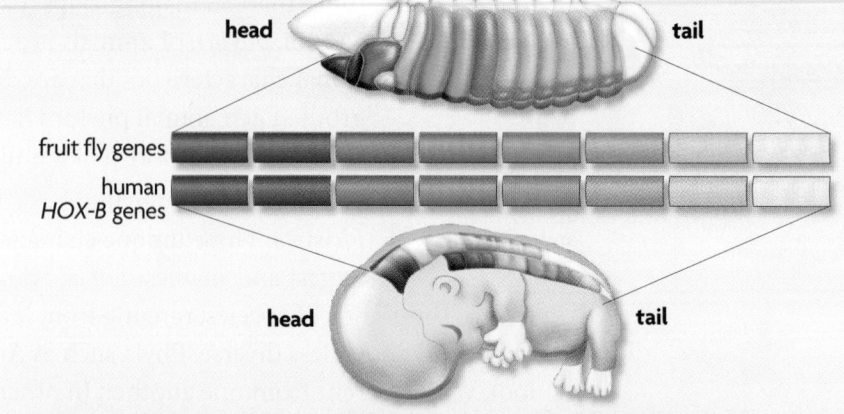

Analyze In both fruit flies and humans, *Hox* genes occur in a similar order on chromosomes. How does the illustration emphasize this point?

▶ MAIN IDEA

Animals are grouped using a variety of criteria.

Like other organisms, animals are placed in separate groups based on certain characteristics. Three criteria used to categorize animals are body plan symmetry, number of tissue layers, and developmental patterns.

Body Plan Symmetry

Symmetry refers to how similar an object is across a central axis. For example, if you draw a line down the middle of a square, both sides are equal in shape and size. An object is asymmetrical if the two sides are not mirror images of one another. Most animal body plans fall into one of two types of symmetry.

- Animals with **bilateral symmetry** can be divided equally along only one plane, which splits an animal into mirror-image sides.
- Animals with **radial symmetry** have body parts arranged in a circle around a central axis.

Bilateral animals have distinct heads and tails, which are called the anterior (head) and posterior (tail) ends. These animals also have distinct backs and bellies, which are called the dorsal (back) and ventral (belly) surfaces. Each of these regions can become specialized. For example, structures that an animal uses to move, such as legs, are usually found on its ventral surface. Active hunters that often travel in one direction in search of food have a head region with a concentration of nervous tissue that forms a brain and with sensory organs such as eyes.

Tissue Layers

Bilateral animals have three distinct layers of tissue. Animals with three tissue layers are triploblastic. These layers are the ectoderm, endoderm, and mesoderm. The ectoderm is the outer layer that develops into both the skin and the brain and nervous system. The endoderm is an inner layer that lines the animal's gut. The mesoderm is a middle layer that develops into internal tissues and organs. Complex organ systems resulted from the evolution of this third tissue layer.

Most radial animals have only two distinct layers of tissue. These layers are an inner endoderm and an outer ectoderm. Radial animals do not have a mesoderm layer, and therefore they lack the complex internal tissues and organs found in triploblastic animals.

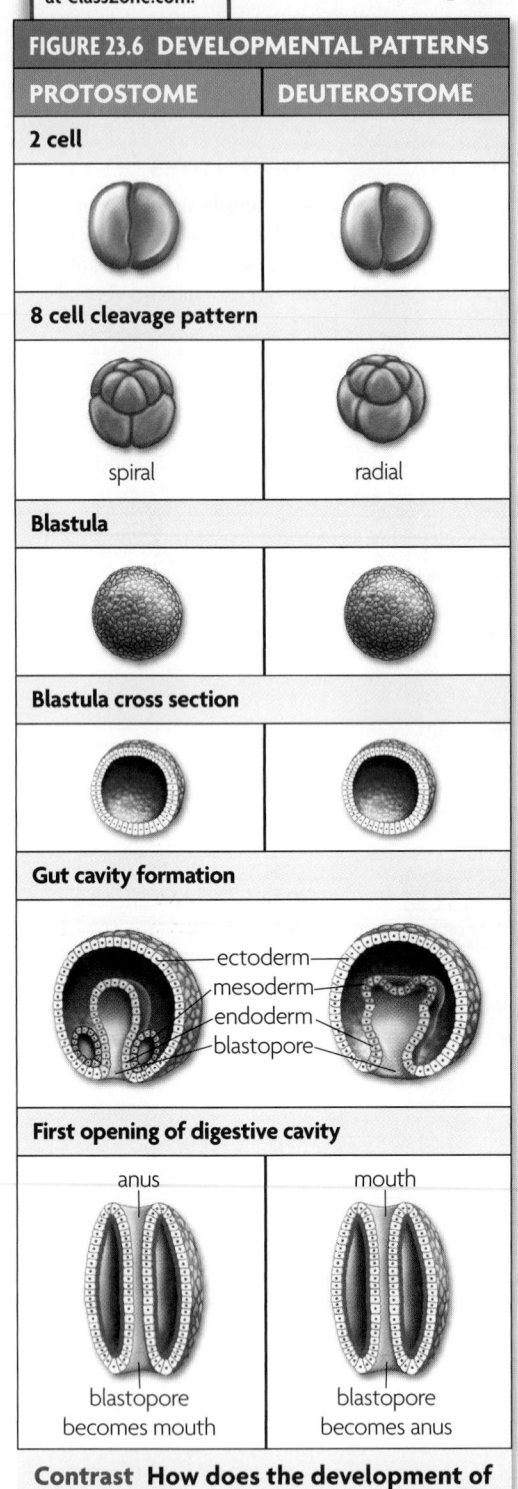

FIGURE 23.6 DEVELOPMENTAL PATTERNS

PROTOSTOME	DEUTEROSTOME

2 cell

8 cell cleavage pattern

spiral | radial

Blastula

Blastula cross section

Gut cavity formation

ectoderm
mesoderm
endoderm
blastopore

First opening of digestive cavity

anus | mouth

blastopore becomes mouth | blastopore becomes anus

Contrast How does the development of protostomes and deuterstomes differ?

Developmental Patterns

Animals are separated into two major divisions: the protostomes and the deuterostomes. As shown in **FIGURE 23.6**, protostome and deuterostome development differs in a number of ways:

- **First opening of the digestive cavity** The major difference between protostomes and deuterostomes is the structure that develops from the first opening of the digestive cavity. In **protostomes** (PROH-tuh-STOHMZ), the mouth is formed first, and the anus second. In **deuterostomes** (DOO-tuh-roh-STOHMZ), the first opening forms the anus, and the mouth is formed second.
- **Gut cavity formation** In protostomes, the gut cavity is formed from separations in the mesoderm. In deuterostomes, the gut cavity forms from pouches created by the folds in the gut tube.
- **Cleavage pattern** In most protostomes, early cell divisions lead to an eight-celled embryo in a twisted arrangement called spiral cleavage. In deuterostomes, cells divide into eight-celled embryos with cells that are lined up one atop the other in an arrangement called radial cleavage.

Connect Is the symmetry of the human body bilateral or radial?

▶ MAIN IDEA

A comparison of structure and genetics reveals the evolutionary history of animals.

Work by the American zoologist Libbie Hyman in the mid-1900s provided the basis for scientists' understanding of the relationships between invertebrate species. Hyman based her phylogeny, or evolutionary history, on major events in development. The ability to compare ribosomal DNA and *Hox* genes has helped to both confirm and rearrange some relationships among invertebrate animal groups.

The presence of tissues is one characteristic that separates one animal group from another. Sponges, which lack tissues, are the simplest members of the animal kingdom, followed by animals with two tissue layers, such as jellyfish and corals. Whether an animal has radial or bilateral symmetry is another defining characteristic. As shown in **FIGURE 23.7**, the two major radiations, or phylogenetic branches, are the protostomes and the deuterostomes.

Protostomes Protostomes are further divided into the Lophotrochozoa (flatworms, annelids, and mollusks) and Ecdysozoa (roundworms and arthropods). All members of the Lophotrochozoa have either a specialized feeding structure made of hollow tentacles or a free-swimming ciliated larval form. Members of the Ecdysozoa must shed their outer skin to grow.

Deuterostomes Deuterostomes include members of the Echinodermata (such as sea stars and sand dollars) and the Chordata (such as birds, mammals, and all other vertebrates). As a member of the Chordata, you are a deuterostome.

FIGURE 23.7 **Phylogeny of Animals**

Comparisons of genetic sequences were used to modify the phylogenetic tree of animals.

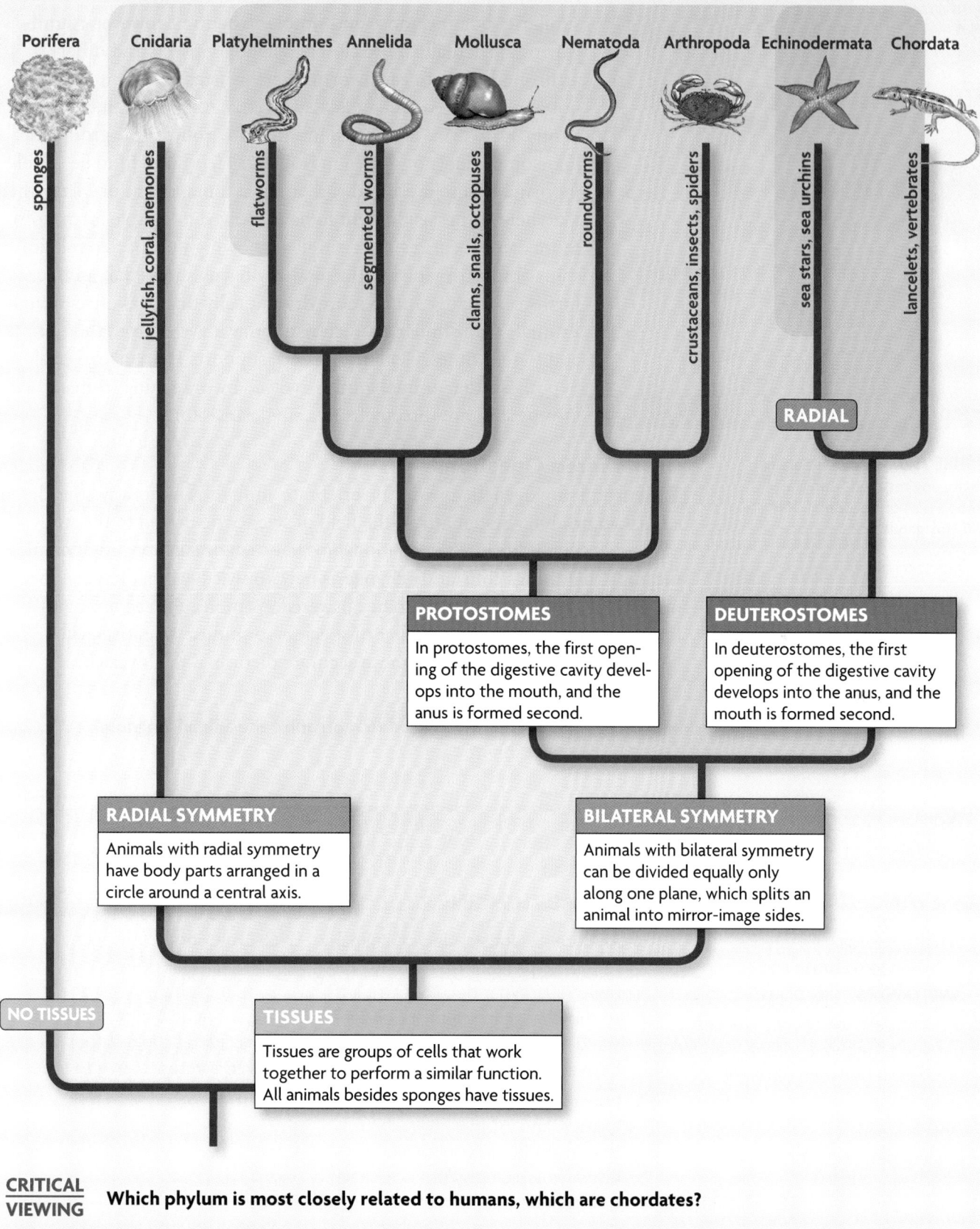

PROTOSTOMES

In protostomes, the first opening of the digestive cavity develops into the mouth, and the anus is formed second.

DEUTEROSTOMES

In deuterostomes, the first opening of the digestive cavity develops into the anus, and the mouth is formed second.

RADIAL

RADIAL SYMMETRY

Animals with radial symmetry have body parts arranged in a circle around a central axis.

BILATERAL SYMMETRY

Animals with bilateral symmetry can be divided equally only along one plane, which splits an animal into mirror-image sides.

NO TISSUES

TISSUES

Tissues are groups of cells that work together to perform a similar function. All animals besides sponges have tissues.

Porifera — sponges
Cnidaria — jellyfish, coral, anemones
Platyhelminthes — flatworms
Annelida — segmented worms
Mollusca — clams, snails, octopuses
Nematoda — roundworms
Arthropoda — crustaceans, insects, spiders
Echinodermata — sea stars, sea urchins
Chordata — lancelets, vertebrates

CRITICAL VIEWING **Which phylum is most closely related to humans, which are chordates?**

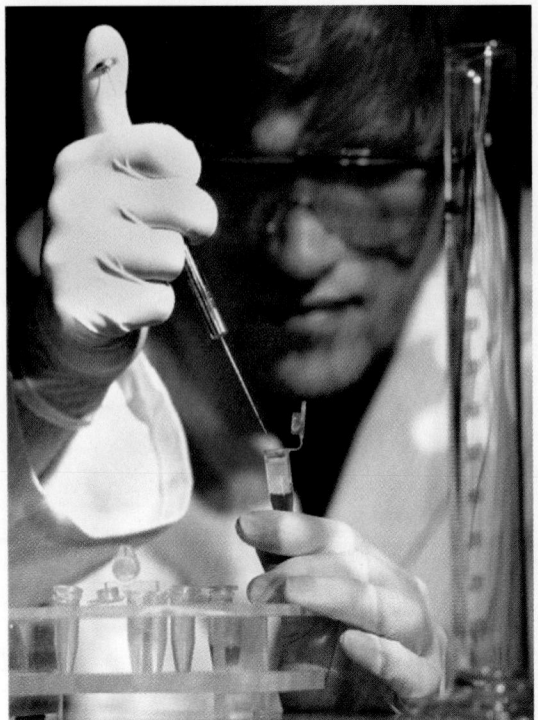

Unexpected Evolutionary Relationships

The new organization of the animal kingdom shows relationships between animals that were previously unexpected. Originally, roundworms and earthworms were grouped together due to their similarity in appearance and simple structure. However, roundworms are actually more closely related to insects and other arthropods than to earthworms. Earthworms and arthropods are not closely related and, in fact, evolved segmentation independently. Flatworms are now split into two groups. One group, the Acoelomorpha (not shown in **FIGURE 23.7**), is thought to be simple in form because it evolved early in the animal radiation. The other, Platyhelminthes, is thought to have evolved its simple form from more complex ancestors. As well as showing unexpected relationships among organisms, the new phylogeny shows that animal forms can change much more dramatically than was once thought. Animals with similar characteristics may have evolved those traits at different times. Genetic evidence supports Hyman's original hypothesis that animal groups evolved by branching from earlier groups, and not directly from a single ancestor.

FIGURE 23.8 The current animal phylogeny resulted from the comparison of ribosomal DNA and *Hox* genes.

Unanswered Questions

The current phylogenetic tree for invertebrate animals is in no way considered a finished product. Systematics—the field of science dedicated to the study of the diversity of life and the relationships between organisms—is dynamic, meaning that things constantly change as new knowledge is gathered. A large number of questions still need to be answered. As molecular technologies improve, and an increased number of species are studied, scientists will be able to put together an even more accurate picture of the invertebrate evolutionary tree.

Summarize What evidence was used to reorganize the animal kingdom?

23.2 ASSESSMENT

ONLINE QUIZ
ClassZone.com

REVIEWING ▶ MAIN IDEAS

1. What is the main difference between **vertebrate** and **invertebrate** body plans?

2. List and describe the differences between the three criteria used to distinguish between different animal groups.

3. What evidence is used to create the phylogenetic tree for animals?

CRITICAL THINKING

4. **Analyze** Scientists' view of animal relationships has changed since the mid-1900s. What development led to this change in scientists' understanding of the relationships between animals?

5. **Provide Examples** Think again about animals, and list five invertebrates that might live in your neighborhood. To which **phylum** does each invertebrate belong?

Connecting CONCEPTS

6. **Evolution** A phylogeny is a hypothesis of evolutionary relationships. What does the current animal phylogeny say about the relationship of vertebrates to invertebrates?

23.3

Sponges and Cnidarians

KEY CONCEPT Sponges and cnidarians are the simplest animals.

▶ MAIN IDEAS

- Sponges have specialized cells but no tissues.
- Cnidarians are the oldest existing animals that have specialized tissues.

VOCABULARY

sessile, p. 705   **mesoglea,** p. 707
filter feeder, p. 706   **nematocyst,** p. 707
polyp, p. 707   **gastrovascular**
medusa, p. 707   **cavity,** p. 708

MICHIGAN STANDARDS

B2.4C Explain how different organisms accomplish the same result using different structural specializations (gills vs. lungs vs. membranes).

VOCABULARY

Sessile comes from a Latin word meaning "to sit." The opposite of sessile is mobile. *Mobile* comes from a Latin word meaning "to move."

FIGURE 23.9 Sponges are among the simplest animals that still exist today.

Connect Imagine you are snorkeling beneath the clear blue waters surrounding Australia's Great Barrier Reef. In addition to schools of tropical fish and sharks, covering the ocean floor are brightly colored sponge and coral species. Sponges and corals are members of two of the simplest animal phyla, the Porifera and the Cnidaria.

▶ MAIN IDEA

Sponges have specialized cells but no tissues.

Sponges have long been considered the most primitive animals on Earth because their body plan is much like what scientists would expect for an early multicellular organism. Two lines of recent evidence have strengthened this hypothesis.

- Sponge fossils more than 570 million years old were found in Australia, making sponges one of the most ancient groups of known animals.
- Molecular evidence confirms that sponges are closely related to a group of protists called choanoflagellates. Choanoflagellates are very similar in size and shape to certain cells found within a sponge. These protists are considered the most likely ancestors of all animals.

Sponge Characteristics

Sponges lack muscle and nerve cells. So not surprisingly, they are **sessile,** meaning they are unable to move from where they are attached. As **FIGURE 23.9** shows, sponges attach to hard surfaces. They secrete toxic substances that prevent other sponges from growing into their area and also protect them from hungry predators and parasites. Some of these chemicals have been used in the development of medicines to treat forms of cancer such as lymphoma.

Sponge Reproduction

Sponges reproduce both sexually and asexually. In sexual reproduction, some species release eggs and sperm into the water, and fertilization occurs there. In other species, sperm is released into the water, and the egg is fertilized within the female sponge. The fertilized egg develops into a free-swimming larva that attaches to a surface, where it remains and develops into its adult form.

Some sponges reproduce asexually by budding. Buds break off from the adult sponge and float in the water until they attach to an underwater surface, where they grow into their adult form.

Sponge Anatomy

Sponges do not have mouths. As you can see in **FIGURE 23.10,** their cells are arranged around a network of channels that let water flow directly through the sponge's body. Water is pulled into the sponge though tiny pores in its body wall, and used water is ejected from a larger hole at the top of the sponge called the osculum. Of the thousands of known species of sponges, most are marine filter feeders. **Filter feeders** eat by straining particles from the water.

Sponges can be found in many colors and shapes. Some sponges are shaped like tubes, while others lie flat against the ocean floor. Regardless of their shape, all sponge bodies are made up of two layers of cells that cover a framework of collagen-like fibers, called spongin. The skeleton is usually reinforced with hard calcium- or silicon-based crystals called spicules. While sponges do not have tissues, they do have several types of specialized cells.

- **Pinacocytes** These thin and leathery cells form the sponge's outer layer.
- **Choanocytes** These cells, also called "collar cells," form the inner layer of the sponge. Each has a long flagellum surrounded by a collar of tiny hairlike structures called microvilli. These cells pull water through the sponge by beating their flagella. As the water passes the choanocytes, tiny food particles are trapped in the mucus on the microvilli.
- **Amoebocytes** These are mobile cells found in the jellylike material sandwiched between the two cell layers. Amoebocytes absorb and digest the food particles caught by the choanocytes and move the nutrients to other parts of the sponge. They also transport oxygen and wastes in the sponge. Because of their mobility, amoebocytes are important to a sponge's growth and repair of injuries.

Summarize **What characteristics make sponges the simplest animals?**

Connecting CONCEPTS

Symbiosis Recall from **Chapter 14** that symbiosis is a close relationship between two or more species living in close contact. Sponges form symbiotic relationships with many different animals. Shrimps, crabs, and worms have been found living within the cavities of a sponge.

FIGURE 23.10 Sponges are animals that have specialized cells but lack tissues. This cutaway shows the internal organization of the sponge.

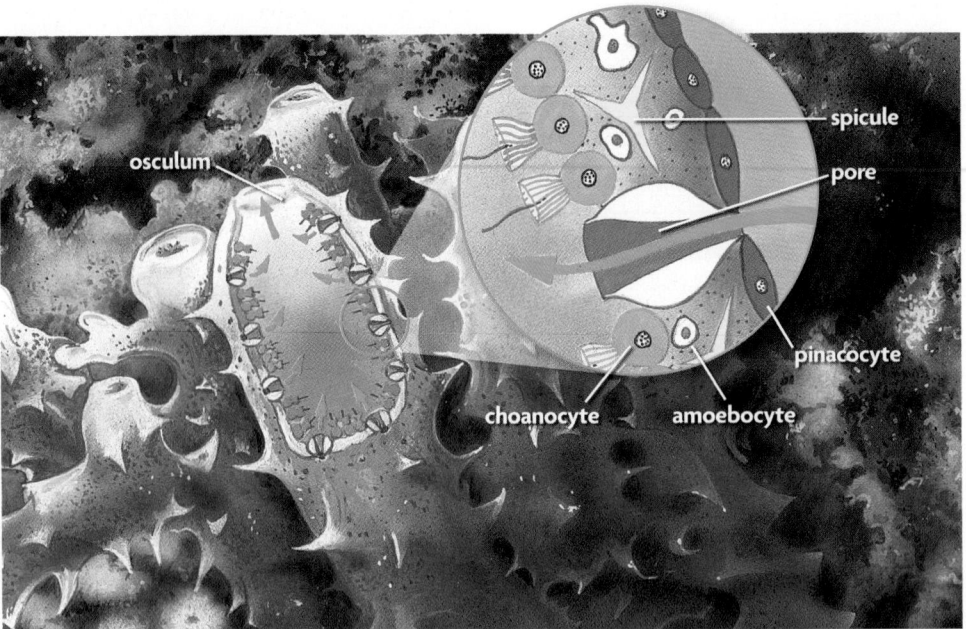

> **MAIN IDEA**

Cnidarians are the oldest existing animals that have specialized tissues.

In contrast to sponges, cnidarians (ny-DAIR-ee-uhnz) can move. A jellyfish pulsing through the water and an anemone waving its tentacles make deliberate movements using simple nerves and muscles.

Cnidarian Characteristics

Cnidarians have two body forms: the polyp and the medusa, both of which are shown in **FIGURE 23.11. Polyps** (PAHL-ihps) are cylindrical tubes with mouth and tentacles facing upward. This form is characteristic of cnidarians such as corals. **Medusas** are umbrella-shaped, with their mouth and tentacles on the underside. This form is characteristic of free-swimming cnidarians such as the jellyfish. Many cnidarian species alternate between the two forms during their life cycle. Both polyps and medusas have radial symmetry, a characteristic of all cnidarians.

Cnidarian Reproduction

A cnidarian may reproduce both asexually and sexually during its life cycle. Polyps reproduce asexually by budding. This method produces genetically identical offspring. In the medusa form, cnidarians reproduce sexually by releasing gametes into the water. The fertilized egg develops into a free-swimming larva, called a planula. The planula then develops into the polyp stage.

Cnidarian Anatomy

Cnidarian bodies have two tissue layers separated by a non-cellular jellylike material called **mesoglea** (MEHZ-uh-GLEE-uh). The outer layer of tissue is made up of three types of cells.

- **Contracting cells** Contracting cells cover the surface of the cnidarian and contain muscle fibers.
- **Nerve cells** Nerve cells interconnect and form a network over the entire animal. They send sensory information around the animal and coordinate muscular contractions. Cnidarians do not have brains.
- **Cnidocytes** (NY-duh-SYTS) Cnidocytes are specialized cells that contain stinging structures used for defense and capturing prey. They are unique to cnidarians. Cnidocytes are found all over a cnidarian's body, but most of them are on the tentacles.

One type of stinging structure found in both sea anemones and jellyfish is the nematocyst. A **nematocyst** (NEHM-uh-tuh-SIHST) is a capsule containing a thin, coiled, harpoon-shaped tubule with a poisonous barb at one end.

FIGURE 23.11 In the polyp form of a coral (top), the tentacles and mouth face upward. In the medusa form of a jellyfish (bottom), the tentacles and mouth face downward.

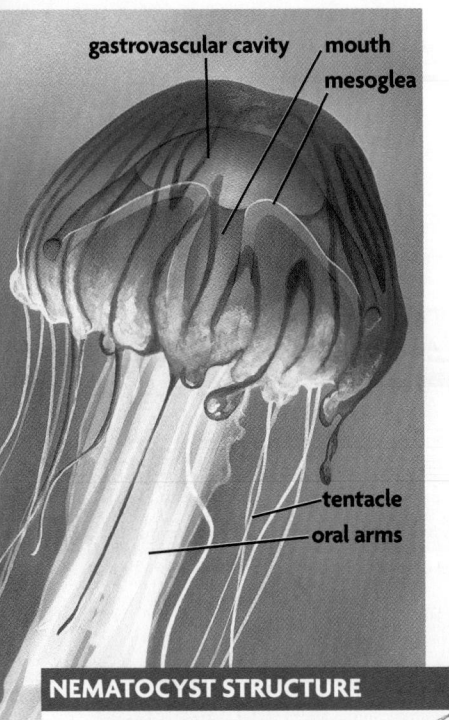

gastrovascular cavity mouth
mesoglea

tentacle
oral arms

NEMATOCYST STRUCTURE

discharged
nematocyst

barbs

coiled nematocyst

FIGURE 23.12 Cnidarians such as this jellyfish use nematocysts, a type of stinging structure found on their tentacles, to both capture prey and defend themselves against predators.

Nematocysts, shown in **FIGURE 23.12**, usually do not fire on contact unless a chemical signals the presence of prey or a predator. When they fire, nematocysts uncoil rapidly to spear and poison prey. Prey captured by nematocysts on the tentacles are stuffed through the animal's mouth into a saclike digestive space called the **gastrovascular cavity.** The cavity is lined with the cnidarian's inner tissue layer, which has cells that secrete digestive enzymes and absorb nutrients. Cnidarians do not have an anus, which in other animals is a separate exit for wastes. In cnidarians, wastes are pushed out through the mouth.

The gastrovascular cavity also moves oxygenated water to internal cells. When the animal's mouth is closed, water in the cavity becomes pressurized and provides skeletal support to the tissue, similar to a balloon full of water. Muscular contractions can work against the pressurized fluid and change the animal's shape.

Cnidarian Classes

There are four major groups, or classes, of cnidarians. Each class is defined in part by which body form is dominant during the animals' lives.

- **Anthozoa** (AN-thuh-ZOH-uh) include sea anemones and corals. The polyp form is dominant in these animals. There is no medusa stage.
- **Hydrozoa** (HY-druh-ZOH-uh) include fire corals, the Portuguese man-of-war, and hydras. These animals alternate between polyp and medusa forms. Medusas reproduce sexually, producing gametes that fuse to produce larvae. Larvae settle to the seafloor and grow into polyps. Most polyps are asexual.
- **Scyphozoa** (SY-fuh-ZOH-uh) are jellyfish. The medusa form is dominant in these animals. Some species have either a very short polyp stage or none at all.
- **Cubozoa** (KYOO-buh-ZOH-uh) include the tropical box jellyfish and sea wasps. These animals also have a dominant medusa form. Unlike the Scyphozoa, they have a cube-shaped body and well-developed eyes with retinas, corneas, and lenses—though how an animal with no brain interprets visual data is still unknown.

Contrast How do the polyp and medusa forms differ?

23.3 ASSESSMENT

ONLINE QUIZ
ClassZone.com

REVIEWING ▶ MAIN IDEAS

1. What is the main function of each of the three types of cells that make up a sponge's body?
2. What are the functions of the inner and outer tissue layers in a cnidarian?

CRITICAL THINKING

3. **Infer** What are the advantages of a **gastrovascular cavity** to the body functions of a cnidarian?
4. **Contrast** How do sponges and cnidarians defend themselves against predators? What is different about the methods used by each?

Connecting CONCEPTS

5. **Evolution** Some sponges have the remarkable ability to reassemble themselves after they are experimentally broken down into individual cells. What might this suggest about the origin of multicellularity in animals?

MATERIALS

- 2 large eyedroppers
- culture of *Hydra*
- petri dish
- drop of bottled spring water
- hand lens or dissecting microscope
- toothpick
- culture of *Daphnia magna*

PROCESS SKILLS

- **Observing**
- **Collecting Data**

B1.1C Conduct scientific investigations using appropriate tools and techniques (e.g., selecting an instrument that measures the desired quantity—length, volume, weight, time interval, temperature—with the appropriate level of precision).

B2.6a Explain that the regulatory and behavioral responses of an organism to external stimuli occur in order to maintain both short- and long-term equilibrium.

Feeding *Hydra*

Hydra belong to the phylum Cnidaria, which includes jellyfish and coral. These animals have thin body walls that are only a few cells thick. They eat small groups of microorganisms, called plankton, that include single-celled animals and protists. In this investigation, you will observe the *Hydra*'s anatomy, responses to touch, and feeding behavior.

PROBLEM   What are the behaviors of a *Hydra*?

PROCEDURE

1. Using the eyedropper, place a drop of water from the culture containing a *Hydra* into a petri dish. Be careful not to damage the *Hydra*. Cover the *Hydra* with spring water.

2. Observe the *Hydra* using a hand lens or dissecting microscope. Draw the *Hydra* and label its parts.

3. Using a toothpick, gently touch the side of the *Hydra* and note its response. Record your observations in your lab notebook.

4. Using a toothpick, gently touch the tentacles of the *Hydra* and note its response. Record your observations in your lab notebook.

5. Using a new eyedropper, transfer a drop of water containing *Daphnia* to the petri dish with the *Hydra*. Note all the events that happen as the *Hydra* catches and eats the *Daphnia*. Write all of your observations in your lab notebook. Wash your hands when you are finished with your work.

Hydra (LM; magnification 20×)

ANALYZE AND CONCLUDE

1. **Analyze**   Did the *Hydra* have a head or tail end? If so, explain how you could tell the difference.

2. **Describe**   Where was the *Hydra*'s mouth?

3. **Infer**   How do you think a *Hydra* removes wastes from its body? Explain your answer.

4. **Analyze**   What was the most sensitive part of the *Hydra*? Why do you think this part was sensitive?

5. **Analyze**   Describe the feeding behavior of the *Hydra*. How did it react to the presence of *Daphnia*?

6. **Apply**   From your observations of the *Hydra*'s feeding behavior, what do you think the small, rounded cells on the *Hydra*'s tentacles do? Explain your answer.

23.4 Flatworms, Mollusks, and Annelids

KEY CONCEPT Flatworms, mollusks, and annelids belong to closely related phyla.

MAIN IDEAS
- Flatworms are simple bilateral animals.
- Mollusks are diverse animals.
- Annelids have segmented bodies.

VOCABULARY
complete digestive tract, p. 712
radula, p. 712
hemocoel, p. 712
segmentation, p. 714
coelom, p. 714

MICHIGAN STANDARDS

L2.p1E Compare and contrast how different organisms accomplish similar functions (e.g., obtain oxygen for respiration, and excrete waste). (prerequisite)

L3.p2A Describe common relationships among organisms and provide examples of producer/consumer, predator/prey, or parasite/host relationship. (prerequisite)

Connect Imagine if you had no stomach or lungs. Just like a flatworm, you would have to be rather flat and thin in order to get the oxygen and food you need to survive. While some flatworms can grow up to 20 meters long, they are never more than a few millimeters thick.

MAIN IDEA
Flatworms are simple bilateral animals.

Based on molecular studies, most flatworms, mollusks, and annelids are classified together as members of the Lophotrochozoa. These animals have either a feeding structure made of hollow tentacles called a lophophore, or a distinctive free-swimming ciliated larva called a trochophore. The name Lophotrochozoa is taken from these two anatomical features.

Flatworms have a solid body and an incomplete or absent gut. A flatworm's shape is the direct result of having no circulatory system. Flatworms can only move oxygen to their cells by diffusion, so all their cells must be close to the outside environment. Complex characters such as gut tubes were probably lost at a later stage of evolution, often as the flatworms became parasitic on other animals. The three classes of flatworms include the planarians, flukes, and tapeworms.

Planarians

Planarians are free-living, nonparasitic flatworms. Planarian worms have a head with eyespots and a simple brain built of a cluster of nerve tissue. As shown in **FIGURE 23.13**, the mouth is found on the animal's ventral surface rather than in its head, and it leads to a gut cavity. A muscular tube called the pharynx extends from the mouth to collect food. These worms actively hunt for food using chemoreceptors to detect odors in the water or in the air. They usually move using the cilia on their ventral surface, but they also have bands of muscle that let them twist their bodies.

FIGURE 23.13 Planarians, such as this zebra flatworm, have a solid body that lacks a complete gut.

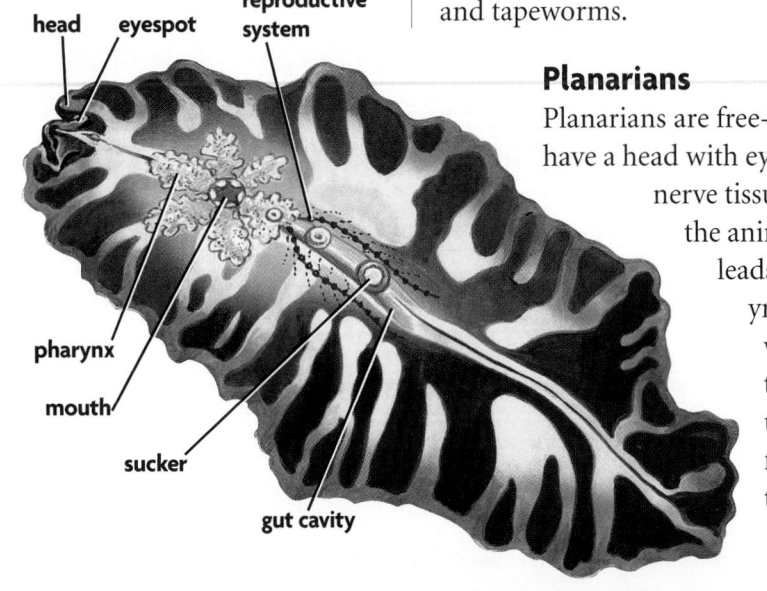

head eyespot reproductive system
pharynx
mouth
sucker
gut cavity

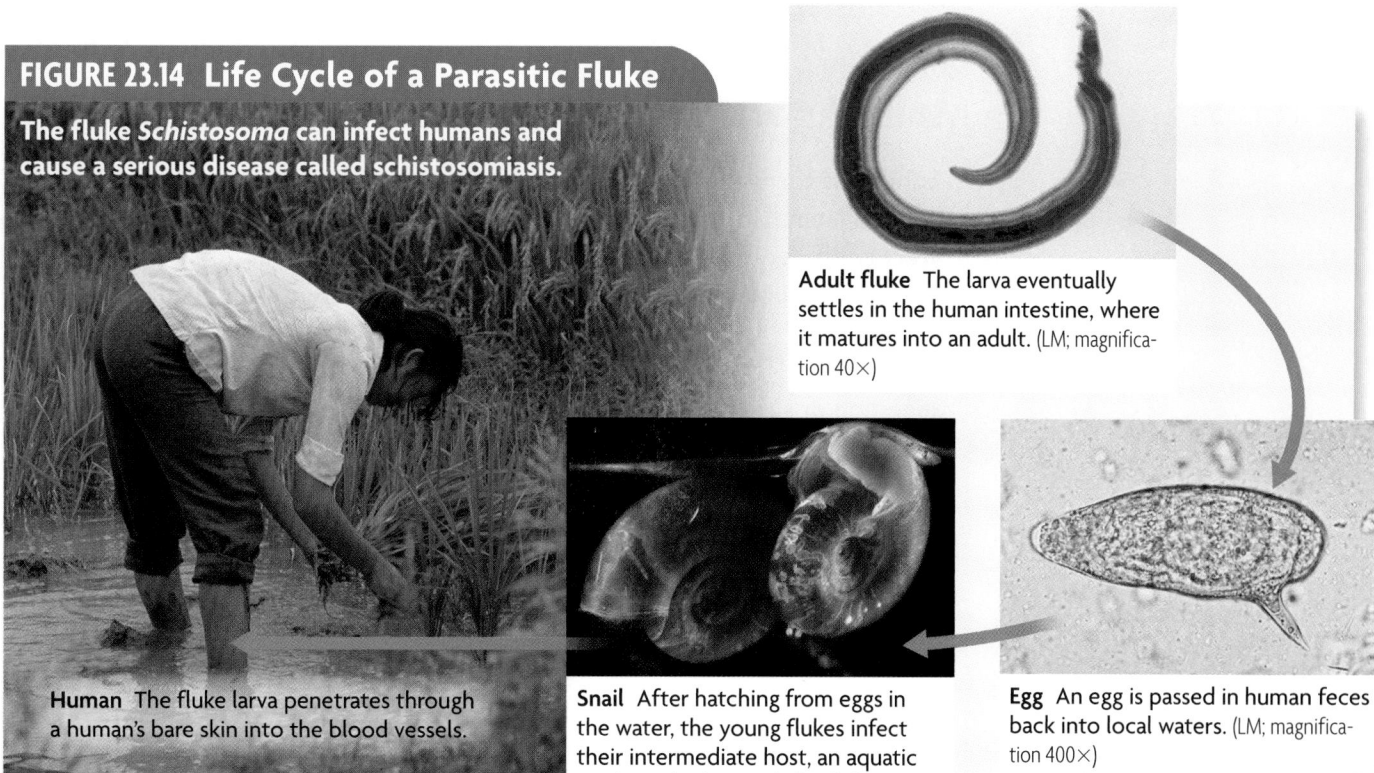

FIGURE 23.14 Life Cycle of a Parasitic Fluke

The fluke *Schistosoma* can infect humans and cause a serious disease called schistosomiasis.

Adult fluke The larva eventually settles in the human intestine, where it matures into an adult. (LM; magnification 40×)

Human The fluke larva penetrates through a human's bare skin into the blood vessels.

Snail After hatching from eggs in the water, the young flukes infect their intermediate host, an aquatic snail. Inside the snail, the flukes develop into tadpolelike larvae.

Egg An egg is passed in human feces back into local waters. (LM; magnification 400×)

Flukes

Flukes are parasites that feed on the body fluids of other animals. Flukes have a mouth with a pharynx that opens into a gut cavity. They are found in both invertebrate and vertebrate hosts. Many species of flukes have life cycles that involve more than one host. **FIGURE 23.14** shows the life cycle of one fluke, *Schistosoma* (SHIHS-tuh-SOHM-uh), which can infect humans and cause a serious disease called schistosomiasis. This disease affects about 200 million people in areas such as Africa and Southeast Asia. The disease is contracted by wading in or drinking fresh water contaminated with fluke larvae. Symptoms of the disease include the onset of fever and muscle pain within one to two months of infection. The disease is treated by an anti-parasitic medicine.

Tapeworms

Tapeworms are parasites that live in vertebrate guts. They have a small head with suckers or hooks used to attach to the host. Their long ribbonlike body has no gut. Instead of swallowing food, these animals absorb nutrients from the digested food in which they live. An adult tapeworm's body is made up of segments containing both male and female sexual organs. When these segments fill with fertilized eggs, they break off and are excreted with the host's feces.

Many tapeworms have complex life cycles involving multiple hosts. The life cycle of a dog tapeworm begins when an egg is passed with a dog's feces. A flea eats the egg, and the egg develops into a larva within the flea's body. The tapeworm infects another dog when it accidentally eats the infected flea while licking its fur. The tapeworm develops into an adult within the dog's intestines, and the cycle begins again.

Contrast How are planarians different from flukes and tapeworms?

Connecting CONCEPTS

Structure and Function The simple structure of a tapeworm reflects that as an adult it does not have to move or digest food. The lack of complex internal systems allows for a simpler body plan.

▶ MAIN IDEA

Mollusks are diverse animals.

While flatworms have a digestive sac with only one opening, mollusks and all other bilateral animals have a complete digestive tract. A **complete digestive tract** consists of two openings—a mouth and an anus—at opposite ends of a continuous tube. Because food moves one way through the gut, animals with complete digestive tracts can turn their guts into disassembly lines for food. As food moves down the gut, it travels through areas that are specialized for digestion or absorption. Animals with complete digestive tracts can eat continuously. This efficient and frequent digestion allows animals to be more active.

Mollusk Anatomy

Mollusks include animals as different-looking as oysters, garden snails, and giant squid. Mollusks may be sessile filter feeders, herbivores that graze on algae, or predators. Despite this variety of form and lifestyle, all mollusks share at least one of three features, shown in **FIGURE 23.15**.

- **Radula** The **radula** is a filelike feeding organ. Mollusks eat by scraping the radula over their food. The hard teeth of the radula pick up tiny particles that the animal swallows.
- **Mantle** The mantle is an area of tissue covering the internal organs. In most mollusks, the mantle secretes a hard calcium-based shell that protects the animal from predators.
- **Ctenidia** (tih-NIHD-ee-uh) The ctenidia are flat gills found in a pocket of the mantle tissue called the mantle cavity. The gills absorb oxygen from water that enters this cavity. In the land-dwelling snail shown below, the gills have been lost, and oxygen is absorbed from air rather than from water in the cavity.

While the gills contain blood vessels, blood is also pumped through the hemocoel. The **hemocoel** (HEE-muh-SEEL) consists of spaces between cells within the animal's tissues. This circulatory system extends into a large muscular foot. Snails and slugs crawl on the foot, while clams and scallops dig with the foot. In cephalopods, such as squids and octopuses, the foot forms a muscular siphon, parts of the tentacles, and head.

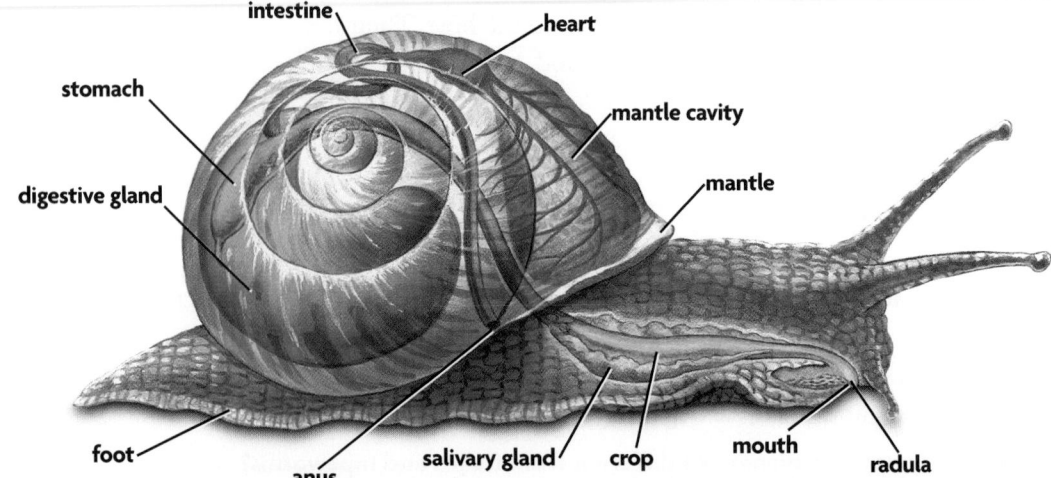

FIGURE 23.15 The anatomy of a common garden snail includes a radula and a mantle, both of which are features shared by most mollusks.

Classes of Mollusks

There are seven classes of mollusks. The majority of species, however, are found within three classes: the gastropods, pelecypods (bivalves), and cephalopods.

- **Gastropoda** This class includes snails, nudibranchs, abalones, and limpets. This class includes over half of the species found in the Mollusk phylum. Gastropods live in both land and aquatic ecosystems. This class includes species that are herbivores, carnivores, and scavengers.

- **Pelecypoda** This class includes clams, oysters, mussels, and scallops. Pelecypods, which are also called bivalves, have a soft body that is protected by two hard shells that are hinged together. Most bivalves are filter feeders that live in marine ecosystems.

- **Cephalopoda** This class includes squid, as shown in **FIGURE 23.16**, octopuses, nautiluses, and cuttlefish. Among the mollusks, the nervous system and eye of the cephalopod are the most well-developed. Cephalopods are carnivores that eat animals such as crustaceans, fish, and other mollusks.

- **Scaphopoda** This class is also called the tusk shells, so named because their shells resemble the shape of an elephant's tusks. These mollusks live at the bottom of water bodies, where they feed on detritus.

- **Polyplacophora** This class is also called the chitons, which are animals that have a shell with overlapping plates. These marine mollusks spend most of their lifetime clinging to rocks, where they feed by using their radula to scrape algae and plant matter from the rocks.

- **Aplacophora** This class includes small wormlike animals that, unlike most mollusks, do not have shells. These mollusks live in deep water. Some feed on small marine invertebrates, while others are parasites of coral.

- **Tryblidia** This class of mollusks was once believed to be extinct, but they were rediscovered in 1952. Little is known about these marine mollusks that live in deep water.

FIGURE 23.16 The Humboldt, or jumbo, squid may grow to nearly 2 meters (6 ft) in length.

Connecting CONCEPTS

Convergent Evolution Much like the human eye, the cephalopod eye is made up of a lens, retina, iris, and pupil. However, the evolution of cephalopod and human eyes occurred independently. Recall from **Chapter 11** that convergent evolution is the evolution of similar structures in unrelated species.

Mollusk Reproduction

Mollusks use a variety of reproductive strategies. Garden snails, for example, are hermaphrodites. Hermaphrodites are organisms that have both male and female reproductive organs. Reproduction usually involves cross-fertilization. Just before mating, the impregnating snail fires a "love dart" into the other. This calcium-rich, mucus-covered dart causes the recipient snail's reproductive system to store more sperm. During mating, a packet of sperm is transferred into the recipient snail. This packet of sperm is used to fertilize the eggs. These eggs are laid in underground nests. After a period of two to four weeks, juvenile snails hatch from the eggs.

Summarize **What common features are shared by mollusks?**

Anatomy of a Clam

A clam is a bivalve mollusk. In this lab, you will explore the parts and systems of a clam.

PROBLEM What are the internal organs and systems of a clam?

PROCEDURE

1. Place the clam in the dissecting tray and follow the instructions on the drawing to carefully open the shell.
2. Look for the gills, and use your probe to study them.
3. Observe and note the shape of the foot. Locate the palps.
4. Follow the instructions to peel away the muscle layer to see the internal organs.
5. Locate the reproductive organs, and then find the digestive system.
6. Dispose of your specimen as instructed by your teacher.

ANALYZE AND CONCLUDE

1. **Infer** What organ does the clam use to breathe?
2. **Infer** The clam is a filter feeder. Based on your observations of the digestive system, how does the clam eat?
3. **Infer** The arteries and veins are not attached to each other. How might the circulatory system work?

MATERIALS

- preserved clam specimen
- dissecting tray
- Anatomical Clam Drawing
- screwdriver
- scalpel
- probe
- scissors
- forceps
- 12 dissecting pins
- hand lens
- paper towels

▶ MAIN IDEA

Annelids have segmented bodies.

All annelids share more similarities in their body plans than mollusks do. Three groups of annelids—earthworms, marine worms, and leeches—are characterized by segmentation. **Segmentation** refers to the repeated sections of an annelid's long body that contain a complex set of body structures.

Annelid Anatomy

The features of an annelid's segmented body are shown in **FIGURE 23.17.** A typical annelid segment contains part of the digestive tract, nerve cord, and blood vessels that carry blood to the worm's tissues. Annelids have a closed circulatory system, where blood travels in a closed circuit inside blood vessels. Each body segment also contains organs that collect and excrete wastes, bands of longitudinal and circular muscle, and a coelom.

The **coelom** (SEE-luhm) is a fluid-filled space that is completely surrounded by muscle. The coelom is divided by partitions called septa (singular, *septum*). The fluid inside the coelom acts as a hydrostatic skeleton. To understand how a hydrostatic skeleton works, think of a water balloon. When you squeeze one end, the water moves to the opposite end. An annelid uses its hydrostatic skeleton in a similar way to move from one place to another. When the longitudinal muscles contract, the segment shortens. When circular muscles contract, the segment lengthens. Alternating waves of contractions move from head to tail, producing the worm's characteristic crawling motion.

VOCABULARY

Coelom comes from a Greek word meaning "cavity." *Septum* comes from a Latin word meaning "partition."

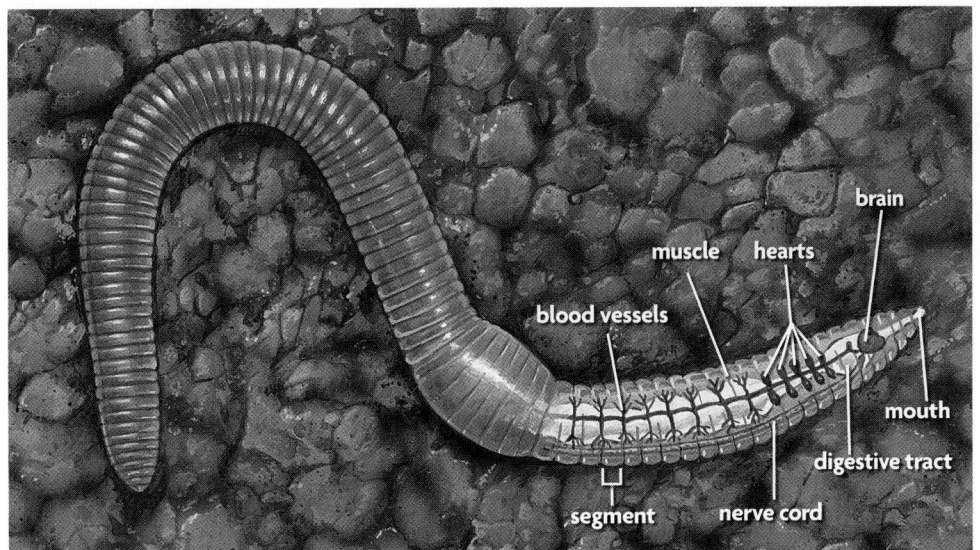

FIGURE 23.17 Annelids, such as earthworms, have similar body plans, characterized by segmentation.

brain
muscle   hearts
blood vessels
mouth
digestive tract
segment   nerve cord

Annelid Diet

Earthworms and marine worms eat organic waste material. Earthworms excrete digested material, called castings, into the soil. Castings help maintain a nutrient-rich soil. While most people think of leeches as blood-feeders, a number of leech species are actually predators that feed on invertebrates such as snails and aquatic insect larvae.

Annelid Reproduction

Annelid reproduction may be either asexual or sexual. Asexual reproduction results from fragmentation. In this method, a portion of the posterior end of the annelid breaks off and forms a new individual. Some annelids, such as earthworms, are hermaphrodites. Just as in land snails, reproduction occurs by cross-fertilization. Other annelids, such as marine worms, have separate males and females. Fertilized eggs of marine annelids initially develop into free-swimming larvae. Larvae grow in size by the formation of new segments.

Contrast In what ways are annelids different from mollusks?

23.4 / ASSESSMENT

ONLINE QUIZ ClassZone.com

REVIEWING ▶ MAIN IDEAS

1. Describe the characteristics that separate the three groups of flatworms.
2. What is the function of a mollusk's **radula**?
3. What are the three groups of annelids? Describe their body plan, using the word **coelom.**

CRITICAL THINKING

4. **Apply** How might a community prevent *Schistosoma* infections?
5. **Infer** What adaptations might mollusks without shells use to defend against predators?

Connecting CONCEPTS

6. **Evolution** Free-living flat-worms have pairs of sensory organs in their heads. What might make two sense organs set on either side of the head more adaptive than a single central organ?

23.5 Roundworms

KEY CONCEPT Roundworms have bilateral symmetry and shed their outer skeleton to grow.

▶ MAIN IDEAS

- Roundworms shed their stiff outer skeleton as they grow.
- Many roundworms are parasites.

VOCABULARY

cuticle, p. 716
pseudocoelom, p. 716

MICHIGAN STANDARDS

L2.p1E Compare and contrast how different organisms accomplish similar functions (e.g., obtain oxygen for respiration, and excrete waste). (prerequisite)

L3.p2A Describe common relationships among organisms and provide examples of producer/consumer, predator/prey, or parasite/host relationship. (prerequisite)

Connect Imagine grabbing a handful of soil. In that single handful, there may be thousands of roundworms. These animals are found in nearly every ecosystem on Earth, including mountaintops and deep ocean trenches. They are also found within extreme environments such as hot springs and Arctic ice.

▶ MAIN IDEA

Roundworms shed their stiff outer skeleton as they grow.

Roundworms, also called nematodes, are one of the most numerous kinds of animals, in terms both of numbers and of species diversity. The more than 15,000 species of roundworms vary in size from less than a millimeter to over 10 meters in length.

Roundworms are part of the group Ecdysozoa, which also includes arthropods—crustaceans, spiders, and insects. Like mollusks and annelids, members of the Ecdysozoa are protostomes and have bilateral symmetry. All Ecdysozoans have a tough exoskeleton called a cuticle. The **cuticle** (KYOO-tih-kuhl) is made of chitin, and must be shed whenever the animal grows larger. When the animal sheds its cuticle, its soft body is exposed to predators until its new skeleton hardens.

Roundworm Anatomy

As shown in **FIGURE 23.18**, a roundworm is cylindrical, with a blunt head and tapered tail. It is covered with a tough cuticle that lies over a layer of muscle. Muscle in the roundworm is laid out lengthwise. This arrangement means that a roundworm moves by bending its body side-to-side. Rather than crawling like other types of worms, a roundworm's movement is more whiplike.

Muscle within the roundworm is separated from the central gut tube by a fluid-filled space. This fluid-filled space is called a **pseudocoelom** (soo-duh-SEE-luhm) because it is not completely lined by muscle. (The prefix *pseudo-* means "false.") Roundworms do not have circulatory or respiratory systems. However, they do have a digestive system, which includes a mouth, pharynx, intestine, and anus. Food that is eaten, such as plant matter, algae, or bacteria, travels the length of the roundworm, from the mouth at one end to the anus at the other.

FIGURE 23.18 Roundworms have a cylindrical shape and must shed their tough outer cuticle to grow in size.

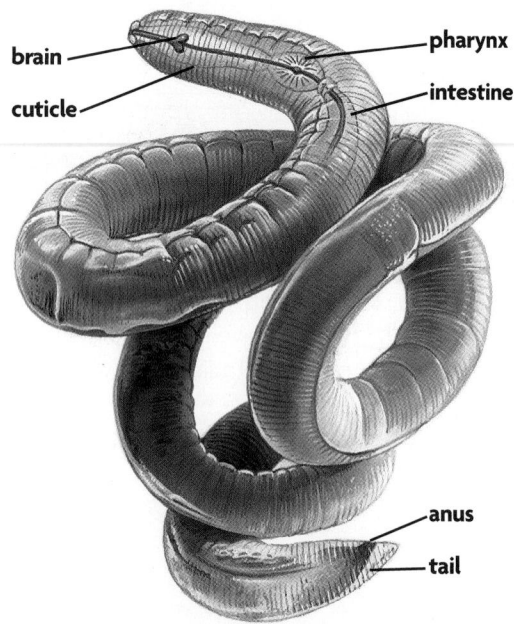

brain
cuticle
pharynx
intestine
anus
tail

Roundworm Reproduction

Most roundworms reproduce sexually. In some cases, female roundworms bear live young after eggs hatch within the female's reproductive tract. In most cases, however, larvae develop from eggs laid by the female. Roundworms grow into their adult form by molting.

Contrast How does growth differ in a roundworm and in a human?

▶ MAIN IDEA

Many roundworms are parasites.

Roundworms are parasites of nearly every plant and animal species. These animals cause a lot of damage to the crop species they infect. Such a widespread loss of crops can seriously harm the economy of farming communities. Other roundworms infect humans. These roundworms include hookworms, pinworms, and Guinea worms.

"So much for being the early bird, you've got worms."

Source: CartoonStock.com

- **Hookworms** A hookworm is found within the digestive tract of its host. This parasite feeds on its host's blood. A hookworm infects its human host when a person walks barefoot over contaminated soil. Over 1 billion people are infected with hookworms. Such infections are common in the tropics and subtropics.
- **Pinworms** A pinworm is found in the gut of its host. Pinworm infections often occur when the host accidentally swallows eggs picked up from contaminated surfaces.
- **Guinea worms** Guinea worms are found in the guts and connective tissues of their hosts. Guinea worm infections occur when a person drinks contaminated water. Work by global health organizations has helped to eliminate this disease from most of the world.

Infer Why might most parasitic roundworms live in the gut of their host?

23.5 ASSESSMENT

ONLINE QUIZ
ClassZone.com

REVIEWING ▶ MAIN IDEAS

1. Why do roundworms molt? Use the term **cuticle** in your answer.

2. What are three parasitic roundworms that infect human hosts?

CRITICAL THINKING

3. **Contrast** How are earthworm and roundworm body cavities different?

4. **Apply** How might Guinea worm infections be prevented?

Connecting CONCEPTS

5. **Parasitism** Many species of roundworms are parasites of plants and animals. How is a roundworm's body plan related to its function as a parasite?

23.6 Echinoderms

KEY CONCEPT Echinoderms are on the same evolutionary branch as vertebrates.

MAIN IDEAS
- Echinoderms have radial symmetry.
- There are five classes of Echinoderms.

VOCABULARY

ossicle, p. 718

water vascular system, p. 718

MICHIGAN STANDARDS

L2.p1E Compare and contrast how different organisms accomplish similar functions (e.g., obtain oxygen for respiration, and excrete waste). (prerequisite)

L3.p2A Describe common relationships among organisms and provide examples of producer/consumer, predator/prey, or parasite/host relationship. (prerequisite)

Connect If you have ever seen a tide pool, you may have noticed several creatures clinging to the pool's rocky bottom and sides. Brightly colored sea stars and spiky sea urchins are just two of the echinoderms that are often found in these habitats.

MAIN IDEA

Echinoderms have radial symmetry.

Adult echinoderms are slow-moving marine animals that have radial symmetry. In contrast, echinoderm larvae have bilateral symmetry. This difference suggests that echinoderms had bilateral ancestors and that radial symmetry is a derived character.

Echinoderm Anatomy

The anatomy of a sea star is shown in **FIGURE 23.19.** Note that each arm of a sea star contains both digestive glands and reproductive glands. For clarity, they are shown separately in different arms in the illustration.

All echinoderms have an internal skeleton made up of many tiny interlocking calcium-based plates called **ossicles.** These ossicles are embedded within the skin. The plates are joined together by a unique catch connective tissue with adjustable stiffness. Catch connective tissue allows echinoderms to change their consistency, going from very flexible to very stiff in a matter of seconds. The combination of a firm skeleton and a surface covered with spiny projections (often poisonous) helps to fend off predators.

Echinoderms have a **water vascular system,** which is a series of water-filled radial canals that extend along each arm from the ring canal surrounding the central disk. The radial canals store water that is used for circulation and for filling tiny suckerlike appendages along the arms called tube feet. Changes in water pressure extend and retract the tube feet. On its own, a tube foot is small, but many of them working together can exert large forces. Tube feet are used to grab objects and to move around.

FIGURE 23.19 Echinoderms, such as sea stars, are radially symmetrical animals with an internal skeleton made of interlocking plates embedded under the skin. Three arms of this sea star have been "cut away" to show internal anatomy.

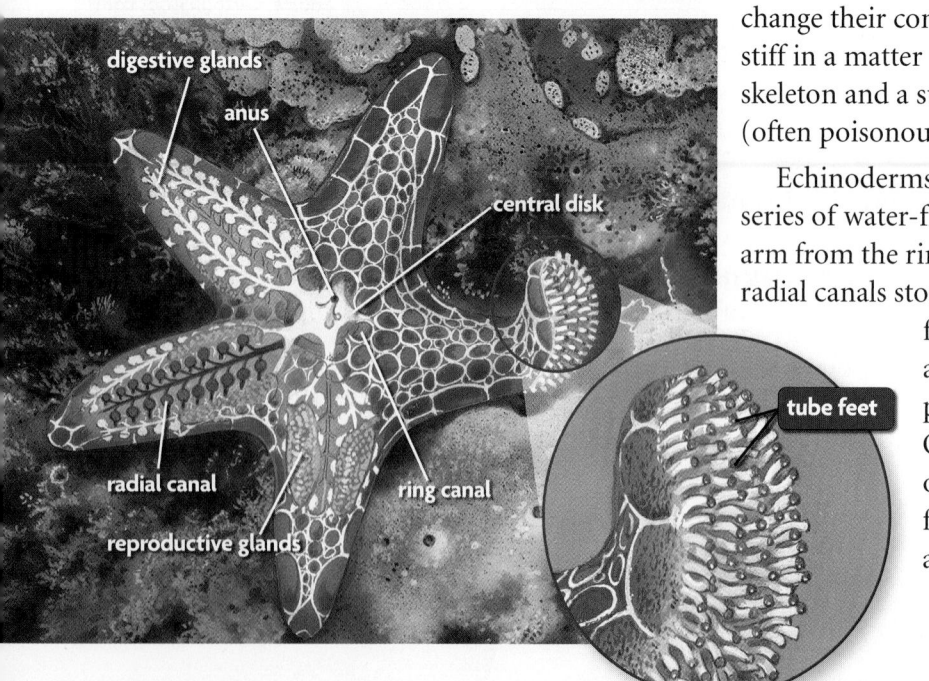

digestive glands
anus
central disk
radial canal
ring canal
reproductive glands
tube feet

A sea star has a complete digestive system made up of a mouth, stomach, a small length of intestine, and an anus. To eat a clam, a sea star grabs hold of the clam with its tube feet and uses pressure to pull apart the clam's shell. Sea stars are able to push their stomach out of their mouths. The stomach enters the narrow space between the two shells of a clam, and digestive juices from the digestive glands dissolve the clam's body. The clam is completely digested in the stomach. Waste material exits out the anus.

Echinoderms such as sea stars can regenerate, or regrow, their limbs, as shown in **FIGURE 23.20**. Sea cucumbers can regenerate a portion of their digestive system, which they sometimes eject when disturbed. For regeneration to occur, certain body parts, such as a portion of a sea star's central disk, must still remain.

FIGURE 23.20 Sea stars and other echinoderms are able to regenerate, or regrow, limbs.

Echinoderm Reproduction

Most echinoderms reproduce sexually. Adult sea stars, for example, release sperm and eggs from the reproductive glands in their arms into the water. The fusion of these gametes results in fertilization of the egg. The fertilized egg develops into a free-floating, planktonic larva that matures in the water. As it matures, an echinoderm undergoes a complex series of changes into its adult form. The left side of its body begins to form the tube feet, while the right side forms the ossicle plates that will protect its outer surface. Eventually, the echinoderm settles onto the ocean floor, where it develops into an adult.

Connect A sea star specimen has bilateral symmetry. Is it an adult or a larva? Why?

FIGURE 23.21 Feather stars are members of the class Crinoidea. These animals are filter feeders.

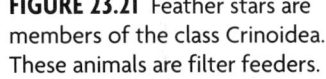 **MAIN IDEA**

There are five classes of Echinoderms.

Echinoderms have a variety of body plans, ranging from the spiny round sea urchin to the oblong and the well-named sea cucumber.

Feather Stars and Sea Lilies

Feather stars and sea lilies are members of the class Crinoidea (kry-NOY-dee-uh). A feather star, shown in **FIGURE 23.21**, can move with its arms, but it is usually attached to a surface. Sea lilies are sessile. They are attached to the ocean bottom by a stalk on one side of their bodies. These animals filter feed by using the tube foot–like extensions covering their arms to collect and transfer food to the mouth.

Sea Stars

Sea stars are members of the class Asteroidea (AS-tuh-ROY-dee-uh). Some sea stars are filter feeders, while others are opportunistic feeders, meaning that they will eat whatever food source they happen to come upon. Other sea stars are carnivorous predators.

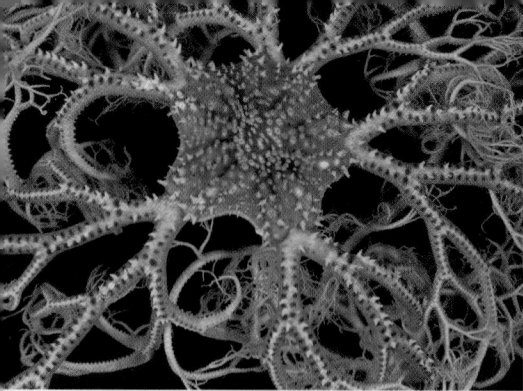

FIGURE 23.22 Basket stars (left) use their long, branched arms to capture plankton. Sea urchins (middle) are covered in long, sharp spines that protect them from predators. Sea cucumbers (right) are fleshy animals that live on the ocean floor.

Brittle Stars and Basket Stars

Brittle stars and basket stars are both members of the class Ophiuroidea (AHF-ee-yuh-ROY-dee-uh). Brittle stars have long spindly arms and are fast movers. Because their tube feet lack suckers, brittle stars use their arms to move. Some brittle stars are scavengers that feed on detritus on the ocean floor. Others are predators. Basket stars, shown in **FIGURE 23.22**, also have long arms, although with many branches. Basket stars filter feed by capturing plankton with their arms.

Sea Urchins, Sea Biscuits, and Sand Dollars

Sea urchins, sea biscuits, and sand dollars are all members of the class Echinoidea (EHK-uh-NOY-dee-uh). The bodies of sea biscuits and sand dollars are covered with tiny projections, which the animals use for movement and for burrowing on the ocean floor. Sea urchins, which do not burrow, do not have these projections. Instead, these animals are covered in long, sharp spines. Burrowing animals feed on waste matter on the ocean floor. Most sea urchins graze on algae by trapping it on sticky tentacles found on their ventral side.

Sea Cucumbers

Sea cucumbers are the only members of the class Holothuroidea (HAHL-uh-thu-ROY-dee-uh). Sea cucumbers are fleshy animals that have a long, bilateral shape. Instead of arms, sea cucumbers have thick, fleshy tentacles. These tentacles are used to capture particles of food, which the animal eats by pulling its tentacles through its mouth. Sea cucumbers, which live on the ocean floor, are also sediment feeders. These animals absorb food items in their digestive tract, and eject nonfood particles through their anus.

Contrast How do feeding behaviors differ between sea stars and sea cucumbers?

23.6 ASSESSMENT

REVIEWING ▶ MAIN IDEAS

1. How does the **water vascular system** enable echinoderms to move?

2. Describe the differences in body plans between the five classes of echinoderms.

CRITICAL THINKING

3. **Contrast** How do the feeding habits of sessile echinoderms differ from those that are mobile?

4. **Infer** How does an echinoderm benefit from the ability to regenerate limbs?

Connecting CONCEPTS

5. **Bioindicators** Sea urchins live on rock- and sand-covered areas of the ocean floor. What changes in an ocean ecosystem might be indicated by an increase in the sea urchin population?

DATA ANALYSIS
ClassZone.com

Correlations Among Invertebrate Data

A **scatterplot** is a type of graph used to identify a trend or a correlation between two variables.

- The independent variable is usually graphed on the *x*-axis.
- The dependent variable is usually graphed on the *y*-axis.
- The data points are plotted but not connected.

Three types of correlations between variables can be shown on a scatterplot.

- Positive—as one variable increases or decreases, the other variable increases or decreases respectively.
- Negative (inverse)—as one variable increases, the other decreases.
- No correlation—there is no change in one variable as the other variable either increases or decreases.

EXAMPLE

Graph 1, a scatterplot of butter clam shell length and width, shows that as the width of the clam's shell increases, the length of the shell increases as well. This is a positive correlation, because as width increases, length increases. If it were an inverse correlation, one of the variables would increase as the other decreased.

Graph 2, a scatterplot of zooplankton feeding rates, shows no correlation between the feeding rates of zooplankton and the concentration of dinoflagellates. You can infer that there is no correlation from the graph, because the data is scattered across the graph and does not form a pattern.

ANALYZE A SCATTERPLOT

Scientists measured the heart rate and shell diameter of snails. These data are shown in the graph at the right. Use the graph to answer the following three questions.

1. **Analyze** Describe the correlation between the shell diameter and the heart rate in this species of snail.

2. **Predict** If a snail shell were to grow past 14 mm, what do you think would happen to the snail's heart rate?

3. **Infer** Suggest a possible explanation for the correlation between heart rate and shell diameter.

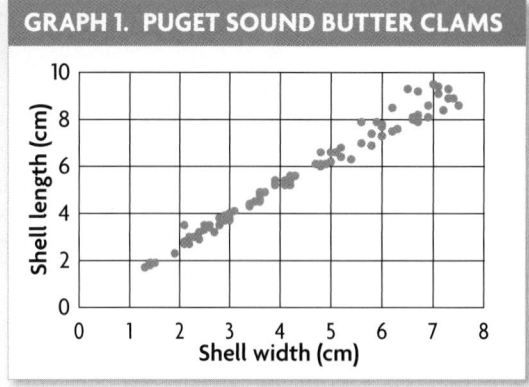

GRAPH 1. PUGET SOUND BUTTER CLAMS

Source: Seattle Central Community College

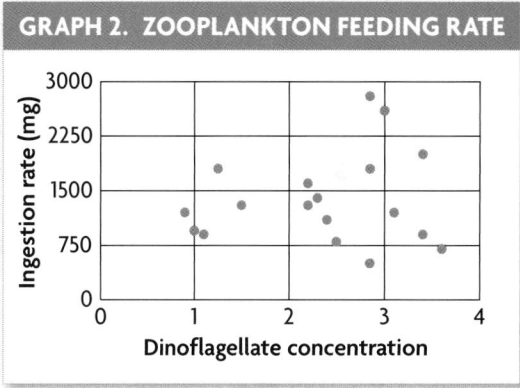

GRAPH 2. ZOOPLANKTON FEEDING RATE

Source: Calbet, A. et al. *Journal of Aquatic Microbial Ecology* 26

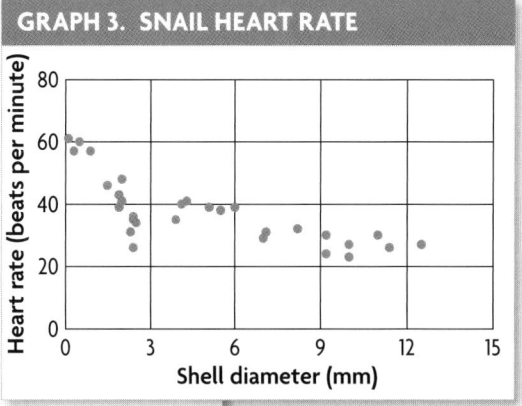

GRAPH 3. SNAIL HEART RATE

Source: Iowa State University

Use these inquiry-based labs and online activities to deepen your understanding of invertebrates.

MICHIGAN STANDARDS

B1.2C Develop an understanding of a scientific concept by accessing information from multiple sources. Evaluate the scientific accuracy and significance of the information.

L2.p1D Explain how the systems in a multicellular organism work together to support the organism. (prerequisite)

INVESTIGATION

Anatomy of a Sea Star

A sea star is a saltwater echinoderm in the same phylum as sea urchins and sand dollars. In this lab, you will dissect and explore the parts of a sea star.

SKILL Observing

PROBLEM What organs and systems are inside a sea star?

MATERIALS

- preserved sea star specimen
- dissecting tray
- scissors
- forceps
- dissecting needle
- 12 dissecting pins
- hand lens or dissecting microscope
- paper towels
- Anatomical Sea Star Drawing

PROCEDURE

1. Remove the sea star from its container and place it in the dissecting tray.
2. Examine the external anatomy of the sea star.
3. Follow the instructions on the sea star drawing as you complete steps 4–8.
4. Use scissors to cut off the end of one ray about one inch from the tip. Use the scissors to cut a long circular flap of skin along the length of one ray to expose the organs underneath. Look closely in the ray on either side of the groove.
5. With forceps and scissors, lift and cut the skin closer to the center (within half an inch). There, on either side of the groove, you will see the gonads, or reproductive organs, of the sea star.
6. The water-filled space in each ray is called the coelom. Notice that the sea star has no heart or circulatory system.
7. When finished, dispose of your sea star according to instructions from your teacher. Be sure to wash your hands thoroughly before leaving the lab.

ANALYZE AND CONCLUDE

1. **Apply** What type of symmetry does the sea star have?
2. **Analyze** What type of texture does the dorsal surface have? What is it covered with?
3. **Infer** How do the eyespots compare with eyes of other animals?
4. **Predict** A sea star does not have teeth. How does it eat?

EXTEND YOUR INVESTIGATION

You have learned about the different structures and their functions within a sea star. How would you design an experiment to determine what food items sea stars prefer? Use the library or Internet to research which food items sea stars eat, and then design your experiment. Include in your experimental design your control, independent variables, and dependent variables.

Anatomy of an Annelid

The California blackworm (*Lumbriculus variegatus*) lives in sediments and organic debris on the edges of freshwater ponds, marshes, and lakes. In this investigation, you will observe a blackworm's anatomy and behavior, and observe and measure blood flow.

SKILL Observing

PROBLEM What are the features of an annelid?

MATERIALS

- 6–10 filter paper disks
- forceps
- petri dish
- 10 mL spring water
- California blackworm
- eyedropper
- dissecting microscope

PROCEDURE

1. Place a filter paper disk in the petri dish and moisten it with water at room temperature.
2. Carefully transfer a blackworm to the petri dish using the eyedropper.
3. Observe the blackworm at low (40×) and high (400×) powers with the microscope.
4. Draw what you see. What structures can you identify? How many segments does the blackworm have? Can you see the large blood vessels running along the worm? Draw them.
5. Observe the blood vessels more closely. Do they change over time? If so, what happens?

ANALYZE AND CONCLUDE

1. **Analyze** Does the worm have a head end and tail end? Explain.
2. **Infer** What causes blood to flow in the worm?
3. **Experimental Design** Write a procedure to measure the blood flow using a ruler and a watch.

CLASSZONE.COM

ANIMATED BIOLOGY
Shared Body Structures

Animals that look very different can have similar body structures. Compare structures and organs of four different invertebrates to explore shared characteristics.

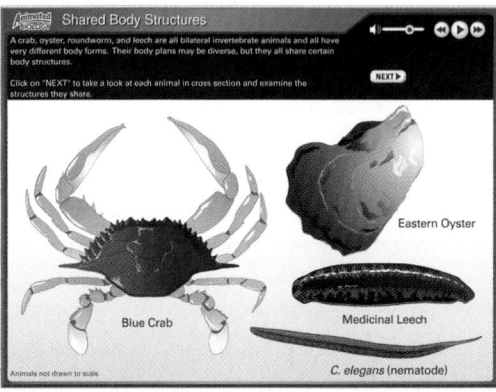

WEBQUEST

Parasites. Just the word can make your skin crawl. In this WebQuest, you will explore one parasite, the tapeworm. You will learn about its lifecycle and how to keep from becoming a host yourself! (colored SEM; magnification 40×)

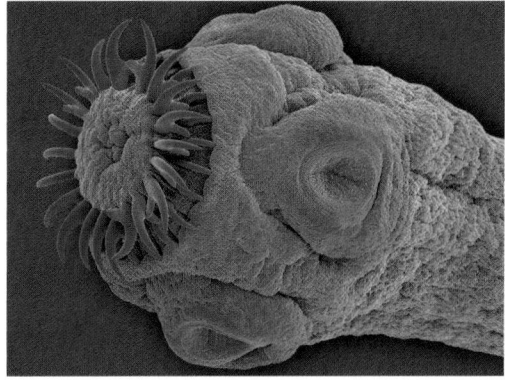

BIOZINE

Stories about invertebrates—such as "Sea Snails' Slime Holds Healing Properties" and "Designer Dogs: Get the Mix You Want"— are often in the headlines. Read the latest news about animals in the BioZine.

23.1 Animal Characteristics

Animals are diverse but share common characteristics. Animals are the most physically diverse kingdom of organisms. All animals share a set of characteristics.
- All animals are multicellular heterotrophs.
- Animal cells are supported by collagen.
- Animals that reproduce are diploid and usually reproduce sexually.
- Most animals have *Hox* genes.

23.2 Animal Diversity

More than 95 percent of all animal species are invertebrates. Each animal phylum has a unique body plan. Scientists have constructed an invertebrate phylogenetic tree supported by anatomy comparisons and molecular evidence.

Bilateral symmetry　　　**Radial symmetry**

23.3 Sponges and Cnidarians

Sponges and cnidarians are the simplest animals. Sponges are aquatic animals that have specialized cells but lack tissues. These animals were among the first to evolve during the Cambrian explosion. Cnidarians, which include jellyfish, corals, and sea anemones, are the most primitive animals still in existence today with specialized tissues.

23.4 Flatworms, Mollusks, and Annelids

Flatworms, mollusks, and annelids belong to closely related phyla. Flatworms are simple bilateral animals. They include planarians, flukes, and tapeworms. Mollusks share at least one feature in common: a radula, a mantle, or ctenidia. Common mollusks include snails, bivalves such as clams, and squid. Annelids have segmented bodies and include earthworms, leeches, and marine polychaete worms.

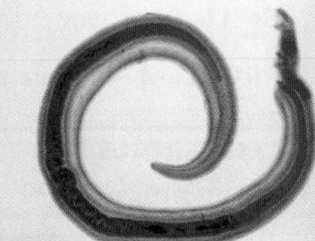

23.5 Roundworms

Roundworms have bilateral symmetry and shed their outer skeleton to grow. Roundworms are cylindrical, with a blunt head and tapered tail. They are covered with a tough cuticle that lies over a layer of muscle. Roundworms may be free-living or parasitic. Common human parasites include hookworms, pinworms, and Guinea worms.

23.6 Echinoderms

Echinoderms are on the same evolutionary branch as vertebrates. Echinoderms and vertebrates are both deuterostomes. Like cnidarians, echinoderms have radial symmetry. These animals have body parts arranged in a circle around a central axis and use a water vascular system to move and transport nutrients. Some echinoderms can regenerate portions of their body, and sometimes they use regeneration as a way to produce offspring.

Synthesize Your Notes

Concept Map Use a concept map to summarize what you know about animal phylogeny.

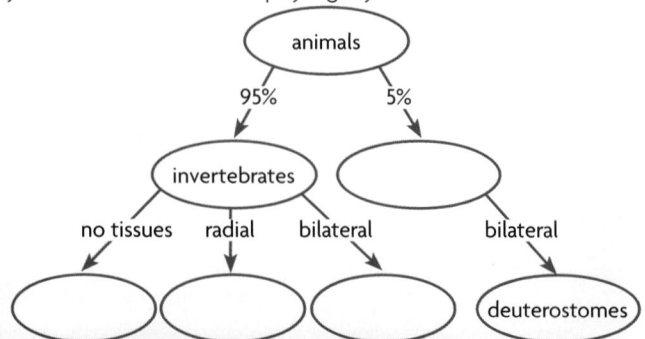

Content Frame Use a table to synthesize notes on the characteristics of the different invertebrate phyla.

Phyla	Features	Symmetry	Examples
Cnidaria	Tissues	Radial	Jellyfish, coral
Flatworms			

Chapter Assessment

Chapter Vocabulary

23.1 collagen, p. 697
homeotic, p. 698
homeobox, p. 698

23.2 vertebrate, p. 699
invertebrate, p. 699
phylum, p. 699
bilateral symmetry, p. 701
radial symmetry, p. 701
protostome, p. 702
deuterostome, p. 702

23.3 sessile, p. 705
filter feeder, p. 706
polyp, p. 707
medusa, p. 707
mesoglea, p. 707
nematocyst, p. 707
gastrovascular cavity, p. 708

23.4 complete digestive tract, p. 712
radula, p. 712
hemocoel, p. 712
segmentation, p. 714
coelom, p. 714

23.5 cuticle, p. 716
pseudocoelom, p. 716

23.6 ossicle, p. 718
water vascular system, p. 718

Reviewing Vocabulary

Visualize Vocabulary

For each word or word pair below, use simple shapes, lines, or arrows to illustrate the meaning. Label each picture, and write a short caption.

1. collagen
2. segmentation
3. mesoglea
4. gastrovascular cavity
5. polyp, medusa
6. radial symmetry, bilateral symmetry
7. radula
8. hemocoel

Greek and Latin Word Origins

Using the Greek or Latin word origins of the terms below, explain how the meaning of the root relates to the definition of the term.

9. The word *phylum* comes from the Greek word *phūlon*, which means "class."

10. The word *sessile* comes from the Latin word *sedere*, which means "to sit."

11. The word *segment*, as in *segmentation*, comes from *segmentum*, from the Latin word *secāre*, which means "to cut."

12. The word *radula* comes from the Latin word *radere*, which means "to scrape."

13. The word *pseudocoelom* comes from the Greek words *pseudes*, which means "false," and *koilos*, which means "hollow."

Reviewing MAIN IDEAS

14. What four characteristics are common to members of the animal kingdom?

15. What is the difference between an invertebrate and a vertebrate?

16. Describe three different criteria used to classify animals into groups.

17. What types of evidence are used to put together the evolutionary history of the animal kingdom?

18. What characteristic makes sponges the simplest animals?

19. Describe the two general body forms of cnidarians, which include jellyfish and corals.

20. What are the three types of flatworms? Describe the main features of each.

21. Mollusks have a complete digestive tract. What is one benefit of having this feature?

22. Describe what a segmented body plan looks like. Which phylum includes animals with segmented bodies?

23. Why must roundworms shed their outer skeleton?

24. Several species of roundworms are parasites with human hosts. Name one and explain how it affects human health.

25. What is the function of an echinoderm's water vascular system?

26. How does the ability to regenerate help an echinoderm escape from predators?

27. Analyze How are the functions of *Hox* genes related to the diversity of body plans and characteristics within the animal kingdom?

28. Contrast How is development different for an echinoderm and a mollusk? Use a table to summarize their different development patterns.

29. Infer While both sponges and cnidarians are simple animals, cnidarians have specialized tissues. What might be some advantages of having specialized tissues?

30. Infer Why is the ability to secrete toxic substances important to the survival of a sponge?

31. Synthesize How has molecular biology played a critical role in our understanding of animal relationships and phylogeny?

32. Infer Even when an annelid is cut in half, it can often still survive. What anatomical feature enables an annelid to remain alive when half of its body is gone?

33. Apply What is the function of an echinoderm's catch connective tissue?

34. Compare and Contrast Animals exhibit variety in their digestive systems. What do you think are the advantages and disadvantages of having a gastrovascular cavity compared with a complete digestive tract?

Interpreting Visuals

Use the *Hox* gene diagram below to answer the next two questions.

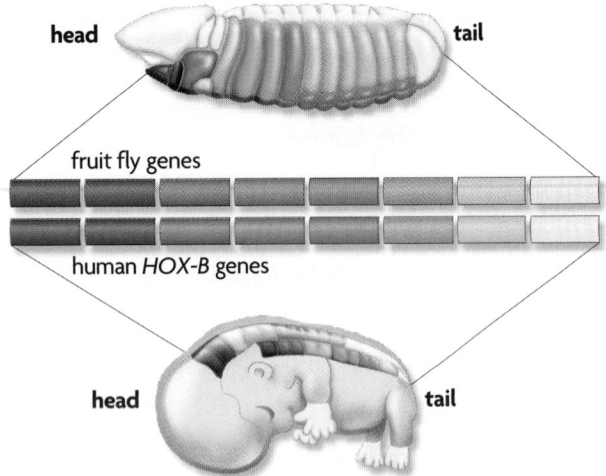

35. Apply How do the two organisms above display the pattern seen in all *Hox* genes?

36. Synthesize How does the diagram support the idea that all animals share a common ancestor?

Analyzing Data

Scientists measured the depth and velocity of water in the Columbia River in Washington. These data are shown on the scatterplot graph below. Use the graph to answer the next three questions.

COLUMBIA RIVER DEPTH AND VELOCITY

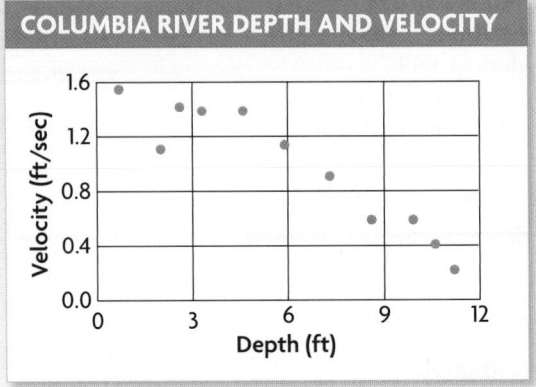

Source: USGS

37. Analyze What type of relationship exists between the depth and the velocity of the water? Explain your answer.

38. Predict Make a prediction about the velocity of the water if the depth were 14 feet.

39. Infer In what way might a species adapted to living at lower depths differ from a species adapted to living in shallow water?

Connecting CONCEPTS

40. Write a Travel Brochure Imagine you are an advertising director for a travel agency. Choose an invertebrate from this chapter, and create a brochure to entice your chosen invertebrate to visit a vacation spot. Remember that each invertebrate species has specific requirements for survival. In your brochure, include a description of the location (and why it is the perfect place for your invertebrate), the menu of local restaurants, and other features that would make your chosen invertebrate feel at home.

41. Connect In addition to storing poisonous chemicals from their food, nudibranchs also are very colorful. In other colorful animals, such as birds, fish, and insects, colors are important for a variety of reasons. What might be the adaptive advantage of a nudibranch's bright coloration?

MICHIGAN STANDARDS-BASED ASSESSMENT

✓ **Test Practice**
For more test practice, go to ClassZone.com.

1. A scientist needs to measure one hundred snails of a particular species to get an average measurement of the length of their shells. The most useful unit of measurement would most likely be **B1.1.C**

   A kilometer.

   B centimeter.

   C meter.

   D decameter.

2. Sponges are made up of three types of cells that cover a hard framework. Pinacocytes form a thin, leathery covering. Choanocytes pull water through the sponge. Amoebocytes absorb and digest food particles. This example shows that cells in multicellular organisms **L2.p1D**

   A can work in different ways to support an organism.

   B have only the genes that code for the proteins they need.

   C need more organelles than do single-celled organisms.

   D do not regulate ion concentrations at the cellular level.

   THINK THROUGH THE QUESTION

   Do not get caught up in the different names of the cells. This information is irrelevant to the question at hand. Instead, consider what having different types of cells, each with a different function, means to a multicellular organism.

3.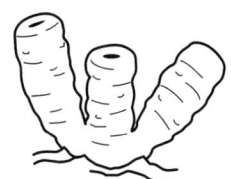

   Sponges have tiny pores in their body walls that they use to pull water in and a large hole at the top of the sponge from which water is ejected. These structures perform a similar function as what structure of most animals? **B2.4C**

   A nostril

   B eye

   C ear

   D mouth

4. Jellyfish and anemones are both classified as cnidarians. One similarity between these two types of organisms is that they both **B2.4d**

   A have the same polyp body form.

   B reproduce by budding.

   C swim in mid-ocean water.

   D have bodies with two tissue layers.

5. Flatworms, mollusks, and annelids look very different from each other. However, they are classified together in the same phyla. What type of evidence is this classification based upon? **B2.4A**

   A molecular

   B physical

   C functional

   D historical

6. Invertebrates have a diverse array of structures that help protect them from predators. For example, many sponges and flatworms can secrete toxic chemicals. Most mollusks, on the other hand, simply have a hard shell to protect their soft bodies. Cnidarians protect themselves by using **L2.p1E**

   A jelly-like mesoglea.

   B stinging nematocysts.

   C trapping tentacles.

   D biting mouthparts.

CHAPTER

24 A Closer Look at Arthropods

KEY CONCEPTS

24.1 Arthropod Diversity
Arthropods are the most diverse of all animals.

24.2 Crustaceans
Crustaceans are a diverse group of ancient arthropods.

24.3 Arachnids
Arachnids include spiders and their relatives.

24.4 Insect Adaptations
Insects show an amazing range of adaptations.

24.5 Arthropods and Humans
Arthropods and humans interact in many ways.

Online BIOLOGY CLASSZONE.COM

Animated BIOLOGY
View animated chapter concepts.
• Molting Cicada
• Insect Metamorphosis
• Insect and Crime Scene Analysis
• What Type of Arthropod?

BIOZINE
Keep current with biology news.
• Featured stories
• News feeds
• Strange Biology

RESOURCE CENTER
Get more information on
• Ancient Arthropods
• Crustaceans
• Insects

What is the relationship between these two insects?

Connecting CONCEPTS

Arthropod predators such as this digger wasp help to keep an important balance among Earth's invertebrates. This digger wasp has captured a meal not for itself but for its young. The wasp will deposit the live, but paralyzed, grasshopper into a burrow she has constructed. She will then lay a single egg next to the grasshopper so when the egg hatches the larva will have a fresh meal.

Animal Behavior Unlike the solitary digger wasp, many insects live in large social colonies. This paper wasp nest has been carefully constructed of wood pulp mixed with the insects' saliva. Within the colony, all insects are related to one another. A single queen lays eggs, which are raised by workers. Wasps will aggressively defend their nests from predators to ensure that the colony survives.

24.1 Arthropod Diversity

KEY CONCEPT Arthropods are the most diverse of all animals.

▶ MAIN IDEAS

- Arthropod features are highly adapted.
- Arthropod exoskeletons serve a variety of functions.
- Arthropod diversity evolved over millions of years.

VOCABULARY

arthropod, p. 730
exoskeleton, p. 730
chitin, p. 730
appendage, p. 730

segmentation, p. 730

Review
cuticle

MICHIGAN STANDARDS

B2.4B Describe how various organisms have developed different specializations to accomplish a particular function and yet the end result is the same (e.g., excreting nitrogenous wastes in animals, obtaining oxygen for respiration).
B2.4C Explain how different organisms accomplish the same result using different structural specializations (gills vs. lungs vs. membranes).

Connect Earth is truly ruled by bug-eyed monsters. In just about every way, arthropods are the most successful animal phylum on Earth. More than three-fourths of all known animals—more than 1 million species—are arthropods. They play an important role in every ecosystem on the planet. What makes this phylum so interesting? Arthropods are as diverse in shape and size as any life form on Earth, and are the result of millions of years of adaptation.

▶ MAIN IDEA
Arthropod features are highly adapted.

Without knowing it, almost everywhere you go, you are interacting with arthropods. They can be found in the carpet you walk on and in the bed where you sleep. An **arthropod** is an invertebrate animal with an exoskeleton made of chitin; a series of paired, jointed appendages; and segmented body parts.

Arthropod Characteristics

The entire surface of an arthropod's body is covered by a protective exoskeleton. An **exoskeleton** is an external skeleton that supports the animal's tissues against gravity. Arthropods, such as the rhino beetle in **FIGURE 24.1,** have exoskeletons made of proteins and chitin. **Chitin** (KYT-uhn) is a long organic molecule made of sugars—similar to plant cellulose—that is arranged in layers. In each layer, fibers are laid out parallel to one another. But fibers in different layers point in different directions, forming a biological "plywood" that is very tough and strong. Like armor, chitin also protects the animal from predators.

Jointed appendages were an important adaptation during the evolution of arthropods. An **appendage** is an extension of an organism's body. It can be used for walking, swimming, sensing, manipulating food, or chewing. Arthropods can have six, eight, ten, or even hundreds of appendages. The appendages can be shaped like rakes, tweezers, nutcrackers, hammers, or paddles.

Arthropods have an incredible variety of body forms. Some are microscopic, while others are quite large. For example, some tropical stick insects and millipedes can reach 30 centimeters (1 ft) in length, and spider crabs can have an arm span of 3.6 meters (12 ft). But all arthropod bodies are segmented for specific functions. **Segmentation** describes how an arthropod's body parts are divided into similar sections that have each evolved for a different function.

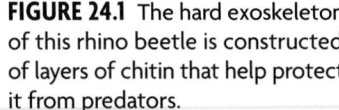

FIGURE 24.1 The hard exoskeleton of this rhino beetle is constructed of layers of chitin that help protect it from predators.

Arthropod Groups

Classifying animals with so many differences might seem difficult, but most fossil and living arthropod species can be placed into one of five groups.

- **Trilobites** Trilobites are now extinct but were an important part of Paleozoic marine ecosystems for nearly 300 million years. As you can see in **FIGURE 24.2**, their bodies were divided into three long vertical sections, or lobes. A central body and outgrowths of shell on each side covered their many delicate legs. Most of the 4000 known species were bottom feeders, sucking up muck, algae, or soft animals from the sea floor.

- **Crustaceans** Among the most familiar arthropods, crustaceans (kruh-STAY-shuhnz) are found in all of the oceans, freshwater streams, and even on land. Crustaceans are a diverse group that includes huge king crabs and lobsters, microscopic copepods, oysterlike barnacles, and armored pill bugs.

- **Chelicerates** The group known as chelicerates (kih-LIHS-uh-RAYTS) includes horseshoe crabs, scorpions, spiders, mites, ticks, and the extinct sea scorpions. These animals share a set of specialized daggerlike mouthparts that are used for tearing their food.

- **Insects** Insects account for 80 percent of all known animal species. Familiar animals such as ants, bees, butterflies, moths, cockroaches, flies, and mosquitoes are all insects. Though this group is very diverse, most insects are terrestrial and have six legs.

- **Myriapods** The most commonly known myriapods (MIHR-ee-uh-PAHDS) are centipedes and millipedes. Their long bodies and many pairs of legs are the most distinctive characteristics of the myriapods. The largest species can grow up to a foot long. They generally live in humid environments, such as leaf litter, decaying wood, or moist soil. The first pair of legs in centipedes bear poisonous fangs for capturing prey.

Infer How did the evolution of jointed appendages lead to the wide variety of arthropods we see today?

FIGURE 24.2 Trilobite fossils such as this one show the exoskeleton, segmentation, and jointed appendages. These features led scientists to suggest that trilobites were one of the first marine arthropods.

TAKING NOTES

Use a main idea diagram to outline the unique features of each arthropod group.

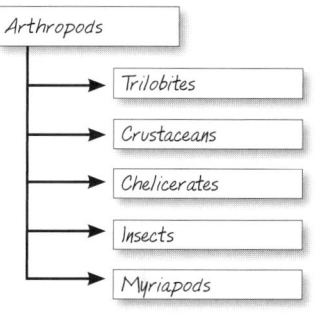

FIGURE 24.3 Arthropod Diversity

Arthropods are a diverse group of animals. Millions of years of evolution has led to many different body forms and functions.

CRUSTACEANS	CHELICERATES	INSECTS	MYRIAPODS

Crab As aquatic arthropods, crabs have appendages adapted for both swimming and walking.

Scorpion The carnivorous scorpions have sharp appendages for tearing apart their prey.

Butterfly Insects have three pairs of jointed appendages that are used for many different functions.

Centipede Many pairs of legs make centipedes suited to a wide variety of biomes.

MAIN IDEA

Arthropod exoskeletons serve a variety of functions.

Connecting CONCEPTS

Chemistry of Life Recall that in **Chapter 2**, you learned about the plant structure cellulose. The molecular structure of chitin forms a polymer similar to plant cellulose. This rigid structure contributes to the strength of an insect's exoskeleton.

All arthropods have an exoskeleton and its structure determines how an arthropod lives. Recall that an exoskeleton is made of many layers of chitin. Chitin is not living tissue, and having a living body crammed into a hard exoskeleton is similar to how a medieval knight would wear a suit of armor. Despite the protective benefits, an exoskeleton makes important functions, such as movement, growth, and maintaining internal and external equilibrium, difficult. Over millions of years, arthropods have developed ways of managing normal functions that are both efficient and effective.

Movement and Growth

Movement Two types of cuticle plates assist in movement. Stiff cuticle plates of the exoskeleton are separated by sections of more flexible cuticle that form joints in the hard armor. When muscles stretching across exoskeleton joints contract, they bend the joint so the arthropod can move. The cuticle supporting arthropod legs acts as a spring, efficiently storing and releasing energy as the animal moves.

Molting Arthropod cuticle cannot grow along with the animal, so an arthropod must shed its exoskeleton in a process called molting. This process of shedding and reforming a new exoskeleton is illustrated in **FIGURE 24.4.**

1. Before molting, the animal secretes a new layer of cuticle underneath its exoskeleton. The new cuticle layer will actually be larger than the layer of cuticle covering it.
2. The animal secretes enzymes that begin to digest and weaken the old cuticle, allowing the exoskeleton to split open and the animal to crawl out of it. This is as extreme as it sounds—the animal must shed every surface of its body, including the entire lining of its gut and tracheae. Some animals die in the process.
3. The new exoskeleton is filled with fluid while it is still soft, making the animal larger than it was before the molt. However, the exoskeleton takes time to harden. During this time, the animal is very vulnerable to predators.

FIGURE 24.4 Molting

Arthropods must molt their old exoskeletons in order to grow.

Animated BIOLOGY
Watch a cicada molt at ClassZone.com.

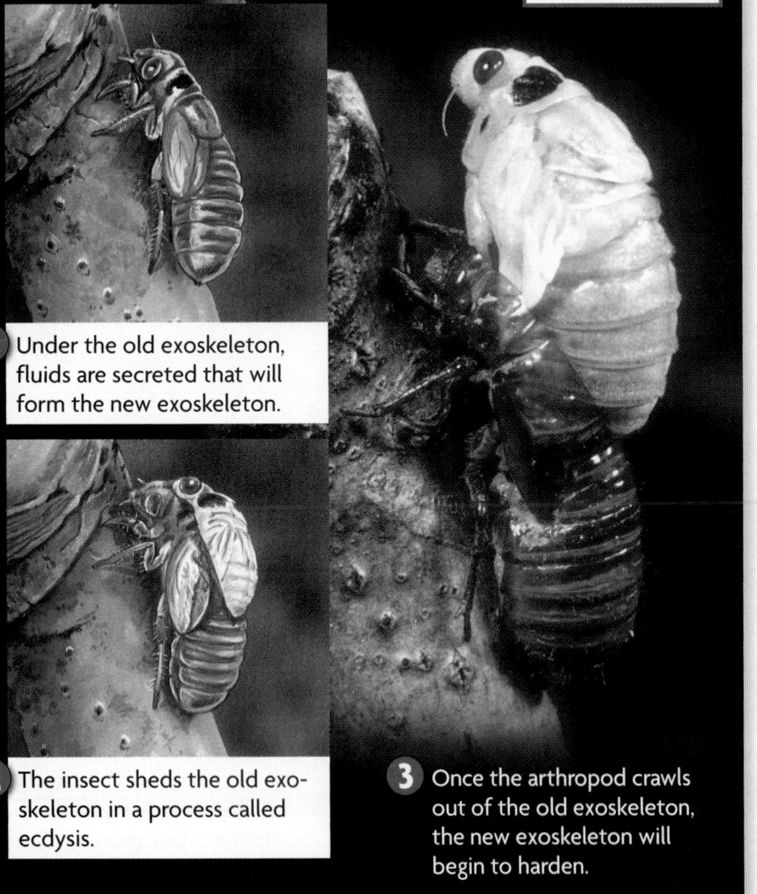

1. Under the old exoskeleton, fluids are secreted that will form the new exoskeleton.
2. The insect sheds the old exoskeleton in a process called ecdysis.
3. Once the arthropod crawls out of the old exoskeleton, the new exoskeleton will begin to harden.

Apply **What are the advantages and disadvantages of going through the process of molting?**

Managing Internal and External Functions

Circulation Arthropods have an open circulatory system, in which blood is pumped through a tubelike heart and out into the body cavity. In comparison, vertebrates have a closed circulatory system, in which blood is contained inside a system of arteries, veins, capillaries, and a heart. In an open circulatory system, blood is pumped through the heart and into the body, where it comes in direct contact with organs and tissues. The stiff exoskeleton of arthropods also helps control blood pressure. Because an exoskeleton does not change shape, when the heart pumps blood out into the body, the exoskeleton keeps the blood contained, while body movements keep it circulating.

Senses Most arthropod sensory organs, including antennae, are made of modified cuticle. Hard cuticle would otherwise block environmental stimuli. Antennae and body hairs allow an arthropod to sense its surrounding environment, including temperature, touch, sound, and smell.

Most arthropods also have compound eyes. Unlike mammalian eyes, which have a single lens that collects all visual information, arthropod eyes have thousands of tiny individual lenses that interpret only a small portion of the field of view. The image in **FIGURE 24.5** gives an idea of how many individual eyes form a single compound eye. When all of these individual images come together, they form a rough mosaic of an object that resembles a newspaper or magazine image.

Summarize How does an exoskeleton make functions such as movement and growth difficult?

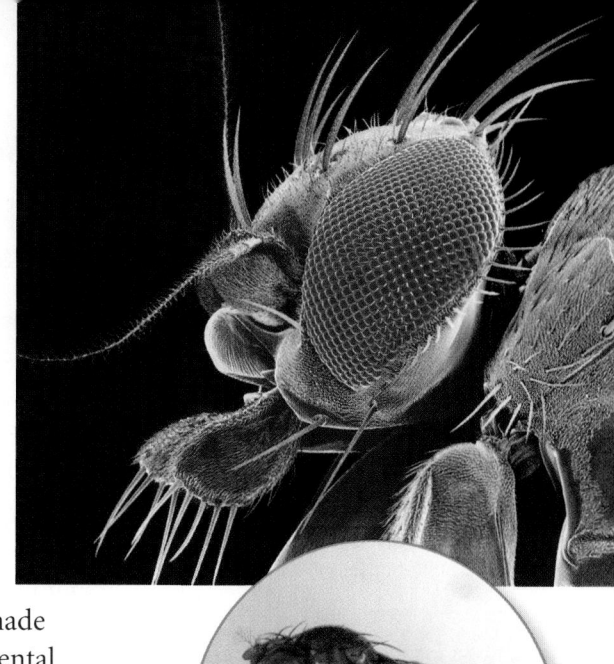

FIGURE 24.5 The compound eye of this fruit fly contains 800 individual eye units. These eyes are highly sensitive to movement and can also determine colors.

QUICK LAB   COMPARING

Comparing Arthropods

In this lab you will examine and compare the structures of different arthropods.

PROBLEM How do arthropods differ from one another?

PROCEDURE

1. Choose one of the four arthropod slides. Observe one organism under low power. Switch to high power and draw and label the structures of each organism.

2. Repeat the process with a second slide and compare features such as appendages, antennae, and body segments between the two organisms.

3. Find another group who viewed different specimens. View and note any differences between their specimens and yours.

MATERIALS
- slide of tick
- slide of mite
- slide of spider
- slide of mosquito
- microscope

ANALYZE AND CONCLUDE

1. **Observe** What unique structures did you notice on the slide specimens? Predict what uses these structures may have for the survival of each organism.

2. **Evaluate** What similar features do the organisms share? Based on your observations, how closely related do you think the specimens are?

▶ MAIN IDEA

Arthropod diversity evolved over millions of years.

FIGURE 24.6 The velvet worm (top) and the water bear (below) belong to two phyla thought to be the closest relatives of arthropods. (colored SEM water bear; magnification 200×)

All of the major arthropod groups are incredibly old. The oldest arthropod fossils are trilobites from the early Cambrian period, about 540 million years ago. The oldest known chelicerates and crustaceans appeared a few million years later, during the Cambrian explosion. The oldest known myriapod fossils are younger—about 415 million years old—but trace fossils from rocks in Pennsylvania suggest myriapods are older than this. During the next 100 million years, rapid diversification of arthropod species resulted in the appearance of all the major groups of arthropods. Many of today's arthropods are very similar to the arthropods that lived hundreds of millions of years ago. Because the major groups of arthropods appeared so long ago, relationships between them are difficult to determine, and many questions about classification still exist.

Based on similarities in body structures, some scientists think that arthropods are most closely related to annelid worms. Because both groups have segmented bodies, some scientists hypothesize they share a similar ancestry. Recent molecular evidence indicates that annelids and arthropods may have evolved segmentation independently. Two other members of the Ecdysozoa, velvet worms and water bears, are thought to be the closest living relatives of the arthropods. You can see these animals in **FIGURE 24.6**.

- **Velvet worms** (phylum Onchyophora) are soft-bodied carnivorous invertebrates that can grow up to 10 centimeters in length and are covered with a thin cuticle layer. They roam about the tropical forest floor on many unjointed legs, hunting for termites and small mollusks.
- **Water bears** (phylum Tardigradia) are microscopic invertebrates, less than one millimeter in length. Water bears are commonly found in the mud of marine, freshwater, and terrestrial environments. They are omnivores, feeding on plants, algae, dead organic matter, and other organisms.

Analyze Explain how ancient fossils can be used to determine relationships between modern arthropods.

24.1 ASSESSMENT

ONLINE QUIZ
ClassZone.com

REVIEWING ▶ MAIN IDEAS

1. What are the five main groups of **arthropods**?

2. What characteristics make the phylum Arthropoda unique?

3. Why are the relationships between arthropod families so difficult to determine?

CRITICAL THINKING

4. **Contrast** How are the structures used for supporting organs different in arthropods and humans?

5. **Synthesize** Fossils reveal that arthropods have been walking the planet for nearly 500 million years. How have arthropods survived for so long? What features have allowed them to be so successful?

Connecting CONCEPTS

6. **Anatomy** In contrast to arthropods, humans have an internal skeleton. What advantages and disadvantages does this type of support system have, as compared with an **exoskeleton**?

24.2

Crustaceans

KEY CONCEPT Crustaceans are a diverse group of ancient arthropods.

▶ MAIN IDEAS

- Crustaceans evolved as marine arthropods.
- Crustacean appendages can take many forms.
- There are many different types of crustaceans.

VOCABULARY

crustacean, p. 735
cephalothorax, p. 735
abdomen, p. 735
carapace, p. 735

mandible, p. 737

Review
filter feeding, sessile

MICHIGAN STANDARDS

B2.4C Explain how different organisms accomplish the same result using different structural specializations (gills vs. lungs vs. membranes).

L3.p2A Describe common relationships among organisms and provide examples of producer/consumer, predator/prey, or parasite/host relationship. (prerequisite)

Connect If you have ever eaten a shrimp, you may have an idea of what a crustacean looks like. But this large group of arthropods is surprisingly diverse. Shrimp and lobsters are crustaceans, but so are the tiny brine shrimp better known as "sea monkeys." Tadpolelike copepods, oysterlike barnacles, and the pill bugs that live under damp rocks in your garden are also crustaceans.

▶ MAIN IDEA

Crustaceans evolved as marine arthropods.

Crustaceans are a group of arthropods that have two distinct body sections, a hard exoskeleton, two pairs of antennae, and one pair of appendages per segment. Crustaceans evolved in the oceans, and today most crustaceans still live in saltwater environments. But there are also many freshwater species, and a few have evolved to survive on land.

Crustaceans come in a variety of shapes and sizes. They are vital to the stability of aquatic ecosystems. Some species, such as the violet-spotted reef lobster in **FIGURE 24.7,** are predators of marine fish, mollusks, and worms, while others scavenge dead animals and plants. Most importantly, crustaceans are a significant food source for larger animals. Large crustaceans such as shrimp, lobsters, and crabs are a primary food source for fish, birds, seals, and even humans. But there are also numerous species of microscopic crustaceans. Zooplankton, krill, and copepods are very small as adults but are so abundant that they constitute an important food source for fish, whales, and many species of filter-feeding crustaceans.

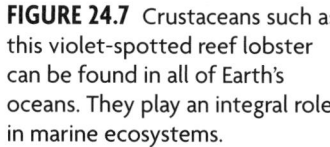

FIGURE 24.7 Crustaceans such as this violet-spotted reef lobster can be found in all of Earth's oceans. They play an integral role in marine ecosystems.

Crustacean bodies are made up of two distinct body sections, a cephalothorax and an abdomen. The **cephalothorax** (SEHF-uh-luh-THAWR-aks) is the region of an organism in which the head and trunk region are combined into one long section. The **abdomen** refers to the rear portion of the organism. The cephalothorax is covered by a shieldlike section of cuticle called the carapace. The **carapace** (KAR-uh-PAYS) covers the sides of the body and protects the gills. The largest crustaceans have a cuticle layer with calcium deposits that make the carapace a hard shell.

Connect Describe how a decrease in marine crustacean populations could affect an ocean ecosystem.

FIGURE 24.8 Crustacean Anatomy

The anatomy of a crustacean is well suited to its underwater habitat. Crustacean appendages are adapted for many different purposes.

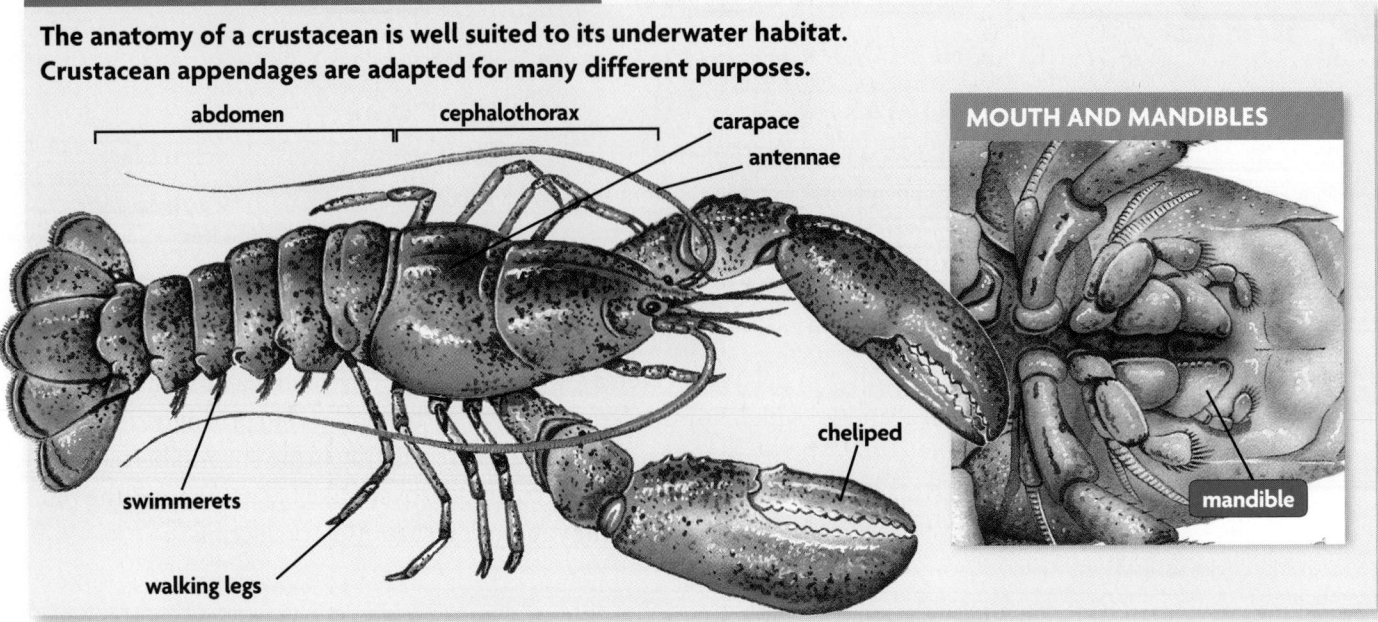

abdomen cephalothorax carapace antennae

MOUTH AND MANDIBLES

swimmerets

walking legs

cheliped

mandible

▶ MAIN IDEA
Crustacean appendages can take many forms.

All crustacean appendages are homologous structures. Anatomical structures are homologous when they share a common origin. For example, your arm is homologous to a bat wing because long ago, humans and bats shared a common ancestor. As the ancestors of bats and humans evolved, different uses for the same appendage structures developed. In bats, the appendage evolved into a winglike structure, while in humans, the appendage evolved into the arm structure we have today.

Long ago, crustacean appendages probably all looked the same. Today, crustacean appendages have been modified for a variety of different functions. Crustacean appendages are used for sensing the environment, defending against predators, walking, feeding, and even attracting mates.

FIGURE 24.9 The mantis shrimp is a crustacean that spends most of its time scavenging for food. Many species of shrimp and prawn inhabit the coastlines of every continent.

Crustacean appendages are adapted to an underwater habitat and are essential for survival. The illustration in **FIGURE 24.8** shows many of the different types of crustacean appendages. Probably the best known of crustacean appendages are the large claws that are found on many species of crabs and lobsters. Lobsters' claws, or chelipeds (KEE-luh-PEHDZ), are used for collecting and manipulating food. But chelipeds can be specialized for other jobs. Male fiddler crabs have large claws that are used to attract females. Some hermit crabs use their claws to block the entrance to the shells in which they live. There are also some mantis shrimp, such as the one shown in **FIGURE 24.9**, that have hunting claws shaped like clubs. The clubs are attached to spring-loaded limbs that can strike at more than 22 meters per second (50 mph), letting the shrimp break through snail shells to feed.

All crustaceans have two pairs of antennae on their head. These appendages have a covering of tiny hairs packed with chemical sensors. As antennae flick through the water, crustaceans use these appendages to smell food, locate mates, and avoid predators. Some crustaceans, such as the tiny water flea *Daphnia,* use the hairy antennae as oars to move around. Many species of spiny lobsters rub antennae against their cephalothorax to make loud calls that are thought to startle predators.

Crustaceans, like other arthropods, have mouths composed of a pair of hard appendages called mandibles. **Mandibles** are highly adapted appendages that crush and bite food before ingestion. Other appendages near the mouth can act as additional jaws and tear food into bits. In copepods, they can collect food from the water and push it toward the animal's mouth.

Appendages such as walking legs allow a crustacean to move along the ocean floor as it scavenges for food. Swimming requires additional specialized appendages called swimmerets, which move in wavelike motions to propel the crustacean through the water.

As their appendages changed shape over time, crustaceans were able to use them for more than movement. This diversification of appendages allowed crustaceans to specialize and move into different ecological niches. The speciation of crustaceans through changes to their appendages is a good illustration of the process of natural selection.

Summarize Give three examples of crustacean appendages and how they are used.

TAKING NOTES
Use a main idea web to describe the many ways arthropods use jointed appendages.

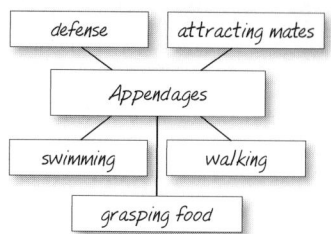

⊙ **MAIN IDEA**
There are many different types of crustaceans.

Crustaceans vary in both anatomy and structure. However, they are all similar in how they develop into the adult form.

Decapods
When you think of a crustacean, you are probably thinking of a decapod. This familiar group includes lobsters, crabs, and shrimp, as well as hermit crabs, their cousins the king crabs, and many others. Decapods live primarily in saltwater environments, but species such as crayfish have invaded fresh water. Some crabs, such as the coconut crab shown in **FIGURE 24.10**, even venture onto land to look for food.

Decapods have characteristic features that distinguish them from other crustaceans. The name *decapod* means "ten legs," so all decapods have five pairs of jointed appendages that are used for many different purposes. Decapods also have fused body segments that contain two regions, the cephalothorax and abdomen.

FIGURE 24.10 This coconut crab is the largest terrestrial arthropod in the world, and can have a leg span of almost 1 meter. Primarily a nocturnal creature, this arthropod feeds on coconuts it cracks open using a powerful cheliped.

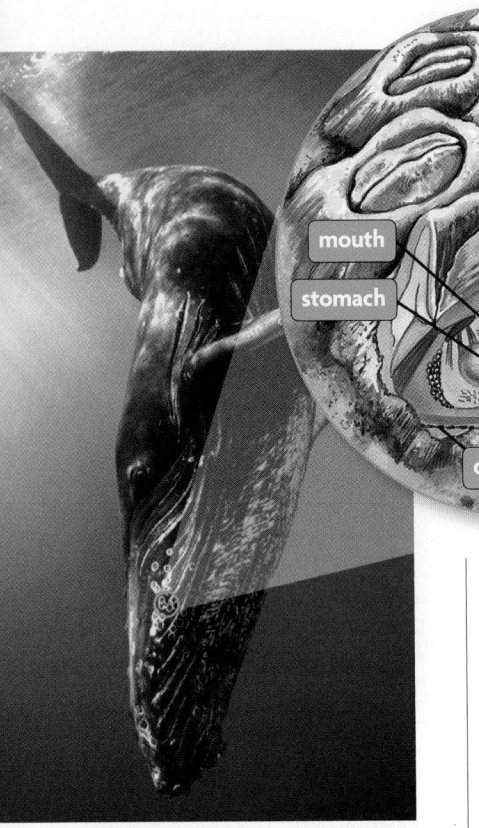

Barnacles, Isopods, and Tongue Worms

Other species of crustaceans look nothing like a "typical" decapod. Although these species are different in structure from other crustaceans, scientists discovered from developmental evidence that most crustaceans pass through similar phases as they grow into adults. Almost all juvenile crustaceans pass through a free-swimming planktonic larval stage. The most common of these larva forms is the nauplius larva. A nauplius larva has a carapace and six long, feathery limbs. When scientists looked at newly hatched barnacles and tongue worms, they found nauplius larvae. Only crustaceans have nauplius larvae, so both groups are recognized as crustaceans. But as they grow into their adult form, these crustaceans look very different from any other crustacean.

- **Barnacles** Barnacles are sessile, or nonmoving, filter feeders wrapped in a heavily calcified shell. They live attached to the surface of rocks, boats, sea turtle shells, and even the skin of humpback whales, such as the one shown in **FIGURE 24.11**. Barnacles have turned their carapace into a saclike "mantle" (similar to that found in a mollusk) that secretes a calcium shell. Inside the shell, the animal sits on its head and sweeps food into its mouth with its legs.

- **Isopods** Isopods have flattened bodies and seven pairs of legs. Most species are marine and freshwater scavengers. Pill bugs and wood lice belong to a group of isopods that have become completely terrestrial. These animals usually live in damp habitats and eat rotting plants.

- **Tongue worms** Tongue worms are parasites that live in the lungs and nasal passages of vertebrates. They have no eyes, mandibles, or antennae, and they have lost most of their limbs. Despite this, molecular evidence shows tongue worms to be most closely related to crustaceans.

Analyze What evidence helped scientists to classify barnacles and tongue worms as crustaceans?

FIGURE 24.11 Attached to the skin of this humpback whale, thousands of barnacles use the whale's constant movement through the water to filter food from the water.

24.2 ASSESSMENT

REVIEWING ▶ MAIN IDEAS

1. What characteristics make **crustaceans** different from other arthropods?

2. What are some of the different functions of arthropod appendages?

CRITICAL THINKING

3. **Summarize** Draw a food web that includes at least three different types of arthropods.

4. **Infer** How did the discovery of nauplius larvae allow scientists to categorize barnacles and tongue worms as crustaceans?

Connecting CONCEPTS

5. **Evolution** Lobster claws can grow extremely large. What selective pressures may have led to the evolution of such large appendages?

MATERIALS

- clear plastic cups
- 100-mL graduated cylinder
- 400 mL sea salt solution
- 0.1 g brine shrimp eggs
- plastic spoon
- balance
- clear plastic wrap
- aluminum foil
- clear plastic bottles with lids
- vinegar
- baking soda
- pH duo-test paper
- 2 eyedroppers
- 10 petri dishes
- hand lens or dissecting microscope
- lamp

PROCESS SKILLS

- **Designing Experiments**
- **Collecting Data**
- **Analyzing**
- **Predicting**

B1.1C Conduct scientific investigations using appropriate tools and techniques (e.g., selecting an instrument that measures the desired quantity—length, volume, weight, time interval, temperature—with the appropriate level of precision).

B1.2f Critique solutions to problems, given criteria and scientific constraints.

Hatching Brine Shrimp

Brine shrimp are small arthropods found in oceans, salt lakes, estuaries, and tidal ponds. Brine shrimp are used primarily for fish food, especially on fish farms where natural food sources are unavailable. Their eggs can be harvested and hatched under controlled conditions by biologists working in an aquaculture facility. In this investigation, you will design an experiment to determine the best conditions for hatching brine shrimp eggs.

PROBLEM What are the best conditions for hatching brine shrimp eggs?

PROCEDURE

1. Choose one factor to investigate. Some factors to consider are the presence or absence of light, aeration (open container versus air-tight container), and pH (6–8). Make a hypothesis about that factor, and design an experiment to test your hypothesis. Have your teacher approve your design.

2. The conditions of the hatching (temperature, pH, light conditions, and so on) will depend upon your independent variable. If you are testing pH, use vinegar to adjust the pH of the sea salt solution to pH 6.0 or baking soda to adjust the pH to 8.0 as measured with the pH test paper.

3. Determine the number of cups of brine shrimp needed based on your experimental design. Be sure to include a control. Hatch the brine shrimp eggs by filling each cup with 200 mL sea salt solution and 0.1 g brine shrimp eggs. Cover the cups with plastic wrap or aluminum foil depending upon your experiment. If you are testing aeration, use bottles with lids instead of cups.

4. Once you have set up your cups or bottles, remove 5 mL from each with an eyedropper and place each volume in a separate clean petri dish.

step 4

5. Examine each dish with a hand lens or microscope. Count the number of eggs and the number of hatched brine shrimp. Note these numbers.

6. Repeat steps 4 and 5 each day for five days and note the numbers of hatched shrimp and eggs each day.

ANALYZE AND CONCLUDE

1. **Analyze** Graph the data with the number of shrimp hatching or number of shrimp hatching rate (shrimp hatching divided by number of eggs) on the y-axis and the days on the x-axis.

2. **Analyze** On what day did you observe the most shrimp hatching? Was this day consistent with the findings of other members of your group? List possible reasons for inconsistent results.

3. **Experimental Design** Identify possible sources of error in your experiment and give reasons why they might have occurred.

4. **Analyze** How did your factor affect the hatching of brine shrimp?

5. **Infer** Compare your team's result with other teams in your group. Identify conditions that had the most positive effect on the hatching of brine shrimp.

6. **Experimental Design** Explain why it was important to have a control in your experiment.

24.3 Arachnids

KEY CONCEPT Arachnids include spiders and their relatives.

▶ **MAIN IDEAS**
- Arachnids are the largest group of chelicerates.
- Arachnids have evolved into a diverse group.

VOCABULARY

chelicerate, p. 740
arachnid, p. 740
book lung, p. 740
spiracle, p. 741
trachea, p. 741

FIGURE 24.12 The bright coloration of the spiny spider actually attracts insects to the spider's web, where they are trapped and made into an easy meal.

Connect At first, the bump on Emily's back looked like an insect bite. But soon the rash grew into a bulls-eye that was six inches wide. Emily began complaining of aches, and her temperature shot up to 102 degrees. A trip to the doctor gave her parents a startling surprise—Emily had Lyme disease. This disease is caused by bacteria that is carried and spread by a tiny arachnid called a deer tick.

▶ **MAIN IDEA**

Arachnids are the largest group of chelicerates.

Deer ticks are chelicerates—arthropods without mandibles. **Chelicerates** (kih-LIHS-ur-AYTS) are arthropods that lack antennae and have six pairs of appendages, which include four pairs of walking legs. One set of highly modified appendages form fanglike mouthparts called chelicerae, which are used to mash up food and shove it into a holelike mouth. A second set of appendages, called pedipalps, are used to grasp and subdue prey. Chelicerate bodies have two sections: a cephalothorax and an abdomen.

There are three main groups of chelicerates. The horseshoe crabs and sea spiders are two of these groups. Arachnids are the third group, representing more than 80 percent of all chelicerate species. **Arachnids,** such as the spiny spider shown in **FIGURE 24.12,** are a terrestrial group of chelicerates characterized by eight legs, fanglike pincers that inject venom, and the ability to produce silk.

Evidence from fossils nearly 400 million years old suggests that arachnids evolved adaptations that allowed them to conserve water and live on land. Arachnids have four different adaptations that reduce water loss.

- **Waterproof cuticle** An arachnid's cuticle is waterproof, so water cannot evaporate across the skin.
- **Book lungs** Some arachnids have specialized respiratory structures called book lungs that allow them to breathe air. **Book lungs** are structures built of many thin, hollow sheets of tissue that look like the pages of a book. They provide a large surface for gas exchange but also create a very large surface for water loss. To prevent water loss, book lungs are enclosed in a humid chamber covered by a plate of abdominal cuticle.
- **Malpighian tubules** Excretory structures called Malpighian (mal-PIHG-ee-uhn) tubules allow spiders to minimize loss of water while excreting metabolic wastes.

FIGURE 24.13 Arachnid Anatomy

Arachnids have many unique adaptations for catching and consuming their prey.

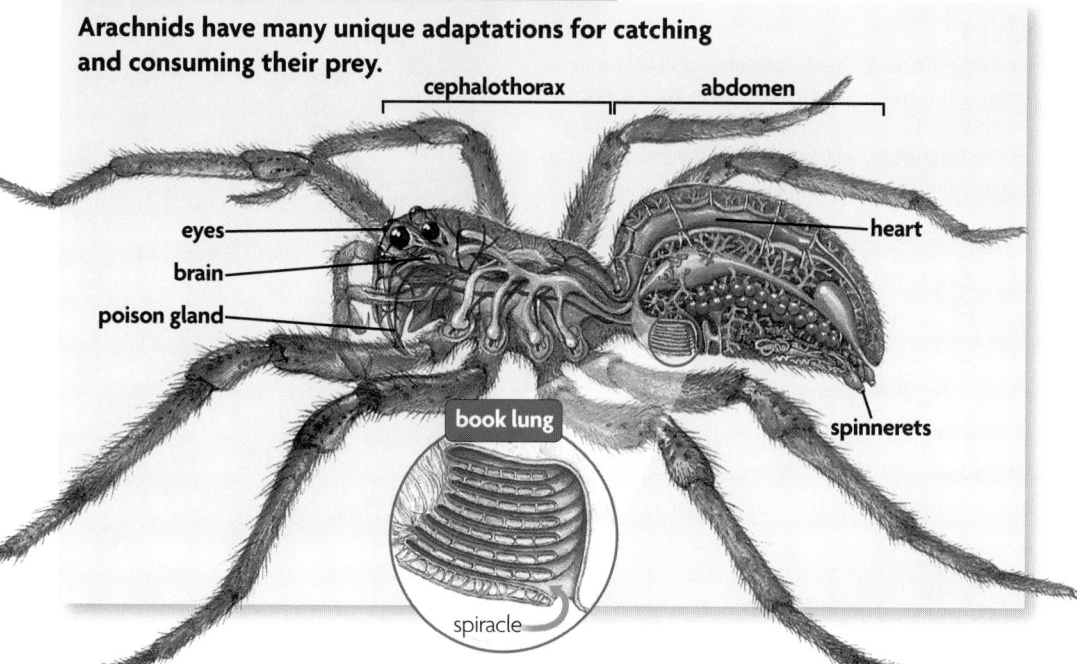

cephalothorax | abdomen

eyes
brain
poison gland
heart
book lung
spinnerets
spiracle

- **Spiracles** Some species of arachnid use spiracles to breathe. **Spiracles** are tiny holes on the abdomen that open and close to allow oxygen to enter. Oxygen flows through a series of tubes called tracheae. **Tracheae** (singular, *trachea*) carry oxygen directly to the arachnid's tissues.

Explain How do the features of an arachnid allow it to live on land?

▶ MAIN IDEA
Arachnids have evolved into a diverse group.

Spiders make up half of the more than 60,000 known arachnid species. They are predators that hunt or trap their prey. All spiders have the ability to make silk and produce venom. Silk is made by glands in the spider's abdomen and released by modified appendages called spinnerets. Spiders use silk for building webs, wrapping prey and egg cases, building shelters, and producing drag lines that anchor the animal like a climber's safety line.

All spiders produce venom. Spiders inject venom into their prey through modified chelicerae. Neurotoxic proteins paralyze the victim by attacking the central nervous system, and digestive enzymes in the venom begin to dissolve the prey from the inside. Among North American spiders, only the black widow and brown recluse spiders have venom that can affect a human, but many species around the world have venom that can paralyze or even kill humans.

Mites, ticks, and chiggers are a large group of very small arachnids. Some species are less than 0.25 millimeters long. Many are parasites of plants and animals, sucking up sap or blood through their needlelike mouthparts. Scorpions are arachnids with huge pincers for grabbing their prey after it has been injected with venom from a stinger at the end of their tail. Scorpions hunt at night by feeling the vibrations made as their prey moves.

Connecting CONCEPTS

Neurotransmitters Neurotoxins in the venom of spiders disrupt neurotransmitter function and lead to paralysis of a victim. You will learn more about the nervous system and neurotransmitters in **Chapter 29**.

DATA ANALYSIS

CONSTRUCTING SCATTERPLOTS

Spiders produce silk for a wide variety of purposes. Some spiders build webs to capture prey, or to safely wrap their eggs. It is important that silk be strong enough to support the spider as it moves from one place to another. Scientists studying spider silk measured the diameter of silk strands in relationship to the body length of the spider. Their results are summarized in the table below.

1. **Graph Data** Construct a scatterplot using the data from the table. Be sure to label the axes and to include a title for your graph. Refer to page 721 in Chapter 23 on how a scatterplot is constructed.

2. **Interpret** What is the relationship between silk diameter and spider length?

3. **Interpret** Does your scatterplot data show any outliers? How might a larger data set help in interpreting the validity of outliers?

TABLE 1. SPIDER LENGTH AND SILK DIAMETER

Body length (mm)	7	8	10	11	12	15	16	17	18	20	25	26	26	35	40	45
Silk diameter (mm)	.02	.03	.03	.04	.04	.06	.05	.08	.06	.05	.08	.09	.10	.18	.14	.15

Most scorpions eat insects, spiders, and other scorpions, while some of the largest species eat lizards and small rodents.

Arachnids are important prey species for vertebrates, but they are even more important as predators. Spiders are some of the most widespread predators on the planet and play an important role in most terrestrial food webs. The mass of the insects they eat each year is larger than the combined mass of all human beings. Mites and ticks also have a major impact on ecosystems. Spider mites are serious pests of fruit trees, cotton, and other crops. Ticks can transmit serious human diseases such as Rocky Mountain spotted fever and Lyme disease.

NSTA SCiLINKS
scilinks.org
To find out more about arachnids, go to scilinks.org.
Keycode: MLB024

Infer How might the loss of many arachnid species affect an ecosystem?

24.3 ASSESSMENT

ONLINE QUIZ
ClassZone.com

REVIEWING ▶ MAIN IDEAS

1. What unique features do all **arachnids** share?

2. What four adaptations do arachnids have for conserving water?

3. Why are spiders such an important part of an ecosystem?

CRITICAL THINKING

4. **Summarize** How do **book lungs** help arachnids to reduce water loss?

5. **Infer** Spiders use different kinds of silk for different purposes. What might a spider build with sticky silk?

Connecting CONCEPTS

6. **Ecology** Describe a situation in which spiders would be a secondary consumer. What species might prey on a spider? Draw a simple food web to illustrate your answer.

24.4 Insect Adaptations

KEY CONCEPTS Insects show an amazing range of adaptations.

▶ MAIN IDEAS

- Insects are the dominant terrestrial arthropods.
- Insects undergo metamorphosis.
- Insects have adapted to life on land.

VOCABULARY

incomplete metamorphosis, p. 744

complete metamorphosis, p. 744

pupa, p. 744

MICHIGAN STANDARDS

B5.1e Explain how natural selection leads to organisms that are well suited for the environment (differential survival and reproduction of chance inherited variants, depending upon environmental conditions).

Connect Everywhere you turn, there are more of them. They are under your feet, flying over your head, nestled in your clothing fibers, and waiting for you to go to bed. Insects are virtually everywhere, and many times you may not even know it. With more than 900,000 known species, insects are the single largest and most diverse group of animals on the planet.

▶ MAIN IDEA
Insects are the dominant terrestrial arthropods.

Insects are an incredible success story. Like the arachnids, they invaded land around 400 million years ago. They have many of the same adaptations for terrestrial life as arachnids do. Insects have moved into virtually every ecological niche, which has helped them diversify into the largest group of animals.

Insects can be found in the most extreme places, including hot sulphur springs and the soil of Antarctica. They are also found in streams and ponds. Though some species live in the marine intertidal zone, they are largely absent in the seas, where crustaceans are the dominant arthropods. Due to such a wide distribution, scientists are discovering new species of insects each day.

All insects have a body with three parts: a head, a central region called the thorax (THAWR-aks), and an abdomen, as shown in **FIGURE 24.14**. The thorax has three pairs of legs, and most adult insects also have two pairs of wings. Insects usually have one pair of antennae and one pair of compound eyes. Many have mandibles that they use to chew up their food, but others have modified mouthparts for more specialized feeding behaviors.

Some insect species live in colonies of hundreds or thousands of individuals. Within these colonies, complex social structures exist. Individuals perform specific jobs that help the colony be successful. Scientists believe that an insect's genetic code determines what role it will play in a colony.

Compare and Contrast **How are insects similar to and different from crustaceans and arachnids?**

FIGURE 24.14 This potter wasp illustrates the three-part body structure of all insects: head, thorax, and abdomen.

abdomen · thorax · head

▶ MAIN IDEA

Insects undergo metamorphosis.

VOCABULARY is a sidebar

VOCABULARY

The word *metamorphosis* comes from the Greek word *metamorphoun*, which means "to transform."

Insects do not develop the same way you do. When you were first born, you had all of the same body parts as an adult. The same is not true of most insects. Some insects, such as butterflies and mosquitoes, go through dramatic physical changes between their immature and mature forms.

Some insects, such as grasshoppers and cockroaches, look like miniature adults when they hatch. This pattern of development, illustrated in **FIGURE 24.15**, is **incomplete metamorphosis** (мент-uh-MAWR-fuh-sihs), or direct development. These immature insects are often called nymphs. They have six legs and a head, thorax, and abdomen, but they do not have wings or sex organs. Nymphs get larger with each molt, but only grow wings and sexual organs during the later molting stages.

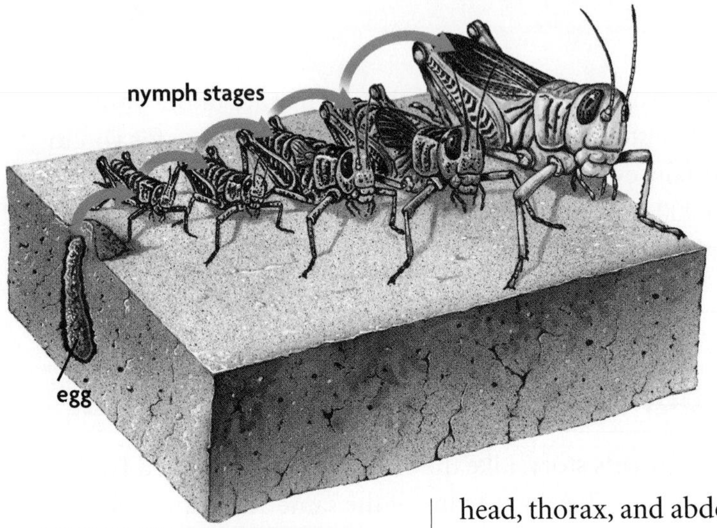

In the process of **complete metamorphosis**, illustrated in **FIGURE 24.16**, young insects do not look like adults but molt and change their form as they mature. Young insects hatch out of eggs as wormlike larvae whose bodies are not clearly divided into a head, thorax, and abdomen, and they often lack legs or antennae. As they grow, larvae pass through several molts, getting bigger each time, until they molt into an inactive form called a **pupa.** Inside the pupa, some tissues are broken down for energy and others are reorganized to produce a completely new body form. When the adult insect emerges from the pupa, it looks very different from a larva. It has wings, legs, and compound eyes, and is ready to fly away and begin its search for a mate.

Connect **Which type of metamorphosis more closely resembles human development? Explain.**

FIGURE 24.15 In the process of incomplete metamorphosis, a nymph appears to be a miniature copy of the adult insect. But on closer inspection, these immature insects lack important features such as wings and sex organs.

▶ MAIN IDEA

Insects have adapted to life on land.

Connecting Concepts is a sidebar

Connecting CONCEPTS

Plants Recall from **Chapter 21** that stomata are holes in the leaves of plants that open and close to control transpiration and gas exchange. Many arthropods use spiracles in the same way, opening and closing them to control water and gas exchange.

Insects have several adaptations that allow them to be successful terrestrial species. Just like arachnids, insects retain water for survival using exoskeletons, Malpighian tubules, spiracles, and tracheae. Gases move through the tracheae by diffusion, and spiracles can close to prevent water loss. Some insects can also pump air through their bodies by rapidly squeezing and expanding the tracheae. The water-conserving characteristics that are shared by insects and arachnids are an example of convergent evolution. In both groups, individuals that could survive longer without water were better able to reproduce. In this way, natural selection independently moved both groups toward similar features that allowed them to carry out similar water-conserving functions.

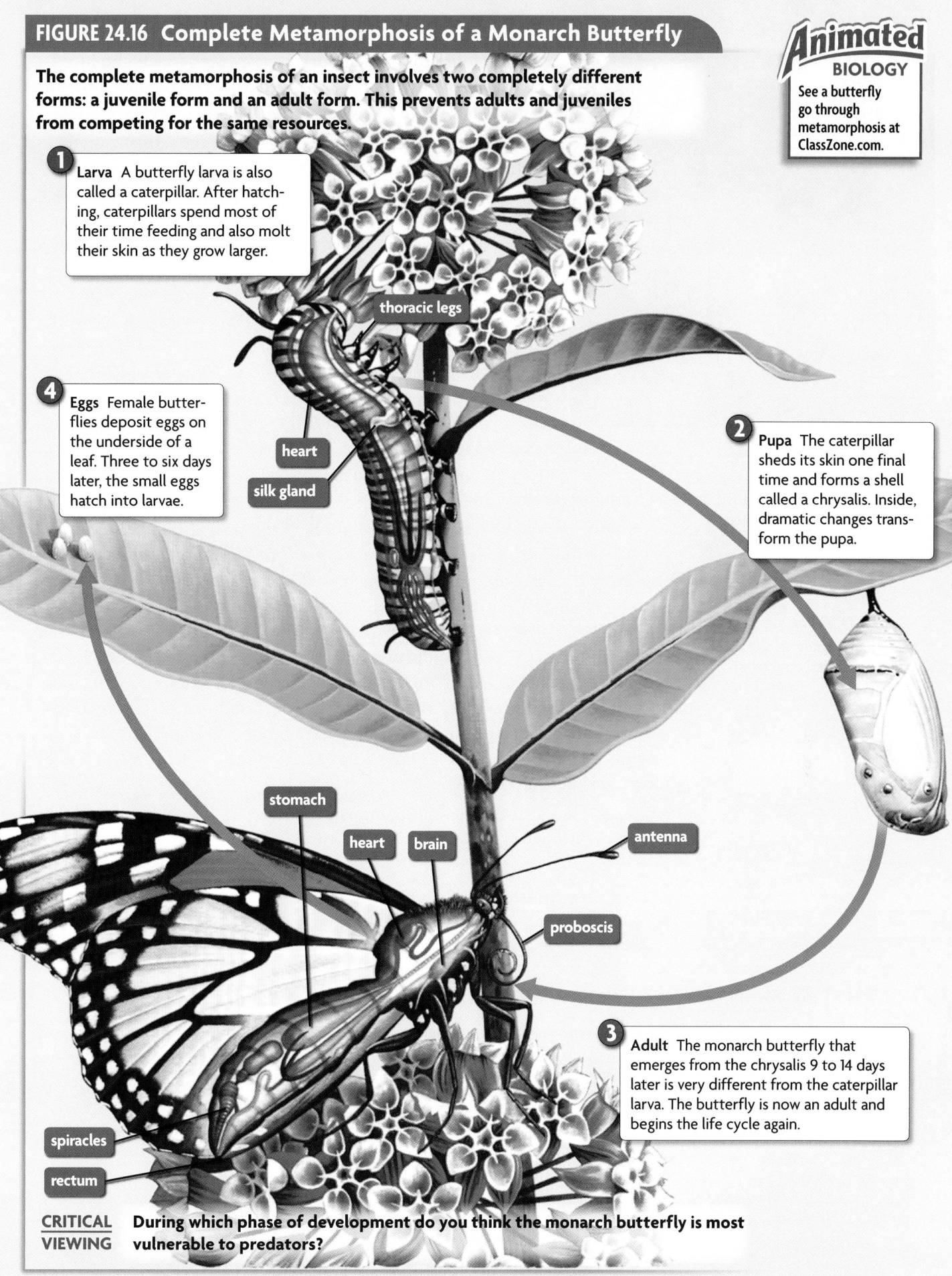

FIGURE 24.16 Complete Metamorphosis of a Monarch Butterfly

The complete metamorphosis of an insect involves two completely different forms: a juvenile form and an adult form. This prevents adults and juveniles from competing for the same resources.

Animated BIOLOGY
See a butterfly go through metamorphosis at ClassZone.com.

1 Larva A butterfly larva is also called a caterpillar. After hatching, caterpillars spend most of their time feeding and also molt their skin as they grow larger.

thoracic legs

4 Eggs Female butterflies deposit eggs on the underside of a leaf. Three to six days later, the small eggs hatch into larvae.

heart

silk gland

2 Pupa The caterpillar sheds its skin one final time and forms a shell called a chrysalis. Inside, dramatic changes transform the pupa.

stomach

heart   brain

antenna

proboscis

3 Adult The monarch butterfly that emerges from the chrysalis 9 to 14 days later is very different from the caterpillar larva. The butterfly is now an adult and begins the life cycle again.

spiracles

rectum

CRITICAL VIEWING   During which phase of development do you think the monarch butterfly is most vulnerable to predators?

FIGURE 24.17 Bees can beat their wings 200 times per second. This ability allows them to hover in one place while looking for food.

TAKING NOTES

Use a Venn diagram to categorize insects based on their mouth parts.

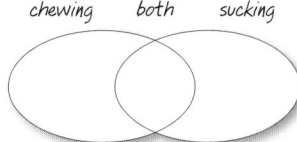

chewing   both   sucking

Only four groups of animals have evolved true flight: insects, the extinct pterosaurs, bats, and birds. Insects conquered the air first and have been flying for nearly 400 million years.

Insect wings are long, flat extensions of the exoskeleton that stick out of the animal's back. At the base of each wing are muscles that move the wing up and down, allowing insects, such as the bee in **FIGURE 24.17**, to fly. But it takes a great deal of energy to move a wing up and down. The insect exoskeleton has evolved in ways that conserve the energy needed for flight. By enabling the insect to reuse the stored kinetic energy created by wing movement, muscles attached to wings do only part of the work. For example, when a diver uses a springboard, the diver's mass creates kinetic energy as the board flexes. When the board rebounds, this energy is released and the diver is shot into the air. Like a springboard, insect cuticle is slightly flexible. As the wing moves, it exerts force on the exoskeleton, causing it to flex and slightly deform. When the cuticle rebounds, the stored kinetic energy moves the wing back to its original position. In this way, an insect reduces the amount of energy needed for flying, leaving more energy available for feeding and reproduction.

Insects feed on many different foods. Over time, insect mouth shapes have taken on a variety of forms according to their diets. Generally speaking, insects eat by either chewing or sucking. Insects such as butterflies and moths that feed on plant nectar and fruits have a long, strawlike mouth called a proboscis (proh-BAHS-sihs). A mosquito also has a proboscis, but instead it uses its mouth to suck blood from other animals. Other insects feed by chewing their food. Ants, beetles, and dragonflies have chewing mouthparts, which consist of mandibles adapted either to crushing leaves and plant stems, or to tearing apart flesh. Bees, wasps, and some flies are insects that have adapted to feed by both sucking and chewing.

Contrast How might the chewing mouthparts of carnivorous and herbivorous insects be different?

24.4 / ASSESSMENT

ONLINE QUIZ
ClassZone.com

REVIEWING ▶ MAIN IDEAS

1. What features make insects different from other arthropods?
2. What is the difference between **complete metamorphosis** and **incomplete metamorphosis**?
3. What are two major adaptations that helped insects to survive on land?

CRITICAL THINKING

4. **Hypothesize** How might the spiracles of a desert insect be different from the spiracles of a tropical rain forest insect?
5. **Infer** Give two reasons why flight has enabled insects to be so successful.

Connecting CONCEPTS

6. **Evolution** Hundreds of millions of years ago, spiders began to use silk around the same time insects began to fly. Explain how natural selection affected these changes.

24.5 Arthropods and Humans

KEY CONCEPT Arthropods and humans interact in many ways.

MAIN IDEAS

- Arthropods and humans share many of the same resources.
- Some arthropods can spread human diseases.

VOCABULARY

insecticide, p. 747

vector, p. 748

Review
biomagnification

MICHIGAN STANDARDS

B2.3C Explain how stability is challenged by changing physical, chemical, and environmental conditions as well as the presence of disease agents.

Connect People have a love-hate relationship with arthropods. Some arthropods are important pollinators that fertilize human crops. Others are pests that destroy crops and infest our homes. Still others are predators that eat pests. Insect species are used for food and fibers in many human cultures, but other insect species spread human diseases. Over time, the unavoidable interactions between arthropods and humans have created many conflicts.

MAIN IDEA

Arthropods and humans share many of the same resources.

Many arthropods are herbivores, and many of them eat the same plants people use for food, textiles, and building materials. These arthropods compete with humans for the same resources. Competition is stiff, because there are far more arthropods than people. For example, when you look under the leaves of apple trees or pepper plants, you may see clusters of tiny bumps. These bumps are insects called aphids. Aphids, shown in **FIGURE 24.18,** use their needlelike mouthparts to pierce the cell walls of a plant and suck up the sugary liquid inside. A single aphid is small and cannot do much damage on its own. But aphids live in large colonies. Hundreds of aphids on a plant can remove enough sap to damage or kill the plant.

FIGURE 24.18 Aphids devour plant tissues, often killing the host plant. Arthropod pest species can cause damage to crops, forests, and even homes.

Each year, arthropods cause millions of dollars in damage to crops such as corn, wheat, and cotton. To prevent costly infestations, farmers use insecticides to control arthropod populations. An **insecticide** is a chemical compound that kills insects and other arthropods. But spraying toxic chemicals on plants can have unwanted side effects. Many insecticides are toxic to other animals, including people. Some, such as chlordane and DDT, do not break down quickly. They can accumulate in predator species through the process of biomagnification. Arthropods can also become resistant to insecticides through natural selection. This resistance causes humans to use even larger doses of the toxin.

To avoid the potential hazards of using insecticides, scientists have discovered ways to use the unique characteristics of arthropods to find safer ways of controlling pest populations.

- Insecticides can be developed to be specific to arthropods. One example is a neurotoxin that blocks a particular receptor that is common in arthropod nerves but not found in other animal nerves.
- Integrated pest management, or IPM, reduces the number of insect pests on a plant crop by managing their ecology. By using a variety of other methods including insect traps, physical barriers, and introduced predators such as ladybugs and parasitic wasps, IPM helps to control pest species.
- Genetically modified plants can be made to resist particular pest species. For example, Bt corn has been engineered to include a gene from a soil bacterium, *Bacillus thuringiensis*, artificially inserted into its DNA. The gene makes a protein that kills caterpillar pests such as the European corn borer but is harmless to most other animals.

Infer **What would be a disadvantage to introducing a predator insect for pest management?**

FIGURE 24.19 Many arthropods are important pollinators. In addition to getting a nectar meal, this Eastern tiger swallowtail butterfly helps to pollinate flowers by carrying pollen from one flower to another.

▶ **MAIN IDEA**

Some arthropods can spread human diseases.

Humans are a source of food to arthropods such as mosquitoes, biting flies, fleas, and ticks. **FIGURE 24.20** shows how arthropods can also be vectors that carry diseases. A **vector** is an organism that carries a disease from one host to another.

Diseases spread by arthropods can have serious effects on human populations. Many methods for controlling arthropod vectors have been developed. Vaccinations have been developed to protect individuals from many types of diseases by delivering small doses of the pathogen to the immune system, which can then fight off future pathogen invasions. The use of pesticides targeted to specific arthropods can also help slow the spread of disease.

- **Bubonic plague** is caused by a bacterium carried by a flea. The disease normally affects rodents such as prairie dogs, squirrels, and rats. Human infections occur when a flea that has fed on an infected rat feeds on a human. Outbreaks of bubonic plague devastated European cities between the 1300s and the 1600s. The largest of these epidemics, between 1347 and 1350, killed between one-third and one-half of the people living in Europe. Today, bubonic plague is controlled by antibiotics and improved hygiene.
- **Yellow fever** is caused by a virus and normally affects monkeys, but it can be carried to humans by mosquitoes. The virus causes fever and bleeding. It was common in the United States until the early part of the 1900s and is still common in Africa and South America. Yellow fever epidemics killed nearly 20,000 people during the construction of the Panama canal before mosquito eradication programs brought the disease under control.
- **Malaria** is caused by a protozoan parasite carried by mosquitoes. The parasites enter red blood cells to breed, periodically emerging and destroying them. Like yellow fever, malaria was once common in the United States and Europe. Malaria was largely eliminated in temperate countries during the 1950s by a program of DDT spraying. It is still common in tropical regions of Africa, Asia, and Central and South America.

TAKING NOTES

Use a main idea diagram to list the diseases carried by arthropod vectors.

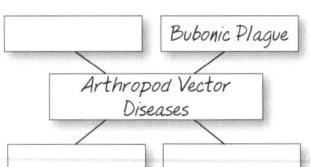

FIGURE 24.20 Arthropod Vectors

Arthropods are vectors for carrying diseases such as Lyme disease.

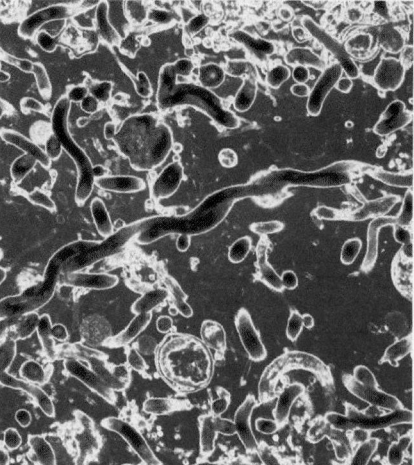

① As the tick feeds on the host's blood, microscopic pathogens pass from deer to tick. (colored SEM tick; magnification 15×)

② Inside the tick, the pathogens are stable and do not affect the tick. (LM; magnification 4000×)

③ When the tick feeds on another host, pathogens are passed from the tick to the new host.

Analyze Though vectors can bring disease into human populations, explain why diseases carried by arthropods spread more quickly through the populations of other animals.

- **West Nile virus** is contracted from mosquito carriers that have previously fed on birds infected with the virus. Originally discovered in Africa, West Asia, and the Middle East, the virus has spread throughout the world and has been identified in 46 of the United States. Fever, headache, and skin rashes are some of the minor symptoms, but the virus can lead to meningitis or encephalitis, potentially fatal diseases. Scientists are currently working to control the spread of the virus.

Infer Explain how an organism other than an arthropod could be a vector.

Connecting CONCEPTS

Immune System Vaccines can only work to prevent a disease; they cannot cure a person who is already sick. The human immune system has specifically designed cells which work to fight diseases in your body.

24.5 ASSESSMENT

ONLINE QUIZ
ClassZone.com

REVIEWING ▶ MAIN IDEAS

1. What are three effective ways of managing insect pest populations?

2. How does a **vector** spread a disease such as malaria?

CRITICAL THINKING

3. **Analyze** What are the potential costs and benefits of using an introduced predator to control a pest population?

4. **Connect** What effect, if any, would the development of a vaccine against a tick-borne disease have on the tick population? Explain.

Connecting CONCEPTS

5. **Natural Selection** Describe a situation in which natural selection could lead to an arthropod population that is resistant to pesticides.

Use these inquiry-based labs and online activities to deepen your understanding of arthropods.

INVESTIGATION

Daphnia and Heart Rate

The water flea, or *Daphnia*, is a tiny crustacean that lives in fresh water. Biologists often use *Daphnia* to study the effects of various chemicals, such as hydrogen peroxide, on freshwater ecosystems.

SKILLS Collecting Data, Graphing, Analyzing

PROBLEM How does hydrogen peroxide affect *Daphnia* heart rate?

PROCEDURE

1. Make a ring of petroleum jelly on a slide and make wet mount with a *Daphnia* sample.

2. Observe the *Daphnia* under low and high power.

3. Looking through the microscope, measure the heart rate of the *Daphnia* by tapping a pencil on the desk once for each heartbeat. Your partner should count the number of taps in 15 seconds. Calculate the number of beats per minute by multiplying this number by 4. Take the average of three trials, and record the data in a data table.

4. Predict the effect of adding hydrogen peroxide to the *Daphnia* environment, and record it in your notebook.

5. Place two drops of one of the hydrogen peroxide solutions on one side of the wet mount. Draw the liquid under the cover slip by placing the edge of a tissue on the opposite edge of the cover slip.

6. Repeat step 3 to measure the *Daphnia* heart rate.

7. Calculate the change in heart rate by subtracting the average heart rate observed after adding hydrogen peroxide from the average heart rate observed in water.

8. Collect average heart rate data from other groups who used different hydrogen peroxide concentrations.

ANALYZE AND CONCLUDE

1. **Analyze** Using your own data and the data collected by your classmates using different hydrogen peroxide concentrations, construct a graph with the change in heart rate on the *y*-axis versus hydrogen peroxide concentration on the *x*-axis.

2. **Interpret** How did hydrogen peroxide affect the heart rate of *Daphnia*? At what concentration was the effect greatest?

3. **Experimental Design** What are possible reasons for error in the experimental design?

MATERIALS

- cotton swab
- tissues
- petroleum jelly
- microscope slide
- culture of *Daphnia magna*
- 2 eyedroppers
- cover slip
- stopwatch
- microscope
- hydrogen peroxide solutions

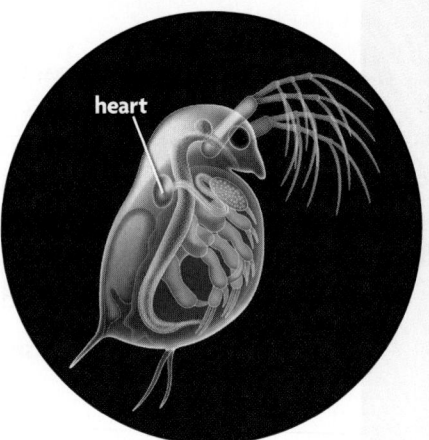

Daphnia

Inside a Crayfish

A crayfish is a freshwater crustacean similar to shrimp, crabs, and lobsters. In this lab, you will dissect and examine the parts of a crayfish.

SKILL Observing

PROBLEM How do the form and function of crayfish organs help it survive in a marine environment?

MATERIALS

- dissecting tray
- scissors
- forceps
- dissecting needle
- 12 dissecting pins
- preserved crayfish specimen
- hand lens or dissecting microscope
- paper towels
- paper and pencil
- Anatomical Crayfish Drawings

PROCEDURE

1. Examine the external anatomy of the crayfish. Draw and label a picture of the crayfish anatomy, using illustrations in your handout. Label the structures listed on the drawing.

2. Turn the crayfish on its side and remove the legs below the carapace.

3. Using the forceps and scissors, lift and cut the carapace to expose the featherlike gills.

4. Carefully remove the gills and the joints. Cut the remaining plates from the top (dorsal) midline to the base of each leg to expose the internal organs. Examine the inside of the crayfish and identify as many internal organs as you can.

ANALYZE AND CONCLUDE

1. **Infer** What do you think the antennae and antennules do?

2. **Analyze** How does the feathery structure of the gills help with their function?

3. **Infer** Why do you think the gills are attached to the legs?

VIRTUAL LAB
Insects and Crime Scene Analysis
How can bugs help solve a crime? In this interactive lab, you will examine insects found on a corpse to determine how long the body was lying in a field.

ANIMATED BIOLOGY
What Type of Arthropod?
Can you tell what group an arthropod belongs to just by looking at it? Examine a series of arthropod images and try to categorize them. Be careful—looks can be very deceiving!

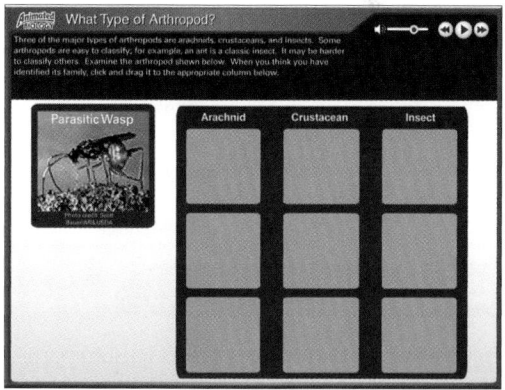

WEBQUEST
Arthropods live in almost any environment. As a class, develop a field guide of arthropods in your area. Research and report on each arthropod's habitat, feeding habits, life cycle and evolutionary history.

KEY CONCEPTS | Vocabulary Games | Concept Maps | Animated Biology | Online Quiz

24.1 Arthropod Diversity

Arthropods are the most diverse of all animals. The five major groups of arthropods are trilobites, crustaceans, chelicerates, insects, and myriapods. Each group has unique features that have evolved over millions of years, but all share features—including an exoskeleton made of chitin, and jointed appendages.

24.2 Crustaceans

Crustaceans are a diverse group of ancient arthropods. Most crustaceans are aquatic arthropods with segmented bodies, a hard exoskeleton, two pairs of antennae, and one pair of appendages per segment that set crustaceans apart from other arthropods. The recognizable decapods have two major body segments: a cephalothorax and an abdomen. Isopods, barnacles, and tongue worms appear very different but share the same characteristic features. The appendages of crustaceans are highly adapted to each species' habitat and niche.

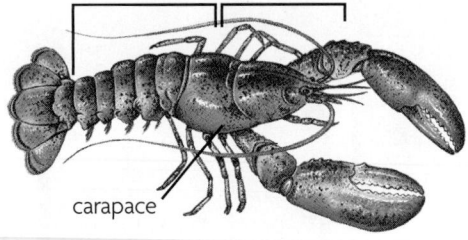
abdomen cephalothorax
carapace

24.3 Arachnids

Arachnids include spiders and their relatives. Chelicerates are arthropods that are distinguished by four pairs of walking appendages and two pairs of modified appendages used for feeding. The arachnids are terrestrial chelicerates that have evolved book lungs and other adaptations for survival on land. The most common arachnids are spiders, but mites, ticks, chiggers and scorpions are also members of this family. They play an important ecological role as invertebrate predators.

24.4 Insect Adaptations

Insects show an amazing range of adaptations. Insects are the dominant terrestrial arthropods and are found in all of Earth's biomes. All insects have three body segments—a head, thorax, and abdomen—as well as wings, compound eyes, and three pairs of legs. Insects grow through either complete or incomplete metamorphosis. Breathing through a system of tracheae and spiracles helps insects to conserve water.

24.5 Arthropods and Humans

Arthropods and humans interact in many ways. Humans and arthropods often compete for the same resources. Pesticides are a common way in which humans control arthropod populations. Arthropods are also vectors for many different diseases, carrying viruses and bacteria from one species and infecting another.

Synthesize Your Notes

Concept Map Use a concept map to summarize the features of arthropods.

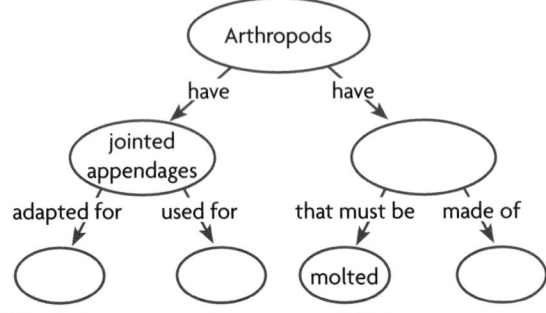

Process Diagram Use a process diagram to explain arthropod vectors.

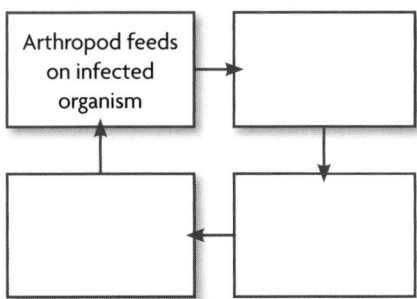

Chapter Assessment

Chapter Vocabulary

24.1 arthropod, p. 730
exoskeleton, p. 730
chitin, p. 730
appendage, p. 730
segmentation, p. 730

24.2 crustacean, p. 735
cephalothorax, p. 735
abdomen, p. 735

carapace, p. 735
mandible, p. 737

24.3 chelicerate, p. 740
arachnid, p. 740
book lung, p. 740
spiracle, p. 741
trachea, p. 741

24.4 incomplete metamorphosis,
p. 744
complete metamorphosis,
p. 744
pupa, p. 744

24.5 insecticide, p. 747
vector, p. 748

Reviewing Vocabulary

Vocabulary Connections

For each pair of words below, write a sentence or two that clearly shows how the terms are connected. For example, for *appendage* and *chelipeds,* you could write, "A cheliped is a type of appendage that looks like a large claw."

1. pupa, metamorphosis
2. cephalothorax, carapace
3. chitin, exoskeleton
4. mandible, chelicerae

Keep It Short

Write a short, precise phrase that defines each vocabulary term below. For example, a short phrase to describe *exoskeleton* could be "hard, outer covering."

5. segmentation
6. chelicerae
7. book lung
8. metamorphosis
9. spiracle

Word Origins

10. The term *appendage* comes from the Latin word *appendere,* which means "to cause to hang (from something)." Explain how this meaning relates to what an appendage is.

11. The term *carapace* is a French word that means "tortoise shell." Explain how this meaning relates to what a carapace is.

Reviewing MAIN IDEAS

12. Each of the thousands of known arthropod species can be placed into one of five groups. What features do arthropods in all five groups have in common?

13. Your skeleton is inside your body, and it grows along with you. How does an arthropod's exoskeleton differ in both its location and its response to growth?

14. Explain how scientists can determine relationships between ancient arthropods that lived 500 million years ago and arthropods of today.

15. Crustaceans, such as crabs and shrimp, are found in nearly all aquatic food chains. Describe the significance of crustaceans to these ecosystems.

16. Arachnids were some of the first land animals. How did the development of methods for conserving water allow them to colonize land?

17. What important function do arachnids serve in an ecosystem?

18. What features set insects apart from other arthropods?

19. What stages does a butterfly go through during metamorphosis?

20. Insects evolved from ancestors that lived in water. What adaptations did insects develop that allowed them to live on land?

21. Insects and humans interact in many ways. Give two ways in which insects are beneficial to humans, and two ways in which they are harmful to human societies.

Critical Thinking

22. Classify You turn over a rock and several long, thin animals with many sets of legs scurry away into the leaves. To what group of arthropods do they likely belong? What do they likely eat?

23. Apply If you walk along a rocky shoreline, you will likely see many barnacles attached to rocks. But barnacles can also be found attached to large whales that never swim up on the shore. How do these barnacles get onto whales?

24. Compare and Contrast The tracheae of insects branch out throughout the body. Humans can only breathe through their mouth or nose. What are the advantages and disadvantages of having tracheae instead of a mouth or nose?

25. Apply Termites are a pest species that feed on the cellulose found in wood. They live in large colonies and can destroy houses over the course of a few years if left untreated. What are some ways in which a homeowner might eliminate a termite colony?

26. Infer The world's largest spider is the goliath bird-eating spider of South America, which can be as large as a dinner plate. What anatomical features may prevent spiders from growing any larger than this?

Interpreting Visuals

Use the diagram to answer the next two questions.

27. Apply What type of metamorphosis is illustrated in the diagram?

28. Identify Name and describe each phase of metamorphosis shown above. What adaptive advantage does this type of metamorphosis give this species?

Analyzing Data

Use the data below to answer the next three questions.

Crab nets have to be designed to capture crabs of varying lengths. The data below show the efficiency of crab nets at capturing crabs of varying carapace length.

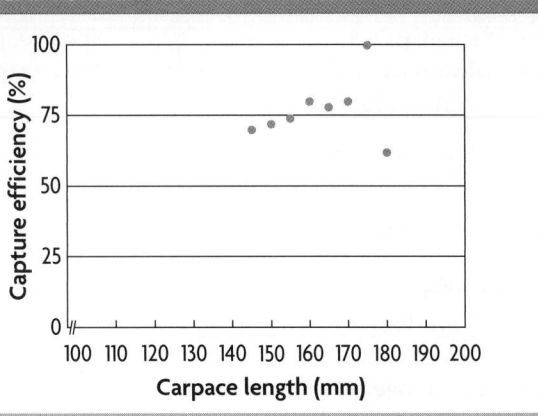

CAPTURE EFFICIENCY AND CARAPACE LENGTH

29. Interpret What is the relationship between capturing efficiency and carapace length?

30. Interpret Does the scatterplot have any outliers? If so, what explanation might explain the outlier?

Connecting CONCEPTS

31. Write Science Fiction Create your own species of arthropod. Imagine that you are sampling arthropod species 1 million years into the future. Arthropods are very different than they are today. Draw and label the appendages and other features of this new species. Write a brief description of the species, and include your hypothesis on its ancestors, what environmental pressures selected for its features, and describe its habitat, food, and lifestyle.

32. Compare and Contrast Insect predators such as the potter wasp hunt numerous species of arthropods. In what ways are the hunting styles of arachnids and wasps similar and different?

MICHIGAN STANDARDS-BASED ASSESSMENT

✓ **Test Practice**
For more test practice,
go to ClassZone.com.

1. Whereas vertebrates have internal skeletons made of bone, and cnidarians use water as a skeleton to support their structures, arthropods have **B2.4C**

   A an internal skeleton made of chitin.

   B an external skeleton made of chitin.

   C an internal skeleton made of cellulose.

   D an external skeleton made of cellulose.

2. In order for respiration to occur, there must be a surface available in an organism for gas exchange to occur. In humans, this occurs in the lungs. For some arachnids, this specialized surface is many sheets of thin, hollow tissue called **B2.4B**

   A spiracles.

   B tracheae.

   C gills.

   D book lungs.

3. Yellow fever is caused by a virus that is transmitted by mosquitoes. The virus causes symptoms in humans such as fever and bleeding. A human's immune system can work against the virus to prevent these symptoms if the human **B2.3C**

   A has already been exposed through vaccination.

   B does not itch the area where bitten.

   C immediately kills the mosquito after a bite.

   D consumes vitamin C at the first sign of symptoms.

4. Walking sticks are insects that look like parts of a plant. They are eaten by birds, lizards, and other predators. Over many generations, natural selection has *most* likely favored individual walking sticks that **B5.1e**

   A cannot be easily seen by predators.

   B look the most frightening to predators.

   C stand out the most to predators.

   D do not have any predators.

   THINK THROUGH THE QUESTION

   Remember that natural selection favors individuals with adaptations that allow them to survive and reproduce.
   ---

5. Both arachnids and insects are able to conserve water using their exoskeletons. They did not evolve this ability at the same time, however. Instead, natural selection worked on both groups independently by favoring **B5.3A**

   A individuals that could survive longer without water.

   B individuals that needed the constant presence of water.

   C populations that could survive in desert conditions.

   D populations that needed an aquatic environment.

6.

Trilobite Abundance in the Fossil Record	
Millions of Years Ago (MYA)	Fossil Record
540 MYA	trilobite fossils appear
500 MYA	peak of trilobite diversity
450 MYA	trilobite diversity drops
300 MYA	trilobites uncommon
245 MYA to Present	no trilobites

Scientists have generated the above data based on hundreds of thousands of trilobite fossils that have been identified and dated in the fossil record. What conclusion can be drawn from these data? **B1.1h**

   A Scientists must look longer for trilobite fossils.

   B Trilobite fossils began to decay 300 MYA.

   C Trilobite speciation peaked about 300 MYA.

   D Trilobites went extinct about 245 MYA.

25 Vertebrate Diversity

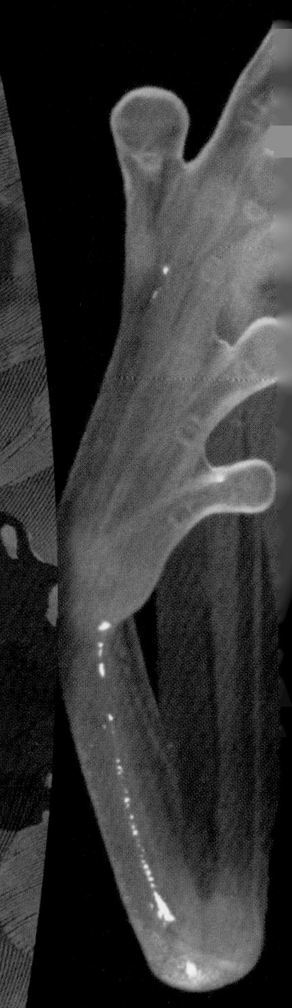

KEY CONCEPTS

25.1 Vertebrate Origins
All vertebrates share common characteristics.

25.2 Fish Diversity
The dominant aquatic vertebrates are fish.

25.3 A Closer Look at Bony Fish
Bony fish include ray-finned and lobe-finned fish.

25.4 Amphibians
Amphibians evolved from lobe-finned fish.

25.5 Vertebrates on Land
Reptiles, birds, and mammals are adapted for life on land.

Online BIOLOGY CLASSZONE.COM

Animated BIOLOGY

View animated chapter concepts.
- Gas Exchange in Gills
- What Type of Fish Is It?
- Frog Metamorphosis

BIOZINE

Keep current with biology news.
- News feeds
- Careers
- Polls

RESOURCE CENTER

Get more information on
- Chordates
- Fish
- Amphibians

Why is this frog see-through?

The Fleischmann's glass frog is one of several members of the family Centrolenidae. Glass frogs lack pigment on their undersides, making their skin transparent. The skin on the top portion of their body has a pigment that reflects the same wavelength of light as plants, helping them to blend in with the green leaves on which they live.

Connecting CONCEPTS

Reproduction In some species of glass frogs, the male protects the eggs from predators. Seahorses, such as the one shown at left, also exhibit male parental care. The seahorse's role is even more extreme than that of the glass frog. A female deposits eggs into the male's brood patch, where they are fertilized and left to develop. After two to four weeks, the male seahorse gives birth to live young.

25.1 Vertebrate Origins

KEY CONCEPT All vertebrates share common characteristics.

MAIN IDEAS

- The phylum Chordata contains all vertebrates and some invertebrates.
- All vertebrates share common features.
- Fossil evidence sheds light on the origins of vertebrates.

VOCABULARY

chordate, p. 758
notochord, p. 758
endoskeleton, p. 759

MICHIGAN STANDARDS

B2.4A Explain that living things can be classified based on structural, embryological, and molecular (relatedness of DNA sequence) evidence.

B2.4d Analyze the relationships among organisms based on their shared physical, biochemical, genetic, and cellular characteristics and functional processes.

Connect Just like the glass frog, you too are a vertebrate. So are birds, tigers, lizards, and squirrels. While the vertebrates you most often see are those that live on land like us, the group first evolved in the ocean. The first vertebrates were fish, and even today the vast majority of vertebrates are still fish.

MAIN IDEA

The phylum Chordata contains all vertebrates and some invertebrates.

The phylum Chordata is made up of three groups. One group includes all vertebrates. Vertebrates are large, active animals that have a well-developed brain encased in a hard skull. The other two groups are the tunicates and lancelets, which are both invertebrates. Tunicates, or the urochordates, include both free-swimming and sessile animals such as sea squirts. Lancelets, or the cephalochordates (SEHF-uh-luh-KAWR-DAYTS), are small eel-like animals that are commonly found in shallow tropical oceans. Although lancelets can swim, they spend most of their lives buried in sand, filtering water for food particles.

Despite their enormous differences in body plans and ways of life, all **chordates** share the four features illustrated in **FIGURE 25.1** at some stage of their development.

FIGURE 25.1 A sea squirt shows all four features of a chordate as a larva.

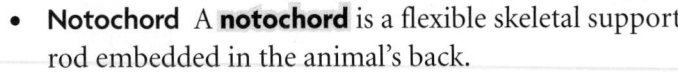
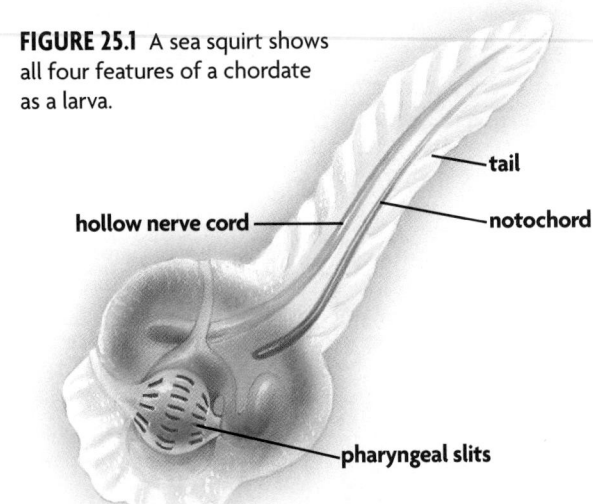

tail
hollow nerve cord
notochord
pharyngeal slits

- **Notochord** A **notochord** is a flexible skeletal support rod embedded in the animal's back.
- **Hollow nerve cord** A hollow nerve cord runs along the animal's back. The nerve cord forms from a section of the ectoderm that rolls up during development.
- **Pharyngeal slits** Pharyngeal (fuh-RIHN-jee-uhl) slits are slits through the body wall in the pharynx, the part of the gut immediately beyond the mouth. Water can enter the mouth and leave the animal through these slits without passing through the entire digestive system.
- **Tail** A tail extends beyond the anal opening. The tail, as well as the rest of the animal, contains segments of muscle tissue used for movement.

Most chordate groups lose some or all of these characteristics in adulthood, but they are present in their larvae and embryos. For example, the larval form of sea squirts have all four chordate characteristics. However, an adult sea squirt, shown in **FIGURE 25.2**, retains only one chordate characteristic, the pharyngeal slits. Adult sea squirts use the pharyngeal slits for filter feeding. Similarly, vertebrate embryos have a notochord that is for the most part replaced by the vertebrae during later development. The fluid-filled disks between adjacent vertebrae are remnants of the notochord.

Compare and Contrast How are humans similar to sea squirts? How are they different?

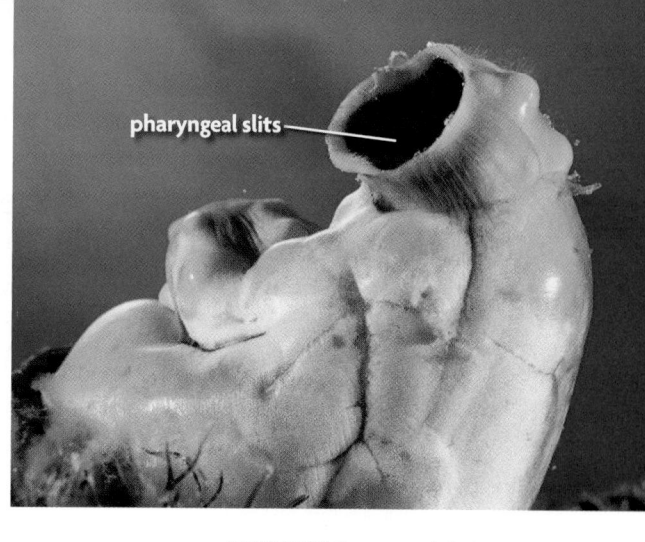

pharyngeal slits

FIGURE 25.2 In its adult form, the only chordate feature a sea squirt retains is the presence of pharyngeal slits (located within the sea squirt's body).

▶ MAIN IDEA
All vertebrates share common features.

Vertebrates tend to be large, active animals. Even the smallest living vertebrate, an Indonesian carp smaller than a fingernail, is larger than most invertebrates.

Vertebrate Endoskeleton
One characteristic that allows vertebrates to grow to large sizes is the endoskeleton. An **endoskeleton** is an internal skeleton built of bone or cartilage. Bone and cartilage are both dense connective tissues. Each tissue is made of collagen fibers that are embedded in a matrix, or combination, of harder materials.

Vertebrate endoskeletons can be divided into distinct parts. Some of these parts are shown on the ape skeleton in **FIGURE 25.3**.

FIGURE 25.3 Every vertebrate has an endoskeleton, such as the one you see in this x-ray of a small ape.

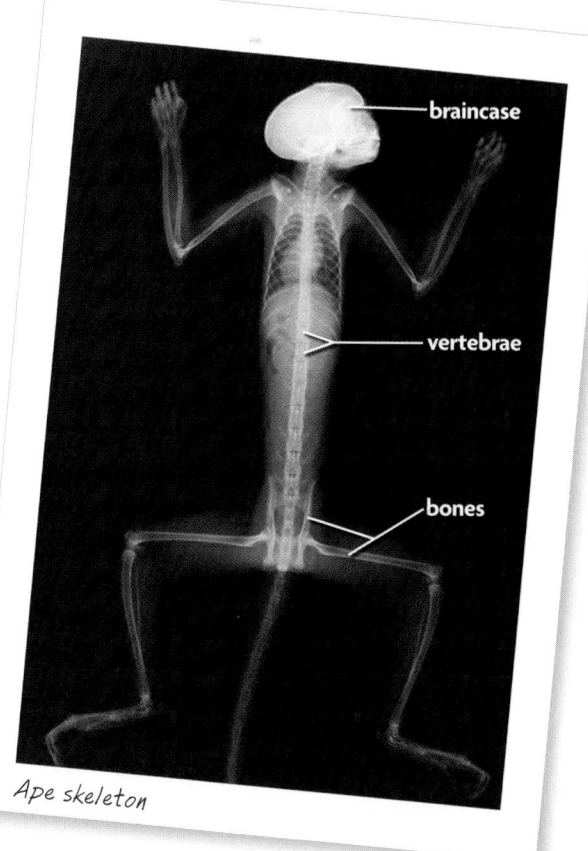

braincase

vertebrae

bones

Ape skeleton

- **Braincase** A braincase or cranium protects the brain.
- **Vertebrae** A series of short, stiff vertebrae are separated by joints. This internal backbone protects the spinal cord. It also replaces the notochord with harder material that can resist forces produced by large muscles. Joints between the vertebrae let the backbone bend as the animal moves.
- **Bones** Bones support and protect the body's soft tissues and provide points for muscle attachment.
- **Gill arches** Gill arches, found in the pharynx of fish and some amphibians, support the gills.

The endoskeleton forms a framework that supports muscles and protects internal organs. It contains cells that can actively break down skeletal material and rebuild it. This characteristic means a vertebrate endoskeleton can slowly change size and shape. It can grow as a vertebrate changes size, unlike arthropod exoskeletons, which must be shed as the animal grows. It can also change shape in response to forces on a vertebrate's body. Bones subjected to large forces get thicker.

Vertebrate Classes

The phylogenetic tree shown in **FIGURE 25.5** shows the probable evolutionary relationships among the seven classes of vertebrates.

Agnatha The Agnatha are the oldest class of vertebrates. These jawless animals include lampreys, a type of fish.

Chondrichthyes The Chondrichthyes, or cartilaginous fish, have skeletons made of cartilage. These animals include sharks, rays, and chimeras.

Osteichthyes The Osteichthyes, or bony fish, have skeletons made of bone. Ray-finned fish, a type of bony fish, are the most diverse group of vertebrates.

Amphibia The Amphibia were the first vertebrates adapted to live both in water and on land, although they reproduce in water or on moist land. These animals include salamanders, frogs (including toads), and caecilians.

Reptilia The Reptilia are able to retain moisture, which lets them live exclusively on land. Reptiles produce eggs that do not have to develop in water. Reptiles include snakes, lizards, crocodiles, alligators, and turtles.

Aves The Aves are birds. Aves are distinguished by the presence of feathers, along with other features.

Mammalia The Mammalia are animals that have hair, mammary glands, and three middle ear bones.

Contrast How does growth differ between an animal with an endoskeleton and an animal with an exoskeleton?

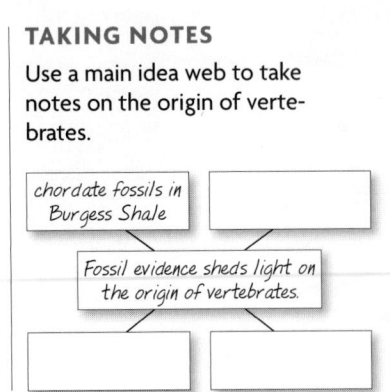

FIGURE 25.4 Box turtles, members of the class Reptilia, are just one of the many different animals found in the vertebrate subphylum.

▶ MAIN IDEA
Fossil evidence sheds light on the origins of vertebrates.

TAKING NOTES

Use a main idea web to take notes on the origin of vertebrates.

> chordate fossils in Burgess Shale

> Fossil evidence sheds light on the origin of vertebrates.

Much of what we know about early vertebrates comes from fossil evidence found in the Burgess Shale located in the Canadian Rocky Mountains. This fossil site, discovered in the early 1900s, was not fully explored until the late 1960s. Fossils found within the Burgess Shale date from the Cambrian explosion and include preserved exoskeletons, limbs, and in some cases, gut contents and muscles. Fossils of sponges, worms, and arthropods are among the invertebrate remains found at the quarry site. Other fossils with traces of notochords provide evidence of the earliest chordates.

Closest Relatives of Vertebrates

In the past, scientists thought that lancelets were more closely related to vertebrates than tunicates were. They based this on fossil evidence, along with anatomical comparisons and molecular evidence. However, recent research indicates that tunicates may actually be the closest relatives of vertebrates. All vertebrate embryos have strips of cells called the neural crest, which develops into parts of the nervous system, head, bone, and teeth. Scientists have found that tunicates have cells that resemble the neural crest, but lancelets do not have such cells. This evidence could indicate that either lancelets secondarily lost these cells, or tunicates are indeed the closest relatives to vertebrates.

FIGURE 25.5 Vertebrate Phylogenetic Tree

Each vertebrate class has unique characteristics that separate one class from another.

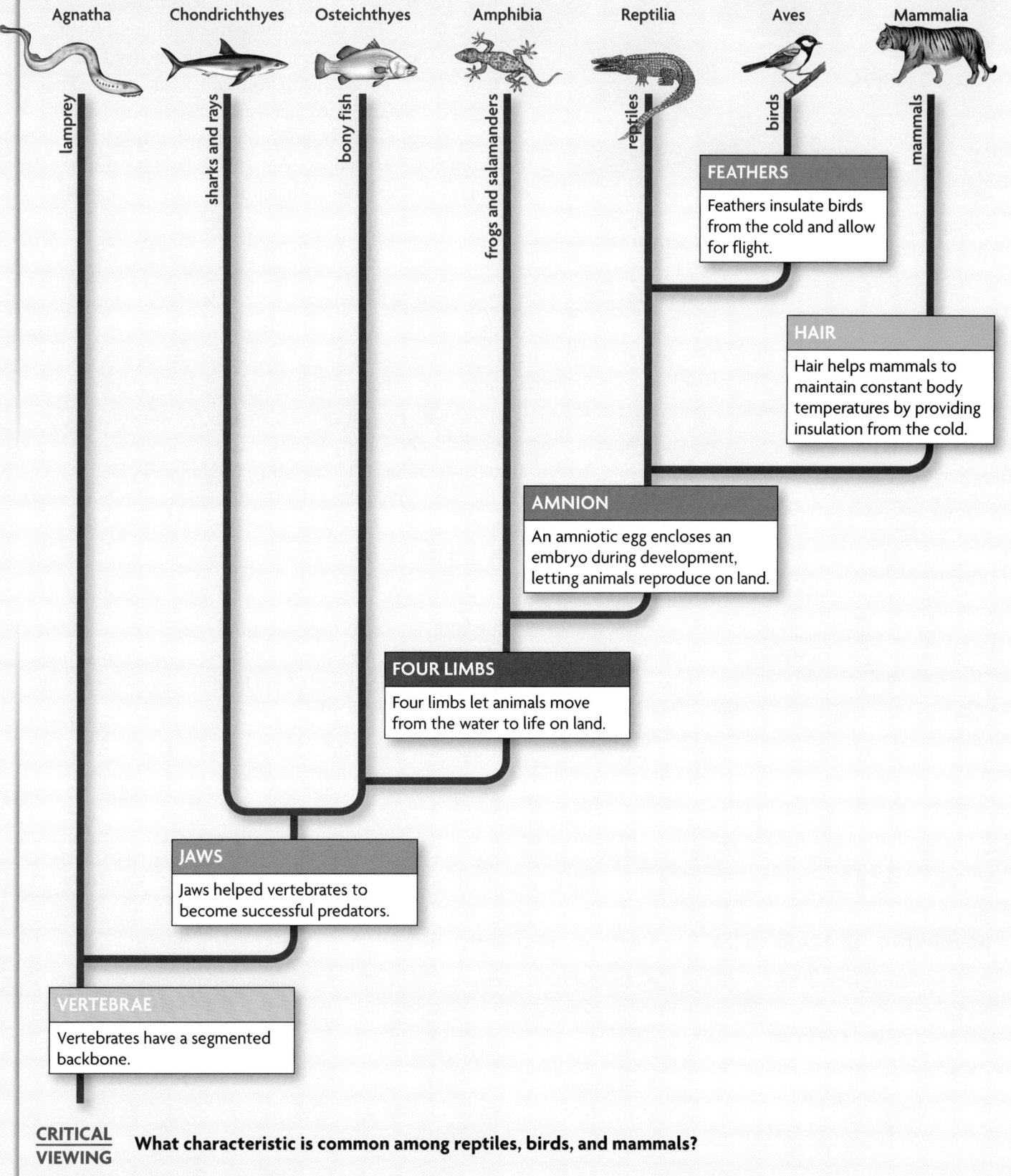

Agnatha — lamprey

Chondrichthyes — sharks and rays

Osteichthyes — bony fish

Amphibia — frogs and salamanders

Reptilia — reptiles

Aves — birds

Mammalia — mammals

FEATHERS
Feathers insulate birds from the cold and allow for flight.

HAIR
Hair helps mammals to maintain constant body temperatures by providing insulation from the cold.

AMNION
An amniotic egg encloses an embryo during development, letting animals reproduce on land.

FOUR LIMBS
Four limbs let animals move from the water to life on land.

JAWS
Jaws helped vertebrates to become successful predators.

VERTEBRAE
Vertebrates have a segmented backbone.

CRITICAL VIEWING What characteristic is common among reptiles, birds, and mammals?

FIGURE 25.6 Hagfish are thought to be the chordates most closely related to vertebrates.

Early Vertebrates

The first recognizable vertebrates were fish. The oldest fossil fish are found in 530-million-year-old rocks from China. Early fish were small, jawless bottom-feeders that sucked soft-bodied prey and detritus off the ocean floor. Jawless fish radiated into many different forms during the Paleozoic era. Some had bony head shields. Others were covered with bony plates and scales. Their heavy armor may have been a defense against predators such as giant sea scorpions. Most jawless fish were extinct by 360 million years ago. Today, two groups of jawless fish remain: the lampreys and the hagfish.

Lampreys

There are more than 35 species of lampreys. Most of these species are highly specialized fish parasites. Their physical characteristics include

- long and slender body plans that lack paired fins
- mouths surrounded by a large sucker
- tongues covered by horny toothlike projections

Lampreys hold on to fish with their suckers, then use their tongues to scrape holes in their prey. Substances in their saliva keep blood flowing by preventing clotting as they feed. The accidental introduction of sea lampreys into the Great Lakes in the early 1900s had a devastating impact on the fishing industry. Ongoing control programs have helped to restore the fisheries by reducing the sea lamprey population by 90 percent.

Hagfish

A hagfish, shown in **FIGURE 25.6**, is a jawless eel-like animal with a partial skull but no vertebrae. It uses a notochord for support. Although both hagfish and lampreys have primitive characteristics, none of the living species are ancient. They are recent animals that happen to be the living remnants of very ancient, mostly extinct groups.

Summarize How have scientists' views on the origins of vertebrates changed?

Connecting CONCEPTS

Defense Mechanisms Hagfish secrete massive amounts of slime when disturbed by potential predators. Hagfish rid themselves of their slime cocoon by tying their body into a knot and sliding off the slime. You will learn more about defensive behaviors in **Chapter 27.**

25.1 ASSESSMENT

 **ONLINE QUIZ**
ClassZone.com

REVIEWING ▶ MAIN IDEAS

1. What features are shared by all members of the phylum Chordata?
2. How is an **endoskeleton** involved in an animal's movement?
3. What evidence places fish as the first vertebrates?

CRITICAL THINKING

4. **Compare and Contrast** What are the advantages of having an endoskeleton instead of an exoskeleton? Are there any disadvantages? Why?
5. **Summarize** Draw a phylogenetic tree that shows the relationships between hagfish, lampreys, and all other fish.

Connecting CONCEPTS

6. **Adaptations** How is the structure of a lamprey's body related to the lamprey's function as a parasite?

25.2 Fish Diversity

KEY CONCEPT The dominant aquatic vertebrates are fish.

MAIN IDEAS

- Fish are vertebrates with gills and paired fins.
- Jaws evolved from gill supports.
- Only two groups of jawed fish still exist.

VOCABULARY

gill, p. 763
countercurrent flow, p. 764
lateral line, p. 767
operculum, p. 767

MICHIGAN STANDARDS

B2.4B Describe how various organisms have developed different specializations to accomplish a particular function and yet the end result is the same (e.g., excreting nitrogenous wastes in animals, obtaining oxygen for respiration). **B2.4C** Explain how different organisms accomplish the same result using different structural specializations (gills vs. lungs vs. membranes).

Connect In order to move in a swimming pool, you need to push your body through a thick, heavy blanket of water. Swimming for a long time is tiring. Long-distance swimming requires endurance and a lot of energy. Fish spend their entire lives moving through water, but adaptations to an aquatic environment make their movements through water much more energy-efficient than yours.

MAIN IDEA
Fish are vertebrates with gills and paired fins.

You get the oxygen you need by breathing in the air that surrounds you. Because fish live underwater, the way that they get oxygen is completely different from the way you breathe. Fish use specialized organs called gills to take in the oxygen dissolved in water. **Gills** are large sheets of thin frilly tissue filled with capillaries that take in dissolved oxygen from the water and release carbon dioxide. As shown in **FIGURE 25.7**, gills have a very large surface area, which increases the amount of gases they can exchange with the water. Muscles in the body wall expand and contract, creating a current of water that brings a steady supply of oxygen to the blood.

Just like you, fish have body systems that provide their cells with oxygen and nutrients and also remove waste products. Fish circulatory systems pump blood in a single circulatory loop through a heart with two main chambers. An atrium collects blood returning from the body and moves it into the ventricle. The ventricle pumps blood through the gills, where carbon dioxide is released and oxygen is picked up by the blood. The blood then carries the oxygen directly to the tissues and picks up more carbon dioxide. The blood returns to the heart, and the process begins again.

Animated BIOLOGY
Explore oxygen and carbon dioxide exchange in gills at ClassZone.com.

FIGURE 25.7 Fish use the large surface area of their gills to exchange carbon dioxide and oxygen with the water in which they live.

water flow

Countercurrent Flow

Arteries in the gills carry blood to the exchange surfaces. The arteries are arranged so that blood flows in the opposite direction of the current of water entering the gills. **Countercurrent flow** is the opposite movement of water against the flow of blood in the fish's gills. Because oxygen dissolved in the water is at a greater concentration than the oxygen in the fish's blood, countercurrent flow maximizes the amount of oxygen the fish can pull from the water by diffusion. In countercurrent flow, blood is always passing by water that contains more oxygen than it does. Both well-aerated water entering the gills and depleted water leaving the gills pass by blood with an even lower oxygen load. Oxygen diffuses into the blood along the entire length of the gill.

VISUAL VOCAB

Countercurrent flow maximizes the amount of oxygen the fish can pull from the water.

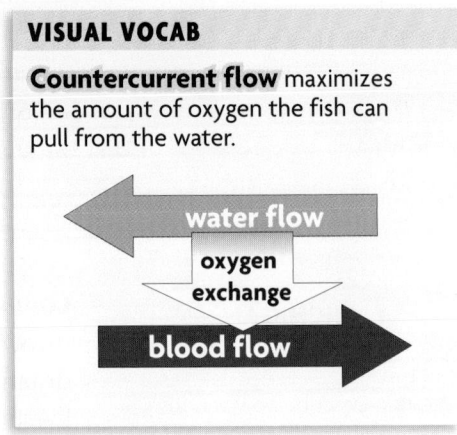

Swimming and Maneuvering

Most fish swim by contracting large segmented muscles on either side of their vertebral column from the head to the tail. These muscle segments power the contractions that produce a series of S-shaped waves that move down the fish's body and push it through the water. These waves also tend to nudge the fish from side to side. Such horizontal movements waste energy, so fish counteract them with their fins.

As you can see in **FIGURE 25.8,** fins are surfaces that project from a fish's body. Most fish have dorsal fins on their backs and anal fins on their bellies. Most fish also have two sets of lateral paired fins. One set, the pectoral fins, are found just behind the head. The other set, the pelvic fins, are often found near the middle of the belly. The caudal fin is another name for the tail fin. Fin tissue is supported by part of the endoskeleton, and its associated muscles let fish actively move their fins as they swim.

Fins keep fish stable. Their movements redirect water around the fish as it swims, producing forces that keep it from rolling, pitching up and down, and moving from side to side. The dorsal and anal fins keep the fish from rolling over. The caudal fin moves the fish in a forward direction. The pectoral and pelvic paired fins help the fish to maneuver, stop, and hover in the water.

Infer What is the connection between countercurrent flow and a fish's movement in the water?

TAKING NOTES

Draw a simple picture of a fish in your notes and label the five kinds of fins found on most fish.

FIGURE 25.8 This clown anemone fish shows the main types of fins commonly found in fish.

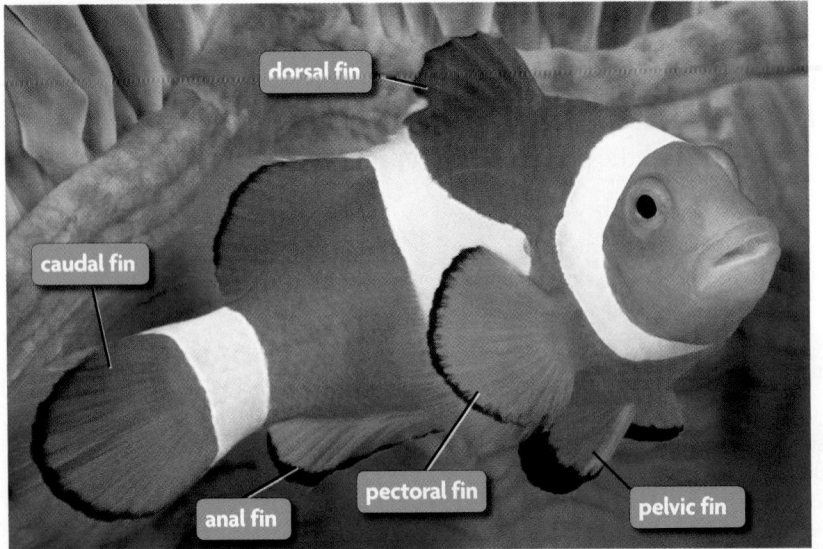

dorsal fin

caudal fin

anal fin

pectoral fin

pelvic fin

MAIN IDEA

Jaws evolved from gill supports.

Jaws evolved from gill arches. Located on both sides of the pharynx, gill arches are structures made of bone or cartilage that function as a support for a fish's gills. As shown in **FIGURE 25.9**, jaws developed from gill arches near the mouth, which fused to the cranium. The upper section of the third gill arch attached to the cranium, forming the upper jaw. Because the gill arches are jointed, the bottom part of the gill arch could bend to open and close the mouth, forming the lower jaw.

In most fish, the fourth set of gill arches are also fused to the cranium. In these animals, the upper part of the gill arch reinforces the jaws. The gill arch's lower part supports the tissue inside the floor of the mouth. Most jawed vertebrates have teeth on their upper and lower jaws. Teeth are used to capture and process food. They evolved from the armored scales that covered early jawless fish.

As a result of natural selection, jaws gave vertebrates a huge advantage as predators and quickly pushed them to the top of the food chain. But the original function of jaws may not have been to help fish capture food. Evidence suggests that the earliest jaws prevented backflow as a fish pumped water over its gills. Clamping the front pair of arches together prevented oxygen-rich water from escaping through the mouth, ensuring that it all flowed over the gills. The fact that they also kept prey from escaping was a happy accident.

Compare What advantages are provided to an animal that has jaws, compared with an animal that does not have jaws?

MAIN IDEA

Only two groups of jawed fish still exist.

Jawed fish diversified very quickly after their first appearance about 440 million years ago. Four groups of fish appeared at this time.

- **Acanthodians** Acanthodians were fish covered with spines. They became extinct about 250 million years ago.
- **Placoderms** Placoderms were heavily armored with huge bony plates. They became extinct about 350 million years ago.
- **Cartilaginous fish** Cartilaginous fish are one of the two groups of fish that survive today. The cartilaginous fish include sharks, rays, and chimeras.
- **Bony fish** Bony fish are the group that includes all other living fish, and is the other group of fish still in existence.

FIGURE 25.9 JAW EVOLUTION

Evidence from animal development studies supports the idea that jaws evolved from gill arches.

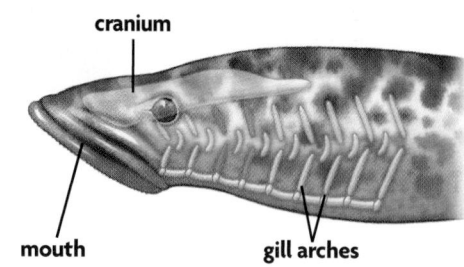

Agnatha Jawless fish such as lampreys evolved from filter-feeding ancestors. In jawless fish, the filters were modified to function as gills.

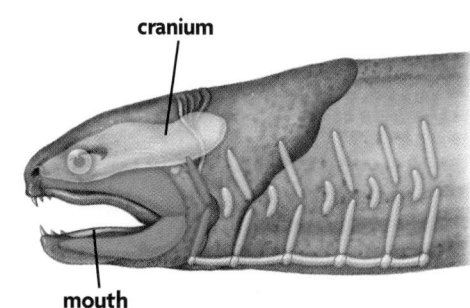

Placoderms Jaws developed from what was the third gill arch in Agnatha.

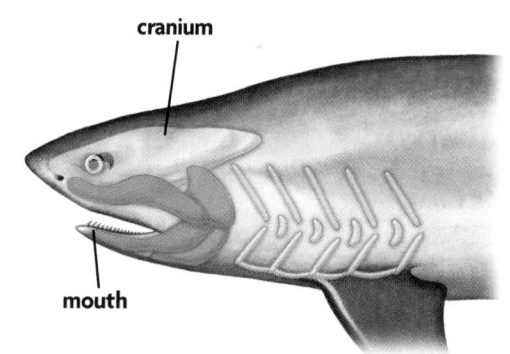

Modern fish In modern fish such as sharks, the fourth set of gill arches fused to the cranium.

FIGURE 25.10 The grey reef shark is found in the tropical waters surrounding coral reefs. When pursuing prey, some shark species may swim at speeds up to 48 km/h (30 mph).

FIGURE 25.11 The blue-spotted ray lives on sandy ocean bottoms beneath coral reefs. If threatened, the ray will use a venomous barb at the base of its tail to inject poison into its attacker.

Cartilaginous Fish

Members of the class Chondrichthyes, or cartilaginous fish, have skeletons made of cartilage, while their ancestors had skeletons made of bone. This characteristic means that their cartilaginous skeleton is not a primitive trait. These fish have lost the ability to make bone. In fact, the type of cartilage found in their skeletons is unique. It contains calcium deposits that make it stiffer than the squishy stuff found in human joints. Even though they have relatively flexible skeletons, cartilaginous fish have a strong bite, and they are major predators in every ocean. There are two groups within the Chondrichthyes—Holocephali and Elasmobranchs.

The Holocephali include chimeras, or ratfish. Chimeras are a small group of deep-sea fish with platelike grinding teeth. They feed on crustaceans and other invertebrates.

The Elasmobranchs include sharks, rays, and skates. There are more than 300 species of sharks and nearly 400 species of rays and skates. Most sharks, such as the grey reef shark shown in **FIGURE 25.10**, hunt other fish, although some species eat seals and sea lions. The biggest sharks, the whale sharks and basking sharks, are both filter feeders that eat plankton.

Rays and skates have flattened bodies and large pectoral fins that they use to "fly" through the water. Most rays, such as the blue-spotted ray shown in **FIGURE 25.11**, crush invertebrates such as crustaceans for food. Others, such as the huge manta rays, are planktonic filter-feeders. Most rays have poisonous venom in their barbed tails, which they use to defend themselves against predators. Skates do not have poisonous venom, but instead use thorny projections on their backs to fight off attackers.

While the cartilaginous fish as a group may be ancient, they have many advanced features. They have internal fertilization, and many species give birth to live young. They are actually denser than water, but oil stored in their livers provides buoyancy that keeps them from sinking.

Cartilaginous fish are incredibly efficient hunters. They are powerful swimmers with good eyesight and an excellent sense of smell. They can also sense their prey's movements at a distance with a sensory system called the lateral line.

All fish have a **lateral line** system, which is a series of shallow canals on the sides of the fish made up of cells that are sensitive to small changes in water movement. The lateral line gives fish a sense of "distant touch," letting them feel the movements in the water currents created by more distant animals as they swim.

Many fish also have sensory organs that detect the electrical currents made by muscular contractions in other animals. These sensory organs are called electroreceptive cells because they receive electric signals. In cartilaginous fish, the electroreceptive cells are clustered on the snout, and they are extremely sensitive. In experiments in which all other senses are blocked, a shark can still detect the electric currents generated by the heartbeat of a hiding animal.

FIGURE 25.12 The operculum is a protective plate that covers a fish's gills, as shown on this white margate, a bony fish.

Bony Fish

All other living fish have skeletons made of bone. These bony fish are called the Osteichthyes (*oste-* comes from a Greek word meaning "bone"). There are more than 20,000 species of bony fish living in nearly every aquatic environment on Earth, including tropical freshwater streams, Antarctic oceans, and deep-sea trenches. Some have become parasites of other fish. One group of bony fish can even spend short periods of time on land.

The gills of all bony fish are in a chamber covered by a protective plate called the **operculum** (oh-PUR-kyuh-luhm), shown in **FIGURE 25.12**. Movements of the operculum help bony fish move water over their gills by creating a low-pressure area just outside the gills. Water flows from the high-pressure area in the mouth through the gills toward the low-pressure area by the operculum.

Some of these characteristics have been modified or lost in some species of bony fish. In Section 25.3, Osteichthyes will be examined in more detail.

Contrast What is the difference between cartilaginous and bony fish?

NSTA
scilinks.org
SCI LINKS

To learn more about jaw evolution, visit scilinks.org.
Keycode: MLB025

25.2 / ASSESSMENT

ONLINE QUIZ
ClassZone.com

REVIEWING ▶ MAIN IDEAS

1. What is the function of **countercurrent flow** in a fish's **gills**?

2. What key changes took place in the evolution of fish jaws?

3. Name the four groups of jawed fish that evolved during the Paleozoic. Which groups are still alive today?

CRITICAL THINKING

4. **Infer** How might fin shape differ in a fish with a torpedo-shaped cylindrical body and a fish with a flattened body?

5. **Analyze** How would you expect the **lateral line** system to differ in fish that live in rivers with strong currents?

Connecting CONCEPTS

6. **Evolution** A shark's jaw is lined with several rows of teeth. How is this adaptation related to a shark's effectiveness as a predator?

25.3 A Closer Look at Bony Fish

KEY CONCEPT Bony fish include ray-finned and lobe-finned fish.

▶ MAIN IDEAS

- Ray-finned fish have a fan of bones in their fins.
- Lobe-finned fish have paired rounded fins supported by a single bone.

VOCABULARY

ray-fin, p. 768
swim bladder, p. 769
lobe-fin, p. 770

MICHIGAN STANDARDS

B2.4A Explain that living things can be classified based on structural, embryological, and molecular (relatedness of DNA sequence) evidence.

Connect Most of the fish you are familiar with are bony fish. Perhaps you won a goldfish at a carnival or ate a tuna fish sandwich for lunch. Or maybe you fish at a local lake for trout or bass. All of these fishes are examples of bony fish.

▶ MAIN IDEA

Ray-finned fish have a fan of bones in their fins.

All ray-finned fish, such as goldfish and tuna, have fins supported by a fan-shaped array of bones called a **ray-fin.** Ray-fins are embedded in a thin layer of skin and connective tissue. The muscles that move the bones are found in the fish's body wall. This arrangement of bones and muscles makes the fin light, collapsible, and easy to move. Ray-finned fish can quickly change a fin's shape, making the fish more maneuverable in the water. But the fins' maneuverability also means that they are thin and too weak to provide support out of water. They would buckle under the fish's weight. It would be like trying to stand on a few soda straws. Some ray-finned fish such as mudskippers have thickened ray-fins that let them shuffle around slowly on land.

Diversity of Body Plans

The ray-finned fish are the most diverse group of living vertebrates, making up nearly half of all vertebrate species. Most familiar species, such as tuna, have streamlined torpedo-shaped bodies that make it easier to swim through the water. But others can look quite different. As a result of natural selection, the bodies of bony fish are specialized for specific swimming and feeding strategies.

- Long, torpedo-shaped fish, such as the barracuda shown in **FIGURE 25.13**, are ambush predators that can accelerate quickly and surprise their prey.
- Fish that are flattened from side to side, such as butterflyfish, cannot swim quickly but are very maneuverable. They are usually found on coral reefs, in dense algae beds, or in large schools of their own species.
- Fish that feed on the surface of the water, such as some killifish, have flattened heads and mouths that point up. This body plan allows them to slurp up invertebrates from the surface while avoiding being seen by predators lurking above the surface.

FIGURE 25.13 A barracuda's torpedo-shaped body is adapted for quick swimming and ambushing prey.

- Flatfish, such as the plaice shown in **FIGURE 25.14**, are flat-shaped and lie on the sea floor waiting for their prey to swim by. During development into its adult form, one eye migrates to the top of its head as its body flattens out.
- Some slow-swimming fish use camouflage to hide from predators or prey. For example, a leafy sea dragon has dozens of fleshy flaps on its body that make it look like the seaweed it lives in.

Staying Afloat

Most ray-finned fish have lungs modified into a buoyancy organ called a **swim bladder.** The swim bladder, shown in **FIGURE 25.15**, helps a fish float higher or lower in the water. The swim bladder lets the fish save energy, because a neutrally buoyant fish does not have to swim to keep from sinking or floating toward the surface. But if the fish changes depth, it must either add or remove air from the swim bladder to maintain neutral buoyancy. Adding oxygen from the bloodstream increases buoyancy the same way inflating a life vest makes you more buoyant. Reabsorbing oxygen into the bloodstream reduces buoyancy. Some species have adapted the swim bladder for use as an amplifier, picking up sound waves and transmitting them to the inner ear through a series of bones. A few fish even use the swim bladder to make sounds by vibrating it like a loudspeaker.

Some ray-finned fish still have lungs. One example is the bichir, which lives in stagnant streams in West Africa. These fish have gills, but can also breathe air and survive out of water for several hours at a time.

Explain What is a swim bladder, and how does it work?

FIGURE 25.14 A plaice's flat-shaped body helps it to blend in with the sea floor, where it lies and waits for prey to swim by.

Connecting CONCEPTS

Buoyancy You may recall from physical science that buoyancy is the upward force that a fluid exerts on an object. To rise to the surface, a fish fills its swim bladder with oxygen, increasing its volume but not its mass, causing it to float upwards.

FIGURE 25.15 Bony Fish Anatomy

The unique features of the anatomy of a bony fish include a swim bladder that maintains buoyancy and gills used to breathe.

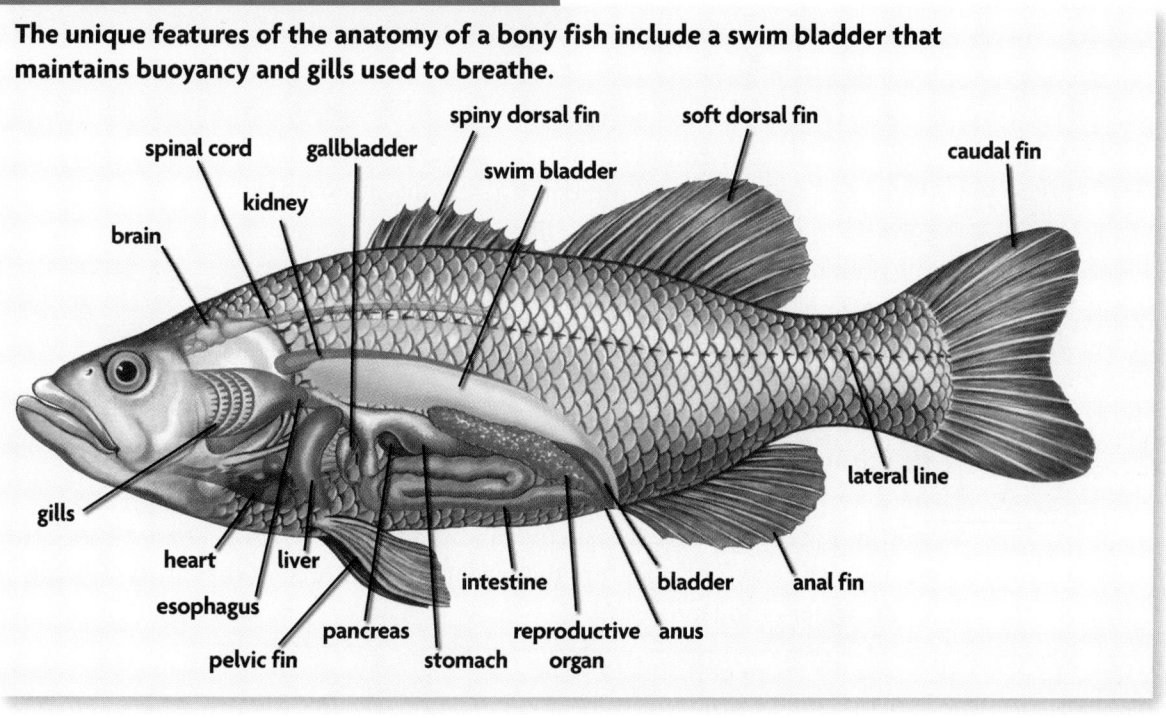

DATA ANALYSIS

CONSTRUCTING SCATTERPLOTS

In order to analyze the relationship between two variables, scientists graph their data. The table below contains data about the length and age of largemouth bass in two lakes in Washington state.

1. **Graph** Construct a graph of the data in the table. Remember, for scatterplots you do not connect the data points.
2. **Analyze** What is the relationship between length and age in largemouth bass?
3. **Infer** An additional fish is measured with a length of 250 millimeters. What might be the age of this fish? Explain your answer.

TABLE 1. LARGEMOUTH BASS LENGTH AND AGE												
Length (mm)	295	310	310	355	365	405	390	400	410	430	470	450	442
Age (years)	5	4	3	5	5	8	8	7	8	9	11	12	12

Source: Washington State Department of Ecology

▶ MAIN IDEA

Lobe-finned fish have paired rounded fins supported by a single bone.

The lobe-finned fish include the ancestors of all terrestrial vertebrates. But most species of lobe-finned fish are extinct. Only seven species remain today. These fish first appeared about 400 million years ago in the Devonian period. Despite their early presence in the fossil record, the lobe-finned fish have never been as diverse as the ray-finned fish, which first appeared in the Devonian period as well.

Lobe-fins are paired pectoral and pelvic fins that are round in shape. These fins are arranged around a branching series of bony struts, like the limb of a land vertebrate. There is always one bone at the base of the fin. It is attached to a pair of bones, which are attached to a fan of smaller bones. Muscles extend into the fin and stretch across the bones, making the fin thick and fleshy. Lobe-fins cannot change shape as quickly as ray-fins can, and they provide less maneuverability in the water. But they are excellent at supporting weight, a feature that eventually let some of these fish walk out of the water onto land.

VISUAL VOCAB

Lobe-fins are paired limblike fins that are round in shape.

lobe fins

Coelacanths

Coelacanths (SEE-luh-KANTHS) are distinctive-looking fish with thick, fleshy fins and a tail with three lobes. They breathe with gills. Their swim bladders are filled with fat and provide buoyancy. There are two species of coelacanth. Both live in deep water in the Indian Ocean.

Coelacanths were first known from fossils. They are found in freshwater and shallow marine deposits from the Devonian until the late Cretaceous periods (410 to 65 million years ago), and then completely disappear from the fossil record. Before 1938, scientists assumed that they had gone extinct at the same time as the dinosaurs. In 1938, a modern coelacanth was caught off the coast of South Africa. Another was discovered near Indonesia in 1997.

Lungfish

Lungfish, such as the one shown in **FIGURE 25.16**, live in streams and swamps in Australia, South America, and Africa. They can breathe with either gills or lungs. This characteristic means that they can live in stagnant, oxygen-poor water that other fish cannot tolerate. Lungs even keep some species alive when their ponds dry up. They make burrows in the mud, which hardens as the water dries up. Then they breathe air until the next rain refills their pond.

The relationships between lungfish, coelacanths, and the terrestrial vertebrates are controversial. Recent studies of mitochondrial DNA suggest that lungfish are the closest living relatives of terrestrial vertebrates. Anatomical evidence also supports this idea. For example, lungfish and terrestrial vertebrates are the only animals with separate blood circuits for the lungs and the rest of the body. However, this characteristic does not mean that modern lungfish are the direct ancestors of terrestrial vertebrates. Both groups are descended from ancient lungfish, and they have changed in different ways over time.

Infer How are lobe-fins related to vertebrate evolution?

VOCABULARY
The name *coelacanth* comes from the combination of the Greek word *koilos*, which means "hollow," and the Greek word *akantha*, which means "spine."

FIGURE 25.16 Lungfish are lobe-finned fish that are able to breathe with either gills or lungs.

25.3 ASSESSMENT

ONLINE QUIZ
ClassZone.com

REVIEWING ▶ MAIN IDEAS

1. How are the bones arranged in a **ray-fin**? How is the arrangement related to the fin's function?

2. What are two examples of living **lobe-finned** fish? How are lobe-finned fish different from ray-finned fish?

CRITICAL THINKING

3. **Infer** You are looking at a long, torpedo-shaped fish with a flat head and a mouth that points upward. What do you predict about the hunting style of this fish?

4. **Predict** Any animal that is underwater is under pressure. Diving exposes animals to higher pressures. How would this affect a fish's **swim bladder**?

Connecting CONCEPTS

5. **Genetics** Early coelacanth fossils have a single dorsal and a single anal fin. Second sets of dorsal and anal fins appear suddenly in the fossil record and persist in modern species. Explain how *Hox* genes could be responsible for the sudden appearance of this novel feature.

MATERIALS
- 20 colored beads
- 1 large bowl
- 100 clear beads
- graph paper
- ruler
- calculator

PROCESS SKILL

Modeling

L4.p1A Compare and contrast the differences between sexual and asexual reproduction. (prerequisite)
L4.p1B Discuss the advantages and disadvantages of sexual vs. asexual reproduction. (prerequisite)

Fish Reproduction

For many species of fish, reproduction usually occurs outside the body. Male and female fish must come together in one place where the females lay eggs and the males release sperm to fertilize the eggs. Some female fish lay as many as 9 million eggs at a time. In this lab, you will model the reproduction method of egg-laying fish.

PROBLEM Why must fish produce so much eggs and sperm?

PROCEDURE

1. With your lab partner, decide who will represent the male fish and who will represent the female fish.
2. If you represent the female obtain beads of a single color. Each bead represents an egg released by the female.
3. Obtain a bowl with 100 clear beads. If you are the female fish, place one bead into the bowl and mix them up.
4. If you are the male, draw one bead from the bowl without looking. If you draw a colored bead, then you have had a successful fertilization. Record whether the attempt was successful. Replace the bead and repeat this step four more times.
5. If you represent the female, add four more eggs to the bowl (total = 5).
6. If you are the male fish, choose five beads from the bowl without looking. Record the number of successful fertilizations. Replace the beads and repeat this step four more times.
7. If you represent the female, add five more eggs to the bowl.
8. If you are the male fish, choose ten beads from the bowl, for a total of five trials.
9. If you represent the female, add ten more eggs to the bowl.
10. If you are the male fish, choose twenty beads from the bowl. Repeat for a total of five trials.

CALCULATE

1. Calculate the average number of successful fertilizations for each condition (1, 5, 10, and 20 eggs released).

ANALYZE AND CONCLUDE

1. **Graph Data** Plot the average successful fertilizations versus the number of eggs released.
2. **Analyze** What were the chances of a single egg becoming fertilized?
3. **Analyze** How might the chances of an egg becoming fertilized change as a male produces more sperm?
4. **Infer** What might be the connection between the production of a large number of eggs and the survivorship of hatched fish?
5. **Hypothesize** How might the situation change if fertilization occurred internally?

25.4 Amphibians

KEY CONCEPT Amphibians evolved from lobe-finned fish.

MAIN IDEAS

- Amphibians were the first animals with four limbs.
- Amphibians return to the water to reproduce.
- Modern amphibians can be divided into three groups.

VOCABULARY

tetrapod, p. 773
amphibian, p. 773
tadpole, p. 774

MICHIGAN STANDARDS

B5.1c Summarize the relationships between present-day organisms and those that inhabited the Earth in the past (e.g., use fossil record, embryonic stages, homologous structures, chemical basis).

Connect What would it really be like to be a "fish out of water"? On shore, the air does not support your body. Gravity pulls on you and makes it hard to move. Your lateral line does not work. You are deaf, because your body absorbs sound waves before they reach your ear. The air is too thin to let you suck food into your mouth, and it is so dry that you start losing water through your skin. These are just a few of the conditions animals faced when they first moved onto land.

MAIN IDEA

Amphibians were the first animals with four limbs.

Connecting CONCEPTS

History of Life In 2006, scientists uncovered the fossil remains of a transitional species between fish and tetrapods. *Tiktaalik roseae* has fins and scales like a fish. However, it also has the beginnings of limbs, including digits, proto-wrists, elbows, and shoulders along with a functional neck and ribs similar to a tetrapod's.

One of the oldest known fossils of a four-limbed vertebrate was found in 360-million-year-old rocks from Greenland. We know that *Acanthostega* had lungs and eight-toed legs. But it also had gills and a lateral line system, neither of which work in air. These features suggest that the earliest animals with four limbs were aquatic and used their limbs to paddle underwater.

All of the vertebrates that live on land, as well as their descendants that have returned to aquatic environments, are tetrapods. A **tetrapod** is a vertebrate that has four limbs. Each limb evolved from a lobe-fin. Tetrapod legs contain bones arranged in the same branching pattern as lobe-fins, except that the fan of bones at the end of the fin is replaced by a set of jointed fingers, wings, or toes. Animals such as snakes, which do not have four limbs, are still considered to be tetrapods because they evolved from limbed ancestors.

Limbs and lungs were features that made these animals successful in an oxygen-poor, debris-filled underwater environment. But, over time, these adaptations let tetrapods climb out of the water to search for food or escape predators. These animals gave rise to the first amphibians. **Amphibians** are animals that can live both on land and in water. In the word *amphibian*, the root *amphi* comes from a Greek word meaning "on both sides," while the suffix *-bian* comes from a Greek word meaning "life."

A number of adaptations help amphibians to live on land. Large shoulder and hip bones help support more weight, while interlocking projections on the vertebrae help keep the backbone from twisting and sagging. A mobile, muscular tongue allows amphibians to capture and manipulate food. Development of a middle ear helps some amphibians to hear out of the water.

Some amphibians can hear sound due to the development of a tympanic membrane attached to a bone called the stapes. The stapes evolved from the top part of the second gill arch. Sound waves moving through the air vibrate the tympanic membrane, or eardrum, which transfers the sound waves further into the ear cavity to the middle and inner ear.

Depending on the species, amphibians breathe through their skin or with the use of gills or lungs. The balloonlike lungs of an amphibian are simple in structure. An amphibian uses its lungs to breathe by changing the amount and pressure of air in its mouth. Unlike fish, which have a two-chambered heart, amphibians have a three-chambered heart. An amphibian heart is made up of two atria and one ventricle. Oxygenated and deoxygenated blood are partially separated by the two atria. Blood is pumped through the heart on a double circuit. Blood pumped through the pulmonary circuit goes to the skin and lungs. Blood pumped through the systemic circuit brings oxygen-rich blood to the organs, and returns oxygen-poor blood to the heart.

Over time, amphibian species evolved with adaptations that allowed them to live on land. But they did not evolve ways to keep themselves or their eggs from drying out in the air.

Analyze **What adaptations helped amphibians move from water to live on land?**

⊙ MAIN IDEA
Amphibians return to the water to reproduce.

An amphibian's skin is thin and wet. Water constantly evaporates from it, and amphibians risk drying out if they move too far from a source of water. This need for moisture is why you rarely find an amphibian in arid habitats. A few species live in deserts, where they burrow underground, emerging only during the brief rainy season. Desert-living species can absorb large amounts of water through their skin when it is available and store it for the dry season.

FIGURE 25.17 This female pygmy marsupial frog keeps her eggs moist by tucking them into a pouch under the skin of her back.

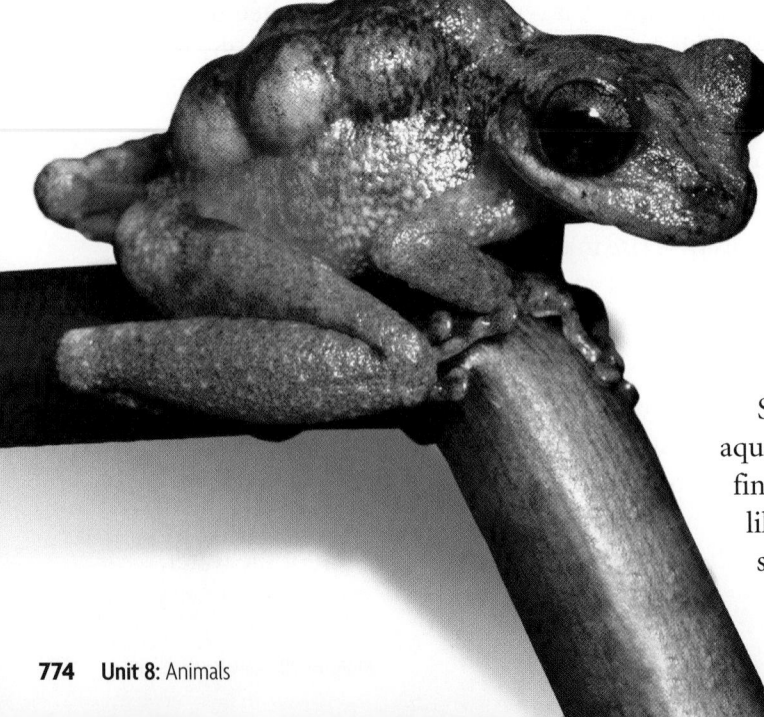

Reproduction Strategies
Amphibians need a source of water to reproduce. Their eggs do not have a shell, and the embryos will dry out and die without a source of moisture. Amphibians use many strategies to keep their eggs wet, including

- laying eggs directly in water
- laying eggs on moist ground
- wrapping eggs in leaves
- brooding eggs in pockets on the female's back, as shown in **FIGURE 25.17.**

Some frogs start their lives as tadpoles. **Tadpoles** are aquatic larvae of frogs. Tadpoles have gills and a broad-finned tail, and swim by wiggling their limbless bodies like fish. They typically eat algae, but some may eat small invertebrates or even other tadpoles.

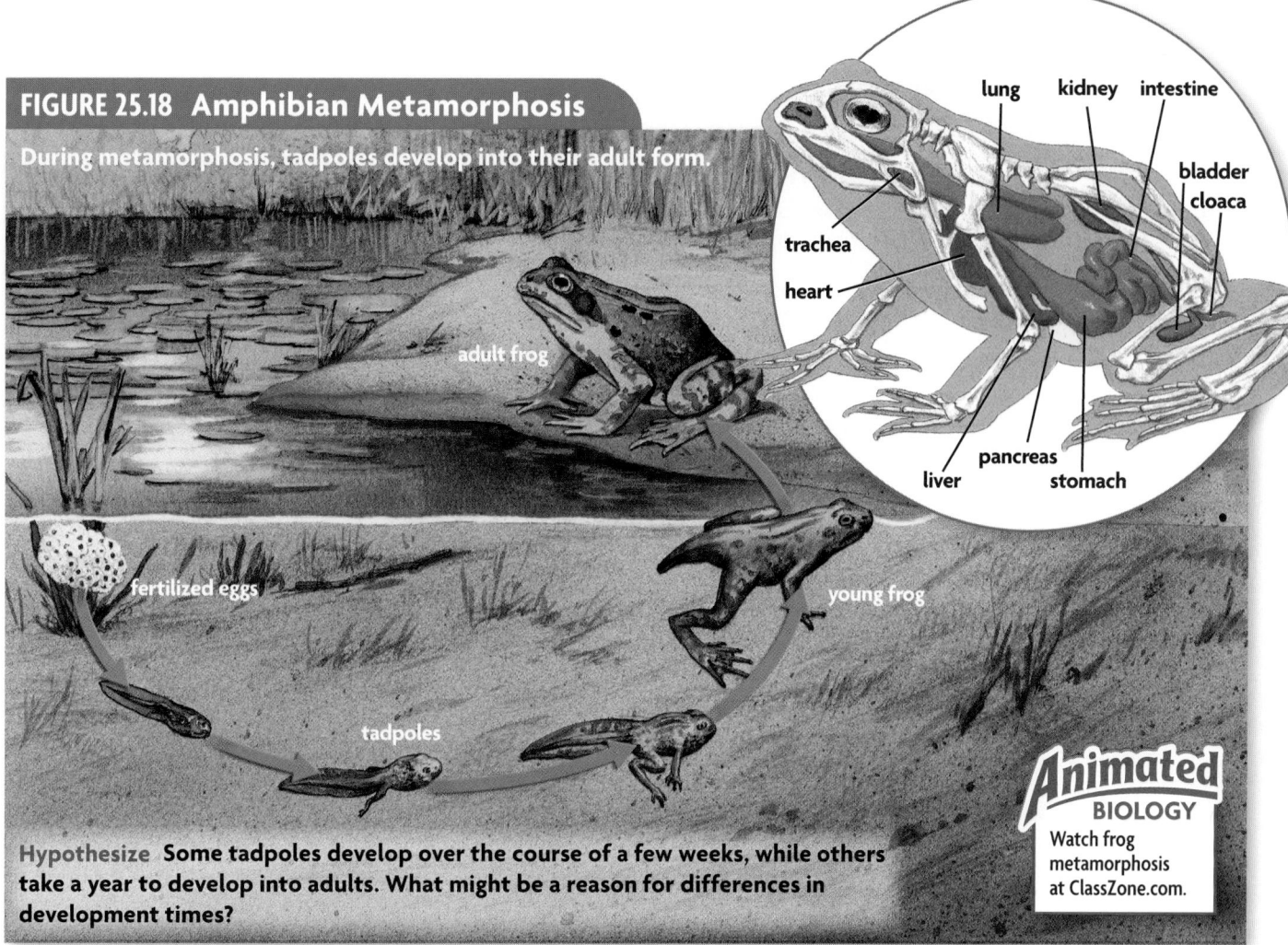

FIGURE 25.18 Amphibian Metamorphosis

During metamorphosis, tadpoles develop into their adult form.

lung   kidney   intestine

bladder
cloaca

trachea

heart

liver   pancreas   stomach

adult frog

fertilized eggs

young frog

tadpoles

Animated
BIOLOGY
Watch frog
metamorphosis
at ClassZone.com.

Hypothesize Some tadpoles develop over the course of a few weeks, while others take a year to develop into adults. What might be a reason for differences in development times?

Amphibian Metamorphosis

To grow into terrestrial adults, tadpoles must undergo metamorphosis. Recall from Chapter 24 that metamorphosis is the change in form and habits of an animal. Similar to the metamorphosis of a butterfly, the metamorphosis of a tadpole into an adult frog affects nearly every organ in the tadpole's body. It produces enormous changes in the animal's body form, physiology, and behavior. The stages of amphibian metamorphosis, in which a tadpole transforms into its adult form, are shown in **FIGURE 25.18**.

During metamorphosis, the tadpole undergoes many changes. The gills are reabsorbed and lungs develop, shifting the frog from a water-breathing to an air-breathing mode of life. The circulatory system is reorganized to send blood to the lungs. The tail fin (if not the entire tail) is reabsorbed. The body grows limbs and completely reorganizes its skeleton, muscles, and parts of the nervous system. The digestive system is rebuilt to handle a carnivorous diet. In the adult amphibian, digestion occurs in the animal's stomach, and wastes are expelled through the cloaca. The cloaca is also a part of the reproductive system.

Many amphibians do not undergo metamorphosis. Adult females lay eggs on the ground or keep them in their bodies, and the young develop directly into their terrestrial forms.

Infer Describe the stages of amphibian metamorphosis.

TAKING NOTES

Draw a simple diagram of amphibian metamorphosis in your notes. At each step, label the changes that occur as the amphibian changes from an egg to its adult form.

Frog Development

Every vertebrate starts off as a fertilized egg or zygote. In this lab, you will identify and sequence the various stages of development of a frog from embryo to adult.

PROBLEM In what order should the specimens be placed to trace the development of the frog?

PROCEDURE

1. Use a spatula to place each coded specimen in a petri dish.
2. Observe each specimen with either a hand lens or a dissecting microscope.
3. Make a drawing of each specimen.
4. When finished, return the specimens to the coded jar.
5. Label your drawings, and put them in the proper sequence.

ANALYZE AND CONCLUDE

1. **Analyze** What stage of development most resembles a fish?
2. **Analyze** Explain how the breathing mechanism changes during frog development.
3. **Identify** What change occurs in the circulatory system to accommodate the change in the breathing mechanism?
4. **Infer** What is the correct sequence of your drawings from the earliest to the latest stages of development?

MATERIALS

- preserved specimens of frog embryos and tadpoles
- petri dish
- spatula
- hand lens or dissecting microscope

▶ MAIN IDEA

Modern amphibians can be divided into three groups.

FIGURE 25.19 The mud salamander lives in swamps, bogs, springs, and streams of the southeastern United States.

The three groups of modern amphibians are salamanders, frogs, and caecilians. The body plans of the amphibians in each of these groups is adapted to the feeding habits and requirements of the habitats in which they live.

Salamanders

There are more than 300 species of salamanders. As shown in **FIGURE 25.19**, salamanders have a long body, four walking limbs, and a tail. They walk with a side-to-side movement biologists think is similar to the way ancient tetrapods probably walked. But appearances can be deceiving. Salamanders have a number of adaptations specific to their way of life. Some salamander species, such as the axolotl (AK-suh-LAHT-uhl), retain some juvenile features as they mature, growing into aquatic adults that look like giant tadpoles with legs. Members of the largest family of salamanders do not have lungs and exchange gases through the lining of their skin and mouth.

Salamander larvae and adults are carnivorous. They eat invertebrates such as insects, worms, and snails. Large species eat smaller vertebrates such as fish and frogs. Salamander larvae and some aquatic adults suck food into their mouths as fish do. On land, a salamander hunts by flinging its sticky tongue at its prey and pulling it back into its mouth.

Frogs

Frogs make up the largest group of living amphibians, with more than 3000 species. Adult frogs are physically distinctive, with tailless bodies, long muscular hind limbs, webbed feet, exposed eardrums, and bulging eyes. Their bodies are adapted for jumping. Elongated bones in their hips, legs, and feet increase their speed and power. Their hind legs have fused bones that absorb the shock of landing.

Toads are actually one family of frogs. They have rougher and bumpier skin than do other frogs, as well as relatively shorter legs that make them poor jumpers. Glands in the bumpy skin of toads and the smooth skin of tropical frogs make toxins that protect the animals from predators. Many species of these poisonous frogs and toads have bright coloration that warns predators that they are deadly.

Frogs live in every environment on Earth except at the poles and in the driest deserts. Although most tadpoles eat algae, adult frogs are predators and will eat any animal they can catch.

FIGURE 25.20 The Wallace's flying frog is able to glide up to 15 meters (50 ft) using its webbed feet and skin folds as mini-sails to float through the air.

Caecilians

Caecilians (suh-SIHL-yuhnz), such as the one shown in **FIGURE 25.21**, are legless, burrowing amphibians that live in the tropics. There are 160 species, ranging in length from about 10 centimeters (4 in.) to 1.5 meters (5 ft). Caecilians have banded bodies that make them look like giant earthworms, and they are specialized for a life burrowing through the soil.

Like other amphibians, caecilians are predators. They burrow through the soil searching for earthworms and grubs. Because they have no legs, they cannot dig through the soil the way a mole would. Instead, like an earthworm, a caecilian uses a hydrostatic skeleton to stiffen its body and drive its head forward like a battering ram.

FIGURE 25.21 Caecilians, common to South America, are legless amphibians that live in underground burrows.

Contrast How are caecilians different from other amphibians?

25.4 ASSESSMENT

ONLINE QUIZ
ClassZone.com

REVIEWING ▶ MAIN IDEAS

1. What evidence suggests that the first **tetrapods** were **amphibians**?

2. List two reasons why amphibians must live in moist environments.

3. In what ways are the three groups of amphibians similar? different?

CRITICAL THINKING

4. **Connect** Like poisonous dart frogs, monarch butterflies are brightly colored. What might be the adaptive advantage of bright coloration?

5. **Apply** Amphibians are very sensitive to changes in their environment. Why might this be?

Connecting CONCEPTS

6. **Evolution** Caecilians have no legs. Neither do snakes or whales. Why, then, do we call them all tetrapods? (Hint: consider their evolutionary histories.)

25.5 Vertebrates on Land

KEY CONCEPT Reptiles, birds, and mammals are adapted for life on land.

▶ **MAIN IDEAS**
- Amniotes can retain moisture.
- Amniotes do not need to return to water to reproduce.

VOCABULARY

amniote, p. 778
keratin, p. 778
amniotic egg, p. 779
placenta, p. 779

MICHIGAN STANDARDS

B5.1c Summarize the relationships between present-day organisms and those that inhabited the Earth in the past (e.g., use fossil record, embryonic stages, homologous structures, chemical basis).

Connect Around 350 million years ago, one group of ancient amphibians evolved traits that let them walk away from the water forever. Over time, they diversified into the types of vertebrates you are most familiar with, including reptiles, birds, and mammals—the class that includes you.

▶ **MAIN IDEA**
Amniotes can retain moisture.

An **amniote** is a vertebrate that has a thin, tough, membranous sac that encloses the embryo or fetus. Amniotes first appeared as small, lizardlike creatures in the late Carboniferous period. Since that time, amniotes have evolved into thousands of different forms and have invaded nearly every ecosystem on Earth. They have become predators in the tropics, the most arid deserts, the Arctic, and in any number of freshwater and marine environments. They have become burrowers, sprinters, sit-and-wait predators, and slow trackers. Some species never leave the trees. Some specialize in eating plants and have evolved symbiotic relationships with bacteria that can break down cellulose. Some have also developed powered flight.

When you look at the phylogenetic tree of amniotes, it is clear that many of the species we see today are survivors of larger radiations that have gone extinct. Mammals are survivors of a huge line of animals that went extinct about 245 million years ago. Birds are survivors of the dinosaur radiation and extinction. You will learn more about amniote diversity in Chapter 26.

All amniotes share a set of characteristics that prevent water loss. Skin cells are waterproofed with keratin. **Keratin** is a protein that binds to lipids inside the cell, forming a hydrophobic—or water repellent—layer that keeps the water inside the animal from reaching the skin. The presence of this hydrophobic layer means that amniotes lose less water to evaporation than amphibians do. Waterproofing also means that amniotes cannot exchange gases across their skin. They rely on their lungs for respiration.

Kidneys and large intestines are bigger in amniotes than in amphibians. These organs contain tissues that reabsorb water. The increased surface area of these tissues enables amniotes to absorb more water internally, so they lose less to excretion than do amphibians.

Connecting CONCEPTS

Extinction Recall from **Chapter 11** that a mass extinction is an intense period of extinction that occurs on a global scale. In the Permian-Triassic extinction, 95 percent of all species and over 50 percent of all families disappeared.

Connect **What makes your skin cells waterproof? Why is this important?**

MAIN IDEA

Amniotes do not need to return to water to reproduce.

With adaptations that limit water loss, amniote adults could move into drier environments on land. But it was the evolution of the amniotic egg that let them stay there. The **amniotic egg** is an almost completely waterproof container that keeps the embryo from drying out as it develops. After it evolved, amniotes did not have to return to a wet environment to reproduce.

An amniotic egg, shown in **FIGURE 25.22**, is essentially a private pool that the mother builds for her embryo. Like any swimming pool, the egg is expensive. In egg-laying amniotes, the mother must make enough yolk and white to feed the embryo until it hatches, then build the shell around the fertilized egg. Each egg represents a large investment of energy. For example, a bird may lose 5 to 30 percent of its body weight as it makes an egg.

Other amniotes, such as rattlesnakes and garter snakes, make eggs but do not lay them. Instead, they keep their eggs in their oviduct until they hatch. Retaining eggs protects them from predators. Some amniotes have evolved the ability to give birth to living, well-developed young.

Most mammal embryos develop inside of the mother's reproductive tract. Their eggs have no shells, but their embryos make the same series of membranes found in a typical amniotic egg. The **placenta** is a membranous organ that develops in female mammals during pregnancy. It lines the uterine wall and partially envelops the fetus. The placenta carries nutrients from the mother to the embryo and also removes metabolic wastes from the embryo.

FIGURE 25.22 Amniotes, such as this gecko, develop within an amniotic egg.

Summarize How is an amniotic egg protected from water loss?

25.5 ASSESSMENT

ONLINE QUIZ ClassZone.com

REVIEWING ▶ MAIN IDEAS

1. What characteristics help an **amniote** retain moisture?

2. Why don't amniotes need to return to water to reproduce?

CRITICAL THINKING

3. **Infer** If eggshells were thicker, the egg would lose even less water to the environment. Why are eggshells thin?

4. **Infer** What is an advantage of giving birth to live young, rather than having young that hatch from eggs?

Connecting CONCEPTS

5. **Evolution** Most mammals and at least some lizards and snakes have evolved live birth by keeping the eggs inside the mother until they hatch. However, no bird species has ever retained its eggs. Suggest a possible explanation for this fact.

Use these inquiry-based labs and online activities to deepen your understanding of vertebrate diversity.

INVESTIGATION

B1.2C Develop an understanding of a scientific concept by accessing information from multiple sources. Evaluate the scientific accuracy and significance of the information.

B2.4A Explain that living things can be classified based on structural, embryological, and molecular (relatedness of DNA sequence) evidence.

Anatomy of a Bony Fish

A perch is a bony fish. There are several freshwater species and a saltwater species of perch. In this lab, you will dissect and explore the anatomy of a perch.

SKILL Observing

PROBLEM What is the relationship between the structure and functions of the organ systems of a fish?

PROCEDURE

1. Place the perch in the dissecting tray.

2. Examine the external anatomy of the fish. Use the Anatomical Perch Drawing to explore the fish's external anatomy.

3. Use the scalpel to make a cut from the anal opening forward 2 centimeters. Take the scissors and cut through the body wall along the underside to the pelvic fin. Use the scissors to cut vertically from the anal region to the lateral line. Use the scalpel to make a cut along the lateral line toward the operculum. Use the scissors to cut vertically from the pelvic fin to the lateral line (you may remove the pelvic fins).

4. Look in the body cavity at the internal organs. Follow the handout instructions to explore the fish's internal anatomy.

5. Cut a small flap of skin from the rear dorsal fin down to the lateral line to expose the underlying muscles. The muscles are arranged in groups called myotomes.

6. When finished, dispose of your perch according to instructions from your teacher. Be sure to clean and dry your instruments and tray. Wash your hands thoroughly.

MATERIALS
- dissecting tray
- preserved perch specimen
- Anatomical Perch Drawing
- hand lens
- scalpel
- scissors
- forceps
- dissecting needle
- 12 dissecting pins
- paper towels

ANALYZE AND CONCLUDE

1. **Analyze** What type of symmetry does the fish have?

2. **Analyze** What is the function of the operculum?

3. **Analyze** How many gill arches does the perch have? Would you expect a lamprey to have more or fewer gill arches? Explain.

4. **Infer** Which structure did you observe that allows fish to sense prey in the distance? Describe it.

5. **Analyze** What organ in humans is homologous to the swim bladder?

6. **Apply** If the fish's swim bladder was damaged and could not hold air, would the fish sink or float? Explain.

7. **Infer** How does the shape of the perch's body help it to maneuver through the water?

INVESTIGATION

Vanishing Amphibian—an Indicator Species

Indicator species are species that can be used as a measure, or indicator, of the overall health of an ecosystem. In this activity, using the Internet and other resources, you will research the role of amphibians as ecological indicators.

SKILL Researching

MATERIALS

- map of the United States
- colored pencils

PROBLEM What characteristics make amphibians a good choice as ecological indicators?

RESEARCH

1. **Apply** Why are amphibians good indicators of ecological health?

2. **Analyze** Are populations of amphibians increasing or decreasing?

3. **Analyze** What are the reasons for the change in amphibian populations?

4. **Apply** On the map, shade in areas of the United States where changes in amphibian populations are occurring, and cite specific examples and possible reasons for the changes in populations.

Online BIOLOGY
CLASSZONE.COM

ANIMATED BIOLOGY
What Type of Fish Is It?
Can you tell a ray-finned fish from a cartilaginous fish? Use physical characteristics to categorize a set of jawed fish.

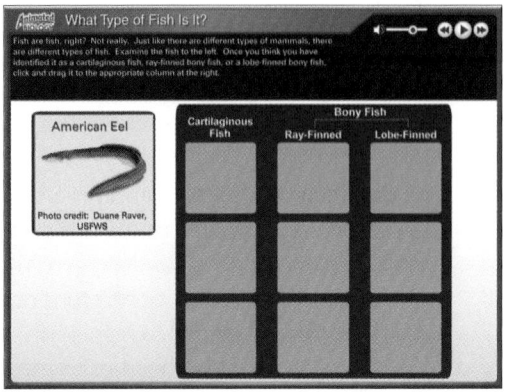

WEBQUEST
Worldwide, more than 70 percent of marine fisheries have been fished to their sustainable limits or overfished. At the same time, an increasing number of people depend on fish for food. In this WebQuest, you will explore the problems facing fisheries and what is being done to save them.

DATA ANALYSIS ONLINE
Lake Malawi in Africa has a great diversity of fish. However, the fish aren't distributed evenly throughout the lake. One factor that determines where fish can live is availability of oxygen. Graph the number of species and the amount of dissolved oxygen at specific depths and determine the relationship.

KEY CONCEPTS | Vocabulary Games | Concept Maps | Animated Biology | Online Quiz

25.1 Vertebrate Origins

All vertebrates share common characteristics. At some point during development, all chordates have a notochord, a hollow nerve cord, pharyngeal slits, and a tail. All vertebrates have an endoskeleton made of bone or cartilage. The first recognizable vertebrates were fish. Lampreys and hagfish are two primitive jawless fish still in existence today.

25.2 Fish Diversity

The dominant aquatic vertebrates are fish. Fish use the large surface area of their gills to exchange carbon dioxide and oxygen with the water in which they live. Countercurrent flow maximizes the amount of oxygen a fish can pull from the water. Fish use their fins to move around in the water. Cartilaginous fish include sharks, rays, and chimeras. All other living fish are categorized as bony fish.

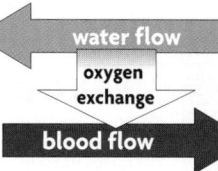

water flow
oxygen exchange
blood flow

25.3 A Closer Look at Bony Fish

Bony fish include ray-finned and lobe-finned fish. Ray-finned fish have a fan of bones in their fins. Most ray-finned fish use an organ called a swim bladder to stay neutrally buoyant, which means they neither sink nor float in the water. Lobe-finned fish have a series of bones in their fins. Lobe-finned fish include the ancestors of all land vertebrates. Coelacanths and lungfish are two types of lobe-finned fish.

25.4 Amphibians

Amphibians evolved from lobe-finned fish. Amphibians were the first vertebrates with four limbs. Amphibians can live both on land and in water. However, they must live in moist environments, as they need a source of water to reproduce. Modern amphibian groups include salamanders, frogs, and caecilians.

adult frog
fertilized eggs
young frog
tadpoles

25.5 Vertebrates on Land

Reptiles, birds, and mammals are adapted for life on land. During embryonic or fetal development, an amniote is enclosed within a thin, tough, membranous sac. This waterproof container allows amniotes to reproduce outside of water. Some amniotes give birth to live young, while others lay hard-shelled eggs.

Synthesize Your Notes

Concept Map Use a concept map like the one below to summarize what you know about fish diversity.

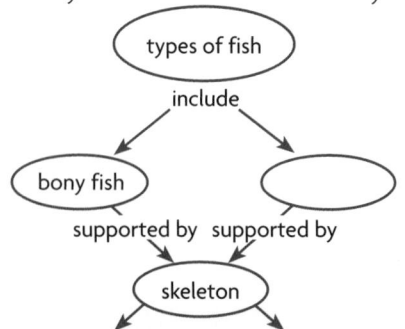

types of fish
include
bony fish
supported by   supported by
skeleton

Process Diagram Use a process diagram like the one below to make a detailed summary of the steps that occur during amphibian metamorphosis.

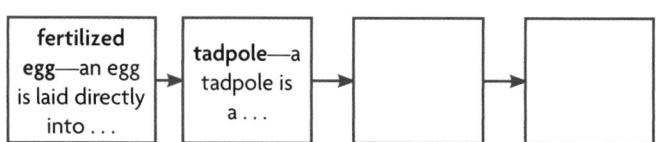

fertilized egg—an egg is laid directly into . . .
tadpole—a tadpole is a . . .

Chapter Assessment

Reviewing Vocabulary

Compare and Contrast

Describe one similarity and one difference between the two terms in each of the following pairs.

1. invertebrate, vertebrate
2. endoskeleton, exoskeleton
3. gill, lung
4. ray-fin, lobe-fin
5. tetrapod, amphibian
6. amniotic egg, placenta

Greek and Latin Word Origins

Using the Greek or Latin word origins of the terms below, explain how the meaning of the root relates to the definition of the term.

7. The word *operculum* comes from the Latin word *operire,* which means "to cover."
8. The term *caecilian* comes from the Latin word *caecus,* meaning "blind." (**Hint:** Consider where a caecilian lives.)
9. The word *notochord* comes from a combination of the Greek words meaning "back" and "gut or string."
10. In the term *tetrapod,* the prefix *tetra* means "four."
11. In the term *chondrichthyes,* the word part *chondr-* comes from a Greek word meaning "cartilage." Why is a shark a member of the group Chondrichthyes?

Visualize Vocabulary

For each term below, use simple shapes, lines, or arrows to illustrate their meaning. Below each picture, write a short caption. Here's an example for *operculum.*

An operculum is a protective plate that covers the gills of a bony fish.

12. countercurrent flow
13. lateral line

Reviewing **MAIN IDEAS**

14. Sea squirts and dogs are both chordates, but they are very different kinds of animals. What four features do these animals share at some point in their development?
15. All vertebrates have an endoskeleton. What are the main parts of an endoskeleton?
16. What are the seven classes of living vertebrates?
17. How does countercurrent flow contribute to the function of a fish's gills?
18. What evidence indicates that jaws were once gill arches?
19. Barracuda and flatfish have very different body shapes and methods of finding food, yet both have ray-fins. How does the structure of their fins help them to survive?
20. What is the function of the swim bladder in a ray-finned fish?
21. What feature of a lobe-fin fish makes it the closest relative to terrestrial vertebrates?
22. List two adaptations of amphibians and briefly describe why each is important for life on land.
23. Why does amphibian reproduction require a moist environment?
24. What are the three types of modern amphibians?
25. How does the presence of keratin in skin cells affect where an amniote can live?
26. Mammals and birds have very different methods of reproduction, but both are able to reproduce on land. Explain why amniotes do not need to return to water to reproduce.

27. Analyze Describe the structure and function of the notochord and the internal backbone of an endoskeleton.

28. Analyze Gas exchange in fish occurs in the gills using a countercurrent flow. Imagine that there are five stations in a gill at which gas exchange takes place. Describe what happens and why as the water and blood pass each other at each station.

29. Apply Submarines rise and sink using a mechanical system that works much like a swim bladder. Use your knowledge of how a swim bladder works to explain how submarines use these systems to rise and descend in the water.

30. Infer Frogs have bodies that are specialized for jumping, yet they have webbed feet. How are webbed feet beneficial for frogs?

31. Connect How would your kidneys help you survive for a couple of days without water better than the type of kidneys that frogs have?

Interpreting Visuals

Use the image below to answer the next three questions.

32. Classify This mudskipper has climbed out of the water and is resting on a rock. Based on the physical characteristics of the mudskipper's fin shape, to which group of fish does the mudskipper belong? Explain your reasoning.

33. Analyze When it is out of the water, how might the lungless mudskipper breathe?

34. Apply If mudskippers were to evolve into a terrestrial animal, what body part might function as a limb?

Analyzing Data

Use the data below to answer the next three questions. The calling activity, body size, and body temperature were recorded for a population of Fowler's toads. Below is a scatterplot that shows the relationship between a male toad's body temperature and calling effort, measured as the number of seconds the male called per minute of time.

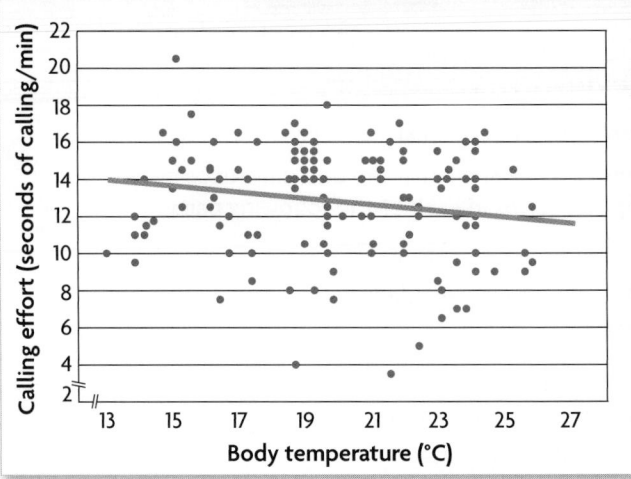

BODY TEMPERATURE AND CALLING EFFORT

Source: Given, M. *Copeia* 2002:04.

35. Analyze What is the relationship between the body temperature of the Fowler's toad and calling efforts?

36. Analyze Is this data an example of positive correlation, negative correlation, or no relationship?

37. Predict Would you expect a toad with a body temperature of 15° Celsius to have a higher or lower calling effort than a toad with a body temperature of 21° Celsius? Explain.

Connecting CONCEPTS

38. Write a Letter Imagine you are a green frog, adapted to life both in water and on land, and one of your best friends is a fish that lives in a nearby lake. Write a letter to the fish, explaining what adaptations he would need to survive outside of the water on land. In the letter, be sure to compare any similar characteristics and contrast differing characteristics.

39. Connect Take another look at the glass frog on page 757. Its translucent skin helps it to blend in with the green leaves on which it lives. How could natural selection have played a role in the development of this trait common among all glass frogs?

MICHIGAN
STANDARDS-BASED ASSESSMENT

✓ **Test Practice**
For more test practice, go to ClassZone.com.

1. **A scientist observes an unusual organism in the deep ocean. Because she is not familiar with this organism and suspects it has never been identified before, she wants to give it a scientific name. But first, she must** `B1.2C`

   A study Latin to determine an appropriate scientific name.

   B collect many specimens to determine if there is a population.

   C sketch the organism and label all the identifiable parts.

   D research many sources to determine if it is a new discovery.

2. **A human heart has four chambers consisting of two atria and two ventricles. In contrast, a fish has a heart with** `B2.4C`

   A one chamber.

   B two chambers.

   C three chambers.

   D is solely related to the ancestor species.

3.

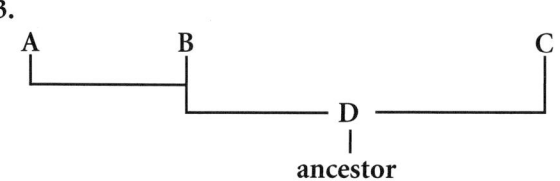

   After studying fossils of fish in one region, scientists developed this family tree to describe how the various species they found are related. If live specimens of species A, B, and C can all be found today, it is safe to say that species D `B5.1c`

   A is an ancestor of present-day fish.

   B is also a living species of fish.

   C has no relatives that still exist today.

   D is solely related to the ancestor species.

4.

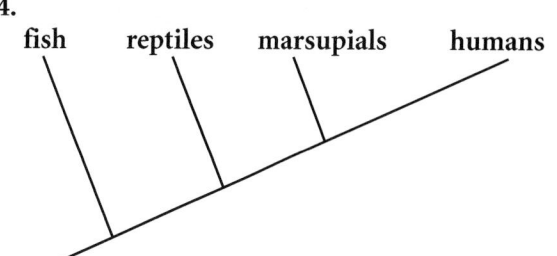

   According to this cladogram, which of the following statements is true? `B2.4A`

   A Fish are more closely related to humans than reptiles.

   B Reptiles are more closely related to marsupials than fish.

   C Marsupials and fish do not share a common ancestor.

   D Marsupials and humans share a common ancestor.

   THINK THROUGH THE QUESTION

   Recall that cladograms are based on common ancestory, and they are read from left to right.
   ---

5. **Countercurrent flow in a fish's gills allows blood to efficiently release carbon dioxide into the water and absorb oxygen from the water. This maintenance of oxygen levels in the fish's body is an example of** `B2.4B`

   A homeostasis.

   B bioregulation.

   C nutrient cycling.

   D biomagnification.

6. **Amphibians need a source of water to reproduce. They may keep their fertilized eggs wet by laying them directly in water, on moist ground, wrapped in leaves, or in pockets on the female's back. No matter where they are kept, however, the eggs of amphibians are all a product of** `L4.p1A`

   A asexual reproduction.

   B sexual reproduction.

   C tadpole metamorphosis.

   D internal fertilization.

26 A Closer Look at Amniotes

KEY CONCEPTS

26.1 Amniotes
Reptiles, birds, and mammals are amniotes.

26.2 Reptiles
Reptiles were the first amniotes.

26.3 Birds
Birds have many adaptations for flight.

26.4 Mammals
Evolutionary adaptations allowed mammals to succeed dinosaurs as a dominant terrestrial vertebrate.

Online BIOLOGY CLASSZONE.COM

Animated BIOLOGY

View animated chapter concepts.
- Bird Flight
- Beak Shape and Diet

BIOZINE

Keep current with biology news.
- Featured stories
- News feeds
- Careers

RESOURCE CENTER

Get more information on
- Body Temperature
- Reptiles
- Birds

Is this a monkey or a mouse?

The large eyes and ears of this eastern tarsier make it an excellent nocturnal hunter. These unusual mammals are primates and are closely related to modern monkeys. About the same size as a kitten, a tarsier has strong hind legs similar to those of frogs. The tarsier's eyes cannot move but it has a full range of view because it can rotate its head almost 360 degrees.

Connecting CONCEPTS

Biomes Tarsiers are exceptional climbers that live only in the tropical rain forests of southeastern Asia. Deep within these jungles are areas of the highest biodiversity on Earth. High above the ground, an entire community of species have adapted to become arboreal. They live almost their entire lives in the treetops, or forest canopy, very rarely setting foot on the dense forest floor.

26.1 Amniotes

KEY CONCEPT Reptiles, birds, and mammals are amniotes.

▶ MAIN IDEAS

- Amniote embryos develop in a fluid-filled sac.
- Anatomy and circulation differ among amniotes.
- Amniotes can be ectothermic or endothermic.

VOCABULARY

pulmonary circuit, p. 789
systemic circuit, p. 789
ectotherm, p. 791
endotherm, p. 791

MICHIGAN STANDARDS

B2.4A Explain that living things can be classified based on structural, embryological, and molecular (relatedness of DNA sequence) evidence.

B2.4B Describe how various organisms have developed different specializations to accomplish a particular function and yet the end result is the same (e.g., excreting nitrogenous wastes in animals, obtaining oxygen for respiration).

Connect When you were about nine weeks into your development, you had a mass of about 2 grams and measured about 18 millimeters long, roughly the size of a dime. Over the next seven months, you grew and developed while living safely inside a fluid-filled membrane, or amniotic sac. There are many different types of amniotes, but each of them, like you, begins life inside an amniotic sac.

▶ MAIN IDEA

Amniote embryos develop in a fluid-filled sac.

Reptiles, birds, and mammals are all amniotes. Recall from Chapter 25 that amniotes develop in a sac inside the mother's abdomen. This sac contains everything an embryonic vertebrate needs to grow and prepare for the world outside. In some amniotes, the sac is contained inside the mother's body. In other amniotes, a tough outer shell protects embryos as they develop outside of the mother. This shell is semipermeable, which means that it allows gases such as oxygen and carbon dioxide to pass through but prevents the embryo from drying out by holding water inside.

An egg is a completely self-sustaining container that provides enough energy and nutrients to enable the embryo to mature. The illustration in **FIGURE 26.1** shows the different membranes found inside an amniotic egg. The egg you may have eaten for breakfast this morning was formed with all of the necessary membranes and nutrient stores to support a chicken embryo. But because the egg was never fertilized, the genetic composition of the egg remained haploid and did not develop into an embryo.

The development of the amniotic egg was an important adaptation because it allowed vertebrates to reproduce on land. Without the self-contained source of energy and water, an egg needed to develop in water or else the embryo would dry out.

Predict What happens when all of the resources that are stored inside the egg are used?

FIGURE 26.1 Amniotic Egg

Inside the shell of an amniotic egg, four membranes perform specific functions during development of the embryo.

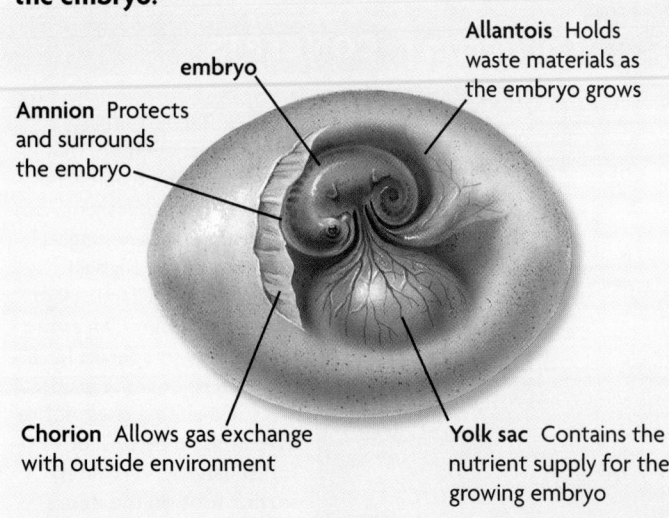

embryo

Amnion Protects and surrounds the embryo

Allantois Holds waste materials as the embryo grows

Chorion Allows gas exchange with outside environment

Yolk sac Contains the nutrient supply for the growing embryo

● MAIN IDEA
Anatomy and circulation differ among amniotes.

Over time, amniotes have evolved many different body shapes and sizes, resulting in many differences in anatomy and blood circulation.

Anatomy

The first amniotes walked in a sprawl similar to that of the lizard in **FIGURE 26.2**. A lizard's legs stick out on either side of its body. It walks with its elbows and knees bent. Muscles around the ribs help propel the body forward, and their contractions make the lizard's body sway from side to side with each step. Because these same muscles also inflate the lungs, many animals with a sprawling stance cannot run and breathe at the same time. However, some reptiles have adaptations that allow them to breathe while running.

FIGURE 26.2 The sprawling walking style illustrated by this Komodo dragon is very different from the upright stance of a cat. Anatomical features make breathing easier and more efficient for upright walkers.

Amniotes such as mammals, dinosaurs, and birds evolved a more upright stance. The cat in **FIGURE 26.2** has straighter limbs than the lizard. Its legs are underneath its body and hold it far away from the ground. When it walks, its legs swing back and forth like pendulums, and its body does not wiggle from side to side. An upright stance uses less energy than a sprawling one. It also separates the muscles the animal uses to breathe from the muscles it uses to walk and run. The evolution of the diaphragm, an independent muscle used to expand the chest cavity and force air into the lungs, separated the muscles needed for walking and breathing. A diaphragm enables amniotes with an upright stance to run and breathe at the same time.

Circulation

As amniotes evolved, their bodies required more energy for movement and growth. To get this energy, their tissues demanded more energy and needed highly efficient ways of delivering this oxygen. This need led to the development of many different types of circulatory systems. All amniotes have a centralized heart that moves blood through a complex system of blood vessels to deliver nutrients to tissues and organs.

All amniotes have two circuits of blood vessels. Because the circuits are separate, amniotes can conserve energy more effectively. The two circuits of blood vessels are the pulmonary and systemic circuits.

- The **pulmonary circuit** moves oxygen-poor blood from the heart to the lungs, and oxygen-rich blood back to the heart.
- The **systemic circuit** moves oxygen-rich blood from the heart to the rest of the body.

The differences in amniote circulatory systems evolved over millions of years. As you will see, these differences affect the efficiency of an organism's everyday functions and behavior.

TAKING NOTES

Use a two-column chart to take notes on the pulmonary and systemic blood circuits.

Pulmonary Circuit	Systemic Circuit

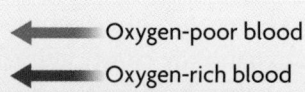
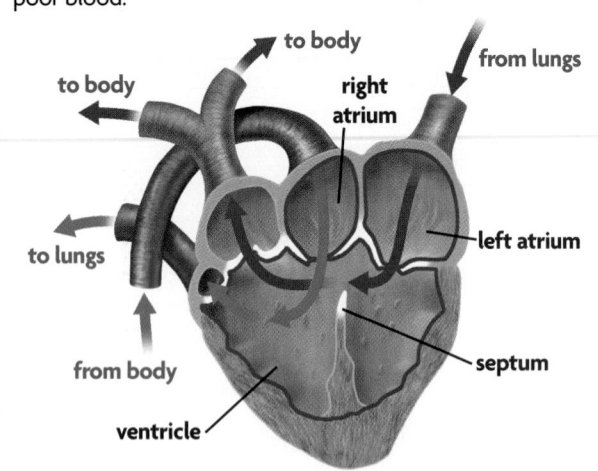
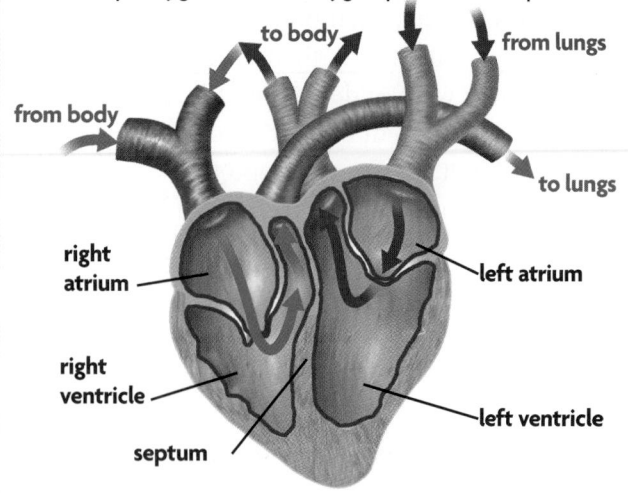

MAIN IDEA
Amniotes can be ectothermic or endothermic.

Like all organisms, amniotes are more active when they are warm. Enzymes that speed up the chemical reactions inside cells are more active at higher temperatures. A warm amniote digests food faster and can send more nutrients to its tissues. It can also move faster because its muscles contract more quickly and more often. All living organisms absorb heat from the environment and release heat as a byproduct of metabolism. But all animals manage heat in different ways.

You may have heard the term "cold-blooded" to describe a snake or a lizard. This term does not accurately describe reptiles and amphibians, because their blood is not actually cold. Instead, scientists use the term **ectotherms** to refer to organisms whose body temperatures are determined by their surrounding environment. These organisms' body temperature fluctuates with the temperature of their environment. They have higher body temperatures in a warm environment than in a cool one.

Ectotherms regulate their body temperature through their behavior. For example, many reptiles, such as the chameleon in **FIGURE 26.4**, bask in sunny places to warm their tissues when they are cold. Similarly, desert lizards move into shady burrows when outside temperatures climb too high. Large animals have a harder time shedding heat than small animals. If an ectothermic animal is massive enough, it will take a long time to cool down. Large ectotherms, such as crocodiles, can stay warm even when the environment is relatively cool.

On the other hand, you have probably heard humans and other mammals described as "warm-blooded." But to describe these organisms more accurately, scientists use the term *endotherm*. **Endotherms** are organisms that use their own metabolic heat to keep their tissues warm. More specifically, endotherms regulate their metabolic activity in ways that keep their body temperature relatively constant all of the time. They may shiver when they get too cold, contracting their muscles to generate extra heat. If they get too hot, they may cool down by sweating or panting. Many endotherms, such as the polar bear in **FIGURE 26.4**, are covered with insulation in the form of hair, fat cells, or feathers, which helps them control heat loss.

FIGURE 26.4 As an ectotherm, a chameleon increases its body temperature by basking in sunlight. Endotherms such as this polar bear can maintain a relatively constant body temperature even in cold environments.

You can think of endotherms and ectotherms as having two different strategies for managing energy use. There is a trade-off between an animal's body temperature and the amount of energy it uses. Warm tissues work quickly and require more ATP, which requires an animal to eat more. For example, lions and crocodiles are both large predators, but a crocodile can survive on much less meat than a lion can. In short, ectotherms are less active when it is cold but can survive on less food than endotherms. Endotherms are active all the time but must eat more than ectotherms eat.

CHOOSING GRAPHS

Choosing an appropriate type of graph to represent data collected in an experiment is an important part of the scientific process.

The table to the right contains data that show the differences in energy requirements for endotherms and ectotherms. Despite having similar sizes, endotherms and ectotherms use energy in different ways and therefore require different amounts of food.

TABLE 1. BODY MASS AND FOOD INTAKE

Organism	Mass (kg)	Food Intake (kg/yr)
Nile crocodile	150	750
Grey kangaroo	45	1108
Komodo dragon	45	250
Koala	8	252
Monitor lizard	8	93

Source: Nagy, K.A. *Nutrition Abstracts and Reviews* Series B:71.

1. **Graph** Choose and construct one graph that can represent both sets of data.

2. **Analyze** Explain why there is a difference in energy requirements between endotherms and ectotherms.

The ability to regulate their own temperature served as an important function in the early stages of endotherm evolution. This adaptation gave endotherms a distinct advantage over ectotherms as Earth's climate changed millions of years ago. Because they could stay warm in colder weather, endotherms were able to exploit resources that the ectotherms could not. Many scientists believe that the ability to regulate their own body temperature allowed endotherms to survive the catastrophic events that led to the extinction of dinosaurs.

Analyze As you move away from Earth's equator into colder latitudes, why are there fewer ectotherms and more endotherms?

26.1 ASSESSMENT

ONLINE QUIZ
ClassZone.com

REVIEWING ▶ MAIN IDEAS

1. How did the development of an amniotic egg allow vertebrates to reproduce on land?

2. How does anatomy and circulation differ among amniotes?

3. What is the difference between an **endotherm** and an **ectotherm**?

CRITICAL THINKING

4. **Infer** A 30-gram shrew will die if it cannot eat for a few hours. A 30-gram gecko thrives on a few crickets every other day. Why might shrews need food more often?

5. **Compare** Illustrate the path of blood through a three-chambered heart when the animal is breathing. Show how the pathway changes when the animal is not breathing.

Connecting CONCEPTS

6. **Survivorship** When eggs are laid by a species of reptile or bird, they generally stay in a nest that is closely guarded by a mother. How does this behavior affect the chances for offspring to survive to adulthood? What type of survivorship strategy does this represent?

26.2 Reptiles

KEY CONCEPT Reptiles were the first amniotes.

▶ MAIN IDEAS

- Reptiles are a diverse group of amniotes.
- Reptiles have been evolving for millions of years.
- There are four modern groups of reptiles.

VOCABULARY

reptile, p. 793
oviparous, p. 793
viviparous, p. 793

MICHIGAN STANDARDS

B2.4A Explain that living things can be classified based on structural, embryological, and molecular (relatedness of DNA sequence) evidence.

VOCABULARY

The name *reptile* comes from the Latin word, *reptilis*, which means "creeping."

FIGURE 26.5 As a reptile, this eastern water dragon must use energy from sunlight to maintain its body temperature. From its perch atop a rock, it can also spot predators or look for prey.

Connect Basking on the sunny banks of the river, the lizard may look slow, but it has a top speed of almost 20 kilometers per hour, and strong jaws filled with sharp teeth. It is a daunting predator. The eastern water dragon may only grow to 80 centimeters in length and may never compare to a crocodile as a threat to humans, but it hunts, kills, and eats its prey in the same way that its larger cousins do. What makes reptiles unique?

▶ MAIN IDEA

Reptiles are a diverse group of amniotes.

About 200 million years ago, a mass extinction resulted in the loss of many of Earth's plant and animal species. One group of organisms that survived— the reptiles—have thrived for millions of years. **Reptiles** are ectotherms that are covered with dry scales or plates and reproduce by laying amniotic eggs covered with a tough outer shell.

Unlike amphibians, reptiles produce a completely self-sustaining, amniotic egg that allows an embryonic reptile to develop fully before it is born. There are two ways that reptile eggs develop.

- **Oviparous** reptiles deposit their eggs into an external nest, and the eggs develop completely independent of the adult reptile.
- **Viviparous** reptiles hold the eggs inside their body through the duration of development and give birth to live offspring.

The shapes and sizes of modern reptiles vary widely. Some reptiles have no legs. Other reptiles run swiftly on land or spend much of their time in the water. The oddly shaped turtles and tortoises carry their homes on their backs. Each reptile group has adapted different features that allow it to be successful. But despite these differences, all reptiles share a few similarities.

All living reptiles are ectotherms. Recall that an ectotherm's body temperature changes based on the surrounding environment. Similar to the eastern water dragon in **FIGURE 26.5**, many reptiles spend a great deal of time basking, or sunbathing, to absorb energy from sunlight. In addition, reptiles have dry scales or plates that absorb energy and help contain heat needed to maintain normal body functions.

Analyze What advantages does a self-sustaining egg give reptiles?

MAIN IDEA

Reptiles have been evolving for millions of years.

Fossil evidence suggests that reptiles began to emerge from the water during the late Paleozoic era, almost 350 million years ago. They became the dominant vertebrate during the Mesozoic era.

Synapsids, Anapsids, and Diapsids

Scientists discovered that, over time, amniotes evolved into three different groups. This discovery was based on temporal holes that are found on the sides of the amniote skull.

Synapsids Reptiles that had one hole in each temporal region were synapsids. The synapsids eventually gave rise to modern mammals.

Anapsids Reptiles that have skulls with no temporal holes are anapsids. Scientists do not know why anapsids have no skull holes. Some think that they may still have the same skull anatomy as the first amniotes or that they may have lost skull holes through natural selection. The anapsids of today are turtles and tortoises, with skulls similar to the one shown in **FIGURE 26.6**.

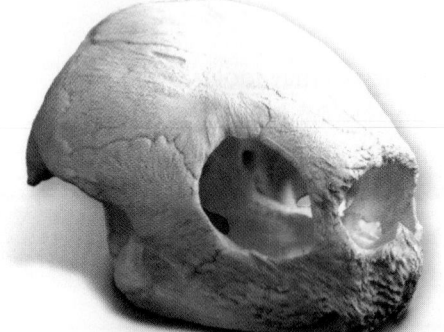

FIGURE 26.6 Turtles and tortoises are anapsids. Aside from the holes for eyes and nose, this skull of a modern turtle has no temporal holes.

AMNIOTE SKULL TYPES		
SKULL TYPE	NUMBER OF HOLES	EXAMPLE
Anapsid	0	turtles
Synapsid	1	mammals
Diapsid	2	birds, lizards, crocodilians

Diapsids Reptiles that have two holes in each temporal region, one above the other, are diapsids. Diapsid skulls came about as reptiles began to colonize land. For the next 200 million years, diapsid reptiles ruled Earth. Eventually, this group gave rise to many of the modern reptiles and birds of today.

Skull holes may have started out as a weight-reducing adaptation. Less bone would have made the skull lighter and easier to move and given more space for muscle attachments, allowing jaw muscles to get larger. The phylogenetic tree in **FIGURE 26.7** shows how the ancient and now extinct groups of reptiles may have evolved.

Diversity of Extinct Amniotes

Pelycosaurs were synapsids that first appeared during the late Carboniferous period. This group included both carnivores and herbivores. Some pelycosaurs had a distinctive "sail-back" made of elongated vertebral spines. Most pelycosaurs died in a mass extinction 245 million years ago, but some of their descendants later gave rise to the mammals.

Ichthyosaurs were some of the first diapsid reptiles. An ichthyosaur's sleek body, flipper-shaped limbs, and fleshy dorsal fin were similar to those of the modern day dolphin. Ichthyosaurs swam by beating their fishlike tails back and forth in the water, and their peglike teeth suggest that they ate fish. Fossil evidence indicates that ichthyosaurs first appeared about 250 million years ago and went extinct about 90 million years ago.

Plesiosaurs were some of the strangest prehistoric marine reptiles. They "flew" through the water like sea lions, using four limbs like elongated flippers. Some plesiosaurs had small heads and very long necks, which were likely used to help them catch fish. Others had short necks and long heads and probably chased down larger prey. Fossils show the plesiosaurs first appeared around 220 million years ago and then died out around 80 million years ago.

FIGURE 26.7 Phylogenetic Tree of Reptiles

The diversification of ancient reptiles eventually led to the evolution of modern animals.

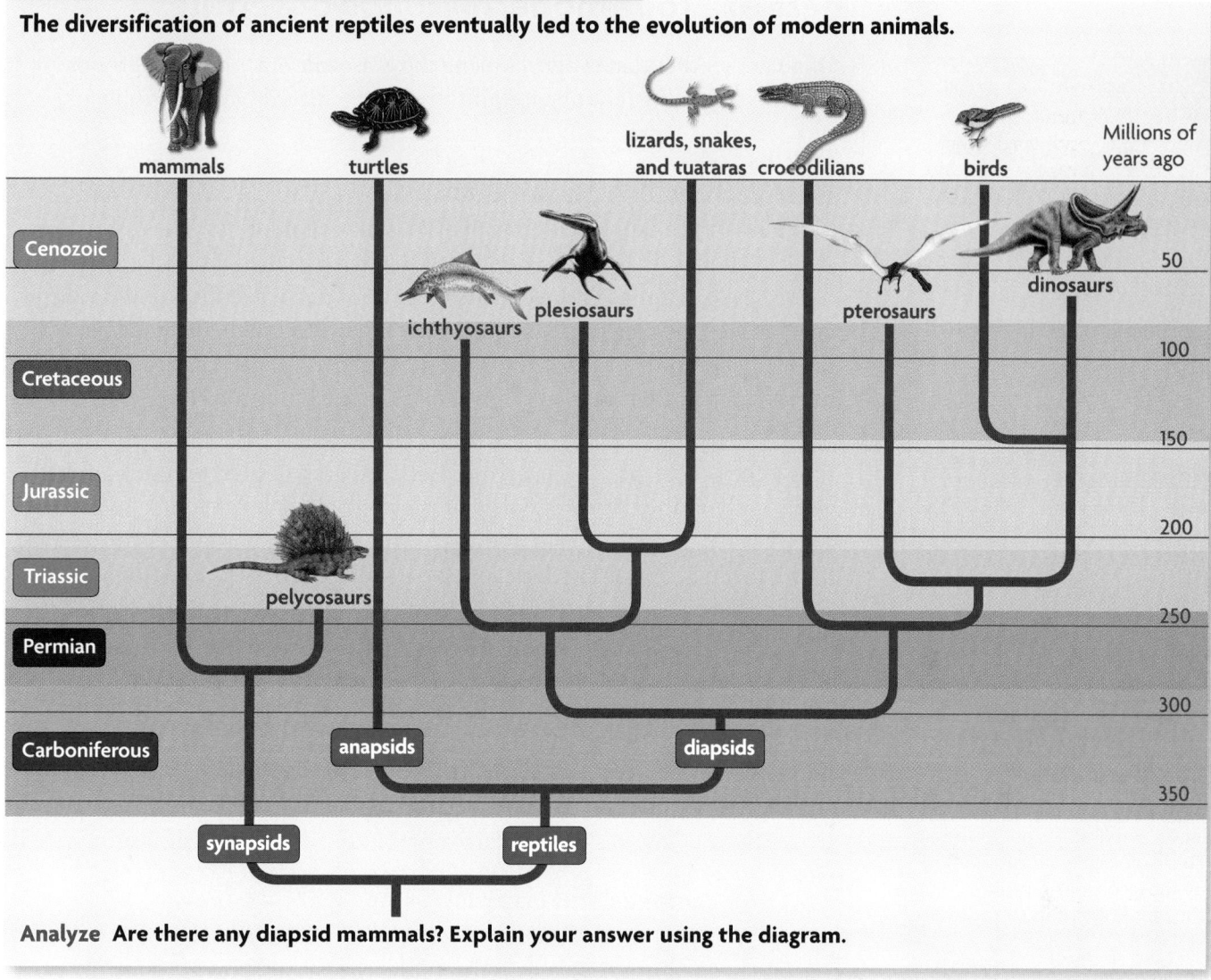

Analyze Are there any diapsid mammals? Explain your answer using the diagram.

Dinosaurs were the second great radiation of the amniote family. They appeared 230 million years ago and were the dominant land vertebrates for the next 150 million years. Many kinds of dinosaurs evolved during that time. Herbivorous species included huge sauropods, tanklike ceratopsians, and duck-billed dinosaurs. They were hunted by carnivorous theropod dinosaurs, which eventually gave rise to birds. All of the nonavian, or walking, dinosaurs went extinct 65 million years ago.

Pterosaurs were the first vertebrates to evolve powered flight. Their wings consisted of skin supported by an extremely elongated fourth finger. The earliest species, from the end of the Triassic, were small animals with long tails. Later species, such as *Pteranodon* lost their tails and grew as large as small airplanes. Recent fossils show that pterosaurs may have been covered with hair, suggesting that they were endothermic. They went extinct at the end of the Cretaceous along with the dinosaurs.

Apply How did the discovery of temporal skull holes help scientists determine phylogeny of amniotes?

Connecting CONCEPTS

Phylogeny Recall from **Chapter 17** that a phylogeny is a type of evolutionary tree that illustrates how different species are related to each other. The relationships between modern animals and ancient reptiles help scientists understand evolution.

There are four modern groups of reptiles.

Of all the reptiles that evolved during the Mesozoic era, only four groups are alive today: turtles, sphenodonts, snakes and lizards, and crocodilians.

Turtles

There are about 200 living species of turtles today. Turtles, tortoises, and terrapins are the only remaining anapsid group of amniotes. The distinctive shape of a turtle is actually a bony shell that encases the reptile's body. The domed back of a turtle's shell is called the carapace, while the smooth ventral part is called the plastron. This shell is covered with tough, flattened plates made of keratin that are fused to the turtle's rib cage and vertebrae. Many turtles can pull their head and limbs into the shell for protection.

Turtles are toothless and have sharp, horny beaks. Most turtles are omnivorous—they eat plants as well as animals. They are found in terrestrial, freshwater, and marine environments. Fully terrestrial turtles are called tortoises. They have high domed shells and thick stumpy limbs. Freshwater turtles have flatter shells. Some species have lost the bone in their shells to become "soft shell" turtles. The sea turtle in **FIGURE 26.8**, like most marine turtles, has forelimbs that are large flippers that let it "fly" underwater.

Sphenodonts

The only living sphenodonts are two species of tuatara that live on a few small islands off the coast of New Zealand. They are closely related to lizards and snakes, and look similar to a spiny iguana. Tuataras have primitive characteristics, such as a diapsid skull and an eyespot in the center of their head.

Snakes and Lizards

Snakes and lizards are very closely related and share a number of features. Snakes and lizards all shed their skin at regular intervals. They also have flexible skulls that let them capture and swallow prey larger than their head. All snakes and lizards use a highly developed organ that allows them to "taste" the air. As shown in **FIGURE 26.9**, when a snake or lizard flicks its forked tongue out of its mouth, the tongue collects particles out of the air. Particles are interpreted by a sensory receptor called the Jacobson's organ, which is found in the top of the reptile's mouth. This organ allows lizards and snakes to locate prey and avoid predators.

Most lizards are carnivorous. Small species hunt insects, but large species such as the Komodo dragon prey on mammals. Some species, such as iguanas, are strict herbivores. Snakes are a group of legless lizards. All snakes are predators. Some snakes kill their prey by constriction, wrapping their body around their prey and squeezing. Others use poisons that are injected into their prey through modified teeth.

FIGURE 26.8 Sea turtles live in tropical ocean waters all over the world.

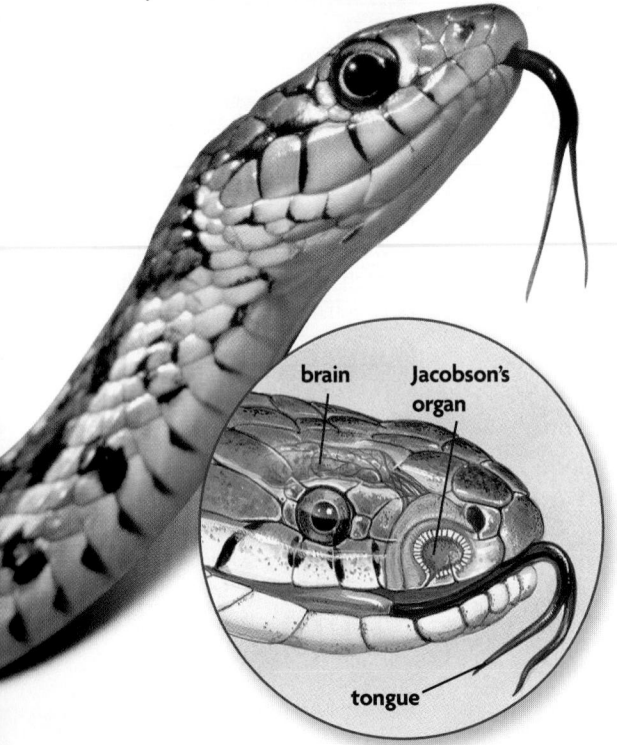

FIGURE 26.9 Snakes and lizards protrude a forked tongue to collect tiny molecules out of the air. These molecules are interpreted by the Jacobson's organ to inform the reptile about its surroundings.

brain   Jacobson's organ

tongue

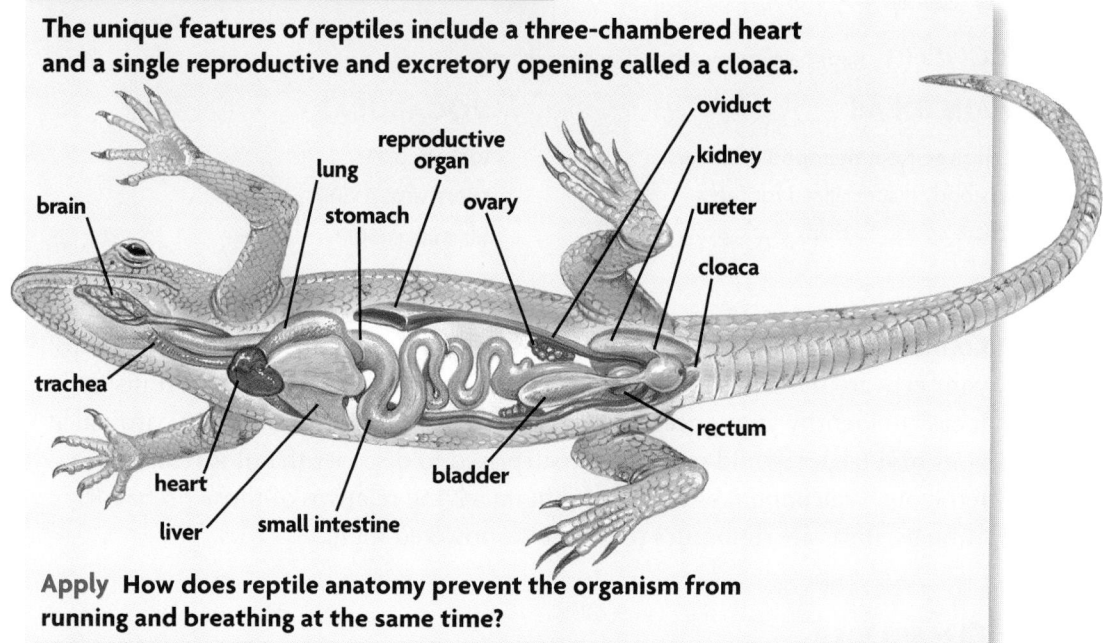

FIGURE 26.10 Reptile Anatomy

The unique features of reptiles include a three-chambered heart and a single reproductive and excretory opening called a cloaca.

brain
lung
reproductive organ
stomach
ovary
oviduct
kidney
ureter
cloaca
trachea
heart
liver
small intestine
bladder
rectum

Apply How does reptile anatomy prevent the organism from running and breathing at the same time?

Crocodilians

There are 23 species of crocodilians, including alligators, crocodiles, and caimans. They are all semiaquatic predators that live in swamps and rivers in the tropics and subtropics. They are ambush predators, waiting underwater to surprise other animals. Their sprawling resting posture makes them look slow, but they are capable of lifting up their bodies and running at up to 27 kilometers per hour (17 mph).

Crocodilians are one of two groups of archosaurs that survived the mass reptile extinction 65 million years ago. Archosaurs were a large group of reptiles that included crocodiles, dinosaurs, and modern-day birds. Based on fossil evidence, crocodilians are actually more closely related to birds than they are to lizards and snakes. Many of the body shapes and structures of ancient crocodilians are similar to the features of modern crocodilians.

Summarize What features do all reptiles share?

26.2 ASSESSMENT

ONLINE QUIZ
ClassZone.com

REVIEWING ▶ MAIN IDEAS

1. How is a **viviparous** reptile different from an **oviparous** reptile?
2. What are the major groups of extinct **reptiles**?
3. What features do modern reptiles share?

CRITICAL THINKING

4. **Classify** You find a fossil of a reptile that has a long neck and four long flippers for limbs. It is in marine sediments. To which group of ancient reptiles could it belong?
5. **Infer** Explain why there are no reptiles found in the Arctic.

Connecting CONCEPTS

6. **Amphibians** Amniotes emerge from their shell fully developed. Amphibians must go through metamorphosis to reach their adult form. What is the advantage of direct development for amniotes?

26.3 Birds

KEY CONCEPT Birds have many adaptations for flight.

MAIN IDEAS

- Birds evolved from theropod dinosaurs.
- A bird's body is specialized for flight.
- Birds have spread to many ecological niches.

VOCABULARY

airfoil, p. 799

sternum, p. 801

air sac, p. 801

MICHIGAN STANDARDS

B2.4B Describe how various organisms have developed different specializations to accomplish a particular function and yet the end result is the same (e.g., excreting nitrogenous wastes in animals, obtaining oxygen for respiration).
B2.4C Explain how different organisms accomplish the same result using different structural specializations (gills vs. lungs vs. membranes).

FIGURE 26.11 Fossil evidence of *Archaeopteryx* shows features such as feathers and a beaklike structure not seen in dinosaurs. *Archaeopteryx* is an important link between dinosaurs and modern-day birds.

Connect You may share certain features with your parents or siblings. Perhaps your eyes are the same color or your nose is the same shape. Certain traits make it easy to identify your ancestors. Birds have a bit more trouble. That cardinal at your bird feeder would probably be surprised to discover that it is related to a ferocious *Velociraptor*, but birds are the surviving relatives of those prehistoric animals. Birds are dinosaurs that evolved powered flight.

MAIN IDEA
Birds evolved from theropod dinosaurs.

Most paleontologists agree that birds are the descendants of one group of theropod dinosaurs. Theropods were bipedal, or two-legged, dinosaurs that evolved during the Triassic period of the Mesozoic era. Most were carnivorous, and some, such as *Allosaurus* and *Tyrannosaurus*, were enormous. Theropod fossils support the hypothesis that these dinosaurs are closely related to birds. They show that birds and many theropods share anatomical features, including

- hollow bones
- fused collarbones that form a V-shaped wishbone, or furcula
- rearranged muscles in the hips and legs that improve bipedal movement
- "hands" that have lost their fourth and fifth fingers
- feathers

In the 1990s scientists discovered theropod fossils with feathers. This important discovery showed that feathers did not originate as an adaptation for flight. These theropods were covered with feathers, but they did not have wings. They were running animals. This means that feathers originally had another function in the theropods. They may have been insulation that trapped air to keep the animals warm. Or they may have been used in courtship or territorial displays. As birds evolved, they used the feathers they had inherited from their theropod ancestors to form wings.

The oldest undisputed fossil bird is shown in **FIGURE 26.11**. *Archaeopteryx* was a chicken-sized animal that lived about 150 million years ago. Like all modern birds, it had feathered wings and a furcula. But it also had many reptilian features, including clawed fingers, a long tail, and teeth. Because of its features, *Archaeopteryx* was classified as a dinosaur. However, its feathers made it an important link between flightless dinosaurs and avian, or flying, dinosaurs, as well as the birds of today.

Scientists have two hypotheses for the origin of flight in birds. The "trees-down" hypothesis suggests that birds evolved from animals that used their feathers to glide down to the forest floor. In contrast, the "ground-up" hypothesis suggests that birds evolved from running animals that used their feathered arms for balance.

The fossil evidence showing a close relationship between theropods and birds tends to support the "ground-up" hypothesis. Many theropods were bipedal carnivores that hunted by running down their prey. Scientists still do not know how these dinosaurs moved from running and grabbing to flapping and flying. Some recent research suggests that small theropods could have flapped their feathered arms to run up trees and escape predators. Whether they also used those feathered arms to glide back down to the ground is unknown, but future fossil discoveries may provide an answer.

FIGURE 26.12 The broad wings of an eagle owl are adapted for silent flight, making this nocturnal bird a quiet and deadly predator.

Infer How might hollow bones have helped theropods move more efficiently?

◉ MAIN IDEA
A bird's body is specialized for flight.

Birds such as the eagle owl in **FIGURE 26.12** have many specialized adaptations for powered flight. Some of them are modifications of features inherited from their theropod ancestors. Others are unique to birds. These adaptations include

- wings that produce flight
- strong flight muscles that move the wings
- an active metabolism that provides energy to the muscles
- hollow bone structure that minimizes weight
- reproductive adaptations

Wings

Wings are structures that enable birds to fly. Bird wings are curved similar to the shape of an airplane wing. This kind of curved surface is called an airfoil. An **airfoil** is curved down on the top (convex) and curved up on the bottom (concave). The curved shape makes air move faster over the top of the airfoil than underneath it.

VISUAL VOCAB

An **airfoil** is convex on the top and concave on the bottom. Differences in air pressure above and below the airfoil create lift.

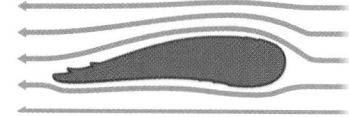

The difference in air speed above and below the airfoil produces a pressure difference that lifts the wing up. In birds, the airfoil is constructed of limbs that are homologous to human arms and covered by large feathers.

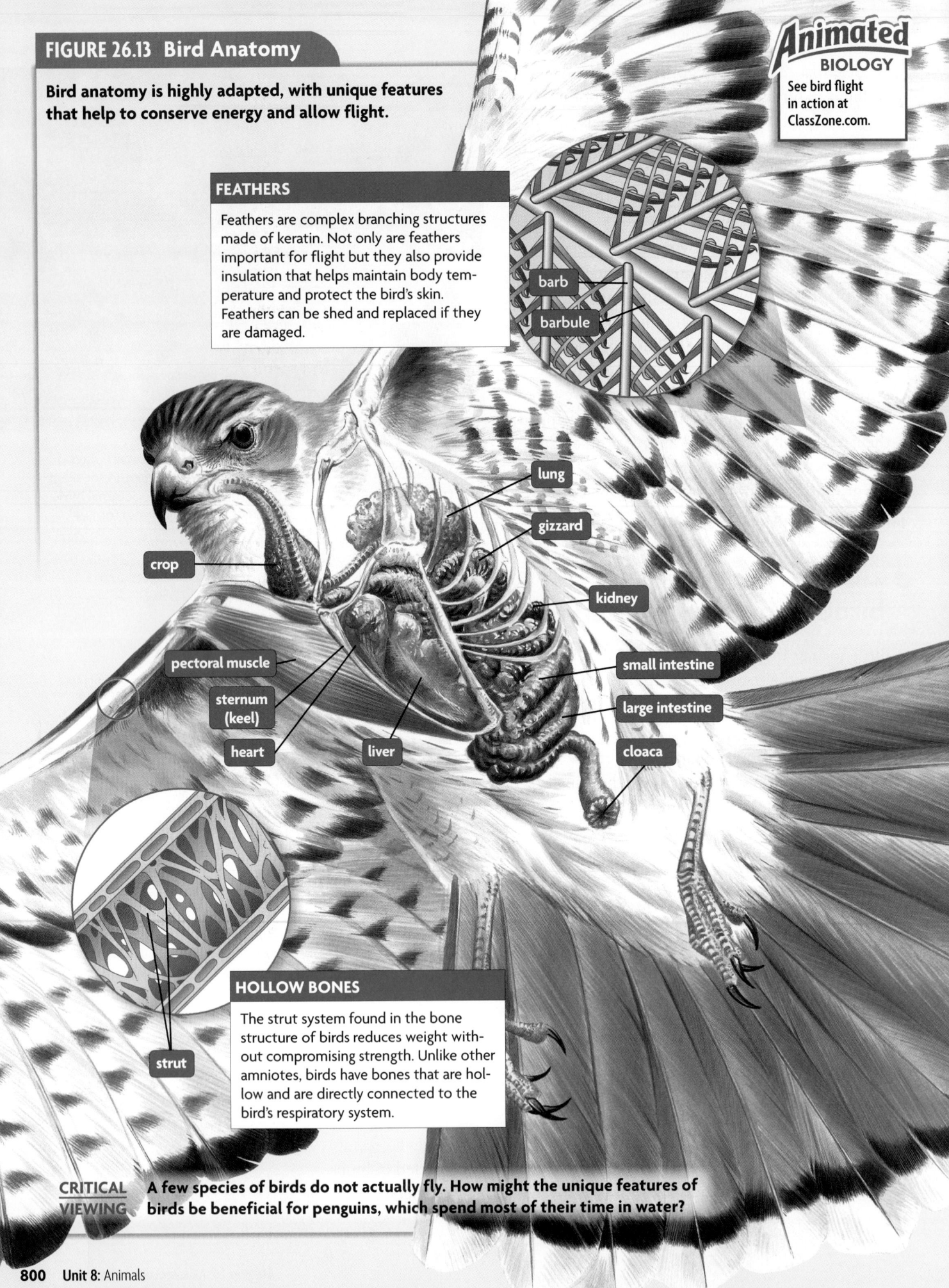

FIGURE 26.13 Bird Anatomy

Bird anatomy is highly adapted, with unique features that help to conserve energy and allow flight.

Animated BIOLOGY
See bird flight in action at ClassZone.com.

FEATHERS

Feathers are complex branching structures made of keratin. Not only are feathers important for flight but they also provide insulation that helps maintain body temperature and protect the bird's skin. Feathers can be shed and replaced if they are damaged.

barb

barbule

lung

gizzard

crop

kidney

pectoral muscle

small intestine

large intestine

sternum (keel)

heart

liver

cloaca

HOLLOW BONES

The strut system found in the bone structure of birds reduces weight without compromising strength. Unlike other amniotes, birds have bones that are hollow and are directly connected to the bird's respiratory system.

strut

CRITICAL VIEWING   A few species of birds do not actually fly. How might the unique features of birds be beneficial for penguins, which spend most of their time in water?

Muscles

A bird's chest muscles provide the power for flight. In almost all vertebrates, chest muscles attach to the arms and the breastbone, or **sternum.** But anyone who has carved a chicken knows that a bird's chest muscles are enormous. They are so large that the sternum has evolved a large keel, or ridge, that supports the muscles. The keel provides a large attachment surface for the chest muscles, and serves as an anchor that they can pull against to flap the wings.

When birds fly, their chest muscles contract to pull their wings backward and down. The downstroke moves the wings to produce lift and propel the animal forward. Deeper chest muscles contract during the upstroke, moving the wings forward and up until the bird starts another downstroke.

Metabolism

Flying takes a lot of energy. Birds are endotherms and have active metabolisms that can produce large amounts of ATP for the flight muscles. But maintaining an active metabolism during flight requires an enormous amount of oxygen. Birds meet this challenge with a respiratory system that increases the amount of oxygen they can take out of the air.

A bird's body is filled with a series of **air sacs** that connect to the lungs. Air sacs store air as the bird breathes. During flight, movements of the furcula help push air through the air sacs and lungs. Inhaled air travels through the lungs and air sacs in such a way that oxygen-rich air is always available. In other vertebrates, oxygen-rich air mixes with oxygen-poor air inside the lungs during respiration. But because only oxygen-rich air flows through a bird's lungs, the amount of oxygen that can be absorbed into the bloodstream is dramatically increased and maximizes a bird's metabolism.

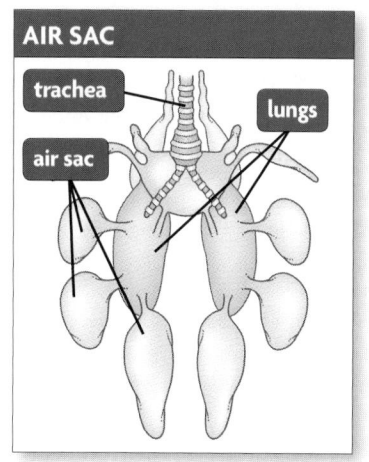

AIR SAC

trachea

lungs

air sac

TAKING NOTES

Use a main idea diagram to take notes on how the features of birds help them to achieve flight.

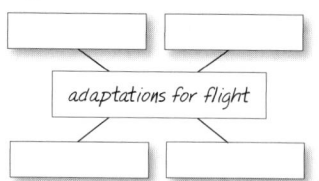

adaptations for flight

Connecting CONCEPTS

Cellular Respiration Birds require large amounts of ATP to provide the energy needed for flight. Recall from **Chapter 4** that cellular respiration needs oxygen and glucose to produce ATP. Air sacs provide a great deal of oxygen, but birds must also consume large amounts of food to support their active metabolism.

Bone Structure

The structure of a bird's skeletal system is different than that of other amniotes. Birds have evolved bones that are hollow. As you can see in **FIGURE 26.13,** inside bird bones, a system of struts and support structures maintain the bird's bones to meet the demanding requirements of flight. In all birds, many bones are connected to the air sacs, and air fills the cavities in the bone, aiding in flight. This adaption further increases the amount of air in a bird's body, and makes flying easier. It also helps to decrease the mass of the bird. In fact, a bird's skeleton makes up only five percent of its overall body mass.

Reproductive Adaptations

The reproductive organs of both male and female birds are only active for the two to three months of the mating season. During the rest of the year, the unused organs shrink to reduce the mass of the bird. This weight-reducing adaptation serves to decrease the amount of energy needed for flight.

Summarize **How are bird bodies adapted to flying?**

Comparing Feathers

Feathers are features that allow birds to adapt to a unique way of life. In this lab, you will examine three different types of feathers.

SKILL Observing

PROBLEM How do the structures and functions of different feathers compare?

PROCEDURE

1. Obtain a large quill feather and study its overall shape, structure and weight. Draw the features.

2. Examine the central shaft of the feather. Hold the end of the shaft with one hand. With your other hand, gently try to bend the upper third of the feather without breaking it.

3. Observe the vane, the flat part of the feather on either side of the shaft. Separate some of the barbs of a vane. Join them again with your fingers.

4. Hold the end of the shaft and wave the feather so that it catches the air. Note the resistance you feel as you move the feather through the air.

5. Repeat steps 1–4 with the contour and down feathers.

ANALYZE AND CONCLUDE

1. **Analyze** What is the function of the shaft?

2. **Analyze** How are down feathers different from contour and quill feathers?

3. **Infer** Describe the function of each type of feather.

4. **Apply** What characteristics make quill feathers well suited for their function?

5. **Apply** How are contour feathers designed to make a bird streamlined?

6. **Infer** How do you think the structure of down feathers helps to insulate a bird?

MATERIALS
- purchased quill feather
- purchased contour feather
- purchased down feather

▶ MAIN IDEA

Birds have spread to many ecological niches.

Birds first evolved during the Mesozoic era, but most Mesozoic bird species went extinct with the dinosaurs. All modern birds are the descendants of the one group that survived the mass extinction. This group diversified into the more than 9000 species of bird we see today. Through natural selection, birds have adapted to many different habitats and methods of feeding. This has led to visible physical differences in the shapes of the wings, beaks, and feet.

Differences in Wing Shape

The shape of a bird's wing reflects the way it flies. Most birds have short, broad wings that allow them to maneuver very easily. In contrast, albatrosses and gulls, such as the blue-footed booby in **FIGURE 26.14,** have long, narrow wings specialized for soaring long distances over water. Hawks, eagles, and condors have wide, broad wings specialized for soaring at low speeds over land. Many types of songbirds, including woodpeckers, finches, and robins, have stout, tapered wings that help them to maneuver through tight spaces. Penguins have short wings adapted to "fly" in water. Flightless birds, such as ostriches and emus, have wings that are too small to let them fly at all.

Differences in Beak Shape

The shape of a bird's beak reflects how it eats. A bird's beak is a sheath of keratin that covers the jaw bones. As Charles Darwin observed in the many finch species of the Galapagos Islands, beak shapes are adapted for many different functions. For example, the blue-footed booby uses its long, spearlike beak to capture fish on the bird's dives into the ocean. The beak of the bald eagle is hooked to tear flesh from its prey. Birds that catch insects often have thin, pointed bills. Woodpeckers have beaks like chisels to pry insects out of trees. Other birds, such as hummingbirds, have long, thin beaks that can reach deep into flowers for nectar. Pelicans have large pouches of skin attached to their beaks for scooping fish out of the water. Parrots use their thick, strong beaks for ripping open fruits and cracking nuts.

Differences in Foot Shape

With few exceptions, bird feet have four toes. But as **FIGURE 26.14** shows, their feet can look very different. The blue-footed booby and other aquatic birds have webbed feet, with skin connecting the toes to form paddles. Predatory birds such as the bald eagle have heavy claws that they use to capture and kill prey. Birds that live in trees have feet that can grab onto branches and tree bark. Woodpeckers, for example, have two toes pointing forward and two pointing backward, which lets them cling to vertical tree trunks. Sparrows and crows have three toes pointing forward and one pointing backward, which lets them perch on horizontal tree limbs.

Infer Where would you expect to find a bird with webbed feet and very long and narrow wings?

FIGURE 26.14 Birds' features are specifically adapted to their habitat and niche. Natural selection has led to a wide array of wings, beaks, and feet.

blue-footed booby

bald eagle

green woodpecker

26.3 ASSESSMENT

ONLINE QUIZ ClassZone.com

REVIEWING ▶ MAIN IDEAS

1. What are three anatomical features that birds share with their theropod ancestors?

2. What adaptations do birds have that help them with flight?

3. Describe how the wings, beak, and feet of an eagle are well adapted to its niche.

CRITICAL THINKING

4. **Analyze** The red-headed wood-pecker has an unusually long tongue and a stout, pointed beak. How are these features related to the woodpecker's feeding habits?

5. **Connect** Reptiles and birds are closely related. Why is the evolution from being an ectotherm to being an endotherm so important for bird evolution?

Connecting CONCEPTS

6. **Selection** Male cardinals have bright red feathers, whereas females have dull brown feathers. What type of selection likely caused these differences?

MATERIALS

- balance
- 100 mL graduated cylinder
- 50 mL water
- boiled chicken bone (flightless bird)
- boiled duck or turkey bone (flying bird)
- boiled cow bone (mammal)
- hammer
- hand lens

PROCESS SKILLS

- **Observing**
- **Measuring**
- **Analyzing**

B1.1C Conduct scientific investigations using appropriate tools and techniques (e.g., selecting an instrument that measures the desired quantity—length, volume, weight, time interval, temperature—with the appropriate level of precision).

A Bird's Airframe

Wings were an important adaptation for birds. The structure of wings gave birds the ability to fly and move great distances in search of resources. But for some birds, flight was not necessary for survival. In this lab, you will investigate the differences and similarities between flying and flightless birds, and compare them with mammals.

PROBLEM Besides wings, what major adaptation is beneficial for flight?

PROCEDURE

1. Measure the mass of each bone (chicken, duck, cow) using the balance. Record the mass for each.

2. Pour the water in the graduated cylinder and note the volume. Add one of the bones to the cylinder and record the volume again. To find the volume of the bone, subtract the original volume from the second reading.

3. Repeat step 2 for each bone used.

4. Attempt to break the bone by hand and note how easy or difficult it is. (If you can't break the bone by hand, it is okay.)

   Caution: Wearing your safety goggles, carefully break each experimental bone with the hammer (watch out for flying pieces).

5. Examine the internal structure of each bone with the hand lens. Make a labeled drawing for each bone.

ANALYZE AND CONCLUDE

1. **Predict** Which bone do you think has the greatest density? Which bone is the least dense?

2. **Calculate** Calculate the densities for each bone (density = $\frac{mass}{volume}$).

3. **Apply** What can you conclude about bone density and the ability to fly?

4. **Observe** How does the structure of the flightless bird bone compare with that of the flying bird bone? with the cow bone?

5. **Infer** What bones are easier to break by hand than others? Explain why you think this is true.

6. **Analyze** What features of the bird bones might be adaptations for flight?

7. **Contrast** Were there any significant differences between bones from flying birds and those from flightless birds? Why might one bird be able to fly while another cannot fly?

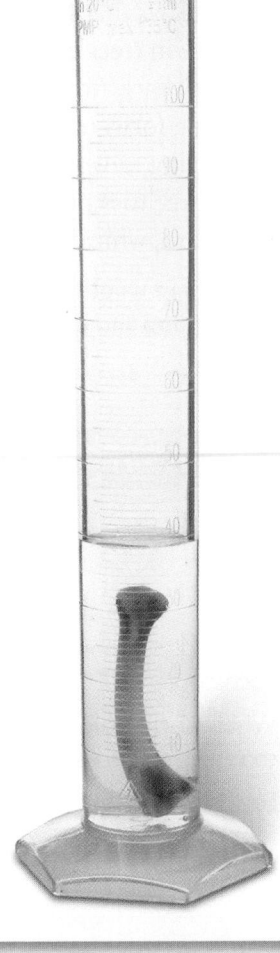

100 mL graduated cylinder

26.4

Mammals

KEY CONCEPT Evolutionary adaptations allowed mammals to succeed dinosaurs as a dominant terrestrial vertebrate.

▶ MAIN IDEAS

- All mammals share several common characteristics.
- Modern mammals are divided into three main groups.

VOCABULARY

mammal, p. 805
mammary gland, p. 806
monotreme, p. 807
marsupial, p. 808
eutherian, p. 809

MICHIGAN STANDARDS

B2.4B Describe how various organisms have developed different specializations to accomplish a particular function and yet the end result is the same (e.g., excreting nitrogenous wastes in animals, obtaining oxygen for respiration).

B2.4C Explain how different organisms accomplish the same result using different structural specializations (gills vs. lungs vs. membranes).

Connect Each time you get your hair cut, you are having a feature clipped off that sets humans and other mammals apart from reptiles, birds, amphibians, and fish. In addition to hair, what other traits make mammals unique?

▶ MAIN IDEA

All mammals share several common characteristics.

All **mammals** are active, large-brained, endothermic animals with complex social, feeding, and reproductive behaviors. Modern mammals—such as the bat in **FIGURE 26.15**—come in many shapes, but they share a set of four anatomical characteristics.

- hair
- mammary glands
- a middle ear containing three bones
- a jaw that lets them chew their food

Mammals are as ancient as dinosaurs and are the only group of synapsids alive today. They are descended from a group of carnivorous synapsids. Many of the characteristics we now see only in mammals were actually inherited from these reptilian ancestors. Earth's first mammals appeared more than 200 million years ago, when dinosaurs were already on their way to becoming the top predators and herbivores on the planet. During the Cretaceous period, while *Tyrannosaurus rex* was hunting *Triceratops,* tiny rodentlike mammals had found a niche as nocturnal insect eaters.

FIGURE 26.15 This Yuma myotis bat has all of the basic mammalian features. Bats are the only mammals that can fly.

Fossil evidence suggests that early mammals had long noses and short legs. They may have looked similar to modern-day shrews. They probably lived underground, reproduced by laying eggs, and nursed their young on nutrient-rich milk produced by highly adapted glands. The ability to regulate their own body temperature was an important adaptation that gave mammals a distinct advantage over reptiles. When the dinosaurs went extinct, mammals survived and filled their vacant ecological niches. In time, mammals succeeded dinosaurs as a dominant terrestrial life form.

Connecting CONCEPTS

Natural Selection All mammals have hair or, more accurately, hair follicles. Whales are mammals, but most adult whales do not have hair. Recall from **Chapter 10** that natural selection favors traits that increase the fitness of individuals. In the underwater environment of whales, hair causes resistance and may be obstructions in catching prey, thus making them less likely to survive and reproduce.

Hair

Mammals are furry. Most species are covered with a layer of hair that helps them retain heat. Each hair is a long, thin shaft of dead, keratinized cells that grows out of a follicle in the skin. The hair traps a layer of air next to the skin, which insulates the animal, much like a down vest insulates you. When mammals get cold, muscles around the follicles pull the hair upright. When you get "goose bumps," your insulating air layer is thickening to help keep you warm.

Hair also has other functions. Anyone who has watched a frightened cat fluff up knows that mammals can use hair for behavioral displays. Patterns of pigmented hairs provide camouflage for many mammals. Porcupines and hedgehogs have modified hairs that form stiff protective quills. And many mammals have long, stiff whiskers that collect sensory information. Even mammals that have lost most of their hair, such as whales, retain some sensory bristles.

Mammary Glands

All mammals take care of their babies after they are born. Females feed them a specialized fluid called milk. **Mammary glands** are specialized glands that produce milk. Milk contains water, sugars, protein, fats, minerals, and antibodies that help young animals grow and develop.

Mammary glands are unique to mammals. They are present in both males and females but produce milk only in females. Some mammals, such as pigs or dogs, have a series of glands along the belly. Other mammals have glands only in specific areas, such as udders in a cow's groin or the pair of glands on a primate's chest. Mammary glands contain masses of milk-producing tissues that are connected to a series of ducts. The ducts bring milk to the surface of the skin. In most mammals, the ducts empty into nipples or teats that young mammals, such as the piglets in **FIGURE 26.16**, can hold in the mouth and suckle.

FIGURE 26.16 Mammals produce milk in mammary glands to provide nutrients to their offspring. These piglets will nurse from their mother for three to eight weeks.

Middle Ear

Mammals have three small bones in their middle ear. One of the bones, the stapes, is also found in other tetrapods. The other two, the malleus and incus, are unique to mammals. They were derived from reptilian jaw bones.

The top part of the hyoid arch became modified to form the stapes in early tetrapods. Bones that supported the jaws in fish became bones that transferred vibrations to the inner ear in tetrapods. A similar shift, illustrated in **FIGURE 26.17**, occurred as mammals evolved from their reptilian ancestors.

Synapsids such as the pelycosaur had jaws that were made of many bones fused together. The middle ear of these reptiles contained only one bone, the stapes, which transmitted sound to the inner ear, where it was converted to nerve impulses and interpreted by the brain. This is the same configuration of bones we see in reptiles today.

Over time, the formation of these bones changed. Two bones, the quadrate and the articular bones, once formed the joint between the jaws of reptiles. These bones evolved to serve a different function—hearing. In mammals, the quadrate and articular bones are now tiny and are incorporated into the middle ear as the malleus and the incus. Sounds collected in the ear canal vibrate the eardrum. These vibrations are transferred through the malleus and incus bones to the stapes. These tiny vibrations are converted into nerve impulses in the inner ear and then interpreted by the brain. The ability to detect small vibrations allowed mammals to hear higher-pitched sounds.

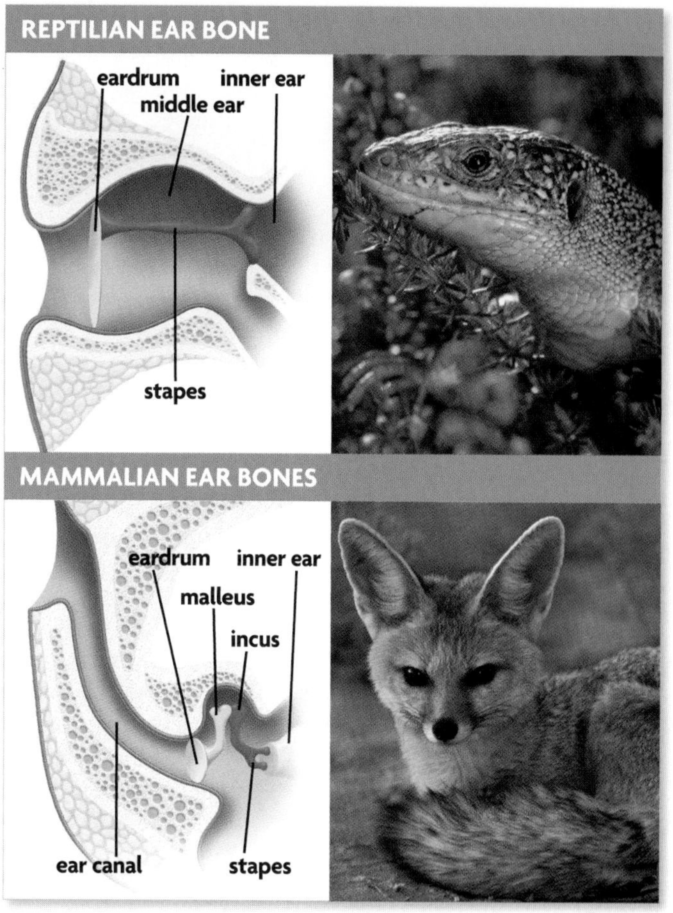

Chewing

Mammals developed the ability to chew their food. Amphibians, reptiles, and birds usually bite off large chunks of food or swallow it whole. Most of their mechanical processing occurs inside their digestive tract. Mammals, in contrast, start to break up their food as soon as it enters the mouth.

A set of adaptations in the mammalian jaw makes chewing possible. While food is in the mouth, a secondary palate separates the nasal and oral cavities. It keeps the passages for air and food separate, so mammals can chew and breathe at the same time. In addition, complex muscles can move the jaw from side to side.

Infer Hair was an important adaptation for mammals. How might hair and other adaptations have enabled mammals to survive where reptiles could not?

REPTILIAN EAR BONE

eardrum inner ear
middle ear
stapes

MAMMALIAN EAR BONES

eardrum inner ear
malleus
incus
ear canal stapes

FIGURE 26.17 As mammals evolved, the structures of the inner ear changed. The incus and malleus bones that were once part of reptilian jaw structures evolved in ways that enhanced hearing.

▶ **MAIN IDEA**

Modern mammals are divided into three main groups.

More than 4500 species of mammal are alive today. They can be classified into three groups: monotremes, marsupials, and eutherian mammals.

Monotremes

The **monotremes** are mammals that lay eggs. They are remnants of an ancient group of mammals that have characteristics of both mammals and reptiles. The group split off from the line that led to the other living mammals sometime during the Mesozoic. Their fossils suggest that they once lived throughout the Southern Hemisphere. But today only three species of monotreme survive. The duck-billed platypus is found only in Australia and Tasmania. Two types of echidna live in Australia, Tasmania, and New Guinea.

VOCABULARY

The name *monotreme* comes from a Greek word that means "single opening," referring to the cloaca opening, which these mammals have in common with birds and reptiles.

FIGURE 26.18 The shovel-like bill of the duck-billed platypus is tightly packed with nerve endings. The platypus uses this bill to scrape the bottom of rivers and lakes in search of food.

Monotremes such as the platypus in **FIGURE 26.18** have a mix of ancestral mammalian and reptilian features. Monotremes have retained reptilian characteristics such as

- a sprawling posture
- a single external opening, called the cloaca, for their urinary, digestive, and reproductive tracts
- amniotic eggs with leathery shells that develop outside the body

Monotremes also have characteristic mammalian features, including mammary glands. When monotreme babies hatch, their mothers feed them milk. But monotremes do not have nipples. Their babies lick milk from pools on their mother's belly.

Marsupials

Kangaroos, wombats, koalas, and opossums are a few of the 282 living species of marsupial. **Marsupials** are mammals that give birth to immature, underdeveloped live young that grow to maturity inside a marsupium, or pouch. After fertilization, marsupial embryos begin to develop internally, attached to a placenta that exchanges nutrients and wastes with the mother. But the amount of time the embryo develops inside the mother is very short. Most marsupial species give birth only a few weeks after fertilization. The immature babies, such as the one seen in **FIGURE 26.19,** attach themselves to a nipple inside the marsupium and nurse for up to six months before emerging from their mother's pouch.

FIGURE 26.19 The red kangaroo of Australia gives birth to tiny babies that develop within a pouch in the mother's abdomen. Inside the pouch, the infant attaches to a mammary gland, where it will stay until it is mature.

Fossil evidence shows marsupials once lived all over the world. They have gone extinct over most of their former range. Most living species are found only in Australia and New Guinea. A few live in South America. One species, the Virginia opossum, lives in North America. Australian marsupials have diversified into many forms, and there are many examples of convergent evolution between these marsupials and eutherian mammals. In each case, the animals share similar ecological roles. For example, Australia is home to mouselike, molelike, anteating, and gliding marsupials that are physically similar to unrelated mice, moles, anteaters, and flying squirrels.

Eutherian Mammals

All the mammals most familiar to you are eutherians. **Eutherian** mammals give birth to live young that have completed fetal development. Eutherian mammals are commonly called placental mammals, but this term is misleading because most marsupials also use a placenta during embryo development. In most eutherian development, an embryo is attached to the mother's uterine wall. The connection between the fetus and the mother forms an organ called the placenta. Through the placenta, the mother delivers oxygen and nutrients to the embryo and removes waste products. The placenta only forms during gestation and leaves the mother's body following birth. The placenta is the only example of a disposable organ.

Eutherian gestation lasts longer than in marsupials—often months—and the babies are born at a more advanced stage of development. In some species, including the Bengal tiger in **FIGURE 26.20**, newborns are still relatively helpless and need extensive parental care until they can survive on their own. In others, such as deer or horses, the time shortly after birth is when the newborn is most vulnerable to predators, so it is important that they are able to get up and run within hours of birth.

After the extinction of the dinosaurs, eutherians quickly filled vacant ecological niches, and the modern groups of mammals appeared quickly. Rodents and carnivores appeared about 55 million years ago, and the first known species of bat, elephant, manatee, and horse appeared soon afterwards. Modern eutherians include fast carnivores such as cheetahs, and massive herbivores such as elephants. Three groups of aquatic eutherians—whales, manatees, and seals—evolved from land-dwelling mammals. Bats evolved powered flight. And one group of primates, the humans, evolved the ability to think about their ancestors.

FIGURE 26.20 The cubs of this Bengal tiger will stay with their mother for up to 18 months until they are able to hunt on their own. Many eutherian mammals care for their young after birth.

To find out more about mammals, visit scilinks.org.
Keycode: MLB026

Compare and Contrast Compare and contrast the advantages and disadvantages of marsupial and eutherian mammal reproduction.

26.4 ASSESSMENT

ONLINE QUIZ ClassZone.com

REVIEWING ▶ MAIN IDEAS

1. What features make **mammals** different from reptiles?

2. How does fetal development differ among the three living groups of mammals?

CRITICAL THINKING

3. **Summarize** How did the mass extinction that ended the reptile reign help lead to today's mammal diversity?

4. **Classify** **Monotremes** were confusing to early scientists because they had both reptilian and mammalian features. How might scientists have classified monotremes differently?

Connecting CONCEPTS

5. **Ecology** A sea turtle may lay up to 200 eggs in a nest, then leave and return to the ocean. When the young turtles hatch they must fend for themselves. How do mammals differ in the number of offspring produced and in the role of parental care of offspring?

Use these inquiry-based labs and online activities to deepen your understanding of amniotes.

INVESTIGATION

The Parts of an Egg

Birds, some reptiles, and even a few mammals lay eggs. In this lab, you will dissect and identify the parts of an egg.

SKILL Observing

PROBLEM What are the parts of an egg, and what are their functions?

PROCEDURE

1. Use colored pencils to illustrate and label the structures you observe.

2. With the various dissecting tools, carefully chip away at the eggshell without breaking the delicate membranes beneath the shell or the yolk. Make observations with the hand lens and record them.

3. In an unfertilized egg, you will find several structures, including the vitelline membrane, which surrounds the yolk; a white spot on the yolk called the germinal disk; and two cordlike strands on either side of the yolk, called chalazae.

4. In a fertilized egg, you may find an embryo attached to the yolk and two additional membranes within the yolk: the amnion and the allantois. Surrounding the yolk is chorion.

5. Use the Egg Drawing to identify and illustrate additional structures.

6. When you have identified all structures and investigated both fertilized and unfertilized eggs, dispose of the eggs and wash your hands.

ANALYZE AND CONCLUDE

1. **Infer** What do you think would happen to the yolk if the egg were to become fertilized?

2. **Infer** What is the function of the vitelline membrane and the albumen? Explain.

MATERIALS

- chicken egg
- dissecting tray
- Egg Drawing
- colored pencils
- fine scissors
- dissecting needle
- dissecting forceps
- hand lens

INVESTIGATION

Migration and Range

Each year, when the days begin to get shorter and the temperature begins to drop, you may notice flocks of birds flying across the sky. The seasonal movement of birds is called migration. Birds use a great deal of energy to migrate.

Tiny ruby-throated hummingbirds, for example, spend much of the spring and summer in the eastern United States and Canada. But each year, they make an incredible migration, flying south around the Gulf of Mexico to Central America, and some go as far south as Panama. Compare this to the Arctic tern, which travels over 32,000 kilometers (20,000 mi) per year.

In this activity, you will research aspects of bird migration.

SKILL Researching

MATERIALS
- pencil
- North America map

PROBLEM Why do birds migrate?

PROCEDURE
Choose three of the following questions to research and help explain bird migration.

1. Why do birds migrate?
2. How do birds know when to start migrating?
3. How do migrating birds navigate?
4. What methods do scientists use to monitor bird migration?
5. What problems do migrating birds face?
6. What are the major routes of bird migrations in North America? On the attached map, shade in areas of major flyways over the United States.

ANIMATED BIOLOGY
Beak Shape and Diet

The shape of a bird's beak allows it to take advantage of specific food sources. Examine a set of bird images and use the shape of each beak as a clue to identify the food source.

WEBQUEST

There are seven species of sea turtles on Earth; all are endangered or threatened. In this WebQuest, you will explore the threats sea turtles face and the actions people are taking to save them. Find out if we can reverse the sea turtles' paths to extinction.

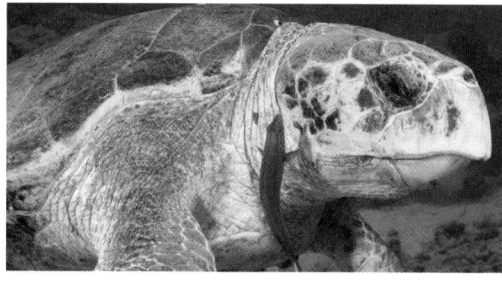

DATA ANALYSIS ONLINE

Internal body temperature can provide information about an unknown amniote. Graph and compare body temperatures of four hypothetical animals over a range of environmental temperatures. Use data in the graphs to make inferences about the animals.

26.1 Amniotes

Reptiles, birds, and mammals are amniotes. Organisms that develop inside an amniotic sac are called amniotes. Inside this sac, an embryo is provided with the necessary nutrients to help it develop and prepare for life. Amniotes pump blood through pulmonary and systemic circuits and use lungs to exchange essential gases with the environment and provide for the body. In ectotherms, the external environment plays an important role in maintaining body temperature, while endotherms control their body temperature by regulating their metabolism.

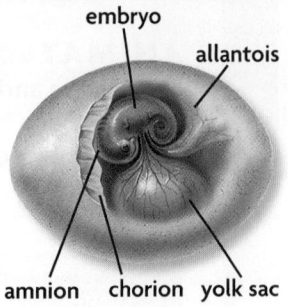

embryo
allantois
amnion   chorion   yolk sac

26.2 Reptiles

Reptiles were the first amniotes. Reptiles come in many shapes and sizes, but all have a three-chambered heart and are ectotherms. Oviparous reptiles lay eggs externally, and viviparous reptiles retain eggs internally to full development. Scientists have traced the ancestors of modern reptiles based on skull anatomy and have determined how modern birds, reptiles, and mammals are descended from ancient reptiles. Today, turtles, sphenodonts, snakes and lizards, and crocodilians are the major reptile groups.

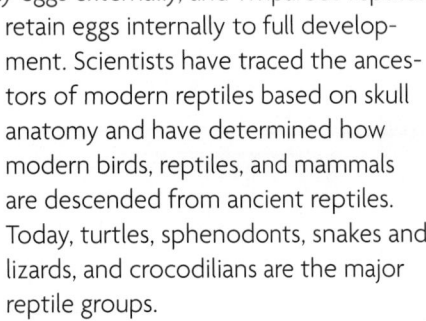

26.3 Birds

Birds have many adaptations for flight. All birds share unique features such as hollow bones, a highly modified circulatory system, and feathers. Bird wings have a convex curved shape, called an airfoil, to enable flight. Their strong chest muscles are attached to a large sternum, or keel. Birds have a very high metabolism and a unique one-way breathing system that is highly efficient. Birds are directly descended from dinosaurs. Birds come in many shapes and sizes, and features such as wings, beak, and feet are highly adapted to each species' niche.

26.4 Mammals

Evolutionary adaptations allowed mammals to succeed dinosaurs as a dominant terrestrial vertebrate. Mammals evolved while dinosaurs were walking Earth. After the dinosaurs went extinct, many new species of mammals evolved and filled the vacant niches. Mammals share four features—hair, mammary glands, a modified middle ear, and a jaw that lets them chew food. Mammals are endotherms, and hair plays an important role in keeping their body temperature stable. Mammary glands produce nutrient-rich milk, which is the primary food source for growing infant mammals. There are three major groups of mammals: monotremes, marsupials, and eutherians.

Synthesize Your Notes

Concept Map Use a concept map like the one below to summarize distinctive amniote characteristics.

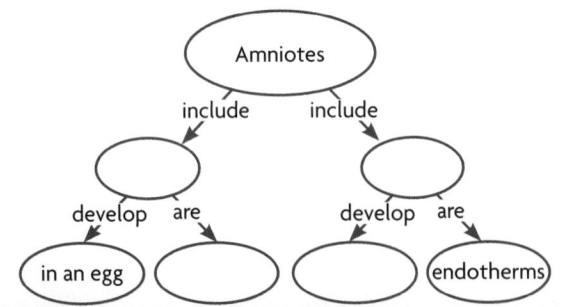

Amniotes
include   include
develop   are   develop   are
in an egg   endotherms

Main Idea Web Use a main idea web like the one below to summarize the features of mammals, birds, and reptiles.

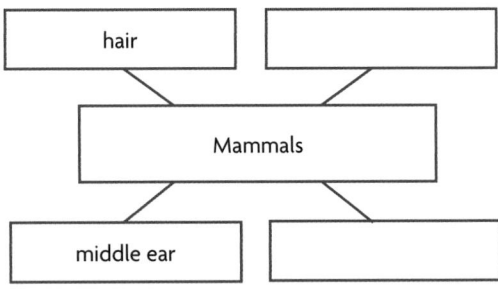

hair
Mammals
middle ear

Chapter Assessment

Chapter Vocabulary

26.1 pulmonary circuit, p. 789
systemic circuit, p. 789
ectotherm, p. 791
endotherm, p. 791

26.2 reptile, p. 793
oviparous, p. 793
viviparous, p. 793

26.3 airfoil, p. 799
sternum, p. 801
air sac, p. 801

26.4 mammal, p. 805
mammary gland, p. 806
monotreme, p. 807
marsupial, p. 808
eutherian, p. 809

Reviewing Vocabulary

Vocabulary Connections

Write a sentence or two to clearly explain how the vocabulary terms in this chapter are connected. For example, for the terms *mammal* and *mammary gland,* you could write, "The mammary gland is one of the unique characteristics of a mammal."

1. endotherm, mammal
2. reptile, viviparous
3. marsupial, eutherian

Greek and Latin Word Origins

Use the definitions of the word parts to answer the following questions.

Part	Meaning
pulmo-	lung
endo-	inner
-parous	to give birth

4. Explain why the prefix *pulmo-* is used to describe blood circuits.
5. Why is the prefix *endo-* used to describe the temperature regulation strategy of mammals and birds?
6. How is the meaning of the suffix *-parous* related to its use in the word *oviparous*?

Compare and Contrast

Describe one similarity and one difference between the two terms in each of the following pairs.

7. pulmonary circuit, systemic circuit
8. oviparous, viviparous
9. endotherm, ectotherm

Reviewing MAIN IDEAS

10. Name the four membranes found in an amniotic egg and explain the function of each.

11. Describe one similarity and one difference between the functions of a three-chambered heart and those of a four-chambered heart.

12. The desert tortoise, an ectotherm, spends as much as 95 percent of its time in underground burrows. Even in a predator-free environment, why might it have to do this?

13. Birds live in hot deserts and in Antarctica. How is it possible for birds to live in hot and frigid environments where reptiles cannot survive?

14. What are two ways that reptiles can reproduce?

15. Summarize the relationships between modern birds, reptiles, and mammals and their ancient ancestors.

16. Compare how snakes and lizards find prey with how crocodiles find prey.

17. What five pieces of evidence indicate that birds evolved from theropod dinosaurs?

18. What is the sternum? How does it help make flight possible for birds?

19. How is the reproductive system of a bird adapted for flight?

20. What three parts of a bird's body can indicate what ecological niche the bird fills?

21. How is the mammalian middle ear different from that of reptiles?

22. How does development differ among the three groups of mammals?

23. Analyze A person goes out for a jog wearing a jacket because the morning is cool. After about 15 minutes, the person feels very warm and has to take off the jacket, even though the temperature hasn't changed. Explain what is happening.

24. Classify Imagine that a new animal has been discovered in the rain forest. It has four limbs and a tail. Scientists observe that it can swallow prey larger than its head. It gives birth to live young. Based on this information, how would you classify this animal? Explain your answer.

25. Apply Explain why the number of native reptile species decreases as you move away from Earth's equator.

26. Analyze Feathers are one of the most important adaptations for birds. Why are feathers a more useful adaptation for flying than hair?

27. Infer Elephants and leopards both live in Africa, where it is hot. But elephants have very little hair, and leopards have a full coat of hair. Explain why this might be.

28. Analyze Though it is bad manners, why is it possible for a person to talk while chewing a mouthful of food?

Interpreting Visuals

Use the following illustration to answer the next three questions.

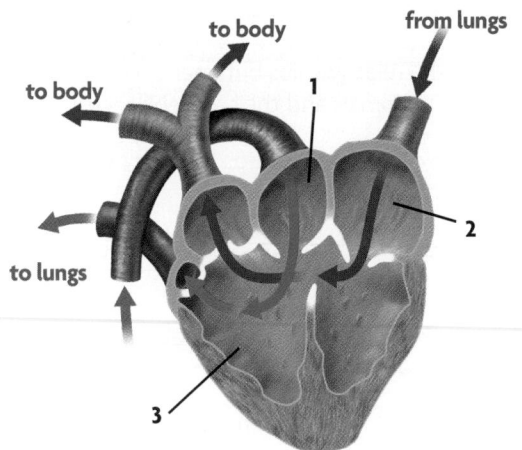

29. Analyze Blood coming from the lungs enters which part of this heart? Give the number and identify the part.

30. Analyze Blood going to the body comes from which part of the heart? Give the number and identify the part.

31. Synthesize Is this a three-chambered heart or a four-chambered heart? Explain how you know.

Analyzing Data

The table below shows the weight loss of two box turtles during hibernation. A box turtle should lose only about 1 percent of its body weight during each month of hibernation and no more than 5 percent during the entire hibernating period. Use the data to answer the next two questions.

WEIGHT LOSS DURING HIBERNATION					
Turtle	**Nov**	**Dec**	**Jan**	**Feb**	**Mar**
No. 1	600g	594g	588g	582g	576g
No. 2	600g	590g	585g	580g	576g

32. Graph Which type of graph would best represent both sets of data in the table? Why?

33. Evaluate Based on the differences in mass over the course of hibernation, which turtle will be healthier at the end of hibernation? Explain your reasoning.

Connecting CONCEPTS

34. Write a Script Birds, reptiles, and mammals coexist in many environments on Earth. But many times their paths cross and confrontations occur. Perhaps while a lion is feeding, a vulture may fly down to try and get a bite to eat, or maybe a bird's nest is being invaded by a reptile. Choose a place where two very different amniotes might interact, and write a script of their conversation. Using what you have learned about birds, reptiles, and mammals and how they function, have them discuss advantages and disadvantages of each other's lifestyles and how their conflict could be resolved.

35. Apply Look again at the picture of the tarsier on page 787 and read the description. Despite body parts that might remind you of other types of animals, why are scientists sure that the tarsier is a mammal?

MICHIGAN STANDARDS-BASED ASSESSMENT

✓ **Test Practice**
For more test practice, go to ClassZone.com.

1. A researcher studies dairy cows to determine if feed type affects milk production. The researcher gives each cow one of the three types of feed for a month and measures milk production. Which of the following sources of error were unavoidable in this experiment? **B1.1B**

   A the genetic make up of cows in each group

   B the average age of cows in each group

   C the number of cows in each group

   D the types of cows in each group

2. A student wanted to find the volume of various types of bird bones. The tool that would be most helpful to do this is a **B1.1C**

   A metric ruler.

   B graduated cylinder.

   C electronic balance.

   D dissecting forceps.

3. All organisms need to manage the absorption and release of heat from their bodies. Animals use various methods to do this. Whereas a reptile's temperature is determined by its surrounding environment, a mammal uses its own metabolic heat to keep its tissues warm. A mammal can correctly be described as a(n) **B2.4B**

   A ectotherm.

   B endotherm.

   C marsupial.

   D sphenodont.

4. Amniotes are multicellular animals whose embryos develop in an enclosed membrane. What else must be true of *all* amniotes? **B2.4A**

   A They can only reproduce asexually.

   B Fertilization is always external.

   C They lay eggs during their life cycle.

   D Half of their DNA comes from each parent.

   ### THINK THROUGH THE QUESTION

   First, think about what an embryo is. Can an embryo be produced asexually? Next, eliminate answer choices that could be true for some amniotes, but may not be true for all amniotes.

5. Many organisms lay eggs that are simply membranes for their young to develop within. In contrast, reptiles, birds, and mammals all have four membranes that each perform specialized functions during development of their young. This distinction makes reptiles, birds, and mammals all classified as **B2.4C**

   A vertebrates.

   B animals.

   C amniotes.

   D chordates.

6.

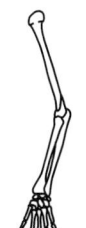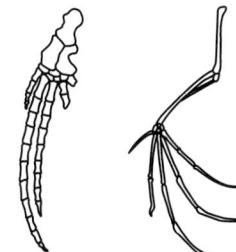

   These illustrations show the bones of the forelimbs of three organisms. The similarities in bone arrangement supports the hypothesis that these organisms **B2.4A**

   A are members of one species.

   B descended from a common ancestor.

   C have adaptations for similar environments.

   D have the same genetic information.

CHAPTER
27 Animal Behavior

KEY CONCEPTS

27.1 Adaptive Value of Behavior
Behavior lets organisms respond rapidly and adaptively to their environment.

27.2 Instinct and Learning
Both genes and environment affect an animal's behavior.

27.3 Evolution of Behavior
Every behavior has costs and benefits.

27.4 Social Behavior
Social behaviors enhance the benefits of living in a group.

27.5 Animal Cognition
Some animals other than humans exhibit behaviors requiring complex cognitive abilities.

Online BIOLOGY CLASSZONE.COM

Animated BIOLOGY
View animated chapter concepts.
• Spider Mating Habits
• Animal Cognition
• Interpreting Bird Response
• Behavioral Costs and Benefits

BIOZINE
Keep current with biology news.
• News feeds
• Strange Biology
• Bio Bytes

RESOURCE CENTER
Get more information on
• Courtship Behaviors
• Animal Tools

What can be learned from this chimpanzee's behavior?

This chimpanzee is using a leaf to drink water. Chimpanzees use a variety of tools. Bunched up leaves might serve as a sponge to sop up water for drinking or for cleaning themselves. Some chimpanzees also use twigs to dig termites out of their mounds and rocks to crack open hard-shelled nuts or fruits. Tool use is considered an example of complex behavior.

Connecting CONCEPTS

Scientific Methods Modern animal behavior studies are conducted with the aid of a variety of tools, including computers. For example, a keyboard that allows for speech synthesis was developed for language acquisition studies with bonobos. Data from these experiments have helped scientists to understand the cognitive abilities of primates, such as their ability to understand spoken words.

Adaptive Value of Behavior

KEY CONCEPT Behavior lets organisms respond rapidly and adaptively to their environment.

▶ MAIN IDEAS

- Behavioral responses to stimuli may be adaptive.
- Internal and external stimuli usually interact to trigger specific behaviors.
- Some behaviors occur in cycles.

VOCABULARY

stimulus, p. 818   **circadian rhythm,** p. 820

kinesis, p. 819   **biological clock,** p. 820

taxis, p. 819

MICHIGAN STANDARDS

B2.6a Explain that the regulatory and behavioral responses of an organism to external stimuli occur in order to maintain both short- and long-term equilibrium.

TAKING NOTES

Use a cause-and-effect diagram to take notes on stimuli.

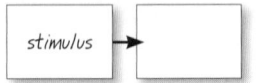

FIGURE 27.1 When threatened, a pufferfish responds by inflating itself with water until its spines stick out from its rounded body.

Connect Animal behavior can be simple, such as a moth flying toward a light, or it can be complex, such as a chimpanzee using a leaf as a tool to drink water from a stream. At its most basic level, however, every animal behavior demonstrates the adaptive advantage of an organism's ability to detect and respond to stimuli.

▶ MAIN IDEA

Behavioral responses to stimuli may be adaptive.

A houseplant bends its leaves toward a sunny window. A lizard moves into the shade on a hot day. A pufferfish inflates when threatened by a predator, as shown in **FIGURE 27.1**. Your cat comes running when it hears a can opener. What do these four observations have in common? They are all examples of organisms responding to stimuli in a beneficial way. A plant can only bend toward light by growing in its direction, but organisms such as the lizard, the pufferfish, or your cat have mechanisms that let them gather and actively respond to information. Behavior can be quite complex, especially in animals with complex nervous systems, but the adaptive nature of behavior can be seen in the relationship between a stimulus and a response.

Stimulus and Response

A **stimulus** (plural, *stimuli*) is a type of information that has the potential to make an organism change its behavior. Internal stimuli tell an animal what is occurring in its own body. For example,

- Hunger signals a need for more energy and causes an animal to search for food.
- Thirst signals a loss of internal fluid and causes an animal to look for water.
- Pain warns an animal that some part of its body may be subject to injury and causes it to take some action to avoid injury.

External stimuli give an animal information about its surroundings. For example,

- The sound of a predator can cause an animal to hide or run away to avoid being caught.
- The sight of a potential mate can trigger courtship behaviors.
- Changes in day length can trigger reproductive behaviors or migration.

Animals detect sensory information with specialized cells that are sensitive to changes in specific kinds of physical or chemical stimuli. These sensory cells may detect things such as light, sound, or chemicals. They transfer information to an animal's nervous system. The nervous system, in turn, may activate other systems in the animal's body that generate a response to the stimulus. For example, a stimulus may cause a gland to increase or decrease its production of a hormone. When you are startled or scared, your adrenal glands release a hormone called epinephrine that causes many other systems in your body to react in what is known as the "fight-or-flight" response. The most obvious organs activated in response to nervous activity are muscles. An animal's ability to move is what lets it behave in response to stimuli.

FIGURE 27.2 The attack by a lioness activates the "flight" response in this kudu, helping it try to evade its predator.

The Function of Behavior

One way to look at an animal's behavior is to consider it as a kind of high-level homeostatic mechanism. Recall that homeostasis refers to the maintenance of constant internal conditions. Many animal behaviors are responses to stimuli—both internal and external—that affect an individual's well-being. For example, temperature receptors cause a lizard to move to a sunnier spot if it is too cold, or to a shadier spot if it becomes too warm. The lizard's body has an ideal temperature, and when its actual temperature differs from its ideal temperature, the lizard behaves in a way that returns its body to its ideal temperature.

Connecting CONCEPTS

Plant Biology Plants also react to stimuli. Recall from **Chapter 22** that tropism is the movement of a plant in response to an environmental stimulus.

Kinesis and taxis are two simple types of movement-related behaviors that illustrate behavior's adaptive nature. Both behaviors cause an animal to go from a less desirable location to a more desirable location. **Kinesis** is an increase in random movement that lasts until a favorable environment is reached. For example, when a pill bug begins to dry out, its activity increases until it happens upon a moist area, after which its activity decreases again. **Taxis** is a movement in a specific direction, either toward or away from a stimulus. For example, *Euglena* are light-sensitive and will move toward a light source.

VISUAL VOCAB

Kinesis is an increase in random movement.

Like a taxi that takes you directly from one location to another, **taxis** is a movement in a particular direction induced by a stimulus.

Like any trait, the way an animal behaves can vary from individual to individual. A kudu that waits too long to run may wind up being a lion's dinner, as shown in **FIGURE 27.2**. A male mockingbird with a weak repertoire of songs may not attract a mate. Animals with more successful behaviors tend to have more offspring. If the behaviors are heritable, their offspring will likely behave in similar ways. Just like any of an animal's characteristics, behaviors can evolve by natural selection.

Analyze **How is taxis or kinesis an example of the adaptive nature of behavior?**

▶ MAIN IDEA

Internal and external stimuli usually interact to trigger specific behaviors.

Some behaviors can be triggered by a single stimulus, but most behaviors occur in response to a variety of internal and external stimuli. For example, an external signal, such as a change in day length, might cause an animal to secrete specific hormones. These hormones act as internal signals that cause other physiological changes. These changes, in turn, make the animal more likely to respond to another external stimulus, such as the mating display of an individual of the opposite sex. This kind of interaction can be seen in the reproductive behavior of green anoles.

Green anoles are small lizards that live in the woodlands of the southeastern United States. During most of the year, female anoles ignore males. However, their behavior changes each spring, when males begin to aggressively guard territories and court females. Two external stimuli trigger the females' change in behavior. First, females must be exposed to long days and short nights. Females must also see reproductively active males.

To court females, males that are ready to mate bob their bodies up and down while extending their dewlap. The dewlap, shown in **FIGURE 27.3**, is a flap of bright red skin under the lizard's chin. Seeing the red dewlap during the spring makes females release sex hormones into their bloodstream. Sex hormones are an internal signal that make females reproductively receptive.

Experiments with female anoles have shown that their reproductive behavior depends on the presence of both external and internal signals. Females that do not have sex hormones do not respond to courtship. And hormones are not released unless females are exposed to both external stimuli.

Connect **What might be internal and external stimuli that cause you to wake up in the morning?**

FIGURE 27.3 The extended red dewlap of this male green anole announces to females that it is ready to mate. The dewlap is also used in territorial defense as a "keep out" signal to other males.

▶ MAIN IDEA

Some behaviors occur in cycles.

Many environmental changes are predictable, especially those that occur on a daily, monthly, or yearly basis. Animals often use cues such as differences in day length to keep track of these changes, triggering adaptive changes in their behavior. For example, in order to be active during the day, your body requires a period of sleep every night. This daily pattern of activity and sleep is an example of a circadian rhythm. A **circadian rhythm** (suhr-KAY-dee-uhn) is the daily cycle of activity that occurs over a 24-hour period of time.

These activity patterns are controlled by an internal mechanism called a **biological clock.** Evidence indicates that an organism's biological clock is run by a combination of melatonin secretions by the pineal gland in the brain and proteins in the body that can detect changes in light.

VOCABULARY

The term *circadian* comes from a combination of the Latin words *circa*, meaning "around," and *dies*, meaning "day."

Hibernation

Hibernation is a behavior in which an animal avoids cold winter temperatures by entering into a dormant state. During hibernation, an animal, such as the dormouse shown in **FIGURE 27.4**, has a lower body temperature, reduced heartbeat, and a slowed breathing rate. Hibernating animals prepare for the winter by eating large amounts of food and storing it as fat. This layer of fat not only provides a food source for the animal but also provides additional insulation from the cold.

External factors such as light intensity and temperature determine when an animal enters and leaves hibernation. Shorter days and cooler temperatures cause animals to enter hibernation in the fall. In the spring, increasing day length and warmer temperatures cause the secretion of hormones that awaken the animal out of its dormant state.

FIGURE 27.4 During hibernation, the dormouse's blood temperature drops from 36°C (97°F) to just above 0°C (32°F).

Migration

Many kinds of animals migrate, but you are probably most familiar with bird migration. If you've ever seen—or heard—a flock of geese flying southward during the fall, you've seen bird migration in action. Migratory Canada geese typically spend the spring and summer in Canada and the northern United States. They spend the winter in the southern United States and northern portions of Mexico. Like hibernation, migratory behavior allows animals to avoid harsh conditions in their home range for a part of the year.

Migration is set in motion by a variety of internal and external stimuli. A change in day length during the spring and fall stimulates a change in the portion of the bird's brain that controls hunger. This change causes birds to gain weight. An increase in fat storage is needed to fuel the bird's long-distance migration.

Infer How might climate change affect animal migration patterns?

27.1 / ASSESSMENT

ONLINE QUIZ
ClassZone.com

REVIEWING ◉ MAIN IDEAS

1. Why are behavioral responses to **stimuli** considered to be adaptive?

2. What internal and external stimuli might signal to Alaskan caribou that it is time to migrate?

3. What is the connection between a **circadian rhythm** and the **biological clock**?

CRITICAL THINKING

4. **Analyze** What is the relationship between an animal's behavior and homeostasis?

5. **Predict** How might an animal's behavior be affected if its pineal gland is destroyed?

Connecting CONCEPTS

6. **Sexual Selection** A peacock uses its colorful train of feathers to attract a mate. What factors might control how large a peacock's train of feathers may grow to be?

Instinct and Learning

KEY CONCEPT Both genes and environment affect an animal's behavior.

▶ MAIN IDEAS

- Innate behaviors are triggered by specific internal and external stimuli.
- Many behaviors have both innate and learned components.
- Learning is adaptive.

VOCABULARY

instinct, p. 822
innate, p. 822
releaser, p. 822
habituation, p. 823
imprinting, p. 824

imitation, p. 825
classical conditioning, p. 826
operant conditioning, p. 826

MICHIGAN STANDARDS

B2.6a Explain that the regulatory and behavioral responses of an organism to external stimuli occur in order to maintain both short- and long-term equilibrium.

Connect Why are some families filled with good athletes? Is athleticism passed on from parent to child? Or are younger generations repeating behaviors they watched while they were growing up? You may have heard this "nature versus nurture" debate about many human behaviors, including musical ability, addiction, and thrill seeking. But research shows that genetic and environmental factors interact in most behaviors. "Nature versus nurture" is a false division. Most behaviors represent a mixture of both nature *and* nurture.

▶ MAIN IDEA

Innate behaviors are triggered by specific internal and external stimuli.

FIGURE 27.5 After hatching from its egg, a leatherback sea turtle hatchling instinctively makes its way to the ocean, where it will remain until maturity.

Nothing teaches a spider to build a web. It builds it correctly the first time it tries. This kind of complex inborn behavior is called an **instinct.** Instinctive behavior is characterized as being innate and relatively inflexible. An **innate** behavior is performed correctly the first time an animal tries it, even when the animal has never been exposed to the stimulus that triggers the behavior. An inflexible behavior is performed in a similar way each time.

Instinctive behaviors are typically found where mistakes can have severe consequences. Baby mammals that do not suckle die of starvation. Newly hatched sea turtles, such as those shown in **FIGURE 27.5,** that do not race to the ocean will be eaten by predators. By having set reactions to particular stimuli, animals can automatically respond correctly in a life-or-death situation.

Instinctive behavior is especially important in newborns, who have had no time to learn any behaviors. Performing certain innate behaviors is key to both the animal's survival and its ability to pass its genes on to future generations. Animals that do not perform a necessary innate behavior will likely die.

Many innate behaviors are triggered by a simple signal. The signal is called a **releaser** because it makes the animal run through a behavior. Releasers can be any kind of stimulus: a visual sign, a sound, a scent, or a touch. When a releaser signal has been detected, the animal's nervous system triggers the expression of a specific behavior. Sometimes the triggered behavior is fixed, and the animal runs through a set sequence of movements each time the behavior is performed.

Dutch zoologist Niko Tinbergen's experiments with herring gulls showed how simple releasers can be. Hungry herring gull chicks will peck at a red spot at the tip of a parent's bill. The parent usually responds by coughing up a bit of half-digested fish for the chick to eat. Very young chicks do not actually recognize their parent when they beg for food. Instead, the behavior is triggered simply by the sight of a long bill with a red dot near its tip. The chicks will beg from any long object with a red dot, including cardboard cutouts of a herring gull head and the end of a painted stick. Other gull species, such as the lesser black-backed gull shown in **FIGURE 27.6**, also have red-dotted bills.

Biologists think that innate behaviors are hard-wired into an animal's nervous system, but they have studied the details for only a few invertebrate species. Innate behaviors are heritable and are strongly affected by gene expression. But they can also be changed by environmental factors. For example, during its lifetime, a honeybee moves through a sequence of innate behaviors that help to maintain the hive. The behaviors are regulated by different sets of genes. As a bee ages, its brain cells express different genes and its behavior changes. But gene expression is also affected by the hive's social environment. If a hive has few older foragers, some of the younger bees will mature faster. Even the bill-pecking behavior of gulls has been shown to improve with age, as young herring gulls become more accurate in their ability to aim their pecks at the red spot on their parent's bill.

FIGURE 27.6 Some gull species, such as this lesser black-backed gull, have a red-dotted bill. The red dot is the releaser that causes the gull chick to beg for food.

Apply Why is behavior considered to be a mixture of both nature and nurture?

▶ MAIN IDEA

Many behaviors have both innate and learned components.

Animals often change their behavior as they gain real-world experience. In other words, animals learn. Learning takes many forms, ranging from simple changes in an innate behavior to problem-solving in new situations. In each case, learning involves the strengthening of nerve pathways. Most animal behaviors are not simple reactions to stimuli using preset pathways in the animal's brain. Instead, they represent a combination of innate tendencies influenced by learning and experience.

Habituation

Garden shops sell plastic owls that are supposed to frighten away birds. But a gardener who doesn't move the owls every few days may soon see birds sitting on top of them. This is an example of habituation. **Habituation** occurs when an animal learns to ignore a repeated stimulus, even if it has features that trigger innate behaviors. The habit of seeing owls in the exact same place in the garden every day causes the birds to get used to, and therefore ignore, the stimulus.

Connecting CONCEPTS

Brain Chemistry Research indicates that during learning, some neurons undergo structural and molecular changes that allow for the easier flow of information. You will learn more about the structure and function of neurons in **Chapter 29**.

Human Behavior

Have you ever wondered what might explain a particular kind of behavior you observe in people? In this lab, you will observe some aspect of human behavior and form a hypothesis that explains the behavior.

PROBLEM What is the behavior of people in certain situations?

MATERIALS
- paper
- pencil

PROCEDURE

1. Choose a question that you have about human behavior that can be answered by observing people. For instance, you could ask, "Where do people sit in a cafeteria?"

2. Determine which behavior you will observe.

3. Determine how you will quantitatively measure the behavior. For example, you may record how many people are in the cafeteria, where people are sitting, and the number of full, partially full, and empty tables.

4. Make your observations and record your data.

ANALYZE AND CONCLUDE

1. **Analyze** Present your results in a table or graph. What can you conclude?

2. **Hypothesize** Form a hypothesis that could explain the behavior pattern you saw.

3. **Extend** Create an experiment to test your hypothesis.

Imprinting

Imprinting is a rapid and irreversible learning process that only occurs during a short time in an animal's life. During this critical period the animal may, for example, learn to identify its parents, its siblings, its offspring, characteristics of its own species, or the place it was born.

Austrian zoologist Konrad Lorenz's studies with graylag geese are among the most famous studies of imprinting. Newly hatched graylag geese normally imprint on their mother during the first two days after hatching. After this period, the goslings will follow their mother and eventually grow up to mate with other graylag geese. Lorenz divided a clutch of goose eggs in half, leaving some with the mother and raising the rest himself. The goslings that stayed with their mother behaved normally. Their siblings, which stayed with Lorenz during their critical period, did not recognize other geese as members of their own species. They followed Lorenz as goslings, and tried to mate with humans when they matured. This experiment showed that imprinting is an innate and automatic process, even though the behavior's stimulus is learned.

When working to reintroduce species into the wild, it is important to avoid having the animals imprint on their human handlers. For example, when working with endangered whooping cranes, scientists try to minimize the birds' contact with humans. When humans need to interact with the cranes, they wear costumes that cover their entire bodies. They use puppets painted to look like adult cranes to feed the young, as shown in **FIGURE 27.7**.

FIGURE 27.7 To avoid having cranes imprint on their human handlers, biologists use puppets painted to resemble the head of an adult crane to feed young birds raised in captivity.

Imitation

In **imitation,** animals learn by observing the behaviors of other animals. The initial behavior becomes a model that the other animals try to copy. Young male songbirds learn to sing by listening to adult males and trying to repeat what they hear. By trial and error, over time they begin to sing the species-specific song they heard from adults. Human babies also imitate adults in a number of ways, such as when they learn to speak their native language.

Not all imitative behaviors are passed from adult to younger animals, however. For example, consider the potato washing behavior among Japanese macaques, or snow monkeys, shown in **FIGURE 27.8**. A juvenile female monkey, named Imo by researchers, discovered that it was easier to wash sand off a potato by dipping it in water rather than by brushing it off with her hands. At first, only her brothers and sisters imitated the behavior, followed by her mother. Over a period of time, a number of individuals in the troop adopted the potato washing behavior.

Infer What would be the harm of having a captive animal intended for release imprint on its human handlers?

FIGURE 27.8 Snow monkeys learn to wash their potatoes before eating them by imitating the behavior of other individuals.

⦿ MAIN IDEA
Learning is adaptive.

Animals that are able to learn can modify, or change, their behavior to better adapt to new situations. This ability to learn can give animals an edge in survival and reproduction, allowing them to pass their genes on to future generations.

Associative Learning

In associative learning, an animal learns to associate a specific action with its consequences. For example, an experiment with young blue jays showed that the birds do not identify prey instinctively. Instead, they ate every new insect that was offered to them. Insects that tasted good, such as grasshoppers, they ate again and again. But it only took one experience with a bad-tasting monarch butterfly to make the jays avoid them for the rest of their lives. The jays learned to associate the monarch's distinctive orange and black markings with its bad taste. Such trial-and-error learning can help animals to survive within their environments.

One type of associative learning studied by animal behavior scientists is conditioning. Conditioning is a way to modify an animal's behavior in response to certain stimuli. When teaching an animal by conditioning, two stimuli are paired together, and an animal is conditioned to give a specific response to these stimuli. The two main types of conditioning are called classical conditioning and operant conditioning.

Classical Conditioning

Classical conditioning is a process in which an animal learns to associate a previously neutral stimulus with a behavior that was once triggered by a different stimulus. Ivan Pavlov, a Russian physiologist, was studying digestion in dogs when he realized that salivation, or drooling, is an automatic behavior. Pavlov created an experiment to determine if external stimuli are involved in this behavior.

- Normally, the presence of food makes a dog salivate.
- A bell is rung when food is presented to the dog.
- The dog salivates because of the presence of the food.
- After constantly being presented with both food and the ringing bell at the same time, when only the bell is rung, the dog salivates even though the food is not present.

In this experiment, the ringing bell is initially a neutral stimulus. The response in which the dog salivates upon hearing the ringing bell is the conditioned response. Because the dog was given food at the same time the bell rang, the dog has been conditioned to salivate when the bell is rung because it also expects to be given food.

Operant Conditioning

Operant conditioning is a process in which the likelihood of a specific behavior is increased or decreased by positive or negative reinforcement. Positive reinforcement refers to the presence of something pleasurable, such as a food reward as shown in **FIGURE 27.9**, while negative reinforcement refers to the removal of something pleasant.

B. F. Skinner, an American psychologist, created "Skinner boxes" to study operant conditioning. A Skinner box is a cage that has a bar or pedal on one wall. When an animal such as a rat pushes down on the bar, a food pellet pops out. The rat then associates the behavior of pressing the bar with the food reward, even if not rewarded every time. If the behavior is no longer rewarded, the rat will, over time, stop performing it.

Apply How might you train a dog to do a trick using positive reinforcement?

"AND THEN INSTEAD OF FEEDING ME HE WOULD RING A LITTLE BELL."

Source: CartoonStock.com

FIGURE 27.9 Teaching a pet a trick, such as how to shake, often involves giving it a reward after it performs the correct behavior.

27.2 / ASSESSMENT

ONLINE QUIZ
ClassZone.com

REVIEWING ▶ MAIN IDEAS

1. What is the difference between an **instinct** and a learned behavior?
2. Describe a behavior that you learned by **imitation.**
3. Using either **classical** or **operant conditioning** as an example, explain how learning can be adaptive.

CRITICAL THINKING

4. **Apply** Ducklings that are shown a paper silhouette of a hawk initially freeze and cower. After repeated exposure to the silhouette they stop responding. What is this lack of response called?
5. **Summarize** What is the connection between neurons in the brain and learning?

Connecting CONCEPTS

6. **Evolution** Monarch butterflies are toxic. Viceroy butterflies, which look like monarch butterflies, are not toxic, but birds avoid them anyway. Explain how the bird behavior described in this section could have influenced the evolution of viceroys.

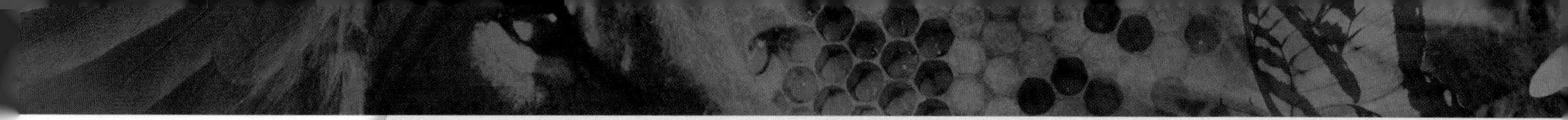

27.3 Evolution of Behavior

KEY CONCEPT Every behavior has costs and benefits.

▶ MAIN IDEAS

- Even beneficial behaviors have associated costs.
- Animals perform behaviors whose benefits outweigh their costs.

VOCABULARY

survivorship, p. 827
territoriality, p. 828
optimal foraging, p. 829

MICHIGAN STANDARDS

B2.6a Explain that the regulatory and behavioral responses of an organism to external stimuli occur in order to maintain both short- and long-term equilibrium.

Connect The zebra was very thirsty. It flicked his ears to and fro as it walked toward the water hole, listening carefully for any sign of a hungry lioness. Nothing looked out of the ordinary. But as it neared the edge of the water, it saw a crocodile lurking in the shallows. The zebra quickly retreated and trotted back to its herd. It needed water, but the risk to its life was too great.

▶ MAIN IDEA

Even beneficial behaviors have associated costs.

Every behavior has benefits and costs. Shorebirds travel thousands of miles during their spring and fall migrations, burning through an enormous amount of energy in the process. But migration increases a bird's chances of survival by escaping from cold seasonal temperatures to warmer locations.

Benefits of Behavior

From an evolutionary standpoint, the most important benefits of a behavior include increased survivorship and reproduction rates. **Survivorship** refers to the number of individuals that survive from one year to the next. Certain behaviors reduce the chance that an animal will die in a given time period. Similarly, some behaviors increase the number of offspring that an animal will have during its lifetime.

Behaviors that increase an individual's survival or reproduction are behaviors that increase its fitness. These behaviors will be favored by natural selection, but they still have associated costs. For instance, when a sea star touches a sea anemone called *Stomphia*, the anemone stops feeding, wrenches free of the sea bottom, and swims away. Escape behaviors such as this are expensive in terms of energy in the short term. The animal stops eating and uses up stored energy. But dead animals cannot reproduce. The long-term benefit of the behavior is the increase in the animal's survival and reproduction rates.

FIGURE 27.10 These male Siberian tigers are very territorial. Fights over territory can lead to serious injury or even death.

Costs of Behavior

Behavioral costs can be broken down into three basic categories.

Energy costs Every animal behavior, such as running away from a predator, uses up ATP. When an animal uses metabolic energy for one behavior, such as searching for a mate, that energy is not available for other needs, such as searching for food.

Animated
BIOLOGY
Watch the unusual mating habits of the Australian redback spider at ClassZone.com.

FIGURE 27.11 While mating with the female, the smaller male Australian redback spider somersaults directly over the female's mouth, offering himself as her next meal.

Opportunity costs Every animal behavior takes time. When an animal spends time doing one behavior, it loses the opportunity to do a different behavior. For example, when a songbird defends its territory from rivals, it is using time that could have been spent eating or mating.

Risk costs Many behaviors expose an individual to possible injury or death. All animals have to look for food, but foraging also increases the chance that an animal will meet a predator. In many species, males risk injury by fighting for access to females during the breeding season.

Some behaviors that seem harmful may have surprising benefits for an animal. For example, while most male spiders go to great lengths to avoid getting eaten by their mates, a male Australian redback spider deliberately flips his abdomen over the female's mouth, as shown in **FIGURE 27.11**. As they mate, she literally eats him alive. His behavior clearly does not increase his survival. But because it lets him fertilize more of her eggs, it has the benefit of increasing his reproductive success.

Analyze **What is the benefit of bird migration? The cost?**

▶ MAIN IDEA
Animals perform behaviors whose benefits outweigh their costs.

It is difficult to determine if animals make conscious decisions about their actions. Whether behavioral responses are automatic or reflect more complex cognitive processes, they evolve only if they improve the fitness of those individuals that perform them. Territoriality and optimal foraging are just two examples that demonstrate how animal behaviors are expressed if their benefits outweigh their costs.

Territoriality

Territoriality refers to the control of a specific area—or territory—by one or more individuals of an animal species. The benefit of territorial behavior is the ability to control the resources within the animal's territory, such as food or access to potential mates. The costs associated with territorial behavior include the energy and time that could have been used for feeding or mating. That time is instead spent protecting territory from invasion by other animals.

Consider the territorial behavior of the Hawaiian honeycreeper. This bird feeds on the nectar of flowers, and it defends a territory that has the flowers from which it feeds. The benefit of holding a territory can be measured in the amount of nectar the bird can get from the flowers located in its territory. An individual should only defend a territory if that territory holds enough flowers to provide the food it needs to at least offset the energy cost of defense. Studies of honeycreeper behavior have shown that individuals stop defending territories when the number of flowers falls below a certain minimum or exceeds a certain maximum number. Individuals only defend a territory in which there is a benefit from excluding other individuals, and in which the energy benefit from the nectar outweighs the energy cost of the defensive behavior.

Connecting CONCEPTS

Competition Recall from **Chapter 14** that competition occurs when two organisms fight for the same limited resources. Interspecific competition occurs when members of different species fight for access to resources. Intraspecific competition is the fight for resources between members of the same species.

Optimal Foraging

When animals search for food, they must make decisions about what they should eat. The benefits of foraging are measured in the amount of energy gained. The costs of foraging include the energy used to search for, catch, and eat food; the risk of capture by a predator while foraging; and the loss of time to spend on other activities. The theory of **optimal foraging** states that natural selection should favor behaviors that get animals the most, or optimal amount of, calories for the cost.

The foraging methods of oystercatchers, a type of shorebird shown in **FIGURE 27.12,** have been the subject of many studies. As the birds' name suggests, they eat bivalves such as oysters and mussels. Some birds sneak up on relaxed bivalves and quickly stab out the meat. Others use their chisel-shaped beak to hammer a hole through the shells.

Hammering oystercatchers get a benefit from eating the mollusks, but at the cost of the time and energy it takes to break open their shells. Small mussels are easy to open, but don't contain much meat. Larger mussels are meatier but harder to open. Scientists first hypothesized that oystercatchers would prefer to eat the largest mussels they could find. These mussels contained the most meat for the time the birds spent opening them.

When the biologists observed oystercatchers in the wild, they found that the birds did not eat the largest mussels they could find. Their experiment showed that there was another cost to eating mussels. Their first model assumed that the birds could open any mussel given enough time. However, their experiment showed them that the birds also faced a "handling cost" when they hunted. Birds that picked very large mussels lost time handling bivalves they could not open. They actually got less meat on average than birds that ate smaller mussels. Oystercatchers that learn to hunt medium-sized mussels get the most food for their efforts. Better-fed birds have higher survivorship and their chicks, in turn, learn this behavior.

Apply How does optimal foraging improve an individual's overall fitness?

FIGURE 27.12 The oystercatcher uses its long, sharp beak to break open the shells of bivalves such as oysters.

27.3 ASSESSMENT

ONLINE QUIZ
ClassZone.com

REVIEWING ▶ MAIN IDEAS

1. Compare the three categories of behavior costs.

2. Any animal behavior has a cost and a benefit. Explain this statement using **optimal foraging** as an example.

CRITICAL THINKING

3. **Infer** What might be a stimulus that triggers a songbird's **territorial** behaviors?

4. **Analyze** Some species of cichlid fish hold their fertilized eggs inside their mouths until they hatch. What might be the costs and benefits of this behavior?

Connecting CONCEPTS

5. **Scientific Process** Some spiders build webs that include visible zigzag lines of silk. But more visible webs catch fewer insects than do less visible webs. Hypothesize what benefits the spider gets by building such a visible web.

MATERIALS

- pet or classroom animal
- watch
- calculator
- graph paper
- ruler

PROCESS SKILLS

- **Observing**
- **Graphing Data**

B1.2C Develop an understanding of a scientific concept by accessing information from multiple sources. Evaluate the scientific accuracy and significance of the information.

B2.6a Explain that the regulatory and behavioral responses of an organism to external stimuli occur in order to maintain both short- and long-term equilibrium.

Using an Ethogram to Describe Animal Behavior

An ethogram is a catalog of the types of behaviors an animal may perform. For example, in a 24-hour period, male and female chimpanzees may display behaviors such as hunting, eating, sleeping, grooming, caring for young, and defending territory. After making initial observations, a scientist might make further observations and collect data to create a time budget of the observed behaviors. The time budget shows how much time individuals spend in each type of behavior. Among other uses, data from a time budget can be used to compare behavior patterns between males and females of the same species or members of different species. In this investigation, you will create an ethogram by observing an animal of your choice.

PROBLEM How much time do animals spend on specific behaviors?

Jane Goodall's studies with chimpanzees involved many long hours in the field observing behavior.

PROCEDURE

1. Decide which animal you are going to study.

2. You must be able to observe active animal behavior for at least one hour. Conceal yourself so your presence does not influence its behaviors. For example, your family pet may respond to your presence and want attention.

3. Predict what types of behaviors the animal will engage in, and create a table to record your data. For example, behaviors might include sleeping, eating, or playing.

4. Observe your animal for at least one hour. Record the specific behaviors of the animal, the order in which the animal carries out those behaviors, the number of times the behavior occurs, and the length of time of each behavior.
Caution: If the animal you are observing becomes agitated, stop observing it.

ANALYZE AND CONCLUDE

1. **Categorize** Make a list of the most common behaviors that your animal carried out. Was each behavior isolated, or were some behaviors carried out in a specific order? Explain.

2. **Graph Data** Determine the percentage of the total time spent in each behavior. Make a bar graph from the data.

3. **Analyze** Use your bar graph to determine which behavior was the most frequent. Which behavior was least frequent? Explain.

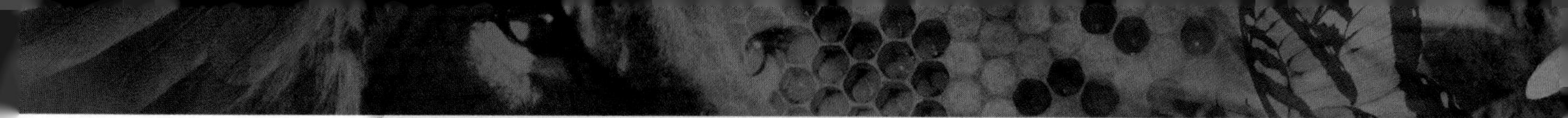

27.4 Social Behavior

KEY CONCEPT Social behaviors enhance the benefits of living in a group.

MAIN IDEAS

- Living in groups also has benefits and costs.
- Social behaviors are interactions between members of the same or different species.
- Some behaviors benefit other group members at a cost to the individual performing them.
- Eusocial behavior is an example of extreme altruism.

VOCABULARY

pheromone, p. 832
altruism, p. 833
inclusive fitness, p. 834
kin selection, p. 834
eusocial, p. 834

MICHIGAN STANDARDS

B2.6a Explain that the regulatory and behavioral responses of an organism to external stimuli occur in order to maintain both short- and long-term equilibrium.

TAKING NOTES

Use a two-column chart to take notes on the costs and benefits of social behavior.

costs	benefits

FIGURE 27.13 During the breeding season, emperor penguins live in huge colonies made up of between 200 and 50,000 pairs.

Connect Many factors determine if a species lives alone or in a group. Even closely related species have different living patterns. Such is the case with marmots. Woodchucks (*Marmota monax*), found in the eastern United States, live alone. Yellow-bellied marmots (*Marmota flaviventris*), which live out west, live in colonies.

MAIN IDEA

Living in groups also has benefits and costs.

Some species, such as the emperor penguins shown in **FIGURE 27.13**, live together in groups. These groups may have a definite social structure or they may have a constantly changing membership. Social behaviors evolve in species in which the benefits of group living outweigh its costs.

Benefits of Social Behavior

Living in a social group provides significant benefits to individuals within the group. Living in a group may lead to improved foraging, as an individual can follow other members of the group to good feeding sites. Immature or nonreproductive members of the group can provide assistance to those who do reproduce by helping to gather food for or protecting newborn members. Living in a group can lead to a reduced chance of predation. Having more eyes and ears in the group helps in detecting predators. Although groups of animals are easier for predators to spot, a predator can usually capture only one member of a group in any attack, letting the others escape.

Costs of Social Behavior

Living in a group also comes at some cost to an individual. Living together in large groups leads to increased visibility. A group of animals cannot hide from predators as easily as an individual can. Group living also leads to increased competition. A limited amount of resources, such as food or mates, can lead to conflicts between group members. Animals that live together in groups also have an increased chance of contracting diseases or passing parasites to each other. As group size increases, so does the risk.

Connect What is the benefit of doing group work in class? Are there any drawbacks?

FIGURE 27.14 Male satin bower-birds decorate their bowers with shiny and brightly colored objects (including human-made items) to attract a mate.

Connecting CONCEPTS

Evolution Recall from **Chapter 11** that sexual selection is a factor that violates Hardy-Weinberg equilibrium. When certain traits improve mating success, alleles for these traits increase in frequency within a population, causing the population to evolve over time.

▶ MAIN IDEA

Social behaviors are interactions between members of the same or different species.

Social behaviors are behaviors animals use when interacting with members of their own or other species. These behaviors help to make interactions such as mate selection easier, and they often involve specialized signals.

Communication

Animals use communication as a way to keep in contact with one another, raise alarm in the presence of danger, and attract a mate.

Visual Gestures or postures, such as the submissive posture of a dog with its tail between its legs, may help to identify an animal's status in the group.

Sound Animals often use calls to identify offspring, such as the specific call shared between a young penguin and its parents. Alarm calls and distress calls alert others to the presence of a threat. Mating calls are also used to advertise an animal's readiness to mate.

Touch Bees use their antennae, for example, to interpret the waggle dance performed by a scout bee in order to locate a food source outside the hive.

Chemical Some animals communicate by using pheromones. **Pheromones** are chemicals released by an animal that affect the behavior of other individuals of the same species. Often, these chemicals announce an animal's readiness to mate. Odors are also used to identify group members and mark territory.

Mate Selection

Courtship displays are behaviors most often used by male members of a species to attract females. Scientists theorize that females use courtship displays to judge the condition of their potential mate or the quality of his genes. By being choosy about a mate, a female can help ensure that her offspring have the best chance of survival. While some behaviors may be simple in nature, such as the leg-waving dance display of the jumping spider, other behaviors are more elaborate. For example, as shown in **FIGURE 27.14**, the male satin bowerbird of Australia constructs a nest site, called a bower, that is decorated with brightly colored and shiny objects. Females inspect the bowers when choosing a mate.

Defense

Defensive behaviors include aggressive actions to protect both the individual and the group. For example, when threatened, an elephant herd will form a protective circle surrounding the younger members of the family group. Another defensive behavior is mobbing by birds. When a predator is spotted, flocks of birds, often of the same species, will join together to harass the intruder to force it to leave. Keeping watch is another defense tactic. For example, while foraging, one or more members of a giraffe herd will serve as a lookout for the group. While vigilant individuals forage less, they also benefit themselves and other members of their group by keeping an eye out for predators.

Infer How might the size of a group affect its defense?

Some behaviors benefit other group members at a cost to the individual performing them.

Individuals that live in a social group often help one another. They may share food or warmth or warn others about an approaching predator. But remember that animals typically perform behaviors that aid their own fitness. In some cases, however, social behaviors seem to reduce the fitness of the individuals that perform them. How could such behaviors evolve?

Types of Helpful Social Behavior

Most social interactions between animals improve the survival and reproduction of both individuals. The three kinds of helpful social behavior are cooperation, reciprocity, and altruism.

Cooperation involves behaviors that improve the fitness of both individuals. For example, lionesses hunt in a group and share the prey they catch, even though only one member of the pride may have made the kill.

Reciprocity involves behaviors in which individuals help other group members with the expectation that they will be helped in return. For example, vampire bats form feeding relationships with one another. Bats that have fed will regurgitate blood for other bats that are hungry. The cost to the donor bat is small. But there is a large benefit for the hungry bat, because vampire bats starve if they do not eat every few nights. By giving up some food, the donor ensures that it will be fed when it is hungry.

Altruism is a kind of behavior in which an animal reduces its own fitness to help other members of its social group. In other words, the animal appears to sacrifice itself for the good of the group. Consider the behavior of Belding's ground squirrels. A Belding's ground squirrel, shown in **FIGURE 27.15,** is a small rodent that lives in large colonies on the open grasslands such as the alpine grasslands surrounding the Sierra Nevada mountains in California. When ground squirrels are active during the late spring and summer, they are hunted by predators from the air and on the ground. When an individual spots a predator, it may give an alarm call to alert the rest of the colony. But alarm calls are costly. A calling ground squirrel is twice as likely to be killed as a ground squirrel that does not call. Calling benefits other colony members because it gives them time to escape, but it is harmful to the caller.

Evolution of Altruism

How can we explain the evolution of altruism if behavior is supposed to increase fitness? British evolutionary biologist William Hamilton addressed this puzzle by asking how alleles involved in altruistic behavior could spread through a population. He realized that alleles can be transmitted and therefore spread in a population two ways, either directly from an individual to its offspring or indirectly by helping close relatives survive.

VOCABULARY

Reciprocity can be thought of in a "You scratch my back, I'll scratch yours" kind of way. Each animal performing the behavior will eventually benefit when another animal performs it in return.

FIGURE 27.15 An adult female Belding's ground squirrel gives an alarm call to alert her relatives to the presence of a predator.

When an animal reproduces, its offspring gets half of its alleles. But its relatives also share some of the same alleles, in the following proportions:

- Parents and siblings share 50 percent of the animal's alleles.
- Nephews and nieces share 25 percent of its alleles.
- First cousins share 12.5 percent of its alleles.

The total number of genes an animal and its relatives contribute to the next generation is called its **inclusive fitness.** It includes both direct fitness from reproduction and indirect fitness from helping kin survive. When natural selection acts on alleles that favor the survival of close relatives, it is called **kin selection.**

If kin selection explains the squirrels' altruism, callers should be closely related to others in the group. Ground squirrel colonies are made up of closely related females and unrelated males. Males do not call much. Nor do adult females foraging alone. The ones that risk their lives are adult females foraging near their daughters, siblings, and nieces. They are warning their relatives.

Infer **Why is altruistic behavior not very common?**

⊙ MAIN IDEA
Eusocial behavior is an example of extreme altruism.

VOCABULARY

The term *eusocial* comes from the Greek prefix *eu-*, which means "good, well, or true" and the Latin word *socius,* which means "companion."

Relationships within populations of some social animals are very specialized. **Eusocial** species live in large groups made up of many individuals, most of whom are members of nonreproductive castes such as workers or soldiers. All of the young in the colony are the offspring of one female, called the queen. Other adults look for food, defend the colony, care for the queen, and raise her offspring. Eusocial behaviors likely evolve by kin selection.

Social Insects

Many social insects, such as bees, ants, and wasps, are haplodiploid, which means their sex is determined by the number of chromosome sets in an individual. Males are haploid and females are diploid. Female social insects use sperm to produce only daughters. They lay unfertilized eggs to produce sons. In these animals, daughters share half of their mother's alleles but all of their father's alleles. Sisters therefore share up to 75 percent of their alleles overall with one another, compared with 50 percent in humans and most other animals. The very close relationship between sisters in a colony may influence the evolution of eusociality in these insects.

As shown in **FIGURE 27.16,** weaver ants are one example of a eusocial insect species. The three main castes of this species are a queen, major workers, and minor workers. The worker ants work together to weave their nests from leaves that hang from branches throughout one tree or several trees located next to one another. The ants communicate by secreting pheromones. For example, the queen secretes pheromones that induce workers to groom or feed her. If threatened, soldier ants may release pheromones to call in reinforcements to help protect the nest.

FIGURE 27.16 Social Behavior of Ants

Ants live together in colonies. Each ant has an important part to play within the colony.

COOPERATION

After pulling together two leaves, weaver ants attach one leaf to another by using their mandibles to gently squeeze a larva, which produces a silk that glues the leaf edges to each other.

ANT CASTES

Queen The queen lays eggs inside the nest.

Minor worker The smaller minor worker spends most of its time within the nest tending the larvae and egg chambers.

Major worker The larger major worker defends the territory surrounding the nest, tends the queen, and forages for food.

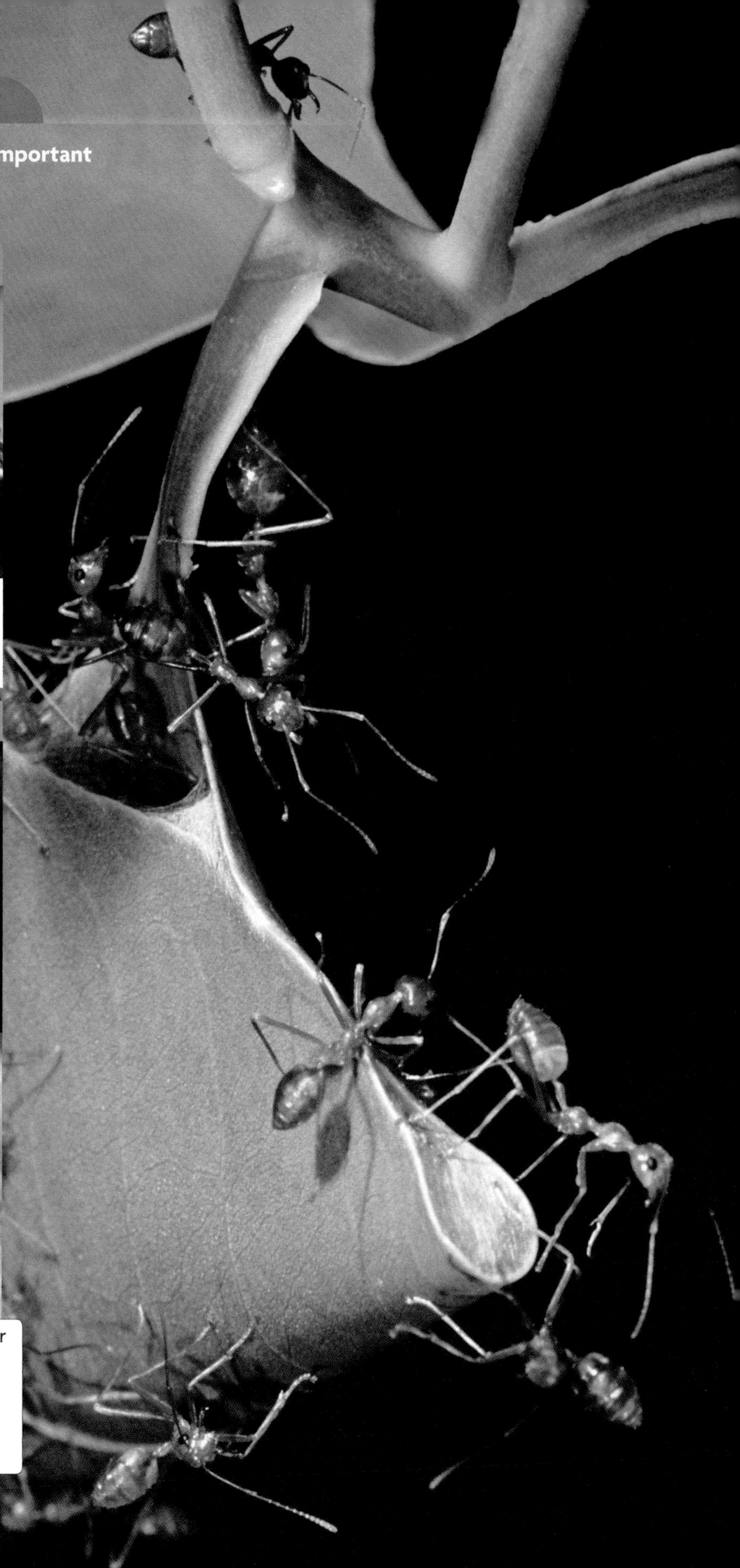

CRITICAL VIEWING **What genetic benefit does a worker ant receive by taking care of its siblings?**

CONSTRUCTING BAR GRAPHS

As you learned earlier in this chapter, an ethogram is a catalogue of the types of behaviors an animal may perform. A time budget shows how much time organisms spend engaged in each type of behavior. Scientists can use these time budgets to compare patterns of behavior between different species, or between different sexes or age groups of the same species.

TABLE 1. KITE BEHAVIOR	
Behavior	Time (min)
Active perching	162
Hunting flight	194
Cruising flight	4
Other flight	7
Feeding nestlings	26

Source: Jaksic et al. *The Condor* 89:4.

Table 1 contains data that were recorded through observations of male and female black-shouldered kites, a type of hawk, during the summer.

1. **Graph Data** Construct a time budget that shows the percent of time (per 24-hour period) the hawks spent in each behavior. (**Hint:** Remember to convert the amount of time to a percent before graphing.)

2. **Analyze** What behavior did the hawks spend the most time engaged in? Why do you think this behavior was most common?

Other Eusocial Animals

Eusocial termites, snapping shrimp, and naked mole rats are all normal, diploid animals. But their colonies are still made up of closely related animals. These animals often live in areas where it is difficult for individuals to survive on their own. For example, naked mole rats live in colonies of 70 to 80 individuals dominated by a single queen and a few fertile male "kings." Most of the colony are the queen's siblings or offspring. Nonreproducing adults are either soldiers or workers. Soldiers defend the colony, while workers work together as a chain gang to dig through the soil to find edible tubers. This eusocial behavior may have evolved due to the amount of work needed to find food. If leaving the colony leads to starvation, kin selection may favor staying in the burrow to work together as a group instead.

NSTA *SCiLINKS*
scilinks.org
To learn more about animal communication, go to scilinks.org.
Keycode: MLB027

Apply How are eusocial behavior and a species' level of relatedness connected?

27.4 ASSESSMENT

ONLINE QUIZ
ClassZone.com

REVIEWING ▶ MAIN IDEAS

1. Outline the costs and benefits of living in a group.

2. Use an example to explain what social behavior is.

3. What are the three types of helpful behavior?

4. What characteristic makes a social group **eusocial**?

CRITICAL THINKING

5. **Connect** Give an example of reciprocal behavior from everyday life.

6. **Analyze** Why might a juvenile scrub jay help its parents raise a new brood of chicks instead of building its own nest?

Connecting CONCEPTS

7. **Genetics** How is a haplodiploid species different from a diploid species?

27.5 Animal Cognition

KEY CONCEPT Some animals other than humans exhibit behaviors requiring complex cognitive abilities.

▶ MAIN IDEAS

- Animal intelligence is difficult to define.
- Some animals can solve problems.
- Cognitive ability may provide an adaptive advantage for living in social groups.

VOCABULARY

cognition, p. 837
insight, p. 838
cultural behavior, p. 839

MICHIGAN STANDARDS

B2.6a Explain that the regulatory and behavioral responses of an organism to external stimuli occur in order to maintain both short- and long-term equilibrium.

Connect No one would deny that humans are intelligent animals. We surround ourselves with invented objects, from the clothes we wear to the buildings in which we live. But from where did human cognition come? And do other animals share aspects of this ability to think about the world?

▶ MAIN IDEA

Animal intelligence is difficult to define.

In the first half of the 20th century, the focus of many animal intelligence studies was determining whether a certain animal was "intelligent" according to human standards. Today, learning how an animal's level of intelligence compares with a human's is no longer a focus of research. Instead, as shown in **FIGURE 27.17**, scientists study an animal's cognitive abilities. **Cognition** is the mental process of knowing through perception or reasoning. Cognitive behavior also includes awareness and the ability to judge. Animals with a higher level of cognition can solve more complex problems.

In contrast to intelligence, which is difficult to define and measure, cognitive abilities can be more objectively described and measured. However, even an animal's cognitive abilities can be difficult to distinguish from other factors that might be affecting an animal's behavior.

For example, in the early 1900s, a horse in Germany nicknamed Clever Hans seemed to be able to solve math questions by using its hoof to tap out the correct answer. However, upon closer inspection it was found that the horse's ability to tap out the correct answer had nothing to do with mathematical skills. Instead, it was relying on changes in the posture or facial expressions of its trainer. The horse was able to perceive the increased tension in its trainer when it neared the correct answer, and would stop tapping its hoof. This example illustrates how difficult it can be to determine the cognitive abilities of animals. While the horse was unable to solve mathematical problems, it can be argued that its ability to perceive changes in its trainer's posture is an example of cognition on a different level.

Analyze Why do scientists focus on an animal's cognitive abilities rather than its "intelligence" when studying animal behavior?

FIGURE 27.17 While considered to have fewer cognitive abilities than other primates, studies have shown that lemurs have the ability to remember long sequences of images and can place images in the correct order.

MAIN IDEA
Some animals can solve problems.

Scientists sometimes study how animals think by giving them problems to solve. If cognition involves the ability to invent new behaviors in new situations, then animals with cognitive abilities should be able to solve problems they have never encountered before. Different species react to new situations with varying amounts of success.

Problem-Solving Behavior

Researchers have observed extremely complex problem-solving behavior in primates, dolphins, and the corvids—a group of birds that includes crows, ravens, and jays. In one classic study, a chimpanzee was placed in a room containing boxes, sticks, and a banana hung out of reach. At first, the chimp sat around and did nothing. But after a while it suddenly piled up the boxes and climbed up to knock down the fruit with a stick. This ability to solve a problem mentally without repeated trial and error is called **insight.**

Tool Use

Tools are inanimate objects that help an animal accomplish a task, such as collecting hard-to-reach foods. A number of different animals use tools. For example, Australian bottlenose dolphins use pieces of sponge to cover their snouts when foraging. Not only does this method protect them from being stung on their noses by stonefish but it also helps to scare up fish from the ocean floor. Some primates and New Caledonian crows have been observed making tools. Chimpanzees trim sticks to make termite probes. As shown in **FIGURE 27.18,** brown capuchin monkeys use rocks to crack open palm nuts. In one experiment, crows given straight wires bent the wire to make a hook, then used it to fish food out of a tube. Tool use itself is not a sign of cognitive ability. But making tools suggests that an animal can understand cause and effect, and can make predictions about its own behavior.

Contrast **What is the difference between insight and associative learning?**

FIGURE 27.18 Brown capuchin monkeys use a rock to crack open the hard shells of palm nuts.

MAIN IDEA
Cognitive ability may provide an adaptive advantage for living in social groups.

Animals we recognize as the most "intelligent" often have two things in common. They have relatively large brains for their body size, and they live in complex social groups. More neurons may mean more interconnections and greater opportunities for complex behaviors to emerge. But evidence suggests that it is just as important to live in a group with a complex social system.

FIGURE 27.19 Elephants are social animals that form close bonds within their group.

Animals that live in large groups with a definite social structure, such as the elephants shown in **FIGURE 27.19**, are surrounded by politics. Surviving and reproducing depends on remembering and being able to use a vast amount of information to the individual's advantage. These animals must be able to

- identify other individuals in the group
- remember which individuals are their allies and rivals
- keep track of the constantly changing state of affairs among individuals
- use this information to their own advantage

Cultural behavior is behavior that is spread through a population by learning, rather than by selection. The key to cultural behavior is that the behavior is taught to one generation by another. The development of cultural behavior does not require living in complex societies. For example, some scientists would argue that the transmission of birdsong is an example of cultural behavior. However, living close together in social groups may help to enhance the transmission and expression of cultural behaviors.

Connect   What is an example of cultural behavior from your life?

27.5 / ASSESSMENT

ONLINE QUIZ
ClassZone.com

REVIEWING ▶ MAIN IDEAS

1. Why is animal intelligence difficult to define?
2. Use an example to explain what solving a problem by using **insight** means.
3. Explain how living in a complex social group might select for increased cognitive abilities.

CRITICAL THINKING

4. **Apply** In Section 27.2, you learned about the potato-washing behavior of snow monkeys. Is this an example of **cultural behavior**? Explain your reasoning.
5. **Analyze** There are three keys on a table. How might you use insight to determine which key opens a nearby door?

Connecting CONCEPTS

6. **Scientific Process** Why are scientists so interested in studying primate behavior? What might scientists learn about human behavior?

Use these inquiry-based labs and online activities to deepen your understanding of animal behavior.

DESIGN YOUR OWN INVESTIGATION

Pill Bug Behavior

Pill bugs (*Armadillidium vulgare*) are terrestrial crustaceans that feed on decaying plant and animal matter. As scavengers and composters, they even eat their exoskeleton when it sheds, to recycle the calcium. As crustaceans, they have two pairs of antennae, breathe through gills, and have seven pairs of legs on their abdomen and thorax. In this investigation, you will design an experiment to determine how manipulating a variable changes the behavior of pill bugs.

PROBLEM How does the behavior pattern of pill bugs change when their environment is manipulated?

1. Formulate a question to ask about pill bug behavior by looking at the materials list and determining how you can manipulate their environment.

2. Determine a control setting. Create a data table to record your observations of 12 pill bugs in the control setting.

3. Choose a variable to manipulate. Create a data table to record your observations of pill bug behavior in the manipulated environment. Remember to treat all living things carefully.

4. Make a list of all the conditions you will hold constant in your experiment.

5. Formulate a hypothesis to your question.

6. Have your teacher approve your experimental design.

7. Conduct your experiment.

8. If time permits, conduct three trials, using a new set of pill bugs for each trial.

9. Wash your hands when you are done.

MATERIALS

- shoebox lid
- marker
- 12 pill bugs
- 25 cm piece of foil
- light source
- 10-mL graduated cylinder
- 10 mL water
- 4 paper towels
- sheet dark-colored paper
- sheet light-colored paper

ANALYZE AND CONCLUDE

1. **Analyze** Compare your data to your hypothesis. Explain whether your data supported your hypothesis or not.

2. **Conclude** What effect did manipulating the environment have on pill bug behavior?

3. **Experimental Design** Identify possible sources of unavoidable experimental error in your design.

4. **Experimental Design** List possible reasons for inconsistent results you may have observed.

5. **Predict** How might pill bug behavior be different in a more natural environment? Why might this occur?

Animal Cognition

With technology such as remote-controlled cameras, scientists can observe the behavior of animals in their natural environment. This allows them to learn more about how animals communicate with each other, their mating rituals, how they compete with each other, and problem-solving skills they may have.

SKILL Researching

PROBLEM What are scientists learning about animal cognition?

RESEARCH

1. Choose an animal to research in the field of animal cognition, such as the African elephant, the New Caledonian crow, the Australian bottlenose dolphin, the octopus, the humpback whale, or the chimpanzee.

2. Investigate, using library and/or Internet resources, what research is being done to learn more about the cognitive abilities of the animal. Include
   - methods for data collection
   - data obtained
   - conclusions drawn

EXTEND YOUR INVESTIGATION

Based on information from your research, form a hypothesis that is relevant to the topic of animal intelligence and design an experiment to test the hypothesis.

Online BIOLOGY
CLASSZONE.COM

VIRTUAL LAB
Interpreting Bird Response

Does a male song sparrow react to other song sparrows in the same way? In this interactive lab, you will determine how male song sparrows respond to the songs of local and foreign song sparrows.

WEBQUEST

How smart is a dolphin? In this WebQuest, you will learn about the study of animal cognition. Explore examples of animal cognition as well as experiments used to test the mental capabilities of animals.

ANIMATED BIOLOGY
Behavioral Costs and Benefits

Can you balance the energy costs and benefits of behaviors? Have a hummingbird use optimal foraging and defensive strategies to maximize its limited energy supply.

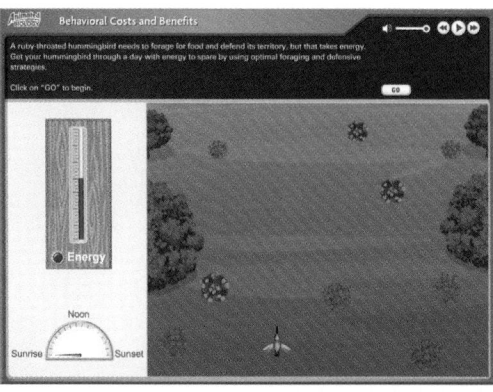

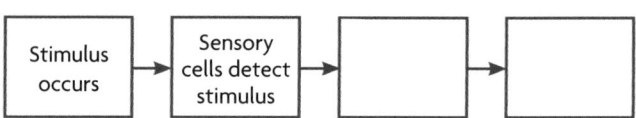
KEY CONCEPTS | Vocabulary Games | Concept Maps | Animated Biology | Online Quiz

27.1 Adaptive Value of Behavior

Behavior lets organisms respond rapidly and adaptively to their environment. A stimulus is a type of information that has the potential to make an organism change its behavior. An animal's behavior can be considered as a way of maintaining homeostasis. Many animal behaviors are responses to stimuli that affect an individual's well-being. Internal and external stimuli interact to trigger specific behaviors. Some behaviors occur in cycles. Hibernation and migration are two behaviors that are controlled by an animal's biological clock.

27.2 Instinct and Learning

Both genes and environment affect an animal's behavior. Innate behaviors are inborn instinctive behaviors. Many behaviors have both innate and learned components. Animals that are able to learn can modify their behavior to adapt to new situations. Classical conditioning and operant conditioning are two examples of associative learning.

27.3 Evolution of Behavior

Every behavior has costs and benefits. Benefits of certain behaviors include increased survivorship and rates of reproduction. Three categories of behavioral costs include energy costs, opportunity costs, and risk costs. Animals perform behaviors for which the benefits outweigh the costs.

27.4 Social Behavior

Social behaviors enhance the benefits of living in a group. Social behaviors are interactions between members of the same species. Altruistic behaviors benefit other group members at the cost to the individual performing them. Eusocial behaviors are an example of extreme altruism.

27.5 Animal Cognition

Some animals other than humans exhibit behaviors requiring complex cognitive abilities. Animal intelligence is difficult to define, but animal behavior scientists are able to study the cognitive abilities of animals. Characteristics of animal cognition include awareness, perception, reasoning, and judgment. Some animals can solve problems through the use of insight. Cultural behavior is behavior that is spread through a population by learning rather than by selection.

Synthesize Your Notes

Concept Map Use a concept map like the one below to summarize your notes on cyclical behaviors.

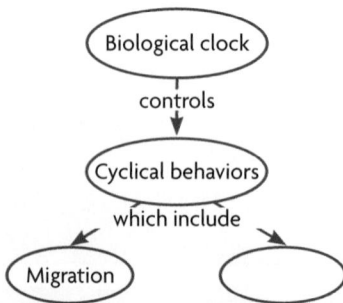

Process Diagram Use a process diagram like the one below to summarize your notes on an animal's response to a stimulus.

| Stimulus occurs | → | Sensory cells detect stimulus | → | | → | |

Chapter Assessment

Chapter Vocabulary

27.1 stimulus, p. 818
kinesis, p. 819
taxis, p. 819
circadian rhythm, p. 820
biological clock, p. 820

27.2 instinct, p. 822
innate, p. 822
releaser, p. 822

habituation, p. 823
imprinting, p. 824
imitation, p. 825
classical conditioning, p. 826
operant conditioning, p. 826

27.3 survivorship, p. 827
territoriality, p. 828
optimal foraging, p. 829

27.4 pheromone, p. 832
altruism, p. 833
inclusive fitness, p. 834
kin selection, p. 834
eusocial, p. 834

27.5 cognition, p. 837
insight, p. 838
cultural behavior, p. 839

Reviewing Vocabulary

Compare and Contrast

Describe one similarity and one difference between the two terms in each of the following pairs.

1. classical conditioning, operant conditioning
2. cultural behavior, imitation
3. territoriality, optimal foraging

Vocabulary Connections

The vocabulary terms in this chapter are related to each other in various ways. For each group of words below, write a sentence or two to clearly explain how the terms are connected.

4. stimulus, taxis
5. survivorship, territoriality
6. altruism, eusocial
7. instinct, innate

Greek and Latin Word Origins

8. The term *stimulus* comes from a Latin word, *stimulare,* which means "to goad, prod, or urge." Explain how this meaning relates to *stimulus.*

9. The term *habituation* comes from the Latin word *habitus,* which means "condition or habit." Explain how this meaning relates to *habituation.*

10. The term *pheromone* comes from a combination of the Greek words *pherein,* meaning "to carry," and *horme,* meaning "impulse." How do these words relate to the meaning of *pheromone*?

11. The term *altruism* comes from the Latin word *alter,* meaning "other." How is this meaning related to the definition of an altruistic individual?

12. The term *kinesis* comes from the Greek word *kinein,* meaning "to move." Explain this connection.

Reviewing MAIN IDEAS

13. What is the role of the nervous system in an animal's response to a stimulus?

14. Identify the internal and external factors that are likely to lead to migration in songbirds.

15. What are some of the characteristics of innate behaviors?

16. When does habituation occur?

17. How is the ability to adapt behaviors to new situations important to an animal's survival?

18. Describe the benefits and costs of migratory behavior.

19. The territory of a pack of gray wolves can be more than 3000 square kilometers. The alpha male marks the boundaries of the territory with urine. Explain why a wolf would engage in this time-consuming behavior.

20. Groups of small songbirds will often mob an owl or a hawk. They fly around it and call loudly. What is the cost and benefit of this behavior to the songbirds? Explain your answer.

21. Arctic ground squirrels live in groups and forage for food during daylight. What is the cost of foraging in a group?

22. What information might be provided to potential mates by a courtship display such as the competitive performances of sage grouses?

23. In the meerkat group, one animal always stands guard and sounds an alarm call if a bird of prey is sighted. Why is this an altruistic behavior?

24. What are the characteristics of eusocial behavior?

25. What is the connection between cognitive ability and insight?

Critical Thinking

26. Connect Your alarm clock wakes you up and you get ready for school. You eat breakfast but then eat one more slice of toast. After stepping outside, you go back in to get a lighter jacket. Identify all the stimuli in this scene and whether they are internal or external.

27. Apply A zookeeper needs to use a scale to measure the weight of an otter. How might she use operant conditioning to get the otter onto the scale?

28. Analyze Gray wolves live in packs with about 6 to 15 members. Young pups remain behind while the older animals hunt for prey as a group. They often seek out old, sick, and slower prey animals. All of the adults regurgitate food for the pups. Suggest two costs and two benefits of gray wolf feeding behavior.

29. Infer The unison call is performed by a pair of whooping cranes. The male and female each have their own notes and perform this call often when they arrive at their nesting area. Suggest some reasons why the birds perform this call.

30. Apply You buy a bag of raisins. There are no directions how to open the bag. There is no tab to pull. You do not have a scissors to cut the bag open. You examine the bag for a few seconds and then pull the seams of the sealed top apart to open it. What type of problem-solving behavior did you demonstrate? Explain your answer.

Interpreting Visuals

Use the photograph to answer the next three questions.

31. Infer Why do you think the baby elephants are traveling between the adults?

32. Analyze For which elephants might there be a benefit for this type of behavior and for which elephants might there be a cost?

33. Evaluate If there is a benefit, does it outweigh the cost? Explain your answer.

Analyzing Data

The graph below shows a time budget for different behaviors exhibited by grizzly bears in a national park in the Yukon Territory, Canada. Use the data to answer the next three questions.

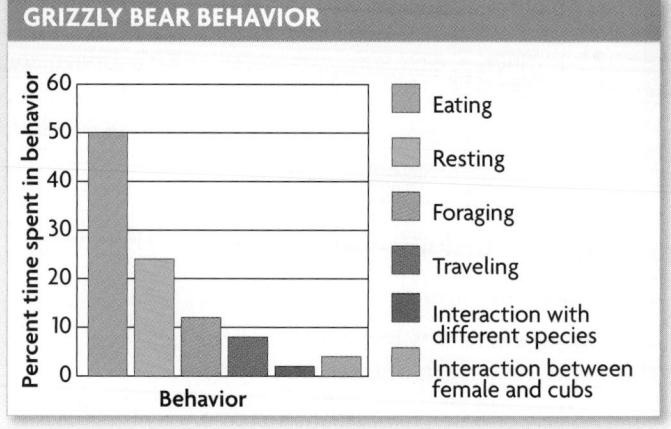

GRIZZLY BEAR BEHAVIOR

Legend:
- Eating
- Resting
- Foraging
- Traveling
- Interaction with different species
- Interaction between female and cubs

Source: MacHutchon *Ursus* 12:2001.

34. Analyze What behavior did the bears engage in most of the time?

35. Analyze Do the bears interact more often with other bears or with other species in this park?

36. Infer What can you infer about the habitat based on the data for foraging and eating?

Connecting CONCEPTS

37. Write a Fable You may remember reading Aesop's fables as a child. A fable is a story that ends with a moral, or lesson, such as "the early bird gets the worm." This chapter described reasons for animal behaviors, various types of responses, and the situations in which behaviors might occur. Write a short fable about an animal's behavior, in which the moral of the story illustrates the adaptive value of the behavior.

38. Analyze Consider again the chimpanzee shown on page 817. Why might scientists be interested in studying tool use in primates such as chimpanzees?

MICHIGAN STANDARDS-BASED ASSESSMENT

✓ **Test Practice**
For more test practice, go to ClassZone.com.

1. Students plan an experiment to determine whether fish exhibit different feeding behaviors when presented with food flakes of different colors. They determined that the fish chose the brightest color of flakes, and concluded it was because the fish could see bright colored flakes most easily. If this conclusion is true, then fish fed in the dark should **B1.1f**

   A still prefer the brightest flakes.

   B then prefer the dullest color of flakes.

   C eat all the colors of flakes equally.

   D prefer a pellet form of food rather than flakes.

2. A female ground squirrel may send out a call warning her offspring that a predator is near. Often, the mother sacrifices her own life since the predator can more easily locate her from the call. Even though this behavior results in death, it is beneficial to her in that **B2.6A**

   A half of her alleles are preserved in each offspring.

   B all of her alleles are preserved in each offspring.

   C the predator may be less likely to attack the population again.

   D the alleles that caused her behavior will no longer be in the gene pool.

3.

   This action illustrated above will *most* likely result in a response produced by the **B2.3d**

   A nervous system.

   B respiratory system.

   C endocrine system.

   D immune system.

4. When a frog hunts, it catches its prey with one flick of its long, sticky tongue. Energy obtained from eating the insect that is *not* stored in newly made body structures is **B3.2B**

   A lost to the environment as heat.

   B converted into sugars.

   C passed on to offspring.

   D recycled within the frog.

   ### THINK THROUGH THE QUESTION
   Consider the flow of energy though an energy pyramid. In which directions does energy flow?

5. A scientist is interested in a research topic that he has not studied before. A good first step for him would be to **B1.2C**

   A research relevant information from multiple sources.

   B jump right in and perform some experiments.

   C leave it to scientists more familiar with the topic.

   D return to school to learn more about the topic.

6.

Alleles for Rabbit Fur Color	
Allele	Trait
F	gray fur
f	brown fur

   In a hypothetical rabbit species, females prefer to mate with brown males over gray males. Fur color is a trait controlled by one gene that can occur in a dominant form *(F)* or a recessive form *(f)*. A gray female *(Ff)* mates with a gray male *(Ff)*, and they produce a brown male offspring. How is this possible? **B5.3A**

   A Since brown fur is preferred by females, male offspring are more likely to be brown.

   B During fertilization, a mutation for brown fur color formed.

   C A new combination of alleles *(FF)* formed in the offspring during fertilization.

   D A new combination of alleles *(ff)* formed in the offspring during fertilization.

Go online for the latest biology news and updates on all BioZine articles.

Expanding the Textbook

News Feeds

- Science Daily
- CNN
- BBC

Careers

Bio Bytes

Opinion Poll

Strange Biology

Emperor tamarins are omnivores that eat fruits, insects, flowers, and nectar. As seed dispersers for a variety of plant species, these primates are important to the health of the tropical rain forest ecosystems in which they live.

The Loss of Biodiversity

Extinction is occurring at a rate that is 1000 times faster than any time in the past 100,000 years. Wide swathes of rain forest are being destroyed as humans develop the land for agriculture and other human needs. Because rain forests are areas with high biodiversity, each time an acre of land is lost, species that once lived there may be lost as well. Why is biodiversity important? How does its loss affect you?

Biodiversity at Risk

At present, we are losing more species than we are finding. Across the globe, animal species that are known to be threatened with extinction include

- 12 percent of all birds
- 30 percent of all fishes
- 24 percent of all mammals
- 20 percent of all amphibians

Biologists think that there are least 10 million, and possibly as many as 100 million, species of plants and animals. At current rates of extinction, over half of these species will be gone by the end of this century. Extinction is a natural process and is always occurring. Using evidence from the fossil record, the background extinction rate is calculated to be between 10 and 100 species per year. However, the current rate of extinction greatly exceeds that number. Hundreds of thousands of species will disappear before we are even aware of their existence.

Does Biodiversity Really Matter?

Some people might suggest that biodiversity belongs in a zoo and the rest of the world belongs to humans to develop. Arguments in favor of development include the following:

- The rise and fall of species is part of nature. No species lives forever. New species replace old ones.
- Economic development provides jobs to people who are living in poverty.
- Land set aside as wilderness could be better used as farmland to provide more food for a rapidly increasing human population.

Conservation biologists view the pro-development arguments as shortsighted. Their view is that the Earth must be maintained for future generations, not simply harvested to provide for the needs of its current population. In fact, they argue that biodiversity plays an important part in ecosystem stability.

TECHNOLOGY

Bioremediation

Microorganisms can be used to clean up wastes that are spilled. Some bacteria can eat substances that would be fatal to humans and most other animals. Using microorganisms to clean up a polluted environment is called bioremediation.

1. Toxic waste, such as crude oil, is spilled on soil or in water.

2. The waste kills most bacteria, but a few survive and adapt.

3. Surviving bacteria feed on the toxins that were spilled and break them down. They may change the toxin to another form that is not dangerous, break the compound into smaller parts, or completely degrade it into inorganic molecules such as carbon dioxide and water.

4. Oxygen and nutrients are added so that more bacteria will survive to help break down the toxins.

5. When the spill has been completely broken down, bacteria die because they have run out of food.

Sometimes the needed microbes do not naturally occur in the contaminated site. When this is the case, the clean-up crew adds the specialized microbes to the site to break down the toxins.

Read More >> *at* CLASSZONE.COM

Clean-up crews use the *Pseudomonas putida* bacteria (inset) to decontaminate soil polluted by oil spills.
(colored SEM; magnification 300×)

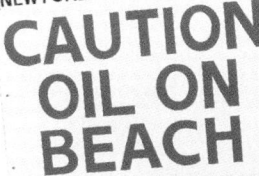

NEW FOREST DISTRICT COUNCIL
CAUTION OIL ON BEACH

The Value of Biodiversity

Ecosystems provide human communities with a number of services free of charge, including air and water purification, flood and drought control, pollination of crops and other vegetation, dispersal of seeds, and nutrient cycling. These services have an economic value. If it were possible for humans to pay for ecosystem services based on their market value, biologists estimate that the cost would be approximately $33 trillion annually.

In general, the more species that live in an ecosystem, the more efficient and stable that ecosystem will be. For example, a rain forest can produce much more oxygen than an orchard full of apple trees. Also, many plants, including 75 percent of the world's staple crop plants, need animal pollinators such as birds and insects to help them reproduce.

In addition, 40 percent of all medicines are derived from plants, animals, and microbes. For example, biologists are developing a painkiller based on an extract from the skin of an Ecuadorian frog. The painkiller is 200 times stronger than morphine, but is not addictive. Every time a plant, animal, or microbe becomes extinct, biologists lose whatever knowledge they might have been able to gain by studying it.

> *In general, the more species that live in an ecosystem, the more efficient and stable that ecosystem will be.*

Unanswered Questions

As you have learned, biodiversity is very valuable. Yet questions remain about how best to protect biodiversity. Two of these unanswered questions include

- How can we slow down the current extinction rate?
- Some of the areas with the highest amount of biodiversity are located in developing countries. How can biodiversity be preserved without harming the country's economic growth?

Read More >> *at* CLASSZONE.COM

By the mid-1970s, peregrine falcon populations had declined between 80 and 90 percent. Today, their numbers have rebounded. They were taken off the endangered species list in 1999.

CAREERS

Conservation Biologist in Action

ANGEL MONTOYA

TITLE Senior Field Biologist, The Peregrine Fund

EDUCATION M.S., Wildlife Science, New Mexico State University

In 1990 Angel Montoya was a student intern working at Laguna Atascosa National Wildlife Refuge in Texas. He became interested in the Aplomado falcon, a bird of prey that disappeared from the southwestern United States during the first half of the 20th century. Montoya decided to go looking for the raptors, and he found a previously unknown population of Aplomados in Chihuahua, Mexico. His work helped to make it possible for the falcons to be reintroduced to an area near El Paso, Texas.

Restoration of the Aplomado falcon became Montoya's life work. He has monitored and researched the falcon since 1992. He helps release falcons that have been raised in captivity back into the wild, and monitors falcons that have already been released. It isn't easy to keep tabs on a falcon, however. "Their first year they are pretty vulnerable because they haven't had parents," Montoya says. "Just like juveniles, they're always getting into trouble. But I think they will do just fine."

Read More >> *at* CLASSZONE.COM

UNIT 9
Human Biology

CHAPTER 28
Human Systems and Homeostasis   850

CHAPTER 29
Nervous and Endocrine Systems   872

CHAPTER 30
Respiratory and Circulatory Systems   908

CHAPTER 31
Immune System and Disease   938

CHAPTER 32
Digestive and Excretory Systems   970

CHAPTER 33
Protection, Support, and Movement   998

CHAPTER 34
Reproduction and Development   1022

BIOZINE

INTERNET MAGAZINE
Brain Science—We Are Wired to Learn!   1050
    TECHNOLOGY Scanning the Brain
    CAREER Neuroscientist

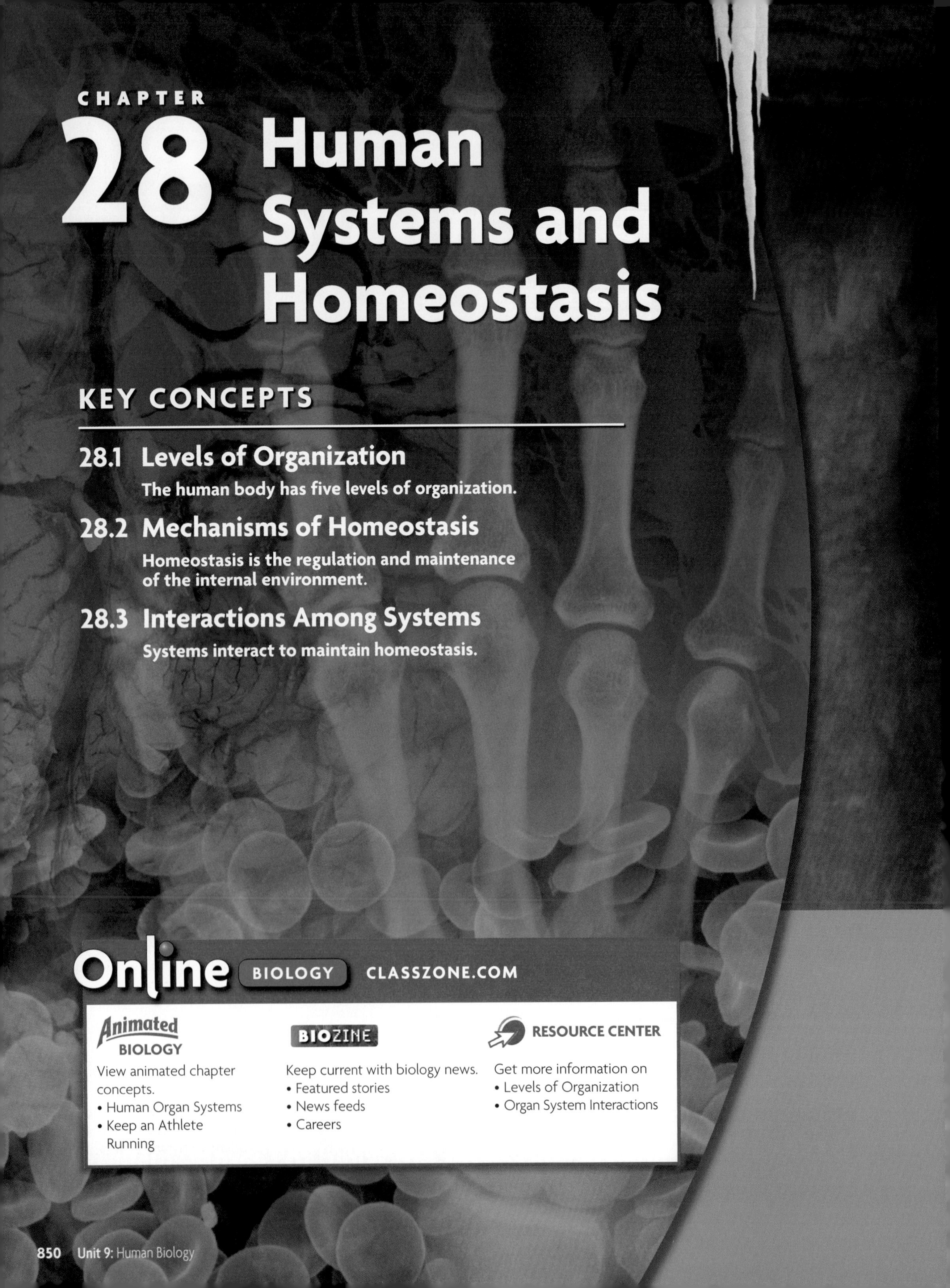

CHAPTER
28 Human Systems and Homeostasis

KEY CONCEPTS

28.1 Levels of Organization
The human body has five levels of organization.

28.2 Mechanisms of Homeostasis
Homeostasis is the regulation and maintenance of the internal environment.

28.3 Interactions Among Systems
Systems interact to maintain homeostasis.

Online BIOLOGY CLASSZONE.COM

Animated BIOLOGY
View animated chapter concepts.
• Human Organ Systems
• Keep an Athlete Running

BIOZINE
Keep current with biology news.
• Featured stories
• News feeds
• Careers

RESOURCE CENTER
Get more information on
• Levels of Organization
• Organ System Interactions

How does this ice climber hang on to his body temperature?

This climber has to concentrate on every move—one slip could mean serious injury or even death. His body is working just as hard on the inside to provide energy and to maintain a stable body temperature. The climber's clothes help prevent heat loss, while his body's internal systems increase his body heat.

Connecting CONCEPTS

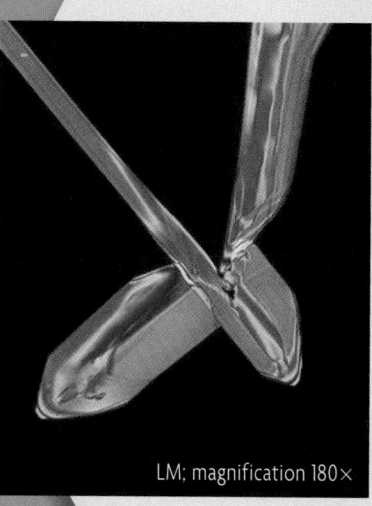

LM; magnification 180×

Biochemistry Recall that the metabolic processes in cells release energy stored in nutrients. The thyroid gland produces hormones that regulate cell metabolism. One hormone, thyroxine (shown here under polarized light), stimulates cells to produce more energy when needed. In this chapter, you will learn about the body's organ systems and the control mechanisms that maintain homeostasis.

28.1 Levels of Organization

KEY CONCEPT The human body has five levels of organization.

MAIN IDEAS
- Specialized cells develop from a single zygote.
- Specialized cells function together in tissues, organs, organ systems, and the whole organism.

VOCABULARY

determination, p. 852
differentiation, p. 853
tissue, p. 854

organ, p. 854
organ system, p. 854

Review
cell, stem cell, zygote

Connect Climbing a wall of ice requires careful interaction among all parts of the body. You probably know that the brain and muscles work together to coordinate the climber's movements. The heart and lungs also have to work together to help provide energy for the climb. Yet every human body starts out as a single cell, a fertilized zygote. How does a single cell give rise to all the different types of cells, tissues, and organs in the human body? Further, how do such different parts coordinate their activities to keep the body functioning?

MAIN IDEA
Specialized cells develop from a single zygote.

If you were to watch an emergency medical team in action, you would quickly notice that each person has a special job. One keeps in radio contact with the main hospital. Another monitors the patient's vital signs. Still others perform life-saving procedures. All emergency teams are made up of people, but each person within the group has a different job.

Likewise, multicellular organisms are made up of cells, but different cells in the organism have different functions. Take a moment to study the images of the blood cells and nerve cells, or neurons, in **FIGURE 28.1.** You will notice that the red blood cells are round with a concave center. This structure gives them more surface area to help deliver oxygen to all parts of the body. In contrast, neurons develop extensions that transmit and receive messages from other neurons.

Humans, like almost all multicellular organisms, are collections of specialized cells that work together. These cells arise from a single cell, the zygote, which is formed by the union of an egg and sperm. The zygote divides and differentiates into more than 200 different types of human cells. These cells allow you to do everything from lifting a glass, to learning people's names, to maintaining your body temperature on a cold day. Cell specialization involves two main steps: determination and differentiation.

Determination

The cells produced during the first few divisions of the zygote are known as embryonic stem cells. These cells have the potential to become any type of specialized cell in the body. Within a few weeks, however, a process called **determination** occurs in which most stem cells become committed to develop

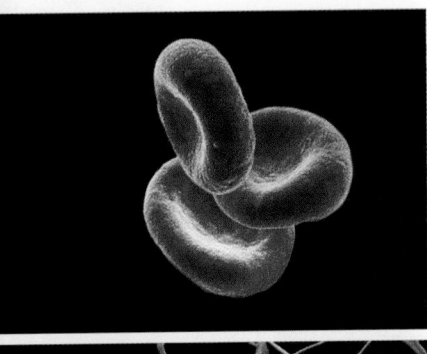

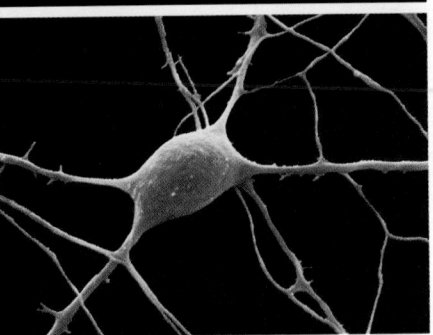

FIGURE 28.1 The disk-shaped red blood cells (top) carry oxygen to all parts of the body. The neuron (bottom), through its extensions, receives and transmits messages from and to other neurons.
(colored SEMs; magnifications: blood cells 2800×; neuron about 1600×)

into only one type of cell. For instance, a stem cell might become a cardiac muscle cell or a spinal neuron. These committed cells still retain all of the genetic information needed to build an entire organism. However, during determination, they lose their ability to express some of this information.

Once a cell is committed to becoming a specialized cell, it will develop into only that type of cell. For instance, a cell that will become a neuron can only be a neuron, even if it is transplanted into another part of the body. During normal development, determination cannot be reversed.

Differentiation

Differentiation is the process by which committed cells acquire the structures and functions of highly specialized cells. Differentiation occurs because specific genes in each cell are turned on and off in a complex, regulated pattern. The different structures of these specialized cells, such as those shown in **FIGURE 28.2**, allow them to perform specific functions within the body.

The function of muscle cells, for example, is to produce movement by contracting and relaxing. However, skeletal muscle and smooth muscle cells have different structures. Skeletal muscle cells align in bands of orderly rows and contain many nuclei. They are responsible for nearly all voluntary muscle movements, such as lifting your foot to kick a ball. In contrast, smooth muscle cells are shorter and have only one nucleus. They perform involuntary movements, such as raising the hairs on your arms and legs.

Other cells have even more specialized structures and functions. Sperm cells, for instance, develop whiplike tails that enable them to swim. Cells lining the gut are elongated and tightly packed to provide more surface area for the absorption of nutrients.

Not all cells continue to develop into specialized cells. The process of programmed cell death, called apoptosis (AP-uhp-TOH-sihs), is also a normal part of development. For example, when your hands first formed, your fingers resembled a mitten. The death of cells between the fingers allowed individual fingers to develop.

Analyze What are some of the reasons that multicellular organisms need specialized cells?

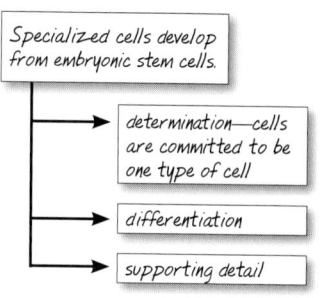

Specialized cells develop from embryonic stem cells.

determination—cells are committed to be one type of cell

differentiation

supporting detail

FIGURE 28.2 Cell Differentiation

Cells develop specialized structures and functions during differentiation.

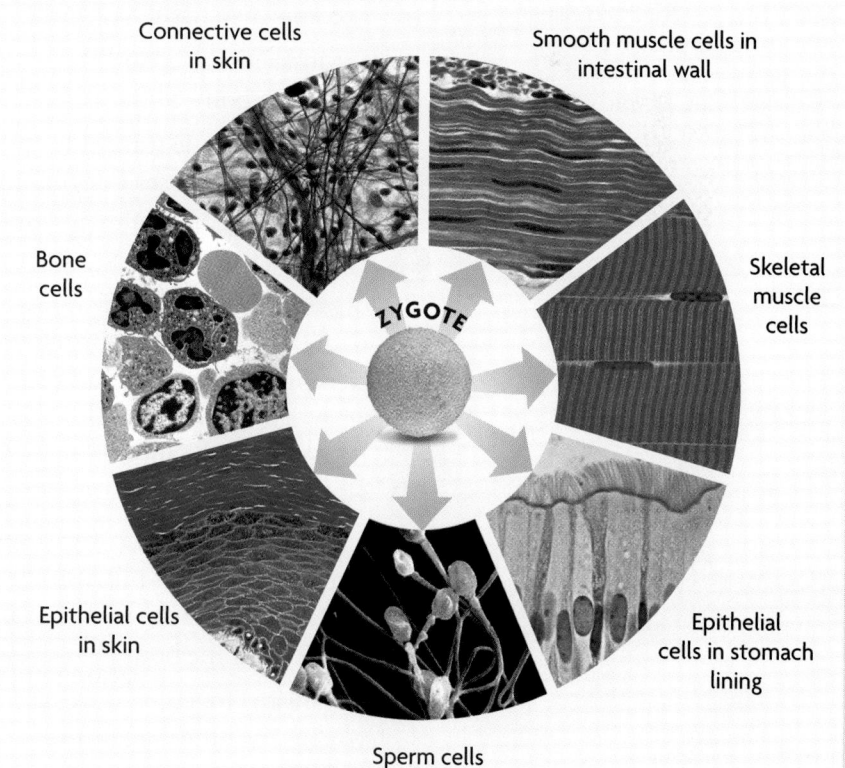

Connective cells in skin

Smooth muscle cells in intestinal wall

Bone cells

ZYGOTE

Skeletal muscle cells

Epithelial cells in skin

Epithelial cells in stomach lining

Sperm cells

Contrast How do the structures of sperm cells and epithelial cells in the stomach differ?

▶ MAIN IDEA

Specialized cells function together in tissues, organs, organ systems, and the whole organism.

Specialized, or differentiated, cells are only the first level of organization in a multicellular organism. Scientists organize multicellular structures into five basic levels, beginning with cells and moving to increasingly complex levels—tissues, organs, organ systems, and the whole organism. These five levels in the human body are shown in **FIGURE 28.3**.

1 **Cells** Each type of specialized cell has a particular structure and a chemical makeup that enable it to perform a specific task. Some cells in the lungs, for instance, are involved in the exchange of gases. Others secrete mucus that helps to trap foreign particles and to protect the lungs from pathogens, such as bacteria and viruses.

2 **Tissues** Groups of similar cells that work together to perform a specialized function are known as **tissues.** The human body is made up of four general types of tissues.

- Epithelial tissue consists of protective sheets of tightly packed cells connected by special junctions. The skin and the membranes that line the stomach, the lungs, and other organs are epithelial tissues.

- Connective tissue serves to support, bind together, and protect other tissues and organs. Tendons, ligaments, bone, and cartilage are all connective tissues.

- Muscle tissue is capable of contracting to produce movement. The human body contains skeletal, cardiac, and smooth muscle tissues.

- Nervous tissue transmits and receives impulses in response to stimuli, processes information, and regulates the body's response to its environment.

3 **Organs** Different types of tissue that function together form an **organ.** For example, the lungs are organs composed of all four types of tissues. Muscle and connective tissues expand and contract the lungs. Nervous tissue sends and receives messages that help regulate gas exchange in the lungs and the rate at which a person breathes. Epithelial tissue forms the inner lining of the lungs.

4 **Organ systems** Two or more organs working in a coordinated way form an **organ system.** The organ system that allows you to breathe includes not only the lungs but also the sinuses, the nasal passages, the pharynx, and the larynx (the voice box). Organ systems perform the most complex activities in the body.

5 **Organism** Together, the organ systems make up the entire organism. For you or any other organism to stay alive, all of the systems must interact and work together. As a result, anything that harms one organ or organ system will affect the health of the entire body.

Connecting CONCEPTS

Digestion and Elimination In addition to serving as a protective layer, epithelial tissue can absorb materials and secrete special types of fluids. Your ability to digest food and eliminate waste depends in part on the specialized functions of epithelial tissue, as you will learn in **Chapter 32.**

FIGURE 28.3 Five Levels of Organization

All levels of organization interact and work together to maintain the body's health.

BIOLOGY
Explore the human organ systems at ClassZone.com.

1 CELLS

Epithelial lung cell
These cells have tiny hairlike structures (cilia) at the top.

2 TISSUES

Epithelial lung tissue
Cells with cilia are packed together in the lung's inner lining. They act like a conveyor belt to move foreign particles and pathogens out of the lungs.

3 ORGANS

Lungs
The lungs are composed of four types of tissue. The lungs are the site where gases are exchanged.

4 ORGAN SYSTEMS

Respiratory system
This system includes the lungs, trachea, larynx, pharynx, sinuses, and nose. The nose and sinuses filter, moisten, and warm the air before it enters the lungs.

5 ORGANISM

Human
The respiratory system is one of several organ systems that work together to keep the human body functioning properly.

CRITICAL VIEWING How might a sinus infection affect the rest of the respiratory system?

FIGURE 28.4 Major Organ Systems

SYSTEM	MAJOR TISSUES AND ORGANS	PRIMARY FUNCTION
Circulatory	heart, blood vessels, blood, lymph nodes, lymphatic vessels	transports oxygen, nutrients, wastes; helps regulate body temperature; collects fluid lost from blood vessels and returns it to circulatory system
Digestive	mouth, pharynx, esophagus, stomach, small/large intestines, pancreas, gallbladder, liver	breaks down and absorbs nutrients, salts, and water; eliminates some wastes
Endocrine	hypothalamus, pituitary, thyroid, parathyroid, adrenals, pancreas, ovaries, testes	influences growth, development, metabolism; helps maintain homeostasis
Excretory	skin, lungs, kidneys, bladder	eliminates waste products; helps maintain homeostasis
Immune	white blood cells, thymus, spleen	protects against disease; stores and generates white blood cells
Integumentary	skin, hair, nails, sweat and oil glands	acts as a barrier against infection, injury, UV radiation; helps regulate body temperature
Muscular	skeletal, smooth, and cardiac muscles	produces voluntary and involuntary movements; helps to circulate blood and move food through digestive system
Nervous	brain, spinal cord, peripheral nerves	regulates body's response to changes in internal and external environment; processes information
Reproductive	*male:* testes, penis, associated ducts and glands *female:* ovaries, fallopian tubes, uterus, vagina	produces reproductive cells; in females, provides environment for embryo
Respiratory	nose, sinuses, pharynx, larynx, trachea, lungs	brings in O_2 for cells; expels CO_2 and water vapor
Skeletal	bones, cartilage, ligaments, tendons	supports and protects vital organs; allows movement; stores minerals; serves as the site for red blood cell production

The major organ systems in the human body, including their main parts and primary functions, are listed in **FIGURE 28.4.** Keep in mind that all of the organs in these systems developed from specialized cells and tissues that arose from a single cell, the zygote. The major parts and functions of each organ system are examined in greater detail in Chapters 29 through 34.

How do these complex organs and organ systems keep functioning and working together properly? As you will read in Section 28.2, the body has sophisticated mechanisms for maintaining a stable internal environment.

Compare and Contrast How do tissues differ from organs and organ systems?

28.1 ASSESSMENT

ONLINE QUIZ
ClassZone.com

REVIEWING ▶ MAIN IDEAS

1. How does the process of cell **determination** differ from the process of cell **differentiation**?

2. Briefly define and give an example of each of the five levels of organization in multicellular organisms.

CRITICAL THINKING

3. **Apply** What **organ systems** must work together to bring oxygen to the body's cells?

4. **Predict** A cell has undergone determination to become an endocrine gland cell. If it is transplanted to a leg muscle, what do you think will happen to this cell?

Connecting CONCEPTS

5. **Cell Cycle** In the spring, tadpoles lose their tails as part of their life cycle. At a certain stage in development, the human fetus acquires individual fingers and toes. What occurs in some cells of both species to explain these changes?

MATERIALS
- jump rope
- stop watch

PROCESS SKILLS
- **Observing**
- **Collecting data**

MICHIGAN STANDARDS

B2.3B Describe how the maintenance of a relatively stable internal environment is required for the continuation of life.

B2.3e Describe how human body systems maintain relatively constant internal conditions (temperature, acidity, and blood sugar).

Homeostasis and Exercise

Your body's temperature, heart rate, and blood pressure need to remain within certain set ranges. In this lab, you will work in groups to examine the effects of exercise on the circulatory and respiratory systems and on perspiration level.

PROBLEM How does exercise affect a person's heart rate, breathing rate, and perspiration level?

PROCEDURE

1. Choose one person to jump rope. Measure the person's heart rate by taking his or her pulse for 15 seconds. Multiply this number by four to calculate beats per minute. (**Caution:** If the person exercising feels discomfort at any time, stop the experiment and inform your teacher.)

2. Measure the person's breathing rate by counting the number of breaths taken in 15 seconds. Multiply this number by four to calculate breaths per minute.

3. Rate the person's perspiration level from 1 to 5 (1 = none; 5 = droplets dripping down the face).

4. Design a data table like the one shown below. Write a hypothesis about the effect of exercise on the dependent variables that you are measuring.

5. Have the person jump rope for 2 minutes. When the person stops, measure heart rate, breathing rate, and perspiration level and record the data. Repeat step 5 three more times and record your data at each point.

6. After the final recording of the dependent variables, wait 1 minute and measure all of the variables again.

TABLE 1. EFFECTS OF EXERCISE			
Time (Min)	Heart Rate (Beats/Minute)	Breathing Rate (Breaths/Minute)	Perspiration Level
0			
2			
4			
6			
8			
9			

ANALYZE AND CONCLUDE

1. **Identify Variables** What is the independent variable in this experiment?

2. **Organize Data** Graph the relationship between the independent and dependent variables. You may choose one graph to display all of your data, or you may use separate graphs for each of the dependent variables. Explain your graph choice.

3. **Summarize** What are the effects of exercise over time on the circulatory and respiratory systems and on perspiration level?

4. **Synthesize** What other processes could you have measured to determine the external and internal effects of exercise on the body?

5. **Infer** How is perspiration level related to body temperature? How is perspiration related to homeostasis?

28.2 Mechanisms of Homeostasis

KEY CONCEPT Homeostasis is the regulation and maintenance of the internal environment.

▶ MAIN IDEAS

- Conditions within the body must remain within a narrow range.
- Negative feedback loops are necessary for homeostasis.

VOCABULARY

homeostasis, p. 858
feedback, p. 859
negative feedback, p. 860
positive feedback, p. 861

Review
tissue, organ, organ system

MICHIGAN STANDARDS

B2.3B Describe how the maintenance of a relatively stable internal environment is required for the continuation of life.

B2.3e Describe how human body systems maintain relatively constant internal conditions (temperature, acidity, and blood sugar).

VOCABULARY

The word *homeostasis* is formed from two Greek words: *homos*, meaning "similar," and *stasis*, meaning "standing" or "stopping."

Connect The complex tissues, organs, and organ systems in your body must respond to a wide variety of conditions. For instance, during the summer, you might walk out of a cold, air-conditioned store into a stifling hot summer day. Your body temperature has to remain the same under both conditions in order for you to survive. In fact, your life depends on your body's ability to maintain the delicate balance of your internal chemistry.

▶ MAIN IDEA
Conditions within the body must remain within a narrow range.

During every moment of your life, trillions of chemical reactions are taking place in your body. The enzymes that control these reactions work best within a narrow range of conditions. One of these conditions is your internal body temperature, which should remain between 36.7°C and 37.1°C (98.2°F and 98.8°F). If it rises only a few degrees, you could easily die from overheating. At temperatures over 41°C (106°F), many enzymes stop functioning. If your internal temperature falls below 27°C (80°F), your heart may fail.

Likewise, the levels of trace minerals in your body must stay within strict limits. For instance, if calcium levels are too high, you can slip into a coma. If they are too low, your heartbeat becomes irregular.

You live in a constantly changing environment. Your body must cope not only with temperature changes but also with pollution, infection, stress, and many other conditions. Every change is a challenge to your body. What keeps the human body from breaking down every time the internal or external environment changes?

Homeostasis and the Internal Environment

Fortunately, the body has many control systems that keep its internal environment stable. Together, these control systems are responsible for maintaining homeostasis. **Homeostasis** (HO-mee-oh-STAY-sihs) is the regulation and maintenance of the internal environment—temperature, fluids, salts, pH, nutrients, and gases—within the narrow ranges that support human life. Your internal control systems respond quickly to change, whether from outside conditions or internal ones, as shown in **FIGURE 28.5**.

Control Systems in the Body

Internal control systems require sensors, a control center, communication systems, and targets.

Sensors Sensors, also called receptors, gather information about conditions inside and outside of the body. In cold or hot weather, for instance, sensors in your skin and nasal passages gather data about air temperatures. The body has thousands of internal sensors and other specialized sensors that detect changes in the outside world.

Control center A control center, often the brain, receives information from the sensors. It then compares this information to the set points, or ideal values, at which the body functions best. When conditions move above or below a set point, the control center responds by sending messages through a communication system.

Communication systems Communication is controlled by the nervous system and the endocrine system, which carry messages to all parts of the body. These messages, in the form of nerve impulses or hormones, tell targets in the body how to respond to internal or external changes.

Targets A target is any organ, tissue, or cell that changes its level of activity in response to a message. For instance, in a cold environment, a message might cause the muscles to start shivering to generate more body heat.

Draw Conclusions Why is it so important to maintain homeostasis within the body?

FIGURE 28.5 Homeostasis and Change

Control systems in the skin help reduce or conserve body heat.

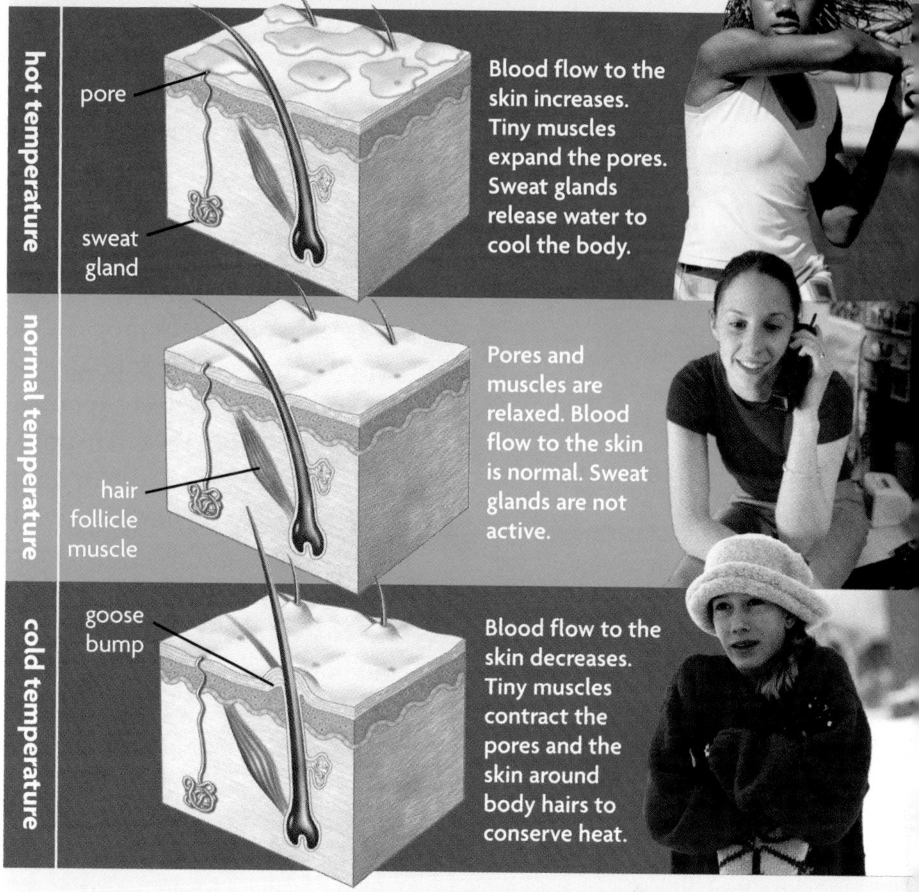

hot temperature
pore
sweat gland

Blood flow to the skin increases. Tiny muscles expand the pores. Sweat glands release water to cool the body.

normal temperature
hair follicle muscle

Pores and muscles are relaxed. Blood flow to the skin is normal. Sweat glands are not active.

cold temperature
goose bump

Blood flow to the skin decreases. Tiny muscles contract the pores and the skin around body hairs to conserve heat.

Apply If the girl in cold temperature starts jogging, how would the control mechanisms in her skin respond as she runs?

▶ MAIN IDEA

Negative feedback loops are necessary for homeostasis.

Sensors, control centers, communication systems, and targets work together in what is known as a feedback loop. **Feedback** is information from sensors that allows a control center to compare current conditions to a set of ideal values. In a feedback loop, information moves continuously among sensors, a control center, and a target. Most functions in the body are regulated by negative feedback loops.

Negative Feedback

In **negative feedback,** a control system counteracts any change in the body that moves conditions above or below a set point. Negative feedback loops help keep the internal environment stable. A thermostat is a good example of how a negative feedback loop works. A sensor in the thermostat continuously measures air temperature in a room. A control mechanism then compares the current room temperature to a set point, say 21°C. When the temperature falls below 21°C, the thermostat sends an electronic message that turns on the furnace. When the sensor indicates the air temperature is at or just above 21°C, the thermostat sends another message that turns off the furnace. As a result, the room always stays within a few degrees of the desired temperature.

Negative feedback loops in the body work in a similar way. They are the reason why you cannot hold your breath for a long time. The control systems involved in this feedback loop are shown in **FIGURE 28.6.** As you hold your breath, sensors in the circulatory and respiratory systems send information to the brain stem, the body's respiratory control center. Sensors signal a gradual increase in carbon dioxide (CO_2) and a decrease in oxygen (O_2). The control center compares this information with the set points for these gases. When the change becomes too great, the control center takes steps to counteract it. Messages are sent to the muscles of the diaphragm and the rib cage to relax and then contract, forcing you to exhale and then inhale deeply. At this point, you cannot stop these muscles from moving. You will continue to breathe rapidly and deeply until the gas levels return to their set points.

Connecting CONCEPTS

Biochemistry As you read in Chapter 4, cells require a constant supply of oxygen to maintain cell metabolism. Oxygen is not stored in the human body in any great amounts. Once oxygen reserves have been used up, the body must have a fresh supply of oxygen to prevent cell death.

FIGURE 28.6 Negative Feedback Loop

Negative feedback counteracts any change in the body that moves conditions away from a set point.

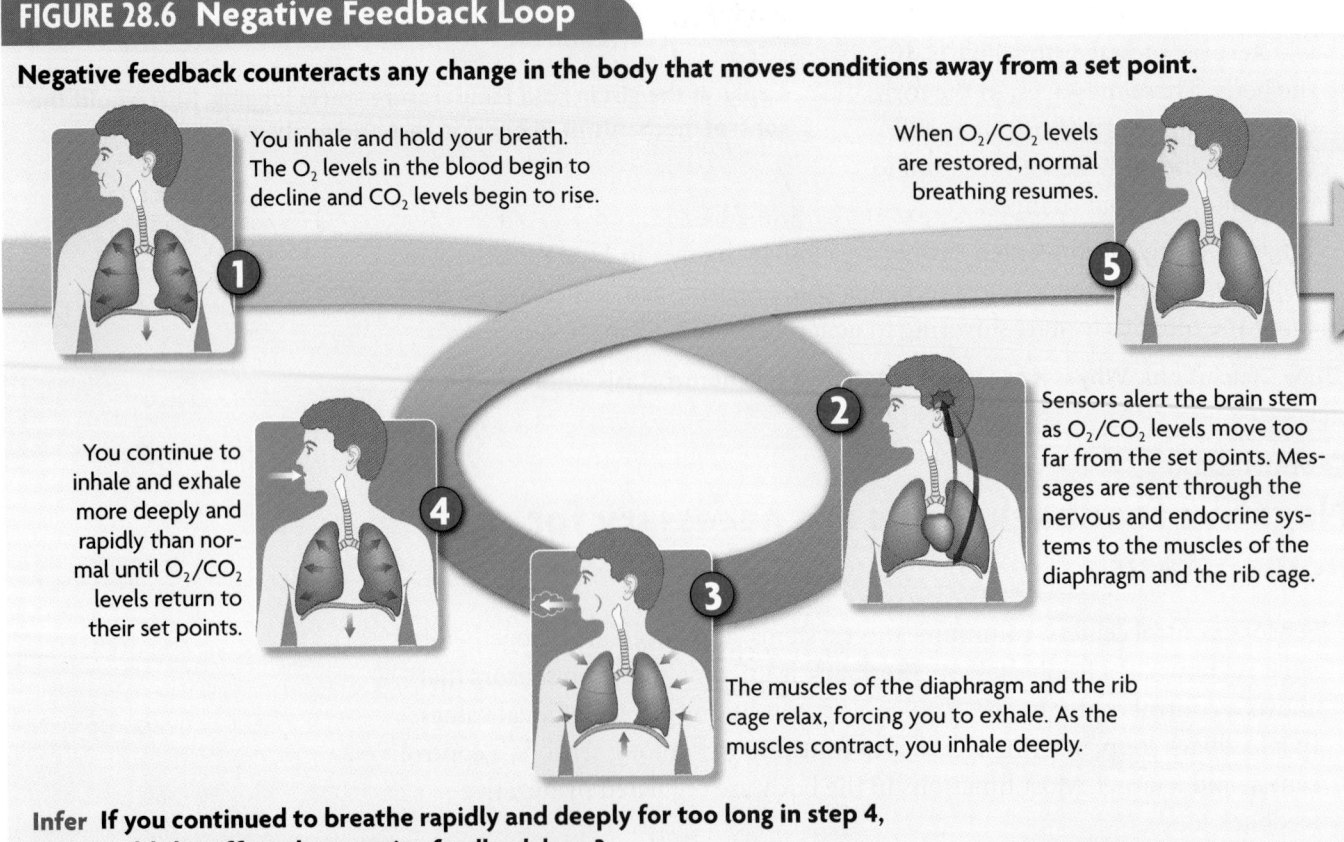

1. You inhale and hold your breath. The O_2 levels in the blood begin to decline and CO_2 levels begin to rise.

2. Sensors alert the brain stem as O_2/CO_2 levels move too far from the set points. Messages are sent through the nervous and endocrine systems to the muscles of the diaphragm and the rib cage.

3. The muscles of the diaphragm and the rib cage relax, forcing you to exhale. As the muscles contract, you inhale deeply.

4. You continue to inhale and exhale more deeply and rapidly than normal until O_2/CO_2 levels return to their set points.

5. When O_2/CO_2 levels are restored, normal breathing resumes.

Infer If you continued to breathe rapidly and deeply for too long in step 4, how would this affect the negative feedback loop?

QUICK LAB   MODELING

Negative Feedback Loop

You can experience a negative feedback loop by doing a simple demonstration.

MATERIALS
hardcover book at least 6" × 9"

PROBLEM How does a negative feedback loop work?

PROCEDURE

1. Balance the hardcover book on your head.
2. Walk 3 meters forward and backward—once with eyes open, then with eyes closed.

ANALYZE AND CONCLUDE

1. **Analyze** Describe the negative feedback loop that helped keep the book balanced on your head. How did closing your eyes affect your ability to balance the book?
2. **Connect** Think of another example of a negative feedback loop that you might observe in your everyday life. Explain how you think this loop works.

Positive Feedback

Negative feedback loops maintain homeostasis by counteracting, or reversing, change to return conditions to their set points. In some cases, however, the body actually needs change to accomplish a specific task. In **positive feedback,** a control center uses information from sensors to increase the rate of change away from the set points. Though not as common in the body, this type of feedback is important whenever rapid change is needed.

For example, if you cut your finger, positive feedback mechanisms increase the rate of change in clotting factors in the blood until the wound is sealed. Once the injury heals, another positive feedback loop occurs as chemicals are released to dissolve the clot. Positive feedback also occurs in the release of certain growth hormones during puberty. Your body needs higher levels of these hormones to accomplish all of the changes that take place at this time.

Infer Why are most of the functions of the body regulated by negative, rather than by positive, feedback mechanisms?

scilinks.org
To find out more about homeostasis, go to scilinks.org.
Keycode: MLB028

28.2   ASSESSMENT

ONLINE QUIZ
ClassZone.com

REVIEWING ▶ MAIN IDEAS

1. A system to maintain **homeostasis** must have at least four parts that function together. Name these parts and briefly explain what each one does.

2. What is the main difference between the way **negative feedback** and **positive feedback** mechanisms regulate change in the body?

CRITICAL THINKING

3. **Predict** When a newborn baby nurses, the mother's body is stimulated to produce milk. What would happen to the milk supply if the mother chose to bottle feed rather than breast feed? Why?

4. **Sequence** Suppose you go on a long hike in hot weather. Describe a possible negative feedback loop that would keep your body from overheating.

Connecting CONCEPTS

5. **Zoology** Reptiles regulate their body temperature by changing their environment. A snake, for instance, must lie in sunlight to warm its body. Mammals, on the other hand, can regulate their internal environment to gain or lose heat. How might this ability give mammals an advantage over reptiles?

28.3 Interactions Among Systems

KEY CONCEPT Systems interact to maintain homeostasis.

▶ MAIN IDEAS
- Each organ system affects other organ systems.
- A disruption of homeostasis can be harmful.

VOCABULARY
thermoregulation, p. 863

Review
homeostasis, feedback, negative feedback

MICHIGAN STANDARDS

B2.3d Identify the general functions of the major systems of the human body (digestion, respiration, reproduction, circulation, excretion, protection from disease, and movement, control, and coordination) and describe ways that these systems interact with each other.

B2.3f Explain how human organ systems help maintain human health.

Connect The moment a race car pulls in for a pit stop, the pit crew springs into action. Each person has a special role that must be coordinated with the efforts of the team. As one member jacks up the car, others are changing the tires, putting in fuel, and checking the engine. If anyone fails to do a job properly, it affects the entire team and places the driver at serious risk.

▶ MAIN IDEA
Each organ system affects other organ systems.

At its most basic level, the body is a community of specialized cells that interact with one another. On a larger scale, all of the organ systems form a type of community regulated by feedback mechanisms. This interaction among organ systems means that what affects a single organ system affects the entire body.

Like highly trained crew members, each organ system in your body must do its own special job. But for you to remain healthy, each system also must coordinate with other organ systems through chemical messages and nerve impulses. The relationship among your organs and organ systems is not always obvious—for example, when the body produces a substance such as vitamin D. In other cases, you are more aware that some organs are affecting others, as in the regulation of your body temperature in hot or cold weather.

Vitamin D Production
You may know that sunlight plays a part in the production of vitamin D in your body. You may not know that the liver, kidneys, circulatory system, and endocrine system are necessary for this process as well. The skin contains a substance that in the presence of ultraviolet light is changed into an inactive form of vitamin D. As **FIGURE 28.8** shows, this form enters the blood and is carried to the liver. The liver changes the inactive form of vitamin D into another compound, which is then carried to the kidneys. Here, this compound is converted into active vitamin D.

The blood transports active vitamin D throughout the body, where it interacts with hormones that regulate the amount of calcium and phosphorus in the body. These two minerals are essential for building strong bones. If any organ along this path fails to do its job, the level of vitamin D in the body decreases. Without enough vitamin D, children's bones do not develop normally. Adults lose bone mass, which means their bones break more easily.

FIGURE 28.7 Precision teamwork is the secret to a pit crew's success. Likewise, your life depends on every organ system doing its job at the right time and in the right order.

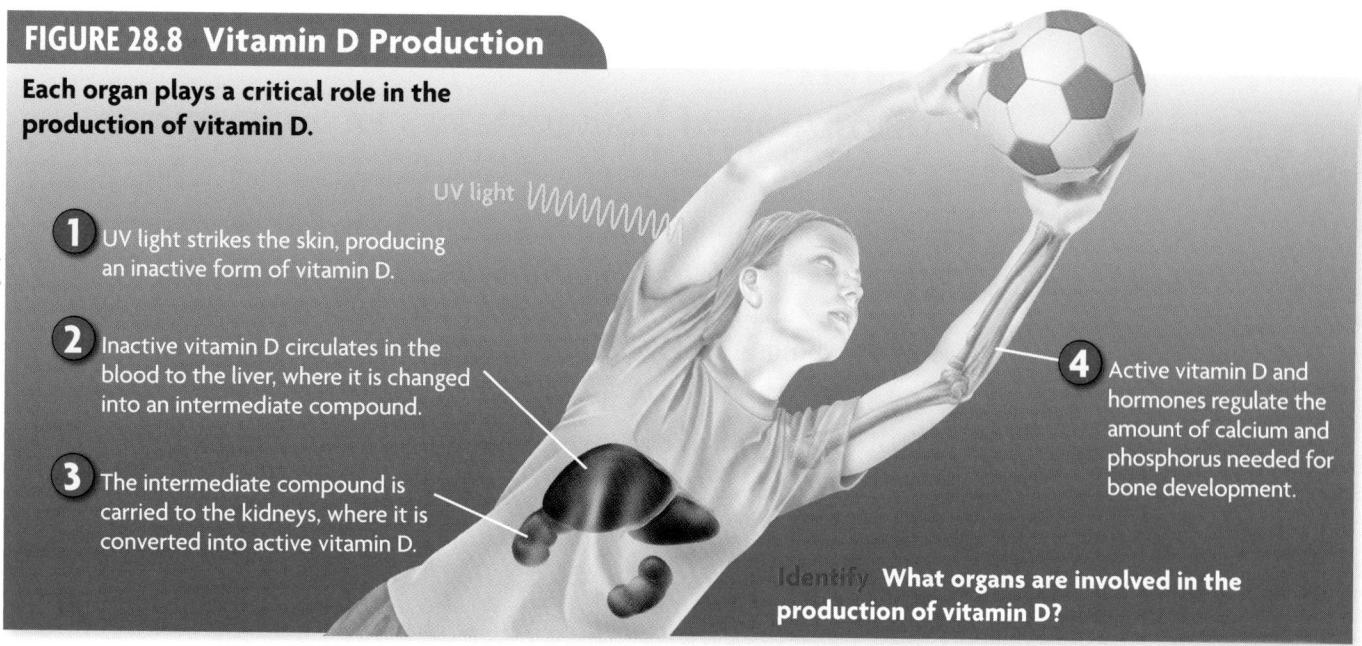

FIGURE 28.8 Vitamin D Production

Each organ plays a critical role in the production of vitamin D.

1 UV light strikes the skin, producing an inactive form of vitamin D.

2 Inactive vitamin D circulates in the blood to the liver, where it is changed into an intermediate compound.

3 The intermediate compound is carried to the kidneys, where it is converted into active vitamin D.

UV light

4 Active vitamin D and hormones regulate the amount of calcium and phosphorus needed for bone development.

Identify What organs are involved in the production of vitamin D?

Regulation of Body Temperature

The process of maintaining a steady body temperature under a variety of conditions is known as **thermoregulation** (THUR-moh-REHG-yoo-LAY-shuhn). The most obvious organ systems involved in maintaining body temperature are the skin and muscles. You sweat in hot weather and shiver when you are cold. However, far more is going on than what you can see on the surface. Thermoregulation requires the close interaction of the respiratory, circulatory, nervous, and endocrine systems.

Sensors in the skin and blood vessels provide information about body temperature to a control center in the brain called the hypothalamus. The hypothalamus protects the body's internal organs by monitoring temperature. When the hypothalamus receives information that the temperature of the blood is rising, it sends messages through the nervous and endocrine systems. These messages activate the sweat glands, dilate blood vessels in the skin, and increase both heart and breathing rates. All of these activities carry heat away from the center of the body to the surface, where excess heat can escape.

When the temperature of the blood falls too low, the hypothalamus sends another set of signals to the skin and to the muscular, respiratory, and circulatory systems. Blood vessels in the skin constrict, reducing blood flow to prevent loss of heat. Muscles in the skin contract around the pores, reducing their size. Rapid, small contractions of skeletal muscles cause shivering. The thyroid gland releases hormones that increase metabolism. All of these activities increase body heat and reduce the loss of heat to the environment.

VISUAL VOCAB

Thermoregulation maintains a stable body temperature under a variety of conditions, just as a thermostat regulates a furnace. Both mechanisms use feedback to keep temperatures within set ranges.

control
THERMOSTAT
messages
FURNACE
info to control
target

Connecting CONCEPTS

Animals In **Chapter 26** you learned that animals have many ways of regulating their body temperatures. For example, some animals stay cool by panting, by being active only at night, or by getting rid of excess heat through their body structures, such as large ears or thin skins.

Infer If a person's circulatory system does not function well, how might thermoregulation in his or her body be affected?

MAIN IDEA

A disruption of homeostasis can be harmful.

Some changes may be too great or too rapid for your body to control through feedback mechanisms. Homeostasis can be disrupted for several reasons.

- Sensors fail to detect changes in the internal or external environment.
- Wrong messages may be sent or the correct ones fail to reach their targets.
- Serious injuries can overwhelm the homeostatic mechanisms.
- Viruses or bacteria can change the body's internal chemistry.

Disruption of homeostasis can begin in one organ or organ system and result in a chain reaction that affects other organs and organ systems. These effects can be harmful to your body over the short or long term.

Short-Term Effects

Short-term effects usually last a few days or weeks. For example, when a cold virus first enters your body, your immune system may not be able to prevent the virus from multiplying. As a result, you develop a sore throat, runny nose, and dry cough, and your muscles and joints become inflamed. However, within a few days, your body's immune system begins to kill the virus and to restore homeostasis. Usually, there is no lasting harm to your body.

Long-Term Effects

A long-term disruption of homeostasis, as in the case of diabetes, can cause more damage. Diabetes occurs when the body fails to control the amount of glucose circulating in the blood.

Normal glucose control Glucose levels are controlled by two hormones—insulin and glucagon—which are released by the pancreas. When glucose in the blood rises above a set point, beta cells in the pancreas release insulin. Insulin causes cells to take in more glucose from the blood and causes the liver to store glucose as glycogen. When blood glucose levels fall below the set point, alpha cells in the pancreas release glucagon. This hormone stimulates the liver to break down stored glycogen into glucose and release it until levels in the blood rise to the set point.

Type 1 and Type 2 diabetes What if the pancreas fails to do its job? The result can be diabetes mellitus, a condition in which the body can no longer regulate glucose levels. There are two types of diabetes. Type 1 occurs when the body's immune system destroys the ability of beta cells to produce insulin. Type 2 is caused when insulin production decreases or when insulin cannot move glucose into cells.

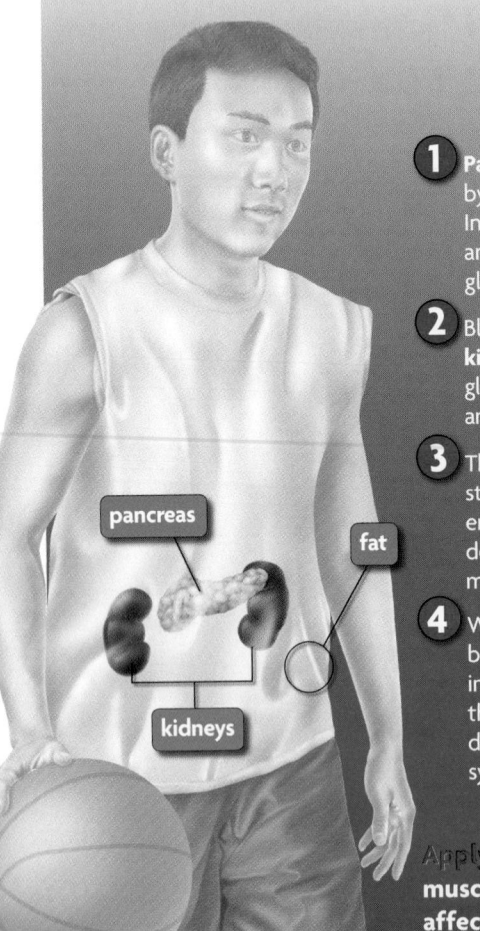

FIGURE 28.9 Type 1 Diabetes

Failure to control glucose levels affects the entire body.

1 **Pancreas** cells are attacked by the immune system. Insulin production decreases, and cells cannot remove glucose from the blood.

2 Blood glucose levels rise. The **kidneys** excrete the excess glucose along with large amounts of water.

3 The body begins to use **fat** stored in the tissues as an energy source. As fat breaks down, the blood becomes more acidic.

4 With changes in pH and fluid balance, cell metabolism is impaired. Cells throughout the body function poorly or die, affecting every organ system.

pancreas

fat

kidneys

Apply How do you think the muscular system might be affected by Type 1 diabetes?

DATA ANALYSIS

INTERPRETING INVERSE RELATIONSHIPS

Two variables are inversely related if an increase in the value of one variable is associated with a decrease in the value of the other variable. For example, the level of insulin decreases the longer a person exercises. Therefore, insulin levels have an inverse relationship with exercise time. The graphs at right show the levels of insulin, glucose, and glucagon during moderate exercise over 250 minutes. Use the graphs to answer the questions.

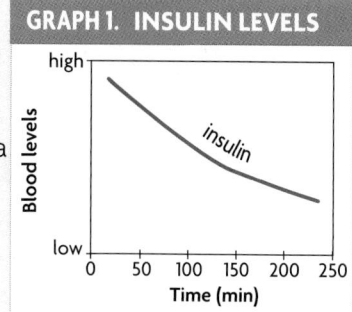

GRAPH 1. INSULIN LEVELS

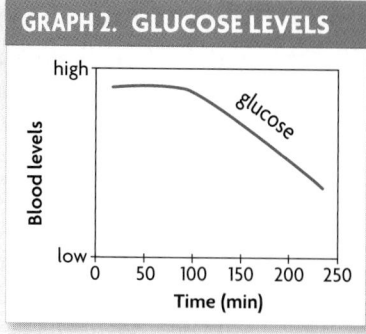

GRAPH 2. GLUCOSE LEVELS

GRAPH 3. GLUCAGON LEVELS

1. **Analyze** Which variable(s) has/have an inverse relationship with time?

2. **Conclude** What relationship exists between glucagon and the other two variables (insulin and glucose)? Explain.

In Type 1 diabetes, the failure of the pancreas sets up a destructive chain reaction in other organ systems, as shown in **FIGURE 28.9.** As glucose builds up in the blood, the kidneys must remove it along with large amounts of water. Also, since the body is unable to use glucose as an energy source, it must use stored fat instead. As the fat breaks down, the blood becomes more acidic. This altered pH disrupts the metabolism of the cells in every organ and every system in the body. The long-term effects can result in heart disease, blindness, nerve damage, kidney damage, and even coma and death.

In Type 2 diabetes, the pancreas cannot produce enough insulin, or the insulin cannot be used to move glucose into the cells. As a result, blood glucose levels rise, and the cells starve. Risk factors for developing Type 2 diabetes include chronic obesity, a family history of diabetes, and aging.

Connect **Why might diabetes be a particular problem for an athlete?**

28.3 ASSESSMENT

ONLINE QUIZ
ClassZone.com

REVIEWING ▶ MAIN IDEAS

1. Why do the organ systems in the body need to work so closely together?

2. Explain why a long-term disruption of homeostasis can often be more damaging to the body than a short-term disruption is.

CRITICAL THINKING

3. **Analyze** Why would giving synthetic insulin to people with Type 1 diabetes restore their glucose homeostasis?

4. **Predict** If you lived in Alaska for the whole year, what changes might occur in your calcium and phosphorus levels during the winter versus the summer? Explain.

Connecting CONCEPTS

5. **Evolution** Some animals can store more glucose—in the form of glycogen—in their bodies than can other animals. What might be the evolutionary advantage of having these extra energy stores?

Use these inquiry-based labs and online activities to deepen your understanding of human systems and homeostasis.

MICHIGAN STANDARDS

B2.3C Explain how stability is challenged by changing physical, chemical, and environmental conditions as well as the presence of disease agents.

B2.3d Identify the general functions of the major systems of the human body (digestion, respiration, reproduction, circulation, excretion, protection from disease, and movement, control, and coordination) and describe ways that these systems interact with each other.

INVESTIGATION

Examining Human Cells

In this lab, you will examine different types of human body cells under the microscope. As you study the cells, think about how the structure of each type of cell is related to its function.

MATERIALS
- slide of skeletal-muscle cells
- slide of bone cells
- slide of nerve cells
- microscope

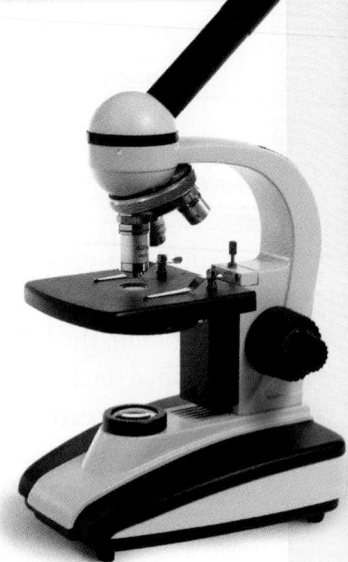

SKILL Observing

PROBLEM How can you identify different types of specialized cells?

PROCEDURE
1. Examine the first slide under low power and high power on the microscope.
2. Make a data sheet to draw and label one cell and its structures.
3. Repeat steps 1 and 2 for the remaining slides.

ANALYZE AND CONCLUDE
1. **Describe** What is the general shape of a muscle cell? How does this shape differ from the shape of a bone cell or a nerve cell?
2. **Evaluate** How can the differences in the shapes of cells be explained?
3. **Compare** What structures do all of the cells viewed have in common?
4. **Apply** Sometimes, due to inherited disorders, nerve cells in the muscular system do not function properly. What problems might a person have if he or she had one of these disorders?
5. **Infer** Find a diagram on the Internet showing bone cells embedded within bone tissue. Explain how nutrients and oxygen might reach bone cells that are surrounded by hardened bone tissue.

EXTEND YOUR INVESTIGATION
Find examples on the Internet of muscle cells or bone cells that have been damaged by disease or injury or that did not develop properly. How do these changes affect the cells' structure and function? What effect might these cells have on the tissues they are part of?

Hormones and Homeostasis

Endocrine glands release chemical messengers (hormones) that help regulate functions throughout the body. Sometimes these glands fail to respond to normal feedback loops, resulting in a disruption of homeostasis. For example, the pituitary gland, located in the brain, secretes human growth hormone. If cells in the gland produce too much of this hormone, a person will continue to grow far above average height. The result is a condition known as gigantism, as shown in the photograph.

If the cells produce too little of the hormone, a person will grow to far less than average height. This condition is known as dwarfism.

Robert Wadlow stands 2.6 meters (8 ft 9 in.) in this 1938 photo. The two people next to him are average size.

SKILL Researching

PROBLEM How does the disorder of a particular endocrine gland affect the rest of the body?

RESEARCH

Choose one of the glands below and one of the disorders listed under it.

Thyroid Gland
- hypothyroidism
- Graves' disease
- myxedema

Adrenal Gland
- Cushing's syndrome
- Addison's disease

1. Describe the function of the gland and the hormones it releases.
2. What happens to the functioning of the gland in the disorder that you have chosen?
3. How does the disorder affect the rest of the body?
4. How is the disorder diagnosed? What treatments or lifestyle changes are necessary?
5. What are the long-term health effects if the disorder remains untreated?

Online BIOLOGY
CLASSZONE.COM

ANIMATED BIOLOGY
Keep an Athlete Running
Regulate a runner's homeostasis to get her to the end of a course in the best time without stopping.

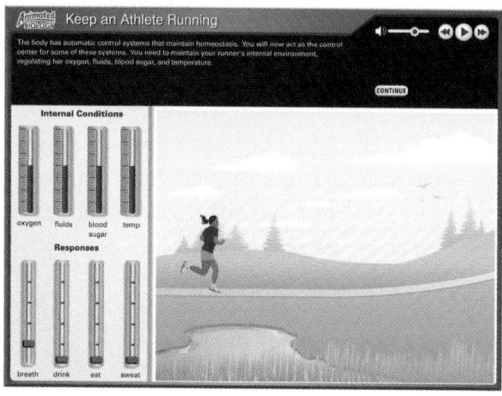

WEBQUEST
When you are cold, the systems in your body respond in ways that maintain your body temperature. In this WebQuest, you will learn about hypothermia and its potentially life-threatening consequences. Find out what happens when you get so cold that homeostasis breaks down.

BIOZINE
Stories about human biology—such as "Researchers Test Vaccine for Emerging Flu Virus" and "Obesity a Growing Problem for Kids and Teens"—are often in the headlines. Catch the latest news about human biology in the BioZine.

28.1 Levels of Organization

The human body has five levels of organization.
Specialized cells in multicellular organisms arise from the zygote. Most embryonic stem cells go through determination, during which they are committed to becoming specialized cells. During differentiation, cells develop their specialized structures and functions.

Groups of similar specialized cells form tissue. Different types of tissues form an organ, and various specialized organs together form an organ system. All of the organ systems together make up an entire organism.

Differentiated Cells

28.2 Mechanisms of Homeostasis

Homeostasis is the regulation and maintenance of the internal environment. Conditions within the body must remain within the narrow ranges that support human life. Homeostasis is maintained by internal control systems composed of sensors, a control center, communication systems, and target tissues or organs. The control centers use feedback to keep the internal environment stable. In a negative feedback loop, control systems counteract change to maintain conditions within a narrow range. In a positive feedback loop, control systems increase change away from set points.

28.3 Interactions Among Systems

Systems interact to maintain homeostasis.
Each organ system affects other organ systems. For example, thermoregulation depends on the interaction of the circulatory, respiratory, endocrine, and skin systems. If one organ system fails, it can affect other systems in a chain reaction. Long-term disruptions of homeostasis, as in diabetes, are more serious than temporary short-term disruptions because more organ systems can be damaged over time.

Synthesize Your Notes

Cycle Diagram Use this note-taking strategy to summarize what you know about how control systems work to maintain homeostasis.

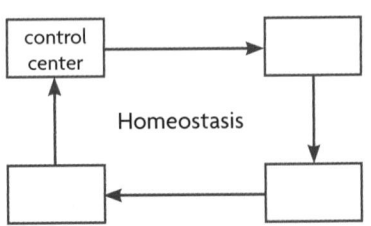

Concept Map Draw a concept map to help you remember the developmental steps of cells.

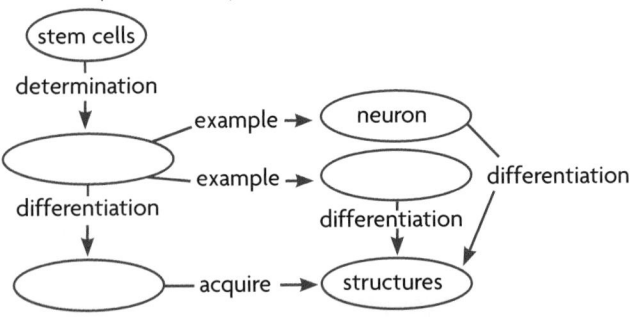

Chapter Assessment

Chapter Vocabulary

28.1 determination, p. 852
differentiation, p. 853
tissue, p. 854
organ, p. 854
organ system, p. 854

28.2 homeostasis, p. 858
feedback, p. 859
negative feedback, p. 860
positive feedback, p. 861

28.3 thermoregulation, p. 863

Reviewing Vocabulary

Keep It Short

For each vocabulary word that follows, write a short phrase that defines its meaning. For example: *cell—the basic unit of life.*

1. tissue
2. organ
3. organ system
4. determination
5. differentiation
6. negative feedback
7. positive feedback
8. thermoregulation

Word Origins

9. The word *organ* comes from the Latin word *organum,* meaning "instrument" or "implement." Describe how this meaning relates to the definition of a living organ.

10. *Homeostasis* can be broken into two parts: *homos,* meaning "similar," and *stasis,* meaning "standing" or "stopping." Write a brief definition of *homeostasis* based on the meaning of these two parts.

11. A thermos is a container for keeping liquids hot. The word comes from the Greek *thermos,* which means "hot" or "warm." How does this meaning relate to the term *thermoregulation?*

12. The word *feedback* originally comes from the field of electrical engineering. Feedback occurs when part of a signal put out by an amplifier returns to its source. It's that loud squeal you sometimes hear when someone is using a microphone. Explain how this meaning of feedback relates to what happens in a feedback loop.

Reviewing MAIN IDEAS

13. Embryonic stem cells have the potential to become any type of cell in the body. What happens to these cells during the process of determination?

14. Once a cell goes through the process of determination, what happens next as the cells develop in the embryo?

15. Briefly explain how cell differentiation and cell death are both needed to develop such structures as human hands and feet.

16. A human being is composed of five levels of organization. Name each of the levels of organization and give an example of each one.

17. Organs have many specialized cells and tissues that enable them to carry out their functions. Describe two specialized cells in the respiratory system that enable the lungs to function well.

18. Your body has control systems that keep its internal conditions within the narrow ranges that support life. On a hot day, how do your body's control center and sensors work together to help you stay cool?

19. Your body has many feedback loops to help maintain homeostasis. Explain the difference between a negative feedback loop and a positive feedback loop.

20. Explain how the failure of one organ can lead to the failure of other organs or of an entire organ system.

21. When glucose levels in the blood rise above a set point, hormones are released that cause the glucose levels to decline. Is this process an example of a positive or a negative feedback loop? Explain your answer.

22. Give two example of what can happen to a person if the body's homeostasis is not maintained.

23. **Compare** Explain how the cells in the human body might be similar to various building materials in a house.

24. **Infer** Scientists are investigating methods to use embryonic stem cells to repair any tissue in the human body. What characteristic of embryonic stem cells could make this type of treatment possible?

25. **Analyze** Review the chart of organ systems on page 856. Identify some interconnections between the immune system and the circulatory system.

26. **Apply** Describe which organ systems you think would be involved in maintaining homeostasis when a person gives a major speech or presentation. Include what may be happening within the person just before, during, and after the speech.

27. **Synthesize** For various specialized cells to work together, they must communicate with one another. Use the information you learned in Chapter 3 about cell parts to describe how you think a neuron might communicate with a muscle cell.

28. **Compare and Contrast** Explain how the difference between negative and positive feedback makes negative feedback more effective in maintaining homeostasis in the body.

29. **Infer** People with weak or damaged hearts often have trouble regulating their body temperatures in a hot or a cold environment. Explain why an impaired heart might make a person less able to maintain homeostasis.

Analyzing Visuals

Use the diagram of the digestive system to answer the next three questions.

30. **Analyze** Why is this considered an organ system?

31. **Infer** How do you think the nutrients released from food leave the digestive system and travel throughout the body?

32. **Predict** When a person has the flu and is vomiting, how does this condition affect the organ system and its ability to provide nutrients to the body?

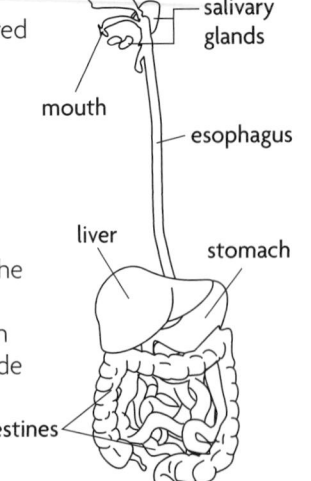

salivary glands

mouth

esophagus

liver

stomach

intestines

Analyzing Data

The graph below shows the relationship between different types of energy yield during exercise. Use the graph to answer the next three questions.

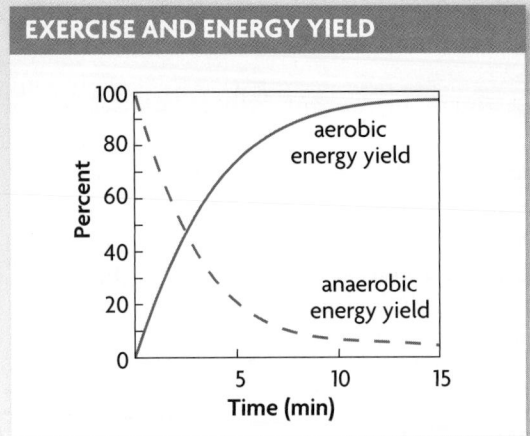

EXERCISE AND ENERGY YIELD

aerobic energy yield

anaerobic energy yield

Percent

Time (min)

33. **Compare and Contrast** Within what time period does the greatest amount of change occur in both variables?

34. **Analyze** Which variable is inversely related to time? Explain.

35. **Conclude** What relationship do the two variables have to each other at the beginning and at the end of the exercise period?

Connecting CONCEPTS

36. **Blog Your Morning Wake-Up Call** Blogs have become a popular form of communicating personal experiences online. Think about the changes that occur in your body when you wake up in the morning—changes in your heart rate, in your breathing, and in the movements of your arms and legs. Describe in a blog entry some of the environmental and physical changes that you experience. Which organ systems seem to be involved? What feedback loops might be working to make sure such changes do not become too great?

37. **Apply** Extreme sports test the limits of the human body. Describe one extreme condition, other than temperature, facing the ice climber in the photograph on page 851. Explain how feedback mechanisms in the climber's body can maintain homeostasis under the extreme condition you choose to describe.

MICHIGAN
STANDARDS-BASED ASSESSMENT

✓ **Test Practice**
For more test practice, go to ClassZone.com.

1. A group of scientists investigates how the blood pressure of students changes while taking an exam. To properly control their experiment, the scientists must first measure the **B1.1B**

   A number of questions on the exam.

   B students' grade point averages.

   C temperature and humidity of the exam room.

   D students' blood pressure before the exam.

2. Hormones released by the pancreas control glucose levels in the body. The hormone glucagon increases blood sugar levels while the hormone insulin reduces blood sugar levels. When blood sugar becomes too high, what is *most* likely to happen to insulin and glucagon levels for the body to maintain homeostasis? **B2.5B**

   A Insulin levels increase and glucagon levels decrease.

   B Insulin and glucagon levels remain the same.

   C Glucagon levels increase and insulin levels decrease.

   D Insulin and glucagon levels decrease.

3. Why is it important that oxygen and carbon dioxide levels be closely regulated in the human body? **B2.3B**

   A Both gases are needed for the proper functioning of cell processes.

   B Oxygen is needed for cell processes and carbon dioxide is a waste product.

   C Both gases are waste products that need to be removed from cells.

   D The carbon and oxygen from the gases are needed to build new molecules.

4. No matter what the temperature is outside, your body temperature stays relatively constant at about 98.6°F. This is part of your body's ability to maintain **B2.3e**

   A osmoregulation.

   B homeostasis.

   C negative feedback loops.

   D positive feedback loops.

5. The kidneys filter wastes and excess salts from the blood. If salt concentrations are low, negative feedback mechanisms would *most* likely **B2.3C**

   A decrease the amount of salts removed.

   B increase the amount of salts removed.

   C slow down overall kidney function.

   D increase the rate of kidney function.

THINK THROUGH THE QUESTION

Think about what the body needs to do to maintain homeostasis in this situation. Remember, the feedback mechanism should affect only salt concentration.

6.

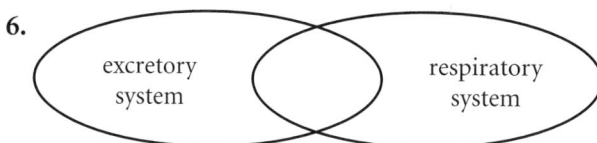

excretory system   respiratory system

Which characteristic *best* fits in the overlapping area of this Venn diagram? **B2.3D**

A absorbs nutrients

B brings in oxygen

C transports oxygen

D removes wastes

CHAPTER

29 Nervous and Endocrine Systems

KEY CONCEPTS

29.1 How Organ Systems Communicate

The nervous system and the endocrine system provide the means by which organ systems communicate.

29.2 Neurons

The nervous system is composed of highly specialized cells.

29.3 The Senses

The senses detect the internal and external environments.

29.4 Central and Peripheral Nervous Systems

The central nervous system interprets information, and the peripheral nervous system gathers and transmits information.

29.5 Brain Function and Chemistry

Scientists study the functions and chemistry of the brain.

29.6 Endocrine System and Hormones

The endocrine system produces hormones that affect growth, development, and homeostasis.

Online BIOLOGY CLASSZONE.COM

Animated BIOLOGY

View animated chapter concepts.
• Nerve Impulse Transmission
• Reflex Arc
• Diagnose a Hormone Disorder

BIOZINE

Keep current with biology news.
• Featured stories
• News feeds
• Bio Bytes

 RESOURCE CENTER

Get more information on
• Senses
• Nervous System

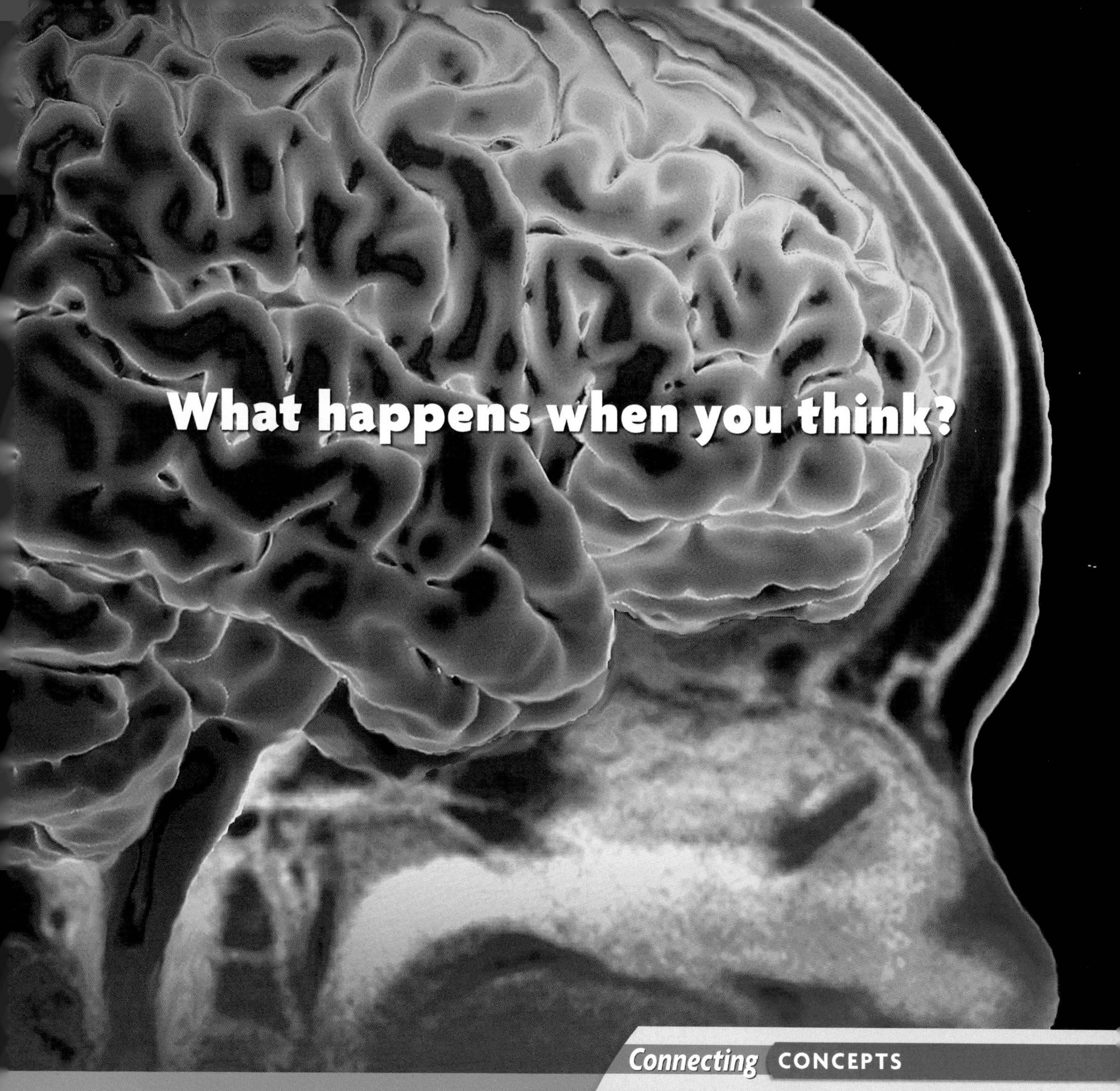

What happens when you think?

Some technology allows researchers to look into the body of a living person. As recently as the 1970s, there was no way for doctors and scientists to see inside of the body without putting a patient through surgery. Today, researchers and others use magnets and computer technology, such as the MRI scan above, to look at the internal organs of live patients.

Connecting CONCEPTS

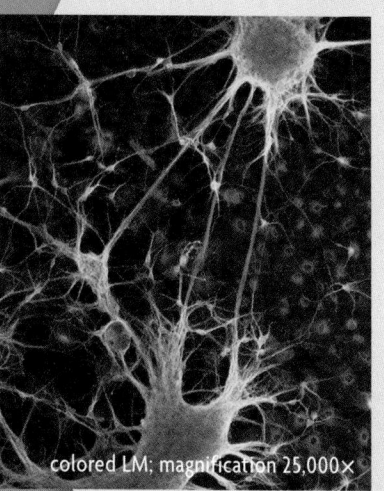

colored LM; magnification 25,000×

Animals Although only vertebrates have a spinal column, most animals have neurons. Neurons are specialized cells that send signals to different organ systems throughout the body. Neurons connect the brain to muscles and other tissues, and some neurons send such fast signals that they can make a person blink in less than one one-hundreth of a second.

29.1 How Organ Systems Communicate

KEY CONCEPT The nervous system and the endocrine system provide the means by which organ systems communicate.

▶ MAIN IDEAS

- The body's communication systems help maintain homeostasis.
- The nervous and endocrine systems have different methods and rates of communication.

VOCABULARY

nervous system, p. 874
endocrine system, p. 874
stimulus, p. 874
central nervous system (CNS), p. 875
peripheral nervous system (PNS), p. 875

MICHIGAN STANDARDS

B2.3d Identify the general functions of the major systems of the human body (digestion, respiration, reproduction, circulation, excretion, protection from disease, and movement, control, and coordination) and describe ways that these systems interact with each other.

Connect Scientists try to find new ways, such as MRI scans, to study the brain because the brain is so important. Your brain lets you think and move. It controls digestion, heart rate, and body temperature. Your brain does these things with help from the endocrine system and the rest of the nervous system.

▶ MAIN IDEA
The body's communication systems help maintain homeostasis.

Homeostasis depends on the ability of different systems in your body to communicate with one another. To maintain homeostasis, messages must be generated, delivered, interpreted, and acted upon by your body. The nervous system and the endocrine system are the communication networks that allow you to respond to changes in your environment countless times each day.

- The **nervous system** is a physically connected network of cells, tissues, and organs that controls thoughts, movements, and simpler life processes such as swallowing. For example, when you walk outside without sunglasses on a sunny day, your nervous system senses the bright light coming into your eyes. It sends a message that tells your pupils to shrink and let in less light.
- The **endocrine system** (EHN-duh-krihn) is a collection of physically disconnected organs that helps to control growth, development, and responses to your environment, such as body temperature. For example, when you are outside on a hot day or you exercise, your body starts to feel warm. Your endocrine system responds by producing messages that tell your body to sweat more so that you can cool down.

Both of these systems, which are shown in **FIGURE 29.1**, let you respond to a stimulus in your environment and maintain homeostasis. A **stimulus** (STIHM-yuh-luhs) is defined most broadly as something that causes a response. In living systems, a stimulus is anything that triggers a change in an organism. Changes can be chemical, cellular, or behavioral.

Analyze What stimuli cause you to sweat and cause your pupils to shrink?

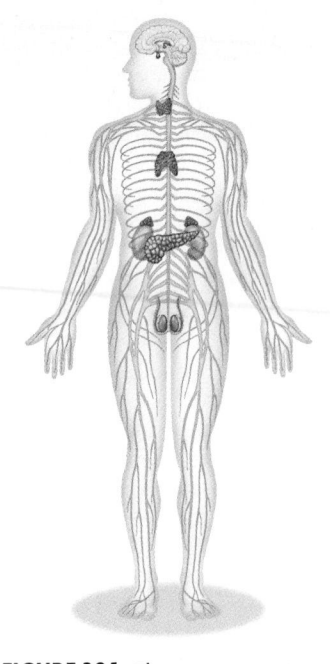

FIGURE 29.1 The nervous system (yellow) is a physically connected network, while the endocrine system (red) is made up of physically separated organs.

MAIN IDEA

The nervous and endocrine systems have different methods and rates of communication.

You can think about your endocrine system as working like a satellite television system. A satellite sends signals in all directions, but only televisions that have special receivers can get those signals. Your endocrine system's chemical signals are carried by the bloodstream throughout the body, and only cells with certain receptors can receive the signals. On the other hand, your nervous system is like cable television. A physical wire connects your television to the cable provider. Similarly, your nervous system sends its signals through a network of specialized tissues.

The nervous and endocrine systems also have different rates of communication. Your endocrine system works slowly and controls processes that occur over long periods of time, such as hair growth, aging, and sleep patterns. The endocrine system also helps regulate homeostatic functions such as body temperature and blood chemistry. For example, as the day gradually warms, your endocrine system responds by releasing chemicals that stimulate sweat glands. The change in the temperature over the course of a day is slow so you do not need a rapid response from your body.

Your nervous system works quickly and controls immediate processes, such as heart rate and breathing. If you touch your hand to a hot stove, an immediate response from the nervous system causes you to jerk your hand away. Without a quick reaction, your hand would be badly burned.

Signals move from the skin on your hand to the muscles in your arm by passing through the two parts of the nervous system: the central and the peripheral. The **central nervous system (CNS)** includes the brain and spinal cord. The CNS interprets messages from other nerves in the body and stores some of these messages for later use. The **peripheral nervous system (PNS)** is a network of nerves that transmits messages to the CNS and from the CNS to other organs in the body. You can see some of the nerves of the PNS extending from the spinal cord toward the neck and shoulders in **FIGURE 29.2**.

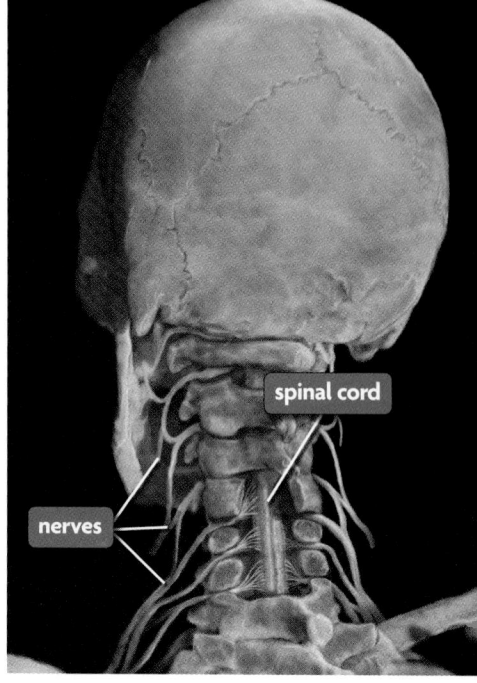

FIGURE 29.2 This medical illustration shows how the spinal cord connects the brain to the nerves that run throughout the body.

Infer Which system controls the rate at which your fingernails grow?

29.1 / ASSESSMENT

ONLINE QUIZ
ClassZone.com

REVIEWING ▶ MAIN IDEAS

1. Why does your body need a communication system?

2. What are three differences between the ways in which the **endocrine system** and the **nervous system** work?

CRITICAL THINKING

3. **Apply** Which system, the endocrine or the nervous, controls the rate at which you blink? Explain.

4. **Predict** How might a clogged blood vessel affect the nervous system's and the endocrine system's abilities to deliver signals?

Connecting CONCEPTS

5. **Cell Structure** What structures on a cell membrane might ensure that the endocrine system's signals only affect the cells for which they are intended?

Chapter 29: Nervous and Endocrine Systems **875**

29.2 Neurons

KEY CONCEPT The nervous system is composed of highly specialized cells.

▶ MAIN IDEAS

- Neurons are highly specialized cells.
- Neurons receive and transmit signals.

VOCABULARY

neuron, p. 876
dendrite, p. 876
axon, p. 876
resting potential, p. 877
sodium-potassium pump, p. 877

action potential, p. 878
synapse, p. 879
terminal, p. 879
neurotransmitter, p. 879

MICHIGAN STANDARDS

B2.1d Describe how, through cell division, cells can become specialized for specific function.

Connect When you eat a snack, you might flick crumbs off of your fingers without giving it much thought. The specialized cells of your nervous system, however, are hard at work carrying the messages between your fingers and your brain.

▶ MAIN IDEA

Neurons are highly specialized cells.

A **neuron** is a specialized cell that stores information and carries messages within the nervous system and between other body systems. Most neurons have three main parts, as shown in **FIGURE 29.3**.

① The cell body is the part of the neuron that contains the nucleus and organelles.

② **Dendrites** are branchlike extensions of the cytoplasm and the cell membrane that receive messages from neighboring cells. Neurons can have more than one dendrite, and each dendrite can have many branches.

③ Each neuron has one axon. An **axon** is a long extension that carries electrical messages away from the cell body and passes them to other cells.

FIGURE 29.3 Structure of a Neuron

A **neuron** is a specialized cell of the nervous system that produces and transmits signals.

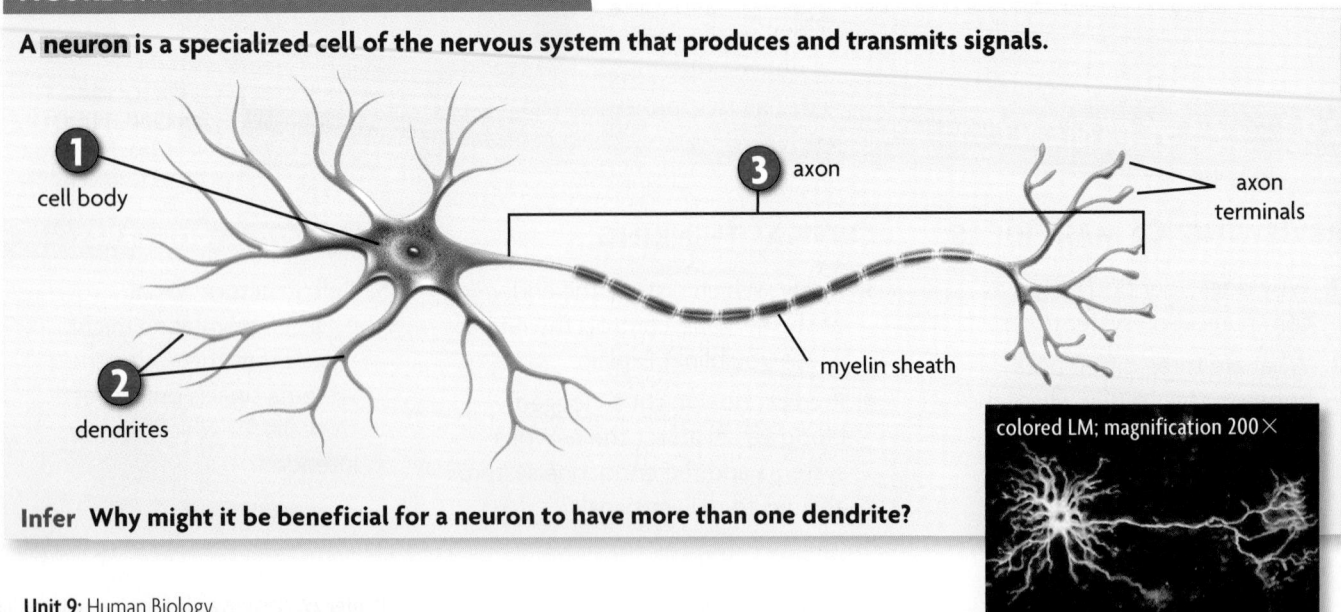

① cell body
② dendrites
③ axon
axon terminals
myelin sheath
colored LM; magnification 200×

Infer Why might it be beneficial for a neuron to have more than one dendrite?

There are three types of neurons: (1) sensory neurons, (2) interneurons, and (3) motor neurons. Sensory neurons detect stimuli and transmit signals to the brain and the spinal cord, which are both made up of interneurons. Interneurons receive signals from sensory neurons and relay them within the brain and the spinal cord. They process information and pass signals to motor neurons. Motor neurons pass messages from the nervous system to other tissues in the body, such as muscles.

The nervous system also relies on specialized support cells. For example, Schwann cells cover axons. A collection of Schwann cells, called the myelin sheath, insulates neurons' axons and helps them to send messages.

Analyze How does a neuron's shape allow it to send signals across long distances?

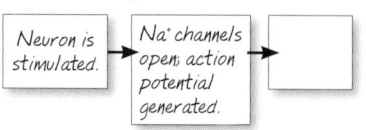
▶ MAIN IDEA
Neurons receive and transmit signals.

When your alarm clock buzzes in the morning, the sound stimulates neurons in your ear. The neurons send signals to your brain, which prompt you to either get out of bed or hit the snooze button. Neurons transmit information in the form of electrical and chemical impulses. When a neuron is stimulated, it produces an electrical impulse that travels only within that neuron. Before the signal can move to the next cell, it changes into a chemical signal.

Before a Neuron Is Stimulated
When a neuron is not transmitting a signal, it is said to be "at rest." However, this does not mean that the neuron is inactive. Neurons work to maintain a charge difference across their membranes, which keeps them ready to transmit impulses when they become stimulated.

While a neuron is at rest, the inside of its cell membrane is more negatively charged than the outside. The difference in charge across the membrane is called the **resting potential,** because it contains the potential energy needed to transmit an impulse. The resting potential occurs because there are unequal concentrations of ions inside and outside the neuron.

Two types of ions—sodium ions (Na^+) and potassium ions (K^+)—cause the resting potential. More Na^+ ions are present outside the cell than inside it. On the other hand, there are fewer K^+ ions outside the cell than inside it. Notice that both ions are positively charged. The neuron is negative compared with its surroundings because there are fewer positive ions inside the neuron.

Proteins in the cell membrane of the neuron maintain the resting potential. Some are protein channels that allow ions to diffuse across the membrane—Na^+ ions diffuse into the cell and K^+ ions diffuse out. However, the membrane has many more channels for K^+ than for Na^+, so positive charges leave the cell much faster than they enter. This unequal diffusion of ions is the main reason for the resting potential. In addition, the membrane also has a protein called the **sodium-potassium pump,** which uses energy to actively transport Na^+ ions out of the cell and bring K^+ ions into the cell. This process also helps maintain the resting potential.

Connecting **CONCEPTS**

Active Transport Recall from **Chapter 3** that energy and specialized membrane proteins are required to move molecules and ions against the concentration gradient.

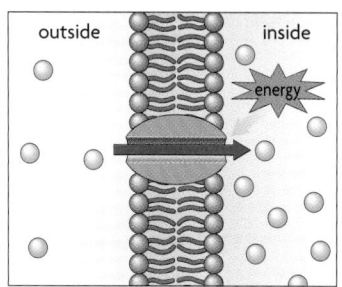

FIGURE 29.4 **Transmission Through and Between Neurons**

Once a neuron is stimulated, a portion of the inner membrane becomes positively charged. This electrical impulse, or **action potential**, moves down the axon. Before it can move to the next neuron, it must become a chemical signal.

Animated BIOLOGY
View an animation of transmission at ClassZone.com.

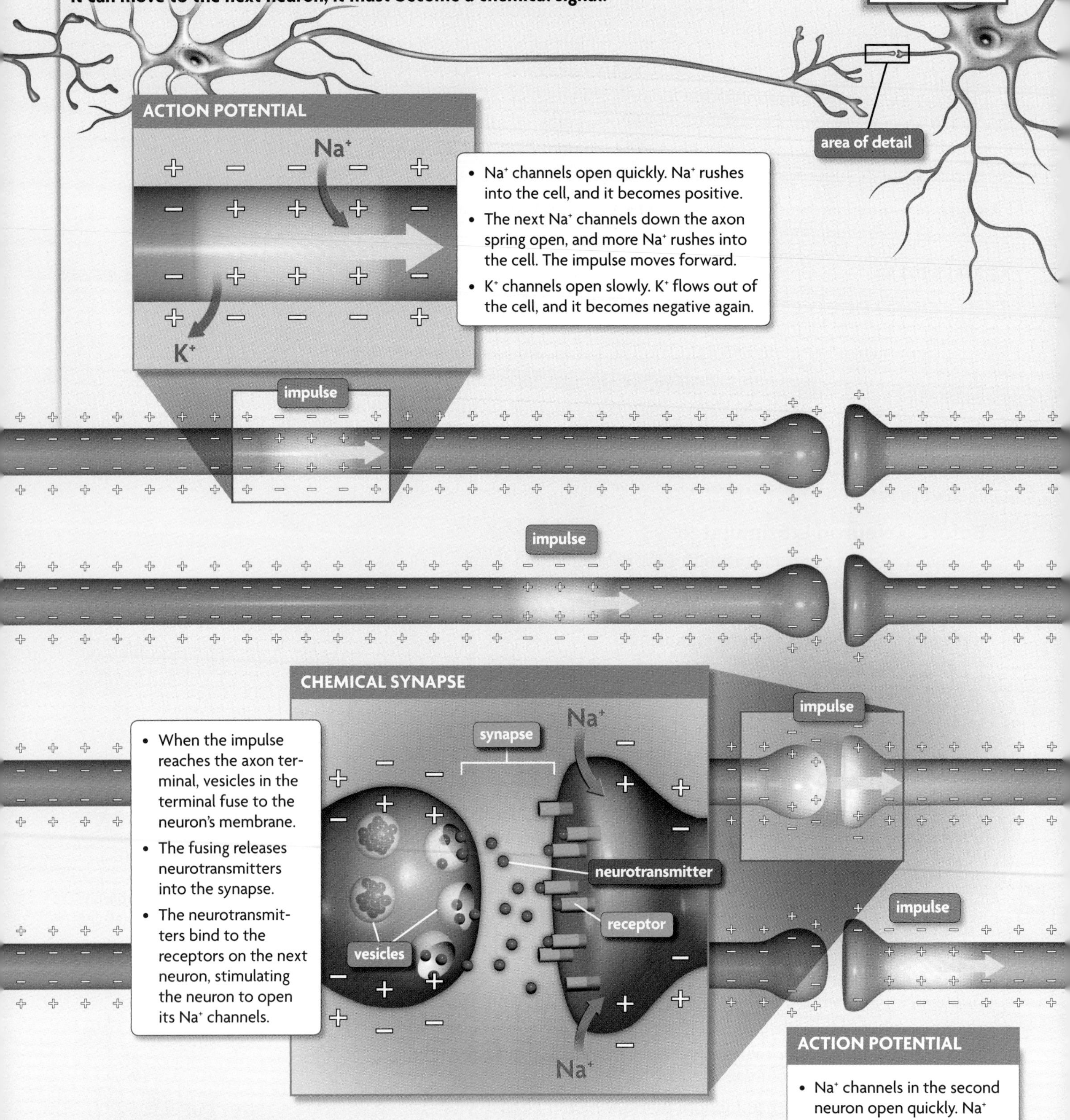

area of detail

ACTION POTENTIAL

Na^+

K^+

- Na^+ channels open quickly. Na^+ rushes into the cell, and it becomes positive.
- The next Na^+ channels down the axon spring open, and more Na^+ rushes into the cell. The impulse moves forward.
- K^+ channels open slowly. K^+ flows out of the cell, and it becomes negative again.

impulse

impulse

CHEMICAL SYNAPSE

synapse

Na^+

impulse

neurotransmitter

receptor

vesicles

Na^+

impulse

- When the impulse reaches the axon terminal, vesicles in the terminal fuse to the neuron's membrane.
- The fusing releases neurotransmitters into the synapse.
- The neurotransmitters bind to the receptors on the next neuron, stimulating the neuron to open its Na^+ channels.

ACTION POTENTIAL

- Na^+ channels in the second neuron open quickly. Na^+ rushes into the cell.
- A new impulse is generated.

CRITICAL VIEWING How is an action potential generated, and how does it move down the axon?

Transmission Within a Neuron

As you tap your finger on a desk, pressure receptors in your fingers stretch. The stretching causes a change in charge distribution that triggers a moving electrical impulse called an **action potential,** shown in **FIGURE 29.4**.

An action potential requires ion channels in the membrane that have gates that open and close. When a neuron is stimulated, gated channels for Na^+ open quickly, and Na^+ ions rush into the cell. This stimulates adjacent Na^+ channels down the axon to spring open. Na^+ ions rush into the cell, and then those ion channels snap shut. In this way, the area of positively charged membrane moves down the axon.

At the same time Na^+ channels are springing open and snapping shut, K^+ ion channels are opening and closing more slowly. K^+ ions diffuse out of the axon and cause part of the membrane to return to resting potential. Because K^+ channels are slow to respond to the change in axon's charge, they appear to open and close behind the moving impulse.

Transmission Between Neurons

Before an action potential moves into the next neuron, it crosses a tiny gap between the neurons called a **synapse.** The axon **terminal,** the part of the axon through which the impulse leaves that neuron, contains chemical-filled vesicles. When an impulse reaches the terminal, vesicles bind to the terminal's membrane and release their chemicals into the synapse. **Neurotransmitters** (NUR-oh-TRANS-miht-urz) are the chemical signals of the nervous system. They bind to receptor proteins on the adjacent neuron and cause Na^+ channels in that neuron to open, generating an action potential.

Typically, many synapses connect neurons. Before the adjacent neuron generates an action potential, it usually needs to be stimulated at more than one synapse. The amount a neuron needs to be stimulated before it produces an action potential is called a threshold.

Once neurotransmitters have triggered a new action potential, they must be removed from the synapse so that ion channels on the second neuron will close again. These neurotransmitters will be broken down by enzymes in the synapse, or they are transported back into the terminal that released them.

Contrast How does signal transmission within and between neurons differ?

29.2 ASSESSMENT

REVIEWING ▶ MAIN IDEAS

1. What are the roles of the three types of **neurons**?

2. Draw a picture to illustrate **resting potential,** and explain how it helps transmit signals in neurons.

CRITICAL THINKING

3. **Infer** How does a threshold prevent a neuron from generating too many **action potentials**?

4. **Predict** What might happen if a drug blocked **neurotransmitter** receptors?

Connecting CONCEPTS

5. **Cell Chemistry** Hyponatremia occurs when people have very low amounts of sodium in their body. How might the nervous system be affected if a person had this condition?

29.3 The Senses

KEY CONCEPT The senses detect the internal and external environments.

MAIN IDEAS
- The senses help to maintain homeostasis.
- The senses detect physical and chemical stimuli.

VOCABULARY
rod cell, p. 881
cone cell, p. 881
hair cell, p. 882

MICHIGAN STANDARDS

B2.3f Explain how human organ systems help maintain human health.

Connect You may think that you hear sounds with your ear, smell with your nose, or taste with your tongue, but that is not true. Your sensory organs only collect stimuli and send signals to your brain. Your brain interprets these signals. Together, your sensory organs and your brain allow you to perceive stimuli as various sounds, sights, smells, tastes, and so forth.

MAIN IDEA

The senses help to maintain homeostasis.

You rely on your sensory organs to collect information about the world around you. Once your brain has information from sensory organs, it triggers a response that will maintain homeostasis. For example, eyes adjust to bright and dim light by changing the size of your pupils, as shown in **FIGURE 29.5**. If your skin feels cold, you might shiver. You might get goose bumps, or your arm hairs might stand up, trapping the heat that would otherwise escape from your skin.

Your sensory organs also influence your behavior. Although homeostasis is strictly defined as the regulation and maintenance of the body's internal condition, you could also think of behaviors that prevent death or injury as a kind of homeostatic mechanism.

Imagine that you are getting ready to cross a street, and you look both ways to see if it is safe. Light enters your eyes and the light receptors in your eyes are stimulated to produce impulses. The impulses travel down bundles of axons to your brain. Your brain filters these impulses and forwards some of them to the specific area of your brain that interprets visual information. Your brain then combines this information with that from your other sense organs. Your brain interprets the light that entered your eyes as a large truck speeding your way. With the help of your eyes, you will wait for the truck to pass before walking into the street.

Your senses influence many other behaviors that help protect your tissues from damage. For example, if automatic responses such as shivering and goose bumps don't warm you up, you might decide to put on a jacket. If the sun is too bright, you might decide to put on sunglasses. If a room is too dark, you might decide to turn on a light.

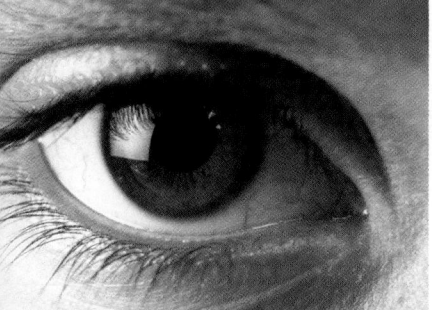
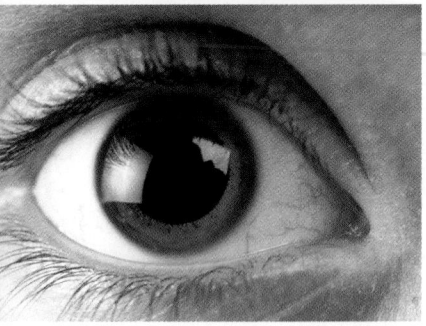

FIGURE 29.5 The size of your pupil changes depending on the amount of light around you. In bright light, your pupil constricts. In dim light, the pupil expands.

Summarize How do your sensory organs help you to maintain homeostasis?

▶ MAIN IDEA

The senses detect physical and chemical stimuli.

Humans have specialized sensory organs that detect external stimuli. The information these organs collect helps to make up the five senses: vision, hearing, touch, taste, and smell. Five different types of sensory receptors help humans to detect different stimuli.

- Photoreceptors sense light.
- Mechanoreceptors respond to pressure, movement, and tension.
- Thermoreceptors monitor temperature.
- Chemoreceptors detect chemicals that are dissolved in fluid.
- Pain receptors respond to extreme heat, cold, and pressure, and to chemicals that are released by damaged tissues.

Vision

Humans rely on vision more than any of the other senses. In fact, the eye contains about 70 percent of all the sensory receptors in the body. Most of these are photoreceptors on the back inside wall of the eye. This layer of tissue, called the retina, is shown in **FIGURE 29.6**. Specialized cells called rods and cones are the photoreceptors. **Rod cells** detect light intensity and are used in black and white vision. **Cone cells** detect color. Rod cells are sensitive to low amounts of light, and cone cells need bright light to function. This is why you have difficulty seeing color when it is dark.

Because sight depends on the amount of light available, the eye must have a way to limit the amount of light from a bright source or allow more light to enter from a dim light source. Muscles around the iris—the colored part of the eye—control the size of the hole at its center, the pupil. The eye adjusts the amount of light that enters it by changing the size of the pupil. The larger the pupil, the more light that can enter.

Before light can stimulate the rod and cone cells in the retina, it must pass through structures at the front of the eye. Light enters the eye through a protective transparent layer called the cornea and moves through the pupil. After the pupil, light passes through the lens. The lens is behind the iris, and it focuses the light onto the retina. The light stimulates the rod and cone cells, which generate nerve impulses. The impulses travel along the bundle of axons that form the optic nerve. The nerve carries the impulses to the brain, where they are interpreted as images.

VOCABULARY

You can remember what kind of stimuli each receptor receives by remembering what their prefixes mean:
photo- = light
mechano- = machine, movement
thermo- = heat
chemo- = chemical

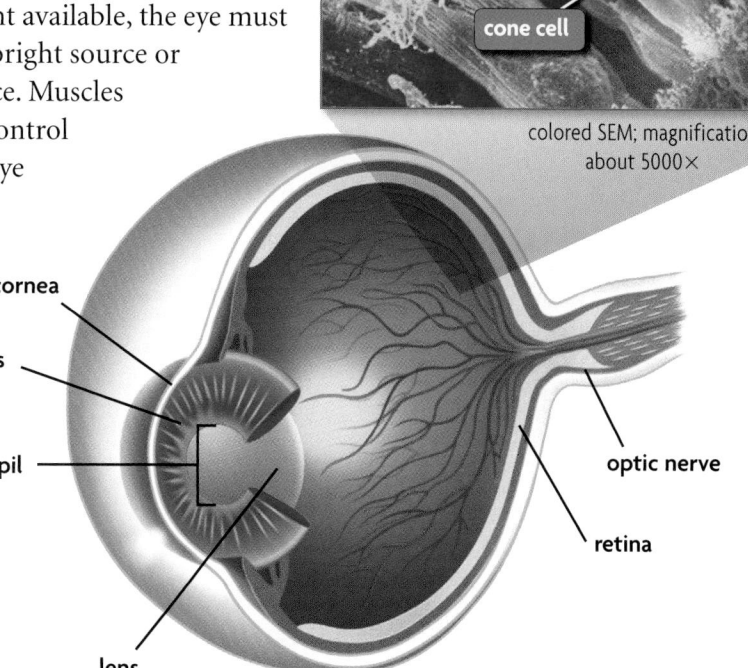

colored SEM; magnification about 5000×

FIGURE 29.6 Light is focused by the lens onto the retina, where rod and cone cells generate impulses. These impulses travel through your optic nerve to your brain, where they are interpreted as images.

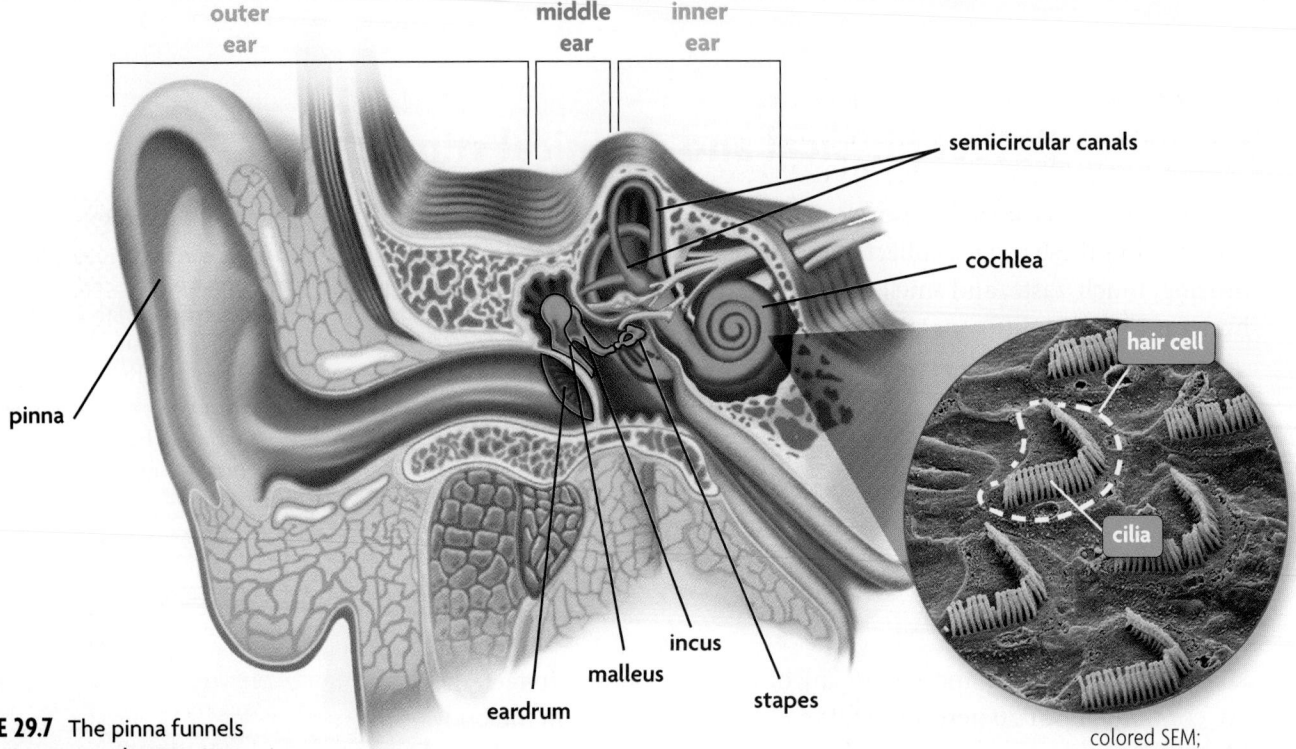

outer ear   middle ear   inner ear

semicircular canals

cochlea

hair cell

cilia

pinna

incus

malleus

eardrum

stapes

colored SEM;
magnification 3400×

FIGURE 29.7 The pinna funnels vibrations, or sound waves, into the ear. Hair cells convert vibrations into impulses that are sent to the brain for interpretation.

Connecting CONCEPTS

Animal Behavior Sensory organs collect stimuli that influence human and animal behavior, as you read in **Chapter 27**.

Hearing

The ear collects vibrations—sound waves—from the air, amplifies them, and converts them into nerve impulses that are interpreted in the brain as sounds. **Hair cells** are specialized cells in the inner ear that contain mechanoreceptors that detect vibrations. Hair cells produce action potentials when they are bent.

Sound waves enter the body through the outer ear. The pinna, the part of the ear you can see, collects sound and funnels it into the auditory canal. Sound waves in the auditory canal hit the eardrum, or tympanic membrane, causing it to vibrate like the head of a drum. The vibrations are amplified by three small bones in the middle ear—the malleus, the incus, and the stapes.

As **FIGURE 29.7** shows, the amplified vibrations are transferred to the cochlea. The cochlea is a structure of fluid-filled canals in the inner ear where hair cells are located. The fluid in the cochlea moves in response to vibrations. This movement causes the hair cells to bend. When the hair cells bend, an impulse is produced. The impulse is carried by the auditory nerve to the brain, where it is perceived as a sound.

The ear also has organs that regulate balance. Balance is controlled by an organ in the inner ear called the semicircular canals. When your head moves, fluid inside the semicircular canals moves. The movement bends the hair cells in the canals. As the cells bend, they generate impulses that are transmitted to the brain.

Smell and Taste

You may have noticed that food seems to have less flavor when you have a cold. If you haven't, you can try holding your nose the next time you eat. It will have a similar effect. Your sense of taste is less sensitive when your nose is stuffed up because your smell and taste senses are closely related. Both the nose, which senses odors, and the tongue, which senses flavors, have chemoreceptors. These receptors detect molecules that are dissolved in liquid.

In smell, small airborne chemicals enter the nose. These chemicals dissolve in mucus in the nose, and they are detected by olfactory cells, which generate impulses. The olfactory nerve takes impulses to the brain.

Taste buds are chemoreceptors that detect tastes. They are found in bumps on the tongue called papillae. As in the nose, chemicals must be dissolved before they can be detected. The chemoreceptors generate impulses that are sent to the brain. Although your tongue can only detect five basic tastes—sweet, sour, salty, bitter, and savory—your brain interprets combinations of these as complex flavors.

Touch, Temperature, and Pain

Your skin contains receptors that sense touch, temperature, and pain. Touch is sensed by mechanoreceptors that detect pressure, movement, and tension. The skin has two general types of mechanoreceptors. Mechanoreceptors that detect gentle touch are located in the upper layer of the skin. Some of these are wrapped around hair follicles. They help you feel when these hairs move, as they might when a small fly lands on your arm. Mechanoreceptors that recognize heavy pressure are found deeper within the skin, as you can see in **FIGURE 29.8.**

Temperature and pain are sensed by thermoreceptors and pain receptors. Thermoreceptors detect heat and cold. Pain receptors detect chemicals that are released by damaged cells. Some pain receptors detect sharp pains, such as the pain you would feel by stepping on a nail. Other pain receptors sense blunt or throbbing pain, such as that caused by a bruise.

Summarize To which senses do mechanoreceptors contribute?

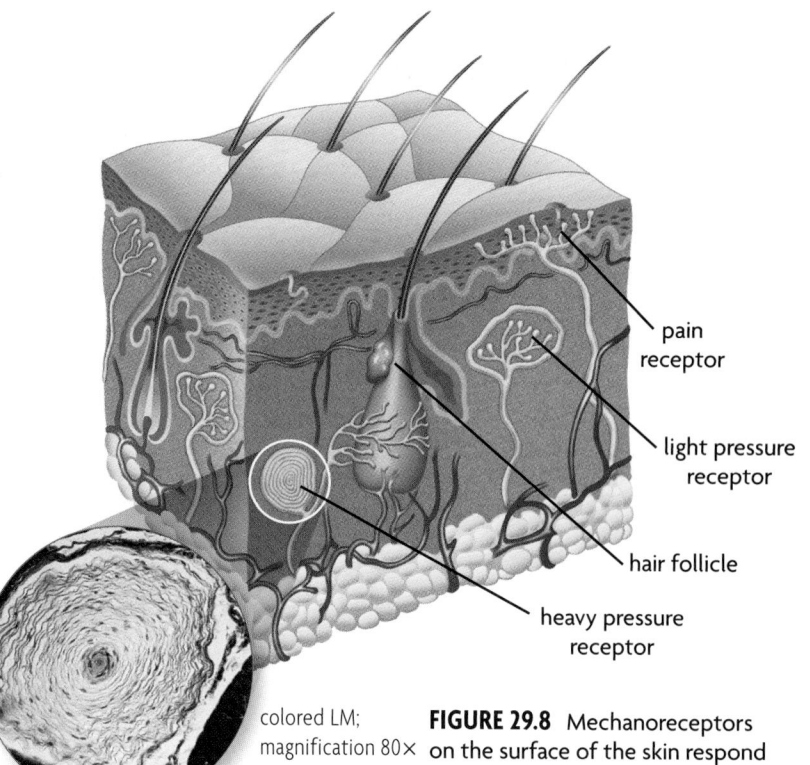

colored LM; magnification 80×

FIGURE 29.8 Mechanoreceptors on the surface of the skin respond to gentle pressure, and those deep in the skin respond to hard pressure. Pain receptors are close to the skin's surface.

pain receptor

light pressure receptor

hair follicle

heavy pressure receptor

29.3 ASSESSMENT

ONLINE QUIZ ClassZone.com

REVIEWING ▶ MAIN IDEAS

1. How do your sensory organs work with your brain to help you perceive the world around you?

2. What kinds of receptors are **hair cells, rod cells,** and **cone cells,** and to which of your senses do these cells contribute?

CRITICAL THINKING

3. **Connect** Why do you think that you can perceive some sounds as loud and others as very soft?

4. **Predict** In the human eye, there are 20 rod cells for every 1 cone cell. How would your vision be different if you had 5 rod cells for every 20 cone cells?

Connecting CONCEPTS

5. **Evolution** For some invertebrates that live in water, the sense of taste and the sense of smell are identical. Why do you think separate organs for taste and smell might have evolved in animals that live on land but not in some animals that live exclusively in water?

MATERIALS

watch with second hand

PROCESS SKILLS

- **Observing**
- **Collecting Data**
- **Inferring**

B1.1C Conduct scientific investigations using appropriate tools and techniques (e.g., selecting an instrument that measures the desired quantity—length, volume, weight, time interval, temperature—with the appropriate level of precision).

The Stroop Effect

Psychologist John Stroop studied the processing of words and how these thought processes affected other mental tasks. He found that the brain must override an automatic response when it receives conflicting information, or interference. This is now called the Stroop Effect. In this lab, you will complete a task that demonstrates the Stroop Effect.

PROBLEM How does interference affect the completion of a task?

PROCEDURE

1. Have your partner time and record how long it takes for you to say aloud the color of ink in which each word in column 1 is printed (say the color, not the word itself). Give your responses as quickly as possible. Also record the number of incorrect responses.

2. Have your partner time and record how long it takes for you to say aloud the color of ink in which each word in column 2 is printed (say the color, not the word itself). Give your responses as quickly as possible. Also record the number of incorrect responses.

3. Switch roles and repeat steps 1 and 2.

TABLE 1. STROOP EFFECT COLOR TEST	
COLUMN 1	**COLUMN 2**
blue	red
yellow	gray
red	orange
green	blue
black	black
purple	yellow
gray	green
orange	purple

ANALYZE AND CONCLUDE

1. **Analyze** Compare the times for naming the ink colors in both column 1 and column 2. Was there a difference between the two times? Explain why this difference exists.

2. **Infer** How many incorrect responses did you give for column 1? for column 2? Explain why incorrect responses might have occurred.

3. **Experimental Design** Design your own Stroop Effect test. For example, you could draw outlines of animals and write the name of a different animal in the drawing and test if interference occurs.

29.4 Central and Peripheral Nervous Systems

KEY CONCEPT The central nervous system interprets information, and the peripheral nervous system gathers and transmits information.

▶ MAIN IDEAS

- The nervous system's two parts work together.
- The CNS processes information.
- The PNS links the CNS to muscles and other organs.

VOCABULARY

cerebrum, p. 886
cerebral cortex, p. 887
cerebellum, p. 888
brain stem, p. 888
reflex arc, p. 889
somatic nervous system, p. 889

autonomic nervous system, p. 890
sympathetic nervous system, p. 890
parasympathetic nervous system, p. 890

Review
central nervous system (CNS),
peripheral nervous system (PNS)

MICHIGAN STANDARDS

B2.3d Identify the general functions of the major systems of the human body (digestion, respiration, reproduction, circulation, excretion, protection from disease, and movement, control, and coordination) and describe ways that these systems interact with each other.

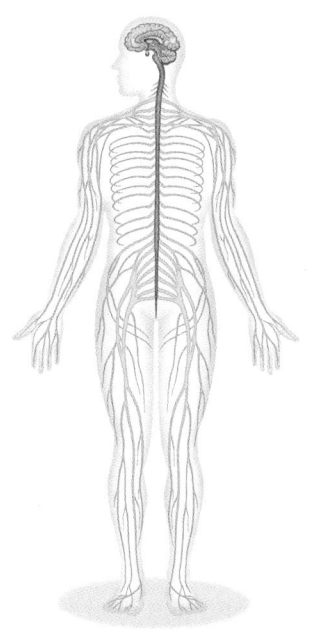

FIGURE 29.9 Your central nervous system (orange) and peripheral nervous system (yellow) are connected.

Connect Imagine that you're watching television, and you want to turn up the volume. Without taking your eyes off the screen, you reach for the remote control on a table next to you. When you touch a glass of water or your homework that is sitting on the table, you will not pick it up because you know that it does not feel like the remote. Your brain is interpreting the stimuli gathered by your sense of touch. If you had no way to interpret each stimulus, you might pick up every item on the table before finding the remote.

▶ MAIN IDEA

The nervous system's two parts work together.

Earlier in this chapter you read that your nervous system is divided into two parts—the central nervous system and the peripheral nervous system—which are shown in **FIGURE 29.9**.

- The central nervous system (CNS) includes the brain and spinal cord. The CNS is composed of interneurons that interact with other nerves in the body. The CNS receives, interprets, and sends signals to the PNS.
- The peripheral nervous system (PNS) is the collection of nerves that connects the CNS to all of your organ systems. The PNS uses sensory neurons to detect stimuli from inside and outside your body, and it uses motor neurons to carry signals from the CNS to other parts of the body and stimulate your muscles or other target organs.

Both the CNS and the PNS are made of several smaller parts. For example, the brain has several areas that control different functions. Divisions of the PNS influence voluntary responses, such as muscle contractions that occur while you walk, and involuntary responses, such as those that occur during digestion.

Summarize How do the neurons of the CNS and PNS work together to produce responses to stimuli?

The Primary Sensory Cortex

The primary sensory cortex is the part of your cerebrum that receives information about your sense of touch from different parts of your body. Each body part sends information to a different place in your primary sensory cortex. In this lab, you will determine the relationship between different body parts and the amount of space the brain devotes to receiving touch information from those body parts.

MATERIALS
- 3 toothpicks
- soft blindfold/bandana

PROBLEM Does your finger or your forearm have more space devoted to it in the primary sensory cortex?

PROCEDURE

1. Hypothesize which area will be more sensitive. Make a data table to record the information you gather during the lab.

2. Have your partner close his or her eyes. Gently, touch the tip of your partner's index finger with the tip(s) of one, two, or three toothpicks at the same time.

3. Ask your partner how many points he or she feels. Write down the number your partner says next to the number of toothpicks you used. Repeat three more times, varying the number of toothpicks used.

4. Repeat steps 2 and 3 on your partner's forearm.

ANALYZE AND CONCLUDE

1. **Analyze** Did your partner's finger or forearm receive more sensory information? Do your data support your hypothesis? Why or why not?

2. **Infer** Which area likely has more space in the primary sensory cortex?

TABLE 1. PRIMARY SENSORY CORTEX DATA		
Area Tested	Number of Toothpicks	
	Used	Reported

▶ MAIN IDEA
The CNS processes information.

TAKING NOTES

Use a main idea diagram to study the parts of the brain.

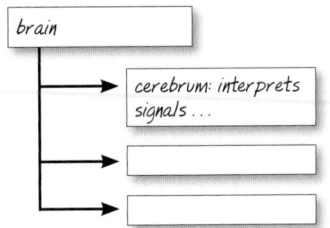

The interneurons of the brain and spinal cord are arranged in a particular way. All of the neuron cell bodies are clustered together, and all of the axons are clustered together. The collection of neuron cell bodies is called gray matter because of its dark gray color. The collection of axons is called white matter because the myelin sheath on the axons give them a white appearance. In the brain, the gray matter is on the outside, and the white matter is on the inside. The spinal cord has the opposite arrangement.

The Brain

The entire brain weighs about half as much as a textbook and has more than 100 billion neurons. The brain is protected by three layers of connective tissue, called meninges (muh-NIHN-jeez), that surround it. Between the layers of meninges is a fluid. The fluid cushions the brain so that the brain will not bang up against the skull. The brain itself has three main structures: the cerebrum, the cerebellum, and the brainstem.

The **cerebrum** (SEHR-uh-bruhm) is the part of the brain that interprets signals from your body and forms responses such as hunger, thirst, emotions, motion, and pain. The cerebrum has right and left halves, or hemispheres.

Each hemisphere controls the opposite side of the body. For example, the right hemisphere of your brain processes all of the stimuli received by your left hand. Similarly, the left side of your brain controls the muscles that kick your right leg. When the spinal cord brings a signal from the body, the signal crosses over to the opposite hemisphere in the corpus callosum. The corpus callosum is a thick band of nerves that connects the two hemispheres.

The outer layer of the cerebrum, called the **cerebral cortex,** interprets information from your sensory organs and generates responses. The cerebral cortex is about as thick as a pencil. Yet its size is deceptive because its folds give it a larger surface area than you might expect. If the cerebral cortex were unfolded, it would cover a typical classroom desk. This surface area is large enough to hold more than 10 billion neurons.

The neurons in the cerebral cortex are arranged in groups that work together to perform specific tasks. For example, movement is initiated by an area of the brain called the motor cortex, and the sense of touch is received by the sensory cortex. Scientists divide the cerebral cortex into different areas, or lobes, based on function. Each hemisphere of the human brain can be divided into four lobes—frontal, parietal, occipital, and temporal. The lobes and the cortical areas they contain are shown in **FIGURE 29.10**.

FIGURE 29.10 Lobes of the Brain

The various areas of the cerebral cortex process different types of information.

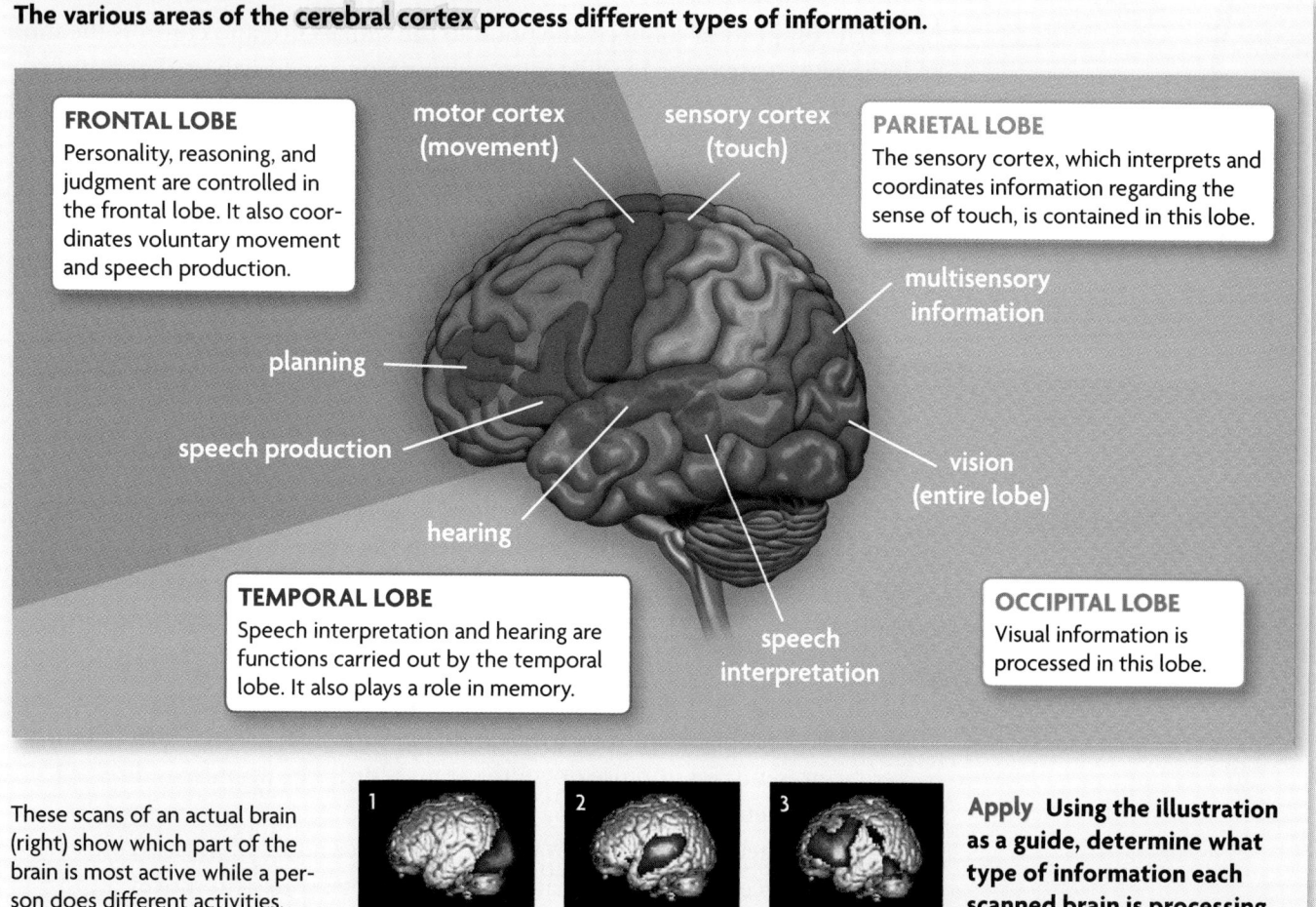

FRONTAL LOBE
Personality, reasoning, and judgment are controlled in the frontal lobe. It also coordinates voluntary movement and speech production.

motor cortex (movement)

sensory cortex (touch)

PARIETAL LOBE
The sensory cortex, which interprets and coordinates information regarding the sense of touch, is contained in this lobe.

multisensory information

planning

speech production

vision (entire lobe)

hearing

TEMPORAL LOBE
Speech interpretation and hearing are functions carried out by the temporal lobe. It also plays a role in memory.

speech interpretation

OCCIPITAL LOBE
Visual information is processed in this lobe.

These scans of an actual brain (right) show which part of the brain is most active while a person does different activities.

Apply Using the illustration as a guide, determine what type of information each scanned brain is processing.

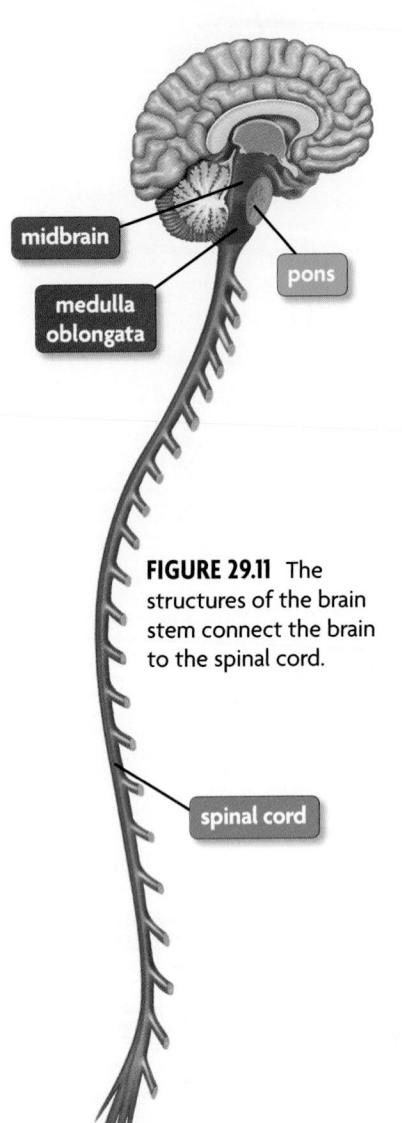

FIGURE 29.11 The structures of the brain stem connect the brain to the spinal cord.

Underneath the cerebral cortex are many smaller areas with different functions. The limbic system, for example, is involved in learning and emotions and includes the hippocampus and the amygdala. The thalamus sorts information from your sensory organs and passes signals between the spinal cord and other parts of the brain. The hypothalamus gathers information about body temperature, hunger, and thirst. Then it sends signals that help the body adjust and maintain homeostasis, as you will see in Section 29.6.

The **cerebellum** (sehr-uh-BEHL-uhm) is the part of the brain that coordinates your movements. It helps you maintain your posture and balance, and it automatically adjusts your body to help you move smoothly. For example, when you brush your teeth, your cerebellum gets information about where your arm is positioned compared with the rest of your body. Your cerebellum plans how much your arm would need to move in order to brush your teeth. It sends this information to the motor cortex in your cerebrum, which signals your arm to move.

VISUAL VOCAB

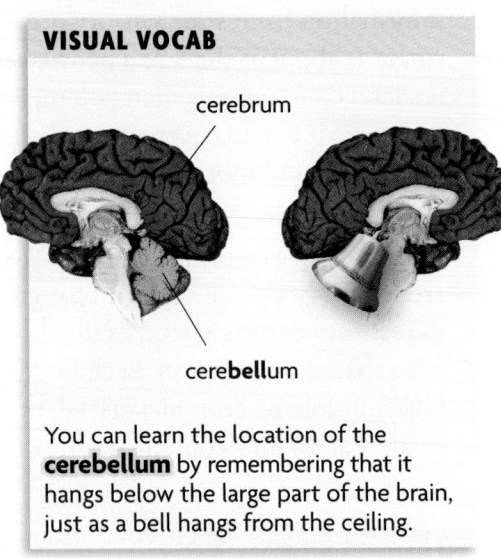

You can learn the location of the **cerebellum** by remembering that it hangs below the large part of the brain, just as a bell hangs from the ceiling.

The **brain stem** connects the brain to the spinal cord and controls the most basic activities required for life, such as breathing and heartbeat. The brain stem has three major parts—midbrain, pons, and medulla oblongata—which are shown in **FIGURE 29.11**.

- The midbrain controls some reflexes, such as changing the size of the pupil to control the amount of light entering the eye.
- The pons regulates breathing and passes signals between the brain and the spinal cord.
- The medulla oblongata connects the brain to the spinal cord. It controls basic life-sustaining functions, such as heart function, vomiting, swallowing, and coughing.

The Spinal Cord

The spinal column consists of vertebrae, fluid, meninges, and the spinal cord. The spinal cord is a ropelike bundle of neurons that is about as wide as your thumb. It connects the brain to the nerves that are found throughout the body. All signals that go to or from the brain pass through the spinal cord.

Although movement is controlled by your cerebrum and cerebellum, your brain depends on your spinal cord to deliver messages to the proper muscles. When you are brushing your teeth, and you want to move your arm, the cerebrum sends an impulse down the spinal cord. The impulse is directed by an interneuron to the motor neuron that connects to the arm muscles. The motor neuron then carries the impulse to receptors in the arm muscle. When the receptors are stimulated by the impulse, your arm moves.

Connecting CONCEPTS

Chordates The spinal cord is one anatomical feature that defines the phylum Chordata, which includes humans and many other animals. You can read more about chordates in **Chapter 25**.

If the spinal cord is damaged, messages cannot move between the brain and the rest of the body. This results in paralysis.

The spinal cord also controls involuntary movements called reflexes. **Reflex arcs,** as shown in **FIGURE 29.12,** are nerve pathways that need to cross only two synapses before producing a response. Because the signal never has to travel up the spinal cord to the brain, you react quickly.

For example, when the doctor taps your knee, tissues that connect your kneecap to your leg muscles stretch and stimulate a sensory neuron in your leg. The sensory neuron sends an impulse to your spinal cord. An interneuron in the spinal cord directs the impulse into motor neurons that cause your leg to jerk.

Reflex arcs play an important role in protecting your body from injury. When you put your hand on a hot stove, for example, you will jerk your hand away before you even have the chance to say "Ouch!" You do not feel the pain until moments after you jerk your hand away. If you did not have reflex arcs, your hand would remain on the stove until your brain interpreted the heat detected by thermoreceptors in your skin. Your hand would be badly burned before you ever reacted.

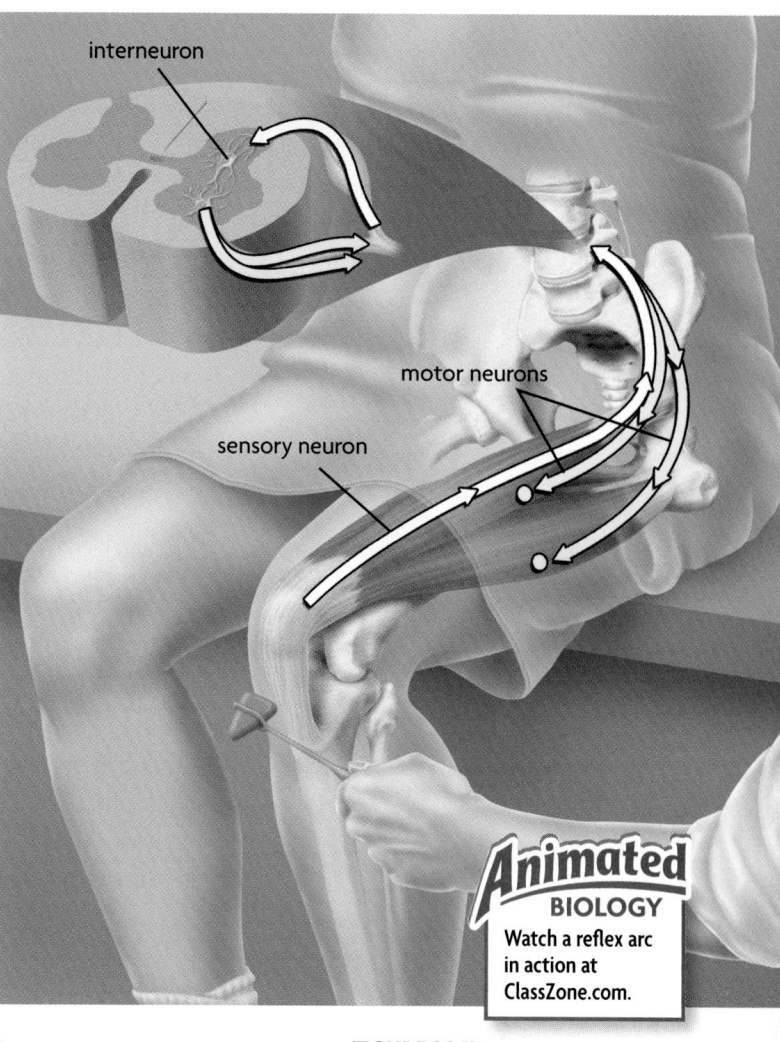

Animated BIOLOGY
Watch a reflex arc in action at ClassZone.com.

FIGURE 29.12 Reflex arcs allow your body to respond quickly and without thinking, as when your leg jerks after your doctor taps your knee with a mallet.

Summarize How is a muscle movement caused by a reflex arc different from a voluntary muscle movement?

▶ MAIN IDEA
The PNS links the CNS to muscles and other organs.

The peripheral nervous system (PNS) includes 12 pairs of nerves in the head, such as the facial and olfactory nerves, and 31 pairs of spinal nerves. Most nerves contain axons from both sensory and motor neurons that carry information to and from the CNS. In general, the PNS is made up of a sensory system and a motor system. The system of sensory nerves collects information about the body and its surroundings. The system of motor nerves triggers voluntary and involuntary responses within the body.

When you are running, walking, or even sitting, you rely on your somatic nervous system to stimulate your muscles to maintain your movement, posture, and balance. The **somatic nervous system** is the division of the PNS that regulates all of the movements over which you have voluntary control. It connects the CNS to target organs.

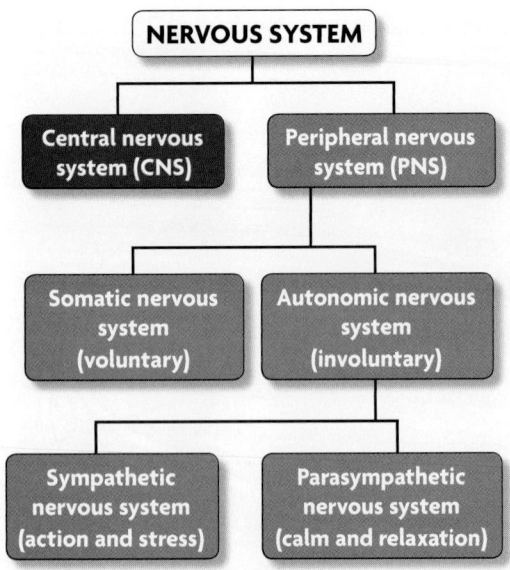

NERVOUS SYSTEM

- Central nervous system (CNS)
- Peripheral nervous system (PNS)
  - Somatic nervous system (voluntary)
  - Autonomic nervous system (involuntary)
    - Sympathetic nervous system (action and stress)
    - Parasympathetic nervous system (calm and relaxation)

FIGURE 29.13 The nervous system can be divided into subsystems based on their functions.

The **autonomic nervous system** is the division of the PNS that controls automatic functions that you do not have to think about. For example, involuntary muscles help you to digest food by pushing it through your intestines. The autonomic nervous system is also important in maintaining homeostasis. It takes messages from the hypothalamus to organs in the circulatory, digestive, and endocrine systems.

Within the autonomic nervous system are two subdivisions: the sympathetic nervous system and the parasympathetic nervous system. **FIGURE 29.13** shows how these two systems relate to the rest of the nervous system. Although the two systems have opposite effects on the body, they both function continuously. If something happens to cause one system to produce more signals, the other system will become more active to balance the effects of the first. Together, the sympathetic and parasympathetic nervous systems help your body to maintain homeostasis.

The **sympathetic nervous system** is the part of the autonomic nervous system that prepares the body for action and stress. This is called the "fight or flight" response. When you become frightened or you are preparing to compete in a sport, your sympathetic nervous system is stimulated. Blood vessels going to the skin and internal organs contract, which reduces blood flow to those areas. Meanwhile, blood vessels going to the heart, brain, lungs, and skeletal muscles expand, increasing the blood supply in those areas. Heart rate increases. Airways enlarge, and breathing becomes more efficient. These changes improve your physical abilities and allow you to think quickly.

If something frightens you, your sympathetic nervous system activates. When the danger passes, the parasympathetic nervous system takes over to bring your body back to normal. The **parasympathetic nervous system** is the division of the autonomic nervous system that calms the body and helps the body to conserve energy. It does this by lowering blood pressure and heart rate. It is active when the body is relaxed.

Analyze Are reflex arcs part of the somatic or autonomic nervous system? Explain.

29.4 ASSESSMENT

ONLINE QUIZ
ClassZone.com

REVIEWING ▸ MAIN IDEAS

1. How do the types of neurons found in the CNS and PNS differ in their functions?

2. How does the **cerebral cortex** differ from the rest of the **cerebrum**?

3. What are some similarities and differences between the **somatic nervous system** and **autonomic nervous system**?

CRITICAL THINKING

4. **Apply** Why might a person with a brain injury be able to understand the speech of others but not be able to speak?

5. **Synthesize** You step on a sharp rock, your leg jerks upward, and a moment later you feel pain in your foot. Use the words *motor neuron*, *sensory neuron*, and *interneuron* to explain what happened.

Connecting CONCEPTS

6. **Evolution** Which part of the brain—the cerebrum, **cerebellum**, or **brain stem**—probably evolved first? (**Hint:** Consider which part is most important for basic life processes.)

29.5 Brain Function and Chemistry

KEY CONCEPT Scientists study the functions and chemistry of the brain.

▶ MAIN IDEAS

- New techniques improve our understanding of the brain.
- Changes in brain chemistry can cause illness.
- Drugs alter brain chemistry.

VOCABULARY

addiction, p. 893
desensitization, p. 893
tolerance, p. 893
sensitization, p. 893

stimulant, p. 894
depressant, p. 894

Review
neurotransmitter, action potential

MICHIGAN STANDARDS

B1.2k Analyze how science and society interact from a historical, political, economic, or social perspective.

Connect When you take medicine for a headache, the drug alters your brain's chemistry. Aspirin, for example, stops your brain from making certain chemicals. In small amounts, it is beneficial to your health. However, even nonprescription drugs can cause permanent damage to your nervous system if taken incorrectly.

▶ MAIN IDEA

New techniques improve our understanding of the brain.

For many years, the only way scientists could study brain function was by observing changes that occurred in people who had accidental brain injuries or by dissecting the brains of people who had died. A live patient would have to undergo surgery in order for scientists to learn about brain function.

Today, scientists use imaging technologies such as CT, MRI, and PET scans to study the brain in living patients without the need for surgery. These methods use x-rays, magnetic fields, or radioactive sensors and computer programs to form images of the brain, as shown in **FIGURE 29.14.**

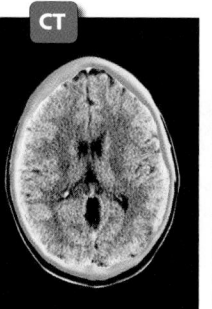
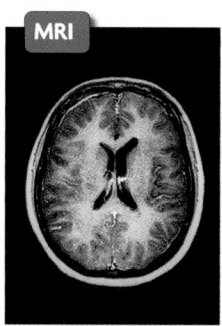
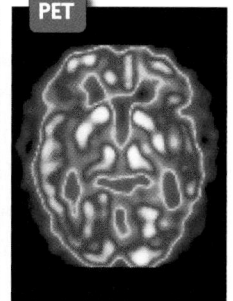

Computerized tomography (CT) scans use x-rays to view the brain. Magnetic resonance imaging (MRI) uses magnetic fields and radio waves. Both CT and MRI scans make images that show the structure of the brain. These scans are used to examine the brain's physical condition.

Positron emission tomography (PET) scans show which areas of the brain are most active. During PET scans, a person is injected with radioactive glucose. Recall from Chapter 4 that cells use glucose for energy. By measuring where the radioactive glucose collects in the brain, scientists can see which areas of the brain are using the most energy. In the image shown above, the bright red and yellow areas are the most active, and the dark blue areas are the least active.

FIGURE 29.14 Modern technologies use computers and sensing devices to observe the brain without the need for surgery.

Infer Why are modern technologies for studying the brain safer for the patients being studied?

▶ MAIN IDEA

Changes in brain chemistry can cause illness.

Connecting CONCEPTS

Enzymes In **Chapter 2** you read that enzymes are like locks because only certain shaped molecules can fit into them. Neurotransmitters only affect certain areas of the brain because they are like keys that can only fit into certain neurons' receptors.

In Section 29.2, you learned that your nervous system cannot work without neurotransmitters. These chemicals regulate different functions in different areas of the brain. Neurotransmitters are specific to some areas of the brain because, like hormones, they only affect cells that have specific receptors. The function of neurotransmitters relates to the functions of the cells they stimulate.

- Acetylcholine is involved in learning and memory.
- Dopamine primarily influences your emotional behavior, but it also plays some role in stress and voluntary muscles.
- Serotonin is mainly found in the hypothalamus and midbrain. It also influences mood, some muscle functions, and hunger.
- Glutamate affects learning, memory, and brain development.
- Gamma amino butyric acid (GABA) is found throughout the brain. Unlike other neurotransmitters, when GABA binds to a neuron's membrane, it prevents the neuron from generating an impulse.

When your brain produces the correct amount of these neurotransmitters, homeostasis is maintained. If your body produces too much or too little of a neurotransmitter, the areas of your brain that are targeted by that chemical will be more or less active than normal. Because all of the areas of your brain work together, abnormal activity in one part of the brain can affect the whole brain and change the way you move, behave, and think. **FIGURE 29.15** shows that the brain activity of a healthy patient differs from that of patients with depression or schizophrenia, which are associated with chemical imbalances in the brain.

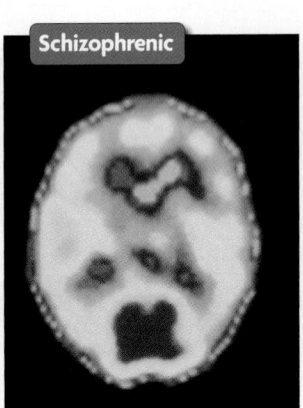
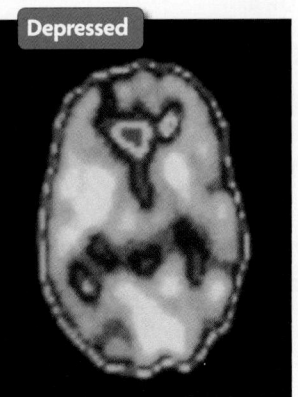

Normal | Schizophrenic | Depressed

FIGURE 29.15 These PET images show the activity of a normal, a schizophrenic, and a depressed brain. Blue and green areas have low activity, and red areas are the most active.

Illnesses such as Parkinson's disease and schizophrenia are linked to abnormal amounts of dopamine. Parkinson's disease is caused by low amounts of dopamine in certain areas of the brain. People with Parkinson's disease have difficulty controlling their movements, maintaining their balance, and starting movements. Many patients with Parkinson's take drugs that increase the amount of dopamine in the brain. On the other hand, schizophrenia sometimes occurs when a person has too much dopamine. Schizophrenia is a mental disorder that causes hallucinations, irrational behavior, and illogical speech. It is treated with drugs that block dopamine receptors in the brain.

Depression is linked to low amounts of serotonin in parts of the brain. Depression causes extended periods of intense sadness, inability to sleep, and feelings of helplessness. One treatment for clinical depression uses drugs that extend the time that serotonin remains active in nerve synapses.

Summarize How do treatments for neurological illnesses alter brain chemistry?

MAIN IDEA
Drugs alter brain chemistry.

You may have noticed that some medicines come with warnings that say they may cause drowsiness so they should only be taken at night. People who use prescription, illegal, or other types of drugs can experience behavioral changes, such as changes in appetite, aggression, or sleep cycles. Drugs also cause changes in coordination or sensitivity to pain. Drugs might return one system in the body to homeostasis while pushing another system further out of balance. These changes occur because drugs change the way the brain works.

Many drugs affect the amount of neurotransmitter in synapses. Remember from Section 29.2 that a certain amount of neurotransmitter must be in the synapse before the threshold is reached and an action potential is generated. If a drug increases the amount of neurotransmitter released, impulses are more likely to occur. If a drug decreases the amount of neurotransmitter, action potentials are less likely to occur.

Some Drugs Cause Addiction

Many illegal, recreational, and prescription drugs can lead to addiction. **Addiction** is the physiological need for a substance. Through feedback loops, a person becomes addicted to a substance when the body changes the way it works so that it needs the drug in order to function normally. The brain adapts to drug exposure so that neurons will generate normal amounts of impulses despite abnormal levels of neurotransmitter.

Brain cells undergo **desensitization** when there is more neurotransmitter present in the synapse than usual. When a drug increases the amount of neurotransmitter in the synapses, the neuron generates more impulses than normal. The neuron responds by reducing the number of receptors on its cell membrane, as shown in **FIGURE 29.16**. With fewer receptors, less neurotransmitter can bind to the cell membrane and impulses are less likely to generate. Desensitization builds a person's tolerance. When someone has a **tolerance,** it takes larger doses of the drug to produce the same effect.

Sensitization occurs when low amounts of a neurotransmitter are in the synapses. When drugs lower the amount of a neurotransmitter, fewer action potentials are generated than normal. With less neurotransmitter than normal, brain cells adapt by increasing the number of receptors for them, also shown in **FIGURE 29.16**. By producing more receptors, cells increase the amount of neurotransmitter that bind to the cell. This causes the cell to generate more action potentials, just as if the normal amount of neurotransmitter were in the synapse.

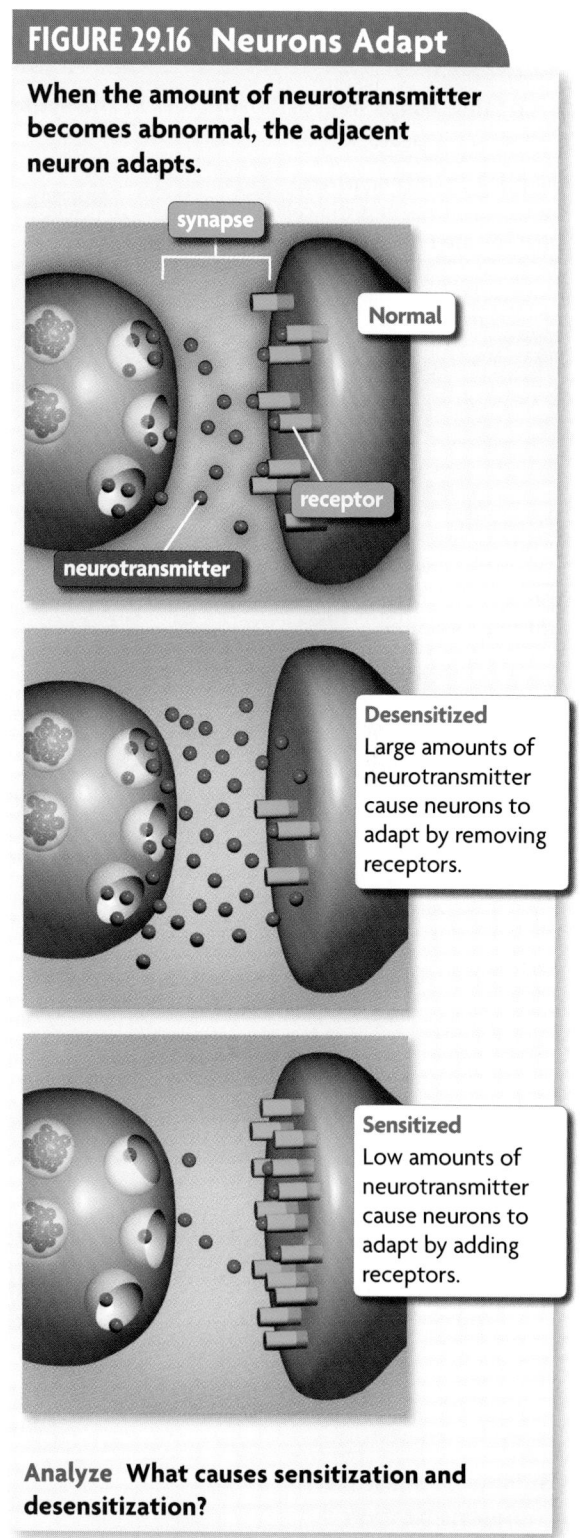

FIGURE 29.16 Neurons Adapt

When the amount of neurotransmitter becomes abnormal, the adjacent neuron adapts.

synapse

Normal

receptor

neurotransmitter

Desensitized
Large amounts of neurotransmitter cause neurons to adapt by removing receptors.

Sensitized
Low amounts of neurotransmitter cause neurons to adapt by adding receptors.

Analyze What causes sensitization and desensitization?

How Drugs Work

In order for drugs to have an effect on your behavior, they must change the number of action potentials your neurons generate.

Some drugs make a person feel happy, energetic, and alert. **Stimulants** are drugs that increase the number of action potentials that neurons generate by increasing the amounts of neurotransmitter in the synapses. Methamphetamine, for example, causes neurons to produce and release more neurotransmitters, especially serotonin and dopamine. However, there are other ways that stimulants can increase the amount of neurotransmitter.

Some drugs have almost the same chemistry as neurotransmitters, and they bind directly to the receptors on neuron membranes. Other drugs slow the removal of neurotransmitters from the synapses. These drugs can bind to enzymes that break down the neurotransmitters and make them unable to work. Drugs such as cocaine, however, bind to transport proteins on the axon terminal, as shown in **FIGURE 29.17**. Normally, these proteins would allow neurotransmitters to flow back into the cell that released them. If a drug is blocking the protein, the neurotransmitter remains in the synapse and an action potential is more likely to occur.

Depressants are drugs that make a person feel relaxed and tired. The person may react slowly or seem out of touch with the world around them. Depressants reduce the ability of neurons to generate impulses. Some depressants block neuron receptors so that neurotransmitters cannot produce an impulse. Other depressants, such as methaqualone, can make a person feel relaxed or sleepy by increasing in the synapses the amount of GABA, which prevents neurons from generating impulses.

Analyze How do stimulants and depressants affect a neuron's ability to generate impulses?

FIGURE 29.17 How Cocaine Works

Cocaine keeps neurotransmitters in the synapse.

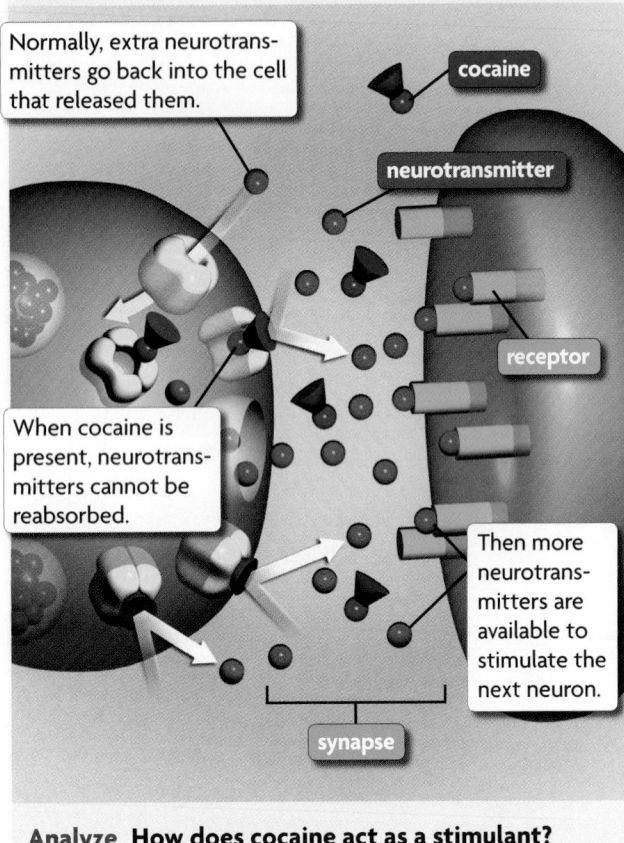

Normally, extra neurotransmitters go back into the cell that released them.

cocaine

neurotransmitter

receptor

When cocaine is present, neurotransmitters cannot be reabsorbed.

Then more neurotransmitters are available to stimulate the next neuron.

synapse

Analyze How does cocaine act as a stimulant?

REVIEWING ▸ MAIN IDEAS

1. How are CT and MRI scans different from PET scans?

2. Why is it important that neurotransmitters are balanced in the brain?

3. How do **sensitization** and **desensitization** differ?

CRITICAL THINKING

4. **Synthesize** Draw before and after pictures to explain why a person whose neurons were sensitized by drug use experiences opposite symptoms when they quit.

5. **Analyze** How does desensitization relate to drug **tolerance**?

Connecting CONCEPTS

6. **Feedback Loops** What kind of feedback loops are sensitization and desensitization? Explain. (**Hint:** What causes these processes to begin and end?)

DATA ANALYSIS   CORRELATION OR CAUSATION

Relationships Between Variables

When scientists analyze their data, they must remember that just because two variables are related, it does not mean that one caused the other to change. A **causation** occurs when a change in one variable was caused by the other. Sometimes the cause of change in a variable may be the result of a third, unknown variable. A **correlation** occurs when scientists find that two variables are closely related, but the change in one variable did not definitely cause the change in the other. When a strong correlation exists between two variables, scientists will conduct other experiments to discover exactly how the variables are related.

EXAMPLE

Scientists studied the memory of people who regularly used the illegal drug ecstasy. They found that ecstasy users were more forgetful than people who didn't use ecstasy. Therefore, ecstasy use and memory loss are correlated. However, scientists do not know that ecstasy *causes* forgetfulness. It could be that people who are forgetful use ecstasy.

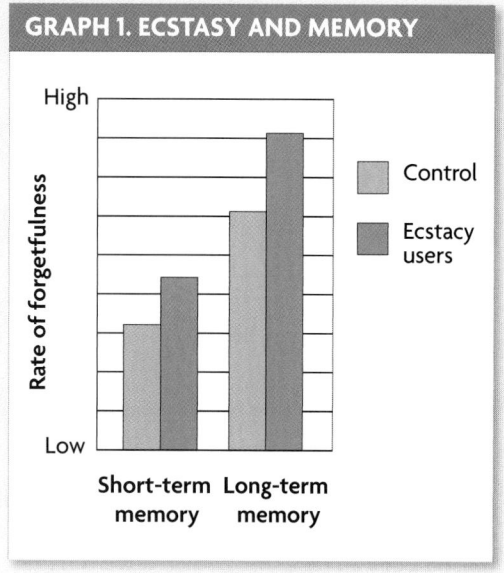

GRAPH 1. ECSTASY AND MEMORY

Source: T. M. Heffernan, et al., *Human Psychopharmacol Clinical Experiments* 2001:16.

DETERMINE CORRELATION OR CAUSATION

A panic attack is characterized by a sudden increase in pulse and anxiety. The graph on the right shows hypothetical data for the incidence of panic attacks in the general population and in a population of people who have a disorder called mitral valve prolapse, in which a heart valve does not work properly.

1. **Analyze** Does a correlation or a causation exist between mitral valve prolapse and panic attacks? How do you know?

2. **Evaluate** Can you conclude that mitral valve prolapse causes panic attacks? Why or why not?

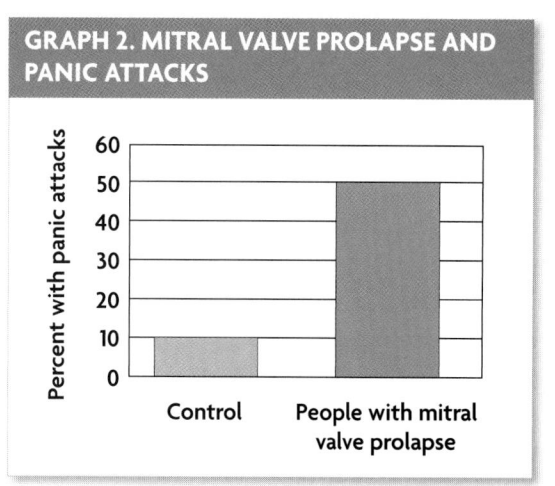

GRAPH 2. MITRAL VALVE PROLAPSE AND PANIC ATTACKS

The Endocrine System and Hormones

KEY CONCEPT The endocrine system produces hormones that affect growth, development, and homeostasis.

▶ MAIN IDEAS

- Hormones influence a cell's activities by entering the cell or binding to its membrane.
- Endocrine glands secrete hormones that act throughout the body.
- The hypothalamus interacts with the nervous and endocrine systems.
- Hormonal imbalances can cause serious illness.

VOCABULARY

hormone, p. 896
gland, p. 896
hypothalamus, p. 898
pituitary gland, p. 898
releasing hormones, p. 900

MICHIGAN STANDARDS

B2.2f Explain the role of enzymes and other proteins in biochemical functions (e.g., the protein hemoglobin carries oxygen in some organisms, digestive enzymes, and hormones).

Connect If you hear a loud BANG, your brain tells your body that you could be in danger. You might need to run away or defend yourself. Your brain alerts your endocrine system to send out chemicals that will speed up your heart rate, increase blood flow to your muscles, and get you ready for action.

▶ MAIN IDEA

Hormones influence a cell's activities by entering the cell or binding to its membrane.

The endocrine system makes chemical signals that help the body grow, develop, and maintain homeostasis. Some of these chemicals control processes such as cell division, cell death, and sexual development. Others help you maintain homeostasis by affecting body temperature, alertness, or salt levels.

The chemical signals made by the endocrine system are called **hormones.** Hormones are made in organs called **glands,** which are found in many different areas of the body. Glands release hormones into the bloodstream, as shown in **FIGURE 29.18.** As a hormone moves through the body, it comes into contact with many different cells. But it will interact only with a cell that has specific membrane receptors. If the hormone touches a cell that does not have a matching receptor, nothing happens. If it touches a cell that has the correct receptors, it binds to the cell and prompts the cell to make certain proteins or enzymes. Cells that have receptors for a hormone are called the target cells of that hormone.

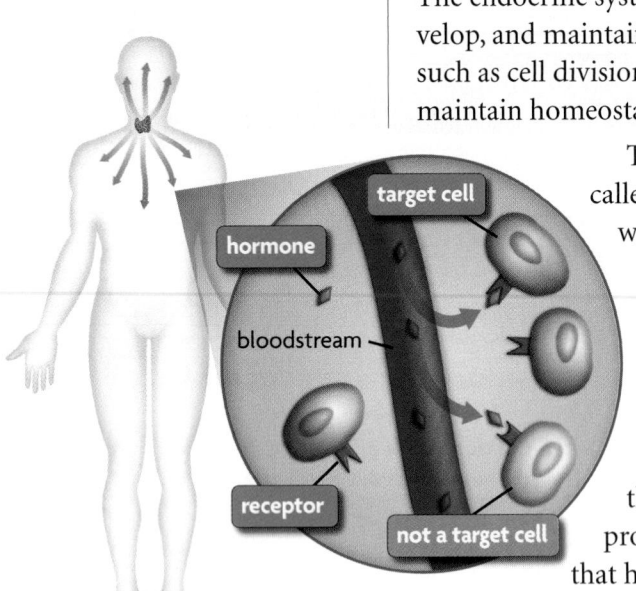

FIGURE 29.18 Glands release hormones into the bloodstream, but hormones will only affect cells that have receptors for those hormones.

All hormones belong to one of two categories: steroid hormones and nonsteroid hormones. All steroid hormones are made of cholesterol, a type of lipid. On the other hand, there are three types of nonsteroid hormones that are made up of one or more amino acids.

As **FIGURE 29.19** shows, steroid hormones and nonsteroid hormones influence cells' activities in different ways. A steroid hormone can enter its target cells by diffusing through the cell membrane. Once inside, the steroid hormone attaches to a receptor protein, which transports the protein into the nucleus. After it is inside, the steroid hormone binds to the cell's DNA. This binding causes the cell to produce the proteins that are coded by that portion of DNA.

Nonsteroid hormones do not enter their target cells. These hormones bind to protein receptors on a cell's membrane and cause chemical reactions to take place inside the cell. When nonsteroid hormones bind to receptors, the receptors change chemically. This change activates molecules inside the cell. These molecules, called second messengers, react with still other molecules inside the cell. The products of these reactions might initiate other chemical reactions in the cell or activate a gene in the nucleus.

Apply **Why do hormones only affect some cells?**

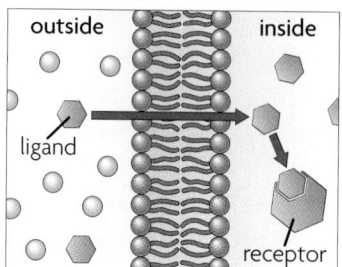
FIGURE 29.19 Hormone Action

Steroid hormones enter the cell, but nonsteroid hormones do not.

STEROID HORMONE

steroid hormone

1 Steroid hormone diffuses through the cell membrane.

receptor

2 Steroid hormone binds to a receptor within the cell.

nucleus

3 The hormone and receptor enter the nucleus and bind to DNA.

DNA

4 Steroid hormone causes DNA to make proteins.

proteins

INTERACTS WITH MEMBRANE

GETS MESSAGE INTO CELL

CAUSES CHEMICAL REACTIONS

MAKES PRODUCTS

NONSTEROID HORMONE

non-steroid hormone

1 Nonsteroid hormone binds to receptor on the cell membrane.

receptor

2 Receptor stimulates a second messenger within the cell.

second messenger

3 Second messenger starts a series of chemical reactions in the cytoplasm.

chemical reactions

nucleus

4 Second messenger reactions activate enzymes.

activated enzymes

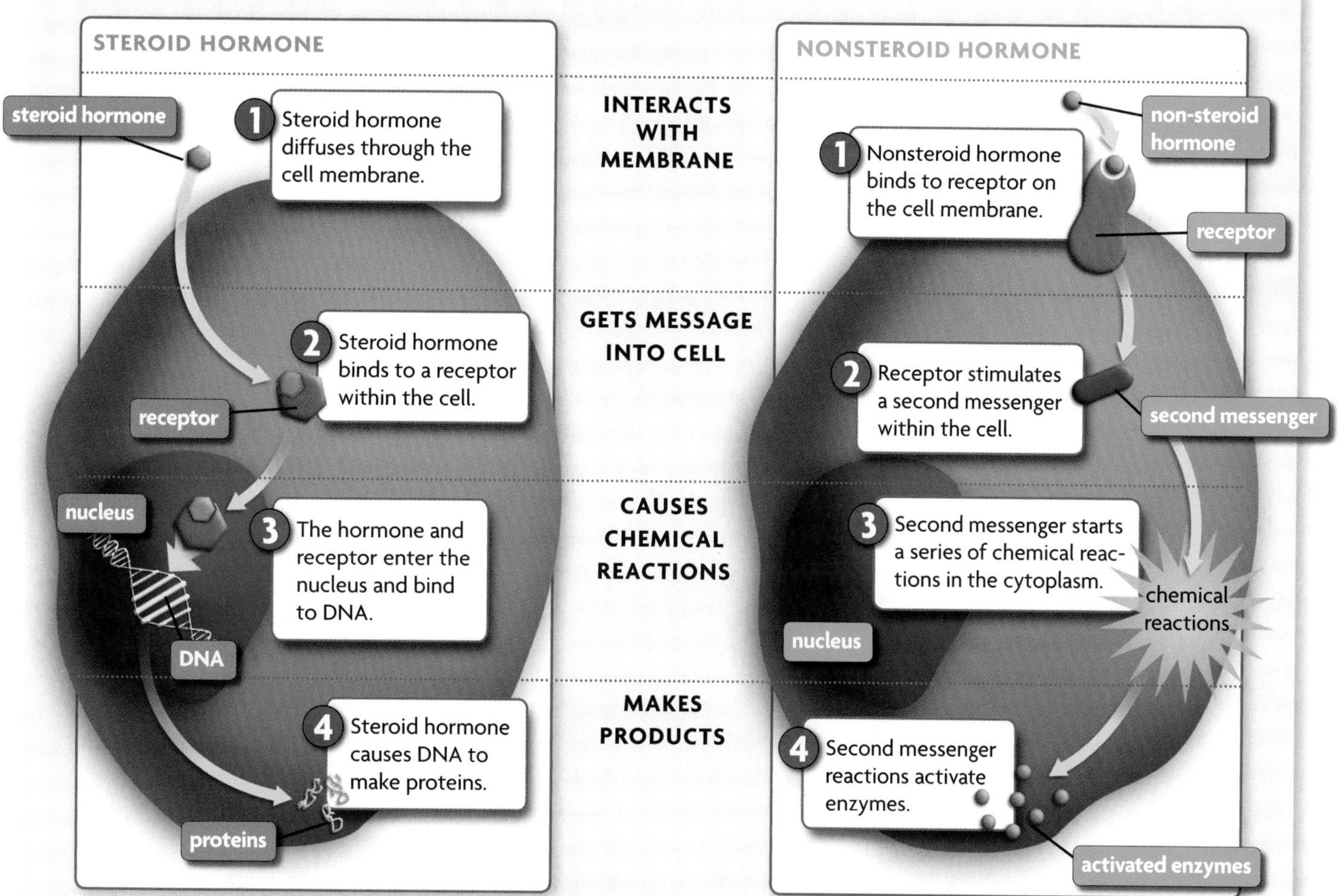

Contrast **How do the ways in which steroid and nonsteroid hormones affect a cell differ?**

▶ MAIN IDEA

Endocrine glands secrete hormones that act throughout the body.

Unlike the nervous system, the endocrine system does not have its own connected network of tissues. However, its chemical messages can still travel where they need to go. Hormones travel in the bloodstream to all areas of the body to find target cells.

The endocrine system has many glands. Each gland makes hormones that have target cells in many areas of the body. Some of these glands make hormones that prompt other endocrine glands to make and release their hormones. Other glands affect different body systems. Their hormones prompt cells to divide or to take up nutrients. Other hormones keep the body's blood pressure within a set limit. Some of the major glands, along with a few of the hormones that they make, are described below and in **FIGURE 29.20**.

1 The **hypothalamus** is a small area of the middle of the brain, as you might recall from Section 29.4. It makes hormones that stimulate the pituitary gland to release hormones. It also stimulates the production of hormones that control growth, reproduction, and body temperature. You will read more about the hypothalamus later in this section.

2 The **pituitary gland** is also in the middle of the brain. It makes and releases hormones that control cell growth as well as osmoregulatory hormones that regulate the concentration of water in the blood. Some pituitary hormones stimulate the adrenals, thyroid, and gonads. The pituitary also acts as a gateway through which hypothalamus hormones pass before they enter the bloodstream.

3 The **thyroid gland** wraps around the windpipe on three sides. Its hormones regulate metabolism, growth, and development.

4 The **thymus** is in the chest. It makes hormones that cause white blood cells to mature. It also stimulates white blood cells to fight off infection.

5 The **adrenal glands** are above the kidneys. The adrenals secrete hormones that control the "fight or flight" response when stimulated by the parasympathetic nervous system. Adrenal hormones increase breathing rate, blood pressure, and alertness.

6 The **pancreas** lies between the stomach and intestines. It makes digestive enzymes as well as hormones that regulate how much glucose the body stores and uses.

7 The **gonads**—ovaries in women and testes in men—make steroid hormones that influence sexual development and functions. Gonads of men and women make the same hormones. However, men and women make them in different amounts, which gives men and women different sexual characteristics.

Summarize What body processes do each of the main endocrine glands influence?

Connecting CONCEPTS

Reproduction You can read more about how chemical signals in the body affect growth, development, and reproduction in **Chapter 34.**

FIGURE 29.20 Glands and Some of the Major Hormones

Endocrine glands are found throughout the body, and they influence whole-body processes. Some of the hormones they make are listed here.

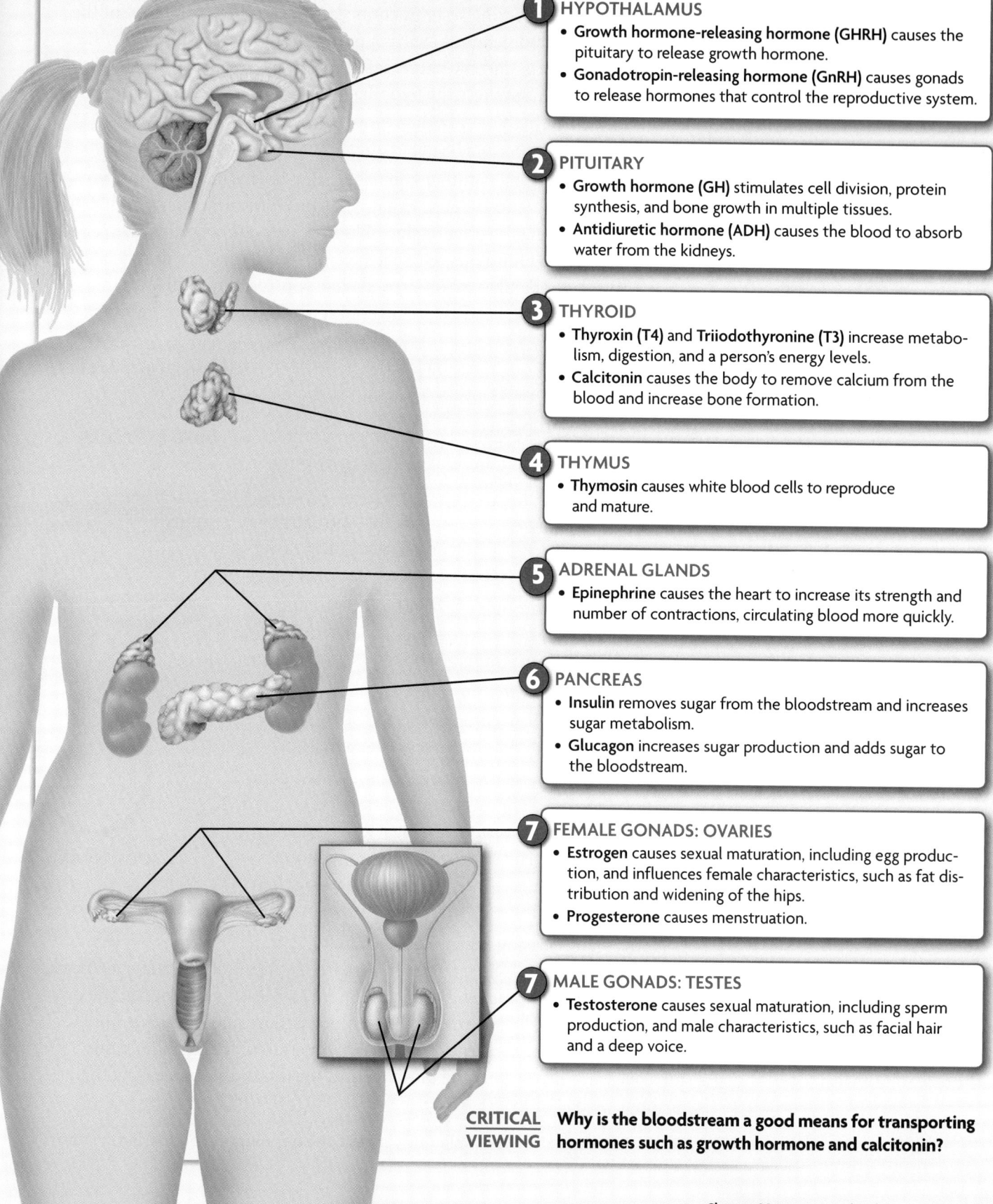

1 HYPOTHALAMUS
- **Growth hormone-releasing hormone (GHRH)** causes the pituitary to release growth hormone.
- **Gonadotropin-releasing hormone (GnRH)** causes gonads to release hormones that control the reproductive system.

2 PITUITARY
- **Growth hormone (GH)** stimulates cell division, protein synthesis, and bone growth in multiple tissues.
- **Antidiuretic hormone (ADH)** causes the blood to absorb water from the kidneys.

3 THYROID
- **Thyroxin (T4)** and **Triiodothyronine (T3)** increase metabolism, digestion, and a person's energy levels.
- **Calcitonin** causes the body to remove calcium from the blood and increase bone formation.

4 THYMUS
- **Thymosin** causes white blood cells to reproduce and mature.

5 ADRENAL GLANDS
- **Epinephrine** causes the heart to increase its strength and number of contractions, circulating blood more quickly.

6 PANCREAS
- **Insulin** removes sugar from the bloodstream and increases sugar metabolism.
- **Glucagon** increases sugar production and adds sugar to the bloodstream.

7 FEMALE GONADS: OVARIES
- **Estrogen** causes sexual maturation, including egg production, and influences female characteristics, such as fat distribution and widening of the hips.
- **Progesterone** causes menstruation.

7 MALE GONADS: TESTES
- **Testosterone** causes sexual maturation, including sperm production, and male characteristics, such as facial hair and a deep voice.

CRITICAL VIEWING Why is the bloodstream a good means for transporting hormones such as growth hormone and calcitonin?

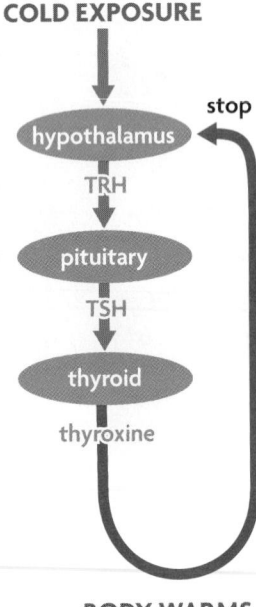

▶ MAIN IDEA

The hypothalamus interacts with the nervous and endocrine systems.

The nervous and endocrine systems connect to each other at the base of the brain, where the hypothalamus acts as a part of both systems. As part of the CNS, it receives, sorts, and interprets information from sensory organs. As part of the endocrine system, the hypothalamus produces releasing hormones that affect tissues and other endocrine glands. **Releasing hormones** are hormones that stimulate other glands to release their hormones.

Many of the hypothalamus's releasing hormones affect the pituitary gland. These glands can quickly pass hormones back and forth to each other. A series of short blood vessels connects the two, as you can see in **FIGURE 29.21**. These two glands work together to regulate various body processes. When the nervous system stimulates the hypothalamus, it releases hormones, which travel to the pituitary.

Together, the hypothalamus and pituitary regulate many processes. The diagram below shows how releasing hormones help glands to "talk with" one another to maintain body temperature.

FIGURE 29.21 The hypothalamus stimulates the pituitary to secrete hormones into the bloodstream.

COLD EXPOSURE

1 When the body becomes cold, thermoreceptors in the nervous system send a signal that stimulates the hypothalamus.

2 The hypothalamus responds to this stimulus by secreting a releasing hormone called TRH (TSH-releasing hormone).

3 TRH travels through a short blood vessel and stimulates the pituitary to release TSH (thyroid-stimulating hormone).

4 TSH travels through the bloodstream to the neck, where it stimulates the thyroid to release thyroxine, a hormone that increases cells' activity.

5 As cells become more active, the body's temperature increases. Thermoreceptors signal the hypothalamus to stop releasing TRH. In the absence of TRH, the other glands are no longer stimulated. One by one, they stop releasing their hormones, and the cycle is turned off.

BODY WARMS

Notice that releasing hormones, such as TRH and TSH, act as a type of feedback on the glands they target. In Chapter 28, you learned that a feedback is something that stimulates a change. As long as releasing hormones are present, each target gland will continue to make more and more hormones. However, when the body reaches its ideal temperature, the hypothalamus stops releasing TRH. Then the pituitary and the thyroid stop releasing their hormones too.

Analyze **How does the hypothalamus connect the nervous and endocrine systems?**

Hormonal imbalances can cause severe illness.

Because hormones play an important role in maintaining homeostasis, too much or too little of a hormone will affect the entire body. In Chapter 28, you learned that diabetes occurs when the pancreas does not make the right amounts of insulin and glucagon, hormones that regulate sugar concentration in the blood. When other glands do not function properly, a person may get other diseases. For example, if the thyroid does not make enough hormones, a person will develop hypothyroidism. In children, this condition slows growth and mental development. In adults, hypothyroidism causes weakness, sensitivity to cold, weight gain, and depression. Hyperthyroidism, or the condition of having too many thyroid hormones, produces opposite symptoms.

The wrong amount of adrenal hormones also affects the entire body. Cortisol is an adrenal hormone that helps the body break down and use sugars and control blood flow and pressure. If the adrenal glands produce too much cortisol, the body cannot metabolize sugars properly, and a person can develop Cushing's syndrome. This syndrome causes obesity, high blood pressure, diabetes, and muscle weakness. It occurs when the pituitary, which releases hormones that stimulate the adrenal glands, is not working the way it should. Steroids, a pituitary tumor, or some prescription drugs can make the pituitary overactive and indirectly cause Cushing's syndrome.

On the other hand, in Addison's disease the adrenal glands do not make enough cortisol. Usually, Addison's disease occurs because the immune system attacks the adrenal glands. The disease causes loss of appetite, weight loss, and low blood pressure. Although hormonal imbalances can cause serious illnesses and may even be fatal, many hormonal imbalances can be treated with surgery or medicine.

NSTA **SC*i*LINKS**
scilinks.org
To learn more about the endrocrine system, visit scilinks.org.
Keycode: MLB029

Infer Why might a problem with a person's pituitary gland lead to problems in other body systems?

29.6 ASSESSMENT

ONLINE QUIZ
ClassZone.com

REVIEWING ▶ MAIN IDEAS

1. What determines whether a particular **hormone** will act on a target cell?

2. What two main hormones does the **pituitary gland** produce?

3. How do **releasing hormones** of the **hypothalamus** connect the nervous and endocrine systems?

4. Why do hormonal imbalances affect the entire body?

CRITICAL THINKING

5. **Predict** How might your body be affected if a certain **gland** made too much releasing hormone that stimulates the thyroid? What if it made too little releasing hormone?

6. **Apply** What two body systems does the endocrine system rely on to generate and transport signals?

Connecting CONCEPTS

7. **Cell Biology** Steroid hormones are made of cholesterol, which is a type of lipid. Using what you know about cell membranes, why do you think steroids can diffuse into a cell, while nonsteroid hormones cannot?

Use these inquiry-based labs and online activities to deepen your understanding of nervous and endocrine systems.

MICHIGAN STANDARDS

B1.2C Develop an understanding of a scientific concept by accessing information from multiple sources. Evaluate the scientific accuracy and significance of the information.

DESIGN YOUR OWN INVESTIGATION

Reaction Time

In this lab you will test reaction time during the completion of simple sorting tasks. You will first find a baseline, or "normal" level, of time needed to complete the tasks. Then you will repeat the tasks when distracting stimuli are also present.

MATERIALS
deck of cards

SKILLS Collecting Data, Analyzing Data, Graphing Data

PROBLEM How does a distraction affect task completion?

PROCEDURE

1. Measure and record the amount of time it takes to finish each of the following tasks. The deck of cards should be shuffled before the beginning of each task.

   a. Separate a deck of cards into two even piles.

   b. Sort a deck of cards into two piles, with one pile for each card color.

   c. Separate a deck of cards into four even piles.

   d. Sort a deck of cards into four piles, with one pile for each suit of cards.

2. Design your own experiment to test how a distraction will change the amount of time needed to complete a task. Distractions could include listening to music or a video in the background, tapping a ruler on the desktop, talking to the person, or having the person say the alphabet aloud while completing the task.

3. Determine what the independent variable is in your experiment. Form a hypothesis about how manipulating your independent variable may affect reaction time. Create a data table in which to record your data. One possible data table is shown below.

TABLE 1. TIME TAKEN TO COMPLETE TASK		
Task	Baseline Time (sec)	Time with Distractor (sec)
Two even piles		
Two piles (by color)		
Four even piles		
Four piles (by suit)		

4. Have your teacher approve your procedure. Conduct your experiment.

ANALYZE AND CONCLUDE

1. **Analyze** Draw a graph to present your data.

2. **Analyze** What are the trends in your data regarding the completion of tasks without a distraction? What effect did the distraction have on reaction time?

3. **Experimental Design** What are some possible sources of unavoidable experimental data in your design?

Brain-Based Disorders

Scientists do not always know what causes many brain-based diseases or disorders because the scientific study of the brain is relatively new. Sometimes doctors find that drug treatments are effective, but they do not understand exactly how or why these treatments work.

SKILL Researching

PROBLEM Choose one of the following disorders or diseases to research: Autism, Tourette syndrome, obsessive-compulsive disorder, or migraine headaches.

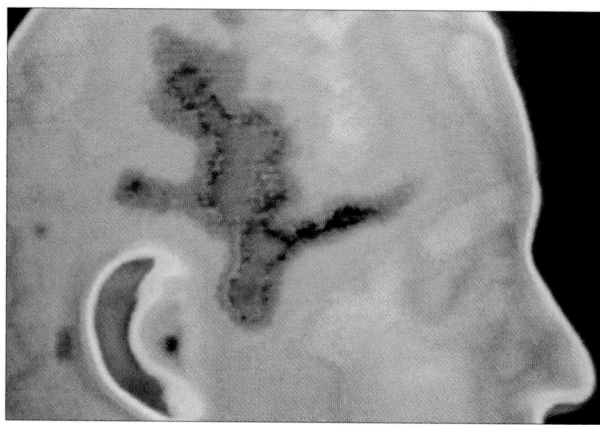

This PET scan shows a person who is experiencing a migraine headache.

RESEARCH

1. What are the symptoms of this disorder?
2. What do scientists believe causes this disorder?
3. How is the disorder treated?
4. What are the trends in diagnosis of the disorder over the past 10 to 15 years?
5. What could explain the trends?
6. What new discoveries and discussions have been in the news over the past year that indicate how scientists' understanding of this disorder is changing?

Online BIOLOGY
CLASSZONE.COM

ANIMATED BIOLOGY
Diagnose a Hormone Disorder
Can you diagnose and correct a hormone imbalance? Review three patient histories and compare each to a set of hormone disorders. Diagnose the patients' disorders to get them, and their hormones, back on track.

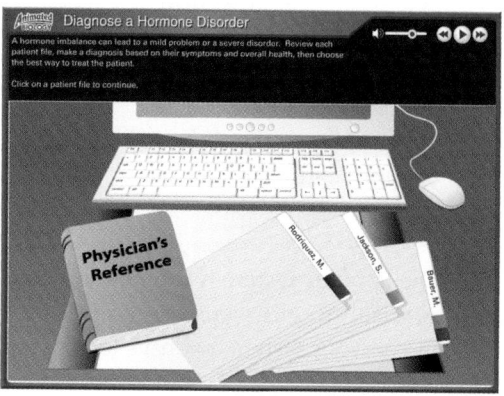

WEBQUEST
A drug addiction is not just life-altering—it alters the brain as well. In this WebQuest, you will learn about the biology of addiction. Find out how different drugs affect neurons and neurotransmitters, creating dependency.

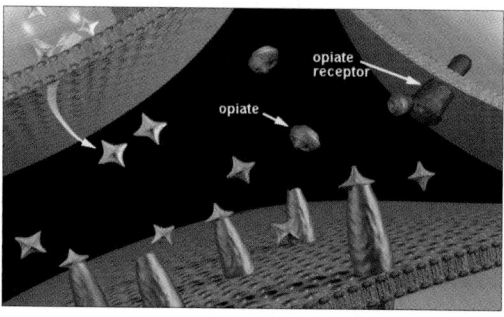

DATA ANALYSIS ONLINE
Cortisol is powerful hormone. Its many actions include metabolizing fats and proteins and managing stress. Graph cortisol levels in the body throughout the day and hypothesize why the body needs high amounts of cortisol at a specific time.

29.1 How Organs Systems Communicate

The nervous system and the endocrine system provide the means by which organ systems communicate. The body's nervous system and endocrine system generate, interpret, and deliver messages that help to maintain homeostasis. The two systems have different rates of communication because they send their signals by different methods.

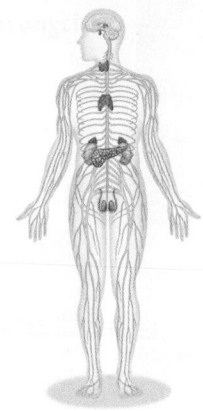

29.2 Neurons

The nervous system is composed of highly specialized cells. Neurons are specialized cells of the nervous system that have long extensions for transmitting signals over long distances. These cells produce, receive, and transmit impulses called action potentials.

29.3 The Senses

The senses detect the internal and external environments. The senses gather information about the body's internal and external environments. The senses use five types of receptors and many specialized cells, including rod, cone, and hair cells, that detect physical and chemical stimuli.

29.4 Central and Peripheral Nervous Systems

The central nervous system interprets information, and the peripheral nervous system gathers and transmits information. The CNS and PNS work together. In the CNS, the cerebrum controls conscious thought and interprets sensory signals from throughout the body. The PNS delivers messages from the body toward and away from the CNS.

29.5 Brain Function and Chemistry

Scientists study the function and chemistry of the brain. Imaging techniques allow scientists to look at the brain without having to have a patient undergo surgery. This technology can show chemical and physical changes in brains that have severe illnesses. Both prescription drugs and illegal drugs alter brain chemistry and neuron structure.

29.6 Endocrine System and Hormones

The endocrine system produces hormones that affect growth, development, and homeostasis. The glands of the endocrine system produce chemical signals called hormones that act throughout the body. The hypothalamus is a gland that interacts with the nervous and endocrine systems. Hormone imbalances can cause severe illnesses, such as hypothyroidism, diabetes, and Addison's disease.

Synthesize Your Notes

Concept Map Summarize your notes about the nervous system by drawing a concept map.

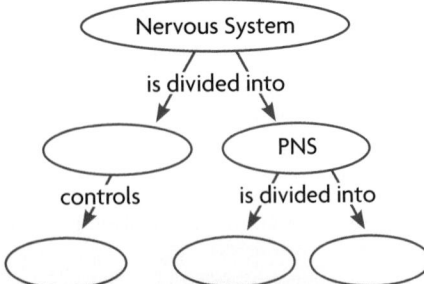

Three-Column Chart Make a chart to organize the information you learned about the senses.

Sense	Receptor Type	Receptor Name
sight	photoreceptor	

Chapter Assessment

Chapter Vocabulary

29.1 nervous system, p. 874
endocrine system, p. 874
stimulus, p. 874
central nervous
  system (CNS), p. 875
peripheral nervous
  system (PNS), p. 875

29.2 neuron, p .876
dendrite, p. 876
axon, p. 876
resting potential, p. 877
sodium-potassium pump, p. 877
action potential, p. 878
synapse, p. 879
terminal, p. 879
neurotransmitter, p. 879

29.3 rod cell, p. 881
cone cell, p. 881
hair cell, p. 882

29.4 cerebrum, p. 886
cerebral cortex, p. 887
cerebellum, p. 888
brain stem, p. 888
reflex arc, p. 889
somatic nervous system, p. 889
autonomic nervous system,
  p. 890
sympathetic nervous system,
  p. 890
parasympathetic nervous
  system, p. 890

29.5 addiction, p. 893
desensitization, p. 893
tolerance, p. 893
sensitization, p. 893
stimulant, p. 894
depressant, p. 894

29.6 hormone, p. 896
gland, p. 896
hypothalamus, p. 898
pituitary gland, p. 898
releasing hormones, p. 900

Reviewing Vocabulary

Compare and Contrast

Describe one similarity and one difference between the two terms in each of the following pairs.

1. somatic nervous system, autonomic nervous system
2. rod cell, cone cell
3. sensitization, desensitization

Greek and Latin Word Origins

4. *Dendrite* comes from the Greek word *dendron,* which means "tree." Explain how the root word relates to the meaning of *dendrite.*

5. *Addiction* comes from the Latin word *addicere,* which means "deliver, yield, devote." How does this meaning relate to addiction?

6. *Endocrine* comes from the Greek word *krinein,* which means "to distinguish, separate." Explain how the root word relates to the meaning of *endocrine.*

Keep It Short

For each vocabulary term below, write a short, precise phrase that describes its meaning. For example, a short phrase to describe *stimulus* could be "causes change."

7. action potential
8. reflex arc
9. hormone
10. axon

Reviewing MAIN IDEAS

11. Name two differences between the way in which the nervous and endocrine systems communicate.

12. How does the structure of a neuron make it effective in carrying out the functions of the nervous system?

13. Draw pictures to show how Na^+ ions, K^+ ions, and electrical charges are distributed across a neuron's membrane during resting and action potential.

14. What type of receptor do each of your five senses have?

15. If you have a question, you will raise your hand to ask it. How do your CNS and PNS work together to allow you to raise your hand?

16. What types of information do the occipital lobe and the temporal lobe process?

17. What are the differences between the sympathetic and the parasympathetic nervous systems?

18. How can a PET scan give clues about the activity of different neurotransmitters in the brain?

19. Why do hormones act only on some cells?

20. How do releasing hormones help glands to communicate with one another?

21. How are a target cell's activities changed if a gland produces too much of a particular hormone?

Critical Thinking

22. Apply You wake up at night and turn on the light next to your bed. The light seems very bright at first, but soon your eyes adjust. Describe how your senses and your brain interact to let your eyes adjust to the light level.

23. Infer Research on babies shows that a certain part of a neuron gets longer as the babies interact with more stimuli. Which part do you think it is? Why?

24. Analyze How does the inside of a neuron become positively charged during an action potential, even though both potassium (K^+) and sodium (Na^+) ions are positively charged?

25. Predict An eye disease called macular degeneration damages the light-sensitive cells in the eye. How might this disease affect the ability of the eye to communicate with the brain?

26. Compare What are three similarities between neurotransmitters, used in the nervous system, and hormones, which are used in the endocrine system?

27. Apply The part of your brain that processes touch devotes more space to interpreting signals from your hands than from other parts of your body. Why might this be beneficial?

Interpreting Visuals

The toxin in the diagram is commonly known as Botox. It is a cosmetic treatment used on the muscles under skin to reduce wrinkles. Use the diagram below to answer the next two questions.

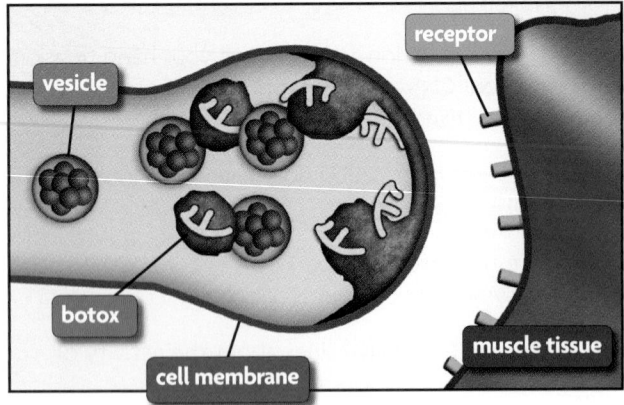

receptor

vesicle

botox

cell membrane

muscle tissue

28. Apply What structures of the nervous system are being shown in the diagram?

29. Analyze Botox affects the normal functioning of nerve cells. According to the diagram, what part of the normal process is Botox affecting?

Analyzing Data

Cataracts can impair a person's vision, making objects appear fuzzy. Cataracts occur when the lens in a person's eye becomes cloudy, or less transparent. This happens when the proteins that make up the lens clump. Use the graph below to answer the next three questions.

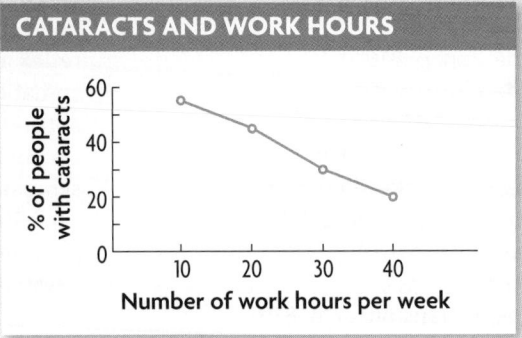

CATARACTS AND WORK HOURS

% of people with cataracts

Number of work hours per week

30. Analyze Does a correlation exist between incidents of cataracts and work hours? Explain.

31. Evaluate Can you conclude for sure that the number of hours worked causes cataracts? Explain your reasoning.

32. Infer If a correlation exists between cataracts and work hours, what might explain it?

Connecting CONCEPTS

33. Write a Script Imagine you have a friend who wanted to try drugs, and you wanted to tell your friend about the effects that drugs have on the nervous system. Write a conversation that you could have about addiction and the negative effects of drug use.

34. Connect The image on page 873 shows some of a person's internal organs. Write a paragraph that discusses which division of the nervous system is shown in this picture. Also, discuss how the cells of this body system allow you to rapidly pull your hand off of a hot pan before your hand is burned.

MICHIGAN
STANDARDS-BASED ASSESSMENT

✓ **Test Practice**
For more test practice,
go to ClassZone.com.

1. A scientist investigates the toxic effects of a chemical on the brain. Which of the following experimental design elements would *most* likely lead to inconsistent results? **B1.1B**

    A using the same method to measure toxicity

    B having a sample size that is very large

    C keeping the chemical at a constant temperature

    D running the tests in different locations

2.

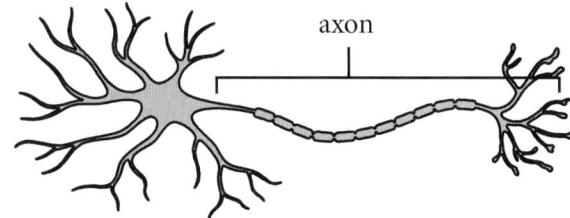

An axon, illustrated above, is most like **B2.3g**

    A the wire between a light switch and a lamp.

    B an open circuit.

    C a leaky garden hose.

    D a ladder.

3. The hypothalamus releases antidiuretic hormone, which causes the kidneys to release less water from the body. Under which condition might the hypothalamus produce more antidiuretic hormone? **B2.3d**

    A having high levels of antidiuretic hormone

    B having excess water in the body

    C drinking a bottle of juice

    D sweating due to exercise

THINK THROUGH THE QUESTION

Think carefully about each answer choice. Under which condition would the body respond by conserving water?

---

4. Anabolic steroids are drugs that mimic specific hormones in the body. As athletes abuse anabolic steroids in hopes of becoming stronger, their bodies produce less natural hormone. This effect can be *best* described as a(n) **L2.p1C**

    A form of negative feedback.

    B reflex arc.

    C conditioned response.

    D osmoregulatory response.

5. The chemical signals of the nervous system are called **B2.2f**

    A axons.

    B dendrites.

    C neurotransmitters.

    D neurons.

6.

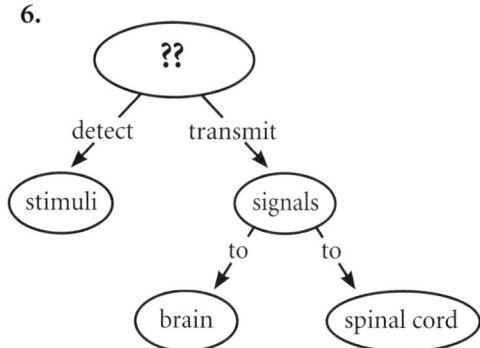

Which of the following *best* completes this concept map? **B2.3f**

    A motor neurons

    B interneurons

    C electric neurons

    D sensory neurons

CHAPTER

30 Respiratory and Circulatory Systems

KEY CONCEPTS

30.1 Respiratory and Circulatory Functions
The respiratory and circulatory systems bring oxygen and nutrients to the cells.

30.2 Respiration and Gas Exchange
The respiratory system exchanges oxygen and carbon dioxide.

30.3 The Heart and Circulation
The heart is a muscular pump that moves the blood through two pathways.

30.4 Blood Vessels and Transport
The circulatory system transports materials throughout the body.

30.5 Blood
Blood is a complex tissue that transports materials.

30.6 Lymphatic System
The lymphatic system provides another type of circulation in the body.

Online BIOLOGY CLASSZONE.COM

Animated BIOLOGY
View animated chapter concepts.
• How You Breathe
• How the Heart Pumps Blood
• Blood Typing
• Build the Circulatory and Respiratory Systems

BIOZINE
Keep current with biology news.
• News feeds
• Strange Biology
• Careers

RESOURCE CENTER
Get more information on
• Circulatory System
• Blood
• Lymphatic System

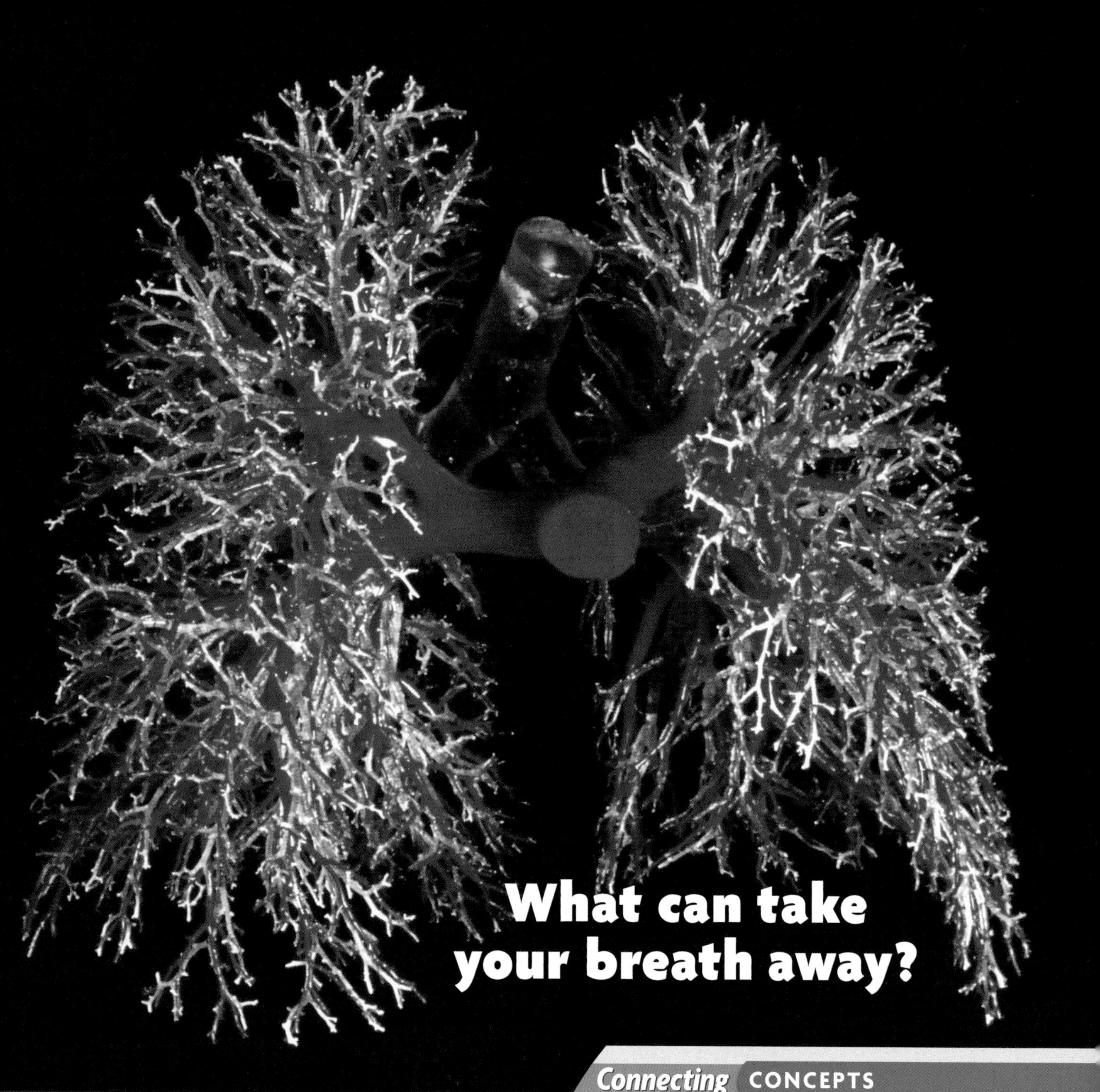

What can take your breath away?

This photograph shows a resin cast of the thousands of vessels that supply blood and air to your lungs. As you take a breath every three to five seconds, this network takes in oxygen and expels carbon dioxide. Pollution, disease, or injury can damage this intricate network, literally taking your breath away.

Connecting CONCEPTS

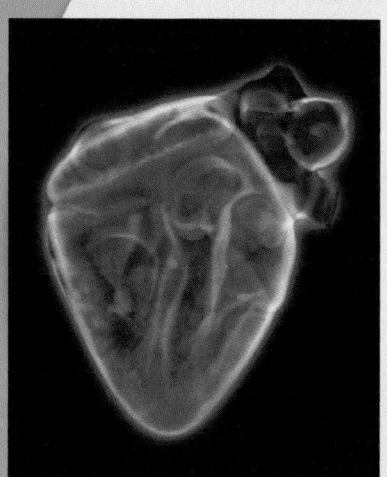

Nervous System The heart shown to the left is a model that has been x-rayed to reveal the inner chambers. Your heart is a muscular pump that moves blood through your body, bringing carbon dioxide to the lungs and picking up oxygen. When your body's needs for oxygen change, signals from the nervous system speed up or slow down your heartbeat and breathing rate.

30.1 Respiratory and Circulatory Functions

KEY CONCEPT The respiratory and circulatory systems bring oxygen and nutrients to the cells.

MAIN IDEAS

- The respiratory and circulatory systems work together to maintain homeostasis.
- The respiratory system moves gases into and out of the blood.
- The circulatory system moves blood to all parts of the body.

VOCABULARY

circulatory system, p. 910

respiratory system, p. 910

trachea, p. 911

lung, p. 911

alveoli, p. 911

diaphragm, p. 912

heart, p. 912

artery, p. 913

vein, p. 913

capillary, p. 913

MICHIGAN STANDARDS

B2.3d Identify the general functions of the major systems of the human body (digestion, respiration, reproduction, circulation, excretion, protection from disease, and movement, control, and coordination) and describe ways that these systems interact with each other.

B2.3e Describe how human body systems maintain relatively constant internal conditions (temperature, acidity, and blood sugar).

Connect You have thousands of kilometers of blood vessels in your body and several hundred *million* tiny air sacs in your lungs. Blood circulates constantly through the vessels, while air continually fills and empties from the tiny air sacs. Your heart keeps beating and your lungs keep working 24 hours a day, every day of your life. Even more amazing, everything works without your having to think about it.

MAIN IDEA

The respiratory and circulatory systems work together to maintain homeostasis.

Every cell in your body needs nutrients and oxygen to function and needs to get rid of its waste products. The **circulatory system** is the body system that transports blood and other materials. It brings vital supplies to the cells and carries away their wastes. The blood vessels of the circulatory system also keep oxygen-poor blood from mixing with oxygen-rich blood. The **respiratory system** is the body system in which gas exchange takes place. You can think of your respiratory system as a major supply depot where the blood can pick up oxygen (O_2) and deposit excess carbon dioxide (CO_2). The lungs of the respiratory system are the only place in your body where gases in the blood are exchanged with gases from the atmosphere.

The respiratory and circulatory systems work closely together to maintain homeostasis in the face of constant change. Every time you exercise, lie down to rest, or simply stand up, you change your needs for oxygen and nutrients. As a result, your heart speeds up or slows down and you breathe faster or slower, depending on your activity. This section gives you an overview of the major structures of the respiratory and circulatory systems and their functions. Sections 30.2 to 30.5 provide a closer look at the organs of each system, how they work, and what can damage them.

Apply When you stand up after lying down, why do your heart rate and breathing rate increase?

TAKING NOTES

Use a supporting main ideas strategy to help you remember the respiratory and circulatory structures and their functions.

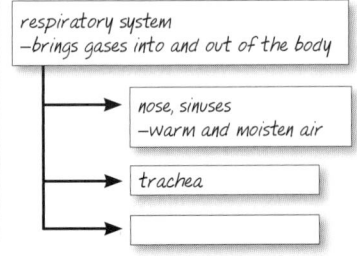

respiratory system
—brings gases into and out of the body

nose, sinuses
—warm and moisten air

trachea

FIGURE 30.1 Respiratory Organs and Tissues

Specialized structures move air into and out of the body.

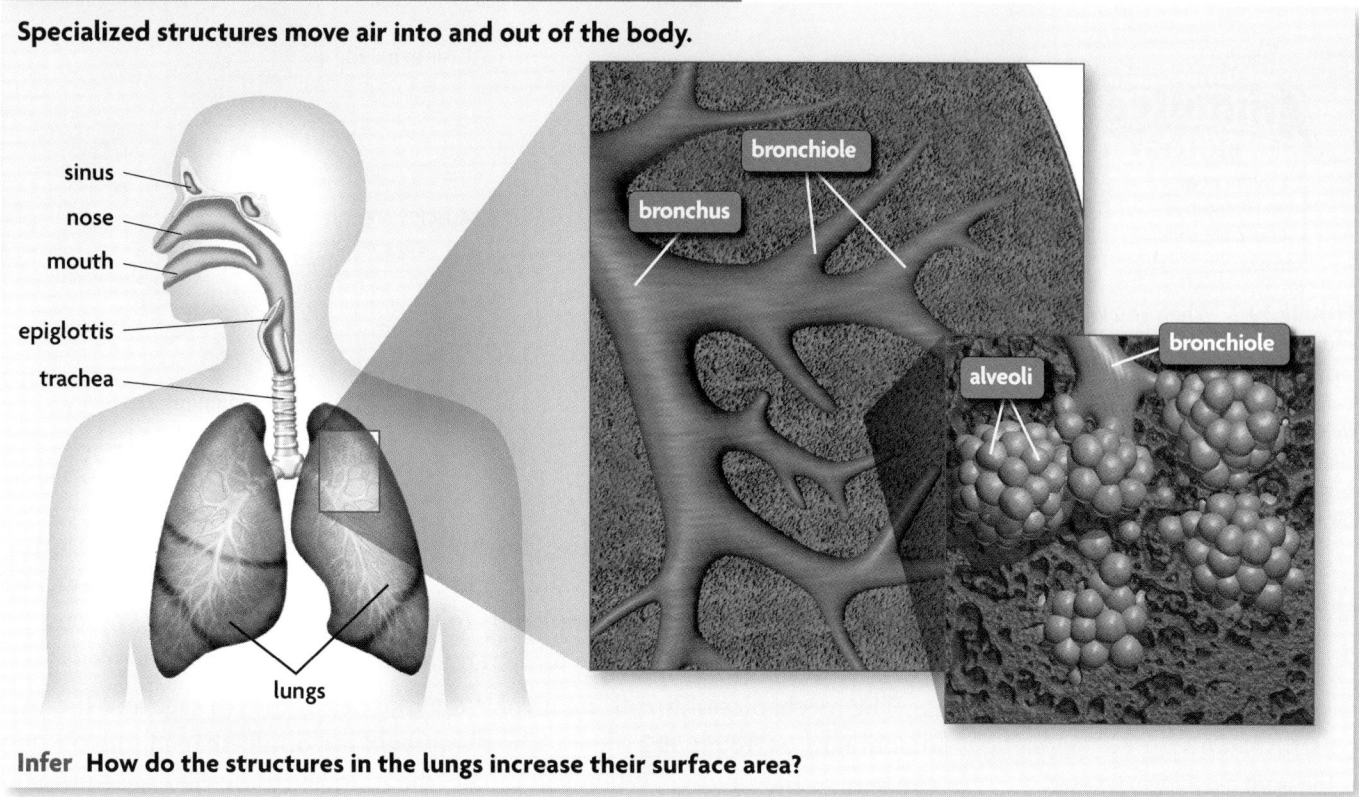

sinus
nose
mouth
epiglottis
trachea
lungs

bronchiole
bronchus
bronchiole
alveoli

Infer How do the structures in the lungs increase their surface area?

▶ MAIN IDEA

The respiratory system moves gases into and out of the blood.

The function of the respiratory system is to bring O_2 into the body and to expel CO_2 and water vapor. The structures of this system bring the gases in close contact with the blood, which absorbs O_2. The circulatory system then carries O_2 to all of the body's cells and transports CO_2 from the rest of the body to the lungs, where it is exhaled.

The specialized structures of the respiratory system are shown in **FIGURE 30.1.** The nose and mouth are the entry points to the system. When air enters the nose, mucus that lines the nasal passages warms and moistens the air. The mucus and tiny hairs called cilia help filter dust and pathogens from the air. At the back of the throat, a small piece of tissue, the epiglottis, regulates airflow into the trachea, or windpipe. The **trachea** (TRAY-kee-uh) is a long structure made of soft tissue reinforced with C-shaped rings of cartilage. It resembles the hose of a vacuum cleaner. When you swallow, the epiglottis closes the entrance to the trachea to keep food or saliva from entering the airways. The trachea divides into the two bronchi, with one branch going to each lung.

The **lungs** are the organs that absorb O_2 from the air you inhale. Inside the lungs, the bronchi divide into smaller and smaller branches that resemble the limbs and twigs of a tree. The smallest branches, the bronchioles, end in clusters of tiny air sacs called **alveoli** (al-VEE-uh-LY). One air sac is called an alveolus. The lungs have a huge number of alveoli—from 300 to 600 million.

Connecting CONCEPTS

Cellular Respiration You learned in **Chapter 4** that eukaryotic cells require a constant supply of oxygen to produce ATP, which is the main energy source for cells.

BIOLOGY

Explore how you breathe at ClassZone.com.

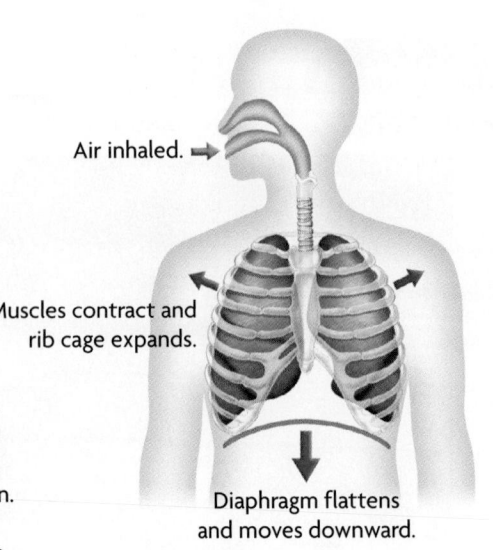

Air inhaled. →

Muscles contract and rib cage expands.

Diaphragm flattens and moves downward.

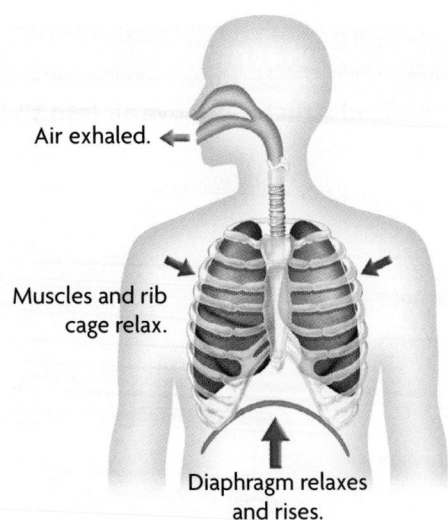

Air exhaled. ←

Muscles and rib cage relax.

Diaphragm relaxes and rises.

FIGURE 30.2 When you inhale, movements of the rib cage and diaphragm produce lower pressure in the lungs, and air flows in. When you exhale, rib cage and diaphragm movements produce higher pressure in the lungs, and air flows out.

VOCABULARY

The word *diaphragm* is based on the Latin *diaphragma,* which means "midriff." The midriff extends from below the breast to the waist. The diaphragm is located in this area.

This huge number of alveoli gives the lungs a massive surface area for absorbing O_2 and releasing CO_2 and water vapor. Lung tissue is spongy and elastic, which allows the lungs to expand and contract as you breathe. Lung mucus and cilia help trap and remove foreign materials and pathogens.

The mechanics of breathing involve the muscles of the rib cage and the diaphragm, as **FIGURE 30.2** shows. The **diaphragm** is a dome-shaped muscle at the base of the rib cage. When you inhale, the muscles of the rib cage contract, causing the rib cage to expand. The diaphragm then flattens and moves downward. The volume of your lungs increases, and the air pressure decreases, falling below the air pressure outside your body. Gases move from areas of greater pressure to areas of lower pressure, so air flows into the lungs.

When you exhale, the rib cage muscles relax, and the rib cage becomes smaller. The diaphragm also relaxes, causing it to rise and regain its domelike shape. Now the air pressure inside your lungs is greater than the air pressure outside your body, so air flows out.

Predict **How might damaged alveoli affect the oxygen level in the blood?**

▶ **MAIN IDEA**

The circulatory system moves blood to all parts of the body.

The function of the circulatory system is to transport O_2 and nutrients to body cells and to carry oxygen-poor blood and CO_2 back to the heart and lungs. To do its job, the system must keep blood constantly circulating.

The main parts of the circulatory system are the heart, the blood, and the blood vessels. The **heart** is a muscular pump, about the size of your fist, that keeps the blood moving to every part of the body. The blood circulates through a closed system—that is, blood in the circulatory system stays inside the vessels. The average adult body contains about 5 liters (more than 5 qt) of blood. On average, your blood circulates from your heart, throughout your body, and back to your heart about every 60 seconds.

The circulatory system has three types of blood vessels: arteries, veins, and capillaries. **Arteries** are blood vessels that carry blood away from the heart to the rest of the body. **Veins** are blood vessels that carry blood from the rest of the body back to the heart. As illustrated in **FIGURE 30.3**, arteries carry oxygen-rich blood (red) and veins carry oxygen-poor blood (blue). Blue is used for illustration purposes only. In your body, oxygen-poor blood is not actually blue but a darker red color. You can think of arteries and veins as a system of roads. Large arteries and veins are like major highways. Smaller arteries and veins are like streets that route traffic through local neighborhoods.

Arteries and veins are connected by a system of capillaries. **Capillaries** are the tiny blood vessels that transport blood to and from the cells of the body. These vessels are so small that blood cells must move through them in single file. The walls of these tiny blood vessels are only one cell thick. Materials can easily diffuse into and out of them.

In addition to transporting vital supplies to the cells, the circulatory system performs two other important functions that maintain homeostasis.

- The circulatory system collects waste materials produced by digestion and cell metabolism, and delivers them to the liver and kidneys to be filtered out of the body. For example, muscle cell activity produces a waste product known as urea. As blood moves past the muscle cells, urea is moved into the bloodstream and carried to the kidneys to be excreted.

- The circulatory system helps maintain body temperature by distributing the heat that cells produce in the muscles and internal organs. When you are active, your organs and muscles produce more heat. The heart pumps harder, and the blood vessels dilate to bring excess heat to the skin, where it can escape. In cold weather, the blood vessels constrict to conserve heat.

The heart, the blood vessels, and the blood are described in more detail in Sections 30.3 to 30.5.

Infer If a person has a weak heart, how might his or her ability to maintain a stable body temperature be affected?

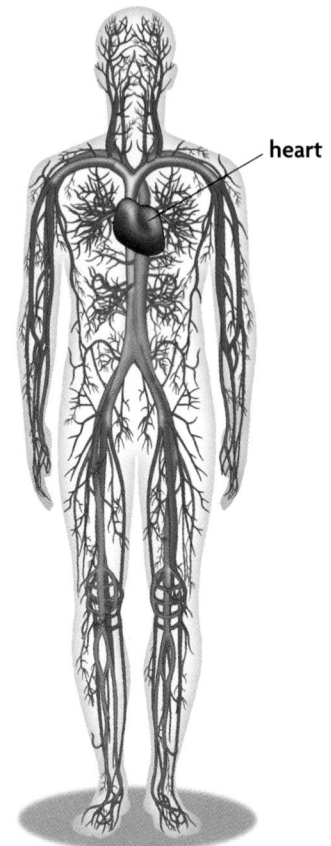

FIGURE 30.3 The circulatory system is composed of the heart, arteries carrying oxygen-rich blood (red), veins carrying oxygen-poor blood (blue), and capillaries.

30.1 / ASSESSMENT

ONLINE QUIZ
ClassZone.com

REVIEWING ▶ MAIN IDEAS

1. How do the **respiratory** and **circulatory systems** help maintain homeostasis in the body?

2. List the main parts and functions of the respiratory system.

3. Describe the basic parts and functions of the circulatory system.

CRITICAL THINKING

4. **Apply** Why can't you breathe through the mouth while you are swallowing food? What would happen if you could do this?

5. **Infer** **Arteries** and **veins** are equally distributed throughout the body. How does this arrangement help to maintain the functions of each cell?

Connecting CONCEPTS

6. **Science and Technology** A mechanical ventilator breathes for a paralyzed person. During inhalation, the machine forces air under pressure into the **lungs.** During exhalation, the pressure drops and air moves out of the lungs. How does this machine compare with natural breathing?

30.2 Respiration and Gas Exchange

KEY CONCEPT The respiratory system exchanges oxygen and carbon dioxide.

MAIN IDEAS

- Gas exchange occurs in the alveoli of the lungs.
- Respiratory diseases interfere with gas exchange.

VOCABULARY

red blood cell, p. 915
hemoglobin, p. 915
emphysema, p. 916
asthma, p. 916

Review
alveoli, lung, capillary, diffusion

MICHIGAN STANDARDS

B2.3d Identify the general functions of the major systems of the human body (digestion, respiration, reproduction, circulation, excretion, protection from disease, and movement, control, and coordination) and describe ways that these systems interact with each other.

B2.3e Describe how human body systems maintain relatively constant internal conditions (temperature, acidity, and blood sugar).

Connect Nearly every winter, newspapers carry stories of people killed by carbon monoxide (CO) gas in their homes. This colorless, odorless gas escapes from leaks in furnaces that burn fossil fuels. What makes CO so deadly? Your body readily absorbs it into the blood, which means less O_2 is absorbed. Within a short time, your cells become oxygen starved. You must quickly get to an area where you can breathe fresh air.

MAIN IDEA

Gas exchange occurs in the alveoli of the lungs.

Recall that the cells in your body carry out cellular respiration, which requires O_2 and produces CO_2 as a waste product. Thus, every cell in the body needs O_2 and must get rid of CO_2. However, the alveoli and their capillaries are the only places where gas exchange with the atmosphere occurs. The lungs bring in a steady supply of O_2 and expel excess CO_2. Gas exchange in the lungs is based on three principles:

- O_2 and CO_2 are carried by the blood.
- Gases move by diffusion—that is, they move from an area of higher concentration to an area of lower concentration.
- The lining of the alveoli must be moist to help gases diffuse.

Diffusion of O_2 and CO_2

In the alveoli, the respiratory and circulatory systems come together in the process of gas exchange. When you inhale, air flows from the bronchi to the bronchioles and finally to the alveoli. A cross-section of a bronchiole and several alveoli is shown in **FIGURE 30.4**. Each alveolus is about the size of a grain of sand, but all of the alveoli together give the lungs a surface area of about 100 square meters. Without this huge area for gas exchange, the lungs would be unable to extract enough O_2 from the air to keep you alive.

A complex network of capillaries surrounds and penetrates the alveoli, as shown in **FIGURE 30.5**. Blood entering these capillaries contains a lower concentration of O_2 than does the air in the alveoli. As a result, the O_2 diffuses from an area of high concentration in the alveoli to an area of low concentration in

FIGURE 30.4 This micrograph shows a bronchiole and several alveoli. Alveoli walls are about one cell thick, which allows O_2 and CO_2 to diffuse easily across them. (colored SEM; magnification 150×)

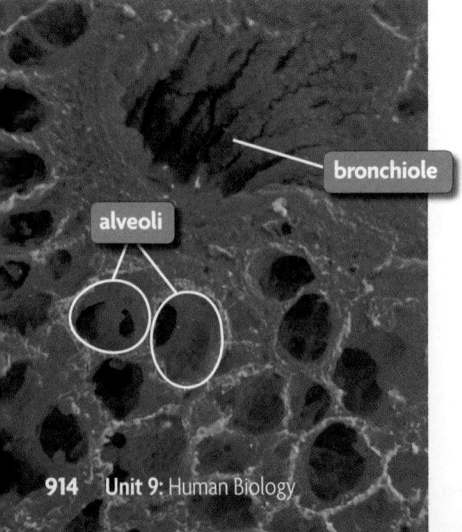

FIGURE 30.5 Gas Exchange in the Alveoli

Diffusion of gases into and out of the alveoli maintains O_2 and CO_2 homeostasis.

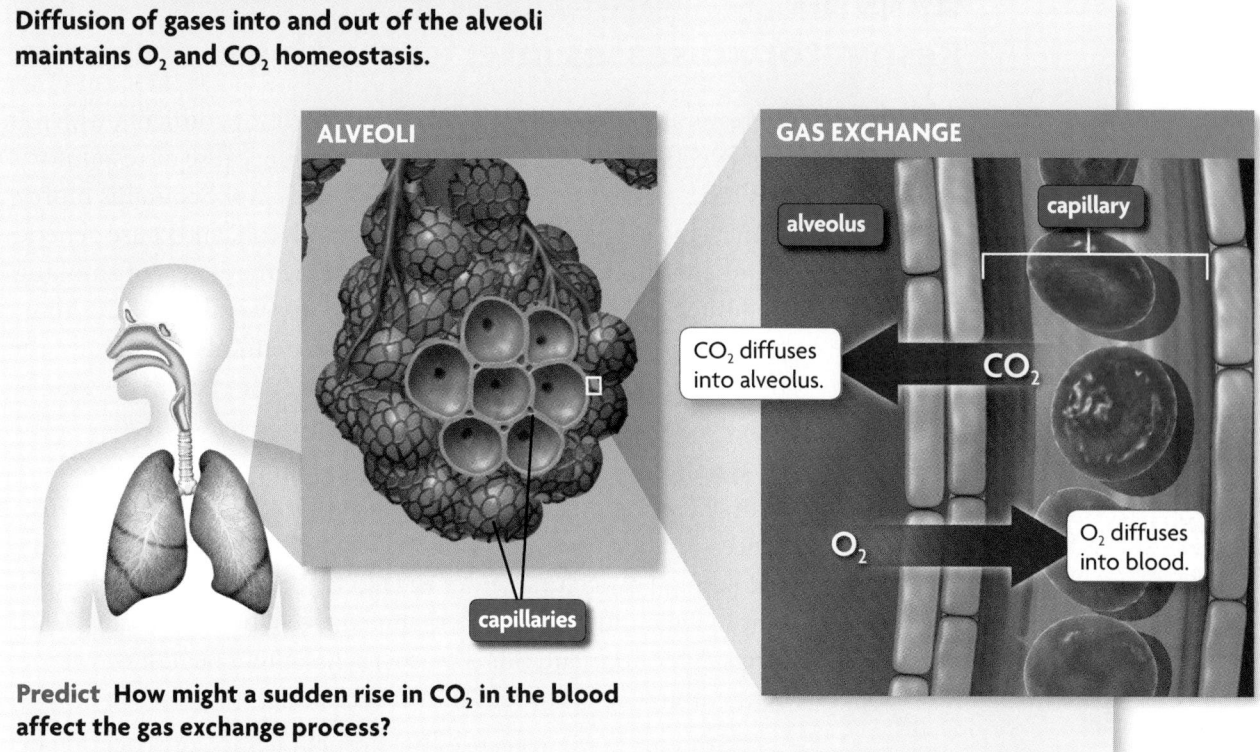

ALVEOLI

GAS EXCHANGE

alveolus

capillary

CO_2 diffuses into alveolus.

CO_2

O_2

O_2 diffuses into blood.

capillaries

Predict How might a sudden rise in CO_2 in the blood affect the gas exchange process?

the capillaries. The blood in the capillaries contain **red blood cells,** a type of cell that picks up oxygen in the lungs and delivers it to all of the body's cells. In red blood cells, most of the O_2 molecules bind to an iron-rich protein called **hemoglobin** (HEE-muh-GLOH-bihn). Each molecule of hemoglobin binds with four O_2 molecules. The iron in hemoglobin is what gives blood its reddish color. Blood becomes bright red only when it absorbs oxygen. The blood leaving the alveoli carries almost three times the amount of O_2 that it had coming into the lungs.

In contrast, CO_2 concentrations are higher in the blood than in the alveoli. As a result, CO_2 diffuses into the alveoli. The higher concentration of CO_2 in the blood is due to the fact that every cell produces CO_2 and water as waste products. The CO_2 and water combine in the blood to form the compound carbonic acid. The more carbonic acid there is in the blood, the more acidic the blood becomes. When carbonic acid diffuses into the alveoli, the compound separates into CO_2 and water, which are exhaled.

Gas Exchange and the Nervous System

Gas exchange is so critical to the body that it is an autonomic function regulated by the medulla and pons in the brain stem. These centers monitor dissolved gases in the blood, particularly CO_2 concentrations. As you become more active, CO_2 levels increase and the blood becomes more acidic. Sensors in the respiratory and circulatory systems signal this change to the brain stem. The medulla sends messages through the nervous and endocrine systems that stimulate the diaphragm and rib cage muscles to work harder. The medulla regulates how often and how deeply you breathe based on your activity.

Analyze How does the alveoli's structure relate to the function of gas exchange?

Connecting CONCEPTS

Nervous System As you read in Chapter 29, the brain stem is located at the base of the brain. The brain stem is involved in regulating breathing and other autonomic functions that help maintain homeostasis.

▶ MAIN IDEA

Respiratory diseases interfere with gas exchange.

FIGURE 30.6 Healthy lung tissue is free of any deposits. When a person smokes for several years, black tar deposits first invade and then choke the tissue, and greatly reduce gas exchange. (LM; magnification 250×)

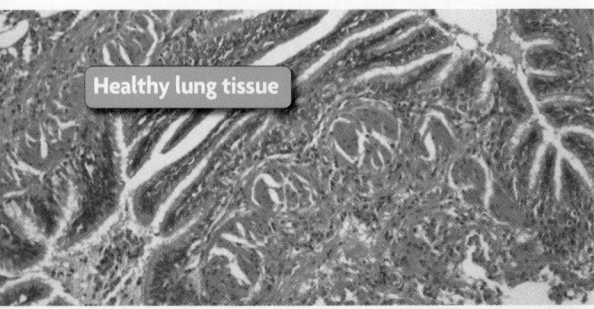
Healthy lung tissue

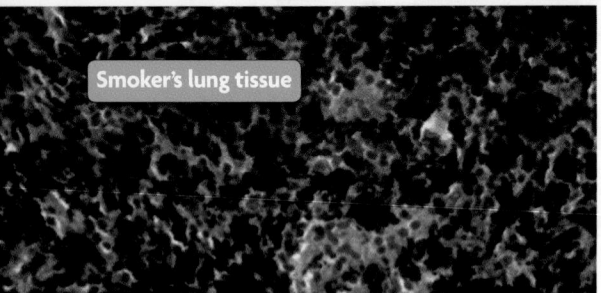
Smoker's lung tissue

NSTA scilinks.org *SCLINKS*
For more information on the respiratory system, go to scilinks.org.
Keycode: MLB030

Damage to the respiratory system makes gas exchange more difficult, which in turn affects every cell in the body. Smoking is the leading cause of respiratory diseases such as lung cancer and emphysema. Tobacco smoke contains more than 4800 chemicals that can paralyze cilia, damage alveoli, and cause genetic mutations leading to cancer. In **FIGURE 30.6,** you can see the effects of smoking on lung tissue. When a person smokes for several years, the lung tissue is slowly coated by tars and other chemicals. Eventually, the tissue becomes almost solid black. The sooner people stop smoking, the sooner such damage to the lungs can be reversed.

Emphysema (EHM-fih-SEE-muh) is a lung disorder caused mainly by smoking. Over time, many alveoli are destroyed. This process gradually reduces the surface area for gas exchange, and not enough oxygen can enter the blood. People with advanced emphysema must use supplemental oxygen, but eventually their lungs fail. At present, this disease has no cure. The best way to prevent emphysema is to refrain from smoking.

Asthma (AZ-muh) causes the bronchioles to constrict due to muscle spasms. This condition makes it hard to move air in and out of the lungs. A person having a severe asthma attack can die from lack of oxygen. Attacks may be triggered by allergies, stress, exposure to smoke and chemicals, or exercise. The attacks can be relieved by drugs that relax the bronchioles.

Cystic fibrosis (CF) is a genetic disease that causes the lungs to produce a thick, sticky mucus. This mucus blocks the airways and allows microorganisms to thrive in the lungs. People with CF have frequent, sometimes fatal, lung infections. Treatments focus on preventing the mucus from building up.

Synthesize How does smoking affect gas exchange?

30.2 ASSESSMENT

ONLINE QUIZ ClassZone.com

REVIEWING ▶ MAIN IDEAS

1. Explain how diffusion allows gases to move into and out of the alveoli of the lungs. Use the term **red blood cell** in your explanation.

2. In what ways can respiratory diseases reduce the level of O_2 in the blood?

CRITICAL THINKING

3. **Synthesize** Explain how your breathing rate would change if your blood became more acidic.

4. **Apply** People poisoned by CO are often given 100 percent O_2 in a room with two to three times normal atmospheric pressure. Explain why more oxygen would enter their blood under these conditions.

Connecting CONCEPTS

5. **Forensic Science** When police find a body in a lake or river, they must determine if the person was drowned or was killed in some other way and then thrown into the water. How would examining the lungs of the person help them to solve the mystery?

30.3 The Heart and Circulation

KEY CONCEPT The heart is a muscular pump that moves the blood through two pathways.

▶ MAIN IDEAS

- The tissues and structures of the heart make it an efficient pump.
- The heart pumps blood through two main pathways.

VOCABULARY

atrium, p. 917
ventricle, p. 917
valve, p. 917
pacemaker, p. 918

pulmonary circulation, p. 920
systemic circulation, p. 920

Review
heart, artery, vein

MICHIGAN STANDARDS

B2.3d Identify the general functions of the major systems of the human body (digestion, respiration, reproduction, circulation, excretion, protection from disease, and movement, control, and coordination) and describe ways that these systems interact with each other.

B2.3e Describe how human body systems maintain relatively constant internal conditions (temperature, acidity, and blood sugar).

Connect *Lub-dub, lub-dub.* This is the sound of your heart beating. The *lub* sound occurs when the valves between the upper and lower chambers of the heart snap shut. The *dub* sound is made by valves closing the two arteries that carry blood out of the heart. If a valve does not close properly and allows blood to leak backward, the sound of the heart changes. A heart with a leaky valve might sound like this: *Lub-dub-shhh, lub-dub-shhh.* The sounds your heart makes can tell a physician a great deal about how it is performing.

▶ MAIN IDEA

The tissues and structures of the heart make it an efficient pump.

Each day your heart beats about 100,000 times, circulating blood through nearly 96,000 kilometers of blood vessels—roughly one-quarter of the distance to the moon. Over 70 years, your heart will beat about 2.5 *billion* times. How can it keep going? One reason is that cardiac muscle tissue, unlike skeletal muscle tissue, can work continuously without becoming tired. Also, the structures of the heart make this organ an efficient pump.

FIGURE 30.7 HEART CHAMBERS AND VALVES

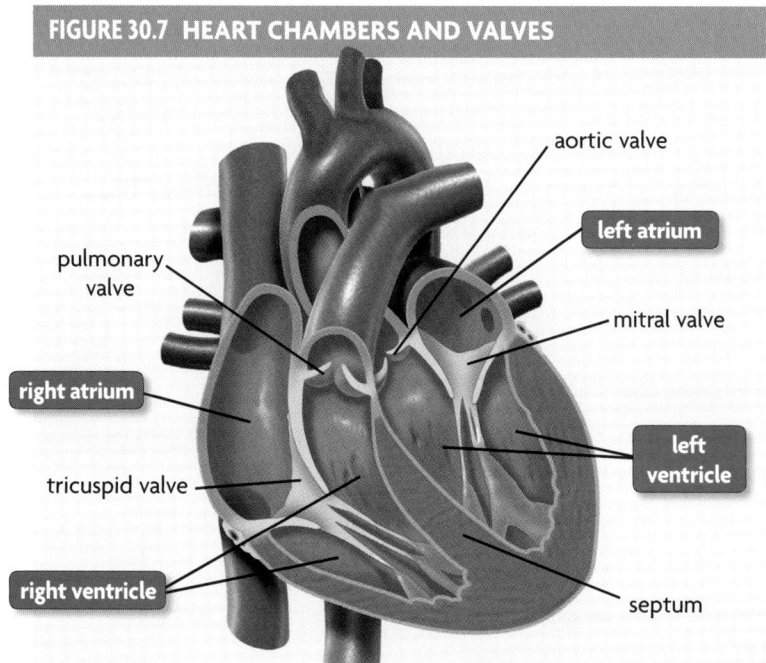

- aortic valve
- left atrium
- pulmonary valve
- mitral valve
- right atrium
- left ventricle
- tricuspid valve
- right ventricle
- septum

Structures of the Heart

The largest structures in your heart are the four chambers. As shown in **FIGURE 30.7**, the two smaller chambers are the right **atrium** and left atrium (plural, *atria*), and the two larger chambers are the right and left **ventricles.** The ventricles are separated by the septum, a thick wall of tissue. The heart **valves** are flaps of tissue that prevent blood from flowing backward. They open when the atria or ventricles contract, and close when the atria or ventricles relax.

After blood fills a chamber, the cardiac muscle contracts and pumps the blood out of the chamber. The heart is an amazingly powerful pump.

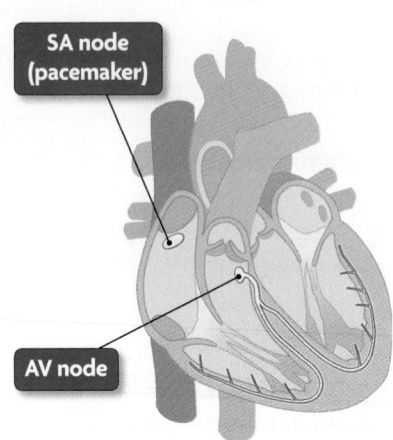

FIGURE 30.8 An electrical signal from the SA node causes both atria to contract. The AV node then picks up the signal and transmits it to both ventricles, causing them to contract.

SA node (pacemaker)

AV node

The reason has to do with the small size of the heart, which allows the strong cardiac muscles to exert a great deal of force on the chamber. The combination of small size and large force results in a powerful pumping action. The heart is also an efficient, self-regulating pump. It can respond to signals from the nervous system to change the speed and force of its pumping action. For example, if you increase your level of activity, your heart will pump faster.

The Heartbeat

The heartbeat consists of two contractions: the first takes place in the atria and the second in the ventricles. The contractions occur partly because the cardiac muscle fibers of the chambers have a unique property. Whenever one fiber is stimulated to contract, all of the fibers contract at the same time.

The first contraction of the heart begins in the right atrium at a signal from the sinoatrial (SA) node, shown in **FIGURE 30.8**. The SA node is known as the heart's **pacemaker** because the cells in this node generate an electrical signal that starts the wave of contractions. Once the atria have contracted, the electrical signal spreads through conducting fibers to the atrioventricular (AV) node, located in the wall of the right ventricle. The AV signal stimulates both ventricles to contract at the same time.

If the SA node is seriously damaged by injury or disease, it can be replaced with an artificial pacemaker that is implanted into the heart. This device, like the SA node, sends electrical signals to the muscle fibers of the atria.

Blood Flow in the Heart

Once you know the basic structures and actions of the heart, you can follow how oxygen-rich and oxygen-poor blood flow through this organ. Study **FIGURE 30.9,** which illustrates this pathway. Notice that blood always enters the heart through an atrium and leaves the heart through a ventricle. The contractions of the atria and then of the ventricles keep blood moving in this sequence.

1 Oxygen-poor blood from the body enters the right atrium. The SA node signals the atria to contract, and blood flows into the right ventricle.

2 When the AV node signals the ventricles to contract, blood is pumped from the right ventricle into the pulmonary artery. This artery, which goes to the lungs, is the only artery in the body that carries oxygen-poor blood. The blood enters the lungs, where CO_2 and water vapor diffuse into the alveoli and O_2 diffuses into the blood.

3 Oxygen-rich blood returns to the heart through the pulmonary vein and enters the left atrium. This is the only vein in the body that carries oxygen-rich blood. As the atria contract, blood is pumped into the left ventricle, the largest chamber in the heart.

4 When the ventricles contract, blood is pumped from the left ventricle into a large artery, the aorta, and is circulated to the rest of the body.

After oxygen has been delivered to the cells, the oxygen-poor blood returns through the veins to the heart, and the sequence begins again.

Analyze **The left ventricle is the largest chamber of the heart. How is its size related to its function?**

VOCABULARY

The word *pulmonary* comes from the Latin root *pulmo*, meaning "lung." The suffix *-ary* means "belonging to or connected with." Therefore, *pulmonary* means something "belonging to or connected with the lung."

FIGURE 30.9 Blood Flow in the Heart

The structures of the heart keep oxygen-poor blood separated from oxygen-rich blood.

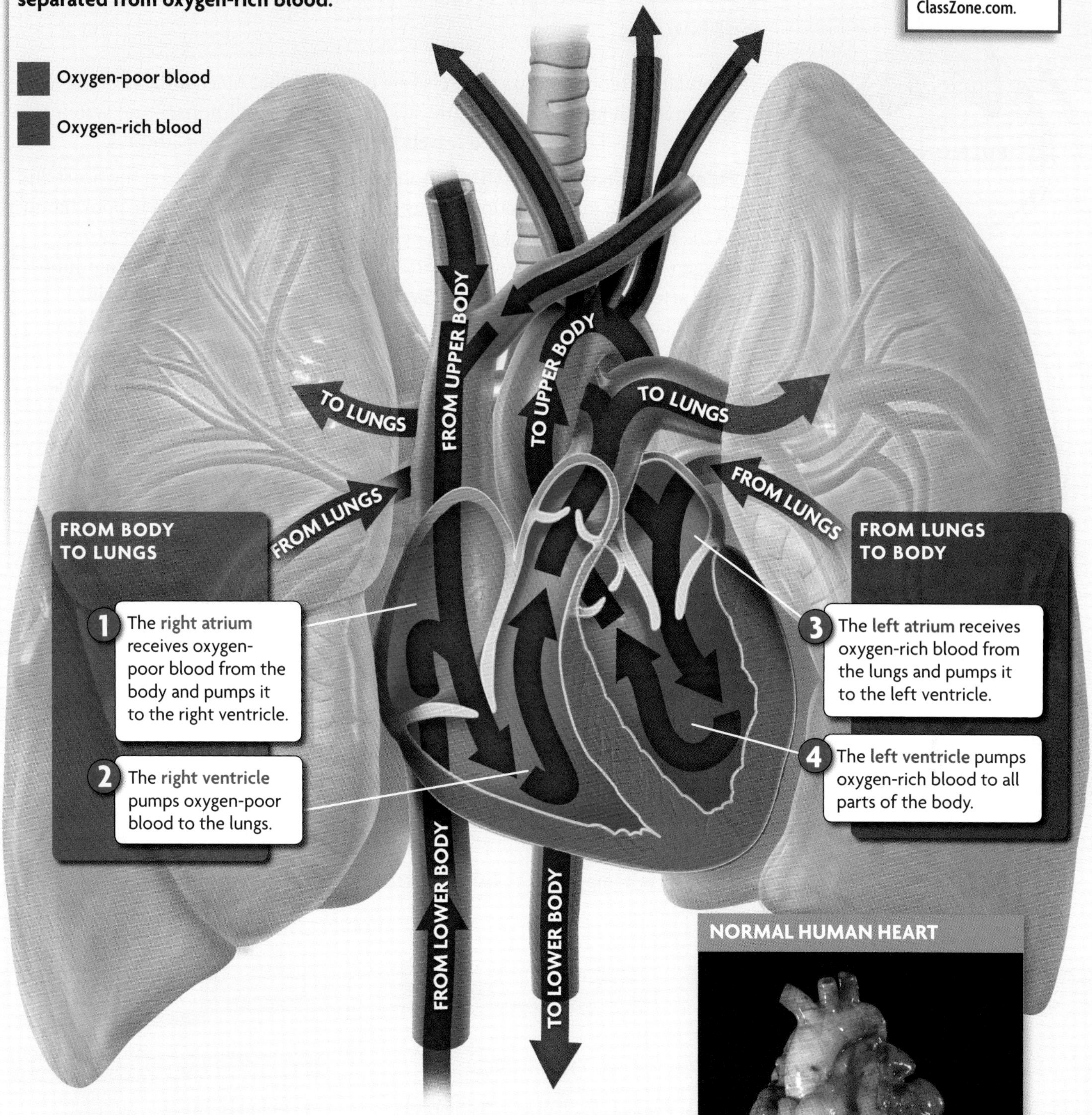

Animated BIOLOGY
See how the heart pumps blood at ClassZone.com.

■ Oxygen-poor blood

■ Oxygen-rich blood

FROM UPPER BODY

TO UPPER BODY

TO LUNGS

FROM LUNGS

TO LUNGS

FROM LUNGS

FROM BODY TO LUNGS

1 The right atrium receives oxygen-poor blood from the body and pumps it to the right ventricle.

2 The right ventricle pumps oxygen-poor blood to the lungs.

FROM LOWER BODY

TO LOWER BODY

FROM LUNGS TO BODY

3 The left atrium receives oxygen-rich blood from the lungs and pumps it to the left ventricle.

4 The left ventricle pumps oxygen-rich blood to all parts of the body.

NORMAL HUMAN HEART

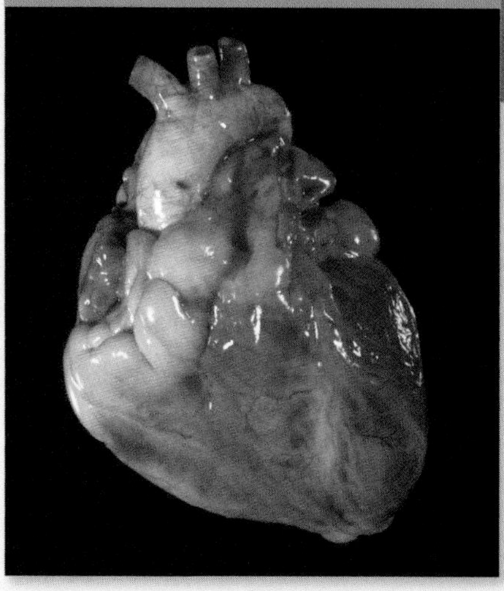

CRITICAL VIEWING If the valves in the right ventricle do not close properly, where in the body might circulation be affected the most?

MAIN IDEA
The heart pumps blood through two main pathways.

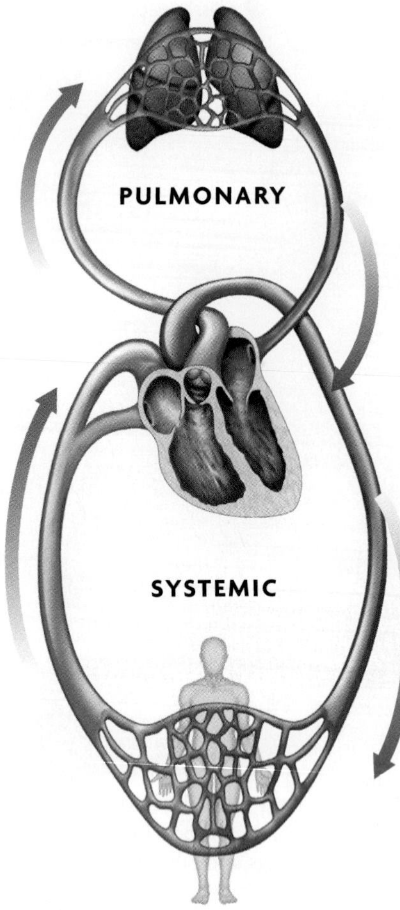

Circulating blood follows two separate pathways that meet at the heart, as shown in **FIGURE 30.10**. These pathways are called the pulmonary and systemic circulation. All of your blood travels through both of these pathways.

Pulmonary circulation (PUL-muh-NEHR-ee) occurs only between the heart and the lungs. The main function of this circulation is to carry oxygen-poor blood to the lungs, where it picks up O_2, expels excess CO_2 and water, and carries oxygen-rich blood back to the heart. Each lung is supplied by its own pulmonary artery and pulmonary vein. **Systemic circulation** (sihs-STEHM-ihk) occurs between the heart and the rest of the body, except for the lungs. The main function of this circulation is to carry oxygen-rich blood to all cells and transport oxygen-poor blood back to the heart. Systemic circulation begins when blood leaves the left ventricle, the largest chamber of the heart. The blood then circulates through the torso, arms, legs, and head, and then returns to the heart.

As the body's need for oxygen changes, sensors in the walls of major arteries in the pulmonary and systemic pathways send information to the medulla in the brain stem. The medulla coordinates this information with signals from the respiratory system. Homeostasis is maintained by matching heart rate and respiration rate with the oxygen needs of the body.

In extreme conditions, such as severe cold, the pulmonary and systemic circulation systems serve another vital function—making sure the body's brain, heart, and other major organs remain at a constant temperature. When the body is exposed for any length of time to a cold environment, blood vessels to the arms and legs begin to constrict. The blood flow to the arms and legs is reduced in order to keep the torso and head warm. Once you reach a warmer environment, these blood vessels dilate and normal circulation resumes.

PULMONARY

SYSTEMIC

FIGURE 30.10 The circulatory system has two general pathways. Pulmonary circulation moves blood between the heart and the lungs. Systemic circulation moves blood between the heart and the rest of the body.

Infer Why is it important to have two separate pathways for circulation?

30.3 ASSESSMENT

ONLINE QUIZ
ClassZone.com

REVIEWING ▶ MAIN IDEAS

1. What structures make the heart an efficient pump? In your answer, describe the direction of blood flow into and out of the heart.

2. Briefly describe the **pulmonary** and **systemic circulation** pathways.

CRITICAL THINKING

3. **Predict** Explain how leaky heart **valves** might damage the heart over time.

4. **Predict** How might a high fever affect a person's heart and breathing rates? Explain your answer.

Connecting CONCEPTS

5. **Animals** Unlike a human heart, an amphibian heart has two **atria** but only a single **ventricle.** How might living in a watery environment help reduce the work that an amphibian heart needs to do?

MATERIALS

- 100-mL graduated cylinder
- 250-mL beaker
- 800 mL water
- eyedropper
- bromothymol blue solution
- straw
- 50 mL 0.4% sodium hydroxide solution
- clock with second hand

PROCESS SKILLS

- **Observing**
- **Measuring**
- **Analyzing**

B1.1C Conduct scientific investigations using appropriate tools and techniques (e.g., selecting an instrument that measures the desired quantity—length, volume, weight, time interval, temperature—with the appropriate level of precision).

Carbon Dioxide and Exercise

In this lab you will examine the effects of exercise on how much carbon dioxide is released by your respiratory system. Bromothymol blue turns yellow in the presence of carbon dioxide when sodium hydroxide is added to the solution. The more sodium hydroxide that needs to be added to turn the bromothymol blue solution yellow, the more carbon dioxide there is in the solution.

PROBLEM How does exercise affect the release of carbon dioxide from the lungs?

PROCEDURE

1. Fill the graduated cylinder with 100 mL of water and pour the water into a beaker.
2. Add four drops of bromothymol blue solution to the water.
3. Place one end of the straw in the water and blow into the water for one minute. **Caution:** Do not inhale from the straw.
4. Add one drop at a time of the sodium hydroxide solution to the water. Swirl the water while adding the drops. Count the number of drops needed for the solution in the cylinder to turn yellow and remain yellow for one minute.
5. Record your data in a table similar to the one below.
6. Empty the beaker. Repeat steps 1 and 2.
7. Perform three types of exercise during your experiment: one that is low impact, such as walking; one that is medium impact, such as running in place; and one that is high impact, such as jumping jacks.
8. Perform each type of exercise for two minutes. At the end of each two-minute exercise period, repeat steps 3 through 6.

TABLE 1. THE EFFECT OF EXERCISE ON CARBON DIOXIDE RELEASE	
Exercise	**Number of 0.4% Sodium Hydroxide Solution Drops**
Rest	
Exercise 1 (walking)	
Exercise 2 (running in place)	
Exercise 3 (jumping jacks)	

ANALYZE AND CONCLUDE

1. **Graph Data** Construct a graph that represents your data.
2. **Analyze** How does the amount of carbon dioxide exhaled change with different types of exercise? What mechanisms in the body explain these results?
3. **Hypothesize** Suppose you had subjects exercise for 15 minutes, and every 5 minutes they increased their rate of exertion. If you measured the amount of carbon dioxide exhaled every 5 minutes, what results would you expect? Explain your answer.

30.4 Blood Vessels and Transport

KEY CONCEPT The circulatory system transports materials throughout the body.

▶ MAIN IDEAS

- Arteries, veins, and capillaries transport blood to all parts of the body.
- Lifestyle plays a key role in circulatory diseases.

VOCABULARY

blood pressure, p. 923
systolic pressure, p. 923
diastolic pressure, p. 923

Review
artery, vein, capillary, ventricle

MICHIGAN STANDARDS

B2.3d Identify the general functions of the major systems of the human body (digestion, respiration, reproduction, circulation, excretion, protection from disease, and movement, control, and coordination) and describe ways that these systems interact with each other.

B2.3e Describe how human body systems maintain relatively constant internal conditions (temperature, acidity, and blood sugar).

TAKING NOTES

A two-column chart can help you organize your notes about different blood vessels and circulatory pathways.

arteries	- Thicker, more muscular than veins - Blood under greater pressure

Connect In the 1600s, most scientists thought that the lungs, not the heart, moved the blood, and that blood was consumed and produced by the internal organs. William Harvey, court physician to the king of England, challenged these ideas. He showed that the heart was the true pump for the blood and that blood circulated in two pathways: one between the heart and the lungs, and another between the heart and the rest of the body. Harvey's work on circulation is regarded as one of the greatest advances in the history of medicine.

▶ MAIN IDEA

Arteries, veins, and capillaries transport blood to all parts of the body.

As you read in Section 30.1, the circulatory system includes three types of blood vessels—arteries, veins, and capillaries—that act as transportation networks for the blood. Each of the three vessels has its own structure and function, as illustrated in **FIGURE 30.11**.

Arteries

Arteries need to be strong and flexible because the blood they carry from the heart is under great pressure. An artery's thick wall is composed of three layers. The innermost layer consists of endothelium coated with a protein that prevents blood from clotting. The middle layer is a thick band of smooth muscle and elastic fibers. The outer layer consists of connective tissue and elastic fibers. The elastic fibers allow the arterial walls to expand and contract to help move blood through the arteries. Arterioles, or smaller arteries, contain the same three layers, but the outer and middle layers are much thinner.

Veins

The structures of veins reflect the fact that blood is under much less pressure when it is returning to the heart. Veins have larger diameters and thinner walls than do arteries and contain valves that prevent blood from flowing backwards. Veins do not have a thick layer that expands and contracts to keep blood moving. Instead, they need the activity of skeletal muscles to help maintain circulation. For example, as you walk, skeletal muscles in your legs push against the veins. The valves open, and blood moves toward the heart. If you sit for too long, the lack of exercise makes it harder for the blood to move upward. Venules are small veins that join larger veins to capillaries.

FIGURE 30.11 Three Types of Blood Vessels

Arteries, veins, and capillaries transport the blood to every cell.

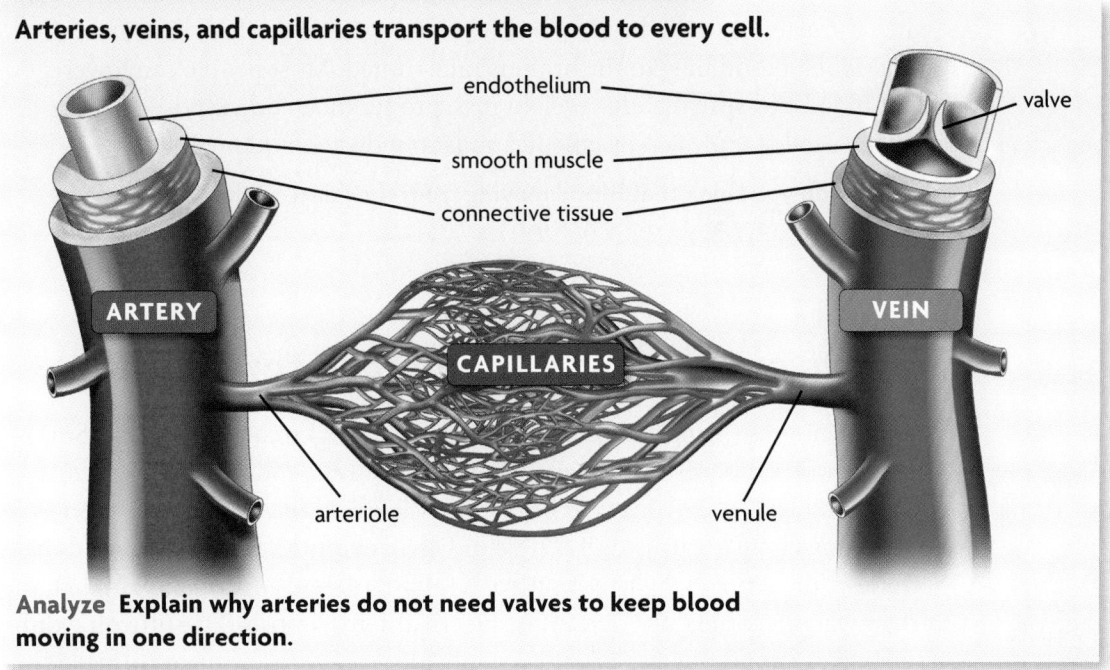

Analyze **Explain why arteries do not need valves to keep blood moving in one direction.**

Capillaries

Capillary walls are made of epithelium, but they contain no muscle cells or elastic fibers. The thinness of capillary walls allows materials to diffuse into and out of the blood quickly and easily. In areas of high metabolic activity, such as the lungs, kidneys, and liver, capillaries form dense networks called capillary beds. These beds move a great deal of blood into and out of these organs.

Circulation and Blood Pressure

Blood pressure is the force with which blood pushes against the wall of an artery. A healthy resting blood pressure for a young adult is around 120/70 mm Hg (read as "120 over 70 millimeters of mercury"). The top, and higher, number is known as the **systolic pressure** (sih-STAHL-ihk). This is the amount of pressure on the walls of an artery when the left ventricle contracts to pump blood through the body. The bottom, and lower, number is known as the **diastolic pressure** (DY-uh-STAHL-ihk). This is the pressure in the artery when the left ventricle relaxes.

Blood pressure depends on how elastic and unblocked the arteries are and on the strength of the heart contraction. The less elastic the arteries and the more blockages that reduce blood flow, the harder the heart must pump. As a result, blood pressure rises. Blood pressure also rises naturally with activity, stress, and strong emotions, but it should drop again with rest. If the pressure remains high, there could be a problem in the circulatory system.

Connecting CONCEPTS

Differentiated Cells In **Chapter 28**, you learned that epithelial cells line most organs and structures in the body. These cells provide a protective layer that helps each organ or structure to do its job.

VISUAL VOCAB

Systolic pressure occurs when the left ventricle contracts. **Diastolic pressure** occurs when the ventricle relaxes. You can write these numbers as a fraction in which systolic pressure is always on top.

$$\frac{120}{70}$$

120 **systolic** = numerator

70 **diastolic** = denominator

People with permanently high blood pressure have a condition called hypertension, which can lead to a heart attack or stroke. A heart attack occurs when the arteries to the heart muscle are damaged or blocked. A stroke can occur when blood flow to the brain is interrupted. Most people can lower their blood pressure through weight loss, proper diet, and exercise. If these remedies fail, people can use medications to reduce blood pressure.

Infer Why do you think that blood moving from the heart to the lungs must be carried by an artery and not by a vein?

▶ MAIN IDEA

Lifestyle plays a key role in circulatory diseases.

Lifestyle choices strongly influence the health of your circulatory system. Smoking, lack of exercise, excessive weight, long-term stress, and a diet low in fruits and vegetables but high in saturated fats are all linked to an increased risk of developing circulatory diseases. These diseases mainly affect the heart and the arteries. For example, in arteriosclerosis (ahr-TEER-ee-oh-skluh-ROH-sihs), the artery walls become thick and inflexible. In atherosclerosis (ATH-uh-roh-skluh-ROH-sihs), blood flow is partially or fully blocked by sticky material, called plaque, that collects on the walls of the arteries, as **FIGURE 30.12** shows. High blood pressure is often the only warning sign of these problems.

Both diseases can lead to a heart attack, stroke, or kidney damage. Some blocked arteries supplying the heart muscle can be opened using a surgical technique known as a balloon angioplasty (AN-jee-uh-PLAS-tee). A device is threaded into the artery and then inflated so that it squeezes the obstruction against the artery wall. If this procedure does not work, bypass surgery may be necessary. In this operation, a healthy blood vessel from another part of the body (usually the leg) is attached to the artery on either side of the blockage. Blood can then bypass the obstruction.

To reduce the risk of circulatory diseases, physicians urge people either not to smoke or to quit smoking, to maintain a healthy weight, and to exercise regularly. Medications can also help reduce the risks of heart disease.

Provide Examples How can lifestyle choices affect the function of the arteries?

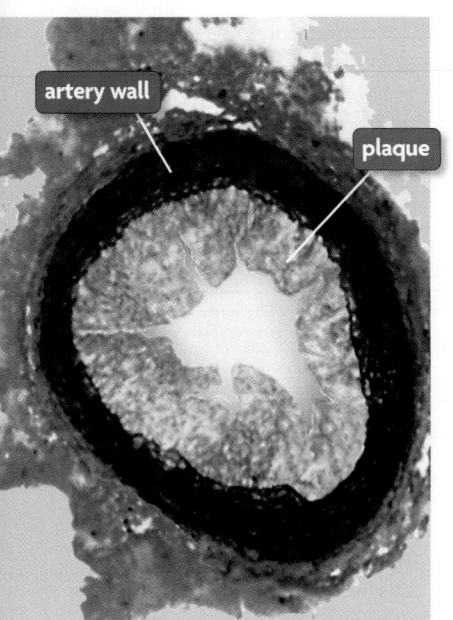

FIGURE 30.12 This micrograph clearly shows fatty deposits, called plaque, building up on an artery wall. If such deposits block blood flow, they can cause a heart attack or stroke. (LM; magnification 25×)

30.4 ASSESSMENT

ONLINE QUIZ
ClassZone.com

REVIEWING ▶ MAIN IDEAS

1. How do the structures of arteries, veins, and capillaries relate to their functions?

2. How can lifestyle choices help reduce the risk of heart disease?

CRITICAL THINKING

3. **Infer** People who smoke often have cold hands and feet. What might explain this condition in terms of blood flow?

4. **Apply** Explain why narrowing of the arteries decreases blood flow but increases **blood pressure.**

Connecting CONCEPTS

5. **Arthropods** The hard exoskeleton of an arthropod exerts pressure on the animal's circulatory system. In what way does the exoskeleton serve the same function as the heart does in mammals?

Age Group and Disease

When scientists investigate some type of phenomenon, such as when they are trying to determine the cause of a disease, they often need to rule out variables that may or may not be important. This is especially helpful when many factors might play some role in the phenomenon, as is often the case, in the causes of disease.

The formation of a **null hypothesis** is useful during these types of investigations. The null hypothesis states that there is no difference among study groups for the independent variable being tested. The null hypothesis is always stated in the negative: one variable does *not* have an effect on the other variable. The null hypothesis is accepted or rejected based on the data. If the investigation shows that the one variable *does* affect the other, the null hypothesis is rejected. If the investigation shows that the one variable *does not* affect the other, then the null hypothesis is accepted.

EXAMPLE

A scientist investigates the rate of death from heart disease among different age groups. The null hypothesis for this investigation would be, "There is no difference in the rate of death from heart disease among different age groups." Consider the results listed below for the rate of death from heart disease per 100,000 people.

- Rate for ages 55–64 is 246.9
- Rate for ages 65–74 is 635.1
- Rate for ages 75–84 is 1725.7

In this case, the null hypothesis would be rejected because there is an obvious difference in the rate of death due to heart disease among different age groups. As people get older, the rate of death increases.

Exercise is an important factor in preventing heart disease.

ACCEPT OR REJECT THE NULL HYPOTHESIS

The graph at right shows the results of an investigation about differences in the rate of asthma based on age.

1. **Hypothesize** Form a null hypothesis for this investigation.

2. **Evaluate** Explain whether you accept or reject the null hypothesis, based on the data.

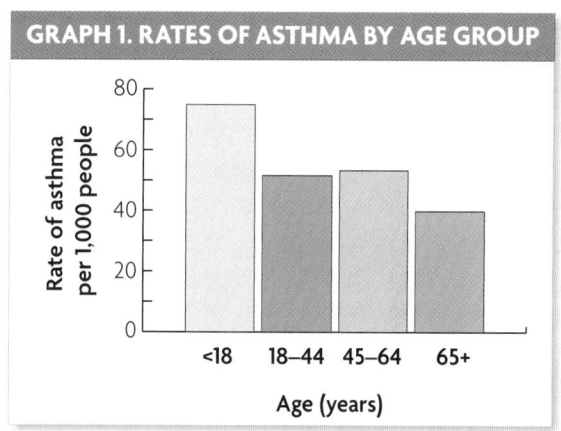

GRAPH 1. RATES OF ASTHMA BY AGE GROUP

Source: National Health Interview Survey, National Center for Health Statistics

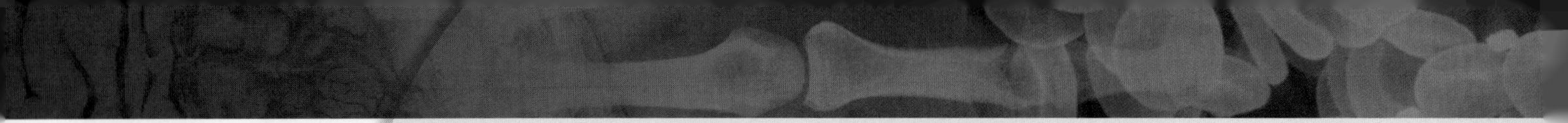

30.5 Blood

KEY CONCEPT Blood is a complex tissue that transports materials.

▶ MAIN IDEAS

- Blood is composed mainly of cells, cell fragments, and plasma.
- Platelets and different types of blood cells have different functions.

VOCABULARY

platelet, p. 926
plasma, p. 926
ABO blood group, p. 927
Rh factor, p. 928
white blood cells, p. 928

Review
hemoglobin, red blood cell

MICHIGAN STANDARDS

B2.3d Identify the general functions of the major systems of the human body (digestion, respiration, reproduction, circulation, excretion, protection from disease, and movement, control, and coordination) and describe ways that these systems interact with each other.

B2.3e Describe how human body systems maintain relatively constant internal conditions (temperature, acidity, and blood sugar).

Connect The adult human body contains about 5 liters (more than 5 qt) of blood. This fluid supplies your organs with gases and nutrients, helps you keep warm or cool off, and gets rid of waste products from your cells. Blood also has other components that help fight infections and control bleeding from damaged blood vessels. How can one substance accomplish all of these functions?

▶ MAIN IDEA
Blood is composed mainly of cells, cell fragments, and plasma.

When you look at blood with the naked eye, it appears to be a single substance. Whole blood is actually a sticky mixture of cells, cell fragments, and fluid, along with particles of fat, other nutrients, and dissolved gases. If you put blood in a test tube and spin it in a centrifuge, it will separate into two main parts, as shown in **FIGURE 30.13**. At the bottom, a reddish-brown band contains red blood cells, white blood cells, and platelets. **Platelets** are cell fragments, produced in bone marrow, that help in blood clotting.

At the top of the tube is **plasma,** a clear pale-yellow fluid that makes up about 55 percent of the blood. Plasma is roughly 90 percent water. Many types of molecules dissolve in plasma and can be transported throughout the body. These molecules include amino acids, glucose, hormones, vitamins, salts, and waste products.

Why is plasma important? The concentration of molecules dissolved in plasma determines which substances will diffuse into and out of the blood that moves through the capillaries. The movement of water, gases, nutrients, and ions between the capillaries and the cells plays a critical role in maintaining homeostasis. For instance, as the concentration of glucose increases in the capillaries, it moves outward to an area of lower concentration and eventually enters the cells.

Plasma proteins such as albumin, fibrinogen, and immune proteins also help maintain homeostasis. Albumin, the same substance as in egg white, is the most abundant plasma protein. Its main role is to stabilize blood volume so that fluid in the blood does not leak out of the vessels. Fibrinogen is a clotting factor that works with platelets to stop the bleeding after an injury.

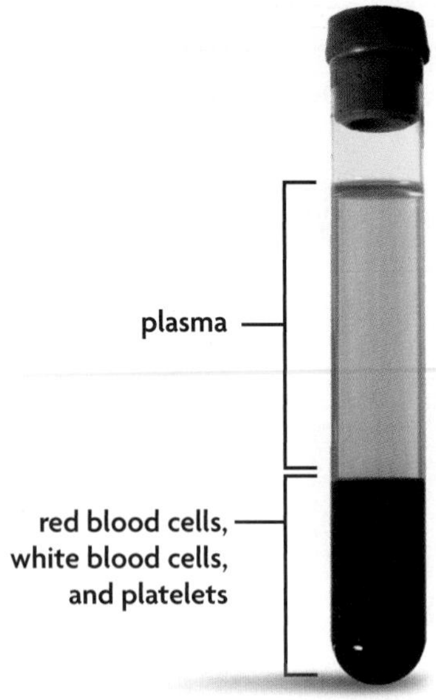

plasma

red blood cells, white blood cells, and platelets

FIGURE 30.13 Whole blood is composed of several parts that help to fight infections, control bleeding, and transport gases, nutrients, waste products, and hormones.

A group of specialized proteins made by the immune system fights infection or attacks foreign materials in the blood. You will learn more about these proteins in Chapter 31.

Predict **What do you think might happen to your blood if you become dehydrated?**

▶ MAIN IDEA

Platelets and different types of blood cells have different functions.

Blood contains red blood cells, several types of white blood cells, and platelets, as the photograph in **FIGURE 30.14** shows. These three blood components are manufactured mostly in the bone marrow. Each one has a specialized shape and function.

Red Blood Cells

Red blood cells make up 40 to 45 percent of all cells in the blood. Mature red blood cells are shaped like an inner tube with a solid center. They are produced from stem cells in bone marrow. As these cells mature, they gradually fill with hemoglobin and lose their nuclei and other organelles. Without nuclei, they cannot undergo cell division. Red blood cells circulate through the body for about 120 days before they begin to degrade. Degraded cells are carried to the liver and spleen, which break up the cells and recycle them.

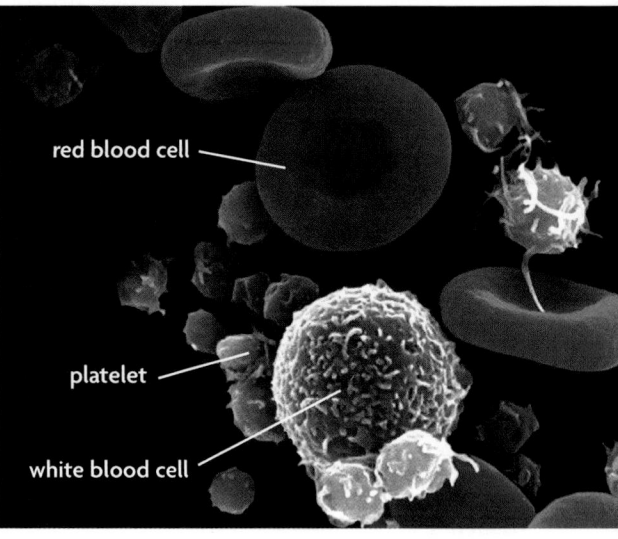

The most important function of red blood cells is to transport O_2 to the cells and carry CO_2 away from them. As you read in Section 30.3, O_2 binds to the hemoglobin in red blood cells and is transported to all cells. When blood is returning to the heart, it picks up CO_2 and carries it to the lungs.

If red blood cells are damaged or misshapen, they cannot transport O_2 effectively. In sickle cell disease, for example, red blood cells are distorted into crescent shapes, as shown in **FIGURE 30.15.** They transport less O_2, last only 10 to 20 days, and tend to clump in blood vessels. This genetic disorder is most commonly found in people of African descent.

ABO Blood Group and Rh Factors

Red blood cells have surface protein markers that define your blood type. Blood type is very important when people give or receive blood for transfusions. If you receive blood with a protein marker different from your own, your immune system will attack the foreign blood cells, causing them to clump. The clumped blood can block vital blood vessels and result in death.

Protein markers exist for about 26 different blood types. The most common markers are A and B, which produce four blood types: A, B, AB, and O, also known as the **ABO blood group.** Type O has no protein marker and can be donated to a person with any other blood type. Type AB blood has both protein markers and can accept any type of blood. People with Type A and Type B blood can receive only their own blood type or type O blood.

FIGURE 30.14 Red blood cells transport gases, white blood cells defend the body against pathogens and foreign materials, and platelets help seal wounds. (colored SEM; magnification 2500×)

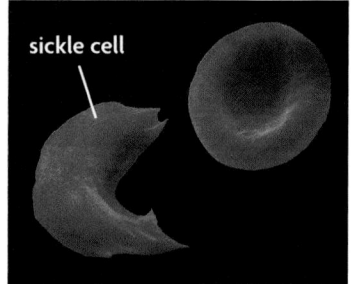

FIGURE 30.15 Sickle cell anemia is an inherited blood disease in which hemoglobin proteins clump together. This causes red blood cells to stiffen and curl into a crescent shape. (colored SEM; magnification 2500×)

Blood Cells

In this lab, you will examine different types of blood cells under the microscope.

MATERIALS
- slide of blood cells
- microscope

PROBLEM What are the different characteristics of blood cells?

PROCEDURE

1. Examine the slide under low power and high power on the microscope. Identify a red blood cell, a white blood cell, and a platelet. Notice the proportion of each type of cell on your slide.

2. Draw each type of cell and label its structures.

ANALYZE AND CONCLUDE

1. **Explain** What is the general shape of a red blood cell? How is this shape related to the function of a red blood cell?

2. **Infer** Based on the proportion of each type of cell on your slide, which type of cell is the most numerous in the blood of a healthy person? Which is least numerous?

Connecting CONCEPTS

Genetics In **Chapter 7**, you read about the alleles that produce the different phenotypes in the ABO blood group.

Another blood protein, known as the **Rh factor,** is also critical in making a successful transfusion. People either are Rh positive (Rh⁺) and have this protein or are Rh negative (Rh⁻) and do not have it. Anyone can receive Rh⁻ blood without harm. However, if you are Rh⁻ and receive Rh⁺ blood, your immune system will make proteins that cause the Rh⁺ blood cells to swell and burst. As a result, blood must be matched for both the ABO group and the Rh group. The possible ABO/Rh blood combinations are shown in **FIGURE 30.16**.

FIGURE 30.16 ABO Rh BLOOD COMBINATIONS

BLOOD TYPE	CAN DONATE TO	CAN RECEIVE FROM
A	A, AB	A, O
B	AB, B	B, O
AB	AB	A, B, AB, O
O	A, B, AB, O	O
Rh FACTOR	CAN DONATE TO	CAN RECEIVE FROM
Rh⁺ factor	Rh⁺	Rh⁺, Rh⁻
Rh⁻ factor	Rh⁺, Rh⁻	Rh⁻

White Blood Cells

White blood cells, which contain no hemoglobin, are cells that defend the body against infection and that remove foreign material and dead cells. Different kinds of white blood cells defend the body in different ways. Some surround and ingest microorganisms. Others produce proteins that act to destroy pathogens. Unlike red blood cells, white blood cells are not limited to the circulatory system. Some of these cells are able to pass through capillary

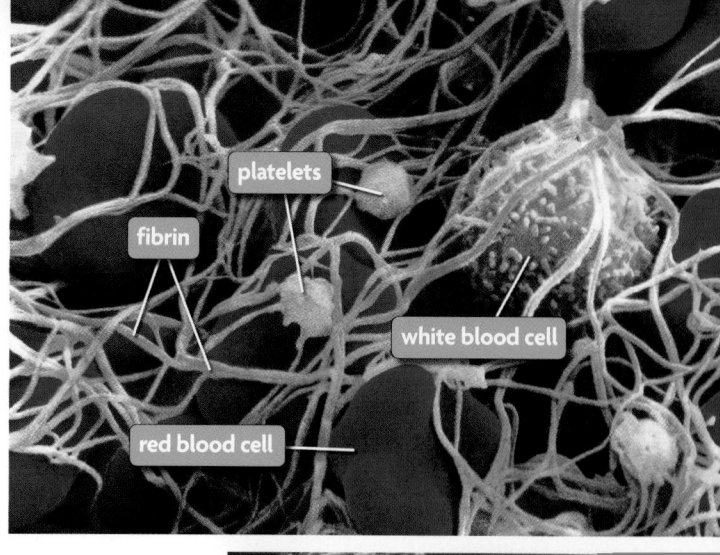

walls into the lymphatic system and attack pathogens in the body's tissues. For this reason, white blood cells are also considered part of the immune system.

Platelets and Blood Clotting

Platelets are cell fragments that help form clots that control bleeding. When you cut or tear a blood vessel, platelets quickly cluster around the wound.

Repairing injuries At the site of an injury, platelets form spiky extensions that intertwine into a complex net. The platelets then release proteins known as clotting factors, which begin the process of repair. One of the factors converts prothrombin, a plasma protein, into thrombin. Thrombin, in turn, converts fibrinogen into fibrin. Sticky threads of fibrin form a web that traps platelets and white blood cells, as the top photo shows in **FIGURE 30.17.**

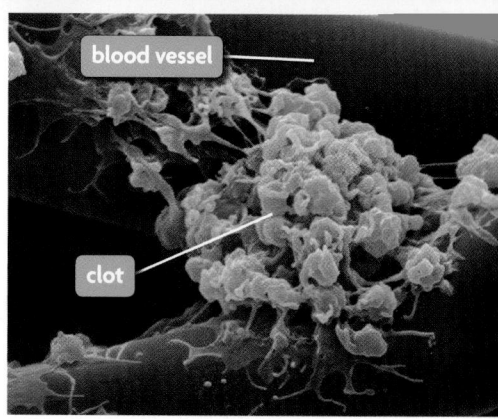

The bottom photo shows how the tangle of fibrin, platelets, and blood cells has grown to form a plug, or clot, on the blood vessel. The clot seals the wound and prevents any further loss of blood. The steps in blood clotting are a good example of a positive feedback loop. The body increases the rate of change in clotting until the wound is sealed. Once the injury heals, other chemicals are released that dissolve the clot.

Blood clotting disorders Blood clots can also form inside blood vessels and present serious risks to a person's health. For example, clots that block arteries to the heart or brain can cause a heart attack or stroke. Medications that thin the blood or dissolve clots can help prevent these circulatory problems.

FIGURE 30.17 The top photograph shows platelets clustering at the site of a wound. Fibrin threads trap more cells until a plug, or clot, forms (bottom) and stops the bleeding from a blood vessel. (colored SEMs; magnifications: platelets and fibrin 6000×; clot 1900×)

The inability to form clots can be equally serious. For example, hemophilia is a genetic disorder in which a key clotting factor is missing in the blood. For people with hemophilia, even a minor cut can cause life-threatening bleeding. As a result, they must guard against the slightest scrape or bruise. When injured, they must have the missing clotting factor injected into their blood to help seal the wound.

Apply Why might it be important for white blood cells to be part of a clot that seals an injury?

30.5 ASSESSMENT

ONLINE QUIZ
ClassZone.com

REVIEWING ▶ MAIN IDEAS

1. List some of the substances dissolved in **plasma** and describe how they help maintain homeostasis.

2. What are the primary roles of red blood cells, **white blood cells,** and **platelets**?

CRITICAL THINKING

3. **Apply** What would happen if a person with type A Rh⁻ blood were transfused with type A Rh⁺ blood?

4. **Infer** Some people must take medications that interfere with clotting factors. How might they need to change their activities?

Connecting CONCEPTS

5. **Chemistry** Water is the most abundant component in human blood. What characteristic of water allows glucose, hormones, and many other materials to dissolve into it?

30.6 Lymphatic System

KEY CONCEPT The lymphatic system provides another type of circulation in the body.

MAIN IDEAS

- Lymph is collected from tissues and returned to the circulatory system.
- The lymphatic system is a major part of the immune system.

VOCABULARY

lymphatic system, p. 930
lymph, p. 930
node, p. 930
lymphocyte, p. 931

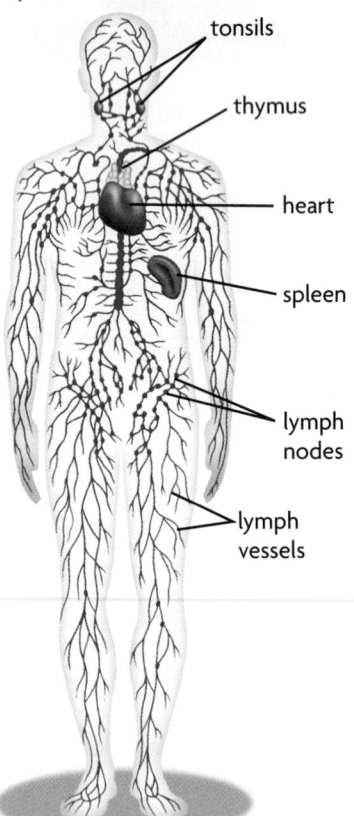

FIGURE 30.18 The lymphatic system collects fluid that leaks from the blood vessels and returns it to the heart. The spleen recycles old red blood cells; white blood cells mature in the thymus.

Connect Your body has two transport networks that circulate fluids. The first is the circulatory system, which brings gases and nutrients to every cell. The second is the lymphatic system. While this system also helps to distribute nutrients, its main jobs are to absorb excess fluid, to fight disease, and to carry waste products away from the cells. These two systems work so closely together that almost everywhere there are blood vessels, there are also lymph vessels.

MAIN IDEA

Lymph is collected from tissues and returned to the circulatory system.

The **lymphatic system** (lihm-FAT-ihk) consists of a complex network of organs, vessels, and nodes throughout the body, as shown in **FIGURE 30.18**. The system collects excess fluid that leaks out of the blood capillaries into the area between the cells. This fluid, called interstitial (IHN-tuhr-STIHSH-uhl) fluid, brings nutrients to the cells and removes their wastes.

Although 90 percent of the fluid returns to the capillaries, up to 3 liters (3 qt) per day remain outside the blood vessels. Without the lymphatic system, your body would begin to swell as more fluid becomes trapped in your tissues. The system prevents this problem through a two-step process:

- It collects the fluid and filters it to remove dead cells and microorganisms.
- It returns the cleaned fluid to the circulatory system.

Lymphatic circulation begins when the fluid between the cells enters the lymphatic capillaries, where it becomes known as **lymph.** The lymph then flows into larger vessels within the lymphatic system. Without a heart to pump the fluid, the vessels rely on contractions of skeletal and smooth muscles to circulate the lymph. One-way valves similar to those in veins keep the fluid from flowing backwards.

From the vessels, lymph collects in small rounded structures called lymph **nodes.** The nodes filter the lymph and trap bacteria, viruses, fungi, and cell fragments. Specialized immune cells ingest and destroy this organic material. Vessels then carry the lymph out of the nodes. In the last stage of the journey, the lymph returns to the circulatory system. Two large vessels, one on either side of the body, enter veins located just under the collarbones. The lymph is returned to the blood and becomes part of the circulatory system again.

When lymphatic tissues and nodes are damaged or removed, lymph cannot drain normally from that area. The result is swelling as fluid accumulates. The swelling can be controlled by exercise, pressure bandages or garments, and massage. These treatments exert pressure on the tissues and nodes to "push" lymph into the vessels.

Predict How would sitting for a long time affect the lymphatic circulation?

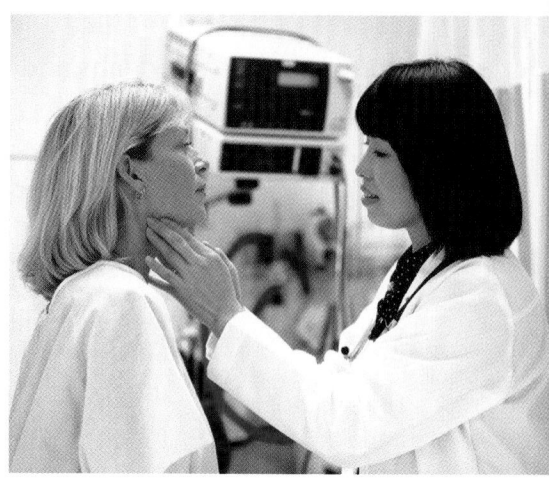

FIGURE 30.19 Doctors check your lymph nodes during a routine physical examination. Enlarged or lumpy nodes might indicate that your body is fighting an infection.

◗ MAIN IDEA

The lymphatic system is a major part of the immune system.

Three structures in the lymphatic system—the tonsils, thymus, and spleen—also function as part of the immune system. Each of these structures has specialized functions that help the body to defend itself. The tonsils are lymph nodes set in the back of the throat on either side. These nodes help to filter out bacteria and viruses that have escaped the body's outer defenses. When too many pathogens collect in the tonsils, these nodes become swollen and infected and may have to be removed.

The thymus, located behind the breastbone, is important in developing certain types of white blood cells known as **lymphocytes** (LIHM-fuh-SYTS). These cells help the body fight pathogens, parasites, and other types of foreign organisms. Some immature lymphocytes migrate from the bone marrow to the thymus, where they develop the ability to recognize specific microorganisms. Most of these cells leave the thymus and circulate through the lymphatic and circulatory systems to protect the body.

The spleen is the largest organ in the lymphatic system. Its main job is to filter and clean the lymph of cell fragments and abnormal tissue. This organ also contains many lymphocytes and other white blood cells that destroy harmful bacteria and foreign organisms.

Predict If the spleen is removed, how might the immune and lymphatic systems be affected?

Connecting CONCEPTS

Immune System You will read more in **Chapter 31** about how the body uses lymphocytes and other types of cells to fight pathogens.

30.6 ASSESSMENT

ONLINE QUIZ
ClassZone.com

REVIEWING ◗ MAIN IDEAS

1. Describe the main organs and functions of the **lymphatic system.**

2. Give three examples of organs that are part of both the immune and lymphatic systems, and briefly describe their functions.

CRITICAL THINKING

3. **Compare and Contrast** How are the structures of an artery and a vein different from or similar to the structure of a **lymph** vessel?

4. **Infer** The circulatory system of the blood is a closed system. Is the lymphatic system a closed or an open system? Explain your answer.

Connecting CONCEPTS

5. **Immunology** Mononucleosis is a disease that causes the body to greatly increase the number of **lymphocytes** circulating in the blood and lymph. If you felt the spleen and looked at the tonsils of someone with mononucleosis, what might you observe and why?

Use these inquiry-based labs and online activities to deepen your understanding of how the lungs respond when you exercise.

INVESTIGATION

Making and Using a Respirometer

In this lab you will make a model respirometer, an instrument that measures your lung capacity. You will use your model to measure your lung capacity before and after different types of exercise.

SKILL Modeling

PROBLEM How might exercise affect a person's lung capacity?

PROCEDURE

1. Use the materials to construct a model like the one shown. In your finished model, you should be able to breathe into the straw and raise the cup.

2. Construct a data table in which to record your data.

3. Measure your lung capacity at rest. Take a deep breath and blow into the straw until the bottom of the cup reaches between 2 cm and 6 cm. Your partner will time how long you can keep the cup between these two points.

4. Decide on three types of exercises to perform during your investigation. You will perform each exercise for two minutes. After two minutes, immediately blow into your respirometer. Have your partner time how long you can keep the bottom of the cup between the 2 cm and 6 cm mark. Rest for three minutes, then start the next exercise.

MATERIALS

- 1 liter bottle with a hole in the bottom
- scissors
- white paper
- marker
- metric ruler
- 15 cm clear tape
- small paper cup
- plastic straw that bends
- clock with a second hand

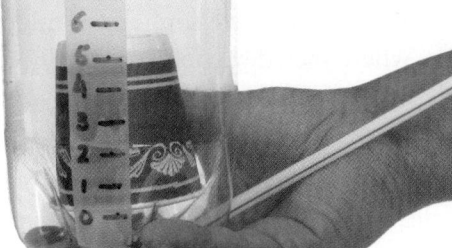

ANALYZE AND CONCLUDE

1. **Graph Data** Construct a bar graph to represent your data. What differences occurred in your lung capacity before and after you exercised?

2. **Contrast** What were the differences in your lung capacity after each type of exercise?

3. **Predict** How would you expect a person's lung capacity to change one week, two weeks, and three weeks after recovering from a minor cold?

EXTEND YOUR INVESTIGATION

Ask a sprinter and a long-distance runner, someone who plays a trumpet or trombone, and someone who is a singer to do this experiment. Which person would you expect to have the greatest lung capacity? After conducting the experiment, form a hypothesis based on your observations for further testing.

INVESTIGATION

Stimuli and Heart Rate

In this lab, you will test how different stimuli affect heart rate. You will expose the subject to two different stimuli—one that is intense and exciting and one that is calming and relaxing. You will then measure how the heart rate is affected before and after each stimulus.

SKILL Designing Experiments

PROBLEM How would the heart rate respond to two different types of stimuli?

MATERIALS

- CD player
- VCR or DVD player
- videos, DVDs, or CDs
- clock with a second hand (or stopwatch)

PROCEDURE

1. Determine a procedure for your experiment. You may want to compare the difference in results between music with a fast beat and music that is more relaxing. Or you may want to compare the difference between a video or DVD of an exciting sports competition and a video or DVD that shows beautiful scenery.

2. Identify your independent and dependent variables. How long will you expose the subject to each stimulus? How will you measure heart rate? At what points in the experiment will you measure the subject's heart rate?

3. Predict how the independent variables will affect the dependent variable. Construct a data table in which to record your data.

4. Have your teacher approve your procedure. Carry out your experiment.

ANALYZE AND CONCLUDE

1. **Analyze** Construct a graph to represent your data. What is the relationship between the independent and dependent variables? Was your prediction supported by the data?

2. **Evaluate** How could you improve the design of your experiment to obtain more accurate results? What variables could you control better?

Online BIOLOGY
CLASSZONE.COM

VIRTUAL LAB
Blood Typing

How does a doctor find out the blood type of a blood sample? In this interactive lab, you will learn how to identify blood types, and then work on your own to identify the blood types of several samples.

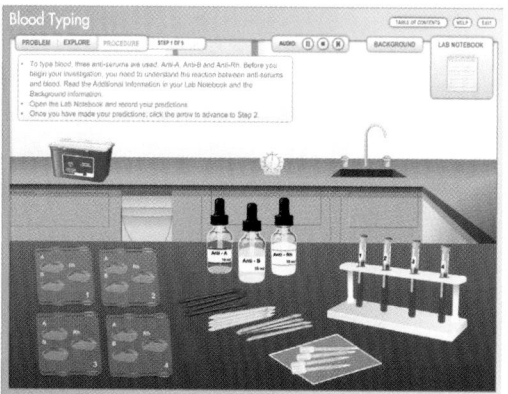

ANIMATED BIOLOGY
Build the Circulatory and Respiratory Systems

The respiratory system and circulatory system are closely connected. Build the two systems to get a better understanding of how they work together.

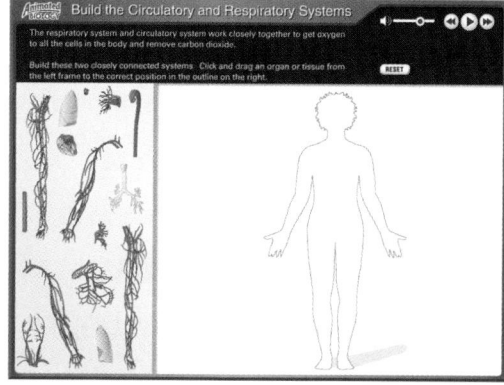

WEBQUEST

Asthma rates are increasing steadily across the country. Complete the WebQuest to learn what causes asthma, what triggers an episode, and why people with asthma can still live healthy, active lives.

KEY CONCEPTS | Vocabulary Games | Concept Maps | Animated Biology | Online Quiz

30.1 Respiratory and Circulatory Functions

The respiratory and circulatory systems bring oxygen and nutrients to the cells. These two systems work together to maintain homeostasis. The respiratory system moves gases into and out of the blood. The circulatory system transports blood to all parts of the body.

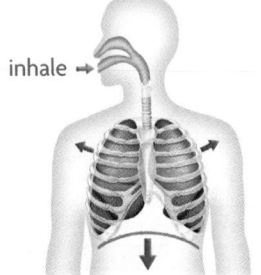 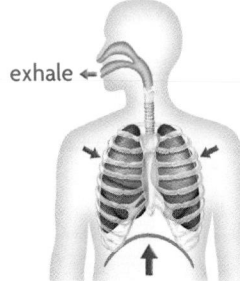

inhale →   exhale ←

30.2 Respiration and Gas Exchange

The respiratory system exchanges oxygen and carbon dioxide. Gas exchange occurs in the alveoli of the lungs, where oxygen and carbon dioxide diffuse into and out of the blood. Respiratory diseases such as emphysema and asthma interfere with gas exchange.

30.3 The Heart and Circulation

The heart is a muscular pump that moves the blood through two pathways. The tissues and structures of the heart make it an efficient pump and allow it to work continuously. The heartbeat consists of two contractions that move blood from the atria to the ventricles. Blood circulates through the pulmonary and systemic pathways.

30.4 Blood Vessels and Transport

The circulatory system transports materials throughout the body. Arteries, veins, and capillaries transport blood to all the cells. The force with which blood pushes against the wall of an artery is known as blood pressure. The health of the circulatory system can be supported or harmed by lifestyle choices.

30.5 Blood

Blood is a complex tissue that transports materials. Blood is composed mainly of cells, platelets, and plasma. Red blood cells transport gases, white blood cells help fight diseases, and platelets help seal wounds. Proteins in blood determine blood type and Rh+ and Rh- factors. The ABO group is the most commonly used of all the blood grouping systems.

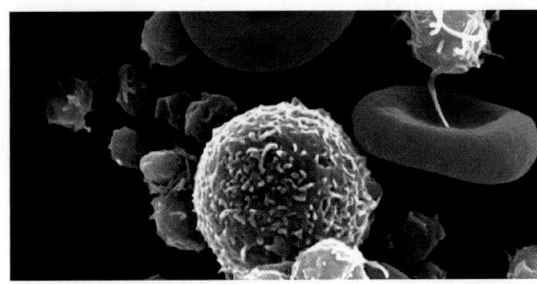

30.6 Lymphatic System

The lymphatic system provides another type of circulation in the body. The lymphatic system collects excess fluid between the cells, filters it, and returns it to the circulatory system. The lymphatic system is also an important part of the immune system.

Synthesize Your Notes

Venn Diagram Use a Venn diagram to help you compare structures in the respiratory and circulatory systems.

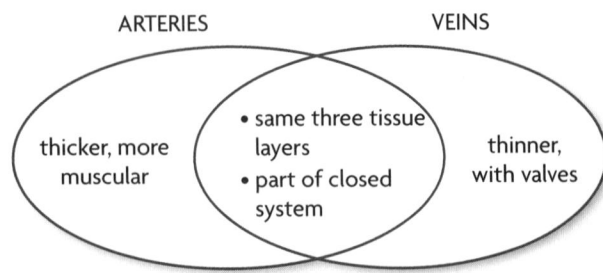

ARTERIES   VEINS

thicker, more muscular | • same three tissue layers • part of closed system | thinner, with valves

Concept Map A concept map is a good way to organize your notes on topics such as the components of blood.

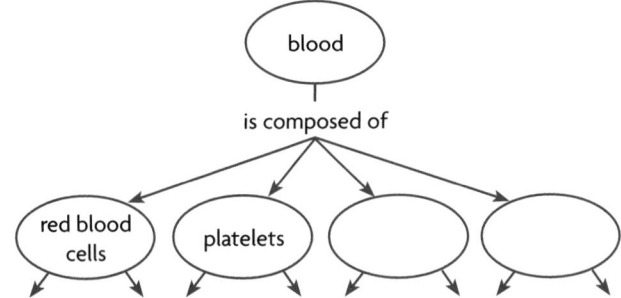

blood
is composed of
red blood cells   platelets

Chapter Assessment

Chapter Vocabulary

30.1 circulatory systems, p. 910
respiratory systems, p. 910
trachea, p. 911
lung, p. 911
alveoli, p. 911
diaphragm, p. 912
heart, p. 912
artery, p. 913
vein, p. 913
capillaries, p. 913

30.2 red blood cell, p. 915
hemoglobin, p. 915
emphysema, p. 916
asthma, p. 916

30.3 atrium, p. 917
ventricle, p. 917
valve, p. 917
pacemaker, p. 918
pulmonary circulation, p. 920
systemic circulation, p. 920

30.4 blood pressure, p. 923
systolic pressure, p. 923
diastolic pressure, p. 923

30.5 platelet, p. 926
plasma, p. 926
ABO blood group, p. 927
Rh factor, p. 928
white blood cells, p. 928

30.6 lymphatic system, p. 930
lymph, p. 930
node, p. 930
lymphocyte, p. 931

Reviewing Vocabulary

Term Relationships

For each pair of terms below, write a sentence that describes or explains a relationship between the two terms. For example, *oxygen, carbon dioxide:* All cells use oxygen and produce carbon dioxide as a waste product.

1. vein, capillary
2. atrium, ventricle
3. artery, heart
4. systemic circulation, pulmonary circulation
5. systolic pressure, diastolic pressure
6. platelet, plasma
7. lung, trachea
8. lymph, lymphocyte

Word Origins

For each term below, describe how its Latin or Greek meaning relates to its definition.

9. *Alveolus* comes from the Latin term *alveus*, which means "small hollow space."

10. *Emphysema* comes from the Greek term *emphysan*, which means "to inflate."

11. *Hemoglobin* is a combination of the Greek term *haima*, which means "blood," and the word *globin*, which refers to a protein.

12. *Plasma* comes from the Greek term *plassein*, which means "to mold or spread thin."

Reviewing MAIN IDEAS

13. When you exercise, your need for O_2 rises. How do your respiratory and circulatory systems react to maintain homeostasis in your body?

14. Describe how the diaphragm and muscles of the rib cage help bring air into and out of the lungs.

15. Explain how, in normal respiration, CO_2 and O_2 are able to diffuse in opposite directions through the alveolar and capillary walls.

16. How does damage to the alveoli from injury or disease affect the exchange of gases in the lungs?

17. Describe how the structures of the heart make it an efficient pump.

18. Explain how the circulatory system keeps oxygen-poor blood separate from oxygen-rich blood.

19. Compare the functions of arteries and veins.

20. Advice for maintaining a healthy circulatory system always includes proper diet and exercise. Explain what impact these two factors can have on the arteries.

21. Describe the main components of blood and the function of each component.

22. Explain what happens after a blood vessel is torn.

23. Why might it be important to know your blood type?

24. Explain what the lymphatic system is and why it is considered part of the immune system.

25. Infer When people lift or push a heavy weight, their veins often puff up and become visible under their skin. Why do you think this happens?

26. Synthesize A person who is exposed to high levels of smoke during a fire may be taken to a hospital for a test to determine whether he or she has enough oxygen in the blood. Would you test the blood from an artery or a vein in this case? Explain your answer.

27. Analyze In volcanic areas, certain depressions in the ground are filled with high levels of CO_2. Animals wandering into these areas die so quickly that they have no chance of getting out. Use your knowledge of diffusion and circulation to explain why death might occur so quickly.

28. Apply If someone has a heavy weight on his or her chest, explain why after a short time it becomes difficult to breathe, even though the person's mouth and nose are not affected.

29. Predict A stroke occurs when the blood supply to the brain is interrupted. What immediate impact would this event have on the brain cells?

Interpreting Visuals

Use the diagram of the heart to answer the next three questions.

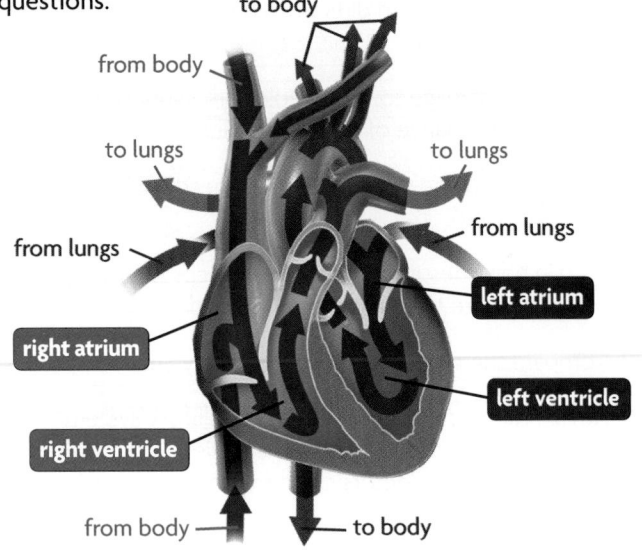

30. Identify Describe the path of blood in the heart.

31. Infer Why does the heart need two openings leading into the right atrium?

32. Analyze Which chamber(s) and valve(s) do you think would be under the most stress from high blood pressure? Explain.

Analyzing Data

A scientist is investigating the relationship between age and rates of smoking—light, medium, or heavy. Use the graph below about age and smoking rates to answer the next two questions about accepting or rejecting a null hypothesis.

AGE GROUPS AND RATES OF SMOKING

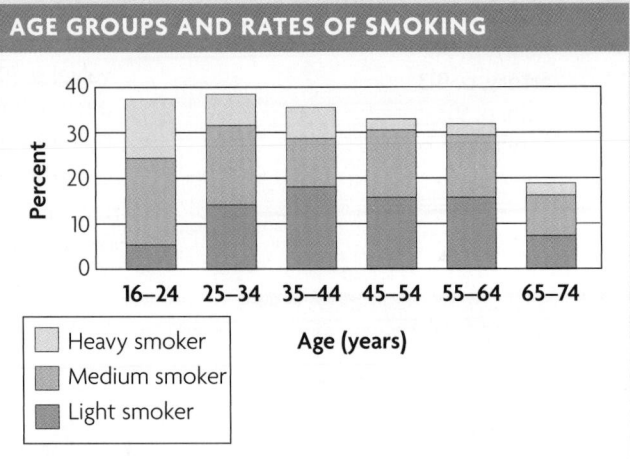

33. Evaluate One null hypothesis for this investigation might be: "There is no relationship between age and smoking rates." Based on the data, would you accept or reject this null hypothesis? Explain your answer.

34. Apply Form another null hypothesis for this investigation based on age and smoking rates. Explain whether the data would cause you to accept or reject your hypothesis.

Connecting CONCEPTS

35. Write a Proposal Suppose you are asked to make an animated film about the journey of an oxygen molecule from the time it is inhaled until it reaches a cell. Write a proposal describing your concept for the film. Include in your description the names of structures in the circulatory and respiratory systems, such as *trachea, alveoli, atrium, ventricle,* and so on.

36. Synthesize The heart and lungs work very efficiently, but they can be strengthened by exercise to work even better. For instance, the heart rate of an athlete at rest is actually lower than the resting heart rate of a person who does not regularly exercise. Why do you think this is so? Use your knowledge of the muscular, circulatory, and respiratory systems in your answer.

MICHIGAN STANDARDS-BASED ASSESSMENT

1.

Blood Type Compatibility	
Blood Type	**Can Receive Blood From**
A	A or O
B	B or O
AB	A, B, AB, O
O	O

This chart shows compatibility between different blood types. What would happen if a person with type O blood received a blood transfusion of any other blood type? **B1.1E**

A There would be no complications because any blood type can be exchanged for another.

B Complications would result as the immune system attacks the foreign blood cells.

C A larger amount of the different blood type would be needed to supply the missing protein.

D There would be complications only if type AB were given.

2. The circulatory and respiratory systems work together to provide cells with oxygen and nutrients and remove waste products such as carbon dioxide. When you need more oxygen, how does the circulatory system respond? **B2.3d**

A More blood is sent to the lungs and less to the rest of the body.

B The blood vessels to the arms and legs constrict to conserve oxygen.

C The heart beats faster to match the rise in breathing rate.

D Blood moves more slowly through the organs to carry away more wastes.

3. In order for the body to maintain homeostasis, the intake of oxygen into the lungs must be followed by **B2.3e**

A an increase in blood pressure.

B the exhalation of carbon dioxide.

C a decrease in gas exchange.

D a decrease in blood flow.

4.

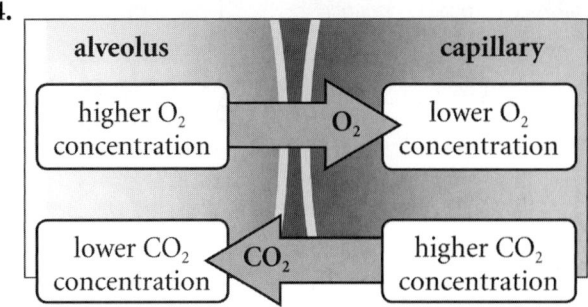

As shown above, gas exchange occurs between the alveoli and the capillaries of the lungs. What process is this diagram illustrating? **B2.3d**

A circulation

B absorption

C diffusion

D exhalation

5. At higher elevations, the air has a lower concentration of oxygen. What effect would living at higher elevations have on a person's lung capacity? **B2.3d**

A It would be larger to take in more oxygen.

B It would be smaller because the lungs need less oxygen.

C It would be larger because there is more carbon dioxide.

D It would be the same regardless of elevation.

> **THINK THROUGH THE QUESTION**
>
> Think about what *concentration* means in this context. At higher elevations, a standard breath of air would contain less oxygen than would the same volume of air at lower elevations.

6. The circulatory system helps to maintain a stable body temperature as you exercise. Which statement *best* describes this process? **B2.3e**

A Heat produced by the muscles is absorbed by the surrounding blood, where it cools.

B Blood carries excess heat from the muscles to the skin, which allows heat to escape.

C The circulatory and lymphatic systems work together to remove heat from the muscles.

D Excess heat from the muscles is transported to the heart and lungs, where it cools.

31 Immune System and Disease

KEY CONCEPTS

31.1 Pathogens and Human Illness
Germs cause many diseases in humans.

31.2 Immune System
The immune system consists of organs, cells, and molecules that fight infections.

31.3 Immune Responses
The immune system has many responses to pathogens and foreign cells.

31.4 Immunity and Technology
Living in a clean environment and building immunity help keep a person healthy.

31.5 Overreactions of the Immune System
An overactive immune system can make the body very unhealthy.

31.6 Diseases That Weaken the Immune System
When the immune system is weakened, the body cannot fight off diseases.

Online BIOLOGY CLASSZONE.COM

Animated BIOLOGY

View animated chapter concepts.
• Vaccines and Active Immunity
• Destroy the Invaders

BIOZINE

Keep current with biology news.
• Featured stories
• News feeds
• Bio Bytes

RESOURCE CENTER

Get more information on
• Immune Response
• Allergies
• Autoimmune Disorders

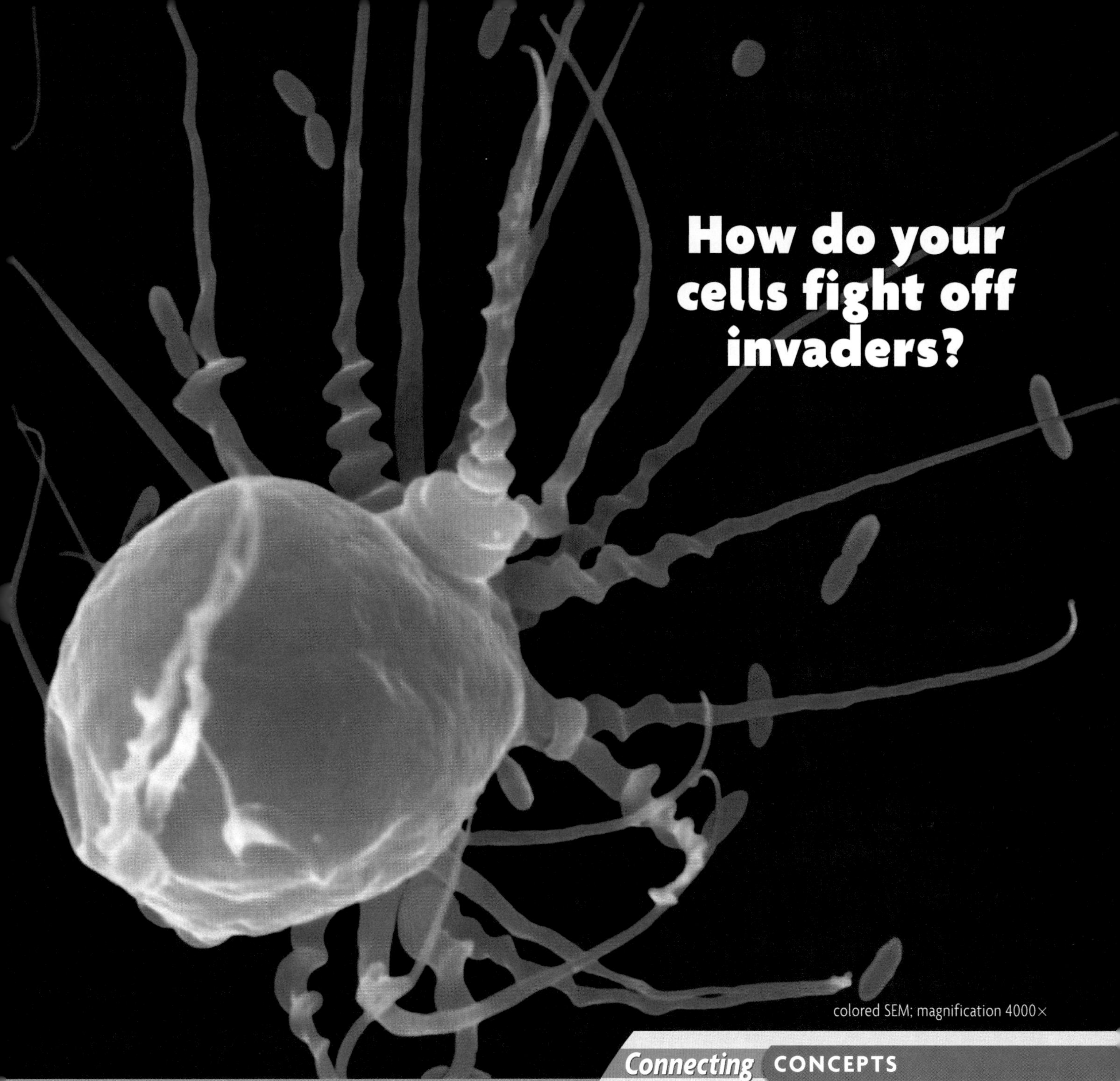

How do your cells fight off invaders?

colored SEM; magnification 4000×

Yyou do not get sick every time disease-causing germs invade your body. Sometimes white blood cells, like the one in blue above, attack and destroy invaders without your feeling ill. Other times, you get sick because germs, such as the purple *E. coli* above, start winning. Fortunately, a healthy immune system can overpower many different types of germs—even when the germs temporarily gain the upper hand.

Connecting CONCEPTS

Plants Spots on a plant's leaves are evidence that the plant's immune system is fighting an infection. When a germ invades a plant, the infected cells release chemicals that kill the neighboring plant cells. With the surrounding cells dead, the germ is isolated and cannot infect the rest of the plant. Here, an English oak tree leaf has responded to a parasitic infection by causing its own cells around the infection sites to die (orange).

31.1 Pathogens and Human Illness

KEY CONCEPT Germs cause many diseases in humans.

▶ MAIN IDEAS

- Germ theory states that microscopic particles cause certain diseases.
- There are different types of pathogens.
- Pathogens can enter the body in different ways.

VOCABULARY

germ theory, p. 941
pathogen, p. 941
vector, p. 944

MICHIGAN STANDARDS

B2.3C Explain how stability is challenged by changing physical, chemical, and environmental conditions as well as the presence of disease agents.

B2.r6e Analyze the body's response to medical interventions such as organ transplants, medicines, and inoculations. (recommended)

Connect Diseases caused by germs, such as the *E. coli* bacteria on the previous page, can be fatal. From 1330 to 1352, the bacteria that caused the Black Death killed 43 million people worldwide, or 13 percent of the population at the time. In 1918, a viral disease called the Spanish flu killed between 20 and 50 million people worldwide, or as much as 3 percent of the population. Because diseases can have devastating effects, scientists become concerned whenever a new disease such as HIV, SARS, or avian flu appears.

▶ MAIN IDEA

Germ theory states that microscopic particles cause certain diseases.

A disease can be either infectious or noninfectious. Infectious diseases, such as flu and polio, can be passed from one person to another because infectious diseases are caused by germs. In contrast, cancer and heart disease are non-infectious diseases. These diseases are called noninfectious because a sick person cannot pass the disease to, or infect, a healthy person. Noninfectious diseases are not caused by germs; they result from a person's genetics or lifestyle.

FIGURE 31.1 History of Medicine

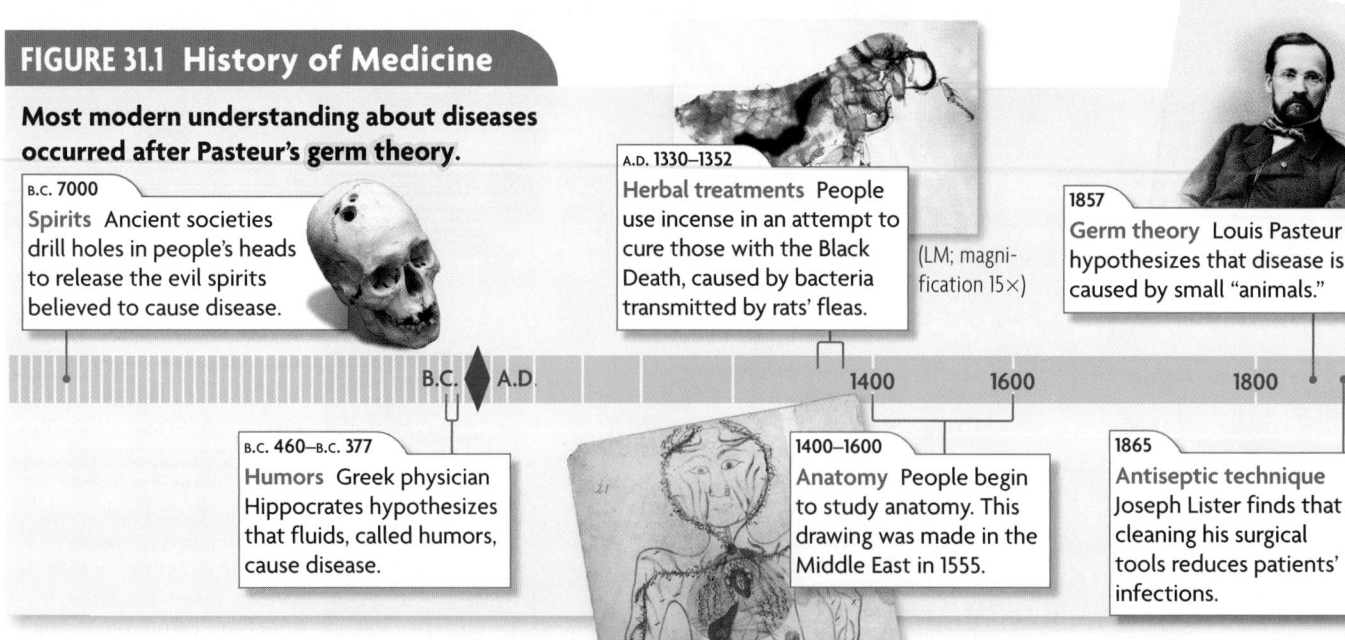

Most modern understanding about diseases occurred after Pasteur's germ theory.

B.C. 7000
Spirits Ancient societies drill holes in people's heads to release the evil spirits believed to cause disease.

A.D. 1330–1352
Herbal treatments People use incense in an attempt to cure those with the Black Death, caused by bacteria transmitted by rats' fleas.

(LM; magnification 15×)

1857
Germ theory Louis Pasteur hypothesizes that disease is caused by small "animals."

B.C. 460–B.C. 377
Humors Greek physician Hippocrates hypothesizes that fluids, called humors, cause disease.

1400–1600
Anatomy People begin to study anatomy. This drawing was made in the Middle East in 1555.

1865
Antiseptic technique Joseph Lister finds that cleaning his surgical tools reduces patients' infections.

B.C. | A.D. ... 1400 1600 1800

On the other hand, infectious diseases can be passed from one person to another because infectious diseases are caused by germs.

Today, it seems obvious that some germs cause infectious disease, but this concept is only a little more than 100 years old. It was not until the 1850s that French scientist Louis Pasteur helped make the connection between micro-organisms and disease. His theory, called the **germ theory** of disease, proposed that specific microorganisms caused diseases. These disease-causing agents are called **pathogens.** Pasteur hypothesized that if pathogens were eliminated from the body, a person would not get sick.

Pasteur's germ theory led to rapid advances in our understanding of disease, as shown in **FIGURE 31.1.** But at the time, germ theory was not immediately accepted. It took the work of two other scientists to bring about the complete acceptance of Pasteur's germ theory.

Between 1861 and 1865, about half of British surgeon Joseph Lister's patients died from infections after otherwise successful operations. After hearing Pasteur's germ theory, Lister began using a weak acid to clean his operating tools and his patients' wounds before surgery. The number of his patients who died from infection dropped dramatically to near zero.

Meanwhile, German scientist Robert Koch found that he could make a healthy animal sick by injecting it with pathogens from a sick animal. From his experiments, he concluded that four conditions must be met before one can say that a certain pathogen causes a disease. These conditions are called Koch's postulates.

- The pathogen thought to cause the disease must be present in every case in which the disease is found.
- The pathogen must be isolated and grown outside the body in a pure, uncontaminated culture.
- Healthy animals infected with the pure culture must develop the disease.
- The pathogen must be re-isolated and cultured from the newly sick animals and must be identical to the original pathogen.

Contrast **How is germ theory different from earlier theories about disease?**

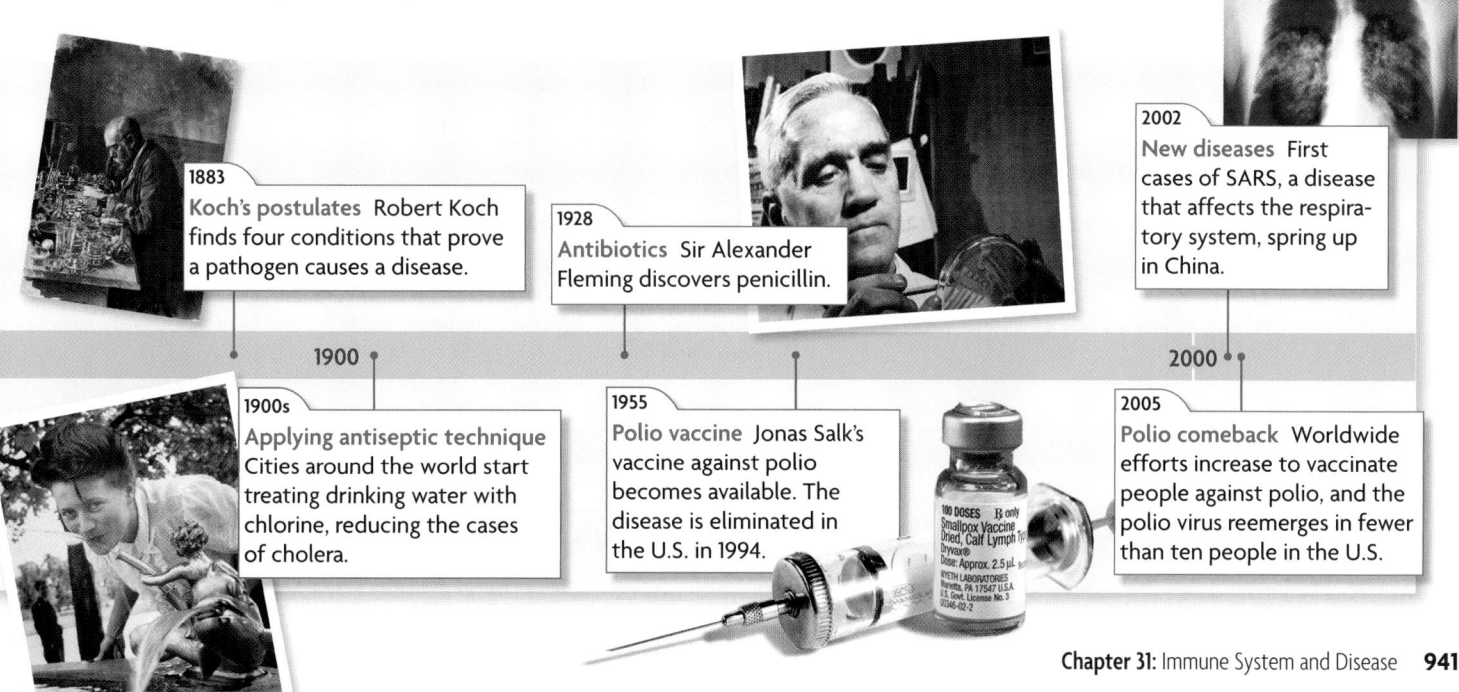

1883
Koch's postulates Robert Koch finds four conditions that prove a pathogen causes a disease.

1900s
Applying antiseptic technique Cities around the world start treating drinking water with chlorine, reducing the cases of cholera.

1900

1928
Antibiotics Sir Alexander Fleming discovers penicillin.

1955
Polio vaccine Jonas Salk's vaccine against polio becomes available. The disease is eliminated in the U.S. in 1994.

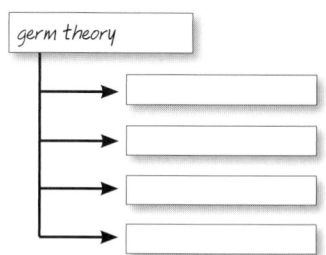

2002
New diseases First cases of SARS, a disease that affects the respiratory system, spring up in China.

2000

2005
Polio comeback Worldwide efforts increase to vaccinate people against polio, and the polio virus reemerges in fewer than ten people in the U.S.

> MAIN IDEA
There are different types of pathogens.

Traditionally, bacteria and larger pathogens were isolated by straining them through a ceramic filter with tiny pores. The disease-causing bacteria would remain on the filter, and the solution that passed through the pores was harmless.

Sometimes, however, there were no visible pathogens on the filter, and the solution caused disease. By 1898, scientists had hypothesized that some disease-causing agents must be smaller than bacteria. They called these agents filterable viruses. As better technology was developed, scientists discovered a huge variety of tiny new pathogens, which are outlined below and in **FIGURE 31.2**.

Connecting CONCEPTS

Pathogens You can read more about microorganisms and viruses that cause disease in **Chapters 18** and **19**.

- **Bacteria** are single-celled organisms. They can cause illness by releasing chemicals that are toxic to the host or by destroying healthy body cells. Food poisoning, which causes a person to become nauseous, is a sickness caused by bacteria-released toxins.
- **Viruses** are disease-causing strands of DNA or RNA that are surrounded by protein coats. Viruses are so small that they could not be seen until the invention of the electron microscope in the 1930s. These particles enter and take over a healthy cell, forcing it to stop its normal activities and produce more viruses. Viruses cause illnesses such as flus, colds, and AIDS. You will learn more about AIDS in Section 31.6.
- **Fungi** can be multicellular or single-celled organisms, such as those you read about in Chapter 19. The fungi that cause disease do so by piercing healthy cells and taking the cell's nutrients. Fungal infections usually occur in places that are warm and damp. Athlete's foot, for example, is a fungus that invades the skin cells between the toes.

FIGURE 31.2 Common Infectious Diseases Worldwide

DISEASE	PATHOGEN TYPE	HOW IT SPREADS	AFFECTED BODY SYSTEMS	DEATHS ANNUALLY
HIV	virus	body fluids	immune	3,100,000
Pneumonia	virus, bacteria	airborne	respiratory	2,000,000
Tuberculosis	bacteria	airborne	respiratory, digestive	1,800,000
Malaria	protozoa	mosquito bite	digestive, circulatory, muscular	1,000,000
Hepatitis B	virus	contaminated food/water	digestive, immune	1,000,000
Measles	virus	airborne	respiratory, nervous	500,000
Influenza	virus	airborne, direct contact	respiratory	400,000

Source: World Health Organization

- **Protozoa** are single-celled organisms that prey on other cells. Like viruses, protozoa need healthy cells to complete their life cycles. Malaria is a blood disease that is caused by a protozoan. Chapter 19 includes a description of how the protozoan that causes malaria uses red blood cells to complete its life cycle.
- **Parasites** are organisms that grow and feed on a host. Some parasites kill the host, while others drain the body's resources without killing the host. **FIGURE 31.3** shows a filaria, a parasitic worm found in tropical climates. Filaria will rarely kill its host, although some forms, such as heartworm, can be fatal in mammals. You can read more about parasitic worms in Chapter 23.

Although each of these pathogens is different, they all cause disease by attacking healthy cells. However, the way by which they attack varies.

Summarize What do all of these pathogens do that makes a person sick?

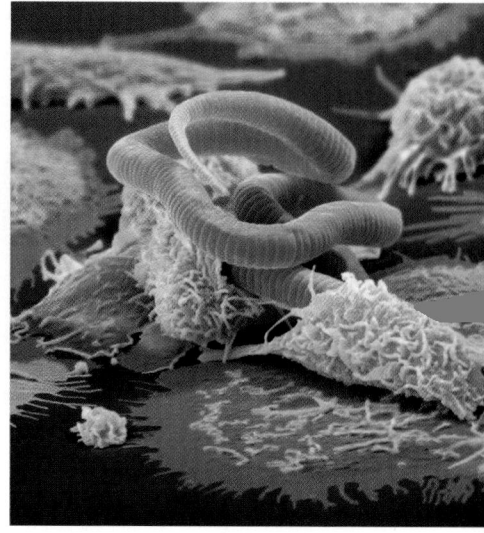

FIGURE 31.3 Filaria, such as this one, enter the body through contaminated food and can grow to be a meter long. (colored SEM; magnification 2500×)

⏵ MAIN IDEA
Pathogens can enter the body in different ways.

Before a pathogen can make a person sick, it must get inside the body. Some pathogens can be transferred by direct or indirect contact. Pathogens that spread by direct contact are those that require an infected person or animal to physically touch a healthy person. Rabies, for example, is transferred when an infected animal bites a healthy animal. HIV is transmitted through an exchange of bodily fluids, such as during sexual intercourse or sharing of infected needles. It can also be transmitted from a mother to her child through the placenta or breast milk.

QUICK LAB   MODELING

How Pathogens Spread
Pathogens are disease-causing particles. In this lab, you will model how a pathogen spreads through a population.

PROBLEM From whom did the pathogen originate?

PROCEDURE

1. Obtain a cup filled with an unknown solution. Pour half your solution into a classmate's cup. Then pour the same amount from your classmate's cup back into your cup. Now your cup contains a mixture of the two solutions.
2. Repeat step 1 two more times with different classmates. Keep a record of with whom you exchanged solutions and in which order.
3. After you have exchanged solutions with three classmates, add three drops of "pathogen"-detecting solution to your cup. If your solution becomes pink, your cup contains the pathogen.

ANALYZE AND CONCLUDE

1. **Analyze** If your cup contained the pathogen, can you identify its origin? If your cup did not contain the pathogen, is it possible that any of the other solutions poured into your cup contained the pathogen?
2. **Analyze** Only one person in your class began with the pathogen in his or her cup. How can you determine whose cup had it?

MATERIALS
- 8-oz cup
- 100 mL unknown solution
- eyedropper
- 3 drops "pathogen"- detecting solution

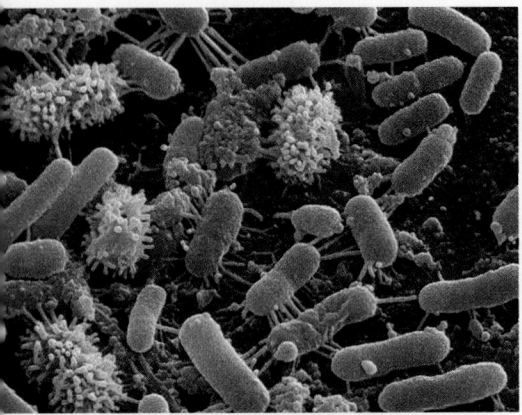

FIGURE 31.4 Sometimes even surfaces that we think are clean are covered with pathogens. Here you can see different types of pathogens clinging to a kitchen sponge. (colored SEM; magnification 6000×)

Pathogens that are spread by indirect contact can survive on nonliving surfaces, such as tables, door knobs, or kitchen sponges—as shown in **FIGURE 31.4**. Some parasitic worm larvae live in the soil and can burrow through the skin of a victim's bare foot. Once inside the body, the larvae travel into the victim's intestines. Species that remain in the intestines throughout their life cycle can cause discomfort, nausea, and diarrhea.

Other pathogens are spread through the air. When you cough or sneeze, you release droplets into the air around you. When you are sick, these droplets might contain pathogens. Other airborne pathogens are lightweight and hearty enough that they can survive in the air on dry particles. Respiratory diseases such as tuberculosis and SARS are examples of airborne diseases.

Still other pathogens are spread by vectors. A **vector** is anything that carries a pathogen and transmits it into healthy cells. Insects are examples of vectors. Insects can transmit bacteria, viruses, and protozoa. The Black Death, which killed millions of people in the 1300s, is caused by a bacterium that lives in the stomach of a rat's flea. People got sick with the Black Death when they were bitten by a contaminated flea. Mosquitoes can also pass diseases between animals. The protozoan that causes malaria, for example, completes a part of its life cycle in the gut of a mosquito. Mosquitoes can also transmit diseases between species. West Nile virus originally affected birds, but when an infected mosquito bites a person with a weak immune system, the virus can cause the person's brain to swell. However, insects cannot transmit pathogens, such as HIV, that die when the insect digests the infected human blood cells.

Pathogens can also be transmitted through food. Some diseases are caused by pathogens that were alive when the food-animal lived. Mad cow disease, which causes neurological problems in humans, is caused by an abnormal protein that is found in some beef cattle. Salmonella, which causes vomiting, is found in the intestines of some pigs and other animals. Most parasitic worm eggs enter the body through the mouth, as when a person eats contaminated food. Other diseases, such as various types of food poisoning, are caused by bacteria or fungi that decompose food.

Infer Why are some diseases only spread by insect bites?

31.1 ASSESSMENT

ONLINE QUIZ
ClassZone.com

REVIEWING ▶ MAIN IDEAS

1. What conditions must be met before a specific **pathogen** is proved to cause a disease?

2. Name five general types of pathogens.

3. What are some ways in which pathogens spread?

CRITICAL THINKING

4. **Contrast** How do bacteria and viruses differ in the ways they affect cells in the body?

5. **Synthesize** How did the work of Lister and Koch support Pasteur's **germ theory** of disease?

Connecting CONCEPTS

6. **Viruses** Viruses infect healthy cells by injecting their genetic material into them. How are viruses similar to **vectors**? If the virus is the vector, what is the pathogen?

31.2 Immune System

KEY CONCEPT The immune system consists of organs, cells, and molecules that fight infections.

MAIN IDEAS

- Many body systems protect you from pathogens.
- Cells and proteins fight the body's infections.
- Immunity prevents a person from getting sick from a pathogen.

VOCABULARY

immune system, p. 945
phagocyte, p. 946
T cell, p. 946
B cell, p. 946
antibody, p. 947

interferon, p. 947
passive immunity, p. 948
active immunity, p. 948

Review
pathogen, lymphocyte

MICHIGAN STANDARDS

B2.3g Compare the structure and function of a human body system or subsystem to a nonliving system (e.g., human joints to hinges, enzyme and substrate to interlocking puzzle pieces).
B2.r6e Analyze the body's response to medical interventions such as organ transplants, medicines, and inoculations. (recommended)

Connecting CONCEPTS

Hypertonic You learned in **Chapter 3** that when the environment has more solutes than a cell, water will diffuse out of the cell and the cell could die.

FIGURE 31.5 Cilia that line the throat (yellow) capture foreign particles. (colored SEM; magnification 7500×)

Connect Think of your body as a heavily guarded castle. When pathogens come to invade, they must first break down the outer wall or find a way around it. If the intruders get past the physical barriers, they must face your body's fighters in hand-to-hand combat. When the invaders gain the upper hand, you become sick. When the body's defenses are winning the war, you remain healthy.

MAIN IDEA

Many body systems protect you from pathogens.

The **immune system** is the body system that fights off infection and pathogens. Just as a castle has several lines of defense, so does your body's immune system. The immune system relies on physical barriers to keep pathogens out. However, when pathogens get past the physical barriers, the warrior cells of the immune system travel through the lymphatic and circulatory systems to reach the site of infection.

Your skin is your body's first line of defense. Like a castle's outer wall, the skin surrounds and protects your insides. The skin physically blocks invading pathogens. The skin also secretes oil and sweat, which make the skin hypertonic and acidic. Many pathogens cannot survive in this kind of environment.

Just as a castle's walls have doors and windows, your skin also has openings. For example, your eyes, nose, ears, mouth, and excretory organs are open to the environment, and so they need extra protection. Mucous membranes in these organs use hairlike cilia that are covered with a sticky liquid to trap pathogens before they move into the body, as shown in **FIGURE 31.5.**

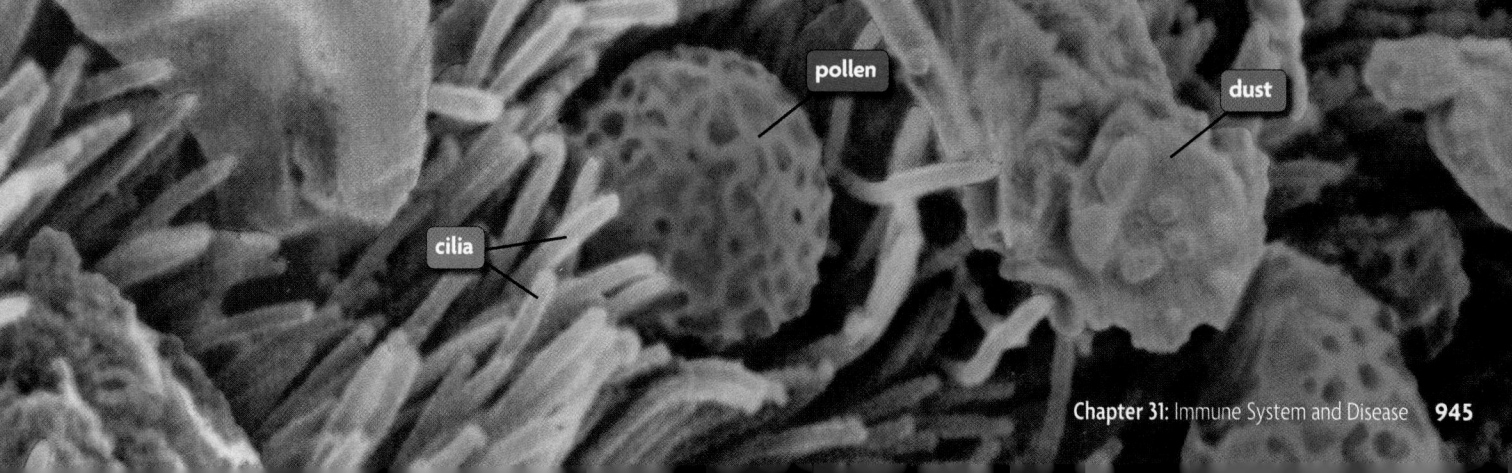

Even with skin and mucous membranes to protect you, some pathogens still get into the body. Once pathogens are inside, the immune system relies on the circulatory system to send chemical signals to coordinate an attack and to transport specialized cells to the infection.

Summarize **Name some of the tissues that help to prevent and fight infection.**

▶ MAIN IDEA
Cells and proteins fight the body's infections.

Once pathogens get past all of your outer defenses, the cells of your immune system spring into action. Just as a castle has many fighters and weapons, your immune system has many types of white blood cells and proteins.

White Blood Cells
White blood cells find and kill pathogens that have gotten past the body's external barriers. The six main types of white blood cells and their roles in fighting infection are summarized in **FIGURE 31.6**.

When a pathogen enters the body, basophils in the blood stream or mast cells found in other tissues release chemical signals. These signals attract other white blood cells to the site of the infection. If the pathogen is a parasite, eosinophils come and spray the parasite with poison. If the pathogen is a virus, bacterium, or fungus, neutrophils and macrophages go to work. These cells are phagocytes. A **phagocyte** (FAG-uh-SYT) is a cell that destroys pathogens by surrounding and engulfing them.

VISUAL VOCAB

A **phagocyte** is a cell that engulfs and destroys other cells. It comes from Greek words that translate to mean "cell eater."

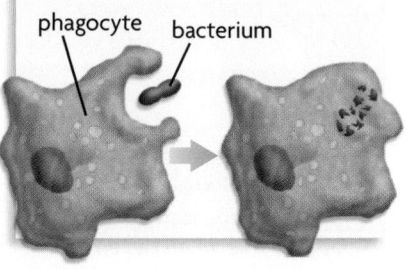

phagocyte   bacterium

After phagocytes, lymphocytes reach the infection. Lymphocytes are white blood cells that initiate the specific immune responses, which you will read about in Section 31.3. There are two types of lymphocytes: T-lymphocytes and B-lymphocytes, also called T cells and B cells. **T cells** destroy body cells that are infected with pathogens. **B cells** produce proteins that inactivate pathogens that have not yet infected a body cell.

Connecting CONCEPTS

Lymphocytes Recall from **Chapter 30** that lymphocytes are cells of the lymphatic system that attack disease-causing particles.

FIGURE 31.6 White Blood Cells

NAME	FUNCTION
Basophil	makes chemicals that cause inflammation in the bloodstream
Mast cell	makes chemicals that cause inflammation in other body tissues
Neutrophil	engulfs pathogens and foreign invaders; phagocyte
Macrophage	engulfs dead or damaged body cells and some bacteria; phagocyte
Lymphocyte	destroys infected body cells or produces proteins that inactivate pathogens
Eosinophil	injects poisonous packets into parasites, such as protozoa

IDENTIFYING EXPERIMENTAL DESIGN FLAWS

Sometimes scientific investigations can be flawed as a result of how the experiments were designed. Such design problems could include having a sample that is not representative of the population or one that is too small. This can result in the collection of invalid data, incorrect conclusions, and the release of misleading information.

To study how common certain diseases are in the United States, a student interviews 100 people as they exit a small Midwestern hospital. The student asks them if they have ever had any of five specific infectious diseases. He calculates the percent of people who responded "yes" to each question and puts the data in the graph to the right.

Based on his data, the student concludes that chickenpox is the most contagious disease of the five diseases studied. He also concludes that people in the United States no longer get tuberculosis.

1. **Evaluate** What problems exist with the sample population in this investigation?

2. **Analyze** Are the conclusions drawn from this data accurate? Why or why not?

3. **Evaluate** How could this investigation be redesigned to produce valid results?

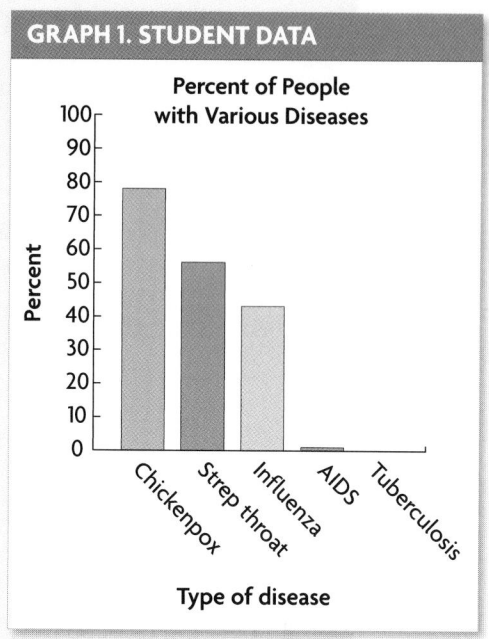

GRAPH 1. STUDENT DATA

Percent of People with Various Diseases

(bar graph: y-axis "Percent" from 0 to 100; x-axis "Type of disease" with categories Chickenpox, Strep throat, Influenza, AIDS, Tuberculosis)

Proteins

The immune system uses three types of proteins to fight off invading pathogens: complement proteins, antibodies, and interferons.

- Complement proteins are made by white blood cells and by certain organs. Some complement proteins weaken a pathogen's cell membrane, allowing water to enter the cell and cause it to burst. Others attract phagocytes to the infected area. Still others cause microbes to stick to the walls of blood vessels, where they can more easily be found and destroyed by circulating phagocytes.

- **Antibodies** are proteins made by B cells. Antibodies destroy pathogens in one of three ways. Antibodies might make the pathogen ineffective by binding to the pathogen's membrane proteins. As **FIGURE 31.7** shows, antibodies might also cause pathogens to clump, making them easier for phagocytes to engulf and destroy. Other antibodies activate complement proteins that weaken the pathogen's cell membrane.

- **Interferons** (ihn-tuhr-FEER-ahnz) are proteins produced by body cells that are infected by a virus. Cells release interferons, which stimulate uninfected body cells to produce enzymes that will prevent viruses from entering and infecting them. If viruses cannot enter healthy cells, they cannot reproduce. Other interferons stimulate an inflammation response.

Compare and Contrast What are some differences between the ways white blood cells and proteins fight infections?

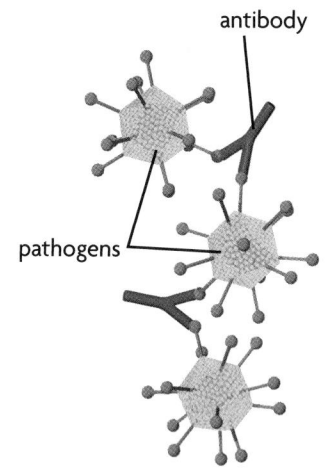

antibody

pathogens

FIGURE 31.7 Antibodies help the immune system. Some types of antibodies cause pathogens to clump, making them easier to engulf and destroy.

▶ MAIN IDEA

Immunity prevents a person from getting sick from a pathogen.

If you are immune to a pathogen, it means that you will not get sick when that pathogen invades your body. There are two types of immunity—passive and active.

Passive Immunity

Passive immunity is immunity that occurs without the body's undergoing an immune response. Passive immunity is transferred between generations through DNA and between mother and child.

Some viruses can be spread between different species. A pathogen that infects a bird might infect a person as well. However, some viruses only make members of a specific species sick. Genetic immunity is immunity that a species has because a pathogen is not specialized to harming that species. Infants have another type of immunity. Inherited immunity occurs when pathogen-fighting antibodies in a mother's immune system are passed to the unborn baby through the umbilical cord or the mother's milk.

Active Immunity

Active immunity is immunity that your body produces in response to a specific pathogen that has infected or is infecting your body. Acquired immunity is a type of active immunity that occurs after your immune system reacts to a pathogen invasion. Acquired immunity keeps you from becoming sick by a particular pathogen more than once. We will look more closely at how the immune system produces acquired immunity in the next section.

Sometimes people get the same colds or flus over and over again throughout their lifetimes. This occurs because the viruses that cause these sicknesses mutate very quickly. Each time a different strain of virus invades, your immune system has to start from the beginning again. On the other hand, your immune system destroys repeat invaders before you get sick.

Contrast How do passive and active immunity differ?

NSTA *SCiLINKS*
scilinks.org
To find out more about the immune system, go to scilinks.org.
Keycode: MLB031

31.2 ASSESSMENT

REVIEWING ▶ MAIN IDEAS

1. How does the **immune system** work with other body systems to prevent and fight disease?

2. How do **phagocytes** help to fight infections?

3. Which of the two types of immunity requires white blood cells? Explain.

CRITICAL THINKING

4. **Contrast** How do complement proteins differ from **antibodies**?

5. **Predict** If a person had a disease that prevented lymphocytes from maturing, how would the immune system's response to infection change?

Connecting CONCEPTS

6. **Protein Synthesis** How might a person's immune system be affected if a portion of the DNA that codes for **interferons** has mutated?

MATERIALS

- slide of normal lymph tissue
- slide of diseased lymph tissue
- slide of normal lung tissue
- slide of diseased lung tissue (lung cancer or pneumonia)
- slide of normal red blood cells
- slide of anemic red blood cells
- slide of healthy stomach tissue
- slide of ulcer cells
- slide of normal liver
- slide of sclerosis of the liver
- microscope

PROCESS SKILLS

- **Observing**
- **Analyzing**

B1.1C Conduct scientific investigations using appropriate tools and techniques (e.g., selecting an instrument that measures the desired quantity—length, volume, weight, time interval, temperature—with the appropriate level of precision).

Observing Normal and Diseased Tissue

In this lab, you will examine different cells and tissues under the microscope and compare the appearance of normal tissue with that of diseased tissue.

PROBLEM How do diseased tissues differ from normal ones?

PROCEDURE

1. Choose three slides of different healthy tissues and three slides of the same types of tissues with disease.

2. Examine a slide of normal tissue under low power and high power on the microscope. Draw the cells that you see.

3. Examine a slide of the same kind of tissue, but diseased, under low power and high power on the microscope. Draw the cells that you see.

4. Repeat steps 2 and 3 with each of the remaining slides that contain the different types of tissues.

ANALYZE AND CONCLUDE

1. **Contrast** How do each of the diseased tissues you observed differ from the normal tissues?

2. **Compare** What do the diseased tissues have in common with one another?

3. **Infer** Using what you know about pathogens, why do you think a tissue's appearance changes when it is infected?

4. **Infer** Using what you know about the function of each tissue, how do you think each of the diseased tissues is affected by the pathogen?

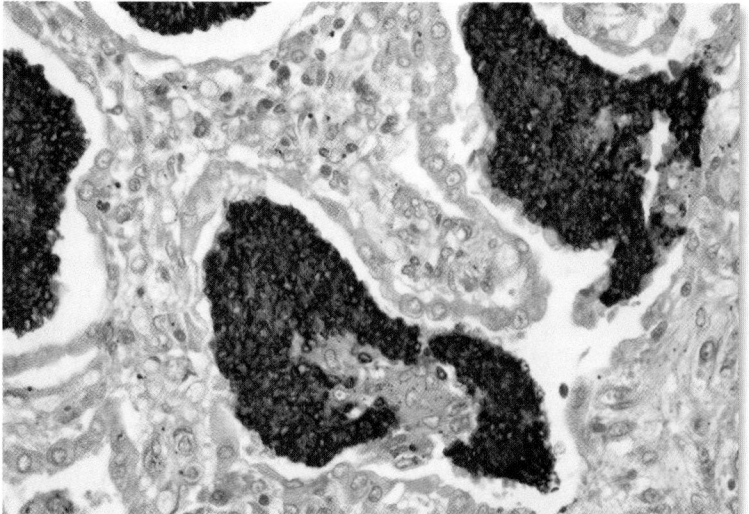

Many different viruses, bacteria, and fungi can cause pneumonia, a disease characterized by inflammation of the lungs. In this photograph, fungi (brown) have filled the aveolar spaces of the lungs (purple). (colored LM; magnification: 300×)

31.3 Immune Responses

KEY CONCEPT The immune system has many responses to pathogens and foreign cells.

▶ MAIN IDEAS

- Many body systems work to produce nonspecific responses.
- Cells of the immune system produce specific responses.
- The immune system rejects foreign tissues.

VOCABULARY

inflammation, p. 950
antigen, p. 951
memory cell, p. 951
cellular immunity, p. 952
humoral immunity, p. 953
tissue rejection, p. 954

Review
T cell, B cell

MICHIGAN STANDARDS

B2.3d Identify the general functions of the major systems of the human body (digestion, respiration, reproduction, circulation, excretion, protection from disease, and movement, control, and coordination) and describe ways that these systems interact with each other.

Connect Your body responds to pathogens in several different ways. For example, when you get a mosquito bite, your skin might swell and itch. After you are bitten, the skin around the bite becomes swollen, and the cells of your immune system attack the pathogens that entered the skin through the bite.

▶ MAIN IDEA

Many body systems work to produce nonspecific responses.

The body responds to pathogens and foreign particles with specific and nonspecific responses. Responses that occur on the cellular level are called specific defenses. Specific responses are slightly different for each pathogen. Nonspecific immune responses are those that happen in the same way to every pathogen. Some examples of nonspecific defenses are inflammation and fever.

Inflammation

Inflammation is a nonspecific response that is characterized by swelling, redness, pain, itching, and increased warmth at the affected site. Inflammation occurs when a pathogen enters the body or when the body's other tissues become damaged. For example, if you scrape your knee, it swells up. This occurs because the body is trying to head off pathogens that enter the body through the newly broken skin.

An inflammation response begins when mast cells or basophils release chemicals called histamines in response to a pathogen invasion. Histamines cause the cells in blood vessel walls to spread out. When this happens, fluids can move out of the blood vessel and into the surrounding tissues. White blood cells squeeze out of the capillary and move toward the site of infection, as shown in **FIGURE 31.8**. Once outside of the circulatory system, the white blood cells fight off the infection. When the pathogens are defeated, swelling stops, and tissue repair begins. Inflammation is a normal body response, but sometimes it occurs in response to things other than pathogens, as you will read in Section 31.5.

FIGURE 31.8 When pathogens invade your body, white blood cells squeeze through the capillary wall and move toward the infection. (LM; magnification 6500×)

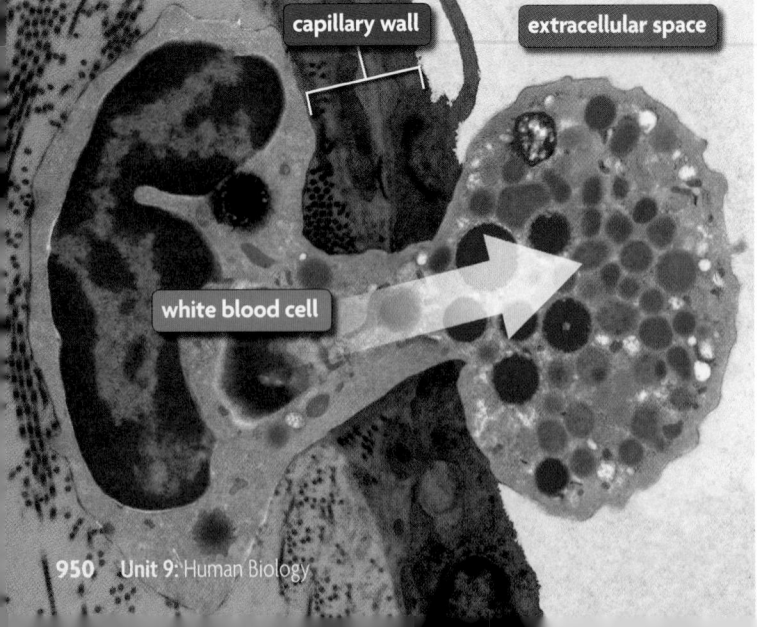

Fever

Fevers develop when mast cells or macrophages release chemicals that cause the hypothalamus to increase the body's temperature. When the infection is controlled and the mast cell's chemicals are no longer being made, the body temperature returns to normal.

Fever is a response that affects the entire body. Low fevers, around 37.7°C (100°F), stimulate the production of interferons. Recall that interferons are proteins that prevent viruses from reproducing. Low fevers also increase the activity of white blood cells by increasing the rate at which they mature, as shown in **FIGURE 31.9**. Having many mature white blood cells is important because only mature cells can destroy pathogens. The more mature white blood cells in the body, the more quickly the body can fight off an infection.

While low fevers speed up pathogen destruction, high fevers—more than 39°C, or 103°F—are dangerous. Under high fever conditions, the hypothalamus can no longer regulate body temperature. Enzymes that control chemical reactions in the body stop functioning. High fever can cause seizure, brain damage, and even death.

Connect What body systems, other than the immune system, help to produce inflammation and fever?

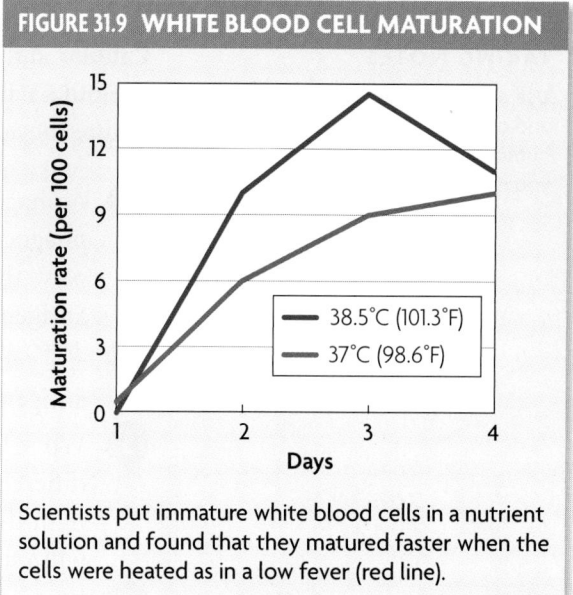

FIGURE 31.9 WHITE BLOOD CELL MATURATION

Scientists put immature white blood cells in a nutrient solution and found that they matured faster when the cells were heated as in a low fever (red line).

Source: Roberts, N. J. Jr. and R. T. Stergbigel. *American Society of Microbiology*

● MAIN IDEA

Cells of the immune system produce specific responses.

Specific immune defenses lead to acquired immunity, and they occur on the cellular level. For these specific immune defenses to work, the body must be able to tell the difference between its own healthy cells and foreign or infected cells. **Antigens** (AN-tih-juhnz) are protein markers on the surfaces of cells and viruses that help the immune system identify a foreign cell or virus. If pathogens are the invading army that is waging war on the immune system, then you can think of antigens as the pathogens' uniforms.

When the immune system detects a pathogen, it triggers an immune response. There are two types of specific immune system responses: cellular and humoral immune responses. Although the two responses are different, as you will read on the next page, they both produce acquired immunity. Immunity is acquired when your body produces memory cells after fighting off an infection. **Memory cells** are specialized T and B cells that provide acquired immunity because they "remember" an antigen that has previously invaded your body. So when memory cells come across this antigen a second time, they quickly destroy the pathogen before the body has a chance to get sick. You will learn more about how memory cells work in Section 31.4, when you read about vaccines. Now, we will discuss how the immune system fights a pathogen that it is encountering for the first time.

Connecting CONCEPTS

T cells and B cells Recall from the previous section that T and B cells are lymphocytes that are specialized to fight off pathogens.
- T cells destroy infected body cells.
- B cells produce proteins that inactivate pathogens.

TAKING NOTES

Use a Venn diagram to compare and contrast the cellular and humoral immune responses as you read this section.

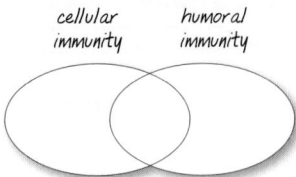

cellular immunity   humoral immunity

Cellular Immunity

Cellular immunity is an immune response that depends on T cells. As shown in **FIGURE 31.10**, T cells attach to infected body cells and cause them to burst. Before they can do this, however, T cells must become activated.

1 A phagocyte recognizes a foreign invader and engulfs it. Once inside the phagocyte, the invader's antigens are removed, and the phagocyte displays them on its cell membrane. A phagocyte that displays foreign antigens on its membrane is called an antigen-presenting cell.

2 A T cell encounters the antigen-presenting cell and binds to it. The antigen-presenting cell releases proteins that activate the T cell.

3 When a T cell is activated, it begins to divide and differentiate into two different types of T cells: activated and memory. The activated T cells will fight the current infection, but the memory T cells act as reserves that will wait for future invasions.

4 The activated T cells bind to and destroy infected body cells.

FIGURE 31.10 Cellular Immunity

In cellular immunity, T cells destroy infected body cells.

1 Phagocytes engulf pathogens and display the pathogens' antigens on their membrane surface.

pathogen

antigens

antigens

2 A T cell binds to the antigen-presenting cell. The antigen-presenting cell activates the T cell.

T cell

receptors

3 The T cell divides and differentiates into memory T cells and activated T cells.

memory T cells

4 The activated T cells bind to infected body cells and cause them to burst.

activated T cells

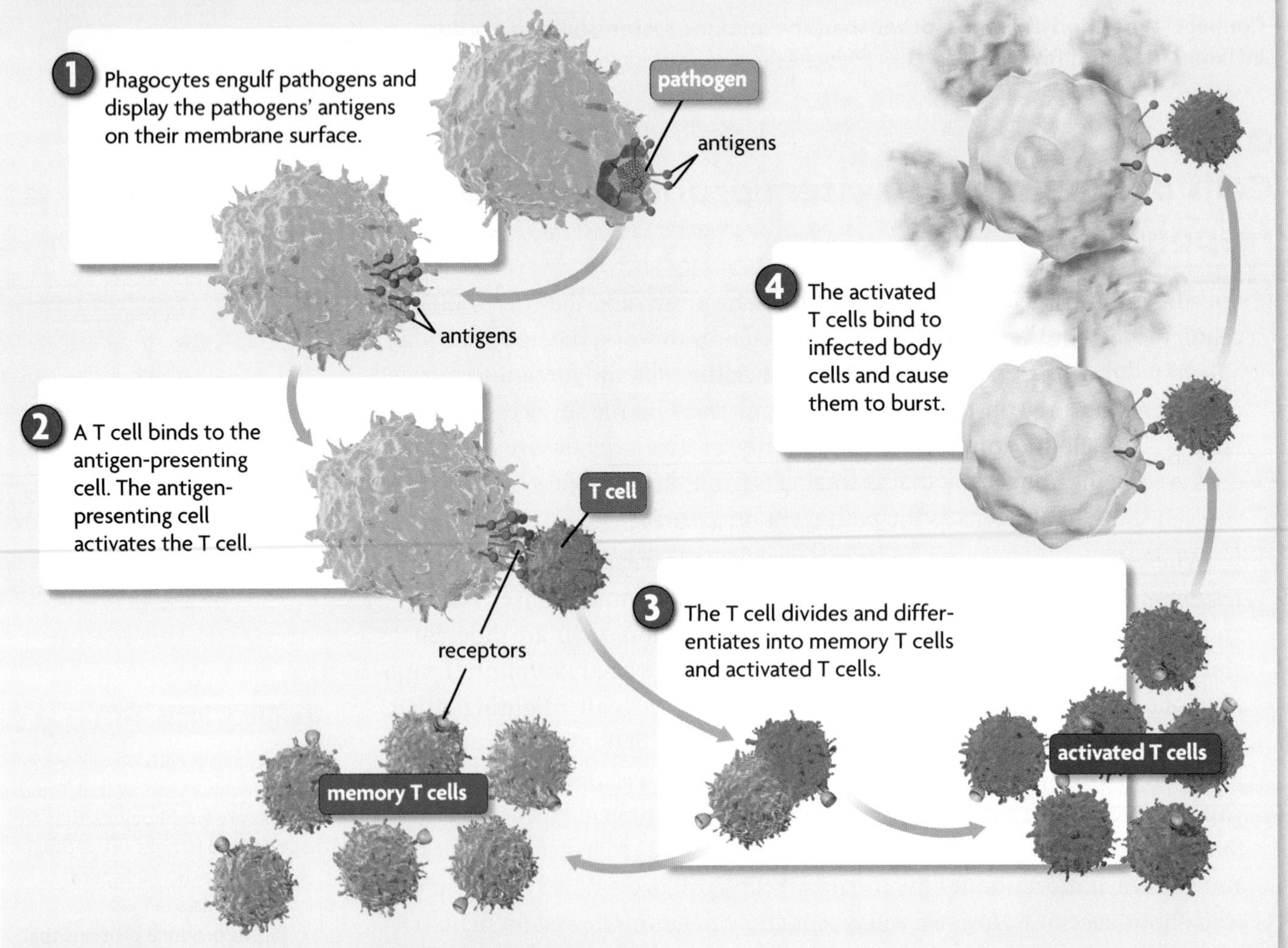

Analyze What allows T cells to identify infected body cells?

Humoral Immunity

Humoral immunity is a type of immune response that depends on antibodies. Different types of antibodies fight pathogens by either causing them to burst, inactivating them, or causing them to clump, as shown in **FIGURE 31.11**.

1 A pathogen binds to a B cell. The B cell engulfs the pathogen and puts part of the antigen onto its surface.

2 When a T cell encounters the antigen-presenting B cell, it binds to the antigens. Then the T cell releases proteins that activate the B cell.

3 Once activated, the B cell divides and differentiates into activated B cells and memory B cells.

4 Activated B cells produce as many as 2000 pathogen-specific antibodies per second. In some cases, antibodies cause pathogens to clump.

5 Phagocytes engulf and destroy the pathogen clumps.

Compare What are some similarities between the cellular and humoral responses?

VOCABULARY

Humoral immunity comes from the Latin word *humor,* which means "fluid." *Humoral immunity* refers to the immunity given by antibodies that travel in the blood and other body fluids.

FIGURE 31.11 Humoral Immunity

In **humoral immunity**, B cells produce antibodies that help destroy pathogens.

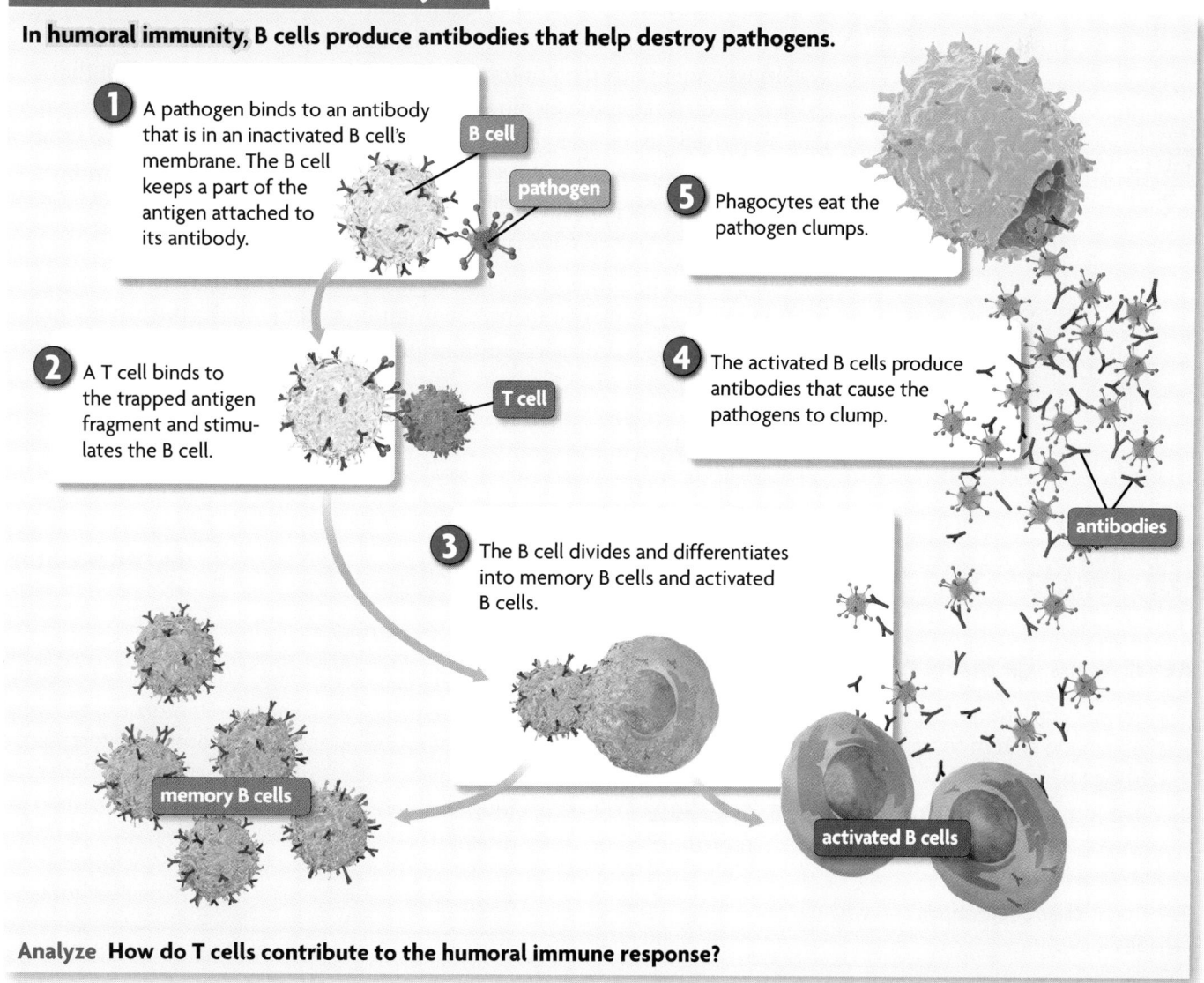

1 A pathogen binds to an antibody that is in an inactivated B cell's membrane. The B cell keeps a part of the antigen attached to its antibody.

B cell

pathogen

5 Phagocytes eat the pathogen clumps.

2 A T cell binds to the trapped antigen fragment and stimulates the B cell.

T cell

4 The activated B cells produce antibodies that cause the pathogens to clump.

antibodies

3 The B cell divides and differentiates into memory B cells and activated B cells.

memory B cells

activated B cells

Analyze How do T cells contribute to the humoral immune response?

▶ MAIN IDEA

The immune system rejects foreign tissues.

Connecting CONCEPTS

Blood Typing Blood cells have different proteins, called Rh factors, on their cell walls. Review **Chapter 30** for more information on how blood types affect a person's ability to receive blood transfusions.

All cells have protein markers on their surfaces. Your body must constantly decide whether your healthy cells are, in fact, your own or foreign cells. Sometimes you do not want your body to be able to identify foreign tissues and cells. For example, when you receive a blood transfusion or an organ transplant, you want to fool your body into ignoring the foreign tissues' protein markers. If protein markers on donated tissue differ from your cells' proteins, an immune response can occur and the transplanted tissue will be attacked and rejected. **Tissue rejection** occurs when the recipient's immune system makes antibodies against the protein markers on the donor's tissue.

Antigen receptors on the surface of your white blood cells determine whether your immune system will attack or ignore a transplanted tissue. Cells with protein markers that fit into the white blood cells' receptor molecules are foreign. Cells with protein markers that do not interact with white blood cells' receptor molecules are not detected by the immune system.

People have thousands of different combinations of protein markers on their cells. The fewer of these protein markers that differ between a donor's tissue and a recipient's, the better the chance that the recipient's immune system will not attack the donor tissue. For this reason, it is important that tissues are analyzed to determine whether a donor and recipient are compatible. To prevent tissue rejection, recipients must take drugs that decrease the activity of their immune system. These drugs weaken the person's immune response against all pathogens. This leaves the recipient less able to fight off infections from viruses, bacteria, and fungi.

Other times, the immune system loses the ability to recognize the body's healthy cells. When this happens, the immune system attacks the healthy body cells. These diseases are called autoimmune diseases, and you will read more about them in Section 31.5.

Infer **Why might it be beneficial for a person to get blood or tissues donated from a relative instead of a non-related donor?**

31.3 ASSESSMENT

ONLINE QUIZ
ClassZone.com

REVIEWING ▶ MAIN IDEAS

1. How does **inflammation** help the immune system to fight pathogens?

2. What is the main difference between **cellular immunity** and **humoral immunity**?

3. What is **tissue rejection,** and why does it occur?

CRITICAL THINKING

4. **Contrast** What are the differences between a specific and a nonspecific immune response?

5. **Synthesize** Explain how the proteins on the surface of white blood cells, pathogens, and transplanted tissues interact to produce an immune response.

Connecting CONCEPTS

6. **Genetics** Doctors can test a person's blood to determine what types of proteins are on the surface of the person's blood cells. This is called blood typing. Why does blood typing reduce the likelihood of tissue rejection in blood transfusions?

31.4 Immunity and Technology

KEY CONCEPT Living in a clean environment and building immunity help keep a person healthy.

MAIN IDEAS
- Many methods are used to control pathogens.
- Vaccines artificially produce acquired immunity.

VOCABULARY
antiseptic, p. 955
antibiotic resistance, p. 955
vaccine, p. 956

MICHIGAN STANDARDS

B2.r6e Analyze the body's response to medical interventions such as organ transplants, medicines, and inoculations. (recommended)

Connect Because infectious diseases are spread from person to person, the risk of getting sick increases when there are many people in one area. Luckily, scientists have developed many different ways to control the spread of disease. Cleaning supplies, medicines, and vaccines are technologies that help to prevent against sickness or treat people who are already sick.

MAIN IDEA

Many methods are used to control pathogens.

Because pathogens can have such a negative effect on health, scientists have developed many ways to kill pathogens that our immune system might otherwise have a hard time fighting off. One way to prevent infection is to keep your environment clean. Cleaning can kill pathogens before they ever have a chance to enter your body and make you sick.

Heat and chemicals kill pathogens that are outside of the body. **Antiseptics** (an-tih-SEHP-tihks) are chemicals, such as soap, vinegar, and rubbing alcohol, that kill pathogens. Rubbing alcohol, for example, weakens cell membranes. Without a strong cell membrane, the microbe's nutrients leak out, and the microbe bursts. Antiseptics are not specific, meaning that they can kill many different types of pathogens.

FIGURE 31.12 Antibiotics have killed the bottom cell by weakening its cell wall and causing it to burst. (colored TEM; magnification 55,000×)

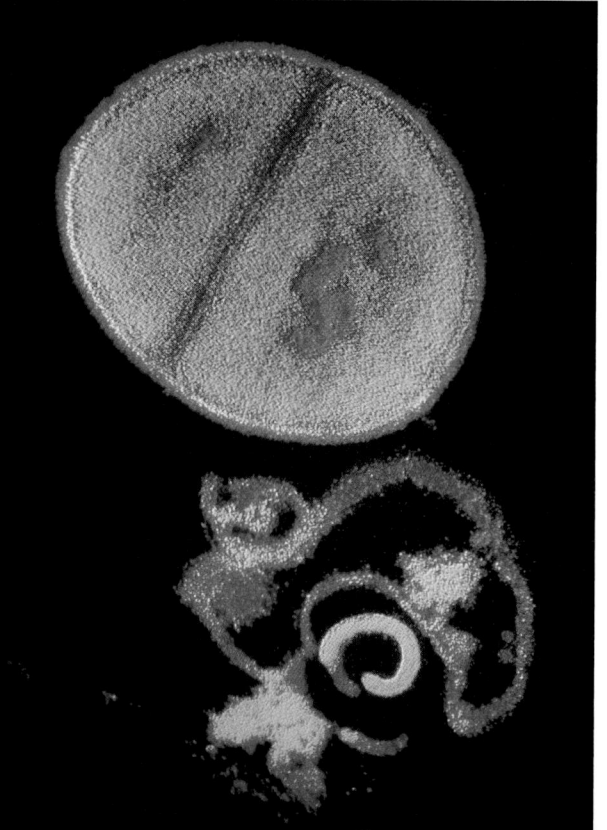

Once pathogens enter the body, sometimes they can be killed with medicines. Antibiotics are medicines that target bacteria or fungi and keep them from growing or reproducing. Antibiotics work in a variety of ways. For example, penicillin makes bacteria unable to form cell walls. The bacteria cannot divide successfully, and they burst, as shown in **FIGURE 31.12**.

Unlike antiseptics, antibiotics target one type of bacterium or fungus. As antibiotic use has become more common, antibiotic-resistant bacteria have evolved. As you read in Chapter 18, **antibiotic resistance** occurs when bacteria mutate so that they are no longer affected by antibiotics. Mutations make the bacteria resistant to the effects of antibiotics. When bacteria become resistant, scientists must find new medicines that can kill these mutant bacteria.

Compare and Contrast What are the similarities and differences between antiseptics and antibiotics?

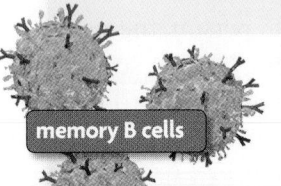

▶ MAIN IDEA

Vaccines artificially produce acquired immunity.

Vaccination cannot cure a person who is sick because vaccines only work to prevent infection. Vaccination allows a person to develop memory cells and acquired immunity against an illness without actually contracting the disease.

A **vaccine** is a substance that contains the antigen of a pathogen. The antigen causes your immune system to produce memory cells, but you will not get sick. You do not get sick because the pathogen is weakened, and it cannot reproduce or attack your cells. When you are exposed to a pathogen and have not been vaccinated, you get sick because the pathogen reproduces faster than your immune system can respond. You stop being sick when your B or T cells win the fight over the infection.

If the pathogen enters your body after you are vaccinated, your memory B cells make antibodies right away, as shown in **FIGURE 31.13**. If you have not been vaccinated, your body must go through the entire humoral immune response, and the pathogen has enough time to make you feel sick.

There are four main types of vaccines.

- Some vaccines contain whole dead bacteria or viruses.
- Live attenuated vaccines contain weak living pathogens.
- Component vaccines use only the parts of the pathogen that contain the antigen, such as the protein coat of a virus that has had its genetic material removed.
- Toxoid vaccines are made from inactivated bacterial toxins, which are chemicals a bacterium produces that causes a person to become ill.

Apply Why do you think that some vaccines, such as the flu vaccine, need to be given every year?

FIGURE 31.13 Vaccine Response

Vaccines stimulate an immune response so that you will not get sick if the real pathogen infects you.

memory B cells

1 Antigens in a vaccine trigger an immune response, and memory B cells are made.

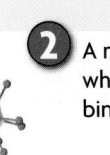

2 A memory B cell is stimulated when the real pathogen binds to it.

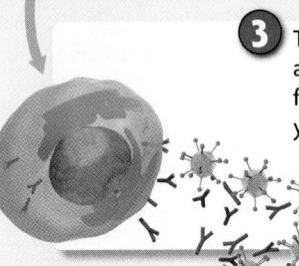

3 The B cell quickly activates and makes antibodies that fight the pathogens before you get sick.

Animated BIOLOGY
Watch how vaccines and active immunity work at ClassZone.com.

Compare How do memory cells cause a faster immune response?

31.4 ASSESSMENT

ONLINE QUIZ
ClassZone.com

REVIEWING ▶ MAIN IDEAS

1. Under what circumstances might antibiotics not be useful in treating a disease caused by a pathogen?

2. How does the immune system respond to a pathogen that the person has been vaccinated against?

CRITICAL THINKING

3. **Summarize** Write out and describe the steps that your immune system takes when you are vaccinated.

4. **Apply** Why is the immune response faster after vaccination than the response that occurs the first time a pathogen invades?

Connecting CONCEPTS

5. **Evolution** Explain why **antibiotic resistance** is considered to be evidence of evolution. (**Hint:** Review Chapter 18 and the information about natural selection.)

31.5 / Overreactions of the Immune System

KEY CONCEPT An overactive immune system can make the body very unhealthy.

► MAIN IDEAS

- Allergies occur when the immune system responds to harmless antigens.
- In autoimmune diseases, white blood cells attack the body's healthy cells.

VOCABULARY

allergy, p. 957
allergen, p. 957
anaphylaxis, p. 958

Connect Eating a peanut can be deadly for a person who has an allergy. People who are allergic to peanuts can have their immune response activated by eating just one peanut or some peanut butter. An allergy is an overreaction in which the immune system produces an extreme response to a harmless protein marker. Other times, the immune system overreacts because it loses its ability to recognize the body's own healthy tissues.

► MAIN IDEA

Allergies occur when the immune system responds to harmless antigens.

More than half of all Americans have an allergy. You probably know someone who is allergic to something—dogs, bee stings, or drugs, such as penicillin. An **allergy** is an oversensitivity to a normally harmless antigen. When someone has an allergy, the immune system produces antibodies in response to an allergen. **Allergens** are antigens that cause an allergic reaction.

When an allergen enters the body, mast cells or basophils release histamine, as shown in **FIGURE 31.14**. Histamine is a chemical that causes nonspecific immune responses, such as inflammation. Another type of white blood cell, eosinophils, also seems to have a role in allergic reactions. Eosinophils normally release poisonous chemicals that kill parasites that they encounter. These chemicals can also cause an inflammation response. Recall from Section 31.3 that in a normal inflammation response, cells release histamine. When histamine is released in response to a pathogen, the inflammation helps fight infection. When inflammation occurs in response to an allergen, the inflammation is unnecessary because it provides no benefit to the individual.

Scientists and doctors do not know why some individuals have allergies but others do not. Research suggests that some allergies are triggered by the overabundance of a certain type of antibody, and that a person's genetic makeup determines if a person has allergies. Other studies suggest that allergies are triggered when an allergen, such as one found in food, is given to a child at a certain stage in life.

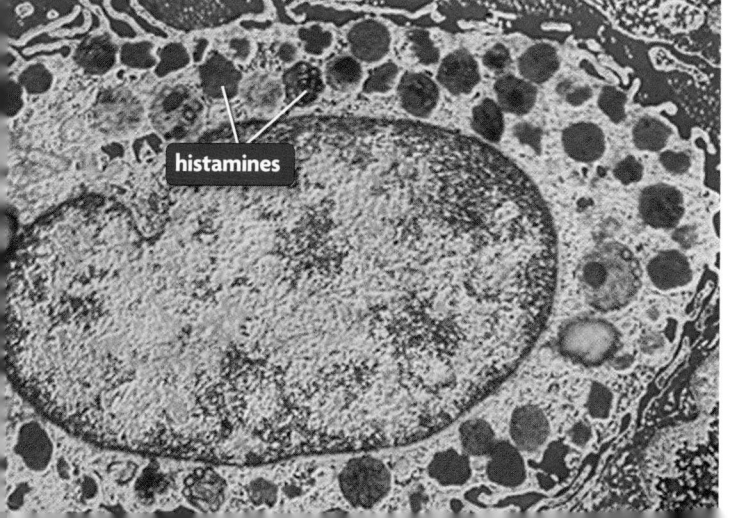

FIGURE 31.14 A basophil cell produces histamine, a chemical that triggers inflammation. (colored TEM; magnification 11,500×)

histamines

Food Allergens

An allergic reaction can occur when a person eats a specific type of food. In the United States, one to two adults in every 100 have a severe allergy to at least one type of food, and five to eight children out of 100 have a food allergy. Although any type of food can cause an allergy, the most common food allergens are milk, eggs, peanuts and tree nuts, soy, wheat, fish, and shellfish.

If a person's allergic response is severe, he or she may experience anaphylaxis. **Anaphylaxis** (AN-uh-fuh-LAK-sihs) is a condition that occurs when the immune system releases a large amount of histamine, which causes airways to tighten and blood vessels to become porous. When the airways tighten, air cannot enter the lungs or other tissues. When blood vessels become porous, blood leaks out of the circulatory system, causing the body to shut down. If not treated immediately, anaphylaxis can cause death.

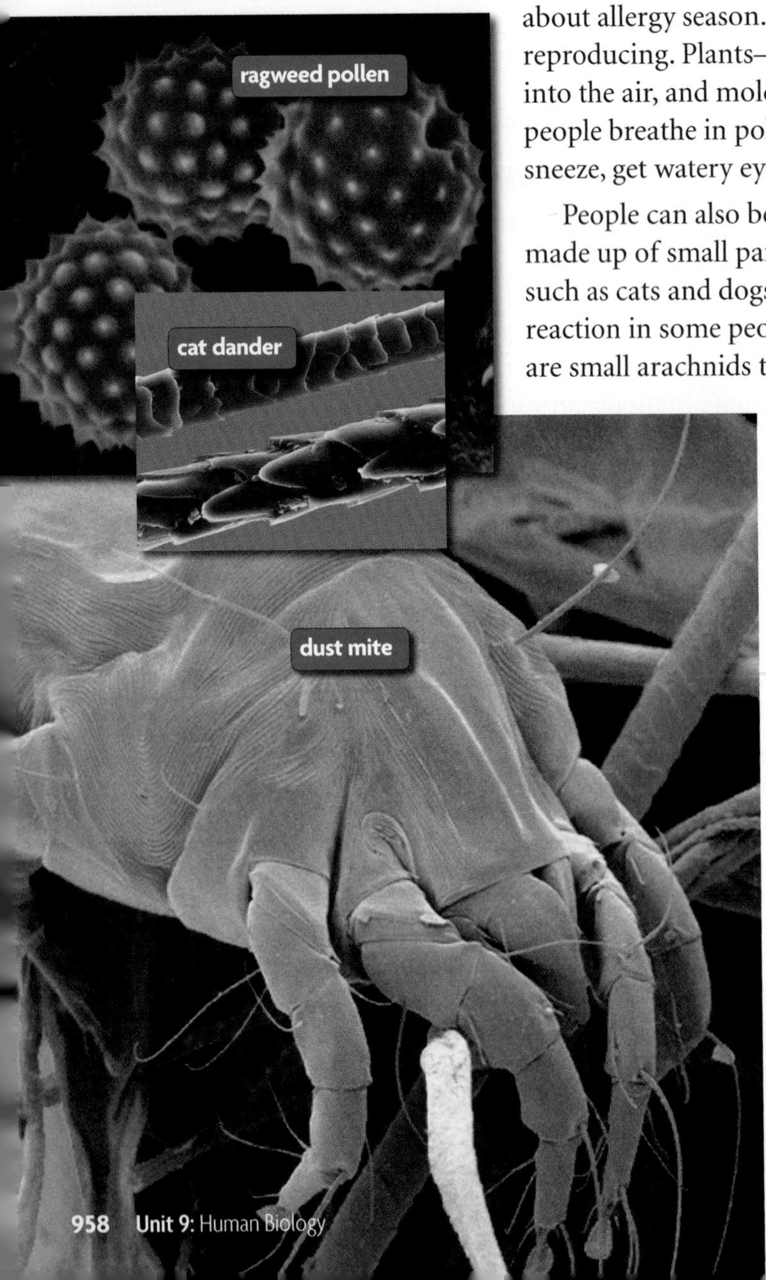

Airborne Allergens

Airborne allergens, such as the ones shown in **FIGURE 31.15,** are those that cause allergic responses when they are breathed in. You may have heard people talk about allergy season. Allergy season occurs when certain plants and molds are reproducing. Plants—such as ragweed, dandelions, and grass—release pollen into the air, and molds release spores as part of their reproductive cycle. When people breathe in pollen or spores, the histamine response may make them sneeze, get watery eyes, or become congested.

People can also be allergic to things that are indoors. Dander, which is made up of small particles in animal hair, makes some people allergic to pets, such as cats and dogs. Chemicals in animal saliva can also trigger an allergic reaction in some people. Others are allergic to the feces of dust mites, which are small arachnids that live in dust balls and cloth. In some cases, allergic reactions to airborne allergens can cause asthma. During an asthma attack the airways tighten, and breathing becomes difficult. Some people with asthma carry inhalers containing medicine that opens up the airways, reversing the effects of an asthma attack.

Chemical Allergens

Chemical allergens include metals that come in contact with the skin or those that enter the blood through injection or digestion. In metal allergies, people develop rashes when certain types of metal rest on their skin for too long. Ten percent of people in the United States are allergic to nickel, a metal that is common in jewelry.

Other chemicals, such as the venom from bee stings or drugs such as penicillin, can cause allergic reactions. These chemicals can cause anaphylaxis in a person with a severe allergy.

Compare and Contrast How is an allergic response the same as and different from a normal inflammation response?

FIGURE 31.15 Common airborne allergens include pollen, animal dander, and dust mite wastes. (colored SEMs; magnifications: ragweed 1000×; cat dander about 300×; dust mite 300×)

ragweed pollen

cat dander

dust mite

In autoimmune diseases, white blood cells attack the body's healthy cells.

Autoimmune diseases are those that occur when the immune system cannot tell the difference between the body's healthy and unhealthy cells. Normally, immune system cells attack only foreign substances, such as pathogens and infected or abnormal cells. With auto-immune diseases, the body treats its own cells as though they are foreign invaders.

In Type 1 diabetes, the immune system destroys cells in the pancreas. As a result, the pancreas makes less insulin. Without insulin, the body cannot remove glucose from the blood. Type 1 diabetes can cause death if a person does not get extra insulin into the body. There are more than 60 other autoim-mune diseases. Some of the most common ones are described in **FIGURE 31.16.**

Scientists do not know why some people develop autoimmune diseases. Research suggests that a person's genes may make them more likely to get an autoimmune disease, but that the actual immune system attack is triggered by another factor—a virus, a drug, or an environmental toxin. Currently, doctors cannot cure autoimmune diseases, but they can provide treatments that lessen the diseases' effects.

FIGURE 31.16 Common Autoimmune Diseases

AUTOIMMUNE DISEASES	BODY SYSTEMS AFFECTED	THE IMMUNE SYSTEM ...	HOW MANY AFFECTED
Rheumatoid arthritis	integumentary	breaks down tissues that line joints, making movement difficult	70 in 10,000
Type 1 diabetes mellitus	endocrine, digestive	attacks the pancreas, stopping the digestion of sugars	60 in 10,000
Hashimoto's thyroiditis	endocrine	attacks the thyroid gland, causing it to make fewer hormones	15 in 10,000
Multiple sclerosis (MS)	nervous	breaks down myelin sheaths, disrupting nerve communication	10 in 10,000
Graves' disease	endocrine	stimulates the thyroid gland, causing it to make more hormones	5 in 10,000

Apply How do autoimmune diseases disrupt other body systems?

31.5 ASSESSMENT

ONLINE QUIZ
ClassZone.com

REVIEWING ● MAIN IDEAS

1. Under what conditions is an antigen called an **allergen**?

2. Why might an autoimmune disease be considered a failure of the immune system?

CRITICAL THINKING

3. **Infer** Some **allergies** are treated with drugs called antihistamines. How do you think antihistamines might work?

4. **Analyze** Why does someone experiencing **anaphylaxis** need to receive medicine through injection instead of swallowing a pill?

Connecting CONCEPTS

5. **Ecology** Bee stings can be deadly for people who are allergic to them, but in most people, a bee sting simply hurts and warns the person to leave the insect alone. How are stingers beneficial to the survival of bee species?

31.6 Diseases That Weaken the Immune System

KEY CONCEPT When the immune system is weakened, the body cannot fight off diseases.

▶ MAIN IDEAS

- Leukemia is characterized by abnormal white blood cells.
- HIV targets the immune system.

VOCABULARY

leukemia, p. 960
opportunistic infection, p. 961
human immunodeficiency virus (HIV), p. 961
acquired immune deficiency syndrome (AIDS), p. 963

Review

T cells

MICHIGAN STANDARDS

B2.3C Explain how stability is challenged by changing physical, chemical, and environmental conditions as well as the presence of disease agents.

Connect There is no cure for AIDS. But people who are infected with HIV do not die directly from it—some people don't know that they're infected for more than ten years. Instead, as HIV weakens the immune system, they become sick with other diseases. Illnesses that weaken the immune system, such as an AIDS infection, make it easy for other pathogens to infect the body and take over.

▶ MAIN IDEA

Leukemia is characterized by abnormal white blood cells.

Bone marrow is a tissue found within bones. Red bone marrow makes red and white blood cells and platelets. In healthy marrow, new blood cells replace mature ones that die. Sometimes, blood cells do not mature properly.

Leukemia is cancer of the bone marrow. Unlike other cancers, leukemia does not form tumors. Instead, it prevents the bone marrow from functioning properly. In one type of leukemia, the bone marrow produces white blood cells that do not develop properly. Because the cells are immature, they cannot fight infections. Here is how leukemia weakens the immune system.

- Bone marrow produces white blood cells that don't mature. These cells are smaller and have less cytoplasm than mature ones, as shown in **FIGURE 31.17**.

- In effort to replace the defective white blood cells, the bone marrow produces more and more white blood cells. However, none of these new cells mature into effective white blood cells.

- Eventually, the bone marrow spends all of its time making white blood cells. As a result, it makes fewer red blood cells and platelets than are needed to replace those that die or become damaged.

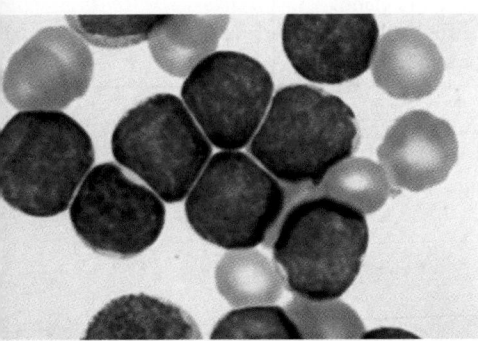
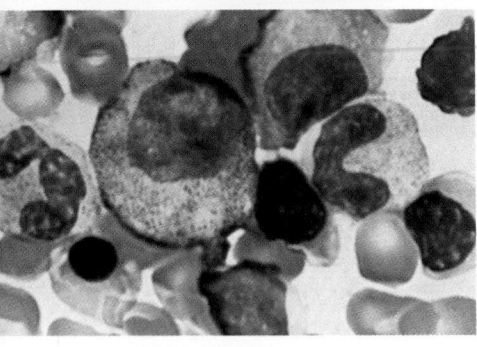

FIGURE 31.17 The cells affected by leukemia (top) do not have a ring of cytoplasm around the organelles, as the healthy blood cells (bottom) do. (magnification unknown)

To cure leukemia, the cancerous bone marrow must be replaced with healthy marrow from a donor. Before a bone marrow transplant takes place, the recipient is given large doses of radiation and chemotherapy to kill all the abnormal bone marrow cells. Then the donor marrow is put into the body. If the transplant is successful, the donor marrow will make healthy blood cells.

However, problems can arise from bone marrow transplants. In graft-versus-host disease (GVHD), the donor marrow makes antibodies against the host's healthy tissues. Chemotherapy and radiation treatments also kill both cancerous cells and healthy cells, leaving the immune system weak and open to opportunistic infections. An **opportunistic infection** is an infection caused by a pathogen that a healthy immune system would normally be able to fight off. When the immune system is weakened, an opportunistic infection can make a person very sick.

Analyze **Shortness of breath and inability to form blood clots are common symptoms of leukemia. How does the disease lead to these symptoms?**

▶ MAIN IDEA
HIV targets the immune system.

The World Health Organization estimates that more than 40 million people in the world have HIV/AIDS. During the 1980s, fewer than 2 million people had the virus. The **human immunodeficiency virus (HIV),** illustrated in **FIGURE 31.18,** is a retrovirus that attacks and weakens the immune system. A retrovirus is a type of virus that contains RNA instead of DNA. HIV is a retrovirus that has nine genes. HIV weakens the immune system, and the body is likely to get opportunistic infections.

HIV Transmission
Although HIV is a very dangerous pathogen, it can only live in human blood cells and thus will not survive for long outside of the human body. For this reason, HIV is not transmitted through shaking hands with an infected individual, or swimming in a pool with an infected person. HIV cannot be transmitted through insect bites either. Insects that suck blood, such as ticks or mosquitoes, quickly digest the blood cells in their guts. Once the blood is digested, HIV dies.

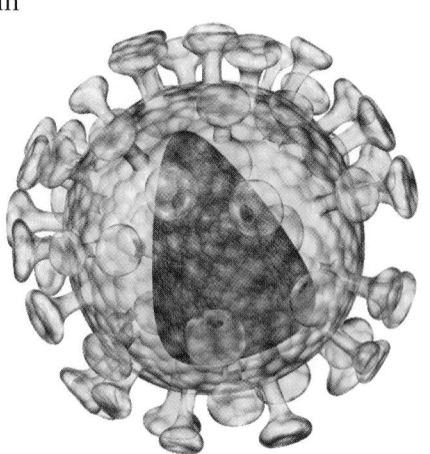

FIGURE 31.18 HIV is a small retrovirus that is covered with bumps, which are its antigens. This illustration shows an HIV about 500,000 times its actual size.

A person becomes infected with HIV when the virus enters his or her bloodstream. HIV is passed from person to person through the mixing of blood and other body fluids. HIV is transmitted through sexual intercourse with an infected individual. It can also be passed from mothers to their unborn babies through the umbilical cord. A person might also get HIV if his or her skin is pierced by a needle that an infected individual recently used. Hypodermic needles used for injecting some illegal drugs and needles used for body piercing and tattooing have transmitted HIV between individuals. However, needles that your doctor uses to give shots or take blood do not transmit HIV because doctors use a new needle for every patient.

HIV Reproduces in T Cells
HIV infects T cells, the white blood cells that trigger the body's immune responses. When HIV enters a T cell, the T cell becomes ineffective and can no longer stimulate an immune response. While the T cell cannot function in the immune system, it remains alive as a host and produces new HIV. A single T cell can give rise to thousands of HIV viruses before it eventually dies.

FIGURE 31.19 HIV Destroys T cells

HIV reproduces within T cells, killing T cells and weakening the immune system.

1 HIV ENTERS THE BODY

When HIV first enters the body, T cells activate B cells, and the activated B cells make antibodies against HIV.

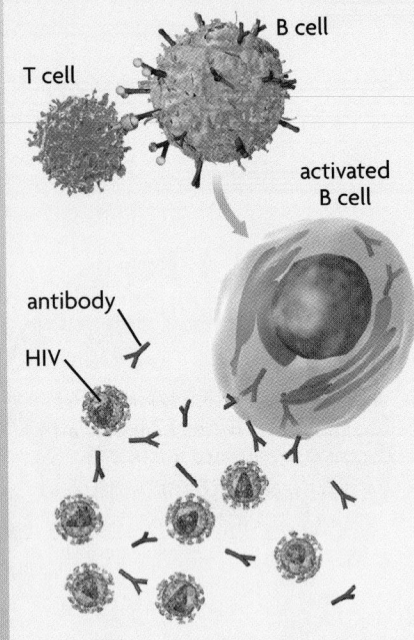

2 HIV DESTROYS T CELLS

Because HIV kills T cells and reproduces more quickly than T cells, as HIV continues to reproduce, fewer and fewer T cells remain in the body.

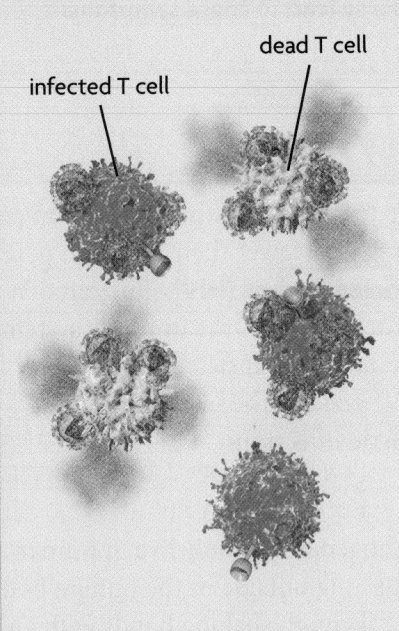

3 HIV OVERPOWERS THE IMMUNE SYSTEM

With fewer T cells, B cells cannot be activated to make antibodies. HIV and pathogens that cause opportunistic diseases take over the body.

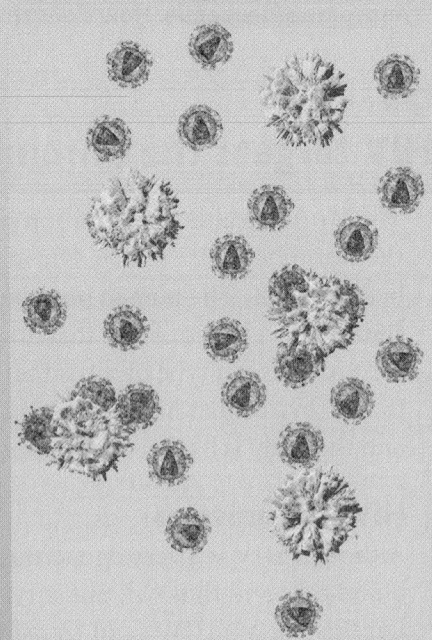

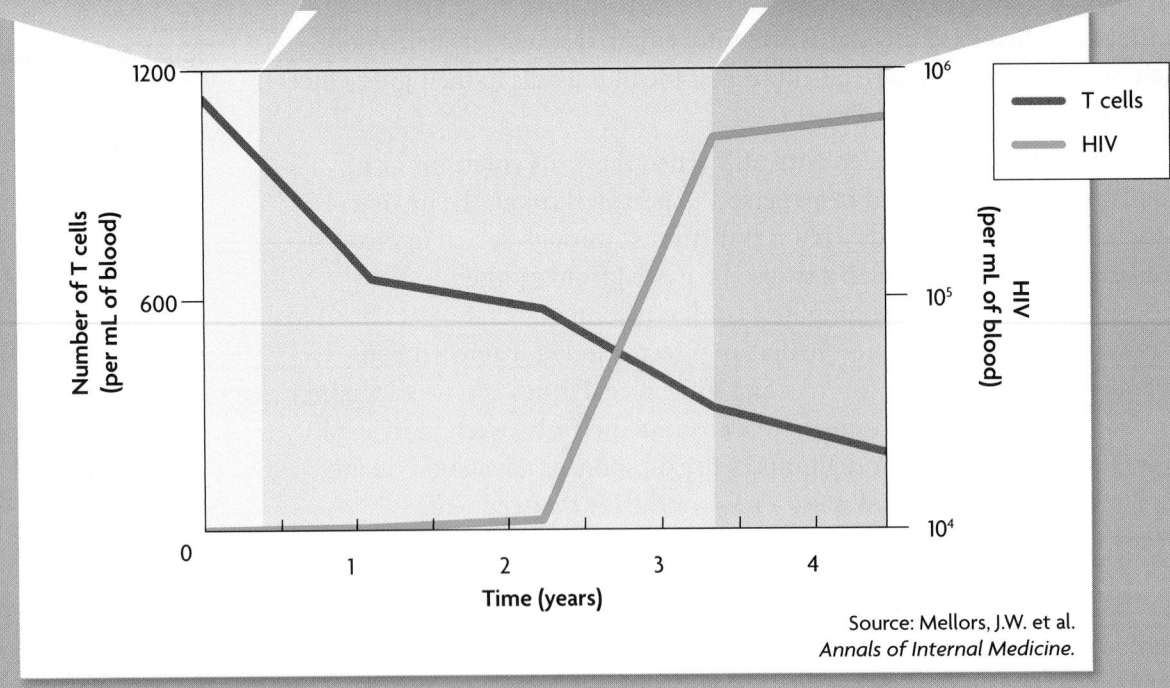

Source: Mellors, J.W. et al. *Annals of Internal Medicine.*

CRITICAL VIEWING Why might a graph comparing HIV and antibodies have a similar shape to the one above, which compares HIV and T cells?

As HIV reproduces, the body cannot make replacement T cells fast enough. As the immune system weakens, opportunistic infections begin to take over.

During the first few weeks of infection, a person usually does not feel sick. Although HIV is infecting some T cells, there are still enough healthy T cells that B cells can be activated to produce antibodies against HIV, as shown in **FIGURE 31.19**. At this stage, HIV is diagnosed by determining whether a person's blood contains antibodies against HIV.

After the initial infection, an infected person can have HIV for ten years or more without experiencing any symptoms. During this stage, more and more T cells become infected, and each cell produces thousands of HIV cells, as shown in **FIGURE 31.20**. Soon, the bone marrow cannot replace dead T cells quickly enough, and the body develops opportunistic infections and AIDS.

HIV Leads to AIDS

Acquired immune deficiency syndrome (AIDS) is the final stage of the immune system's decline due to HIV. Whereas HIV is a virus, AIDS is the condition of having a worn-out immune system. A person with AIDS can have several opportunistic infections—such as fungal infections, tuberculosis, pneumonia, viral infections, and cancers—and very few T cells. AIDS always results in death because a person's body cannot fight off its many infections.

Treatment of an HIV infection is expensive, complicated, and only slows—but does not cure—the disease. Treatment involves a combination of three to four antiviral drugs that are taken as often as five times each day. These drugs can cause many unpleasant side effects and can be very expensive. What's more, as HIV mutates, a patient might need to use many different drug combinations to keep the infection under control. Also, HIV mutates rapidly, and so far no vaccine has provided complete protection against the new strains of HIV that are constantly evolving.

Apply **How does the destruction of T cells lead to the failure of the overall immune system?**

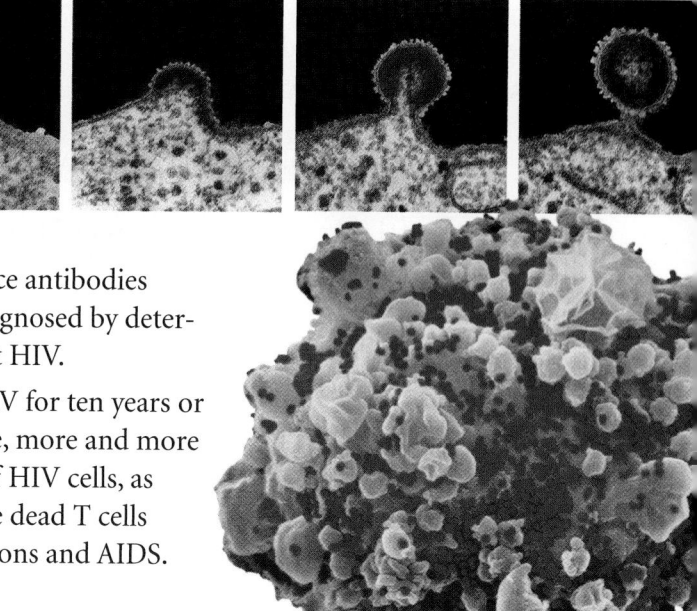

FIGURE 31.20 Thousands of HIV, shown in red, will bud off a T cell before the T cell dies. (top: colored TEM, magnification 105,000×; bottom: colored SEM, magnification 5000×)

31.6 ASSESSMENT

ONLINE QUIZ
ClassZone.com

REVIEWING ▶ MAIN IDEAS

1. How does **leukemia** affect a person's entire body?
2. How do **HIV** and **AIDS** differ?

CRITICAL THINKING

3. **Analyze** Why won't people who take multiple medications to treat HIV infections ever be cured?
4. **Compare and Contrast** Which cells of the immune system are affected by HIV and leukemia, and what parts of the immune response do these cells influence?

Connecting CONCEPTS

5. **Antibiotics** You learned in Chapter 18 that viruses cannot be treated with antibiotics. Why, then, might doctors prescribe antibiotics to patients with HIV anyway?

Use these inquiry-based labs and online activities to deepen your understanding of immune system response.

INVESTIGATION

Modeling T Cell Activation

In this lab, you will make a model that shows how a T cell becomes activated. Recall that T cells have receptors on the cell membrane surface that recognize and react with antigens. In a process similar to the lock-and-key method used by enzymes and the substrates they act on, each T cell reacts specifically with only one antigen.

MATERIALS
- sheet of white paper
- 5 colors of construction paper
- colored markers
- glue
- scissors

SKILL Modeling

PROBLEM How does a T cell become activated?

PROCEDURE

1. Decide how you will model each of the components involved in T cell activation. Keep in mind that
   - You will need to represent a T cell with receptors on the surface of the cell membrane.
   - You will also need to represent a macrophage that has ingested an antigen and has antigen fragments on its cell surface.
   - You will also need to represent chemicals released by the macrophage and the T cell that lead to the production of more T cells.

2. Refer to Section 31.3 for more information and diagrams about T cell activation as you determine which materials you will use for constructing your models.

3. Make your model.

ANALYZE AND CONCLUDE

1. **Evaluate** What are the limitations of your model?

2. **Evaluate** How would your model change if you wanted to show how a T cell is involved in the activation of a B cell?

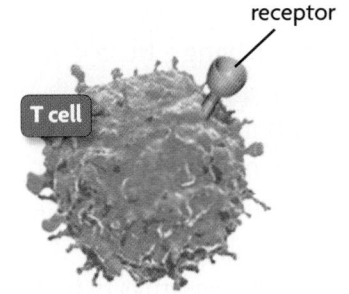

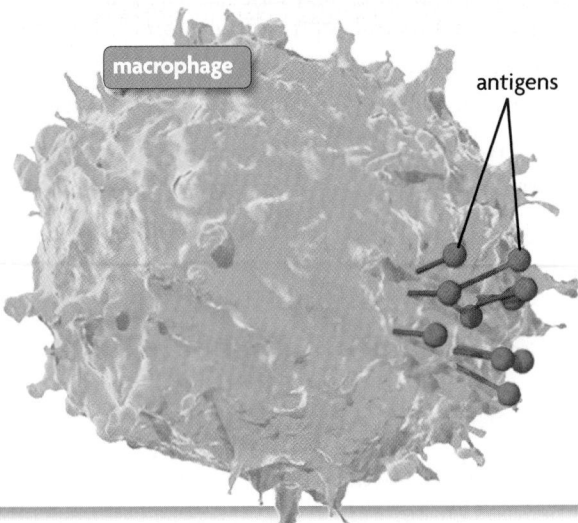

MICHIGAN STANDARDS

B1.2C Develop an understanding of a scientific concept by accessing information from multiple sources. Evaluate the scientific accuracy and significance of the information.

B2.3C Explain how stability is challenged by changing physical, chemical, and environmental conditions as well as the presence of disease agents.

INVESTIGATION

What Is an Autoimmune Disease?

Sometimes the immune system attacks and damages the body's own healthy tissues. An autoimmune disorder is a disease that occurs when the immune system can no longer tell the difference between the body's own cells and foreign cells. Graves' disease, a disorder in which antibodies attach to receptors on cells in the thyroid gland, results in an overactive thyroid gland that must be treated with medication, surgery, or radiation.

SKILL Researching

PROBLEM What is the nature of the autoimmune disease?

PROCEDURE

1. Choose one of the following autoimmune diseases:
   a. Myasthenia gravis
   b. Lupus
   c. Rheumatoid arthritis
   d. Rheumatic fever
2. Perform research to find the cause of the disease.
3. How does the disease progress?
4. What are the possible treatments?

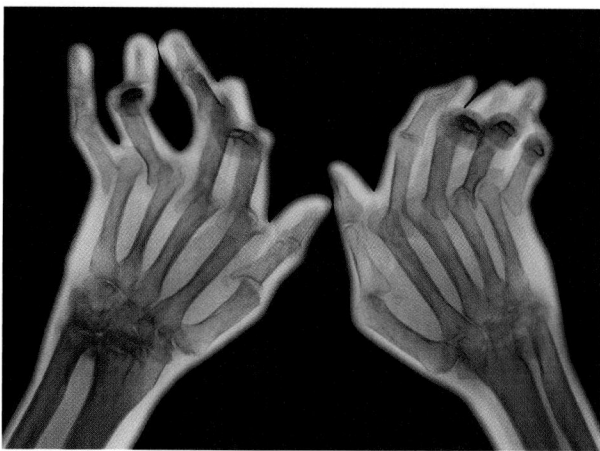

This x-ray image shows the hands of a person who is affected with rheumatoid arthritis.

Online BIOLOGY
CLASSZONE.COM

ANIMATED BIOLOGY
Destroy the Invaders
Can you keep someone from contracting an illness? Use a set of immune cells to mount attacks against a variety of pathogens to keep the person healthy.

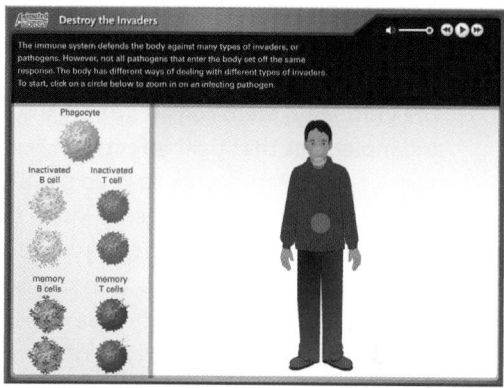

WEBQUEST
HIV infects people all over the world. You will learn more about how this deadly virus works and causes AIDS. Explore how HIV is treated and look into ongoing research devoted to overcoming HIV.

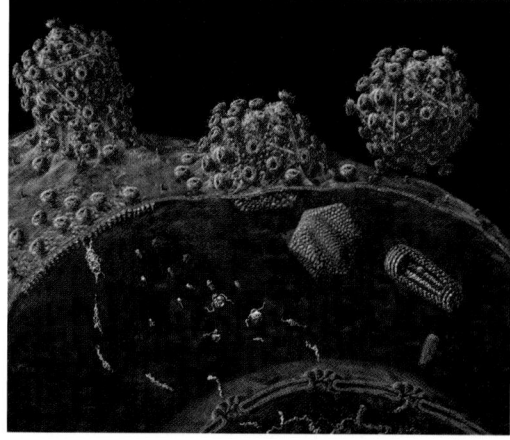

DATA ANALYSIS ONLINE
The West Nile virus first appeared in North America in 1999. The first reported infections were in the New York City area. Since then, it has spread across the United States. Graph the number of West Nile virus cases and discover just how quickly the virus spread.

Interactive ◄ Review @ CLASSZONE.COM

KEY CONCEPTS | Vocabulary Games | Concept Maps | Animated Biology | Online Quiz

31.1 Pathogens and Human Illness

Germs cause many diseases in humans. Germ theory hypothesized that microbes—not spirits—caused disease. Viruses, bacteria, fungi, protozoa, and parasitic worms are examples of pathogens. These pathogens can be spread through physical contact, the air, or vectors.

31.2 Immune System

The immune system consists of organs, cells, and molecules that fight infections. Skin and mucous membranes work to keep pathogens out of the body. Once a pathogen is inside the body, the circulatory and lymphatic systems transport white blood cells to the infection site. Some microbes and viruses do not cause illness because a person has some type of immunity.

31.3 Immune Responses

The immune system has many responses to pathogens and foreign cells. Nonspecific responses, such as inflammation and fever, are those that react the same to every pathogen. Specific responses, such as the cellular and humoral responses, are different for every pathogen. The immune system might initiate a specific response against transplanted tissues.

31.4 Immunity and Technology

Living in a clean environment and building immunity help keep a person healthy. Antiseptics destroy pathogens outside of the body, and antibiotics destroy pathogens inside of the body. Vaccines activate an immune response without getting a person sick. When the pathogen does invade, a vaccinated person's immune response is so quick that the person will not get sick.

31.5 Overreactions of the Immune System

An overactive immune system can make the body very unhealthy. Allergies occur when the immune system responds to a harmless antigen. In autoimmune diseases, white blood cells attack the body's healthy cells.

31.6 Diseases That Weaken the Immune System

When the immune system is weakened, the body cannot fight off diseases. Leukemia is characterized by immature white blood cells. HIV attacks T cells so that other pathogens can take over the body. When a person has very few T cells and several opportunistic diseases, the person has a condition called AIDS.

Synthesize Your Notes

Concept Map Use a concept map to organize your notes about lymphocytes.

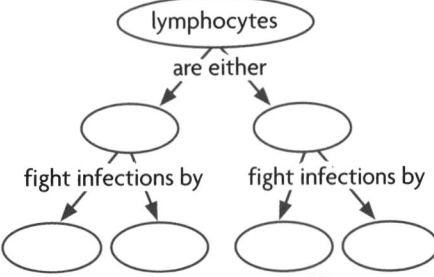

Chart Use a three-column chart to compare similar concepts.

Word	Definition	How It Is Different from Others
antigen		
allergen		
protein marker		

Chapter Assessment

Chapter Vocabulary

31.1 germ theory, p. 941
pathogen, p. 941
vector, p. 944

31.2 immune system, p. 945
phagocyte, p. 946
T cell, p. 946
B cell, p. 946
antibody, p. 947
interferon, p. 947
passive immunity, p. 948
active immunity, p. 948

31.3 inflammation, p. 950
antigen, p. 951
memory cell, p. 951
cellular immunity, p. 952
humoral immunity, p. 953
tissue rejection, p. 954

31.4 antiseptic, p. 955
antibiotic resistance, p. 955
vaccine, p. 956

31.5 allergy, p. 957
allergen, p. 957
anaphylaxis, p. 958

31.6 leukemia, p. 960
opportunistic infection, p. 961
human immunodeficiency
virus (HIV), p. 961
acquired immune deficiency
syndrome (AIDS), p. 963

Reviewing Vocabulary

Vocabulary Connections

For each group of words below, write a sentence or two to clearly explain how the terms are connected. For example, for the terms *HIV* and *AIDS*, you could write, "HIV weakens the immune system and leads to AIDS."

1. pathogen, vector

2. T cells, B cells

3. antibody, antigen

Keep It Short

For each vocabulary term below, write a short, precise phrase that describes its meaning. For example, a short phrase to describe *leukemia* could be "cancer of the bone marrow."

4. interferon

5. inflammation

6. cellular immunity

7. antiseptic

Greek and Latin Word Origins

8. The term *phagocyte* comes from the Greek word *phagos*, meaning "to eat." Explain how this meaning relates to the word *phagocyte*.

9. The word *antibiotic* contains the prefix *anti-*, from a Greek word meaning "opposite," and the Greek word *bios*, meaning "life." Explain how, together, these meanings relate to the term *antibiotic resistance*.

Reviewing MAIN IDEAS

10. Why do Koch's postulates and germ theory apply to infectious diseases but not noninfectious diseases?

11. What are some types of pathogens, and how do they attack the body?

12. What are some ways that pathogens spread?

13. How do other body systems help the immune system respond to infections?

14. How do phagocytes, antibodies, and interferons help to fight pathogens?

15. How are passive immunity and active immunity similar and different?

16. How does fever help to fight infections?

17. How do specific immune responses lead to active immunity?

18. How might organ transplants, which are meant to save a person's life, endanger the person?

19. People say, "Too much of a good thing can be bad." How does this statement relate to the use of antibiotics?

20. How does a vaccine produce active immunity without making a person sick?

21. How do autoimmune diseases disrupt homeostasis?

22. How does leukemia weaken the immune system?

23. What is the difference between HIV and AIDS?

Critical Thinking

24. Apply In 1918, scientists found a bacterium in the lungs of some people who died of flu. The bacteria were given to healthy volunteers, but only some volunteers developed flulike symptoms. Using germ theory, decide whether this bacterium caused flu.

25. Connect How does the evolution of pathogens, specifically bacteria and viruses, negatively affect humans' ability to stay healthy?

26. Synthesize If you get stung by a bee, the skin around the bite will swell. Explain the process that produced the swelling. Use and define the terms *vector, allergen, inflammation,* and *white blood cell* in your answer.

27. Compare and Contrast How can the humoral immune response both help and hurt the body?

28. Analyze People infected with HIV are said to be HIV-positive because they have the antibodies for the virus. Why don't antibodies, which normally protect the body against pathogens, protect people who are HIV-positive from developing AIDS?

29. Explain Summarize the process by which a vaccine helps the body fight off pathogens. Begin with what happens when a person gets vaccinated, and conclude with the destruction of the invading pathogen.

30. Infer Compare the normal humoral immune response to the response after someone is vaccinated. Which steps of the humoral response probably take the longest, allowing the pathogen to make the body sick?

Interpreting Visuals

Use the diagram below to answer the next three questions.

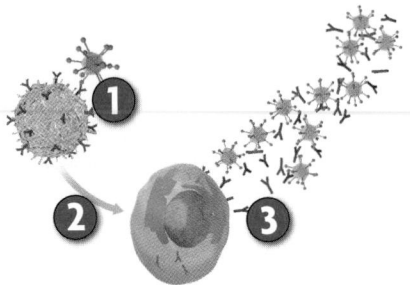

31. Summarize What is happening in each numbered part of the process shown above?

32. Apply Before this process could take place, one of two events must have occurred. What are the two events?

33. Analyze What kind of immunity is shown here?

Analyzing Data

Use the graph below to identify data flaws and answer the next two questions.

A researcher designs an experiment to determine what dose of a new antibiotic must be given to patients to kill the bacteria that cause pneumonia. The researcher infects three groups of mice with three different strands of pneumonia bacteria. Group 1 is not given any antibiotic. The researcher gives Groups 2 and 3 different doses of the antibiotic. The results are shown below.

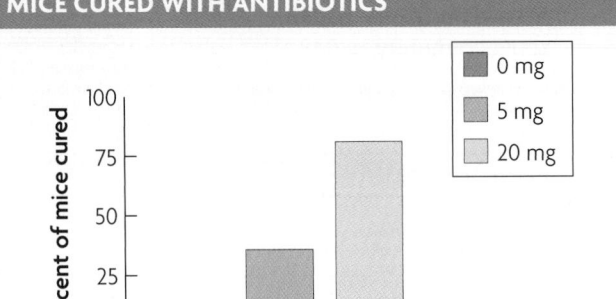

34. Analyze Can the researcher conclude that the largest dose of antibiotic is necessary to cure pneumonia? Why or why not?

35. Evaluate How could this investigation be redesigned to better answer the researcher's question?

Connecting CONCEPTS

36. Design a Video Game Imagine that you are creating a video game in which the player can choose to be a T cell or a B cell. Describe the player's goals for each version of the game. How will the player direct the cells in their mission to seek out and destroy the invading pathogens?

37. Design an Experiment One fall, children who live in a wooded area become ill. They develop an itchy rash, a hacking cough, and a sick feeling in their stomachs. One local doctor tells concerned parents that their children had an allergic reaction to something in the woods and advises that the children rest in bed. Another doctor thinks that a bacterium causes the sickness and prescribes medicine for the children. Design an experiment to determine who is correct. (**Hint:** What evidence do you need to prove a pathogen caused a disease?)

MICHIGAN
STANDARDS-BASED ASSESSMENT

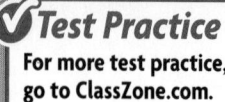

✓ **Test Practice**
For more test practice,
go to ClassZone.com.

1. In the 1850s, Louis Pasteur conducted many experiments and based on his results, proposed that specific microorganisms cause disease. This proposal is an example of a scientific **B1.2h**

   A hypothesis.

   B guess.

   C theory.

   D experiment.

2.

Set Up for Chicken Pox Experiment		
Volunteer	Injected with Dead Chicken Pox Virus	Injected with Distilled Water
A	X	
B		X
C	X	X

A scientist studies three volunteers who never had chicken pox by injecting each with a dead virus, distilled water, or a combination of the two. The experimental design is described in the table above. After the injection, whose blood stream would *most* likely contain antibodies for the chicken pox virus? **B1.1E**

   A volunteer A only

   B volunteer B only

   C volunteers A and B

   D volunteers A and C

3. A substance that provides acquired immunity is called **B2.r6e**

   A a vector.

   B an antihistamine.

   C an antibiotic.

   D a vaccine.

4. Mucous membranes and the skin are nonspecific defenses against infection. The functions of the skin in immunity are to block the entry of pathogens and to **B2.3d**

   A release white blood cells.

   B produce antibodies.

   C secrete sweat and oil.

   D activate active immunity.

5.

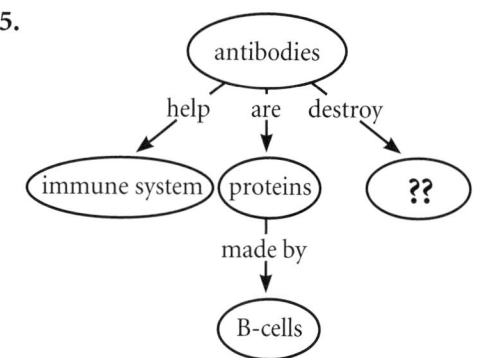

Which word *best* completes this concept map? **B2.3C**

   A white blood cells

   B red blood cells

   C pathogens

   D vectors

6. Some interferons stimulate noninfected cells to produce thick coats that prevent viruses from infecting the cells. Which statement *best* explains why interferons are effective against viruses but not bacteria? **B2.2f**

   A Bacteria are living microorganisms, but viruses are not.

   B Interferons affect viral DNA, but do not affect bacterial DNA.

   C Bacteria have a cell wall, but viruses only have a protein coat.

   D Viruses need to enter a cell to reproduce, but bacteria do not.

THINK THROUGH THE QUESTION

To answer this question, think about how bacteria and viruses are different. Which of these differences is related to the way interferons act?

CHAPTER

32 Digestive and Excretory Systems

KEY CONCEPTS

32.1 Nutrients and Homeostasis
Cells require many different nutrients.

32.2 Digestive System
The digestive system breaks down food into simpler molecules.

32.3 Absorption of Nutrients
Nutrients are absorbed and solid wastes eliminated after digestion.

32.4 Excretory System
The excretory system removes wastes and helps to maintain homeostasis.

Online BIOLOGY CLASSZONE.COM

Animated BIOLOGY

View animated chapter concepts.
• Digestive System
• Run the Digestive System

BIOZINE

Keep current with biology news.
• Featured stories
• Strange Biology
• Polls

RESOURCE CENTER

Get more information on
• Nutrition
• Urinary System

What is that gut feeling inside you?

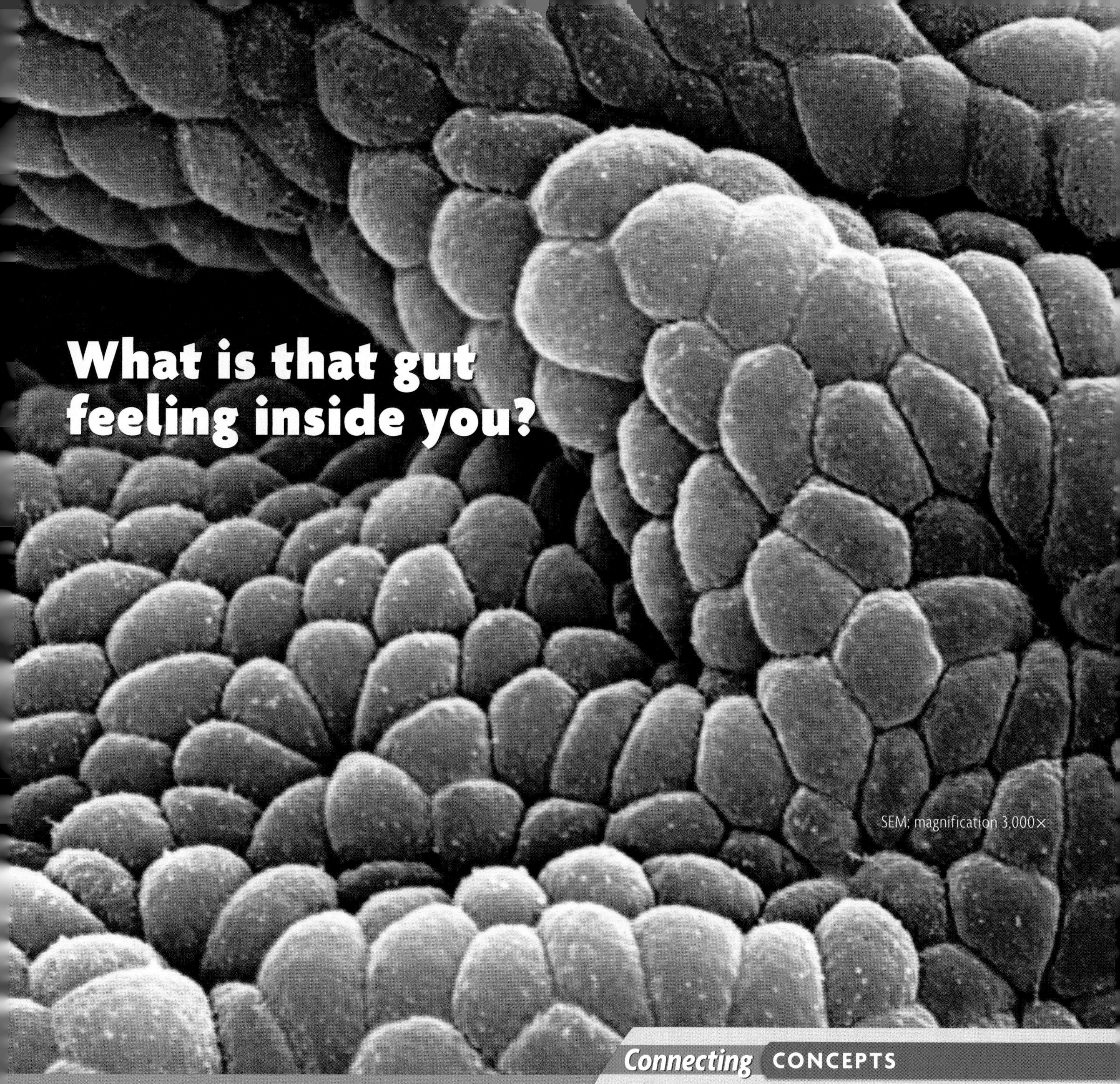

SEM; magnification 3,000×

A lot is going on in your stomach when you eat. For instance, epithelial cells, shown in the close-up above, secrete four types of substances: stomach acid; a protective mucus that keeps the stomach from digesting itself; enzymes that break down many types of food; and hormones that control the process.

Connecting CONCEPTS

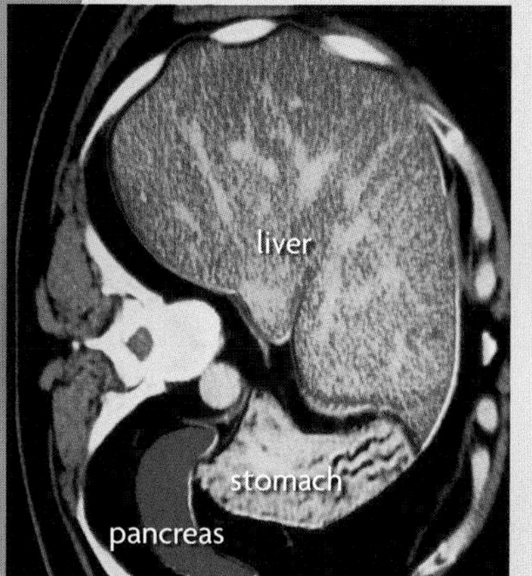

Organ Systems This colored CT scan is a cross-section of the digestive system as seen from above. The vertebrae and rib bones (white) help to protect the liver, stomach, and pancreas. The small and large intestines (not shown) are below these organs. The whole system breaks down food into simpler molecules that the body can absorb and use.

32.1 Nutrients and Homeostasis

KEY CONCEPT Cells require many different nutrients.

▶ MAIN IDEAS
- Six types of nutrients help to maintain homeostasis.
- Meeting nutritional needs supports good health.

VOCABULARY
mineral, p. 973
vitamin, p. 974
Calorie, p. 975

Review
carbohydrate, protein, fat

MICHIGAN STANDARDS

B2.3e Describe how human body systems maintain relatively constant internal conditions (temperature, acidity, and blood sugar).

Connect Until the 1740s, British sailors on long voyages were crippled by scurvy, an illness that produced weakness, bruising, bleeding gums, and painful joints. British physician James Lind learned that Dutch sailors who ate oranges at sea never got scurvy. He hypothesized that citrus fruits might not only cure the illness but prevent it as well. To test his ideas, Lind divided the crew of one ship into six groups and gave each group different foods. Only the sailors eating oranges and lemons remained healthy. By simply adding vitamin C to the sailors' diets, Lind had shown the British navy how to wipe out scurvy at sea.

▶ MAIN IDEA

Six types of nutrients help to maintain homeostasis.

Today, scientists and health experts know a great deal more about how important nutrients are to maintain homeostasis in your body. You need to consume six types of nutrients every day to keep your body in good health: water, carbohydrates, proteins, fats, minerals, and vitamins. If any one of these nutrients is missing for too long, your body's cells will stop working properly, which also affects your organs.

Water
Your body is made up of 55 to 60 percent water. As a natural solvent, water is involved in nearly every chemical reaction in every cell of your body. It also helps you to digest food and eliminate waste products, maintain your blood volume, regulate your body temperature, and keep your skin moist. To maintain your fluid balance, you need to drink about 2 liters (8 cups) of water a day to replace the amount you lose through sweat, urine, and respiration.

Carbohydrates
Carbohydrates, shown in **FIGURE 32.1**, are the main source of energy for your body. Simple carbohydrates are sugars found in sugar cane, honey, and fruits. Complex carbohydrates are starches found in vegetables, grains, and potatoes. To be absorbed by your body, starches must be broken down during digestion into simple sugars, such as glucose. Excess supplies of glucose are converted to glycogen and are stored in the liver and muscle tissues for future use. Many grains, fruits, and vegetables also contain cellulose, a dietary fiber. Fiber cannot be digested, but it helps move food through your digestive system.

FIGURE 32.1 Complex carbohydrates (whole grains, potatoes, vegetables) must be broken down into sugars to be used as fuel. Simple carbohydrates, such as those found in fruits, do not need to be broken down as much.

Proteins

Proteins are the raw materials used for the growth and repair of the body's cells and tissues. In addition, proteins make up all enzymes and many hormones that are vital for cell metabolism. Proteins are composed of chains of amino acids. Your body can make only 12 of the 20 amino acids it needs to build proteins. The other 8, called essential amino acids, must come from the foods you eat. Foods such as meat, cheese, and eggs contain all eight essential amino acids. However, most plant proteins lack at least one essential amino acid. Vegans—people who do not eat meat, dairy products, or eggs—must eat plant foods in combination to obtain all the amino acids they need. For example, red beans and rice together contain all 20 amino acids.

Fats

Fats provide energy and key components in cell membranes, myelin sheaths for neurons, and certain hormones. Fats consist of long chains of fatty acids hooked to glycerol molecules. Your body can make some fatty acids, but you must obtain all of the essential fatty acids from the foods you eat. Fats are classified as either saturated or unsaturated, depending on the structure of their fatty acid chains. Saturated fats are solid at room temperature and are found in animal products. Most unsaturated fats are liquid at room temperature and are found in plant oils, such as corn or olive oils, and in some fish, such as cod or salmon. In general, unsaturated fats are considered more beneficial to people's health than are saturated fats.

Minerals

Small amounts of minerals and vitamins are also needed to maintain homeostasis. **Minerals** are inorganic materials the body uses to carry out processes in cells and to build or repair tissues. Some of the more common minerals are listed in **FIGURE 32.3**. Calcium, for example, is essential for bone and tooth formation, muscle contraction, and nerve transmission. Sodium and potassium help to maintain the body's fluid homeostasis. You are constantly losing minerals in sweat, urine, and other waste products. You can replace them by eating a variety of plant foods or by combining plant and animal foods.

FIGURE 32.2 Proteins and fats are often found in the same foods. Beef, chicken, and eggs contain protein and saturated fats. Fish, nuts, beans, and seeds contain protein and unsaturated fats.

TAKING NOTES

Use a two-column chart to organize your notes about different nutrients and their functions.

Water	- makes up 55 to 60% of body - maintains blood volume

FIGURE 32.3 Important Minerals

MINERALS	SOURCES	IMPORTANT FOR
Calcium	dairy products, salmon, sardines, dark leafy greens	blood clotting, bone/tooth formation; muscle/nerve function
Iron	liver, dark leafy greens, whole grains	component in hemoglobin
Iodine	iodized salt, seafoods, sea vegetables	component in thyroid hormones
Magnesium	nuts, whole grains, leafy green vegetables	bone/tooth formation; coenzyme in protein synthesis
Phosphorus	meats, dairy products, nuts, dried peas and beans	bone/tooth formation; active in many metabolic processes
Potassium	meats, dairy products, many fruits and vegetables	regulation of pH, fluid balance, and muscle/nerve function
Sodium	table salt, seafoods, processed foods	regulation of pH, fluid balance, and muscle/nerve function
Zinc	meats, seafoods, grains	activation of many enzymes in metabolic processes

Vitamins

Vitamins are organic molecules that work with enzymes to regulate cell functions, growth, and development. As shown in **FIGURE 32.4,** these nutrients are divided into fat-soluble vitamins and water-soluble vitamins. Fat-soluble vitamins dissolve in fatty acids. The fat-soluble vitamins A, D, E, and K can be stored in the body's fatty tissues for future use. For this reason, taking high doses of these vitamins can actually create harmful, or toxic, levels in the body.

Water-soluble vitamins dissolve in water. The water-soluble vitamin C and the B vitamins cannot be stored and are excreted in urine and feces. As a result, you need to eat foods rich in these nutrients to keep replenishing them. The National Academy of Sciences publishes recommended daily amounts of minerals and vitamins based on your age, gender, and level of activity.

Apply **Would a diet higher in protein or in complex carbohydrates give you more energy? Explain your answer.**

FIGURE 32.4 Essential Vitamins

VITAMIN	SOURCES	IMPORTANT FOR
Fat-Soluble (Dissolves in Fat)		
A (retinol)	dark green, yellow, and orange vegetables, fortified milk, fish and liver oils	healthy skin, mucous membranes, vision
D (calciferol)	fortified dairy and whole grain products, egg yolks, fish and liver oils	bone and tooth formation, increase in calcium and phosphorus absorption
E (tocopherol)	vegetable oils, nuts, fish oils, meats, leafy green vegetables	prevention of cell damage
K	leafy green vegetables, egg yolks, liver; also made by intestinal bacteria	blood clotting and synthesis of clotting factors
Water-Soluble (Dissolves in Water)		
B_1 (thiamine)	pork and red meats, whole grains, dried beans and peas, eggs	metabolism of carbohydrates
B_2 (riboflavin)	dairy products, liver and organ meats, enriched whole grains	metabolism of carbohydrates and proteins, normal growth in skin, lips, and mucous membranes
B_3 (niacin)	meats, dried peas and beans, whole grains	metabolism of glucose, fats, and proteins
B_6 (pyridoxine)	meats, fish, peanuts, eggs, bran cereal	metabolism of amino acids
B_{12}	liver, meats, eggs, dairy products	protein synthesis and red blood cell production
C (ascorbic acid)	citrus fruits, berries, tomatoes, broccoli, cabbage, potatoes, melons	antioxidant, maintenance of cartilage and bone, iron absorption, tissue repair, wound healing, healthy gums
Pantothenic acid	meats, dairy products, whole grains	metabolism of glucose, fats, and proteins
Folic acid	leafy green vegetables, liver, nuts, oranges, broccoli, peas, fortified cereals	amino acid synthesis and metabolism, prevention of neural tube defects in fetuses
Biotin	egg yolks, liver, soybeans	metabolism of carbohydrates, proteins, and fats
Choline	egg yolks, liver, whole grains	production of phospholipids and neurotransmitters

▶ MAIN IDEA
Meeting nutritional needs supports good health.

A balanced diet is important throughout your life, but particularly during pre-teen and early teen years. During these years, you are growing and developing faster than at any other time since the first two years of your life. Your bone mass is increasing nearly 40 percent, you are gaining most of your adult body mass, and you are developing sexual characteristics.

To fuel this growth spurt, your body requires considerably more nutrients and more energy in the form of Calories consumed, as shown in **FIGURE 32.5**. A calorie, with a small *c,* is the amount of energy required to raise one gram of water one degree Celsius. One **Calorie** (capital *C*) from food equals one kilocalorie, or 1000 calories. Different foods contain different amounts of energy. One gram of protein or carbohydrate yields four Calories, while one gram of fat yields nine Calories.

Calories alone are not the whole story, however. The rapid changes in your body require adequate amounts of all six nutrients. Dietary experts recommend that most of your Calories come from eating whole grains, fruits, and vegetables, which are rich in fiber, vitamins, and minerals. Also, experts suggest drinking more low-fat milk or soy drinks and water, and fewer high-sugar soft drinks and juices. High-sugar foods provide Calories but very little nutritional value. Dietary experts also recommend eating more lean meats and fish, while cutting down on foods high in saturated fat.

It is also important to find a balance between food and physical activity so that you use about as many Calories as you consume. The U.S. Department of Agriculture (USDA) Web site provides information on how to develop a balanced diet.

Connecting CONCEPTS

Cellular Respiration You read in **Chapter 4** about the different ways that plant and animal cells obtain energy. In nearly all plant and animal cells, mitochondria use molecules broken down by digestion to build ATP, the main power source for cells.

FIGURE 32.6 Your food choices can help you consume high-quality energy and nutrients at a time when your body needs them the most.

FIGURE 32.5 Growth and Energy Needs

During rapid growth, the body requires significantly more energy.

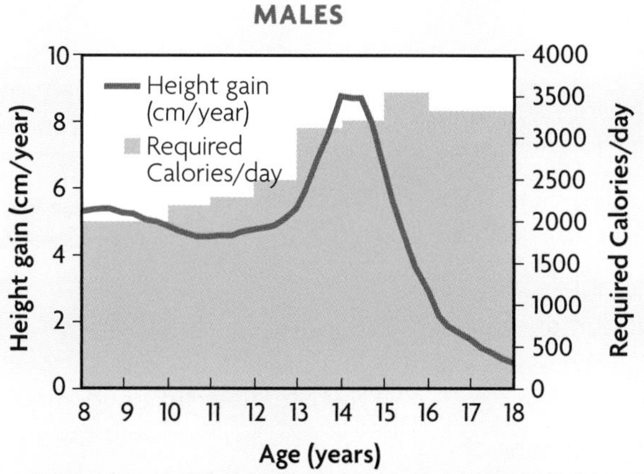

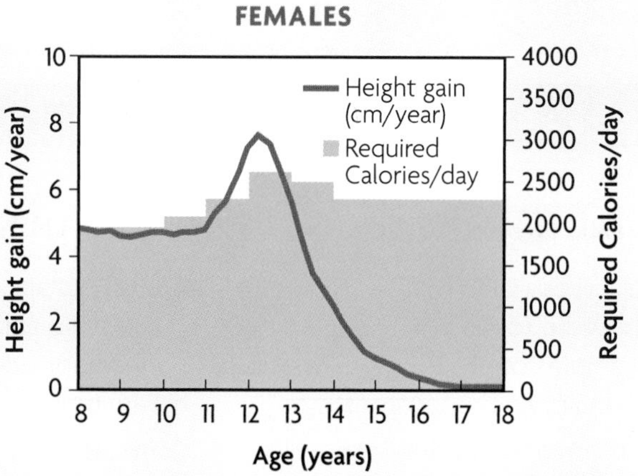

MALES

Height gain (cm/year)
Required Calories/day

FEMALES

Height gain (cm/year)
Required Calories/day

Contrast What differences do you notice between the two charts?

Sources: Adapted from JM Tanner: *Growth at adolescence,* ed.2, Oxford; Food and Nutrition Board: *Recommended dietary allowances,* ed. 10, National Academy Press; Institute of Medicine, Food and Nutrition Board, *Dietary reference,* National Academies Press.

FIGURE 32.7 READING A FOOD LABEL

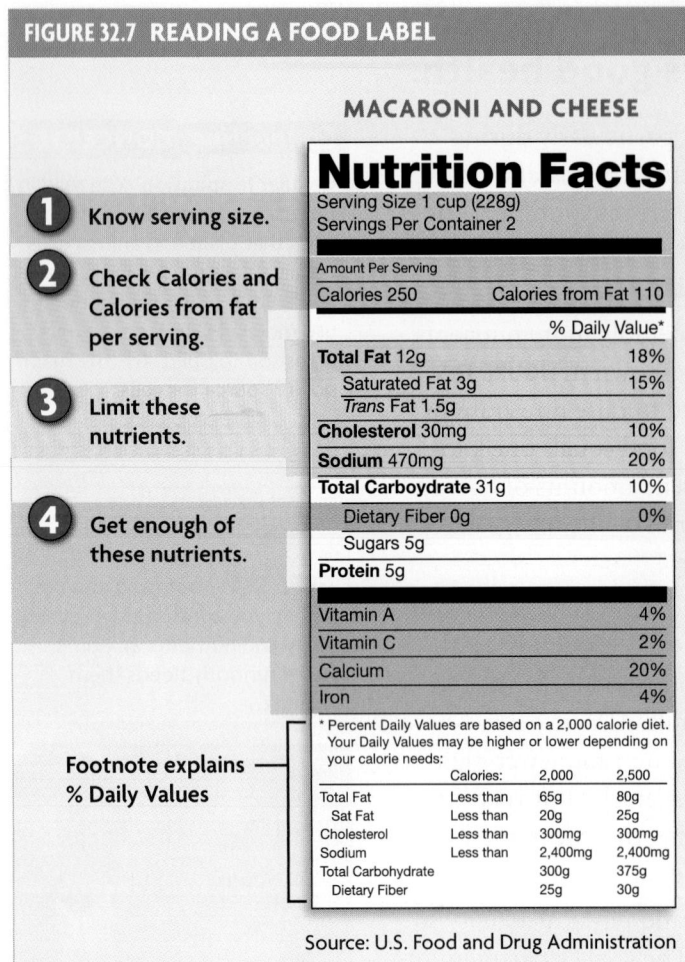

MACARONI AND CHEESE

Nutrition Facts

Serving Size 1 cup (228g)
Servings Per Container 2

Amount Per Serving

Calories 250	Calories from Fat 110

	% Daily Value*
Total Fat 12g	18%
Saturated Fat 3g	15%
Trans Fat 1.5g	
Cholesterol 30mg	10%
Sodium 470mg	20%
Total Carboydrate 31g	10%
Dietary Fiber 0g	0%
Sugars 5g	
Protein 5g	

Vitamin A	4%
Vitamin C	2%
Calcium	20%
Iron	4%

* Percent Daily Values are based on a 2,000 calorie diet.
Your Daily Values may be higher or lower depending on
your calorie needs:

		Calories:	2,000	2,500
Total Fat	Less than		65g	80g
Sat Fat	Less than		20g	25g
Cholesterol	Less than		300mg	300mg
Sodium	Less than		2,400mg	2,400mg
Total Carbohydrate			300g	375g
Dietary Fiber			25g	30g

Source: U.S. Food and Drug Administration

1 Know serving size.

2 Check Calories and Calories from fat per serving.

3 Limit these nutrients.

4 Get enough of these nutrients.

Footnote explains
% Daily Values

The information on a food label, such as the one in **FIGURE 32.7**, can help you make good choices and compare the values of different foods. The label shown here is from a box of macaroni and cheese.

1 **Serving size and number** This measurement varies from one product to another. In this case, one serving equals one cup. Notice that this container holds *two* servings.

2 **Calories and Calories from fat** The numbers listed on the label are for *one serving only*. If you eat both servings, you are actually getting 500 Calories, nearly half from fat.

3 **Nutrients to limit** Americans usually consume too much saturated fat, trans fat, cholesterol, and sodium. Trans fat is a type of fat that can cause cell damage. A diet high in these nutrients is linked to obesity, which affects more and more Americans of all ages. Too much sodium can raise blood pressure by causing the body to retain water.

4 **Nutrients to target** Americans need to consume enough of these nutrients each day. Notice that this product is low in vitamins and minerals, except for calcium, and has no dietary fiber. The wheat used in the macaroni has been processed until there is no fiber left.

As the label shows, if you eat this product, you will also need to eat whole grains, vegetables, and fruits during the day to obtain the nutrients that are missing from this food.

Analyze **What nutritional advantages do unprocessed foods offer over processed foods?**

32.1 ASSESSMENT

ONLINE QUIZ
ClassZone.com

REVIEWING ▶ MAIN IDEAS

1. What six types of nutrients must you consume to stay healthy? Give two examples of how nutrients help to maintain homeostasis.

2. What information besides the number of **Calories** can help you make good food choices?

CRITICAL THINKING

3. **Apply** Explain why vegans—people who eat no animal products—may have trouble getting all the essential amino acids from their diet.

4. **Contrast** How do the functions of **vitamins** and **minerals** differ from the functions of proteins and carbohydrates?

Connecting CONCEPTS

5. **Cellular Respiration** All cells need ATP to power their metabolic processes. Explain why eating carbohydrates is so important to the process of cellular respiration.

32.2 Digestive System

KEY CONCEPT The digestive system breaks down food into simpler molecules.

▶ MAIN IDEAS

- Several digestive organs work together to break down food.
- Digestion begins in the mouth and continues in the stomach.
- Digestion is completed in part of the small intestine.

VOCABULARY

digestion, p. 977
digestive system, p. 977
sphincter, p. 977
esophagus, p. 978
peristalsis, p. 978

stomach, p. 978
chyme, p. 979
small intestine, p. 980
bile, p. 980

MICHIGAN STANDARDS

B2.3d Identify the general functions of the major systems of the human body (digestion, respiration, reproduction, circulation, excretion, protection from disease, and movement, control, and coordination) and describe ways that these systems interact with each other.

Connect In June 1822, Alexis St. Martin was shot in the stomach and treated by William Beaumont, an Army surgeon. The 28-year-old St. Martin recovered, but the bullet wound left a small hole in his stomach. Beaumont covered the hole and persuaded St. Martin to let him observe the digestive process by tying foods to a string, dropping them into the stomach hole, and retrieving them at different times to see how quickly different foods were digested. Over ten years, the experiments yielded a wealth of information about the digestive process. St. Martin married, had children, and lived to the age of 86.

▶ MAIN IDEA

Several digestive organs work together to break down food.

Digestion is the process by which the large complex molecules in food are broken down into smaller molecules that can be used by the body. The **digestive system** is a collection of organs that breaks down food into energy that can be used in cells. It is like a factory that takes things apart instead of putting them together. The major organs of this "disassembly line" include the mouth, esophagus, stomach, pancreas, liver, gallbladder, large and small intestines, rectum, and anus, as shown in **FIGURE 32.8**. Rings of muscle, called **sphincters** (SFIHNGK-tuhrs), separate one section from another. The opening and closing of these sphincters and the contractions of smooth muscle in the walls of the organs keep food moving in one direction.

Digestion takes place through the interactions of enzymes, stomach acid, hormones, bile from the liver, and a network of nerves and muscles throughout the digestive system. Each organ contributes to breaking food down. For instance, in the mouth, salivary glands secrete an enzyme that helps to digest starches. The stomach releases enzymes that break down proteins.

Once digestion is complete, nutrients are absorbed by the body and transported by the circulatory system and lymphatic system to all the cells. Finally, undigested materials are eliminated as liquid and solid wastes. The entire process—from food entering the mouth to wastes leaving the body—takes about 24 to 33 hours per meal.

Predict **What might happen if the digestive sections were not divided by sphincters?**

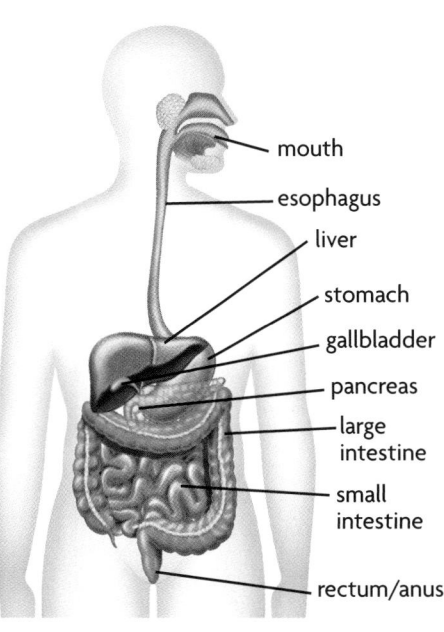

FIGURE 32.8 The major digestive organs are separated by sphincters, which help keep food moving in one direction.

mouth
esophagus
liver
stomach
gallbladder
pancreas
large intestine
small intestine
rectum/anus

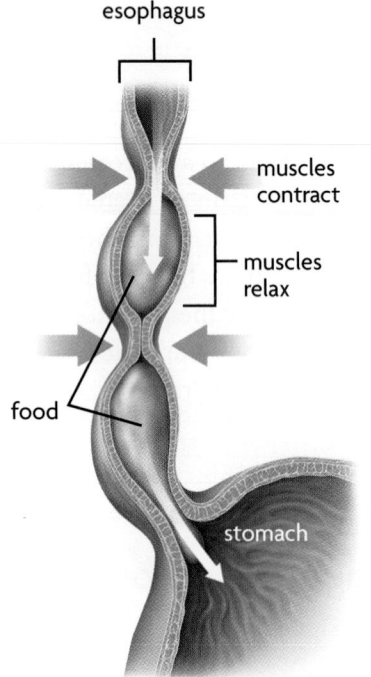

esophagus

muscles contract

muscles relax

food

stomach

FIGURE 32.9 As food enters the esophagus, muscles behind the food contract, pushing it forward, while the muscles in front of the food relax. This rhythmic squeezing, called peristalsis, keeps food moving in one direction.

> ▶ MAIN IDEA

Digestion begins in the mouth and continues in the stomach.

You may have heard someone telling their children, "Chew your food—don't just gulp it!" This is actually good advice, because the first step in breaking down food is mechanical and chemical digestion in the mouth.

Digestion in the Mouth

You unwrap the sandwich you brought for lunch and bring it up to your mouth. Mechanical digestion begins the moment you bite into the sandwich and start chewing. Your teeth shred and grind the food into smaller pieces. Your tongue keeps the pieces positioned between your teeth. Chemical digestion, on the other hand, involves the action of enzymes. As you chew your food, the salivary glands release saliva that moistens the food and contains an enzyme called amylase (AM-uh-LAYS). Amylase begins the breakdown of complex starch molecules into sugars.

Once food has been chewed and mixed with saliva, the tongue pushes it to the back of the mouth. As you swallow, the food moves into the **esophagus** (ih-SAHF-uh-guhs), a tube that connects the mouth to the stomach. Food is kept moving down the esophagus by the action of peristalsis, as **FIGURE 32.9** shows. **Peristalsis** (PEHR-ih-STAWL-sihs) is the rhythmic, involuntary contraction of the smooth muscles in the walls of digestive organs.

Digestion in the Stomach

The next stop for your thoroughly chewed sandwich is the stomach. The **stomach** is a muscular sac that can stretch to nearly twice its original size and holds up to 2 liters (2 qt) of food. The stomach continues the digestion that began in the mouth. Proteins are digested in the stomach and small intestine, but fats and sugars are digested only in the small intestine. Major enzymes and their functions in the digestive system are listed in **FIGURE 32.10**.

The walls of the stomach contain three layers of smooth muscle that contract about every 20 seconds. This churning action breaks food into even smaller pieces and mixes the food with the stomach's digestive juices.

FIGURE 32.10 Major Digestive Enzymes

ENZYME	DIGESTIVE ORGAN	FUNCTION
Salivary amylase	mouth	breaks down starches into simpler sugars
Pepsin	stomach	breaks down proteins
Maltase, lactase, sucrase	small intestine	breaks down sugars into simpler molecules
Peptidase		breaks down proteins into amino acids
Trypsin	small intestine, pancreas	continues breakdown of proteins
Amylase		continues breakdown of starches
Lipase		aids in breaking down fats

As **FIGURE 32.11** summarizes, chemical digestion occurs along with the churning of mechanical digestion. The stomach lining secretes gastric juice containing hydrochloric acid (HCl) and the digestive enzyme pepsin. Gastric juice is acidic enough to kill most bacteria found on food and to break the bonds between protein molecules. Pepsin also breaks some chemical bonds between the amino acids in proteins. Digestive juices and enzymes turn your partly digested sandwich into a semi-liquid mixture called **chyme** (kym).

The stomach empties as peristaltic actions push the chyme against the sphincter that separates the stomach from the small intestine. With each contraction, the sphincter opens slightly, and chyme squirts into the small intestine, where digestion continues. It takes from two to six hours to empty the stomach after a meal.

Once the stomach is empty, the production of gastric juice stops. What keeps the stomach from digesting itself? First, pepsin is active only when there is food to digest. Second, the stomach secretes a layer of mucus to protect itself from its own acidic environment. Even so, cells in the stomach lining are replaced every few days to maintain the protective layer of mucus.

Apply If you ate a meal of spaghetti and meatballs, where would digestion of the pasta and meat begin?

Connecting CONCEPTS

Chemistry Hydrochloric acid (HCl) is so strong that it can dissolve an iron nail in a matter of hours. To protect your stomach lining, specialized epithelial cells secrete bicarbonate, a base substance. Bicarbonate neutralizes the acid to keep it from burning through your stomach lining.

FIGURE 32.11 Mechanical and Chemical Digestion

The digestive organs use mechanical and chemical digestion to break food down into simple molecules.

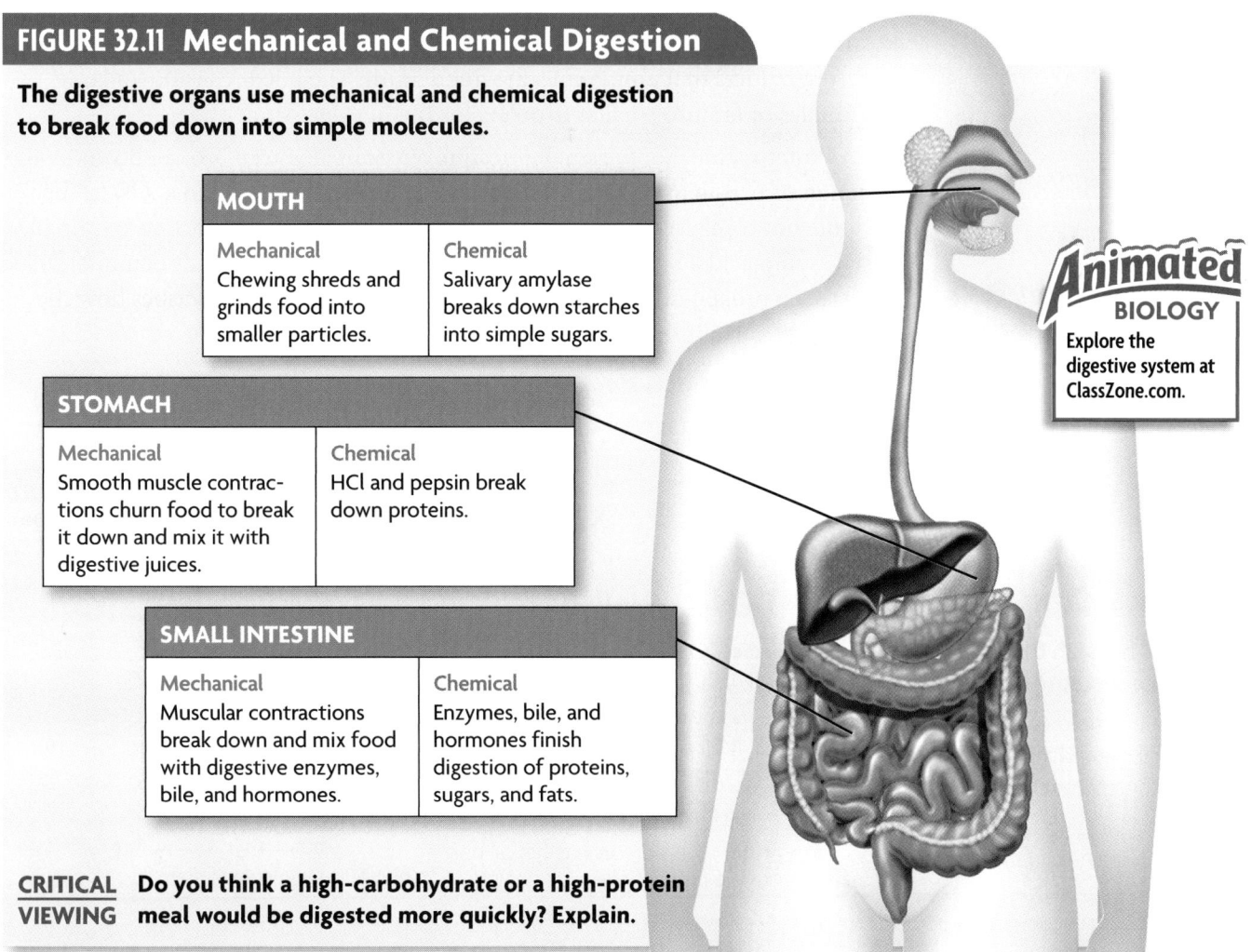

MOUTH

Mechanical	Chemical
Chewing shreds and grinds food into smaller particles.	Salivary amylase breaks down starches into simple sugars.

STOMACH

Mechanical	Chemical
Smooth muscle contractions churn food to break it down and mix it with digestive juices.	HCl and pepsin break down proteins.

SMALL INTESTINE

Mechanical	Chemical
Muscular contractions break down and mix food with digestive enzymes, bile, and hormones.	Enzymes, bile, and hormones finish digestion of proteins, sugars, and fats.

Animated BIOLOGY
Explore the digestive system at ClassZone.com.

<u>CRITICAL VIEWING</u> Do you think a high-carbohydrate or a high-protein meal would be digested more quickly? Explain.

● MAIN IDEA

Digestion is completed in part of the small intestine.

FIGURE 32.12 The liver and pancreas help digest fats, carbohydrates, and proteins in the small intestine. The liver secretes bile through the gallbladder, and the pancreas secretes an alkaline fluid and digestive enzymes.

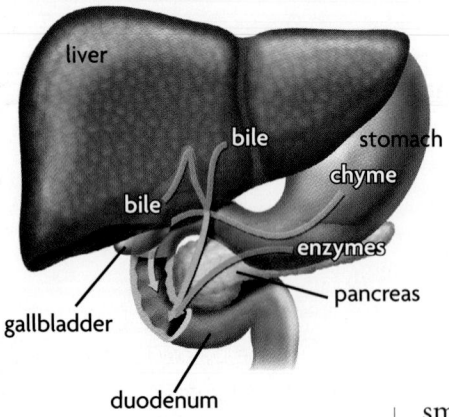

To learn more about digestion, visit scilinks.org.
Keycode: MLB032

The remaining carbohydrates, proteins, and fats from your sandwich are digested in the duodenum (DOO-uh-DEE-nuhm), the section of small intestine closest to the stomach. The **small intestine** is a long, narrow tube in which most digestion takes place. Smooth muscle contractions churn the food, and chemical digestion further breaks down the complex molecules. As shown in **FIGURE 32.12**, enzymes and hormones from the pancreas, liver, and gallbladder flow through ducts into the duodenum to help complete the digestive process.

The pancreas is a small gland located behind the stomach. When chyme first enters the small intestine, the pancreas releases an alkaline fluid to help neutralize the acid and stop the action of pepsin. The pancreas also releases enzymes to break down starches further into simple sugars. For example, lactase is an intestinal enzyme that breaks down lactose, a sugar found in milk. The pancreas also produces an enzyme, lipase, that splits fat into fatty acids and smaller molecules.

The liver, which filters blood, is also a digestive organ. It produces a chemical substance, **bile,** that helps to digest fats. Bile is stored in a smaller organ, the gallbladder. When bile is needed to digest fats, it is released through ducts that empty into the duodenum. The bile breaks down large globules of fat into smaller droplets for further digestion.

Proteins entering the small intestine have already been broken down by the action of pepsin and gastric juice into smaller chains of amino acids. In the duodenum, enzymes finish the process by breaking these chains into individual amino acids. By the time chyme has passed through the duodenum, food has been broken down into small molecules. Section 32.3 describes how these molecules are absorbed by the body.

Apply How would the pancreas and liver help to digest ice cream?

32.2 ASSESSMENT

REVIEWING ● MAIN IDEAS

1. What is the main function of the **digestive system**?
2. Give an example of mechanical and chemical **digestion** in the mouth and in the **stomach.**
3. What organs help to continue digestion in the **small intestine**?

CRITICAL THINKING

4. **Predict** One person eats a beef steak in a few bites, while another chews the same amount of beef well. If all other conditions are equal, will both people digest their beef at the same rate? Explain.
5. **Predict** If a person has his or her gallbladder removed, what changes in diet should be made? Why?

Connecting CONCEPTS

6. **Cell Structure** The cells of the stomach lining produce a great deal of mucus. If you were to view such a cell under a microscope, what type of organelle would you expect to see in abundance?

MATERIALS

- 4 100-mL beakers
- 10 cm tape
- marker
- 2 100-mL graduated cylinders
- 160 mL water
- 80 mL 1% hydrochloric acid solution
- 80 mL pepsin
- 4 pecans
- balance
- 4 pieces of potato
- 4 pieces of beef jerky
- warm water bath
- clock

PROCESS SKILL

Analyzing Data

MICHIGAN STANDARDS

B1.1f Predict what would happen if the variables, methods, or timing of an investigation were changed.

B2.2f Explain the role of enzymes and other proteins in biochemical functions (e.g., the protein hemoglobin carries oxygen in some organisms, digestive enzymes, and hormones).

Testing a Digestive Enzyme

In this lab, you will test the effectiveness of the digestive enzyme pepsin under different conditions. You will also determine whether pepsin acts on carbohydrates, fats, or proteins.

PROBLEM Under which conditions is pepsin most effective?

PROCEDURE

1. Label the beakers A, B, C, and D. Add 80 mL of water to beaker A.
2. Add 40 mL of water and 40 mL of the hydrochloric acid solution to beaker B.
3. Add 40 mL of water and 40 mL of pepsin to beaker C.
4. Add 40 mL of the hydrochloric acid solution and 40 mL of pepsin to beaker D.
5. Measure and record the mass of four pecans. Find the average of the four masses. Obtain four pieces each of potato and beef jerky that are about the same mass as the average mass of the pecans.
6. Place one of each piece of food in beaker A. Repeat this step with beakers B, C, and D.
7. Place the beakers in a warm water bath at a temperature of about 37°C.
8. Observe and record the condition of the food in each beaker after 15 minutes, 30 minutes, 45 minutes, and 24 hours. Create a data table like the one below for each beaker. Use the following phrases to describe your observations of the condition of each piece of food: "not dissolving," "beginning to dissolve," "partly dissolved," "mostly dissolved," "completely dissolved." If the condition does not change at all, write "nothing happened."

TABLE 1. CONDITIONS OF FOOD PIECES			
Beaker A	**Potato**	**Pecan**	**Beef Jerky**
15 min			
30 min			
45 min			
24 hr			

ANALYZE AND CONCLUDE

1. **Experimental Design** What were the independent and dependent variables in this experiment? Which beaker was the control? Why were the beakers placed in the warm water bath?
2. **Analyze** Compare the condition of each of the same pieces of food in each beaker. Which piece of food in which beaker was the most digested?
3. **Analyze** Hydrochloric acid has a low pH. What conclusion can you draw about the relationship between the effectiveness of pepsin and pH?
4. **Infer** Potatoes are about 90 percent carbohydrate and 10 percent protein. Pecans are about 87 percent fat, 5 percent protein, and 8 percent carbohydrate. Beef jerky is about 80 percent protein and 20 percent carbohydrate. On which molecule does pepsin act?
5. **Predict** If you were to repeat this experiment, replacing the pepsin with salivary amylase, which breaks down carbohydrates, how would you expect your results to change? The pH of saliva is about 7.4.

32.3 Absorption of Nutrients

KEY CONCEPT Nutrients are absorbed and solid wastes eliminated after digestion.

▶ MAIN IDEAS

- Most absorption of nutrients occurs in the small intestine.
- Water is absorbed and solid wastes are eliminated from the large intestine.

VOCABULARY

absorption, p. 982
villi, p. 983
microvilli, p. 983

MICHIGAN STANDARDS

B2.3d Identify the general functions of the major systems of the human body (digestion, respiration, reproduction, circulation, excretion, protection from disease, and movement, control, and coordination) and describe ways that these systems interact with each other.

B2.3e Describe how human body systems maintain relatively constant internal conditions (temperature, acidity, and blood sugar).

Connect Suppose you tried to wipe up spilled water with a "sponge" made of solid plastic. Without the ability to absorb water, your sponge is useless. People with celiac disease face a similar, but more life-threatening, problem. Celiac disease is an autoimmune disorder that makes people unable to tolerate the protein gluten found in wheat, rye, and barley. Their immune systems produce antibodies to destroy it. The antibodies also damage the surfaces of cells lining the small intestine. This means that no matter how much a person eats, the body cannot absorb the food and becomes malnourished. The only treatment is to eliminate all gluten from the diet to protect the lining of the small intestine.

▶ MAIN IDEA

Most absorption of nutrients occurs in the small intestine.

Food moving through the "disassembly line" of the digestive system is only part of the process. Your body must absorb the nutrients in order for the food you digest to do you any good. **Absorption** is the process by which nutrients move out of the digestive organs into the circulatory and lymphatic systems. As shown in **FIGURE 32.13,** the small intestine has three main structures—the lining, villi, and microvilli—that absorb most of the nutrients from chyme.

FIGURE 32.13 Small Intestine Structures

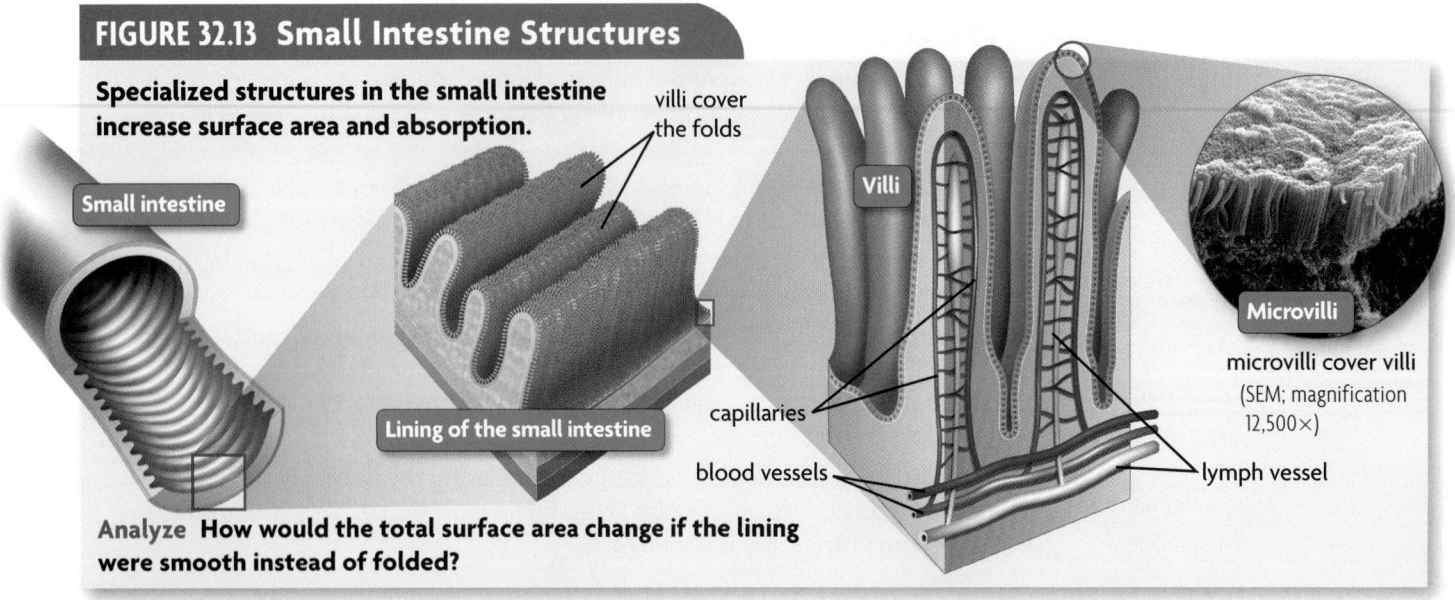

Specialized structures in the small intestine increase surface area and absorption.

villi cover the folds

Villi

Small intestine

Lining of the small intestine

capillaries

blood vessels

Microvilli

microvilli cover villi
(SEM; magnification 12,500×)

lymph vessel

Analyze How would the total surface area change if the lining were smooth instead of folded?

Specialized Structures for Absorption

As you look over the diagram in **FIGURE 32.13,** notice that the lining of the small intestine is ridged and folded. These structures increase the surface area and slow the passage of material through the intestine. Slower motion allows more time for nutrients to be absorbed. The folds of the lining are covered with villi. **Villi** (VIHL-eye) are small fingerlike projections, covered with epithelial cells, that absorb nutrients.

In turn, every epithelial cell on the villi has thousands of tiny projections called **microvilli** that add even more surface area to absorb nutrients. Each microvillus is smaller than the period at the end of this sentence. The photograph in the diagram shows microvilli covering the epithelial cells like a dense carpet.

TAKING NOTES

Use a main idea and supporting detail diagram to help you remember the facts about absorption.

absorption occurs in small intestine

→ *folds, villi, microvilli increase surface area, absorption*

→

Absorption of Different Nutrients

As digestion is completed, nutrients are absorbed in each of the three parts of the small intestine: the duodenum, the jejunum, and the ileum. Together, these parts measure about 6 meters (about 20 ft) long. Villi in each of the three sections absorb different nutrients.

Duodenum Most simple sugars, amino acids, and minerals such as calcium and iron are absorbed by villi in the duodenum. These nutrients diffuse into the circulatory system and are carried to the liver.

Jejunum The villi in the jejunum (juh-JOO-nuhm) absorb glucose along with some amino acids, vitamin C, most B vitamins, and some water. These nutrients diffuse into the circulatory system to be distributed throughout the body.

Ileum The villi in the ileum (IHL-ee-uhm) absorb fat-soluble vitamins and vitamin B_{12}, fatty acids, cholesterol, and some water. The nutrients empty into lymph and blood vessels and are distributed to the cells.

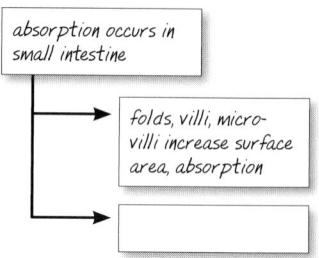

Connecting CONCEPTS

Cell Structure As you read in **Chapter 3,** plant cell walls are made of cellulose, or fiber. These tough cell walls cannot be broken down or absorbed in the small intestine. Instead, fiber moves through the small intestine to the large intestine.

QUICK LAB **DESIGN YOUR OWN INVESTIGATION**

Villi in the Small Intestine

In this lab, you will design a model of the villi in the lining of the small intestine.

PROBLEM How can you model the function of villi in the small intestine?

PROCEDURE

1. Use a paper cup, water, and paper towel to make a model of the villi in the lining of the small intestine.
2. Make three new models that are different. To do this, change one material to determine which model most effectively shows the action of the villi.
3. Determine which of your models most effectively models the villi.

ANALYZE AND CONCLUDE

1. **Summarize** Explain how this experiment models the action of the villi in the small intestine.
2. **Apply** Write a definition to describe how you measured each model's effectiveness.
3. **Analyze** Which model was most effective? How do you know?

MATERIALS

- 4 large paper cups
- water
- 8 paper towels
- timer

Absorbed Nutrients and the Liver

Nutrient-rich blood leaves the small intestine and enters the liver. Enzymes in the liver use some nutrients to build more complex molecules that are needed by cells. The liver also stores some nutrients in liver tissues. For example, excess glucose is turned into glycogen and stored for future use. When you need large amounts of energy, glycogen can be converted back into glucose to keep the glucose levels in your blood relatively stable.

Analyze Explain how the microvilli add more surface area to the small intestine to absorb nutrients.

▶ MAIN IDEA

Water is absorbed and solid wastes are eliminated from the large intestine.

The large intestine, or colon, is 1.5 meters (5 ft) long and about twice the diameter of the small intestine. The large intestine absorbs about 1 liter of water a day, along with some salts, which helps to maintain the body's fluid balance. The remaining undigested material forms into a solid mass, called feces. This material is partly composed of undigested fiber from plant foods, dead bacteria, and traces of undigested fat and protein. Bile pigments from the liver give feces its brownish color. The feces is stored in the rectum, a tube that connects the large intestine to the anus. Feces is then eliminated through the anus.

The large intestine also contains many types of bacteria. Some synthesize a few B vitamins and vitamin K (a blood-clotting factor). Other bacteria, such as *Escherichia coli*, shown in **FIGURE 32.14**, live harmlessly in the colon until some disturbance, such as an illness, allows them to overgrow other bacteria. An overgrowth of *E. coli* can reduce water absorption and cause severe diarrhea.

Your sandwich has taken roughly 24 to 33 hours to move through your digestive system. Now some of the water absorbed by the large intestine must be filtered through the kidneys and excreted, as described in Section 32.4.

Infer A diet high in which types of foods might help the colon to function well?

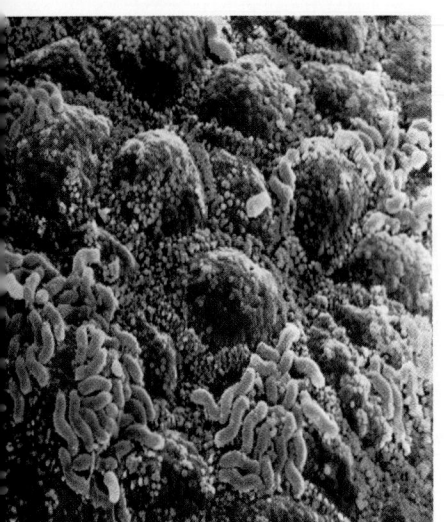

FIGURE 32.14 This micrograph shows the surface of the large intestine colonized by normally harmless bacteria, such as *Escherichia coli* (shown in pink clusters). (colored SEM: magnification 2500×)

32.3 ASSESSMENT

ONLINE QUIZ
ClassZone.com

REVIEWING ▶ MAIN IDEAS

1. Explain the purposes of the lining, **villi,** and **microvilli** in the small intestine.

2. What are the main functions of the large intestine?

CRITICAL THINKING

3. **Contrast** Explain the difference between digestion and **absorption.** What role does each process play in maintaining homeostasis?

4. **Apply** Which nutrients would take longer to digest and absorb: sugars, proteins, or fats? Explain.

Connecting **CONCEPTS**

5. **Animals** The desert kangaroo rat in Arizona eats plants but doesn't drink water. Yet even in summer, it doesn't suffer from dehydration. How do you think the rat's digestive system helps it to obtain water to maintain homeostasis?

Outliers in Data Sets

Sometimes in a scientific investigation, one or more unusual data points are recorded. A data point that is outside of the pattern of data is called an **outlier.** Outliers can result from human error in reading or recording data, from equipment failure, or from rare events such as a 31°C (70°F) day in Wisconsin in January.

To rule out the possibility that the outlier is a valid data point, scientists check their equipment, the laboratory set-up, and the recording process. If the outlier seems to be valid, further research may be needed. Simply ignoring or deleting outliers are not appropriate ways of handling these data.

EXAMPLE

A scientist measured the body temperatures of 1 person over time. As shown in the scatterplot at the right, nearly every temperature was between 36.9°C (98.4°F) and 37.8°C (98.6°F). Notice, however, that one temperature was recorded at 36.8°C (98.2°F). This outlier could be the result of equipment failure or human error. In cases of outliers, scientists must always ask, "What other explanations could there be for the data point? Do these data warrant further investigation?" Investigating the outlier further might lead to new discoveries.

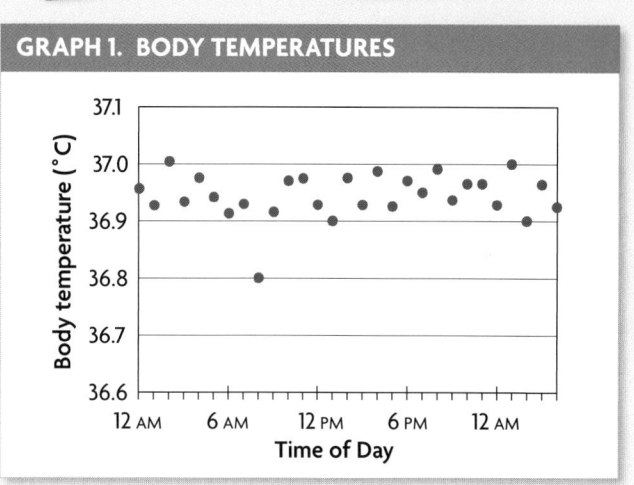

GRAPH 1. BODY TEMPERATURES

IDENTIFY OUTLIERS

Scientists investigated how the mass of an antacid affects its ability to raise the pH of gastric juices in the stomach. They recorded their data in the graph below. Examine the graph, and answer the questions that follow.

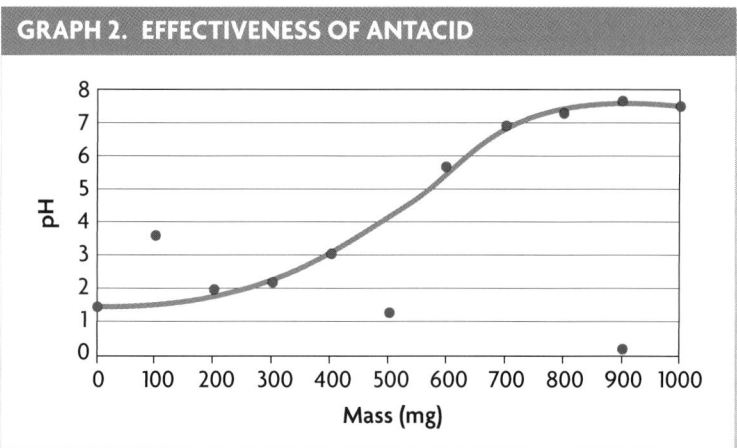

GRAPH 2. EFFECTIVENESS OF ANTACID

1. **Analyze** What is the trend in the data? Which points might be the outliers?

2. **Evaluate** What are some possible explanations for these outliers? How should the scientists proceed?

32.4 Excretory System

KEY CONCEPT The excretory system removes wastes and helps maintain homeostasis.

MAIN IDEAS

- The excretory system eliminates nonsolid wastes from the body.
- The kidneys help to maintain homeostasis by filtering the blood.
- Nephrons clean the blood and produce urine.
- Injury and disease can damage kidney functions.

VOCABULARY

excretory system, p. 986
kidney, p. 986
ureter, p. 986
urinary bladder, p. 986
nephron, p. 987
glomerulus, p. 988
dialysis, p. 991

MICHIGAN STANDARDS

B2.3C Explain how stability is challenged by changing physical, chemical, and environmental conditions as well as the presence of disease agents.

B2.3d Identify the general functions of the major systems of the human body (digestion, respiration, reproduction, circulation, excretion, protection from disease, and movement, control, and coordination) and describe ways that these systems interact with each other.

Connect In 1943, Dutch physician Willem Kolff, who treated kidney patients, constructed the first machine to filter the blood of patients whose kidneys had temporarily stopped functioning. Kolff circulated their blood through synthetic sausage skins submerged in a saltwater bath. The high concentration of salt in the water drew metabolic wastes out of the blood through tiny pores in the synthetic skins. The filtered blood was then returned to the patients. However, Kolff's machine worked well only for people with temporary kidney failure. Today, modern kidney machines can help people even when their kidneys have permanently failed.

MAIN IDEA

The excretory system eliminates nonsolid wastes from the body.

If the digestive system is like a disassembly and distribution line, the excretory system is a like a group of waste treatment and disposal facilities. The **excretory system** is the body system that eliminates nonsolid wastes through sweat, urine, and exhalation to help maintain homeostasis in the body. The waste products include toxic materials, excess water, salts, CO_2, urea, minerals, and vitamins. The main organs of this system are the skin, lungs, kidneys, ureters, urinary bladder, and urethra, as shown in **FIGURE 32.15.**

The lungs remove excess CO_2 and some water vapor through exhalation. This action maintains the balance of O_2 and CO_2 in your blood. Sweat glands in the skin release excess water and salts. Sweat not only removes wastes but also cools the body to maintain a stable internal temperature.

The **kidneys** are organs that eliminate wastes by filtering and cleaning the blood to produce urine. The urine moves through the ureter, the bladder, and the urethra. The **ureter** (yu-REE-tuhr) is a tube that carries urine from each kidney to the bladder. The **urinary bladder** is a saclike organ that can store up to half a liter (over 2 cups) of urine at one time. The urine is released through a single tube, the urethra, into the outside environment.

Connect When you are exercising, what organs of the excretory system are eliminating wastes?

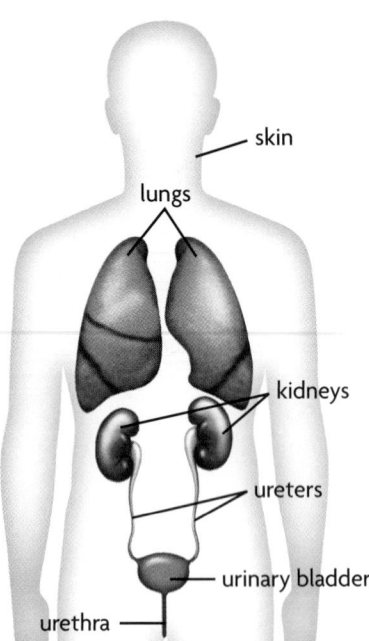

FIGURE 32.15 The excretory system not only excretes nonsolid wastes but also maintains the body's homeostasis.

The kidneys help to maintain homeostasis by filtering the blood.

The kidneys are among the main organs responsible for maintaining fluid and chemical balances in your body within the limits that support life. One quarter of your blood supply passes through your kidneys every minute. Once the blood is filtered, cleaned, and chemically balanced by the kidneys, it is returned to the circulatory system.

Structure of the Kidneys

Your kidneys are a pair of bean-shaped organs, each about the size of your fist. They are located on the right and left sides of the lower back. Each kidney weighs about as much as a baseball. Most people are born with two kidneys. However, if one is damaged or must be removed, you can still live comfortably with only one kidney.

The main parts of the kidney are illustrated in **FIGURE 32.16**. Each kidney has an inner layer, called the medulla, and an outer layer, called the cortex. The cortex is packed with nephrons, which extend through the cortex and partly into the medulla. A **nephron** (NEHF-rahn) is the individual filtering unit of the kidney. Each of your kidneys contains about 1 million nephrons.

A large volume of blood continually enters the kidneys through the renal artery and exits through the renal vein. The word *renal* means "relating to the kidneys." The function of the kidneys is largely controlled by how much water, salts, and other materials are concentrated in the blood. Hormones released in response to these concentrations help to regulate kidney function.

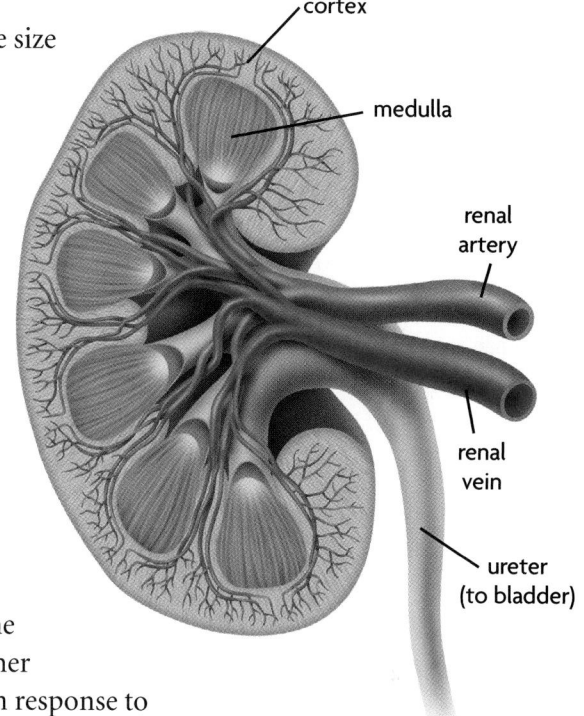

cortex

medulla

renal artery

renal vein

ureter (to bladder)

FIGURE 32.16 The bean-shaped kidneys are the main blood filtration and chemical balancing organs in the body. The cortex and medulla layers contain over 1 million nephrons, which are the kidneys' main filtering units.

Kidneys and Homeostasis

The kidneys have three basic functions in maintaining homeostasis.

- They remove waste products from the blood, such as those produced from digestion and cell respiration.
- They help to maintain electrolyte, pH, and fluid balances in the body.
- They release hormones that help to keep bones healthy, to produce red blood cells, and to regulate blood pressure.

What if the kidneys fail to work properly? Waste products quickly build up in the blood, causing serious disruptions in homeostasis in many organ systems. For example, imbalances in electrolytes such as sodium and potassium could disrupt the rhythm of the heart, causing the organ to fail. A buildup of toxic substances such as ammonium salts in the blood can impair the functioning of neurons in the brain. Someone with this condition would quickly become confused and disoriented.

Infer What might be one reason why so many nephrons are needed in the kidneys?

> ▶ **MAIN IDEA**

Nephrons clean the blood and produce urine.

The nephrons clean the blood in a three-step process: filtration, reabsorption, and excretion. First, water and other materials move out of the capillaries and into the nephron. Next, some of these materials are reabsorbed and returned to the blood. Finally, the remaining waste products are excreted in the urine.

Filtration

As shown in **FIGURE 32.17**, each nephron is supplied with blood through an arteriole, a venule, and a tangled ball of capillaries that is known as the **glomerulus** (gloh-MEHR-yuh-luhs). Each glomerulus is tucked into a cup-shaped structure called Bowman's capsule.

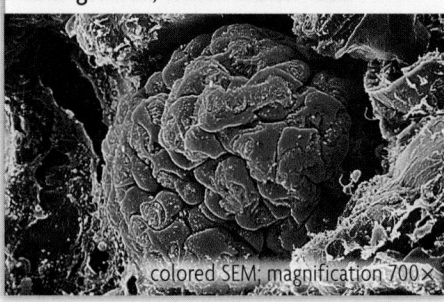

VISUAL VOCAB

Glomerulus, a tangled ball of capillaries, is a word based on the Latin *glomus*, which means "ball."

colored SEM; magnification 700×

When the blood enters the kidneys, it flows into the arterioles and then moves into the glomerulus of each nephron. Because the blood is under pressure, small molecules such as water, amino acids, salts, glucose, electrolytes, and urea are pushed out of the capillaries and into Bowman's capsule. Urea is a waste product produced by the breakdown of proteins. Anything too large to move out of the capillaries—such as blood cells, plasma proteins, and platelets—stays in the blood.

Reabsorption of Materials

The materials in Bowman's capsule are called the filtrate. The nephrons process about 180 liters (48 gal) of filtrate every day, yet only about 1 percent is excreted as urine. What happens to the other 99 percent?

Most of the filtrate is reabsorbed into the capillaries and returns to the blood. This process ensures that nutrients such as water, amino acids, glucose, and sodium (Na^+) are made available to the body. The reabsorption of water and Na^+ helps to maintain your fluid balance. For example, if you drink too much water, the nephrons will reabsorb less of the fluid and produce more urine. If you drink too little water, the nephrons will reabsorb more fluid and produce less urine.

Excretion of Materials

Finally, the waste products that are not reabsorbed are excreted in the urine. Urine is made up of water, urea, excess salts, and other materials that remain in the filtrate. These materials include ions such as potassium and hydrogen. Removal of some of these ions helps to maintain homeostasis by keeping the pH of the blood within normal limits. Filtrate moves out of Bowman's capsule and is concentrated in the loop of Henle. The loop of Henle is where water is removed one final time to reduce the volume of urine.

FIGURE 32.17 Structures and Functions of the Nephron

The nephron filters the blood and produces urine through a three-step process.

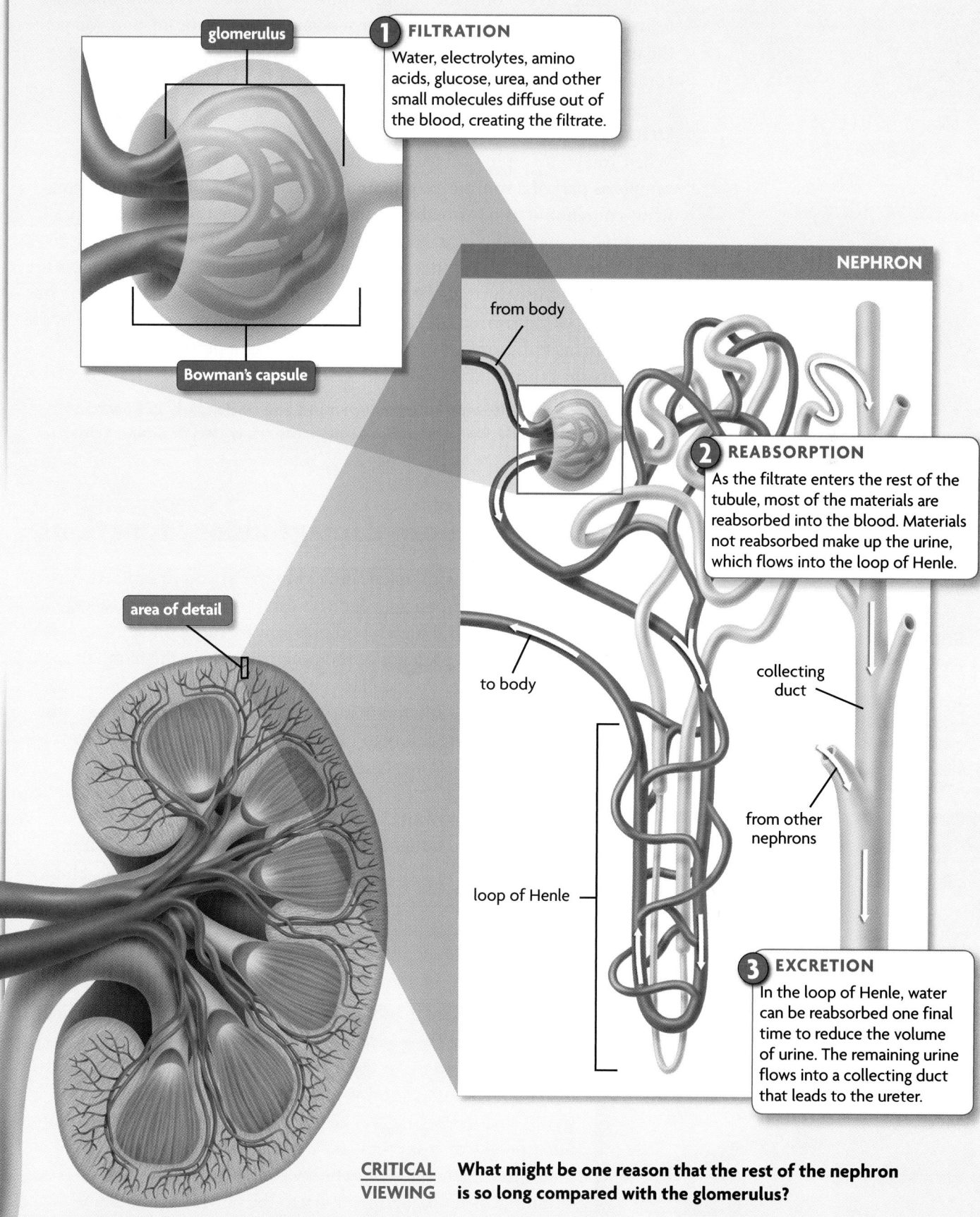

glomerulus

1 FILTRATION
Water, electrolytes, amino acids, glucose, urea, and other small molecules diffuse out of the blood, creating the filtrate.

Bowman's capsule

NEPHRON

from body

2 REABSORPTION
As the filtrate enters the rest of the tubule, most of the materials are reabsorbed into the blood. Materials not reabsorbed make up the urine, which flows into the loop of Henle.

area of detail

to body

collecting duct

from other nephrons

loop of Henle

3 EXCRETION
In the loop of Henle, water can be reabsorbed one final time to reduce the volume of urine. The remaining urine flows into a collecting duct that leads to the ureter.

CRITICAL VIEWING What might be one reason that the rest of the nephron is so long compared with the glomerulus?

The urine then moves into the collecting ducts. From there it flows through the ureter and into the urinary bladder. The adult bladder can hold about 1 liter (16 oz) of urine before it must be emptied. When the bladder is full, nerves in the walls of the bladder send signals to the brain, and you get the urge to urinate. In a healthy person, urine is a clear, pale-yellow fluid containing about 95 percent water and 5 percent waste products.

Urine Testing

When you go for a physical checkup, the doctor may ask you for a urine sample as part of a routine examination. The doctor is checking for normal urine content but also for materials that should not be there. For example, urine that contains sugar, protein, or blood may indicate that the nephrons have been damaged by an infection or injury. Ordinarily, these substances are too large to diffuse through the glomerulus. Also, any drugs that a person has taken are broken down in the liver, filtered by the kidneys, and excreted in the urine. A urine test is one way to determine whether a person is abusing drugs, and, if so, the types of drugs that may be involved.

Apply **Which of the following substances would you find mainly in Bowman's capsule: red blood cells, Na⁺, glucose, plasma proteins, water, or amino acids?**

> ▶ **MAIN IDEA**
> ## Injury and disease can damage kidney functions.

You can live comfortably with one healthy kidney, but you cannot live without any kidney function. Although your kidneys can be damaged in an accident or by an infection, diabetes and high blood pressure are more often the causes of damage to nephrons. The presence of too much glucose in the blood or high blood pressure can damage the capillary walls in the glomerulus and make them more porous. As a result, too many substances pass through the walls, and the nephrons lose their ability to filter the blood. The only treatments for kidney failure are a kidney transplant or the use of dialysis.

FIGURE 32.18 Maria Alverez (center) received a kidney from her daughter, Rosario Proscia, and part of a liver from her son, José Alvarez. The close tissue matches between mother and children made the organ transplants possible.

Kidney Transplant

As described in **FIGURE 32.18**, a patient who needs a kidney transplant can receive a kidney from a close relative, such as a sibling, parent, or child. The tissues of both people are similar enough that the patient's body will accept the new kidney more easily than a kidney from someone who is not related. Once the new kidney begins to function, the patient can live a fairly normal life.

Both the recipient and the donor must live with some restrictions, however. The recipient will have to take drugs that suppress the immune system for the rest of his or her life to guard against the possibility of the body's rejecting the new organ. This also means that the person will be more vulnerable to infections from other people or from ordinary cuts and bruises. Both recipient and donor must generally avoid heavy contact sports, such as hockey, wrestling, or football. Any injury to the one kidney could be fatal.

Kidney Dialysis

If a kidney donor is not available or the patient cannot have surgery, dialysis can save the person's life. **Dialysis** is a treatment in which a patient's blood is cleaned and chemically balanced through a mechanical process. The blood is then returned to the patient's body.

The main unit of a dialysis machine, as shown in **FIGURE 32.19**, acts like the glomerulus. Blood moves from a vein in the arm into the filtering unit. The tubing in the unit is porous, like the capillary walls, which allows waste materials to diffuse into the dialysis fluid. The fluid is continually replaced to carry wastes out of the unit. The chemical makeup of the fluid is as close to normal blood as possible. The process takes 3 to 5 hours and is done three times a week in the hospital or with a smaller dialysis machine in a patient's home.

A few patients may prefer not to use a dialysis machine. Instead, they may be given peritoneal (PEHR-ih-tuhn-EE-uhl) dialysis, in which the lining of the patient's abdomen acts as a blood filter. Dialysis fluid is pumped through tubing into the abdomen. Waste products and excess fluid move from the bloodstream into the dialysis solution. The waste-filled fluid is drained from the abdomen and replaced several times until the blood is cleaned and chemically balanced.

Summarize Explain why people without kidney function would need to have dialysis at least three times a week.

FIGURE 32.19 Dialysis Process

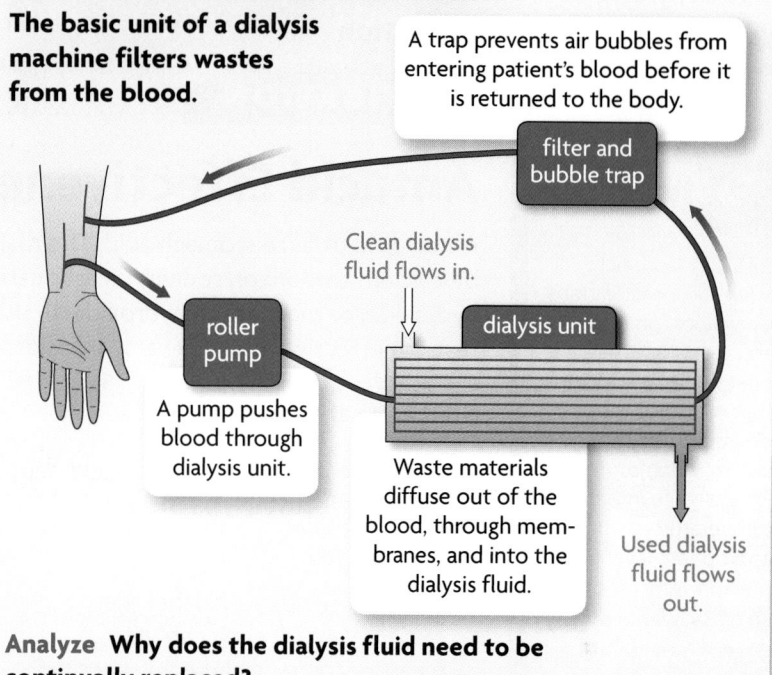

The basic unit of a dialysis machine filters wastes from the blood.

A trap prevents air bubbles from entering patient's blood before it is returned to the body.

filter and bubble trap

Clean dialysis fluid flows in.

roller pump

dialysis unit

A pump pushes blood through dialysis unit.

Waste materials diffuse out of the blood, through membranes, and into the dialysis fluid.

Used dialysis fluid flows out.

Analyze Why does the dialysis fluid need to be continually replaced?

32.4 ASSESSMENT

ONLINE QUIZ
ClassZone.com

REVIEWING ▶ MAIN IDEAS

1. How do the main organs of the **excretory system** get rid of wastes?

2. Give two examples of how **kidneys** help to maintain homeostasis.

3. Describe the main structures of the **nephron** and their functions.

4. Explain how the process of **dialysis** is similar to the way the kidneys filter the blood.

CRITICAL THINKING

5. **Apply** When kidney function is impaired, the pH level in the blood is disrupted. How would this loss of homeostasis affect the body's cells?

6. **Explain** Briefly explain the following sentence: "Filtration of the blood is relatively nonselective, but reabsorption of materials is selective."

Connecting CONCEPTS

7. **Respiration** Compare the alveoli in the lungs to the nephrons in the kidneys. List the ways in which their structures and functions may be similar.

Use these inquiry-based labs and online activities to deepen your understanding of digestion.

MICHIGAN STANDARDS

B1.1C Conduct scientific investigations using appropriate tools and techniques (e.g., selecting an instrument that measures the desired quantity—length, volume, weight, time interval, temperature—with the appropriate level of precision).

B2.3d Identify the general functions of the major systems of the human body (digestion, respiration, reproduction, circulation, excretion, protection from disease, and movement, control, and coordination) and describe ways that these systems interact with each other.

INVESTIGATION

Antacid Effectiveness

Antacids neutralize stomach acid. The main ingredient may be calcium carbonate, sodium bicarbonate, aluminum hydroxide, or magnesium hydroxide. In this lab, you will test the effectiveness of several antacids.

SKILL Analyzing Data

PROBLEM Which type of antacid neutralizes stomach acid most effectively?

MATERIALS

- 4 large paper cups
- marker
- 50-mL graduated cylinder
- 100 mL white vinegar
- 8 pH test strips
- antacid A
- antacid B
- antacid C
- antacid D
- knife
- mortar and pestle
- scale
- stirrer
- timer

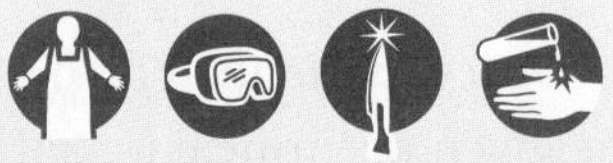

PROCEDURE

1. Obtain four cups and label them A, B, C, and D, respectively. Fill each cup with 25 mL of vinegar and measure and record the vinegar's pH in each cup.
2. Read the ingredients label and identify the active ingredient in each antacid. Determine how much of the active ingredient is in one dosage.
3. Your teacher will tell you the amount of each active ingredient you will be testing. Determine how much of each antacid you will need in order to test equal amounts of the different active ingredients. You might need to cut tablets into halves or quarters to make the amounts equal. Place tablet antacids in the pestle and grind them into powder. Design a data table like the one shown to the right.
4. Add antacid A to cup A. Stir the solution thoroughly. Wait one minute, then measure and record the pH in your data table. Record any observations of what occurs in the cup as the antacid dissolves. Clean the stirrer and the mortar and pestle (if needed).
5. Repeat step 4 with antacid B and cup B, antacid C and cup C, and antacid D and cup D, respectively.

TABLE 1. ANTACID OBSERVATIONS

Antacid	A	B	C	D
Active ingredient (__mg)				
pH of vinegar before adding antacid				
pH of vinegar after adding antacid				
Observations				

ANALYZE AND CONCLUDE

1. **Analyze** Which antacid was most effective in neutralizing the acid in the vinegar? How do you know? What is the active ingredient in that antacid?
2. **Experimental Design** Identify the independent and dependent variables in this experiment. What is the operational definition of the dependent variable? What variables were constants in the experiment?
3. **Infer** Why is it important for the environment of the stomach to be acidic? What health effects might a person experience if too little hydrochloric acid were released in the stomach?

Digesting Milk

In this lab, by testing two types of milk, you will try to determine why some people cannot digest milk.

SKILL Analyzing Data

PROBLEM Why are some people unable to digest milk?

MATERIALS

- 2 test tubes
- 5 cm tape
- marker
- 2 eye droppers
- 20 drops of milk A
- 20 drops of milk B
- 4 glucose test strips
- 2 drops of unknown solution
- 2 stirrers
- timer

PROCEDURE

1. Label one test tube A and one test tube B. Fill test tube A with 20 drops of milk A. Using a new dropper, fill test tube B with 20 drops of milk B.

2. Use a glucose test strip to test and record the concentration of glucose in test tube A. Use a new strip to test and record the concentration of glucose in test tube B.

3. Add one drop of the unknown solution into test tube A. Mix the milk and solution with a stirrer. After one minute, measure the concentration of glucose in the solution.

4. Using a new stirrer, repeat step 3 with test tube B.

ANALYZE AND CONCLUDE

1. **Contrast** What is the difference between milk A and milk B before the unknown solution was added? What happened to the milk in test tube A after the unknown solution was added?

2. **Infer** The unknown solution is not glucose. What could it be? (**Hint:** Identify the type of sugar naturally found in milk.)

3. **Analyze** What type of milk is milk B?

4. **Summarize** Explain why some people cannot digest regular milk.

ANIMATED BIOLOGY
Run the Digestive System
The digestive system must get nutrients and water from food to the rest of the body. Move a snack from the mouth through the large intestine and get as much nourishment out of the food as possible.

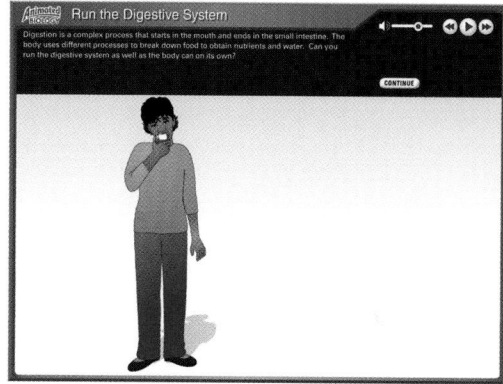

WEBQUEST
Obesity is on the rise, but is the answer as simple as "eat less and exercise more"? In the WebQuest, you will examine the causes and health risks of obesity. How can people take control of their weight?

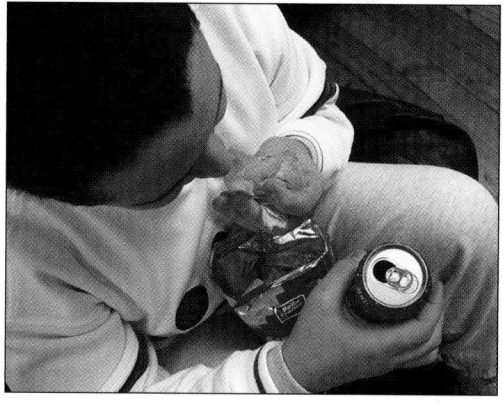

DATA ANALYSIS ONLINE
The hormone insulin helps to regulate glucose levels in the bloodstream. Graph the rate at which the pancreas releases insulin in response to changing glucose levels to see how quickly insulin acts to maintain homeostasis.

32.1 Nutrients and Homeostasis

Cells require many different nutrients. Six types of nutrients are important to maintain homeostasis in the body: water, carbohydrates, proteins, fats, minerals, and vitamins. These nutrients help to maintain fluid balance, cell processes, functions such as digestion and elimination, and tissue building and repair. A balanced diet and adequate Calories are especially important during puberty, a time of rapid growth and development.

32.2 Digestive System

The digestive system breaks down food into simpler molecules. The digestive system includes the mouth, esophagus, stomach, pancreas, liver, gallbladder, large and small intestines, rectum, and anus. Sphincters and the action of peristalsis keep food moving in one direction through the digestive system. Mechanical and chemical digestion help to break down food into simpler molecules. The process of digestion begins in the mouth and is completed in the duodenum of the small intestine.

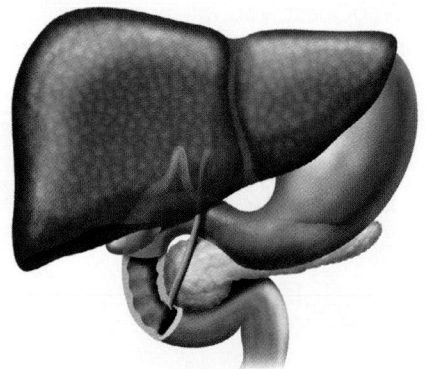

32.3 Absorption of Nutrients

Nutrients are absorbed and solid wastes eliminated after digestion. Most absorption of nutrients occurs in the small intestine. The small intestine has specialized structures—folds, villi, and microvilli—that increase the surface area so that more nutrients can be absorbed. Nutrients diffuse into the circulatory and lymphatic systems and are carried to all the cells. The large intestine absorbs water and eliminates the solid wastes that are the byproducts of digestion.

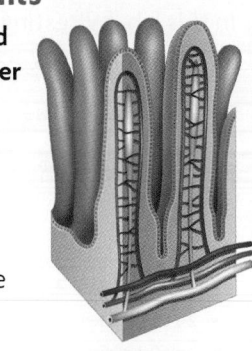

32.4 Excretory System

The excretory system removes wastes and helps maintain homeostasis. The excretory system includes the skin, lungs, kidneys, ureter, bladder, and urethra. The nephrons in the kidneys filter the blood, reabsorb needed materials, and excrete waste materials in the urine. A person whose kidneys stop functioning must have a kidney transplant or dialysis treatment to maintain the body's homeostasis.

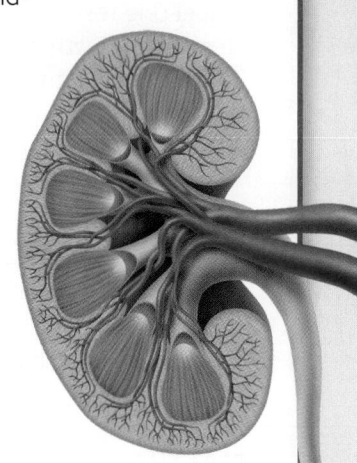

Synthesize Your Notes

Concept Map Use this graphic organizer to help you recall the functions of each of the six types of nutrients.

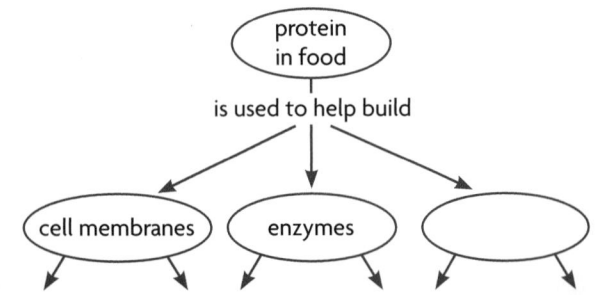

Flow Chart A flow chart like the one below can help you remember the steps in digestion.

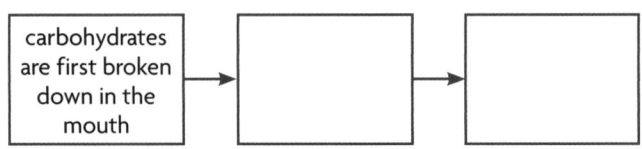

Chapter Assessment

Chapter Vocabulary

32.1 mineral, p. 973
vitamin, p. 974
Calorie, p. 975

32.2 digestion, p. 977
digestive system, p. 977
sphincter, p. 977
esophagus, p. 978
peristalsis, p. 978

stomach, p. 978
chyme, p. 979
small intestine, p. 980
bile, p. 980

32.3 absorption, p. 982
villi, p. 983
microvilli, p. 983

32.4 excretory system, p. 986
kidney, p. 986
ureter, p. 986
urinary bladder, p. 986
nephron, p. 987
glomerulus, p. 988
dialysis, p. 991

Reviewing Vocabulary

Vocabulary Connections

For each pair of words below, write a sentence to clearly show how the terms are connected. For example, for the terms *stomach* and *chyme*, you might write, "Digestive juices in your stomach turn food into a semiliquid substance called chyme."

1. esophagus, peristalsis
2. absorption, villi
3. ureter, urinary bladder
4. digestion, bile
5. small intestine, microvilli

Keep It Short

For each vocabulary term below, write a short phrase that describes its meaning. For example, a short phrase to describe *sphincter* might be "ring of muscle separating digestive sections."

6. vitamin
7. Calorie
8. nephron
9. glomerulus

Word Origins

10. The term *chyme* comes from the Greek word *khūmos*, meaning "juice." Using this meaning, explain how it relates to what chyme is.

11. The term *dialysis* is based on the Greek word *dialūein*, meaning "to break up or to dissolve." Explain how this meaning relates to the process of dialysis.

Reviewing MAIN IDEAS

12. List the six types of nutrients the body needs to maintain homeostasis. Which nutrients are the main sources of energy for the body?

13. Explain why meeting nutritional needs is particularly important during pre-teen and teen years.

14. Explain the main purpose of the digestive system. In which organs does the digestion of carbohydrates, proteins, and fats take place?

15. What is the difference between mechanical and chemical digestion? Give three examples of enzymes involved in chemical digestion.

16. Describe how the digestion of food is completed in the duodenum. What digestive organs are involved in this process?

17. How are the nutrients from digested foods transported from the small intestine to the body's cells?

18. What are the two main functions of the colon? How can diet affect the functions of this organ?

19. List the main organs of the excretory system. Give two examples of how this system helps the body maintain homeostasis.

20. The main functions of the kidneys are to maintain fluid and chemical balances in the body. Explain how the structure of the kidney helps it carry out these functions.

21. The nephrons filter the blood and produce urine. Describe the steps involved in this process.

22. How does diabetes or high blood pressure affect kidney function?

Critical Thinking

23. Analyze A deficiency in calcium can cause spasms in the calf muscles at night. A woman complains to her doctor about this problem, yet she gets plenty of calcium in her diet. The doctor wants to check her kidney functions. Why would he suspect a problem with her kidneys?

24. Infer A gastric ulcer is a type of sore that appears in the stomach lining. The ulcer can be caused by infection or by overuse of products like aspirin or ibuprofen. How might a gastric ulcer affect a person's ability to digest food in the stomach?

25. Infer A teenager wants to build muscle so he can compete better on the wrestling team. He decides to eat a diet of mostly meat and fruit juices. Within a week, he is constipated. What probably happened, and how can the problem be corrected?

Interpreting Visuals

Molecules move across a membrane by means of active or passive transport. In active transport, molecules can be pumped across a membrane into areas of higher or lower concentration. In passive transport, molecules can move only from an area of higher concentration to an area of lower concentration. Use the following diagram to answer the next three questions.

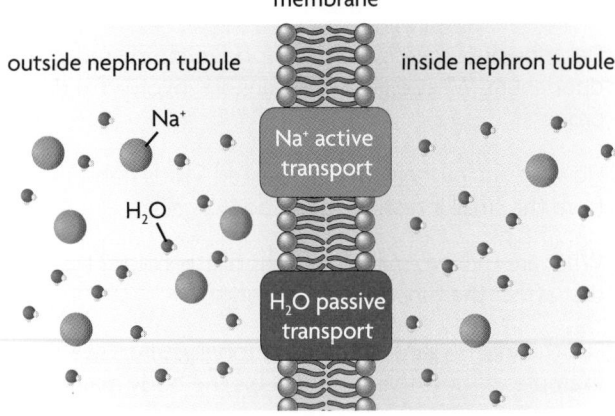

26. Analyze Look at the concentrations of Na⁺ ions and H_2O in the diagram. Can more Na⁺ ions move out of the tubule? Explain your answer.

27. Infer The membrane can change to let more or less water through. If a person were dehydrated, how might the membrane change? Explain.

28. Evaluate If the body contains too much fluid, which way would H_2O molecules move across the membrane? Explain your answer.

Analyzing Data

To educate young people about diet and health, a local hospital offered glucose testing so teenagers could learn more about how their bodies were functioning. Testing was done one to two hours after each meal so that the food was digested and nutrients were absorbed into the body. In a healthy person, glucose levels should be 80–120 mg/dL of blood before a meal and less than 180 mg/dL after food is digested. The graph below shows the results for one teenager. Use the graph to answer the next two questions.

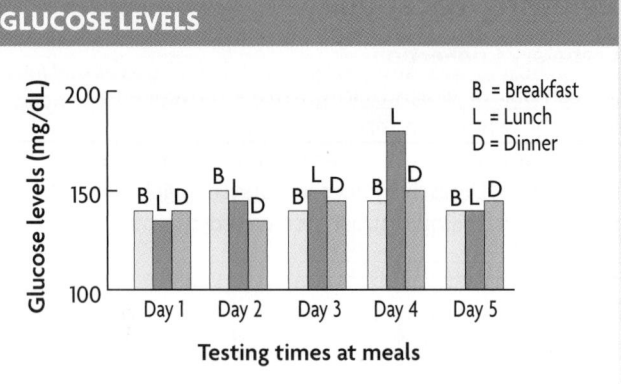

29. Analyze What is the typical glucose range for this teenager after meals? Which point is the outlier in this data set?

30. Evaluate What are some possible explanations for the outlier data? How should the scientists proceed?

Connecting CONCEPTS

31. Blog a Snack-Food Challenge More companies are offering alternative, "healthier" snack foods, such as protein bars or fruit strips. Your challenge: Use your knowledge of food labels to compare the nutritional information on these products with other snack foods such as candy bars and potato chips. Write a blog entry on your findings, including each product's nutritional content, its cost, and where you can buy it.

32. Synthesize The photo on page 971 shows the specialized cells in the lining of the stomach. Use what you know about the digestive process and the digestive tract to explain why the processes that occur in the stomach could not occur anywhere else.

MICHIGAN STANDARDS-BASED ASSESSMENT

✓ *Test Practice*
For more test practice,
go to ClassZone.com.

1.

Effect of Diet on Weight Loss and Heart Disease			
Type of Diet	No Prescribed Diet	Diet A	Diet B
Weight loss	4%	6%	5%
Heart disease reduction	7%	15%	8%
Drop-out rate	0%	50%	35%

Scientists studying the effects of two different diets monitored three groups of people for one year. The first group was not asked to change the way they ate. The second group followed Diet A. The third group followed Diet B. The first group was asked not to change their diets in the study because **B1.1B**

A scientists knew that people would drop out.

B scientists knew this group would lose weight.

C the group acted as a control for the study.

D the group acted as a model for the study.

2. A student made a simple model to demonstrate digestion. A plastic bag and mallet were used to represent the chewing action of teeth in the mouth. A deflated balloon that could be twisted to churn food represented the stomach. Pantyhose that could be squeezed and stretched were used as a small intestine. One limitation of this model is that **B1.1B**

A it does not include chemical digestion.

B it does not include mechanical digestion.

C the order of the organs is incorrect.

D model parts are each made of the same thing.

3. Malnutrition occurs when necessary nutrients do not reach the body's cells. In order for cells of the body to receive nutrients from the food that we eat, digestion must be followed by **B2.3C**

A excretion.

B fluid retention.

C respiration.

D absorption.

4. Chemical digestion occurs throughout the digestive tract. The stomach releases pepsin, the liver and gallbladder release bile, the salivary glands release amylase, and the pancreas releases an alkaline fluid. Together, these processes are an example of **B2.2f**

A the release of unnecessary chemicals.

B coordinated function within an organ system.

C a positive feedback loop between organs.

D a negative feedback loop between organs.

5. Lungs are part of both the respiratory system and the excretory system. In their function as excretory organs, the lungs help remove which waste products from your body? **B2.3d**

A oxygen and water vapor

B oxygen and carbon dioxide

C carbon dioxide and water vapor

D water vapor only

> **THINK THROUGH THE QUESTION**
>
> Think about what is present in the air that is not required by the respiratory system, and therefore would be removed by the excretory system.

6.

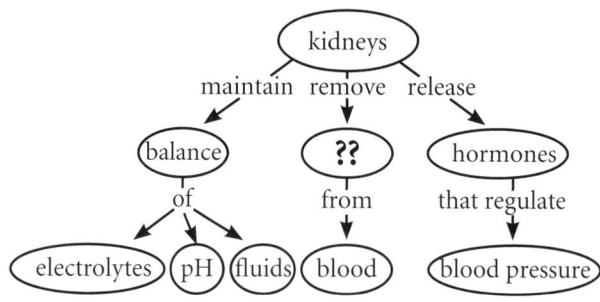

Which of these terms *best* completes this concept map? **B2.3e**

A nutrients

B water

C waste products

D red blood cells

33 Protection, Support, and Movement

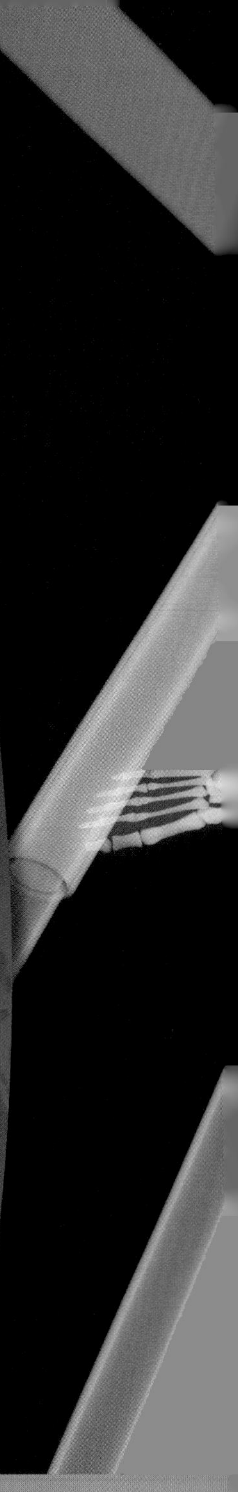

KEY CONCEPTS

33.1 Skeletal System

The skeletal system includes bones and tissues that are important for supporting, protecting, and moving your body.

33.2 Muscular System

Muscles are tissues that can contract, enabling movement.

33.3 Integumentary System

The integumentary system has many tissues that protect the body.

Online BIOLOGY CLASSZONE.COM

Animated BIOLOGY

View animated chapter concepts.
• Muscle Contraction
• What Kind of Joint Is It?

BIOZINE

Keep current with biology news.
• News feeds
• Strange Biology
• Bio Bytes

RESOURCE CENTER

Get more information on
• Skeletal System
• Muscular System
• Integumentary System

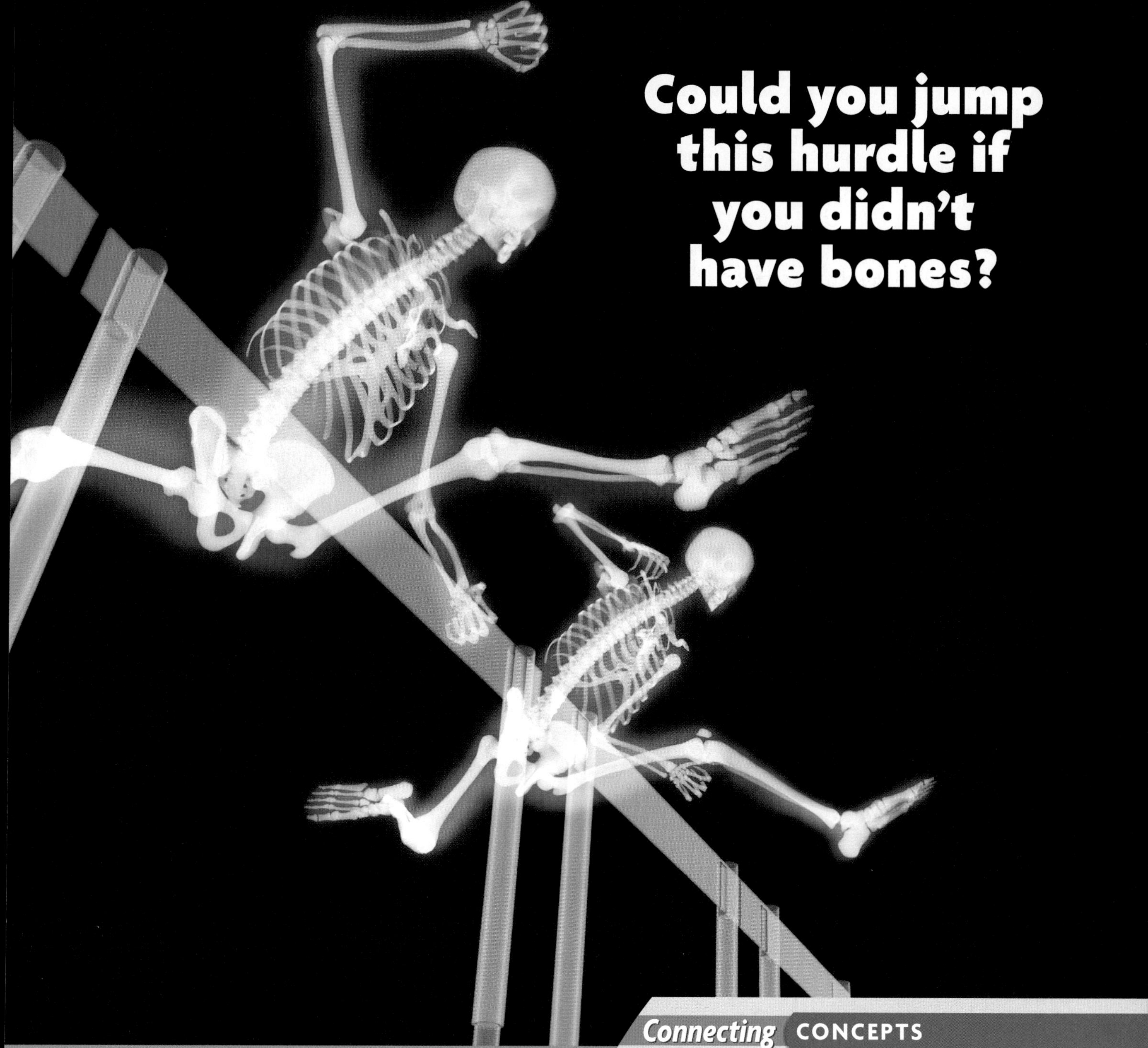

Could you jump this hurdle if you didn't have bones?

This dramatic image of the skeletal system is a composite of many x-ray images. As you can see, your bones form a system of levers to which your muscles attach. Without this system of bones, you would not be able to move around the way that you normally do.

Connecting CONCEPTS

Exoskeleton You don't have to take an x-ray to see an insect's skeleton. Unlike people and other vertebrates, an insect has a skeleton on the outside of its body. The exoskeleton, which is red and black on the red lily beetle to the left, is a hard protective covering. Muscles attached to the inside of the jointed exoskeleton pull at it, allowing movement.

33.1 Skeletal System

KEY CONCEPT The skeletal system includes bones and tissues that are important for supporting, protecting, and moving your body.

▶ **MAIN IDEAS**

- Your skeletal system is made up of the appendicular and axial skeletons.
- Bones connect to form joints.
- Bones are living tissue.

VOCABULARY

skeletal system, p. 1000
appendicular skeleton, p. 1000
axial skeleton, p. 1001
vertebrae, p. 1001

cartilage, p. 1001
joint, p. 1001
ligament, p. 1002
calcification, p. 1005

MICHIGAN STANDARDS

B2.3d Identify the general functions of the major systems of the human body (digestion, respiration, reproduction, circulation, excretion, protection from disease, and movement, control, and coordination) and describe ways that these systems interact with each other.

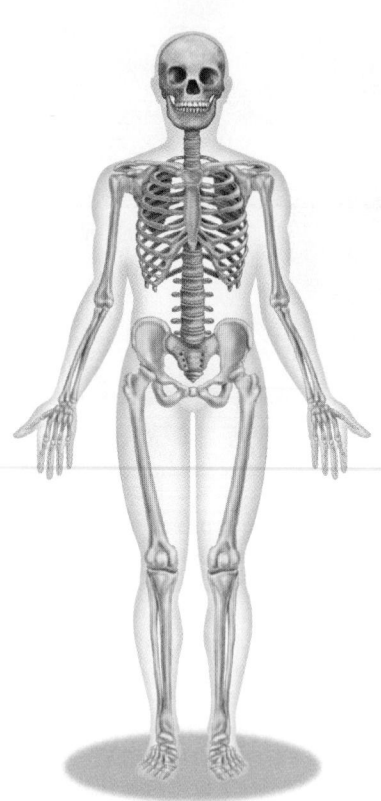

FIGURE 33.1 The skeletal system is composed of an appendicular skeleton (white) and an axial skeleton (red).

Connect Your bones and muscles must be strong enough to support more than your body's weight. Each time you move, whether walking or running, your bones and muscles must absorb the force of the ground pushing upward on your foot. How much force do your bones need to absorb? When you jog, your body absorbs a force of more than twice your body weight with each step. When you jump and land, this force is about 12 times your body weight.

▶ **MAIN IDEA**

Your skeletal system is made up of the appendicular and axial skeletons.

Imagine a tree. The wood fibers support the tree and protect the tree's internal tissues. As wood fibers support a tree, your skeletal system protects your organs and supports your body, allowing your body to keep its shape. Unlike the wood in a tree, however, your skeletal system allows you to move.

The **skeletal system,** shown in **FIGURE 33.1,** is an organ system that includes the bones and the connective tissues that hold the bones together. The human skeleton has 206 bones, which can be categorized as part of either the appendicular or axial skeletons.

Appendicular Skeleton

Unlike the branches of a tree, which cannot move much, parts of your skeleton allow for wide ranges of movement. The **appendicular skeleton** is the part of your skeleton that is adapted to allow the body to move. It includes the bones in the limbs that extend from the trunk of your body—your legs, arms, feet, and hands.

The appendicular skeleton also includes two sets of bones, called girdles, that connect your limbs to your body. The girdles attach the bones of the arms and legs to the body loosely enough that these limbs have a wide range of motion. Your arm, for example, can rotate from the floor to the ceiling, as when a swimmer does the backstroke or a baseball pitcher "winds up" during a pitch. Your leg is connected loosely enough that your knee can be raised high in front of your body, as when you are running, or it can move away from your body, as when a basketball player shuffles sideways down a court.

Axial Skeleton

The **axial skeleton** is made up of the bones found in the trunk and head of the body. The bones of the axial skeleton support the weight of the body and protect the internal tissues. The axial skeleton includes the 27 bones in the skull, the 33 bones that form the spine, the 12 pairs of ribs, and the breastbone, the flat bone in the front of the chest that connects the ribs.

The bones of the axial skeleton cover most of the body's vital organs. **Vertebrae** are the bones that surround the spinal cord. The bones of the skull protect the brain, and the ribs and breastbone protect the heart and lungs, as shown in **FIGURE 33.2**.

Although the main functions of the axial skeleton are protection and support, it also provides some limited movement. The ribs are connected with flexible tissue that allows the chest to expand while breathing. Flexible tissue in the spine allows people to bend or to turn and look behind them.

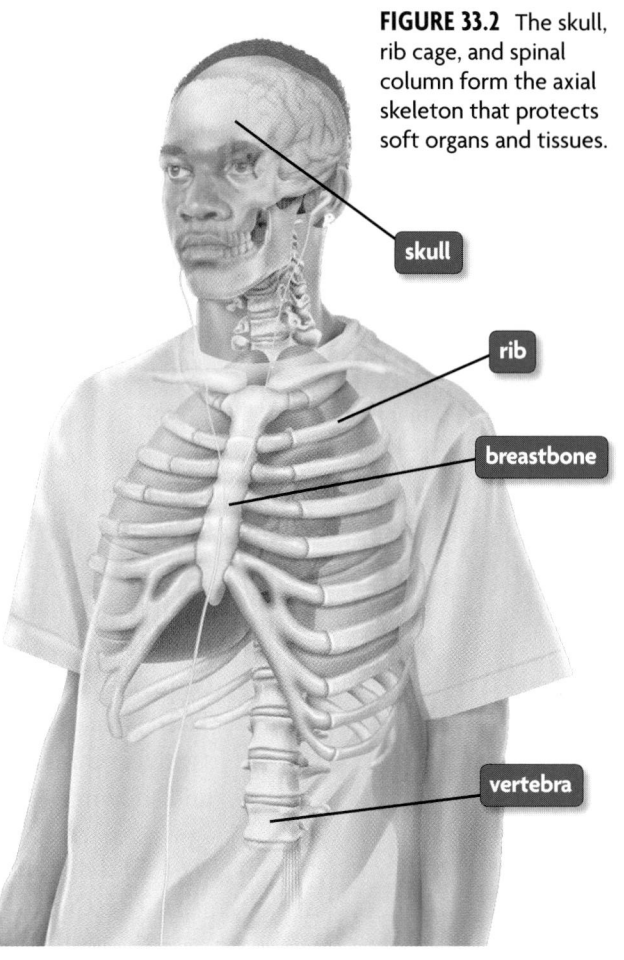

FIGURE 33.2 The skull, rib cage, and spinal column form the axial skeleton that protects soft organs and tissues.

skull

rib

breastbone

vertebra

Cartilage

Bones are very hard organs. If two bones in your finger fused into one, your muscles would not be able to move your finger. But if the two bones were in contact with one another, they would rub together every time you moved, and eventually, the ends of the bones would wear down. Fortunately, the ends of your bones are protected from wear by cartilage.

Cartilage is flexible connective tissue that is found between your bones. It cushions your bones and allows for smooth movements. Sometimes cartilage physically connects two bones. The cartilage found in your chest, for example, holds neighboring ribs together into one strong rib cage. Because the ribs are held together with cartilage and not bone, the rib cage is flexible too. Cartilage is also found between neighboring bones that move relative to one another.

Analyze Why is it important that the ribs are connected by cartilage?

▶ MAIN IDEA

Bones connect to form joints.

A **joint** is the place where two bones meet. Joints allow for different amounts of movement. Some joints are made of very strong fibers that do not allow movement. These joints, called fibrous joints, are made of the same dense material that bone is made of, and they act like a tough glue that connects the bones and holds them in place. Fibrous joints in your jawbone hold your teeth in your mouth. Fibrous joints also connect the plates of your skull into one large structure that surrounds your brain.

TAKING NOTES

Use a main idea diagram to organize your notes about joints.

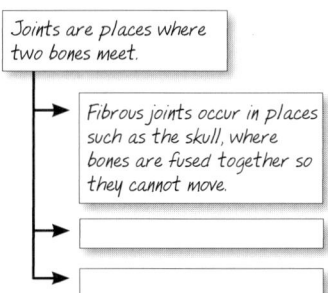

Joints are places where two bones meet.

Fibrous joints occur in places such as the skull, where bones are fused together so they cannot move.

Cartilaginous (KAHR-tuhl-AJ-uh-nuhs) joints allow partial movement. In these joints, cartilage physically holds bones together. Discs of cartilage between the vertebrae keep the bones stacked on top of one another and give the spine some flexibility. A person can bend slightly to one side at the waist. However, a person cannot fold in half by bending to the right or left.

Cartilaginous joints are also found where the breastbone and ribs meet. Because of cartilage's flexibility, these joints allow the chest to expand and contract while you breathe. But there is a limit to how far your chest can expand. Taking in a deep breath will cause the circumference of your chest to expand by only about 7 cm (3 in.).

Other joints, called synovial joints, are cushioned with cartilage and held together by ligaments. A **ligament** is a long, flexible band of connective tissue that connects two bones across a joint. Ligaments keep bones physically connected while remaining loose enough that the bones can move. There are several different types of synovial joints, which are listed below and shown in **FIGURE 33.3**.

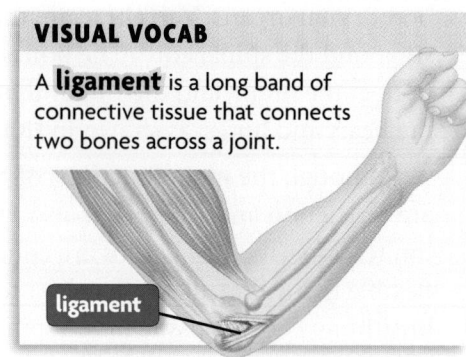
1. **Gliding joints** allow the flat surfaces of bones to slide over each other. These joints give flexibility to the ankle and wrist. These joints give you the ability to walk on uneven surfaces and move your hand to the right and left.

2. **Pivot joints** are found where two bones turn on each other and allow rotation. The top two vertebrae that support the skull form a pivot joint that allows the head to turn to the right and left.

3. **Ball-and-socket joints** are found in the hip and shoulder. In these joints, the knoblike end of an arm or thigh bone fits into a bony cup in the shoulder blade or hip bone. Ball-and-socket joints allow the arm or leg to move in almost any direction.

4. **Saddle joints** allow a bone to move front to back and left to right. Your thumbs are connected to your hands by saddle joints. The saddle joint in your thumb is what gives your thumb the ability to reach across the palm of your hand and touch your other fingers.

5. **Hinge joints** allow bones to move in one direction, like a swinging door. These joints are found in the knees, fingers, and toes.

Some bones in the body are connected by more than one type of synovial joint. These are called compound joints. In your elbow, for example, a hinge joint connects your forearm to your upper arm and allows you to extend and retract your forearm. Your elbow also has a pivot joint that allows the arm to rotate so that your hand can face up or down.

Infer Why do you think that ligaments are found in the appendicular skeleton but not the axial skeleton?

Connecting CONCEPTS

Levers Recall from your physical science courses that a lever is like a door that moves by pivoting at the hinges. Joints are similar to levers in that the bone is the rigid object, and the ligaments and joints allow the bone to pivot.

FIGURE 33.3 **Joints**

Some joints allow for movement.

1 **GLIDING JOINT**
Gives flexibility to the wrist and ankle

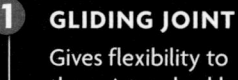

2 **PIVOT JOINT**
Allows the bones in the neck to move a short distance to the left or right

3 **BALL-AND-SOCKET JOINT**
Holds the upper arm and leg to the trunk of the body and allows these bones to move in almost any direction

4 **SADDLE JOINT**
Gives bones in the fingers the ability to move in all directions but in a much more limited way than a ball-and-socket joint

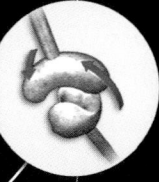

5 **HINGE JOINT**
Lets many different bones in the body move toward or away from one another

CRITICAL VIEWING How does the range of motion of a saddle joint in the thumb differ from the hinge joint in the finger?

▶ MAIN IDEA
Bones are living tissue.

In addition to their role in providing support, allowing movement, and protecting internal organs, bones are living tissue that produce blood cells and act as a storage bank for minerals. Bones are covered by a layer of connective tissue called periosteum (PEHR-ee-AHS-tee-uhm), which holds and protects blood vessels that run alongside of the bone tissue. Just like any other tissue in the body, bones rely on blood vessels to bring nutrients and remove wastes.

Bone Structure

There are two types of bone tissue: compact and spongy. Compact bone is the hard, dense layer that protects against jolts and bumps. It is found inside the periosteum but on the outside of the spongy bone. Compact bone is made up of several calcium-rich rings. These rings are maintained by bone cells called osteocytes, which are scattered in small spaces throughout the rings. At the center of the rings are channels called Haversian canals, each of which contains a small blood vessel.

Spongy bone is the less dense bone that is surrounded by compact bone. Spongy bone is a porous tissue that holds and protects red or yellow bone marrow, as shown in **FIGURE 33.4**. When a person is young, most of the spongy bone is filled with red bone marrow. Red marrow is a part of the circulatory system. It produces blood cells. As a person matures and grows, some of the red bone marrow in their bones is replaced with yellow bone marrow.

FIGURE 33.4 Bone Structure

Bones have many layers for protection and transport.

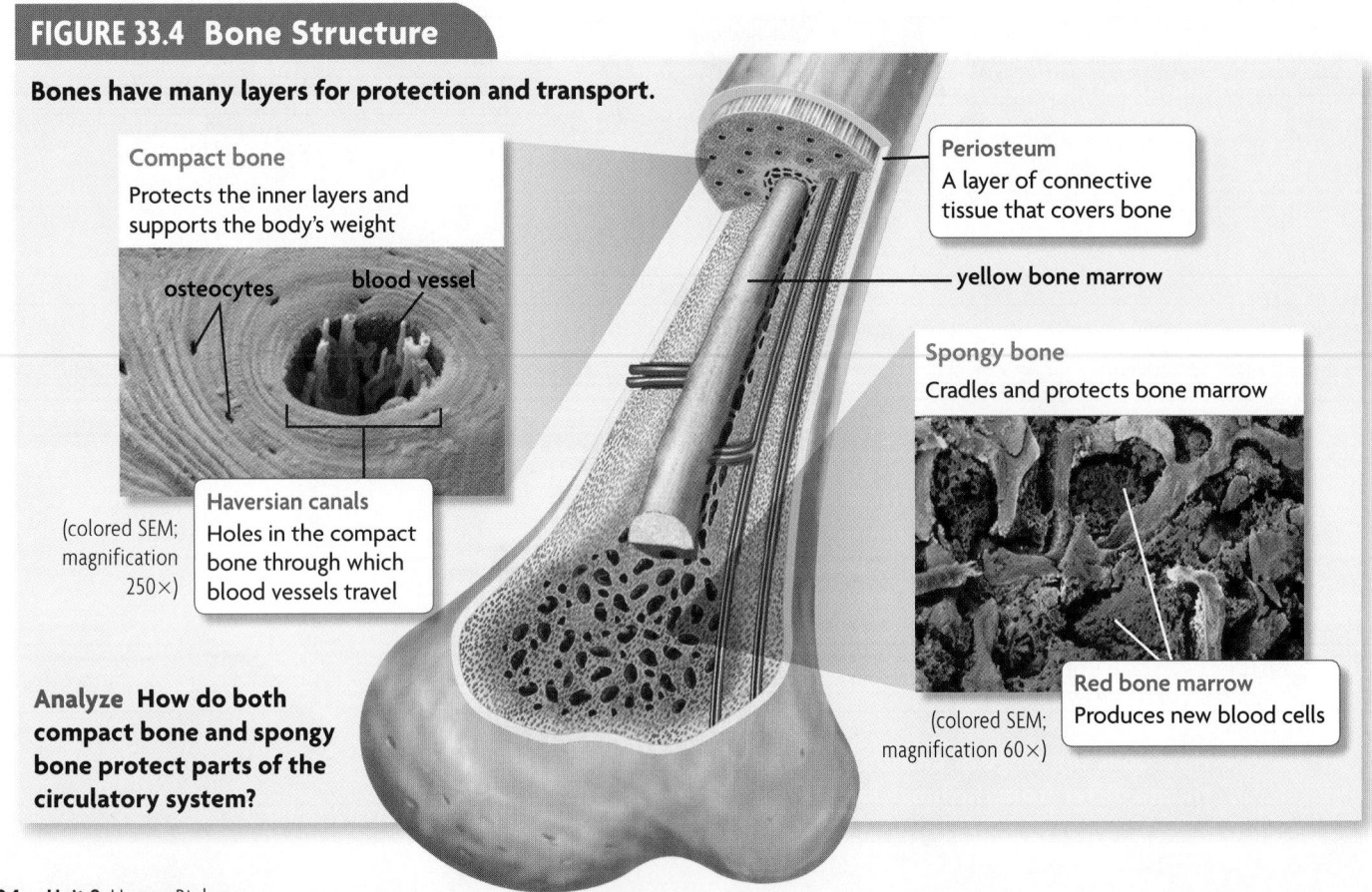

Compact bone
Protects the inner layers and supports the body's weight

osteocytes   blood vessel

(colored SEM; magnification 250×)

Haversian canals
Holes in the compact bone through which blood vessels travel

Periosteum
A layer of connective tissue that covers bone

— yellow bone marrow

Spongy bone
Cradles and protects bone marrow

(colored SEM; magnification 60×)

Red bone marrow
Produces new blood cells

Analyze How do both compact bone and spongy bone protect parts of the circulatory system?

Yellow marrow is mostly fat, but it can change back into red marrow and produce blood cells if the body suddenly loses blood.

Bone Growth

Human embryos do not have bones at first. Instead, when they are developing, their skeletal system is made mostly of cartilage. Over time, the flexible cartilage becomes hardened bone.

Bones form when cells called osteoblasts secrete chemicals that cause cartilage to harden. Osteoblasts release a mixture of collagen, a strong fibrous connective tissue, and calcium phosphate, a mineral that hardens the collagen. The process of creating hard bone by combining collagen and calcium phosphate is called **calcification.** Once bone calcifies, the trapped osteoblast is called an osteocyte, shown in **FIGURE 33.5.**

Bones grow from their ends, where the cartilage is located. After birth, two bands of cartilage remain at either end of the bone. Until puberty, children's bones grow longer, wider, and thicker. In adolescence, sex hormones stimulate bones to become more dense. Bones are strongest when a person is between 18 and 30 years old. After that, bones lose density because calcium is taken from the bones and used elsewhere in the body.

Depositing and removing calcium from bones is a continual process that reshapes bones and helps maintain chemical homeostasis in the body. New bone can be created by osteoblasts to heal fractures even after a person matures and the bones stop growing. Bones also serve as storage areas for calcium that the body uses in many metabolic activities such as muscle movement, which you will read about in Section 33.2. Calcium removal from and deposit into bones is regulated by calcitonin, a hormone produced by the thyroid gland, and parathyroid hormone (PTH), which is produced by the parathyroid gland. Calcitonin stimulates osteoblasts to remove calcium from the blood and deposit it in bone. PTH stimulates other bone cells called osteoclasts to remove calcium from bone and make it available for use in the body.

Infer How are Haversian canals important to the function of spongy bone?

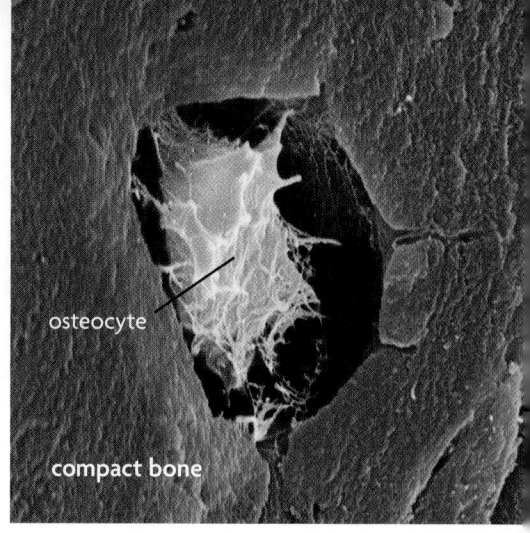

FIGURE 33.5 Osteocytes are specialized bone cells that have produced compact bone.
(colored SEM; magnification 4500×)

To find out more about joints, go to scilinks.org.
Keycode: MLB033

33.1 ASSESSMENT

ONLINE QUIZ
ClassZone.com

REVIEWING ▶ MAIN IDEAS

1. What are the differences between the **axial skeleton** and the **appendicular skeleton**?

2. How are **ligaments** and **cartilage** functionally similar in **joints**?

3. How is **calcification** important for growth and protection?

CRITICAL THINKING

4. **Analyze** Some scientists say that a person's bones will never contain more calcium than they had when the person was 18 years old. How might they explain this hypothesis?

5. **Compare and Contrast** How are the joints of the axial skeleton similar to and different from the joints of the appendicular skeleton?

Connecting CONCEPTS

6. **Nervous System Vertebrae** protect the spinal cord, the organ that sends messages to and gets messages from the brain. Why do you think it is beneficial for vertebrae to have cartilaginous joints that limit movement?

33.2 Muscular System

KEY CONCEPT Muscles are tissues that can contract, enabling movement.

▶ MAIN IDEAS

- Humans have three types of muscle.
- Muscles contract when the nervous system causes muscle filaments to move.

VOCABULARY

muscular system, p. 1006	**cardiac muscle**, p. 1008
muscle fiber, p. 1006	**myofibril**, p. 1008
skeletal muscle, p. 1006	**sarcomere**, p. 1008
tendon, p. 1006	**actin**, p. 1008
smooth muscle, p. 1007	**myosin**, p. 1008

MICHIGAN STANDARDS

B2.3d Identify the general functions of the major systems of the human body (digestion, respiration, reproduction, circulation, excretion, protection from disease, and movement, control, and coordination) and describe ways that these systems interact with each other.

Connect Make a muscle with your arm. The biceps you see is one type of muscle. Your beating heart is another. You also have muscles that line other organs. Some of these muscles push food through your digestive organs. Others change the size of the blood vessels to allow more oxygenated blood to reach the other muscles of the body that are doing hard work.

▶ MAIN IDEA

Humans have three types of muscle.

The **muscular system** is the body system that moves bones at joints and pushes substances such as blood, food, and fluids throughout the body. Muscle fibers perform a lot of hard work, and so they contain many mitochondria to power their contractions. Your muscle contractions also help regulate your body temperature. While you're at rest, as much as 25 percent of your body heat comes from the energy used as your various muscles contract. When your body temperature falls below a set point, you shiver. The involuntary muscles that cause shivering generate even more heat that helps raise your body temperature. The part of your muscular system that moves your bones and allows you to shiver is shown in **FIGURE 33.6**.

All muscles are longer than they are wide, and they are divided into fibers. **Muscle fibers** are muscle cells that contract, or shorten, when they are stimulated by the nervous system. Because muscle fibers can only shorten and not elongate, muscles only work in a pulling action. There are three types of muscle tissue: skeletal muscle, smooth muscle, and cardiac muscle.

Skeletal Muscle

The muscles you are most familiar with are skeletal muscles. **Skeletal muscle** is a type of muscle that attaches to the skeleton by tendons. A **tendon** is a connective tissue that begins within the muscle and continues into the bone or other muscle tissue. It physically connects the two, allowing for movement.

Skeletal muscle cells are rectangular and have many nuclei. Under a microscope, skeletal muscle appears striped, or striated, as you can see in **FIGURE 33.7**. The stripes result from a regular pattern of the protein filaments that cause skeletal muscle contraction, as you will read later in this section.

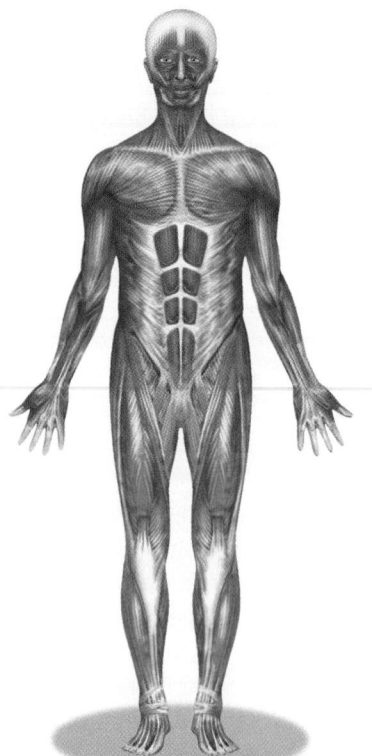

FIGURE 33.6 Muscle tissue moves matter in the body.

FIGURE 33.7 TYPES OF MUSCLE

SKELETAL MUSCLE
Muscle that moves bones has dark bands across it and is rectangular in shape.

colored TM; magnification 150×

CARDIAC MUSCLE
Muscle in the heart has dark bands and oval-shaped cells.

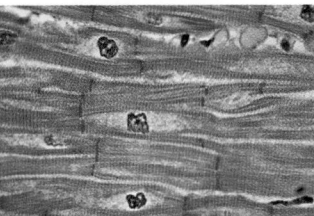

colored TM; magnification 300×

SMOOTH MUSCLE
Muscle in the arteries and intestines has spindle-shaped cells and no bands.

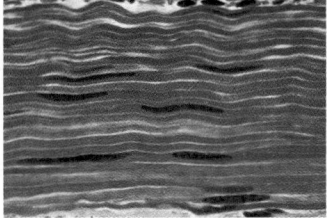

colored TM; magnification 400×

Skeletal muscles are mostly under voluntary control, which means that you can tell yourself to move your arm or wiggle an eyebrow, and it will happen. Some skeletal muscles, such as those in the spinal column, are involuntary. Muscles in your spine help maintain your posture, and muscles in your legs and feet allow you to remain balanced without your needing to think about it.

Skeletal muscles are made of two different types of muscle fibers: fast-twitch fibers and slow-twitch fibers. Fast-twitch fibers respond quickly to nerve impulses, and they make quick, sudden movements. Slow-twitch fibers respond slowly and are responsible for sustained movements. Your eye, for example, contains the quickest fast-twitch fiber. It can make you blink in less than one one-hundredth of a second. On the other hand, muscles in your leg can take several seconds to contract when you walk slowly.

A person with a high percentage of fast-twitch fibers would be a good sprinter, while a person with more slow-twitch fibers would do better as a distance runner. Individuals are born with certain amounts of fast-twitch and slow-twitch fibers. These amounts cannot be changed. With exercise, however, both fiber types can develop more mitochondria and become more efficient.

Smooth Muscle

Smooth muscle is found in many body systems and, unlike striated muscle, it is not striped. Smooth muscle moves food through the digestive system, empties the bladder, and helps push out a baby during birth. It also plays an important homeostatic role by controlling blood flow by regulating the width of blood vessels, as shown in **FIGURE 33.8**. When the smooth muscle cells surrounding a blood vessel contract, the blood vessel becomes narrow. When the muscle cells relax, the blood vessel becomes wider, and more blood can pass through. Smooth muscle cells are spindle-shaped, meaning they are wide in the middle and taper at the ends. Also, smooth muscle cells have only one nucleus.

No smooth muscle is under voluntary control. Hormones or the nervous system stimulate smooth muscle, as you read in Chapter 29. The contractions of smooth muscle are slower than those of skeletal muscle, but they can be sustained for longer periods of time.

FIGURE 33.8 Smooth muscle around this artery allows the artery to regulate blood flow by shrinking and expanding. (colored SEM; magnification 1430×)

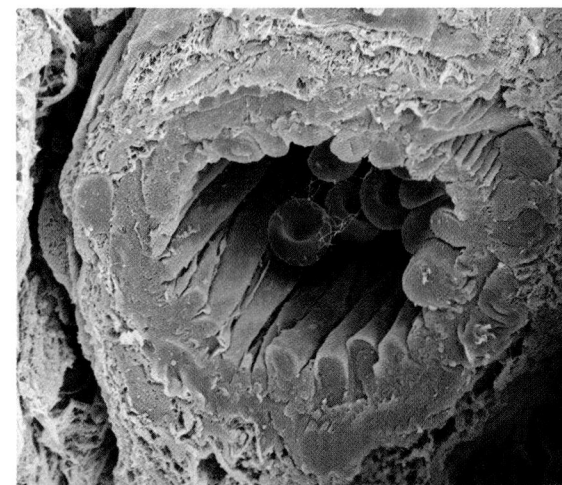

Cardiac Muscle

Your heart is a muscle that pumps blood throughout your body, and it uses a specific kind of muscle cell. **Cardiac muscle** is muscle that is found only in the heart, and it looks like a combination of the two other muscle types. It is striated, like skeletal muscle, but its cells are oval-shaped and have multiple nuclei. Cardiac muscle cells use a huge amount of ATP and have more mitochondria than do skeletal muscles.

Cardiac muscle cells are under involuntary control. The impulse to contract comes from a pacemaker within the heart, and signals from the brainstem can only modify the rate at which the pacemaker causes contractions.

Compare and Contrast How are the three types of muscle both similar and different in their functions?

Connecting CONCEPTS

Pacemaker The pacemaker is the part of the heart that stimulates contractions. To learn more about how the heart works, review Section 30.3.

▶ MAIN IDEA

Muscles contract when the nervous system causes muscle filaments to move.

When you play tug-of-war, your team must hold on to a rope and pull the other team toward you. Each player on your team reaches down to the rope, grabs onto it, and pulls. The filaments in muscles work in a similar way during contractions. Some filaments act like the players in a game of tug-of-war and pull at other filaments, which are like the ropes that connect the teams. To understand how these filaments work, let's take a look at the smallest functional unit of a muscle, which is called a myofibril.

Muscle Structure

Myofibrils are long strands of protein found within a muscle fiber, as shown in **FIGURE 33.9**. Each myofibril contains a complex set of filaments that are arranged in a regular pattern. The protein filaments within these myofibrils cause muscle contraction.

Myofibrils can be further divided into sarcomeres. A **sarcomere** is a section of a myofibril that contains all of the filaments necessary to make that section of the muscle contract. You can see sarcomeres if you look at muscle tissue under a microscope; they are bounded by a dark stripe on each side.

The dark stripes occur where the filaments are located in the muscle cell. These filaments are called actin filaments. **Actin** filaments are thin protein fibers that are pulled to cause muscle contraction. The ends of the actin filaments are anchored to the sarcomere by a plate of structural protein called a Z line. Because actin filaments are attached to the sarcomere, when they are pulled, they drag the ends of the sarcomere along with them.

In the center of the sarcomere are thick filaments, called myosin. **Myosin** filaments are protein fibers that pull actin. The myosin is anchored to the middle of the sarcomere at the M line. By being anchored to the center of the of the sarcomere, myosin can pull the actin without moving itself.

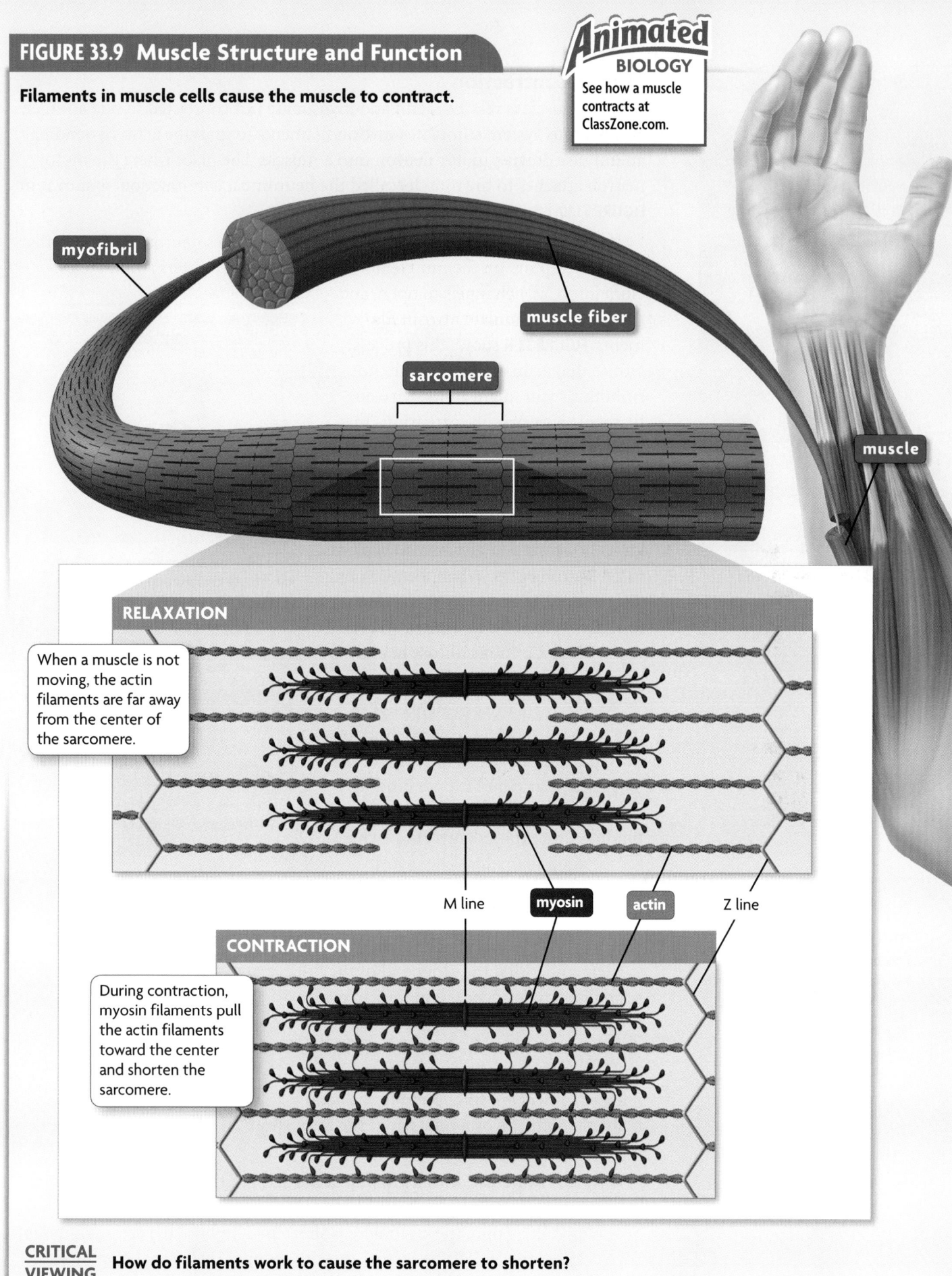

FIGURE 33.9 Muscle Structure and Function

Filaments in muscle cells cause the muscle to contract.

Animated BIOLOGY See how a muscle contracts at ClassZone.com.

myofibril

muscle fiber

sarcomere

muscle

RELAXATION

When a muscle is not moving, the actin filaments are far away from the center of the sarcomere.

M line   myosin   actin   Z line

CONTRACTION

During contraction, myosin filaments pull the actin filaments toward the center and shorten the sarcomere.

CRITICAL VIEWING   How do filaments work to cause the sarcomere to shorten?

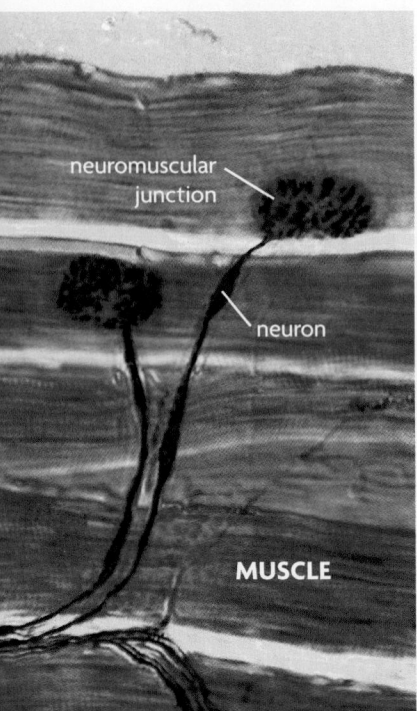

FIGURE 33.10 Neurons send electrical impulses that stimulate muscle contractions. (colored LM; magnification 150×)

Muscle Contraction

When a muscle is relaxed, actin and myosin are not connected to one another. The nervous system stimulates myosin filaments to grab the actin by sending an impulse down a motor neuron into a muscle. The place where the motor neuron attaches to the muscle, called the neuromuscular junction, is shown in **FIGURE 33.10**.

At the neuromuscular junction, the neuron releases neurotransmitters that bind to receptors on the muscle fiber. The neurotransmitters stimulate calcium ion (Ca^{2+}) channels to open, and the Ca^{2+} ions stimulate myosin filaments. **FIGURE 33.11** shows this process. Notice that actin and myosin are not smooth, as you might think. Myosin filaments have armlike extensions that act like little hands. These hands grab onto and pull the actin filaments. Actin filaments also have bumps on their surface. These bumps act like knots in a rope and give myosin a place to get a strong grip. When the nervous system stimulates a muscle, calcium ion (Ca^{2+}) channels in the sarcomere open. Then, Ca^{2+} ions diffuse in and bind to regulatory proteins.

At rest, regulatory proteins tightly hug actin. But when Ca^{2+} ions bind to the regulatory proteins, the proteins loosen their grip and expose binding sites on the actin filament. With the binding sites exposed, myosin reaches for the actin filaments. The myosin binds to and pulls the actin. When the myosin has moved as far as it can, it uses ATP to break its bond with actin. As long as Ca^{2+} ions are bound and binding sites are exposed, the myosin will grab and pull the actin filament.

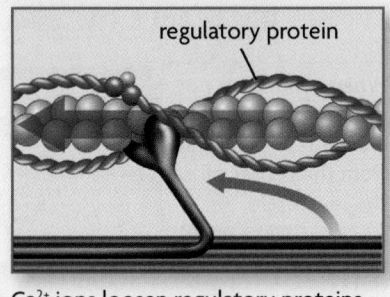

FIGURE 33.11 FILAMENT ACTION

actin   Ca²⁺

myosin

The nervous system causes Ca^{2+} ions to diffuse toward and bind to actin.

regulatory protein

Ca^{2+} ions loosen regulatory proteins. Now, myosin can grab and pull actin.

TAKING NOTES

Use a cause-and-effect diagram to explain how muscles contract.

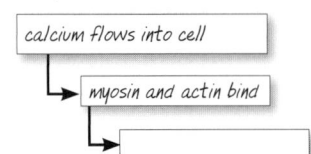

Remember that the other end of the actin filament is anchored in the sarcomere at the Z line. However, the actin filament does not slip when one myosin bulb lets go, because although one myosin bulb has released, others are still bound to the actin filament. Some myosin bulbs hold the actin steady, while other myosin arms reach farther down the actin filament.

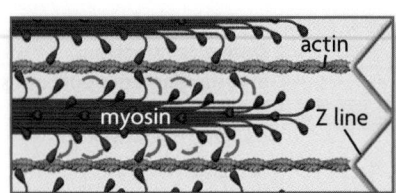

actin

myosin

Z line

Myosin filaments continue to pull at the actin in this hand-over-hand type of motion until the actin filaments have moved as far into the center as possible. At this point, the sarcomere is shortened because the actin filaments have dragged the end of the sarcomere with them as they were being pulled. Once the sarcomere is shortened, the muscle is contracted.

Muscles and Bones of the Skull

In this lab, you will learn about the muscles that attach to the skull.

PROBLEM What is the arrangement of muscles and bones in the skull?

PROCEDURE

1. Place your fingers on the side of your jaw. Clench and unclench your jaw several times. You can feel your masseter muscle moving beneath your finger.
2. Place your fingers on either side of your mouth. Open and close your mouth and smile several times. You can feel your orbicularis ori moving beneath your fingers.
3. Place your fingers under your eye. Wink several times. You can feel your obivularis oculi moving beneath your fingers.
4. Look at the model skull and the muscle drawings. Identify the muscles you felt, and to which bones they were attached.

ANALYZE AND CONCLUDE

1. **Analyze** What type of muscles (skeletal or smooth) are the three muscles you identified in this lab? How do you know?
2. **Infer** What do you think the word *orbicular* means?
3. **Evaluate** What are some of the limitations to using models and illustrations in this lab?

MATERIALS
- model skull
- Muscle and Bone Drawings

The contraction stops when the nervous system stops stimulating the muscle tissue. When this happens, the Ca^{2+} ions unbind and are actively transported away from the actin. The myosin binding sites on the actin filament become covered and myosin can no longer grab the actin. So the actin filaments slide outward to where they began before the contraction.

The contraction of a muscle fiber is an all-or-nothing event. This means that an entire muscle will move only when many individual muscle fibers contract. Muscle contractions require the shortening of millions of sarcomeres. The coordination of these multiple sarcomeres is controlled by the nervous system.

Apply **Explain why getting enough calcium in your diet is important for muscle function.**

33.2   ASSESSMENT

ONLINE QUIZ
ClassZone.com

REVIEWING ▶ MAIN IDEAS

1. How do **skeletal muscle, cardiac muscle,** and **smooth muscle** differ in their structure and function?
2. How do **actin** and **myosin** filaments work together to cause muscle contractions?

CRITICAL THINKING

3. **Synthesize** How does muscle help keep the body warm?
4. **Synthesize** How does the number of mitochondria in a muscle cell relate to the amount of work the cell can do?

Connecting CONCEPTS

5. **Nervous System** Sensory neurons gather information. Interneurons process information. Motor neurons produce responses. Which type of neuron stimulates each of the three types of muscle tissue? Explain.

MATERIALS
- tennis ball
- timer with a second hand

PROCESS SKILLS
- **Collecting Data**
- **Analyzing Data**
- **Graphing**

B1.1f Predict what would happen if the variables, methods, or timing of an investigation were changed.

Muscle Fatigue

In Chapter 4, you learned that as your muscles do continuous activity, they will eventually begin to feel tired and fatigued. Muscles get fatigued because they need more oxygen than the blood vessels can supply them with, and they begin to work anaerobically, or without the necessary oxygen. In this lab, you will measure how long it takes before muscle fatigue begins.

PROBLEM How much time does it take for muscles to become fatigued?

PROCEDURE
1. Construct a data table like the one shown below. Extend the table to at least 120 seconds.
2. Hold a tennis ball in your nonwriting hand. When your partner tells you to begin, start squeezing the tennis ball as fast as you can, and count the number of squeezes.
3. Every 10 seconds, your partner will record the number of times you squeezed the tennis ball during that 10-second interval. Continue the activity for at least 120 seconds.
4. Switch roles with your partner and repeat steps 1–3.

| TABLE 1. TIME AND NUMBER OF BALL SQUEEZES ||
Time (sec)	Number of Squeezes
0–10	
11–20	
21–30	
31–40	

ANALYZE AND CONCLUDE
1. **Graph Data** Construct a graph that displays your data. How did the number of squeezes change over time?
2. **Infer** How long did it take for your forearm muscles to become fatigued?
3. **Predict** How might your data be different if you performed the experiment with your writing hand instead of your nonwriting hand?

33.3 Integumentary System

KEY CONCEPT The integumentary system has many tissues that protect the body.

▶ MAIN IDEAS

- The integumentary system helps maintain homeostasis.
- The integumentary system consists of many different tissues.

VOCABULARY

integumentary system, p. 1013
keratin, p. 1013
epidermis, p. 1014
dermis, p. 1015
hair follicle, p. 1015

MICHIGAN STANDARDS

B2.3d Identify the general functions of the major systems of the human body (digestion, respiration, reproduction, circulation, excretion, protection from disease, and movement, control, and coordination) and describe ways that these systems interact with each other.

B2.3e Describe how human body systems maintain relatively constant internal conditions (temperature, acidity, and blood sugar).

Connect Have you ever noticed that when you are warm, your face becomes reddish? This is not an optical illusion. It is your skin helping you to maintain a constant body temperature. When you are warm, nerves in your skin signal blood vessels to expand and rise to the surface of the skin. At the surface, blood vessels release heat into the environment. When your body temperature drops, the blood vessels sink into your skin, keeping the heat in your body.

▶ MAIN IDEA

The integumentary system helps maintain homeostasis.

Skin is a part of your integumentary system. The **integumentary system** is the body system that surrounds all of your other organ systems, and it includes the skin, hair, nails, oil glands, and sweat glands. Together, these tissues protect your body and help your body maintain homeostasis.

Your integumentary system consists of many tissues that protect your body. Oil glands in the skin release acidic oils that stop fungi and bacteria from growing on the skin, thereby preventing infection. Your fingernails and hair also have protective qualities. Fingernails and hair are made up of keratin. **Keratin** is a tough, waterproof protein that gives your hair and nails the ability to grow away from the body but still maintain their shape and sturdiness. In nails, keratin allows your nails to absorb some of the impact if you accidentally stub your toe. The microscopic view of a fingernail in **FIGURE 33.12** shows that these structures are actually many layers of thin, dead cells that are stacked on top of one another. In hair, keratin proteins are long and twisted around one another. Hair on top of the head shades your skin and keeps you cool.

Nerves in your skin can help maintain temperature homeostasis, but your integumentary system maintains homeostasis in other ways as well. It removes water, salts, and urea from the bloodstream. Sweat glands help maintain homeostasis by cooling the body as the sweat evaporates off the skin. The average person has 2,600,000 sweat glands. During an intense hourlong workout, these glands allow your body to sweat out more than a liter of water.

Connect When have your fingernails helped to protect you from injury?

FIGURE 33.12 Fingernails are dense layers of dead cells that protect the fingers from injury. (colored SEM; magnification 650×)

▶ MAIN IDEA

The integumentary system consists of many different tissues.

Connecting CONCEPTS

Immune System You read in **Chapter 31** that the skin and its various tissues are also part of the immune system; they help keep germs out of the body.

All of the tissues of your integumentary system are housed in the skin. Your skin is the largest organ in your body. It covers from 1 to 2 square meters (10 to 15 ft²) and makes up about 15 percent of your body mass. The skin has three layers: the epidermis, the dermis, and the subcutaneous fat. The skin layers and the structures contained in them are shown in **FIGURE 33.13**.

The **epidermis** is the outermost layer of the skin, and it provides the first layer of protection for the tissues that are in deeper skin layers. The epidermis also contains pores through which sweat, salts, and oils can leave the body. The surface of the epidermis consists mostly of dead cells that continually flake off. Below the surface are new, living cells that are constantly dividing. The new cells pile on top of one another and push up to the surface over a period of two to four weeks to replace old, dead cells.

Cells in the epidermis also produce protective proteins, such as keratin and melanin. Almost every type of cell in the epidermis produces keratin. Keratin causes the skin to feel thick or hard, and it builds thicker layers in areas of the skin that come into frequent contact with the outer environment. The soles of your feet, for example, have a thick layer of keratin, and so the skin on your feet is tougher than the skin on your face. Although keratin is produced by almost every epidermal cell, only specialized cells, called melanocytes, produce melanin. Melanin is a dark pigment that absorbs harmful ultraviolet sunlight that would otherwise reach and damage internal organs. When a person's skin is exposed to more and more sunlight, melanocytes produce more melanin to block the additional rays. In other words, the skin tans.

DATA ANALYSIS

ANALYZING TRENDS IN DATA

Analyzing trends in data is a critical component of a scientific investigation. The graph below shows data about the incidence of basal cell skin cancer in men and women ages 26–30.

1. **Evaluate** What is the trend in the data for the incidence of this type of cancer in men in this age group? What is the trend for women of this age group?

2. **Compare and Contrast** How are these trends similar and different?

3. **Infer** Give a possible explanation for the trends.

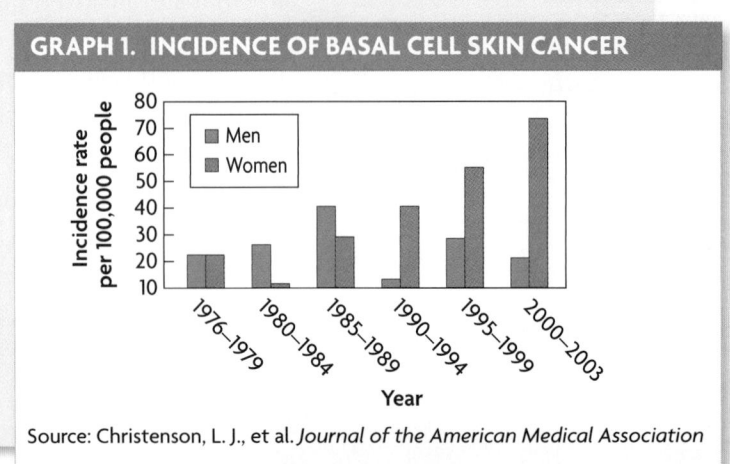

GRAPH 1. INCIDENCE OF BASAL CELL SKIN CANCER

Source: Christenson, L. J., et al. *Journal of the American Medical Association*

The next layer of skin, the **dermis,** contains glands and the cells that maintain the skin's structure by producing elastin and collagen. Elastin is a protein that gives the skin flexibility, allowing it to stretch without tearing. Collagen is a dense protein that gives skin its shape. As a person ages, collagen molecules become weak and clump. Clumping collagen is one factor that contributes to wrinkles.

The dermis also contains sweat glands, oil glands, and hair follicles. A **hair follicle** is an elongated pit under the skin's surface that contains cells that produce the keratin that forms hair. Each hair follicle has a pain receptor associated with it, which is why it hurts when you pull out a hair.

Sweat and oil glands in the dermis also protect your body. Each person has 2 to 5 million glands—that's more than 10 glands for every square millimeter of skin. Sweat glands are called eccrine glands. Eccrine glands are found all over the body and help control body temperature. They also produce sweat that prevents damage that might occur when a person moves. When a person sweats from their armpits, for example, this sweat is protecting the skin by preventing the skin under the arm from rubbing too hard on the skin around the rib cage. Other glands, called sebaceous glands, produce oils that lubricate the skin and keep it waterproof.

Beneath the epidermis and dermis is a layer of subcutaneous fat. This layer of fat cells protects and cushions larger blood vessels and neurons. It also insulates the muscles and internal organs from temperature changes in the body's surrounding environment. These cells are connected to the muscles and bones by a layer of connective tissue.

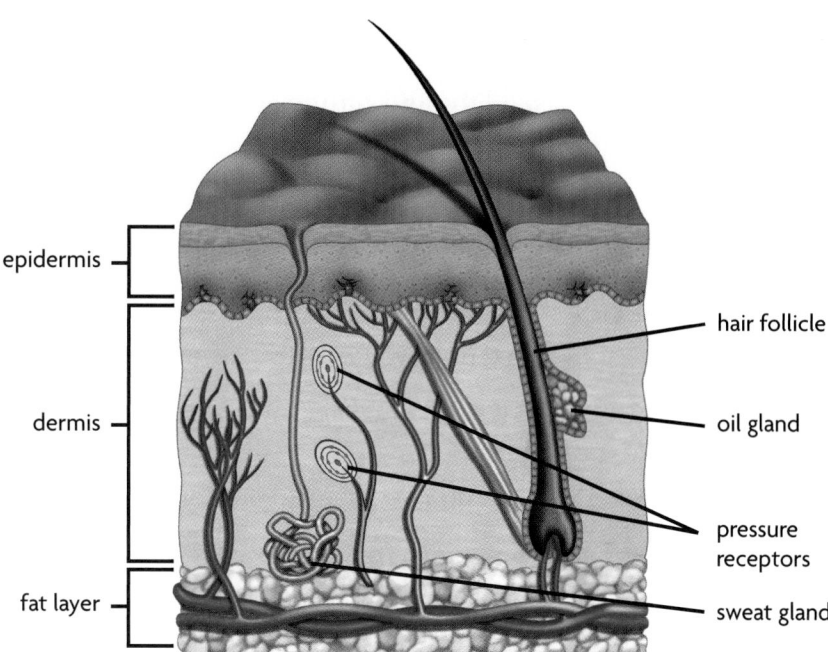

FIGURE 33.13 Skin has many structures that protect internal organs and sense the world around you.

Summarize What structures are found in each of the three layers of skin?

33.3 ASSESSMENT

ONLINE QUIZ
ClassZone.com

REVIEWING ▶ MAIN IDEAS

1. How does the **integumentary system** help your body maintain homeostasis?

2. What are three types of tissue that can be found in the **dermis**?

CRITICAL THINKING

3. **Infer** Why might it be beneficial to have dead skin cells on the outermost layer of the **epidermis**?

4. **Infer** What kind of sensory receptors are associated with **hair follicles**?

Connecting CONCEPTS

5. **Plants** Although the epidermises of plants and humans have different structures, some of these structures have the same function. How are pores in human skin functionally similar to stomata on plants?

Use these inquiry-based labs and online activities to deepen your understanding of muscles and bones.

INVESTIGATION

Muscles in Action

In this lab, you will illustrate muscles in action.

SKILLS Analyzing Relationships, Interpreting, Modeling

MATERIALS
Muscle and Bone Charts

PROBLEM Which muscles are used in an action?

PROCEDURE

1. Choose an appropriate action to illustrate, such as a person getting ready to kick a soccer ball, throw a football, or hold a guitar.

2. Determine which bones, muscles, and tendons are involved in the motion. Identify which muscles are contracting and which are extending.

3. Illustrate the part of the body frozen in the motion. Draw and label the relevant bones, muscles, and tendons involved in the action. Indicate the role of each structure in the action.

ANALYZE AND CONCLUDE

1. **Analyze** What is the function of a tendon? What would happen if one of the tendons involved in the action were torn?

2. **Infer** Suppose one of the muscles used in the action were stretched. How might that affect the performance of that muscle as the action is repeated?

3. **Infer** How does the overall structure of the body part (including the type of joint and the shapes of the bones and muscles) you drew allow for the motion that it made?

Bone and Muscle Cells

Imagine an injured athlete undergoing knee surgery. In this lab, you will use a microscope to examine the skin, the compact bone cells, and the different types of cells that the surgeon will see.

SKILL Modeling

MATERIALS

- slide of smooth muscle
- slide of skeletal muscle
- slide of bone cells
- slide of tendon tissue
- slide of ligament tissue
- slide of skin cells
- compound light microscope

PROBLEM What differences exist between different types of cells?

PROCEDURE

1. Examine the first slide under low power and high power on the microscope.
2. Draw and label one cell and its structures.
3. Repeat steps 1 and 2 for the remaining slides.

ANALYZE AND CONCLUDE

1. **Compare and Contrast** What are the similarities and differences in the structures of the two types of muscle cells you viewed?
2. **Analyze** How do nutrients and oxygen reach bone cells that are surrounded by calcitic bone?
3. **Contrast** How do the slides of ligament and tendon tissue differ from skeletal muscle tissue?
4. **Summarize** Draw and label in the correct order the layers of the skin that the surgeon will cut through to reach the kneecap.

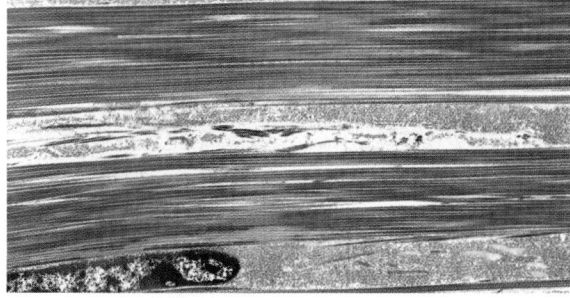

Tendon tissue, pictured above, connects muscles to bones.
(colored TEM; magnification 15,000×)

Online BIOLOGY
CLASSZONE.COM

ANIMATED BIOLOGY
What Kind of Joint Is It?
Can you tell a gliding joint from a hinge joint? Explore different joints in the body and learn how they move. Then categorize each joint based on its movement and structure.

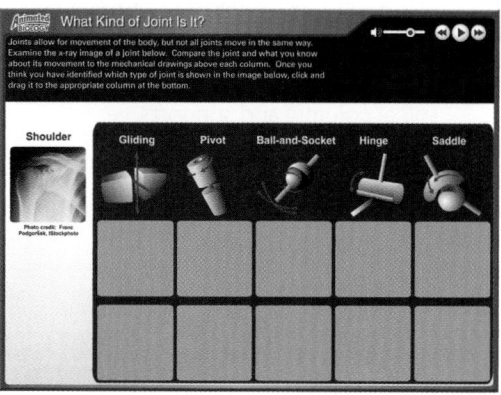

WEBQUEST

Every year there is a telethon to raise money for muscular dystrophy. What exactly is muscular dystrophy? Why should we worry about money for research? Complete this WebQuest to find out. Learn the causes and symptoms of muscular dystrophy, and the treatment options available to those afflicted with it.

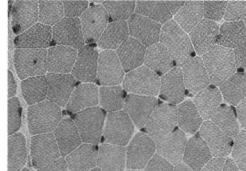 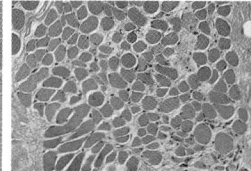

Healthy muscle
(LMS; magnification 25×)

Muscle affected by muscular dystrophy
(LMS; magnification 25×)

DATA ANALYSIS ONLINE

Some runners can run a mile in less than 4 minutes, while others might take 13 minutes to run the same distance. Graph the speed at which different people move their legs versus each person's top speed. Determine whether fast runners move their legs more quickly than slow runners.

33.1 Skeletal System

The skeletal system includes bones and tissues that are important for supporting, protecting, and moving your body. The skeletal system has two parts: the appendicular skeleton and the axial skeleton. The appendicular skeleton is responsible for most of the body's movements and includes the arms and legs. The axial skeleton includes bones such as the skull, rib cage, and spinal column, and supports the body and protects internal organs. Individual bones are connected to one another by joints. Each individual bone is living tissue that contains specialized cells and blood vessels.

33.2 Muscular System

Muscles are tissues that can contract, enabling movement. Humans have three types of muscles: skeletal, smooth, and cardiac. Skeletal muscle attaches to bones. Smooth muscle surrounds blood vessels and the organs of the digestive system. Cardiac muscle is only found in the heart. The various types of muscles contract when the nervous system stimulates muscle filaments to move. The nervous system causes Ca^{2+} to enter the sarcomere, allowing myosin filaments to bind to actin filaments. The muscle contracts when the myosin filaments pull the actin toward the sarcomere's center.

33.3 Integumentary System

The integumentary system has many tissues that protect the body. The integumentary system is the body system that acts as a barrier between the body's internal and external environments. It helps to maintain homeostasis by regulating the body's temperature and blocking out pathogens. The skin has three layers: the dermis, the epidermis, and the layer of subcutaneous fat. The skin also contains proteins, such as keratin and melanin, that protect the skin's cells and maintain its structure.

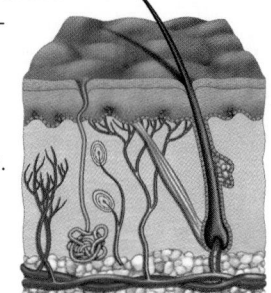

Synthesize Your Notes

Concept Map Organize your notes on the skeletal system using a concept map like the one below.

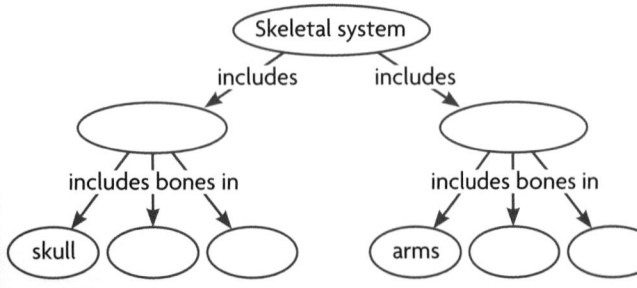

Three-Column Chart Study the integumentary system using a three-column chart like the one below.

Parts of the Integumentary System

Parts	Structures	Functions
skin	dermis epidermis	
nails		
hair		

Chapter Assessment

Reviewing Vocabulary

Write Your Own Questions

Write a question about the first term that uses the second term as the answer. For the pair *skeletal system, appendicular skeleton,* the question could be, "What part of the skeletal system is responsible for most of your movements?"

1. hair follicle, keratin
2. joint, ligament
3. tendon, skeletal muscle
4. myosin, actin

Category Clues

For each clue, list the appropriate vocabulary term from the chapter.

Category: Types of Muscle

5. found only in the heart
6. regulates width of blood vessels

Category: Parts of the Skin

7. consists mostly of dead cells
8. contains glands

Keep It Short

For each vocabulary term below, write a short, precise phrase that defines it. For example, a short phrase to describe *vertebrae* could be "protect spinal cord."

9. axial skeleton
10. sarcomere
11. calcification

Reviewing MAIN IDEAS

12. Which organs do each of the three collections of bones in the axial skeleton protect?

13. How does cartilage protect bones from wearing out while allowing muscles to move bones?

14. What type of joint is found in the hips and shoulders? How does this type of joint allow these body parts to move the way that they do?

15. How do compact and spongy bone interact with the circulatory system?

16. Bone is formed when flexible cartilage is transformed into hard bone. How do specialized cells create compact bone from cartilage?

17. Ligaments and tendons are connective tissues that help the body move. What are some differences between ligaments and tendons?

18. Humans have three types of muscle: skeletal, smooth, and cardiac. How are the three types of muscle cells different from one another?

19. Both the Z line and the M line have important roles in muscle contraction. What are the differences in the function and placement of the Z line and the M line in the sarcomere?

20. How do actin and myosin work together to produce muscle contractions?

21. How does the integumentary system help to maintain homeostasis?

22. What are the three layers of skin, and how do they work to protect the body?

23. What roles do elastin and collagen play in the connective tissue of the dermis?

Critical Thinking

24. Connect Neurons are specialized cells of the nervous system. Sensory neurons sense the internal and external environments. Motor neurons cause the body to respond to a stimulus. Which neurons do you think are found in the integumentary system? the muscular system? How do you know?

25. Infer A hair on your arm emerges through a pore and onto the surface of your skin. Within your skin, the hair follicle has an oil-secreting gland associated with it. Why might hair follicles be good targets for infections? How do glands prevent hair follicles from becoming infected?

26. Infer Calcium is an important nutrient in the body. It allows for the nervous, muscular, and skeletal systems to work. How do Haversian canals work with bone cells to maintain calcium homeostasis?

27. Connect What is the relationship between ATP and the number of mitochondria in muscle cells?

28. Summarize Several things must happen to make a sarcomere shorten and a muscle contract. Describe the steps involved in contracting and relaxing a muscle. In your answer, discuss the following: sarcomeres, actin filaments, myosin filaments, M lines, and Z lines.

29. Predict Your body stores extra calcium in your bones. What might happen to your bones if there weren't enough calcium in your muscle fibers to stimulate muscle contractions?

Interpreting Visuals

Use the diagram to answer the next three questions.

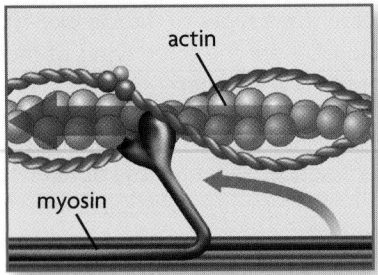

30. Analyze What is happening in the diagram?

31. Apply What will result from the action shown in the diagram?

32. Infer Assume that the actin filament is moving to the left. On which side of the picture would the Z line be? The M line? How do you know?

Analyzing Data

For a research project, a student asked 200 students at her school to record some of their physical activities. Each student recorded if they walked, rode a bicycle, or went swimming at least three times a week. The recording sheets were handed out in March and collected shortly after the students returned to school in the fall. Use the data to answer the next three questions.

STUDENTS' ACTIVITIES EACH MONTH

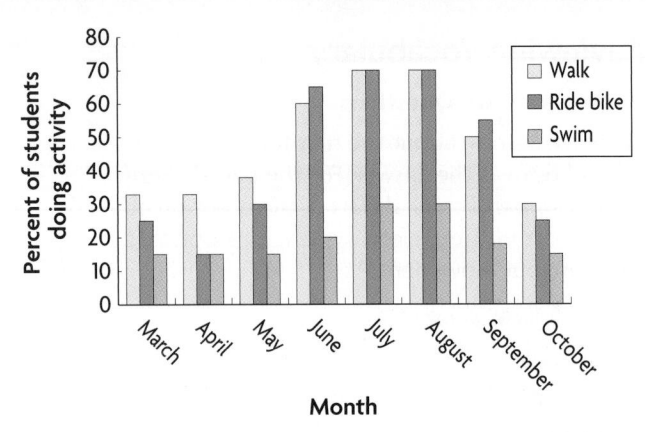

33. Evaluate What are the trends for physical activities from spring through early fall?

34. Contrast How do the trends differ between activities?

35. Hypothesize What might be possible explanations for these trends and differences?

Connecting CONCEPTS

36. Write a Help Wanted Ad Figure 33.3 on page 1003 shows the different types of joints and describes how they work. Write Help Wanted ads for two of the joints. Each ad should include the type of joint that is needed, what it must be able to do (job description), and the kinds of tasks it should expect to perform.

37. Compare Look at the pictures on page 999. How do an insect's skeletal and muscular systems compare with those of humans? (**Hint:** Consider the physical structures of the skeletons, their types of movement, and their relationships to the animal's muscles.)

MICHIGAN
STANDARDS-BASED ASSESSMENT

✓ *Test Practice*
For more test practice,
go to ClassZone.com.

1.

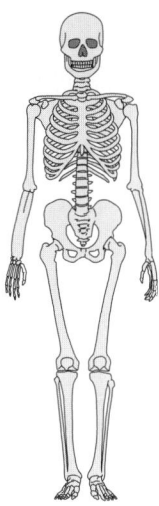

Three-dimensional models of human skeletons are useful learning tools. However, they do *not* help to show how the B1.1B

A axial and appendicular skeletons join.

B vertebrae form the spinal column.

C bones meet to form joints.

D bones adjust to support the body's weight.

2. **When you run a race, the muscles in your legs need extra oxygen. To get oxygen to your muscles, your lungs breathe harder. Your heart pumps more blood. The muscles that line your blood vessels change the size of the blood vessel to direct more blood to the active muscles and less blood to the inactive muscles. This situation is an example of** B2.3d

A positive feedback.

B operant conditioning.

C multiple body systems working together.

D anaerobic respiration.

3. **Which of these is the *best* example of the skin maintaining the body's stable environment, or homeostasis?** B2.3e

A becoming sunburned after a day in the sun

B releasing acidic oils that prevent infection

C breaking out in acne after eating certain foods

D freckles appearing after sun exposure

4. skin ⟶ sensory neuron ⟶ interneuron ⟶ motor neuron ⟶ **?**

Imagine you place your finger on a hot pan. A sensory neuron generates an impulse that is passed along as shown in the diagram. Which of the following *best* describes the role of the motor neuron in this example? B2.3d

A The motor neuron stimulates the brain to feel a burning sensation.

B The motor neuron stimulates the sensory neuron to jerk the hand off of the hot pan.

C The motor neuron stores and processes the signal in the brain.

D The motor neuron stimulates a muscle to jerk the hand off of the hot stove.

5. **In amyotrophic lateral sclerosis (ALS), or Lou Gehrig's disease, motor neurons lose their ability to send impulses. Which of the following is *most* likely to occur due to this disease?** B2.3C

A The patient will lose sensory ability.

B The patient will lose memory ability.

C The patient will lose thought ability.

D The patient will lose speaking ability.

6. **Calcium is an important nutrient that is involved in stimulating muscle contraction and sending nerve impulses. Depositing and removing calcium from bones is a continual process that reshapes bones and sends calcium to other parts of the body where it is needed. Which of the following events would *most* likely result in calcium moving into bones?** B2.3C

A bone injury

B intense exercise

C digestion

D thinking

THINK THROUGH THE QUESTION

Read the first part of the question carefully. Then consider which one of the answer choices would not require calcium to be sent to another part of the body.

34 Reproduction and Development

KEY CONCEPTS

34.1 Reproductive Anatomy
Female and male reproductive organs fully develop during puberty.

34.2 Reproductive Processes
Human reproductive processes depend on cycles of hormones.

34.3 Fetal Development
Development progresses in stages from zygote to fetus.

34.4 Birth and Development
Physical development continues through adolescence and declines with age.

Online BIOLOGY CLASSZONE.COM

Animated BIOLOGY
View animated chapter concepts.
• Embryonic Development
• Human Aging
• Developmental Timeline

BIOZINE
Keep current with biology news.
• Featured stories
• Careers
• Polls

RESOURCE CENTER
Get more information on
• Gametes, or Sex Cells
• Fetal Monitoring
• Human Development

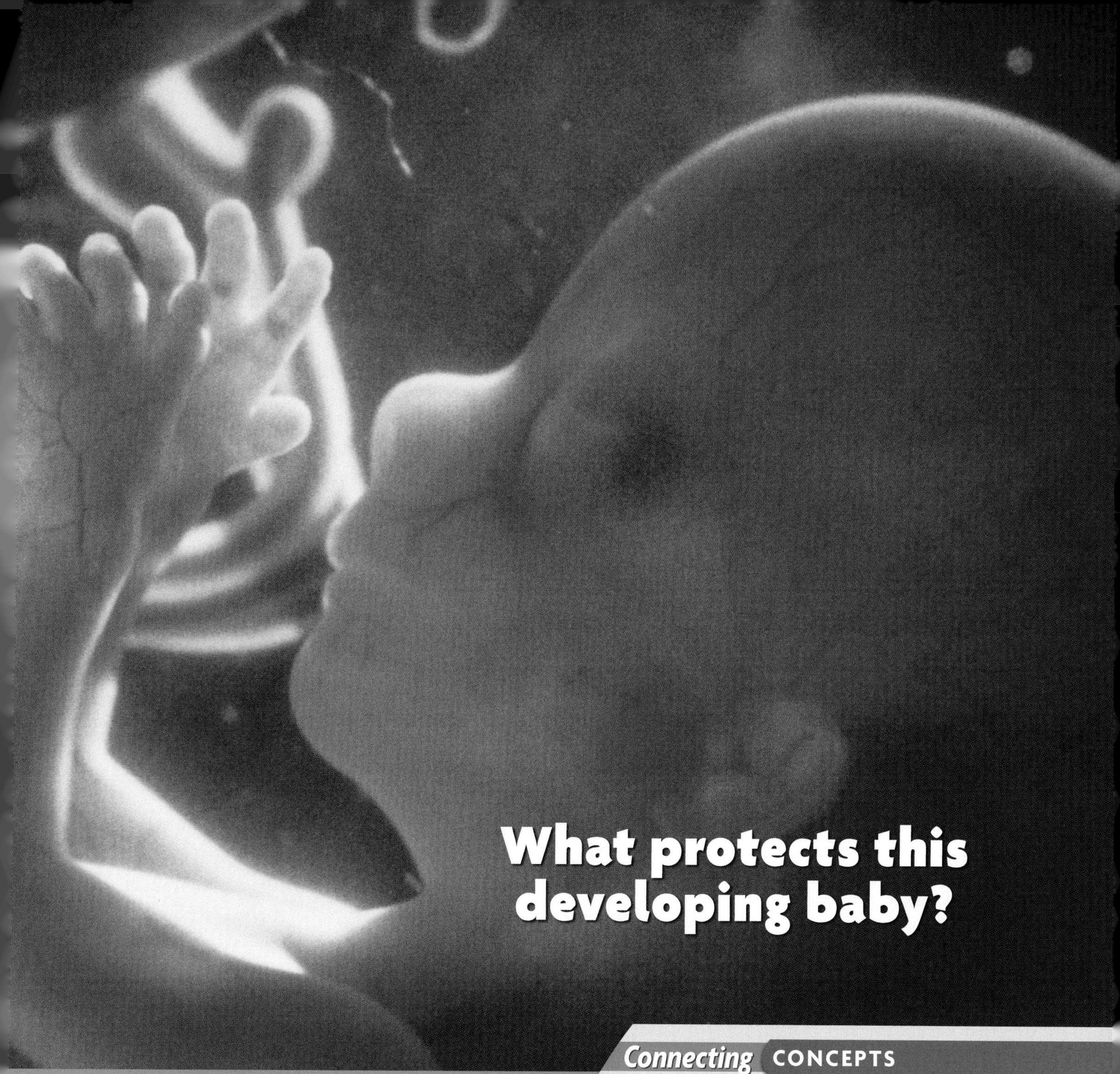

What protects this developing baby?

This developing baby, only about four months old, floats in a liquid world, receiving all its oxygen and nutrients from its mother's body. The journey from a single cell to a fully developed human being is guided by genetic instructions, environmental influences, and the complex actions of hormones in both mother and baby.

Connecting CONCEPTS

Amphibians This photograph shows a cluster of nine-day-old embryos of a tree frog. Unlike human babies, these embryos do not develop completely within the mother's body. Instead, they are deposited in special underwater nurseries. Once these eggs hatch, the tiny tadpoles are left to fend for themselves.

34.1 Reproductive Anatomy

KEY CONCEPT Female and male reproductive organs fully develop during puberty.

▶ MAIN IDEAS

- The female reproductive system produces ova.
- The male reproductive system produces sperm.

VOCABULARY

reproductive system, p. 1024	**uterus,** p. 1024	**scrotum,** p. 1026
puberty, p. 1024	**estrogen,** p. 1024	**epididymis,** p. 1026
ovum, p. 1024	**fallopian tube,** p. 1024	**vas deferens,** p. 1026
ovary, p. 1024	**testis,** p. 1025	**semen,** p. 1026
	testosterone, p. 1025	

MICHIGAN STANDARDS

B2.3d Identify the general functions of the major systems of the human body (digestion, respiration, reproduction, circulation, excretion, protection from disease, and movement, control, and coordination) and describe ways that these systems interact with each other.

Connecting CONCEPTS

Endocrine System You read in **Chapter 29** that the hypothalamus and pituitary glands are part of the endocrine system. These two glands are considered "master" glands because the hormones they secrete affect other glands that play key roles in human reproduction, growth, and development.

Connect You have something in common with every person ever born. Like everyone else, you began life as a single cell, produced when one male sex cell joined with one female sex cell. Sexual reproduction is the means by which the human species passes on genetic information to each generation.

▶ MAIN IDEA

The female reproductive system produces ova.

The **reproductive system** is a collection of specialized organs, glands, and hormones that help to produce a new human being. Females and males reach sexual maturity, or the ability to produce offspring, only after puberty. **Puberty** marks a time in your life when your hypothalamus and your pituitary gland release hormones, such as follicle-stimulating hormone (FSH) and luteinizing hormone (LH). Such hormones begin the process of developing your sexual characteristics and reproductive system.

The main functions of the female reproductive system are to produce ova (singular, **ovum**), or egg cells, and to provide a place where a fertilized egg can develop. Unlike males, females have all of their reproductive organs located inside their bodies. This organization helps to protect a fertilized egg while it develops. The egg cells are produced in the ovaries. The **ovaries** are paired organs located on either side of the **uterus,** or womb, as shown in **FIGURE 34.1.** When a female baby is born, she already has about 2 million potential egg cells stored in her ovaries.

In the ovaries, FSH and LH stimulate the release of another important hormone, estrogen. **Estrogen** is a steroid hormone that has three main functions. First, it controls the development of female sexual characteristics, including widening the pelvis, increasing fat deposits and bone mass, and enlarging the breasts. Second, it is needed for egg cells to develop fully before they leave the ovaries. Third, estrogen helps to prepare the uterus for pregnancy every month and helps to maintain a pregnancy when it occurs.

When an egg cell matures each month, it is released from an ovary and enters the fallopian tube. The **fallopian tube** (fuh-LOH-pee-uhn) is an organ about 10 centimeters (4 in.) long that ends in the uterus. An egg takes several days to travel through this tube. During that time, it can be fertilized by sperm

FIGURE 34.1 FEMALE REPRODUCTIVE ANATOMY

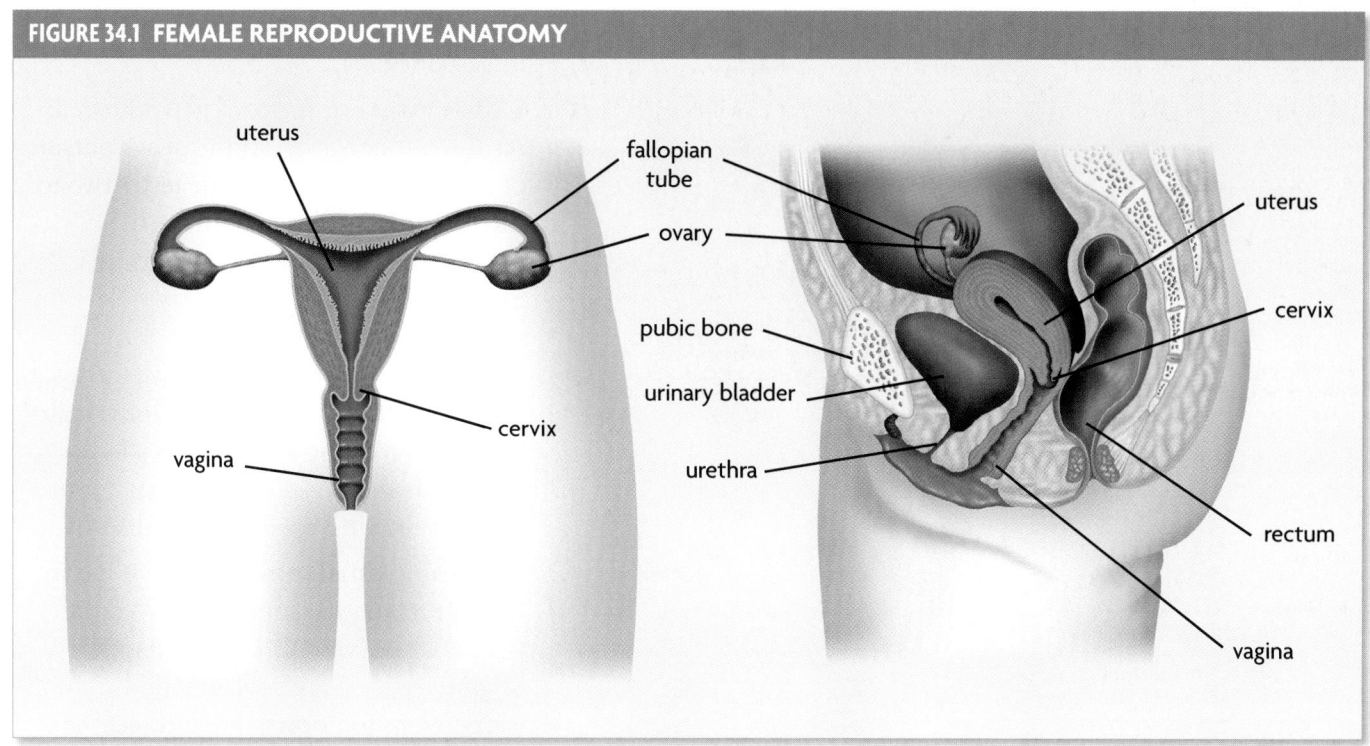

that enter the tube. A fertilized egg will attach to the wall of the uterus, but an unfertilized egg will eventually be broken down and discarded.

The uterus is about the size and shape of a pear. It is composed of three layers: a thin inner layer of epithelial cells, a thick middle layer of muscle, and an outer layer of connective tissue. The lower end of the uterus is called the cervix, which opens into the vagina. In a normal birth, a baby is pushed down the canal of the vagina to exit the mother's body. The complex processes of fertilization and human development are described in Sections 34.2 and 34.3.

Analyze How does the release of estrogen affect the female reproductive system during puberty?

TAKING NOTES

Use a two-column chart to list the major parts and functions of the female and male reproductive anatomy.

Female	Male
Ovaries — Paired organs where eggs are produced	Testes — Paired organs that produce sperm cells

▶ MAIN IDEA
The male reproductive system produces sperm.

The main functions of the male reproductive system are to produce sperm cells and to deliver them to the female reproductive system. The diagram in **FIGURE 34.2,** on the following page, shows the organs in which sperm are produced and stored and the organs that deliver the sperm.

Males do not produce sperm until puberty but afterward can produce sperm all their lives. Sperm production takes place in the testicles, or **testes** (TEHS-teez), which are paired organs. Each testis (singular of testes) contains hundreds of tiny tubules where millions of sperm cells are produced. In the testes, LH stimulates the release of testosterone. **Testosterone** (tehs-TAHS-tuh-ROHN) is a steroid hormone that, along with FSH, stimulates the production of sperm cells. Testosterone also controls the development of male sexual characteristics. These include a deeper voice than a female's, more body hair,

FIGURE 34.2 MALE REPRODUCTIVE ANATOMY

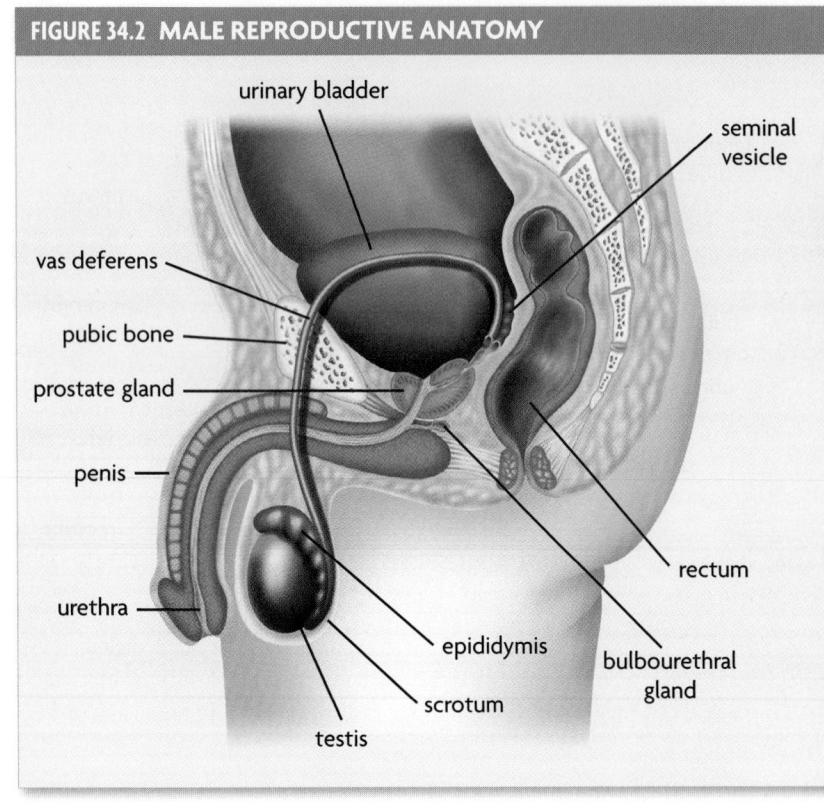

- urinary bladder
- seminal vesicle
- vas deferens
- pubic bone
- prostate gland
- penis
- urethra
- epididymis
- scrotum
- testis
- rectum
- bulbourethral gland

greater bone density, and increased muscle mass.

The testes are enclosed in a pouch, the **scrotum.** It hangs below the pelvis outside of the body, which keeps the testes two to three degrees cooler than the core body temperature. The lower temperature is important because sperm cannot develop if the temperature in the testes is too high. When the immature sperm leave the testes, they travel through a duct to a long, coiled tube known as the **epididymis** (EHP-ih-DIHD-uh-mihs). Here the sperm mature and remain until expelled or reabsorbed.

During sexual stimulation, the sperm travel into another long duct called the **vas deferens** (vas DEHF-uhr-uhnz). Secondary sex glands secrete fluids into the vas deferens to nourish and protect the sperm. The prostate gland, which surrounds the urethra, produces a fluid that helps sperm move more easily. The bulbourethral gland (BUHL-boh-yu-REE-thruhl) and the seminal vesicle secrete basic fluids that help to neutralize the acidity in the urethra and in the female's vagina. The fluids from all three glands, together with the sperm, form a milky white substance known as **semen.**

During sexual arousal, blood flows into the penis, making it rigid. Semen moves from the vas deferens into the urethra, which runs the length of the penis. When ejaculation occurs, a muscle closes off the bladder to prevent urine from mixing with the semen in the urethra. Smooth muscle contractions then propel the semen along the urethra and eject it from the penis.

Apply Why might having a high fever affect sperm production?

34.1 ASSESSMENT

ONLINE QUIZ
ClassZone.com

REVIEWING ▶ MAIN IDEAS

1. Explain the function of the following parts of the female reproductive system: **ovary, fallopian tube, uterus**.

2. Explain the function of the following parts of the male reproductive system: **testes, scrotum, epididymis, vas deferens**.

CRITICAL THINKING

3. **Compare** In what ways are the effects of **testosterone** on males and **estrogen** on females similar?

4. **Infer** Both males and females have paired organs that produce sex cells. What survival advantage for our species might this pairing of organs provide?

Connecting CONCEPTS

5. **Plants** You read in Chapter 22 that flowering plants reproduce sexually. The stamen produces pollen grains, and the carpel contains an ovary where eggs are produced. How do these structures compare with human reproductive organs?

34.2 Reproductive Processes

KEY CONCEPT Human reproductive processes depend on cycles of hormones.

▶ MAIN IDEAS

- Eggs mature and are released according to hormonal cycles.
- Sperm production in the testes is controlled by hormones.
- Fertilization occurs when a sperm cell joins an egg cell.
- Sexually transmitted diseases affect fertility and overall health.

VOCABULARY

follicle, p. 1028
ovulation, p. 1028
menstrual cycle, p. 1028
endometrium, p. 1028
corpus luteum, p. 1029
menopause, p. 1029

zygote, p. 1031
infertility, p. 1031
sexually transmitted disease, p. 1032

Review
meiosis, ovary, uterus, ovum, fallopian tube, sperm, vas deferens

MICHIGAN STANDARDS

B2.2f Explain the role of enzymes and other proteins in biochemical functions (e.g., the protein hemoglobin carries oxygen in some organisms, digestive enzymes, and hormones).

Connect You may have heard the phrase "Timing is everything." In football, for instance, precise timing between players can mean the difference between catching or dropping a key pass. Likewise, timing is everything for the hormones that regulate the reproductive processes in your body. Numerous feedback loops among these hormones help ensure that each process occurs at the right time and in the right order.

▶ MAIN IDEA

Eggs mature and are released according to hormonal cycles.

A female's reproductive cycle is controlled by hormones released by the hypothalamus, the pituitary gland, and the ovaries. Each month, the levels of these hormones rise and fall in well-timed feedback loops that regulate the development and release of an egg and prepare the uterus to receive it.

Production of Eggs

The production of eggs, or ova, begins before a female is born, as described in Section 34.1. Recall from Chapter 6 that meiosis is a type of cell division that produces sex cells, or gametes. After the chromosomes in each of the cells are duplicated, meiosis I can begin. The potential eggs then enter a resting phase that lasts until puberty. At birth, a female has about 2 million of these partially developed eggs in her ovaries. Before puberty begins, many of these cells break down until only about 400,000 are left.

At puberty, a monthly hormone cycle begins the second stage of egg production. Every 28 days or so, an increase in FSH stimulates a potential egg to complete meiosis I, as shown in **FIGURE 34.3**. The potential egg divides unevenly, producing two sex cells. The larger cell receives most of the organelles, cytoplasm, and nutrients an embryo will need when an egg is fertilized. The smaller cell, or polar body, simply breaks down. The larger sex cell completes meiosis II only after a sperm enters it. The cell divides again to produce an ovum, or egg, and a second polar body that also breaks down. Both the ovum and the second polar body contain 23 chromosomes from the mother.

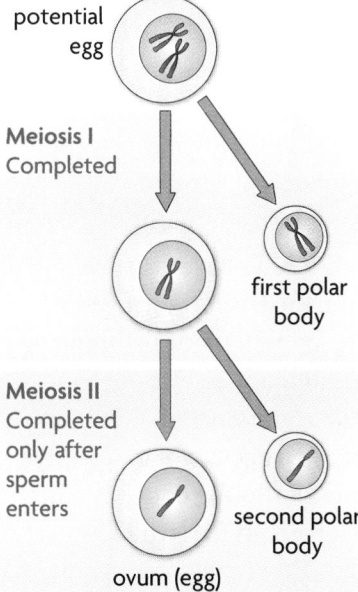

FIGURE 34.3 Potential eggs go through meiosis I and II to produce mature ova, or eggs with 23 chromosomes each.

potential egg

Meiosis I Completed

first polar body

Meiosis II Completed only after sperm enters

ovum (egg)

second polar body

FIGURE 34.4 Release of Egg

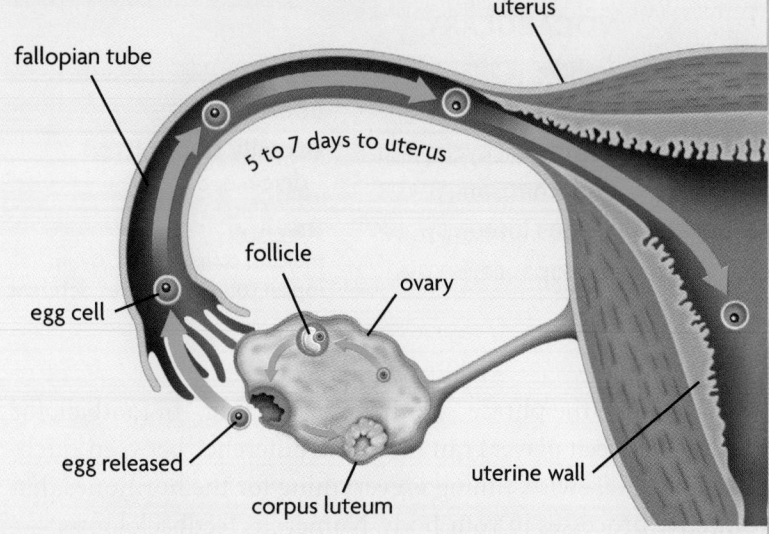

After an egg is released, it travels through the fallopian tube, where it might be fertilized.

uterus

fallopian tube

5 to 7 days to uterus

follicle

ovary

egg cell

egg released

corpus luteum

uterine wall

Infer Why might it be an advantage that the egg takes several days to travel through the fallopian tube?

Release of Egg

Each developing sex cell, which you can think of as an egg, is surrounded by a group of cells called a **follicle** that helps the egg to mature. When an egg is ready to be released, the follicle ruptures, and the egg breaks through the ovary wall, as shown in **FIGURE 34.4**. The release of an egg from the ovary is called **ovulation.** The egg is swept into the fallopian tube, where it can be fertilized by a sperm. Over the next five to seven days, the egg moves through the tube to the uterus. An unfertilized egg is discarded during menstruation.

In most cases, only one egg is released during ovulation. About 400 to 500 eggs are released over a female's reproductive life. Which ovary releases an egg each month is entirely random. If one ovary is damaged, however, the other may take over and release an egg each month.

The Menstrual Cycle

The **menstrual cycle** is a series of monthly changes in the reproductive system that include producing and releasing an egg and preparing the uterus to receive it. The length of the cycle is slightly different for each female, but averages about 28 days. The cycle has three main phases—flow phase, follicular phase, and luteal phase, as **FIGURE 34.5** shows. The timing of each phase is regulated by specific hormones.

1 **Flow phase** Day 1 of the menstrual cycle is the first day that the menstrual flow begins. The flow occurs when the lining of the uterus, or **endometrium** (EHN-doh-MEE-tree-uhm), detaches from the uterine wall and passes through the vagina to the outside of the body. Some blood, mucus, and tissue fluid are also expelled. The muscles of the uterus contract to help expel the lining. These contractions, known as "cramps," can be painful for some females. During this phase, the level of FSH starts to rise, and another follicle in the ovaries begins to mature.

2 **Follicular phase** The follicular (fuh-LIHK-yuh-luhr) phase lasts from about day 6 to day 14. At the start of this phase, the level of estrogen in the blood is relatively low. Hormones from the hypothalamus stimulate the pituitary to release more FSH and LH. Recall that a rise in FSH and LH causes the egg and follicle to mature. Ovulation occurs at about day 14. As the egg is developing, the follicle releases estrogen, which steadily increases over the next few days. This hormone causes the endometrium to thicken. Estrogen also stimulates a sharp increase in LH, which causes the follicle to rupture, releasing the egg.

Connecting CONCEPTS

Animal Behavior As you read in **Chapter 27,** hormone cycles control more than reproduction. Certain glands and proteins in some animals detect seasonal changes in temperature and in the hours of daylight. As a result, the glands secrete hormones that control when an animal will hibernate or migrate.

3 **Luteal phase** In the luteal (LOO-tee-uhl) phase, the release of hormones is now timed to stop egg production and to develop the endometrium to receive a fertilized egg. After ovulation, the empty follicle turns yellow and is called the **corpus luteum** (KAWR-puhs LOO-tee-uhm), or "yellow body." The corpus luteum releases estrogen and another hormone, progesterone, which limits the production of LH. Progesterone and estrogen also increase the number of blood vessels in the endometrium. If the egg is not fertilized, rising levels of estrogen and progesterone cause the hypothalamus to stop releasing FSH and LH. The corpus luteum then breaks down and stops secreting estrogen and progesterone. As a result, the uterus lining begins to shed, and the next flow phase starts.

For most women, the menstrual cycle continues throughout their reproductive years, which may last from preteen years to the late 50s. Eventually, however, the levels of hormones decline with age. This decline disrupts the normal timing of the menstrual cycle. In a process called **menopause,** the cycle gradually becomes more and more irregular and finally stops altogether. Menopause can occur as early as a woman's mid-30s.

Summarize What are the main functions of estrogen and progesterone during the follicular and luteal phases?

FIGURE 34.5 Menstrual Cycle

Hormones cause changes in the follicle, egg, and lining of the uterus.

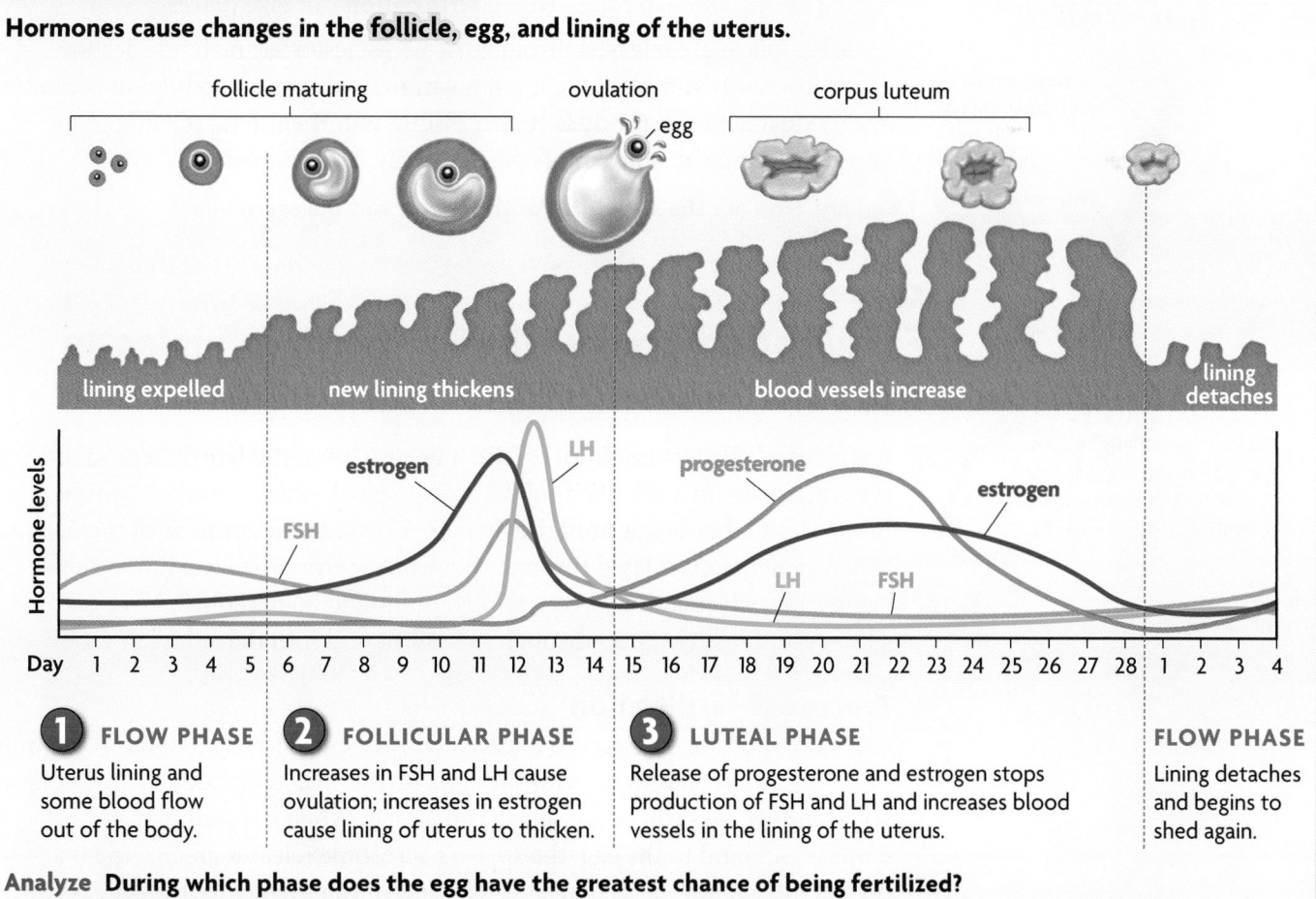

1 FLOW PHASE
Uterus lining and some blood flow out of the body.

2 FOLLICULAR PHASE
Increases in FSH and LH cause ovulation; increases in estrogen cause lining of uterus to thicken.

3 LUTEAL PHASE
Release of progesterone and estrogen stops production of FSH and LH and increases blood vessels in the lining of the uterus.

FLOW PHASE
Lining detaches and begins to shed again.

Analyze During which phase does the egg have the greatest chance of being fertilized?

FIGURE 34.6 Each potential sperm cell that undergoes meiosis produces four mature sperm cells with 23 chromosomes each. A mature sperm has a head, midpiece, and whiplike tail that enables it to move.

SPERM PRODUCTION

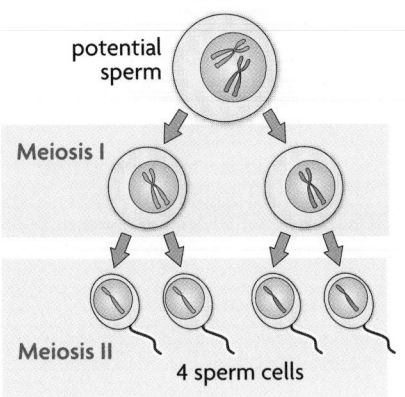

potential sperm

Meiosis I

Meiosis II

4 sperm cells

SPERM CELL

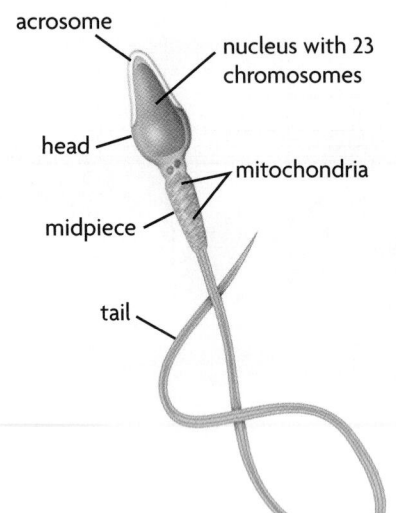

acrosome

nucleus with 23 chromosomes

head

mitochondria

midpiece

tail

▶ MAIN IDEA

Sperm production in the testes is controlled by hormones.

The reproductive cycles for males and females are different in two ways. First, females begin to produce eggs before they are born, but males do not produce sperm until they reach puberty. Second, females usually produce only one egg a month to be fertilized, while males produce millions of sperm almost daily.

The production of sperm begins when hormones from the hypothalamus stimulate the pituitary to release FSH and LH, which circulate to the testes. The testes start releasing testosterone, which causes specialized cells to go through meiosis to develop into mature sperm. As the levels of testosterone rise, the levels of FSH and LH begin to decline. This feedback loop among the hormones helps to control the number of sperm that are produced.

Unlike eggs, which produce polar bodies, the developing sperm divide into four equal sperm cells, as shown in **FIGURE 34.6**. Each cell is haploid, with 23 chromosomes. Sperm cells then fully mature in the epididymis. As the diagram shows, each sperm has a head, midpiece, and tail. The head contains a nucleus and a cap region called the acrosome. When a sperm cell contacts an egg, the acrosome releases enzymes that allow the sperm to penetrate the egg's membrane. The midpiece holds the mitochondria that supply the sperm with ATP for the energy it needs. The tail, or flagellum, propels the sperm from the vagina to the fallopian tubes, where fertilization can take place.

After sperm are released through the penis, testosterone levels decline. These low levels stimulate the hypothalamus, and sperm production increases again. Most men can produce sperm throughout their lives, starting in puberty. However, the number of sperm usually declines with age.

Compare How are the structures of the sperm and the egg similar?

▶ MAIN IDEA

Fertilization occurs when a sperm cell joins an egg cell.

For an egg to be fertilized, sperm must be present in the female reproductive system, usually in a fallopian tube. During sexual intercourse, the penis is inserted into the vagina until the tip comes close to the opening of the uterus. When semen is ejaculated through the penis, sperm are released into the vagina. One ejaculation can contain 50 million to 500 million sperm cells. The sperm must swim up through the uterus and into the fallopian tubes.

Process of Fertilization

Out of millions of sperm cells released, only one will fertilize an egg. Why only one? The answer has to do with the egg's membrane—a protective layer filled with binding sites where the sperm can attach. When a sperm manages to contact and bind to the egg, the sperm's acrosome releases an enzyme that digests the membrane at that spot. The sperm can then enter the egg, as shown in **FIGURE 34.7.** Once the egg is penetrated, its surface changes to form a barrier that stops other sperm from entering. In effect, the egg lets in one sperm, then closes the door on the others. The egg then completes meiosis II. Then the 23 chromosomes of the sperm join with the 23 chromosomes of the egg to form a fertilized egg called a **zygote.** This combination of chromosomes helps preserve genetic diversity because chromosomes in a pair often have different alleles of genes. This is one reason children are never exact genetic copies of their parents.

In rare cases, more than one egg may be released into the fallopian tubes. If two eggs are fertilized, they will develop into fraternal twins. Fraternal twins are not genetically the same. They are just like any other siblings who are born separately.

Genetically identical twins occur only when a single fertilized egg splits into two zygotes, each one with 46 chromosomes. As a result, two identical but separate embryos develop in the uterus. In even rarer cases, a fertilized egg may split into three, four, or more zygotes. If they all develop, the mother will give birth to several genetically identical babies.

Problems in Fertilization

Infertility refers to any condition that makes reproduction difficult or impossible. In the male, for instance, the vas deferens may be too narrow or blocked, which prevents sperm from leaving the body. If the sperm count is too low or the sperm are weakened or deformed, fertilization may not occur. Certain illnesses, such as mumps in adults, can destroy the testes' ability to produce sperm. In females, diseases that damage the ovaries or fallopian tubes can prevent eggs from being produced or reaching the uterus. The eggs themselves may have defects that keep the sperm from getting through the membrane. Many infertility problems can be corrected through treatments such as medications, surgery, or even dietary changes.

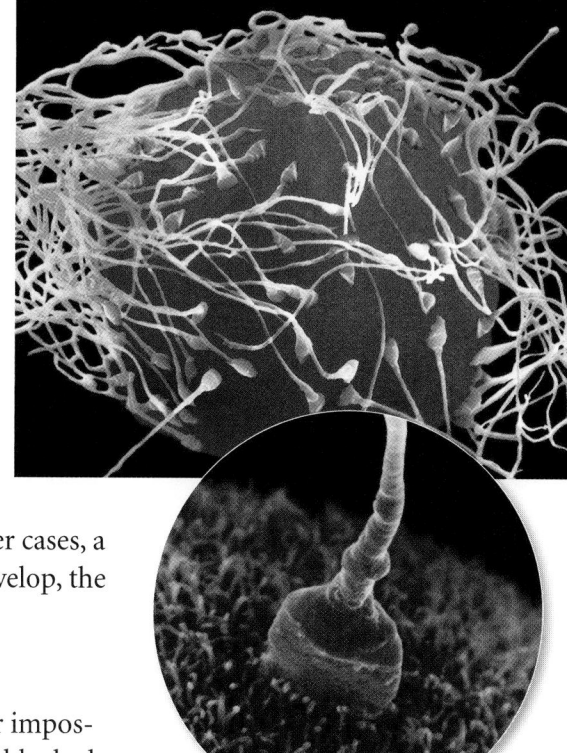

FIGURE 34.7 In the top image, sperm surround an egg. The bottom image shows one sperm penetrating an egg's membrane. (colored SEM; magnifications: egg with sperm 3500×; sperm detail 13,000×)

Apply **If twins are born and one is a boy and one is a girl, are they identical or fraternal siblings? Explain your answer.**

○ MAIN IDEA

Sexually transmitted diseases affect fertility and overall health.

Diseases passed from one person to another during sexual contact are called **sexually transmitted diseases,** or STDs. These diseases affect millions of people in their peak reproductive years and cause thousands of deaths. Some STDs in the early stages produce few symptoms. People do not realize they are carrying the disease and continue to infect others through sexual contact.

Bacterial STDs include chlamydia, syphilis, and gonorrhea. Chlamydia is the most common infection in the United States. Bacterial STDs attack the reproductive organs, such as the ovaries, and often cause infertility. In the case of syphilis, an untreated infection can even be fatal. Another infection, trichomoniasis, is caused by a parasite, shown in **FIGURE 34.8**. Trichomoniasis and chlamydia mostly affect young women aged 15 to 24 and can cause a serious condition known as pelvic inflammatory disease. People with these infections show few symptoms at first. This may be one reason why rates for trichomoniasis and chlamydia are increasing. Most parasitic and bacterial STDs can be treated with antibiotics.

Viral STDs include hepatitis B, genital herpes, human papillomavirus (HPV), and human immunodeficiency virus (HIV), which causes AIDS. Although medications can control these diseases, there are no cures. Antibiotics have no effect on viruses. HPV has been linked to cervical cancer, and AIDS has caused millions of deaths worldwide.

People can avoid STDs, just as they avoid other diseases. The surest ways are to abstain from sexual contact before marriage and for partners who do not have STDs to remain faithful in a committed relationship. Using a condom is the next safest choice; however, a condom can break or tear.

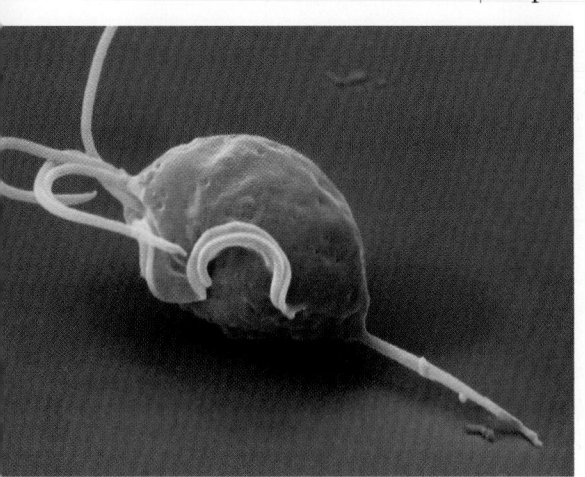

FIGURE 34.8 The parasite *Trichomonas vaginalis* causes a common STD infection, trichomoniasis, that can affect fertility. (colored SEM; magnification 9000×)

Infer **How might a bacterial STD infection affect the reproductive cycle of a male or female?**

34.2 / ASSESSMENT

ONLINE QUIZ
ClassZone.com

REVIEWING ○ MAIN IDEAS

1. What is the main function of each phase in the **menstrual cycle**?
2. How does the structure of the sperm cell aid its function?
3. Describe how an egg is fertilized.
4. **Sexually transmitted diseases** can affect fertility. Explain why.

CRITICAL THINKING

5. **Contrast** Name two ways that the production of eggs differs from the production of sperm.
6. **Apply** A woman gives birth to quadruplets, or four infants. Two of her children are identical twins. The other two are fraternal twins. How could this have happened?

Connecting CONCEPTS

7. **Developmental Biology** Every egg contains one X chromosome. Each sperm contains either one X or one Y chromosome. Explain why the sperm always determines a baby's gender.

MATERIALS
- graph paper
- colored markers
- Hormone Blood Levels Datasheet

PROCESS SKILLS
- **Graphing**
- **Interpreting Graphs**

B2.2f Explain the role of enzymes and other proteins in biochemical functions (e.g., the protein hemoglobin carries oxygen in some organisms, digestive enzymes, and hormones).

Hormones in the Human Menstrual Cycle

Hormones, including follicle-stimulating hormone (FSH), luteinizing hormone (LH), estrogen, and progesterone, play critical roles in the human menstrual cycle. As blood levels of these hormones rise and fall, the follicle, the egg, and the lining of the uterus go through different stages of development. In this lab, you will graph and analyze the changes in the blood levels of these four hormones during a menstrual cycle.

PROBLEM How do the blood levels of hormones change during the menstrual cycle?

PROCEDURE
1. Using the data sheet, construct a graph that shows the changes in the blood levels of hormones during a 28-day menstrual cycle in which fertilization does not occur.
2. Plot all hormones on one set of axes, and use different colors to represent the different hormones.

ANALYZE AND CONCLUDE
1. **Summarize** Describe the changes in levels that occur in each of the hormones throughout the month.
2. **Analyze** On what day of the cycle does LH peak? What is the significance of this fact?
3. **Analyze** When does the level of estrogen peak? What is the source of estrogen during this time?
4. **Explain** What is the significance of the rise in levels of estrogen and progesterone between days 10 and 22 of the cycle?
5. **Predict** How would the levels of hormones be affected if the egg were fertilized?

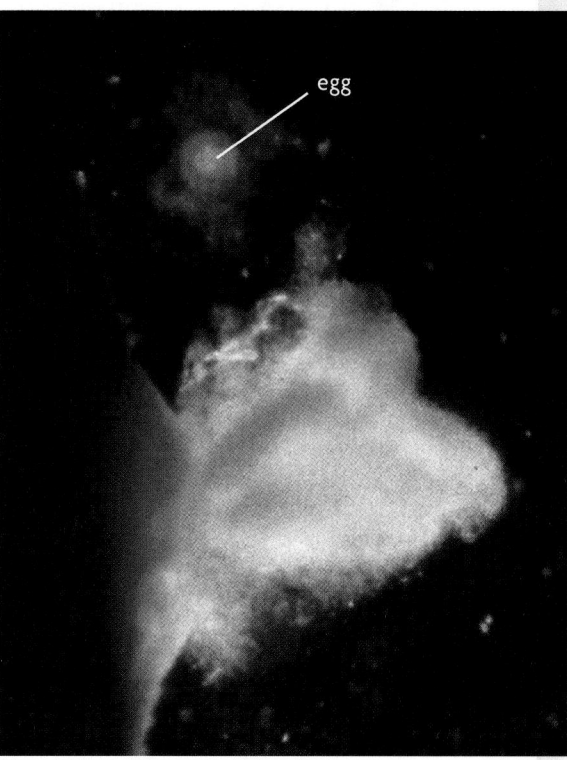

This micrograph captures the process of an egg breaking free from a rupturing follicle in the ovary. (LM; magnification unknown)

34.3 Fetal Development

KEY CONCEPT Development progresses in stages from zygote to fetus.

▶ MAIN IDEAS

- The fertilized egg implants into the uterus and is nourished by the placenta.
- A zygote develops into a fully formed fetus in about 38 weeks.
- The mother affects the fetus, and pregnancy affects the mother.

VOCABULARY

blastocyst, p. 1034	**umbilical cord**, p. 1035
embryo, p. 1034	**trimester**, p. 1036
amniotic sac, p. 1035	**fetus**, p. 1036
placenta, p. 1035	

REVIEW AT CLASSZONE.COM

Connect A human zygote develops from a single cell into a fully formed human in about nine months. The rate of growth in the first few weeks is astonishing. If you grew at the same rate after birth, you would be 4 meters (13 ft) tall at one month of age. The zygote's growth is directed by its DNA. However, the environment of the uterus and the mother's overall health also have a strong impact on how well the zygote develops.

▶ MAIN IDEA

The fertilized egg implants into the uterus and is nourished by the placenta.

After fertilization, the zygote begins to divide through mitosis as it travels down the fallopian tube. During this time, the corpus luteum continues to secrete progesterone and some estrogen. These hormones increase the number of blood vessels in the lining of the uterus and prepare it to receive the fertilized egg. After the zygote reaches the uterus, another chain of events takes place that helps it to develop.

Implantation in the Uterus

The zygote continues to undergo cell division until a hollow ball of cells called the **blastocyst** is formed. Cells on the surface of the blastocyst attach, or implant, into the uterine lining, as shown in **FIGURE 34.9**. Once the blastocyst is implanted, it goes through another stage in which three cell layers develop: the ectoderm, the mesoderm, and the endoderm.

The ectoderm layer develops into the skin and nervous system. The mesoderm layer forms many of the internal tissues and organs. The endoderm layer develops into many of the digestive organs and the lining of the digestive system. Once these structures begin to form, the ball of cells is known as an **embryo.**

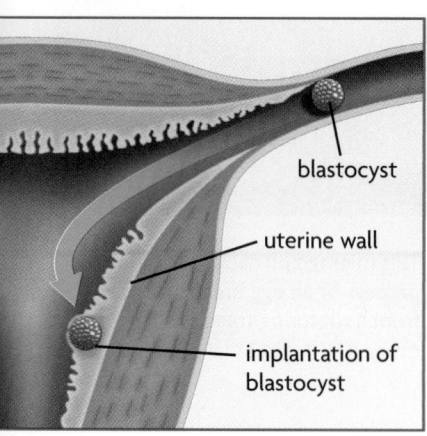

FIGURE 34.9 About seven days after fertilization, the blastocyst enters the uterus and attaches, or implants, into the uterine wall. Implantation is the beginning of a pregnancy.

blastocyst
uterine wall
implantation of blastocyst

VISUAL VOCAB

The **blastocyst** is a hollow ball of cells that implants in the uterus.

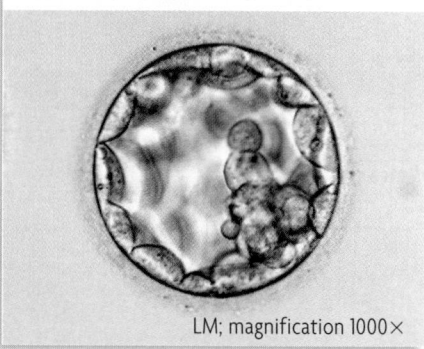

LM; magnification 1000×

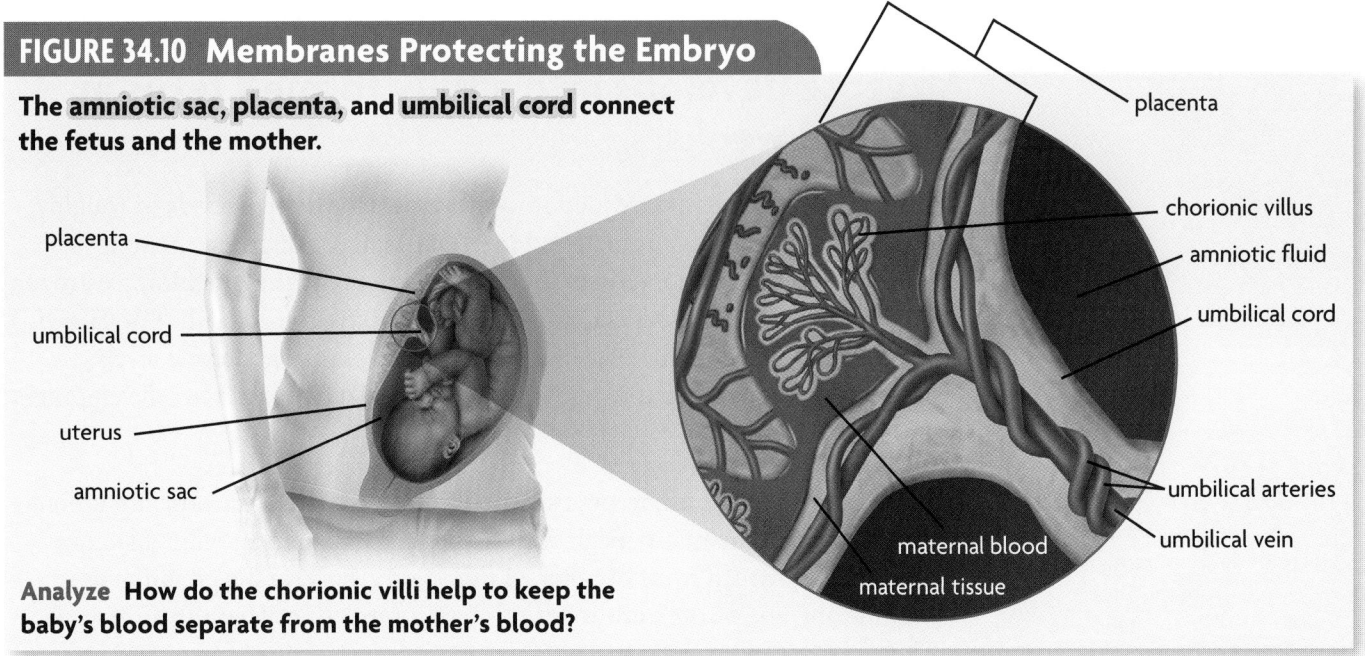

FIGURE 34.10 Membranes Protecting the Embryo

The **amniotic sac, placenta, and umbilical cord** connect the fetus and the mother.

placenta

umbilical cord

uterus

amniotic sac

placenta

chorionic villus

amniotic fluid

umbilical cord

umbilical arteries

umbilical vein

maternal blood

maternal tissue

Analyze How do the chorionic villi help to keep the baby's blood separate from the mother's blood?

Embryonic Membranes

As the pregnancy continues, membranes form that nourish and protect the developing embryo, as shown in **FIGURE 34.10**. One membrane, the amnion, becomes filled with fluid and is called the **amniotic sac** (AM-nee-AHT-ihk). This sac cushions the embryo within the uterus and protects it from sudden temperature changes. The amniotic sac surrounds the embryo until birth. Another membrane, the chorion (KAWR-ee-AHN), also begins to form. The chorion helps to nourish the embryo as it develops. The outer surface of the chorion has small projections called chorionic villi that extend into the uterine lining.

Together, the chorionic villi and the lining of the uterus form an important organ called the placenta. The **placenta** (pluh-SEHN-tuh) connects the mother and embryo to allow for the exchange of oxygen, nutrients, and wastes between them. Another structure, the **umbilical cord,** consists of two arteries and a vein that are twisted together. This cord connects the embryo inside the amniotic sac to the placenta. Nutrients and oxygen from the mother's blood diffuse into the chorionic villi, which contain blood from the embryo. The nutrients are carried to the embryo along the umbilical cord. In turn, wastes from the embryo are carried back along the umbilical cord to the chorionic villi. From there, the wastes diffuse into the mother's blood and are excreted in her urine.

The blood flows of the mother and the embryo move past each other but never mix. The placenta keeps the two flows separated. If proteins from the embryo leaked into the mother's circulatory system, they might be detected as foreign invaders by her immune system. The mother's immune system would then attack the proteins, which could end the pregnancy. The placenta provides a protective barrier for the embryo as it develops.

Apply Why might a pregnant woman need to be concerned about what she eats or drinks during pregnancy?

Connecting CONCEPTS

Circulatory System Like the pulmonary arteries and veins that you read about in **Chapter 30**, the umbilical arteries carry oxygen-poor blood and the umbilical vein carries oxygen-rich blood. The umbilical arteries carry blood away from the fetus's heart, and the umbilical vein carries blood to the fetus's heart.

▶ MAIN IDEA

A zygote develops into a fully formed fetus in about 38 weeks.

Human pregnancies are divided into **trimesters,** or three periods of roughly three months each, as summarized in **FIGURE 34.11.** Throughout the nine months, several hormones help to maintain the pregnancy, including estrogen, progesterone, and human chorionic gonadotropin (goh-NAD-uh-TROH-pihn), which is produced by the placenta to help maintain progesterone levels. Thyroid hormones from the mother help to regulate the embryo's development.

First Trimester

In the first trimester, embryonic stem cells undergo determination and differentiation to form the many specialized tissues and organs that will make up a human body. Recall from Chapter 28 that stem cells have the potential to become any one of the hundreds of different types of cells in the human body. The embryo can be more easily damaged during this trimester as the result of genetic errors or mutations, nutritional deficiencies in the mother, and any toxic chemicals, such as alcohol or drugs, that the mother may consume.

Even at this early stage, the complete body plan is already becoming visible. The heart begins beating at about five weeks. The early structures for the vertebrae and spinal cord have been formed. The brain is developing, many internal organs have appeared, and the arms and legs are evident. The embryo at nine weeks—now called a **fetus**—is only about 3 centimeters (about 1 in.) long, but is beginning to look like a small human being.

Second Trimester

The second trimester is a time of continuing development and increased physical activity. The heartbeat can now be heard by placing a stethoscope over the uterus. As the fetus flexes its muscles, the mother can feel movement within her uterus. During these three months, the uterus expands enough to make the mother's pregnancy noticeable. As the fetus develops, the uterus continues to expand until it reaches four to five times its original size. At the end of the second trimester, the fetus may be only 30 centimeters (12 in.) long, but it looks more and more like a full-sized baby. Even its fingers and toes are fully formed, as shown in **FIGURE 34.11.**

Third Trimester

In the third trimester, the fetus grows to its largest size. At birth, most babies weigh about 3 to 4 kilograms (7 to 9 lb) and are about 50 centimeters (20 in.) long. Babies born prematurely at the beginning of the third trimester have a difficult time surviving. Their organs, especially their lungs, are often too immature to function well. Babies born prematurely toward the middle of the third trimester often survive and thrive. In the last month, the lungs are strengthened as the fetus sucks in and pushes out the amniotic fluid.

Infer **Why might a fetus be more easily damaged by genetic errors or toxic chemicals during the first trimester than during any other trimester?**

VOCABULARY

The words *zygote, embryo,* and *fetus* describe different stages of development.

• **Zygote**—from the Greek word *zugotos,* meaning "yoked," or "joined," as when the sperm joins the egg and cell division begins

• **Embryo**—from the Greek word *embruon,* meaning "to be full to bursting." This stage covers weeks 1 to 8 when the entire body plan is developed.

• **Fetus**—from the Latin word *fetus,* meaning "offspring." This stage covers weeks 9 to 36.

TAKING NOTES

Use a timeline to help you take notes on early fetal development.

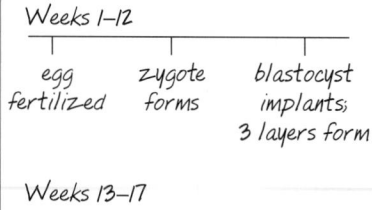

Weeks 1–12

egg fertilized | zygote forms | blastocyst implants; 3 layers form

Weeks 13–17

FIGURE 34.11 Trimesters of Development

During each **trimester**, the **fetus** goes through different stages of growth and development.

Animated BIOLOGY
See embryo development in action at ClassZone.com.

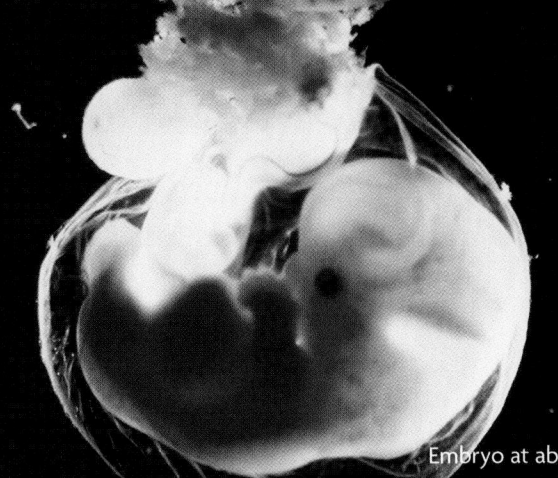

Embryo at about 8 weeks

FIRST TRIMESTER: WEEKS 1–12

Heart, brain, intestines, pancreas, kidneys, liver are forming.

Heartbeat can be detected after week 5.

Arms and legs begin to develop.

Lenses of the eye appear; eyelids will later fuse shut to allow irises to develop.

Individual fingers and toes begin to form.

Hair, fingernails, and toenails develop.

Cerebral hemispheres begin to form.

Early structure of bronchi begin to develop.

External sex organs show sex of the fetus.

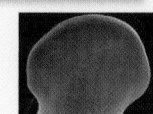

Hand at week 6

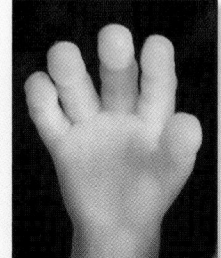

Hand at week 12

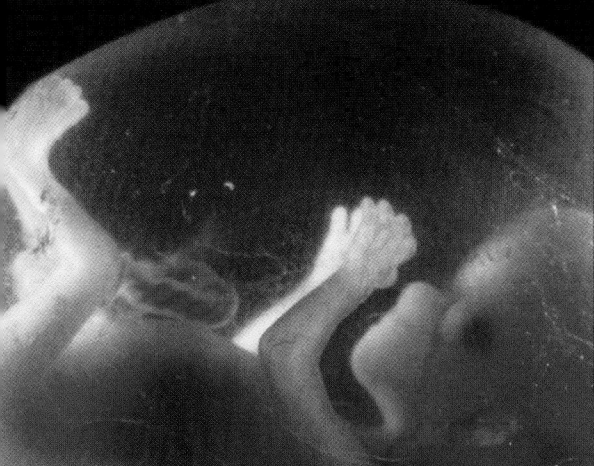

Fetus at about 25 weeks

SECOND TRIMESTER: WEEKS 13–27

Most joints and bones have started to form.

Skin is protected by fine hair and waxy substance.

First movements are felt by mother.

Wake and sleep cycles are more regular.

Brain begins a stage of rapid growth.

Eyes open and blink; eyebrows and eyelashes have formed.

Fetus breathes in amniotic fluid, which strengthens lungs.

Fetus swallows amniotic fluid and makes urine.

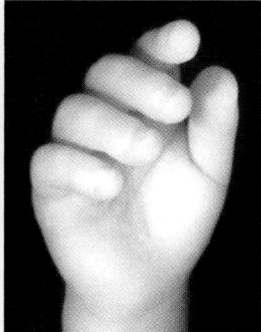

Hand at week 20

THIRD TRIMESTER: WEEKS 28–40

Fetus responds more strongly to light and sound outside the uterus.

Fetus has periods of dreaming; eyes are open when awake and closed when asleep.

Fine body hair thins and scalp hair grows in.

Bones are growing and hardening.

Synapses between neurons form in huge numbers.

Lungs complete development.

Fetus turns to head-down position.

Fetus at about 32 weeks

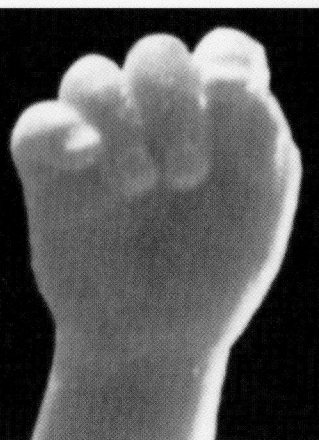

Hand at week 32

CRITICAL VIEWING Study the pictures of the embryo and fetus. What are some of the structural changes that have taken place from week 8 to week 32?

INTERPRETING GRAPHS

Scientists collected data on the amounts of thyroid-stimulating hormone (TSH) in mothers and in their developing fetuses. Researchers wanted to determine the point at which a fetus's own endocrine system begins to work independently of its mother's. The *x*-axis shows the different times during the pregnancy that levels of TSH were measured.

- The *y*-axis shows the amount of TSH in microliters per milliliter (μL/mL).
- The blue bar represents the fetus's levels of TSH.
- The orange bar represents the mother's levels of TSH.

1. **Analyze** What happens to both the mother's TSH levels and the fetus's TSH levels as the pregnancy progresses?

2. **Analyze** What is the relationship between the week of pregnancy and fetal TSH levels?

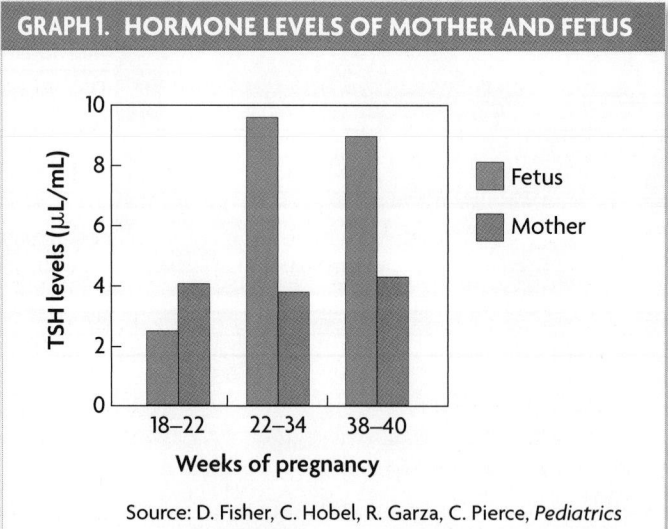

GRAPH 1. HORMONE LEVELS OF MOTHER AND FETUS

Source: D. Fisher, C. Hobel, R. Garza, C. Pierce, *Pediatrics*

▶ MAIN IDEA

The mother affects the fetus, and pregnancy affects the mother.

Throughout pregnancy, the mother and the fetus continually affect each other's health. For the most part, whatever the mother eats or drinks, the baby is exposed to through the placenta and the umbilical cord. On the other hand, the hormones released during pregnancy and the nutritional needs of the fetus present their own challenges to the mother's health.

Health of the Fetus

The fetus depends on the mother for all its nutrition. As a result, it is vitally important that the mother eat well throughout pregnancy. Her diet must include all the essential amino acids, vitamins, minerals, fats, and carbohydrates that the developing fetus needs. Vitamin and mineral supplements can provide extra amounts of these nutrients. For example, folic acid is an important B vitamin that can significantly lower the risk of serious birth defects in a fetus's brain and spinal cord. Folic acid is found in such foods as poultry, oranges, and dark green leafy vegetables. In contrast, toxic chemicals in alcohol, tobacco, and many other drugs can diffuse through the placenta and harm the fetus. These substances often interfere with fetal development and can cause many types of birth defects and produce learning disabilities in a child.

Studies have shown that many of these problems can be completely prevented if the mother avoids alcohol, tobacco, and drugs during the pregnancy. Even some over-the-counter medications can harm the fetus. As a result, the mother must check with a health care provider to be sure any medications she needs to take are safe for the fetus.

Health of the Mother

The mother's health is affected by pregnancy in a number of ways. To supply enough energy for herself and her baby, the mother must add roughly 300 more Calories a day to her diet after the first trimester. During pregnancy, most women will gain on average about 12 kilograms (26 lb). However, gaining too much or too little weight can affect the fetus. Women who gain too little weight often have underweight babies who may have impaired immune systems, learning disabilities, and delayed development.

FIGURE 34.12 Routine medical tests can be used to check the mother's blood pressure, glucose levels, nutrition, and other factors. The baby's growth and development in the uterus can also be monitored.

Hormone levels also fluctuate, affecting the mother's ability to maintain homeostasis. For example, some pregnant women are unable to control their glucose levels and may develop pregnancy-related diabetes. This type of diabetes normally disappears after the pregnancy is over. Hormones may also affect the digestive tract, causing what is known as morning sickness, or vomiting, for a time. This condition generally clears up as the pregnancy progresses. After the baby is born, some women may experience some depression during the time that their hormone levels are stabilizing. To help ensure a healthy pregnancy, the mother should have regular physical checkups. The normal challenges of pregnancy can be managed through proper diet, exercise, and medical care.

Infer When a woman first learns that she is pregnant, what lifestyle changes might she need to make?

34.3 ASSESSMENT

ONLINE QUIZ
ClassZone.com

REVIEWING ▶ MAIN IDEAS

1. Explain the main functions of the **placenta** during a pregnancy.

2. List two milestones of fetal growth and development achieved in each **trimester.**

3. Give two examples of how the mother and **fetus** affect one another during pregnancy.

CRITICAL THINKING

4. **Apply** A woman doesn't want to gain more than 6 kg (13 lbs) during her pregnancy. What effects might this decision have on the fetus?

5. **Infer** A baby is born 12 weeks premature. The organs are developed, but the baby must breathe using a ventilator. Explain why this treatment is necessary.

Connecting CONCEPTS

6. **Tissue Rejection** A woman with type O Rh⁻ blood is pregnant for a second time. During her first pregnancy, she developed antibodies for Rh⁺ factor. Her second baby's blood is type O Rh⁺. What might happen if some fetal blood leaks into the mother's blood?

34.4 Birth and Development

KEY CONCEPT Physical development continues through adolescence and declines with age.

▶ **MAIN IDEAS**

- Birth occurs in three stages.
- Human growth and aging also occur in stages.

VOCABULARY

infancy, p. 1042
childhood, p. 1042
adolescence, p. 1042
adulthood, p. 1043

REVIEW AT CLASSZONE.COM

Connect After birth, you will spend nearly two decades learning how to live on your own. Until recently, scientists thought that the most important learning period happened in the first three years of life. Now they have discovered that in adolescence the brain goes through a second period of development. During this time, you are maturing emotionally and mentally, not just physically. This may be one reason why humans take so long to grow up.

▶ **MAIN IDEA**

Birth occurs in three stages.

When the fetus has fully developed, the placenta can no longer provide enough nourishment. The time has come for the baby to be born. The birth process involves three stages: dilation of the cervix, emergence of the baby, and expulsion of the placenta, as shown in **FIGURE 34.13.** The physical changes that the mother's body goes through are known as labor.

Dilation of the Cervix

Labor begins with regular contractions of the uterus. The hormone oxytocin (AHK-sih-TOH-sihn), released by the mother and the fetus, stimulates the muscles in the wall of the uterus. However, not all contractions mean that the baby is about to be born. Expectant mothers are usually taught to count the number and strength of these contractions. When they become more frequent, intense, and painful over time, then true labor has begun. The amniotic sac usually breaks in the early stages of labor, although it can break earlier. The amniotic fluid is released through the vagina, which is also called the birth canal.

The contractions serve to push the walls of the cervix apart. The baby cannot leave the uterus until the cervix dilates, or widens, to at least 10 centimeters (4 in.). This space allows most babies to pass through. If the cervix does not dilate, the doctor must make an incision through the abdominal wall to remove the baby, a procedure called a cesarean section, or c-section.

Emergence of the Baby

This stage of the birth process is often the most stressful for the mother and the baby. If everything goes well, the powerful contractions of the uterus help rotate the baby so that its head is toward the cervix. In some cases, the baby

Connecting CONCEPTS

Marsupials In **Chapter 26**, you read about marsupial mammals that give birth to young that are little more than embryos. These tiny life forms must then find their way into the mother's pouch to complete their development. In contrast, human babies are born at an advanced stage of development.

FIGURE 34.13 Three Stages of Birth

Birth begins with contractions and continues until the baby and placenta emerge.

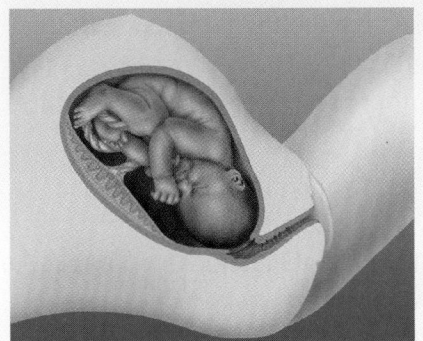

STAGE 1
As regular, strong contractions occur, the cervix dilates and the baby turns.

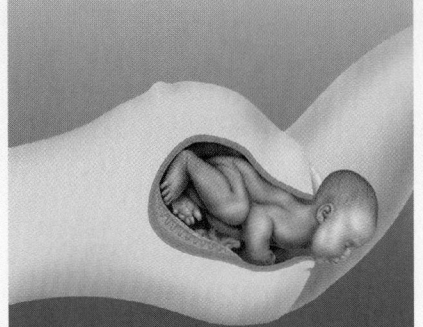

STAGE 2
The baby is pushed through the cervix and out of the vaginal canal.

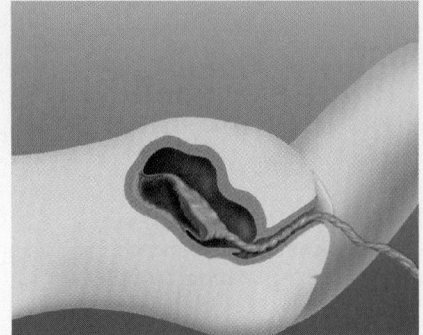

STAGE 3
Contractions continue, expelling the placenta and helping to control bleeding.

Predict At what point might the baby begin to breathe on its own?

does not turn and is born feet first, which is a more difficult birth process. Usually, however, the baby is in the right position. The muscles of the uterus then push the baby into the birth canal. Once the head emerges, the rest of the body usually slips out quickly. Within a short time, the baby is breathing on its own. The hormone oxytocin also stimulates the mother's breasts to produce milk and increases her desire to bond with her infant. This bond helps to ensure that she will care for the baby after it is born.

Expulsion of the Placenta

The third stage of birth happens soon after the baby emerges. As the uterine contractions continue, the placenta detaches from the wall of the uterus and is expelled. These contractions also help to constrict blood vessels and reduce the amount of bleeding the mother experiences. The baby's umbilical cord is clamped and cut a few inches from the abdomen. This bit of cord eventually dries up and falls away, leaving a scar called the navel, or belly button.

Infer Why might a head-first delivery be the safest for both mother and baby?

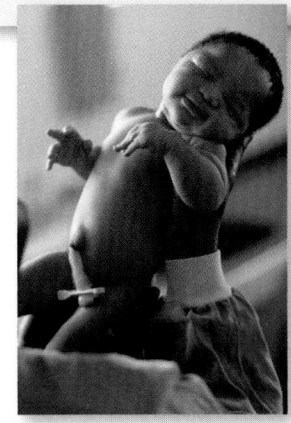

After living in the uterus for nine months, this newborn is breathing air for the first time. From now on it must live outside the protected environment of its mother's body.

▶ MAIN IDEA

Human growth and aging also occur in stages.

Just as hormones regulate human reproduction, they are also involved in human growth after birth. Most children follow the same pattern of growth and development, but each child matures at his or her own pace. Rates of growth are also affected by factors such as genetics, nutrition, and environment.

Key hormones involved in growth include thyroxin, estrogen, testosterone, and human growth hormone (hGH), which is secreted by the pituitary gland. Human growth hormone increases the body's rate of fat metabolism and protein synthesis. These processes cause all body cells to divide, particularly bone and skeletal muscle cells. However, as a person ages, the pituitary secretes less and less hGH.

Infancy and Childhood

Infancy lasts from birth to about age 2. When babies are born, their homeostatic mechanisms are not completely developed. As a result, a newborn's body temperature, heart rate, and breathing rate vary more than they do in older children. Also, an infant's kidneys are less efficient at reabsorbing water, which can lead to rapid dehydration. As infancy progresses, homeostatic mechanisms mature and these variations decrease.

The first year of life is a period of rapid growth. Both male and female infants usually triple their weight and grow about 25 centimeters (10 in.) by their first birthday. Other changes are equally dramatic. Rapid development of the brain and nervous system occurs, and vision improves as babies learn to focus their eyes. They begin to coordinate muscle groups to sit, stand, and finally walk. By the end of infancy, children usually have a vocabulary of several words and may even express themselves using short sentences.

Childhood begins at age 2 and extends to about age 12. During childhood, physical growth slows down. Each year, most children grow only about 6 centimeters (3 in.) and gain about 4 kilograms (6 lb). Childhood is a time during which muscle skills and coordination improve as the nervous system matures. The continued development of sensory receptors, nerves, and muscles mean that children can learn both fine-motor skills such as writing and large-motor skills such as walking, as shown in **FIGURE 34.14.** Language and abstract reasoning abilities improve. Children begin to express more complex and varied emotions and become better able to understand the emotions of others.

Puberty and Adolescence

Puberty marks the beginning of sexual maturity and the development of sexual characteristics. As you read in Section 34.1, puberty begins when the hormones FSH and LH are released by the pituitary gland. For girls, the average age range for the onset of puberty is 10 to 14. For boys, the average age range is 10 to 16. During this time, young people experience a period of rapid growth stimulated by the release of testosterone and estrogen. Growth averages 5 to 7 centimeters (2 to 3 in.) and can reach up to 15 centimeters (6 in.) in one year. Young people often feel clumsy as they adjust to their changing bodies. They also experience rapid changes in their emotions and in their reasoning abilities as the brain continues to make new neural connections.

Adolescence begins at sexual maturity. In girls, sexual maturity is marked by ovulation and the first menstrual cycle. Although boys can ejaculate before sexual maturity, sexual maturity is indicated by the presence of sperm in the semen. During adolescence, bone growth continues until about age 15 in girls and about age 17 in boys. Adolescent boys and girls often experience greater strength and physical endurance in these years, and their coordination often improves. Although the brain stops increasing in size, the rearrangement of neural connections continues. In a very real sense, the adolescent brain is being "rewired" in preparation for adulthood.

FIGURE 34.14 The child (top) is learning to control major muscle groups in her legs in order to walk. The adolescent skater (below) is adapting her knowledge of walking to learn a more sophisticated skill.

Adulthood and Aging

You might think that **adulthood** marks a time when people reach their peak in terms of skills and abilities. For the most part, you would be right. During these years, most people establish independent lives, and many raise their own families. However, adulthood, like other life stages, also marks a time of distinct physical changes, as you can see in **FIGURE 34.15**.

Scientists are only now beginning to unlock the mysteries of how the body ages. As a person grows older, some of the most important changes include a decline in immune functions and in the production of many key hormones, such as growth hormone, testosterone, and estrogen. Most women around age 50 or so go through menopause. In men, the sperm count gradually decreases. For both sexes, the body's rates of metabolism and digestion slow down. Skin becomes thinner and less elastic, bones lose calcium, and muscle mass decreases and is replaced by fat deposits.

However, scientists are also finding that how one experiences the aging process may depend as much on genetics, lifestyle, and environment as it does on chronological age. In general, those who eat a healthy diet, remain physically active, and keep learning may be able to slow down or even counter-act many of the changes that aging brings about. For example, regular weight-bearing exercise such as walking several miles a week can help to maintain bone and muscle mass. Also, studies have shown that if a person keeps learning throughout life, the brain continues to make new neural connections just as it did when the person was younger.

Compare Describe some of the ways that the process of aging is the reverse of the processes that occur during puberty and adolescence.

1 ½ years
11 years
17 years
48 years
71 years

BIOLOGY
Watch how a person ages at ClassZone.com.

FIGURE 34.15 These photos show the changes that occur in the same person's face from childhood to the 70s.

34.4 ASSESSMENT

ONLINE QUIZ ClassZone.com

REVIEWING ▶ MAIN IDEAS

1. Briefly describe the three stages of the birth process. What are the signs that true labor has begun?

2. What are the basic stages of development after birth? During which stage(s) does the greatest amount of physical growth usually occur?

CRITICAL THINKING

3. **Compare and Contrast** What are some similarities and differences between the first year of life and the first year of puberty?

4. **Connect** Most large prey species, such as elk or antelope, are eutherian (placental), and not marsupial. What survival advantage might this give the offspring of the prey species?

Connecting CONCEPTS

5. **Reproductive Strategies** Many insects and fish give birth to hundreds of young at one time but do little to care for them. Most birds and mammals give birth to only one or a few young, but care for them until they are independent. What are some advantages and disadvantages to each type of reproduction?

Use these inquiry-based labs and online activities to deepen your understanding of reproductive systems.

MICHIGAN STANDARDS

B1.1C Conduct scientific investigations using appropriate tools and techniques (e.g., selecting an instrument that measures the desired quantity—length, volume, weight, time interval, temperature—with the appropriate level of precision).

B1.2C Develop an understanding of a scientific concept by accessing information from multiple sources. Evaluate the scientific accuracy and significance of the information.

INVESTIGATION

Development of an Embryo

Animals from echinoderms to humans go through three main stages of development after fertilization. In the first stage, cleavage, the embryo in an echinoderm divides to form the blastula, called a blastocyst in mammals. In the second stage, the blastula develops three distinct layers and becomes known as the gastrula. In the third stage, the embryo's internal organs begin to form. In this lab, you will examine slides of sea stars in the first two stages of embryonic development.

MATERIALS
- slide of sea star embryo in early cleavage
- slide of sea star embryo in late cleavage
- slide of sea star blastula
- slide of sea star gastrula
- microscope

SKILLS Observing, Analyzing

PROBLEM How does a sea star embryo develop?

PROCEDURE

1. Obtain the slide of a sea star embryo in early cleavage and examine it under low power and high power on the microscope. Draw and label the cell and its structures.

2. Repeat step 1 with each of the remaining slides.

ANALYZE AND CONCLUDE

1. **Describe** What does a sea star embryo look like in the early stages of cleavage?

2. **Analyze** What type of cell division occurred to produce the multicellular embryo after fertilization?

3. **Compare** How does the appearance of the cells in the late stages of cleavage compare with the appearance of the cells in the blastula?

4. **Contrast** Sketch the different cell layers in the gastrula. What differences do you see among them?

5. **Compare** How are the developmental stages of a sea star embryo similar to the stages of development in a human embryo?

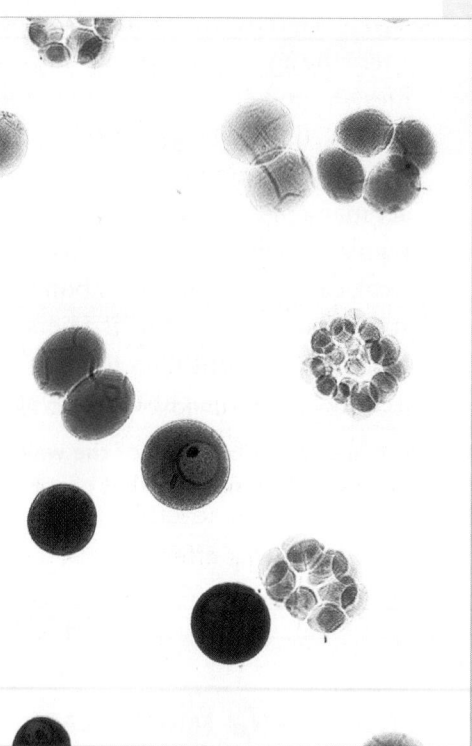

This slide shows sea star embryos in different stages of development. Sea stars become larvae before they metamorphose into five-limbed sea stars. (LM; magnification 100×)

Effects of Chemicals on Reproductive Organs

Like other organs in the human body, including the liver, kidneys, and lungs, reproductive organs can be harmed by chemicals. Exposure to certain chemicals or toxins through the use of alcohol, tobacco, or drugs or from the environment can affect the structure and functioning of both the male and female reproductive systems.

SKILL Researching

PROBLEM What effects do certain toxic chemicals have on the male and female reproductive systems?

PROCEDURE

1. Choose one of the substances listed below to research.
   - Anabolic steroids
   - Alcohol
   - Cocaine
   - Tobacco
   - Pesticides (herbicides and/or insecticides)
   - Environmental toxins (benzene, toluene)

2. Describe the chemical's effects on male and female reproductive organs.

3. Explain whether scientists know if the effects are permanent or reversible.

4. Identify what effects, if any, the chemical might have on future offspring.

Toxic chemicals sprayed on fruits and vegetables to control pests may remain inside the plants. When a mother eats these foods, some of these toxic chemicals could harm her growing fetus.

Online

ANIMATED BIOLOGY
Developmental Timeline

Does the heart develop in the first month or second month of pregnancy? When do fingers form? Use physical changes and other clues to place images along a developmental timeline.

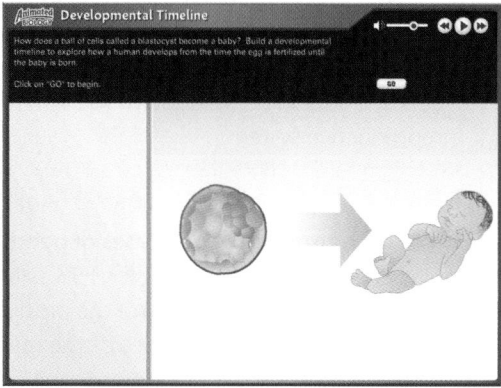

WEBQUEST

Developing fetuses depend on their mothers for nutrition. In this WebQuest, you will find out why expectant mothers must get balanced, proper nutrition. Explore what a pregnant woman should eat and what she should avoid.

DATA ANALYSIS ONLINE

Graph the rise and fall of human growth hormone through adolescence for both girls and boys.

34.1 Reproductive Anatomy

Female and male reproductive organs fully develop during puberty. Puberty in both males and females begins with the release of two hormones: FSH and LH. These two hormones stimulate the release of estrogen in females and of testosterone in males. The female reproductive system produces ova, or egg cells, and provides an environment for a fertilized egg to develop. The male reproductive system produces sperm cells and delivers sperm to the female reproductive system.

34.2 Reproductive Processes

Human reproductive processes depend on cycles of hormones. In females, FSH, LH, estrogen, and progesterone control the production of egg cells and the three phases of the menstrual cycle. Females usually release only one egg a month until menopause.

In males, FSH, LH, and testosterone control the production of sperm cells. Males release millions of sperm on ejaculation and can continue to produce sperm all their lives. When a sperm penetrates an egg and the two nuclei fuse, fertilization occurs. Reproductive organs can be damaged or destroyed by STDs.

34.3 Fetal Development

Development progresses in stages from zygote to fetus. The fetus is nourished and protected by the amniotic fluid, placenta, and umbilical cord, which connect the mother and fetus. Development takes roughly nine months, divided into three trimesters. To ensure the health of her baby, a mother needs to eat well, exercise, and have regular medical checkups.

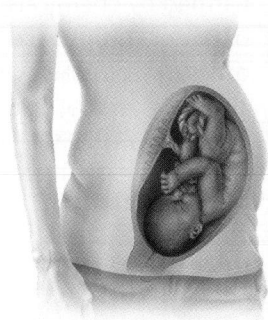

34.4 Birth and Development

Physical development continues through adolescence and declines with age. The birth process takes place in three stages: dilation of the cervix, emergence of the baby, and expulsion of the placenta. Key hormones regulate human growth and development throughout infancy, childhood, adolescence, and adulthood.

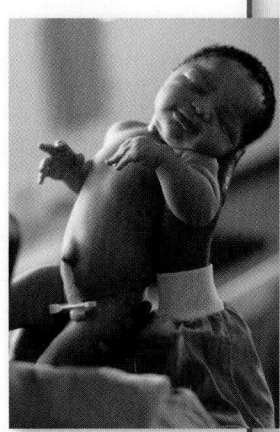

Synthesize Your Notes

Concept Map   Use a concept map like the one below to take notes on topics such as puberty.

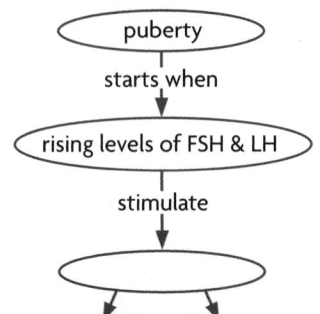

puberty
↓ starts when
rising levels of FSH & LH
↓ stimulate

Process Diagram   A process diagram like the one below is a good way to remember the steps in reproductive processes.

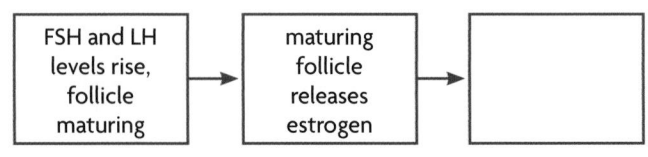

| FSH and LH levels rise, follicle maturing | → | maturing follicle releases estrogen | → | |

Chapter Assessment

Reviewing Vocabulary

Term Relationships

For each pair of terms below, write a sentence that contains both terms and shows a relationship between them. For example, *fetus, umbilical cord: The fetus obtains nutrients through the umbilical cord.*

1. puberty, testosterone
2. follicle, ovulation
3. menstrual cycle, endometrium
4. embryo, amniotic sac
5. menopause, adulthood

Label Diagrams

In your notebook, write the vocabulary term that matches each item pointed out in the diagrams below.

MALE

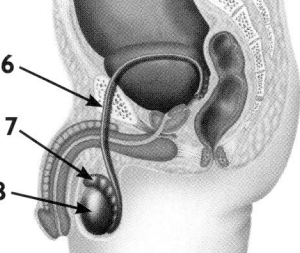

6
7
8

FEMALE

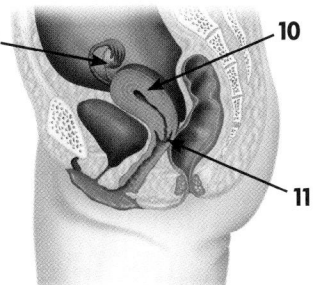

9
10
11

Reviewing MAIN IDEAS

12. Describe the three main functions of estrogen.

13. The sperm move from the testes to the epididymis to the vas deferens as they develop. What happens at each location?

14. Explain what happens to the endometrium during the three phases of the menstrual cycle.

15. What process of cell division do eggs and sperm undergo to become mature sex cells?

16. What happens to their chromosomes when one sperm joins with an egg?

17. Why can chlamydia and syphilis be cured with antibiotics, but genital herpes and HIV cannot?

18. Explain how nutrients and oxygen from the mother's blood are transported to the embryo.

19. A premature baby is born near the end of the second trimester. Why would it have a harder time surviving than one born during the middle of the third trimester?

20. Discuss two ways in which a fetus's health could be harmed by a mother's actions during pregnancy.

21. Describe what marks the beginning of the birth process and what marks the end of the process.

22. In what two phases of human development might human growth hormone be the most active? Explain.

Critical Thinking

23. **Infer** A young woman discovers that she is not ovulating. What endocrine glands might a doctor suspect are not functioning well? Explain your answer.

24. **Analyze** Alcohol and drug abuse can damage the brain, including the hypothalamus. How would this condition affect sperm production?

25. **Synthesize** In a bird egg, the developing embryo is inside the *amnion,* which contains fluid. The embryo gets nourishment from the *yolk.* The *chorion* lines the inside of the shell and helps protect the embryo. What structures in a human provide the same functions as these structures in the bird egg?

26. **Connect** How do you think your ability to express complex emotions and use abstract reasoning changed between the ages of 5 and 15?

Interpreting Visuals

The structures shown below supply a fetus with oxygen and nutrients and remove its waste products. Use the diagram to answer the next three questions.

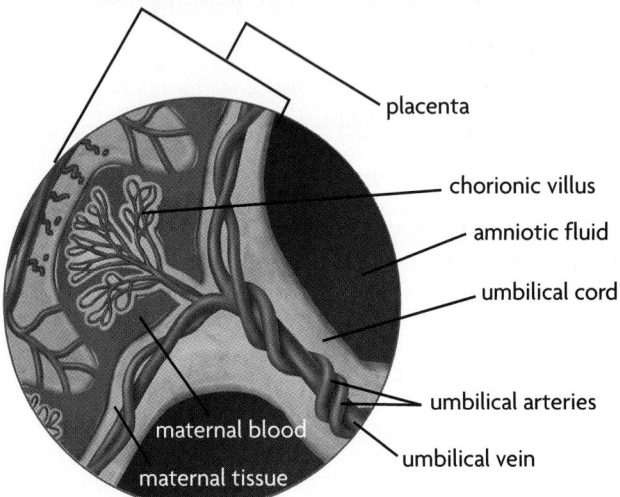

placenta

chorionic villus

amniotic fluid

umbilical cord

umbilical arteries

umbilical vein

maternal blood

maternal tissue

27. **Apply** Explain how the chorionic villi help move nutrients from the maternal blood to the fetus.

28. **Analyze** Look carefully at the umbilical arteries and vein. Which of these carries oxygen to the fetus? Explain.

29. **Predict** Suppose the umbilical arteries became blocked. Describe one way this condition would immediately affect the health of the fetus.

Analyzing Data

Puberty is a time of rapid physical development. The graph below shows average height increases for boys and girls in centimeters per year from ages 8 to 19. Study the data to answer the next two questions.

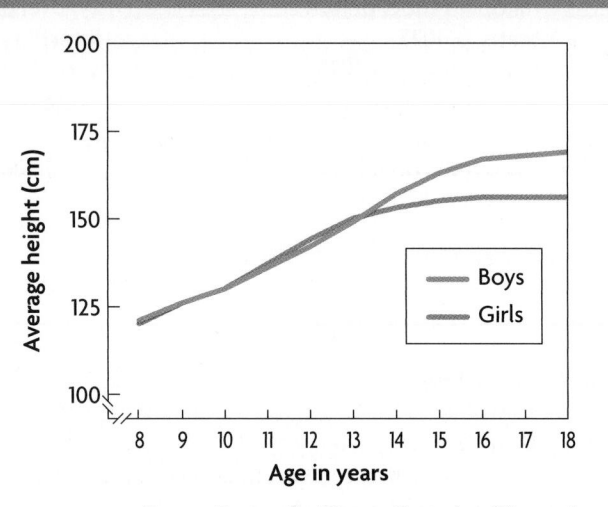

GROWTH RATES IN BOYS AND GIRLS

Average height (cm)

Age in years

Boys
Girls

Source: Centers for Disease Control and Prevention

30. **Analyze** What does the graph show about the growth rates of boys and girls?

31. **Analyze** According to the graph, at about what age does the growth rate peak for boys? for girls?

Connecting CONCEPTS

32. **Write a Brochure** This chapter explained how a pregnant woman can affect the health of her fetus. Write the text for a brochure that gives women information on how to promote their own health and the health of their babies during pregnancy. Include a list of what to do and what to avoid and the reasons why. Be sure to cover the topics of food, checkups, and unhealthy activities.

33. **Synthesize** Look again at the picture of the fetus on page 1023. Use what you have learned in this chapter to explain how the fetus can live without breathing while it is in the uterus.

MICHIGAN
STANDARDS-BASED ASSESSMENT

✓ **Test Practice**
For more test practice, go to ClassZone.com.

1.

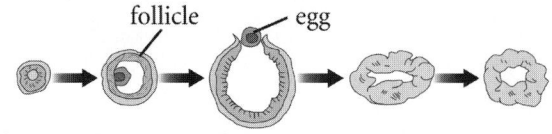

Stage 1   Stage 2   Stage 3   Stage 4   Stage 5

The release of an egg from the ovary is called ovulation. A female's body temperature typically rises significantly when ovulation occurs. Above is an illustration of the development of the follicle and egg. At which stage would you expect to plot the highest temperature?   **B1.1E**

A Stage 2

B Stage 3

C Stage 4

D Stage 5

2. Each month, the levels of hormones in the female's reproductive system rise and fall. The precise coordination of these hormone levels is responsible for the timing and release of an egg. These hormones are coordinated through a series of   **B2.2f**

A mitotic divisions.

B meiotic divisions.

C feedback loops.

D fallopian tubes.

3. During most months of a woman's life, no egg is fertilized. Estrogen and progesterone hormone levels then both decline, and the uterus lining is shed in the process of menstruation. If an egg is fertilized, which of the following happens?   **B2.3C**

A The levels of these hormones still decline.

B The levels of these hormones remain high.

C Another egg will soon be released.

D Hormones are no longer needed.

THINK THROUGH THE QUESTION

Think about the importance of the uterus to a developing embryo. What needs to happen to prevent its lining from being shed?

4. Sex cells are produced during a specific type of cell division known as   **B4.3A**

A mitosis.

B meiosis.

C ovulation.

D implantation.

5.

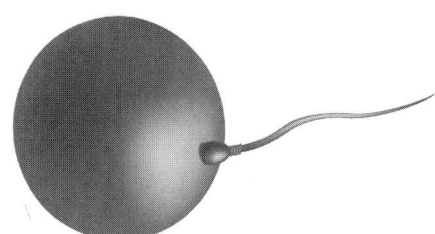

During fertilization, a sperm enters an egg, and the two join to form a zygote. Which statement is true regarding the combination of alleles in the zygote?   **L4.p1A**

A All of the alleles come from the mother's egg.

B All of the alleles come from the father's sperm.

C New combinations of alleles are formed.

D Allele combinations depend on when the egg is fertilized.

6. The placenta is an organ that allows for the exchange of oxygen, nutrients, and wastes between the mother and the developing embryo. In other words, the placenta is responsible for   **B2.3d**

A allowing the mother and the embryo to maintain homeostasis at the same time.

B repairing genetic damage due to mutation in the embryo.

C ensuring that no fluids leave or enter the uterus.

D serving as a barrier to keep out all toxic materials.

BIOZINE

at **CLASSZONE.COM**

Go online for the latest biology news and updates on all BioZine articles.

Expanding the Textbook

News Feeds

- Science Daily
- CNN
- BBC

Careers

Bio Bytes

Opinion Poll

Strange Biology

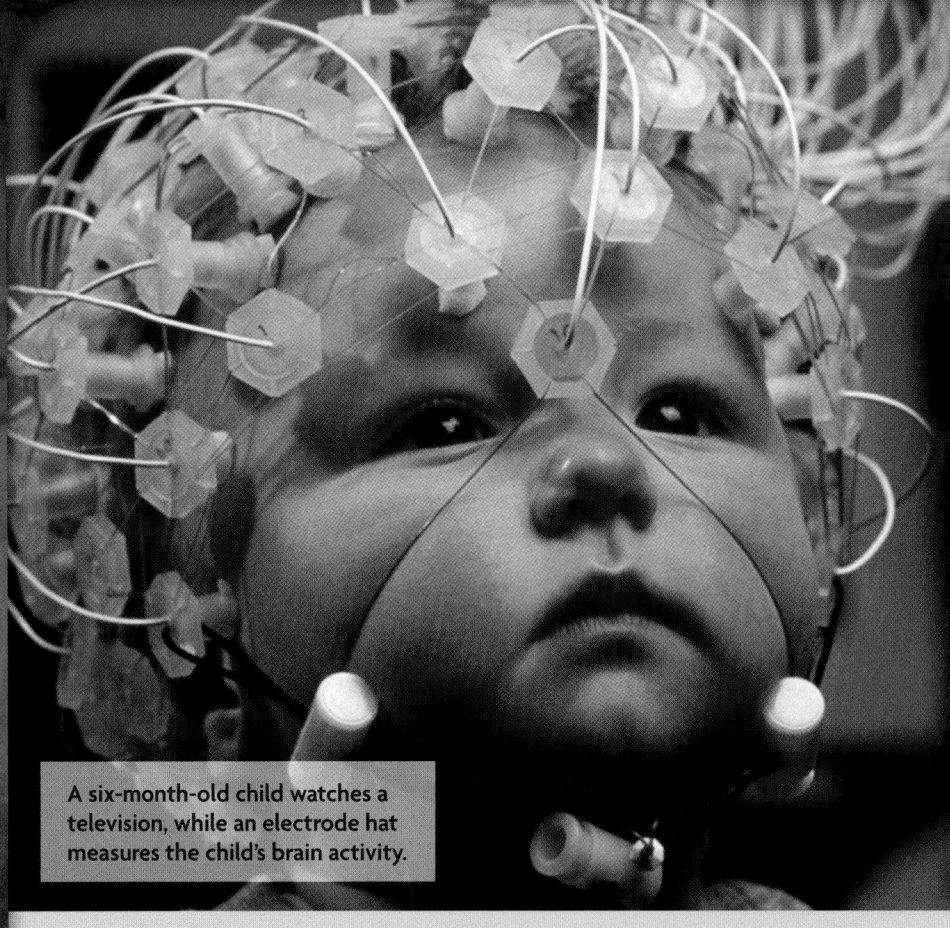

A six-month-old child watches a television, while an electrode hat measures the child's brain activity.

Brain Science— We Are Wired to Learn!

Your brain has more than 100 billion cells, called neurons. Together, the neurons in your brain are so powerful that they can process more information than the most powerful existing computer can in the same amount of time. Your brain can accomplish so much because you've spent years— every second of your life—learning from and interpreting the world around you.

Plasticity of the Brain

What factors affect the brain's plasticity, or ability to learn new things? How does the brain change with age? These are some of the questions neuroscientists addressed in the early years of brain research.

During the first three years of life, the neurons in the brain rapidly form connections, or synapses, between each other. Neurons and synapses are overproduced in babies' brains because their brains are taking in a lot of new information. At three years old, the brain begins to prune, or reduce the number of, these connections so that only the most used connections are intact. On average, three-year-olds have two times more synapses than adults have.

Of course, the brain does not lose all of its plasticity after the age of three. Even adults can learn a new skill, such as how to speak a foreign language. But neuroscientists have recently found a surprising second wave of brain growth and plasticity that begins just before puberty, similar to that observed in infants. Then, during the teenage years, some connections are pruned. The remaining connections become stronger and more efficient by the addition of more insulation around the neurons. This period of pruning and strengthening continues until a person is about 30. Connections that are used least are pruned away, and connections that are used the most are strengthened.

So how teenagers spend their time can affect their brain's wiring. One researcher says, "If a teen is doing music or sports or academics, those are the cells and connections that will be hard-wired. If they're lying on the couch or playing video games . . . those are the connections that are going to survive."

Although researchers agree that playing video games affects the brain, they do not agree on how the brain is affected. Some studies suggest that video games could strengthen beneficial connections. Other studies imply that some beneficial connections could become weakened.

TECHNOLOGY

Scanning the Brain

Much of today's research on brain function uses functional magnetic resonance imaging (fMRI). In a traditional MRI, computers use information from a magnetic field to make a three-dimensional image of the brain. An fMRI uses an MRI machine together with computer software that can analyze which part of the brain is active while a person performs different tasks.

A person lies in an MRI machine and thinks about something, observes images, listens to music, or does arithmetic. While the person thinks, the largest quantity of oxygenated blood gets directed to the part of the brain that is doing the most work.

The magnets detect molecules of hemoglobin, which bind oxygen in red blood cells. The hemoglobin contains atoms of iron, a metal that is attracted to magnets. When the magnetic field encounters the iron in hemoglobin, the magnetic field bends slightly.

Sensors in the MRI machine record the bending and send the information to a computer. The computer calculates, based on the amount of bending in the magnetic field, how much oxygen is present and calculates where in the brain the oxygen is located.

The computer maps this information on a three-dimensional model of the brain as shown in the photograph. The orange highlighted area on the model indicates the area of the brain that the person was using during the experiment.

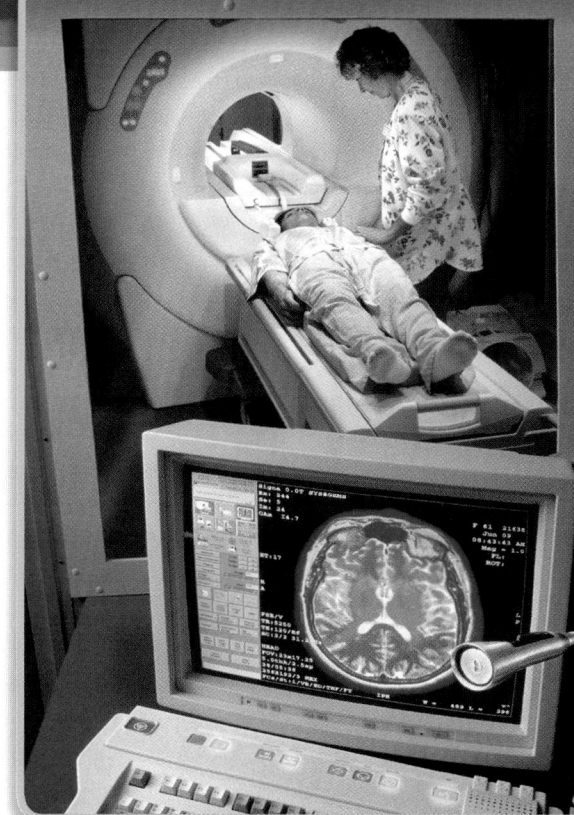

A patient emerges from an MRI machine as a computer maps oxygen (orange) in the patient's brain.

Read More >> *at* CLASSZONE.COM

The Multitasking Brain

How can some video games strengthen connections in your brain? Some video games present the player with complicated puzzles and patterns. The player must take in visual messages from the computer or television screen, while using problem-solving skills to analyze patterns at the same time. This multitasking requires the player to use different areas of the brain at the same time. Using language has a similar effect on the brain as playing video games in that both activate many areas of the brain at the same time.

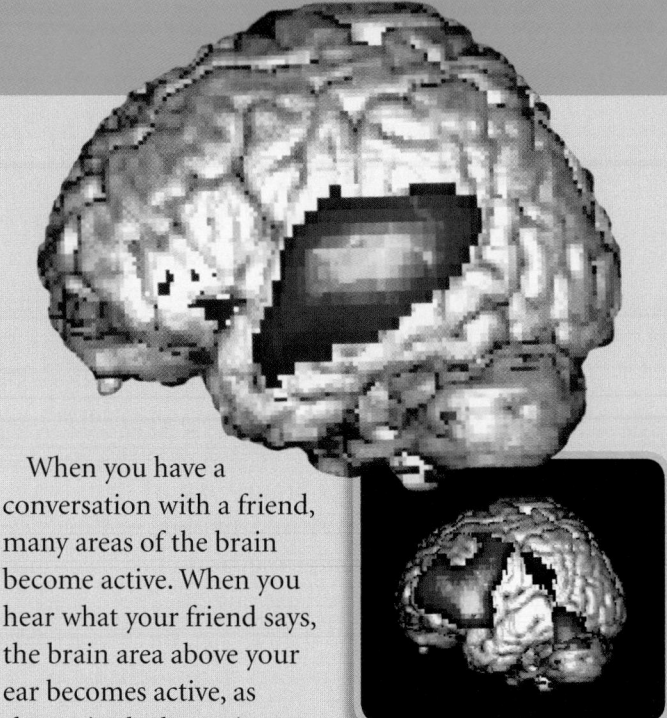

CAREERS

Neuroscientist in Action

DR. RAE NISHI

TITLE Director, Neuroscience Graduate Program, University of Vermont

EDUCATION Ph. D., Biology, University of California, San Diego

Dr. Rae Nishi's research proves that you do not need complicated technology, such as fMRIs, to make discoveries in neuroscience. Through observation and experiment, Dr. Nishi's research tries to answer the question: What causes brain cells to die?

Although the question is too broad to answer completely, Dr. Nishi has discovered a molecule that seems to keep alive brain cells in dying chick embryos. She also found that by blocking a certain receptor on the surface of neurons, dying neurons will stop showing signs of decline. Studies of how and why brain cells might die are important in understanding Alzheimer's and Parkinson's diseases, which cause certain areas of the brain to become inactive.

"There is no profession as exciting as being a scientist," Dr. Nishi says. "You get to learn new things every day. You get to make discoveries. You get to solve puzzles." Dr. Nishi is currently working to determine how the molecules released during one neuron's death might trigger the growth of new, neighboring neurons.

Read More >> *at* **CLASSZONE.COM**

When you have a conversation with a friend, many areas of the brain become active. When you hear what your friend says, the brain area above your ear becomes active, as shown in the larger image above. When you form a response and speak, different brain areas become activated, as shown in the smaller image at right. The front of the brain is activated when you interpret your friend's words and form a response. When you begin to respond, an area in the back of the brain becomes active. This area becomes more and more active as you talk.

As a person listens (top) and then speaks (bottom), different areas of the brain become active (red and yellow).

Reading is another complicated activity. The same areas of your brain that are active when you talk to your friend are active when you read. But another area is also activated. This third area is farther back in the brain. It allows you to see and interpret the printed words in front of you. Even people who read Braille use the visual part of their brain to interpret what is on the page.

Unanswered Questions

Every new discovery in neuroscience brings with it new questions. Some of these include the following:

- Can the plasticity of an adult brain be used to help adults recover from brain injuries and diseases?
- Can neuroscientists find ways to treat, or even cure, disorders such as Alzheimer's disease?
- Why are humans, and not other primates, good at learning words and systems of grammar?

Read More >> *at* **CLASSZONE.COM**

Student Resources

LAB HANDBOOK   R2

Safety   R2
Safety Symbols   R4
The Metric System and SI Units   R5
Measuring in the Lab   R6
Using a Light Microscope   R8
Designing Experiments   R11

MATH AND DATA ANALYSIS HANDBOOK   R14

Calculating Mean, Median, and Mode   R14
Significant Figures and Scientific Notation   R14
Data Tables and Line Graphs   R15
Bar Graphs and Combination Graphs   R16
Histograms, Scatterplots, and Circle Graphs   R17

VOCABULARY HANDBOOK   R18

Greek and Latin Word Parts   R18
Academic Vocabulary   R20

NOTE-TAKING HANDBOOK   R22

Process and Cycle Diagrams and Supporting Main Ideas Notes   R22
Main Idea Webs, Two-Column Notes, Cause-and-Effect Diagrams, and Content Frames   R23
Venn Diagrams, Y Diagrams, and Concept Maps   R24

APPENDICES   R25

A Classification   R25
B Life Cycles   R32
    Moss   R32
    Fern   R33
    Conifer   R34
    Flowering Plant   R35
C Periodic Table   R36
D Biology Careers   R38

Lab Handbook

Safety

Before you work in the laboratory, read these safety rules. Ask your teacher to explain any rules that you do not completely understand. Refer to these rules later on if you have questions about safety in the science classroom.

Directions

- Know where the fire extinguisher, fire blanket, shower, and eyewash are located in your classroom.
- Read all directions and make sure that you understand them before starting an investigation or lab activity. If you do not understand how to do a procedure or how to use a piece of equipment, ask your teacher.
- Do not begin any investigation or touch any equipment until your teacher has told you to start.
- Never experiment on your own. If you want to try a procedure that the directions do not call for, ask your teacher for permission first.
- If you are hurt or injured in any way, tell your teacher immediately.

Dress Code

- Wear goggles when using glassware, sharp objects, or chemicals; heating an object; or working with anything that can easily fly up into the air and hurt someone's eye.
- Tie back long hair or hair that hangs in front of your eyes.
- Remove any article of clothing—such as a loose sweater or a scarf—that hangs down and may touch a flame, chemical, or piece of equipment.
- Observe all safety icons calling for the wearing of eye protection, gloves, and aprons.

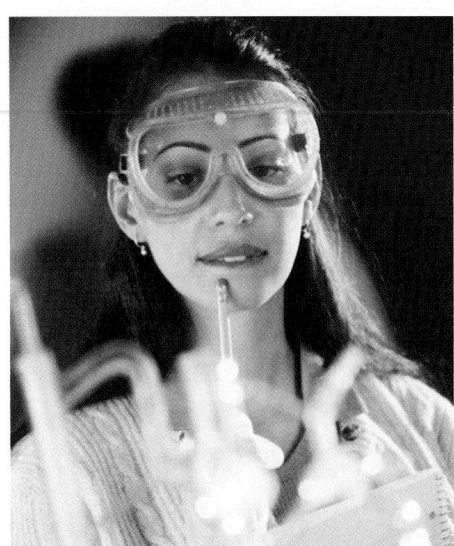

Heating and Fire Safety

- Keep your work area neat, clean, and free of extra materials.
- Use only borosilicate glass for heating substances.
- Never reach over a flame or heat source.
- Point objects being heated away from you and others.
- Never heat a substance or an object in a closed container.
- Use oven mitts, clamps, tongs, or a test tube holder to hold heated items.
- Never touch an object that has been heated. If you are unsure whether something is hot, treat it as though it is.
- After heating test tubes, place them in a test tube rack.
- Do not throw hot substances into the trash. Wait for them to cool and dispose of them in the container provided by your teacher.

Chemical Safety

- Always wear goggles when working with any type of chemical, even household items such as baking soda.
- Stand when you are working with chemicals. Pour them over a sink or your work area, not over the floor. If you spill a chemical or get it on your skin, tell your teacher right away.
- If you get a chemical in your eye, use the eyewash immediately.
- Never touch, taste, or sniff any chemicals in the lab. If you need to determine odor, waft. To waft, hold the chemical in its container 15 cm (6 in.) away from your nose, and use your fingers to bring fumes from the container to your nose.
- Keep lids on all chemicals you are not using.
- Use materials only from properly labeled containers.
- Never use more chemicals than the procedure calls for.
- When diluting acid with water, always add acid to water.
- Never put unused chemicals back into the original containers. Dispose of extra chemicals in the container provided by your teacher.
- Always wash your hands after handling chemicals.

Electrical Safety

- Never use lamps or other electrical equipment with frayed cords.
- Make sure no cord is lying on the floor where someone can trip over it.
- Do not let a cord hang over the side of a counter or table so that the equipment can easily be pulled or knocked to the floor.
- Never let cords hang into sinks or other places where water can be found.
- Turn off all power switches before plugging an appliance into an outlet.
- Never touch electrical equipment with wet hands.
- Never try to fix electrical problems. Immediately inform your teacher of any problems.
- Unplug an electrical cord by pulling on the plug, not the cord.

Glassware and Sharp-Object Safety

- Use only clean glassware that is free of chips and cracks.
- If you break glassware, tell your teacher right away.
- If you use a microscope that has a mirror, do not aim the mirror directly at the sun as you can damage your eyes.
- Use knives and other cutting instruments carefully. Always wear eye protection and cut away from yourself.
- Clean glassware according to your teacher's instructions after you use it.
- Use an appropriately sized test tube for the quantity of chemicals you are using, and store test tubes in a test tube rack.

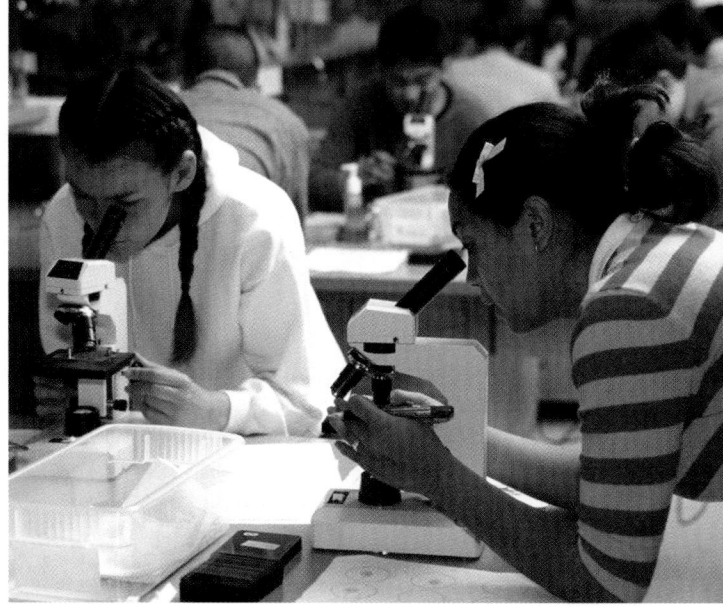

Animal Safety

- Never hurt an animal.
- Touch animals only when necessary. Follow your teacher's instructions for handling animals.
- Wear gloves when handling animals or preserved specimens.
- Specimens for dissection should be properly mounted and supported.
- Do not cut a specimen while holding it in your hands.
- Do not open containers of live microorganisms unless you are directed to do so.
- Dispose of preserved specimens as directed by your teacher.
- Always wash your hands with soap and water after working with animals or specimens.

Cleanup

- Follow your teacher's instructions for the disposal or storage of supplies.
- Clean your work area and pick up anything that has dropped to the floor.
- Wash your hands.

Safety Symbols

Safety is the priority in the science classroom. In all of the activities in this textbook, safety symbols are used to alert you to materials, procedures, or situations that could be potentially hazardous if the safety guidelines are not followed. Learn what you need to do when you see these icons, and read all lab procedures before coming to the lab so you are prepared. Always ask your teacher if you have questions.

 ANIMAL SAFETY Never injure an animal. Follow your teacher's instructions for handling specific animals or preserved specimens. Wash your hands with soap and water when finished handling animals or preserved specimens.

 APRON Wear an apron when using any substance that could cause harm if spilled on you. Stand whenever possible to avoid spilling in your lap.

 BREAKAGE Use caution when handling items that may break, such as glassware and thermometers. Always store test tubes in a test tube rack.

 CHEMICAL SAFETY Always wear goggles when working with chemicals. Stand whenever possible when working with chemicals to avoid spilling on your lap. Tell your teacher immediately if you spill chemicals on yourself, the table, or floor. Never taste any substance or chemical in the lab. Always wash your hands after working with chemicals.

 DISPOSAL Follow your teacher's instructions for disposing of all waste materials, including chemicals, specimens, or broken glass.

 ELECTRICAL SAFETY Keep electrical cords away from water to avoid shock. Do not use cords with frayed edges. Unplug all equipment when done.

 FIRE SAFETY Put on safety goggles before lighting flames. Remove loose clothing and tie back hair. Never leave a lit object unattended. Extinguish flames as soon as you finish heating.

 FUMES Always work in a well-ventilated area. Bring fumes up to your nose by wafting with your fingers instead of sniffing.

 GENERAL SAFETY Always follow the safety rules and ask your teacher if you are unsure about something. If you are designing your own experiment, get your teacher's approval on your plan before you start. Think about which safety rules you must follow in your experiment.

 GLOVES Always wear gloves to protect your skin from possible injury when working with substances that may be harmful or when working with animals.

 HAND WASHING Wash your hands with soap and water after working with soil, chemicals, animals, or preserved specimens.

 HEATING SAFETY Wear goggles and never leave any substance while it is being heated. Use tongs, hot pads, or test tube holders to hold hot objects. Point any materials being heated away from you and others. Place hot objects such as test tubes in test tube racks while cooling.

 HOT/GLOVE Always wear gloves such as oven mitts when handling larger hot materials.

 POISON Never touch, taste, or inhale chemicals. Most chemicals are toxic in high concentrations. Wear goggles and wash your hands.

 SAFETY GOGGLES Always wear safety goggles when working with chemicals, heating any substance, or using a sharp object or any material that could fly up and injure you or others.

 SHARP OBJECTS Use scissors, knives, or razor tools with care. Wear goggles when cutting something with scalpels, knives, or razor tools. Always cut away from yourself.

The Metric System and SI Units

Scientists around the world use the metric system of measurement. The official name for the metric system is the International System of Units (SI). The short name SI comes from the French name, Système International d'Unitès.

SI Units

SI includes units for measuring length, mass, volume, temperature, and many other properties. The most commonly used SI units are shown in Table 1.

The relationships between all SI units are based on powers of 10. In most cases, an SI unit has a prefix that shows its relationship to the base unit. For example, 1 kilometer is 1000 meters, and 1 centimeter is one-hundredth of a meter. Table 2 lists the commonly used SI prefixes along with their symbols and values.

TABLE 1: COMMON SI UNITS

PROPERTY	NAME
Length	meter (m)
Volume	liter (L)
Mass	kilogram (kg)
Temperature	Kelvin (K)

TABLE 2: SI PREFIXES

PREFIX	SYMBOL	VALUE
giga-	G	1,000,000,000
mega-	M	1,000,000
kilo-	k	1000
hecto-	h	100
deca-	da	10
deci-	d	0.1
centi-	c	0.01
milli-	m	0.001
micro-	μ	0.000001
nano-	n	0.000000001
pico-	p	0.000000000001

For your reference, the mass of a paper clip is about 1 g. The diameter of a red blood cell is very small—about 10 μm.

Mass of paper clip = 1 g

Diameter of a red blood cell = 10 μm

Customary to SI Conversion

Although all scientists use the metric system, in the United States the customary system of measurements is still widely used. Table 3 provides useful equivalents for making conversions between these two systems of measurement.

TABLE 3: CUSTOMARY AND SI EQUIVALENTS

U.S. CUSTOMARY	SI
1 inch (in.)	2.54 centimeters (cm)
39.37 inches (in.)	1 meter (m)
0.62 miles (mi)	1 kilometer (km)
1.06 quarts (qt)	1 liter (L)
1 fluid ounce (oz)	236 milliliters (mL)
2.2 pounds (lb)	1 kilogram (kg)
1 ounce (oz)	28.3 grams (g)

Temperature

Use the formulas at right for converting between Celsius and Fahrenheit temperatures.

$$°C = \frac{5}{9} \times (°F - 32)$$

$$°F = \left(\frac{9}{5} \times °C\right) + 32$$

Measuring in the Lab

Collecting accurate and precise data in the lab requires the skillful use of some basic lab equipment. Be sure that you know how to use all equipment correctly in the lab, not only to obtain accurate results but also to ensure your safety.

Metric Rulers

- Use metric rulers or meter sticks to measure length.
- Because the end of a meter stick or ruler is often imperfect, begin the measurement from the 1 cm mark.
- Lay a ruler flat on top of the object so that the 1-centimeter mark lines up with one end. Make sure the ruler and the object do not move between the time you line them up and the time you take the measurement.
- Estimate the reading to one place value beyond what is marked on the ruler. The ruler is marked to the tenths place value, so estimate to the hundredths. The stem of the leaf hits the ruler about halfway between the 4.2 and 4.3 cm marks, so it is estimated at 4.25 cm. However, it is necessary to subtract 1 cm from the edge of the ruler not used in the measurement, so the leaf measures 3.25 cm.

Graduated Cylinder

- Use a graduated cylinder to measure the volume of a liquid.
- You can use a graduated cylinder to find the volume of a solid object by measuring the increase in a liquid's level after you add the object to the cylinder.
- Be sure that the graduated cylinder is on a flat surface. Your eye level should be even with the surface of the liquid.
- Read the volume of the liquid at the bottom of the curve, or meniscus (muh-NIHS-kuhs).
- The volume of liquid is on the 96 mL mark. Estimate to one place value beyond what is marked on the graduated cylinder. The volume of liquid is 96.0 mL.

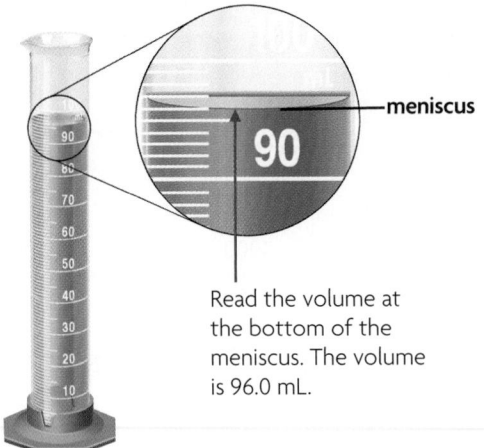

Read the volume at the bottom of the meniscus. The volume is 96.0 mL.

Thermometer

- To measure the temperature of a liquid, place a thermometer into the container without letting the thermometer touch the bottom of the container. Attach a clip to hold the thermometer in place, especially if the liquid is hot.
- As the liquid moves up or down inside the thermometer, rotate the thermometer for more accurate results.
- Stop recording measurements when the liquid in the thermometer stops moving. Take note of the highest point of liquid by estimating to the nearest tenth of a degree.
- The temperature on this thermometer is 24.5°C.

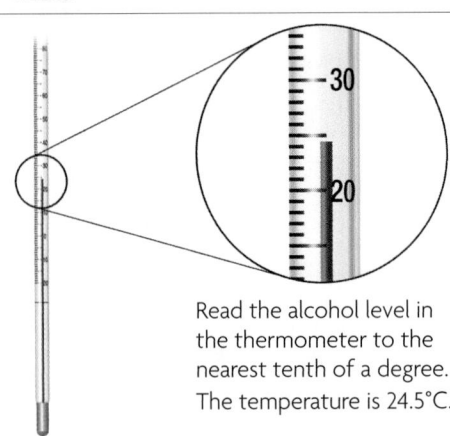

Read the alcohol level in the thermometer to the nearest tenth of a degree. The temperature is 24.5°C.

Triple-Beam Balance

This balance has a pan and three beams with sliding masses, called riders. Each beam is calibrated to a different level of mass, allowing the balance to be accurate to a tenth of a gram. At one end of the beams, a pointer indicates whether the mass on the pan is equal to the masses shown on the beams.

1. Place the balance on a stable, level surface.

2. Make sure the balance is zeroed before measuring the mass of an object. The balance is zeroed if the pointer is at zero when nothing is on the pan and the riders are at their zero points. Use the adjustment knob under the pan of the balance to zero it.

3. Place the object to be measured on the pan. Do not place a hot object or chemical on the pan. The changing temperature may have a direct impact on your measurement and can also be dangerous.

4. Move the riders one notch at a time away from the pan. Begin with the largest rider. If moving the largest rider one notch brings the pointer below zero, move the mass back and then begin measuring the mass of the object with the next smaller rider.

5. Change the positions of the riders until they balance the mass on the pan and the pointer is at zero. Then add the readings from the three beams to determine the mass of the object.

6. The balance below is being used to measure a beaker of water. To find the mass of the water inside the beaker, a student moved the riders to the positions shown. The total mass of the beaker and water is 163.0 g, but you must also subtract the mass of the empty beaker from the total.

Mass of water = Mass of beaker + water   = 163.0 g
– Mass of beaker =   63.0 g
_____
Mass of water   = 100.0 g

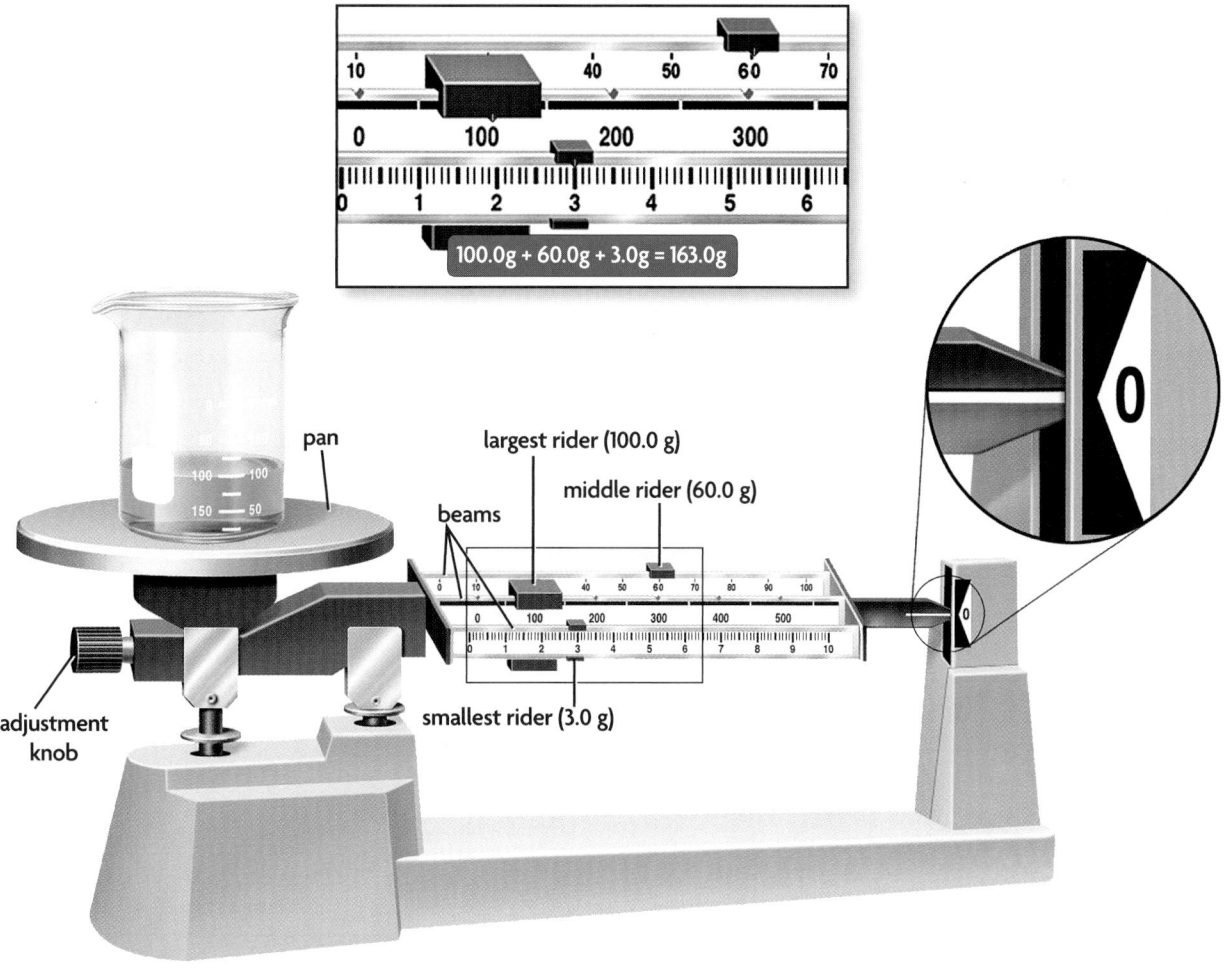

100.0g + 60.0g + 3.0g = 163.0g

pan

largest rider (100.0 g)

middle rider (60.0 g)

beams

smallest rider (3.0 g)

adjustment knob

Lab Handbook

Using a Light Microscope

Microscopes are used to view objects too small to be seen with the naked eye.

Viewing an Object

Use these directions to view your specimen.

1. Use the coarse adjustment to raise the body tube.
2. Adjust the diaphragm so that you can see a bright circle of light through the eyepiece.
3. Place the slide on the stage. Be sure to center it over the hole in the stage and secure it with the stage clips.
4. Turn the nosepiece to click the scanning objective lens into place.
5. Using the coarse adjustment knob, slowly lower the lens and focus on the specimen being viewed. Be sure not to touch the slide or object with the lens.
6. When using the high power lens, use only the fine adjustment knob.
7. Move the slide on the stage with very small movements to view other parts of it. You may need to refocus using the fine adjustment.

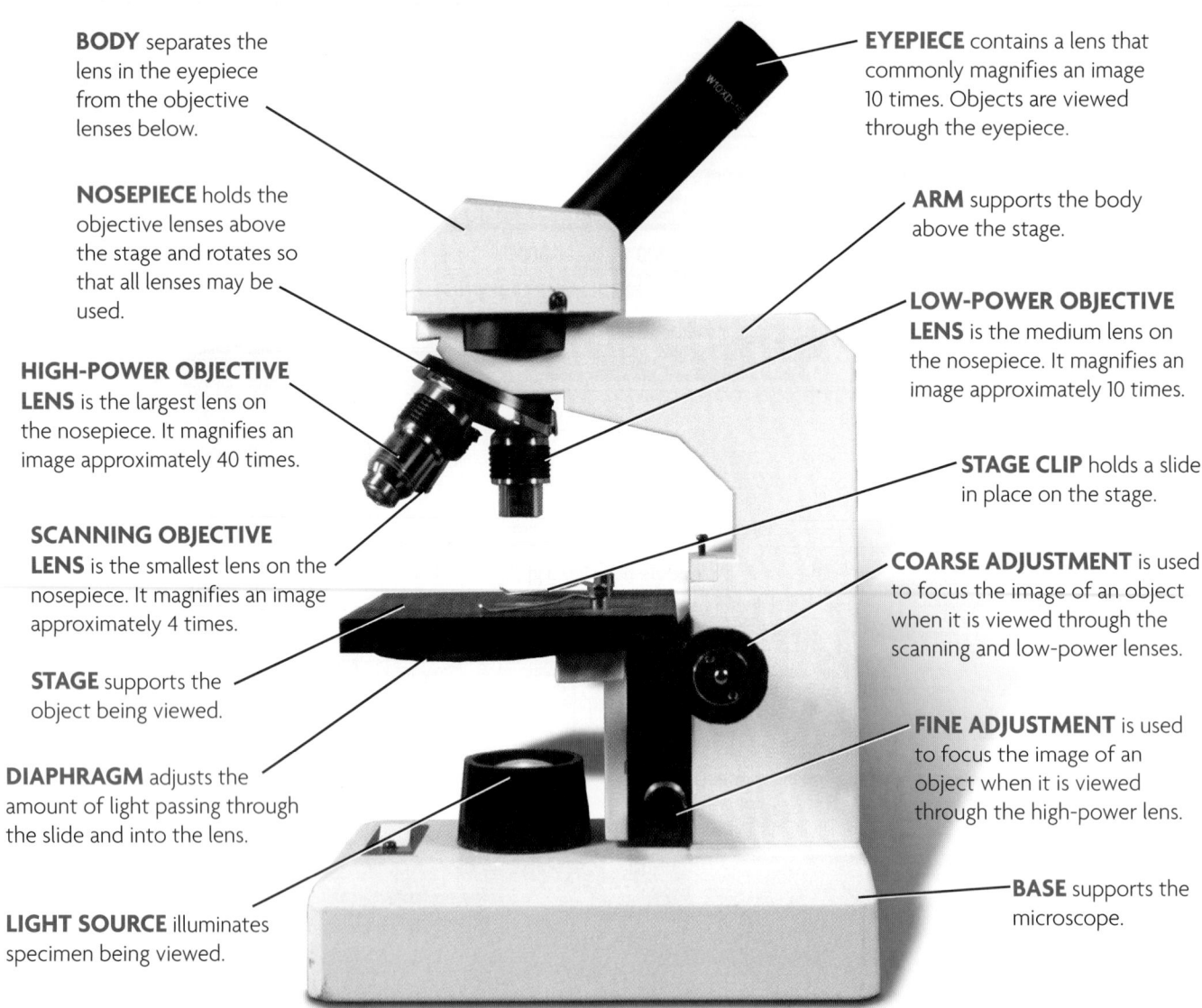

BODY separates the lens in the eyepiece from the objective lenses below.

NOSEPIECE holds the objective lenses above the stage and rotates so that all lenses may be used.

HIGH-POWER OBJECTIVE LENS is the largest lens on the nosepiece. It magnifies an image approximately 40 times.

SCANNING OBJECTIVE LENS is the smallest lens on the nosepiece. It magnifies an image approximately 4 times.

STAGE supports the object being viewed.

DIAPHRAGM adjusts the amount of light passing through the slide and into the lens.

LIGHT SOURCE illuminates specimen being viewed.

EYEPIECE contains a lens that commonly magnifies an image 10 times. Objects are viewed through the eyepiece.

ARM supports the body above the stage.

LOW-POWER OBJECTIVE LENS is the medium lens on the nosepiece. It magnifies an image approximately 10 times.

STAGE CLIP holds a slide in place on the stage.

COARSE ADJUSTMENT is used to focus the image of an object when it is viewed through the scanning and low-power lenses.

FINE ADJUSTMENT is used to focus the image of an object when it is viewed through the high-power lens.

BASE supports the microscope.

Making a Wet Mount

Use these steps to prepare a specimen to be viewed under a microscope.

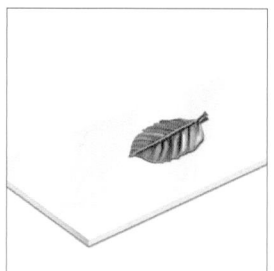  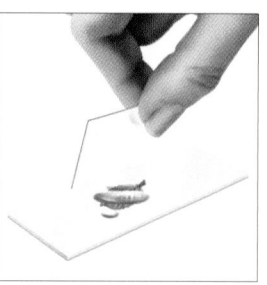 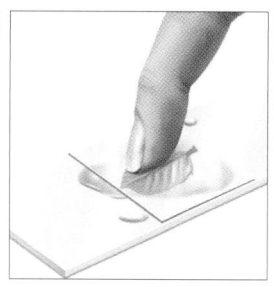 

Place the specimen in the center of a clean slide.

Place a drop of water on the specimen.

Place a cover slip on the slide. Put one edge of the cover slip into the drop of water, and slowly lower the cover slip over the specimen.

Remove any air bubbles from under the cover slip by gently tapping the cover slip.

Dry any excess water before placing the slide on the microscope stage for viewing.

Staining a Specimen

After you make a wet mount, use these steps to stain the specimen.

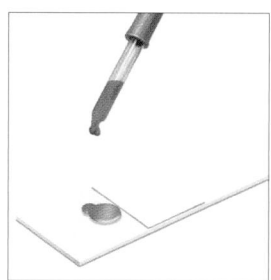 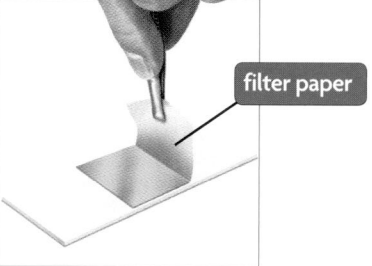

filter paper

Place a drop of stain at one end of the cover slip.

Hold a piece of filter paper with forceps at the other end of the cover slip. The stain will flow underneath the cover slip and stain the specimen.

Calculating Magnification

When you look through a microscope, you see a magnified image of the specimen on the slide. Magnification describes how much larger an object appears when viewed through a microscope than its actual size. Calculating the magnification of the image will give you an idea of the sizes of its features.

There are two magnifying features of every microscope: the eyepiece and the objective lens. The **eyepiece** has a lens that magnifies the image 10× (times) its actual size. The objective lenses magnify the image by different levels.

	Scanning Objective	4×
Eyepiece 10× •	Low-Power Objective	10×
	High-Power Objective	40×

The total magnification of the image is the product of multiplying the eyepiece magnification by the objective lens magnification.

The examples below show how to calculate the total magnification of the daphnia under each lens.

EXAMPLE
Eyepiece • Scanning Objective = Total Magnification
  (10×)   •   (4×)   = 40×
This image is magnified 40× its actual size.

EXAMPLE
Eyepiece • Low-Power Objective = Total Magnification
  (10×)   •   (10×)   = 100×
The image is magnified 100× its actual size.

EXAMPLE
Eyepiece • High-Power Objective = Total Magnification
  (10×)   •   (40×)   = 400×
This image is magnified 400× its actual size.

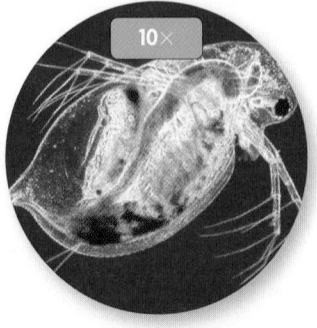
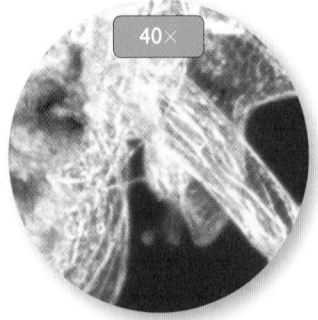

Calculating Specimen Size

The field of view is the area seen through the microscope eyepiece. You can calculate the estimated size in micrometers (μm) of a specimen or object you are viewing based on the size of the field of view. Since many specimens viewed are smaller than a millimeter, the sizes of specimens are usually written in micrometers. Use these steps to calculate specimen size.

1. Place a ruler on the microscope stage and use the coarse adjustment to focus the image in the 4× objective lens.

2. Look at the markings on a ruler viewed in the eyepiece, as shown in the image below.

3. Estimate the diameter of the field of view to the nearest millimeter, which is approximately 4 mm in this example.

4. Remove the ruler and put the slide specimen on the stage.

5. Adjust the slide so the specimen is at one side of the field of view. Estimate the size of the specimen based on the field of view. The length of the daphnia specimen viewed under the scanning objective lens is about 2 mm.

6. Convert mm to μm.

length of specimen • 1000 μm/mm = ?
         2 mm   • 1000 μm/mm = 2000 μm

Designing Experiments

Biologists continually make observations about the natural world around them and raise questions about these observations. Designing experiments to answer these questions serves as the basis of scientific discovery.

An **experiment** is a test under controlled conditions that is made to find a cause-and-effect relationship between variables. Every well-designed experiment has a purpose and an organized, step-by-step procedure.

Determining a Purpose

A simple observation that sparks your interest can lead to a purpose for an experiment. An observation can lead to many questions, but you should choose just one question to study. From that starting point, you can do background research and examine the results of previous experiments.

- Write the purpose of your experiment as a question or problem that you want to investigate.
- Write down specific questions that you will research to find information that will help you design your experiment.

EXAMPLE

Suppose you notice that different patches of plants appear to grow better in different areas around your school. How could you use this observation to design an experiment?

Problem: How does fertilizer affect plant growth?

Research Questions
    What nutrients do plants need?
    Which fertilizers contain those nutrients?

Writing a Hypothesis

A **hypothesis** is a tentative explanation for an observation. A hypothesis leads to testable predictions of what would happen if the hypothesis is valid.

An experiment is designed to test a hypothesis, not to prove that a hypothesis is correct. An experiment cannot prove a hypothesis; data from the experiment can only support it or fail to support it. Keep in mind that there are no "good-or-bad, right-or-wrong" experimental results. Even when results fail to support a hypothesis, they can lead to an idea for another experiment. Hypotheses can be written in several ways.

EXAMPLE

Hypothesis: Nitrogen is a nutrient that plants need for growth.

Testable prediction: If plants are given fertilizer that contains nitrogen, plant growth will increase.

Formalized hypothesis: If plants need the nutrient nitrogen to grow, then plants given fertilizer with nitrogen will experience an increase in growth.

Identifying Variables and Constants

All experiments include constants and variables. **Constants** are all of the factors that are kept the same—held constant—during the entire experiment. A variable is any factor that changes. The **independent variable** is the factor that you are testing and that you manipulate, or change. The **dependent variable** is the factor that you measure. The dependent variable changes, or "depends on," the independent variable. In the example below, plant growth (the dependent variable) is measured and depends on the amount of fertilizer with nitrogen (the independent variable) the plant is given.

EXAMPLE

Independent variable: amount of fertilizer with nitrogen

Dependent variable: plant growth

Constants: temperature, amount of light, intensity of light, type of plant, amount of water, frequency and time of watering, time when dependent variable is measured, amount of soil, type of soil

Lab Handbook

Determining Experimental and Control Groups

An experiment to determine how two factors are related always has at least two groups—a control group and an experimental group.

- The control group is exactly the same as the experimental group—except for the factor that is being tested.
- An experiment can have one or more experimental groups. With one experimental group, you are testing whether the independent variable has an effect. With more than one experimental group, you are testing the presence of the independent variable and different amounts of it.

EXAMPLE

In our example, there are three experimental groups—each tests a different amount of fertilizer.

Experimental Groups

   5 g fertilizer
   10 g fertilizer
   15 g fertilizer

Control Group
   0 g fertilizer

Identifying Types of Data

There are two types of data: qualitative and quantitative.

- **Qualitative data** are descriptions of the dependent variable, such as color, or sound. Qualitative data can also be a simple "yes-or-no" observation about whether something happens, such as whether a plant grows.
- **Quantitative data** are numerical measurements of the dependent variable. Quantitative data include measurements of size, mass, frequency, temperature, rate, and many other factors.

Qualitative data are useful, but they cannot be statistically analyzed. No experiment is based on qualitative data alone.

Forming Operational Definitions

An **operational definition** is a description of the exact way in which you will measure the dependent variable. Your operational definition will help you determine how you will do your experiment.

EXAMPLE

Quantitative operational definition: Height of the plant's main stem (in mm) is the operational definition for the effect of fertilizer on plant growth.

Writing a Procedure

All experiments need a step-by-step written procedure. The procedure should be detailed and clear so that someone else could exactly repeat the experiment. You can think of your procedure as a cookbook recipe that has to be followed exactly. A procedure should include

- a detailed materials list
- how and when to make observations

Even if you are planning to collect only quantitative data, you can still make qualitative observations. These observations may help you to explain your data and can provide clues toward a new experiment.

If something goes wrong during your experiment, make sure you record and report it. Not following the procedure exactly can produce errors in your results that you will need to explain.

Analyzing Data

You have carried out your experiment and collected data. Do the data support your hypothesis? You cannot answer that question by looking at a list of numbers and making a guess at what they show. Without organizing and analyzing your data, it is difficult to draw conclusions from your experiment.

- Organize all of the individual measurements, or data points, in a table. Data tables provide a person evaluating your experiment with a summary of your data.
- Analyze the raw data that you organized in your table. Calculate the mean, median, mode, and range for each group in the experiment. Use whatever type of statistics are appropriate for your data.

EXAMPLE

TABLE 1. PLANT GROWTH – CONTROL GROUP			
Day	Plant 1 Height (cm)	Plant 2 Height (cm)	Plant 3 Height (cm)
0	12.40	11.30	11.90
3	12.45	11.40	12.20
6	13.25	12.00	13.10
9	14.75	12.75	14.25
12	15.35	13.40	15.65
15	16.85	14.95	16.95
18	18.00	15.90	17.25
21	19.75	16.50	17.80
Total growth	7.35	5.20	5.90

Mean Growth = 6.15 cm

Presenting Results

To present your results, look at your organized and analyzed data. Look for ways to most accurately and effectively show your results. You might make a graph to show and compare the groups' means. You might make several graphs that show each group separately. When possible, use spreadsheet software to present your data.

EXAMPLE

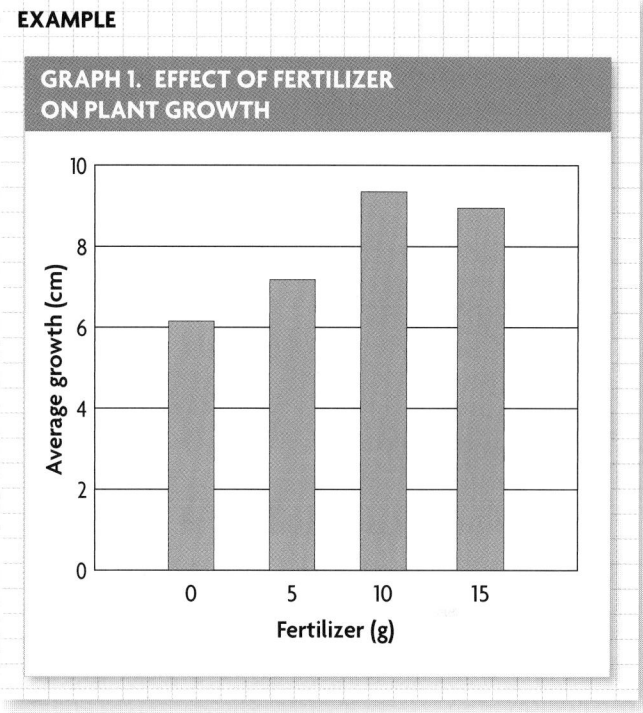

GRAPH 1. EFFECT OF FERTILIZER ON PLANT GROWTH

Drawing Conclusions

Compare your results with your hypothesis to determine whether your results support your hypothesis. Discuss what your results show about a relationship between the independent variable and the dependent variable. It is important to draw conclusions from your results, but do not make inferences about factors that you did not test.

EXAMPLE

Adding a fertilizer with nitrogen to soil tends to increase plant growth. Both high and moderate amounts of fertilizer tend to increase plant growth more than a low amount of fertilizer. However, high and moderate amounts of fertilizer appear to have the same effect on growth.

Common Math Skills Used in Science
Some math skills that are often used in science are presented below.

Calculating Mean
The **mean** of a data set is the average: the sum of the values divided by the number of values.

> **EXAMPLE**
> To find the mean of the data set {14, 6, 10, 8, 4, 11, 6, 3, 5, 13}, add the values and then divide the sum by the number of values.
>
> ANSWER $\dfrac{14 + 6 + 10 + 8 + 4 + 11 + 6 + 3 + 5 + 13}{10} = \dfrac{80}{10} = 8$

Calculating Median
The **median** of a data set is the middle value when the values are ranked in numerical order. Half of the values fall above the median value, half below. If a data set has an even number of values, the median is the mean of the two middle values.

> **EXAMPLE**
> To find the median value of the data set {582, 133, 207, 87, 164, 290, 98, 155, 196, 278 }, arrange the values in order from least to greatest. The median is the middle value.
>
> 87, 98, 133, 155, 164, 196, 207, 278, 290, 582
>
> ANSWER The median is the mean of the two middle values, $\dfrac{164 + 196}{2} = 180.$

Finding Mode
The **mode** of a data set is the value that occurs most often. A data set can have more than one mode if two or more values are repeated the same number of times. A data set can have no mode if no values are repeated.

> **EXAMPLE**
> To find the mode of the data set {6, 7, 6, 4, 4, 4, 3, 6, 4, 6}, arrange the values in order from least to greatest and determine the value that occurs most often:
>
> 3, 4, 4, 4, 4, 6, 6, 6, 6, 7
>
> ANSWER There are two modes, 4 and 6.

Using Significant Figures
The number of **significant figures** in a measurement or calculation is equal to the number of digits that are known with some degree of confidence plus the next digit, which is an estimate. When multiplying or dividing measurements, the answer should have only as many significant figures as the value with the fewest significant figures.

> **EXAMPLE**
> A density calculation is made in which 5.31 g is divided by 22 mL. The calculator output was 0.2413636 g/mL.
>
> ANSWER There are three significant figures in the mass, but only two in the volume measurement. The density should have two significant figures: 0.24 g/mL.

Using Scientific Notation
Scientific notation is a shorthand way to write very large or very small numbers as a product of a number times a power of 10.

> **EXAMPLE**
> To convert from standard form to scientific notation:
>
> | Standard Form | Scientific Notation |
> |---|---|
> | 720,000 | 7.2×10^5 |
> | 5 decimal places left | Exponent is 5 |
> | 0.000291 | 2.91×10^{-4} |
> | 4 decimal places right | Exponent is -4 |
>
> To convert from scientific notation to standard form:
>
> | Scientific Notation | Standard Form |
> |---|---|
> | 4.63×10^7 | 46,300,000 |
> | Exponent is 7 | 7 decimal places right |
> | 1.08×10^{-6} | 0.00000108 |
> | Exponent is -6 | 6 decimal places left |

Presenting Data

Scientists often communicate results of their experiments through tables and graphs. Tables and graphs organize and display information so that it can be easily interpreted.

Data Tables

A **data table** is used to organize and record data that are collected. Data tables can also help identify trends in data. Tables are organized according to the independent and dependent variables in the experiment. The **dependent variable** changes as a result of a change in the **independent variable.** The independent variable is listed in rows. The dependent variable is in columns. When repeated trials are conducted, they are recorded in subdivisions of the dependent variable column. When recording data in a table, the values of the independent variable are ordered. Most data are arranged from the smallest to largest.

The information given in each column is identified with a heading at the top of each column. When units are used, they are also included at the top of the column. Data tables should always have a title that clearly communicates what is being shown in the table. The title should make reference to the variables in the experiment.

TABLE 2. EFFECT OF HORMONES ON CELL GROWTH		
Concentration of Hormone Solution (%)	Diameter of Cell Clump After 24 Hours (mm)	
	Trial 1	Trial 2
0	3	4
25	4	4
50	8	7
75	9	8

EXAMPLE

Table 2 shows data from a hypothetical experiment in which growth hormones were added to clumps of cells in a laboratory. The growth of the cell clumps was measured. In this example, the independent variable is the concentration of hormone solution. The values of the independent variable are listed in rows from lowest to highest concentration. The dependent variable, the diameter of the cell clumps after 24 hours, is in columns.

Line Graphs

A **line graph** is used to show a relationship between two variables. Line graphs are particularly useful for showing changes in variables over time. Line graphs are used when variables are continuous—that is, they can have any value including fractional values. For example, the height of a growing plant changes continuously. As a plant grows from 10 cm to 11 cm, its height can be 10.2 cm, 10.537 cm, or any other value between 10 and 11.

Line graphs are useful for representing trends. Two values are inversely related or have a **negative correlation** if an increase in the value of one variable is associated with a decrease in the value of the other variable. If an increase in one variable is associated with an increase in another variable, there is a **positive correlation** between the two variables. If there is no relationship between the two variables, they are said to have **no correlation.**

EXAMPLE

The level of the hormone insulin and length of exercise time have a negative correlation. As length of time increases, levels of insulin decrease.

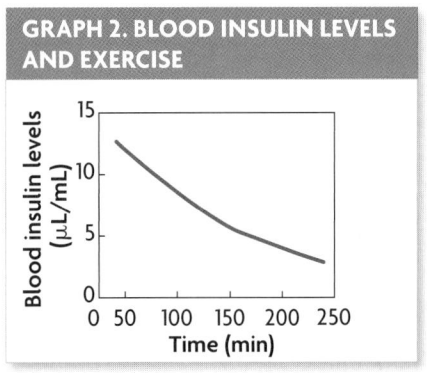

GRAPH 2. BLOOD INSULIN LEVELS AND EXERCISE

Math and Data Analysis Handbook

The level of the hormone glucagon and length of exercise time have a positive correlation. As length of time increases, levels of glucagon increase.

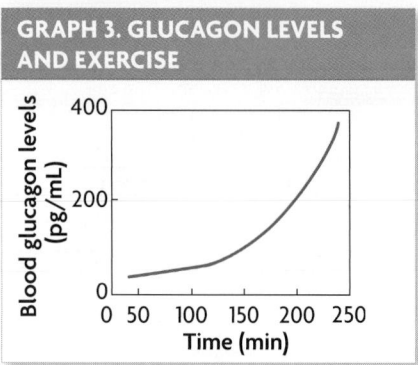

GRAPH 3. GLUCAGON LEVELS AND EXERCISE

The level of the hormone ghrelin and length of exercise time have no correlation. The levels of ghrelin do not increase or decrease over time.

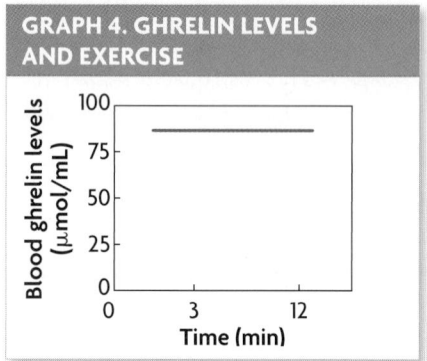

GRAPH 4. GHRELIN LEVELS AND EXERCISE

Bar Graphs

A **bar graph** is a type of graph in which the lengths of the bars are used to represent and compare data. A numerical scale is used to determine the lengths of the bars. Bar graphs can be used with either continuous or discrete data. **Discrete data** can have only whole-number values, such as the number of people or trees in a neighborhood.

EXAMPLE

The bar graph at the top of the next column contains data about the frequency of various genetic disorders in the human population. For each syndrome on the x-axis, the bar extends vertically on the y-axis to represent the incidence per 100,000 births. For example, out of 100,000 births, 111 children are born with Down syndrome.

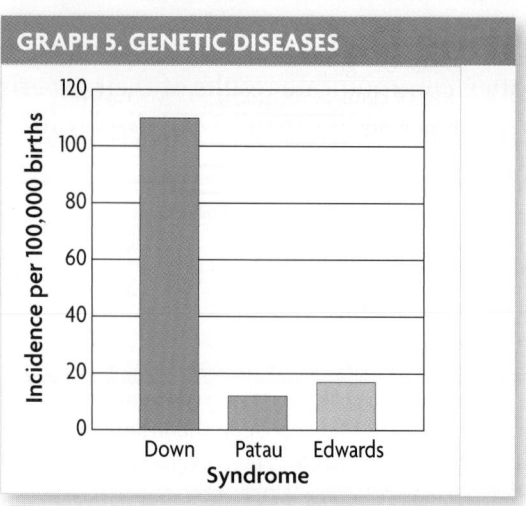

GRAPH 5. GENETIC DISEASES

Combination Graphs

Combination graphs show two sets of data on the same graph. One set of data may be shown as a bar graph, and the other set may be shown as a line graph. The two data sets must share the same independent variable on the x-axis. Sharing the same independent variable makes it possible to determine if a relationship exists between two dependent variables.

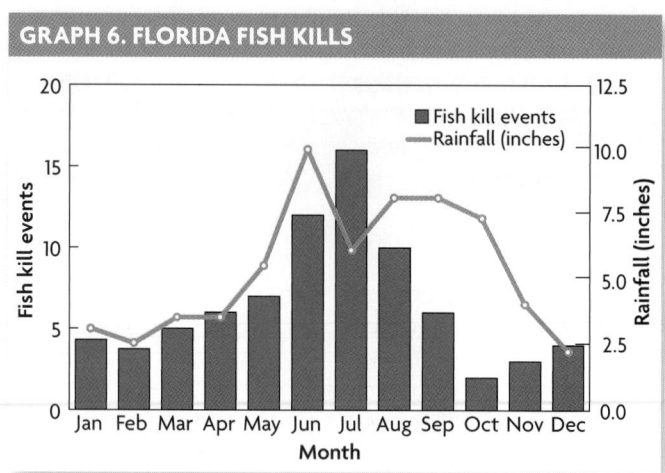

GRAPH 6. FLORIDA FISH KILLS

EXAMPLE

The combination graph above displays data about fish kill events and monthly rainfall in Florida.
- The y-axis on the left side of the graph represents the number of fish kill events.
- The y-axis on the right side of the graph represents rainfall amounts.
- The x-axis shows the month of data collection.

For example, the graph shows that in January there were four fish kill events and about 2.7 inches of rain.

Histograms

A **histogram** is a type of bar graph used to show the frequency distribution of data. A **frequency distribution** displays the number of cases that fit into each category of a variable.

EXAMPLE

The histogram below shows the frequency distribution of body fat in adult men. According to the histogram, the percentage body fat with the greatest frequency is 20 percent. When interpreting histograms, it is important to note that how the histogram is constructed can affect how the data are interpreted.

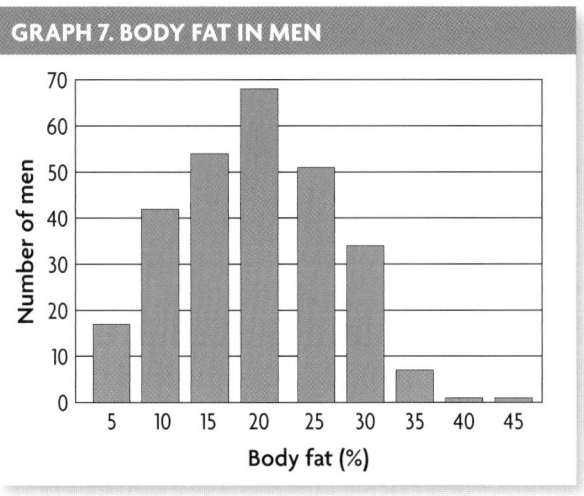

GRAPH 7. BODY FAT IN MEN

Scatterplots

A **scatterplot** is a type of graph used to identify a trend or correlation between two variables. The origin is usually at zero on both the *x*-axis and the *y*-axis. On a scatterplot, the data points are plotted but not joined together as they are on a line graph. Three types of relationships between variables that can be shown on a scatterplot are positive, negative, and no relationship. In a positive relationship, as one variable increases or decreases, the other variable increases or decreases, respectively. In a negative relationship, as one variable increases, the other variable decreases. For some variables, there is no consistent change in one variable as the other variable increases or decreases. Thus, there is no relationship between those two variables.

EXAMPLE

The scatterplot below of butter clam shell measurements shows that as the width of the clam's shell increases, its length also increases. This is a positive relationship, because as the value of one variable increases, the value of another variable increases. If it were a negative relationship, one of the variables would increase as the other decreased.

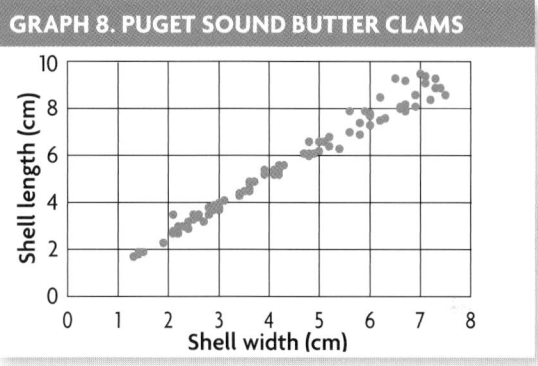

GRAPH 8. PUGET SOUND BUTTER CLAMS

Circle Graphs

A **circle graph,** or pie chart, is a type of graph used to represent parts of a whole. It is made of a circle divided into sections that represent the frequency of each category's occurrence. To determine how much of the circle each section should cover, divide the number of occurrences for that category by the total number that the circle represents. When the result is multiplied by 100, it gives the percentage of the circle covered by the category.

EXAMPLE

In the circle graph below, the diversity of invertebrates is illustrated. Notice that all of the percentages for each category of invertebrate can be added together to equal 100. This is always the case in a circle graph, unless the values have been rounded after calculation.

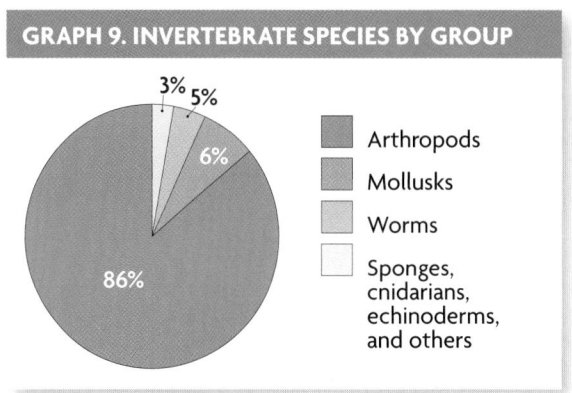

GRAPH 9. INVERTEBRATE SPECIES BY GROUP

Vocabulary Handbook

Greek and Latin Word Parts

Many words in the English language developed from Greek and Latin words. If you know some common Greek and Latin word parts, you can decode the meanings of other unknown words.

Suppose you read a magazine article that says, "If you see this plant, don't touch it! It's phototoxic and could cause a skin rash." How can you predict what the word *phototoxic* means without looking it up in a dictionary? To decode a word, follow the steps to the right.

Break the word into parts. Try to find the Greek or Latin word parts within the word. In the word *phototoxic,* you can find two word parts: *photo-* and *tox-*.

Look up the word parts in the table below. You will find that *photo-* means "light" and *tox-* means "poisonous."

Analyze the clues to determine a definition. In this example, your word clues are "light" and "poisonous." But there is also a clue in the sentence, "skin rash." You might guess that a phototoxic plant is one that can poison a person's skin when a chemical in the plant reacts with sunlight, and that's just what it means!

WORD PART	DEFINITION	EXAMPLE
a-	not, without	**a**biotic: factor in an ecosystem that is not alive
ab-	away, apart	**ab**sorption: movement away from one system and into another
ad-	to, toward	**ad**hesion: attraction that pulls molecules of the same substance toward one another
anti-	against	**anti**biotic: chemical that acts against bacteria
-ase	enzyme	DNA polymer**ase**: enzyme that builds DNA polymers
bi-	two	**bi**nary fission: asexual reproduction in which a cell divides into two cells
bio-	life	**bio**engineering: process by which life forms are changed using technology
cardio-	of or relating to the heart	**cardi**ac muscle: muscle in the heart
cerebr-	brain	**cerebr**al cortex: part of the brain that controls voluntary functions
chloro-	green	**chloro**phyll: green pigment in photosynthetic organisms that absorbs light
-cide	kill	insecti**cide**: chemical that kills insects
con-, co-, com-	with, together	**co**dominance: both genes expressed together
cyto-	cell	**cyto**plasm: jellylike substance within a cell
di-	two	**di**cot: plant whose seeds have two cotyledons
diplo-	double	**diplo**id: having double genetic information
ecto-	outer, outside	**ecto**therm: organism that uses the outer environment to regulate body temperature
endo-	inner, inside	**endo**skeleton: skeleton found inside of the body
-gram	write, record	clado**gram**: record of proposed evolutionary relationships
hetero-	different	**hetero**zygous: having two different alleles
homo-, homeo-	the same	**homo**zygous: having two of the same alleles
hydro-	water	**hydro**logic cycle: water cycle

WORD PART	DEFINITION	EXAMPLE
hyper-	above, over	**hyper**tonic: having a concentration above that of another solution
hypo-	below, under	**hypo**tonic: having a concentration below that of another solution
im-, in-	with, into	**im**migration: movement of individuals into a population
iso-	equal	**iso**tonic: having a concentration equal to that of another solution
-itis	inflammation	appendic**itis**: inflammation of the appendix
-lysis	decomposition, dissolving	glyco**lysis**: breakdown of glucose
meso-	middle	**meso**phyll: layer of tissue in the middle of the plant leaf
mono-	one	**mono**hybrid cross: mating that examines inheritance of one trait
-morph	form	meta**morph**osis: change in body form
neuro-	neuron	**neuro**transmitter: chemical that signals neurons
-osis	condition or process	mit**osis**: process of cell division
path-	disease	**path**ogen: disease-causing agent
peri-	around	**peri**pheral nervous system: nerves found around, or outside, the central nervous system
phago-	to eat	**phago**cytosis: engulfing, or eating, of bacteria or foreign bodies by phagocytes
-philic	having a preference for	hydro**philic**: having an attraction to water
-phobic	having an aversion for	hydro**phobic**: having an aversion to water
photo-	light	**photo**synthesis: process that uses light to make sugars
phyto-	plants	**phyto**plankton: plantlike plankton
-pod	foot	pseudo**pod**: fake foot
poly-	many	**poly**genic trait: trait resulting from the interaction or many genes
re-	again, new	**re**generation: regrowth of lost or destroyed parts or organs
sperma-	relating to sperm or seeds	**sperma**togenesis: process that forms sperm
tel-, telo-	end	**telo**phase: ending phase of mitosis
-therm	heat	endo**therm**: animal that uses its internal tissues to produce its body heat
tox-	poisonous	**tox**in: poisonous substance that can destroy cells
trans-	across	**trans**genic: an organism that contains a gene from a different species
-troph	nutrition	auto**troph**: organism that makes its own source of nutrition
-tropism	response	geo**tropism**: growth response to gravity
uni-	single, one	**uni**cellular: organism made up of one cell
zoo-	animal	**zoo**logy: study of animals

Vocabulary Handbook

Academic Vocabulary

Academic vocabulary words are words that occur frequently in textbooks, instructions, and standardized tests. The words can have many meanings. Some of these words are defined below and grouped into categories. These words appear in all subject areas. The simple definitions below give only one meaning of each word, the way it might be used in this book. Learn to recognize and understand these words.

Words Used in Lab Instructions

affect to produce a change
alter to change
analyze to study the parts
assemble to put together
characteristic a distinct part or feature
component part
conduct to manage or control
confirm to use data to support a statement
consequence a result
constraint a limit
control a part of the experiment that keeps all variables constant
criteria standards for judging
demonstrate to show
dominant having the most influence or control
emerge to rise from or to come forth
extract to draw or pull out
factor an individual part of a combination, ingredient
function a job, duty, or activity
indirect not direct or to the point
method a way of doing something
model a small object made to look like the real one
modify to change
monitor to watch closely
objective a goal
obtain to get

parameter a measurable factor that can vary
potential possible but does not yet exist
process a series of actions
produce to bring forth or create
property a trait or characteristic
prove to show as true by using evidence
purpose a reason to do
represent to stand for
restrict to keep within limits
reveal to show, to make known
signal a sign for communicating
source the origin or place something began
spatial having to do with space
structure the way the parts are put together
sufficient enough, as much as needed
technique a procedure, the way something is done
trace tiny amount
trait a feature
transfer to move from one to another
variation the result of changing
vary to change or to show change

Words About Math and Measuring

approximate nearly
compile to put together into one
convert to change something to another form
cumulative increasing by adding
derive to arrive at by reasoning
dimension measurement of one part
diminish to make less or smaller
equivalent equal to
pace the rate of speed
proportion an equation stating that two ratios are equal
range the difference between the smallest and largest amounts
reduce to make smaller
solve to find the answer to a problem

Words About Importance

core the center part
crucial a must-have, extremely important
essential necessary or basic
regular usual or normal
requisite necessary, required
significance the importance
standard the usual and accepted measure for comparing

Words Found in Test Directions

analyze to study the parts
apply to put on; to be relevant
assess to figure out the value of
clarify to make clear
compose to create or write something new
critique to judge carefully
define to tell what it means
demonstrate to show
develop to add detail, to fill out
evaluate to judge or decide the value of
exhibit to show or display
indicate to point out
interpret to explain the meaning of
relate to tell; to hook to something else
revise to review and change for the better
summarize to reduce to the main points in a few words
synthesize to combine parts into a whole

Other Words Used in Tests

alternative another choice
analogy a comparison to something similar
approach to come near; the way of getting near
articulate to say or write clearly
aspect appearance from one point of view
background the knowledge behind something
concise in a few words
confirm to make sure it's true
convey to communicate or show
correspond to be similar in nature
detail an individual part
detect to discover or learn about
determine to learn the facts; to decide
emphasize to stress
establish to set up
explicit fully and clearly expressed
focus to direct to one point
general about the whole or entire thing
imply to express indirectly
optional left to a person's choice
refer to direct to a source for help
specific definite and particular
succinct in a few words
symbolize to act as a sign that stands for something else
technical used in a special job or subject
topic a subject
transition the words that link one part to the next
valid correct or well-grounded
verify to prove the truth of

Words About Organization

category a class or special division
compile to put together
consist to be made up of
correlate to put into relation to something else
differentiate to separate by differences
dominant the strongest
integrate to put together
organize to put in order
primary first or most important
sequence order
series one after another
subsequent ones coming after

Words About Ideas

abstract cannot be touched
analogy a comparison to something else
authentic real
claim a statement that says something is a fact
complex not simple
conceive to form an idea
concept an idea
concrete actual or real
credible believable
deduce to figure out by reasoning
devise to form, plan, or design
discover to notice or learn; to be the first to learn
innovation a new idea or thing
irrelevant off the point
logical reasoning in a clear manner
origin the beginning; where something began to exist
principle a basic truth, rule, or standard
relevant to the point
strategy a plan of action
subjective depends on a person's viewpoint
topic the subject of writing or speech

Words About Time

intermittent off and on
invariably always, every time
prior before
typically usually

Note-taking Handbook

Graphic organizers are tools to help you take notes. Some graphic organizers are best used as you read to help you understand concepts. Others are best used to summarize or review information. Using a variety of graphic organizers will help you to understand and remember what you have learned.

During Reading

Use these graphic organizers while you are reading. They help you organize ideas in paragraphs and sections as you read them.

Process Diagrams

What is it? A process is series of steps that produces a result. Process diagrams show these steps.

How do you make it? Start with the first step, and then draw each step, one after the other, and connect them with arrows.

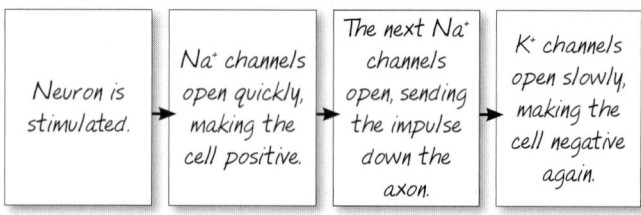

Cycle Diagrams

What is it? A cycle, such as the cell cycle, is a repeating series of events that happen one after another. Cycles do not have a beginning or an end. Cycle diagrams identify the steps in a cycle or process that repeat regularly.

How do you make it? Draw a cycle diagram to show processes that repeat without a beginning or ending. Use the arrows between the boxed steps to show the direction or order in which the cycle happens.

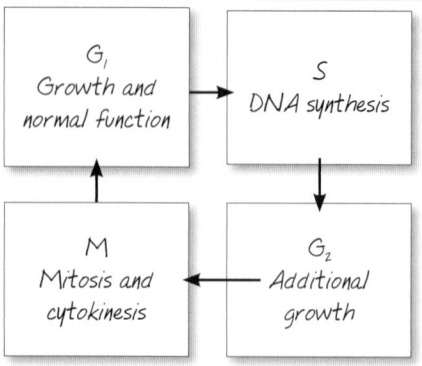

Supporting Main Ideas Notes

What is it? A main idea graphic helps separate and organize reading material into important concepts and related details of support. You can choose the main idea graphic that best fits the material. The first strategy is useful when details follow some type of order.

How do you make it? First, find the main idea. The main idea may be the title of the section, it may be labeled "main idea" or "key concept" in your book, or it may be the topic sentence in a paragraph. Write the main idea in the top box. Next, summarize or paraphrase details that help explain that idea in the boxes that follow.

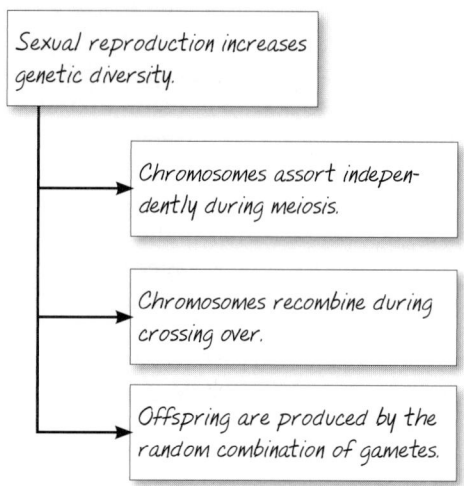

Main Idea Webs

Another way you can take notes on main ideas is to draw a web. Write the main idea in the center and the details in the web around it. This is useful when the details do not occur in any particular order.

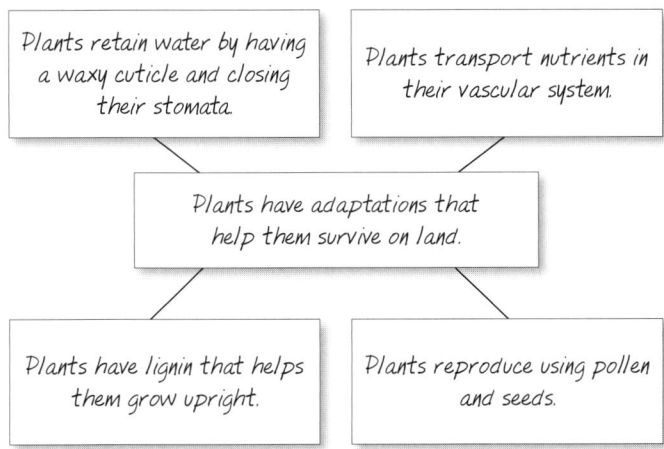

Two-Column Notes

What is it? Two-column notes is a strategy for taking notes to show

- vocabulary and their definitions
- processes or cycles and their steps
- main ideas and supporting details
- questions and possible answers
- causes and effects
- comparisons and contrasts

How do you make it? List processes, concepts, main ideas, or vocabulary in the left column of a two-column table. Write the description or explanation of the words or concepts in the right-hand column across from the words in the left column. You can also draw pictures in the right-hand column.

Leave enough space between words or concepts in the left-hand column so that you can write notes in the right column.

To study for quizzes and tests, fold your two-column notes in half vertically so you can only see the left column. Ask yourself to describe and explain the word in the left column.

Cellular Respiration	produces ATP occurs in mitochondria $C_6H_{12}O_6 + 6O_2 \rightarrow 6CO_2 + 6H_2O$
Photosynthesis	absorbs sunlight occurs in chloroplasts $6CO_2 + 6H_2O \rightarrow C_6H_{12}O_6 + 6O_2$

After Reading

Use these graphic organizers after you have read material and have taken notes on it. These organizers help you summarize the most important concepts and relate them to each other.

Cause-and-Effect Diagrams

What is it? This strategy shows cause and effect relationships. In the diagram below, several effects result from a single cause. Those effects can cause more effects. A cause-and-effect diagram can also be drawn to show how multiple causes can produce a single effect.

How do you make it? Write the cause in the first box, and write the effects in the boxes connected to the cause. Then think about what effects can result from the first effects, and connect them.

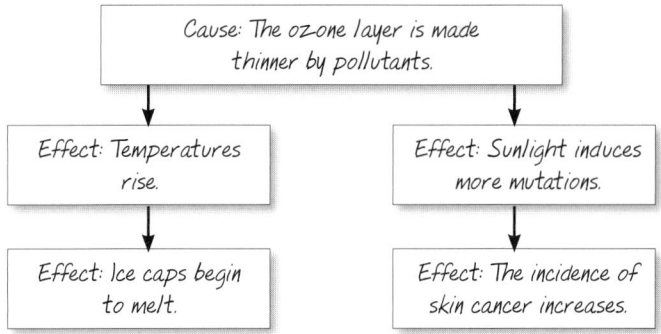

Content Frames

What is it? Content frames are tables that help you organize and condense large amounts of information.

How do you make it? To make a content frame, make a table. Label the rows along the side with characteristics. Label the columns with the topics or categories. You can also include a column for drawings or sketches.

Biome	Tropical	Temperate	Tundra
Climate	Warm and rainy	Hot summers, cold winters	Cold and dry
Vegetation	Lush, thick forests	Broadleaf forests	Mosses and similar
Example	Manaus, Brazil	Burlington, Vermont	Barrow, Alaska

Note-taking Handbook

Venn Diagrams

What is it? Venn diagrams help you show how two processes, ideas, or things are alike and different.

How do you make it? Draw two circles that overlap, such as the ones below. Write one of the words or processes that you are going to compare in each circle. For example, the word *arteries* is written in the left circle and the word *veins* is written in the right circle. Under *arteries*, list characteristics or traits that only arteries possess. Under *veins*, list characteristics or traits that only veins possess. In the intersection of the two circles, list the traits that both arteries and veins share.

When you finish the diagram, write a sentence to summarize the similarities and differences: "Both veins and arteries have three-tissue layers and are each part of the closed circulatory system, but arteries are thicker and more muscular, and veins are thinner and have valves."

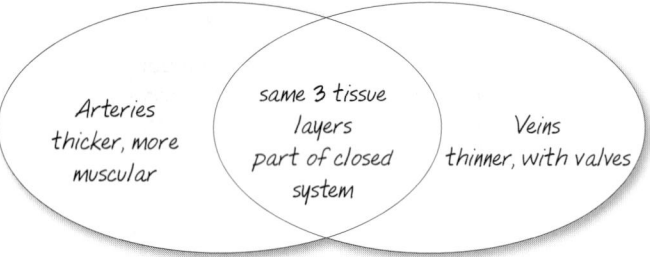

Y Diagrams

What is it? Y diagrams can be used instead of Venn diagrams to show how two processes, ideas, or things are alike and different.

How do you make it? On the top parts of the Y, list the characteristics of each topic separately. Then find the characteristics that are the same in both halves. Write them at the bottom part of the Y, and cross them out from the top half. When you finish, the top limbs of the Y show differences, and the bottom part shows similarities between the two topics.

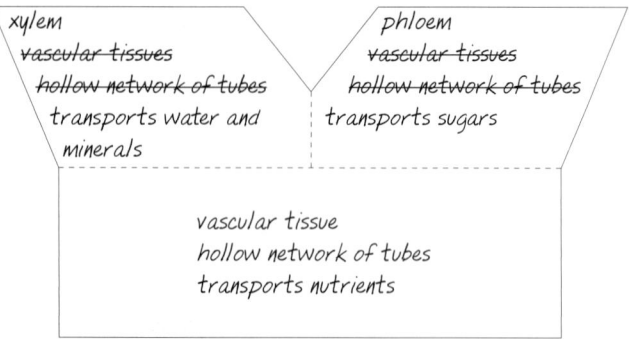

Concept Maps

What is it? A concept map is a diagram that shows the main concepts from a passage you've read as well as the relationships between those concepts. Concept maps are useful tools for organizing and reviewing information.

How do you make it? First, identify the concepts in the section you've read. A concept is a single word or short phrase that represents an idea, process, or important characteristic. Next, identify the major concept and place it at the top of your concept map. Then arrange the other concepts from the most general to the most specific. Each concept should be enclosed in an oval or box. Finally, use lines to connect concepts and write linking words on the lines. Linking words are usually verbs, verb phrases, or prepositions that show the relationship between the concepts.

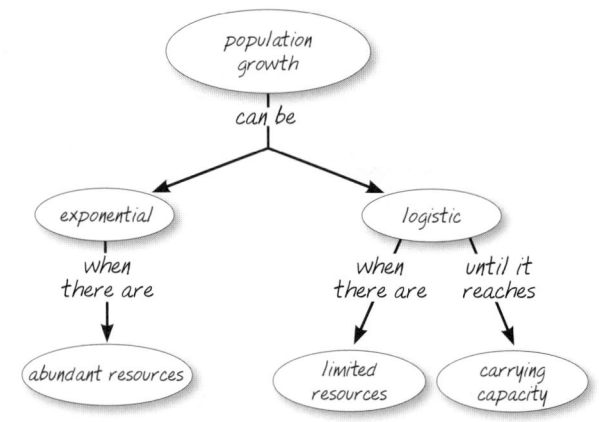

Appendix A: Classification

Living things are classified into three domains. These domains are further divided into kingdoms, and then phyla. Major phyla are described in the table below, along with important features that are used to distinguish each group.

KINGDOM	COMMON NAME AND DESCRIPTION
DOMAIN ARCHAEA	
ARCHAEA *Pyrococcus*	**Archaea** Single-celled prokaryotes (no nucleus or other membrane-bound organelles) with distinct rRNA sequences. Lack peptidoglycan cell walls. Reproduce asexually. Live in some of Earth's most extreme environments, including salty, hot, acidic, and the deep ocean. They are often grouped according to where they live. Examples: *Sulfolobus solfataricus, Pyrococcus.*
DOMAIN BACTERIA	
BACTERIA *Escherichia*	**Bacteria** Single-celled prokaryotes (no nucleus or other membrane-bound organelles), most with peptidoglycan cell walls. Live in all types of environments, including the human body. Reproduce by binary fission or budding. Examples: blue-green bacteria (cyanobacteria), *Streptococcus, Bacillus, Escherichia.*

KINGDOM	PHYLUM	COMMON NAME AND DESCRIPTION
DOMAIN EUKARYA		
		Eukaryotes Cells are larger than archaea or bacteria and are eukaryotic (have a nucleus containing DNA, as well as other membrane-bound organelles). Can be single-celled, colonial, or multicellular.
PROTISTA		**Protists** Usually single-celled, but sometimes multicellular or colonial. Many phyla resemble animals, plants, or fungi but are usually smaller or simpler in structure.
Animal-like Protists: Unicellular, heterotrophic, most can move.		
Paramecium	Ciliophora	**Ciliates** Have many short, hairlike extensions called cilia, which they use for feeding and movement. Example: *Paramecium.*
	Zoomastigophora	**Zooflagellates** Have usually one or two long, hairlike extensions called flagella. Sometimes called Zoomastigina. Example: *Trichomonas.*
	Apicomplexa	**Sporozoans** Parasites that can move by body flexion or gliding. Cause diseases in animals such as birds and humans. Example: *Plasmodium.*

Appendix A: Classification

KINGDOM	PHYLUM	COMMON NAME AND DESCRIPTION
PROTISTA (continued)	Rhizopoda	**Rhizopods** Use footlike extensions called pseudopods to move and feed. Phylum sometimes called Sarcodina. Example: *Amoeba*.
	Foraminifera	**Forams** Use footlike extensions called pseudopods to move. Have multi-chambered shells made of organic material. Most are marine. Example: *Rosalina globularis*.

Plantlike Protists: Many are photosynthetic autotrophs, but none have roots, stems, or leaves.

	Euglenozoa	**Euglenoids** Single-celled, with one or two flagella. Most live in fresh water. Some are heterotrophs, others are photosynthetic autotrophs. Examples: *Euglena, Trypanosoma*.
	Dinoflagellata	**Dinoflagellates** Single-celled, with two flagella that allow cell to turn over and change direction. Some species are autotrophic, some are heterotrophic. In great numbers, some species can cause red tides along coastlines. Example: *Noctiluca*.
	Chrysophyta	**Chrysophytes** Also called yellow algae or golden-brown algae. Single-celled. Named for the yellow pigments in their chloroplasts (*chrysophyte*, in Greek, means "golden plant"). Example: *Thallasiosira*.
	Bacillariophyta	**Diatoms** Single-celled with glasslike shells made of silica. Shells serve as external skeleton. Example: *Amorpha ovalis*.
	Chlorophyta	**Green algae** May be single-celled, colonial, or multicellular. Contain both chlorophyll-*a* and chlorophyll-*b*, which are the same photosynthetic pigments found in land plants. Examples: *Pediastrum, Ulva, Spirogyra*.
	Phaeophyta	**Brown algae** Multicellular, photosynthetic. Live mainly in salt water. Contain the pigment fucoxanthin, which is the source of their brown color. Includes kelp. Example: *Sargassum*.
	Rhodophyta	**Red algae** Multicellular, photosynthetic. Most live in salt water. Contain a red pigment called phycoerythrin that makes these organisms red, purple, or reddish-black. Example: coralline algae.

Funguslike Protists: Most are decomposers that can move during part of their life cycle.

	Acrasiomycota	**Cellular slime molds** Live partly as free-living single-celled organisms, often in the soil. When food is scarce, they can fuse together to form a many-celled mass that moves as if it's one organism. Example: *Dictyostelium*.

Euglena

Diatom

Red Algae

KINGDOM	PHYLUM	COMMON NAME AND DESCRIPTION
	Myxomycota	**Plasmodial slime molds** Live most of their lives as a mass of cytoplasm that is actually one large, slimy cell with many nuclei. Example: *Physarium* (dog-vomit slime mold).
	Oomycota	**Water molds and downy mildews** Produce thin, cottonlike extensions called hyphae. Feed from dead or decaying material, often in water. Some are parasites of plants or fish. Example: *Phytophthora infestans* (cause of potato blight).
FUNGI		**Fungi** Eukaryotic, heterotrophic, usually multicellular but some are single-celled. Cells have a thick cell wall usually containing chitin. Obtain nutrients through absorption. Often function as decomposers.
	Chytridiomycota	**Chytrids** Oldest and simplest fungi, usually aquatic. Have flagellated spores. Some are decomposers, some are parasitic. Example: chytrid frog fungus.
	Ascomycota	**Sac fungi** Reproduce with spores formed in an ascus. Includes single-celled yeasts as well as morels, truffles, and molds. Example: *Penicillium*.
	Zygomycota	**Bread molds** Obtain food by decomposing dead or decaying matter. Mold hyphae grow into food source and digest it. Some are parasitic. Example: black bread molds.
	Basidiomycota	**Club fungi** Multicellular with club-shaped fruiting bodies. Examples: mushrooms, puffballs, bracket fungi, rusts, smuts.
PLANTAE		**Plants** Multicellular photosynthetic autotrophs. Most have adapted to life on land. Cells have thick cell walls made of cellulose.
	Bryophyta	**Mosses** Nonvascular plants. Gametophyte generation is a grasslike plant. Most live in moist environments. Example: sphagnum (peat) moss.
	Hepatophyta	**Liverworts** Nonvascular plants named for the liver-shaped gametophyte generation. Most live in moist environments. Example: *Marchantia*.
	Anthocerotophyta	**Hornworts** Nonvascular plants named for the visible hornlike structures with which they reproduce. Live in moist, cool environments. Example: *Dendroceros*.
	Lycophyta	**Club mosses** Seedless vascular plants. Some resemble tiny pine trees. Live in wooded environments. Example: *Lycopodium* (ground pine).

Slime mold

Sac fungus

Toad stool mushroom

Appendix A: Classification

KINGDOM	PHYLUM	COMMON NAME AND DESCRIPTION
PLANTAE (continued)	Pterophyta	**Ferns, whisk ferns, and horsetails** Seedless vascular plants. Most have fringed leaves. Whisk ferns sometimes classified in phylum Psilotophyta; horsetails sometimes classified in phylum Sphenophyta. Example: *Psilotum* (whisk fern).
	Cycadophyta	**Cycads** Gymnosperms; reproduce with seeds produced in large cones. Slow-growing, palmlike plants that grow in tropical environments. Example: sago palms
	Ginkgophyta	**Ginkgo biloba** Only species in phylum, a tree often planted in urban environments. Gymnosperm; reproduces with seeds that hang from branches.
	Coniferophyta	**Conifers** Gymnosperms; reproduce with seeds produced in cones. Usually evergreen. Examples: pines, spruces, firs, sequoias.
	Anthophyta	**Flowering plants** Also called angiosperms. Reproduce with seeds produced in flowers. Seeds are surrounded by fruit, which is the ripened plant ovary. **CLASS: Monocotyledonae** Monocots. Embryos have one cotyledon. Leaves with parallel veins, flower parts in multiples of three, and vascular bundles scattered throughout the stem. Examples: irises, tulips, grasses. **CLASS: Dicotyledonae** Dicots. Embryos have two cotyledons. Leaves with netlike veins, flower parts in multiples of four or five, and vascular bundles arranged in rings. Examples: roses, daisies, deciduous trees, foxgloves.
ANIMALIA		**Animals** Multicellular, eukaryotic heterotrophs with cells supported by collagen. Cells lack cell walls. Most have cells that are organized into specialized tissues, which make up organs. Most reproduce sexually.
	Porifera	**Sponges** Spend most of their lives fixed to the ocean floor. Feed by filtering water (containing nutrients and small organisms) through their body. Reproduce sexually and asexually. Example: *Euplectella* (Venus's flower basket).
	Cnidaria	**Cnidarians** Aquatic animals with a radial (spokelike) body shape; named for their stinging cells (cnidocytes). Have two basic body forms: the polyp and the medusa. May produce sexually and asexually. **CLASS: Hydrozoa** Alternate between polyp and medusa stages. Medusas reproduce sexually, polyps reproduce asexually. Example: hydras. **CLASS: Scyphozoa** Dominant medusa form. Example: jellyfish. **CLASS: Anthozoa** Dominant polyp form; there is no medusa stage. May be colonial or solitary. Central body surrounded by tentacles. Examples: sea anemones, corals. **CLASS: Cubozoa** Dominant cube-shaped medusa form with well-developed eyes. Examples: tropical box jellyfish, sea wasps.

Sago palm

Foxglove

Giant anemone

KINGDOM	PHYLUM	COMMON NAME AND DESCRIPTION
	Ctenophora	**Comb jellies** Resemble jellyfish; named for the comblike rows of cilia (hairlike extensions) that are used for movement. Example: *Pleurobrachia*.
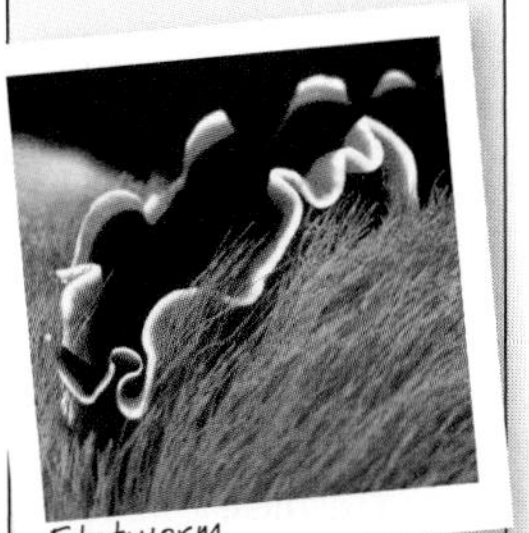 Flatworm	Platyhelminthes	**Flatworms** Thin, flattened worms with simple tissues and sensory organs. Includes planaria and tapeworms, which cause diseases in humans and other hosts. **CLASS: Turbellaria (turbellarians)** Free-living carnivores or scavengers that move with cilia. Example: planarians. **CLASS: Trematoda (flukes)** Internal parasites; life cycle often includes alternation of hosts. Example: *Schistosoma*. **CLASS: Cestoda (tapeworms)** Internal parasites; segmented body and head with suckers or hooks for attaching to host. Example: dog tapeworm.
 Nautilus	Mollusca	**Mollusks** Soft-bodied aquatic animals that usually have an outer shell. **CLASS: Gastropoda (gastropods)** Use muscular foot for movement. Have a distinct head and complete digestive tract. Most have a chambered shell. Examples: snails and slugs. **CLASS: Pelecypoda (bivalves)** Soft body protected by two hard shells that are hinged together. Most are filter feeders. Examples: clams, oysters, mussels, scallops. **CLASS: Cephalopoda (cephalopods)** Carnivores with well-developed eyes and nervous systems. Examples: squids, octopuses, nautiluses.
 Leeches	Annelida	**Segmented worms** Body is made of many similar segments. **CLASS: Polychaeta (polychaetes)** Marine worms with a pair of appendages on each segment. Have many setae. Examples: fan worms, featherduster worms. **CLASS: Oligochaeta (oligochaetes)** Earthworms; live in soil or fresh water. Have no appendages. Have few setae. Example: *Tubifex tubifex* (sludge worm). **CLASS: Hirudinea (leeches)** Most live in fresh water. Have flattened body with no appendages. Suckers at both ends; carnivores or blood-sucking parasites. Example: *Macrobdella decora* (medicinal leech).
	Nematoda	**Roundworms** Small, round worms; many species are parasites, causing diseases in humans, such as trichinosis and elephantiasis. Example: *Trichinella*.

Appendix A: Classification

KINGDOM	PHYLUM	COMMON NAME AND DESCRIPTION
ANIMALIA (continued) *Scorpion* *Dragonfly*	Arthropoda	Animals with an outer skeleton called an exoskeleton, and jointed appendages such as legs or wings. **SUBPHYLUM: Trilobita (trilobites)** Includes the trilobites, which are all extinct. Important part of the Paleozoic marine ecosystems for 300 million years. Bodies divided into three lobes. Bottom feeders. **SUBPHYLUM: Crustacea (crustaceans)** Live in all of the oceans, freshwater streams, and on land. Have chewing mouthparts and two pairs of antennae. Examples: crabs, lobsters, copepods, pill bugs. **SUBPHYLUM: Chelicerata (chelicerates)** First pair of appendages specialized as daggerlike mouthparts that are used for tearing food; no antennae. Examples: horseshoe crabs, scorpions, spiders, mites, ticks. **SUBPHYLUM: Uniramia** Most live on land. Have one pair of antennae and chewing mouthparts. **CLASS: Insecta (insects)** Have three body segments with three pairs of legs attached to second segment. Examples: ants, bees, butterflies, cockroaches, flies, mosquitoes. **CLASS: Chilopoda (centipedes)** Body divided into many segments with one pair of legs per segment. Carnivores; first pair of legs bears fangs for capturing prey. Example: *Scutigera coleoptrata* (common house centipede). **CLASS: Diplopoda (millipedes)** Body divided into many segments with two pairs of legs per segment. Most are herbivores. Example: *Glomeris* (pill millipede).
Sea star	Echinodermata	Adults are slow-moving marine animals with radial symmetry; larvae have bilateral symmetry. Have an internal skeleton, a water vascular system, and a complete digestive system. Some can regenerate limbs. **CLASS: Crinoidea (crinoids)** Filter feeders that remain attached to a surface such as the ocean floor. Examples: feather stars, sea lilies. **CLASS: Asteroidea (sea stars)** Star-shaped bottom dwellers that may be suspension feeders, opportunistic feeders, or carnivorous predators. Example: *Acanthaster planci* (crown-of-thorns starfish). **CLASS: Ophiuroidea** Most have five long spindly arms that they use to help move and feed; tube feet lack suckers. Examples: brittle stars, basket stars. **CLASS: Echinoidea** Have a five-part body plan but no arms; body covered with projections or spines. Most graze for food on ocean floor. Examples: sea urchins, sea biscuits, sand dollars. **CLASS: Holothuroidea (sea cucumbers)** Fleshy animals with long, cylindrical shape. Tentacles are used to capture food; also feed on sediment from ocean floor. Example: *Holothuria*.

KINGDOM	PHYLUM	COMMON NAME AND DESCRIPTION
	Chordata	**Chordates** Have bilateral symmetry, a notochord, a hollow nerve tube, pharyngeal slits, and a tail at some point in development.

Sea squirt

Stingray

Salamander

Kingfisher

Elephant

Chordates Have bilateral symmetry, a notochord, a hollow nerve tube, pharyngeal slits, and a tail at some point in development.

SUBPHYLUM: Urochordata (tunicates) Marine animals whose larvae have features of phylum chordata. Some adults are free-swimming, others are sessile. Example: sea squirts.

SUBPHYLUM: Cephalochordata (lancelets) Eel-like marine animals with no internal skeleton. Spend much of life buried in sand; filter feeders. Example: *Branchiostoma*.

SUBPHYLUM: Vertebrata (vertebrates) Have an internal skeleton, usually including a backbone made of vertebrae, which protects the nerve cords. Distinct head with well-developed brain encased in hard skull.

CLASS: Myxini (hagfish) Part of superclass Agnatha. Jawless with poorly developed eyes. Have cartilaginous skeleton and tentacles around mouth used for scavenging food. Lack scales and paired fins. Ectothermic. Example: *Myxine glutinosa* (Atlantic hagfish).

CLASS: Cephalaspidomorphi (lampreys) Part of superclass Agnatha. Jawless with cartilaginous skeleton. Larvae are filter feeders and adults are parasites with a mouth surrounded by a sucker. Lack scales and paired fins. Ectothermic. Example: *Petromyzon marinus* (sea lamprey).

CLASS: Chondrichthyes (cartilaginous fish) Fish with true jaws, paired fins, and a cartilaginous skeleton. Have gills, usually with several gill slits. Have no swim bladder. Ectothermic. Examples: sharks, skates, rays, sawfish.

CLASS: Osteichthyes (bony fish) Fish with bony skeleton. Have jaws, paired fins, and swim bladder. Most have gills attached to gill arch. Marine and freshwater. Ectothermic. Examples: lobe-finned fish such as lungfish and coelacanth; ray-finned fish such as bass, goldfish, sea horses.

CLASS: Amphibia (amphibians) Gills usually present in larval stage; eggs usually laid in water and fertilized externally. Adults aquatic or terrestrial, most adapted to wet environments, respiring through moist skin and/or lungs. Ectothermic. Examples: frogs, toads, salamanders.

CLASS: Reptilia (reptiles) Adapted to life on land, although some live in water. Breathe using lungs at all stages. Have dry skin covered in scales. Lay amniotic eggs that are fertilized internally. Ectothermic. Examples: snakes, lizards, turtles, crocodiles, dinosaurs (extinct).

CLASS: Aves (birds) Body mostly covered with feathers. Forelimbs modified into wings, most often used for flight. Hollow, lightweight bones, well-developed lungs and air sacs. Lay shelled, amniotic eggs. Four-chambered heart. Endothermic. Examples: robins, eagles, ducks, penguins, owls, chickens.

CLASS: Mammalia (mammals) Have hair on part of body. Young nourished with milk from mother's mammary glands. Jaw allows for chewing of food. Middle ear contains three bones. Breathe using lungs. Have four-chambered heart. Endothermic. Three main groups include monotremes, which lay eggs; marsupials, or pouched mammals; and eutherian mammals, which give birth to live young. Examples: duckbill platypus (monotreme); koala (marsupial); bats, squirrels, rabbits, whales, bears, monkeys, elephants, pigs, horses, humans (eutherian).

Appendix B: Life Cycles

Moss Life Cycle

This diagram illustrates the life cycle of moss in detail. The life cycle of mosses is discussed in Chapter 22.

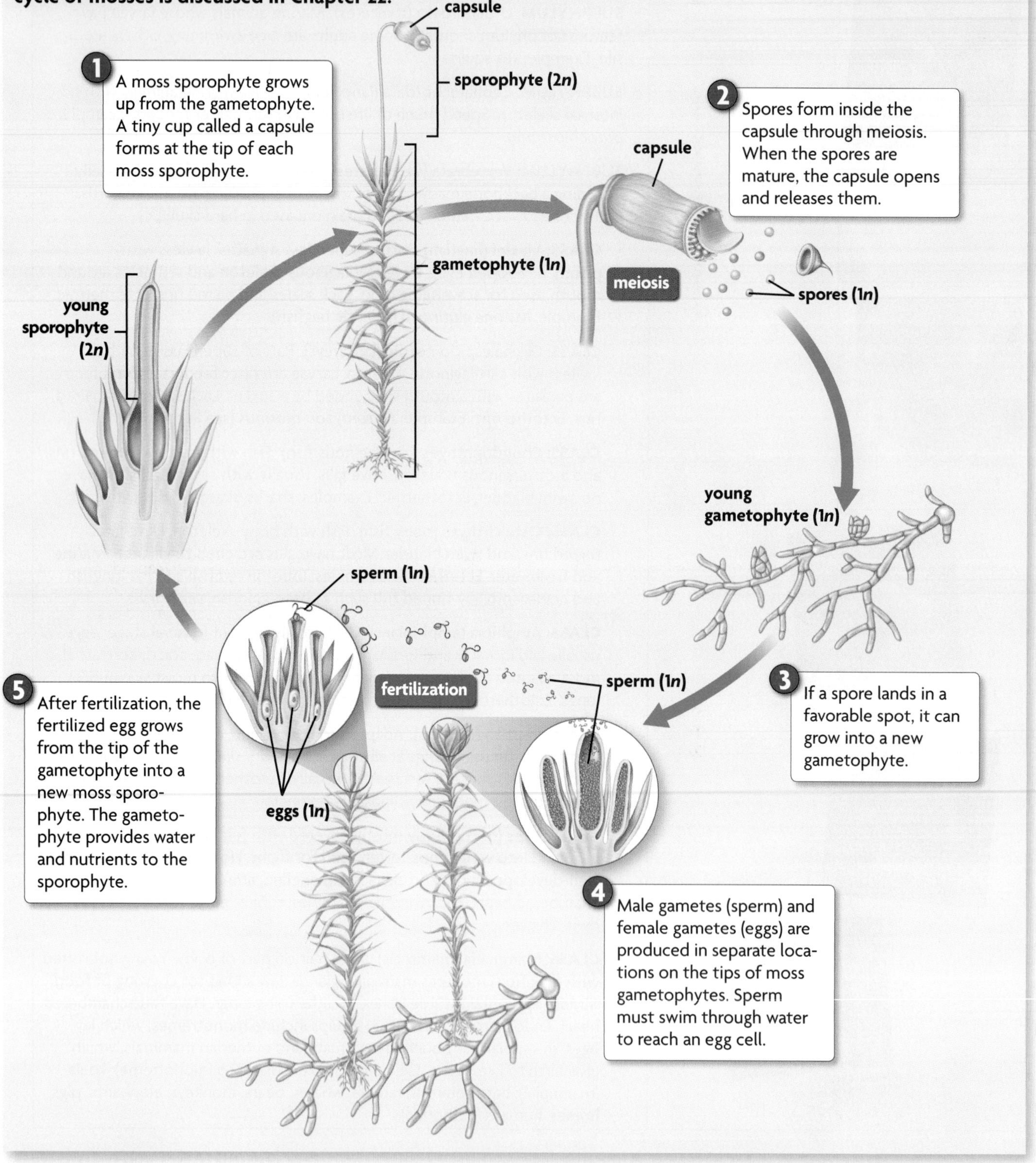
capsule
sporophyte (2n)
gametophyte (1n)
1 A moss sporophyte grows up from the gametophyte. A tiny cup called a capsule forms at the tip of each moss sporophyte.
capsule
2 Spores form inside the capsule through meiosis. When the spores are mature, the capsule opens and releases them.
meiosis
spores (1n)
young gametophyte (1n)
3 If a spore lands in a favorable spot, it can grow into a new gametophyte.
sperm (1n)
fertilization
sperm (1n)
eggs (1n)
4 Male gametes (sperm) and female gametes (eggs) are produced in separate locations on the tips of moss gametophytes. Sperm must swim through water to reach an egg cell.
5 After fertilization, the fertilized egg grows from the tip of the gametophyte into a new moss sporophyte. The gametophyte provides water and nutrients to the sporophyte.
young sporophyte (2n)

Fern Life Cycle

This diagram illustrates the life cycle of ferns in detail. The life cycle of ferns is discussed in Chapter 22.

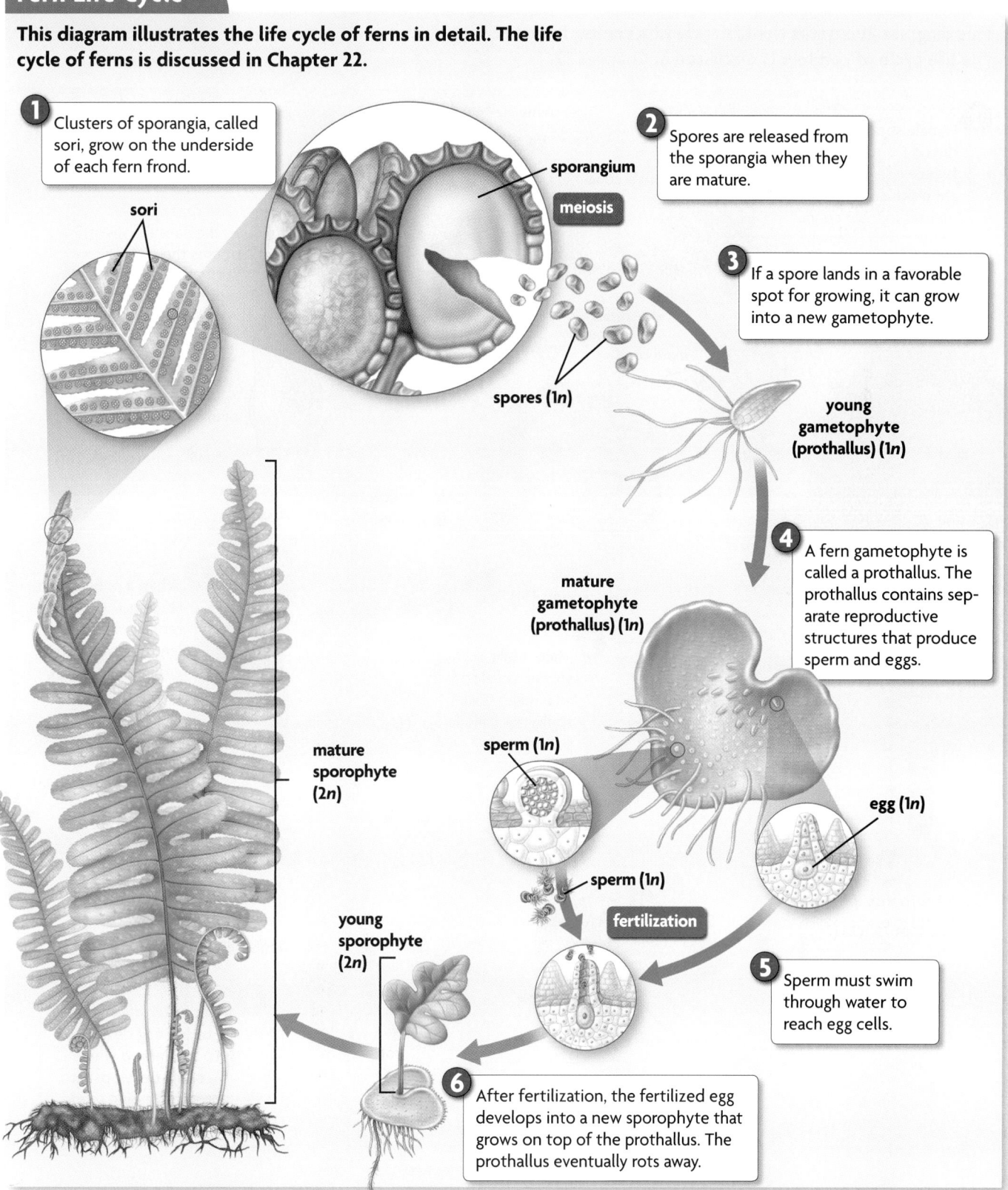

1 Clusters of sporangia, called sori, grow on the underside of each fern frond.

sori

sporangium

meiosis

2 Spores are released from the sporangia when they are mature.

spores (1*n*)

3 If a spore lands in a favorable spot for growing, it can grow into a new gametophyte.

young gametophyte (prothallus) (1*n*)

4 A fern gametophyte is called a prothallus. The prothallus contains separate reproductive structures that produce sperm and eggs.

mature gametophyte (prothallus) (1*n*)

mature sporophyte (2*n*)

sperm (1*n*)

sperm (1*n*)

egg (1*n*)

fertilization

5 Sperm must swim through water to reach egg cells.

young sporophyte (2*n*)

6 After fertilization, the fertilized egg develops into a new sporophyte that grows on top of the prothallus. The prothallus eventually rots away.

Appendix B: Life Cycles

Conifer Life Cycle

This diagram illustrates the life cycle of a conifer in detail.
The life cycle of conifers is discussed in Chapter 22.

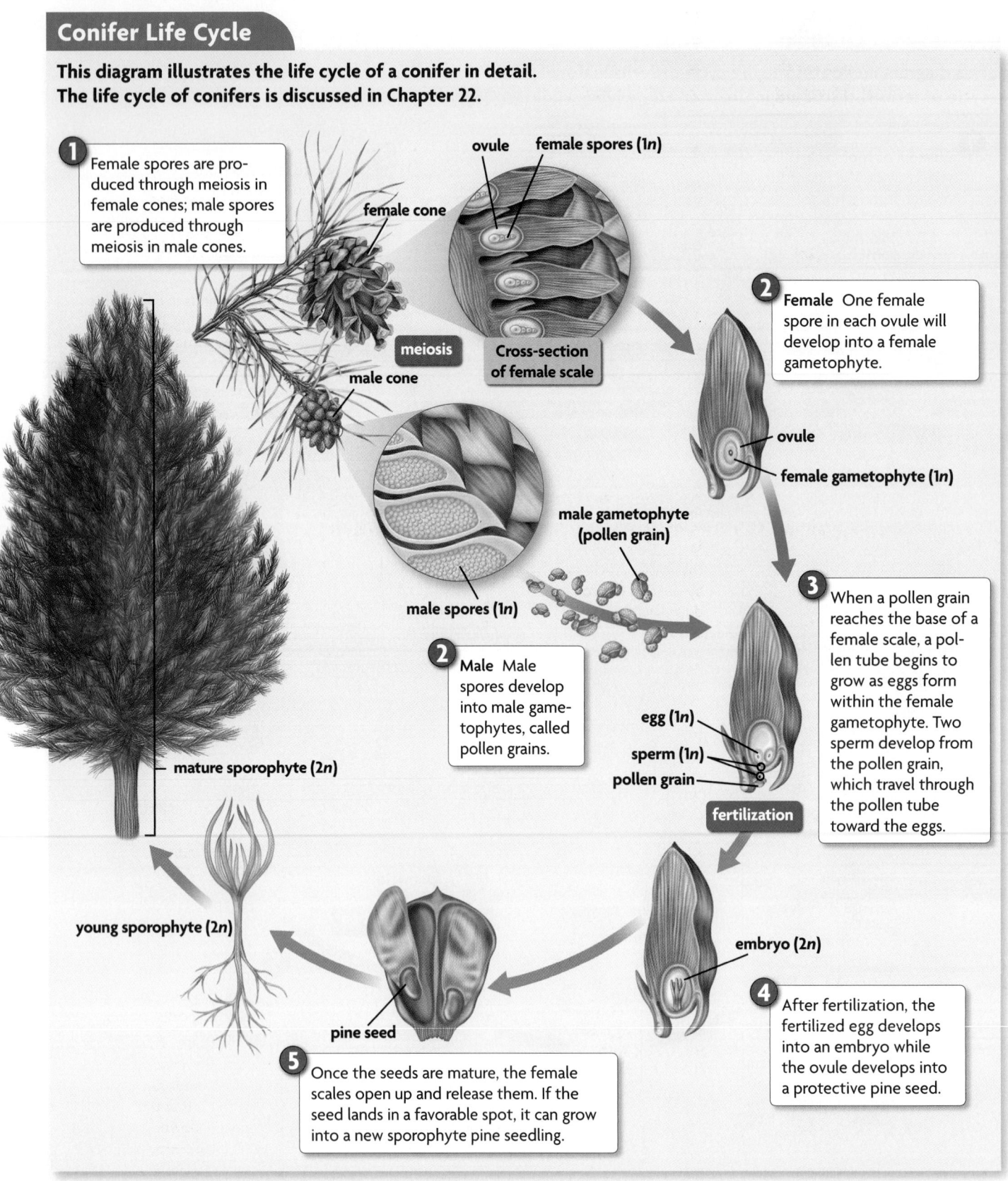

1 Female spores are produced through meiosis in female cones; male spores are produced through meiosis in male cones.

ovule   female spores (1*n*)

female cone

meiosis   Cross-section of female scale

male cone

male gametophyte (pollen grain)

male spores (1*n*)

2 Male Male spores develop into male gametophytes, called pollen grains.

2 Female One female spore in each ovule will develop into a female gametophyte.

ovule
female gametophyte (1*n*)

3 When a pollen grain reaches the base of a female scale, a pollen tube begins to grow as eggs form within the female gametophyte. Two sperm develop from the pollen grain, which travel through the pollen tube toward the eggs.

egg (1*n*)
sperm (1*n*)
pollen grain

fertilization

mature sporophyte (2*n*)

embryo (2*n*)

young sporophyte (2*n*)

pine seed

4 After fertilization, the fertilized egg develops into an embryo while the ovule develops into a protective pine seed.

5 Once the seeds are mature, the female scales open up and release them. If the seed lands in a favorable spot, it can grow into a new sporophyte pine seedling.

Flowering Plant Life Cycle

This diagram illustrates the life cycle of a flowering plant in detail.
The life cycle of flowering plants is discussed in Chapter 22.

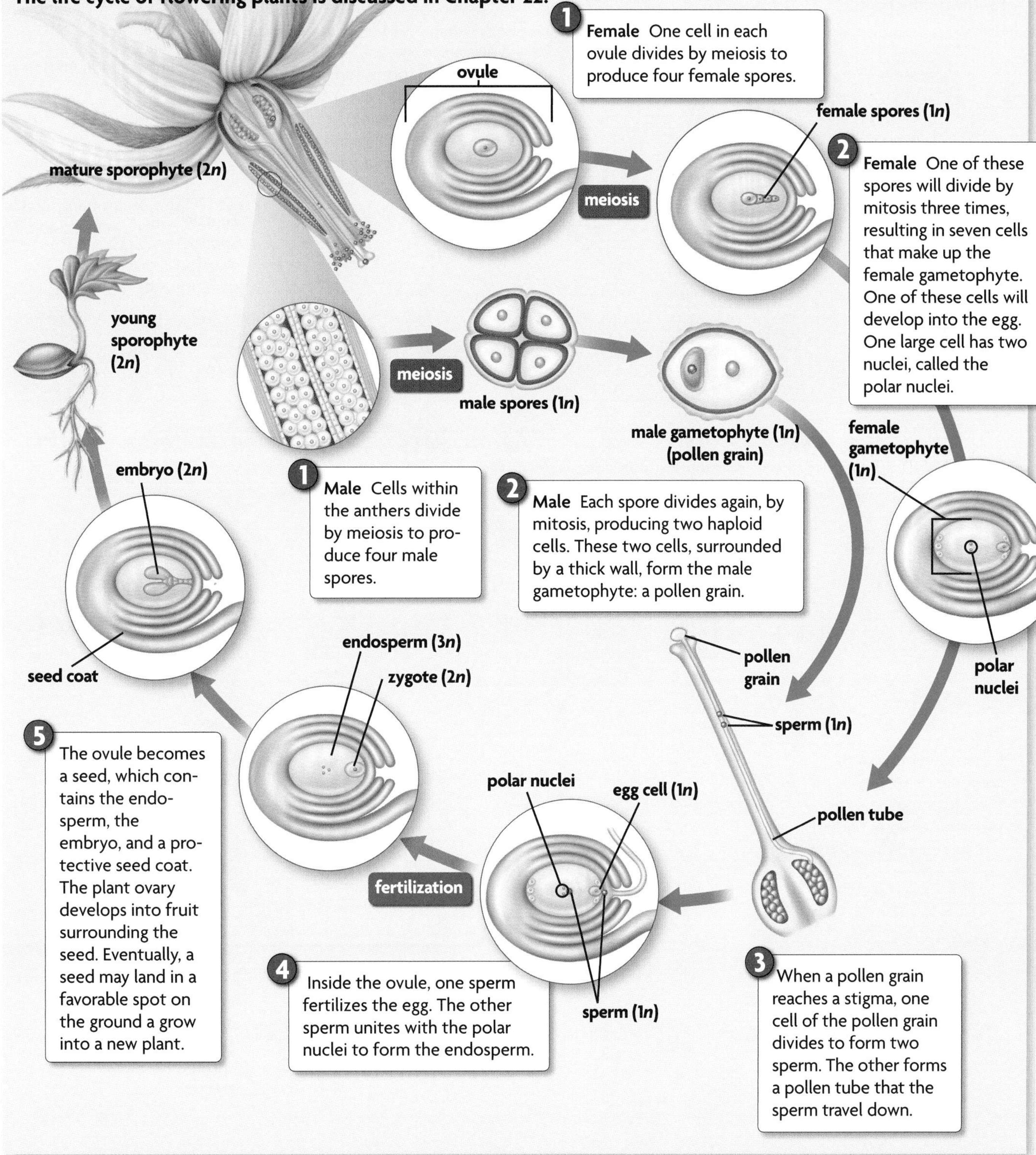

1 **Female** One cell in each ovule divides by meiosis to produce four female spores.

ovule

female spores (1n)

meiosis

2 **Female** One of these spores will divide by mitosis three times, resulting in seven cells that make up the female gametophyte. One of these cells will develop into the egg. One large cell has two nuclei, called the polar nuclei.

mature sporophyte (2n)

young sporophyte (2n)

meiosis

male spores (1n)

male gametophyte (1n) (pollen grain)

female gametophyte (1n)

embryo (2n)

1 **Male** Cells within the anthers divide by meiosis to produce four male spores.

2 **Male** Each spore divides again, by mitosis, producing two haploid cells. These two cells, surrounded by a thick wall, form the male gametophyte: a pollen grain.

pollen grain

polar nuclei

seed coat

endosperm (3n)

zygote (2n)

sperm (1n)

5 The ovule becomes a seed, which contains the endosperm, the embryo, and a protective seed coat. The plant ovary develops into fruit surrounding the seed. Eventually, a seed may land in a favorable spot on the ground a grow into a new plant.

fertilization

polar nuclei

egg cell (1n)

pollen tube

4 Inside the ovule, one sperm fertilizes the egg. The other sperm unites with the polar nuclei to form the endosperm.

sperm (1n)

3 When a pollen grain reaches a stigma, one cell of the pollen grain divides to form two sperm. The other forms a pollen tube that the sperm travel down.

Appendix C: Periodic Table

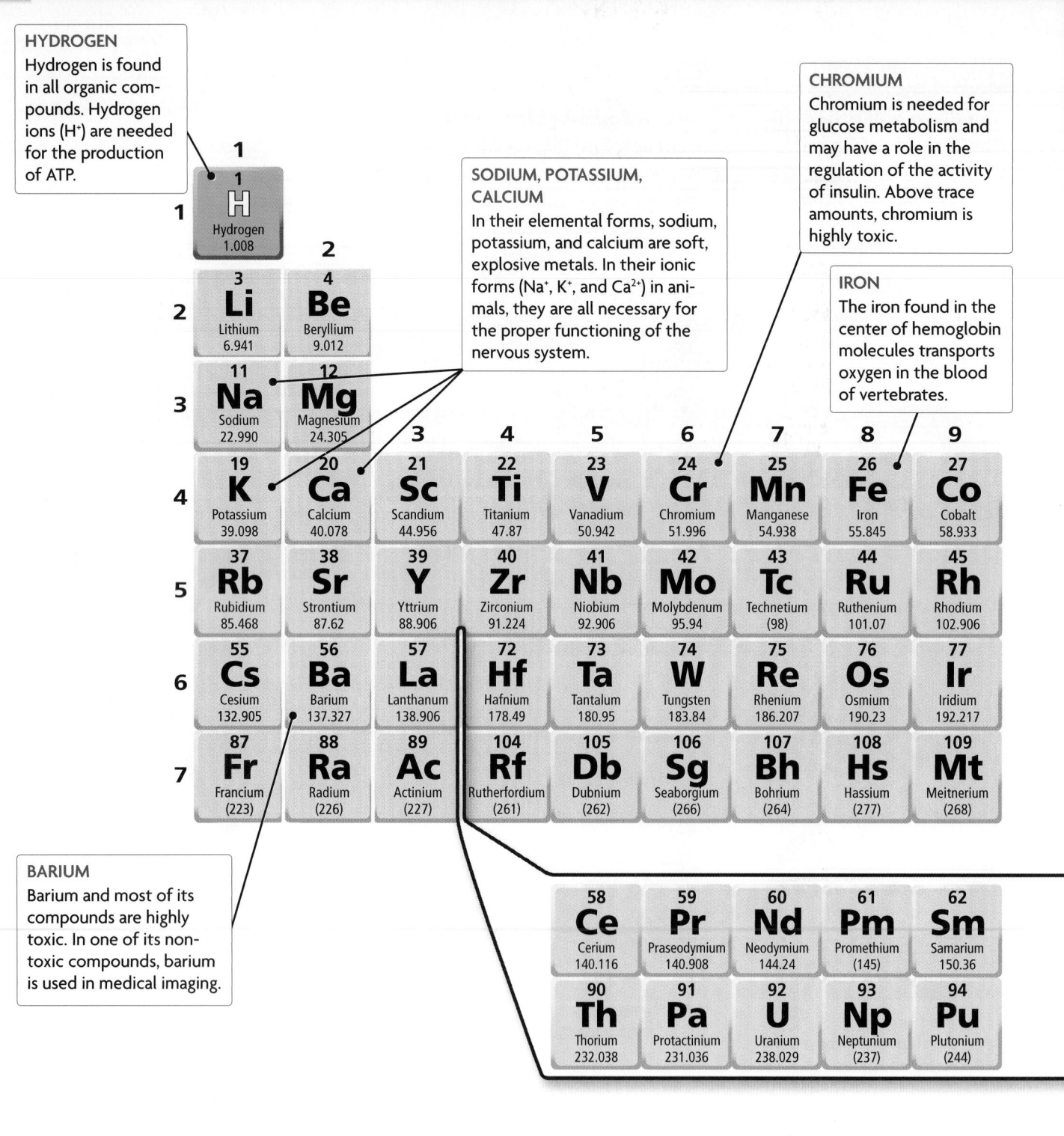

HYDROGEN
Hydrogen is found in all organic compounds. Hydrogen ions (H^+) are needed for the production of ATP.

SODIUM, POTASSIUM, CALCIUM
In their elemental forms, sodium, potassium, and calcium are soft, explosive metals. In their ionic forms (Na^+, K^+, and Ca^{2+}) in animals, they are all necessary for the proper functioning of the nervous system.

CHROMIUM
Chromium is needed for glucose metabolism and may have a role in the regulation of the activity of insulin. Above trace amounts, chromium is highly toxic.

IRON
The iron found in the center of hemoglobin molecules transports oxygen in the blood of vertebrates.

BARIUM
Barium and most of its compounds are highly toxic. In one of its non-toxic compounds, barium is used in medical imaging.

1	H Hydrogen 1.008
3 Li Lithium 6.941	4 Be Beryllium 9.012
11 Na Sodium 22.990	12 Mg Magnesium 24.305
19 K Potassium 39.098	20 Ca Calcium 40.078	21 Sc Scandium 44.956	22 Ti Titanium 47.87	23 V Vanadium 50.942	24 Cr Chromium 51.996	25 Mn Manganese 54.938	26 Fe Iron 55.845	27 Co Cobalt 58.933
37 Rb Rubidium 85.468	38 Sr Strontium 87.62	39 Y Yttrium 88.906	40 Zr Zirconium 91.224	41 Nb Niobium 92.906	42 Mo Molybdenum 95.94	43 Tc Technetium (98)	44 Ru Ruthenium 101.07	45 Rh Rhodium 102.906
55 Cs Cesium 132.905	56 Ba Barium 137.327	57 La Lanthanum 138.906	72 Hf Hafnium 178.49	73 Ta Tantalum 180.95	74 W Tungsten 183.84	75 Re Rhenium 186.207	76 Os Osmium 190.23	77 Ir Iridium 192.217
87 Fr Francium (223)	88 Ra Radium (226)	89 Ac Actinium (227)	104 Rf Rutherfordium (261)	105 Db Dubnium (262)	106 Sg Seaborgium (266)	107 Bh Bohrium (264)	108 Hs Hassium (277)	109 Mt Meitnerium (268)

| 58 Ce Cerium 140.116 | 59 Pr Praseodymium 140.908 | 60 Nd Neodymium 144.24 | 61 Pm Promethium (145) | 62 Sm Samarium 150.36 |
| 90 Th Thorium 232.038 | 91 Pa Protactinium 231.036 | 92 U Uranium 238.029 | 93 Np Neptunium (237) | 94 Pu Plutonium (244) |

Metal   Metalloid   Nonmetal   **Fe** Solid   Hg Liquid   ⃝ Gas

OXYGEN
Oxygen is found in many organic molecules, and is needed for the aerobic stages of cellular respiration. Oxygen is also a waste product of photosynthesis and in some cases it is even toxic to cells.

NITROGEN
Proteins and nucleic acids both contain nitrogen. Although nitrogen makes up almost 80 percent of Earth's atmosphere, plants and animals cannot directly use nitrogen gas.

CARBON
All organic molecules, which are the basic building blocks of life, contain carbon.

ZINC
Zinc is found in many enzymes. Zinc is also important for maturation of human reproductive systems.

CHLORINE
Chlorine gas is a deadly poison. Chloride ions (Cl^-) are necessary for the transmission of certain types of signals in the nervous system.

PHOSPHORUS
Phosphorus is found in the lipids that make up all cell membranes. It is a part of the "backbone" of both DNA and RNA molecules. On a larger scale, both bones and teeth contain phosphorus.

10	11	12	13	14	15	16	17	18
								2 He Helium 4.003
			5 B Boron 10.811	6 C Carbon 12.011	7 N Nitrogen 14.007	8 O Oxygen 15.999	9 F Fluorine 18.998	10 Ne Neon 20.180
			13 Al Aluminum 26.982	14 Si Silicon 28.086	15 P Phosphorus 30.974	16 S Sulfur 32.066	17 Cl Chlorine 35.453	18 Ar Argon 39.948
28 Ni Nickel 58.69	29 Cu Copper 63.546	30 Zn Zinc 65.39	31 Ga Gallium 69.723	32 Ge Germanium 72.61	33 As Arsenic 74.922	34 Se Selenium 78.96	35 Br Bromine 79.904	36 Kr Krypton 83.80
46 Pd Palladium 106.42	47 Ag Silver 107.868	48 Cd Cadmium 112.4	49 In Indium 114.818	50 Sn Tin 118.710	51 Sb Antimony 121.760	52 Te Tellurium 127.60	53 I Iodine 126.904	54 Xe Xenon 131.29
78 Pt Platinum 195.078	79 Au Gold 196.967	80 Hg Mercury 200.59	81 Tl Thallium 204.383	82 Pb Lead 207.2	83 Bi Bismuth 208.980	84 Po Polonium (209)	85 At Astatine (210)	86 Rn Radon (222)
110 Ds Darmstadtium (281)	111 Rg Roentgenium (272)	112 Uub Ununbium (285)	113 Uut Ununtrium (284)	114 Uuq Ununquadium (289)	115 Uup Ununpentium (288)	116 Uuh Ununhexium (292)		

63 Eu Europium 151.964	64 Gd Gadolinium 157.25	65 Tb Terbium 158.925	66 Dy Dysprosium 162.50	67 Ho Holmium 164.930	68 Er Erbium 167.26	69 Tm Thulium 168.934	70 Yb Ytterbium 173.04	71 Lu Lutetium 174.967
95 Am Americium (243)	96 Cm Curium (247)	97 Bk Berkelium (247)	98 Cf Californium (251)	99 Es Einsteinium (252)	100 Fm Fermium (257)	101 Md Mendelevium (258)	102 No Nobelium (259)	103 Lr Lawrencium (262)

1 H Hydrogen 1.008

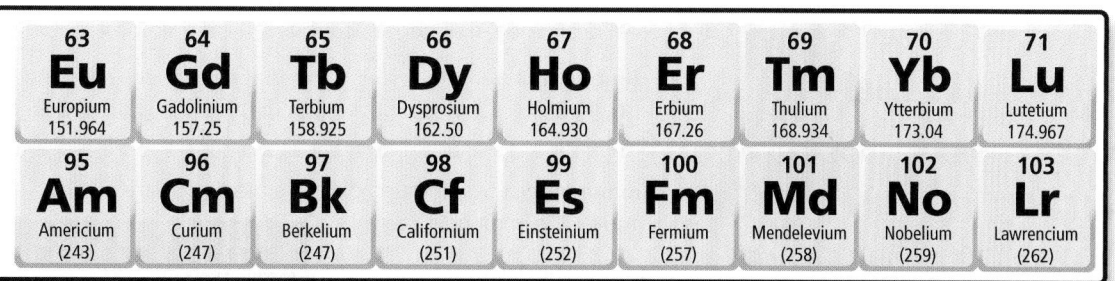

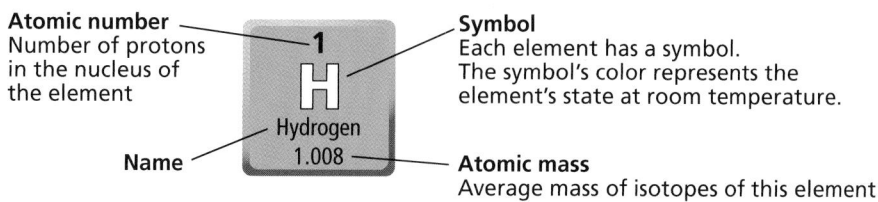

Atomic number
Number of protons in the nucleus of the element

Symbol
Each element has a symbol.
The symbol's color represents the element's state at room temperature.

Name

Atomic mass
Average mass of isotopes of this element

Careers in Biology

A number of careers require a background knowledge of biology. Some of these career choices may be more obvious than others, such as that of a biology teacher, doctor, or zookeeper. But there are many more careers that may be less familiar to you. While your image of someone who uses their knowledge of biology might be that of a scientist who works in a laboratory, you just might be surprised to discover what other jobs require a background in the biological sciences.

To learn more about careers in the biological sciences, go to the BioZine at ClassZone.com.

Agronomist An agronomist is an expert in soil management who advises farmers on how to manage their crops.

Anthropologist An anthropologist studies the origin, behavior, and social and cultural development of humans.

Bioinformatics Professional A bioinformatics professional uses computers, laboratory robots, and software to develop, manage, and interpret complex biological data.

Biological Illustrator A biological illustrator provides scientifically accurate hand-drawn or computer-aided illustrations for clients, ranging from web sites to publications such as textbooks, newspapers, or magazines.

Biomedical Engineer A biomedical engineer develops devices and procedures that solve medical and health-related problems.

Conservation Biologist A conservation biologist manages, improves, and protects natural resources.

Ecotourism Guide An ecotourism guide leads groups of tourists on trips to natural areas to promote conservation and sustain the livelihood of local people.

Emergency Medical Technician An emergency medical technician provides emergency medical services to critically ill and injured persons.

Environmental Economist An environmental economist uses the principles of economics to determine the impact of such things as species loss, pollution, and climate change.

Environmental Health Professional An environmental health professional inspects the health and safety of establishments such as restaurants and housing areas.

Environmental Journalist An environmental journalist writes articles or books on environmental topics, frequently in an investigatory manner.

Epidemiologist An epidemiologist studies causes and control of diseases.

Exercise Physiologist An exercise physiologist develops exercise routines and educates people about the benefits of exercise.

Ethologist An ethologist studies animal behavior.

Farm Manager A farm manager manages the day-to-day activities of one or more farms, focusing on the business aspects of running a farm.

Fish and Wildlife Manager A fish and wildlife manager manages the populations of fish and/or wildlife on public or private lands.

Forensic Scientist A forensic scientist analyzes biological, chemical, or physical samples taken as evidence during a criminal investigation.

Forester A forester manages and protects forests and supervises tree harvesting.

Genetic Counselor A genetic counselor is a health professional who specializes in telling families about the nature and risks of inherited conditions and syndromes.

Geneticist A geneticist specializes in the study of genes and their influence on health, as well as the treatment of genetic disorders.

Immunologist An immunologist is a medical scientist who studies the immune system.

Landscape Architect A landscape architect plans the location of buildings, roads, and walkways along with the placement of plants so that the designs are not only functional but also compatible with the natural environment.

Medical Transcriptionist A medical transcriptionist listens to dictated recordings made by doctors and other health care workers and transcribes them into medical reports.

Medical Device Sales Representative A medical device sales representative sells medical devices to health professionals.

Molecular Biologist A molecular biologist studies the structure and function of biological molecules, such as DNA and proteins.

Nature Photographer
A nature photographer takes photographs of natural settings and wildlife for publication online and in print material such as books and magazines.

Neuroscientist
A neuroscientist specializes in the study of the structure and function of the brain and nervous system.

Nutritionist A nutritionist plans food and nutrition programs and provides advice to those with food allergies or those seeking weight loss.

Oceanographer An oceanographer studies the world's oceans and their inhabitants.

Park Ranger A park ranger supervises, manages, and performs work in the conservation and use of resources in national, state, and city parks.

Pharmacist A pharmacist distributes drugs prescribed by doctors and other health workers and provides information to patients about medications and their use.

Phlebotomist
A phlebotomist collects blood samples.

Physician Assistant
A physician assistant takes medical histories, examines and treats patients, orders and interprets laboratory tests and x-rays, and makes diagnoses, all under the supervision of a doctor.

Physical Therapist A physical therapist provides services that help restore function, improve mobility, relieve pain, and prevent or limit permanent physical disabilities of patients suffering from injuries or disease.

Radiologist A radiologist is a doctor who specializes in the interpretation of x-rays and other medical images.

Respiratory Therapist
A respiratory therapist evaluates, treats, and cares for patients with breathing or other cardiopulmonary disorders.

Science Editor A science editor edits scientific writing, ranging from academic journals to works meant for a general audience.

Science Museum Curator A science museum curator oversees the development and management of museum exhibits.

Science Patent Lawyer A science patent lawyer represents clients in legal proceedings, draws up legal documents, and advises clients on legal transactions.

Science Policy Analyst A science policy analyst advises lawmakers with regard to legislation focused on scientific issues such as biomedical research or environmental regulations.

Science Writer A science writer specializes in writing about scientific topics for both academic and general audiences.

Speech-Language Pathologist A speech-language pathologist tests, diagnoses, treats, and helps to prevent speech, language, and other voice-related disorders.

Sports Trainer A sports trainer helps athletes in the prevention of injury and provides initial management of a sports-related injury.

Surgical Technician A surgical technician assists in surgeries by preparing the surgical room, providing support to surgical workers, and monitoring the patient during surgery.

Ultrasound Technician An ultrasound technician operates an ultrasound machine, which collects reflected echoes and forms an image that may be videotaped, transmitted, or photographed for interpretation and diagnosis by a doctor.

X-Ray Technician An x-ray technician takes x-rays and administers nonradioactive materials into patients' bloodstreams for diagnostic purposes.

Glossary

A

abdomen part of an arthropod's body that is behind the thorax. (p. 735)
abdomen parte del cuerpo de un artrópodo situada detrás del tórax.

abiotic nonliving factor in an ecosystem, such as moisture, temperature, wind, sunlight, soil, and minerals. (p. 402)
abiótico factor inerte de un ecosistema, como la humedad, la temperatura, el viento, la luz solar, el suelo y los minerales.

ABO blood group four common blood types (A, B, AB, and O) and the protein markers that distinguish them. (p. 927)
grupo sanguíneo ABO sistema que contiene los cuatro tipos de sangre comunes (A, B, AB y O) y los marcadores proteicos que los distinguen.

absorption process by which nutrients move out of one system and into another. (p. 982)
absorción proceso mediante el cual los nutrientes pasan de un sistema del organismo a otro.

abyssal zone (uh-BIHS-uhl) depth of the ocean that lies below 2000 meters and is in complete darkness. (p. 469)
zona abisal región del océano por debajo de los 2000 metros de profundidad que se encuentra en total oscuridad.

acid compound that donates a proton (H⁺) when dissolved in a solution. (p. 42)
ácido compuesto que cede un protón (H⁺) al ser disuelto en una solución.

acid rain precipitation produced when pollutants in the atmosphere cause the pH of rain to decrease. (p. 489)
lluvia ácida precipitación que se produce cuando los contaminantes de la atmósfera hacen que el pH de la lluvia disminuya.

acquired immune deficiency syndrome (AIDS) condition characterized by having several infections and very few T cells; caused by HIV. (p. 963)
síndrome de inmunodeficiencia adquirida (SIDA) enfermedad caracterizada por falta de defensa contra varias infecciones y muy pocas células T; causada por el VIH.

actin filament that is pulled by myosin filaments to cause muscle contraction. (p. 1008)
actina filamento que al ser accionado por los filamentos de miosina provoca una contracción muscular.

action potential fast, moving change in electrical charge across a neuron's membrane; also called an impulse. (p. 878)
potencial de acción cambio rápido en la descarga eléctrica a lo largo de la membrana de las neuronas; también llamado impulso.

activation energy energy input necessary to initiate a chemical reaction. (p. 53)
energía de activación energía necesaria para iniciar una reacción química.

active immunity immunity that occurs after the body responds to an antigen. (p. 948)
inmunidad activa inmunidad que se produce después de que el cuerpo haya respondido a un antígeno.

active transport energy-requiring movement of molecules across a membrane from a region of lower concentration to a region of higher concentration. (p. 89)
transporte activo desplazamiento de moléculas a través de una membrana desde un medio de baja concentración a un medio de alta concentración.

adaptation inherited trait that is selected for over time because it allows organisms to better survive in their environment. (pp. 10; 302)
adaptación rasgo heredado durante un periodo de tiempo mediante selección natural, que facilita la supervivencia de los organismos en su medio ambiente.

adaptive radiation process by which one species evolves and gives rise to many descendant species that occupy different ecological niches. (p. 351)
radiación adaptativa proceso evolutivo mediante el cual una especie da lugar a varias nuevas especies que ocupan distintos nichos ecológicos.

addiction uncontrollable physical and mental need for something. (p. 893)
adicción necesidad física y mental incontrolable de alguna sustancia o actividad.

adenosine diphosphate (ADP) low-energy molecule that can be converted to ATP. (p. 101)
adenosín difosfato (ADP) molécula con poca energía que puede convertirse en ATP.

adenosine triphosphate (ATP) high-energy molecule that contains, within its bonds, energy that cells can use. (p. 100)
adenosín trifosfato (ATP) molécula de alta energía en cuyos enlaces se almacena energía para las células.

adhesion attraction between molecules of different substances. (p. 41)
adhesión atracción que se produce entre moléculas de diferentes sustancias.

adolescence period of life beginning at puberty and ending at adulthood. (p. 1042)
adolescencia periodo de la vida que comienza en la pubertad y que termina en la edad adulta.

ADP *see* adenosine diphosphate. (p. 101)
ADP *véase* adenosín difosfato.

adulthood period of life when a person is fully developed and physical growth stops. (p. 1043)
edad adulta período de la vida en el que un individuo alcanza su completo desarrollo y en el que cesa el crecimiento.

aerobic (ay-ROH-bihk) process that requires oxygen to occur. (p. 113)
aeróbico proceso que requiere la presencia de oxígeno para ocurrir.

airfoil surface, such as a bird's wing, whose shape moves air faster over the top than underneath it, allowing for flight. (p. 799)
superficie aerodinámica superficie de ala cuya forma, como en el caso de las aves, permite que el aire se mueva más rápido por arriba que por abajo, facilitando así el vuelo.

air sac air-filled space that connects to a bird's lungs, aiding in breathing. (p. 801)
sacos aéreos órganos llenos de aire conectados a los pulmones de las aves para facilitar la respiración.

algae (singular: *alga*) photosynthetic plantlike protists. (p. 581)
alga protista fotosintética de aspecto vegetal.

alkaloid chemical produced by plants that contains nitrogen, many of which are used in medicines. (p. 631)
alcaloide compuesto químico, producido por las plantas, que contiene nitrógeno y es usado en muchos medicamentos.

allele (uh-LEEL) any of the alternative forms of a gene that occurs at a specific place on a chromosome. (p. 180)
alelo cualquier variante de un gen que ocupa la misma posición en un cromosoma.

allele frequency proportion of one allele, compared with all the alleles for that trait, in the gene pool. (p. 328)
frecuencia alélica proporción de un alelo determinado con respecto a los demás alelos del mismo rasgo en una misma población.

allergen antigen that does not cause disease but still produces an immune response. (p. 957)
alérgeno antígeno que, si bien no causa una enfermedad, produce una respuesta inmune.

allergy immune response that occurs when the body responds to a nondisease-causing antigen, such as pollen or animal dander. (p. 957)
alergia respuesta inmune producida cuando el organismo responde a aquellos antígenos que no causan enfermedades, como el polen o la caspa de ciertos animales.

alternation of generations plant life cycle in which the plant alternates between haploid and diploid phases. (p. 664)
alternancia generacional ciclo de vida de las plantas en el que la planta alterna fases haploides y diploides.

altruism behavior in which an animal reduces its own fitness to help the other members of its social group. (p. 833)
altruismo patrón de comportamiento animal, en el cual un individuo sacrifica su integridad para beneficiar a otros miembros de su grupo social.

alveolus (al-VEE-uh-luhs) (plural: *alveoli*) tiny, thin-walled structure across which oxygen gas is absorbed and carbon dioxide is released in the lungs. (p. 911)
alvéolo pequeña estructura de paredes delgadas a través de la cual se absorbe oxígeno gaseoso y se libera dióxido de carbono en los pulmones.

amino acid molecule that makes up proteins; composed of carbon, hydrogen, oxygen, nitrogen, and sometimes sulfur. (p. 47)
aminoácido molécula que forma las proteínas; está compuesta de carbono, hidrógeno, oxígeno, nitrógeno y, a veces, de azufre.

amniote vertebrate whose embryo or fetus is enclosed by a thin, tough membranous sac. (p. 778)
amniota vertebrado cuyo embrión o feto está envuelto en un saco membranoso delgado y resistente.

amniotic egg waterproof container that allows an embryo to develop out of water and externally from the mother without drying out. (p. 779)
huevo amniótico envoltura impermeable que permite el desarrollo del embrión fuera del agua y de la propia madre sin que éste se deshidrate.

amniotic sac fluid-filled organ that cushions and protects the developing embryo of some vertebrates. (p. 1035)
saco amniótico membrana que contiene líquido y que amortigua y protege el embrión de ciertos vertebrados.

amphibian vertebrate that can live on land and in water. (p. 773)
anfibio vertebrado que puede vivir en el agua y en tierra firme.

anaerobic process that does not require oxygen to occur. (p. 113)
anaeróbico proceso que no requiere oxígeno para ocurrir.

analogous structure body part that is similar in function as a body part of another organism but is structurally different. (p. 313)
estructura análoga parte del cuerpo que cumple una función similar a la parte del cuerpo de un organismo diferente, pero que tiene una estructura diferente.

anaphase third phase of mitosis during which chromatids separate and are pulled to opposite sides of the cell. (p. 140)
anafase tercera fase de la mitosis, en la cual las cromátidas se separan y se dirigen hacia los polos opuestos de la célula.

anaphylaxis (AN-uh-fuh-LAK-sihs) severe allergic reaction that causes airways to tighten and blood vessels to leak. (p. 958)
anafilaxis reacción alérgica grave que produce rigidez de las vías aéreas y el drenaje de líquido de los vasos sanguíneos.

angiosperm (AN-jee-uh-SPURM) seed plant whose embryos are enclosed by fruit. (p. 621)
angiosperma planta cuyos embriones se encuentran encerrados en el fruto.

Glossary

anthropoid humanlike primate. (p. 380)
   antropoide primate semejante al ser humano.

antibiotic chemical that kills or slows the growth of bacteria. (p. 564)
   antibiótico compuesto químico que mata o inhibe el desarrollo de las bacterias.

antibiotic resistance process by which bacteria mutate so that they are no longer affected by an antibiotic. (p. 955)
   resistencia antibiótica proceso mediante el cual una bacteria sufre mutaciones y para hacerse resistente a los antibióticos.

antibody protein produced by B cells that aids in the destruction of pathogens. (p. 947)
   anticuerpo proteína producida por las células B que contribuye a la destrucción de los patógenos.

anticodon set of three nucleotides in a tRNA molecule that binds to a complementary mRNA codon during translation. (p. 245)
   anticodón grupo de tres nucleótidos de la molécula de ARNt que se acopla a un codón complementario de ARNm durante la traslación.

antigen (AN-tih-juhn) protein marker that helps the immune system identify foreign particles. (p. 951)
   antígeno marcador proteico que ayuda al sistema immune a identificar sustancias extrañas tales como los virus.

antiseptic (AN-tih-SEHP-tihk) chemical, such as soap, vinegar, or rubbing alcohol, that destroys pathogens outside of the body. (p. 955)
   antiséptico compuesto químico, como el jabón, el vinagre o el alcohol, que destruyen los patógenos fuera del cuerpo.

apoptosis (AP-uhp-TOH-sihs) programmed cell death. (p. 145)
   apoptosis muerte celular programada.

appendage extension, such as an antenna or arm, that is attached to the body. (p. 730)
   apéndice prolongación del cuerpo, como una antena o un brazo, unida o contigua al mismo.

appendicular skeleton part of the skeletal system that allows for most of the body's movements; includes bones of the arms, shoulders, legs, and pelvis. (p. 1000)
   esqueleto apendicular parte del sistema esquelético que permite la mayor parte de los movimientos del cuerpo; consta, entre otros, de los huesos de los brazos, hombros, piernas y la pelvis.

arachnid terrestrial chelicerate, such as a spider. (p. 740)
   arácnido quelicerado terrestre, como la araña.

Archaea one of the three domains of life, containing single-celled prokaryotes in the kingdom Archaea. (p 534)
   Arqueas uno de los tres dominios de la vida, compuesto de procariontes unicelulares del reino Archaea.

artery large blood vessel that carries blood away from the heart. (p. 913)
   arteria gran vaso sanguíneo que transporta la sangre desde el corazón.

arthropod invertebrate with an exoskeleton, jointed appendages, and a segmented body. (p. 730)
   artrópodo invertebrado con exoesqueleto, apéndices articulados y cuerpo segmentado.

artificial selection process by which humans modify a species by breeding it for certain traits (p. 304)
   selección artificial proceso mediante el cual los seres humanos modifican una especie al criarla para obtener ciertos rasgos.

asexual reproduction process by which offspring are produced from a single parent; does not involve the joining of gametes. (p. 148)
   reproducción asexual proceso mediante el cual se producen descendientes de un solo progenitor, sin necesidad de la unión de gametos.

asthma (AZ-muh) condition in which air pathways in the lungs constrict, making breathing difficult. (p. 916)
   asma enfermedad que, al estrechar las vías aéreas de los pulmones, dificulta la respiración.

atmosphere air blanketing Earth's solid surface. (p. 456)
   atmósfera envoltura de aire que rodea la superficie sólida de la Tierra.

atom smallest basic unit of matter. (p. 36)
   átomo unidad básica más pequeña de la materia.

ATP *see* adenosene triphosphate. (p. 100)
   ATP *véase* adenosín trifosfato.

ATP synthase enzyme that catalyzes the reaction that adds a high-energy phosphate group to ADP to form ATP. (p. 110)
   ATP sintetasa enzima que cataliza la reacción para enlazar un grupo fosfato de alta energía al ADP y formar así el ATP.

atrium (plural: *atria*) small chamber in the human heart that receives blood from the veins. (p. 917)
   aurícula pequeña cavidad del corazón humano que recibe sangre de las venas.

autonomic nervous system division of the peripheral nervous system that controls involuntary functions. (p. 890)
   sistema nervioso autónomo parte del sistema nervioso periférico que controla las funciones involuntarias.

autosome chromosome that contains genes for characteristics not directly related to the sex of the organism. (p. 169)
   autosoma cromosoma cuyos genes no rigen los rasgos relacionados directamente con el sexo del organismo.

autotroph organism that obtains its energy from abiotic sources, such as sunlight or inorganic chemicals. (p. 406)
   autótrofo organismo que obtiene su energía a partir de fuentes abióticas como, por ejemplo, la luz solar o sustancias inorgánicas.

auxin (AWK-sihn) plant hormone that stimulates the lengthening of cells in the growing tip. (p. 681)
auxina hormona vegetal que estimula la elongación de las células y regula el crecimiento de las plantas.

axial skeleton part of the skeletal system that supports the body's weight and protects the body's internal tissues; includes the bones of the skull, spinal column, and rib cage. (p. 1001)
esqueleto axial parte del sistema esquelético que da soporte al peso corporal y que protege los tejidos internos del organismo; consta de los huesos del cráneo, la columna vertebral y la caja torácica.

axon long extension of the neuron membrane that carries impulses from one neuron to another. (p. 876)
axón prolongación de la membrana de la neurona que transmite impulsos eléctricos de una neurona a otra.

B

Bacteria one of the three domains of life, containing single-celled prokaryotes in the kingdom Bacteria. (p. 534)
Bacteria uno de los tres dominios en los que se dividen los seres vivos, que consta de procariontes unicelulares del reino Bacteria.

bacteriophage virus that infects bacteria. (pp. 228; 549)
bacteriófago virus que infecta a las bacterias.

bacterium (plural: *bacteria*) organism that is within the kingdom Bacteria. (p. 534)
bacteria organismo perteneciento al reino Bacteria.

base compound that accepts a proton (H^+) when dissolved in solution. (p. 42)
base compuesto que al disolverlo en una solución acepta un protón (H^+).

base pairing rules rule that describes how nucleotides form bonds in DNA; adenine (A) always bonds with thymine (T), and guanine (G) always bonds with cytosine (C). (p. 232)
reglas de apareamiento de bases regla que describe cómo se enlazan los nucleótidos en el ADN; la adenina (A) siempre se enlaza con la timina (T), y la guanina (G) siempre se enlaza con la citosina (C).

bathyal zone (BATH-ee-uhl) zone of the ocean that extends from the edge of the neritic zone to the base of the continental shelf. (p. 469)
zona batial region oceánica que se extiende desde el límite de la zona nerítica hasta la base de la plataforma continental.

B cell white blood cell that matures in the bone marrow and produces antibodies that fight off infection; also called a B-lymphocyte. (p. 946)
célula B glóbulo blanco que madura en la médula osea y que produce los anticuerpos que combaten las infecciones; también se conoce como linfocito B.

behavioral isolation isolation between populations due to differences in courtship or mating behavior. (p. 345)
aislamiento etológico aislamiento entre poblaciones debido a diferencias en los rituales de cortejo o apareamiento.

benign having no dangerous effect on health, especially referring to an abnormal growth of cells that are not cancerous. (p. 146)
benigno que no tiene efectos graves sobre la salud; se refiere particularmente al crecimiento anormal de células que no son cancerosas.

benthic zone lake or pond bottom, where little to no sunlight can reach. (p. 474)
zona béntica fondo de un lago o estanque, adonde llega poca o ninguna luz.

bilateral symmetry body plan of some organisms in which the body can be divided equally along only one plane. (p. 701)
simetría bilateral se observa en los organismos que pueden dividirse en partes iguales a lo largo de un plano único.

bile fluid released by the liver and gallbladder into the small intestine that aids in the digestion and absorption of fats. (p. 980)
bilis fluido segregado por el hígado y almacenado en la vesícula biliar, y que es liberado al intestino delgado para facilitar la digestión y la absorción de las grasas.

binary fission (BY-nuh-ree FIHSH-uhn) asexual reproduction in which a cell divides into two equal parts. (p. 148)
fisión binaria reproducción asexual en la que una célula se divide en dos partes iguales.

binomial nomenclature naming system in which each species is given a two-part scientific name (genus and species) using Latin words. (p. 519)
nomenclatura binomial sistema de denominación de especies mediante el cual se les otorga un nombre científico que consta de dos palabras en latín (género y especie).

biodiversity variety of life within an area. (pp. 5; 403)
biodiversidad variedad de las formas de vida en una zona determinada.

biogeochemical cycle movement of a chemical through the biological and geological, or living and nonliving, parts of an ecosystem. (p. 413)
ciclo biogeoquímico movimiento de una sustancia química a través de los componentes biológicos y geológicos, o vivos e inertes, de un ecosistema.

biogeography study of the distribution of organisms around the world. (p. 311)
biogeografía estudio de la distribución de los organismos en el mundo.

bioinformatics use of computer databases to organize and analyze biological data. (p. 282)
bioinformática utilización de bases de datos de computación para organizar y analizar datos biológicos.

Glossary

biological clock internal mechanism that controls an animal's activity patterns. (p. 820)
reloj biológico mecanismo interno que controla el ritmo de actividad de un animal.

biology scientific study of all forms of life. (p. 5)
biología estudio científico de todas las formas de vida.

biomagnification condition of toxic substances being more concentrated in tissues of organisms higher on the food chain than ones lower in the food chain. (p. 495)
biomagnificación condición en la cual la concentración de sustancias tóxicas en los tejidos de los organismos que pertenecen a eslabones más altos de la cadena alimentaria es mayor que la concentración en los organismos de los eslabones más bajos.

biomass total dry mass of all organisms in a given area. (p. 417)
biomasa masa deshidratada total de todos los organismos de un área determinada.

biome regional or global community of organisms characterized by the climate conditions and plant communities that thrive there. (p. 397)
bioma comunidad regional o global de organismos caracterizada por las condiciones climáticas y el tipo de vegetación del área.

bioremediation process by which humans use living things to break down pollutants. (p. 561)
biorremediación proceso mediante el cual los seres humanos emplean organismos vivos para descomponer sustancias contaminantes.

biosphere all organisms and the part of Earth where they exist. (pp. 4; 456)
biosfera todos los seres vivos y las partes de la Tierra en las que existen.

biota collection of living things. (p. 456)
biota conjunto de seres vivos.

biotechnology use and application of living things and biological processes. (p. 26)
biotecnología aprovechamiento y aplicación de los seres vivos y de sus procesos biológicos.

biotic living things, such as plants, animals, fungi, and bacteria. (p. 402)
biótico referente a los seres vivos, tales como las plantas, los animales, los hongos y las bacterias.

bipedal animal that walks on two legs. (p. 381)
bípedo animal que camina sobre dos patas.

blade broad part of a leaf where most of the photosynthesis of a plant takes place. (p. 652)
lámina parte ancha de la hoja donde ocurre la mayor parte de la fotosíntesis de una planta.

blastocyst stage of development during which the zygote consists of a ball of cells. (p. 1034)
blastocisto fase de desarrollo en la que el cigoto consta de células apelotonadas.

blood pressure force with which blood pushes against the wall of an artery. (p. 923)
presión sanguínea fuerza que ejerce la sangre contra las paredes de las arterias.

bond energy amount of energy needed to break a bond between two particular atoms; or the amount of energy released when a bond forms between two particular atoms. (p. 51)
energía de enlace energía necesaria para romper un enlace entre dos partículas atómicas; energía liberada al formarse un enlace entre dos átomos determinados.

book lung respiratory organ that has several membranes that are arranged like the pages in a book. (p. 740)
pulmón en libro órgano respiratorio compuesto por una serie de membranas dispuestas como las páginas de un libro.

botany study of plants. (p. 629)
botánica estudio de las plantas.

bottleneck effect genetic drift that results from an event that drastically reduces the size of a population. (p. 336)
efecto de cuello de botella deriva genética resultante de un acontecimiento que reduce drásticamente el tamaño de una población.

brain stem structure that connects the brain to the spinal cord and controls breathing and heartbeat. (p. 888)
tronco del encéfalo estructura que conecta el cerebro con la médula espinal y que controla la respiración y los latidos del corazón.

C

calcification process that hardens bones by adding calcium phosphate and collagen. (p. 1005)
calcificación proceso que endurece los huesos mediante depósitos de fosfato cálcico y colágeno.

Calorie measure of energy released from digesting food; one Calorie equals one kilocalorie of heat. (p. 975)
caloría medida de energía liberada al digerir la comida; una caloría equivale a una kilocaloría de calor.

Calvin cycle process by which a photosynthetic organism uses energy to synthesize simple sugars from CO_2. (p. 111)
ciclo de Calvin proceso mediante el cual un organismo fotosintético usa energía para sintetizar monosacáridos a partir del CO_2.

Cambrian explosion earliest part of the Paleozoic era, when a huge diversity of animal species evolved. (p. 376)
explosión Cámbrica periodo inicial de la era paleozoica, en la que surgió una enorme diversidad de especies animales.

cancer common name for a class of diseases characterized by uncontrolled cell division. (p. 146)
cáncer nombre común de una clase de enfermedades caracterizadas por una división descontrolada de las células.

canopy dense covering formed by the uppermost branches of trees. (p. 464)
cobertura arbórea tupido entramado formado por las ramas más altas de los árboles.

capillary tiny blood vessel that transports blood between larger blood vessels and other tissues in the body. (p. 913)
capilar diminuto vaso sanguíneo que transporta la sangre entre vasos sanguíneos más grandes y otros tejidos del cuerpo.

capsid protein shell that surrounds a virus. (p. 547)
cápsida cubierta proteica que envuelve al virus.

carapace (KAR-uh-PAYS) plate of exoskeleton that covers the head and thorax of a crustacean. (p. 735)
caparazón parte del exoesqueleto de los crustáceos que cubre la cabeza y el tórax.

carbohydrate molecule composed of carbon, hydrogen, and oxygen; includes sugars and starches. (p. 45)
carbohidrato molécula compuesta de carbono, hidrógeno y oxígeno; incluye los azúcares y los almidones.

carcinogen substance that produces or promotes the development of cancer. (p. 146)
carcinógeno sustancia que estimula o contribuye a inducir el cáncer.

cardiac muscle muscle tissue that is only found in the heart. (p. 1008)
músculo cardíaco tejido muscular, también conocido como miocardio, que sólo se halla en el corazón.

carnivore organism that obtains energy by eating only animals. (p. 409)
carnívoro organismo que obtiene energía al alimentarse únicamente de otros animales.

carpel female structure of flowering plants; made of the ovary, style, and stigma. (p. 668)
carpelo estructura reproductora femenina de las plantas con flor; consta de ovario, estilo y stigma.

carrier organism whose genome contains a gene for a certain trait or disease that is not expressed in the organism's phenotype. (p. 201)
portador organismo cuyo genoma contiene un gen de cierto rasgo o enfermedad que no se encuentra expresado en el fenotipo de dicho organismo.

carrying capacity number of individuals that the resources of an environment can normally and persistently support. (p. 442)
capacidad de carga de población número de individuos que los recursos de un ambiente pueden sustentar normalmente de manera continua.

cartilage tough, elastic, and fibrous connective tissue found between bones. (p. 1001)
cartílago tejido conectivo resistente, fibroso y elástico que se encuentra entre los huesos.

catalyst (KAT-uhl-ihst) substance that decreases activation energy and increases reaction rate in a chemical reaction. (p. 54)
catalizador sustancia que disminuye la energía de activación y aumenta la tasa de reacción de una reacción química determinada.

catastrophism theory that states that natural disasters such as floods and volcanic eruptions shaped Earth's landforms and caused extinction of some species. (p. 301)
catastrofismo teoría según la cual la configuración actual de los accidentes geográficos de la Tierra y la extinción de algunas especies se debió a inundaciones, erupciones volcánicas y otras catástrofes naturales.

cell basic unit of life. (p. 5)
célula unidad básica de la vida.

cell cycle pattern of growth, DNA replication, and cell division that occurs in a eukaryotic cell. (p. 134)
ciclo celular proceso de crecimiento, replicación de ADN y división celular que ocurre en las células eucarióticas.

cell differentiation processes by which unspecialized cells develop into their mature form and function. (p. 152)
diferenciación celular proceso mediante el cual las células no especializadas adquieren una forma y una función determinada.

cell membrane double-layer of phospholipids that forms a boundary between a cell and the surrounding environment and controls the passage of materials into and out of a cell. (p. 81)
membrana celular capa doble de fosfolípidos que forma una barrera entre la célula y el medio que la rodea, y que controla el flujo de materiales hacia dentro y hacia fuera de la célula.

cell theory theory that states that all organisms are made of cells, all cells are produced by other living cells, and the cell is the most basic unit of life. (p. 71)
teoría celular establece que todos los organismos están formados por células, que todas las células proceden de otras células vivas y que la célula es la unidad básica de la vida.

cellular immunity immune response that relies on T cells to destroy infected body cells. (p. 952)
inmunidad celular respuesta inmune que depende de las células T para atacar las células infectadas del cuerpo.

cellular respiration process of producing ATP by breaking down carbon-based molecules when oxygen is present. (p. 113)
respiración celular proceso de producción de ATP mediante la descomposición de moléculas de carbono en presencia de oxígeno.

cell wall rigid structure that gives protection, support, and shape to cells in plants, algae, fungi, and bacteria. (p. 79)
pared celular estructura rígida que proteje, sustenta y da forma a las células de las plantas, algas, hongos y bacterias.

Glossary

Cenozoic geologic time period that began 65 million years ago and continues today. (p. 378)
  Cenozoico período geológico que empezó hace 65 millones de años y que se extiende hasta la actualidad.

central dogma theory that states that, in cells, information only flows from DNA to RNA to proteins. (p. 239)
  dogma central teoría que formula que la información en las células siempre fluye del ADN al ARN y luego a las proteínas.

central nervous system (CNS) part of the nervous system that interprets messages from other nerves in the body; includes the brain and spinal cord. (p. 875)
  sistema nervioso central parte del sistema nervioso encargada de interpretar los mensajes recibidos de otros nervios del cuerpo; consta del cerebro y de la médula espinal.

centriole (SEHN-tree-OHL) small cylinder-shaped organelle made of protein tubes arranged in a circle; aids mitosis. (p. 78)
  centriolo orgánulo celular con forma de pequeño cilindro formado por una serie de tubos de proteínas en disposición circular; participa en la reproducción celular.

centromere (SEHN-truh-MEER) region of condensed chromosome that looks pinched; where spindle fibers attach during meiosis and mitosis. (p. 139)
  centrómero región de condensación del cromosoma donde se une el huso durante la meiosis y la mitosis.

cephalothorax (SEHF-uh-luh-THAWR-AKS) region of a crustacean body where the head and thorax meet. (p. 735)
  cefalotórax región del cuerpo de los crustáceos donde se unen la cabeza y el tórax.

cerebellum (SEHR-uh-BEHL-uhm) part of the brain that coordinates and regulates all voluntary muscle movement and maintains posture and balance. (p. 888)
  cerebelo parte del encéfalo que coordina y regula todos los movimientos musculares voluntarios, y que permite mantener la postura y el equilibrio.

cerebral cortex layer of gray matter on the surface of the cerebrum that receives information and generates responses. (p. 887)
  corteza cerebral capa de material gris situada en la superficie del cerebro que se encarga de recibir información y de generar respuestas.

cerebrum (SEHR-uh-bruhm) largest part of the brain, coordinating movement, thought, reasoning, and memory; includes the cerebral cortex and the white matter beneath it. (p. 886)
  cerebro la parte más grande del encéfalo que se encarga de coordinar el movimiento, el pensamiento, el razonamiento y la memoria; incluye la corteza cerebral y la materia blanca que se encuentra debajo de ésta.

chaparral (SHAP-uh-RAL) biome characterized by hot, dry summers and cool, moist winters; also called Mediterranean shrubland. (p. 466)
  chaparral bioma caracterizado por veranos secos y calurosos e inviernos frescos y húmedos; también se conoce como matorral mediterráneo.

chelicerate arthropod that lacks antennae and has four pairs of walking legs and a pair of fanglike mouth parts. (p. 740)
  quelicerado artrópodo sin antenas con cuatro pares de patas y una boca de dos piezas en forma de colmillos.

chemical reaction process by which substances change into different substances through the breaking and forming of chemical bonds. (p. 50)
  reacción química proceso mediante el cual una sustancia se transforma en otra sustancia diferente al romperse sus enlaces químicos y formarse otros nuevos.

chemosynthesis (KEE-mo-SIHN-thih-sihs) process by which ATP is synthesized by using chemicals as an energy source instead of light. (pp. 102, 407)
  quimiosíntesis proceso de síntesis del ATP cuya fuente de energía no es la luz, sino determinadas sustancias químicas.

childhood period of life from age two until puberty. (p. 1042)
  infancia periodo de la vida comprendido entre los dos años y la pubertad.

chitin tough, protective polysaccharide that makes up arthropod skeletons and the cell walls of some fungi. (pp. 589; 730)
  quitina polisacárido duro que forma los exoesqueletos de los artrópodos y las paredes celulares de algunos hongos.

chlorophyll (KLAWR-uh-fihl) light-absorbing pigment molecule in photosynthetic organisms. (p. 103)
  clorofila molécula pigmentaria de los organismos fotosintéticos que absorbe la luz.

chloroplast (KLAWR-uh-PLAST) organelle composed of numerous membranes that are used to convert solar energy into chemical energy; contains chlorophyll. (p. 79)
  colorplasto orgánulo compuesto de numerosas membranes cuya funcción es transformer la energía solar en energía química; contiene clorofila.

chordate any animal having, at some stage in development, a hollow nerve cord, pharyngeal slits, and tail. (p. 758)
  cordado todo tipo de animal que en alguna fase de su desarrollo tiene un cordón nervioso dorsal, hendiduras faríngeas y cola.

chromatid (KROH-muh-tihd) one half of a duplicated chromosome. (p. 139)
  cromátida mitad de un cromosoma duplicado.

chromatin loose combination of DNA and proteins that is present during interphase. (p. 139)
  cromatina conjunto de ADN y proteínas que se manifiesta durante la interfase.

chromosome long, continuous thread of DNA that consists of numerous genes and regulatory information. (p. 138)
  cromosoma un largo y continuo filamento de ADN formado por numerosos genes y que almacena información genética.

chyme (kym) partially digested, semi-liquid mixture that passes from the stomach to the small intestine. (p. 979)
quimo mezcla semi líquida parcialmente digerida que pasa del estómago al intestino delgado.

cilia (singular: *cilium*) short hairlike structures that cover some or all of the cell surface and help the organism swim and capture food. (p. 578)
cilios estructuras en forma de pelillos cortos que cubren total o parcialmente la superficie de determinadas células y que ayuda a los organismos a nadar y capturar alimentos.

circadian rhythm daily cycle of activity that occurs over a 24-hour period of time. (p. 820)
ritmo circadiano ciclo diario de actividad que abarca 24 horas.

circulatory system body system that transports nutrients and wastes between various body tissues; includes heart, blood, and blood vessels. (p. 910)
sistema circulatorio sistema corporal encargado de transportar nutrientes y desechos entre diversos tejidos corporales; consta del corazón, la sangre y los vasos sanguíneos.

citric acid cycle *see* Krebs cycle. (p. 115)
ciclo del ácido cítrico *véase* ciclo de Krebs.

cladistics method of organizing species by evolutionary relationships in which species are grouped according to the order that they diverged from their ancestral line. (p. 525)
cladismo método de clasificación de las especies según su parentesco evolutivo en el que las especies son agrupadas en el orden en que se separaron de su linaje ancestral.

cladogram diagram that displays proposed evolutionary relationships among a group of species. (p. 525)
cladograma diagrama en el que se presentan los parentescos evolutivos propuestos de un grupo determinado de especies.

classical conditioning process by which an organism learns to associate a previously neutral stimulus with a reward or punishment. (p. 826)
condicionamiento clásico proceso mediante el cual un organismo aprende a asociar un estímulo, que previamente había sido neutro, con un premio o castigo.

climate average long-term weather pattern of a region. (p. 458)
clima promedio de valores del tiempo en una región a largo plazo.

clone genetically identical copy of a single gene or an entire organism. (p. 275)
clon copia genéticamente exacta de un gen o de un organismo completo.

codominance heterozygous genotype that equally expresses the traits from both alleles. (p. 205)
codominancia genotipo heterocigoto que expresa equitativamente los rasgos de ambos alelos.

codon sequence of three nucleotides that codes for one amino acid. (p. 243)
codón secuencia de tres nucleotides que codifica un aminoácido.

coelom fluid-filled space that is completely covered by muscle. (p. 714)
celoma cavidad llena de líquido cubierta enteramente por el músculo.

coevolution process in which two or more species evolve in response to changes in each other. (p. 349)
coevolución proceso mediante el cual dos o más especies evolucionan a consecuencia de cambios producidos en cada uno de ellas.

cognition mental process of knowing, including aspects such as awareness, perception, reasoning, and judgment. (p. 837)
cognición conjunto de procesos mentales cuya función es el conocimiento y que incluyen la conciencia, la percepción, el razonamiento y el juicio.

cohesion attraction between molecules of the same substance. (p. 41)
cohesión atracción entre moléculas de una misma sustancia.

cohesion tension theory theory that explains how the physical properties of water allow it to move through the xylem of plants. (p. 643)
teoría de la tensión-cohesión teoría que explica el modo en que las propiedades físicas del agua permiten que ésta fluya a través del xilema de las plantas.

collagen three-stranded protein, unique to animals, that combines to form strong, flexible fibers. (p. 697)
colágeno proteína animal compuesta por tres cadenas que se enlazan para formar fibras resistentes y flexibles.

collenchyma cell elongated cells with unevenly thick walls that form a supportive tissue of plants. (p. 640)
célula del colénquima célula alargada con paredes de grosor irregular que forma el tejido de sostén de las plantas.

commensalism ecological relationship in which one species receives a benefit but the other species is not affected one way or another. (p. 432)
comensalismo relación ecológica entre dos especies en la que una se beneficia sin perjudicar ni beneficiar a la otra.

community collection of all of the different populations that live in one area. (p. 397)
comunidad conjunto de todas las poblaciones que viven en un área determinada.

competition ecological relationship in which two organisms attempt to obtain the same resource. (p. 431)
competencia relación ecológica en la que dos organismos tratan de obtener el mismo recurso.

competitive exclusion theory that states that no two species can occupy the same niche at the same time. (p. 429)
exclusión competitiva teoría según la cual dos especies distintas no pueden ocupar el mismo nicho al mismo tiempo.

complete digestive tract digestive system that has two openings, a mouth and an anus, that are at opposite ends of a continuous tube. (p. 712)
tubo digestivo completo sistema digestivo con dos aperturas, la boca y el ano, situadas en los extremos opuestos de un tubo continuo.

complete metamorphosis process by which immature organisms change their body form before becoming an adult. (p. 744)
metamorfosis completa proceso mediante el cual se van produciendo cambios en los organismos inmaduros antes de llegar a adultos.

compound substance made of atoms of different elements that are bonded together in a particular ratio. (p. 37)
compuesto sustancia formada por átomos de diversos elementos combinados en una proporción determinada.

concentration gradient difference in the concentration of a substance from one location to another. (p. 85)
gradiente de concentración diferencia en la concentración de una sustancia entre un lugar y otro.

cone reproductive structure of gymnosperms inside of which the female gamete is fertilized and seeds are produced. (p. 621)
cono estructura reproductora de las gimnospermas en cuyo interior se fertiliza el gameto femenino y se producen semillas.

cone cell sensory neuron in the eye that detects color. (p. 881)
cono (célula) neurona sensorial del ojo que detecta el color.

coniferous tree that retains its needles year-round and reproduces with cones. (p. 465)
conífera árbol que mantiene sus hojas durante todo el año y que se reproduce mediante conos.

conjugation process by which a prokaryote transfers part of its chromosome to another prokaryote. (p. 558)
conjugación proceso mediante el cual un procarionte transfiere parte de su cromosoma a otro procarionte.

constant condition that is controlled so that it does not change during an experiment. (p. 16)
constante condición controlada de un experimento que no varía en el transcurso del mismo.

consumer organism that obtains its energy and nutrients by eating other organisms. (p. 406)
consumidor organismo que obtiene su energía y nutrientes mediante la ingestión de otros organismos.

convergent evolution evolution toward similar characteristics in unrelated species, resulting from adaptations to similar environmental conditions. (p. 348)
evolución convergente evolución hacia características similares en especies no relacionadas, que resulta de adaptaciones a condiciones ambientales similares.

coral reef ocean habitat found in the shallow coastal waters in a tropical climate. (p. 470)
arrecife de coral hábitat oceánico que se encuentra en aguas costeras poco profundas de climas tropicales.

corpus luteum (KAWR-puhs LOO-tee-uhm) follicle after ovulation; also called a yellow body because of its yellow color. (p. 1029)
cuerpo lúteo folículo que aparece después de la ovulación; se conoce también como cuerpo amarillo a causa de su color.

cotyledon (KAHT-uhl-EED-uhn) embryonic leaf inside of a seed. (p. 625)
cotiledón hoja embriónica que se forma en el interior de la semilla.

countercurrent flow flow of water opposite that of the flow of blood in a fish's gills. (p. 764)
flujo contracorriente flujo de agua en sentido opuesto al flujo de la sangre en las branquias de los peces.

covalent bond chemical bond formed when two atoms share one or more pairs of electrons. (p. 39)
enlace covalente enlace químico que se forma cuando dos átomos comparten uno o más pares de electrones.

cross mating of two organisms. (p. 178)
cruzamiento apareamiento de dos organismos.

crossing over exchange of chromosome segments between homologous chromosomes during meiosis I. (p. 190)
entrecruzamiento intercambio de segmentos de cromosomas entre cromosomas homólogos durante la meiosis I.

crustacean any of the aquatic arthropods, such as lobsters, crabs, and shrimps, that has a segmented body, an exoskeleton, and paired, jointed limbs. (p. 735)
crustáceo artrópodo acuático, como las langostas, los cangrejos y los camarones, que se caracteriza por tener un cuerpo segmentado, un exoesqueleto y pares de extremidades articuladas.

cultural behavior behavior that is passed between members of the same population by learning and not natural selection. (p. 839)
comportamiento cultural comportamiento que se transmite entre los miembros de una misma población, no por selección natural, sino mediante un proceso de aprendizaje.

cuticle in plants, a waxy layer that holds in moisture; in insects, a tough exoskeleton made of nonliving material. (pp. 614; 716)
cutícula en las plantas, es una capa de cera que mantiene la humedad; en los insectos, exoesqueleto duro de material inerte.

cyanobacteria (singular: *cyanobaterium*) bacteria that can carry out photosynthesis. (p. 372)
cianobacteria bacteria capaz de realizar la fotosíntesis.

cytokinesis (SY-toh-kuh-NEE-sihs) process by which the cell cytoplasm divides. (p. 135)
citocinesis proceso mediante el cual el citoplasma celular se divide.

cytokinin (sy-tuh-KY-nihn) plant hormone that stimulates the final stage of cell division, cytokinesis; also involved in the growth of side branches. (p. 681)

citoquinina hormona vegetal que estimula la última fase de la división celular: la citocinesis; también participa en el crecimiento de las ramas laterales.

cytoplasm jellylike substance inside cells that contains molecules and in some cells organelles. (p. 72)

citoplasma sustancia gelatinosa del interior de las células que contiene diversos tipos de moléculas y, en algunas células, orgánulos.

cytoskeleton network of proteins, such as microtubules and microfilaments, inside a eukaryotic cell that supports and shapes the cell. (p. 73)

citoesqueleto red proteica, como los microtúbulos y los microfilamentos, dentro de una célula eucariótica que da soporte y define la forma de la célula.

D

data (singular: *datum*) observations and measurements recorded during an experiment. (p. 14)

datos observaciones y medidas registrados en el transcurso de un experimento.

deciduous tree that has adapted to winter temperatures by dropping its leaves and going dormant during the cold season. (p. 465)

caducifolio árbol que pierde su foliaje y entra en un período de letargo para adaptarse a las temperaturas invernales.

decomposer detritivore that breaks down organic matter into simpler compounds, returning nutrients back into an ecosystem. (p. 409)

descomponedor detritívoro que, al descomponer la materia orgánica en compuestos más sencillos, devuelve al ecosistema sus nutrientes básicos.

dendrite branchlike extension of a neuron that receives impulses from neighboring neurons. (p. 876)

dendrita prolongación ramificada de la neurona que recibe impulsos eléctricos de las neuronas adyacentes.

density-dependent limiting factor environmental resistance that affects a population that has become overly crowded. (p. 443)

factor limitativo dependiente de la densidad resistencia ambiental que afecta a una población sometida a una densidad demográfica excesiva.

density-independent limiting factor environmental resistance that affects a population regardless of population density. (p. 444)

factor limitativo independiente de la densidad resistencia ambiental que afecta a una población sin importar su densidad demográfica.

dependent variable experimental data collected through observation and measurement. (p. 16)

variable dependiente datos de una investigación recolectados por medio de la observación y de la medición.

depressant drug that causes fewer signals to be transmitted between neurons. (p. 894)

depresor medicamento que reduce la transmisión de señales entre las neuronas.

derived characteristic trait that differs in structure or function from that found in the ancestral line for a group of species; used in constructing cladograms. (p. 525)

caracter derivado rasgo que difiere, en su estructura o función, del hallado en un linaje ancestral de un grupo de especies; se usa para crear cladogramas.

dermal tissue tissue system that covers the outside of plants and animals. (p. 642)

tejido dérmico sistema de tejidos que cubre la superficie de los animales y las plantas.

dermis second layer of skin that includes structural proteins, blood vessels, glands, and hair follicles. (p. 1015)

dermis segunda capa de piel formada por proteínas estructurales, vasos sanguíneos y folículos capilares.

desensitization process by which neurons in the brain break down neurotransmitter receptors in response to a larger amount of neurotransmitter in the synapse than usual. (p. 893)

desensibilización proceso mediante el cual las neuronas del cerebro inactivan los receptores de los neurotransmisores como respuesta a una cantidad de neurotransmisores mayor de lo habitual en la sinapsis.

desert biome characterized by a very dry climate. (p. 464)

desierto bioma caracterizado por un clima muy seco.

determination process by which stem cells become committed to develop into only one type of cell. (p. 852)

determinación celular proceso mediante el cual las células madre se desarrollan en un tipo específico de célula.

detritivore organism that eats dead organic matter. (p. 409)

detritívoro organismo que se alimenta de materia orgánica muerta.

deuterostome animal development in which the animal's anus develops before the mouth. (p. 702)

deuterostomia desarrollo animal en el que el ano del animal se desarrolla antes que la boca.

dialysis treatment in which a patient's blood is filtered through a machine, the waste is removed, and the cleaned blood is returned to the patient's body. (p. 991)

diálisis tratamiento médico que consiste en filtrar la sangre del paciente mediante una máquina que elimina los desechos y devuelve la sangre purificada al cuerpo del paciente.

diaphragm thin muscle below the rib cage that controls the flow of air into and out of the lungs. (p. 912)

diafragma músculo delgado situado debajo de la caja torácica que controla el flujo de aire hacia el interior y el exterior de los pulmones.

Glossary

diastolic pressure (DY-uh-STAHL-ihk) pressure in an artery when the left ventricle relaxes. (p. 923)
presión diastólica presión en la artería en el momento en que se relaja el ventrículo izquierdo.

dicot (DY-KAHT) flowering plant whose embryos have two cotyledons. (p. 626)
dicotiledónea planta con flor cuyos embriones tienen dos cotiledones.

differentiation process by which committed cells acquire the structures and functions of highly specialized cells. (p. 853)
diferenciación celular proceso mediante el cual ciertas células adquieren estructuras y funciones altamente especializadas.

diffusion movement of dissolved molecules in a fluid or gas from a region of higher concentration to a region of lower concentration. (p. 85)
difusión movimiento de las moléculas disueltas en un líquido o gas desde una región de alta concentración a otra región de menor concentración.

digestion process by which large, complex molecules are broken down into smaller molecules that can be used by cells. (p. 977)
digestión proceso mediante el cual grandes y complejas moléculas se descomponen en moléculas más pequeñas que pueden ser absorbidas por las células.

digestive system body system that digests food; includes mouth, esophagus, stomach, pancreas, intestines, liver, gallbladder, rectum, and anus. (p. 977)
sistema digestivo sistema corporal encargado de la digestión de los alimentos; consta de la boca, el esófago, el estómago, el páncreas, los intestinos, el hígado, la vesícula biliar, el recto y el ano.

dihybrid cross cross, or mating, between organisms involving two pairs of contrasting traits. (p. 186)
cruzamiento dihíbrido cruzamiento o apareamiento entre organismos que tienen dos pares de rasgos opuestos.

diploid (DIHP-LOYD) cell that has two copies of each chromosome, one from an egg and one from a sperm. (p. 170)
diploide celula que tiene dos copias de cada cromosoma, una proveniente de un óvulo y la otra de un espermatozoide.

directional selection pathway of natural selection in which one uncommon phenotype is selected over a more common phenotype. (p. 331)
selección direccional proceso de selección natural en el que se favorece un fenotipo menos común sobre un fenotipo más común.

disruptive selection pathway of natural selection in which two opposite, but equally uncommon, phenotypes are selected over the most common phenotype. (p. 333)
selección disruptiva proceso de selección natural en el que se favorece a dos fenotipos opuestos, pero igualmente poco comunes, sobre el fenotipo común.

divergent evolution evolution of one or more closely related species into different species; resulting from adaptations to different environmental conditions. (p. 348)
evolución divergente evolución de una o más especies afines que lleva a la formación de especies diferentes como resultado de adaptaciones a diversas condiciones ambientales.

DNA; deoxyribonucleic acid (dee-AHK-see-RY-boh-noo-KLEE-ihk) molecule that stores genetic information in all organisms. (p. 6)
ADN (ácido desoxirribonucleico) molécula que almacena la información genética de todos los organismos.

DNA fingerprint unique sequence of DNA base pairs that can be used to identify a person at the molecular level. (p. 272)
identificación por ADN secuencia única de pares de bases de ADN que permite la identificación de una persona a nivel molecular.

DNA microarray research tool used to study gene expression. (p. 282)
micromatriz de material genético (biochip) instrumento de investigación usado para estudiar la expresión de los genes.

DNA polymerase (PAHL-uh-muh-RAYS) enzyme that makes bonds between nucleotides, forming an identical strand of DNA during replication. (p. 236)
ADN polimerasa enzima que establece enlaces entre los nucleótidos y que permite la formación de cadenas idénticas de ADN durante el proceso de replicación.

dominant allele that is expressed when two different alleles are present in an organism's genotype. (p. 181)
dominante el alelo que se expresa de entre dos alelos diferentes que integran el genotipo de un organismo determinado.

dormancy state of inactivity during which an organism or embryo is not growing. (p. 674)
letargo periodo de inactividad durante el cual un organismo o embrión no crece.

double fertilization process by which two sperm of a flowering plant join with an egg and a polar body, forming an embryo and endosperm. (p. 670)
fertilización doble proceso mediante el cual dos gametos masculinos de una planta angiosperma se combinan con un óvulo y un núcleo polar para dar lugar al embrión y al endosperma.

double helix model that compares the structure of a DNA molecule, in which two strands wind around one another, to that of a twisted ladder. (p. 232)
doble hélice modelo mediante el cual se representa la estructura molecular del ADN como dos cadenas que giran sobre sí mismas, como una escalera espiroidal.

E

ecological equivalents organisms that share a similar niche but live in different geographical regions. (p. 430)
equivalentes ecológicos organismos que tienen nichos ecológicos similares, pero que viven en diferentes zonas geográficas.

ecological footprint amount of land necessary to produce and maintain enough food, water, shelter, energy, and waste. (p. 487)
huella ecológica espacio que requiere una población humana para producir y mantener suficiente alimento, agua, alojamiento y energía, y para contener sus desperdicios.

ecological niche all of the physical, chemical, and biological factors that a species needs to survive, stay healthy, and reproduce in an ecosystem. (p. 428)
nicho ecológico conjunto de factores físicos, químicos y biológicos que una especie requiere para sobrevivir de manera saludable y reproducirse en un ecosistema determinado.

ecology study of the interactions among living things and their surroundings. (p. 396)
ecología estudio de las interacciones entre los seres vivos y su entorno.

ecosystem collection of organisms and nonliving things, such as climate, soil, water, and rocks, in an area. (pp. 7; 397)
ecosistema conjunto de organismos y factores físicos, como el clima, el suelo, el agua y las rocas, que caracterizan una zona determinada.

ectotherm organism that regulates its body temperature by exchanging heat with its environment. (p. 791)
poiquilotermo organismo que regula su temperatura corporal mediante el intercambio de calor con el ambiente.

egg female gamete. (p. 176)
óvulo gameto femenino.

electron transport chain series of proteins in the thylakoid and mitochondrial membranes that aid in converting ADP to ATP by transferring electrons. (p. 109)
cadena de transporte de electrones serie de proteínas de las membranas de las mitocondrias y los tilacoides que contribuyen a transformar ADP en ATP mediante la transferencia de electrones.

element substance made of only one type of atom that cannot be broken down by chemical means. (p. 36)
elemento sustancia formada por un solo tipo de átomo que no se puede descomponer por medios químicos.

embryo stage of development after the fertilized cell implants into the uterus but before the cells take on a recognizable shape. (p. 1034)
embrión fase de desarrollo a partir de la implantación del óvulo fertilizado en el útero, anterior a la etapa en que las células adquieren una forma reconocible.

emigration movement of individuals out of a population. (p. 440)
emigración flujo de individuos que abandonan una población.

emphysema (EHM-fih-SEE-muh) condition of the lungs in which the surface area of alveoli decreases, making breathing difficult. (p. 916)
enfisema enfermedad de los pulmones que causa una reducción en la superficie de los alvéolos y, en consecuencia, dificulta la respiración.

endocrine system (EHN-duh-krihn) body system that controls growth, development, and responses to the environment by releasing chemical signals into the bloodstream. (p. 874)
sistema endocrino sistema corporal que controla el crecimiento, el desarrollo y las respuestas al entorno, mediante la liberación de señales químicas al torrente sanguíneo.

endocytosis (EHN-doh-sy-TOH-sihs) uptake of liquids or large molecules into a cell by inward folding of the cell membrane. (p. 90)
endocitosis captación celular de líquidos o de grandes moléculas mediante una invaginación de la membrana hacia el interior de la célula.

endometrium (EHN-doh-MEE-tree-uhm) lining of the uterus. (p. 1028)
endometrio recubrimiento interior del útero.

endoplasmic reticulum (EHN-duh-PLAZ-mihk rih-TIHK-yuh-luhm) interconnected network of thin, folded membranes that produce, process, and distribute proteins. (p. 76)
retículo endoplasmático red de finas membranas interconectadas y plegadas que producen, procesan y distribuyen proteínas.

endoskeleton internal skeleton built of bone or cartilage. (p. 759)
endoesqueleto esqueleto interno formado por huesos y cartílagos.

endosperm tissue within seeds of flowering plants that nourishes an embryo. (p. 670)
endosperma tejido de reserva dentro de las semillas de las plantas con flor que abastece el embrión.

endospore prokaryotic cell with a thick, protective wall surrounding its DNA. (p. 558)
endospora célula procariótica cuyo ADN está protegido por una gruesa pared.

endosymbiosis ecological relationship in which one organism lives within the body of another. (p. 373)
endosimbiosis relación ecológica en la que un organismo vive en el interior de otro.

endotherm organism that produces its own heat through metabolic processes. (p. 791)
endotermo organismo que regula la temperatura de su cuerpo mediante sus propios procesos metabólicos.

Glossary

endothermic chemical reaction that requires a net input of energy. (p. 53)

endotérmica reacción química que requiere un aporte neto de energía.

energy pyramid diagram that compares energy used by producers, primary consumers, and other trophic levels. (p. 418)

pirámide de energía diagrama mediante el cual se compara la energía usada por los productores, los consumidores primarios y otros niveles tróficos.

enzyme protein that catalyzes chemical reactions for organisms. (p. 55)

enzima proteína que cataliza reacciones químicas para los organismos.

epidemic rapid outbreak of a disease that affects many people. (p. 553)

epidemia aparición repentina de una enfermedad que afecta a muchas personas.

epidermis outermost layer of skin that consists mainly of dead skin cells, and provides a barrier to pathogens. (p. 1014)

epidermis primera capa de piel, que consta principalmente de células epiteliales muertas y que constituye una barrera para los patógenos.

epididymis coiled tube through which sperm leave the testes and enter the vas deferens. (p. 1026)

epidídimo tubo enrollado a través del cuál los espermatozoides salen de los testículos y pasan al conducto deferente.

epoch smallest unit of geologic time, lasting several million years. (p. 367)

época unidad más pequeña de tiempo geológico, que dura varios millones de años.

equilibrium (EE-kwuh-LIHB-ree-uhm) condition in which reactants and products of a chemical reaction are formed at the same rate. (p. 51)

equilibrio químico estado en el que los reactivos y los productos de una reacción química se forman a la misma velocidad.

era second largest unit of geologic time, lasting tens to hundreds of millions of years and consisting of two or more periods. (p. 367)

era segunda unidad más amplia de tiempo geológico; que abarca entre decenas y cientos de millones de años y consta de dos o más períodos.

esophagus (ih-SAHF-uh-guhs) tube-shaped tissue of the digestive system that connects the mouth to the stomach. (p. 978)

esófago tejido en forma de tubo del sistema digestivo que conecta la boca con el estómago.

estrogen steroid hormone that is found in greater quantities in women than men and contributes to female sexual characteristics and development. (p. 1024)

estrógeno hormona esteroide que abunda más en las mujeres que en los hombres, y que contribuye al desarrollo de las características sexuales femeninas.

estuary partially enclosed body of water found where a river flows into the ocean. (p. 471)

estuario masa de agua parcialmente cerrada donde un río desemboca en el océano.

ethnobotany study of how various cultures use plants. (p. 629)

etnobotánica estudio del conocimiento que tienen las culturas sobre el uso de las plantas.

ethylene (EHTH-uh-LEEN) plant hormone that is produced in fruits and causes them to ripen. (p. 681)

etileno hormona vegetal que se produce en las frutas y que las hace madurar.

Eukarya one of the three domains of life, contains all eukaryotes in kingdoms Protista, Plantae, Fungi, and Animalia. (p. 534)

Eukarya uno de los tres dominios de la vida; consta de todos los eucariotas de los reinos protistas, plantashongos y animales.

eukaryotic cell (yoo-KAR-ee-AHT-ihk) cell that has a nucleus and other membrane-bound organelles. (p. 72)

célula eucariota célula que consta de un núcleo y de otros orgánulos limitados por una membrana.

eusocial organism population in which the role of each organism is specialized and not all of the organisms will reproduce. (p. 834)

eusocial población de organismos en la que todos tienen una función especializada y en la que algunos de ellos no se reproducen.

eutherian mammal that gives birth to live young that have completed fetal development. (p. 809)

euterio mamífero cuyas crías nacen tras un desarrollo fetal completo.

evolution change in a species over time (p. 10); process of biological change by which descendents come to differ from their ancestors. (p. 298)

evolución proceso de cambio de las especies a través del tiempo; proceso de cambios biológicos a través del cual los descendientes se diferencian de sus ancestros.

excretory system body system that collects and eliminates wastes from the body; includes the kidneys and bladder. (p. 986)

sistema excretor sistema corporal que recoge y elimina los desechos del organismo; consta de los riñones y la vejiga urinaria.

exocytosis (EHK-soh-sy-TOH-sihs) release of substances out a cell by the fusion of a vesicle with the membrane. (p. 91)

exocitosis expulsión de sustancias de una célula mediante la fusión de una vesícula citoplasmática con la membrana celular.

exon sequence of DNA that codes information for protein synthesis. (p. 251)

exón secuencia de ADN que codifica la información para la síntesis de las proteínas.

exoskeleton hard outer structure, such as the shell of an insect or crustacean, that provides protection and support for the organism. (p. 730)

exoesqueleto estructura exterior dura como, por ejemplo, el caparazón de un crustáceo, que protege y sustenta al organismo.

exothermic chemical reaction that yields a net release of energy in the form of heat. (p. 53)

exotérmica reacción química que, al producirse, libera energía en forma calor.

experiment process that tests a hypothesis by collecting information under controlled conditions. (p. 16)

experimento procedimiento mediante el cual se trata de comprobar una hipótesis mediante la recolección de datos bajo condiciones controladas.

exponential growth dramatic increase in population over a short period of time. (p. 441)

crecimiento exponencial intenso incremento de población en un breve espacio de tiempo.

extinction elimination of a species from Earth. (p. 350)

extinción desaparición de una especie o grupo de especies de la Tierra.

F

facilitated diffusion diffusion of molecules assisted by protein channels that pierce a cell membrane. (p. 87)

difusión facilitada difusión de moléculas asistida mediante canales de proteínas que perforan la membrana celular.

facultative aerobe organism that can live with or without oxygen. (p. 555)

aerobio facultativo organismo capaz de vivir con o sin oxígeno.

fallopian tube tube of connective tissue that attaches the ovary to the uterus in the female reproductive system and in which fertilization occurs. (p. 1024)

trompa de Falopio conducto de tejido conjuntivo que conecta el ovario con el útero en el sistema reproductor femenino, y donde se produce la fertilización.

fatty acid hydrocarbon chain often bonded to glycerol in a lipid. (p. 46)

ácido graso cadena de hidrocarbono que suele enlazarce con los glicéridos de un lípido.

feedback information that is compared with a set of ideal values and aids in maintaining homeostasis. (p. 859)

retroalimentación información que se compara con un grupo de valores ideales y que contribuye al mantenimiento de la homeóstasis.

fermentation anaerobic process by which ATP is produced by glycolysis. (p. 122)

fermentación proceso anaeróbico que da lugar al ATP mediante la glicólisis.

fertilization fusion of an egg and sperm cell. (p. 170)

fertilización fusión de un gameto masculino y uno femenino.

fetus unborn offspring from the end of the eighth week after conception to the moment of birth. (p. 1036)

feto cría no nacida desde el final de la octava semana después de la concepción hasta el momento del nacimiento.

fibrous root root system made up of many threadlike members of more or less equal length. (p. 649)

raíces fibrosas sistema radical compuesto de una multitud de filamentos que tienen una longitud aproximadamente igual.

filter feeder animal that eats by straining particles from water. (p. 706)

organismo filtrador animal que se alimenta mediante la filtración de partículas del agua.

fitness measure of an organism's ability to survive and produce offspring relative to other members of a population. (p. 307)

aptitud biológica capacidad de un organismo determinado para sobrevivir y producir descendencia en relación con los demás miembros de una población.

flagellum (plural: *flagella*) whiplike structure outside of a cell that is used for movement. (p. 556)

flagelo estructura en forma de látigo del exterior de determinadas células que les permite moverse en su medio.

flower reproductive structure of an angiosperm. (p. 622)

flor sistema reproductor de una angiosperma.

fluid mosaic model model that describes the arrangement and movement of the molecules that make up a cell membrane. (p. 82)

modelo de mosaico fluido modelo que describe la disposición y movimiento de las moléculas que conforman la membrana celular.

follicle collection of cells that surrounds and nourishes an egg while it is in the ovary. (p. 1028)

folículo conjunto de células que rodean y nutren al óvulo mientras éste permanece en el ovario.

food chain model that links organisms by their feeding relationships. (p. 408)

cadena alimentaria modelo que relaciona los organismos según sus interacciones alimentarias.

food web model that shows the complex network of feeding relationships within an ecosystem. (p. 411)

red alimentaria modelo que representa una red compleja de relaciones alimentarias en un ecosistema determinado.

fossil trace of an organism from the past. (p. 300)

fósil huella de un organismo del pasado.

Glossary

founder effect genetic drift that occurs after a small number of individuals colonize a new area. (p. 336)
 efecto fundador deriva genética que se produce cuando un pequeño número de individuos coloniza una nueva región.

frameshift mutation mutation that involves the insertion or deletion of a nucleotide in the DNA sequence. (p. 252)
 mutación del marco de lectura mutación que implica la incorporación o la eliminación de un nucleótido en una secuencia de ADN.

fruit fertilized and mature ovary of a flower. (p. 622)
 fruto ovario fertilizado y maduro de una flor.

fruiting body spore-producing structure of a fungus that grows above ground. (p. 590)
 esporocarpo estructura productora de esporas de un hongo que crece sobre la tierra.

G

gamete sex cell; an egg or a sperm cell. (p. 168)
 gameto célula sexual; óvulo o espermatozoide.

gametogenesis (guh-MEE-tuh-JEHN-ih-sihs) process by which gametes are produced through the combination of meiosis and other maturational changes. (p. 176)
 gametogénesis proceso de producción de gametos mediante una combinación de meiosis y otros cambios de maduración.

gametophyte (guh-MEE-tuh-FYT) haploid, gamete-producing phase in a plant life cycle. (p. 664)
 gametofito fase de producción de gametos o células sexuales haploides en el ciclo de vida de las plantas.

gastrovascular cavity saclike digestive space. (p. 708)
 cavidad gastrovascular espacio digestivo en forma de bolsa.

gel electrophoresis (ih-LEHK-troh-fuh-REE-sihs) method of separating various lengths of DNA strands by applying an electrical current to a gel. (p. 266)
 electroforesis en gel método de separación de fragmentos de ADN mediante la aplicación de una corriente eléctrica a un gel.

gene specific region of DNA that codes for a particular protein. (pp. 23; 180)
 gen parte específica del ADN con información codificada para sintetizar una proteína.

gene flow physical movement of alleles from one population to another. (p. 335)
 flujo génico desplazamiento físico de alelos de una población a otra.

gene knockout genetic manipulation in which one or more of an organism's genes are prevented from being expressed. (p. 279)
 supresión génica manipulación genética mediante la cual se anula la capacidad de expresarse de uno o más genes de un organismo determinado.

gene pool collection of alleles found in all of the individuals of a population. (p. 328)
 acervo genético colección de alelos de todos los individuos de una población determinada.

generalist species that does not rely on a single source of prey. (p. 409)
 generalista especie que no depende de un solo tipo de presa.

gene sequencing process of determining the order of DNA nucleotides in genes and genomes. (p. 280)
 secuenciación génica proceso de determinación del orden de los nucleótidos de ADN en los genes y en los genomas.

gene therapy procedure to treat a disease in which a defective or missing gene is replaced or a new gene is inserted into a patient's genome. (p. 285)
 terapia génica procedimiento para el tratamiento de una enfermedad en el que un gen defectuoso o ausente se reemplaza por uno sano que se inserta en el genoma del paciente.

genetic drift change in allele frequencies due to chance alone, occurring most commonly in small populations. (p. 336)
 deriva genética cambio en las frecuencias de alelos que se produce, sobre todo, en poblaciones pequeñas.

genetic engineering process of changing an organism's DNA to give the organism new traits. (p. 276)
 ingeniería genética proceso de modifación del ADN de un organismo con el fin de dotarlo de nuevos rasgos.

genetic linkage tendency for genes located close together on the same chromosome to be inherited together. (p. 191)
 ligamiento genético tendencia de los genes que se encuentran muy próximos en un cromosoma a ser transmitidos juntos a la descendencia.

genetics study of the heredity patterns and variation of organisms. (p. 177)
 genética estudio de los patrones hereditarios y de la variación de los organismos.

genetic screening process of testing DNA to determine the chance a person has, or might pass on, a genetic disorder. (p. 284)
 análisis genético proceso de análisis de ADN para determinar las probabilidades que tiene una persona de contraer o transmitir una enfermedad genética.

genome all of an organism's genetic material. (p. 181)
 genoma todo el material genético de un organismo determinado.

genomics (juh-NOH-mihks) study and comparison of genomes within a single species or among different species. (pp. 23, 280)
 genómica estudio comparativo de los genomas de una misma especie y de especies diferentes.

genotype (JEHN-uh-TYP) collection of all of an organism's genetic information that codes for traits. (p. 181)
 genotipo conjunto de todos los rasgos codificados en la información genética de un organismo.

genus first name in binomial nomenclature; the second-most specific taxon in the Linnaean classification system that includes one or more physically similar species, which are thought to be closely related. (p. 519)
género primera palabra de la nomenclatura binomial; segundo taxón más específico del sistema de clasificación de las especies de Linneo, que consta de dos o más especies físicamente semejantes consideradas muy próximas.

geographic isolation isolation between populations due to physical barriers. (p. 346)
aislamiento geográfico separación entre poblaciones debido a barreras físicas.

geologic time scale time scale representing the history of Earth. (p. 367)
escala de tiempo geológico escala de tiempo para representar la historia de la Tierra.

geosphere features of Earth's surface—such as continents and the sea floor—and everything below Earth's surface. (p. 456)
geosfera componentes de la superficie de la Tierra, es decir, los continentes, el suelo oceánico y el interior mismo de la Tierra.

germination process by which seeds or spores sprout and begin to grow. (p. 675)
germinación proceso mediante el cual las semillas o esporas brotan y empiezan a crecer.

germ theory theory that states that diseases are caused by microscopic particles called pathogens. (p. 941)
teoría de los gérmenes teoría según la cual las enfermedades son causadas por unas partículas microscópicas llamadas patógenos.

gibberellin (JIHB-uh-REHL-ihn) plant hormone that stimulates cell growth. (p. 680)
giberelina hormona vegetal que estimula el crecimiento celular.

gill respiratory organ of aquatic animals that allows breathing underwater. (p. 763)
branquia órgano respiratorio de numerosos animales acuáticos que permite respirar bajo el agua.

gland organ that produces and releases chemicals that affect the activities of other tissues. (p. 896)
glándula órgano que produce y secreta compuestos químicos que afectan el funcionamiento de otros tejidos.

global warming worldwide trend of increasing average temperatures. (p. 492)
calentamiento global incremento del promedio de la temperatura en toda la Tierra.

glomerulus (gloh-MEHR-yuh-luhs) tangled ball of capillaries that circulates blood in the kidneys. (p. 988)
glomérulos ovillo de vasos capilares por los que circula la sangre en los riñones.

glycolysis (gly-KAHL-uh-sihs) anaerobic process in which glucose is broken down into two molecules of pyruvate and two net ATP are produced. (p. 113)
glicólisis proceso anaeróbico en el que la glucosa se descompone en dos moléculas de piruvato y se producen dos moléculas de ATP.

Golgi apparatus (GOHL-jee) stack of flat, membrane-enclosed spaces containing enzymes that process, sort, and deliver proteins. (p. 76)
aparato de Golgi conjunto de sacos apilados y aplanados rodeados de una membrana que contienen enzimas que procesan, clasifican y distribuyen proteínas.

gradualism principle that states that the changes in landforms result from slow changes over a long period of time. (p. 301)
gradualismo principio que postula que los cambios en los accidentes geográficos resultan de pequeños cambios graduales durante extensos períodos de tiempo.

grassland biome in which the primary plant life is grass. (p. 464)
pradera bioma en la que las forma de vida vegetal predominante son las hierbas y los pastos.

gravitropism growth of plants in response to gravity; plant stems grow upward, against gravity, and roots grow toward the gravitational pull. (p. 682)
gravitropismo crecimiento de las plantas condicionado por la gravedad; el tallo crece hacia arriba, en sentido inverso a la fuerza de gravedad, y las raíces crecen hacia abajo, en el mismo sentido que la gravedad.

greenhouse effect normal warming effect produced when gases, such as carbon dioxide and methane, trap heat in Earth's atmosphere. (p. 490)
efecto invernadero calentamiento producido cuando ciertos gases, como el dióxido de carbono y el metano, atrapan el calor en la atmósfera terrestre.

ground tissue tissue system that makes up the majority of a plant. (p. 642)
tejido fundamental sistema de tejidos que comprende la parte principal del cuerpo de la planta.

growth factor broad group of proteins that stimulate cell division. (p. 144)
factor de crecimiento grupo numeroso de proteínas que estimulan la división celular.

guard cell one of a pair of cells that controls the opening and closing of a stoma in plant tissue. (p. 653)
células oclusivas las dos células que controlan la apertura y cierre de los estomas en el tejido vegetal.

gymnosperm (JIHM-nuh-SPURM) seed plant whose seeds are not enclosed by fruit. (p. 621)
gimnosperma planta productora de semillas que no están encerradas en una fruta.

Glossary

H

habitat combined biotic and abiotic factors found in the area where an organism lives. (p. 428)
hábitat conjunto de factores bióticos y abióticos de la zona donde vive un organismo determinado.

habitat fragmentation process by which part of an organism's preferred habitat range becomes inaccessible. (p. 499)
fragmentación del hábitat proceso mediante el cual una parte del hábitat de un organismo se hace inaccesible.

habituation process of eventually ignoring a repeated stimulus. (p. 823)
habituación proceso que eventualmente conduce a ignorar un estímulo que se repite.

hair cell mechanoreceptor in the inner ear that detects sound waves when bent. (p. 882)
célula ciliada mecanoreceptor del oído interno que detecta las ondas sonoras que lo accionan.

hair follicle pit in the dermis of the skin that contains cells that produce hair. (p. 1015)
folículo piloso estrecha cavidad de la piel que contiene células que forman el cabello.

half-life amount of time it takes for half of the isotope in a sample to decay into its product isotope. (p. 362)
vida mitad intervalo de tiempo necesario para que la mitad de los átomos de una muestra de isótopos se desintegren.

haploid (HAP-LOYD) cell that has only one copy of each chromosome. (p. 170)
haploide célula que sólo tiene una copia de cada cromosoma.

Hardy-Weinberg equilibrium condition in which a population's allele frequencies for a given trait do not change from generation to generation. (p. 340)
equilibrio de Hardy-Weinberg condición en la que las frecuencias alélicas de un rasgo determinado en una población determinada se mantienen constantes de una generación a otra.

heart muscle in the chest that moves blood throughout the body. (p. 912)
corazón músculo situado en el pecho que hace circular la sangre por el cuerpo.

hemocoel open space between cells in animal tissues. (p. 712)
hemocele cavidad intracelular de los tejidos animales.

hemoglobin (HEE-muh-GLOH-bihn) iron-rich protein in red blood cells that allows the cell to absorb oxygen gas. (p. 915)
hemoglobina proteína rica en hierro de los glóbulos rojos que permite a las células absorber oxígeno gaseoso.

herbivore organism that eats only plants. (p. 409)
herbívoro organismo que sólo se alimenta de plantas.

heritibility ability of a trait to be passed from one generation to the next. (p. 304)
heredabilidad propiedad de un rasgo determinado de ser transmitido de una generación a la siguiente.

heterotroph organism that obtains its energy and nutrients by consuming other organisms. (p. 406)
heterótrofo organismo que obtiene su energía y sus nutrientes alimentándose de otros organismos.

heterozygous characteristic of having two different alleles that appear at the same locus of sister chromatids. (p. 180)
heterocigoto característica que consiste en tener dos alelos diferentes en el mismo locus de cromátidas hermanas.

histone protein that organizes chromosomes and around which DNA wraps. (p. 139)
histona proteína que ordena los cromosomas y alrededor de la cual se enrolla el ADN.

homeobox (HOH-mee-uh-BAHKS) genes that define the head-to-tail pattern of development in animal embryos; also called *Hox* genes. (p. 698)
homeobox genes que definen el desarrollo de los embriones animales organizado de cabeza a cola; también se conocen como genes *Hox*.

homeostasis (HOH-mee-oh-STAY-sihs) regulation and mainte-nance of constant internal conditions in an organism. (pp. 9; 858)
homeostasis regulación y mantenimiento de condiciones internas constantes en un organismo determinado.

homeotic (hoh-mee-AH-tihk) genes that control early develop-ment in animals. (p. 698)
homeóticos genes que controlan la primera fase del desarrollo de los animales.

hominid primate that walks upright, has long lower limbs, thumbs that oppose the other four fingers, and a relatively large brain. (p. 380)
homínido primate que camina erguido, que tiene extremi-dades inferiores largas, pulgar desarrollado y alineado con los cuatro dedos restantes y un cerebro relativamente grande.

homologous chromosomes chromosomes that have the same length, appearance, and copies of genes, although the alleles may differ. (p. 169)
cromosomas homólogos cromosomas de la misma longitud, aspecto y secuencia de genes, aunque los alelos de uno y otro cromosoma pueden ser distintos.

homologous structure body part that is similar in structure on different organisms but performs different functions. (p. 312)
estructura homóloga estructura anatómica similar de organismos diferentes pero que cumplen funciones diferentes.

homozygous characteristic of having two of the same alleles at the same locus of sister chromatids. (p. 180)
homocigoto característica que consiste en tener los mismos alelos en el mismo locus de cromátidas hermanas.

hormone chemical signal that is produced in one part of an organism and affects cell activity in another part. (pp. 680; 896)
hormona señal química producida en una parte del organismo que afecta a la actividad celular en otra parte del cuerpo.

Human Genome Project project whose goal is to map, sequence, and identify all of the genes in the human genome. (p. 281)
Proyecto Genoma Humano proyecto cuya meta consiste en cartografiar un mapa, identificar y hallar la secuencia de todos los genes del genoma humano.

human immunodeficiency virus (HIV) virus that weakens the immune system by reproducing in and destroying T cells; causes AIDS. (p. 961)
virus de inmunodeficiencia humana (VIH) virus que debilita el sistema inmune al reproducirse en las células T y destruirlas; causa el SIDA.

humoral immunity immune response that relies on B cells to produce antibodies to help fight infection. (p. 953)
inmunidad humoral respuesta inmune basada en los anticuerpos producidos por las células B para combatir las infecciones.

hydrogen bond attraction between a slightly positive hydrogen atom and a slightly negative atom. (p. 41)
enlace de hidrógeno atracción entre un átomo de hidrógeno con una carga parcial positiva y otro con una carga parcial negativa.

hydrologic cycle pathway of water from the atmosphere to Earth's surface, below ground, and back. (p. 412)
ciclo hidrológico movimiento del agua desde la atmósfera hasta la superficie de la Tierra, al subsuelo y de vuelta a la atmósfera.

hydrosphere collection of Earth's water bodies, ice, and water vapor. (p. 456)
hidrosfera conjunto de las masas de agua líquida, sólida y gaseosa de la Tierra.

hypertonic solution that has a higher concentration of dissolved particles compared with another solution. (p. 86)
hipertónica solución con una concentración mayor de partículas disueltas que otra solución.

hypha (plural: *hyphae*) threadlike filament forming the body and mycelium of a fungus. (p. 589)
hifa filamento que forman el cuerpo y el micelio de los hongos.

hypothalamus small area of the midbrain that plays a role in the nervous and endocrine systems. (p. 898)
hipotálamo área reducida del cerebro medio que participa en las funciones de los sistemas nervioso y endocrino.

hypothesis (plural: *hypotheses*) proposed explanation or answer to a scientific question. (p. 14)
hipótesis proceso de explicación o respuesta a una pregunta científica.

hypotonic solution that has a lower concentration of dissolved particles compared with another solution. (p. 87)
hipotónica solución con una concentración menor de partículas disueltas que otra solución.

I

imitation process by which an organism learns a behavior by observing other individuals. (p. 825)
imitación proceso mediante el cual un organismo aprende un determinado comportamiento mediante la observación de otros individuos.

immigration movement of individuals into a population. (p. 440)
inmigración desplazamiento de individuos hacia una población establecida.

immune system body system that fights off infections. (p. 945)
sistema inmune sistema encargado de combatir las infecciones.

imprinting process by which a newborn animal quickly learns to recognize another animal, such as a parent. (p. 824)
impronta filial proceso mediante el cual un animal recién nacido aprende rápidamente a reconocer a otro como, por ejemplo, su progenitor.

inclusive fitness total number of genes an animal contributes to the next generation. (p. 834)
aptitud inclusiva número total de genes que un animal transmite a la siguiente generación.

incomplete dominance heterozygous phenotype that is a blend of the two homozygous phenotypes. (p. 204)
dominancia incompleta fenotipo heterocigoto que resulta de la mezcla de dos fenotipos homocigotos.

incomplete metamorphosis process by which immature arthropods look similar to their adult form. (p. 744)
metamorfosis incompleta proceso mediante el cual los especímenes jóvenes de los artrópodos son muy similares en forma a los adultos.

independent variable condition or factor that is manipulated by a scientist during an experiment. (p. 16)
variable independiente condición o factor que es manipulado en el transcurso de un experimento científico.

index fossil fossil of an organism that existed during only specific spans of geologic time across large geographic areas. (p. 365)
fósil índice fósil de un organismo que existió en el pasado geológico durante un intervalo corto con una amplia distribución geográfica.

indicator species species whose presence in an ecosystem gives clues about the condition of that ecosystem. (p. 494)
especies indicadoras especies cuya presencia en un ecosistema proporcionan claves sobre el estado en que se encuentra dicho ecosistema.

Glossary

infancy period of life from birth until the ability to walk has been acquired. (p. 1042)
infancia periodo de vida comprendido entre el nacimiento y los primeros pasos.

infertility persistent condition in which offspring cannot be produced. (p. 1031)
esterilidad incapacidad recurrente de un individuo para reproducirse.

inflammation immune response that is characterized by swelling, redness, pain, and itching. (p. 950)
inflamación respuesta inmune caracterizada por hinchazón, rubor, dolor y picazón.

innate behavior that is not learned through experience. (p. 822)
innato comportamiento que no se aprende a través de la experiencia.

insecticide chemical that is used to kill insects. (p. 747)
insecticida compuesto químico usado para matar insectos.

insight ability to solve a problem without repeated trial and error. (p. 838)
perspicacia capacidad para resolver un problema sin necesidad de pasar por procesos reiterados de prueba y error.

instinct inborn pattern of behavior that is characteristic of a species. (p. 822)
instinto patrón innato de comportamiento característico de cada especie.

integumentary system body system that separates the other body systems from the external environment; includes the skin and the tissues found within it. (p. 1013)
sistema tegumentario sistema que delimita los sistemas corporales del medio exterior; consta de la piel y de los tejidos que la conforman.

interferon type of protein, produced by body cells, that prevents viruses from replicating in infected cells. (p. 947)
interferón tipo de proteína generada por las células corporales que impide la replicación de los virus en el interior de las células infectadas.

intertidal zone strip of land between the high and low tide lines. (p. 468)
zona intermareal banda de tierra comprendida entra las líneas de pleamar y de bajamar.

introduced species species that is not native and was brought to an area as a result of human activities. (p. 500)
especie introducida especie no autóctona que llega a otras regiones como resultado de actividades humanas.

intron segment of a gene that does not code for an amino acid. (p. 251)
intrón región de un gen que no participa en la codificación de amino ácidos.

invertebrate animal without a backbone. (p. 699)
invertebrado animal sin columna vertebral.

ion atom that has gained or lost one or more electrons. (p. 38)
ión átomo que ha ganado o perdido uno o más electrones.

ionic bond chemical bond formed through the electrical force between oppositely charged ions. (p. 38)
enlace iónico enlace químico que se establece mediante la fuerza eléctrica ejercida entre dos iones de cargas opuestas.

isotonic solution that has an equal concentration of dissolved particles compared with another solution. (p. 86)
isotónica solución que tiene la misma concentración de partículas disueltas que otra solución.

isotope form of an element that has the same number of protons but a different number of neutrons as another element. (p. 362)
isótopo átomo de un elemento químico que tiene el mismo número de protones, pero una cantidad diferente de neutrones que otro átomo del mismo elemento.

J

joint location in the body where two bones meet. (p. 1001)
articulación área del cuerpo en la que se unen dos huesos.

K

karyotype (KAR-ee-uh-TYP) image of all of the chromosomes in a cell. (p. 217)
cariotipo imagen de todos los cromosomas de una célula.

kelp forest ocean habitat that exists in cold, nutrient-rich shallow coastal waters, composed of large communities of kelp, a seaweed. (p. 470)
bosques de quelpo hábitat oceánico de frías aguas costeras de poca profundidad que son ricas en nutrientes y en las que abundan grandes comunidades de algas pardas llamadas quelpos.

keratin protein that binds to lipids inside a skin cell, forming a waterproof layer within the skin. (pp. 778; 1013)
queratina proteína que se enlaza con los lípidos dentro de las células epiteliales creando una capa impermeable en el interior de la piel.

keystone species organism that has an unusually large effect on its ecosystem. (p. 403)
especie clave organismo que tiene una rol dominante en su ecosistema.

kidney organ of the excretory system that removes waste from the blood and helps to maintain stable water levels in the body. (p. 986)
riñón órgano del sistema excretor que elimina los desechos de la sangre y contribuye a mantener niveles estables de agua en el organismo.

kinesis random movement that results from an increase in activity levels due to a stimulus. (p. 819)
quinesia movimiento aleatorio que resulta de un incremento en los niveles de actividad producidos por un estímulo.

kin selection when natural selection acts on alleles that favor the survival of close relatives. (p. 834)
nepotismo selección natural de los alelos que favorece la supervivencia de los familiares más próximos.

Krebs cycle process during cellular respiration that breaks down a carbon molecule to produce molecules that are used in the electron transport chain. (p. 115)
ciclo de Krebs proceso de respiración celular en el que se desintegra una molécula de carbono para generar moléculas que intervienen en la cadena de transporte de electrones.

L

lactic acid product of fermentation in many types of cells, including human muscle cells. (p. 123)
ácido láctico producto de fermentación de muchos tipos de células como, por ejemplo, las células musculares humanas.

lateral line sensory system in fish that allows them to sense distant movements in the water. (p. 767)
línea lateral sistema sensorial de los peces que les permite captar movimientos lejanos en el agua.

law of independent assortment Mendel's second law, stating that allele pairs separate from one another during gamete formation. (p. 186)
ley de transmisión independiente segunda ley de Mendel, según la cual los pares de alelos se separan durante la formación de los gametos.

law of segregation Mendel's first law, stating that (1) organisms inherit two copies of genes, one from each parent, and (2) organisms donate only one copy of each gene in their gametes because the genes separate during gamete formation. (p. 179)
ley de la segregación primera ley de Mendel, según la cual (1) los organismos heredan dos copias de cada gen, una de cada progenitor, y (2) que los organismos sólo reciben una copia de cada gen de los gametos de sus progenitores ya que los genes se separan durante la formación de gametos.

leukemia cancer of the bone marrow that weakens the immune system by preventing white blood cells from maturing. (p. 960)
leucemia cáncer de la medula ósea que debilita el sistema inmune al impedir que maduren los glóbulos blancos.

lichen fungus that grows symbiotically with algae, resulting in a composite organism that grows on rocks or tree trunks. (p. 598)
liquen organismo compuesto por un hongo y una alga que viven en y que crece sobre las rocas y los troncos de los árboles.

ligament long, flexible band of connective tissue that joins two bones across a joint. (p. 1002)
ligamento tira alargada y flexible de tejido conjuntivo que une dos huesos a través de una articulación.

light-dependent reactions part of photosynthesis that absorbs energy from sunlight and transfers energy to the light-independent reactions. (p. 105)
reacciones lumínicas etapa de la fotosíntesis en la que se absorbe energía solar para luego usarse en las reacciones oscuras.

light-independent reactions part of photosynthesis that uses energy absorbed during the light-dependent reactions to synthesize carbohydrates. (p. 105)
reacciones oscuras etapa de la fotosíntesis en que se aplica la energía absorbida durante las reacciones lumínicas para la síntesis de carbohidratos.

lignin (LIHG-nihn) complex polymer that hardens cell walls of some vascular tissues in plants. (p. 614)
lignina polímero complejo que endurece las paredes celulares de determinados tejidos vasculares de las plantas.

limiting factor environmental factor that limits the growth and size of a population. (p. 443)
factor limitante factor ambiental que limita el crecimiento y tamaño de una población determinada.

limnetic zone open water of a lake or pond that is located away from shore. (p. 474)
zona limnética aguas abiertas de un lago o estanque alejadas de las orillas.

linkage map diagram that shows the relative locations of genes on a chromosome. (p. 210)
mapa de ligamiento diagrama que representa la situación relativa de los genes en un cromosoma determinado.

lipid nonpolar molecule composed of carbon, hydrogen, and oxygen; includes fats and oils. (p. 46)
lípido molécula apolar compuesta de carbono, hidrógeno y oxígeno; las grasas y los aceites son lípidos.

littoral zone area between the high and low water marks along the shoreline of a lake or pond. (p. 474)
zona litoral área de aguas de profundidad intermedia a lo largo de la orilla de un lago o estanque.

lobe-fin paired limblike fin that is round in shape. (p. 770)
aleta lobulada tipo de aleta de forma redondeada que se presenta en pares y que se asemeja a una extremidad.

logistic growth population growth that is characterized by a period of slow growth, followed by a period of exponential growth, followed by another period of almost no growth. (p. 441)
crecimiento logístico crecimiento de población que se caracteriza por un período de crecimiento lento, seguido por un período de crecimiento exponencial al que le sigue un período de crecimiento insignificante.

lung organ that absorbs oxygen gas from air that an organism inhales. (p. 911)
pulmón órgano que absorbe el oxígeno gaseoso que inhala un organismo.

Glossary

lymph collection of interstitial fluid and white blood cells that flows through the lymphatic system. (p. 930)
linfa conjunto de los fluidos intersticiales y de glóbulos blancos que circulan por el sistema linfático.

lymphatic system (lihm-FAT-ihk) body system that consists of organs, vessels, and nodes through which lymph circulates. (p. 930)
sistema linfático sistema corporal que consta de órganos, vasos y nódulos a través de los cuales circula la linfa.

lymphocyte (LIHM-fuh-SYT) white blood cell that plays a role in an immune response; *see* B cell and T cell. (p. 931)
linfocito glóbulo blanco que participa en la respuesta inmune; *véanse* célula B y célula T.

lysogenic infection infectious pathway of a virus in which host cells are not immediately destroyed. (p. 551)
infección lisogénica infección vírica en la que las células huésped no son destruidas de inmediato.

lysosome (LY-suh-SOHM) organelle that contains enzymes. (p. 78)
lisosoma orgánulo que contiene enzimas.

lytic infection infectious pathway of a virus in which host cells are destroyed. (p. 551)
infección lítica infección vírica en la que se destruyen las células huésped.

M

malignant cancerous tumor in which cells break away and spread to other parts of the body, causing harm to the organism's health. (p. 146)
maligno tumor canceroso en el que las células se desprenden y se diseminan a otras partes del cuerpo provocando daños a la salud del organismo.

mammal endothermic organism that has hair, mammary glands, bones in the ear that allow for hearing, and a jaw for chewing food. (p. 805)
mamífero organismo endotérmico que tiene pelo y glándulas mamarias, además de huesos en el oído que le permiten oír y una mandíbula para masticar.

mammary gland gland that produces milk. (p. 806)
glándula mamaria glándula productora de leche.

mandible appendage that is used to crush and bite food. (p. 737)
mandíbula apéndice empleado para triturar y morder la comida.

marsupial mammal whose young complete fetal development in the mother's external pouch. (p. 808)
marsupial mamífero cuyas crías terminan su desarrollo fetal en una bolsa exterior de la madre.

medusa umbrella-shaped body form of a cnidarian in which the mouth and tentacles are on the underside. (p. 707)
medusa organismo cnidario en forma de paraguas que tiene la boca y los tentáculos en la superficie cóncava.

meiosis (my-OH-sihs) form of nuclear division that divides a diploid cell into haploid cells; important in forming gametes for sexual reproduction. (p. 170)
meiosis forma de división nuclear en la que una célula diploide se divide en células haploides; importante en la formación de gametos para la reproducción sexual.

memory cell specialized white blood cell that contributes to acquired immunity by acting quickly to a foreign substance that infected the body previously. (p. 951)
célula de memoria glóbulo blanco que participa en el proceso de inmunización mediante una respuesta rápida ante una sustancia extraña que ya había infectado el organismo anteriormente.

menopause period of life when the female reproductive system permanently stops the menstrual cycle. (p. 1029)
menopausia período de la vida en que el sistema reproductor femenino deja de producir el ciclo menstrual.

menstrual cycle series of changes in the female reproductive system that takes place over the course of one month. (p. 1028)
ciclo menstrual sucesión de cambios en el sistema reproductor femenino que ocurre en el plazo de un mes.

meristem undifferentiated plant tissue from which new cells are formed. (p. 648)
meristemo tejido indiferenciado de las plantas en el que se forman nuevas células.

mesoglea jellylike material that separates the two tissue layers of a cnidarian. (p. 707)
mesoglea matriz gelatinosa que separa las dos capas de tejidos de un cnidario.

mesophyll photosynthetic tissue of a leaf, located between the upper and lower epidermis. (p. 652)
mesófilo tejido fotosintético de la hoja, situado entre la epidermis superior y la epidermis inferior de la hoja.

Mesozoic era during which dinosaurs roamed Earth (from 248 million years ago to 65 million years ago). (p. 377)
Mesozoico era de la Tierra que se inició hace unos 248 millones de años y que finalizó hace 65 millones de años en la que abundaron los dinosaurios.

messenger RNA (mRNA) form of RNA that carries genetic information from the nucleus to the cytoplasm, where it serves as a template for protein synthesis. (p. 240)
ARN mensajero (ARNm) forma de ARN que transporta la información genética del núcleo al citoplasma, donde sirve de patrón para la síntesis de las proteínas.

metabolism all chemical processes that synthesize or break down materials within an organism. (p. 6)
metabolismo conjunto de procesos químicos que sintetizan o descomponen sustancias en el interior de los organismos.

metaphase second phase of mitosis when spindle fibers align the chromosomes along the cell equator. (p. 140)
metafase segunda fase de la mitosis en la que las fibras de los husos alinean los cromosomas en el plano ecuatorial de la célula.

metastasize (mih-TAS-tuh-SYZ) to spread by transferring a disease-causing agent from the site of the disease to other parts of the body. (p. 146)

metástasis diseminación de una enfermedad causada por un agente patógeno del foco en que se origina a otras partes del cuerpo.

microclimate climate of a specific location within a larger area. (p. 458)

microclima clima de un lugar específico enclavado en un área más extensa.

microevolution observable change in the allele frequencies of a population over a few generations. (p. 331)

microevolución cambio observable en las frecuencias alélicas de una población en el transcurso de unas pocas generaciones.

microscope tool that provides an enlarged image of an object. (p. 19)

microscopio instrumento que permite ver una imagen amplificada de un objeto.

microvillus (plural: *microvilli*) small hairlike projection on the surface of a villus in the small intestine. (p. 983)

microvellosidad proyección pilosa muy pequeña que recubre las vellosidades del intestino delgado.

mineral inorganic material, such as calcium, iron, potassium, sodium, or zinc, that is essential to the nutrition of an organism. (p. 973)

mineral material inorgánico, como el calcio, el hierro, el potasio, el sodio o el zinc, que resulta esencial en la nutrición de los organismos.

mitochondrial DNA DNA found only in mitochondria, often used as a molecular clock. (p. 532)

ADN mitocondrial ADN propio de las mitocondrias que suele actuar a modo de reloj molecular.

mitochondrion (MY-tuh-KAHN-dree-uhn) (plural: *mitochondria*) bean-shaped organelle that supplies energy to the cell and has its own ribosomes and DNA. (p. 77)

mitocondria orgánulo en forma de fríjol que suministra energía a la célula y que tiene sus propios ribosomas y ADN.

mitosis (my-TOH-sihs) process by which a cell divides its nucleus and contents. (p. 135)

mitosis proceso en el cual tanto el núcleo como los demás elementos de la célula se duplican.

molecular clock theoretical clock that uses the rate of mutation to measure evolutionary time. (p. 530)

reloj molecular reloj teórico que emplea la tasa de mutación para medir el tiempo evolutivo.

molecular genetics study of DNA structure and function on the molecular level. (p. 23)

genética molecular estudio de la estructura y función del ADN a nivel molecular.

molecule two or more atoms held together by covalent bonds; not necessarily a compound. (p. 39)

molécula dos o más átomos unidos mediante enlaces covalentes; no forman necesariamente un compuesto.

monocot (MAHN-uh-KAHT) flowering plant whose embryos have one cotyledon. (p. 626)

monocotiledónea planta angiosperma cuyos embriones tienen un solo cotiledón.

monohybrid cross cross, or mating, between organisms that involves only one pair of contrasting traits. (p. 184)

cruzamiento monohíbrido cruzamiento o apareamiento entre dos organismos que sólo involucra un par de rasgos diferentes.

monomer molecular subunit of a polymer. (p. 45)

monómero subunidad molecular del polímero.

monotreme mammal whose offspring complete fetal development in laid eggs. (p. 807)

monotrema mamífero que pone huevos donde sus crías completan su desarrollo fetal.

muscle fiber cell of the muscular system that shortens when it is stimulated by the nervous system. (p. 1006)

fibra muscular célula del sistema muscular que se contrae al ser estimulada por el sistema nervioso.

muscular system body system that moves bones within and substances throughout the body. (p. 1006)

sistema muscular sistema corporal que mueve los huesos y que hace circular sustancias a través del cuerpo.

mutagen agent that can induce or increase the frequency of mutation in organisms. (p. 255)

mutágeno agente que puede inducir mutaciones en un organismo o incrementar la frecuencia de éstas.

mutation change in the DNA sequence. (p. 252)

mutación cambio en la secuencia de ADN.

mutualism ecological relationship between two species in which each species gets a benefit from the interaction. (p. 432)

mutualismo relación ecológica entre dos especies que resulta beneficiosa para ambas.

mycelium vegetative part of a fungus, consisting of a mass of branching, threadlike hyphae that grows underground. (p. 590)

micelio parte vegetativa del hongo compuesta de un entramado de filamentos ramificados, llamados hifas, que crece bajo tierra.

mycorrhizae ecological relationship between the mycelium of a fungus and the roots of certain plants. (p. 591)

micorriza relación ecológica entre el micelio de un hongo y las raíces de determinadas plantas.

myofibril long strand of protein within a muscle fiber. (p. 1008)

miofibrilla larga cadena proteica dentro de una fibra muscular.

Glossary

myosin filament that pulls actin filaments to cause muscle contraction. (p. 1008)
miosina filamento que al tensar los filamentos de actina causa la contracción muscular.

N

natural selection mechanism by which individuals that have inherited beneficial adaptations produce more offspring on average than do other individuals. (p. 305)
selección natural mecanismo mediante el cual los organismos que han heredado adaptaciones beneficiosas producen un promedio más alto de descendientes que los demás individuos.

nebula rotating cloud of gas and dust. (p. 368)
nebulosa nube giratoria de polvo y gases.

negative feedback control system for homeostasis that adjusts the body's conditions when the conditions vary from the ideal. (p. 860)
retroalimentación negativa sistema de control de la homeostasis que regula las condiciones del cuerpo cuando éstas no son óptimas.

nematocyst capsule containing a thin, coiled tubule with a poisonous barb at one end. (p. 707)
nematocisto cápsula que contiene un fino túbulo enrollado con un aguijón venenoso en la punta.

nephron (NEHF-rahn) individual filtering unit of the kidney that removes waste from the blood. (p. 987)
nefrona unidad de filtración del riñón que retira los desechos de la sangre.

neritic zone zone of the ocean that extends from the intertidal zone out to the edge of the continental shelf. (p. 468)
zona nerítica zona del océano que se extiende desde la zona intermareal hasta el límite de la plataforma continental.

nervous system body system that controls sensation, interpretation, and response; includes the brain, spinal cord, and nerves. (p. 874)
sistema nervioso sistema corporal que controla las sensaciones, las interpretaciones y las respuestas; incluye el encéfalo, la médula espinal y los nervios.

neuron cell of the nervous system that transmits impulses between the body systems as well as interprets and stores some messages in the brain. (p. 876)
neurona célula del sistema nervioso que transmite impulsos entre los diversos sistemas del organismo y que, además, interpreta y almacena información en el cerebro.

neurotransmitter (NUR-oh-TRANS-miht-uhr) chemical that transmits a nervous system's signal across a synapse. (p. 879)
neurotransmisor compuesto químico que transmite una señal del sistema nervioso a través de la sinapsis.

nitrogen fixation process by which certain types of bacteria convert gaseous nitrogen into nitrogen compounds. (p. 415)
fijación del nitrógeno proceso mediante el cual ciertos tipos de bacterias transforman el nitrógeno gaseoso en compuestos nitrogenados.

node organ located along the lymphatic vessels that filters bacteria and foreign particles from lymph. (p. 930)
ganglio linfático órgano situado a lo largo de los vasos linfáticos encargado de filtrar bacterias y sustancias extrañas de la linfa.

nonrenewable resource natural resource that is used more quickly than it can be formed. (p. 485)
recurso no renovable recurso natural que se consume con más rapidez de la que se puede reponer.

normal distribution distribution in a population in which allele frequency is highest near the mean range value and decreases progressively toward each extreme end. (p. 330)
distribución normal distribución de la población en la que la frecuencia alélica es mayor en la zona de valor medio y disminuye progresivamente hacia ambos extremos.

notochord flexible skeletal support rod embedded in an animal's back. (p. 758)
notocordio bastón esqueletal flexible que proporciona sostén y que está situado en el dorso de los animales.

nucleic acid polymer of nucleotides; the genetic material of organisms. (p. 48)
ácido nucleico polímero de nucleótidos; material genético de los organismos.

nucleotide (NOO-klee-oh-TYD) monomer that forms DNA and has a phosphate group, a sugar, and a nitrogen-containing base. (p. 230)
nucleótido monómero que forma el ADN y que tiene un grupo fosfato, un azúcar y una base nitrogenada.

nucleus (NOO-klee-uhs) (plural: *nuclei*) organelle composed of a double membrane that acts as the storehouse for most of a cell's DNA. (p. 75)
núcleo orgánulo compuesto de una doble membrana que almacena la mayor parte del ADN de la célula.

O

obligate aerobe prokaryote that cannot survive without the presence of oxygen. (p. 555)
aerobio obligado procariota que no puede sobrevivir en un entorno sin oxígeno.

obligate anaerobe prokaryote that cannot survive in the presence of oxygen. (p. 555)
anaerobio obligado procariota que no puede sobrevivir en un entorno oxigenado.

observation using the senses to study the world; using tools to collect measurements; examining previous research results. (p. 13)
observación utilización de los sentidos para estudiar el mundo; uso de instrumentos de medición; análisis de resultados de investigación.

omnivore organism that eats both plants and animals. (p. 409)
omnívoro organismo que se alimenta tanto de animales como de plantas.

operant conditioning process by which a behavior increases or decreases as the result of a reward or punishment. (p. 826)
condicionamiento operante proceso mediante el cual varía la frecuencia de un comportamiento como resultado de un premio o un castigo.

operculum protective bony plate that covers a fish's gills. (p. 767)
opérculo placa protectora ósea que recubre las branquias de los peces.

operon section of DNA that contains all of the code to begin transcription, regulate transcription, and build a protein; includes a promotor, regulatory gene, and structural gene (p. 248)
operon sección de ADN que contiene todos los códigos necesarios para iniciar y regular el proceso de transcripción y para sintetizar una proteína: consta de un promotor, de un gen regulador y de un gen estructural.

opportunistic infection infection caused by a pathogen that a healthy immune system would normally be able to fight off. (p. 961)
infección oportunista infección causada por un patógeno que un sistema inmune saludable podría combatir con eficacia.

optimal foraging theory that states that natural selection will favor organisms that have behaviors that can gather the best food sources. (p. 829)
abastecimiento óptimo teoría según la cual la selección natural favorece a aquellos organismos cuyos comportamientos les permiten acceder a las mejores fuentes de alimento.

organ group of different types of tissues that work together to perform a specific function or related functions. (pp. 151; 854)
órgano grupo de diversos tipos de tejidos que funcionan de manera coordinada para desarrollar una función específica o funciones relacionadas.

organelle membrane-bound structure that is specialized to perform a distinct process within a cell. (p. 72)
orgánulo estructura intracelular que se especializa en una función específica.

organism any individual living thing. (p. 5)
organismo cualquier ser vivo.

organ system two or more organs that work in a coordinated way to carry out similar functions. (pp. 151; 854)
sistema de órganos dos o más órganos que funcionan de manera coordinada para realizar funciones similares.

osmosis diffusion of water molecules across a semipermeable membrane from an area of higher water concentration to an area of lower water concentration. (p. 86)
ósmosis difusión de moléculas de agua a través de una membrana semipermeable, desde un área de mayor concentración de agua a otra de menor concentración de agua.

ossicle small bone, especially one of the three found in the middle ear of mammals. (p. 718)
huesecillo en los mamíferos, cada uno de los tres huesos pequeños que se encuentran en el oído medio.

ovary organ in which female gametes develop prior to fertilization. (pp. 668; 1024)
ovario órgano en el que se desarrollan los gametos femeninos antes de la fertilización.

oviparous reproductive strategy in which the embryos develop outside of the mother's body. (p. 793)
ovíparo organismo que se reproduce mediante un sistema en el que los embriones se desarrollan fuera del cuerpo materno.

ovulation process by which an egg is released from the ovary and becomes available for fertilization. (p. 1028)
ovulación proceso mediante el cual se libera un óvulo del ovario, quedando susceptible a ser fertilizado.

ovum (plural: *ova*) egg cell that is produced by the female reproductive system. (p. 1024)
óvulo ovocito producido en el sistema reproductor femenino.

P

pacemaker collection of cells that stimulates the pumping action of the heart. (p. 918)
nódulo sinusal conjunto de células que estimula los latidos del corazón; también conocido como marcapaso natural.

paleontology study of fossils or extinct organisms. (p. 316)
paleontología estudio de los fósiles o de los organismos extintos.

Paleozoic era of geologic time (from 544 to 248 million years ago) during which members of every major animal group alive today evolved. (p. 376)
Paleozoico era geológica (desde hace 544 a 248 millones de años) durante la cual evolucionaron especies de los principales grupos de animales de la actualidad.

parasitism ecological relationship in which one organism benefits by harming another organism. (p. 432)
parasitismo relación ecológica en la que un organismo se beneficia perjudicando al otro organismo.

parasympathetic nervous system division of the peripheral nervous system that calms the body and helps the body to conserve energy. (p. 890)
sistema nervioso parasimpático parte del sistema nervioso periférico encargado de mantener un estado corporal de descanso y ayudar al cuerpo a conservar energía.

Glossary

parenchyma cell cell with thin walls that forms tissues within leaves, roots, stems, and fruit of plants. (p. 640)
célula del parénquima célula de paredes delgadas que forma tejidos en el interior de las hojas, raíces, tallos y frutas de las plantas.

particulate microscopic bits of dust, metal, and unburned fuel produced by industrial processes. (p. 488)
materia particulada partículas microscópicas de polvo, metal y combustibles sin quemar, que se generan en los procesos industriales.

passive immunity immunity that occurs without the body undergoing an immune response. (p. 948)
inmunidad pasiva inmunidad que tiene lugar sin que el cuerpo experimente una reacción inmune.

passive transport movement of molecules across the cell membrane without energy input from the cell. (p. 85)
transporte pasivo movimiento de moléculas a través de la membrana celular, que se produce sin aporte de energía celular.

pathogen agent that causes disease. (pp. 544; 941)
patógeno agente que causa una enfermedad.

pedigree chart of the phenotypes and genotypes in a family that is used to determine whether an individual is a carrier of a recessive allele. (p. 214)
pedigrí diagrama de los fenotipos y genotipos de una familia que se emplea para determinar si un individuo es portador de un alelo recesivo.

period unit of geologic time that lasts tens of millions of years and is associated with a particular type of rock system. (p. 367)
periodo unidad de tiempo geológico que abarca decenas de millones de años y que suele asociarse a tipos determinados de formaciones rocosas.

peripheral nervous system (PNS) division of the nervous system that transmits impulses between the central nervous system and other organs in the body. (p. 875)
sistema nervioso periférico (SNP) división del sistema nervioso que transmite impulsos entre el sistema nervioso central y otros órganos del cuerpo.

peristalsis (PEHR-ih-STAWL-sihs) wavelike involuntary muscle contractions that push food through the organs of the digestive system. (p. 978)
peristaltismo contracciones involuntarias en forma de ondas que impulsan los alimentos a través de los órganos del sistema digestivo.

petal modified leaf that surrounds a flower's reproductive structures. (p. 668)
pétalo hoja modificada que rodea las estructuras reproductivas de la flor.

petiole stalk that attaches a leaf blade to a stem. (p. 652)
peciolo rabillo que une la lámina de la hoja al tallo.

pH measurement of acidity; related to free hydrogen ion concentration in solution. (p. 42)
pH medida de acidez; relacionada con la concentración de los iones libres de hidrógeno en una solución.

phagocyte cell that destroys other cells by surrounding and engulfing them. (p. 946)
fagocito célula que destruye a otras células rodeándolas y engulléndolas.

phagocytosis (FAG-uh-sy-TOH-sihs) uptake of a solid particle into a cell by engulfing the particle; *see* endocytosis. (p. 90)
fagocitosis absorción de una partícula sólida por parte de una célula que la envuelve: *véase* endocitosis.

pharmacology study of drugs and their effects on the body. (p. 631)
farmacología estudio de los medicamentos y de los efectos que causan en el cuerpo.

phenotype collection of all of an organism's physical characteristics. (p. 181)
fenotipo conjunto de todas las características físicas de un organismo determinado.

pheromone chemical released by an organism that stimulates a behavior in other organisms of the same species. (p. 832)
feromona compuesto químico liberado por un organismo que estimula ciertos comportamientos en otros organismos de la misma especie.

phloem tissue that transports sugars in vascular plants. (p. 642)
floema tejido transportador de azúcares en las plantas vasculares.

phospholipid molecule that forms a double-layered cell membrane; consists of a glycerol, a phosphate group, and two fatty acids. (p. 81)
fosfolípido molécula que forma una membrana de capa doble; consta de glicerol, un grupo fosfato y dos ácidos grasos.

photoperiodism response of an organism to changes in the length of the day. (p. 683)
fotoperiodismo respuesta de un organismo a las variaciones de luz en un período de 24 horas.

photosynthesis process by which light energy is converted to chemical energy; produces sugar and oxygen from carbon dioxide and water. (p. 103)
fotosíntesis proceso mediante el cual la energía del sol se convierte en energía química; produce azúcar y oxígeno a partir de dióxido de carbono y agua.

photosystem series of light-absorbing pigments and proteins that capture and transfer energy in the thylakoid membrane. (p. 108)
fotosistema conjunto de pigmentos y proteínas que capturan y transfieren energía en la membrana tilacoide.

phototropism growth of a plant toward a light source. (p. 682)
fototropismo crecimiento de la planta hacia la luz.

phylogeny evolutionary history of a group of related species. (p. 524)
filogenia historia evolutiva de un grupo de especies relacionadas.

phylum group of animals defined by structural and functional characteristics that are different from every other animal phylum. (p. 699)
división grupo de animales definidos por una serie de características estructurales y funcionales que se diferencian de cualquier otra división; también se conoce como filum.

phytoplankton photosynthetic microscopic protists, such as algae. (p. 469)
fitoplancton colonia de protistas microscópicas fotosintéticas, como las algas.

pioneer species organism that is the first to live in a previously uninhabited area. (p. 446)
especie pionera primer organismo que vive en una zona hasta entonces deshabitada.

pituitary gland area in the middle of the brain that makes and releases hormones that control cell growth and osmoregulation, water levels in the blood. (p. 898)
glándula pituitaria zona en el centro del cerebro que produce y segrega hormonas que controlan el crecimiento celular y la osmorregulación, es decir, la regulación de los niveles de líquidos en la sangre.

placenta (pluh-SEHN-tuh) organ that develops in female mammals during pregnancy and carries nutrients from the mother to the embryo. (pp. 779; 1035)
placenta órgano que se desarrolla en las hembras de los mamíferos durante la gestación y que lleva nutrientes de la madre al embrión.

plankton microscopic, free-floating organisms, which may be animals or protists, that live in the water. (p. 469)
plancton organismos microscópicos, animales o protistas, que flotan libremente en el agua.

plant multicellular eukaryote that produces its own food through photosynthesis. (p. 612)
planta organismo eucariota multicelular que produce su propio alimento mediante la fotosíntesis.

plasma clear yellowish fluid, about 90 percent water, that suspends cells in the blood. (p. 926)
plasma líquido de color amarillento pálido que consisten en un 90 por ciento deagua en el que están suspendidas las células sanguíneas.

plasmid circular piece of genetic material found in bacteria that can replicate separately from the DNA of the main chromosome. (pp. 276; 556)
plásmido cadena de material genético en forma circular que se encuentra en las bacterias y que se replica independientemente del ADN cromosómico.

platelet cell fragment that is produced in the bone marrow and is important for blood clotting. (p. 926)
plaqueta fragmento celular que se produce en la médula ósea y que cumple una función importante en la coagulación de la sangre.

point mutation mutation that involves a substitution of only one nucleotide. (p. 252)
mutación puntual mutación que involucra la sustitución de un solo nucleótido.

polar body haploid cell produced during meiosis in the female of many species; these cells have little more than DNA and eventually disintegrate. (p. 176)
cuerpo polar célula haploide producida durante la meiosis en las hembras de muchas especies; esta célula tiene poco más que ADN y termina por desintegrarse.

pollen grain two-celled structure that contains the male form of the plant's gamete. (p. 614)
grano de polen estructura formada por dos células que contiene el gameto masculino de la planta.

pollination process by which seed plants become fertilized without the need for free-standing water. (p. 620)
polinización proceso mediante el cual las plantas con semillas se fertilizan sin depender del agua del suelo.

pollution anything that is added to the environment and has a negative affect on the environment or its organisms. (p. 488)
contaminación cualquier sustancia que se libera en el medio ambiente con efectos negativos para los organismos que lo habitan y su entorno.

polygenic trait trait that is produced by two or more genes. (p. 206)
rasgo poligénico rasgo producido por dos o más genes.

polymer large, carbon-based molecule formed by monomers. (p. 45)
polímero gran molécula de carbono formada por monómeros.

polymerase chain reaction (PCR) method for increasing the quantity of DNA by separating it into two strands and adding primers and enzymes. (p. 269)
reacción en cadena de la polimerasa (RCP) método para obtener un gran número de copias de ADN separándolo en dos hebras y añadiendo cebadores y enzimas.

polyp tube-shaped body form of a cnidarian in which the mouth and tentacles face upward. (p. 707)
pólipo cuerpo de forma tubular de un cnidario con la boca y los tentáculos orientados hacia arriba.

population all of the individuals of a species that live in the same area. (p. 306)
población conjunto de individuos de la misma especie que viven en la misma zona.

population crash dramatic decline in the size of a population over a short period of time. (p. 442)
colapso poblacional reducción drástica del tamaño de una población en un breve período de tiempo.

Glossary

population density measure of individuals living in a defined area. (p. 436)
  densidad de población cantidad de habitantes que viven en un área determinada.

population dispersion way in which individuals of a population are spread out over an area or volume. (p. 437)
  dispersión de población manera en la que los individuos de una población determinada se han distribuido en una área o en un volumen.

positive feedback control system in which sensory information causes the body to increase the rate of change away from homeostasis. (p. 861)
  retroalimentación positiva sistema de control mediante el cual la información sensorial estimula el cuerpo a incrementar la tasa de cambio, alejándola de valores homeostáticos.

predation process by which one organism hunts and kills another organism for food. (p. 431)
  predación proceso mediante el cual un organismo acecha, mata y se come a otro organismo.

pressure-flow model model for predicting how sugars are transported from photosynthetic tissue to the rest of a plant. (p. 645)
  modelo de flujo de presión modelo para predecir la forma en que los azúcares son transportados del tejido fotosintético al resto de una planta.

primary growth growth in vascular plants resulting in elongation of the plant body. (p. 651)
  crecimiento primario crecimiento de las plantas vasculares que resulta de la elongación del cuerpo de la planta.

primary succession establishment and development of an ecosystem in an area that was previously uninhabited. (p. 446)
  sucesión primaria establecimiento y desarrollo de un ecosistema en una zona hasta entonces deshabitada.

primate mammal with flexible hands and feet, forward-looking eyes, and enlarged brains relative to body size. (p. 379)
  primate mamífero de manos y pies flexibles, mirada frontal y un cerebro grande en relación con el tamaño del cuerpo.

primer short segment of DNA that initiates replication by DNA polymerase. (p. 271)
  cebador pequeño segmento de ADN que inicia la replicación mediante ADN polimerasa.

prion infectious agent that consists of a protein fragment that can cause other proteins to fold incorrectly. (p. 545)
  prión agente infeccioso que consta de una partícula proteica que induce a otras proteínas a plegarse de forma incorrecta.

probability likelihood that a particular event will happen. (p. 187)
  probabilidad posibilidad de que ocurra un suceso en particular.

producer organism that obtains its energy from abiotic sources, such as sunlight or inorganic chemicals. (p. 406)
  productor organismo que obtiene su alimento de fuentes abióticas, como la luz solar o compuestos inorgánicos.

product substance formed by a chemical reaction. (p. 50)
  producto sustancia formada por una reacción química.

prokaryotic cell (proh-KAR-ee-AHT-ihk) cell that does not have a nucleus or other membrane-bound organelles. (p. 72)
  célula procarionta célula que no tiene núcleo ni orgánulos limitados por membranas.

promoter section of DNA to which RNA polymerase binds, starting the transcription of mRNA. (p. 248)
  promotor sección de ADN a la que se enlaza el ARN polimerasa al inicio del proceso de transcripción de ARNm.

prophage DNA of a bacteriophage inserted into a host cell's DNA. (p. 551)
  profago ADN de un bacteriófago insertado en el ADN de la célula huésped.

prophase first phase of mitosis when chromatin condenses, the nuclear envelope breaks down, the nucleolus disappears, and the centrosomes and centrioles migrate to opposite sides of the cell. (p. 140)
  profase primera fase de la mitosis, en la que la cromatina se condensa, la membrana nuclear se desintegra, el nucleolo desaparece y los centrosomas y los centriolos migran a lados opuestos de la célula.

prosimian oldest primate group that includes mostly small, nocturnal primates such as lemurs. (p. 379)
  prosimio grupo de primates más antiguo que consta, principalmente, de pequeños primates nocturnos, como los lemures.

protein polymer composed of amino acids linked by peptide bonds; folds into a particular structure depending on bonds between amino acids. (p. 47)
  proteína polímero compuesto de aminoácidos unidos por enlaces peptídicos; se pliega formando una estructura determinada según sean los enlaces que hay entre los aminoácidos.

proteomics (PROH-tee-AH-mihks) study and comparison of all the proteins produced by an organism's genome. (p. 283)
  proteómica estudio y comparación de todas las proteínas producidas por el genoma de un organismo determinado.

protist eukaryote that is not an animal, plant, or fungus. (p. 574)
  protista organismo eucariota que no es un animal, una planta, ni un hongo.

protostome animal development in which the animal's mouth develops before the anus. (p. 702)
  protóstomo animal en el que la boca se desarrolla antes que el ano.

protozoa animal-like protist. (p. 577)
  protozoo protista con características animales.

pseudocoelom fluid filled space with mesoderm only on one side of the space. (p. 716)
  pseudoceloma cavidad llena de fluido que tiene mesodermo en un solo lado de la cavidad.

pseudopod temporary extension of cytoplasm and plasma membrane that helps protozoa move and feed. (p. 578)
pseudópodo extensión temporal del citoplasma y de la membrana plasmática que permite a los protozoos moverse y alimentarse.

puberty stage of adolescence that is marked by the production of hormones involved in reproduction. (p. 1024)
pubertad fase de la adolescencia marcada por la producción de hormonas involucradas en la reproducción.

pulmonary circuit (PUL-muh-NEHR-ee) collection of blood vessels that carries blood between the lungs and heart. (pp. 789; 920)
circuito pulmonar conjunto de vasos sanguíneos que transporta sangre entre los pulmones y el corazón.

pulmonary circulation *see* pulmonary circuit.
circulación pulmonar *véanse* circuito pulmonar.

punctuated equilibrium theory that states that speciation occurs suddenly and rapidly followed by long periods of little evolutionary change. (p. 351)
equilibrio puntuado teoría según la cual la especiación se produce repentinamente y va seguida de largos períodos de escasa actividad evolutiva.

Punnett square model for predicting all possible genotypes resulting from a cross, or mating. (p. 183)
cuadrado de Punnet modelo de predicción de todos los genotipos posibles que se pueden obtener a partir de un determinado cruzamiento o apareamiento.

pupa stage of metamorphosis in which the organism reorganizes into a completely new body form. (p. 744)
pupa fase de la metamorfosis en la que el organismo adopta una nueva forma corporal.

purebred type of organism whose ancestors are genetically uniform. (p. 178)
pura raza organismo de ancestros con uniformidad genética.

R

radial symmetry arrangement of body parts in a circle around a central axis. (p. 701)
simetría radial disposición de las partes del cuerpo en un círculo que rodea un eje central.

radiometric dating technique that uses the natural decay rate of isotopes to calculate the age of material. (p. 362)
fechado radiométrico técnica para medir la tasa natural de decaimiento de los isótopos para calcular la edad de los materiales.

radula filelike feeding organ found in mollusks. (p. 712)
rádula órgano raspador con el que se alimentan los moluscos.

ray-fin fan-shaped arrangement of bones in a fish's fin. (p. 768)
aleta radial disposición en abanico de las espinas de una aleta de pez.

reactant substance that is changed by a chemical reaction. (p. 50)
reactante sustancia que cambia a consecuencia de una reacción química.

receptor protein that detects a signal molecule and performs an action in response. (p. 84)
receptor proteína que detecta la señal de una molécula y responde con una acción concreta.

recessive allele that is not expressed unless two copies are present in an organism's genotype. (p. 181)
recesivo alelo que no se expresa, a menos que en el genotipo del organismo en cuestión estén presentes dos copias de dicho gen.

recombinant DNA (ree-KAHM-buh-nuhnt) genetically engineered DNA that contains genes from more than one organism or species. (p. 276)
ADN recombinante ADN manipulado geneticamente que contiene genes de más de un organismo o especie.

red blood cell cell that carries oxygen gas from the lungs to the rest of the body. (p. 915)
glóbulo rojo célula encargada de transportar oxígeno gaseoso de los pulmones al resto del cuerpo.

reflex arc nerve pathway in which an impulse crosses only two synapses before producing a response. (p. 889)
arco reflejo circuito nervioso en el que un impulso sólo atraviesa dos simpasis antes de producir una respuesta.

regeneration process by which a new plant can grow from a fragment of a nonreproductive structure, such as a root, stem, or leaf. (p. 678)
regeneración proceso mediante el cual una nueva planta puede desarrollarse a partir de un fragmento de una estructura no reproductora, como una raíz, un tallo o una hoja.

relative dating estimate of the age of a fossil based on the location of fossils in strata. (p. 362)
datación relativa estimación de la edad de un fósil según la ubicación de los fósiles en los estratos.

releaser stimulus that triggers a specific behavior. (p. 822)
estímulo liberador que suscita un comportamiento específico.

releasing hormone chemical that stimulates other glands to release their hormones. (p. 900)
hormona liberadora sustancia química que estimula otras glándulas para que secreten hormonas.

renewable resource resource that replenishes itself quickly enough so that it will not be used faster than it can be produced. (p. 485)
recurso renovable recurso natural que se restablece a un ritmo superior del ritmo al que se consume.

replication process by which DNA is copied. (p. 235)
replicación proceso mediante el cual se copian las moléculas de ADN.

Glossary

reproductive isolation final stage in speciation, in which members of isolated populations are either no longer able to mate or no longer able to produce viable offspring. (p. 344)
aislamiento reproductor fase final de la especiación en la que los miembros de poblaciones aisladas pierden la capacidad de aparearse o no pueden producir crías viables.

reproductive system body system that allows for sexual reproduction; includes testes, ovaries, uterus, and other male and female sex organs. (p. 1024)
sistema reproductor sistema corporal que permite la reproducción sexual; consta de testículos, ovarios, útero y otros órganos sexuales masculinos y femeninos.

reptile ectotherm that is covered with dry scales, breathes with lungs, and reproduces by laying eggs. (p. 793)
reptil vertebrado ectotermo con la piel cubierta de escamas, que respira con pulmones y que pone huevos para reproducirse.

respiratory system body system that brings oxygen into the body and removes carbon dioxide; includes the nose, trachea, and lungs. (p. 910)
sistema respiratorio sistema corporal que lleva oxígeno al cuerpo y elimina el dióxido de carbono; consta de nariz, tráquea y pulmones.

resting potential difference in electrical charge between the inside and outside of a neuron; contains the potential energy needed to transmit the impulse. (p. 877)
potencial de reposo diferencia de carga eléctrica entre el interior y el exterior de una neurona; energía potencial necesaria para transmitir un impulso.

restriction enzyme enzyme that cuts DNA molecules at specific nucleotide sequences. (p. 265)
enzima de restricción enzima que fragmenta moléculas de ADN en secuencias específicas de nucleótidos.

restriction map diagram that shows the lengths of fragments between restriction sites in the strand of DNA. (p. 267)
mapa de restricción diagrama que representa las longitudes de los fragmentos entre los sitios de corte de una hebra de ADN.

retrovirus virus that contains RNA and uses the enzyme called reverse transcriptase to make a DNA copy. (p. 553)
retrovirus virus que contiene ARN y que usa una enzima llamada transcriptasa para hacer una copia del ADN.

Rh factor surface protein on red blood cells in the ABO blood group; people can be Rh$^+$ or Rh$^-$. (p. 928)
factor Rh proteína de la superficie de los glóbulos rojos de los grupos sanguíneos ABO; el factor Rh de las personas puede ser Rh$^+$ o Rh$^-$.

ribosomal RNA (rRNA) RNA that is in the ribosome and guides the translation of mRNA into a protein; also used as a molecular clock. (pp. 240; 532)
ARN ribosómico (ARNr) ARN presente en los ribosomas que guía el proceso de síntesis de las proteínas a partir del ARNm; también denominado reloj molecular.

ribosome (RY-buh-SOHM) organelle that links amino acids together to form proteins. (p. 76)
ribosoma orgánulo que enlaza las moléculas de aminoácidos para formar proteínas.

ribozyme RNA molecule that can catalyze specific chemical reactions. (p. 370)
Ribozima molécula de ARN que tiene la capacidad de catalizar determinadas reacciones químicas.

RNA nucleic acid molecule that allows for the transmission of genetic information and protein synthesis. (p. 239)
ARN molécula de ácido nucleico encargada de la transmisión de información genética y de la síntesis de las proteínas.

RNA polymerase enzyme that catalyzes the synthesis of a complementary strand of RNA from a DNA template. (p. 240)
ARN polimerasa enzima que cataliza la síntesis de una hebra complementaria de ARN a partir de un patrón de ADN.

rod cell photoreceptor in the eye that detects light intensity and contributes to black and white vision. (p. 881)
bastoncillo célula fotosensible del ojo que detecta la intensidad de la luz y contribuye a la visión en blanco y negro.

root cap mass of cells that covers and protects the tips of plant roots. (p. 648)
ápice de la raíz masa de células que cubre y protege las puntas de las raíces de las plantas.

root hair thin hairlike outgrowth of an epidermal cell of a plant root that absorbs water and minerals from the soil. (p. 648)
pelos radicales finas extensiones de la célula epidérmica en las raíces de una planta encargada de absorber agua y minerales del suelo.

S

sarcomere section of a muscle fiber that contains all of the filaments necessary to cause muscle contraction. (p. 1008)
sarcómero sección de fibra muscular con todos los filamentos necesarios para generar una contracción muscular.

sclerenchyma cell thick-walled, lignin-rich cells that form a supportive plant tissue. (p. 641)
esclereida célula rica en lignina que constituye el esclerénquima, un tejido de sostén de las plantas.

scrotum skin that encloses the testes outside of the male body. (p. 1026)
escroto piel que envuelve las gónadas masculinas en el exterior del cuerpo.

secondary growth growth in woody plants resulting in wider roots, branches, and stems. (p. 651)
crecimiento secundario crecimiento de las plantas que produce un engrosamiento de las raíces, de las ramas y de los tallos.

secondary succession reestablishment of a damaged ecosystem in an area where the soil was left intact. (p. 447)
sucesión secundaria desarrollo de un ecosistema dañado en una zona donde el suelo permanece inalterado.

seed structure used by some land plants to store and protect the embryo. (p. 614)
semilla estructura empleada por algunas plantas para almacenar y proteger al embrión.

segmentation repeated sections of an annelid's long body that contain the same set of body structures, apart from its distinct head and tail region. (pp. 714; 730)
segmentación secciones repetidas del cuerpo alargado de un anélido, cada una de las cueles contiene el mismo conjunto de estructuras corporales, con excepción de la cabeza y de la cola.

selective permeability condition or quality of allowing some, but not all, materials to cross a barrier or membrane. (p. 83)
permeabilidad selectiva condición o cualidad que permite discriminar el flujo de determinados materiales a través de una membrana o barrera.

semen white substance that contains sperm and fluids produced by sex glands of the male reproductive system. (p. 1026)
semen sustancia blanca que contiene espermatozoides y fluidos generados por las glándulas sexuales del sistema reproductor masculino.

sepal modified leaf that covers and protects the flower while it develops. (p. 668)
sépalo hoja modificada que cubre la flor durante su desarrollo.

sensitization process by which a neuron adds more receptors to its surface in response to consistently lower amounts of a neurotransmitter in the synapse. (p. 893)
sensibilización proceso mediante el cual una neurona incorpora a su superficie más receptores en respuesta a una insuficiencia sostenida de neurotransmisores en el espacio sináptico.

sessile unable to move from a fixed point. (p. 705)
sésil fijo a un punto, que no se mueve.

sex chromosome chromosome that directly controls the development of sexual characteristics. (p. 169)
cromosoma sexual cromosoma que controla directamente el desarrollo de las características sexuales.

sex-linked gene gene that is located on a sex chromosome. (p. 201)
gen ligado al sexo gen ubicado en un cromosoma sexual.

sexually transmitted disease (STD) disease that is passed from one person to another during sexual contact. (p. 1032)
enfermedad de transmisión sexual (ETS) enfermedad que se transmite de una persona a otra durante el contacto sexual.

sexual reproduction process by which two gametes fuse and offspring that are a genetic mixture of both parents are produced. (p. 170)
reproducción sexual proceso mediante el cual se unen dos gametos que dan lugar a crías cuyo genoma es una mezcla del de los dos progenitores.

sexual selection selection in which certain traits enhance mating success; traits are, therefore, passed on to offspring. (p. 338)
selección sexual selección en la que determinados rasgos incrementan el éxito del apareamiento; en consecuencia, tales rasgos se transmiten a las crías.

skeletal muscle muscle tissue that is attached to the skeletal system and, when contracted, moves bones. (p. 1006)
músculo esquelético tejido muscular adherido al sistema esquelético que, al contraerse, mueve los músculos.

skeletal system body system that includes bones and the connective tissues that hold the bones together in the body. (p. 1000)
sistema esquelético sistema que consta de los huesos y de los tejidos conjuntivos que mantienen unidos a los huesos.

slime mold protist with a slimelike amoeboid stage that grows on decaying vegetation and in moist soil. (p. 587)
moho mucoso protista de aspecto gelatinoso con una fase ameboide, que crece en material vegetal en descomposición y en la tierra húmeda.

small intestine organ of the digestive system that connects the stomach to the large intestine and in which chemical digestion takes place. (p. 980)
intestino delgado órgano del sistema digestivo que conecta el estómago al intestino grueso y en el que se produce la digestión química.

smog air pollution in which gases released from burning fossil fuels form a fog when they react with sunlight. (p. 488)
smog contaminación atmosférica en la que los gases liberados por la combustión de hidrocarburos reaccionan con la luz creando una niebla.

smooth muscle muscle tissue that moves substances, such as food and blood, through organs and tissues, such as the digestive system organs and blood vessels. (p. 1007)
músculo liso tejido muscular que mueve los alimentos y la sangre por los órganos y los tejidos como, por ejemplo, los órganos del sistema digestivo y los vasos sanguíneos.

sodium potassium pump active transport protein in neurons that carries sodium (Na^+) ions out of the cell and bring potassium (K^+) ions into the cell. (p. 877)
bomba sodio-potasio transporte activo de proteínas en las neuronas, en el que se extrae de la célula iones de sodio (Na^+) y se mete iones de potasio (K^+).

solute substance that dissolves in a solvent and is present at a lower concentration than the solvent. (p. 42)
soluto sustancia que se disuelve en un solvente y que aparece en menor concentración que éste.

solution mixture that is consistent throughout; also called a homogeneous mixture. (p. 42)
solución mezcla uniforme en toda su extensión; también se conoce como mezcla homogénea.

Glossary

solvent substance in which solutes dissolve and that is present in greatest concentration in a solution. (p. 42)

solvente sustancia en la que se disuelve un soluto y que se presenta en mayor concentración que éste.

somatic cell (soh-MAT-ihk) cell that makes up all of the body tissues and organs, except gametes. (p. 168)

célula somática célula que conforma todos los tejidos y órganos del organismo, excepto los gametos.

somatic nervous system division of the peripheral nervous system that transports signals from the brain to the muscles that produce voluntary movements. (p. 889)

sistema nervioso somático parte del sistema nervioso periférico que transporta señales del encéfalo a los músculos para producir los movimientos voluntarios.

specialist consumer that eats only one type of organism. (p. 409)

especialista consumidor que se alimenta de un solo tipo de organismo.

speciation evolution of two or more species from one ancestral species. (p. 344)

especiación evolución de dos o más especies a partir de una sola especie ancestral.

species group of organisms so similar to one another that they can breed and produce fertile offspring. (pp. 5; 298)

especie grupo de organismos tan semejantes entre sí que pueden reproducirse y tener descendencia fértil.

sperm male gamete. (p. 176)

espermatozoide gameto masculino.

sphincter (SFIHNGK-tuhr) ring of muscle that separates the different organs of the digestive system. (p. 977)

esfínter músculo en forma de anillo que separa a los diversos órganos del sistema digestivo.

spiracle (SPIHR-uh-kuhl) hole on the body of an insect's exoskeleton through which air can be taken in or released. (p. 741)

espiráculo orificio en el cuerpo del exoesqueleto de los insectos a través del cual entra y sale aire.

sporangia spore-forming structures found in fungi, algae, and some plants. (p. 592)

esporangio estructura que produce esporas y que se encuentra en los hongos, las algas y algunas plantas.

sporophyte (SPAWR-uh-FYT) diploid, spore-producing phase of a plant life cycle. (p. 664)

esporofita fase diploide de producción de esporas en el ciclo de vida de una planta.

stabilizing selection pathway of natural selection in which intermediate phenotypes are selected over phenotypes at both extremes. (p. 332)

selección estabilizadora proceso de selección natural en el que se da preferencia a los fenotipos intermedios sobre los fenotipos de ambos extremos.

stamen male structure of flowering plants; includes the stalk and anther, which produces pollen. (p. 668)

estambre estructura floral masculina de las gimnospermas; consiste de una antera productora de polen unida a un pedicelo.

start codon codon that signals to ribosomes to begin translation; codes for the first amino acid in a protein. (p. 244)

codón de iniciación codón que da la señal a los ribosomas para que inicien el proceso de traducción; codifica el primer aminoácido de la proteína.

stem cell cell that can divide for long periods of time while remaining undifferentiated. (p. 153)

célula madre célula capaz de dividirse durante largos periodos de tiempo sin diferenciarse.

sternum long, flat bone that connects the ribs in front of the chest and to which the chest muscle attaches. (p. 801)

esternón hueso plano y alargado que conecta las costillas a la altura del pecho y al que van adheridos los músculos pectorales.

stimulant drug that increases the number of impulses that neurons generate. (p. 894)

estimulante droga que incrementa el número de impulsos que generan las neuronas.

stimulus (STIHM-yuh-luhs) (plural: *stimuli*) something that causes a physiological response. (pp. 818; 874)

estímulo cualquier cosa capaz de provocar una respuesta fisiológica.

stomach muscular sac in the digestive system that breaks down food into a liquidlike mixture. (p. 978)

estómago saco muscular del sistema digestivo donde se descompone la comida en una mezcla líquida.

stomata (singular: *stoma*) pores in the cuticle of a plant through which gas exchange occurs. (p. 614)

estoma poro en la cutícula de una planta a través del cual se produce el intercambio gaseoso.

stop codon codon that signals to ribosomes to stop translation. (p. 244)

codón de terminación codón que indica a los ribosomas que detengan el proceso de traducción.

substrate reactant in a chemical reaction upon which an enzyme acts. (p. 56)

sustrato reactivo de una reacción química sobre el que actúa un enzima.

succession sequence of biotic changes that regenerate a damaged community or start a community in a previously uninhabited area. (p. 445)

sucesión secuencia de cambios bióticos que regeneran una comunidad dañada o que crean una nueva comunidad en una zona hasta entonces deshabitada.

survivorship probability of surviving to a particular age. (p. 827)

supervivencia probabilidad de sobrevivir hasta una edad determinada.

survivorship curve graph showing the surviving members of each age group of a population over time. (p. 438)
curva de sobrevivencia gráfica que representa los sobrevivientes de una población por grupos de edad durante un periodo determinado.

sustainable development practice of not using natural resources more quickly than they can be replenished. (p. 502)
desarrollo sostenible práctica que consiste en no utilizar los recursos naturales más rápidamente de lo que pueden ser generarlos.

swim bladder buoyancy organ that helps fish to swim at different depths in the water. (p. 769)
vejiga natatoria órgano de flotación que permite a los peces nadar a diferentes profundidades.

symbiosis ecological relationship between members of at least two different species that live in direct contact with one another. (p. 432)
simbiosis relación ecológica en la que los miembros de al menos dos especies diferentes viven en contacto directo.

sympathetic nervous system part of the autonomic nervous system that prepares the body for action and stress. (p. 890)
sistema nervioso simpático sistema que forma parte del sistema nervioso autónomo y que se encarga de preparar el cuerpo para situaciones de acción y de estrés.

synapse tiny gap between neurons through which chemical signals are sent. (p. 879)
sinapsis pequeño espacio entre las neuronas a través del cual se envían señales químicas.

system changing, organized group of related parts that interact to form a whole. (p. 7)
sistema conjunto organizado y dinámico de partes que interactúan entre sí para formar un todo.

systemic circuit (sihs-STEHM-ihk) collection of blood vessels that carries blood between the heart and the rest of the body, except for the lungs. (pp. 789; 920)
circuito sistémico conjunto de vasos sanguíneos que transporta la sangre entre el corazón y el resto del cuerpo, excepto los pulmones.

systemic circulation *see* systemic circuit.
circulación sistémica *véanse* circuito sistémico.

systolic pressure (sih-STAHL-ihk) measure of pressure on the walls of an artery when the left ventricle contracts to pump blood through the body. (p. 923)
presión sistólica medida de la presión de las paredes arteriales cuando el ventrículo izquierdo se contrae para bombear sangre a través del cuerpo.

T

tadpole aquatic larva of frogs or toads. (p. 774)
renacuajo larva acuática de las ranas y los sapos.

taiga (TY-guh) biome with long and cold winters, lasting up to six months; also called a boreal forest. (p. 465)
taiga bioma propio de zonas de largos y fríos inviernos de hasta seis meses de duración; también se conoce como bosque boreal.

taproot main root of some plants, usually larger than other roots and growing straight down from a stem. (p. 649)
raíz pivotante raíz principal de determinadas plantas, normalmente más grande que las demás raíces y que crece en en lína recta hacia abajo a partir del tallo.

taxis movement in a particular direction, either toward or away from a stimulus. (p. 819)
taxismo movimiento en una dirección determinada, ya sea hacia un estímulo o en sentido opuesto a éste; conocido también como taxis.

taxon (plural: *taxa*) level within the Linnaean system of classification (kingdom, phylum, class, order, family, genus, or species) that is organized into a nested hierarchy. (p. 518)
taxón cualquiera de los niveles del sistema de clasificación jerárquico de Linneo, (reino, división, clase, orden, familia, género o especie).

taxonomy science of classifying and naming organisms. (p. 518)
taxonomía ciencia dedicada a la clasificación y nomenclatura de los organismos.

T cell white blood cell that matures in the thymus and destroys infected body cells by causing them to burst; also called a T-lymphocyte. (p. 946)
célula T glóbulo blanco que madura en el timo y que destruye las células infectadas haciéndolas reventar; también se conoce como linfocito T.

telomere (TEHL-uh-MEER) repeating nucleotide at the ends of DNA molecules that do not form genes and help prevent the loss of genes. (p. 139)
telómero extremo de la molécula de ADN compuesto de nucleótidos repetidos que no producen genes pero que ayudan a prevenir la pérdida de éstos.

telophase last phase of mitosis when a complete set of identical chromosomes is positioned at each pole of the cell, the nuclear membranes start to form, the chromosomes begin to uncoil, and the spindle fibers disassemble. (p. 140)
telofase última fase de la mitosis en que un conjunto completo de cromosomas idénticos se sitúa en los polos opuestos de la célula; empiezan a formarse las membranas nucleares; los cromosomas empiezan a desenrollarse y el huso mitótico se desintegra.

temporal isolation isolation between populations due to barriers related to time, such as differences in mating periods or differences in the time of day that individuals are most active. (p. 346)
aislamiento temporal aislamiento entre poblaciones que se produce por motivos de índole temporal como, por ejemplo, diferencias en los períodos de apareamiento o de las horas del día en que los individuos son más activos.

Glossary

tendon band of connective tissue that joins a muscle to the bone that it moves. (p. 1006)
tendón banda de tejido conjuntivo que conecta cada músculo con el hueso que mueve.

terminal end of the neuron's axon from which neurotransmitters are released to stimulate an adjacent cell. (p. 879)
terminal extremo del axón de la neurona desde el cual se segregan neurotransmisores para estimular a la célula adyacente.

territoriality behavior pattern in which an organism controls and defends a specific area. (p. 828)
territorialidad patrón de comportamiento mediante el cual un organismo determinado controla y defiende un área específica.

testcross cross between an organism with an unknown genotype and an organism with a recessive phenotype. (p. 185)
cruzamiento de prueba cruzamiento entre un organismo de genotipo desconocido y un organismo de fenotipo recesivo.

testis (plural: *testes*) organ of the male reproductive system that produces sperm. (p. 1025)
testículo órgano del sistema reproductor masculino encargado de la producción de espermatozoides.

testosterone (tehs-TAHS-tuh-ROHN) steroid hormone that is found in greater quantities in men than women and contributes to male sexual characteristics and development. (p. 1025)
testosterona hormona esteroide que se encuentra en mayor cantidad en el hombre que en la mujer y que contribuye al desarrollo de las características sexuales masculinas.

tetrapod vertebrate with four limbs. (p. 773)
tetrápodo vertebrado con cuatro extremidades.

theory proposed explanation for a wide variety of observations and experimental results. (p. 16)
teoría explicación de un fenómeno a partir de una amplia gama de observaciones y resultados experimentales.

thermoregulation (THUR-moh-REHG-yoo-LAY-shuhn) process of the body maintaining a stable internal temperature under various conditions. (p. 863)
termorregulación proceso que permite mantener una temperatura interna constante bajo diferentes condiciones.

thigmotropism turning or bending of a plant in response to contact with an object. (p. 682)
tigmotropismo giro o flexión de una planta como respuesta al contacto con un objeto.

thylakoid (THY-luh-KOYD) membrane-bound structure within chloroplasts that contains chlorophyll and other light-absorbing pigments used in the light-dependent reactions of photosynthesis. (p. 104)
tilacoide estructura de la membrana interna de los cloroplastos que contiene clorofila y otros pigmentos fotoabsorbentes que intervienen en las reacciones captadoras de luz de la fotosíntesis.

tissue group of cells that work together to perform a similar function. (pp. 151; 854)
tejido grupo de células similares que trabajan juntas para desempeñar la misma función.

tissue rejection process by which a transplant recipient's immune system makes antibodies against the protein markers on the donor's tissue; can result in the destruction of the donor tissue. (p. 954)
rechazo de tejidos proceso mediante el cual el sistema inmune de un individuo receptor de un transplante genera anticuerpos contra los marcadores proteicos del tejido donante; puede producir la destrucción del tejido donante.

tolerance drug resistance that occurs when cells adapt, requiring larger doses of the drug to produce the same effect. (p. 893)
tolerancia resistencia a una droga producida cuando las células se adaptan a ella, lo cual requiere un aumento de la dosis para producir el mismo efecto.

toxin poison released by an organism. (p. 563)
toxina sustancia tóxica producida por un organismo.

trachea (TRAY-kee-uh) (plural: *tracheae*) long structure made of soft tissue that connects the mouth and nose to the lungs in humans (p. 911); a system of thin branching tubes in the bodies of insects that allow for breathing. (p. 741)
tráquea tubo alargado de tejido blando que conecta la boca y la nariz con los pulmones de los humanos; sistema de finos tubos ramificados en el cuerpo de los insectos que les permite respirar.

trait characteristic that is inherited. (p. 177)
rasgo característica heredada.

transcription process of copying a nucleotide sequence of DNA to form a complementary strand of mRNA. (p. 240)
transcripción proceso donde se copia una secuencia de ADN para formar una cadena complementaria de ARNm.

transfer RNA (tRNA) form of RNA that brings amino acids to ribosomes during protein synthesis. (p. 240)
ARN de transferencia (ARNt) tipo de ARN que transporta aminoácidos a los ribosomas durante el proceso de síntesis proteica.

transgenic organism whose genome has been altered to contain one or more genes from another organism or species. (pp. 26; 277)
transgénico organismo cuyo genoma ha sido alterado mediante la incorporación de uno o más genes de otro organismo o especie.

translation process by which mRNA is decoded and a protein is produced. (p. 243)
traducción proceso mediante el cual se decodifica el ARNm y se produce una proteína.

transpiration release of vapor through the pores of the skin or the stomata of plant tissue. (p. 645)
transpiración liberación de vapor a través de los poros de la piel o, en los tejidos vegetales, de los estomas.

trimester one of three periods of approximately three months each into which a human pregnancy is divided. (p. 1036)

trimestre uno de los períodos de aproximadamente tres meses en que se divide la gestación humana.

trophic level level of nourishment in a food chain. (p. 409)

nivel trófico nivel de alimentación de la cadena trófica.

tropism movement or growth of a plant in response to an environmental stimulus. (p. 681)

tropismo movimiento o crecimiento determinado por un estímulo ambiental.

tundra biome found at far northern latitudes where winters last as long as ten months per year. (p. 466)

tundra bioma de latitudes septentrionales extremas donde los inviernos duran hasta diez meses.

U

umbilical cord structure that connects an embryo to its mother and provides the embryo with nourishment and waste removal. (p. 1035)

cordón umbilical estructura que conecta el embrión con su madre y que le suministra alimento y un sistema de eliminación de residuos.

umbrella species species whose being protected under the Endangered Species Act leads to the preservation of its habitat and all of the other organisms in its community. (p. 503)

especie paraguas especie protegida por la Ley de Especies en Peligro de Extinción cuya salvaguarda conlleva la protección de su hábitat y la de todos los otros organismos que viven en él.

uniformitarianism theory that states that the geologic processes that shape Earth are uniform through time. (p. 301)

uniformitarismo teoría según la cual los procesos geológicos que dan forma a la Tierra se producen de manera uniforme a lo largo del tiempo.

ureter (yu-REE-tuhr) tube of connective tissue that carries urine from each of the kidneys to the bladder. (p. 986)

uréter tubo de tejido conjuntivo que transporta la orina desde los riñones hasta la vejiga.

urinary bladder saclike organ that collects and stores urine before it is excreted from the body. (p. 986)

vejiga urinaria órgano en forma de bolsa donde se recoge y se almacena la orina antes de ser excretada del cuerpo.

uterus organ of the female reproductive system in which a fertilized egg attaches and a fetus develops. (p. 1024)

útero órgano del sistema reproductor femenino al que se adhiere el huevo fertilizado y dónde se desarrolla el feto.

V

vaccine substance that stimulates an immune response, producing acquired immunity without illness or infection. (pp. 553; 956)

vacuna sustancia que estimula una respuesta inmune y que proporciona inmunidad ante una enfermedad o infección determinada sin provocarla.

vacuole (VAK-yoo-OHL) organelle that is used to store materials, such as water, food, or enzymes, that are needed by the cell. (p. 77)

vacuola orgánulo encargado de almacenar diversos materiales necesarios para la célula, como el agua, nutrientes o enzimas.

valve flap of tissue that prevents blood from flowing backward into a blood vessel or heart chamber. (p. 917)

válvula tejido membranoso encargado de evitar que la sangre refluya por el vaso sanguíneo en que circula o hacia una cavidad del corazón.

variation differences in physical traits of an individual from the group to which it belongs. (p. 302)

variación diferencia en rasgos físicos que presenta un individuo con respecto al grupo al que pertenece.

vascular cylinder center of a root or stem that contains phloem and xylem. (p. 648)

cilindro vascular cilindro en el centro de una raíz o tallo que contiene el floema y el xilema.

vascular system collection of specialized tissues in some plants that transports mineral nutrients up from the roots and brings sugars down from the leaves. (p. 614)

sistema vascular conjunto de tejidos especializados de determinadas plantas que transportan nutrientes minerales desde las raíces hacia arriba y que conducen el azúcar de las hojas hacia abajo.

vascular tissue supportive and conductive tissue in plants, consisting of xylem and phloem. (p. 642)

tejido vascular tejido conductor y de sostén de las plantas que consta de xilema y de floema.

vas deferens duct in which sperm mixes with other fluids before reaching the urethra. (p. 1026)

conducto deferente conducto en el que el esperma se mezcla con otros fluidos antes de alcanzar la uretra.

vector organism, such as a mosquito or tick, that transfers pathogens from one host to another. (pp. 748; 944)

vector organismo, como o el mosquito o la garrapatas que puede transferir patógenos de un huésped a otro.

vegetative reproduction asexual reproduction in which a stem, leaf, or root will produce a new individual when detached from a parent plant. (p. 678)

reproducción vegetativa reproducción asexual en la que un tallo, una hoja o una raíz producen un nuevo individuo cuando se separan de la planta de la cual forman parte.

Glossary

vein large blood vessel that carries blood from the rest of the body to the heart. (p. 913)
vena vaso sanguíneo de gran caudal que transporta la sangre desde todas las partes del cuerpo hasta el corazón.

ventricle large chamber in the heart that receives blood from an atrium and pumps blood to the rest of the body. (p. 917)
ventrículo amplia cámara del corazón que recibe sangre de la aurícula y la impulsa al resto del cuerpo.

vertebra (plural: *vertebrae*) bone that makes up the spinal column. (p. 1001)
vértebra hueso que compone la columna vertebral.

vertebrate animal with an internal segmented backbone. (p. 699)
vertebrado animal con una columna vertebral interna y segmentada.

vesicle (VEHS-ih-kuhl) small organelle that contains and transports materials within the cytoplasm. (p. 77)
vesícula pequeño orgánulo que contiene y transporta materiales en el interior del citoplasma.

vestigial structure remnants of an organ or structure that functioned in an earlier ancestor. (p. 314)
estructura vestigial restos de algún órgano o estructura en una especie determinada que cumplieron alguna función en un ancestrode ésta.

villus (VIHL-uhs) (plural: *villi*) small fingerlike projection in the small intestine that absorbs nutrients. (p. 983)
vellosidades pequeñas proyecciones en forma de dedo del intestino delgado encargadas de absorber los nutrientes.

viroid infectious particle made of single-stranded RNA without a protein coat, that almost always use plants as their host. (p. 544)
viroide partícula infecciosa que consta de un solo filamento de ARN sin envoltura de proteínas, que casi siempre se hospeda como parásito en las plantas.

virus infectious particle made only of a strand of either DNA or RNA surrounded by a protein coat. (p. 544)
virus partícula infecciosa que consta de un sólo filamento de ADN o ARN y rodeado por una envuelta de proteína.

vitamin organic molecule that works with enzymes to regulate cell function, growth, and development. (p. 974)
vitamina molécula orgánica que funciona con enzimas para regular el funcionamiento, el crecimiento y el desarrollo de las células.

viviparous reproductive strategy in which the embryo develops within the mother's body. (p. 793)
vivíparo modalidad de reproducción en la que los embriones se desarrollan en el interior de la madre.

W

water mold fungus that is either a parasite or decomposer and lives in fresh water or moist soil. (p. 588)
moho acuático hongo acuático o de suelos húmedos que actúa como parásito o descomponedor de materia orgánica.

watershed region of land that drains into a river, river system, or other body of water. (p. 473)
cuenca hidrográfica área terrestre que vierte sus aguas hacia un río, una red fluvial o cualquier otra masa acuática.

water vascular system system of water-filled canals that extend down each arm of a echinoderm, such as a sea star. (p. 718)
sistema ambulacral sistema formado por una serie de tubos llenos de agua que se prolongan por los brazos de los equinodermos como, por ejemplo, la estrella de mar.

white blood cell cell that attacks pathogens. (p. 928)
glóbulo blanco célula cuya funcíon es atacar a los patógenos.

wood fibrous material made of dead cells that are part of the vascular system in some plants. (p. 627)
madera material fibroso formado por células muertas que forman parte del sistema vascular de algunas plantas.

X

X chromosome inactivation process that occurs in female mammals in which one of the X chromosomes is randomly turned off in each cell. (p. 203)
inactivación X proceso en los mamíferos del sexo femenino en que uno de los cromosomas X de cada célula se desactiva aleatoriamente.

xylem tissue that transports water and dissolved minerals in vascular plants. (p. 642)
xilema tejido de las plantas vasculares que transporta agua y sales minerales disueltas.

Z

zooplankton animal plankton. (p. 469)
zooplancton plancton animal.

zygote cell that forms when a male gamete fertilizes a female gamete. (p. 1031)
cigoto célula formada cuando un gameto masculino fertiliza un gameto femenino.

Index

Page numbers for definitions are printed in **boldface** type. Page numbers for illustrations, maps, and charts are printed in *italics*.

A

abdomen, **735**
abiotic factor, **402**–405, 457, 458
ABO blood group, **927**–928, *928*
absorption, *644*, 649, **982**
abyssal zone, **469**
acacia, 349, *349*
Acanthodian, 765
Acanthostega, 773
acetylcholine, 892
acid, **42**–43
acid rain, *483*, **489**, *489*, 493
acne, *564*
Acoelomorpha, 704
acquired characteristics, inheritance of, 299. *See also* heredity.
acquired immune deficiency syndrome (AIDS), 960, **963**, 965, 1032
acquired immunity, 948, 951
Acrasiomycota, 587
acrosome, 1030
actin filament, **1008**–1011, *1009, 1010*
action potential, *878*, **879**, 893–894
activation energy, *52*, **53**, *54*, 54–55
active immunity, **948**
active transport, **89**–90, *89*, 877, *877*
adaptation, 10–11, **302**–303, *307*, 353
    and animal behavior, 818–821, 825–826
    of birds, 799–803
    to climate, 461
    as compromise, 309
    to ecosystem, 473
    environmental, 305–306, 321
    of finches, 308–309, 311
    of freshwater organisms, 473
    of insects, 744–746
    of leaves, 655
    online animation, 477
    of plants, 613–614, *615*, 624–625, *625*, 657
adaptive radiation, **351**, 367
addiction, **893**, 903
Addison's disease, 901
adenine, 230–233, *231, 233*, 240
adenosine diphosphate, 101
adenosine triphosphate, 100
adhesion, **41**, *41*, 643–645, *644*
adolescence, 1042
ADP, 101, *102*
adrenal gland, **898**, *899*, 901
adulthood, 1043
adult stem cell, 154
advantageous characteristics. *See* natural selection.
aerobic process, **113**
aflatoxin, 590
African swallowtail, 334
African violet, 679
agar, 584

agave plant, 680, *680*
aging, 1043
Agnatha, 760, *765. See also* jawless fish.
agriculture, 565, 567, 629–630
AIDS, 960, **963**, 965, 1032
Ailurus fulgens, 521
airfoil, **799**
air movement, 460
air quality, 488–492
air sac, **801**
alanine, 244
albatross, 436
albinism, 59, 207, *207*
albumin, 926
alcoholic fermentation, 124–125
aldosterone, 84
algae, *410*, 411, **581**–586, 601
    green, 612–613, *613*
    limiting nutrients for, 448
    photosynthetic, 99, *99*
    red, 584, *R26*
    and pollution, 494
alkaloid, **631**
allele, **180**–184, 187. *See also* genetics.
    codominance, 205–206, *205*, 208
    dominant/recessive, 341
    in gene pool, 328–329
    and genetic disorders, 201
    incomplete dominance, **204**–205, *205*, 219
    and phenotypes, 204–207
    and probability, 193
allele frequency, **328**–331, *329*, 341–343
allergen, **957**–958
allergy, 692, **957**
Allosaurus, 798
aloe vera, 631
alternation of generations, **664**, *664*
Altman, Sidney, 370
altruism, 833–836
Alvarez, José and Maria, *990*
alveolus, **911**–912, *914*, 914–916, *915*
Alzheimer's disease, 1052
amber-preserved fossil, 360
Ambulocetus natans, 318
amino acid, **47**–48, *47*, 369
    essential, 973
    and molecular clocks, 530–531, *531*
    and species' relatedness, 529
    and translation, 243–247
Amish communities, 336
ammonia, 415
ammonification, 415
amniote, **778**–779, 786–809
    anatomy and circulation, 789–790, *790*
    birds, 798–804
    body temperature regulation, 791–792
    embryos, 788, *788*
    mammals, 805–809
    reptiles, 793–797

amniotic egg, **779**, 788, *788*
amniotic sac, 526, 788, **1035**, *1035*
amoeba, 578, *578*
amoebocyte, 706
Amphibia, 760
amphibian, 430, 526, **773**–777, 781
    online animation, 477
amygdala, 888
amylase, 55, 56, 978, *978*
anaerobic process, **113**
analogies, drawing, 353
analogous structure, **313**, *313*
analyzing data. *See* data analysis.
anaphase, **140**, *141*
anaphylaxis, **958**
anapsid, 794
ancestry, common, 244, 299, 310–313, 317, 524–525
Andes mountains, 303
anemone, sea, 150, 468, 707–708, 827, *R28*
angioplasty, 924
angiosperm, **621**, 622. *See also* flowering plant.
anhinga, 395, *395*
animal
    and allergies, 958
    arthropods, 704, 716, 728–749, **730**
    body structures, 696, *696*, 699–700, 723
    body temperature regulation, 863, 875, 900, 913
    cells, 74, 78, 113, 140
    characteristics of, 696–698
    classification of, 701–702
    developmental patterns of, 702, *702*
    embryo growth, 153, *153*
    and fungi, 697
    genetic engineering in, 278–279
    invertebrates, **699**, 705–720
    and neurons, *873*
    online animation, 723
    phyla, 699, 703–704, *761*
    and sensory organs, 882
    vertebrates, **699**, 756–779
animal behavior, 816–839
    adaptive value of, 818–821, 825–826
    and cognition, **837**–839
    costs of, 827–828, 831, 833–834
    evolution of, 827–829, 833–834
    and hormone cycles, 1028
    instinct and learning, 822–826
    mate selection, 832
    online animation, 841
    problem-solving, 838
    social, 831–836, 838–839
animalcule, *71*
animal fat, 46
Animalia, *R28–R31*

Index

Animated Biology, 21, 29, 41, 52, 59, 74, 93, 104, 114, 127, 157, 175, 182, 193, 219, 233, 237, 246, 257, 266, 270, 287, 307, 321, 337, 342, 353, 373, 385, 406, 421, 430, 449, 474, 477, 484, 491, 507, 531, 537, 550, 567, 579, 583, 601, 633, 644, 657, 685, 723, 732, 745, 751, 763, 775, 781, 800, 811, 828, 841, 855, 867, 878, 889, 903, 912, 919, 933, 956, 965, 993, 1017, 1037, 1043, 1045

anino acid, 243
annelid, 714–715, *715*, 734. *See also* segmented worm.
annual plant, 627
anole lizard, 352, 820, *820*
Anopheles mosquito, 580
ant
    honeypot, 4, *4*
    leafcutter, 599, *599*
    social behavior of, 834, *835*
    stinging, 349, *349*
    weaver, 834
antacid, 992
Antarctica, 467
antelope, 429
antenna, 733, 736
Antennapedia, 698
anther, 668
Anthocerophyta, 617
Anthophyta, 622
anthozoa, 708
anthrax, *564*
anthropoid, **380**, *380*
antibiotic, **564**, *941*, **955**, *955*
    and fungi, 597, 599
    online animation, 567
    resistance, 331, 353, 391–392, 565, **955**
antibody, **947**, *947*, 953, *953*
anticodon, 245
antidiuretic hormone (ADH), 993
antigen, **951**
antigen-presenting cell, 952, *952*
antiseptic, *941*, **955**
anus, 984
aorta, 918
ape, 380, *380*
aphid, 747, *747*
aphotic zone, 468
apical meristem, 648, 651
Apicomplexa, 580
aplacophora, 713
Aplomado Falcon, 848
apoptosis, 145, 157, 853
appendage, **730**
appendicular skeleton, **1000**, *1000*
apple, 679, 681
apple snail, 409, *409*
arachnid, 740–742, *741*
Archaea domain, **534**–535, *535*, 555–557, *R25*
Archaeopteryx, 798, *798*
archosaur, 797
Arctic, 467

Arctic Sea, 492, *492*
Arctic tern, 811
Armadillidium vulgare, 840
armadillo, 303, *524*, 525
Armidillidium vulgare, 519
Armillaria ostoyae, 589
arteriole, 922
arteriosclerosis, 924
artery, **913**
arthropod, 376, 528, 704, 716, 728–749, **730**
    and annelid worms, 734
    arachnids, 740–742, *741*
    characteristics of, 730–734
    crustaceans, 731, *731*, **735**–738
    fossils, 359
    groups, 731, 751
    and humans, 747–749
    insects, 313, 731, *731*, 743–746
    online animation, 751
articular bone, 807
artificial selection, **304**–305, 308, 630
Ascomycota, 590, 594
ascorbic acid, *974*
ascus, 591, 594
asexual reproduction, **148**–150, 373, 678–679
    of algae, 584–585
    of animals, 698
    of fungi, 591–594
    of invertebrates, 705–707, 715
Aspergillis flavus, 590
aspirin, 631
associative learning, 825
Asteroidea, 719
asthma, **916**, 933
athlete's foot, 942
atmosphere, **456**
atom, **36**–37, *37*
    and bond energy, 51
    covalent bonds, **39**, *39*
ATP, **100**–102, *102*, 975
    and active transport, 90
    and cellular respiration, 113, 115, 117–118, 120
    and photosynthesis, 108, 110–111
ATP synthase, **110**, *110*
atrioventricular (AV) node, 918
atrium, **917**
Australia, *441*
australopithecine, 382
Australopithecus afarensis, 382, *383*
autoimmune disease, 959, *959*, 965
autonomic nervous system, **890**
autosome, **169**, 200–201, *201*, 214, *215*
autotroph, **406**
auxin, **681**–682
Avery, Oswald, 227, 229
Aves, 760. *See also* birds.
avian flu, 553, 608
axial skeleton, **1000**, **1001**, *1001*
axillary bud, 652

axolotl, 776
axon, **876**, *876*
azalea, 43

B

Bacillariophyta, 583
bacillus, 556
Bacillus anthracis, 564
Bacillus thuringiensis, 748
background extinction, 350, *350*, 847
bacteria, 79, 544. *See also* prokaryote.
    and antibiotics, 564–565
    cyanobacteria, *366*, 372
    and digestion, 125
    and disease, 942
    drug-resistant, 149, 331, 353, 391–392, 565
    and endosymbiosis, 373
    in esophagus, *543*
    generation times of, 375
    and genetics, 227–228, 276–278
    growth of, *149*
    and humans, 11
    and infections, 563–564, *564*
    in intestine, *559*
    leaf print, 562
    and oil, 561, 566
    online lab, 157, 287, 567
    and plants, 616
    and restriction enzymes, 265, *265*
    shapes of, *556*
    and viral infection, 549
Bacteria domain, **534**–535, *535*, 555–557, *R25*
bacteriophage, **228**, *228*, 391, **549**
bald eagle, 335, *335*, 504
ball-and-socket joint, 1002, *1003*
bandicoot, 190, *190*
band 3 protein, 84
banyan fig, 639
baobab tree, *650*
bar graph, 172, 210, 339, 497, 836, 895, 1038, R16
bark, 650, *651*
barnacle, 311, *311*, 738
barn owl, 519, *519*
barracuda, *768*
base, 42–43
base pair, 230–233, 265
basidia, 592
Basidiomycota, 590, 592
Basilosaurus isis, 316, *316*
basket star, 720, *720*
basophil, 957, *957*
bat
    vampire, 833
    wings of, *312*, 312–313, *313*
    Yuma myotis, *805*
Bateson, William, 209
bathyal zone, 469
B cell, **946**, 947, 951, 953, *953*
beak, 321, 803, 811

bear
  grizzly, *396*
  polar, 9, *9*, 467, *467*, *512*
Beaumont, William, 977
beaver, 403
bee, *429*, *432*, *669*, *746*, *823*, *832*
beetle
  elm bark, 597, *597*
  red leaf, *696*
  red lily, *999*
  rhino, *730*
  snout, *8*, 9
behavior, animal. *See* animal behavior.
behavioral isolation, 345
Beijerinck, Martinus, 547
Belding's ground squirrel, *833*, 833–834
beluga whale, 496
Bengal tiger, *809*
benign tumor, **146**
benthic zone, 468, **474**
best-fit line, 142
betta fish, 205, *205*
bichir, 769
biennial plant, 627
bighorn sheep, 338
bilateral symmetry, **701**, *701*, *703*
bile, 980
binary fission, **148**–149, *149*, 558
binomial nomenclature, **519**
biochemistry. *See* chemistry of life.
biochip, 293
biodegradable material, 561
biodiversity, 5, 11, **403**, 498–501, 846–848
  and genetics, 276
  online analysis, 29, 537
bioethics, 26–27, 29, 63–64
biogeochemical cycle, **413**, 587
biogeography, **311**
bioindicator, 494
bioinformatics, **282**–283
biological clock, **820**
biology, **5**
  characteristics of organisms, 5–6
  and ethics, 26–27
  and health, 24–25
  and scientific thinking, 13–17
  tools and technology, 19–23
  unifying themes of, 7–11
biomagnification, **495**–496, *495*
biomass, **417**–418, *418*, 470
biome, **397**, *397*, 462–467, 476
bioreactor, 26
bioremediation, *561*, 847
biosphere, 4, 454–474, **456**
  biomes, **397**, *397*, 462–467, 476
  and climate, **458**–461
  and Earth's systems, 456–457
  estuaries and freshwater ecosystems, 471–474
  marine ecosystems, 411, 468–471
biota, **456**

biotechnology, **26**, 262–285. *See also* DNA.
  and bacteria, 543
  bioinformatics, **282**–283
  gene therapy, **285**, 293–294
  genetic engineering, 275–279, **276**, 286
  genetic screening, 63–64, **284**, 287
  genomics, **280**–281
biotic factor, **402**–405, 457
biotin, *974*
BioZine, 62–64, 162–164, 292–294, 390–392, 512–514, 606–608, 690–692, 846–848, 1050–1052
bipedal animal, 381
bird, 798–803
  adaptation of, 799–803
  anatomy of, *800*
  beaks of, 321, 803, 811
  bones of, *800*, 801
  competition, 431
  and estuaries, 472
  evolution of, 798–799
  flight hypotheses, 799
  heart of, 790, *790*
  migration, 811, 821
  mobbing by, 832
  online animation, 800, 811
  radiation of, 378
  response, 841
  wings of, 799, 802, 804
bird flu, 553, 608
birth, human, 1040–1041, *1041*
Bishop pine, 346
bivalve, 713
Black Death, 940, *940*, 944
black-footed ferret, 398
black widow spider, 741
bladder, urinary, **986**, 990
blade, **652**
blastocyst, **1034**, *1034*
blood, 926–929
  and carbonic acid, 51, *51*
  circulation, 917–920
  clotting, 861, 929, *929*
  and kidney function, 987–991
  online lab, 933
  plasma, 42, *51*
  pressure, **923**–924
  and smooth muscle, 1007
  types, 205–206, 927–928, *928*, 933, 954
  vessels, 922–923, *923*
blood cell
  and erythropoietin, 145
  microscopic observation of, 928
  red, 8–9, *852*, **915**, 927, *927*
  white, 55, 553, 898, **928**, 931, *939*, 946, *946*, *950*, 950–951, 959–960
blue-footed booby, 803, *803*
blue-spotted ray, *766*
bluestem, *627*
blue whale, 696, *696*

B-lymphocyte, 946, 947, 951, 953, *953*
body heat, 851
body temperature
  of amniotes, 791–792
  and blood, 920, 1013
  homeostasis, 858, 859, *859*, 867, 1013
  and human skin, 883
  and muscular system, 1006
  online graphing, 811
  regulation of, 9, 863, 875, 900, 913
bog, 359
Bohr, Niels, *37*
bond energy, 51
bonding, chemical, 50–51, *51*
  online animation, 59
bone, 759, *800*, 801, 1000–1005, *1004*. *See also* skeletal system.
bone marrow, 145, 960–961, *1004*, 1004–1005
bony fish, 765, 767, 768–771, *769*, 780. *See also* Osteichthye.
booby, blue-footed, 803, *803*
book lung, **740**
boreal forest, 465
Borlaug, Norman, 691
Borrelia Burgdorferi, *564*
botany, **629**
bottleneck effect, **336**
bottlenose dolphin, 838
botulism, 563
bovine spongiform encephalopathy (BSE), 545
bowerbird, satin, 832, *832*
Bowman's capsule, **988**, *989*
box turtle, *760*
bracket fungus, 591
braconid wasp, 432, *433*
brain, 886–888, *887*, 1050–1052. *See also* nervous system.
  cell, 317
  chemistry of, 891–894
  disorders of, 892, 903
  and drugs, 893–894
  lobe, *887*
  multitasking, 1052
  plasticity of, 1051
  size, 382–383
  stem, **888**, 915
braincase, 759
bread mold, 591–592, *592*, *593*
breast cancer, 146, 294
breathing, 860, *860*, 912, *912*
breeding, 193, 304–305, 308
brine shrimp, 739
bristlecone pine, 622
brittle star, 720
bronchiole, 911, *911*, *914*, 916
bronchus, 911, *911*
brown algae, 584, *584*
brown pelican, 471
brown recluse spider, 741

Index

Bryophyta, 617
Bt, 278, 692
bubonic plague, 748
budding, 150, 591
buffer, 43
Buffon, Georges Louis Leclerc de, 299, *299*
bugeye squid, *53*
bulb, 679
bulbourethral gland, 1026, *1026*
bull-thorn acacia, 349, *349*
buoyancy, 769
Burgess Shale, 359, 376
Burmese python, 500, *500*
burr, 673, *673*
butterfly, *429, 731*
   monarch, 616, *745*
   swallowtail, 334, *748*
bypass surgery, 924

C

cactus, 465, 640, 650, *650*, 655, *678*
caecilian, 777, *777*
calciferol, *974*
calcification, **1005**
calcitonin, **1005**
calcium, 38, 973, *973*, 1005
calculating, 106–107, 188, 218, 384. *See also* data analysis.
Calorie, **975**
calorimetry, 59
Calvin cycle, 105, **111**
Cambrian explosion, **376**, 700, 734
Cambrian period, 366
Canada goose, 821
cancer, **146**
   breast, 146, 294
   cell, *133, 144, 146,* 147
   cervical, 146
   lung, 133, *133*
   online animation, 157
   and plant compounds, 631
   skin, 256
   treatments for, 705
cancer geneticist, 294
Candida, 597
Canis lupis, 520, 521
canopy, **464**
Cape sugarbird, *611*
capillary, **913**
capillary action, 645
capsid, **547**
capuchin monkey, 838, *838*
carapace, **735**
carbohydrate, **45**–46, *46*, 101–102
   in cell membrane, 82, *82*
   complex/simple, 972
carbon
   atom, 44
   and fatty acids, 46
   radiometric dating, **362**–363
   sinks and sources, 414

carbon-based molecule, *44,* 44–48
   and ATP, 101–102
   and cellular respiration, 118
   chains and rings, 44, *44*
   and energy, 100
   and photosynthesis, 111
carbon cycle, 112, 414, *414,* 499
   online lab, 127
carbon dioxide, **39**, *39,* 414, 457
   and carbonic acid, 51
   and exercise, 921
   and photosynthesis, 105, 112
   and respiratory and circulatory systems, 50, 911, 914–915
   and temperature change, *490,* 490–492, 514
carbonic acid, 51, 915
Carboniferous period, 366, *376,* 377, 619, 794
carcinogen, **146**
cardiac muscle, 917–918, *1007,* **1008**
careers
   in Biology, R38–R39
   cancer geneticist, 294
   cell biologist, 164
   conservation biologist, 848
   epidemiologist, 608
   evolutionary biologist, 392
   geneticist, 64
   neuroscientist, 1052
   oceanographer, 514
   research engineer, 692
carnivore, **409**
carotenoid, **584**
carpel, **668**
carrageenan, 584
Carribean Sea, 402
carrier, **201**
carrying capacity, **442**, 484–485
Carson, Rachel, *255,* 502
cartilage, **1001**
cartilaginous fish, 765–767. *See also* Chondrichthye.
cartilaginous joint, 1002
cast, natural, 360
cat, 203, *203,* 275, *275,* 789, *789*
catalase, 57
catalyst, **54**–55, *54*
catastrophism, *300,* **301**
caterpillar, hornworm, 432, *433*
Caulerpa taxifolia, 601
causation, **895**
Cech, Thomas, 370
cecum, **314**
celery, 640
celiac disease, 982
cell, 5–6, 68–91, 98–125. *See also* blood cell; cellular respiration; somatic cell.
   active transport, **89**–90, *89*
   ADP, 101, *102*
   animal, *74, 113*
   ATP, 90, **100**–102, *102*

binary fission, **558**
brain, 317
   cycle, 235
   determination, **852**–853
   differentiation, **152**–153, *153,* **853**–854, *853*
   diffusion, **85**–88
   diploid, **170**–171, 664
   endocytosis and exocytosis, **90**
   eukaryotes, 373–374
   and fermentation, 118, **122**–125, 127
   formation of first cells, 370
   haploid, **170**–171, 175–176, 664
   host, 373
   membrane, 8, 47, **81**–84, *82,* 88, 93, 370, 897, 988
   metabolism, 851, 860
   microscopic examination of, 866
   multicellular organisms, 376
   online animation, 93
   organelles, **72**, 73–79, 93
   osmosis, **85**–87, *86*
   and photosynthesis, 102, *103*–112
   plant, *71, 74,* 100, 640, 640–642, *641*
   prokaryotes, 372–374
   sex, 1031
   size, 136–137, *137,* 156
   sperm, 853, *1030*
   stem, **153**–155, 852–853
   structure and function, 8–9, 35, 38, 46, 92–93, 148
   theory, **70**–72, **71**
   wall, **79**, *79,* 87, 142, 983
   zygote, 852, **1031**, 1034
cell biologist, 164
cell division, 132–150, 173. *See also* meiosis.
   and asexual reproduction, **148**–150
   and cancer, 146–147, *146*
   cell cycle, **134**–137, *134, 140,* 140–142, *142*
   cytokinesis, **135**, 138–142, *141*
   and growth factors, 144–145
   mitosis, 134, **135**, 138–142, *141,* 143
   rate of, 136, *136*
   regulation of, 144–147
cellular immunity, **952**, *952*
cellular respiration, 50, 53, **113**–121, *114,* 126, 417
   and ATP, 113, 115, 117–118, 120
   of birds, 801
   and electron transport, *114,* 119–121, *120*
   and glycolysis, 113, 117–118, 122–123
   and Krebs cycle, *114,* **115**, 118–*119*
   and photosynthesis, 112, 114–115, *115,* 121, *121*
cellular slime mold, 588
cellulose, 45–46, 112, 314
   in cell walls, 79
   in food, 972
   plant, 732
Celsius
   conversion to Fahrenheit, R5

Cenozoic era, 366–367, **378**
centipede, *731*
central dogma, **239**, *239*
central nervous system (CNS), **875**, *885*, 885–890
central tendency, **628**
centriole, **78**, *78*
centromere, **139**, *139*
centrosome, 78
cephalochordate, 758
cephalopoda, 713
cephalothorax, **735**
cerebellum, **888**
cerebral cortex, **887**
cerebrum, **886**–887, *887*
cervical cancer, 146
cervix, 1025, 1040
Cesarean section, 1040
chaparral, **466**, *466*
Chara, 612
Chargaff, Erwin, 231, 257
Chargaff's rules, 231, 257
charophycean, 612, *612*
Chase, Martha, 228, 230, 231
cheese, 123, *125*
chelicerate, 731, *731*, 734, **740**
cheliped, 736
chemical energy, 6, 100–102. *See also* cellular respiration; photosynthesis.
chemical reaction, 50–53
chemiosmotic gradient, 110
chemistry of life, 34–56
    atoms, ions, and molecules, 36–39
    bonding, 50–51
    carbon-based molecules, *44*, 44–48
    catalysts, 54–55, *54*
    chemical reactions, **50**–53
    enzymes, 54–56, **55**
    isotopes, 362
    water, 40–43
chemoreceptor, 881
chemosynthesis, **102**, 407
chemotherapy, 147, 163
chickenpox, *554*
chigger, 741
childhood, **1042**
chimera, 766
chimpanzee, 380, *380*, 817, 838
chitin, 79, **589**, **730**, 732
chiton, 713
chlamydia, 1032
Chlamydomonas, *584*, 584–585, *585*
chloride ion, 38, *38*
chlorine, 38
chlorophyll, 79, **103**–105, 582, 584
    fluorescence, 654
    and green algae, 612
Chlorophyta, 584
chloroplast, **79**, *79*, 80, *103*, 103–104, *104*, 114, 373

choanocyte, 706
choanoflagellate, 705
cholesterol, 82, *82*
choline, *974*
Chondrichthye, 760, 766. *See also* cartilaginous fish.
Chordata, 702, 758
chordate, **758**, 888
chorion, 1035
chromatid, **139**, *139*, 173, *173*, 175, *175*, 190
chromatin, **139**, *139*
chromosomal mutation, 253–254
chromosome, **138**–139, *138*, *139*, 168–171. *See also* genetics.
    autosomes, **169**, 200–201, *201*, 214, *215*
    cross-overs, **190**–191, *190*, 210–211, *211*
    for eye color, *199*
    and fertilization, 1031
    homologous, **169**, *173*, 173–174, *174*, 190
    and linked genes, 209
    mapping, 216–217
    and phenotype, 200–203
    sex, **169**, 200–201, *201*
    X and Y, 169, 201–203, 213, *213*
    X chromosome inactivation, **203**
chyme, **979**
chytrid, 590
Chytridiomycota, 590
cigarette smoke, 25, 916
cilia, 78, 578–579, *855*, 911, 945, *945*
ciliate, 578–579
Ciliophora, 579
circadian rhythm, **820**
circle graph, R17
circulatory system, 614, *856*, **910**–913, *913*
    of amniotes, 789–790, *790*
    of amphibians, 774
    of arthropods, 733
    and blood transport, 922–924
    diseases of, 924
    of fish, 763
    and gas exchange, 914–915
    and heart, 917–920
    and lymphatic system, 930
    online animation, 933
citric acid, 118, 599
citrus fruit, 972
clade, 525–526, *527*
cladistics, 525
cladogram, 525–526, *527*
    online animation, 537
clam, 714
classical conditioning, **826**
classification, *R25–R31*
    of animals, 701–702
    domains and kingdoms, 533–535, 575
    and evolutionary relationships, 524–528
    genus, 383
    Linnaean, 298, 518–521
    and molecular evolution, 530–532
    of plants, 617–622, 632
    of vertebrates, 758–760, *761*

classifying, 522, 525. *See also* data analysis.
class taxon, *520*, 520–521
Clean Air Act, 504
cleaner shrimp, *7*
Clever Hans, 837
climate, **458**–461
cloaca, *797*, 808
clone, **275**–276, 287
Clostridium botulinum, 563, 563–564
Clostridium tetani, 564
clotting, blood, 861, 929, *929*
clover, 561, *561*
clown anemone fish, *764*
club fungus, 591–592, *592*, *593*
club moss, 619, *619*
clumped dispersion, **437**, *437*
cnidarian, *707*, 707–708, *708*
cnidocyte, 707
coal, 377
coastal ecosystem, 470
cocaine, *894*
cocci, 556
cochlea, 882
coconut, 673
coconut crab, *737*
codominance, **205**–206, *205*, 208
codon, **243**–245
coelacanth, 771
coelom, **714**
coenzyme A, 118
coevolution, 349
cognition, animal, **837**–839, 841
cohesion, 41, *41*, 643–645, *644*
cohesion-tension theory, **643**–645
cold desert, 465
cold virus, 552, *552*, 864
collagen, **697**, *697*, 1015
collecting data, 28, 57, 126, 143, 405, 493, 497, 647, 709, 739, 750, 857, 884, 902, 1012. *See also* data analysis.
collenchyma cell, **640**, *641*
colon, 984, *984*
Colorado River, *473*
colorblindness, 214–216, *215*
combination graph, 442, R16
commensalism, **432**, *433*, 663
common ancestor, 244, 299, 310–313, 317, 524–525
communicating, 59, 157. *See also* data analysis.
communication
    animal, 832
    in human organism, 859
    nervous and endocrine systems, 875
community, **397**, *397*
compact bone, 1004, *1004*
comparing, 92, 147, 477, 506, 733. *See also* data analysis.
competition, 306, 429, **431**, 443, 639, 828
competitive exclusion, **429**–430
complement protein, 947

Index

complete metamorphosis, **744**, *745*
complex tissue, 643
component vaccine, 956
compound, **37**
   buffer, 43
   ionic, 38, 42
   online animation, 59
compound joint, 1002
compound microscope, 70, *70*
computerized tomography (CT), 891, *891*
computer modeling, 3, 22, 282
concentration gradient, **85**, 89–90
conclusions, drawing, 320. *See also* data analysis.
conditioning, behavioral, 825–826
cone, **621**, 666–667, *667*
cone cell, *881*
conidia, 594
conifer. *See also* gymnosperm.
   life cycle, *R34*
Coniferophyta, 621
coniferous tree, 465, **622**, *622*, 666–667, *667*
conjugation, 391, **557**
connective tissue, 854
conservation, 502–505, 847–848
conservation biologist, 848
constant, **16**, R11
consumer, **406**, 409
continuous data, **497**
control center, 859
control group, **16**, R12
convergent evolution, **348**, *348*, 517, 744
coordination. *See* muscular system; skeletal system.
Copeland, Herbert, 533
copepod, 735, 737
coral, 583, *707*, 707–708
coral larva, 586
coral reef, 402, *410*, 411, **470**, *470*
Cordyceps, 594
cork, 70
corn, 188, *630*, 748
cornea, 881
coronary artery disease, *254*
corpus callosum, 887
corpus luteum, 1029
correlation, 895
cortisol, 901, 903
cotyledon, **625**, 672, 675
countercurrent flow, **764**
covalent bond, **39**, *39*, 232
cow, *555*
coyote, 438
crab, 311, *311*, 349, *731*
   coconut, *737*
   fiddler, 736
   hermit, 736
   spider, 730
crane
   sandhill, 444
   whooping, 824, *824*

crayfish, 751
Cretaceous period, 351, 366, 795
Creutzfeld-Jakob disease (CJD), 545
Crick, Francis, 231–232, *232*, 235, 239, 264
crinoid, *360*
Crinoidea, 719
crocodile, 432, *433*
crocodilian, 797
cropper, *305*
cross, genetic, **178**–179, *178*, *179*, 184–186
crossing over, chromosome, **190**–191, *190*, 210–211, *211*
crustacean, 731, *731*, **735**–738
ctenidia, 712
CT scan, 891, *891*
cubozoa, 708
cultural behavior, 383, **839**
Curry, Eddy, 63
Curry, Ruth, 514
curly-tail lizard, 352
Curvier, Georges, 300–301
Cushing's syndrome, 901
cuticle, **614**, *615*, 652, **716**, 732, 740
cutting, plant, 679
cyanobacteria, *366*, *372*, 560–561
cycad, 621, *621*
Cycadophyta, 621
cyclin, 145
cycling of matter, 412–416
cypsela, *673*
cystic fibrosis (CF), 201, *252*, 916
cytokinesis, **135**, 138–142, *141*, 175
cytokinin, **681**
cytoplasm, **72**, *72*, 75
cytosine, 230–233, *231*, *233*
cytoskeleton, **73**
cytosol, 75

D

daffodil, 679
dander, 958
Daphnia, 737, 750
Darwin, Charles, 298–306, *302*, 309–312, 316, 803
data, **14**, R15–R17
   continuous, R15
   discrete, R16
   qualitative, R12
   quantitative, R12
data analysis, 18, 58, 88, 92, 116, 147, 156, 185, 188, 192, 202, 208, 218, 229, 268, 287, 435, 438, 448, 475, 506, 525, 529, 536, 546, 562, 566, 586, 600, 623, 632, 647, 654, 656, 674, 676–677, 709, 714, 722, 723, 733, 739, 751, 804, 824, 857, 866, 884, 886, 949, 964, 981, 992, 993, 1016, 1017, 1044. *See also* graphing.
   bioinformatics, 282–283
   causation, 895
   central tendency, **628**

collecting and interpreting data, 28, 57, 126, 143, 405, 493, 497
   correlation, 895
   dichotomous keys, 522
   frequency distributions, 234
   identifying patterns, 320, 339
   identifying variables, 28, 49, 57, 256
   inverse relationships, 865
   null hypothesis, 925
   online, 29, 219, 257, 321, 353, 449, 477, 507, 601, 781, 811, 903, 965, 993, 1017, 1045
   operational definitions, 80
   outliers, **985**
   qualitative and quantitative data, 12, 14, 497
   repeated trials, 649
   sampling, 398–399, 401, 420, 947
   trends, 1014
   types of, 12
data mining, 23
data tables, **R15**, R15–R17
dating, fossil, 362–365, 385
daughter cell, 140–142, *141*, 149
DDT, 502
decapod, 737
deciduous forest, *463*, **465**
decomposer, **409**, 471, 474, 596
deep-sea sediment coring, 513
deep-sea vent, 102, 407
deer, 436
deer tick, 740
definition, operational, R12
demodicid, 432, *433*
dendrite, **876**, *876*
density-dependent limiting factor, **443**
density-independent limiting factor, **444**
deoxyribonucleic acid (DNA). *See* DNA.
deoxyribose, 230
dependent variable, **16**, R11, R15
depressant, **894**
depression, 892
derived character, **525**–526, *527*, 528
dermal tissue, **642**
dermis, 1015
descent with modification, **306**, *307*
desensitization, **893**, *893*
desert, 408, *463*, **464**–465
desert cottontail, *408*, 408–409
designing experiments, 28, 88, 106–107, 124, 127, 493, 566, 586, 600, 674, 933. *See also* data analysis.
determination, 852–853
detritivore, **409**
deuterostome, **702**, *702*, *703*
Devonian period, 366, 621, 770
dewlap, 820
diabetes mellitus, 864–865, 959, *959*
   pregnancy-related, 1039
   and stem cell research, 155

dialysis, **991**, *991*
diaphragm, 789, **912**
diapsid, 794
diastolic pressure, **923**
diatom, 99, *99*, 583, *583*, R26
dichtomous key, 522
dicot, **626**, *626*, 632, 650
Didinium, *573*, 574
diet, 973
differential survival. *See* natural selection.
differentiation, 853–854, *853*
diffusion, 85–88, 764
digestion, **977**
digestive system, *856*, *971*, **977–984**, *977*
    digestive enzymes, *978*
    and fermentation, 125
    online animation, 993
digestive tract, complete, **712**
digger wasp, *729*
dihybrid cross, **186**, *186*
Dimetrodon, *360*
Dinoflagellate, 582–583, *583*
dinosaur, 795
    Dimetrodon, *360*
    extinction of, 351
    ichthyosaurs, 377, 794
    Mononykus, *366*
    online animation, 321
    pterosaurs, *377*, 795
    Velociraptor, *360*, 798
diploid cell, **170–171**, 664
diploid organism, 698
directional selection, **331**, *331*
discrete data, **497**
disease, 443, *940*, **940–941**, *941*
    and arthropods, 748–749
    germ theory of, 17
    and kidney function, 990–991
    and protists, 580
dispersion, population, **437**, *437*
disruptive selection, **333**, *333*
dissecting, 669, 685, 722, 780
divergent evolution, **348**, *348*
division, 617
division taxon, **520**, *520*
DNA, 6, 23, 48. *See also* gene; RNA.
    base pairing rules, 230–233, **232**, 265
    blunt/sticky ends, 265–266
    and cell nucleus, 75
    chromosomes in, **138–139**, *138*, *139*, *169*
    copying, 269–271
    and evolutionary tree, 528
    extracting, 229
    fingerprinting, 236, *263*, **272–274**, *272*, *273*
    and gametes, 168
    and gene expression, 248–251
    as genetic material, 228
    and genetic variations, 199
    hybridization, 536

    manipulating, 264–267
    microarray, 282–283, *283*
    mitochondrial, **532**, *532*
    mutations, 252–255
    nuclear, 532
    online animation, 233, 237, 241, 257
    polymerase, **236**, 269–271
    and proteins, 138–139
    recombinant, **276–277**, *277*, 287
    replication, 135, **235–238**, *237*, *238*, 242, 255, 271
    sequencing, 280–281, 317
    structure of, 230–233
    transcription, **239–242**, **240**, *241*, *242*, 248–251
    as transforming principle, 226–227, *227*
    and translation, **243–247**, *246*
    of ungulates, *318*
    and viral infection, 551
    of whales, *318*
Dobzhansky, Theodosius, 319, 353
dog-vomit slime mold, *574*, *574*, 587
dogwood, *624*
dolphin, 12, *12*, 348, *348*, 838
domain, 520, **533–535**, R25
domed tortoise, 302, *303*
dominant allele, **181–182**, 187, 201, 204
dopamine, 892
dormancy, **674**, 683
dormouse, *821*
dorsal surface, 701
Dorudon, *318*
double fertilization, **670**, *671*
double helix, *139*, 232
Down syndrome, 172, 217, *217*
downy woodpecker, 332, *332*
dragonfly, R30
drawing conclusions, 320, 656, 865. *See also* data analysis.
Drosophila melanogaster, 209, 344. *See also* fruit fly.
drug reaction, 292–293
drug-resistant bacteria, 149, 331, 353, 390–392, 565
drug treatment, 392, 893–894
Duchenne's muscular dystrophy (DMD), 284, *284*
duck-billed platypus, 807–808, *808*
duodenum, 980, 983
dust mite, 958
Dutch elm disease, 597, *597*
dwarfism, 336
dynamic equilibrium, **85**

E

eagle, bald, 335, *335*, 504
eagle owl, *799*
ear, 806–807, 882, *882*
Earth. *See also* evolution.
    age of, 299–301, 303, 363
    biomes of, 462–467

    biosphere, **456**
    climate zones of, *459*, 459–460
    geologic time scale, **365–367**, *366*, 381
    multicellular life on, 376–378
    natural resources of, 485–487, 504–505
    origin of life on, 368–371
    and photosynthesis, 112
    and population growth, 484–486
    single-cellular organisms on, 372–375
    systems of, 456–457
earthworm, 704, **714–715**, *715*
Easter Island, 486, *486*
eccrine gland, 1015
Ecdysozoa, 702, 716, 734
echinoderm, 718, **718–720**, *719*, *720*
Echinodermata, 702
Echinoidea, 720
E. coli, 265, 375, *375*, 544, 549, *549*, *939*, 984
ecological equivalent, **430**
ecological footprint, **487**, *487*
ecological niche, 315, **428–429**, 697
ecology, 395–400, **396**
    levels of organization, **397**, *397*
    research methods, 398–401
ecoparasite, **434**, *434*
ecosystem, 7–8, **397**, *397*, 402–419, 427–447. *See also* biosphere.
    air quality, 488–492
    biodiversity, **403**, 498–501, 847–848
    biotic and abiotic factors, **402–405**, 457, 458
    community interactions, 431–434
    competitive exclusion, **429**–430
    conservation of, 502–505
    cycling of matter, 412–416
    ecological equivalents, **430**
    ecological niche, 351, **428–429**
    energy in, 406–407, 417–418
    food chains and webs, **408**–411
    freshwater, 471–474
    and fungi, 596–599
    habitat, **428–429**, 499
    marine, 411, 468–471
    modeling, 400, 417–419, 421
    online animation, 477
    population density of, **436–439**
    population growth in, 440–444, 484–487
    and prokaryotes, 560–561
    pyramid models, 417–419
    water quality, 494–496, 506, 507
    wetland, 404, *404*
ectoderm, 701, 1034
ectotherm, **791–793**
eel, *7*
egg
    amniotic, **788**, *788*, 810
    human, *167*, **176**, 1024, *1027*, 1027–1028, *1028*, 1030–1031, *1031*
Egyptian plover, 432, *433*
ejaculation, 1026

Index

Elasmobranch, 766
elastin, 1015
Eldredge, Niles, 351
electron, 36–37, 108
electron microscope, 3, 19–20
electron tomography, 607
electron transport, *114*, 119–121, *120*
electron transport chain, **109**
   online animation, 127
electroreceptive cell, 767
element, **36**–37
   cycling of, 413
   in organisms, 37
elephant, *400*, 832, 839, *839*, *R31*
elephant seal, 336, 436
elk, Irish, 338
Ellis-van Creveld syndrome, 336
elm bark beetle, 597, *597*
embryo
   amniote, 788, *788*
   and cell differentiation, 152–153
   human, 145, *145*, 167, 176, *1023*, **1034**–
     1035, *1035*, 1044
embryology, 311–312, 318
embryonic membrane, 1035, *1035*
embryonic stem cell, 154–155, *155*, 852–853,
   1036
embryo sac, 670
emigration, **440**
emperor penguin, *831*
emperor tamarin, *846*
emphysema, 916
Endangered Species Act, 503–504
endocrine system, *856*, **874**, *874*
   glands of, 896, *896*, 898–900, *899*
   and homeostasis, 874–875
   and hormones, 896–901
   and hypothalamus, 900, *900*
endocytosis, **90**
endoderm, 701, 1034
endometrium, **1028**
endoparasite, 434, *434*
endoplasmic reticulum, **76**, *76*
endoskeleton, **759**
endosperm, **670**
endospore, **558**
endosymbiosis, **373**, *373*
endotherm, **791**–792
endothermic reaction, *52*, 53
energy
   atomic, 37
   bond, 51
   chemical, 6, 50–53, *52*, 100–102
   in ecosystems, 406–407, 417–418
   and food, *102*
   and natural resources, 485–486
energy pyramid, **417**–**418**, *418*, 495
Enterococcus faecalis, *331*, 556
environment, response to, 6
Environmental Protection Agency, 504

enzyme, 8, 54–57, **55**, 59, *371*
   as catalyst, 236
   digestive, *978*, 978–979, 981
   and germination, 675
   lysosomes, 78
   restriction, **265**–266, *265*, *266*, 278
eosinophil, 957
epidemic, *553*
epidemiologist, 608
epidemiology, 22
epidermis, 642, **1014**
epididymis, **1026**
epiglottis, 911, *911*
epinephrine, 819
epiphyte, 464
episodic speciation, **351**, 367
epistatic gene, 206–207
epithelial cell, 923, *971*, 983
epithelial tissue, **854**, *855*
epoch, geologic, 367
equilibrium
   chemical, 51
   dynamic, 85
era, geologic, 367
erythropoietin, 145
Escherichia coli, *265*, 375, *375*, *544*, 549, *549*,
   939, 984, *R25*
esophagus, *543*, *978*, 978
estrogen, 494, **1024**, 1028–1029, 1036
estuary, **471**–472, *471*
ethnobotany, **629**
ethogram, 830
ethylene, **681**, 684
euglena, 582, *582*, 819, *R26*
euglenoid, 582
Euglenophyta, 582
Eukarya domain, **534**, *535*, 575, *R25–R31*
eukaryote, 373–374, 534
   and protists, 575–576, *576*
   and viral infection, 549
eukaryotic cell, **72**, *72*, 73–75, 135, 150
   and DNA, 239, 249–251
European rabbit, 441, *441*
eusocial species, **834**–836
eutherian mammal, **809**
eutrophication, 494, *494*
evaporation, 412
Everglades, *397*
evolution, **10**–11, 296–319, *298*, 328–351,
   359–383. *See also* adaptation.
   age of Earth, 299–301, 303, 363
   of altruism, 833–834
   of animals, 702–704, 827–829, 833–834
   of arthropods, 734
   and classification, 524–528
   coevolution, 349
   convergent/divergent, *348*, 348, 517, 744
   descent with modification, 306
   evidence of, 310–319
   and fossils, **300**, 310, 316, 360–364

   and genetic variation, 328–329
   geologic time scale, **365**–**367**, *366*, 381,
     385
   Hardy-Weinberg equilibrium, 340–343
   human, 378–383
   of mammals, 377–378
   mechanisms of, 335–339, *342*, 343
   microevolution, **331**
   molecular, *530*, 530–532
   of multicellular life, 376–378
   by natural selection, 304–309, **305**, 330–
     334, *342*, 343
   online animation, 353
   and origin of life, 368–371
   patterns in, 347–351
   of plants, 455, 612–616, *613*
   pre-Darwinian theories of, 298–301
   primate, 379–383, *380*
   of reptiles, 794–795
   of sexual reproduction, 374
   of single-celled organisms, 372–375
   speciation, 344–346, 351
   and species varation, **302**, 306, *307*,
     308–309
evolutionary biologist, 392
evolutionary biology, 316–319
evolutionary response, 429
excretory system, *856*, **986**, 986–991
experiment, R11. *See also* lab experiment.
   designing an, R11–R13
experimental group, R12
exercise, 921
exocytosis, **90**
exon, **251**
exoskeleton, **730**, 732–733, *999*
exothermic reaction, *52*, 53
experiment, 16, 399
exponential growth, **441**
extinction of species, 299–301, **350**–351, *350*
   background, **350**, *350*, 847
   mass, 367, 377, 778
eye, *880*, 880–881, *881*, 1007
   of arthropod, 733
   of cephalopod, 713
   color, *199*, 206, *206*
   of vertebrates, 317
eyelash mite, 432, *433*

F

facilitated diffusion, **87**, *87*
facultative aerobe, **555**
Fahrenheit
   conversion to Celsius, R5
falcon, 848
fallopian tube, **1024**
family taxon, *520*, 520–521
fantail, *305*
farming, 629–630
fast-twitch fiber, 1007

fat, 46
    and homeostasis, 973
    trans, 976
fatty acid, **46**, *46*, 973
feather, 798, *800*, 802
feather star, 719, *719*
feces, 984
feedback, 859–861, 900, 903
feedback loop, 457
female reproductive system, 1024–1025,
    1025, 1038. *See also* human reproduc-
    tion.
fermentation, 118, **122**–125, 127, 559
fern, 619, *619*, 666, *666*
    life cycle, *R33*
ferret, black-footed, 398
fertilization, **170**, 184, **670**, *671*, 1030–1031
fetal development, 1034–1039
fetus, **1036**
fiber, dietary, 972
fibrin, 929
fibrinogen, 926
fibrous joint, 1001
fibrous root, **649**
Ficus, 639
fiddlehead, 619, *619*, 666
fiddler crab, 736
field experiment, 399
field guide, 449
field mice, 315, *315*
fight-or-flight response, 819, 890, 898
fig tree, *639*
filaria, 943, *943*
filter feeder, **706**
filtrate, 988
fin, 764, *764*
finch, Galapagos, 302, 308–309
    cactus finch, *311*
    tree finch, *311*
fingernail, 1013, *1013*
fingerprinting, DNA, 236, *263*, **272**–274, *272*,
    273
fire, *447*, 464, 466
firefly, 345
fish, 763–771
    bony, 765, 767, 768–771, *769*, 780
    characteristics of, 763–764
    early, 762, 771
    fin shape in, *341*, 348
    gill slits in, 312
    groups of, 765–767
    jaw evolution of, 762, 765, *765*
    jawless, *366*, 376
    lobe-finned, 770–771
    online animation, 781
    radiation of, 378
    ray-finned, 768–769
    schools of, *437*
fishing industry, 503
fission, 558, 591

fitness, **307**
flagellum, 78, **556**, 577, 1030
flamingo, *472*
flatfish, 769
flatworm, 150, 704, *710*, 710–711, *711*, *R29*
flea, 434, 750
Fleming, Sir Alexander, *941*
flight
    bird, 799–801
    insect, 746
Florida snail kite, 409, *409*
flower, **622**, 624, *668*
flowering plant, 378, 622, 624–627, 668–672
    life cycle, *671*, *R35*
flow phase, 1028, *1029*
fluid mosaic model, **82**
fluke, 711, *711*
fluorescence, 654
"fluropig", *62*
flu virus, 607–608
flying frog, *777*
folic acid, *974*, 1038
follicle, 1015, *1015*, **1028**
follicle-stimulating hormone (FSH), 1024,
    1025, 1028–1030
follicular phase, 1028, *1029*
food, 973
    allergen, 958
    and energy, 100–102
    labels, 976, *976*
    and photosynthesis, 113
    poisoning, 563–564, 942
food chain, **408**–409, *408*, 417
food web, *410*, **411**, 513
    online animation, 421, 507
foot
    of birds, 803
    human, *9*
    length, 384
foraging, 828–829
foram, 578, *578*
foraminifera, 578, *578*
forensic model, 268
forest
    conservation of, 502–503
    deciduous, *463*, **465**
    rain, 403, 455, *455*, 463, 464, 499
Forsteronia refracta, 633
Forster's tern, 495
fossil, **300**, 310
    amber-preserved, 360
    arachnid, 740
    arthropod, 734
    bird, 798–799
    in bogs, 359
    fish, 762, 771
    footprints, 384
    of hominids, 382
    index, **365**
    and molecular clocks, 531
    plant, *366*, 613, 619

    record, *360*, 360–364
    sponge, 705
    stromatolites, 372, *372*
    trace, 360
    transitional, 316
    types of, 360
    of vertebrates, 760–762, 773
    whale, 318
fossil fuel, 485, 488
founder effect, 336, *337*
four-chambered heart, 790, *790*
four o'clock plant, 204
fox, 348, *348*
foxglove, 627, *R28*
fragmentation, 150
frameshift mutation, **252**
Franklin, Rosalind, 231, *231*
frequency distribution, 234, R17
freshwater ecosystem, 473–474
frigate bird, 338
frog, *531*, 774–777
    anatomy of, *775*
    deformities, 25, *25*
    flying, *777*
    glass, *757*
    as indicator species, 494
    leaf nesting, 498, 499
    mantella, 430, *430*
    metamorphosis of, 775, *775*
    poison dart, 430, *430*
    pygmy marsupial, *774*
    red-legged, 438–439
    water-holding, 461, *461*
frond, 619, 666
frontal lobe, *887*
fructose, 45
fruit, 621, **622**, 625, 672–673
fruit fly, *209*, 209–211, *211*, 281, 344–345,
    345, *700*, *733*
fruiting body, **590**
Fu, Tong-Jen, 692
Fuligo septica, 574, *574*, 587
functional MRI, 20, 1051
fungicide, 597
Fungi, *R27*
fungus, 79, 409, 533, 589–599, *R27*
    and animals, 697
    and disease, 942
    online animation, 601
    and plants, 589, 597, 616
    reproduction of, 591–594, *592*, *593*
    types of, 590–591
fur color, 206–207
furcula, 798
fusulinids, 365, *365*

G

Gaia hypothesis, 457
Galapagos finch, 302, 308–309
    cactus finch, *311*
    tree finch, *311*

Index

Galapagos Islands, 302
gall fly, 332, *332*
gamete, 148, **168**, 170, 664
gametogenesis, 152, 176, **176**
gametophyte, **664**–667, 670
gamma amino butyric (GABA), 892
gannet, *437*
gap 1 stage, 135
gap 2 stage, 135
gas exchange, 914–916, *915*
gasoline engine, *118*
gastropoda, 713
gastrovascular cavity, **708**
gecko, *779*
gel electrophoresis, **266**–267, *267*
   online animation, 287
gene, **23**, **180**–182. *See also* DNA.
   autosomal, **169**, 200–201, *201*, 214, *215*
   bacterial, 692
   brain-related, 383
   duplication, 253
   epistatic, 206–207
   expression and regulation, 248–251, 823
   homeobox, 250, 317, **698**, 700, *701*
   knockout, **279**
   mutations, 252–254, 267, 329
   pesticide resistant, 692
   and phenotypes, 330
   pool, 328–329
   pseudogene, 317
   recombination, 329, 374
   sequencing, **280**–281
   sex-linked, **201**–203, 213–216, *215*
   therapy, **285**, 293–294
gene flow, **335**, *342*, 343–344, 436
gene frequency. *See* allele frequency.
gene gun, 691
generalist, **409**, 573
genetic drift, **336**–337, *342*, 343
genetic linkage, **191**, 209–211
geneticist, 64
genetics, **177**, 278–279. *See also* allele; chromosome.
   and biodiversity, 276
   genetically modified (GM) crops, 278–279, 294, 690–692
   genetic disorders, 200–201, 212–213, 284, 287
   genetic engineering, 62, 275–279, **276**, 286
   genetic immunity, 948
   genetic screening, 26–27, 63–64, 214, **284**, 287
   genetic variation, 189–191, 254, 328–329, 337, 374
   heredity, **177**–179, 181, 183–187, 204–207
   meiosis, **170**–176, 189–191
   Mendelian, 340
   molecular, **23**
   and natural selection, 319
   online lab, 287
   and pedigrees, 214–218, *215*

genome, **181**, 273, 280, *281*
genomics, **23**, **280**–281
genotype, **181**, 183–185, 207
   frequency, 341
   online animation, 219
   and phenotypes, 214–216, *215*
genus, 383, **519**–521, *519*, *520*
Geochelone elephantopus, 303
geographic dispersion, 437
geographic isolation, 346, *346*
geologic time scale, 365–**367**, *366*, 381
   online animation, 385
geosphere, **456**
germ cell, 140, 168
germination, **675**–676, *675*
germ theory, 17, **941**
giant anemone, *R28*
giant panda, 521
Giardia, 580
gibberellin, **680**
gibbon, 380, *380*
gigantism, 867, *867*
gill, **763**
gill arch, 759, 765
gill slit, 312
ginger, *650*
Ginkgo biloba, 621, *621*
giraffe, 299, *696*, 832
girdle, 1000
Glacier Bay, *446*
gland, **896**, *896*, 898–900, *899*, 1015
glass frog, *757*
gliding joint, 1002, *1003*
global warming, 491, **492**, *492*, 512–514
glomerulus, **988**, *988*, *989*
glucagon, 864
glucose, 45, *45*, 50, 105, 113, 984
   and diabetes, 864–865
   and PET scans, 891
   in plasma, 926
glutamate, 892
glycerol, 46
glycogen, 45, 984
glycolysis, 113, 117–118, 122–123
Glyptodon, 303, *524*, 525
Glyptotherium arizonae, *524*
golden rice, 691
goldenrod, 332, *332*
gold-specs jawfish, 6, *6*
Golgi apparatus, **76**, *76*, 142
gonad, **898**, *899*
gonadotropin, *1036*
Goodall, Jane, *830*
Goodman's mouse lemur, *29*
goose
   Canada, 821
   graylag, 824
gorilla, 13, *13*, 380, *380*
Gould, Stephen Jay, 351
GPS transmitter, *400*

graduated cylinder, R8, *R8*
gradualism, *300*, *301*, 303
grafting, 679
graft versus host disease (GVHD), 961
grama grass, *408*
Gram staining, 557, *557*
Grant, Peter and Rosemary, 308, 321
granum, 104, *104*
grape, 680
graphic organizers. *See* note-taking strategies.
graphics, interpreting, 1011
graphing, 29, 106–107, 126, 364, 601, 649, 750, 804, 902, 1012, 1033. *See also* data analysis.
   bar graph, 830, 836, R16, *R16*
   bar graphs, 172, 210, 339
   best-fit lines, 142
   choice of graph, 792
   combination graphs, 442, 461, R16, *R16*
   continuous data, R15, *R15*
   discrete data, R16
   histograms, 234, 282, R17, *R17*
   line graphs, 308, 334, 1038
   online, 29, 219, 257, 321, 353, 449, 477, 507, 601, 781, 811, 903, 965, 993, 1017, 1045
   scales of axes, 375
   scatterplots, 721, 742, 770, R17, *R17*
   survivorship curves, 438
grass, grama, *408*
grasshopper, 442
grassland, *463*, **464**
Graves' disease, 959, 965
gravitropism, **682**
gravity, 682
graylag goose, 824
gray matter, 886
gray mold, 597
gray squirrel, 429
gray wolf, 400, 406, 409, 443, *443*, 520, 521
Greek word parts, R18
green algae, 584, 584–585, *585*, 612–613, *613*
green fluorescent protein (GEP), *225*
greenhouse effect, **490**, *491*
Green Revolution, 691
green woodpecker, 803, *803*
grey reef shark, 766, *766*
Griffith, Frederick, 226–227
grizzly bear, *396*
ground-level ozone, 488–489
ground tissue, **642**
"ground-up" hypothesis, 799
group
   control, R12
   experimental, R12
growth, human, 975, *975*, 1041–1043
growth factor, cell, 144–145
growth hormone, 145
guanine, 230–233, *231*, *233*

guard cell, **653**, *653*
Guinea worm, 717
gull
    black-backed, 823, *823*
    herring, 823
guppy, 339
gymnosperm, 621. *See also* conifer.

H

habitat, **428**–429
habitat fragmentation, **499**
habituation, **823**
Hadean eon, 368
Haeckel, Ernst, 396, 533
hagfish, 762, *762*
hair, 1013
    cell, *882*
    follicle, **1015**, *1015*
    line, 212, *212*, 214, *215*
    of mammals, 806
    texture, *200*
half-life, **362**
Hamilton, William, 833
hand, human, 312, *312*, 853
hantavirus, 608
haplodiploid species, 834
haploid cell, **170**–171, 175–176, 664
HapMap, 281
Hardy, Godfrey, 340
Hardy-Weinberg equilibrium, **340**–343
Harris's hawk, *408*, 408–409
Harvey, William, 922
Hashimoto's thyroiditis, *959*
Haversian canal, 1004, *1004*
Hawaiian honeycreeper, 828
Hawaiian Islands, 445
hawk
    Harris's, *408*, 408–409
    sparrow, 803, *803*
hawk moth, 616, *616*
hearing, 882
heart, **912**, 917–920
    amniote, 790, *790*
    attack, *22*
    blood flow in, 918–920, *919*
    cardiac muscle, 1008
    coronary artery disease, *254*
    and nervous system, *909*
    structures of, *917*, 917–918
heartwood, 650, *651*
hedgehog, *207*
HeLa cell, 147
helicase enzyme, 269, *371*
hemocoel, **712**
hemoglobin, 48, *48*, 530–531, **915**
hemophilia, 213, 929
Henle, loop of, 988, *989*
hepatitis A, *554*
hepatitis B, *942*, 1032

Hepatophyta, 617
herbaceous plant, 627, 650
herbicide, 681
herbivore, **409**, 432, 616
heredity, 177–179, 181, 183–187, 204–207.
    See also genetics.
heritability, 299, **304**
hermaphrodite, 713
hermit crab, 736
herpes, 1032
herring gull, *495*, 823
Hershey, Alfred, 228, 230, 231
heterotroph, **406**, 575, 697
heterozygous allele, **180**, 182, 184–185, 201,
    204
hibernation, 821
hinge joint, 1002, *1003*
hippocampus, 888
Hippocrates, *940*
hippopotamus, *318*, 319
histamine, 950, 957, *957*, 958
histogram, **234**, 282, **R17**
histone, **139**, *139*
history of life. *See* evolution.
HIV, 553, *553*, *942*, 943, **961**–963, *961*, *962*,
    965, 1032
Holocephalus, 766
Holothuroidea, 720
homeobox gene, 250, 317, **698**, 700, *700*
homeostasis, **9**, 43, 83, 151, 327, **858**–865
    and animal behavior, 819
    body temperature, 858, 859, *859*, 867
    disruption of, 864–865
    and exercise, 857
    and hormones, 867
    and integumentary system, 1013
    and kidneys, 987
    mechanisms of, 858–861
    and nervous and endocrine systems,
        874–875
    and nutrients, 972–976
    online animation, 867
    and organ systems, 862–865
    and respiratory and circulatory systems,
        910, 913
    and senses, 880
homeotic gene, **698**
hominid, **380**–383, *380*, *383*
hominoid, 380, *380*
    online animation, 385
Homo habilis, 382, *383*
homologous chromosome, **169**, *173*, 173–
    174, *174*, 190
homologous structure, **312**–313, 736
Homo neanderthalensis, 382, *383*
Homo sapiens, 378, 382, *383*
homozygous allele, **180**, 182, 184–185, 201,
    204
honeybee, 429, 432, 669, 746, 823, 832
honeycreeper, 828
honeypot ant, 4, *4*

Hooke, Robert, 70, *71*
hookworm, 434, *434*, 717
hormone, **680**, **896**, *896*
    and endocrine system, 896–901
    feedback loop, 903
    and fetal development, 1036
    and glands, 898, *899*
    and growth, 145, 1041, 1045
    and homeostasis, 867
    and illness, 901
    and menstrual cycle, 1024, 1027–1029,
        1033
    online animation, 903
    plant, 680–681, 684
    and pregnancy, 1039
    releasing, **900**
    and sperm production, 1030
    steroid and nonsteroid, 897, *897*
hornworm caterpillar, 432, *433*
hornwort, 618
horse, 378, 837
horsetail, 619, *R28*
host, 434
host cell, 373
hot desert, 464
Hox gene, **698**, 700, *700*
H. pylori, 17
human. *See also* hominid.
    appendix, 314
    behavior, 824
    brain size of, 382–383
    evolution of, 378–383
    hands of, 312, *312*
    ice-preserved remains of, *360*
    parasites, *433*, 434
human biology
    circulatory system, *856*, **910**–913, *913*,
        917–924
    digestive system, *856*, *971*, **977**–984, *977*
    endocrine system, *856*, **874**–875, *874*,
        896–901
    excretory system, *856*, *986*, 986–991
    fetal development and birth, 1034–1041
    homeostasis, 858–865, 972–976, 987
    immune system, *856*, **945**–963
    integumentary system, *856*, **1013**–1015
    lymphatic system, **930**–931, *930*
    muscular system, *856*, **1006**–1011, *1006*
    nervous system, *856*, **874**–894, *874*
    online news, 867
    reproductive system, *856*, 898, **1024**–1032
    respiratory system, *855*, *856*, **910**–916
    skeletal system, *865*, *999*, **1000**–1005,
        1000, *1001*, *1003*
human body. *See also* human biology.
    control systems, 859–860
    development of, 1041–1043
    growth and energy needs, 975, *975*
    levels of organization, 852–855
human embryo, 145, *145*, *167*, 176, *1023*,
    1034–1035, *1035*, 1044

Human Genome Project, 181, **281**, *281*
human growth hormone (hGH), 1041
human immunodeficiency virus (HIV), 553, *553, 942*, 943, **961**–963, *961, 962*, 965, 1032
human papillomavirus (HPV), 1032
human population growth, 484–487
human reproduction, 1022–1043, **1024**
  anatomy of, 1024–1026, *1025, 1026*
  birth and development, 1040–1043
  and exposure to chemicals, 1038–1039, 1045
  fertilization, 1030–1031
  fetal development, 1034–1039
  and hormones, 1024, 1027–1029, 1030, 1033, 1036, 1039
  menstrual cycle, **1028**, 1028–1029, *1029*
  online animation, 1045
hummingbird, ruby-throated, 811
humoral immunity, **953**, *953*
humpback whale, 99, *99, 318, 319*, 738, *738*
Huntington's disease, 201
hurricane, *444*, 472
Hutton, James, 301
hybridization, 298, 329
hydra, 150, *150*, 698, 708, 709, *709*
hydrochloric acid, 979
hydrogen, 36, *37*
  and fatty acids, 46
  ions, 38, 42–43
  in water, 40
hydrogen bond, 40–41, 48, 81
  and cohesion, 643
  and protein shape, 75
hydrologic cycle, **412**, 486
hydrosphere, **456**
hydrostatic skeleton, 714
hydrothermal pool, 407, *407*
hydrothermal vent, 102
hydrozoa, 708
Hyman, Libbie, 702, 704
hypertension, 924
hypertonic solution, **86**, *86*
hypha, 589–590
hypothalamus, 888, **898**, *899, 900, 900*
  and reproduction, 1024
  temperature regulation, 863
hypothermia, 867
hypothesis, 14–16, 925, R11
  online animation, 29
hypothyroidism, 901
hypotonic solution, *86*, **87**, 945

I

Iberian lynx, *350*
ice, 40, 513
ice cap, 467
Iceland, 64
ice-preserved man, *360*
ichthyosaur, 377, 794
ileum, 983

imaging, 20
imitation, **825**
immigration, **440**
immortal cell, 133
immune system, *856*, **945**–963
  autoimmune diseases, 959, *959*, 965
  cells of, 951–952
  and circulatory system, 946
  and cold virus, 864
  diseases of, 960–963
  and lymphatic system, 931
  online animation, 965
  overreactions of, 957–959
  and pathogens, 945–946
  of plants, 939
  and proteins, 947
  responses, 950–954
  and skin, 1014
  and technology, 955–956
  and vaccines, 554, 564
immunity, **948**, 951–953
imprinting, **824**
inclusive fitness, **834**
incomplete dominance, **204**–205, *205*, 219
incomplete metamorphosis, **744**
incus, 806–807, 882
independent assortment, law of, **186**, 191
independent variable, 16, 18, R11, R15
index fossil, **365**
indicator species, **494**, 781
industrialization, *483. See also* conservation; pollution.
infancy, **1042**
infant mortality, 439, 485
infectious disease, 391–392, 940–941, *942*
  bacterial, 563–564, *564*
  and protists, 580
  types of, 549–551, *550*
  viral, 544–546, 552–554, *554*
inferring, 28, 58, 106–107, 156, 185, 208, 218, 313, 320, 321, 384, 595, 857, 884. *See also* data analysis.
infertility, **1031**
inflammation, **950**, 957
influenza, 553, 607–608, *942*
inheritance. *See also* genetics; heredity.
  of acquired characteristics, 299
  patterns of, 177–179, 181, 183–187, 204–207
inherited immunity, 948
innate behavior, **822**–823
Innocence Project, 274
inoculation, 946, *946, 950*, 950–951, *951*
insect, 731, *731*, 743–746. *See also* arthropod.
  flight and feeding, 313, *313*, 746
  and fungi, 599
  online lab, 751
  social, 834, *835*
  as vector, 944
insecticide, 747–748

insight, **838**
instinct, **822**
insulin, 91, 277
  and diabetes, 864–865
integrated pest management (IPM), 748
integumentary system, *856*, **1013**–1015
interferon, **947**, 951
International System. *See* SI units.
interneuron, **877**
interphase, 134, 140, *141*
interpreting data, 364, 384. *See also* data analysis.
interstitial fluid, **930**
intertidal zone, **468**
intestine
  large, 984, *984*
  small, *979, 980, 982*, 982–984
introduced species, 429, 441, 444, **500**, 507
intron, **251**
invertebrate, **699**, *699*, 705–720. *See also* arthropod.
  annelids, 714–715, *715*, 734
  cnidarians, *707*, 707–708, *708*
  echinoderms, *718*, 718–720, *719, 720*
  flatworms, 704, *710*, 710–711, *711*
  larval stage of, 469
  marine, 376
  mollusks, *712*, 712–713, *713*
  online news, 723
  roundworms, 704, *716*, 716–717
  sexual reproduction of, 705–707, 713, 715, 717, 719
  sponges, *695, 705*, 705–706, *706*
iodine, *973*
ion, 38, *38*
ionic bond, 38, *38*, 42
iris, *627*, 678
Irish elk, 338
iron, *973*
iron sulfide, 370
isolation, population, 344–346
isopod, 738
isotonic solution, **86**, *86*
isotope, 362, *362*
Ivanovksy, Dmitri, 547
ivory-billed woodpecker, 5

J

jackal, 12, *12*
jacobin, *305*
Jacobson's organ, 796, *796*
jaguar, 306–307, *307*
Janssen, Hans and Zacharias, 70
jaw, mammalian, 807
jawfish, 6, *6*
jawless fish, 366, 376. *See also* Agnatha.
jejunum, 983
jellyfish, *410, 707*, **707**, *707, 708*, 708
joint, **1001**–1002, *1003*
  online animation, 1017
jumping spider, 832
Jurassic period, 366, 377, 621

K

kangaroo, red, *808*
kangaroo rat, 409, 471
karyotype, **217**, *217*
Kawaoka, Yoshihiro, 607
kelp, 584
kelp forest, **470**
keratin, **778**, **1013**–1014
key, dichotomous, 522
keystone species, 403–404, *404*, 472
    online animation, 421
kidney, 84, 986–987, *987*, 990–991
kinase, 145
kinesis, **819**
kingdom, *520*, 520–521, 533–536, 575,
    R25–R31
kingfisher, *R31*
king penguin, *327*, 327–328
kin selection, **834**
kit fox, 348, *348*
knee, human, *20*
Koch, Robert, 941, *941*
Kolff, Willem, 986
Komodo dragon, *789*
Krebs cycle, *114*, **115**, *118–119*
krill, 99, 735
kudu, *819*
kudzu, 501, *501*

L

lab equipment, R6–R9
    graduated cylinder, R6, *R6*
    light microscope, R8, *R8*
    metric ruler, R6, *R6*
    thermometer, R6, *R6*
    triple-beam balance, R7, *R7*
lab experiment, 399
lab safety, R2–R4
    animal, R3
    chemical, R2
    clean up, R3
    directions, R2
    dress code, R2
    electrical, R3
    glassware and sharp-object, R3
    heating and fire, R2
    symbols, R4, *R4*
labor, birth, 1040
laboratory methods. *See* Virtual Lab.
Lacks, Henrietta, 147
lac operon, **248**–249
lactase, *978*, 980
lactic acid, **123**–124
Lactobacilli, *556*
lactose, 249, 980
lake, 474
lake trout, *495*
Lamarck, Jean-Baptiste, *299*, 299–300
lamprey, *529*, 762
lancelet, 758, 760

land bridge, 499, *499*
land management, 502–505. *See also* natural
    resource.
landmass, 460
large intestine, 984, *984*
larva, 311, *311*, 744, *745*
lateral growth, 681
lateral line, **767**
lateral meristem, **648**, 651
Latin word parts, R18
lava flow, *445*
lazuli bunting, 333, *333*
leaf, *5*, *21*, *103*, *547*, 652–655, *655*
    characteristics, 653, *653*
    online animation, 657
    and photoperiodism, 683
    print, 562
    stomata, **614**, *615*, 647, 652–653, *653*
leafcutter ant, 599, *599*
leaflet, 653
leaf nesting frog, *498*, 499
learning, animal, 822–826
leech, 434, *434*, 714, *R29*
Leeuwenhoek, Anton van, 70, *71*
leg length, 384
legume, 561
lemur, *29*, *379*, *837*
Lenski, Richard, 392
leucine, 244
leukemia, **960**, *960*
levels of organization, *151*, *152*, 852–855, *855*
lever, 1002
lichen, **598**, *598*
ligament, **1002**
ligand, 84, *84*
ligation, 277
liger, 537, *537*
light, *103*
light-dependent reaction, *104*, **105**, 108–110,
    109
light-independent reaction, *104*, **105**, 110–
    112, *111*
lightning, 415
lignin, **614**, *615*
lily, *668*
limbic system, 888
limiting factor, **443**
limnetic zone, **474**
limpet, 522, *523*
Lind, James, 972
line graph, 116, 308, 375, 497, 865, **R15**
linkage map, 210–211
Linnaean system of classification, **298**,
    518–521
Linnaeus, Carolus, 298, *299*, 518
lion, *428*, 428–429, *819*
lipase, *978*
lipid, **46**–47, *47*, 102
lipid membrane, 370
liposome, *370*

Lister, Joseph, *940*, 941
littoral zone, **474**
liver, 980, *980*, 984
liverwort, 617, *617*
lizard, 789, 796, *796*, 819
    anole, 352, 820, *820*
    curly-tailed, 352
    whiptail, 698
lobe, brain, *887*
lobe-fin, **770**
lobe-finned fish, 770–771
lobster, 735, *735*, 736, *736*, 737
lock-and-key model, 56
locus, genetic, 180
logistic growth, **441**
loop of Henle, 988, *989*
Lophotrochozoa, 702, 710
Lorenz, Konrad, 824
loris, 379
Lovelock, James, 457
lumen, 76
lung, 854, *909*, 910–913, **911**, *911*
    cancer, 133, *133*
    effects of smoking on, 916, *916*
    epithelial cells, 855
    and waste elimination, 986
lungfish, 771, *771*
luteal phase, 1029, *1029*
luteinizing hormone (LH), 1024, 1025,
    1028–1030
Lycophyta, 619
Lycopodium, 619, *619*
Lyell, Charles, 299, 301, 302, 303
Lyme disease, *564*
lymph, **930**
lymphatic system, **930**–931, *930*
lymphocyte, 136, **931**, 946
lynx, Iberian, *350*
lysogenic infection, *550*, **551**
lysosome, **78**, *78*, 90
lytic infection, *550*, **551**

M

macaque, Japanese, 825, *825*
macronucleus, 579
macrophage, 69, 90
Madagascar periwinkle, 631, 633
mad cow disease, 545, 944
magnesium, 649, *973*
magnetic resonance imaging (MRI), *20*, *873*,
    891, *891*, 1051
malaria, 580, 748, *942*, 943
male reproductive system, 1025–1026, *1026*.
    See also human reproduction.
malignant tumor, **146**
malleus, 806–807, 882
malpighian tubule, 740
maltase, *978*
Malthus, Thomas, 305, 484

Index

mammal, 805–809
  characteristics of, 805–807
  early, 351
  evolution of, 377–378
  gill slits of, 312
  heart of, 790, *790*
  placental, 378
  types of, 807–809
Mammalia, 760
mammary gland, **806**
manatee, West Indian, *503*, 503–504
mandible, **737**
mangrove tree, 402, *402, 631*
mantella frog, 430, *430*
mantis shrimp, 736, *736*
mantle, **712**
manzanita, 471
mapping chromosomes, 216–217
Margulis, Lynn, 373, 457
marine ecosystem, 411, 468–471
marine worm, 317, *317*
mark-recapture, 398
marmot, yellow-bellied, 831
Marmota flaviventris, 831
Marmota monax, 831
marsupial, 377, **808**, 1040
marsupium, **808**
Martin, Gail, 164
Martin, William, 370
mass extinction, 350, *350*, 367, 377, 778
mating, 338. *See also* reproduction.
mean, 628, **R14**
measles, *942*
measuring, 18, 57, 126, 384, 506, 676–677,
  804, 921. *See also* data analysis.
mechanoreceptor, **881**
median, 628, **R14**
medicine, history of, *940, 941, 941*
Mediterranean shrubland, 466
medulla, 915, 920
medulla oblongata, **888**, *888*
medusa, **707**, *707*
meiosis, 170–176, 179, 329, 670. *See also*
  genetics.
  crossing over, **190**–191, *190*
  and genetic variation, 189–191
  and human reproduction, 1027, *1027*
  meiosis I, 174, *174*
  meiosis II, 175, *175*
  and mitosis, 170–171, *171*
  modeling, 192
  and probability, 187, 193
melanin, 59, 1014
melanocyte, 1014
membrane
  amniotic, 788, *788*
  cell, 47, **81–84**, *82*, 88, 93, 897, 988
  channels, 8
  embryonic, 1035, *1035*
  online animation, 93

memory cell, **951**
memory deficit, 895
Mendel, Gregor, *177*, 177–182, 191, 193,
  200–201, 204, 209
Mendelian genetics, **340**
Mendel's laws, **179**, **186**, 191
meninge, 886
meniscus, R6, *R6*
menopause, **1029**
menstrual cycle, **1028**, 1028–1029, *1029*,
  1033
meristem, **648**, 650–651
mesoderm, **701**, 1034
mesoglea, **707**
mesophyll, **652**, 654, *655*
Mesozoic era , 366–367, **377**, 621, 802
mesquite, 465
messenger RNA (mRNA), **240**, *243*, 243–247,
  244, 250–251, *251*
metabolism, **6**, 417, 801. *See also* cellular
  respiration; chemistry of life.
metamorphosis, **744**, *744, 745, 775, 775*
metaphase, **140**, *141*
metastasis, **146**
meteorite, 363, 369
methamphetamine, 894
methane worm, 27, *27*
methaqualone, 894
metric system, R5, *R5*
  prefixes, *R5*
microarray, 282–283
microclimate, **458**, *458*, 460
microevolution, **331**
microfilament, **73**, *73*
micrograph, *21*
microgravity, 685
micronucleus, 579
microscope, 3, **19**–20, *19*, 22, 70, 70–71
  calculating magnification, R10, *R10*
  calculating specimen size, R10, *R10*
  light, R8, *R8*
  making a wet mount, R9, *R9*
  parts of, *R9*
  staining specimen for, R9, *R9*
  viewing objects, R9
microtubule, **73**, *73*, 78
microvilli, *982*, **983**
midbrain, **888**, *888*
middle ear, 806–807
migration, 513, 811, 821
milk, 993
milk products, 123
milkweed, 616
Miller, Stanley, 369
Miller-Urey experiment, 369, *369*
millipede, 409, 730
mimosa, 683
mineral, **973**, *973*
mineral nutrient, 649
miotic reproduction, 150

Mississippian period, 455
mite, 432, *433*, 741–742, 958
mitochondrial DNA, **532**, *532*
mitochondrion, **77**, *77, 113*, 113–115, *114*,
  119–120, 373
mitosis, 134, **135**, 138–142, *141*, 143, 631
  and binary fission, 148–149, *149*
  and meiosis, 170–171, *171*
  online animation, 157
mockingbird, 819, *819*
mode, 628, **R14**
modeling, 3, 18, 83, 93, 156, 192, 257, 268,
  278, 282, 286, 315, 334, 337, 352, 364,
  381, 385, 400, 417–419, 421, 435, 476,
  496, 507, 536, 567, 772, 861, 932, 943,
  964, 1016, 1017. *See also* data analysis.
mold, 600, R27. *See also* fungi; protist.
mole, 312
  forefoot of, 312, *312*
  star-nosed, 297, *297*
molecular clock, 530–532
molecular fingerprinting, 317
molecular genetics, **23**
molecule, **39**
  carbon-based, 44–48
  polar and nonpolar, 40–42
  water, 40, 40–41
mole rat, 836
mollusk, *712*, 712–713, *713*
molting, arthropod, 732, *732*
monarch butterfly, 616, *745*
Monera kingdom, 533–534
monkey, 380, *759*
  capuchin, 838, *838*
  snow, 825, *825*
monoamine oxidase, 25
monocot, **626**, *626*, 632, 650
monohybrid cross, **184**
monomer, **45**
Mononykus, 366
monosaccharide, **45**
monotreme, 378, **807**–808, 1035
Monterey pine, 346
Montoya, Angel, 848
moose, *443*
moray eel, *7*
morel, 590, *590*
Morgan, Thomas Hunt, 209–210
morning sickness, 1039
Morowitz, Harold, 370
Morro Bay estuary, 471, *471*
mortality, infant, 485
mortality rate, **439**
mosaic disease, 547
mosquito, 3, *42*, 580, 748, 944
moss, 617–619, *618, 619, 665, 665*
  life cycle, R32
moss cup fungus, *590*
moth orchid, *663*
motor cortex, 887, *887*
motor neuron, **877**

mountain climate, 460, 467
mountain habitat, 419, *419*
mouse, 206–207, 278–279, *279*, 315, *315*, *500*, 501, *821*
mouse lemur, *29*
mouth, 978, *979*
MRI scan, 20, *873*, 891, *891*, 1051
mRNA, **240**, *243*, 243–247, *244*, 250–251, *251*
mucus, 911
Mullis, Kary, 269, *269*
multicellular life, 376–378
multicellular organism, 5, 151–155
    algae, 581
    fungi, 592–594
    levels of organization, 852–856
multiple sclerosis (MS), *959*
multipotent stem cell, 154, *154*
multitasking, 1052
mumps, *554*
Muneta, Ben, 608
murex snail, 349
muscle
    of birds, 801
    cells, 853
    fatigue, 1012
    and fermentation, 122–123
    microscopic examination of, 1017
    online animation, 127
    structure and function, 1008–1011, *1009*, 1016
    tissue, 854
    types of, 1006–1008, *1007*
muscle fiber, **1006**, *1009*
muscular dystrophy, 284, *284*
muscular system, *856*, **1006**–1011, *1006*
mushroom, *458*, 589, *589*, 595, *R27*
mutagen, **255**
mutation, **252**–255, *342*, 343
    and cancer, 146
    gene, 252–254, 267
    in homeotic genes, 698, 700
    and molecular clocks, 530–532
    online lab, 193
    and phenotypes, 329, 330
    and reproductive isolation, 344–345
    silent, 254
    types of, 252–253, *253*
mutualism, **432**, *433*, 616
mutualist, 598–599
mycelium, **590**, 598
Mycobacterium tuberculosis, 563
Mycomycota, 598
mycorrhizae, **591**, 598
myelin sheath, 877, 886
myofibril, **1008**, *1009*
myosin filament, **1008**–1011, *1009*, *1010*
myriapod, 731, *731*, 734
Myxomycota, 587

N

NADH, 117–118
NADPH, 108, 110–111

naked mole rat, 836
names, scientific, 519, *519*. *See also* classification.
nanoball, 392
natural resource, 485–487, 504–505
natural selection, 10, 304–309, **305**, *307*
    and artificial selection, **304**–305, 308
    and fishing techniques, 503
    forms of, 330–333
    and genetics, 319
    and genetic variation, 190, 308–309
    and mammals, 806
    and mutations, 254
    online animation, 321
    patterns in, 347, *347*
    and phenotypes, 328, 330–334
    and population evolution, *342*, 343
    principles of, 306
    and sexual reproduction, 374
nauplius larva, 738
Nautilus, *R29*
navel, 1041
Neanderthal, 382
nebula, **368**, *368*
nectar, 624
negative feedback, 9, **860**, *860*, 861
negative reinforcement, 826
nematocyst, **707**–708, *708*
nematode, 716
nephron, **987**–990, *989*
neritic zone, **468**
nerve cell. *See* neuron.
nerve cord, 758
nervous system, 856, **874**–894, *874*
    and brain chemistry, 891–894
    central and peripheral, **875**, *885*, 885–890
    and gas exchange, 915
    and homeostasis, 874–875
    and hypothalamus, 900, *900*
    and interference, 884
    subsystems of, 889–890, *890*
    tissue of, 854
neural crest, 760
neuromuscular junction, 1010
neuron, *852*, *873*, **876**–879, *876*, 1052
    adaptation of, 893, *893*
    and cell division, 136
    exocytosis, 91
    and learning, 823
    and muscle contractions, 1010, *1010*
    types of, 877
neuroscientist, 1052
neurotransmitter, *878*, **879**, 892, *893*, 893–894
    and muscular contraction, 1010
    and spider venom, 741
neutron, 36
new world monkey, 380, *380*
niacin, *974*
niche, ecological, 351, **428**–429, 559, 697
niche partitioning, 429

Nile crocodile, 432, *433*
nine-banded armadillo, *524*
Nishi, Rae, 1052
nitrate, 415
nitrification, 415
nitrogen, 649
nitrogen cycle, 415, *415*
nitrogen fixation, **415**
nitrogen-fixing bacteria, 560–561, *561*
nitrogen oxide, 415, 489
node, cladogram, 526, *527*
node, lymph, **930**–931
nondisjunction, 192
noninfectious disease, 940
nonnative species, 429, 441, 444, 500, 507
nonpolar molecule, 40, 42
nonrenewable resource, **485**–486
nonspecific immune response, 950
nonsteroid hormone, 896–897, *897*
nonvascular plant, 620, 665
nori, 584
normal distribution, 330
North Atlantic current, 514
northern pike, *507*
note-taking strategies
    cause-and-effect diagram, 361, 818, 1010, **R23**, *R23*
    combination notes, 654, 665
    concept map, 30, 60, 94, 128, 158, 220, 258, 288, 322, 354, 379, 386, 422, 450, 478, 508, 538, 568, 602, 634, 686, 752, 782, 812, 842, 868, 904, 934, 941, 966, 994, 1018, 1046, **R24**, *R24*
    content frame, 30, 44, 724, **R23**, *R23*
    cycle diagram, 135, 194, 236, 568, 686, 868, **R22**, *R22*
    diagrams, 414, 429, 456, 485, 697, 775, 842
    examples, 432
    flow chart, 877, 994
    levels of organization, 397, 422
    main ideas, 36, 60, 94, 101, 139, 220, 264, 322, 450, 478, 518, 538, 602, 613, 658, 681, 731, 737, 748, 801, 812, 853, 886, 910, 983, 1001, **R23**, *R23*
    mind map, 24, 123, 280, 328
    outlining, 70
    process diagram, 508, 752, 782, 1046, **R22**, *R22*
    sketches, 701, 764
    summarizing, 258, 306
    supporting main ideas notes, **R22**, *R22*
    tables, 226, 831
    three-column chart, 534, 574, 634, 641, 658, 904, 966, 1018
    timeline, 386, 1036
    two-column chart, 5, 75, 128, 168, 202, 288, 298, 354, 545, 789, 922, 973, 1025
    Venn diagram, 158, 173, 556, 746, 934, 952, **R24**, *R24*
    Y diagram, 194, **R24**, *R24*

Index

notochord, **758**–759
nuclear division, 170–171, 173
nuclear DNA, 532
nuclear transfer, 163, 275
nucleic acid, **48**, 138. *See also* DNA; RNA.
nucleolus, 75
nucleotide, 48, 138–139, **230**, 232–233, 240
nucleus, 36, **75**, *75*
null hypothesis, 925
nutrient
    absorption, 89, 982–984
    and homeostasis, 972–976
    limiting, 448
nutrition, 1045
nymph, 744

O

oak, 519, *519*, *627*, *939*
obesity, 976, 993
obligate aerobe, **555**
obligate anaerobe, **555**
obligate pathogen, 597
observing, **13**, 15, 28, 57, 58, 92, 143, 147,
    229, 315, 398, 449, 460, 522, 560, 562,
    579, 595, 623, 632, 647, 656, 657, 676–
    677, 709, 714, 722, 723, 751, 776, 780,
    802, 804, 824, 830, 857, 866, 884, 921,
    928, 1031, 1044. *See also* data analysis.
occipital lobe, *887*
ocean
    deep-sea vents, 407
    online animation, 477
    plankton, 444
    sediment coring, 513
    zones of, 468–470
oceanographer, 514
oil, 46
old world monkey, 380, *380*
olfactory cell, 883
Olopade, Olufunmilayo, 294
omnivore, **409**
Onchyophora, 734
oncogene, 146
oncomouse, 278–279
onion, 679
online lab. *See* Virtual Lab.
On the Origin of Species, 306
operant conditioning, **826**
operational definition, **80**, R12
operator, 248
operculum, **767**, *767*
operon, **248**–249
Ophiuroidea, 720
opossum, Virginia, 808
opportunistic infection, **961**, 963
opportunity cost, 828
optimal foraging, **829**
orange, 679
orangutan, 380, *380*
orchid, 10, *10*, *663*

order taxon, *520*, 520–521
Ordovician period, 366
organ, **151**, *152*, **854**
organelle, **72**, 73–79, 93
organic life, 369
organism, **5**, 397, *397*, 854
organ system, **151**, *152*, **854**, 856, *856*, 874–
    875. *See also* human biology.
organ transplant, 990
origin of life, 368–371. *See also* earth; evolu-
    tion.
    early cell structure hypotheses, 370
    organic molecule hypotheses, 369
    RNA hypothesis, 370–371
osculum, 706
osmosis, 85–87, **86**, *86*, 646
ossicle, 718
Osteichthye, 760, 767. *See also* bony fish.
osteoblast, 1005
osteocyte, 1004–1005, *1005*
ostrich, 314, *314*
otter, sea, 421
outgroup, 525
outlier, 985
ovary, **668**, 898, 899, **1024**
overproduction, 306, *307*
oviparous reptile, **793**
ovulation, **1028**
ovum, 168, **1024**, *1027*, 1027–1028, *1028*,
    1030–1031, *1031*
owl, 315, *315*, 799
oxygen, 36, *37*
    and cell metabolism, 851, 860
    and cellular respiration, 117–118, 120,
    122
    cycle, 413, *413*
    diffusion of, 86
    and energy, 50
    molecules, 39
    and ozone, 489
    and prokaryotes, 555
    and respiratory and circulatory systems,
    911, 914–915, 920
    in water, 40
oxytocin, 1040, 1041
Oxytricha, 575, *575*
oystercatcher, 829, *829*
ozone, ground-level, 488–489
ozone layer, 489

P

Pace, Betty, 285, *285*
pacemaker, **918**, *918*, 1008
Pacific salmon, 396, *396*
Pacific yew, 631
pain receptor, 881, 883
Pakicetus, 318
paleontology, 316
Paleozoic era, 366–367, **376**–377
palisade mesophyll, 654, *655*

Panama, Isthmus of, 346
pancreas, 91, 864–865, **898**, *899*, 980, *980*
panda, 309, *309*
    giant, 521
    red, *521*
pandemic, 606–607
pangolin, *517*
panic attack, 895
pantothenic acid, *974*
paper wasp, *729*
papilla, 883
Paramecium, *573*, 574, 579, *579*, R25
parasite, 943
    flukes and tapeworms, 711, *711*
    online animation, 723
    roundworms, *716*, 716–717
    tongue worms, 738
parasitic wasp, 332, *332*
parasitic worm, 943, *943*, 944
parasitism, **432**–434, *433*, 443
parasympathetic nervous system, **890**
parathyroid hormone (PTH), 1005
parenchyma cell, **640**, *641*
parietal lobe, *887*
Parkinson's disease, 892, 1052
parrot, 803
parrotfish, *410*, 411
particulate, **488**
passive immunity, **948**
passive transport, **85**, *85*
Pasteur, Louis, *940*, 941
pathogen, 544, 940–944, **941**, 947, 955. *See*
    also bacteria; virus.
    fungi as, 597
    and immune system, 945–946
    and white blood cells, 946, *946*, 950,
    950–951, *951*
patterns
    identifying, 339
    predicting from, 320
Pauling, Linus, 231, 530
Pavlov, Ivan, 826
PCB, 495, 496
peach scab, 597
peacock, 338
peanut, 626, 957
pea plant, 178
peat, 618
Pediastrum, 575, *575*
pedigree, **214**–218, *215*, 287
pedipalp, 740
peer review, 14–15
pelagic zone, 468, 474
pelecypoda, 713
pelican, 471, 803
pellicle, 582
Pelomyxa palustris, 578
pelvic inflammatory disease, 1032
pelycosaur, 794
penguin
    emperor, *831*
    king, *327*, 327–328

penicillin, 955

Penicillium, 590

pepsin, *978*, 979, 981

peptidase, *978*

peptide bond, 47, *47*

peptidoglycan, 79, 557, *557*

peregrine falcon, *848*

perennial plant, 627

period, geologic, 367

periodic table, *R36–R37*

periosteum, 1004, *1004*

peripheral nervous system (PNS), **875**, *885*, 885–890

peristalsis, **978**

peritoneal dialysis, 991

permafrost, 466

Permian period, 366

permineralization, 360–361, *361*

pesticide, 278

petal, **668**

petiole, **652**

PET scan, 891, *891, 892*

pH, **42**–43, *43*, 58

   and acid rain, 489

   and enzymes, 55

Phaeophyta, 584

phage, 228

phagocyte, **946**

phagocytosis, **90**, 578

pharmacogenomics, 293–294

pharmacology, **631**

pharming, 276

pharyngeal slit, 758–759

pharynx, 710

phenotype, **181**–186, 328

   in ABO blood group, 928

   and alleles, 204–207

   and chromosomes, 200–203

   and genotypes, 214–216, *215*

   and mutations, 254, 329, 330

   and natural selection, 330–334

   online animation, 219

pheromone, 344, **832**

phloem, **642**, *645*, 645–646, *646*

phosphate group, 100–101, 416

phospholipid, 47, *47*, **81**–82, *82*

phosphorus, *973*

phosphorus cycle, 416, *416*

photic zone, 468

photon, 42

photoperiodism, **683**

photoreceptor, 881

photosynthesis, 53, 102, **103**–112, 372, 407, 413, *413*, 469

   Calvin cycle, **111**

   and cellar respiration, 112, 114–115, *115*, 121, *121*

   and cynobacteria, 560

   and diatoms, 583

   functions of, 112

   and leaves, 654–656

   light-dependent reactions, *104*, **105**, 108–110, *109*

   light-independent reactions, *104*, **105**, 110–112, *111*

   overview of, 103–105, *104*

   and phloem, 645

   rates of, 106

   and sugars, 105, 110–111

photosynthetic algae, 99, *99*

photosystem, **108**–110, *109*

phototropism, **682**, *682*

Photuris fairchildi, 345

Photuris frontalis, 345

Photuris hebes, 345

phycoerythrin, 584

phylogeny, **524**, 702–704, *703*

phylum, *520*, 520–521, **699**, *R25–R31*

Phytophthora infestans, 588, *588*

phytoplankton, *410, 411,* 444, **469**, *495*, *495*, 513, 581

Picrophilus, 43

pigeon, 304, *305*

piglet, *806*

pigment, flower, 182

pili, 556

pill bug, 519, 738, 819, 840

pinacocyte, 706

pine, 655, 666–667, *667*

   Bishop, 346

   bristlecone, 620

   Monterey, 346

   Ponderosa, 622

pinna, 882

pinworm, 717

pioneer species, **446**

pistil, 668

pitcher plant, 655

pituitary gland, **898**, *899,* 900, *900,* 901

   and growth, 1041

   and reproduction, 1024

pivot joint, 1002, *1003*

placenta, 779, 809, **1035**, *1035,* 1041

placental mammal, 378

Placoderm, 765, *765*

plaice, *769*

planarian, 710, *710*

plankton, **469**, 582

plant, **612**–631, 638–655

   abiotic factors, 405

   adaptation, 613–614, *615*, 624–625, *625*, 657

   and allergies, 958

   and carbon cycle, 414

   and cell differentiation, **152**–153

   cells, *71, 74, 77, 77,* 78–79, *100, 483,* 640, 640–641, *641*

   and chlorophyll, 103

   classification, 617–622, 630

   cloning, 275

   epiphytes, 464

   evolution of, 455, 610–614, *611*

   flowering, 378, 622, 624–627, 668–672, *R35*

   fossils, *366,* 611, 617

   and fungi, 589, 597, 616

   genetic engineering in, 277–278

   habitat, 623

   herbaceous, 627, 650

   and herbivores, 616

   hormones, 680–681, 684

   and human culture, 629–631

   insect repelling, 692

   life cycle and lifespan, 170, 627, 664–667, *R32. R33, R34, R35*

   medicinal uses of, 631, 633

   online animation, 633, 685

   organ systems, 151

   origins of, 612–616

   and phosphorus, 416

   and photosynthesis, 102, 112

   population sampling, 398

   purebred, **178**, *178*

   reproduction, 614, 620, 668–679

   roots, *639, 648,* 648–649, *649*

   seeds, 620–622

   stems, *650,* 650–651

   structure and function, 657

   tissues, 151, 641–642, *642*

   vascular system of, **614**, *615,* 620, 643–646

Plantae, *R27–R28*

planula, 707

plaque, 924, *924*

plasma, 42, 51, **926**, *926*

plasma membrane, 81

plasmid, **276**–278, *276, 277,* 391, **556**

plasmodesmata, 641

plasmodial slime mold, *587,* 587–588

Plasmodium, 580, *580*

platelet, 145, **926**

Platyhelminthes, 704

platypus, duck-billed, 807–808, *808*

plesiosaur, 794

plover, Egyptian, 432, *433*

plumule, 675

pluripotent stem cell, 154, *154*

pneumonia, *942, 949*

poinsetta, 683

point mutation, 252

poison dart frog, 430, *430*

polar bear, 9, *9,* 467, *467, 512*

polar body, **176**

polar climate, *459,* 467

polar ice cap, 467, 492, *492*

polar molecule, 40–42

polar nucleus, 670

polio, *941*

pollen grain, **614**, *615,* 669, 669–670

pollination, **620**, 624, 669

   online animation, 633

Index

pollution, **488**
  air, 488–493
  water, 494–496
polychlorinated biphenyl (PCB), 495, 496
polydactyly, *181*
polygenic trait, **206**
polymer, **45**
polymerase
  DNA, **236**, 269–271
  enzyme, *371*
  RNA, **240**, *241*, 242
polymerase chain reaction (PCR), **269**–271, *270*
polyp, **707**
polypeptide, *47*, 47–48, 239, 243
polyplacophora, 713
polysaccharide, **45**
pond ecosystem, 418, *418*, 474
Ponderosa pine, 622
pons, 888, *888*, 915
population, 397, *397*. *See also* evolution.
  crash, **442**
  density, **436**–439
  dispersion, **437**
  evolving, 352, 392
  growth, 305, **306**, 440–444, 449
  Hardy-Weinberg model, 340–343
  human, 484–487
  isolation, 344–346
  online animation, 353, 421, 449
  sampling, 398, 401, 421
Portuguese man-of-war, 708
positive feedback, **861**, 929
positive reinforcement, 826
positron emission tomography (PET), 891, *891*, 892
potassium, 973, *973*
potato, 150, *650*, 679, *679*
potato blight, 588
potter wasp, *743*
power consumption, 485–486
PPFM bacteria, 562
prairie dog, 398, 417
prairie ecosystem, 418, *418*
Precambrian time, 366
precipitation, 412, 460, 464–466
predation, 431–432, 435, 443
predator-prey pursuit, 315
predicting, 202, 208, 219, 268, 315, 320, 595, 739. *See also* data analysis.
pregnancy, 1038–1039
preserved remains, 360
pressure-flow model, 645–646, *646*
prickly pear, 678, *678*
primary growth, **651**
primary sensory cortex, 886
primary succession, **446**, *446*, 598, 618
primate, *366*, **379**
primate evolution, 379–383, *380*
primer, **271**
primitive fungus, 590
Principles of Geology, 301

prion, 17, 59, **545**
probability, **187**, 193, 218, 273–274
problem-solving behavior, 838
proboscis, 746
process skill. *See* data analysis.
producer, 103, **406**–407
product, **50**
progesterone, 1029, 1036
prokaryote, 372–374, 533–534, 544, *544*, 555–561
  flagella of, 577
  functions of, 559–561
  structure of, 556–557, *557*
prokaryotic cell, **72**, *72*, 136
  and DNA, 239, 248
promoter, **248**
prophage, **551**
prophase, **140**, *141*
Propionibacterium, 564
prop root, *639*
prosimian, **379**, *380*
prostate gland, 1026, *1026*
protea, *611*, 612
protein, 8, **47**–48, *47*, 102
  and blood types, 927–928, 954
  in cell membrane, 82, *82*
  complement, 947
  and DNA, 138–139
  and homeostasis, 973
  molecular fingerprinting, 317
  online animation, 59, 257
  and organelles, 75–77
  and pathogens, 947
  and prions, 545
  as transforming principle, *227*, 227–228
  translation, **243**–247, *246*
  transport, 87, 89–90
proteomics, **283**
prothallus, 666
protist, 572–588, *573*, **574**, 697
  animal-like, 577–579
  choanoflagellates, 705
  funguslike, 587–588
  online animation, 601
  and other eukaryotes, 575–576, *576*
  plantlike, 581–585
  types of, 575
Protista kingdom, 533, 574, 575, *R25–R27*
proton, 36
proton pump, 90
protostome, **702**, *702*, *703*
protozoa, **577**–579, 943
pseudocoelom, **716**
pseudogene, 317
Pseudomonas putida, 847
Pseudomyrmex ferrugineus, 349
pseudoplasmodium, 588
pseudopod, **578**
Pteranodon, 795
Pterophyta, 619
pterosaur, *377*, 795
puberty, 861, **1024**, 1042

puffball, 591, *591*
pufferfish, 818, *818*
pulmonary ciculation, 920, *920*
pulmonary circuit, **789**
pumpkin, 672, *672*
punctuated equilibrium, **351**
Punnett, R. C., 183, *183*, 209
Punnett square, **183**–188, *183*, *184*, *185*, *187*, 340
pupa, **744**, *745*
pupil of eye, *880*
purebred plant, **178**, *178*
pygmy marsupial frog, *774*
pyramid, energy, **417**–**418**, *418*, 495
pyramid model, 417–419
pyramid of numbers, 419, *419*
pyridoxine, *974*
pyrococcus, *R25*
Pyrococcus furiosus, 534
pyruvate, 117–118
python, Burmese, 500, *500*

Q

quadrate bone, 807
quadrat sampling, 398–399
qualitative data, 12, 14, **R12**
quantitative data, 12, 14, **R12**
Quaternary period, 366, 378
Quercus alba, 519, *519*

R

rabbit, 441, *441*
rabbit-eared bandicoot, 190, *190*
rabies, **554**, 943
racoon, 521
radial symmetry, **701**, *701*, *703*
radiation, adaptive, **351**, 367
radiation therapy, 147
radicle, 675
radioactive decay, 364
radiometric dating, **362**–363, *363*
radio telemetry, 398, *398*
radula, **712**
rainfall, 412, 460, 464–466
rain forest, 403, 455, *455*, *463*, 464, 499, 846
random dispersion, **437**, *437*
random event, 347
random sampling, 420
rat, kangaroo, 409, 471
ratfish, 766
ray, 766, *766*
ray-fin, **768**–769
R bacteria, 226–227
reactant, **50**
reaction time, 902
reading frame, 244
receptor, **84**, *84*, *167*, 552, 680, 859, 881
recessive allele, **181**–182, 187, 201, 204
recombinant DNA, **276**–277, *277*
recombination, 329, 374
rectum, 984
red algae, 584, *R26*

redback spider, 828, *828*
red blood cell, 8–9, *852*, **915**, 927, *927*
red fox, 348, *348*
red leaf beetle, *696*
red-legged frog, 438–439
red lily beetle, *999*
red panda, *521*
red squirrel, 429
red tide, 583, *583*
reduction division, 171
reef shark, *410*, 411
reflex arc, **889**
regeneration, **678**
reindeer, 443
relative dating, 362
releaser, 822
releasing hormone, **900**
renal function, 987
renewable resource, **485**–486
replication, DNA, **235**–238, *237*, *238*, 242, 255, 271
repressor protein, 249
reproduction, 6. *See also* asexual reproduction; human reproduction; sexual reproduction.
    of algae, 584–585
    of amphibians, 774
    of birds, 801
    of fish, 772
    of fungi, 591–594, *592*, *593*
    miotic, 150
    of plants, 614, 620, 668–679
    and stimulus, 820
    strategy, 438–439
    vegetative, **678**–679
reproductive isolation, **334**, **344**, *345*
reptile, 377, **793**–797
    anatomy of, *797*
    ear bone of, *807*
    heart of, 790, *790*
    phylogenic tree of, 794, *795*
Reptilia, 760
research engineer, 692
researching, 29, 601, 633, 781, 811, 841, 867, 903, 965, 1045. *See also* data analysis.
respiration, 413, *413*, 414. *See also* cellular respiration.
respiratory system, *855*, *856*, **910**–916
    of birds, 801
    and cellular respiration, 911
    diseases of, 916
    and gas exchange, 914–916
    online animation, 933
    organs and tissues, *911*
respirometer, 932
resting potential, **877**
restriction enzyme, **265**–266, *265*, *266*, 278
restriction map, 267, *267*, 272
restriction site, 265
retina, 881

retinol, *974*
retrovirus, 553, *553*, 961
reverse transcriptase, 553
rheumatoid arthritis, *959*
Rh factor, **928**, 954
rhino beetle, *730*
rhizoid, 618
rhizome, 619, 678
Rhizopoda, 578
Rhodophyta, 584
riboflavin, *974*
ribonucleic acid (RNA). *See* RNA.
ribosomal RNA (rRNA), **240**, **532**
ribosome, 75, 76, 245, *245*, *247*
ribozyme, 370–371
rice, 691
risk cost, 828
river ecosystem, 457, 473
RNA, 48. *See also* DNA.
    base pairing, 240
    and DNA, 239–240, 370–371, *371*
    and gene expression, 248–251
    hypothesis, 370–371
    mRNA, **240**, *243*, 243–247, *244*, 250–251, *251*
    online animation, 246
    polymerase, **240**, *241*, 242
    rRNA, **240**, **532**
    translation, 243–247, *246*
    tRNA, **240**, *245*, 245–247
    and viral infection, 553
rod cell, *881*
root, *639*, *648*, 648–649, *649*
root cap, **648**
root hair, **648**, *648*
rotifer, 696, *696*
roundworm, 704, *716*, 716–717
Royal, Charmaine, 64
rRNA, **240**, **532**
ruby-throated hummingbird, 811
runner, plant, 150, 678
Russell, Michael, 370

S

Saccharomyces cerevisiae, 590
sac fungus, 590, *590*, *592*, 594, *594*, *R27*
saddle-back tortoise, 302, *303*
saddle joint, 1002, *1003*
safety, R2–R4
sago palm, *R28*
Sahelanthropus tchadensis, 382
St. Martin, Alexis, 977
salamander, 776, *776*, *R31*
salicin, 631
salinity, 472
saliva, 55, 826, 978
salmon, Pacific, 396, *396*
salmonella, 944
salt, 38
samara, *673*

sampling, 947. *See also* data analysis.
    and population size, 398, 401
    quadrat, 398–399
    random, 420
sand dollar, 720
sandhill crane, 444
Sanger, Frederick, 280
sap, 645
sapwood, 650, *651*
sarcomere, **1008**–1011, *1009*
SARS, 553, *941*
saturated fat, 46, 973
savanna, 464
S bacteria, 226–227
scanning electron microscope (SEM), 3, 20, 21, 69
scaphopoda, 713
scarlet elf cup, *590*
scatterplot, 721, 742, 770, R17
schistosomiasis, 711
schizophrenia, 892
Schleiden, Matthias, 71, *71*
Schwann, Theodor, 71, *71*
Schwann cell, 877
scientific inquiry, 399. *See also* data analysis.
    computers in, 817
    scientific thinking, 13–17, *15*
    surveys, 398
    terminology, 519, *519*
    and theories, 299, 301
scientific notation, R14
sclerenchyma cell, **641**, *641*
scorpion, *731*, 741–742, *R30*
scrotum, 1026
scurvy, 972
scyphozoa, 708
sea. *See* ocean.
sea anemone, 150, 468, 707–708, 827
sea biscuit, 720
sea cucumber, 537, 720, *720*
sea dragon, 769
seahorse, *757*
sea ice, 513
seal, elephant, 336, 436
sea lily, 719
sea otter, 421
sea slug, *695*
season, climatic, 459
sea sponge, *410*
sea squid, 713, *713*
sea squirt, *758*, 759, *759*, *R31*
sea star, *718*, 718–719, *719*, 722, *R30*
sea turtle, 207, *410*, 796, *796*, 811, 822, *822*
sea urchin, 720, *720*
sea wasp, 708
sebaceous gland, 1015
secondary growth, **651**
secondary succession, **447**, *447*
second messenger, 897
sediment coring, 513

Index

seed, 614, *615*, 620, 625–626, 672
seed dispersal, 673–674
   online animation, 685
seedling, 675
seed plant, 620, *620*, 620–622
segmentation, 714, **730**
segmented worm, 528. *See also* annelid.
segregation, law of, **179**, 186
selective permeability, **83**
semen, **1026**
semiarid desert, 465
seminal vesicle, **1026**, *1026*
semipermeable membrane, **83**
sensitization, **893**, *893*
sensor, 859
sensory cortex, 887, *887*
sensory neuron, 877
sensory organs, 880–883
sepal, **668**
septum, 714
sequoia tree, 622
serine, *47*
serotonin, 892
sessile, **705**
severe acute respiratory syndrome (SARS), 553
sex chromosome, **169**, 200–201, *201*
sex-linked gene, 201–203, 213, 214–216, *215*
sexually transmitted disease (STD), **1032**
sexual reproduction, 148, **170**
   of algae, 584–585
   of animals, 698
   and chemical signals, 898
   evolution of, 374
   of fungi, 591–594
   and genetic variation, 189–190
   hermaphroditism, 713
   of invertebrates, 705–707, 713, 715, 717, 719
   meiosis, 329
   and reproductive strategy, 438–439
sexual selection, **338–339**, *342*, 343, 832
shark, 348, *348*, 766, *766*
   reef, *410*, 411
sheep, bighorn, 338
shrimp, *7*, *410*, 411
   brine, 739
   mantis, 736, *736*
   snapping, 346, *346*, 836
Siberian tiger, *827*
sickle cell anemia, 48, *48*, 208, *208*, 927, *927*
Sierra Nevada, 460, *460*
significant figures, R14
Silent Spring, 502
silk, 741
Silurian period, 366
single-celled organism, 5, 372–375, 533
   algae, 581
   fungi, 591
sinoatrial (SA) node, 918

sister chromatid, 173, *173*, 175, *175*, 190
SI units, R5, *R5*
   conversion from customary system, R5
skate, 766
skeletal muscle, **1006**–1007, *1007*
skeletal system, *865*, 999, **1000**–1005, *1000*, *1001*, *1003*
   of birds, *800*, 801
   comparisons, 312–313, 383, *383*
skepticism, 13
skin, 883, *883*, 1013–1015, *1015*
   cancer, 146, *146*, 157, 256
   color, 206
   and pathogens, 945
Skinner, B. F., 826
Skinner box, 826
skull
   hominid, 383, *383*
   muscles of, 1011
   of reptiles, 794, *794*
sleeping sickness, 580
slime mold, 574, *574*, **587**–588, *R27*
sloth, tree, 437
slow-twitch fiber, 1007
small intestine, *979*, 980, *982*, 982–984
smell, 882–883
smelt, *495*
Smith, William, 365
smog, *488*, 488–489
smooth muscle, 1007, *1007*
snail, *712*
   apple, 409, *409*
   murex, 349
snail kite, 409, *409*
snake, 314, 796, *796*
   timber rattlesnake, *431*, 432
snapping shrimp, 346, *346*, 836
snout beetle, *8*, 9
snow monkey, 825, *825*
social behavior, animal, 831–836, 838–839
sodium, 38, *38*, 973, *973*, 976
sodium chloride, 38, *38*
sodium-potassium pump, 90, **877**–879
soil, 477
solar car, *108*
solar system, 368
solute, **42**
solution, **42**
solvent, **42**
somatic cell, 140, 163, **168**, 170
somatic cell nuclear transfer (SCNT), 163
somatic nervous system, **889**
somatic stem cell, 154
sonic hedgehog, 250
sorus, 666
Spanish flu, 607
sparrow hawk, 803, *803*
Spassky, N. P., 353
specialist, **409**, 573

speciation, 344–346. *See also* evolution.
   adaptative radiation, **351**, 367
   online animation, 353
   patterns in, 351
species, 5, **298**
   coevolution, 349
   common ancestors of, 299, 310–313, 317, 524–525
   and competition, 429, **431**, 443
   defining, 537
   ecological equivalents of, **430**
   endangered, 503–504
   extinction of, 299–301, *350*, 350–351, 367, 377
   indicator, **494**, 781
   introduced, **500**, 507
   keystone, **403**–404, *404*, 421, 472
   in Linnaean system, 518–521, *519*, *520*
   nonnative, 429, 441, 444
   pioneer, **446**
   survival strategies of, 438–439
   symbiotic relationships among, 432–434
   umbrella, 503–504
   variation, **302**, 306, *307*, 308–309
specific immune response, 950
sperm, 1025–1026, 1030–1031
spermatozoa, 168
sperm cell, *167*, **176**, 853, *1030*
sphagnum, 618
sphenodont, 796
sphincter, **977**
spice, 630, *630*
spider, 695, 740–742. *See also* arachnid.
   Australian redback, 828, *828*
   black widow, 741
   brown recluse, 741
   jumping, 832
   spiny, 740, *740*
spider crab, 730
spinal cord, *875*, 888, 888–889
spiny spider, 740, *740*
spiracle, **741**, 744
spirillus, 556
Spirochaeta, 556
spirochete, 556
spleen, 931
sponge, 695, 705, 705–706, *706*
spongin, 706
spongy bone, 1004, *1004*
spongy mesophyll, 654, *655*
sporangia, 592, 666
spore, fungus, 594
sporophyte, **664**–667
sporozoan, 580
squid, *53*, 713, *713*
squirrel
   Belding's ground, *833*, 833–834
   gray, 429
   red, 429
Sri Lanka, 499

stabilizing selection, **332**, *332*
stamen, **668**
standards-based assessment, 33, 63, 97, 131,
    161, 197, 223, 261, 291, 325, 357, 389,
    425, 453, 481, 511, 541, 571, 605, 637,
    661, 689, 727, 755, 785, 815, 845, 871,
    907, 937, 969, 997, 1021, 1049
stapes, 774, 806–807, *807*, 882
staph infection, 391
Staphylococcus aureus, 391, 563
starch, 45, 56, 112
starfish, 150
star-nosed mole, 297, *297*
start codon, 244
statistical analysis, 14
Steller's jay, *696*
stem cell, **153**–155, *154, 155,* 162–164, 852–
    853, 1036
    embryonic, *162*
sternum, **801**
steroid hormone, 896–897, *897*
stewardship, 504–505
stick insect, 730
stigma, **668**
stimulant, **894**
stimulus, 818–820, **874**, 933
stinging ant, 349, *349*
sting ray, *R31*
stolon, 678
stoma, *21*, 151, **614**, *615,* 647, 652–653, *653,*
    744
stomach, 978–979, *979*
stomach ulcer, 17
Stomphia, 827
stonefly, 473
stop codon, 244
strangler fig, *639*
strawberry, 150, *650,* 678
Streptococcus, 564, *564*
stride inference, 384
stroma, 104, *104*
stromatolite, 372, *372*
Stroop, John, 884
Sturtevant, Alfred, 210
style, **668**
subcutaneous fat, 1015
substrate, **56**
succession, **445**–447
sucrase, *978*
sugar, 45, 103
    and photosynthesis, 105, 110–111
    sources and sinks, 645–646, *646*
sulphur atom, 48
sunflower, 624
sunlight, 102, 368, 407, 417. *See also* photo-
    synthesis.
    and climate, 459
    and plants, 681–682
    in tropical rain forest, 464
superbug, 565
superposition, law of, 300

surface tension, 41, *41*
survey, scientific, 398
survival strategy, 438–439
survivorship, **827**
survivorship curve, **438**–439
sustainable development, 502–503
swallowtail butterfly, 334, *748*
sweat, 986, 1013
sweat gland, 1015, *1015*
swim bladder, **769**
swimmeret, 737
swimming, 764
symbiosis, **432**, 433, 706
    lichens, 446
    mutualistic, 559
symmetry, animal, **701**, *701*
sympathetic nervous system, 890
synapse, *878,* **879**
synapsid, 794, 805, 806
synovial joint, 1002
synthesis stage, 135
syphilis, 1032
system, 7–8
systematics, 704
systemic ciculation, **920**, *920*
systemic circuit, **789**
systolic pressure, **923**

T

tadpole, 473, **773**–774, *774, 1023*
taiga, *463,* **465**
tail, 758
tamarin, *846*
tapeworm, 711
taproot, **649**
Tardigradia, 734
target, 859, 896
tarsier, 379, *379, 787*
taste, 882–883
TATA box, 250
taxis, **819**
taxol, 631
taxon, **518**
taxonomy, **518**
T cell, **946**, 951–952, *952,* 961–963, *962, 963,*
    964
technology, 485
Tejo Estuary, *472*
telomere, **139**, *139*
telophase, **140**, *141*
temperate climate, *459, 463,* 465
temperature, 460. *See also* body tempera-
    ture.
    and enzymes, 55
    global warming, *491,* **492**, *492,* 512–514
    greenhouse effect, **490**, *490*
    and hydrogen bonds, 41
temporal isolation, 346
temporal lobe, *887*
tendon, **1006**, *1017*

teosinte, *630*
tepal, 668
terminal, **879**
termite, 578, 836
tern, Arctic, 811
terrapin, 796
terrarium, 421
territoriality, **828**
Tertiary period, 366, 378
testcross, **185**
testes, *898, 899,* **1025**–1026, 1030
testicle, 1025
testoterone, **1025**, 1030
tetanus, *564*
tetraploidy, 170
tetrapod, 312, 526, *527,* **773**
thalamus, 888
thallose liverwort, 617, *617*
theory, 16–17
therapeutic cloning, 163
thermoreceptor, 881
thermoregulation, **863**
thermostat, 860
Thermotoga maritima, 535
theropod, 798–799
thiamine, *974*
thigmotropism, **682**
thorn bug, 10, *10*
threatened species, 503–504
three-chambered heart, 790, *790*
threshold, neuron, 879
thylakoid, 79, **104**–105, 110
thymine, 230–233, *231, 233,* 240
thymus, *898, 899,* 931
thyroid gland, *898, 899,* 901
thyroid hormone, 91, 1036
thyroxine, *851*
tick, 434, 740–742, *749*
tide pool, *468*
tiger, *827*
    Bengal, *809*
Tiktaalik roseae, 773
timber rattlesnake, *431,* 432
time, geologic, 365–367, *366,* 381, 385
Tinbergen, Niko, 823
tissue, 151, *152,* **854**
    animal, 701, *703*
    of integumentary system, 1014
    leaf, 652
    microscopic observation of, 949
    rejection, 954
    system, 641–642, *642*
titan arum plant, *663*
T-lymphocyte, 946, **946**, 952, *952,* 961–963,
    962, 963, 964
toad, 777
toadstool mushroom, *R27*
tobacco, 916
tobacco mosaic virus (TMV), *547*
tocopherol, *974*

Index

tolerance, **893**
Tollund Man, 359, *359*
tomato, *671*, 681, *681*
tongue worm, 738
tonsil, 931
tool use, 383, 838
tooth decay, *564*
tortoise, *263*, 796
    domed, 302, *303*
    saddle-back, 302, *303*
    skull of, 794, *794*
totipotent stem cell, 154, *154*
touch, 883
toxin, 563
toxoid vaccine, 956
trace fossil, 360
trachea, **741**, **911**, *911*
tracheid cell, 643, *643*
trait, **177**, 181, 183–187. *See also* phenotype.
transcription, 239–242, **240**, *241*, *242*, 248–251, 257
transcription factor, 250
transdifferentiation, 154
trans fat, 976
transfer RNA (tRNA), **240**, *245*, 245–247
transgenic organism, **26**, 257, **277–279**, 294
transitional fossil, 316
translation, **243**–247, *246*
translocation, 253
transmission electron microscope (TEM), 20, *21*
transpiration, 412, **644**, **645**
    online animation, 657
transplant, kidney, 990
transport
    active, **89**–90, *89*
    electron, **109**, *114*, 119–121, *120*, 127
transport protein, 87, 89–90
tree
    and acid rain, 489, *489*
    coniferous, 465
    deciduous, 465
    ecosystem, 419
    rings, 651, *651*
tree of life. *See* classification.
"trees-down" hypothesis, 799
tree sloth, *437*
Triassic period, 366, 377
tribolite, *310*, *366*, 731, *731*, 734
Trichomonas vaginalis, 1032, *1032*
trichomoniasis, 1032
triggerfish, *410*, 411
triglyceride, 46–47, *47*
trimester, **1036**, *1037*
triploblastic animal, 701
tRNA, **240**, *245*, 245–247
trochophore, 710
trophic level, **409**, 418–419
tropical climate, *459*, 463
tropical rain forest, 403, 455, *455*, 463, 464

tropism, **681**, 819
trout, 473
tryblidia, 713
Trypanosoma, 580
trypsin, *978*
tsetse fly, 580
tsunami, 444
tuatara, 796
tube foot, 718
tuber, 679
tuberculosis (TB), 563, *942*
tube worm, *696*
tulip, 679
tumor, 146
tundra, *463*, **466**
tunicate, 758, 760
turtle, *760*, 796
    sea, 796, *796*, 811, 822, *822*
    skull of, 794, *794*
tusk shell, 713
tympanic membrane, 882
type 1 diabetes, *864*, 864–865
type 2 diabetes, 864–865
Tyrannosaurus rex, 798, 805
Tyto alba, 519, *519*

U

ultraviolet (UV) radiation, 255, 256
umbilical cord, **1035**, *1035*, 1041
umbrella species, 503–504
ungulate, *318*
uniform dispersion, **437**, *437*
uniformitarianism, *300*, **301**, *301*
unsaturated fat, 973
uracil, 240
urea, 913
ureter, **986**
urethra, **986**, 1026, *1026*
Urey, Harold, 369
urinary bladder, **986**, 990
urine, 986, 988–990
urochordate, 758
uterus, **1024**–1025, 1036

V

vaccine, 294, **553**, 554, 564, 749, *941*, **956**, *956*
vacuole, **77**, *77*, 578
vagina, 1025, 1040
valve, **917**
vampire bat, 833
vancomycin, 391
variable, 49
    dependent, R10, R15
    independent, R10, R15
variation, **302**, 306, *307*
    in bird beaks, 321, 811
    genetic, 189–191, 254, 328–329, 337, 374
    and natural selection, 308–309
vascular cylinder, **648**

vascular system
    of plants, **614**, *615*, 620, 640–646
    water, 718
vascular tissue, **642**
vas deferens, **1026**
vector, **748**, *749*, **944**
vegan, 973
vegetative propagation, 679
vegetative reproduction, 150, **678–679**
vein, **913**
Velociraptor, 360, 798
velvet worm, 734, *734*
ventral surface, 701
ventricle, **917**
Venus flytrap, *35*, 54, 683, *683*
vertebra, 759, **1001**
vertebrate, **395**, **699**, 756–779
    amniotes, **778**–779, 786–809
    amphibians, 773–777, 781
    cell differentiation in, 153
    classification, 758–760, *761*
    eye of, 317
    fish, 763–771
    land, 778–779
    origins of, 760–762, 773
vesicle, **77**, *77*, 90–91
vessel, blood, 922–923, *923*
vessel element, 643, *643*
vestigial structure, **314**, *314*, 318
Victoria, Queen, 213
villi, *982*, 983
vinblastine, 633
vincristine, 633
violet, 679
violet-spotted reef lobster, 735, *735*
Virchow, Rudolf, 71, *71*
virion, 547
viroid, 544
Virtual Lab, 59, 127, 157, 193, 287, 385, 421, 567, 657, 685, 751, 841, 933
virus, *3*, 17, **544**–554, 606–608
    and disease, 942
    genetic material of, 548–549
    and infection, 544–546, 552–554, *554*
    shapes and sizes of, *545*, 548
    structure and reproduction, 547–551, 567
vision, 881
vitamin, **974**, *974*
vitamin D production, 862, *863*
viviparous reptile, 793
vocabulary. *See* word parts.
    academic, R20–R21
Volvocales, 581
Volvox, 581, *581*

W

Wadlow, Robert, 867
walking upright, 381
Wallace, Alfred Russel, 306

wasp
  amber-preserved, *360*
  braconid, 432, *433*
  digger, *729*
  paper, *729*
  parasitic, 332, *332*
  potter, *743*
waste elimination, *856*, *986*, 986–991
waste production, 486–487
  air pollution, 488–493
  water pollution, 494–496
water
  and algae, 613
  and cells, 22
  cohesion-tension theory, 643–645
  heating and cooling, 477
  and homeostasis, 972
  hydrologic cycle, **412**, *413*
  ice, 40
  molecules, *40*, 40–41, 51
  movement of, 460
  and nutrient absorption, 984, 988
  osmosis, 86–87
  plant absorption of, *644*, 649
  properties of, 40–43, 412
  and temperature change, 475
water bear, 734, *734*
water dragon, 793, *793*
water flea, 737, 750
water-holding frog, 461, *461*
water lily, 655
water mold, **588**
water quality, 494–496, 506, 507
watershed, **473**
water vascular system, **718**
Watson, James, 231–232, *232*, 235, 264
weather, 444
  online animation, 449
weaver ant, 834
Webquest, 29, 59, 93, 127, 157, 193, 219, 257,
  287, 321, 353, 385, 421, 449, 477, 507,
  537, 567, 601, 633, 657, 685, 723, 751,
  781, 811, 841, 867, 903, 933, 965, 993,
  1017, 1045
Weinberg, Wilhelm, 340
West Nile virus, *554*, 749, 944, 965
wetland ecosystem, 404, *404*, 473, 499
whale, 319
  Basilosaurus isis, 316
  beluga, 496
  blue, 696, *696*
  evolution of, *318*
  humpback, 99, *99*, *318*, *319*, 738, *738*

wheat, *627*
whiptail lizard, 698
whisk fern, 619
white blood cell, *55*, 553, 898, **928**, 931, *939*
  autoimmune diseases, 959, *959*
  and leukemia, 960
  and pathogens, 946, *946*, *950*, 950–951,
  951
white matter, 886
white oak, 519, *519*
white stork, 15
Whittaker, Robert, 533
whooping crane, 824, *824*
widowbird, 339
widow's peak, 212, *212*, 214, *215*
wildtype fly, 698, *698*
Wilkins, Maurice, 231
willow tree, 631
wind turbine, 485, *485*
wing, bird, 799, 802, 804
Woese, Carl, 532, 533–534
wolf, gray, 400, 406, 409, 443, *443*, 520, 521
wood, **627**
woodchuck, 831
wood lice, 738
woodpecker
  downy, 332, *332*
  green, 803, *803*
  ivory-billed, 5
word parts, R18, *R18–R19*
  Greek, R18–R19
  Latin, R18–R19
world population, *484*, 484–485
worm
  marine, 317, *317*
  methane, 27, *27*
  parasitic, 943, *943*, 944
  segmented, 528
  velvet, 734, *734*

X

X chromosome, 169, 201–203, 213, *213*
X chromosome inactivation, **203**
x-ray, 20
x-ray crystallography, 231
xylem, **642**, 643–645, *644*, *645*, *646*

Y

Y chromosome, 169, 201–203, 213, *213*, 219
yeast, 125, 135, 150, *150*, 281, 590–591, *591*,
  599
yellow fever, 748
Yellowstone ecosystem, 400, 407
yew, Pacific, 629
yogurt, 560
Yosemite National Park, *504*, 504–505
Yuma myotis bat, *805*

Z

zebra, *427*, 427–428
zebra flatworm, *710*
zinc, *973*
zooflagellate, *577*, 577–578
Zoomastigophora, 577
zoonose, 608
zooplankton, *410*, 444, **469**, 495, *495*, 735
zoospore, 584
Zuckerkandl, Emile, 530
Zygomycota, 590, 592
zygote, 852, **101**, 1034

Acknowledgments

PHOTOGRAPHY

Unit Openers 1 *Chapter 1 image* © Eye of Science/Photo Researchers, Inc.; *Chapter 2 image* © OSF/Photolibrary.com; *red blood cells, banner* © Royalty-Free/Corbis; *red blood cells, background* © William Fowle/Electron Microscopy *Center*, Northeastern University; *all others* © Getty Images; **67** *Chapter 3 image* © Dennis Kunkel/Phototake; *Chapter 4 image* © Andrew Syred/Photo Researchers, Inc.; *Chapter 5 image* © SPL/Photo Researchers, Inc.; *rabbit colon cell* © 2006 JupiterImages Corporation; *red blood cells, background* © Royalty-Free/Corbis; *onion cell* © Getty Images; *neuron* © Dr. Paquet-Durand/Nikon Small World; *amoeba* © www.micrographia.com; *red blood cells, banner* © William Fowle/Electron Microscopy *Center*, Northeastern University; **165** *Chapter 6 image* © David M. Phillips/Photo Researchers, Inc.; *Chapter 7 images, left to right* © Jupiter Images; © Getty Images; © Gazimal/Getty Images; © Kaz Mori/Getty Images; © Diana Koenigsberg/Getty Images; © Getty Images; © James Woodson/Getty Images; © Kaz Chiba/Getty Images; © Nancy Honey/Getty Images; © Blend Images/Alamy; © Hans Neleman/Getty Images; © Navaswan/Getty Images; *bottom* © CNRI/Photo Researchers, Inc.; *Chapter 8 image* © Eye of Science/Photo Researchers, Inc.; *Chapter 9 image* © Getty Images; *DNA sequence* © Royalty-Free/Corbis; *DNA GATTACA* Image used under license from Shutterstock, Inc.; *fruit fly* © Dwight Kuhn; **295** *Chapter 10 image* © Ken Catania; *Chapter 11 image* © Theo Allofs/Corbis; *Chapter 12 image* © Silkeborg Museum, Denmark; *fossil fish, archaeopteryx* Images used under license from Shutterstock, Inc.; *all others* © Getty; **393** *Chapter 13 image* © www.richardettlinger.com; *Chapter 14 image* © Anup and Manoj Shah; *Chapter 15 image* © Andrew Brown/Photo Researchers, Inc.; *Chapter 16 image* © Simon Fraser/Photo Researchers, Inc.; *all others* © Getty; **515** *Chapter 17 image* © Frans Lanting/Minden Pictures; *Chapter 18 image* © Steve Gschmeissner/Photo Researchers, Inc.; *Chapter 19 image* © Eye of Science/Photo Researchers, Inc.; *filaments, diatoms* © University of Wisconsin-Madison; *lichen* © Sue Baugh; *mushrooms* Image used under license from Shutterstock, Inc.; **609** *Chapter 20 image* © Martin Harvey/Corbis; *Chapter 21 image* Paul Chesley/National Geographic Image Collection; *Chapter 22 image* Image used under license from Shutterstock, Inc.; *all others* © Getty; **693** *Chapter 23 image* © Jez Tryner 2005/Image Quest Marine; *Chapter 24 image* © Dan Tenaglia Photography/missouriplants.com; *Chapter 25 image* © Gregory G. Dimijian/Photo Researchers, Inc.; *Chapter 26 image* © F. Stuart Westmorland/Photo Researchers, Inc.; *Chapter 27 image* © Cyril Ruoso/JH Editorial/Minden Pictures; *reptile skin* © Royalty-Free/Corbis; *wing, honeybee* © Getty; *all others* Images used under license from Shutterstock, Inc.; **849** *Chapter 28 image* © Ken Redding/Corbis; *Chapter 29 image* © ISM/Phototake; *Chapter 30 image* © Martin Dohrn/Royal College of Surgeons/Photo Researchers, Inc.; *Chapter 31 image* © Dr. Dennis Kunkel/Visuals Unlimited; *Chapter 32 image* © Dr. Michael Webb/Visuals Unlimited/Getty Images; *Chapter 33 image* © Gusto/Photo Researchers, Inc.; *Chapter 34 image* © Nestle/Petit Format/Photo Researchers, Inc.; *skull* © Artville; *red blood cells, banner* © Royalty-Free/Corbis; *red blood cells, background* © William Fowle/Electron Microscopy *Center*, Northeastern University; *brain, x-ray* Images used under license from Shutterstock, Inc.; *all others* © Getty.

Unit 1 **2–3** © Eye of Science/Photo Researchers, Inc.; **3** Provided by Michael G. Rossman and Richard J. Kuhn of the Department of Biological Sciences, Purdue University; **4** *left* © Mitsuhiko Imamori/Minden Pictures; *bottom* © Leo Meier/Australian Picture Library/Corbis; **5** *bottom* © R.B. Taylor/Photo Researchers, Inc.; *top* © Getty Images; **6** © David Fleetham/Bluegreen; **7** © Doug Perrine/naturepl.com; **8** *left* © Dr. David Phillips/Visuals Unlimited; *right* © Steve Gschmeissner/Photo Researchers, Inc.; **9** *bottom* © Fritz Polking/Peter Arnold, Inc.; *center right* © Andrew Syred/Photo Researchers, Inc.; **10** *left* © Martin Gabriel/naturepl.com; *right* © Bill Beatty/Visuals Unlimited; **12** *top* © Doug Perrine/naturepl.com; *bottom* © Laurent Geslin/naturepl.com; **13** Michael Nichols/National Geographic Image Collection; **14** © Colin Cuthbert/Photo Researchers, Inc.; **17** *top inset* © Dr. E. Walker/Photo Researchers, Inc.; *top* © Veronika Burmeister/Visuals Unlimited; **19** Photograph by Sharon Hoogstraten; **20** *left* © SPL/Photo Researchers, Inc.; *right* © Susan Leavines/Photo Researchers, Inc.; **21** *top left* © ISM/Phototake; *bottom left, right* © Dr. Jeremy Burgess/Photo Researchers, Inc.; *background* © Aflo/naturepl.com; **22** *top right* Photograph by Sharon Hoogstraten; *left, bottom left* © James King-Holmes/Photo Researchers, Inc.; **23** *top* © David Parker/Photo Researchers, Inc.; *right* © Kevin Curtis/Photo Researchers, Inc.; **25** *bottom* © Frans Lanting/Minden Pictures; *top* Courtesy of Brookhaven National Laboratory; **26** *top* © Pascal Goetgheluck/Photo Researchers, Inc.; *center left* © Pascal Goetgheluck/Photo Researchers, Inc.; **27** Charles Fisher, The Pennsylvania State University; **29** © Robert Zingg/Zoo Zurich; **30** *left* © Martin Gabriel/naturepl.com; *right* © Bill Beatty/Visuals Unlimited; **32** © Martin Harvey/Foto Natura/Minden Pictures; **34–35** © OSF/Photolibrary.com; **35** James Mauseth, University of Texas; **41** *top right* © Robert Calentine/Visuals Unlimited; *bottom right* © Sinclair Stammers/Photo Researchers, Inc.; **42** *center left* © Roger Eritja/Alamy; **45** *bottom right* © Mike Powell/Getty Images; **46** © ISM/Phototake; **48** *top left* © Eye of Science/Photo Researchers, Inc.; **49** *top right* © Tom and Dee Ann McCarthy/Corbis; **50** *bottom left* © AFP/Getty Images; **51** *bottom right* © Rapho Agence de Presse/Phototake; *top* Photograph by Sharon Hoogstraten; **53** *right* © Peter Batson/ExploreTheAbyss.com; **55** *center right* © Biology Media/Photo Researchers, Inc.; *bottom right* © Dr. Gopal Murti/Photo Researchers, Inc.; **57–59** Photographs by Sharon Hoogstraten; **64, 65** AP/Wide World Photos; **66** © Ron Ceasar.

Unit 2 **68–69** © Eye of Science/Photo Researchers, Inc.; **69** © Eye of Science/Photo Researchers, Inc.; **70** © Science Museum London/HIP/The Image Works; **71** *center right* © HIP/Art Resource, New York; *top* Library of Congress, Prints and Photographs Division, #LC-USZ62-95187; *second from left* The Granger Collection, New York; *second from right* The Granger Collection, New York; *bottom left* The Granger Collection, New York; *center* The Granger Collection, New York; *bottom right* The Granger Collection, New York; **72** *top left* © Dr. Gopal Murti/Visuals Unlimited; *center left* © Dr. Kari Lounatmaa/Photo Researchers, Inc.; **73** *bottom left* © Albert Tousson/Phototake; **75** *bottom right* © Dr. Elena Kiseleva/Photo Researchers, Inc.; **76** *top left* © Dennis Kunkel/Phototake; *bottom left* © Dennis Kunkel/Phototake; **77** *center* © Bill Longcore/Photo Researchers, Inc.; *top* © Don W. Fawcett/Photo Researchers, Inc.; *bottom right* © ISM/Phototake; **78** *top left* © CNRI/Photo Researchers, Inc.; *bottom* © Don W. Fawcett/Photo Researchers, Inc.; **79** *top* © ISM/Phototake; *center right* © George Chapman/Visuals Unlimited; **80** *top* © Herman Eisenbeiss/Photo Researchers, Inc.; *bottom* © Herman Eisenbeiss/Photo Researchers, Inc.; **83** Photograph by Sharon Hoogstraten; **86** *bottom left* © David M. Phillips/Photo Researchers, Inc.; *bottom center* © David M. Phillips/Photo Researchers, Inc.; *bottom right* © David M. Phillips/Photo Researchers, Inc.; *top left* Photograph by Sharon Hoogstraten; **88** Photograph by Sharon Hoogstraten; **90** DoD/US Air Force; **92** Photograph by Sharon Hoogstraten; **93** *bottom right* © P. Motta & T. Naguro/Photo Researchers, Inc.; **98–99** © Andrew Syred/Photo Researchers, Inc.; **99** © Francois Gohier/Photo Researchers, Inc.; **100** *bottom left* © Dr. Martha Powell/Visuals Unlimited; **102** *top left* © 2006 JupiterImages Corporation; **103** *center left* © ISM/Phototake; *bottom left* © Royalty-Free/Corbis; **106** Photographs by Sharon Hoogstraten; **108** *bottom left* Photo by Stefano Paltera/North American Solar Challenge; **110** *both* © Medical Research Council, UK; **113** © Dr. Gopal Murti/Visuals Unlimited; **116** *top* © Tommaso Guicciardini/Photo Researchers, Inc.; *right* © Tommaso Guicciardini/Photo Researchers, Inc.; **118** © Yellow Dog Productions/Getty Images; **121** AP/Wide World Photos; **122** AP/Wide World Photos; **125** © Rob Fiocca/FoodPix/JupiterImages; **126** Photograph by Sharon Hoogstraten; **132–133** © SPL/Photo Researchers, Inc.; **133** *right* © Ralph Hutchings/Visuals Unlimited; *left* © Science Source/Photo Researchers, Inc.; **136** *top left* © Jose Luis Pelaez, Inc./Corbis; **138** *bottom right* © Science VU/Visuals Unlimited; **141** *all* © Michael W. Davidson at Florida State University; **143** *bottom left* © Robert Calentine/Visuals Unlimited; **145** *center right* © Ralph Hutchings/Visuals Unlimited; *bottom right* © Royalty-Free/Corbis; **146** © CNRI/Photo Researchers, Inc.; **149** *top* © Dr. Gopal Murti/Photo Researchers, Inc.; **150** *both* © Dr. Stanley Flegler/Visuals Unlimited; **152** *top left* © 2004 Dennis Kunkel Microscopy, Inc.; *second from left* © Dr. Richard Kessel & Dr. Gene Shih/Visuals Unlimited; *third from left* © Ken Davies/Masterfile; **153** *left* © Andrew Syred/Photo Researchers, Inc.; *center* © Susumu Nishinaga/Photo Researchers, Inc.; *right* © David Scharf/Photo Researchers, Inc.; **157** *bottom left* © Dr. Gopal Murti/Visuals Unlimited; *animated bio, left* © Michael Abbey/Photo Researchers, Inc.; *animated bio, second from left* © Carolina Biological Supply Company/Phototake; *animated bio, third from left* © Carolina Biological Supply Company/Phototake; *animated bio, third from right* © Carolina Biological/Phototake; *animated bio, second from right* © Carolina Biological/Phototake; *animated bio, right* © Carolina Biological Supply Company/Phototake; **160** © Biodisc/Visuals Unlimited; **162** © Professor Miodrag Stojkovic/Photo Researchers, Inc.; **164** *top right* © Chris Stewart/San Francisco Chronicle/Corbis; *bottom left* © 2006 Seth Affoumado.

Unit 3 **166–167** © David M. Phillips/Photo Researchers, Inc.; **167** © K.H. Kjeldsen/Photo Researchers, Inc.; **169** *top* © CNRI/Photo Researchers, Inc.; **172** © CNRI/Photo Researchers, Inc.; **174** © Adrian T. Sumner/Photo Researchers, Inc.; **177** © Bettmann/Corbis; **178** *all purple flowers* © David Hosking/Alamy; *snow pea flowers* © George D. Lepp/Corbis; **181** © CNRI/Photo Researchers, Inc.; **182** © Gilbert S. Grant/Photo Researchers, Inc.; **183** © John Innes Archives courtesy of the John Innes Foundation; **184** *all purple flowers* © David Hosking/Alamy; *snow pea flower* © George D. Lepp/Corbis; **185** *top left* © David Hosking/Alamy; *top right* © George D. Lepp/Corbis; **187** *all* Photograph by Sharon Hoogstraten; **188** © Phototake Inc./Alamy; **189** © Chuck Savage/Corbis; **190** © Martin Harvey/Peter Arnold, Inc.; **192, 193** Photograph by Sharon Hoogstraten; **198** *top* © 2006 JupiterImages Corporation; *center* © Diana Koenigsberg/Getty Images; *bottom* © Gazimal/Getty Images; **199** *first row, left* © Getty Images; *first row, center* © Blend Images/Alamy; *third row, right* © Navaswan/Getty Images; *second row, left* © Getty Images; *second row, right* © Kaz Chiba/Getty Images; *second row, center* © James Woodson/Getty Images; *first row, right* © Kaz Mori/Getty Images; *third row, center* © Hans Neleman/Getty Images; *third row, left* © Nancy Honey/Getty Images; *bottom* © CNRI/Photo Researchers, Inc.; **200** © Dimitri Vervits/Getty Images; **202** Photograph by Sharon Hoogstraten; **203** © John Daniels/Ardea London Limited; **205** *top right* Photo by Atison Phumchoosri; *top left* Photo by Atison Phumchoosri; *top center* Photo by Atison Phumchoosri; **206** *second row, left* © BSIP, Chassenet/Photo Researchers, Inc.; *second row, right* © Martin Dohrn/Photo Researchers, Inc.; *first row, left* © Matthew Wiley/Masterfile; *first row, center* © David Greenwood/Getty Images; *first row, right* © Steve Dunwell/Getty Images; *second row, center* © Jon Feingersh/zefa/Corbis; **207** © Jose Fuste Raga/zefa/Corbis; **208** © Eye of Science/Photo Researchers, Inc.; **209** *both* © Dwight Kuhn; **211** © Dennis Kunkel Microscopy, Inc.; **212** Photograph by Sharon Hoogstraten; **213** © Biophoto Associates/Photo Researchers, Inc.; **216** *both* © Reuters/Corbis; **217** *right* © Leonard Lessin/Peter Arnold, Inc.; *top* Courtesy of Professor Christine Harrison/University of Southampton, UK; *center* © CNRI/Photo Researchers, Inc.; **219** *bottom right* © Biophoto Associates/Photo Researchers, Inc.; **220** *left* © John Daniels/Ardea London Limited; *right, both* © Dwight Kuhn; **224–225** © Eye of Science/Photo Researchers, Inc.; **225** © Kenneth Eward/BioGrafx/Photo Researchers, Inc.; **227** © Bettmann/Corbis; **228** © Biozentrum, University of Basel/Photo Researchers, Inc.; **229** *all* Photograph by Sharon Hoogstraten; **231** © Jewish Chronicle Ltd/HIP/The Image Works; **232** *top left* © A. Barrington Brown/Photo Researchers, Inc.; *top right* © SPL/Photo Researchers, Inc.; **234** © Ted Spiegel/Corbis; **237** © Dr. Gopal Murti/Visuals Unlimited; **242** © O. L. Miller, B. R. Beatty, D. W. Fawcett/Visuals Unlimited; **250** © "Steve Paddock, Jim Langeland & Sean Carroll"/Visuals Unlimited; **252** © Janie Airey/Getty Images; **254** *both* © SPL/Photo Researchers, Inc.; **255** © Time Life Pictures/Getty Images; **256** Photograph by Sharon Hoogstraten; **257** *bottom right* © U. S. Grains Council; **262–263** © Getty Images; **263** © 2005 Peter Menzel/Menzelphoto.com; **265** © Torunn Berge/Photo Researchers, Inc.; **267** © Eurelios/Phototake; **268** Photograph by Sharon Hoogstraten; **269** © MarkRobertHalper.com; **272** © David Parker/Photo Researchers, Inc.; **274** © Tek Image/Photo Researchers, Inc.; **275** AP/Wide World Photos; **276** © Professor Stanley Cohen/Photo Researchers, Inc.; **277** © Dr. Gopal Murti/Photo Researchers, Inc.; **278** From The Beast That Ate the Earth. © Chris Madden; **279** © **1995** Amgen, Inc.; **281** © Alfred Pasieka/Photo Researchers, Inc.; **283** Arnold Greenwell/Environmental Health Perspectives; **284** © National Centre for Medical Genetics, Dublin, Ireland; **285** © John Scott Glass; **286** Photograph by Sharon Hoogstraten; **292** © Bernardo Bucci/Corbis; **293** © Sam Ogden/Photo Researchers, Inc.; **294** *left* © Dan Dry/University of Chicago; *right* © Jim Richardson/Corbis.

Unit 4 **296–297, 297** © Ken Catania; **299** *bottom left* Plant Sexual System, Carl Linnaeus. Natural History Museum, London. © The Bridgeman Art Library; *second from right* Portrait of Dr. Erasmus Darwin, Joseph Wright of Derby. Oil on canvas. 76.2 cm x 63.5 cm. Private collection. © The Bridgeman Art Library; *second from left* Histoire Naturelle des Oiseaux - Le Courly Rouge, Georges de Buffon. Christie's Images. © The Bridgeman Art Library; *third from left* Skunk, from Histoire Naturelle, Georges Louis Leclerc Buffon. Colored engraving. Bibliotheque Nationale, Paris. © Lauros/Giraudon/The Bridgeman Art Library; *bottom right* © The Granger Collection, New York; **300** *bottom right* © Richard Hamilton Smith/Corbis; *bottom left* © Jim Sugar/Corbis; *bottom center* © David Muench/Corbis; **301** © Richard Hamilton Smith/Corbis; **302** *bottom left* © The Granger Collection, New York; **303** *top left* © Stephen Frink/Corbis; *top right* © Mark Jones/Roving Tortoise Photography; **305** *bottom left* © Lynda Richardson/Corbis; *second from right* © Australian National Pigeon Association; *second from left* © Australian National Pigeon Association; *bottom right* © Australian National Pigeon Association; **309** *bottom right* © Keren Su/Corbis; *top right* AP/Wide World Photos; **310** *bottom* AP/Wide World Photos; *top left* AP/Wide World Photos; **311** *bottom left* © Brandon Cole/Visuals Unlimited; *bottom right* © Wim van Egmond/Visuals Unlimited; **312** *center right* © Science Photo Library/Photo Researchers, Inc.; *center* © Dietmar Nill/naturepl.com; **313** *bottom right* © Gusto/Photo Researchers, Inc.; *bottom left* © Dietmar Nill/naturepl.com; **314** *top left* © Tony Heald/naturepl.com; **315** *top right* © Joe McDonald/Corbis; **316** *bottom left* © Philip D. Gingerich/University of Michigan; **317** *right* © Douglas P. Wilson/Frank Lane Picture Agency/Corbis; **318** *bottom left* From The Life History and Ecology of the Gray Whale (Eschrichtius robustus) by Dale W. Rice and Allen A. Wolman. © 1971 by The American Society of Mammologists; *top right* © Will Darnell/Animals Animals–Earth Scenes; **319** *top right* © Paul A. Souders/Corbis; **320** Photograph by Sharon Hoogstraten; **321** *bottom right* © James L. Amos/Corbis; **322** *left* © Stephen Frink/Corbis; *second from left* © Mark Jones/Roving Tortoise Photography; *center, second from right* © Science Photo Library/Photo Researchers, Inc.; *right* © Dietmar Nill/naturepl.com; *bottom right* © Will Darnell/Animals Animals–Earth Scenes; **326–327** © Theo Allofs/Corbis; **327** © Laura Riley/Bruce Coleman, Inc.; **331** © Mark Thomas/Photo Researchers, Inc.; **332** *bottom right* © Gary W. Carter/Corbis; *center* © M.F. Claridge; *top left* photo by W. Abrahamson; *top left, inset* © Peter Harris, Agriculture and Agri-Food Canada/www.forestryimages.org; **333** *center right* © C. Allan Morgan/Peter Arnold, Inc.; **334** © Patti Murray/Animals Animals–Earth Scenes; **335** *left* © Randy Wells/Corbis; **337** *bottom right* Photograph by Sharon Hoogstraten; **338** © Pete Oxford/naturepl.com; **339** © Peter Blackwell/naturepl.com; **345** *top left* © Royalty-Free/Corbis; *top center* © Royalty-Free/Corbis; *flies* © Oliver Meckes/Nicole Ottawa/Photo Researchers, Inc.; **346** © Fred Bavendam/Minden Pictures; **348** *second from right* © Kolar, Richard/Animals Animals–Earth Scenes; *right* © Bennett, Darren/Animals Animals–Earth Scenes; *second from bottom left* © Alexis Rosenfeld/Photo Researchers, Inc.; *bottom left* © Jeffrey L. Rotman/Corbis; **349** *top right* © Phil Savoie/Nature Picture Library; **350** *top left* © John Cancalosi/Nature Picture Library; **353** *bottom right* © NaturePics/Alamy Images; **358–359** © Silkeborg Museum, Denmark; **359** Waptia fieldensis. Photo © Chip Clark/National Museum of Natural History/Smithsonian Institution; **360** *left* © Louie Psihoyos/Corbis; *second from left* © Jim Jurica,

2006. Used under license from Shutterstock, Inc.; *center* © Lester V. Bergman/Corbis; *second from right* © Barry Runk/STAN/Heilmanphoto; *right* © Corbis; **364** *top right* © James King-Holmes/Photo Researchers, Inc.; **365** *center left* © Ron Sturm; **366** *top* © Nick Garbutt/Nature Picture Library; *second from top* © Louie Psihoyos/Corbis; *third from top* © James L. Amos/Corbis; *second from bottom* © OSF/Paling, J./Animals Animals–Earth Scenes; *bottom* © James L. Amos/Corbis; *bottom left* © S. Stammers/Photo Researchers, Inc.; **368** *bottom left* © David A. Hardy/Photo Researchers, Inc.; **370** *bottom left* © David McCarthy/Photo Researchers, Inc.; *center right* Emory Kristof/National Geographic Image Collection; **372** *bottom left* © Mitsuaki Iwago/Minden Pictures; **373** Courtesy of David H. Walker, M.D. an Vsevolod L. Popov, Ph.D.; **375** *top right* © Photo Researchers, Inc.; **377** *center right* © Murray Alcosser; **378** *center* Hyracotherium vasacciensis. Photo © Chip Clark/National Museum of Natural History/Smithsonian Institution; **379** *right* © Michael & Patricia Fogden/Corbis; **380** *left* © Pete Oxford/Nature Picture Library; *third from left* © David A. Northcott/Corbis; *second from left* © Pete Oxford/Nature Picture Library; *fourth from left* © Sohns, Juergen and Christine/Animals Animals-Earth Scenes; *fourth from right* © Kenneth W. Fink/Ardea London Ltd.; *right* © Wegner, Jorg and Petra/Animals Animals-Earth Scenes; *second from right* © Anup Shah/Nature Picture Library; *third from right* © PictureQuest; **381** © Brand X Pictures/Alamy Images; **382** *bottom* © MPFT; *top* © MPFT; **384** *top right* © Tom Bean/Corbis; **385** *top* Illustration by Six Red Marbles; **390** *top* © Francisco Leong/AFP/Getty Images; *bottom* © Hannah Gleghorn, 2006. Used under license from Shutterstock, Inc.; **391** © Hank Morgan/Photo Researchers, Inc.; **392** *left* Photo courtesy of Bruce Fox, MSU; *right* © Gary Gaugler/The Medical File/Peter Arnold, Inc.

Unit 5 **394–395** © www.richardettlinger.com; **395** *bottom right* © Jeff Gynane/Alamy; **396** *bottom left* © Hal Beral/Corbis; **398** *top left* © Gary Will/Visuals Unlimited; **399** Photograph by Sharon Hoogstraten; **400** © Reuters/Corbis; **401** *top right* © Paul Glendell/Peter Arnold, Inc.; **402** *bottom left* © Louise Murray/Getty Images; **405** Photograph by Sharon Hoogstraten; **406** *center left* gene@seawifs.gstc.nasa.gov; **407** *right* © Dennis Frates/Alamy Images; **408** *bottom left* © Frank Oberle; *center* © D. Robert & Lorri Franz/Corbis; *right* © Tom Brakefield/Corbis; **409** *top right* © Arthur Morris/Corbis; **426–427** © Anup and Manoj Shah; **427** *bottom right* © Jeremy Woodhouse/Masterfile; **428** *bottom left* © Paul A. Souders/Corbis; **429** *bottom* © WizData, Inc./Alamy; **430** *top left* © David A. Northcott/Corbis; *top right* © Michael & Patricia Fogden/Corbis; **431** *bottom left* © Bianca Lavies/National Geographic Image Collection; **433** *bottom* © Merlin D. Tuttle/Bat Conservation International; *center* © Steve Gschmeissner/Photo Researchers, Inc.; *bottom* © Scott Camazine/Alamy; **434** *top left* © Martin Dohrn/Photo Researchers, Inc.; *top right* © David Scharf/Peter Arnold, Inc.; **435** *top right* © Lynn M. Stone/Nature Picture Library; **437** *left* © Franklin Viola/Animals Animals; *center* © Wolfgang Kaehler/Corbis; *right* © Buddy Mays/Corbis; **441** *bottom right* © M. W. Mules/CSIRO; **443** *center right* © Rolf O. Peterson; **444** AP Photo by Michael Spooneybarger, Tampa Tribune; **445** *bottom left* © 2006 Frans Lanting/www.lanting.com; *bottom right* © **2006** Frans Lanting/www.lanting.com; **446** *top right* © Getty Images; **447** *top right* © Raymond Gehman/National Geographic Image Collection; **448** Photograph by Sharon Hoogstraten; **449** *bottom right* © Jacques Descloitres, MODIS Rapid Response Team, NASA/GSFC; **450** © M. W. Mules/CSIRO; **454–455** © Andrew Brown/Photo Researchers, Inc.; **455** © Frank Krahmer/zefa/Corbis; **457** © Corbis; **458** © Frank Zullo/Photo Researchers, Inc.; **459** NASA; **460** *top* © Andrew Brown; Ecoscene/Corbis; *bottom* © Dennis Flaherty/Photo Researchers, Inc.; **461** © Jason Edwards/Getty Images; **463** *first from top left* © Corbis; *fifth from top left* © Ed Reschke/Peter Arnold, Inc.; *seventh from top left* © John Cancalosi/Peter Arnold, Inc.; *ninth from top left* © Getty Images; *eleventh from top left* © Comstock; *thirteenth from top left* © Getty Images; *fifteenth from top left* © Getty Images; *second from top left* © Michael Fogden/Animals Animals; *fourth from top left* © Frank Krahmer/zefa/Corbis; *eighth from top left* © Andrew Brown; Ecoscene/Corbis; *sixth from top left* © Layne Kennedy/Corbis; *fourteenth from top left* © Getty Images; *sixteenth from top left* © Wolfgang Kaehler/Corbis; *third from top left* © Corbis; *twelfth from top left* © Getty Images; *tenth from top left* © Brand X Pictures; **466** © Andrew Brown; Ecoscene/Corbis; **467** © Norbert Rosing/National Geographic Image Collection; **468** © Don Geyer/Alamy Images; **470** *top left* © Wolf Hilbertz/Global Coral Reef Alliance; **471** © Morro Bay National Estuary Program; **472** *center left* © John R. MacGregor/Peter Arnold, Inc.; *top* © Paulo Magalhaes/Getty Images; **473** *top* © David Muench/Corbis; *bottom* © Royalty-Free/Corbis; **474** © NHPA/David Woodfall; **475** © Anthony Edgeworth/Corbis; **476** Photograph by Sharon Hoogstraten; **477** *bottom* © Susan Berg/SJB Photography; **478** *bottom left* NASA; **482–483** © Simon Fraser/Photo Researchers, Inc.; **483** © Alfred Pasieka/Photo Researchers, Inc.; **485** © Alan Sirulnikoff/Photo Researchers, Inc.; **486** © Bill Bachmann/Alamy Images; **488** © Nik Wheeler/Corbis; **489** © Adam Hart-Davis/Photo Researchers, Inc.; **491** © G. Baden/zefa/Corbis; *bottom left* © Dennis MacDonald/Alamy Images; **492** NASA © 2005 NRDC; **493** Photograph by Sharon Hoogstraten; **494** © Chris Howes/Wild Places Photography/Alamy Images; **496** © age fotostock/SuperStock; **497** © Michael & Patricia Fogden/Corbis; **498** AP Photo/Courtesy Wild Life Heritage Trust, HO; **499** © Joel Sartore; **500** *bottom* © John Mitchell/Photo Researchers, Inc.; *top* © CSIRO; **501** © Cameron Marlow; **502** © China Tourism Press/Getty Images; **503** © Brandon D. Cole/Corbis; **504** © Susan Berg/SJB Photography; **505** © Raymond Gehman/Corbis; **507** *bottom* © Wil Meinderts/Foto Natura/Minden Pictures; **508** *top right* AP Photo/Courtesy Wild Life Heritage Trust, HO; *bottom right* © Raymond Gehman/Corbis; **512** *top right* © Thomas Nilsen/Science Photo Library/Photo Researchers, Inc.; *bottom left* © Tom Van Sant/Photo Researchers, Inc.; **513** AP/Wide World Photos/ Katsumi Kasahara; **514** *top left* © Peter Essick/Aurora/Getty Images; *top right* Photo by Tom Kleindinst/Woods Hole Oceanographic Institution.

Unit 6 **516–517** © Frans Lanting/Minden Pictures; **517** © Jen & Des Bartlett/Oxford Scientific/Jupiter Images; **519** *top right* © Digital Vision/Robert Harding; *bottom right* © Larry Michael/naturepl.com; **521** *top right* © Sohns, Juergen and Christine/Animals Animals–Earth Scenes; **523** *all* Photograph by Sharon Hoogstraten; **524** *bottom left* © The Natural History Museum; *bottom right* © Pontier, John/Animals Animals–Earth Scenes; **529** © Gary Meszaros/Photo Researchers, Inc.; **531** © Michael Durham/Minden Pictures; **534** © Eye of Science/Photo Researchers, Inc.; **536** Photograph by Sharon Hoogstraten; **537** *bottom left* © Bill Dow/Shambala Preserve; *bottom right* © Fred Bavendam/Minden Pictures; **538** *bottom left* © The Natural History Museum; *bottom center* © Pontier, John/Animals Animals–Earth Scenes; **542–543** © Steve Gschmeissner/Photo Researchers, Inc.; **543** © Andrew Syred/Photo Researchers, Inc.; **544** © Dr. Linda Stannard, UCT/Photo Researchers, Inc.; **547** *top* © Duncan Smith/Photo Researchers, Inc.; *bottom* © Norm Thomas/Photo Researchers, Inc.; **548** *center left* © Nibsc/Photo Researchers, Inc.; *center* © Em Unit, CVL Weybridge/Photo Researchers, Inc.; *center right* © Alfred Pasieka/Photo Researchers, Inc.; **549** *top* © Eye of Science/Photo Researchers, Inc.; *top, inset* © Eye of Science/Photo Researchers, Inc.; **552** © Dr. Steve Patterson/Photo Researchers, Inc.; **553** *center* © Reuters/Corbis; **553** *bottom right* © Nibsc/Photo Researchers, Inc.; **555** © Stephen Ausmus/Agricultural Research Service/USDA; **556** *bottom left* © SciMAT/Photo Researchers, Inc.; *bottom center* © SciMAT/Photo Researchers, Inc.; *bottom right* © Eye of Science/Photo Researchers, Inc.; **557** *bottom left* © Dr. Gladden Willis/Visuals Unlimited; *bottom right* © Dr. Gladden Willis/Visuals Unlimited; **558** *center right* © Dr. L. Caro/Photo Researchers, Inc.; **559** *right* © Dr. Gary Gaugler/Photo Researchers, Inc.; **561** *top right* © Dr. Jeremy Burgess/Photo Researchers, Inc.; *center* © Dr. Jeremy Burgess/Photo Researchers, Inc.; **562** Photograph by Sharon Hoogstraten; **563** © Dr. Gary Gaugler/Photo Researchers, Inc.; **564** *bottom left* © Dr. Ken Greer/Visuals Unlimited; **568** *center* © Eye of Science/Photo Researchers, Inc.; **572–573** © Eye of Science/Photo Researchers, Inc.; **573** *all three bottom* © Biophoto Associates/Photo Researchers, Inc.; **574** © Rob & Ann Simpson/Visuals Unlimited; **575** *top right* © Dr. Gopal Murti/Visuals Unlimited; *center right* © SPL/Photo Researchers, Inc.; **577** © SPL/Photo Researchers, Inc.; **578** *all four top left* © Michael Abbey/Visuals Unlimited; *bottom right* © Astrid & Hanns-Frieder Michler/Photo Researchers, Inc.; **579** © Eric Grave/Photo Researchers, Inc.; **581** © Roland Birke/Peter Arnold, Inc.; **582** © Andrew Syred/Photo Researchers, Inc.; **583** *top inset* © Dr. David M. Phillips/Visuals Unlimited; *top right* © Bill Bachman/Photo Researchers, Inc.; *bottom left* © Andrew Syred/Photo Researchers, Inc.; *bottom center, bottom right* © Susumu Nishinaga/Photo Researchers, Inc.; **584** *bottom* © Andrew Syred/Photo Researchers, Inc.; *top* © Gary Bell/oceanwideimages.com; **587** *left* © Eye of Science/Photo Researchers, Inc.; *right* © Dr. Richard Kessel & Dr. Gene Shih/Visuals Unlimited; **588** *inset* © Andrew Syred/Photo Researchers, Inc.; *top left* © Scott Bauer/USDA/Agricultural Research Service; **590** *top* © Royalty-Free/Corbis; *bottom* © Vaughan Fleming/Photo Researchers, Inc.; **591** *top* © Bill Keogh/Visuals Unlimited; *bottom* © J. Forsdyke/Gene Cox/Photo Researchers, Inc.; **592** *top* © Orla, 2006. Used under license from Shutterstock, Inc.; *center* © Mauritius, GMBH/Phototake; *bottom* © Vaughan Fleming/Photo Researchers, Inc.; **593** *top left* © Orla, 2006. Used under license from Shutterstock, Inc.; *center* © Mauritius, GMBH/Phototake; **594** *top left* © Ray Coleman/Photo Researchers, Inc.; *inset* © Dr. John D. Cunningham/Visuals Unlimited; **596** © Merryl Brackstone, **2006**. Used under license from Shutterstock, Inc.; **597** *center* © Roger Tidman/Corbis; *center right* © E.R. Degginger/Animals Animals–Earth Scenes; **598** © Pat O'Hara/Corbis; **599** © Michael & Patricia Fogden/Corbis; **601** *bottom right* © Eye of Science/Photo Researchers, Inc.; **602** *right* © Orla, 2006. Used under license from Shutterstock, Inc.; **606** *top right* © age fotostock/SuperStock; *center right* © Pasieka/Photo Researchers, Inc.; **607** *top left* © The Art Archive/Culver Pictures; *top right* © By Ian Miles–Flashpoint Pictures/Alamy; *bottom right* Courtesy of Drs. Takeshi Noda and Yoshihiro Kawaoka; **608** *top left* Photo of Dr. Ben Muneta courtesy of Jana Muneta; *top right* © Ali Imam/Reuters/Corbis.

Unit 7 **610–611** © Martin Harvey/Corbis; **611** © Nigel J. Dennis; Gallo Images/Corbis; **612** © Ken Wagner/Phototake; **613** *top left* © Ken Wagner/Phototake; *second from top left* © Stuart Westmorland/Corbis; *top center* © Gusto/SPL/Photo Researchers, Inc.; *second from top right* © Stephen P. Parker/Photo Researchers, Inc.; *top right* © Lynn Watson, 2006. Used under license from Shutterstock, Inc.; **615** *top left* © Magdalena Bujak, 2006. Used under license from Shutterstock, Inc.; *top right* © Brad Mogen/Visuals Unlimited; **616** *top left* © Colin Keates/Dorling Kindersley, Courtesy of the Natural History Museum, London; *left* © Paul Harcourt Davies/Photo Researchers, Inc.; **617** *bottom right* © Harold Taylor/PictureQuest; **618** *top right* Olympic National Park Site/National Park Service, U.S. Dept.of the Interior; *bottom* © Stuart Westmorland/Corbis; **619** *top right* © Philip Gould/Corbis; *bottom right* © Gusto/SPL/Photo Researchers, Inc.; *bottom* © Steve Kaufman/Corbis; **620** © Martha Cooper/Peter Arnold, Inc.; **621** *center* © Chris Jones/PictureQuest; *bottom left* © Science Pictures Limited/Photo Researchers, Inc.; *bottom right* © Joseph Malcolm Smith/Photo Researchers, Inc.; **622** *inset* © Stephen P. Parker/Photo Researchers, Inc.; *top left* © Andrew Brown; Ecoscene/Corbis; **623** Photograph by Sharon Hoogstraten; **624** © Royalty-Free/Corbis; **625** *top left* © Michael and Patricia Fogden/Corbis; *top right* © Michael Quinton/Minden Pictures; **627** *left* © Lynn Watson, **2006**. Used under license from Shutterstock, Inc.; *second from top left* © Yare Marketing, 2006. Used under license from Shutterstock, Inc.; *top second from right* © BananaStock/PictureQuest; *top right* © Matt, 2006. Used under license from Shutterstock, Inc.; *bottom center* © Tom Bean/Corbis; **628** © Royalty-Free/Corbis; **629** © Charles O'Rear/Corbis; **630** *top left* © Science VU/Visuals Unlimited; *center left* © Helmut Partsch/Photo Researchers, Inc.; *bottom* © Hanan Isachar/Corbis; **631** © Bojan Brecelj/Corbis; **633** *bottom left* © Chris Hellier/Corbis; *bottom right* © Gunter Marx Photography/Corbis; **634** *top left* © Ken Wagner/Phototake; *top right* © BananaStock/PictureQuest; *bottom right* © Hanan Isachar/Corbis; **638–639** © Paul Chesley/National Geographic Image Collection; **639** © Walter H. Hodge/Peter Arnold, Inc.; **641** *top left* © Lester V. Bergman/Corbis; *top center* © B. Runk/S. Schoenberger/Grant Heilman Photography; *top right* © Dr. Dennis Drenner/Visuals Unlimited; **643** © Dr. Richard Kessel & Dr. Gene Shih/Visuals Unlimited; **646** *left* © Olga Shelego, 2006. Used under license from Shutterstock, Inc.; *top* © Laurin Rinder, **2006**. Used under license from Shutterstock, Inc.; **648** *left* © M.I. Walker/Photo Researchers, Inc.; *right* © Andrew Syred/Photo Researchers, Inc.; **649** *top right* © Scott Sinklier/Alamy Images; *center right* © David Wasserman/Alamy Images; **650** *top left* © Nick Garbutt/naturepl.com; *top center* © B.S.P.I./Corbis; *center left* © Dwight R. Kuhn; *center* © Ron Chapple/Alamy Images; *top right* © TPH/Alamy Images; *bottom left* © Ed Reschke/Peter Arnold, Inc.; *second from bottom left* © B. Runk/S. Schoenberger/Grant Heilman Photography; **651** *center right* © Alan Linn, 2006. Used under license from Shutterstock, Inc.; **652** © B. Runk/S. Schoenberger/Grant Heilman Photography; **653** *top center, top right* © Dr. Jeremy Burgess/Photo Researchers, Inc.; *simple, compound, double, toothed, entire, lobed* © B. Runk/S. Schoenberger/Grant Heilman Photography; *parallel* © Brian Tan, **2006**. Used under license from Shutterstock, Inc.; *pinnate* © Adam Hart-Davis/Photo Researchers, Inc.; **656** Photograph by Sharon Hoogstraten; **657** *bottom* © LEAF—Wisconsin's K-12 Forestry Education Program; **658** *top right* © Scott Sinklier/Alamy Images; **660** © Alan Linn, 2006. Used under license from Shutterstock, Inc.; **662–663** Image used under license from Shutterstock, Inc.; **663** © Reuters/Corbis; **665** *bottom left* © Ed Reschke/Peter Arnold, Inc.; *bottom right* © Dwight R. Kuhn; **666** *top left inset* © Grant Heilman Photography; *center left* © Dr. Richard Kessel & Dr. Gene Shih/Visuals Unlimited; *top left* © Craig Tuttle/Corbis; **667** *top right* © Darrell Gulin/Corbis; *right* © Dr. Jeremy Burgess/Photo Researchers, Inc.; **669** *top right* © Darwin Dale/Photo Researchers, Inc.; *top left* © Susumu Nishinaga/Photo Researchers, Inc.; *bottom right* © Archie Young/Photo Researchers, Inc.; **672** *bottom right* © Ingram Publishing/Alamy Images; *top left* © Scott Camazine/Photo Researchers, Inc.; *top center* © Tonis Valing, 2006. Used under license from Shutterstock, Inc.; *top right* © Royalty-Free/Corbis; **673** *bottom left* © Scott Camazine/Alamy Images; *bottom right* © Anette Linnea Rasmussen, **2006**. Used under license from Shutterstock, Inc.; *bottom center* © Dwight R. Kuhn; **675** *top left* © Andrew Syred/Photo Researchers, Inc.; *second from top left* © Andrew Syred/Photo Researchers, Inc.; *second from top right* © Andrew Syred/Photo Researchers, Inc.; *top right* © Andrew Syred/Photo Researchers, Inc.; **676** Photographs by Sharon Hoogstraten; **677** © Dwight R. Kuhn; **678** © Joseph Sohm/Corbis; **679** *top* © Dwight R. Kuhn; *bottom* Photograph by Sharon Hoogstraten; **680** © Richard Cummins/Corbis; **681** *top right* © Stockbyte Platinum/Alamy; *center right* © Chris Howes/Wild Places Photography/Alamy; **682** © Grant Heilman/Grant Heilman Photography; **683** © Dr. Jeremy Burgess/Photo Researchers, Inc.; **684** Photograph by Sharon Hoogstraten; **686** *top right* © Dwight R. Kuhn; **688** © Dan Rosandich/www.CartoonStock.com; **690** *top* © Nick Cobbing/Peter Arnold, Inc.; *bottom left* © Anastassios Mentis/FoodPix/Jupiter Images; **691** *top right* © Leonard Lessin/Peter Arnold, Inc.; *bottom right* © Matt Meadows/Peter Arnold, Inc.; **692** *top left* Photo courtesy of Dr. Tong-Jen Fu; *bottom right* Noah Berger/AP/Wide World Photos.

Unit 8 **694–695** © Jez Tryner 2005/Image Quest Marine; **695** © SeaPics.com; **696** *first row left* © Wim van Egmond/Visuals Unlimited; *first row right* © George Grall/National Geographic Image Collection; *second row left* © Mike VanDeWalker/Alamy; *first row center* © D. Allen Photography/Animals Animals; *second row right* © SeaPics.com; *second row center* © Jurgen Freund/naturepl.com; **697** *bottom right* © David M. Phillips/The Population Council/Photo Researchers, Inc.; *bottom right inset* © Kenneth Eward/Photo Researchers, Inc.; **698** *both* © F. R. Turner, Indiana University; **701** *bottom* © Sue Daly/naturepl.com; *top* © National Geographic/Getty Images; **704** © Deco/Alamy Images; **705** © Carlos Villoch 2004/Image Quest Marine; **707** *bottom* © Phillip Colla/www.OceanLight.com; *top* © Jeff Rotman/naturepl.com; **709** *top right* © Biophoto Associates/Photo Researchers, Inc.; *center right* © Image Source/Getty Images; **711** *top left* © Alan Towse; Ecoscene/Corbis; *top right* © E. R. Degginger/Photo Researchers, Inc.; *right* © John Durham/Photo Researchers, Inc.; *second from top left* © Peter Arnold, Inc./Alamy Images; **713** © Brian J. Skerry/National Geographic Image Collection; **717** © David Cooney/www.CartoonStock.com; **719** *top* © Alexis Rosenfeld/Photo Researchers, Inc.; *bottom* © Fred Bavendam/Minden Pictures; **720** *top left* Southeastern Regional Taxonomic Center/South Carolina Department of Natural Resources; *top center* © Flip Nicklin/Minden Pictures; *top right* © Fred Bavendam/Minden Pictures;

Acknowledgments

721 © Dynamic Graphics Group/IT Stock Free/Alamy; **723** *bottom* © 2004 Dennis Kunkel Microscopy, Inc.; **724** *left* © National Geographic/Getty Images; *center* © Sue Daly/naturepl.com; *top right* © E. R. Degginger/Photo Researchers, Inc.; **729–730** © Dan Tenaglia Photography/Missouriplants.com; **729** © Bartomeu Borrell/Age Fotostock; **730** © Hans Christoph Kappel/naturepl.com; **731** *top* © Sinclair Stammers/Photo Researchers, Inc.; *second from bottom right* © Holger Wulschlaeger, 2006. Used under license from Shutterstock, Inc.; *bottom right* © Tom McHugh/Photo Researchers, Inc.; *bottom left* © Pete Oxford/naturepl.com; *second from bottom left* © Stephen Dalton/Photo Researchers, Inc.; **732** © Breck P. Kent/Animals Animals; **733** *inset* © Holt Studios International Ltd/Alamy; *top* © Susumu Nishinaga/Photo Researchers, Inc.; **734** *bottom* © Andrew Syred/Photo Researchers, Inc.; *top* © Dr. Morley Read/Photo Researchers, Inc.; **735** © Roger Steene/Image Quest Marine; **736** © Peter Lange/www.fotofish.at; **737** © Pete Oxford/naturepl.com; **738** © Wayne Levin/Getty Images; **739** Photographs by Sharon Hoogstraten; **740** © Piotr Naskrecki/Minden Pictures; **742** © The Garden Picture Library/Alamy; **743** © Gary Meszaros/Visuals Unlimited; **746** © Mitsuhiko Imamori/Minden Pictures; **747** © Mike Wilkes/naturepl.com; **748** © Bruce Marlin/cirrusimage.com; **749** *top left* © Volker Steger/Photo Researchers, Inc.; *second from left* © Rod Planck/Photo Researchers, Inc.; *second from right* © Chu Tours-Joubert/Photo Researchers, Inc.; *right* © Scott Camazine/Photo Researchers, Inc.; **751** *bottom inset* Photo by Scott Bauer/Agricultural Research Service, USDA; **752** *top left* © Hans Christoph Kappel/naturepl.com; *top right* © Piotr Naskrecki/Minden Pictures; **756–757** © Gregory G. Dimijian/Photo Researchers, Inc.; **757** © Dr. Paul A. Zahl/Photo Researchers, Inc.; **759** *top* © Robert Yin/Corbis; *bottom* © Untitled/Alamy; **760** © Ingram Publishing/Alamy; **762** © Tom McHugh/Photo Researchers, Inc.; **764** © David Fleetham/Bluegreen; **766** *top* © David Fleetham/Bluegreen; *bottom* © blickwinkel/Alamy; **767** © Roberto Rinaldi/Bluegreen; **768** © Eric Haucke/Photo Researchers, Inc.; **769** © 2006 Kåre Telnes/Image Quest Marine; **770** © E. R. Degginger/Photo Researchers, Inc.; **771** © Reg Morrison/Auscape/Minden Pictures; **772** © blickwinkel/Alamy; **773** © AFP/Getty Images; **774** © Michael & Patricia Fogden/Corbis; **776** © Gary Meszaros/Photo Researchers, Inc.; **777** *bottom* © Michael & Patricia Fogden/Minden Pictures; *top* © Stephen Dalton/Photo Researchers, Inc.; **779** © Leszczynski, Zigmund/Animals Animals–Earth Scenes; **781** *left* © 2006 S. K. Sessions; *bottom right* © Jeffrey L. Rotman/Corbis; *top right inset* Duane Raver/U.S. Fish and Wildlife Service; **784** © Jane Burton/naturepl.com; **786–787** © F. Stuart Westmorland/Photo Researchers, Inc.; **787** © Fabio Liverani/naturepl.com; **789** *top right* © Cyril Ruoso/JH Editorial/Minden Pictures; *top left* © Aaron Shimer; **791** *top* © David R. Parks (http://www.mobot.org/mobot/madagascar); *bottom* © Flip Nicklin/Minden Pictures; **793** © Michael Maconachie/Alamy Images; **794** © California Academy of Sciences Department of Ornithology and Mammalogy/Valley Anatomical Preparations; **796** *top* © Gerard Soury/Oxford Scientific Films Ltd.; *bottom* © Joe McDonald/Corbis; **799** © Dietmar Nill/Foto Natura/Minden Pictures; **802** © Nguyen Thai, 2006. Used under license from Shutterstock, Inc.; **803** *left bottom* © dkimages.com; *left center* © Arthur Morris/Corbis; *right bottom* © William Osborn/naturepl.com; *right center* © Royalty-Free/Corbis; *top left* © Frans Lanting/Minden Pictures; *top right* © Pete Oxford/naturepl.com; **804** Photograph by Sharon Hoogstraten; **805** © Michael Durham/Minden Pictures; **806** © Jose Azel/Getty Images; **807** *top* © John Cancalosi/naturepl.com; *bottom* © Tony Heald/naturepl.com; **808** *top* © Tom McHugh/Photo Researchers, Inc.; *bottom left* © Charles Philip Cangialosi/Corbis; *bottom center* © Mitsuaki Iwago/Minden Pictures; **809** © Terry Whittaker; Frank Lane Picture Agency/Corbis; **810** Photograph by Sharon Hoogstraten; **811** *top right* John J. Mosesso/NBII; *bottom right* © Fred Bavendam/Minden Pictures; *top left* © Tim Davis/Corbis; **812** *center right* © Terry Whittaker; Frank Lane Picture Agency/Corbis; *left* © Joe McDonald/Corbis; **816–817** © Cyril Ruoso/JH Editorial/Minden Pictures; **817** © Frans Lanting/Minden Pictures; **818** © Jeffrey L. Rotman/Corbis; **819** *top right* © Martin Harvey/Foto Natura/Minden Pictures; *center* © Dwight Kuhn; *bottom* © Alan Schein Photography/Corbis; **820** Max Feken; **821** © George McCarthy/naturepl.com; **822** © Mike Parry/Minden Pictures; **823** © John Cancalosi/Ardea London Limited; **824** © NHPA/Martin Harvey; **825** © Heather Angel/Natural Visions; **826** *center* © Elmer Parolini/www.CartoonStock.com; *top* © Scott Tysick/Masterfile; **827** © Steve Bloom/Alamy; **828** © Ken Jones/MCB Andrade 2003; **829** © Martin Woike/Foto Natura/Minden Pictures; **830** © Michael Neugebauer/mine@netway.at; **831** © Doug Allan/naturepl.com; **832** © Staffan Widstrand/naturepl.com; **833** © Marie Read; **835** background © Brian Rogers/Visuals Unlimited; *bottom* © Alex Wild 2006; *center left* © Richard Seaman; *top* © D. Clyne/OSF/Animals Animals; **837** © Jim Wallace/Duke University Photography; **838** © Pete Oxford/Minden Pictures; **839** © Joe McDonald/Visuals Unlimited; **840** *both* © Dwight Kuhn; **841** *top left* © Nigel J. Dennis/Photo Researchers, Inc.; **842** *left* © Scott Tysick/Masterfile; *right* © Staffan Widstrand/naturepl.com; **844** © Gallo Images/Corbis; **846** © Claus Meyer/Minden Pictures; **847** *top right* © Gerry Ellis/Minden Pictures; *bottom right* © Sally A. Morgan; Ecoscene/Corbis; *center right* © Manfred Kage/Peter Arnold, Inc.; cleanup © Getty Images; **848** *center right* © The Peregrine Fund; *top right* © blickwinkel/Alamy.

Unit 9 **850–851** © Ken Redding/Corbis; **851** © Dennis Kunkel/Phototake; **852** *top left* © Susumu Nishinaga/Photo Researchers, Inc.; *bottom* © David McCarthy/Photo Researchers, Inc.; **853** *center* © Dr. Yorgos Nikas/Photo Researchers, Inc.; *1 o'clock position, 3 o'clock position, 4 o'clock position, 7 o'clock position,* © Ed Reschke/Peter Arnold, Inc.; *9 o'clock position* © Dr. Gopal Murti/Visuals Unlimited/Medical-On-Line; *11 o'clock position* © Educational Images/Custom Medical Stock Photo; *bottom* © CNRI/Photo Researchers, Inc.; **855** *top* © SPL/Photo Researchers, Inc.; *second from top* © Dr. Gladden Willis/Getty Images; *right* © RubberBall/Alamy Images; **857** *bottom left* © WidStock/Alamy Images; **859** *bottom right* © Steve Mason/Getty Images; *center right* © age fotostock/SuperStock; *top right* © Lori Adamski Peek/Getty Images; **862** © Kevin Fleming/Corbis; **866** © Ken O'Donoghue; **867** *top left* © Bettmann/Corbis; *bottom right* © Michael Krasowitz/Getty Images; **868** *center* © Dr. Yorgos Nikas/Photo Researchers, Inc.; *1 o'clock position, 3 o'clock position, 4 o'clock position, 7 o'clock position,* © Ed Reschke/Peter Arnold, Inc.; *9 o'clock position* © Dr. Gopal Murti/Visuals Unlimited/Medical-On-Line; *11 o'clock position* © Educational Images/Custom Medical Stock Photo; *bottom* © CNRI/Photo Researchers, Inc.; **872–873** © ISM/Phototake; **873** *bottom right* © Francois Paquet-Durand/Photo Researchers, Inc.; **875** © Anatomical Travelogue/Photo Researchers, Inc.; **876** © James Cavallini/Photo Researchers, Inc.; **880** *top* © Custom Medical Stock Photo; *bottom* © Custom Medical Stock Photo; **881** © Omikron/Photo Researchers, Inc.; **882** © Steve Gschmeissner/Photo Researchers, Inc.; **883** © CNRI/Photo Researchers, Inc.; **887** *bottom left* © Wellcome Dept. of Cognitive Neurology/Photo Researchers, Inc.; *bottom center* © WDCN/Univ. College London/Photo Researchers, Inc.; *bottom right* © Wellcome Dept. of Cognitive Neurology/Photo Researchers, Inc.; **888** *top center* © Dr. Fred Hossler/Getty Images; bell, *top right* © Fotolistic, 2006. Used under license from Shutterstock, Inc.; *top right* © Dr. Fred Hossler/Getty Images; **891** *bottom left* © Du Cane Medical Imaging Ltd./Photo Researchers, Inc.; *bottom center* © ISM/Phototake; *bottom right* © Tim Beddow/Photo Researchers, Inc.; **892** *all* © Science VU/Visuals Unlimited/Mediscan; **903** *left* © Howard Sochurek/Corbis; *bottom right* Courtesy of National Institute of Drug Abuse/National Institutes of Health; **908–909** © Martin Dohrn/Royal College of Surgeons/Photo Researchers, Inc.; **909** © David Arky/Corbis; **914** © Photo Insolite Realite/Photo Researchers, Inc.; **916** *top* © Dachez/Photo Researchers, Inc.; *bottom* © Kent Wood/Photo Researchers, Inc.; **919** © Custom Medical Stock Photo; **921** © SW Productions/Getty Images; **924** © ISM/Phototake; **925** © Paul Barton/Corbis; **926** © Yoav Levy/Phototake; **927** *top* © Dr. Dennis Kunkel/Visuals Unlimited; *bottom* © Dr. Stanley Flegler/Visuals Unlimited; **929** *center right* © CNRI/Photo Researchers, Inc.; *top* © SPL/Photo Researchers, Inc.; **931** © Dynamics Graphics Group/Creatas/Alamy Images; **932** Photograph by Sharon Hoogstraten; **934** *right* © Dr. Dennis Kunkel/Visuals Unlimited; **938–939** © Dr. Dennis Kunkel/Visuals Unlimited; **939** © Ross Hoddinott/naturepl.com; **940** *bottom left* © Science Museum/Science and Society Picture Library; *third from left* © Science Source/Photo Researchers, Inc.; *second from left* Ms Pesan 1555 Anatomical diagram of the human circulatory and digestive system (1425–1450), Mansour b. Eliyas Chirazi. Vellum. 26.5 x 18. Biblioteque Nationale, Paris. © Bridgeman Art Library; *bottom right* © Archivo Iconografico, S.A./Corbis; **941** *center* © Bettmann/Corbis; *bottom right* © CDC/Photo Researchers, Inc.; *right* © Garo/Photo Researchers, Inc.; *center left* © Bettmann/Corbis; *bottom left* © Yale Joel/Time Life Pictures/Getty Images; *bottom right* © pixelman, 2006. Used under license from Shutterstock, Inc.; **943** © Oliver Meckes/Nicole Ottawa/Photo Researchers, Inc.; **944** © David Scharf/Photo Researchers, Inc.; **945** © E. Gray/Photo Researchers, Inc.; **949** © Dr. G. W. Willis/Visuals Unlimited; **950** © Dr. David Philips/Visuals Unlimited; **955** © CNRI/Photo Researchers, Inc.; **957** © Dr. Dorothea Zucker-Franklin, M.D./Phototake; **958** *top* © Ralph C. Eagle Jr./Photo Researchers, Inc.; *center* © Dennis Kunkel/Phototake; *bottom* © A. Syred/Photo Researchers, Inc.; **960** *bottom* © Courtesy of Scientific Data Registry, Atomic Bomb Disease Institute/Nagasaki University, Japan; *center* © Courtesy of Scientific Data Registry, Atomic Bomb Disease Institute/Nagasaki University, Japan; **963** *top* © Eye of Science/Photo Researchers, Inc.; *bottom* © Nibsc/Photo Researchers, Inc.; **965** *bottom left* © CNRI/Photo Researchers, Inc.; *bottom right* © Russell Kightley Media, rkm.com.au; **970–971** © Dr. Michael Webb/Visuals Unlimited/Getty Images; **971** © Alfred Pasieka/Science Photo Library/Photo Researchers, Inc.; **972** © Louis B. Wallach, Inc./The Image Bank/Getty Images; **973** © Comstock Production Department/Alamy Images; **975** © David Young-Wolff/PhotoEdit; **982** © Eye of Science/Photo Researchers, Inc.; **984** © Professors P. Motta & F. Carpino/University "La Sapienza", Rome/Science Photo Library/Photo Researchers, Inc.; **985** © Jason Smith, 2006. Used under license from Shutterstock, Inc.; **988** © Susumu Nishinaga/Photo Researchers, Inc.; **990** © Vince Bucci/AFP/Getty Images; **993** *bottom* © BSIP/Phototake; **998–999** © Gusto/Photo Researchers, Inc.; **999** © Steve Hopkin/Ardea London Limited; **1003** © Anatomical Travelogue/Photo Researchers, Inc.; **1004** *bottom left* © Andrew Syred/Photo Researchers, Inc.; *bottom right* © SPL/Photo Researchers, Inc.; **1005** © SPL/Photo Researchers, Inc.; **1007** *top all* © Ed Reschke/Peter Arnold, Inc.; *bottom right* © SPL/Photo Researchers, Inc.; **1010** © Kent Wood/Photo Researchers, Inc.; **1012** ball © Nina Shannon, **2006**. Used under license from Shutterstock, Inc.; timer © Hannah Gleghorn, 2006. Used under license from Shutterstock, Inc.; **1013** © Andrew Syred/Photo Researchers, Inc.; **1016** © Anatomical Travelogue/Photo Researchers, Inc.; **1017** *webquest left* © Siebert/Custom Medical Stock Photo; *webquest right* © Siebert/Custom Medical Stock Photo; *bottom left* © Steve Gschmeissner/Photo Researchers, Inc.; *top right inset* © Franc Podgorsek/istockphoto.com; **1022–1023** © Nestle/Petit Format/Photo Researchers, Inc.; **1023** © Francois Gohier/Ardea London Limited; **1031** *top* © Dr. David M. Philips/Visuals Unlimited; *bottom* © D. Philips/Photo Researchers, Inc.; **1032** © Eye of Science/Photo Researchers, Inc.; **1033** © Claude Edelmann/Photo Researchers, Inc.; **1034** © Liz Sanders/Mississippi Fertility Institute; **1037** *top left* © Claude Edelmann/Photo Researchers, Inc.; *center left* © Claude Edelmann/Photo Researchers, Inc.; *bottom left* © Petit Format/Photo Researchers, Inc.; *top right* © SPL/Photo Researchers, Inc.; *top right* © SPL/Photo Researchers, Inc.; *center right* © Mediscan/Visuals Unlimited; *bottom right* © Petit Format/Photo Researchers, Inc.; **1039** © Jose Luis Pelaez, Inc./Corbis; **1041** © David Turnley/Corbis; **1042** *center left* © Tom & Dee Ann McCarthy/Corbis; *bottom left* © Bob Daemmrich/PhotoEdit; **1043** *all* Courtesy of the Peel Family, Chicago, IL; **1044** © Biodisc/Visuals Unlimited; **1045** *bottom left* © Paul Grebliunas/Getty Images; *bottom right* © Marnie Burkhart/Masterfile; **1046** *bottom left* © D. Philips/Photo Researchers, Inc.; *bottom right* © David Turnley/Corbis; **1050** © Cary Wolinsky/National Geographic Image Collection; **1051** © Lester Lefkowitz/Corbis; **1052** *top right* © WDCN/Univ. College London/Photo Researchers, Inc.; *left* © Raj Chawla/UVM College of Medicine; *center right* © Wellcome Dept. of Cognitive Neurology/Photo Researchers, Inc.

Backmatter **R2** © Comstock Images/Age Fotostock America, Inc.; **R3** *top right* © Michael Newman/PhotoEdit; *bottom left* © Andrew Lambert Photography/Photo Researchers, Inc.; **R5** *top right* © davies & starr/Getty Images; *center right* © MicroScan/Phototake; **R8** © Kevin and Betty Collins/Visuals Unlimited; **R10** *all* © M. I. Walker/Photo Researchers, Inc.; **R11** © Cathlyn Melloan/Getty Images; **R12** © Martyn Chillmaid/Oxford Scientific; **R25** *top* © Eye of Science/Photo Researchers, Inc.; *center* © NIAID/CDC/Photo Researchers, Inc.; *bottom* © M. I. Walker/Photo Researchers, Inc.; **R26** *top* © Wim van Egmond/Visuals Unlimited; *center* © Dr. Stanley Flegler/Visuals Unlimited; *bottom* © Robert F. Myers/Visuals Unlimited; **R27** *top* © Bill Beatty/Visuals Unlimited; *center* © Bryan Eastham, 2006. Used under license from Shutterstock, Inc.; *bottom* © Galina Dreyzina, 2006. Used under license from Shutterstock, Inc.; **R28** *top* © David Hughes/Photo Researchers, Inc.; *center* © Cindy Haggerty, 2006. Used under license from Shutterstock, Inc.; *bottom* © Norbert Wu/Minden Pictures; **R29** *top* © Gary Bell/oceanwideimages.com; *center* © Norbert Wu/Minden Pictures; *bottom* © Kim Taylor/naturepl.com; **R30** *top* © F. Collet/Ardea London Limited; *center* © Rene Krekels/Foto Natura/Minden Pictures; *bottom* © Gary Bell/oceanwideimages.com; **R31** *top* © Gary Bell/oceanwideimages.com; *second from top* © eStock Photo; *center* © Joseph T. Collins/Photo Researchers, Inc.; *second from bottom* © Jeremy Early/FLPA/Minden Pictures; *bottom* © Frans Lanting/Minden Pictures; **R38** *bottom left* © Peter Oxford/naturepl.com; *top right* © Scott Bauer/USDA/Agricultural Research Service; *bottom right* © Aaron Haupt/Photo Researchers, Inc.; **R39** *top left* © Kim Heacox/Getty Images; *top right* © Ron Levine/The Image Bank/Getty Images; *bottom left* © Geoff Tompkinson/Photo Researchers, Inc.

ILLUSTRATIONS

Illustration by Argosy **029, 093, 127, 157, 193, 257, 321, 353, 385, 421, 449, 477, 507, 537, 567, 601, 633, 685, 723, 751, 781, 841, 867, 903, 933, 965, 993, 1017, 1045;** Illustration by Thomas Bayley/Sparks Arts & Literary Agents **307;** Illustration by Richard Bonson/Wildlife Art Ltd. **397** *bottom*, **446–447, 595, 732;** Illustration by Robin Boutell/Wildlife Art Ltd. **741;** Illustration by Peter Bull **83, 85, 87, 89, 90–91, 94, 139, 325, 357, 361, 495, 520, 538, 541, 576, 580, 589, 598, 603, 605, 642, 646, 655, 658–659, 700, 702–703, 726, 750, 761, 763, 765, 769–770, 859–860, 874, 876–878, 885, 896, 904, 911–913, 915, 920, 923, 930, 934, 977, 979, 980, 982, 986, 994, 1000, 1002, 1004, 1006, 1010, 1015, 1018, 1025–1026, 1028–1029, 1034, 1047;** Illustration by Robin Carter/Wildlife Art Ltd. **708, 710, 715–716, 738, 758, 788, 796–797, 812;** Illustration by Stuart Carter /Wildlife Art Ltd. **348, 404, 706, 712, 718;** Illustration by Dan Cole/Wildlife Art Ltd. **800;** Illustration by Barry Croucher/Wildlife Art Ltd. **790, 814;** Illustration by Stephen Durke **37–48, 60, 104, 114, 128, 146, 165, 233, 237, 241, 258, 260, 318, 369, 386, 545, 548–549, 557, 579, 582, 585, 602, 643, 911, 915, 947, 952–953, 956, 961–962, 964, 966, 968, 1030;** Illustration by Luigi Galante/Sparks Arts & Literary Agents **152, 329, 354, 644, 775, 782;** Illustration by Garth Glazier **550, 565, 568, 570, 881–883, 887–888, 890;** Patrick Gnan **311;** Illustration by Sharon & Joel Harris **855, 863–864, 889, 899, 978, 987, 989, 994, 1001, 1009–1010, 1018, 1035, 1041, 1046;** Illustration by Inklink Studio/Sparks Arts & Literary Agents **413, 414, 415, 416, 418–419, 422, 469;** Illustration by Joel Ito **383;** Illustration by Ian Jackson/Wildlife Art Ltd. **744;** Illustration by Virge Kask **592–593;** Elliott Kimmel, Science Teacher **219;** Illustration by Debbie Maizels **178, 182, 615, 626, 644-645, 658, 664, 667–668, 671, 682, 686, 800–801, R32–R35;** Illustration by Alan Male **376, 377–378, 527, 795, 798;** Courtesy of National Institute of Drug Abuse/National Institutes of Health **903** *bottom right*; Illustration by Steve Oh/KO Studios **140–141;** MapQuest.com, Inc. **303, 311, 335, 346, 354, 397, 430, 462;** Illustration by Jun Park **52;** Illustration by Mick Posen/Wildlife Art Ltd. **349, 410;** Illustration by Six Red Marbles **59, 127, 193, 287, 567, 657, 685, 751, 841, 933;** Illustration by Mick Stevens **169;** Dan Stuckenschneider (Uhl Studios) **R2, R6–R7, R9;** Illustration by Myke Taylor/Wildlife Art Ltd. **341, 736, 744, 752;** Illustration by Bart Vallecoccia **73–79, 82, 94–96, 104, 109, 111, 113–115, 119–120, 128, 130, 311, 373, 386, 640, 897, 917–919, 936;** Illustration by Jane Watkins/Wildlife Art Ltd. **615.**

R100 McDougal Littell Biology

The Periodic Table

HYDROGEN
Hydrogen is found in all organic compounds. Hydrogen ions (H⁺) are needed for the production of ATP.

SODIUM, POTASSIUM, CALCIUM
In their elemental forms, sodium, potassium, and calcium are soft, explosive metals. In their ionic forms (Na⁺, K⁺, and Ca²⁺) in animals, they are all necessary for the proper functioning of the nervous system.

CHROMIUM
Chromium is needed for glucose metabolism and may have a role in the regulation of the activity of insulin. Above trace amounts, chromium is highly toxic.

IRON
The iron found in the center of hemoglobin molecules transports oxygen in the blood of vertebrates.

BARIUM
Barium and most of its compounds are highly toxic. In one of its non-toxic compounds, barium is used in medical imaging.

Period	1	2	3	4	5	6	7	8	9
1	**1** **H** Hydrogen 1.008								
2	**3** **Li** Lithium 6.941	**4** **Be** Beryllium 9.012							
3	**11** **Na** Sodium 22.990	**12** **Mg** Magnesium 24.305							
4	**19** **K** Potassium 39.098	**20** **Ca** Calcium 40.078	**21** **Sc** Scandium 44.956	**22** **Ti** Titanium 47.87	**23** **V** Vanadium 50.942	**24** **Cr** Chromium 51.996	**25** **Mn** Manganese 54.938	**26** **Fe** Iron 55.845	**27** **Co** Cobalt 58.933
5	**37** **Rb** Rubidium 85.468	**38** **Sr** Strontium 87.62	**39** **Y** Yttrium 88.906	**40** **Zr** Zirconium 91.224	**41** **Nb** Niobium 92.906	**42** **Mo** Molybdenum 95.94	**43** **Tc** Technetium (98)	**44** **Ru** Ruthenium 101.07	**45** **Rh** Rhodium 102.906
6	**55** **Cs** Cesium 132.905	**56** **Ba** Barium 137.327	**57** **La** Lanthanum 138.906	**72** **Hf** Hafnium 178.49	**73** **Ta** Tantalum 180.95	**74** **W** Tungsten 183.84	**75** **Re** Rhenium 186.207	**76** **Os** Osmium 190.23	**77** **Ir** Iridium 192.217
7	**87** **Fr** Francium (223)	**88** **Ra** Radium (226)	**89** **Ac** Actinium (227)	**104** **Rf** Rutherfordium (261)	**105** **Db** Dubnium (262)	**106** **Sg** Seaborgium (266)	**107** **Bh** Bohrium (264)	**108** **Hs** Hassium (277)	**109** **Mt** Meitnerium (268)

58 **Ce** Cerium 140.116	**59** **Pr** Praseodymium 140.908	**60** **Nd** Neodymium 144.24	**61** **Pm** Promethium (145)	**62** **Sm** Samarium 150.36
90 **Th** Thorium 232.038	**91** **Pa** Protactinium 231.036	**92** **U** Uranium 238.029	**93** **Np** Neptunium (237)	**94** **Pu** Plutonium (244)

 Metal  Metalloid   Nonmetal  **Fe** Solid  **Hg** Liquid   Gas